SEVENTH-DAY ADVENTIST

ENCYCLOPEDIA

SECOND REVISED EDITION

A-L

COMMENTARY
REFERENCE
SERIES
Volume 10

SEVENTH-DAY ADVENTIST

ENCYCLOPEDIA

SECOND REVISED EDITION

A-L

Review and Herald® Publishing Association
Hagerstown, MD 21740

The contributors assume full responsibility for the accuracy of all facts and quotations as cited in this book.

PRINTED IN U.S.A.

00 99 98 97 96 5 4 3 2 1

R&H Cataloging Service

Seventh-day Adventist encyclopedia. Second
revised edition

1. Seventh-day Adventists—Dictionaries.

286.732

IISBN 0-8280-0918-X

EDITORS

Contributors

Abdul-Shereeff, P.
Abel, L. Marcel
Abraham, Dittu
Abrahamsen, Karl
Acosta-Muñiz, Eloy
Adams, R. R.
Adams, W. Melvin
Adeogun, Caleb
Aeschlimann B., Alfredo
Afenir, J. O.
Aga, Negassa
Agdon, Solomon S.
Aguadera, Rogelio J.
Aikman, James A.
Aimonetti, Michel
Airey, Wilfred J.
Aitken, Dorothy
Aittala, W. E.
Alagusundaram, K.
Alalade, A. A.
Aldridge, Richard A.
Allen, David
Allen, Jane
Allen, Ken
Allen, Sydney
Alonso, Ramiro P.
Alsaybar, B. B.
Alway, Raymond
Amelung, Erich
Amoah, John Kenneth
Ampuero Matta, Victor E.
Amundsen, Wesley
Andersen, G. E.
Andersen, Howard C.
Anderson, Carl Dicmann
Anderson, Carl P.
Anderson, G. T.
Anderson, J. P.
Anderson, John David
Anderson, Lyle C.
Anderson, Roy Allan
Andrade Guerra, Segundo Eloy
Anduik, Helge
Anniss, George L.
Anspach, Helen B.
Anthony, W. D
Anttila, Simo
Appave, S. W.
Appenzeller, R. E.
Aritonang, Urbanus H.
Armer, E.
Armour, Eugene
Arnold, Rhonda
Arnold, Rudolf
Arthur, Errol M.
Ashbaugh, Kraid I.
Åsheim, Frithjof
Åsheim, Trygve
Ashlock, J. F.
Astner, Margaret M.
Atherton, Herbert
Atkins, Mrs. Lloyd
Attakora, Kwasi
Avendano, Nelson U.
Ayala, Manuel G.
Azevedo, Roberto Cesar de
Aziz, Basim

Ba Khin
Baasch, David H.
Babalola, David O.
Babcock, Fern Gibson
Baden, P. G.
Badenas, Roberto
Baduza, S.B.M.
Bahr, O.
Bailey, Carl M.
Bailie, Ira E.
Bairagee, A.
Baker, H. C.
Baker, Sue Ellen
Baldwin, Jennifer M.
Balharrie, Gordon
Ballew, Daniel A.
Bangloy, J. A.
Banks, Rosa T.
Banyie, Lawrence
Bara, John M.
Barayuga, Petronilo J.
Barbuscia, Ignazio
Barger, R. Curtis
Barnes, Belvina
Barnett, Paulene
Barnett, Richard J.
Baro, Saul Perez
Barrow, R. M.
Barrus, Iva May
Bartlett, Alvin M.
Bartlett, V. L.
Basanta, Febo
Bascom, Mrs. V. E.
Bassham, W. S.
Batoebara, Damin
Battle, Maurice T.
Battye, Walter E.
Bauman, Herman
Bautista, Jose O.
Beach, B. B.
Beach, W. R.
Beardsell, Derek C.
Beardsell, S. W.
Becerra, Enrique
Bechtel, James J.
Beck, Edwin C.
Beck, Reuben
Becker, Madeleine
Beebe, Jan
Beeler, Charles R.
Bell, Anthony William
Bell, Arthur F.
Bell, DeLona L.
Bell, G. Martin
Bendall, Suzanne K.
Bentancor, Juan C.
Benton, Pat
Bera, Filimoni K.
Berg, Henrique
Berg, Orley M.
Bergland, Karl J.
Berkeley, S. P.
Beskow, Oldemar I.
Bhattacharjee, Anil
Bhosale, Bakul B.
Bigham, Ervin H.
Bilima, K. D.
Bingcang, Marie E.
Biraro, Sam
Birbeck-Robinson, H. A.
Bird, Irene Couch
Birkenstock, C. J.
Birkenstock, David
Bissell, H. LeVerne
Bjarnason, Sigurdur
Bjerkan, Ole-Chr.
Blackburn, C. C.
Blewett, Larry E.
Blodgett, Ralph
Blomdahl, Rune
Blomstedt, Norman
Bocala, Violeto F.
Boehm, Eric A.
Boehm, Roy R.
Bohme, W. H.
Bohr, Harold
Boice, Ben R.
Bokovoy, A. P.
Bolling, Per
Bolst, Toni
Bond, Verlyn D.
Bonney, C. R.
Booker, Robert L.
Boram, Arnold

Borges dos Santos, Jose
Bork, Norma K.
Borm, Erna
Bornert, M.
Borton, Harvey Dale, Jr.
Böttcher, Manfred
Bouit, Jean-Jacques
Bowen, Dorothy O.
Bowers, Marshall
Boyatt, Ed
Boyle, James W.
Bracho, Gilberto
Bradfield, James T.
Bradford, C. E.
Bradley, Thomas J.
Bradley, W. P.
Branster, G.
Breedt, G.J.A.
Bremer, Oswald
Brendel, Harold J.
Brendel, Gary
Brenneman, Duane
Brennwald, F. W.
Brinkman, Jan
Bristow, A. H.
Bristow, W. B.
Brody, Ronald W.
Brogden, Aaron N.
Brooks, C. L.
Brothers, Greg
Brown, Carla
Brown, Donald L.
Brown, Graeme H.
Brown, Henry F.
Brown, K. S.
Brown, Ken
Brown, R. H.
Brown, R. R.
Brown, Richard C., Sr.
Brown, Walton J.
Browning, Pearl
Brownsberger, Elsie
Bruce, James A.
Bruington, Harry S.
Bruinsma, R.
Bryson, G. E.
Buckley, Robert M.
Bulli, K. J.
Bullock, K. J.
Burchard, R. W.
Burgess, Reginald
Burgos, Nelson V.
Burke, I. E.
Burkhard, A.
Burrell, Natelkka E.
Burrill, Russell
Burton, Shirley
Bustamante, Eliseo
Bustamante, Gilberto
Butler, A. B.
Butler, Everett C.
Butler, George
Butler, L. L.
Butler, Maria A.
Butscher, Lothar

Cabaluna, Reuben L.
Cadavero, David A.
Camagay, Ulysses
Campbell, J. N.
Campbell, Mike W.
Campbell, Nonnie H.
Cannon, W. John
Canosa, Louis
Capobres, E. A.
Capule, Bienvenido E.
Carey, Richard G.
Cargill, Ireno E.
Carlson, Dennis N.
Carman, Eldon E.
Carr, Dalles L.
Carson, Ruby Leach
Carter, C. A.
Carter, G. Tom
Carter, Ralph T.
Carter, Robert H.
Casaca, Armando
Caslow, Daniel E.
Castillo, Nelson G.
Castrejon, Jaime
Castro, Gabriel
Catolico, Jonathan C.
Cavil, James A.
Cayrun, Oswaldo R.
Celestre, Jimmy A.
Chaffin, Deborah
Chaij, Enrique
Chalmers, Charles
Chalupka, Roman
Chambugong, Edward P.
Chan Yun Ko
Chang Ki Hyun
Chapman, Ruth R.
Chartier, Gary
Chase, James A.
Cherian, Maliakal E.
Chimoga, F. V.
Cho, Hanson
Cho, Paul
Choi E Kwon
Choo Yau Fong
Chow, Dowell
Christensen, Beulah L.
Christensen, Carl D.
Christensen, Donald W.
Christensen, Otto H.
Christian, C. Dionisio
Christian, Johnson S.
Christian, Percy W.
Christie, E. B.
Christman, Don R.
Christman, Harry K.
Christo, Gerald J.
Christo, John
Christoforides, C. A.
Chu, T. M.
Chun Jung Kwon
Chun Se Won
Chuquimia Condori, Federico
Clack, L. H.
Clarke, J. W.
Claus, Wilbur H.
Claveria, M. M.
Clifford, Gerald Francis
Clifford, H. E.
Clouzet, Gaston
Coe, Gary
Coe, W. O.
Coen, Warren
Coetzee, A. O.
Coetzee, G.J.E.
Coetzee, J. D.
Coetzee, Pieter H.
Coffen, Richard
Coffey, Cecil
Coffin, G. H.
Cole, Roy
Cole, Samuel E.
Collins, Mario A.
Comstock, Darryl L.
Conteh, J.S.B.
Cook, Charles F.
Cook, LaRue L.
Cooks, J. B.
Cooks, W. M.
Coolen, Margaret
Coolidge, L. E.
Coombe, Raymond
Cooper, Lowell C.
Copiz, Pietro E.
Cordas, D. L.
Corkum, Donald W.
Cornforth, Leon
Corrales, Luis C.
Cortes, Daniel
Cosendai, A. H.
Cossentine, E. E.
Cottrell, Raymond F.
Cozens, M. P.
Craig, F. C.
Craig, Jeanie
Craig, R. D.
Craig, Wanda
Crandall, Walter T.
Crane, Donald E.
Crawford, R. E.
Crays, Laurinda
Cress, James A.
Cripps, Jean
Cronte, Kenneth B.
Crook, D. S.
Crook, Harold
Cross, Sherman
Crumbly, Faith
Cumbo, Everett E.
Cunningham, Winston D.
Curameng, Dottie R.
Currie, H. Carl
Curtis, Rena A.

Cuthbert, Maurice W.

Dabrowski, S.
Dake, Myrl E.
Dalaguan, Joel Y.
Dale, Robert G.
Dale, Robert L.
Dalisay, Flaviano
Daniel, James F.
Danielsen, Jens
Dare, Enoch O.
Darnell, Robert
Dart, Archa O.
Dart, G. Charles
Dasher, Ron
Dassenko, Geo. W.
Daugherty, Frank J.
Davidson, Lawrence
Davidson, Ralph M.
Davis, Glen W.
Davis, J. M.
Davis, Roger
Davis, Thomas A.
Davy, Eric
Dawson, Ira F.
Dayson, Nestor D.
de Abreu, Nepomuceno S.
de Armas, Juan C.
de Beer, J. N.
De Chavez, Nelson D.
De los Santos Mena, Abner
De Parra, Nury
Delafield, D. A.
Delgrado, E. H.
Delice, Ohanis
DeMeo, Giuseppe
Demie, Djeffar
Demkaso, Yohanis
Dennis, David
Dennis, W. R., Jr.
DePaula, Marenus
Dessain, Willard A.
Deucher, Zildomar
Devins, René M.
Dhason, Manickam
Dialektakis, E.
Dias, Joaquim
Dick, Everett
Dick, W. G.
Dien, Arie
Dietrich, F.
Digneo, E. J.
Dimara, John S.
Disasa, Abebe
Ditta, Maxwell
Dixon, Robert D.
Dobbs, Keith T.
Dobroskay, Desmond
Dodd, L. Elaine
Donald, J. Robert
Donga, David Q.
dos Santos, J. B.
dos Santos, Valdir M.
Doss, G. R.
Doss, Norman L.
Doyle, Norise
Drachenberg, Dora G. de
Drejnar, Jiri
Duarte, Mark P.
Dudley, C. E.
Dudley, Roger L.
Duerksen, Richard
Duffy, J. E.
Dumba, H.
Dumitrescu, Nelu
Dunfield, D. L
Dunlop, W. C.
Dunn, L. D.
Dunn, Norman W.
Dunton, Hugh I.
Dwyer, Audley L.
Dyason, A. P.
Dyer, Mercedes H.
Dykes, James E.

Eagan, John T.
Eager, Hedley J.
Easterbrook, W. F.
Eaton, Mark M.
Eberhardt, W.
Ebner, Franz
Eccles, Floyd W.
Edwards, J. E.
Edwards, Otis B.
Edwards, Rex D.
Edwards, Ronald
Edwardy, Fredrik W.
Eichman, H. G.
Elam, Mary Elizabeth
Eldridge, Paul H.
Eliot, D. R.
Elmadjian, Moses
Emmerson, J. O.
Emmerson, W. L.
Engelbrecht, L. H.
Engelkemier, Betty
Engroff, Richard L.
Entima, Israel G.
Epperson, K. J.
Erdmann, Lydie
Erdmann, Robert
Erickson, H. D.
Esteb, Adlai Albert
Eva, Gloria
Eva, W. Duncan
Evans, A. H.
Evans, I. M.
Evans, R. A.
Evard, Henri
Evert, John G.

Fafale, George
Fagal, Virginia M.
Farah, Raja D.
Fasnacht, Jean-Pierre
Faull, R. S.
Fay, Jocelyn R.
Fearing, Andrew
Fedorenko, T.
Fenn, Richard Lee
Fenner, G. R.
Fenz, Giovanni
Ferguson, Vilma M.
Fernando, C. A.
Fernánez, Christina
Ferraro, G.
Ferreira, Ernesto
Ferreira, T. V.
Ferrer, Sergie B.
Fields, O. I.
Figueroa, J. H., Jr.
Finck, Ernest F.
Fiscalini, Jean
Fisher, C. Gerry
Fisher, George
Fitch, J. D. Victor
Flaiz, Theodore R.
Flanigan, Veronica M.
Fleary, Leo T.
Flórez Q., Luis J.
Flory, Vernon
Flowers, Ron
Fokuoh, J. K.
Foo, Doris
Forbes, A. H.
Ford, Heidi
Ford, Merle E.
Ford, Mrs. Orley
Forde, K. Eugene
Foster, E. H.
Foster, Ray
Foster, Mrs. Ray
Fowler, Allen
Fralick, William
Franz, C. O.
Fraser, Colin H.
Fraser, Raymond J.
Freiman, A. O.
French, B.G.O.
Friesen, Henry P.
Frikart, Ulrich
Froom, Fenton E.
Froom, LeRoy E.
Fulfer, James G.
Futcher, W.G.A.

Gaban, Charles S.
Galang, William P.
Galicia, Agustin
Gallagher, Ed
Gallant, E. A.
Ganson, Reo
Garbi, Ermanno
Garcia, Emily N.
Garcia, Loreto R., Jr.
Garcia-Marenko, Emilio
Garcia Robayna, Nathaniel
Garland, Alex
Garne, G. E.

Garsin, André
Gasapo, Rufo G.
Gatchet, John F.
Gay, David
Gearing, Catherine
Geeroms, Jean
George, C. K.
Geraty, T. S.
Gerber, Robert
Gerhart, R. B.
Germanis, Nick
Geslani, F. T.
Giao, Le cong
Gibb, A. E.
Gibb, Earl
Gibson, George
Gibson, Jessie O.
Gibson, Leota
Giddings, Philip E.
Gidlund, C.
Gilbert, Donald F.
Gilbert, Flossie M.
Gilson, W. J.
Giordano, Oscar
Girard, Paul
Gjertsen, Øivind
Glants, Marvin E.
Glass, James
Gmehling, O.
Gnass, Arturo E.
Goertzen, C. H.
Goh, Boon Chay
Goh, Joshua M.
Goldstein, Clifford R.
Golubic, Mirko
Gomes, Juvenal
Gomez, Jose L.
Gonzalez, Guillermo
Gonzalez, Israel
Gonzalez, Oskar
Gordon, A. J.
Gorle, Ruth
Gorski, Nevil
Gosse, William H.
Graham, G. A.
Graham, O. O.
Graham, Roy E.
Gray, K. J.
Greaves, Norma E.
Greek, Ramona
Green, Carlyle
Green, Ian
Greene, Margaret O.
Gregory, Ronald C.
Greive, Constance M.
Greive, S. C.
Grellmann, Lauro
Grenberg, Allise
Griffin, Charles J.
Griffin, L. B.
Griffith, Joyce
Griffiths, Carol Joy
Gudday, Tebedje
Gudmundsen, G.
Gudmundsson, Eric
Gudmundsson, Julius
Gueho, Daniel
Guenther, C. E.
Guild, Cecil B.
Gullon, Roberto
Guptill, Stephen R.
Gustavsson, Bo
Gustavsson, Ulf
Gutekunst, Daniel
Gutman, M. M.
Guy, Fritz
Guy, G. Herman

Haapasalo, Erkki O.
Haas, Gideon A.
Hackett, Willard
Hadley, Mary Ann
Hagele, Lowell C.
Hain, Dieter
Hairston, R. B.
Halder, Swapon
Hall, Richard C.
Halladay, H. K.
Hallam, Keith L.
Halliday, H. G.
Halliwell, Leo B.
Haloviak, Bert
Hamel, C. H.
Hamilton, R. E.
Hämmerly, Daniel
Hammerly, Marcelo A.
Hammill, Richard
Hammill, Roger
Hammond, Richard J.
Hancock, John
Handysides, Dan J.
Hanhardt, Mrs. W. H.
Hannah David
Hansen, Alice
Hansen, Eskild
Hansen, Joseph C.
Hanson, Ernest D.
Hanson, Herbert M.
Harcombe, J. D.
Harcombe, J. Neville
Harden, Hal D.
Harder, Frederick E. J.
Hardy, Gretchen E.
Hare, Eric B.
Harris, H. J.
Harrison, Roy A.
Hartman, Carl
Hartmann, Walder
Hartshorn, Robin
Harvey, Myron
Harvey, Norman K.
Harvey, R. J.
Hass, Herbert E.
Hatzinger, E.
Haubeil, H.
Haugsted, Ruby
Hawkins, James A., Jr.
Hawley, D. T.
Hawrylak, Christine
Hay, David E.
Haycock, L.
Hayden, Georgiana
Hayes, Douglas
Heald, B. M.
Heath, H. J.
Hecketsweiler, Jean J.
Hecketsweiler, Marc
Hedges, Allan G.
Hefren, A. L.
Heggie, R. N.
Hegstad, Roland R.
Heijkoop, N.
Heinrichs, David C.
Heinz, Daniel
Heise, Paul A.
Heisler, E. J.
Helm, Rudolf
Hennig, E.
Henning, Heinz
Henri, C. D.
Henrickson, Roy L.
Henriksen, Glenn F.
Henriksen, J. D.
Henriquez, Clayton V.
Heppenstall, Edward
Herbert, Raleigh D.
Herin, Mazie A.
Herman, James K.
Hermann, P. H.
Herrera, Jose M.
Hetke, E. A.
Hetzell, M. Carol
Hibbert, J. G.
Hicks, Debra J.
Higgins, D. A.
Higgins, Edward W., Jr.
Higgins, W. A.
Hilgert, Earle
Hill, G. Walter
Hills, Desmond B.
Hirota, Minoru
Hirvonen, Leo
Hodges, A. D.
Hoffman, Jay M.
Hofmann, Paul
Hogganvik, Kristian
Hogganvik, V.
Holland, Kenneth J.
Holbrook, Delmer
Holland, Lee D.
Holt, B. Russell
Holzer, Gunther
Hood, John R., Sr.
Hope, Lorraine M.
Hopp, Joyce W.
Hopps, John
Horn, Siegfried H.
Howard, Grace Clifford
Howell, L. I.

CONTRIBUTORS

Howlett, R. H.
Hubert, William J.
Hudgins, Franklin W.
Huff, Barbara
Hugo, Adolfo Lista
Hunt, Dean
Hunt, J. N.
Hurlow, W. A.
Hurlow, W. H.
Huse, George
Huu, Le
Hyatt, Helen M.
Hyde, Gordon M.
Hyde, J. Ashford
Hyde, J. J.
Hyde, William T.

Idaosos, C. F.
Imo, Z. N.
Inada, Minoru
Ingersoll, Jim
Injety, Roy J.
Iredale, David
Irvine, James Keith
Itin, R. A.
Iversen, J. O.

Jackson, Carleton G.
Jackson-Hall, Barbara
Jacobs, James J.
Jacobs, Ray L.
Jacobsen, Henning
Jacobson, Alfred
Jacobson, Arthur G.
Jacques, Oliver
Jaecks, Lenard D.
Janes, John
Janssen, Carol
Jaqua, Mrs. C. L.
Jarry, T. Kudar
Jean-Elie, Serge B.
Jean-Pierre, Emmanuel A.
Jemson, W. D.
Jenkins, H. R.
Jensen, E. E.
Jensen, Marenus H.
Jensen, Marjorie
Jensen, W. Svarre
Jepson, Robert E.
Jepthas, Alex. D.
Jeremiah, M. S.
Jewell, E. L.
Jimeno, Eliseo A.
Jochmans, François
Johannsson, Johann E.
Johansen, Svein B.
John, Elaine M.
Johns, Alger Francis
Johnson, A. J.
Johnson, C. Delmar
Johnson, Cleo V.
Johnson, Duane S.
Johnson, George C.
Johnson, I. J.
Johnson, Jeannette
Johnson, Mildred Lee
Johnson, Patricia
Johnsson, William G.
Johnston, Bruce
Johnston, Carl S.
Johnston, Patricia
Joiner, James
Jones, Esther
Jones, Ralph H.
Jordal, Odd
Jordon, Richard D.
Joseph, Manasseh
Juberg, Morten
Juriansz, Ralph B.

Karr, Eldyn
Keizer, Ivor
Kempf, J.
Kennedy, Betsy
Kesler, Mervin
King, Debra L.
Kinjo, Kenyu
Kirstein, William
Kiser, Jerry
Kisku, Manick
Kline, Fylvia F.
Klooster, Judson
Knott, Harald
Knowles, George
Knowles, Lillian
Kohls, Tom
Koleada, Helen
Koo Hyun Suh
Kromann, L. G.
Krushenitsky, V.
Kudo, Shojiro
Kuen, Joseph N.P.
Kuma-Korante, Charles
Kusekwa, George M.
Kyte, Robert E.

Laco, Gustavo A.
Lahti, Matti J.
Lall, Prem H.
Lampeang, Pieter
Lanares, Pierre
Landa, Eugene J.
Landis, Erma L.
Lane, Bruce
Lange, O. W.
Larson, Lewis J.
Larwood, Lens G.
Laspe, William L.
Lauda, Caris H.
Lavooy, Humberto
Lawson, H. D.
Layman, Rachel K.
Leadbetter, Ray M.
Lecklider, Mrs. J. D.
Lee, Anna S.
Lee, Clinton W.
Lee, Don H.
Lee, Gordon A.
Lee, Howard M.
Lee, John R.
Lee, Mrs. Milton
Lee, W. S.
Lee Yung Lin
Lehmann, Richard
Leichner, Donaldo
Leiska, Wolfgang
Lemke, E. C.
Lemon, Duane
Lemon, P. F.
Lempinen, Heimo
Lenz, Mercedes E.
Leonhardt, Russell
Leonie, Andrew
Lessa, Rubens S.
Leung, H. S.
Lew, John M.
Lewis, Stephen T.
Lewis, Virgil K.
Liebelt, Ben J.
Liebelt, Peggy
Lighthall, Wallace J.
Lim, C. B.
Lim, Michael
Lind, M. E.
Liscombe, George W.
Lister, Robert L.
Litchfield, Neil W.
Litster, J. G.
Litster, W. G.
Litten, Lowell
Liu, Richard
Liwidjaja, Elisha
Llaguno, Perfecto L.
Llaguno, S. L.
Lloyd, George
Lloyd, Marjorie Lewis
Lo Hing So
Loasby, Roland E.
Lock, Lester N.
Lock, William Norman
Loewen, Marvin E.
Loewen, Sam C.
Lohne, Alf
Lombart, Claude A.
Londis, Dolores
Long, A. M.
Long, Henri
Longhofer, Wayne
Longway, E. L.
López, José
Lorenz, Felix
Lorenzo, Nicole
Louis, S. O. Jean
Lowe, Alice
Lowe, H. W.
Lowry, Morris C.
Lubis, Johnny
Lucas, Theodore
Luce, Carolyn V.

Lucero, Mariano Renedo
Ludescher, Edwin
Ludgate, T. Kenneth
Luepke, Siegfried
Luke, Handel
Lukk, Heino
Lumingkewas, Henky
Lutz, Evelyn Bigford
Luxton, Andrea
Lyko, Zachariasz
Lynd, A. L.
Lynsdale, Joan
Lyu, H. H.

Määttänen, Onni
McAdams, D. A.
McClintock, David
McClure, A. C.
McClure, Charlotte P.
McCumber, Robert A.
McCune, R. Dale
McCutcheon, O.D.F.
McDowell, E. G.
Mace, Grace D.
McFadden, Elisabeth S.
McFarland, J. Wayne
McFarlane, Milton
McGlawn, Van S.
Machamire, Paminus R.
McKee, A. C.
McKee, A. D.
McKenzie, L.
McKeone, Steven D.
Mackert, Keith
Mackett, C. H.
Mackie, Esther M.
McKinney, S. N.
McMillan, J. A.
McNutt, D. Wayne
Maddock, Dean
Madigan, Geoffrey A.
Madsen, Jens
Maganga, Joseph M.
Magee, George P.
Magi, Eduard
Magi, Trina J.
Mahele, Clement
Mahon, Jack
Mahorney, Sharryn
Maiorov, Eduardo
Makowski, M.
Malaka, Hanna
Malcolm, Roy E.
Manalaysay, Reuben G.
Manassian, Johnny
Manchur, Fred
Mangkei, Herman E.
Manley, M. O.
Manoram, Charles
Manrique, Alcibiades
Manrique, Walter
Mansell, Don
Manuel, P. W.
Manzolli, Italo
Marais, Agnes B.
Marley, E. L.
Marsh, Larry D.
Marshall, D. N.
Marshall, Sue
Marter, E. W.
Martin, Charles
Martin, T. K.
Martin, Wayne A.
Martinsen, Thure
Martinson, Arthur J.
Marx, R. A.
Mashingaidze, W. H.
Masitise, Peete
Masoka, Wenson L.
Mason, Alice S.
Mataya, Ron H.
Mathay, Mrs. C. A.
Mathews, George M.
Mathy, L. A.
Matthews, Elizabeth E.
Mattison, B. W.
Mattison, Kenneth R.
Maxwell, Arthur S.
Maxwell, C. Mervyn
Maxwell, Lawrence
Maxwell, S. G.
May, W. R.
Mayer, Edwin I.
Mayeur, M.
Mayeur, Edgar
Mayr, Werner
Medanich, J. F.
Menegusso, Eliseu
Mensah, C. B.
Meredith, Glynne
Merrow, Roberta
Mesa, Carlos
Meyer, Sylvain
Meyers, Daryl
Meyers, Samuel D.
Mhosva, Absalom
Michael, Darren L.
Midkiff, Marvin C.
Miettinen, Yrjö
Millard, Walter
Miller, C. A.
Miller, G. R.
Miller, Joseph H. D.
Miller, K. R.
Miller, Leslie M.
Millet, Garland J.
Mills, Merle
Milne, R. M.
Milne, Mrs. R. M.
Minchin, Gerald H.
Minder, Nick E.
Minder, Warren
Missud, Yvon
Mitchell, D.E.G.
Mitosva, A. M.
Mittleider, Kenneth J.
Miyashiro, James S.
Moahi, B.
Moi, John A.
Mole, Robert
Moline, Olof T.
Monnier, S.
Monod, Daniel
Montaña, Leodegario E.
Monteith, Ernest J.
Mooa, Baraniko
Mookerjee, Noney G.
Moon, Bud
Moon, Robert D.
Moor, Edith James
Moor, Fred B.
Moore, Archie
Moore, Lawrence F.
Moore, Mary Hunter
Moore, Roberta J.
Moore, Wesley A.
Moralde, Reuben P.
Morales, Carlos
Morel, Grace
Morenings, H. E.
Moreno, Francisco J.
Morey, Peter
Morgado, J. A.
Morgado, Rolando
Morgan, Clyde N.
Morgan, J. N.
Morita, Matsumi
Morton, Roger W.
Moses, I. K.
Moses, M. D.
Mostert, T. J., Jr.
Mubonenwa, Libonina
Muderspach, H.
Mugemana, Manasse
Munoz, Miguel
Murdoch, W. G.
Murray, Eric John
Murray, Milton
Murray, W. E.
Murrill, W. L.
Musgrave, Andrew R.
Musonda, Rashford
Mutentu, Kyambala
Mwamukonda, Lame

Naenny, Edouard
Nagakubo, Senzo
Nagel, Sherman A., Jr.
Nagele, Charles J.
Napitupulu, Immanuel R.
Nash, James R.
Nation, Ira Murl
Navamaratna, Salinee
Navarose, J. S.
Nazirian, M. N.
Neall, Ralph E.
Negri, Urban D.
Nelson, A. L.
Nelson, Lawrence M.

Nelson, Raymond
Nelson, W. Edwin
Nelson, W. G.
Nembhard, M. G.
Neri, Abraham O.
Nestares, Daniel
Neufeld, Mary
Newball, Jorge D.
Newball, Nancy
Newman, J. David
Nichol, F. D.
Nicholls, John H.
Nicholson, W. G.
Niedermaier, Johann
Nielsen, A. Falk
Nielsen, Bent
Nielsen, Elisabeth
Nielsen, Mae Mathews
Niemann, Henry
Niininen, Joel
Nishino, M.
Nishiura, K.
Nix, James
Nixon, Robert W.
Nixon, Roger R.
Noack, Walter
Nobuo, Willy
Noland, Boardman
Noltze, Ronald
Norcliffe, Lillian
Norman, R. Steven III
Norris, G. E.
Norwood, William Frederick
Nowak, Karel

Obeng, D. K.
Oberg, Renato Emir
Odom, R. L.
Oduro, Joseph
Oemcke, D. C.
Oh Man Kyu
Ojalis, D.
Olafsson, Gudmundur
Oldenhoff, W.
Olin, Reijo R.
Oliveira, Enoch de
Oliveira, Gideon de
Oliver, C. G.
Oliver, John B.
Ollivierre, Anthony
Olmstead, C. R.
Olsen, V. Norskov
Olson, A. V.
Olson, L. H.
Olson, Mildred Thompson
Olson, Wayne E.
Omans, Clarence D.
Ombuyi, P. M.
Onsoe, Kaleb
Oosterwal, Gottfried
Opsahl, Finn H.
Ornopia-Upsales, Annabelle
Ortner, Clifford A.
Osborn, Dick
Osborn, Robert
Osborn, Tom
Osmunson, E. R.
Oster, Kenneth
Osundina, Samuel Folorunso
Oswald, Caron
Otter, G. A.
Owusu-Mensa, Kofi
Ozanne, Gaye

Padilla, Guido Medina
Pairo Cusi, Mariano
Pak, C. U.
Pala, Ernst
Palange, L.
Palm, Erik H.
Palm, H. W.
Palma, Violeta C.
Palmer, C. E.
Palmer, L. R., Jr.
Palmer, Margaret E.
Palvie, S. T.
Pamplona, Jorge D.
Pang, T. S.
Parchment, John A., Jr.
Park, Lester E.
Parker, N. L.
Parmenter, Vernon B.
Parnell, Michael
Parr, R. H.
Parrish, Ann
Parsons, Leona Chew
Parsons, Roy B.
Paschal, L. A.
Pascoe, C.
Pascoe, W. L.
Patten, Rebecca
Patterson, Gary B.
Paypa, Joshua S.
Paytee, Lorenzo W.
Pearson, R. G.
Pearson, William D.
Pease, Norval F.
Peckham, D. H.
Peckham, Lori Tripp
Pedernal, Mrs. R. D.
Pedersen, Emanuel W.
Pedersen, John
Peeke, J. W.
Pein, Kyi
Peixoto da Silva, D.
Peltonen, Onni
Pengilley, R. E.
Pérau, Marcel
Percy, V. Hannibal
Perepelitza, A. W.
Pérez, Víctor Alfonso
Perkins, Curtis L.
Perkins, Malcolm W.
Perla, Juan Otoniel
Perrin, Roy E.
Peter, Kingsley C. J.
Peters, Andrew
Peterson, Laurell M.
Peterson, Myrna
Petrie, Ivor
Pettibone, Dennis
Peverini, Héctor J.
Pfeiffer, Baldur Ed
Pharo, Joe
Philip, Matthew K.
Phillips, Irma
Phillips, W. E.
Phoon Chek Yat
Pieringer, Ferdinand
Pierson, Robert G.
Piez, E. R.
Pifer, George
Pilar, Oseas C.
Pingho, B. F.
Pinkney, Addison V.
Pitt, Arthur A.
Pitter, Colin A.
Pizarro, Alejo
Plaatjes, Philip
Plantier, Anthony J.
Platner, C. Elwyn
Platt, Evelyn
Plubell, Dennis L.
Plummer, P. E.
Poddar, D. S.
Pogue, Oliver J.
Pohl, Helmuth
Poirier, Timothy
Poole, Loren E.
Pooley, Burt
Popa, D.
Porter, George C.
Postrero, J. J.
Pothier, Dominique
Poublan, Gerard
Powell, B. J.
Powers, C. L.
Powers, Sylvia P.
Powis, Beth
Powrie, L. N.
Pozo Moras, Luis del
Praestiin, Bent
Prall, Jay E.
Prasad, K. Johnendra
Predoljak, Vladimir
Preston, Calvin E.
Prince, M. Webster
Prior, Donald G.
Provonsha, Jack W.
Puyol, Carlos Buil

Quaile, Leonard D.
Quirante, L. L.

Rabello, Roberto Mendes
Rabuka, Mickey M.
Raelly, L. D.
Raethel, E. A.
Rafanan, David R.

Ranzolin, Leo
Rajoelison
Raju, Venkataswamy V.
Ramamonjisoa, J.
Ramos, Joaquim Nunes
Rampton, Howard F.
Randolph, C. E.
Rao, A. Prasada
Rao, K. Gopala
Raposo, Albert F.
Rappetta, SuzAnn
Raranta, Walter
Rau, Eugene W.
Read, W. E.
Rebok, Denton E.
Rector, James
Redding, Hubert
Reed, Martha
Rees, Don R.
Reid, F. G.
Reile, Harry C.
Reimche, D. S.
Reimche, Kenneth Dale
Reiner, R. L.
Reis, S.
Rema, D. P.
Remboldt, Erwin J.
Rene, Donovan
Renedo, Mariano
Retzer, Fernon
Reye, Arnold C.
Reye, Raymond
Reynolds, Donald G.
Reynolds, Louis B.
Reynolds, Robert L.
Rhoads, Gayle E.
Rice, Frank E.
Richards, H.M.S.
Richardson, Reginald W.
Richardson, Stephen A. L.
Richli, Alfred
Richter, R. W.
Rick, Rowena R.
Rider, Hattie Lee
Riegler, Otto
Rieseberg, Marilyn
Riffel, A. H.
Riffel, Oleva Atwood
Rigsby, G. Robert
Rimoldi, Ismaele
Rios, Felix
Ritchie, C. J.
Ritland, R. M.
Rittenhouse, Judy
Rivas, Augusto
Rivera, Carmen de
Robbins, Carrie J. A.
Roberts, Cassie C.
Roberts, Olive Lindberg
Robeson, V. Martin
Robinson, A. W., Jr.
Robinson, Leonard C.
Robinson, Virgil E.
Robinson, W. B.
Rock, C. B.
Roda, A. Z.
Rodgers, A. George
Rodriguez, Angel Manuel
Rodríguez, Eleodoro
Rodriguez, Tito
Rodríguez, Vicente
Rosales, Irineu
Rose, Leo S.
Ross, Charlotte
Rossi, Gianfranco
Roth, Ariel A.
Roth, Don A.
Rouhe, Olavi
Rouhe, U. K.
Rozema, Eunice
Ruby, William
Rudatsikira, Mitsindo
Rudisaile, H. A., Jr.
Rudy, Henry L.
Rue, George H.
Rue, Mrs. G. H.
Ruff, Stephen
Ruffcorn, John D.
Ruhaya, Ntwali
Ruiz B., Rubén
Rumble, Beverly J.
Runyan, Warren
Russell, Elsie M.
Russell, L. E.
Ryan, Michael J.

Sackett, John
Sackett, R. L.
Sackey, Ebenezer D.
Saejeng, Rungsit
Sage, Royal
Sager, William C.
Saint-Villiers, Paul F.
Saito, T.
Saliba, Slimen
Sample, Eugene
Samson, L. S.
Samuel, Hewton M.
Sanchez, Hector G.
Sand, Nestor
Sandberg, Lars
Sandy, Sahr D.
Sanes, Manuel S.
Sang Ok Shim
Santa Cruz, Oscar
Santini, Franco
Saulsbury, Everett
Saunders, K. W.
Schantz, Borge
Schaffner, M. H.
Scheidegger, Kurt
Schmidt, Ronald G.
Schneebauer, L.
Schneider, E. H.
Schoen, V. W.
Schomburg, William
Schranz, Roland
Schuenemann, B. E.
Schultz, I. E.
Schutter, Louis
Schwartz, Mike
Schwarz, Richard W.
Schwisow, Edwin A.
Scott, Bob
Scoggins, T. Henry
Scragg, Walter R. L.
Scriven, Wayne A.
Scully, J. V.
Scurry, Joyce
Seamount, Robert
Seiler, Ricky
Seligmann, K.
Seltzer, Sheldon D. H.
Seng, Gustav
Senkomo, Silas
Serns, Dan
Seybold, Blossom E.
Shahine, Samir
Shain, Jacquelyn Brown
Shawver, J. R.
Shepard, Evelyn
Shepard, James A., Jr.
Sheron, Carole A.
Shipowick, L. A.
Short, Donald K.
Shorter, Roland W.
Shultz, M. W.
Siagian, Edmund
Sibil, J. H.
Sica, Philip T.
Sierra, Rolando Montoya
Silva, Kevin F.
Simanungkalit, L.
Simmonds, W. H.
Simon, John D.
Simons, Norman G.
Singleton, H. D.
Sipkens, Ruth E.
Sircar, Nelson N.
Siregar, S. N.
Sispman, Milton
Skinner, L. A.
Skoretz, Bernard
Skoretz, Frank
Sládek, O.
Small, Mary
Smårs, Gunnar
Smit, Herman J.
Smit, S.
Smith, C. Roy
Smith, Clark
Smith, David B.
Smith, Derrell K.
Smith, Donald R.
Smith, Dunbar W.
Smith, E. Kenneth
Smith, George E.
Smith, George Fraser
Smith, Myrtle Neff

Smith, S. R.
Smith, William E.
Smyk, Andreas
Söderberg, Eric
Sohlmann, Charles J.
Soloniuk, W. G.
Soneda, Kenji
Sonestam, Egon
Sonnenberg, Lydia M.
Sonter, Allen
Soper, Francis A.
Soper, G. R.
Sorajjakool, Sunti
Sorensen, Chris P.
Soto, Atanasio
Soto, Victor
Southcott, L.D.W.
Sowers, W. A.
Sox, Aileen Andres
Spangle, R. E.
Spangler, J. R.
Spangler, Marie C.
Sparks, Vernon C.
Spaulding, Earl
Specht, Walter F.
Speh, Kathryne
Spradley, Jean
Spruill, Karen
Staples, A. W.
Staples, Warren E.
Stauffer, J. Paul
Stavnem, M. K.
Steed, Lincoln
Steenberg, Hendrik F.
Stenbakken, R. O.
Stephenson, J. M.
Sterner, Jerry L.
Stevens, James L.
Stevenson, E. G.
Stevenson, E. J.
Stevenson, G. S.
Stevenson, H. W.
Stevenson, John
Stevenson, Michael
Steveny, Georges
Stewart, A. G.
Stewart, Constance B.
Stewart, Kenneth
Sticker, Elton
Stiles, Jack C.
Stockhausen, Allan C.
Stokes, R. F.
Stoltz, Garth "Duff"
Stoneburner, Ella May
Storz, W. F.
Stout, Lewis A.
Stovall, Samuel W.
Streeter, E. R.
Streithorst, Walter J.
Stricker, Valerie L.
Strickland, Doris
Sturges, J. Hubert
Sturges, Keith W.
Sturzenegger, Karl
Summerton, Mildred
Sumpter, Ward D.
Sundaram, S.
Sundin, Carl
Supunavong, Nursia
Šušljić, Milan R.
Sutcliffe, David C.
Sutherland, Adeline Victoria
Svenson, Ragnar
Swanepoel, D. H.
Swannell, R. J.
Swanson, Evan
Swanson, Mildred
Sweetland, Loraine F.
Szakacs, J.
Szigeti, Jeno

Tabingo, Remelito A.
Tabuenca, Juan
Tachmissjan, Agop
Taggi, Ursula
Tahay T., R. Moises
Tambunan, E. H.
Tambunan, P. L.
Tan, Daniel
Tang, C. H.
Tarr, W. Claude
Tasa, Piuki
Tauran, R. H.
Taylor, Charles R.
Taylor, Clifton L.
Taylor, June
Taylor, R. W.
Taylor, William H.
Taylor, William Holmes
Teesdale, W. Homer
Teeuwen, J. Frank
Tejel, A.
ter Horst, T. A.
Terry, J. B.
Tetteh, E. C.
Teubert, Holger
Tew, Norman L.
Thappa, Deep Bahadur
Tharp, Paul R.
The, James
Thomas, Boban
Thomas, Don H.
Thomas, F. G.
Thomas, F. H.
Thomas, K. E.
Thomas, Thambi
Thomas, Y. G.
Thompson, G. Ralph
Thompson, Thomas P.
Thompson, W. A.
Thomsen, Eugene V.
Thomsen, Marilyn
Thomson, Alec C.
Thomson, S. G.
Thomson, W. W.
Thorpe, Alayne D.
Thorvaldsson, Johann
Thrift, E. G.
Thrift, L. R.
Thrower, Aubrey B.
Thurber, Merwin R.
Tidwell, Charles H., Jr.
Tilghman, K. W.
Tilstra, K.
Tilstra, R. K.
Timple, A. B.
Tinkler, Desmond E.
Tippett, Harry M.
Tobler, Gustav
Toews, Mary R.
Tolhurst, Athal H.
Tompkins, J. O.
Toop, Charles L.
Torkelsen, Max C. II
Torkelson, T. R.
Torres, Jose
Torrey, C. L.
Towery, Mable H.
Townend, B.H.R.
Townend, M. G.
Traeder, Lothar E.
Treiyer, H. R.
Tressler, H. J.
Tsai, Samuel S.
Ts'ao, James Tsun-kai
Tucker, Bill
Tung, Peter
Turambi, Wim
Turner, Louis
Turner, W. G.
Turpen, Kenneth
Twist, O. H.
Tyner, Mitchell A.

Uebersax, Otto
Uhl, Henry A.
Unhola, Aarne
Uren, T. H.
Uruma, Masao
Utt, Richard H.
Utt, Walter C.
Utterbäck, Bertil

Vail, W. R.
van der Merwe, Johannes Carolus
van der Ploeg, C. E.
Van Der Veken, Henri
Van Dolson, Bobbie Jane
Van Dolson, Leo R.
Van Heerden, W.S.J.
Van Lange, Ivan
van Oossanen, Karel C.
van Putten, C. G.
Vande Vere, Emmett K.
Vandenvelde, Georges
Vandermark, Maybelle E.
Varona, Orvillo B.
Vaucher, Alfred
Vaughan, Anna May

Vasquez, Manuel
Vázquez López, Miguel
Veitch, W. R.
Veloso, Mario
Verfaillie, Maurice
Vervoort, Eugeen
Vetne, Olaf
Vetter, H. G.
Vine, R. D.
Vink, D.
Vogel, Emilio
von Pohle, Berit
Voorthuis, F. J.
Voth, Harvey E.
Vyhmeister, Werner

Waber, Karl
Waddell, Ralph F.
Wade, Kenneth R.
Wade, Loron T.
Wagenblast, Arne
Wagiran, Jonathan W. S.
Wakeham, Irene
Wale, Nathaniel M.
Walalangi, R. H.
Walde, E. R.
Walker, Lisa S.
Wallace, Gaston W.
Waller, John O.
Waller, W. H.
Walter, Marvin
Walters, H. S.
Walther, Daniel
Wang, H. C.
Ward, F. Percival
Warren, Donald M.
Wart, Paula J.
Washington, James A.
Waterman, Rita
Waters, Keith D.
Watson, C. D.
Watts, K. E.
Wawondatu, Robert
Waynne, Harold M.
Webb, Donna
Weber, William
Webster, Athol M.
Webster, F. C.
Webster, K. G.
Weddle, Robert S.
Wedin, Goran
Weeks, Howard B.
Weick, Elie
Weir, M. E.
Weis, Carl C.
Weis, Theofield G.
Weithers, W. W.
Welch, Donald W.
Welch, Howard J.
Wendth, Ernest N.
Wensell, Egil H.
Werekeitzen, Cristobal
Werner, Hans
Werner, Mayr B.
Werner, P. G.
Wernick, Francis W.
Westerlund, H.
Wetmore, Thomas E.
Whea, David Z.
Wheaton, John
Wheeler, Gerald
Whelpley, J. Elmer
Whelpley, Theresa A.
White, Arthur L.
White, E. F.
White, Edward E.
White, Herb
White, S. E.
Whitmill, Marolyn
Whitney, K. W.
Whitworth, Gary C.
Wick, Palmer G.
Wick, Ted
Wickham, Carol J.
Wieland, R. J.
Wiggins, Ronald C.
Wiklander, Bertil
Wilcox, Wendell L.
Wild, W. A.
Wilday, Lawrence A.
Wilkinson, R. K.
Will, Stanley S.
Will, Walter T.
Williams, Gerald
Williams, Roy F.
Williams, Sylvia
Wilson, Colin
Wilson, Mrs. Howard C.
Wilson, Kenneth W.
Windeyer, H. Julian
Wines, E. C.
Wing, Carlos
Winn, Ted
Winslow, Grover C.
Winter, Thelma
Wise, Boni
Wisel, Lee Marie
Wisener, Maureen M.
Wogu, Joseph W.
Wolff, Edir Kern
Wolfkill, Marilyn
Wondim, Agegnehu
Wong, James
Wood, James R.
Wood, Kenneth H.
Wood, Miriam
Wood, Peter R.
Woodruff, G. M.
Woodruff, W. L.
Wood-Stotesbury, V.
Woolley, David D.
Woolsey, Raymond
Woysch, Martin
Wright, Carol
Wright, Donald E.
Wright, Lunett
Wright, Ruth
Wu Chook Ying
Wu Sze Fai, James
Wynne, Harold M.

Yamamoto, Tetsuya
Yamanishi, Teru
Yanami, Hidesada
Yanami, Yasutsugu
Yeatts, Roy O.
Yoon Choong Yuh
Yost, F. Donald
Young, Ethel
Young, Samuel C.
Youngberg, Russel E.

Zackrison, James W.
Zarka, D.
Zgerya, Ivan I.
Ziegler, Cesar Roberto
Zilgalvis, Valdis
Ziprick, Lottie
Zurcher, Adi
Zurcher, E.
Zurcher, Jean

Preface

The *Seventh-day Adventist Encyclopedia* is a compendium of facts about Seventh-day Adventists (in this work sometimes abbreviated SDAs)—their work, beliefs, organization, methods, and philosophies. The work is intended to inform not only church members but non-SDAs as well who may be inquiring about the church's work and beliefs.

The present volume is the church's first attempt to systematize information concerning Seventh-day Adventists in encyclopedic form. The idea of a denominational encyclopedia was conceived in 1959 and was suggested to the Review and Herald Publishing Association by Earle Hilgert, professor of New Testament literature at Andrews University, Berrien Springs, Michigan. The immensity of the undertaking led the leaders of the publishing house to set aside the idea at the time. However, the plan was again suggested in 1962, upon the completion of the *Seventh-day Adventist Bible Students' Source Book,* volume 9 of the Commentary Reference Series. At that time the publishing house was looking for a suitable volume with which to complete the series, and the conclusion was reached that a denominational encyclopedia would fittingly round out the series and represent a worthy climax to the reference volumes. Action was taken by the board of the house on April 4, 1962, that the project be launched immediately.

Don F. Neufeld, who had been an associate editor on the first seven volumes and the editor of volumes 8 and 9, was asked to be editor in chief; Julia Neuffer, who had been assistant editor and associate editor of the previous volumes, was asked to be associated with him; and Martha Reed was appointed as editorial secretary. Later several assistant editors were added to the staff—Raymond F. Cottrell to edit the articles on theology; Donald E. Mansell; and George A. Selivanoff. There were in addition two part-time assistant editors—Gerald H. Minchin and Virgil E. Robinson.

I. Planning and Production. The project was announced to the church leaders assembled in the Spring Meeting of 1962; they commended the publishing house for its undertaking and pledged their cooperation.

The announcement of the plan to the church at large was made at the General Conference session in July 1962. At that time contacts were made with the heads of conferences, institutions, and the various divisions, whose help would be needed in so large an enterprise. They accepted willingly their assignments of providing articles on their respective areas of administration.

1. *How the Articles Were Obtained.* The more than 2,000 articles in the present volume were obtained as follows: In the North American Division the articles on the history and development of Seventh-day Adventist work were assigned to writers by the presidents of the various local conferences, who took the responsibility for these articles; the articles on institutions, such as schools, hospitals, and publishing houses, were provided by the institutions themselves. For articles covering the history and development of SDA work in the various countries and institutions of the rest of the world field, the presidents of the various divisions accepted the task of selecting competent writers, who would be responsible to these leaders and would submit their articles to them. These division leaders were L. C. Naden (Australasian), O. Gmehling (Central European), C. P. Sorensen (Far Eastern), C. L. Powers (Inter-American), R. A. Wilcox (Middle East), E. E. Roenfelt (Northern European), J. J. Aitken (South American), R. S. Lowry (Southern Asia), Marius Fridlin (Southern European), and R. H. Pierson (Trans-Africa). They were asked to have the manuscripts widely read and to revise them before submitting them.

The various departments and branches of the General Conference likewise furnished the articles on their work, as did editors of periodicals on their papers. Their contributions are gratefully acknowledged.

These various organizations bore the expense of preparing these articles, enabling the price of the book to be kept within a reasonable figure. Their contributions are greatly appreciated.

In the area of theology, those competent in their fields were chosen to write the various articles. In these articles it was aimed to present not only what the church believes but how it came to adopt these beliefs. This feature of tracing the development of doctrine, where such occurred, in addition to the doctrine itself, is a unique contribution of this volume of the Commentary Reference Series. The range of topics was chosen after counsel with Bible teachers of SDA universities and colleges, who met in convention at Pacific Union College, Angwin, California, immediately after the 1962 General Conference session in San Francisco, California. The selection of writers was made in counsel with W.G.C. Murdoch, dean of the SDA Theological Seminary, Andrews University, and Earle Hilgert, originator of the encyclopedia idea, both of whom contributed a number of articles.

The biographies were written by various writers. The majority were prepared by the editorial staff, who had access to various sources, such as the personnel and retirement files of the General Conference, and to various periodicals. In many instances they sent questionnaires to those who had access to sources not available in the editorial office.

The editorial staff also contributed many articles of a miscellaneous nature.

2. *Editorial Procedure.* After the manuscripts were received they were carefully checked and rechecked editorially. Then two copies of the material were sent to the division presidents, local conference presidents, heads of North American institutions, General Conference department heads, and periodical editors. They were asked to update the articles and to make any final revisions. All efforts were made to have the material as accurate as possible.

In addition to those who had read various manuscripts before submission to the publishers, two readers were chosen to read the entire volume. These were Walter R. Beach, secretary of the General Conference, and Walter E. Murray, one of the general vice presidents of the General Conference. Their efforts and suggestions are greatly appreciated. Two others were asked to read the articles on theology—Harry W. Lowe, general field secretary of the General Conference, and Merwin R. Thurber, book editor of the Review and Herald Publishing Association. Their contributions too are gratefully acknowledged.

To all who contributed to this project in any way—to the more than 700 authors scattered throughout the world, to those who accepted responsibility for providing the various articles, to those in the division and other offices upon whom the responsibility was placed for collecting, processing, and revising the manuscripts, to the hundreds of readers who read the articles in their various stages, to those in the churches in the North American Division who filled out questionnaires to provide background information for writing the history of Seventh-day Adventist work in the various conferences, and to those who lent encouragement and counsel in a difficult and challenging task—we express our heartfelt gratitude.

II. Contents. This reference work on a worldwide denomination necessarily covers a wide variety of articles, yet the contents may be summarized in a few principal categories—church history, organization, institutions, biographies, beliefs, practices, methods, definitions, and activities.

1. *Church History.* For the North American Division (the United States, Canada, and Bermuda) each article dealing with the history and statistics of the church covers a conference (the church unit comprising one or a few states or provinces). In the other divisions, covering the rest of the world, each article deals with a country, an island or island group, or other geographical unit. Length of treatment is roughly proportionate to the SDA membership, but there are variations.

For each country a descriptive and historical introductory section has been included—not a comprehensive survey, but a sketch derived from general reference books, intended to furnish a few basic facts on the land, the people, and the historical and religious background that will form an introduction to the story of Seventh-day Adventist work in that country. For more information the reader may consult a general encyclopedia and an atlas.

This pattern has not been followed for the United States and Canada, because most of the readers are presumed to be in those two countries. This is also the reason the church history is dealt with in smaller units—the conferences.

2. *Church Organization and Operation.* Besides a general article on organization, which describes the history and structure of the denominational organization, there are articles on topics ranging from the local church—its membership, officers, services, and auxiliary organizations and societies—through the conference (or mission, or section, or other unit composed of local churches) and the union (or union conference, or union mission), to the worldwide administrative body, the General Conference. There are also articles on the worldwide territorial divisions of the General Conference, and its functional departments and other bureaus and agencies.

3. *Institutions.* There are articles on many of the church-owned and -operated colleges, secondary schools, sanitariums and hospitals, publishing houses, health food factories, orphanages, and retirement homes. The clinics and dispensaries are only listed, and with regard to the nearly 5,000 elementary schools, only the number in particular areas is given in statistics on that area. Generally, only schools on at least the senior high school level are included.

4. *Biographies.* The encyclopedia contains hundreds of biographical sketches of men and women who played a notable part in the work of the church or were "first" in various parts of the world (it does not include any living persons). The list of names was drawn from SDA historical works and accounts in the church papers, and from the lists and data submitted by the various divisions. A few who were not Seventh-day Adventists are included because they have been mentioned or quoted in SDA works and therefore need identification. The length of the sketch is not necessarily an index of the subject's importance. Some who accomplished much seldom took time to write reports to the church papers, and hence little is known of them; some required a longer account because they happened to work in many different places; some of the variation is because of the difference in the style of the authors of the sketches.

5. *Beliefs and Practices.* Since Seventh-day Adventists find themselves in harmony with other conservative Christians on the basic doctrines, such as salvation through faith, and Christ's preexistence, deity, and atonement, it was not thought necessary to include lengthy articles on these topics. A longer treatment was thought necessary on doctrines on which SDAs differ from the majority—such as the nature of the millennium, immortality only in Christ (not originated by Seventh-day Adventists), or the seventh-day Sabbath (shared with the Seventh Day Baptists, but approached somewhat differently). The Sabbath, for example, is treated at length from different angles. Occasionally a minor doctrine of an obscure or once-controversial nature (such as the "daily" of Dan. 8 and 11) required a disproportionately long discussion to clarify its historical background. Views on the prophecies of Daniel and the Revelation are summarized under Daniel, Interpretation of, and Revelation, Interpretation of. Because this book is a part of a reference series containing a seven-volume Bible commentary, the reader is referred to the *Commentary* for detailed exposition of Bible doctrines.

6. *Miscellaneous Topics.* Definitions are required to explain various names or phrases of organizations, methods, and activities—such as church school (a church-operated elementary school), Ingathering (an annual appeal for funds), Bible studies (a method of personal evangelism), Pathfinder Clubs (the SDA equivalent of Scouting, with religious emphasis), and Medical Cadet Corps (those in training for noncombatant medical military service).

Some articles that were planned have been omitted because the historical information is lacking or insufficient, or because of insufficient space.

III. Sources of Information. Except for the descriptive and historical introductions to the articles on the countries, which have been taken mostly from standard encyclopedias and reference works (such as the *Encyclopaedia Britannica, World Almanac,* and *National Geographic Atlas),* original sources have been used whenever possible either in writing or in verifying the articles. These sources include everything from personal reminiscences and local church records to newspaper clippings to firsthand accounts in the files of the union or division periodicals and the *Review and Herald,* also school bulletins, yearbooks, statistical reports, and official minutes of conference sessions or of institutional boards, retirement records, and obituaries. Not surprisingly, in the assembling of thousands of articles from around the globe, written by hundreds of contributors using a wide variety of sources, occasional discrepancies have appeared in spelling, names, dates, and facts. The discrepancy may be genuine, indicating an error, either in one of the articles or in one of various sources used by the several writers. However, it may be only apparent—a difference in date between an individual's appointment and arrival; between the beginning of construction and the completion of a building; or the difference between the founding of an institution as a clinic and of the same institution, later, as a hospital.

The *SDA Encyclopedia* staff and the Review and Herald copy editors have checked facts as far as possible from the materials available in either the Review and Herald or the General Conference, which includes most of the sources mentioned above except the personal accounts and the local records and local periodicals. Some of the discrepancies have been resolved through checking original sources, and others through correspondence. (Certain authors, correspondents in the division offices, General Conference personnel, and others deserve commendation for service beyond the call of duty for their aid to the inquiring editors.)

The best that the editors could do was to sift with care, taking into account the probable relative trustworthiness of the source material used. Experience has shown that a person's recollections in afteryears (and even more an individual's obituary, written by someone else, probably in haste and under stress) will often disagree with that individual's own firsthand account submitted at the time of the events to the *Review and Herald* or to some other church paper. Even official contemporary sources can be misleading: a *Yearbook,* a school bulletin, or the minutes of a conference session may list an appointment that was rescinded before it went into effect. In one case, the contemporary records trace a couple through their appointment to a mission field, their arrival in the country, and their travel en route to their location; yet they never actually served there, for the wife's sudden illness turned them back before they reached their station.

In many articles there is a possible uncertainty of one year in the terms of presidents of conferences or heads of schools because they are based only on the *Yearbook* listing, from which one cannot always be certain in what year a person is replaced by a successor. (In general, the *Yearbook* of a certain year gives the information for the preceding year.) Also the date of the organization of an institution or a conference may be recorded differently in two sources because the organization was voted, and the officers elected, late in the year, but the organization began to function the next year.

The editors have in many articles added early historical information derived from contemporary sources, such as firsthand accounts in early files of the *Review and Herald,* that were not available to the original writer of the article. In some cases, when two conflicting accounts appear in different sources, both have been included and the reader is left to decide between them.

The spelling of place names has in general been determined by the usage in the *National Geographic Atlas of the World.*

Denominational statistics have generally been taken from the *Statistical Report,* and the listing of territories under each division article has been taken from the *Seventh-day Adventist Yearbook.*

1976
REVISED EDITION

The *Seventh-day Adventist Encyclopedia* was first revised 10 years after the original appeared in 1966. During those years the work of the church developed rapidly, and many changes took place. The 1976 edition of the *SDA Encyclopedia* reflected that development and those changes, and presented a picture of the church as it was at the time of the 1975 General Conference session in Vienna. Changes in organization effected at that time appeared in the Revised Edition. Information with respect to all organizations and institutions of the church was also updated. Biographical sketches of outstanding leaders who had died since 1966 were also included. Otherwise the articles remained as they were in the original edition.

For the revised *SDA Encyclopedia,* copies of the original articles were sent to the leaders in the various fields for reappraisal and updating. Articles on new institutions and organizations were written by authorized individuals in the field and submitted to the editors.

1996
SECOND REVISED EDITION

During the past two decades remarkable growth and change has taken place in the Seventh-day Adventist Church. Illustrative of this is the country of Mozambique, which in 1976 had 44 churches attended by 13,236 members. In 1993 nearly 80,000 members attend 473 churches. In the light of what has happened since 1976, General Conference president Robert Folkenberg invited the division presidents and institutional leaders in the worldwide church to submit revisions and new articles to the editors. Nearly all responded with material gathered from officers and leaders in their respective fields. Six hundred fifty men and women contributed to the Second Revised Edition. The youngest was a student of 14 and the oldest a retiree of 80.

Because of the almost overwhelming amount of information received, the editorial process encompassed approximately two years. In the case of the few who did not respond, the editors drew upon the *Seventh-day Adventist Yearbook* and the *World Almanac* to update the articles.

After the revised copy was submitted to the publisher, Richard W. Coffen served as in-house editor, and the Review and Herald copy editors carefully checked the material for accuracy and consistency in style.

This edition was done entirely on computer, a method nearly unheard-of at the time of the first revision.

The world field was invited to submit additional biographies of people who made considerable contribution to the church during their lives. Some 200 new biographical sketches are included. There are undoubtedly many others who should have been added, but the editors had no way of knowing of these.

As far as possible, this new edition of the *SDA Encyclopedia* reflects the changes in the church through 1994. However, even as we go to press, progressive changes are taking place.

List of Abbreviations

1. ***Books of the Bible***

Gen. Ex. Lev. Num. Deut. Joshua Judges Ruth 1 Sam. 2 Sam. 1 Kings 2 Kings 1 Chron. 2 Chron. Ezra Neh. Esther Job Ps. Prov. Eccl. S. of Sol. Isa. Jer. Lam. Eze. Dan. Hosea Joel Amos Obadiah Jonah Micah Nahum Hab. Zeph. Haggai Zech. Mal. Matt. Mark Luke John Acts Rom. 1 Cor. 2 Cor. Gal. Eph. Phil. Col. 1 Thess. 2 Thess. 1 Tim. 2 Tim. Titus Philemon Heb. James 1 Peter 2 Peter 1 John 2 John 3 John Jude Rev.

2. ***Other Abbreviations***

AA	*The Acts of the Apostles,* by Ellen G. White
ADRA	Adventist Development and Relief Agency International
AJY	Adventist Junior Youth (Society)
AMC	Adventist Media Center
ANF	*Ante-Nicene Fathers*, edited by Alexander Roberts and James Donaldson (10 vols.; New York, 1885-1896).
APHS	Adventist Professional Health Services in South Africa
art.	article
ASI	Adventist-Laymen's Services and Industries
ATS	Adventist Theological Society
ATS	American Temperance Society
AU	Andrews University
AUC	Atlantic Union College
AUSS	*Andrews University Seminary Studies*
AVS	International Audio Visual Service
AWR	Adventist World Radio
AY	Adventist Youth (Society)
b.	born
c.	circa, "about"
cf.	confer, "compare"
ch(s).	chapter(s)
CH	*Counsels on Health*, by Ellen G. White
CHL	Christian Home Library Series
CME	College of Medical Evangelists, Loma Linda University
COL	*Christ's Object Lessons*, by Ellen G. White
CUC	Columbia Union College
CRS	Christian Record Services
CS	*Counsels on Stewardship*, by Ellen G. White
CT	*Counsels to Parents, Teachers, and Students*, by Ellen G. White
CW	*Counsels to Writers and Editors*, by Ellen G. White
d.	died

DA	*The Desire of Ages*, by Ellen G. White
Ed	*Education*, by Ellen G. White
ed.	edition, editor, edited
EMC	Emmanuel Missionary College
enl.	enlarged
est.	estimate, estimated
Ev	*Evangelism*, by Ellen G. White
EW	*Early Writings of Ellen G. White*
f., ff.	following page, pages
FE	*Fundamentals of Christian Education*, by Ellen G. White
fl.	flourished
fol., fols.	folio, folios
GC	General Conference of Seventh-day Adventists
GC	*The Great Controversy*, by Ellen G. White
Gr.	Greek
GW	*Gospel Workers,* by Ellen G. White
Heb.	Hebrew
ibid.	*ibidem,* "in the same place" (referring to the preceding reference)
i.e.	*id est,* "that is"
JMV	Junior Missionary Volunteer (Society)
Jos. *Ant.*	Josephus, *Antiquities*
Jos. *War*	Josephus, *Wars of the Jews*
KJV	King James Version
LLU	Loma Linda University
LS	*Life Sketches of Ellen G. White*
LSU	La Sierra University
LXX	Septuagint
MB	*Thoughts From the Mount of Blessing*, by Ellen G. White
MH	*The Ministry of Healing*, by Ellen G. White
MM	*Medical Ministry*, by Ellen G. White
MS, MSS	manuscript, manuscripts
MV	Missionary Volunteer (Society)
MYP	*Messages to Young People*, by Ellen G. White
n.	footnote
NKJV	New King James Version
no(s).	number(s)
NPNF	*A Select Library of Nicene and Post-Nicene Fathers,* ed. by Philip Schaff and others. 1st series, 14 vols.; 1905-1917. 2nd series, 14 vols.; 1890-1900. Both series reprinted by Eerdmans.
N.S.	new series
NT	New Testament
OT	Old Testament
p., pp.	page, pages
passim	here and there
PG	J.-P. Migne, ed., *Patrologia . . . Graeca.* 161 vols. in 166. Paris, 1857-1866.
PK	*The Story of Prophets and Kings*, by Ellen G. White
PP	*Patriarchs and Prophets*, by Ellen G. White

PPPA	Pacific Press Publishing Association
pub.	published, publishing
PUC	Pacific Union College
1QS	The Sectarian Rule of the Community (from Qumran cave 1)
1QSa	Adjunct to the Rule of the Community (from same cave)
4Q Test	Sheet of testimonia (from Qumran cave 4)
r	recto (obverse side of a folio, right-hand page)
rev.	revised
RH, R&H	Review and Herald® Publishing Association
RSV	Revised Standard Version
SB	*Seventh-day Adventist Bible Students' Source Book*
S.B.	systematic benevolence
SC	*Steps to Christ*, by Ellen G. White
SDA	Seventh-day Adventist
SDACom	*Seventh-day Adventist Bible Commentary*
SDADic	*Seventh-day Adventist Bible Dictionary*
SDB	Seventh Day Baptist
sec.	section
1SG (2SG, etc.)	*Spiritual Gifts* (4 vols.), by Ellen G. White
sic	"thus"
1SM (2SM, etc.)	*Selected Messages* (3 vols.), by Ellen G. White
SPA	Southern Publishing Association
SR	*The Story of Redemption*, by Ellen G. White
1T (2T, etc.)	*Testimonies to the Church* (9 vols.), by Ellen G. White
T. & M.	Tract and Missionary (Society)
Te	*Temperance*, by Ellen G. White
TM	*Testimonies to Ministers and Gospel Workers*, by Ellen G. White
tr.	translator, translated
UC	Union College
UN	United Nations
USSR	Union of Soviet Socialist Republics
v	verso (reverse side of a folio, left-hand page)
v.	verse
v.	versus
vs.	verses
vol(s).	volume(s)
WCTU	Woman's Christian Temperance Union
WM	*Welfare Ministry*, by Ellen G. White
WWC	Walla Walla College

A

AALBORG, DON L. (1929-1989). Minister, conference administrator. Born Feb. 2, 1929, at Hurley, South Dakota, he was a graduate of Campion Academy and Union College, and in 1975 he graduated from Georgia State University with an M.Ed. degree in school administration. He was married May 27, 1951, to Viva Carol Ellis.

He served a ministerial internship in the Oklahoma Conference, and began his own first pastorate in Vinita, Oklahoma, in 1954. Continuing pastoral work in Oklahoma, he was ordained there in 1956. In 1959 he became youth director and educational superintendent of the conference.

The Georgia-Cumberland Conference called him in 1965 to be youth director. During the five years he spent in that work, he directed in the rebuilding of the conference's Camp Cumby-Gay. In 1970 he became the conference superintendent of education, and in 1978 he was elected secretary of the conference. During the 10 years of his service in that capacity he coordinated the development of the conference's Cohutta Springs Adventist Center.

Aalborg became president of the Texas Conference in 1988, and served in that capacity until his death Sept. 8, 1989.

AB ESDAKOST. *See* Esdakost Food Company.

AB HALSANS KOK. *See* Healthy Kitchen Food Company.

AB SVENSKA NUTANA. *See* Swedish Nutana Food Company.

ABA HEALTH CENTRE AND MOTHERLESS CHILDREN'S HOME. A 50-bed facility that serves most of east Nigeria. It was dedicated on March 25, 1984. The East Nigeria Conference had operated a motherless babies' home before the center was opened. After the center was dedicated, it took over the administration of the babies' home.

The Motherless Babies' Home cares for 20-25 children from birth or soon afterward until they become 2 years old; then they are sent to foster homes. The health center contributes part of its profit to add to conference and public donations to cover the expense of running the home.

The center also has used part of its profits to expand the facilities. As of 1993 the center has three buildings for wards, an outpatient clinic, and a laboratory. There also is a mortuary and two duplexes that are being used for medical doctors. In 1992 the center admitted 2,533 patients and treated 17,354 outpatients.

Medical Directors: E. N. Nzotta, 1984; N. P. Mosqueda, 1985-1990; E. E. Enyinna, 1991- .

ABBOTSFORD ADVENTIST VILLA. A retirement villa located in Abbotsford, British Columbia, built by the British Columbia Conference in 1981 to provide low-cost housing in the lower mainland for church members. The facility contains six two-bedroom suites and 21 single-bedroom suites. Unlike Okanagan Manor, a personal-care facility operated by the British Columbia Conference, the suites were for sale to church members. Many were sold, but the remainder retained by the conference were rented. Plans called for the development of phase 2 as a personal-care or nursing home that would provide a dining room large enough to serve all the residents. Because the application for government funding was not approved, phase 2 was not completed.

ABBOTT, GEORGE KNAPP (1880-1959). Physician, administrator. A graduate of the American Medical Missionary College (1903), he began the practice of medicine in Burbank, California. In 1906 he married Dr. Cora Richards, and the two went to Loma Linda Sanitarium to assist in developing a medical school. He was president of the Loma Linda College of Evangelists (1907-1910), and then dean of the College of Medical Evangelists and medical superintendent of the sanitarium (1911-1914).

After his service at Loma Linda he continued in denominational work for 32 years, serving as medical director of St. Helena

Sanitarium, Washington Sanitarium, and Glendale Sanitarium.

Among his many writings are the books *The Witness of Science, Hydrotherapy and Electrotherapy for Nurses,* and *Technique of Hydrotherapy and Massage.*

ABC. *See* Adventist Book Center.

ABELLA, JOSÉ (JOSEPH) (1892-1928). Pioneer colporteur in Algeria, and minister in Portugal. He was born at Grañena de las Garrigas in the province of Lérida, Spain. When he was a young boy his parents moved to the town of Sabadell, where he was enrolled among the first students in the school opened by the pioneer SDA workers in Spain, the brothers Frank and Walter Bond. He and his mother, baptized by B. G. Wilkinson in 1904, were among the first Seventh-day Adventist converts baptized in Spain. After studying at the missionary school at Gland, Switzerland, for a time, Abella was sent from there with Ulysse Augsburger to Algeria, in North Africa, as a colporteur. About a year and a half later he was sent to Lisbon, Portugal, where he worked with Charles Rentfro until 1910. He then returned to North Africa and worked as a colporteur and evangelist until about 1920. In 1918 he married Antonia Mateu. In 1920 he was ordained to the ministry at the Latin Union session, held in Geneva, Switzerland. Afterward he went to Porto, Portugal, where his dedicated service brought many converts into the church. He died in May 1928 from tuberculosis, only a few months after contracting the disease.

ABERNATHY, WILLIAM EARL (1886-1964). Departmental secretary, treasurer, sanitarium manager, missionary. A native of Georgia, he was baptized as a result of evangelistic meetings held by F. C. Webster in Charleston, South Carolina. While employed at the Southern Publishing Company he was called to serve as home missionary and Sabbath school secretary, and treasurer of the Georgia-Cumberland Conference.

During his years of service he was treasurer of the Southeastern and Lake Union conferences, assistant auditor of the General Conference, and manager of two sanitariums. He also did treasury work in the Southwestern and North Pacific unions. After World War II he was sent to China to help in the rehabilitation of the work there, returning to the United States in 1948.

ABOMINATION OF DESOLATION. A cryptic designation found in Matt. 24:15, borrowed from Daniel (11:31; 12:11), where the corresponding phrase appears as "abomination that maketh desolate." Daniel predicted a great desecration of the Temple by an alien power in an attempt to substitute a false system of worship for that of the true God. The Gr. *bdelugma tēs erēmōseōs,* "abomination of desolation," in Matt. 24:15 is identical with the LXX translation (MS 88) of the Heb. *shiqqûṣ shomem* in Dan. 12:11. In Dan. 11:31 *shiqqûṣ meshômem* is rendered *bdelugma erēmōseōs* (MS 88). (Compare the LXX *bdelugma tōn erēmōseōn,* "the abomination of desolations," in Dan. 9:27; and *hamartia erēmōseōs,* "transgression of desolation," in Dan. 8:13; both of which doubtless are to be identified with the *bdelugma tēs erēmōseōs* of Dan. 11:31 and 12:11.) The Heb. *shiqqûṣ,* "abomination," is a common OT term describing an "idol deity" (e.g., Deut. 29:17; 2 Kings 23:24; 2 Chron. 15:8; Eze. 37:23). Such idol "abominations" set up in the Temple at Jerusalem in OT times were said to defile, or pollute, it (Jer. 7:30; Eze. 5:11). The Heb. *shamem,* a form of which is translated "desolation" (more literally, "something that makes desolate"), is used of the devastation caused by an invading army (Jer. 12:11), a scene that creates a sense of horror in a person beholding it (Jer. 18:16). The Heb. *pesha',* "transgression," in the parallel expression "transgression of desolation" in Dan. 8:13, is used of acts of apostasy and rebellion against God (see Amos 2:4, 6; Micah 1:5).

Interpretation. About 100 B.C. the writer of 1 Maccabees (see 1:54, 59; cf. 6:7) identified the "abomination of desolation (*bdelugma erēmōseōs*)" as an idol altar erected by Antiochus Epiphanes upon the altar of burnt offering at the Temple in Jerusalem in 168 B.C. Josephus, about A.D. 70, similarly applied Daniel's prophecy to "an idol altar" built "upon God's altar" (Jos. *Ant.* x. 11. 7 [Loeb, 272-276]; xii. 5 [Loeb, 253]). In Matt. 24:15 (cf. Luke 21:20-22) Christ applies it to the Romans, who, 40 years later, in A.D. 70, invested Jerusalem and burned the Temple, and in A.D. 130 ordered a shrine to Jupiter Capitolinus to be erected in its place (*Cambridge Ancient History,* Vol. XI, p. 313). Medieval Jewish expositors such as Ibn Ezra likewise applied it to the work of the Romans in the first century A.D. (L. E. Froom, *Prophetic Faith of Our Fathers,* vol. 2, pp. 210, 213). Irenaeus, Origen, and other Christian writers of the early centuries applied it to a future antichrist *(ibid.,* vol. 1, pp. 247, 320, 366), as did later medieval Catholic writers such as Villanova and Olivi *(ibid.,* pp. 752-754, 773). Pseudo Joachim applied it to the popes of his day *(ibid.,* p. 728). Wyclif *(ibid.,* vol. 2, p. 58), Huss *(ibid.,* p. 118), Luther *(ibid.,* pp. 272, 277, 280), and numerous Protestant commentators identified it with the papacy or with doctrines or practices of the papal church. William Miller and probably most Millerite preachers did the same. Most modernist Protestant commentators apply the "abomination of desolation" to the idolatrous worship instituted by Antiochus Epiphanes, while fundamentalist commentators regard Antiochus Epiphanes as a prototype of the man of sin to come in the future.

Seventh-day Adventist Interpretation. Uriah Smith, pioneer SDA expositor, applied *(Review and Herald* 37:84, Feb. 28, 1871) the "overspreading of abominations" in Dan. 9:27 to the events of A.D. 70 under pagan Rome, and the "abomination of desolation" to the papacy. Specifically identifying "the daily" of Dan. 8:11; 11:31; 12:11 as "paganism" in the Roman Empire, and the "abomination of desolation" as the papacy, Smith applied the taking away of "the daily" and the setting up of "the abomination of desolation" in its place to the establishment of papal supremacy upon the dissolution of the Roman Empire, a process he considered to be complete by A.D. 538 and a state of affairs continuing for 1,260 years, to the imprisonment of Pope Pius VI in 1798 (on the basis of Dan. 7:25 and 12:7). Smith identified the little horn of Dan. 8 as Rome in its two phases, pagan and papal (*Daniel and the Revelation* [1882 ed.], p. 202).

Contemporary SDA expositors of prophecy similarly identify the "abomination of desolation" with unscriptural papal teachings and practices—such as the Roman sacrifice of the mass, the confessional, the veneration of the virgin Mary, priestly celibacy, and hierarchical structure of the church—but, while some hold Smith's view of "the daily," others understand "the daily," for which these unscriptural practices were substituted, to refer, in the application of Daniel's prophecy to Christian times, to the ministry of Christ as our great high priest in the heavenly sanctuary. They equate the "little horn," or "king of fierce countenance" (Dan. 8:9-14, 23), who sets up the "transgression of desolation," and the "king of the north" of Dan. 11 and 12, who sets up the "abomination of desolation," with the "man of sin," "mystery of iniquity," or "Wicked [one]" of 2 Thess. 2:2-12; with the "antichrist" of 1 John 2:18; with the leopardlike beast of Rev. 13, and with "mystery, Babylon the great, the mother of harlots and abominations of the earth" of Rev. 17. The "abomination" set up by the apostate power thus referred to consists of its unscriptural teachings and practices that cause a "falling away" (literally, "apostasy") from the truth revealed in Scripture (2 Thess. 2:3, 9-12); of its "blasphemies" (Rev. 13:1, 5, 6); and of the "wine" of Babylon (Rev. 17:2). In the historic Protestant tradition, SDAs understand that the Church of Rome and its unscriptural teachings constitute the fulfillment in history of these prophecies.

ABORIGINAL MISSION. *See* Australia.

ACADEMIA ADVENTISTA CENTRO-AMERICANA. *See* Central American Adventist University.

ACADEMIA ADVENTISTA DEL NOROESTE. *See* Northwestern Adventist Academy.

ACADEMIA ADVENTISTA DEL NORTE. *See* North Adventist Academy.

ACADEMIA ADVENTISTA DEL OESTE. *See* West Adventist Academy.

ACADEMIA ADVENTISTA HISPANO-AMERICANA. *See* Central American Adventist University.

ACADEMIA ADVENTISTA METROPOLITANA. *See* Metropolitan Adventist Academy (Puerto Rico).

ACADEMIA ALENZA. *See* Spain.

ACADEMIA ARTURO ROTH. *See* Enriquillo Adventist Secondary School.

ACADEMIA COLOMBO-VENEZOLANO. *See* Colombia Adventist University.

ACADEMIA METROPOLITANA ADVENTISTA. *See* Metropolitan Adventist Academy (Santo Domingo).

ACADEMIA REGIONAL ADVENTISTA CENTRAL. *See* Central Adventist Academy.

ACADEMIA REGIONAL ADVENTISTA DEL ESTE. *See* East Adventist Academy.

ACADEMIA REGIONAL ADVENTISTA DEL NORTE. *See* North Adventist Academy Puerto Rico.

ACADEMY. A name applied by Seventh-day Adventists to most of their secondary schools. *See* Schools, Seventh-day Adventist; also names of institutions.

ACCENT. *See Youth Ministry ACCENT.*

ACHENBACH, CLINTON V. (1875-1935). Missionary, a graduate nurse from the Battle Creek Sanitarium (1903). He with his wife (nee Minnie Branson) established treatment rooms in Orlando, Florida. He was called to the ministry in 1909, and from 1912 to 1914 was president of the South Carolina Conference. For five years he engaged in medical missionary work in the Lake Titicaca Indian Mission (1915-1920) and then was director successively of the Puerto Rico Mission, the Venezuela Mission, the Cuba Mission, and the Santo Domingo Mission. Returning to Puerto Rico, he conducted evangelistic work from 1928 to 1934.

ACTION. *See Church Ministries Worker;* Sabbath School Action Units.

ACTION FOR BETTER LIVING. The monthly news and promotional bulletin of the International Temperance Association and American Temperance Society. *Activities*, begun by W. A. Scharffenberg in 1951, was continued until *Action for Better Living* replaced it in 1966, edited by E.H.J. Steed.

An eight-page two-color English publication, it provides guidelines for pastors and temperance leaders on temperance principles and programs, gives world reports of activities, and announces availability of aids and materials.

ACTION UNITS. *See* Sabbath School Action Units.

ACTIVITIES (1951-1964; monthly; Temperance Department; 1964 circulation, c. 10,000; files in dept.; superseded 1965 by *Listen News,* a supplement to *Listen,* and by *Secretaries' Exchange*). A now-suspended organ of the International Temperance Association, intended to keep church officers and temperance leaders informed as to the plans, policies, and programs of the association and serving as an exchange bulletin for conference and church temperance secretaries, chapter leaders, and Action Unit officers promoting temperance in local communities. First appearing Jan. 1, 1951, as an eight-page magazine, it was on special occasions enlarged to 16 or 32 pages. *See Action for Better Living.*

ADAMS, ANDERSON GRANT (fl. late 1890s). Recording secretary and treasurer of the General Conference of Seventh-day Adventists from 1897 to 1898 and treasurer from 1898 to 1900; treasurer of the General Conference Association in 1898 and its secretary and treasurer from 1899 to 1900. He had been treasurer of the Minnesota Conference in 1894.

ADDIS ABABA TRAINING SCHOOL FOR BOYS. *See* Akaki SDA School.

ADDIS ABABA TRAINING SCHOOL FOR GIRLS. *See* Kabana Mission School.

ADDIS ALAM TRAINING SCHOOL FOR BOYS. *See* Akaki SDA School.

ADELAIDE ADVENTIST HIGH SCHOOL. *See* Prescott College.

ADELAIDE SANITARIUM. *See* Australia.

ADELPHIAN ACADEMY. Instituted as a boarding school on the senior high school level, it was a member of the Association of SDA Institutions of Higher Education and Secondary Schools, and was accredited with the University of Michigan. The enrollment in the years before it was closed averaged 250, with a faculty and staff numbering 24. A mill producing garden trellises and outdoor furniture provided student labor. The campus and farm covered 325 acres (132 hectares).

In September 1904 the president and superintendent of education of the East Michigan Conference, E. K. Slade and J. G. Lamson, respectively, were authorized to look for a suitable location for an academy. Their search led to the purchase of a 77-acre (31-hectare) farm near Holly, situated almost halfway between Flint and Pontiac and about 50 miles (80 kilometers) from Detroit. The new academy, named Adelphian, opened with six students in January 1905, in the house that was on the farm. Later that year the enrollment reached 17. J. G. Lamson and his wife, the founders also of Cedar Lake Academy, were the first teachers at Adelphian.

The farmhouse soon filled with girls and some faculty members, a nearby farmhouse was rented as a boys' dormitory, and a temporary tar paper-covered building 20' x 54' (6.1 cm. x 16.5 cm.) was erected for classes and offices. It became known familiarly as the Black Chapel. In February 1906 the rented home burned, and the boys were forced to crowd into the attic of the Black Chapel until the fall of 1907, when two new buildings were completed, one housing a chapel, classrooms, offices, and a boys' dormitory; the other a girls' dormitory, kitchen, dining room, and guest rooms.

Adelphian Academy reached full 12-grade status in 1917. Growth was slow for the first 25 years. The farm, gradually enlarged, served as the main industry until about 1927, when an industrial program that aided in a rapid development of the school was introduced. In 1927-1928 the principal, John Z. Hottel, established a student woodworking industry in an unused chicken house and in the first year sold $20,000 worth of garden trellises. Later a wood structure was erected for the industry. In 1931 one of the teachers, A. E. Mobley, devoted much time to giving business instruction and to supervising this growing project.

In 1931, when the East and West Michigan conferences were combined, it was proposed that Cedar Lake Academy, in the West Michigan Conference, could be enlarged to care for the enrollment of both schools. In protest, a procession of cars carried to Lansing a delegation from the larger churches in the eastern area, along with the Adelphian principal, George H. Simpson, and members of the faculty and student body. As a result, the Michigan Conference committee decided to keep both schools operating.

In 1934 E. P. Weaver, a 1912 graduate, returned as principal. In 1938, when asked to devote more time to the mill, he gave up his duties as principal and from then until his death in 1956 operated the Adelphian Mill as a successful business enterprise, providing work for increasing numbers of students. A large cement-block two-story mill building was constructed with 35,000 square feet (3,255 square meters) of floor space (enlarged in 1953). Under Weaver's management the production of garden goods increased greatly.

After World War II the following were constructed: (1) two large fireproof dormitories to accommodate a tripled student body; (2) a central heating plant, a modern laundry, the Adelphian Press, and shop and maintenance facilities; and (3), in 1955-1956, the E. P. Weaver Auditorium-gymnasium, seating 1,500. A food services center and cafeteria seating 325 occupied its ground floor.

Another building program was begun in May 1966, when construction of a $500,000 classroom and administration complex was approved. This was followed in 1970 by a new industrial arts building with $30,000 worth of new equipment. The structure consisted of two classrooms, a ceramics lab, and a machine and woodworking shop. During the same period a 30' x 60' (9 m. x 18 m.) greenhouse was erected to provide laboratory facilities for advanced biology classes. In 1970 a new 17,000-square-foot (1,581-square-meter) addition to the mill was begun, which increased production capacity of their redwood products to more than $1 million worth (market value) a year. During that same year a new 2,100-foot (640-meter) airstrip was constructed by the students and staff, who also in the spring of 1974 erected a 50' x 100' (15 m. x 30 m.) metal barn for the school farm. Several pieces of farm equipment and a small irrigation system were purchased, classes in agriculture were added to the curriculum, and the farm reactivated its student work program. During the period from 1966 to 1974 five new faculty homes were also added to the campus.

A special constituency meeting of the Michigan Conference voted on November 2, 1986, to merge Adelphian Academy and Cedar Lake Academy. This led to the establishment of Great Lakes Adventist Academy on the grounds of what was formerly Cedar Lake Academy. *See* Cedar Lake Academy and Great Lakes Adventist Academy.

Principals: J. G. Lamson, 1905-1907; Robert B. Thurber, 1907-1909; Eugene F. Dresser, 1909-1911; Clifton L. Taylor, 1911-1913; Thomas W. Steen, 1913-1918; Robert B. Thurber, 1918-1919; W. L. Avery, 1919-1922; W. C. Hannah, 1922-1927; John Z. Hottel, 1927-1931; G. H. Simpson, 1931-1934; E. P. Weaver, 1934-1938; M. S. Culver, 1938-1945; V. E. Garber, 1945-1953; R. W. Pratt, 1953-1968; Henry Wooten, 1968-1970; Stephen Young, 1970-1974; Joshua Swinyar, 1974-1975; Erich Bekowies, 1976-1977; Duane Barnett, 1977-1979; Jack Stiles, 1980-1983; Keith Dowell, 1984-1985; George Parry, 1986-1987.

ADMINISTRATION. *See* Church, (local); Conference; Division; General Conference; General Conference Constitution and Bylaws; General Conference Executive Committee; Mission; Organization; Union.

ADMIRALTY ISLANDS. *See* Papua New Guinea.

ADOBENCHISUTO MEDEKARU SENTA. *See* Adventist Medical Center.

ADOBENCHISUTO RAIFU ("Adventist Life") (1972- ; successor to *Shimei no Otozure* ["Tidings of the Message"], 1913-1920; *Shimei* ["Message"], 1921-1943, 1946-1971; monthly). Official organ of the Japan Union Conference. Until 1981 it was published by Japan Publishing House, except for the few years that its publication was suspended by the military government toward the end of World War II. Since 1981 it has been published by the Japan Union Conference. It carries articles and discussions on doctrinal, devotional, health, and practical subjects. It also includes church news, translations of Ellen G. White books in serial form, daily devotional readings, and exchange of views and experiences, all geared to enrich and uplift the lives of Adventists in Japan.

ADORNMENT. *See* Dress.

ADRA. *See* Adventist Development and Relief Agency International.

ADVANCED BIBLE SCHOOL. *See* Andrews University, III.

ADVENT AWAKENING. *See* Advent Movement.

ADVENT CORRESPONDENCE SCHOOL. An institution in the Australasian Division that was operated for a time, offering instruction on the secondary and collegiate level for Seventh-day Adventist young people, workers, and church officers. It was listed in the *Yearbook* from 1947 to 1953. Its work was taken over by Home Study International of Washington, D.C.

ADVENT HARBINGER. *See Voice of Truth* [1].

ADVENT HERALD. A Millerite journal (March 1840-February 1844 as *The Signs of the Times*) edited and published for many years by J. V. Himes, Boston, and considered the leading voice of the majority group of the post-1844 Millerites, who were sometimes therefore referred to as the *"Advent Herald* party." This meant, especially after a split in the 1850s, the Adventists who did *not* accept the doctrine of conditional immortality. (The conditionalists among the non-Sabbatarian Adventists rallied under the banner of the *"World's Crisis* party," and *World's Crisis* became the organ of the Advent Christian Church, which originated about that time; *see* Adventist Bodies.) Early Seventh-day Adventist periodicals often quoted from or replied to articles in the *Advent Herald* (for example, *Review and Herald* 7:84, Dec. 11, 1855). Some years later it became *Messiah's Herald,* then *Herald of the Coming One*. Files 1840-1863 in AU.

ADVENT MESSENGER. *See Messenger* [2].

ADVENT MIRROR. A non-Seventh-day Adventist paper, published at Boston in at least one issue, volume 1, Number 1, January 1845, written by "A. Hale and J. Turner, editors" (photostat in Review and Herald). Possibly no further numbers were issued, since this one was devoted entirely to one topic, a controversial view that was not long held by the authors, an explanation of the Millerite disappointment by a new interpretation of the parable of the ten virgins. This explanation was that the coming of the bridegroom to the wedding was not the Second Advent, which they had expected, but Christ's reception of His kingdom, the heavenly Jerusalem (p. 2), "some change of work or office" "within the veil"; and that His people were to "wait and keep themselves ready till they pass in to the marriage supper" at His "return from the wedding" (p. 3). This mode of independent publication was adopted because both authors were on the editorial staffs of other periodicals that did not share their view—Apollos Hale on the *Advent Herald* and Joseph Turner on the *Hope of Israel.* However, the *Advent Herald* (9:17-19 and 26-28, Feb. 26 and Mar. 5, 1845) published the pro and con on the subject, reprinted in *Review and Herald* 2:26, 27, Sept. 16, 1851. William Miller's remarks on the *Advent Mirror* exposition are quoted in the first issue of the *Advent Review* 1:10, August 1850.

ADVENT-MISSIONSSEMINAR. *See* Baltic Union School.

ADVENT MOVEMENT. A term often used variously to mean: (1) in expressions such as "great Advent movement of 1843-4" (*Review and Herald* 42:180, Nov. 18, 1873), the Millerite movement, principally in America; (2) the Seventh-day Adventist movement (W. A. Spicer, *Certainties of the Advent Movement*); or (3) the whole international movement, sometimes referred to as the "Advent awakening," beginning in Europe during the early decades of the nineteenth century (*see* Premillennialism), in which thousands of people of varying views and in many countries were expecting the Second Advent and/or the millennium to occur shortly on the basis of certain time periods of Bible prophecies.

ADVENT ORION PUBLISHING HOUSE. *See* Czecho-Slovakian Publishing House.

ADVENT PERS. *See* Netherlands Adventist Publications.

ADVENT PRESS (Ghana). A publishing house with printing facilities operated by the Africa-Indian Ocean Division with a staff of 66 national workers. It prints Sabbath school lesson quarterlies, tracts, and books in Twi, English, Ga, and Hausa languages, and some tracts and books in French.

The Advent Publishing House, earlier known as the Nigerian Advent Press, West African Union Press, and Advent Press, began when W.T.B. Hyde, principal of the Ibadan Training School, West Nigeria, purchased a small hand press and began producing vernacular tracts in Ibadan. In 1935 a cylinder press, purchased with the help of the Stanborough Press in England, was erected in a converted garage, where full-time printing operations were begun by the Nigerian Advent Press (after 1937 called the Advent Press). Production included Sabbath school lessons in the Yoruba language, tracts, training booklets, and a Yoruba hymnal. Upon the recommendation of the West African Union executive committee, the press was moved from Nigeria to Accra, Gold Coast (now Ghana) about 1951. Its new building was officially opened Jan. 3, 1954, by Dr. Kwane Nkrumah, who later became president of the republic of Ghana.

During the period 1971-1973, the Advent Publishing House changed from letterpress machinery to litho machines. In 1993 the pressroom was equipped with the following presses: a two-color Heidelberg Speedmaster, a one-color SOR, a one-color SORD, a one-color KORD, a two-color GTOZP, and a single-color GTO. The photo offset department is equipped with one Kodak camera, five printing frames, one layout table, and one platemaker. The composing room has two Intertype machines, one proof press, and desktop publishing equipment. The Advent Press has the best equipped bindery in the country, with two cutters, two folding machines, three sewing machines, two three-knife trimmers, a gathering pony, a gang stitcher, a stitcher, a pressing machine, a casemaker, a bundler, a flowline, an endsheeting machine, and a laminating machine.

In order to keep up with the demand of literature evangelists in both anglophone and francophone countries, the Advent Publishing House has produced more than 12 subscription books over the past five-year period.

Managers (Accra): H. S. Pearce, 1948-1957; C. G. Meredith, 1957-1965; Alfred Berger, 1965-1967; Leland R. Shultz, 1968-1972; Bent Praestiin, 1972-1975; Luther Talley, 1976-1982; Brent Praestiin, 1982-1983; Dieter Gramkow (Ag), 1983-1984; T. R. Rojas, 1984-1985; S. A. Armah, 1985-1988; E. C. Tetteh, 1988- .

ADVENT PRESS (Kenya). *See* Africa Herald Publishing House.

ADVENT PUBLISHERS (Switzerland). A publishing firm, without printing plant, the property of the German Swiss Conference, which comprises the German- and Romansh-speaking territory of Switzerland and Liechtenstein.

In 1928 the German Swiss Conference, formerly a part of the Central European Union Conference, under the old European Division, was transferred to the newly formed Southern European Division. Soon thereafter (1929), the Internationale Traktatgesellschaft (International Tract Society) in Basel, which had operated as a branch of the German Advent-Verlag of Hamburg, was transferred to Zurich. In the *Statistical Report,* it is listed as a depository (1937-1946), then as the Zurich Advent-Verlag, an independent publishing house, in 1947. In 1966 the publishing house was moved to new quarters in Krattigen, overlooking Lake Thun.

In 1944 a literary committee (to select manuscripts) was appointed for the first time, with Robert Gerber, Hans Struve, and H. F. Schuberth as members.

Since the setback of World War II, which seriously handicapped the publishing work in Switzerland, there has been a steady and encouraging growth. In 1992 literature evangelist sales amounted to about 1.3 million Swiss francs. The monthly *Leben und Gesundheit* ("Life and Health"), published since 1920, has an average edition of 23,000 copies.

Managers: Jacob Bollier, 1929-1943; Charles Wehrli, 1943-1947; Gustav Tobler, 1947-1968; Alfred Burkhard, 1968-1985; Hans Huegli, 1985-1989; Paul Hofmann, 1990- .

ADVENT PUBLISHING HOUSE. A plant established in 1989 in Budapest, Hungary. In 1994 Laszlo Erdelyi was manager. *Sabbath School Lessons* and *Ministers' Review* were being published in Hungarian.

Managers: Laszlo Ferdelyi, 1989-1994; Istvan Fekete, 1994- .

ADVENT PUBLISHING HOUSE (Ghana). *See* Advent Press (Ghana).

ADVENT REVIEW (August-November 1850; irregular issue; published by James White, with a committee, in Auburn, N.Y., Paris, Maine; reprinted complete in *Facsimiles of the Two Earliest SDA Periodicals*). For a description of the *Advent Review, see Adventist Review.*

ADVENT REVIEW AND SABBATH HERALD. *See Adventist Review.*

ADVENT, SECOND. *See* Second Advent.

ADVENT SHIELD (May 1844-April 1845; irregular issue; published by Joshua V. Himes, Boston; volume in the Review and Herald). A Millerite journal edited by J. V. Himes, S. Bliss, and A. Hale. It was published in magazine rather than newspaper style, with long articles and no news items or fillers. Its contents defended the Millerite positions, contained a historical sketch of the movement, and, after the disappointment of October 1844, contained a statement of "our position," a narrative of the "Seventh Month Movement," and book reviews discussing various opposing views. (See articles in SDA periodicals citing the *Advent Shield in Present Truth* 1:47, December 1849; *Advent Review* 1:55, September 1850.)

ADVENT SURVEY. *See Light.*

ADVENT TIDENDE. *See* Denmark.

ADVENTES MISIJAS SEMINARS. *See* Latvian Conference School.

ADVENTHAUS FREUDENSTADT (Freudenstadt Adventist Retreat). An institution affording facilities for a meeting place and a youth hall for the Freudenstadt church and accommodations for 40 guests, operated by the South German Union in the town of Freudenstadt in the Black Forest, a natural park area in southwestern Germany. The town of Freudenstadt is a mountain resort at an elevation of about 2,600 feet (792 meters) in the midst of some 94 miles (150 kilometers) of wooded footpaths.

Construction was begun in 1953 and the center was opened and dedicated in the summer of 1954. At first the property was used mainly as a site for junior and senior camps, but since 1958 the building has been used chiefly as a retreat, for recreation camps, and as a place for committee meetings and special courses offered by the church.

The Adventhaus also serves the German Health Association (Deutscher Verein für Gesundheitspflege) as a locale for conducting health seminars, and as a rehabilitation health resort.

Superintendents: F. Streit, 1954-1955; A. Altenberger, 1955-1956; F. Ebner, 1956-1984; W. Oldenhoff, 1984- .

ADVENTHAVEN. A housing facility for the aged, situated on the campus of the Sedaven High School, five miles (eight kilometers) from Heidelberg, Transvaal, South Africa, that opened on May 11, 1960. Operated by the Transvaal Conference, this institution serves the constituency of the conference, but accepts applicants from other areas in South Africa as well.

In 1993 there were 26 houses, accommodating 40 persons, who provided their own meals. There were also 28 rooms providing accommodation for 54 persons who eat in the dining room.

ADVENTHEIM STEGLITZ. *See* Berlin-Steglitz Old People's Home.

ADVENTIST. (a) Originally, and properly, a member of the Adventist (or Millerite) movement or of any one of the six (now five) Adventist church bodies (SB, no. 6) that sprang from it; (b) in Seventh-day Adventist usage, a short term for "Seventh-day Adventist"; (c) in some dictionaries, any believer in "Adventism," which they define loosely as the doctrine of the nearness of the Second Advent and the end of the world, or age. The terms *Adventist* and *Adventism* were coined by the Millerites (SB, no. 7). Hence these terms are most correctly employed in the framework of Millerite eschatology, which included not only the teaching of the near, personal advent of Christ but also a distinctive body of doctrine concerning the events connected therewith. Understood in this way, Adventism was and is distinct from and should not be confused with other views of the Second Advent; the differences are discussed under Premillennialism.

Defined in the loose sense of believing in the nearness of the Second Advent, "Adventism" originated neither in the U.S. nor with the Millerite movement. In the early nineteenth century in the British Isles and on the Continent there was a great revival of interest in the return of Christ as near, in contrast with the then-dominant view that Christ would come only after a future millennium. The Millerites in America were a distinctive part of this general "Advent awakening," and looked upon all those who held "the Advent near" as brothers and sisters, despite differences in other areas of doctrine *(see* Premillennialism). Later, when representatives of the Sabbathkeeping branch of the Adventists in America went abroad, first to Europe, they found others looking for the Second Advent. In many languages, the term *Adventist* has come to be used by those who do not know the origin of the word, to mean specifically the church that teaches both the keeping of the seventh-day Sabbath and preparation for the coming of the Lord, namely the Seventh-day Adventist Church.

ADVENTIST ACADEMY (Australia). *See* Lilydale Adventist Academy.

ADVENTIST AGRICULTURAL-INDUSTRIAL ACADEMY (Instituto Adventista Agro-Industrial). A coeducational boarding school situated on 6,250 acres (2,500 hectares) of virgin jungle, donated by the governor of Amazonas, about 47 miles (74 kilometers) from Manaus (pop. 600,000), the capital city of Amazonas, on the first paved highway in the state—opened in 1964. The school is owned and operated by the North Brazil Union, whose headquarters are in Belém, Pará. Students come from all over the northern part of Brazil. All are industrial students, and almost all work their way through school.

The founder, Robert H. Habenicht a departmental secretary in the Central Amazon Mission, first entered the area in January of 1964. By June a road was opened into the industrial part and a few hired workers and volunteers began clearing land, planting trees and crops, and building thatch shelters, a boys' dormitory, and the first teacher's house.

The first primary classes began in 1967 with a national teacher and 12 boys in one half of the boys' dormitory, which also served as the church. The entire staff, consisting of a Brazilian teacher, Luiza Kettle; the director, Robert Habenicht, and family; the treasurer-agronomist, Marvin Glantz, and family, lived in one house. By 1968 a small house was constructed for a girls' dormitory, and in 1969 a new dining room, part of which was a *farinha* (mandioca flour) factory, replaced the thatch shelter. A generator provided electricity three hours in the evening.

Official title to the land was granted in November 1970. Construction of simple wood-frame houses continued as more workers were added to the staff.

A simple irrigation system consisting of a series of plastic movable pipes brought water, pumped from the small river that runs through the land, to irrigate crops during the dry season. A small seedling house was built but soon was replaced by another twice as large. In 1971 the first plastic-covered greenhouse was put up. Laboriously, almost all by hand, the jungle was pushed back and crops of soybeans, peanuts, corn, sweet potatoes, as well as banana plantations increased. Charcoal ovens began to turn discarded logs into charcoal to sell to a steel factory. The 1970s saw continued growth in enrollment and expansion of the school plant. By 1980 a new campus was in use. In 1993 there was a faculty and staff of 11.

Principals: Robert H. Habenicht, 1964-1973; Nelson O. Duarte, 1973-1981; João Kuntze, 1981-1983; Willer C. Prego, 1983-1985; Orlando G. Ferreira, 1985-1986; Wilson Schenfeld, 1986-1990; Selso A. Kern, 1991- .

ADVENTIST ATLANTIC SECONDARY SCHOOL (Colegio Max Trummer). A school in Colombia located in Boston, the northern suburb of the city of Barranquilla. It was founded on Feb. 15, 1925. The school has grades from kindergarten through six years of secondary studies and has been approved by the Colombian government. It is owned and operated by the Atlantic Colombia Mission. Beginning with one teacher and 16 students, it had 18 teachers and 460 students in 1993. It previously operated under the names Barranquilla Secondary School, Boston School, Max Trummer School, and Atlantic School.

Principals: Victoria Davila, 1925-1930; Justina Colon, 1931-1933; Sara Escandon, 1934-1936; Graciela Rodriquez, 1937-1938; Elias Garcia, 1939-1943; Ignacio Carrillo, 1943; Jose Pereira del Rio, 1944; Narcisa Moreno, 1945; Ines Mejia, 1946; Ana Teresa Perez, 1947; Lola Escandon, 1948; Judith Escandon, 1949-1953; Zita Robinson, 1953-1956; Rosalbina Hereira, 1960-1961; Conchita Pacheco, 1962; Hernando Sierra, 1963; Augusto Ferrer, 1964; Lola Escandon de Gelvis, 1966-1970; Mariela Miranda, 1971-1972; Jorge Sanchez, 1973; Jorge Robinson, 1974; Trinidad de Leyva, 1975-1976; Eunice Zabarain, 1977; Enoc Iglesias, 1978-1982; Eunice Zabarain de Robinson, 1983-1987; Lixberth Ruiz, 1988-1989; Nelson Utria Avendano, 1990- .

ADVENTIST BIBLE SEMINARY (Teologicky Seminar CASD). A training school for evangelistic workers in Lodenice, near Prague, Czech Republic, that was operated by the Czechoslovakian Union Conference from 1925 until World War II. After the war, plans were made to reestablish and enlarge the school at Prague, and in 1948 the erection of buildings was begun. A new government sequestered the property, and the school was closed. The earlier school is listed in the *Yearbook* from 1926 to 1935. The postwar school is listed from 1947 to 1955 under the name of Czechoslovakian Bible School.

Reopened in 1968 under the name Czechoslovakian Bible Seminary, it existed from 1973 on as only a correspondence school. In 1990 a new school for training future workers was established under its present name.

Principals: Josef Simon, 1926-1935; T. Zigmund, 1946-1970; Miloslav Sustek, 1970-1983; Alois Barta, 1983-1990; Jiri Moskala, 1990-1994; Miloslav Zalud, 1994- .

ADVENTIST BODIES. Denominations derived from the Millerite movement of the 1840s in the United States include:

1. *Evangelical Adventists,* organized about 1858 under the name American Millennial Association. Originally the main body of the earlier Millerites, by 1858 they constituted those who held the view that the dead are conscious and that the lost suffer eternally, as distinguished from group 2. Their organ was the periodical called the *Advent Herald,* later *Messiah's Herald* (originally *Signs of the Times).* The Evangelical Adventists, dwindling by 1906 to 481 members, soon disappeared as an organized group.

2. *Advent Christians,* who separated from the main body after the failure of an 1854 expectation of the Second Advent, and were largely composed of those who held to conditional immortality as a principal doctrine. The group was organized in 1860. The *World's Crisis* was its organ.

3. *Seventh-day Adventists,* a group that separated from the aforementioned two groups in 1845, and organized as a denomination in 1860 and 1863. It is distinguished chiefly by its observance of the seventh-day Sabbath. It shares with the Advent Christians the doctrine of conditional immortality, but holds a distinctive view of the cleansing of the sanctuary and the millennium.

4. *Church of God (Adventist),* organized 1866, an offshoot from the Seventh-day Adventist Church, retaining the seventh-day Sabbath, but differing in some other views *(see* Marion Party).

5. *Church of God (Adventist).* Unattached congregations.

6. *Life and Advent Union,* originating from a group led by John T. Walsh and George Storrs. It is differentiated from the other conditionalists by the belief that the unsaved are never resurrected and by holding that the millennium is past.

7. *Churches of God in Christ Jesus,* sometimes called "age-to-come Adventists," differing from the other bodies in expecting the Second Advent to usher in an age of "restitution" on earth, and a millennial kingdom with the restored "Israelitish nation" in the most favored position, to be gradually extended from Jerusalem to embrace all nations. This was the older "Literalist" view *(see* Messenger Party; Premillennialism).

ADVENTIST BOOK CENTER (ABC). A distribution and service outlet for Seventh-day Adventist publishing house products and other church-approved materials, including Bibles, audiovisual aids, all church department needs, public evangelism supplies, and often special dietary health products. Generally there is one or more in each conference territory, selling either subscription literature wholesale to literature evangelists and/or subscription and trade literature at retail to individuals—subscription literature being the type produced for door-to-door gospel sales by literature evangelists; trade literature, usually with fewer illustrations, being the type of literature produced for Seventh-day Adventist church member home-and-neighborhood evangelism purposes.

North American subscription literature is handled by Home Health Education Service offices, which also finance literature evangelist credit sales to the public. These offices may be conference-, union-, or publishing house-owned. Australia, New Zealand, South Africa, and many European conferences/unions operate a similar plan.

Conference Adventist Book Centers often establish branch book centers in major cities and operate well-equipped bookmobiles, which regularly visit the denomination's churches and all major church gatherings.

Before 1924 the name Tract Society was used. For the origins, *see* Tract and Missionary Societies. Soon after 1870, when S. N. Haskell organized the New England Tract and Missionary Society, every conference had its own Tract Society, with local churches active in evangelism through the distribution of tracts and papers. For supplying their members the conference Tract Societies soon proved themselves convenient centers for handling not only tracts but also a complete line of books and other denominational publications. They also furnished various types of printed supplies by the churches and the different departments of the conferences, and functioned as wholesale outlets supplying the colporteurs.

The denomination-wide International Tract Society was replaced in 1901 by a publication committee, which a little later became the Publishing Department of the General Conference. The local societies, as important evangelizing agencies, eventually became the church missionary societies, fostered by the Home Missionary Department.

This left the conference Tract Societies with the specialized function of serving as distributing outlets for the publishing houses. In 1924, their scope of influence having long since reached beyond the small literature stage, the name was changed to Book and Bible Houses. In 1972 the name Adventist Book Center was adopted. These agencies are now established throughout North America and in most parts of the world field. Each is operated by an experienced manager elected by the conference constituency, with appropriate personnel to handle the business of the field in which the center is situated. The influence of the Adventist Book Centers extends to all departments of the church through supplying materials for use in every phase of Christian endeavor. Adventist Book Center managers, as spiritual leaders of the church, encourage church members to build a library of good books in their homes as a means of nurturing their Christian experience.

ADVENTIST CHAPLAINCY MINISTRIES. The denominational agency that provides support and supervision to Seventh-day Adventist chaplains serving in hospitals, prisons, the armed forces, the Veterans Administration, industries, and on campuses. When the matter of Seventh-day Adventist ministers serving in the armed forces of the United States arose early in World War II, the General Conference Committee questioned whether the church should favor such service on the grounds of separation of church and state. However, at the Spring Meeting of the committee in 1942, in response to the urging of some ministers, a compromise action was passed that tended to discourage ministers from entering the chaplaincy, yet allowed that if a person felt the call to serve, the decision be left up to individual conscience. It was subsequently learned that the government would commission only a person who had ecclesiastical endorsement. Thus matters stood until Floyd E. Bresee became the first Seventh-day Adventist chaplain to enter the U.S. Army on Sept. 28, 1942, on the recommendation of the Central Union Conference. W. H. Bergherm became the second such chaplain the next year. Robert L. Mole became the first SDA chaplain in the U.S. Navy in March 1953, while Christy M. Taylor was the first in the U.S. Air Force in September 1953.

Because Army chaplains were of considerable help to SDA service personnel during the war years, the Autumn Council in 1950 voted to place no barrier in the way of those who felt called upon to serve as chaplains. Those who chose to serve in this capacity were to receive their credentials from the General Conference. The National Service Organization was asked to look after the needs of these chaplains who were issued ministerial credentials by the General Conference. The National Service Organization now is part of the Adventist Chaplaincy Ministries. *See* National Service Organization.

After World War II the various military forces made available openings for chaplains based on the ratio of the church's membership to the population of the country. At the peak of

U.S. military strength in 1989, 50 chaplains served in the military in ranks ranging from lieutenant to full colonel, and in assignments including troop units, aircraft carriers, paratroops, and staff assignments at the Pentagon.

There is no general denominational policy respecting SDA chaplains in the armed forces of countries other than the United States. So far as is known, there has been only one such chaplain—a Belgian minister, Daniel Peyffer, who served his country in the Korean War.

Chaplains serve in the U.S. military as part of the uniqueness of the U.S. Constitution, which mandates the free exercise of religion for all citizens, including those serving in the armed forces.

ADVENTIST COLLEGE OF BEIRUT. *See* Middle East College.

ADVENTIST COLLEGE OF MUNGULUNI. *See* Mozambique Adventist Training School.

ADVENTIST COLLEGE OF THEOLOGY PUBLISHING (Izdavastro Adventistickog teoloskog Marusevec). *See* Croatian-Slovenian Publishing House; Yugoslavian Publishing House.

ADVENTIST COMMUNICATION NETWORK. A live satellite connection begun in 1994. It enables groups in many metropolitan areas to see and hear church-sponsored programs live. Two events were scheduled for March 1994—a VBS workshop and a pastors' planning conference. Beginning Apr. 6, a regular news and information briefing was provided monthly. A total of 20 live events were scheduled for ACN in 1994, with more than twice that number in 1995, including a division-wide evangelistic campaign conducted by Mark Finley and originating in Chattanooga, Tennessee. A growing number of churches and conference offices are obtaining downlink packages.

ADVENTIST DEVELOPMENT AND RELIEF AGENCY INTERNATIONAL (ADRA). An agency established in 1983 after the reorganization of Seventh-day Adventist World Service, Incorporated (SAWS). As the humanitarian arm of the Seventh-day Adventist Church ADRA works in more than 90 countries around the world.

The values that have shaped the agency are the traditional Christian values of the potential of each individual to reflect the image of God, the dignity that is inherent in every person, and the importance of quality in human life. ADRA approaches humanity as an integrated entity comprised of physical, mental, social, and moral facets. ADRA works on behalf of the poor. It regards them with respect, as partners with whom it works in a learning and sharing relationship.

ADRA is legally incorporated in Silver Spring, Maryland, and is one of the largest international nongovernmental organizations distributing food to underdeveloped countries. Independent ADRA offices in nearly 100 countries provide the agency with a network that reaches the world. ADRA is registered with the U.S. Agency for International Development (USAID) of the United States government and is eligible to receive food for distribution to needy people in developing countries. It also receives reimbursement for ocean freight for shipment of food, clothing, bedding, medicines, and hospital and vocational equipment. ADRA's programs include agricultural training, mother/child health care, commodity-supported development, small enterprise development, water resources, and disaster relief.

ADRA also works with other governments and humanitarian organizations around the world, including the Australian Development Assistance Bureau, Canadian International Development Agency, CARE, Church World Service, Danish International Development Agency, the European Community, United Nations High Commission for Refugees, United Nations International Children and Education Fund, and World Vision, among others.

ADRA is also a member of Interaction, an association of U.S. private voluntary organizations engaged in international humanitarian efforts, and the International Council of Voluntary Agencies (ICVA).

ADRA received 1.2 million pounds (450,000 kilograms) of food from the World Food Program and USAID for distribution in 1992. This food was distributed in Russia, Albania, Romania, Yugoslavia, Jamaica, Trinidad, Mexico, Colombia, and Argentina.

More than 15 ADRA offices around the world act as donor countries whose primary goal is to raise and distribute funds for ADRA projects. Donor countries include Japan, Germany, Italy, Australia, Switzerland, the Netherlands, Canada, Sweden, Norway, Denmark, and Ireland. Donor countries work closely with their governments and local relief organizations to deliver donated funds and goods to ADRA projects internationally.

Funding for ADRA comes from several government and international humanitarian agencies and public support. In 1992 ADRA received $41,302,207 from the U.S. government in commodities, excess property, ocean and inland freight, and grants.

ADRA also receives funds from the annual Disaster and Famine Relief Offering, which is collected in Seventh-day Adventist churches around the world each spring. In 1992 ADRA received more than $1,875,000 from the offering.

The board of directors consists of up to 60 members elected from the General Conference Committee including representation from the executive, secretarial, and other departments of the church. The board meets once a year at the time of the Annual Council of the Executive Committee of the General Conference of Seventh-day Adventists.

ADRA maintains warehouses in Germany, Australia, Japan, Canada, the Philippines, and the United States (California and Maryland). These warehouses process, store, and ship supplies such as clothing and food to ADRA projects around the world.

Since the emergence of ADRA from SAWS, development has become the main focus of the agency's work. At the heart of ADRA's development work are projects that benefit mothers and children. These include activities that stress growth monitoring, oral rehydration therapy, breast-feeding, and immunization; parent education in nutrition, hygiene, child spacing, and child care; and supplementary food aid for pregnant women, preschool children, and nursing mothers. ADRA also aids in the distribution of food to undernourished schoolchildren.

The development of deep-water wells, water reservoirs, irrigation systems, sewage and storm drainage projects, and potable water projects is part of ADRA's efforts to make abundant water accessible to all.

Small enterprise development projects teach individuals skills that they can use to support themselves. Often ADRA will give them a loan to start a business after they have gone through a training program.

ADRA is involved in agricultural training. Farmers are taught new farming methods intended to increase crop production as well as improve the soil. This not only brings families better nutrition, but can increase family income. These types of development projects give people an opportunity to improve their immediate situation and bring a permanent change to their lives.

The agency's worldwide infrastructure enables ADRA to respond quickly and efficiently to disasters around the world. ADRA has brought relief to victims of natural and human-made disasters in Africa, South Asia, Central America, South America, the South Pacific, and North America.

Whenever possible, ADRA carries out long-term rehabilitation in disaster situations. Once the immediate needs of food, clothing, and shelter have been provided, ADRA often stays in the area to help victims become reestablished in homes, jobs, and life.

ADRA's roots and the beginnings of the church's dedication to humanitarian overseas service were first seen in 1918. A special offering was taken to assist church workers, missionaries, and members in difficult circumstances resulting from the Great War. World War II brought unprecedented devastation to Europe, parts of Asia, and North Africa. Entire nations were threatened by starvation and diseases. In 1944 and 1945 warehouses were established in New York and San Francisco to process materials for overseas shipment.

During the 1940s 2.8 million pounds (1.04 million kilograms) of clothing were shipped to 41 countries and island groups.

In 1956 the General Conference established the Seventh-day Adventist Welfare Service, Incorporated. The agency became known as SAWS. In 1973 the name was modified to Seventh-day Adventist World Service. The total value of all SAWS activities in the three years from 1960 to 1962 is recorded as $5,533,470. The Disaster and Famine Relief Offering was taken every two years during that time. In 1963 the total North American offering for Disaster and Famine Relief was $232,319.

In 1980 the SAWS budget was $19,931,179, and SAWS was active in 26 countries. The total estimated value of all SAWS activities in 1980 was close to $28 million.

In 1983, when ADRA was officially organized by the church, it was in the context of activities that were ongoing between funders in North America, Australia, and Europe, and beneficiaries in the Americas, the Far East, and Africa.

By 1980 the church already had a 20-year history with USAID, with projects dating back to 1960 in South America, and with ASHA grants dating back to 1978 in Haiti and Thailand. The Australian Development

Assistance Bureau and the Canadian government also were heavily involved in funding for ADRA. In Europe, Odd Jordal was instrumental in obtaining grants from European funders as early as 1978, with money coming in from Holland, EZE, SIDA, and DANIDA, and going to projects in Inter- and South America. The first grant from European funders to Africa was in 1980 to Rwanda, Ethiopia, and Zambia. Eventually grants were extended to countries in the western part of the continent as well as to other East African countries.

Directors of SAWS and ADRA: C. W. Bozarth, 1956-1962; W. E. Phillips, 1962-1970; Theodore Carcich, 1970-1974; Howard Burbank, 1974-1980; Richard O'Fill, 1980-1983; Robert Drachenberg, 1983-1985; R. S. Watts, 1985- .

ADVENTIST EDITORS INTERNATIONAL (formerly International Association of Seventh-day Adventist Editors). A professional association for Seventh-day Adventist editors whether employed by the denomination or not. Originally established at the World Editorial Council meeting on the campus of Columbia Union College, Takoma Park, Maryland, in 1986, this organization offers networking, a newsletter called *Headlines,* an annual conference, and an evaluation process for periodicals. It was instrumental in conducting the World Editorial Council in Frankfurt, Germany, in October 1993. Enquiries about membership should be addressed to the membership director, Adventist Editors International, 12501 Old Columbia Pike, Silver Spring, MD 20904.

Presidents: William G. Johnsson, 1986-1988; David Newman, 1988-1990; Roy Adams, 1990-1991; Marvin Moore, 1991-1992; Gary B. Swanson, 1992-1993; Penny Wheeler, 1993-1994; Myron Widmer, 1994-1995; Ted Jones, 1995-1996.

ADVENTIST EDUCATIONAL CENTER (Centro Educacional Adventista). A coeducational boarding school on the high school level operated by the continental Honduras Mission. The school is located at Peña Blanca, 40 miles (65 kilometers) south of San Pedro Sula. It was established as a self-supporting institution by Dr. J. L. DeWitt on Feb. 8, 1962, and was transferred to mission administration on Jan. 11, 1964. In 1966 the Central American Union took over management of the school. Classes are taught in the Spanish language.

In recent years, dormitories, a cafeteria, a laundry, a new church, and a classroom laboratory building have been erected. More than three miles (five kilometers) of pipeline bring a permanent supply of water to the campus. In 1993 a new administration and library building were being constructed. High school degrees are given with emphasis on bilingual secretarial skills and computer science.

Principals: James Bechtel, 1964-1966; L. T. Wade, 1966-1968; James Zackrison, 1969-1970; Larry Huston, 1970; James Zackrison, 1971; Vicente Rodriguez, 1972; Felix Fernandez, 1973-1975; Mario Munoz, 1976-1979; Eliseo Escalante, 1980; Daniel Medina, 1981-1982; Irvin Haylock, 1983; Oscar Villeda, 1984; Eugenio Vallejos, 1985-1987; Jose A. Moran, 1988-1991, Ismael Rojas, 1992- .

ADVENTIST EKAMAI SCHOOL/ EKAMAI INTERNATIONAL SCHOOL. A coeducational day school operated by the Thailand Mission on a five-acre (two-hectare) tract of land off Ekamai in Bangkok, Thailand. There are two separate accredited schools on the campus, one a Thai school called the Ekamai Adventist School and the other an English language school called Adventist English School. The Thai section offers Pratom I through Matayom Sueksa III (10 years of study). The English section offers courses based on the North American curriculum leading to a high school diploma (twelfth grade). In 1974 the total enrollment was 913, about equally divided between the Thai and the English sections, with 48 teachers and staff members in the two sections.

Most of the students are Chinese Thai, with approximately 10 percent of the students coming from Seventh-day Adventist homes. A few of the others come from a Christian background, while the rest are Buddhists.

The Thai and English sections of the school originated separately. The first Adventist church in Bangkok (organized 1921) opened a primary school with 16 pupils, but discontinued it after one year. In 1925 the school reopened in another place. In 1932, when the Chinese church was built, a new school building was erected. The enrollment continued to increase, finally reaching 500. Fires sweeping the neighborhood destroyed the school buildings twice.

An English school, known as the Child Training Center, was opened in October 1946, with four students, who met in the garage of Dr.

Ralph F. Waddell, medical director of the Bangkok Sanitarium and Hospital. Mrs. R. M. Milne was the principal for the first year. Because of the great demand for English education, this mission school grew rapidly and became financially self-supporting. By 1951, having outgrown the garage, the school was moved to the hospital compound, first to a mat shed, then to three rooms in back of the church; later it occupied three rooms above the laundry.

In 1956 buildings were erected on five acres (two hectares) of newly purchased land near Ekamai, seven miles (11 kilometers) from the sanitarium. The English classes, together with the upper grades of the Thai school from the Chinese church compound (called thereafter the Ekamai Adventist School), began at the new site in May 1957. By 1959 all classes in Thai and in English were accommodated on the new campus.

The school continued to grow rapidly, and in 1964 the auditorium-library building was dedicated. It was named Milne Auditorium, after the founder of the Adventist Ekamai School. Following this, many changes took place in the next few years: 1965—duplex apartment building; 1968—annex of four new classrooms for the Thai section; 1969—cafeteria and classroom structure; 1970-1971—three-story administrative and classroom building for the English section; 1971—modern Sony language laboratory. In 1993 the English section was upgraded by the Thai government's Department of Education to a 12-grade international school with the legal name changed to Ekamai International School.

The first three teachers hired locally for the English school were Mrs. Paz Peng (1947), Mrs. M. K. Ee (1948), and Mrs. Beatrice Chia (1950). All three have dedicated much of their lives to the Adventist educational work in Thailand.

Principals and Administrators: Alma M. Milne, 1946-1947; Esther M. Feltus, 1947-1949; A. P. Ritz, 1949-1950; Alma M. Milne, 1950-1958; C. E. Ondrizek, 1958-1961; Alma M. Milne, 1961-1964; J. B. Falconbridge, 1964-1968; J. F. Harris, 1968-1969; J. B. Falconbridge, 1969-1972; A. F. Penstock, 1972; A. F. Bell, 1973-1979; Donald Sahly, 1980-1981; Ronald Anderson, 1981-1985; Paul Essig, 1986-1987; Earl Adams, 1988-1989; Don Duncan, 1990-1994; John Baldwin, 1994- .

ADVENTIST ENGLISH CONVERSATION SCHOOL (AECS). An institution whose headquarters are located in Jakarta with branches at Bandung and Surabaya. This institution is operated by the West Indonesia Union Mission under the direct control of a Board of Directors elected by the constituency at its quinquennial session.

The school was started in 1970. M. E. Thorman, who was the director of the union's Education Department, was appointed to organize the first program. One of the main objectives of the school is to introduce the Lord and communicate the gospel to the students through English, helping them to apply its meaning to their own life.

When the school was being established, Edwin L. Moore, an English teacher and a student missionary from Andrews University, was called to Jakarta to teach.

Directors: M. E. Thorman, C. G. Oliver, D. Matacio, H. Sitompul, T. L. Tobing, E. H. Tambunan.

ADVENTIST FOUNDATION FOR THE BLIND (Stiftung Blindendienst der Advent-Mission). A publishing institution founded in 1963 in Basel, Switzerland, near where the borders of Switzerland, Germany, and France meet. The staff of the "Blindendienst" encompasses six associates, including both sighted, sight-impaired, and blind persons. Transcriptions are made from German and French into braille, and printed matter is produced for distribution to those with no sight, with a paper volume output of nearly six tons (five metric tons) per year. As of 1993 braille publications, in the German and French languages, are mailed out to 1,200 readers, in 30 countries, on three continents. Ninety-seven percent of those receiving braille publications are not members of the Seventh-day Adventist Church.

The work began when W. Schenk saw the need for transcribing the adult Sabbath school quarterly into German braille for three blind church members, and met it. Shortly after that, other blind church members from Germany and Austria heard about the work being done in Basel and requested braille Sabbath school lessons. From Elder Schenk's desire to help his fellow church members a braille publishing service was established with international readership. As requests began to increase over the years, French language braille publications were added to the growing publishing line, first to the French-speaking part of Switzerland and then to other French language areas worldwide.

The publishing technology of the "Blindendienst" has progressed with the increase of readership. From a beginning in 1963, with two manually operated braille typewriters, the typewriters were supplemented in 1969 with a braille Thermoform duplicating machine. In 1973 a second duplication machine was added. In 1975 the continual rise in production surpassed the capability of the equipment. At that time a braille embossing machine was purchased to produce braille dots on aluminum plates. These plates were taken to a commercial printer for duplication. In 1978 a rotation press was purchased and all the printing was again done at the "Blindendienst." In 1989 the printing process was computerized, and all braille transcription was produced through a new system of computer software. In 1991 a new embossing machine was purchased with the capability of producing 11 braille characters per second.

The following German language periodicals are available in braille: *Zeichen der Zeit* ("Signs of the Times"), *Leben und Gesundheit* ("Life and Health"), and *Studienanleitung für die Bibel* ("Adult Sabbath School Lessons"). Also published in braille for the French language readers are: *Signes des Temps* ("Signs of the Times") and *Vie et Santé* ("Life and Health"). Currently the adult Sabbath school lessons in French are not available in braille, but they are distributed on audiocassette.

Some of the E. G. White publications that have been translated into the German language have also been transcribed into German braille. Currently these include *Der Bessere Weg* ("Steps to Christ") and other extracts from translated materials; there are plans for more of these materials to be made available in the future. *Der Bessere Weg* is also published in large print, in both German and French, for those who still enjoy part of their visual acuity.

Several booklets and pamphlets, as well as courses on various topics, such as Christian education, Bible study, and health reform topics are transcribed into German braille. All literature is given without charge to the blind or visually impaired readers.

Managers: Werner Schenk, 1963-1969; Georges Lutz, 1970-1984; Paul Clerc, 1985- .

ADVENTIST FRONTIER MISSIONS (AFM). A supporting ministry developed and founded by Clyde and Cathy Morgan in 1985, along with a small group of seminarians, and mission instructors Russell Staples and Gottfried Oosterwal. At the time, Clyde was a student at the Seventh-day Adventist Theological Seminary.

AFM focuses exclusively on establishing new churches among people groups as yet unreached by the SDA Church and, in many cases, yet unreached by Christianity. It is funded by voluntary contributions, yet works closely with church leadership at every level. Working agreements are signed with each division of the church in which AFM projects are located. AFM also works closely with the Global Mission program.

The first project launched was among the Ifugao people of northern Luzon in the Philippines in April 1987, with Marc and Aunie Scalzi serving as missionaries. A church and several companies were established among this previously unreached group. Other projects in the Philippines, Papua New Guinea, Cambodia, Mongolia, Albania, Guinea, Burkina Faso, and India were started in the late 1980s and early 1990s.

AFM sends out missionaries under several categories. Career missionaries form the backbone of a new project and stay six years or longer until a church is established. Short-term missionaries include student missionaries who help out in an existing project for 9-12 months as well as nonstudent volunteer missionaries who serve for one to two years. Prior to service, all missionaries receive training at the Summer Institute of Frontier Missions conducted by AFM in Berrien Springs, Michigan.

AFM's goal is to establish the work, train indigenous leaders, then turn the work over to the local mission or conference. Missionaries seek to use methods that can be reproduced and maintained by the people they reach.

A monthly magazine, *Adventist Frontiers*, is published by AFM and sent free to those requesting it. It primarily contains accounts and photographs submitted by the missionaries of the work they are doing.

ADVENTIST GIRLS' VOCATIONAL INSTITUTE. *See* Ghana.

ADVENTIST GRAMMAR SCHOOL. A boarding school on the secondary level established in 1960 and located at Ede, Nigeria. E. O. Dare was principal in the mid-1970s.

ADVENTIST HEALTH CENTER (Centro Adventista de Saúde). A health center that was officially opened in 1989 and is connected with the Penfigo Adventist Hospital. It is located in the city of Pôrto Alegre, Rio Grande do Sul, in south Brazil. On September

14, 1987, the hospital conducted a How to Stop Smoking in Five Days program. The live-in participants took part in such daily activities as exercises, walks, hydrotherapy and physiotherapy, lectures, and group dynamics. The success of this program led to the development of a new wing of the hospital in which nine beds were consigned to patients developing new lifestyles.

This center is dedicated to reeducation in eating habits, weight control, diabetes control, stress management, and recovery from smoking and alcoholism. It operates uninterruptedly with no vacancies. In addition to the hydrotherapy and physiotherapy services, there is a pool in which patients are trained in exercise hydrogymnastics.

Medical Director: João Kiefer, Jr., 1989- .
Administrator: Waldomiro Klu, 1989- .

ADVENTIST HEALTH CENTRE LILONGWE. A dental and optometry practice situated on the Presidential Highway in Lilongwe, the capital city of Malawi. Previously this was an extension of Blantyre Adventist Hospital

In 1983 Dr. M. A. Rue started the dental practice. One year later he was joined by a second dentist, Dr. E. R. Russell. The dental practice is largely patronized by officials from the various embassies in Lilongwe.

In 1989 Dr. Gary Peterson arrived to start the optometry department. Besides fitting eyeglasses and contact lenses, the optometrist carries out simple eye treatements.

In 1992, 4,800 dental patients and 1,947 optometry patients were treated. Trywell J. Ndoliro has been chief administrator since the separation of the institution from Blantyre Adventist Hospital supervision.

Dental Directors: M. A. Rue, 1983-1988; E. R. Russell, 1988-1990; W. B. Seasly, 1991-1994; C. Aba, 1994- .

ADVENTIST HEALTH EDUCATION FOUNDATION (Egypt Food Factory). A Seventh-day Adventist vegetarian food factory operated by the church in the Middle East and founded in 1976. It is located in Matariah, on the outskirts of Cairo.

The idea of establishing an Adventist food factory in this area was conceived in 1972 under the leadership of Robert Darnell, then president of the Middle East Union. Dr. Darnell realized that the Adventist health message could serve as a bridge between Seventh-day Adventists and Islam, and believed that an SDA vegetarian food factory could spearhead the formation of such a bridge. The General Conference provided funds for purchasing the land, building the factory, equipping it, and paying the workers.

In spite of financial difficulties encountered in the beginning, it is now a growing business venture with a staff of 33 workers (1993) that facilitates contacts with Muslims and Christians of other churches.

Managers: Habib Banna, 1975-1983; Tom Staples, 1983-1984; Mokhtar Nashed, 1984- .

ADVENTIST HEALTH SYSTEM (AHS) (Adventist Health Care Association). The Seventh-day Adventist Church's health-care work in the United States, including 60 acute-care hospitals, plus nursing homes, retirement centers, home health agencies, medical offices, walk-in clinics, and many other related activities and diversified businesses.

The first SDA health-care facility opened in 1866 in Battle Creek, Michigan. Founders of the young Seventh-day Adventist denomination saw the need for a health-care work that emphasized physical, mental, and spiritual wholeness. The center stressed prevention as well as scientific treatment of disease.

By the turn of the century, additional SDA health-care facilities were established across the United States and abroad, creating a need for trained medical workers. To meet this need, the church established a training center in Loma Linda, California, in 1905. *(See* Loma Linda University.)

Health care changed dramatically with the introduction of vaccines, antibiotics, and other medical advances. Health insurance and Medicare brought even more changes in the health-care delivery system. By the mid-1970s the church had formed five regional organizations to manage its health-care work. A system organization gave the church's hospitals the corporate strength of a larger organization's resources and expertise.

A national organization was formed in 1982. The union of five SDA health-care corporations into Adventist Health System/United States (AHS/US) created the largest not-for-profit multiinstitutional health-care system in the country. Donald W. Welch was president of AHS/US from 1982 to 1991.

The system was reorganized in 1991 with regional systems operating independently of a national corporation.

In 1993 the church's health-care work in the United States was operated by nine regional corporations. These corporations and the hospitals in each follows. (Some have separate entries in the *Encyclopedia.*)

Adventist Health System/Loma Linda, Inc. (est. 1982), Loma Linda, Calif.: Barstow Community Hospital (50 beds), Barstow, Calif.; Loma Linda Community Hospital (120 beds), Loma Linda, Calif.; Loma Linda University Medical Center (546 beds), Loma Linda, Calif.

Adventist Health System/Sunbelt Health Care Corporation (est. 1973), Orlando, Fla.: Central Texas Medical Center (109 beds), San Marcos, Tex.; East Pasco Medical Center (85 beds), Zephyrhills, Fla.; Florida Hospital (1,462 beds) with campuses in Altamonte Springs, Apopka, East Orlando, Kissimmee, and Orlando, Fla.; Florida Hospital/Waterman (182 beds), Eustis, Fla.; Gordon Hospital (65 beds), Calhoun, Ga.; Highland Hospital (48 beds), Portland, Tenn.; Huguley Memorial Medical Center (185 beds), Fort Worth, Tex.; Jellico Community Hospital (50 beds), Jellico, Tenn.; Lake Placid Medical Center (50 beds), Lake Placid, Fla.; Medical Center Hospital (200 beds), Punta Gorda, Fla.; Memorial Hospital (63 beds), Manchester, Ky.; Metroplex Hospital (78 beds), Killeen, Tex.; Park Ridge Hospital (103 beds), Fletcher, N.C.; Rollins Brook Community Hospital (36 beds), Lampasas, Tex.; Sierra Vista Hospital (34 beds), Truth or Consequences, N.Mex.; Smyrna Hospital (100 beds), Smyrna, Ga.; Takoma Adventist Hospital (115 beds), Greeneville, Tenn.; Tennessee Christian Medical Center (307 beds), Madison, Tenn.; Walker Memorial Medical Center (101 beds), Avon Park, Fla.; Walker Memorial Medical Center/Wauchula (50 beds).

Adventist Health System/West (est. 1980), Roseville, Calif.: Castle Medical Center (160 beds), Kailua, Hawaii; Feather River Hospital (121 beds), Paradise, Calif.; Hanford Community Medical Center (54 beds), Hanford, Calif.; Monument Valley Hospital (20 beds), Monument Valley, Utah; Paradise Valley Hospital (228 beds), National City, Calif.; Portland Adventist Medical Center (302 beds), Portland, Oreg.; St. Helena Hospital and Health Center (188 beds), Deer Park, Calif.; San Joaquin Community Hospital (178 beds), Bakersfield, Calif.; Sonora Community Hospital (143 beds), Sonora, Calif.; Southern California Healthcare Network—Glendale Adventist Medical Center (464 beds), Glendale, Simi Valley Hospital and Health Care Services (215 beds), Simi Valley, and White Memorial Medical Center (377 beds), Los Angeles; Tillamook County General Hospital (49 beds), Tillamook, Oreg.; Ukiah Valley Medical Center (116 beds), Ukiah, Calif.; Walla Walla General Hospital (72 beds), Walla Walla, Wash.

Adventist Healthcare Mid-Atlantic Corporation (est. 1989), Rockville, Md.: Hackettstown Community Hospital (106 beds), Hackettstown, N.J.; Reading Rehabilitation Hospital (90 beds), Reading, Pa.; Shady Grove Adventist Hospital (253 beds), Rockville, Md.; Washington Adventist Hospital (300 beds), Takoma Park, Md.

Atlantic Adventist Healthcare Corporation (est. 1991), Stoneham, Mass.: Fuller Memorial Hospital (82 beds), South Attleboro, Mass.; New England Memorial Hospital (191 beds), Stoneham, Mass.

Hinsdale Health System (est. 1990), Hinsdale, Ill.: Chippewa Valley Hospital (30 beds) and Oak View Care Center (60 beds), Durand, Wisconsin; Glen Oaks Medical Center (186 beds), Glendale Heights, Ill.; Hinsdale Hospital (459 beds), Hinsdale, Ill.

Kettering Adventist Healthcare (est. 1982), Kettering, Ohio: Kettering Memorial Hospital (503 beds), Kettering, Ohio; Sycamore Hospital (191 beds), Miamisburg, Ohio.

Midwest Adventist Health Services Corporation (est. 1990), Shawnee Mission, Kans.: Moberly Regional Medical Center (120 beds), Moberly, Mo.; Shawnee Mission Medical Center (383 beds), Shawnee Mission, Kans.

Rocky Mountain Adventist Healthcare (est. 1990), Denver, Colo.: Avista Hospital (50 beds), Louisville, Colo.; Littleton Hospital (105 beds), Littleton, Colo.; Platte Valley Medical Center (58 beds), Brighton, Colo.; Porter Memorial Hospital (368 beds), Denver, Colo.

ADVENTIST HERITAGE MINISTRY. An educational and evangelistic corporation organized in 1981 to assist in preserving the heritage of the Seventh-day Adventist Church through the purchase, restoration, and, where appropriate, replication of properties significant to the denomination's founding and development. Sponsored by the North American Division, Adventist Historic Properties is supported mainly by direct contributions.

Historical Background. Early in the twentieth century interest was first shown in the historic sites connected with the beginning of the Seventh-day Adventist Church. The denomination's first history book, *Rise and Progress of the Seventh-day Adventists*, by J. N. Loughborough, had been printed in 1892. In 1909 Ellen G. White, on her final visit to Portland, Maine, manifested a keen interest in visiting the various local sites associated with her own childhood. Later M. E. Olsen tried to locate historic sites so they could be photographed to illustrate his thoroughgoing book, *A History of the Origin and Progress of Seventh-day Adventists*, published in 1925. During the 1930s and 1940s several individuals continued the attempt to locate historic sites associated with early Adventist history. Two men prominent in this endeavor were Elders A. W. Spalding and W. C. White. In 1947 Spalding's research led to the publication of his *Footprints of the Pioneers*, a helpful guide that provided not only information about the sites, including photographs, but also general directions to help travelers find them.

In the 1950s the Ellen G. White Estate began organizing annual denominational history tours to New England Adventist sites. Later members of the Tabernacle church in Battle Creek, Michigan, began conducting weekly Sabbath afternoon tours to the historic Adventist sites in their city.

In 1956 the Pacific Union Conference acquired Elmshaven in northern California, Ellen G. White's final home, 1900-1915. Later, in 1960, the Australasian (now South Pacific) Division acquired and restored Sunnyside, Ellen White's home in Australia, 1895-1900. In 1966 the Battle Creek (Michigan) tabernacle purchased the Wood Street home, where James and Ellen White lived from 1855 to 1863.

Organization of Adventist Historic Properties. By 1980 several Adventist historians and lay members had become actively concerned about the ever-diminishing number of historic sites. When Garth H. "Duff" Stoltz, an outstanding local historian in Battle Creek, learned that the Battle Creek home of Deacon John White, James White's father, was soon to be demolished, he decided it was time to put a stop to the trend. Duff Stoltz contacted James R. Nix, then director of the Heritage Room at Loma Linda University, and the two men raised the funds needed to buy the property.

Adventist Historic Properties, Inc., was organized on May 8, 1981, in Battle Creek. Shortly thereafter, its motto, "The Past With a Future," was adopted. Founded by lay members, the organization did not come under church ownership until February 22, 1988. Its first president and board chair was Lawrence E. Crandall, also of Battle Creek.

Almost immediately after Adventist Historic Properties' organization, the two White homes in Battle Creek were deeded to it. In 1982 what had traditionally been thought to be the J. N. Loughborough home in Battle Creek was purchased. Later it was discovered that this home actually belonged to John N. Daigneau, an early Adventist believer, so in 1992 Adventist Historic Properties purchased the actual J. N. Loughborough home, which still stood next door. In 1982 property adjacent to the Washington, New Hampshire, church was purchased and deeded to the Northern New England Conference.

On September 25, 1984, Adventist Historic Properties purchased 25 acres (10 hectares) that originally were part of William Miller's farm in Low Hampton, New York. Included in this acquisition were Miller's house that he built in 1815 and Ascension Rock, where local Millerite Adventists are reported to have waited for the Lord's return on October 22, 1844.

In 1985 the first issue of *AHP Bulletin* appeared, containing reports on the activities of Adventist Historic Properties. The following year a Michigan State historical marker, sponsored by Adventist Historic Properties, was erected in Oak Hill Cemetery in Battle Creek near the graves of James and Ellen White. During the years 1987-1990 Adventist Historic Properties worked closely with the North American Division's Office of Education to promote Seventh-day Adventist history in elementary and secondary schools throughout the division.

Starting in 1988, Adventist Historic Properties began sponsoring volunteer work bees at its various historic sites. Several of these have involved Adventist young people, thus enabling them to learn about their Adventist roots while helping to preserve them.

On January 26, 1989, Adventist Historic Properties purchased 17 acres (7 hectares) that were originally part of Hiram Edson's farm near Port Gibson, New York. Three years later the organization purchased a barn that originally belonged to Luther Edson, Hiram's father, dismantled it, and transported it to the Hiram Edson farm to be reerected there.

With sesquicentennial commemoration events planned for the William Miller farm in 1994, extensive restoration work was carried out on Miller's house during 1993 and 1994.

At the same time, and with the encouragement of the city of Battle Creek, Adventist Historic Properties is moving ahead with development of a small Advent village consisting, at least initially, of the two White houses, the Loughborough home, and the surrounding area. In 1994 the organization's name was changed to Adventist Heritage Ministry.

Board Chairs: Lawrence E. Crandall, 1981-1988; Robert L. Dale, 1988- .

Presidents: Lawrence E. Crandall, 1981-1991; James R. Nix, 1991- .

Secretaries: Delbert L. Brown, 1982-1983; James R. Nix, 1983-1985; C. Mervyn Maxwell, 1985- .

Treasurers: Herbert W. Pritchard, 1981- .

ADVENTIST HOSPITAL OF HAITI (Hôpital Adventiste d'Haiti). A 68-bed medical institution founded in 1978 and located in Port-au-Prince. When started, under the management of Halden Ritz, it had 33 beds and 54 employees. In 1993 157 employees staffed the hospital. Since 1989 the general manager has been Dr. Jude Jean-Baptiste, and the treasurer has been Kelly Joseph.

ADVENTIST INFORMATION MINISTRY (AIM). A 24-hour-per-day telephone answering and literature request service operated by the North American Division. Its priorities also include follow-up of interests from outreach telecasts, radiobroadcasts, and literature ministries, and helping such interests become involved with a local Seventh-day Adventist church. AIM also contracts to provide 24-hour registration services for local evangelistic campaigns and Revelation seminars, answers coupons placed in outreach periodicals, and raises funds for church agencies through telephone solicitation.

The follow-up process begins when AIM answers a viewer's call on an 800 number phone line. Most requests are for free literature offered on the program. When a viewer requests Bible studies or a pastoral visit, an AIM chaplain confirms the request, compiles a record of the individual's prior requests, then makes a referral to the nearest Adventist pastor. The chaplain monitors the progress made by the interested person and reports when a baptism occurs.

AIM was established on the Andrews University campus in 1982 by the North American Division as the result of planning efforts by Desmond Cummings, Jr., Robert Dale, and Robert Moon. Approximately half the funds used at AIM benefit the NAD churches three ways. First, they provide a service for the church. Second, they provide seminary and other students contact opportunities and experience in the church's outreach and follow-up programs. Third, they provide students funds to help with educational expenses. A small full-time staff oversees the work of a large number of student employees and volunteers.

ADVENTIST INTERNATIONAL INSTITUTE OF ADVANCED STUDIES. An educational institute established in 1987 at Pasay City, Philippines, serving the Far Eastern Division, as well as accepting students from other areas. The school offers limited graduate work in its own name. The 1994 *Yearbook* listed John C. Pesulima as president, with an administrative staff of 12. Jairyong Lee was listed as dean of the Theological Seminary, with a staff and faculty of 14.

ADVENTIST INTERNATIONAL MEDICAL SOCIETY (AIMS). A nonprofit church-related professional organization of Seventh-day Adventist physicians, medical students, and other health-care workers desiring fellowship, scientific exchange, and mutual encouragement in Christian service. Many local chapters have been organized in the Caribbean and Latin America, Europe, Asia, and Africa since the initiation of AIMS at Loma Linda in 1977. A major project of AIMS has been the publishing of the *Health Evangelism Study Guide*, which was developed as an introduction to a distinctive SDA lifestyle and method of medical practice, and as a beginning guide to work in health evangelism. It has been, or is currently being, translated from English into Spanish, German, Russian, and French. Although affiliated with the LLU SM Alumni Association, AIMS is organizationally separate, as it attempts to serve the many health professionals around the world who are not LLU graduates. Further information is available from AIMS, 11245 Anderson St., Suite 200, Loma Linda, California 92354.

ADVENTIST LAYMAN (1972-1986; quarterly). Formerly the official organ of the General Conference Department of Laymen's Activities. It promoted the department's activities, and contained the programs and guidance for the monthly special occasion services, the materials for the weekly 10-minute missionary services, articles and hints on successful lay soul-winning methods and experiences, and other features of Christian service. It replaced *GO* in 1972.

Editors: L. A. Shipowick, 1972-1973; V. W. Schoen, 1974-1977; George E. Knowles, 1977-1986.

ADVENTIST-LAYMEN'S SERVICES AND INDUSTRIES (ASI). A church-sponsored organization for the promotion of the interests of Seventh-day Adventist privately owned and operated supporting enterprises in North America, formerly known as the Association of SDA Self-supporting Institutions and as the Association of Privately Owned SDA Services and Industries. It continues to be referred to by the initials ASI.

This organization, originally known as the North American Commission for Self-supporting Missionary Work, was established in 1946 with the vice president for the North American Division, N. C. Wilson, as chair, and E. A. Sutherland, M.D., of Madison Institution, as secretary. Six General Conference representatives were appointed as members of the operating committee.

The Association of SDA Self-supporting Institutions was organized at a special meeting held in Cincinnati, Ohio, in 1947, with 25 charter members. E. A. Sutherland, M.D., was elected president; W. E. Mahlin, M.D., vice president; Wayne McFarland, M.D., secretary-treasurer. This action was ratified at the 1947 Annual Council.

Merger and Reorganization. At its Fourth Annual Convention at Grand Ledge, Michigan, Sept. 3, 1951, ASI voted to amalgamate with the General Conference Commission for Self-supporting Missionary Enterprises (the latter organization had succeeded the Commission on Rural Living, created in 1946 by a merger of the Committee on Country Living and the North American Commission for Self-supporting Missionary Work).

Association Objectives. The purpose of the ASI is:

1. To foster and promote the interests of businesses and supporting enterprises operated by Seventh-day Adventists throughout the North American Division.

2. To encourage Seventh-day Adventist church members in privately owned enterprises of various types to unite their efforts with those of denominationally operated enterprises in the furtherance and extension of the gospel to their immediate communities, and to the ends of the earth, according to their abilities and opportunities.

3. To encourage such businesses and enterprises to commit themselves to work in full and complete harmony with the standards and policies of the denomination in their relationships with conference and church administrations, ministers, and church members, and with the people of their communities.

Membership. The membership of ASI may be classified under the following types of institutions or enterprises: businesses; industries; educational; nursing homes; retirement centers; community and convalescent hospitals; medical and dental clinics; foundations of various types; and personal members. Membership is limited to businesses, personalized enterprises, and institutions operated by SDA church members in harmony with denominational standards and principles, and according to professional and ethical standards, and recommended by local and union conference administrations and their ASI secretaries.

Memberships are subject to a biennial review by the ASI board. An annual membership fee is set for each member according to the size of the enterprise.

Officers and ASI Board consist of a president, a general vice president, four other vice presidents, an executive secretary, and a treasurer, who are elected by the constituency of the association and approved by NADCOM. The ASI board consists of 26 members, consisting of 20 laypersons and six church administrators appointed by NADCOM.

The General Conference provides office space and an annual budget for office, secretarial, and travel expense. It also provides the salary and general expense of the executive secretary and treasurer of the ASI, since that individual is considered a member of the General Conference Executive Committee.

Conventions. Formerly held quarterly, then biennially, conventions are now held annually. Nationwide conventions provide professional training and Christian fellowship for the thousands who attend, all at their own expense.

Statistics: As of July 1993, ASI had 1,021 members.

ASI News and *ASI Magazine.* In 1947 a mimeographed news bulletin, called *News Letter*, was founded. In 1951 this publication was issued in printed form and the name was changed to *News and Views*. In 1953 it became known simply as *News;* in 1961 the name was changed to *ASI News*. In 1993 a new four-color bimonthly 16-page magazine titled *ASI Magazine* was launched, edited by Ralph Blodgett. At that time the *ASI News* was changed into a two-color newsletter and published on alternating months.

Projects. Lately a program has been instituted whereby various worthy enterprises are chosen as recipients of help extended by special offerings from ASI members. Numerous schools and hospitals in mission lands have thus been aided.

Chapters. Upon vote of the ASI board, any union conference may organize its own ASI chapter. Chapters may call meetings whenever it is feasible and may recruit members as they see fit. The Pacific Union and the Lake Union were the first unions to so organize.

Presidents: E. A. Sutherland, M.D., 1947-1949; W. E. Straw, 1949-1951; L. A. Senseman, M.D., 1951-1966; Allan R. Buller, 1966-1973; Roger F. Goodge, 1973-1979; Harold Lance, 1979-1983; Philip Winsted, 1983-1987; Henry Martin, 1987-1989; Raymond Hamblin, 1989- .

Executive Secretaries: Wayne McFarland, M.D., 1947-1951; Wesley Amundsen, 1951-1968; Caris H. Lauda, 1968-1975; J. J. Aitken, 1975-1981; Kenneth H. Livesay, 1981-1985; William C. Arnold, 1985-1991; G. Edward Reid, 1991-1993; Dwight Hilderbrandt, 1994- .

ADVENTIST LIFE. *See Adobenchisuto Raifu.*

ADVENTIST MEDIA CENTER (Seventh-day Adventist Radio, Television, and Film Center) (AMC). A broadcast and film production center that includes radio and television studios, central service departments, and the offices and Bible schools for Breath of Life, Faith for Today, It Is Written, La Voz de la Esperanza, and the Voice of Prophecy, as well as the Adventist Evangelistic Association.

In 1969 study began to determine the advisability of establishing a denominational center for broadcast and film production. During 1970 production problems in New York led Faith for Today to request a transfer to California. The 1971 Annual Council voted the establishment of the center and appointed a board of trustees, with R. R. Bietz, chair, and Walter R. L. Scragg, secretary. Alvin G. Munson was elected president of the center.

The center was incorporated in 1972. Construction of the first building to house services for the ministries began in 1973 on a 19-acre (7.7-hectare) site in Newbury Park, California. Following the death of Munson, the first president, this building was named in his memory.

Two additional buildings were completed and occupied in 1978. These are named in memory of William Fagal, founder of Faith for Today, and H.M.S. Richards, founder of the Voice of Prophecy.

The structure of the center organization maintains a large measure of creative and management independence for the various ministries, but provides centralized services that include video and audio recording studios, printing, computer services, mailing and warehouse, plant operations, human resources, accounting, marketing, trust services, and administration.

The Adventist Media Center includes an in-house advertising agency, TRANSDA, which places Adventist broadcasts on the air on stations around the world, as well as arranging print advertising, billboards, and direct mail. TRANSDA is dedicated to finding the best time periods available for the best price, and has saved the church millions of dollars over the years in airtime and advertising costs.

Television and radio programs produced at the Adventist Media Center are aired not only in North America but also around the world. Persons in nearly every country can tune in an AMC production. The ministries of the center collectively influence more non-Adventists favorably for Christ, every week, than attend all Seventh-day Adventist churches worldwide.

In 1994 the Adventist Media Center included 145 full-time workers, 30 part-time employees (including academy and college students), and 152 volunteers. These workers had come from 20 countries, and represented a wide variety of ethnic origins.

Presidents: Alvin G. Munson, 1971-1976; Robert Frame, 1977-1985; B. E. Jacobs, 1986-1990; Glenn Aufderhar, 1990- .

ADVENTIST MEDICAL CENTER (Okinawa Medical Center). A 48-bed general hospital at Nishihara, Okinawa, owned and operated by the Japan Union Conference.

The medical center is the outgrowth of a small clinic opened at Shuri, then the mission headquarters, in November of 1953, with a part-time physician and an Okinawan nurse in charge. Shortly afterward a nurse was called from Japan to assist in caring for the increasing number of patients seeking its services.

On Mar. 1, 1959, the clinic became the outpatient section of a new, modern, 15-bed hospital named the Adventist Medical Center, built on the outskirts of the capital city of Naha. In June of 1960 the inpatient department was ready for service. The physician in charge was George M. Tolhurst, and the director of nursing service was Norma Eldridge, R.N. The hospital was later expanded to 24 beds when a five-room addition was completed in 1965. A dental department was added in 1968, and in 1974 three dentists were employed.

The facilities soon became inadequate for the growing number of patients. In December 1984 a modern four-story 70-bed hospital, five doctor's residences, and a 10-unit nurses apartment were built on the hilltop at Nishihara.

The hospital has medical, dermatological, surgical, obstetrical and gynecological, and family practice specialties, with a staff of 123 workers. In 1993 there were seven physicians and three dentists. The hospital cares for 110 inpatient admissions and 6,500 outpatients monthly, with emphasis on dermatology.

Medical Directors: George M. Tolhurst, 1960-1961; Ralph F. Meinhardt, 1961-1963; Evert E. Kuester, 1963-1968; James R. Wood, 1968-1985; James S. Miyashiro, 1985- .

ADVENTIST MEDICAL SERVICES IN SOUTH AFRICA. *See* Adventist Professional Health Services in South Africa.

ADVENTIST MEN. A men's service organization that was intended to give direction and strength to church lay leaders, lay preaching, and other lines of Christian service, such as prison ministry, civil defense, and certain types of Community Services projects.

The original society was authorized by the 1937 Annual Council of the General Conference and called the Society of Missionary Men. The name "Adventist Men" was adopted and the service program was recommended at the Lay Activities Advisory Council in 1961. To give guidance to the organization and train the Adventist men for service, an Adventist Men's Seminar program was developed and widely used on the conference level.

Adventist Men's organizations worked within the framework of the former church lay activities program, under the direction of the Church Evangelism Council. Officers were a leader (who was a member of the Church Evangelism Council) and a secretary-treasurer. Membership was open to male members of the church.

"ADVENTIST MISSIONS FACING THE 21ST CENTURY." *See* European Institute of World Mission.

ADVENTIST MUSLIM REVIEW, THE. *See* Adventist Global Centre for Islamic Studies.

ADVENTIST NURSES' HOME. A hostel formerly maintained and operated by the South African Union Conference in Mowbray, a suburb six miles (10 kilometers) from Cape Town, for housing Seventh-day Adventist women who were taking the course in nursing at Groot Schuur Hospital. In the absence of an SDA hospital in South Africa providing training in nursing, arrangements were made with the Groot Schuur Hospital for Sabbath privileges for SDA student nurses. The home, supervised by W. H. Hurlow and his wife, was opened on Aug. 1, 1957, offering accommodations to 15. It occupied the building formerly housing the offices of the Voice of Prophecy. Student nurses came from all the provinces of the Republic of South Africa and from Zambia and Rhodesia. Mrs. A. B. Mayais took charge of the home in 1961 and remained in that position until it closed in 1967.

ADVENTIST PORT ACADEMY. (Cologio Porteño Adventista). A coeducational day academy organized in 1965 at Puerto Cabezas, Zelaya, Nicaragua, by LeRoy Haughton and Peter Wood to provide low-cost education to the coastal population. It last appeared in the *Yearbook* in the early 1980s.

Principals: Alfredo Ordonez, 1970-1971; Norton Perilla, 1971-1977; Gabriel Jeffries, 1977-1979; Jaime Bordas, 1979-1981.

ADVENTIST PRINTING HOUSE (MADAGASCAR) (Imprimerie Adventiste) (Trano Fanontam-Printy Adventista). A publishing house with printing plant, established in 1930 in Antananarivo, the capital of Madagascar, by the Indian Ocean Union Mission at Soamanandrariny, Antananarivo. The house serves six islands of the Indian Ocean, with a population of about 14 million.

In 1951 the first publication began with five employees. The work made good progress from the start and increased in volume. By 1956 the plant was able to buy a stitcher, and in 1962 a folding machine was purchased. In May 1993 a new modern stitcher was purchased from Germany.

The publishing house operates four presses and employs 25 Malagasy workers. The five volumes of the Conflict of the Ages series have been translated into Malagasy. The plant serves the denomination first. Canvassers are satisfied with the 20 bookshops spread throughout Madagascar that are served by the publishing house. Outside of the church, the Malagasy Bible Society is the main customer.

The press issues the Sabbath school quarterly and the mission quarterly in Malagasy and French. Two other periodicals, *Adventist Standard* (in both Malagasy and French), and *The Witness* (in Malagasy), are also published. All materials needed by the churches, schools, and the mission; the manual of religious instruction; hymnbooks; tracts and books; and materials needed for evangelistic work are printed at Imprimerie Adventiste.

The plant is now too small for the challenges. In 1993 it was decided that the publishing house should move to a larger place near the union office, into an enlarged and remodeled building. Workers' homes are to be built.

In 1991 the sales amounted to FMG 118,442,546 (about $65,881), representing more than 15 million pages.

Managers: H. L. Henriksen, 1950-1954; René Villeneuve, 1954-1955; Marc Hecketsweiler, 1955-1975; Robert Roeland, 1975-1984; Michel Chaigne, 1984-1991; Velomanantsoa Rajaonarison, 1991-1992; John Ravelomanantsoa, 1992-1993; Francine Razafindrabe, 1993- .

ADVENTIST PROFESSIONAL HEALTH SERVICES IN SOUTH AFRICA. Established December 1982 as an interunion organization falling under the South African Affairs Committee of the General Conference with headquarters in Bethlehem, South Africa.

The forerunner organization, Adventist Medical Services, was disbanded and the private practice medical work of the South African Union Conference and the Southern Union Conference was united in one organization under the leadership of W. E. Staples, M.D.

The aims of APHS are:

1. To help finance the establishment of Seventh-day Adventist private medical, dental, and paramedical practices within its territories to serve the church, particularly where the church is struggling.
2. To support and encourage young people to prepare for service in southern Africa and also other mission appointments.
3. To assist in the planning and establishment of medical institutions and clinics where the need should arise.
4. To conduct spiritual retreats for medical, dental, and paramedical workers and students.
5. To assist in the establishment of a blended ministry program with the territory of southern Africa. A number of doctors have been ordained to the gospel ministry and are assisting in the pastoral work of the church.
6. To provide pastoral care for all Seventh-day Adventist medical, dental, and paramedical professionals and students.

ADVENTIST PUBLISHING HOUSE IN RUSSIA. *See* Source of Life Publishing House.

ADVENTIST RADIO, TELEVISION, AND FILM CENTER. *See* Adventist Media Center; Communication, Department of.

ADVENTIST RESOURCE MANAGEMENT SERVICE (ARMS). An agency that matches volunteers in the church with mission and service opportunities. Established in 1992, ARMS serves as a clearinghouse for mission opportunities, providing volunteer resources to fill the needs of ministries and organizations sharing the mission of the church.

The first Global Mission project in North America was initiated by ARMS in 1992, utilizing volunteer resources to establish a new congregation in the inner city of Baltimore, Maryland, and to carry out evangelism in 10 other churches in the surrounding area. Since that time, ARMS has continued to provide new opportunities for mission-minded church members and necessary volunteer resources for a wide variety of ministries.

Although ARMS focuses on the North American Division as its volunteer base, the opportunities for service are worldwide. Many other church entities and supporting ministries utilize the services of ARMS to further the ministry and mission of the Seventh-day Adventist Church.

Executive Director: Tony E. Finch, 1992- .

ADVENTIST RETIREMENT VILLAGE, INC. (formerly known as Kressville Home for the Aged). A retirement village incorporating Kressville Home Units, Kressville Resident-funded Units, Alton Villas Resident-funded Units, Charles

Harrison Memorial Home, and Kressville Hostel. It is owned and operated by the North New South Wales Conference. Because it was once the site of the Avondale Health Retreat, served by Drs. D. H. and Lauretta Kress, the estate on which the homes and hostel stand has been named Kressville.

The first eight self-care units of brick construction were built under a grant from the government. These units were officially opened on Oct. 9, 1960. Over the next 14 years 54 more units were built.

In 1980, 36 resident-funded units were added, bringing the total number of units at Kressville to 98. On Aug. 16, 1964, the 72-bed Charles Harrison Memorial Home was opened on the estate. In 1982 the 35-bed Kressville Hostel was opened, and in 1993 an additional 40-bed hostel was constructed.

In 1990 an additional 32 resident-funded units were completed in Alton Road, Cooranbong. By 1993, 18 more resident-funded units were added, making a total of 50 units in the facility known as Alton Villas.

Managers: E. J. Garrard, 1960-1964; R. Craig, 1964-1967; O. H. Twist, 1963-1981; A.W.J. Shirley, 1981-1989; K. A. Allen, 1989- .

ADVENTIST RETIREMENT VILLAGES (South Queensland Conference). Four modern retirement complexes sponsored by the South Queensland Conference in Australia. These are:

Redlands (Victoria Point). The head office of the care of the aged work in the conference, Redlands is located 12 miles (20 kilometers) east of Brisbane, overlooking beautiful Moreton Bay. The village contains 155 one- and two-bedroom units, a hostel of 54 rooms, a 33-bed nursing home, a chapel, a workshop/hall, and other amenities. A staff of 70 cares for the residents.

Melody Park (Nerang). A partly established retirement complex acquired by the conference in 1992, located 50 miles (80 kilometers) south of Brisbane. It contains 30 units, with manager's residence, pool/spa, and a library/games room. A 60-bed hotel complex is planned.

Capricorn (Yeppoon). Located 375 miles (600 kilometers) north of Brisbane at a coastal resort. In response to the need of a facility for care of the aged in the northern part of the South Queensland Conference, 10 units had been completed by 1993. Altogether, 60 one- and two-bed units are planned.

Caloundra Retirement Village (Sunshine Coast). Located 55 miles (90 kilometers) north of Brisbane. In 1993 this newest of the retirement villages was still in the early construction stage. The first stage planning envisages 50 units.

Two other aged care facilities are supervised and maintained by local churches:

Hervey Bay contains three independent living units.

Toowoomba contains four two-bedroom units and is located 60 miles (100 kilometers) west of Brisbane, in the Darling Downs region.

ADVENTIST REVIEW (1850- ; successor to *Present Truth,* 1849-1850; title changes noted below; weekly; published by the General Conference of Seventh-day Adventists, printed by RH; January 1994 circulation, 250,000, first issue of each month; other issues, 40,000; files in RH, AU, AUC; also available in microcard form). It originated as a semimonthly (issued with some irregularities at first), formed by the merging of *The Present Truth* and *The Advent Review.*

Background. The historical setting of the *Review* was in the experiences of a small group of Adventists who had belonged to the Millerite movement, which met deep disappointment on Oct. 22, 1844, the day on which its adherents had expected the prophecy of the cleansing of the sanctuary at the end of the 2300 prophetic days (Dan. 8:14) to be fulfilled by the second coming of Christ. After 1844 those who still retained belief in the basic Millerite teachings divided into two main groups: first, those who felt that their 1844 movement had erred in the prophetic time reckoning; second, those who felt that the error lay not in their expectation of the cleansing of the sanctuary in 1844, but in their concept of what the cleansing of the sanctuary meant. One distinctive group of the latter began to keep the seventh-day Sabbath and became the embryo Seventh-day Adventist Church. This small group claimed to be the true spiritual successors of the Millerites, because the main group was denying its past experience in the 1844 movement. To support their claim they proceeded to publish two periodicals, the forerunners of the *Review:*

1. Between July 1849 and November 1850 they published 11 issues of a little paper, *The Present Truth,* which placed a major emphasis on the seventh-day Sabbath but also included an ardent defense of their view of what

the sanctuary cleansing really involved.

2. After the tenth issue of *The Present Truth* appeared (May 1850), they issued, at irregular intervals between August and November 1850, vol. 1, nos. 1 to 5, of *The Advent Review,* a publication so named because it reprinted and reviewed certain views advocated in the Advent movement of 1844. The opening sentence of the first issue reads: "Our design in this review is to cheer and refresh the true believer, by showing the fulfillment of Prophecy in the past wonderful work of God, in calling out, and separating from the world and nominal church, a people who are looking for the second advent of the dear Saviour." Also carrying the title *The Advent Review* was an Extra, issued following no. 4, bearing a date of September 1850, and a 48-page reprint of certain articles from earlier issues, bearing simply the date "1850."

The Church Paper. In November 1850, from the same printing house, G. L. Mellen & Co. of Paris, Maine, came the last issue of each of these two parent publications and vol. 1, no. 1, of the *Second Advent Review and Sabbath Herald.* The editor states:

"TO OUR READERS.—The REVIEW AND HERALD is designed to be strictly confined to those important truths that belong to the present time. We hope to be able to send you this enlarged size of the paper quite often, containing a simple and clear exposition of those great and sanctifying truths embraced in the message of the third angel [embodying the Sabbath in the last-day setting]" (p. 7).

"The paper," in its "enlarged size," apparently was considered by its publishers as the continuation of *The Present Truth,* or perhaps *The Advent Review,* or possibly both. Certainly it was larger in size than either of the two. Its prime policy, as its name suggests, was to review the Advent experience of 1843-1844, and to herald the Sabbath doctrine. With vol. 2, Aug. 5, 1851, it became *The Advent Review and Sabbath Herald.* This lengthy name, with minor variations, was employed until May 4, 1961, when it was formally contracted to *Review and Herald.* The original name was restored on Mar. 18, 1971, but, with the first issue of 1978, the name was changed to *Adventist Review,* its present name. (In fact, throughout its history the paper has been commonly referred to simply as the *Review.)*

From the first issue onward until 1939 there appeared under the title on the front cover, or under the name on page 3, the words: "Here is the patience of the saints; here are they that keep the commandments of God and the faith of Jesus." From 1909 to 1961 the following statement appeared either on the cover or on the masthead: "General Church Paper of the Seventh-day Adventists." In 1961 this was changed to read "Official Organ of the Seventh-day Adventist Church," but in 1967 the statement reverted to "General Church Paper of the Seventh-day Adventists." The paper was changed in format and design with the first issue of 1986 (see below), and since that time has carried "weekly news and inspiration for Seventh-day Adventists," and the statement "General Paper of the Seventh-day Adventist Church" on the masthead.

Places of Publication. Vol. 1 (November 1850 through June 9, 1851) was published at Paris, Maine; vol. 2 (July 21, 1851, through Mar. 23, 1852) at Saratoga Springs, New York; vol. 3 through vol. 7, no. 9 (May 6, 1852, through Oct. 30, 1855), at Rochester, New York; vol. 7, no. 10, through vol. 80, no. 32 (Dec. 4, 1855, through Aug. 11, 1903), at Battle Creek, Michigan; vol. 80, no. 33 through vol. 166, no. 26 (Aug. 20, 1903, through June 29, 1989), at Washington, D.C.; and vol. 166, no. 27 (July 6, 1989, onward), at Silver Spring, Maryland.

Printing Office Set Up. For the first two years the paper was printed at one and then another printing house. Then, while still at Saratoga Springs, James White set forth a series of reasons for his dissatisfaction with the printing arrangements. He thought it inappropriate to have the journal that advocated the Sabbath printed on the Sabbath day, as might easily be the case. He reasoned that if they had their own office this would not only ensure that the paper would not be printed on the Sabbath, but would also reduce costs. Furthermore, he could hire those "who are keeping the Sabbath, who would take an interest in the paper that cannot be expected of others" (*Review and Herald* 2:104, Mar. 2, 1852). The publication of the *Review* was the first collective endeavor on the part of the emerging SDA Church, and the first general offering solicited from the scattered groups of Sabbathkeepers was this fund to establish a publishing office and to purchase a printing press.

In the spring of 1852 James and Ellen White moved to Rochester, New York. There they soon rented a building, at $175 a year, which provided living quarters for them and a printing office—the first office headquarters the denomination had, and for a time, the only one. Nothing could better reveal how closely the church has been connected with our publishing work from the beginning. When the *Review* office was moved to Battle Creek in 1855, it entered a building erected and owned by church members. From the time the General Conference was organized in 1863, the offices that served as denominational headquarters were situated in a Review and Herald building until headquarters were transferred to Washington in 1903.

The General Conference Becomes Publisher. From 1863 to 1983, the Review and Herald Publishing Association and the General Conference were located together. Throughout this period the Review and Herald Publishing Association functioned as publisher of the church paper. However, during 1982 and 1983 the Review and Herald Publishing Association moved to a new facility at Hagerstown, Maryland, some 70 miles (112 kilometers) away from Washington, D.C. The impending move led to careful consideration of the role of the church paper and who should be its publisher. These discussions resulted in the General Conference's assuming the role of publisher in 1983, with the editorial staff of the *Adventist Review* located at Washington, D. C., as part of the General Conference. The Review and Herald Publishing Association was assigned responsibility for printing, marketing, design, and list fulfillment.

An *Adventist Review* editorial board was established at this time to guide the editors in general policies for the paper and to handle the hiring and firing of editors. The General Conference president has served as chair of this board from its inception. A large, broad-based *Adventist Review* advisory council was also set up in 1983 but was discontinued in 1990.

By June 30, 1989, the relocation of the General Conference in Silver Spring, Maryland, was completed. This became the legal place of publication of the *Review*.

In 1991 a commission of the General Conference was set up to clarify the roles of the General Conference and the Review and Herald Publishing Association with regard to the *Review*. This commission's recommendation reiterated the division of responsibilities that went into effect in 1983. However, an adjustment to the finances was made so that from Jan 1, 1993, the General Conference and Review and Herald Publishing Association share equally in any profits from the *Review* operation.

Size and Circulation. The *Review* in the early years was eight pages, about 10" x 14" (25 cm. x 36 cm.) in size. In the later years of the nineteenth century the page size was much larger, and the average number of pages per issue slowly increased to about 24, an average rather steadily maintained for years. From 1953 onward the number of pages has varied, usually being either 24 or 32, but occasionally 48, depending on the number of pages devoted to advertising. Page size is 8⅛" x 10⅝" (20.6 cm. x 30 cm.). Since 1986 at least 26 issues per year have included four-color pages.

Early circulation figures are not known, though stray news items reveal that 1,000 or 2,000 copies of certain of the earliest issues were printed. This slowly grew, as funds became available, for the *Review* was at first sent to all who desired it, and the readers were requested to give, as they were able, to support it. After a time the paper was put on a subscription basis. The paid circulation gradually increased, until in the 1940s it passed the 40,000 mark, and in the 1950s it exceeded 50,000. In 1963 because of a drastic cut in subscription price and aggressive promotion, the circulation reached 96,000, but has since declined. The current circulation includes about 280,000 for the first issue of each month (see below), with about 40,000 subscribers to the other weekly issues. The circulation is confined largely to North America, although subscribers are to be found in almost every country of the world, wherever there are Seventh-day Adventists.

Frequency of Issue. As might be expected, the early issues were not published regularly. Lack of funds, lack of time, and frequent changes of residence made any kind of schedule difficult to follow. Vol. 1 had 13 numbers, and ran from November 1850 through June 9, 1851; vol. 2, 14 numbers, July 21, 1851 (the first issue was an Extra; the first regular issue bore the same number and was dated Aug. 5, 1851), through Mar. 23, 1852; vol. 3, 26 numbers, May 6, 1852, through May 12, 1853; vol. 4, 26 numbers, May 26, 1853, through Jan. 10, 1854; vol. 5, 26 numbers, Jan. 24, 1854, through Aug. 1, 1854; vol. 6, 32 numbers, Aug. 15, 1854, through June 26, 1855; vol. 7, 26 numbers, July 10, 1855, through Mar. 27, 1856; vol. 8, 26 numbers, Apr. 10, 1856, through Oct. 30, 1856. Beginning with vol. 9 the volumes ran uniformly for six months each, and almost without exception contained 26 issues until vols. 46 through 58 (July 1, 1875, through Dec. 20, 1881) regularly contained 25 numbers each.

Beginning with vol. 59 (Jan. 3, 1882), the volume length was changed from the half year to the calendar year, 50 numbers; from vol. 72 (Jan. 1, 1895) to the present time 52 numbers have appeared annually, with several exceptions as noted in the following paragraph.

Extras and Supplements. Not infrequently through the years, Extras or Supplements have been published, most of them outside the regular sequence of weekly numbers. These have sometimes dealt with some timely issue, such as critical attacks by offshoots or other enemies; often with lay missionary work and distribution of publications.

Then two Extras on current events in 1914 and a series of 24 in 1915-1916 (in addition to the weekly issues but numbered as part of the regular sequence), each on a single doctrinal topic, were published for general distribution. These were continued in 1917 as a separate periodical. *(See Present Truth* [2], 1917-1955.)

The *Review* originally published the proceedings of the General Conference sessions, which at first were held annually. Later separate *General Conference Bulletins* contained these special reports. In 1905 and from 1926 on, the *Review* again incorporated them, thus making them available to all subscribers. These reports currently require about 10 extra issues.

In recent years the *Review* has published two or three special issues each year devoted to a single topic, such as last-day events, Adventist women, and the family. These special issues are part of the regular sequence, but usually are undated to provide for longer shelf life.

Special Editions. The first few annual Ingathering magazines (1908-1910, 1913, 1914) were *Review* specials issued in extra quantities for distribution. The *Review* has an annual special containing the readings for the Week of Prayer each autumn. From 1948 to 1960 one number each quarter, printed in two colors and presenting a special array of general articles, was issued in increased quantities to provide copies to all SDA families in North America who were not subscribers. The total press runs on these quarterly color numbers, as they were called, averaged about 140,000. The cost of the extra copies for nonsubscribers was borne by the General Conference and local conferences.

In 1985 the editors, in conjunction with design and marketing personnel from the Review and Herald Publishing Association, gave major study to recasting the *Review* in an endeavor to attract young adult readers. These discussions led to a new format and design introduced with the Jan. 2, 1986, issue. The first of each month was shaped also to fit the needs of a North American Division paper and was labeled "NAD edition." A cost-sharing plan involving the General Conference, North American Division, and each NAD union and conference was introduced in order to provide this edition free to each Adventist home in North America. Almost all conferences have chosen to participate in this plan, and circulation of the NAD edition has ranged from 240,000 to the current 280,000.

Editions. From 1947 to 1953 a monthly 16-page English language World Edition of the *Review* was published for countries outside North America. For English-speaking countries the magazine was printed in Washington, D.C., and shipped abroad. For other countries copies of the English language edition were mailed to certain publishing houses overseas for translation and printing. The cost of this World Edition was borne entirely by the General Conference.

In 1971 the monthly edition was revived and placed on a subscription basis. This edition, which was subsidized by the General Conference, was printed at Stanborough Press in England through 1974, but in 1975 was transferred to the Review and Herald Publishing Association. With the introduction of the NAD edition in 1986, the monthly, often referred to as the "Monthly Digest," was discontinued.

The *Review* also serves as the church paper for other divisions. As *Revista Adventista* it is published in separate Portuguese and Spanish editions for readers in the South American Division. The Inter-American Division publishes the *Review* for English readers, *Revista Adventista* for Spanish-speaking readers, and *Revue Adventiste* for French-speaking readers. These editions at first were edited from the *Review* office, but for some years have been edited in the respective divisions. The Africa-Indian Ocean Division also calls its paper *Adventist Review* and publishes separate editions in English and French. For all these division papers the parent *Review* serves as the base: division editors draw upon its doctrinal and inspirational articles, and news of the world church.

In 1990 a quarterly edition in Spanish, *Revista Adventista*, was introduced for Spanish-speaking readers in North America. This edition, which likewise is built on articles selected from issues of the parent *Review,* is edited and published at the Pacific Press in Boise, Idaho.

A quarterly braille edition, made up of material selected from the weekly *Review*, was begun in January 1965. It is published by Christian Record Services in Lincoln, Nebraska.

In 1972 the Columbia Union Conference discontinued its union paper as a separate publication and entered into an arrangement with the Review and Herald to send the *Review* free to every family in its territory. In 1978 the Southwestern Union Conference began a similar arrangement for its union paper. The Columbia Union discontinued the plan in 1982; the Southwestern Union in 1985.

In 1991 the *Review* expanded its outreach beyond print with the introduction of a quarterly video magazine, *OnLine Edition*. Each program consists of six or seven short segments and aims to fulfill through the medium of video the same purposes as the printed *Review*—news and inspiration for SDAs. *OnLine Edition* is subsidized by the General Conference and in January 1993 had a circulation of 5,000, with 3,400 copies sent each quarter to churches in the NAD.

The World Edition of the *Review* was revived in March 1993 in response to several requests from divisions outside the NAD. The current World Edition consists of 16 pages, but, unlike the earlier one, is printed in the divisions from negatives supplied by the Review and Herald Publishing Association. This edition is edited in the *Review* office and is drawn entirely from articles appearing in the regular issues of the *Review*. Currently the FED, SAD, EAD, and SPD print and circulate the World Edition.

Editorial Policy and Range. The designation "General Paper of the Seventh-day Adventist Church" suggests both policy and range. From the first the *Review* has sought in two ways to unify the thinking of the members: by its presentations on doctrine and by its news of the activities of various SDA congregations and individuals. As the church began to grow rapidly overseas the news portion of the journal became increasingly important. From its very beginning the *Review* has been the church's one unbroken record of all notable events throughout SDA history, including the life sketches of all who have been leaders in the movement.

The *Review* is one of the oldest continuously published religious journals in America.

Editors. For most of the years the record is clear as to the editorship. For limited periods, when a group of names is listed under the title "editors," only the first named is here given—the available evidence indicates that that person was *the* editor. Beginning with the first issue, November 1850, the list reads: "Publishing Committee" (including James White), 1850-1851; James White, 1851-1855; Uriah Smith, 1855-1861; James White, 1861-1864; Uriah Smith, 1864-1869; J. N. Andrews, 1869-1870; Uriah Smith, 1870-1871; James White, 1871-1872; Uriah Smith, 1872-1873; James White, 1873-1877; Uriah Smith, 1877-1880; James White, 1880-1881 (died, Aug. 6, 1881); Uriah Smith, 1881-1897; A. T. Jones, 1897-1901; Uriah Smith, 1901-1903 (died Mar. 6, 1903); W. W. Prescott, 1903-1909; W. A. Spicer, 1909-1911; F. M. Wilcox, 1911-1944; W. A. Spicer, 1945 (six months); F. D. Nichol, 1945-1966; Kenneth H. Wood, 1966-1982; William G. Johnsson, 1982- .

ADVENTIST REVIEW PUBLISHING HOUSE (Romania). *See* Romanian Adventist Publishing House.

ADVENTIST SANITARIUM AND HOSPITAL (Addis Ababa, Ethiopia). *See* Empress Zauditu Memorial Adventist Hospital.

ADVENTIST SEMINARY (CROATIA) (Adventisticki Seminar Dvorac Marusevec; Adventistieko Uciliste Marusevec). An educational institution established for the purpose of preparing youth for the ministry, operated by the Croatian-Slovenian Conference. Seventh-day Adventist leaders in Yugoslavia early on recognized the need for a training school. Circumstances prevented the fulfillment of this goal until 1931, when J. F. Huenergardt established a small school in rented quarters in Belgrade. The next year the school was transferred to a property that belonged to the church in Zagreb. It operated there until 1942, with Robert Schillinger as principal and F. Zupancic, Albin Mocnik, Siegfried Ludewig, Mirko Golubic, Dragisa Stojcevic, and K. Semkovic as teachers.

By the end of the 1934-1935 school year, 55 students had obtained their training there, 15 of whom were employed by the organization. During World War II the school was closed.

Some time after the war, the Yugoslavian Union committee laid plans to reestablish the training school. In 1955 the school was reopened on a small property bought in Rakovica, near Belgrade. Dragisa Stojcevic was the first principal, succeeded by Jovan Slankamenac and Jovan Lorencin. The expansion of Belgrade and the cutting of a road through the property, together with the probable requisition of the estate, caused the transfer of the seminary to Marusevec in September 1974. In this latter area near Varazdin, in the north, a secondary school had been opened in September 1970, in a historic castle. Mirko Golubic was the director, and from an initial enrollment of 67, the number of students in the four secondary grades increased to 142 in 1974. That same year a dormitory for 80 young men and a similar building for 80 young women were constructed on land adjoining the castle. An apartment house for six faculty families was also completed by the time the seminary was merged with the secondary school. Jovan Lorencin was the first president of the seminary at Marusevec, assisted by 10 other full-time teachers and 15 part-time instructors. Successors include Jovan Slankamenac, Jovan Mihaljcic, and, at present, Franjo Wagenhofer, with a faculty and staff of more than 30.

In 1992 the seminary was reorganized, the Adventist Theological Seminary (Adventisticki Teoloski Fakultet) moving to Belgrade. In 1994 its president was Miroslav Pujic, the staff numbered 20. The secondary school (Srednja Vjerska Skola) remained at Marusevec.

ADVENTIST SEMINARY OF HEALTH EVANGELISM. A school of public health that served the Tanzania Union area. It was located on the campus of Heri Hospital. It began as a field station, operated by the Division of Public Health and Tropical Medicine of Loma Linda University. Workers and other interested members were brought in for two years of public health training, the first class graduating in 1962.

C. R. Stafford arrived in 1963 as the first permanent director, and was at different times assisted by R. G. Lorenson and J. Thompson and several student missionaries. By 1974 a total of 124 graduates had completed this course, among them pastors, evangelists, nurses, and teachers. The principles of healthful living and preventive medicine were spread through all areas of church influence in Tanzania.

Late in 1974 the school, still under the direction of C. R. Stafford, was moved to Arusha, where it was hoped that the evangelists in training at the seminary would be able to benefit simultaneously from the public health course. By 1993 it was no longer in existence.

ADVENTIST SEMINARY OF WEST AFRICA. A coeducational boarding institution on the senior college level, situated in Nigeria, on a 370-acre (150-hectare) tract near the town of Ilishan, midway between Lagos and Ibadan, state capitals in western Nigeria. Under the direction of the Africa-Indian Ocean Division, it serves a constituency of approximately 355,000 in Nigeria, Ghana, Côte d'Ivoire, Liberia, and Sierra Leone. A governing board of 18 members representing the division, West African Union, Nigerian Union, and local conference and mission headquarters is responsible for the operation of the seminary. The president of the division is the chair of this board, and the president of the Nigerian Union is the vice chair.

The seminary has been affiliated with Andrews University since 1975 and offers a liberal arts education leading to the Andrews B.A. degree in two majors (religion and theology) and eight minors (biology, business administration, English, health and wellness, history, computer science, and French). Since 1988 the seminary has offered the Andrews M.A. degree in pastoral ministry and religion. Forty candidates received these degrees in 1992, and 13 in 1993. These students came from all the unions of the division and the Burundi Mission. The Adventist faculty is international.

The campus is situated in the beautiful tropical rain forest region of Nigeria. It receives electricity from government sources, but has its own standby generators, water supply, and plumbing system; church building; plant services building; thriving farm with large agricultural building, storage, equipment offices, and classroom; married students housing; and 22 faculty housing units. A spacious library and assembly complex was begun in 1975. The farm, bakery, and peanut butter industries are successful and greatly assist the public image of the seminary. A 12-bed hospital operated by the Adventist Health Services in Nigeria is located on the southwestern part of the seminary property.

History and Development. Plans for the development of the school were first made in 1954 by D. V. Cowin, educational secretary of the West African Union Mission. By June 4, 1958, a definite decision was reached to lease a 370-acre (150-hectare) tract at Ilishan for 99 years. The first classes opened in October 1959, with an enrollment of seven, all ministerial postsecondary students. Until buildings were ready on the new site, classes met in rented quarters in town. Grover C. Winslow, the first president, taught some classes, assisted by Roger W. Coon, later joined by Fred

Riley. The college continued to develop curriculum and expand its facilities into a junior college, with a B.A. in theology first offered in 1966. In 1975 it became a senior college. During the 1992-1993 academic year there were 35 teachers and 476 students.

Presidents: Grover C. Winslow, 1959-1961; Howard J. Welch, 1961-1967; Jan Paulsen (acting), 1967-1968; S. P. Berkeley, 1968-1971; K. F. Mueller (acting), 1971; Percy Paul, 1971-1975; S. Gustavson (acting), 1975-1976; J. Korgan, 1976-1980; R. McKenzie, 1981-1983; A. A. Alalade, 1983- .

ADVENTIST SOCIETY FOR RELIGIOUS STUDIES. A scholastic society. Its purpose is "to provide intellectual and social fellowship among its members and encourage scholarly pursuits in all religious studies disciplines, particularly with reference to the Seventh-day Adventist tradition." It was formally organized in New York City in 1979.

In 1972 Adventist religion scholars agreed to meet in conjunction with the annual meetings of the American Academy of Religion (AAR) and Society of Biblical Literature (SBL). Biblical Research Institute (BRI) agreed to sponsor and plan these meetings. After BRI ceased their sponsorship in 1978, Adventist scholars met informally at New Orleans. AAR/SBL informed the Adventist group that it could not provide meeting rooms nor announce the meetings in its printed program unless the group officially organized and adopted a distinctive name that did not have a denominational identifier. At the New York meeting the group officially organized, selected the name Andrews Society for Religious Studies (ASRS), and elected officers. The name Andrews referred to J. N. Andrews, who is considered to have been the first Adventist religion scholar. In 1993 the society unanimously voted to change its name to Adventist Society for Religious Studies. This became possible when AAR/SBL lifted the restrictions on denominational identifiers.

Presidents: William Johnsson, 1979; Fritz Guy, 1980; Robert M. Johnston, 1981; George Reid, 1982; Walter Douglas, 1983; Richard Coffen, 1984; Doug Clark, 1985; Sakae Kubo, 1986; Alden Thompson, 1987; James Londis, 1988; Richard Rice, 1989; Russell Staples, 1990; Pedrito U. Maynard-Reid, 1991; Gerald R. Winslow, 1992; Warren Trenchard, 1993; Madelynn Haldeman, 1994; Roy Branson, 1995; Jon Dybdahl, 1996.

ADVENTIST THEOLOGICAL SEMINARY. *See* Adventist Seminary (Croatia); Nile Union Academy.

ADVENTIST THEOLOGICAL SOCIETY (ATS). A society formed for the encouragement of Seventh-day Adventists who hold to the divine inspiration of Scripture as the infallible revelation of propositional truth, who have accepted Christ as their Lord and Saviour, who endorse the use of historical-grammatical biblical interpretation, who believe in a literal Creation week of seven 24-hour days and a worldwide flood, who affirm a real sanctuary in heaven and the pre-Advent judgment of believers, who subscribe to the rest of the 27 fundamental beliefs of the Seventh-day Adventist Church, and who are committed to upholding and supporting the church.

Largely the brainchild of Jack Blanko, the society was organized at Southern College in October 1988. Four of those present for this meeting were from Andrews University, and eight were from Southern College. They adopted a tentative constitution that was finalized at the first annual session at Wheaton College in November 1988. At the time of the formulation of the society at Southern College, Jack Blanco was elected president. At the annual meeting in Lincoln, Nebraska, in the spring of 1989, the society voted to publish a scholarly journal known as the *Journal of the Adventist Theological Society*. Leo Van Dolson was elected editor. C. Mervyn Maxwell was asked to desktop-publish the *Journal,* and Gerhard Hasel did much to oversee production. Sometime after the first 1988 meeting, then General Conference president Neal Wilson stated that he did not object to the use of the name "Adventist Theological Society."

The society holds two annual meetings: a general session in the spring or early summer, which includes the annual business meeting; and a "research" or scholarly session at the same time as the Evangelical Theological Society meetings in the fall. The president serves a two-year term. After Jack Blanco's term, Gerhard Hasel, C. Raymond Holmes, and E. Edward Zinke were elected to that office. In 1994 Richard M. Davidson agreed to serve as vice president and president-elect.

Besides the *Journal,* the society has published a newsletter, *ATS Occasional Papers, ATS Monographs,* and the *ATS Dissertation Series.* In 1991 the society donated $38,000 toward the development of a seminary in

Czechoslovakia. Since then $10,000 was donated to Griggs University, and a computer and CD-ROM of Ellen White writings were presented to the seminary at Zaokski in Russia. After the death of Enoch Oliveira, who had been a staunch supporter of ATS, a ministerial scholarship fund was started in his name.

As of 1994, six chapters had been organized: four in North America, one in Europe, and one in Africa. As of 1994, membership was 1,400. Home office: P.O. Box 551, Collegedale, Tennessee 37315.

ADVENTIST TRAINING SCHOOL (formerly Assam Training School). A coeducational boarding school operated by the Northeast India Union of the Southern Asia Division in the Jaintia Hills of Meghalaya near Jowai. In 1991 the enrollment was 495, and a staff of 41 included 24 teachers. The school prepares students for entrance into Spicer Memorial College.

The students come from a score of language areas, mostly from the northeastern states. More than half the present staff (1993) are alumni of the school. Formerly this school was known as Assam Training School. The name was changed in 1974.

The school is an outgrowth of an elementary church school that was opened in Shillong soon after Seventh-day Adventists came to Assam in 1935 to establish permanent work. In 1942 construction started in the current location.

Principals: O. W. Lange, 1941-1942; C. Jensen, 1942-1943; O. W. Lange, 1943-1948; D. S. Laursen, 1948-1949; Albert Schimke, 1949-1951; I. R. Thomas, 1951-1952; W. C. Rick (acting), 1952-1953; B. J. Williams, 1953-1955; H. D. Erickson, 1955-1959; F. H. Nash, 1959-1967; C. A. Boykin, 1967-1969; D. R. Bankhead, 1970-1973; J. I. Khonghat, 1973-1974; D. S. Poddar, 1974-1975; L. K. Neitham, 1976-1977; B. Luikham, 1978-1980; D. Nongtdu, 1980-1983; H. Dkhar, 1983-1985; L. Colney, 1985-1988; Mrs. D. Sangma, 1989- .

ADVENTIST TRAINING SCHOOL OF EL SALVADOR (Escuela de Capacitacion Adventista Salvadorena). A coeducational high school in El Salvador. Until this school was established in 1983, there were only eight primary schools in this field, three of which provided junior high level education. Besides administration and classroom facilities, two dormitories and a cafeteria and kitchen had been built when school opened in February 1983. In 1992, 275 students were enrolled, served by 24 faculty members.

Principals: Elden Ford, 1982-1986; Donaldo Clarke, 1986-1988; Eliseo Martinez, 1988-1994; Noel Ruiloba, 1994- .

ADVENTIST UNION COLLEGE. *See* Kambubu Adventist High School.

ADVENTIST UNIVERSITY OF CENTRAL AFRICA (Universite Adventiste d'Afrique Centrale). A coeducational boarding school on the baccalaureate level, situated in Gisenyi Prefecture of northwestern Rwanda on 290 acres (118 hectares) overlooking beautiful Lake Kivu. It is located on the slopes of Mount Karisimbi, an extinct volcano that frequently is crowned with a light blanket of snow. In all directions there is a beautiful panorama of mountains. To the west, across the western arm of the Great African Valley, in which Lake Kivu is located, the Mitumba Mountains in Zaire can be seen. The university is located 77 miles (124 kilometers) from Kigali, the nation's capital, and 19 miles (30 kilometers) by road from the resort town of Gisenyi, on the shores of Lake Kivu.

The Adventist University of Central Africa (AUCA) serves the entire francophone constituency of the Africa-Indian Ocean Division. This includes the French-speaking countries of western and central Africa, Zaire, Rwanda, and Burundi, as well as Madagascar, Reunion, Mauritius, and the Seychelles Islands in the Indian Ocean. The board of directors, made up of 23 members representing the division, each francophone union, the North Rwanda Association, and the Adventist Seminary of West Africa, is responsible for the operation of the university. The president of the division is the board chair, and the president of the Rwanda Union Mission is the vice chair.

The university offers a liberal arts education leading to the B.A. degree. There are five faculties (schools) presenting majors in accounting, information science, education, construction, public health, biology-chemistry, and theology. The university is recognized (accredited) by the Ministry of Higher Education of the Rwandan government. Andrews University is presently offering an M.A. in religion on the AUCA campus each summer. The AUCA faculty and staff are highly international, with five continents being represented. The student body also is quite cosmopolitan in origin.

Even though the university is located about 60 miles (100 kilometers) south of the equator, it enjoys a springlike, tropical climate. Temperatures average 50° F (10° C) every night of the year and 70° F (21° C) each day. Precipitation averages about 55 inches (1,400 milimeters) per year, with rain falling any time of the year except for the big dry season in July and August and the little dry season that normally comes over the year's end. AUCA's rich volcanic soils and mild climate contribute to a thriving farm. Crops such as corn, vegetables of all kinds, and such fruits as oranges, grapefruit, lemons, avocados, mountain papayas, strawberries, and Cape gooseberries thrive. A small dairy and poultry ranch also serve the needs of the institution.

The university receives its electricity (220 volts) from the national grid; however, it has four generators that provide power in emergency situations. Water comes from nonvolcanic mountains some 9 miles (15 kilometers) away. A local purification plant on campus prepares the water for consumption. A campus telephone system provides local communication, and three outside lines connect the school with the rest of the world.

The main buildings on campus are the administration building, one women's dormitory, two men's dormitories, the science building and auditorium, the cafeteria, the chapel, the library, a primary school, and two technology buildings. Thirty faculty homes and 14 married-student houses also are located on campus. A small bakery and food processing plant is attached to the kitchen. A new library was being constructed in 1993. The university also operates an important dispensary on the edge of the campus.

History and Development. The Adventist University of Central Africa was founded on Oct. 17, 1978. On that date President Juvenal Habyarimana approved the creation of the university at Mudende in northwestern Rwanda. Dr. Elton Wallace, the first rector of the university, directed the beginning of construction in 1979. During the five succeeding years a small team of workers constructed most of the homes and major buildings that now make up the university.

On Oct. 15, 1984, the young university opened its doors for the first time. Relations with the Ministry of Higher Education have always been cordial and productive. On Feb. 22, 1988, the ministry sent a team of evaluators to inspect the university. As a result, AUCA was granted recognition (accreditation) by the government of Rwanda. Enrollment reached 445 students in October 1992, and several buildings—a primary school, science building, a duplex, and two dormitories—have since been completed.

Rectors: Elton Wallace, 1979-1990; Robert Pierson, 1990- .

ADVENTIST VOCATIONAL COLLEGE. *See* Belize Adventist College.

ADVENTIST VOCATIONAL INSTITUTE. *See* Ghana.

ADVENTIST VOCATIONAL SCHOOL OF NICARAGUA (Colegio Vocacional Adventista de Nicaragua). A coeducational boarding and day school at the high school level, situated on 105 acres (43 hectares) of volcanic fertile land near the Andes Mountains, located eight miles (13 kilometers) from the capital city, Managua.

The school opened in 1982 in a remote location on the Atlantic coast and was moved three times before it was located on its present site. From the beginning it received official recognition by the government.

Its excellent farm supplies the school with a large variety of fruits and vegetables. The school has a capacity of 320 boarding students, with two dormitories and a cafeteria that can seat up to 700 persons. A printing shop provides work for the students. The 1993 enrollment was 330.

Principals: Jaime Bordas, 1981-1982; Napoleon Beteta, 1982-1983; Roberto Brown, 1983-1986; Kessle Hodgson, 1987- .

ADVENTIST WORLD PURCHASING SERVICE. *See* Institutional Services/ESDA.

ADVENTIST WORLD RADIO (AWR). An institution of the General Conference devoted to international broadcasting of the gospel, particularly for countries where local broadcasting by the church is not possible.

Adventist World Radio began broadcasting on Oct. 1, 1971, under the direction of the Radio and Television Department of the General Conference, using a 250-kilowatt transmitter leased from Radio Trans-Europa in Lisbon, Portugal. The initial broadcasts were supplemented by leasing time on Radio Mediterranean (Malta) in 1975 and Radio Andorra in 1980; both efforts were short-lived. AWR continued to lease time on Radio Trans-

Europa until 1992, when broadcasts from Russia replaced its use.

AWR-Europe releases broadcasts for Europe, the Commonwealth of Independent States, North Africa, the Middle East, and South Asia. On Feb. 2, 1985, AWR activated a 12.5-kilowatt shortwave facility in Forli, Italy. In May 1991 AWR went on the air in Mazara del Vallo, Sicily, using a 300-watt medium-wave transmitter. In 1992 AWR-Europe became the programming partner of the Voice of Hope Media Center in Tula, Russia. Programs from Novosibirsk on Mar. 1, 1992, using a leased 200-kilowatt transmitter were the first Christian broadcasts to originate from within Russia for external broadcast. On May 3, 1992, broadcasts from Moscow, Ekaterinburg, and Samara increased AWR-Europe releases to 238 hours a week from Russia, 32 from Forli, and 84 from Mazara del Vallo, using 19 languages.

General Managers: Allen R. Steele, 1971-1976; Ronald Myers, 1976-1981; Mike Wiist, 1981-1985; Greg Hodgson, 1985- .

AWR-Latin America. On Aug. 17, 1979, the Central American Union began broadcasts from Union Radio in Guatemala City in shortwave, AM and FM. The shortwave operation was transferred to AWR-Latin America in 1979. In 1986 AWR-Latin America headquarters were transferred to Alajuela, Costa Rica, and on Oct. 22, 1986, began transmissions. In 1990 additional transmitters were purchased at Cahuita, Costa Rica, and new antennas installed. AWR-Latin America operates three 50-kilowatt and two 20-kilowatt transmitters at Cahuita, a 5-kilowatt transmitter at Alajuela, and a 10-kilowatt transmitter at Guatemala City, all of them shortwave. It broadcasts 322 hours a week from Costa Rica and 57.5 hours from Guatemala, using five languages.

General Manager: Dave Gregory, 1986- .

AWR-Africa began broadcasting in October 1983 using time on a 250-kilowatt transmitter of Africa One, a station located in Gabon. AWR-Africa has responsibility for the continent of Africa south of the Sahara and broadcasts seven hours a week using French and English.

General Manager: Daniel Grisier, 1985- .

AWR-Asia: In 1985 the General Conference session offering launched a major initiative to begin broadcasts that would reach China. As a result, AWR-Asia was established on Guam, using the call sign KSDA. Broadcasts began on Mar. 6, 1987, using two 100-kilowatt shortwave transmitters and four curtain antennas. In 1993 AWR-Asia purchased a third 100-kilowatt shortwave transmitter. AWR-Asia broadcasts to China, East and Southeast Asia, Burma, and India. The major language used is Mandarin (nine hours a day). AWR-Asia broadcasts a total of 235 hours a week in 19 languages.

General Managers: Allen R. Steele, 1985-1992; Ben Sumicad (acting), 1992-1993; Gordon Retzer, 1993- .

AWR-Russia was established in 1992 to manage the release of programs from Russia. AWR-Russia is a programming partner of the Voice of Hope Media Center located in Tula, Russia *(see AWR-Europe* above). The Voice of Hope has contracted for the use of two 250-kilowatt and two 200-kilowatt shortwave transmitters. AWR-Russia broadcasts 238 hours a week in 19 languages.

General Manager: Peter M. Kulakov, 1993- .

The Global Mission Committee of the General Conference has requested AWR to assume responsibility for broadcasting in more than 80 languages, *each* spoken by more than 10 million people. By 1993 AWR was broadcasting more than 900 hours per week in 31 languages and was authorized to increase to 1,100 hours and 43 languages.

Until October 1990, AWR operated in conjunction with the Radio and Television (1971-1972) and Communication (1973-1990) departments of the General Conference, under the control of a board whose membership included all division presidents, North American lay representation, and General Conference leadership. Stations were operated by local boards, with representation from the divisions being served.

In 1990 the AWR board assumed direct control of all its stations, with the AWR director appointed by the board and serving as chief executive officer. Area broadcast committees provide for planning and programming within the divisions. The 1992 Annual Council established AWR as an institution of the General Conference, with a president/executive director appointed by the board.

AWR is funded through General Conference appropriation, an annuual worldwide offering, and donations that come largely from North America.

Directors: James J. Aitken, 1971; Walter Scragg, 1971-1975; Carol Hetzell, 1975-1977; James Chase, 1977-1980; Tulio Haylock, 1980-1990; Walter Scragg, 1990-1992.

President/Executive Director: Walter Scragg, 1992- .

ADVENTIST YOUTH CAMPSITES. *See* Youth Campsites.

ADVENTIST YOUTH BOOK CLUB. Originally a plan in which book selections were recommended annually for Adventist Youth (AY) Society members and others on senior, junior, and primary levels, paralleling the membership age divisions of 16-30; 10-15; and school age under 10. The local conference youth department issued a certificate to the reader upon completion of the book club selections for any one year. The club (originally called a reading course) was inaugurated in 1907, the year that the Missionary Volunteer (MV) Department was organized.

In 1970 a change was made in the book club plan to allow individual selection of book titles in the three age categories from a selected book list prepared by the publishing houses in North America. Certificates are still issued by the local conference upon the completion of required reading from selected subjects.

ADVENTIST YOUTH CLASSES. Attainment levels denoting development in spiritual, physical, mental, and social areas, the dignity of labor, and the nobility of service. The first three classes, introduced by the General Conference Youth Department in 1922 for junior youth (10-15 years of age), were those of Friend, Companion, and Comrade (now Guide). In 1928 a class on the leadership level, Master Comrade (now Master Guide), was introduced for senior youth. In 1930 four preparatory pre-Friend classes (called Adventurer classes since 1979) were developed for boys and girls 6 to 9 years old: Busy Bee, Sunbeam, Builder, and Helping Hand. In 1950, at the same time the Comrade name was changed to Guide, a fourth class, Explorer, was added after the Companion class. In 1968 the classes were revised to include the following classes: Friend, Companion, Explorer, Pioneer, Guide and for leadership, Master Guide. In 1970 the name Pioneer was changed to Ranger. A complete revision of requirements of the AY classes from Busy Bee to Ranger was made in 1975.

In 1979 the terms Missionary Volunteer (MV) and Junior Missionary Volunteer (JMV) were changed to Adventist Youth (AY) and Adventist Junior Youth (AJY). In addition, the term MV classes was changed to Pathfinder/AJY classes. In 1982 the Voyager class was added between the Ranger and the Guide classes. The Pathfinder curriculum was revised in 1988. Two manuals were produced: *Teacher's Resource Manual for Juniors* and *Teacher's Resource Manual for Teens.* The next year the *Pathfinder Honors Manual* (international version) was revised. These manuals contain all the requirements for the Pathfinder classes and honors.

In 1979 the pre-JMV classes were changed to Adventurer classes, and in 1989 the Adventurer classes were completely revised and the Adventurer Club was started. The new publications included the *Adventurer Administrative Manual,* with requirements and teachers' resources for the Adventurer classes, and the *Adventurer Award Manual,* with 46 Adventurer awards to go along with the Adventurer curriculum. The service or ceremony for presenting pins, honors, and awards for the Pathfinder and Adventurer classes is called an Investiture.

ADVENTIST YOUTH COMMUNITY SERVICE (changed from MV Community Service in 1979). The name adopted in July 1957 by the MV Advisory Committee, meeting in Mount Vernon, Ohio, for the wide range of activities by the local AY Society in meeting community needs. Some of the most notable records have been made by youth at SDA colleges: being first on the job after a disaster; participating in, and even initiating, community cleanup and improvement campaigns; and distributing food, clothing, and toys at Christmastime.

Some of the services recommended to young people are visiting shut-ins, the bereaved, the handicapped; using their training in AY Honors to help other young people; giving special services to the aged, blind, and deaf; making scrapbooks for children in hospitals; conducting Story Hours for children; presenting programs in sanitariums, orphanages, old people's homes, and prisons; collecting and distributing food and clothing; making contacts with displaced persons, burned-out families, flood victims, unemployed, and families of prisoners; making home improvements for the needy; distributing evangelistic publications; writing missionary letters; helping existing community welfare organizations; conducting classes in storytelling; and directing a specialized ministry to the underprivileged living in the inner city.

ADVENTIST YOUTH GOLD AWARD. A special award presented to college-age youth who complete a set of requirements dealing with physical and cultural excellence. The award was introduced in 1964 by the Youth Department of the General Conference and is a gold medallion.

ADVENTIST YOUTH HONORS. *See* Pathfinder Honors.

ADVENTIST YOUTH SERVICE (AYS). An organization whose motto "From Everywhere to Everywhere" is demonstrated in its objective of offering opportunities of intradivision and interdivision volunteer missionary service to the youth of the worldwide Seventh-day Adventist Church.

The AYS program began in 1959 as the Student Missionary program for college students. In 1982 the Student Missionary program was expanded to allow all qualified Seventh-day Adventist youth, students or nonstudents, from 18 to 30 years of age to have the opportunity to serve God and others in many of the countries of the world. Most service requests do not require bilingualism, a college degree, or specialized training in a given field.

All applicants must be baptized Seventh-day Adventists in good and regular standing. If they are students in an Adventist college or university, they are approved by the college/university screening committee. If they are students in institutions of higher learning other than an Adventist institution, or if they are nonstudents, they must receive approval from the local church in which they hold membership.

Each year thousands of Adventist youth enter the AYS program from many of the countries located within the divisions of the world church. They commit themselves to a term of service that is agreeable to the call, which ranges from several weeks up to one year in duration. AYS service requests include work opportunities as teachers, assistant dormitory deans, office secretaries, assistant chaplains, teachers of English as a second language in language schools owned and operated by the church, musicians, and maintenance workers, as well as positions in the fields of agriculture, medical services, business, evangelism, youth ministry, and construction.

If applicants know what type of volunteer service project they wish to engage in and the country in which they would like to work, there is a possibility that it can be arranged. The work assignments of the AYS volunteer are chosen to be compatible with the applicant's level of education, skills, and talents.

Generally, upon completion of their term of service, AYS volunteers return home or to the campus to visit churches to report about their volunteer missionary experience and the impact it has had on their life, and to encourage other young people to "go . . . and do likewise."

The comment made by the majority of returned AYS volunteers is "I will never be the same person I was prior to my mission service."

ADVENTIST YOUTH SILVER AWARD. A special award presented to high school-age youth who complete a set of requirements dealing with physical and cultural excellence attainments. The award was introduced in 1962 by the General Conference Youth Department and is a silver medallion.

ADVENTIST YOUTH SOCIETIES (formerly MV Societies). The young people's organizations, senior and junior, in the local Seventh-day Adventist churches, called Adventist Youth (AY) or Adventist Junior Youth (AJY) Societies, sponsored and guided by the General Conference and union and local conference youth directors.

Youth ministry in the Seventh-day Adventist Church has gone through several phases, always evolving into a more specialized ministry to a narrower segment of the church's population. This evolution has taken the church from the early beginnings, when youth work was blended with Sabbath school, to the present, when youth ministry is divided into clearly defined areas of interest but pursues the same goals.

Three levels of ministry to youth are active in youth ministry today:

Adventurers Ministry. To reach and help children 6-9 years of age.

Pathfinder Ministry. To reach, help, and train youth 10-15 years old.

Senior Youth Ministry. To work with youth and young adults 16-30 years of age.

Activities. The AY Society's objectives are best revealed by the variety of features in the Seven Modules of Youth Leadership:

Organization. The organization module presents the history and organization of youth ministry in the Seventh-day Adventist Church. The strong emphasis is on youth ministry based in the local church, not a ministry based on conference-organized activities. Responsibilities of the leaders at the local church level are also covered in this module.

Leadership. This module incorporates aspects of training and actual practice of those activities required for senior leadership, and includes both philosophical base and practical practices. Emphasis is placed on qualities of ideal leadership, the psychology of leadership, leadership styles and functions, and practical matters such as how to chair a committee or business meeting.

Commitment. The commitment module primarily revolves around those activities and programs that are devotional in nature and that provide for special affirmation and celebration opportunities. Weeks of Prayer or Weeks of Spiritual Emphasis are outlined in which a seven-day period of time is selected for a concentrated thrust of personal relationships with the Lord through fellowship, intense scriptural study, and communion. Also featured are Bible conferences, with ideas and helps for church and school youth groups.

Discipleship. This module deals with how to help youth become disciples and stay committed to that way of life. Extensive presentation on the psychological aspect of youth leadership is given. Growth and nurture group leaders specializing in the spiritual well-being of their members will find resources in this module to accomplish all that might be desired, whether in youth or family situations. The ultimate objective is discipling others to the Lord and equipping them to share in this experience.

Worship. Worship is not merely attending church. The religious exercise of worship includes learning to live in God's presence and integrating those things learned at church into one's daily living. The purpose of this module is to help SDA young people discover the joy of worship and how to adopt a worshipful spirit while attending church.

Witnessing. Witnessing, the sharing of our own individual experience in the Lord, is among the first and foremost ministries in which the discipled Christian will want to engage.

Fellowship. This module is designed to guide in finding resources to help provide meaningful recreation for the AY Society. Youth must be guided to discover and take part in meaningful recreation, in addition to learning how to deal with their leisure time. Recreation and entertainment must be defined, and proper practices that reflect the SDA lifestyle adopted.

Aim, Motto, and Pledge. The blueprint for AY activities is found in the Aim, Motto, and Pledge. For the Senior Society these are:

Aim. The Advent Message to All the World in This Generation.

Motto. The Love of Christ Constraineth Us.

Pledge. Loving the Lord Jesus, I promise to take an active part in the work of the Adventist Youth Society, doing what I can to help others and to finish the work of the gospel in all the world.

Pledge and Law: The AJY/Pathfinders are guided by a Pledge and Law.

The AJY/Pathfinder Pledge: By the grace of God, I will be pure and kind and true. I will keep the AJY/Pathfinder Law. I will be a servant of God and a friend to man.

The AJY/Pathfinder Law: The AJY/Pathfinder Law is for me to—1. Keep the Morning Watch. 2. Do my honest part. 3. Care for my body. 4. Keep a level eye. 5. Be courteous and obedient. 6. Walk softly in the sanctuary. 7. Keep a song in my heart. 8. Go on God's errands.

History: AY Societies date from 1907. In that year plans for a Young People's Department were made in a General Conference council at Gland, Switzerland; and later in the same year at Mount Vernon, Ohio, the new department was named the Young People's Missionary Volunteer Department. *See* MV Societies. This department gave the societies their present organization. However, this was not the beginning of young people's societies in the church; for earlier history, *see* Youth Department of Missionary Volunteers. In 1972 the name of the department was officially changed to Youth Department of Missionary Volunteers. The term Missionary Volunteers was changed to Adventist Youth in 1979.

In 1985 the General Conference Youth Department was merged with four other departments of the General Conference (Home and Family Service, Lay Activities, Sabbath School, and Stewardship) to form the Church Ministries Department.

ADVENTIST YOUTH TO YOUTH (AY2Y). An organization begun in Ohio in 1982 as a high school program. Its goal was to support and encourage teenagers to be drug-free. By 1984 the program had received much attention and an overwhelming number of requests for help from all over the United States. In response the first national Youth to Youth conference was developed. The annual conference in Ohio spread to regional conferences in California, Idaho, Ohio, and New York.

Adventist Youth to Youth was first promoted in the North American Division in 1988 in the Southern Union, where the first SDA Y2Y conference was held. That conference was such a success that it led to further conferences throughout North America. In February 1990 the Health and Temperance Department of the General Conference adopted Adventist Youth to Youth as its official prevention program for the 1990s.

AY2Y is a positive program that uses local clubs led by youth supported by adult sponsors to reach other youth and children with a drug-free message from their peers. Clubs are started by participants who have attended a four-day conference and have made a commitment to be drug-free. The program focuses on positive alternatives to handling problems so that the use of alcohol, tobacco, and other drugs is seen as unnecessary and undesirable.

The five elements of the AY2Y program are: information, family groups, fun events, community change and outreach, and leadership training.

ADVENTIST YOUTH WEEK OF PRAYER (formerly called MV Week). A week listed in the church calendar in March, observed in the local churches around the world, during which the church gives its entire interest to the spiritual welfare of its youth. The week is sponsored by the General Conference. It was named Missionary Volunteer Week in 1932. A special *Youth Ministry Accent* for the Adventist Youth Week of Prayer, containing a complete format of suggestions and sermon materials for use in every church during this special week, is distributed annually. As a result of Adventist Youth Week of Prayer, thousands of baptisms of youth have taken place around the world.

A week of devotions began in 1915 as a spring Week of Prayer in SDA schools. This proved so successful that the Autumn Council of 1920 recommended that each union arrange for an Adventist Youth Week in every church. The first Sabbath of Adventist Youth Week is designated as Adventist Youth Day.

ADVENTISTICKA KNJIZARA "PREPOROD." *See* Yugoslavian Publishing House.

ADVENTISTICKI SEMINAR DVORAC MARUSEVEC. *See* Adventist Seminary (Croatia).

ADVENTISTICKI TEOLOSKI FAKULTET. *See* Adventist Seminary (Croatia).

ADVENTISTICKO UCILISTE MARUSEVEC. *See* Adventist Seminary (Croatia).

ADVENTKIRKENS ELDRESENTER, NORDAS. *See* Nordås Retirement Center.

ADVENTTIARUT. *See Nykyaika.*

ADVENTTIKIRKON VANHAINKOTI. An old people's home, situated in Tampere, Finland, eight miles (13 kilometers) from the center of the city, in a rural area. The home has a capacity of 45 residents and a staff of 17. The original main building and grounds for the home, situated near a large lake, were part of an estate purchased by the Finland Publishing House. After enlargement and improvements the home was dedicated on May 29, 1956. Additions with modern facilities were added in 1965 and 1968. Residents of the home come from various parts of Finland.

ADVENTURER CLUB. A Seventh-day Adventist church-sponsored ministry open to all children ages 6-9, in which the church, home, and school join together to help children grow joyfully "in wisdom and stature, and in favour with God and man."

The Adventurer Club is offered to assist parents in making the development of their child richer and more meaningful. In some ways the Pathfinder and Adventurer Clubs are similar, but the Adventurer program is to be unique in its own way and should be kept separate. One of the Adventurer Club objectives is to provide a meaningful and exciting experience as the children look forward with anticipation to being a Pathfinder in the future.

ADVENTUSUÜHINGUTE USUTEADUSE KOOL. *See* Estonian Mission School.

ADVOCATE OF CHRISTIAN EDUCATION (1899-1905; 1899-1901 as *Training School Advocate;* 1902-1903 absorbed *Sabbath School Worker;* monthly; pub. Battle Creek, then Berrien Springs, Mich.; incomplete files at GC). A periodical published at first by Battle Creek College and later by Emmanuel Missionary College for the promotion of educational work under the name *Training School Advocate.* In 1901 it was transferred to the General Conference to become a joint organ of the Education and Sabbath School departments. From January 1902 to the end of 1903 it carried Sabbath school lessons and other Sabbath school study helps. Afterward its masthead ceased to carry the General Conference name. It seems to have ceased publication after the January 1905 number.

Editors: Edward A. Sutherland, 1899-1904; M. Bessie DeGraw, 1904; N. W. Kauble and J. H. Haughey, 1904-1905.

ADVOCATE PUBLISHING COMPANY. *See* University Printers.

AECS. *See* Adventist English Conversation School.

AESCHLIMANN, ALFREDO (1904-1992). Educator, pastor, administrator. A native of Chile, he entered denominational service in the South American Division, where he labored many years.

In 1955 he accepted the call of the Inter-American Division to serve as president of Antillian College in Cuba. He was there until 1961. He then became president of the Mexican Union, and in 1970 was called to be ministerial secretary of the Inter-American Division. While in this position he served one year as interim president of the Central American Union.

After retirement in 1975 he remained active, assisting with the organization of the university at Montemorelos and also serving for a year as interim president of the Chile Union.

AFARS AND ISSAS, TERRITORY OF. *See* Djibouti.

AFGHANISTAN. A republic in central Asia, bordered by Iran on the west, Turkmenistan, Tajikistan, and Uzbekistan on the north, and Pakistan on the south and east. The northeast tip touches China. It has an area of about 250,000 square miles (647,500 square kilometers) and is populated (1994) by about 17 million Muslims of mixed descent, most of whom are tribal villagers (though there are some nomads). The main language spoken is Dari. Another official language is Pushtu, which is spoken particularly in the east and north.

Loma Linda University, in cooperation with Indiana University, supplied medical personnel for the training of Afghans at the medical college in Jalalabad. American physicians Bernard Briggs, Emmett Tetz, Benjamin Herndon, and J. E. Peterson served for varying periods of time. Dr. Gordon Hadley served as project chief of party and O. W. Lange was general administrative officer for the medical team and for the Seventh-day Adventist organization in general. Two Indians, Japes Fowler and R. Sajjano Rao, medical technologists, along with their nurse wives, were part of this mission, as were Zenaida Querol and Rachael Gayoba, nurses from the Philippines. At present no work is being carried on.

The territory of Afghanistan is part of the Pakistan Union Section, which in turn is part of the Trans-European Division.

AFM. *See* Adventist Frontier Missions.

AFRICA. *See* names of countries in Africa.

AFRICA HERALD PUBLISHING HOUSE (formerly East African Publishing House). A publishing house at Kendu Bay, Kenya, owned and operated by the Eastern Africa Division, but having an interunion board because it serves the East African and Tanzania unions. It is situated on land belonging to Gendia Station, which overlooks Kendu Bay of Lake Victoria. In 1993 the staff consisted of four European and 40 African workers. Printing is done in 16 languages, one of which, Swahili, is common throughout East Africa, besides being widely used in Rwanda, Burundi, and Zaïre (formerly the Democratic Republic of the Congo), which territories order supplies from this publishing house. Total sales for 1993 amounted to more than $110,000.

The history of the publishing house goes back to 1913, when A. A. Carscallen returned from furlough late in the year, bringing with him a small platen press and a few pounds of type. Among the workers who had come to East Africa from England in 1912 was L.E.A. Lane, who previously had done some printing. In 1914 the newly arrived press was set up at Gendia, and Lane taught three Africans, E. Nyalando, E. Owano, and E. Singa, to set type. He printed Luo spelling and grammar books, which Carscallen, who was the first to reduce that language to writing, had prepared. He also published a small monthly paper called *Jaote Luo* ("The Luo Messenger"). The press was first known as the South Kavirondo Press. About 1930 the name was changed to the Advent Press. In 1925 a former cowshed was renovated and adapted, enlarging the press's floor space. A secondhand power press, brought from England by F. H. Thomas, and a Davis typecaster were installed. The African staff was increased to five. From the first,

Africans have been trained to do most of the printing work. Some of them have given a lifetime of service to the publishing house. Today (1993) a well-educated group, operating modern machinery, make their contribution to the work of evangelizing their fellow Africans. Funds from the 1937 Missions Extension Offering made possible the addition of another building and more equipment.

In addition to textbooks, hymnbooks, and Sabbath school lessons, the press has produced many small books for sale by colporteurs. These were issued in four main languages (Swahili, Luganda, Gusii, and Luo), some passing through many editions. Colporteur work began in Kenya in 1932 with Y. Odongo as the first colporteur. Sometime later R. A. Carey wrote, "Our chief difficulty in the colporteur work is not finding men, but territory. East Africa has hundreds of square miles and millions of people, but the small percentage of people who can read means that a colporteur cannot stay long in one place with one book." In more recent years opportunities for universal primary education and selective secondary education in East Africa have greatly raised the level of literacy, and at the same time better and more attractive books have been produced. Recent publications include full-color illustrations.

The translation of English books and selections from English books has always been a major task. Much credit for this work must be given to such overseas workers as Grace Clarke and W.C.S. Raitt, and also to many African workers.

In 1956 the press was reorganized and the name changed to the East African Publishing House. Financial help from the General Conference Publishing Rehabilitation Fund made possible the purchase of much-needed equipment. In 1958 R. E. Gardner was called to be the works superintendent. The installation of additional new equipment to meet the demands of a larger colporteur force serving an expanding reading public increased the facilities of the institution. The enlargement of the factory from 4,200 square feet (390 square meters) to 14,000 square feet (1,300 square meters) was completed in 1961. In 1965 the name was changed to Africa Herald Publishing House, with further reorganization taking place in 1968. Since then, $66,000 worth of new equipment has enabled the same number of staff to quadruple production.

The years since 1974 have presented the greatest challenge the publishing house work has faced in East Africa. With the great increase in education there has been a phenomenal demand for literature. In 1992 the Africa Herald Publishing House experienced its greatest loss in sales because of inadequate facilities. Plans are being laid to increase sales.

Managers: L.E.A. Lane, 1913-1925; F. H. Thomas, 1925-1932; R. A. Carey, 1933-1947; R. L. Wangerin, 1947-1949; E. J. Trace, 1949-1951; D. K. Short, 1951-1960; A. M. Webster, 1960-1963; R. E. Gardner, 1964-1968; D. C. Swan, 1968-1983; Neal Scott, 1984-1988; Ted Proud, 1988-1989 (acting); David Vanderwelt, 1989-1991; Ted Proud, 1991-1992; Bent Praestiin, 1992- .

AFRICA-INDIAN OCEAN DIVISION. A large unit of church organization to which is allotted the following territory: Benin, British Indian Ocean territory, Burkina Faso, Burundi, Cameroon, Cape Verde, Central African Republic, Chad, Comoro Islands, Congo, Côte d'Ivoire, Equatorial Guinea, Gabon, Gambia, Ghana, Guinea, Guinea-Bissau, Kerguelen Islands, Liberia, Madagascar, Mali, Mauritania, Mauritius, Niger, Nigeria, Reunion, Rwanda, Senegal, Seychelles, Sierra Leone, Togo, and Zaire. It is divided into the Central African, Indian Ocean, Nigeria, Rwanda, Sahel, West African, and Zaire union missions, and the Burundi Association. Statistics (1992): churches, 3,769; members, 890,017; church or elementary schools, 429; secondary schools and colleges, 23; ordained ministers, 861; licensed ministers, 525; Bible instructors, 9; elementary teachers, 1,584; secondary and college teachers, 462; medical institutions, 14; publishing houses, 3; dispensaries, 57; retirement homes, 3. Headquarters: 22 Boite Postale 1764, Abidjan 22, Côte d'Ivoire. Official organ: *Adventist Review*.

The Africa-Indian Ocean Division was voted into existence at the 1980 General Conference session and began to function officially that year. It is comprised of a merger of countries formerly administered by the Euro-Africa, Northern Europe-West African, and the Trans-African divisions.

For the history of Seventh-day Adventist work in the Africa-Indian Ocean Division, see specific names of countries and island fields in the area.

Constituent Organizations. The Africa-Indian Ocean Division is comprised of seven union missions and one attached field.

1. *Central African Union Mission* (orga-

nized 1949). Territory: Cameroon, Central African Republic, Chad, Congo, Equatorial Guinea, and Gabon; comprising the Central African Republic, Central-South Cameroon, Chad, East Cameroon, Equatorial Guinea, Gabon, North Cameroon, and West Cameroon missions, and the Republic of Congo Mission Station. Statistics (1992): churches, 629; members, 55,143; ordained ministers, 93; licensed ministers, 69; schoolteachers, 120; elementary schools, 25. Headquarters: Boite Postale 401, Yaounde, Republic of Cameroon.

Constituent organizations and their territories—*Central African Republic Mission* (organized 1970): Central African Republic; *Central-South Cameroon Mission* (organized 1971): Dja and Lobo, Haut Nyong (parts), Lekie, Mbam, Mefou, Mfoundi, Mvila, Ntem, Nyong-Kelle, Nyong-Mfoumou, and Nyong-Soo circumscriptions of Cameroon; *Chad Mission* (organized 1973; reorganized 1987): Chad; *East Cameroon Mission* (organized 1949; reorganized 1966, 1970): Boumba et Ngoko, Haut-Nyong, Haute-Sanaga, Kadei, and Lom et Djerem; *Equatorial Guinea Mission* (established 1986): Equatorial Guinea; *Gabon Mission* (organized 1947; reorganized 1978): Gabon; *North Cameroon Mission* (organized 1933; reorganized 1967, 1970): Adamaoua, north Cameroon, and extreme North provinces of Cameroon; *Republic of Congo Mission Station* (established 1972): Congo; *West Cameroon Mission* (established 1962; reorganized 1972): littoral, northwest, southwest, west, and ocean district of Cameroon.

2. *Indian Ocean Union Mission* (organized 1938; reorganized 1960). Territory: British Indian Ocean territory, Comoro Islands, Kerguelen Islands, Madagascar, Mauritius, Reunion, Rodrigues, and Seychelles; comprising the Mauritius and Reunion conferences, and the Central Malagasy, North Malagasy, Seychelles, and South Malagasy missions. Statistics (1992): churches, 212; members, 36,491; ordained ministers, 73; licensed ministers, 29; schoolteachers, 39; elementary schools, 9. Headquarters: P.K 6 Route de Toamasina, Soamanandrainy, Antananarivo, Madagascar, Indian Ocean.

Constituent organizations and their territories—*Central Malagasy Mission* (organized 1949; reorganized 1960, 1972) provinces of Tamatave and Tananarivo in Madagascar; *Mauritius Conference* (organized 1958; reorganized 1984): Mauritius, including Rodrigues; *North Malagasy Mission* (organized 1949; reorganized 1958, 1966, 1972): provinces of Antsiranana and Mahjanga in Madagascar; *Reunion Conference* (organized 1947): Reunion Island; *Seychelles Mission* (organized 1947): Seychelles; *South Malagasy Mission* (organized 1949; reorganized 1960, 1972): provinces of Fianarantsoa and Tulear.

3. *Nigeria Union Mission* (organized 1972). Territory: Nigeria; comprising the East Nigeria, Rivers, and West Nigeria conferences, and the East Central, Edo-Delta, North East, North West, and South East missions. Statistics (1992): churches, 480; members, 99,080; ordained ministers, 149; licensed ministers, 117. Headquarters: Ikorodu Road (opposite Maryland bus stop), Ikeja.

Constituent organizations and their territories—*East Central Mission* (organized 1986): assigned local government areas of Abia, Anambra, and Imo states; *East Nigeria Conference* (organized 1930; reorganized 1971, 1977, 1986): portions of Abia, Anambra, and Imo states; *Edo-Delta Mission* (organized 1977): Edo and Delta states; *North East Mission* (organized 1954; reorganized 1993): Abuja (Federal Capital Territory), Andamawa, Bauchi, Borno, Plateau, Taraba, and Yobe states; *North West Mission* (established 1932; organized 1993): Jigawa, Kaduna, Kano, Katsina, Kebbi, Niger, and Sokoto states; *Rivers Conference* (organized 1971): Rivers state; *South East Mission* (established 1980): Akwa Ibom and Cross River states; *West Nigeria Conference* (organized 1930): Kogi, Kwara, Lagos, Ogun, Ondo, Osun, and Oyo states.

4. *Rwanda Union Mission* (organized 1960; reorganized 1984). Territory: Rwanda; comprising the East Rwanda, North Rwanda, and South Rwanda fields. Statistics (1992): churches, 787; members, 243,242; ordained ministers, 161; licensed ministers, 28; schoolteachers, 208; elementary schools, 34. Headquarters: Avenue de la Paix, Kigali, Rwanda.

Constituent organizations and their territories—*East Rwanda Field* (organized 1965; reorganized 1984): Byumba, Kibungo, and Kigali prefectures; *North Rwanda Field* (organized 1956; reorganized 1960): Gisenyi, Kibuye, and Ruhengeri prefectures; *South Rwanda Field* (organized 1921; reorganized 1960, 1972, 1984): Butare, Cyangugu, Gikongoro, and Gitarama prefectures.

5. *Sahel Union Mission* (organized 1981). Territory: Benin, Burkina Faso, Cape Verde, Côte d'Ivoire, Guinea, Guinea-Bissau, Mali, Mauritania, Niger, Senegal, and Togo; com-

prising the Benin, Burkina Faso, Cape Verde, Côte d'Ivoire, Guinea-Bissau, Senegal, and Togo missions, and the Guinea, Mali, and Niger mission stations. Statistics (1992): churches, 55; members, 7,138; ordained ministers, 28; licensed ministers, 20; elementary teachers, 28; Headquarters: 3 Rue Curie, Quartier des Etoiles, Lome, Togo.

Constituent organizations and their territories—*Benin Mission* (established 1964, reorganized 1987): Benin; *Burkina Faso Mission* (organized 1973): Burkina Faso; *Cape Verde Mission* (reorganized 1981): Cape Verde; *Côte d'Ivoire Mission* (organized 1952): Côte d'Ivoire; *Guinea Mission Station* (established 1991): Guinea; *Guinea-Bissau Mission* (organized 1981): Guinea-Bissau; *Mali Mission Station* (organized 1982): Mali; *Niger Mission Station* (established 1986): Niger; *Senegal Mission* (reorganized 1981): Senegal; *Togo Mission* (established 1964; reorganized 1987): Togo.

6. *West African Union Mission* (organized 1943). Territory: Gambia, Ghana, Liberia, and Sierra Leone; comprising the Central Ghana and South Ghana conferences; the Liberia, Mid-West Ghana, North Ghana, and Sierra Leone missions; and the Gambia Mission Station. Statistics (1992): churches, 499; members, 168,908; ordained ministers, 114; licensed ministers, 104; schoolteachers, 2,627; elementary schools, 288. Headquarters: 55 Fifth Avenue, Accra, Ghana. Official organ: *Advenit Messenger*.

Constituent organizations and their territories—*Central Ghana Conference* (organized 1933; reorganized 1970, 1977): Ashanti region and part of the Brong Ahafo, Eastern, and Western regions; *Gambia Mission Station* (established 1977): Gambia; *Liberia Mission* (organized 1933): Liberia; *Mid-West Ghana Mission* (organized 1933; reorganized 1986): the Brong Ahafo region (excluding Atebubu district), and all Mo-speaking areas of the Northern region; *North Ghana Mission* (organized 1968): the Northern, Upper East, and Upper West regions, and portions of the Volta Region north of the Asukawkaw and Volta rivers; *Sierra Leone Mission* (organized 1913): Sierra Leone; *South Ghana Conference* (organized 1933; reorganized 1987): Anyinam, Asunafo, Ayiribi, Bogoso, Foso, Midland Insu, and Twifu Prasu, portions of Assini and Samraboi, all the coastal areas from East Anum to West Axim, and the Volta region to Kete Krachi.

7. *Zaire Union Mission* (organized 1925). Territory: Zaire; comprising the East Kasai, East Zaire, North Shaba, North Zaire, South Kivu, South Shaba, Upper Zaire, West Kasai, West Zaire, and Zaire Equatorial fields. Statistics (1992): churches, 1,003; members, 246,720; ordained ministers, 211; licensed ministers, 148; schoolteachers, 489; elementary schools, 64. Headquarters: 765 Avenue de la Revolution, Lubumbashi, Zaire Republic.

Constituent organizations and their territories—*East Kasai Field* (organized 1993): East Kasai province; *East Zaire Field* (organized 1955; reorganized 1960): North Kivu province (except Beni and Lubero territories); *North Shaba Field* (organized 1954; reorganized 1974): Kabambare and Kasongo territories in Kivu province, and Tanganyika and Upper Lomami districts in Shaba province; *North Zaire Field* (organized 1956): Beni and Lubero territories in North Kivu province, and Kibali-Ituri district in Upper Zaire province; *South Kivu Field* (organized 1988): South Kivu province; *South Shaba Field* (organized 1974): Shaba province (except Tanganyika and Upper Lomami districts); *Upper Zaire Field* (organized 1974): Lubutu and Punia zones in Kivu Maniema Territory, and Upper Zaire province (except Kibali-Ituri district); *West Kasai Field* (organized 1993): West Kasai province; *West Zaire Field* (organized 1956; reorganized 1962): Bandundu, Bas-Zaire, Kinshasa City; *Zaire Equatorial Field* (organized 1989): Equator province.

8. *Attached field* (under the direct supervision of the division)—*Burundi Mission* (organized 1931; reorganized 1960, 1964, 1984): Burundi.

Institutions. The following institutions are located in the Africa-Indian Ocean Division.

Educational Institutions. Adventist Seminary of West Africa (Nigeria); Adventist University of Central Africa (Rwanda); Adventist Vocational Institute (Ghana); Agona Seventh-day Adventist Secondary School (Ghana); Antarandolo Adventist School (Madagascar); Asokore Seventh-day Adventist Teacher Training College (Ghana); Bazega Horticultural Training Center (Burkina Faso); Bekwai Seventh-day Adventist Secondary School (Ghana); Bouake Adventist Secondary School (Côte d'Ivoire); Dogba Secondary School (Cameroon); Gitwe Adventist Secondary School (Rwanda); Konola Academy (Liberia); Lukanga Adventist Institute (Zaire); Mugonero School of Nursing

Science (Rwanda); Nanga-Eboko Adventist Secondary School (Cameroon); Peninsula Secondary School (Sierra Leone); Phoenix Adventist Secondary School (Mauritius); Rwamiko Institute (Zaire); Rwankeri Adventist Secondary School (Rwanda); Soamanandrariny Adventist Secondary School (Madagascar); Songa Institute (Zaire); Valley View College (Ghana); Yele Seventh-day Adventist Secondary School (Sierra Leone).

Hospitals and Sanitariums. Aba Health Centre and Motherless Children's Home (Nigeria); Andapa Adventist Hospital (Madagascar); Asamang Seventh-day Adventist Hospital (Ghana); Batouri Adventist Hospital (Cameroon); Dominase Adventist Hospital (Ghana); Inisha Community Medical Centre (Nigeria); Jengre Seventh-day Adventist Hospital (Nigeria); Koza Adventist Hospital (Cameroon); Masanga Leprosy Hospital (Sierra Leone); Mugonero Hospital (Rwanda); Seventh-day Adventist Cooper Memorial Hospital (Liberia); Seventh-day Adventist Hospital Ile-Ife (Nigeria); Songa Adventist Hospital (Zaire).

Publishing Houses. Advent Press (Ghana); Adventist Printing House (Madagascar); Central African Publishing House (Cameroon).

Retirement Homes. Rosie Le Meme Home (Mauritius).

Presidents: R. J. Kloosterhuis, 1980-1985; J. J. Nortey, 1985- .

AFRO-MIDEAST DIVISION. A former large unit of church organization to which was allotted the following territory: Arab Republic of Egypt, Bahrain, Cyprus, Djibouti, Ethiopia, Iran, Iraq, Jordan, Kenya, Kuwait, Lebanon, Libya, People's Democratic Republic of Yemen, Qatar, Saudi Arabia, Somalia, Sudan, Sultanate of Oman, Syria, Tanzania, Turkey, Uganda, United Arab Emirates, and Yemen Arab Republic. Headquarters were located first in Beirut, Lebanon, then in Nicosia, Cyprus. The official organ was the Afro-Mideast Division *Impact.*

The division was organized in 1970 with a membership of 124,382 in 662 churches, being formed by uniting the East African Union (which had functioned as a detached union mission under the General Conference in 1969 and 1970), the Ethiopian Union from the Northern European Division, the former Middle East Division, and the Tanzania Union from the Trans-Africa Division, into one organization. In 1981 a territorial realignment of African divisions took place. The Eastern Africa Division was formed, and the Middle East Union became attached to the General Conference.

Constituent Organizations. The Afro-Mideast Division comprised four union missions:

1. *East African Union Mission* (organized originally 1921; dissolved 1933, Tanganyika going to Central European Division, Section 2; reorganized 1942 [Tanganyika made a separate union in 1960]). The Seychelles Islands were transferred to Euro-Africa Division in 1974.

2. *Ethiopian Union Mission* (organized 1923; reorganized 1945). Territory: Ethiopia and Somalia.

3. *Middle East Union Mission* (organized in 1941; reorganized in 1970, having functioned as a division from 1951 to 1970). Territory: Arab Republic of Egypt, Bahrain, Cyprus, Iran, Iraq, Jordan, Kuwait, Lebanon, Libya, People's Democratic Republic of Yemen, Qatar, Saudi Arabia, Sudan, Sultanate of Oman, Syria, Turkey, United Arab Emirates, and Yemen Arab Republic.

4. *Tanzania Union Mission* (organized 1903; reorganized 1960). Territory: Tanzania.

Institutions. The institutions located in the Afro-Mideast Division were the following:

Educational Institutions. Adventist Seminary of Health Evangelism (Tanzania); Akaki SDA School (Ethiopia); Amman Adventist Secondary School (Jordan); Bawshrieh Adventist Secondary School (Lebanon); Beirut Overseas School (Lebanon); Bishmezzine Adventist School (Lebanon); Bourj-Hammoud Adventist School (Lebanon); Bugema Adventist College (Uganda); Dar-es-Salaam School (Iraq); Ethiopian Adventist College; Ikizu Seventh-day Adventist Seminary (Tanzania); Iran Adventist Academy; Kamagambo Secondary School and Teachers' College (Kenya); Middle East College (Lebanon); Museitbeh Adventist Secondary School (Lebanon); Nile Union Academy (Coptic Adventist Theological Seminary); University of Eastern Africa (became the senior college for the division in 1978); Wollega Adventist Academy (Ethiopia).

Hospitals and Sanitariums. Empress Zauditu Memorial Adventist Hospital (Ethiopia); Gimbie Hospital (Ethiopia); Haile Selassie I Hospital (Ethiopia); Heri Mission Hospital (Tanzania); Ishaka Hospital (Uganda); Kendu Mission Hospital (Kenya); Taffari Makonnen Hospital (Ethiopia).

Publishing Houses. Africa Herald

Publishing House (Kenya); Ethiopian Advent Press (Ethiopia); Middle East Press (Lebanon).

Orphanage. Matariah Mercy Home (Arab Republic of Egypt).

History. For the history of the work in the Afro-Mideast Division, see specific names of countries in the area of the division. *See also* Middle East Division.

Presidents: M. E. Lind, 1970-1974; E. W. Pedersen, 1974-1975; C. D. Watson, 1975-1980; Bekele Heye, 1980-1981.

AFRO-MIDEAST DIVISION *IMPACT* (1971-1981; monthly; English; files in GC). A periodical that was the official organ of the Afro-Mideast Division. It was published by both the Middle East Press and the Africa Herald Publishing House. Total circulation was approximately 2,000.

"AGE-TO-COME" THEORY. *See Messenger* Party.

AGED, HOMES FOR. *See* Retirement Homes and Orphanages.

AGONA SEVENTH-DAY ADVENTIST SECONDARY SCHOOL. A coeducational boarding and day school jointly managed by the Ministry of Education and the Seventh-day Adventist Church in Ghana. It was established in 1963 as a four-year teacher training college with an initial enrollment of 80 students. The church provided the initial infrastructure for the opening of the school.

In October 1972 the Secondary School Department was established on the same campus with the training college, until the latter was completely phased out in 1974. The school operates on two campuses: the old site, which is located in the northern part of the town along the Kumasi-Mampong Motorable Road, contains the administrative block, the classrooms, girls' domitory, dining hall, and residences for the tutors; the new site, which is located on the northeastern part of the town, on the Agona-Effiduasi Motorable Road, houses the boys' dormitory and additional housing for the tutors.

In 1993 the school was running two programs concurrently, namely the General Certificate of Education (GCE), and the Senior Secondary School (SSS) programs. The GCE was to be phased out completely in 1994. The school pursues three programs in the SSS course: general science, general arts, and vocational studies. The subjects taught in the SSS program include: English language, English literature, Bible knowledge, history, government, economics, Twi, mathematics, physics, chemistry, biology, food and nutrition, management in living, clothing and textiles, and art.

The school operates an institutional church with a full-time chaplain. Sabbath afternoon programs include doctrinal teachings; stewardship; and health and temperance studies, such as drug abuse, drug addiction, and sex education.

Principals: L. H. Berlin, 1963-1965; I. K. Ansong, 1965-1976; C. A. Mensah, 1976-1984; Seth Okrah, 1984-1986; F. Boadi, 1986-1989; D. K. Obeng, 1989-1991; Kwasi Attakora, 1991- .

AGRO-INDUSTRIAL ADVENTIST TRANS-AMAZON ACADEMY (Instituto Adventista Transamazonico Agro-Industrial). A boarding academy located in Uruara, Para, north Brazil. Begun in 1978, it is under the jurisdiction of the Lower Amazon Mission and the North Brazil Union. It started as an elementary school, but became a secondary school in 1982, offering courses for teachers and technicians in farming and husbandry. In 1993 the 286 students in attendance were served by 26 teachers.

Directors: Joel Fernandes, 1978-1982; Benedito Alves, 1983; Orlando Ferreira, 1984; Salon da Costa, 1985-1988; Daniel Costa, 1989; Esteban Gusman Leyva, 1989-1990; Waldemar Lauer, 1991- .

AHEF. *See* Adventist Health Education Foundation.

AHNBERG, BETTY (1931-1986). Radio personality, administrator. She was born in Ohio. While attending Andrews University, she became interested in the *Your Story Hour* broadcast. She volunteered 35 years of service to the program, starting as a character actor in 1950 and becoming known as Aunt Sue. She directed the Community Services in Medina, Ohio, for 24 consecutive years and served as a lay representative on various committees. In June 1986 she was awarded a Doctor of Humane Letters degree from Andrews University.

ÅHRÉN, EMIL J. (1865-1936). Preacher, editor, author. Born in Vermland, Sweden, he became a Seventh-day Adventist about 1880. Arriving in Battle Creek, Michigan, in 1882, he began working in the Swedish department of the Review and Herald publishing house. To earn funds to enable him to attend Battle Creek College, he did colporteur work, being the first Swede to sell SDA Swedish subscription books. On completion of his studies he entered the ministry and was ordained in the late eighties.

In 1890 he returned to Sweden, but two years later came back to America. With a growing conviction that he should work for the people of his homeland he sailed back to Sweden in 1894, and for 38 years was editor of *Tidens Tecken* ("Signs of the Times"). Two of his brothers were also SDA ministers. Åhrén was a man of culture, humble and sincere. He was a good preacher and an able editor.

AHS. *See* Adventist Health System.

AIBLING SEMINARY. *See* Marienhoehe Seminary.

AIM. *See* Adventist Information Ministry.

AIRPLANES. *See* Mission Aviation.

AKAKI SEVENTH-DAY ADVENTIST SCHOOL. A coeducational 12-grade boarding school operated under the direction of the Central Ethiopia Field at Akaki, near Addis Ababa. The 1973 enrollment was 450 students (about 300 of them boarders), ranging in age from 6 to 18, with 22 full- and part-time teachers for the 12 grades.

Forerunner of the school was a boys' school opened under the leadership of W. Kölling and R. Stein in 1921 on rented land near the village of Addis Alam, about 40 miles (65 kilometers) west of Addis Ababa. Manuel J. Sorensen and his wife, who arrived in Ethiopia in 1922, took charge of the school in 1923 and continued with it till 1929. Carl Jensen and his wife, from Denmark, were there for about a year before moving to western Ethiopia. P. M. Myhre from Norway was there from 1930 to 1933 and made many improvements on the school plant. In 1934, after the school had been without a foreign teacher for about a year, Herbert M. Hanson and his wife arrived. The Italian administration, which took control of Ethiopia in 1936, allowed the Addis Alam school to be operated on a limited scale until 1938, when it was ordered closed. This school is listed in the *Yearbook* from 1933 to 1940, first as the Boys' Training School, then as Addis Ababa Training School for Boys, Addis Alam Training School for Boys, and Ethiopian Union Training School for Boys.

After the Italians left in 1941, Hanson organized a boys' school in rented quarters in Addis Ababa, but in March 1943 moved it to its present site, about 12 miles (20 kilometers) south of the city near the village of Akaki, where some ground and 15 dilapidated stone and mud buildings, which had housed an Italian dynamite factory, were leased from the Ministry of Education for 51 years with the sanction of Emperor Haile Selassie I. This school was listed in the *Yearbook* as Ethiopian Mission Training School for Boys.

Known as Akaki Boys' School, the institution opened with about 70 students, mostly boarders, ranging in age from about 10 to well over 21. A few girls attended as day students. Teachers were few, and most of them had a limited education. From about 1950, girls were accepted as boarding and day students, and the school was renamed the Akaki Mission School. By 1954, classes ranged from grades 1 to 11.

In 1955 the secondary section was moved to Kuyera, the secondary school for Ethiopia (Ethiopian Adventist College), leaving Akaki an eight-grade school. But in 1967 the school was upgraded to its present level of 12 grades.

The boarding fee in 1993 was $50 per month. Paying students are required to work 10 hours a week. Some work in the school garden and kitchen; others help to maintain the grounds and buildings; still others care for the plumbing and electrical work. Rugmaking and other handcrafts provide salable articles.

In 1993 the school had an enrollment of 1,500 students and employed 28 teachers. It rates high academically in Ethiopia.

Principals: H. M. Hanson, 1941-1955; C. Z. Nielsen, 1955-1958; Ato Negassa Aga, 1958-1971; Truneh Wolde-Selassie, 1971-1985; Negaro Djaleta, 1985-1994; Fonta Chaleabo, 1994- .

ALABAMA. *See* Gulf States Conference; South Central Conference.

ALABAMA-MISSISSIPPI CONFERENCE. *See* Gulf States Conference.

ALARM. *See Alert.*

ALASKA CONFERENCE. The unit of church organization comprising the territory of the state of Alaska. Statistics (1993): churches, 27; members, 2,498; church or elementary schools, 9; ordained ministers, 15; licensed ministers, 6; church school teachers, 17.

Headquarters: 6100 O'Malley Road, Anchorage, Alaska. The conference forms part of the North Pacific Union Conference.

Local churches: Aleknagik, Anchorage (Abundant Life, Community, Jewell Lake, Northside, O'Malley), Craig, Delta Junction, Dillingham, Eagle River, Fairbanks, Gambell, Juneau, Kenai, Ketchikan, Kodiak, Nome, North Pole, Palmer, Safe Harbor, Savoonga, Sitka, Sunshine, Valdez, Wasilla, Wrangell.

Companies: Bethel, Copper Basin, Homer, Korean, Kotzebue, Petersburg. Groups meeting: Selawik, Shungnak, Spanish, Togiak, Toko.

There are nine schools, one offering 10 grades.

Alaska is about one fifth the area of the rest of the United States, stretches across the boundaries of two time zones, and reaches beyond the Arctic Circle. The people are separated by great distances and live in modern cities, in logging camps, in floating villages, on homesteads, on farms, and in native villages. The population (1992) is 580,861.

Principal income is from fisheries, minerals (especially North Slope oil), wood products, tourism, and furs. Military bases also form a significant part of the Alaska economy. Salmon, halibut, herring, cod, and shellfish are frozen and canned.

History of Beginnings of Seventh-day Adventist Work. In 1895 there was in Alaska one known SDA, Mrs. J. W. Young, in Ketchikan. According to the *Review and Herald* (74:91, Feb. 9, 1897), in 1896 a colporteur, with another layperson, met some Indians in Alaska who requested a missionary to teach them the Bible. The account does not identify either of these. In the 1898 gold rush an SDA miner-blacksmith, Jasper N. Sylvester (grandfather of H.M.S. Richards, Sr., of the Voice of Prophecy), came to Alaska and gave away tracts wherever he went. George E. Henton, a layman who came to Skagway in 1898, wrote to the *Review and Herald* in 1900 appealing for missionaries to come. He reported one convert and said that SDAs were favorably known.

The first Seventh-day Adventist missionaries to Alaska were A. M. Dart and T. H. Watson, who in 1901 came to Juneau and Douglas (at that time a mining community situated across the Gastineau Channel from Juneau). It is not known how long Watson stayed (he was still there in 1902), but Dart returned to California in 1904 because of poor health. In 1905 J. M. Estes, of Nome, Alaska, reported working among the Eskimos, several of whom had begun to observe the Sabbath (*Review and Herald* 82:18, Aug. 17, 1905). Possibly it was to this work that John Spoon, the father of an Inuit tribe, referred in 1930 when he told S. C. Hanson who was teaching in a government school at Ugashik, that he had attended SDA meetings "in Nome years ago" (*North Pacific Union Gleaner* 25:4, Dec. 2, 1930).

In the summer of 1905 Dart was back again in Alaska, holding meetings in a tent in Ketchikan. He was assisted by R. S. Greaves, a student on vacation from Walla Walla College, and by local lay members "Brother and Sister Sparhawk and Sister [J. W.] Young, who are engaged in mercantile business here" *(ibid.* 1:8, July 24, 1906). They established a Sabbath school of 11 members. In the autumn a store building was fitted up as a meeting place, and Dart held Sunday night meetings attended about equally by indigenous people and settlers. In the spring of 1907 an SDA Indian preacher from British Columbia, Henry Pierce, came temporarily to work among the interested Indians around Ketchikan. After spending the summer in Skagway and visiting the small number of SDAs in Juneau, Douglas, and other places, Dart returned to Ketchikan for the winter. The work in Skagway, which consisted mostly of distributing publications among the travelers coming through, yielded no permanent results. On this trip Dart visited "Sister Carter," who had "held the fort at Douglas for about ten years" *(ibid.* 2:4, Nov. 6, 1907), and therefore must have been one of the earliest SDAs in Alaska.

Alaska Mission Church. By 1907 the *Yearbook* names Dart as superintendent and minister of the Alaska Mission, which had a membership at that time of 25. For the next three years no worker is listed, but the 1911 *Yearbook* names Fred W. Temple, in Ketchikan, as missionary licentiate for Alaska. In June 1909 he and William Furber had been sent from Walla Walla College as student colporteurs by the North Pacific Union Conference. The two purchased a launch, the *Evangel,* and used it to travel among the islands until winter set in. In 1910 Temple, who stayed on until 1913 or 1914, had a larger boat built, a 36-foot (11-meter) cruiser called *Searchlight,* and used it as a "marine relief ship" on emergency missions. In 1915 and again in 1916 the *Yearbook* names no missionary for Alaska, but in 1916 D. H. Hanson, a minister from Montana sent by the North Pacific Union Conference, arrived at Juneau in April.

Visiting Skagway and Eagle River, he held meetings at the latter place and established a Sabbath school of 11. At that time there were two SDA nurses working in the Juneau hospital and "a sister living at Ketchikan."

In September came another minister, William T. Hilgert, with his wife and Dorothy Rice. Shortly afterward he organized a mission church of 10 members. Evangelistic meetings at Ketchikan resulted in six converts. Before the end of the year, work had begun among the Indians, and one convert, a Tsimshean from Metlakahtla, had been won. Weekly meetings were held at a native Thlinglet village where "sister Young, who has been in Alaska for many years, taught . . . a number of years ago" and where the villagers asked the missionaries to return in the autumn (*North Pacific Union Gleaner* 11:1, Jan. 25, 1917). In the spring and summer of 1917, meetings at Skagway resulted in five converts. The secretary-treasurer of the North Pacific Union Conference, S. J. Lashier, came during the summer of 1917 and assisted Hanson with meetings at Douglas.

By early 1918 Hanson reported that in the entire mission field there was only one church, with 16 members, who were widely scattered (all of them in southeastern Alaska). Some had moved to the continental United States. There were three Sabbath schools, at Ketchikan, Douglas, and Skagway (*ibid.* 12:2, Feb. 14, 1918).

By the summer, W. T. Hilgert had returned to Oregon, and F. A. Lashier was assisting Hanson in holding evangelistic meetings at Haines. Late in 1919, after Hanson had returned to the continental U.S., O. W. Herwick, from North Dakota, went to Alaska. He assisted Lashier in evangelistic meetings at Sitka. The Lashiers returned to the continental U.S., while Herwick remained until 1963, though retired from the active ministry in 1929. In the spring of 1921 T. H. Watson, who had spent some time in Alaska at the beginning of the century, returned to work among the natives, but first assisted Herwick in evangelistic meetings in southeastern Alaska and in organizing a church at Ketchikan, which met in the home of Mrs. Young (*ibid.* 16:3, May 26, 1921). That same year Herwick, with the help of a few members, began to erect a small church building at Ketchikan, a two-story structure with the chapel on the upper level.

In 1922 the North Pacific Union Conference bought a boat for the Alaska Mission, the 50-foot (15-meter) *Dixie*. The decision to purchase was made when H. W. Cottrell, president of the union conference, and S. J. Lashier, treasurer, came to Alaska at the request of Herwick to plan for mission work for the Inuits and Indians as well as the settlers.

Work in Western Alaska. Watson traveled among the islands of southeastern Alaska, meeting with natives and other fishers. In 1923 he worked far to the north and west of the SDA base in southeast Alaska. He established and taught in the government school at Kulukuk, and worked in an outpost station among primitive natives untouched by Christianity. By his example he taught Christianity to the Inuits living around Bristol Bay, in western Alaska, even though he could not teach his religion formally in a government school. "It is said that when he was first asked to go to Alaska, Ellen G. White talked with him about the work in that vast territory and advised him, 'Let no man take you from that field'" (Fern Royer Owens, *Sky Pilot of Alaska,* p. 48). He continued working for Inuits and Indians, with periodic returns to California for his health, until his death, in January 1927.

From time to time (1924-1927) the *North Pacific Union Gleaner* mentions several SDA members who did lay missionary work among the Inuits at the Kanakanak orphanage and elsewhere in the Bristol Bay area (Watson, the L. D. McGhees, the Howard Hansens, and Josie Moody). The V. P. Dicksons worked in a school at Shishmaref, in the far northwest. In 1929 S. F. Nance worked in Valdez, Fairbanks, and Anchorage. As a result, in that year one woman was baptized at Valdez and two men at Anchorage.

Mission Organization. In 1929 H. L. Wood was sent to superintend the Alaska Mission and to organize the mission as nearly as possible like the organized conferences in the continental U.S. He was appointed secretary-treasurer, Book and Bible House manager, Sabbath School Department secretary, and Home Missionary Department secretary. He soon repaired and remodeled the *Dixie,* which he renamed the *Messenger.* Assuming the role of captain and his wife that of deck hand, they followed the fishing fleet "fishing for men," and sailed from village to village holding meetings and preaching the gospel.

According to the records there were 24 members in Alaska at the close of 1928, and four Sabbath schools, with five members of the extension division scattered throughout the territory. Wood set up the mission office in his home in Ketchikan; his wife handled the correspondence. Letters were sent to the isolated members each quarter.

After evangelistic meetings were held at Juneau in 1931, 10 were baptized. A church was organized there the same year under the leadership of Vernon Gyes and his wife, who came to Alaska in 1930.

Through the influence of Frank Waskey (Alaska's first delegate to the United States Congress, and a convert of L. D. McGhee and T. H. Watson), Ray Smith with his family of 10 left Washington in 1930, moved to the Bristol Bay area, and settled at Mosquito Point on Lake Aleknagik, near Dillingham. As the years went by, relatives and friends moved in, until the Aleknagik church was established in 1934, with 25 charter members, the first in the Bering Sea region.

In 1935 the mission headquarters were moved from Ketchikan to Juneau, and an old trading post in the downtown area was purchased and remodeled into a church. A later addition housed the mission offices.

Wood broadcast on Sunday evenings over the Juneau radio station, with the Gyeses helping with the music. The following year M. J. Jackson preached on the radio at Anchorage, in south central Alaska, where in 1934 there had been only one known SDA *(North Pacific Union Gleaner,* Dec. 11, 1934), and where he organized a Sabbath school in April 1936. In 1974 this old church was replaced by a new one.

With the opening up of Matanuska Valley to homesteaders, there soon was a small group of believers at Palmer. Through the efforts of Jackson, a church of 23 was organized and a new log church building was dedicated there Apr. 19, 1936. This was the first church of any denomination in the Matanuska Valley. This church was sold in 1971 and replaced by a new one, which was completed early in 1975.

The first Alaskan general meeting was held in April 1934 at Ketchikan. Fifty of the 91 members were present, and 10 converts were baptized.

At this time the *Messenger* was sold and a coast guard patrol boat was purchased from the government and named *Messenger II.* Later, during World War II, when invasion threatened Alaska, the Navy requisitioned *Messenger II,* leaving the mission without transportation. On Wood's appeal the North Pacific Union Conference purchased an airplane for the mission. On his fifty-second birthday, May 1, 1942, Wood enrolled as a student pilot. On one two-month trip around the field he logged 11,000 air miles. But death came suddenly on Sept. 24, 1944, apparently from a heart attack, as he flew over the inland waters of southeastern Alaska, approaching the Owens logging camp.

In 1924 Sam Hance canvassed southeast Alaska, covering Ketchikan, Petersburg, Juneau, and Sitka. In 1925 he took Harold Peckham from Walla Walla College with him across the Gulf of Alaska to Kodiak Island, then back to Anchorage, Valdez, and Seward; then they hiked the approximately 500 miles (800 kilometers) from Seward to Fairbanks to reach the men building the Alaska railroad. They found a small group of men about every 12 miles (19 kilometers). After reaching Fairbanks, they canvassed about three weeks before they were told to obtain a $200 permit or desist. So Hance hiked another 380 miles (600 kilometers) over Chitna Creek and on to Cordova, while Peckham hiked to Valdez and on to Cordova, where they took a boat to southeast Alaska and canvassed the islands from the mission boat.

In 1926 Harold Peckham and Robert Wirth, from Walla Walla College, canvassed in southeastern Alaska, then went north. They hiked 150 miles (240 kilometers) inland to the head of the Yukon River, then traveled by boat down the river, and later hiked the more than 500 miles (800 kilometers) from Seward to Fairbanks, selling SDA publications. In 1927 Wirth returned with Edd Norwood and covered the same territory.

Elmer Henderson, called a veteran colporteur, lost his life in 1930 on the Shismaref Shoal when the mailboat *Good Hope* was wrecked in a storm.

In 1948 A. L. Zumwalt, in Alaska since 1946, became the first president of the Alaska Mission. He concluded that church schools were the answer to the problem of helping the Alaska Mission grow. New members who moved into the territory or who were baptized locally would soon leave in order to secure a Christian education for their children. In the summer of 1953 the mission office was moved to the Anchorage church building, and two years later to a new office at 718 Barrow Street. Before Zumwalt's retirement in 1961, every church had a church school, as did the company on Vank Island.

In 1946, while Jack Provonsha served as pastor at Fairbanks, a church was organized there. A new building was erected in 1960, but it was severely damaged by the flooding of the Chena River in 1967. This building was replaced by a new church at College, near the University of Alaska, under the leadership of Dr. A. V. Pflugrad and Pastor James Stagg.

Evangelism Among the Inuits. Work among Inuits in the north above the Arctic Circle began in 1949. Interested people were found at Selawik by Marvin Troutman, Merle Smith and his wife, and the mailing band of the Dillingham church. Beginning in 1955, Glenn Murphy and his wife lived and worked there for seven years. With Inuit help, Murphy logged with dog teams in the winter and by summer floated the logs 80 to 100 miles (128 to 160 kilometers) down the rivers to build the church and apartment at Selawik. In 1962 John Topkok and his wife, Naomi, became the first Inuit workers, traveling among their own people for hundreds of miles around the Selawik area in their own small airplane.

At Gambell, on St. Lawrence Island, Frank Daugherty and his wife were lay members stationed there from 1938 to 1945. Because of this couple's personal Christian witnessing, Wood came and baptized Robert Tungiyan and John Walunga on June 20, 1944. Two years later, on Aug. 29, 1946, 12 young people and adults were baptized by Fred Wagner. A church building was erected at Gambell by Glenn Murphy. In 1970 Pastor and Mrs. Bernie Willis were assigned as the first permanent workers at this most isolated place. In March 1972 a church was organized at Gambell. This was the first Inuit church in the North American Division.

Village Work. Mr. and Mrs. Clyde Harris made funds available in 1965 for the establishment of chapels in Inuit villages. Later a year-round student missionary program was begun in Shungnak, Selawik, Savoonga, and Togiak. Each village has a chapel and adequate housing for arctic conditions. At the small town of Craig, in southeastern Alaska, the mission owned an abandoned church building and school. Seeing the success of the arctic student missionary work, Murray Gildersleeve renovated the Craig property in 1971. A year later work was begun by David Brown, a colporteur, and his wife. The Craig church building now serves as a central meeting facility for the community. A full-time pastor is located there.

Messenger III. In southeast Alaska SDAs are scattered in many logging camps and villages. There are also Indian villages in the area. To serve this area the people in the camps raised funds to build a 53-foot (16-meter) motor vessel. In 1970 the *Messenger III* was launched. It serves as a parsonage, chapel, and mobile evangelistic outreach center.

New Groups. Laymembers have established the work at Valdez, Kodiak, and the Kenai Peninsula. In 1959 Milford Taylor moved to Valdez and served the community as a schoolteacher and later as a principal. He established a Sabbath school that grew, and in 1973 a small group organized into a company. The town of Valdez was completely demolished by the tidal wave following the great Alaska earthquake in 1964. The town has been completely relocated and is the terminus for the Alaska oil pipeline. The church in Valdez was completed in 1972 under the direction of Glen Mills. Dr. A. V. Pflugrad, of Fairbanks, was also one of the motivating influences encouraging the building.

In 1972 Douglas Cooper and his family moved to Kodiak for the purpose of establishing a church in Alaska's fifth-largest city. He began by canvassing to find interested people. Families were also encouraged to move to the area. In 1973 a company was officially organized and land purchased for a building site. There now is a new church/school combination building that houses 12 students and 55 church members.

In 1968 Bert McCool moved his family from Palmer to the Kenai Peninsula. At that time there was no organized work on all of the peninsula. The McCools held Sabbath school in their home and gradually gathered together other interested people and Sabbathkeepers. By 1973 the group was officially organized as a church to serve the twin cities of Kenai-Soldotna.

In 1982 the Alaska mission officially became the Alaska Conference.

Youth Camps. Because of the immense size of Alaska and the scattered membership, the conference operates three youth camps: Camp Tukuskoya, to serve south central Alaska; Camp Polaris, to serve the west; and Camp Lorraine, to serve the southeast. A new lodge was built at Tukuskoya, near Anchorage, during the summer of 1974. Elder Harold Dawson began work on Camp Lorraine, on Vank Island, in 1970 and completed seven cabins and a four-story A-frame lodge. The camp was dedicated the summer of 1974. Much of the work and material was donated by people living in the city of Wrangell and area logging camps. The camp is also used in community service for the young people and adults of that area.

Superintendents and Presidents: A. M.

Dart, 1906- ?; Fred W. Temple, 1910-1917; D. H. Hanson, 1917-1919; F. A. Lashier, 1919-1921; O. W. Herwick, 1921-1929; H. L. Wood, 1929-1944; E. E. Jensen, 1944-1949; A. L. Zumwalt, 1949-1961; J. C. Hansen, 1961-1974; F. M. Beavon, 1974-1977; W. L. Woodruff, 1977-1985; S. L. McPherson, 1985-1988; D. R. Watts, 1988-1991; J. L. Stevens, 1991- .

ALBANIA. A republic in the western part of the Balkan Peninsula, having an area of 11,100 square miles (28,750 square kilometers) and a population (1994) of 3.4 million. Albanians are considered to be descendants of the ancient Illyrians, who may have migrated into the Balkans even before the Greeks. The area was later controlled by the Romans, Slavs, and Normans. Then in the fifteenth century came the Turks, who introduced Islam. In 1912 the country was proclaimed independent. The people of the country are predominantly Albanians, but there are small groups of Greeks, Vlachs, Bulgarians, and Serbs. The Albanians speak a language not related closely to any other European language. Their religions are: Muslim (more than 70 percent), Greek Orthodox (about 17 percent), and Roman Catholic (about 10 percent). All public worship and religious institutions were outlawed in 1967. In 1990 the right to practice religion was restored.

Seventh-day Adventist Work. Perhaps the first Albanian converts (who lived, however, in an area now in Greece) were three of the Brakas family, who became SDAs through reading denominational publications and were baptized in 1909 by R. S. Greaves. There was no development of the work in Albania itself for many years.

In 1932 E. Hennecke, director of the Grecian Mission, who was forced to leave Greece, moved to Tiranë, the capital of Albania, hoping to continue to direct the mission from there. He sought and obtained permission to establish medical work in Albania, and received authorization for two trained nurses from Germany to enter the country. This experiment lasted less than a year, for in a few months all the foreign workers had to leave the country. However, as the result of some meetings held during that year, one woman was baptized.

In 1938 D. C. Lewis, an Albanian returning to his country after having learned the SDA message in America, was baptized en route in Saloniki, Greece. After settling in Albania, he shared his faith, with the result that four converts were baptized in 1940 by C. A. Christoforides, director of the Grecian Mission, who had the responsibility for members in Albania.

During World War II contact with Albania was lost. D. C. Lewis, as was learned later, died soon after the end of the war.

When contact was reestablished in 1991, it was discovered that there had been two believers who had remained faithful during this period of isolation. ADRA and the Communication/Public Affairs and Religious Liberty departments of the Trans-European Division were the entering wedge in reestablishing contact. They developed a good working relationship with the government and local authorities.

In the spring of 1992 a team of evangelists under the direction of David Currie, Ministerial Association secretary of the Trans-European Division, began a series of evangelistic campaigns in Tiranë and Korçë. This resulted in the first baptisms in Albania in 50 years.

In a special ceremony on Oct. 10, 1992, the first church was formally organized in Tiranë. A prominent feature of the church program is its children's ministries. More than 100 enthusiastic children attend each week. By the end of 1992 there were 124 baptized members in Albania.

In 1993 ADRA was able to lease a portion of land (approximately 1.25 acres [5,000 square meters]) from the local council in Tiranë for the future development of a warehouse, community center, health center, and micro industrial units.

The territory of Albania is a part of the Trans-European Division.

Albanian Mission Organized. Just three years after Albania opened its doors, Seventh-day Adventists formally established church organization in that country. Seventy delegates representing believers from Tiranë, Korea, Shkodra, and Elbasan, convened April 14-16, 1994, in Tiranë and voted to adopt a church constitution and form the Albanian Mission.

The international church made its first contacts with Albania in decades during April 1991. Today there are 155 baptized members in Albania. According to Ron Edwards, mission president, the number worshiping on Sabbath is much greater. They are now preparing 80 for baptism and have an objective of tripling their membership by 1997.

ALBANIAN MISSION OF SEVENTH-DAY ADVENTISTS. *See* Albania; Trans-European Division.

ALBANY CONFERENCE. *See* Millerite Movement, III, 9.

ALBERTA CONFERENCE. The unit of church organization comprising the province of Alberta and a portion of the Northwest Territories in Canada. Statistics (1993): churches, 55; members, 7,607; church schools, 11; ordained ministers, 37; licensed ministers, 9. Headquarters: Willow Street, South Red Deer, Alberta. The conference forms part of the Seventh-day Adventist Church in Canada.

Institutions. Canadian Union College, Chinook Winds Adventist Academy, Parkview Adventist Academy, Sherwood Park Nursing Home.

Local churches: Airdrie, Beauvallon, Beiseker, Bentley, Bonnyville, Boyle, Brooks, Calgary (Asian, Bridgeland, Central, Mountain View, Pineridge, Spanish), Camrose, College Heights, Consort (Loyalist), Drumbeller, Edmonton (Central, South, Spanish, West), Edson, Fairview, Fort McMurray, Grande Prairie, Hanna, Innisfree, Lacombe, Leduc, Lethbridge, Lloydminster, Medicine Hat, Myrnam, Okotoks (Foothills), Olds, Peace River, Ponoka, Red Deer, Rimbey, Rocky Mountain House, Ryley, Sedgewick, Sherwood Park, Smokey Lane, St. Albert, Stettler, Stony Plain, Sylvan Lake, Vegreville, Wanham (Peoria-Smoky), Warburg, Wetaskiwin, Yellow.

Companies: Calgary (Korean), Edmonton (Korean), Edson (Hinton), Fort Vermilion (Morning Star), Lae La Biche, Lethbridge (Taber), Ponoka (Maskwachees), Red Deer (Northwest), Spirit River.

History. *Beginnings of the Work.* Seventh-day Adventist teachings were introduced into Alberta in May 1895 by two colporteurs, Thomas Astleford and George W. Sowler. Astleford, preceding Sowler by two weeks, began working in Edmonton. Sowler sold 200 copies of *Bible Readings* in Calgary. He also canvassed north of Calgary and in the towns along the Canadian Pacific Railroad to the east, and among the ranchers from Calgary to Fort MacLeod, and from the Bow River to the foothills of the Rockies. On one trip he traveled in the saddle 25 miles (40 kilometers) without seeing a house.

Astleford, working in Edmonton and in the towns along the railroad to the south, was responsible for the first converts in the province. These included Gustave Litke of Leduc (the *Northern Union Gleaner* [1:1, Aug. 14, 1906] calls him John), and Dr. Menzel and his family, of Stony Plains. Litke shared his new faith with his German friends, and soon H. J. Dirksen was sent from Manitoba, who organized a church at Leduc on May 14, 1898, the first Seventh-day Adventist church in the Northwest Territories.

The first SDA pastor to settle in Alberta was Henry Block, who arrived in October 1899. His charge was the German congregation at Leduc. Next came J. W. Boynton, who made his headquarters in Ponoka in the summer of 1901. He estimated that in all there were some 35 German-speaking and 12 English-speaking members in Alberta. He held meetings about 15 miles (24 kilometers) west of Olds, a community in which a few SDAs had settled, which resulted in the Harmattan church.

Persecution came to Seventh-day Adventists in Alberta as early as 1902 and 1903. J. L. Hamren, of Wetaskiwin, was fined $2 and costs for doing farmwork on Sunday, even though the law prohibiting work on that day was not applicable to farmers. Later a blacksmith in Leduc named Gebanus was fined $10.70 for operating his shop on Sunday. Hamren appealed his case and won a dismissal. Later the attorney general at Regina, the center from which the Northwest Territories were then governed, ordered the Royal Canadian Mounted Police not to disturb SDAs or Jews doing work on Sunday.

Alberta Mission Organized. The first general meeting in Alberta was held in July 1903 at the home of J. H. Lowry in Ponoka, and a year later, also in Ponoka, the first camp meeting was held, with about 50 present, reported Boynton. At that time Alberta, which had formed a mission field of the Northern Union, was organized into a mission, with J. W. Boynton as first superintendent. There were then in Alberta one German, one Scandinavian, and two English churches. In the next two years two more churches were organized, one at Leavings (July 1905) and the other, an English congregation, at Leduc (Feb. 23, 1906).

Alberta Conference Organized. By the time of the third camp meeting, held in Red Deer in July 1906, the number of churches had risen to six. At this meeting, with R. A. Underwood, Dr. P. T. Magan, and C. A. Burman present, the Alberta Mission was made a conference, with C. A. Burman as president, J. W. Boynton, vice president, and Stella B. Lowry, secretary-treasurer. After remaining more than a year longer under the Northern Union Conference (Minnesota, the Dakotas,

Manitoba, and Alberta), the Alberta Conference joined with Manitoba, Saskatchewan, and British Columbia in October 1907 to form the Western Canadian Union Conference (since 1932 part of the SDA Church in Canada). During the first decade of the conference's history, almost 800 members were added and 20 new churches were organized. Contributing to this rapid growth were immigration of SDAs from the U.S. and the establishment in 1907 of an industrial school at Leduc (*see* Canadian Union College).

In 1907 new congregations were established in Calgary (May 26) and Edmonton (Apr. 28) and one at Vermilion Lake (Sept. 1), composed almost entirely of English-speaking SDAs from the U.S. who had taken advantage of land available at low cost in this country of opportunity. In 1908 one such group, consisting of 13 German families from North Dakota, came on an immigrant train, with their livestock and equipment on a special freight train, to settle in virgin territory in what is now Rosebud. They arrived so late in the year that they were forced to spend the winter in tents and to subsist on frozen potatoes and beef. As they met for Sabbath services they expressed their feelings in one of the old German songs, "Gäste und Fremdlinge sind wir" ("We Are Guests and Strangers"). Later C. A. Burman, conference president, and Henry Block, another minister in Alberta, organized the group into a church with 20 charter members, over which H. H. Humann was elected local elder. The congregation met in the home of Henry Kindopp. In 1910 they founded a church school of which some of the first teachers were C. C. Neufeld, Teddy Roth, A. C. Harder and his wife, and Dan Ochs. Neufeld taught his 55 students in German in the morning and in English in the afternoon.

Work in the Peace River district began in 1904 or 1905 with Cornelius D. Holdeman, a colporteur. The first converts, the Knutsons and Keillors, were won through papers distributed by a former SDA, Doc Chase, who operated a stopping place on Lesser Slave River. In May 1918 H. A. Niergarth opened a series of public meetings at Clairmont. In August Calvin D. Smith and his wife settled in the town of Peace River. In September E. S. Stanley (later well known for his column Dad's Philosophy in the Peace River *Record)* arrived in Swan River and established a school. During the influenza epidemic the Smiths went from place to place ministering to the sick. When they moved to southern Alberta the next year, Peter Rick, Mrs. Smith's brother, took over their missionary work. Rick was responsible for the first SDA church in the area, the Bluesky church, organized on July 17, 1921.

In the Beauvallon district it was many years before the English-speaking members of the Vermilion Lake church won any of their predominantly Catholic Ukrainian neighbors. The first such convert was a lad who fled to a family named Philbrick to escape from a cruel father. This lad, later known as M. H. Philbrick, became an SDA minister. The second Ukrainian convert, George Soloniuk, also became an SDA minister. Soloniuk and his wife became interested in the study of the Bible through a report emanating from one Ripka, a Baptist, to the effect that worship of images was unbiblical. Their friend, Elia Tkachuk, was equally roused and sought for a Ukrainian Bible. On learning that a Mrs. Tym had one in her possession, he went to borrow it. Mrs. Tym consented to lend it, but while she was upstairs searching for it, her baby sat down in a pan of boiling water she had left on the floor. The baby's cries ended her search and Tkachuk's visit, but a Mrs. Smith, an SDA, saved the child's life. After the child's recovery, Tkachuk went back for the Bible, and this time got it. He began at once to read it, but found he could not understand it. He confided his dilemma to Mr. Smith, husband of the woman who saved the child's life. Smith requested help from the conference office, and finally Joe Walshy, a Polish worker, was sent. Walshy studied with the Soloniuks and in the Tkachuk home. The Soloniuks were the first to be baptized (Aug. 12, 1918).

At first the meetings at the Tkachuk home were well attended, but when Walshy began using charts, his audience became frightened and ceased to attend. Then the conference sent T. T. Babienco, who baptized 34 and organized the Pobida (Victory) church on Aug. 3, 1919.

To be baptized by the SDAs was a bold step to take. At one baptism of 23, conducted by Peter Yakavenko, it was necessary to post three husky men at the gate to keep out potential troublemakers. Even so, when one lad went into the water, his uncle had to be forcibly restrained from interfering. This baptism was followed by the organization of the second Ukrainian church, the Myrnam church.

Many Alberta congregations, such as those at Clive and Cassils, were composed almost exclusively of immigrants. The Cassils church, formed in 1919, owed its existence to a pseudo-SDA who had induced SDAs from the U.S. to enter the country by promising to build a 10-grade school. The congregations at Peoria, Belloy, and Cluny were composed of German settlers.

The Alberta Conference has always been a "little Europe." Formerly there were Scandinavian churches in Edmonton, Donalda, and Camrose; Russian churches in Coronation and in Loyalist; a Romanian company in Hamlin. There have been numerous German and Ukrainian congregations.

Seventh-day Adventist schools early became a feature of the church in Alberta. The little log building constructed in 1902 at Harmattan was erected to serve as both a church school and a place of worship. Its first teacher was Addie Tifel, and the second, LaRena Carpenter, later Mrs. F. L. Hommel. By 1921 provincial laws in Alberta barred church schools.

Membership in the Alberta Conference has grown steadily. From 1,000 members in 1916 it has increased to 7,600 in 1993. The number of churches has varied little since 1916. A few churches have ceased to exist; others have changed their names and locale, or have combined or divided.

For the medical work in Alberta, *see* Bethel Sanitarium.

Further Developments. After World War II many new church buildings were erected in Alberta, such as those in Edmonton, Lacombe, and Calgary. Representative church schools have been built and staffed with provincially certified teachers. A youth camp was established near Banff, fittingly named Camp Rundle, after the towering mountain that overlooks it. Provincial zoning regulations prevented a necessary expansion of the camp in 1971. This situation led to the purchase of almost 180 acres (73 hectares) of land along the Little Red Deer River west of Bowden. The former Camp Rundle properties were sold, and the present site has been developed for year-round use. Officially opened July 8, 1973, the new facilities are used for the conference camping programs, the annual camp meeting, and workers' meetings, as well as many other meetings and conventions. The camp name, as seen on highway direction signs, is "Seventh-day Adventist Camp."

Canada's Northland has been largely untouched in terms of Seventh-day Adventist witnessing. In 1969 the Alberta Conference took a significant step in this direction by establishing a mission work in Yellowknife, Northwest Territories, under the leadership of Henry Bartsch. Beginning primarily with Community Services programs and *Signs of the Times* distribution, Pastor Bartsch was able to gain the people's confidence in the Seventh-day Adventist Church. Lay members moving to Yellowknife and assistance from student missionaries have enabled the mission work to reach many communities surrounding Yellowknife. In 1973, with valuable help from Maranatha Flights International, a mission complex was built. The facility provides a worship center, an auditorium, the manse, and guest rooms. The opportunities for extending mission work in the Northwest Territories were greatly enhanced by acquiring a Cessna 180H airplane in 1974. Christened *Arctic Arrow* (in honor of C. S. Cooper's missionary foray up the Mackenzie River with a boat named *Arctic Arrow),* the plane came as a gift from the Quiet Hour and its supporters. Seventh-day Adventists in Yellowknife are members of the Alberta Conference church.

In recent years an increasing number of physicians, dentists, and optometrists, as well as other medical and paramedical personnel, have located in the conference. Annual health evangelism conferences are held to maintain a close team relationship among medical professionals and the ministry.

During the decade of the 1980s a significant work was established among the native Indian population in central Alberta. A church was established on the reservation at Hobbema with a full-time pastor. A strong educational work was established for native children. Between 1984 and 1993 one or two schools were operated each year on the reservation. In 1991 a new school with approximately 100 students opened off the reservation. It is the only school for native children operated by the church in Alberta.

Presidents: C. A. Burman, 1906-1914; H. H. Humann, 1914-1918; A. J. Haysmer, 1918-1920; J. J. Reiswig, 1920-1928; A. V. Rhoads, 1928-1935; W. B. Ochs, 1935-1936; H. L. Rudy, 1936-1937; C. W. Degering, 1938-1946; E. H. Oswald, 1947-1949; A. E. Millner, 1949-1951; G. E. Taylor, 1952-1957; H. D. Henriksen, 1957-1958; J. W. Bothe, 1959-1962; P. Moores, 1962-1966; A. W. Kaytor, 1966-1974; J. W. Wilson, 1974-1980; H. Larsen, 1980-1987; D. W. Corkum, 1987- .

ALBERTA INDUSTRIAL ACADEMY. *See* Canadian Union College.

ALBERTA MISSION. *See* Alberta Conference; Northern Union Conference.

ALBERTA SANITARIUM. *See* Bethel Sanitarium.

ALCOHOL. *See* Temperance.

ALENZA ACADEMY. *See* Spain.

ALERT. The title (registered U.S. Patent Office) that was used by the International Health and Temperance Association to strengthen the temperance work around the world by providing information not only for church leaders but for prominent men and women in government, medicine, law, education, and other professions. It also provided material that national temperance societies could use in their own temperance papers in various geographical and language areas.

This editorial service was sent out on a regular basis under the title *Alert* International News Service (AINS).

ALGERIA. A North African country independent since 1962; formerly a French colony and province from 1830. The country is bounded on the west by Morocco and Mauritania, on the north by the Mediterranean Sea, on the east by Tunisia and Libya, and on the south by Niger and Mali. It has an area of 920,000 square miles (2,382,800 square kilometers) and a population (1994) of about 28 million, mainly Arabs, and 90 percent Muslim. Agriculture is the principal occupation, with wine, cereals, olive oil, and alfalfa the chief products. Large deposits of oil have been found in Algeria in recent years.

Statistics. The territory of Algeria is part of Mission and Services to Muslims (MISSERM) (which includes Tunisia and Morocco), which is part of the Euro-Africa Division. Statistics (1993) for *Algeria:* church members, 12.

For a former institution, *see* Algerian Publishing House.

Seventh-day Adventist Work. The first SDA in Algeria was Joseph Gomis, who had been born into a Spanish Catholic family but had become a Protestant at the age of 16. During a trip to Switzerland he became acquainted with SDAs through reading the magazine *Les Signes des Temps,* and was baptized. About 1886 he established himself as a baker in the town of Relizane, in the province of Oran, Algeria. While working at his trade he shared his faith with several members of his family and others, some of whom accepted the new doctrines. About 1889 J. D. Comte and Albert Vuilleumier visited these new converts, and Vuilleumier baptized them. Many of the early converts emigrated to South America, while those who remained continued to be faithful in Sabbath observance though they were not visited for many years.

In 1905 S. Jespersson and his wife were sent to Algiers to do medical missionary work. In September 1907 Paul Steiner arrived to assist them in evangelistic work, but for health reasons he had to leave before completing his first year. Before the end of 1908 Ulysse Augsburger, a minister, and Joseph Abella, a colporteur, arrived. In April 1909 four women were baptized. Thus was laid the foundation for a church in the capital.

At the time of the Latin Union Conference session in 1909, Albert Guyot was invited to go to Algeria. He went first to Algiers, then in October 1910 to Oran. In Oran he renewed contact with the early adherents of Relizane, met the founder of the group, Joseph Gomis, then 77 years old, and found four large families keeping the Sabbath.

As a result of the work of Paul Badaut, J. C. Guenin, R.T.E. Colthurst, W. E. Hancock, and others, the work spread gradually to the different sections of Algeria. In 1912 the field was assigned directly to the General Conference. Then after World War I it again became a part of the Latin Union Conference. In 1921 the Algerian Mission was organized, with Albert Meyer in charge, and with a membership of 61.

When the North African Union Mission was organized in 1928, the headquarters were placed in Algiers. By 1933 there were 207 members in the Algerian Mission. Colporteur work contributed substantially to evangelism in Algeria. The medical work was represented by the Vie et Santé Institute of Algiers (established 1933) and dispensaries at Mostaganem and Bel-Hacel in the region of Relizane-Oran. In 1950 a church and headquarters building was dedicated in the center of Algiers.

In 1958 the Algerian-Tunisian Mission had 12 churches or companies, with a membership of 540. At that time 15 evangelistic and other workers and two colporteurs were at work in this vast territory. When Algeria became independent in 1962, more than a million Europeans left, and with them nine tenths of the SDA members.

A school for boys aged 12 to 17 in Algiers was closed by the government in 1968. The clinic, Vie et Santé, was taken over by the government. Our other properties were classified as "available for possession," although our office was endeavoring to function In 1993 there were six members in Algiers and six in the rest of the country.

Evangelistic efforts are confined to Arabic radiobroadcasts, and the Bible correspondence course originating in France.

ALGERIAN PUBLISHING HOUSE. A former publishing house without printing facilities, operated from 1932 to 1952 by the North African Union Mission at Algiers, Algeria. In the *Statistical Report* it is listed from 1933 to 1939 as a depository only, though from 1935 on, both book and periodical sales were reported. In 1940 it was designated as a publishing house, but there were no new reports on the house's activity until 1948, when its sales of books and one periodical title were given at $25,000. In 1950 it reached its highest volume of sales, nearly $40,000, but since then the sales declined, and after 1952 the house was no longer listed.

ALGERIAN-TUNISIAN MISSION. *See* Algeria; Euro-Africa Division; Tunisia.

ALIMENTOS CREAPE. *See* River Plate College Food Factory.

ALIMENTOS COLPAC. *See* Inter-American Health Food Company, Mexico-Navojoa Branch.

ALIMENTOS GRANIX. *See* South American Division Health Food Company.

ALINSA. *See* Inter-American Health Food Company.

ALLEGHENY EAST CONFERENCE. A unit of church organization comprised of predominantly Black congregations within the Columbia Union Conference; that is, that portion of Pennsylvania east of Potter, Clinton, Centre, Mifflin, Huntingdon, and Fulton counties; that portion of Virginia east of Clarke (including the town of Berryville in Clarke county), Warren, Rappahannock, Madison, Greene, Albemarle, Fluvanna, Cumberland, Prince Edward, Lunenburg, and Mecklenburg counties (except the city of Gordonsville in Orange county); and Berkeley and Jefferson counties in West Virginia; all of Maryland (except Garrett and Allegany counties); all of New Jersey; all of Delaware; and the District of Columbia. The estimated Black population within these areas totals approximately 4 million. Headquarters of the Allegheny East Conference of Seventh-day Adventists (on Pine Forge Road): P.O. Box 266, Pine Forge, Pennsylvania 19548. Statistics (1993): churches, 84; companies, 9; members, 23,406; church schools, 10; ordained ministers, 71; licensed ministers, 9; Bible instructors, 13; church school teachers, 75; literature evangelists (credentialed), 10; literature evangelists (licensed), 10; commissioned minister credentials, 9; commissioned teacher credentials, 48; missionary credentials, 46; commissioned minister licenses, 9; missionary licenses, 31.

Institutions. Pine Forge Academy.

Local churches—*Maryland:* Annapolis, Baltimore (Berea Temple, Cherry Hill, Edmondson, Liberty, Maranatha, Miracle Temple, Sharon), Bladensburg, Brinklow, Bryans Road (Pisgah), Cambridge, Fort Washington, Gaithersburg, Hyattsville, Prince Frederick, Rockville (Korean), Salisbury. *Delaware:* Dover, Harrington, Millsboro, Wilmington (Sharon Temple, Spanish). *New Jersey:* Asbury Park (French), Bridgeton, Camden, East Orange (French), Elizabeth (French), Englewood, Glassboro, Hillside, Jersey City, Montclair, Neptune, New Brunswick, Newark (Salem French, Trinity Temple), Newtonville, Orange (Spanish), Paterson, Plainfield, Pleasantville, Salem, Teaneck, Trenton (Ephesus, Mount Sinai), Washington, Whitesboro. *Pennsylvania:* Chester, Coatesville, Harrisburg (Hillside, Spanish), Norristown, Philadelphia (Ebenezer, Germantown, Jerusalem French, Mizpah, New Life, North, Southwest, West), Pine Forge, Pottstown, Willow Grove, York. *Virginia:* Alexandria, Berryville, Brandy Station, Crewe, Franklin, Newport News, Norfolk, Petersburg, Portsmouth, Richmond (Ephesus), Suffolk, Williamsburg. *Washington, D.C.:* Capitol Hill, DuPont Park, First, Fourth Street Friendship, Hadley.

Companies—*Maryland:* Frederick, Langley Park (Haitian). *Delaware:* Wilmington (Mount Zion). *New Jersey:* Trenton (Mount Sinai French), West Orange (French). *Pennsylvania:* Reading. *Virginia:* Richmond (Cornerstone),

Tappahannock. *West Virginia:* Martinsburg.

History. *Allegheny East Conference Organized.* The Columbia Union Conference committee voted July 9, 1966, to approve a reorganization of the Allegheny Conference. The present organization began in January 1945 and grew to such proportions that a commission was established to study the plan for organization of two conferences within the Allegheny Conference territory. The membership at this time was 11,144.

May 1, 1966, the Allegheny Conference constituency recommended that the new conferences begin their operation Jan. 1, 1967. Also voted at this time: the time and place for the two constituencies to meet and elect their officers.

The western section of the conference held its election Nov. 13, 1966, in Columbus, Ohio; and the eastern section held its election Nov. 20, 1966, in Baltimore, Maryland, at which time W. A. Thompson was elected as president; Edward Dorsey, secretary-treasurer; D. L. Davis, lay activities and MV director; C. L. Brooks, Sabbath school and education director; and T. S. Barber, publishing secretary of the Allegheny East Conference. The manager of the Book and Bible House was to be supplied by the Allegheny East Conference executive committee. R. W. Newman, the pastor of the Oberlin-Toledo, Ohio, district, was called to the managerial post of the Allegheny East Conference Book and Bible House Jan. 8, 1967.

Further Developments. In 1970 W. A. Thompson, the president, accepted a call to the Columbia Union Conference as secretary. The Allegheny East Conference executive committee on June 28, 1970, elected Edward Dorsey as the president and C. W. Laurence as secretary-treasurer.

In July 1971 Laurence's automobile overturned and he was fatally injured. The executive committee met on Aug. 1, 1971, and elected M. C. Van Putten, who was serving as secretary-treasurer of the Lake Region Conference, to become the secretary-treasurer of the Allegheny East Conference; the executive committee met Aug. 26, 1971, and decided to separate the two offices, calling L. R. Palmer, Jr., to be the conference's first executive secretary. Allegheny East Conference has experienced near phenomenal growth, going from 44 churches and 7,745 members in 1967 to 84 churches and 23,406 members in 1993. The conference has nine active companies. The Allegheny East Conference jointly operates Pine Forge Academy in partnership with the Allegheny West Conference. It is fully accredited. Recent improvements include a church, gymnasium, industrial building, and swimming pool. The enrollment in the elementary school system was 1,330 in 1993.

Presidents: W. A. Thompson, 1967-1970; Edward Dorsey, 1970-1975; L. R. Palmer, 1975-1981; M. C. Van Putten, 1981-1988; A. M. Kibble, 1989- .

ALLEGHENY WEST CONFERENCE. A unit of church organization comprising the Black congregations of the Columbia Union Conference, that is, that portion of Pennsylvania west of and including Potter, Clinton, Centre, Mifflin, Huntingdon, and Fulton counties; Garrett and Allegany counties in Maryland; that portion of Virginia west of and including Clarke, Warren, Rappahannock, Madison, Green, Albermarle, Fluvanna, Cumberland, Prince Edward, Lunenburg, and Mecklenburg counties and the city of Gordonsville in Orange County; all of West Virginia (except Berkeley and Jefferson counties); and all of Ohio. Headquarters of the Allegheny West Conference of Seventh-day Adventists is at 1339 East Broad Street, Columbus, Ohio 43205. *Statistics* (1992): churches, missions, or companies, 53; members, 10,291; church schools, 3; ordained ministers, 29; licensed ministers, 11; lay pastors, 5; credentialed missionaries, 6; licensed missionaries, 6; literature evangelists, 12; teachers, 10.

Local churches—*Ohio*: Akron (Bethel, Twinsburg), Ashtabula (Berean), Canton (New Hope), Chillicothe Prison Institute, Cincinnati (Emmanuel, Maranatha, Revelation, Shiloh), Cleveland (Bethel, Glenville, Southeast), Columbus (Central, Ephesus, Hilltop), Dayton (Ethan Temple, Hillcrest), Delaware (Victory), Germantown, Hamilton (Mount Olive), Lima (Gospel Tabernacle), Lorain (Lakeview), Newark, Oberlin, Springfield (South Fountain), Toledo (Parkwood Avenue), Warren (Oak Street), Youngstown (Temple Emmanuel), Zanesville (Hillside). *Pennsylvania:* Eau Claire, Erie (Mount Zion), Franklin, Meedville, Pittsburgh (Hillcrest), Uniontown (Berean), Wilkinsburg. *Virginia:* Afton, Charlottesville (Bethany), Covington, Danville (Ross Street), Gordonsville, Lynchburg (Smyrna), Martinsville (Ephesus), Roanoke (Melrose), South Boston (Emmanuel), Staunton (Bethel). *West Virginia:* Beckley (East Beckley), Charleston (Berea), Huntington (Shiloh), Kimball (Bethel).

Because of the unprecedented growth of the

original Allegheny Conference, the constituents felt that they could be served better by becoming two conferences. After a feasibility study was conducted by the Columbia Union Conference, plans were laid for the reorganization.

In two separate constituency meetings held in Columbus, Ohio, on Nov. 13, 1966, and in Baltimore, Maryland, on Nov. 20, 1966, it was voted to organize two new conferences in Allegheny territory. The Allegheny West Conference was officially established by vote of the constituents of the western section of the old Allegheny Conference in the constituency meeting held on Nov. 13, 1966, in Columbus, Ohio. Walter M. Starks, stewardship secretary of the Allegheny Conference, was elected as the first president, and Aaron N. Brogden as secretary/treasurer. Other personnel elected included Henry Freeman, publishing secretary; N. K. Jenkins, associate publishing secretary; D. B. Simons, lay activities and Sabbath school director; A. T. Westney, education and MV secretaries. Elected as members of the executive committee were: W. M. Starks, Aaron N. Brogden, N. A. Bliss, J. A. Washington, A. L. Jones, D. B. Simons, and Charles Anderson.

The membership of the conference at the time of organization was 4,299. The conference territory included 30 churches.

In 1988 a 72-acre (30-hectare) campground at Thornville, Ohio, was purchased and paid for within two years for $250,000. A 5,000-seat pavilion was built in 1991 for $350,000. The campground is about 55 miles (88 kilometers) southeast of Columbus, Ohio.

Presidents: W. M. Starks, 1966-1967; D. B. Simons, 1967-1972; H. L. Cleveland, 1972-1983; H. M. Wright, 1983-1988; W. J. Lewis, 1988- .

ALLEN, ALVIN NATHAN (1880-1945). Missionary in Latin America, minister, teacher, and administrator. He was born in a Seventh-day Adventist family and was educated at Union (1898-1899) and Battle Creek (1900-1901) colleges. In 1901 he married Luella Goodrich, who with her parents was a missionary in the Bay Islands and Honduras. He too went there as a missionary. Together they taught, preached, and engaged in colporteur work until 1907, when they returned on furlough and he attended Washington Missionary College. In 1908 he was ordained and soon thereafter was sent to Peru to superintend the field. Between 1914 and 1917 he headed the Cuban Mission, then was president of the South Carolina Conference in 1917 and also assumed responsibility for the war service relations in the Southern Union and preached in Tennessee and Kentucky. Later he went to Mexico, where he worked in Mexico City and among the Indians of Tehuantepec. Upon his return to the United States he organized and for a while directed the Spanish-American Training School (a training school for the Spanish-speaking people at Phoenix, Arizona). In 1926 he went to South America and taught Bible at the Brazilian Seminary (Colegio Adventista). Volunteering to begin work among the Indians on the Araguaya River, he superintended the Goyaz and Araguaya Indian missions from 1927 until about 1933. At that time he resigned the leadership, but continued in the ministry until 1938. Returning to the United States, he pastored churches in Virginia and Florida until a few weeks before his death.

ALLRED, IVAN LAMAR (1918-1985). Minister, publishing director, trust services director. He was born in Greenville, Michigan. He entered denominational service in 1951 as assistant publishing director in the Michigan Conference. Three and a half years later he became the conference's publishing director and was ordained to the gospel ministry on Aug. 26, 1955. In 1960 he accepted a call to direct the Texas Conference Publishing Department, where he served for nearly eight years.

In 1968 he entered the church's trust services work, first as secretary of the Oklahoma Conference Corporation from 1968 to 1972, then as associate trust services director in Michigan for five years and in Ohio for a short time. Finally he was trust services director in the Texas Conference from 1977 until his retirement in 1983.

ALLUM, FRANCIS ARTHUR (1883-1948). Minister, evangelist, and administrator in China and Australia. As a result of hearing a mission talk on China in his native England at the age of 14, he dedicated his life to Christian service and planned to go to China as a missionary. Later he with his family moved to Australia, where a missionary-minded woman acquainted them with the Seventh-day Adventist beliefs. With his mother and sister he was baptized in 1900. Afterward he attended Avondale School (1901-1905), and, after completing the course of training, engaged in tent evangelism in New South Wales. In 1905 the Mission Board invited him to join the pioneer

SDA workers in China, but it could not provide him with fare to reach his post. He earned passage for himself and his young bride (the former Eva Osborne) by colporteur work in New Zealand. In China his first station was in the province of Honan. In 1908 or 1909 he was ordained at Shanghai by I. H. Evans, and afterward superintended the North Central China Mission (1910-1912), assisted in the supervision of the China Union (1912), directed the West China Mission (1914-1915), and presided over the North China Union Conference (1918-1919) and the Central China Union Mission (1919-1922). Ill health caused his return to the homeland after 16 years of service in China. In Australia he became secretary (1923) and later vice president (1924-1926) of the Australasian Union Conference, and later served as president of the Victoria-Tasmania Conference. He retired because of poor health and went first to Port Macquarie and then to Warrawee, New South Wales, but continued to carry pastoral and evangelistic work. In retirement he designed and distributed Bible text cards.

ALPINE CONFERENCE. *See* Austria.

ALTAR. *See* Church Buildings.

ALTERSHEIM BAD AIBLING. *See* Haus Wittelsbach Old People's Home.

ALTERSHEIM BENSHEIM-AUERBACH. *See* Bensheim-Auerbach Old People's Home.

ALTERSHEIM BERLIN-STEGLITZ. *See* Berlin-Steglitz Old People's Home.

ALTERSHEIM FRIEDENSAU. *See* Friedensau Old People's Home.

ALTERSHEIM NEANDERTAL. *See* Neandertal Old People's Home.

ALTERSHEIM UELZEN. *See* Uelzen Old People's Home.

ALTMAN, ROGER (1895-1992). Editor, teacher, administrator. Born in Colorado, he served the church for more than 40 years, most of them in the Far Eastern Division. He served as secretary to the General Conference president and as an associate secretary of the General Conference. His last position before his retirement was as secretary-treasurer of the Southeast Asia Union Mission. He passed to his rest in Virginia.

ALTO PARANÁ MISSION. *See* Argentina.

ALTON VILLAS. *See* Adventist Retirement Village, Inc.

ALVARADO, EMILIA HERLINDA (1933-1991). Teacher. Born in Peru, she distinguished herself with her dedicated work for children. She began to teach in 1954, and officially finished her own training in 1957. She was involved in the development of hundreds of children, many of whom are now professionals serving in the Lord's vineyard. She retired in 1985 after 31 years of fruitful labor. In retirement she, along with her sister, established a private school patterned after the model of true education.

AMADON, GEORGE WASHINGTON (1832-1913). Publishing house worker. He was educated at Oberlin College, joined the Review and Herald office when it was in Rochester, New York, and moved with it to Battle Creek in 1855. For 50 years he served the publishing house in various capacities, such as typesetter, foreman in charge of the foreign language publications, and part-time, then full-time, editor of the *Youth's Instructor* (1858-1864). After the Review and Herald plant was destroyed by fire in 1902, he was for several years visiting pastor of the Battle Creek church, and was ordained when 72 years of age.

AMADON, GRACE (1872-1945). Teacher, bacteriologist, and research worker, daughter of G. W. Amadon. Educated at Battle Creek College and the American Medical Missionary College, she taught Greek, Latin, mathematics, and music in Claremont Union College, South Africa, from 1893 to 1900, and biology in the Chicago Veterinary College from 1907 to 1911. During 25 years of caring for her invalid mother, she worked as a bacteriologist in a public health laboratory, did technical illustrating, and carried on research in biblical chronology. Beginning in 1939 she was employed as a researcher by the General Conference.

AMADON, MARTHA D. (BYINGTON) (1834-1937). The eldest daughter of John Byington, the first teacher of a school established at Buck's Bridge, New York, by her father in 1853, which is held to be the first school organized for Seventh-day Adventist children. In 1860 she married George W. Amadon. She was the first president of the first Dorcas Society, and held many sewing bees in her living room at Battle Creek.

AMAZING FACTS. Amazing Facts began as a daily radio program on WEMD in Baltimore in the spring of 1966. The radio show was developed by the Chesapeake Conference as a way to sow seeds for public evangelism. This new approach to soul winning quickly became popular under the direction of pastor and evangelist Joe Crews.

Each radiobroadcast opened with an amazing scientific or historical fact, and a brief biblical message followed. Hundreds and then thousands of listeners began sending for the free Bible lessons offered at the end of each broadcast. Christians and non-Christians alike praised the colorful and attention-grabbing Amazing Facts That Affect You lessons written by Bill May.

Realizing the enormous soul-winning potential of the fledgling program, the Chesapeake Conference began paving the way for Amazing Facts to become a nationwide ministry. First, it was legally incorporated as a nonprofit organization in the fall of 1966. Shortly thereafter, Amazing Facts became officially recognized as an authorized ministry of the Seventh-day Adventist Church. Today it continues to operate as a ministry of the Chesapeake Conference, and thus as part of the Columbia Union. All Amazing Facts employees are licensed or issued credentials by the Chesapeake Conference, and the ministry is audited yearly by the General Conference. However, because of the generous donations of supporters, Amazing Facts is totally self-funding. This unique relationship makes Amazing Facts a one-of-a-kind Adventist media ministry.

Originally located at the Chesapeake Conference office, Amazing Facts moved its headquarters to Frederick, Maryland, in 1980. This move enabled the ministry to expand in both form and function. Its Bible correspondence course continued to grow, serving students from around the world. Then, to meet a growing need within the church for affordable public evangelism, Amazing Facts began training young men to join the ministry's team as full-time evangelists. In 1987 the ministry added television programming to its communication chain. A 27-night evangelistic series held by Joe Crews was filmed live and aired on selected stations around the country. Audience response was enthusiastic, as it had been with the radio program more than 20 years earlier. The clear, Bible-based messages and straightforward delivery gained immediate acceptance by countless people nationwide.

Sensing the urgency of the gospel imperative, Amazing Facts in 1993 added two more elements to its outreach agenda. The first was a program for equipping laypersons and pastors with the skills necessary to hold successful evangelistic campaigns. These hands-on training seminars have enabled hundreds of dedicated and energetic individuals to conduct public crusades worldwide.

The second element was a church preparation coordinator to teach churches how to do prework and follow-up for each Amazing Facts evangelistic meeting. A model timeline includes one year of preparation for each reaping series, followed by a six-month program to nurture new converts and those still making decisions. Pastors, laypersons, and church leaders alike have applauded these two new programs as long overdue.

Amazing Facts has grown from a local broadcast to a soul-winning center with worldwide scope. Today its radio programs are broadcast from 81 stations around the world, and its telecast airs 45 times each week. From its beginning with one evangelist it has grown to a team of 15 ministers dedicated to spreading this last-day message. Furthermore, the original 12 Amazing Facts That Affect You Bible lessons have been expanded to 27, and their appeal remains unprecedented. More than 10,000 students are enrolled in its Bible correspondence school.

Amazing Facts also publishes a monthly magazine, *The Inside Report,* which is free upon request. A free catalog of evangelistic resource materials is also available. Both may be obtained through Amazing Facts' corporate headquarters.

AMAZON AGRICULTURAL SCHOOL. *See* Agro-Industrial Adventist Trans-Amazon Academy.

AMBATOHARANANA DISPENSARY. *See* Madagascar.

AMBON ACADEMY. *See* Maluku Academy.

AMBON MISSION. *See* Indonesia.

AMBS, KARL FREDERICK (1903-1970). Missionary, administrator, treasurer. A native of Wisconsin, he entered denominational work in 1925. In 1932 he married Glenna Muriel Tatro and soon after went to Union Springs Academy in New York, where he served as treasurer. This was followed by a term of service at Forest Lake Academy in Florida, where he served in the same capacity, and a period at Pine Tree Academy in New England, where he was principal.

In 1940 he began administrative work at the Gitwe Training School in Rwanda, Africa. During the following 18 years he held various administrative positions, from president of the Congo Union Mission to treasurer of the South African Division.

Returning to the United States in 1958, he served as business manager of Andrews University until 1962, when he was elected assistant treasurer of the General Conference, which position he held for seven years until his death.

AMERICAN CLINIC. *See* Quito Adventist Clinic.

AMERICAN HEALTH AND TEMPERANCE ASSOCIATION. An organization dedicated to the advocacy of temperance. On Feb. 13, 1826, the American Health and Temperance Association, then called the American Temperance Society, was incorporated in Boston, Massachusetts. The *Christian Examiner* at that time declared: "The greatest enterprise and the most hopeful omen of the age, perhaps, is the temperance reform." By 1827 more than 7,000 temperance societies had been established and were active, composed of one and a quarter million members and claiming more than 10,000 reclaimed drunkards.

This organization was reconstituted and established by the General Conference in 1932.

Joseph Bates, one of the Seventh-day Adventist pioneers, had long been a temperance reformer. Toward the end of his years as a seaman, he discarded the use of all alcoholic drinks and tobacco. On the day of his baptism into the Christian church in 1827, he expressed his determination to organize a temperance society, and invited the minister who had baptized him to assist in this, but the minister refused to become involved in the project.

Bates therefore approached a minister of the Congregational church, and was successful in securing his support. In addition to the Congregational minister, two of his deacons, several former sea captains, and a few others whom Bates had persuaded to assist him met and organized the Fairhaven Temperance Society at Fairhaven, Massachusetts. The charter members of the society took a pledge against gin, rum, brandy, and whiskey. Later the society amended the pledge by including all intoxicating beverages, thus putting the ban on fermented as well as distilled liquors, except for medicinal purposes.

The New Bedford Society, the Bristol County Society, and then the Massachusetts State Society were organized in due course. Thus, Joseph Bates was among the earliest pioneers in organizing a temperance society and in promoting and fostering the total-abstinence movement in the United States.

Bates later devoted his full time to the Adventist movement of the 1840s, and following the disappointment in 1844 became one of the principal founders of the Seventh-day Adventist Church.

Early Seventh-day Adventist Advocacy of Temperance. The original SDA leaders were abstainers, but not until 1862 was a more thoroughgoing reform inaugurated. Chiefly through the writings of James and Ellen G. White, emphasis was given to the fact that the moral nature is largely affected by physical nature, and that success in appealing to people spiritually is more effective if they can first be turned from those habits that undermine their physical powers and benumb their moral sensibilities.

The first united move was made among Seventh-day Adventists in behalf of a broad temperance program in 1863, but Ellen White had already warned of the dangers of not only liquor and tobacco but also tea and coffee.

The years of the Civil War in the United States and the subsequent period of reconstruction witnessed a serious setback to the cause of temperance reform that had flourished in the earlier part of the century. During the 1870s several temperance organizations appeared, including the Woman's Christian Temperance Union. Mrs. White actively cooperated with the national temperance movements, frequently speaking on their behalf and addressing on numerous occasions large audiences on the subject of temperance. On one occasion, during the summer of 1876, she spoke to some 20,000 people on a campground at Groveland, Massachusetts. The next day she repeated her address to the Haverhill Reform Club.

American Health and Temperance

Association. A great forward movement to enlist the rank and file of Seventh-day Adventists began in December 1878. A meeting was held in the publishing house chapel in Battle Creek, Michigan, on Dec. 30 "to consider the propriety of organizing a national health and temperance society." At a second meeting, held on New Year's Day, 1879, further steps were taken, and on Jan. 5 the organization of the American Health and Temperance Association was completed. J. H. Kellogg, M.D., of the Battle Creek Sanitarium, was elected president. Some 133 persons signed the teetotalers' pledge, discarding tea and other stimulants and narcotics, as well as alcohol, and 22 signed the anti-rum and tobacco pledge.

Another action was taken on Nov. 24, 1879, by vote of the General Conference, emphasizing that it is "the duty of all members of this denomination to become members of the American Health and Temperance Association, and to use their influence in inducing others to unite in this reformatory effort."

At this time the membership program was inaugurated as the basis of temperance organization. Any person of good moral character could become a member of the association by paying an initiation fee of 25 cents, and thereafter a minimum of 10 cents a year, and signing a teetotal pledge.

Also the basis was laid for general support of the temperance cause by ministers and church leaders. "*Resolved,* That the conference committee of each conference be requested to encourage proper persons to fit themselves to engage in the health and temperance work; and we especially urge all ministers to prepare themselves to present the subject of health and temperance in an efficient and practical manner, and make it a part of their work in their various fields of labor."

During the next few years the subject of temperance was presented actively in the camp meetings, and all SDAs were invited to become members of the organization and to take an active part in temperance endeavor.

International Health and Temperance Association. By 1881 the American Health and Temperance Association had 9,819 members, according to the minutes of a meeting held that year. In that year a children's pledge was prepared for circulation among the younger people. In 1889 at the eleventh annual session, the society was renamed the International Health and Temperance Association.

The association continued its activities until 1893, when the SDA Medical Missionary and Benevolent Association was organized. The specific purpose of the original organization became subordinated in the general health program promoted by the church.

Specific counsel had been given by Ellen G. White on the necessity of establishing temperance societies and clubs, printing temperance literature, and appointing workers who would go to the cities and bear the message of temperance.

Temperance activity of Seventh-day Adventists followed the national trends during the period leading up to the enactment of the Eighteenth Amendment, with some church leaders, such as C. S. Longacre, taking part in the public education that resulted in the passage in 1917 of the prohibition amendment and its ratification by the states in 1919. SDAs oppose church participation in politics; but they have always considered legislation against alcohol and other similar poisons to be not a political but a moral issue.

When the Volstead Act of 1919 made national prohibition effective, Seventh-day Adventists relaxed their public efforts, as did the other organizations that had pushed for prohibition. In the meantime the anti-prohibition forces became active to nullify prohibition, until in 1933 the Twenty-first Amendment, to repeal the Eighteenth, was passed by Congress and became effective on Dec. 5, 1933, after the required number of states had ratified it.

American Temperance Society Reorganized. Already in 1932, discerning the increasing tragedy of intemperance in the nation as repeal approached, SDAs had organized the American Temperance Society of Seventh-day Adventists. During the following 15 years a modest temperance program was carried on. The chief organ for the society was the *Temperance Bulletin,* an informational sheet of four pages. Special annual temperance editions of the *Signs of the Times,* circulated in millions of copies, made a major impact on the public. Anti-narcotic issues of *Our Little Friend* were published for the children.

After the 1946 Autumn Council, the General Conference appointed representative committees to review the church's temperance objectives and to formulate a program of world action along temperance lines, with a view to setting up an organization through which an aggressive effort could be promoted both within and outside the church.

American Temperance Society Again Reorganized. Two constitutions were planned, one for the organization that was to serve the world to be known as the International Temperance Association, and the other a new constitution for the American Temperance Society. The latter would serve as the model for the organizing of a temperance society in every country. The constitution of the American Temperance Society was adopted by the General Conference Committee on Jan. 27, 1947, with J. L. McElhany, the General Conference president, being elected as president of the society and W. A. Scharffenberg as executive secretary. The constitution of the International Temperance Association was adopted at the Autumn Council of 1947.

Methods, Projects, and Publications. About this time a compilation was made from Ellen G. White's writings on the subject. Published under the title *Temperance,* this book serves as the blueprint for the church's temperance program.

The first major project of the American Temperance Society was the launching of the magazine *Listen* in 1948. This was the first of an increasing number of temperance publications that have served during subsequent years as the major stimulus for the society's growing program.

The American Temperance Society was set up as a membership organization, following the instruction and personal example of Mrs. White herself in the early temperance work of the church. Various memberships offered were junior and student memberships for the children and young people, as well as regular, family, contributing, sustaining, supporting, and life memberships for adults. Each member was to receive benefits for the respective membership, these benefits consisting mainly of the publications such as *Listen, Alert, Smoke Signals, Activities,* and *The Winner.* The annual pledge-signing campaign and membership drive provided opportunity for all church members to enroll as temperance members; this took place on Temperance Commitment Sabbath, designated at the time in the church calendar as the last Sabbath in February.

Financial support for the society came from four major sources: membership dues; sale of publications, films, and other materials; contributions from interested donors; and the annual Temperance Offering, received on World Temperance Day, the fourth Sabbath in October.

By 1964 four national conventions of the American Temperance Society had been held, two in Washington, D.C., the others in Denver, Colorado, and Kansas City, Missouri. These served as training schools for church temperance secretaries and other laypersons interested in temperance activity, and provided opportunity to present nationally known authorities in person and to publicize widely the church's temperance program.

Chapters of the American Temperance Society were organized in SDA schools. Active projects, including oratorical, essay, jingle, and poster contests, were encouraged for the young people. Many student participants presented their orations before civic and business clubs, and before other church and youth organizations. Chapters sponsored annual Temperance Weeks for the students, and engaged in community literature distribution to aid in local option elections.

Currently such activity is directed by Collegiate Adventists for Better Living and (on the elementary and academy level) Adventist Youth for Better Living.

Program. The program of the American Temperance Society can be summarized under three major headings, as follows:

1. *Education:* the producing and making effective use of attractive magazines, pamphlets, posters, films, public lectures, and all other means to focus the attention of the church and the public on problems of intemperance, but emphasizing the principles of better living from a positive approach, in order to present appealingly, especially to youth, the advantages of abstinence as the genuine alternative.

2. *Legislation:* cooperating with civic and government agencies in making the community and nation a safer place in which to live, and pressing for the passage of laws to restrict, control, or ban the production, sale, distribution, and consumption of liquor, tobacco, and illegal narcotics, also urging church members and all others to make use of their vote at every opportunity on temperance issues.

3. *Reformation:* helping those who are victims of intemperance, pointing them back to normal living, through the use of natural means and dependence on divine aid. Spiritual emphasis is a real part of such projects.

To reflect more accurately the fusion of the Health and Temperance departments into one department in 1980, the American Temperance Society's name was change to the American Health and Temperance Society. In the early 1990s the name was changed again to the American Health and Temperance Association.

Presidents: J. L. McElhany, 1947-1950;

H. L. Rudy, 1951-1960; M. V. Campbell, 1961-1962; R. S. Watts, 1963-1968; M. S. Nigri, 1968-1975; F. W. Wernick, 1975-1980; Mervyn G. Hardinge, 1980-1981; C. E. Bradford, 1981-1990; A. S. McClure, 1990- .

Executive Secretaries/Directors: W. A. Scharffenberg, 1947-1964; E. J. Folkenberg, 1965-1968; E.H.J. Steed, 1968-1981; Rudolf E. Klimes, 1981-1985; S. E. Proctor, 1985-1990; D. S. Williams, 1990- .

AMERICAN MEDICAL MISSIONARY COLLEGE. A coeducational medical school operated from 1895 to 1910 in Chicago, Illinois, and Battle Creek, Michigan, incorporated separately but sponsored by the Battle Creek Sanitarium. It offered a four-year course leading to the M.D. degree. Students were to be "those who desire to devote their lives to altruistic work," with preference given to "those who are preparing themselves for medical missionary activity in home or foreign fields" *(The Battle Creek Schools* [1905-1906 bulletin], p. 43).

The school's president was John Harvey Kellogg, M.D., who continued to serve as the pivotal administrative and professional figure in the Battle Creek Sanitarium. From 1899 to 1910, 194 Doctor of Medicine degrees were conferred. The faculty included the staff of Battle Creek Sanitarium and several eminent Chicago physicians who gave clinical instruction to students while assigned to Cook County Hospital, St. Luke's Hospital, and the college's dispensary in Chicago. The lack of strong financial support and the failure of the college to provide a hospital in Chicago under the control of its own staff, the plan of the denomination to develop Loma Linda as a center of medical education along with lesser problems, brought about its dissolution in 1910. Prior to the closing of the American Medical Missionary College the stockholders of the Battle Creek Sanitarium had chosen to decline official denominational ownership and control. The college dropped out of the denominational *Yearbook* in 1907.

AMERICAN SAMOA. *See* Samoa and Takelau Islands.

AMERICAN SENTINEL. *See Sentinel of Christian Liberty.*

AMERICAN TEMPERANCE SOCIETY. *See* American Health and Temperance Association.

AMES ACADEMY. *See* Gem State Adventist Academy.

AMILLENNIALISM. *See* Premillennialism.

AMMAN ADVENTIST SECONDARY SCHOOL. A coeducational secondary school situated in Jabal Amman, Amman, Jordan, operated by the East Mediterranean Field. The school was begun by Naim Awais in 1942. It follows the curriculum prescribed by the Jordanian Ministry of Education augmented by the Seventh-day Adventist religion program. The enrollment in 1993 was 170 students.

Principals: Naim Awais, 1942-1943; Farid Srour and Mousa Azar, 1943-1946; Ruby Williams, 1946-1948; Hana Nasr, 1948-1957; Rose Katrib, 1957-1959; Hana Nasr, 1959-1963; Rose Katrib, 1963-1965; Hana Nasr, 1965-1969; Faiz Haddad, 1969-1972; Tawfic Madanat, 1972-1977; Faiz Haddad, 1977-1986; Tawfic Madanat, 1986- .

AMUSEMENTS. *See* Recreation and Amusements.

AMYES MEMORIAL HOSPITAL. *See* Kukudu Adventist Hospital.

ANA STAHL ADVENTIST CLINIC (Clínica Adventista Ana Stahl). A general 50-bed hospital (originally operated as an obstetrical hospital under the name Ana Stahl Clinic), owned and operated by the Inca Union Mission, situated in Iquitos, Peru.

From the time the East Peru Mission was founded in 1927, F. A. Stahl had a vision of a medical institution serving the sick of the Upper Amazon area. In 1930 a wooden building to be used as a clinic was erected on the mission property in the city of Iquitos. However, except for one room, which was used as the medical room, the building stood more than 30 years before being put to the use for which it was intended, although during much of that time it was used as the mission office. In that room Stahl and his wife, Ana, carried on an extensive and well-known medical work.

In 1953 plans were formulated for a maternity clinic under the nursing direction of Mrs. S. C. Pritchard. In 1957 Mrs. Bernice Larrabee was called to take charge of the clinic, and through her efforts the building was reconditioned and equipped, and a class of nurse's aides was trained.

On May 18, 1960, Dr. Rodolfo Alfaro from Argentina came to Iquitos, opened a medical office, and as first medical director presided on May 18, 1961, at the official opening of the clinic. Under his leadership the Stahl Clinic initiated an active public health program in the little jungle villages surrounding Iquitos.

In 1963 a new brick building to house the doctors' offices, administration and other offices, X-ray, and laboratory was completed, increasing the space for patient beds in the old building. At the same time the clinic was made a general hospital. During 1974 the Ministry of Health approved plans for the construction of a modern, well-equipped clinic, at a cost of US$750,000, which was financed by the German Evangelical Agency for Development and the Inca Union.

Medical Directors: Rodolfo Alfaro, 1961-1962; Erwin O. Beskow, 1962-1964; E. C. Lanz, 1965; E. E. Rippey, 1966; G. A. Gilkes, 1967-1970; J. H. Lund Victoria, 1971-1973; Walter León, 1973; Moisés Rojas Shapiana, 1974-1977; Daniel Florian Ortiz, 1978-1979; Moisés Rojas Shapiana, 1980-1981; Daniel Florian Ortiz, 1982; Juan Barrientos Morales, 1982-1987; Emiliano Contreras Castro, 1988-1989; Alejandro Medina Vilca, 1990-1991; Elmer Ribeyro, 1991-1993; Jose Medina Garcia, 1993- .

ANACAPA ADVENTIST HOSPITAL. A 48-bed general acute hospital that was incorporated in September 1974 and became affiliated with Adventist Health Services, Inc., a forerunner of Adventist Health System/West, on Jan. 1, 1975. Originally Bellinda Hospital, it was founded by Dr. A. H. Crites. This modern medical facility is a single-story cement block building. Originally 30 beds, additional construction in 1964 increased the occupancy. In 1974 a two-story medical building was completed on the same site to support the hospital's operations. Later known as Port Hueneme Adventist Hospital, the facility now is leased as a behavioral treatment center for adults as well as adolescents. The hospital is located on the coast of California near a deep draft harbor, in the city of Port Hueneme.

ANDAMAN AND NICOBAR ISLAND REGION. *See* Andaman and Nicobar Islands; Southern Asia Division.

ANDAMAN AND NICOBAR ISLANDS. A group of islands in the Bay of Bengal toward the Myanmar coast, forming one of the Union territories of India, with a total area of about 3,200 square miles (8,300 square kilometers) and a population (1991) of 188,741. For almost a century the archipelago served as a penal colony for the government of India, and descendants of the prisoners constitute a large segment of the population, which is augmented by some recent immigrants resettled from Bangladesh. The indigenous inhabitants have retired into the interior and avoid all contact with civilization. Hindi is the main language, while southern India languages are in use in the interior.

An interest in Seventh-day Adventist teachings was created in these islands through the Voice of Prophecy Bible correspondence courses. In 1951 evangelistic work was administered from Sri Lanka, but in 1953 it was transferred to the Northeast India Union. Between 1952 and 1960 S. Daniel and his wife worked on the islands as literature evangelists. In 1959 N. G. Mookerjee conducted Voice of Prophecy and temperance meetings. In 1974 there were a few scattered members on the islands. C. C. Joseph carried on evangelistic work from 1975 to 1986. From 1985 to 1988 Dudley Poneah served as an attached field director. Simon Amrithraj served as literature evangelist from 1986 to 1988. In 1987 G. Devadass began serving as an evangelist and continues to the present.

Kindergarten-level schools were started in 1986. The Andaman and Nicobar Islands are an attached field of the Southern Asia Division. The 1989 year-end committee meetings voted to designate this territory as the Andaman and Nicobar Island Region and appointed J. H. Sibil as director. In 1992 there were 89 Seventh-day Adventist members and two companies in this region.

ANDAPA ADVENTIST HOSPITAL. A 55-bed institution started in 1976 by Brazilian and European missionaries. It is situated in the northern region of Madagascar. In 1982 Dr Michel Lachenal, a Belgian physician, served as director, assisted by Dr. Ratsioharana Mahatana. In 1992 the hospital had a staff of 27. The ratio of employees to occupied beds is one to one or less, and there is a high morale among the employees. The hospital is self-supporting. There are approximately 12,000 outpatients and 350 surgeries per year.

Medical Directors: Lutero Marques de Oliveira, 1976-1982; Michel Lachenal, 1982-1988; Ratsioharana Mahatana, 1988- .

ANDERSEN, A. (1883-1965). Physician and medical director. He was born in Ålborg, Denmark, and began an illustrious medical career as a physician at Skodsborg Sanitarium in 1915. He was asked to become the director of that institution in 1936. Through his efforts the physiotherapy course at the sanitarium was approved by the authorities, and much goodwill in medical circles was developed.

ANDERSEN, ALMA (c. 1869-1956). Pioneer Seventh-day Adventist health worker in Norway. The place of her birth is not known. She became an SDA about 1890 and in 1896 graduated from the nursing course at Battle Creek Sanitarium. In that same year she went to Norway, where she opened treatment rooms at Frederickshald. The next year, she joined the faculty of the mission school at Frederikshavn, Denmark *(see* Danish Junior College). In 1898 she and her sister were asked to establish a denominational medical institution in Norway, and opened Kurbadet treatment rooms in Oslo (listed in the *Yearbooks* as Oslo Health Home and also as Christiania Health Home; *see* Kurbadet). She died in Norway.

ANDERSON, ALBERT W. (1868-1949). Minister, musician, editor, author. He served with the Echo Publishing Company (Melbourne, Australia) and the Signs Publishing Company (Warburton), becoming editor of the Australian *Signs of the Times* and *Life and Health.* From 1916 he gave strong leadership, at various times at the union level, to the Education, Sabbath School, Home Missionary, and Religious Liberty departments. His published works include *The Battle for Freedom* and *Through Turmoil to Peace.*

ANDERSON, ALFONSO NILS (1887-1958). Missionary in Japan, administrator, teacher, and editor. He was reared in a Seventh-day Adventist home and prepared for the ministry at Healdsburg and Union colleges. In 1913, the year of his graduation, he married Maytie Olive Landis, and together they went to Japan, where he took charge of a mission station at Hiroshima (1915-1917), after which he assisted in the publication of *Toki no Shirushi* ("Signs of the Times"; later called *Jicho*) and *Shimei no Otozure* ("Tidings of the Message"). He served as secretary of the Japan Union's Home Missionary Department (1919-1920) and as field missionary secretary (publishing secretary) of the union (1919-1921). He was ordained in 1924. In addition to his other duties, from 1921 to 1927 he taught Bible and history at Japan Mission Training School. Between 1928 and 1934 he served as director of the Tohoku Mission, and from 1934 to 1936 he taught Bible at Japan Union College. In 1937 he entered evangelistic work among the Japanese in Davao, Philippines, and with the coming of World War II was interned. The privations of internment undermined his health, and after liberation in 1945, he retired (1946) from active service.

ANDERSON, BENJAMIN L. (1873-1962). Missionary in China. He was born in Denmark, came to America, and received his education at Battle Creek College, Union College, and the University of Colorado. After ministerial work in Wisconsin and his ordination in 1905, he served for more than 40 years in south China in evangelistic and administrative work. Among offices held were those of educational secretary for the China Division and president of the South China Union. During World War II he was interned in Amoy; his wife, Julia Peterson Anderson, was interned in Hong Kong.

ANDERSON, CLIFFORD RUSSELL (1905-1967). Evangelist, missionary, medical writer, "Your Radio Doctor." A native of Melbourne, Australia, Anderson began his service to the church in 1924 when he joined his brother Roy in an evangelistic effort in New Zealand. After working with the Sanitarium Health Food Company in Australia, he conducted evangelistic work in north Queensland. In 1930 he and his wife went to England, where he did evangelistic work in London. He was ordained to the gospel ministry and in 1937 enrolled at the College of Medical Evangelists in Loma Linda. After his graduation he began medical practice in Washington, D.C., and in 1944 he and his family answered a call to Jamaica, where Dr. Anderson was responsible for the development and construction of the Andrews Memorial Hospital at Kingston. He also served as medical secretary for the Inter-American Division. Later he located in Worthington, Ohio, at Harding Hospital, specializing in neurology and psychiatry. Following this he served on the staff of Washington Sanitarium and Hospital. During this time Dr. Anderson conducted the series of broadcasts known as *Your Radio Doctor.* Later he connected with the teaching staff of Loma Linda University.

He is the author of a correspondence course entitled "Radiant Health" and the book *Modern Ways to Health.*

ANDERSON, EMMA THOMPSON (1865-1909). Educator, Bible worker, missionary, author. Born in Wisconsin, she began teaching in 1882. In 1887 she became a Bible worker in Wisconsin. In 1892 she was invited to serve as Sabbath school secretary and president of the Sabbath School Association for Wisconsin. She married teacher-preacher J. N. Anderson in 1896, and four years later the family, including 4-year-old Stanley and Emma's sister, Ida, embarked on a mission to China. They stayed with Abram La Rue in Hong Kong while studying Chinese. Although surrounded by the danger of disease, they witnessed the firstfruits of their ministry when 11 were baptized. In 1903 the family moved to Canton and opened a training school. Emma became well acquainted with Chinese culture as she worked with the women and children and served as mission bookkeeper. The family was forced to return to the United States when Emma became ill in 1909. Still burdened for the Chinese, she wrote *A'Chu and Other Stories.*

ANDERSON, GODFREY T. (1909-1986). Physician, administrator. Born in Chicago, as a young man he taught history at Kingsway College for two years. In 1939 he accepted the chair of the History Department at Atlantic Union College and was later appointed academic dean. He served as president of La Sierra College for eight years and as president of the College of Medical Evangelists (now Loma Linda University).

ANDERSON, JACOB NELSON (1867-1958). Danish-born educator, the first commissioned Seventh-day Adventist missionary in China. He obtained a B.S. degree from a Seventh Day Baptist college, entered the SDA ministry in Wisconsin, and was ordained in 1899. In 1901 he received a B.D. degree from the University of Chicago and volunteered for service in China. Forced to return to America because of illness (1909), he taught Bible at the Washington Foreign Mission Seminary (now Columbia Union College) from 1910 to 1915, and classes in missions and Greek from 1924 to 1928. He taught classes in missions and biblical languages (1915-1924) and in religion and biblical languages (1934-1943) at Union College, and after 1943 retired as professor emeritus.

ANDERSON SCHOOL. A multiracial and coeducational boarding school offering full primary and four years of secondary work, situated 10 miles (16 kilometers) from Gweru, Zimbabwe, and operated by the Zambesi Union. By 1993 the enrollment had reached 111 students in the secondary school and 93 in the primary school. There was a staff of 11 teachers in the secondary school and four in the primary.

The school was opened by J. R. Burns in 1950 on a farm called Christmas Gift, near the conference headquarters in Gweru. It was then called Rhobecon Preparatory School, Rhobecon being a contraction of Rhodesia-Bechuanaland Conference, the name of the conference at that time. In 1952 the school was moved to its present 20-acre (eight-hectare) site at Thorngrove Farm on the Umvuma Road, which during World War II had been an airfield for the Royal Rhodesia Air Force.

Forty acres (16 hectares) have been added to the property, giving it a total of 60 acres (24 hectares). This has made it possible to run a dairy farm. Camp meeting facilities that were used by the former Zambesi Conference are to be used by the English-speaking churches in the Zambesi Union.

In 1960 the school was renamed Anderson Memorial School in commemoration of W. H. Anderson, a pioneer missionary. In 1963 the first class beyond the first eight years of schoolwork was added, and in 1972 the fourth year of high school was offered. In 1993, through the help of ADRA, a secretarial skills training center was established.

The plant includes a church building, boys' and girls' dormitories, administrative offices, two school buildings, a dining room and kitchen unit, auditorium, library, laboratory, woodwork shop, and dwellings for the staff. A swimming pool is also provided.

Principals: J. R. Burns, 1950-1952; Mrs. G.A.C. Ellingworth, 1952-1955; P. B. Fairchild, 1955-1959; T. A. ter Horst, 1960-1964; R. Fuss, 1965; R. A. Tarr, 1966-1968; D. H. Thomas, 1969-1970; R. Strasdowsky, 1971-1972; A. Tredoux, 1973-1976; K. B. Cronje, 1976-1981; J. E. Marter, 1982-1985; R. G. Pearson, 1986-1988; P. J. Birkenstock, 1989-1993; F. R. Oberholster, 1993- .

ANDERSON, WILLIAM HARRISON (1870-1950). Pioneer missionary to Africa, 1895-1944. He was born in Mexico, Indiana. Harry Anderson, as he was affectionately known to his friends, graduated in 1895 from

Battle Creek College, where he was converted. At the school he took a prominent part in the formation of the first student foreign mission band, and from early youth felt a strong pull toward the mission field.

In 1895, several months before his graduation (in absentia), he joined G. B. Tripp and Dr. A. S. Carmichael to form the party of missionaries who operated the first permanent Seventh-day Adventist mission for the people of Africa. (For two earlier short-lived attempts, *see* Ghana; James, George.) Before leaving the homeland, Anderson was married to Nora Haysmer. Arriving in South Africa, the party proceeded by train to Mafeking, and then spent six weeks traveling by ox wagon (the railroad had not yet been built) to the site of the Solusi Mission, near Bulawayo, Southern Rhodesia.

The Andersons, with the other workers at Solusi, had trying experiences. During the Matabele rebellion the following year, they spent several months in Bulawayo. In 1898 they watched several of their group die of malaria and others leave the country. A second larger party was likewise stricken, and in 1901 the Andersons were the only workers left at Solusi.

In 1919 the Andersons began pioneer work among the Bechuanas, through whose country he had passed nearly 25 years before en route to Solusi. In 1922 he opened work in Angola, and during the next eight years he established several mission stations.

His last 15 years in Africa were spent as a member of the African Division (and later of the Southern African Division) staff, locating new mission stations, visiting camp meetings, holding institutes, and giving advice to new missionary recruits.

In 1944 Anderson took part in the Golden Jubilee celebrations at Solusi Mission, driving an ox wagon onto the very ground on which he had first begun mission work nearly 50 years before. The following year he returned to the United States, having served for 50 years in Africa. Anderson's book, *On the Trail of Livingstone* (1919), did much to stimulate interest in African missions.

ANDES ADVENTIST ACADEMY (Instituto Adventista de Los Andes). In 1936 in La Paz, government seat of the republic of Bolivia, the Chijini Adventist School was opened with 40 students. In 1939 it moved from Los Andes Street and became known as the Fernando Stahl School.

In 1966, by resolution of the Education Ministry, it was made an academy, and in 1976 the name was changed a second time to Los Andes Adventist Academy. In 1986 it became simply Andes Adventist Academy.

Even though it was located in a highly populated area, it had acquired a good reputation. But land was purchased in a more secure area that provided a better climate for the students. In 1991 a five-story building was constructed. In 1993, 405 students were enrolled and 22 teachers served the school.

Principals: Felipe Alcón, 1966-1967; Miguel Ramos, 1968-1970; Elías Ticona, 1971-1972; Samuel Coronal, 1973-1975; Wilfredo Condemayta, 1976-1982; Adalberto Ticona, 1983; Alcides Limachi, 1984-1985; Adalberto Ticona, 1985-1992; Arturo Chambilla, 1992-1993; Elías Ticona, 1993- .

ANDORRA. An autonomous principality (area, 185 square miles [480 square kilometers]; population [1994], 64,000), situated between France and Spain. The people are of Catalan stock and language, and are Roman Catholics. Andorra is noted for its powerful privately owned radiobroadcasting station. Several literature evangelists have worked in Andorra, but so far there is no organized work.

Its territory is assigned to the Spanish Union, which is a part of the Euro-Africa Division.

ANDRÉ, HATTIE (1865-1952). Missionary, teacher, dean of women. She entered Battle Creek College (1884), but left soon to become a Bible instructor in Ohio. Returning to the college five years later, she was graduated in 1892 and spent the following summer studying hydrotherapy and cooking. In company with seven other Seventh-day Adventist missionaries she sailed from San Francisco to Pitcairn Island (1893) on the second voyage of the ship *Pitcairn*. She remained on the island while the other missionaries went to various parts of the South Pacific. There she organized and conducted a school, remaining until June 1896, when she returned to America.

For one year Miss André worked as a Bible instructor in Kentucky, and then was appointed to the faculty of Oakwood College. In 1899 Ellen G. White invited her to join the staff of the Australasian Missionary College (now Avondale College), at Cooranbong, Australia. From 1900 to 1908 she gave devoted service to that institution and strongly influenced the growth of SDA education in Australia.

Miss André then spent 11 years as dean of

women and taught certain courses at Pacific Union College. In 1920 she resigned to care for her aged mother, but at the same time she taught Bible in the School of Nursing at Hinsdale Sanitarium and was a member of the faculty of Hinsdale Academy. She retired from institutional work in 1929 but remained active in church work. Altogether she gave more than 60 years of dedicated service to the church.

ANDREASEN, MILIAN LAURITZ (1876-1962). Danish-born administrator, educator, author; A.B., University of Nebraska (1920); M.A., University of Nebraska (1922). Following his ordination in 1902 he held varied administrative positions: president of the Greater New York Conference (1909-1910), president of Hutchinson Theological Seminary (1910-1918), dean of Union College (1918-1922), dean of Washington Missionary (now Columbia Union) College (1922-1924), president of the Minnesota Conference (1924-1931), president of Union College (1931-1938), and field secretary of the General Conference (1941-1950). From 1938 to 1949 he taught at the SDA Theological Seminary in Washington, D.C.

Andreasen wrote numerous articles and at least 13 books, including *The Sanctuary Service, The Epistle to the Hebrews, A Faith to Live By, What Can a Man Believe?* and *Saints and Sinners.* He gave special study to the doctrine of the sanctuary and was considered an authority in that field.

ANDREWS ACADEMY. *See* Andrews University, I, 7; V.

ANDREWS HIGH SCHOOL. A coeducational nonresident high school situated at 65 Real Street, San Juan, Trinidad, West Indies. The school was opened in September 1964 under Mrs. Veronica Grimshaw as principal at its first location in the church welfare center, on Mission Road, San Juan. It was at first operated by the San Juan church but came under conference operation in 1969.

It is under the direction of a board of management, which meets annually to establish policies, and an executive board, which meets monthly.

In the 1992-1993 school year there was a staff of 12 and an enrollment of 200. The school offers five years in academic preparation for the Caribbean Examination Council and the General Certificate of Education examinations at ordinary level. In 1992 it was accredited for three years by the Inter-American Division commission on accreditation and the General Conference Board of Regents.

Principals: Veronica Grimshaw, 1964-1969; John Thompson, 1969-1970; Veronica Grimshaw, 1970; Melvin Gadsby, 1970-1973; Prettilal Sawh, 1973-1975; Fulmer Walker, 1975-1976; Hugh Mitchell, 1976-1977; Ludrick St. Bryce, 1977-1978; Hillman St. Bryce, 1978-1979; Harrihar Sonoo, 1979-1983; Paul Phillip, 1983- .

ANDREWS, JOHN NEVINS (1829-1883). First Seventh-day Adventist missionary sent to countries outside North America. He was born in Poland, Maine, and died at Basel, Switzerland, at the age of 54. In 1856 he married Angeline S. Stevens; their children were Charles (b. 1857), Mary (b. 1861), and two who died in infancy. Few details are available on his childhood and youth. At 13 he "found the Saviour." He enjoyed "severe study" much more than physical activity; in later years he could read the Bible in seven languages and claimed the ability to reproduce the New Testament from memory. At the age of 17 he began to observe the seventh-day Sabbath. He began his work as a minister at 21, in 1850, and was ordained in 1853.

During those three years he conducted evangelistic meetings in 20 different localities throughout Maine, New Hampshire, Vermont, New York, Ohio, Michigan, and eastern Canada, and published 35 articles, totaling some 170,000 words. As a result of this intense program of writing and public ministry, in five years he was "utterly prostrated"; his voice failed, and his eyesight was injured. To recover his health, he went to Waukon, Iowa, in 1855 and worked on his parents' farm. Returning to ministerial work in 1859, Andrews conducted public meetings for several years in Michigan, Massachusetts, Minnesota, and New York.

In 1864 he became a member of the New York Conference committee and the next year a member of the General Conference Executive Committee. In 1867 he became the third president of the General Conference, a position he held for two years. He was an editor of the *Review and Herald* from May 1869 to March 1870. On Sept. 15, 1874, in company with his children, Charles and Mary (his wife had died Mar. 18, 1872), he sailed from Boston for Liverpool, England, en route to Switzerland. His first work in Switzerland was to visit and organize the converts already there and to do personal work with interested persons. Then he wrote tracts and laid plans for the publication of a paper. In April 1876 the General Conference voted $10,000 for a printing house in Europe. In July 1876 Andrews issued the first number of *Les Signes des Temps,* a monthly covering a wide range of subject material, such as world events, prophecy, Bible doctrines, and health and temperance, and containing articles from American newspapers and magazines. The absorption of his time in the publication of this paper caused the General Conference leaders to express apprehension that he was neglecting personal work and public ministry, to which Andrews replied that he never planned to shut himself up in a printing office and that in the future he would aim for a better balance in his program, but that at heart he was a writer, and since his health was not very good, he was doing his best under the circumstances. He died in Basel nine years after he first went to Europe.

As a theologian Andrews made significant contributions to the development of various doctrines of the Seventh-day Adventist denomination. For example, for some time after Sabbatarian Adventists had begun to observe the biblical Sabbath, the seventh day, there was difference of opinion among them as to when they should begin the Sabbath. Joseph Bates in 1851 held that the Sabbath should begin at 6:00 Friday evening. Others held that the Sabbath should be observed from sunset to sunset, as was the custom of the Seventh Day Baptists. In 1855 James White requested Andrews to give the subject a thorough investigation. Andrews published his findings in an article in which he showed on biblical evidence that the Sabbath begins at sunset Friday evening. His conclusions became the accepted position of the church.

Andrews' extensive writings on the subject of the seventh-day Sabbath in history were published in October 1861 in a book of 340 pages entitled *History of the Sabbath and the First Day of the Week.* Later editions of this work were issued in 1873 and 1887, and in 1912 the book, revised and enlarged (864 pages) by L. R. Conradi, was republished under the names of Andrews and Conradi. Andrews was the first among the church leaders to publish an article that applied the two-horned beast of Revelation 13 to the United States of America. He also led in a study of what the Scriptures taught concerning the support of the ministry, as a result of which the plan of Systematic Benevolence was adopted. In 1878 Andrews served on the committee that recommended the tithing system.

Andrews also was active helping in the development of church organization. Early pioneer Adventists were opposed to organization, but they recognized that without it the church could not legally hold property. Andrews proposed the formation of an association that he claimed would "not be a church incorporated by law." "Not a legal church organization, but a legal business association" was his recommendation. Andrews was chair of a committee of three to suggest a plan of organization for the denominational publishing house (1860), also chair of a committee to draft a constitution and bylaws for the central organization of the church (1863). During the Civil War, when the Conscription Act went into effect, Andrews represented the church in Washington, D.C., to explain why SDAs believe that participation in combat is contrary to Christian principles, with the result that SDA draftees could apply for noncombatant service (*see* Noncombatancy).

ANDREWS MEMORIAL HOSPITAL. A 45-bed general acute hospital located in Kingston, Jamaica, owned and operated by the West Indies Union, with Medical, Surgical, Obstetrical, and Physiotherapy departments and a dental clinic, a medical laboratory, and an X-ray laboratory. The hospital's staff consists of two physicians, seven graduate nurses, two other registered nurses, four practical nurses, nine enrolled nurses, and 60 other employees.

In 1944 Sulgrave Manor, a property with a large dwelling house, on Hope Road in an attractive suburb of the city of Kingston, was purchased as the site for a hospital. The Loma Linda medical college contributed $12,500 to this new hospital. Toward the end of 1944 a physician, C. R. Anderson, arrived with a nurse, Ruth M. Munroe, her parents, C. R. Munroe and his wife, and R. E. Gibson and his wife, to build and organize what was to be the first Seventh-day Adventist hospital in the Inter-American Division. In 1945 a clinic building with five wards, housing 22 beds, was built on James Street in the heart of the city.

In January 1945, while Sulgrave Manor was being remodeled, Ruth Munroe began a prenursing class at West Indian Training College (now West Indies College). In May 1945 the Andrews Memorial School of Nursing was officially opened with seven students.

In December 1946 the cornerstone for a

two-story concrete building of 21 rooms was laid at the Hope Road property. In 1953 the clinic was moved from James Street to Hope Road, and the hospital-clinic has operated as one unit since. In the first 18 years of operation the institution was patronized by 165,000 patients. Six nurses were graduated in 1948 and 22 in the next three years. However, in 1952 the school was closed because the hospital did not have the required minimum number of beds according to the new regulations for nursing schools. For some time annually a class of eight girls was trained as practical nurses to assist graduate nurses at the hospital, but this has been discontinued.

In 1971 Dr. Cuthbert Arthur, who was then the medical director of the hospital, reopened the School of Nursing. It is currently affiliated with the West Indies College in Mandeville. In June 1974 six nursing students graduated with their Bachelor of Science degree. They were the first to receive a degree from the School of Nursing.

Medical Directors: C. R. Anderson, 1945-1949; A.W.N. Druitt, 1949-1950; E. J. Horsley, 1950-1951; A. R. Parchment (acting), 1951-1952; Martin R. Hoehn, 1952-1956.

Administrators: E. H. Heisler, 1956-1964; B. G. Arellano, 1965-1966; R. L. Hendrickson, 1966-1969; A. B. Marshalleck, 1969-1974; M. C. Alana, 1975-1977; A. B. Marshalleck, 1977-1986; P. A. Jorgensen, 1986-1987; H. A. Newman (acting), 1988-1990; J. G. Bennett, 1990-1991; G. A. James, 1991-1994; H. A. Newman (acting), 1994- .

ANDREWS MEMORIAL SCHOOL OF NURSING. *See* Andrews Memorial Hospital.

ANDREWS SOCIETY FOR RELIGIOUS STUDIES. *See* Adventist Society for Religious Studies.

ANDREWS UNIVERSITY. An institution operated jointly by the General Conference and the Lake Union Conference, the first university to be organized by the Seventh-day Adventist Church. It is situated on a 1,600-acre (650-hectare) campus near Berrien Springs, Michigan, on the St. Joseph River, 15 miles (24 kilometers) east of Lake Michigan.

The university comprises seven schools: the College of Arts and Sciences, the College of Technology, the School of Business, the School of Education, the School of Graduate Studies, the SDA Theological Seminary, and the University School.

The Theological Seminary and the School of Graduate Studies, which were formerly operated in Washington, D.C., under the name of Potomac University, were moved to Berrien Springs in 1959-1960 by action of the 1958 General Conference Autumn Council. At first it was planned that the three schools would be affiliated under one president but would otherwise remain distinct institutions. When this plan was found to be impracticable under the corporation procedures of the state of Michigan, it became necessary to incorporate as a single institution. This action was voted Apr. 7, 1960, and the name Andrews University (honoring John Nevins Andrews, the first missionary to extend SDA work outside North America) was chosen. Andrews University originally had a single board of trustees but two executive committees, one of which conducted the between-session affairs of the undergraduate school and the other those of the two graduate branches. On advice of the North Central Association of Colleges and Schools, the regional accrediting body, it was voted, on June 20, 1962, to replace the two executive committees with a single executive committee responsible for all three branches.

The net capital worth of the university in 1993 was more than $38 million.

The university operates several industries, including a supermarket, a farm and dairy, and a greenhouse, where students may learn useful skills while earning money to defray educational expenses. There are residence halls for unmarried men and women and furnished apartments for married students and unmarried graduate students.

All university programs are accredited by the Board of Regents of the General Conference of Seventh-day Adventists. The university (as Emmanuel Missionary College) has been on the accredited list of the North Central Association of Colleges and Schools (NCA) since 1922, at which time it was accredited at the junior college level. Accreditation at the bachelor's degree level was granted by the NCA in 1939, for master's level programs in 1968, and at the doctoral level in 1979. The university has made concerted efforts to have its professional programs accredited by appropriate bodies. This has resulted in the following accreditations: teacher training and school services programs by the National Council for the Accreditation of Teacher Education, Theological Seminary programs by the Association of Theological Schools in the

United States and Canada, the Chemistry Department by the American Chemical Society, the coordinated program in dietetics by the American Dietetics Society, the program in clinical laboratory sciences by the Committee on Allied Health Education and Accreditation in cooperation with the National Accrediting Agency for Clinical Laboratory Sciences, the speech-language pathology and auditory programs by the American Speech-Language-Hearing Association, the physical therapy program by the Commission of Accreditation in Physical Therapy Education of the American Physical Therapy Association, the graduate and undergraduate programs in nursing by the National League of Nursing and the Michigan Board of Nursing, the architecture programs by the National Architectural Accrediting Board, the social work program by the Council on Social Work Education, the graduate and undergraduate programs in music by the National Association of the Schools of Music, and the School of Education's counseling programs by the Counsel for Accreditation of Counseling and Related Educational Programs.

Andrews University holds membership in the American Association of Colleges for Teacher Education; the American Association of Collegiate Registrars and Admissions Officers; the American Schools of Oriental Research; the American Theological Library Association; the American Assembly of Collegiate Schools of Business; the Association of Collegiate Schools of Architecture; the Council of Graduate Schools in the United States; the Michigan Academy of Science, Arts, and Letters; the National Association of Foreign Students Affairs; the National Collegiate Honors Council; and the Upper Midwest Honors Council. The university has a local chapter of the interdisciplinary National Honor Society, Phi Beta Kappa, as well as chapters of 15 honor societies in specific subject areas.

I. Component Schools. 1. *College of Arts and Sciences.* The original undergraduate school, which must be considered as the successor to Battle Creek College (founded 1874), is the oldest college in the denomination. As of 1993 it offers Bachelor of Arts (B.A.) degrees in 22 areas, Bachelor of Science (B.S.) degrees in 32 areas, and minors in 33 areas, with courses adaptable to a wide variety of educational goals. The college also offers professional bachelor degrees in art education, dietetics, fine arts, medical technology, music, radiologic technology, and social work. Associate of Science (A.S.) degrees are available in child development and medical laboratory technology. The college also offers preprofessional programs in 14 areas. On the graduate level the college offers Master of Arts (M.A.) degrees in English, history, home economics, interdisciplinary studies, and music; the Master of Music degree; Master of Science (M.S.) degrees in biology, human nutrition, interdisciplinary studies, and nursing; and the professional M.S. degrees in medical technology and physical therapy.

2. *College of Technology.* The College of Technology was established in 1974 to consolidate the offerings in the technical and job-oriented areas. The college offers (1993) the five-year professional Bachelor of Architecture degree, the B.S. degree in engineering in five areas, the B.S. in industrial technology in six areas, the Bachelor of Technology in five areas, and the B.S. in interiors. The two-year Associate of Engineering Technology degree is available in three areas and the Associate of Technology in 11 areas. Nondegree certificates in aircraft airframe, flight, and powerplant are also offered.

3. *School of Business.* The School of Business, which evolved from the College of Arts and Sciences' Department of Business Administration, was established in 1980. In 1993 the school offered the following degrees: professional Master of Business Administration with emphasis in management, accounting, or computer information science; M.S. in administration or computer science (two areas); Bachelor of Business Administration; B.S. in computer information systems or computer sciences; B.A. in economics; and A.S. in three areas. A minor in business administration and a second major in business are offered for students in the Colleges of Arts and Sciences and Technology.

4. *School of Education.* The School of Education traces its origins to the Normal Department, which enrolled a large share of students in Battle Creek College. Graduate programs in education were an original part of the offerings of Potomac University. These were continued and expanded when it merged to form Andrews University. Undergraduate and graduate programs were combined into the School of Education in 1983. In 1993 the school offered the following degrees: B.S. in elementary education (seven areas); B.A. with elementary certification; and either the B.S. or

B.A. with secondary certification (26 areas). The school's graduate programs lead to the M.A., the M.A. degree in teaching, the Educational Specialist, and the Ed.D. and Ph.D. degrees.

5. *School of Graduate Studies.* The School of Graduate Studies originally was part of Potomac University and became operative at Berrien Springs when Andrews University was formed. Until 1987 it granted all the university's degrees except those offered in the SDA Theological Seminary. Since 1987 the various graduate degrees were offered by the school or college that housed the department of instruction. The School of Graduate Studies then became a coordinating and quality control entity that gave particular attention to admission and graduation requirements. It is governed by a graduate council composed of representatives from the schools and colleges that have graduate programs and members of the university administration.

6. *SDA Theological Seminary.* The Theological Seminary's primary purpose is to prepare candidates for effective leadership in the church's gospel ministry in the world. This ministry is grounded in the biblical, historical, and theological witness of the church, and is made proficient and effective by careful development of the ministering arts (preaching, teaching, pastoral care, and leadership).

The Theological Seminary offers the Master of Divinity degree, the M.A. degree in pastoral ministry, M.A. degree in religion (nine areas), the Master of Theology degree (six areas), the Doctor of Ministry degree (two areas), the Doctor of Philosophy degree in religion (five areas), and the Doctor of Theology degree (two areas). A major part of the course work for the M.A. degree in pastoral ministry is offered in intensives, both on and off campus. The M.A. degree in religion is offered both on campus and at selected affiliation and extension centers.

The Theological Seminary has offered a number of short-term extension schools in the various world divisions for those who cannot take advantage of Theological Seminary training elsewhere.

7. *The University School.* The University School, a coeducational day school operated by the university, is the successor to the original secondary departments of Battle Creek College and Emmanuel Missionary College, and later the separate elementary and secondary schools operated by the university. The University School consists of the Ruth Murdoch Elementary School (preschool through grade 8) and Andrews Academy (grades 9 through 12). The University School is governed by the University board of trustees and administered by the director, who is responsible to the university president and who is assisted by the principals of each of the school's divisions, and by assistants in admissions and records, instructional media, and student personnel services. Andrews Academy grants college preparatory and general curriculum diplomas and is accredited by the General Conference Board of Regents and the University of Michigan Bureau of School Services.

II. History of the College of Arts and Sciences. 1. *Origin as Battle Creek College.* This college, founded in 1874, evolved from a "select" private school established in 1868 by G. H. Bell and conducted successively in the building that first housed the Review and Herald printshop, in the church building, and in a new Review and Herald building. The school was adopted as a General Conference project in May 1872. By 1873 enrollment was more than 100, and Sidney Brownsberger, a graduate of the University of Michigan, was the new principal, Bell staying on as a teacher.

In March 1873 the General Conference, then in session, encouraged by James and Ellen White, voted to form an Educational Society (legally incorporated in March 1874) and to raise money for a college building. Vigorous efforts by G. I. Butler, S. N. Haskell, and others raised $54,000 in cash or pledges by the end of the year.

The society, acting against the advice of the Whites, who favored a 40-acre (16-hectare) former fairgrounds outside Battle Creek, purchased a 12-acre (five-hectare) estate in the city near the Western Health Reform Institute. In 1874 a three-story building was erected, which was dedicated Jan. 4, 1875. Battle Creek College opened, meanwhile, on Aug. 24, 1874, with 100 students.

Despite Ellen White's early counsels favoring a large measure of manual and religious education, the curriculum in the early years to a considerable degree followed the conventional college pattern of the day. In 1877-1878, for example, there were three students taking the classical course (Latin, Greek, mathematics, "natural science," rhetoric, elocution, geology); 16 the three-year "English course" (mathematics, science, a year of English, and two of a foreign language—Latin, Greek,

French, or German); 235 the "normal" (teacher training) course, 111 the "special course" for those preparing for missionary work (arithmetic, grammar, history, two terms of biblical lectures, and one year of biblical Greek); 48 the school of hygiene (conducted that year by physicians from the sanitarium, but apparently discontinued the next year). Notable, from the later SDA point of view, is the presence of a classical course. Even more notable is the absence of regular Bible courses in the curriculum. The "Biblical Department" was a series of daily lectures by Uriah Smith during two of the three terms of the school year; this was required of none but those in the "special course"; others could elect it. In 1877-1878 only 75 took the Bible lectures. That year the college-level enrollment was 413; the total, including elementary grades, 478 Because there were no church schools in which they could work, most of the graduates of the Teacher Training Department, the largest, entered nondenominational service. The ministerial training was weak. When the "special course" was raised to a three-year "biblical course" with one, then two, years of biblical languages, the enrollment dropped; it was 42 in 1879-1880.

The lack of student residence halls occasioned various administrative problems; most students boarded in private homes, some banded together into clubs for group feeding, and many boarded themselves.

James White, president of the Educational Society, was nominal president of the college until 1880, when on his recommendation the college presidency went to Brownsberger, the principal. By 1880 the enrollment had climbed to 490. Leading teachers during those years included G. H. Bell, Uriah Smith, and Dr. John Harvey Kellogg.

In 1881, the year of James White's death, Brownsberger was succeeded by Alexander McLearn, a recent convert who knew little of SDA educational ideals. The 1881-1882 term, marred by unrest and dissension in faculty ranks, ended with the dismissal of McLearn and the temporary closing of the college through the 1882-1883 term.

After reopening in 1883 under Wolcott H. Littlejohn, the college attempted to follow more closely the counsels of Ellen White. Curricula were revised to emphasize short courses for denominational workers. A new three-story boarding hall, occupied first in 1883, partially solved the student residence problem; a second dormitory, including improved dining quarters, was built in 1886. Under William W. Prescott, who succeeded Littlejohn in 1885, the school-home system flourished, the president and his wife setting a pattern of etiquette by dining regularly with the students. Attempts to establish manual training and college industries, for which space was provided in a building constructed in 1885, foundered and were abandoned by 1889. For several years, beginning in 1888, ministerial institutes *(see* General Conference Bible Schools) during the winter months brought 150 to 300 ministers and other church workers to the college.

The early 1890s were years of deepening spiritual emphasis at the college. By 1894-1895 all students were required to take at least one year of Bible, and all classes were given a more spiritual tone. The classical course, already broadened to include history, English literature, and other subjects, gradually introduced biblical Greek and ecclesiastical Latin and diminished the classical literature. Throughout the decade revivalism marked college activities. A study made in 1897 showed that 38 percent of all ordained ministers in the denomination had received some training at Battle Creek College. The highest enrollment to be recorded at Battle Creek was reached in 1893-1894 (768, including 337 in the preparatory departments).

In 1894 the presidency passed to George W. Caviness, whose educational ideas were similar to Prescott's. In 1897 a movement for drastic curricular changes replaced Caviness with Edward A. Sutherland. Led by Alonzo T. Jones, Dr. John Harvey Kellogg, and Percy T. Magan, the reformers supporting Sutherland were resolved to abolish classical studies (by 1898 this was accomplished, and only New Testament Greek, New Testament [Vulgate] Latin, and medical Latin were taught), to expunge all traces of apparently worldly educational thought, to base all studies closely on the Bible, to establish college industries, and to prepare denominational workers, especially church school teachers, more speedily. An 80-acre (32-hectare) farm was purchased, various manual enterprises were begun, the playground was plowed and set to potatoes, and in several classes standard textbooks were largely supplanted by the Bible and denominational religious volumes. The movement was crowned when in 1898-1899 the college, operating under a new charter, discontinued the granting of academic degrees. It likewise abolished enrollment statistics, but estimates indicate that by 1900-

1901 enrollment had declined noticeably.

During this period the training of teachers to staff the rapidly expanding denominational church school system became a major concern at the college. By 1899 there were 150 church schools in the United States, with two thirds of their teachers having studied at Battle Creek.

The cramped and urban campus was not well suited to the educational concepts of Sutherland, who desired a spacious rural setting like that of the recently founded Avondale College in Australia. Following the counsel of Ellen White, who had wanted a rural site from the first, the 1901 General Conference session approved the decision of the Educational Society to move the college. The property was sold to the Battle Creek Sanitarium. A "Battle Creek College" continued to operate, beginning in 1903, controlled by Dr. Kellogg's board, but it had no connection with the original institution except the use of the same buildings.

2. *Emmanuel Missionary College.* After a search throughout southwestern Michigan a site was chosen near Berrien Springs, an area Sutherland had favored since 1899. Two tracts, the Richardson and Garland farms, totaling 272 acres (110 hectares), were purchased for about $18,000. The site extended along the banks of the St. Joseph River, near a passenger boat landing. The relocated institution was named Emmanuel Missionary College.

During the summer of 1901 a denomination-wide summer school for about 150 to 200 active and prospective church school teachers was held under trying conditions in tents beside the river near the village. During the regular 1901-1902 term, while the new campus was being developed, the school occupied the former county courthouse, the sheriff's home and jail, an office building, and a summer hotel overlooking the river. Enrollment reached 100. The plan was that the college would not be allowed to exceed 250; beyond that figure a new college would be started.

During 1902 and 1903, with student labor, a group of four modest frame buildings was erected. Sutherland deliberately kept buildings dispersed and plain, to discourage the growth of pride and institutional spirit. One building was to be kept warm enough for student study; others were to be left with a minimum of heat or light, to simulate conditions in the mission fields.

Fund-raising for the new school was a major problem. Though the change was not heralded, financial responsibility for the college was passing from the General Conference into the hands of the newly established Lake Union Conference. P. T. Magan and President Sutherland tirelessly solicited donations from the laity of the area. Ellen White, the General Conference, and the Review and Herald had dedicated all proceeds from her book *Christ's Object Lessons* (1900) to the support of denominational schools, and the college became a major beneficiary. Classes were suspended on four extended occasions as teams of teachers and students spread out, selling the book in communities throughout the union. Thus Emmanuel Missionary College became known as "the college in the country built by a book."

To encourage self-government and a salutary group spirit, faculty and students assembled weekly for frank discussion of college problems of all kinds. Spirituality and evangelical fervor pervaded the campus. A considerable proportion of the academic instruction was conducted in the evenings, since many students worked all day. A novel and controversial feature of Sutherland's program was limiting the student to one major academic subject each of the three terms.

The Sutherland regime ended in the spring of 1904, in the wake of the broad-reaching controversies between General Conference leaders and Dr. Kellogg. Sutherland went on in 1906 to pioneer SDA higher education in the South, at Madison College, Tennessee *(see* Madison Institutions). His successor, Nelson W. Kauble, eliminated the "one-study plan," but continued the emphasis upon practical education, with special attention to developing the farm.

In 1910, under the presidency of Otto J. Graf, the college secured a new charter permitting the granting of academic degrees. The new charter also recognized the college as a Lake Union Conference institution, which in fact it had been since 1908. Through sound financial policies, a $60,000 debt of 1908 was cleared by 1916. Enrollment moved from 138 (including preparatory students) in 1908-1909 to 228 in 1913-1914 and 349 in 1917-1918. By 1924 the enrollment exceeded 500.

During these years of growth zeal for building an outstanding institution and for spreading the gospel through missions continued high. A 30-day student campaign in 1919 raised $6,000 to erect a music building. Student solicitation also contributed greatly to raising funds for the chapel building and a pipe organ, which were dedicated in 1928. During the virulent influenza epidemic of 1918 the college was closed for more than a month, and four students died. During the influenza epidemic of 1919-1920, 160 students went out to nurse victims in the surrounding area, and the Berrien Springs Chamber of Commerce responded in 1923 by sponsoring a fund-raising campaign on behalf of the college. Practical education continued to flourish alongside the strengthening academic program. The farm was expanded and an agricultural curriculum was added; the College Wood Products was established. A pioneering radio station, WEMC, was in operation from 1923 to 1931; it was heard as far away as southern California, and its broadcasts included evangelistic programs. Efforts to ensure standards of collegiate excellence in both teaching staff and student performance were intensified in the late 1920s. For the first time in SDA education, funds were specifically set aside to finance graduate education of faculty members.

Its pioneering years behind it, the college, from 1930, progressively improved its physical plant and strengthened its academic offerings. Despite a period of declining enrollments and considerable financial strain, and with the help of a reserve of nearly $30,000 built up during G. F. Wolfkill's administration, the school survived the Depression. During those same years it was struggling to attain accreditation for its full college program. The North Central Association of Colleges and Schools had accredited the first two college years in 1922, but further accreditation necessitated drastic improvements. For example, as recently as 1935 every building on the campus was of wood, and each was rated as substandard. Policies for supporting graduate education of college teachers and encouraging their attendance at professional meetings had to be greatly liberalized.

Under a long-range overall plan for campus improvement, a succession of brick or stone buildings was begun. The first was occupied in 1937, as students and faculty in only four hours moved 20,000 volumes into the newly erected James White Library (now superseded by the newer university library building of the same name, dedicated in 1962).

College accreditation was attained in 1939. Meanwhile, in 1934, on discontinuation of its college-level work, Broadview College had transferred its college records to Berrien Springs. While World War II restricted the active building program, the board continued through the war years to add to the building fund and to stockpile bricks so that construction could be readily resumed. Surprisingly, the college enrollment during the war dropped by only 20 (503 full-time college students in 1941-1942, 483 in the low-enrollment year of 1943-1944), although nearly one fifth of the male enrollment was inducted into the armed forces during the year 1942-1943. By 1944-1945 a few discharged veterans were returning to classes, presaging the flood of enrollees soon to appear.

The enrollment of 29 veterans in the fall of 1945, when applicants were turned away for lack of housing facilities, swelled to 341 one year later. The 1944-1945 total enrollment (502) was doubled by 1947-1948 (1,093), and a peak of 1,119 was reached in 1949-1950. Single men and those with families were housed in various residential annexes, including quonset-type dwellings for 72 men, 16 four-room duplex houses and 17 trailer houses secured by the college, and 65 privately owned trailer houses. Throughout the emergency an only slightly augmented faculty assumed unusually heavy teaching loads. During these years and since, the new construction program has proceeded steadily, as building after building of modern permanent construction has been erected.

With the arrival of the first contingent of Theological Seminary and Graduate School students in 1959-1960, and through most of the 1960-1961 term while Seminary Hall was being completed, the already-crowded college buildings provided classroom and office space for the entire new university. From 1959 to 1962 the college was administered largely by the vice president for undergraduate affairs, Fabian A. Meier. From 1962 there was a greater centralization of administration under the university president.

III. History of the Seventh-day Adventist Theological Seminary. In the Autumn Council of 1932 the General Conference Committee voted to establish a school of theology, but the action proved on further study to be premature. The Autumn Council of 1933, expressing principal concern for the training of Bible teachers for colleges, academies, and schools of nursing, voted a substitute proposal, that "successive summer schools of 12 weeks' duration be operated at designated colleges under the auspices of the General Conference, the first session to be opened June 6, 1934, at Pacific Union College." In addition to the special lecturers provided by the General Conference, a faculty equivalent to four full-time instructors, two to be from elsewhere than the host college, were to be employed.

The first of these summer schools—named the Advanced Bible School—was held as planned at Pacific Union College, with a staff of 13, an enrollment of 71, and Milton E. Kern as dean. Twenty courses were offered.

The Autumn Council of 1934 recommended that course offerings be expanded to include the fields of history and education, to benefit history teachers and school principals. Editors and ministers were also invited to enroll, and plans now included a master's degree. The 1935 session was again held at Pacific Union College, with its faculty increased by two. For the 10-week session, at the same place, during the General Conference session in the summer of 1936, the staff had added three more, and 93 students registered.

In 1936 the General Conference voted to organize a permanent seminary separate from any other institution. There was to be a 1937 summer school and a three-month winter session in 1937-1938. Seminary faculty members, when not occupied in the school, could be sent to overseas divisions to assist in ministerial institutes. Erection of a suitable building was approved.

With Kern as president (1937-1943), an initial faculty of 11, and an enrollment of 38, the sessions were opened in temporary quarters in Takoma Park, Washington, D.C. Majors were offered in Bible and religious history (either church history or Near Eastern antiquity); minors included Greek and Hebrew. The new building, planned for 100 to 125 students, was begun in August 1938 and dedicated on Jan. 21, 1941. By 1942 the winter quarter enrollment had reached 65. In April 1942 came authorization to confer the degree of Master of Arts in religion. A new calendar announced winter, spring, and summer sessions.

From 1943 to 1947 a division of missions and Christian leadership offered intensive instruction in the Arabic, French, German, and Russian languages. A fourth quarter of instruction for the Theological Seminary was instituted in 1944-1945. In 1945 a program was announced for the Bachelor of Divinity (B.D.) degree; the first Master of Theology degree was conferred in 1959. Four apartment buildings, accommodating 24 families, were erected in Takoma Park in 1947. The Theological Seminary's library collection grew rapidly, doubling between 1944 (15,000 books) and 1947 (32,000 books), by which time it was said to rank among the upper one fourth of seminary libraries in the United States in total acquisitions. When the institution was moved to Berrien Springs in 1960, the collection had grown to more than 50,000 books.

An action by the Autumn Council of 1953 called for a fifth year at the Theological Seminary for all ministerial students immediately after completion of their college work. The Autumn Council of 1954 revised this action and prescribed a one-year field internship before the Theological Seminary year. In 1956 this latter action was rescinded and the 1953 Autumn Council action reaffirmed. An Autumn Council action in 1962 called for a three-year ministerial internship plan whereby the then-present two-year internship plan was extended to include an additional year of internship of study at the Theological Seminary. This plan was revised in 1964 so that, upon completion of college work, the intern would study two years at the Theological Seminary and receive the B.D. degree and spend a third year of internship in the field.

In 1971 the Bachelor of Divinity degree was changed to Master of Divinity (M.Div.).

IV. History of the School of Graduate Studies and Potomac University. In 1956 the Autumn Council authorized the establishment of a university-type institution to include with the Theological Seminary a School of Graduate Studies, with Washington Missionary College (now Columbia Union College) to be affiliated as the undergraduate school. Potomac University was organized in 1957, consisting of the School of Graduate Studies, with an enrollment of 31, and the Theological Seminary; but the plan to affiliate with Washington Missionary College encountered problems in finding an adequate campus site. Finally the Autumn Council of 1958 voted to move the graduate institutions to Berrien Springs, Michigan, and to affiliate them with Emmanuel Missionary College. During the 1959-1960 term, instruction by both graduate divisions was given at both Washington, D.C., and Berrien Springs, but the 1960-1961 term was conducted entirely at Berrien Springs. In 1960 the entire institution, including Emmanuel Missionary College as the undergraduate school, became Andrews University.

The Emmanuel Missionary College faculty formed the nucleus of the School of Graduate Studies faculty, which was augmented by a number of new appointees. Initially members of the Theological Seminary faculty assisted in the School of Graduate Studies. In 1961 the Theological Seminary stopped granting the Master of Arts degree. It was relocated in the School of Graduate Studies until 1987, when it was returned to the Theological Seminary.

V. History of the University School. In 1901 Battle Creek College was moved to Berrien Springs and was given the name Emmanuel Missionary College. When Emmanuel Missionary College opened, the curriculum consisted largely of secondary school courses. The first class, graduated in 1908, consisted of all secondary students. In 1922 the academy was organized as a department with a faculty of its own. The academy was accredited by the state of Michigan in 1916 and by the North Central Association of Colleges and Schools in 1922 under the name Emmanuel Missionary College Academy.

The name Andrews University Laboratory School was voted by the board of trustees in 1963, and in 1964 the university board of trustees voted to accept the Laboratory School as its responsibility. In 1974 the board of trustees voted to adopt the name The University School.

VI. Growth of the University From 1959 to 1974. 1. *Physical Plant.* In 1959 a development program was begun to improve and enlarge the campus, as a result of the move of the university to Berrien Springs.

To provide additional housing for married students the university erected six apartment buildings for graduate students, with a total of 118 apartments (1959) and another unit with 10 apartments and 30 additional sleeping rooms (1963). In 1966 and 1967 another apartment complex was added, and again in 1970 and 1973, making a total of 268 apartments for married students. A new men's residence hall, Meier Hall, for single men students was completed in 1964, and an addition to Lamson Hall, residence hall for single women, was completed in 1968.

Seminary Hall was dedicated in 1961. The year 1961 also saw the completion of the campus center, which houses the food service and student center, as well as the FM radio station, which was completed in 1970. The James White Library building, housing the combined libraries of the university, was dedicated in 1962.

When the new administration building was completed in 1966, the old administration building (Nethery Hall) was transformed into additional classroom space. The new dairy complex was completed in 1967 and helped the university to become the largest producer of milk in southwestern Michigan. The year 1968 saw the completion of the swimming pool and gymnasium addition. In 1969 the elementary grades were moved from the main campus to a new building near the campus, and the former building was transformed into a home for the School of Education.

Auxiliary departments were not forgotten in the development plan. The book bindery (1959), laundry (1959), press building addition (1962), custodial services (1965), sewage treatment plant (1968), College Wood Products warehouse (1969), airport (1971), and the airport terminal building (1974) added to the growth of the campus. Construction on a new plant service building and the enlargement of the heating plant were started in 1973 and were completed in 1975.

The science complex, composed of three buildings that house the Departments of Chemistry, Biology, Physics, Mathematics, Engineering, Engraving Technology, and Medical Technology, was dedicated in 1974. The net capital worth of the university in 1993 was about $39 million, and the campus had expanded to more than 1,600 acres (650 hectares).

2. *Enrollments.* The university's opening enrollment during its centennial year (1974-1975) totaled 2,314, of which 546 were involved in graduate programs. By the 1991-1992 school year, enrollment had increased to 3,057, with 988 enrolled at the graduate level. Over the 18 years from 1974 to 1992, only the opening enrollment in 1981-1982 (3,083) surpassed that of a decade later. Graduate enrollments peaked at 1,141 in 1986-1987, while the high point of undergraduate enrollments (2,087) came in 1979-1980.

3. *Affiliations.* In 1975 the university began making its degrees available on the campuses of affiliated Seventh-day Adventist colleges outside the United States. This involved careful inspection and continued monitoring of facilities, faculty, and instruction at each institution. The first year (1975), undergraduate programs in approved subject areas were begun at the Adventist Seminary of West Africa in Nigeria and at Helderberg College in the republic of South Africa. Courses in these programs are taught almost entirely by faculty of the host college, although occasionally an exchange teacher might be supplied from the Michigan campus. Eventually master's degrees in religion and pastoral ministry were added in Nigeria and in religion in South Africa.

Graduate courses were taught almost entirely by instructors from the home campus or by visiting instructors from another SDA college.

Following this pattern, course work toward master's degrees in religion and education were initiated in 1979 at West Indies College in Jamaica and in Religion at Montemorelos University in Mexico, with classes being taught primarily during the summer months. The next year course work toward a graduate degree in religion was begun at Antillian College in Puerto Rico and at Avondale College in Australia. In 1980 Andrews also extended its granting of undergraduate degrees to students at the new University College of Eastern Africa in Kenya. This program was continued until the Kenyan government was satisfied that the University College of Eastern Africa had developed enough academically to offer its own degrees.

In 1983 Andrews added Newbold College in England to the colleges at which certain undergraduate degrees could be earned. Later master's programs in religion and pastoral ministry were added. The year 1983 also saw the start of master's programs in education and religion at Spicer Memorial College in India. Solusi College in Zimbabwe was added as an affiliated college for undergraduate degree programs in 1984. A similar program was established at Caribbean Union College, Trinidad, in 1985. The graduate program in pastoral ministry was subsequently instituted at Solusi College.

Prior to 1988, all affiliations were with SDA institutions outside the United States. In 1988, however, an agreement was reached with Kettering Medical Center in Ohio to offer the Andrews' B.S. in nursing at that institution. The most recent Andrews' affiliation, established in 1992, provides for the university's M.A. in religion to be offered at Zaokski Theological Seminary in Russia.

VII. Andrews University in Its Second Century. In 1974 Andrews University celebrated the one hundredth anniversary of its founding as Battle Creek College with a variety of special convocations and conferences. These conferences (on the arts, missions, evangelism, and family life) were in many ways indicative of the emphases that would develop over the next two decades. The international aspect of the university's student body received visual acknowledgment in 1974 with the dedication at alumni homecoming of that year of the international flag walk between the Pioneer Memorial SDA Church and the James White Memorial Library. During the 1991-1992 academic year, students were enrolled from all 50 states and from 88 other countries. The first student from Russia had arrived in 1978 and from mainland China in 1980. The University operates an English Language Institute, in which students whose native language is not English may, through intensive classwork, rapidly acquire the language proficiency necessary to handle classes satisfactorily.

The undergraduate Honors Program, begun in 1966, demonstrates the university's strong commitment to intellectual excellence. It stresses the close cooperation of academically talented students with faculty in a variety of special courses, seminars, and research projects. An interdisciplinary emphasis avoids narrow specialization. Subject departments have been encouraged to form chapters of National Honor societies in their disciplines. In 1987 an Academic Support and Advising Service was begun to aid students in developing their potential more quickly. That year the emphasis on academic excellence was demonstrated when two undergraduates were accepted to work during the summer in the famed Argonne National Laboratory. In 1985 a Gifted Student Program was developed to allow local high school seniors to take one university class per quarter. Three years later, a Summer Scholars Program was initiated to stimulate the academic interests of talented academy juniors and seniors. These programs paid off; by 1991 the undergraduate student body included 57 National Merit scholars. The University School also was demonstrating academic excellence. In 1985 Andrews Academy was one of only 65 private schools in the country to be designated as an "exemplary school" by the United States Department of Education.

Recognizing that many students' special talents lie more in vocational lines than in the traditional academic areas, the university established a Center for Occupational Education in 1971. This center offered courses ranging from carpentry to automobile radiator repair in programs stretching from 10 weeks to 30 months. In 1974 these programs were combined with engineering, aviation, computer science, photography, graphic arts, and other vocationally oriented departments to form the College of Technology. From its inception this college has stressed cooperative work-study programs with appropriate industries. The university's traditionally strong Agriculture

Department eventually was relocated in the College of Technology. The College of Technology proceeded to develop strong programs in engineering technology and media technology, and in 1983 launched the five-year Bachelor of Architecture program.

The university's 1974 Conference on Missions highlighted a variety of activities that developed to support the spread of Seventh-day Adventism around the world. That year the College of Arts and Sciences' Modern Languages Department began offering courses in French and Spanish for workers assigned to countries in which these languages were dominant. The Institute of World Mission, established in 1966 in the Theological Seminary, began holding sessions, eventually three or four times per year, to aid missionaries under appointment in preparing for more effective service by broadening their understanding of cultural differences and challenges. A strong student missionary program and an active chapter of Maranatha Flights International, which regularly promotes student involvement during vacations in church building projects in Mexico, El Salvador, and the Dominican Republic, have kept students in all the university's subdivisions aware of the challenges of world missions. In 1976 the General Conference designated Andrews University as the center for preparing pilots for mission aircraft, and the Aviation Training and Service Center was established. During the Christmas recess in 1991 and again in 1992, the Institute of World Mission sponsored conferences aimed at preparing young people from all parts of the nation. These "Go" conferences attracted more than 400 individuals, inspiring them with a vision of what they could do to aid in fulfilling the Great Commission.

In June 1974 Andrews hosted one of the three Bible conferences sponsored by the North American Division. Theological Seminary faculty were major speakers at all three conferences. That same year, the Theological Seminary developed a joint Master of Divinity-Master of Science in Public Health program with Loma Linda University. When the North American Division opened its Evangelism Institute in Chicago, the Theological Seminary faculty included a quarter of work at this institute or a similar facility as part of every M.Div. program. In 1980 the university established the Institute of Church Ministry within the Theological Seminary. This later was followed by the addition of the Center for Continuing Education for Ministry and a Youth Resource Center, all designed to harness the talents of Theological Seminary faculty and students in preparing more effective ways to aid the church in reaching the various publics that make up the modern secular world. In 1984 an Institute of Hispanic Ministry was established to better meet the needs of this rapidly expanding segment of the church.

Better preparation for effective ministry lay behind the Theological Seminary's launching of a Doctor of Ministry program in 1973 and the Doctor of Theology program in 1974. This also served as a major reason for the continuing support of periodic archaeological "digs," begun at ancient biblical Heshbon in 1968 and continued after 1984 at Tell el-ᶜUmeiri in Jordan. In 1980 the university established an Institute of Archaeology to coordinate the development of the Horn Archaeological Museum and the continuation of university-sponsored archaeological expeditions. A better understanding of Christianity's roots became possible for interested Theological Seminary students with the start of an on-location study quarter at the Adventist Center in Jerusalem in 1987.

Two other activities demonstrate that the 1974 Conference on Evangelism was not just an academic exercise: the heavy involvement of the Theological Seminary faculty in the preparation of the Statement of Fundamental Beliefs adopted at the 1980 General Conference session and the establishment of the Adventist Information Ministry.

The year following the university's centennial year Conference on Family Life, the university sponsored the first of what were to become annual summer family life workshops. These became very popular as they brought together leading authorities on the modern family and its problems with scores of denominational workers dedicated to meeting the challenges of eroding family life. By 1992 Drs. John and Millie Youngberg, who directed these workshops, had conducted more than 100 Marriage Enrichment seminars, involving more than 2,000 couples, in a continuing effort to strengthen Christian homes.

Andrews University has become heavily involved in meeting another late-twentieth-century problem: drug dependency. In 1971 as an ancillary to the Department of Chemistry, the university established a Drug Identification Laboratory. This laboratory has been widely utilized by local law enforcement officials, who rely on it to identify samples of suspected illicit drugs. In 1984 the university established the Institute of Alcoholism and Drug Dependency to research further what had become a critical national problem. In 1989 the university received a federal government grant of $118,000 to fund the development of a comprehensive drug prevention program.

In 1987 the university began a Community Service Assistance Program with the aid of another federal grant. Under this program interested students are given modest financial assistance as they provide a variety of social services in connection with established agencies in nearby Benton Harbor, Michigan, one of the state's most critically depressed areas economically. By 1992 students had put in more than 100,000 hours in projects as varied as literacy programs and counseling of welfare applicants. In 1988 the state of Michigan recognized the university's commitment to aiding energetic persons who had been unable to complete their education by granting $28,000 for a pilot program for single parents wishing to complete a degree program. These funds are used in part to provide child care for the students enrolled under this "Genesis Program."

The university has attempted to reach out to its local community in a variety of ways. In 1987 an Intercultural Seminar was developed and offered for employees of the Whirlpool Corporation about to take overseas assignments. In 1986 university staff who were bicycle enthusiasts began promoting an annual springtime metric century bicycle event that attracts hundreds of exercise "buffs" from a tri-state area. That same summer it began hosting an annual International Music Festival that drew students, from the elementary grades up, from all over the nation. In 1989 the university Physical Education Department hosted the national championships for the United States Sports Acrobatics Federation. University facilities were made available during the summer of 1990 and thereafter for state baseball and basketball camps and for a number of state high school bands' preseason practice weeks.

Constantly expanding programs demanded increased and improved facilities. In 1975 Apple Valley Market, a modern supermarket that was soon to be a major employer of student labor and a magnet for healthful shoppers in the area, was opened. The year 1978 saw the completion of a new Andrews Academy and an expansion to the university library that more than doubled its storage capacity while providing new quarters for the Ellen G. White Research Center and temporary quarters for the developing Horn Archaeological Museum. The expanded library also housed a Teaching Materials Resource Center and a growing Adventist Heritage Center. By 1993 the university library housed more than 1.2 million bibliographic items, nearly 3,000 periodical subscriptions, thousands of musical recordings and scores, and 75,000 maps and other non-book items. Following years of planning, the library's holdings became more accessible through the installation of an on-line catalog in 1993. In 1979 two new instructional buildings were added at the Andrews Airport to accommodate the expanding aviation program. A new men's residence hall was completed in 1982, substantially adding to student housing on campus. In 1983 the former Geoscience Institute building was reopened as the Horn Archaeological Museum. Other university buildings were converted to new uses: in 1985 a former president's residence became the Honors House, and the laundry building (discontinued as an industry in 1982) became a converted laboratory for the new physical therapy program. The expanding architecture program demanded its own new building (1984), while another former president's home was converted in 1987 to an alumni house. That same year the restored Sutherland House (home of Emmanuel Missionary College's first president after the move to Berrien Springs) became the headquarters of the Institute of World Mission.

As the result of a generous grant of $1.5 million from SDA philanthropist Chan Shun, $100,000 from the Whirlpool Corporation, and a number of other gifts, Chan Shun Hall was opened in 1989 as headquarters for the School of Business. This was the first new university building to be opened with an operating endowment for its continued maintenance. Similar generous funding from the Harrigan family allowed the opening in 1991 of Harrigan Hall as the principal center of the College of Technology. The expanding campus facilities required the erection of a new 135-foot (41-meter), 250,000-gallon (946,000-liter) water tank in 1988 and a new power plant in 1992.

Expanded facilities and programs demanded increased financial support. In the early 1980s extensive efforts were made to solicit gifts from alumni, foundations, industry, and the general public. By the 1984-1985 academic year, gifts to the university exceeded $1.1 million. In 1986 an extensive campaign was begun to raise a $10 million endowment for the university, part to be used to establish student scholarships, part for general operations. That year a gift of $925,000 established the Frank and Dolly DeHaan Work Excellence Scholarships. For the next several years the university annually received gifts exceeding $2 million. The high point of such contributions came to the university in the 1989-1990 academic year when the total surpassed $3 million.

Student life during the last quarter of the twentieth century differed markedly from the early days in Berrien Springs. The increased availability of student loans and grants coupled with more rigorous academic demands lessened students' desire to "earn while they learned." By 1987 the university trustees decided to sell off longstanding industries that had become increasingly unprofitable. The University Laundry had been closed in 1982; now it was the turn of the University Printers, the University Bindery, and the College Wood Products.

All students were being expected to be computer-literate. Major computer laboratories were established in Bell Hall, Nethery Hall, and Chan Shun Hall, with minor facilities available in most other instructional buildings. By 1992 many occupants of the residence halls had their own personal computers and telephones, complete with answering machines.

The Andrews University Press, established with minimum funding in 1969, began a considerable expansion of publishing in 1979 with the appointment of a permanent director. By 1992 it had published more than 80 titles, principally in the fields of theology, archaeology, and education. A Museum of Natural History, begun in 1960 with a small collection of teaching specimens, by 1993 included more than 30,000 marine shells, 1,600 birds, 1,400 mammals, and hundreds of butterflies and insects. This museum's herbarium section houses more than 5,000 botanical specimens. The most complete skeleton of a woolly mammoth to be found in Michigan is a popular attraction. More and more faculty attract outside funding for research projects, although few have been as successful as biology professor John Stout, funded for more than 10 years by the National Science Foundation. By 1987 attendance at commencement exercises was so great that separate services were begun for graduates and undergraduates.

The university's alumni have been taking an increasing role in the university's affairs. Not only do they make major contributions to the annual giving campaigns, but they are taking a larger role in the university's governance. In 1987 an alumni "shadow program" was instituted in which a number of alumni in various professions allow undergraduate seniors to observe their participation in the work world.

VIII. Presidents: *Battle Creek College:* Sidney Brownsberger (1874)-1881; Alexander McLearn, 1881-1882; W. H. Littlejohn, 1883-1885; W. W. Prescott, 1885-1894; G. W. Caviness, 1894-1897; E. A. Sutherland, 1897-1901.

Emmanuel Missionary College: E. A. Sutherland, 1901-1904; N. W. Kauble, 1904-1908; O. J. Graf, 1908-1917; C. L. Benson, 1917-1918; Frederick Griggs, 1918-1924; G. F. Wolfkill, 1924-1930; Lynn H. Wood, 1930-1934; T. W. Steen, 1934-1937; H. J. Klooster, 1937-1943; A. W. Johnson, 1943-1950; P. W. Christian, 1950-1955; F. O. Rittenhouse, 1955-1959 (thereafter the college was incorporated into the university).

SDA Theological Seminary: M. E. Kern, 1937-1943; D. E. Rebok, 1943-1951; V. E. Hendershot, 1951-1952; E. D. Dick, 1952-1957 (the Theological Seminary was incorporated under Dick into Potomac University, not including Emmanuel Missionary College).

Potomac University (including the Theological Seminary and newly established School of Graduate Studies): E. D. Dick, 1957-1958.

Andrews University (including Emmanuel Missionary College, School of Graduate Studies, and Theological Seminary; incorporated 1960): F. O. Rittenhouse, 1958-1963; Richard Hammill, 1963-1976; J. G. Smoot, 1976-1983; W. Richard Lesher, 1984-1994; Niels-Erik Andreasen, 1994- .

ANDREWS UNIVERSITY LABORATORY SCHOOL. *See* Andrews University, V.

ANDREWS UNIVERSITY SEMINARY STUDIES (AUSS) (1963-). The scholarly journal of the Seventh-day Adventist Theological Seminary at Andrews University. After two yearly issues AUSS was published twice a year until 1981, when the journal began to come out three times a year. In 1995 semiannual publication resumed, with a circulation of 600.

A refereed journal, AUSS provides a scholarly venue, within the context of biblical faith, for the presentation of research in the area of religious and biblical studies. AUSS publishes research articles and brief notes on the following topics: biblical archaeology and history of antiquity; Hebrew Bible; New Testament; church history of all periods; historical, biblical, and systematic theology; ethics; history of religion and mission; and selected research articles on ministry and Christian education.

Reports of the Andrews University archaeological digs appear regularly in AUSS. Abstracts of AU dissertations in religion are also published. Articles usually appear in English, but occasionally an article may be in another major Western language. Most of the articles are written by SDA scholars, many of them Theological Seminary professors. However, subject to the refereeing process, AUSS may accept articles by authors of other persuasions. Since 1967 AUSS has included reviews of significant new scholarly books in the same areas as its research articles. Articles are indexed in several scholarly bibliographical works, among which are *Religion Index One* and *Elenchus of Biblica.*

Siegfried H. Horn began the journal almost single-handedly, editing it from 1963 to 1974. Kenneth A. Strand followed him as editor until 1988. At that time, editorial responsibilities were divided between two coeditors: Strand with George R. Knight until 1991; Strand with Nancy J. Vyhmeister, 1991-1994. In 1994 Vyhmeister assumed the editorship, and Jerry Moon became associate editor and book review editor.

Editorial office: Seminary Hall, Andrews University, Berrien Springs, Michigan.

ANDROSS, ANNA MATILDA (ERICKSON) (1880-1957). Assistant secretary of the Missionary Volunteer Department of the General Conference, author, and editor. She was born in Denmark and in her early childhood heard the Seventh-day Adventist message preached by J. G. Matteson, pioneer of the SDA Scandinavian work, who held meetings in her home. Shortly after this, she emigrated to America. She received an education in nursing at Nebraska Sanitarium, and in liberal arts at Union College (B.A., 1907). Later she took graduate studies at the University of Nebraska and Columbia University.

Having taught for several years, she was chosen in 1907 as the first secretary (under chairmanship of M. E. Kern) of the Young People's Missionary Volunteer Department of the General Conference. Then in 1922 she went with her husband, E. E. Andross, whom she had married in 1920, to the Inter-American Division. There she served as the Missionary Volunteer and Sabbath school secretary of the division. She helped to found and, until her return in 1936 to the United States, edited the *Inter-American Division Messenger* and the *Mensajero.* She wrote several pamphlets and books, among them, *Alone With God, The Life That Wins, Life's Greatest Things, Sunshine and Shadow in Southern Europe,* and a substantial history of the Seventh-day Adventist Church, *Story of the Advent Message,* for the use of the MV Department. She also wrote a handbook, *Missionary Volunteers and Their Work.*

ANDROSS, ELMER ELLSWORTH (1868-1950). Evangelist and administrator. After engaging in evangelistic work from 1888 to 1894, he served as Bible teacher at Healdsburg College for two years. Back in evangelistic and pastoral work, he spent three years in San Francisco, then was called (1899) to evangelism in England. After three years he was appointed president of the North England Conference, and later (1905 to 1908) served as president of the British Union Conference. Returning to America, he served terms as president of the Southern California Conference and the Pacific Union Conference, and was vice president of the General Conference for North America (1918-1922). In 1917 his wife, née Sophie P. Miller, died, and in 1920 he married Matilda Erickson. A new and important phase of his lifework began in 1922 when he organized the Inter-American Division. Fourteen years of service as president of that field was followed by a term as a field secretary of the General Conference, and a brief period as president of the Caribbean Union.

ANERLEY PLACE. A home for the aged operated by the Orange-Natal Conference at Anerley, approximately 75 miles (120 kilometers) south of Durban, South Africa, on a 2.5-acre (one-hectare) property donated early in 1962 by an elderly Seventh-day Adventist member. The site overlooks the Indian Ocean, is adjacent to the Missionary Volunteer youth camp, and is within a five-minute walk of a shop, a post office, and a beach. The home was officially opened with 14 residents on Apr. 15, 1963. Besides the original residence, which provides some accommodations, facilities for a large kitchen, and a community dining room, there were 45 self-contained single and double apartments, with veranda and garden space for each occupant, and a community library-lounge. Anerley church, just across the road, provides the residents with a place of worship. A conference-appointed pastor cares for their spiritual needs.

ANG, TAU KIET (c. 1864-1936). Minister, one of the early Seventh-day Adventists in China. In his early life, he joined the Baptists and became an ordained elder in charge of an independent Baptist congregation in the town of Chiaoon, in eastern Kwangtung. Through his contact with N. P. Keh, a pioneer national SDA minister in China, he accepted the SDA beliefs and devoted his life and means to their propagation in his native province. Ang began to observe the seventh-day Sabbath, together with many members of his congregation, on the Chinese New Year's Day which fell on a Saturday that year. His church building became the first property owned by the Swatow Mission. An enthusiastic leader, he immediately began to spread through his province the good news of Christ's soon coming. He opened new stations, distributed publications, and even employed others at his own expense to preach the gospel before the SDA mission provided financial aid for his work. He continued in evangelistic work for about a quarter of a century, opening schools and establishing churches in seven of the 12 districts in the Swatow Mission. In 1915 he became the second Chinese national to be ordained to the SDA ministry. In 1928 his health failed and his right side was paralyzed. He died in 1936 and was buried in his native village of Peh-tah.

ANGERVO, OSCAR (1885-1958). Minister, teacher, editor, and administrator in Sweden and Finland. As a young man of 17 he attended the Nyhyttan school in Sweden, where he finished the ministerial course. He began working as a colporteur, then in 1905 entered evangelistic work and the same year was called to Finland. Being adept at learning languages, he soon learned to speak Finnish. After two years he returned to Sweden, where he preached in different places for a number of years. For a while he was departmental secretary in the South Swedish Conference; then he taught Bible at Nyhyttan (1919-1921). In 1922 he was ordained and in 1925 went to Vasa, Finland, as a minister. Then he was called to be president and Bible teacher at the Finland SDA Mission School (now Finland Junior College). In 1932 he became editor of the Swedish *Tidens Tecken* and editor in chief of the Stockholm Publishing House. He served there till his retirement in 1952.

ANGLO-CHINESE ACADEMY. *See* Hawaiian Mission Academy.

ANGOLA. An independent republic situated on the west coast of Africa a short distance south of the equator; it is composed of two units, Angola proper and Cabinda, a small coastal area separated from the rest by a strip belonging to Zaire. The Portuguese first established bases in Angola in the 1500s. The area is 481,351 square miles (1,246,699 square kilometers); the population (1994) is 9.8 million. Agriculture is the principal occupation of the people, the chief products being coffee, corn (maize), sugar, palm oil, and palm kernels. There are 13 separate ethnic groups, speaking 65 languages and dialects. Of the population, 38 percent are Catholic, 15 percent Protestant.

Seventh-day Adventist Statistics. The territory of Angola constitutes four of the five missions that form the Angola Union Mission, a part of the Euro-Africa Division (the fifth being São Tomé and Príncipe Mission). Statistics (1992) for *Angola:* churches, 551; members, 136,154; ordained ministers, 88; licensed ministers, 159. Headquarters: Rua Teixeira da Silva, Huambo.

Statistics (1992) for the missions: *Central Association Mission:* churches, 198; members, 55,847; ordained ministers, 25; licensed ministers, 67. Headquarters: Huambo. *East Association Mission:* churches, 111; members, 29,925; ordained ministers, 14; licensed ministers, 15. Headquarters: Luena, Moxico. *North Association Mission:* churches, 126; members, 29,759; ordained ministers, 18; licensed ministers, 33. Headquarters: Luanda. *South Association Mission:* churches, 111; members, 24,001; ordained ministers, 17; licensed ministers, 40. Headquarters, Lubango.

Institutions. Angola Publishing House; Bongo Mission Hospital.

History. The first Seventh-day Adventist to enter Angola was W. H. Anderson, who, coming from South-West Africa in 1922, explored the country to study the possibilities of establishing mission work. Later he, with T. M French, field secretary for the African Division, and J. D. Baker, who had been released by the South African Union Conference for work in Angola, was sent in 1923 to choose the site for the first mission station. After traveling for a month, they selected the district of Lepi, on the central plateau of Angola. In 1924, after overcoming several legal difficulties, Anderson, Baker, and O. O. Bredenkamp settled in the country.

Lepi became the temporary headquarters of the South Atlantic United Missions, which included South-West Africa and Angola. In 1925 South-West Africa was transferred to the South African Union Conference, and Angola later became part of the Equatorial Union Mission. Angola was divided on the basis of ethnic and linguistic groups into four mission fields: Ovimbundu, Kimbundu, Huila, and Chokwe. In 1928 Angola itself was detached and organized as the Angola Union Mission. (Briefly between 1955 and 1957, when Portuguese East Africa was temporarily added to it, this union was named the Portuguese African Union Mission.) Anderson was president of these three successive organizations from 1924 to 1933. He endured great hardships, spending most of his time traveling, choosing the sites for the Angola mission stations.

Shortly after their arrival, Baker and Bredenkamp opened a mission station at Bongo, in the heart of the Umbumbu tribe, 10 miles (16 kilometers) from Lepi. They lived in a mud-and-pole hut while constructing houses for their families. With the arrival of D. P. Harder in 1925, they erected a school building (*see* Bongo Adventist Seminary). Dr. A. N. Tonge from California arrived in 1926 and practiced medicine under the most primitive conditions, until the first unit of a hospital was built in 1928 (*see* Bongo Mission Hospital). In 1927, during the dry season, evangelistic meetings were conducted in four villages, as a result of which 48 persons joined the hearers' classes. By the end of that year five village Sabbath schools were functioning regularly in addition to the one on the mission, with a total average Sabbath school attendance of 500. Bongo became the most important center of SDA influence in Angola.

In August 1925 Bredenkamp opened the Luz Mission, in the northeastern part of Angola. He built two missionaries' homes, and a school building (1927) with a capacity of 200 students. A dispensary built in 1929 was placed in charge of Nurse M. Fourie. A church building was built in 1937, and in 1950 the old school building was replaced.

In 1927 a building for the union headquarters was erected in Nova Lisboa in the west central section. Other construction followed, and by 1961 there were homes for three missionary families, a primary school, which began functioning in 1961, a spacious church dedicated in the same year, and a secondary school, which opened in the autumn of 1963.

In 1928 a mission station was opened by Baker at Namba. (A permanent structure for the school was built in 1956, and the church was dedicated in 1961.) In 1932 Bredenkamp established the Lucusse Mission among the difficult Luena tribe in eastern Angola. In addition to the residence for the director, he erected a temporary school building (replaced in 1952 by a permanent structure) and a dispensary. From Lucusse the work spread to the Rhodesian border, reaching the Bunda and Luchaze tribes.

At Cuale, to the north, E. A. Buckley in 1934 opened work among the Kimbundu, a hitherto-unreached tribe. The work here grew rapidly. A school was opened in 1953, a hospital in 1962, and a new church building in 1963.

At the General Conference session held in San Francisco in 1950, the Angola Union Mission was transferred to the Southern European Division. The union was then redivided into six mission fields, of which Ovimbundu had by far the largest membership.

In 1952 José de Sá was sent to open a station at Quicuco, in the south, on property acquired in 1931. This meant the beginning of work for a new tribe, the Quilengues. Two residences, a church, and various other buildings were erected, and in 1957 a dispensary (operated by two experienced nurses) was built. The Quilengues Mission was organized in 1958 with 136 members.

Until recently the work among the Africans in the Angola Union Mission was carried out primarily by teachers graduated from the Bongo Adventist Seminary, while conversions among the European population were to a large extent the result of the influence of the Bongo Mission Hospital. The first European Seventh-day Adventist church was formed in Benguela in 1947. The European Mission within the Angola Union was organized in 1959 with 193 members.

The first Adventist radio programs in Angola went on the air in 1953. In 1963 the Voice of Prophecy programs were being broadcast weekly from Benguela, Nova Lisboa, Sá da Bandeira, Moçamedes, Malanje, and Luso. A Bible correspondence course was offered for the first time in 1958. In 1964 the

Luanda station began to broadcast the Angola Voice of Prophecy.

A building was constructed at Bongo in 1958 to house the plant printing for the Angola Publishing House, which has produced SDA publications in Portuguese and various African languages.

Since 1975, when political independence was achieved, the country has been suffering from a terrible civil war. All missionaries have been forced to leave the country. In spite of these difficulties, the church has been growing rapidly.

ANGOLA ACADEMY (Colegio Adventista do Huambo). A secondary boarding school that was owned and operated by the Angola Mission and situated in Nova Lisboa, Angola.

The problems of Sabbath classes and a worldly environment presented such serious problems to the Seventh-day Adventist youth of Angola that, in 1964, the union committee, under the leadership of Ernesto Ferreira, opened a secondary school in Nova Lisboa. Legal authority for its existence was obtained and its official name, Colegio Adventista do Huambo, was taken from the district where it is situated.

The school began with a few students, two teachers offering two grades of secondary work, but the quality of instruction gained a good reputation for the institution and it progressed rapidly. In 1974 a full five-year secondary course was given, preceded by a complete five-year preparatory and elementary section. The school closed in the mid-1970s, when civil war broke out in Angola.

Principals: Ernesto Ferreira, 1964-1969; J. N. Ramos, 1970-1976.

ANGOLA PUBLISHING HOUSE (Casa Publicadora Angolana). A publishing firm, with printing plant, operated by the Angola Union Mission at Nova Lisboa, Angola. The problem of providing publications in the vernacular, especially for Sabbath schools, was first solved by the use of a duplicator. When this means became inadequate, a Multigraph press was obtained in 1937, and a printshop was set up as a department of the Bongo Training School at Lepi, Angola. From this small printshop, during its 20 years of service, came many thousands of pages of Sabbath school material and other printed matter, including schoolbooks and songbooks.

As early as 1947 plans were laid for the purchase of a larger press, but it was apparent that soon more than a printshop would be required. At a meeting of the union committee held at headquarters in Nova Lisboa, Feb. 8-15, 1951, the organization was set up for the establishing of a publishing house, with E. L. Jewell as manager. Because of certain legal technicalities it was at first linked to the publishing house in Portugal and was named Publicadora Atlantico Limitada—Filial de Angola ("Atlantic Publishers Limited—Angola Branch"). After a building in Nova Lisboa was selected and a Babcock cylinder press and a paper trimmer were ordered, the city council decided to widen the street, making it necessary to alter and reduce the building to a size that made it inadequate as a printing plant.

Although an active business was carried on with the sale of denominational books, both directly and with the aid of colporteurs, the lack of a building and of funds delayed the establishment of the new printing plant until 1957. On Aug. 5 of that year plans were laid to erect a building for the proposed plant at the Bongo Mission, thus providing an opportunity for students from the mission school to learn the printing trade. The building was completed in 1958. In the meantime, a small Victoria press, a power plant, and other equipment were purchased, and before the end of 1957 the plant was in operation, with J. da Silva Botelho as superintendent. In 1965 the division and the General Conference assisted in the purchase of an Ala press, and in 1972 of an automatic folding machine and hydraulic vulcanizing molding machine. The printing plant was enlarged in 1973.

In 1959 a legal organization, independent of the publishing house in Portugal, was set up under the name Casa Publicadora Angolana (S.A.R.L.), that is, Angola Publishing House, with headquarters in Nova Lisboa and the printing plant still at Bongo Mission. The management remained the same, and Ernesto Ferreira was chosen as editor.

The first main project, completed in 1961, was the preparation and printing of hymnbooks in the Umbundu and Chokwe languages, paralleled in each case with the Portuguese. This was followed in 1962 by Ellen G. White's *Steps to Christ* in the same languages, and in January 1963 by the first issue of the local union mission monthly periodical. In the late 1970s the publishing house was moved to Huambo.

Managers: E. L. Jewell, Juvenal Gomes, Joaquin Sabino, Bella Vista Felix, Jorge Agostinho, Joao Valerio, Autunes Filipe.

ANGOLA UNION MISSION. *See* Angola; Euro-Africa Division; São Tomé and Príncipe.

ANGUILLA. *See* Inter-American Division; Leeward and Windward Islands.

ANIMALS, CLEAN AND UNCLEAN. *See* Diet.

ANKAZAMBO ADVENTIST SCHOOL (École Adventiste d'Ankazambo). A coeducational boarding school on the secondary level that was operated by the Indian Ocean Union Mission near Befandriana-Nord, Madagascar.

The site of the school was chosen in 1951 by Henri Pichot, David Riemens, and Edgard Villeneuve, when they were on a prospecting and canvassing trip. In 1952 René Villeneuve arrived to supervise construction of buildings. A primary school was opened under the direction of Robert Rasamimanana. In 1953 more buildings were erected, and Henri Long and his family arrived and opened a small boarding school for boys. Also a girls' boarding school was opened. A church was organized and evangelistic work carried on in the villages by students and teachers. In 1958 five young men graduated.

The school was closed in 1990.

Principals: Henri Long, 1953-1957; Michel Grisier, 1958-1961; Jacques de Laere, 1961-1963; René Villeneuve, 1963-1966; Claude Villeneuve, 1966-1971; Paul Pichot, 1972; Jacques Gallis, 1972-1977; Nilton Amorim, 1977-1978; Louise Razafindrakalo, 1978-1984; Lyla Herimanitra, 1984-1985; Samuel Ravonjiarivelo, 1985-1986; Ernestine Rabesalama, 1986-1990.

ANKOLE HOSPITAL. *See* Ishaka Hospital.

ANNIHILATION. *See* Hell.

ANNUAL COUNCIL. An annual meeting of the Executive Committee of the General Conference, held in October of each year at such time and place as shall be determined by the Executive Committee. The General Conference Executive Committee exercises full administrative power on behalf of the General Conference during the intervals between General Conference sessions.

The Annual Council reviews annually, in the form of reports, resolutions, and general planning, the work pursued under the general supervision of the headquarters organization. The budgets submitted on behalf of fields, institutions, and general organizations are given careful consideration, and yearly budgetary appropriations are voted. Business pertaining to the general policy of the worldwide work is transacted. Policy items intended for insertion in the General Conference *Working Policy* must have Annual Council approval.

The Annual Council gives approval for all general departmental councils, advisory committees, and other general meetings involving attendance from several unions and/or institutions. The boundaries between divisions can be adjusted at Annual Council provided no divisional territorial line is changed when the division or divisions involved are not represented at the council by one of their executive officers or when such division or divisions have not given consent. Emergency conditions such as war would be an exception, in which case the General Conference Executive Committee makes such provisions as are necessary for the conduct of the work.

The members of division executive committees act to a degree as the General Conference Committee in their respective division territories. In case of appeal from a division committee action, the matter may be referred for counsel to the General Conference Committee. In case of any needed adjustment of differences of opinion arising between the division committee and the General Conference Committee, the matter is referred to the next Annual Council of the General Conference Executive Committee.

The Annual Council appoints a number of standing committees to prepare the regular business of the council and to process items or recommendations that are to come before the council. Ad hoc committees can also be appointed to deal with specific problems or certain aspects of the General Conference operation. The work of these committees comes to the Annual Council likewise through regular channels.

Before 1968 Annual and Midterm Council meetings were all held in the United States of America. In 1968 the Midterm Council was held outside the United States for the first time, in Toronto, Canada. Subsequently it has been held in the following cities outside the United States: 1972, Mexico City, Mexico; 1982, Manilla, Philippines; 1986, Rio de Janeiro, Brazil; 1988, Nairobi, Kenya; 1991, Perth, Australia; 1993, Bangalore, India.

See also Spring Meeting.

ANNUAL STATISTICAL REPORT (1906- ; annual, GC; limited circulation). An annual statistical summary of the Seventh-day Adventist Church activities issued as a separate publication since 1906 (reporting for the year 1905), at first apparently as a reprint from the *Review and Herald.*

Statistical reports for the denomination date from the fifth annual session of the General Conference, held in 1867, when a brief table of nine lines and one column in width was published in the *Review and Herald.* This was done in accordance with a resolution passed at the preceding session that statistics from conferences were to be furnished by the delegates to the General Conference from each local conference. At that time there were 28 ministers, 160 churches, and 4,320 members in the Michigan, New York and Pennsylvania, Wisconsin and Illinois, Iowa, Ohio, Vermont, and Minnesota conferences and in the New England Mission, all in North America. The reports were published in the *Yearbook* for the years 1882 to 1893, and in the *General Conference Bulletin* for the years 1892 to 1902, and even after the separate publication began, the statistics, at least in summary, continued to be published in the *Review and Herald* for some years, into the 1920s.

This report devotes 22 pages to the main table, which gives 35 items of information about church membership, contributions, church workers, and etc., for each conference, mission, union, and division. The remaining pages provide historical statistics, departmental statistics, and summary tables.

ANNUITIES. *See* Trust Services; Wills, Charitable Gift Annuities, Trusts, Life Income and Other Charitable Agreements.

ANOINTING OF THE SICK. *See* Healing, Faith.

ANTARANDOLO ADVENTIST SCHOOL (Collège Adventiste d'Antarandolo). A coeducational day school on the secondary level operated by the South Malagasy Mission. It first opened its doors in 1962 at Manaotsara before being transferred. This school served both primary and secondary levels under Eugene Vervoort as its first headmaster. In 1972 it became the Ivoamba School; in 1985 its name again became Antarandolo. The enrollment has steadily increased. More than 600 students were enrolled in 12 classes in 1988. The enrollment is now 960. The teaching staff has 18 teachers, with a pastor serving as the Bible teacher.

Principals: Eugene Vervoot, 1963-1968; Othon Metz, 1968-1971; J. J. Henriot, 1971-1973; Roland Schranz, 1973-1975; Alain Menis, 1975-1978; Jean Razafindrabe, 1978-1980; Zacharie Razafimahafaly, 1980-1982; Salomon Mazava, 1982-1984; Albert Ranaivomanana, 1984-1986; Raphael Andrianjakazafy, 1986-1992; Mamisoa Ravelonandrasana, 1992- .

ANTHONY, THEODORE (c. 1838-1895+?). First Seventh-day Adventist missionary in Turkey. He was a Greek of Turkish speech and nationality, born in Asia Minor. After his conversion in California (1888) he sold his business and returned to Turkey (1889) at his own expense to spread his faith. When his money was spent he made his living at his shoemaker's trade. He met violent opposition and was imprisoned repeatedly, most often at the instigation of other Christians. But he made a number of converts, including Z. G. Baharian, who became a minister. Anthony's first name is mentioned as Theodore by his associate, Baharian (*Review and Herald* 69:390, June 21, 1892), and in the 1894 *Yearbook;* references to him as R. S. Anthony appear to indicate confusion with R. S. Anthony of South Africa, a colporteur who became a physician.

ANTICHRIST. A word appearing only in Christian contexts, and in the NT only in 1 John 2:18, 22; 4:3; 2 John 7; hence probably coined by the author of these Epistles. In these passages the term has a historical application to false teachers, especially Gnostics (cf. 1 John 4:2, 3), in the churches of Asia Minor in the last part of the first century, who appear to have taught the Docetic doctrine that Christ was only an appearance and not truly human. However, the theme of an antichrist is much broader, and the term has been used to refer to powers that set themselves in opposition to the plan of salvation (cf. Ellen G. White, in SDACom 7:950). The figure of a great antagonist of God appears elsewhere, for example in 2 Thess. 2:1-4 and in the prophecies of Revelation. Repeatedly Christ is portrayed as victor over this power at His second coming (2 Thess. 2:8; Rev. 17:14; 19:19, 20).

The concept of a supernatural and primeval antagonist of Yahweh is found in the OT in figures such as leviathan, Rahab, and the multi-headed dragon (as in Isa. 27:1). This antagonist is both primeval and eschatological, and is symbolic of Satan (see SDADic 278, 649, 901). Similar figures are carried on into Jewish apocalyptic; thus in the Dead Sea scrolls two personalities appear oriented against God—the Evil Priest and the Man of the Lie (oldest evidence probably in 4Q Test). Possibly these parallel, negatively, the two messianic figures also found in that literature, the messiahs of Aaron and Israel, and thus may have been a kind of "anti-messiah" or "antichrist."

In Christian history the epithet "antichrist" has been applied to a variety of historical personages and institutions, for example, to Nero, to various popes and emperors, and to vague figures expected to arise in the East. Not infrequently he has been anticipated as a Jew from the tribe of Dan. The identification with the papacy goes back at least to Archbishop Eberhard II of Salzburg (1200-1246), during the controversy between Frederick II and Gregory IX. A similar point of view was popular among the spiritual Franciscans, influenced by the prophetic interpretations of Joachim of Floris (who expected the antichrist to be a false, heretical pope). John Wycliffe and Jan Hus adopted this interpretation, which appears also among the Waldenses. With the Reformation the idea that the papacy was the antichrist became a general Protestant tenet. Luther wrote it into the Articles of Schmalkald (1537). It remained a characteristic article of Protestant prophetic interpretation from the sixteenth to the nineteenth centuries.

Seventh-day Adventists similarly have applied the word "antichrist" to the papacy (for example, J. N. Andrews, in *Signs of the Times* 7:463, Oct. 13, 1881). They call "spiritualism" the "manifestation of antichrist" (PP 686). They regard Satan, the author of rebellion in heaven, as the antichrist par excellence (9T 229, 230), and identify him as the "mystery of iniquity" (TM 365; cf. 2 Thess. 2:7), who will claim to be God and deceive people by his miracles (5T 698; 6T 14; 8T 27, 28; 9T 16; TM 62, 364, 365; GC 624; SDACom 7:975).

ANTIGUA AND BARBUDA. A constitutional monarchy located in the eastern Caribbean about 30 miles (50 kilometers) north of Guadeloupe. The population (1994) of 65,000 is largely of African descent.

Colonized by the British in 1632, the island achieved independence in 1981.

The territory of Antigua and Barbuda is part of the North Caribbean Conference in the Caribbean Union of the Inter-American Division. *See also* Leeward and Windward Islands.

ANTIGUA SEVENTH-DAY ADVENTIST SCHOOL. A secondary educational institution located in St. John's, Antigua, West Indies. It opened in the mid-1980s. Vera James has been its only principal; currently there is a staff and faculty of 15.

ANTILLEAN ADVENTIST HOSPITAL (Antilliaans Advent Ziekenhuis). A 40-bed hospital and clinic operated by the Venezuela-Antilles Union. In 1969 a building was purchased from the Netherlands government for the purpose of beginning Seventh-day Adventist medical work in the Netherlands Antilles. The building was transformed into a 40-bed hospital. On Apr. 2, 1970, the hospital was officially opened by the minister of health.

From the beginning, Loma Linda University Medical School graduates have been recognized by the governments of the Netherlands and the Netherlands Antilles.

ANTILLES GUYANE ADVENTIST SECONDARY SCHOOL (College Adventiste Antilles-Guyane). A boarding secondary school located in Martinique in the Sainte-Luce area. The school opened in 1974. Enrollment was 313 in the 1992-1993 school year.

Directors: Maurice Roseau, 1974-1983; Daniel Milard, 1983-1989; Patrick Griffith, 1989-1991; Pierre Milard, 1991- .

ANTILLIAANS ADVENT ZIEKENHUIS. *See* Antillean Adventist Hospital.

ANTILLIAN ADVENTIST UNIVERSITY (Universidad Adventista de las Antillas). A coeducational boarding school operated by the Antillian Union Conference in the environs of Mayagüez, Puerto Rico. The 1992 college enrollment was 854. Total school staff numbered 150. Instruction is given in Spanish. Secondary accreditation has been granted by the Puerto Rican Department of Education. The nursing and elementary education programs are accredited by the Puerto Rican Council on Higher Education, and with the Commission of Higher Education of the Middle States Association. In 1964 the General Conference gave its approval for the offering of full college work in liberal arts. At that time, degrees were being offered in the fields of religion and general, primary, and secondary education it offered junior college courses in Bible instructors' training, and in commercial and secretarial fields. The school is noted for the cosmopolitan composition of its student body.

Antillian Adventist University in Puerto Rico is a successor of the Antillian College that operated at Santa Clara, Cuba, from 1955 to 1961, when because of political conditions in Cuba the college department was transferred to Puerto Rico *(see* Cuba Adventist Seminary).

Seventh-day Adventist educational work in Puerto Rico began in 1920 with the establishment of a school in Aibonito *(see* Puerto Rico). In 1946 a 12-grade academy was established in Santurce, Puerto Rico *(see* Metropolitan Adventist Academy [Puerto Rico]) This school, called Puerto Rico Academy, was moved in 1957 to a 284-acre (115-hectare) site near Mayagüez, a port and industrial city in the extreme western part of Puerto Rico.

In May 1961 the school was authorized to offer the college courses formerly offered at Antillian College in Santa Clara, Cuba, and in September 1961 began to function under the name of Puerto Rico Adventist College. In March 1962 its name was changed to Antillian College, and the institution was recognized as the advanced school in the Spanish-Caribbean area of the Inter-American Division. In August 1989 the Higher Education Council in Puerto Rico authorized the name Antillean Adventist University.

Principals: Donovan W. Olson, 1956-1959; G. B. Harper, 1959-1961; F. G. Drachenberg, 1961-1966; Robert Woods, 1966-1967; R. H. Howlett, 1967-1974; Conrad Visser, 1974-1975; Israel Recio, 1975-1980; Stuart Berkeley, 1980-1982; Angel M. Rodriguez, 1982-1987; James Unger, 1987-1989; Moises Velazquez, 1989-1990; Miguel A. Munoz, 1990- .

ANTILLIAN COLLEGE ACADEMY. *See* West Adventist Academy.

ANTILLIAN UNION CONFERENCE. *See* Cuba; Dominican Republic, Puerto Rico.

ANTINOMIANISM. From *anti,* "against," and *nomos,* "law," and meaning an attitude of hostility toward law, specifically, of Christians toward the Law, including the Decalogue. Traces of antinomianism were evident among Gnostic Manicheans of the third century, and throughout the Middle Ages. It originated as a distinct theological phenomenon with Johannes Agricola (1492-1566), in Germany, whose views were condemned by the Formula of Concord in 1577. During the sixteenth and seventeenth centuries it appeared in England, where its advocates were known as "the Ranters." It is found today in certain forms of dispensationalism.

The antithesis of antinomianism is nomism, which manifests itself as legalism, that is, the idea that salvation can be obtained by strict compliance with legal requirements instead of by faith in Jesus Christ. Seventh-day Adventists believe that legalism and antinomianism are equally contrary to the spirit of the gospel. They see the Ten Commandment law on the one hand, and grace on the other hand, not as mutually exclusive, but as complementary (Rom. 1:17; 3:31; 5:1; 7:12). To SDAs, salvation is by grace alone, but obedience to all of God's revealed will, including the Decalogue, is the fruit of faith (see DA 126). The function of the Decalogue is to convict of sin, but law has no power to pardon. Pardon comes exclusively by justification through faith in Christ (*Review and Herald* 3:24, June 10, 1852). *See* Law; Law and Grace; Righteousness by Faith.

ANTOFAGASTA ADVENTIST ACADEMY (Colegio Adventista de Antofagasta). A secondary school located in the North Chile Mission territory. It began functioning as a secondary school in 1990 with 45 students enrolled. From 1990 to 1993, 225 students have attended classes at the academy. There are 15 teachers serving in a school building that has three floors and a cellar. The small library is limited to 645 volumes.

Principals: Jose Antenor Parra, 1990-1991; Víctor Pérez, 1992- .

AORE ADVENTIST HIGH SCHOOL. A coeducational boarding school situated at Aore, Vanuatu. The 1993 enrollment was 252.

The school opened on Oct. 27, 1927, as the Aore training School, a training institution for national teachers and missionaries, with 25 students. After the land was cleared, indigenous-style houses were built for the students. In 1928 J. C. Radley arrived as engineer, builder, and sawmiller, and instructed the students in these lines of work.

About 1950 the institution became known as the Parker Missionary School, in honor of

C. H. Parker, the pioneer Seventh-day Adventist missionary to the New Hebrides.

During the visit in 1955 of Sir Christopher Cox (the adviser on education in the colonies to the British government), warm commendation was given to the mission for the high standard of the school.

Until the end of 1972 the school offered a full primary curriculum and only one year of high school study. At the beginning of 1974 the primary school was removed from the campus. Simultaneously the name was changed to Aore Adventist High School. Five years of high school study are now offered and the sixth senior year is soon to be added.

Principals: J. R. James, W. O. Broad, A. R. Barrett, G. H. Engelbrecht, C. F. Hollingsworth, J. H. Miller, L. R. Harvey, A. C. Thomson, J. Cernik, A. R. Hiscox, M. P. Cozens, D. H. Powell, N. Hughes, G. Harrington, B. Hamilton, A. Smith, C. Crawford, D. Iredale, D. Rogers, T. Rore.

APHS. *See* Adventist Professional Health Services in South Africa.

APIA CENTRAL SCHOOL *See* Samoa Adventist College.

APOCRYPHA. A term used by Protestants of a group of writings found in the Septuagint and the Vulgate (with minor differences), which do not appear in the Hebrew canon of Scripture. Catholics designate at least 12 of these books as "deuterocanonical" and use "Apocrypha" to refer to the Judeo-Christian religious writings between 200 B.C. and A.D. 200 that Protestants generally refer to as the "pseudepigrapha."

Originally the Apocrypha appeared in the King James Version, but in the nineteenth century the Bible societies insisted on removing these books from the Bibles they printed, and it became customary to omit them from most printings of this version.

Seventh-day Adventists, though recognizing some historical and literary value in the Apocrypha, agree with Protestants generally in denying that it is either inspired or an authoritative source of doctrine.

APOSTASY. *See* Church Discipline.

APOSTATE MOVEMENTS. Since the beginning of the Seventh-day Adventist Church various offshoots from it have appeared. Dr. J. H. Kellogg and prominent ministers such as A. T. Jones, D. M. Canright, and A. F. Ballenger, who left the SDA Church, did not lead organized movements of their own, although they did disagree with, and even oppose, some of the denomination's teachings and policies. For information concerning these persons, see their biographical sketches. The following offshoot organizations, listed here in the order of the dates of their rise, are discussed in other articles: the *Messenger* Party and "Age to Come" Defection (1853-1855); the *Hope of Israel* and Marion Party (1858-1863); the SDA Reform Movement—German (1915); the Reformed SDAs—Rowenite (1916); the Shepherd's Rod movement, or Davidian SDAs (1929); the United Sabbath Day Adventists (1930).

APPLES OF GOLD LIBRARY (1893-1915; monthly until October 1899, then quarterly; after 1903 irregular; PPPA; partial files at AU, LLU, LSU, PUC, R&H, UC, CoUC). A series of small pamphlets (4 to 32 pages) dealing with health, temperance, religious liberty, and doctrine designed as helps to personal evangelism. The small size—3½" x 6" (8.9 cm. x 15.2 cm.)—made it possible to enclose the pamphlets with personal correspondence. There were 97 titles in this series. It was listed in the *Yearbooks* up to 1908 as a periodical and afterward only as a collection of tracts. It was discontinued in 1915. Some of its titles, such as "How Esther Read Her Bible," were included in other series. Among those serving on the editorial committee were M. C. Wilcox, W. N. Glenn, C. M. Snow, O. A. Tait, M. H. Brown, H. H. Hall, J. F. Beatty, and A.J.S. Bourdeau.

APPROPRIATIONS AND EXPENDITURES. *See* Budget.

AR. *See Adventist Review.*

ARAB REPUBLIC OF EGYPT. *See* Egypt, Arab Republic of.

ARABIA. *See* Bahrain; Egypt, Kuwait; Oman; Qatar; Saudi Arabia; United Arab Emirates; Yemen.

ARABIC LITERATURE SOCIETY. *See* Middle East Press.

ARABIC UNION MISSION. *See* Egypt, Arab Republic of.

ARAKI, AI (1890-1982). Born in Japan, she was blinded in her teens. She was a believer in Tenrikyo, a branch of Shintoism, when she met Shu Kuniya, one of the first SDA ministers in Japan. Four years later at the age of 30 she became a paid Bible instructor. In the midst of World War II, with the church in disrepute, Ai, along with 41 Seventh-day Adventist lay and church leaders, was arrested. Most were imprisoned, but Ai had her Braille Bible confiscated and was ordered not to speak about Christianity. She and others did their best to contact the scattered members, praying for them and repeating memorized scriptures to them. The church in her city of Kagoshima was locked, but Ai continued to meet with the flock when she could. At the end of the war hers was the only congregation in Japan to remain virtually intact.

ARCHAEOLOGY, BIBLICAL. The scientific study of material remains of human life and activity relating to the Bible or Bible times.

History and Purpose. The purpose of biblical archaeology is the recovery of the history, culture, and religion of the ancient peoples of all Bible lands from Persia in the east to Italy in the west, with special interest in Palestine and the neighboring regions of Egypt Syria, and Mesopotamia, which played a major role in Bible history. The archaeological exploration of Egypt began in 1798, when 120 artists and scientists accompanied Napoleon on his Egyptian campaign to study and report on Egypt's ancient remains. Exploration in Assyria began in 1842 with the excavation of Nineveh by the French consul E. Botta; and that of Palestine, with topographical explorations conducted by the American scholar Edward Robinson, in 1838.

Hand in hand with the fieldwork of excavation went the recovery of dead languages, such as the deciphering of Egyptian hieroglyphic script by J. François Champollion in 1822, and of Babylonian cuneiform writing by Henry Rawlinson and others around the middle of the nineteenth century. Since that time several other ancient scripts and languages have been recovered. Thus a wealth of ancient literature has become available for study, including historical records and annals, religious and mythological texts, prayers and hymns, laws, and documents of a judicial, economic, and scientific character.

Excavations carried on at hundreds of sites in virtually every area of the ancient Bible lands have uncovered cities, temples, palaces, tombs, and graves, and brought to light objects of daily use such as weapons and tools, musical instruments, and works of art, as well as tens of thousands of written texts. Many biblical cities—for example, Babylon, Jerusalem, Nineveh, Shushan, Shechem, and Bethel—have been diligently explored. All of this—the labors of the field archaeologist and those of the scholar who deciphers and publishes ancient texts—has provided a veritable wealth of information about Bible times and thus about the Bible itself. It has clarified numerous formerly obscure passages of Scripture, supplemented information provided by the Bible, and confirmed many historical statements. Biblical archaeology thus has a threefold purpose and value for students of the Bible: 1. It provides contemporary illustrations of customs and practices mentioned in the Bible and clarifies obscure statements. 2. It furnishes much supplementary material, especially to the historical portions. 3. It corroborates the accuracy of the Bible record.

Seventh-day Adventist Interest in Biblical Archaeology. For more than a century Seventh-day Adventists have taken note of archaeological discoveries that tended to confirm the credibility of the Scriptures. Beginning with volume 10 (1857), the *Review and Herald* occasionally carried articles and notes of archaeological news, taken mostly from newspapers and therefore not always altogether reliable. Sometimes articles written by prominent scholars were reprinted. Of these, the earliest appeared in the issue for Apr. 29, 1884 (pp. 275-277). It was written by the American Assyriologist William Hayes Ward for the *Sunday School Times,* from which it was reprinted. Later, when archaeological material became more plentiful, series of articles, sometimes illustrated with pictures, appeared in SDA journals. One of these was M. E. Kern's series of seven articles entitled "The Bible and the Ancient Monuments," which ran in the *Review and Herald* during August and September 1905 and covered archaeological discoveries in Egypt, Babylonia, Assyria, and Palestine.

Writers of SDA books also made use of new historical knowledge obtained through archaeological discoveries. For instance, in his earliest editions of *Thoughts on the Book of Daniel,* Uriah Smith referred to King Belshazzar of Dan. 5 as a grandson of Nebuchadnezzar. In reply to a reader's query, he explained in the *Review and Herald* for

Mar. 11, 1873, that he had followed Prideaux in equating Belshazzar with Nabonidus, known from ancient sources as the last king of Babylon. In 1888, however, he published an article in the *Review and Herald* for Dec. 4 of that year in which he referred to texts found at Tell el-Muqaiyar (Ur) indicating that Belshazzar was Nabonidus' firstborn son. He therefore accepted a coregency for Nabonidus and Belshazzar during the last years of Babylon's history. Later editions of Smith's work on Daniel set forth this new information.

Books on ancient history and the fulfillment of prophecy such as those by A. T. Jones, which enjoyed great popularity among SDAs around the turn of the century, also utilized new historical knowledge in a limited way, but were based mainly on classical Greek and Roman sources.

The first book of a purely archaeological nature written by an SDA was W. W. Prescott's *The Spade and the Bible* (Revell, 1933), a book of 216 pages. For many years an educator and later an editor of the *Review and Herald,* the author made use of a large amount of archaeological material that shed light on various phases of Old Testament history. Since the author was neither a professional archaeologist nor a linguist, and had to rely on secondhand sources for information, it is no surprise to find the material in his book not everywhere reliable, and, of course, rather out-of-date. The same can be said with regard to other, usually small, books on archaeology issued by SDA publishing houses, such as Roy F. Cottrell's *The Spade and the Book* (1947). Not directly on the subject of archaeology, but utilizing archaeological documents, was a book on the chronology of Judah and Israel, *The Mysterious Numbers of the Hebrew Kings* (1951; revised 1965), written by Edwin R. Thiele, of Emmanuel Missionary College, and published by the University of Chicago. Unlike the preceding above-mentioned books, which were written on the popular level, this was a scholarly treatment (based on his doctoral dissertation) harmonizing the biblical figures for the reigns with the generally accepted Assyrian and Babylonian chronology, and it achieved recognition among Old Testament scholars and contributed to increased respect for the accuracy of the Hebrew historians.

Archaeology and the SDA Theological Seminary. The SDA Theological Seminary, founded in 1934 as "The Advanced Bible School," lists Lynn H. Wood for the first time in its 1937 catalog as "Professor [of] Eastern Antiquities and Archaeology." During the following seven years various archaeological courses were continuously offered, but in 1944 a regular Department of Archaeology and History of Antiquity was organized with Wood as chair. This enabled students to obtain their master's degree in this field of studies. In 1951 Siegfried H. Horn became chair of this department, and in 1952 Wood retired from active teaching. When the seminary was reorganized in 1955, Horn became chair of the Department of OT Studies, but remained professor of archaeology and history of antiquity and continued to devote most of his time to the teaching of courses in this area. The first master's degree with a major in archaeology and history of antiquity was conferred in 1947; by 1967 a total of 43 such degrees had been conferred. Beginning in 1966, the Master of Arts in Religion with a concentration in archaeology was taken over by the School of Graduate Studies of Andrews University.

In 1975 Gerhard Hasel was asked to direct the Ph.D./Th.D. program at the seminary. One of the cognate areas of this new doctoral program, Biblical Archaeology and History of Antiquity, has been selected by a large number of doctoral students since this program began. Also, a number of doctoral dissertations have dealt specifically with archaeological topics. These include "The Hellenistic and Roman Strata of Hesban," by Larry A. Mitchell (1980), "Archaeology in Adventist Literature Between 1937-1980," by Lloyd A. Willis (1982), and "The Byzantine Strata of Hesban," by J. Bjornar Storfjell (1983). Most of these dissertations have been published by Andrews University Press and the Institute of Archaeology.

Not only has archaeology expanded in the seminary's academic program, but Andrews University has provided important research facilities for archaeology. In 1970 an archaeological museum was opened on the campus of Andrews University. In 1978 it was named the Horn Archaeology Museum in honor of its founder and first curator. The museum was housed in the James White Library until 1982, when it moved into its own three-story building (the former headquarters building for the Lake Union Conference and the Geoscience Research Institute) in close proximity to the SDA Theological Seminary. The museum contains some 7,000 artifacts of art and utility from the ancient Near East. Many objects such as coins, pottery, cuneiform tablets, sculptures, tools, weapons, figurines, jewelry, seals, and glass vessels have come to this collection through purchase or as gifts. Nearly 2,000 artifacts were obtained during the archaeological expeditions to Heshbon. These objects serve as visual aids for a better understanding of certain biblical passages of a historical, religious, or cultural nature. This museum houses also the Hartford Seminary Foundation Cuneiform Tablet Collection, consisting of about 3,000 ancient clay tablets ranging from the Sumerian period to Neo-Babylonian times. They are being studied with the aim of eventually publishing their contents. Curators of the Horn Archaeology Museum have included Lawrence T. Geraty, J. Bjornar Storfjell, and David Merling.

In 1980 the board of trustees established the Andrews University Institute of Archaeology, under the administration of the theological Seminary, to coordinate and direct the archaeological programs and activities of the university. The institute is housed in the same building as the Horn Archaeology Museum and contains offices, workrooms, storage rooms, a darkroom, and the Horn Archaeological Library. Its first director was Lawrence T. Geraty, who served in this capacity from 1980 until 1986. William H. Shea served as director from 1986 to 1987, and was followed by J. Bjornar Storfjell, who assumed this role from 1987 to 1988 Randall W. Younker has served as director of the institute since 1988. In 1991 P. David Merling and Øystein S. LaBianca were appointed as associate directors of the institute. Ralph Hendrix was appointed that same year to serve as managing editor of archaeological publications.

Seventh-day Adventist Archaeologists. For further information on Lynn H. Wood (1887-1976) and Siegfried H. Horn (1908-1993), *see* Wood, Lynn H., and Horn, Siegfried H.

Lawrence T. Geraty (1940-) received his B.A. in Theology from Pacific Union College, his M.A. in Old Testament from Andrews University, where he also received a B.D. degree, and his Ph.D. in Hebrew Bible and Syro-Palestinian Archaeology from Harvard University under G. Ernest Wright in 1972. His dissertation was on "Third and Fourth Century B.C. Ostraca From Khirbet el Kom." From 1972 to 1985 Geraty served as professor of archaeology and history of antiquity at the SDA Theological Seminary. From 1976 to 1985 Geraty also functioned as the curator of the Horn Archaeology Museum. In 1981 he founded the Institute of Archaeology at Andrews University and served as its first director from 1981 until 1985. He was on the Heshbon dig staff from its beginning and spent a year in Jerusalem (1970-1971), during which time he participated in several archaeological expeditions sponsored by the Albright Institute of Archaeological Research, where he served as Thayer fellow. Geraty directed the 1974 and 1976 excavation seasons at Hesban, Jordan (taking over this position from Horn); functioned as senior adviser for archeological investigations at Ein-Gedi, Israel (1979), Tell Jalul, Jordan (1992), and initiated the Madaba Plains Project, Jordan, as senior project director in 1984. Geraty has continued in this role during the subsequent excavation seasons in 1987, 1989, 1992, and 1994. In 1985 Geraty accepted an invitation to become president of Atlantic Union College with the rank of professor of archaeology. He continued in this position until 1993, when he accepted the offer to become president of La Sierra University with the rank of professor of archaeology. In spite of his duties as a president of an academic institution, Geraty continued to be active in scholarly circles, serving on numerous committees for the American Schools of Oriental Research and as vice president and acting president of the American Center of Oriental Research in Amman, Jordan. He has served as coeditor for both the Hesban and Madaba Plains final publication series and has published numerous articles in church and scholarly journals.

Larry G. Herr (1946-) received his Ph.D. in Near Eastern Studies from Harvard University in 1971. His dissertation dealt with scripts of ancient northwest Semitic seals. Herr taught at the Seventh-day Adventist Theological Seminary, Far East, from 1978 to 1984. Since 1984 he has been a professor at Canadian Union College. Herr has done extensive archaeological fieldwork. He was an area supervisor at Hesban during the 1974 and 1976 seasons, director of the Amman Airport Project in 1976, chief archaeologist of the Hesban North Church Project in 1978, and chief archaeologist and director of excavations at Tell el-ᶜUmeiri during the 1984, 1987, 1989, and 1992 seasons. Herr also is a codirector of the Madaba Plains Project and wrote the excavation manual for that project. Herr has been active in professional archaeological circles, especially the American Schools of Oriental Research (ASOR), where he has served as an editor for some of their publication series. Herr also has been an American Schools of Oriental Research (ASOR) fellow (1974-1975) and a resident scholar at the Albright Institute of Archaeological Research in Jerusalem (1993-1994). Herr has numerous publications in church and scholarly journals and has served as senior coeditor of the final publication series for the Madaba Plains Project.

Øystein S. LaBianca (1949-) received his Ph.D. from Brandeis University in 1987 in anthropology. He has been a professor of anthropology at Andrews University since 1980. He also served as chair of the Behavioral Science Department from 1981 to 1992. With Geraty, LaBianca helped establish the Institute of Archaeology at Andrews and initiated the Madaba Plains Project in Jordan. In 1991 he was appointed associate director of the Institute of Archaeology at Andrews University. LaBianca's archaeological fieldwork includes serving as staff anthropologist (intially with Robert Little of Andrews University) for the Hesban excavations (1971, 1973, 1974, and 1976 seasons), chief anthropologist of the Wadi Tumilat Project in Egypt in 1979-1985, and director of regional survey for the Madaba Plains Project during the 1984, 1987, 1989, and 1992 seasons. He also has overseen the ecolab and initiated careful analysis of bone remains that provided the foundation for his food systems theory. LaBianca has been active in professional archaeological and anthropological societies, in which he has organized and chaired several sessions. He has been an Albright fellow at the American Center for Oriental Research (ACOR) in Amman, Jordan. He also has been active in archaeological publications. In addition to publishing numerous scholarly articles, he is coeditor for both the Hesban and Madaba Plains final publication series. His dissertation "Sedentarization and Nomadization" (vol. 1 of the Hesban series) provided an anthropological framework for interpreting the history of Heshbon.

Randall W. Younker (1953-) graduated from Pacific Union College with a B.A. in religion in 1975 and an M.A. in biology from that same school in 1977. After additional graduate studies in archaeology and anthropology at California State University, Sacramento, and Andrews University, Younker joined the Old Testament Department of the SDA Theological Seminary in 1986 as an assistant professor of Old Testament and Biblical Archaeology. That same year, he was appointed director of the Institute of Archaeology at Andrews University. Since then Younker has continued his doctoral work in Near Eastern archaeology at the University of Arizona under William G. Dever. His archaeological fieldwork includes five seasons on the staff of Tell Dor in Israel (1980-1984), staff ecologist and surveyor for Tell el-ᶜUmeiri in 1984 and 1987, cordirector of the Madaba Plains Project (MPP), in charge of excavations at Tell Jawa and El-Dreijat in 1989, associate director of excavations at Tell Gezer, Israel, with William G. Dever in 1990, and director of excavations at the MMP's newest site in Jordan, Tell Jalul in 1992. In addition to fieldwork, Younker served on the board of the Albright Institute of Archaeological Research in Jerusalem as a corporate trustee for the 1992-1994 term. Younker has coedited two books and published more than 30 scholarly articles and reviews dealing with archaeology.

Douglas R. Clark (1947-) received his doctorate in 1984 from Vanderbilt University. He has served as Old Testament professor at Southwestern Adventist College (1975-1987) and Walla Walla College (1987-). Since 1990 he has been dean of the School of Theology at Walla Walla and professor of Old Testament and Archaeology. Clark has been active in archaeological fieldwork. He served on the staff of the Hesban excavation as a square supervisor during the 1973 and 1976 seasons and was a field supervisor at Tell el-ᶜUmeiri during the 1984, 1987, 1989, and 1992 seasons. He has overseen the excavation of the most extensive ancient fortification system in Jordan. Clark also has been the consortium director for the Madaba Plains Project in Jordan. He has published a number of archaeological articles in both church and scholarly journals and is a contributor to the Madaba Plains Project final publication series.

David P. Merling (1948-) received his B.A. and M.Div. from Andrews University, where he also has pursued doctoral studies with an emphasis in archaeology. From 1984 to 1986 Merling was the assistant curator of the Horn Archaeological Museum. Since 1986 he has been the curator for the museum and assistant professor of Archaeology and History of Antiquity at the SDA Theological Seminary. In 1991 he was appointed an associate director of the Institute of Archaeology at that institution. Merlings' archaeological fieldwork includes serving as a square supervisor at Hesban in 1974 and at Tell el-ᶜUmeiri during the 1984 and 1987 seasons, field supervisor at Tell Gezer in 1990, and associate director at Tell Jalul in 1992. Merling has been responsible for completing the renovation of the Horn Archaeology Museum. He has also been responsible for setting up the Horn Archaeological Library at the Institute of Archaeology, a research library with more than 5,000 scholarly volumes. Merling has published several articles on archaeology in church and scholarly journals. Most recently he has served as coeditor and contributor of the 25-year anniversary volume of the Hesban excavations published by the Institute of Archaeology at Andrews University.

Boguslaw Dabrowski (1964-) is a doctoral student in archaeology at the University of Krakow in Poland. He teaches at Polish Spiritual Seminary, Podkowa Lesna, Poland. His fieldwork includes excavation with the Madaba Plains Project during the 1987, 1989, and 1992 seasons. After the 1992 season Dabrowski was appointed field director of the tomb excavation for Tell el-ᶜUmeiri. He founded the Levant Foundation Poland in order to further Polish archaeological research in the Middle East. He also has published several scholarly articles in both Polish and English.

S. Douglas Waterhouse (1931-) completed his Ph.D. in 1965 at the University of Michigan. His dissertation is entitled "Syria in the Amarna Age: A Borderland Between Conflicting Empires." He has taught at Andrews University since 1963. His archaeological fieldwork includes participation in all five seasons at Hesban and the 1992 season at Tell el-ᶜUmeiri. Waterhouse was responsible for starting the Hesban survey, which was then taken up by others, and the excavation of the Roman period tombs near Hesban. He has published several articles on archaeology in various journals, including *Ministry* and *Andrews University Seminary Studies.* He also is publishing an article on the Hesban tombs for the final publication series.

J. Bjornar Storfjell (1944-) received his Ph.D. from Andrews University in 1983. His dissertation dealt with the Byzantine strata at Hesban. Since 1980 Storfjell has been a professor of archaeology and history of antiquity in the Old Testament Department of the SDA Theological Seminary. He also has held both the position of curator of the Horn Archaeology Museum and director of the Institute of Archaeology at Andrews University. His archaeological fieldwork includes staff positions with the Hesban excavation during the 1976 season, the Tell el-Hesi Project in 1981, administrative director of the Tell el-ᶜUmeiri excavation in 1987, and ceramicist for the Wadi es-Siah Project during the 1988-1989 seasons. In addition to various articles he has written for church and scholarly journals, Storfjell's dissertation on the Byzantine period at Hesban has been published as part of the Hesban final publications series by Andrews University Press and the Institute of Archaeology.

Since 1972 Loma Linda University also has become involved in archaeological fieldwork by participating in the excavations of Caesarea, Israel, as one of the sponsoring institutions of a consortium. Kenneth L. Vine (1923-), chair of the Department of Religion of the College of Arts and Sciences (now retired), and James H. Stirling (1921-), associate chair of the Department of Sociology and Anthropology of the same college, took part in the excavations. Vine was granted a Ph.D. in Near Eastern studies from the University of Michigan in 1965 with a dissertation entitled "The Establishment of Baal at Ugarit." He had participated also in the excavations of biblical Ai in 1966, and was president of Middle East College from 1965 to 1971. Vine continued to participate in the Caesarea expedition again in 1974, while Stirling transferred to the Heshbon expedition, which Loma Linda University also supported during the 1974 season.

Vine's publications include "Byzantine Written Lamps From Caesarea Maritima," in the *Robert Bull Festschrift* (1986); "Ceramic Lamps From the Hippodrome of Caesarea Maritima, 1974," in the *Horn Festschrift* (1986), and "Terracotta Lamps of Caesarea Maritima, 1971-1976," preliminary report in *The Joint Expedition to Caesarea Maritima* (1982).

Another important SDA archaeological scholar is William H. Shea (1932-), who received his Ph.D. in ancient Near Eastern studies from the University of Michigan in 1976. He joined the Old Testament faculty of the SDA Theological Seminary at Andrews in 1972. In addition to various Old Testament classes, Shea taught courses in ancient Near Eastern history, archaeology, and languages. During the 1985-1986 academic year, Shea also directed the Institute of Archaeology. Since 1986 Shea has been an associate director of the Biblical Research Institute at the General Conference of Seventh-day Adventists. His responsibilities there have included, among other things, continued research on important biblical, historical, and archaeological issues and the direction of biblical studies and archaeologica tours of the

Holy Land out of the church's Jerusalem study center. In addition to field seasons at Gezer (1966-1967) and Hesban (1971), Shea has written extensively on archaeological topics in almost every major scholarly journal dealing with ancient Near Eastern studies. Some of his important publications include "Sennacherib's Second Palestinian Campaign," in *Journal of Biblical Literature;* "The Eblaite Letter to Hamazi," in *Oriens Antiquus* (1984); "Date of the Exodus," in the *International Standard Bible Encyclopedia* (1982); "Menahem and Tiglath-Pileser III," in the *Journal of Near Eastern Studies* (1978); and "The Date and Significance of the Samaria Ostraca," in the *Israel Exploration Journal* (1977).

Paul F. Bork (1924-) received his Ph.D. from the California Graduate School of Theology in 1971. He began his college teaching career at Pacific Union College in 1967, where he was a professor of Old Testament and Archaeology. He chaired the Religion Department at PUC from 1986 to 1989. Bork also participated in several archaeological projects in the Middle East, including the 1971 and 1972 seasons at Tell Gezer, the 1976 season at Mount Zion area in the old city of Jerusalem, and the 1978 and 1979 seasons at the City of David. Bork also began and directed the PUC Religion Department extension program at Jerusalem, which continued for five years until taken over by the General Conference. Bork followed Horn's tradition of making archaeological discoveries accessible to the average SDA layperson and minister by numerous publications in the *Adventist Review* and *Ministry* magazines. He also published several books on archaeology including *The World of Moses* (1978) and *Out of the City, Across the Sands* (1982).

Udo Worschech (1947-) studied theology and biblical archaeology at Andrews University (M.A., 1971). He has taught at the Marienhoehe SDA Theological Seminary, Darmstadt, Germany, since 1972 and the J. W. Goethe-Universitat since 1984. He directed several seasons of excavations at Tell Balu'a, an Iron Age Moabite site in Jordan. His publications include *Die Beziahungen Moabs zu Israel und Agypten in der Eisenzeit*, a scholarly work on the emergence of the Moabite polity in Jordan, and *Das Land Jenseits des Jordan: Biblische Archaologie in Jordanien,* a popular work on biblical archaeology in Jordan.

Archaeological Fieldwork. Beginning with the summer of 1968, Andrews University sponsored an archaeological expedition to biblical Heshbon in Jordan. The first three seasons of excavations (1968, 1971, 1973), which were supported also by the American Center for Oriental Research in Amman and by Calvin Theological Seminary in Grand Rapids, Michigan, were directed by Siegfried Horn.

The excavations brought to light remains of the ancient city of Heshbon from the twelfth century to the fourteenth century A.D. Among them were parts of the ancient city's fortifications; a huge water reservoir, probably one of the pools mentioned in Song of Solomon 7:4; the remains of a Roman cult center consisting of a *via sacra,* a monumental stairway leading to a temple on the summit of the mound, and the foundations of that temple; ruins of the Christian church of the early Christian centuries when Heshbon was the seat of a bishop; and remains of later structures, including the only complete Mamluk bath ever found in Jordan.

Several early Roman and Byzantine tombs, some containing rich contents, were also discovered and excavated, among them two family tombs of the first century A.D., each closed with a rolling stone. The excavations have brought to light no remains earlier than the twelfth century B.C., which leads to the conclusion that the Heshbon of King Sihon of the Amorites, conquered by the Israelites under Moses, must have been located at another site, from which it was transferred after its conquest by the Israelites to the site that for the past 3,000 years has carried the name of Heshbon *(Esbus* in Greek and Latin, and *Ḥesbân* in Arabic).

Beginning with the fourth season of excavations (1974), the directorship of the Heshbon expedition was taken over by Lawrence T. Geraty, who was then assistant professor of Old Testament studies at the seminary. Preliminary reports on the results of the Heshbon expedition have regularly been published in popular form in the *Adventist Review,* and since 1969 in a more scientific form in the *Andrews University Seminary Studies*. About half of the dozen or so final report volumes of the Hesban Project have been published by Andrews University Press and the Institute of Archaeology.

The successor to the Heshbon excavation, and the first project to be coordinated by the new Institute of Archaeology at Andrews University, was the Madaba Plains Project, begun in 1984 with additional seasons in 1987, 1989, 1992, and 1994. Leadership of this project includes Lawrence Geraty, senior project director; Larry Herr, director of the Tell el-ᶜUmeiri excavations; Øystein LaBianca, director of hinterland surveys; Randall Younker, director of the Tell Jalul excavation; and Doug Clark, consortium director. The archaeological findings of the Madaba Plains Project include impressive settlement remains from Tell el-ᶜUmeiri, including an Iron Age II (Assyrian and Babylonian periods) citadel and fortification systems, a Late Bronze Age occupation, and an Early Bronze Age (patriarchal period) residential area. The survey discovered numerous Iron Age farmsteads with features similar to those described in Isaiah 5:1-7. Important Ammonite inscriptions have been found, including one that has the impression of a servant of Baalis, an Ammonite king mentioned in Jeremiah 40:14 (discovered by Lloyd Willis, of Southwestern Adventist College). Another Ammonite inscription testifies to the presence of an Ammonite province during the Persian period. New excavations at Jalul have found evidence of the city gateways of the ninth and eighth centuries B.C., as well as evidence of destruction from the premonarchal period (Iron Age I). There also is evidence of Late Bronze Age occupation from the period of Israel's wandering and conquest.

In addition to the Madaba Plains Project, the Institute of Archaeology sponsored a single season dig at Tell Gezer, Israel, in 1990. Randall Younker and David Merling, along with a number of graduate students from Andrews University, joined William G. Dever and a number of his graduate students from the University of Arizona for this excavation. This dig brought additional evidence for the existence of Solomonic building activity described in 1 Kings 9:17. Specifically, it seems certain that, based on new stratigraphic and ceramic evidence, the famous "six-chambered gateway" and adjoining palace were indeed built by Solomon during the tenth century B.C. This building activity at Gezer was preceded by a dramatic destruction layer that can be associated with the sack of Gezer by an Egyptian pharaoh mentioned in 1 Kings 9:16.

Contribution of SDA Archaeological Scholarship. Careful fieldwork and prompt and unbiased publication of the results have created respect for Andrews University archaeologists on the part of the scholarly community at large. For example, Phil King, former president of the American Schools of Oriental Research, writes in his *American Archaeology in the Mideast: A History of the American Schools of Oriental Research* (1983): "The archaeology of Jordan owes an extraordinary debt of gratitude to the Hesban expedition, especially for its pioneering efforts in many areas of archaeological research." "Through its field school, Hesban has touched almost every dig in Jordan by serving as the training ground for scores of graduate students, several of whom now direct their own projects." Similarly, William G. Dever, former editor of the *Bulletin of the American Schools of Oriental Research* (BASOR) and a leading Syro-Palestinian archaeologist, writes: "This combined project has long since become one of the most sophisticated and truly interdisciplinary of all American archaeological excavations in the Middle East. While others talk ad nauseam about 'research design,' 'holistic approaches,' 'total retrieval,' 'ecology,' and the 'new archaeology'. . . these people do it. The publication of the Hesban excavations has propelled Seventh-day Adventist archaeology—against all the odds—into the very forefront of Near Eastern archaeology" (BASOR 190-191, 1991).

While these accomplishments can give the SDA Church a certain amount of pride, we must never lose sight of the fact that our ultimate goal in pursuing this specialized area of biblical research is to help make God's Word, which gives the world the good news of salvation, more understandable to those of us who are separated by time and distance from the world to which God originally communicated.

ARCHANGEL MICHAEL. *See* Michael, the Archangel.

ARCHITECTURE. *See* Church Buildings.

ARCHIVES. The General Conference Archives serves as "the headquarters depository for documents, records, correspondence, publications, photographs, recordings, films, etc., that have historical and cultural value to the Seventh-day Adventist Church, . . . particularly materials produced or collected by the General Conference as an institution" (General Conference Committee minutes, Nov. 8, 1973). Established July 1, 1973, this office functions under the guidance of the Archives and Statistics Committee, chaired by the General Conference secretary. For about 70 years prior to 1973, the statistical secretary of the General Conference preserved special documents and reports, minutes, and printed items, including many of the church's publications. As early as the 1940s or 1950s, members of the General Conference Secretariat spoke of having an archives, but it was not until late 1972 and early 1973, when urgings of SDA historians and the proposal to develop overseas Ellen G. White-SDA research centers converged, that action was taken to establish a General Conference Archives. The archivist also functions as records manager of the General Conference, and is a consultant for the archival functions of the world divisions and of General Conference institutions.

Records housed at the GC Archives span the years from the 1830s to the present. Most are the files of the General Conference as the central administrative body of the Seventh-day Adventist Church. The vast percentage of the more than 9,000 feet (2,750 meters) of records are available to responsible researchers and church leaders for research use.

At the 1975 General Conference session it was voted to combine Archives with the Statistical Office, henceforth to be known as Archives and Statistics.

F. Donald Yost was archivist from 1973 to 1975. In 1975 he became the director of Archives and Statistics.

ARCHIVES AND STATISTICS. An office of the General Conference, under the direction of the GC secretary, established at the General Conference session of 1975 to combine the work of statistical secretary and archivist.

Director: F. Donald Yost, 1975- .

ARCHIVIST (1973-1975). A member of the General Conference administrative staff charged with the responsibility of preserving historical records of the GC and making them available for administrative and research use. Since 1975, when the position was combined with that of the statistical secretary to become director of Archives and Statistics, the director has been elected at the General Conference session and is responsible to the General Conference Committee. *(See* Archives; Statistical Secretary.)

Archivist: F. Donald Yost, 1973-1975.

ARDMORE ADVENTIST HOSPITAL. A general hospital of 104-bed capacity owned and operated by the Oklahoma Conference at Ardmore, Oklahoma, from May 1959 to April 1992. In 1947 Drs. J. B. McConnell, A. W. Truman, Floyd Bates, and Ethel Walker secured the old Von Keller Hospital and incorporated the Ardmore Sanitarium and Hospital as a nonprofit, self-supporting institution.

Although privately owned, the hospital maintained close connections with the church organization. In 1949 the Southwestern Union Conference president and the Oklahoma Conference president were invited to participate in the board meetings, and this participation continued until an arrangement was made in 1957 for the ownership of the hospital to be assumed by the Oklahoma Conference, under the leadership of W. A. Dessain, president.

A new $400,000 hospital building was opened on May 10, 1959. In 1960 a women's auxiliary was organized, whose volunteers from the community donated many hours, performing extra services for the patients. Two workers especially, Mrs. Eldora Taylor of the office staff and Roy M. Johnson of the board, worked untiringly and at personal sacrifice to build up the institution. Early managers and administrators, in the period of private ownership, were William G. Nelson, Robert Trimble, Sam Bailey, W. H. Wineland, and Myron Lysinger.

From 1980 to 1987 Ardmore Adventist Hospital was operated by Adventist Health System/Sunbelt. After that it was managed by the Oklahoma Conference. It was closed in April 1992.

Administrators: Earl Nelson, 1956-1958; Kent Griffin, 1958-1959; Robert E. Trimble, 1959-1962; Charles Martin, 1962-1965; W. V. Wiist, 1965-1971; John Koubs, 1971-1974; James C. Culpepper, 1974-1976; W. C. McConnell, 1976-1977; Sam C. Loewen, 1978-1990; William Straight, 1990-1992.

ARGENTINA. A federal republic situated in the southern part of South America. It is bounded on the west by the Andes Mountains, which separate it from Chile; rivers provide a large section of its boundaries with Uruguay, Brazil, Paraguay, and Bolivia on the north and east. It has an area of 1,065,189 square miles (2,758,840 square kilometers), and an estimated population (1994) of 34 million. The inhabitants of Argentina are largely of Latin and Germanic origin, with full-blooded Indians representing less than 1 percent of the population. Illiteracy is low.

More than 90 percent of the people profess Catholicism. The Roman Catholic Church is supported by the state, but all other churches are granted freedom of worship.

Argentina has mountain ranges to the west, extensive plains to the east, and vast plateaus to the south. The climate is moderate, but with the greater part of the rainfall in the east. Two thirds of the country is arid. Because of the scarcity of commodities that arose during the two world wars, light and medium-heavy industries were added to the cattle raising and agriculture that had always been the backbone of the economy.

Historical Background. Argentina probably was discovered by Juan Diaz de Solís, who about 1515 claimed for Spain the Río de la Plata, the estuary at the confluence of the Paraná and Uruguay rivers, on whose bank Buenos Aires is situated. In 1536 Pedro de Mendoza, leader of a large expedition, founded a settlement where the city now stands, which, repeatedly attacked by the Indians, was later abandoned. Eventually the territory of Argentina was settled, not from the Atlantic side but from Peru, by settlers who came from the conquered Inca Empire. Argentina, along with much of the territory of the present republics of Uruguay, Paraguay, and Bolivia, was made subject to the viceroyalty of Peru, and the settlers were forced to trade with Europe by way of Lima. The *criollos,* the area's inhabitants of Spanish extraction, felt that Spain, through this viceroyalty, intended to exploit their land solely for her benefit. This policy produced smuggling and considerable unrest. Finally, in 1776 the new viceroyalty of Río de la Plata was created for this eastern territory, with the privilege of free commerce with Spain granted to it. The salutary effect of this policy was immediately felt in the increased prosperity of the country.

As part of this viceroyalty, Argentina was under Spanish domination until the beginning of the nineteenth century. On May 25, 1810, a junta consisting of nine men was set up, which professed to rule in the name of the king of Spain, but which actually ruled independently. This pretense was dropped on July 9, 1816, when independence was declared. A series of civil wars disturbed the country for the next 37 years.

In 1853 a national constitution was ratified, which, with certain reforms, is still in force. In spite of political instability since 1930, the religious liberty that was guaranteed by article 14 of the national constitution has not been restricted.

Seventh-day Adventist Statistics. The territory of Argentina is part of the Austral Union Conference (which also includes Paraguay and Uruguay) in the South American Division, and is divided into three conferences and two missions. Statistics (1992) for *Argentina:* churches, 501; members, 62,698; church or elementary schools, 57; ordained ministers, 153; licensed ministers, 50; Bible instructors, 5; full-time teachers, 434. Headquarters for the Austral Union Conference are at Calle Echeverria 1452, 1602 Florida, Buenos Aires, Argentina.

Statistics for the conferences and the missions—*Buenos Aires Conference:* churches, 122; members, 15,642; church or elementary schools, 6; ordained ministers, 35; licensed ministers, 14; Bible instructors, 3; full-time teachers, 77. Headquarters: Uriarte 2429, 1425 Capital Federal, Buenos Aires, Argentina. *Central Argentine Conference:* churches, 140; members, 17,833; church or elementary schools, 18; ordained ministers, 35; licensed ministers, 14; Bible instructors, 1; full-time teachers, 90. Headquarters: Avenida Sabattini 1662, Barrio Maipu, 5014 Cordoba, Argentina. *North Argentine Conference:* churches, 114; members, 14,029; church or elementary schools, 23; ordained ministers, 16; licensed ministers, 10; full-time teachers, 124. Headquarters: Mexico 830, Barrio Yapeyu, 3400 Corrientes, Argentina. *Northwest Argentine Mission:* churches, 43; members, 7,793; church or elementary schools, 3; ordained ministers, 7; licensed ministers, 4; full-time teachers, 140. Headquarters: Avenida Mate de Luna 2399, 4000 San Miguel de Tucuman, Argentina. *South Argentine Mission:* churches, 82; members, 7,401; church or elementary schools, 7; ordained ministers, 17; licensed ministers, 5; Bible instructors, 1; full-time teachers, 57. Headquarters: Villarino 39, 8000 Bahia Blanca, Buenos Aires, Argentina.

Institutions. Balcarce Adventist Academy; Belgrano Adventist Medical Clinic; Buenos Aires Adventist Academy; Buenos Aires Old People's Home; Buenos Aires Publishing House; Loma Linda Adventist Sanitarium; Los Polvorines Adventist Academy; Morón Adventist Academy; Northeast Argentine Academy; Northeast Argentine Sanitarium; Resistencia Adventist Academy; River Plate Adventist University; River Plate Sanitarium and Hospital; Santa Fe Adventist Academy; South American Division Health Food Company (Alimentos Granix); Velez Sarsfield Adventist Academy; Victor Ampuero Matta Adventist Academy.

Beginnings of Seventh-day Adventist Work. *Forerunners.* Long before Seventh-day Adventists entered Argentina, a book on the second coming of Christ was circulated in the country—*La Venida del Mesías en Gloria y Magestad* ("The Coming of the Messiah in Glory and Majesty"), written by a Chilean

Jesuit, Manuel Lacunza (1731-1801). It was Manuel Belgrano, an Argentinian, who had financed a London edition of Lacunza's book in 1816 for distribution in Argentina. Among those who read this work and were influenced by it was a prominent Argentinian patriot, Francisco Ramos Mexía (1773-1828), who also kept the seventh-day Sabbath, having learned of it through reading the Bible. Ramos Mexía encountered considerable opposition from the Roman clergy when some of his friends joined with him in his beliefs and many Indians living on his estates began to observe the Sabbath. Other prominent men who knew and appreciated Lacunza's book were Dean Gregorio Funes and Domingo Faustino Sarmiento.

Pre-SDA Sabbathkeepers. By 1886 there were two groups of Sabbathkeepers in Argentina, one at the colony of Esperanza and the other at a colony near Reconquista, both in Santa Fe Province. There are at least three slightly different versions of how the group at Esperanza began to observe the Sabbath, and two of how the group near Reconquista became interested in the SDA message. These accounts come from the 1890s after SDAs had entered South America.

Writing from Buenos Aires on Feb. 3, 1892, C. A. Nowlen and E. W. Snyder, who with A. B. Stauffer were the first SDA canvassers in South America, reported: "Before closing we would speak of an experience of Brother Stauffer, who left us three weeks ago for the German colonies of Santa Fe Province. Having notified our brethren at Esperanza of his coming, he was met at the depot on his arrival there and taken to this brother's home. Through the kindness of a German neighbor who acted as an interpreter, he learned something of their history.

"It seems that about three years since, four men there—all heads of families—were at church one Sunday, and taking up the study of the Sabbath question, they soon came to the conclusion that the seventh day is the Sabbath, and at once with their families began its observance. This occurred before they had received a line of literature from the Seventh-day Adventists" *(The Home Missionary* 4:91, 92, April 1892).

In 1896 Jean Vuilleumier, visiting the Sabbathkeepers at the colony of Esperanza, reported that the "first Sabbathkeeping families" in Argentina had been members of the Baptist Church *(Review and Herald* 73:527, Aug. 18, 1896). Speaking of the group a few months before, he said: "This is where, 10 or 11 years ago, three heads of families, a Belgian, a Swiss, and a native of Swiss parentage, embraced the Sabbath after reading, in a Baptist paper, an account of Seventh-day Adventist baptisms in Switzerland" *(ibid.* 73:236, Apr. 14, 1896).

Writing many years later in the *Revista Adventista,* E. W. Thomann recounted a somewhat different version of these Sabbathkeepers as told to him by Mrs. Anna Dupertuis. He wrote: "In 1885 a group of Swiss-French Baptist colonists living in the vicinity of Felicia in the province of Santa Fe . . . discovered spontaneously, through the study of the Bible, that God commands the keeping, not of Sunday, the first day of the week, but of the Sabbath or seventh day. This subject so impressed them that they could not hide it, and upon being visited by their pastor, Mr. Pablo Besson, they told him of their discovery. However, he did not attach much importance to the subject, and tried in vain to dissuade them from keeping the Sabbath" (translated from *Revista Adventista* 34:6, June 18, 1934).

Thomann went on to say that Besson informed the group that the SDAs in Switzerland published a periodical in French entitled *Les Signes des Temps* ("The Signs of the Times"). Their curiosity was aroused by the discovery that they were not the only people who kept the Sabbath, and they begged Besson to send for a copy of *Les Signes* for them. He finally agreed, with much reluctance, to send for the periodical. Through the influence of this periodical the families of Jules (Julio) Dupertuis, Alberto Arn, and Floris Mathieu soon began observing the Sabbath *(Review and Herald* 66:710, Nov. 12, 1889). These and the Arnold Pidoux and Dobanton families of Grütly, Santa Fe, were baptized by Vuilleumier in 1896.

Some of the differences in Snyder's, Vuilleumier's, and Thomann's reports may be accounted for through errors in transmission, or possibly through confusing the basic story of how the colonists of Esperanza came to keep the Sabbath with a somewhat similar story of the colonists living near Reconquista.

Concerning the latter group, there are two versions. Relating in 1896 the story of how the Peverini family became Sabbathkeepers, Vuilleumier said: "The husband, Brother Peverini, was a Catholic, but embraced the Sabbath several years ago, after his wife [a Waldensian] had sent for *Les Signes,* of which she saw mention in the religious organ of the

Waldenses, while the journal was opposing the work of Brother Bourdeau and Sister [Ellen G.] White in the Piedmont Valleys. Sister Peverini handed *Les Signes* to a [Waldensian], Daniel Rostan, 18 miles (29 kilometers) farther north, who also began to keep the Sabbath" *(Revew and Herald* 73:541, Aug. 25, 1896).

A slightly different version of this story is related by N. Z. Town. Writing in 1899, he said that "about 13 years ago" Peverini saw, in a paper that came from Italy, an adverse criticism of Bourdeau, who was then preaching that the end of the world was near, suggesting that if his doctrine be true it hardly seemed necessary for the brethren in Basel to print *Les Signes des Temps* on such durable paper.

Being an ungodly man, Brother Peverini felt somewhat frightened to hear that the end might be near, and was anxious to see what the paper had to say about the matter, so Mrs. Peverini ordered the French *Signs* through her brother in Italy, and from their study of the truths presented therein, they began the observance of the true Sabbath *(The Missionary Magazine* 11:118, March 1899).

The members of both these groups of Sabbathkeepers were baptized into the SDA Church in 1896 by Jean Vuilleumier and Francis (Frank) H. Westphal *(Home Missionary,* 8:285, 286, December 1896). It appears impossible to determine which of the two groups began to observe the Sabbath first.

First Seventh-day Adventists. Early in 1890 four SDA families, comprising a total of 10 persons, came to Diamante, Entre Ríos Province, from Tampa, Kansas, U.S.A., and formed a colony nearby at Crespo. These were German farmers who had been colonists in Russia and had become SDAs while in the United States. The head of one of these families, Jorge Riffel, had been in Argentina several years before he lived in the United States. When he decided to return to Entre Ríos to share his faith with his neighbors, the families of Osvaldo Frick, Augusto Yanke, and Adam Zimmermann, who had emigrated directly from Russia to the United States, decided to accompany him. On their arrival they were met at Diamante by Reinhardt Hetze, a colonist of the same origin who had become an SDA after hearing something about SDAs in Russia. The next day they held the first Sabbath school service in South America, in a village near Diamante.

During this same year the General Conference assigned funds for beginning the work in South America and named a commission, subordinate to the Board of Foreign Missions, to study methods for beginning work in South America, Mexico, the East Indies, and Africa. It was this commission that sent the three colporteurs, Nowlen, Snyder, and Stauffer, who arrived in Buenos Aires in December 1891. They were joined a little later by a convert, Lionel Brooking. Over them was R. B. Craig, sent from the United States in March 1893 to take charge of the canvassing work. One of the members of the commission, L. C. Chadwick, made a trip to Argentina in July 1892. It was his reports and letters from the five colporteurs and from the SDA families in Entre Ríos and Santa Fe that resulted in the sending of Westphal, the first ordained SDA minister in South America. His task was to organize the East Coast Mission (Argentina, Uruguay, Paraguay, and Brazil). Arriving at La Plata, Buenos Aires, on Aug. 18, 1894, and leaving his family in Buenos Aires, he left for Entre Ríos Aug. 26, 1894, where on Sept. 9, 1894, he organized the first SDA church in what is now the South American Division (one of the earliest on that continent), in Crespo with 36 members. The following month he organized two other churches, one in San Cristóbal, Santa Fe, with 13 members, in the home of the Mangold family, and the other in Buenos Aires with 12 members. In 1895 and 1896 other ministers, Jean Vuilleumier, John McCarthy (superintendent of a seamen's mission, who had become an SDA in 1893), and Nelson Z. Town; a Bible instructor, Lucy Post; and a male nurse, Ole Oppegard, arrived.

In July 1896 the first SDA camp meeting in Argentina was held in Crespo, Entre Ríos, with 150 persons attending, and Westphal and McCarthy serving as speakers. By the end of 1900 the number of workers in the country had increased to 13—5 pastors, 1 licentiate, and 7 missionary licentiates, who took care of 11 churches (with 367 members), 4 companies (with 19 members), and 31 Sabbath schools (with 524 members). The headquarters of the East Coast Mission were in Buenos Aires.

Early Organization. The organized work in South America began with the arrival in 1894 of Westphal and his organizing of the East Coast Mission. In 1895, after a trip to Brazil, Westphal saw the desirability of setting apart Brazil as a separate mission. Upon his return on furlough to the United States in 1901, he recommended to the General Conference that such reorganization be made. His recommendation was accepted, but because of ill health he was unable to return to South America for several years. His place was filled by his brother, Joseph W. Westphal, who became president of the newly created South American Union Mission, with headquarters in Buenos Aires. The mission was divided into three fields: the Chilean Mission Field (changed to West Coast Mission in May 1902), the Brazil Mission Field (changed to Brazilian Conference in October 1901), and the Argentine Mission Field (which was called the River Plate Conference after November 1901).

At the first session of the newly established union, held in Palmar, Entre Ríos, from Nov. 10 to 20, 1901, the Argentine Mission Field became the River Plate Conference, with Nelson Z. Town as first president and Rodolfo Diriwaechter as secretary-treasurer. A period of rapid expansion followed.

In March 1906 the South American Union Mission was reorganized as the South American Union Conference in a meeting held in Paraná, Entre Ríos, Argentina. J. W. Westphal, who already had been president of the union mission since 1901, became the first president of the union conference, which office he held until 1916. After the formation of the South American Union Conference a new territorial distribution was made. In meetings held in Alberdi, Santa Fe, Argentina, from Oct. 25 to Nov. 4, 1906, the River Plate Conference was divided into the Uruguay Mission, the Alto Paraná Mission (Paraguay and the province of Misiones, Argentina), and the Argentine Conference. A further adjustment of territory was made in February 1912, when the Argentine Conference transferred the provinces of Chaco, Formosa, and half of Corrientes to the Alto Paraná Mission.

On Feb. 6, 1916, the South American Union Conference became the South American Division, with O. Montgomery as its first president, and with headquarters in Buenos Aires. Immediately after this, in a meeting held in La Plata, Argentina, the Austral Union was created, which comprised the Uruguay Mission, the Alto Paraná Mission, the Chile Mission, and the Argentine Conference.

Subsequent Reorganizations. The territory comprising the Austral Union, of which Argentina forms a part, has been reorganized several times since 1916. In that year the Argentine Conference comprised all of the republic of Argentina with the exception of the provinces of Formosa, Chaco, and the upper half of Corrientes, and the territory of Misiones, which belonged to the Alto Paraná Mission. In 1920 the Mendoza Mission was formed, consisting of the province of Mendoza.

The first major reorganization took place in 1921. According to a report by C. E. Krieghoff (former secretary and treasurer of the Argentine Conference), which appeared in the Mar. 28, 1921, issue of the *Revista Adventista* (21:8, 9): "It was voted during the conference that the provinces of San Juan and San Luis be transferred to form part of the Mendoza Mission; the territories of Río Negro and Neuquén will form the South Argentine Mission; the new Buenos Aires Conference will include the territory from Tigre to La Plata and Ensenada, including the city of Buenos Aires and its suburbs; the Central Argentine Mission will embrace the territories of La Pampa and that portion of Buenos Aires Province not included in the Buenos Aires Conference; the extant Argentine Conference will continue under the name of the North Argentine Conference and will embrace the provinces of Entre Ríos, Santa Fe, Córdoba, La Rioja, Santiago del Estero, Tucumán, Catamarca, Salta, Jujuy, and the territory of Los Andes."

According to the *Yearbook* (1922, pp. 123, 124), a further adjustment was made in 1921: Apparently the South Argentine Conference was dissolved and the provinces of Río Negro and Neuquén, which it comprised, were transferred to the Central Argentine Conference. About 1926 the Central Argentine Conference was disbanded, the whole of its territory becoming part of the Buenos Aires Conference (*Yearbook,* 1927, p. 183). About 1926 the Magellan Mission, consisting of the territories of Chubut, Santa Cruz, Tierra del Fuego, Magellan (belonging to Chile), and the Falkland Islands, was established *(ibid.,* p. 186).

In 1931 the North Argentine Conference was divided, the provinces of Entre Ríos, Santa Fe, and Córdoba going to make up a new Central Argentine Conference, and the provinces of Tucumán, Salta, Santiago del Estero, Catamarca, Jujuy, La Rioja, and the territory of Los Andes becoming the new Northwestern Argentine Mission. This mission was disbanded in 1934, and the provinces of Catamarca and La Rioja were transferred to the Mendoza Mission, which had been renamed Cuyo Mission about 1932; Santiago del Estero, Tucumán, Salta, Jujuy, and the territory of Los Andes became part of the Alto Paraná Mission, which was later renamed North Mission, or North Argentine Mission. In December 1947, Paraguay was detached from the North Mission to form the new Paraguay Mission.

Another important change occurred in 1943, when the Magellan Mission was absorbed into the Buenos Aires Conference.

In 1961 and 1971 major reorganizations occurred. In April 1961 the provinces of Chubut, Río Negro, Santa Cruz, Tierra del Fuego, and the Malvinas (Falkland) Islands were detached from the Buenos Aires Conference and became the Patagonia Mission. In December 1971 a general change took place in the administrative division of Argentina: a new South Argentine Conference was formed, comprising the provinces that formerly formed the Buenos Aires Conference and the Patagonia Mission, i.e., the Federal Capital, Buenos Aires, La Pampa, Neuquén, Río Negro, Chubut, Santa Cruz, Tierra del Fuego, and Malvinas (Falkland) Islands. Joining the provinces under the Central Argentina Conference and almost all of the Cuyo Mission, the new Central Argentina Conference was organized: Entre Ríos, Santa Fe, Córdoba, San Luis, Mendoza, San Juan, and La Rioja. In 1985 the South Argentine Mission was organized to include half the Buenos Aires Province and all the territories to the south of it, and the Falkland Islands. That which was not included is now part of the Buenos Aires Conference. In 1988 the North Argentine Conference was reorganized. It includes Corrientes, Misiones, Chaco, Formosa, and North Santa Fe provinces. Also the Northwest Argentine Mission was formed, which includes Catamarca, Jujuy, Salta, Santiago del Estero, and Tucumán provinces.

Departmental Work. 1. *Publications.* The first colporteurs came in 1891. The first colporteur director was R. B. Craig, 1893-1895 (*The Home Missionary* 7:270, December 1895; 7:100, June 1895). In 1894 a Tract Society was organized (called Sociedad Argentina de Tratados, 1896, and Sociedad Adventista de Tratados del Plata, 1908). Four years later three divisions of the society were formed to care for Uruguay, Argentina, and Alto Paraná. The first colporteur director appointed by the Argentine Conference was E. Max Trummer, in 1909. In 1912 there were 26 colporteurs. In 1994 there were 33 literature evangelists.

2. *Sabbath School.* The first Sabbath schools were organized in 1894 in Crespo, Entre Ríos, and in Buenos Aires; the lessons appeared in *El Faro,* later in *Las Señales de los Tiempos* and *La Revista Adventista;* and, after 1904, in separate form, under various names, until the present name, *Lecciones de la Escuela Sabática,* was adopted. Ottena Fulton was the first director of the Sabbath School Department in the South American Union (1907-1910). Beginning with 1914, the plan of the General Conference for the distribution of the offerings has been accepted. In 1992 there were 56,582 Sabbath school members.

3. *Home Missionary.* The first resolution designed to stimulate lay missionary activity was made in the biennial session held in Lehmann, Santa Fe, in 1904. In 1907 it was decided to organize home missionary societies in each church. In 1914 a Home Missionary Department was organized, with Mrs. Luisa P. Everest as director. The Ingathering plan was approved in 1924, although it had been occasionally practiced several years previously. Different activities were encouraged and organized later, until the establishing in 1960 of the Obra Filantropica y Asistencia Social Adventista ("SDA Welfare and Philanthropic Work"), abbreviated OFASA. Since 1992 it has been known as ADRA-OFASA.

4. *Radio.* Radio evangelism began in Argentina Sept. 2, 1933, on L.U.7, Radio General San Martin, of Bahia Blanca, in the form of lectures delivered by Andres Ascione, assisted by several coworkers. In June 1943 it was resumed under the name of La Voz de la Profecía (later changing to La Voz de la Esperanza), through records broadcast by L.T.8, Radio Rosario. At the same time, the radio correspondence school was begun with Lylon H. Lindbeck as director; Edgar Brooks prepared the first correspondence course (1943) and Juan Ferri and others the later courses, such as *Tesoros de Vida* ("Treasures of Life"), *Curso Juvenil* ("Youth Course"), and *Felicidad en el Hogar* ("Happiness in the Home"). In June 1964 a new radio program was begun under the leadership of Enrique Chaij, *Una Luz en el Camino* ("A Light in the Way"). Starting with just one radio station, it is now transmitted by 140 stations from Monday to Friday and 650 television channels, once a week in Argentina, without any charge. The original program, *La Voz de la Esperanza,* is heard weekly on 15 radio stations. There are 2,300 active students in the correspondence school.

5. *Educational.* The Colegio Adventista del Plata (River Plate College) began to operate in Las Tunas, Santa Fe, at the beginning of 1899,

and was transferred the next year to Puiggari, Entre Ríos, its present campus. Its present name is Universidad Adventista del Plata (River Plate Adventist University). Instituto Adventista Florida (Buenos Aires Adventist Academy) began operating in 1914 as a primary school and in 1938 as a secondary school. Instituto Adventista Juan Bautista Alberdi (Northeast Argentine Academy) began as a primary school in 1923 and as a secondary school in 1946. Instituto Adventista de Balcarce (Balcarce Adventist Academy) began as a secondary school in 1986. Instituto Adventista Los Polvorines (Los Polvorinas Adventist Academy) was established in 1983. Instituto Adventista de Resistencia (Resistencia Adventist Academy) was established in 1989.

6. *Medical.* Argentina has four SDA medical institutions: Sanatorio Adventista del Plata (River Plate Sanitarium and Hospital), founded in 1908 at Puiggari, Entre Ríos (since 1983 a Healthful Living Center has neen located on the premises); Clínica Médica Adventista de Belgrano (Belgrano Adventist Medical Clinic), founded in 1959 in Buenos Aires; Sanatorio Adventista Loma Linda (Loma Linda Sanitarium and Hospital), founded in 1966 at Presidencia Roque Sáenz Peña, Chaco (with its own building since June 1972); and Sanatorio Adventista del Noreste Argentino (Northeast Argentine Sanitarium), inaugurated in April 1972 at Leandro N. Alem, Misiones.

ARIANISM. *See* Christology.

ARIZONA ACADEMY. *See* Thunderbird Adventist Academy.

ARIZONA CONFERENCE. The unit of church organization comprising the territory of the state of Arizona. Statistics (1992): churches, 60; members, 9,347; elementary church schools, 18; ordained ministers, 45; licensed ministers, 7; commissioned ministers, 5; church school teachers, 61. Headquarters: 13405 North Scottsdale Road, Scottsdale, Arizona 85267. The conference forms part of the Pacific Union Conference.

Institutions. Thunderbird Adventist Academy; Holbrook Seventh-day Adventist Indian Mission School.

Local churches: Ahwatukee, Apache Junction, Benson, Bisbee, Buckeye, Bullhead City, Camp Verde, Casa Grande, Chandler, Chinle, Coolidge, Cottonwood, Dewey, El Mirage (Spanish), Flagstaff, Globe, Holbrook, Kingman, Lake Havasu City, Mesa (East Mesa, Mesa), Monte Vista (Spanish), Nogales, (Nogales, Spanish), Oracle, Parker, Patagonia, Payson, Peoria-Sun Cities, Phoenix (Beacon Light, Camelback, Central, Glendale, Maryvale, Monte Vista Spanish, North Valley, North Valley Spanish, Paradise Valley, South Mountain, Spanish, West Baseline, West Valley Spanish), Prescott, Safford, Scottsdale (Thunderbird), Sedona, Show Low, Sierra Vista, Springerville, Tempe (Tempe, Spanish), Tucson (Desert Valley, Esperanzo Spanish, Midvale Park, Sharon, Spanish), Wickenberg, Willcox, Yuma (Central, Spanish).

Companies: Douglas, Kinlichee, Marana (Spanish), Window Rock.

History. The work of Seventh-day Adventists in Arizona can be traced back to the 1880s. According to a letter from A. J. Potts, the origin of the Phoenix church goes back to 1887. Its formal organization in 1890 was noted in the conference president's report to the 1891 session of the California Conference, which in 1889 had taken Arizona as a mission territory. The same report says that "Arizona was entered more than one year ago" by "Brother [D. C.] Hunter and Brother Merrill and wife," who worked in three places. In 1895 Arizona became a General Conference mission field. In 1897 George O. States and W. L. Iles went in as evangelists, and later, W. L. Black, C. D. M. Williams, and J. E. Evans. In the next several years the *Review and Herald* carried reports of early evangelism in the state. Tent meetings were held at Prescott and in neighboring Peeples Valley and Skull Valley, in Phoenix and nearby Mesa (a Mormon district), and in Flagstaff. By June 1899 a new (still-unfinished) church was occupied at Phoenix, and a church school was opened in October with 15 pupils, taught by Martha Neilson. Williams and Black worked several months at Tucson among English- and Spanish-speaking people. A church was organized in Tucson Dec. 31, 1899, with a membership of 23. About the same time, a church was organized at Solomonville, a Spanish language group. Elder R. M. Kilgore, superintendent of District No. 5 of the General Conference, came especially for the organization of both groups. In January 1900 the Flagstaff church was organized with a membership of 12.

About that time States traveled on his bicycle through the Verde Valley, distributing tracts and visiting places in which meetings had been held before. His trip to Peeples

Valley illustrates some of the difficulties of evangelism in Arizona. His visit two and a half years before had carried him, with tent and equipment, 35 miles (55 kilometers) south of Flagstaff on a grueling three-day journey, during which his wagon broke down and there were long treks between water supplies. But he had been successful in gathering and instructing a handful of converts. Now upon his return he found only one family of converts left. The others had either given up or moved away. A drought had caused a considerable migration. Aside from the sparseness and the transient nature of the population and the vast distances of mountain and desert to be traversed, living expenses were exorbitant. Freight rates were high, and the local foodstuffs had to be raised in relatively small irrigated areas. Large numbers of the settlers were gold seekers, and many, according to the local saying, had left their religion behind at the Missouri River. This was a common frontier condition among westward migrants who had outrun the church.

At the beginning of 1901 there were churches at Phoenix, Flagstaff, Tucson (13 Spanish-speaking; nine English-speaking, including four workers; one Chinese), and a Spanish-speaking church at Solomonville. Meetings were being held at Bisbee, on the southern border. In April, Arizona was made a mission of the newly formed Pacific Union Conference, which appointed the mission executive committee. E. W. Webster was the first superintendent of the Arizona Mission. At this time, Arizona, with an area of about 113,000 square miles (290,000 square kilometers), had a population of only 122,931, and 128 SDA members. By Dec. 31, 1901, the mission had one ordained minister, three licensed ministers, two Bible instructors, a colporteur, and a church school teacher.

The Arizona Sanitarium was operated (1903-1906) at Phoenix, first by the Arizona Medical Missionary and Benevolent Association (according to 1904 *Yearbook*), then by the Arizona Conference (1905 *Yearbook*). The 1906 *Yearbook* contains information that it changed hands. Afterward it operated as a private institution. It was housed in a rented two-story 40-room building.

In 1902 the mission became the Arizona Conference, with E. W. Webster as the first president. Then in 1932, because of economic depression, on the recommendation of the union conference the Arizona Conference was united with the Southeastern California Conference and remained part of the Southeastern California-Arizona Conference until 1936, when the Arizona Conference, with a membership of 1,107, was reorganized, with W. E. Atkin as president. Offices were at 1230 N. First Street, Phoenix; then from 1949 until mid-1974 offices were at 2601 East Thomas Road. In July 1974 an executive office-book center complex was occupied at 322 North 44th Street. Later an organization wishing to build an office complex and hotel on that site purchased the property for enough money to pay off the mortgage, build a new facility, and have $100,000 left over for evangelism, besides establishing a $500,000 education trust fund. The new office and Adventist Book Center is located in Scottsdale, adjacent to Thunderbird Adventist Academy, and has been occupied since 1983.

One aspect in the development of Seventh-day Adventism in southern Arizona was the Spanish language work. As a result of work in Tucson in the late 1890s, Marcial B. Serna, a Mexican-American minister, serving a Spanish language Methodist church, and most of his congregation accepted SDA doctrine and joined the church. Some were baptized in 1899 and others in years that followed. The church organized in Tucson in 1899 was largely a Spanish language group, and virtually the first Spanish church in the U.S.A. The Methodist church building in Tucson was deeded to the SDA Church by Serna's former congregation. Serna converted a group of Methodists at Solomonville to the Sabbath, and a church was organized there in 1899. Early in 1900 colporteur work began in Phoenix for the Spanish-speaking settlers by brothers Frank and Walter Bond, prior to their departure as missionaries to Spain. By 1917 Juan Garcia was giving Bible studies among the Spanish-speaking people in Phoenix.

In 1920, when the Arizona (later Thunderbird) Academy was established at Phoenix, a Spanish Language Department was set up as the Spanish-American Training School. It served its purpose well as the first training school for Spanish workers, but closed in 1933. The Phoenix Spanish church was organized in 1922. In 1923 Frank Bond returned from Spain to continue the work among the Spanish-speaking people. In 1993 there were 10 Spanish churches and two Spanish companies in Arizona, with a combined membership of 1,470.

Until a few years ago Indians and Mexican-

Americans comprised a large percentage of the population in Arizona. In 1933 the first Indian from the Maricopa Reservation, 15 miles (25 kilometers) southwest of Phoenix, was baptized, during a series of meetings held by John Ford in Phoenix. The next year the Orno Follett family began work among the Maricopas through public meetings. Later a school and church were established and work expanded to several other Southern tribes.

In 1941 Marvin Walter and his wife began working among the Navajos in northern Arizona. The Seventh-day Adventist Indian Mission School at Holbrook, begun in 1946, conducted evangelism among the various tribes in Arizona. Many Indians have been baptized, some of whom have gone to an SDA academy or college for training to work among their own people. A former student now serves his people on the Navajo Reservation as an SDA minister. The school earned an enviable reputation in local government circles. Enrollment at the Holbrook SDA Indian School in 1993 exceeded 100. Three Native American churches and companies were in operation on the reservation.

In October 1951 eight acres (3.2 hectares) on Iron Springs Road near Prescott were secured as a campground site. Additional campground area has since been obtained, increasing the camp to 170 acres (70 hectares). Permanent buildings, including a large open-air pavilion, have been erected, providing year-round camping facilities.

On Sept. 6, 1961, the privately operated Tempe Clinic-Hospital at 1500 S. Mill Avenue, Tempe, Arizona, was turned over to the Arizona Conference. It was then renamed the Tempe Community Hospital. In 1974 the Pacific Union Conference assumed operation of the acute-care hospital in newly expanded and remodeled facilities. The Adventist Health System/West, upon its establishment, took over management of the hospital. But the hospital was sold in 1981.

Presidents: E. W. Webster, 1902-1903; A. J. Howard, 1903-1904; C. E. Knight, 1904-1905; F. I. Richardson, 1905-1907; H. G. Thurston, 1907-1912; G. W. Reaser, 1912-1914; J. E. Bond, 1914-1919; A. R. Sandborn, 1919-1926; C. S. Prout, 1926-1927; Adolph Johnson, 1927-1930; T. L. Oswald, 1930-1932; (combined Southeastern California-Arizona Conference) C. S. Prout, 1932-1934; E. F. Hackman, 1934-1936; (Arizona separated from Southeastern California Conference) W. E. Atkin, 1936-1939; C. E. Andross, 1939-1949; Carl Becker, 1949-1950; G. H. Rustad, 1950-1959; D. C. Butherus, 1959-1967; W. D. Blehm, 1967-1968; John V. Stevens, 1968-1974; E. Frank Sherrill, 1974-1988; Herman Bauman, 1988- .

ARIZONA INTERMEDIATE SCHOOL. *See* Thunderbird Adventist Academy.

ARIZONA MISSION. *See* Arizona Conference.

ARKANSAS. *See* Arkansas-Louisiana Conference; Southwest Region Conference.

ARKANSAS CONFERENCE. *See* Arkansas-Louisiana Conference.

ARKANSAS-LOUISIANA CONFERENCE. A unit of church organization comprising the territory of Arkansas, Louisiana, and the city of Texarkana in Texas *(see also* Southwest Region Conference). Statistics (1993): churches, 82; members, 7,709; church schools, 19; ordained ministers, 41; licensed ministers, 46; credentialed Bible instructors, 1; church school teachers, 36. Headquarters: 7025 Greenwood Road, Shreveport, Louisiana 71105. The conference forms part of the Southwestern Union Conference.

Institutions: Ozark Adventist Academy; West Shores Medical Clinic.

Local churches—*Arkansas:* Amity, Batesville, Benton, Bentonville, Berryville, Blytheville, Bonnerdale, Booneville, Camden, Chapel Valley, Clarksville, Clinton, Conway, Decatur, DeQueen, El Dorado, Fayetteville, Forrest City, Fort Smith, Gentry (Gentry, Gentry Home), Hardy (Spring River), Harrison, Hope, Hot Springs (Hot Springs, Sharon), Huntsville, Jonesboro, Lincoln, Little Rock (Little Rock, Sharon), Magnolia, Malvern, Mammoth Spring, Mena (Chapel Valley, Mena), Monroe (Twin Pines), Monticello, Mountain Home, Mountain View, North Little Rock (Sylvan Hills), Ozark, Pine Bluff (Northside, Pine Bluff), Plainview, Pocahontas, Rogers, Russellville, Searcy, Siloam Springs, Springdale, Sulphur Springs, Umpire, West Helena, West Memphis (New Life, West Memphis), Winslow (Brentwood), Yellville; *Louisiana:* Alexandria (Alexandria, Smyrna), Baton Rouge (Baton Rouge, Baton Rouge-Faith, Berean), Bogalusa, Coushatta, Covington (Ephesus-Covington), De Ridder,

Denham Springs, Gonzales, Gray (Houma), Gretna (West Bank), Hammond (Emmanuel-Hammond, Hammond), Jonesboro, Lafayette, Lake Charles (Lake Charles, Sharon), Mandeville, Mansfield (Memorial), Marrero (Thibodaux-Central), Marthaville, Meraux (Saint Bernard), Metairie (Kenner), Minden (Minden, New Start), Monroe (Macedonia, Monroe Westlakes), Natchitoches (First), New Iberia, New Orleans (Caffin Avenue, Central, East, Ephesus, First, Metairie Spanish, Spanish, Westbank United), Shreveport (Cedar Grove, Conference, First, Philadelphia, South), Slidell (Glad Tidings, Slidell), Tallulah, Thibodoux (Central), Vivian, Zachary; *Texas:* Texarkana (Bethel, Texarkana).

Earlier Conferences. The following three organizations have preceded the present Arkansas-Louisiana Conference: (1) Arkansas Conference, 1888 to 1932; (2) Louisiana Conference, 1901 to 1920; (3) Louisiana-Mississippi Conference, 1920 to 1932.

Arkansas Conference. The early history of Arkansas is marked by struggles with poverty and Sunday law persecutions. The history of Seventh-day Adventism in the state goes back to at least 1877, when J. H. Cook held a week's meetings at Smith Chapel, two miles (three kilometers) south of Elm Springs, Arkansas. He also held meetings at Wildcat schoolhouse, where he preached to a congregation of "age to come" believers and their minister, with the result that five members accepted the Sabbath. Sometime later J. G. Wood came to Arkansas and at Hindsville visited a couple named McAlexander, who had been keeping the Sabbath about three years. He also held meetings, as a result of which there were 10 who signed the covenant and three who were baptized. J. H. Cook reported the same year (1882): "The people of Arkansas are hospitable and kind, always willing to share with you the comforts of their homes; but at present they are in very straitened circumstances" *(Review and Herald* 59:330, May 23, 1882). J. N. Bunch, of Oakland, California, held meetings at Casa and Ola in 1883. In 1884 J. W. Scoles and his wife and D. A. Wellman worked at Little Rock and Springdale, where the first organizations were effected.

A climax in state Sunday law prosecution came in 1886 and 1887 after the Arkansas legislature in 1885 had repealed the exemption clause for those who observed another day. A statement of policy on Sunday laws was drawn up at the first Arkansas camp meeting, held at Springdale, Arkansas, in the summer of 1886, and in the same year the General Conference in session voted to offer financial help for members sick because of long prison terms. They also voted to appeal a test case, that of J. W. Scoles, to the United States Supreme Court, and to employ suitable counsel and public relations help. At the same time they invited S. H. Lane to return from England to work in Arkansas because of the spirit of persecution in the state.

Relief came soon, for in January 1887 Senator Robert H. Crockett, grandson of famed David Crockett, introduced into the Arkansas General Assembly a bill exempting Sabbathkeepers from the state Sunday law. After an impassioned plea by the senator, the bill passed with only two dissenting votes. One sentence from that plea reads as follows: "On next Monday, at Malvern, six as honest, good, and virtuous citizens as live in Arkansas are to be tried as criminals for daring to worship God in accordance with the dictates of their own consciences." (For this speech and for accounts of prosecutions of SDAs, see *American State Papers . . . on Freedom in Religion* [1949], pp. 458-465, 477-484.) Despite this victory, 10 years later C. A. Gordon and his wife, from Little Rock, were listed among many others from several states who were imprisoned.

Arkansas Conference Organized. The Arkansas Conference was organized May 21, 1888, with 10 churches and 226 members. J. P. Henderson, the only ordained minister on the staff, was president; licentiates included E. B. Young, secretary; William Martin, treasurer; and W. J. Kerr. A camp meeting was held at Rogers, Aug. 20-27, 1889. Ellen G. White attended a meeting at Springdale in March 1890.

R. M. Kilgore reported in 1898: "The finances of the conference are so meager that it was thought best to ask all ministers and licentiates, except the president of the conference, to engage in the canvassing work, thus becoming self-supporting missionaries" *(Review and Herald* 75:575, Sept. 6, 1898). Despite these difficulties, converts were won. Sidney Scott, a Black minister, in 1901 reported the acceptance of the Sabbath by an entire Black non-SDA church (Monarch). For Black SDA churches in Arkansas, *see* Southwest Region Conference.

A small institution called the Little Rock Sanitarium was established in 1900 and operated by W. C. Green, M.D. It was last listed in the *Yearbook* of 1906.

The Arkansas Conference Association was

chartered Mar. 23, 1902. Conference headquarters were successively at Springdale, Fayetteville, and Little Rock. Not until 1922, when it moved into quarters next to the church, at 1215 Marshall Street, Little Rock, did it own its offices. Membership grew from the 226 members in 1888 to 1,189 in 1932, when the Arkansas Conference and Louisiana section of the Louisiana-Mississippi Conference were united.

Louisiana Conference. The first Sabbathkeeper in Louisiana appears to have been Mary A. Nugent in New Orleans in 1866. In 1883 George W. Winn returned to his home near Marthaville from Texas, having been a Sabbathkeeper about one year. The next year he won Dr. T. B. Sellers. A church was organized there in January 1887 by T. H. Gibbs, then of New Orleans. In the meantime a church, the first in the state, had been organized in New Orleans.

The interest that resulted in this church was aroused by R. M. Kilgore and H. W. Cottrell, who, during the exposition held in New Orleans in 1884-1885, set up an exhibit of SDA publications. This interest was followed up by SDA members canvassing and giving Bible readings. The few converts that resulted were baptized and organized into a church by G. K. Owen, of Michigan. By December 1885 about 45 had begun to observe the Sabbath. With the help of S. N. Haskell and J. H. Waggoner a city mission was established, in which "parlor services" were held. Later the mission was moved to other addresses. In 1939, while J. Lee Neil was the pastor, the first Louisiana church moved to a new building at 3500 St. Charles Avenue, in New Orleans. This building served the congregation until 1974, when the present New Orleans First church was built at 4201 W. Esplanade Ave. in Metairie.

Additional churches were established at Evergreen, Galvez, Hope Villa, Shreveport, and Welsh before 1891. The Hope Villa (later Hobart and now Gonzales) church had a threefold increase in members within a year, and erected the first SDA church building in Louisiana. M. D. Broussard donated the site and much of the building materials.

Annual camp meetings and literature and tent evangelism were the principal factors contributing to growth in church membership. The first camp meeting was held in a grove outside the city limits of Alexandria in July 1898; the second in H. E. Heald's grove at Welsh, Louisiana, in July 1899; and the third at Marthaville in 1900. In 1899 the first church school was organized at Marthaville, with Mrs. C. F. Dart in charge.

Louisiana Conference Organized. Louisiana was a mission field in General Conference District No. 2 until, at the fourth camp meeting, at Crowley in 1901, the Louisiana Conference was organized and became part of the new Southern Union Conference. At the end of the year it reported six churches, 178 members, one company, and two ordained ministers (*General Conference Bulletin,* first quarter 1902, p. 596). Officers were as follows: S. B. Horton, president; W. T. Hartsock, Medical and Missionary departments; Frank Peabody, treasurer; C. F. Dart, state (canvassing) agent; Ruby Roach, superintendent of schools and Sabbath School Department. Conference committee: S. B. Horton, C. A. Watkins, E. S. Abbott, Solomon Broussard, J. R. Hudson. Conference headquarters were in New Orleans. Office space at first was rented, but in 1908 property at 810 Jackson Street was purchased and used until 1920. Contributing substantially to the growth in membership in the conference was the work of Mrs. Frances Goodwin, a Bible instructor, which dated back to 1886 and continued many years. The conference also carried on an active colporteur work, developing strong leaders.

For evangelism among Blacks in Louisiana, *see* Southwest Region Conference. Evangelism for the French-speaking people of Louisiana was undertaken at various times. Notable was the work of Louis F. Passebois about 1915 in and around New Orleans.

Louisiana-Mississippi Conference. A new conference was organized in Jackson, Mississippi, in 1920 by combining the SDA churches and members of Louisiana and Mississippi. Each state had functioned as a single conference since organization in 1901. To this union of conferences Louisiana brought 13 churches, 4 ordained and 2 licensed ministers, and 673 members; 7 church schools, with 8 teachers and 116 pupils; 7 conference-owned buildings valued at $28,000, and a 1920 tithe of $30.06 per capita, totaling $20,231.26. The new Louisiana-Mississippi Conference, in an area with a population of 3,587,182, was organized with 30 churches, 1,144 members, 8 ordained ministers, 5 licentiates, and 12 teachers. W. R. Elliott was elected president, and N. L. Taylor secretary-treasurer. The conference headquarters were at 703 S. Gallatin Street, Jackson, Mississippi. (For the history of Seventh-day Adventist beginnings in Mississippi, *see* Gulf States Conference.)

Arkansas-Louisiana Conference Organized. In 1932, when the economic depression necessitated adjustments in administration, major territorial changes were effected in several union conferences. Louisiana, after its 12-year union with Mississippi, was transferred to the Southwestern Union Conference and joined to Arkansas. The Louisiana Conference was reluctant to break its ties with Mississippi and the Southern Union, but once the transfer was effected, a good spirit of solidarity developed.

The Arkansas-Louisiana Conference, in an area with a population of 3,956,075, was organized Feb. 23, 1932, with 33 churches, 2,078 members, 9 ordained ministers, 5 licentiates, and 18 teachers. The president was R. P. Montgomery; the secretary-treasurer, Ella M. Winn. The conference headquarters were established at 1215 Marshall Street, Little Rock, Arkansas. There were 3,266 members in 1946, the year when the Southwestern Mission (later the Southwest Region Conference) was organized, subtracting 12 Black churches and 850 members.

Ozark Academy, although located geographically off center in the northwest corner of Arkansas (Gentry, Arkansas), serves both states, and the Oklahoma Conference also.

In 1960, during the administration of I. M. Evans, president, and P. I. Nosworthy, secretary-treasurer, the conference office was moved from Little Rock, Arkansas, to Shreveport, Louisiana, a more central location. The membership grew to 3,945, as of Jan. 1, 1965, in 49 churches and 9 companies.

On Sept. 15, 1965, Camp Yorktown Bay was officially transferred from the U.S. Navy League of Hot Springs to the Arkansas-Louisiana Conference. This camp consists of 113 acres (45 hectares) on Lake Ouachita. When the camp was received it could accommodate 80 campers; now it accommodates more than 200.

Presidents: Arkansas Conference: J. P Henderson, 1888-1889; J. G. Wood, 1889-1891; C. McReynolds, 1891-1893; J. M. Rees, 1893-1894; J. B. Beckner, 1894-1896; J. A. Holbrook, 1896-1899; C. McReynolds, 1899; A. E. Field, 1899-1903; J. A. Sommerville, 1903-1904; Urbanus Bender, 1904-1907; V. B. Watts, 1907-1909; J. W. Norwood, 1909-1914; W. E. Baxter, 1914-1917; J. I. Taylor, 1917-1922; H.M.J. Richards, 1922-1926; R. P. Montgomery, 1926-1932.

Louisiana Conference: S. B. Horton, 1901-1908; E. L. Maxwell, 1908-1912; R. W. Parmele, 1912-1916; C. N. Sanders, 1916-1920; D. P. Wood, 1920; W. K. Smith, 1920.

Louisiana-Mississippi Conference: W. R. Elliott, 1921-1926; R. H. DeVinney, 1926-1932.

Arkansas-Louisiana Conference: R. P. Montgomery, 1932; W. H. Heckman, 1932-1933; H. C. Hartwell, 1933-1937; I. C. Pound, 1937-1943; F. D. Wells, 1943-1948; F. O. Sanders, 1948-1954; I. M. Evans, 1954-1964; O. D. Wright, 1964-1966; E. F. Sherrill, 1966-1974; W. H. Elder, Jr., 1974-1982; Don C. Schneider, 1982-1985; William L. Woodruff, 1985-1994; James Gilley, 1994- .

ARMAGEDDON. (From the Greek transliteration of an unknown Hebrew phrase usually thought to be *Har-megiddo,* "Mount Megiddo.") The word "Armageddon" occurs in the Bible only in Rev. 16:16, as the Hebrew name for a "place" to which three "unclean spirits" (v. 13) gather "the kings of the earth" to "the battle of that great day of God Almighty" (v. 14)—John's designation for what is popularly called the battle of Armageddon.

The gathering to Armageddon is the principal feature of the sixth plague (vs. 12-16). The sixth angel pours out his "bowl" upon "the great river Euphrates," whose "water was dried up, to prepare the way for the kings from the east." Then three "demonic spirits" resembling frogs go forth from the mouths of the "dragon," the "beast," and the "false prophet" to "the kings of the whole world, to assemble them for battle on the great day of God the Almighty" (vs. 13-16, RSV). The sixth plague closes with the nations of the earth gathered for battle, and the context implies that battle is joined as the seventh angel pours out the vial of the seventh plague.

In popular usage "Armageddon" means any major military conflict involving many nations, though usually without reference to the biblical meaning of the term. Armageddon was not given specific emphasis by earlier Protestant interpreters, but in the first four decades of the nineteenth century, the increased emphasis on the imminence of the end of several prophetic periods in the prophecies of Daniel and the Revelation led to increased interest in the subject of Armageddon. A large group of expositors taught that events foretold in Rev. 16:12-16 paralleled those of Dan. 11:44, 45, since in both instances the establishment of Christ's eternal kingdom follows almost immediately. Furthermore, it was pointed out that the "king of the north" of Dan. 11:40-

45, whom many identified as the Ottoman Empire, occupied the area drained by the Euphrates River, which is mentioned in Rev. 16:12. Their belief that the Turks were referred to by "the great river Euphrates" under the sixth trumpet (Rev. 9:14) strengthened the conviction that the Euphrates mentioned under the sixth plague must refer to the same power. The fact that throughout the nineteenth century the territory of the Ottoman Empire *was* progressively being diminished ("dried up"), coupled with belief in the imminence of the event foretold, tended to confirm this interpretation. Politically and in the public press the Turkish Empire was referred to as "the sick man of the East," and its demise was supposed to be imminent. Contemporary events were construed as part of the drying-up process to which Rev. 16:12 referred. The "Eastern question" occupied the continuing attention of political leaders throughout the century, and of the interpreters of Bible prophecy as well.

History of Seventh-day Adventist Interpretation. Millerite interpreters had held varying views on Armageddon. For example, William Miller taught that the sixth plague was a diminishing or taking away, of "the Turkish power" and was then (1836) in the process of fulfillment, "so that the way now appears to be prepared for the kings to come up to the battle of the great day" (*Evidence . . . of the Second Coming of Christ* [1836], p. 185). Josiah Litch, who placed the plagues "in the future, and after the second advent" *(Prophetic Expositions,* [1842], vol. 1, p. 175), believed that *'the great river Euphrates'* will be as literally dried up to make way for kings of the Eastern world to come up to Jerusalem and Palestine to that battle, as the same river was dried up before Cyrus, when he entered and took the city of Babylon; or as the Red Sea and the river Jordan were dried up to make a highway for Israel through their bed. The effects of the sixth vial will be, *first,* to dry up the waters of the river, to make a highway; and *secondly,* to send forth the spirit of devils to deceive, by miracles, the kings of the whole earth, and their armies, and gather them" *(ibid.,* p. 183).

SDA publications contained little on the subject of Armageddon until the 1850s. In an article in 1852 in the *Review and Herald,* G. W. Holt contended that the plagues were "real and literal," as were the plagues of Egypt. After quoting Rev. 16:12, Holt declared, "This doubtless will be literal, and better understood about the time of its fulfillment" (2:105, Mar. 23, 1852). Whether by this statement he wished merely to affirm that the sixth plague would, like the others, be literal, or whether by "literal" he meant that the prophetic symbols in this verse were to be literally understood (for example, that the river Euphrates would be literally dried up, as Litch had held), is not clear. Interpreting verses 13 and 14, he comments: "This work of deception will probably increase until the great majority are led captive, and so deceived by it as to engage in the great battle against the Lamb and his humble followers. By this means they are led to resist the truth, and make war upon those that keep the commandments of God and the faith of Jesus. Thus Pharaoh and his host were deceived by the magicians and led on until they were overwhelmed in the water of the Red Sea" *(ibid.,* p. 106).

A similar view was expressed by R. F. Cottrell in the *Review and Herald* in 1853: "But the last work of the spirits will be to gather the nations to the battle of the great day of God Almighty (Rev. 16:14). They are now preparing the way, and gaining an influence over kings and subjects, and when the sixth vial of the wrath of God shall be poured out, they will gather them to the battle. . . . Notwithstanding men are crying peace and safety, while sudden destruction is hanging over their heads; and the spirits of devils are arrayed against God and his truth; yet that truth will triumph" (4:157, Nov. 22, 1853).

An early SDA hymnal included a hymn entitled "Armageddon." With phraseology based on Rev. 14:14-20 and 19:11-21, it emphasized the role of Christ and the angels in the battle of Armageddon, in defeating the wicked powers of earth and delivering God's beleaguered people immediately prior to the resurrection and the appearance of Christ in the clouds of heaven (*Hymns for Second Advent Believers Who Observe the Sabbath of the Lord* [1852], pp. 23, 24).

Early in the Civil War certain individuals, obviously not the responsible leaders of the church, declared that the battle of the great day of God was beginning. James White, as editor of the *Review and Herald,* pointed out in the issue for Jan. 21, 1862 (19:61) that "preparations for that battle do not commence until the time of the pouring out of the sixth vial," and that battle is joined only as the Son of God, accompanied by the angel armies of heaven, descends to earth. "The great battle is not between nation and nation," he wrote, "but between earth and heaven," between Satan and Christ.

The first formal exegesis of Rev. 16:12-16 in SDA literature appeared during the course of a series of articles entitled "Thoughts on the Revelation," by Uriah Smith, which ran in the *Review* intermittently from June 3, 1862, to Feb. 3, 1863. In the issue for Dec. 2, 1862 (21:5), Smith identified the symbolic drying up of the river Euphrates as "the consumption of the Turkish empire," which power, he said, would cease to exist altogether under the sixth plague. He considered the dissolution of the Ottoman Empire a necessary prelude to the battle of Armageddon, inasmuch as that battle, he said, would be fought at Jerusalem, and Jerusalem was then in the hands of the Turks. The dissolution of the Turkish Empire, he said, would prepare the way for "the kings of the East"—by which he understood nations to the east of Palestine—to fight in the battle at Jerusalem. He identified the three "unclean spirits" that gather the nations to Armageddon as "Paganism, Catholicism, and Protestantism." These, the great religious organizations of the world, would gather the nations to "an unequal warfare . . . against the Lord of hosts." The gathering of the nations he assigned to the sixth plague, and the battle itself, which he identifies with the judgment of Babylon in vs. 17-19, to the seventh. This exposition was retained when the series of articles appeared in book form in 1867 and became the standard SDA pattern of interpretation for the next three quarters of a century. About this time Smith also began to identify the king of the north (Dan. 11:40-45) with Turkey. Earlier he had identified this king with the Papacy *(Review and Herald* 19:192, May 13, 1862).

The international situation that culminated in the Russo-Turkish War (1877-1878) led to expectation of the imminent end of the Ottoman Empire, with Armageddon following immediately. In the *Review and Herald* for Mar. 28, 1871 (37:116, 117), Uriah Smith wrote: "All eyes are now turned with interest toward Turkey; and the unanimous opinion of statesmen is that the Turk is destined soon to be driven from Europe. . . . Time will soon determine this matter; and it may be but a few months." (See also *Thoughts on Daniel* [1881], pp. 361-372.)

But James White was never reconciled to this view. While admitting that there was "general agreement upon this subject, and that all eyes are turned toward the war now in progress between Turkey and Russia as the fulfillment of that portion of prophecy which will give great confirmation of faith in the soon loud cry and close of our message," he concluded: "What will be the result of this positiveness in unfulfilled prophecies *should things not come out as very confidently expected is an anxious question" (Review and Herald,* 50:172, Nov. 29, 1877; italics supplied).

The armament race that led to World War I revived interest in Armageddon. In a *Review and Herald* article entitled "The Gathering for Armageddon," W. A. Spicer wrote of the evil spirits of Rev. 16:13, 14 stirring up the nations for war, and gathering all the world to Armageddon. He said: "Men who know the pulse of international affairs see just before us a world-conflict, which they describe as the Armageddon of the nations. . . . The sure word of prophecy says that it is the gathering to the battle of the last great day. . . . With express speed the world is rushing on to the great Armageddon. Before our very eyes the prophecy is fulfilling. Men of the world bear witness to it. The rest will surely come, and the time is near at hand" *(ibid.* 80:6, 7, Oct. 22, 1903).

In the Feb. 6, 1913, *Review and Herald* (90:127) W. H. Branson commented: "It is astonishing to note how the idea of Armageddon is taking hold of thinking people of every country, and how the world is awaiting with fear and trembling the great crisis that Armageddon stands for, and that is so sure and so soon to come."

In the issue for Dec. 25 of the same year (90:1240) F. M. Wilcox asked, "What will be the end of all this great preparation for war?" and answered: "The end of it all will be that foretold by the prophet, the end looked for by far-seeing statesmen—the battle of Armageddon, the last great conflict of earth just preceding the coming of the Lord."

Six years before the outbreak of World War I, S. N. Haskell wrote: "Even the Turks themselves are looking forward to the time when they will have to remove their capital from Constantinople to Jerusalem. . . . All know that when the Turk steps out of Constantinople, there will be a general breaking up of Europe. They may not name the impending conflict the battle of Armageddon, but God has so named it" *(The Story of Daniel the Prophet* [1908 ed.], pp. 282, 283).

A few weeks after the beginning of World War I, F. M. Wilcox commented: "The Scriptures indicate that eventually the site of government will be removed to the glorious holy mountain between the seas, referring evidently to Jerusalem. . . . The river Euphrates, representing the Ottoman government, is rapidly being dried up that the way of the kings of the East may be prepared to take part in the great battle of Armageddon" *(Review and Herald* 91:9, Oct. 15, 1914).

In the issue for Sept. 17 (91:7) C. M. Snow suggested that if Turkey should enter the war, "then this [World War I] is the first stage of the Armageddon battle. But that is yet to be determined. The outcome of this war we cannot forecast. Its relation to Armageddon depends upon the aligning and shifting of the nations themselves. Will those shiftings and alignings so dry up that power designated as the Euphrates that the way will be prepared for the forces of heathenism and Mohammedanism to come up to the common battleground of the world? Time will tell. But if this war does not do it, another must follow soon that will."

When Turkey did declare war, six weeks later, G. B. Starr wrote: "'The Ottoman Empire in Europe will soon be merely a memory' (London *Times,* Oct. 30, 1914). . . . For nearly forty years the writer has watched with deepest interest the movements in the Near East with reference to the fulfilment of the predictions relating to the Eastern question, and rejoices in the clear evidences that the last step, the last act of the drama, is at hand" *(Review and Herald* 91:3, Nov. 26, 1914).

The outbreak of hostilities in 1914 inspired cautious admonitions not to consider that war the biblical Armageddon. A. O. Tait counseled: "The furious way in which this European war has broken out, and the rapidity with which it is spreading from one nation to another, is causing many people to ask the question, 'Is this the beginning of Armageddon?'

"To this question we can clearly say, No, the war of Armageddon has not commenced; for it will be observed, in the prophecy already quoted, that that war of Armageddon takes place under the pouring out of the sixth of the seven last plagues, and these plagues have not begun to fall, as everyone knows" *(Signs of the Times* 40:7, Aug. 18, 1914).

Said C. M. Snow: "The war now being fought in Europe is not Armageddon, but it is entirely possible that it may lead into that battle" *(Review and Herald* 91:7, Sept. 17, 1914). W. W. Prescott wrote: "This great war is not Armageddon. It is not surprising that that word appears in the papers, but it is not Armageddon. This war is not the end" *(ibid.* 91:6, Oct. 1, 1914).

The armament race culminating in World War I was paralleled by other developments that introduced the nations of the Far East into the Armageddon picture. The awakening of Japan under the enlightened rule of the great emperor Meiji (1852-1912), the Sino-Japanese War (1894-1895), the Boxer Rebellion in China (1900), a brilliant Japanese victory in the Russo-Japanese War (1904-1905), and the Chinese Revolution (1911) gave birth to the idea that Armageddon would be essentially a battle between the nations of the Orient (the "kings of the East") and the Occident. The king of Sweden is said to have declared as early as 1896 that "the Occident will be conquered by the Orient" (see R. C. Porter, "The World's Armageddon Battle in Prophecy," *Review and Herald* 90:748, 749, Aug. 7, 1913). The Boxer Rebellion led to the coining of the popular phrase "Yellow Peril" (London *Daily News,* July 21, 1900, quoted in *The Oxford English Dictionary,* art. "Yellow"). A series of four articles by R. C. Porter in the *Review and Herald* during July and August 1913 was based on the idea of Armageddon as essentially an East-West struggle. In his Aug. 7 article (90:749) Porter wrote of the great world color problem as a challenge to the White man's supremacy, and of "the battle of Armageddon as the probable result of present conditions in the East." He quoted Archibald R. Colquhoun, F.R.G.S., as saying in the *Daily Mail Year Book* (1908), "There is no question that the victory of Japan over Russia [in 1905] raised the question of relations between white and yellow in an entirely new form, and moreover that a spirit of renaissance is at work throughout Asia, which *is destined to challenge the vaunted supremacy of the white man"* (emphasis his). Following World War I, Lothrop Stoddard popularized such phrases as "Yellow Peril" and "the rising tide of color" in a series of books, including one entitled *The Rising Tide of Color* (1920). C. B. Haynes used both of these expressions in his book *On the Eve of Armageddon* (1946), p. 54.

Decreasing emphasis on the role of Turkey in Armageddon, between World War I and World War II, was paralleled by greatly increased emphasis on the role of Japan and other Asian nations. But with the decisive defeat of Japan in World War II, this emphasis also disappeared. Under the title "Japan and the Kings of the East" *(Ministry* 19:10, June 1946) Andrew N. Nelson emphatically denied that Japan had anything to do with "the kings of the East." As world developments made the application of Dan. 11:45 and Rev. 16:12 to Turkey increasingly improbable after World War I, and likewise that of Rev. 16:12 to Japan after the close of World War II, there developed in SDA exegesis a trend toward eliminating both Turkey and Japan from consideration in connection with these prophecies and toward returning to the more general view of the pioneers. Hence there are many today who hold that the battle of Armageddon is the conflict between the forces of good and the forces of evil that will culminate in the destruction of the wicked at the second coming of Christ. Others, however, hold that the battle will be of a military character, waged between nations of the earth, and that this military battle will be terminated at the second coming of Christ.

The word "Armageddon" seldom appears in Ellen G. White's writings. See, for example, 6T 406 and several passages printed in SDACom, 7:967, 982, 983.

ARMED FORCES, SEVENTH-DAY ADVENTISTS IN. *See* Adventist Chaplaincy Ministries; Noncombatancy.

ARMENIA. An ancient country, parts of which now are in Turkey and Iran. It occupies an area of 11,306 square miles (29,783 square kilometers). The 1994 population is 3.5 million. It is bordered by Georgia, Azerbaijan, Iran, and Turkey. Present-day Armenia was set up as a Soviet republic on Apr. 2, 1921. Armenia became a consituent republic of the USSR on Dec. 5, 1936. An earthquake struck Armenia on Dec. 7, 1988, killing some 25,000 people and destroying several cities and towns. Armenia became an independent republic when the USSR disbanded on Dec. 26, 1991.

Development of Seventh-day Adventist Work. As far back as the 1830s, many Molokans settled in the area of Mount Ararat in Armenia to await the millennium. In 1886 several Seventh-day Adventists from the Stavropol region were exiled to the same place because of their religious beliefs. When some families in the village of Bazarchar became interested in Sabbathkeeping, they sent V. Zhukov and I. Kasmynin to the Stavropol Seventh-day Adventist Church, where both were baptized. As a result of these developments, several companies and local churches had been organized in Armenia by 1908.

In 1925 two families (the Sperlings from Persia and the Galodzhevs from Tiflis) moved to Yerevan. That same year Elder Galodzhev baptized nine Armenians.

In 1993 there were nine churches and four companies in Armenia serving 365 members. Elder A. Kachikyan directs the work. Armenia is part of the Trans-Caucasian Field, in an attached field of the Euro-Asia Division.

ARMENIAN ADVENTIST SCHOOL. A 10-grade coeducational school that was located in Bourj-Hammoud, Lebanon, and operated by the East Mediterranean Field of Seventh-day Adventists. It was founded by Neshan Hovhannessian in Khalil Badawy, Beirut, Lebanon, in 1939 as a church school to meet the educational needs of Armenian SDA children. Because of hostile political conditions the school was moved to a new building in Bourj-Hammoud in 1963. The curriculum was presented in three languages, Arabic, Armenian, and English, and was designed to prepare the students for the Brevet examination of the Lebanese government. The school was closed in 1984.

Principals: Yepraxe Gomig, 1939-1941; Hosanna Ayoub, 1941-1946; Sella Nazirian, 1946-1950; Haigouhi Delice, 1950-1952; Hagop Keushguerian, 1952-1953; Sella Nazirian, 1953-1962; Nourhan Ouzounian and Mary Bitar, 1962-1963; Sella Nazirian, 1963-1967; Jirayr Kourouyan, 1967-1968; Aram Aghassian, 1968-1971; H. Cowles, 1971-1972; Minas Megurdichian, 1972-1975; Sella Nazirian, 1975-1984.

ARMINIANISM. A theological position in regard to salvation founded by Jacobus Arminius (Hermansz) (1560-1609), professor at the University of Leiden, Netherlands. Focusing his attack principally on the Calvinist position that God has predestined some to salvation and others to damnation, Arminius declared that salvation is theoretically possible for all. As the Arminian doctrine developed, his followers (known in Holland as Remonstrants), denied that any guilt pertains to a child before the age of accountability and that because individuals are not completely depraved they can cooperate with God. Conversely, they also can fall from grace. Probably the most significant theological tenet of Arminianism is that election is based on the foreknowledge of God concerning individuals' choice, rather than upon the sovereign decree of God, as taught by Calvin. At this point, it has been objected, too great stress on the Arminian position runs the risk of making salvation primarily a question of human decision and thus underemphasizing the sovereignty of God, as manifested in the election of Jesus Christ. Although condemned by the Calvinists at the Synod of Dort in 1619, Arminianism lived on. In some areas it developed far beyond Arminius' original doctrine. The basic evangelical form of Arminianism later became the soteriological position of Wesley and the Methodist Church. While Seventh-day Adventists do not formally identify themselves as Arminians, the general Arminian point of view has come to characterize their doctrine.

ARMITAGE, FRANK BENJAMIN (1864-1952). Pioneer missionary to Africa. Born into a Seventh-day Adventist family in Wisconsin, he attended Battle Creek College. In 1884 he married Annie Olsen, sister of O. A. Olsen. For several years he taught at Union College and other places in the Midwest.

The Armitages went to southern Africa as members of the second party of American missionary workers to Solusi Mission. They arrived there in 1897, at the height of an epidemic of malaria. Within a year Mrs. Armitage died. Shortly thereafter Armitage married the widow of G. B. Tripp. Tripp had been the first superintendent of the Solusi Mission.

In 1901 new recruits arrived at Solusi. Then the Armitages went nearly 200 miles (320 kilometers) northeast to establish the Somabula Mission. Through five long hard years they slowly won the confidence of the tribal people. Mrs. Armitage opened a school for girls. Briefly they were aided by Mrs. W. S. Hyatt, Armitage's sister, who remained and helped at Somabula when her husband, superintendent of the union, passing through, visited other missions in the north and in Nyasaland.

After their daughter Irene had suffered her fifth attack of blackwater fever the Armitages left Somabula. By this time they had greatly endeared themselves to the people. Not without reason was Armitage known as *Matand' Abantu* ("the man who loves people").

For nearly 20 years longer the Armitages worked in the Union of South Africa, building up the work at Maranatha, Bethel, Kolo (in Basutoland, now Lesotho), and Spion Kop missions. Then because of the failing health of Mrs. Armitage, the family returned to the United States in 1925. For a number of years after his return, Armitage pastored in California.

ARMONA UNION ACADEMY. A coeducational senior high school sharing the campus with an elementary school in the San Joaquin Valley town of Armona, California. It is accredited by the SDA Board of Regents and is a charter member of the Western Association of Secondary Schools and Colleges through 1999. The day school is owned by the Central California Conference and operated jointly by the conference and five constituent churches.

The school began in 1903 in Nis Hansen's home, with Nellie Brown as teacher. When the enrollment increased from 4 to 13, it was transferred to Hansen's buggy house, and later to a small cottage on his ranch. By October 1906 it became known as the Central California Intermediate and Church School under the direction of B. L. Howe.

Nis Hansen donated a five-acre (two-hectare) tract of land on which a church and the old Armona Library were built. Approximately 70 students enrolled that first year. Community homes boarded nonresident students during the week. When the enrollment reached 90 in 1909, a new schoolroom was added. Myrtle B. Hudson, a physician from Battle Creek Sanitarium, joined the staff as a science teacher and conducted temperance and health clinics in the community.

During the summer of 1911 J. L. Jones arrived from Union College, and instruction was offered through grade 12. In the spring of 1912 Armona Academy graduated five students. In the summer of 1913 the Pacific Union Conference requested that academies restrict their curriculums in order to strengthen the Pacific Union College program. Armona Academy was reduced to a 10-grade school and placed under local control. In 1925 the constituent churches of Island, Laguna, Lemoore, Hanford, and Armona consolidated their small schools, bought two buses, and united as the Armona Union Intermediate School.

This school operated in the old academy building and became accredited with the General Conference Department of Education in 1928. The school expanded to include ninth-, tenth-, and eleventh-grade subjects. The 1935 enrollment of 94 filled the school to capacity.

On Feb. 24, 1936, a fire destroyed the old wooden building. Only the piano and a few books and maps were salvaged. Within two weeks plans were approved to rebuild a larger unit accommodating 100 students. The community and constituents rallied with pledges exceeding $5,000, plus materials and time. The classes met in tents and in the Armona church for the rest of the year. By the fall of 1936 four classrooms and the office were readied for the beginning of the school year. By the following year, a 300-seat auditorium and a mechanical drawing and woodworking facility were completed.

Armona Union Academy again began offering 12 grades in 1939-1940, enrolling 135. In 1949 three new classrooms and a cafeteria were added for the elementary school, and two teachers' duplexes and a metal shop building for vocational subjects. The vocational complex was named for W. A. Johnstone. In 1955 the school was accredited by the General Conference Department of Education. In 1956, under the direction of Paul Plummer, school buses were provided, the grounds were landscaped, and the school building was painted. In 1957 Lambert Flory and others purchased and donated to the school 10 acres (four hectares) across the street.

During Dallas Carr's administration, a four-room office complex, complete with intercom system and air-conditioning, was moved in behind the administration building. The old elementary building was remodeled and transformed into academy classrooms and a science laboratory. Then two classrooms in the administration building were combined into a spacious library, complete with carrels, a listening center, and a conference room.

During the summer of 1978 the foundation was laid for a new gymnasium, multipurpose room, and kitchen. The old gymnasium was remodeled into a chapel that was named to honor L. A. Hansen, whose family has consistently supported the school for 90 years.

The Armona church is located on the academy campus along with the King's Crusaders Pathfinder Building, which serves the five area churches.

Principals of the 12-Grade Academy: J. L. Jones, 1911-1913; R. N. Gardner, 1938-1941; R. Shephard, 1941-1944; W. F. Storz, 1944-1946; Theophil Fischer, 1946-1947; B. C. Clark, 1947-1948; Helen Morris, 1948-1949; B. E. Schaffner, 1949-1953; M. A. Smith, 1953-1956; P. E. Plummer, 1956-1964; W. E. Minder, 1964-1966; Norman Morris, 1966-1968; E. F. Judy, 1968-1969; Dallas Carr, 1969-1973; Richard Stafford, 1973-1974; James A. Hawkins, 1974-1977; Curtis Church, 1977-1982; Bob Evans, 1982-1985; Ron Turner, 1985-1987; Earl Spalding, 1987-1990; Lon Gruesbeck, 1990-1992; Sam Geli, 1992-1993; Donald Olson, 1993- .

ARMS. *See* Adventist Resource Management Service.

ARMSTRONG, ALBERT KINGSLEY (1884-1965). Pastor and composer. Born Feb. 19 in Ulceby, England, he was probably the first child born to Seventh-day Adventist parents in Britain, his parents having been baptized the previous year. He was baptized in 1901 and graduated from Stanborough College in 1908. After his marriage that same year, he and his wife went to Ireland and began lifelong service to the church. In 1913 he was transferred to the North England Conference, where he served in many churches during the next 16 years. The last 35 years of his life were spent working among the churches of the South England Conference, his last charge being the headquarters church at Stanborough Park, where he served for 17 years. He was gifted with musical talent, and two of his hymns appear in *The New Advent Hymnal.*

A prominent minister of another denomination volunteered the information that he found more fellowship of the spirit with Pastor Armstrong than with his fellow ministers.

ARMSTRONG, HARRY E. (1873-1920). Minister, administrator, missionary. He began work with the British publishing house in 1890, entered the ministry in 1895, and was ordained in 1898. In 1901 he conducted evangelistic work in Glasgow.

After one year as superintendent of the Scottish mission he went to India, and in 1904 was sent on a preaching mission to Ceylon. While there, certain Sabbathkeeping Tamils from Tinnevelly met him. As a result, evangelistic work was begun in their village in 1908.

After three years' service in India and Ceylon, Armstrong returned to England because of ill health. He was president of the Welsh Conference for six years, and of the North England Conference for six more. On retiring from administrative responsibilities, he conducted evangelistic work on the Isle of Wight until near the time of his death.

ARMSTRONG, WALTER WORSLEY (1895-1970). Missionary, administrator. He was born in north London into a second-generation Seventh-day Adventist family. Baptized in 1910, he suffered persecution for his faith during World War I, but his stalwart witness, along with that of others, paved the way for a better understanding of the SDA noncombatant in Britain. He was married in 1920, and with his wife, Madge, went to Kenya, where they labored for 19 years.

In 1946 Pastor Armstrong was elected to the presidency of the South England Conference, a position he held until called to the presidency of the British Union in 1950. Because of ill health, he retired in 1958.

ARNESEN, ERIK (1868-1960). Editor, educator, administrator. Born in Öyer, Gudbransdalen, Norway, in 1888 he left his homeland for America, and found work and a home at Gelckrist, Minnesota, with a Seventh-day Adventist Norwegian farmer named Hilde. Accepting the SDA faith, he was baptized at the Minnesota camp meeting in 1891 by J. M. Erickson. That same year he enrolled as a student of the Scandinavian Department of Union College, where he spent two years. The next two years he served as secretary to J. G. Matteson, who was editor of *Evangeliets Sendebud* and teacher in the Danish-Norwegian Department of Union College. In the school year of 1895-1896 he taught at Union College. At the end of the school year he was called to Battle Creek to serve as a secretary in the General Conference office.

In 1897 Arnesen was called to Denmark to serve as secretary to Dr. J. C. Ottosen, who had been chosen as medical superintendent of the Skodsborg Sanitarium, which opened its doors in 1898. In addition to his secretarial duties he took the nursing course, giving the first treatment to the first male patient. He remained at Skodsborg 11 years.

In 1908, when J. C. Raft was elected president of the Scandinavian Union Conference, Arnesen was elected secretary, a position he held for 24 years, until 1932, when the one union was divided into two. Also in 1908 he was appointed head of the union training school (established at that time in Skodsborg) and the next year, Bible teacher. He also served as editor of *Evangeliets Sendebud* and translated books and tracts.

In March 1917 Arnesen was released from the school to become the manager of the publishing house (Norsk Bokforlag) in Christiania (now Oslo), Norway, and to devote his time to editorial and other literary work. Three years later he was called back to Denmark to head the training school, which was then in Naerum *(see* Danish Junior College). In 1925 he was again asked to return to the publishing house in Christiania to assume his old post as editor of *Evangeliets Sendebud,* which in 1928 had its name changed to *Tidens Tale.*

In February 1929 Arnesen suffered a near-fatal attack of pneumonia, which made it necessary for him to relinquish his editorial work. For the school year 1930-1931 he taught Bible in the Onsrud mission school. This was his last official post before he retired.

For Arnesen retirement did not mean inactivity. Until the time of his death he continued his writing. During his long and active life he wrote numerous articles for SDA papers. He also edited a large songbook, of which 200 songs were composed by him. In addition, he translated nine of Ellen G. White's books. The last one, *The Desire of Ages,* was finished in his eighty-seventh year.

ARNOLD, DAVID (1805-1889). Colleague of James White in publishing the *Advent Review* (1850), and first president of the New York Conference. He was a Millerite who accepted the Sabbatarian position soon after 1844. The first conference of Sabbathkeeping Adventists in New York State was held in his barn (or, as some say, carriage house) at Volney on Aug. 18, 1848. He wrote rather extensively for the early Adventist papers. His expositions of the Bible were essentially standard, although he held a few views that differed slightly from the rest at first—such as that the "daily" represented literal Jewish sacrifices. *(See* L. E. Froom, *Prophetic Faith of Our Fathers,* vol. 4, pp. 1022, 1086, 1087.)

ARNOLD, WILLIAM (1854-1922). Pioneer colporteur. He was born in New York State, and as early as 1882 decided to make colporter work his career. He went as a self-supporting worker to Australia in 1885, and three years later was invited to work in London. He made five trips in 10 years to the West Indies, canvassing on many of the islands and in British Guiana. He worked in Ontario, Canada, and canvassed with success in Alabama and Tennessee. Ill health forced his retirement in 1919.

ART IN THE SEVENTH-DAY ADVENTIST CHURCH. Art in all its disciplines has played an increasingly significant role within the Seventh-day Adventist Church. William Miller and other pioneers who preceded the organization of the church used charts and graphs to clarify the complicated truths of Daniel and Revelation. But these were amateurish and limited. Eventually woodcuts, simple renderings, and then more finished illustrations were used in SDA work and publications as cost permitted.

The great themes of the Bible have challenged artists throughout the centuries, but simple line renderings have been used to communicate volumes of truth that carry eternal consequences.

Today the use of contemporary design, full-color illustrations, and photography are viewed as necessities rather than luxuries as SDAs communicate spiritual truths to a visually literate world.

Art in Evangelism. In the early days of the Seventh-day Adventist Church, illustrative material was extremely limited. Chiefly charts and illustrated diagrams were available, but with these the early evangelists sought to make their preaching effective.

James White, who had probably used the Millerite "1843 chart," picturing the metallic image of Dan. 2, the four beasts of Dan. 7, the ram and he-goat of Dan. 8, the beasts of Revelation, and the three angels of the fourteenth chapter, initiated the printing of SDA prophetic charts. Others using such charts were Joseph Bates, J. N. Loughborough, George I. Butler, and M. E. Cornell. The quality of the art on these early charts tended to be poor.

As evangelism and evangelistic audiences became more sophisticated, the quality of art used for charts was improved. Ingenious visual methods were used both to advertise evangelistic meetings and to illustrate the messages presented. For example, around 1900 William Ward Simpson used life-sized painted papier-mâché sculptured models of the symbolic beasts of prophecy with his evangelistic work, and on a truck displayed them through the streets to advertise his meetings. Ellen White commended his ingenuity. Other evangelists used attractive handbills with many strongly appealing cartoons and posters. Later many evangelists made use of hand-colored glass lantern slides to illustrate gospel songs and biblical topics. Beginning in the 1930s, Kodachrome slides, color movies, overhead projectors, black light, and video presentations have been used.

One- and two-color handbills, posters, and promotional materials proved to be effective forms of advertising through the 1950s and 1960s. But as four-color advertising and trendy design became more widely used, SDA evangelists have needed to use full color in presenting their campaigns. New illustration and contemporary news and stock photos help keep evangelistic campaign promotions current.

Art in Education. In 1887 a course in drawing and painting was offered at Healdsburg College, California, and by 1900 in other SDA colleges. Today most SDA colleges maintain art departments and offer majors and/or minors in art. The courses emphasize basic design, drawing, painting, ceramics, computer graphics, graphic design, sculpture, and photography to enable students to develop a creative use of these mediums. Courses are offered also in art education, art appreciation, and the history of art. Art galleries in some of the colleges have facilitated exposing the students and community to artists' works.

The need for more professionally trained artist-teachers has arisen in both elementary and secondary schools because of the positive aesthetic and therapeutic value of such programs.

A pre-art therapy program presently is being offered at Andrews University. There is an ongoing need by the denomination's publishing houses for skilled graphic designers, photographers, and illustrators. Supplying such professionals who can comprehend fully the church's publishing mission necessitates the training of as many as possible within the SDA educational system.

Illustration in Publishing. The first illustration used in Seventh-day Adventist literature appeared in the *Review and Herald* of Mar. 23, 1852, a reproduction of a tree with the two tables of the law hanging from its branches. It was hand-engraved on wood by Uriah Smith. A similar engraving appeared in the first number of the *Youth's Instructor,* illustrating Sabbath school lessons in August 1852. Later periodicals made somewhat regular use of engraved reproductions of pictures that had appeared elsewhere, as well as some originals.

As demands have increased and scanning, separating, and printing techniques have improved, more full-color work is being used. The use of process color is recognized today as vital to the success of SDA publications, although many still are limited by budgets to one or two colors.

Recognizing the usefulness of pictures to convey a vital truth, James White, in 1876, had a picture prepared entitled *The Way of Life, From Paradise Lost to Paradise Restored,* which he offered for sale with an explanatory leaflet for $1. It showed Jesus on the cross in the center; at the left was the angel expelling

Adam and Eve from Eden. To the right of the cross were pictured the Last Supper and baptism, and in the top right corner the Holy City. It was about 14" x 20" (36 cm. x 50 cm.) in size. Six years later an improved version of the picture appeared. This was copyrighted in 1889 by Ellen G. White with a new title, *Christ, the Way of Life.*

There was a period about 1900, as illustrations were used more plentifully in SDA books and periodicals, when pictures were used that poorly and sometimes falsely represented the facts of the textual matter. Regarding this, Ellen G. White counseled: "I am troubled in regard to the use of pictures in our publications. . . . Some of the cuts used are very inferior, and poorly illustrate the subjects represented. I hope our publications will not come to resemble a comic almanac. I would not altogether condemn the use of pictures, but let fewer be used, and only such as are good illustrations of the subject. . . . If you choose to have a few pictures and good ones, I do not object. Let illustrations be choice rather than numerous" (CW 172).

Yet she also pointed out that "God Himself employed pictures and symbols to represent to His prophets lessons which He would have them give to the people, and which could thus be better understood than if given in any other way. He appealed to the understanding through the sense of sight" (2SM 319).

The first Seventh-day Adventist subscription book on doctrinal subjects, *Thoughts on Daniel and the Revelation,* by Uriah Smith, issued 1882, was illustrated with reproductions from steel engravings of biblical and historical subjects and some wood engravings of prophetic symbols overprinted in flat colors. The foundations of the New Jerusalem were illustrated in colors. A few of the "abundantly illustrated" books of that period were *Bible Readings* (1888) and Ellen G. White's *Steps to Christ* (1892), *Thoughts From the Mount of Blessing* (1896), *Christ's Object Lessons* (1900), and *The Desire of Ages* (1898). The last named, republished in 1900 in two large volumes, 7¾" x 11" (20 cm. x 28 cm.), by the Pacific Press, was undoubtedly the best example, up to that time, of SDA bookmaking and illustration. *The Coming King,* by J. E. White (1898), contained a number of illustrations by the art staff of the Review and Herald, whose Art Department was staffed by Peter J. Rennings, William Robinson, Harry Goodrich, Fred Roberts, Pedro Lemos, Sanford M. Harlan (an apprentice), and a file clerk. However, many of the best pictures were done by freelance illustrators F. Louis Mora and W. B. Davis. Some work was also done by Charles Mente, of Congers, New York.

When the Review and Herald moved to Washington, D.C., in 1906, Sanford Harlan became the nucleus of the Art Department, which was built up by T. K. Martin, who came in 1920 and served through 1968.

In the 1940s a major step forward was taken in the production of a new edition of Uriah Smith's *Daniel and the Revelation.* The illustrating of this book, under the direction of T. K. Martin, introduced a number of original paintings by noted illustrators, giving the prophecies a stronger pictorial presentation. It was about that time that an illustrator of national reputation, Harry Anderson, who had recently joined the SDA Church, began contributing to the Review and Herald publications, and two other SDA illustrators, Clyde Provonsha and John Steel, were commissioned to produce several illustrations for the Southern Publishing Association and the Pacific Press, respectively.

As offset printing came into general use, greater flexibility in the reproduction and use of pictures became possible. Books formerly limited to black and white and a few color tip-ins could now be profusely illustrated in full color. The first successful attempt to produce an all-color set of subscription books was the publication of *The Bible Story,* by Arthur S. Maxwell, in 10 volumes. Twenty-one illustrators were employed to supply pictures for *The Bible Story,* including such outstanding artists as Harry Anderson, Harry Baerg, Jes Schlaikjer, N.A., Vernon Nye, and Russell Harlan (son of Sanford Harlan and great-grandson of John N. Andrews). The quality of art in *The Bible Story* has contributed to the phenomenal sale of the set not only in North America but also abroad.

About the beginning of the 1970s, art in SDA publications assumed a new appearance in keeping with the fast-changing trends and tastes in society. With the new and uninhibited use of the principles of design, an influx of new typefaces, and fresh use of color and textures, the designer's skills were given full freedom of expression.

With constantly changing desktop and litho technology, today's graphic designers enjoy seemingly limitless options. Photos and artwork are created and viewed instantly on desktop computers. Design skills, coupled with new technology, are bringing fresh visual direction to old themes.

Photography in Publishing. Photography plays a large part in the overall account of SDA art, not only for documentary purposes but for promotion of literature and in editorial presentations and book illustrations, both black and white and color. Both U.S. publishing houses have a full-time photographer.

The bridge between photography and computers is narrowing. Photos are being scanned directly into desktop systems for sizing, position, and design. Nevertheless, the eye of the skilled photographer will always have its place in publishing, as photography adds authenticity to printed materials.

Art in Church Departmental Activities. Graphic design, illustration, and photography are making strong contributions to the departmental activities of the church through the use of books, magazines, brochures, videos, and many other promotional and outreach materials. These provide a significant link between the various departments, unions, conferences, and laypersons to which they are sent in the SDA world.

Sculpture. Of the space, or visual, arts, SDAs have made least use of sculpture. William Ward Simpson's papier-mâché models of the prophetic beasts were imitated by other evangelists, who elaborated on his idea, one using a plaster of Paris model of the image of Dan. 2. For years, very little if any sculpture appeared on SDA architecture except as borders and in connection with adapted Gothic design motifs. In 1963 British sculptor Alan Collins, A.R.C.A., A.R.B.S. did a 14-foot (4.3-meter) representation of the three angels of Rev. 14 in high relief, in fiberglas, for the Trans-European Division headquarters building in St. Albans, England. While on the faculty of Andrews University (1971-1978), Collins designed the 22-foot (6.7-meter) abstract sculpture *Regeneration,* adjacent to the College of Technology building. Subsequently, he has made larger-than-life figure groups in stone and bronze—*The Good Samaritan* (1981) for Loma Linda University, and *Christ Our Healer* (1992) for Paradise Valley Hospital. Other works for churches or church institutions are at Bay Knoll church, Rochester, New York; North Hills church, Claremont, California; Atlantic Union College; and Union College. In the planning stage are figure groups for Andrews University (depicting J. N. Andrews and his two children embarking as the first missionaries for the SDA Church) and for the General Conference headquarters *(The Watchers,* eight figures of different ethnic origin, typifying the races of the world in anticipation of the Second Advent).

Another artist, Wayne Hazen, has carved a large wood relief for Founders' Hall at Atlantic Union College and has built a large abstract construction in concrete for the campus of Andrews University. More recently he carved a wood relief sculpture 17 feet (5 meters) long by 7 feet (2 meters) high of the healing hands of Christ for Hinsdale Hospital.

ARUBA. *See* Inter-American Division; Netherlands Antilles.

ARUSHA SDA SEMINARY. *See* Ikizu Secondary School.

A/S HELSEKOST. A small health food store located in Tromsø, Norway, owned and run by the North Norway Rehabilitation Center and the Norwegian Union Conference. Founded in 1973, its sales in 1992 were about $500,000.

Director: Odd Maeland.

ASAMANG SEVENTH-DAY ADVENTIST HOSPITAL. A medical institution in Ghana, operated by the Central Ghana Conference. It was started as a clinic in 1984 by the people of Asamang in the Ashanti region in the Afigya Sekeyer district and is situated on 35 acres (14 hectares) of land donated by the chief and people of Asamang. The Central Ghana Conference provided money for the completion of the building, and it was officially inaugurated in November 1984. The first medical director was Owusu-Achew, assisted by Offeh Gyima, administrator; and Mary Owusuaa, medical assistant.

Equipment, hospital supplies, and a Nissan Urvan bus were donated to the hospital by the SIMANYUI in 1985.

The main hospital building is made up of a single block containing three in-patient wards, a labor ward, operating theater, injection and dressing room, consulting, accounting, and administration sections. Phase one of a building project, which was started in 1991, has been realized with the completion of the maternity block. The construction of a new operating theater will start in 1994.

Medical Directors: Owusu-Achew, 1984-

1987; E. E. Nyatepe-Coo, 1987-1988; J. Oduro, 1988- .

ASDAN-NAD. *See* Association of Seventh-day Adventist Nurses.

ASI. *See* Adventist-Laymen's Services and Industries.

ASIA. *See* names of countries in Asia.

ASIATIC DIVISION. A former unit of church organization that was in existence from 1909 to 1918. It was composed originally of China, India, Japan, Korea, Malay Peninsula, Philippine Islands, and Straits Settlements (the territory of the later China, Far Eastern, and Southern Asia divisions). In 1910 India, Burma, and Ceylon were formed into the India Union Mission, which in a reorganization in 1915 was reunited with the Asiatic Division. In the same year, the Australasian Union Conference also became a part of the division. At the General Conference session of 1918 these units were separated again. The India Union Mission and the Australasian Union Conference (with its island mission territory) were both placed under the supervision of J. E. Fulton (former president of the Asiatic Division), whereas the Far Eastern section, including the East Asian Union, the North China Union, the South China Union, and the Philippine Union, was placed under the supervision of I. H. Evans, with headquarters in the old division headquarters at Shanghai. At the council of the Far Eastern section, held in March 1919, this Far Eastern section adopted the name "Far Eastern Division of the General Conference of Seventh-day Adventists"; from this the China Division was later separated. In 1920 the India Union Mission became the Southern Asia Division of the General Conference, at first called the Eastern Asia Division. In 1922 the Australasian Union Conference became the Australasian Division.

ASOCIACIÓN CASA EDITORA SUDAMERICANA. *See* Buenos Aires Publishing House.

ASOCIACIÓN CIVIL FILANTROPICA Y EDUCATIVA. *See* Mexico, IV, 2.

ASOCIACIÓN PUBLICADORA INTERAMERICANA. *See* Inter-American Publishing Association.

ASOKORE SEVENTH-DAY ADVENTIST TEACHER TRAINING COLLEGE. An institution established in 1962 and operated at Asokore-Kofondua, Ghana, West Africa. The original name, according to the *Yearbook,* was Koforidua Day-Teacher Training College. It became a boarding institution in 1964 and is a postsecondary teacher training institution.

The total student enrollment in 1993 was 640, which represents a 15 percent increase over previous years.

A serious effort is made on the part of staff to maintain high academic standards, which has resulted typically in 99 percent success in the external examinations. The spiritual aspect of the school is emphasized. In addition to the regular Week of Prayer, a special one is organized to coincide with the beginning of the external exams. In 1993 more than 30 students were baptized into the Adventist faith.

Presently under construction is an assembly hall-church building. It is being financed solely by the college church community, made up of students and staff. Future projects for the school include the construction of an ultramodern administration and library complex and additional staff housing.

In 1994 the college was to become a "polytechnic"—one of the regional colleges of arts, science, and technology.

Principals: C. Y. Kyereme, 1962-1967; I. T. Agboka, 1967-1976; J. A. Manu, 1976-1982; M. E. Duodu, 1982-1991; C. Kuma-Korante, 1991- .

ASSAM REGION. *See* India; Southern Asia Division.

ASSOCIATION OF ADVENTIST PARENTS (AAP). An organization developed as a specific means of helping meet the increasing drug problem in the Seventh-day Adventist Church, especially for those who may already be involved in chemical or other dependencies.

Initiative for AAP as an organization came from the grass roots level, beginning with an informal group of 13 parents meeting in Washington, D.C., to discuss forming a parent support movement within the church. Exploratory meetings determined the feasibility of such an organization and climaxed in a mass rally of parents, educators, and church leaders who called for immediate action.

Formal organization was completed on Apr. 27, 1985, in Atlanta, Georgia, at which time bylaws were adopted and a board of directors was chosen, along with a panel of educational and professional advisors. The basic aim of AAP is described in its statement of philosophy: "The use and abuse of both legal and illegal drugs in the Seventh-day Adventist Church have reached challenging proportions. Such use has extended into many segments of our church, bringing with it individual loss, spiritual degeneration, and disregard for law and regulation. With the ever younger age of drug and alcohol users, even extending to elementary school children, we as parents feel that we must join together to accomplish the changes necessary to ensure a drug-free environment to today's and the children yet to come. . . . We are committed to work in a productive, nonjudgmental manner to create positive change in the church, home, school, and community."

The AAP works in close cooperation with other parent groups and community efforts to encourage recovery from and to prevent addictive problems. It helps provide resources for parents and youth to prevent, reduce, or eliminate drug use. Another aim of the AAP is to provide referral for those needing information as to places or persons who can help families in crisis.

A major project of AAP is the Celebration of Recovery, which is a weekend spiritual retreat for Adventists with dependency problems. These celebrations explore spiritual resources for recovery and provide opportunity for participants to share experiences, strength, and hope, and to offer praise to God for the gift of continuing sobriety.

The AAP is a membership organization open to anyone desirous of furthering the purposes of the organization, benefiting from its services, or contributing (financial or otherwise) to its program. Where feasible, AAP encourages the formation of local parent support groups to help families and youth facing addiction and dependency problems.

ASSOCIATION OF ADVENTIST PHYSICISTS. An organization developed in 1976 with the purpose of facilitating communication among its members and fostering a sense of community, promoting the science of physics and its responsible application to human endeavors, providing a forum for the continued development of an integrated view of science and theology, providing a common voice of its members to other individuals and organizations, and coordinating efforts and initiating programs of interest to the group.

The association publishes the *Newsletter of the Association of Adventist Physicists* four times a year. It is sent free to all physicists who request it and to all SDA academy and college campuses.

Presidents: Milo Anderson, 1976-1978; Bob Kingman, 1978-1980; Clark Rowland, 1980-1982; Ed Karlow, 1982-1984; Terry Anderson, 1984-1986; Ivan Rouse, 1986-1988; Ken Thomson, 1988-1990; Bill Mundy, 1990-1992; Milo Anderson, 1992-1994; Ed Karlow, 1994-1996.

ASSOCIATION OF PRIVATELY OWNED SEVENTH-DAY ADVENTIST SERVICES AND INDUSTRIES. *See* Adventist-Laymen's Services and Industries.

ASSOCIATION OF SDA HISTORIANS. An organization founded in San Francisco on Dec. 28, 1973, designed, according to its constitution, to "provide intellectual and social fellowship among its members, encourage scholarly pursuits in all the historical disciplines, identify Seventh-day Adventist teachers of history both within and without the church's educational system as well as researchers and graduate students working in historical fields, [and] acquaint others with our contributions as historians."

The association meets annually in conjunction with the convention of the Organization of American Historians. Its newsletter and directory have provided members with networking information about fellow historians.

ASSOCIATION OF SDA INSTITUTIONS OF HIGHER EDUCATION AND SECONDARY SCHOOLS. An association of denominationally owned and controlled institutions of higher education and secondary schools throughout the world that (1) have been approved and registered by, or accredited with, state, regional, or national associations or by the Board of Regents of the Department of Education of the General Conference, and (2) are operated in harmony with the aims and policies approved by the General Conference and by the educational boards and executive committees of the union conferences and divisions in which the schools are situated.

It was brought into existence in 1929 as the Association of Seventh-day Adventist Colleges and Secondary Schools to deal with common problems in the North American Division confronting denominationally owned and operated schools in their relationship with university, state, and regional accrediting organizations. Membership consisted of the Board of Regents of the General Conference Department of Education (the executive committee of the association), qualifying SDA educational institutions, certain honorary members, secretary and associate secretaries of the General Conference Department of Education, and union conference secretaries of education. The secretary of the Department of Education is the president (formerly chair) of the association. In 1943 the name of the association was changed to Association of SDA Institutions of Higher Education and Secondary Schools. By 1954 the organization was enlarged beyond North America to include institutions of higher education, training schools, and secondary schools of the overseas divisions, and duties were expanded. The organization aimed "to assist member institutions in identifying, reaching, and maintaining adequate standards in administration, management, teaching, scholarship, Christian worship and service and citizenship, character training, and health education, and to assist the church in understanding and giving support to its system of schools," and to assist the educational institutions of the church in interpreting and meeting the needs of the denomination and its young people. In 1962 the constitution and bylaws were revised, enlarging the Board of Regents, making provision for representation on it from college departments of education and additional representation from academy principals and union conference secretaries of education. The association became inactive in 1970 when the Association of Seventh-day Adventist Educators was organized.

ASSOCIATION OF SDA NURSES. A church-sponsored organization for promoting the ideals and principles of Seventh-day Adventist nursing, to encourage SDA young people to enter the nursing profession, to keep members informed as to the need for SDA nurses in denominational work and other places, to encourage practicing nurses to give spiritual assistance to patients while caring for their physical needs according to the instructions and teachings of the denomination, and to advance the standards of SDA nurses and nursing, the care of the sick, and the honor and character of the nursing profession. The organization is commonly referred to as ASDAN.

On May 7, 1967, 45 registered nurses of the North American Division met at the New York Center, to organize an association of SDA nurses. The following officers were elected for a two-year term: president, Maureen Maxwell; president-elect, Alice E. Smith; secretary-treasurer, Marjorie Cornor; board members at large, Naomi Gowan and Ellen Gibson; executive director, Mazie A. Herin.

ASDAN holds an annual meeting usually preceding or following the meetings of the American Nurses' Association or the National League for Nursing.

ASDAN awards honors to outstanding SDA nurses through the Nurse of the Year and the Hall of Fame programs. At the 1974 annual meeting the president recognized 18 chapters of ASDAN located in various sections of the North American Division. The secretary reported a total of 1,879 members in the association. ASDAN publishes the *Forum* four times a year as its official organ.

Other divisions have formed or are planning to organize associations for SDA nurses. The British Adventist Nurses Association (BANA) was organized Apr. 1, 1972. Tabitha Abel was elected the first president; Ruth Balderstone, secretary; Ann Marie Kelly, treasurer. This association publishes the *BANA Newsletter* several times a year.

The Pan American SDA Nurses Association was organized in November 1972, and the nurses of the Mexican Union organized in 1973. For a number of years SDA nurses in Germany have had an association called Friedensauer Schwesternschaft. The nurses in Brazil and Argentina are working on separate organizations for SDA nurses in these countries.

ASDAN ceased to exist as a membership organization in 1993 and became ASDAN-NAD, an official committee of the North American Division. The mission remains the same.

Chair: R. L. Dale, 1993- .

President: M. Ringer, 1993- .

ASSOCIATION OF SDA OPTOMETRISTS. An organization established by a group of practicing optometrists of the Seventh-day Adventist Church in June 1958 at the White Memorial Hospital in Los Angeles, California. Its purpose is sixfold: to aid in spiritual development of its members; to promote greater missionary activities through their offices and their churches; to encourage active participation in foreign mission service; to encourage students in SDA academies and colleges to study optometry; to stimulate members in current scientific developments; to encourage members to attend the annual meetings for spiritual and social development.

The members of this organization are confined to individuals that subscribe to the code of ethics of the American Optometric Association and who are members in good standing in the SDA Church. Student membership may be granted to individuals of accredited schools and colleges of optometry who also are members in good standing in the SDA Church. They may be entitled to all rights and privileges of regular members except the right to vote or hold office. Meetings of the association shall be held annually during the months of June, July, or August, usually just prior to the annual meeting of the American Optometric Association or at such other time and place as shall be determined by the president and the board of directors. In August 1973 the first SDA optometrist, Dr. Robert Baker, was given mission appointment by the General Conference to the island of Guam in the Far Eastern Division. Since then, this clinic has been expanded with the addition of two more optometrists and an opthamologist. Eye clinics also have been established in Manzini, Swaziland; Lilongwe, Malawi; and on the islands of Palau and Saipan.

The organization is a member of the Health Advisory Commission for the General Conference of Seventh-day Adventists. In 1993 Clarence D. Omans was serving as assistant director for vision affairs in the Health and Temperance Department of the General Conference.

ASTRONOMY. From the beginning Seventh-day Adventists have had an interest in certain elements of astronomy as they relate to certain aspects of their teaching: 1. *Chronology.* Seventh-day Adventists inherited their chronology of the 2300 prophetic days from the Millerites, who had cited for it the canon, or king list, of the ancient astronomer Ptolemy as well as the ancient lunisolar calendar. 2. *The Sabbath.* Advocacy of the Sabbath often evokes the demand for an explanation of certain problems, such as the phenomenon of the day beginning at the date line and traveling with sunset round the rotating globe; of the sunset reckoning of the Sabbath in the polar regions, which is connected with the inclination of the earth's axis; of the continuity of the week *(see* Sabbath, VI; Week).

Astronomical cycles cannot identify the first Sabbath (or the year of Creation or the day of the Crucifixion); but there are certain dates in OT history that have been fixed by astronomical computation (for example, in Nebuchadnezzar's reign; see SDADic, "Chronology," V, 3; SDACom 2:152; SB, No. 452). On the other hand, the very absence of any astronomical basis for a seven-day cycle is cited by SDAs as strengthening the case for the Mosaic account of the origin of the week (see SB, Nos. 1762, 1766; also *Encyclopaedia Britannica (*11th ed.), vol. 4, p. 988). 3. *Cosmic-theological concept.* Beginning with Ellen G. White's early references to other planets (2SG 83; EW 39, 40), which influenced the pioneer leader Joseph Bates, SDAs developed a sort of cosmic-theological concept of the earth as a planet—indeed, a revolted planet—among other worlds in an orderly universe sustained by the Creator. They see world history as a cosmic demonstration of both the results of sin on a rebel world and the redemptive power of God's love; and they envision the re-creation of this globe as Paradise restored *(see* Home of the Redeemed).

In addition, evangelists have often employed popularized descriptions of the heavenly bodies as examples of the obedience of the cosmos to God's natural law, and as evidence of His creative and sustaining power.

ASUNCIÓN ADVENTIST ACADEMY (Colegio Adventista de Asunción). A coeducational secondary school that specializes in Japanese language education as well as Spanish. Part of the Paraguay Mission, it is located in Asunción, capital of Paraguay, in the heart of South America.

It was built in 1971, with a small dormitory for Japanese students and a school building to be used for teaching in the Japanese language. In 1993, 145 students attended the Japanese school.

In 1975 an elementary school in Spanish was opened, and in 1980 the initial high school classes were taught. In 1982 the full high school program of six years training was added. The academy has been accredited by the Board of Regents since 1986.

In 1993, 185 off-campus students were in attendance, served by 17 teachers. The library contains 3,350 volumes.

Principals: Segio Sosa, 1980-1982; Eugenio Di Dionisio, 1983-1990; Osvaldo Ruben Cayrus, 1991- .

ASUNCIÓN ADVENTIST SANITARIUM (Sanatorio Adventista de Asunción) (formerly Paraguay Adventist Sanitarium and

Hospital). A general acute hospital owned and operated by the Austral Union Conference, situated in the capital city of Asunción on the principal road leading to the interior (Pettirossi 372). The brick building (its interior portion three stories high), with 25 adult beds, two pediatric beds, five bassinets, and an Isolette incubator, provides care for private as well as charity patients and has facilities for surgical, obstetrical, medical, and pediatric cases. The staff consists of two physicians, an administrator, 14 nurses, a physiotherapist, and 10 auxiliary personnel.

The forerunner of the sanitarium was the Fisioterapia Mayo (Asunción Treatment Rooms), which was opened under the auspices of the Paraguay Mission in August 1945 and was staffed by Miguel Esparcia and his wife and Arnol Treiyer, graduate nurses from the River Plate Sanitarium in Argentina. In April 1954 Ira E. Bailie, M.D., a graduate from Loma Linda, arrived to direct the medical work in Asunción. Plans were drawn up, and construction was begun on a hospital building on land previously purchased. The building was completed in February 1957, at which time the Fisioterapia Mayo was transferred to its new headquarters, but it was not until 1959 that equipment arrived making inpatient care possible. On May 18, 1959, the first patient was admitted, the next day the first surgery was performed, and a few days later the first baby was born. Though the hospital was functioning, it was not inaugurated until a few months later, July 26, 1959.

It was not long until the sanitarium bed capacity was inadequate, and in November 1960 land adjoining the original plot was purchased and plans were laid to increase the bed capacity and to modernize the outpatient facilities. The first stage of this expansion project was begun in August 1962, and was completed in 1964. An expansion project being planned will bring the capacity to 50 beds. The second stage of the expansion now in progress will add 1,076 square yards (900 square meters), which will permit relocation of surgery, intensive care, and other facilities. The space now used for these services will provide room for 10 new beds. The planned expansion will require the services of four additional doctors (a general physician, a surgeon, a gynecologist, a pediatrician), four nurses, two nurse's aides, a biochemist, a chaplain, and an administrative employee. This hospital serves all economic classes; more than two thirds of the patients come from low-income groups.

Medical Directors: Ira E. Bailie, 1959-1972; Juan Carlos Drachenberg, 1972-1975; Alcides Cairus, 1975-1978; Guillermo Richards, 1978-1980; Haroldo Janetzko, 1980-1984; Enrique Manrique, 1984- .

ATHENS INTERNATIONAL ACADEMY. An English language secondary school that operated from 1972 to 1982 under the direction of Home Study Institute. From an enrollment of 12 in 1972 the number of students rose to a peak of 35. During its existence more than 80 young people enrolled in the school, and a significant number of these made their decision for baptism. A total of 10 student missionaries gave invaluable assistance in math and science classes.

After a decade of operation, the school was closed; it was a unique experience for the students, teachers, and the Greek Mission.

Principals: Nick Germanis, 1972-1982.

ATLANTA ADVENTIST ACADEMY. A college preparatory high school serving the Seventh-day Adventist youth of the Greater Atlanta area. The academy has been in operation as a senior academy since 1979 and has an average enrollment in the nineties. A high percentage of the students are enrolled in a college preparatory course. Ten constituent churches support this high school. In the past two years, approximately $500,000 has been spent in expansion and refurbishing. Buildings on campus include an administration building, chapel, elementary school, music building, and gymnatorium.

Principals: Keith Gibbons, 1979; David Fardulis, 1980; William Worth, 1981-1982; Victor Kostenko, 1983-1987; William Ruby, 1987-1991; Dean Maddock, 1991- .

ATLANTIC COLOMBIA MISSION. *See* Colombia; Inter-American Division.

ATLANTIC CONFERENCE. A former unit of church organization existing in North America from 1889 to 1902. It originally embraced New York City, Long Island, New Jersey, Delaware, Maryland, and the District of Columbia. In 1899 it was reduced to Greater New York, Long Island, and New Jersey, when the southern portion was formed into the Chesapeake Conference. In 1902 the Atlantic Conference was divided into the Greater New York (including Long Island) and New Jersey conferences.

ATLANTIC SCHOOL. *See* Adventist Atlantic Secondary School.

ATLANTIC UNION COLLEGE (AUC). A coeducational four-year undergraduate liberal arts college operated by the Atlantic Union Conference. With more than a century of recognized academics behind it, the small New England college has an international student body. It first opened in 1882 as an academy. Its strategic location in South Lancaster, Massachusetts, 40 miles (65 kilometers) west of Boston, 15 miles (25 kilometers) north of Worcester, and 190 miles (305 kilometers) northeast of New York City, allows for cultural outings to museums and concert halls, as well as to nearby historic landmarks.

Incorporated under the laws of Massachusetts, it is authorized to grant the degrees of Bachelor of Arts, Bachelor of Science, Bachelor of Arts in Music, Master of Education, and Associate in Science. AUC is a member of the New England Association of Colleges and Secondary Schools, is on the approved list of the Board of Regents of the University of the State of New York, and is a member of the Association of American Colleges.

The faculty of Atlantic Union College has adopted a master plan that emphasizes traditional and nontraditional academic programs. Besides the on-campus program, the college offers other programs for those interested. Continuing education coordinates degree programs for people who live within commuting distance of the college, particularly in afternoon and evening courses. The adult degree program, begun in 1972, is open to adults 25 or older and is arranged as the student proposes a semester's plan for earning 16 credits. The electronic distance learning program offers college courses via computers for unserved segments of the population, such as residents of correctional facilities and mental institutions. Enrollments in these programs in 1993 were: on-campus program, 653; continuing education, 143; adult degree program, 109; and electronic distance learning, 543.

On Atlantic Union College's tree-lined, 330-acre (133-hectare) campus tradition and technology not only coexist but thrive. The college's book collection, consisting in 1993 of more than 110,000 volumes, has been housed since 1970 in the G. Eric Jones Library. The present college administration building, Haskell Hall, first occupied in the autumn of 1951, is named for the founder of the college, S. N. Haskell.

In 1975 the college restored its first administration building, the oldest academic building at an SDA college still standing on its original site. Now called Founders Hall, the 107-year-old building contains a chapel, classrooms, and offices for the Department of Theology and Religion. On display are Bundy's portraits of Mr. and Mrs. William Miller, a pulpit used by Miller, and other Adventist memorabilia.

The Bartlett Art Gallery is a local museum landmark purchased by the college in 1973, named for Mabel R. Bartlett, professor emeritus of art, and renovated as the headquarters of the college's Art Department. The Thayer Conservatory of Music is housed in an elegant nineteenth-century mansion once owned by New England's prestigious Thayer family.

In 1993, under the coordination of Lawrence Geraty, then college president, ground was broken for the Chan Shun Dining Commons, named in honor of its major donor, an SDA philanthropist.

The college's two main dormitories are Rachel Preston Hall and Lenheim Hall. In addition, the college maintains apartments for married students.

History. Early in 1882 S. N. Haskell called the quarterly meeting of the New England Tract and Missionary Society to meet in Lancaster to consider the "propriety of establishing a Seventh-day Adventist school at some point in New England," also to find out how many would patronize the school if established, and whether the members were ready to support such a venture.

At the meeting, held Feb. 4 and 5, 1882, most of those who spoke on the subject were strongly in favor of the project. Resolutions were passed indicating approval, Dores A. Robinson and F. W. Mace were named to meet with the conference committee (S. N. Haskell, C. W. Comings, J. C. Tucker) to act as a school committee.

The school committee chose South Lancaster as the place for the new institution and announced that the school would open about the first of April. G. H. Bell, of Battle Creek College, was chosen as the first principal.

The first term opened on Apr. 19, 1882, with 19 pupils. The teachers included S. N. Haskell, G. H. Bell, Dores A. Robinson, Edith Sprague, and Maria Huntley. For a time the small new school went unnamed; frequent articles about the new educational project appearing in the *Review and Herald* referred to it simply as "that New England school," a name that indicated neither its educational level nor its specific locality in New England.

The enrollment continued to increase so that the school had to be moved from its original one room to the basement of the South Lancaster church, which it occupied from September 1882 until June 1884.

At the close of the fall term, on Nov. 29, 1882, the New England Conference, in a meeting in South Lancaster, voted to form a permanent school organization according to the laws of the state and to raise $15,000 to purchase and erect buildings and purchase land in South Lancaster or elsewhere. On Dec. 12, 1883, a board of managers was elected and the school was incorporated under the laws of Massachusetts as South Lancaster Academy. Land was purchased and permanent academy buildings were erected, which were dedicated on Oct. 29, 1884.

Although advanced courses were offered for some years in several departments, it was not until 1918, during the administration of M. E. Olsen, that the school became a full-fledged junior college, and the name was changed to Lancaster Junior College.

In 1922, under the presidency of Benjamin F. Machlan, the college was granted the right to confer the Bachelor of Theology degree to those finishing a new four-year course. At the same time, the name was changed to Atlantic Union College.

In 1926 permission was granted to give a Bachelor of Religious Education degree. In 1927 the Atlantic Union College Alumni Association was organized. In 1933 permission was granted by Massachusetts to confer the Bachelor of Arts degree. Regional accreditation was achieved in 1945. Permission was granted to confer the Bachelor of Science degree in 1954.

The college paper, *The Lancastrian,* had earlier predecessors. *The True Educator*, beginning in April 1884, was published by South Lancaster Academy. At first an eight-page monthly, it was enlarged during the administration of C. C. Ramsay to 16 pages, and the subscription list reached about 800. In 1890 the academy students began to publish a new monthly paper called *The Kaleidoscope*, but there were only five issues. In December 1907 the students began another paper called *The Student Idea*, which in October 1926 became *The Lancastrian*.

Presidents (for principals from the beginning, *see* South Lancaster Academy): *Lancaster Junior College:* Mahlon E. Olsen, 1918-1920; George R. Lehman, 1920-1921; Benjamin F. Machlan, 1921-1922.

Atlantic Union College: Benjamin F. Machlan, 1922-1928; Otto M. John, 1928-1936; G. Eric Jones, 1936-1948; Lewis N. Holm, 1948-1953; Lawrence M. Stump, 1953-1960; Robert L. Reynolds, 1960-1968; Herbert E. Douglass, 1968-1970; William G. Nelson, 1970-1975; R. Dale McCune, 1975-1980; Larry M. Lewis, 1980-1985; Lawrence T. Geraty, 1985-1993; James Londis, 1993- .

ATLANTIC UNION CONFERENCE. A unit of church administration in North America comprising the following conferences: Bermuda, Greater New York, New York, Northeastern, Northern New England, and Southern New England. Headquarters are at South Lancaster, Massachusetts. Official organ: *Atlantic Union Gleaner*. Statistics (1992): churches, 399; members, 74,130; church or elementary schools, 71; ordained ministers, 279; credentialed commissioned ministers, 17; licensed ministers, 47; licensed commissioned ministers, 20; Bible instructors, 36; credentialed commissioned ministers of teaching, 134; licensed commissioned ministers of teaching, 130.

Institutions. Adventist Healthcare Corporation, which includes Boston Regional Medical Center and Fuller Memorial Hospital; Atlantic Union College; Bermuda Institute; Greater Boston Academy; Greater New York Academy; Northeastern Academy; Parkview Memorial Hospital; Pine Tree Academy; South Lancaster Academy; Union Springs Academy; Victory Lake Nursing Home.

The Atlantic Union Conference, originally called the Eastern Union Conference, was formed Apr. 16, 1901, at the General Conference session. At that time it was made up of nine conferences (Maine, Vermont, New England, New York, Pennsylvania, Atlantic, Chesapeake, Virginia, and Quebec) and two mission fields (the Maritime Provinces and Newfoundland).

Later, at the first biennial session of this union, held Nov. 27 to Dec. 5, 1901, the name was changed to Atlantic Union Conference. At this meeting the territories of Quebec, the Maritime Provinces, and Newfoundland were separated from the Atlantic Union and made part of the Canadian Union Conference.

In 1907 the southern part of the union (the New Jersey, East and West Pennsylvania, Chesapeake, Virginia, and West Virginia conferences) was given over to the then-forming Columbia Union Conference. About 1915 the Bermuda Mission was added to the Atlantic Union Conference.

Presidents: H. W. Cottrell, 1901-1906; E. W. Farnsworth, 1906-1909; W. B. White, 1909-1913; R. D. Quinn, 1913-1919; E. K. Slade, 1919-1932; J. K. Jones, 1932-1936; W. H. Heckman, 1936-1938; M. L. Rice, 1939-1951; L. E. Lenheim, 1951-1958; W. J. Hackett, 1958-1964; F. R. Millard, 1964-1969; K. W. Tilghman, 1969-1971; J. L. Dittberner, 1971-1979; E. A. Amundson, 1979-1985; P. S. Follett, 1986-1992; D. L. Taylor, 1992-1994; Theodore T. Jones, 1994- .

ATLANTIC UNION GLEANER (1902- ; monthly; files in GC). Official organ of the Atlantic Union Conference; 24 pages circulated to 8,500 constituent church members.

ATOIFI ADVENTIST HOSPITAL. A 100-bed general hospital with facilities for midwifery, surgery, and treatment of tropical diseases. It is situated in East Kwaio on the east coast of Malaita Island in the Solomon Islands, and is owned and operated by the Western Pacific Union of Seventh-day Adventists. The first buildings were funded by the fourth quarter 1965 Thirteenth Sabbath Offering overflow. The first carpenter, Michael, a Solomon Islander, arrived at Atoifi on July 12, 1963, 11 days after his 11-year-old daughter, Linda, died of dysentery.

Brian and Valmae Dunn from Australia were the first nurses appointed to serve at Atoifi Hospital. Eleven days after their arrival, Dec. 19, 1965, while caring for an outpatient, Brian met his death when he was speared by a hostile native. Lens Larwood was appointed in 1966 to take Brian's place. He died in a tractor accident on Aug. 15, 1979.

The hospital was officially opened on Aug. 25, 1966, and has X-ray and laboratory facilities, with power being supplied by a hydro generator.

For many years the *M.V. Dani,* a 28-foot (8.5-meter) medical launch, was used for medical patrols and infant and maternal welfare clinics. It has been replaced by motorized canoes.

No roads link Atoifi to the outside world. The main contact is through the mission-owned airline. Occasionally the island is served by small passenger or cargo boats. Most patients arrive by canoe or by walking down from the hills.

Two permanent clinics are operated from Atoifi at Honoa and Sango, and village health workers are trained in elementary medical and health care and work in some villages.

Ian Cameron began the nurse training program in 1973, but accreditation of the program was opposed; the first official general nurse program began in 1981. Graduates from this program serve in the 14 Seventh-day Adventist clinics in the Solomon Islands as well as those in Kiribati and Vanuatu. The graduates also are in demand for service in the government's health service.

In 1992 the hospital had 1,602 admissions, treated 23,000 outpatients, and performed 600 surgical procedures. Also, 2,002 patients were treated on patrols and 2,004 were examined in infant welfare clinics.

Medical Superintendents: Dr. L. H. McMahon, 1966-1969; Dr. H. Posala, 1969-1982; Dr. D. Pikacha, 1982-1984; Dr. J. Chee, 1986-1989; Dr. C. Kuma, 1989- .

Directors of Nursing: B. Dunn, 1965; L. Larwood, 1966-1979; R. Leet, 1980-1981; B. Robinson, 1982-1986; B. Vavozo, 1986- .

Directors of School of Nursing: I. Cameron, 1973-1978; L. Doble, 1979-1981; G. Evans, 1982-1984; G. Wilson, 1985; J. Jays, 1986-1989; J. Tutuo, 1989-1991; L. Hope, 1992- .

ATONEMENT. Hebrew *kippurîm,* from *kaphar,* "to make atonement," generally believed to have the basic meaning of "to cover." The Greek *katallagē,* "reconciliation," is translated "atonement" once (Rom. 5:11) in the KJV. Theologically atonement is the process by which a sinner is reconciled to God or brought into a state of at-one-ment with Him. Christ's vicarious sacrifice upon the cross is the central, decisive, effective act in this process, and without it all else would be insufficient to atone for sin. The atonement there provided was perfect and complete. It was "once for all" in the sense that it would never have to be repeated. Having made the atonement on the cross, Christ ascended to heaven as our great high priest, there to be our intercessor and to minister on our behalf the benefits of the atonement made available at the cross (Heb. 7:27; 9:12, 26; 10:10). Since His ascension Christ ever lives to make intercession for us, and this intercession is part of the work of reconciliation, or atonement, in its larger sense (Heb. 7:25; 8:1, 2; 9:11, 12; 10:12-14, 21, 22). Accordingly He invites us to draw near to the throne of grace with confidence, "that we may obtain mercy, and find grace to help in time of need" (Heb. 4:16).

Some early Adventists, basing their definition of the term on its OT meaning with reference to the ancient sanctuary service, and believing that the ancient priests served "unto the example and shadow of heavenly things" (Heb. 8:5), stressed this high-priestly aspect of Christ's atoning ministry to the point of seeming to deny that His sacrifice on the cross could properly be called a work of atonement. William Miller, for instance, wrote that Christ's shedding of His blood on Calvary for a sinful world was "the propitiatory sacrifice to God," but that the atonement "is made by his life and intercession in heaven (Heb. 7:25)," "so that through his intercession we can be saved by his life (Rom. 5:10; 1 John 5:11)" (letter of Nov. 22, 1844, in *Western Midnight Cry* 4:26, Dec. 21, 1844).

The misunderstanding arising from the denial by Miller and by some early SDA writers that atonement was made on the cross is a matter of semantics. None of those who denied this denied either the fact or the efficacy of Christ's sacrifice made on the cross, nor did they believe that He offered another sacrifice in heaven. They were simply using the word "atonement" in its original, biblical sense rather than in the popular theological sense. They pointed out that in the ancient sanctuary service atonement was made for the sinner, not by the slaying of the sacrificial offering, but by the *priestly ministry* performed within the sanctuary *after* the sacrifice had been slain: "And he [the penitent] shall lay his hand upon the head of the sin offering, and slay the sin offering in the place of the burnt offering.

"And the priest shall take of the blood thereof. . . . And the priest shall burn it [the fat] upon the altar for a sweet savour unto the Lord; and the priest shall make an atonement for him, and it shall be forgiven him" (Lev. 4:29-31; cf. v. 27).

They contended that the atoning ministry of Christ in the heavenly sanctuary since His ascension—and not His sacrifice on Calvary—was the biblical counterpart of the atoning ministry of the priest in the earthly sanctuary after the sacrifice had been slain (Heb. 9:11-15, 23-26; 10:11-14; cf. Lev. 4:27-31, etc.). Thus when Miller and other early Adventists spoke of the atonement as being made *not* on the cross, but by Christ after His ascension to heaven, they were technically correct insofar as the use of the word "atonement" in ritual law was concerned. However, contemporary theological usage of the word "atonement" does not include its biblical application to the priestly *ministration* of the blood of a sacrifice that had already been slain. This is the reason the Seventh-day Adventist position on the atonement has sometimes been misunderstood and misrepresented. In any discussion of the atonement, it is important that this distinction between biblical and modern theological use of the word be recognized.

The relationship between Christ's sacrifice on the cross and His priestly ministry in heaven since His ascension is explained thus by Ellen G. White: "The intercession of Christ in man's behalf in the sanctuary above is as essential to the plan of salvation as was His death upon the cross. By His death He began that work which after His resurrection He ascended to complete in heaven" (GC 489).

"The great sacrifice had been offered, and had been accepted, and the Holy Spirit which descended on the day of Pentecost carried the minds of the disciples from the earthly sanctuary to the heavenly, where Jesus had entered by His own blood, to shed upon His disciples the benefits of His atonement" (EW 260; first published in 1858 in 1SG 170).

But that this position in no sense depreciates the atonement provided at the cross is evident from her further comments: "The sacrifice of Christ as an atonement for sin is the great truth around which all other truths cluster" (Ellen G. White, in SDACom 5:1137).

"The cross must occupy the central place because it is the means of man's atonement and because of the influence it exerts on every part of the divine government" (6T 236).

"Christ's words on the mountainside [in Galilee after the Resurrection] were the announcement that His sacrifice in behalf of man was full and complete. The conditions of the atonement had been fulfilled; the work for which He came to this world had been accomplished" (MS 138, 1897).

When SDAs speak of Christ's work of atonement in the heavenly sanctuary, they refer to the application to each individual believer, according to his/her need, of the benefits of salvation provided for all at Calvary.

In the ancient sanctuary the solemn services of the annual Day of Atonement brought the yearly ritual cycle to a close (Lev. 16). The work of atonement, or reconciliation, performed on that day brought to completion all that the sanctuary and the priests could do for repentant sinners, and cleansed the sanctuary and the people. On the basis of the clear analogy drawn by the inspired writer of Hebrews between the earthly sanctuary and that in heaven, SDAs recognize in the final phase of the heavenly ministry of Christ a counterpart of the earthly Day of Atonement service. SDAs refer to this concluding phase of Christ's ministry of reconciliation as the "great antitypical day of atonement," and the "investigative judgment" *(see also* Sanctuary).

The need for a reconciliation, or atonement, between God and humanity derives from the fact that when Adam sinned "sin entered into the world, and death by sin; and so death passed upon all men, for that all have sinned" (Rom. 5:12; cf. 3:23). Disobedience separated human beings from their Maker, and the outraged divine law demanded the death of the transgressors. God's justice required that all imperfection must be eradicated. But since humans were the offspring of a loving Creator, almighty love planned a way of escape for those who had fallen into the trap of sin set for them by Satan.

Being a reflection of the character of God, the moral law is immutable. There is nothing sinners can do to recommend themselves to God or to bring about reconciliation. Accordingly God made provision for reconciling sinners to Himself should the need arise. The plan was devised before the creation of Adam (1 Peter 1:20), and explained to him before his expulsion from Eden (Gen. 3:15). This plan called for the Son of God to lay aside His divine power, to be clothed with a human body, to meet temptation as humans must meet it, yet without sin, and to die a vicarious death in the sinner's place. He would be treated as the worst of sinners, and experiencing separation from the love and presence of the Father, He would suffer for all sinners. He paid the price of sin and offered humanity His righteousness.

John 3:16 summarizes the plan of the atonement: "For God so loved the world, that he gave his only begotten Son, that whosoever believeth in him should not perish, but have everlasting life." The love of God is free, but it must be believed and accepted voluntarily. It is available to all, but not all accept it. There can be no atonement for those who "neglect so great salvation" and refuse to "live by faith" (Heb. 2:3; Rom. 1:17). A complete atonement must not only afford pardon for past sins but also provide human beings with power to overcome temptation. For this reason Christ lived among humans as their example and also offers them the Holy Spirit to enable them to live sinless lives.

ATONEMENT, DAY OF. *See* Investigative Judgment; Sanctuary; Scapegoat.

ATS. *See* American Temperance Society.

AUBURN ADVENTIST ACADEMY. A coeducational boarding school on the senior high school level, situated 4.5 miles (7.2 kilometers) southwest of Auburn, Washington, between the Olympic Mountains and the Cascade Range, on a plateau overlooking the Green River Valley. The school serves the constituency of the Washington Conference and is accredited by the SDA Board of Regents, the Washington State Board of Education, and Northwest Association of Schools and Colleges.

The academy replaced two conference schools, one at Mount Vernon and the other near Battle Ground. Under the leadership of George F. Enoch, funds were raised at the 1919 camp meeting to complete a single-unit administration building with classrooms, chapel, kitchen, dining room, and girls' and boys' dormitories; also to erect an apartment dwelling for faculty and workers. The school (called Western Washington Missionary Academy until 1930) opened in 1919 under the principalship of Lyle C. Shepard. In 1930 the name was changed to Auburn Academy and in 1971 to Auburn Adventist Academy.

On May 6, 1921, fire destroyed the administration building; in 1922 a new administration building and a separate 40-student girls' dormitory, Regina Hall, were erected (Regina Hall was enlarged in 1926 and 1937). The boys moved into East Hall, the former apartment dwelling.

A dormitory accommodating 80 boys (and boasting hot and cold water) was constructed in 1931-1932 of lumber produced by a student-operated sawmill, using trees from the academy property. The dormitory was named in honor of Olaf Gibson, a retired halibut fisherman, who donated liberally to the project. East Hall became a gymnasium in 1933-1934, and in 1943, a girls' dormitory and Manual Arts Department.

Several buildings were erected during the administration of A. J. Olson: a new building of 21,000-square-foot (1,950-square-meter) capacity, to replace the woodshop, which burned in 1942; a 9,000-square-foot (850-square-meter) gymnasium in 1943; a two-story service building containing a pasteurizing plant, laundry, cannery, Home Economics Department, and extra classrooms in 1945, to which were added in 1947 a new power plant, metal shop, and Maintenance Department (the power plant was moved to a separate location in 1949; the service building burned down in 1988); and South Hall, a three-story girls' dormitory and cafeteria, completed by stages, 1946-1949. After extensive remodeling, South Hall was renamed Ruby E. Nelson Hall in 1965.

Regina Hall, changed to a boys' dormitory in 1949, was renamed Manous Hall, in memory of N. L. Manous, teacher of music and Spanish from 1945 to 1947, who died while teaching at the Chile Training School. This building was razed in 1965.

The woodshop burned in 1951 and was rebuilt in 1952. In 1953 the woodworking and mechanical drawing classes moved from East Hall to the service building, and the Music Department moved to East Hall.

In 1958 a concrete shower room was added to Gibson Hall, and the Washington Conference built a 28,000-square-foot (2,600-square-meter) camp meeting auditorium that supplemented the school gymnasium. In 1959 a maintenance garage was constructed, and architectural studies for a long-range building program were instituted.

By the 1962-1963 school year a masonry-and-steel boys' dormitory was ready for use. It accommodated 180 students and included two deans' apartments, a recreation room, and a chapel. In 1965 it was renamed C. L. Witzel Hall.

In 1965 construction was completed on a one-level masonry-and-steel administration building (C. A. Scriven Hall, with classrooms, learning resources center, and chapel accommodations for 500 students) and a chapel for the girls' dormitory (with a seating capacity of 178). With a new cafeteria, Rudolph Hall, in 1963 and the remodeling of the girls' dormitory the same year, the academy's three-year expansion program (1963-1965) cost more than $1 million.

In 1966 operation of the academy furniture factory, established by C. L. Witzel in 1926, was transferred to the General Conference industrial organization Harris Pine Mills. This organization employed approximately 200 students annually.

During the 1968-1969 school year approximately $40,000 was spent in remodeling Gibson Hall, an overflow girls' dormitory. During the following year the Land Improvement District installed water and sewer lines throughout the campus at a cost of $43,000. A storm sewer system was installed in 1991 in order to eliminate standing surface water during the rainy season.

A 2,100-square-foot (195-square-meter) swimming pool, with lockers, shower rooms, and physical education personnel offices, adjacent to the school gymnasium, Rainier Auditorium, was opened in 1969.

In 1974 the Music Department transferred from the former administration building to a single-level brick structure designed for that purpose, immediately west of C. A. Scriven Hall. During the same year, the students and staff raised more than $150,000 in cash, materials, and labor to construct a 16,000-square-foot (1,500-square-meter) industrial arts building. This complex, completed in the spring and summer of 1974, was named Spady Hall in 1986. During 1974 construction of a three-bedroom home for the girls' dean, adjoining Nelson Hall, was completed.

A 17,300-square-foot (1,600-square-meter) church building seating 850 was ready for services in 1981 and was dedicated in 1986. In 1985 the Loving to Learn Day-Care Center for ages 1-10 was opened. In 1993 an addition to accommodate children from 6 months to 12 years of age was being planned.

In July 1993, prior to the Maranatha International convention being held on campus, more than 100 Maranatha volunteers made major renovations in the administration building, music building, faculty housing, and other areas.

Since the founding of the school more than 5,500 students have graduated. Graduation classes have grown from five members in 1920 to more than 100 per year.

Yearly enrollments that fluctuated between 300 and 400 since the mid-1940s rose sharply in 1968 to 547 and peaked in 1974 with 595. Since then enrollment averages between 350 and 400 students.

Principals: Lyle C. Shepard, 1919-1920; L. C. Wilcox, 1920-1922; H. H. Hamilton, 1922-1925; Claude A. Shull, 1925-1928; Leon B. Losey, 1928-1930; Albert E. Green, 1930-1932; J. Z. Hottel, 1932-1935; J. Z. Hottel and H. B. Wilcox, 1935-1936; R. L. Hubbs, 1936-1941; A. J. Olson, 1941-1949; William Lay, 1949-1951; R. W. Fowler, 1951-1954; Clifford L. Witzel, 1954-1960; L. E. McClain, 1960-1965; V. Fullerton, 1965-1968; J. V. Peters,

1968-1969; C. W. Jorgenson, 1969-1976; Edward Wines, 1976-1985; Wayne Wentland, 1985-1991; D. Wayne Culmore, 1991- .

AUCA. *See* Adventist University of Central Africa.

AUCKLAND ADVENTIST HOSPITAL. A 62-bed surgical and medical hospital owned and operated by the Trans-Tasman Union Conference, situated at St. Heliers, a suburb of Auckland, New Zealand. The hospital is built on an elevated site overlooking the nearby harbor and gulf. Although the hospital project was conceived as early as 1963, it was not until 1972 that work began on its construction. On July 30, 1972, Ralph F. Waddell, M.D., unveiled a plaque commemorating the beginning of building. The hospital was officially opened by the mayor of Auckland on Jan. 20, 1974.

Medical Directors: R. J. Swannell, 1974-1977; A. D. Laughlin, 1978-1991; D. Rankin, 1992- .

AUCKLAND ADVENTIST HIGH SCHOOL. A coeducational day school on the senior high school level, operated by the North New Zealand Conference. It is situated in Mangere, Auckland, New Zealand, approximately six miles (10 kilometers) from the center of the city. In 1993 the enrollment of the high school was 160, with a staff of 12 teachers. The students are drawn from all the Auckland suburban Seventh-day Adventist churches.

The school developed from a primary school established in 1945 at the rear of the Balmoral church. In 1949, shortly after the Remuera church school began to offer high school studies, the two schools amalgamated, and the Balmoral Adventist High School came into being. Then in 1956, when the Royal Oak Primary School combined with it, the Balmoral High School became the Auckland Adventist Central School, with 43 primary and 23 secondary pupils. In 1958 an adjoining property was purchased, on which extra classrooms and staff facilities were erected. Membership growth led the Balmoral church to rebuild on a completely new site, where it became known as the Brentwood Avenue church. The school took over the old church building (1961), converting it into a library, a commercial room, and a classroom.

In 1970 the secondary school was separated from the primary department and moved to a new location at Mangere. The new site provides ample space for playing fields and tennis and basketball courts, as well as a new classroom and administration building with library, science laboratory, home economics room, commercial room, and woodwork shop.

Between 1981 and 1985 additional buildings added were: a design technology and chapel complex; a new administration wing; and extensions to the library.

The Auckland Adventist High School, registered as a high school with the New Zealand Ministry of Education, offers both an academic course and a commercial course, and prepares for the University Entrance Examination.

Principals: V. Herbert, 1950-1952; W. Whisker, 1953; R. Blair, 1954-1955; D. R. Kent, 1956-1960; W. C. Dunlop, 1961-1963; I. R. Harvey, 1964-1969; J. H. Eager, 1970-1974; B. Howell, 1975-1976; D. W. Reye, 1977-1980; W. G. Litster, 1981-1984; D. J. Harvey, 1985-1986; A. S. French, 1987-1989; G. R. Williams, 1990- .

AUDIOVISUAL SERVICES OF THE GENERAL CONFERENCE. *See* Adventist Media Center; Communication, Department of; International Audio-Visual Service.

AUDITING SERVICE. An organization that makes a systematic audit of financial records of all organizations in the Seventh-day Adventist body from the local church to the General Conference.

From the time the General Conference was organized in 1863, provision was made by the General Conference Executive Committee for the appointment of an auditing committee annually to audit the books of account. As the General Conference grew and its constituent organizations and institutions multiplied, the annual appointment of a committee was superseded by the election of an auditor of the General Conference and associates as required by the increasing volume of work.

Each overseas division committee followed the pattern by electing a division auditor and by appointing auditors for the union missions. In North America each union conference elected an auditor and such associates as were necessary. Auditors on the union level were responsible for financial audits of local conferences/missions in their respective territories and of union institutions—publishing, educational, and health care.

The responsibility for audits of local

churches, church schools, and other entities under the direction of the local conference has throughout the period rested with the local conference executive committee, which elects or appoints the local conference auditor.

The General Conference auditor and staff audited the records of the General Conference and its legal corporations, as well as those of all divisions and General Conference institutions. In all cases, annual reports were submitted by the auditor to the organization's executive committee and, as scheduled meetings of constituencies took place, to the assembled constituency. In the case of the General Conference, this meant an annual report to the full General Conference Committee and a report by the General Conference auditor to the General Conference session on a four-year and later a five-year basis.

As membership in all divisions grew, and as the financial activity of the various organizations became more significant and more diversified, it was seen that, from considerations of objectivity and independence, it was wise to distance the auditing function on all levels from the controlling committees at those levels. Thus in 1976 the General Conference Committee in the Annual Council authorized the establishment of a unitary Auditing Service as a part of the General Conference structure. The Auditing Service was organized with a director and associate directors, and the North American Division territory was set up in three areas, each with several district offices corresponding, in most cases, to the territories of the union conferences. The same pattern was expected to be followed in other divisions, and this reorganization has been going forward since 1977.

Under the new plan the responsibility for all audits, down to the local conference level, rests directly with professionally qualified individuals elected or appointed by the General Conference and under the day-to-day guidance of the director of the General Conference Auditing Service. This step has led to the application of uniform standards of reporting and disclosure for all organizations, and to the development of higher standards of training and proficiency in all members of the worldwide auditing staff. It has made it possible to raise the standards of auditing around the world to more nearly meet those of the business community in developed countries.

At the time of the establishment of the Auditing Service in 1976, a policy was also enunciated that placed the responsibility for auditing the General Conference itself, and its related legal organizations, on a firm of independent Seventh-day Adventist certified public accountants selected by the General Conference Executive Committee.

Under the unitary plan, all audits of all denominational organizations, from the local conference level through to the General Conference itself, are performed by professional auditors independent of their employing organizations. Audits of local churches and entities operated by local churches remain under the aegis of the local conference constituency, which names the local conference auditor with counsel from the director of the General Conference Auditing Service.

Auditors: J. J. Ireland, 1914-1932; Claude Conard, 1932-1942; W. E. Phillips, 1942-1955; H. W. Barrows, 1956-1958; E. L. Becker, 1958-1964; R. J. Radcliffe, 1964-1968; R. M. Reinhard (acting), 1968-1970; R. M. Davidson, 1970-1976; David D. Dennis, 1976-1994; Eric A. Korff, 1994- .

AUFRANC, LOUIS (1842-1906). One of the pioneers of Seventh-day Adventist work in Europe. He was a teacher at a school in Le Locle, Switzerland, when he became acquainted with SDAs through a series of evangelistic meetings that D. T. Bourdeau held in that community in 1876. Convinced that the SDA interpretation of Christianity was correct, he resigned his position as an elder of a local Protestant church, accepted baptism, and moved to Basel. There he assisted in the founding of *Les Signes des Temps* and in publishing SDA materials generally. He translated many articles and also wrote his own. Being a good linguist, he translated into French *The Life of Christ* and *The Great Controversy,* both by Ellen G. White. He was employed full-time by the church for only a short time and later studied and practiced dentistry in Basel and its vicinity.

AUGER, EMERY P. (1864-1922). Pioneer Seventh-day Adventist colporteur in France. Born in Ayer, Massachusetts, he went to France about 1888. There he made an attempt to sell SDA publications, but apparently was not there long enough to develop the work, which had a new beginning some eight or nine years later. After his return to the United States he was a self-supporting missionary in the South.

AUGSBURGER, ULYSSE (1878-1963). Minister, pioneer missionary in North Africa, and conference administrator. A Swiss national, he was baptized into the Seventh-day Adventist Church in 1891, and was one of the first French-speaking young men to be trained for the ministry at the Geneva and Paris training institutes (1901-1903). In 1907 he was ordained to the ministry. In 1908 he went to Algeria, where, with the help of José Abella, he established a church. He was president of the Leman Conference (1917-1923; 1932-1938), the North France Conference (1923-1929), and the South France Conference (1929-1932). He continued being listed until 1950 in the *Yearbook* as an active minister in the Leman Conference. He was a successful evangelist and a good pastor, rather conservative in his outlook, but a staunch supporter of the church program in all its facets. He was married twice, first to Ruth Jeanlouis, who died in 1934, and then to Clementine Fankhauser.

AUSTIN, LINDA HYACINTH (1903-1980). Educator, administrator. Born in Trinidad, she was taken to Panama at the age of 9. She was among the first students enrolled at the Adventist school in the Canal Zone. In 1926 she graduated and was baptized. A year later she was among the first teachers to arrive at Caribbean Union College, where she served for 40 years. She was the first West Indian to serve in a leadership role at that school, acting as teacher, matron, and head of the Secretarial Department, as well as treasurer. Although a strict disciplinarian, she exemplified Christian grace. Her exemplary role caused the school to name the women's residence in her honor. After retiring in 1967, she served for 12 years as manager of the Voice of Prophecy Bible School of the South Caribbean Conference.

AUSTRAL ISLANDS. *See* French Polynesia; South Pacific Division.

AUSTRAL UNION CONFERENCE. *See* Argentina; Paraguay; South American Division; Uruguay.

AUSTRALASIAN DIVISION. *See* South Pacific Division.

AUSTRALASIAN INTER-UNION CONFERENCE. *See* Australia; South Pacific Division.

AUSTRALASIAN MISSIONARY COLLEGE. *See* Avondale College.

AUSTRALASIAN RECORD AND ADVENT WORLD SURVEY. *See Record.*

AUSTRALASIAN UNION CONFERENCE. *See* Australia; New Zealand; South Pacific Division.

AUSTRALIA. A self-governing country comprising geographically the continent of Australia (the smallest continent in the world) and the island of Tasmania to the south—a total land area of 2,966,151 square miles (7,682,300 square kilometers), slightly smaller than that of the United States of America, all lying south of the equator, between the Indian Ocean and the South Pacific Ocean. It is divided into six states (New South Wales, Victoria, Queensland, South Australia, Western Australia, and Tasmania) and two territories (Northern and Australian Capital). Its population (1994) is 18 million.

The country has hundreds of species of eucalyptus and acacia trees. About 1,000 flowering plants are indigenous to the country. The fauna peculiar to Australia includes the emu, wallaby, koala, kangaroo, and duck-billed platypus (a creature that has a facial projection resembling the bill of a duck, lays eggs, is covered with hair, and suckles its young). The country has a variety of bright-plumaged birds; there are no fierce beasts of prey.

The continent has an equable climate and is well watered by lakes and rivers along its great coastal belts, with the exception of the Great Australian Bight. The longest rivers are the Murray and its tributary, the Darling. The Murray rises in the Snowy Mountains, near Mount Kosciusko (7,316 feet [2,230 meters] in elevation and Australia's highest), and forms the border between Victoria and New South Wales for a distance of 1,200 miles (1,930 kilometers).

Primary products include wool, coal, beef, sheep, steel, dairy products, and wheat. Australia's mineral wealth includes gold, bauxite, uranium, silver, and lead, and the recently discovered large oil deposits. The estimated population of Australia in 1992 was approximately 17.6 million, predominantly of European descent and basically of British extraction. The indigenous people are the Aborigines. After a period of decline, their numbers are increasing. Their heritage and nomadic lifestyle have contributed to major cultural clashes between them and the Caucasian population. However, significant moves toward reconciliation and integration are now taking place.

Universal manhood suffrage was conceded to the Australian colonies in the 1850s, and secret voting (the "Australian ballot") was first adopted by Victoria in 1856. Woman suffrage was enacted in 1902. A number of benevolent social service schemes are administered by the government, such as pensions for the aged, child endowments, maternity allowances, and sickness and unemployment benefits. Australia regulates its basic wage and maximum hours of work.

Historical Background. Dutch explorers visited the northern coast of Australia in the early seventeenth century and named it New Holland. Captain James Cook explored the east coast and took formal possession of that portion on behalf of the English Crown on Aug. 23, 1770, calling it New South Wales. The first settlement was a British colony founded in 1788. In the nineteenth century the continent became known as Australia and was claimed in its entirety by Great Britain.

Through the activities of courageous explorers and the rapid expansion of the parent colony of New South Wales after the discovery of gold in 1851, four new colonies were formed: Victoria, Tasmania, South Australia, and Queensland. These became self-governing by 1860. Western Australia, founded in 1829, did not have self-government until 1890. In 1901 the six colonies federated themselves as states into the Commonwealth of Australia, governed by a federal parliament consisting of a Senate and a House of Representatives, with a governor-general acting for the sovereign. Each of the six states has its own constitution, governor, and parliament (bicameral except in Queensland, which in 1922 ceased to operate the upper house). The federal capital is Canberra, in the Australian Capital Territory, which lies within the state of New South Wales.

The federal government administers the Northern Territory (which came under its control in 1911) and several overseas territories such as Norfolk Island and Christmas Island. Australia claims a large portion of the Antarctic regions to the south, an estimated 2,472,000 square miles (6,402,000 square kilometers).

Seventh-day Adventist Statistics. The territory of Australia constitutes the Trans-Australian Union Conference and part of the Trans-Tasman Union Conference (which also includes New Zealand), under the South Pacific Division, and is divided into nine conferences. Statistics (1992) for *Australia:* churches, 397; members, 47,594; church or elementary schools, 59; ordained ministers, 256; licensed ministers, 56; Bible instructors, 1; teachers, 388. Headquarters for the South Pacific Division are at 148 Fox Valley Road, Wahroonga, New South Wales, Australia.

Statistics (1992) for the *Trans-Australian Union Conference* (entirely in Australia): churches, 188; members, 20,381; church or elementary schools, 30; ordained ministers, 114; licensed ministers, 29; teachers, 166. Headquarters for the Trans-Australian Union Conference are at Surrey Hills (a suburb of Melbourne), Victoria, Australia. Statistics (1992) for the *South Australian Conference:* churches, 29; members, 2,946; church or elementary schools, 3; ordained ministers, 15; licensed ministers, 1; teachers, 20. Headquarters for the South Australian Conference are at Adelaide, South Australia. Statistics (1992) for the *South New South Wales Conference:* churches, 29; members, 2,433; church or elementary schools, 6; ordained ministers, 16; licensed ministers, 5; teachers, 15. Headquarters for the South New South Wales Conference are at Canberra, A.C.T. Statistics (1992) for the *Tasmanian Conference:* churches, 13; members, 1,282; church or elementary schools, 2; ordained ministers, 7; licensed ministers, 6; teachers, 11. Headquarters for the Tasmanian Conference are at Hobart, Tasmania. Statistics (1992) for the *Victorian Conference:* churches, 71; members, 8,602; church or elementary schools, 11; ordained ministers, 41; licensed ministers, 10; teachers, 58. Headquarters for the Victorian Conference are at Nunawding, Victoria. Statistics (1992) for the *Western Australian Conference:* churches, 46; members, 5,082; church or elementary schools, 8; ordained ministers, 26; licensed ministers, 7; teachers, 40. Headquarters for the Western Australian Conference are at Gosnells, Western Australia.

Statistics (1992) for the Australian portion of the *Trans-Tasman Union Conference:* churches, 209; members, 27,213; church or elementary schools, 29; ordained ministers, 142; licensed ministers, 27; Bible instructors, 1; teachers, 222. Headquarters for the Trans-Tasman Union Conference are at Gordon, New South Wales, Australia. Statistics (1992) for the *Greater Sydney Conference:* churches, 55; members, 7,743; church or elementary schools, 8; ordained ministers, 46; licensed ministers, 11; teachers, 74. Headquarters for the Greater

Sydney Conference are at Strathfield, New South Wales. Statistics (1992) for the *North New South Wales Conference:* churches, 66; members, 9,386; church or elementary schools, 11; ordained ministers, 39; licensed ministers, 12; teachers, 86. Headquarters for the North New South Wales Conference are at Wallsend, New South Wales. Statistics (1992) for the *Northern Australian Conference:* churches, 23; members, 2,113; church or elementary schools, 3; ordained ministers, 13; licensed ministers, 2; teachers, 8. Headquarters for the North Australian Conference are at Aitkenville, Townsville, Queensland. Statistics (1992) for the *South Queensland Conference:* churches, 65; members, 7,971; church or elementary schools, 7; ordained ministers, 38; licensed ministers, 2; teachers, 54. Headquarters for the South Queensland Conference are at Brisbane, Queensland.

Institutions. Adventist Retirement Village (Kings Langley, New South Wales); Adventist Retirement Village (Normanhurst, New South Wales); Adventist Retirement Village (Victoria Point, Queensland); Adventist Retirement Village (Morphett Vale, South Australia); Alawara Retirement Village; Alstonville Adventist Retirement Village; Alton Villas; Avondale Adventist High School; Avondale College; Brisbane Adventist High School; Capricorn Adventist Retirement Village; Carmel Adventist College; Charles Harrison Memorial Home; Coronella Retirement Village/Nursing Home; Fernleigh Retirement Village; Home Study International (South Pacific Branch); Kressville Hostel and Homes for the Aged; Lilydale Adventist Academy; Macquarie College; Maranatha Homes for the Aged; Melody Park Adventist Retirement Village; Mountain View Retirement Village and Hostel; Murwillumbah Seventh-day Adventist High School; Nunawading Adventist College; Pine Rivers Adventist High School; Prescott College; Sanitarium Health Food Company; Seventh-day Adventist Retirement Village; Signs Publishing Company; South Pacific Adventist Media Centre; Sydney Adventist College; Sydney Adventist Hospital; Warburton Hospital.

Seventh-day Adventist Work. *Beginnings.* Seventh-day Adventist teachings were first preached in Australia by Alexander Dickson, of Melbourne, Australia, who accepted them while serving as a missionary in Africa, where he came in contact with Hannah More, another missionary, and heard from her what she had learned of SDAs on visiting New England about 1861. When Dickson returned to his homeland, he published tracts and traveled about preaching the new doctrine to people. Although his work aroused considerable favorable interest, he did not succeed in developing any visible results, and became discouraged (S. N. Haskell, in *Historical Sketches,* p. 94). The next move to introduce SDA doctrines into Australia was made from the United States.

As early as 1874 Ellen G. White urged the SDA Church to spread the message widely, and made particular mention of the continent of Australia (LS 209). At a General Conference session in Battle Creek in 1884 an action was taken to send S. N. Haskell to Australia. On May 10, 1885, a party consisting of Haskell, J. O. Corliss, M. C. Israel, William Arnold, and Henry Scott, with their families, sailed from San Francisco, and upon arrival in Australia settled in the city of Melbourne, Victoria. That country thus became the first in the Southern Hemisphere to be entered by SDA missionaries. While Haskell, Corliss, and Israel engaged in evangelistic work, Arnold devoted himself to selling books, disposing of 2,168 during his brief stay in Australia. Scott was occupied in organizing the equipment to print literature.

The first Sabbath school in Australia was held on July 4, 1885, and the first public discourse by an SDA was delivered a week later by Corliss in the Temperance Hall in Richmond, a suburb of Melbourne. Four weeks later the first SDA convert in Australia, J. H. Stockton, with his two children, joined the Sabbath school. The first tent meetings were conducted by Corliss in North Fitzroy, a northern suburb of Melbourne, with meetings held every night from Oct. 25, 1885, to January 1886. On Jan. 10, 1886, the first SDA church in the Southern Hemisphere was organized. Then meetings were held in South Melbourne. By the time these meetings ended, further accessions brought the number to 55; by May this church recorded a membership of 90, and within five years a membership of more than 200.

In January 1886 Corliss and Haskell began editing and publishing a 16-page monthly, *The Bible Echo and Signs of the Times.* Beginning in January 1889, it was published weekly.

Israel visited Ballarat, Victoria, in May and held cottage meetings every night for three weeks, awakening a keen interest. Corliss followed him, conducting public meetings from June 20 to Aug. 8, when a Sabbath school of 50 was organized. Within a few weeks a church of 20 members was established in Ballarat.

South Australia was entered when, in September 1886, Corliss opened a series of meetings in Norwood, Adelaide. Within 12 weeks, on Nov. 27, an initial company of 34 members was organized, which developed into a strong church.

Early in 1887 additional workers from the United States, W. D. Curtis, Byron Belden, W.L.H. Baker, and their families, arrived in Melbourne. During 1887, meetings were held in Geelong, Daylesford, Trentham, Wychitella, and Kyneton, where groups of converts were gathered.

Curtis' first appointment was to the town of Castlemaine, Victoria, where a church was established. Later he built up churches in the suburbs of Melbourne and Adelaide, using a large pavilion for his meetings. It was necessary at times to hold double sessions to accommodate his audiences. He returned to the United States in 1892, after a ministry of five and a half years.

Tasmania was entered after an interest had been created there through the distribution of publications. A tent mission was conducted by Israel and Baker in Sandy Bay, Hobart, beginning late in February 1888. They moved to the Federal Hall when cold weather set in. In a short time 60 had enrolled in the Sabbath school, and a church of 24 members was organized in June of that year. In July 1889 there were 50 members and about 100 Sabbathkeepers reported. Early in 1889 David Steed entered Bismarck (Collinsvale), a rural community about 12 miles from Hobart, and established a church of 33 members. Churches were established also in Latrobe and Launceston.

Australian Conference Organized. At a general meeting held in the Rae Street Temperance Hall, North Fitzroy, Melbourne, the Australian Conference was organized about the first of September 1888. G. C. Tenney was elected president and Stephen McCullagh secretary. At the same meeting the Australian Tract and Missionary Society was organized, with M. C. Israel as president and Josie L. Baker as secretary. Delegates were present from the Adelaide, Ballarat, Hobart, and Melbourne churches, and a representative from the company at Wychitella. At that time 335 Sabbathkeepers were reported in Australia and Tasmania, 266 of whom were church members.

In 1888 a three-story building was erected in Melbourne, and the Echo Publishing Company opened that same year. Here was published monthly *The Bible Echo and Signs of the Times,* which became a bimonthly and ultimately a weekly periodical. *See* Signs Publishing Company.

In 1889 E. M. Morrison arrived in Australia with his family, to be the leader of the bookselling work in that country. In the following year, 1890, there were 28 colporteurs; these made monthly sales of more than £1,000. In 1895 a new leader, E. R. Palmer, arrived in Sydney from the United States to manage this important work. From 1914 to 1954 $5.5 million worth of books were sold. Deliveries from 1955 to 1964 amounted to $5.25 million (almost as much in one decade as in the four previous decades), while from 1965 to 1974 book sales reached $6.5 million.

In the latter part of 1889 David Steed was transferred from Tasmania to Victoria and joined Stephen McCullagh in evangelistic tent meetings in Sandhurst (Bendigo). There a church of 22 members was organized with the assistance of Robert Hare, of New Zealand.

The work in New South Wales began in Sydney in 1890 through Steed's ministry. Before the close of the year a church was organized. The meetings continued in a large pavilion in the suburbs of Burwood and Newton. For a brief period in 1891, A. G. Daniells, who had recently been transferred from New Zealand to Australia, was associated with the mission. In 1892 Robert Hare joined Steed in a tent series in Parramatta, one of the outlying suburbs of Sydney, which resulted in a church of 50 members. A church building was erected in five and a half weeks at a cost of £420, and dedicated on Dec. 10, 1892.

Meetings were opened a few miles from Parramatta in the village of Kellyville in 1893. A suitable church building was erected, and within six months a membership of 30 was reported. The movement spread rapidly as interests sprang up in the suburbs and outlying areas of Sydney.

In May 1894 two orchardists, members of the Kellyville church, were charged in court under a statute of Charles II (about 1675) for doing manual work on Sunday, for which the penalty was to forfeit five shillings or, in default, to be set publicly in the stocks for two hours. They were convicted and fined. Three months later another SDA who was similarly sentenced to pay a fine of two shillings and sixpence, with costs, or to spend two hours in the stocks, said, "I will prefer the stocks to paying." The attorney general ultimately recommended remission of the sentence—because there were no stocks. Much public interest and press comment favorable to SDAs was created by these cases.

Ellen G. White in Australia. In 1891 the General Conference arranged for Ellen G. White, her son W. C. White, G. B. Starr and his wife, and other helpers to visit Australia. Her gifts, her spiritual insight, and her counsels brought great blessing and lasting benefit to this field in its formative years. Mrs. White lived in Australia almost 10 years. She made her home on land adjoining the property of the school that is now Avondale College, whose founding she encouraged.

Mrs. White's group arrived in time to attend the fourth session of the Australian Conference, which opened in the Federal Hall, North Fitzroy, on Dec. 23, 1891, with 40 delegates in attendance, in addition to a large number of church members from New South Wales, Victoria, Tasmania, and South Australia. Two new churches, one at Geelong and the other at Latrobe, were received into the conference, and A. G. Daniells was elected president.

A Bible training school was opened at a temporary location on St. Kilda Road, Melbourne, on Aug. 24, 1892, with L. J. Rousseau as principal and G. B. Starr the Bible teacher. The school, which opened the first year with 25 students, was the forerunner of Avondale College.

In 1892 A. G. Daniells organized the first Young People's Society in Adelaide, one of the earliest in the denomination *(see* Adventist Youth Societies; MV Societies).

The first camp meeting in Australia, with more than 100 tents, was held at Middle Brighton, Victoria, from Jan. 5 to 22, 1894. O. A. Olsen, president of the General Conference, Ellen G. White, and her son W. C. White were in attendance. It was at this camp meeting, with 40 delegates from nine churches, that the Australasian Union Conference was organized, the first union conference in the denomination, which became a pattern for those later organized. W. C. White was elected president; A. G. Daniells, vice president; and L. J. Rousseau, secretary. Headquarters were in Melbourne (in 1898 they were transferred to Sydney).

This conference decided that G. B. Starr and A. S. Hickox should conduct public evangelism in Rockhampton, Queensland, where there were 10 adherents. Hickox, recently from the United States, was holding meetings in the Seven Hills district, an outlying area of Sydney. He was ordained at the camp meeting on Jan. 20, 1894. The evangelistic meetings in Rockhampton yielded the first church in Queensland, with 48 members.

The following year, G. B. Starr conducted meetings in Toowoomba, where another church of 32 members was organized. In 1898 two more churches, one in South Brisbane and the other in North Brisbane, resulted from the work of S. N. Haskell.

During the inception of the work in Australia, camp meetings drew large and responsive audiences. This invariably led to a keen interest in the proceedings and in the ultimate establishment of a church in the area. For example, a camp meeting held in Ashfield, a suburb of Sydney, in 1894, resulted in a church of 66 members.

During 1894 and 1895, as the work expanded in Sydney, it grew also in the suburbs of Melbourne. Churches were established in Middle Brighton, Williamstown, and Hawthorn. These, with North Fitzroy and Prahran, brought to five the number of Melbourne suburbs in which SDA services were being conducted.

Western Australia Entered. The first series of meetings in Western Australia was opened in the city of Perth on Feb. 9, 1896, by J. O. Corliss. Within a few months a church was established. When Corliss became ill, Robert Hare succeeded him. The membership continued to increase.

About 17 miles (27 kilometers) from Perth, in the Darling Range area of Western Australia, a boarding academy was opened in 1907 to assist students to obtain a secondary education, preparatory to entering Avondale College *(see* Carmel Adventist College).

Church Schools. Around the turn of the century there was an awakening consciousness of the need not only for denominational higher education but also for church day schools for primary education. On June 10, 1900, it was reported that there was a church school at North Fitzroy, Melbourne, with two teachers and more than 60 pupils in attendance.

Other schools soon followed in the various conferences. Schools and junior colleges have also been established in the fields of the Pacific Island union missions, and today most of the administrative responsibility is being placed upon the island nationals in these areas.

Health Institutions. In her counsels Ellen G. White urged upon the constituency the need for a medical institution for the treatment of the sick. In 1896 treatment rooms were opened in a seven-room house in Ashfield. The work was later transferred to Summer Hill. These were replaced by the Sydney Sanitarium (now Sydney Adventist Hospital) at Wahroonga, a suburb of Sydney, established in 1903. At Adelaide a 10-bed institution called the Adelaide Sanitarium was operated from 1908 to 1919. Warburton Sanitarium (now Warburton Hospital) was established in 1910 in a bush setting in a valley 45 miles (70 kilometers) from Melbourne.

The Sanitarium Health Food Company, now with headquarters at Wahroonga, New South Wales, was opened in Melbourne, registered in 1898, and has established a chain of factories, wholesale distributing depots, and cafés and retail stores in the main cities of Australia and New Zealand. The company's earnings are used to bring assistance to the educational, benevolent, and missionary enterprises sponsored by the church.

Later Organization. The Australasian Union Conference, organized at the conclusion of the Australian Conference session held during the first camp meeting in 1894, comprised the Australian Conference and the New Zealand Conference. In 1895 the Australian Conference was divided into two conferences: the New South Wales Conference, with W. C. White as president, comprised the colony of New South Wales; and the Central Australian Conference, with A. G. Daniells as president, comprised Victoria, South Australia, and Tasmania. In 1899 Queensland, which with West Australia had been administered as a mission by the union, was organized as a conference, with 211 members and with G. C. Tenney as president. South Australia was organized as a separate conference in 1899, with a membership of 190, and with J. H. Woods as president. Tasmania became a separate conference in 1901, with a membership of 150 and with E. Hilliard as the first president. In 1902 the West Australian Conference was organized, with a membership of 152 and with J. Pallant as president.

In 1920 the New South Wales Conference was divided into the North New South Wales Conference and the South New South Wales Conference. In 1949 the South New South Wales Conference was divided into the Greater Sydney Conference and the South New South Wales Conference. The latter had its headquarters originally in Wagga Wagga, but in 1965 moved them to Canberra, the federal capital.

The Queensland Conference was divided in 1929. Its northern area was designated the North Queensland Mission under the direction of, and subsidized by, the Australasian Union Conference, with headquarters in Townsville. At that time it had four churches and a membership of 161.

In the same area, some 35 miles (55 kilometers) northwest of Cairns, a mission station had been established for the Aborigines in 1913, called Mona Mona Mission, with P. B. Rudge and J. L. Branford as its first administrators. In 1949 the North Queensland Mission, which had been separated from the Queensland Conference in 1929, was transferred, together with the Mona Mona Mission, from the control of the Australasian Union Conference to the control of the newly formed Trans-Tasman Union Conference. In 1955 the North Queensland Mission was constituted the North Queensland Conference, and the Mona Mona Mission was taken over by this conference. With this additional membership of 112, the conference had a total of 711 members. In 1984 the territory of the North Queensland Conference and that part of the South Australia Conference within the boundaries of the Northern Territory were joined to form the Northern Australian Conference.

In 1953 the Trans-Commonwealth Union Conference (now Trans-Australian Union Conference), formed in 1949, sponsored an Aboriginal Mission at Karalundi, some 500 miles (800 kilometers) north of Perth, Western Australia, under the direction of the West Australian Conference. Another mission was opened in 1956 at Wiluna, 100 miles (160 kilometers) east of Karalundi.

In 1949 the Australasian Union Conference (also administered as the Australasian Division since 1922) was reorganized as the Australasian Inter-Union Conference, composed of two union conferences and two union missions. At that time the conferences of Australia were formed into the Trans-Commonwealth Union Conference (now Trans-Australian Union Conference) and, with New Zealand, into the Trans-Tasman Union Conference.

Progress in Australia. The total number of conferences in Australia increased from six in 1905 to nine in 1955.

In recent decades large numbers of SDAs of Eastern European origin have migrated to Australia.

Sydney Adventist Hospital: The Wahronga site of Sydney Adventist Hospital (formerly

Sydney Sanitarium) was chosen by Ellen White and built in 1903. Sydney Adventist Hospital was the first private hospital in New South Wales to be accredited by the Australian Council on Healthcare Standards and has maintained its accreditation continuously. In 1995 Sydney Adventist Hospital, with a bed capacity of 320, was the largest private hospital in New South Wales.

In 1972 a new School of Nursing was built. In 1973 the Institution was rebuilt and renamed Sydney Adventist Hospital. At a cost of $8.5 million, the main wooden building was replaced by a 10-story brick-and-concrete structure.

In 1980 a tertiary nursing program commenced with Avondale College. The hospital further consolidated its place as a teaching hospital in 1994 with an affiliation with the Faculty of Medicine with the University of Sydney.

In 1990 a 50-bed maternity unit was opened (replacing an existing ward), and a special care nursery was added. In 1992 the Physiotherapy Department was extended, and the lithotripsy service commenced.

In 1995 a $37 million extension opened featuring 12 operating theaters (increased from eight), new day surgery and endoscopy facilities, medical imaging and renal dialysis, new School of Nursing, new Hospital Library and Lecture Theatre (*see* Sydney Adventist Hospital).

SDA Media Centre: In 1966 new offices and studio were opened. Film production for TV began with *Focus on Living* films. In 1971 color movie films with synchronized sound were produced for denominational departments, and in 1973 LP records were produced.

In 1973 a new TV series was produced entitled *Crisis.* In 1974 the studio control room was reequipped with a new mixer control and four program duplicators; "Teac" tape recorder, cassette deck, and two cassette duplicators; 16-millimeter film editing machine for film department.

"Here's Life," a 34-lesson doctrinal Bible correspondence course, was introduced in 1974. By 1974 radio outreach increased to more than 100 programs per week using *These Times* in both the five- and 15-minute format. TV outreach increased to 12 regular 30-minute TV programs per week using *It Is Written* and *Faith for Today.* In 1974 a series of TV one-minute commercials were produced. In 1985 the Video Production Department was set up. More than 30 productions are completed annually. The department is often requested to produce reports for other world divisions.

Since 1991, TV commercials in 60-second and 30-second versions have been produced and screened by television networks. These have been the major source of responses and enrollments for the correspondence school. Some 16,000 reponses are received annually.

TV community service spots (30-second) are screened free of charge. In 1984 a presenter and media evangelist was appointed to reap contacts gained from correspondence school and electronic media contacts. In 1994 an associate was appointed.

At present there are plans to extend the current building.

Education: See Avondale College.

Archives: An archive room was established at Avondale College in 1974. In 1964 Sunnyside, Ellen White's home, was purchased by the denomination, and the South Pacific Museum set up on land adjacent to it.

Builders of the Church in Australia: The earliest leaders came from overseas as pioneers, but soon Australian converts stood side by side with the men and women from the United States. Among the former might be named S. N. Haskell, who led the pioneering party to Australia and New Zealand; J. O. Corliss and M. C. Israel, who did so much to break new ground in these countries; W. D. Curtis, who accomplished much in a short time; G. C. Tenny; A. G. Daniells, who was later to emerge as a great denominational leader in the General Conference; Ellen G. White, whose counsel and help in founding our education system, the sanitarium, and the health food interests made this division the great mission base that it is; E. W. Farnsworth; Drs. Daniel and Lauretta Kress in the medical sphere; G. A. Irwin, W. W. Prescott, and later Lynn Wood in the service of education.

Among Australian and New Zealand denominational employees who have made an outstanding contribution to the work in this division might be named the Hare family, the Stewarts, the Piper brothers, J. H. Woods, J. M. Johanson, and the Kent family. A. W. Anderson and Reuben E. Hare, who hammered out the principles of religious liberty before legislators, military authorities, and trade union executives, leading them to recognize the principles of freedom and helping preserve the priceless heritage of liberty now enjoyed by the church; C. H. Watson, who became head of the church in Australia and then proceeded to fill the wider office of General Conference president. In the Pacific mission fields the names of G. H. Gates, J. M. Cole,

E. S. Butz, J. E. Fulton, and G. F. Jones are remembered along with those of Andrew Stewart, A. H. Piper, H. Steed, R. H. Tutty, S. W. Carr, and many others.

AUSTRIA. A republic situated in the heart of Europe, bounded by Germany, the Czech Republic, Slovakia, Hungary, Slovenia, Italy, Switzerland, and Liechtenstein. Its area is 32,374 square miles (83,847 square kilometers), and the population (1994) is nearly 8 million. Ninety-nine percent of the people are ethnic Germans, with various minority groups, such as Slovenians, Hungarians, and Croatians. Eighty-eight percent of the population are Roman Catholic, 5 percent are Lutheran or Reformed, and the rest belong to religious minorities or are unaffiliated. Austria's economy is chiefly industrial.

Pre-World War I Austria was the center of an empire, from 1867 called the Austro-Hungarian Empire, which included what are now the Czech Republic, Slovakia, Hungary, Slovenia and Croatia, and parts of Romania, Russia, Poland, and Italy. The Austrian imperial house of Hapsburg ruled from the Middle Ages to 1918, and from 1438 to 1806 supplied the monarchs of the so-called Holy Roman Empire. After World War I the monarchy was abolished, and various parts of the heterogeneous empire were incorporated into the states named above. The German-speaking core of Austria became a republic with a democratic constitution. Hitler annexed it to Germany in 1938, but it was restored to independence after World War II. Its present constitution dates from 1955.

Because of the changes in boundaries, the use of the word "Austria" can be confusing. Before 1918, the name was used loosely to refer to the whole Austro-Hungarian Empire. At the same time, it also was used to disignate "Austria proper," or the western segment of the Dual Monarchy, which at that time included several non-Austrian areas that do not now belong to Austria (German Austria).

Seventh-day Adventist Statistics. The territory of Austria constitutes the Austrian Union of Churches, part of the Euro-Africa Division. Statistics (1993) for *Austria:* churches, 44; members, 3,266; ordained ministers, 23; licensed ministers, 8. Headquarters for the Austrian Union of Churches are at Nussdorferstrasse 5, 1090 Vienna.

Institutions: Austrian Publishing House; Bogenhofen Seminary; Haus Stefanie (Retirement Home).

Development of Seventh-day Adventist Work. In 1895 L. R. Conradi conducted the first SDA baptismal service in Austria-Hungary at Klausenburg (Kolozsvár). Christine Pauline Rottmayer joined the SDA Church on that occasion. She was the daughter of Johann Rottmayer, Jr., who worked as a Baptist pastor in Vienna. Her grandparents were converted to Seventh-day Adventism by Conradi as early as 1890. Living in Klausenburg (Kolozsvár), they were the first SDA members in the Hapsburg empire. Upon her return to Vienna, Christine Pauline Rottmayer remained the only SDA church member within the borders of present-day Austria until 1903. The year 1902 marks the beginning of SDA missionary work in Vienna by H. Kokolsky, a well-known sculptor at the turn of the century who had been baptized by G. Perk in Germany. Also in 1902 a German-American pastor, L. Mathe, was sent to Pressburg (Pozsony). Interest in the SDA message had developed in Ratzersdorf (Rac), a village near Pressburg, through a relative's visit from the U.S. In 1903 Mathe succeeded in organizing a small SDA congregation in Ratzersdorf, which is close to the present-day Austrian border. Because his life was threatened on several occasions, Mathe transferred his missionary activity to nearby Vienna, where, on July 1, 1903, he was able to perform the first SDA baptism within the borders of present-day Austria. At that time the distrustful if not hostile mentality of the rural, strongly Catholic population could be easily avoided in the cities in which underground work was possible. In 1902 "Austria proper" was designated as the Austrian Mission. Under the leadership of L. Mathe (1903-1906) and W. Prillwitz (1907-1908) missionary work advanced primarily in Bohemia, Moravia, and Austrian Silesia. Until 1912 these lands, together with German-speaking Austria (German Austria), constituted a single mission field. The breakthrough in missionary work is credited to the efforts of J. Wolfgarten (1909-1918), who had come to Austria from Germany. He was the first to start regular and systematic missionary work in German Austria, searching for a way to make public evangelism possible. Because members of unrecognized religions, such as Seventh-day Adventism, were not allowed to engage in public worship or evangelism, new forms of mission outreach had to be found. Two legal societies (Vereine) were founded: the Society of Christian Men and Women (for Vienna) and the Austrian More-Light Reading

Society (for the entire country). Under the guise of these lecture societies, SDAs in Austria could hold public meetings. The SDA Church in Vienna, the first in present-day Austria, was founded in 1908.

Before World War I, 11 local churches were organized in German Austria, with approximately 250 members. In 1909 the first native Austrian SDA minister, Franz Gruber, was ordained in Vienna. The church made a serious effort to train indigenous missionary workers, as foreign pastors were in constant danger of being deported for "disturbing the peace." Colporteur work was extremely difficult in the face of laws forbidding the circulation of religious literature by loan, sale, or gift.

In 1913 A. G. Daniels, SDA General Conference president, visited Austria a second time. He reported: "Austria is said to be the most intensely Catholic country in all Europe, and possibly in all the world. We have not been permitted to take a religious name, or to hold a regular public religious service. The law forbids religious teaching, baptizing, and the forming of churches. It aims to make it impossible for any religious body, save the Catholic Church, to exist in Austria" *(Review and Herald* 90:1145, 1146, Nov. 27, 1913; see also D. Heinz, *Church, State, and Religious Dissent: A History of Seventh-day Adventists in Austria, 1890-1975* [1993]). A petition sent to Emperor Francis Joseph I by the SDA leaders in Austria in 1914 asking him to stop "systematic religious discrimination," to which SDAs in Austria were continually exposed, remained unnoticed. The repressive situation forced the SDA Church in Austria to work underground until the collapse of the monarchy in 1918. The rise of democracy after 1918 proved a turning point in the mission history of the SDA Church in Austria, inaugurating the era of large-scale public evangelism.

Austrian Conference. As a result of the peace treaty of St.-Germain after World War I, the Austrian republic was established. With religious freedom guaranteed under the democratic constitution, the way was open for the new mission era. In 1920 the Austrian Mission was reorganized as a conference, with a membership of 526, and with offices in Vienna. Also after the war the Hamburg Publishing House opened a Vienna branch, and the colporteur work was promoted. Many new members joined the church. During the 1930s new obstacles appeared, as a result of revolutionary political movements. Then in 1939, with the outbreak of World War II, public mission work was forbidden without exception. The war brought untold destruction. At the end of the war the people rallied, the SDA message was again preached freely, and many were baptized.

Austrian Union of Churches. After World War II the Austrian Conference, which until then had belonged to one or another of the German union conferences or to the Central European Division, was transferred to the Southern European Division but not attached to any union conference. In 1947 it became the Austrian Union Conference and was divided into two conferences: the Danube Conference with headquarters in Vienna, with a membership of 1,138; and the Alpine Conference with headquarters in Salzburg and a membership of 984.

In order to facilitate administrative work, the two conferences were replaced in 1967 by an Austrian "Union of Churches," the first Seventh-day Adventist organization of this kind in Europe. It represented a centralized form of church government with union status, composed of the local churches within a given area. The church organization of 1967 ultimately led to the financial independence of the SDA movement in Austria. The reasons for financial independence include savings realized by a simplified denominational structure and an increase of church offerings as a result of the growing economic prosperity of the country. In later years the Austrian members have ranked second worldwide in terms of the total amount of offerings given to the church.

In 1950 an evangelistic center was purchased that furnishes office space and a hall seating 500, where the largest SDA church in Vienna meets. A publishing house (without a printing plant) was opened in 1948, the colporteur work was revived, and a Bible correspondence course was launched. The Bogenhofen Seminary was established in 1949. In addition to the headquarters building, 14 chapels were built in different cities, and new halls have been rented and equipped.

The General Conference session of 1975 in Vienna, the first ever held outside North America, represented a highlight for the SDAs in Austria. It also marked a new beginning for the SDAs in the Communist countries of Eastern Europe, allowing them to turn gradually to the West. By 1993, because of the secularizing trends of society, SDA Church growth had slowed, but the membership had crossed the 3,000 mark.

AUSTRIAN CONFERENCE. *See* Austria.

AUSTRIAN MISSIONARY SEMINARY. *See* Bogenhofen Seminary.

AUSTRIAN PUBLISHING HOUSE (Wegweiser-Verlag). An incorporated publishing firm (without printing plant) in Vienna, owned and operated by the Austrian Union of Churches.

The predecessor of the Austrian Publishing House was a branch of the Hamburg Publishing House established in Vienna in 1921 for the Austrian Conference, which at that time was under the South German Union Conference. The branch operated with two employees and 20 colporteurs. When it was closed in 1941 by the police, the Hamburg Publishing House assumed responsibility for Austria's colporteurs, who, however, because of the war, had to stop their work. To prevent confiscation, the books in stock were sent to Hamburg and to the Zurich Publishing House.

In 1948, when the Austrian Union Conference became a part of the Southern European Division, an independent publishing house (without printing plant) was established in Vienna, since it was difficult to import books from outside. At first the work had to be carried out in the name of the first manager, Rudolf Ueberbacher. In 1951 the firm became the Wegweiser-Verlag Society. In 1948, with two employees and 10 colporteurs, it had sales amounting to $5,579. Since 1948 the delivery of books to customers has been made directly from the house. Doing so has increased sales considerably. The house published *Zeichen der Zeit,* a 16-page bimonthly, for more than 20 years. Because more and more books were printed for the German-speaking area in Europe, the manager of the Austrian Publishing House was also appointed a member of the planning committee of the Hamburg Publishing House. The sales in 1992 amounted to $1,670,500. At that time there were five employees and 70 literature evangelists. From 1948 to 1992, 673 people have been baptized as a result of this ministry.

Managers: Rudolf Ueberbacher, 1948-1959; Engelbert Hatzinger, 1959-1975; Otto Chrastek, 1975- .

AUSTRIAN-SWISS JUNIOR COLLEGE. *See* Bogenhofen Seminary.

AUSTRIAN UNION OF CHURCHES. *See* Austria; Euro-Africa Division.

AUTUMN COUNCIL. *See* Annual Council.

AVIATION. *See* Mission Aviation.

AVISTA HOSPITAL. A general, acute, 50-bed hospital operated at Louisville, Colorado, by the Mid-America Union Conference. It is accredited by the Joint Commission on Accreditation of Healthcare Organizations, Chicago, Illinois, and has a staff of 250 physicians and 400 employees, approximately 180 of whom are nursing personnel. About half of the individuals employed by Avista were employees at Boulder Memorial Hospital until its closing in March 1989 *(see* Boulder Memorial Hospital). Avista Hospital services include obstetrics and gynecology, pediatrics, medical/surgical services, radiology, cardiopulmonary, rehabilitation, and 24-hour emergency care.

The hospital's Family Life program offers a wide selection of pregnancy, childbirth, and parenting classes tailored to today's active family. In addition, the hospital serves its community with Ask-a-Nurse, a 24-hour, free health information and physician referral service. Avista Hospital is a member of Rocky Mountain Adventist Healthcare (RMAH), the regional corporate organization that also includes Porter Memorial Hospital in Denver, Littleton Hospital in Littleton, and Platte Valley Medical Center in Brighton. The hospital supports Avista Medical Associates, a physician network formed to further encourage relationships with medical insurance companies.

History. Avista Hospital was established in 1990 with funds from the sale of Boulder Memorial Hospital's facility. Ground was broken on Feb. 21, 1989, and nearly 500 visitors looked on as the hospital opened publicly on May 6, 1990. The first patient was admitted on May 7, 1990, and the first baby was born on May 9.

Avista Hospital stood strong through its turbulent first two years of operation, despite a delay in the expected population increase in the area. The hospital's financial performance dramatically improved in 1992 and 1993 because of a large increase in residential building and the hospital's success in medical insurance contracting.

John Sackett, formerly vice president of general services at Boulder Memorial Hospital, has served as the hospital's president since before its opening; Harold T. Dupper, formerly vice president of finance for Heritage Centers of America, is vice president of finance; and Carol Schmidt, R.N., M.H.A., formerly vice president of nursing at Boulder Memorial Hospital, is vice president and chief clinical officer. John Brownlow joined the staff in August 1990 as vice president of operations for Avista Medical Associates. Marvin Dunaway, N.M., has served as the president of Avista Medical Associates since the organization's inception.

AVONDALE ADVENTIST HIGH SCHOOL. A coeducational day school (years 7-12) located near Avondale College, Cooranbong, New South Wales, Australia. In 1993 the school had an enrollment of 368 and employed a staff of 25 full-time and three part-time teachers.

The school began as a primary school in 1897 with 15 students in a room borrowed from Avondale College. By 1899 the school had 42 students and was run in conjunction with the Teacher Training Department of the college. Between 1922 and 1933 the first three years of high school were added.

In 1934 the Avondale Village church began the operation of a full high school, first in the old church in which Ellen White had preached, then in a weatherboard building on the grounds of the church. A brick five-room building was constructed for the primary school in 1937.

The high school gained improved facilities when it moved to a new building on the college campus in 1942 and came under the administration of the college. In the postwar years the college offered a precollege academic course that was operated in conjunction with the high school. When in 1971 the NSW Higher School Certificate became the prerequisite for tertiary-level studies, the high school assumed full responsibility for the years 7-12 program.

During the 1970s the school came under the control of the North New South Wales Conference. A 42-acre (17-hectare) block at the end of Avondale Road was acquired from the Australasian Conference Association. A new primary school complex, caretaker's cottage, and high school complex was built on the site in 1980.

The high school comprises 14 classrooms, two science laboratories, an industrial arts block, library, and administration block. Extensive playing fields and sports courts were developed for physical exercise. In 1992 an auditorium with associated music classroom and music teaching studios was constructed.

Although conference-owned, the school continues its working relationship with Avondale College. Trainee teachers visit the school to observe lessons and practice-teach, as they did in its beginnings.

Principals: H. K. Martin, 1930-1932; G. A. Currow, 1934-1936; W. R. Whisker, 1937; W. A. Westerman, 1938-1941; G. A. Currow, 1942-1947; G. W. Maywald, 1948-1949; C. H. Millist, 1950-1951; E. M. Tonkin, 1952-1957; W. J. Driscoll, 1958-1964; L. R. Thrift, 1965-1968; H. J. Eager, 1969-1970; W. G. Litster, 1971-1974; W. R. Veitch, 1975-1979; E. G. Krause, 1980-1984; R. A. Spoor, 1985-1987; D. W. Reye, 1988-1992; D. D. Tame, 1993- .

AVONDALE COLLEGE. A multidisciplinary residential institution of higher education situated near Cooranbong about 90 miles (145 kilometers) north of Sydney, New South Wales, Australia, with a secondary campus for its School of Nursing on the grounds of the Sydney Adventist Hospital. Avondale is owned by the South Pacific Division of the Seventh-day Adventist Church, and operated by a board of governors constituted in accordance with terms agreed to by the church and the government. In 1993 there was an enrollment of 786, a teaching staff of 77, and a support staff of 61.

Avondale offers six baccalaureate degree programs accredited in Australia, as well as a master's degree in religion offered through an affiliation agreement with Andrews University. An associate diploma is available in aviation, and certificate courses are offered in secretarial studies and pilot training.

History: The predecessor of Avondale College was the first Seventh-day Adventist Bible training school in Australia, operated in rented buildings on St. Kilda Road, Melbourne, Victoria, from Aug. 24, 1892, to September 1894. The school opened with 25 students, increasing to 56 by the following June. L. J. Rousseau served as first principal.

Upon the recommendation of Ellen G. White a more suitable school site was sought in the country, and in 1894 an estate of 1,450 acres (585 hectares) was inspected at Cooranbong. Although it was regarded unfavorably by many of the leaders of the church and by agricultural experts, Mrs. White, after visiting the estate, urged its purchase, being certain that the Lord had led in its discovery. In 1895 the decision was made to establish the school there.

Between 1896 and 1899 the Avondale School for Christian Workers, as the college was originally called, was literally hewn out of the forest. Students and teachers lived in tents and in the Healy Hotel, Cooranbong, which was rented for this purpose. By day, trees were felled and land cleared and drained, and in the evening, classes were conducted in the hotel. The corner brick of the first building, Bethel Hall, was laid by Ellen White on Oct. 5, 1896, and the school opened Apr. 28, 1897, when two buildings were ready for use, at least in part—Bethel Hall and the dining hall, both two-story wood structures. The school opened with only 10 students (two were boarders), who were directed in their studies by four teachers. By the close of the term the enrollment had increased to 60. The first principal was C. B. Hughes. Associated with him were his wife, S. N. Haskell and his wife, and H. C. Lacey and his wife. In 1898 the enrollment was 104; by 1900 it was 158. A third of the students were enrolled in the preparatory grades (equivalent to United States grades 1-8).

The boys' dormitory, a three-story wood building providing accommodation for 60, was completed in 1898. A church was erected at the entrance to the estate, about a mile (1.6 kilometers) from the school buildings. The central building of the school, known as the chapel (used for 60 years as an administration building for classes, and for assembly), was opened in April 1899. By 1908 several smaller buildings, including a press, had been erected.

Ellen White was closely associated with the school during its early days. She raised much of the money required to launch the project and was the guiding spirit behind its establishment. She made her home near the school from 1895 to 1900, living in a cottage named Sunnyside, and was a frequent visitor to the school. Many of her counsels concerning Christian education were written at Cooranbong.

In June 1911 the name of the school was changed to Australasian Missionary College. The new name was suggested in part by the responsibility accepted by the Australasian Union Conference of training missionaries, not only for the South Pacific area but also for Malaya and Indonesia.

Also in 1911 the growth of church school work in Australia and New Zealand led to the reorganization of teacher training at the college. From the early years practical instruction in several lines of manual training had been offered. Class instruction was available in agriculture, carpentry, blacksmithing, printing, sewing, and cooking. However, from 1923 onward strong efforts were made to expand and organize such subjects by introducing a Department of Technical Education and by outlining new courses in carpentry and sewing. In 1924 home economics and cooking were added, and the home economics building was erected. Prior to this expansion into technical education, college courses were restricted to the training of ministers, missionaries, teachers, and office workers.

Music was taught at the college almost from its beginning. The department was strengthened in 1925 when a brick building was erected to house it. The Avondale Symphonic Choir was formed in 1948, and from 1951 a more extensive music course has been offered. Art was introduced in 1903; in 1949 the standard was raised and the department strengthened. Science had been taught in an elementary form from the first, but with the completion of the science building in 1928, that field was given increased emphasis. In common with most subjects, however, none of the work was above senior secondary level.

Until 1951 only two years of tertiary-level work were offered. The advanced courses were based on five years of secondary education, followed by two years of professional study. In 1951 the ministerial course became a three-year program and led to the granting of a Licentiate of Theology (L.Th.). Arrangements were also made at that time for students to take external studies with the University of London for the Bachelor of Science degree. This arrangement continued until 1976, by which time Avondale had achieved accreditation for its Bachelor of Education degree with a science specialty.

The college course was raised to a four-year level when affiliation was effected with Pacific Union College in 1954. The affiliation, which continued until 1990, was valuable to Avondale by enabling it to offer degree courses while local accreditation was being developed, and for providing opportunities for staff exchange. In 1964 the name of the school was changed to Avondale College. In 1974 the college received its first national accreditation, which was for a degree and diplomas in education. Recognition in Australia of other courses has continued, with accreditation being given for Bachelor of Business (1983), Bachelor of Arts (Theology) (1990), Bachelor of Nursing (1991), Bachelor of Arts (1993), and Bachelor of Science (1993).

Additions to the school plant have included: brick primary school building (1937), secondary school building (1942), brick 70-bed women's dormitory (1953), auditorium (1955), new administration building with classrooms and library (1961), hostel for missionaries' children of high school age (1961), brick dormitory for 300 men (1964), food service building (1967), additional lecture theater (1973), library building (1973), married students' units (1974), women's chapel (1980), chemistry building (1981), College church (1986), student fitness center (1984), and an additional women's dormitory (1989).

Presidents: C. B. Hughes, 1897-1898; E. R. Palmer, 1899; C. B. Hughes, 1900-1902; C. W. Irwin, 1903-1908; J. H. Paap, 1909; B. F. Machlan, 1910-1912; G. Teasdale, 1913-1914; J. Mills, 1915; J. M. Johanson, 1916-1917; I.D.A. Lemke, 1918-1920; H. Kirk, 1921; W. W. Prescott, 1922; L. H. Wood, 1923-1927; E. E. Cossetine, 1928-1929; H. K. Martin, 1930-1932; A. E. Speck, 1933-1935; C. S. Palmer, 1936-1937; A. H. Piper, 1938-1939; T. C. Lawson, 1940-1943; B. H. McMahon, 1944; E. E. Rosendahl, 1945-1946; W.G.C. Murdoch, 1947-1952; E. G. White, 1953-1958; E. C. McDowell, 1959-1970; E. A. Magnusson, 1971-1981; J.J.C. Cox, 1981-1984; B. W. Ball, 1984-1990; G. A. Madigan, 1990- .

AVONDALE HEALTH RETREAT. A medical institution operated for a time at Cooranbong, New South Wales, one of the earliest opened by Seventh-day Adventists in the Australasian field. It was built under the direction of Ellen G. White, and opened for patients on Dec. 28, 1899. It was managed first by H. A. Hellier and his wife, of Victoria (with Dr. Silas Rand, of Newcastle, as the physician on call), and after about a year by a couple named Robie, from the United States. After the arrival from the U.S. of the Drs. D. H. and Lauretta Kress in November 1900, a training school for nurses was opened.

After the opening of the Sydney Sanitarium at Wahroonga in 1903, the health retreat lost much of its former significance, and later became an overflow dormitory for young men from the nearby school (now Avondale College). In the early 1930s the building was demolished, and in 1960 the site was used for the erection of the Kressville Home for the Aged.

AVONDALE SCHOOL FOR CHRISTIAN WORKERS. *See* Avondale College.

AVS. *See* International Audio-Visual Service.

AWR. *See* Adventist World Radio.

AY BOOK CLUB. *See* Adventist Youth Book Club.

AY CLASSES. *See* Adventist Youth Classes.

AY COMMUNITY SERVICE. *See* Adventist Youth Community Service.

AY GOLD AWARD. *See* Adventist Youth Gold Award.

AY HONORS. *See* Pathfinder Honors.

AY SILVER AWARD. *See* Adventist Youth Silver Award.

AY SOCIETIES. *See* Adventist Youth Societies.

AY WEEK OF PRAYER. *See* Adventist Youth Week of Prayer.

AYER MANIS SCHOOL. A coeducational boarding school on the secondary level for training national Seventh-day Adventist workers, operated by the Seventh-day Adventist Church of Sarawak on a 114-acre (46-hectare) campus on the main road, 34 miles (54 kilometers) southeast of Kuching, the capital of Sarawak, Malaysia.

Founded in late 1933, when Albert Munson was the president of the Sarawak Mission, the school opened in January 1934 to receive its first Dyak students. Tuition and board was free. A. L. Pauner, a missionary from Indonesia, was the first principal. Because of the danger of malaria, the school was moved from its original 11-acre (4.5-hectare) campus to higher ground on the other side of the road. The enrollment gradually increased, and an academic level of six grades was reached. During the Japanese occupation in World War II the school was closed, but its facilities served as a haven for the mission personnel, who supported themselves by farming the land.

The school was reopened in 1946, with J. T. Pohan as principal. The medium of instruction was Malay, but English classes were taught. Four years later English became the medium of instruction, with classes in the

Malay language. The present dormitories, built since the war, were financed by a Thirteenth Sabbath Offering overflow.

Primary 1 to 6 was taught until 1961. Since that time, three years of secondary education have been provided in English. In 1965 the Sarawak government authorized a five-year program leading up to the Cambridge School Certificate. The school has been accredited by the board of regents of the Far Eastern Division, and following a self-evaluation program in 1974, accreditation was granted for a four-year period. The enrollment was 250 in 1974; the faculty for these grades totaled nine. The students are Chinese, Iban, Land Dyak, and Malay; approximately 33 percent come from non-SDA homes.

Because of free education provided by the government, Ayer Manis enrollment was affected to the extent that the school was closed in 1983. In 1984 it was reopened with 45 students and a staff of two. In 1993, 98 students were enrolled, and there were 10 teachers.

In 1992 a commercial branch school was begun in Serian, a town two miles (three kilometers) from the campus, and 75 were enrolled in typing and computer courses.

Principals: A. R. Musgrave, 1961-1963; Clifford Ortner, 1963-1972; C. H. Goertzen, 1972-1976; G. A. Pauner, 1977; W. Turambi, 1977-1979; Saul Nyungaa, 1980-1982; P. Ngadan, 1983; L. Randig, 1984-1991; Kueh Hong Ewe, 1992- .

AYEYARWADY MISSION. *See* Far Eastern Division; Myanmar.

AYS. *See* Adventist Youth Service.

AZAZEL. *See* Scapegoat.

AZERBAIJAN. An Asian country bordered by Russia, Georgia, Iran, Armenia, and the Caspian Sea. It occupies an area of 33,428 square miles (86,600 square kilometers) and has a population (1994) of 7.7 million. Azerbaijan was conquered by Russia in 1813 and 1828. It joined the USSR on Dec. 30, 1991, and became an independent state when the Soviet Union disbanded in December 1991.

Seventh-day Adventist Statistics. Jacob Klein was the first preacher entering the city of Baku and Caucasian areas in 1894. Several German families had already kept the Sabbath there. He baptized seven people from these families and shared the Lord's Supper with them. After several days Elder Klein was arrested and exiled. Soon after that, those he baptized also had to leave that place.

In 1906 in the village of Novo-Vasiljevka, near the Caspian Sea, a Russian church of 34 former Molokans was organized. In the same year Elder Albert Ozel visited Koryazhno (now Fizuli) and baptized a group of believers. Vasily Zhukov was the first church elder there. Elder G. A. Lepsak visited this group in 1908.

In spite of 70 years of repression and atheistic propaganda, in 1993 there were four local churches and two companies in Azerbaijan, with a total membership of 259. A unique church in Gyandzha consists of 29 Azerbaijanians (formerly Moslems) and 23 Jews. The worship services are held in the Azerbaijan language.

Azerbaijan is part of the Trans-Caucasian Field, an attached field of the Euro-Asia Division.

AZORES. A group of nine islands in the eastern Atlantic Ocean, administered as three districts of Portugal. The total area is 868 square miles (2,250 square kilometers), with a population (1993) of 236,000. Agriculture is the principal occupation.

Seventh-day Adventist Statistics. The territory of the Azores Islands, formerly a mission of the Portuguese Union, is now part of the territory assigned to the newly organized Portuguese Union of Churches of the Euro-Africa Division. Statistics (1992) for *Azores:* churches, 5; members, 174; ordained ministers, 2.

Development of Seventh-day Adventist Work. As early as 1892 G. R. Drew, of England, reported the sending of publications by ship to the island of São Miguel in the Azores *(Review and Herald* 69:230, Apr. 12, 1892). No results were known. Direct SDA work in the Azores began in 1931 when a colporteur sold SDA publications there. E. P. Mansell and his wife, who were transferred there from Madeira in 1934, rented a hall and held meetings in Ponta Delgada on the isalnd of São Miguel. On Dec. 12, 1935, the first six converts were baptized. Other missionary families followed. A church was built on the island of Pico in 1949, a donation from Lidia Madsen, a native of the Azores then resident in California. In the 1930s a Catholic woman on the island of Flores had SDA books that she had not read. She lent some to one of her relatives, who accepted their teachings but was not baptized until 1947.

The Azores Mission appeared first in the

Statistical Report for 1936 with one church of 10 members, and five Sabbath schools totaling 32 members. The converts, having been won largely through SDA publications, were active in distributing tracts.

AZTEC UNION MISSION. A former unit of church organization (1923-1926); its territory included British Honduras (now Belize), El Salvador, Guatemala, Honduras, and Mexico.

B

BAASCH, DAVID HENRY (1921-1987). Missionary, administrator. He was born in Puerto Rico, the son of missionaries. After graduation from Pacific Union College in 1943, he married Iva N. Munson. They had two sons and two daughters. Baasch began his ministry as an intern in the Arizona Conference in 1943 and soon became a departmental director in the Puerto Rico Mission. He was ordained to the ministry in Santurce, Puerto Rico, in 1948. He held the position of departmental secretary in the Colombia-Venezuela Union from 1948 to 1951, after which he was called to be principal of Colombia-Venezuela Union College. He also served as Inter-American youth director for the Inter-American Division, president of the Mexican Union, secretary of the division, and associate secretary of the General Conference before accepting the position of undersecretary of the General Conference, a position he held until his death.

BABCOCK, DAVID CALDWELL (1854-1932). Conference administrator and missionary. He was educated at Battle Creek College and was president of the West Virginia Conference (1892-1895) and the Virginia Conference (1897-1899). He directed the British Guiana Mission (1900-1905) and the British West African Mission (1905-1914); he opened up Seventh-day Adventist work in Nigeria (1914-1917). In 1917, while en route to England seeking treatment for sleeping sickness, he was rescued when the ship was torpedoed. In 1919 he was sent to the Virgin Islands for ministerial work, and again to British Guiana as president of the conference (1925). Two years later ill health forced his return to America.

BABER, GRANVILLE HENDERSON (1852-1936). Pioneer Seventh-day Adventist missionary in Chile, teacher, and conference administrator. He was educated at Battle Creek College and was a member of the first class in Dr. J. H. Kellogg's Health and Temperance Missionary School. In 1895 he was sent to Chile as the first SDA minister to engage in regular evangelistic work. While there he started the missionary paper *Las Señales de los Tiempos* in 1900. In 1902 he returned to the United States and joined the faculty of the Southern Training School (now Southern College) in Tennessee, where he served for 11 years.

BABIENCO, THEOPHIL A. (1850-1943). One of the pioneer Seventh-day Adventists in Russia; lay evangelist. He was a native of the village of Tarashcha in the Ukraine south of Kiev. As a young man he assisted in the services of the Orthodox Church by reading the psalms. His interest in the Bible thus being aroused, he obtained permission to take a copy home. Gathering his neighbors together, he read to them. His study led him to the conclusion that many doctrines believed and taught by his church were not scriptural.

In 1877 Babienco and a group whom he had interested in the Bible left the Orthodox Church and organized themselves into "a community of brethren, believers of the Bible." The community grew and spread to other towns and villages of the Ukraine. Some time later in exile in Stavropol in northern Caucasus he was led, according to his son's account, to keep the seventh day of the week as the Sabbath and to expect Christ's return to this earth in a short time. Correspondence with some of his former associates at Tarashcha led them to join him in his beliefs.

About 1886 or 1887 Babienco, then still in exile at Stavropol, accepted the SDA message, becoming acquainted with the church, probably through a visit by Conrad Laubhan (one of the early SDA workers among the German Protestant settlers in Russia) to Babienco's employer, a Baptist. Through his missionary efforts Babienco gathered a group of Russian converts at Stavropol, which later, in 1890, was organized into a church. Other groups were developed in the vicinity. In 1890, at the first general meeting of the Seventh-day Adventists in Russia, which was held at Eigenheim in the Caucasus, Babienco was ordained as church elder for the Russian group, the first Russian SDA ordained to a church office. Soon after the ordination, Babienco secretly (he was still in exile) visited his former home village and organized a church among his former brethren, with whom he had continued to correspond through the years.

His active work in behalf of the gospel brought persecution. Less than a year after the church was organized at Stavropol, Babienco and seven members of the church were exiled beyond the Caucasus Mountains, to a place named Herusy, near Mount Ararat, at the end of the stagecoach route. But exile did not daunt him. He spoke of his faith to other exiles and to the coachmen, mostly Russian Baptists and Molokans, and soon more than 200 persons were observing the Bible Sabbath in the surrounding villages.

Babienco was threatened with another exile even farther from Russian centers, but the amnesty proclaimed on the accession of the new czar, Nicholas II, prevented this. Nevertheless, his five-year term was increased by another eight years. Separation from his family and continual harassment by the political administration turned his mind to emigration. With the help of English Protestants he went to Romania in 1896, where his family joined him.

In 1903 the family emigrated to Canada, and he settled on a farm in Saskatchewan. His son, Theophil T., became a minister, and preached for many years among the Russian people in Canada, the United States, China, and the Baltic States.

BABYLON, SYMBOLIC. A cryptic designation in Revelation (Rev. 14:8; 16:19; 17:5; 18:2, 10, 21) for apostate religious organizations in opposition to Christ and His people on earth, especially during the closing phase of the agelong conflict between good and evil. Babylon is variously identified as "that great city, which reigneth over the kings of the earth," as "the great whore" and a "mother of harlots" (Rev. 16; 17:1, 5, 18). Adultery is a common OT metaphor for apostate religion (for example, Eze. 16:15ff.; 23:2, 3ff.; Hosea 4:15). The revelator declares that Babylon has "fallen" (Rev. 14:8; 18:2), has seduced "the kings of the earth" to commit fornication with her (Rev. 17:2), has enticed "the inhabitants of the earth" to become "drunk with the wine of her fornication" (Rev. 17:2; 19:2), and has deceived the nations with her "sorceries" (Rev. 18:23). He represents her as "drunken with the blood of the saints, and with the blood of the martyrs of Jesus" (Rev. 17:5, 6; 18:24; 19:2). He sees her "sins" as consisting of pride and arrogance (Rev. 17:4; 18:7, 16), defiance of God, and the persecution of His people on earth (cf. Rev. 16:19; 17:6; 18:24), and an illicit alliance with the political powers of earth (Rev. 17:2, 3; 18:9). He notes that "her sins" eventually reach "unto heaven," and the time comes for God to judge her (Rev. 16:19; 18:5, 6; 19:2). God therefore summons His people to leave Babylon, in order to avoid complicity in her "sins" and the "plagues" He is about to visit upon her (Rev. 18:4). Disillusioned, the kings of the earth turn on Babylon and destroy her (Rev. 17:14, 16, 17; cf. Rev. 18:19, 21; 19:3). In this way God avenges His people on Babylon (Rev. 18:20; 19:2).

Babylon is "a name of mystery" (Rev. 17:5, RSV), that is, a figurative or cryptic title; hence the often-used designation, "mystical

Babylon." This symbolic name connotes the historical fact that in OT times literal Babylon was the archfoe of God's covenant people. Mystical Babylon is to be understood in terms of the role played by its historical counterpart in OT times (see SDACom 7:866, 869). The Babylonian name *Bâb-ilu* (Babel or Babylon) meant "gate of god." In ancient times the city gate was the place where official visitors conducted public business. The name *Bâb-ilu* reflected the belief that Babylon was the place selected by the gods to meet with human beings, and the claim of Babylonian kings that the gods had commissioned them to rule the world. In Hebrew *Bâb-ilu* was disparagingly associated with the term *balal,* "to confuse"—a reminder that God had confused the speech of the Babel builders (Gen. 11:9).

From the time of its founding by Nimrod (Gen. 10:9, 10; 11:1-9), Babylon was characterized by disbelief in the true God and defiance of His will. Its tower was a monument to apostasy, and a citadel of rebellion against Him. Isaiah identifies Lucifer as king of Babylon (Isa. 14:4, 12-14), and implies that Satan made Babylon the center and agent of his master plan to secure control of the human race, even as God purposed to work through Jerusalem to accomplish His plan for this world. Throughout OT times the two cities typified the forces of evil and good at work in the world. In Revelation mystical Babylon stands in contrast with the New Jerusalem, Christ's "bride," who is dressed in "fine linen, clean and white: . . . the righteousness of the saints," in contrast with Babylon's gaudy, voluptuous attire (Rev. 19:8; cf. Rev. 17:4; 18:7, 16).

Nebuchadnezzar II made Babylon one of the wonders of the ancient world, intending his kingdom to be universal and eternal (Dan. 3:1, 4-30). Over the centuries following its destruction by Xerxes, the city gradually lost its glitter and importance, and by the time John wrote Revelation it was virtually a desolate ruin, and thus a graphic illustration of the impending fate of mystical Babylon.

As early as the first century A.D., Christians were referring to Rome by the cryptic title Babylon (see 1 Peter 5:13). The Jews were suffering under Rome as they had previously suffered under Babylon, and Christians were also experiencing sporadic persecution. To avoid reprisal, both Jews and Christians began to use "Babylon" as a secret name for imperial Rome (see the *Sibylline Oracles* 5:155-161; 2 Baruch 11:1; the Jewish Midrash Rabbah on Canticles 1:6 ["They called the place Rome Babylon"] [Soncino ed.], p. 60).

The Church Fathers of the early centuries, as for example Tertullian *(Against Marcion* 3. 13) and Irenaeus *(Against Heresies* 5. 26. 1), applied "Babylon" in the Apocalypse to the city of Rome or to the empire. Joachim of Floris (d. 1202) was among the first to include the Roman Church under "Babylon" (L. E. Froom, *Prophetic Faith,* vol. 1, p. 708). Others of the late Middle Ages who did so were Pierre Jean d'Olivi, a French Spiritual (d. 1298) *(ibid.,* pp. 764, 765); Michael of Cesena *(ibid.,* vol. 2, p. 20); the Lollards *(ibid.,* pp. 78, 79); John Huss *(ibid.,* p. 116); and Savonarola *(ibid.,* p. 152). This identification came to be widespread among Protestants.

William Miller identified mystical Babylon with "Rome under papal rule" (Joshua V. Himes, [William Miller's] *Views of the Prophecies and Prophetic Chronology* [1842], p. 200). Sylvester Bliss, a Millerite editor, held that Babylon is "everything in this world opposed to or varying from the spirit of Christ," or "Satan's Kingdom," and that upon the division of the Roman Empire "the Papal horn succeeded to the supremacy, as the head of Satan's power, and became the Babylon of the world" *(The Advent Shield and Review* [1844], pp. 112, 113, 115, 116). When the Protestant churches rejected the message of Christ's soon coming, Adventists began to include them under "Babylon," along with papal Rome, and interpreted the fall of Babylon to be these churches' rejection of that message. For example, Joseph Bates assigned the fall of Babylon to 1843-1844 and attributed it to the churches' utter rejection of the doctrine of the coming Lord.

"When this subject first began to be introduced in 1843, the most of the professed nominal churches had closed their doors against the Second Advent doctrine, and began to treat the message with scorn and contempt. . . .

"Mystery Babylon . . . represents the organized churches of all descriptions, divided into three parts, Rev. 16, 19, viz, Roman, Greek, and Protestant. . . .

"Our business then is with the Protestant Church, for it will be admitted by all that the Roman and Greek churches are corrupt and anti-Christian" (Joseph Bates, in *Advent Review* 1:66, 67, November 1850).

In 1851 James White wrote: "The woman, which is the great city, called Babylon, symbolizes the fallen apostate churches" *(Review and Herald* 2:3, Aug. 5, 1851). J. N. Andrews similarly defined Babylon as being "all the corrupt religious bodies which ever have existed, or which exist at the present time, united to the world, and sustained by the civil power," including "the corrupt Jewish church," "the corrupt Papal and Greek churches," and "the great body of the Protestant churches" that "imitate the Romish church" *(ibid.* 5:5, Feb. 21, 1854).

Uriah Smith, classic SDA commentator on Daniel and the Revelation, understood "that by this symbol [Babylon] is meant the great mass of confused and corrupt Christianity," and added that "her fall was a moral fall, caused by rejecting the vivifying truths of the first message, or great Advent proclamation. By the wine of the wrath of her fornication we understand her false doctrines and pernicious errors. These she has caused all nations to drink" *(Thoughts on the Revelation* [1865 (i.e., 1867) ed.], p. 233).

He identified the component parts of modern Babylon as "paganism, Catholicism, and Protestantism," and the whore of chapter 17 as the Roman Church. "Other independent religious organizations," are her daughters, and all "belong to the same great family." The Roman segment of Babylon, he wrote, comes to an end in chapter 17, and the Protestant daughters in chapter 18. He quoted contemporary Protestant commentators to the effect that the popular Protestant churches had become Babylon *(ibid.* [1867 ed.], pp. 233-275, *passim).*

Seventh-day Adventist interpretation today is essentially that of Uriah Smith and other early SDA commentators. Modern Babylon is understood to stand for all Christian churches that have departed from the "everlasting gospel" as set forth in the Scriptures, including both the great Roman apostasy of the early Christian centuries and the more recent departure of mainstream Protestantism from God's Word, beginning in particular with its rejection of the 1844 message. The fall is understood to be progressive; it is not yet complete, but it will be so when the major Protestant churches collaborate with the Church of Rome in an attempt to coerce the conscience (Rev. 13). The second angel's message of Rev. 14:8 is a warning that Babylon has fallen, and Rev. 18:1-4 is a call to God's people to come out of Babylon, in order to avoid complicity in her crimes and a share in her "plagues."

BACHELLER, JOHN WARREN (1839-1917). Printer. He worked on the *Review and Herald* when it was published in Saratoga Springs, New York, went with it to Rochester, New York, and to Battle Creek, Michigan, where the first Adventist publishing association was formed. He was a charter member of the Battle Creek Seventh-day Adventist Church.

BÄCKER, FRIEDRICH ALEX (1893-1958). Minister, missionary in Turkey, and departmental secretary in Germany and the Netherlands. The son of a church leader in Frankfort on the Main, he was baptized in 1910 after attending elementary and secondary schools. Five years later he began his service in the church as conference secretary and Sabbath school and tract society secretary of the West German Union Conference (c. 1916-1921). In 1921 he was ordained to the ministry. During the next several years he was secretary for the Sabbath School and Home Missionary departments of the same union. In 1928 he went to Turkey to superintend the mission work and worked there until 1936, when he returned to Germany and served as a pastor in the Hessia-Westphalian Conference. Shortly before World War II he assumed leadership of the Home Missionary, Sabbath School, and Young People's departments of the newly organized Netherlands Union Conference. After the war he was a minister in the Northern Hanover and Southern Hanover conferences until his death in 1958. He married Antonie Henriette Frohmann in 1920.

BACOLOD SANITARIUM AND HOSPITAL. A 100-bed general hospital operated by the Central Philippine Union Mission. It began as a small rented clinic operated by Dr. Gideon Mercurio in downtown Bacolod City in 1961. On Feb. 18, 1958, six acres (2.5 hectares) of land were bought, and construction on a new building began Apr. 29, 1962. The first patient was admitted on Sept. 8, 1966, and on Dec. 8 the hospital was officially opened, with Dr. W. G. Dick as the first medical director. Dr. W. C. Richli, a self-supporting medical missionary, was most helpful during the early years of the hospital's history.

In 1969 Philippine Union College affiliated with the hospital for the medical technology internship training program. In 1970 Dr. R. W. Spalding relieved Dr. Dick. In August 1971 Dr. F. T. Geslani served as the first national medical director. In 1990 Rufo G. Gasapo was appointed president.

In 1972 the government approved and accredited the hospital as a teaching institution for medical interns, and the clinical division began as a facility of the Mountain View College School of Nursing. Later affiliations included the University of Negros Occidental-Recoletos School of Medical Technology, Colegio de San Agustin-Bacolod School of Nursing, Southwestern University School of Medical Technology, and Central Philippine Adventist College School of Nursing.

Under the supervision of Dr. F. T. Geslani, assisted by Chaplain H. V. Gayares, the largest Seventh-day Adventist church in the Philippines was constructed adjacent to the hospital. In 1988 a new dormitory for Central Philippine Adventist College nursing students was completed.

Medical Directors/Administrators. W. G. Dick, 1966-1970; R. W. Spalding (acting), 1970-1971; F. T. Geslani, 1971-1989; Rufo G. Gasapo, 1990- .

BAD AIBLING SANITARIUM AND OLD PEOPLE'S HOME. *See* Haus Wittelsbach Old People's Home.

BADAUT, JEAN PIERRE (1850-1933). Pioneer colporteur and evangelist in France. Of Protestant background, he read J. N. Andrews' French periodical, *Les Signes des Temps,* about 1880, and thus became acquainted with Seventh-day Adventists. Over a period of several years he investigated SDA teachings, accepting them one by one. When his employer refused his request to have Sabbaths free, he left his job at a flour mill, and was baptized into the Seventh-day Adventist Church in 1884. One year later he went out to sell publications that came from the newly established SDA publishing house in Basel, Switzerland. Later he became an evangelist, and was ordained to the ministry in 1908. Two of his sons, Paul and Samuel, distinguished themselves as strong leaders of the SDA Church in France.

BADAUT, PAUL (1880-1948). French evangelist, missionary, and conference administrator. A member of a pioneer French Seventh-day Adventist family (his father, J. P. Badaut, being one of the earliest SDA colporteurs and evangelists in France), he took an active part in the work of the church from an early age. He was baptized in 1897, and in 1900 went to the Institut Sanitaire at Basel, Switzerland *(see* Lake Geneva Sanitarium), where he attended a course for nurses for two years. Meanwhile, in 1901, he attended a short Bible course in Geneva. Afterward he preached at Charleroi, Belgium, then at Mazamet, in southern France, and in several places in Switzerland and again in southern France. In 1903 he married Martha Rose Fontane. He was ordained to the ministry in 1906. In 1909 he went to French North Africa and became one of the pioneers of the SDA work there. In 1914, when a call for a minister came from Mauritius, in the Indian Ocean, Badaut went there, baptized the first SDA converts on the island, organized a church, and for a few years served as director of the Mauritius Mission. In 1920, after his wife's failing health made necessary a return to France, Badaut entered evangelistic work in his homeland. Between 1932 and 1938 he headed the South France Conference. He spent the last years of his working life at Bordeaux. He retired in 1945, but continued to take part in the work until he died from the effects of a cold he caught while on a visit in Switzerland after attending a conference session at Collonges.

BADAUT, SAMUEL (1891-1927). Minister and departmental leader in France. His birth came as a consolation to his parents, a pioneer French Seventh-day Adventist family who previously had lost three children by diphtheria. His father, J. P. Badaut, was one of the early colporteurs and evangelists in France. Samuel was baptized at the age of 14, and after having received secondary education in France, went to Stanborough Park Missionary College in England in 1908. While there he earned his expenses as a colporteur. He also mastered the English language well enough to become a proficient translator. On his return to France in 1910 he worked as a colporteur and in the office of the Latin Union, and assisted in evangelism. When World War I broke out he was drafted for military service and remained in the service until 1917. Successful in obtaining the permission of his superiors to observe the Sabbath, he preached regularly in the Seventh-day Adventist church at Grenoble, in southeastern France. He spent much of the war years as an interpreter with the English Expeditionary Army. In 1917 he returned to the service of the church as an evangelist, an enthusiastic leader, and an administrator. In the same year, he married Madeleine Delahaye. Between 1920 and 1925 he was secretary of the home missionary and young people's work in the Latin Union. In 1924 he was ordained, and from 1925 until his death, the result of a motorcycle accident in 1927, he was a minister in north France.

BADEN-WUERTTEMBERG CONFERENCE. *See* Euro-Africa Division.

BAER, ROSCOE THURMAN (1881-1942). Minister and mission administrator in South America. He grew up in a pioneer environment in the Midwest and was trained for the ministry at Union College. After teaching church school in Nebraska, he pastored churches and taught in South Dakota and Wyoming. He was ordained in 1907. In 1910 he became president of the Chesapeake Conference.

In 1915 he was called to South America as president of the Argentine Conference, and four years later, in 1919, became president of the Chile Conference. The next year he was elected the second president of the Austral Union. In 1927 he returned to the United States, where he pastored the church at College View, Nebraska, for several years and then was in charge of districts in western Nebraska (1932-1936) and western Colorado (1936-1942).

BAESA ADVENTIST ACADEMY. A coeducational day school on the senior high school level operated by the Central Luzon Conference, situated on a 1.2-acre (.5-hectare) campus at Baesa, Caloocan City, adjacent to the former site of Philippine Union College (now Eternal Garden Memorial Park). Begun as the Baesa church school in 1968, with 135 pupils and three teachers, it soon swelled to an enrollment of 506, with 12 teachers, in 1971. In 1971-1972, the first two years of academy were offered, and the school became known as Baesa Junior Academy. With the assistance of friends, local and abroad, a two-story building was constructed, housing six classrooms, offices, and a library.

In 1974-1975 the Baesa church turned over the operation of the school to the Central Luzon Mission upon the addition of the third year of the academy. Enrollment in 1993 was 423, with 20 staff members.

When Philippine Union College moved to Silang, Cavite, the school became Baesa Adventist Academy and shares the campus with Baesa Elementary School. After government recognition in 1986, the academy has graduated an average of 100 students yearly. Typing and computer classes are being taught to augment practical arts subjects.

Principals: R. G. Evangelista, 1971-1973; R. D. Pedernal, 1973-1974; R. A. Budayao, 1974-1975; R. G. Evangelista, 1975-1980; J. V. Afenir II, 1980-1981; A. A. Arit, 1981-1982; B. C. Casi, 1982-1984; R. S. Barizo, 1984-1986; B. A. Bico, 1987-1988; J. C. Afenir III, 1988-1990; A. T. Amada, 1990-1993; J. C. Afenir III, 1993- .

BAHAMAS ACADEMY. A coeducational day school on the senior high school level situated on a four-acre (1.6-hectare) plot on Wulff Road in Nassau, Bahamas. Operated by the Bahamas Conference, it serves a constituency of 12,000. The academy offers a secondary program leading to the BGCSE examination. The secondary enrollment is 377, with a faculty of 16. Graduates may go on to the West Indies College, from which they may enter denominational work.

Bahamas Academy developed from a church school established by James H. Smith, who came to the Bahamas in 1913. The school first met in Aurora Hall of the Odd Fellows Building, with G. G. Coffin and his wife as principal and teacher. After several moves it began to occupy the present Wulff Road building in 1948. In that year the school became a junior academy; it achieved senior academy status in 1955.

Principals: G. G. Coffin, 1914-1916; C. G. Howell, 1916-1918; Enid Wright, 1923-1925; O. J. Lawrence, 1926-1927; Mrs. H. E. Beddoe, 1927-1928; H. T. Saulter, 1928-1929; A. R. Haig, 1930-1931; L. S. Crawford, 1931-1933; D. B. Reid, 1933-1938; Eulalie Lawrence, 1938-1949; O. P. Jones, 1949-1950; Eulalie Lawrence, 1950-1952; W. W. Liskie, 1953-1957; E. Mullings, 1957-1958; Mrs. T. O. Shaw, 1958; Ruth White, 1958-1959; H. A. Roach, 1959-1968; John Carey, 1968-1977; Ruth White, 1977-1992; Cheryl McMillan-Rolle, 1992- .

BAHAMAS CONFERENCE. *See* Inter-American Division; The Bahamas.

BAHAMAS, THE. A former British colony that became independent July 10, 1973, and is presently known as The Bahamas. This chain of islands, cays, rocks, and reefs extends some 750 miles (1,200 kilometers) southeast, beginning some 50 miles (80 kilometers) off the Florida peninsula. One of the islands, San Salvador, was the first landfall of Columbus in the New World. Thirty of the islands are inhabited, with a total population (1994) of 275,000.

Seventh-day Adventist Statistics. The

territory of the Commonwealth of the Bahamas constitutes the Bahamas Conference, formerly (until 1968) the Bahamas Mission, which is part of the West Indies Union Conference, which in turn is part of the Inter-American Division. Statistics (1993) for the *Bahamas:* churches, 39; members, 12,589; ordained ministers, 15; licensed ministers, 2. The Bahamas Conference office is in Nassau, Bahamas.

Institutions. Bahamas Academy.

Development of Seventh-day Adventist Work. SDA work in the Bahamas was begun by colporteurs. According to the *Review and Herald* (71:293, 294, May 8, 1894) C. H. Richards, a colporteur, and his wife arrived in Nassau, Bahamas, late in 1893. In April of the following year they wrote of a young police officer who had "been a local preacher among the Methodists" and who was interested in SDA teachings but could "not yet" see "his way clear to leave his position on account of his family." Richards and his wife returned to the United States a few months later *(Home Missionary* 6:192, August 1894), and early in 1895 Charles F. Parmele, a former canvassing agent, came to the Bahamas to sell books. He reported in the *Review and Herald* (72:827, Dec. 24, 1895) that when he arrived, "no real fruit then appeared," but that the first Sabbath after he landed, one brother for whom Richards and his wife had labored "began to keep the Sabbath." This brother had a wife and four children, and Parmele went on to report that "thus far our Sabbath school consists of these."

The story of the beginnings of SDA work in the Bahamas has also been related as follows: A colporteur by the name of Richards began selling books in the Bahamas in 1893. The first to accept the SDA beliefs were William Charles Antonio and his wife. Antonio, at the time the superintendent of a Baptist church, searched his Bible in an endeavor to refute the teachings found in the books sold to him by Richards, and later by Parmele, but the more he searched, the more he became convinced that the SDA doctrines were correct. A Sabbath school, begun in Antonio's home immediately after he and his wife were baptized, continued for approximately 10 years. All the members of the Antonio family became Seventh-day Adventists.

In 1909 the first full-time SDA missionary to the Bahamas, W. A. Sweany, was sent to Nassau. The new mission was placed under the Southeastern Union Conference, an arrangement that proved temporary (it can be found only in the 1910 *Yearbook*). Sweany conducted evangelistic meetings, established a Sabbath school in the Odd Fellows Lodge Hall on Meeting Street, and soon after the first baptisms in 1911 organized a church. After Sweany left the islands, his work was continued by J. H. Smith, who came in 1913. The first Seventh-day Adventist church in the Bahamas, known as the Shirley Street church, was built in Nassau under his direction in 1914. Not confining his efforts to Nassau alone, Smith journeyed to Andros and Eleuthera, the second and third islands entered by SDAs in the Bahamas. He also held evangelistic meetings on Cat Island and on San Salvador. From this small beginning the SDA teachings have spread through the Bahamas.

In the early 1930s R. J. Sype established a second church in the Bahamas, on the island of San Salvador. By this time colporteurs were selling SDA books throughout the archipelago, and lay evangelism through self-supporting work and branch Sabbath schools was playing an important part in the growth of the work in the Bahamas. In 1940 the Bahamas Mission embraced 17 churches, with 545 members, and operated two elementary schools, with a total enrollment of 96 students. During the next 10 years the membership increased to 718, and though the number of churches increased only by two, the number of church buildings increased by six, giving the mission 22 places of worship in 1950. In 1955 the school at Nassau became a senior academy *(see* Bahamas Academy). By the early 1960s all the islands of the Bahamas could hear the weekly broadcast of the Voice of Prophecy programs over station ZNS in Nassau, the only radio station in the Bahamas at that time. A branch of the Voice of Prophecy Bible correspondence school had been opened by the mission office, and a welfare center established in the mission office building, from which thousands of persons were being helped every year.

The decade of the 1960s can be characterized as the decade when the changing of the guard occurred in the leadership of the then-burgeoning mission. In 1964 Silas N. Mckinney became the first Bahamian minister to assume the presidency of the mission. Under his leadership the mission became a conference and experienced phenomenal membership growth.

In 1993 the educational institutions in the conference included three academies and two church schools with a total enrollment of more than 1,200 students. The conference also was sponsoring the *Breath of Life* telecast and a local radio program called *Family Forum.*

BAHARIAN, ZADOUR G. (d. 1915). Armenian evangelist and missionary. While attending college at Aintab, Turkey, he received tracts from his father, in whose home Theodore Anthony, the first Seventh-day Adventist in Turkey, was staying. At home for the summer of 1890, he read Uriah Smith's *Daniel and the Revelation* and J. N. Andrews' *History of the Sabbath,* and accepted the SDA faith. He then went to Basel for two years' training in SDA teachings and while there began to translate Bible readings and tracts; then in 1892 he returned to Turkey to proclaim his faith.

He was associated at first with Theodore Anthony, and together they gained six converts, one of whom became his wife. Many times he was imprisoned and threatened with death, both by mobs and by officials, all of which he met with unflinching courage. In addition, he encountered strong opposition from other Protestants in the country. He was ordained in 1894, and shortly after found himself in the thick of the Armenian-Turkish conflict of 1896. He worked for Armenian Christians and Muslims alike, and for some years was superintendent of the Armenian Mission. He sent frequent reports to the *Review and Herald* between 1893 and 1905.

In 1915, while traveling to Constantinople, he was killed and robbed by his Kurdish driver.

BAHIA ADVENTIST ACADEMY. *See* Northeast Brazil; Northeast Brazil College.

BAHIA CONFERENCE. *See* Brazil; South American Division.

BÄHLER, ROBERT (1885-1954). Swiss evangelist and administrator. He became acquainted with Seventh-day Adventist teachings in Zurich in 1906, was baptized in the same year, and attended Friedensau Missionary Seminary between 1909 and 1912. He afterward served as an evangelist, first holding meetings in Belgium, and later preaching in the cities of Halle, Ulm, and Stuttgart in Germany. When World War I broke out he returned to Switzerland and worked in Zurich, but after having received permission from the military authorities to preach in Germany, he went there again. Shortly thereafter, in 1916, he was called to Hungary, and worked in that country until 1921, despite the troubled conditions. He was ordained to the ministry in 1919, and the same year married Violette Bourquin. After the war he preached in Bavaria and Württemberg and then returned to Switzerland, where he was president of the German-Swiss Conference from 1926 to 1930. From then until his retirement in 1950, he preached in various cities of his native land.

BAHRAIN. A sheikdom situated midway along the Persian Gulf, about 20 miles (32 kilometers) off the eastern shore of the Arabian Peninsula, with an area of 231 square miles (600 square kilometers) and a population (1994) of 586,000. The population consists mainly of Arabs, but also includes Indians, Pakistanis, Persians, Europeans, and Americans. Half the Arab population are Sunni Muslims and the other half Shiite Muslims. Long a British Protected State, it became independent in 1971.

Bahrain is a territory in the Gulf Section in the Middle East Union of Seventh-day Adventists.

In 1971 it was learned that four Seventh-day Adventists from Seychelles, including Eghbert Fred and his wife, had moved to Bahrain. Mrs. Fred was employed as nurse for the daughter of the ruler, Sheik Isaibn Sulman Al Khalifah. Through her witness the sheik became interested in SDAs and welcomed anti-smoking clinics, the first of which was conducted by K. S. Oster and H. N. Sheffield. Clinics have been held periodically since then.

The first converts on Bahrain were Don Yettie and his wife and three children. They had been in contact with SDAs before moving to Bahrain. They were baptized in 1972. Through the efforts of Eghbert Fred, Nima Shring, a young Buddhist, was baptized in 1973. Mona Nicette was baptized later that year and joined the company that was organized in Bahrain.

After being inactive for many years, the company was reorganized in 1993 with 17 members. Benjamin Flaiz from India is the company leader.

BAILEY, DOUGLAS ALFRED (1892-1962). Publishing manager. He was successively assistant business manager of the Wabash Valley Sanitarium, Book and Bible House manager in the Indiana and New York conferences, manager of the Review and Herald branch at Peekskill, New York, and from 1938 to 1962 associate manager of the Book Department of the Review and Herald.

BAJA CALIFORNIA CONFERENCE. *See* Mexico; Inter-American Division.

BAKER, JOSEPH (fl. 1852). Minister of Lebanon, New Hampshire. He had been a worker in the Millerite movement, and was brought into Adventist ranks by Joseph Bates in 1850. He served on the publishing committee of the Review and Herald between 1852 and 1854.

BAKER, WILLIAM LEMUEL HENRY (1858-1933). Iowa-born teacher and evangelist. He was connected with the publishing work at the Pacific Press (1882) and in Australia (1887). After entering evangelistic work, he became president of several Australian conferences, and in 1914 Bible teacher at the Australasian Missionary College. Returning to the United States (1921), he was chaplain at the Washington Sanitarium, then Bible teacher at Oakwood Junior College (1923-1927). While seeking to regain his health, he was chaplain at Dr. T. J. Evans' sanitarium at Colorado Springs, Colorado.

BAKERSFIELD ADVENTIST ACADEMY. A coeducational day school on the senior high school level, with an elementary school and on-site preschool, serving a number of Bakersfield area churches. It is owned by the Central California Conference and is operated by a board consisting of representatives of the Pacific Union Conference, Central California Conference, and the constituent churches. Bakersfield Academy is accredited with the SDA Board of Regents and the Western Association of Schools and Colleges. The enrollment in 1993 was 287, with 66 high school and 221 elementary students.

The school began in 1902, at the corner of 8th and Eye streets. There were nine pupils, and Minnie Miller was the first teacher. Ninth- and tenth-grade work was begun in 1940, and the school operated as a full 12-grade academy for the first time during the 1968-1969 school year. The cost of the new academy building was $279,000.

The academy is situated on a 20-acre (eight-hectare) site at 3333 Bernard Street, and consists of a high school building, a Discoveryland preschool, three buildings for the elementary school, a gymnasium, a maintenance building, and a cottage.

Principals: Charles Hanson, 1968-1971; H. D. Lawson, 1971-1975; Roy Larsen, 1976; Lester Devine, 1977-1979; G. Bronson, 1980-1982; Bob Taylor, 1983-1984; Ernie Unruh, 1985-1986; Everett Perry, 1986-1987; Samir Berbawy, 1988-1993; Myron Wareham, 1993-1994; Malcolm Hutchinson, 1994- .

BAKSH (BAKHSH), J. ALI (1864-1937). Minister, author, editor, and translator. He was born at Una, in Hoshiarpur district, in eastern Punjab, India, in the family of a Muslim zamindar. In his youth he embraced Christianity and joined the Church of England. He was educated in India and England and early showed ability and scholarship. He began his career as a teacher at the Baring High School at Batala. However, he soon developed into a religious leader and author. He was called to the pastorate of the Holy Trinity Church in Lahore (now in Pakistan), and at the same time he was professor at the Divinity College in Madan Mohan Singh Bagh, Lahore, and wrote and edited several books and pamphlets. He assisted a committee on the revision of the translation of the Bible. He also was a member of the executive committee of the Punjab Religious Book Society. He was one of the first Indians to become a canon in the Church of England. In 1923 he listened to a Seventh-day Adventist evangelist, N. C. Burns, and accepted the SDA beliefs. Afterward he served as headmaster of the Punjab Boys' School (now Pakistan Adventist Seminary) and then as evangelist in the Punjab; editor of *Amad* ("Advent"), *Qasid-i-Jadid* ("New Messenger") (the official organ of the mission), and Urdu language periodicals; and translator (1926-1937). His writings in Urdu included *Zabur ki Kitab ki Tafsir* ("A Commentary on the Book of Psalms"), *Ahd Jadid ki Kitaben* ("Books of the New Testament"), *Peshingoyian Masih ke bare men* ("Prophecies Concerning Christ"), *Tafsir-i-Quran* ("Commentary of the Koran"), *Markus ki Injil ki Tafsir* ("Commentary on the Gospel of Mark").

BALADA, ENRIQUE (fl. 1896-1915). Minister; one of the early Seventh-day Adventist converts in Chile. He was born in Spain and came to Chile in the mid-1890s as a Baptist missionary. In Chile he became acquainted with the SDA beliefs through the work of F. W. Bishop and T. H. Davis, pioneer colporteurs there, and soon joined the small group of SDAs in Chile, becoming one of their leaders and a minister. He traveled extensively and organized numerous churches, and was sent in 1902 to open work in Lima, Peru. He also preached in Argentina and Bolivia. He is not listed in the *Yearbook* after 1916.

BALCARCE ADVENTIST ACADEMY (Instituto Adventista de Balcarce). An educational institution located in kilometer 79 of the 226 National Road, near the city of Balcarce, in the Buenos Aires province of Argentina. It belongs to the Buenos Aires Conference.

It began as a secondary school Mar. 19, 1986. It received its accreditation that same year. Its secondary course lasts five years, and the students are trained to proceed to the university of their choice. In 1993 there were 239 students and 22 teachers.

The institution fills an area of 570 acres (230 hectares). The buildings provide 43,000 square feet (4,000 square meters) of space. The library has 5,872 books.

Principals: Heriberto Müller, 1986-1988; Héctor Pérez, 1989-1991; Carlos Mesa, 1992- .

BALDWIN, WILTON OAKES (1910-1970). Educator, missionary. A native of California, he received his education in Western schools, Walla Walla and Pacific Union colleges, the University of Portland, and the University of Southern California. He began his career in 1932 as a teacher, and in the following years served in that capacity at Vallejo, California, as principal of the St. Helena Sanitarium School and Pacific Union College Preparatory School, as boys' dean at Lodi Academy, and principal of Golden Gate Academy. He and his wife, Ruth, were missionaries in the Far East for a time. He also served as educational superintendent in the Southeastern California, Central California, and Oregon conferences. In 1959 he joined the staff of the Pacific Union Conference.

Baldwin was instrumental in the establishment of two major educational institutions—San Pasqual Adventist Academy (in southern California), and Mountain View College (in the Philippines).

BALEARIC ISLANDS. *See* Spain.

BALL, DEXTER A. (1851-1906). Pioneer worker in the West Indies; minister. He was the seventh child of a poor farm family in southwestern New York. While working as a farmhand he was converted and joined the Baptist Church in 1873, and preached on occasion. Embracing Seventh-day Adventist beliefs in 1874, he actively propagated them by word of mouth and through the sale of publications. He became a full-time preacher in New York and Pennsylvania and formed a number of churches. In 1890 he and William Arnold, a colporteur, were sent to do pioneer self-supporting work in the West Indies. Ball spent two years in the islands and established churches on Barbados and Antigua before a developing cancer of the stomach made his return to the United States necessary. Recovering somewhat, he preached and sold books and periodicals for the remainder of his life. He was a staunch supporter of church educational and medical programs and personally sold hundreds of copies of Ellen G. White's *Christ's Object Lessons* in support of the schools. He was married twice: first to Martha Clark, a teacher from Pennsylvania; and then, after her death in 1901, to Hattie M. Buckland. His daughter by the first marriage became the wife of Roy F. Cottrell.

BALLENGER, ALBION FOX (1861-1921). A one-time Seventh-day Adventist minister, who later apostatized. He was born on a farm near Winslow, Illinois, the son of J. F. Ballenger, an SDA minister. After completing his public school education he taught for four years. Then the conference granted him a ministerial license and sent him out to preach. He became a fluent preacher and an able writer. After entering the ministry, he attended Battle Creek College for parts of two years.

In 1890 he was chosen secretary of the National Religious Liberty Association, with headquarters in Chicago. Three years later he was invited to serve as assistant editor of the *American Sentinel*, published in New York City. Eager to get back into public work, he resigned his editorial post after about a year. He attended camp meetings and other important gatherings in nearly all the conferences in North America. Outstanding among his sermons was the one entitled "Receive Ye the Holy Ghost." About this time he wrote the book *Power for Witnessing.*

About the turn of the century he was called to Great Britain, where he worked in several of the large cities of England. For a time he served in the Welsh Mission and later the Ireland Mission.

It was while leading the work in these missions that he began to entertain erroneous views regarding the work of Christ in the heavenly sanctuary. He submitted a manuscript on his views to a committee selected to examine them, who pointed out the errors and counseled him not to print the manuscript. He rejected their counsel and proceeded to propagate his views by voice and by pen. This naturally led to a separation from the organized work. His name appeared for the last time in the 1905 *Yearbook* as superintendent of the Ireland Mission. He returned to the United States, where he became active in proclaiming his erroneous views.

Beginning in 1914 he sought to bring his views before the church by means of a publication called *The Gathering Call,* which he took over from one Eylar of Bache, Oklahoma, and transferred to Riverside, California. He won sympathizers here and there, but did not develop an organized offshoot movement.

He was successful in influencing his aged father, J. F. Ballenger, a retired SDA minister, to embrace his erroneous views and to lend his influence in disseminating them. His brother, E. S. Ballenger, an ordained minister, also joined him, and as a result lost his credentials in 1913 or 1914. When Albion died, August 1921, E. S. Ballenger became the editor of *The Gathering Call,* with Mrs. A. F. Ballenger as associate editor.

BALLENGER, JOHN FOX (1834-1921). Minister. He was born on a farm where the city of Columbus, Ohio, now stands, the son of Asa Ballenger, a Methodist circuit rider and farmer. When John was 2 years old the family moved to a farm near Winslow, Illinois. His religious experience began in early childhood, and later he became a class leader in the Methodist Church. Shortly before the Civil War he accepted the Seventh-day Adventist faith as the result of tent meetings conducted by W. S. Ingraham in Onesco, Illinois. Recognizing the abilities of the young farmer, Ingraham urged him to enter the ministry. Ballenger gladly accepted the call, planted his rented farm to small grain, said goodbye to his family, and joined Ingraham in a series of tent meetings in St. Cloud, Minnesota. He was ordained Oct. 14, 1893, in the Battle Creek Tabernacle. For more than 50 years he preached in Minnesota, Illinois, Wisconsin, Michigan, Canada, and California, retiring in 1910 or 1911.

In his old age he was influenced by his son Albion to embrace and propagate certain erroneous views regarding the work of Christ in the heavenly sanctuary. When he refused to accept the counsel of the leaders to renounce the false teachings, he was asked to surrender his credentials. His monthly sustentation allowances were, however, continued until the time of his death.

BALMORAL ADVENTIST HIGH SCHOOL. *See* Auckland Adventist High School.

BALTIC UNION CONFERENCE. *See* Euro-Asia Division; Estonia; Latvia; Lithuania.

BALTIC UNION SCHOOL. A school established in 1923 for the training of church workers. It was operated by the Baltic Union at Suschenhof estate near Riga, Latvia. It is listed in the *Yearbook* from 1924 to 1937. The estate was situated in a picturesque area near Lake Stintsee and included a main building, referred to as a castle, and several auxiliary dwellings and farm buildings. The main building contained classrooms, a 120-seat chapel, a dining room for 100 persons, and a young women's dormitory. Other buildings housed faculty members and married students. A dormitory for male students, housing two or three in a room, was erected in 1924. Instruction began under the direction of L. F. Oswald, who came from the United States. Other early faculty members were A. Eglit and M. Oswald, wife of the principal.

The school had a multilingual student body and offered courses in German, Latvian, Estonian, and Russian. About two thirds of the enrollment came from Latvia, about a third from Estonia, and a few from Lithuania. The school was also known by the German names Missions-Schule Suschenhof and Advent-Missionsseminar. In 1935 the Estonian Conference established its own school, Estonian Mission School (Adventusuühingute Usuteaduse Kool). From 1938 the only school listed as near Riga was the Latvian Conference School (Adventes Misijas Seminars).

BANA NEWSLETTER. *See* Association of SDA Nurses.

BANAT CONFERENCE. *See* Euro-Africa Division; Romania.

BANDUNG ACADEMY (Sekolah Lanjutan Advent). A day school situated in Bandung, Java, Indonesia. Church members in the Bandung area of Indonesia began a church school on July 30, 1948. This became a junior academy on Aug. 4, 1963, with M. L. Tobing as principal. When the children graduated from the junior academy in 1966, the church members and the West Java Mission staff opened the present senior academy as a day school on Aug. 4, 1966, with an enrollment of 22 students. R. K. Siahaan was the principal. Since that time enrollment increased until it reached 450 students. The academy has been self-supporting since it opened. The present location is adjacent to the Seventh-day Adventist church, 63 Jalan Karyawan, Bandung, Java, Indonesia.

Principals: E. T. Mangunsong, 1968; R. K. Siahaan, 1969-1971; M. R. Manurung, 1972-1976; W. Hutapea, 1977-1978; H. Sitompul, 1979-1981; W. Hutapea, 1982-1986; B. Bangun, 1987-1991; B. Hutasoit, 1991-1994; K. A. Siregar, 1994- .

BANDUNG ADVENTIST HOSPITAL (Rumah Sakit Advent). A 200-bed general hospital operated by the West Indonesia Union Mission in Bandung, Java, Indonesia.

Seventh-day Adventists began conducting medical work in Indonesia soon after establishing their mission work there. The Java Health Retreat at Sumber Wekas, in eastern Java, was opened in 1908. It was put in the charge of Anna Nordstrom (later Mrs. G. A. Wood), a nurse from the Wahroonga Sanitarium, who arrived in Surabaja on Oct. 20, 1907, and Ethelbert Thorpe and his wife, both nurses, who arrived in Surabaja from Australia late in 1908. Wood and his wife operated a clinic at Pangungsen Colony in central Java from 1909 to 1912. Tena Judge did medical missionary work in Padang, Sumatra, from 1909 to 1914; she was joined in 1910 by Victoria Whitton, also a graduate of the Wahroonga Sanitarium in Australia.

In 1920 when D. S. Kime was appointed to take charge of the work in Batakland, Sumatra, he immediately opened a clinic in connection with an English school at Sipogu, Sipirok, Tapanuli, which continued to operate until the Japanese occupation; Mrs. G. A. Wood opened a mobile clinic in Tandjung Medan, Sumatra, in April 1930.

Maria Muster, a midwife from Germany, opened medical work in Palembang, Sumatra, in May 1932, but the clinic closed in 1936 when she married. A clinic was opened adjacent to the Batavia (now Jakarta) church on Apr. 19, 1938. Mrs. S. H. Horn, a graduate nurse from Holland, operated the clinic with the help of J. E. Sinambela, a national nurse, and under the medical supervision of Dr. Tan Tjoe Han, a member of the church. This clinic later became a maternity clinic, first employing Mrs. P. Loth as midwife and later Anna Kalangi in the same capacity. This maternity clinic continued to function until 1947, when, during the revolution, it was taken over by the Red Cross and never returned to the denomination.

Dr. N. Twijnstra opened a dental clinic, which is still in operation, in Medan, Sumatra, in 1950.

In October 1920 J. E. Gardner, M.D., had sailed from the United States under appointment to begin medical work in Indonesia, but because he was not given permission to do so by the Dutch government, he later began medical work in Penang, Malaya.

In 1949 Donald N. Holm, M.D., from the United States, came to Indonesia with the understanding that if he would work in the government health department for three years, he would be allowed to open up denominational medical work thereafter. However, as he studied the contract he discovered that the law under which foreign doctors were allowed to practice in mission hospitals made no mention of the necessity of serving the government first. The church, therefore, requested permission for Dr. Holm to open an SDA mission hospital immediately. Providentially, since the Dutch were preparing to transfer the government to the people of Indonesia, they consented.

As a result, on Apr. 24, 1950, a clinic was opened in south Bandung, Java, at Kiaratjondong, and in October 1950 the Rumah Sakit Advent (Bandung Adventist Hospital) was officially opened at Taman Sari 40. This 20-bed hospital occupied a dwelling converted into crowded but efficient quarters for providing the multiple type of services required.

In October 1952 the first class of seven nursing students was admitted. In 1953 a second house adjacent to the hospital was purchased, renovated, and enlarged to increase the bed capacity to 70, as well as to provide more suitable quarters for the School of Nursing, kitchen, and dining room. Later remodeling increased the bed capacity to 110, including the bassinets. In 1953 Dr. Jess C. Holm arrived with his family to join the hospital staff.

Wilma Leazer, from the United States, a nurse with special training and experience in nursing education, devoted herself to strengthening the scholastic program of the School of Nursing. She arranged collegiate cooperation with Indonesia Union Seminary, and in 1957 sponsored a postgraduate program of nursing education with the cooperation of the Indonesia Union Seminary faculty and others qualified to teach these advanced subjects. A large building was purchased to house the School of Nursing.

Plans for building a representative medical institution were largely in the hands of Dr. D. N. Holm. Shortly before he left on furlough in 1960, the groundbreaking ceremony was held (Mar. 1) on the 2.5-acre (one-hectare) plot he had purchased in a choice location of the city of Bandung. The erection of the new three-story hospital building began a short time later under the supervision of A. L. Sherman, a builder from the United States, who had arrived from Bangkok. When Sherman returned to the United States, the hospital's business manager, Tan Peng Hong, who had solicited millions upon millions of rupiahs for its construction, supervised the building of the new plant. The new Bandung Adventist Hospital, containing 200 beds and costing nearly $4 million, was officially opened on Jan. 24, 1963, with Dr. Jess C. Holm as the medical director.

Medical Directors: Donald Holm, 1950-1960; Neil Thrasher, 1960-1961; Jess C. Holm, 1962-1966; Neil Thrasher, 1966-1968; Henry A. Novak, 1968-1970; E.B.K. Supit, 1970-1971; A. M. Mamora, 1971-1976. Paiyan L. Tambunan, 1976-1982; Simon Tomarere, 1982- .

BANGALORE SEVENTH-DAY ADVENTIST HIGHER SECONDARY SCHOOL. A coeducational day school offering instruction up to the twelfth standard, or School Leaving Certificate. It is operated at Bangalore, Karnataka state, by the Karnataka Section of the South India Union of the Southern Asia Division. Enrollment in 1993 was 2,000.

The school was opened in 1941 as an elementary church school, with 30 students and Edna Dyer as teacher. In 1954 additional classrooms were constructed, along with an auditorium and boys' and girls' dormitories. In January 1955 the Bangalore Middle School was opened as a coeducational English language boarding school with the equivalent of 10 grades. In 1961 the boarding section was closed and the school operated as a day school only. In 1967 the school was accredited with the Council for the Indian School Certificate examination, which is affiliated with the University of Cambridge Examination Syndicate, London. At present (1993) there are two sections in the high school classes, one for the Secondary School Leaving Certificate and government examination, and the other for the Indian Certificate of Secondary Education examination, conducted by the Council for the Indian School Certificate board, New Delhi.

In 1971 additional classrooms and a science laboratory were added, thus giving more accommodation for better classroom facilities.

In 1989 computer classes were started with 10 computers in the classroom.

Principals: R. E. Stahlnecker, 1955-1957; Mrs. E.H.J. Scott, 1957-1958; E. N. Simon, 1958; Joan Lynsdale, 1959-1960; T. R. Potts, 1960; J. S. Christian, 1961-1963; Y. G. Thomas, 1964; Joan Lynsdale, 1965-1968; K. Bhaskara Rao, 1968-1969; Monickam Dhason, 1970-1971; K. I. Varghese, 1972-1973; K. S. Rassalam, 1974-1976; Sharatn Chandra, 1976; Kamala Jagadeesan, 1976-1983; Moses E. Joseph, 1983-1984; Daniel Thomas, 1984-1992; J. S. Navarose, 1992- .

BANGALORE SEVENTH-DAY ADVENTIST HOSPITAL. *See* Seventh-day Adventist Hospital (Bangalore).

BANGKOK ADVENTIST HOSPITAL (formerly Bangkok Sanitarium and Hospital). A general hospital with a capacity of 180 beds and 24 bassinets, situated at 430 Pitsanuloke Road, Bangkok, Thailand, owned and operated by the Christian Medical Foundation of Seventh-day Adventists, Thailand.

Bangkok Mission Clinic. The present institution is an outgrowth of the Bangkok Mission Clinic, opened in rented quarters at 4986 Plabplachai Road, on May 2, 1937, with funds contributed by a philanthropist sea captain, Thomas Hall, of Mexico. Dr. Ralph F. Waddell and his wife, Ellen; Nai Pleng Vitiamyalaksna; and Kon Vui-leong directed the development of the original 12-bed hospital with an Outpatient Department into a 50-bed clinic.

As the medical work in Bangkok grew, expanded facilities were needed. In late 1940 a large house about a mile (1.6 kilometers) from the original clinic was leased and remodeled to provide an additional 30 beds, and became known as the Annex. This increased the hospital's capacity to 80 beds and made possible the opening of a School of Nursing in May of 1941 under the direction of Ruth Munroe.

World War II and After. When war came to Southeast Asia, Dr. G. G. Innocent (the medical director) and Dr. D. P. LaTourette, with their families, and Ruth Munroe were interned. The Annex was closed, but the clinic continued to operate under the direction of Nai Pleng, a medical assistant, and a Romanian physician, S. Bene, was employed to attend the patients. During the war years the clinic's income supplied funds for the mission budget.

Bangkok Sanitarium and Hospital. With the cessation of hostilities, the overseas staff returned to Thailand. On Dec. 25, 1946, the former Annex and surrounding buildings, occupying a six-acre (2.4-hectare) tract of land at the corner of Pitsanuloke and Lan Luang roads, were purchased for the development of the Bangkok Sanitarium and Hospital. The former Annex, remodeled again, became the initial building of the Bangkok Sanitarium and Hospital. Another building was converted into quarters for the School of Nursing, which was reopened July 1, 1947. Thirty-three students of the first postwar class were capped Oct. 30, 1947. Some of these still work at the hospital and its related institutions.

Medical activities of the Bangkok Sanitarium and Hospital were extended into the provinces of Thailand in 1949, when the institution sponsored the opening of mission clinics at Ubol, Phuket, and Haad Yai, under Drs. J. E. Sandness, F. N. Crider, and R. C. Gregory, respectively. The clinics at Ubol and Haad Yai have since been closed.

On Aug. 3, 1949, the cornerstone of the new Bangkok Sanitarium and Hospital building was laid. A joint church community financial campaign provided funds for a modern four-story hospital building, which was officially opened by L. Pibulsonggram, Thailand's premier, on Mar. 19, 1951. During the ensuing years, the clinic was departmentalized and the number of staff members increased accordingly.

In July 1955 the wife of the premier officially opened the new building for the School of Midwifery. Gertrude Green, an American midwife, directed the development of the obstetrical clinic, which serves the poor and also provides clinical experience for midwifery students. Green retired in 1980 and returned to the United States in 1992 after a total of 51 years of service, 43 of them at the Bangkok Adventist Hospital.

Near the end of 1957 a dental clinic was developed by M. C. Lamberton, D.D.S., who later moved to Chingmai and opened a dental clinic there. The original clinic was sold, and a new one has been built on a different site.

In mid-1958 a much-needed addition to the sanitarium building increased the total bed capacity to 180. At that time the work that had been conducted in the city clinic was transferred to the sanitarium.

On Dec. 2, 1958, Queen Sirikit of Thailand opened a modern three-story concrete building for the School of Nursing, with dormitory space for 120 student nurses, administrative offices, library, and classrooms. A new administrative building for the nursing training program was opened in 1989, and the administrative section of the original building (along with the library and classrooms) was transferred to this new building. Training schools in nursing, medical and X-ray technology, anesthesia, and midwifery were conducted at that time, but now midwifery has been absorbed by the college program, and training in X-ray and laboratory skills are being run by the government and other universities. Nurse anesthetists are no longer being trained.

March 1969 marked the opening of a midwifery clinic at Chiengkhong. An attractive four-story dormitory to house graduate nurses was completed in 1972 in Bangkok.

The name Bangkok Adventist Hospital was officially adopted in January 1973. In 1983 a new wing was opened, built into the original hospital building, in order to increase much-needed outpatient, operating room, and patient room facilities. This wing was named after Ralph Waddell. In 1987 the Pleng Vitimalaksna building was opened on the fiftieth anniversary of the hospital to provide beds for obstetric and pediatric patients, a new food and bakery service, and much-needed car parking space.

In 1990 a lifestyle center called the Mission Health Promotion Center, capable of housing 60 people, was opened in the hamlet of Muak Lek in the province of Saraburi. This facility is designed to present preventive medicine in harmony with the traditional SDA "sanitarium" concept.

All the Seventh-day Adventist medical institutions in Thailand are operated under the auspices of the Christian Medical Foundation.

Clinical Activity: In 1992 the Bangkok Adventist Hospital admitted 8,000 patients, treated 118,000 outpatients, and provided $161,000 worth of charity care. In that year there were more than 500 employees working at the hospital, in Muak Lak, at the college, and in the hospital store.

Other Features: Besides admitting and treating patients, the hospital also runs a mobile clinic that is equipped with an X-ray unit.

Medical Directors/Administrators: R. F. Waddell, 1937-1942, 1946-1951; L. G. Ludington, 1951-1952; R. F. Waddell 1952-1953; L. G. Ludington, 1953-1955; R. T. Nelson, 1955; R. F. Waddell, 1955-1960; L. G. Ludington, 1960-1965; G. J. Wiesseman, 1965-1969; G. C. Ekvall, 1969-1970; G. L. Dybdahl, 1970-1973; R. C. Thompson, 1973-1974; D. L. Brown, 1974-1977; Jonathan Kon, 1977-1980; Russell R. Standish, 1980-1984; Ronald W. Brody, 1984-1994; T. Y. Billones, 1994- .

BANGKOK ADVENTIST SCHOOL. A school listed in the *Yearbook* from 1941 to 1952 and in 1959 with the address 1325 Rama IV Road, Bangkok, Thailand, operated by the Thailand Mission. It was listed in the *Yearbook* under the names Bangkok Mission School or Bangkok SDA Mission School and in 1959 as Bangkok Adventist School. According to the *Yearbook* it was either established in 1934 or reorganized then. *See* Adventist Ekamai School.

BANGLADESH. A republic comprising what was formerly known as East Pakistan. It gained independence from Pakistan in December 1971. Bangladesh covers an area of 55,813 square miles (144,556 square kilometers) bounded by India on its northern, eastern, and western borders, the Bay of Bengal to the south, and Myanmar in the southeastern corner. The population (1994) is about 125 million, the majority of whom are Bengalis in ethnic origin, with smaller groups of tribal people, such as Garo, Santali, Mog, and Chakma, found mostly in the border areas. The country is probably the most densely populated area of the world, with about 2,150 persons per square mile (830 per square kilometer). The climate is warm and humid, with high rainfall during the monsoon season, but drier weather during the winter months. Much of the land, which includes the vast delta areas of the Padma, Meghna, and Jamuna rivers, is subject to seasonal flooding. Consequently, when this is excessive, crops can be seriously damaged. The country is periodically battered by severe cyclones coming from the Bay of Bengal. These sometimes whip up tidal waves, as was the case in 1970 and 1991, killing tens of thousands of people. The official language of the area is Bengali, but other languages, including English, are used. More than 85 percent of the people are Muslim, about 12 percent Hindu, and the rest are Christians, Buddhists, and animists.

Seventh-day Adventist Statistics. The Bangladesh Union Mission, comprised of the entire territory of Bangladesh and made up of the East Bangladesh Region, the North Bangladesh Mission, the South Bangladesh Mission, and the West Bangladesh Mission, is part of the Far Eastern Division. Statistics (1993) for *Bangladesh:* churches, 67; members, 8,500; elementary schools, 94; ordained ministers, 23; licensed ministers, 18. Headquarters for the Bangladesh Union Mission: Adventpur, 149, Mirpur Road No. 1, Shah Ali Bagh, Dhaka 1216, Bangladesh.

Statistics (1993) for the missions—*East Bangladesh Region:* churches, 2; members, 734; ordained ministers, 3; licensed ministers, 3. Headquarters: Dhaka. *North Bangladesh Mission:* churches, 23; members, 3,392; ordained ministers, 36; licensed ministers, 5. Headquarters: Mymensingh. *South Bangladesh Mission:* churches, 30; members, 3,232; ordained ministers, 37; licensed ministers, 4. Headquarters: Gopalgonj. *West Bangladesh Mission:* churches, 12; members, 1,202; ordained ministers, 18; licensed ministers, 3. Headquarters: Joypurhat.

Institutions. Bangladesh Adventist Publishing House, Bangladesh Adventist Seminary and College, Kellogg-Mookerjee Memorial Seminary.

Development of Seventh-day Adventist Work. Seventh-day Adventists began work in the territory of Bangladesh in the last decade of the nineteenth century, when colporteurs from Calcutta entered the area. In 1906 Lal Gopal Mookerjee, an early convert in India and a descendant of William Carey's first convert, opened the first SDA mission station in East Bengal (now Bangladesh) at Gopalganj. With his own funds he paid for the mission buildings, his own dwelling, a church, a dispensary, and a residence for other national workers. A few years later he left because of his wife's failing health, and in 1909 A. G. Watson, an Anglo-Indian, was placed in charge of the station, while Mookerjee went to develop the city work in Calcutta and to edit a newly established Bengali language evangelistic magazine, *Juga Lakshan.*

In 1909 the first general meeting of adherents was held, and at that time the first SDA communion was celebrated in East Bengal. Late in that year J. C. Little, who had been assigned to the East Bengal field, went to the city of Barisal. A few months later, in February 1910, a second annual meeting was held, at which about 40 members were present and 20 persons were baptized. The first SDA church in Bangladesh was organized at Barisal with 26 members. Unfortunately, Little died in August 1910, while itinerating during a cholera epidemic. Nevertheless, the work continued to grow. In 1910 the General Conference appropriated funds for a 25-foot (7.6-meter) mission launch to ply the rivers and canals of East Bengal (M. E. Olson, *Origin and Progress,* p. 524; in *Our Story of Missions,* p. 315, W. A. Spicer mentions a houseboat, *The Canal Friend,* as being there about the same time). Much work was also done by colporteurs, among whom R. C. Dey, A. Mundel, and B. A. Nath were pioneers.

In 1921 a boarding school for boys was opened at Gopalganj. Mrs. L. G. Mookerjee, whose husband was superintendent of the field, was principal of the school. In 1926 A. G. Youngberg became field superintendent and principal of the school. In 1929 a physician, C. F. Schilling, came as dispensary doctor and his wife as principal of the school. In the same year, a girls' school (called the Bengali Girls' School), which had been established in 1916, was transferred from Hooghly, West Bengal, to Gopalganj and was combined with the boys' school in 1932. In 1939 the school was transferred to Jalirpar, about 19 miles (30 kilometers) north of Gopalganj *(see* Kellogg-Mookerjee Memorial Seminary.

Organization and Growth. Until 1910 SDA work in British India, Ceylon, and Burma was administered by the India Mission, organized in 1895, with headquarters at Calcutta. In that year, at the fourth biennial meeting of the mission held at Lucknow, India, October-November 1910, SDA work in India was organized along the language lines into four missions, among them the Bengali Mission, with headquarters at Calcutta, including the part that later became Bangladesh. L. G. Mookerjee, A. G. Watson, W. A. Barlow, and W. W. Miller were assigned to work in East Bengal. W. R. French, who had recently arrived from the United States, was given supervision of the work in that area. He was succeeded by L. G. Burgess in 1915, and by L. G. Mookerjee in 1919. In this year the Northeast Union was formed, with East Bengal Mission as a part. From Aug. 15, 1947, it was known as East Pakistan Local Mission, still under the Northeast Union. Then, from 1956, it continued as the East Pakistan Section under the Pakistan Union, with R. S. Fernando as president. After independence, in December 1971, the area was renamed the Bangladesh Section.

Still later, because of upgrading, the name was changed to the Bangladesh Union Mission. In 1993 a new seminary was under construction in the West Bangladesh Mission to meet the needs of a fast-growing field.

BANGLADESH ADVENTIST PUBLISHING HOUSE. A printing establishment begun in 1952 under the name Seventh-day Adventist Mission Press, at what is now Kellogg-Mookerjee Memorial Seminary. At that time only a letter press was in use. An electric press was purchased in 1963. In 1966 the press was transferred to church headquarters at Dhaka. In the 1970s the name was changed to Bangladesh Adventist Press and Publishing House. Its main mission was to print books for literature evangelists.

In 1988 the Bangladesh Union Mission purchased a flatbed press from Japan, but because of financial difficulties, the press had to be sold. In 1991 the union mission purchased a computer and laser printer that enables the publishing house to prepare materials for printing on an offset press.

In 1993 there were 40 literature evangelists distributing the literature produced by the publishing house in Bangladesh.

Managers: S. K. Sircar, 1952-1962; N. N. Sircar, 1962-1963; P. B. Dass, 1964-1968; N. N. Sircar, 1969-1972; E. P. Baroya and P. B. Dass, 1972-1990; Rawesh K. Biswas, 1990; N. N. Sircar, 1991-1994; S. Halder, 1994- .

BANGLADESH ADVENTIST SEMINARY AND COLLEGE (formerly Bangladesh Adventist Academy). A coeducational boarding college and seminary located about 30 miles (50 kilometers) north of Dhaka near the town of Kaliakoir, on the Dhaka-Tangail Highway. It is situated on 60 acres (25 hectares) of rural land. The college offers majors in education, religion, business, and office management, with minors in health as well as in the areas mentioned. In 1993 the institution had approximately 585 students, including about 120 in college.

The kindergarten through standard 10 program is taught in the Bengali language with a strong emphasis on English. The college program is taught in English.

In 1964 several plots of land were purchased near Kaliakoir with the plan of starting an educational program. The spot was remote and almost uninhabitable at the time. Thick jungle covered most of the high ground. The road to Dhaka was not much more than a dirt track. By 1969 the education needs for the young people were critical, and so a junior high school was established under the direction of D. P. Rema. He worked with the students and faculty to build "Kutchal" houses and cleared a portion of jungle. In 1970, 30 students enrolled in the pioneer school.

Students traveled from the north and south to attend the new school. Most were from poor families in villages where they could not obtain the education they needed. By 1973 the program was upgraded to the high school level under the leadership of Sunith K. Dass. A two-year seminary program beyond high school also was introduced at this time. Several of the early brick buildings were constructed during these years. As the land was cleared slowly, the campus took shape.

A special agricultural program, following the Mittleider method, was begun under the direction of W. L. Fuller in 1975. The goal was not only to feed the students but to train them in effective agricultural methods so that when they returned to their homes they could help improve the health and prosperity of their villages.

In 1976 B. H. Stickle succeeded Sunith K. Dass as principal. Under his leadership the physical plant improved considerably. In 1981 R. G. Burton returned as principal and continued to improve the program in preparation for future college status.

By 1983 Bangladesh Adventist Seminary was ready to consider offering higher seminary and college level classes. A visiting evaluation team from the Board of Higher Education encouraged the institution to press forward with a college program, and set about to meet the many challenges this step would require.

Sukrit K. Dass was called to be the first president of Bangladesh Adventist Seminary and College, and in June 1983 the junior college program was begun. Programs were offered in business, religion, education, and office management. The college program thrived and grew under S. K. Dass's leadership.

In 1988 I. P. Bairagee came and began preparations for upgrading the institution to a four-year program. In 1989 E. P. Rema became acting president. The college board prepared for another visit of the evaluation team with the hope of approval for a four-year program. The four-year senior college program was inaugurated in August 1990 with the arrival of Dr. S. R. Guptill, the new college president. Four-year programs were started in business, religion, and education.

This led to a time of rapid growth for the campus physical plant. A new church was built, followed by a new women's hostel. A new deep well was dug and several married student houses were made. A three-story shower and latrine facility was constructed for the men's hostel, and a water tank was built on top of the administration building. A metal workshop was started through the efforts of ADRA, and a new gate was built at the entrance. A dining hall/gymnasium was constructed in 1993, and paved walks and benches were added to the campus landscape. Also at this time a playing field was constructed for students' use.

Principals: D. P. Rema, 1969-1973; Sunith K. Dass, 1973-1975; B. H. Stickle, 1976-1977; R. G. Burton, 1977; C. E. Ondrizek, 1977-1981; R. G. Burton, 1981-1982; Sukrit K. Dass, 1983-1987; I. P. Bairagee, 1988-1989; E. P. Rema, 1989-1990; Stephen R. Guptill, 1990- .

BANGLADESH UNION MISSION. *See* Bangladesh; Far Eastern Division.

BANKS, EDWARD C. (1907-1993). Pastor, educator, counselor. A native of Georgia, he pastored churches in Tennessee, Kentucky, Florida, and Illinois. He taught at Southern Missionary College (now Southern College) for 12 years, and served as professor of evangelism at Andrews University for 28 years. He and his wife, Letah, founded the Adventist Marriage Enrichment program. He passed to his rest in Florida.

BANKS ISLANDS. *See* Vanuatu.

BAPTISM. (Gr. *baptisma,* from *baptizō* "to dip," "to immerse.") The Christian ceremony of initiation, traditionally either by immersion, pouring, or sprinkling. Seventh-day Adventists "belive in baptism by immersion," and that baptism "typifies the death, burial, and resurrection of Christ, and openly expresses faith in His saving grace and the renunciation of sin and the world, and is recognized as a condition of entrance into church membership" (*Church Manual* [1990], pp. 42, 182). Accordingly, baptism is administered only to those who have reached an age of accountability. It "is usually conducted by an ordained minister, but in his absence the local church elder may officiate," only, however, with the approval of the conference president *(Manual for Ministers* [1992], p. 84). Persons entering the SDA Church who have been baptized by immersion in other religious communions are accepted without rebaptism, unless they desire to be rebaptized; however, "it is recognized that rebaptism is desirable" *(Church Manual,* p. 51).

When members have apostatized, the *Church Manual* recommends rebaptism: "When members have fallen away in apostasy and have lived in such a manner that the faith and principles of the church have been publicly violated, they should, in case of reconversion and application for church membership, enter the church as in the beginning, by baptism" (p. 51).

Seventh-day Adventists believe that candidates for baptism should be thoroughly instructed in the Christian faith, in order that they may take the step intelligently and with resolute purpose. To this end, special classes are conducted in which instruction on the principal articles of faith and on the Christian way of life is given. In non-Christian lands candidates may remain in baptismal classes for as long as one or two years, until they have demonstrated both a theoretical and a practical understanding of the Christian faith. Immediately prior to baptism, candidates are asked to affirm, publicly before the church, their assent to the teachings of the church, and their intent to order their lives in harmony with their beliefs.

Origin and Development of the Seventh-day Adventist View. The question of baptism naturally arose early among SDAs, coming as they did largely from membership in other churches. In 1857 J. H. Waggoner declared that a person should be rebaptized after coming to have a correct understanding of the law of God, since that individual cannot have truly been baptized until having died to sin; in baptism that person "puts on Christ, . . . and takes His name," but we "cannot live unto God and walk in newness of life, while we continue to transgress the law," regardless of whether the sin was committed in ignorance *(Review and Herald* 9:173, Apr. 2, 1857; 9:181, Apr. 9, 1857). The question of baptism was further discussed by James White in 1867, who listed several conditions that call for rebaptism: not having truly died to sin; having been baptized by an unholy minister or one who opposed "Bible purity" or spiritual gifts, or the work of SDAs; having been baptized before accepting "the truth"; having apostatized and turned to iniquity *(ibid.* 30:114 f., Aug. 6, 1867). Although there is evidence that the question of the character of the minister was an issue in the early years, this has not generally typified SDA doctrine. The question of whether rebaptism of converts is necessary, however, continued to be an issue until the General Conference session of 1886, when the policy essentially as it stands today (see above) was formally adopted (EW 99; Ellen G. White, *Sketches From the Life of Paul,* p. 133; Ev 375; *Yearbook* [1887], p. 45).

Meanwhile, the theological dimensions of baptism were developed in a series of articles by Waggoner in 1878, followed by four more articles from J. N. Andrews in 1880 *(Review and Herald,* Feb. 14-June 6, 1878; Jan. 15, 22, Feb. 5, 26, 1880). Emphasis was placed on the relation of baptism to the law: baptism is the outward act signifying that the sinner has died with Christ, i.e., has been united with Him in His atoning death; he or she dies to the transgression of the law and thus is forgiven of past sins; he or she rises to a new life of obedience to God's will, a life of consecration. In a later series appears a new emphasis on the importance of faith and the work of the Spirit, particularly in connection with baptism as a symbol of resurrection: O. Davis writes in 1893 that in baptism "God . . . raises us up as He raised Jesus up a new creature, if we have faith in the operations of God." "We are reckoned new creatures, born of the Spirit" *(ibid.* 70:595, Sept. 19, 1893; 70:614, Oct. 3, 1893). Ellen G. White portrays baptism as an oath of allegiance on the part of the one baptized (Ev 307 [1903]) and represents that individual as having received "a pledge from the . . . Father, the Son, and the Holy Spirit" (SDACom 6:1074 [1900]). "If we are true to our [baptismal] vow, there is opened to us a door of communication with heaven—a door that no human hand or satanic agency can close" (*ibid.* 1075 *[Review and Herald* 83:20, May 17, 1906]). In more recent years C. B. Haynes wrote: "When the believer . . . rises from the baptismal waters, he testifies that his only hope of a life that will give him victory over his old sinful nature is in a risen Lord and the new spiritual and resurrection life which his Lord alone can give" *(These Times* 67:19, September 1958).

Historical Backgrounds of Baptism. The OT background of baptism is to be found in the ceremonial washings with water specified for the ancient Hebrew rituals. It included both sprinkling and bathing the entire body (Lev. 14:8, 9; 16:4; cf. Zech. 13:1). Compare also "Purge me with hyssop" (Ps. 51:7); in the ancient services of purification hyssop was dipped in water and used for sprinkling the people (Lev. 14:6, 7; Num. 19:17-19).

In late Judaism at least three developments are relevant to a background for baptism:

1. According to the Talmud *(Tractate Mikwaoth),* virtually all the washings prescribed in the sanctuary rituals were to be accomplished by complete immersion in a pit filled with water (a *Mikweh*). This makes understandable the variant reading of Mark 1:4, where even beds are spoken of as being baptized, a ceremony provided for in the Talmud.

2. There is evidence from the Talmud *(Yebamoth* 46*a-b)* that from the end of the first century of the Christian Era at least, baptism along with circumcision and sacrifice was required for the admission of a proselyte to Judaism. While some have questioned that this was practiced as early as the time of John and Jesus, it is now generally conceded by scholars that it must have been. (See Frank A. Moran, "Jewish Elements in Christian Baptism," pp. 10-13, where the problem is discussed and the evidence presented for the antiquity of a proselyte baptism.)

3. Josephus mentions daily ritual washings of the Essenes *(War* 2. 19. 5, 10), and there are repeated references in the Dead Sea scrolls to some kind of ritual washing (1QS, III, 4-6, 8-10; IV, 18-21). In addition, a number of cisterns have been found at the Qumran monastery, at least one of which is well suited for baptism (W. H. Brownlee, "John the Baptist in the Light of Ancient Scrolls," *The Scrolls and the New Testament,* ed. Krister Stendahl [1957], pp. 38, 39).

A development may be observed in Jewish, Johannine, and Christian baptism: Jewish baptism was largely a cleansing from ritual defilement and, at least at Qumran, was also connected with rectitude of life and granting of "a holy spirit" by God (1QS, III, 6-10; IV, 18-20).

John the Baptist seems to place an even greater emphasis upon repentance and also looks forward to a connection between baptism and "spirit." With John the emphasis seems to be much more directly upon cleansing spiritually and upon ethical rectitude, while at Qumran there is a stronger ritual orientation upon the cleansing of the "flesh."

Particularly significant is the fact also that while the Qumran ritual was highly exclusive, limited only to members of the community—the "elect"—John's baptism was open to all who repented.

As contrasted with that of John, Christian baptism is "in the name of Jesus" and associated with the reception of the Holy Spirit (see Acts 19:1-6). Also in contrast with Qumran, the Holy Spirit in the New Testament is divine and not simply "a holy spirit" granted by God to an individual. Furthermore, Christian baptism is connected with the death, burial, and resurrection of Christ (Rom. 6:1-11).

Infant Baptism. Seventh-day Adventists reject infant baptism, asserting that there is no Scripture warrant for such a practice. They believe that active faith on the part of the participant is a prerequisite for baptism, and since infants cannot exercise such kind of faith their baptism would be entirely without meaning.

Historically clear evidence of infant baptism first appears in the Christian church during the second half of the second century. Whether it arose first in the East or in the West is not clear. However, our earliest testimony to it is in the West, and the two major factors that seem to have contributed to its appearance are first attested there: an identification of baptism as "spiritual circumcision" (Justin Martyr *Dialogue With Trypho* 43, in ANF, vol. 1, p. 216); and the belief that baptism cleansed from original sin.

Infant baptism is probably referred to by Irenaeus *(Against Heresies* 2. 22. 4, in ANF, vol. 1, p. 391), and is testified to from the beginning of the third century by Tertullian *(On Baptism* 18, in ANF, vol. 3, p. 678). The fact that in the East infant baptism apparently was practiced before the doctrine of original sin was introduced suggests that the latter may have been introduced in explanation, at least partially, of the practice of infant baptism. Thus, Origen (d. c. 254) supported infant baptism as an apostolic tradition and used it as an evidence for the doctrine of original sin, which he strongly taught *(Commentaria in Epistolam ad Romanos* 5. 9, in PG, vol. 14, p. 1047; *In Lucam Homilia* 14, in PG, vol. 13, p. 1835; *In Leviticum Homilia* 8, in PG, vol. 12, p. 496). However, the doctrine of original sin was never as deeply rooted in the East as in the West.

Mode of Baptism. From the beginning Seventh-day Adventists have practiced baptism by immersion. While it is unsafe to make the meaning of *baptizō* a final argument for the mode of baptism, it does seem clear that as used in ancient literature, at least to A.D. 100, *baptizō* never departs from the basic meaning of "to dip," "to overwhelm." At the same time it cannot be proved beyond all doubt that *bap-*

tizō never refers to a rite performed by sprinkling or pouring, in view of the wide variety of figurative uses in which the word is employed. The strongest argument for baptism by immersion is a theological one—Paul's symbolism of baptism as representing death, burial, and resurrection, which would have had no significance if the apostolic church had practiced a mode of baptism other than immersion.

Significance of Baptism. From the beginning Seventh-day Adventists, in common with their Protestant heritage, have rejected any view of baptism as an *opus operatum,* that is, as an act that, in and of itself, imparts grace and effects salvation. Historically, the beginnings of such a view of baptism—the idea that ritual washing had some kind of supernatural power—are very early and may well be a part of the early Christian heritage from Judaism. This already seems to be suggested in *Hermas,* book 3, similitude 9, 16. Tertullian is the first writer to refer to baptism as a *sacramentum.* However, this in itself cannot be taken as proof that he thought of baptism as a sacrament in the sense of an *opus operatum,* for he expresses disapproval of the belief of some who expected from baptism a magical cleansing of sin without true repentance. This in itself testifies to the extent to which baptism, in some minds, had come to be considered an *opus operatum* by the early third century (Tertullian *On Repentance* 6). However, in another treatise he comes very close to the idea that the water of baptism has a special power after the invocation of God has been made over it *(On Baptism* 4). Later in the fourth century the Donatist controversy was settled in favor of baptism as an *opus operatum* as against an *opus operantis.* Augustine's victory over Pelagius on the side of the doctrine of original sin did much to enhance a sacramentalist view of baptism.

BARBADOS. An independent state occupying the most easterly of the Caribbean islands, with an area of 166 square miles (430 square kilometers) and a population (1994) of 256,000. In general appearance the island is reminiscent of the English countryside, and the people follow many English customs. The elected House of Assembly, an organ of popular government on the island, dates from 1639. The Church of England is the established church, to which about 70 percent of the people adhere. About 80 percent of the population is of African descent, 16 percent of mixed descent, and about 4 percent of European descent.

Seventh-day Adventist Statistics. The territory of Barbados is a part of the East Caribbean Conference (which includes also Dominica, the Grenadines, St. Lucia, and St. Vincent) in the Caribbean Union Conference, which is part of the Inter-American Division. Statistics (1992) for *Barbados:* churches, 45; members, 10,777; church schools, 2; ordained ministers, 9; Bible instructors, 1; elementary teachers, 7. The East Caribbean Conference headquarters are situated at Bryden's Avenue, St. Michael, Barbados, West Indies.

Institutions. Barbados Seventh-day Adventist Secondary School.

Development of Seventh-day Adventist Work. SDA work in Barbados had its beginning when Anna Alleyne became acquainted with SDA teachings through reading magazines sent to her by her sister from British Guiana some time in the 1880s. She shared her magazines with her neighbors with the result that several others began to keep the seventh-day Sabbath. In 1889 an SDA went from British Guiana to Barbados, scattering SDA publications and arousing widespread interest in SDA teachings.

As a result, Sabbathkeepers began meeting in Bridgetown, the island's capital. On Sept. 21, 1891, a group of 17, including Anna Alleyne, C. D. Adamson, Hannah Holder, and Miriam Blenman, was organized by D. A. Ball into the Bridgetown SDA Church. Four years later the church membership had grown to 40. Later James Morrow (1897) and A. J. Haysmer (1900) preached there. At that time the Barbados church served as a base for SDA work in the other East Caribbean islands.

In June 1900 land was purchased in Bridgetown at a cost of WI$250, on which the first SDA church building was erected. A mission school at Bridgetown was reported in the 1904 *Yearbook.* During the following three decades churches were organized at Gardens, Cave Hill, Checker Hall, and Mile-and-a-Quarter. In the early 1920s a sanitarium was reported on Barbados. A church school was opened in Bridgetown in July 1922. In 1932 the Government Hill church was organized, which at present has 597 members. In 1953 a secondary school was opened.

The territory of Barbados was organized in 1903 as a part of the East Caribbean Conference. Subsequently the administration of the work on the island was transferred through several conferences until in 1930 it was placed with the Leeward Islands Conference.

In 1934, because of administrative advantages, Barbados was chosen as a working base for the conference, which previously had had its headquarters in Antigua. Financial problems arising out of World War II forced the conference to accept mission status in 1945, but with improved conditions conference status was restored in July 1960 under the name of the East Caribbean Conference.

The Cave Sanitarium, which was located on Culloden Road, was transferred to a 2.3-acre (.9-hectare) property on Britton's Hill comprising a commodious two-floor building providing 14 rooms for patients, and two cottages. On this property the new spacious conference headquarters was erected. The old office building was converted into a senior citizens' home. In 1974 an assembly hall was built in back of the Ephesus church to house general gatherings.

BARBADOS SEVENTH-DAY ADVENTIST SECONDARY SCHOOL. A coeducational day school on the senior high school level, situated at Dalkeith Road, Bridgetown, Barbados, West Indies. The school prepares students for the General Certificate of Education Examination of the Oxford and Cambridge Examination Board and also for college entrance.

The school was established in 1953 by the Leeward Islands Mission (now the East Caribbean Conference) in rented quarters at "Flodden," Culloden Road, not far from its present site. In January 1961 it was moved to its present property.

The school was founded primarily to provide secondary Christian education for SDA young people in Barbados and the Leeward Islands, but pupils of other faiths are also accepted. In 1993 the school had a staff of 17.

Principals: B.G.O. French, 1953-1959; L. L. Lawrence, 1959-1963; J. R. Hill, 1963-1966; I. Bayne, 1966-1978; L. Jones, 1978-1984; N. Niles, 1984- .

BARCELONA PUBLISHING HOUSE. *See* Safeliz Publishing House.

BARLOW, WILLIAM ALEXANDER (1862-1942). One of the pioneers of Seventh-day Adventist work in India. He was born in Garston, near Liverpool, England, and spent four years in a parish school there. After working as an office boy, he served as captain's boy on several cruises to North America. When he was about 21 years old he was converted, joined the Salvation Army, and worked with the rank of captain as a self-supporting missionary in the villages of Kent and in the slums of Liverpool. Later he went to India, where he joined an independent Baptist mission working among the Santals in the northeastern part of India. Several years later he became convinced of SDA teachings through reading and was baptized in 1900 at Simultala by G. K. Owen. He then established a self-supporting Seventh-day Adventist mission among the Santals at Simultala, about 30 miles (50 kilometers) west of Karmatar, in the state of Bihar. He retired from active service about 1914, although he remained in India and, almost to the time of his death, continued to make missionary visits and to distribute publications.

BARNES, EDWIN (fl. 1884-1900). Music teacher and composer of hymns. He headed the Music Department and taught vocal and instrumental music at Battle Creek College (1884-1900), and was coeditor of *Hymns and Tunes* (1886). Seven of his hymn tunes, written in classic style, appear in the *Church Hymnal,* among them Winterbourne, Southampton, and Morton.

BARNES, ROGER W. (1897-1982). Urologist. Born in Littleton, Colorado, he attended the College of Medical Evangelists (now Loma Linda University), graduating in 1922. After his residency, he accepted an appointment to the faculty of the school and served there until his death. One of his most noted accomplishments was involvement in the development of trans-urethral resections of the prostate, a procedure in which he was unsurpassed. At the School of Medicine he served as chairman of the Department of Urology for several years. He and his wife, Oca, accepted assignments to various parts of the world, including the Middle East, Far East, Australia, South America, and Southern Asia, where they helped establish and organize teaching programs in urology.

BARQUISIMETO ADVENTIST CLINIC (Clínica Adventista de Barquisimeto). A health-care institution owned and operated by West Venezuela Mission of Seventh-day Adventists for some time, then taken over by the Venezuela-Antilles Union Mission.

It was begun in 1978 in a dwelling bought by the West Venezuela Mission to be used as the mission office, and was remodeled for hospital use and surgery with a capacity of 10 beds. The mission office moved to another building, leaving more space for the clinic. The clinic was administered by mission presidents Ernesto Santos and Nathaniael Garcia from 1978 to 1981. Since 1982 official administrators were appointed.

New services were gradually added and by 1993 a strong outpatient service had been developed, including laboratory, X-ray, ultrasonic, dentistry, ophthalmology, 24-hour emergency, general surgery, internal medicine, gynecology, laparoscopic surgery, reconstructive surgery, pediatric, urology, and other services. In 1993 the clinic was planning a new building that would increase the number of beds to 45, responding to the needs of the thousands of patients that come to the institution each year.

Administrators: Pacifico Merchan, 1982-1984; Gonzalo Carreno, 1985-1989; Franklin Caicedo, 1989-1990; George Newball, 1990- .

BARRANQUILLA ADVENTIST SCHOOL. *See* Adventist Atlantic Secondary School.

BARRON, RICHARD CLINTON (1925-1972). Evangelist. He was born and reared in California. When very young he dedicated his life to the Lord and was baptized at the age of 9. As a child he would line up chairs on the front porch and "preach" to the "congregation" on Sabbath afternoons.

After his graduation from La Sierra College in 1945, he married Jeanne Bickett and began his work as pastor of the Hawthorne, California, church. After attending an evangelistic workshop in Texas, he joined with his brother in full-time evangelism. In 1960 the Barron-Turner evangelistic team was formed. The following year he suffered back pain, which ultimately led to surgery and divine healing. This was followed by a decade of successful evangelistic work.

He died in the crash of a small plane he was piloting near Walla Walla College in Washington.

BARRY, A. (d. 1914). One of the earliest Black Seventh-day Adventist ordained ministers. He worked in Tennessee, Michigan, and Kentucky. *See* South Central Conference.

BARTLETT, WILLIAM T. (1870-1947). Minister, missionary, church administrator, editor, and teacher. He was born in London, England, and trained for the law. He was baptized into the Seventh-day Adventist Church in 1888, and soon thereafter joined the staff of the Chaloners Mission in north London. After having canvassed for two years, he entered employment with the SDA publishing house in England in 1892. He began his work with the International Tract Society in 1896, and from 1897 to 1901 managed a health food business. Between 1897 and 1920 he served first as an assistant editor and later as editor of the British *Present Truth.* Concurrently he taught Bible at, and for two years served as principal of, the Stanborough Missionary College (predecessor of Newbold College). He was ordained to the ministry in 1907 in Nottingham, England, by L. R. Conradi and E. E. Andross. In 1916, in the course of World War I, the SDA Church in Great Britain appointed him to look after the interests of SDA young people in the armed services. In 1920 he was called to Africa, where he superintended British East African missions until his return to England in 1930. From 1930 to 1932 Bartlett served as president of the North England Conference; between 1932 and 1941 he was field secretary of the Northern European Division, and for some time after 1933 was its Sabbath school division secretary. His last place of service was Newbold College, where he taught Bible for six years.

BASEL PUBLISHING HOUSE. *See* Life and Health Publishing House (France).

BASEL SANITARIUM. *See* Lake Geneva Sanitarium.

BASS MEMORIAL ACADEMY. A coeducational boarding school on the senior high school level, operated by the Gulf States Conference and located near Lumberton, Mississippi. The school includes grades 9-12 and is fully accredited by the state and the denomination. On the campus are the following buildings: administration, music, domestic science, natural science, industrial arts, chapel, library, pecan building, laundry, maintenance, elementary school, six separate classrooms, two dormitories (for 160 students), cafeteria, 11 faculty homes, and a gymnasium-auditorium seating 2,000.

Bass Memorial Academy was envisioned in 1957 when Mr. Bass, of the Bass pecan-oil-timber family, decided to donate 356 acres (144 hectares) of his 25,000-acre (10,000-hectare) property to the SDA Church for this purpose. Although not a Seventh-day Adventist, he had read about the church and was acquainted with various members, including Ralph Hendershot, a layman in the Talowah, Mississippi, church, whom he had met in the Ingathering campaign several years earlier. He admired the clean-living principles of SDAs, which paralleled his own nondrinking and nonsmoking code, and was especially interested in the SDA program of industrial training.

At Bass's invitation LeRoy J. Leiske, conference president; Oscar L. Heinrich, educational secretary; and L. E. Aldrich, conference treasurer (later replaced by J. Henson Whitehead), selected a choice site of 356 acres (144 hectares)—including a pecan grove of 20 acres (eight hectares), about 80 acres (32 hectares) of cleared land, and 250 acres (101 hectares) of pines—a tract evaluated at $100,000. On Aug. 25, 1957, the conference voted to accept the gift. About a year later, in July 1958, the first board meeting was held.

The churches in the conference undertook separate fund-raising projects for specific buildings or rooms. Members donated calves for the dairy farm. Pathfinder clubs raised funds for the school entrance sign, which was dedicated on Sept. 14, 1958, in the presence of J. P. Coleman, governor of Mississippi.

A "Million Penny Campaign" for the administration building culminated on Apr. 5, 1959, when members of the national guard shoveled the 1,242,221 coins into buckets before loading them onto a truck for a widely publicized four-ton (3.6-metric ton) bulk deposit in a New Orleans bank.

O. O. Smith was the original architect and supervising engineer. Later O. L. Heinrich became full-time contractor and superintendent of development. His son, Jerry, thereafter did most of the architectural drawing and Mrs. O. L. Heinrich the interior decorating. S. A. Brown did much of the building. The academy opened on schedule Sept. 10, 1961.

On Aug. 18, 1969, the academy was badly damaged by Hurricane Camille. Even though the total cost of repairing the damage reached almost $100,000, the opening of school was delayed only one week.

May 29, 1971, marked the dedication of the academy with the burning of a $70,000 note, leaving the academy plant with no indebtedness.

A committee of 100, organized in 1969, by 1974 had raised more than $50,000 for school equipment and improvements.

The continued interest of the Bass family in the school and its operation was evidenced by an unrestricted gift of 80 acres (32 hectares) of prime land in 1974. This was officially appraised at $76,000.

Construction of a new $200,000 church was completed in 1975 with a seating capacity of more than 400.

Butler Industries, which arranges silk flowers, was established in 1981 and employs 15 or more students. The Adventist Health Center, a primary-care nursing home, was constructed in 1981 and also employs 15 or more students.

Major remodeling was done in 1988-1989 to the cafeteria, dorms, administration building, and gymnasium. New tennis facilities and a swimming pool were added.

Enrollment in 1992 was 108.

Principals: Clifford L. Jaqua, 1961-1966; R. P. Bailey, 1966-1968; John Mayhew, 1968-1969; L. A. Stout, 1969-1974; K. J. Epperson, 1974-1978; Cyril Connely, 1978-1980; Dallas Carr, 1980-1982; Gerald Kovalski, 1982-1985; Kenneth Kirkham, 1985-1987; Ted Winn, 1987-1990; Jerrell Gilkeson, 1990-1993; Tui Pitman, 1993- .

BASUTOLAND. *See* Lesotho.

BATA, RUDOLPH ANDREW (1922-1974). Pastor, evangelist, departmental secretary. A native of Ohio, he received his early education in a small church school. He attended Broadview Academy and later Columbia Union College.

While still in college he met and married Margaret Ellis. After graduation he interned in the Ohio Conference and then served in a pastoral capacity in several Midwest and Southern states. Later he became lay activities secretary of the Texas Conference. He also served as secretary-treasurer of the Kentucky-Tennessee Conference and then moved to the Potomac Conference, where he was lay activities secretary. In 1973 he moved back to Tennessee, where he became secretary of the conference and also served as ministerial secretary.

During his 29-year ministry he baptized personally more than 1,000 persons.

BATAKLAND ENGLISH SCHOOL. A school operated for a time at Sipogu, Sipirok, in northwest Sumatra, under the direction of the North Sumatra Mission. It was established in 1921, along with a clinic, by Dallas S. Kime and his wife, both nurses, and Albinus

Mamora, interpreter and teacher of English. After the school opened, with an enrollment of 175, several other national teachers were added. In 1925, because of the help given the local people by the clinic and school, government officials proposed that the community be known as Huta Kime (Village of Kime). The school was changed later into a Dutch language school. In 1937 it was closed and replaced by a colony for the blind. During World War II the buildings were destroyed.

BATES, JOSEPH (1792-1872). Mariner, reformer, Advent preacher, one of the founders of the Seventh-day Adventist Church. He was born July 8, 1792, at Rochester, Massachusetts, near New Bedford. At the age of 15 he set out from his home to follow the sea. He experienced shipwreck, capture, and forced service in the British Navy, and was for two and a half years a prisoner of war in England, being released in 1815. After being restored to his home and family, he continued his career as a merchant seaman, becoming a captain in 1820.

In 1818 he married Prudence Nye, a childhood friend. "Prudy" proved to be an exceptionally patient and loyal wife, and a godly influence upon her husband and family. To them were born five children: one son who died in infancy, another son who died at sea at the age of 35, and three daughters who survived to maturity.

In 1821 Bates gave up the drinking of ardent spirits. The following year he resolved to drink no wine, and soon after gave up smoking and chewing tobacco, as well as the use of profane language. Before 1838 he had abandoned the use of tea and coffee, and in 1843 he discontinued the use of flesh foods. Previously he had stopped using butter, grease, cheese, pies, rich cakes, and spices. Thus, before Seventh-day Adventists were organized into a religious group, Joseph Bates was an enthusiastic supporter of the health principles that this body eventually came to embrace.

After Bates's conversion to Christianity in the middle 1820s, he commanded a temperance ship on which he allowed no intoxicants, no swearing, and no washing and mending of clothes on Sunday. He conducted morning and evening worship, but in spite of these rigid rules the rough crew adapted themselves very well to this strict regimen. Earlier, in 1824, a New Testament that his wife had placed in his trunk stimulated the beginning of a spiritual awakening. Sobered by the death of a crew member, he surrendered his life to Christ and began daily Bible study and prayer. Upon reaching home, he was baptized and attended religious meetings, and in 1827 he joined the Fairhaven Christian church, to which his wife belonged. It was in this year that he went on his temperance voyage, which lasted almost a year, with which he ended his career as a seaman.

Bates now settled in Fairhaven, fairly well fixed financially with what was known as "a competency" of about $11,000. For the next dozen years, until the Millerite movement attracted his full attention and participation, Joseph Bates dealt with local affairs, such as his father's properties, civic matters, and a variety of reforms of which the air was full at this particular period in American history. These included temperance, antislavery, tract distribution, vocational education, and the level of morality among seamen in general.

In 1839 Bates accepted William Miller's views on the Second Advent and from that time forward devoted his whole attention to the Millerite movement, eventually giving all his means to this cause. The following year he served on the committee that issued a call for the first general conference at Boston on the Second Advent. He became an exceptionally active and successful Millerite minister and in May 1842 served as chair of one of the most important of the Millerite conferences. In 1844 he sold his home and most of his other real estate, settled all his debts, and prepared to go wherever necessary to herald the second coming of Christ. Accompanied by H. S. Gurney, an evangelistic singer and formerly a blacksmith, he went into Maryland and preached on Kent Island in the Chesapeake Bay, where he had once been shipwrecked. There he was opposed, particularly for his antislavery views, but he stood up courageously to those who threatened to do him bodily harm.

Bates experienced the disappointment of 1844 without losing his faith. After reading T. M. Preble's article on the seventh-day Sabbath, published in *The Hope of Israel* in February 1845, and checking the Bible evidence with his customary thoroughness, he made his decision to observe the seventh-day Sabbath. Five years later Prudence joined him in this. Characteristic of the man was his reply when, on the bridge between Fairhaven and New Bedford, upon being hailed by James Madison Monroe Hall, his neighbor and fellow Adventist, with the question "What's the news, Captain Bates?" he replied, "The news is that the seventh day is the Sabbath."

The years between 1846 and 1850 were difficult ones for the early Advent believers. It was a time of bewilderment and recapitulation, of looking back and looking forward, of trying to figure how events and prophecies could fit together to give a clear picture of what had happened and where events were leading. Bates was eminently fitted to lead out in this work. He was a careful student of the Scriptures, having spent much time on his later long sea voyages with his Bible.

In 1846 Bates published a tract dealing with the Sabbath. In this 48-page tract entitled "The Seventh-day Sabbath, a Perpetual Sign," he presented the case of the Sabbath almost exclusively on the basis of the Ten Commandments as the moral guide and rule for all humanity, including Christians. He touched only briefly on the prophesied change of the Sabbath by the papal little horn of Dan. 7.

In the second edition of the tract, published the following year, Bates emphasized the place of the third angel's message in the Sabbatarian movement. On the basis of the long-accepted Protestant identification of the beast with the Papacy, he held that the change of the weekly day of worship from Saturday to Sunday was the badge of papal power. To explain this he issued his tract entitled "A Seal of the Living God," which set forth the Sabbath as the seal.

In 1847 Bates published the longest of his pamphlets, entitled "Second Advent Waymarks and High Heaps, or a Connected View of the Fulfillment of Prophecy by God's Peculiar People From the Year 1840 to 1847." In this he gave an overview of the Advent message for this period, proposing to give its readers a view of their journey to the Promised Land and a survey of things they had passed and things still to come.

These pamphlets, six in all in this period, gave evidence of Bates's sincere desire to know the truth, and of his willingness to search for it diligently. His interpretations of prophecy, tentatively given, indicate a willingness to change with the coming of new light, but on cardinal points of Bible teaching he was adamant and not disposed to compromise.

Bates played a prominent part in the "Sabbath Conferences" that began in 1848 and were intended to clarify the Sabbath teaching and bring it into harmony with other basic concepts of doctrine.

In 1849 Bates's pioneering spirit led him west to Michigan, where in time he gathered a company of converts in Jackson. In 1852 he went on to Battle Creek and pioneered the work in this city, which was to be for many decades the center and headquarters of the Seventh-day Adventist denomination. His first convert here, Presbyterian David Hewett, by his prompt and enthusiastic acceptance of the Advent truths, led Bates and other Adventist leaders in 1852 to abandon the "shut door" position, which had been accepted after the disappointment of 1844.

During the 1850s Bates spent an increasing amount of his time in Michigan and the adjoining states and in Canada. In 1858 he moved permanently from Fairhaven and settled for the rest of his days in Monterey, in western Michigan.

A striking feature of Bates's activities for the last two decades of his life was his constant itinerating, first in New England and later in Michigan and neighboring states. A good share of his life he spent on the move, first by sea and later by land, seemingly a compulsive traveler. These itineraries, after 1845 in particular, reveal that after he had given his modest fortune to the Adventist movement he was almost totally dependent upon the financial largesse of interested friends and of those to whom he ministered.

As the church moved toward formal organization, which came in May 1863, Bates was called upon regularly to assume the leadership of conferences of church leaders. He presided at the conference in Battle Creek when the name Seventh-day Adventist was adopted to designate the body of Sabbathkeepers who were looking for the coming of Christ.

After the Ellen White vision of June 1863, dealing with health reform, Bates felt a compulsion to advocate more openly and aggressively the health principles that he had long practiced. In 1865, when practically all the church leaders were incapacitated because of serious illness, and when for nearly a year it was not possible to gather a quorum to transact church business, Bates carried on in good health, encouraging the others and setting an example in healthful living.

At the first camp meeting, held at Wright, Michigan, in 1868, Bates, then 76 years of age, was one of the speakers. His lifetime companion, "Prudy," passed to her rest in 1870, but Bates continued his ministry, though at a more restricted pace. In 1871, the year before his death, he held at least 100 meetings, besides those at his local church in Monterey and the conferences that he faithfully attended. He died at the Western Health Reform Institute in

Battle Creek on Mar. 19, 1872. He was buried by the side of his wife in Poplar Hill Cemetery in Monterey, where about 100 of his SDA brethren also await the call of the Life-giver.

Bates's contribution—as one of the triumvirate, with James and Ellen White, that founded the Seventh-day Adventist Church—was extensive and varied. He won many to the Lord by his personal efforts and contributed significantly to the shaping of the body of Adventist beliefs and teachings.

BATES MEMORIAL HIGH SCHOOL. A coeducational day school on the senior high school level, operated at Sangre Grande, Trinidad, West Indies. It is under the direction of a board of management that meets annually and an executive board that meets monthly. During the 1992-1993 academic year the school had a staff of 13 and an enrollment of 268. Instruction is offered in five-year secondary courses in preparation for the Caribbean Examination Council and is approved by the Trinidad and Tobago government.

The forerunner of the school was the Sangre Grande Intermediate School, established in January 1948 with an enrollment of 14, and taught by J. R. Hill and M. McKenzie. Because its growth was slow, it was not until October 1952 that the secondary section was separated from the elementary grades and named Bates Memorial High School. At first the school operated under the control of the local church, with the assistance of the conference. However, in March 1962, when its enrollment had reached 100, it came under direct conference control.

The school was moved to a new location on Adventist Street, Sangre Grande, Trinidad, in April 1974. In 1992 it was accredited for three years by the Inter-American Division Commission on Accreditation and the General Conference Board of Regents.

Principals: A.C.W. Haynes, 1952-1954; Oliver Hosten, 1954-1956; Eric George, 1956-1958; Leslie Carrington (acting), 1958-1960; Claude Pierce, 1960-1961; Merille McKenzie, 1961-1967; John Thompson, 1967-1969; Carlos Duncan (acting), 1969; E. Bernard, 1970-1971; Robert Melville (acting), 1971; Willie Joseph, 1971-1980; Althea Cordner, 1980-1984; Hamil Tobias, 1984-1989; Aaron Smith, 1989- .

BATOURI ADVENTIST HOSPITAL. An institution owned and operated by the East Cameroon Mission. It was established as a dispensary Mar. 10, 1962, under the direction of Akamba Roger, a male nurse.

In 1966 it was operated under the supervision of Mrs. Maurice Zehnacker, and from 1970 to 1974, by Mrs. Adolphe Kinder, who was helped by nurse aides Bekolo David and Samba Gaston. Unfortunately, it was closed in 1987.

The dispensary was reopened by Paul Gheorghe in 1990, and by January 1991 it was converted into a hospital. The stone-laying ceremony for the construction of the surgery block was held May 15, 1991. On June 28, 1992, the teachers' houses were converted into temporary medical quarters. The hospital has two modern units with a capacity of 70 beds.

The administrator, Paul Gheorghe, is assisted by his wife, Renée Sansfamille, a qualified nurse, as well as two local helpers.

There have been approximately 1,500 patients registered at the hospital. Among them are Muslims (Bororo, Kakou), Catholics, and Presbyterians. Funds that have helped develop construction came from private donations contributed by non-Adventist medical institutions in the United States, and the CIBA-Geigy Association of Switzerland.

Plans include adding a maternity unit. This is the only hospital unit in the region where cataract surgery is performed.

BATTLE CREEK ACADEMY. A coeducational day school on the senior high school level, with associated grade school, operated at Battle Creek, Michigan, by a board consisting of the Lake Union educational secretary, the Michigan Conference president, secretary, treasurer, and educational superintendent, together with the school principal, the pastors and other representatives from each of the five area churches (Battle Creek [Berean, Tabernacle, Urbandale], Delton, and Marshall), with a total constituency (1992) of 1,404. Students also are enrolled from other Seventh-day Adventist churches. The school is accredited with the University of Michigan and with the SDA Board of Regents.

The enrollment of the high school for 1992-1993 was 64, with another 147 enrolled in the kindergarten and grades 1 through 8. The school employed eight academy teachers, seven elementary teachers, and five nonteaching staff members.

Battle Creek Academy offers strong college preparatory courses. Instruction is given in English, mathematics, physics, science, history, business education, Spanish, technology education, physical education, music, and other fields.

SDA schools began to operate in Battle Creek as early as 1856, a year after the Review and Herald was moved to Battle Creek. In that year a church school was opened in a private home, the teacher receiving 25 cents a week for each pupil. This school ran for several years, with a succession of teachers. Then after an interval of several years without a school, another was opened by G. H. Bell, first in a little cottage, then in a room in the Review and Herald building. Later the school came under General Conference auspices.

When Battle Creek College was founded in 1872, a day school was operated that became a church school when the college moved to Berrien Springs, Michigan, in 1902. In 1904 the Battle Creek Industrial Academy, as the school was then named, opened in a new building on Sept. 6. This was a school supported by the church, and operated by the church board, M. B. Miller being the pastor. B. E. Nicola was the principal and in charge of secondary grades; elementary teachers were Pearl Hallock, seventh and eighth grades; Frances L. Case, fifth and sixth; Mrs. Ella King Sanders, third and fourth; Mrs. L. Flora Williams, first and second. Part of the time the school had 10 grades. Before many years had passed, the word "industrial" was dropped, and it took its present name of Battle Creek Academy.

When the academy building on North Kendall Street, endeared to many students during 40 years, was damaged by fire in 1945, classes met at the municipal airport for a time. Then a new, modern school building was erected on a 44-acre (18-hectare) plot at 180 Welch Avenue (now renamed 480 Parkway Drive), and dedicated on Sept. 6, 1948, by E. L. Pingenot, former pastor of the Battle Creek Tabernacle, who, with V. E. Garber, a former principal, had begun the planning for the new school building. Several local business and professional men led in the promotion and financing of the project, including H. M. Babcock, William Heffley, D. B. Wildman, Sr., and Dr. William Kenzie, the latter leaving a sizable sum of money that was given to the school. M. D. Hannah was the first principal of the new Battle Creek Academy.

In 1953 an auditorium-gymnasium was completed; by 1959 three new classrooms were added for the sixth, seventh, and eighth grades; and in the fall of 1961 a new chapel. During 1968 two additional rooms were constructed, and in 1970 two more, which serve as a kindergarten room and an elementary media center. A year later a three-bay garage with an automatic hoist was added to the shop area, and in 1974 a three-room primary unit complex was completed, making two additional classrooms available for secondary use. In 1985 a new addition was completed to serve as the band room.

Principals: Frederick Griggs, 1889-1898; J. G. Lamson, 1903-1904; B. E. Nicola, 1904-1907; Mrs. Flora Williams, 1907-1908; C. A. Russell, 1908-1912; Mrs. William Heffley, 1912-1913; Don Ludington, 1913-1914; W. J. Blake, 1914-1920; F. S. Everest, 1920-1921; T. S. Copeland, 1921-1923; J. G. Lamson, 1923-1924; B. H. Phipps, 1924-1928; C. Roy Smith, 1928-1932; A. J. Skeels, 1932-1934; H. J. Alcock, 1934-1940; V. E. Garber, 1940-1945; D. N. Hartman, 1945-1948; M. D. Hannah, 1948-1951; F. M. Miller, 1951-1952; Donald E. Jacobs, 1952-1953; D. Lorne Jones, 1953-1955; J. H. Rhoads, 1955-1956; Ralph P. Bailey, 1956-1958; Stephen W. Young, 1958-1964; La Rue L. Cook, 1964-1967; Erich Bekowies, 1967-1972; Ralph A. Darrough, 1972-1977; T. Alvin Astrup, 1977-1980; Robert M. Mead, 1980-1988; John M. Deming, 1988-1992; Sunimal Kulasekere, 1992- .

BATTLE CREEK ADVENTIST HOSPITAL. *See* Battle Creek Sanitarium.

BATTLE CREEK COLLEGE. *See* Andrews University, II, 1.

BATTLE CREEK SANITARIUM. A pioneer Seventh-day Adventist medical institution at Battle Creek, Michigan, in which SDA concepts of health and healing were given their first public demonstration. It was owned, controlled, and operated by the Seventh-day Adventist Church from 1866 to 1908 (when control of the institution was taken over by its medical director, J. H. Kellogg); from 1957 to 1974 it was operated as an SDA self-supporting institution; and from 1974 to 1993 it was fully owned and operated by the church. In 1959 its name was changed to Battle Creek Health Center, and in 1966 its name was again changed to the Battle Creek Sanitarium Hospital. The name was changed once again on Dec. 10, 1981, to Battle Creek Adventist Hospital.

History of the Sanitarium. *The Sanitarium Founded in 1866.* The need for a health institution based on health principles newly advocated by the developing SDA Church was presented by Ellen White at the fourth session of the General Conference, which convened in Battle Creek, Michigan, in May 1866. It was decided to establish such an institution at Battle Creek, where the headquarters of the church were situated at that time. The site was considered to be midway between the East and the West, and easily accessible by means of the Michigan Central Railroad, which operated between Detroit and Chicago and ran through Battle Creek. The leaders of the church, among them James White and J. N. Loughborough, decided that the proposed institution should be organized as a stock company. In mid-June an appeal to the people to subscribe to the stock was made in the *Review and Herald.* By that time the members of the church at Battle Creek and at Olcott, New York, had already subscribed more than $2,500, with J. P. Kellogg and James White heading the list with a subscription of $500 each. With these and other funds that came in, a residence with seven or eight acres (about three hectares) of land, situated in Battle Creek, was purchased from Benjamin Graves, a judge of the Michigan Superior Court. During that same summer a two-story addition was built and treatment rooms were equipped, allowing the institution to open for patients on Sept. 5, 1866, under the supervision of Dr. Horatio S. Lay. In less than two years, the stockholders voted to forgo any future profits in their investment and to turn any realized proceeds back to the hospital's directors to use for charity.

A note in the *Review and Herald* of Sept. 11 called attention to the rapidity with which the enterprise was conceived and carried out: "We have only to look back to our conference in May last, less than four short months ago, for the time when this matter first began to take practical shape among our people. Now we behold an elegant site secured, buildings ready for operation, a competent corps of assistants on the ground, . . . a sum bordering on $11,000 already subscribed for stock in the enterprise, and the institute opened and operations actually commenced. In no enterprise ever undertaken by this people has the hand of the Lord been more evidently manifested than in this thing" *(Review and Herald* 18:116, Sept. 11, 1866).

The opening of the institution, named the Western Health Reform Institute, marked a new era in SDA history. The building was situated on high ground in Battle Creek, a flourishing manufacturing town of about 5,000 people. Screened from the street in front by a grove of trees, the institute looked out in the rear on a landscape of hill, valley, and stream. It was in a location suitable for inculcating the principle of right living as a means of recovering and preserving the health through the "correct application of water, the right use of air, and a proper diet." The equipment was meager but adequate for the immediate needs.

Said M. E. Olsen, a later church historian: "It not only gave tangible outward expression to the health principles as a definite phase of denominational belief but it supplied an effective instrumentality for the propagation of those principles. It represented, on the side of the Adventists, a new and enlarged vision of the world's need, and of the duty resting upon the Christian church to supply that need. The healing ministry of Christ was seen to be a manifestation of divine love which should be continued in the world through the instrumentality of the church. The practice of health principles and the use of simple hydropathic means of treating disease were regarded as a means of cooperating with the divine power, which alone can truly heal. Disease was seen to be the result of transgression of natural law; and the duty and privilege of Christians to obey all these laws, and teach others to obey them, appeared to be a part of the everlasting gospel" *(Origin and Progress of Seventh-day Adventists,* pp. 269, 270).

When the pioneers of the SDA medical work decided to establish a corporation, they discovered that Michigan law had no provision for benevolent institutions of their kind. Consequently, the institute property was held in trust until the legislature could authorize the corporation (in an amendment to an act authorizing mining and manufacturing enterprises). The Western Health Reform Institute was legally incorporated on Apr. 9, 1867. The unfortunate result of its incorporation under a law for business companies was the limiting of its charter to 30 years, a provision that later caused many difficulties over the administration and control of the institution and that eventually led to the separation of the sanitarium from the church.

During the first 10 years, the institution had a struggle financially. James White, the leader in the enterprise, was away from his office much of the time, and also suffered from overwork. Without his business counsel, the institute came close to financial ruin. Furthermore, its medical staff, which at first did not represent the best medical schools, failed to inspire the public with confidence. Despite noble attempts on the part of the entire staff to carry on as best they could, attempts that on the whole were reasonably successful, the patronage wavered. However, fortunes changed after John Harvey Kellogg, M.D., a graduate of Belleview Hospital Medical College, New York City, joined the staff in 1875, and the next year was appointed medical superintendent of the institute. About the same time, James White returned to leadership of the enterprise. By 1877 increased patronage made the erection of another building necessary. In the same year, the institution was renamed the Medical and Surgical Sanitarium; however, it later was commonly called the Battle Creek Sanitarium. When someone remarked that the word "sanitarium" was not in the dictionary, Dr. Kellogg replied that it soon would be. Although the Battle Creek institution was not the first one in the world to use the word "sanitarium," it made the term well known, and for many years afterward SDA medical establishments were distinguished by this name. The Battle Creek institution soon became known affectionately as the "San" and gradually achieved an international reputation growing from its one-patient status at its opening to 1,200 patients and guests at the height of its fame in 1929. It has played an integral and lively part in two great histories—the beginning of both a worldwide medical ministry of the Seventh-day Adventist Church and of the cereal industry, which still is an important part of Battle Creek's economy.

Expansion of Buildings and Facilities. Late in the spring of 1877 construction began on a four-story brick veneer building 136 feet (41 meters) in length. It was dedicated in April 1878 and constituted the central portion of what later became known as the main building. Its cost was $115,000.

The equipment of the new building included new apparatus, the policy of management being to keep up with the scientific and sanitary developments in America and abroad. The improvements increased the efficiency of the institution. With a continued growth in patronage, new additions were made: In 1884 a five-story addition containing a gymnasium, dining facilities for 400, serving room and kitchen, and a storeroom was built to the south at a cost of $50,000. In 1887 a separate five-story hospital structure, 60' x 100' (18 m. x 30 m.) was built for surgical and charitable work. This was dedicated in 1888. Two years later another five-story extension on the north was added to the main building at a cost of $50,000, and the original section was raised one story. In 1894 a five-story brick dormitory, 90' x 120' (27 m. x 37 m.) was erected to accommodate 150 or more women nurses. In 1895 further additions were made, the hydrotherapy space was enlarged, and a chapel seating about 400 was built.

In 1895, in line with the program of health education that the sanitarium had sponsored since its inception, the American Medical Missionary College was established. While not formally a part of the sanitarium itself, this school used the sanitarium facilities for clinical instruction, and had Dr. Kellogg as its president and moving spirit.

By the end of the century the sanitarium employed more than 900 workers, not only to provide health care, but also to operate the farms that supplied produce, milk, and eggs for the patients. The acreage was about 1,000 acres (405 hectares), including several farms—one of 150 acres (60 hectares), northwest of the sanitarium; one of 125 acres (50 hectares), northeast, devoted entirely to vegetables and fruits; and another of 120 acres (49 hectares) on the south side of Lake Goguac, where a large amount of produce was raised.

In 1893 the Seventh-day Adventist Medical Missionary and Benevolent Association was brought into being as the legal embodiment of the medical arm of the denomination, and Dr. Kellogg placed at its head. As the number of institutions under its control grew, and spread outside the United States (by the turn of the century there were institutions in such countries as Switzerland, Germany, Mexico, South Africa, Palestine, and Egypt), the name of the association was changed (1896) to the International Medical Missionary and Benevolent Association. The absence of "Seventh-day Adventist" in the name made it easier for Dr. Kellogg later to divorce the medical and humanitarian work of the association from the church that gave it birth.

Reorganization of the Corporation. When the charter of the Western Health Reform Institute expired in 1897, the assets of the corporation were sold for an amount equal to the corporation's indebtedness at a public auction to a new body, the Michigan Sanitarium and Benevolent Association, organized by the International Medical Missionary and Benevolent Association to hold the property of the sanitarium and its associated enterprises.

The constituency of the new association was considerably larger than the number of stockholders of the old corporation. The number of members was made equivalent to the number of shares in the old corporation—650 instead of about 150. The new members were nominated by the former stockholders and the board of directors, although still from among members of the SDA Church, and mostly from its ministry.

Several changes were also made in the articles of the association. Whereas in the past only members of the church could be stockholders, the membership of the new association was not expressly so limited; the control over the activities of the association was given to the members meeting annually, each of whom now had only one vote and could exercise it only in person; and the statement of objectives contained the provision that the institution was to perform acts "of an undenominational, unsectarian, humanitarian, and philanthropic nature." There were some questions raised over the insertion of these words, which might be interpreted as divorcing the institution from denominational control, but Dr. Kellogg explained that they were meant to refer only to the application of the benevolence of the institution without regard to creed. This explanation was accepted in good faith. Later this provision was to play the key role in Kellogg's claim that the Battle Creek Sanitarium was not under denominational control.

Repeated Warnings From Ellen G. White. As the work at the sanitarium developed, numerous and repeated warnings came from Ellen G. White that this institution, created and nurtured under the guidance of God, should ever be managed in the spirit of service and in humility, and should always be kept distinguishable from secular institutions. This instruction, however, was not always welcomed by the management. At the same time, the church at Battle Creek also was being warned of its indifferent spiritual condition and of the danger that the initial success of the Battle Creek enterprises would lead to courting the favor of the public through compromises in the standards and principles on which the institutions were originally founded. At times the warnings were heeded, and at other times, they were disregarded. Mrs. White especially counseled against concentrating much investment in one place and drawing the best workers there, as well as concentrating in a few hands the power and control over the various medical institutions serving the church. This latter instruction ran directly counter to the plans of Dr. Kellogg, whose dream it was to create a network of SDA health and welfare institutions under his leadership.

By this time it was evident that in his speeches and articles Dr. Kellogg was setting himself and the medical work in opposition to the General Conference and was seeking independence in matters of administration and policy. At the time of the reorganization of the Seventh-day Adventist work effected in the 1901 General Conference session *(see* Organization, IV, 2, 3), the conflict came into the open, but it was temporarily assuaged. Then in the early morning of Feb. 18, 1902, the main sanitarium building and the hospital burned down. The question immediately arose as to whether to rebuild them, at what cost, and in what size. In a meeting held in March, which was attended by the president of the General Conference, union conference presidents, and other leaders of the denomination then in Battle Creek, the sanitarium board recommended the erection of only one building, which was not to exceed five stories in height and 450 feet (137 meters) in length.

But when the building was actually put under construction, it became apparent that Dr. Kellogg had proceeded independently and had ordered an elaborately equipped building five stories in height and 550 feet (168 meters) in length, with extensions aggregating another 500 feet (152 meters) on the sides, ornamented with marble and mosaic work supervised by the master craftsman who had supervised the mosaic work in the Library of Congress in Washington, D.C. Although the break between the denomination and the sanitarium was not yet openly declared, the action of the medical director made it impossible for the church to support the project, since it was being carried out in disregard of denominational counsel.

Final Break With the Denomination. The final break with the denomination came several years later through legal technicalities in the organization of the Michigan Sanitarium and Benevolent Association. The charter taken out in 1897, at the expiration of the original charter of the Western Health Reform Institute, contained a provision (thought useful at the time to safeguard denominational control over the property in case some members of the association should leave the church) that any member who was out of harmony with the principles of the association could be dropped at an annual meeting by a two-thirds vote of the members present. Now this provision was used to drop from membership those loyal SDA members and leaders who opposed the plans and projects of Dr. Kellogg. This maneuver became possible because, after the denominational headquarters were removed from Battle Creek to Washington, D.C., many members of the association, the majority of whom were faithful working ministers of the church, found it inconvenient to attend the meetings of the association that earlier had usually been held in conjunction with the General Conference sessions. Since no quorum was provided for in the charter or the bylaws, in 1908 most of the active SDA leaders were dropped from the sanitarium association by a small group of members, most of whom were connected with the management of the sanitarium, and the institution was effectively taken away from denominational ownership and control.

Later History. After the alienation of the sanitarium from the denomination, the sanitarium board became its practical owner. Elected by the small minority of the remaining association members who attended the annual meeting, it represented a limited base of support. The medical school faltered and was closed in 1910. The welfare institutions under the control of the sanitarium in Chicago and elsewhere closed one after another. A grandiose building program in 1927, which included a 15-story tower with an elaborately decorated lobby and dining room added to the main part of the sanitarium at a cost of $4 million, put the institution into debt that the prolonged depression of the 1930s made impossible to repay. For a number of years the institution operated with heavy annual deficits. Finally, in 1933, after it defaulted on the payment of interest and principal on its outstanding obligations, it went into receivership.

Following this, representatives of the sanitarium (which still had many members of the SDA Church holding responsible positions on its administrative and operating staff) approached the General Conference Committee and invited the denomination to collaborate in planning for future operation of the sanitarium. After due consideration, the officers of the General Conference declined to assume the heavy financial burden that the mammoth institution would have required.

In 1938 the sanitarium association was reorganized under Section 77B of the National Bankruptcy Act, and with the approval of the court the Battle Creek Sanitarium and Benevolent Association was formed to take over the assets and obligations of the enterprise. In 1942 the main building of the sanitarium was sold to the United States government, and the indebtedness of the association was paid in full. There remained in the hands of the association the annex building across the street, about $1 million in cash and other assets, and certain real estate in the vicinity of Battle Creek.

The disbursement of these assets sparked a controversy that ended in court action. Dr. Kellogg, then more than 90 years old, proposed that the assets be turned over to a new organization to be created from a merger of the Battle Creek Sanitarium and Benevolent Association with the Race Betterment Foundation (of which Dr. Kellogg was the head), and be left in the hands of a named and self-perpetuating board of trustees for the purpose of conducting "a charitable hospital or other charitable asylum within the state of Michigan or elsewhere." Certain other members of the association, desiring to perpetuate the then-existing Battle Creek Sanitarium, appealed to the General Conference Committee to rally the surviving members of the association, the great majority of whom were SDAs, to an annual meeting. This was arranged, and a large representation of members gathered at a meeting presided over by Dr. Kellogg. He strenuously objected to the proceedings, and when the members decided to perpetuate the association and duly elected a new board of trustees, including Dr. Kellogg and several of his associates, he refused to recognize the action of the constituency and obtained an injunction from the court against the General Conference Corporation, against W. H. Branson, who acted as the representative of the General Conference and as coordinator of the meeting, and against the newly elected members of the board. The dispute was settled by a division of assets, of which about $650,000 reverted to the denomination. The sanitarium association remained in existence, and it carried on its medical activities independently of the SDA organization, in the building called the Annex, across the street from the original sanitarium building.

Return to Seventh-day Adventists—The Battle Creek Health Center. In May of 1957 the sanitarium went into receivership that terminated when its board resigned and was superseded by a board of SDA physicians representing the Hospital Service Foundation, of Glendale, California. At the time the receivership was established, the civic leaders of Battle Creek began a campaign to return the institution to the control of the SDAs.

At that time the property of the sanitarium was valued at about $1 million and consisted of a 236-bed sanitarium, a 59-bed hospital located a short block away on Emmett Street, doctors' offices, and an auditorium. Considerable renovation and reequipping was done, and in 1959 the institution was renamed the Battle Creek Health Center, operating as an acute-care hospital and sanitarium. It operated under its 1938 charter as a nonprofit institution and as a member of the Association of SDA Self-supporting Institutions (now Adventist-Laymen's Services and Industries). Organizationally, it had an SDA constituency and was operated by an independent board, of which the chair was the president of the Michigan Conference. Of its 13 members, 12 were SDAs.

Although a "sanitarium" type practice was continued, it soon became evident that the days of this type of treatment were passing, and the hospital board focused its attention on other areas. In 1958 a 28-bed mental health unit had been established, and in 1965 an inpatient and outpatient alcoholism rehabilitation program. Services were expanded in 1972 to include a similar program in drug rehabilitation. Sanitarium functions were closed on Mar. 1, 1972, as was the health center. The sanitarium thus became solely an acute-care hospital with medical, surgical, and mental facilities.

In January 1971 patients were moved into the first and second floors of a modern $2 million four-story brick Jeffrey Building, named after a former sanitarium janitor, James R. Jeffrey, who went on to get his medical degree and who, upon Dr. Kellogg's death in 1943, became the sanitarium's medical director. The new building featured a 39-bed mental health unit on the first floor and a 37-bed medical-surgical unit with a four-bed intensive coronary care unit on the second. Another patient unit on the second floor of the old building was continued until August 1973, when the third floor of the Jeffrey Building was finished and patients moved into its 34-bed unit.

On Oct. 1, 1974—for the first time in its 108 years of service—the Battle Creek Sanitarium Hospital's constituency voted to come under the ownership of the SDA Church. Thus, this institution, which was the forerunner of the medical work of Seventh-day Adventists, became the church's 394th medical facility.

The study to change the status of the hospital from a member of the ASI to a denominationally owned facility was begun in 1973 by a special commission under the direction of Francis W. Wernick, president of the Lake Union Conference. At the constituency meeting he was named chair of the board, and Robert D. Moon, president of the Michigan Conference, the vice chair.

In January of 1975 the hospital began a $3.5 million expansion program incorporating a new administrative and reception center, a new area for the Pharmacy, Physical Therapy, and Laboratory departments, and the completion of the fourth floor of the Jeffrey Building to increase the hospital's bed capacity to 155.

A highlight in the history of the hospital came during the celebration of its 100 years of service. When Battle Creek Sanitarium was founded Sept. 5, 1866, President Johnson was in the White House—Andrew Johnson. One hundred years later to the day, another President Johnson signed the guest registry—this time Lyndon B. Johnson. He was accompanied by his wife, Lady Bird, who, in her remarks to a crowd estimated at 15,000, indicated that at the age of 11 she had visited the sanitarium with an aunt, Mrs. Effie Patillo. She added that she remembered Dr. Kellogg practicing what he preached as he rode his bicycle to and from the san. "It was here that I first heard about the importance of vitamins, sunshine, and exercise," she recalled. Louis Gordon, administrator, presented Mrs. Johnson with her original sanitarium admission card as a memento of her visit on its centennial day.

In 1979, when the Michigan Bed Reduction Plan mandated more efficient use of existing health-care facilities, the Battle Creek Sanitarium Hospital, supported by more than 25 years of mental health treatment, began phasing down medical/surgical intensive care programs, emphasizing, in its place, chemical dependency and psychiatric care. In 1983 surgery was closed. When the last medical unit was closed in December 1987, the change from a general hospital to a specialty mental hospital was complete. With inpatient and outpatient psychiatric services and substance abuse programs, Battle Creek Adventist Hospital continued to deliver one of the most comprehensive ranges of psychiatric services available in southwest Michigan. The hospital was sold in September 1993.

Administrators of Battle Creek Sanitarium since it was taken over by Adventist laity include: Dunbar Smith, 1957-1958; William G. Simmons, 1958-1961; S. J. Ruskjer (consultant administrator), 1961-1962; Clifford Eckman, 1961; Louis E. Gordon, 1961-1967; Clarence Simmons (acting administrator), 1967; Richard E. Lane, 1967-1972; H. H. Hill, 1972-1974; Vernon L. Small, 1974-1981; Thomas K. Williams, 1981-1983; Teddric J. Mohr, 1983-1991; Don L. Platt, 1991-1992; Ronald C. Brown, 1992- .

BATTLEFORD ACADEMY. A coeducational secondary boarding school formerly operated at Battleford, Saskatchewan, from 1916 to 1931 by the Saskatchewan Conference. The school was housed in one of the most historic buildings in the province—a building that had housed the government of the Northwest Territories from 1876 to 1883. Originally leased from the government at one cent an acre (.405 hectare), the property, containing about 600 acres (243 hectares), was finally purchased by the conference. The enrollment, beginning with 114 in 10 grades, in 1918 reached a peak of 166 in 12 grades. Then, after a decade of fluctuation between 121 and 150, it dropped to 90, and in 1930-1931, as the economy became more severely depressed, to 65. With such a small enrollment it seemed inadvisable to continue operating the school, especially since Canadian Junior College in neighboring Alberta, which also was suffering a decline in enrollment could absorb the Saskatchewan students. In 1931 the school was closed. Its demise was considered a severe blow to the work in the Saskatchewan Conference. The property was sold to the Oblate Fathers.

Principals: Cassius B. Hughes, 1916-1918; W. G. Foreshaw, 1918; Thomas D. Rowe, 1918-1919; Reginald E. Noble, 1919-1921; Charles O. Smith, 1921-1922; Hubert K. Martin, 1922-1926; Claude W. Degering, 1926-1930; Arthur J. Skeels, 1930-1931.

BAUER, CLIFFORD LAWRENCE (1891-1964). Conference worker, missionary, administrator. Bauer was a native of Michigan. He joined the church in 1917 and entered its employ in 1920, serving as secretary-treasurer of the West Virginia Conference. He then served in the Virginia Conference and spent 12 years in mission service in South America, serving in the São Paulo Conference, the Austral Union, and the division office. He returned to the United States to labor in the Southwestern and Pacific union conferences, serving as president of the latter for 11 years. He retired in California in 1957.

BAUTAMA CENTRAL SCHOOL. *See* Mount Diamond Adventist High School and Agriculture Centre.

BAWSHRIEH ADVENTIST SECONDARY SCHOOL. *See* Boushrieh Adventist Secondary School.

BAXTER, WILLIAM EDGAR (1881-1973). Pioneer missionary. A native of Indiana, he entered the ministry in 1901 in the Oklahoma Conference. He was one of the founders of the Inter-American Division, having first served there in 1909 as pastor in Kingston, Jamaica, returning later as Venezuela Mission superintendent in 1917. At the time of the division organization, he became Caribbean Union president, and later filled a similar post in Central America. He also served as president of the Arkansas Conference for the four-year period from 1913 to 1917.

During his 34 years of overseas mission service he worked in Jamaica, Venezuela, Costa Rica, Colombia, Panama, Puerto Rico, and Cuba. His trek with C. B. Sutton to Mount Roraima in search of the Davis Indians sparked the imagination of Seventh-day Adventists around the world.

BAY ISLANDS MISSION. *See* Honduras; Inter-American Division.

BAZEGA HORTICULTURAL TRAINING CENTER. *See* Burkina Faso.

BEACH, WALTER RAYMOND (1902-1993). Church administrator, preacher, writer. Born in St. John, North Dakota, he was educated at Gem State Academy and Walla Walla College, where he received a bachelor's degree in 1923. He married Gladys I. Corley, an elementary school teacher, to whom he was married for 70 years.

He began his denominational employment as Bible teacher and dean of boys at Auburn Academy. He was ordained in New York City in 1926 on his way to Europe. He and his wife spent 28 years in service on that continent. After French culture and language study at the Sorbonne, he served as a departmental director in the old Latin Union from 1927-1928, president of both the Belgian Conference (1929-1932) and the Franco-Belgian Union (1932-1936). In 1936 he was elected secretary and in 1946 president of the Southern European Division. This period included the difficult years of World War II, when the division office was cut off from much of its territory. During this time Beach served also as editor of the French *Life and Health,* and together with his wife broadcast in the English overseas radio programs of the Swiss Broadcasting Corporation.

His period as division president marked a remarkable postwar rebuilding and expansion of the worship and educational facilities of the church in Europe. Beach concluded his overseas service in 1954 when he was elected secretary of the General Conference, in which position he served until 1970. During this period he was instrumental in launching the first Global Mission program, entitled "From Everywhere to Everywhere."

He retired in 1975 as a general vice president, after 52 years of active service. He was a member of the General Conference Executive Committee for 44 years.

Beach was known as an inspiring preacher, an administrator with a cosmopolitan bent of mind, and a prolific writer. His best-seller, *Nous et Nos Enfants*, originally written in French, was translated into a dozen languages. His best-known books in English are *Dimensions in Salvation* and *Light From God's Lamp*. Together with his son Bert he authored his last book, *Pattern for Progress* (1985), dealing with church organization. He died in Loma Linda, California.

BEASTS, SYMBOLIC, OF DANIEL. *See* Daniel, Interpretation of.

BEASTS, SYMBOLIC, OF REVELATION. *See* Mark of the Beast; Number of the Beast; Revelation, Interpretation of.

BECHUANALAND. *See* Botswana.

BECKER, VERNON W. (1908-1989). Evangelist, pastor, administrator. Born in Kansas, he began evangelistic work in Texas in 1929 and received his degree from Union College in Nebraska in 1932. He spent the next five years teaching and was ordained in 1936. He became superintendent of education and youth director of the Texas Conference in 1937 and later held that position in the Greater New York Conference. In 1944 he became principal of Campion Academy in Colorado. In 1951 he was elected director of education and youth for the Northern Union Conference and served there until 1955, when he moved to the same work in the Atlantic Union. In 1972 he earned the Citation of Excellence, the church's highest award for educational service. Throughout retirement, he was on the board of Becker Adventist School in Decatur, Georgia, an institution named in his honor.

BECKNER, ROBERT A. (1886-1941). Missionary to Burma. A graduate of South Lancaster Academy in 1908, he began evangelistic work in Pennsylvania but left the same year for service in Burma. He worked in Rangoon and Mandalay, spending much time distributing publications. He was ordained in 1919, and, beginning in 1925, served for three and one-half years as principal of the Meiktila Training School. He then became editor of the Burmese *Watchman* magazine, a post he held until his return to the United States in 1941. While editor, he also for a time was the director of the Delta district.

BEDDOE, BENJAMIN E. (1884-1931). Conference administrator, department secretary. Educated at Missouri State University and Emmanuel Missionary College, he began ministerial work in the Missouri Conference, serving that conference from 1903 to 1905. From 1905 to 1909 he preached in the California Conference and then served as its Missionary Volunteer secretary from 1910 to 1911. Later he was pastor of the Oakland church (1912-1913), president of the Central California Conference (1914-1915), and president of the Southern California Conference (1915-1916). From 1917 to 1918 he was employed by the Pacific Union Conference. After that, he was pastor of the San Francisco church (1919), president of the Southeastern California Conference (1920), and president of the South African Union Conference (1921-1923). In 1923 he was called to the General Conference, serving first as an associate secretary of the Sabbath School Department, then as an associate secretary of the General Conference (1924).

BEECHWOOD MANUAL TRAINING ACADEMY. *See* Indiana Academy.

BEEM, KENNETH C. (1912-1992). Treasurer, auditor. Born in Arkansas, he was married to Thelma Grace Imler in 1936, and they taught school for four years. He then was employed as manager of the Arkansas-Louisiana Book and Bible House. After taking correspondence courses in accounting, he sat for the CPA test and passed. He was believed to be the first Seventh-day Adventist worker to attain the CPA certificate.

In 1945 he was called to the Atlantic Union Conference as auditor. Seven years later he moved to Georgia-Cumberland, where he served as secretary-treasurer for two years before becoming auditor and later treasurer of the Southern Union Conference, a position he held for 11 years. The Beems then moved to Southwestern Union, where he served as treasurer for six years.

Five years after the death of his wife, Beem married Florence May Baker Slepnikoff. In 1974 they retired from the Central Union, where he had served for four years. In retirement he was employed by the Southwestern Union on a part-time basis for seventeen years, making a total of 56 years of denominational service. He passed to his rest in Keene, Texas.

BEEVILLE MEMORIAL HOSPITAL ASSOCIATION. *See* Memorial Hospital of Bee County.

BEGEMDER MISSION SCHOOL. *See* Debre Tabor Adventist Church School.

BEIRUT COLLEGE. *See* Middle East College.

BEIRUT OVERSEAS SCHOOL. A 12-grade coeducational day school on the senior high school level, operated by the former Afro-Mideast Division in Beirut. The purpose of the school was to provide a fully accredited secondary school for the children of missionaries living in the Beirut area. It began operation in 1953 as the Beirut English Church School. When in 1965 grades 9 and 10 were added it was called Beirut Overseas School. The school was further upgraded to 12 grades in 1967. The school was closed in 1984.

Principals: Izella Stuivenga, 1965-1966; J. R. Stephan, 1966-1967; G. J. Unger, 1967-1973; F. N. Chase, 1973-1974; L. R. Kuhn, 1974-1977; Dwight Rose, 1977-1984.

BEIRUT TRAINING SCHOOL. *See* Middle East College.

BEKWAI SEVENTH-DAY ADVENTIST SECONDARY SCHOOL. A coeducational boarding school with a curriculum leading to the advanced level general certificate in education. The school is situated on a tract of land near the town of Bekwai, in the Ashanti region of Ghana, about 25 miles (40 kilometers) south of Kumasi.

History. The school began as a six to nine months' basic evangelistic training course for capable national workers, offered at the mission established in 1931, a half mile (.8 kilometer) north of the town of Bekwai, by Jesse Clifford, from England. In 1939 Charles A. Bartlett arrived from the United Kingdom to become the first principal of a new teacher-evangelist one-year training program, which continued through 1944.

Bekwai Training School appears for the first time in the *Statistical Report* in 1940, which reports three finishing the course and three entering the work. The 1940 *Yearbook* lists the school as established in 1939, "formerly the Agona Training School." However, the latter, situated at the Agona Mission Station, about 22 miles (35 kilometers) northeast of Kumasi, continued as an elementary school, as it had operated since about 1915. It appeared in these annual records from 1930 (with H. K. Munson as the first principal) through 1939. In one year (1934) the *Statistical Report* listed 28 pupils in grades 9-11; then the school disappeared from the record in 1940 and Bekwai Training School came into the list.

In 1944 Bekwai Training School received official permission from the Ministry of Education to offer the two-year Certificate B teacher's course. Fifteen students enrolled in the first class on Jan. 26, 1945. With the enrollment in 1947 of three girls as teacher trainees, the school became coeducational.

A further two-year training course leading to Certificate A was authorized in 1948. In that year James C. Vetter arrived from the United States to assist in this higher training program, which began with four students. Demonstration primary and middle schools, where trainees could observe and practice, were operated on the compound. An advanced evangelistic training course was also offered for promising workers. The four-year training college was completely phased out in August 1974 to make room for the expansion of the secondary school.

Under the direction of H. J. Welch, who had arrived from the United States in 1949 to become the principal, the first class enrolled for a new five-year secondary school program. In 1953 a concrete secondary school building housing five classrooms, an assembly hall, and administrative offices was built. N. C. Maberly became the first headmaster of the newly opened secondary school. Other headmasters were H. I. Dunton, W. L. Parker, and E. B. Christie. With an increase in the enrollment, more buildings were erected, such as a science laboratory in 1956. A third stream was added to the school in September 1973.

The school offers arts, science, and business for the Ordinary Level GCE/School Certificate Examination. In 1974 the teacher training program was phased out and the sixth form course was added, which offers arts and sciences at the advanced level, making the school the largest SDA school in the country. Agricultural and vocational courses are also offered. The enrollment in 1993 was 1,212. The school celebrated its fortieth anniversary in October 1993.

Headmasters: N. C. Maberly, 1955-1956; H. I. Dunton, 1957-1961; W. L. Parker, 1961-1962; E. B. Christie, 1963-1964; J. D. Dorland, 1965-1967; C. Y. Kyereme, 1967-1976; I. T. Agboka, 1976-1981; I. K. Boateng, 1981-1984; S. Okrah, 1984-1985; C. A. Mensah, 1985-1987; J. A. Manu, 1987-1990; F. Boadi-Suadwa, 1990-1992; D. K. Obeng, 1992- .

BELARUS. A republic that is a sovereign independent state of eastern Europe. It borders Poland on the west, Latvia and Lithuania on the north, Russia on the east, and Ukraine on the south.

Belarus occupies an area of 80,309 square miles (208,000 square kilometers) and has a population (1994) of 10.4 million. Byelorussians are in the majority. Byelorussia was divided into two parts: the eastern part belonged to Russia, and the western part was Polish territory. In 1939 it was united into one republic. It became an independent state known as Belarus when the USSR was disbanded on Dec. 26, 1991.

Seventh-day Adventist Statistics. The territory of Belarus comprises the Belarus Conference, an attached field of the Euro-Asia Division. Statistics (1994) for *Belarus:* churches, 18; members, 3,071; ordained ministers, 8. Conference headquarters are at Minsk.

Development of SDA Work. The SDA message came to Byelorussia in 1924 and the first company was organized in the village of Zhoekino, Pinsk, Brest region. In 1925 the message penetrated into other parts of Byelorussia as well. By 1930 the republic had 6 churches with a membership of 215.

By 1960 the membership of the Seventh-day Adventist Church in Byelorussia numbered 550. There was no church organization.

In 1990 at the General Conference session, the Euro-Asia Division was organized, and the Belarus Conference became part of the Baltic Union. By the end of 1992 the conference had 18 churches and 2,610 members. In 1993 the Baltic Union Conference became part of the Trans-European Division, with the Belarus Conference remaining in the Euro-Asia Division as an attached field.

BELARUS CONFERENCE. *See* Belarus; Euro-Asia Division.

BELCHAMBERS, MARION HULDA (c. 1886-1949). Conference office worker and teacher in India, one of the early Seventh-day Adventists in India. As a child she attended the first Sabbath school in Calcutta, which had been opened by the pioneer group of SDA missionaries to India. She attended the first SDA school in India, which opened in 1899. In 1903 she was baptized and began her work with the mission, first as a church school teacher at Karmatar and Calcutta, and then as assistant to Mrs. M. M. Quantock, who was then treasurer of the India Mission. Later she served as secretary-treasurer successively of the Northwest India Union, Northeast India Union, and Western India Union. Her last years of service were spent in the office of the publishing house at Poona and in the division office.

BELDEN, FRANKLIN E. (1858-1945). Publishing house worker and songwriter, nephew of Ellen G. White. With Edwin Barnes he was musical editor of *Hymns and Tunes* (1886); later he was a superintendent at the Review and Herald Publishing House. He wrote hundreds of Sabbath school songs and hymns, in most cases both words and music. Although it has been remarked that the volume of his output exceeded its quality, the present *Seventh-day Adventist Hymnal* retains 16 of his tunes and a dozen of his lyrics. At the turn of the century he entered into certain business transactions relating to songbook publishing, which, although faithfully carried out by the publishers, led him to feel that he had been unfairly treated. This supposed grievance laid the foundation for a course of action that led to his separation from the church about 1907.

BELÉM ADVENTIST HOSPITAL (Hospital Adventista de Belém). A 100-bed general hospital owned by the North Brazil Union Mission and operated by an administrator and a medical director appointed by an administrative committee formed by members of the union and three missions. It is housed in a two-story brick and concrete structure situated in Belém, capital of Pará, Brazil, on the Belém-Brasília Highway. Built with funds from the Thirteenth Sabbath Offering overflow for the fourth quarter of 1949, it was opened on Apr. 10, 1953. With a capacity of 27 beds, it offered a laboratory, pharmacy, and X-ray facilities.

In 1962 the number of beds was increased to 40, even though the building was not enlarged, and the same year a first-aid service and a blood bank were added. In 1964 there were four doctors, eight graduate nurses, and 16 nurse's aides employed at the hospital. The Belém Hospital enjoys a good reputation among local doctors and the public.

In 1970 a new wing was inaugurated, increasing the hospital's capacity to 120 beds. New equipment was acquired, and the institution became one of the best equipped hospitals in north and northeast Brazil.

In 1993 the hospital medical staff included 22 missionary physicians and 23 missionary nurses. It has an ICU, children's ICU, and five modern surgery rooms.

Medical Directors: Elmer Bottsford, 1953-1955; Gunther Ehlers, 1955-1956; Oséas Florencio, 1956; Russell T. Smith, 1956-1957; Jetro Carvalho, 1958-1961; Zildomar Deucher, 1962-1972; Daniel J. dos Reis, 1972-1973; Rene Gross, 1974-1976; Alaor Jose Toledo, 1977-1984; Merari Reinert, 1985- .

BELGIAN FLEMISH PUBLISHING HOUSE. A publishing house (without a printing plant) formerly operated in Brussels by the Belgian-Luxembourg Conference.

At the turn of the century, pioneers published and used the evangelistic journal *Tekenen des Tijds* and the health magazine *Leven en Gezondheid* to arouse interest in the third angel's message. Publications were later supplied by the Netherlands Publishing House, but because of Belgium's predominantly Catholic population, with its different needs, an independent Belgian-Flemish Publishing House was established in 1966.

Educational books—*Praktische Gids voor de Vorming van de Personnlijkheid*—were published, in addition to the monthly health journal, *Leven en Gezondheid.* Dutch translations of various Ellen White books, including *The Great Controversy,* were published in close collaboration with the Netherlands Publishing House.

The publishing house closed in 1989.

Managers: Roger Merckx, 1969-1974; Jean Geeroms, 1974-1986; Henri Van Der Veken, 1986-1989.

BELGIAN-LUXEMBOURG CONFERENCE. *See* Belgium; Euro-Africa Division.

BELGIUM. A constitutional monarchy in Western Europe with an area of 11,779 square miles (30,500 square kilometers) and an estimated population (1994) of 10 million, divided between the Germanic Flemings and the French-speaking Walloons. Both French and Flemish are used as official languages. The religion of the people is mainly Roman Catholic, but there are a few Protestants and Jews. The constitution guarantees civil and religious liberty.

At the time of the Reformation the territory that is now Belgium and the Netherlands (the Low Countries) was controlled by Spain. Spain's attempts to eradicate Protestantism among the Dutch of the northern part of this territory led to their revolt and the establishment of the Netherlands. The southern part of this area remained Catholic and was later controlled by Austria. In 1815 the Low Countries were again united under the Dutch sovereignty, but in 1830 Belgium declared its independence from the Netherlands.

Seventh-day Adventist Statistics. The territory of Belgium constitutes part of the Belgian-Luxembourg Conference, which is part of the Franco-Belgian Union Conference, which, in turn, is part of the Euro-Africa Division. Statistics (1993): churches, 25; members, 1,532; ordained ministers, 10; credentialed missionaries, 3; licensed ministers, 7; licensed missionaries, 5. Headquarters for Belgian-Luxembourg Conference: Rue Ernest Allard 11-13, 1000 Brussels, Belgium.

Institutions. Maison de Retraite.

Development of Seventh-day Adventist Work. In 1897 the first French-speaking SDA missionary, C. Augsburger, entered Belgium from Switzerland and established himself in Angleur, near Liège. C. Grin joined him in 1898. As a result of their work, several families accepted the SDA message, and in July 1899

J. Erzberger organized a church of 10 members in Jemeppe, a suburb of Liège. In 1901 Augsburger returned to Switzerland, and in 1902 Grin died. In 1903 J. Curdy took charge of the work in Belgium, and in 1907 Gustave Roth replaced him. During this time Brussels, Charleroi, and Narmur were entered. Until 1904, when R. G. Klingbeil began to work with success in the Flemish language in Antwerp, all work had been done in the French-speaking part of the country.

At first the work in the French section of Belgium was under the direction of the Central European Conference; later it was under the Latin Union. The work in Flemish was under the West German Union Conference. In 1910 the two sections were united as a part of the West German Union. As the work progressed, the colporteur work was organized, evangelistic meetings were held, baptisms took place, and churches were organized. The Sabbath School, Home Missionary, and Young People's departments were so well organized that despite many privations brought on by the German occupation of 1914-1918 the activities of these various departments continued.

In 1919 the territory of Belgium was organized as the Belgian Conference under the Latin Union, with Jacob Wibbens as president, and with a membership of 257. The work prospered in the years between the two world wars. The Antwerp church built the first Seventh-day Adventist chapel in Belgium. In 1926 the conference purchased a large building in Brussels with halls for two churches (French and Flemish), and with offices for the conference and for the Book and Bible House. Ingathering was introduced with excellent results. Missionaries were sent to different countries. By Dec. 30, 1940, there were 15 churches, with 624 members, in the conference.

World War II was a period of great trial because of the bombings. At Liège the church and the pastor's home were completely destroyed. The work was hindered, and the departments had to be reorganized.

Since the war, the SDA message has been preached in unentered cities, and a number of new churches have been added to the conference. Work is carried on through Flemish and French Bible correspondence courses, with encouraging results. Since the 1960s, stop-smoking programs have been held in most of the large cities. Most evangelistic campaigns begin with Bible and archaeology multivision slide shows. By this means much prejudice is broken down. The territory of Luxembourg was attached to Belgium in 1968, thus forming the Belgian-Luxembourg Conference (*see* Luxembourg).

BELGRANO ADVENTIST MEDICAL CLINIC (Clínica Médica Adventista Belgrano). A 14-bed general acute hospital owned by the Austral Union Conference, situated in the residential district of Belgrano, in Buenos Aires, Argentina. It began operation in 1959, and represents Seventh-day Adventist medical work in an area of approximately 10 million people. It is administered by a medical director and a business manager responsible to an administrative board that includes representatives of the union conference, the Belgrano Clinic, and the local conference.

The hospital has specialists in ophthalmology, orthopedics, otorhinolaryngology, and dentistry, a room for major surgery, and offices for general practitioners. It also offers services in obstetrics, urology, pediatrics, gynecology, cardiology, and hematology.

When the clinic was opened in 1959, services were limited to outpatients (doctors' consulting offices, laboratory, X-ray, and hydrotherapy), but soon it was expanded to accommodate surgery and some beds for inpatients. In 1979 a total of 28,525 square feet (2,650 square meters) were added. In 1980 and 1981 a tower of 11,840 square feet (1,100 square meters) was added that requires the services of several more physicians and nurses.

The first medical director was C. E. Drachenberg, who worked alone for a while accompanied solely by two nurses, until Dr. Klinton Weiss and more nurses joined the clinic. The first head nurse was Mercedes Peverini.

Medical Directors: C. E. Drachenberg, 1959-1963; Oldemar Beskow, 1963-1978; Pedro Tabuenca, 1978-1983; Oldemar Beskow, 1983-1993; René A. Leichner, 1993- .

BELIZE (formerly known as British Honduras). A parliamentary democracy situated on the east coast of Central America, bordered by Mexico on the north and Guatemala on the west and south. Its area is 8,867 square miles (22,965 square kilometers). The population (1994) is 209,000. There is a complex racial mixture of European, Maya, Creole, Carib, Syrian, and Chinese elements. English is the official language. However, Spanish is widely used, and Carib and Maya are used on a lesser scale. On Aug. 3, 1970, Belmopan became the new capital of the country. It is situated in the very center of the nation. The site is about 50 miles (80 kilometers) from Belize City, 55 miles (88 kilometers) from Stann Creek, and 30 miles (50 kilometers) from Benque Viejo del Carmen, in the Cayo district, which borders on Guatemala. One major contrast to the former capital is that it nestles 200 feet (61 meters) above sea level.

Seventh-day Adventist Statistics. The territory of Belize constitutes the Belize Mission, part of the Central American Union Mission, which in turn is part of the Inter-American Division. Statistics (1992) for *Belize:* churches, 33; members, 12,308; ordained ministers, 10; credentialed missionaries, 31; licensed ministers, 3; licensed missionaries, 61. Mission headquarters are at Belize City, Belize.

Institutions. Belize Adventist College.

Development of Seventh-day Adventist Work. *Beginnings.* SDA teachings were introduced into British Honduras by means of SDA publications. About 1885 Mrs. E. Gauterau, from the republic of Honduras, who had joined the SDA Church while in California, distributed publications in her home area and apparently went into British Honduras also. According to reports, T. H. Gibbs, a minister from New Orleans, visited Belize in 1887 and placed a reading rack on one of the principal streets, securing the services of one of the interested readers to keep it supplied with tracts. In December 1891 L. C. Chadwick, then president of the International Tract Society, visited Belize and found a small group of converts there. About this time F. J. Hutchins was sent to settle in the Bay Islands of the republic of Honduras; he came to Belize from time to time and in 1894 reported holding evangelistic meetings there. In 1893 J. C. Brooks canvassed there. In 1895 James A. Morrow settled in Belize and held regular weekly meetings at his house, reporting that he hoped to organize a church in the city soon.

Organization and Growth. From the beginning of the mission work in the area, British Honduras and the republic of Honduras, including the Bay Islands, were administered as a single mission field, and the statistics were reported together. At the turn of the century the headquarters for SDA work in the area (referred to as the Central American Mission) and a book depository were situated in Belize. The regular church congregation at Belize was reported to be about 50 persons in 1902.

In 1905 the combined membership for both countries, most of it in the Bay Islands, in Honduras, was reported at 160, organized in five churches and five companies. In 1906 the field was included in the West Indian Union Conference. In 1908 the Central American Mission was extended to include Guatemala and El Salvador, and the whole was organized as the Central American Conference, with 333 Sabbathkeepers. In 1913 the Central American Conference was reduced to the size of the original mission, and the next year it, along with some other areas, was transferred to the General Conference as a detached mission, the whole group being named the Northern Spanish American Missions. In 1918 the Honduras Mission (including both British Honduras and Honduras) was organized with a membership of 267. After several administrative transfers within the Inter-American Division, the mission was divided in 1930, and British Honduras and the Bay Islands were formed into a separate mission field. At that time British Honduras had only one church, with a membership of 56. By the time the mission was reorganized in its present territory in 1937, the membership had increased to 385, with the addition of seven churches. At the end of 1944 there were 12 churches and 422 members in this mission, which earlier that year had been attached to the British West Indies Union Mission. In 1952 the British Honduras Mission, which at the beginning of that year had 15 churches and 486 members, was returned to the Central American Union.

Laypersons have played a prominent part in the growth of the SDA Church in British Honduras. In 1930 I. D. Sabido, a member of the Belize church, sold books and gave Bible studies at San Pedro, a small fishing village on Ambergris Cay. The fishermen carried the new doctrine to Pembroke Hall on the northern mainland, where they sold fish. In 1931 two lay members, Mrs. Amy Campbell and Mrs. C. A. Gill, held meetings at Pembroke Hall. As a result of this work almost the entire village was won. Some families from there later moved to another village called Calcutta, which today is composed mainly of SDAs and has a large church school. In 1934 Mrs. Gill organized a Sabbath school at Corozal, near the Mexican border. The work in the Stann Creek area in the south was opened by another laymember, C. E. Overstreet.

In the Cayo district, in the western part of the country, the seed of Seventh-day Adventism was first sown by Violet James and a couple by the name of Raisin. In 1968 Aquilino Jesse was sent to look after the interest and help advance the work. He immediately organized a branch Sabbath school. This was followed a few months later by an evangelistic effort, after which six persons were baptized. Today there are a large number of believers. In April of 1972 Petronilo Romero, an active laymember, was asked to leave his hometown in Progresso to reside in Punta Gorda for the purpose of beginning SDA work in an organized way. When he arrived, he began preaching. Today many persons are members of the church as a result of his efforts in this southern district of the country.

BELIZE ADVENTIST COLLEGE. A coeducational school on the secondary level located about 10 miles (16 kilometers) northeast of Belize City in Central America. It is connected to the city by a paved highway. Belize International Airport is located about 10-12 miles (16-20 kilometers) from Belize City on the Belize-Corozal road, about two hours' ride by car from the college campus. The school was established in 1969.

About five miles (eight kilometers) to the north of BAC is the beautiful coastal town of Corozal, this being the main shopping center of the district. The college campus covers an area of about 80 acres (32 hectares) of flat, rocky but fertile land, of which about one third is under sugarcane cultivation. However, efforts are now being made to cultivate the remaining land with vegetables and fruit trees.

A primary school had been in operation in the Calcutta Village area for approximately 20 years before this institution came into being. The need for a Christian education center was felt as early as 1960, but it was not until the early part of 1968 that things began to take some shape when a meeting was held between a representative of the Department of Education of Belize and the local leaders of the Calcutta Seventh-day Adventist Church. A positive agreement was reached, and in the second half of the year the clearing of the site was begun.

Under the leadership of Elder Winston D. Cunningham, president of the mission at that time, the members of the district churches began the construction of classrooms early in 1969. In September of the same year, the Adventist Vocational College (now Belize Adventist College), proudly opened its doors to 53 students, becoming also the fifty-third secondary school in the Inter-American Division of Seventh-day Adventists. Since then Belize Adventist College has welcomed an ever-increasing number of students each year.

Principals: James Bechtel, 1970-1972; Wilbert Oliver, 1972-1974; R. Elden Ford, 1977-1979; Arnold McLean, 1980-1982; Donaldo Clarke, 1983-1986; Carlos Edwards, 1987-1988; Ellis Coe, 1989-1994; Aquilino Jesse, 1994- .

BELIZE MISSION. *See* Belize; Inter-American Division.

BELL, GOODLOE HARPER (1832-1899). Educator and author. He was born, the eldest of 12 children, at Watertown, New York, and studied at Oberlin College.

At 19 he taught his first country school, but overwork placed him in the Battle Creek Sanitarium, where he accepted the Seventh-day Adventist faith, having been earlier a Baptist, and, for a time, a Disciple. After his health improved he began a private school for SDA children in the community. In 1872 he opened a school, under the auspices of the General Conference, which later became Battle Creek College. The following year Sidney Brownsberger was made principal. Subsequently Bell became head of the English Department. In 1881 Bell, who was considered a severe disciplinarian and who strongly advocated the principles of education set forth by Ellen G. White, clashed sharply with the principal, Alexander McLearn, on the operation of the college. As a result, the school was closed for a year, and Bell resigned and became principal of the newly established South Lancaster Academy in Massachusetts. After two years there he returned to Battle Creek and established a monthly called *The Fireside Teacher,* gave private instruction, particularly in English, and devoted considerable time to the preparation of textbooks in that subject. His wide interests led him to original field research in botany and natural history, and he was interested in painting, architecture, and music.

Bell made a noteworthy contribution to the development and molding of Sabbath schools, modeling them after the day school, with recitations, records, and thorough scholarship. He prepared a series of eight books for class use. When the General Sabbath School Association was formed in 1878, he was made the first recording secretary, and later the president. Among his published works are *Natural Method in English, Rhetoric and Higher English,* and a series of three grammar textbooks.

BELLA VISTA ADVENTIST ACADEMY. A coeducational day school with grades K-12. It is operated by Bella Vista Hospital as an Antillian Union school. It is accredited by the Puerto Rico Department of Education. The school opened in 1955 in Dr. Dunscombe's home with 10 students. William Barney was the first teacher for the one-room school.

The school continued expanding and now is located in three buildings that have 15 classrooms, three offices, and the library. The campus is on the Bella Vista Hospital grounds. Student enrollment in 1993 totaled 286. There are 21 faculty members composed of principal, librarian, guidance counselor, secretary, Spanish elementary teacher, music teacher, seven elementary teachers, and eight secondary teachers.

Principals: William Barney, 1955-1956; Ralph E. Williams, 1956-1962; G. L. Olsen, 1962-1965; Martha Duncan, 1965-1967; R. D. Hayden, 1967-1968; Maude Pearson, 1968-1971; Joseph L. Miller, 1971-1978; Aaron Moon, 1978-1980; Flora Alvarez, 1980-1982; Eli Toro, 1982-1983; Esther Brugnoni, 1983- .

BELLA VISTA HOSPITAL. A 157-bed general hospital situated at an elevation of 1,000 feet (305 meters) on a mountain ridge about two miles (three kilometers) from the city of Mayagüez on the western coast of the island of Puerto Rico. It is owned and operated by the Antillian Union. The hospital is fully accredited by the Joint Commission on Accreditation of Health Care Organizations and the Department of Health of the commonwealth of Puerto Rico.

The property consists of a modern four-story hospital building of reinforced concrete, a nurses' home, staff apartments, family residences, a new church building, and an academy. In 1960 an auditorium, seating about 300, was added.

In 1972 construction began on a new wing that doubled the capacity of the hospital. In addition to more beds, new surgery suites, a new pharmacy, a new central supply area, a new intensive care unit, a new kitchen and cafeteria, and other new services were added. Remodeling of the original building is taking place. In 1992 there were 550 employees, including 14 physicians, two dentists, and 220 graduate nurses, in the hospital and its clinics.

The institution is operated on an open-staff basis, with an administrator. About 200 qualified physicians and specialists use its facilities, which include medical, surgical, obstetrical, X-ray with CT scan, nuclear medicine, bone densitometry, cardio respiratory therapy, clinical laboratory, health education, one-day surgery, endoscopy, and physical therapy units. There also is an invasive digital substraction catheterization/angiography laboratory.

The minimum daily census of patients in 1992 was 77, with a maximum of 156. In that year 8,779 patients were admitted, and 44,779 patient days of care were given. More than 2,366 major operations and 4,147 minor operations were performed, and 686 babies were delivered. An additional 36,006 patients were treated at the polyclinic that is operated by the hospital in the city. In May 1993 the hospital opened a pediatric satellite outpatient clinic in San Sebastian. It also operates a satellite dental clinic in Ponce, on the southern part of the island. Many patients come from the nearby islands to be treated at the hospital.

The site for the hospital was chosen in 1947. A group of Seventh-day Adventist physicians (including Colby William Dunscombe and Charles B. Moore) were already practicing in Mayagüez, operating a regular polyclinic and a charity clinic. L. L. Dunn, the first administrator, supervised the construction of the hospital building and the purchase of equipment, which were partially financed by Hill-Burton funds. The hospital accepted its first patient on Jan. 1, 1954. During the first 10 years of its operation 27,600 patients were admitted.

On Aug. 15, 1965, a three-year accredited School of Nursing was opened in affiliation with Antillian College (about four miles [six kilometers] away). In 1972 the associate degree program was begun at Antillian College. In 1973 the hospital three-year diploma program was terminated. The hospital and the local church share in the support of a nine-grade school for English-speaking students. Along with Antillian Adventist University, the hospital has developed a four-year nursing program, a two-year respiratory therapy technician program, and a two-year medical technician degree. It also has its own internship program for physicians.

Medical Directors: C. W. Dunscombe (acting), 1954; C. B. Moore, 1955; C. M. Donaldson, 1956; C. W. Dunscombe, 1957; C. M. Donaldson, 1958; H. F. Evans, 1959; R. L. Horner, 1960-1961; B. H. Westphal, 1962; C. M. Donaldson, 1963-1971; Benjamin LeDuc, 1972- .

BELLAH, CHARLES GREELEY (1873-1964). Literature evangelist leader, administrator, author. At the beginning of the century he and his wife spent four years in colporteur work, and by 1906 he was directing the book work in the Missouri Conference. From 1907 to 1914 he directed the colporteurs in the Central Union, which in those days led in book sales. Following this, Bellah did evangelistic work in Missouri and for several years was pastor of the Central church in St. Louis. From 1922 to 1924 he served as president of the Kansas Conference, and for the following seven years carried heavy pastoral responsibilities.

Because of serious illness he retired in 1931, settling in Fredricktown, Missouri, chosen because there were no Seventh-day Adventists in town. The Bellahs aided in the establishment of a debt-free church there in 1950. He authored nine books.

BELLEAU, GEORGE S. (1895-1964). Departmental secretary, administrator. A native of Quebec, he first came in contact with the teachings of the Seventh-day Adventist Church in 1913. He immediately enrolled at Canadian Union College to prepare for the ministry. In 1918 he began his service to the church in the Idaho Conference, following which he worked among the French-speaking people of eastern Canada and served for a time as mission superintendent in Brazil.

After graduation from the ministerial and educational course at Walla Walla College in 1927, he served in various capacities in the Oregon Conference and as MV and educational secretary in the North Pacific Union. He later served as president of the Idaho and Northern New England conferences.

BELLINDA HOSPITAL. *See* Anacapa Adventist Hospital.

BELZ, FRANCISCO (1866-1948). Pioneer teacher and evangelist in Brazil. He was born in Germany and emigrated with his family to Brazil, where his father was among the first in that country to join the Seventh-day Adventist Church. In 1899 he was baptized, and two years later, in 1901, entered denominational work as a teacher of a primary school. He received his education at the SDA Brusque missionary training school at Gaspar Alto (near Brusque), Santa Catarina, in Brazil. His name appears in the *SDA Yearbook* between 1909, when he was listed as a licentiate in the Santa Catarina and Paraná Conference, and 1928, when he was listed as an ordained minister in the Rio-Espirito Santo Mission. In between these dates he is listed also in the Rio Grande do Sul and Espirito Santo missions.

BELZ, WILHELM (GUILHERME) (fl. 1895). Reported to be the first Seventh-day Adventist in Brazil. As a child in Pomerania, he learned that according to the Bible the seventh day is the Sabbath. However, when he questioned his minister and his mother about the matter, he was led to dismiss the subject from his mind by the reply that Christ had changed the day of rest. Many years later, after the family had moved to Brazil, he found in the home of his elder brother, Carl, a copy of Uriah Smith's *Gedanken über das Buch Daniel* ("Thoughts on the Book of Daniel"), in which he read that the papacy had changed the Sabbath. He began an investigation, read and reread his Bible, and finally came to the conclusion that there was no divine authority for the change and that the seventh-day Sabbath was still the day appointed by God for worship. After a while he determined to observe it even though he was not aware of other Christians' doing so. His influence led several others in the neighborhood to begin keeping the seventh-day Sabbath some years before SDA missionaries reached Brusque, near Gaspar Alto, Santa Catarina, where he lived. He joined the SDA Church about 1895 and was "elected librarian of the [Brusque] tract society" *(Review and Herald* 72:636, Oct. 1, 1895).

BENDER, URBANUS (1877-1959). Minister, educator, and administrator in South Africa, West Indies, and the United States. He became a Seventh-day Adventist while still in his teens through reading. Upon graduation from Union College he assisted in city missions in Nebraska as cook, nurse, and general helper. Later he worked in Arkansas, first as a minister, and then as conference president (1901-1906). He was the first president of the West Indian Union (1907-1913), president of the Montana Conference (1913-1916), successively principal of Spion Kop College, administrator of Solusi Mission, and president of Cape Conference (1916-1927), teacher at Oakwood College (1927-1928), teacher at Mount Pisgah and Fletcher academies, minister in the North Carolina Conference (1928-1939), and minister in the Michigan Conference (1939-1946).

BENEVOLENCE, SYSTEMATIC. *See* Systematic Benevolence; Tithe.

BENGALI BOYS' SCHOOL. *See* Raymond Memorial High School.

BENGALI GIRLS' SCHOOL. *See* Kellogg-Mookerjee Memorial Seminary.

BENGEL, JOHANN ALBRECHT (1687-1752). German Lutheran theologian, textual scholar, and commentator. He predicted that "the appearance of the coming of Jesus Christ," the destruction of the beast, and the imprisonment of Satan would take place about 1836, and would be followed by *two* millenniums, the first a golden age on earth, the second the reign of the saints in heaven (Bengel, *Gnomon of the New Testament,* ed. Andrew R. Fausset, vol. 4, p. 226; vol. 5, pp. 365, 367, 368, 373). He described this "appearance" of Christ's coming as separate from the "one coming of Christ in glory, at the last day" *(ibid.,* vol. 5, p. 363). Yet for many in Europe who did not necessarily follow his elaborately contrived chronology or his double millennium and double Second Advent, his writings served as a call to prepare for "the appearance of His coming," which he called "the first dawn of the brightness of His actual coming" *(ibid.,* vol. 4, p. 232). His predictions for 1836 led many in Germany and Russia, for example, to look for "the advent near." In fact, during the time of the Millerite movement in America, Bengel's doctrine in summary was published in an English translation, in which a table listed the beast's "overthrow at the appearing of the Lord" for 1836 (John C. F. Burk, *A Memoir of the Life and Writings of John Albert Bengel,* trans. R. F. Walker, p. 294). Bengel is mentioned in a Millerite paper as "looking for the advent about this time" *(The Signs of the Times* 6:36, Sept. 20, 1843), and referred to similarly by J. N. Andrews *(Review and Herald* 55:10, Jan. 1, 1880).

BENGHAZI ADVENTIST HOSPITAL. A 32-bed general hospital formerly operated by the Middle East Division in Benghazi, Cyrenaica, Libya, immediately east of the main commercial section of the city. It was administered by a medical director. The institution operated Medical, Surgical, and Obstetrical departments, and provided laboratory, X-ray, and pharmaceutical services. In 1964 a school of nursing was opened for training registered nurses and nurse's aids.

The institution was opened in 1956 by Dr. Roy S. Cornell, who had arrived Feb. 2, 1955, and had supervised the remodeling of a war-damaged hotel building secured for the hospital, purchased equipment, and arranged for a staff, while assisting the Libyan government as chief surgeon at the government hospital in Benghazi. The hospital was formally opened May 21, 1956. A year later Dr. Cornell contracted acute paralytic poliomyelitis, which left him completely paralyzed and unable to continue directing the project that he had pioneered.

The hospital was operated by the Nile Union Mission, until, at the end of 1958, it came under the direct control of the Middle East Division. Fakhry Naguib was the first business manager; the first nurses were Mrs. Rafic Issa and Dallal Kotaira (later Mrs. Munir Masloub), who, with Rafic Issa, business office assistant, and Munir Masloub, laboratory and X-ray technician, were active in establishing the work of the hospital. Miriam Bruce was the first director of nurses (from September 1956).

By 1963 minor construction provided for expanded laboratory and kitchen facilities and increased the patient capacity from 27 to 32. However, already by late 1961, because of the need for expanded medical services, it had been decided to relocate the hospital. A member of the royal family made available for purchase 10 acres (40,000 square meters) of choice property. Community support was enlisted, and oil companies operating in the area contributed $750,000. Construction on the project began in 1964, and on Jan. 17, 1968, the 60-bed hospital, valued at US$1.4 million, was dedicated and opened to the public, with a staff of 105. On Nov. 23, 1969, the new Revolutionary Command Council, whose policy required that all medical services be owned and administered by the government, nationalized the hospital. The expatriate staff, consisting of 48 families and single workers from the United States, the Philippines, Indonesia, India, and several Arab countries of the Middle East, were relocated outside the country.

Medical Directors: Roy S. Cornell, 1956-1957; J. P. Munsey (acting), 1957-1960; William Wagner, 1960-1963; D. Clifford Ludington, 1963-1968; G. N. Benson, 1968-1969.

BENIN (formerly Dahomey). A republic in West Africa, formerly colonized by France. It received its independence on Aug. 1, 1960. It has an area of 43,483 square miles (112,621 square kilometers) and a population (1994) of 5.3 million. It is bounded on the north by Niger, on the east by Nigeria, on the west by

Togo and Burkina Faso, and on the south by the Gulf of Guinea. Agriculture is the principal occupation, the chief exports being palm kernels, palm oil, groundnuts, cotton, and coffee. Most of the people are animists, with some Muslims and Christians.

Seventh-day Adventist Work. The territory of Benin constitutes the Benin Mission, which is part of the Sahel Union Mission and thus part of the Africa-Indian Ocean Division. The country, then known as Dahomey (its name was changed to Benin in 1975), was first entered by an SDA in 1957 when Georges Vaysse, a European colporteur, canvassed there for about two years. As a result of his efforts, two men accepted the SDA message.

In 1963 the West African Union asked H. Kempf, president of the Ivory Coast Mission, to make a tour of Dahomey and Togo to explore the possibilities of establishing permanent work there. In 1964, while working in Togo, he visited Dahomey and won converts. The Togo-Dahomey Mission was established the same year. Work progressed gradually. In 1986 Benin became an organized mission. At the end of 1992 there were 1 church, 10 companies, and 551 members.

BENIN MISSION. *See* Africa-Indian Ocean Division; Benin.

BENJAMIN, WILLIAM ANTHONY (1884-1969). Pioneer in General Conference insurance. He was a native of Michigan and entered denominational employ in 1931, serving as business manager of Southern Missionary College. Four years later he inaugurated the insurance service of the General Conference, and was in charge of it until his retirement in 1957.

BENSHEIM-AUERBACH OLD PEOPLE'S HOME. A home that had 20 apartments for the aged, situated at Bensheim-Auerbach, south of Darmstadt, in the famous "Bergstrasse," the part of Germany with the mildest climate. It was established on May 1, 1960. There was a chapel in the home that also served as a place of assembly for the local church members. This institution was closed in 1979.

Superintendents: O. K. Fuchs, 1960-1962; Karl Koehler, 1962-1963; J. Buerger, 1963-1968; Hans Graf, 1969-1979.

BENSON, HARRY FARMER (1882-1947). Missionary, teacher. He was baptized in 1901, entered the ministry in 1904, taught at Beechwood Academy (1905), and in 1906 began 35 years of mission service in Japan, Korea, and Malaya. He was at various times secretary-treasurer, district mission director, and union mission superintendent. During furloughs he taught at Mount Vernon Academy and Atlantic Union College. He was transferred in 1940 from Japan Junior College to Penang, Malaya, for pastoral work, and returned to the United States in 1942.

BEQUESTS, ANNUITY CONTRACTS, TRUSTS, AND LIFE INCOME AGREEMENTS. *See* Wills, Charitable Gift Annuities, Trusts, Life Income, and Other Charitable Agreements.

BEQUIA SEVENTH-DAY ADVENTIST SECONDARY SCHOOL. A coeducational nonboarding high school, situated at Port Elizabeth, Bequia, St. Vincent and the Grenadines, West Indies. The school was begun in September 1950, with L. A. Gittens as principal. It is operated by the East Caribbean Conference. The school offers five years of secondary instruction in academic preparation for examinations administered by the Caribbean Examinations Council (CXC). The school was accredited as a secondary school by the Board of Regents of the General Conference of Seventh-day Adventists, and the relevant certificate was issued July 9, 1990.

Principals: Anthony Ollivierre, 1990- .

BEREAN LIBRARY. A set of books selected for the training of lay evangelistic workers through individual or group reading in accordance with a plan called the Missionary Reading Circle and conducted through the pages of the *Review and Herald,* the *Missionary Magazine,* and the *Youth's Instructor,* under the title "Berean Library Studies." The idea first appeared in the *Review and Herald* (76:776, Nov. 28, 1899). The Berean Library is first listed in the *General Conference Bulletin* for the third quarter of 1899 (p. 65). It was published by the Review and Herald Publishing Association, although the early titles carried the imprint Berean Library, Battle Creek, Michigan. At first the plan was to issue the selected titles, usually reprints in paperbound form, quarterly, and the library was advertised as a periodical (annual subscription 75 cents), but apparently the plan was abandoned, and only 12 numbers had been listed by 1915. The series was carried as a separate set in the Review and Herald catalog until 1921 and was afterward discontinued.

The library as listed in 1905 included: (1) *Steps to Christ,* by Ellen G. White; (2) *Thoughts on Daniel,* and (3) *Thoughts on Revelation,* both by Uriah Smith; (4) *Christian Principles,* by S.M.I. Henry; (5) *Looking Unto Jesus,* by Uriah Smith; (6) *History of the Sabbath,* by J. N. Andrews; (7) *Great Nations of Today* (pamphlet), by A. T. Jones; (8) *Battle of the Century* (pamphlet), by P. T. Magan; and (9) *Miraculous Powers* (pamphlet), by M. E. Cornell. The 1915 catalog listed numbers (10) *Our Paradise Home,* by S. H. Lane; (11) *Religious Liberty in America,* by C. M. Snow; and (12) *The Coming King,* by J. Edson White. The catalog listed the following substitutions for the original selections: (4) *His Glorious Appearing* [James White?]; (5) *Sabbath in the Scriptures,* and (6) *Sabbath in History,* two parts of a two-book reprint of the *History of the Sabbath,* by J. N. Andrews; (7) *Conflict Between Capital and Labor,* by E. T. Russell; (8) *Here and Hereafter,* by Uriah Smith; and (9) *Bible Footlights,* by William H. Granger. The 1916 and later catalogs listed *Religious Liberty in America* as number 4 of the set, which by then had only seven or eight titles. Several volumes included in the series are in print at the present time.

In its early period the editorial committee included L. A. Hoopes, S. N. Haskell, A. T. Jones, W. C. Sisley, and S. H. Lane.

BERGER, ALBERTO (fl. 1895). One of two brothers (the other was J. Frederico) who were among the earliest Seventh-day Adventist colporteurs in Brazil. Apparently they were originally from Germany and emigrated first to the United States and then to Brazil, where they arrived in August 1895 and worked among the German settlers in Rio Grande do Sul for a short time, after which they returned to Germany.

BERGER, J. FREDERICO. *See* Berger, Alberto.

BERGHEIM MÜHLENRAHMEDE (Mühlenrahmede Retreat Center). A property consisting of about five acres (two hectares) of land, with a building completed in 1961 by the Grundstückverwaltung der Siebenten-Tags-Adventisten in Westdeutschland (the Seventh-day Adventist Building Corporation in Western Germany) providing accommodations for 215 guests, a large dining room and meeting hall seating 150 (which can be enlarged, if necessary, by opening the sliding doors to the vestibule), and also a library and a music room. It is situated on the hillside above the Rahmede Valley in the Sauerland forests near the town of Altena in North Rhine-Westphalia, western Germany, about 40 miles (64 kilometers) east of Düsseldorf. The center is owned and operated by the North German Union.

The institution provides opportunities for rest and recreation for church members and their friends. Its facilities are used also for ministerial meetings, colporteur institutes, church officers' and laypersons' meetings, Bible schools for youth and adults, children's and veterans' camps, and courses in diet.

The institution originated in 1953 when the Hessia-Westphalian Conference established in Evingsen, near Altena, Westphalia, a small recreation camp for SDA young people, which consisted of three small wooden houses. Later these buildings were moved to Mühlenrahmede, where, about 1960, the construction of the present structure was begun. After several alterations in 1993, 104 persons can be accommodated. The meeting hall seats 120. In the 1980s a sports field, a playground for children, and a small animal precinct were added. In 1993 the property covered 8.4 acres (3.4 hectares).

Managers: Ernst August Schulz, 1961-1964; Helmut Gaffron, 1964-1973; Wolfgang Thieme, 1973-1980; Wolfgang Oldenhoff, 1980-1984; Reinhard Fuchs, 1984- .

BERGMAN, GEORGE CLYDE (1898-1957). A Loma Linda graduate (1924), first Seventh-day Adventist missionary doctor sent to Ethiopia (1927). He married Gertrude Katherine Nelson in 1921. Largely because of Emperor Haile Selassie's confidence in him, he established the Taffari Makonnen Hospital in Dessie. To reach Dessie he, his wife, and baby had to travel 300 miles (500 kilometers) by horseback and mule caravan, and then he had to build the mission hospital himself. In 1932 he founded the Empress Zauditu Memorial Hospital in Addis Ababa, with his sister, Esther Bergman, as director of nursing education. She died there in 1935.

Bergman was called to serve in the United States Army in 1942, and received distinguished service medals for his services in inter-American affairs. In 1946 he entered private practice.

BERLIN HOSPITAL (Krankenhaus Waldfriede). A 230-bed acute-care hospital operated by the Euro-Africa Division in Berlin. It has six departments—internal medicine, surgery, gynecology, obstetrics, anesthesiology, and radiology—each headed by a department chief.

Founded on Apr. 15, 1920, the institution was called Waldfriede Sanitarium and Clinic. When in 1930 the sanitarium was enlarged, the name was changed to Waldfriede Hospital because of the requirements of the government health insurance program. From then on, it has been a registered hospital with three departments, each with two wards. Recognition as a sanitarium had already been granted by the regency of Potsdam, where the hospital was situated at the time. After the area was incorporated into Greater Berlin, the hospital came under municipal authorities (at that time, the public health office) of the metropolitan area of Berlin.

The institution was opened with 39 beds; later the number increased to 60; and through an extension in 1922-1923, to 110. Further enlargement in 1927-1928 brought the number of beds to 134 and later, in 1959, to 186, and in 1991 120 beds were registered by the senate of Berlin.

Many patients prefer the Waldfriede Hospital to other institutions because of the excellent care they receive and because of the friendly spirit evident there. The hospital runs internship and residency programs in each of the departments, and works with a closed staff program.

Up to 300 physicians from all over the city refer their patients to Waldfriede Hospital.

Since 1923 the hospital has had a nursing school with 65 students. The diploma is recognized by the German authorities.

In July 1993 a health center opened its doors. It is the first center attached to an acute-care hospital within the European Seventh-day Adventist health-care system and is under the leadership of a specialist in public health.

Medical Directors: L. E. Conradi, 1920-1955; G. R. Fenner, 1955-1975; A. Schwarz, 1975-1983; R. Noltze, 1983- .

Managers: E. A. Behrens, 1924-1928; Johannes Seefried, 1928-1935; Ernst Müller, 1935-1961; Hermann Leue, 1961-1970; Rudolf Arnold, 1970-1986; E. Scharfschwerdt, 1986- .

BERLIN-BRANDENBURG CONFERENCE. *See* Euro-Africa Division; Germany.

BERLIN-STEGLITZ OLD PEOPLE'S HOME. A 55-bed old people's home operated in Berlin, Germany, by the Berlin-Brandenberg Conference of the North German Union.

The need for a home for aged Seventh-day Adventists of the Berlin area became apparent after World War II. In 1956 a suitable house at 39 Grunewald Street, Berlin-Steglitz, was purchased and remodeled. The first patients moved in on June 1, 1957, and the home was opened officially on June 6, 1957, with 36 patient beds. Capacity in 1993 was 755 patient beds. At present (1993) the manager is Gerd Mollack, and the head nurse is Manda Brala.

BERMUDA CONFERENCE. The unit of church organization comprising the territory of Bermuda, and forming part of the Atlantic Union Conference, which in turn is part of the North American Division. Statistics (1993): churches, 8; members, 2,883; church schools, 1; ordained ministers, 7; licensed ministers, 2; teachers, 28. Headquarters: 41 King Street, Hamilton HM 19, Bermuda.

Institutions. Bermuda Institute.

Local churches: Devonshire, Hamilton (Hamilton, Pembroke), Hamilton Parish (Midland Heights), Somerset, Southampton, St. George's, and Warwick.

History. Seventh-day Adventist work began in Bermuda early in the 1890s when two SDAs, Marshall Enoch and his wife, emigrated from Nova Scotia. About the same time two brothers, Frank and Marquis Pogue, came from Minnesota as colporteurs. The first Bermudan converts were the R. T. Munroe family, who began observing the Sabbath after studying SDA publications bought from one of the Pogue brothers. In 1895, when Marshall Enoch heard of the Munroes, he visited them and arranged to hold weekly services in their home. From this Munroe family came a minister, several missionaries, Bible instructors, and nurses.

From 1901 until Bermuda was made a part of the Atlantic Union Conference in 1915, the work in the islands was directed by the General Conference as one of the "miscellaneous missions." The mission was fully organized in 1959, and was incorporated by an act of the Bermuda Parliament in 1960. In 1986 the Bermuda Mission became the Bermuda Conference.

The first Seventh-day Adventist minister sent to Bermuda was J. W. Bartlett, who organized a company in Hamilton on Mar. 16, 1901. During the pastorate of J. A. Morrow, the first permanent pastor (1903-1909), the first little church was built in Hamilton. This has been replaced since by a larger church on King Street. The new building, dedicated in 1949, and serving also as an evangelistic center, has been an important factor in the growth of the work in the islands.

The second church, begun in Southampton in 1926, was a small chapel erected on land donated by Profirio Gomez, and later enlarged. A new church building was erected and was dedicated on Dec. 19, 1964.

Another church was organized in St. George's in 1935. The members met in rented quarters until 1954. They bought the historic Cooper estate on York Street and remodeled the building into a church auditorium and Sabbath school rooms, and dedicated it free of debt in 1957. In 1984 a larger edifice was erected on Secretary Road in St. George's. A portion of the York Street church is being used as a Community Services center.

In 1965 the Warwick church was dedicated; in 1978 the Midland Heights church was dedicated. The new Somerset church was completed in 1983 and dedicated debt-free in the same year. In 1987 and 1990 new churches were opened in Devonshire and Pembroke, respectively.

Special emphasis was placed on evangelism following the 1950 General Conference session, when W. H. Branson, the newly elected General Conference president, challenged the world field to double the church membership during the coming quadrennium. The Bermuda Mission doubled its membership in less than two years: the 1950 total was 288; the 1952 total was 607.

Evangelism in Bermuda has been fostered in many ways through a number of radio and television programs. Tent, church, and school evangelism continue to constitute the thrust of witness to the island.

Since 1989 administrative posts have been filled by Bermudans.

Mission Superintendents/Conference Presidents: J. A. Morrow, 1903-1909; H. F. Taylor, 1913-1914; Eugene Leland, 1914-1919; E. C. Rowell, 1919-1921; H. W. Carr, 1921-1926; W. A. Sweany, 1926-1930; Alexander Houghton, 1930-1933; Joseph Capman, 1933-1938; O. R. Snipes, 1938-1939; J. F. Knipschild, Sr., 1939-1945; J. A. Toop, 1945-1949; Beaman Senecal, 1949-1956; H. R. Jenkins, 1956-1964; V. E. Kelstrom, 1964-1965; R. R. Adams, 1965-1968; H. C. Currie, 1968-1971; F. R. Aldridge, 1971-1974; R. H. Carter, 1974-1977; A. R. Goulbourne, 1977-1986; E. L. Richardson, 1986-1992; Carlyle C. Simmons, 1992- .

BERMUDA INSTITUTE. A coeducational elementary and secondary school located in Southampton, Bermuda. In 1898 a school was opened by the Enoch family, with Winnie M. Peebles as teacher. This was before a church was organized in Bermuda. In 1942 J. F. Knipschild, Sr., superintendent of the mission, was granted permission by the government to establish a school in Southampton Parish. Classes were conducted in rooms at the back of the old Southampton church until 1953, when an old homestead known as Sandringham was secured and remodeled into two classrooms. Another classroom was added in 1956.

On Nov. 16, 1961, Governor Major General Sir Julian Gascoigne officially opened a modern two-room primary department. June 9, 1965, saw the groundbreaking for a new library, science laboratory, assembly hall, kitchen, and classrooms to accommodate the increased enrollment.

With the introduction of the tenth grade in September of 1966, the enrollment rose to 200 and the faculty increased to nine. In 1967 a full secondary school year began with some 210 students and 11 teachers.

A third modern and fully equipped building valued at $125,000 was dedicated free of debt in March 1972. The phenomenal growth and excellent quality of its teaching soon resulted in full denominational accreditation for Bermuda Institute.

In 1981 ground was broken for the construction of an administration building and classrooms for the elementary school. It was completed in 1983.

In 1984 a building to facilitate vocational arts for the high school was added. To meet further expanding enrollment, the administration converted the assembly hall in the elementary school to three classrooms. In April 1993 a new elementary and administration building was opened free from debt.

Principals: R. E. Malcolm, 1967-1968; C. B. Skinner, 1968-1970; William Brown, Jr., 1970-1974; Howard Pires, 1974-1976; Gladwin R. Trott, 1976-1979; Mrs. Joseph Dixon (acting), 1980; Joseph Redcross, 1981-1982; Ian Kelly, 1982-1986; Rosemary Tyrrell, 1987-1991; Clayton McKnight, 1991- .

BERNSTEIN, OTTO O. (1874-1965). Evangelist, teacher, administrator. After hearing

Ellen White and other speakers at the 1888 General Conference session, he was inspired to become an evangelist. He enrolled in Union College during 1891, its opening year, and became known as an orator. He became a minister in the Minnesota Conference and was called to evangelism in England. Back in the United States he conducted a total of 77 major evangelistic campaigns during terms of service in Pennsylvania, Colorado, Kansas, and Nebraska. He was the first principal of Maplewood Academy, where he also taught Bible. He served as president of the New Jersey Conference and the Southern California Conference.

During 1934 Bernstein was in charge of a booth at the World's Fair in Chicago, where the worldwide work of the church was presented to the public and more than 500,000 pieces of literature were distributed.

BETHEL ACADEMY. *See* Wisconsin Academy.

BETHEL COLLEGE. A coeducational boarding school on the academy level, operated by the Southern Africa Union Conference, located in southern South Africa. It provides secondary training for a student body representing the African population in the territory of the union.

In 1993 enrollment was 551 (56 secondary, 495 junior college). The faculty numbered 27. About 52 percent of the students were from Seventh-day Adventist families and the rest from Christian backgrounds.

The college is affiliated with the local University of the Transkei and registered with the government. Students sit for external government examinations after the tenth and twelfth years, reaching a university entrance standard.

History. *Maranatha Mission.* The forerunner of Bethel College was the school at Maranatha Mission, situated in the Eastern Cape Colony 25 miles (40 kilometers) from Grahamstown, on 500 acres (200 hectares) of land donated by a layperson, Charles Sparrow. It was the first Seventh-day Adventist mission among the African people.

The school was opened by G. A. Ellingworth, its first principal, in 1909 with an enrollment of 60 students. The first among many trained during those early years were Amos Magalela, Agrippa Mzozoyana, Stanford Ntwana, Banford Scott, Shadrach Pikoli, Douglas Ntsikeni, Dode Kobe, and Griffiths Mayaba, all of whom later occupied responsible positions in the work. In 1910 the first four converts were baptized.

In 1916, when W. Claude Tarr was director of Maranatha Mission, the committee decided, because the African population was moving eastward, to move Maranatha Mission to the Transkei, an area of teeming African population.

Bethel Mission. In 1917 approximately 300 acres (120 hectares) of partly cultivated farmland, five miles (eight kilometers) from Butterworth, were purchased for £1,100. The first building was a small pole-and-mud church with a thatch roof. Soon other buildings were added, and the school was moved from Maranatha Mission. The new mission took the name Bethel.

One year after the opening of the work in the Transkei 30 converts were baptized, one of them being 100 years old. It was necessary for I. B. Burton and W. C. Tarr to work without the assistance of African teachers, inasmuch as none had yet completed their training. The first graduation from the Theological Department took place in 1920. The school served as the Bethel Training School for all African workers within the Union of South Africa.

Spion Kop Missionary Institution. From 1928 to 1937 the training school was operated in Natal and became known as the Spion Kop Missionary Institution, occupying the buildings vacated when the European training school, Spion Kop College, was moved to Helderberg.

Bethel College. At the end of 1937 the institution was transferred again to Bethel Mission, and was established on its present site. Its name was changed to Bethel Training College and changed again at the end of 1961 to Bethel College.

Beginning in 1955 the plant and facilities were expanded in order to provide for doubling the enrollment. Additions included a new church and a basement recreation hall (1955), a new cafeteria and a domestic science unit (1958), a remodeling of the administration building with a two-story frontage (1960), and extensive additions to the boys' dormitory (1962).

In 1974 additions to the girls' dormitory were made and a new science block was built.

The industrial program includes operating a dairy with a registered Friesland herd; also kitchen cabinet making. Bethel farm is productive, supplying milk to neighboring villages as well as to the Bethel community. By 1993 poultry farming was proving to be the backbone of the farming program.

Also by 1993 many of the old buildings had

been modernized and converted to new uses. A magnificent new administration building had been erected at the center of the college.

Principals—Spion Kop Missionary Institution: J. G. Siepman, 1928-1929; F. E. Thompson, 1930-1933; R. E. Ansley (acting), 1933-1934; E. D. Hanson, 1935-1937.

Bethel College: E. W. Tarr, 1938-1940; P. H. Mantell, 1941; E. W. Tarr, 1942-1944; A. V. Edwards, 1945-1947; S. W. Beardsell, 1948-1957; W. A. Hurlow, 1957-1963; R. G. Pearson, 1963-1970; R. A. Marx, 1971-1973; M. R. Siepman, 1973-1978; I. du Preez, 1979-1980; J. J. Mdakane, 1981-1990; T. H. Langeni, 1990-1992; S.B.M. Baduza (acting), 1992-1993; S. Lebese, 1993- .

BETHEL SANITARIUM (1917-1925). A health institution, earlier called the Alberta Sanitarium, operated by the Alberta Conference and the Western Canadian Union Conference between 1917 and 1925 at Calgary, Alberta, Canada. It occupied a two-story main building with 31 rooms and a number of outbuildings on a 23-acre (nine-hectare) property at Bowness Park, eight miles (13 kilometers) west of Calgary. Between 1920 and 1924 it treated between 200 and 400 patients a year, was supervised by a physician, and had a staff of nurses numbering from 5 to 20. Until 1922 the sanitarium operated a Physiotherapeutic Department in the city of Calgary. For some time it also offered nursing training in affiliation with one of the Seventh-day Adventist schools of nursing in the United States.

The sanitarium was an outgrowth of treatment rooms opened in Edmonton in 1903 by Frank L. Hommel, a graduate of Battle Creek Sanitarium. His work prospered so well that in 1908 a 28-room house, one of the largest in town, was rented to house his establishment, which had become known as the Alberta Sanitarium. According to the 1909 *Yearbook* (pp. 176, 190) an institution under the name of Alberta Sanitarium was opened in 1908 at Lacombe, on the campus of the present Canadian Union College (see *Western Canadian Tidings* 13:3, 4, Mar. 14, 1923; 13:1, Mar. 28, 1923). The *Yearbook* lists its assets at $4,000, capacity at 20 patients, and the number of patients treated in the preceding year is given as 250. In the 1910 *Yearbook* there is a notation that the sanitarium is not under conference control, though the *Yearbook* still lists the conference president as a member of the governing board. In 1911 Hommel went to Calgary and opened treatment rooms there. In June 1917 the Alberta Conference took over the management of the establishment. About that time two physicians, Hans and Dale Bonde, recent Loma Linda medical graduates, came to Calgary and apparently set up a small hospital, which soon required more space. The conference then provided property first in town and later at Bowness Park, to which the treatment rooms and the doctors' offices were transferred. On Aug. 1, 1923, the institution, which had been called Alberta Sanitarium, changed its name to Bethel Sanitarium to avoid confusion with government-operated Alberta Sanitarium situated nearby. In 1919 the operation of the sanitarium was assumed by the Western Canadian Union Conference, but later it was returned to the Alberta Conference.

BETHEL SCHOOL. *See* Hong Kong Adventist College.

BETHEL TRAINING SCHOOL. A school at the Bethel Mission near Butterworth, Transkei, South Africa, listed in the *Yearbook* from 1925 to 1927 and included in the list of African Division institutions from 1925 to 1929. Its faculty included E. E. Ladd and his wife; Miss A. V. Sutherland; A. P. Tarr and his wife; Ross Ansley; and three national teachers. *See* Bethel College.

BETHESDA ADVENTIST HOME AND HOSPITAL. A home for senior citizens situated at 27 Esplanade Road, Mount Eden, Auckland, New Zealand. The property is conveniently located about two miles (three kilometers) from the center of Auckland, on the base of Mount Eden, an extinct volcanic cone. The institution is owned and operated by the North New Zealand Conference.

The original two-story building was for many years the conference office and was converted to form the administrative section of the home, providing an office, kitchen, dining room, chapel, and staff quarters. To this was added a new wing that provided a bed capacity of 28. Alterations to the two-story building, together with the construction of the new wing, were financed by the church in North New Zealand and generously subsidized by the New Zealand government. The home was officially opened on July 4, 1965.

Additional extensions were opened in 1971, increasing the accommodations of the home to 38.

BETIKAMA ADVENTIST HIGH SCHOOL. A coeducational boarding school on the seventh-standard (approximately junior high school) level, owned and operated by the Western Pacific Union Mission, situated on the banks of the Lunga River, about eight miles (13 kilometers) from Honiara, capital of the island of Guadalcanal, Solomon Islands. The school was founded in 1948 by A. L. Thrift, an Australian missionary, using the facilities of an abandoned World War II American base camp, which included, among other things, dormitories, a light plant, and water systems.

The school originally accepted only boys, but it was made coeducational in 1950, the first such school in the eastern Solomon Islands. Students come from all the islands of this group. Instruction is conducted in English, and high standards are maintained in all subjects of the curriculum. Besides high academic standards, strong evangelistic outreach and Pathfinder programs have been carried on through the years.

In 1962 more than 100 boys and nearly 100 girls were in academic classes ranging from preparatory to standard 7. In 1963 a European woman teacher was appointed to help train the girls, making a teaching staff of two Europeans and nine nationals.

Form 1, the first year of high school, was added in 1965. The high school program developed over the years until in 1973 the first group of form 5 students sat for the Cambridge Overseas School Certificate. The 1993 enrollment was 364, with an academic staff of eight.

The operational costs of the school, apart from the salaries of overseas missionaries, are largely met from two major industries—Betikama School Farm and Betikama Carvings, the latter providing a worldwide outlet for Solomon Island woodcarving and other local handcrafts. A girls' sewing industry is currently being expanded.

Prior to 1963 the school building complex consisted of American wartime Quonset huts, except for two classroom blocks and the chapel, with a seating capacity of 300. From 1963 onward a vigorous building program has been carried on to replace the wartime buildings. A Thirteenth Sabbath Offering overflow started this program. By 1974 the only wartime buildings remaining in the greatly expanded high school complex were the woodwork classroom and the boys' kitchen-dining room.

Principals: R. W. Richter, 1948-1959; K. F. Silva, 1959-1962; L. M. Miller, 1962-1968; M. J. Ward, 1968-1971; R. H. Smith, 1971-1975; G. Hawke, 1976-1977; D. Cowley, 1977-1978; N. D. Tosen, 1978-1979; R. Woolley, 1980-1985; T. Rore, 1986-1989; M. Katovai, 1990-1991; C. Viva, 1992- .

BEULAH COLLEGE. A coeducational boarding school offering 12 grades of secondary education, situated on 327 acres (132 hectares) of flat leasehold land at Vaini, nine miles (14.5 kilometers) east of the administrative capital of Nuku'alofa, on the island of Tonga.

A school in the area was opened in 1895 by Mrs. E. Hilliard, who arrived in Tonga with her husband, a Seventh-day Adventist minister, a few months before. Classes were at first conducted in their home. When the enrollment increased, instruction was transferred to a 14' x 24' (4.3 m. x 7.3 m.) schoolhouse. The next year Mrs. E. S. Butz, who came with her husband and child from Pitcairn, assisted in the school, which numbered up to 28 pupils. However, the school did not continue.

On Nov. 28, 1904, a school was established on the Nuku'alofa Mission site with 12 pupils, and Ella Boyd, from Australia, as teacher. Nellie Sisley, Myra Ford, and Mrs. E. Thorpe followed her as teachers. The school was patronized by the European trading community, as well as by the Tongan royal family and local chiefs.

In 1921 a boarding school was opened at Houma, with E. E. Thorpe in charge. In 1924 C. S. Palmer arrived as the school's first principal. The enrollment increased steadily to about 50 pupils, four of whom were girls. Joni Latu, recently returned from Avondale College, assisted.

Toward the close of 1923 the first lease, 80 acres (32 hectares), of the present property was secured by R. W. Smith. The Houma school was moved to the new campus in 1925. When C. S. Palmer returned to Australia in 1926 because of ill health, Mrs. R. W. Smith assumed leadership of the school and continued until H. L. Tolhurst arrived in 1927, acting as both field superintendent and principal.

Beulah was officially recognized by the government's Education Department as a college in 1937.

For some years the school struggled against difficulties, such as lack of facilities, which restricted enrollment. Gradually conditions improved, and capable national staff were added. Henele Moala, Steven Fine, and Ilaisa Teaupa were assisting J. Cernik in 1948. The Tongan government, the director of education, the secretary to the premier, and other officials spoke highly of the educational contribution made by Beulah College during the 1940s.

During the principalship of A. E. Watts (1938-1940), a new European-style school building was erected that was opened by Queen Salote in 1939. During the Japanese invasion of the Pacific, Paul Fua led the college. Another 100 acres (40 hectares) of fertile land was secured during J. Cernik's administration, while in 1955 a third lease of 147 acres (60 hectares) of coconuts was obtained. To cope with increased enrollment and advanced levels of education, a second expatriate was added to the staff, commencing in 1958 with R. N. Sutcliffe. In 1972, 11 grades were offered, and 12 in 1985. An excellent brass band has operated since 1966, and in recent years two dormitories, additional classrooms, a kitchen and dining room, and a library have been added. Enrollment in 1993 was 310.

Principals: C. S. Palmer, 1924-1926; Mrs. R. W. Smith (acting), 1926-1927; H. L. Tolhurst (acting), 1927; B. E. Hadfield, 1928-1933; H. L. Tolhurst, 1933-1937; A. E. Watts, 1938-1940; A. W. Martin, 1940-1942; Paul Fua, 1943; J. Cernik, 1943-1950; A. H. Dawson, 1950-1956; D. Powell, 1956-1958; E. M. Arthur, 1959-1965; A. Sonter, 1966-1968; Peter Truscott, 1969-1970; D. Edgeworth, 1972; G. Hawke (acting), 1973; L. Hughes, 1974-1975; D. C. Sutcliffe, 1976-1977; Nemani Tausere, 1978; D. A. Caldwell, 1979-1981; Tesimale Latu, 1982-1987; E. Butler, 1988; Apisai Mahe, 1989-1991; R. M. Hansen, 1992-1993; K. A. Rowe, 1993-1994; T. Latu, 1994- .

BHUKET MISSION HOSPITAL. *See* Phuket Mission Hospital.

BHUTAN. An autonomous kingdom lying on the southeastern slopes of the Himalayas. It is bordered on the west by Sikkim, on the north by Tibet, and on the south and east by India. It has an area of 19,305 square miles (5,000 square kilometers) and an estimated population (1994) of 1.7 million. In the eighteenth and nineteenth centuries Bhutan resisted British efforts to open trade; in 1866 it accepted a settlement by which the British undertook to protect it from outside interference. After 1949 its foreign affairs were administered by India. Bhutan is ruled by a hereditary maharajah. The people of Bhutan are mostly of Tibetan stock, with a significant minority of Nepalese in western Bhutan. There are also Lepchas from Sikkim, and Paharis. The Bhutanese speak a Tibetan dialect. They are predominantly Lamaistic Buddhists. The preaching of Christianity has been forbidden by a royal decree.

The hill people are graziers and herders, the inhabitants of the valleys industrious farmers. Primitive and virtually roadless Bhutan was first opened up to the outside world in 1959, and now has three roads. In 1962 the country had two doctors and 20 pharmacists and was issuing its own passports and postal stamps.

Seventh-day Adventist influence is restricted to the sale of health and religious books by student literature evangelists. There are several hundred students of the Voice of Prophecy Bible Correspondence School. Five Bhutanese were baptized on Oct. 24, 1993, as a result of evangelistic meetings conducted by P. D. Kujur and his team at Raimatan Forest Camp, near the Bhutan border.

Bhutan is assigned to the Himalayan region, which is a part of the Southern Asia Division. In 1993 this region, which includes Nepal, had three Seventh-day Adventist churches.

BIBLE. The collection of sacred writings accepted by conservative Christians as being of divine origin and therefore possessing divine authority. The OT consists of 39 books written before the first advent of Christ, while the NT, written since Christ's time, consists of 27 books. (Seventh-day Adventists, in common with Protestants in general, hold that the Apocrypha is not a part of the canon of Scripture.)

Bible in the Seventh-day Adventist Church. SDAs believe that "the Holy Scriptures, Old and New Testaments, . . . given by divine inspiration" and that they "are the infallible revelation of His will" *(Church Manual* [1990], p. 23). All theological beliefs must be measured by them; any teaching that is contrary to them is to be rejected.

Early SDAs affirmed that the Bible alone was the source of their beliefs. Every matter was to be decided by the Bible, which is the test of all doctrine. They believed it to be the duty of all members to search the Scriptures for themselves and to know the reason for their faith. In 1847 James White declared, "The Bible is a perfect, and complete revelation. It is our only rule of faith and practice" *(A Word to the "Little Flock,"* p. 13).

In 1849 he reaffirmed his position: "The Bible is our chart—our guide. It is our only rule of faith and practice, to which we would closely adhere" *(Present Truth* 1:46, December 1849). In this position he was supported by his wife, who said, "The Bible and the Bible alone is to be our rule of faith" (Ellen G. White, in *Sabbath School Worker* 2:4, October 1886).

When, in 1889, Seventh-day Adventists for the first time included in their *Yearbook* a list of fundamental principles, they prefaced the list with the statement "Seventh-day Adventists have no creed but the Bible." Their declaration on the Bible reads as follows: "That the Holy Scriptures of the Old and New Testaments were given by inspiration of God, contain a full revelation of His will to man, and are the only infallible rule of faith and practice" (pp. 147, 148).

Bible Study Encouraged. In a great variety of ways Seventh-day Adventists encourage the reading and study of the Bible, both among members and nonmembers. The Bible is the focal center of the young minister's seminary training. Bible courses are required in every university and college curriculum of denominationally operated schools, both graduate and undergraduate, and in each year of the elementary and secondary levels. In the weekly Sabbath school, which is attended not only by children but by adults of all ages, the lesson is devoted exclusively to a study of the Bible, and all members are encouraged to attend Sabbath school regularly and to study the lesson each day. Senior and youth Morning Watch calendars present selected passages for daily meditation, and a devotional book published each year provides a three-minute comment on each passage. Church members, especially young people, are encouraged to read the Bible through each year.

Because of the emphasis Seventh-day Adventists have placed on individual Bible study, they have stood high in contests involving knowledge of the Bible. For example, at the Second International Bible Contest (1961) sponsored by the Israel Bible Society, and held at Jerusalem, Israel, Mrs. Yolanda da Silva, a teacher and homemaker of Brazil, came so close to first place that the judges reconsidered and awarded her a gold medal similar to the first prize. In 1964 at the Third International Bible Contest, Graham Mitchell, an accountant at the Sanitarium Food Company, Australia, took first prize. Several other Seventh-day Adventists from other countries also ranked high in the same contest.

SDA publishing houses around the world produce millions of dollars' worth of literature each year, most of which is related in one way or another to the Bible. In addition to evangelistic periodicals and tracts, there are many Bible-related books, including *The Seventh-day Adventist Bible Commentary,* a seven-volume, 8,000-page commentary on the entire Bible; the *Seventh-day Adventist Bible Dictionary,* a matching 1,200-page work, and *The Bible Story,* a 10-volume work profusely illustrated in color to which has been added a companion volume for adults, *Your Bible and You;* Bible readings, in book or pamphlet form in various languages (outline or question-and-answer Bible study guides with comment on Scripture topics); and materials for Sabbath schools and Vacation Bible Schools.

Bible Evangelism. Public evangelism consists essentially of the exposition of the Bible. In some instances good-quality Bibles are given away by the hundreds and thousands to those attending a specified number of meetings, at which the audience marks the texts used by the evangelist. Full-time evangelistic assistants called Bible instructors conduct Bible studies with individuals and groups. Training courses and institutes are conducted regularly to instruct laypersons how to teach the Bible to others through Bible studies.

From time to time Bible conferences, at which the youth participate in discussing selected Bible topics, are held for the young people of the church. Radio and television programs highlight the Bible, and a number of local, regional, or national Bible correspondence schools enroll registrants by the hundreds of thousands.

Seventh-day Adventists also cooperate with the Bible societies by official, direct contributions, by participation in translation projects, and by assisting in the circulation of the Bible.

See also Bible, Interpretation of; Inspiration of Scripture.

BIBLE CONFERENCE. A term Seventh-day Adventists have applied to a series of regular meetings, convened by the General Conference since 1919, for the purpose of in-depth study of biblical and theological issues.

Bible conferences had their beginning in the formative years of the church, when the leaders met to pray and to study the Bible so as to arrive at doctrinal unanimity on the basis of the Bible's being the only rule of faith and practice *(see* Sabbath Conferences).

A significant Bible conference was held in Washington, D.C., from July 1 to 21, 1919. This was a closed conference and was attended only by denominational editors, Bible and history teachers from Seventh-day Adventist colleges, and members of the General Conference Committee. The objective of the conference was "to unite in a definite, practical, spiritual study of the Word of God" in order "to gain more light and greater unity" *(Review and Herald* 96:3, 4, Aug. 21, 1919). The following topics were discussed at this Bible conference: (1) The Person and Mediatorial Work of Christ, (2) The Nature and Work of the Holy Spirit, (3) The Two Covenants, (4) The Principles of Prophetic Interpretation, (5) The Eastern Question (Turkey and Armageddon in Bible Prophecy), (6) The Beast Power in Revelation, (7) The 1260 Days, (8) The United States in Prophecy, (9) The Seven Trumpets, (10) Matthew 24, and (11) The Identification of the 10 Kingdoms. There is a stenographic transcript of this conference in the denominational archives in Washington, D.C.

The announced result of this conference was that "the Bible and history teachers, the editors, and the members of the General Conference Committee, who came together from all parts of North America, rejoiced to find themselves in agreement on all the great fundamental truths of the Bible" *(ibid.,* p. 4).

A second SDA Bible conference was held in Washington, D.C., Sept. 1-13, 1952. Much larger than the previous Bible conference, it was attended by members of the General Conference Committee; in North America, two Bible teachers from each senior college, one Bible teacher from each junior college, from one to several evangelists from each union conference, editors of leading periodicals, book editors of leading publishing houses, representatives from the SDA Theological Seminary; and the presidents and a minimum of three others from the overseas divisions.

A transcript of this conference is preserved in the denominational archives in Washington, D.C., and photostatic copies of this transcript are available at the Andrews and Loma Linda universities' heritage rooms.

The purpose of this conference was threefold: (1) to study together the doctrines that made Seventh-day Adventists a distinct people and that justified their continued existence, (2) to set forth Seventh-day Adventist doctrines in a way that most fully explained the meaning of the times and most effectively challenged the attention and response of the public, and (3) to keep "in step" in areas of prophetic interpretation "heretofore but dimly discerned," but "now . . . seen more clearly" *(Our Firm Foundation* [1953], vol. 1, p. 17). The following topics were presented at the conference: (1) Recent Discoveries Confirm the Bible, (2) Christ the Center of All True Preaching, (3) The Spirit of Prophecy and the Remnant Church, (4) The Gospel in Type and Antitype, (5) The Atonement and the Cross, (6) The Covenants and the Law, (7) Life Only Through Christ, (8) The Increasing Timeliness of the Threefold Message, (9) Antichrist in History and Prophecy, (10) The Mediatorial Ministry of Jesus Christ, (11) The Advent Message Built Upon the Foundation of Many Generations, (12) The Imminence of Christ's Second Coming, (13) The Great Controversy, (14) Health and the Gospel Message, (15) The Companions of the Lamb, (16) The Gospel Commission and the Remnant Church, (17) World Evangelism Our Basic Task, (18) The Place of Prophecy in Our Preaching, (19) The Lord Our Righteousness, and (20) The Holy Spirit and the Latter Rain.

Reporting on the results of the conference, D. A. Delafield wrote: "The General Conference Committee did not anticipate that the Bible conference should simply reaffirm our faith in the great truths of the third angel's message. They also encouraged, and looked forward to, a great spiritual revival at the meetings that would reach out through the 450 delegates to our churches in all the world. The greater, more compelling result of sanctification of life through the truth was realized to a highly gratifying extent by the meetings" *(Review and Herald* 129:1, Oct. 2, 1952).

In May and June 1974 three identical eight-day Bible conferences drew 2,000 delegates of the North American Division to the campuses of Southern Missionary College, Andrews University, and Pacific Union College. The conference program was built around the work being done by the Biblical Research Committee in the area of biblical hermeneutics (principles of interpretation). Small group discussions of the topics presented, and panel discussions of group questions, attempted maximum interaction.

A Symposium on Biblical Hermeneutics (Gordon M. Hyde, ed., 1974), written primarily by members of the Biblical Research Committee, was distributed to delegates in advance of the conferences as a means of orientation to the Bible conference papers. The latter covered: (1) Biblical Archaeology as an Aid to Biblical Exegesis, (2) Biblical Authority: A Study of Religious Trends From the Apostolic Church to the Present Time, (3) Toward a Seventh-day Adventist Theology of

Revelation-Inspiration, (4) The Relationship Between the Bible and the Writings of Ellen G. White, (5) General Principles of Biblical Interpretation, (6) Principles of Interpretation of the Prophetic and Apocalyptic Literature of the Bible, (7) "The Song of the Vineyard," a Case Study in Biblical Interpretation, (8) Preaching the Bible, (9) The Use of Tools in the Study of the Bible, (10) The Role of the Holy Spirit in Biblical Interpretation, (11) Issues in Current Theology, (12) The Interrelation of the Bible and Science With Particular Consideration of Issues Related to Creation, (13) The Everlasting Gospel and Righteousness by Faith, (14) The Unique Contribution of Adventist Eschatology, (15) The Role of the SDA Church in the Great Controversy in the End-time.

Morning Bible study series were presented on the Epistles of Ephesians, Galatians, and Colossians, respectively. Reports were presented on a proposed biography of Ellen G. White and on the Andrews University Heshbon dig.

The delegations were primarily drawn from the preaching and Bible teaching ministries of the church, with representation of all departments, institutions, administrative branches, and laypersons. World divisions sent observers to the conferences.

The primary objectives were to review the Seventh-day Adventist concept of the revelation-inspiration basis for the authority of inspired writings; to present a sound SDA system of interpretation principles for the study of inspired messages; and to attempt application of such principles in key eschatological subject areas.

Reporting on the Bible conferences, Kenneth H. Wood wrote, "The . . . editors of the *Review* . . . consider these conferences one of the most constructive influences within the church during this generation" (*Review and Herald* 151:33, Aug. 15, 1974, p. 3).

After 1974 Bible conferences were conducted in Europe (1977), Australia (1978), and South America (1979). The biblical and theological subjects discussed were the same ones presented in North America in 1974. However, allowance was made for the discussion of subjects of particular relevance and interest to each region.

The Euro-Africa Division was the location of another Bible conference in 1982. The main focus of discussion was prophecy and eschatology. The papers presented were published in French (*Prophétie et Eschatologie* I-II [France: Seminaire Adventiste du Saleve, 1982]) and German (*Prophetie und Eschatologie* I-II [Marienhöhe, 1982]). The same subjects were discussed in two other Bible conferences held in the Southern Asia Division (1983) and in the Far Eastern Division (1984).

It has been the practice of the Euro-Africa Division to organize and direct Bible conferences every five years in its territories. One of those was held in 1988 on the book of Revelation (*Études sur l'Apocalypse* [Conférences Bibliques Division Eurafricane, 1988]), and another one in 1993 on ecclesiology.

See also Youth Bible Conference.

BIBLE CORRESPONDENCE SCHOOLS. Organizations conducting evangelistic correspondence courses in Bible subjects, operated by various union or local conferences or missions and by broadcasting organizations; often promoted in connection with radio or television programs. The courses, which carry no school credit and are offered free of any obligation, are intended to lead the student to Christ through a study of the Bible. They are designed for various age levels and prepared in several degrees of difficulty. The majority are biblical courses, but there are also health courses and a special course for alcoholics. They are issued in many languages and in braille.

The largest of the schools in North America are those conducted in connection with radio and television programs. There are many Voice of Prophecy Bible Correspondence schools outside the North American Division and others connected with the various national broadcasts in other lands, or conducted without any broadcast at all, publicized by word of mouth or by newspaper or other advertising.

Many of these schools are conducted under the name Voice of Prophecy or the equivalent national name for the local broadcast or organization, some offering courses in many languages.

The first of these Bible correspondence schools originated in connection with a local radiobroadcast. In 1939 Dallas Youngs, pastor of the Williamsport, Pennsylvania, church, needed a method of following up interests resulting from his broadcasts over station WRAK. Conceiving the idea of offering a free Bible correspondence course, he announced a 23-lesson course, for which he used an already available series of Bible lessons written by J. L. Shuler and published in loose-leaf form for use in evangelistic Bible classes conducted in churches. When this series proved successful as a correspondence course, another evangelist, A. E. Lickey, wrote a new set of correspondence lessons that became the Twentieth Century Bible Course; and the *Voice of Prophecy* broadcast began to issue its own correspondence courses, as did the telecast *Faith for Today* later *(see* the articles on these two programs).

As Bible correspondence schools came to be operated by various conferences, the General Conference recommended in the Autumn Council of 1947 that the Home Missionary Department foster the organization and direction of the conference-operated Bible correspondence schools in the North American Division. In 1961 the securing of enrollments in regularly established Bible schools, the distribution of radio-TV logs, etc., was assigned to the Home Missionary Department on all levels in North America.

At the time of the 1954 General Conference session a total of 44 conference Bible schools were in operation in North America, resulting in many baptisms. In the preceding four years 6,682 students had been baptized.

By 1968 the responsibility for Bible correspondence schools in North America operated under the lay activities departments in local conferences and unions had been transferred to the *Voice of Prophecy* and *Faith for Today*. Some small schools have been operated in connection with local broadcasts such as those of Amazing Facts (Chesapeake Conference). The Church Ministries Department has the responsibility for securing enrollments in courses.

Beginning in 1970, the *Voice of Prophecy* and *Faith for Today* began revising their major courses. Specialized courses are offered such as health, nutrition, and youth. Revised and new courses maintain enrollments and results at a high level.

In Latin America, eastern Asia, Australia, and the South Pacific, Bible correspondence courses form an essential part of door-to-door evangelism. Laypersons act as letter carriers, taking the lessons to students and returning the test sheets for grading and offering spiritual help during their visits. Large graduations of students often have been a feature of follow-up of courses.

BIBLE ECHO PUBLISHING HOUSE. *See* Signs Publishing Company.

BIBLE EXPOSITOR (listed in the *Yearbook* from 1935 to 1954; monthly; the Christian Record Benevolent Association, Lincoln, Nebraska). An evangelistic magazine for the visually impaired printed in revised braille and New York point. It began as a 12-page publication but later reached 42 pages. It was discontinued in the 1950s, and its place was taken by various Bible correspondence courses for the visually impaired.

BIBLE IN THE CURRICULUM. *See* Education, Seventh-day Adventist Philosophy of; Schools, Seventh-day Adventist.

BIBLE, INSPIRATION OF. *See* Inspiration of Scripture.

BIBLE INSTRUCTOR. In the Seventh-day Adventist program of evangelism, a person who dedicates himself or herself to the teaching of the Scriptures, generally to individuals or to small groups. Such persons may be assigned to local churches or to institutions, or may be asked to work with evangelists. Generally personal Bible instruction is given in the homes of interested people. Most of the Bible instructors in the church have been women. Through the centuries of the Christian Era gifted women have played their part in spreading the good news of salvation in Christ.

Before the church provided a system of training in its Christian schools and colleges, ministers' and colporteurs' wives (for example, Angeline Cornell) volunteered their services for personal Bible instruction.

In 1883, the same year that S. N. Haskell promoted a new method of evangelism by the Bible reading plan *(see* Bible Studies), the Battle Creek Tabernacle Institute gave great impetus to the training of workers in this method of Bible instruction. At first referred to variously as Bible readers or Bible reading workers, these became known as Bible workers, now called Bible instructors. About the same time large-city missions began to prepare women through in-service training for house-to-house Bible teaching. (Mrs. A. T. Robinson, née Loretta Farnsworth, is reputed to have been the first woman Bible instructor.) At the turn of the century a large number of women skilled in the knowledge and use of the Scriptures were associated with large-city public evangelism. Thus a place for the profession was made in the church organization.

In time some dedicated young women took

the undergraduate ministerial course, thus qualifying themselves to be of even greater service to evangelists in gaining decisions and in establishing new believers in doctrinal truth. Some of these skilled instructors assumed the responsibility of training gifted young people in the churches, thus recruiting new Bible instructors. Later, courses for Bible instructors were offered in SDA colleges and in the SDA Theological Seminary.

BIBLE, INTERPRETATION OF. From the first, Seventh-day Adventists have stressed the importance of following sound principles of exegesis when interpreting Scripture. They recognize that interpretation is necessary because of the diverse literary forms found in the Bible; because the languages in which it was originally written, the modes of thought and expression, the customs, and the historical setting are unfamiliar to the modern reader; and because human language is at best an imperfect medium for the communication of divine thought.

As to literary forms, the language of Scripture may be in the form of poetry or prose; it may be literal or figurative; it may be historical, prophetic, or apocalyptic. As to language, it is often difficult if not impossible to translate an idea expressed in one language into another without loss or modification of the thought. The customs and modes of thought and expression of people of a foreign culture that ceased to exist many centuries ago are easily susceptible to being misunderstood today. The messages of Scripture were often given with respect to a particular historical situation, which must be known and understood before their original import and their application today can be accurately determined. The fact that human language is at best an imperfect vehicle for conveying divine thought calls for caution, and the guidance of the Holy Spirit.

The early SDA leaders, such as James White and Joseph Bates, who had no formal seminary training, brought a natural strength of intellect, deep earnestness, and diligent effort to their study of the Bible. Despite their lack of formal theological training, they discovered and followed sound principles of exegesis. Their expositions of Scripture have, accordingly, at nearly every significant point stood the test of the years. They stressed that the Scriptures were to be taken literally unless the context made it obvious that a figure of speech was being used by the sacred writer. In this they followed William Miller, who "concluded from his study of the Bible that it should be understood literally unless there is clear proof that figurative language is being employed by the inspired writer. That is, the words of Scripture ought to be understood in their ordinary historical and grammatical sense, even as with secular writing, except in those instances where the writer used figurative language. In thus viewing the Scriptures literally, Miller was simply following the path of conservative theologians from the very beginnings of Protestantism" (F. D. Nichol, *The Midnight Cry* [1944], p. 32).

Of the literal method of interpretation Ellen G. White wrote (1888): "The truths most plainly revealed in the Bible have been involved in doubt and darkness by learned men, who, with a pretense of great wisdom, teach that the Scriptures have a mystical, a secret, spiritual meaning not apparent in the language employed. These men are false teachers. . . . The language of the Bible should be explained according to its obvious meaning, unless a symbol or figure is employed" (GC 598, 599).

In general, early SDAs followed the method of Scripture interpretation characteristic of conservative Protestantism, which viewed all Scripture as divinely inspired. To find truth, early SDAs believed it was necessary to compare all relevant Scripture passages. They pointed to Isa. 28:10, "line upon line; here a little, and there a little," as authority for using the proof-text method. They were convinced that when correctly understood, the Bible is consistent throughout.

Emphasis was also given to the matter of understanding biblical passages in their context. Mrs. White urged *(Review and Herald* 60:1, Oct. 9, 1883): "Make the Bible its own expositor, bringing together all that is said concerning a given subject at different times and under varied circumstances." The introduction to the book *Bible Readings for the Home Circle* (1888) called for a careful study of the context in order to determine the meaning of a statement of Holy Writ.

The antithesis of the literal method is the allegorical method, a system of interpretation that arose early in the Christian Era, minimizing the literal sense of Scripture. This method of interpretation seems to have originated with the Greeks, who in the sixth century before Christ invented it to reinterpret the ancient gods and their cruel and immoral actions, as depicted by the poet Homer, in order to save Homer for the more enlightened ethical philosophy of a more sophisticated age.

The Jewish philosopher Philo, of Alexandria (c. 20 B.C.-after A.D. 40), borrowed the allegorical method from the Greeks and applied it to the OT. He did not deny the literal meaning altogether, but considered it only shadow. He took the figurative or allegorical meaning to be the real substance or meaning of the text. By this process of reinterpreting the OT he harmonized Scripture with his eclectic Greek philosophy. The Christian scholar Origen (c. A.D. 185-c. 254), also of Alexandria, introduced the allegorical method to Christian hermeneutics, which method dominated interpretation for more than a millennium. Origen found three meanings in Scripture corresponding to the human body, soul, and spirit—literal and moral meanings for the simple-minded, and the more profound allegorical mysteries for the discerning few.

Meanwhile, beginning at least as far back as Theophilus of Antioch at the end of the second century after Christ, a more conservative hermeneutic developed in opposition to Alexandria, emphasizing a literal, historical, and grammatical exegesis. Only with caution in Antioch were OT prophecies and types applied to Christ; allegory was despised. Great names in the "school" of Antioch included Diodorus of Tarsus (d. A.D. 394), John Chrysostom (c. 345-407), and above all Theodore, bishop of Mopsuestia (392-428). The Antiochene hermeneutic did not deny the validity of spiritual meanings but attempted to derive them from the literal meanings. Antiochene principles were not totally lost during the Middle Ages, and came to new life in Luther's emphasis on the grammatical sense of Scripture and in the literalistic comments of Calvin. Conservative Protestant theology, including that of Seventh-day Adventists, has tended to follow this approach.

See also Daniel, Interpretation of; Revelation, Interpretation of; Symbol.

BIBLE-READING GAZETTE (1 vol., 1884; monthly; R&H; vol. in R&H). A monthly periodical containing Bible studies, published from January to December 1884, in accordance with the resolution of the General Conference session of 1883. The subscription price was set at $1 for those who submitted one or more studies for publication, and at $5 for others. The 12 numbers contained 162 lessons in all, written by many ministers and lay evangelistic workers on a wide range of scriptural topics covering the cardinal points of the doctrines held by Seventh-day Adventists. Although more than 12,000 copies were distributed in 1884, there was a large inventory still left at the end of the year. As an experiment the series was bound in book form and sold by colporteurs in Ohio. The book, containing Bible lessons in a form not available elsewhere, met with a large degree of success, and was reprinted. Later the Review and Herald prepared a similar series of studies, again by various authors, under the name *Bible Readings for the Home Circle,* which replaced the *Gazette* volume and which is still in print.

BIBLE READING PLANS. Several plans for systematic Bible reading that were promoted by the former Young People's Missionary Volunteer Department.

Bible Year. A plan of reading the Bible through in one year. The idea was suggested at the 1920 MV Secretaries' Council held in Indianapolis. For those who completed this reading within the year the General Conference MV Department issued Bible Year certificates, the first of which were awarded in 1922. Various Bible reading checklists in leaflet form subsequently appeared.

Correlated Reading Plans. Plans for daily reading of the Bible along with character-building books. The 1946 Advisory Committee introduced the Character Classics, daily readings in the five books of the Conflict of the Ages Series (Ellen G. White's *Patriarchs and Prophets, Prophets and Kings, The Desire of Ages, The Acts of the Apostles,* and *The Great Controversy)* correlated with selected chapters of the Bible. Outlines were provided for four different years of reading. In 1957 a similar plan was introduced for the reading of Ellen White's *Messages to Young People* along with certain correlated Bible references.

MV Bible Marking Plan. Sets of Bible references printed on gummed paper that could be cut apart and pasted beside Bible verses, thus guiding the reader from text to text in 20 different Bible studies. During its first three years of use (1959-1962) 86,500 sets of the MV Bible Marking Plan were distributed through the local MV departments.

BIBLE READINGS. *See Bible-Reading Gazette;* Bible Studies.

BIBLE SCHOOLS AND INSTITUTES. Seventh-day Adventists use the term *Bible School* mostly in combination, as in Branch

Bible School, Community Bible School, or Bible Correspondence School. However, in earlier years, when there were few Seventh-day Adventist colleges and academies, many short-term schools or institutes were held in various places, called Bible schools, biblical institutes, Bible reading institutes, or Bible training schools. These schools offered instruction in doctrines and evangelistic methods for ministers, Bible instructors, colporteurs, and laypeople wishing to enter such work. *See* Workers' Institutes.

BIBLE STUDENTS' LIBRARY (1889-1915; monthly 1889-1899, quarterly 1899-1908, then irregular to 1915; PPPA). A series of pamphlets, designed for the public, containing brief and pointed essays on Bible doctrines, the fulfillment of prophecy, and other aspects of Seventh-day Adventist teachings. The 1915 catalog of publications listed 209 titles. Later the tracts were renumbered. In 1922 the series, which then contained 42 titles, was discontinued. M. C. Wilcox was chair of the editorial committee for a number of years.

BIBLE STUDIES (or Bible readings). Topical presentations, usually in question (sometimes in outline) form with the answers read from the Bible—a method of Bible evangelism practiced extensively in the Seventh-day Adventist Church. From the 1880s the method was used systematically by ministers and Bible instructors, and also by lay members, in house-to-house visitation.

A Bible study may be completely informal, given in response to an inquiry on a specific subject; or it may be, and more often is, one of a progressive series of studies planned for the purpose of systematic instruction in Bible doctrines and Christian living or of preparation for baptism. Since Bible studies are usually given to an individual or a small group, they can be constructed with reference to the problems and questions of the individual and varied in order and difficulty according to the circumstances and the skill of the instructor. On the other hand, there are various series of published Bible studies, either in printed form or recorded on sound tape, complete with the Bible answers, which may be used along with filmstrips and portable projectors, and, more recently, on videotapes. These aids, which enable even inexperienced laypersons to present standardized courses of Bible study, include filmstrips and tapes keyed to the Twentieth Century Bible Correspondence Lessons, Friendship Bible Study Cards, Better Life Picture Roll, a Bible chain-marking plan, and the "My Bible Says" series of printed studies.

In 1883 the plan of conducting Bible studies was introduced to SDAs as a major method of evangelism, by S. N. Haskell, the "father of the Tract and Missionary Societies," who at that time was the president of the California Conference. As he later told the story, he gave his first "Bible reading" during a southern California camp meeting held near Lemoore in May 1883. When a downpour of rain prevented his holding one of the regular meetings, he gathered a group around him in the center of the tent and began to announce texts of Scripture to be read by various persons in response to questions related to the subject under discussion. This method of communicating Bible teachings and Christian faith was received with enthusiasm and was endorsed by church members and leaders.

Two months later, also in southern California, two ministers, E. A. Briggs and M. C. Israel, joined with several colporteurs each morning for a Bible class, training themselves to use this new method. Haskell quotes one of these men as follows: "We have been having a drill on different subjects, and each person has a short form of Bible reading questions in his Bible, so when the Sabbath question or any other subject comes up, each one makes it a point to have the person or family visited get a Bible, and have the subject cleared up right from the Scriptures. In this way a controversy never arises; but the people are in almost every case convinced that the Bible teaches that doctrine. . . . I do not see why very many of our brethren and sisters may not be educated in this way to make efficient workers. By practice they could soon get so they would not have to look at the questions. They could get companies of neighbors together, and have prayer with them, and Bible readings" *(Review and Herald* 60:486, July 31, 1883).

Haskell recommended that every family study the Bible in this way, and thus teach their children and others. When Haskell attended the Michigan Conference in September, and reported the success of Bible readings in California, Nebraska, and elsewhere, the conference voted approval of the plan for use by colporteurs, and a 10-day Bible Reading Institute was announced for Battle Creek, to begin Oct. 30, preceding the General Conference session. Haskell reported: "The subject of Bible readings has been one of interest on the Pacific Coast, and has been considered of that importance that there is a special department in that College [Healdsburg College] devoted to it. Those who have adopted this method in their colporteur work speak of it in the highest terms, as it avoids all discussion, and simply calls the attention of the people to the Word of God" *(ibid.* 60:649, Oct. 16, 1883).

To this institute Haskell invited ministers and licentiates, licensed colporteurs, and church officers, at least one from each church. He conducted such Bible studies at the institute and during the General Conference session.

The conference voted to recommend the Bible study method and proposed the publication, by a "Bible reading Bureau," of a monthly sheet containing one or more lessons for each week, to be sent out to those who would pay $1 a year and furnish one or more original readings each month; others were to pay $5 for the publication. This *Bible-Reading Gazette* was issued monthly through the year 1884. Afterward it was bound and sold as a book, and later was replaced by the much larger book still published, after many editions, as *Bible Readings for the Home.*

This same 1883 General Conference session recommended the establishment of "Missions" in the principal cities *(see* City Missions) as centers of evangelism. In the 1880s a number of these were opened, containing combination reading room, lecture hall, Tract and Missionary Society depot, and colporteur headquarters. In these missions the new method of giving Bible studies was used with excellent results, and the missions became training centers for workers, especially young women, in this method. Referred to as "Bible workers," they became what are now known as Bible instructors, full-time assistants to evangelists or pastors, carrying on personal evangelism mainly through Bible studies with individuals. Bible instructor training came to be offered in SDA colleges, and the giving of Bible studies by lay members has been encouraged, and training courses for laypersons have been offered in the churches.

BIBLE TRAINING SCHOOL. A 16-page monthly devoted to the interests of house-to-house evangelism, edited by S. N. Haskell, first at New York, and afterward at South Lancaster, Massachusetts. It is listed in the *General Conference Bulletin,* second-third quarter 1902, as a denominational publication. The *Yearbook* lists it as a privately sponsored periodical from 1907 to 1913, after which the *Yearbook* no longer listed private periodicals.

BIBLE WORKER. *See* Bible Instructor.

BIBLE WORKERS' TRAINING SCHOOL FOR FOREIGNERS. A school established in 1910, appearing in the *Yearbook* only in 1911. It was conducted at 1831 Gates Avenue, Brooklyn, New York, by the Greater New York Conference under direction of the North American Foreign Department of the General Conference. Its teacher was H. R. Johnson.

BIBLE YEAR. *See* Bible Reading Plans.

BIBLICAL ARCHAEOLOGY. *See* Archaeology, Biblical.

BIBLICAL INSTITUTES. *See* Workers' Institutes.

BIBLICAL RESEARCH INSTITUTE. A service department of the General Conference established by action of the GC Committee on Sept. 25, 1975 (GCC 75-274). The purpose and goals of the institute are to (1) identify areas in which biblical research is needed in the Seventh-day Adventist Church; (2) conduct research in the Bible and related areas; (3) communicate the results of this research to the appropriate audiences; (4) assist the GC administration on matters of biblical interpretation, doctrines, and church trends; (5) serve the world field as a resource in the areas of biblical interpretation and doctrine; (6) evaluate manuscripts referred to it by the North American unions and the overseas divisions; (7) provide educational services in biblical studies and theology for pastors, Bible teachers, administrators, and other interested workers; (8) maintain contact with SDA seminaries; (9) foster and maintain contact and good relationships with the community of SDA scholars in biblical studies, theology, and related areas; and (10) provide a forum for the presentation and discussion of papers on biblical studies (BRIAD Committee, Feb. 13, 1980).

The historical roots of the institute go back to two committees that functioned for many years independent of each other: the Biblical Study and Research Committee and the Defense Literature Committee. The Biblical Study and Research Committee was appointed by the Autumn Council on Sept. 24, 1952. The purpose of this committee was to encourage, organize, and coordinate biblical research and exegesis; to give guidance to persons who made what they considered to be significant discoveries of truth; and to examine manuscripts submitted to it for evaluation (*Ministry,* February 1953).

The Biblical Study and Research Committee was established when the Biblical Research Fellowship was being dissolved, and was to a certain extent to take its place. The fellowship was a self-appointed society of SDA Bible teachers organized in 1940 with the purpose of deepening the understanding of known truth and exploring other areas in which additional knowledge was needed. The new committee was to foster that interest in biblical research.

The Defense Committee, established in 1943, had basically an apologetic function answering publications against the church. In 1969 this committee and the Biblical Study Research Committee merged under the name Biblical Research Committee (Officers' Meeting 69-135). The objectives of this committee were stated as follows:

"a. To explore new areas of truth.

"b. To study question of biblical interpretation.

"c. To review problems of biblical chronology.

"d. To study and analyze problems of biblical translations.

"e. To provide an agency for the examination of theological interpretations, ideas, and theories presented by laymen and/or church scholars.

"f. To prepare materials as needed by the church in defense of truth and to recommend individuals for specific field assignments" (Officers' Meeting, Mar. 31, 1969 [69-135]).

This committee was only a study committee and did not have "final authority to speak for the church on theological or doctrinal matters" *(ibid.).*

The change from Biblical Research Committee to Biblical Research Institute facilitated employing persons trained in theology to work full-time with the director of the institute as associate directors. The institute is under the leadership of a GC field secretary and three other associate directors. All of them are trained in biblical or theological studies. In addition to an administrative committee, the institute works with two subcommittees. One of them deals with biblical and theological matters (BRICOM) and the other with the interaction of science and religion (BRISCO).

Since its inception, the institute has organized many Bible conferences around the world and in North America. The institute's work on biblical hermeneutics became the foundation of the North American Bible Conference in 1974. Under the leadership of the director of the institute, seven volumes were published, called the Daniel and Revelation Series (1982-1992). They address issues raised against the Adventist doctrine of the sanctuary and its prophetic interpretation during the late seventies and early eighties.

Chair/Secretaries/Directors: W. E. Read, 1952-1959; H. W. Lowe, 1959-1969; G. M. Hyde, 1969-1979; W. R. Lesher, 1979-1984; G. W. Reid, 1984- .

BIBLICKY SEMINAR CASD. *See* Adventist Bible Seminary.

BIESDA (BORDER INSTITUTE OF ENGLISH, SEVENTH-DAY ADVENTIST) LANGUAGE PROGRAMS. An evangelistic outreach school that teaches conversational English and Spanish to youth and adults along the Texas-Mexico border in Brownsville, Texas. It is part of the Texas Conference of Seventh-day Adventists.

In 1977 while conducting an evangelistic campaign in Korea, Cyril Miller, then president of the Texas Conference, became acquainted with the concept of English language school evangelism with student missionaries Dan Serns and Jeff Brown.

Two years later, in June 1979, the Texas Conference rented a building one block from Mexico in Brownsville, Texas, and began renovations. Within two weeks after the grand opening August 30, 1980, youth and adults had registered for the first two-month term. The original staff consisted of director Dan Serns, Bible worker Lillian Gonzalez, and student missionaries Jeff Brown, Danny Payan, and Bill Serns.

In 1980 BIESDA summer camp operated on the campus of Valley Grande Academy with 112 campers. In August a second school was opened in Hidalgo, followed by a third in Laredo in 1981. BIESDA was selected as one of the Sabbath school Investment projects in 1980, and money received was used to purchase the Brownsville school and office building.

Three students were baptized in BIESDA's first baptism in May of 1982. During the next three years BIESDA was productive evangelistically but suffered financially as the Mexican peso plunged in value more than 1,000 percent. BIESDA experimented with schools operated in Adventist churches in Houston, San Antonio, El Paso, Pharr, and Del Rio, Texas, as well as Reynosa and Mexico City, Mexico.

As the Mexican peso continued to decline in value in the late 1980s, all operations were closed except the Flagship School in Brownsville. In spite of difficulties during its first decade (1979-1988) BIESDA gave 110 student missionaries an opportunity to share their faith with 18,000 students, seeing 120 of them baptized into area churches.

Directors: Dan Serns, 1979-1984; Jeff Brown, 1984-1989; Rudy Juarez, 1989-1991; Jan Yakush, 1991-1992; Harvey Kornegay, 1992-1993; Randy Hart, 1993- .

BIG WEEK. An annual one-week campaign devoted to the sale of Seventh-day Adventist publications by colporteurs. Originally church leaders and laypersons were encouraged to participate, and to turn over at least half, and if possible all, of the proceeds of their sales to missions; colporteurs were asked to contribute the sales of their biggest day. This plan was first tried in North Dakota in 1913 and was gradually adopted by other conferences in North America. In 1920 the Spring Council made it a part of the denomination's worldwide program. During the 1920s and early 1930s this week usually came during the month of April or May. It became associated with the Missions Extension Fund for important special projects in the worldwide work of the church. Big Week was discontinued about 1935 as a fund-raising project and became a week during which colporteurs were encouraged to put forth extra time and effort in the sale of SDA publications. In the churches a Missions Extension Offering, no longer necessarily derived from the sale of publications, is taken annually—now in the month of September (*see* Church Calendar). About 1944 Big Week was shifted from a week in April or May to a week in the first half of September.

BIGGS, LLOYD E. (1893-1973). Treasurer and administrator. In 1915 after his graduation from Walla Walla College he became secretary-treasurer of the Upper Columbia Conference. He served in this capacity in several conferences in the succeeding years, including a term with the Zambesi Union in South Africa. In 1938 he became treasurer of the Southeastern California Conference, and two years later was elected president of that field. In 1944 he was called to serve as comptroller of Loma Linda University, in charge of financial affairs. Four years later he was elected president of the Oregon Conference, which position he held until 1959. From that time until his retirement, he was religious liberty secretary of the North Pacific Union.

BIHAR MISSION HIGH SCHOOL OF SEVENTH-DAY ADVENTISTS. *See* Raymond Memorial Higher Secondary School.

BÊNH-VIÊN CO'-DÔC. *See* Saigon Adventist Hospital.

BIRKENSTOCK, CARL FREDERICK (1897-1958). Medical administrator, missionary. Born in Natal, South Africa, he went to the United States and entered Pacific Union College (1918), and graduated from the College of Medical Evangelists (1923). After qualifying with the Royal College of Physicians and Surgeons, Edinburgh, he served as medical secretary in the South African Division (1924-1928). He also served as medical administrator of the Cape Sanitarium and Hospital and in 1925 was the first physician at the Malamulo Mission, where he established the first leper hospital in that part of Africa. On returning to the U.S., he was chief surgeon and medical administrator of the Hinsdale Sanitarium and Hospital (1928-1930). For the next 24 years he was in private practice in San Diego, California.

BIRTHDAY-THANK OFFERING. *See* Sabbath School Offerings.

BISHOP, FREDRICK W. (1864-1929). One of the pioneer colporteurs who opened Seventh-day Adventist work in Chile. He was born in England, and as a small child was brought to the United States by his mother. He became acquainted with SDA beliefs when someone invited him to attend the SDA church in San Francisco sometime in the 1880s. Soon after joining the church, he began selling books and then attended Healdsburg College. While there, F. L. Mead asked him if he would be willing to go to Chile, and without any knowledge of Spanish, he sailed there in 1894 in company with Thomas Davis. In 1897 he married a Chilean and remained in Chile, retiring from active canvassing in 1921.

BISMARCK ARCHIPELAGO. *See* Papua New Guinea.

BISMARCK-SOLOMONS UNION MISSION. *See* South Pacific Division.

BLACK ROCK JUNIOR ACADEMY. *See* Highland View Academy.

BLACK SEVENTH-DAY ADVENTISTS IN NORTH AMERICA. *See* Human Relations, Office of.

BLAKE, LOTTIE C. ISBELL (1876-1976). Physician. She began a career in teaching in Columbus, Ohio, in 1896, where she became a Seventh-day Adventist. Later, while studying nursing at Battle Creek, she was encouraged to become a doctor. She trained at the American Medical Missionary College, graduating in 1902. She began practicing in Nashville, Tennessee, as director of Rock City Sanitarium. A year later she organized a nurses' training program in Huntsville. In 1904 she was the only Black female physician practicing in Birmingham. The Blakes, parents of five children, engaged in team medical work in Central America and the Caribbean. After her husband's death, she moved back to Columbus, Ohio, and worked in general practice until 1957. She was honored by the AMA for 50 years of medical service.

BLAND, WILLIAM THOMAS (1862-1953). Educator and administrator. A Seventh-day Adventist since his youth, he was teaching in a public school when he was called to teach English language and literature at Battle Creek College about 1889. In 1893 he became the first principal of Mount Vernon Academy, Ohio, and in 1896 took charge of the Graysville, Tennessee, academy. From 1898 to 1901 he was president of Union College. In 1903 he was appointed acting treasurer of the General Conference and was placed in charge of the business transactions connected with the transfer of the Seventh-day Adventist headquarters to Washington, D.C. He assisted in the establishment of Washington Missionary College, Washington Sanitarium, and the Review and Herald Publishing Association. After that, he was principal of Fox River Academy for about a year until his retirement. His wife, Flora H. Bland, was acting secretary of the Sabbath School Department of the General Conference in 1903, and for many years was an active and inspiring leader in the educational and religious activities promoted by the SDA Church.

BLANTYRE ADVENTIST HOSPITAL. A 45-bed hospital started in 1956 as an outpatient extension of the Malamulo Hospital, 40 miles (65 kilometers) south of Blantyre, Malawi. It began in Limbe, five miles (eight kilometers) from Blantyre and moved to the present location in 1958. From being a single-doctor outpatient facility it has now grown to seven full-time staff physicians and four courtesy staff.

In 1964 a dental practice was started by Dr. Ben Nelson. This was carried on in temporary quarters on the second floor of the clinic building. In 1968 an extension to the existing facility was added and a compact two-operatory dental unit was located on the main floor. In 1974 a second dentist arrived, and the clinic was extensively remodeled to provide four dental operatories.

In 1974 Drs. Elton and Rheeta Stecker purchased a house that they converted into a 10-bed hospital, with one bed in the labor ward and operating room. This brought a lot of professional satisfaction, as the doctors could not admit their patients anywhere else. In 1983, 14 more beds were added, and another doctor was called to make it a two-physician practice. There was a felt need for a health education building, and funding was sought. The Scandinavian ADRA provided the funds.

Today adjacent to the hospital is a beautiful building where "Breathe Free, weight control, stress control, vegetarian cooking, and prenatal classes" are held.

The hospital provides X-ray services, ultrasound diagnostics in both medicine and obstetrics/gynecology, endoscopy services, and general medical care.

A large donation was received from the Blantyre business community for the expansion of the in-patient facility. In 1993 this project was in progress. It would provide the hospital with an additional 14 beds.

Administrators: R. G. Garner, 1989; C. Koester, 1990- .

BLIND PERSONS, WORK AMONG. *See* Christian Record Services, Inc.

BLISS, SYLVESTER (1814-1863). Ablest of the Millerite editors, first assistant editor, then editor, of the Millerite journal *The Signs of the Times.* He was a Congregationalist from Hartford, Connecticut, with a liberal education and was a member of the Historical Society of Boston. He was also an editor of the *Advent Shield* and later edited the *Memoirs of Miller* (1853). Among his works are *Commentary on the Revelation, The Time of the End,* and *Analysis of Sacred Chronology.* He remained until his death the editor of the *Advent Herald* (a later name of *The Signs of the Times),* which remained the organ of the group of ex-Millerites who did not accept the doctrine of conditional immortality (see L. E. Froom, *The Prophetic Faith of Our Fathers,* vol. 4, pp. 631, 632).

BLUE, IRVIN F. (1885-1966). Missionary and teacher. He was a native of Nebraska. Following his education at Union College he became chaplain of the Nebraska Sanitarium. In 1914 he went to India, where he devoted many years in Christian service to the people of that country. Back in his homeland, he occupied the chair of theology at Union College from 1940 to 1945.

BLUE LAWS. *See* Sunday Laws.

BLUE MOUNTAIN ACADEMY. A coeducational secondary school for boarding students situated on 750 acres (300 hectares) of rolling farm and woodland at the base of the Blue Mountain Range of the Appalachians, three miles (five kilometers) west of Hamburg, Pennsylvania. It is owned and operated by the Pennsylvania Conference. The student enrollment in 1993 was 210; total school staff, 36 (teachers and administration, 25; industry management, vocational and clerical staff, 11). The school is approved by the Department of Public Instruction for the state of Pennsylvania, and is accredited by the Middle State Association of Colleges and Secondary Schools.

Industries include the farm, dairy, cafeteria, and literature evangelism. In 1990 an on-campus industry was added and housed in an expanded industrial arts building for the express purpose of providing student employment. The students fold, price-tag, and package garments and plasticware. This industry employs half the student body.

The forerunner of Blue Mountain Academy was Philadelphia Academy, established as a senior academy in 1939 and operated until the spring of 1945 in the German church building. In the autumn of 1946 the school was moved to a newly purchased property in Overbrook. The last class graduated from Philadelphia Academy in the spring of 1955. Blue Mountain Academy opened its doors to students that fall.

The history of Blue Mountain Academy goes back to July 4, 1948, when the East Pennsylvania Conference, at its fifteenth biennial session, voted to establish and maintain a boarding academy. It created an educational expansion committee, which appointed three committees (locating, financing, and publicity) to execute the establishment of the academy. In August 1948 the actions of the educational committee were presented to the churches of the East Pennsylvania Conference for approval. When the plans were approved, the constituency pledged 96 percent of the needed amount to build.

On January 28, 1954, groundbreaking ceremonies took place, and construction began on the cafeteria building. In the autumn of 1955 the school opened with the following buildings: the south wing of the girls' dormitory, the north and south wings of the boys' dormitory, the cafeteria building, a sewage disposal plant, and a Quonset building. The north wing of the boys' dormitory was used as a temporary administration building, classrooms, library, chapel, and music studios. Opening enrollment was 143.

Additional construction since 1955 includes a new farm shop (1959); administration building containing classrooms, auditorium, library, Music Department, administrative offices (1961); three new faculty homes (1961); remodeling of the north wing of the boys' dormitory to be used as residence hall, second floor for the boys and the first floor for girls (1961); additional faculty home (1963); a 10-acre (four-hectare) athletic field (1964); a north wing of the girls' dormitory (1966); a gymnasium/auditorium (1967); an airfield and new dairy complex (1970).

The 2,800-foot (850-meter) sod runway, located south of the gymnasium and the athletic fields, is lighted and has tie-down facilities. Flight training is given in the academy-owned Cessna 150. After 23 years the flight program has logged 8,000 accident- and incident-free hours and has produced 67 private pilots.

The dairy farm cultivates 400 acres (160 hectares); it milks 130 head, with a yearly production average per cow of 18,500 pounds. The Industrial Arts Department was established in 1965.

Beginning in 1974, a vocational and career

diploma was established. Vocational and career certificates are offered in several areas and are designed to provide the basic experience, knowledge, and skills necessary for a student to be able to obtain at least an entry-level position upon graduation. Each student completes up to 37.5 semester hours of additional classwork and as many as 350 hours of work experience to earn a certificate. Certificates offered are: Private Pilot, Office Skills, Auto Mechanics, and Auto Body.

In 1991 the school established a service program to enhance its mission statement objective of providing a Christ-centered Seventh-day Adventist education that leads youths into lives of service for God. The student body participates in 15 different community outreach projects throughout the year by dividing the student body into 15 family groups.

Principals: T. H. Jemison, 1954-1955; R. R. Adams, 1955-1959; G. C. Dart, 1959-1964; M. W. Shultz, 1964-1978; Wayne Longhofer, 1978-1981; Richard J. Emery, 1981-1985; Hamlet Canosa, 1985-1988; Stan Rouse 1988- .

BLUNDEN, HAROLD M. (1885-1974). Departmental secretary, administrator, pastor. A native of Australia, he was educated at Avondale College in that country. In 1907 he married Nellie Mountain. At this time he was serving as publishing secretary of South Australia. A year later he began teaching at Darling Range School in West Australia. In 1910 he became publishing secretary for the New South Wales Conference. Two years later he became manager of the *Signs* magazine and in 1914 accepted the position of publishing secretary of the China Union Mission, where he pioneered in the work of training Chinese colporteurs. In 1916 he served as superintendent of the Hupeh Mission in north China, and the following year became superintendent of the North China Union. In 1919 he was appointed lay activities secretary for the Australian Division. In the years that followed, he served as secretary of the Pacific Island Union Mission, president of the North New Zealand Conference, publishing secretary of the Pacific Union Conference, and chaplain of the Glendale Sanitarium and Hospital.

In 1937 he became the first manager of the Voice of Prophecy and associate speaker for the broadcast. Following this he served as president of the Antillian Union Mission until 1941, when he became secretary of the General Conference Publishing Department.

In 1947 he was appointed field secretary of the General Conference. In 1951 he became pastor of three churches in northern California and, five years later, was appointed field secretary of northern California. He retired in 1963 after 56 years of service to the denomination.

BOA VISTA CLINIC (Good View Clinic). *See* Brazil; São Paulo Adventist Hospital.

BOARD OF EDUCATION, SDA INTERNATIONAL. *See* Education, Department of.

BOARD OF REGENTS. The denominational accrediting body for the academies, colleges, and universities in the world church. It was established in 1928 by authority of the General Conference, and it functions as an agent of the Department of Education in accordance with General Conference policies concerning denominational aims, standards, and the application of the Christian philosophy of education to curricula and methods. The board is composed of the director and associate directors of the General Conference Department of Education, with the director serving as chair and one of the associate directors as executive secretary, the General Conference vice presidential advisor for education, the division/attached union directors of education, the union directors of education, and members who serve for terms of five years and include one university/college board chair, college and university presidents, one university/college academic vice president or dean, one university/college registrar or admission officer, one university/college finance officer, one university/college department of education chair, one conference/mission superintendent or director of education, and two persons engaged in education not employed by the church. Ex officio members are the General Conference president, secretary, and treasurer.

As the agent of the Department of Education, the board, in cooperation with the regional educational associations of America, visits schools and evaluates their programs. *See also* Education, Department of (General Conference).

BOATS, MISSIONARY. *See* Missionary Vessels.

BOEKENHUIS "VERITAS." *See* Netherlands Adventist Publications.

BOETTCHER, JULIUS THEODOR (1865-1931). Minister, administrator. He was born in Lindenwerder, Germany, and at the age of 14 was confirmed a member of the Lutheran Church. He came to the United States in 1881. Influenced by his sister and W. B. Hill, he accepted the Seventh-day Adventist faith in 1885. He spent the school year 1885-1886 in Battle Creek College and began preaching in the Ohio Conference. In 1889 he accepted a call to work in Germany. In 1890 he was ordained in Oberweil, Switzerland.

In 1894 Boettcher returned to America. For a short time he carried on evangelistic work in Minnesota and Ohio, then became head of the German Department in Union College, where he remained for seven years. In 1901 he was invited to return to Europe as president of the German-Swiss Conference, transferring in 1905 to the South German Conference, and in 1907 he was appointed leader of the work in Russia. Beginning in 1911, he served as vice president of the European Division.

Boettcher remained in Russia until forced to leave by the exigencies of World War I in 1916. Soon after his return to the United States, he was invited to teach Bible in the Clinton Theological Seminary at Clinton, Missouri. At the 1918 General Conference session in San Francisco he was appointed head of the German work in North America. He held this position until 1930, when failing health forced him to retire.

BOGENHOFEN SEMINARY (Seminar Schloss Bogenhofen). A coeducational boarding school on the secondary level, but offering programs on the junior/senior college level in theology and in German as a foreign language. The school, which is operated by the Austrian and the Swiss unions, in the Euro-Africa Division, is located in the small upper Austrian village of Bogenhofen, close to Braunau am Inn at the German border, 40 miles (65 kilometers) from Salzburg, 80 miles (130 kilometers) from Munich, and 180 miles (290 kilometers) from Vienna. It serves not only the Austrian Union but also, since 1953, the Swiss Union, by accepting students from the German Swiss Conference. The average enrollment is 100, with a staff of 12.

The school accommodates students from countries all over the world, and since 1968 has been connected with the ACA (Adventist Colleges Abroad) Program.

The following programs are offered: theology and religion (four years); Bible for high school graduates and lay workers (one year); high school (four years), leading to the Matura or Abitur, necessary for entrance into any European university; German for foreigners (one or two years). Since 1961 the German Language Department has been authorized by the Goethe Institute in Munich to teach German to foreign students and to award diplomas on three levels.

The 18-acre (7.3-hectare) school property, purchased in 1949 by the Austrian Union Conference with help from the then Southern European Division, includes a fifteenth-century castle under state protection as a historical monument. Classes opened on Nov. 30, 1949, with 22 students and a four-year curriculum consisting of the following programs: theology, general education, commercial courses, prenursing, and home economics.

The school has also owned a farm, vegetable gardens, and a factory (Optimo), manufacturing bedsteads and mattresses, enabling students to learn useful skills while earning money to defray educational expenses. F. Pieringer, the first principal of the institution, established a program combining the religious aspect of learning with the manual. The rural setting of the school helped to implement this goal. The growing enrollment necessitated the erection of various school buildings in the late 1950s and 1960s. Two modern dormitories were built recently. The Theological Seminary, established by F. Pieringer and H. Heinz, now offers classes at the senior college level on a provisional basis until full accreditation is granted. More than 80 percent of the Seventh-day Adventist pastors in Austria and more than 50 percent of those in German-speaking Switzerland have received their ministerial training at Bogenhofen Seminary. A number of pastors who attended the school have served as missionaries in French-speaking central Africa.

During the summer vacations the school is open for junior camps, conferences, and offers an intensive six-week German language course at different levels for foreigners. The summer language program is also affiliated with ACA.

Principals: Ferdinand Pieringer, 1949-1954; Paul Steiner, 1954-1957; Herbert Stöger, 1957-1961; R. J. Buyck, 1961-1963; Hans Heinz, 1963-1970; Horst Herrnstein, 1970-1974; Otto Riegler, 1974-1983; Klaus Zachhuber, 1983-1990; Franz Nusime, 1990- .

BOGGSTOWN MANUAL TRAINING ACADEMY. *See* Indiana Academy.

BOHEMIAN CONFERENCE. *See* Czech Republic; Euro-Africa Division; Slovakia.

BÓKAFORLAG ADVENTISTA. *See* Iceland Publishing House.

BOLIU HOSPITAL. A 24-bed medical institution located on Mussau Island, Papua New Guinea. It was established in 1955. The 1977 *Yearbook* listed two workers, Samuel and Esther Kangai. At that time it operated only as a small clinic and, in 1978, was taken over by the government.

BOLIVIA. A landlocked republic situated in the heart of the South American continent, bounded on the east and north by Brazil, on the west by Peru and Chile, and on the south by Argentina and Paraguay. It has an area of 424,160 square miles (1,100,000 square kilometers) and a population (1994) of 7.7 million.

About 55 percent of the people are Indians (largely Aymarás and Quechuas), 30 percent are mixed European and Indian (called cholos), and 15 percent are European, mainly of Spanish descent. This division is largely cultural; an Indian leaving a tribe and learning Spanish is classed as a cholo, and many classed as European have traces of Indian ancestry.

In general, the cholos are tradespeople, skilled workers, and minor civil servants; and the Indians are mainly laborers. Spanish is the official language of the country, but Aymará and Quechua are spoken by large numbers of Indians in the mountainous region around Lake Titicaca. Besides these two principal Indian languages, there are 28 tribal dialects that have been discovered by the Wycliffe Bible Translators. La Paz, where the executive and legislative branches of government reside, is the de facto capital, though the legal capital, where the judiciary branch resides, is Sucre. The state recognizes and supports the Roman Catholic religion, but since 1906 the constitution has provided for religious toleration. Ninety-five percent of the population professes Roman Catholicism, and of the remaining five percent more than 87,000 (1992) are Seventh-day Adventists, the rest being principally Presbyterians, Methodists, and Baptists.

There are three distinct and widely divergent geographical regions: (1) the Altiplano plateau between two ranges of the Andes Mountains, averaging 12,000 feet (3,650 meters) in elevation, comprising about two fifths of the land area of the republic, but containing three fourths of the population; (2) the yungas region, consisting of small valleys and steep mountain slopes on the eastern side of the Andes; and (3) the lowland plains, occupying the eastern portion of the country. Although Bolivia is entirely within the tropics, differences in elevation result in climates that may be described as arctic in the Altiplano, temperate in the yungas, and tropical in the lowlands. Bolivia is chiefly a mining country and is one of the world's largest exporters of tin. However, less than two percent of the population engage in tin mining. Most of the people (about two thirds) are agricultural workers.

Historical Background. The earliest history of what is now Bolivia is a matter of dispute, but it seems certain that in pre-Inca times a highly developed civilization flourished around the region of Lake Titicaca, as is evidenced by the ruins of Tiahuanaco. The Incas extended their empire into Bolivia long before the arrival of the Spaniards. Upper or Alto Peru, as it was called until 1559, fell to Gonzalo and Hernando Pizarro in 1538. The discovery of enormous silver deposits at Potosí brought a great influx of Spaniards, so that Potosí became the largest city in the Western Hemisphere and held this distinction until Mexico City surpassed it in the eighteenth century. The rule of the Spaniards was so oppressive that revolts erupted from time to time, the most notable one occurring in 1780. All of them except the last one were ruthlessly suppressed by the Spaniards. In 1776 Bolivia (called the *audiencia* of Charcas from 1559 to 1776) was transferred to the vice-royalty of La Plata, with headquarters in Buenos Aires. An uprising in 1809, led by José Domingo Murillo, was crushed, but the country did win independence Aug. 6, 1825, under the leadership of Gen. Antonio de Sucre, with the assistance of Gen. Simón Bolívar and Gen. José de San Martín. The new republic was named Bolivia in honor of Bolívar, and Sucre became its first president. The ensuing history of the country was disturbed by corrupt and autocratic administrations and disastrous military adventures. A war with Chile from 1879 to 1883 ended in the loss of Bolivia's region along the coast. A revolt of Brazilian rubber workers in 1899 led to the ceding of the territory of Acre to Brazil in 1903. But the costliest campaign of all was the Chaco War with Paraguay from 1932 to 1935, in which Bolivia lost most of the Chaco. Recent years have seen progress toward a stable democratic government and economic self-sufficiency.

Seventh-day Adventist Statistics. The territory of Bolivia constitutes the East Bolivia Mission and West Bolivia Mission, a part of the Inca Union Mission, which in turn is part of the South American Division. Statistics (1992): *East Bolivia Mission:* churches, 37; members, 19,161; elementary schools, 9; ordained ministers, 14; licensed ministers, 5; credentialed missionaries, 10. Headquarters are at Santa Cruz de la Sierra. *West Bolivia Mission:* churches, 149; members, 67,883; elementary schools, 80; ordained ministers, 27; licensed ministers, 18; credentialed missionaries, 9. Headquarters are at La Paz.

Institutions. Andes Adventist Academy; Bolivia Adventist Educational Complex; La Paz Adventist Clinic.

SDA Work. *Beginnings.* Bolivia was the last of the countries of the South American Division in which SDAs established their work (*Revista Adventista* 7:5, June 1907). However, as early as the middle of 1897, SDA literature was being sold in that country by Juan S. Pereira, a former Presbyterian colporteur. The *Missionary Magazine* for January 1899 reported: "The last message has been taken to Bolivia by a colporteur named Pereira. He took of our [SDA] books, *Patriarchs and Prophets* and *Steps to Christ.* He was a former colporteur for the Presbyterians who have a Bible Society established in Valparaiso, but he was discharged from their service for propagating Seventh-day Adventist doctrine, as was made public in the annual calendar of the society. Brother Pereira went to Bolivia at his own expense. He was arrested at the instigation of a priest for selling bad books. At his request the books were examined and pronounced not bad, whereupon he was released with the official advice to leave the country. However, he remained and continued his work for 18 months. Word has just arrived that he has returned to the north of Chile. I hope to give fuller particulars later. This brother has not yet fully identified himself with us, not having received baptism yet, as he said he was not ready."

Sometime later, after Pereira had left Bolivia, it came to light that while in that country, he had been imprisoned and condemned to death through the influence of the Roman clergy, but had miraculously escaped death through the help of a judge. Dr. J. Suárez Mirando, who later became interested in SDA teachings (*Revista Adventista* 7:5, 6, June 1907; 35:8, November 1935).

The next attempt at conducting colporteur work was made in the fall of 1902, when Edward W. Thomann and José Luis Escobar went to Bolivia to canvass in La Paz, Cochabamba, and Oruro. Although persecution broke out, the itinerary was a success, the canvassers selling about 1,000 copies of *Señales de los Tiempos* ("Signs of the Times") in La Paz alone. However, the work was not followed up, probably because of lack of religious freedom (*ibid.* 2:8, November 1902; 35:8, Dec. 9, 1935). In 1906 toleration of all religions was guaranteed by the Bolivian constitution, and in March of that year plans were laid for establishing work in Bolivia (*ibid.* 6:3, April 1906). Pereira, who had nearly lost his life a few years before, was among the first to volunteer "to lift the banner of God there" (*ibid.* 6:3, August 1906; 6:4, October 1906) through the sale of books.

First Missionaries. Early in June 1907, Thomann and his wife were sent to Bolivia to direct the work. They arrived in Oruro, Bolivia, where they met several persons who had become interested in the SDA doctrines through the reading of books they had purchased from Pereira (*ibid.* 7:4, August 1907). From Oruro the Thomanns went to Cochabamba, where they settled and worked not only for the Spanish people but also for the Quechua and Aymará Indians (*ibid.* 9:13, September 1909; 11:10, August 1909). At the end of July 1909 they left for Chile (*ibid.* 9:13, September 1909). Ferdinand A. Stahl, the new mission superintendent, arrived in La Paz with his wife and daughter about a week before the Thomanns left (F. A. Stahl, *In the Land of the Incas,* p. 62). Although he was unable to speak the language, Stahl began medical work among the higher class Bolivians before the end of the year (*Revista Adventista* 9:13, December 1909). Later he and Mrs. Stahl opened medical work among the Indians of Bolivia (*ibid.* 11:10, August 1911).

About a year after the Stahls arrived in La Paz, Otto H. Schulz came from the United States to do canvassing work (*ibid.* 11:9, January 1911). A few months later Ignacio Kalbermatter and his wife arrived from Paraguay to canvass as well as to assist the Stahls in medical work (*ibid.* 11:10, April 1911; 11:10, August 1911; 14:13, 14, February 1914).

Early in 1911 Stahl held an open-air meeting with Juan Huanacca, an SDA Indian from Peru, who served as his interpreter (*ibid.* 11:10, 11, May 1911; 11:10, June 1911; 11:10, 11,

August 1911). As a result, a widow, Rosa N. Doering, was baptized on Aug. 7, 1912, as the first Bolivian to become a Seventh-day Adventist *(ibid.* 11:11, 12, August 1911; 11:12, September 1911; 11:10, October 1911; 12:14, November 1912; 13:12, February 1913). A Baptist youth *(ibid.* 11:12, September 1911; 13:12, February 1913), José Cristobal Gómez, attended the same meetings and later joined the SDA Church by profession of faith. In 1913 Gómez canvassed with Schulz in the villages of Viacha and Corocoro and in the cities of Oruro and Cochabamba, selling the book *Salud y Hogar* ("Health and Home") and the magazine *Salud y Vida* ("Health and Life") *(ibid.* 13:12, September 1913; 13:14, November 1913; 14:14, January 1914).

In July 1911 Stahl was temporarily assigned to Plateria, Peru, to develop medical work among the Aymará Indians, while Kalbermatter remained in La Paz, apparently as acting superintendent *(ibid.* 11:16, July 1911; 11:10, August 1911; 11:12, September 1911; 11:16, October 1911; 15:9, June 1915). Later that same year Stahl's temporary assignment became permanent *(ibid.* 11:16, October 1911), but it was two years before a new director could be sent to take his place in La Paz. In 1914 W. R. Pohle replaced Stahl as the new director of the Bolivia Mission *(ibid.* 14:10, July 1914).

The first Sabbath school in the Aymará dialect was organized in 1913, on Potosí Street in the city of La Paz. However, because of the harmful effects of the high elevation of the Altiplano on the health of many of the missionaries, several of the workers were forced to leave Bolivia *(ibid.* 16:16, April-May 1916), resulting in a much smaller increase in membership than had been hoped, an increase from seven to only 15 between 1914 and 1919.

Indian Work. In 1920 Reid Shepard, who had been working at Puno, Peru, with F. A. Stahl, was sent to work among the Indians of Bolivia *(ibid.* 19:7, November 1919; 20:13, June 3, 1920). A few weeks after his arrival, he introduced himself to the minister of public instruction. In the course of the conversation the minister said, "I have in Pucarani [near Lake Titicaca] a normal school I have established to train teachers for the Indians. I will gladly turn over this school to your mission" *(ibid.* 20:13, June 3, 1920). Thinking that perhaps the minister did not fully understand the objectives of SDA work, Shepard replied, "You must remember, Mr. Minister, that as Protestants we cannot teach the Catholic religion in our educational work. Instead of it we teach the religion of our church" *(ibid.).* To this the minister replied, "I don't mind that; on the contrary, it [the SDA religion] is much better" *(ibid.).* The result of this interview was that at Rosario within six months the first SDA mission school in Bolivia was established *(ibid.* 21:11, Jan. 21, 1921; 29:8, January 1929). But severe opposition, which characterized the next 12 years of work in Bolivia, arose immediately. The first national missionaries in Bolivia came from the school at Rosario. Among these were Feliciano Chuquimia, Manuel Mamani, Domingo Chuquimia, Ignacio Mamani, and Ramón Chuquimia, who went out to preach the gospel in various provinces of the Department of La Paz.

Persecution and Hardships. In 1924 in response to a request by Chipana, Juan Pati, Francisco Mamani, and Melchor Mamani, Indians from the village of Collana, that a missionary be sent to them, Isaac C. Schneider went to open the mission station of Collana, assisted by an interpreter, Marcos Zenteno. This was the second Seventh-day Adventist mission station to be established in Bolivia. As the work progressed, persecution again arose. The wells of the mission were filled with dirt, and the buildings were either destroyed or damaged. In response to a request for help, a unit of cavalry was sent by the government to supervise the rebuilding of the damaged buildings by those who had harmed them. The worker's house and the storeroom reconstructed at that time are still in use. Chief Pedro Tambo, urged on by religious leaders, brought suit against the SDAs, claiming that the work was prejudicial to the community. His sudden death ended his opposition.

In 1926 an incident took place that left an indelible mark on the memory of Bolivian SDAs. One night a mob led by religious fanatics beat into unconsciousness Manuel Quilca, the teacher of the school in Arca in Inquisivi province, and burned down his home. His wife likewise was beaten until she was unconscious. C. H. Baker, an SDA missionary who visited the Quilca family about a week after the incident, reported that "alone in the house, which was already ablaze, was the daughter of the teacher. She also had been wounded, but before the fire reached her, she was rescued. Beaten and bruised by clubs, the little body welcomed death as a sweet release, and the end came the following morning" *(South American Bulletin* 2:6, October 1926).

In the following years, as Quilca reflected

upon this experience he found compensation in the fact that some of those who burned his house and murdered his daughter had accepted Christ.

About three years after the founding of Collana Mission Station, David E. Dalinger and his wife established a station near the village of Quime in the valley of Inquisivi, the third mission station to be established in Bolivia. Although they were beset by hardships and the loss of one of their children through disease, they were able to gain many friends and converts among the Indians. Other missionaries have also lost children while engaged in mission service. In little more than a year the Schneiders lost their two little daughters.

At the beginning of 1929 the Colegio Adventista de Bolivia (the Bolivia Training School) was organized on the grounds of the Collana Mission Station, with Leon Replogle as its first director and with Mariano E. Huayllara as a teacher. After two years the school was moved to Carcajes and then to Vinto in the Department of Cochabamba. From its beginning, this institution has provided the Bolivian field with workers and teachers.

The same year that the Bolivia Training School was established, the first Seventh-day Adventist camp meeting was held at Collana Mission Station and was attended by some 600 SDAs, who lived as far away as four days' walking distance from the campgrounds. This number represented nearly half the SDA membership of 1,400 in Bolivia that year. Nearly all related experiences of persecution through which they had passed *(Revista Adventista* 29:6, Mar. 25, 1929).

Medical Work. Seventh-day Adventist medical work was placed on a firm footing with the arrival of Dr. H. E. Butka in 1929, who was put in charge of Chulumani Mission Station, the fourth SDA mission station to be established in Bolivia. His subsequent medical and missionary work became well known throughout the nation and did much to lessen the persecution that had impeded SDA work in Bolivia *(ibid.* 29:8, October 1929; 31:9, Aug. 10, 1931). The local authorities were so impressed by his work that they built a hospital for him in 1931, which has been called Hospital Adventista Chulumani.

In 1937 the Ministry of Public Health of Bolivia assumed ownership of the hospital and leased it to the Bolivia Mission, which operated it until 1970, when it was returned to the government.

The beginning of the Chaco War (1932-1935) marked the end of active persecution of SDAs in Bolivia, and as a result SDAs began to make significant gains. In 1919 there was but one church and 15 members in Bolivia. By 1931 these figures had increased to seven churches and 1,905 members. But in 1936, only five years later, these figures had increased to 20 churches and a total of 2,801 members.

In 1936 Hospital Chulumani was closed because the Bolivia Mission thought it advisable to discontinue operating the hospital under existing arrangements with the government. The mission offered instead to lease it for 25 years. On hearing of these plans, a Roman Catholic priest secured a German medical doctor and offered to pay the Bolivian government 12 times as much for the lease as the SDAs had offered. Nevertheless, SDAs got the lease. Contracting acute appendicitis three years later, the priest was operated on by an SDA doctor at Chulumani Hospital. Recovering, he was so impressed by the Christian treatment he had received from the doctor and the nurses that he stopped his opposition and later publicly offered a dinner to the doctor and his family as a gesture of grateful appreciation. This change of attitude is typical of the change that has come over many former enemies of SDA work in Bolivia *(ibid.* 38:10, June 13, 1938; 38:9, July 11, 1938; 41:12, June 9, 1941; 45:15, Oct. 29, 1945).

In 1946 Dr. Harry T. Pitman, then medical director of the Chulumani Hospital, took charge of the newly built Guayaramerin Hospital (Hospital Adventista Guayaramerin) at Guayaramerin (Puerto Sucre) on the Mamore (Madera) River. In order to take care of these two hospitals so far apart, he purchased two war surplus airplanes. On his first flight he and his Polish pilot were killed instantly when their plane crashed on the side of Tunari Mountain, near Cochabamba. Dr. Pitman was buried at Cochabamba, and later a cenotaph was built at Bolivia Training School at Vinto in his honor and as a reminder of his sacrifice. The Guayaramerin Hospital was then leased by the Bolivia government to Dr. Elmer Bottsford, a missionary doctor who operated it until 1951. It was leased later to the Bolivia Mission from 1961 to 1967.

Recent Developments. After several attempts to establish a medical missionary institution in the Bolivian territory, the La Paz Adventist Clinic opened its doors in 1989, occupying a three-story building purchased for this purpose in the district of Miraflores. In

Santa Cruz de la Sierra, in east Bolivia, a small ambulatory clinic was opened in 1990.

Other events that demonstrate recent progress:

1. The increase in baptisms, reaching a total of 87,044 members in 1992.

2. At the end of 1992, there was one SDA for every 89 in the population.

3. An increase in academic preparation of Bolivian workers through higher education.

4. The development of a solid SDA educational system, including maintaining many elementary schools, and since 1991 the founding of an SDA University.

5. An outstanding increase in social assistance through ADRA, distributing each year hundreds of tons of food and clothing to the destitute.

6. The development of a mission launch program in the wide northeast area of Bolivia.

7. The emphasis on developing urban work, which should help reach those in higher socioeconomic levels, thus providing greater resources to this field where the work has developed largely in rural areas.

BOLIVIA ADVENTIST EDUCATIONAL COMPLEX (Complejo Educativo Adventista de Bolivia). A coeducational boarding school on the secondary level situated on 80 acres (32 hectares) of land at an elevation of 9,000 feet (2,750 meters) above sea level, at Vinto, Province of Quillacollo, Department of Cochabamba, Bolivia. It is owned and operated by the Bolivia Mission and serves the Seventh-day Adventist constituency in Bolivia. In 1993 there were 399 students and 36 teachers.

The school was created on Oct. 24-26, 1928, in the Bolivia Mission. It began its activities on Apr. 2, 1929, in Collana in La Paz, and was named Bolivia Adventist Industrial Institute. On July 9, 1931, it received official accreditation for the operation of an elementary school. In 1932 it was moved to Carcajes in Cochabamba, where it operated for 16 years, relocating in 1949 to Vinto, where it still is. Its name was changed to Colegio Adventista de Bolivia (Bolivia Training School).

On Mar. 16, 1952, by a resolution of the Ministry of Education, the Teacher Training School authorized the operation of a normal rural private school, by which six years of secondary instruction are offered, as well as six years of primary instruction. A later agreement in 1957 allowed the school board to create an Industrial Department, in conjunction with the work plan, which embraces training (largely practical) in carpentry, plumbing, mechanics, tractor farming, cattle raising, culinary art, sewing, and decorating. A four-year teachers' course was offered, following the primary course, for those preparing to teach in the rural SDA schools. Later, the school was authorized to offer, instead of the rural normal course, a three-year college-level course in elementary education. In 1987 an accounting and secretary school was added.

In 1991 the institution became Bolivia Adventist University (BAU) by Supreme Court Resolution. BAU began its activities on Aug. 27, 1991. In 1992 the church changed the name to Bolivia Adventist Educational Complex (BAEC).

Principals: Leon Replogle, 1929-1931; H. C. Morton, 1931-1937; C. E. Fillman, 1937-1940; E. U. Ayars, 1940-1942; D. J. von Pohle, 1943-1944; Eduardo Flores, 1945-1948; R. V. Vinglas, 1949-1952; Angels Foppiano, 1953-1955; Edmundo Alva, 1956-1959; José Bernhardt, 1960-1962; George Burgdorff, 1963; E. G. Meyer, 1964-1968; John B. Youngberg, 1969-1970; Arturo Carcagno, 1971-1973; Febo Basanta, 1974; Claudio Martín, 1975-1979; Félix Bendezú, 1980-1981; Guido Medina, 1982-1986; Juan Medina, 1987-1989; Miriam de Rodríguez (secondary school coordinator), 1990-1991; Mary Arcos Wills (secondary school), 1992; Martín Beltrán, 1993- .

BAEC Presidents: Miguel A. Salomón, 1990-1992; Gonzalo Monroy, 1993- .

BOLIVIA MISSION. *See* Bolivia.

BOLLMAN, CALVIN P. (1853-1943). Editor. He preached in Nebraska from 1881 to 1884, then served on the staff of the Pacific Press from 1884 to 1896, the latter part of the time being spent in editorial work at the branch office in New York City. On the *American Sentinel* staff he served as associate editor from 1896 to 1900, and 1901 to 1903 as associate editor of the *Southern Watchman.* During 1902 and 1903 he also served as editor of the *Gospel Herald.* From 1904 to 1914 he was successively secretary of the Southern Missionary Society, secretary-treasurer of the Southern Union, religious liberty secretary of the Southern Union, president of the Tennessee River Conference, and associate editor of the *Watchman Magazine* (1909-1914).

Joining the staff of the Review and Herald

Publishing Association in 1914, he was soon afterward appointed associate editor of the *Liberty* magazine. From 1920 until 1938 he was an associate editor of the *Review and Herald.* He was the author of *Why I Am a Seventh-day Adventist; Sunday: Origin of Its Observance in the Christian Church;* and *Heralds of the King.*

BOMBAY UNION TRAINING SCHOOL. *See* Seventh-day Adventist Higher Secondary School, Lasalgaon.

BONAIRE. *See* Netherlands Antilles.

BOND, C. LESTER (1888-1971). Youth leader, administrator. Bond was a native of California and received his education at Pacific Union College. Upon graduation he began his ministry in the Arizona Conference, and later served in several California conferences and Cuba. He joined the General Conference Missionary Volunteer Department in 1927 and served as an associate secretary until 1946. Under his leadership the JMV classes and the MV Honors were expanded and refined. He wrote the *JMV Handbook,* which was for many years the official guidebook for the JMV classwork. He became known as "Mr. JMV" because of his untiring work for juniors and his interest in the junior camp program. His book, *Ideals for Juniors,* an extremely popular volume, expands and explains the JMV Pledge and Law.

After 18 years of service to youth, Bond accepted a call to the Upper Columbia Conference, where he served first as Book and Bible House manager and then as president for eight years until his retirement in 1957.

BOND, FRANK STARR (1876-1924). Pioneer Seventh-day Adventist worker in Spain. He was a member of a family that contributed several workers to the church, among them C. Lester Bond, youth leader and author. His father, James Monroe Bond, a descendant of Oregon pioneers, was a farmer in Stanislaus County in California when his uncle, Seth, a convert of J. N. Loughborough, came to tell his brother of his new beliefs. Joining the SDAs, James Bond left farming and became a physician. His son Frank determined early in life to become a minister. After graduation from Healdsburg College, California, where he studied theology (1893-1899), he preached in Arizona and worked among Spanish-speaking settlers. In 1902 he and his brother Walter volunteered to pioneer SDA work in Spain, arriving there in 1903. In 1905 he returned to the U.S. to marry Mrs. Martha Farnsworth, then continued serving in the Iberian field as an evangelist and as a leader until 1923, when poor health caused his retirement. He was ordained to the ministry in 1907 in Gland, Switzerland.

BOND, WALTER GUY (1879-1914). Pioneer Seventh-day Adventist worker in Spain. He was born in California, where his parents became SDAs when he was a child. Near the turn of the century he was preaching in California and, as some reports indicate, among the Spanish-speaking settlers in Arizona. In 1902 he and his brother Frank volunteered to go to Spain to pioneer SDA work there. Before leaving the U.S., he married Leola Gerow. They arrived in Barcelona, Spain, in June 1903, and later that year he with his brother Frank opened a boys' school in the town of Sabadell nearby. From then until his death in 1914, with the exception of one year (1904-1905), he directed SDA work in Spain, establishing churches in several places and preaching in many places. He died from peritonitis while on a missionary journey.

BONFOEY, CLARISSA M. (1821-1856). Housekeeper for Ellen G. White. On the death of her parents in 1849, she proposed that she share with the Whites the furniture she had inherited, live with them, and assist in the housework. For eight years she gave devoted service, traveling with them on occasion, and sometimes caring for the children while the Whites were away. Ellen G. White writes of her in most appreciative terms (LS 123; 2SG 113).

BONGO ADVENTIST SEMINARY (formerly Bongo Mission Training School). A former coeducational boarding school on the junior high school level, operated by the Angola Union Mission in the Euro-Africa Division. It shared the same campus with the Bongo Mission and the Bongo Mission Hospital.

The forerunner of the Bongo Mission Training School was an elementary school opened soon after the founding of the Bongo Mission in April 1924. During the first year, 15 to 20 students from 5 to 50 years of age attended classes for an hour each day on a porch that served as a shelter for the carpenters. In 1925 after the arrival of D. P. Harder, the Bongo school was conducted in a more organized way. A temporary building was constructed in which Artur de Oliveira taught classes four hours a day.

In January 1927 the school moved into a brick building, and a class in teaching methods, conducted by Mrs. A. N. Tonge, was begun. This same year a student named Daniel Cahangala took the government examination and became the first African Seventh-day Adventist worker in Angola.

Because of increasing enrollments, a new school building was erected in 1941. New girls' (1954) and boys' (1962) dormitories replaced the old adobe buildings. From the beginning, agriculture held an important place in the curriculum. From this source students could earn almost enough to meet their expenses.

In addition to five years of elementary schooling, the teachers' course included two years of secondary training plus three years of Bible instruction and related subjects. The average attendance was 300.

Because of the political situation, the school was moved to Huambo. In January 1992, during the terrible events of the war, the buildings were totally destroyed. There are plans to rebuild Bongo Adventist Seminary as soon as peace is established.

Principals: D. P. Harder, 1925-1927; Mrs. A. N. Tonge, 1927-1931; O. I. Fields, 1931-1942; I. D. Higgins, 1942-1944; W. M. Webster, 1944-1948; E. V. Hermanson, 1948-1950; E. L. Jewell, 1950-1951; A.J.S. Casaca, 1951-1952; J. M. Miranda, 1952-1954; J. A. Morgado, 1954-1955; M. S. Castro, 1955-1956; Dr. Roy B. Parsons, 1956-1959; Frank Dietrich, 1959-1964; A. C. Lopes, 1964-1965; J. E. Rodrigues, 1965; A. Mauricio, 1965-1969; J.P.F. Sincer, 1969-1971; Dr. David Parsons, 1971-1972; D. L. Cordas, 1972-1975; Teodoro Elias, 1984-1992.

BONGO MISSION HOSPITAL. Operated until 1975 as a 101-bed general hospital, located at Bongo Mission, Lépi, Angola, and organized as an institution of the Angola Union.

In October 1926 Dr. A. N. Tonge arrived to begin the medical work among the Ovimbundu people, where the Lépi mission station had been opened only two years before by J. D. Baker and his wife. Mrs. Baker, a nurse, had begun a small dispensary for the local people. Dr. Tonge treated his first patients on the veranda of the director's house. Later, when his own house was ready, the doctor used his bathroom, which had an outside entrance, as the dispensary. In 1928 the first building was finished, housing the office and a dispensary. Two small separate buildings were added later. These served as wards and were followed by a new dispensary. All these facilities were permanent.

Dr. Tonge remained at Bongo until February 1930, when he was called to serve as medical secretary of the Southern African Division.

Bongo Dispensary and Hospital remained under the care of nurses, first Ina Moore and then, for a short time, Ruth Johnson, until the arrival of Dr. Roy B. Parsons on Dec. 1, 1931. He had spent 18 months in Portugal learning the language and getting his Portuguese degree to practice medicine.

In 1938 construction was begun to enlarge the patient accommodations, a program that continued until 1955. The original buildings were incorporated into new structure, with additional construction, to bring the bed capacity up to 101. A new dispensary was built in 1945. The new unit included separate buildings for a kitchen, laboratory-pharmacy, laundry, electric-light plant, surgical unit, and dairy. Except for the surgical unit of the hospital, funds for construction were all furnished by income from the European patients and small donations by friends.

The financial maintenance of the hospital and dispensary continued to depend on income from patients. This included all salaries and expenses, except the director's salary, since 1950. In 1973 the dispensary had an average of 10,249 new African patients a year, and the European consultations averaged 4,524 new patients annually. The hospital admissions for 1973 totaled 3,369.

In 1968, after more than 35 years of medical work in Angola (many of those who came from all parts of the country to seek his professional skill became SDAs), Dr. Roy Parsons retired, and his son, Dr. David Parsons, who also held a Portuguese degree, became medical director. Another son, Robert Parsons, was a laboratory technician. Mrs. David Parsons was the director of nurses. In 1972 Dr. Gideon Marques, followed by Dr. Helio Rocumback in 1973, joined the staff. Both doctors were from Brazil. In 1974 the new X-ray Department began to function, with James Holder as technician.

Because of political circumstances, the hospital was closed in 1975. Until 1980 medical care was provided by qualified nurses because of the lack of doctors. In 1980 Dr. Ferran Sabate, from Spain, his wife, and nurse Victoria Duarte reopened and ran the hospital until 1983, when they were kidnapped by the UNITA. The hospital was closed, and local nurses continued offering treatment to the population.

In 1985 Dr. Otello Vergeres from Switzerland and Dr. Roberto Va from Germany resumed medical service at Bongo. Both were forced to leave the country in 1987. Since then the hospital has been operated only as a dispensary.

Medical Directors: A. N. Tonge, 1926-1930; R. B. Parsons, 1931-1968; David Parsons, 1968-1975; Ferran Sabate, 1980-1983; Pedro Balanca de Freitas, 1983-1986; Otello Vergeres, 1986-1987.

BONGO MISSION TRAINING SCHOOL. *See* Bongo Adventist Seminary.

BOOK AND BIBLE HOUSE. *See* Adventist Book Center.

BOOKS (of record in heaven). *See* Investigative Judgment.

BOOKSELLING. See Adventist Book Center; Literature Evangelists.

BORLE, LOUIS EDWARD (1860-1943). Publishing house manager successively in Mexico, Switzerland, Spain, and France. Borle's parents were among the first in Switzerland to become Seventh-day Adventists (about 1870), and so he had an SDA home background. In 1876 he was baptized, and two years later, at the age of 18, he began working at the SDA publishing and printing office in Basel, where he learned the printing trade. In 1888 he came to America and worked at the Pacific Press Publishing Association for 20 years. In 1908 he went to Mexico to work in the SDA publishing house there. About 1910 he returned to Switzerland and took charge of the Latin Union Publishing House. In 1915 he went to Barcelona, Spain, as the first manager of the Barcelona Publishing House, and remained there until 1921. From 1923 to 1925 he again managed the Latin Union Publishing House, which by that time had been transferred to France.

BORNEO. For northern Borneo, *see* Brunei; Malaysia, Federation of; for southern Borneo, *see* Indonesia.

BORNEO-BRUNEI-SARAWAK MISSION. *See* Malaysia, Federation of.

BOSE, KHERODA (d. 1948). Nurse, personal worker. Probably the first Seventh-day Adventist convert in India. She was a teacher in a Baptist school, and came to assist Georgia Burrus, who was teaching the first Seventh-day Adventist school for girls in Calcutta, India, which was opened soon after the arrival of D. A. Robinson in 1895. The transfer was made by recommendation of Baptist missionaries on the basis of the school's increasing enrollment. After a short time with the school, she accepted SDA beliefs and joined the young church in Calcutta despite the reproach and separation from her former Christian friends. After spending some time in schoolwork, she took training in nursing at the Calcutta sanitarium and served as a nurse in the sanitarium with Dr. O. G. Place and Drs. R. and O. Ingersoll. When the sanitarium was closed, she helped in the treatment rooms that succeeded it, and in later years, as long as her strength permitted, she went from house to house speaking of her faith to Indian women. Gentry G. Lowry wrote a book about her entitled *Korada, a Child Widow of India* (1931).

BOSNIA AND HERZEGOVINA. A republic in southeastern Europe whose neighbors are Croatia and Yugoslavia. Bosnia and Herzegovina covers an area of 19,736 square miles (51,100 square kilometers) and has a population (1994) of 4.7 million, made up primarily of Muslims, Serbs, and Croats. The principal language is Serbo-Croatian; religions include Islam, Serbian Orthodoxy, and Roman Catholicism.

For more than 500 years Bosnia and Herzegovina was under Turkish, Austrian, and Hungarian influence. In 1918 it became part of the Kingdom of the Serbs, Croats, and Slovenes, which became Yugoslavia in 1929. Bosnia and Herzegovina became independent from Yugoslavia in 1992.

Seventh-day Adventist Statistics. Bosnia and Herzegovina is part of the Southwest Conference, which in 1993 had 19 churches and 604 members. The Southwest Conference is part of the South-East European Union, which in turn is part of the Trans-European Division.

BOSTON REGIONAL MEDICAL CENTER (formerly New England Memorial Hospital). A 195-bed general hospital in Stoneham, Massachusetts, nine miles (14 kilometers) north of Boston. Ellen White referred to the hospital as the "Melrose Sanitarium" because of its proximity and former access at the railroad station in Melrose, an adjoining city.

The hospital is located on a 45-acre (18-hectare) plot overlooking Spot Pond, in the midst of a beautiful, natural, woodland park of 5,000 acres (2,025 hectares) known as the Middlesex Fels (watershed) reservation.

It is operated by the Atlantic Union Conference of Seventh-day Adventists. A general board of trustees appoints an administrator and an executive board and approves appointments to the medical and administrative staffs.

Approval for operation is granted by the Public Health Department of the Commonwealth of Massachusetts, and accreditation by the Joint Commission on Accreditation of Hospitals; membership is held in the Seventh-day Adventist Hospital Association, American-Protestant Hospital Association, American Hospital Association, Massachusetts Hospital Association, and the North Shore Health Planning Council. The institution is a participating hospital in the Massachusetts Hospital Service.

History. A charter was granted Apr. 28, 1899, to Hampton W. Cottrell, William A. Wilcox, Edgar Kelsey, Horace B. Tucker, Frank W. Mace, Joseph H. Haughey, Charles R. Brown, and Wilbur L. Payne, a group organized for the purpose of founding a hospital, under the name New England Sanitarium and Benevolent Association. The hospital was located near the present campus of Atlantic Union College, in South Lancaster, Massachusetts, as the eastern branch of the Battle Creek Sanitarium. (In 1907 the constitution was amended to relate the hospital directly to the New England Conference—now the Atlantic Union Conference.)

The year 1901 records more than 600 patients from 26 states, Canada, and the West Indies. It was sometimes necessary to find additional accommodations for the patients in the village. Expansion was needed but was impossible on the original site.

In August 1902 C. C. Nicola, M.D., superintendent, wrote to Ellen White regarding local conditions that confirmed warnings she had given (7T 88, 89) against locating sanitariums near wealthy homes.

The search for a new site, in response to a vision of Ellen White *(Review and Herald,* Sept. 29, 1904), resulted in the acquisition of the Langwood Hotel property in Stoneham—then a hotel building—plus several detached buildings, with its own electric lighting and steam heating system. It was purchased from a Dr. Coggswell, formerly port physician of Boston, who had planned to convert it into a hospital or sanitarium. This property, assessed at $98,000, was bought for $40,000.

The final transfer of patients was made from South Lancaster on Oct. 9, 1902, when a railroad car with 25 passengers, 12 of whom were patients, was routed to Melrose. The buildings on the South Lancaster property were torn down and portions were moved to the Stoneham property.

After a visit, Ellen White wrote that the transfer of the sanitarium to "a place much nearer Boston, and yet far enough removed from the busy city so that the patients may have the most favorable conditions for recovery of health," was in God's providence *(Special Testimonies,* Series B, No. 13, p. 3).

In 1906 a new main building was completed. (The original structure was repaired after a fire and used as a residence for student nurses.) A gymnasium and physical-therapy treatment rooms were added in 1908.

An additional stucco hospital wing was constructed in 1924, and was used as a surgical unit. Another wing, the Ruble Memorial, a more modern, four-story brick building, was completed in 1952, and named in honor of Dr. Wells A. Ruble, medical director from 1929 to 1943.

In March 1967 the name of the hospital was changed to New England Memorial Hospital to better reflect the full line of services offered in surgery, medicine, and maternity, and in memory of the early pioneers of the Advent movement. In August 1967 construction was begun on a major modernization and expansion program. All of the buildings, except the brick Ruble Memorial Wing, were demolished after the October 1969 opening of the first phase of a 300-bed hospital. A 16-suite medical arts building, adjacent to and north of the main hospital, was opened in early 1971; and phase two of the rebuilding program was completed in early 1973, thereby offering a completely modern facility for a witness to the community, with up-to-date technology and facilities for health care, and an expanded outreach in health-education evangelism. Another medical office building was added in 1988.

In the five-year period between preconstruction (1969) and after-construction (1974), the inpatient load increased from 5,000 to 9,000 patients per year; and the emergency room load increased from nearly 6,000 to more than 20,000 patients. In the 1990s, inpatient admissions stand at approximately 8,000 per year. Outpatient admissions and visits surpass 171,000.

The hospital is affiliated with schools, colleges, and universities in the following programs: Schools of Nursing—Atlantic Union College and Northern Essex Community College; School of Radiologic Technology—Northeastern University; School of Medical Technology—Atlantic Union College and Framingham State College; Health Education, Physical and Occupational Therapy—Loma Linda University; Physical Therapy—Northeastern University and the North Shore Community College; OR Technician Program—Northeastern Metropolitan Regional Vocational School. (The School of Nursing was operated at the hospital from 1899 to 1966, when it was transferred to Atlantic Union College, 45 miles [70 kilometers] distant.)

The hospital church was organized on Oct. 14, 1903, with 35 members. A Sabbath school was formed on Oct. 22, 1902. A second church was organized in the town of Stoneham, two miles (three kilometers) from the hospital, on Dec. 9, 1942. Both churches attest to the growth of Seventh-day Adventist membership—primarily in affiliation with the hospital—which bears a constant personal witness of Jesus in this area.

Building on the pioneer missionary endeavors of the early workers, two full-time hospital chaplains, one full-time health education worker, and nearly 1,200 full- and part-time employees continually pursue with the help of the lay and medical staff a course of health education, one-to-one and group-witnessing evangelism, and Bible studies leading to baptism.

The present staff is endeavoring to meet the objectives set for the institution in *Special Testimonies,* Series B, No. 13, page 12: "Boston has been pointed out to me repeatedly as a place that must be faithfully worked. The light must shine in the outskirts and in the inmost parts. The Melrose Sanitarium is one of the greatest agencies that can be employed to reach Boston with the truth."

In 1995 New England Memorial Hospital became Boston Regional Medical Center.

Medical Directors/Superintendents: C. C. Nicola, 1899-1907; C. O. Prince, 1907-1908; W. E. Bliss, 1908-1922; L. E. Elliott (acting), 1922; W. C. Dunscombe, 1922-1924; V. L. Fisher, 1924-1929; W. A. Ruble, 1929-1943; C. E. Parrish, 1943-1948; J. S. Kootsey, 1949-1951.

Business Managers/Administrators: W. A. Wilcox, 1899-1903; W. M. Lee, 1903-1908; J. B. Huguley, 1908-1909; J. G. White, 1909-1916; H. B. Steele, 1916-1917; H. K. Presley, 1917-1918; E. J. Baker, 1918-1920; R. Hook, Jr., 1920-1921; V. MacPherson, 1921-1924; S. E. McNeill, 1924-1927; E. L. Place, 1927-1941; H. E. Rice, 1941-1949; A. C. Larson, 1950-1954; R. G. Manuel, 1954-1957; V. D. Dortch, 1957-1961; K. W. Tilghman, 1961-1962; R. L. Pelton, 1963-1970; T. O. Moore, 1970-1975.

Presidents: E. L. Wall, 1975-1981; Wolfgang von Maack, 1981-1988; F. J. Perez, 1988-1994; Charles S. Ricks, 1994- .

BOSTON SCHOOL. *See* Adventist Atlantic Secondary School.

BOTSWANA. An African republic situated in southern Africa, bounded on the west by Namibia (formerly South-West Africa), on the north by Zambia, on the east by Zimbabwe, and on the south by South Africa. It has an area of 231,804 square miles (600,400 square kilometers) and a population (1994) of 1.4 million.

The Botswana people, mainly of Bantu origin, migrated, for the most part, from what is now the Republic of South Africa and the territories of Lesotho and Swaziland. Large areas in the northwest are uninhabited because of sleeping sickness. Arid conditions prevail during much of the year, particularly in the west, in the Kalahari Desert. The principal occupation of the people is raising cattle, sheep, and goats, but during the years 1960-1980 the mining of nickel, copper, and diamonds developed greatly. During the 1980s and after, diamonds have become the backbone of the country's mining resources.

Seventh-day Adventist Statistics. The territory of Botswana constitutes two fields: the South Botswana Field, with headquarters in Gaborone, the capital city; and North Botswana Field, with headquarters in Francistown. These fields are attached to the Eastern Africa Division. Statistics (1992) for the *North Botswana Field:* churches, 16; members, 6,271; ordained ministers, 7; credentialed missionaries, 2. *South Botswana Field:* churches, 11; members, 5,909; ordained ministers, 8; licensed ministers, 7; credentialed literature evangelists, 3.

Institutions. Kanye Hospital.

Development of SDA Work. Permission to open a hospital in Kanye village was granted on the understanding that no preaching be done. W. H. Anderson in 1921 received this in an interview with the queen mother, Gagoangwe, regent for the then-16-year-old chief, Bathoen II. The work of Dr. A. H. Kretschmar in the new hospital broke down prejudice, and subsequently he received permission to preach. In 1922 J. R. Campbell was allowed to enter Kanye and hold meetings. In 1927 H. Walker was permitted to conduct regular mission work there and also at Mauyana, a village some 30 miles (50 kilometers) away, where David Livingstone once worked. After 1928 SDA work in Botswana was administered by the Zambesi Union, except for a short period when it was under the South African Union Conference.

In 1951 Botswana was organized into a field within the Zambesi Union, with headquarters at Kanye. W. M. Webster was president. From 1954 to 1959 work in Botswana was administered by the Zambesi Union, then the territory was reorganized as a field in 1959, with W. M. Cooks as president. At that time the headquarters were established at Francistown, with permanent housing and an office building. In 1962 the first SDA school in Botswana opened in the small village of Ramokgoname, 40 miles (65 kilometers) from Palapye, and soon had a substantial enrollment. In 1984 the Botswana Field was organized into two fields, the North and South, which are attached directly to the Eastern Africa Division.

BOTSWANA FIELD. *See* Botswana.

BOUAKÉ ADVENTIST SECONDARY SCHOOL (Collège Adventiste de Bouaké). A coeducational day and boarding school on the secondary level, situated on the outskirts of Bouaké in the central Côte d'Ivoire, approximately 250 miles (400 kilometers) from Abidjan. It is operated by the Sahel Union Mission. The school developed from an elementary school whose buildings (three classrooms and a house), begun by J. R. Buzenet, who arrived at Bouaké in 1952, were finished in 1955 by G. M. Ellstrom. On Mar. 7 the school opened, offering the first primary class, which was taught by Ba Amadou. In October 1956 Buzenet opened two other classes. With three more added in 1957, the school offered the entire primary school course.

In 1958 G. Gutekunst and H. Kempf opened the first year of the secondary school. The second and third years of the secondary school were added in 1960 and 1961, respectively. A primary school of six classes, housed in temporary quarters, was opened for mass education.

In 1962 the secondary school added the fourth year, as well as the first year, of a commercial course. The straw huts were replaced by classrooms, and the secondary school was transferred to a new building containing four classrooms and two offices, erected on a new compound separated from the old by a road.

In 1971 a seminary was opened, offering three years of theology leading to the diploma of evangelist. An extensive building program was launched in 1973, with projects for lavatories, a new classroom building with a science laboratory, a new primary school, and a boys' dormitory. There are six staff houses and a church seating 1,000.

In 1991 Salomon Assiene became the first national principal. In 1993 the school had a capacity of 1,300 students, with an enrollment of 819.

Principals: H. Kempf, 1958-1959; P. A. Heise, 1959-1964; P. E. Giddings, 1964-1970; G. Dewinter, 1970-1972; A. M. Vine, 1972-1973; R. L. Joachim, 1973-1978; M. Michel, 1978-1980; D. Dekeuster, 1980-1982; S. Galanth, 1982-1991; S. Assiene, 1991- .

BOUGAINVILLE MISSION. *See* Papua New Guinea.

BOULANGERIE ADVENTISTE. *See* Haiti Food Factory.

BOULDER MEMORIAL HOSPITAL. A 93-bed acute-care general hospital with specialized rehabilitation operated at Boulder, Colorado, until it was sold in 1989. It has been replaced by Avista Hospital.

History. In 1893 a retired minister, John Fulton, visited Boulder, Colorado, in search of health. He was so impressed with the city that he wrote to Dr. J. H. Kellogg urging him to found a medical institution there. As a result, on Dec. 4, 1893, a health boarding home was opened in a dwelling on University Hill, and placed under the direction of Lewis Kleuster and his wife, of the Battle Creek nursing staff. From this small nucleus grew the Colorado Sanitarium, which was built by the General Conference and the Medical Missionary Board of the International Medical Missionary and Benevolent Association under the direction of Dr. Kellogg. Ground was broken on June 10,

1895, on a 90-acre (36-hectare) site on Upper Mapleton Hill, for three buildings, the largest six stories high. The sanitarium was dedicated July 1, 1896. Joseph Hartman, a nurse, became the first business manager, and Dr. O. G. Place was the medical superintendent.

In November 1897 the institution, valued at $76,500, was taken over by the newly organized Colorado Medical Missionary and Benevolent Association, to which the General Conference medical organization gave $31,500 as a working capital; the Colorado association promised to pay $45,000 as the sanitarium became sufficiently prosperous. This debt proved to be a millstone about the neck of the fledgling institution.

Being regarded as a summer resort, the sanitarium was well patronized in the summer, especially by people from the South, such as Texans who came to the mountains to spend the hot-weather period, but it had a lean existence during the long period between summers. By July 1902, however, F. M. Wilcox, the chaplain, was able to report in the *Review and Herald* that the past winter the patronage had been about twice what it had been heretofore, that the summer patronage was excellent, and that the sanitarium now needed additional facilities to care for the summer patronage and also separate facilities to care for consumptive patients. (The sanitarium had so many of these patients that it had become known as an institution for tuberculosis patients.) However, 1902 was a peak season. By 1906 the institution was glad to take advantage of the campaign then launched for the relief of sanitarium debt around the circle of the globe through the sale of Ellen G. White's book *The Ministry of Healing*.

In 1905 the institution was renamed the Boulder-Colorado Sanitarium, and in 1910 it was turned over to the Central Union Conference. From 1937 to 1941 Boulder-Colorado Sanitarium was operated under joint management with Porter Sanitarium at Denver, R. J. Brown managing both.

Beginning about 1897, a health-food factory was operated for many years. In 1912 a health food store was operated in Denver, and at times outlets were distributing the products in other cities. A three-story wing was added to the south end of the old main building in 1918-1919. This section included the pharmacy, laboratory, Maternity Department, operating room, patient rooms, a large parlor, and sun deck. In 1929-1930 a three-story nurses' residence was built northwest of the main building. After the professional nursing school was discontinued in 1955, this building was converted into a senior citizens' center.

Nursing Education and Training. Within three months after the opening of Colorado Sanitarium, a training class of 22 student nurses was reported "well in progress." The two-year course included the medical aspects of the care of the sick, hydrotherapy, massage, laundering, waiting on tables, and cooking. Classes were graduated every year, except one, from 1898 to 1944. In the early 1940s a joint School of Nursing was set up by Porter Sanitarium and Boulder-Colorado Sanitarium. The 1947-1948 *Union College Bulletin* announced that the two sister medical institutions had entered into an arrangement with Union College of Lincoln, Nebraska, to establish the first collegiate nursing program among SDAs, whereby the liberal arts and preprofessional science courses were taken on the Lincoln campus and the clinical experience was offered at Boulder and Porter. On Jan. 15, 1955, Boulder dropped out of this arrangement.

Growth in Organization and Changing Concepts. When the institution was built, according to the old traditional sanitarium concept, a corps of SDA physicians was employed by the institution. It was anticipated that the reputation of the sanitarium would attract the sick from many places, often from a distance, to become patients of the sanitarium physicians and under their care to receive such treatments as would aid the body to work its own healing, aided by hydrotherapy and other natural treatments, rest, proper diet, exercise, and the reform of injurious habits. Horseback riding, mountain climbing, and walks amid the beauties of nature were included in the regimen. Lectures on healthful living and the learning of correct habits were intended to bring about a permanent cure.

As the years went by, the old sanitarium concept passed and it became necessary to rely upon local physicians to bring their patients to the sanitarium, usually for short periods of hospitalization. In harmony with the new type of patronage, it was not necessary to employ a medical superintendent and other physicians. The name of the institution was changed to the Boulder-Colorado Sanitarium and Hospital (1956). Under the new hospital system the staff was organized in the conventional manner from local participating physicians.

Outstanding in medical service to the institution was the career of H. A. Green, who arrived at Boulder on Dec. 4, 1910, and continued as medical superintendent and chief surgeon until 1937, a period of nearly 30 years, when the institution was widely known as Dr. Green's sanitarium. Another long term of service was that of Dr. Kate Lindsay, who came around the turn of the century and remained until 1920.

Later Developments. In the late fifties a rebuilding of the physical plant was begun. The original building was razed and was replaced with a new, modern building in 1957. A new obstetrical wing and new operating rooms were added in 1958. In 1962 the name was changed to Boulder Memorial Hospital. The year 1969 marked the completion of a new million-dollar three-story east wing, and a new entrance and offices were added to this east wing in 1972. At the same time a completely new Radiology Department was added. In 1973 the obstetrical service was closed out and in its place a strong pediatrics service was developed.

Hydrotherapy and other natural remedies, a basic part of the sanitarium's treatment since its inception, were expanded into a full physical medicine and rehabilitation program in the early 1970s. By the early 1980s the hospital was considered to have the best rehabilitation service in Colorado.

In 1986 because of the need for a full-service hospital located in an area of growth at a greater distance from its competition, the hospital acquired 72 acres (30 hectares) of land off the Boulder-Denver Turnpike in Louisville, about 10 miles (16 kilometers) southeast of its location in Boulder. In late 1987 plans were accelerated to build in Louisville. At first it was thought that Boulder Memorial could be retained, but because of mounting financial losses, it was decided to sell to Boulder Community Hospital and to build a replacement hospital at Louisville. The sale was finalized on Mar. 9, 1989, and Avista Hospital opened its doors on May 7, 1990, as a continuation of SDA health care in the Boulder area. *See* Avista Hospital.

Medical Superintendents: O. G. Place, 1895-1896; W. H. Riley, 1896-1902; Kate Lindsay, 1902; H. F. Rand, 1902-1906; J. D. Shively, 1906-1910; L. L. Jones, 1910; H. A. Green, 1910-1937; Myron S. King, 1937-1938; H. A. Green, 1938-1939; C. C. Prince, 1939-1942; Ralph F. Waddell, 1942-1945; R. T. Smith, 1945-1948; Russell H. Hanson, 1948-1956.

Managers: Joseph Hartman, 1895-1901; F. M. Wilcox, 1902-1909; Meade MacGuire, 1909-1910; C. E. Rice, 1910-1912; E. J. Baker, 1913-1918; H. B. Steele, 1918-1920; F. R. Eastman, 1920-1925; L. V. Roberson, 1925-1926; R. J. Brown, 1926-1941; C. L. Torrey, 1941-1942; P. L. Williams, 1942-1943; L. F. Bohner, 1943-1945; H. A. Young, 1945-1951; H. E. Rice, 1951-1957.

Administrators: H. C. Hartman, 1957-1960; J. R. Shawver, 1960-1963; Warren M. Clark, 1963-1969; I. E. Hamilton, 1969-1972; Warren M. Clark, 1973-1987; James C. Culpepper, 1987-1989.

BOURDEAU, AUGUSTIN CORNELIUS (1834-1916). Pioneer French language evangelist, brother of D. T. Bourdeau. Born in Canada, he was reared in Vermont; at 12 he joined the Baptist Church and became a promising preacher, working chiefly among French-speaking people. In 1856 he accepted the Sabbath doctrine, and the following year was baptized as a Seventh-day Adventist, and was ordained.

For eight years he supported himself as a carpenter and joiner, while preaching the SDA message. He helped organize the Vermont Conference in 1862, and later served as its president for several years.

He was sent to Iowa in 1866 to help reorganize SDA churches that had been disaffected by the Snook-Brinkerhoff defection *(see* Marion Party). Later he worked in Illinois, Wisconsin, Missouri, and Vermont. Working in Quebec, he organized the Quebec Conference and served as its president for a time.

From 1884 to 1888 he worked in various parts of Europe, including Italy, France (where he promoted the colporteur work), Romania, and Switzerland. While overseas he contracted black typhoid fever, which left permanent aftereffects. On his return he worked in Canada, Vermont, Michigan, Pennsylvania, and the Dakotas. In his earlier ministry he had been closely associated with James and Ellen G. White.

BOURDEAU, DANIEL T. (1835-1905). Evangelist and missionary, brother of A. C. Bourdeau. At 11 years of age he joined the Baptist Church, and at 16, with his brother, attended a Baptist French language institution at Grand Ligne, Lower Canada. In 1861 he married Marion E. Saxby. Ordained to the SDA ministry in 1858, he, with his brother, spent many years in evangelism in New England and Canada. As far as is known, the two brothers were the first of French descent to accept the Seventh-day Adventist faith.

In 1868, with J. N. Loughborough, he responded to a call from an SDA group in California, headed by M. G. Kellogg, to open SDA work in that state. When he returned to the East in 1870, he resumed work among the French-speaking people and organized churches in Wisconsin and Illinois (1873).

In 1876 he went to Europe to spend a year of evangelistic work in Switzerland, France, and Italy, and associated with J. N. Andrews in editorial work. Again in 1882, with his brother, he took up evangelistic work in Europe, working in France, Switzerland, Corsica, Italy, and Alsace-Lorraine. Altogether he spent seven years overseas. On returning to the U.S. (1888), he continued as a minister and writer, working at first for French-speaking people, and then largely for the English.

BOURJ-HAMMOUD ADVENTIST SCHOOL. *See* Armenian Adventist School.

BOUSHRIEH ADVENTIST SECONDARY SCHOOL. A coeducational day school on the thirteenth-grade (college freshman) level, operated by the East Mediterranean Field. It was first opened under the auspices of the educational department of Middle East College to serve as a laboratory for teacher-training students, with Edith Davis as principal. In 1963 it was upgraded to a high school affiliated with Middle East College. In 1969 it was separated from Middle East College and moved to its present location in Boushrieh, Jdeidet El Matn, Lebanon.

In 1987 a thirteenth-grade class (college freshman equivalent) was added. The school follows the curriculum of the Lebanese Ministry of Education augmented by the Seventh-day Adventist religion program. The enrollment in 1993 was 430.

Principals: Jad Katrib, 1963-1965; E. W. Waring, 1965-1966; Jad Katrib, 1966-1971; Issa Kharma, 1971- .

BÖX, HEINRICH (1876-1942). Leader in the publishing work in central Europe. He became a Seventh-day Adventist through the influence of his wife, née Alma Blote (they were married in 1898), who apparently had become an SDA before him. After he was baptized in 1902 by H. F. Schuberth, he began to sell SDA publications in Germany. Sometime thereafter he attended Friedensau Seminary and, according to one source, was ordained to the ministry and became a leader of colporteurs in 1907. His name first appears in the *Yearbook* in 1910 as canvassing agent of the Middle German Conference, then in 1912 as field agent for the East German Union Conference.

Drafted into the German Army during World War I, he performed noncombatant service. His superiors allowed him to visit and instruct the colporteurs then in the field. A story has been told that when he went on such leaves he was supplied with an official pass endorsed with a request to all concerned to give aid and assistance "to Herr Böx, leader of the Seventh-day Adventist colporteur work."

After the war he served as field missionary secretary of the East German Union Conference. In 1922 he became secretary, and later associate secretary, of the Publishing Department of the European Division. In 1925 the *Yearbook* first lists him among ordained ministers. From 1928 until near the time of his death he was secretary of the Publishing Department of the Central European Division.

He is remembered as playing an important part in the development of SDA book sales in Germany. When he began work, there were only 25 colporteurs in his district; at the time the colporteur work was brought to a standstill in the early 1930s, he had 500 trained booksellers under his charge. Someone has said that he did not know the word "cannot." "With God," he said, "I can do all things." He lived his beliefs and allowed himself little rest and relaxation.

BOYD, MAUD (SISLEY) (1851-1937). Pioneer Bible instructor, colporteur, and the first Seventh-day Adventist woman missionary sent to Europe. She was born in England, but emigrated to the United States when she was 11, where she found her older brother keeping the seventh-day Sabbath. Soon her whole family became SDAs. When at the urging of James and Ellen White they moved to Battle Creek, Maud, age 15, found employment in the composing room of the Review and Herald and attended G. H. Bell's pioneer English classes for Review and Herald employees. With a group of young people from the Review and Herald she attended the first SDA camp meeting (at Wright, Michigan, September 1868). When SDAs began to accept the tithing plan, Maud Sisley is reported to have been one of the first tithepayers in Battle Creek. She became a charter member of the first Tract Society in Battle Creek, which was organized by S. N. Haskell.

She was so enthusiastic about the new opportunities that she asked for a six-month vacation in order to join Elsie Gates in self-supporting missionary work in Ohio.

In 1877 the General Conference sent Maud Sisley to assist the pioneer SDA missionary J. N. Andrews in his publishing work in Switzerland. There, in true pioneer spirit, she set in type the first SDA tract in Italian, even though she did not know the language. In 1879 J. N. Loughborough called her to assist in Southampton, England, as Bible instructor and colporteur. Shortly thereafter, on her return to America, she became the second wife of Charles L. Boyd, the president of Nebraska Conference. Later she helped him pioneer in the Northwest, where he was president of the North Pacific Conference.

In 1887 the Boyds were sent by the General Conference in the first group of missionaries to Africa. They remained in South Africa until 1891, when Boyd's failing health forced their return to U.S., where he died in 1898. Mrs. Boyd continued her Christian service in Australia, as a teacher at Avondale for nine years and then for three years as a Bible instructor in New South Wales and Victoria. Then for 17 years, until her retirement in 1927, she worked as a Bible instructor at the Loma Linda and Glendale sanitariums in California.

BOYS' TRAINING SCHOOL (Ethiopia). *See* Akaki SDA School.

BRACK, AUGUSTO (fl. 1890). One of the pioneer colporteurs in Brazil. He came from Germany in 1898, and later (1902) worked with the Berger brothers in Santa Maria and Taquara, Rio Grande do Sul. Shortly after this he returned to his homeland.

BRAILLE. *See* Christian Record Services, Inc.

BRANCH BIBLE SCHOOL. The equivalent of a branch Sabbath school, but conducted on a day other than the Sabbath. Such schools were formerly called Community Bible Schools, but because similar meetings sponsored by the Home Missionary Department were also called Community Bible Schools, the name branch Bible schools was adopted in 1963.

BRANCH SABBATH SCHOOL. An evangelistic type of service for the benefit of non-Seventh-day Adventists conducted generally as a branch of an established Sabbath school. According to the specifications of the North American Sabbath School Secretaries' Council, 1963, such meetings should be approved by the Sabbath school council, or the assistant superintendent for branch Sabbath schools of a parent school, or by the conference Sabbath school secretary in the case of a school conducted by isolated members; should preferably be conducted on Saturday; and should follow the general pattern of a regular Sabbath school, with any necessary program adaptations during the early development of the school. A similar school conducted on days other than Saturday is called a branch Bible school.

The idea of sharing the Sabbath school program and lessons with others began early. In 1879 Sunday schools were organized, a few of which were changed to Sabbath schools and were instrumental in the formation of new churches. Beginning in 1885, a considerable interest was aroused in conducting Sunday schools; two were reported in California in 1885, and others in 1886 in Allegan County, Michigan; in Wellsville, New York; and in several other places. In 1891 a letter from L. Johnson in Scandinavia told of a woman colporteur who opened a branch Sabbath school with 60 children. At the 1901 General Conference session, Ida M. Walters of Ohio reported on "branch Sabbath schools" before the Sabbath school council, and both the council and, in July, the International Sabbath School Association recommended operating such schools wherever practicable.

In 1927 R. G. Jones and his wife founded numerous branch Sabbath schools in the Dominican Republic in the Inter-American Division, and used these neighborhood Sabbath schools as a means of evangelism. They divided the city of Santo Domingo into several zones and encouraged their church members to conduct the schools on Sabbath afternoons in the areas nearest them.

At the General Conference Sabbath School Department meetings in 1930, many encouraging reports were given about branch Sabbath schools in northern California, Iowa, and other places. Some of these were follow-up work after Ingathering, and many resulted in additions to the church.

In 1933 J. M. Howell reported that a Sabbath school in Chile had, in about 1927, held 11 branch Sabbath schools, with the result that the church membership had grown from about 25 to nearly 100. Another Sabbath school conducted six branch Sabbath schools. In 1933 Mrs. Anna L. Hindson, in Australia, reported a number of Sunday schools held in different places.

The Autumn Council of 1934 commended the establishing of branch Sabbath schools, Sunday schools, and home Sabbath schools in all conferences and churches. From then on branch Sabbath schools sprang up everywhere—in Australia, in the Inter-American Division, in South America, in India, in Africa, in China, and wherever the regular Sabbath schools were found. By 1946 the goal was one branch Sabbath school for every regular Sabbath school.

In 1942 a series of four senior lesson quarterlies was provided for branch Sabbath schools, and in 1948 lessons called "Adventures in the Holy Bible" were prepared for boys and girls by R. R. Breitigam and his wife. Later, filmstrips for these lessons were prepared and also a set of lessons for adults, "Bible Adventures."

In 1953 there were 3,058 branch Sabbath schools in all the divisions; by the end of 1964 there were 27,268 schools, with 203,546 members. In addition, there were 7,976 branch Bible schools, with an attendance of 53,307 around the world.

In 1989 there were 66,879 branch Sabbath schools, with 543,650 members. Since then, no statistics have been recorded. *See* Branch Bible School.

"BRANCH, THE." A splinter group from the Davidian Seventh-day Adventists. *See* Davidian Seventh-day Adventists.

BRANCH, THOMAS H. (1856-1924). Missionary. He began his ministry in Pueblo, Colorado, in 1901. The next year he was sent to the newly acquired Plainfield Mission station (renamed Malamulo Mission station in 1907), in Nyasaland (now Malawi), one of the first Seventh-day Adventist Black Americans to be sent overseas as a missionary. His wife gave simple treatments and his daughter was in charge of the school. He returned to the United States in 1908 because of ill health and engaged in pastoral work.

BRANSON, ERNEST LLOYD (1906-1960). Missionary in the Middle East. He was educated at Spion Kop College in South Africa, Emmanuel Missionary College, Atlantic Union College (B.Th., 1927), and the SDA Theological Seminary. In 1926 he married Ardyce Detamore. He served as pastor and evangelist in southern New England (1927-1934) and in Missouri (1934-1935), and then as president of the Missouri Conference (1935-1938). In 1938 he became superintendent of the Egyptian Mission and then superintendent of the Middle East Union Mission (1942-1950). After his return to the United States he pastored at Oakland, California, then became president of the Greater New York Conference (1950-1958), and again pastor in California (1958-1960). He was the son of W. H. Branson.

BRANSON, WILLIAM HENRY (1887-1961). Evangelist, author, conference administrator, General Conference president. He was educated at Battle Creek College (1901-1903) and Emmanuel Missionary College (1903-1904). His denominational service of almost 50 years began in 1906 when he entered the colporteur work. Evangelism in Florida in 1908-1910 was followed by pastoral work in South Carolina in 1910-1911, and ordination to the ministry (1910). In 1911 he was called to the presidency of the South Carolina Conference, and for the next 43 years he held administrative posts. He was president of the Cumberland Conference (1913-1915), and of the Southeastern Union Conference (1915-1920).

He was appointed president of the African Division in 1920 and continued to administer that fast-growing field until 1930, when he became a vice president of the General Conference.

In 1938 Branson served as head of the Central European Division, Section II, and from 1938 to 1940 as head of the China Division. In 1946, in a period of great stress in China, he was sent to direct the rehabilitation of the church, and served as president of the China Division from 1946 to 1949.

He became president of the General Conference in 1950, and filled the office until 1954, when he retired because of failing health.

Branson was a strong administrator, an aggressive builder spiritually and materially, and was considered an authority on early missions in southern Africa. In addition to making numerous contributions to the church papers, he wrote a number of books, including *The Way to Christ, Missionary Adventures in Africa, The Holy Spirit, In Defense of the Faith, How Men Are Saved,* and *The Drama of the Ages.*

BRAUN, JOSEF (also spelled Brown, Joseph) (1881-1958). Minister and conference administrator in Germany, Austria, and the United States. He was baptized in 1904 and four years later, in 1908, began denominational service in western Germany. His name appeared in the *SDA Yearbook* for the first time in 1910, when he was listed as a missionary licentiate in the Rhenish-Prussian Conference. He continued to work in that area as licentiate, minister, and administrator until about 1925 (he was ordained earlier, and in 1921 was elected president of the Rhenish Conference). Between 1925 and 1936 he directed the work of the church in Austria. Later he went to the United States, where he worked as minister in the Wisconsin and North Dakota conferences, and retired in Oregon sometime between 1945 and 1950. About 1953 he returned to Germany. The *Yearbook* from 1955 to 1958 lists him among honorary ministers of the Rhenish Conference. He died in Germany in 1958.

BRAZIL. A federal republic situated on the northeast coast of South America, bounded on the southeast, east, and northeast by the Atlantic Ocean, and bordering the French Guiana, Suriname, Guyana, and Venezuela on the north; Colombia and Peru on the west; Bolivia, Paraguay, and Argentina on the southwest; and Uruguay on the south. Therefore, Brazil has a common border with all the countries of South America except Ecuador and Chile. It has a total area of 3,286,470 square miles (8,511,957 square kilometers) and a population (1994) of 159 million.

Brazilian territory extends in both hemispheres, and it is the fifth-largest country in the world, surpassed only by Russia, China, the United States of America, and Canada. Portuguese is the official language. The capital city, Brasilia, was founded on Apr. 21, 1960, for this purpose.

Brazil is a triangular-shaped country occupying half the land area of the South American continent. It lies almost entirely within the tropics and consists of a vast central plateau bordered by lowlands that range in size from the sprawling Amazon basin in the north to a narrow coastal plain in the east and southeast. The mountainous ranges of what is called the maritime system form the eastern part of this plateau, the easternmost range being known as the Serra do Mar (coastal range). In the northeast the coastal plain rises gradually to the interior, but between Bahia and Rio Grande do Sul the Serra do Mar poses a formidable barrier to communication with the hinterland. West of the maritime mountain ranges are the elevated tablelands of the Paraná and São Francisco river systems. To the northwest of these is the immense Amazon basin, which is drained by a vast system of tributaries, many of which are navigable. The Amazon carries the greatest volume of water of any river in the world, and, when it flows into the Atlantic Ocean along an estuary of 200 miles (335 kilometers), still runs more than 185 miles (300 kilometers) inward. As far as length is concerned, it is the second river in the world, with a total of 4,000 miles (6,440 kilometers), 1,950 miles (3,150 kilometers) of which are within Brazil. It is surpassed only by the Nile River, with 4,150 miles (6,680 kilometers). In the Amazon basin, and in those places along the Atlantic coast where the rainfall is heavy, there are tropical rain forests composed of broadleaf evergreen trees, there being as many as 3,000 different species in a square mile (2.59 square kilometers).

The region drained by the Paraná-Paraguay system is a broad flattish plain clad with semideciduous trees and savanna grass, largely devoted to cattle raising. Southern Brazil is an area of humid subtropical forests and coffee plantations. The varying topography and diversified climate of this region have resulted in a wide range of farm and forest products, which have contributed to Brazil's wealth.

Brazil may be divided into climatic zones that extend from north to south, varying from tropical in the north to subtropical in the south. There are not, however, extremes of temperature or rainfall. The annual average temperature in the Amazon region is around 79°F (26°C) most of the year. In the northeast, which is arid, temperatures as high as 100°F (38°C) occur. Southern Brazil, from the tropic of Capricorn to 30° south latitude, has a humid subtropical climate characterized by warm wet seasons and cool dry seasons. Except in the southernmost states, there is no frost.

The economic history of the country has been characterized by a series of cycles of booms and depressions, the result of Brazil's economy being based upon a single product, coffee, for which the country was, at one time, the world's chief source. Later Brazil was unable to compete with other countries that were able to produce coffee, rubber, and other products more efficiently and at a lower cost. In recent years sustained efforts have been made to diversify the economy, and thus reduce dependence on a single commodity for prosperity. Brazilian industry today accounts for more than half of all industry in Latin America.

Historical Background. Brazil was claimed, Apr. 22, 1500, by Pedro A'lvares Cabral, who was commissioned by the king of Portugal to sail to India to open a trade route with the East Indies. Adverse winds drove his expedition onto the coast of Brazil, in the vicinity of what is now Bahia. Supposing the newly discovered land to be a large island, Cabral named it Ilha de Vera Cruz ("Island of the True Cross"), but when later discoveries revealed the continental nature of the new land, it was renamed Terra de Santa Cruz ("Land of the Holy Cross"). Still later, when *pau-brasil,* a red dyewood, was discovered, the newly discovered land was named Brazil. There is historical evidence that others had touched the coasts of Brazil before Cabral, among them the Spanish navigator Vicente Yáñez Pinzón, a former member of Columbus's expedition, who in January 1500 discovered the mouth of the Amazon River, naming it Mar Dulce ("Freshwater Sea").

According to the generally accepted account, Amerigo Vespucci, an Italian navigator, sailed from Lisbon, Portugal, in the employ of the Portuguese king, May 13, 1501, and discovered Guanabara Bay, Jan. 1, 1502, and probably was the one who named the river Rio de Janeiro ("River of January"). The name "America" is derived from a Latinized form of his name.

1. *Portuguese Colony.* Thirty years passed after the discovery of Brazil before serious efforts were made to colonize it (1530). São Vicente, in the state of São Paulo, and São Salvador, in the state of Bahia, were among the first cities established to consolidate Portuguese claims. Portuguese colonial policy consisted largely in exploiting the new land for its natural resources for the benefit of the mother country, so that during a period of nearly 300 years Brazil was practically closed to commerce with the outside world.

In 1549 Tomé de Sousa was appointed royal governor by John III, king of Portugal, and established his headquarters at Bahia. He was accompanied by several Jesuit missionaries, among them Manuel da Nóbrega, first of a long line of Catholic missionaries who devoted their lives to the conversion of the Indians. In 1554 Nóbrega established a college at Piratininga, giving it the name of São Paulo, which is the origin of the largest Brazilian city. There he was joined by José de Ancheta, another Jesuit missionary who had just arrived and whose labors among the Indians won him the title "Apostle of Brazil."

In 1555 Nicolas de Villegagnon, a French adventurer and soldier of fortune, enlisted the support of Admiral Coligny, leader of French Protestants, and even of John Calvin, for the establishment of a Huguenot colony in Brazil that would be an asylum for Huguenots and other Protestants. Henry II of France approved the project, but after establishing the colony, Villegagnon went back on his promise of toleration and attempted to force the conversion of the colonists to Roman Catholicism. Rumors of this episode reached Europe and checked what might have become a great migration from France and Switzerland.

From 1580 to 1640 Brazil, with Portugal, was under the rule of Spain. This was the time when the colonists, especially those who lived around the village of São Paulo, organized the famous *bandeiras,* expeditions for the purpose of finding gold. Since all of South America belonged to Spain, these expeditions went beyond the frontiers of the Tordesilhas Treaty, signed by the kings of Portugal and Spain in 1494, and took possession of the land they were going through. When Portugal recovered its autonomy again, Brazil had tripled its area. During the Spanish dominion the Dutch tried to occupy part of the country.

In 1624 the Dutch seized and held briefly Bahia, and in 1630 the Dutch East India Company gained control of Pernambuco in northeastern Brazil. The company chose for governor of its new possession Count Maurice of Nassau-Siegen, an able statesman and administrator. However, the directors of the company refused to support him, and he resigned in 1644. When his successors proved unable to cope with an uprising led by João Fernandes Vieira, the Dutch were expelled from Brazil in 1654, and control reverted to the Portuguese.

In 1693 gold was discovered in Minas Gerais ("General Mines"), and in 1729 diamonds were found in the same state, giving new impetus to the growth of the country, and resulting in the removal of the colonial capital from Bahia to Rio de Janeiro (1763).

In 1789 the first rebellion against Portuguese authority was led by Joaquim José da Silva Xavier, popularly known as Tiradentes ("tooth puller"), because he occasionally extracted teeth. The revolt was quelled, and Tiradentes was executed.

2. *Result of Napoleonic Wars.* The Napoleonic invasion of Portugal forced the royal fam-

ily to flee to Brazil in 1808. With the arrival of the queen mother, Maria I, and the prince regent, João, afterward Dom João VI, a new day dawned for Brazil. Brazilian ports were thrown open to foreign commerce, rights were given freely to establish industries, and a royal treasury, a national bank, a supreme court of Justice and Finances, a government press, and an official journal were established.

In 1820 a revolution broke out in Portugal necessitating the return of Dom João VI to his country. The administration of Brazil was left to the king's son, Pedro, assisted by a Council of Four. Meanwhile, in the political ferment of the times, a strong nationalistic sentiment began to lead the people of Brazil toward a struggle for independence. José Bonifácio de Andrada e Silva, known as the "Father of Independence," a man of great prestige in the government of Pedro, persuaded the young prince to cast his lot with the nationalists.

3. *Brazil an Independent Nation.* On Sept. 7, 1822, at Ipiranga, São Paulo, Pedro proclaimed independence and became Dom Pedro I. A constitution was ratified and sworn to early in 1824, and some amendments were added to it in 1835. Strong opposition to the emperor forced Dom Pedro I to abdicate in 1831 in favor of his 6-year-old son, Dom Pedro II. A triple regency held the reins of government through nine stormy years (1831-1840), at the end of which both houses of parliament passed a declaration that Dom Pedro II had attained his majority. Under his enlightened rule Brazil enjoyed 50 years of prosperity and progress.

In 1851 the slave trade was abolished, and in 1871 infants born of slave mothers were declared free. In 1885 slaves more than 60 years of age were freed, and in 1888 an emancipation proclamation abolished slavery, but failed to provide compensation for their owners. This act alienated the rich slaveholders and precipitated the revolution of 1889. Dom Pedro II was dethroned and went into exile, and a republic was declared Nov. 15 of the same year.

The republic was at first ruled by military regimes, but in 1894 constitutional stability was achieved, and the next four presidents, Prudente de Moraes Barros (1894-1898), Manuel Ferraz de Campos Salles (1898-1902), Francisco de Paula Rodrigues Alves (1902-1906), and Affonso Augusto Moreira Penna (1906-1909), gave the country stable administrations.

In 1917 Brazil joined the allies in World War I, shared in the peace settlement, and joined the League of Nations, but withdrew in 1926. Washington Luis Pereira de Souza became president in 1926 and ruled to Oct. 26, 1930, when he was forced to resign by rebels under the leadership of Getúlio Dornelles Vargas, who refused to accept the election results earlier in the year, which showed Julio Prestes to have been elected. Declaring that the election had been won by fraud, Vargas seized control of the country through an armed uprising. Elections were called for in 1933 to establish a constitutional assembly. However, it was not until July 1934 that a new constitution was adopted to supersede that of 1891, and Vargas was chosen constitutional president by the assembly.

Vargas dominated Brazilian politics from 1930 to 1954, with the exception of the period from 1945 to 1951, when Gen. Eurico Gaspar Dutra was president. In 1942 Brazil declared war on Germany and Italy, and in 1944 sent an expeditionary force to Italy. After Vargas's death in 1954, Brazil entered a period of spiraling inflation and political unrest, but after the overthrow of João Goulart (1961-1964), the country has had a stable government.

In 1964 then President João Goulart was removed from office by military coup. During the military regime that followed, there were several presidents. In 1985 a civilian, José Sarney, became president. In 1990 Fernando Collor de Mello was elected president, but resigned in 1992 and was replaced in office by Itamar Franco.

Seventh-day Adventist Statistics. The territory of Brazil is part of the South American Division, and is divided into the Central Brazil Union Conference, the East Brazil Union Conference, the North Brazil Union Mission, and the South Brazil Union Conference. Statistics (1992) for *Brazil:* churches, 2,241; members, 617,919; elementary schools, 405; ordained ministers, 818; licensed ministers, 232; credentialed missionaries, 1,047.

Statistics (1992) for the *Central Brazil Union Conference:* churches, 594; members, 150,809; elementary schools, 119; ordained ministers, 285; licensed ministers, 113; credentialed missionaries, 555. Headquarters are at Artur Nogueira, São Paulo. Statistics (1992) for the missions and conferences—*Central Brazil Conference:* churches, 88; members, 27,456; elementary schools, 25; ordained ministers, 34; licensed ministers, 19; credentialed missionaries, 39. Headquarters are at Goiania, Goiás. *Central São Paulo Conference:* churches, 88; members, 17,762; elementary schools, 13; ordained ministers, 46; licensed ministers, 13; credentialed missionaries, 122. Headquarters are at Campinas, São Paulo. *East São Paulo Conference*: churches, 110; members, 34,429; elementary schools, 14; ordained ministers, 42; credentialed missionaries, 22. Headquarters are at Vila Matilde, São Paulo. *Mato Grosso Mission:* churches, 56; members, 14,397; elementary schools, 20; ordained ministers, 19; licensed ministers, 19; credentialed missionaries, 21. Headquarters are at Cuiaba, Mato Grosso. *São Paulo Conference:* churches, 102; members, 22,441; elementary schools, 20; ordained ministers, 43; licensed ministers, 18; credentialed missionaries, 76. Headquarters are at Campo Belo, São Paulo. *South São Paulo Conference:* churches, 77; members, 22,538; elementary schools, 12; ordained ministers, 27; licensed ministers, 16; credentialed missionaries, 67. Headquarters are at Jardim IAE, São Paulo. *West São Paulo Conference:* churches, 73; members, 13,786; elementary schools, 15; ordained ministers, 30; licensed ministers, 14; credentialed missionaries, 47. Headquarters are at São Jose do Rio Preto, São Paulo.

East Brazil Union Conference: churches, 843; members, 194,420; elementary schools, 124; ordained ministers, 253; licensed ministers, 87; credentialed missionaries, 228. Headquarters are at Niteroi, Rio de Janeiro. Statistics (1992) for the missions and conferences—*Bahia Conference*: churches, 207; members, 43,822; elementary schools, 37; ordained ministers, 48; licensed ministers, 25; credentialed missionaries, 10. Headquarters are at Salvador, Bahia. *Central Minas Conference:* churches, 100; members, 30,673; elementary schools, 14; ordained ministers, 31; licensed ministers, 15; credentialed missionaries, 15. Headquarters are at Belo Horizonte, Minas Gerais. *Espírito Santo Conference:* churches, 147; members, 24,171; elementary schools, 20; ordained ministers, 30; licensed ministers, 11; credentialed missionaries, 13. Headquarters are at Vitoria, Espírito Santo. *Northeast Brazil Mission:* churches, 107; members, 36,024; elementary schools, 27; ordained ministers, 30; licensed ministers, 11; credentialed missionaries, 15. Headquarters are at Recife, Pernambuco. *Rio de Janeiro Conference:* churches, 171; members, 33,911; elementary schools, 18; ordained ministers, 55; licensed ministers, 16; credentialed missionaries, 47. Headquarters are at Rio de Janeiro. *Sergipe-Alagoas Mission:* churches, 40; members, 13,353; elementary schools, 4; ordained ministers, 15; licensed ministers, 2; credentialed missionaries, 3. Headquarters are at Aracuju, Sergipe. *South Minas Mission:* churches, 71; members, 12,466; elementary schools, 4; ordained ministers, 14; licensed ministers, 6; credentialed missionaries, 10. Headquarters are at Juiz de Fora, Minas Gerais.

North Brazil Union Mission: churches, 389; members, 177,234; elementary schools, 62; ordained ministers, 114; licensed ministers, 51; credentialed missionaries, 110. Headquarters are at Belém, Pará. Statistics (1992) for the missions—*Central Amazon Mission:* churches, 94; members, 45,159; elementary schools, 6; ordained ministers, 31; licensed ministers, 11; credentialed missionaries, 36. Headquarters are at Manaus, Amazonas. *Lower Amazon Mission:* churches, 98; members, 56,371; elementary schools, 34; ordained ministers, 28; licensed ministers, 12; credentialed missionaries, 42. Headquarters are at Belém, Pará. *Maranhao Mission:* churches, 95; members, 41,613; elementary schools, 3; ordained ministers, 17; licensed ministers, 3; credentialed missionaries, 5. Headquarters are at São Luis, Maranhao. *North Coast Mission:* churches, 41; members, 12,808; elementary schools, 6; ordained ministers, 11; licensed ministers, 7; credentialed missionaries, 7. Headquarters are at Fortaleza, Ceará. *West Amazon Conference:* churches, 61; members, 21,283; elementary schools, 13; ordained ministers, 18; licensed ministers, 18; credentialed missionaries, 1. Headquarters are at Porto Velho, Rondonia.

South Brazil Union Conference: churches, 415; members, 95,456; elementary schools, 100; ordained ministers, 166; licensed ministers, 74; credentialed missionaries, 154. Headquarters are at Curitiba, Paraná. Statistics (1992) for the missions and conferences—*North Paraná Conference:* churches, 90; members, 19,641; elementary schools, 19; ordained ministers, 35; licensed ministers, 16; credentialed missionaries, 35. Headquarters are at Maringa, Paraná. *Rio Grande do Sul Conference:* churches, 117; members, 33,254; elementary schools, 33; ordained ministers, 39; licensed ministers, 27; credentialed missionaries, 37. Headquarters are at Pôrto Alegre, Rio Grande do Sul. *Santa Catarina Conference*: churches, 66; members, 12,490; elementary schools, 26; ordained ministers, 11; licensed ministers, 11; credentialed missionaries, 19. Headquarters are at Florianópolis, Santa Catarina. *South Mato Grosso Mission:*

churches, 43; members, 10,348; elementary schools, 11; ordained ministers, 20; licensed ministers, 4; credentialed missionaries, 19. Headquarters are at Campo Grande, Mato Grosso. *South Paraná Conference:* churches, 99; members, 19,723; elementary schools, 14; ordained ministers, 34; licensed ministers, 15; credentialed missionaries, 19. Headquarters are at Curitiba, Paraná.

For the respective conference territories, *see* South American Division.

Institutions. Adventist Agricultural-Industrial Academy; Adventist Health Center; Adventist Home for the Elderly; Agro-Industrial Adventist Trans-Amazon Academy; Belém Adventist Hospital; Brazil College; Brazil Publishing House; Brazil Voice of Prophecy Media Center; Central Brazil Academy; Children's Orphanage Center; Cruzeiro do Sul Adventist Academy; Division Health Food Company; Espírito Santo Academy; Grão Pará Adventist Academy; Latin-American Adventist Theological Seminary; Loving Mother Nursery; Manaus Adventist Academy; Manaus Adventist Hospital; Minas Gerais Adventist Academy; Neandertal Children's Home; Northeast Brazil Academy; Northeast Brazil College; Paraná Adventist Academy; Paul Harris Children's Home; Penfigo Adventist Hospital; Petropolis Adventist Academy; São Paulo Adventist Academy; São Paulo Adventist Hospital; São Paulo Old People's Home; São Roque Adventist Clinic; Silvestre Adventist Hospital; Vila Ipe Children's Home; Vitoria Adventist Hospital; Vovo Josephina Children's Home; Xaxim Adventist Home for Boys.

Seventh-day Adventist Work. 1. *Beginnings.* There were Sabbathkeepers in Brazil before the arrival of SDA missionaries. Writing in the *Missionary Magazine* (11:302, July 1899), Friedrich Stuhlman refers to "Brother Kinder, who came here in 1878 as a minister of the Stangnofski [Stangnowsky] [Sabbathkeeping] church" *(see* Germany). Besides Kinder there were others "who observed the Sabbath of the Lord, as the result of [his] labors." Many years later these Sabbatarians were reached by the SDA message, and Kinder, especially, "although much advanced in years, and deprived of the use of his eyes," became an ardent advocate *(ibid.).*

The SDA message first entered Brazil through publications that arrived at the port of Itajaí, Santa Catarina, in 1879. The reason for their arrival centers in the story of a young German named Burchard, who, having violated a local law, fled Brazil as a stowaway on a German ship. Discovered en route to Europe, he was obliged to work out his passage. While on board he conversed with two SDA missionaries, who questioned him regarding religious interest and activities among the people of his community. They learned that the Lutherans were active in evangelistic work among German immigrants, especially in the state of Santa Catarina. Obtaining from Burchard the address of his stepfather, Carlos Dreefke, who lived in Brusque, Santa Catarina, they decided to send him SDA publications.

Almost two years passed before Dreefke received a package of the literature. It was handed to him while he was in a general tavern-grocery shop belonging to David Hort. According to the account of Hort's son Adolf, 9 years old at the time and present, Dreefke was reluctant to open the strange package, which he had not ordered. However, at Hort's insistence he opened it and found 10 copies of the SDA periodical *Stimme der Wahrheit* ("Voice of Truth"), printed in Battle Creek, Michigan. Dreefke kept one paper and gave the rest to Hort and others. As a result, the ten families that received the papers became interested in SDA teachings and asked for more information.

As requests increased for more literature, Dreefke began to fear that the cost of the papers would fall upon him, but a man named Chikrevitowski offered to assume responsibility. In time, however, Chikrevitowski's interest waned.

Later Friederich Dressel, a son of a Lutheran minister, assumed responsibility for ordering and paying for the publications. He had come to Brazil after being banished from his home because he had taken to drink. Settling at Brusque, he taught in an elementary school. In order to quench his thirst for liquor, he supplemented his salary by selling these SDA tracts and magazines. It is said that at times his hands trembled so much that many a tract was dropped quite by chance in a home, in a shop, or on the streets. Many papers were used, after having been read, to wrap groceries, and in this way still others read these SDA publications. Apparently with him was associated a certain Wilhelm Verwiebe, concerning whom nothing is known except that he signed a letter with Dressel asking for more SDA publications *(Review and Herald* 65:157, Mar. 6, 1888).

As orders increased, Dressel continued to make further requests to the International Tract

Society in the United States. Other periodicals were sent, such as the *Christlicher Hausfreund* ("Christian Friend of the Home"), and books, both large and small. In this way hundreds of dollars' worth of SDA publications were scattered among the people in and around Brusque.

2. *Early Converts of German Extraction.* Among the first to begin observing the Sabbath as a result of these scattered publications was Guilherme Belz, a German immigrant of Gaspar Alto, Santa Catarina. While visiting his brother in nearby Brusque, he had seen the book *Gedanken über das Buch Daniel* ("Thoughts on the Book of Daniel"), by Uriah Smith, which his brother had obtained from Dressel. Upon reading it, Belz had become especially impressed by the chapter "The Papacy Changes the Sabbath." This title reminded him of his youth in Germany, when, upon reading the Bible, he found that it only mentioned Sabbathkeeping, though his pastor and mother had explained to him that Christ Himself had made this change. He studied this matter earnestly, and had no more doubts. About the beginning of 1890 he and his family had begun to observe the day. Soon a number of his neighbors, among them the Olm, Lock, and Thrun families, did likewise.

According to extant records, the first Seventh-day Adventist to visit Brazil was L. C. Chadwick, who stopped over in Rio de Janeiro for several weeks in August 1892. In May 1893 came the first SDA colporteur, Albert B. Stauffer, followed soon after by E. W. Snyder and C. A. Nowlen, originally sent from the United States to sell SDA publications in Uruguay and Argentina, and Lionel Brooking, one of their converts from Buenos Aires (*see* Argentina; Uruguay). Stauffer worked first in São Paulo and then successively in Rio de Janeiro and the states of Rio Grande do Sul (1894) and Espírito Santo (1895). Stauffer sold books in German and English, because at this time there were no SDA publications in Portuguese. In Rio Grande do Sul he sold the book *Patriarchs and Prophets* to Germano Preuss, the owner of a hotel in the city of Taquarí, who was baptized with his wife, Claudina, in 1897. When the first missionaries arrived in Rio Grande do Sul, they stayed in his residence, which became a center for evangelism in that state and Brazil. There they founded the first missionary school and the first publishing house. His son, Leopoldo, became a worker, and served for 58 years, many of which were in Brazil Publishing House. In Espírito Santo, Stauffer sold many books in the Santa Maria German colony, which is situated at the head of a river by the same name. And as old Pastor Gustavo Schroeder Storch said: "Harsh persecution started against the 'Verfluchten Sabbatisten' ["cursed Sabbathkeepers"]," but the seed yielded its fruits, and the first baptism took place in December 1895. Later on these SDAs moved to Serra Pelada, to the municipality of Afonso Claudio, where one of the largest churches during the time of the pioneers was established.

At a sailors' home in Rio de Janeiro, Snyder met Alberto Bachmeyer, a young German seaman who some months before had become a Christian while in Liverpool, England (*Review and Herald* 70:665, 666, Oct. 24, 1893). After persuading Bachmeyer to accept the Seventh-day Adventist faith, Snyder instructed him in the art of selling books. Although as yet not baptized, Bachmeyer soon began canvassing in various cities of the state of São Paulo, among them Indaiatuba, Rio Claro, and Piracicaba, where SDA books and papers, chiefly in German, found ready acceptance. Among those who later became SDAs as a result of reading these publications were Guilherme Stein, Jr., and his family, Guilherme and Paulina Meyer, and Guilherme Stein III and his family. Stein III, who had been a Methodist, became convinced about the SDA message after reading *Der Grosse Kampf* ("The Great Controversy"), by Ellen G. White. Guilherme Stein, Jr., abandoned his secular activities and began teaching at the Curitiba International College and the Missionary School of Gaspar Alto. In 1900 he was in Rio de Janeiro, where he published our first missionary magazine, *O Arauto da Verdade* ("Herald of Truth"), and in 1919, the Sociedade Internacional de Tratados no Brazil published the first SDA book written by a Brazilian, *O Sabado* ("The Sabbath Day").

3. *Missionaries Sent In.* In 1894, because of increasing requests for denominational publications, the General Conference sent W. H. Thurston and his wife to establish a book agency in Rio de Janeiro. Receiving no salary from the denomination, he sold books, but being unable to speak Portuguese and knowing no one, he was obliged to canvass with English and German books. At this time the city had a population of nearly 1 million. It was a trying period for the young couple, who faced hunger and hardships, but the Lord provided for their needs. On one occasion a missionary of another

denomination, without having been asked, lent money to the couple, saying, "Here is a little money. I want you to take it and keep it until I call for it, and use it." Later he said, "God told me to give you this money because you needed it" *(General Conference Bulletin,* Apr. 8, 1901, p. 123). Gradually the early obstacles were surmounted, and Thurston became a valuable colporteur agent. He served as chair and treasurer of the Brazil Mission Field from 1895 to 1900. He was ordained to the ministry in 1900 and became director of the Brazil Mission Field during the latter part of the same year.

In 1894 Bachmeyer sold books in the state of Santa Catarina and there discovered Sabbathkeepers at Brusque and Gaspar Alto. Bachmeyer informed Thurston of these interested persons, and Thurston wrote to F. H. Westphal, who had recently (1894) arrived in Argentina from the United States to visit the interested ones. Arriving in Rio de Janeiro in February 1895, Westphal acquainted himself with the progress of the work in that field.

From Rio de Janeiro he and Stauffer left for a trip to the interior of the São Paulo and Santa Catarina states. In March 1895, in the city of Piracicaba, São Paulo, Westphal conducted the first baptismal ceremony in Brazil, baptizing Guilherme Stein, Jr. It is interesting to note that the Indians called Piracicaba the fishing place, and without a doubt Brazil proved to be an extraordinary "piracicaba" of souls for the kingdom. On Sabbath, June 8, 1895, Westphal baptized eight persons, and three days later, three miles (five kilometers) from Brusque, he baptized another 15 people in Gaspar Alto. Guilherme Belz and his wife participated in this baptism, and three generations of workers have come from their family (their son, Francisco Belz; their grandson, Rodolfo Belz, who was president of both South and East Brazil unions; and their great-grandsons Claudio and Otavio Belz). Also baptized was colporteur Bachmeyer, who had not yet had the opportunity. Even though the first regular SDA church was organized in Gaspar Alto, an organized church existed in Rio de Janeiro before this time, but it was composed of newly arrived workers only. By the end of 1895, 35 converts had been baptized into the Seventh-day Adventist Church in Brazil. All the converts were of German birth or descent, or were people who spoke German.

4. *First Brazilian Converts.* Guilherme Stein, Jr., was the first SDA of Brazilian birth to be baptized. Others were being converted at the same time. Writing from Rio de Janeiro on Oct. 15, 1894, Thurston had reported holding Bible readings with "a Portuguese colporteur [a representative of the American Bible Society], whom brother Stauffer interested" *(Review and Herald* 71:725, Nov. 20, 1894). A few months later he wrote: "The Portuguese colporteur [in Rio de Janeiro] has accepted [the SDA message]. . . . Another Portuguese colporteur in São Paulo is interested" *(ibid.* 72:236, Apr. 8, 1895). Finally in the issue of Oct. 1, 1895 (72:636), F. H. Westphal reported: "I have just received a letter from Brother Stauffer and one from Brother Thurston, stating that the Portuguese that took his stand for the truth under Brother Thurston's labor is now at work in connection with Brother Stauffer."

The names of these men are not known.

5. *First Churches Organized.* In order to care for the increasing number of interested persons, Huldreich F. von Graf, a native of Germany, who had been a minister at Good Thunder, Minnesota, was called to Brazil to superintend the Brazil Mission Field *(General Conference Bulletin,* July 1895, p. 547). Soon after his arrival on Oct. 4, 1895, "the first Seventh-day Adventist church in Rio [de Janeiro, and probably the first in Brazil, but consisting entirely of workers from the U.S.] was organized Oct. 27, with H. F. Graf as elder, W. H. Thurston, deacon, and Florence Thurston, clerk" *(Review and Herald* 72:779, Dec. 3, 1895).

At Gaspar Alto (near Brusque), Santa Catarina, in February 1896 Graf supervised the organization of the first Seventh-day Adventist church among the settlers in Brazil. However, it was not until Mar. 23, 1898, that a church building was erected—a structure that served until 1949, when it was replaced by a brick building, the original wood flooring being retained. Graf organized many churches and made many trips into the interior. One of his longest itineraries was made in 1898 and became known as "One Hundred Days on Muleback."

Various groups, such as those at Não-me-Toque and Taquarí in Rio Grande do Sul, Joinvile in Santa Catarina, Curitiba in Paraná, Rio Claro in São Paulo, Teófilo Ottoni in Minas Gerais, and Espírito Santo in the state of Espírito Santo, were organized into Sabbath schools that later became churches.

As the Seventh-day Adventist organization in Brazil developed, the work of ministering the field and directing the workers was assigned to

Frederico Weber Spies, a former colporteur director in Germany, who came to Brazil in 1896. During one four-month period in Brazil, Spies traveled 600 miles (1,000 kilometers) by water, 500 miles (800 kilometers) by rail, and 1,700 miles (2,700 kilometers) by muleback.

Between 1895 and 1904, besides the missionaries already mentioned, others, such as John Hettrick (1895), J. F. and A. J. Berger (1895), John Lipke (1897), Waldemar Ehlers (1898), Augusto Brack (1898), C. W. Barnes (1898), Elsie Strong (1899), and A. L. Gregory, M.D. (1902), came to Brazil. From time to time, as circumstances required, meetings of workers were held. The first meeting at which all the SDA workers then employed in Brazil were present was held in Brusque, Santa Catarina, in May 1898 *(Review and Herald* 76:653, 654, Oct. 9, 1900).

In 1899 the first Seventh-day Adventist service in Portuguese was held. F. W Spies reported: "We had long looked forward to the time when we might begin work [in Rio de Janeiro]. . . . Wm. [Guilherme] Stein [probably III], a native brother, and his family, moved to this place, and on Saturday evening, October 21 [1899], we held the first service in the Portuguese language, in our home" *(ibid.* 76:124, Feb. 20, 1900).

In the same article of the *Review*, Thurston spoke of the urgent need for tracts and magazines in the language of the country. "We have no tract nor paper in the Portuguese tongue, and, in fact, nothing to give the people to read, and they are afraid of the Bible. We are, however, preparing manuscript for the first issue of our Portuguese paper planned long ago. But even when we shall have the matter prepared for the press, we do not know how long we must wait before we can print the first edition, because our funds are low."

In July 1900 the first issue of *O Arauto da Verdade* ("The Herald of Truth"), the first SDA periodical in Portuguese, was published *(General Conference Bulletin,* Apr. 8, 1901, p. 121).

Organization. 1. *Brazilian Conference.* Brazil operated as a mission until 1902. According to the *General Conference Bulletin* (second and third quarters, p. 627) the Brazilian Conference was organized at a meeting held in Gaspar Alto, Santa Catarina, May 10-20 1902, with H. F. Graf as president, A. B. Stauffer, secretary-treasurer, and Johanne Rebling, Sabbath school secretary (cf. *Review and Herald* 79:17, Oct. 21, 1902). The *Bulletin* also gave the following persons as constituting the executive committee: H. F. Graf, F. W. Spies, Abel Gregory, John Lipke, Emílio Schenk, Geo. Wischral, and John Het[t]rick. There were three ordained ministers: H. F. Graf, F. W. Spies, and Ernesto Schwantes; one licentiate: Wm. [Guilherme] Stein; and four missionary licentiates: John Lipke, A. B. Stauffer, A. L. Gregory, and Mrs. Lulu V. Gregory. According to the *Review and Herald* (79:17, Oct. 21, 1902), there were also 8 canvassers, 15 churches, 9 church schools, and about 860 members.

Soon afterward, Abel L. Gregory, a dentist and physician from the United States, opened medical work *(ibid.* 79:16, Nov. 4, 1902; cf. 81:15, July 14, 1904).

2. *Reorganization in Four Parts, 1906.* The South American Union Conference was organized at Paraná, Entre Rios, Argentina, Mar. 15-25, 1906, with the following officers: J. W. Westphal, president; H. F. Graf, vice president; N. Z. Town, secretary-treasurer. Executive committee: J. W. Westphal, H. F. Graf, N. Z. Town, F. W. Spies, Dr. R. H. Habenicht, Arturo Fulton, G. [Wm.] Steele, Jorge Riffel, F. H. Westphal, Juan McCarthy *(Revista Adventista* 6:4, April 1906; cf. *Yearbook* [1907], p. 94).

Soon after, in 1906, the Brazil Conference, which formed part of the South American Union, dissolved and was divided into two conferences, Rio Grande do Sul and Santa Catarina-Paraná, and two missions, São Paulo and North Brazil.

The Rio Grande do Sul Conference was organized Apr. 15, 1906, with headquarters in the city of Taquarí, Rio Grande do Sul, under the following administration: H. F. Graf, president; Abel L. Gregory, vice president; A. Pages, secretary-treasurer; Miona Graf, Sabbath School Department secretary. Executive committee: H. F. Graf, A. L. Gregory, A. Pages, John Lipke, and Emilio Schenk. Ordained ministers: H. F. Graf and Ernesto Schwantes; licensed minister: J. Lipke; missionary licentiates: A. Brack and A. Schwantes *(Revista Trimensal* 1:3, April 1906).

According to the 1906 *Statistical Report,* at the end of the year this conference had 6 churches, 444 members, 1 ordained minister, 1 church school, 1 teacher, 1 colporteur. There were also an industrial school for training future workers and a printing press.

The Santa Catarina and Paraná Conference was organized between May 12 and 15, 1906, with headquarters in Gaspar Alto (near

Brusque), Santa Catarina, with the following officers: Waldemar Ehlers, president; Mary Ehlers, secretary-treasurer and Sabbath School Department secretary. Executive committee: Waldemar Ehlers, Augusto Olm, A. Hort, Jorge Wischral, Rudolph Zimmermann. Minister-evangelist: Waldemar Ehlers; licensed ministers: José Lindermann and Francisco Belz; Bible instructor: Theobald Renk. According to the 1906 *Statistical Report,* there were by the end of the year in this field 12 churches, 427 members, 8 church schools, 8 teachers, 2 colporteurs, and 1 ordained minister.

The São Paulo Mission was established in 1906 in the city of Rio Claro, São Paulo, with 23 members and 1 church. Officers were Emilio Hoelzle, president; Guilherme Stein, secretary-treasurer; Guilherme Meyer, Jr., licensed minister. Executive committee: Emilio Hoelzle, Guilherme Stein, Guilherme Meyer, Jr., João Mosmann, and Walter Meyer. According to the 1906 *Statistical Report,* there were by the end of the year in this field 1 church, 23 members, and 1 ordained minister.

The North Brazil Mission was founded in 1906, with headquarters in Rio de Janeiro, with Frederico W. Spies, president. According to the 1906 *Statistical Report,* by the end of the year this large area, which included 16 states with a population of 7 million, had 5 churches, 176 members, 1 church school, 1 teacher, and 1 minister.

3. *National Association Formed.* The Associação dos Adventistas do Sétimo Dia no Brasil ("Association of Seventh-day Adventists in Brazil"), a legal organization, was established on July 18, 1907, in the worship hall of the church of Rio Claro (São Paulo), having its own constitution and bylaws, which were published in their entirety in the official journal of São Paulo on July 24, 1907. Article III states its objectives: "The purpose of this Association is to diffuse moral and religious education in Brazil, by means of churches, organizations, publishing houses, medical and health institutions, educational institutions, publications, missionary agencies and other instruments and methods appropriate and lawful in reaching these goals, the Association having the right for this to borrow, receive deposits and donations, sign promissory notes, grant annuities, acquire, possess and maintain properties, movable and immovable, within the country, by purchase or donation, and thus to hold mortgages, mortgage and sell properties when it seems best to do so."

4. *Later Reorganizations and Changes.* According to the *Yearbook* four major reorganizations and several lesser changes have been made in SDA work in Brazil since 1906. The first reorganization was voted at a meeting held in Pôrto Alegre, Rio Grande do Sul, Dec. 9-18, 1910 (effective Jan. 1, 1911), by which the territory of Brazil became the Brazilian Union Conference, comprising the following conferences and missions: the Rio Grande do Sul, Santa Catarina, and Paraná conferences and the São Paulo, Rio-Espírito Santo (states of Rio de Janeiro and Espírito Santo and the Federal District), East Brazil (states of Bahia, Sergipe, Alagoas, and Pernambuco), and North Brazil (states of Paraíba, Rio Grande do Norte, Piauí, Ceará Maranhão, Pará, Amazonas, Mato Grosso, Goiás, and Minas Gerais) missions. In 1916 the state of Minas Gerais was separated from the North Brazil Mission and established as the Minas Gerais Mission. The same year Pernambuco was separated from the East Brazil Mission and established as the Pernambuco Mission.

The second major change was made in 1918, when the North Brazil Union Mission, composed of the East Brazil and Pernambuco missions, was separated from the Brazil Union Conference. About a year later this new union mission was named East Brazil Union Mission, and the Brazil Union Conference became the South Brazil Union Conference. At that time several territorial adjustments were made, by which the Minas Gerais Mission was divided into the East Minas and West Minas missions, the former being joined to North Brazil Union Mission, and the latter continuing as a part of the (South) Brazil Union Conference. The same year (1919), the Rio-Espírito Santo Mission was divided into the Rio de Janeiro Mission (state of Rio de Janeiro and the Federal District), and the Espírito Santo Mission, both becoming part of the North Brazil Union Mission. It may be noted that some confusion in names existed during this reorganization period. The church paper, *Revista Mensal,* referred to the South Brazil Union Conference as the Brazil Union Conference, and the *Yearbook* for the same period referred to the East Brazil Union Mission as the North Brazil Union Mission.

The third major reorganization was made in 1927 and 1928. The Paraná Mission and the Santa Catarina Conference were united to form the Santa Catarina-Paraná Mission. The same year the Goiás Mission and in 1928 the

Araguaia Indian Mission were established as part of the South Brazil Union Conference, and the Lower Amazon Mission (states of Ceará, Piauí, Maranhão, Pará, and Amazonas, and the territory of Acre) was established (1928) as part of the East Brazil Union Mission.

In 1931 the Rio de Janeiro Mission was united with the Minas Gerais Mission to form the Rio-Minas Gerais Mission. The next year (1932) the Bahia and Pernambuco missions were joined to form the Northeast Mission.

The fourth major reorganization occurred in 1936 when the Lower Amazon Mission was separated from the East Brazil Union Mission and formed into the North Brazil Union Mission, comprising the Lower Amazon Mission and the North Coast Mission; the same year the Araguaia Indian Mission was disbanded. The next year (1937) the states of Bahia and Sergipe were detached from the Northeast Mission and formed into the Bahia-Sergipe Mission.

Two minor changes were made in 1940: the Santa Catarina-Paraná Mission, which about 1934 had become the Paraná-Santa Catarina Mission, became the Paraná-Santa Catarina Conference, and the state of Amazonas and the territory of Acre in the East Brazil Union Mission were separated from the Lower Amazon Mission and established as the Central Amazon Mission.

The Rio São Francisco Mission, formed in 1945 and organized in 1951, was disbanded in 1955. The Rio-Minas Gerais Mission, which became a conference in 1951, was divided in 1955 into the Rio-Minas Conference and the Minas Mission. That same year (1955) the Rio-Espírito Santo Mission was reorganized as the Espírito Santo Conference.

In 1957 the Paraná-Santa Catarina Conference was divided into the Paraná Conference and the Santa Catarina Mission. The Central Brazil Mission was organized that same year. In 1972 the name of the Espírito Santo Conference was changed to East Conference.

In 1980 the Mato Grosso Mission was divided into the Mato Grosso Mission and the South Mato Grosso Mission. In 1983 the Minas Mission was divided into the Central Minas Mission and the South Minas Mission. In 1986 the South Brazil Union Conference was divided into the South Brazil and the Central Brazil union conferences. In 1988 the Sergipe-Alagoas Mission was formed. In the North Brazil Union in 1988, the Maranhão Mission was formed from the North Coast Mission. In 1989 the Paraná Conference was divided into the North Paraná Conference and South Paraná Conference.

In 1991 the West Amazon Mission became a conference.

Departmental Work. 1. *Publishing.* The need for publications in the Portuguese language was recognized early by SDA workers in Brazil. In September 1898 John Lipke wrote in the *Missionary Magazine* (10:341, September 1898): "We need a paper in this language [Portuguese], and I believe it would be able to accomplish much good here, and then it could be sent to Portugal where we have no one to spread the [SDA] message."

Within a year W. H. Thurston wrote in the same periodical: "We now have three small books in the Portuguese language, *Steps to Christ, Gospel Primer,* and *Bible Lessons for the Sabbath-School, No. I,* and some tracts are in the publisher's hands. *Christ Our Saviour* and a small book of *Bible Readings* will be translated this year, and with these and a Portuguese paper which we are planning to start we hope to teach the natives present truth" *(Missionary Magazine* 11:258, June 1899).

Apparently, these were the first SDA books published in Portuguese.

In July 1900 publication of *O Arauto da Verdade* ("The Herald of Truth"), an evangelistic paper, was begun. According to the *Yearbook* this magazine continued to be published until about 1912. Apparently it was succeeded by a similar paper, *Sinaes dos Tempos* ("Signs of the Times"), which was first published about 1917 as a quarterly and a year later as a monthly, continuing until 1923, when it was superseded by the monthly *O Atalaia* ("The Watchman"), which has continued to be published up to the present time. A church paper, the *Revista Trimensal* ("Quarterly Review"), was begun January 1906; in January 1908 it was changed to *Revista Mensal* ("Monthly Review"); in March 1931 the name of the periodical was again changed, this time to its present title, *Revista Adventista* ("Adventist Review").

In 1902 plans were set afoot "to establish a printing plant in connection with the industrial school [at Taquarí, Rio Grande do Sul]" *(Review and Herald* 79:16, May 13, 1902), but it was not until 1905 that a printing press was secured and the printing plant was established there *(ibid.* 82:15, June 15, 1905; 82:13, July 13, 1905; 83:14, Mar. 22, 1906). In 1907 it was voted to move the printing plant from the school *(Revista Trimensal* 2:1, October 1907), and early in 1908 the press was transferred to São Bernardo, about 10 miles (16 kilometers) from the city of São Paulo *(see* Brazil Publishing House).

2. *Colporteurs.* The story of colporteurs who played a large part in the spread of SDA teachings in the early 1890s has already been told (see above). In August 1895 two brothers, Alberto J. and J. Frederico Berger, arrived from the United States and began colporteur work in the colony of Santa Leopoldina, Espírito Santo state, and later in the state of Santa Catarina. In two and a half months they sold $400 worth of SDA publications, a sizable amount at that time. Later they worked in Mucuri, Minas Gerais, and in southern Bahia state, being pioneers in both regions. In 1897 they began their work in Rio Grande do Sul, and in 1902 they canvassed in Santa Maria and Taquara, Rio Grande do Sul, together with Augusto Brack. Saturnino Mendes de Oliveira, one of the early colporteur directors in Brazil, was associated with the colporteur work for 41 consecutive years before retiring. During that time he is reported to have visited or worked in more than 820 cities and villages in Brazil.

3. *Educational Work.* As in the beginning of the history of our church, the educational work in Brazil started with a private institution, Curitiba International College, which began functioning July 1, 1896, in the city of Curitiba, Paraná. Founded and conducted by dedicated church members such as Paulo Krämer, Vicente Schmidt, and Guilherme Stein, Jr., the school had 117 students in the first year of operation. This number increased later on, surpassing the 400 mark. After some eight years of operation, the school closed about 1904.

The first missionary school was established in 1897 in Gaspar Alto, Santa Catarina, under the direction of Guilherme Stein, Jr., who was succeeded three years later by John Lipke. In 1903 this school was transferred to Taquarí, Rio Grande do Sul, and Emilio Schenk, J. Lipke, and Emanuel Kümpel served as its directors successively. This school continued to operate until 1910.

Finally in 1915 our brethren were able to reopen the missionary school, but in Santo Amaro, São Paulo. The pioneers were John Lipke and John H. Boehm. A Brazilian convert, Pantaleão Theissen, was anxious to see the school functioning, and he sold the necessary land at a very low price. John H. Boehm donated money he received from an inheritance for the same purpose. Originally named Seminario Adventista (Adventist Seminary), it is known as Instituto Adventista de Ensino (Brazil College). In 1943, to facilitate the preparation of workers from the north and northeast, Educandario Nordestino Adventista (Northeast Brazil College) was founded approximately 1,800 miles (2,900 kilometers) north of the college in São Paulo, in the interior of the state of Pernambuco. For many years this college taught the theology course for hundreds of students from the East and North Brazil unions. In 1988 the Theological Seminary was transferred to the Northeast Brazil College in Bahia.

When the government of Brazil took over the property that belonged to Brazil College, the money obtained from the sale was used to purchase a property of 2,000 acres (800 hectares) 110 miles (180 kilometers) from São Paulo, near Artur Nogueira, where a new college called Central Campus already had a student enrollment of 1,300.

4. *Sabbath School.* According to the *Review and Herald* (72:459, July 16, 1895), F. H. Westphal organized what was probably the first Sabbath school in Brazil, sometime in March or April 1895 at Indaiatuba, São Paulo. According to his reports, he established two Sabbath schools in the state of São Paulo and a third in Santa Catarina, between the time of his arrival, about Mar. 11, and his report, May 27. Concerning their organization he wrote: "At Indaiatuba one family began to keep the Sabbath through reading. I baptized seven of the family and organized a Sabbath school [apparently the first in Brazil]. . . . At Piracicaba we held meetings nearly three weeks. . . . [Here] we organized a Sabbath school and a missionary society, and celebrated the ordinances. It was the first quarterly meeting held by Seventh-day Adventists in Brazil. We also baptized five persons in the Piracicaba River. . . . [At Joinvile, Santa Catarina] we organized a Sabbath school of fifteen members, and the second Sabbath of its existence, and my last Sabbath there, the school numbered twenty-eight" *(Review and Herald* 72:459, July 16, 1895).

Shortly before establishing the first Sabbath school at Indaiatuba, Westphal had visited Rio Claro, where he found two families who had accepted SDA teachings. He baptized one person in what probably was the first SDA baptism in Brazil *(ibid.).*

After Westphal's departure, more Sabbath

schools were established. In February 1896 H. F. Graf organized a Sabbath school at Gaspar Alto, Santa Catarina, with Augusto Olm as superintendent, Martha Olm as secretary, and 23 registered members. Four years later (fourth quarter of 1900) there were seven other Sabbath schools: Brusque, Santa Catarina; Taquarí, Rio Grande do Sul; Curitiba, Paraná; Rio Claro, São Paulo; Serra Pelada, Espírito Santo; Mucuri, in the municipality of Teófilo Otoni, in Minas Gerais; and Rio de Janeiro. All the Sabbath schools then existing were supervised by the Sabbath school secretary of the Brazil Union Conference, Mary Ehlers, and included a total of 608 members. The Sabbath school offerings totaled 580 mil and 210 reis, which at the exchange rate at that time would correspond to $193.43 in gold (one gold dollar = 3 milreis).

The subsequent organization of missions and conferences, each with a departmental secretary, made for stronger promotion and supervision of the Sabbath school work. By December 1992 there were 699,480 Sabbath school members in Brazil.

5. *Evangelism.* During the first years of Seventh-day Adventist mission work in Brazil, converts were won principally by colporteur evangelists; later came the regular evangelists. The first ordained ministers in Brazil were foreigners, mostly of German and North American origin, among them W. H. Thurston, H. F. Graf, F. W. Spies, Ernesto Schwantes, J. Lipke, Manuel Kuempel, Max Rohde, Emilio Hoelzle, E. C. Ehlers, Waldemar Ehlers, L. Conrado, C. E. Rentfro, Germano Streithorst, J. L. Braun, Arthur Westphal, Ricardo Suessmann, H. Meyer, and others.

In 1920 the first Brazilian minister, José Amador dos Reis, was ordained, and later others, including Ricardo Wilfart, Henrique Stoehr, and Gustavo Storch. In 1992 there was a total of 818 active ordained ministers in the different missionary fields of the country. Of the 316 active licensed ministers, the majority work as assistant evangelists. Active workers in the country total 9,997.

6. *Voice of Prophecy* ("Voz da Profecia"). The Voice of Prophecy radiobroadcast was launched in Brazil the latter half of 1943, under the direction of Roberto Mendes Rabello, principal speaker of the radio program. The first programs in Portuguese were prepared in Los Angeles under the guidance of W. P. Bradley, secretary of the Radio Commission. At the same time a radio correspondence school was organized at Niterói, Brazil, directed by Ilka Reis, who corrected lessons and answered letters.

Initially some stations were reluctant to broadcast a Protestant program. Because of religious pressures certain others who had signed contracts later canceled them. However, gradually opposition subsided, and the number of stations carrying the program increased, until 295 stations were broadcasting this program in 1973.

From 1943 to the beginning of 1963 the radio correspondence school received 401,362 requests for its course, 133,150 actually enrolling, and 30,234 completing it. During 1973 a total of 20,845 students enrolled. In order to care adequately for this large correspondence, two branches of the Radio Correspondence School were opened, one at Belém, Pará, in the north, the other at Pôrto Alegre, Rio Grande do Sul, in the south. Central offices occupy a building inaugurated October 1962 at Rio de Janeiro, where there are facilities for the recording of the Portuguese programs, including songs by a male quartet.

In 1959 the Brazilian Japanese Voice of Prophecy broadcast was begun with a theology graduate and former tea processor, Kiotaka Shirai, as the principal speaker, and Yoshinobu Omura, announcer and technician. The broadcast uses hymns recorded in Japanese by the King's Heralds of the original Voice of Prophecy in California. The radio correspondence school provides three courses—Youth, Introduction to Christianity, and General (doctrinal). Hundreds of thousands of Japanese are reached each week by the stations broadcasting these programs. Three times a week the Japanese newspaper *Nippaku Shimbun* publishes Voice of Prophecy sermons, prepared by Shirai. The school and studio operate under the auspices of the São Paulo Conference.

In 1960 for the large German-speaking population of southern Brazil, the São Paulo Conference sponsored *Stimme der Hoffnung* ("Voice of Hope"), with Jorge Hoyler, a minister, as speaker.

On Nov. 18, 1962, the SDA television program *Fé para Hoje* ("Faith for Today") was launched in São Paulo, and a little later in Rio de Janeiro. Alcides Campolongo, a minister, with his wife, conducted the program. In November 1991, through the combined effort of some Brazilian businesspeople, the program *It Is Written* is being aired nationally.

7. *Public Affairs and Religious Liberty Department for Brazil* (Deveres Cívicos da Igreja Adventista do Sétimo Dia no Brasil). A

department created in 1951 at Rio de Janeiro to foster good relations between the SDA Church, the public, and governmental authorities in all of Brazil. This department has been instrumental in obtaining government exemption for SDA students from taking school examinations on Saturday and in gaining recognition for the church's medical cadet training. Domingos Peixoto da Silva, general secretary of this department, promoted this activity of the church from its beginning in 1951 until 1968, when Dr. A. A. Nepomuceno was appointed to fill this post until July 1970. Walter J. Streithorst and Assad Bechara have continued this work.

8. *Medical Cadet Training.* In 1945 a medical cadet course was incorporated into the training program of SDA colleges and academies in Brazil. On Mar. 2, 1953, the president of Brazil officially recognized the medical cadet course, called Curso de Formação de Enfermeiro Padioleiro, abbreviated CFEP. The curriculum was approved by the Ministry of War, on Mar. 11, 1954. Thus every young man who has completed the course is automatically assigned, upon induction into the armed forces, to the health corps. Between 1954 and 1974 more than 1,271 young SDA men received diplomas for the medical cadet course.

In 1972 the course underwent some modifications and was again submitted and approved by the armed forces in Brazil. At that time the name was changed to "Curso de Formação de Enfermeiro Socorrista Padioleiro."

Medical Work. 1. *Medical Institutions.* The pioneer missionaries—particularly H. F. Graf, who came to Brazil in 1895—did everything possible to teach the new converts health principles and the advantages of natural treatments, including hydrotherapy.

Seven years after Graf's arrival, Abel L. Gregory, a physician and dentist, came to Brazil from the United States with his wife as a self-supporting missionary, to help develop SDA medical work in Rio Grande do Sul. Working intensively, he did much toward reducing prejudice and in advancing the local church work. He was joined in 1907 by Luisa Wurtz, a physician, and Corina Hoy, a nurse, who arrived from the United States. Both rendered valuable medical and health education service. However, attempts to establish medical work were unsuccessful at this time, and again in 1926, when John Lipke and his wife (a nurse) made another attempt. In 1939, under the leadership of E. H. Wilcox, then president of the South Brazil Union, SDA medical work became firmly established in Brazil, with the foundation of the Boa Vista Clinic (Good View Clinic) under the direction of Dr. Antonio Alves de Miranda. This clinic was substituted in 1942 by the Casa de Saúde Liberdade (São Paulo Adventist Hospital), under the direction of Dr. Galdino Nunes Vieira, a university teacher who left his job to dedicate himself to medical missionary work. At this same time, the São Paulo Conference organized the first Medical Assistance Department, with Renato Emir Oberg as director. In 1942 the Rio de Janeiro Clinic and Rest Home was founded in Rio de Janeiro, with Dr. C. C. Schneider as director. This North American missionary, interested in the right arm of the message, temporarily left his activities to study medicine in Brazil. His assistant was Dr. Artur Oberg, who later became the first SDA medical doctor in the East Brazil Union. In 1948 the Rio de Janeiro Clinic was replaced by Silvestre Adventist Hospital, on a property located under the famous monument of Christ the Redeemer, one of the beauty spots of Rio de Janeiro. In 1953 Belém Adventist Hospital was inaugurated in the capital city of the state of Pará, and in 1959, Pênfigo Adventist Hospital was established in Campo Grande, Mato Grosso, especially dedicated to curing the terrible illness generally known as savage fire, with facilities for ambulatory patients, consultations, and natural treatments, especially hydrotherapy. Until recently a similar clinic was operated in Pôrto Alegre, Rio Grande do Sul, called Clínica Bom Samaritano (Good Samaritan Clinic).

Since then the following institutions have been added: São Roque Adventist Clinic, 60 miles (100 kilometers) from São Paulo, totally dedicated to natural treatments and lifestyle-change programs; Vitoria Adventist Hospital, in Espírito Santo; Manaus Adventist Hospital; Adventist Health Center, located in a residential area of Rio Grande do Sul; São Paulo Adventist Hospital, in the Liberdal district.

2. *Medical Work Among the Indians.* In 1928 with the support of local church leaders, such as Rubens Anderson and Antonio Pereira, of the state of Goiás, A. N. Allen, a missionary from the United States, began welfare work among the Carajá Indians, and established the Rio Araguaia Mission. Later a school was opened. From the beginning until 1934, Ernesto Bergold, assistant to Allen, ministered to the Indians, teaching them such things as agriculture, practical trades, and the Bible,

adapted to the Indian way of thinking. Beginning in 1953, the mission launch *Pioneira* was used to conduct medical work on the Araguaia River. In 1964 this launch was replaced by a new one.

The *Pioneira* was not the first such boat in Brazil; Leo B. Halliwell was the pioneer in launch medical missionary work, beginning his well-known welfare ministry in 1931 with a launch on the Amazon River, designed and built by himself—the first of a series of such craft named *Luzeiro*. There followed others called *Luminar*, on the São Francisco River, beginning in 1946; the *Samaritana*, on the Ribeira River (1955); the *Luzeiro do Sul* (1963), on the coast of Paranaguá; and in 1964 a new medical missionary launch began operation at the Furnas Dam, in the Rio-Minas Conference. As the years have passed, new boats replaced some of the old. Others have been retired as new roads and communication media made them obsolete. In 1993, 10 launches were still in service.

The combined work of these launches gives assistance to thousands of sick persons, besides distributing clothing and food. Malaria, intestinal parasites, malnutrition, skin diseases, general and tropical diseases, and extraction of teeth are the most common problems cared for through this type of medical missionary work. Some literature evangelism also is carried on by the launches.

3. *Social Welfare Work.* Lar da Velhice Adventista ("Adventist Old People's Home"), open to SDAs, was established in the capital of São Paulo in 1950.

Dorcas Societies, established wherever there are Seventh-day Adventist churches, care for the needs of the poor and help with medicines, clothing, food, child care, and the finding of work for the unemployed.

BRAZIL COLLEGE (Instituto Adventista de Ensino) (Central Campus, also known as New Adventist Brazil College). A coeducational senior college located in a rural area in the township of Engenheiro Coelho, 90 miles (144 kilometers) northwest of the city of São Paulo, Brazil.

It is one of the two campuses occupied by Brazil College.

The school is located on a farm that contains 100,000 orange trees. It was bought as a result of the partial expropriation of the institution by the city.

Administered by an interunion board (South and Central Brazil union conferences) and part of the organizational structure of the South American Division, this college was founded with the purpose of becoming the main campus of the new Brazil College, serving a nationwide constituency (1992) of 600,000 members.

The school's atmosphere is characterized by a pollution-free environment, with direct contact with nature. Both the staff and students are involved in practical work, and there is a friendly mixture of young people coming from all over Brazil and from other countries in South America and Africa.

History. The idea of moving the main Brazilian College from São Paulo to a rural area predated the partial expropriation of the land. It was felt that an urban campus was no longer ideal for training young people seeking a Christian education. When attempts to sell the land failed, the expropriation act by the city of São Paulo served as a catalyst for the actualization of the plan. Since then a string of divine providences have shown the moving to be a part of God's plan. From the united action taken by the committee members and the support given by the church to the purchase of prime quality land and the wise use of the resources—all demonstrated that the beginnings of the new Brazil College were not mere coincidence.

Despite fears that the city government might not pay or might underevaluate the expropriated land, the property was paid for in cash at the market value (US$4.3 million). With these resources in hand, a fully equipped, fertile, totally arable, 1,900-acre (770-hectare) farm was purchased. Producing oranges, bananas, and peaches, with an appropriate soil and climate for raising cattle, the farm is self-sufficient and has greatly helped in the development of the institution.

The enthusiasm of church members, private agencies, and foundations has been an added blessing. A gift equivalent to US$1.5 million was donated by an alumnus for the construction and equipment of the library building. The Chan Shun International Foundation is funding half of the construction of the academic complex, estimated at US$2 million. The construction program, begun soon after the land was purchased, totals more than 400,000 square feet (37,200 square meters), including residence halls, kitchen and cafeteria, library, and staff houses.

The enrollment has been larger than expected. Elementary and secondary students, as well as hundreds of college students, looking for a better-quality education apply every year. Today's greatest need is room in the dormitories for college students. As the institution celebrates its tenth anniversary (1983-1993) with a total enrollment of more than 1,500, the Lord's hand can be seen working.

Departments and Industries. The central campus is characterized by the involvement of all boarding students in practical work, allowing them to learn a skill and pay for part or all of their board and tuition costs. This is done in connection with the service departments and industries (New Life Food Factory, Lagoa Bonita Dairy Industry). The quality of what these students do is well known. The cattle they care for and the milk they offer to the market are considered among the best in the country. During vacation they are encouraged to canvass, and experiences gained have been rewarding.

Presidents: Edmer de Oliveira, 1984; Arthur Dassow, 1985-1986; Walter Boger, 1987- .

BRAZIL COLLEGE (Instituto Adventista de Ensino) (São Paulo). One of the two campuses occupied by Brazil College. This is the original site, located 14 miles (22 kilometers) from the center of São Paulo, a city of some 15 million people. The school is now surrounded by the city. The institution maintains three dormitories capable of housing a total of 588 students.

A wide range of courses are offered, including majors in various health fields, language, and literature, and minors in science, mathematics, and biology. It is hoped that by 1995 the school will be authorized to offer courses in data processing, psychology, physiotherapy, nutrition, and physical fitness.

The enrollment in 1993 was 2,735 students on all levels.

Forerunners. The first Seventh-day Adventist mission training school in Brazil, known as the Brusque School, was established late in 1897 at Gaspar Alto (near Brusque), state of Santa Catarina. The founder was Guilherme (Wilhelm) Stein, a teacher, who was among the first converts in Brazil *(Review and Herald* 80:12, Mar. 10, 1903). The first class graduated from this school in 1901; however, it soon became evident that more land was "sadly needed at the Brusque school, to give it proper support" *(Review and Herald* 80:15, July 7, 1903). The school closed in 1903.

In that same year the Taquary School, established at Taquary (near Pôrto Alegre), state of Rio Grande do Sul, by John Lipke, a missionary-teacher, in 1903, seems to have taken over the mission training function of the Brusque School. It was closed in 1910 and sold for $7,000.

There was no mission training school in Brazil for the next few years. However, in 1915 Izadora Spies, wife of F. W. Spies, president of the Brazilian Union Conference, appealed at a ministers' congress for faith to establish a new missionary school, and in the spring an ideal site was found at Santo Amaro, state of São Paulo, which was bought with the $7,000 from the sale of the Taquary School. Work on the new property began on May 6, 1915.

History. The new school, known as the Seminario Adventista da Conferencia União Brazileira dos Adventistas do Sétimo Dia ("Adventist Seminary of the Brazilian Union Conference of SDAs"; Brazilian Seminary), began to function officially with 12 students on July 4, 1915, with John Lipke as principal, J. H. Boehm as manager, and Paulo Henning as teacher. Later five more students enrolled. At first the school faced a serious housing problem, but the Thirteenth Sabbath Offering overflow for the second quarter of 1916, which amounted to $4,318.90, did much to ease the situation by providing funds to build dormitories and homes for teachers.

According to the *Prospecto Annual* (school bulletin) for 1930, "seventeen students enrolled in our seminary during its first year. These spent at least half of their time tending the farm and helping with the construction of the first buildings. The rest of the time was devoted to study. The second year the number of students almost doubled, 33 young people enrolling, and in 1917 the enrollment reached 55" (p. 7). The *Prospecto Annual* goes on to say that "in 1919 there began an era of expansion, including the construction of more buildings and the enlargement of existing structures in order to accommodate a much larger number of students."

In 1922 the first class, consisting of 11 students (four young women and seven young men), graduated. Their motto, "Rumo ao Mar" ("Seaward," or "On to the Sea"), indicates their purpose of carrying the gospel to all the world.

The school has operated under various other names. In 1919 its name was shortened to Seminario Adventista ("Adventist Seminary"). The name was Colégio Adventista ("Adventist College," referred to as Brazilian Seminary or

Brazil Training School in the *Yearbook*) in 1923. This name was retained until 1942, when it became Colégio Adventista Brasileiro ("Brazilian Adventist College," referred to as Brazil College in the *Yearbook*). In 1961 the name was changed to Instituto Adventista de Ensino ("Adventist Training Institute," referred to as Brazil College in the *Yearbook*).

As of 1992, 3,282 college-level students had received diplomas and certificates in seven disciplines. More than half of these have served or are serving the church as workers and missionaries to countries worldwide. In 1993 Brazil College employed 329 faculty and staff members.

Presidents: John Lipke, 1916-1918; Thomas W. Steen, 1919-1927; George B. Taylor, 1928-1931; Ellis R. Maas, 1931-1936; Lloyd E. Downs, 1937-1939; D. Peixoto da Silva, 1939-1947; Dario Garcia, 1947-1950; Jeronimo G. Garcia, 1951-1952; Rodolpho Belz, 1953-1957; Dario Garcia, 1957-1961; Jairo Araujo, 1961-1966; Nevil Gorski, 1966-1975; Oly Ferreira Pinto, 1975-1978; Walter Boger, 1978-1985; Roberto C. de Azevedo, 1985-1993; Nevil Gorski, 1993- .

BRAZIL FOOD FACTORY. *See* South American Division Health Food Company.

BRAZIL OLD PEOPLE'S HOME. *See* São Paulo Old People's Home.

BRAZIL PUBLISHING HOUSE (Casa Publicadora Brasileira). A publishing firm with printing facilities, founded in 1904 in Taquarí (near Pôrto Alegre), Rio Grande do Sul, Brazil, and moved in 1907 to Estação de São Bernardo, 15 miles (25 kilometers) from São Paulo, capital of the state of São Paulo. It is the largest Seventh-day Adventist publishing institution in Latin America, and fourth-largest in sales in the denomination. It is administered by an interunion board representing all the unions in Brazil. Publishing work in Brazil began in 1900 in Rio de Janeiro under the guidance of W. H. Thurston, a missionary from the United States. Under the editorship of Guilherme (William) Stein, a former teacher, *O Arauto da Verdade* ("The Herald of Truth") began to be issued in July of that year. Later John Lipke, a missionary, returned to the United States to appeal for funds for a printing press. A total of $1,500 was raised. In addition, Emmanuel Missionary College donated a handpress salvaged from the Battle Creek fire of 1903.

Jorge (George) Sabeff, then at College View, Nebraska, who had acquired printing experience with the International Tract Society, was called to set up and operate the press in Brazil. In 1905 he was joined by Augusto Preuss, a printer, and his brother, Leopoldo F. Preuss, an apprentice. They set up the press, and on May 10 printed 2,000 16-page issues of *O Arauto da Verdade.* Business to the amount of $667 was done in that year.

At the invitation of the General Conference, Augusto Pages of the Hamburg Publishing House arrived in Brazil in November 1905 to serve as business manager of what had come to be called the Taquarí Branch of the International Tract Society and as secretary of the Rio Grande do Sul Conference.

In January 1906 the first issue of the *Revista Trimestral* ("Quarterly Review"), now *Revista Adventista* ("Adventist Review"), appeared, official organ of SDAs in Brazil. It was also published in German for the large number of German-speaking SDAs in Brazil under the name of *Rundschau der Adventisten* ("Adventist Review"). Besides various leaflets, four books were printed that year: *A Volta de Christo Nesta Geração* ("Return of Christ in This Generation"), Ellen G. White's *Passos a Cristo* ("Steps to Christ"), also *O Glorioso Aparecimento de Jesus* ("Jesus' Glorious Appearing"), and *Sucessos Preditos na História Universal* ("Fulfilled Prophecy in Universal History").

In 1908, after the move to Estação de São Bernardo, the institution received the old handpress from Taquarí, and two smaller gasoline-powered presses, one of which was donated by Hamburg Publishing House in Germany.

At present the Brazil Publishing House has 165 electrically powered machines. There were 16 periodicals published during 1993, among which were *Revista Adventista* ("Adventist Review"), *Decisão* ("Decision"), *Vida e Saúde* ("Life and Health"), *Mocidade* ("Youth"), and *Nosso Amiguinho* ("Our Little Friend"). From 1904 to 1993, 450 different books were published, some in several editions, totaling more than 30 million copies. Among the most popular have been *Vida de Jesús* ("Life of Jesus"), by Ellen G. White, 2,100,000 copies; *O Moço e Seus Problemas* and *A Moça e Seus Problemas* ("On Becoming a Man" and "On Becoming a Woman"), both by Harold Shryock, M.D., 535,000; *O Conflito dos Séculos* ("The Great Controversy"), by Ellen G. White, 1,565,000, including the popular edition; *Nutrição e Vigor* ("Nutrition and Vigor"), by António Miranda, M.D., and Clarita Miranda, M.D., 370,000; *Vereda de Cristo* ("Steps to Christ"), by Ellen G. White, 1,458,969, including pocket edition; *Técnica Moderna de Primeiros Socorros* ("First Aid"), by Dr. Marcelo A. Hammerly, 523,000, including the popular edition; *Pelos Meandros do Mal* ("The Marked Bible"), by C. L. Taylor, 277,000; *Matrimônio Feliz* ("Happy Marriage"), by Luiz Waldvogel, 240,000; *Fumar, ou Não Fumar?* ("To Smoke, or Not to Smoke"), by Dr. Ajax César da Silveira, 265,000; *Escravos do Século XX* ("Slaves of the 20th Century"), 200,000; *Homens que Fizeram o Brasil* ("Men Who Made Brazil"), by Luiz Waldvogel, 195,000; *O Fumo e o Câncer do Pulmão* ("Smoking and Lung Cancer"), 173,000; *A Família Moderna e a Solução de Seus Problemas* ("The Modern Family and the Solution of Its Problems"), 170,000; *Conselheiro Médico do Lar* ("Home Medical Counselor"), by Hubert Swartout, M.D., 170,000; *Felicidade Conjugal* ("Happiness for Husbands and Wives"), by Harold Shryock, M.D., 160,000; *O Destino do Homem* ("The Destiny of Man"), by João Pinho, 152,000. More recently: *Amor, Sexo e Erotismo* ("Love, Sex, and Eroticism"), by Galdino N. Vieira, M.D., 265,000; *A Ilusão das Drogas* ("The Illusion of Drugs"), by Ivan Schmidt, 380,000; *A Cura e a Saúde Pelos Alimnentos* ("Cure and Health Through Food"), by Ernest Schneider, M.D., 560,000. Generally, the more popular books have run through six or seven editions of 30,000 each.

At the present time (1993) more than 73 million Bible study leaflets and other leaflets for missionary distribution are issued annually. From 4 to 5 million periodicals are printed annually. In 1993 gross sales totaled almost US$8.1 million.

Sixty-one Ellen White books have been translated into Portuguese, for a total of 5,406,253 copies for sale to individuals and for church use.

The publishing house presently has 280 employees who supply 2,600 colporteurs, besides 800 students who canvass during school vacations.

In 1985 the Brazil Publishing House was moved to the city of Tatuí, which is 80 miles (130 kilometers) from São Paulo. In 1993 it occupied more than 193,680 square feet (18,000 square meters) of space.

Managers: Augusto Pages, 1905-1921; R. C. Gray, 1921; M. V. Tucker, 1922-1926; C. E. Schofield (acting), 1926; Frederico W. Spies, 1927-1933; J. Berger Johnson, 1933-1937; H. B. Fisher, 1937-1938; Emilio Doehnert, 1938-1949; Domingos Peixoto da Silva, 1949-1951; B. E. Schuenemann, 1951-1977; Wilson Sarli, 1977-1984; Carlos M. Borda, 1985- .

BRAZIL VOICE OF PROPHECY. *See* Brazil.

BREATH OF LIFE. A television ministry featuring the preaching of the gospel by Charles D. Brooks, general field secretary of the General Conference. Excellent music by dedicated musicians augments each program. The *Breath of Life* telecast has wide cross-cultural appeal in the United States and other countries.

In 1973-1974 Breath of Life began operations as a media outreach of the Seventh-day Adventist Church, answering the need for programming targeting Black America. Walter E. Arties, while affiliated with station KHOF-TV in Glendale, California, developed this idea and initiated its acceptance with a pilot and numerous presentations to clergy and laity. Members attending camp meetings and convocations endorsed the concept. The music of the original Breath of Life Quartet—Clyde O. Allen, James L. Kyle, Shelton E. Kilby III, Walter E. Arties—along with Myrna Matthews-Haynes, arranger/accompanist, helped open the way for the telecast. Samuel D. Meyers was the speaker on the pilot program. Brenda Blackmon Wood, news anchor in Atlanta, Georgia, for station WSB, was program announcer and filled this position for several years.

When C. D. Brooks accepted the challenge to be director/speaker, in addition to his elected post, the program's strategy became more focused. In cities where public evangelism was planned, the telecast was aired 13-26 weeks prior to the meetings. The objective was to direct viewers to the meetings and church fellowship. The Washington, D.C., campaigns, conducted consecutively in 1978 and 1979, stand out as the best example of this plan. Church members advertised the telecast and the meetings. Baptisms totaled more than 500, and a new church was organized. Now located in Fort Washington, Maryland, the Breath of Life church bears the name selected by the new converts that commemorates its origin.

More than 12,000 persons rejoice in the blessed hope as a result of crusades from Palau (Micronesian island in the Pacific), across

America to the United Kingdom and the West Indies. Churches have been established in many areas with the first being in Memphis, Tennessee, 1974, and the most recent being in Nassau, Bahamas, 1993. This unique blend of television and public evangelism continues to yield rich dividends.

Scripts for the telecast were written early on by Louis B. Reynolds, associate director of the Sabbath School Department of the General Conference and former editor of *Message* magazine. He particularly assisted with the Heritage Series, which focused on the spiritual connection that our forefathers had with their God and the continued legacy it provides Black Americans today. His contributions added a special quality and dignity to the telecast. Special emphasis was placed on health with a series of programs in which Brooks interviewed physicians and other health professionals. Dr. Samuel L. DeShay provided the spark and substantial financial assistance, through the General Conference Health Department, to produce these programs.

With the emergence of cable TV, the door was opened for *Breath of Life* to become a weekly program in the United States on the Black Entertainment and VISN networks, and in Canada on the VISION Network. Other cable systems air the telecast in local areas to their subscribers. The PTL and ACTS networks carried *Breath of Life* for a substantial period.

With limited resources provided by a relatively faithful few and General Conference appropriations, Breath of Life has made significant strides. In 1981 Dorothy Valcarcel introduced and implemented the direct mail system for consistent contributions. Its steady growth is a principal source of support. Fiscal responsibility is a hallmark of the telecast as well as its high standard for production and spiritual quality. C. D. Brooks continues to set the pace in public evangelism and addresses current spiritual themes on the telecast. Arties serves Breath of Life as ministry coordinator/director of production. In addition to other assignments, he is also assistant to the president of the Adventist Media Center.

To maintain the ministry's growth pattern, Reginald O. Robinson joined the staff in 1982, succeeding Kyle. He is the associate speaker, evangelist, director of field services, fund-raising and development, and several other departments. Also, the rich music of Ron Murphy enhanced outreach engagements. While viewers are asked to write in for free materials (or call via the 800 number), they are also invited to join the Bible school. Thousands have graduated from this course. These names provide a ready source of interests for follow-up and church membership.

A host of people contribute their time and energy to make the actual telecast succeed in its mission, such as program announcers Michael Conner and Maria Anderson, and health professionals Donna L. Willis, M.D., and Gwendolyn L. Foster. The best of music is provided by the Breath of Life Quartet II, namely: Roger C. Smith, Ronald A. Woodfork, Loren Mulraine, and Myron S. Ottley; "Joy" (Deidra Brooks) Tramel, Sharon Brathwaite, and Melvin Bryant; and vocalists Janice Chandler, Ullanda Innocent, and Pastor T. Marshall Kelly. Adrian T. Westney, Jr., serves as music director for the ministry. They offer their expertise on a volunteer basis. Completing the support staff are Mardel Duldulao, administrative secretary; Joyce Shepperd, secretary/departmental assistant; Gerri Banfield, Bible school counselor; and Grayce Grant, trust officer.

BREATHE FREE: THE PLAN TO STOP SMOKING. A program designed to aid the smoker in developing self-assurance and confidence in the cessation process. Breathe Free assists participants in becoming knowledgeable and active in the process of behavior change, opening up to them a vision of personal choice, individual responsibility, freedom to act, and power to direct their own lifestyle. It helps them find confidence in their ability to regain control of their lives.

Breathe Free seeks to empower the individual to reach four major objectives: physical preparation, mental conditioning, social support, and spiritual regeneration. The revised Breathe Free plan consists of nine sessions, one and a half to two hours in length, lasting over a period of four weeks. Periodic home visits and phone or written contacts are very helpful. This includes a minimum of three contacts at least three, six, and 12 months after the initial nine sessions.

The materials provided for the Breathe Free plan consist of nine annotated scripts designed for the expert or the novice in conducting a smoking cessation program. The plan also provides a director's manual giving detailed information on how to plan, promote, and implement the program.

For the participant a number of items are

available to enhance the effectiveness of the program: novelty buttons; a personal plan booklet that guides each participant through each session of the program; diplomas to be given at the end of the nine sessions, at six months, and at one year; a number of posters to be coordinated with each of the nine sessions; nine videos, one for each of the nine sessions; many demonstration devices; new pamphlets designed to accompany each of the sessions, particularly in the area of smoking and the topics of exercise, caffeine, alcohol, heart disease, cancer, secondhand smoke, weight control, stress, diet, and a number of other helpful topics.

The church's first smoking cessation program was designed by Dr. J. Wayne McFarland and Chaplain Elman J. Folkenberg between 1959 and 1961. Called the Five-Day Plan to Stop Smoking, it was one of the first smoking-cessation programs available in the United States. At that time the GC Temperance Department also produced one of the first films on smoking and health—*One in 20,000.* During the next 20 to 25 years this plan was successful in helping many thousands of smokers stop smoking. In 1980 Dr. Mervyn Hardinge set up a commission of smoking-cessation experts to study the feasibility of revising the Five-Day Plan.

In 1984 Stoy Proctor, associate director of the Health and Temperance Department, was commissioned to continue research on revising the Five-Day Plan by conducting a thorough literature search as well as a survey of smoking cessation experts throughout North America. This work was completed in 1984 and a revised Five-Day Plan to Stop Smoking was placed on the market in 1985 and was named the Breathe-Free Plan.

In 1988 the Health and Temperance Department commissioned the Center for Health Promotion at Loma Linda University to study the effectiveness of Breathe Free. Their evaluations and research suggested that the length of the Five-Day Plan should be extended, that the after treatment should be lengthened, and that more time should be allowed for discussion. The small group work should be implemented and given a major part of the program with less attention to be given to the lecture format.

In 1993 Breathe Free was again revised to meet these findings, and the newly revised Breathe Free plan was released. Anyone with successful speaking ability or group dynamics expertise can conduct a successful program because of the comprehensive nature of the self-help material provided by Breathe Free: The Plan to Stop Smoking.

Tobacco is now the leading cause of preventable disease, a major contributor to heart disease, cancer, stroke, and chronic respiratory disease. The surgeon general of the U.S.A. has declared that smoking is an addiction comparable to cocaine addiction. Seventh-day Adventists must continue their efforts to fight this plague.

One of the most successful concepts used by Breathe Free: The Plan to Stop Smoking is found in *Fundamentals of Christian Education:* "If we wish to do good to souls, our success with these souls will be in proportion to their belief in our belief in, and appreciation of, them. Respect shown to the struggling human soul is the sure means through Christ Jesus of the restoration of the self-respect that man has lost" (p. 281).

In 1988 and 1989 Dr. Terry Butler, then a researcher at Loma Linda University involved in the evaluation of the Breathe Free plan, went back to his native Australia and adapted many of the Five-Day and Breathe Free concepts for a program used mainly in the South Pacific Division called "I Quit Now!" The Health and Temperance Department encourages every country to use Breathe Free: The Plan to Stop Smoking as appropriate or to adapt it to the culture and language that are needed in that particular area.

BRENNWALD, FREDERIC (1891-1970). Treasurer and auditor. He was born in Zurich, Switzerland, and after attending college in Berlin, Germany, he began his service to the church as a Bible worker in Germany. Following this, he served as accountant, treasurer, and then manager of the Adventist Publishing House in Hamburg. He served the denomination in Holland, Romania, and Poland, and as auditor of the European Division. He then served as treasurer and auditor of the Southern European Division until 1946. At the end of World War II Brennwald was called to the General Conference, where he served until 1962. When he retired at that time, he had served the church for more than 48 years.

BREWER, NATHAN FALCON (1891-1959). Publishing secretary, administrator. After graduating from South Lancaster Academy (1916), he went to China, and until 1927 led in the publishing and home mission work there. He was superintendent successively of the Central China, Manchuria, and East China union missions, and, in 1940, became president of the China Division.

While visiting Hong Kong in 1942, Brewer was interned, but was repatriated about six months later, and served as a General Conference field secretary until the end of the war. He was then appointed general secretary of the China Division (1946), and returned to America (1948) when the China Division was staffed with Chinese leaders. Again, he served as a General Conference field secretary, and during the last three years of his life was in charge of personnel at the General Conference. He died in an automobile accident.

BRINKERHOFF, WILLIAM H. *See* Marion Party.

BRISBANE ADVENTIST HIGH SCHOOL. A coeducational day school (years 8-12) operated by the South Queensland Conference. The school is located at Mount Gravatt on a 37-acre (15-hectare) campus, which it shares with the Brisbane Adventist Primary School. In 1993 the school had an enrollment of 266 students and a full-time staff of 17. The school opened on its present site in 1973. Since the initial building was constructed, further additions have been made: a four-classroom block in 1977, industrial arts and technology workshops in 1982, an administrative wing in 1985, and a library and fine arts complex in 1989.

The school is registered with the Queensland Department of Education and offers a wide range of subjects leading to the Higher School Certificate. In 1991 the school was registered by the Australian government to educate overseas students.

Principals: D. J. Cooke, 1973-1979; K. R. Dickins, 1980-1982; B. J. Wright, 1983-1991; B. L. Robinson, 1992- .

BRITAIN. *See* Great Britain and Northern Ireland.

BRITISH ADVENT MESSENGER (1897- ;1897-1935 as *Missionary Worker;* every two weeks; Stanborough Press; files in GC). Church paper of the British Union Conference, eight pages, from 1956 to 1981, incorporating each month *Youth,* eight pages (renamed *Encounter* in 1974 and issued bimonthly), organ of the Youth Department of the British Union Conference. *Messenger* was issued free (since July 26, 1922) to church members in the British Isles. It was published at 451 Holloway Road, London, until Oct. 30, 1907; thereafter at the Stanborough Press. The youth paper *Encounter* is published six times per annum. It has been published independently of *Messenger* since 1981.

Editors: (no editor named until 1916); W. E. Read, 1916-1918; W. T. Bartlett, 1918-1920; A. S. Maxwell, 1920-1936; W. L. Emmerson, 1936-1966; R. D. Vine, 1966-1979; D. N. Marshall, 1979- .

BRITISH ADVENTIST NURSES ASSOCIATION. *See* Association for SDA Nurses.

BRITISH COLUMBIA CONFERENCE. The unit of church organization comprising the province of British Columbia, part of the Northwest Territories, and the Yukon. Statistics (1993): churches, 68; members, 5,893; church schools, 25; ordained ministers, 48; licensed ministers, 3; licensed commissioned ministers, 4; church school teachers, 102. Headquarters: 1626 McCallum Road, Abbotsford, British Columbia. The conference forms a part of the Seventh-day Adventist Church in Canada.

Institutions. Caribou Adventist Academy; Fraser Valley Adventist Academy; Kennebec Manor; Okanagan Academy; Rest Haven Lodge.

Local churches: Abbotsford, Aldergrove, Armstrong, Barriere, Bella Coola, Canadian Filipino, Cariboo Central, Cawston-Karemeos, Chetwynd, Chilliwick, Colwood, Comox, Coquitlam, Cranbrook, Creston, Dawson Creek, Duncan, Fort St. John, Fountainview, Golden, Grand Forks, Grandview, Hazelton, Hope, Kamloops, Kelowna, Kitwanga, Langley, Maple Ridge, McBride, Mission, Nakusp, Nanaimo, Nelson, North Shore, Oliver, Open Door, Orchard City, Osoyoos, Penticton, Port Alberni, Port Hardy, Prince George, Quesnel, Rest Haven, Richmond, Rutland (Central, Ukrainian), Salmon Arm, Silver Creek, Silver Hills, Swithers, Surrey (Central, Korean), Terrace, Trail, Vancouver Central, Vancouver Chinese, Vancouver Hispanic, Vanderhoof, Vernon, Victoria, Westbank, Westminster, Whitehorse, White Rock, Wildwood, Williams Lake, Winfield.

Companies: Ashcroft, Campbell River, Cherryville, Conference Church, Gwa'sala Nakwaxda'xw, Horsefly, Lakes District, Lytton, Merritt, Native Indian, 100 Mile House, Pemberton, Powell River, Revelstoke,

Sechelt, Stewart.

History. *Beginnings of the Work in the Conference.* As part of the territory of the North Pacific Conference (U.S.), beginning in 1886, western British Columbia was evangelized by ministers from Oregon. In 1887 a branch of the North Pacific Tract and Missionary Society was established in Victoria, the provincial capital. S. Fulton and G. W. Davis held some meetings there the following winter, baptizing three converts—two of whom had become interested through Bible studies conducted by a man named Robb. In 1889 H. W. Reed, assisted by Baxter and David Fulton, held a tent meeting in Victoria, and before the annual conference session May 27-June 4, 1890, a church was organized in Victoria—the first in British Columbia.

On June 26, 1890, a series of tent meetings was opened in Vancouver by Isaac Morrison and V. H. Lucas. These meetings proved highly fruitful, and on Nov. 30 a church of 16 members was organized by R. A. Underwood. Meetings were also held in Nanaimo at an early date and with some success, for by September 1895 there were a sufficient number of adherents in that place to protest the holding of Saturday elections.

In 1897 J. L. Wilson settled in Vancouver, held a series of meetings, revived the members, and reorganized the church of which the Wolfers and a Mrs. Kenny were charter members.

Early in 1900 W. W. Steward, of the Upper Columbia Conference, began preaching in Rossland; later a church was organized there. Mrs. R. S. Greaves, who had the distinction of being the first public school teacher in the province south of Nelson (1893-1894), and Mrs. Cour-Barron—a convert of the pioneer colporteur Geo. W. Sowler—were two of its members. Other early churches were formed in Mission City and in Cumberland on Vancouver Island. Mrs. C. H. Casey and C. O. Smith, early teachers in British Columbia church schools, came from Cumberland.

The British Columbia Conference Organized. In June 1902 the British Columbia mission field was organized under the superintendency of J. L. Wilson. The following September (1902), at the first camp meeting held in British Columbia, it was reorganized as a conference of five churches (with two church buildings, valued at $3,000), and a membership of about 75. J. L. Wilson became the first president.

The same year treatment rooms were opened in Vancouver at 163 East Hastings Street, with M. Shaffer in charge of the women's treatments and W. H. Davies of the men's. A year later treatment rooms were established in Victoria. Also in Vancouver a pure-food vegetarian restaurant was opened in 1904, at 165 Hastings Street, with A. Ferguson in charge. However, in September of that year it was decided to sell out all these places of business, "freeing . . . hands from the temporal things."

In 1903 William Manson gave land near Vancouver for a school known as Manson Industrial school, which became Manson Academy; it operated from 1904 to 1915.

The work in British Columbia in the early days, with the exception of the two coastal churches at Port Simpson and Bella Coola, was concentrated in three areas: Vancouver Island, the mouth of the Fraser River, and the Okanagan Valley. Before 1902 Vancouver members had built a small church on Keefer Street for $850 (which they sold after eight years for $17,500). In 1909 a church was organized in South Vancouver, and a year later, one in West Vancouver, where a church building with six dwelling rooms below it was purchased. Beginning in April 1910, the conference Tract Society, hitherto situated in Pitt Meadows, was housed in the West Vancouver church. The members in both South Vancouver and East Vancouver built churches of their own, and all three churches were dedicated in December 1911. For many years the Vancouver churches also maintained a Chinese mission, with Lim Ping in charge.

During this same period O. E. Davis began his work among the Indians at Port Simpson, where he established, on Dec. 11, 1903, the first Indian church in the conference. About the same time, A. M. Dart went to the Yukon and worked in White Horse, Dawson, and Bonanza. In 1907 new churches were organized in Bella Coola, where Frank Johnson was the first SDA settler, and at Abbotsford, where the charter members included the Thomas Atkinsons, Pykes, McIlvanias, Hartnells, and Adgates. The conference also owned, successively, three mission launches—the *Evangel,* the *Rambler,* and the *Saturna*—which operated along the coast.

The first SDAs in the Okanagan Valley were a group of immigrants from Great Falls, Montana, who settled in Silver Creek about 1901. They included two Haines families and a McLean family. Soon after, the conference sent William C. Young to hold meetings in Armstrong. Converts from these meetings included W. T. Rogers and his wife, formerly Emma Jane Hoover. Later other members of the Hoover family became SDAs. The result was the organization of the first church in the Okanagan, at Armstrong, with a membership of 13. A year later Young pitched his tent in Salmon Arm, where he numbered among his converts M. E. Toombs, his wife, and their sons George and Harold.

On June 21, 1906, William C. Young and P. P. Adams, with George Toombs as tentmaster, began a series of tent meetings in Vernon, where there were already a few SDAs. From their work emerged a new congregation—the second in the Okanagan—organized Nov. 10, 1906. Twenty-nine miles east of Vernon, at Reiswig (no longer in existence), was a small, unorganized group of German believers, mostly Reiswig families, and there in September 1906 Asa Smith opened the first denominational school in the Okanagan. His 10 pupils ranged in age from 7 to 23.

At Silver Creek E. J. Harvey conducted meetings in the schoolhouse from May to July 1908. In July P. P. Adams moved with his family from Manson Academy to Vernon, where he had worked previously. Several months later he opened a new series of meetings in Silver Creek. In all, he spent two years in this district, working among the members in Salmon Arm, Armstrong, Vernon, Silver Creek, and Reiswig. During his ministry a congregation was organized at Silver Creek, and officers were elected on Jan. 9, 1909; a place of worship at Armstrong, built six years earlier, was dedicated on Oct. 30, 1909; and a church of 21 members was organized at Round Lake by J. G. Walker in the home of William Brown (July 23, 1910), which later became the Grandview church.

The Reiswig families, formerly living east of Vernon, moved into the Grandview area after Adams left the community, in September 1910. Together the members, including the Stickle and Wm. McLeod families, erected a place of worship there, which J. G. Walker dedicated on Dec. 24, 1911—one week after he dedicated a church in Vernon. In this church German services were held in the morning and English in the afternoon. In the church auditorium a church school was begun in the fall of 1911, even before it was dedicated, with Lydia Stickle as teacher. A year later C. O. Smith became the principal, teaching in English at one end of the room while his assistant, Henry Berg, taught in German at the other. There were at that time 16 Reiswigs in Smith's class. In 1913 the English-speaking group separated to form the Lumen church (renamed Lumen Grandview in 1916).

A church in Nanaimo resulted in 1912 from the work of F. H. Conway. That year J. L. Wilson pitched his tent, first in Kamloops and later in Penticton, where resided the Harlow and A. T. Greenslade families. On Mar. 8, 1913, a church was dedicated in Penticton, and the following day a new congregation was organized. In the autumn of 1913, J. G. Walker, the conference president, organized a new church in Vancouver. Two years later C. E. Wood settled in Nelson and E. R. Potter in Kelowna. At Nelson, on Dec. 21, 1915, ten were baptized, and two days later a church was organized. In Kelowna progress was slower, but Potter was successful in making a few converts, Thomas Barber being the first. A church was finally organized there (now Rutland) on Mar. 27, 1919.

By June 1920 there were five ordained ministers and the following churches in the conference: three in Vancouver, two in Grandview, and one each in Armstrong, Vernon, Kelowna, Penticton, Nelson, Firvale (Bella Coola), Victoria, and Nanaimo. On Sept. 3, 1921, W. A. Clemenson organized a new church of 21 members at White Rock as a result of Bible studies conducted there by S. G. White. A year later two new churches appeared—a Russian congregation at Grandview, the work of M. S. Krietzky, and a church at Rest Haven, the result of opening the new sanitarium. In 1923 S. G. White took up residence in Mission City, where there once had been a church. After a systematic distribution of publications followed by tent meetings, he won five converts. On Aug. 8, 1925, the churches in Vancouver united to form one central church with a membership of 139. In 1926 Harry Cameron established himself in Alberni, where one Adventist, Mrs. A. Monks, lived. On Feb. 13, 1927, he organized a new church of 19 members. By the end of 1929 there were 13 churches in British Columbia with a combined membership of 838.

In 1931 new churches were organized in Chilliwack, Aldergrove, and New Westminster. S. J. Shafer was associated with the beginnings of the first two and H. Cameron with the third. Three years later, the church at Silver Creek, which had been disbanded, was reorganized. New churches appeared in Langley (1935), Whalley (1936), Adams Lake (1937), Prince George (1938), and Vancouver (1939)—the last named a Ukrainian church, which owed its existence to S. J. Demchuk, W. Poleshuk, and N. Bodrug. Ainsley Blair was associated with the organization of the church at Prince George, and S. J. Demchuk with the one at Whalley.

About 1939 Fred Blair and his wife, SDAs from Saskatchewan, moved into the Creston Valley. Soon Mrs. Blair began giving Bible studies to her neighbors. Later C. C. Weis followed up the interest. Other SDA settlers joined the group. They purchased and remodeled an old Catholic church and dedicated it on May 15, 1943, when they were organized into a church.

New churches appeared in the interior (often around logging camps operated by SDAs), in the southeast at Oliver, and at Trail; in the far north at Dawson Creek, the most northerly congregation in Canada; and at Hazelton, organized in 1956. In 1962 the only floating church in Canada was dedicated—the Watcher Isle church on Smith Inlet, part of a logging village built on cedar log rafts.

The Golden church, organized in 1970 as a company and in 1973 as a church, purchased the oldest church building in the Kootenays (built c. 1870) from the Catholic diocese. Being a heritage building, the original structure could not be altered, but an extension for school classrooms was permitted.

The British Columbia church school system had its beginning with the organizing of a school in Pitt Meadows in 1904, later becoming the Manson Academy and continuing until 1915. Others followed in Reiswig, Bella Coola, Firvale, Grandview, Penticton, Nanaimo, Silver Creek, Naden Harbor, Kelowna, Nelson, and Mission City. By 1916-1917 the only schools left in the conference were at Grandview and Firvale. From 1918 to 1929 schools were added in Rutland, White Rock, Rest Haven, Vancouver, and Victoria. In 1923-1933 depression brought the number down to four—Vancouver, Rutland, Grandview, and Rest Haven. Later in that decade several had been revived.

The school in Rutland increased its offerings to all grades from 1-12, changing its name to Okanagan Academy. In 1975 the school was relocated on a 13-acre (five-hectare) parcel of land on Hollywood Road. The building was expanded to contain 13 classrooms, library, industrial arts shop, and a large auditorium.

A notable step was taken in 1964 when the Vernon and Armstrong areas began the first consolidated school in the conference. This was called the North Okanagan Academy situated on the Grandview Flats.

The next step in consolidation was the amalgamation of the Vancouver and New Westminster schools in 1965, which became known as the Deer Lake Academy. In 1968 the Rest Haven and Victoria schools united under the name of Van-Isle Academy, located in the Victoria plant. In 1986 property at Elk Lake, midway between Victoria and Sidney, was obtained for the building of a new four-room school with an auditorium. The name was changed to Island Pacific Junior Academy. The most significant consolidation occurred in 1971 when Fraser Valley Academy took in students from Chilliwack, Mission, Abbotsford, Aldergrove, Langley, and White Rock. By 1974 this school had expanded to a senior academy.

Since 1971 the growth rate has accelerated considerably. That year there were 18 schools with 42 teachers. By 1993-1994 there were 25 schools with 102 teachers. In 1971 Cariboo Academy replaced Williams Lake School and expanded to teach all 12 grades. A school was begun in 1983 in Salmon Arm. In 1993 it united with Silver Creek School under the name Shushwap Adventist School. In 1980 a school was built by Maranatha Flights in Whitehorse, Yukon. The Vernon church built the Pleasant Valley School in 1975 for grades 1-8. Beginning with school year 1993-1994, the Riverside SDA School has been operating in a former four-room public school purchased from the Chilliwick School District.

Beginning in 1959 the conference employed a mission launch, the *Northern Light,* to ply the waters off the west coast of Canada. Through the ministry of Ronald Reimche, the first skipper of the boat, and his wife, many persons have been baptized and many isolated members have been strengthened. The original launch was replaced by a modern 52-foot (16-meter) launch specially designed for the task in 1967. This new launch was skippered by Clyde Gildersleeve, assisted by his wife, Nancy. The *Northern Light* outreach initiated a dental health education program for the isolated people of the West Coast and particularly for Native Americans. This dental program has been under the direction of Dr. W. Danielson, with headquarters in Bella Coola. A mission school established in Bella Coola was expanded in 1984 to offer a secondary school program to students with special needs. By this time the *Northern Light* had ceased to operate and was sold in 1975.

The British Columbia Conference also owns a permanent campground at Hope, on the Fraser River, where both the annual camp meetings and the youth camps are held. Camp Hope Lodge, containing 72 motel-like suites, dining hall, auditorium, and recreational area, serves church functions year round. At the eastern end of the campground is Camp Chawuthan, the youth camp. It has its own lodge, pavilion, cabins, and outdoor swimming pool.

Presidents: J. L. Wilson, 1902-1904; E. L. Stewart, 1904-1907; W. M. Adams, 1908-1910; J. G. Walker, 1910-1917; A. C. Gilbert, 1917-1919; W. A. Clemenson, 1920-1926; H. L. Wood, 1926-1928; H. Lukens, 1929-1934; E. A. Beavon, 1934-1941; W. A. Clemenson, 1941-1946; R. E. Finney, Jr., 1946-1950; R. A. Smithwick, 1950-1960; G. O. Adams, 1960-1967; A. N. How, 1967-1974; A. W. Kaytor, 1974-1979; G. E. Maxson, 1979-1984; G. B. DeBoer, 1984-1986; N. C. Sorensen, 1986-1990; E. A. Hetke, 1990-1991; D. R. Watts, 1991- .

BRITISH GUIANA. *See* Guyana.

BRITISH HEALTH FOOD FACTORY. *See* Granose Foods, Limited.

BRITISH HONDURAS. *See* Belize.

BRITISH PUBLISHING HOUSE. *See* Stanborough Press Limited.

BRITISH UNION CONFERENCE. *See* Eire; Great Britain and Northern Ireland; Trans-European Division.

BRITISH VIRGIN ISLANDS. *See* Inter-American Division; Virgin Islands.

BRITISH WEST INDIES UNION VISITOR. *See West Indies Union Visitor.*

BROADCASTING, RELIGIOUS. *See* Faith for Today; It Is Written; Communication, Department of; Voice of Prophecy.

BROADVIEW ACADEMY. A coeducational boarding school on the senior high school level, serving the Illinois Conference. It is now situated on rolling acreage in Kane County, Illinois, five miles (eight kilometers) west of Geneva near Lafox in the Fox River Valley. The 1992-1993 enrollment was 118, and the faculty and staff numbered 21.

The academy is a descendant of the Broadview Swedish Seminary, founded in 1909 on 78 acres (32 hectares) at Broadview, 12 miles (19 kilometers) from Chicago. Through the years this seminary trained many Seventh-day Adventist workers in Swedish, German, and other languages. It graduated its first class in 1914. In 1922 the name of the school was changed to Broadview College and Theological Seminary, and in 1925 the Clinton Theological Seminary was united with it. In 1923 the adjacent Rathe property of 114 acres (46 hectares) was purchased. In 1932 the school became Broadview Junior College and Broadview College Academy. In 1933 it was voted that Emmanuel Missionary College be the one college for the Lake Union Conference and that the Broadview school be operated only as an academy.

At that time Broadview College Academy, with Percy W. Christian as principal, received the highest rating by the Illinois Department of Education and full accreditation by the North Central Association of Colleges and Secondary Schools. In the reorganization as Broadview Academy, the Chicago Academy, the Hinsdale Sanitarium Academy, and the Fox River Academy were merged with Broadview College Academy.

As Chicago and the western suburbs continued their rapid expansion, conference and school officials, aware of the denomination's basic plans for Christian education, became increasingly aware of the problems connected with operating a school in urban surroundings and decided to move the school. The Savage-Marydale farm at Lafox, reputed to be one of the finest and most modernly equipped farms in the state of Illinois, was purchased as the new site. Ground for the new school was broken Nov. 17, 1957.

A new era in Broadview Academy history began in 1958, when two dormitories, an administration building, and a cafeteria were erected. Also constructed were 12 faculty homes; a 12-inch (30-centimeter) well 1,350 feet (410 meters) deep, with a 75,000-gallon (285,000-liter) water tower; and on a nine-acre (3.6-hectare) site on the west side of Geneva, close to shipping facilities, a 45,000-square-foot (4,200-square-meter) building for a branch of the Harris Pine Mills. This building now houses Academy Pak, where students package tractor parts for AGCO, Inc.

When school opened Sept. 8, 1958, nearby communities showed a friendly spirit of welcome toward the new institution. A much-appreciated gift to the academy was a carillon from the Herman Kleist family, installed on the roof of the administration building.

In 1963 an addition to the girls' dormitory and in 1967 an addition to the boys' dormitory were completed, making room for more than 300 students.

In 1971 the camp meeting auditorium was remodeled into a gymnasium and a $100,000 expansion to the warehouse, packaging complex was completed.

Open house for the new $644,000 chapel-music building was held Apr. 29, 1972. This modern two-story octagon-shaped building is air-conditioned and fully equipped, including a three-manual pipe organ.

A $200,000 donation from the Loletta Blaine Estate made possible, during 1974, the building, equipping, and furnishing of the cafeteria-dining room complex.

Principals: Percy Christian, 1932-1933; Arthur J. Olson, 1933-1941; Guy Habenicht, 1941-1942; Duane V. Cowin, 1942-1944; Lewis N. Holm, 1944-1948; Lee Taylor, 1948-1951; John Howell, 1951-1952; Glenn Byers, 1952-1955; Carl W. Jorgensen, 1955-1962; Ralph P. Bailey, 1962-1966; Fred H. Offenbach, 1966-1972; Elwin D. Shull, 1972-1974; Arthur L. Nelson, 1974-1981; Harold Oetman, 1981-1991; William Ruby, 1991-1994; David Rasmussen, 1994- .

BROKEN STONE MISSION. *See* Stahl, Ferdinand Anthony.

BROOKFIELD BRANCH. *See* Pacific Press Publishing Association.

BROOKING, LIONEL (fl. 1892-1904). One of the earliest Seventh-day Adventist converts in Argentina, and later a colporteur in Argentina and in England. He was an evangelist for one of the Protestant churches in Buenos Aires and was connected with the YMCA when, in 1892, he met the first SDA colporteurs in Argentina, E. W. Snyder, A. B. Stauffer, and C. A. Nowlen. After he joined the SDAs, he colporteured in Argentina, chiefly among the French Waldensian settlements, and later went to England, where he also was connected with SDA mission work.

BROOKS, EDGAR (1886-1957). Missionary editor, pastor, and teacher in Argentina. He was born in Plymouth, England, and was converted when about 14 years old. Three years later, in 1903, he began to work at the Caterham Sanitarium as a bellboy. Later he worked as an apprentice typesetter and proofreader at the SDA publishing house in London. From 1904 to 1906 he attended the mission training college there, then worked as a proofreader at the Stanborough Press, and afterward as assistant editor (1908-1911). In 1910-1911 he attended the missionary training college at Watford, England. The next year he accepted a position as a private tutor in Arequipa, Peru. During the four years he spent in that country he engaged in considerable missionary work, organizing a Sabbath school and preaching in Spanish. In 1915 he returned to England, but was called to the Buenos Aires Publishing House as editor. In 1917-1918 he edited *La Revista Adventista* and, from 1917 to 1929, *El Atalaya.* After 1929 he taught Bible at River Plate Junior College, worked as an editor, and preached. He retired after 35 years of service for the church.

BRORSEN, KNUD (1846-1893). Minister. He was born in Norre Farup, Ribe Amt, Denmark. At the age of 22 he came to the United States. The year after his arrival he was converted and accepted the SDA faith in California. Soon after this, he enrolled as a student in Battle Creek College. In 1878 he returned to his homeland to preach, spending the major portion of his time in Denmark, but working also in Norway and attending meetings in Sweden.

In October 1892 Brorsen was invited by the General Conference to attend a health and temperance class at the Battle Creek Sanitarium in order to prepare him to render effective service along these lines in the Scandinavian countries. On May 31, 1893, after the completion of his course, he sailed from New York, in company with S. N. Haskell of the General Conference, to attend a camp meeting in Moss, Norway. From Moss he and Haskell left on June 22 for Sweden to attend a session of the Swedish Conference, in which he took an active part. On June 28, before the session was finished, he died of a hemorrhage of the lungs.

BROUCHY, PEDRO MARIANO (1891-1961). Nurse, masseur, evangelist, president of local fields. He was born in Posadas, Misiones province, Argentina, and was baptized in 1902. In 1913 he graduated from the masseur nurses' school of River Plate Sanitarium, and married Adela Toledo, who graduated the year before, at the first graduation of that school. With her efficient help, he worked the following 14 years in Corrientes, in northeast Argentina, as a self-supporting worker, conducting a physiotherapy treatment center they had established. His dedication to reading in Spanish and English helped him acquire considerable education. He was ordained to the ministry in 1923.

He served as president of the Buenos Aires Conference (1929-1933), of the Uruguay Mission (1934-1941), of the Cuyo Mission (1942-1945), and of the North Argentine Mission (1946-1949). He was an outstanding builder of representative and strategically located churches in big cities. From 1950 to 1952 he was the administrator of River Plate Sanitarium.

BROWN, FREDERICK W. (1860-1899). Pioneer Seventh-day Adventist minister in India. He was a son of a Protestant minister in the state of New York and was dedicated by his parents for service in India in his childhood. At the age of 15 he was baptized in the Free Will Baptist Church. At 17 he determined to become a preacher, and was licensed to preach in 1881. After completing his theological education at Hillsdale College (Michigan), he was invited by the Free Will Baptist Mission Board to go to India, where he went in 1888 as the college's missionary. He served as Indian secretary for his missionary society from 1890 to 1892. While in India he married Kate D. Lawrence, a member of the Disciples Church and a missionary of the Christian Women's Board of Missions. She did zenana work among the women, trained national Bible women, was in charge of two orphanages, and had the oversight of 16 day schools. After they returned to America in 1892, he joined the Disciples Church and was employed by the Christian Women's Board of Missions to travel throughout the United States in the interest of the foreign mission work. In 1895 he enrolled in the Medical Department at the University of Michigan, where he met SDAs and two years later, in 1897, accepted their beliefs, resigned his pastorate of a Disciples congregation, and entered the American Medical Missionary College. He and his wife were baptized into the SDA Church in 1898 and joined the Battle Creek congregation. Soon thereafter they were sent to India. Shortly before leaving in December 1898, he was ordained to the ministry. In India he and D. A. Robinson opened the first Seventh-day Adventist mission station in the interior of the country, at Karmatar, Bihar, where he conducted a medical dispensary until his death in December 1899 during a smallpox epidemic.

BROWN, FREEMAN G. (fl. 1843). Baptist minister of Worcester, Massachusetts, a Millerite preacher, and author of *Views and Experience in Relation to Entire Consecration and the Second Advent* (which was later reprinted by Seventh-day Adventists) and *A Warning to Watchfulness* (1843).

BROWN, GERTRUDE (1879-1974). Social worker, physician, benefactor. Born in Essex, England, she was the youngest of 11 children. She was baptized in 1893 and went to the Seventh-day Adventist sanitarium in Basel, Switzerland, for her nursing diploma. While working in the SDA hospital in Ireland, she met and married Edward Brown, a nurse. She became a social worker for London County Council in Hoxton, where she served before being invited to join the staff of the Battle Creek Sanitarium, working there as matron over 2,000 patients.

Returning to Britain, she qualified as an M.D. in Edinburgh, Scotland. The Browns settled in Scotland and founded Crieff Nursing Home. Upon the death of her husband, she turned the home over to the church with the understanding that it would continue to be developed along the same lines as Battle Creek. Throughout her life she was known as an indefatigable apostle of the remnant church's health message, and was acknowledged as Britain's senior church worker.

BROWNSBERGER, SIDNEY (1845-1930). Educator, administrator. Graduate of University of Michigan (1869), he was the first principal of Battle Creek College (1874-1881), and also of Healdsburg College (1882-1887). His training in the classics led him to view the conventional colleges as suitable patterns for denominational schools, although he did encourage industrial education. He was secretary of the General Conference for a year (1873-1874).

The later years of his life were spent in ministerial work and in self-supporting schools in the South. In 1909 he helped establish the Asheville Agricultural School and Mountain Sanitarium near Fletcher, North Carolina, and for the next 10 years, as his health permitted, he taught the children of the community in a small school.

BRUNEI DARUSSALAM ("Abode of Peace"). A small country located 275 miles (443 kilometers) north of the equator on the northern coast of the island of Borneo. Its land area of 2,226 square miles (5,765 square kilometers) is divided into two parts by the Malaysian state of Sarawak. Brunei is bordered on the north by the South China Sea, and on the other three sides by Sarawak. Bandar Seri Begawan, the capital and main population center, is located nine miles (15 kilometers) from the mouth of the Brunei River. About 110 miles (175 kilometers) from the capital, in the center of the oil and gas industry, are Brunei's other major cities of Seria and Kuala Belait.

Brunei's 1994 population of 285,000 are mainly Muslim Malays, although there are approximately 80,000 Chinese and other non-Malays in the country. Small communities of Britons, Dutch, Americans, and Australians work in commerce and in the oil and gas industry. Oil and gas production give Brunei its revenue, and the population of Brunei enjoy one of the highest per capita incomes in the world.

Brunei has an equatorial tropical climate, with a temperature of about 80°F (27°C) throughout the year. It has consistently high humidity and rainfall. In the fourteenth and fifteenth centuries Brunei was a large empire stretching from north Borneo to the north Philippines. By the end of the nineteenth century Brunei had lost much of its territory and power in the colonial expansion in Southeast Asia. In 1888 Brunei became a British protectorate. On Jan. 1, 1984, Brunei became the world's 159th sovereign state. It is an Islamic nation, a member of the U.N., ASEAN, and the Organization of Islamic Conference.

Seventh-day Adventist Work. As the pioneer Seventh-day Adventist missionaries spread the gospel through the island of Borneo, they encountered the British-administered protectorate of Brunei. It was difficult, if not impossible, to obtain official sanction for church work in Brunei. Only the Roman Catholic and the Anglican churches have official presences in Brunei.

In 1934 the North Sarawak and the South Sarawak mission areas were formed, with Brunei becoming part of the North Sarawak work. Gus Youngberg was assigned to take charge of the work along the Tatau River and was also to have responsibility for the work in Brunei.

In 1936 the minutes of the union committee recorded an action recommending to the upcoming biennial session that Sarawak and Brunei be organized into a regular mission known as the Sarawak Mission of Seventh-day Adventists with headquarters at Kuching. This arrangement was to be effective upon the arrival of a foreign worker who could administer the work in Sarawak and Brunei. Dr. R. T. Morrow was named by the same committee to be in charge and to locate in Bintulu, where the government was eager to turn over its dispensary to the Adventist mission.

In January 1956 it was voted to unite the North Borneo Mission and the Sarawak Mission, effective the first of the year, into a single mission known as the Borneo-Brunei-Sarawak Mission. Five years later Sarawak became a separate mission again.

Because of the difficulty in working in a Muslim area where it was patently illegal to preach the gospel, no real progress was made in Brunei. The country has appeared to be like a volleyball, with its administration alternating back and forth between the Sabah and the Sarawak Mission offices. Though unrecorded, probably the earliest Seventh-day Adventist contact with Brunei was through SDA laity. An SDA member from Kuching, Sarawak, is the longest-standing SDA resident of Brunei. She has been in the country for the past 17 years.

The first recorded attempts by SDAs to enter Brunei officially with literature work date back prior to 1980. Richard Moss, a literature evangelist from Sarawak, and Peter Ching, another literature evangelist from Peninsular Malaysia, both entered Brunei. Moss worked off and on in Brunei, though he was based in Sarawak. Ching was assigned to work in Brunei in 1981 and was given special funding to rent a house to be used also as a meeting place. Ching coordinated the activities and worship services of resident SDAs in Brunei who were entirely foreign workers. Ching continued to work in Brunei until January of 1983. He started two different church groups, which met on a regular basis. The majority of the members in these groups were Malaysians, many of whom were from Sabah and Sarawak. The group also included a number of Filipinos.

After Ching left Brunei to take up leadership in the West Malaysia-Singapore Mission, Richard Moss continued to work until 1984. About this time another literature evangelist, Theresa Chin from Kota Kinabalu, worked for more than six months in the Brunei area on a part-time basis.

In 1986 Colin Choo, a literature evangelist from Sabah, entered Brunei, working out of Kota Kinabalu. He spent more than five months in the country during 1987. In addition, two literature evangelists stationed in Miri, Sarawak, entered Brunei occasionally during the year to sell literature. Choo began to regroup the SDA members he met into Sabbath fellowship groups. His leadership, especially during the weekends, proved invaluable in encouraging the often isolated SDAs who were working in the country.

In 1986 Hulman Sinaga, a university professor and active layman and church elder from the Penang English church, accepted a teaching position at the Universiti Brunei Darussalam. His influence and leadership also breathed life into the membership of the church. Through his work and the work and influence of Colin Choo, and also through the leadership of the administration of the Sabah Mission, today approximately 30 members of the SDA Church meet on a regular basis in three places, namely, Bandar Seri Begawan, Seria, and Kuala Belait. The work done by these dedicated literature evangelists and laypersons has virtually opened up the country to SDA influence and work.

In 1986 a fund of S$50,000 was set aside by the Far Eastern Division and the Southeast Asia Union Mission to enter Brunei with Christian work. These funds were to be spent in opening up SDA work in Kuala Penyu and on the island of Labuan, which is part of Malaysia. Labuan, which is only a short boat trip away from Bandar Seri Begawan, was to serve as a base for gospel work in Brunei. All of these areas—Brunei, Labuan, and Kuala Penyu—were part of the Sabah Mission.

Though the Sabah Mission stationed a worker in both Labuan and Kuala Penyu for a time to develop the work in those areas, and though he made intermittent trips to Brunei to visit members and to start church work, he was unsuccessful because the Bruneian authorities noticed his frequent trips into the country. They warned him not to travel often to the country unless he had official business and a proper visa. It had earlier been visualized that the Southeast Asia Union and the Sabah Mission would have to encourage a "tent-making" type of endeavor in Brunei.

Although the plans laid by church leaders to assign a full-time worker in or near Brunei came to nought, the efforts of dedicated literature evangelists and laymen have opened up the country for Adventists just as the entire Far Eastern Division was opened for the work of the church by pioneers such as Abram La Rue.

In 1991 the Sabah Mission requested the Southeast Asia Union Mission to reassign the territory of Brunei from the Sabah Mission to the Sarawak Mission. The reason for the request was that Sabah had been unable to penetrate Brunei effectively, using Labuan and Kuala Penyu as a base. Most travel to and from Brunei had to be done from Kota Kinabalu by air. Because there is a road link between Miri in Sarawak and Brunei, it was felt that the pastor in Miri could make monthly or periodic visits to the church groups in Brunei, thus strengthening the work.

In 1991 official action was taken by the Far Eastern Division to transfer the responsibility for the work in Brunei to the Sarawak Mission. Since then there has been increased contact between the workers in Sarawak and the SDA members in Brunei. Members continue to meet in private homes. There are regular Sabbath meetings in homes in three locations in the country of Brunei.

BRUSQUE SCHOOL. *See* Brazil College (São Paulo).

BUCARAMANGA SECONDARY SCHOOL. *See* Liberty Secondary School.

BUCKNER, TAZWELL BENJAMIN (1860-1924). Minister; one of the first Black Seventh-day Adventist workers in the South. Beginning as a self-supporting colporteur in 1890, he established numerous companies of SDA believers throughout the South. He was ordained in 1898. Late in life he was pastor of the Hartford Avenue church, Detroit, Michigan.

BUDGET. The method of apportioning the income derived from tithe, offerings, and other sources, for the operation of Seventh-day Adventist world work. The General Conference and subsidiary organizations operate their work on an annual budget system that provides for the intelligent planning of future activities and for making regular measurements of progress.

At its thirty-seventh session, in 1909, the General Conference recommended that "the Executive Committee of the General Conference make appropriations annually to mission fields, equitably distributing the money raised, proportionate to the needs of the fields." These appropriations are voted at each Annual

Council, based on written requests from the respective divisions.

BUDNICK, MICHAEL (1890-1954). Minister and church leader in Germany. He grew up in a Seventh-day Adventist home and was baptized in 1904. After he had attended Friedensau Missionary Seminary he entered denominational service in 1913, working in the eastern part of Germany, around Königsberg. In 1916 he married Helene Krueger. In 1918 he was ordained to the ministry in the East Prussian Conference. About 1924 he assumed leadership of the Young People's, Sabbath School, and Home Missionary departments of that conference. About 1926 he was transferred to the North East Saxon Conference, where he headed the same departments. About 1931 he became president of that conference. From 1936 until his death in 1954, he headed the East German Union, the largest in the country (with almost 20,000 members in 1954).

His coworkers remember him as a talented leader who was devoted to his people and interested in their welfare and in their everyday lives.

BUENA VISTA ACADEMY. *See* Kingsway College.

BUENOS AIRES ADVENTIST ACADEMY (Instituto Adventista Florida). A coeducational day school on the senior high school level situated in Florida, a suburb about a mile from the Buenos Aires city limits, in the province of Buenos Aires. The school is owned and operated by the South Argentine Mission and serves 13 of the 30 Seventh-day Adventist churches of Greater Buenos Aires. The curriculum consists of the five-year official secondary course, accredited by the Argentina Ministry of Education.

The academy originated as a primary school, established in 1913, owned and operated by the Florida church, called Bernardino Rivadavia. Secondary instruction began in 1937 under the direction of David Rhys, the second and third years being added later. A night commercial course was added in 1938, incorporated to the Academia Mercantil Fossa, of the federal capital.

The present course of studies dates from 1944, when the official system of accreditation of the country was initiated. The school continued in the same location until it moved Apr. 7, 1945, into the present building, which was provided by the Buenos Aires Conference. In 1946 the name was changed to Instituto Florida, and in 1974 it was changed again to Instituto Adventista Florida. In English it is known as Buenos Aires Adventist Academy.

The new building had four classrooms and four offices. Since 1955 and before 1971 the following had been added: four more classrooms, a library with reading room, an auditorium, a science laboratory, and other rooms. In 1971, 13,934 square feet (1,295 square meters) of construction were added.

The students publish a school paper *Alma Estudiantil.* The instruction given qualifies the young people to enter River Plate or any university in Argentina. In 1993 the enrollment was more than 900.

Principals: D. H. Rhys, 1937-1943; G. Krieghoff, 1943-1944; V. Ampuero M., 1945-1946; Mrs. H. Mulinari, 1947; J. Meier, 1948; E. Clifford, 1949; G. Krieghoff, 1950-1953; C. Biaggi, 1954-1955; E. H. Wensell, 1956-1963; Jose Bernhardt, 1964-1966; Febo Basanta, 1967-1970; J. C. Priora, 1971-1974; E. Vogel, 1975-1980; Raul Perez, 1981-1985; Carlos Mesa, 1986-1991; Carlos Sapia, 1992- .

BUENOS AIRES CONFERENCE. *See* Argentina; South American Division.

BUENOS AIRES HEALTH FOOD COMPANY. *See* South American Division Health Food Company.

BUENOS AIRES PUBLISHING HOUSE (Asociación Casa Editora Sudamericana). A publishing association with printing facilities, operated at Florida, Buenos Aires, Argentina, to care for the needs of the Austral, Chile, and Inca unions, and North and South Ecuador missions, which comprise the Spanish-speaking portion of the South American Division. The Austral Union encompasses Argentina, Paraguay, and Uruguay, with an area of 1,290,273 square miles (3,341,800 square kilometers) and an approximate population (1993) of 41 million. The Chile Union is comprised of the country of Chile, which has an area of 292,257 square miles (757,000 square kilometers) and an approximate population (1993) of 14 million. A branch of the house is located in Chile. The Inca Union consists of Bolivia and Peru, with an area of 920,437 square miles (2,384,000 square kilometers) and a population (1993) of about 30 million. The North and South Ecuador missions are attached fields with a combined area of 109,483 square miles (283,600 square kilometers) and a population of approximately 10 million.

Development and Organization. In October 1896 authorization was received to publish a magazine in Spanish named *El Faro* ("The Lighthouse") in a commercial printing office in Buenos Aires. The first number of *El Faro* and a monthly leaflet entitled *Carta Mensual* were published in July 1897. On Mar. 17, 1904, the organization that published these periodicals was legally constituted the Casa Editora Sudamericana. The following year the first printing shop for this house was established in Camarero (today Villa Libertador San Martín, Puiggari), Entre Ríos, Argentina, at River Plate College, under the direction of J. W. Westphal. This plant was called Imprenta La Verdad Presente ("Present Truth Printing Office").

On Mar. 22, 1906, the printing office was transferred to Florida, Buenos Aires, and placed under the direction of Juan A. Bonjour, with N. Z. Town and his wife as editors. In 1910 it absorbed the Chile publishing house. In 1913 the publishing house was renamed Casa Editora Unión Sudamericana. In January 1920 the name was registered as Asociación Casa Editora Sudamericana. On Mar. 18, 1920, a branch publishing house was organized in Lima, Peru, which functioned until Dec. 30, 1926, when the Buenos Aires Publishing House began to serve the Inca Union directly. On Jan. 17, 1933, the name was shortened to Casa Editora Sudamericana, and a constitution and statutes were adopted. Sixteen years later, on June 21, 1949, official recognition was obtained.

The publishing house, which employed eight in 1896, employed 84 in 1992. In the latter year it sold almost 214 million pages of books and magazines. The assets of the institution in 1992 included about five acres (30,000 square meters) of land, with buildings in Florida, Buenos Aires, Argentina; two web presses; five presses (two large, two medium-sized, and one small); two folding machines, and various other machines for use in binding books. The operating capital in 1992 was US$3,465,657.

Publications. In 1904 *El Atalaya Americano* ("The American Watchman") replaced *El Faro*. *La Revista Adventista* ("The Adventist Review"), published first (beginning in 1901) in Chile, has been published since 1907 by the Buenos Aires Publishing House. The magazine *Salud* ("Health") was first published in October of 1909. Soon afterward *La Verdad Presente* ("The Present Truth"), which the Buenos Aires Publishing House had published since 1905, was absorbed by *Las Señales de los Tiempos* ("The Signs of the Times"), formerly published in Chile, but thenceforth issued from the Buenos Aires house. The first number of the combined magazine appeared in 1910.

El Centinela ("The Sentinel") was first published in 1915, and in 1918 appeared *El Monitor de la Juventud* ("The Youth's Monitor"), which was published until 1925, and in 1935 was replaced by *Juventud* ("Youth"). The name of *Las Señales de los Tiempos* was changed to *El Atalaya* ("The Watchman") in 1913 and to *Vida Feliz* ("Happy Life") in 1956.

The circulation of the principal magazines in the years 1986-1992 was as follows: *Vida Feliz,* 1,773,425; *Juventud,* 1,070,579; *La Revista Adventista,* 725,897.

Besides the periodicals previously mentioned, the following departmental magazines are published: *El Ministerio Adventista, El Informa Misionero Mundial,* three series of Sabbath school quarterlies (senior, junior, and primary), and *El Colportor Eficiente.* On Feb. 11, 1915, the first book, *La Crisis del Mundo* ("The World Crisis"), was published.

Nearly 463 works of different authors and of various formats have been published on religious themes, morals, health, diet, and the home, in addition to a number of translations of works by Ellen G. White, such as *El Conflicto de los Siglos, El Deseado de Todas las Gentes, Los Hechos de los Apóstoles, El Camino a Cristo, La Educación, Joyas de los Testimonios, Evangelismo,* and others.

Managers: J. W. Westphal, Dr. R. H. Habenicht, and N. Z. Town, 1904-1909; G. E. Hartman, 1909-1920; E. W. Everest, 1920-1925; M. V. Tucker, 1925-1938; J. B. Johnson, 1938-1945; F. Baer, 1945-1954; S. Alberto, 1954-1959; B. C. Kaercher, 1959-1972; O. E. Cesan, 1972-1979; Jose Tabuenca, 1980-1983; Roberto Gullon, 1984- .

Editors in Chief: N. Z. Town, J. W. Westphal, E. W. Thomann, and C. E. Krieghoff, 1905-1916; D. R. Buckner, 1916-1920; E. Brooks, 1921-1929; M. I. Fayard, 1929-1937; E. Brooks, 1937-1946; M. I. Fayard, 1946-1947; F. Chaij, 1947-1960; V. E. Ampuero Matta, 1961-1972; Gaston Clouzet, 1972-1982; Rolando Itin, 1983-1989; Werner Mayr, 1990- .

BUGEMA ADVENTIST COLLEGE. A coeducational boarding school on the junior college level, operated by the East African Union Mission on a 640-acre (260-hectare) tract of land 20 miles (30 kilometers) north of Kampala, the commercial capital of Uganda.

The enrollment in 1993 stood at 120, with 15 percent being women. Bugema College serves the Seventh-day Adventist constituency of Kenya, Uganda, and Tanzania, and is controlled by an interunion board representing the East African, Uganda, and Tanzania unions.

The farm grows much of the food needed in the Boarding Department. Water is supplied from a deep well on the school property, and since 1955 electricity has been available from the public supply.

History. The school was established in 1948 under the name of Bugema Training School, incorporating the East African Union Training School, which, according to the 1947 *Yearbook,* was formerly the Nchwanga Training School. W. N. Andrews was the acting principal, and a staff of six assisted him. Only grades 1 through 8 were offered at that time. By 1950 the plant included an administration building of six classrooms and four offices, a dining hall, and two dormitories, each housing about 80 boys. In 1948 the junior ministerial course was begun. In 1949 a two-year post-grade 6 teachers' course was begun. Although this course was approved, it was not recognized by the Uganda Department of Education; however, it prepared the way for a recognized three-year post-grade 6 course, which was first offered in 1951. In the same year a three-year post-grade 9 teachers' training course (primary teacher training course) was offered. In 1953 the school was registered with the Uganda Education Department as a senior high school, with the first high school students sitting for their Cambridge Overseas School Examination in 1955.

In 1990 the first postsecondary college students were admitted for the Junior of Arts diploma in theology. From 1993 a Bachelor of Theology degree is being awarded.

In 1992 the secondary site was relocated. *See* Bugema Adventist Secondary School.

Principals: W. N. Andrews (acting), 1948; G.J.E. Coetzee (acting), 1949; C.T.J. Hyde, 1950-1959; G. F. Clifford, 1959-1966; M. A. Morford (acting), 1966-1967; J. T. Bradfield, 1967-1971; E. H. Sequeira, 1971-1972; L. L. Nelson, 1972-1973; Y. Gwalamubisi, 1973-1978 (first national); Christian Aliddeki, 1978-1979; E. Lugoye, 1979-1982; J. Villagomez, 1982-1988; N. Walemba, 1988-1991; Moses Golola, 1991- .

BUGEMA ADVENTIST SECONDARY SCHOOL. A coeducational boarding secondary school operated by the Uganda Union mission on a 170-acre (70-hectare) piece of land. The secondary school as a separate institution from the college came into existence at the beginning of 1992, when it was moved from the campus that it had shared with the college since the beginning of the college in 1971.

The enrollment in 1993 was 700 students, with the number of girls equaling that of boys. The school offers programs leading to both the Uganda Certificate of Education and the Uganda Advanced Certificate of Education in both arts and sciences. The staff is comprised of nationals, with Paul Sebiranda as the headmaster.

BUILDINGS, CHURCH. *See* Church Buildings.

BUKOVINSKAYA CONFERENCE (CHERNOVTSKY). *See* Euro-Asia Division; Ukraine.

BULAWAYO ADVENTIST SECONDARY SCHOOL. A coeducational day school that offers four years of secondary education, and is operated by the Zambesi Union. It is situated in the city of Bulawayo next to the Zambesi Union headquarters. The enrollment as of January 1993 was 461 students, 299 of whom were Seventh-day Adventists, and 22 teachers.

History. The property was purchased in 1979 for $150,000, which was raised by different church organizations, with a view to using the premises for operating a secondary school, union offices, medical and dental offices, and a Better Living center. The original name, St. Peter's Diocese School, was changed to Bulawayo Adventist Secondary School after the property was purchased in May 1979. When the school started, it had a total of 18 classrooms, administration offices, and sports grounds that included a swimming pool. Four new classrooms have been added.

The school opened in January 1980 with 160 pupils and eight teachers.

This is the only urban secondary school in the Zambesi Union.

Headmasters: J. N. Gabi, 1980-1989; L. Marandure, 1990- .

BULGARIA. A republic situated in the northeastern part of the Balkan Peninsula bounded by Romania on the north, Yugoslavia and Macedonia on the west, Greece and Turkey on the south, and the Black Sea on the east. It covers an area of

42,818 square miles (1,109,000 square kilometers), and its population (1994) is estimated at 8.8 million, of which 85 percent are Bulgarians (a mixture of Slavs, who in the sixth century A.D. had occupied the area, and Bulgars, Turkic invaders who in the seventh century came around the north shore of the Black Sea). The rest are Turks, Macedonians, Gypsies, Jews, Armenians, Romanians, and Eastern European peoples. The traditional church is the Bulgarian Orthodox, which became independent early in the tenth century. About four fifths of the people belong to this church. The long Turkish rule left its mark on the religion of the country so that there are about 1 million Muslims in Bulgaria. In addition, there are small numbers of Roman Catholics, Armeno-Greeks, and Protestants. The language of Bulgaria belongs to the southern Slavic group, and of the southwestern Slavic languages is probably the closest to the Russian. It uses the Cyrillic alphabet.

The early Bulgarian state successfully challenged the Byzantine Empire, only by the turn of the tenth century to fall under its dominance. It rose again to the rank of a major Balkan power in the twelfth and thirteenth centuries, but in the fourteenth century it was overrun by the Turks. Turkey controlled the land absolutely until 1878, and only in 1908 did Bulgaria attain complete independence. It was a kingdom until 1944, when, in the wake of World War II, a people's republic closely allied to the Soviet Union was proclaimed.

Seventh-day Adventist Statistics. The territory of Bulgaria constitutes the Bulgarian Union of Churches, a part of the Euro-Africa Division. No official reports on the organization and statistics of the Seventh-day Adventist work in Bulgaria have been received, but it has been estimated that there are about 70 churches, with approximately 6,000 members.

Institutions. Bulgarian Adventist Publishing House.

Development of Seventh-day Adventist Work. *Beginnings.* According to extant records, SDA teachings were first introduced into Bulgaria in the early 1890s, when a group of German SDAs who had emigrated from the German settlements in the Crimea, Russia, and had settled in Romania, near the Bulgarian border, apparently spread their beliefs among their Romanian and Bulgarian neighbors. Their minister, G. Wagner, was later listed among the pioneers of Seventh-day Adventist work in Bulgaria *(Review and Herald* 110:12, Feb. 16, 1933). In 1893, L. R. Conradi, the leader of SDA work in Eastern Europe at that time, reported in the *Review and Herald* (70:406, June 27, 1893) that Bulgaria had been recently added to the countries entered by SDAs and that a worker of Bulgarian descent, E. S. Popoff, was soon to go there from America. A few months later he reported that he had heard of one Bulgarian Sabbathkeeper who had learned of the SDA teachings from the SDAs in Romania. In March of 1894 Conradi visited Bulgaria and reported that on that visit he had arranged for the translation and printing of several tracts in the Bulgarian language, the first of which, "Is the End Near?" was ready by the time he wrote, and two others, "The Full Assurance of Faith," and "The Blessed Hope," were being prepared. He also reported that Popoff's sister had accepted SDA doctrines, and that the Bulgarian Sabbathkeeper of whom he had written earlier was teaching his neighbors in Romania. In the spring of 1897 Popoff urged support from the members elsewhere for the work in Bulgaria *(ibid.* 74:267, Apr. 27, 1897).

In 1898 Conradi visited Ruse (Rustchuk) and reported that on Apr. 26 he had conducted the first Seventh-day Adventist baptism in Bulgaria, baptizing two candidates, the fruits of the work carried on by A. Seefried from January of that year. When Conradi arrived, Bible studies were conducted in Bulgarian and Turkish through interpreters on alternate evenings *(ibid.* 75:352, May 31, 1898). At that time there were several SDAs in the city, among them certain Armenian women who had come from Constantinople (Istanbul) in Turkey.

In 1899 Ellen G. White's *Steps to Christ* was translated into Bulgarian, and published in Bulgaria, the first SDA book to be translated into that language.

In the first decade of the present century there were few reports. It appears that although there was liberty for religious work, there was little promotion. It also appears that foreign workers had left the country. However, in 1908, G. Kadaleff, a native Bulgarian, returned to his country after attending an SDA training school in Germany. He worked first in Tutracan and later in Sofia, the capital, where he baptized Anna Kostova on June 3, 1911.

Bulgarian Mission Organized. In 1911 C. Motzer, a minister, came from Germany and in either that year or the next organized the work in Bulgaria (administered at that time as a part of the Balkan Mission of the East German Union Conference) into a separate Bulgarian

Mission under his leadership. Stefan Konstantinoff became secretary of the mission. By 1912 a church of eight members was organized in Sofia.

Despite the difficulties created by the Balkan wars of 1911-1913 and World War I, new converts were added to the church from year to year. Some members of 50 years' standing are alive today. However, when Guy Dail, one of the leaders of the work in Europe, visited Bulgaria in 1920, he reported that at that time there were no ordained ministers or church elders in the country, and that the church, numbering 56 members at the end of 1919 in three churches, at Sofia, Ruse (Rustchuk), and Gabrovo, had only one evangelistic worker, a licentiate, S. Konstantinoff. During this visit he baptized 24 persons, some of whom had waited more than three years for this rite. The church had no literature at all, although they expected to receive whatever publications the Hamburg Publishing House had in stock as a gift. Dail related that one lay leader of the church had expressed his thankfulness for his business success by renting a hall for evangelistic meetings for three years at his expense. Dail also reported that Alfred Thomas, a minister who had been working in Bulgaria for a number of years before World War I, was to return *(Review and Herald* 97:12, 13, Oct. 21, 1920).

Later Developments. In 1924 a publishing house was established in Sofia at mission headquarters (listed in the *Yearbook* as the Bulgarian Publishing House, in Bulgarian, Knigoisdatelstvo "Nov Zhivot"). In 1924 there were nine churches and 205 members in the mission. Growth had been steady but slow. The publications did much to spread the SDA message. For a while there was a missionary journal, *Westitel Na Istinata* ("Herald of Truth"), edited for a time by S. Konstantinoff. At least 20 of Ellen G. White's books were translated into Bulgarian.

In 1933 church membership reached 500. In that year the first workers' meeting was held in Bulgaria, at Varna, on the Black Sea, and was attended by 14 workers. Four years later Charles Sohlmann, the mission director, reported that the church, then numbering 730 members, owned a convenient 250-seat evangelistic hall at the headquarters at Sofia, which was filled to capacity by inquirers twice a week. He also reported that in cooperation with other welfare agencies the welfare department of the church was functioning with great success in ameliorating the conditions of the poor and of those who had suffered in the several earthquakes that had affected Bulgaria. In 1936 the church opened a summer camp for children at Sgove, about a half-hour train ride from Sofia, where many underprivileged boys and girls were taken. But still there was a great shortage of church-owned buildings. In 1938 the Bulgarian Mission had only two church edifices in all the country.

The church's work during and after World War II has not been reported abroad, and no official statistics have been published in denominational sources. It has been made known, however, that the work of the church has been growing in Bulgaria. The membership of the congregation in Sofia was estimated in the early 1960s at about 500.

Recent Developments. In 1959 the Communist authorities abolished the union council and appointed a new council that would work under their direction. In 1965 SDA workers elected a new council, naming Belcho Totev as president. But police came to the office and ordered the council to vacate the premises.

In 1974 Communist authorities appointed a council of two persons and a president. When General Conference president Robert Pierson visited Bulgaria in 1977, he gained permission for three more pastors to be placed on the council. But in 1983 the authorities removed them, and the president assumed responsibility of including whomever he wanted to be on the council. Those were hard years for the church, but it continued to grow.

In 1989, because of political changes in that part of Europe, the authorities gradually lost control over the church. In April of 1990 Euro-Africa Division president Edwin Ludescher officiated at the first election held in accordance with denominational working policy for 42 years. Agop Tachmissjan was elected president of the Bulgarian Union. On Nov. 7, 1990, the Seventh-day Adventist church was recognized officially by the Bulgarian government. In 1992 a publishing house was established in Sofia. The Bulgarian Union has demonstrated the most dramatic membership growth in the Euro-Africa Division since the fall of Communism, having nearly doubled their membership by 1994.

Mission Affiliation. The Bulgarian Mission was at first included in the East German Union Conference, but about a year later was transferred to the Levant Union Mission and remained there until the early 1920s, when it became a detached mission of the European Division. Later, when the Central European Division was organized, it became a detached mission of that division, and in the course of World War II was transferred to the Southern European Division. Now it is part of the Euro-Africa Division.

BULGARIAN ADVENTIST PUBLISHING HOUSE. *See* Bulgaria.

BULGARIAN UNION OF CHURCHES. *See* Bulgaria; Euro-Africa Division.

BUNCH, TAYLOR GRANT (1885-1969). Author, pastor, executive, teacher. Born in Oregon, he attended law school and then felt the call to make the ministry his lifework. He served as pastor of some of the largest Seventh-day Adventist churches in the United States. While pastor in South Lancaster and Takoma Park, he lectured regularly in the Religion departments of Atlantic Union College and Columbia Union College and for five years was the head of the Department of Religion at Atlantic Union College. For seven years he had charge of the Department of Religion at Loma Linda University. He served as president of three conferences, Southern Oregon, Idaho, and Michigan. During his long and active ministry he authored more than 20 books.

BUNOA, PAULIASI (d. 1918). First ordained Fijian Seventh-day Adventist minister. He was a small boy when the first Christian missionaries reached the Fiji Islands. His father was among the first to be converted to Christianity, and for a while it was necessary for him and his family to find refuge in the bush to escape persecution. Pauliasi was educated in a mission school, which he attended for about seven years sometime in the 1870s. After teaching for a while, he was ordained to the ministry in the Wesleyan Methodist Church and spent 10 years as a missionary on the islands of New Ireland and New Britain, where he lost his entire family from malaria. Returning to Fiji, he settled at Suva Vou. After some 20 years in the ministry, he resigned from the service of the church and in the late 1890s came to Fiji. He helped J. E. Fulton write the first Fijian SDA tract on the seventh-day Sabbath. He was baptized into the Seventh-day Adventist Church in 1900, and six years later was ordained to its ministry at Cooranbong, New South Wales, Australia. To the time of his death he preached among his people with great power.

BURDEN, JOHN ALLEN (1862-1942). Administrator. Beginning at 9 years of age he showed a deep interest and regard for the writings of Ellen G. White, and later was closely associated with Mrs. White in the development of sanitariums. In 1874 he joined the Seventh-day Adventist Church, and entered Healdsburg College in 1882. He became manager of the St. Helena Sanitarium in 1891, then from about 1901 to 1904 engaged in sanitarium work in Australia. In 1905, at Ellen White's request, he promoted sanitarium work in southern California.

After assisting in the purchase of the Glendale Sanitarium, he played an important part in the purchase of the Loma Linda property (1905). At Mrs. White's urging, and, in spite of extreme financial difficulties, he gathered together a few students and teachers and began a medical missionary school in 1906, which was incorporated in 1909 as the College of Medical Evangelists (now the Loma Linda University School of Medicine). For a time he was manager of the institution.

From 1916 to 1924 and again from 1925 to 1934 he served as manager of Paradise Valley Sanitarium.

BURDEN, WILLIAM D. (1870-1945). Pioneer Seventh-day Adventist missionary in Japan; founder of the Japan Publishing House (Fukuinsha). Reared on the Pacific Coast, he early chose to become a missionary to the Japanese people. After attending Healdsburg College from 1892 to 1896, he entered city mission work in San Francisco and volunteered to help in the mission school for the Japanese. In 1897 he married Suzanne Margery Grainger, daughter of W. C. Grainger, the first American SDA missionary to Japan, and the next year began a term of service in Japan that lasted 20 years. To foster the publishing work, he set up a small printing shop in his own house and then in 1909 led in the establishment of the Japan Publishing House. He returned to the United States 10 years later.

BUREAU OF PUBLIC RELATIONS. *See* Communication, Department of.

BUREAUD, MICHEL JOSEPH (1895-1958). French minister, missionary, and administrator. He was born in a Catholic home, but became a Seventh-day Adventist at an early age and was baptized into the church in 1909. He studied at the Latin Union School for three years, and in 1914 entered denominational service as a minister and missionary. In 1922 he married Luce Retournat. In 1927 he was ordained to the ministry. From 1927 to 1935 he was president of Madagascar Mission, and from 1936 to 1938 served as the first president of the Indian Ocean Union Mission. After his return to France he served as an evangelist and, between 1949 and 1951, as president of the Southwest France Conference. Called in the early 1950s to the leadership of the St. Lawrence Mission (French) in Canada, he served there from 1952 until his death.

BURESALA TRAINING SCHOOL. *See* Fiji Islands; Fulton Missionary College.

BURGAN, WALTER LEE (1883-1940). Journalist, first director of the General Conference Press Bureau. He began his newspaper career early in life and worked on the *American* and the *Sun* of Baltimore. Shortly after accepting the Seventh-day Adventist faith, he inaugurated the Bureau of Press Relations for the General Conference (1912), and directed it until his death. He promoted friendly relations with the secular press and trained others to present SDA beliefs in the newspapers.

BURGESS, GEORGIA ANNA (BURRUS) (1866-1948). One of the first Seventh-day Adventist missionaries in India, where she spent nearly 40 years. Converted at the age of 16, Georgia Burrus joined the SDA Church over the opposition of her relatives, worked her way through Healdsburg College, and later taught at a Bible Training School held at Oakland. Stirred by the needs of India, she volunteered for service there, and arrived in Calcutta in 1895. She began working as a self-supporting missionary among the secluded women of the country, while studying Bengali. In 1896, with Mae Taylor, she opened a girls' school in Calcutta. In 1903 she was married to Luther J. Burgess, and together they spent 32 years pioneering work among the Bengali-, Hindi-, Urdu-, and Khasi-speaking peoples. So great was their devotion to India that when they were in the United States in 1904 because of the husband's failing health since the mission board had no funds to send them back, they devised a plan to sell 20,000 copies of the *Bible Training School* (at 10 cents each) to defray the travel expenses. They remained in India until 1935, then returned to the United States and retired near the Paradise Valley Sanitarium in National City, California.

BURGESS, LUTHER J. (1874-1946). Missionary. In 1901 he was appointed secretary and treasurer of the India Mission. Two years later he married Georgia Burrus, who had preceded him to India in 1895 as the first Seventh-day Adventist worker among the women of India. The Burgesses pioneered work in the Bengali, Hindi, Urdu, and Khasi languages. Failing health forced his return to the United States in 1935, where he retired in California.

BURKINA FASO (formerly Upper Volta). A military republic in western Africa, independent since 1960, bounded on the south by Côte d'Ivoire, Ghana, Togo, and Benin; on the north and west by Mali, and on the east by Niger. Its area is 105,869 square miles (275,000 kilometers); the population (1994) is about 10 million. About 30 percent are Muslim and 10 percent are Christians (9 percent Catholic and 1 percent Pentecostal). There are many tribal languages, but French is the official language. The area of Burkina Faso was controlled by an African empire of the Mossi people from the eleventh century, before it came under the European influence. It became a French colony in the last decade of the nineteenth century.

It is located in the Sahel area, south of the Sahara, and has suffered many years of drought and famine. The help sent by Seventh-day Adventists to this suffering people has opened many doors and hearts, and made SDAs well known in the country.

The territory of Burkina Faso is assigned to Burkina Faso Mission, part of the Sahel Union Mission, which in turn is in the Africa-Indian Ocean Division.

The country was entered at the end of 1971 by H. Kempf and his family, French missionaries who came from Togo. He secured official recognition from the government for our denomination to work in the country. In 1972 a one acre (one-hectare) piece of land was purchased in the very center of the capital city of Ouagadougou, where SDAs established an open-air evangelistic center. Several evangelistic campaigns were held in 1973, 1974, 1980, 1992, and 1993.

Burkina territory now is an organized mission with three churches, three companies, and 309 church members. An agricultural center, established in 1977, is located at Bazega. ADRA is developing a number of projects in this area.

BURKINA FASO MISSION. *See* Africa-Indian Ocean Division; Burkina Faso.

BURLEY, SERGIUS GREGORY (1884-1941). Evangelist among the Russian and Ukrainian immigrants in North America, educator, editor, and translator. He was born in the town of Boguslav, Ukraine, Russia, in a Greek Catholic family and in his earlier years served as an altar boy, planning to become a priest. He received his earlier schooling in a town school in his native city (1893-1897). His religious inclination led him to search the Bible for himself, and eventually to join the Baptists. In 1903 he was baptized by Johann Perk, and joined the Seventh-day Adventist Church in Boguslav. Because of persecution from his relatives and friends he emigrated to Canada and there attended Portage Plains Academy (1906-1909). Afterward he went to Union College (1909-1910). He was ordained in 1910 and devoted his life to work among the Russian and Ukrainian immigrants in the United States and Canada as an evangelist and teacher. For eight years he conducted a Russian Department at Sheyenne River Academy (1910-1918). During the same time, he established several Russian churches in North Dakota and one at Yale, Virginia (1914). In 1918 he went to Chicago to work for the Russian population there, and while there established a Russian Department at Broadview Theological Seminary. From 1919 to 1921 he edited *Znamenie Vremeni* (the Russian edition of *Signs of the Times)* and prepared Russian translations of Bible lessons and other publications. Later he was sent to Riga, Latvia, to work among the Russian emigrants, and established a church there. After his return to the United States he preached in Virginia, New Jersey, and Illinois. He was married in 1912 to Beatrice Lucinda Tucker, a music teacher at Sheyenne River Academy.

BURMA. *See* Myanmar.

BURMA UNION. *See* Myanmar.

BURMA UNION HIGH SCHOOL. *See* Toungoo High School.

BURMAN, CHARLES A. (1870-1940). Teacher, evangelist, and administrator. He was born near Eau Claire, Wisconsin. His parents became Seventh-day Adventists when he was a child, and through their influence he chose to dedicate his life to the ministry. He was educated in a public school (1882-1887), Minneapolis Conference School (1888-1890), and at Union College, where he attended several semesters between 1892 and 1897. In 1897 he married Leona Summey. He began his evangelistic work as a tent master in 1893 at Jefferson, South Dakota. In 1900 he was ordained to the ministry. He was a recognized administrator and served as president of South Dakota Conference (1904-1906), the first president of Alberta Conference (1906-1914), and the first principal of Alberta Industrial Academy *(see* Canadian Union College), and president of Upper Columbia Conference (1915-1916). Ill health forced him into temporary retirement, but after a year's rest he became instructor in Bible at Walla Walla College and later dean of men at Emmanuel Missionary College *(see* Andrews University). When in 1935 failing health made outdoor work desirable, he undertook the landscaping of the campus at Emmanuel Missionary College while teaching Bible at the academy.

BURNS, NELSON C. (1897-1979). Missionary, Bible teacher. He was head of the Bible Department of Avondale College from 1944 until the 1960s. He was known as a man who inspired Bible study, evangelism, and mission service; one who saw the good and the potential through Christ in every student. After serving widely throughout the Australasian Division (now the South Pacific Division), he retired as honorary chaplain at the Coronella Retirement Homes in Melbourne, still the consummate Christian gentleman who endeared himself to the people.

BURRELL, NATELKKA (1895-1990). Teacher, author. She chaired and taught in the Education Department at Oakwood College for more than 20 years after beginning her career as a church school teacher. She received her doctorate in education and English from Columbia University and served as guest professor at Andrews University. She coauthored 60 basal readers and guidebooks for the General Conference Department of Education. She also wrote an autobiography and many articles that appeared in Seventh-day Adventist periodicals. Burrell received the Citation of Honor from the General Conference

Department of Education in 1972, was included in the Andrews University Hall of Fame in 1973, and in 1975 was cited at the General Conference session in Vienna, Austria, as one of the 10 most outstanding women of the SDA Church.

BURRUS, GEORGIA. *See* Burgess, Georgia Anna (Burrus).

BURRUS, NONI (or NANIBALA) BISWAS (d. 1958). One of the first Seventh-day Adventist converts in India. She was born in a high caste Hindu family in Calcutta, India, was married as a young girl, but by the time the first SDA workers arrived in India she had been widowed and was living in her father's house. There Georgia Burrus, an SDA missionary, while visiting the zenanas (women's quarters) in the neighborhood of the mission, met her and presented Christianity to her. When she accepted the new beliefs, her family threatened to kill her. She escaped during the night and came to the mission school, where she learned to read and write, and soon was baptized, taking the name Burrus after the missionary who introduced her to Christianity. After Dr. Place announced a nursing course at the Calcutta Sanitarium, she was one of the first students. About 1901 she accompanied Dr. Place's family to the United States to continue her education. After training at Battle Creek Sanitarium and in Boston, Massachusetts, she became a registered nurse and a masseuse. For more than 40 years afterward she practiced her calling in the town of Attleboro, Massachusetts.

BURTON ADVENTIST ACADEMY. A coeducational day school offering grades kindergarten through eighth and high school, located in Arlington, Texas. Originally known as Fort Worth Seventh-day Adventist Church School, it began in the early 1900s in the Seventh-day Adventist church at 2020 Hemphill Street, south of downtown Fort Worth. The school later relocated to Lipscomb Avenue and adopted the name Fort Worth Junior Academy. In 1961 Mr. and Mrs. Harry F. Burton graciously donated 10 acres (four hectares) of land, and Fort Worth Junior Academy moved to its present location under the name Harry F. Burton Junior Academy.

In 1985 the school received its present name with the addition of a kindergarten and grades 11 and 12. Burton Adventist Academy is convenient to most areas of the Dallas/Fort Worth Metroplex and has a strong academic program. Three high school levels of transcripts are offered. The campus consists of the main building containing the administrative office, classrooms, library, and cafeteria. Adjacent to the main building are the gymnasium and two fully equipped softball fields. Building began in the summer of 1993 on additional classroom facilities.

In 1969 Harry F. Burton Junior Academy had six teachers, including the school board chair, with an annual budget of $59,000. In 1993 the school today includes 25 staff members with an annual budget of $1 million.

Principals: Lyle Hansen, 1984-1988; John Hopps, 1988- .

BURUNDI. A central African republic, independent since July 1962. Formerly known as Urundi, it had for many years been a part of German East Africa, then after World War I, part of the Belgian mandate called Rwanda-Urundi. Burundi has an area of 10,740 square miles (27,800 square kilometers) and a population (1994) of 6.1 million, almost all Africans. In 1966 the kingdom was replaced by the republic of Burundi. Its capital is Bujumbura. The ruling king at the time independence was granted was Mwami Mwambutsa IV. Two official languages are used, Kirundi, the national language, and French, the diplomatic language. Burundi is mountainous, and agriculture is the chief occupation of the people. Serious famines have devastated the country at times. Burundi is bounded on the north by Rwanda, on the east and south by Tanzania, and on the west by Lake Tanganyika and Zaïre.

Seventh-day Adventist Statistics. The territory of Burundi constitutes the Burundi Mission, which is attached to the Africa-Indian Ocean Division. Statistics (1992): churches, 104; members, 35,471; ordained ministers, 24; licensed ministers, 33. Headquarters: Bujumbura.

Development of Seventh-day Adventist Work. The first SDA worker to enter Burundi (Urundi until 1962) was D. E. Delhove, who came from Rwanda to open a mission in 1925. On a site some 40 miles (65 kilometers) from Usumbura, on a road running north to Cyangugu, he opened the Buganda station. Negotiations leading up to acquiring some 125 acres (50 hectares) of land were concluded in 1936. In 1927 Maxime Duplouy took over the work in Buganda.

In 1936 a concession of 25 acres (10 hectares) was obtained for another mission, in the hills about eight hours' walk to the east of Buganda, at an elevation of 5,905 feet (1,800 meters). This mission, called Ndora, had a climate more suitable for European missionaries, and was still accessible to the schools and church companies built up in connection with Buganda. After the opening of Ndora in 1937 by H. J. Moolman of South Africa, Buganda was operated under an African district leader. Moolman was followed by W. R. Vail (April 1938-February 1941).

During the early years the work in Urundi was conducted as a detached mission in the East Congo Union, and later in the Central African and Congo unions. In 1947 Urundi was joined to Rwanda in an organization known as the Rwanda-Urundi Field, with A. L. Davy as president and H. J. Bennett as secretary-treasurer. Headquarters were at Gitwe, in Rwanda. This relationship continued with varying degrees of change until January 1960, when the country became the Urundi Field, with headquarters at Ndora and with F. L. Bell as president and Labani Biyayire as secretary-treasurer.

Until 1961 the school program in Urundi was limited to the first eight years of school, the last two of which were taught at Ndora Mission only. In April 1961 Ndora Mission was authorized by the Rwanda-Urundi Union to offer the ninth grade.

In January 1961 Mariko Sembagare was called from the North Congo Field to be president of the Urundi Field.

In 1963 the Burundi Field was divided into two parts along the main road running north from the capital, Bujumbura (formerly Usumbura), to Kayanza. The western section, which contained the major portion of the church membership, was known as the West Burundi Field, with the officers as formerly in Urundi Field; the east section was administered directly from the Central African Union office in Bujumbura until 1964, when it was organized as the East Burundi Field.

Because of better communications and improved living conditions, the West Burundi Field headquarters were reestablished at Buganda in 1972.

All Seventh-day Adventist primary schools were taken over by the government in 1980. In 1982 Kivoga, a secondary school, also was taken over, but was given back to the church in September of that year. In 1984 Rwanda became a union, and the two Burundi fields were combined to form the Burundi Mission.

In 1983 all denominations in Burundi were persecuted by the government of that period. The Seventh-day Adventist Church was outlawed, and pastors and believers were prohibited from gathering for worship. In 1987 a new government allowed the churches to be opened again. Since then the Seventh-day Adventist Church has become well known throughout Burundi, and its membership has increased from 17,000 in 1987 to 34,000 at the end of 1992.

BURUNDI MISSION. *See* Burundi; Africa-Indian Ocean Division.

BUSAN ADVENTIST HOSPITAL. *See* Pusan Adventist Hospital.

BUSEGWE STATION. *See* Tanzania.

BUSINESS AND PROFESSIONAL FOUNDATION (BPF). An association begun in 1966 in the Kentucky-Tennessee Conference. Realizing the difficulties encountered by small congregations in constructing suitable church buildings, a group of concerned laypersons, headed by James Ladd, M.D., and E. L. Marley, then president of the conference, organized BPF for the purpose of making low-interest loans to such congregations. Since then, the foundation has assisted with the construction of nearly 40 church buildings and has made loans of nearly $1 million.

In 1993 Dr. Norman Henderson was the president.

BUSINESS MEETINGS. *See* Church (Local Organization), II, 4.

BUTIÁ SCHOOL. *See* Paraná Adventist Academy.

BUTLER, GEORGE IDE (1834-1918). Minister, administrator. His grandfather was a Baptist preacher who had been governor of Vermont (1826-1828). Although the home of Butler's parents had been a center for early Adventist activities, until the age of 22 young Butler had leanings to infidelity, but was upright and honest. In 1859 he settled on a farm near Waukon, Iowa, became a deacon in the local Adventist church, and then an elder. Upon the defection of Snook and Brinkerhoff, president and treasurer, respectively, of the Iowa Conference (*see* Marion Party), Butler was elected president of the conference and threw himself energetically into reviving the church in Iowa, divided by the defection. Two years later he was ordained to the ministry. He was called to the presidency of the General Conference in 1871 and showed a keen interest in the development of the institutions and activities of the church organization. During his first term of office, which extended from 1871 to 1874, he was active in raising funds to establish the first Seventh-day Adventist college in Battle Creek, Michigan, and in establishing the Pacific Press Publishing Company in California. Beginning in 1881 he was for many years president of the SDA Publishing Association, and saw the rapid advance of colporteur work. He served a second time as General Conference president from 1880 to 1888.

On a visit to Europe in 1884 he laid the groundwork for publishing houses in Basel, Switzerland; Christiania (Oslo), Norway; and Grimsby, England. The impetus he gave to the SDA cause in Europe resulted in notable expansion.

In spite of his iron will and strong constitution, he was forced to retire in 1888 for a period. He bought a farm in Florida and planted an orange grove. Because his wife became an invalid the next year, he stayed on in retirement 12 years longer. After her death late in 1901, he was elected president of the Florida Conference, and the next year was called to the presidency of the Southern Union Conference and the Southern Publishing Association. During the last years of his life he held no administrative post, but wrote various articles for SDA periodicals and did some preaching.

BUTTERFIELD, CHARLES LESLIE (1879-1935). Missionary in Korea, conference administrator. He was brought up in a Seventh-day Adventist home and attended the Minneapolis preparatory school and later took the ministerial course at Battle Creek College (1898-1900). After that he canvassed, taught in the winters, and took part in evangelistic meetings in the summers, first in Minnesota and later in western Oregon. Ordained in 1907, he went the next year with his wife (née Mary M. Winnegar) to Korea and served as the first superintendent of the Korean Mission (1908-1922). Because of the failing health of his wife and the educational needs of his children, he returned to America and served as president of the Saskatchewan (1922-1926), Carolina (1926-1932), and Kentucky-Tennessee (1932-1934) conferences.

BUTZ, EDWIN SEBASTIAN (1864-1956). Missionary to Pitcairn and Tonga islands, pastor, teacher, and conference administrator. In 1895 he, his wife, and their daughter sailed on the *Pitcairn* as missionaries to Pitcairn Island. Later he pioneered Seventh-day Adventist work in the Tonga Islands. From 1906 on he worked in Australia, serving as vice president or president of the South Australian, Tasmanian, Queensland, and West Australian conferences successively. Later he was preceptor and teacher of Bible and home nursing at the Australasian Missionary College, and still later he pastored churches in northern New Zealand and southern Australia. His daughter, Alma, married Norman Wiles, who pioneered SDA work in the New Hebrides.

BYELORUSSIA. *See* Belarus.

BYINGTON, JOHN (1798-1887). Pioneer minister and first president of the General Conference. His father, Justus, was a soldier in the Revolutionary War, an itinerant Methodist Episcopal preacher, and later one of the founders of the Methodist Protestant Church, becoming an early president of its Vermont Conference. At 7 years of age John first came under the conviction of sin, and at 18 (1816) was converted. Because his mother was a woman of great diffidence, he conducted family worship when his father was absent. He became active in Methodist laity work, but at 21 years of age his health failed, and for three years he suffered depression. However, encouraged by prayer, he returned to his work, dividing his time between farming and preaching.

Since he was actively antislavery in sentiment, and the leadership of the Methodist Episcopal Church opposed antislavery activities, he withdrew from that denomination and joined the new antislavery Wesleyan Methodist Connection, helping erect a church and parsonage that are still standing at Morley, New York. He went as a lay delegate to the Wesleyan organizational General Conference meeting in Cleveland, Ohio, in 1844; and later became a Wesleyan minister, pastoring the church at Lisbon, New York. He regularly entertained Indians and Blacks in his home, and is said to have maintained a station of the Underground Railroad at Buck's Bridge, New York, where he lived on a farm.

In 1844 he heard a Millerite sermon in Cleveland, Ohio, but was not deeply impressed. In 1852, on reading a copy of the *Review and*

Herald, he began to keep the Sabbath, against bitter opposition from friends. Shortly afterward James and Ellen White visited his home at Buck's Bridge. For three years he conducted Sabbath meetings in his home, then erected and owned a church building on his own property. This may have been the first Seventh-day Adventist-built church, thought to have been completed earlier than the Battle Creek church, built the same year. In a nearby home his daughter Martha (later the wife of G. W. Amadon) taught what has been remembered as the first SDA elementary school (1853). Also, one of the earliest Sabbath schools was conducted in Byington's home.

At the request of James White, Byington moved to Michigan in 1858 and spent 15 years in self-supporting ministerial work, traveling throughout the state. He was closely associated with James White and J. N. Andrews in aggressive planning for the growing church. In 1863, at the initial organization of the General Conference at Battle Creek, Michigan, he became the first president and held that office for two one-year terms. James White, who was elected first, declined the office.

From 1852 until his death Byington served the cause he loved, contributing generously of his means to the cause. Being older in years than his fellow SDA ministers, he became affectionately known as "Father Byington."

BYLAWS. *See* General Conference Constitution and Bylaws.

C

C. C. HANSEN AND COMPANY. *See* Danish Publishing House.

CADY, BENJAMIN JACOB (1863-1927). Missionary. Educated at Battle Creek College, he preached in South Dakota (1884-1887) and in Wisconsin (1887-1892). He was ordained in 1889. In 1893 he sailed on the second trip of the *Pitcairn* for service in the South Pacific. For 17 years he worked mostly in the Society Islands, 16 years as superintendent of the Eastern Polynesian Union Mission, and one year as superintendent of the Central Polynesian Mission. For a time he was chaplain and manager of the Sydney Sanitarium, and then preached in Queensland (1911-1912). On returning to the United States, he worked in Montana (1913-1914), Washington (1914-1917), and Oregon (1917-1923) before retirement.

CADY, MARION ERNEST (1866-1948). Educator and author. A graduate of Battle Creek College (1893), he became head of the Science Department at Union College (1894-1898), president of Healdsburg College (1899-1903), and of Walla Walla College (1905-1911). He also was a Missionary Volunteer and educational secretary on the Pacific Coast for seven years. Later he was educational secretary of the Columbia Union Conference (1921), president of what is now Columbia Union College (1921-1922), and field secretary for the General Conference Educational Department for several years, until 1926. His published works include *Fundamentals of Christian Education, Early Educational Pioneers, Better Voice for Better Speech,* and *The Education That Educates.*

CAGAYAN VALLEY SANITARIUM AND HOSPITAL. A 100-bed general hospital operated by the North Philippine Union at Santiago, Isabela, in the mountains of the northeastern part of Luzon, Philippines. The institution opened on Mar. 16, 1959, in the former Northeast Luzon Mission office building, with equipment and supplies donated by the Loma Linda medical alumni and former American missionaries to the Philippines Dr. B. P. Ingersoll, of Tomah, Wisconsin, and Dr. A. C. Atwood, of Modesto, California.

The original hospital staff consisted of C. A. Fernando, medical director and business manager; Leonardo Rolle, intern; Mrs. A. P. Fernando, head nurse; and Miss E. A. Pasamonte, dietitian. Later another physician, Gideon G. Pilar, joined the staff. A full complement of hospital personnel was soon recruited.

The hospital serves the entire Cagayan Valley, and patients come also from various lowland tribes and mountain peoples. In 1969 a sprawling X-shaped, million-peso, 50-bed-capacity building was opened on an 11-acre (4.5-hectare) lot just outside the town. In 1971 a three-apartment building was constructed on the compound for hospital workers. In 1972 a doctor's residence was added. In 1973 renovations included a new apartment complex, a dormitory, a 50,000-gallon (189,250-liter) water tank, a children's playground, and upgrading of the hospital rooms. In 1976, 12 air-conditioned suites were added. Another 14 suites were added in 1992 and 1993.

Medical Directors/Presidents: C. A. Fernando, 1959-1971; O. C. Pilar, 1971-1972; L. R. Garcia, 1972- .

CALBAYOG SANITARIUM AND HOSPITAL. A 17-bed medical institution operated by the Central Philippine Union Mission in Calbayog City, Samar, third-largest island in the Philippines. A two-story residence was leased for five years by L. E. Montana, then president of the East Visayan Mission, pending the acquisition of a hospital site. Dr. O. B. Varona, former assistant medical director of the Bacolod Sanitarium and Hospital, was appointed as chief of clinic. He arrived with his family on Sept. 13, 1973, bringing 23 crates of medical equipment, supplies, and medicines. Renovation and partition of the rented building started immediately. Dr. William Richli, a self-supporting missionary doctor, helped install the electrical wiring and X-ray.

On Nov. 9, 1973, with only five workers, the clinic was opened. With no adequate seating facilities, patients had to stand in a waiting line. Outpatients averaged 70 daily. Dr. and Mrs. Gaudioso Mabaquiao, as well as medical interns in training at the Miller Sanitarium and Hospital, were lent temporarily to take care of the influx of patients. Later Dr. Roy Day, ophthalmologist and otolaryngologist, joined the staff. Using the clinic as a base, he has done much in projecting a favorable image of Seventh-day Adventist medical and welfare work in Samar and Leyte through the promotion of his Sight for the Curable Blind program, which is sponsored by such civic organizations as the Rotary Club and Kiwanis International.

From its status as a clinic it grew into a hospital and was transferred to a new site in 1984. A five-acre (two-hectare) plot less than two miles from the city center, the structure faces the National Highway, where buses ply the route from the southern Philippines to the northern Philippines.

Staff houses were built to accommodate the workers. In 1988 a guest house was added, with SIMS (Students for International Missionary Service) students being the first guests.

A food factory was opened in 1989 that produces wheat bread, soy milk, and vegetarian products. A Health Food Center building was constructed in 1991 that serves as a canteen and bakeshop for the general public. This was made possible by a donation from Dr. Eliseo and Esther Bautista of Glendale, California.

Hospital facilities were updated by acquiring a 300 MA X-ray machine, a semiautomated chemical analyzer, a cardiac monitor, and a Stateside ambulance.

Medical Directors/Presidents: O. B. Varona, 1973-1982; Lorna N. Madrio (acting), 1983-1984; Manuel S. Daprosa (acting), 1984-1985; Teresa L. Aguilar, 1985-1990; Annabelle O. Ursales, 1990- .

CALCUTTA SANITARIUM. *See* India.

CALDWELL, JOSEPH EDMOND (1855-1923). Physician, missionary. A graduate of the University of Iowa with a Ph.D. degree, and later (1880) with an M.D. degree, he taught at Healdsburg College (1887-1891). After a brief stay in Tennessee, he served at the sanitarium at Claremont, South Africa (1892-1894). Appointed to mission service in the Cook Islands, he sailed on the third voyage of the *Pitcairn* in 1894, and worked for eight years on Rarotonga. Returning to the United States, he worked for eight years in the South, including terms at Graysville Sanitarium (1903-1904); Nashville Treatment Rooms (1904-1905); Knoxville, Tennessee (1905-1906); Florida Sanitarium; and Huntsville, Alabama (1906-1911).

CALDWELL, ROBERT ARCHIBALD (1879-1966). Pioneer missionary to the Philippines. Robert Caldwell was born in Portarlington, Victoria, Australia. He and his mother were among the earliest to accept the

Sabbath truth at Portarlington in the late 1890s, while Ellen White was in Australia. After a period at Avondale College he connected with the colporteur work in Victoria and was appointed publishing secretary of the Western Australian Conference at the turn of the century.

In 1904 he accompanied Pastor G. F. Jones to Singapore, visiting Java and Borneo en route. On his journey to the Philippines in 1905 he traveled through Penang and Bangkok, but in all these places he found it difficult to sell English books. He enjoyed great success in the Philippines because he sold Spanish books. While furloughing in Australia in 1908 he married Mary Schowe, who accompanied him on his return to the Philippines. With the exception of periods spent in China and Japan, he remained in the Philippines until 1919. In 1920 he was preceptor at Avondale College. For a time he was engaged in evangelism with Pastor A. Smart. He was again connected with the colporteur work in Tasmania and Victoria during 1924-1925.

CALENDAR, CHURCH. *See* Church Calendar.

CALENDAR REFORM. A change in an existing calendar. The calendar currently in use in most nations, the Gregorian, is the result of a calendar reform in 1582 that corrected two erroneous suppositions of the Julian calendar, which had been in use since 45 B.C.—namely that the year contains exactly 365¼ days and that 235 lunar months exactly equal 19 solar years. That revision corrected an accumulated error of 10 days and stopped the calendar from slipping farther out of line with the seasons. (See SB, Nos. 360-363, or any standard encyclopedia.)

This article concerns itself only with those attempts to reform the calendar that have occurred during the history of the Seventh-day Adventist Church and that, if adopted, would have disrupted the historic cycle of the week. Calendar reform that would leave intact the weekly cycle is not the concern of the SDA Church. The church's position was defined in a letter from the General Conference Executive Committee to Secretary of State John Foster Dulles in 1955: "We are not opposed to calendar reform per se, but we are opposed to any change that would contribute to national or international disunity, economic perplexity, or religious confusion and distress."

Neither the Julian nor the Gregorian calendar interfered with the weekly cycle.

Concerning the reform of the Julian calendar by Pope Gregory XIII in 1582, we are told: "Thus, every imaginable proposition was made; only one idea was never mentioned, viz. the abandonment of the seven-day week" *(Catholic Encyclopedia,* vol. 9, p. 251, art. "Lilius"). "It is to be noted that in the Christian period the order of days of the week has never been interrupted. Thus, when Gregory XIII reformed the calendar, in 1582, Thursday, 4 October, was followed by Friday, 15 October. So in England, in 1752, Wednesday, 2 September, was followed by Thursday, 14 September" *(ibid.,* vol. 3, p. 740, art. "Chronology").

Among the hundreds of proposals made to improve the Gregorian calendar, only a few have received much attention. Among these are the Edwards Perpetual Calendar, devised by Lt. Com. Willard E. Edwards of the United States Navy, and the World Calendar. Both have 12 months, divided into four equal 91-day quarters of three months each, containing 30-30-31 in the Edwards Perpetual Calendar, and 31-30-30 days in the plan of the World Calendar Association. The 12 months contain 364 days, leaving one "blank day" (two in leap years) outside the count of the months and the weeks. An earlier proposal with strong backing in the 1920s and 1930s was the Moses B. Cotsworth plan, which, because of heavy financial backing by George Eastman, millionaire Kodak manufacturer, came to be called the Eastman Calendar. This calendar had 13 months, each beginning on Sunday and containing exactly four weeks (28 days), making the 13 months contain 364 days.

Advantages claimed by promoters of these calendars are commercial, economic, statistical, and most recently, religious. Adoption of the World Calendar, which was aggressively promoted for a time, will, it is claimed: (1) fix the year in perpetuity; (2) retain and largely equalize the 12 months; (3) retain and equalize the half years; (4) retain and equalize the quarter years; (5) group the months uniformly within the quarters; (6) provide 13 complete weeks within each quarter and uniformly group these weeks; (7) reduce the inequality between months from as much as three days to one day, and establish an equal working month; (8) stabilize the dates of Easter, Christmas, and other religious holidays.

Opponents of the World Calendar, among whom are Seventh-day Adventists, claim it will: (1) upset established religious customs and habits; (2) substitute a spurious or artificial week for the historic seven-day cycle; (3) create new religious controversy; (4) exalt materialism at the expense of religious emphasis and conscience; (5) create working difficulties for millions of conscientious observers of Sabbath and Sunday who would be forced to observe their rest days on working days of the week during most of each seven-year period; (6) compound educational problems for millions of students and teachers who would not attend classes on the seventh or the first day of the historic week.

Two other calendars that have had some backing would achieve most of the objectives of the above proposals without disrupting the weekly cycle. One, called Jubilee Calendar, was proposed by Cecil L. Woods, dean (1948-1954) of Pacific Union College, Angwin, California. The Woods proposal would allow the convenient reckoning of the year at 364 days, and would insert 71 intercalary weeks into the calendar within a 400-year period, according to the following rule: A week is intercalated between the last of December and first of January at the beginning of years divisible by 5, except those ending in 25 or 75, or divisible by 400. This week would have a special name—Jubilee Week, and could be considered the first week of a Jubilee Year, but not as part of any month or of any quarter. Records for the week would be kept separately, making the rest of the year comparable to all other years of 364 days. Another Jubilee Calendar, proposed by a number of Jewish bodies, differs from Woods's proposal in its intercalation of the 71 weeks in 400 years at intervals of five or six years in irregular sequences.

The Woods plan was submitted to the World Calendar Association by Dr. Alvin W. Johnson, secretary of the International Religious Liberty Association, on Jan. 8, 1951, as a compromise plan that might secure the backing of Seventh-day Adventists and Jews and of Sundaykeeping organizations to whom the observance of a particular day is important. The principle of maintaining an unbroken weekly cycle was shrugged aside in a 15-page evaluation of the Jubilee Calendar sent to Johnson and Woods in March 1951. The report quoted Dr. Henry Smith Leiper, associate general secretary of the World Council of Churches: "Shall the World Calendar, which stabilizes our days along scientific and mathematical lines, be denied to the world because of the opposition of minority groups? Must all our days continue to wander throughout the calendar in order to prevent *one* wandering day for the opposition of the minority because of their own particular religion?

"It is difficult to conceive," said the report, "that God would choose one day as of more value and importance than another."

History. Calendar reform in the twentieth century received its impetus, fittingly, from a statistician, Moses B. Cotsworth (1859-1943). Challenged by the uneven distribution of time in the months of the Gregorian calendar, he set out to create a calendar that would lend itself to more exact comparative statistical analysis. His new calendar, described above, received its first endorsement in 1909 from the Canadian Royal Society. Encouraged, Cotsworth organized the International Fixed Calendar League, and in 1923 or 1924 secured the financial support of George Eastman.

Meanwhile other individuals and organizations began to give the subject study. Notable among these were the International Astronomical Union, which in 1922 decided that some revision of the calendar was desirable, though it did not approve a specific plan of revision. About the same time the International Chamber of Commerce approved reform of the calendar and requested that the League of Nations appoint a special committee to study the problem.

When in 1923 such a committee was created, calendar reformers began to send in their plans. Of the some 185 (some sources give 187) plans submitted, only three were deemed worthy of consideration. One of these was the Cotsworth plan. Determining that the next step toward calendar reform must be the arousing of widespread public interest in the question, the committee in 1926 recommended that member nations of the league appoint committees to consider calendar revision, each nation through this medium to report to an international conference at which the final form of a new calendar for the world could be adopted. The committee agreed unanimously "that no reform can be effected without the consent of all, or almost all the important bodies interested, among which 'religious bodies' were placed first."

In 1928 the Pan-American Union, meeting in Havana, recommended not only that member nations appoint national committees on calendar simplification but also that they hold an international conference. Thereupon, in December 1928 a resolution was introduced into the U.S. Congress authorizing the president to call such an international conference or to accept on behalf of the United States an invitation from some other nation to attend such a conference. This bill—known as House Joint Resolution 334—presented the question of revision essentially in terms of Cotsworth's plan.

When extended public hearings on the bill were held before the House Foreign Affairs Committee, SDA leaders joined with other groups to oppose endorsement of a proposal that would upset the weekly cycle. Protests against the "blank day" feature of the plan were so effective that similar resolutions introduced into the House of Representatives on Mar. 15 and Mar. 29, 1929, omitted the preamble favoring the blank day device. Neither of these resolutions was passed. No such resolution has since received public consideration either by Congress or by any of its committees.

In July of 1928 a Calendar Committee was brought into existence, with George Eastman as chairman. Because the United States was not a member of the League of Nations, this committee had no official status. In October 1931 the calendar reform question was submitted to the Fourth General Conference of the Committee on Communications and Transit in Geneva. Present were 111 delegates from 42 nations. Eleven SDA leaders were present to oppose the plan: Charles S. Longacre, secretary of the International Religious Liberty Association; Jean Nussbaum, France; Arthur S. Maxwell, General Conference; L. L. Caviness and S. Rasmussen, southern Europe; R. A. Anderson, Australia; A. Vollmer, Germany; G. E. Nord and P. G. Nelson, Scandinavian countries; T. T. Babienco, Baltic States; and J. I. Robison, Southern African Division. (For an account of the proceedings, including an account of how Longacre produced a letter from Secretary of State Henry Stimson that flatly contradicted the claim of Charles F. Marvin to be the official representative of the United States government, see Nathaniel Krum, *Charles S. Longacre*, pp. 65-68.) The committee took no action, giving three reasons: the troubled state of the world, pronounced religious opposition, and lack of agreement among the calendar revisionists.

Calendar reform from 1930 to 1960 was largely the story of one American woman, Elisabeth Achelis, and the organization she founded in 1930, the World Calendar Association of the United States. A perfervid backer of the "twelve-month equal-quarter plan," which she rechristened the World Calendar, this woman, who claimed to have heard a voice telling her "You must work for this plan," invested her ample fortune and talents in the cause of calendar reform.

During 1930 the World Calendar Association enrolled between 2,000 and 3,000 members, and began to publish a quarterly *Journal of Calendar Reform*. Here was the first attempt to promote continuous study of the calendar on the broadest international basis. By 1956 the association had 10,000 members. Subsidiary organizations had been set up in Argentina, Bolivia, Brazil, Chile, Mexico, Panama, Uruguay, Peru, Colombia, Belgium, England, Germany, France, Denmark, Hungary, Ireland, Italy, Spain, Switzerland, Turkey, and elsewhere.

Miss Achelis resigned as president of the association in April 1956, but only to devote full-time to persuading American authorities to support the World Calendar proposal before the United Nations. In that year also the headquarters were transferred from New York City to Ottawa, Canada, and the organization was renamed the International World Calendar Association.

Notable defeats were suffered by calendar reform backers, with defeat of two bills in the United States House of Representatives during the late 1940s. H. R. 1242, introduced on Jan. 23, 1947, by Joseph R. Farrington, delegate from Hawaii, asked Congress to approve adoption of The Edwards Perpetual Calendar for use in the United States and all its territories, effective Jan. 1, 1950. H. R. 1345, introduced into the House of Representatives on Jan. 27, 1947, by Representative John Kee of the Fifth District of West Virginia, asked Congress to approve adoption of the World Calendar. Both sponsors requested that the president place their projects before the United Nations, with the recommendation that it be approved there by the General Assembly for use in the whole world at the same date, Jan. 1, 1950.

Even more crushing reverses were suffered in 1950, 1954, and 1956 before the United Nations. In 1950 the Committee of Fifteen of the United Nations declined to consider the World Calendar plan. Working with the delegates were the following SDA leaders: Jean Nussbaum for southern Europe, the Netherlands, Poland, and Haiti; Arthur S. Maxwell for the United Kingdom; G. Arthur Keough for the Middle East; C. P. Sorensen for the Far East; B. F. Perez for Mexico, Central America, and South America; H. L. Rudy for Canada; L. G. Mookerjee for Southern Asia; Frank H. Yost for the United States.

In 1954 the Economic and Social Council of the United Nations considered a proposal for calendar revision (the World Calendar) by India and Yugoslavia. The council, in a compromise resolution, referred the question to the governments represented in the United Nations, to "study the problem and furnish their views by some time early in 1955." Views of the governments were then to be considered at the resumed nineteenth session in 1955. Of the 41 governments that replied to the questionnaire, only five favored the plan. This resolution set the stage for an emphatic repudiation of the World Calendar proposal.

Three days before the Economic and Social Council began its twenty-first session in New York on Apr. 17, 1956, the World Calendar Association wrote the president of the council requesting that the calendar item be withdrawn from the agenda. Because of the lack of interest or the disapproval in the replies received from the nations to the questionnaires sent out by the secretary of the United Nations, the association thought it advisable to postpone discussion of the question.

The council, by 15 votes to none, with three abstentions (Czechoslovakia, Canada, and the USSR), adjourned *sine die* without consideration of the plan for a reform of the Gregorian calendar. The proposal for adjournment was made by the representative of the Netherlands, who said there was at present not enough support throughout the world to justify adoption of a new world calendar. Of the 33 nations that replied, three approved: Monaco (if universal), Nepal, and Thailand. Two, Yugoslavia and Iran, recommended further study. Five—Chile, Colombia, Costa Rica, Ireland, and Paraguay—felt no study should be undertaken or proposal approved without the concurrence of the Roman Catholic Church. Twenty-five nations opposed: New Zealand, Union of South Africa, Australia, Burma, Finland, Israel, Italy, Japan, Switzerland, Great Britain, United States, Netherlands, Pakistan, Philippines, Portugal, Canada, China, France, Norway, Sweden, Belgium, Denmark, Lebanon, Mexico, and Syria.

On Mar. 21, 1956, the United States government had presented its position through the following release from the State Department: "The United States government does not favor any action by the United Nations to revise the present calendar. This government cannot in any way promote a change of this nature, which would intimately affect every inhabitant of this country, unless such a reform were favored by a substantial majority of the citizens of the United States acting through their representatives in the Congress of the United States. There is no evidence of such support in the United States for calendar reform. Large numbers of United States citizens oppose the plan for calendar reform which is now before the Economic and Social Council. Their opposition is based on religious grounds, since the introduction of a 'blank day' at the end of each year would disrupt the seven-day sabbatical cycle.

"Moreover, this government holds that it would be inappropriate for the United Nations, which represents many different religious and social beliefs throughout the world, to sponsor any revision of the existing calendar that would conflict with the principles of important religious faiths.

"This government, furthermore, recommends that no further study of the subject should be undertaken. Such a study would require the use of manpower and funds which could be more usefully devoted to more vital and urgent tasks."

The International World Calendar Association became aware that any calendar reform must have strong religious support and shifted its tactics to emphasize the religious rather than the commercial and statistical benefits of the World Calendar.

It was voted to include calendar reform on the agenda of Vatican Council II (opened 1962). Dr. Jean Nussbaum, Dr. B. B. Beach, and Dr. G. Rossi were appointed by the General Conference as a committee to watch the developments at the second Vatican Council regarding calendar reform and oppose any reform that would break the weekly cycle. The objective of the calendar reformers within the Roman Catholic Church was, basically, to stabilize the date of Easter and thus to enhance the chance of reunion, initially between the Papacy and the Eastern Orthodox churches—whose observance of Easter on a different date from that observed by the Roman Church is a stumbling block on the road to unity—and eventually with the rest of Christendom. Stabilizing the Easter date would also greatly facilitate the preparation of the various ecclesiastical calendars used by religious orders and other bodies. The reform submitted to the Central Preparatory Commission for the agenda of the council by Amleto Cardinal Cicognani, acting in his capacity as president of the Preparatory Commission for the Oriental

Churches, was essentially the World Calendar plan. The suggested calendar incorporated the familiar blank days, the extra day of each year being referred to as a "World Holiday," and the extra day of leap years as "Leap Day."

The second session of the council, by a vote of 2,058 to 9 (1 was void), rejected the blank day calendar concept, affirmed the non-interruption of the weekly cycle, and made the following recommendations in the form of amendments to the fifth chapter of the council's schema on the liturgy, here translated from the Latin text.

A Declaration of the Second Ecumenical Council of the Vatican on Revision of the Calendar. The Second Ecumenical Sacred Council of the Vatican, recognizing the importance of the wishes expressed by many concerning the assignment of the feast of Easter to a fixed Sunday and concerning an unchanging calendar, having carefully considered the effects that could result from the introduction of a new calendar, declares as follows:

1. The sacred council would not object if the feast of Easter were assigned to a particular Sunday of the Gregorian calendar, provided that those whom it may concern, especially the brethren who are not in communion with the Apostolic See, give their assent.

2. The sacred council likewise declares that it does not oppose efforts designed to introduce a perpetual calendar into civil society.

But among the various systems that are being suggested to stabilize a perpetual calendar and to introduce it into civil life, the church has no objection only in the case of those systems that retain and safeguard a seven-day week with Sunday, without the introduction of any days outside the week, so that the succession of weeks may be left intact, unless there is a question of the most serious reasons. Concerning these, the Apostolic See shall judge.

Calendar reform continued to be studied at the Vatican after Vatican Council II's action supporting the current weekly cycle. *L'Osservatore Romano* (No. 95 [31.568], p. 3, Apr. 24, 1964) advocates an intercalated day. The writer, Serafino M. Sarb, asserts intercalary days have occurred in the past. *La Civilta Cattolica* (Anno 115, Quaderno 2736, June 20, 1964, pp. 546-560) suggests that Christmas Day be made the "blank" day, outside the week, thereby ensuring religious observance of the extra day. In this way it was thought the disruption of the weekly cycle would not be objectionable to Christian religious authorities. Another article in *L'Osservatore Romano* (No. 155 [31.628], July 8, 1964, p. 7) reviews the calendar problem and the various suggestions without advocating any particular plan although voicing no serious objection to a blank day. The main objective of the Roman Catholic Church is to obtain a fixed date for Easter.

A book, *La Misura del Tempo* (1969), by Prof. G. Imbrighi, a Vatican scholar, gave a history of the calendar and suggested that a "blank" day would solve the problems of the present Gregorian calendar.

Pentecontad Theory. This hypothesis claims there were seven "blank" days in the early Jewish calendar before the reign of Solomon. Propounded by Prof. Julius Lewy and his wife, Dr. Hildegard Lewy, this theory was given wide circulation by Rabbi Julian Morgenstern, former president of the Hebrew Union College in Cincinnati. Dr. Morgenstern included this conjecture in material for *The Interpreter's Dictionary of the Bible* (vol. 4, Articles "Sabbath" and "Week"). The theory, based on Lev. 23:15, 16, postulates seven periods of 50 days plus two weeks of festivals in each Jewish year. Each of the seven periods comprised seven weeks of 49 days, with the fiftieth day outside the weekly cycle. The World Calendar Association has given this assumption wide publicity.

Congressional Proposals. Since 1965 proposals for calendar change have been introduced into each session of the United States Congress. A detailed explanation of a calendar devised by Father Evarist Kleszcz was printed in the *Congressional Record* of Jan. 26, 28, 1965. This calendar does not disturb the weekly cycle, but requires a "leap week" every five or six years. Bills supporting the Edwards Perpetual Calendar died in committee in the Eighty-ninth, Ninetieth, Ninety-first, and Ninety-third Congresses.

Bills for the Adjusted Gregorian Calendar, invented by A. F. Beine, died in committee in the Ninety-first and Ninety-second Congresses. In 1974 Congressman Gilbert Gude (R-Md.) proposed (HR 14092) that the Ninety-third Congress appropriate $100,000 for the study of calendar improvement. The bill was not scheduled for hearings because of a lack of public interest.

Weekday Renumbered. In 1971 the International Organization for Standardization (ISO) of Geneva, Switzerland, recommended (Resolution R2015) "for the purpose of week numbering, the first day of the week shall be

Monday." This plan does not change the Gregorian calendar and maintains the sequence of the traditional weekly cycle without disruption. However, it does disrupt the calendrical numbering of the days of the week by designating Monday as the first day of the week, Sunday as the seventh. In the New Testament, Sunday is consistently referred to as the "first day of the week." Several countries have officially adopted this calendrical method of numbering the days of the week. However, this has been done for commercial standardization, not for religious reasons.

Monday Holidays. President Lyndon Johnson signed the "Monday Holiday" Act, June 28, 1968. Since Jan. 1, 1971, four holidays always fall on Monday. These are: President's Day (third Monday in February), Memorial Day (last Monday in May), Columbus Day (second Monday in October), and Veterans Day (fourth Monday in October).

In March 1970 the World Council of Churches called a consultation in Switzerland regarding calendar reform and fixation of the Easter date. Dr. B. B. Beach served together with the secretary of the archbishop of Canterbury as a drafter of the statement, adopted by the consultation and later approved by the WCC Central Committee, affirming support for fixing the Easter date on the second Sunday after the first Saturday in April, and opposing any civil calendar reform that would break the weekly cycle by introducing blank days.

Psychology. Seventh-day Adventists feel that tampering with the calendar could prepare the minds of people for further change. While neither the "Monday Holiday" law nor the designating of Sunday as the seventh day interferes with the weekly cycle, these changes could condition minds for more substantive changes. People who have become accustomed to change may be inclined to accept even a disruptive "blank" day without critical thought. Since the middle seventies, things have been quiet on the calendar reform front. There seems to be very little public or governmental interest in this matter.

CALEXICO MISSION SCHOOL. *See* Southeastern California Conference.

CALIFORNIA. *See* California Conference; Central California Conference; Northern California Conference; Southeastern California Conference; Southern California Conference.

CALIFORNIA CONFERENCE. A former unit of church organization originally comprising all of the Seventh-day Adventist churches in California. (Later other areas were included or attached at times, as noted hereafter—Nevada, Utah, and Arizona.) The State of California now embraces four conferences, but the present article covers the early development of the churches in the entire state before the division, and in the California Conference as long as it existed as such (until 1932). For the later period see the names of the present conferences: Central California; Northern California; Southeastern California; Southern California.

Perhaps the first SDA in California was Daniel Eaton, who wrote to the *Review* in 1855 and 1857. Merritt G. Kellogg went overland to the state in 1859 and settled in San Francisco. Here he met B. G. St. John and through reading matter and Bible studies persuaded him to accept SDA teachings. The two men interested others and held Sabbath services in the St. John home on Minna Street. In 1865 they raised $133 in gold and sent it to the General Conference with a request for a minister. It was not until 1868, however, that two ministers, J. N. Loughborough and D. T. Bourdeau, were sent. They arrived in San Francisco on July 18. Following a lead furnished by Kellogg, who in 1867 had gone East to study medicine, they found the group of Sabbathkeepers worshiping in San Francisco and preached to them.

Through a newspaper story in the New York press (quoting James White calling for $1,000 to finance a tent in San Francisco), a group of worshipers in Petaluma, near San Francisco, who called themselves Independents, learned of the arrival in San Francisco of the two men with a tent. They prayed, "If these, O Lord, are Thy servants, give them a prosperous journey, and come Thou with them." One of the group went to San Francisco, found the preachers, and brought them to Petaluma. There a tent was pitched and meetings were held from mid-August to mid-October. Despite considerable public prejudice, there were 20 converts.

In the same year, Bourdeau and Loughborough introduced Adventism into other centers in Sonoma County. By January 1869, 50 meetings had been held in Windsor, a dozen persons had accepted the Sabbath, and a Sabbath school had been organized. It was while working for an SDA at Windsor that Abram La Rue, later a pioneer missionary to

Hong Kong, read some of the literature, attended meetings, and became a convert. The tent meetings created much interest in surrounding areas such as Santa Rosa, where a lot and lumber for seats were offered without cost.

On Apr. 11, 1869, Loughborough baptized 15 in the first Seventh-day Adventist baptismal service in California, conducted on the farm of a Mr. Lee, near Santa Rosa. Later the members formed a temporary state organization, but were not as yet organized into churches. They elected as president D. T. Bourdeau; secretary, J. F. Wood; treasurer, J. N. Loughborough; executive committee, D. T. Bourdeau, Merritt G. Kellogg, and John Bowman. When the committee was formed, Bourdeau stated in his report: "When we came to Petaluma we knew of but one in this county who was keeping the Sabbath. Now we know of at least seventy-five."

As a result of the work in this area, a church 30' x 60' (9m. x 18m.) was built in Santa Rosa and dedicated by Bourdeau on Nov. 21, 1869, the first SDA church west of the Rockies. This building stood when the surrounding area was severely damaged by the 1906 earthquake. Work also was conducted in Healdsburg, but with strong opposition. From Healdsburg the tent was moved to Sebastopol, seven miles (11 kilometers) west of Santa Rosa. By 1870 there were more than 100 Sabbathkeepers in California, with four churches established, and the self-sustaining mission had a reserve of several hundred dollars.

In 1871 Loughborough began his first public meetings in downtown San Francisco. Miles Grant, a minister of the Advent Christian Church, from New England, had created some interest with 50 followers, who, not wishing to join the Methodist Church as he advised, had organized into a separate society. San Francisco was favorable to the public meetings, held in a store building at 113 Minna Street. M. E. Cornell from the East joined Loughborough for his campaign. More than 70 new members joined the church, among whom were many from Grant's group. Grant, however, was not a convert. There was a total of $1,100 pledged in tithes in one year, and offerings of $510.

In April 1872 at a regular session of the California state meeting in Santa Rosa, an invitation was sent to James and Ellen White to spend the winter of 1872-1873 in California. Their first appearance, Oct. 2, 1872, was at a small camp meeting held at Windsor, where future plans for evangelism were laid; from there they went with the tent to San Francisco. Their visit did much to bring about a union of the work in the West with that in the East.

In February 1873 a state conference was formed, with seven churches and a total membership of 238; and application was made for admission into the General Conference. The first year's tithe was $2,151.51. Loughborough, the first president, continued in this position until 1878. Offices were in Oakland.

The year 1873 saw the work advance to Red Bluff and the Napa Valley. In May the newly organized conference erected a tent in Napa and established a church of 50 members. The Napa church building was dedicated by the Whites on Apr. 4, 1874. The tent went next to St. Helena.

At the second camp meeting, held at Yountville, near St. Helena, plans were laid for establishing a health institute and a branch publishing house. It was at this meeting that Moses J. Church, a constructor of irrigation ditches, accepted the SDA faith, and, in turn, carried his newfound faith to the San Joaquin Valley. Church was the founder of the irrigation system used in the valley and the one who chose the site of the city of Fresno; he became known as the "father of Fresno." While the work was developing in northern California, Church was using his influence as newspaper editor and businessman to spread his newfound faith in and around Fresno. A church of about 50 members was organized there, and a church building was erected on the corner of Mariposa and O streets.

D. M. Canright joined the working force, beginning meetings in December 1873 in Watsonville, some 100 miles (161 kilometers) south of San Francisco. One of the converts was William Healey, who had learned of the faith in Minnesota, and who later became an outstanding evangelist in southern California.

A few believers had settled in Oakland, including John I. Tay and his wife, who in 1890 sailed from San Francisco on the maiden voyage of the missionary ship *Pitcairn.* Canright and Cornell held meetings in Oakland in 1874, which were well attended. More than 1,500 persons gathered at Lake Merritt on June 14, 1874, when 23 were baptized. They next held tent meetings in San Jose, where 35 accepted the SDA faith, and in Santa Clara, where a church of 25 members was organized.

At the 1874 conference, Healey, Uhl, Carey, Brorsen, Knud Brorsen, Bartlett, Stockton, Howard, and Judson were licensed to preach; others were added later. Tent campaigns were conducted in Stockton, Gilroy, and Hollister. Healey and Stephens took their tent to Sacramento in 1876. In the same year J. L. Wood worked in the San Joaquin Valley, beginning at Kingsburg, where he followed up the interest created by Moses Church.

In 1874 Mrs. White said to her husband, "Somewhere in Oakland is the place to locate the paper," speaking of the proposed missionary paper for the church. After a series of providential developments, the first issue of the *Signs of the Times* came off the press in Oakland, dated June 4, 1874. In 1875 an Oakland site was chosen for the new publishing house, and the Pacific Seventh-day Adventist Publishing Association (later called the Pacific Press Publishing Association) was organized.

In 1876 in order to qualify the laity for more extended missionary work, a Bible institute was conducted in Oakland, Apr. 1-16, the conference providing board and room for the 48 who enrolled. It was led by Uriah Smith and James and Ellen White.

California converts began penetrating other areas—Nevada, Arizona, and the Hawaiian Islands. Abram La Rue went to China, the Tays to Fiji, and William Hunt to South Africa.

In the fall of 1877 two camp meetings were held, one at Yountville, in the north, where 57 were baptized, and the other at Lemoore, in Kings County, which was attended by people from points as distant as San Diego and San Pasqual; 29 were baptized.

With the opening of the Rural Health Retreat (which later became the St. Helena Sanitarium and Hospital) in 1878, the first step was taken to establish health work in the West. It was headed by Merritt G. Kellogg, who had finished an elementary medical course and returned West. In 1885 the *Pacific Health Journal and Temperance Advocate* (an earlier name of *Vibrant Life)* was launched by the medical staff of the sanitarium and printed by the Pacific Press.

At Healdsburg in 1882 a school headed by Sidney Brownsberger was opened with an enrollment of 26—from ages 5 and up—which increased in the first year to 152. At the close of the school year ministerial students were sent out as assistants for the summer tent meetings. Because of financial problems and a need to move to a more rural area, Healdsburg College closed in 1908 and was replaced by Pacific Union College. But during this time nearly 2,000 young people had passed under its influence, 400 of whom became active denominational workers. By 1900 there was a wave of interest in education as attested by an impressive number of church schools conducted by teachers from Healdsburg College and Battle Creek College. There had been early schools in Fresno, San Pasqual, and San Francisco, the first believed to be that opened in Oakland in 1889 taught by a Miss Morrison.

With the arrival in southern California in 1874 of John B. Judson, an ordained minister, SDAs for the first time had an official representative south of the Tehachapis. By this time the state conference had been divided into four Tract and Missionary Society districts, and Judson was made leader of District No. 4, which included the counties of Los Angeles, San Bernardino, and San Diego. The Judsons made their home in San Pasqual Valley, where a church later was organized. J. L. Wood held tent campaigns in Orange in 1879. S. N. Haskell and J. H. Waggoner followed in San Diego, where they found a few Sabbathkeepers as a result of Wood's meetings. They also visited the believers in Los Angeles.

In 1879 William Healey began evangelistic meetings in Los Angeles and organized the first SDA church south of the Tehachapi Pass. This church, at first on Third Street, was moved and became known as the Carr Street church. Several years later it moved to 650 West 21st Street and was renamed the Central church.

The second church group to be organized in southern California, and the first to erect a church building, was the one in Norwalk, organized in 1884. Soon other churches were built in Los Angeles, San Diego, San Pedro, and Pasadena.

In 1887 William Healey held tent meetings in San Diego, where a church was built on 18th and G streets. Treatment rooms were opened in the late nineties by a graduate nurse from Battle Creek, and E. G. Fulton and M. A. Hollister opened a vegetarian restaurant in San Diego.

When in 1889 Merritt G. Kellogg left St. Helena Sanitarium and moved to El Monte, the first American settlement in southern California, he found two members there, and in Pomona a group of 16, who in 1886 had attended tent meetings conducted by E. A. Briggs, a blind SDA evangelist.

In 1896 a vegetarian restaurant and treatment rooms were opened under the direction of a certain Dr. Moran between Broadway and Hill on Third Street, Los Angeles. Besides the group of about 100 meeting in the Carr Street church, there was now another group meeting on the east side of Los Angeles, which was later formed into the Lincoln Park church. The California Conference, sponsoring evangelism in Nevada for some years and having had the members there under its "watch care" since 1878, was enlarged in 1883 to include Nevada. In 1889 it took the responsibility for the largely unentered territories of Utah and Arizona. In 1894 Utah was taken over as a General Conference mission, and Arizona likewise in 1895. The California Conference included Nevada until 1911. In the 1905 and 1906 *Yearbooks* it is called the California-Nevada Conference. In 1901 the California Conference became a member of the newly formed Pacific Union Conference, an area comprising the states of Montana, Idaho, Washington, Oregon, California, the territory of Alaska, Hawaii, British Columbia, Nevada, Utah, and Arizona (1902). At this time C. Santee was president of the California Conference, and offices were at 301 San Pablo Avenue in Oakland.

At the Oakland camp meeting in 1901, the first steps were taken for a division of the California Conference. At that time the area of the state south of the Tehachapi and Santa Ynez mountains was detached and organized into the Southern California Conference. In 1911 when further division was deemed desirable, Inyo and Mono counties, and a portion of Santa Barbara, together with the counties of Clark, Lincoln, Nye, and Esmeralda in Nevada, were added to the Southern California Conference, and the remaining territory in the California Conference was divided into three conferences: the California Conference, the Central California Conference, and the Northern California-Nevada Conference. The California Conference now covered a territory composed only of the following counties: Santa Cruz, Santa Clara, San Mateo, Alameda, Contra Costa, Solano, Marin, Sonoma, San Francisco, Napa, Lake, Mendocino, Trinity, Humboldt, and Del Norte. With a population of 1 million, it had 38 churches and a membership of 2,806, with 21 ministers.

In 1915 the California Conference was divided again, retaining 20 churches and a membership of 1,620 in the area south of the San Francisco Bay and west of the Coast Range (with J. L. McElhany as president); the 21 churches and 1,261 members north of the Bay and west of the mountains to Oregon were organized as the Northwestern California Conference, with J. A. Stevens as president and with offices in Santa Rosa. But in 1918 these two were merged once more under the California Conference, with G. W. Wells, president; H. B. Thomas, secretary-treasurer.

In 1932 the California Conference terminated its separate existence and was divided between the Central and Northern California conferences. For later Seventh-day Adventist history in the state of California, see the separate conferences listed in the first paragraph of this article.

Presidents: Daniel T. Bordeau, 1869-1870; J. N. Loughborough, 1870-1878; no president, 1878-1879; S. N. Haskell, 1879-1887; J. N. Loughborough, 1887-1890; N. C. McClure, 1890-1891; S. N. Haskel, 1891-1894; N. C. McClure, 1894-1896; A. J. Breed, 1896-1897; W. T. Knox, 1897-1900; C. Santee, 1900-1901; A. T. Jones, 1901-1904; A. S. Kellogg, 1904-1906; W. J. Knox, 1906-1908; S. N. Haskell, 1908-1911; E. W. Farnsworth, 1911-1915; J. L. McElhany, 1915-1918; G. W. Wells, 1918-1922; G. A. Roberts, 1922-1932.

CALIFORNIA-NEVADA CONFERENCE. *See* California Conference.

CALKINS, GLENN ALWIN (1889-1962). Evangelist and conference administrator. When he accepted the Seventh-day Adventist faith in 1919 he gave up business interests and entered Pacific Union College to prepare for the ministry. After a period in evangelistic work, he became business manager of the Loma Linda Sanitarium. He served successively as vice president of the Southern California Conference (1927), president of Southeastern California Conference (1927-1930), comptroller of the College of Medical Evangelists (1931-1934), president of the Pacific Union Conference (1933-1941), president of the Inter-American Division (1941-1947, 1951-1954), and a General Conference field secretary (1955-1958).

CAMBODIA. An independent republic situated between Vietnam and Thailand in Southeast Asia, with a population (1994) of 10.3 million living in a geographical area of 70,238 square miles (181,916 square kilometers). From 1863 to 1953 it was a French protectorate.

Buddhism is the state religion, and with the people satisfied with their ancient beliefs, Christian missions have made limited progress.

Seventh-day Adventist Statistics. The territory of Cambodia constitutes the

Cambodia Attached District, in the Southeast Asia Union, which is a part of the Far Eastern Division. Statistics (1994) for *Cambodia* are difficult to verify because of the tremendous growth of our church taking place there and because church officials have not been able to enter some restricted areas of the country. But reports indicate that there are at least 36 groups of believers meeting regularly, with about 185 members (1,500 attending services) and 36 lay pastors being trained to serve these small congregations; ordained ministers, 1. Headquarters for the Cambodia Attached Mission are at Phnom Penh.

Development of Seventh-day Adventist Work. The first Seventh-day Adventist worker to enter Cambodia, then a part of the Indo-China Mission, was Fred L. Pickett, who went there in January 1930. When the government refused to give him permission to build a church, he established a church of 32 Cambodian members at Tinh Bien, a village near Chaudoc, in the neighboring Cochin China (now South Vietnam). Other early workers were Eng Pheng and Svay Sas. In January 1937 Robert Bentz and his wife arrived in Cambodia and from 1939 to 1941 operated a Bible school and maternity clinic in Phnom Penh, the capital. When World War II reached Cambodia, causing other overseas leaders to leave the country, Robert Bentz was called to Saigon, Vietnam, to head the French Indo-China Mission.

In 1957 Ralph E. Neall and his family went to Cambodia—the first postwar SDA workers to arrive there. They were soon followed by Giang Tu Minh and his wife. Later Wong Yew Seng and Manuel G. Tortal joined the staff of workers. On Nov. 1, 1958, the first Seventh-day Adventist church in Cambodia was organized, with 11 charter members of many nationalities. Government recognition of the mission on Aug. 21, 1959, made possible the construction in Phnom Penh of a church building, seating 150, opened Feb. 3, 1962.

Political changes closed down SDA work in 1965, and no overseas workers were allowed in the Khmer Republic until 1972. An English language school was started by Edwin Moore in 1972. In 1975 it had more than 500 students.

The government made an agreement with the SAWS organization for relief commodities to be distributed to refugees in the country. In late 1974 Mr. and Mrs. Matthew Ferguson arrived to serve as volunteer workers with their primary responsibility in the relief area. An overseas family was called from the United States in early 1975. Although there was only one church facility located in the language school building, two services were held every Sabbath, one in a Chinese dialect and the other in the Khmer language.

In 1972 the country was no longer connected with the Vietnam Mission, but became a detached district under the supervision of the Southeast Asia Union Mission. A national missionary couple, Pastor and Mrs. Ng Gan Theow, from Singapore, reactivated the Bible correspondence school, started by Ralph Neall, which offers courses in Chinese and Khmer.

In 1975, after the Khmer Rouge takeover, SDA work, for all practical purposes, ceased.

In late 1978 Vietnam attacked Cambodia and drove the Khmer Rouge from power. During 1979 and 1980 large numbers of Cambodian refugees fled into Thailand and were settled in United Nations-sponsored camps. From 1978 to 1991 Cambodia (known as Kampuchea) remained in a state of civil war. During these years more than 300,000 refugees continued to live in camps inside Thailand.

SAWS was one of the first relief organizations to provide care for these refugees. ADRA carried on active health work for several years, and lay SDA organizations such as Adventist Frontier Missions continued to support workers in the camps until 1993 when repatriation of refugees was completed. As a result of this work, several congregations were started among the refugees living in the camps. More than 14,000 baptisms were reported and at least 600,000 refugees were taken to live in other countries. Many of the Seventh-day Adventists among this group have become active in SDA congregations in their new countries.

Beginning in 1988, ADRA led out in a project that restored an irrigation system near the ancient Angkor Wat ruins. In 1991 ADRA established a country office in Phnom Penh.

In 1991 lay Bible worker training courses were initiated in three of the camps. By April 1992, when repatriation of refugees began, 18 Bible workers had been selected to work inside Cambodia, and in 1994 reports indicate that at least double that number are at work. Attempts to locate pre-1975 members in Cambodia have not been successful so far.

In January 1993 M. Daniel Walter arrived in Phnom Penh to take up responsibilities as administrator of the Cambodia Attached District. In May of that year the Seventh-day Adventist Church was recognized officially by the government of Cambodia.

At a Global Mission rally held at Southern College on Mar. 19, 1994, more than $500,000 was raised to establish and house 63 new congregations in Cambodia.

CAMBODIA ATTACHED DISTRICT. *See* Cambodia; Far Eastern Division.

CAMEROON. An independent republic in West Africa. Cameroon lies between 2° and 13° north latitude and stretches from the tropical jungles in the south to the edge of the Sahara in the north. The country is bounded on the west by the Gulf of Guinea and Nigeria, on the east by Chad, the Central African Republic, and the Congo, and on the south by Gabon and Equatorial Guinea.

First discovered by the Portuguese in 1472, the area was a German colony from 1884 until 1919, when it was made a mandate of the League of Nations and divided between France and Great Britain to administer. On Jan. 1, 1959, that portion assigned to France was granted full autonomy, and complete independence one year later. In a plebiscite held in February 1961 the northern part of the British Cameroons chose to join the Federation of Nigeria, while the southern part voted union with the Cameroon republic and became known as West Cameroon.

The Cameroon republic has an area of 179,714 square miles (465,459 square kilometers) and a population (1994) of 13 million. Agriculture is the principal occupation, the chief products being cacao, palm kernels, coffee, timber, cotton, and rubber. The climate is hot and rainy on the coast, but less hot and humid inland. Thirty-three percent of the population is Christian, 16 percent Muslim, and the rest animist. Christian missions, Catholic and Protestant, entered first in the south.

There is a great contrast between south and north Cameroon, because of differences in climate, and economic, scholastic, and religious development. Those in the north are generally either Muslim or animist. Their staple foods are many varieties of millet and Guinea corn, peanuts, and toward the east, rice. The Muslim Fulani engage in cattle raising and trading; most of the rest are subsistence farmers, raising some sheep and goats. The chief cash crops are cotton and peanuts. In the south the climate is equatorial, and the chief food crops are yams, plantains, cassava, and palm oil.

Seventh-day Adventist Statistics. The territory of Cameroon constitutes the Central-South Cameroon Mission, East Cameroon Mission, North Cameroon Mission, and West Cameroon Mission. It is a part of the Central African Union, which is in turn part of the Africa-Indian Ocean Division. Statistics (1992) for *Cameroon:* churches, 548; members, 56,047; elementary schools, 20; ordained ministers, 75; licensed ministers, 39; teachers, 104.

Statistics (1992) for the missions—*Central-South Cameroon Mission:* churches, 118; members, 9,993; elementary schools, 8; ordained ministers, 23; teachers, 58. Headquarters: Yaoundé-Nlongkak. *East Cameroon Mission:* churches, 234; members, 25,940; elementary schools, 10; ordained ministers, 26; licensed ministers, 17; teachers, 29. Headquarters: Bertoua. *North Cameroon Mission:* churches, 147; members, 15,625; ordained ministers, 14; licensed ministers, 11; teachers, 6. Headquarters: Maroua. *West Cameroon Mission:* churches, 49; members, 4,489; elementary schools, 2; ordained ministers, 12; licensed ministers, 11; teachers, 11. Headquarters, Douala.

Institutions. Batouri Adventist Hospital; Central African Publishing House; Dogba Secondary School; Koza Adventist Hospital; Nanga-Eboko Adventist Secondary School.

Seventh-day Adventist Work. *Beginnings.* SDA work in Cameroon began in November 1926 when W. H. Anderson, founder of several missions in South Africa and in the Congo, chose the site of the first station at Nanga-Eboko, 100 miles (160 kilometers) northeast of Yaoundé, the capital. Early in 1928 Robert L. Jones organized the first Sabbath school and the first primary school. On Jan. 1, 1929, Cameroon was assigned to the Southern European Division, and Marius Raspal, who had pioneered the work in Madagascar, was called. He erected the first brick buildings in Nanga-Eboko and conducted the first baptism there. Daniel Ndi, Josué Medjo, and Antoine Mpfoumi were the first converts. At a second baptism the wives of Ndi and Medjo also joined the church. On Mar. 12, 1930, when 11 persons were baptized, the first Seventh-day Adventist church was organized.

With the arrival of two more missionaries, Serge Yérétzian and Aimé Sallée, the work grew. National evangelists were quickly trained and sent to the following stations: Nsem, Andom, Mbong, Eteké, Ngama, Mbargué, Mbinang, Wall, Sandja, and Menga. The pioneer national workers were Daniel Ndi,

Josué Medjo, Robert Amougou, Thomas Ndongo, Joseph Eto, Samuel Bina, Joseph Assou, Joseph Mimbiang, Antoine Mpfoumi, and Pierre Assamba.

In 1930 a second station was opened in Batouri, and in 1936 a third, in Ndoumbi. The work progressed continuously in that region, and contact was established with the Pygmies several years later, in 1955.

Advance Toward the South. In 1935 Marius Fridlin and his wife arrived to work among the people on the coast. On Nov. 2, 1938, Paul Bénézech and his family opened the first mission station at Grand-Batanga. In 1940 Fridlin baptized the first 18 members, who had been prepared by the African evangelists Adalbert Ekitike, Antoine Mpfoumi, and Adolphe Oyono. In 1950 a new station was opened by A. Cosendai and his wife in Nanganjango, near Kribi.

Around 1940 an interest was awakened among the Boulou tribe, and a mission station was opened in Kongo, 23 miles (37 kilometers) from Sangmélima. In 1944 a main station was opened in Avebe by E. Curmatureanu, assisted by national evangelists Josué Medjo and Daniel Ndi.

In 1946 the district of Babimbi, among the Bassas, was entered. A station was opened in Mandjab by the African pastor Antoine Mpfoumi, and a school was opened by Oscar Nzhie.

In Douala, the port of Cameroon, a Sabbath school was established in 1953, directed by a layman, Antoine Mahelet. In May 1960 Pastor A. Ekitike was transferred to Douala, where he was assisted by K. Waber and his family. The following year a church of 26 members was organized. In 1963 an evangelistic center was bought, which Eliseo Cupertino used in May 1963 for a series of evangelistic meetings, the first in Douala.

North Cameroon. In January 1931 R. Bergström arrived and established a station in Dogba, 15 miles (25 kilometers) from Maroua. Later two other stations were opened, one in Mikiri, the other in Mokio. The first African evangelist, Jean Bikoé, arrived from the south in 1934 and opened a school in Dogba. In March 1935 the first six converts were baptized. In 1949 a second station was opened in Koza, in the heart of the Mandara Mountains, peopled by several Kirdi tribes. In 1954 Koza was chosen as the site for the first SDA hospital, operated by Dr. F. W. Brennwald and his wife.

Central Nyong. From the country of the Yébékolos, watered by the river Nyong and its many tributaries, many pupils went to the primary school at Nanga-Eboko. When they returned home, they taught the SDA message to their parents. In 1940-1941 the first station was established in Niamvoudou by Marius Fridlin, then in charge of the work in Cameroon. Soon, other stations were established in many neighboring villages.

After having operated under the direction of the Nanga-Eboko Mission and then under the Yaoundé Mission, the work in this prosperous section was organized as the Central Nyong Mission in 1962. The principal mission station, Niamvoudou, with its permanent chapel, was chosen as the site of the Collège Biblique Adventiste ("Adventist Bible College," Cameroon Bible School), which opened its doors on Nov. 1, 1963, and began to train ministers and Bible workers.

In 1953, 27 years after SDA teachings were taken to Cameroon, the work was started in Yaoundé, the capital, by Kurt Scheidegger, who undertook evangelistic and construction work. A primary school was opened, which 10 years later had 1,200 pupils. In 1954 a church was organized. A church building and several school buildings were erected on a plot at the edge of the city. This mission station became well known in the capital city.

After the establishment of stations in Obala and Bilomo, north of Yaoundé, the Yaoundé Mission was organized in 1956. It included the territory of the Yébékolos people.

West Cameroon. The area on the eastern border of Nigeria (formerly the southern part of the British Cameroons) was first entered by SDAs when in December 1929 a layman, E. Gji, was sent by the Calabar, Nigeria, church board to investigate in response to a letter from Bekura. He reported that there were 27 interested persons who wished further instruction. In July 1960 M. Gbadiah went from the Calabar area and conducted an evangelistic campaign in West Cameroon. The first overseas missionary to enter the area was Louis Nielsen, who arrived in February 1961. He found a small group of unbaptized converts in Bekura village, who had been faithfully instructed for two years by a Nigerian trader, Okpan Kalu. This trader, formerly a fetish priest at Ikong in Calabar Province, had been converted by an Adventist layman named Chuks, from Calabar, but before he could be baptized he moved to the West Cameroon to set up his own business. There he shared his new faith and organized a Sabbath school. Later S. A. Chicaye, a young minister of the East Nigerian Mission, and S. Giba, a Cameroon national living in Nigeria, came as missionaries to this new territory. Within six months the number of adherents increased and a small church was built.

Development and Organization. Primary schools and, since the arrival of Paul Bernard in 1950, secondary schools have played an important part in advancing the work in Cameroon. Medical work was carried on first in temporary and later in permanent dispensaries at Nanga-Eboko, Bertoua-Ndoumbi, Batouri, Dogba, Kribi, and Niamvoudou. The Cameroon Mission Hospital was established in Koza.

Because of world conditions, Cameroon was placed under the West African Union Mission in 1946, and directed from the General Conference headquarters at Washington, D.C. In 1949 the French West and Equatorial African Union Mission was organized, with headquarters at Nanga-Eboko, Cameroon, under the Euro-Africa Division In 1955 the offices of the union mission were transferred from Nanga-Eboko to Yaoundé, where two buildings were constructed for offices and workers' apartments, on a hillside overlooking part of the city. In addition to the Cameroon republic, the union territory in 1974 embraced the independent states born of the old French Equatorial Africa—the Congo republic (Brazzaville), Gabon, the Central African republic, the republic of Chad—and Equatorial Guinea (Bioko and Río Muni).

Nanga-Eboko Adventist Secondary School has made considerable progress. To prepare well-qualified workers, a training program for evangelists and ministers has been organized on different levels, taking into consideration the varying educational backgrounds. In 1970 a new mission station was opened at Bafang, in West Cameroon, in the Bamiléké district, where there are more than 1 million inhabitants. The first missionaries to that district were René Augsburger and his wife. Recently work, which had been developed largely in the bush, was established in more than 35 cities of the Cameroon. Three new schools were opened: the Bergström School at Dogba, the Adventist school at Niamvoudou, and the Kribi Adventist School.

Radio work has also been organized. Presently the SDA message is being broadcast over Radio-Yaoundé, Radio-Douala, Radio-Maroua, Radio-Bertoua, and Radio-Buéa, which airs a program in English to the area formerly called the British Cameroons. Broadcasts in French are planned for the Central African Republic Mission from Bangui, the capital. In 1977 a dental clinic was opened at Yaoundé, and in 1991 a hospital was constructed at Batouri.

CAMP MEETING. A series of meetings held for a number of days, generally in a rural or semirural setting, with provision for encampment on the grounds; a type of meeting now peculiar to the Seventh-day Adventist Church and a few other denominations. Camp meetings are held in various sections of the world, usually annually, and at times when the weather is suitable for such occasions; customarily a camp meeting is conducted by a conference or an equivalent unit of church organization.

History. Camp meetings originated among the Presbyterians in Kentucky in the early years of the nineteenth century and later flourished especially among the Methodists. SDA camp meetings began in 1868, five years after the General Conference was incorporated in 1863. The background for the SDA gatherings was in the Millerite camp meetings of 1842-1844, in which both James White and Joseph Bates, early leaders of the SDA Church, had participated, and in similar meetings held by the Methodist Church with notable success.

The subject of holding such meetings came up at the General Conference session held at Battle Creek, Michigan, May 12-18, 1868. The minutes of that meeting reported the following: "*Resolved,* That this conference recommend to our people to hold a general camp meeting annually at the time of the sessions of our business associations.

"*Resolved,* That the Gen. Conf. Committee be authorized, at their discretion, to carry this plan into execution" *(Review and Herald* 31:356, May 26, 1868).

Two months later, in an editorial, James White set the matter before the readers *(ibid.* 32:56, 57, July 14, 1868), and made a strong appeal for general camp meetings. He referred to the unsuitability of the business sessions of the General Conference and other business sessions for a spiritual feast.

"This is not a good time for a general gathering of our brethren and sisters to enjoy a spiritual feast. Not understanding this, many have come to our annual conferences, spent a week's time, and gone home disappointed. They had no special interest in the business sessions, thought they occupied too much time, and concluded that their brethren were becoming formal and backslidden."

The issue of Aug. 25 carried the announcement of "Our First General Camp Meeting," to be "held at Wright, Ottawa Co., Mich., Sept. 1-7." This meeting *(ibid.* 32:172, Sept. 15, 1868; 32:197, Oct. 6, 1868), attended by as many as 2,000, was both a revival for the church members and an evangelistic series for the visitors. There were 22 tents, each housing the group from one local church, and two large tents for meetings in case of rain. These were arranged in a circle around the outdoor meeting place, which had a preachers' stand and board benches. There was also a crude stand where books and tracts were sold. Within a month other camp meetings were held at Clyde, Illinois, and Pilot Grove, Iowa *(ibid.* 32:196, 216, Oct. 6, 20, 1868).

From this small beginning camp meetings have become a regular feature of SDA Church life in many countries. The next year several were held; one for New England was held in September 1869 near South Lancaster, Massachusetts. The first SDA camp meeting in the western United States convened Oct. 2, 1872, in Windsor, California. Present were J. N. Loughborough, M. E. Cornell, and James and Ellen White. The meeting lasted six days. In eastern Canada the first SDA camp meeting in Quebec was held at Magog, Aug. 21-26, 1879, with about 90 in attendance; one was held at Ayer's Flat, July 1-6, 1886. In western Canada a camp meeting was held on the banks of the Red River, near Winnipeg, Manitoba, July 2-11, 1897. At this meeting both English and German were used, A. T. Jones being the principal speaker in English. In 1904, the year before the territory of Alberta became a province, the first camp meeting for the Alberta Mission was held in Wetaskiwin.

Camp meetings have been conducted by SDAs outside of North America in various countries. When attention was given to the building up of the SDA Church in Australia, it was decided to hold the first camp meeting in the town of Brighton, Victoria (near Melbourne), in September 1893. Ellen White, who was present, wrote that this Brighton meeting awakened an interest "greater than anything we had witnessed since the movement of 1844."

Open-air encampments, often rather large, are sponsored by the SDA Church in various parts of Africa. In 1939 the Gitwe Mission, then headquarters of the Congo Union, reported a larger attendance at its camp meeting than at any other camp meeting ever held by this denomination. The number exceeded 18,000.

General Pattern for Camp Meeting Procedure. The usual 10-day camp meeting follows a rigorous daily schedule from six in the morning until 10 at night. Each day is filled with sermons, Bible studies, and meetings of various church departments, with some leisure time allotted for meals and rest. Separate meetings are held for young people and for several age groups of children. From early times the programs have included not only doctrinal, devotional, and evangelistic sermons but also instruction on the laws of diet and health, and on temperance. Of a Fresno, California, camp meeting in 1879 S. N. Haskell wrote: "Quite an interest was taken in the temperance question. A goodly number signed the teetotal pledge, thus severing their connection with tea, coffee, and tobacco" *(ibid.* 54:100, Sept. 18, 1879).

From the first, camp meetings have offered not only spiritual help and instruction to the lay members but also evangelistic meetings aimed at the visitors. In earlier times when camp meetings were held in a different locality in the conference each year, the convocations represented major evangelistic campaigns to reach various places.

Steering away from the basically evangelistic nature of the nineteenth-century camp meetings, SDAs today tend more and more to utilize these yearly sectional gatherings as spiritual meetings for the church members, though not ignoring opportunities for neighborhood evangelism. The practice of maintaining permanent camp meeting sites, rather than moving to different locations each year, has become general. In practically all the conferences of North America large permanent pavilions have replaced the former canvas tents as the places of general convocation. A pavilion in Lynwood, California, no longer used for camp meetings, accommodated 10,000 or more people in one meeting. Some campgrounds have cabins; most provide family tents and accommodations for house trailers and recreational vehicles, so that as many campers as may desire can reside on the grounds during the encampment. In recent years many of the conferences have had to hold regional camp meetings because campgrounds can no longer accommodate all who wish to attend.

CAMP MEETING PERMANENT SITES. Many conferences in the North

American Division maintain locations for yearly camp meetings. These often have permanent buildings in which the various age groups meet, though in some cases tents may be pitched to accommodate the series, or existing school buildings are used. Space is available for recreational vehicles, and simple cabins, tents, or dormitory rooms provide living facilities during the sessions. In 1993 the following sites were in operation:

Atlantic Union Conference—Greater New York Conference: Camp Berkshire, Wingdale, New York; *New York Conference:* Union Springs Academy, Union Springs, New York; *Northeastern Conference:* Camp Victory Lake, Hyde Park, New York; *Northern New England Conference:* Pine Tree Academy, Freeport, Maine; *Southern New England Conference:* Southern New England Campground, South Lancaster, Massachusetts.

Seventh-day Adventist Church in Canada—Alberta Conference: Foothills SDA Camp, Olds, Alberta; *British Columbia Conference:* Camp Hope, Hope, British Columbia; *Manitoba-Saskatchewan Conference:* Camp Whitesand, Theodore, Saskatchewan; *Maritime Conference:* SDA Campgrounds, Pugwash, Nova Scotia; *Ontario Conference:* Cloud Lake Camp, Thunder Bay, Ontario; *Quebec Conference:* Bois Francs Adventist Camp, Ste. Clothilde de Horton, Quebec; *Seventh-day Adventist Church in Newfoundland and Labrador:* Woody Acres Camp, Trans-Canada Highway, Newfoundland.

Columbia Union Conference—Allegheny East Conference: Pine Forge Academy, Pine Forge, Pennsylvania; *Allegheny West Conference:* Conference Campsite, Thornville, Ohio; *Chesapeake Conference:* Highland View Academy, Hagerstown, Maryland; *Mountain View Conference:* Valley Vista Adventist Center, Huttonsville, West Virginia; *New Jersey Conference:* Garden State Academy, Tranquility, New Jersey; *Ohio Conference:* Mount Vernon Academy, Mount Vernon, Ohio; *Pennsylvania Conference:* Blue Mountain Academy, Hamburg, Pennsylvania; *Potomac Conference:* Shenandoah Valley Academy, New Market, Virginia.

Lake Union Conference—Illinois Conference: Broadview Academy, LaFox, Illinois; *Indiana Conference:* Indiana Academy, Cicero, Indiana; *Lake Region Conference:* Lake Region Conference Campground, Cassopolis, Michigan; *Michigan Conference:* Great Lakes Adventist Academy, Cedar Lake, Michigan; *Wisconsin Conference:* Camp Go-Seek, Oxford, Wisconsin.

Mid-America Union Conference—Central States Conference: Central States Conference Center, Kansas City, Kansas; *Dakota Conference:* Dakota Adventist Academy, Bismarck, North Dakota; *Rocky Mountain Conference:* Mills Spring Camp, Casper, Wyoming.

North Pacific Union Conference—Alaska Conference: Palmer, Alaska; *Idaho Conference:* Gem State Academy, Caldwell, Idaho; *Montana Conference:* Mount Ellis Academy, Bozeman, Montana; *Oregon Conference:* Gladstone Park Campground, Gladstone, Oregon; *Upper Columbia Conference:* Walla Walla College, College Place, Washington; *Washington Conference:* Auburn Adventist Academy, Auburn, Washington.

Pacific Union Conference—Arizona Conference: SDA Campgrounds, Prescott, Arizona; *Central California Conference:* SDA Campgrounds, Soquel, California; *Nevada-Utah Conference:* SDA Campgrounds, Springville, Utah; *Northern California Conference:* SDA Redwood Area Campgrounds, Redcrest, California.

Southern Union Conference—Carolina Conference: Lake Junaluska Assembly, Junaluska, North Carolina; *Florida Conference:* Forest Lake Academy, Apopka, Florida; *Georgia-Cumberland Conference:* Southern College of Seventh-day Adventists, Collegedale, Tennessee; *Gulf States Conference:* Bass Memorial Academy, Lumberton, Mississippi; *Kentucky-Tennessee Conference:* Highland Academy, Portland, Tennessee; *South Atlantic Conference:* South Atlantic Campground, Orangeburg, South Carolina; *South Central Conference:* Oakwood College, Huntsville, Alabama; *Southeastern Conference:* Hawthorne, Florida.

Southwestern Union Conference—Arkansas-Louisiana Conference: Ozark Adventist Academy, Gentry, Arkansas; *Oklahoma Conference:* Wewoka Woods Adventist Center, Wewoka Woods, Oklahoma; *Southwest Region Conference:* Lone Star Camp, Athens, Texas; *Texas Conference:* Southwestern Adventist College, Keene, Texas; *Texico Conference:* Sandia View Academy, Corrales, New Mexico.

CAMPBELL, ALEXANDER JOHN (1901-1970). South Sea Island missionary. Born in Kalgoorlie, Western Australia, he was instructed in present truth from earliest childhood. Graduating from Avondale College in 1924, he spent a year in colporteur work followed by two years in evangelism in north New South Wales. In 1925 he married Emily Ford. In 1927 he went to Buin in the Solomon Islands for two years and then to Choiseul for another seven years. In 1936 he began a long term in the Eastern Highlands of New Guinea. With the exception of the war years, he worked there until his return to Australia in 1960. From that year until 1967, he was curator of Ellen G. White's old home, Sunnyside, at Cooranbong.

During his retirement, he engaged very actively in furthering the work of the International Educational Recording Organization, headed up by Herbert Ford in California. This group places in the hands of primitive peoples the world over small hand-operated gramophones with gospel recordings in their own tongue.

CAMPBELL, MALCOLM NEAL (1874-1958). Minister, administrator. He was born on Prince Edward Island, Canada, and married Ida Lillian Frohmader in 1897. From 1895 to 1906 he held various pastorates, among them that of the Battle Creek church. With his appointment as president of the Iowa Conference in 1908 began a succession of administrative positions that lasted until his retirement.

He became president of the Eastern Canadian Union (1912), and of the British Union Conference (1917). On his return to North America in 1922, he became assistant secretary of the General Conference until he became secretary of the Bureau of Home Missions (1924). On the uniting of the Eastern and Western Canadian unions in 1932, he became the first president of the Canadian Union. He became president of the North American Division in 1936 and retired in 1939.

CAMPINAS ADVENTIST ACADEMY. *See* São Paulo Academy.

CAMPING. Part of the AY recreational and training program. Organized Seventh-day Adventist youth camps began with a junior boys' camp in the summer of 1926 in Michigan. The next year a girls' camp was added in Michigan and a boys' camp was held in Wisconsin. In 1928 similar camps were first held in California.

The object of these AJY summer camps, conducted by the various conferences, was to invite junior youth to engage in vigorous activity in a healthful Christian environment for the purpose of developing Christian character and habits of usefulness. By 1930 leadership training camps and senior youth camps were being conducted, designed to provide senior young people with the benefits of outdoor life and Christian fellowship. The camping idea began to spread to other divisions of the world field. The greatest growth took place in the 1950s. In 1964 there were 741 junior youth camps conducted in the world field, with an attendance of 46,465.

As conducted in the mid-1960s, the typical daily program at a youth camp begins with reveille, flag raising, and morning watch. After personal inspection, there is breakfast and inspection of quarters. Morning and afternoon sessions are devoted to crafts and MV Honors, with as much swimming, hiking, boating, and horseback riding as time allows.

Religion is given top priority, with early-morning prayer bands, midmorning "camp councils," and campfire devotions. Often an ordained minister serves as camp pastor, speaking each morning at camp council and leading up to a decision for baptism by the end of the camp. The Friday night campfire frequently climaxes with a consecration service.

There is a strong trend toward erecting permanent camp facilities on conference-owned property. Such a camp provides a lodge, a kitchen and dining room, a headquarters building, quarters for staff members, an infirmary, a nature center, cabins for the campers, and where needed, a standard-sized swimming pool; also, wherever possible, one or more outpost camps, where hikers can spend a night or two roughing it.

In addition to junior and senior summer camps there are teenage camps and occasionally adult or family camps; also camps for underprivileged children.

CAMPION ACADEMY. A coeducational boarding school on the senior high school level, operated by the Colorado Conference, and situated four miles (6 kilometers) south of Loveland, Colorado.

The need for a school in the area was sensed in the early 1900s by H.M.J. Richards, who, concerned about a Christian education for his own boys and other young people, obtained conference permission to raise funds for an academy and collected more than $7,000.

The need was also felt in 1904 by W. A. Hankins, who noted that Seventh-day

Adventists near Berthoud, Colorado, had been meeting for some 20 years but had not yet sent out one foreign missionary or Bible instructor. At camp meeting that year he offered any five acres of his homestead for a conference school. A committee consisting of G. F. Watson (conference president), H.M.J. Richards (vice president), G. W. Anglebarger, F. M. Wilcox, Watson Ziegler, E. E. Farnsworth, Elbridge Green, and Horace Williams selected the present site of Campion Academy.

By 1907 a classroom building and a dormitory had been erected, and a modest beginning made. Frank A. Page, the first teacher and principal, had 29 students in grades 1 through 9. The first class, three in number, was graduated in 1911. Called Eastern Colorado Academy at first, the school was later renamed Campion Academy from a nearby stop and spur of the Colorado and Southern Railway. Because expenses of construction and maintenance were met largely by the local church, the earliest years demanded great personal sacrifice on the part of students and teachers. But by 1927, the school's twentieth anniversary, the last of the mortgage papers were burned.

In 1919 the chapel and administration building was destroyed by fire. It was replaced by a brick building, Hankins Hall, which was completed in 1921 and served as administration building and provided classroom, library, chapel, and dining room space.

A notable feature in the early years of the school was the Little Leaven League, a small but influential student organization formed in 1913 to prepare student speakers for missionary activity. John Turner, Roy Miles, Harold M. S. Richards, John Deapen, Kenneth Gant, Charles Stagner, Roger Altman, and Albert E. Hagen began their evangelistic service in this organization.

The school's first dormitory housed both boys and girls and contained the dining room. Then a girls' residence, which included food service, was erected in 1912 of concrete blocks made by students and staff. This dormitory stood nearly 40 years. The original frame dormitory served the boys until a brick home was completed in 1938. Another girls' dormitory was built in 1946. When finally completed in 1953, the dormitory could house 140 girls. In 1980 this dormitory was replaced by a single-story X-shaped building that boasted bathrooms in every suite, a chapel, kitchen, and dean's apartment.

In June of 1951 a gymnasium was erected during camp meeting week and occupied on the last Sabbath. A beautiful new church was completed in December 1966, which serves both the student body and the community. A new classroom-administration building, which combined all instructional facilities under one roof, was completed in 1967. In 1969 a new building was finished that doubled the boys' dormitory space and provided a new cafeteria. Six new homes for faculty had been added also by 1969. In 1974 one more home was built and funds were raised to complete the campus landscape plan.

Although situated in the shadow of the Rockies, Campion Academy depended for water first on a bucket brigade from the Hankins farm home, then on a water wagon, and later on cisterns. In 1937 a four-inch (10-centimeter) water main from the city of Loveland was installed, but by 1956 this was inadequate. In December 1962 connection was made with the Little Thompson Water Association, which provided the school with abundant pure water with good pressure.

Academy industries include Bake 'n' Serve; Silver State Packaging Company, contract packagers and producers of plastic bags; a literature evangelistic ministry; several cabinet shops; a greenhouse; and a graphics business. A press that operated from the earliest years was closed in 1955. The dairy was discontinued in 1974.

Student publications are the school annual, *Mountain Echoes*, and an annual literary journal called *Images*. A monthly newsletter put out by the administration is called the *Campus Communique*. In the past, students also published a paper called *The Frontiersman*, previously known as *The Reflector*, then *The Rocky Mountain Academician*.

Enrollment in 1974 was 324, of whom 256 were in dormitories. The 30-member staff exceeded in number the student enrollment of the first year. Because of demographics, enrollment dropped to about 180 by the 1992-1993 school year, with a third of these attending from the village. Hundreds of the 4,034 alumni graduated by 1993 fulfill the dream of the little group of missionary-minded students of 82 years before.

Principals: F. A. Page, 1907-1908; E. E. Farnsworth, 1908-1911; E. G. Salisbury, 1911-1913; C. L. Taylor, 1913-1915; W. A. Gosmer, 1915-1916; J. B. White, 1916-1917; D. D. Rees, 1917-1919; H. F. Saxton, 1919-1920; C. R. Kite, 1920-1921; H. E. Westermeyer,

1921-1925; W. E. Straw, 1925-1926; E. F. Heim, 1926-1935; G. M. Mathews, 1935-1937; E. E. Bietz, 1937-1941; W. H. Shephard, 1941-1944; V. W. Becker, 1944-1951; O. L. Heinrich, 1951-1955; L. G. Barker, 1955-1959; G. Glenn Davenport, 1959-1965; William Fuchs, 1965-1974; J. A. Shepard, 1974-1976; D. W. McNutt, 1976-1978; Richard Duerksen, 1978-1982; Don R. Keele, 1982-1986; Hal Hampton, 1986-1991; David P. Gillham, 1991- .

CAMPSITES. *See* Youth Campsites.

CANADA. A member nation of the British Commonwealth of Nations and of the United Nations with a land area of 3,851,809 square miles (9.9 million square kilometers) and a population (1994) of 28.1 million. The country is officially bilingual, with French and English as the two principal languages.

The history of the Seventh-day Adventist Church in Canada is given in separate articles under the names of the conferences and missions that compose the Seventh-day Adventist Church in Canada: *see* Alberta Conference; British Columbia Conference; Manitoba-Saskatchewan Conference; Maritime Conference; Ontario Conference; Quebec Seventh-day Adventist Conference; and Seventh-day Adventist Church in Newfoundland and Labrador.

Seventh-day Adventist Statistics. Canada, plus the French possessions of Saint Pierre and Miquelon (two islands off the coast of Newfoundland, with a combined population of 6,000), forms the Seventh-day Adventist Church in Canada, which in turn is part of the North American Division. Statistics (1992) for *Canada:* churches, 328; members, 42,083; church schools, 77; ordained ministers, 216; licensed ministers, 45; Bible instructors, 4; teachers, 330. Headquarters for the Seventh-day Adventist Church in Canada are at 1148 King Street East, Oshawa, Ontario, Canada. For statistics of the conferences and missions, *see* the article under each name.

Institutions. For institutions in Canada, *see* Seventh-day Adventist Church in Canada.

CANADA, SEVENTH-DAY ADVENTIST CHURCH IN. *See* Seventh-day Adventist Church in Canada.

CANADIAN ADVENTIST MESSENGER (1932- ; biweekly; weekly before May 2, 1933; supersedes *Eastern Canadian Messenger* and *Western Canadian Tidings;* files in GC). Official organ of the Canadian Union Conference. It replaced the organs of the two earlier Canadian Union conferences at the time these conferences were united into one in 1932. It began with volume 1, but it bore the same name as the much earlier *Canadian Union Messenger,* the organ of the original Canadian Union Conference (the eastern provinces only), issued from 1901, which was renamed *Eastern Canadian Messenger* in 1913, at the time the union was renamed. The *Western Canadian Tidings* was issued from 1911 to 1932.

In 1977 the name was changed from *Canadian Union Messenger* to *Canadian Adventist Messenger.* It is published monthly at Maracle Press, Limited, in Oshawa.

CANADIAN PUBLISHING ASSOCIATION. *See* Pacific Publishing Association.

CANADIAN SIGNS OF THE TIMES. *See Signs of the Times* (Oshawa, Ontario).

CANADIAN UNION COLLEGE. A coeducational boarding school operated as an accredited high school, as a junior college, and as a senior college in the field of theology by the Seventh-day Adventist Church in Canada at College Heights, in the province of Alberta, Canada, 100 miles (160 kilometers) north of the city of Calgary and two miles (three kilometers) north of the town of Lacombe (7,700 population). The 12 major buildings of the school plant are surrounded by more than 2,000 acres (800 hectares) of farmland belonging to the school. It was known successively as Alberta Industrial Academy (1907-1919), Canadian Junior College (1919-1946), and Canadian Union College (1946-). The 1992-1993 enrollment was 551 (353 college and 198 secondary).

Origin. At the General Conference session of 1901, held at Battle Creek, Michigan, J. W. Boynton, of Nebraska, was assigned to Alberta, then a mission field. At that time Alberta was part of the Northwest Territories (it became a province of the Dominion of Canada in 1905). Of the 50 members found by Pastor Boynton upon arrival, 35 were German believers meeting in a church at Leduc, 60 miles (100 kilometers) north of the present site of Canadian Union College. In 1906 at a camp meeting held in Red Deer, the Alberta Conference was organized, with C. A. Burman as the first conference president. By that time three church schools had been opened in the province, but the growing number of SDA families created a demand for education on higher levels. Upon the recommendation of the conference committee, Burman took charge of the new educational enterprise, and school opened in temporary quarters in the town of Leduc on Jan. 1, 1907. The initial enrollment of nine increased to 27 before the end of the three-month term.

The first faculty consisted of C. A. Burman, principal and Bible teacher; Mrs. C. A. Burman, teacher of the common branches of learning; W. O. James, instructor in methods of selling denominational books; and Mrs. L. T. Heaton, cook. This first school was established primarily to train colporteurs.

During the summer of 1907 the Alberta Conference solicited funds and borrowed money to purchase a farm on which to relocate the school. At a conference held at Lacombe, Alberta, July 1-7, 1907, C. A. Burman, J. W. Boynton, Henry Block, A. C. Anderson, Charles Rick, L. T. Heaton, and H. R. Kitto were chosen to select a site. The place chosen for the school, which was named the Alberta Industrial Academy, was a 160-acre (65-hectare) farm three miles (five kilometers) west of Leduc, on which were two two-story structures, a barn, granary, and other small buildings. The first regular school term of the Alberta Industrial Academy opened on Nov. 9, 1907, and lasted for six months. The enrollment that year was 36.

Relocation in Lacombe. By 1909 need for expansion was so evident that it was proposed to erect two additional buildings—a girls' dormitory with kitchen and dining hall, and a boys' dormitory with chapel and classrooms. Every member in the conference was asked to sell three copies each of Ellen White's books *Christ's Object Lessons* and *The Ministry of Healing* to help defray the expenses to be incurred. However, as a result of the counsel of W. A. Spicer, who visited Alberta in the spring of 1909, it was decided to seek a new location so that a school and a sanitarium might be operated jointly. A gift of $3,000 made possible the purchase of 198 acres (80 hectares) near Lacombe, sold to the conference by Andrew Gilmour. The plan was to move both the school in Leduc and a sanitarium in Edmonton to the new location at Lacombe. However, since greater emphasis was being placed upon the educational work, only the school plant was built on the new site (*see* Bethel Sanitarium).

J. I. Beardsley was chosen as principal of the new school. His arrival from South Dakota in the fall of 1909 permitted Burman to give his entire time to his duties as president of the Alberta Conference. Beardsley, who was connected with the school until 1914, functioned as business manager and teacher as well as principal. Associated with him were I. G. Ortner, preceptor, mathematics and German Bible teacher; Mrs. I. G. Ortner, German language and primary teacher; Mrs. Leona Burman, English teacher; Essie Barber, preceptress and matron; and Mrs. A. J. Beardsley, science and history teacher.

Because the school had neither the funds nor the time in that summer to erect the buildings needed, it was necessary during the first year to hold the school in a large barn. A number of girls lived in tents until the dormitory was ready for occupancy in December. The boys' dormitory was built in 1910. The 81 students who enrolled for the first year on the new campus endured many hardships because of the subzero weather and the primitive living conditions. Grades 7 through 10 were taught, based on the American four-unit high school system. The library consisted of 92 volumes. The first industry was a broom factory established during the 1911-1912 school year. Wages for student labor in those years averaged 10 cents an hour.

In the summer of 1912 construction began on the administration building, and other buildings were added as the school progressed. In 1913 the academy graduated the first class in its history, consisting of one student, Walter A. Clemenson.

Curriculum Changes. In 1915 E. D. Dick, of Lincoln, Nebraska, was elected principal. During his administration study was given to changing the school program from the four-unit plan copied from American schools to the spiral system followed in Canadian public schools; but it was several years before an agreement on this change was reached and the plan implemented.

Canadian Junior College. By 1918 denominational leaders realized that the curriculum should be extended to meet the needs of the growing constituency, and in February 1919 the school, still under Dick's administration, achieved junior college status. At the same time control of the institution was transferred from the Alberta Conference to the Western Canadian Union Conference, comprising the local conferences of British Columbia, Alberta, Saskatchewan, and Manitoba.

On May 28, 1930, a fire of incendiary origin burned three buildings, with a loss of $100,000. Reconstruction began almost at once despite a time of drought and financial depression. School was resumed in October in partially completed buildings.

Impetus for the growth of the school came from the Saskatchewan Conference when in 1931 its academy at Battleford closed and the students came to augment the enrollment of Canadian Junior College.

H. M. Johnson (1940) built large barns and expanded the farming operations.

Senior College Status in Theology. In the summer of 1945, E. E. Bietz, of South Dakota, became president of the institution. On the foundation laid by his predecessors, and with the active support of H. L. Rudy, president of the Canadian Union Conference, Bietz directed further physical and scholastic expansion. Work was begun in 1948 on a new dormitory for the young women, and a cafeteria building was constructed in 1950. Changes were made in the scholastic program; in the summer of 1946, the school was raised to senior college status in the area of theological training, and on Mar. 31, 1947, it was renamed Canadian Union College.

H. T. Johnson, who became president in 1951, undertook to expand the industrial program in order to provide more work for students. A building was erected to house the printing press and the bindery; the farm was enlarged and modernized; and a furniture factory was built, specializing in upholstered furniture. These industries furnish students more than $230,000 worth of work each year.

In 1959 the Canadian Union Conference and the Canadian Union College board voted to launch a 10-year, million-dollar expansion program to provide additional faculty housing and school buildings. A new $300,000 cafeteria, accommodating more than 500 students, and having the dining area and kitchen facilities both on the main floor, was completed in 1964. The former cafeteria building was remodeled to serve as a library.

N. O. Matthews, who became president in 1971, undertook to upgrade the academic program. Negotiations for affiliation with the University of Alberta, begun by the former president, P. G. Miller, were carried to completion; and beginning with the 1971-1972 school year, first-year university-level studies leading to a baccalaureate degree were offered in arts, science, education, business administration, physical education, dentistry, medicine, pharmacy, and household economics. During the summer of 1972, a $200,000 Career Center was constructed to accommodate nonuniversity-bound students in career-oriented areas such as upholstery, bookbinding, fiberglassing, general contracting, industrial management, commercial cooking, business administration, secretarial science, printing technology, and auto mechanics. The Career Center also provided for the needs of high school and college students interested in an industrial arts program, as well as offering adult continuing education courses. Because of decreased enrollment in the career-oriented areas, these programs were terminated.

In March 1982 the academy was separated from the college and named Parkview Adventist Academy.

In September 1991 the college received approval to offer the B.A. degree program (three-year) under the authority of the government of Alberta upon the recommendation of the Private Colleges Accreditation Board (PCAB).

The college has a provincially approved partner campus agreement, begun in 1979, with Union College to offer various four-year degree programs in such areas as Bachelor of Arts, Bachelor of Business Administration, Bachelor of Education, and Bachelor of Science. These degrees are scheduled to become Canadian Union College degrees by 1996.

La Sierra University offers a graduate, professional program through an extended campus program at Canadian Union College. Under this arrangement, which began in 1983, students may complete the requirements for a Master of Arts degree in Elementary Education in four summers. This program, which is accredited by the Western Association of Schools and Colleges, operates with the approval of the Alberta Ministry of Advanced Education.

Since 1989 Loma Linda University has offered a graduate, professional extended campus program at Canadian Union College. Under this arrangement, students may complete the requirements for a Master of Science degree in marriage and family therapy in two academic years. This program, which also is accredited by the Western Association of Schools and Colleges, operates with the approval of the Alberta Ministry of Advanced Education.

During the fall of 1992 the Department of Career and Continuing Education was established, which offers nonacademic career programs in office management.

Physical improvements since 1974 include a gym complex with swimming pool, Lakeview

Hall (college dormitory), a furniture factory, remodeled Education Department facility, remodeled Arts Department facility, additional classrooms in the old Career Center building, and the Chan Shun Science Center.

Principals and Presidents—Alberta Industrial Academy: C. A. Burman, 1907-1909; J. I. Beardsley, 1909-1914; C. A. Burman, 1914-1915; E. D. Dick, 1915-1919. *Canadian Junior College:* E. D. Dick, 1919-1922; C. L. Stone, 1922-1923; H. J. Klooster, 1923-1927; J. I. Beardsley, 1927-1928; C. O. Smith, 1928-1933; H. K. Martin, 1933-1937; L. W. Cobb, 1937-1940; H. M. Johnson, 1940-1945; E. E. Bietz, 1945-1946. *Canadian Union College:* E. E. Bietz, 1946-1951; H. T. Johnson, 1951-1965; R. A. Figuhr, 1965-1967; P. G. Miller, 1967-1971; N. O. Matthews, 1971-1982; Malcolm Graham, 1982-1987; Reo Ganson, 1987-1991; J. D. Victor Fitch, 1991- .

CANADIAN UNION CONFERENCE. *See* Seventh-day Adventist Church in Canada.

CANADIAN WATCHMAN. *See Signs of the Times* (Oshawa, Ontario).

CANADIAN WATCHMAN PRESS. *See* Pacific Publishing Association.

CANAL ZONE. *See* Panama.

CANARY ISLANDS. *See* Euro-Africa Division; Spain.

CANCELE SECONDARY SCHOOL. A coeducational boarding school operated by the Cape Conference, a section of the Southern Africa Union Conference, an attached field of the General Conference. It is situated near Mount Frere in Griqualand East, on 83 acres (35 hectares) of farmland, purchased from the Salvation Army, at the foot of a beautiful range of mountains, which can be seen from the outskirts of Umtata, the capital of the Transkei, 70 miles (110 kilometers) away. In 1974 there were 194 in the secondary classes, with seven teachers. The total enrollment, which included the higher primary, was 275, mainly Xhosa-speaking students.

Cancele was established through the self-sacrificing work of a succession of African and European teachers and missionaries. In 1927 J. N. de Beer and his family, with Charlie Mangcoto and Mountain Yaze, began mission work on the farm. Despite strong opposition, within a few months an elementary school was opened, and on Dec. 22, 1928, a church with a membership of 31 was organized.

The African district pastor who is in charge of the churches and companies in the surrounding district makes his home at the school. With the cooperation of members of the staff and the senior students, he cares for these companies and conducts public evangelism.

In 1954 secondary schoolwork was added and the school became the Cancele Secondary School. The majority of pupils continue their education at Bethel College, where a strong spiritual program is maintained.

Principals: I. J. van Zyl, 1954-1959; G. P. Magee, 1960-1963; A. Koopedi, 1964-1965; K. O. Magenu, 1966-1967; B. B. Mafuya, 1968-1971; P. Ntshangase, 1972-1976; J. J. Mdakane, 1977-1979; G. B. Yaze, 1980-1984; S.B.M. Baduza, 1984-1987; J. M. Skosana, 1988-1990; E. T. Kwanimi, 1990-1992; H. K. Kachoka, 1993- .

CANRIGHT, DUDLEY MARVIN (1840-1919). A onetime Seventh-day Adventist minister and writer who renounced his church affiliation and acquired prominence as the champion of theological opposition to SDA teachings. Ordained to the SDA ministry in 1865, he became a forceful preacher and a polemic writer of considerable ability. He took a prominent part in church administration and for two years was a member of the General Conference Committee. Capable and successful, he became intolerant of the opinions of others and chafed under the administrative control of his fellow ministers and the close guidance of testimonies from Ellen White. He also showed instability of temperament, losing heart and doubting his faith when disagreeable experiences came to him. Several times before his separation from the church he left the ministry, then returned and carried on with great vigor. A vision of greater achievement in the service of a cause more popular than that of SDAs finally led him to resign and sever his connection with the church in February 1887. In April of the same year he was ordained to the ministry of the Baptist church at Otsego, Michigan, his home. Two years later he resigned from this position and devoted his time to writing against SDAs. In 1889 he published a book entitled *Seventh-Day Adventism Renounced.* In it he set forth his arguments against the doctrine of the imminent return of Christ, denied the binding nature of the Ten

Commandments, rejected the ministry of Ellen White, ridiculed the church leaders, and forecast the early disappearance of the SDA movement.

Canright's views are reviewed, analyzed, and refuted in W. H. Branson's book *In Defense of the Faith* (Review and Herald, 1933).

CANTON MIDDLE SCHOOL. *See* Hong Kong Adventist College.

CANTON TRAINING INSTITUTE. *See* Hong Kong Adventist College.

CAP-HAITIEN ADVENTIST ACADEMY (Collège Adventiste Du Cap-Haitien). A coeducational secondary school owned and operated by the North Haiti Mission. In 1963 the North Haiti Mission committee took an action adding the secondary classes to the existing elementary school known as École Toussaint Louverture. At the end of the same year, the Franco-Haitian Union added its approval.

For the school year 1964-1965, the school offered the equivalent to seventh, eighth, and ninth grades, with an enrollment of 40 students. Amos Bossou, the principal of the elementary section, was chosen to be the principal of that new section.

Elie Henry, who became education secretary for the North Haiti Mission in January 1965, succeeded Bossou, who was called to be a district leader. In May 1965 the school was surveyed by Dr. Walton Brown, then Inter-American Division secretary of education. His report was encouraging, and the school was recognized by the Inter-American Division Department of Education. Before the end of 1965 the Haitian government's Department of Education also granted accreditation to the school.

In the beginning the development was slow. But under the leadership of Carolus Augustin the school made appreciable progress and the enrollment continued to increase.

In 1990 a vocational section was added. As of 1993 enrollment in the secondary school was 1,250 with 144 in the vocational section. In 1993 the headmaster was Daniel Calixte.

CAPE CONFERENCE. *See* South Africa, Republic of.

CAPE SANITARIUM. A medical institution operated from 1904 to 1934 about nine miles (14 kilometers) from Cape Town, South Africa, on a piece of property left vacant by the closing of the Plumstead Orphanage. This orphanage, begun in 1895 on another site (Timor Hall Estate), had been donated by the Mrs. E. A. Wessels family, and had cared for from 10 to 20 children for almost 10 years.

Dr. George Thomason, his wife, and his sister, Ida Thomason, arrived in South Africa from the United States in 1904 to operate the new sanitarium. Within a year there were no empty beds. Ida Thomason, who was a graduate nurse, was the matron and organized a nurse's training course. Among the young men and women trained here were some who entered mission service in the countries lying north of the Limpopo River. By 1908 the assets of the institution had risen to £6,270 and the bed capacity had increased to 24. In 1910, 10 more beds were added. In that same year Gen. Louis Botha, then serving as the first prime minister of the Union of South Africa, was a patient in the sanitarium. In addition to its other services, the institution served as a haven of peace for the missionaries who arrived from the north seeking to rebuild their health after arduous years in the tropics.

In 1911 Dr. Thomason was called to become medical secretary of the General Conference. However, Ida Thomason served the sanitarium until 1933.

In the middle 1920s the Cape Sanitarium became the Plumstead Nursing Home. Unable to survive the Depression of the early 1930s, it was closed in 1934.

CAPE VERDE. A republic located in the Atlantic Ocean. An archipelago situated off the westernmost projection of Africa, it was discovered in 1460 by the Portuguese, and is composed of 10 main islands with about 425,000 inhabitants (1994 estimate), most of whom are of Portuguese descent.

Seventh-day Adventist Statistics. In January 1974 the Cape Verde Islands were joined with Guinea-Bissau in forming the Guinea-Cape Verde Mission. The territory of Cape Verde presently constitutes the Cape Verde Mission. It is a part of the Sahel Union Mission, which in turn is a part of the Africa-Indian Ocean Division. Statistics (1992) for *Cape Verde:* churches, 8; members, 1,483; church or elementary schools, 1; ordained ministers, 4; credentialed missionaries, 2; licensed ministers, 2; teachers, 2. The Cape Verde Mission headquarters are in Praia.

Development of Seventh-day Adventist Work. The first SDA to visit Cape Verde appears to have been L. C. Chadwick, who stopped there in October 1892. In 1933 Antonio J. Gomes, who had emigrated to the United States, returned for a visit to his native village of Nossa Senhora do Monte on the island of Brava. Being an SDA, he aroused an interest in the teachings of his church. To follow up the interest, A. F. Raposo and his family were sent to Brava from Portugal, arriving on July 16, 1935. A Sabbath school of about 50 persons was organized in N. S. do Monte, and later another Sabbath school was organized in Vila de Nova Sintra. In March 1936, 15 persons were baptized, and in 1938 Gomes erected a building at N. S. do Monte to serve as a church, school, and residence. Pamphlets were sent from Brava to the other islands, and soon letters were received from São Vicente, São Tiago, and Fogo from those who had become interested in the SDA faith. Other missionary families were sent out, and now SDA work is established on each of these islands as well as on Brava.

CAPE VERDE MISSION. *See* Africa-Indian Ocean Division; Cape Verde.

CAPRICORN ADVENTIST RETIREMENT VILLAGE. *See* Adventist Retirement Village (South Queensland Conference).

CAPRIVI ZIPFEL (also known as Caprivi Strip). A long narrow strip of land extending from the extreme northeast of Namibia (formerly South-West Africa) to the Zambezi River. It measures 300 miles (480 kilometers) in length and is nowhere more than 50 miles (80 kilometers) wide. The 1993 population was approximately 50,000. Its existence results from the aim of the German authorities at the end of the nineteenth century to unite their colony in South-West Africa with that in East Africa. The name is derived from that of Count Leo de Caprivi, who succeeded Prince Bismarck as imperial chancellor in 1890. Under his regime the area was ceded by Britain in 1893. The Caprivi Zipfel is almost dead flat, and having several large rivers, is of potential importance to the possible reclamation of the Kalahari Desert. Because of its isolation from South-West Africa, it was joined to Bechuanaland after World War I, and since 1939 has been administered from Pretoria. During the Bechuanaland administration of Caprivi its people approached the government in Mafikeng to send missionaries to teach the people the gospel and how to read and write. W. H. Anderson, who was then in Mafikeng, received the message and began immediately to respond to the call. He visited two regional chiefs in 1919 and agreed to send teachers. Two were sent from Rusangu Mission in what was then Northern Rhodesia, now Zambia. They were Henry Mabona and Nathan Muyapekwa. A school was opened in 1920 at Ikaba, marking the beginning of Seventh-day Adventist work.

In April 1921 G. L. Willmore was called from Congo (now Zaïre), where he was serving, to go to Caprivi. He was joined by N. Bulgin as the first White missionaries to the country. Schools were opened all over the area with a mission station at Katima Mulilo. Other missionaries were sent as evangelists. The last missionary was P. W. Owen. During his term of service the entire Caprivi work was shut down in 1943. The torch of the gospel continued to shine through dedicated former teachers. Men such as Joel Mwilima, Dickson Mutabelezi, Davison Mubonenwa, and Mixon Fwambi continued to hold believers in the faith for years without pay or encouragement from foreign workers until 1949, when W. M. Cooks began coming back once a year for camp meeting. He continued to strengthen the work until his retirement in 1972.

In that year the Caprivi Mission was organized as a part of the Zambesi Union, which was in turn part of the Trans-Africa Division. In 1975 there were nine churches, with a membership of 1,328.

At the end of 1972 the Caprivi Strip Field was organized. It continued to operate under the Zambesi Union until the end of 1981. In January 1982 the Caprivi Strip Field became the sixth suborganization of the Southern Union (Africa). In 1984 the territory was extended to take in the unentered territories of Kavango, with a population of about 170,000, and Tsumkwe, with about 10,000. These regions have been known as North East Namibia since declaring independence in 1990. In 1993 the field, by the authority of the Southern Africa Union, changed its name to North-East Namibia Field. In that year there were 28 churches with a membership of 6,525.

CARCICH, THEODORE (1905-1988). Administrator. Born in Yugoslavia, he began his service as pastor-evangelist in the New York Conference, eventually moving to the Southern New England Conference, where he became president. He continued his presidency in the Illinois, Washington, and Central union conferences until his election as vice president of the General Conference for the North American Division in 1962. In 1966 he became a general vice president of the General Conference. He died Feb. 12, 1988, near Moscow, Idaho.

CARDEY, ELMER LEE (1884-1973). Pioneer, missionary, evangelist, administrator. A native of Wisconsin, he studied at Bethel Academy in that state and at Emmanuel Missionary College in Michigan. In 1906 he went to the Bay Islands in Central America. The Bay Islands Mission was the first to be organized in the Inter-American Division, and Elder Cardey became its first president. He returned to the United States, and in 1911 worked in the Atlantic Union, where he launched the first Bible correspondence course in the Seventh-day Adventist denomination. He engaged in evangelistic work in New York state and served as chaplain of the New England Memorial Hospital for four years. For a time he served as president of the Southern New England Conference and then went to Lincoln, Nebraska, for pastoral work.

In 1936 he became secretary of the Lay Activities Department of the Central Union Conference and then went to Lincoln, Nebraska, for pastoral work. A year later he was called to evangelism in the Columbia Union.

In 1938 he was appointed to evangelism in South Africa. Three new churches were raised up in Cape Town, the Intermediate School for European Youth was established, and a Bible correspondence school was organized.

In 1950 he returned to the United States, where he established a Bible correspondence school in the Southern Union Conference. More than 1 million students were enrolled during his leadership. He retired in 1963 after 58 years of service to the church.

CAREMARK BEHAVIORAL HEALTH SERVICES provides a full spectrum of psychiatric services in the Portland, Oregon, area. Its main offices are located on the campus of Portland Adventist Medical Center.

Programs offered include admissions coordination, child and adolescent treatment, adult partial hospitalization, adult psychiatric inpatient, ancillary services, chemical dependency treatment, eating disorders, and senior day treatment.

CareMark Behavioral Health Services was created in 1993 and is jointly owned and operated by Adventist Health System/West (Portland Adventist Medical Center's parent organization) and Legacy Health System (the parent organization for five area hospitals).

Medical Director: E. Duncan, 1993- .

Chief Executive Officer: L. D. Dodds, 1993- .

CAREY, ALEXANDER (1882-1970). Treasurer and manager. A native of London, he was among the first 12 to gain a scholarship from London County Council to Sir Walter St. John College.

In 1915 he was introduced to the Seventh-day Adventist message through a tent campaign. When the tent burned to the ground, Carey opened his home for the meetings and soon after took his stand for the truth.

In 1920 he went to Stanborough Park, Watford, beginning denominational service as treasurer in Granose Foods, Ltd. He then served as manager of the Stanborough Sanitarium for a brief period before transferring to the Stanborough College as manager in 1925. Three years later he was asked to serve as secretary-treasurer of the British Union Conference, which position he held for 22 years. When he was nearing 70, he became honorary secretary of Worldwide Advent Missions and served in this capacity for 17 years.

CARIBBEAN UNION COLLEGE. A coeducational boarding school on the college level, with four-year degrees being offered in religion, theology, education, history, social studies, English, business, biology, and home economics. Associate degrees are offered in business, office management, elementary teaching, computer science, and religion. Minors are offered in industrial education, modern languages, music, chemistry, health, and other areas.

The college is located in Trinidad, West Indies. It is situated on 345 acres (140 hectares) of land in the beautiful Maracas Valley in the northwestern part of the island, about nine miles (14 kilometers) northeast of the capital city of Port of Spain. The mission of the college is to develop the whole person—mental, physical, social, spiritual, emotional, and vocational; to provide trained personnel for the church and its institutions as well as the wider community; and to enable students to continue their education at other institutions of higher learning.

The college is operated by the Caribbean Union of Seventh-day Adventists, which has a constituency of 121,882. The college draws students from inside and outside the Caribbean, extending as far as Europe, Africa, and North and South America. These students represent the four major languages of English, Spanish, French, and Dutch. The college curriculum is accredited by the SDA Board of Regents and in 1985 became affiliated with Andrews University through actions by the higher organizations and the boards of both institutions. At the end of 1993 the college enrollment was 660, with 46 faculty members and 30 part-time instructors. A secondary school with an enrollment of 450 and an elementary school are also operated in conjunction with the college.

East Caribbean Training School. The college was established in August 1927 under the name East Caribbean Training School. Its founder and first principal was C. J. Boyd, who was joined the day after his arrival by R.S.J. Hamilton and his wife, together with Eloise Williams and Linda Austin. (In 1963 Ms. Austin completed 36 years of continuous service in the school.) The school opened with five teachers and one student, a Trinidadian. By the middle of October other students had arrived from British Guiana, from some of the northern islands, and from Trinidad itself, increasing the enrollment to 26. At that time the school's main building contained the assembly room, the dining room, the business office, and the women's sleeping quarters. The men slept in tapia huts. Later a men's dormitory was built.

In 1929 the school was renamed Caribbean Training College. The next year two industries were begun—the college press and the broom shop. Agriculture and animal husbandry flourished.

By 1931 an enriched high school program on the American unit system was well established, and in 1935 the first graduating class of three students completed the twelfth grade. In 1938 another three students were graduated. From that time onward, except for 1941, yearly graduating classes became the rule. Also in 1938 the administration building was erected.

Caribbean Training College. A well-defined college preparatory course was organized in 1945, and in 1948 Caribbean Training College was made a junior college with two-year college courses in theology, teacher training, business, and secretarial science. A science department also was begun.

In response to the insistence on a type of education that from a scholastic point of view would meet the needs of an area with British culture, the secondary program was changed from the unit system to the British spiral system, leading to the Cambridge School Certificate or London General Certificate of Education. However, the pattern followed in the postsecondary or junior college section of the school remained unchanged until 1954. At that time the teacher-training program, on its purely professional levels, was modified to meet the requirements of the government of Trinidad and Tobago. The elementary school also was developed at this time, and the institution was then recognized as a teacher-training college qualified to offer candidates for the Trained Teachers' Certificate. The physical plant was enlarged and improved: the chapel was extended, a dining room and teachers' cottages were built, and the dormitories were enlarged. The print shop was expanded and became a profitable school industry. Several years later a laundry was built.

Caribbean Union College. In 1956 the name of the school was changed to Caribbean Union College. In 1957 the offices of president and business manager, until then united in one person, were separated, and B. R. Hamilton was chosen as the first business manager. By 1962 liberal arts, music, and secondary teacher-training courses were added to the junior college curriculum. This last course involves preparation for the London General Certificate of Education (advanced level) in addition to some professional training.

From 1935 to 1962, 370 students graduated from the high school and junior college. The spiritual program is maintained to fulfill the school's purpose to be "a light to the Caribbean." The majority of the ministerial workers and teachers in the union are alumni of the college.

In 1970 the Theology Department of the college was upgraded from a fourteenth-grade program to the sixteenth-grade B.Th. program. The college graduated its first B.Th. graduates in 1972.

In 1973 the college suffered two disastrous fires. The first, in March, destroyed the administration building. This building, which also housed the chapel, was built in 1939. The second fire, which came six months later, in September, completely wiped out such industries as the broom factory, the woodwork and maintenance shops, and the college store. The college program staggered under the heavy loss.

By mid-1974 two new important buildings were constructed—a new industrial arts center for teaching industrial skills, and a new industrial building for housing the new woodworking industry. A new broom industry building was built, and later the woodworking building was renovated to house the College Health Food Industry. The school operates a modern college press. A three-story science complex was completed in 1992. This building also houses the administrative offices.

Principals/Presidents: C. J. Boyd, 1927-1928; L. H. Gardiner, 1928-1930; R.S.J. Hamilton, 1930-1938; M. E. Smith, 1938-1941; C. E. Stenberg, 1941-1944; R. L. Badgley (acting), 1944; A. R. Tucker, 1944-1950; P. W. Manuel, 1950-1957; B. L. Archbold, 1957-1962; B.G.O. French, 1962-1966; K. E. Forde, 1966-1971; W. U. Campbell, 1971-1972; B. W. Benn, 1972-1977; B. N. Josiah, 1977-1980; J. J. Ambrose (acting), 1980-1981; M. O. Manley, 1981-1983; V. E. Andrews, 1983-1990; S. A. Lashley, 1990- .

CARIBBEAN UNION CONFERENCE. *See* Antigua and Barbuda; Barbados; Guyana; Inter-American Division; Leeward and Windward Islands; Netherlands Antilles; Suriname; Trinidad and Tobago; Virgin Islands.

CARIBBEAN UNION GLEANINGS (1930- ; 1930-1943 as *Field Gleanings From the Caribbean Union;* monthly; incomplete files in GC). The official organ of the Caribbean Union Conference, free to constituent church members. Upon the publication of this union paper in December 1930, two earlier local conference papers were discontinued: *Field Gleanings From the South Caribbean* (1922-1930), of the South Caribbean Conference, and *The Outlook,* of the Leeward Islands Conference.

CARIBOO ADVENTIST ACADEMY. A grade K-12 school operated by the Williams Lake and Cariboo Central churches, which have a combined membership of 370. It is located on a 6.5-acre (2.6-hectare) site on South Lakeside Road, two miles (three kilometers) from the city of Williams Lake, in British Columbia. The academy is accredited both denominationally and provincially. Secondary enrollment in 1993 was 63, with a staff of 16.

The school had its beginnings in the logging camps of the D. Basabara and the Jacobson brothers in the 1950s. When they moved their logging companies into the city of Williams Lake, the school opened there in 1959. As the enrollment grew and the program developed, the school became inadequate in physical plant and location. In January 1971 the new school was opened on the present site. By 1973 a fifth classroom and a science room were added. In 1979 an expansion of the existing building provided for home economics classes, an industrial education workshop, and a general purpose room. In 1987 a gymnasium classroom complex was added. The school now has adequate facilities and a well-rounded program.

Principals: Elsie Magoon; Angus Campbell; Ann Friesen; D. Vanderwerff, 1965-1970; C. Nawalkowski, 1970-1971; W. Van Shiek, 1971-1973; R. Martin, 1973-1975; J. Waters, 1975-1982; O. Lofton-Brook, 1982-1988; G. Proctor, 1988-1989; M. Graham, 1990-1991; L. Murrin, 1991- .

CARLSTJERNA, CARL OSCAR (1880-1953). Minister and administrator in Sweden and Finland. He was born in Odensjö, Halland, Sweden, under the name Carlsson and at the age of 19 was baptized by Birger Andersson. In 1902 he completed the three-year worker training course at the Nyhyttan mission school. In 1905 he preached in several places in Sweden and was ordained to the ministry in 1911. In 1912, when the South Swedish Mission was organized, he became its president. Two years later, in 1914, he became president of the Finland Conference. While in Finland he met a general's daughter, Dagmar Tavaststjerna, and married her in 1917. At the same time he adopted the family name Carlstjerna. The same year he returned to Sweden to head the Central Swedish Conference. In 1920 he left the presidency of the conference to assume charge of the Nyhyttan mission school *(see* Swedish Junior College and Seminary), where he remained until 1929. He then became the first president of the Finland-Swedish Conference. From 1932 until about 1940 he was chaplain of Hultafors Sanitarium.

CARMEL ADVENTIST COLLEGE. A coeducational boarding school on the senior high school level, operated by the Trans-Australian Union Conference, near Perth, Australia. The 1993 enrollment was 180, with an instructional staff of 18. This school offers courses leading to the West Australian Higher Secondary certificate, which is a prerequisite to taking advanced studies at Avondale College.

Carmel College began as the Darling Range School, established early in 1907 to provide local educational facilities for secondary students who otherwise would have had to go to the Avondale School for Christian Workers (now Avondale College) at Cooranbong, New South Wales.

On hearing of the search by the West Australia Conference officers for a suitable site for the proposed boarding school, Charles E. Ashcroft, one of the early Seventh-day Adventist converts, offered to donate his holdings situated 17 miles (27 kilometers) east of Perth in the Heidelberg (now Bickley) Valley in the Darling Range. On this property was believed to be the best spring in the district. After an inspection by L. V. Finster, the conference president, H. R. Martin, and the full committee, Ashcroft's offer was accepted and work was begun immediately.

H. R. Martin, who was appointed "teacher and foreman," recalled 19 years later, "I was asked to take charge and build up an intermediate training school, and as a start one pound was given me to buy an ax, grindstone, and digging fork." By the middle of 1907 the unfinished six-room residence already on the land was completed, and an annex built providing a kitchen, dining room, chapel, and recitation room.

Church members demonstrated their interest in the venture by contributing both time and money. The school opened Jan. 13, 1907, with only two students. By the end of the first week the number had grown to five, and by the close of the year to 14.

In 1908 a building program was initiated that was to be completed in three stages, envisaging a central administration block, with two dormitory wings to be built on a more desirable spot higher up the valley. When the 1909 school year opened, the first wing, a two-story wooden building, was sufficiently advanced to accommodate 30 women and a number of staff members. The men continued to occupy the original building. Stage two was completed in 1914—the central portion, containing a dining room and kitchen on the ground floor, and a chapel and classrooms above. Late in 1924 stage three began, when the men's old hall was demolished and the timber used to construct the second wing, completed in 1926, although occupied in 1925. H. R. Martin was both architect and builder. Also erected were several faculty homes and a laundry and bake house at the rear of the main building. In 1926 the school was renamed the West Australian Missionary School, and in 1934 the West Australian Missionary College. The present name dates from 1968.

In 1958 the Charles Ashcroft Hall, a single-story structure in brick and tile, affording accommodations for 50 men, was completed. In 1961 a similar women's dormitory, Kathleen Giblett Hall, was built.

In 1974 plans were laid for the construction of the first stage of a new central administration and classroom block that was erected in 1975.

The college estate was gradually enlarged, until it totaled 138 acres (56 hectares), of which 35 acres (14 hectares) are in orchard, mainly stone-fruit and citrus, and 45 acres (18 hectares) in pasture.

Principals: H. R. Martin, 1907-1910; R. W. Brown, 1911-1912; W. J. Smith, 1913-1916; A. H. Piper, 1917-1918; J. Mills, 1919; E. Rosendahl, 1920-1927; A. E. Speck, 1928-1932; C. S. Palmer, 1933-1934; T. C. Lawson, 1935-1939; A.F.J. Kranz, 1940-1946; A. W. Martin, 1947; C. S. Palmer, 1948-1950; R. Reye, 1951-1958; A. W. Martin, 1959; R. Reye, 1960-1965; H. W. Hammond, 1966-1970; J. G. Litster, 1971-1975; R. S. Bower, 1976-1980; J. Nicholls, 1981-1982; G. R. Shields, 1983-1984; D. W. Reye, 1985-1987; R. T. Skipworth, 1988-1989; D. J. McClintock, 1990-1994; B. L. Mercer, 1994- .

CARO, MARGARET (1848-1938). Dentist, Bible instructor. Born in Wellington, New Zealand, she accepted the Seventh-day Adventist message under the evangelistic ministry of A. G. Daniells in 1888. While attending the first camp meeting in the Southern Hemisphere, she became closely associated with Ellen White. When Mrs. White was holding meetings in Wellington, she sent for Margaret Caro to extract her teeth and fit dentures. Large portions of *The Desire of Ages* were written while her gums were healing. Dr. Caro later attended Avondale College, where she trained under W. W. Prescott and engaged in Bible work in the North New South Wales Conference. She spent the remainder of her life in New Zealand in a continuing advocacy of health reform and was remembered for strength of character, courage, and enthusiasm for God's work.

CAROLINA CONFERENCE. A unit of church organization comprising the territory of North Carolina (except Cherokee County, which is in the Georgia-Cumberland Conference) and South Carolina. *(See also*

South Atlantic Conference.) Statistics (1993): churches, 94; companies, 8; members, 12,121; church schools, 34 (7 junior academies); ordained ministers, 61; licensed ministers, 17; church school teachers, 54. Headquarters: 6000 Conference Drive, Charlotte, North Carolina. The conference forms part of the Southern Union.

Institutions. Mount Pisgah Academy.

Local churches—*North Carolina*: Albemarle, Arden, Asheboro, Asheville, Banner Elk, Brevard, Bryson City, Burlington, Burnsville, Charlotte, Concord, Delco, Durham Five Oaks, Edneyville, Elizabeth City, Elizabethtown, Erwin Hills (Leicester), Fairview, Fayetteville, Fletcher, Franklin, Gastonia, Goldsboro, Greensboro, Greenville, Hendersonville, Hickory, High Point, Hillsborough, Jacksonville, Kernersville, Kinston, Lawndale, Lenoir, Lexington, Lincolnton, Marion, Matthews, Mills River, Mocksville, Morganton, Mount Pisgah Academy, New Bern, Pembroke, Pittsboro, Plymouth, Raleigh, Roanoke Rapids, Rocky Mount, Rutherfordton, Salisbury, Statesville, Sylva, Table Rock, Thomasville, Tryon, Upward, Valle Crucis, Warrensville, Washington, Waynesville, Whiteville, Wilkesboro, Wilmington, Wilson, Winston-Salem. *South Carolina:* Aiken, Anderson, Beaufort, Blythewood, Camden, Charleston, Clinton, Columbia, Columbia (First Korean), Florence, Greenville, Greenwood, Hilton Head, Mount Pleasant, Myrtle Beach, North Augusta, Orangeburg, Pickens, Rock Hill, Salem, South Congaree, Spartanburg, Summerville, Sumter, Union, Westminster, Woodruff, York.

Companies—*North Carolina:* Charlotte (Korean, Spanish), Greensboro (Korean, Spanish), Hickory (Spanish), Highlands, Laurel (Spanish), Rockingham. *South Carolina:* Columbia (Spanish).

History. *Beginnings of the Work in North Carolina.* Seventh-day Adventist work in the Carolinas began in the 1870s in the heart of the North Carolina mountains 50 miles (80 kilometers) and more from the nearest railroad. When SDA papers sent by two women in the north to Watauga County fell into the hands of William Norwood and Larkin Townsend, they became agitated over the Sabbath question, especially when their pastor could give them no Bible proof for Sunday. A mountain preacher, Samuel H. Kime, also received publications. Almost simultaneously these three men, as well as William M. Baird, W. W. Jestes, Columbus (Lum) Fox, and Harrison Clark, began observing the Sabbath. In response to their request for help, C. O. Taylor, who had been one of the first SDA preachers in New York state, visited them as he and his wife traveled south in 1879 and conducted a series of evangelistic meetings at Shull's Mill, six miles (10 kilometers) from Valle Crucis.

That year a church was organized in Watauga County, known as the Watauga church. The next year J. O. Corliss, sent by the General Conference to survey and foster the work in the South, visited the members in the mountains, and on Nov. 21, 1880, he ordained L. P. Hodges and licensed C. F. Fox and Samuel H. Kime. In 1883 he ordained Kime, whose son Stewart later became a president of the conference.

The present Valle Crucis church, originally called the Bethel church, was organized by Hodges in the home of Larkin Townsend on May 15, 1881, with 11 charter members (including some from Banner Elk in an adjoining county, where a separate church was organized in 1912). The Bethel members walked as far as 10 miles (16 kilometers) to help build their church on Dutch Creek in 1882, on land donated by Larkin Townsend. This is believed to be the first church building erected by SDAs in the South.

For many years colporteurs selling Bibles and religious books were the only full-time workers in North Carolina, although occasionally a minister would spend a few months traveling through the state visiting interested groups.

S. H. Kime wrote in 1882 that there was no full-time minister in the state. In 1889, three years after North Carolina had been made a mission field, it had one minister, J. W. Bagby; there were about 80 members, mostly in the western part of the state, a state tract society, and a Sabbath school association.

In 1889 W. L. Killen and another colporteur sold the book *Bible Readings for the Home Circle* to several families in Stokes County. The Toab Young, Will Young, and F. A. Slate families soon became convicted of the Bible truths concerning the seventh-day Sabbath and the return of Christ.

The Slate family sold their lumber business in Stokes County in 1904 and moved to Kernersville, where a printing business was established near the present town square. A few Sabbathkeepers met faithfully in the homes of the Slates, the H. R. Hahns, or often in rooms above the printshop. In 1907 Elder Wood held meetings in the Macy Grove School building.

Other ministers who helped establish the little group were George Thompson, Walter Nash, and George Brown. A number of denominational workers came from this small group. Joe Crews, former speaker of the Amazing Facts radio program, was a grandson of Arch McDowell, one of the first members of the Kernersville church. Joseph Slate spent 28 years in mission service in Africa and a number of the Slate family members gave many years of service in the General Conference or the Review and Herald.

Late in 1890 the General Conference transferred from Kansas City a colporteur and licensed preacher who was afterward ordained—D. T. Shireman (pronounced "Sherman"), of Iowa, a former brickmason, carpenter, and mechanic. Spending the first winter in Watauga County, he preached at Clark's Creek and Bethel, and held meetings on Grandfather Mountain; in 1891 he settled in Asheville. In his house-to-house evangelism he sent names of interested persons to SDAs in the North with a request for papers and personal letters. His reports in the *Review and Herald* record the beginnings of churches at Asheville (organized 1894) and at Greensboro (organized 1895). The latter was not the present Greensboro church established 40 years later; it moved within two years to Lego (and from this Lego church the present High Point church traces its origin). He also reports converts in many places where churches developed much later—in the southeast; at Durham (where there was a company in 1898, a church in 1914); at Raleigh (a company in 1897; a church, from a new start, in 1932).

Beginnings in South Carolina. C. O. Taylor had briefly visited several interested people in Darlington County in 1879, yet as late as 1891 not even a colporteur had been sent in, and there was not one known SDA in South Carolina. Then in 1893 another minister, E. W. Webster, from Wisconsin, was sent to Spartanburg, and soon afterward J. O. Johnston (not yet ordained) arrived at Greenville from North Carolina. Both used Shireman's correspondence method. In the spring of 1894 Webster and Johnston held a series of SDA tent meetings—the first in South Carolina—at Brushy Creek, a rural community near Greenville. The first church was organized at Spartanburg in August 1894. The Brushy Creek church (organized 1895) had the first church building (1897).

Meanwhile in October 1894 I. E. Kimball, a minister from Vermont, settled in Spartanburg, and Webster seems to have returned north. Johnston and Kimball held meetings in many places. They wrote in the *Review and Herald* of encountering kindness and prejudice, much indifference, some deep interest, and few converts. Kimball's report, from Greenwood, of visiting and giving Bible studies, especially among the "aristocratic and wealthy," was not the usual pattern.

Late in 1896 the Kimballs went to Charleston. At first they made personal contacts in churches and homes, then held small meetings in the WCTU chapel. From 1898 they operated night schools for African-Americans and a welfare mission for White unfortunates. In 1899 there was a group of eight White and eight African-American converts, all recipients of "Christian help work" apparently from the mission. A short-lived church of 17 was organized early in 1900 (the present Charleston church had a later beginning; it was organized in 1913). Kimball worked among the African-Americans also in Georgetown, South Carolina, and in Wilmington, North Carolina, early in 1901, then left for Virginia.

Meanwhile, B. F. Gowdy, a newly licensed preacher from Minnesota who replaced Johnston late in 1897, reported various meetings, mostly in the western part of the state. At Chick Springs a church was organized in January 1899, which briefly operated a church school and disbanded after 11 months when all but one family moved away. In February 1900 Gowdy opened an industrial school near Oakwood, Aiken County, in a tenant farmer's cabin, erecting "a substantial building" a year later. By the beginning of 1902, apparently, Gowdy's health broke, and he went West. South Carolina had no SDA worker until 1904.

Conference Organizations. Soon after the General Conference District No. 2 became the Southern Union Conference (spring 1901), the North and South Carolina missions were combined and organized Sept. 1, 1901, as the Carolina Conference, with J. O. Johnston as president. There were three ministers, four licentiates (all in North Carolina after Gowdy left), 10 churches, seven companies, and a total membership of 300. In February 1904 North Carolina was made a conference, and South Carolina, with two churches and 76 members, became a mission under the Southern Union Conference. South Carolina became a conference in 1907, with R. T. Nash as president, with four churches and 100 members. The North Carolina Conference published the *North Carolina Messenger,* which was discontinued in 1907 with the appearance of the Southern Union publication *Report of Progress.*

During the time the Southern Union was divided (1909-1932) the Carolinas belonged to the Southeastern Union Conference. The two conferences were reunited in 1918 as the Carolina Conference, comprising all of South Carolina and that part of North Carolina lying east of Ashe, Watauga, Avery, McDowell, and Henderson counties (from 1933, all of North Carolina except Cherokee County). The conference headquarters were established at Charlotte, North Carolina, and a church was organized there the next year. The conference office maintained its headquarters in Charlotte and built a new office in 1975 at 6000 Conference Drive. The 1990s brought about growth and change with plans for a new office in 1994-1995.

New Beginnings in South Carolina. In 1904 E. W. Webster returned as superintendent of the South Carolina Mission with another minister, R. T. Nash; a licensed preacher, E. W. Carey; and a colporteur, C. F. Dart. They visited the two surviving churches of a decade earlier (Spartanburg and Brushy Creek) and small groups of members and held evangelistic meetings. The next year, when meetings were begun at Columbia, the group included a Bible instructor supported by the Michigan Conference who was "gaining access to some of the best homes with *The Family Bible Teacher*" and holding Bible studies, although the people were "very cautious." The first camp meeting in the state was held near Spartanburg in 1905. In 1907 the Spartanburg church acquired a building, paid for partly by offerings solicited in the *Review and Herald.* With stronger evangelistic help, more churches were established—for example, Charleston in 1913, Columbia and Greenville in 1916. When the two Carolinas reunited in 1918, South Carolina had 22 churches and 495 members, but only seven church buildings and seven church schools.

At that time the outgoing South Carolina president attributed the slowness of progress in that conference to the lack of workers who could stay long enough to build up permanent results; to the difficulty of working for the upper class, who were harder to reach; and to the frequent lack of adaptability to local situations. Spalding writes similarly *(Origin and History of SDAs,* vol. 2, pp. 168-171) of the early SDA difficulties in the South in general. In South Carolina in particular, conservatism and reluctance to accept new and unpopular religious ideas were strong.

Self-supporting Work in North Carolina Mountains. In the first decade of the century SDA work developed in a distinctive form in the rural mountain areas of North Carolina. In contrast to the rich lowlands of the Carolinas, which had been farmed originally in large plantations with slave labor, the mountains had been settled by hardy, independent, small farmers for the most part opposed to slavery (some of whom fought in the Union Army). They cleared their small plots, built their modest cabins, and struggled with the stubborn soil to raise only enough to subsist on. Isolated as they were, they did not have the more favored lowlanders' opportunity for advancement. When Ellen G. White urged SDA families to go south and begin self-supporting work, one result was the founding of small institutions at Hildebran (by D. T. Shireman, 1897), Eufola (by J. O. Johnston, 1908), Glen Alpine, Cowee Mountain, Fletcher (1910), and Pisgah (1914; *see* Mount Pisgah Academy), in North Carolina (and at Math Mountain in South Carolina). Usually one or two families would move in, clear the land, and build up the soil to raise a variety of crops; then they would launch a small school and often a small sanitarium.

Of these, two are at present still operating independently—Fletcher Academy and Mountain Sanitarium. The school (Asheville Agricultural School) was founded by Sydney Brownsberger and A. W. Spalding on a 416-acre (170-hectare) farm 18 miles (30 kilometers) south of Asheville, and the sanitarium (developed from a health cafeteria and treatment rooms in Asheville), by Dr. John Brownsberger and the A. A. Jaspersons, with Lelia Patterson directing the school of nursing.

These mountain institutions endeavored by precept and example to improve the health and standard of living in the community as well as to preach the gospel. For example, Mountain Sanitarium staff members aided their mountain neighbors, who were living on an impoverished diet, by holding home nursing and first-aid classes and by organizing a Good Neighbor Club among the African-Americans to promote gardening and poultry raising. Prizes were awarded—not money but plants, such as strawberries or fruit trees; or sometimes a calf donated by a dairy. As a result of this program, some of the children tasted cow's milk for the first time.

Work Among African-Americans and Indians. Incidental mention has been made of SDA work for African-Americans, but the story of the work by and for African-Americans in the Carolinas belongs to another article. *See* South Atlantic Conference.

A church member with a burden for the North Carolina Indians arranged to have Bible School enrollment cards sent to 2,000 boxholders in Bladen County. There was a good response. P. G. Crestakos, with his wife, responding to students' requests, studied with them in their homes; a few were baptized. Some of these Indians had long believed that the seventh day was the Sabbath without knowing of others who believed it. Later J. O. Wilson carried on the work. In 1962 there were 35 adult believers, and Prestley Lowry, one of the Indian converts, had been trained and was working as an Indian minister. Today the Pembroke, North Carolina, church located in Robeson County serves the Lumbee Indians. A renewed evangelistic effort took place to reach this group in the 1990s.

Through evangelism, SDA work has expanded throughout the Carolina Conference, enabling it to incorporate a more multi-ethnic constituency, including Anglo-American, Hispanic, and Korean cultures. The first African-American pastor began serving the Beaufort, South Carolina, and Hilton Head Island, South Carolina, churches in 1992.

Layperson Involvement in Evangelistic Work. In 1992, using the book *The Great Controversy*, the conference conducted radio campaigns in major cities of the Carolinas. When encouraged to call a toll-free number to receive a free book, more than 10,000 listeners responded. Members of the participating churches hand-delivered most of these 10,000 copies to individual homes. Evangelistic meetings followed in several cities. The combined efforts of this program resulted in a record-breaking year for soul winning, and a renewed commitment to evangelism by the constituency.

Medical-Evangelistic and Welfare Work. Private medical-evangelistic work was carried on by physicians and dentists, for example, by Dr. Kenneth Mathiesen and his wife at Pittsboro, North Carolina, in 1938, joined later by others, resulting in a church of 40 members.

W. R. Winslow Memorial Home is a 146-bed nursing facility that provides skilled and intermediate nursing care. Located in Elizabeth City, North Carolina, the home is owned and operated by the Carolina Conference.

The original facility opened in December 1961 as a 40-bed rest home. W. R. Winslow, a Washington, D.C., businessman, friend of Seventh-day Adventists, and native of Elizabeth City, developed the facility because of his strong desire to help the senior citizens of his hometown. He provided funds for construction and established a "trust" for its continuous operation. Several years after opening the home, Winslow deeded complete ownership to the Carolina Conference.

During the next 12 years the home expanded to 60 beds. In 1973 the nursing home received a Certificate of Need and was enlarged to 121 beds and licensed for a nursing facility. The last addition of 25 beds began in 1991 after the home was awarded another Certificate of Need.

Carolina Living, Inc., is a 24-unit retirement center located adjacent to W. R. Winslow Memorial Home, Inc., in Elizabeth City, North Carolina. At its humble beginning in 1977, the administrator's home was converted to a six-unit retirement facility. In 1990 it was voted to demolish the old home and build a modern 24-unit facility at the same location. Construction was completed and admissions began in May 1991.

Nestled in the mountains of western North Carolina is a beautiful retirement community comprised of Pisgah Manor, a 118-bed skilled and intermediate care nursing facility, a 24-unit assisted living center, and 72 modern condominiums designed for independent living (Pisgah Estates). This retirement campus is located adjacent to Mount Pisgah Academy and provides employment for 60-65 students. The goal of Pisgah Estates, Pisgah Manor Health Care Center, and Pisgah Assisted Living Center is to make retirement an enjoyable and stress-free experience.

Nosoca Pines Ranch, a youth camp and convention center for the Carolina Conference, was purchased in 1971 and the first camp held there in 1974. The 170-acre (70-hectare) camp is located on the shores of Lake Wateree at Liberty Hill, South Carolina, approximately 23 miles (35 kilometers) northwest of Camden, South Carolina. With 18 cabins and a beautifully renovated auditorium/gym, cafeteria, tennis courts, racquetball courts, and lakeside campfire bowl, it offers much for the SDA and other denominational groups that make extensive use of the camp and its natural resources.

Presidents—Carolina Conference: J. O.

Johnston, 1901-1904. *North Carolina Conference:* T. H. Jeys, 1904-1909; G. W. Wells, 1909-1910; G. M. Brown, 1910-1913; Stewart Kime, 1913-1914; J. H. Behrens, 1914-1915; J. B. Locken, 1915-1917; A. H. Evers, 1917-1918; W. H. Branson (acting president), 1918; J. W. MacNeil, 1918. *South Carolina Conference:* R. T. Nash, 1907-1909; T. H. Jeys, 1909-1911; W. H. Branson, 1911-1912; C. V. Achenbach, 1912-1914; J. L. Shuler, 1914-1917; A. N. Allen, 1917; E. W. Wolfe, 1917-1918. *Carolina Conference:* J. W. MacNeil, 1918-1920; L. T. Crisler, 1920-1921; R. I. Keate, 1921-1926; C. L. Butterfield, 1926-1932; E. T. Wilson, 1932-1933; A. S. Booth, 1933-1934; J. L. Shuler, 1934-1937; H. E. Lysinger, 1937-1943; R. S. Blackburn (acting president), 1943; F. O. Sanders, 1943-1948; C. H. Lauda, 1948-1956; G. R. Nash, 1956-1958; H. V. Reed, 1958-1963; Willard B. Johnson, 1963-1968; E. S. Reile, 1968-1977; Malcolm Gordon, 1977-1985; Robert Folkenberg, 1985-1990; Kenneth Coonley, 1990- .

CAROLINE ISLANDS. *See* Guam and Micronesia.

CARR, SEPTIMUS WALFORD (1878-1972). Missionary to Fiji and Papua. S. W. Carr was born in Sweden of British parents and migrated early in life to Sydney. He accepted present truth through reading the book *Rome's Challenge.* At Avondale College he became acquainted with Ellen White, and graduated in 1903 from the Missionary Course. In 1904 he became the first principal of the Buresala Training School (forerunner of Fulton College). In 1905 he married Edith Guilliard. In 1908 in company with a Fijian missionary, Benni Tavodi, he pioneered the work in Papua. He was ordained in 1910. From 1915 to 1916 he was engaged in evangelism in Queensland. The years 1917 to 1919 spent on Niue Island were followed by an extended term in Fiji, in evangelism, education work, and the translating of books, tracts, and Voice of Prophecy lessons. From 1939 to 1946 he served as a pastor in Queensland.

CARSCALLEN, ARTHUR ASA GRANDVILLE (1879-1964). Canadian-born missionary, administrator, and linguist. He was baptized in North Dakota in 1899, and attended Union College in 1900 and 1901. In 1902 he was sent to work as a colporteur in Scotland, Wales, and England. He also assisted in evangelistic meetings, and in 1904 entered Duncombe Hall Training College (now Newbold College), where he completed his course in September 1906.

In 1906 he accepted a call to open up Seventh-day Adventist work in Kenya, East Africa, with the arrangement that his fiancée, Helen Thomson, be sent out the next year. After his ordination, late in 1906, he sailed for Mombasa with Peter Nyambo, an African teacher from Nyasaland who had been attending school in England.

Carscallen spent the next 13 years pioneering in Kenya as superintendent of the British East Africa Mission. Under his direction a string of mission stations was established along the eastern shore of Lake Victoria: Gendia, Wire Hill, Rusinga Island, Kanyadoto, Karungu, Kisii (Nyanchwa), and last, Kamagambo. Returning from furlough in 1913, he brought back a small press and set up a small printing plant at Gendia to publish books, papers, and a small monthly journal (*see* Africa Herald Publishing House).

He mastered the Luo language and was the first to reduce it to writing. The grammar textbook he produced was widely used for many years. He spent more than two years translating portions of the New Testament into the Luo tongue, which were published by the British and Foreign Bible Society.

During World War I many of the missions were looted and damaged, and the workers, except Carscallen and one other, were kept from their stations for nearly two years. Carscallen held the workers together through it all.

In 1921 Carscallen returned with his family to the United States, where his wife died the same year in Oregon. In 1924 he married Anita Johnson. After some years in pastoral work in the Dakotas, he worked in British Guiana from 1931 to 1942. While he was president of the three united Guiana fields he helped demolish the old SDA church building in Georgetown and built another, doing much of the carpentry work himself.

Still a pioneer, he offered himself for work in the interior of British Guiana among the Davis Indians, and went about the close of 1936 to Waramadong, near Mount Roraima, where he opened a mission. Mastering the native dialect, he produced a dictionary and grammar in the local language. In retirement in the United States he settled in La Sierra, California, and continued to visit churches and camp meetings, seeking to kindle a missionary spirit among young and old alike.

CASA EDITORA SUDAMERICANA. *See* Buenos Aires Publishing House.

CASA PUBLICADORA ANGOLANA. *See* Angola Publishing House.

CASA PUBLICADORA BRASILEIRA. *See* Brazil Publishing House.

CASCADE CHRISTIAN ACADEMY. A coeducational day school on the senior high level at Wenatchee, Washington. During the 1992-1993 school year the enrollment was 33, with a faculty of 12.

Principal: Ed Tillotson, 1990- .

CASE, HIRAM S. (fl. 1851-1854). Millerite preacher won to Adventism by S. W. Rhodes in 1851. In 1854 he joined an opposition group that for two years published a paper called the *Messenger of Truth (see Messenger* Party). In a letter to James White published in the *Present Truth* (1:85) he states that light concerning the two-horned beast of Rev. 13 came to him while Rhodes was showing him the third angel's message. His view was that "the image-beast is composed of church and state united—Protestant churches and Republicanism."

CASEBEER, HOMER DAVID (1886-1948). Departmental secretary, missionary. Upon graduating from Pacific Union College in 1916, he was appointed to mission service in the West Indies. He was ordained in 1919. In 1921 he became head of the Spanish Department and later also of the Portuguese and North American Indian departments in the General Conference Bureau of Home Missions *(see* North American Division Multilingual Ministries). With the exception of a short term of service in South America and another in the Illinois Conference, he continued in the General Conference until 1946. Later he served for one year as pastor of the Los Angeles Spanish church.

CASH, ANGELIA VESTA (1881-1953). Teacher, Bible instructor. She taught church school for eight years in Illinois and Wisconsin, and then became the first Bible instructor for Italian-speaking people in the United States, a work to which she devoted 40 years of her life. She worked in the following centers: Chicago (1912-1921, 1945-1952), New York City (1921-1939, 1941-1945), and San Francisco (1939-1941).

"CAST THE NET ON THE RIGHT SIDE." *See* European Institute of World Mission.

CASTLE MEDICAL CENTER. Located in Kailua, Hawaii, a full-service acute-care hospital recognized for both its inpatient care and outpatient programs throughout the state. A nonprofit institution, Castle serves all of Oahu and is the primary health-care facility for windward Oahu. The hospital is operated by Adventist Health System/West.

The 160-bed facility offers a full spectrum of services, ranging from preventive health programs and maternity care to emergency medicine and critical care. Castle is staffed by more than 800 employees, 300 volunteers, and nearly 300 physicians. Each year Castle provides care for 7,000 inpatients.

Castle, which first opened its doors in 1963 with 72 beds, continues to grow and change to keep pace with the community's health-care needs. The most recent expansion and renovation project was a $10 million program that resulted in Hawaii's first single-room maternity-care unit, a progressive-care unit, and a state-of-the-art critical-care unit. Castle is widely recognized for its medical/surgical capabilities, emergency department, laboratory and X-ray facilities, mental health services, and alcoholism and addictions programs.

Many of Castle's most successful programs are focused on preventive care services that promote a healthy lifestyle. The Castle Center for Health Promotion, employee wellness program, and vegetarian restaurant (Pali Gardens), all support this mission. The hospital offers a wide variety of community classes and services, including physical fitness testing, stress management, coronary risk evaluation, smoking cessation, and aerobics.

Castle Quality, the hospital's continuous quality improvement program, earned Castle national recognition in the Commitment to Excellence program, which honors hospitals for their service, excellence, and quality leadership. Castle is the first hospital in the nation to implement patient-focused care—a program to increase efficiency, reduce costs, and improve patient care throughout the facility.

The administrative team includes Terry W. White, president; Ken Finch, senior vice president; Gwen Brownfield, Orvin Fillman, and John Monge, vice presidents; and Don Bieber, Adele Hoe, and Jon Larrabee, administrative directors.

Administrators: William Guthrie, 1963-1966; Marvin Midkiff, 1966-1973; Larry Larrabee, 1973-1978; Robert Carmen, 1978-1983; Herbert Shiroma, 1983-1984; Terry W. White, 1984-1994; Kenneth A. Finch, 1994- .

CAVE MEMORIAL CLINIC AND NURSING HOME. A 29-bed medical institution established in 1970 at Bridgetown, Barbados. The 1993 *Yearbook* listed Mrs. Gillian Howell as matron.

CAVINESS, AGNES ELVIRA LEWIS (1889-1973). Pioneer, dean, teacher, educator, author. She was born in Minnesota and received her education at Union College, Southwestern Union College, Walla Walla College, and Pacific Union College, where she was the first degree candidate. That year she married Leon L. Caviness, and they returned to Union College. The following year they transferred to Columbia Union College. With her husband, she was a founder of the Seminaire Adventiste du Salève, in France, and was dean of women during its first year. Many of her articles appeared in denominational publications. She often wrote under the pen name of Mother Naomi. After serving overseas for 12 years, the family returned to Pacific Union College, where she taught French and German and pioneered in teaching classes in marriage and the family.

She is the author of the book *The Way He Should Go.*

CAVINESS, GEORGE W. (1857-1923). Educator, missionary. A graduate of Battle Creek College (1882), he, with his wife, taught for three years in the Michigan school that developed into Cedar Lake Academy. He was ordained in 1886, and the next year taught at Battle Creek College. He served as principal of South Lancaster Academy from 1888 to 1894, and as president of Battle Creek College, 1894-1897.

Because of his knowledge of Hebrew, Greek, and Latin, he was asked in 1897 to go to Mexico as the Seventh-day Adventist representative on an interdenominational committee to revise the Spanish translation of the Bible. This was the beginning of 25 years of service in Mexico. In 1899 he pioneered SDA work in Mexico City and served in various capacities. For a time he was superintendent of the Mexican field, but perhaps his most important contribution was his work as editor of the Spanish paper. Ill health prevented active service from 1920 until the time of his death.

CAVINESS, LEON LESLIE (1884-1955). Educator, departmental secretary, editor. Educated in Battle Creek, the University of Michigan, the University of Nebraska, and George Washington University (Ph.D.), he taught languages at Union College (1906-1913). Later he was professor of Greek at Washington Missionary Seminary (1913-1915), assistant and later associate editor of the *Review and Herald* (1915-1920), departmental secretary of the Latin Union (1920-1924), director of the Seminaire Adventiste du Salève (1921-1922), Sabbath school and educational secretary of the European Division (1924-1928) and of the Southern European Division (1928-1932), and professor of biblical languages at Pacific Union College from 1932 until his retirement in 1952.

CAYMAN ISLANDS. A crown colony of Great Britain, comprising Grand Cayman, Cayman Brac, and Little Cayman, situated about halfway between Jamaica and the southeast coast of Cuba, contains 102 square miles (264 square kilometers). The population of these islands is approximately 28,000 of whom about 27,000 live on Grand Cayman. The islands were probably named from the caymans (American alligators, genus *Caiman*) that were numerous in Little Cayman and Cayman Brac. These islands were settled mainly by English people from Jamaica, and until Jamaica became independent in 1962, they were regarded as its dependency.

Seventh-day Adventist Statistics. The Cayman Islands form the Cayman Islands Mission, a part of the West Indies Union Conference, which in turn is part of the Inter-American Division. Statistics (1992) for the *Cayman Islands:* churches, 9; members, 1,225; church schools, 1; ordained ministers, 5; church school teachers, 6. Caymen Islands Mission headquarters are at Georgetown, Grand Cayman.

The first Seventh-day Adventist in the Caymans was Gilbert McLaughlin, who had become acquainted with SDA teachings while living at Bonacca, Bay Islands, Honduras, sometime about 1894. Returning to Grand Cayman shortly after that date, he began teaching his newly found faith and erected a small church building. About the same time two colporteurs, F. I. Richardson and B. B. Newman, visited the islands. In 1895 W. W. Eastman, from the United States, arrived to do medical missionary work and remained until 1897, holding evangelistic meetings in the town of Georgetown, the main center.

Working on Grand Cayman from 1905 to 1909, Frank Hall, from Jamaica, baptized about 20 persons and organized Sabbath schools at Georgetown and East End. Cayman Brac learned of Adventist teachings through H. P. Lawson, who in 1925 sold books there and in 1929 held open-air meetings. Seventeen persons were baptized as a result of his work.

In 1929 the Cayman Islands were organized as a separate mission, with two churches comprising 33 members. I. G. Knight became the mission director. In the late 1930s the churches were transferred to the Jamaica Conference, and from there to the West Cuba Conference in the early 1940s. In 1944 they were again organized as a separate mission, but in the early 1950s for a brief period were included in the West Jamaica Conference. In 1954 the present Cayman Islands Mission was formed under the West Indies Union Mission. In 1992 there were seven churches on Grand Cayman and one on Cayman Brac, but no work had been established on Little Cayman, which continues to have a small population of 46.

CAYMAN ISLANDS MISSION. *See* Cayman Islands; Inter-American Division.

CEA ADVENTIST SECONDARY SCHOOL (Centro Educativo Adventista). A coeducational day school located in Santiago, Dominican Republic. It is part of the North Dominican Conference. The Centro Educativo Adventista offers grades K-12 and had an enrollment of 626 students during the 1992-1993 school year. It has received recognition from the Dominican government and the Inter-American Division.

This institution had its beginnings in the year 1920 as a church school with the name Escuela América and was situated on General Valverde Street. Grades 1-6 were taught.

The school went through good and bad times. By 1965 it had 150 students in eight grades, and four teachers who taught double shifts. Shortly after, a lot adjacent to the Central church on Salvador Cucurullo Street was purchased, and a one-story building was constructed. By 1981 the secondary level began functioning on grades 9 and 10 levels.

During the school year 1982-1983, its name was changed to Centro Educacional Adventista and later modified to Centro Educativo Adventista. By 1986 the last two levels, 11 and 12, were added, with a total of 400 students in attendance. The school building was enlarged by the addition of three new classrooms for a total of 10, besides the library, laboratory, physical education facilities, and administration offices.

In 1993 there were 626 students, of which 138 were on the secondary school level. There were eight teachers.

Principals: Mercedes Phipps, 1920; Josefa Contreras, 1946-1947; Dulce Luna, 1950; Irma Gómez, 1965; Esperanza Hidalgo, 1981; Gisela Molina, 1983-1984; Héctor Jiménez, 1985-1986; Carlos Cabrera, 1986-1987; Nereyda Olivo, 1989- .

CEDAR LAKE ACADEMY. A coeducational boarding school on the senior high school level that was operated by the Michigan Conference on a 268-acre (110-hectare) campus at Cedar Lake, Montcalm County, Michigan. It is believed to have been the oldest Seventh-day Adventist boarding academy operating continuously in the same locality.

The school was established Dec. 29, 1898, with the purchase of a two-story public school building on a two-acre (.8-hectare) lot, and was opened as a 10-grade academy Jan. 16, 1899, with three teachers, Justus Grant Lamson, his wife, and H. W. Johnson, and with approximately 30 students in attendance.

During the first term, begun with the one building and makeshift rented quarters, two buildings were bought and moved up from the village. One of these was used as a barn and the other, a store building, was remodeled and enlarged as a dormitory. At first, the students had no separate rooms. The girls' dormitory was the first floor of the old store, with the beds around the walls, separated by curtains; the boys occupied the second floor. Construction of a basement and a front addition was completed little by little while the students lived in the unfinished building. Water was hauled from a spring and stored in a barrel in the basement kitchen.

In 1902, when the academy was incorporated under the name of Cedar Lake Industrial Academy, the curriculum included, in addition to Bible and the basic school subjects, such courses as printing, tentmaking, typing and shorthand, bookkeeping, agriculture, blacksmithing, rugmaking, sewing, food preparation, and carpentry. The school continued as a 10-grade school until the fall of 1919. It graduated its first twelfth-grade class in 1920.

In 1963 the farm shop was remodeled to provide training in woodworking, metalworking, and auto mechanics. The following year an airstrip was constructed and ground school and flight training were initiated.

A major development to improve the campus began in 1964 when the Michigan Conference began an every-member canvass to raise funds for the rebuilding of Cedar Lake Academy as well as to upgrade the conference's two other boarding academies operating at that time, Adelphian and Grand Ledge. By the end of May 1967 Cedar Lake's new brick dormitory housing 120 girls was completed and occupied. By the opening of the 1969 school year a dormitory of the same size and style was ready for the boys. Then followed a cafeteria-service building complex, and early in 1974 a new administration-classroom-chapel complex was completed. This new million-dollar structure completed the major rebuilding of the academy campus, with a total expenditure of more than $3 million.

In 1967 a modern building was erected to house a Rhodes Bake 'n' Serve frozen dough plant, which provided work for 50 students. The academy also owned and operated a woodworking mill, where 37 students earned a portion of their school expenses making redwood lawn furniture. Other buildings on the campus included a gymnasium, a number of farm buildings, and 18 faculty homes.

The enrollment reached a high of 320 students during the 1974-1975 school year.

Cedar Lake Academy officially closed in 1987 when it was merged with Adelphian Academy to become Great Lakes Adventist Academy. *See* Great Lakes Adventist Academy.

Principals: J. Grant Lamson, 1898-1900; H. D. Day, 1900-1901; J. Grant Lamson, 1901-1903; S. M. Butler, 1903-1908; W. C. Mathewson, 1908-1909; W. Leslie Avery, 1909-1911; R. U. Garrett, 1911-1914; J. Grant Lamson, 1914-1915; R. U. Garret, 1915-1918; G. H. Simpson, 1918-1927; T. E. Unruh, 1927-1930; C. M. Gruesbeck, 1930; W. A. Nelson, 1930-1936; W. T. Weaver, 1936-1939; William H. Shephard, 1939-1941; J. R. Shull, 1941-1947; R. O. Stone, 1947-1953; E. E. Burkett, 1953-1954; E. H. Knauft, 1954-1957; B. G. Butherus, 1957-1960; L. C. Strickland, 1960-1961; Herluf L. Jensen, 1961-1967; D. E. Wright, 1967-1971; Oscar Torkelson, 1971-1972; R. K. Lebard, 1972-1977; M. Wesley Shultz, 1978-1983; Donald E. Cochran, 1983-1986; Gregory A. Gerard, 1986-1987.

CELEBRATION (1985-   ; monthly; R&H; March 1995 circulation, 11,043; file in R&H). A 32-page paper for adult church leaders.

Celebration was formally introduced the fourth quarter of 1984 as a pilot publication to fill a need for "caring church" adult Sabbath school program helps. Regular monthly publication as the published voice of the NAD church ministries committee began in 1985.

Celebration nurtures adult local church leaders, providing program helps, resources, instructional material, and networking opportunities that fulfill the paper's motto: "Meeting Needs, Empowering Members, Sharing the Gospel."

Editors: Harold Baasch, 1985; Ginger Church (assistant), 1986; R. R. Watts, 1986-1988; Ginger Church (managing), 1989; Jack Calkins, 1989-1995; Faith Crumbly (managing), 1995- .

CELEBRATIONS OF RECOVERY. Seventh-day Adventists with dependency problems are finding new hope for continuing recovery in a series of weekend spiritual retreats especially for them. These Celebrations of Recovery are planned for SDA addicts and codependents and their families, and are being held annually in major parts of the United States. Gradually the concept is being introduced into other world divisions of the church.

The idea originated with the first celebration held at Andrews University in Berrien Springs, Michigan, in 1987. Since then, celebrations have been held in Washington, D.C., southern California, the Pacific Northwest, and New England. Additional ones are being organized in other areas.

The consistent sponsor of all these is the Association of Adventist Parents (AAP), with cosponsors often being hospitals or local conferences. AAP as an organization that dates from 1985 and was founded to help cope with the growing addiction problems in Adventist churches and families, especially for persons who are already involved in chemical or other dependencies.

The celebration is for the purpose of exploring spiritual resources for recovery; sharing experiences, strength, and hope; and bringing praise to God for the gift of continuing sobriety. Program specifics are directed by local organizing committees.

"The Joy of Serenity and Salvation," as the celebration is titled, is a weekend convention following the guidelines of the Twelve Steps of Alcoholics Anonymous. During open speakers' meetings, recovering persons tell their stories of God's work in their lives. Workshops and closed discussions deal with various aspects of recovery.

"Clean Time" is celebrated with sobriety anniversaries at a Saturday night token ceremony. Concluding the weekend are a "Step Breakfast" and a group consciousness meeting for evaluation and future plans.

Hundreds of SDAs in recent years have found new strength and hope in the celebration.

CENSURE. *See* Church Discipline.

CENTER FOR INTERCULTURAL RELATIONS. *See* Institute of World Mission.

CENTRAL ADVANCE. *See Central Union Outlook.*

CENTRAL ADVENTIST ACADEMY (Academia Regional Adventista Central). A secondary school situated in the city of Caguas, Puerto Rico, some 30 minutes away from the capital of Puerto Rico. It was founded in 1976 as a primary school and through the years grew to become a school offering grades K-12.

In 1993 it had 163 students on the high school level and 10 teachers.

Principals: Carlos Capote, 1988-1989; Carlos Molina, 1989-1990; Juan Cruz, 1990-1991; Ivette Lozada, 1991-1993; Juan E. Milian, 1993- .

CENTRAL AFRICAN PUBLISHING HOUSE (Imprimerie Adventiste "IMA"). A publishing house with printing plant, established in 1954 in Yaoundé, the capital of Cameroon, by the Central African Union Mission, which has its headquarters also in Yaoundé. The house serves five countries, with a population of about 17 million speaking a number of languages.

This plant was established as a self-supporting aid to evangelistic work in a large and difficult field. The beginnings were modest; a secondhand press and other typographical equipment secured from France were installed in a small annex, about 150 square feet (140 square meters), of the newly established primary school of Yaoundé. There was only one workman, Jean Aké, who had been a printer earlier in life.

Soon this place became too small. After moving twice in 1958, the plant was installed in a house next to the union office. After remodeling and enlarging the building, the Central African Union had a well-established printing plant. In 1963 it was equipped with six presses and employed 11 Cameroon workers. In 1968 the first department offset in the union territory was purchased, enabling the plant to print and make separation in four colors. This purchase was made possible by the Publishing House Extension Fund. Since then the department has grown and a new offset machine was added in 1975. Among new equipment acquired since 1975 are two guillotine trimmers, one pasting machine, and one folding machine. The laboratory also is well equipped.

First place is given to denominational publications. The press issues the Sabbath school quarterly in the French language; all blanks needed by the churches, schools, and missions; the manuals of religious instruction, hymnbooks, and tracts for evangelistic work in French as well as the various African languages. Since the publishing department in Cameroon was organized in 1966, the publishing work has grown rapidly.

In 1973 it was decided that the publishing house should print paperback books and tracts for all the French-speaking countries in Africa. The annual sales in 1992 amounted to $327,605. There are 20 Cameroonian workers.

Managers: Kurt Scheidegger, 1954-1962; Jean Lafrancesca, 1962-1964; J. J. Hecketsweiler, 1965-1977; H. Bauder, 1977-1983; R. Bruinsma, 1984-1986; J. Teicheire, 1987-1988; G. Egwakhe, 1988-1991; M. Chaigne, 1991- .

CENTRAL AFRICAN REPUBLIC. An independent African state since Aug. 13, 1960 (formerly a part of French Equatorial Africa), bounded on the north by Chad, on the east by the Sudan, on the south by the Congo and Zaire, and on the west by Cameroon. It has an area of 240,534 square miles (622,983 square kilometers) and supports a population (1994) of 3.1 million, mostly Negroid, the majority of whom are animists. Agriculture is the principal occupation, with cotton the most important export commodity.

Seventh-day Adventist Statistics. The territory of the Central African Republic constitutes the Central African Republic Mission and is a part of the Central African Union Mission, which in turn is part of the Africa-Indian Ocean Division. Statistics (1992) for the *Central African Republic:* churches, 44; members, 2,854; ordained ministers, 3; licensed ministers, 9. Central African Republic Mission headquarters are at Bangui.

Development of Seventh-day Adventist Work. SDAs began their work in the Central African Republic on Jan. 14, 1960, when Jean Kempf and his wife settled on a property near the center of Bangui, the capital. Two additional lots, bought in April, provided land for a school and mission headquarters. In October, Kempf opened the first preparatory Bible course with 17 pupils, seven of whom were later given a special Bible course to train them as evangelists.

With the help of these students three secondary stations were opened in 1961 (in Bangui, Jan. 14; in Alindao, Apr. 8; in Sika, Dec. 31), and in 1962 one in Koukouma-Ngaza (Jan. 2), and two others a little later in Mobaye and in Doukoulou. For the 251 members in five Sabbath schools, lesson quarterlies were mimeographed in the Sango language.

On Mar. 8, 1962, the Association Centrafricaine de lutte contre l'Alcoolisme (Temperance Society) was organized, and the first bulletin was issued in February 1963. The association opened a cultural and social center in Bangui.

In March 1963 Kempf conducted his first baptism and organized the first group of converts.

In 1968 Manuel Martorell, a Spanish missionary, with his family was sent to Zima, a mission station in the eastern part of the country in the Bassekotto area. A Bible school for the training of workers in the Central African Republic functioned successfully. Martorell, then the mission president, opened a small dispensary to minister to the needs of the surrounding population.

A third mission station was founded in 1971 in Bouar, in the western section of the country. Jules Agasson with his wife and two daughters was sent there to carry on evangelistic work. In 1974 a new church building was dedicated in Bangui, the capital of the Central African Republic. This was the first SDA church to be built in the country. In 1989 an evangelistic center and a book center were established in Bangui.

CENTRAL AFRICAN REPUBLIC MISSION. *See* Central African Republic; Africa-Indian Ocean Division.

CENTRAL AFRICAN UNION MISSION. *See* Africa-Indian Ocean Division; Cameroon; Central African Republic; Chad; Congo; Equatorial Guinea; Gabon.

CENTRAL AMAZON MISSION. *See* Brazil; South American Division.

CENTRAL AMERICAN ADVENTIST UNIVERSITY (Universidad Adventista de Centro America). A coeducational boarding school on the college level, situated on a 120-acre (50-hectare) site one mile (1.6 kilometers) from the town of Alajuela, Costa Rica, and 13 miles (20 kilometers) from San José, the capital city. The institution is operated by the Central American Union Mission, which has a constituency of 241,798. It is accredited with the SDA Board of Regents. In 1993 the university enrollment was 498. The secondary enrollment was 215. A total of 45 full-time staff members served in the various teaching and industrial departments.

The forerunners of the Central American Adventist University were the secondary school at Las Cascadas, Panama, opened in 1925; and the Academia Adventista Centroamericana (later Colegio Adventista Latino), founded in 1927 in La Sabana, a suburb of San José, Costa Rica. The latter opened with 16 students and a faculty of three—Glen Ray, principal, and George W. Chapman and his wife. This was a coeducational secondary boarding school, established under the leadership of William E. Baxter, president of the Central American Union at that time, with the purpose of preparing workers to serve in the union.

In 1932 the school was moved to a small farm in the community of Tres Ríos, eight miles (13 kilometers) from the city of Cartago, and named Academia Adventista Hispanoamericana. In 1945 the name Colegio Vocacional de América Central was adopted. The name Centro Adventista de Estudios Superiores was adopted in 1971 and used for the junior college program. In 1987 the Costa Rica government recognized the institution's university status and the name was changed to Central American Adventist University. The secondary section is called Instituto Centroamericana Adventista.

In 1949 two years of study were added above the high school level in the fields of ministerial training, elementary education, and commercial subjects. The teachers' course was affiliated with Union College, Lincoln, Nebraska, until 1990.

Ministerial training was increased to a full baccalaureate program of four years, starting in 1971. In 1972 the secondary section received recognition from the Costa Rican Ministry of Education. During 1973 the college offered the first year of nurses' training in connection with the Adventist Hospital of Nicaragua. In 1974 the teachers' course achieved affiliation with the National University, College of Education. Since 1993, a full nurse's program functions under the authorization of the government and the SDA Board of Higher Education.

In 1950 the school was moved to its present site, which is at an elevation of 2,000 feet (610 meters), where climatic conditions are favorable. The central building, with a frontal structure of 280' x 175' (85 m. x 53 m.) in depth, for more than 40 years housed the women's and men's dormitories, the administration office, the cafeteria, and the assembly hall.

Beginning in 1975 the men's dormitory was relocated in a two-story building, which made space for more classrooms. Later, in 1991, a growth process was initiated on campus that involved the remodeling of the central building to which a lobby was added. The assembly hall was transformed into classrooms and a student center. Computer and nursing labs were added to the already-existing typing lab. The renovation also involved the cafeteria and administration offices.

A new library was inaugurated in 1985, but because of an earthquake in 1991 and the continuous growth of the university population, the library was installed in a two-story building of 24,748 square feet (2,300 square meters). This had been originally built as a men's dormitory. The new men's dorm was relocated in modules with a capacity for 160 students. Also in 1991, 16 rooms were added to the women's dormitory, bringing it to a capacity of 168 students.

The university church building was also seriously damaged by the 1991 earthquake, and it was relocated near the entrance of the campus. The former building was remodeled into an auditorium.

The campus also maintains homes for teachers, housing for married students, an elementary school, a gym and basketball court, football field, laundry, maintenance quarters, and a classroom building for the high school, which will be moved to a new two-acre (one-hectare) property campus.

The Adventist World Radio broadcasting station and the food factory, Fundacion CETEBEDI, administered by the General Conference and the Inter-American Division, respectively, also operate on the campus. The entire site of the Central American Adventist University consists of 120 acres (50 hectares), five acres (two hectares) of which belong to the campus proper, with the rest used for sugarcane, fruit trees, vegetable gardening, and cattle raising.

Principals/Presidents: Glen Ray, 1927-1928; W. H. Wineland, 1929-1935; W. A. Wild, 1935-1940; C. G. Gordon, 1941-1942; C. F. Montgomery, 1943-1945; D. J. Thomann (acting), 1946-1948; A. H. Riffel, 1949-1950; H. A. Habenicht, 1951-1952; Manuel Carballal, 1953-1957; T. J. Harper, 1958-1965; Carlos Ayala, 1965-1969; J. W. Zackrison, 1970; Israel Gonzalez, 1971-1975; Atilio R. Dupertuis, 1976-1978; Hugo Visani, 1978-1979; Francisco Ottati, 1979-1980; Roberto Eubank, 1981-1983; Hector Jurado, 1983-1986; Eustacio Penniecook, 1986-1989; Carlos Molina, 1989-1990; Tevni Grajales, 1990-1995; Ada Barrientias, 1995- .

CENTRAL AMERICAN CONFERENCE. *See* Honduras.

CENTRAL AMERICAN UNION MISSION. *See* Belize; Costa Rica; El Salvador; Guatemala; Honduras; Nicaragua; Panama; Inter-American Division.

CENTRAL AMERICAN VOCATIONAL COLLEGE. *See* Central American Adventist University.

CENTRAL ANDINA MISSION. *See* Peru; South American Division.

CENTRAL ARGENTINE CONFERENCE. *See* Argentina; South American Division.

CENTRAL ASIA CONFERENCE. *See* Euro-Asia Division; Tajikistan; Turkmenistan; Uzbekistan.

CENTRAL ASSOCIATION MISSION. *See* Angola; Euro-Africa Division.

CENTRAL BIBLE SCHOOL (Chicago). *See* Workers' Institutes.

CENTRAL BRAZIL ACADEMY (Instituto Adventista Brasil Central). A boarding and day school with primary and secondary grades. The school is located in Planalmira in the Abadiania district, Goiás, Brazil.

There are 8.7 million square feet (816,750 square meters) of land for agriculture and cattle raising. It was purchased by the Central Brazil Conference in 1981 and is located 19 miles (30 kilometers) from Anápolis, the second-largest city in the state of Goiás.

Construction on the school building began on Apr. 22, 1982, under the leadership of Prof. José Borges dos Santos, the first director. Classes began on May 4, 1985, with 111 boarding students and 38 day school students. In 1993 there were 173 boarding students on the primary level and 149 on the secondary, studying accounting, teaching, and other courses, with a staff of 36.

The fruits and vegetables produced on school property supply most of what is used for the boarding students. The milk produced by the 80 good-quality cows supplies the school's need. There are two sports courts and a semi-Olympic pool that are used by the students for leisure. A large music conservatory of 6,456 square feet (600 square meters) was in the last phase of construction in 1993, along with an auditorium for 500 people.

Directors: José Borges dos Santos, 1983-1985; Enoch da Silva, 1986-1989; José Borges dos Santos, 1990-1994; José R. Machado dos Reis, 1994- .

CENTRAL BRAZIL CONFERENCE. *See* Brazil; South American Division.

CENTRAL BRAZIL UNION CONFERENCE. *See* Brazil; South American Division.

CENTRAL CALIFORNIA CONFERENCE. The unit of church organization comprising the territory of the counties of Fresno, Kern (north of Tehachapi Mountains), Kings, Madera, Mariposa, Merced, Monterey, San Benito, San Francisco, San Luis Obispo, San Mateo, Santa Barbara (west of the 120th meridian), Santa Clara, Santa Cruz, Stanislaus, Tulare, and Tuolumne. Statistics (1993): churches, 123; members, 27,476; ordained ministers, 108; licensed ministers, 12; teachers, elementary 135, secondary 80, total 215; church schools, 32. Headquarters: 2820 Willow Avenue, Clovis, California. The conference forms part of the Pacific Union Conference.

Institutions. Armona Union Academy, Bakersfield Adventist Academy, Fresno Adventist Academy, Hanford Community Medical Center, Modesto Adventist Academy, Monterey Bay Academy, Mountain View Academy, San Joaquin Community Hospital, Sonora Community Hospital.

Local churches: Armona, Arroyo Grande, Arvin, Bakersfield (Central, Hillcrest, Southside, Bilingual, Korean), Burlingame, Cambrian Park, Campbell, Caruthers, Ceres, Chowchilla, Clovis, Coalinga, Corcoran, Cutler (Spanish), Delano (Bilingual), Dinuba, East Palo Alto, Exeter, Fresno (Asian, Central, Central Valley [Filipino], Northwest, Spanish, Sunnyside, Westside), Gilroy (English, Spanish), Greeley Hill, Groveland, Hanford (English, Spanish), Hollister, Kerman, Kern River Valley, Lamont (Spanish), Lemoore, Lindsay, Lindsay (Spanish), Livingston (Spanish), Lompoc, Los Altos (Chinese), Los Banos, Los Gatos, Madera (English, Spanish), Mariposa, Merced Olive East, Milpitas, Modesto (Central, Parkwood, Spanish), Monterey Bay Academy, Monterey (Korean), Monterey Peninsula, Morro Bay, Mountain View (Central, Japanese, Korean, Spanish), North Fork, Oakdale, Oakhurst, Oildale, Orosi, Pacifica, Palo Alto, Pixley, Porterville, Redwood City (Spanish), Redwood Hills, Reedley, Salinas (English, Spanish), San Francisco (Central, Chinese, Filipino, Japanese, Latin-American, Philadelphian, Rainbow, Russian, Samoan, Tabernacle), Sanger, San Jose (Central, Ephesus, Filipino, Samoan, Spanish), San Luis Obispo, Santa Cruz, Santa Maria (English, Hispanic), Seaside Community, Selma, Shafter, Sonora, Soquel, South San Francisco (Latin American), Sunnyvale, Taft, Templeton Hills, Tulare, Turlock West Avenue (Bilingual), Visalia (English, Spanish), Wasco (Bilingual), Waterford, Watsonville (English, Spanish), Woodlake (Spanish), plus the conference church.

Companies: Auberry, Bakersfield East Hills, Merced Bethel, Modesto Westside, San Jose (Vietnamese), Sanger (Spanish), Visalia Hmong.

History. For the beginnings in the area of the present Central California Conference, *see* California Conference.

J. N. Loughborough held meetings in San Francisco in 1871, and a church was formed. In 1873 D. M. Canright conducted evangelistic meetings in Watsonville, and a company of believers was organized. In Lemoore a church was organized in 1878 as a result of tent meetings by J. L. Wood; in 1883 a church at San Jose was organized with 12 charter members. The Fresno church was organized in 1884 as a result of lay preaching by Jackson Ferguson in 1872 and missionary work by Moses Church. The church building that they occupied in 1887 was the largest in the city of Fresno. Meetings held in Arroyo Grande in 1886-1887 by J. G. Smith, R. S. Owen, and Robert Hare resulted in the baptism of nine and the organization of a church in 1888. Other churches followed: Armona in 1888, Bakersfield in 1894, Hanford in 1894, and Modesto in 1902.

In the wake of church organization came church schools. As early as 1897, the Fresno church organized a school, with 25 enrolled. In 1901 the Hanford church started a school. The Bakersfield church operated a school for one year in 1902-1903, then began again in 1911. The San Jose church school came along in 1903 with an enrollment of 12. The Armona church also started its school in 1903.

Because of the steady growth of the work in the central areas of the state, the California Conference in 1911 relinquished the counties of Tulare, Madera, San Benito, Fresno, Kings, San Luis Obispo, Monterey, and the portion of Kern County north of the Tehachapis, in order to form the Central California Conference. The new conference covered an area of 29,850 square miles (77,312 square kilometers), with a population of 200,426; it had 26 churches with a membership of 1,115 served by 11 ministers. J. H. Behrens was appointed first president, and headquarters were located at 1048 O Street in Fresno. In 1932 the conference office was moved to San Jose: first to 85 East San Antonio, later to 685 S. Third Street, and then, in 1941, to 435 N. Third Street, and in 1957 to 1691 The Alameda. In 1984 it moved to its present location in Clovis at 2820 Willow Avenue.

The first 12-grade academy to be opened in central California was at Armona in 1911; the first boarding academy was Monterey Bay Academy, opened in 1949. In February 1932, when the California Conference terminated, the Central California Conference added to its territory counties in the area south of the San Francisco Bay and other territories to make up its present jurisdictional area. Earlier there had been several territorial changes.

In spite of the Depression, rapid strides in conference growth were made in the early thirties. In 1929 a campground of 3.5 acres (1.4 hectares) was purchased for $10,181. In 1931 a conference office was erected in San Jose, and five acres (two hectares) of land was purchased at Wawona for a summer camp. This camp has since been increased to 31 acres (13 hectares) and is within the boundaries of Yosemite National Park.

Several evangelists employed radio. By 1931 this limited working force had baptized 334. Several were baptized as a result of a weekly broadcast on station KMJ in Fresno. A Penny-a-Dish cafeteria made contacts in Fresno during the meager Depression days.

In 1923, through the personal work of Frank Iano, an Italian church was organized in Fresno, with 25 charter members. Frank Iano later became a minister and worked in San Francisco, where in 1928 an Italian company was organized and in February 1941 a church. Later both Italian churches were incorporated into English-speaking churches. Two churches were organized among the Spanish-speaking people. Four German churches were begun, but later discontinued the use of the German language. On Dec. 16, 1950, a church was organized in the largest Chinese community in the United States, San Francisco's Chinatown. As the congregation grew in size, the Chinese church moved in 1973 to a new facility on Geary Boulevard near the Cliff House. J. E. Christensen, P. V. Thomas, and John Oss did much to establish and build the work among the Chinese.

In order to accomplish a more effective evangelism for the Black people scattered throughout San Francisco, the Bay area Black believers requested that they be organized into a church. The original congregation met in Oakland. In 1924 J. E. Cox was called to head this work in San Francisco. Later O. A. Troy conducted public evangelism in San Francisco, and a church of 18 members was organized in 1930.

On Feb. 19, 1947, the Central California Conference purchased a 104-acre (40-hectare) campground site at Soquel, near Santa Cruz, on the coast. The property, first used for camp meeting during the summer of 1948, was later improved by the addition of buildings such as an auditorium, cabins, and dining area.

Hanford Community Medical Center, a 54-bed acute-care hospital, was founded in 1908 by Hanford citizens. It was gifted to the Central California Conference in 1963. The present campus was acquired in 1964.

San Joaquin Community Hospital in Bakersfield was established in 1910 under the noble efforts of two Catholic sisters. By

1937 the hospital had one owner, Dr. Joseph Smith. In 1964 Dr. Smith requested that the hospital be managed by members of the Seventh-day Adventist Church as a nonprofit entity. The hospital was joined with the Adventist Health System/West in 1987. With a bed capacity of 178, it is one of Kern County's largest employers with a full and part-time staff of 825 employees.

The Sonora Community Hospital was started in 1900 as the Bromley Sanitarium and Hospital. The present facility was built in 1957, donated to the conference in 1961, and 10 years later became part of the Adventist Health System/West. In 1971 the hospital merged with the Sierra Hospital. In 1993, with 143 beds, more than 500 employees, and 100 physicians, the institution provides acute- and long-term care services and an urgent care center.

In 1903 Armona Union Academy began as a home school and grew into a 12-grade academy by 1912. However, for 26 years it reduced to a 10-grade school. Since 1939 it has served the constituent churches with 12 grades.

At the beginning of the school year 1968-1969, Bakersfield Academy became a senior academy with 12 grades. A new academy facility has been constructed at a cost of $279,000.

In 1965 Fresno Central church purchased a 40-acre (15-hectare) farm and built a new elementary school at 5397 East Olive. The construction cost including the 40-acre (15-hectare) tract was $380,000. Grades 1-6 were moved to the new location in 1967. The Fresno Adventist constituency funded the building of a new academy facility at a cost of $620,000. Classes began in the new buildings for the school year 1972-1973. Thus the entire school was moved from its West Belmont location to East Olive. Fresno Central church donated 27 acres (11 hectares) of the farm to the academy constituency, plus the elementary school.

A church school was begun in Modesto in 1910. It grew rapidly, resulting in several moves to accommodate the increasing number of students. Currently serving K-12 in a functional facility on 10 acres (four hectares), it even provides a unique training opportunity to those interested in religious broadcasting. This is accomplished at the SDA-owned KADV-FM radio station, which covers the northern part of the San Joaquin Valley.

Established in 1949, Monterey Bay Academy, with 3,000 feet (914 meters) of ocean frontage, has continued to serve as the only boarding academy in the conference. All students are required to be involved in the work program and are employed in one of the many industries on the campus.

A new academy plant was built at a cost of $1,261,764 in 1967 at the same location where Mountain View Union Academy had been in operation since 1922. Subsequently, the gymnasium and church building were destroyed by fire, and a new gymnasium was built and occupied in May 1972 at a cost of $282,000. Later a new multipurpose building was erected and occupied in August 1972 at a cost of $384,000.

On Sept. 5, 1972, Miramonte School was moved from Villa Street to the new school facility. The cost of the new elementary building was $422,000. The new school is located in Los Altos.

Until its move to Nampa, Idaho, in 1984 the Pacific Press Publishing Association was located in Mountain View.

Presidents: J. H. Behrens, 1911-1914; B. E. Beddoe, 1914-1915; N. P. Neilsen, 1915-1919; H. S. Shaw, 1919-1923; E. L. Neff, 1923-1929; H. H. Hicks, 1929-1930; R. S. Fries, 1930-1933; David Voth, 1933-1937; T. L. Copeland, 1937-1942; W. A. Nelson, 1942-1945; R. C. Baker, 1945-1955; D. E. Venden, 1955-1964; Elmer R. Walde, 1964-1968; M. C. Torkelsen, 1969-1970; E. W. Amundson, 1970-1976; Charles F. Cook, 1976-1988; Herbert H. Broeckel, 1988- .

CENTRAL CHIAPAS CONFERENCE. *See* Inter-American Division; Mexico.

CENTRAL CHILE CONFERENCE. *See* Chile; South American Division.

CENTRAL CONFERENCE. *See* Euro-Asia Division; Russia.

CENTRAL DELEGATION. *See* Cuba; Inter-American Division.

CENTRAL DOMINICAN CONFERENCE. *See* Dominican Republic; Inter-American Division.

CENTRAL ETHIOPIA FIELD. *See* Eastern Africa Division; Ethiopia.

CENTRAL EUROPEAN CONFERENCE. An organizational unit formed in the late 1880s (first listed in the 1889 *Yearbook*) to supervise the Seventh-day Adventist work in Eastern, Western, Southern, and Central

Europe, in the Middle East, and in North Africa. In 1891, after Germany and Eastern and Southeastern Europe territories and the Middle East were separated from it, the conference comprised the West European countries that are now in the Euro-Africa Division. In 1902 it was reorganized into the Latin Union.

CENTRAL EUROPEAN DIVISION. A large unit of church organization that functioned from 1929 to 1972, when it merged with the Trans-Mediterranean Division to form the Euro-Africa Division.

The Central European Division, with headquarters in Berlin, was formed when the European Division was divided into four parts in 1928. It then included not only Germany but also Austria, Hungary, and Czechoslovakia; the Balkan States of Albania, Greece, and Bulgaria; territory in the Middle East—Cyprus, Egypt, Iraq, Palestine, Persia (Iran), Sudan, Syria, Transjordan, and Turkey; also Liberia and Spanish and Portuguese colonies in Northwest Africa; and the Netherlands East Indies (Indonesia) in the Far East. Under the Hitler regime, when the German church was not allowed to send mission funds abroad, and so could not support the distant fields, the division was partitioned: Section II, which functioned separately until 1941, included Czechoslovakia (which returned to the German orbit in 1939), Hungary (which went to the Southern European Division in 1941), detached organizations, and mission fields except the Netherlands East Indies (which went to the Far Eastern Division). These missions were supported and administered by the General Conference as detached organizations after 1941, until they were incorporated into other divisions—the Northern European and the Southern European—or organized into a new division (Middle East). At the end of World War II Czechoslovakia and Austria were transferred to the Southern European Division and the Netherlands to the Northern European. Thus the Central European Division, as reorganized in 1948, was comprised only of Germany. It occupied the same territory as the German Inter-Union Association, an organization that had been set up within the area of the former European Division in 1927.

For the history of the SDA work in this area, *see* Germany.

Presidents: Henry F. Schuberth, 1929-1934; George W. Schubert, 1934-1938; Adolf Minck, 1938-1950; Wilhelm Müller, 1951-1962; R. Dettmar, 1962-1964; O. Gmehling, 1964-1970; Heinz Vogel, 1970-1971. (W. H. Branson was president of Section II [the parts outside of Germany] of the division in 1938; and H. L. Rudy, 1939-1941.)

CENTRAL EUROPEAN MISSION. The original organizational unit of the Seventh-day Adventist Church in Europe, which included (1) all of Europe except the British Isles and the Scandinavian countries, (2) the Middle East, and (3) North Africa. It dated from the arrival of J. N. Andrews in Switzerland in 1874 and was succeeded by the Central European Conference in the late 1880s.

CENTRAL EUROPEAN MISSIONARY SEMINARY. *See* Marienhöhe Seminary.

CENTRAL GHANA CONFERENCE. *See* Africa-Indian Ocean Division; Ghana.

CENTRAL INDIA UNION SECTION. *See* India; Southern Asia Division.

CENTRAL JAMAICA CONFERENCE. *See* Inter-American Division; Jamaica.

CENTRAL JAVA MISSION. *See* Indonesia.

CENTRAL KENYA CONFERENCE. *See* Eastern Africa Division; Kenya.

CENTRAL KOREAN MISSION. *See* Korea.

CENTRAL LAKE FIELD. *See* Eastern Africa Division; Malawi.

CENTRAL LUZON ADVENTIST ACADEMY. A coeducational boarding high school located in Bucaran, Bodega, Floridablanca, Pampanga, approximately 75 miles (120 kilometers) west of Manila. The school is located on 104 acres (42 hectares) in a small valley. It is free from noise and pollution, making it ideal for learning activities.

The school site was acquired in 1982. School construction began during the same year under the direction of the administrators of Central Luzon Mission. First to be erected were the administration building, the classrooms, and the dormitories. The academy is still hoping to build a permanent chapel and an auditorium. The supply of electricity comes from a 15 KVA generator powered by a diesel engine that operates five hours every night. There is an ample supply of water from a deep well distributed through an elevated tank. The farm is irrigated year-round by a spring from the mountains.

The academy opened during the school year 1984-1985 with an enrollment of 64 students under 10 teachers. On June 23, 1989, the academy received government recognition. During the 1992-1993 school year, the enrollment rose to 158 students, with 11 teachers. The academy operates a livestock industry and a farm with a banana plantation, a fruit tree plantation, and a vegetable garden.

Principals: Blandino C. Casi, 1985-1987; Antonio Arit, 1987-1989; Nelson G. Castillo, 1989- .

CENTRAL LUZON CONFERENCE. *See* Far Eastern Division; Philippines.

CENTRAL MALAGASY MISSION. *See* Africa-Indian Ocean Division; Madagascar.

CENTRAL MEXICAN CONFERENCE. *See* Inter-American Division; Mexico.

CENTRAL MINAS CONFERENCE. *See* Brazil; South American Division.

CENTRAL MISSION. *See* Mozambique; Euro-Africa Division.

CENTRAL MYANMAR MISSION. *See* Far Eastern Division; Myanmar.

CENTRAL NEW ENGLAND CONFERENCE. A former unit of church organization that comprised, from 1903 through 1909, the territory of New Hampshire and Massachusetts, and from January to October 1910 that of Massachusetts alone. Then its name was changed to the Massachusetts Conference. For the history of Seventh-day Adventist work in these two states, *see* Northern New England Conference; Southern New England Conference; Northeastern Conference.

CENTRAL PACIFIC UNION MISSION. *See* Cook Islands; Fiji Islands; French Polynesia; Niue Island; Pitcairn Island; Samoa and Tokelau Islands; Tonga; Tuvalu; South Pacific Division.

CENTRAL PAPUAN MISSION. *See* Papua New Guinea; South Pacific Division.

CENTRAL PERU CONFERENCE. *See* Peru; South American Division.

CENTRAL PHILIPPINE ADVENTIST COLLEGE. A senior college serving a constituency of more than 124,000 in the Central Philippine Union Mission. It is governed by a college board of 16 members representing the union and the medical institutions, the four missions, and the lay members in the union. The president of the union and the president of the college are the chair and secretary, respectively, of the board.

The college offers six curricula: B.S.A. (Bachelor of Science in Accountancy), B.S.B.A. (Bachelor of Science in Business Administration), B.S.N. (Bachelor of Science in Nursing), B.Th. (Bachelor of Theology), B.A.T. (Bachelor in Agricultural Technology), A.A.T. (Associate in Agricultural Technology), and J.S.C. (Junior Secretarial Course). As soon as government approval is secured, the B.S.E. (Bachelor of Secondary Education) with majors in English and Bible, and B.E.Ed. (Bachelor of Elementary Education), will be offered. With the addition of these two curricula, enrollment is expected to go beyond the present trend of 500-600 students.

Situated in Alegria, Murcia, 14 miles (23 kilometers) east of Bacolod City, on the island of Negros, CPAC rises against a backdrop of the beautiful tall mountains of the Marapara Range. Electricity comes from a government source, and springs on the property supply abundant clear, cool water, which is piped to the campus by gravity.

Industries include sugarcane production, cattle and poultry raising, rice milling, vegetable gardening, and bookbinding. The college also operates a small general store, a bakery, and a copying machine. These industries generate income as well as providing the students with work opportunities.

In 1993 there were 13 permanent buildings on the campus. A large multipurpose building (Noah's Ark) and the Far Eastern Division duplex for expatriates, with a guest apartment behind it, were made available in 1982. The bakery building, which has since been converted into faculty housing, was added in 1983. A rice mill-grain dryer and the motor pool building were erected in 1985. The women's dormitory, the nursing building, and the Quiet Hour clinic were added in 1987. In 1988 a cafeteria was built, and a faculty duplex added in 1991. The day-care center and the clinic have helped considerably in maintaining friendly relationships with the people in the surrounding area, which used to be controlled by rebels fighting against the government.

History and Development. Not long after the organization of Central Philippine Union Mission in 1964, its leaders dreamed of having a college. Years of "site-seeing" activities all over the Visayas, with Negros as front-runner, followed. Finally, in 1979, property was purchased for P600,000, and in 1985 a donation of $64,000 by Mrs. May Chung of Hawaii enlarged the property by 86 acres (35 hectares), bringing the total land purchased to 262 acres (106 hectares).

After 1979 events moved more rapidly. The General Conference set aside the second quarter 1981 Thirteenth Sabbath Overflow Offering for the Central Philippine Union Mission College project, giving it a greatly needed funding boost. On Aug. 12, 1981, 15 years after the dream was born, groundbreaking ceremonies for the college took place. Keynote speaker was Dr. C. D. Hirsch, General Conference director of education; and the guest speaker was the Honorable Alfredo Montelibano, Jr., governor of the province of Negros Occidental. With R. R. Victoriano, a Seventh-day Adventist architect-contractor, donating his services as supervising engineer, actual construction began on Oct. 2, 1981.

When the college first opened its doors to students on June 14, 1982, it was registered with the Department of Education, Culture, and Sports (DECS) as Central Philippine Adventist School; this name was changed to Central Philippine Adventist College upon approval by the DECS of the four-year college agriculture course on Oct. 11, 1985. Initially there was only the one large multipurpose building to house the 100 pioneering students and 17 faculty members and their families, along with space for administrative offices, cafeteria, classrooms, library, and auditorium for chapel, church, and other gatherings (hence the nickname "Noah's Ark"—surrounded by "oceans" of waving sugarcane, it had the likeness of its namesake). The student's rooms had no window shutters, the faculty apartments lacked not only window shutters but also room divisions, and classrooms did not have desirable chairs or acoustics. Classes met as construction continued. At first only two-year courses were offered—rural health, building construction, and an Associate in Agriculture degree.

In September 1984 Typhoon Nitang destroyed the "ark's" plywood walls, which later were replaced with concrete.

The following are milestones in the academic progress of the college. The DECS recognized the B.A.T. degree in 1985, the B.S.A. and the B.S.B.A. in 1989, and the B.S.N. in 1990. In March 1988 the Commission of Higher Education of the General Conference granted four-year senior college status to Central Philippine Adventist College, and in February 1993 the evaluating team of the General Conference Board of Regents recommended five-year accreditation for the college.

Presidents: David J. Recalde, 1981-1983; Mrs. Salvador G. Miraflores, 1983-1985; Eli A. Bingcang, 1985- .

CENTRAL PHILIPPINE UNION MISSION. *See* Far Eastern Division; Philippines.

CENTRAL RHENISH CONFERENCE. *See* Euro-Africa Division; Germany.

CENTRAL SÃO PAULO CONFERENCE. *See* Brazil; South American Division.

CENTRAL SDA PUBLISHING ASSOCIATION. *See* Review and Herald Publishing Association.

CENTRAL-SOUTH CAMEROON MISSION. *See* Africa-Indian Ocean Division; Cameroon.

CENTRAL STATES CONFERENCE. The unit of church organization comprising the Black constituency of Colorado, Iowa, Kansas, Minnesota, Missouri, Nebraska, North Dakota, South Dakota, Wyoming, and San Juan County, New Mexico (the area of the Mid-America Union Conference). Black population (1990), 1 million. Statistics (1993): churches, 37; members, 8,586; primary schools, 3; ordained ministers, 19; licensed ministers, 5; primary school teachers, 10. Headquarters: 3301 Parallel Parkway, Kansas City, Kansas. The conference forms part of the Mid-America Union Conference.

Local churches—*Colorado:* Colorado Springs (Palace of Peace), Denver (Community, Park Hill), Pueblo (Claremont); *Iowa:* Cedar Rapids (Covenant), Davenport (Calvary), Des Moines (Philadelphia); *Kansas:*

Atchison (Bethaven), Coffeyville (Mount Moriah), Independence (South Eighteenth), Kansas City (Bethel, Maranatha, New Life Real Truth), Leavenworth (Shiloh, Zion), Topeka (Highland Crest), Wichita (Grove Heights); *Minnesota:* Minneapolis (Ebenezer Fellowship); *Missouri:* Berkeley (Ebenezer), Charleston (Grand Avenue), Columbia (Breath of Life), Hayti (Emmanuel), Kansas City (Beacon Light, Linwood Temple, Real Truth), Kirkwood (Kirkwood), Pacific (Trinity), St. Joseph (Emmanuel), St. Louis (Agape, Berean, Northside), Sedalia (Sharon Chapel), Sikeston (Compress), Springfield (Providence); *Nebraska:* Lincoln (Allon Chapel), Omaha (Bethesda Temple, Sharon).

History. *Beginnings of the Work.* Kansas was the cradle of the work for the Black race in the area of the Central States Conference. About 1880, in a movement known as the "exodus," thousands of Blacks migrated from the Southern states to Kansas, seeking greater economic freedom, and scattered over the state wherever they could find homes.

On Oct. 12, 1885, C. M. Kinney (Kinny), who later became the first Black ordained minister in the denomination, began work in Topeka and Emporia. In May 1886 he reported in the *Review and Herald* that since October he had made 648 visits and distributed 16,525 tracts, and as a result five women in Emporia were professing to keep the Sabbath and two heads of families were much interested. Although there were few visible results of his work, the pioneer worker continued doggedly on. He began canvassing Nov. 11, 1887, with *The Great Controversy,* by Ellen G. White, in Kansas City, Kansas, and in Atchison, Hannibal, and St. Joseph, Missouri. A number of ministers bought his books, and he preached several times. In 1889 he spent six months canvassing in St. Louis. No churches were organized, but no doubt many of the converts attended services in the White churches.

In 1901 the Black members in Kansas City, Kansas, requested that they have their own meeting place and Sabbath school. In 1902, after meetings held by Sydney Scott and S. S. Ryles had added seven converts, a church of 19 was organized. After renting church space and meeting in halls for two years, the congregation built a church (completed Jan. 24, 1904) with the help of the Kansas Conference. Sydney Scott was the minister in charge at the time. In 1901 it was reported that the St. Louis Black members had formed their own company, which was growing, and that the Kansas City, Missouri, company (dating from 1899) was gaining in numbers. In February 1903 Scott reported two organized churches in Kansas City (Kansas and Missouri) of 16 and 14, respectively, the latter conducting "a Sabbath school of thirty and a Mission Sunday school of fifty." The Kansas City, Kansas, church pioneered the church school work. H. M. Hiatt, educational superintendent of the Kansas Conference in 1909, reported that the Black members of Kansas City, Kansas, "have determined to be in line with the other churches of the conference, and accordingly have organized a school which is doing good work" *(Kansas Worker* 19:2, Oct. 6, 1909). Hiatt noted that this school was perhaps the only SDA school exclusively for Black children north of the Mason-Dixon Line.

The Bethel church, 713 Freeman, Kansas City, Kansas, was built in 1919. A schoolroom was later added in the basement. In 1966 V. Lindsay led out in the purchase of the present church building and parsonage located at 716-720 Nebraska Avenue. The Kansas City, Missouri, group at first met in a rented hall, then bought the lot and building vacated by a branch of the Pacific Press when it left Kansas City in 1926. In 1943 the Beacon Light church was erected on that lot. Elizabeth Hanks, later married to H. J. Miller, of this church, was the first full-time Black Bible instructor in the Central Union Conference. In December of 1972 the church moved its location to Linwood Boulevard and Spruce Avenue, changing its name to Linwood Boulevard Temple, under the pastorate of T. A. McNealy.

The work in Colorado began under the leadership of Charles Lightner and Thomas Branch. At the camp meeting in 1901 a committee of three presented a memorial to the assembled delegates, asking that one or more Black workers be employed to work for their own people. The request was granted by vote of the delegates. The memorial stated that at the time there were about 60 Black members in the conference. Shortly afterward Branch was sent to Pueblo, where he held meetings in a hotel. William North led in building a tabernacle in that city, dedicated Jan. 11, 1903, which was probably the first SDA church building for a Black congregation in the Central States area. This building, which was used for a mission, burned down in 1904. Although Lightner and others worked in Denver, there is no record that a church was organized there until 1909.

In 1910 H.M.J. Richards (father of H.M.S. Richards), while pastor in Denver, sent out a call for money to help the Black members secure a lot on which to build a house of worship. Under the leadership of J. W. Owens a dwelling house was secured in 1913 and made into a comfortable church for the Denver members. This organization, known as the Denver Third church, was later renamed the Beth Haven Seventh-day Adventist Church, and still later the Park Hill Seventh-day Adventist Church.

In St. Louis, Missouri, before U. S. Willis was sent as a permanent worker in 1909, a layperson, M. E. George, had worked among the Black people for years, and through his efforts a company of 13 had been organized in 1904, which grew into the Berean Seventh-day Adventist Church, at the corner of Cook and Sarah avenues. On Sept. 29, 1927, a tornado laid waste about six square miles (16 square kilometers) of St. Louis, causing damages of $50 million and killing 87 persons. It completely demolished the Berean church, with the exception of the bell tower and church sign. The custodian, who was in the building at the time, escaped with minor injuries. The next Sabbath the congregation worshiped in an undertaker's parlor and after services went out visiting the 17 members whose homes had been entirely or partially destroyed. The General, union, and local conferences helped to buy another building. Later (1953) a church seating 700 was purchased. In 1963 a primary school of 60 pupils was taught by two teachers.

In the summer of 1964 E. E. Cleveland, of the General Conference Ministerial Association, conducted a field school of evangelism at St. Louis in cooperation with Andrews University. The evangelistic campaign resulted in the organization of another church, with a membership of 150—the Shreve Avenue church, later named Northside church. In 1974 a church of 38 members, known as Park Avenue, was established on the south side of St. Louis by S. T. Lewis, conference evangelist.

The year 1912 marked a real milepost in the history of the work, when, under the leadership of J. W. Allison, the first camp meeting was held for the Black membership of the Central Union Conference, at Lawrence, Kansas, Aug. 29 to Sept. 8. The next 15 years were marked by a steady growth of churches. Dan Coats and his wife moved from Clinton to Sedalia, Missouri, and opened a Sabbath school in their home; Ella Jackson, a Bible instructor, worked there as well. As a result, a church at Sedalia was organized in 1913. They met in homes and in an improvised storefront hall until 1935, when a frame church, known as the Sharon chapel, was erected. In 1913 J. W. Miller, assisted by local White members, formed a church at Atchison, Kansas, which met in homes for several years, but in time he secured a store, which was made into a meetinghouse.

In 1914 Miller went to Omaha, Nebraska, where the total Black membership consisted of two women who were members of the White congregation. After Bible studies and cottage meetings, a church of 25 was organized. In 1918 the church building formerly used by the White SDAs was purchased for the Sharon church. T. H. Allison pastored this church in 1929 and 1930. The church at Independence, Kansas, which probably was begun by Mrs. Gertrude Johnson, a Bible instructor, was admitted with its 13 members to the Kansas Conference on Aug. 22, 1924. The present building was erected in 1950. The Wabash Avenue church of Wichita, Kansas, received into the conference on Aug. 23, 1925, originated from lay meetings in the home of Charles Greadington in 1918. R. L. Bradford and H. A. Rossin later worked there. S. E. Wight, president of the Central Union Conference, reported in the *Central Union Outlook* in 1927 that the Black work had made great strides in the previous three years. Not only had many been added to the churches but excellent church homes also had been erected in Kansas City and Denver.

The College Avenue church at Topeka, organized Sept. 16, 1928, with 20 members, had its origin in a tent series conducted by the Black evangelist J. H. Lawrence and the White ministers C. S. Wiest and R. L. Boothby. The Philadelphia church at Des Moines came into being in May 1932 with 15 members as a result of meetings held by R. T. Hudson. At St. Joseph, Missouri, several laywomen held meetings in homes, and by 1911 they had gathered a little company. The present congregation, known as the Emmanuel church, was organized June 12, 1937. The Allon Chapel church of Lincoln, Nebraska, originated as a company of eight in 1943, resulting from the work of student colporteurs, with the help of Black Union College students, personal work, and house-to-house visits. It met in a rented hall, then in a building purchased in 1949. From a branch Sabbath school held by the Wichita people, the Wellington, Kansas, church of 12 charter members was organized in 1945.

Central States Mission. In 1946 the leaders among the Black people in the United States recommended that they be allowed to form their own church-governing bodies, in harmony with the new policy of forming Regional conferences. On Jan. 1, 1947, in the Jefferson Hotel in St. Louis, the Central States Mission was organized, with the Black members of the Central Union Conference (a membership of 798) forming the constituency. T. M. Rowe was elected president, and J. H. Jones, secretary-treasurer. The headquarters of the mission were at 2528 Benton Boulevard, Kansas City, Missouri. There followed a tremendous spurt in growth. In five years' time the mission had grown to the stature of a conference, with a membership increase of 76 percent—from 798 in 1947 to 1,408 in 1952, with baptisms averaging more than 100 a year. In 1948 the state of Iowa, of the Northern Union Conference, was added to the territory of the mission, thus adding the church at Des Moines.

The Central States Conference Organized. On Nov. 9, 1952, a constituency meeting held in the Beacon Light church in Kansas City, Missouri, organized the Central States Conference, with F. L. Bland, president, and H. T. Saulter, secretary-treasurer. Churches established since then include those at Kinloch, a suburb of St. Louis (20 members), in 1958; Sikeston, Missouri (22), and Junction City, Kansas, in 1960; Kirkwood, Missouri, in 1961; Springfield, Missouri, in 1962; Charleston, Missouri, in 1967; Coffeyville, Kansas (25 members), in 1972; Hayti, Missouri (16 members), in 1972. Membership rose from 1,408 in 1952 to 2,326 by the close of 1961, and the proportional gain by baptisms and profession of faith in 1961 was the second largest in North America. The number of primary schools is low because the churches are too far apart for consolidated schools, and also because in a number of places the children attend integrated primary schools.

The net gain in membership during the period of 1957-1962 was 524. In the same period eight houses of worship were acquired or constructed, including a quarter-million-dollar church in St. Louis and a modern stone structure in Omaha. In 1963 an intermediate school in St. Louis and a church in Denver were built.

An outstanding campaign was the "Contacts for Christ" program, whereby the laymen of St. Louis averaged 1,000 enlistments a month in the Bible correspondence courses, preparatory for evangelistic meetings by the Voice of Prophecy group. This evangelistic endeavor resulted in 100 baptisms.

In 1965 a new church building and a new elementary school building were erected in St. Louis; also church buildings were purchased in Wichita, Kansas, and Pueblo, Colorado.

Recent Developments. The conference office moved its headquarters in 1970 to 5737 Swope Parkway, Kansas City, Missouri, where a new building valued at more than $150,000 was erected during the administration of W. S. Lee, president, and J. E. Merideth, secretary-treasurer. The present location of the office is in Kansas City, Kansas.

When the Northern and Central unions merged in 1980 to form the Mid-America Union, the territory of the Central States Conference was extended to include Minnesota, North Dakota, and South Dakota.

The conference membership at the close of 1993 was 8,586. During that year more than $2.3 million tithe was returned to God, and total tithe and offerings was almost $4 million.

During the early 1990s Ebony Evangelism Project 2001 was conceived and put into operation as part of a comprehensive decade-long strategy for evangelism and church growth, representing the Global Mission focus of the North American Regional conferences and affirming the African-American heritage, talent, and potential to prepare a people to meet the Lord.

The first major interconference team evangelism activity involved 10 evangelistic efforts in Kansas City, Missouri (two meetings); St. Louis; Omaha; Topeka; Des Moines; Kansas City, Kansas; Denver; and Wichita.

The first Ebony Evangelism meeting was conducted in Wichita, Kansas, where Jerry Lee presented the great truths of the Advent message. As a result, 76 new members joined the Grove Heights church. In Des Moines, Iowa, Gene Donaldson held meetings in which 38 people joined the Philadelphia church there. David King presented the series in Topeka, Kansas, and 36 were baptized. Philip Willis held the Ebony Evangelism meetings in Omaha, Nebraska, and 91 people were baptized. In Denver, Colorado, despite a wave of violence, hundreds came to hear Raymond Sanders, and 156 joined the Park Hill church. In St. Louis, Missouri, Evangelist Calvin Watkins baptized 260 persons. George Rainey's meetings in Colorado Springs were also highly effective.

Taskforce Committee members included Alvin M. Kibble, chairperson; William C. Scales, Jr., cochairperson; DeWitt S. Williams, secretary; Robert Smith, NAD staff representative; Harold L. Lee, planning consultant; Owen A. Troy, communication consultant; Stennett H. Brooks; Willie J. Lewis; R. C. Brown, Sr.; J. Paul Monk, Jr.; Ralph Peay; Joseph W. McCoy; J. M. Doggette; and Robert Lister.

Presidents: T. M. Rowe, 1947-1948; F. L. Bland, 1948-1959; W. W. Fordham, 1959-1966; W. S. Lee, 1966-1971; D. L. Crowder, 1971-1974; S. D. Meyers, 1974-1979; S. Haywood Cox, 1979-1985; J. Paul Monk, Jr., 1985-1994; J. Alfred Johnson, 1994- .

CENTRAL SULAWESI MISSION. *See* Far Eastern Division; Indonesia.

CENTRAL SUMATRA MISSION. *See* Far Eastern Division; Indonesia.

CENTRAL TEXAS MEDICAL CENTER. A 109-bed hospital at San Marcos, Texas. Moved to its current location in 1983, the original hospital was built in 1960 by the commissioners court of Hays County and operated under a lease by the Texas Conference of Seventh-day Adventists. The contract was signed in December 1959 by county judge C. M. Decker, on behalf of Hays County officials, and by B. E. Leach, conference president. The hospital is a result of the reputation established by the Adventist-operated Menard Hospital and Retirement Home in Menard, Texas.

The original hospital location opened on Sunday, Mar. 6, 1960, and the first patients were admitted the next day. It provided 40 beds, a laboratory, an X-ray facility, two operating rooms, and a delivery room. In July of 1964 the facility changed its name to Hays Memorial Hospital. A training school for licensed vocational nurses began in 1966, under the direction of Hazel Kirkpatrick.

A growing community and medical staff, increasing patient needs, and a lack of availability of beds spurred fund-raising efforts to build a larger facility. In 1979 then Hays County judge Walter Burnett and Donald Welch, AHS president, led the way in planning and management of the current hospital. Hays Memorial Hospital opened its new doors in 1983 under a management agreement with AHS/Sunbelt.

In 1987 the name was changed to Central Texas Medical Center in order to reposition the hospital's image within the community and service area. In 1989 Central Texas Medical Center began a push to cut costs, revitalize patient services, and raise quality standards. Partnerships with the community and area businesses were reforged in order to develop strong networks of support. In 1992 Central Texas Medical Center accepted awards from *Hospitals* magazine's Turnaround competition: a nationwide measurement of health-care organizations on the rebound.

During 1992 Central Texas Medical Center added to its campus a three-story physicians' office building that houses a hospital-owned fitness center, magnetic imaging, and remodeled patient service areas (such as cardiopulmonary services) to keep up with the growing outpatient service. The center is accredited by the Joint Commission on Accreditation of Healthcare Organizations and is a member of the American Hospital Society.

Administrators: Herbert Fleenor, 1959-1960; Marvin C. Midkiff, 1960-1963; Bob Scott, 1963-1969; Alfred Tucker, 1970-1971; Jack Northcutt, 1971-1974; Stanley Hatkoff, 1974-1975; George Daschner, 1975-1987; Raymond Carney, 1987-1989; Joel W. Hass, 1989- .

CENTRAL UGANDA FIELD. *See* Eastern Africa Division; Uganda.

CENTRAL UKRAINIAN CONFERENCE. *See* Euro-Asia Division; Ukraine.

CENTRAL UNION CONFERENCE. The North American administrative unit that comprised the Central States, Colorado, Kansas, Missouri, Nebraska, and Wyoming conferences, with headquarters at 4547 Calvert Street, Lincoln, Nebraska. Official organ: *Central Union Reaper.* Institutions situated in the union area included: Boulder Memorial Hospital; Campion Academy; Christian Record Braille Foundation, Inc. (now Christian Record Services); College View Academy; Enterprise Academy; Mile High Academy; Pacific Press Publishing Association; Platte Valley Academy; Porter Memorial Hospital; Shawnee Mission Medical Center; Sunnydale Academy; Union College.

The Central Union Conference was organized in 1902 and took its territory from the Northwestern and Southwestern Union conferences, which had been formed in 1901. The Central Union Conference comprised Colorado, Iowa, Kansas, Missouri, Nebraska, and Wyoming, with a population of 8.7 million. In 1932 the Central Union Conference absorbed the Northern Union Conference (territory: Colorado, Iowa, Kansas, Minnesota, Missouri, Nebraska, North Dakota, South Dakota, and Wyoming). The Northern Union Conference was reorganized in 1937. In 1980 it became part of the Mid-America Union.

Presidents: E. T. Russell, 1902-1914; R. A. Underwood, 1914-1920; S. E. Wight, 1920-1928; J. J. Nethery, 1928-1932; J. F. Piper, 1932-1941; N. C. Wilson, 1941-1946; M. V. Campbell, 1946-1954; J. D. Smith, 1954-1957; Theodore Carcich, 1957-1962; R. H. Nightingale, 1962-1975; W. O. Coe, 1975-1977; Ellsworth Reile, 1977-1980.

CENTRAL UNION OUTLOOK (1911-1932; superseded by *Central Union Reaper;* weekly; files in GC). A former official organ of the Central Union Conference. It had been preceded, 1902-1904, by *Central Advance.*

CENTRAL UNION REAPER (1932-1980; superseded the *Central Union Outlook* and *Northern Union Reaper;* weekly; circulation was free to constituent members; files in GC). Official organ of the Central Union Conference. It was begun in place of the Northern Union and Central Union papers at the time when the Northern Union Conference was merged with the Central Union Conference, a combination that lasted only five years. In 1937, when the Northern Union was organized separately again, the name *Reaper* remained with the Central Union paper, and a new *Northern Union Outlook* was established. These continued until the formation of the Mid-America Union in July of 1980.

CENTRAL VENEZUELA CONFERENCE. *See* Inter-American Division; Venezuela.

CENTRAL VISAYAN MISSION. *See* Far Eastern Division; Philippines.

CENTRAL ZAMBIA FIELD. *See* Eastern Africa Division; Zambia.

CENTRAL ZIMBABWE CONFERENCE. *See* Eastern Africa Division; Zimbabwe.

CENTRE HORTICOLE DE BAZEGA. *See* Burkina Faso.

CENTRO ADVENTISTA DE ESTUDIOS SUPERIORES. *See* Central American Adventist University.

CENTRO ADVENTISTA DE CON VIVENCIA PARA IDOSAS. *See* São Paulo Old People's Home.

CENTRO ADVENTISTA DE SAÚDE. *See* Adventist Health Center.

CENTRO DE MIDIA VOZ DA PROFECIA. *See* Brazil.

CENTRO EDUCACIONAL ADVENTISTA. *See* Adventist Educational Center; Pacific Adventist Secondary School.

CENTRO EDUCACIONAL ADVENTISTA DE CHILE. *See* Chile Adventist Educational Center.

CENTRO EDUCACIONAL ADVENTISTA DE LOS ANGELES. *See* Los Angeles Adventist Academy (Chile).

CENTRO EDUCATIVO ADVENTISTA. *See* CEA Adventist Secondary School.

CENTRO EDUCATIVO ADVENTISTA DE COSTA RICA. *See* Costa Rica Secondary School (Costa Rica).

CENTRO EDUCATIVO ADVENTISTA DE LIMON. *See* Costa Rica Secondary School (Limon).

CENTRO EDUCATIVO IGNACIO MANUEL ALTAMIRANO. *See* Ignacio Manuel Altamirano Educational Center.

CEREMONIAL LAW. *See* Law.

CEYLON. *See* Sri Lanka.

CEYLON ADVENTIST PRESS. *See* Lakpahana Press of Seventh-day Adventists.

CEYLON MISSION SCHOOL. *See* Lakpahana Adventist Seminary.

CHACO SANITARIUM AND HOSPITAL. *See* Loma Linda Adventist Sanitarium.

CHAD. An African republic independent since Aug. 11, 1960. Chad is bounded on the north by Libya, on the east by the Sudan, on the west by Niger, Nigeria, and Cameroon, and on the south by the Central African Republic. It has an area of 495,755 square miles (1.2 million square kilometers), and a population (1994) of about 5.5 million, most of whom are Negroid, speaking Sudanic dialects. Nearly half are Muslims. Most of the people support themselves by agriculture.

The territory of Chad constitutes the Chad Mission, a part of the Central African Union Mission, which in turn is part of the Africa-Indian Ocean Division. Statistics (1992) for *Chad:* churches, 28; members, 788; elementary schools, 3; ordained ministers, 1; licensed ministers, 8. Chad Mission headquarters are at N'Djamena.

Work was begun in Chad in 1967 with the arrival of Albert Bodenmann and his family in Fort-Lamy, the capital, later named N'Djamena. A medical center was constructed in Béré, under the supervision of Armin Krakolinig.

CHAD MISSION. *See* Africa-Indian Ocean Division; Chad.

CHAE TAE HYUN (1888-1943). One of the pioneer Korean evangelists and church leaders. He was a graduate of Won Heung Middle School and studied at Korean Baptist Seminary. He was baptized into the Baptist Church in 1906. In 1910 he joined the Seventh-day Adventist Church and entered evangelistic work, serving as a licensed minister in the Central and West Chosen missions (1910-1922). After his ordination in 1922, he served as district leader of Kando district in Manchuria (1922-1926), president of Central Chosen Mission (1926-1930), Bible teacher at Korean Union Training School at Soonan (1930-1932), president of Central Chosen Mission (1932-1934), president of West Chosen Mission (1934-1940), and president of Chosen Union Mission (1941-1942). He was placed at the head of the SDA Church administration in Korea during World War II, but his service was cut short by the Japanese, who then controlled the country and whose policy it was to suppress Christianity. They imprisoned him along with many other Christian leaders and tortured him to death four months later, on June 2, 1943. He was probably the first SDA martyr in Korea. His name is also transliterated Choi Tai Hyun.

CHAMBERLAIN, E.L.H. (1798-1855). Layperson of Middletown, Connecticut. He and his wife were among the first Seventh-day Adventists in that state who accepted the seventh-day Sabbath. He invited James and Ellen White to visit neighboring Rocky Hill, Connecticut, where the first of a series of "Sabbath Conferences" was held on Apr. 20, 1848, and where the Whites had their headquarters at the time they launched the first SDA periodical, *Present Truth,* in July 1849.

CHAN SHUN INTERNATIONAL FOUNDATION. An international foundation established by Dr. Chan Shun and his sons, Drs. Tom and Caleb Chan, in June 1989. The purpose of this foundation is "to support nonprofit organizations in their pursuit of educational, medical, missionary, and charitable endeavors that substantially reflect the purpose, mission, and philosophy of the Seventh-day Adventist Church." A gift of US$10 million was delivered to the General Conference by the Chan family at the Annual Council of 1989 as initial capital for the new foundation. A similar foundation in Hong Kong, the Chan Shun Foundation, had been set up in 1974 by Dr. Chan Shun.

Before retiring, Dr. Chan Shun was a businessperson in Hong Kong. With a profound gratitude to his Creator and Saviour, who had abundantly blessed him, Dr. Chan decided, from the very beginning of his career, to return to God a significant portion of his wealth as a good steward, and to keep the Sabbath. For 40 years the signs of Sabbath closing on the doors of his garment factories and more than 30 retail stores witnessed to God's love and His commandments before the community. When Dr. Chan Shun retired in the late 1980s, his sons took over and continued to build up the family business.

During the past 20 years the Chan family has from time to time contributed large sums of funds to increase the assets of these foundations, and from them millions of dollars have flowed to scores of Seventh-day Adventist organizations for various projects. From 1989 to 1992 more than US$13.6 million was committed to fund 40 projects. Most of the recipients are universities, colleges, and other educational institutions.

Drs. Tom and Caleb Chan have established other foundations to enhance the functions of the Chan family charities around the world. Major projects by the Chan family foundations in Asia included the full cost of a 400-seat chapel at Hong Kong Adventist College in 1965; HK$1 million to initiate the building fund for the Hongkong Adventist Hospital in 1969;

HK$5 million for the Hong Kong Adventist College Foundation in 1983; HK$10 million for the Tsuen Wan Adventist Hospital from 1982 to 1990; and HK$10 million for the new 1,500-student Adventist school in Macao in 1993.

Other projects supported by the Chan Shun International Foundation included an endowment for Adventist World Radio-Asia; the School of Business at Andrews University; a scholarship endowment for Loma Linda University; the Academic Center at the Adventist International Institute of Advanced Studies; the science complex and an endowment for Pacific Union College; the Dining Commons at Atlantic Union College; the School of Engineering at Walla Walla College; the Science Center at Canadian Union College; and others.

CHANEY, FRANK L. (1872-1963). Missionary, educator, and administrator in Australia, New Zealand, Philippines, West Indies, and Mexico. He was born in Nebraska and educated at Union College. He and his wife, née Bertha Shanks, studied nursing at Battle Creek Sanitarium. In 1901 they went to the Australasian field, and while there established and directed the first Seventh-day Adventist academy in New Zealand. In 1916 he was headmaster at Avondale College.

Returning to the United States, he joined the staff of Washington Missionary College (now Columbia Union College) as dean and teacher of English. Several years later he went to the Philippines, where he was secretary-treasurer and home missionary leader for about four years, until his health failed and he returned home. In 1936 he volunteered to serve in the Inter-American Division as a self-supporting worker and served there as secretary-treasurer of the Antillian Union and of the Jamaica Mission. Between 1942 and 1951 he promoted educational work in northern Mexico, reputedly establishing 13 schools in the Sonora Mountains. After the death of his wife he married Leonora Lacey Warriner.

CHANNEL ISLANDS. *See* Great Britain and Northern Ireland.

CHAPLAINS, CIVILIAN. *See* National Service Organization.

CHAPLAINS, MILITARY. Ordained Seventh-day Adventist ministers assigned as chaplains in the military forces. *See* Adventist Chaplaincy Ministries.

CHAPMAN, MINERVA JANE (LOUGHBOROUGH) (1829-1923). Financial administrator; treasurer of the General Conference (1877-1883); editor of the *Youth's Instructor* (1875-1879, 1884-1889). She was a daughter of Nathan and Minerva Loughborough and a sister of J. N. Loughborough. She became an Adventist early in her life and remained a firm and consistent follower of her religious convictions until her death at nearly 94 years of age. She married Oscar A. Chapman in 1857. In 1866 the couple moved to Battle Creek, where she joined the staff of the Review and Herald as a typesetter. Her ability and faithful service led to her advancement in 1875 to the position of treasurer, and in 1876 to that of secretary of the Central SDA Publishing Association (now the Review and Herald Publishing Association). She held the latter position until 1883. From 1877 to 1883, she was treasurer of the General Conference, and in the 1885, 1886, and 1887 *Yearbooks,* she is listed as corresponding secretary of the General Conference. In 1875 she was elected to her first period of service as editor of the *Youth's Instructor.* In 1884 she returned to the editorial office, from which she retired in 1889, although she continued as editorial contributor. She retired from the Review and Herald in 1893, after 26 years of service.

CHAPTER EXCHANGE (1950-1964; vols. 1-6, 1950-1956, four times during the school year, September to May; vols. 7-15 twice a year, irregular; published by the ATS). A former organ of the American Temperance Society published as a medium of information and coordination among its college and academy chapters. It began as a four-page newspaper-size periodical but later was reduced in size to about one fourth a newspaper-size page. It carried the news regarding oratorical, essay, poster, and jingle contests and promoted temperance activities among the youth, including youth-for-youth activities. In 1965 it was superseded by *Listen News.*

Editors: Don Roth, 1950-1951; Francis A. Soper, 1951-1953; Winton H. Beaven, 1953-1956; James V. Scully, 1956-1964.

CHARITIES. *See* City Missions; Clinics and Dispensaries; Community Services; Adventist Development and Relief Agency.

CHARLES F. KETTERING MEMORIAL HOSPITAL. *See* Kettering Medical Center.

CHARLES HARRISON MEMORIAL HOME. *See* Adventist Retirement Village, Inc.

CHARLOTTE HOSPITAL ASSOCIATION, INC. *See* Medical Center Hospital.

CHARTS, EVANGELISTIC. *See* Art in the Seventh-day Adventist Church.

CHASE, FANNIE M. (DICKERSON) (1864-1956). Teacher, editor, author. She was one of the early students at South Lancaster Academy and taught mathematics and science there from 1884 to 1904. She was editor of the *Youth's Instructor* from 1903 to 1922. Among her published works are *Good Form and Social Ethics, In Starland, God Revealed in the Natural World,* and *Speakers' Manual of Pronunciation.*

CHESAPEAKE CONFERENCE. A unit of church organization comprising the territory of Delaware and Maryland (except Allegany and Garrett counties and certain portions of Montgomery and Prince Georges counties adjoining the District of Columbia, that is, beginning at Mount Vernon, draw a line to Piscataway, continue the line northeast to the junction of highways 301 and 214, from this point continue the line northwest to the junction of highways 650 and 198 [Brown's Corner], then follow highway 650 north to Ednor, from Ednor follow Ednor Road northeast to the Patuxent River); the Virginia counties of Accomac and Northampton; the West Virginia counties of Berkeley, Jefferson, and Morgan. *(See also* Allegheny East and West conferences.) Statistics (1992): churches, 53; members, 8,662; church schools, 15; ordained ministers, 38; licensed ministers, 7; teachers, 54. Headquarters are at 6600 Martin Road, Columbia, Maryland 21044. The conference forms part of the Columbia Union Conference.

Institutions. Highland View Academy.

Local churches—*Maryland:* Atholton, Baltimore (First, Korean, Spanish), Bell Branch, Blythedale, Brooklyn, Cambridge, Catoctin View, Chestertown, Dundalk, Federalsburg, Frederick, Glen Burnie, Grasonville, Hagerstown, Highland View, Linthicum, Middletown Valley, New Hope, Norrisville, Park (Salisbury), Parkville-Essex, Pasadena, Patuxent, Pocomoke, Prince Frederick, Providence, Reisterstown, Rising Sun, Rock Hall, Spencerville (English, Korean), Towson, Triadelphia, Waldorf, Westminster, Williamsport, Willow Brook, Wilna. *Delaware:* Dover (First), Forest Grove, Harrington, Seaford, West Wilmington. *West Virginia:* Berkeley Springs, Charles Town, Martinsburg. *Virginia*: Cornerstone.

Companies—*Maryland:* Aberdeen, Annapolis, Baltimore. *Delaware:* Middletown, Sussex Central.

History. *Beginnings of the Work in the Area.* The Adventist message was preached in the territory of the present Chesapeake Conference as early as 1851 by that hardy pioneer, Joseph Bates. In the *Review and Herald* of that year he reported visiting "Advent believers," that is, former Millerites, in Baltimore for five days and holding several meetings. Seven years earlier, as one of the leaders in the Millerite movement, he had preached the 1843 message on Kent Island, in Chesapeake Bay, accompanied by H. S. Gurney. The two Adventist preachers defied the threat of being ridden out of town on a rail and went on to preach in several places on Maryland's Eastern Shore, which is the portion of the state east of the Chesapeake Bay. At Centreville, Chestertown, Three Corners, and Elkton these preachers made a marked impression on both the Whites and the Black slaves.

Beginning in 1876, the *Review and Herald* carried intermittent reports from preachers and colporteurs, telling of converts made and churches established in Maryland and Delaware. The first baptisms in Maryland were in Calverton, now a portion of Baltimore. The church organized there had a curious beginning. Early in 1876 a Mr. Pope from Washington came teaching the Sabbath but not keeping it himself. He was followed by a fanatical Sabbathkeeper who taught many errors and confused the interested people. In June, D. M. Canright held meetings there for a week, baptized seven, and organized a church, with John F. Jones as elder. Canright crossed to the Eastern Shore to visit five Seventh-day Adventist families who had moved into Caroline County for the purpose of doing missionary work among their neighbors. He preached 15 times and organized 11 members into the second Seventh-day Adventist church in Maryland. The next year Roswell F. Cottrell held meetings at Baltimore and on the Eastern Shore. In 1879, according to reports by I. Sanborn from the region of Baltimore, the brethren requested to be included in what was then the Virginia Mission.

During the next few years the groups in Baltimore and on the Eastern Shore dwindled as families moved away until in 1886, when Victor Thompson arrived, there were only 16 or 18 adherents, including children, in Maryland, and there was no organized church. However, in mid-1888, D. E. Lindsey and D. C. Babcock reported 28 Sabbathkeepers in Maryland and Delaware, and in October a church of 16 members was organized at Baltimore. Evangelism was conducted in several places in northern Maryland and the Eastern Shore and also in Delaware. In 1890 the Pleasant Grove church, near Hollandsville, Delaware, dedicated the first church building in the newly organized Atlantic Conference, a large part of which later became the Chesapeake Conference. Work was conducted by S. J. Hersum in Wilmington, Delaware, in 1891.

In 1892 churches at Rock Hall and Ford's Store, now Grasonville, Maryland, were organized as a result of meetings held by R. D. Hottel, E. E. Franke, and others. In the same year began a series of prosecutions for violation of Sunday laws, and John N. Judefind of Rock Hall was jailed for husking corn on Sunday. The next year there were seven other cases in court at one time, involving six members of the Ford's Store church—Isaac Baker, C. O. Ford, J. Alex. Dodd, George W. Marvel, Milton A. Bryan, and Joseph H. Warran. In 1894 the sixteenth church in the (then Atlantic) conference was organized at Church Hill, Maryland, after evangelistic meetings held by three ministers, S. B. Horton, R. D. Hottel, and H. E. Robinson. Sunday prosecutions continued. By 1896 it was reported that at least one from each church in Maryland had been arrested. In 1898 J. H. Rhodes and John Curlett were jailed in Centreville, and the latter was arrested again in 1907.

Chesapeake Conference Organized. In 1899 in a subdivision of the territory of the Atlantic Conference, the Chesapeake Conference was organized, composed of Delaware, all of Maryland except three of its northwestern counties (which were connected with the West Virginia Conference), and the District of Columbia. K. C. Russell was elected as the first president. At the time of organization the conference, in an area population of 1.5 million, had a membership of more than 700, two ordained ministers, two licentiates, three Bible instructors, four canvassers, and one tentmaster. The largest church, in Baltimore, had 130 members.

When the General Conference of 1901 effected a major administrative reorganization, the Chesapeake Conference became part of the new Eastern Union Conference, which in a redistribution of territory shortly afterward was renamed the Atlantic Union Conference. This union included also all of the present Columbia Union except Ohio.

Subsequent History. In 1901 the first year of the new century, the Chesapeake Conference had 10 churches and five church schools. In the first decade of the twentieth century there were often financial difficulties. Poor years in the Chesapeake Bay fishing industry affected many Eastern Shore members, and some moved away.

In 1903 with the establishment of the General Conference headquarters and of the Review and Herald Publishing Association in Washington, D.C., the churches of the District of Columbia and Takoma Park were placed under General Conference administration. In the same year the counties of Garrett, Allegany, and Washington in western Maryland, and of Morgan, Berkeley, and Jefferson in eastern West Virginia were added to the Chesapeake Conference.

Churches were organized at Cambridge, Maryland (1902), Fairmount, Maryland (1903), and near Cheswold, Delaware (1903). This Cheswold (now Forest Grove) church, described as "the only one of its kind in our country," was composed of "Moors," descendants, according to two traditions, either of a family of Irish and Black origin who intermarried with the Nanticoke Indians, or of shipwrecked Moorish sailors. This mixed group had long remained separate from its White and Black neighbors, attending its own schools. F. H. Seeney, "a Moor from Cheswold," spent many years in evangelistic work among the Blacks.

The work in Baltimore went through several stages of development. The First church, having sold its building in 1904, met in a succession of halls, as did the Second church. In evangelistic endeavors during this time, speakers from the denominational headquarters at Washington assisted in meetings and religious-liberty lectures. A Young People's Society (organized 1906) mailed letters and tracts to ministers and rabbis. Another type of literature work was the distribution of foreign-language tracts aboard ships in the harbor. A one-day meeting (1907) in Glen Burnie opened the way for an evangelistic series that resulted in a church there. Ten campaigns were conducted in Baltimore, some in English, others in German.

The difficulty in reaching the mass of the

White population in segregated Baltimore led, as in Washington and farther south, to the establishment of separate work for and by the Blacks, which resulted in the Third church, organized in 1909. In Dover, Delaware, in 1907 F. H. Seeney found his tent meetings for the Black people filling up with White listeners in such numbers that a minister by the name of Nutter was sent to take care of the additional interest. In 1912 the conference reported one Black church each in Maryland and Delaware, apparently the Baltimore Third and the Wilmington Second.

In 1907 the Chesapeake Conference, and the conferences of Virginia, West Virginia, East Pennsylvania, West Pennsylvania, and New Jersey were taken from the Atlantic Union, and, with the addition of Ohio, were constituted as the Columbia Union Conference. The Chesapeake Conference at this time was not self-supporting, but help was soon provided by other conferences that were. The Iowa Conference sent two young men for two years; Ohio sent two, supporting one for a year while the Northern Union supported the other. In 1909 two ministers held meetings in Baltimore, G. P. Gaede in German and Carlyle B. Haynes in English. Three new churches were organized: Smithsburg, Maryland; Dover, Delaware; and the new Baltimore church, formed by disbanding and recombining the old First and Second churches. In 1910 and 1911 several other churches were admitted: the Baltimore German, Crystal Falls (later Pondsville), Rock Hall (reorganized), and Blythedale.

In 1911 Haynes's Baltimore evangelism continued. A feature of his meetings was Monday night health lectures by doctors from Washington. Another feature was a series of articles that he prepared for the local newspapers under the instruction of a recent convert, Walter L. Burgan of the staff of the Baltimore *American.* Of 88 articles submitted, 84 were accepted.

In 1912 a new evangelistic venture was launched in Baltimore. The purchase of a building on Ellamont Street provided space for the conference headquarters, and for a training center called the City Mission Home, in which lived the city evangelist F. W. Paap, and his helpers, including young Bible instructors in training.

Recent Developments. The conference membership increased by 1916 to 582, and in 1917 to 700. In 1920 there were seven ordained ministers, 21 churches, and a membership of about 1,200, which rose to 1,415 by 1922 and then declined to a low of 1,096 by 1931 (with seven ordained ministers and 23 churches). The total rose to 2,642 (with eight ministers and 35 churches) by the end of 1944. Then the transfer of the Black constituency (728 members) to the new Allegheny Conference (organized 1945) reduced the Chesapeake totals to 1,914 members, five ministers, and 31 churches. But the membership rose again steadily and reached 3,204 in 1960, with 19 ministers and 38 churches.

The development of the work was reflected also in the expansion of facilities. The headquarters building on Ellamont Street had been purchased for $1,700. On Dec. 16, 1924, the old seven-acre (three-hectare) Schermerhorn estate in Catonsville, a western suburb of Baltimore, was purchased for $19,500. This provided a site for a permanent campground until 1971. It was also used for the conference office until it was moved to newer and larger quarters, acquired in 1951 when Dr. Maurice Pincoffs sold his 13-acre (five-hectare) estate to the conference.

In 1942 major improvements were begun on the campground by the erection of a large pavilion. In 1947, with the lifting of the last vestige of old conference debts, a new era of progress began. The acquisition of a 300-acre (120-hectare) tract in the foothills of Mount Aetna, near Hagerstown, furnished a site for a new summer camp, the 12-grade Mount Aetna Academy, and six church-owned residences. In Baltimore a new day academy was established. Throughout the conference several additional 10-grade schools came into being. Four schools were established in as many unentered counties, and work was begun in three others. With 22 new church buildings, these improvements represented, in all, an expenditure of far more than $1 million.

On Sept. 3, 1967, Highland View Academy replaced the former Mount Aetna Academy. The same year a new $400,000 conference office building was completed and opened in Columbia, Maryland, on a seven-acre (three-hectare) site donated to the conference by Mr. and Mrs. Elmer D. Snook. Besides the land, the Snooks gave a sizable sum of cash toward the erection of the buildings.

In 1971 the old Catonsville campgrounds were sold and the campsite was relocated at Highland View Academy, Mount Aetna, Maryland. A new conference warehouse and a complete trailer city were added the same year.

The youth camp was completely rebuilt at Mount Aetna in 1974. In 1991 it was completely demolished and rebuilt in 1992.

Presidents: K. C. Russell, 1899-1900; O. O. Farnsworth, 1900-1906; Morris Lukens, 1906-1908; L. F. Starr, 1908-1909; F. L. Richardson, 1909; R. T. Baer, 1910-1915; M. C. Kirkendall, 1915-1916; J. O. Miller, 1916-1918; A. S. Booth, 1918-1922; J. W. McCord, 1922-1925; R. M. Spencer, 1925-1928; J. A. Leland, 1928-1930; F. H. Robbins, 1931-1934; H. J. Detwiler, 1934; W. C. Moffett, 1934-1940; C. V. Leach, 1940-1947; C. V. Anderson, 1947-1957; M. E. Loewen, 1957-1959; A. B. Butler, 1959-1963; Cyril Miller, 1963-1968; W. R. May, 1968-1976; Philip Follett, 1976-1978; George Woodruff, 1978-1985; Wayne Coulter, 1985- .

CHIANG MAI ADVENTIST EDUCATIONAL CENTER. A coeducational boarding school that includes a tribal adult school for young people, an academy, and a primary church school. The tribal adult school began in 1971 under the direction of Jon Dybdahl as a literacy program for tribal young people above the age of 14, offering grades 1-4. This was later upgraded to grades 1-9.

The Thailand Adventist Academy was established in 1974, offering grades 7-10. Chalaw Artamapadung was the first principal. In 1980 the academy and tribal adult school merged to become Thailand Adventist Educational Center, with Nancy Bassham as administrator. In that same year the academy was upgraded to a full senior academy, offering grades 7-12.

An elementary church school with grades 1-6 was opened in 1992. The combined schools now operate under the name Chiang Mai Adventist Educational Center.

Principals/Administrators: *Tribal School*: Jon Dybdahl, 1971-1974; Roger Kopitzke, 1974-1977; Helton Fisher, 1977-1979; Pat Gustin, 1979-1980. *Thailand Adventist Academy*: Chalaw Artamapadung, 1974-1977; Nancy Bassham, 1977-1980. *Chiang Mai Adventist Educational Center*: Nancy Bassham, 1980-1981; Pat Gustin, 1981-1983; Art Bell, 1983-1991; Merilyn Beveridge, 1991- .

CHICAGO CONFERENCE. *See* Illinois Conference.

CHICAGO MISSION AND BIBLE SCHOOL. *See* City Missions; Workers' Institutes.

CHICAGO SANITARIUM. A medical institution in Chicago, Illinois, established in 1893 and listed in the *Yearbook* until 1905. It was conducted as a branch of the Battle Creek Sanitarium in a building formerly occupied by the Chicago Mission and Bible School (otherwise called Central Bible School) at 28 College Place (apparently later renamed Thirty-third Place). For many years the sanitarium served as a center for various medical missionary activities in the Chicago area. The purchase of the property, held by the American Medical Missionary College, was made possible through a gift of $40,000 by Henry S. P. and Francis H. Wessels, of South Africa, who wanted to see Seventh-day Adventist medical missionary work established in Chicago. Drs. E. H. Mathewson and H. E. Brighouse were in charge in 1896; later David Paulson and Frank J. Otis superintended the work there.

CHICAGO SEVENTH-DAY ADVENTIST ACADEMY. A nonboarding educational institution formerly known as Shiloh Academy. It was started in 1913 at the corner of 48th and D avenues. In 1925 a new church and school was built at 46th and St. Lawrence. High school grades 9-12 were introduced in 1933. In 1942 the institution moved to 39th and Lake Park, and in 1952 the school moved to its present location at 7008 South Michigan Avenue.

Chicago Seventh-day Adventist Academy is recognized by the state of Illinois and accredited with the Board of Regents of Seventh-day Adventists and the North Central Association of Colleges and Schools.

Principals: Ivan Van Lange, 1971-1987; Carolyn Palmer, 1987-1992; Judith Fisher, 1992-199≥4; Benjamin Furman, 1994- .

CHICHOKI MALLIAN HOSPITAL. *See* Pakistan.

CHICHOKI MALLIAN SCHOOL. *See* Pakistan Adventist Seminary.

CHILD DEDICATION. A custom of presenting infants to the Lord in a simple dedication ceremony during a regular worship service in the church. The practice seems to have developed gradually among the church pastors, without official action by the Seventh-day Adventist Church. The purpose is to acknowledge with gratitude the goodness of God, who has brought the children into Christian homes; to help parents recognize the serious responsibility of teaching and training the children from earliest years for the service of God; and to acknowledge the claim the children have upon the prayers and the services of the church.

A typical dedication service might take the following form: Appropriate scriptures, such as Deut. 6:4-7; Matt. 18:10, 5, 14, are read as the parents stand before the pulpit holding their child, or children, and the minister says: "Do you now present this child [or these children] before God in solemn dedication? Do you seriously resolve that, guided by the Spirit of God and seeking the grace of Christ, you will bring him or her up in the nurture and admonition of the Lord, and always regard this as your constant duty and sacred trust? Do you seek so to order your home, your words, your deeds, that this your child shall at all times be encompassed about with pure thoughts, holy living, and Christlike example, so that the child will most naturally come to an open confession of Christ by baptism at the proper age, and thus into the fellowship and the service of the church of Jesus Christ?" Parents may respond in the words of Jesus: "And for their sakes I sanctify myself, that they also might be sanctified through the truth" (John 17:19).

Then the minister prays for God's blessing to be with both child and parents. At the close of the service some ministers present a certificate of dedication to the parents.

The child's name may be officially recorded in the back of the church record book, not as a member but as belonging to the "household of faith."

CHILDREN'S FRIEND (braille). *See* Christian Record Services, Inc.

CHILE. A republic situated on the southwest coast of South America, with Argentina and Bolivia on the east, Peru on the north, the Pacific Ocean on the west, and on the south, the pole.

It has an area of 292,256 square miles (756,945 square kilometers) of continental and insular territory, plus 482,625 square miles (1.2 million square kilometers) of Antarctic territory. The estimated population (1994) is 14 million, 75 percent of Spanish descent, 20 percent from other nationalities, mostly European, and 5 percent Indian. Spanish is the national language. In religion, 89 percent are nominal Roman Catholics. The remaining 11 percent are Protestants (Presbyterian, Baptist, Methodist, Christian and Missionary Alliance, Pentecostal, Assembly of God, Lutheran, Jehovah's Witnesses, and Seventh-day Adventist), Jews, those without religion, and Indians with primitive religious beliefs. The Indians practice an indigenous monotheistic religion that involves shamanism and magic. The country consists of a valley enclosed between two mountain ranges, the Andes on the east and the Coastal Range on the west. The Andes chain, with more than 25 peaks more than 20,000 feet (6,000 meters) in elevation, contains mountains second in height only to the Himalayas. From north to south there are roughly three natural climatic zones: warm deserts in the north, a temperate central valley, and cold channels and archipelagos in the south. Chile is the principal mining country in South America. There are more than 115,000 square miles (297,850 square kilometers) of arable soil, forests, and pastureland.

Historical Background. The aboriginal inhabitants of what is now Chile were Araucanian Indians. During the fifteenth century the Inca Indians from Peru pushed south into northern Chile, but were unable to subjugate the Araucanians of central and south Chile. The first European to land in Chile was Magellan, in 1520. In 1535 the Spaniard Diego de Almagro began a conquest of the country, which was continued under Pedro de Valdivia. Spanish priests introduced Catholicism, which in time became the religion of the majority of people. Spain ruled Chile through Peru for the next three centuries, but on Sept. 18, 1810, the first national government was proclaimed. The struggle for independence led by Bernardo O'Higgins, aided by the Argentine general José de San Martín, ended successfully in 1818. The formative period of the republic took place between 1818 and 1830. In 1823 slavery was abolished, Chile being the first country in South America to do so. When President Prieto took office, he ended a period of anarchy, and together with his minister, Portales, consolidated the republic. A constitution was issued in 1833 that established a presidential type of government. This constitution lasted until 1925, thus permitting a long period of stability and prosperity with reaffirmation of democratic institutions. It established the Catholic Church as the state religion. During Prieto's government there was a war against the Peru-Bolivian Confederation (1836-1839) that ended with the victory of Chile, but did not increase its territory. The discovery of nitrate in the northern pampa later on and the fact that boundary definitions were left in abeyance at the fall of the viceroyship created conflicts with Bolivia. The discussions resulted in the War of the Pacific (1879-1883) when Bolivia, with Peru as an ally, lost. As a consequence Chile received the territory of Tarapaca (Peru) and Antofagasta (Bolivia). Later on (1929), Chile returned Tacna to Peru. Because of the different interpretation given to the constitution of 1833 by the Parliament and the executive power, there was a revolution (1891). The Parliament won, and for more than 30 years a parliamentary government system prevailed until a new constitution was issued (1925). It definitely established the presidential government system, declared separation of church and state, and recognized religious liberty. Chile maintained diplomatic relations with the Vatican.

In 1925 advanced social legislation was begun. Human rights were definitely established in the constitution. After World War II, when the United Nations issued the document entitled "Declaration of Human Rights," Chile was represented. The democratic system became a way of life of the citizen, and made possible the Marxist government that was elected (1970), even against the wishes of almost two thirds of the voters. On Sept. 11, 1973, the armed forces overthrew that government.

Seventh-day Adventist Statistics. The territory of Chile constitutes the Chile Union Mission, which is divided into two local conferences and two local missions. The Chile Union is part of the South American Division. Statistics (1992) for *Chile:* churches, 377; members, 74,396; elementary schools, 33; ordained ministers, 99; licensed ministers, 55; credentialed missionaries, 106.

Chile Union Mission headquarters are at Santiago. Statistics (1992) for the conferences and missions—*Central Chile Conference:* churches, 139; members, 26,142; elementary schools, 7; ordained ministers, 27; licensed ministers, 15; credentialed missionaries, 12. Headquarters: Santiago. *North Chile Mission:* churches, 42; members, 9,271; elementary schools, 5; ordained ministers, 8; licensed ministers, 9; credentialed missionaries, 9. Headquarters: Antofagasta. *Pacific Chile Mission:* churches, 61; members, 9,206; elementary schools, 3; ordained ministers, 14; licensed ministers, 11; credentialed missionaries, 5. Headquarters: Quilpue. *South Chile Conference:* churches, 135; members, 29,777; elementary schools, 18; ordained ministers, 34; licensed ministers, 20; credentialed missionaries, 47. Headquarters: Temuco. *Union and Institutions:* ordained ministers, 16; credentialed missionaries, 33.

Institutions. Antofagasta Adventist Academy; Asociacion Casa Editora Sudamericana, Filial de Chile; Chile Adventist Educational Center; Concepcion Adventist Academy; Las Condes Adventist Academy; Los Angeles Adventist Academy; Los Angeles Adventist Clinic; South Santiago Adventist Academy; Temuco Adventist Academy.

Seventh-day Adventist Work. *Forerunners.* A Chilean Jesuit, Manuel de Lacunza y Diaz (1731-1801), was among the first in the Americas to herald the premillennial second advent of Christ. His book, written in Italy, *La Venida del Mesías en Gloria y Magestad* ("The Coming of the Messiah in Glory and Majesty") was not printed until after his death, but it was circulated in Spain and South America in manuscript form before his death, and aroused widespread interest among both Catholics and Protestants in Europe and the Americas. Lacunza's prophetic interpretation was futurist, a usual Catholic view, but by exalting the Bible above dogmatic tradition and by identifying the second beast of Revelation 13 as the future Catholic priesthood he undermined the authority of, and thus incurred the ire of, the Roman hierarchy. The work was placed on the Index of Prohibited Books (1824), but continued to be circulated and studied surreptitiously in spite of the church. Lacunza was a direct forerunner of modern Protestant futurism, but in one respect he was also the forerunner of the Adventist view—in that he taught that there was to be no millennium before the Second Advent *(see* Premillennialism).

Beginnings (1885-1905). As far as extant records reveal, the first SDAs in Chile were Claude Dessignet and his wife, who accepted the SDA message from D. T. Bourdeau in France, and later emigrated to Chile (1885) and settled near Traiguen, Cautín.

Early Sabbathkeepers in Chile are mentioned in *The Home Missionary* magazine, which in its issue of July 1892 reports: "Some years ago a copy of our French paper *[Les Signes des Temps]* fell into the hands of individuals in North Africa, and resulted in a company of Sabbathkeepers being raised up in Algeria. From this company went out a number of families, who have settled in [Chile], where we may expect to find them preparing the field for the entrance of laborers" (p. 152).

It is not known if there is any connection between the Dessignets and these people, or what part, if any, these people had in the establishing of SDA work in Chile.

Apparently the first SDA missionary to work in Chile was Clair A. Nowlen, a colporteur, who came from Argentina to Valparaiso, Chile, around October 1894. About two months later, on Dec. 10, 1894, he was joined by Fredrick W. Bishop and Thomas H. Davis, who came from San Francisco, California. Shortly after the arrival of Davis and Bishop, Nowlen went to the province of Magallanes in the extreme south to canvass. Davis canvassed in Victoria, Malleco, and Bishop stayed in Valparaiso to look after the ordering of books, while doing what canvassing he could on the side. Nowlen soon returned to Argentina, but Davis prospered in his work and remained in the region around Victoria for "nearly six months" *(Missionary Magazine,* May 1900, p. 217), after which he returned to Valparaiso. Bishop then left for Iquique, Tarapaca, by ship. On the way he met an Englishman who became interested in the SDA message and accepted it some time before November 1895 *(Home Missionary,* November 1895, p. 240). He is apparently the William Springer who became an SDA under the efforts of Bishop at Iquique and was probably the first person to accept the SDA message in Chile *(Review and Herald* 73:284, May 5, 1896).

On Oct. 12, 1895, while Bishop was in Iquique, G. H. Baber arrived as superintendent for the new Chile Mission. A short time later, he began to do missionary work, and his efforts were rewarded when a German woman in Valparaiso "kept her second Sabbath on the 14th" of March 1896. Some time before this, Bishop returned from Iquique, where already there were at least eight or nine interested persons.

While Bishop stayed in Valparaiso, Davis returned to Victoria. On this trip he sold *Bible Readings* to Enrique Balada, "a Bible Society colporteur." After "nearly six months" Davis again returned to Valparaiso, probably around May or June of 1896, where he and Bishop decided to canvass in Santiago together. It was on this trip that Balada and his wife became SDAs *(Missionary Magazine,* May 1900, p. 218). Balada later became a prominent SDA minister in Chile.

About July of the same year, two young immigrants from Switzerland, Edward W. and Victor E. Thomann, were led to become SDAs through a remarkable dream Victor had in which he saw Davis and Bishop on one of the streets of Santiago. Edward in time became editor of the *Revista Adventista* ("Adventist Review," a Spanish language church paper) and *Las Señales de los Tiempos* ("The Signs of the Times"), and Victor became a valuable worker as a canvasser. Some time before Dec. 13, 1896, Baber and Balada went to Iquique, where seven were baptized and a former Methodist lay preacher, Julián Ocampo, was ordained to the SDA ministry. On his return Baber baptized eight persons in San Felipe and organized them into a company. He also baptized 10 persons in Santiago. At the end of 1896 there were some 70 Adventists in Chile. In 1898 the Chilean Mission Field included also the territory of Bolivia, Peru, and Ecuador.

Chile Publishing House. As early as May 1898, Baber was laying plans for the publication of a missionary paper *(Missionary Magazine* 10:184, May 1898). In January 1900 the first issue of *Las Señales de los Tiempos* ("Signs of the Times") was printed at the shop of G. A. Rhode and Co., in Valparaiso. About the middle of that year an old handpress was bought, and in September *Las Señales* was being published in the El Pacifico Press ("The Pacific Press"). Edward Thomann was editor, administrator, pressman, and circulation manager. In 1902, 8,000 copies were printed each month. *La Revista Adventista* was begun in January 1901, and was also published there. Both periodicals were published in Iquique from the middle of 1902 until the middle of 1904. Then the press returned to Valparaiso. The building burned on Nov. 10, 1905, but printing was done by a commercial firm. By December 1906 a cylinder press and other smaller machines had been bought. From 1904 to 1906, the Sabbath school quarterly *(Lecciones Internacionales de las Escuelas Sabáticas)* was published there. In 1904 *La Revista Adventista* became the official organ of the South American Union Mission, and in 1906 the South American Union Conference decided to transfer its publication to Argentina. In 1907 the press and the offices of the Chilean Conference were moved to Lo Espejo, a Santiago suburb. In 1910 the Chile Publishing House was absorbed by the Buenos Aires Publishing House and the press was transferred to Florida, a suburb of Buenos Aires, Argentina.

Through action taken in the middle of 1964 by the Buenos Aires Publishing House, the South American Division, the Austral Union

Conference, the North Chile Mission, and the Chile conferences, it was decided to establish a branch of the Buenos Aires Publishing House in Chile, to print forms, leaflets, Sabbath school lessons, and magazines, and to import and provide subscriptions for the church books to the fields of Chile. These actions were implemented in September 1964, when Roberto Rojas and Aroldo Winkler went to Chile from Buenos Aires to begin work on the Chile branch. The first book imported by the branch entered the country in January 1965, and the first magazines printed in Chile are dated January 1965.

Early Organization. On May 1, 1902, the name West Coast Mission was given to the Chilean mission field. With the River Plate Conference and the Brazil Conference it formed the newly organized South American Union Mission.

The superintendent was H. F. Ketring. The West Coast Mission headquarters were moved to Iquique, then moved back to Valparaiso in 1904. In 1902 the first Seventh-day Adventist primary school in Chile was opened in Santiago, but it was short-lived. In 1905 Victor Thomann established the Filadelfia school among the Araucano Indians of Baja Imperial.

On Nov. 4, 1904, Frank H. Westphal arrived in Chile to be superintendent of the mission, which he directed until 1916. In 1906 the mission had seven churches, 237 members, four ordained ministers, three licensed ministers, three licensed missionaries, and four colporteurs.

In 1906 the West Coast Mission was divided into three parts: the Chile-Bolivian Mission, the Peruvian Mission, and the Ecuador Mission. Also in 1906, the Púa Training School was opened *(see* Chile Adventist Educational Center), and the Pitrufquen church was organized with a total membership of 20.

Later Reorganizations (1907-1950). On Apr. 4, 1907, Bolivia was separated from the Chile-Bolivian Mission, and all of Chile was reorganized as a conference, with headquarters in Valparaiso. Westphal continued as president. At the time there were nine churches, 290 members, three ordained ministers, three licensed ministers, three licensed missionaries, and seven colporteurs. Late that year the press and officers were moved to a recently purchased property in Lo Espejo, a suburb of Santiago. The first Young People's Society in the South American Union was organized at the Púa Training School in 1908, and by 1912 there were three societies. In 1914 the Chilean government officially recognized the corporation of the Seventh-day Adventist Church and the same year the union created the Punta Arenas Mission in the southernmost part of the continent, which was later renamed Magellan Mission.

The Magellan Mission included the Chilean territory of Magallanes, the island of Tierra del Fuego, and the Argentine territories of Santa Cruz, Chubut, and the Falkland Islands. The first superintendent, A. G. Nelson, settled in Punta Arenas, Chile, in 1914. Interest had been aroused in the city by Nowlen, who canvassed there in 1893-1895, and by Bishop, who canvassed there in 1908-1909. In 1918 F. H. Westphal spent about five months in Punta Arenas holding a series of gospel meetings. As a result nine persons were baptized and a church was organized. In 1941 the mission, with headquarters at Punta Arenas, had two churches, 36 members, and one ordained minister. When the mission was reorganized in 1942, the Chilean section of the Magellan Mission became part of the Chile Conference.

In 1919 the Austral Union created a new mission called *North Chile Mission* under direct supervision of the union. It extended from Tacna in the north as far south as Caldera and Copiapó. Its headquarters were in Antofagasta. Abraham A. Berchín was its first missionary. By 1923 a church of 40 members had been organized in Antofagasta. In 1924 the North Chile Mission was administered by the Chile Conference and soon became again an integral part of it.

In 1930 the Chile Conference, with headquarters at Santiago, had 29 churches, 1,771 members, eight church schools, four ordained ministers, eight licensed ministers, 12 licensed missionaries, 26 canvassers, five church buildings, 12 teachers, and 344 students. The Depression affected hundreds of members in Santiago, and in 1931 a special offering was taken to buy food for them.

Work among the Araucano Indians, begun by Victor Thomann in 1905, and subsequently interrupted, was opened again in 1931 at Rucapangue, near Nueva Imperial, where a school was established with Pablo Mora as director. Later (1941), Juan Lefimil worked for the Araucanos near Galvarino, but since that time little has been done to evangelize the Indians.

In 1943 the Voice of Prophecy radio program was first broadcast—in Spanish—on seven stations. Later the name was changed to *La Voz de la Esperanza* ("The Voice of

Hope"). In 1948 the radio correspondence school had 1,773 students in Chile. In 1954 the Chile branch was organized, with offices in Santiago. In 1973 the program was broadcast by 35 radio stations. In November 1974 there were 5,700 active students.

In 1931 Samuel Fayard, a nurse, had opened the Instituto Hidroterápico. This institute did not function in 1935. Later it functioned intermittently until it was definitely closed. In 1958 the Instituto Médico Adventista (Chile Adventist Clinic) was established in Santiago under Dr. Arnaldo Galano. It cared for 204 patients, with two doctors and one nurse. In 1960 there were 1,773 patients, and in 1962 the number was 2,591. In 1973, 6,348 patients received assistance with the help of six doctors, two psychologists, one kinesiologist, one dentist, one nurse's aide, and one secretary. The South Chile Conference, in connection with OFASA (SAWS), established two treatment rooms for tuberculosis patients under the direction of volunteers who provide food and supervise the treatment recommended by the National Health Service. One of these rooms is located in Temuco and the other in Chillán. A dental office in Temuco also gives assistance. At Chile College there is a medical dispensary operated by a physician and a dentist.

In 1963 the Liceo Adventista de Santiago (Santiago Academy) was founded, with Sergio Olivares as director. In 1929 there had been a school in Santiago that offered six years of primary school and some secondary courses. Beginning in 1944, this school offered three years of secondary work, but after some years, because of lack of finances and personnel, it continued as a primary school. The Liceo opened with three years of secondary school, 186 students, and nine teachers.

In 1953 a colporteur found some interested people on the island of Chiloé, and in 1958 Mariano Renedo conducted a short series of meetings, organizing the first Sabbath school in Ancud. In 1962 Andrés Gutiérrez was sent to work there. Some 30 people were soon baptized. Property was purchased and a church established there.

The first youth camp was held in 1941 at the Colegio Adventista de Chile, in Chillán.

In 1959 a Pathfinder Club, the second in the South American Division, was organized in Temuco, Cautin, and by the end of the year there were seven in the conference. The next year, the Voice of Youth was introduced in six churches in the field.

In 1958 the Obra Filantropica y Asistencia Social Adventista, abbreviated OFASA ("Adventist Philanthropic and Social Assistance Work"), under the direction of O. R. Scully, was officially authorized by the government to carry on welfare work. The welfare activities were greatly increased as a consequence of the 1960 earthquake. At the time of the earthquake, trucks, Butler buildings (Quonset-type buildings), food, vitamins, clothing, paints, and tents were received for wider distribution. In July 1963 Adan Mayer was named the first administrator of OFASA for all of Chile to carry on school-lunch and food-distribution programs and all welfare activities. Assistance agreements are maintained with the following institutions: Consejo Nacional de Menores (National Council of Minors); Consejo de Defensa del Niño (Children Defense Council); Carabineros de Chile (Chilean Police); Servicio Nacional de Salud (National Health Service). These agreements cover food, clothing, medicines, equipment, and instruments. They also include temperance programs against tobacco, drugs, and alcohol, with adequate audiovisual equipment; nutrition programs (cooking and nutrition); installation of food processing plants in some centers belonging to the above-mentioned institutions.

In 1971 a request was received to establish work on Easter Island. Because of geographic and administrative reasons the South American Division decided that it should depend directly on the Chile Union. In 1973 Gastón Aguilera and colporteur Eliel Medina were sent to the island. When they returned in June of the same year, 11 persons had been baptized.

Recent Developments. The increase of churches and their extension along a territory of 2,650 miles (4,270 kilometers) made it necessary within a short time to make three reorganizations: the first one took place in 1950, when the Chile Conference was divided into two fields: North Central Conference, with jurisdiction from the Peruvian border to the provinces of Linares and Maule inclusive; and the South Conference, from the province of Nuble to the extreme south of the territory. Both were still part of the Austral Union. The second reorganization took place in 1966, separating the two Chilean conferences from the Austral Union and establishing a new union with three local fields.

The third reorganization took place in 1989 when the Chile Central Conference territory was divided, and the union was left with four fields—two conferences and two missions. Another important event was the creation in 1989 of the Chile Adventist Educational Center, when the old Chile Adventist College was given accreditation by the Education Ministry and became a university.

In the area of evangelism, Francisco Milanovic, a member of a Gypsy tribe, was converted to the gospel in 1978, and five years later an evangelistic campaign was held among the gypsies who lived in the city of Santiago. From this the first Gypsy SDA church was begun in South America, with 40 members. The congregation meets every Sabbath under a tent and the gospel has been preached to 95 percent of all gypsies who live in the country, reaching approximately 1,500 people who are favorable toward the Seventh-day Adventist Church.

CHILE ADVENTIST CLINIC. *See* Chile.

CHILE ADVENTIST EDUCATIONAL CENTER. Foremost educational institution of the Chile Union, located 250 miles (400 kilometers) south of Santiago, the capital city, in a building on 890 acres (360 hectares). It offers preschool, full elementary, high school, a professional institute (college level), and university education. Boarding capacity (1993) is 540 youth, and the total number of students is 1,847.

Tertiary level academic programs. The Adventist Professional Institute, accredited by the government, offers three levels in the area of theology (four years, completing 16 years of study) and five in education (three and a half to four and a half years).

Chile Adventist University offers career preparation of up to six years' duration in engineering, agronomy, agro-industries, administration, and electronics. It also has a postgraduate program in public health.

History. In 1901 Carlos Krieghoff, one of the pioneers in Chile, donated 44 acres (18 hectares) of land that was 185 miles (300 kilometers) south of the present location. He, along with his wife and a handful of students, built the necessary buildings and established courses that provided elementary and secondary education, as well as courses for colporteurs, teachers, and pastors.

The Púa Adventist School, as it was called, opened on Apr. 15, 1906. In 1918 the name was changed to Chilean Adventist Academy. In 1921, because of climatic problems, it was transferred to the present location, seven miles (12 kilometers) from Chillán, adopting the name Chillán Adventist College. In 1928 the name was changed to Adventist Industrial College. Later it assumed the name Chile Adventist College. The accreditation of the higher education program came about when the Adventist Professional Institute was formed in 1982 and the Chile Adventist University in 1990. These institutions, operating on the same campus, form the present Chile Adventist Educational Center.

Facilities. The Las Mariposas campus, where the center operates, has a modern and attractive administration building, independent buildings for the elementary and secondary levels, a classroom building for laboratories for the university and the institute, a library with 35,000 volumes and 160 titles of publications and periodicals, four residences for males and two residences for females, a cafeteria for the boarding students, homes for personnel, and a supermarket and dairy production installations.

Directors: Carlos E. Krieghoff, 1906-1907; George W. Casebeer, 1908-1913; Carlos E. Krieghoff, 1914-1916; J. W. Brower, 1916-1917; Nels Johnson, 1918; William W. Wheeler, 1919-1920; Ernest U. Ayars, 1921-1924; John M. Howell, 1925-1931; W. E. Murray (acting), 1931; George B. Taylor, 1932-1934; Jacob H. Meier, 1935-1941; Andrés Riffel (acting), 1942; Charles D. Christensen, 1943-1945; Werner Aeschlimann, 1946-1947; Merardo León, 1948-1953; Alcides J. Alva, 1954-1956; José Torres, 1957-1960; David H. Rhys, 1961-1964; Mariano Renedo (acting), 1965; Juan Tabuenca, 1966-1969; Sergio Olivares (acting), 1970; Rolando A. Itín, 1970-1974; Enrique Becerra, 1975-1978; Sergio Olivares, 1979-1986; Segundo J. López, 1987-1990; Sergio Olivares, 1991- .

CHILE PUBLISHING HOUSE. *See* Chile.

CHILE UNION MISSION. *See* Chile; South American Division.

CHILIASM. *See* Premillennialism.

CHINA DIVISION. A large unit of church organization that functioned as a division of the General Conference from 1931 to 1951 and comprised the SDA churches in China and adjacent territories. Before 1919 these churches had been a part of the Asiatic Division, and afterward of the Far Eastern

Division. The China Division was organized in 1930, retaining the former Far Eastern Division headquarters at Shanghai and comprising the territory of China (including Manchuria, Mongolia, Tibet, and Sinkiang), and the islands controlled by China, together with Hong Kong and Macao (estimated area population, 480 million), with 150 churches and 9,010 members. It began to function on Jan. 1, 1931. In 1951, when connections with the worldwide church organization were severed, the China Division became an autonomous Chinese church. (For 40 years the denominational *Yearbook* continued to print the last available [1951] statistics for China: 278 churches and 21,168 members.)

After World War II, and while the China Division was still functioning, the territory of Tibet was assigned to the Southern Asia Division. After the separation of the membership in the Chinese People's Republic in 1951, the districts of Hong Kong and Macao, together with Taiwan (Formosa), Pescadores, and other islands in the area, were organized as the South China Island Union Mission, under the Far Eastern Division.

For history of the work in these territories, *see* China, People's Republic of; China, Republic of; Hong Kong; Macao.

Presidents: H. W. Miller, 1931-1936; Frederick Griggs, 1936-1939; W. H. Branson, 1939-1940; N. F. Brewer, 1940-1942; E. L. Longway, 1942-1946; W. H. Branson, 1946-1949.

CHINA MISSIONS TRAINING SCHOOL. *See* China Training Institute.

CHINA, PEOPLE'S REPUBLIC OF. A republic in East Asia bounded by Vietnam and Laos on the south; Myanmar, India, Bhutan, Nepal, Pakistan, and Afghanistan on the southwest; Russia on the northwest and northeast; Tajikistan and Kazakhstan on the west; Mongolia on the north; Korea on the east; and the Pacific Ocean on the east, southeast, and south. China is one of the world's largest countries, with an area about 3.8 million square miles (9.8 million square kilometers), and contains more than one fifth of the world's population: the estimated population of the Chinese mainland (1994) is approximately 1.2 billion.

Ethnically the people are about 94 percent Chinese, with the rest composed of the Zhuang, related to the Thais, in the province of Guangxi; the Uigurs, a Turkic people in Xinjiang; the Hui, Chinese-speaking Muslims of the northwest; the Yi (formerly called Lolo), related to the Tibetans, in the southwest; the Tibetans and the Miao (a distinct group of the Sino-Tibetan family) in the south and southwest; the Mongols, concentrated mainly in Inner Mongolia along the Mongolian border; the Puyi, related to the Thais, in the southwest; and Koreans in the northeast, along the Korean border. There also are numerous smaller ethnic groups numbering less than 1 million persons each.

Chinese, the principal language of the country, is a monosyllabic, tonal language written in ideographs, each of which represents a concept. The script is the same throughout China, but its pronunciation varies greatly from one locality to another, so that its several distinct dialects are incomprehensible outside of their own area. The Mandarin dialect of central China is spoken by about two thirds of the people, and its Beijing branch is recognized as a national language. Among the leading southern dialects are the Shanghai dialect and the Guangdung dialect, the language of many of the Chinese emigrants. The non-Chinese minorities have their own distinctive languages and scripts.

The religion of the Chinese and of most of the ethnic minorities is an eclectic blend of Buddhism and Taoism thoroughly permeated by the ethical and philosophical concepts of Confucianism. In 1953 there were some 10 million Muslims in China, predominantly in the western areas, according to the census figures. Christianity was represented by 3 or 4 million Roman Catholics, who declared independence from the Roman See and about 750,000 Protestants.

Historical Background. *Early History.* China is one of the world's oldest nations, tracing its recorded history from the beginning of the second millennium B.C. The Chinese began to build their civilization on the middle Yangtze River in the third millennium B.C. By the beginning of the Christian Era, the Chinese state reached nearly its present dimensions, and its influence extended into Annam (modern Vietnam). The beginning of the Christian Era was also the time that the Great Wall (which later extended for 1,500 miles [2,400 kilometers] across the mountains and valleys of Northern China) was begun as a defense against the invasions from the nomadic Mongolian tribes. Before A.D. 1000, Chinese civilization reached its greatest brilliance and made notable achievements in sciences and technology: the Chinese invented paper, printing from movable type, and gunpowder (which they used for fireworks); they also made celestial observations with great accuracy.

During the Mongol period (China succumbed to the Mongolian invasion in the thirteenth century) China was the central part of an empire stretching from the Japan Sea to Poland in the west.

European Contacts With China. The Europeans had made contacts with China in the Roman times and then, after the lapse of many centuries, Marco Polo made an overland journey to Beijing, bringing back stories of a fabulous empire. Afterward Catholic missionaries came overland from Europe and established themselves in South China. The Portuguese explorers and traders were the first to make contact with the Chinese by sea, in the sixteenth century. They established an enclave at Macao about 1557, but China followed an isolationist policy until defeated by the British in the Opium Wars, 1840 and 1855, when the first few ports were opened to foreign traders. Near the end of the nineteenth century Taiwan (Formosa) was ceded to Japan, and several Western states likewise obtained important territorial and commercial concessions from the Chinese. In the wake of foreign political penetration came modern Christian missionaries, and in the eyes of many Chinese the two often became associated. This association, at times justified by the behavior of missionaries, impeded the development of Christianity in China.

End of the Monarchy. In 1911 the monarchy fell and was replaced by a republican form of government. However, the political structure of China soon disintegrated, with the result that many areas came to be controlled by local war lords and contending political factions. When, in 1927, a national government was established in Nanjing by Chiang Kai-shek, for a while unification appeared near, but the Japanese attack on China in 1931 in Manchuria and again in 1937, all along the coast, disrupted the social and political development of China. Then at the end of World War II a rival Communist government gained strength. In 1949 it replaced the Nationalist Government (which thereafter operated on the island of Taiwan) and proclaimed a people's republic in mainland China.

Christianity in China. According to Christian tradition, Christianity was first brought to China by the apostle Thomas, but the first historically authenticated evidence of Christianity dates from the middle of the seventh century. In 635 a Nestorian missionary named Alopen, arriving in the capital of China, was received by the emperor, who had some parts of the Scriptures and Christian books translated and placed in the imperial library. Nestorian Christians prospered in China for about two and a half centuries, then unaccountably disappeared for a time, but again reappeared after the Mongols established their empire, which embraced the Christian communities in the Near East. In his account of travels in China, Marco Polo reported the existence of several Nestorian churches there, with a Nestorian metropolitan in the capital of the empire.

Near the end of the thirteenth century, the first Roman Catholic missionaries reached China. However, in succeeding wars evidences of Christianity in China were obliterated. After the Portuguese established an enclave at Macao, in the sixteenth century, Roman Catholic missionaries carried on work from this center, although against resistance from the Chinese.

The first Protestant missionary, Robert Morrison, of England, settled near Guangzhou (Canton) in 1807 and undertook the translation of the Bible into Chinese. But the Chinese opposed the foreign encroachments and interference in their way of life. In the first 35 years of Protestant work, less than 100 converts were won. Although, on the one hand, missionary penetration was aided by the opening of China for trade by Western military power, on the other hand, the defeat of China and its humiliation caused much resentment against all things foreign, including Christianity.

It is interesting to observe, however, that the nucleus of the great T'aip'ing rebellion of the mid-nineteenth century was composed of a society of worshipers of the Supreme Being, who believed in one God, held that Jesus was His Son, and observed the seventh day by ceasing all business on that day and holding services. As the movement developed, leaders and followers went to almost unbelievable lengths in fanaticism, and the outcome of this rebellion created numerous problems for Christians in China. Nevertheless, it is a remarkable coincidence that about the time that a small group of Adventists in America reminded the world that the seventh-day Sabbath is binding upon Christians, a group in China included the observance of the day in its code of beliefs.

The Christians in China increased rapidly

after the opening of the country to trade and the issuance of edicts of toleration in 1844 and 1860. By the time the first interdenominational missionary conference was held in Shanghai in 1877, there were 13,000 Protestants in China. Unlike the early attempts at Christianizing China, the main effort of the Protestant missionaries was directed toward the common people. The church historian Latourette observed that "they founded and maintained some of the best educational institutions in the country. . . . The modern medical and nursing profession owed to them their inception and most of their development. . . . They promoted education in public health, helped in relieving famine, and aided the study of agricultural problems and methods. . . . Protestants prepared and distributed an extensive religious literature" *(The Chinese: Their History and Culture,* p. 484).

Also, in most cases, they placed stress on the development of a strong indigenous ministry and on direct evangelization of the people of the interior provinces.

Seventh-day Adventist Statistics. China, with Outer Mongolia, constituted the territory of the China Division of the General Conference of Seventh-day Adventists until that division became autonomous in 1951. For the next 40 years statistical reports on the Chinese church were not available. In 1951 there were, in *China:* churches, 278; members, 21,168; church or elementary schools, 112; ordained ministers, 134; licensed ministers, 213; teachers, 156.

In 1979 the communication between China and the Outside World took a positive turn with the establishment of diplomatic relations. Therefore the General Conference has been able to obtain information in various ways about the progress of the work there. As of December 1992, it was estimated that there are more than 400 churches and more than 150,000 members in China. Also, since 1979 many opportunities have opened for radio educational work, health education, foreign language teaching, and literature distribution.

Institutions. The 1951 *Yearbook* listed the following institutions: Canton Sanitarium and Hospital; Central China Union Academy; Chiaotou Sanitarium and Hospital; China Training Institute; Chungking Wuhan Sanitarium and Hospital; East China Union Academy; East Lake General Hospital; Honan Junior Academy; Kiangsu Junior Academy; Little Eden Hospital-Dispensary; Nanning Seventh-day Adventist Hospital; North China Sanitarium and Hospital; North China Union Academy; North Fukien Junior Academy; Northeast China Union Academy; Northwest China Sanitarium and Hospital; Northwest China Union Academy; Shanghai Medical Center; Shenyang Clinic-Hospital; Shenyang Sanitarium and Hospital; Signs of the Times Publishing House; South Chekiang Junior Academy; South China Island Union Academy; Southeast China Union Junior Academy; Tibetan Mission Hospital; Tibetan Mission Press; Tsingtao Sanitarium and Hospital; Wai On Hospital-Dispensary; West China Union Academy; West Szechwan Junior Academy; Yencheng Sanitarium-Hospital; Yünnan Junior Academy. Most of these no longer function.

Development of Seventh-day Adventist Work. *Beginnings by Pioneer Layperson.* SDA work in China began as a project of one layperson, Abram La Rue, an American gold miner, sailor, and shepherd, who became an SDA at an advanced age. Perceiving that the Advent message was to be given to the world, he attended Healdsburg College to prepare himself for the gospel work, and requested that he be appointed to China. The Mission Board, considering him too old (he was about 65 at the time), suggested instead that he bear his witness on one of the islands in the Pacific Ocean. He went first to the Hawaiian Islands, where his work led to the establishment of permanent SDA work on the islands. Still longing to carry the SDA message to China, he went, in 1888, to the British colony of Hong Kong, situated on an island scarcely a mile off the South China shore. In the same year, he visited Guangzhou and in 1889 went to Shanghai, in both places selling and distributing SDA publications among the English-speaking residents there.

In 1890 S. N. Haskell, on his missionary tour around the world, visited Hong Kong and Shanghai and was greatly impressed with the need to establish SDA work in the great land of China. During the next decade the subject of mission work in China was held before the leaders and church members through SDA periodicals, but no worker was sent there.

In the meantime, although La Rue never learned Chinese, he requested one of his Chinese acquaintances to translate for him a tract called *The Judgment,* of which he had 2,500 copies printed in 1891. Later he had the chapter "The Sinner's Need of Christ," from Ellen White's *Steps to Christ,* translated and printed. These two tracts represented the beginning of SDA publications in the Chinese language.

First Regular Missionaries. In 1892 what was described by W. A. Spicer (later president of the Mission Board) as the "clear call" from Ellen White to establish missions far and wide was given. She specifically mentioned China as one of the fields that the SDA Church should enter. At a council held at Battle Creek in 1898, it was voted to open work in China in that year, but nothing was done until, at the General Conference session of 1901, J. N. Anderson and his wife, volunteered for service in China. The Andersons and Ida Thompson (Mrs. Anderson's sister) arrived at the British colony of Hong Kong in February 1902. They began the study of the language, meanwhile canvassing among the English-speaking population, and Ida Thompson opened an English school for Chinese children. In December 1902 Edwin H. Wilbur and his wife, the former Susan Haskell, both trained nurses, went to Guangzhou, becoming the first permanent SDA workers in China proper. About that time, an elderly Chinese SDA returned from America to his ancestral home at Sun Ling, not far from Hong Kong, and there aroused interest in SDA teachings among his relatives and neighbors.

Soon after their arrival, the pioneer workers were joined by Eric Pilquist, formerly an employee of the British and Foreign Bible Society in Central China (who had recently become an SDA while on furlough in America, and who had encouraged the Andersons to go to China). Pilquist opened SDA evangelism in Central China in the Mandarin-speaking province of Henan. It appears that, even before he joined the other workers, he had six persons ready for baptism. On Feb. 14, 1903, the first SDA baptism in China took place at Xinyangzhou, about 125 miles (200 kilometers) north of the city of Hankow (Hank'ou, Wuhan), and the next day J. N. Anderson organized the first Seventh-day Adventist church in China, with eight members. Several of these early members became leaders in the church in China.

In April 1903 J. N. Anderson moved to Guangzhou, and made that city the SDA headquarters in China (*Review and Herald* 81:147, June 9, 1904). In response to Pilquist's call for more workers, four physicians, Harry W. and Maude A. Miller and Arthur C. and Bertha E. Selmon, with two nurses, Charlotte Simpson and Carrie Erickson, went in the autumn of 1903 to Central China to develop the work in the province of Henan.

In November 1903, in the first SDA ordination service in China, J. N. Anderson and H. W. Miller ordained Eric Pilquist to the ministry at Xincai, the site of the mission station in Central China. In the middle of 1904, Pilquist moved to a new station at Loshan, where, with the help of national teachers and evangelists, he opened a boys' school. In September 1904 the Millers left Xincai to open another station at Shangcai, and later the Selmons moved to Xiangcheng.

National Missionaries. It was a characteristic of the early Chinese converts that they began immediately to share their faith with their neighbors. As a result, much pioneer work was accomplished even before the missionaries learned enough Chinese to conduct extensive public evangelism. The activities of the laymen resulted in the formation of groups of inquirers in towns and villages where the foreign missionary had not visited.

In 1904 a young Chinese SDA, Timothy Tay, whom R. W. Munson had baptized in Singapore, went to Amoy (Xiamen), a seaport in South China northeast of Guangzhou, to perfect his knowledge of the local dialect so that he could work more effectively among the Amoyese emigrants in Singapore and in the Malay States. There he met a Chinese Protestant minister, Keh Ngo-pit (N. P. Keh), who in an attempt to prove to Tay from the Bible that the seventh-day Sabbath had been changed, himself became converted and joined the SDA workers. Apparently Keh and Tay later went to Swatow (Shant'ou), another large seaport in South China, where they preached to the Christians living there and where they made the acquaintance of a Chinese Christian leader, T. K. Ang, who also attempted to disprove the SDA message, only to accept it himself and enter the work.

When a large interest developed near the port city of Amoy in Fujian, to the northeast of Guangzhou, W. C. Hankins joined Keh and another national preacher there, settling near the city on the island of Gulangyu. The first inland station in the province of Fujian was established in the spring of 1905 at the village of Dogong (Dokong), some 30 miles (50 kilometers) from Amoy, where a meeting place was put in the charge of a national evangelist. The brunt of the work was borne by nationals, some of whom went out preaching even before they were themselves baptized. For their benefit, a training institute was held at Guangzhou in December 1905, the first of its kind.

First Institutions. In the spring of 1904 Ida Thompson opened a Chinese school for girls in Guangzhou, taught by a national woman teacher. She named it Bethel School in honor of Bethel Academy in the Wisconsin Conference, which supported the schoolwork in Guangzhou for a number of years. In the same year, 1904, a school for boys also was opened at Guangzhou.

At the end of 1904 J. N. Anderson summarized the progress of the year's work: two schools opened; regular public preaching begun during the summer; publication inaugurated with the printing of 2,000 copies of a tract written by Keh of Amoy, and a number of new or improved translations of other tracts ready for the printers—among them a tract on the true God, a tract on the Sabbath, a revised translation of the chapter "The Sinner's Need of Christ" from Ellen White's *Steps to Christ,* and school texts prepared by Pilquist. In that year there were 64 members in all of China.

In 1905 a Chinese physician from America, Law Keem, arrived with his family in Guangzhou and began SDA medical work in South China. Also in that year, SDAs established their first printing press in China at Shangcai in Central China, when Dr. Miller set up a small handpress that had been donated to him by a manufacturing firm in Chicago when he left for China. Although he knew little of printing, he planned the production of SDA literature in Chinese. He began publication of a monthly paper, called *Fu Yin Hsuen Pao* ("The Gospel Herald"), first issued in November 1905, also a number of small tracts, and in the spring of 1906, a Chinese hymnbook, printed from wooden blocks.

The early work in China was built through the self-sacrifice of members everywhere. An SDA family in Wisconsin by the name of Peterson wrote to the General Conference in 1904: "Last Sabbath, when reading the *Review and Herald,* we became much impressed by the stirring appeal from China. God has blessed us, and by hard work and economy we have saved up just one thousand dollars, which we have decided to give to this needy mission field. . . . This is about all we own in this world, but we feel assured that God will provide the necessities for us as long as we are to stay here, so we give it cheerfully, and hope and pray that much good may come out of it" *(Review and Herald* 81:5, Feb. 25, 1904).

That the gift came at an opportune time can be seen from the fact that the General Conference appropriation for the year 1905 for China was only $8,400.

In the spring of 1906 J. N. Anderson ordained the first Chinese Seventh-day Adventist worker, N. P. Keh, to the ministry at Amoy. Later in the year SDAs entered the inland province of Hunan, due north of Guangzhou. In September of that year, P. J. Laird, formerly in the service of the Church of England, and his wife, Emma Perrine Laird, M.D., a former SDA missionary in Japan, opened a school and a dispensary at Changsha, the capital of that province. In the same year, B. L. Anderson opened another school at Amoy and laid the foundations for a strong SDA educational center in South China, from which numerous workers later entered the service of the church. In the vicinity of Amoy, the interest in SDA teachings was developing rapidly, and by 1906 there were chapels at Dogong, Tokoe, and Chinchen, with adherents and converts in each place. In that year plans also were made for the work among the Hakka people of Fujian Province (in which Amoy was situated). In preparation for this work, J. P. Anderson, newly arrived from America, began studying the Hakka language.

Early Organization—China Mission. The missionaries in China during the early years received no regular appropriations beyond their salaries. They used their salaries and any other funds they could obtain to care for the needs of the expanding work as best they could. The work throughout China during the earlier days was under the informal administration of J. N. Anderson in Guangzhou, where the distribution of funds and the promotional plans from the General Conference were handled.

As the work grew, it was felt both by the missionaries in China and by the Mission Board that the workers needed to get together and lay concerted plans. In 1906 the General Conference sent W. W. Prescott, then editor of the *Review and Herald,* to China to counsel with the missionaries in the field. After visiting Japan, Korea, and North and Central China, he arrived in Shanghai to attend the first general meeting of the workers in China, which convened in that city from Feb. 10 to 20, 1907.

At this meeting, several resolutions intended to strengthen the work and to ensure its more rapid advance were adopted. The China Mission was more fully organized, with three local missions: Guangdung, Henan, and Fujian. General headquarters were to be established at Shanghai. Committees were formed to foster the Sabbath school, publishing, and other phases of the work, and a general financial plan was adopted. "Actions were taken to maintain high standards for baptism and church membership and the training of national workers. Urgent calls were placed with the Mission Board for workers for the different areas" (John Oss, *Mission Advance in China,* p. 109). Plans were also laid at this meeting for a well-developed organization that could deal with local problems and with various details on the spot instead of referring them to the General Conference Committee at Washington, D.C., as heretofore.

Meanwhile the work continued to grow and develop. In 1907 Keh found a group of about 50 persons some 25 miles (40 kilometers) away from the city of Swatow (Shant'ou), at a place called Chowchowfoo, endeavoring to observe the seventh-day Sabbath to the best of their knowledge; several among them had already given up wine and tobacco. During the year two new stations were opened in the province of Guangdung: one at Fatshan (Fuoshan), some 10 miles (16 kilometers) out from Guangzhou, where Dr. Law Keem opened a clinic, and another at Kongmoon (Jiangmen), some 50 miles (80 kilometers) away, with the Wilburs in charge. Early in 1907 the printing press was moved to Xinyangzhou, on the Beijing-Hankou Railway, where a suitable office building was erected and where H. W. Miller, the manager and editor of the press, F. A. Allum (recently arrived from Australia), Orvie Gibson, and Esta Miller (students from America who had volunteered as missionaries) made their residence. In December of that year the first regional meeting of Seventh-day Adventists held in China was held at Xiangcheng, Henan. About 50 adherents were in attendance, and during the session seven were baptized. A church with 11 members was organized at that place. As a sign of a complete break with the past, the men broke their pipes and women unbound their feet.

Early in 1908 it was decided to sell the press shop at Xinyangzhou and begin printing at the headquarters at Shanghai. After this transfer was made, the title of the monthly paper was changed to *Shi Chao Yueh Pao* ("Signs of the Times"). It was estimated that from 1902 to the end of 1908 a total of 18 million pages of SDA publications was printed and distributed in China. In 1908 there were 128 Seventh-day Adventists in the country. Several new missionaries arrived in the course of that year, among them Roy F. Cottrell, who together with his wife and Pauline Schilberg, the first appointee from the Washington Foreign Mission Seminary, went to the Changsha station; also H. H. Winslow, B. N. Roberts, and Bothilde Miller joined the headquarters and publishing staff.

China Union Mission Organized. In 1909 the second meeting of workers, convened at Shanghai, resulted in the reorganization of the China Mission into the China Union Mission, composed of six mission fields: Eastern, Central, Northwestern, Northern, Western, and Southern. Also the outlying areas of China (Manchuria, Mongolia, Xinjiang, and Tibet) were to become independent mission fields, and plans were made to staff them as rapidly as possible. For this purpose, a call was placed with the General Conference for 40 families for China during 1909 and 1910. Departmental leaders were appointed, and plans were made to enlarge the medical, publishing, and educational activities. At the same time it was decided to purchase sufficient property in Shanghai to allow for the construction of a publishing house to supply the Chinese language literature for SDA work everywhere, a sanitarium, general headquarters offices, and a training school.

China in the Asiatic Division, 1909-1918. At the General Conference of 1909 the work in Eastern and Southern Asia was organized into the Asiatic Division, with headquarters at Shanghai, and was placed under the supervision of I. H. Evans. W. A. Westworth came as superintendent of the China Union, but when he retired soon after, the leadership of the work in China fell to the superintendent of the division.

A Series of Advances. In 1909 SDA work penetrated into the inland province of Anhwei, due west of Shanghai, where Han Tsung-djen, a Chinese Christian pastor at Yingshang, in the western part of the province, and his congregation joined the SDAs. Having received some tracts from a friend in Henan, he had inquired for more information, and was visited by Allum. In 1910 Frederick Lee joined Han at Yingshang. About the same time another Christian minister, in Guangdung, the province in which Guangzhou is situated, also accepted the seventh-day Sabbath; he brought a part of his congregation with him into the SDA Church.

In 1909 J. P. Anderson began to work among the Hakka people in the province of Guangdung, at Waichow (Huizhou), about 75 miles (120 kilometers) east of Guangzhou. From there some years earlier several young people had come to the SDA office in Guangzhou and had asked for a teacher to come to their area. Some of them were baptized at

Guangzhou at the time of their visit. By the end of 1919 there were in the province of Fujian five stations and the following workers: five national evangelists, two colporteurs, two teachers, and two women Bible instructors. There were two schools at Amoy: a boarding school for boys under the direction of B. L. Anderson and a day school for girls directed by Mrs. Anderson. In the province of Hunan the first converts were baptized by Roy F. Cottrell, at Changsha. The printing and distribution of publications also prospered. It was estimated that in 1909 some 40 million pages were produced and circulated in China by the enlarged publishing facilities at Shanghai. Dr. Miller reported that SDA publications had the largest circulation of any Christian publications at that time.

In 1909, in an effort to preserve the health of the workers in the rigorous climate of China, a rest home was built at Mogan Shan in the mountains of Zhejiang Province southwest of Shanghai, and there the first specifically medical institution was established.

In October 1910 a school for the training of Mandarin-speaking workers was opened under the direction of Dr. Miller in a temporary location at Zhoujiakou in the province of Henan, in Central China. Because of its meager facilities and the large proportion of poorer students, it was nicknamed "The Beggars' School." Nevertheless, some of the strongest SDA workers in China were educated there. Later this school, transferred to Nanjing, became the China Union Mission Training School.

The SDA work reached the Gulf of Tonkin in southwestern China in 1910, when a former missionary for another denomination joined the SDAs and began preaching at Pakhoi (Peihai), Guangdung. In the same year public and personal evangelism was begun in the city of Shanghai, where F. E. Stafford, a printer from the city, joined the workers and preached in the first public evangelistic meetings. Bothilde Miller assisted in this work in the city and in the surrounding villages through personal evangelism and the training of national women Bible instructors. The city of Nanjing also was entered in that year when a group of national colporteurs and evangelists led by Allum and Pilquist went there to introduce SDA teachings to the many visitors from around the country who were attending the Chinese National Exposition.

In 1910 or 1911 F. A. Allum and Esta Miller opened the first SDA chapel in the province of Hubei (on the middle Yangtze River), where some Chinese believers from Changsha had scattered SDA publications in the city of Hankou, often called the Chicago of China. By 1913 there was a church of 40 members in that city, and there were several companies in its vicinity. The work also was developing in southern China, where in 1911 W. F. Hills and his wife opened a school at Swatow (Shant'ou), Guangdung. By that time a local Chinese evangelist, T. K. Ang, cared for the work there with only an occasional visit from overseas workers.

In 1911, when the Chinese monarchy was overthrown and the contending factions of the succeeding republican government plunged the country into a period of turbulence that for a number of years unsettled the social, economic, and political life of the people, the orderly development of SDA work in China was greatly hindered, yet it was not halted. In 1911 construction was begun on the headquarters building in Shanghai, voted upon in 1909. In 1912 Dr. Selmon made first use of a tent to hold public evangelistic meetings in China. By 1912, when the worldwide mission work of Seventh-day Adventists had acquired permanence and stability and attention could be turned to the preservation of the health of the workers, the China Union Mission benefited from the "$300,000 fund" raised by the General Conference for the erection of additional schools, hospitals, and workers' homes. Until then the overseas workers in China had used mostly whatever buildings they could find in their territory.

Reorganization of 1912. In 1912 the China Union Mission was dissolved and the missions were placed directly under the Asiatic Division and given responsibility for local matters.

In 1913 a number of advances were made. In the east F. E. Stafford, while recuperating from an illness in the more healthful climate of Shandung (one of the oldest Chinese provinces, where Confucius was born and buried), canvassed in company with a national evangelist, with the *Shi Chao Yueh Pao* ("Signs of the Times"), in the city of Chefoo (Chifu), now Yantai, and thus laid the foundations for future work in that area. In the south, Keh, having mastered the Fuzhou dialect, began work in that part of Fujian province where the Fuzhou dialect was being spoken. Also in the south a call for a minister came from a group in the province of Jiangxi (west of Fujian) who had learned of SDA doctrines through reading literature sold by colporteurs.

A colporteur from the south went to Taiwan (Formosa), even though the island was not a part of China at that time.

During 1912 and 1913 the China Union Training School was operated in rented quarters in Nanjing. During the political disturbances of 1913 it was transferred to the headquarters compound in Shanghai.

In the next year, 1914, SDA work was established in several more provinces. F. A. Allum, M. C. Warren, and two national workers from Henan, Dju Dzi-ih and Shi Yung-gwei, opened the work in the province of Sichuan, in the interior of western China on the upper Yangtze River. For a number of years afterward Warren directed the work there from his station at Chongqing, making journeys through Sichuan, Gueizhou, Yünnan, and the Tibetan borderland.

In 1914 Bernhard Peterson, O. J. Grundset, and Feng Cheng-chun entered Manchuria. Feng had learned of SDA teachings from a Russian SDA at the large railway shops at Harbin and later, when the entry into Manchuria was planned, had gone to the Shanghai school for training. Evangelism in Manchuria began in the city of Shenyang (Mukden), and later it spread to Changchun. The work in Manchuria progressed slowly at first, but the early efforts had built up a strong foundation for later advances.

Also in 1914 Law Keem, M.D., began evangelistic and medical work in the province of Guangxi, west of Guangzhou, establishing a station at Wuzhou, in the eastern part of the province. Because colporteurs had been there previously and had aroused considerable interest in SDA teachings, he was asked to preach immediately upon his arrival, even before he had had an opportunity to settle at his new location. Shortly thereafter he was informed of a group of Sabbathkeepers some distance away, at a place where a convert from Guangzhou had come to live and had shared his knowledge of the Bible with the people.

Other developments in the course of the year were the arrival of the first director of the colporteur work, H. M. Blunden, from Australia; the reestablishment of the work at Pakhoi (Beihai), in the southwest, near the Gulf of Tonkin, by E. H. Wilbur; the use of a houseboat, the *Hayes Gospel Boat,* as a floating chapel and mission station on the many waterways around the city of Swatow (Shant'ou); the organization of a church at Fuzhou by Keh; the first general meeting of SDAs in the Fujian province, held at Fuzhou, at which 47 were baptized, and the membership of the Fuzhou church was enlarged to 55; the opening of boys' and girls' schools at Fuzhou; the extension of the work begun in 1910 in Shanghai to the whole province of Jiangsu; the organization of a church at Nanjing by O. A. Hall and H. J. Doolittle, and a general meeting of members in that area held at Yingshan; and the penetration of the province of Hebei north of Beijing by colporteurs.

In 1915 C. P. Lillie, settling at Yantai, began permanent work in Shantung, Eastern China. That year also marked the ordination of the first Mandarin-speaking workers: Lin Djen-bang and Hwang Dzun-dao. In the same year a boys' school building was erected at Amoy and an Amoyese evangelist ordained; a site for mission homes, school, and chapel was purchased in Swatow; five church schools were opened in Hakkaland and a church building erected at Waichow (Huizhou); in Guangxi province a new station was opened at Nanning, its capital, where Dr. Law Keem established a small hospital; the *Shi Chao Yueh Pao* reached a circulation of more than 60,000 monthly; a call for a minister came from Shanxi, in northern China, where a colporteur gathered a group of inquirers in a Christian community called the Gospel Village; the city church in Shanghai raised funds to build a sanctuary; the workers in the Asiatic Division sent a special memorial to the Mission Board calling for 35 or more missionaries and for $100,000 in funds, in response to which the largest group of SDA missionaries sent out up to that time sailed for the Orient, many of them for China, bringing a new impetus to the work.

In 1916 one of the new arrivals, D. E. Davenport, M.D., opened Yancheng Dispensary-Hospital and a school at Yancheng (Loho) in the province of Henan. Later, that station developed into one of the strongest centers of SDA work in China. Also in 1916, the first subscription book appeared, published by the Signs press in Shanghai. Reports for that year included: more than 200 new converts by the South China Mission; the two training schools in the Central China Mission well filled; homes for missionaries erected at Chongqing; 14 baptized in Mukden (Shenyang), Manchuria.

Reorganization of 1917. In 1917 the territory of China was reorganized into two unions: the North China Union Mission, with work in Zhejiang, Anhwei, Giangsu, Shandung, Henan, Hubei, Hunan, Gianxi, Sichuan; and the South China Union Mission, composed of

Fujian, Guangtung, and Guangxi. The rest of China was considered mission territory in the Asiatic Division. In that year Warren and Andrews made an exploratory visit to Yünnan, far to the west near the borders of Burma. In the southwest, Dr. Law Keem opened a hospital in the capital of Guangxi, Nanning. J. G. White opened a station in the province of Shaanxi, in the central part of China.

The 1918 annual report mirrored the growth of the work. At that time there were two union missions (North and South China) with 14 local missions, 70 churches, 2,862 baptized church members, and 490 workers (including 106 teachers and 86 colporteurs), 67 schools (of which six were secondary schools), with an enrollment of 1,781, one publishing house, and one sanitarium. In that year the second station was opened in the province of Sichuan, at Chengdu, under the leadership of C. L. Blandford; and R. F. Cottrell began preaching in Beijing. About that time an annual campaign soliciting support for SDA welfare and educational work *(see* Ingathering) in China among the people of China themselves was inaugurated in connection with the construction of the Yancheng hospital. Since then contributions from local sources made it possible to expand the work, especially in the medical field, throughout the country much more rapidly than would have been possible from foreign gifts alone.

China in the Far Eastern Division, 1919-1930. When early in 1919 the Asiatic Division was reorganized, China became a part of the newly formed Far Eastern Division. The two Chinese union missions were discontinued, and a number of smaller union missions were organized that became more directly responsible to the division. In 1920 there were six such unions.

New Missions Organized. During 1919 the work in the Zhejiang province, lying immediately south of Shanghai, was organized into a mission under the leadership of G. L. Wilkinson; a mission was established at Jiujiang in the province of Giangxi (inland between Fujian and Hunan), where there had been a group of adherents since 1913, when colporteurs sold SDA publications there. J. N. Andrews, M.D. (grandson of the first SDA worker overseas), opened a dispensary on the border of Tibet, at Dajianlu, Xikang (now included in Sichuan).

On their tour of the western regions of China, Warren and Andrews came upon several people who had become interested in SDA doctrines through colporteurs. From among these people, a Miao tribesman came to Chongqing in 1919 and was baptized, the first from that tribe. At the eastern end of China, the Manchurian Union Mission was organized. According to the *Statistical Report,* by the end of the year there were 3,255 Seventh-day Adventists in China.

Educational Advance. In 1922 advanced training for Chinese and foreign workers was offered in China through the facilities of the Far Eastern branch of the Fireside Correspondence School (now Home Study Institute). In 1925 another step in the development of SDA educational work was taken—the training school was moved from Shanghai to Qiaotouzhen, a rural location about 40 miles (65 kilometers) from Nanjing, and its curriculum was expanded to include vocational training, thus introducing this particular type of education into China. Shortly afterward the Chinese government attempted to introduce a plan of registration and accreditation that would have completely eliminated Bible classes, all religious training, and missionary influence. But the vocational aspects of SDA education saved the school for the church. In harmony with its vocational emphasis, the name of the school was changed to China Training Institute. The institute "was regarded as a school that was 'different,' and officials and educators from all parts of China came to inspect what was looked upon as a 'unique experiment' in the field of education" (John Oss, *Mission Advance in China,* p. 191). Two years later hostilities between warring political factions forced the school to close temporarily. In the same year, 1927, the Shanghai Hospital and Sanitarium building was completed (dedicated in the spring of 1928).

In 1928 C. B. Miller and Dallas White opened the first station in the western province of Yünnan, in the city of K'unming. At the same time a station was opened at Gueiyang, in neighboring Gueizhou province; and permanent work also was established far to the northeast, in north central China, in the province of Shanxi. Also in 1928 the Far Eastern Division office moved into its own new building at Shanghai.

The year 1930 was marked by the establishment of the headquarters for the Mongolian work at Kalgan (Zhangjiakou), north of Beijing. At the end of 1930 there were in China six union missions, 29 local missions, 156 churches, 9,456 church members, 947 workers (76 were ordained ministers, 123 licensed ministers, 364 licensed missionaries, 132 colporteurs, and 152 teachers), 103 church schools, and 3,325 students. There were 17 educational institutions of secondary and college level, one publishing house, two smaller local presses, and 11 medical institutions. About 250 of the 1,900 *hsiens* (counties) had been entered.

Russian SDAs in China. In 1920 for the first time an effort was made to spread the SDA message among the thousands of Russian settlers along the Manchurian part of the Trans-Siberian Railroad and among the Russian *émigrés* who were coming into that country in large numbers after the Russian Revolution of 1917. This work was assigned to the China Division. A Russian mission was established in 1920 at Harbin, Manchuria, under the direction of Theophil T. Babienco (the son of a pioneer Russian minister), from Canada. He was assisted by Max Popow, also from Canada, who, after his arrival, went throughout the Russian communities in Manchuria selling SDA publications. (There had been a church in Harbin by 1912, composed largely of SDAs who had come from Russia, but apparently few were left of the earlier group.) For a while this work was administrated directly by the Russian unions, but in 1925 it was organized as a detached mission, Sungari-Mongolian Mission.

China Division, 1930-1950. In 1930 China was separated from the Far Eastern Division and, together with Hong Kong and Macao, was formed into the China Division. It was felt that the work in China was of sufficiently distinct character that its problems could best be solved on the local level. Furthermore, as the Chinese workers assumed more and more responsibility and came to participate in the division councils, they were confronted with a language barrier in councils where division officers could not understand Chinese. The China Division began to function on Jan. 1, 1931, with H. W. Miller, M.D., a veteran missionary, as its first president. Chinese became the working language of the administrative councils.

Public Evangelism. Public evangelism played an important role in the development of the SDA Church in China. Early evangelists had adapted the custom of public storytelling to attract masses to the message of Christianity. Large-scale meetings were used extensively in the 1920s in the large cities. In the 1930s, after the formation of the China Division, public evangelism received a new impetus and was extended from the large cities to smaller cities and even to remote towns. In 1932 the promotional slogan "Into every *hsien* ["county"]" was adopted.

At the same time economic and social developments were transforming China. The land was awakening out of its age-old sleep, and new and improved means of transport were introduced. As motor roads were built where only footpaths had existed, SDA mission trucks were among the first to roll over them. As air routes were established, SDA workers, flying into distant places establishing the work, were among the first to take advantage of them.

Youth Missionary Movement. The movement to reach every corner of the great land involved not only the workers but the membership as well. The young people at the China Training Institute organized a small group called The Frontier Missionary Band. From this nucleus sprang a strong missionary movement among the young SDAs throughout China. This movement reached into Tibet, the long-closed land, and contributed to the promotion of the work on other borderlands of China, for example, among the Mongols. The first entry had been made earlier, about 1926, by Russian workers who, from a base in northern Manchuria, seem to have penetrated into the areas that became the Mongolian Republic; yet their work later had to be suspended. To renew this work, in 1930 a plot of land was purchased at Kalgan (Zhangjiakou), a town north of Beijing on the borderland between China and Inner Mongolia. In 1931 two Russian workers named Rodionov and Maltsev, under Otto Christensen as leader, opened the work in that area.

Advances on the Frontiers. In the same year two Chinese colporteurs, Beh Djin-djen and Dzeng Hsiang-pu, carried SDA publications deep into Xinjiang, even to its westernmost boundaries at Kashgar (Shufu, K'oshih). In 1932 the territory north of Beijing was entered by Goh Djaoliang, who preached in Chongde; by 1934 another station was opened in that area. Also in 1932 Chen Wen-hsioh, a minister, held public meetings in a tent pitched in the town square at Xining, in the western province of Qinghai; and in November of that year the first baptisms were reported and a church was organized. Many Mongolians, Tibetans, and other non-Chinese people live in that area. In 1932, soon after a new province of Ningxia had been formed in western Inner Mongolia on the edge of the Gobi Desert, Shao Djen-siu began evangelistic meetings there. Only a short while later a group of converts were baptized and a church was formed, and two years later, in 1934, the Ningxia Mission was organized under the direction of Wu Dzeh-shan. By 1934 there was permanent SDA work in 402 *hsiens,* that is, in about one in every five counties of China.

Hospitals and sanitariums were opened or developed in 1931 at Yancheng (Loho), Kalgan (Zhangjiakou), Mukden (Shenyang), and Canton (Guangzhou). In 1935 a mission was organized on the island of Hainan, off the south China coast, where a colporteur had been sent in 1932 by the MV Society of the Guangzhou school. In Yünnan, where C. B. Miller had begun tribal work in 1928, Milton Lee entered a new tribal district in 1937.

China During World War II. As war clouds hung over China in 1937, D. E. Rebok and J. H. Effenberg launched a Medical Cadet Corps program for training SDA youth, which had the sanction of the government. During the summer session at the China Training Institute, about 150 young men took the training. The war ultimately caused the transfer of the division headquarters to Hong Kong. From 1940 to 1942 N. F. Brewer, a seasoned China worker, was president of the China Division with S. L. Frost as secretary and M. D. Howard as treasurer. As the war progressed, he and many other overseas SDA workers were captured and placed in internment camps in Hong Kong, Guangzhou, Shanghai, Amoy, and the Philippines.

In this crisis the Chinese workers took complete charge in the occupied parts of China, operating from Shanghai. In the unoccupied parts of China, E. L. Longway and G. J. Appel carried on from Chongqing, a temporary center.

Postwar Reconstruction. At a general meeting of workers held in the spring of 1946 in Shanghai, the leaders took an inventory of the destruction. Wang Fu-yuan, SDA leader in Manchuria, who had spent 50 grim days in a Japanese prison under torture to compel him to give up his Christian beliefs, summed up the experience of most of the Chinese workers in these words: "We had to sell our clothes, and our land, but we didn't sell our faith or our souls, and thus God brought us through this time of trial."

The Seventh-day Adventist Church came out of its baptism of fire stronger than before. At the end of 1945 there were 22,940 church members, organized in 261 churches, with 10 medical institutions and 1 publishing house. The net gain in church membership during the last five years of the war period was 3,461; there were almost the same number of ordained ministers as there had been in 1930, but the proportion of nationals increased from less than one half to three quarters. By 1948 the China field had been almost fully manned by Chinese and overseas workers and almost all SDA institutions had been reopened.

Postwar Developments. The end of World War II unfortunately did not mean peace in China. In a short time fratricidal civil war swept the country from one end to the other. Nevertheless, in the first few postwar years the work of the SDA Church in China regained almost its prewar magnitude. The church reconstructed most of its medical, educational, and evangelistic institutions, many of which had been ruined and destroyed in the course of many battles and plunderings. Public evangelism, always a prominent part of the work in China, received a tremendous impetus from the turmoil. The *China Division Reporter* from 1947 to 1950 carried accounts of evangelistic campaigns from one end of the country to the other. Because the greatest hindrance to reconstruction and advance was the lack of trained personnel, especially in the medical work, an attempt was made to remedy the lack by offering some medical training at the China Training Institute.

In 1946 Voice of Prophecy broadcasts began in China, first on a station at Shanghai (Nov. 10, 1946), and within one year on 12 other stations, at Nanjing, Hankou, Guangzhou, Changsha, Xian, Lanchow, Shenyang (Mukden), Changchun, and Ningpo. The Signs Bible Correspondence School, operated in conjunction with radiobroadcasts, enrolled about 12,000 students in its first year of operation. In 1950, after temporary interruption in broadcasting caused by the revolutionary war in China and the change in government on the mainland, the Voice of Prophecy again went on the air in the Shanghai area, and the Bible correspondence school reported more than 30,000 active students.

More than 90 percent of the Bible correspondence school enrollment came from persons under 30 years of age. It was believed that social and political upheaval caused the youth of China to become interested in religious things. At the same time the lack of trained evangelists was compensated for by the drive and the dedication of the students from the Chinese training schools who were sent out to preach. The success of the evangelistic work was notable. The last available issue of the

China Division Reporter (for the first quarter of 1951) indicates that in 1950 the total number of baptisms was about 3,000 in the division. As long as they could, colporteurs conducted their work throughout the country.

Soon after the change of government on the mainland, the work there was separated from the rest of the SDA body. After a brief period when the China Division Committee functioned in Hong Kong and the north China provisional division committee of national workers took care of the organization in the country, the provisional division became, on Jan. 1, 1950, the China Division, while the parts of China not under the control of the mainland government, together with Hong Kong and Macao, became the South China Island Union Mission under the Far Eastern Division.

For some time regular relations between the General Conference and Chinese Seventh-day Adventists were not maintained, but it was reported that because of the prevailing antireligious and antimissionary attitudes of the government, SDAs in China underwent severe persecution. As a result, the institutional and organizational structure of the church there was destroyed. In 1979 conditions opened to the extent that the denomination now has contact with the work in China, and a growing work is being administered by the Eastern Asia Administrative Committee of Seventh-day Adventists.

CHINA, REPUBLIC OF (Matsu, Pescadores, Quemoy, Taiwan). Islands off the coast of China administered by the nationalist government of the Chinese republic. The territory of Taiwan is composed of a group of 14 islands with a combined area of approximately 13,900 square miles (36,000 square kilometers). The main island of Taiwan, situated about 110 miles (177 kilometers) from Xiamen, China, is about 240 miles (386 kilometers) long and 90 miles (145 kilometers) wide, and is bisected by the Tropic of Cancer. West of southern Taiwan, and administratively a part of it, are the Pescadores, composed of a group of 64 islands with an estimated area of 49 square miles (127 square kilometers).

Population. An influx of 1.5 million refugees from the mainland after the revolution and a high birth rate contributed to a rapid increase of population from about 5 million in 1945 to almost 12 million in 1962. In 1993 the population was 20.4 million. Density was 1,530 per square mile (590 per square kilometer) at the end of 1992, the highest in the world. Nearly 4 million people live in the capital city of Taipei.

The people of Taiwan are primarily of Chinese origin, and, before the refugee influx the majority were from two language groups, Xiamen and Hakka (both of South China), with the Xiamen group predominant. The refugees, on the other hand, came from all parts of China. Mandarin has been made the official language on the island and, because of the long Japanese occupation, Japanese is understood by most adult Taiwanese. Besides those peoples of Chinese origin, there are scattered in villages throughout the mountain ranges an estimated 265,000 brown-skinned Malayo-Polynesians, the aborigines of Taiwan. Their language, religion, customs, and even facial characteristics differ greatly from the Chinese living in the plains. The religion of the general population has tended lately toward a polytheistic amalgam of Buddhism, Confucianism, and Taoism, whereas animism is the religion of the indigenous tribes.

Historical Background. The first Chinese immigrants settled along Taiwan's coast about A.D. 600. In 1590 Portuguese traders named the island *Ilha Formosa,* meaning "Beautiful Island." In 1624 Dutch traders built a fort near what is now Tainan and operated there about 40 years. Taiwan was officially incorporated into China in 1683. The Treaty of Tientsin (1858) opened Taiwan to foreign trade, and Christian missionaries soon followed. On May 8, 1895, Taiwan was ceded to Japan and for the next 50 years was part of the Japanese Empire. At the close of World War II, Taiwan reverted to China. When the Chinese nationalist government withdrew from the China mainland to Taiwan in 1949, it made Taipei, Taiwan, its capital.

Seventh-day Adventist Statistics. The territory of Taiwan, Pescadores, Matsu, and Quemoy constitute the Taiwan Mission, which is a part of the South China Island Union Mission, which is in turn a part of the Far Eastern Division. Statistics (1992) for *Taiwan Mission:* churches, 43; members, 6,533; church schools, 1; ordained ministers, 28; credentialed missionaries, 14; credentialed literature evangelists, 7. Headquarters: Taichung, Taiwan.

Institutions. Signs of the Times Publishing Association; Taiwan Adventist Hospital; Taiwan Adventist College; Taiwan Adventist Academy.

Development of Seventh-day Adventist Work. *Beginnings.* The first known SDA to enter Taiwan was T. S. Yang, a colporteur from south Fujian, China (Taiwan was then assigned to the South China Union Mission), who went there in 1907. In spite of persecution and occasional imprisonment, he faithfully carried on his work, and, before leaving Taiwan in 1912, had gathered a company of 10 converts. In 1931 at the time the China Division was organized, Taiwan was assigned to the Far Eastern Division and was later made a part of the Japan Union Mission. In 1934 Nagao Wachi was sent to Taiwan to open work in the city of Tainan. There was opposition and the work progressed slowly. The 1938 *SDA Yearbook* lists only six members. When the work came to a standstill in 1942, there was a reported membership of 14.

The Work Reestablished. Sometime after World War II Taiwan reverted to the South China Union Mission under the China Division. In the spring of 1947 K. T. K'ang and C. C. Kuo were sent to Taiwan to find loyal SDAs and to rent housing in preparation for opening mission work on the island. In a three-month survey they found only one Seventh-day Adventist, W. K. Wang, who had arrived from China after the war. Because of high costs, no housing was arranged at that time. In December 1947 the China Division appropriated $10,000 for the purchase of property on the island. The following spring (1948) C. H. Davis, union mission president, T. C. Chin, union mission treasurer, and B. S. Lin visited the island and purchased street chapels in Taipei and Taichung. During the summer of 1948 three Chinese workers, B. S. Lin, T. T. Lee, and T. H. Yang, with their families, arrived. In that first postwar year of SDA missions on Taiwan, about 20 members met in two companies and six baptisms were reported.

Organization and Growth. In December 1948 the Taiwan Mission was organized with H. Carl Currie as its first president and Alva Appel as secretary-treasurer. The Appel and Currie families arrived on Jan. 1, 1949, to become the first overseas SDA missionaries stationed on the island of Taiwan.

Among the million and more refugees from the mainland was a sprinkling of SDAs, who strengthened the fledgling Taiwan church. One of them, a government official, gave valuable assistance in legal matters. Additional help came from two Taiwanese SDAs who had been in Japan during the war. T. O. Su, who came back in December 1949, was sent to school in Hong Kong in 1949 and later became the first Taiwanese ordained SDA minister. R. F. Swen returned to his home in Taiwan in the late spring of 1947, and working as a layperson, contributed much to establishing the work in south Taiwan.

The first Seventh-day Adventist church on the island was organized at Taipei in early 1949, with the majority of its charter members coming from among the refugees from the mainland. In late 1949 the first postwar public evangelistic campaign was conducted in Taipei by H. C. Currie and A. R. Appel, who spoke in Mandarin, with T. C. Lee translating into Taiwanese. This resulted in 16 baptisms.

Reorganization. In 1950 Taiwan was separated from the China Division, and the South China Island Union was organized as a detached union mission under the General Conference, to include Taiwan, Hong Kong, and Macao. Headquarters at first were in Hong Kong, and later, from 1952, on Taiwan. The availability of missionaries evacuated from the Chinese mainland and the stabilization of the political situation on Taiwan made it possible to expand the work on the island in this period. During the summer and fall of 1951, six such missionary families arrived. At the same time funds were appropriated for a training school, a Voice of Prophecy Bible Correspondence School, homes for overseas workers, and budgets for enlarging the national staff. In addition, a Thirteenth Sabbath Offering overflow, previously designated for China, was made available to Taiwan, thus making possible the construction of seven new churches.

Name of Mission Changed. The Taiwan Mission had grown so by 1964 that the island was divided to form two missions: the North Taiwan Mission and the South Taiwan Mission. However, it was necessary to divide again in 1968. The names became Tai An Chyu Hwei (Mountain Mission) and Tai Ping Chyu Hwei (Plains Mission), with all the mountain area in Taiwan, including Orchid Island, being the Tai An Mission territory, and north, south, east plains, and offshore islands of Matsu, Quemoy, and the Pescadores being the Tai Ping Mission territory. The Mountain Mission moved to a new location in Pingtung, South Taiwan, and the Plains Mission remained in Taichung, Central Taiwan. The membership of these missions increased with baptisms totaling 28 and 24, respectively, by the third quarter 1974. In 1975 the missions were combined once again to form the Taiwan Mission. By the end of 1992, membership had increased to 6,594.

Tribal Work. In the spring of 1953 work was begun among the mountain tribal people in the village of Ta She, which had a population of 800 persons. The work grew rapidly in the southern mountains. By 1963 the Ta She church had nearly 200 members and conducted the largest Sabbath school on the island. The tribal work had been extended to seven of the 10 tribes, and more than half of Taiwan's SDA church membership and at least two thirds of the Sabbath school membership were from among the aborigines. In 1963, 36 acres (15 hectares) of land were purchased at the foot of the mountains in southern Taiwan on which to establish a training center specifically for the aboriginal tribes. From this center trained workers have gone to tribes all over the island.

Recent Developments. For several years mission work grew rapidly all over Taiwan. During 1962 an average of one newly organized Sabbath school was added to the total every 11 days, and 69 new Sabbath school members every Sabbath. Vacation Bible Schools were conducted throughout the island.

The Pathfinders organized a strong program in 1971 and in a three-year period increased from one to 293 members. The Sungshan church in Taipei replaced the former meeting area on the second floor of the South China Island Union Mission Office, and began meeting in March 1974 in its beautiful new edifice.

Radio and Television. In 1958 Milton Lee began two broadcasting projects on the island of Taiwan. One was the revival of the weekly Chinese Mandarin Voice of Prophecy program, which had been discontinued after the evacuation from the Chinese mainland. (This program was later released to mainland China.) The other program was the introduction of a daily bilingual program, which presented Christian principles over the air accompanied by the study of a series of English-Chinese booklets. Thousands of students enrolled by purchasing these textbooks from the Voice of Prophecy office as well as from bookstores on the island. This daily broadcast proved so successful that a second set of books was prepared in 1962. In 1968 a weekly broadcast in Taiwanese began, with James Su as speaker. It was later continued by C. H. Yang. By this time the VOP recorded its own programs under the technical supervision of William Yang. In April 1974 a weekly television program was inaugurated over the Chinese Television Company, with Edwin Less as director and producer. The production of local television programs has increased the mail with as many as 10,000 letters received for one broadcast.

CHINA TRAINING INSTITUTE (Chung Hua San Yü Yen Chiu She). An educational institution that was established in 1910 for the training of Mandarin-speaking evangelistic workers in China. It operated until 1951 successively on several campuses and under several names. During most of the period it offered elementary, secondary, and junior college work (approximately grades 1-14). The school opened October 1910, under the name China Union Training School and under the direction of Dr. H. W. Miller. Classes were held in temporary quarters at Zhoujiakou. Because of its meager facilities and the large proportion of needy students, the school was nicknamed "The Beggars' School." Nevertheless, it produced some of the strongest Seventh-day Adventist workers in China.

During the Chinese Revolution of 1911-1912, the school was transferred to Nanjing and there it had about 35 students. Then it was moved to Shanghai about 1913, where it became known as China Missions Training School. In 1919 it was renamed Shanghai Missionary College. As the enrollment swelled toward 300 students in 1925, the college was transferred to Qiaotouzhen, a rural location about 40 miles (64 kilometers) northwest of Nanjing on a property of 125 acres (50 hectares). The school was renamed China Missionary Junior College. Its student capacity varied between 300 and 450 on this campus. In 1927 it was renamed China Theological Seminary, and in the early 1930s it was given the name China Training Institute. At that time its library holdings of 8,000 volumes were the largest among overseas denominational schools. In the late 1930s during the Sino-Japanese conflict, the school was evacuated to Hong Kong, where it was temporarily combined with the South China Training Institute. It then had about 200 students.

Overtaken by World War II, the school was again moved and combined with West China Union Training Institute at Dabao, Tsitsikow, in the Chongqing province of Sichuan. Its enrollment there was 288 in 1944. At the end of the war it was renamed San Yü Theological Seminary. About 1947 it returned to its own campus at Qiaotouzhen and assumed its former name of China Training Institute. In 1948 there were 465 students in 14 grades. When the civil war front reached the province of Jiangxi, the school was again removed to Hong Kong and joined with the South China Island Union Training Institute. After a period there it resumed operations at Qiaotouzhen, but was apparently closed soon thereafter, although the exact time of its closing is not known abroad.

CHINOOK WINDS ADVENTIST ACADEMY. A coeducational secondary institution established in 1945 and located in Calgary, Alberta. In 1994 there was a faculty of 12; the principal was Murray Cooper.

CHISHOLM TRAIL ACADEMY. A coeducational day high school sponsored by the Keene area Seventh-day Adventist churches in Keene, Texas. This academy became independent from Southwestern Union College in 1967 when that school became a senior college. The academy is a member of the Association of SDA Institutions of Higher Education and Secondary Schools and the Texas Education Agency.

Principals: Paul Kilgore, 1967-1968; C. B. Harris, 1968-1969; J. J. Swinyar, 1969-1973; G. Herman Guy, 1973-1975; Lyndon Davis, 1975-1981; Wayne Longhoffer, 1981-1982; Gary Gifford, 1982-1986; Jack Francisco, 1986-1988; Al Beyer, 1988-1992; Mervin Kesler, 1992- .

CHOICE. *See* Free Will.

CHOONG DONG ACADEMY. *See* Wonju Sahmyook Academy.

CHOSEN. *See* Korea.

CHOSEN INDUSTRIAL SCHOOL. *See* Korean Sahmyook University.

CHOSEN UNION TRAINING SCHOOL. *See* Korean Sahmyook University.

CHRISTCHURCH ADVENTIST SCHOOL. A coeducational day school operated by the South New Zealand Conference at Papanui, Christchurch, providing five years of high school work in addition to the full range of primary education. In 1993 the secondary section had an enrollment of 55, with five full-time teachers, and the primary section had an enrollment of 71, with three full-time teachers. The school draws its pupils from all the Christchurch suburban churches.

The school began as the Papanui Private School, under the control of the South New Zealand Conference. It opened in 1925 with an enrollment of 25 children and was taught by Miss M. M. Smart. As the enrollment grew, a three-room open-air type of school was built on adjoining property, and the first year of high school work was added. A second extension provided an extra classroom. In 1933 complete high school courses were offered, and the school's status was changed to that of a central school. Additions in 1959 and in 1961 provided two extra classrooms, a science laboratory, a woodwork room, a library, and a headmaster's office. In 1965 a swimming pool was added.

In 1983 an ultramodern secondary school complex was built, incorporating specialist classrooms, general classrooms, library, staff room, and office facilities.

The Christchurch Adventist School is registered as a high school with the New Zealand government's Education Department, and trains its pupils up to the University Bursary Examination level.

Principals: B. H. McMahon, 1933-1934; Miss J. Eyre, 1935; E. G. McDowell, 1936-1941; H. Millist, 1942; W. Whisker, 1943-1944; Miss M. Smart, 1945-1956; A. H. Dawson, 1957; H. Heath, 1958; W. E. Zanotti, 1959-1962; C. R. Thompson, 1963-1965; S. K. Gillis, 1966-1969; O. L. Hughes, 1970; H. J. Eager, 1971-1976; K. R. Dickens, 1977-1978; P. Truscott, 1979-1983; G. W. Watson, 1984-1985; R.K.L. Woolley, 1986-1988; E. N. King-Adams, 1989- .

CHRISTCHURCH SANITARIUM. A medical institution, operated from 1900 to 1921 at Christchurch, New Zealand, by the New Zealand Conference through the Medical Missionary Benevolent Association formed in 1897. Forerunner of the sanitarium was the Health Home at Christchurch, opened by G. A. Brandstater, of Australia, a nurse, in 1898. After operating in a rented cottage of six rooms for a time, the Health Home moved to a house of 13 rooms at 71 Hereford Street. In 1899 Dr. F. E. Braucht arrived from Samoa to take charge.

In mid-1900 a two-story building with 20 rooms and large grounds, situated on Harewood Road, Papanui, Christchurch, was purchased for a sanitarium for £1,800.

After the addition of treatment rooms and the enlargement of guest accommodations, the Christchurch Sanitarium, accommodating 10 inpatients, was opened on July 1, 1900.

Provision was made for both medical and surgical cases as well as for outpatients from the city. The staff consisted of 12 nurses and helpers receiving training.

Some 12 months after the opening Dr. Braucht returned to Samoa, and Dr. P. N. Keller took charge. Later Dr. G. H. Gibson filled the position of medical superintendent. Largely because of serious financial difficulties the institution closed its doors in September 1921.

CHRISTIAN CENTRE FOR BIOETHICS. A resource center and a Seventh-day Adventist voice in bioethics located at Sydney Adventist Hospital in Australia. Established in 1987, it is the second ethics center in the world operated by the church. Annually it sponsors the National Bioethics Conference, which addresses current ethical issues from a Christian perspective.

CHRISTIAN EDUCATION. *See Home and School.*

CHRISTIAN EDUCATOR (1897-1899; monthly, 10 months a year; Review and Herald, Battle Creek, Michigan; incomplete file in R&H). A journal for parents and teachers. *Editor:* F. W. Howe.

CHRISTIAN EDUCATOR (1915-1922). *See Home and School.*

CHRISTIAN HELP WORK. A phrase used in the Home Missionary Department to cover any sort of otherwise unclassified work done by individuals for anyone in need.

CHRISTIAN, LEWIS HARRISON (1871-1949). Evangelist and administrator. He graduated from Union College in 1896, and in 1897 began preaching in Minnesota. In 1899 he turned to evangelism among the Scandinavians of Chicago, and the next year was ordained. As further preparation for working for the Scandinavians he worked in Denmark from 1902 to 1904. On returning to the United States, he served briefly as president of the Northern Illinois Conference, before taking up responsibilities as secretary of the Danish-Norwegian Department of the North American Foreign Department, a position he held from 1905 to 1913. During this period he helped establish the Danish-Norwegian Seminary in Hutchinson, Minnesota. He was successively president of the Lake Union Conference (1914-1918), secretary of the Bureau of Home Missions of the General Conference (1918-1920), then General Conference associate vice president for Europe (1920-1922), and president of the European Division (1922-1928), where he traveled extensively rebuilding denominational work that had suffered during World War I.

On the separation of the European Division in 1928 into four administrative sections, Christian served as president of the Northern European Division, with headquarters in London. In 1936 he became a general vice president of the General Conference. After serving for 10 years, he was appointed a field secretary of the General Conference. Along with his other duties he taught religion at the SDA Theological Seminary, and devoted time to writing. Among his books are *Facing the Crisis, Modern Religious Trends,* and *The Fruitage of Spiritual Gifts.*

CHRISTIAN LIFESTYLE MAGAZINE. *See Lifestyle Magazine.*

CHRISTIAN, PERCY W. (1907-1989). Educator, administrator. Born in Salt Lake City, he began his teaching career at Broadview Academy in Illinois. Later he taught history at Pacific Union College and at Walla Walla College, where he was chair of the department for nine years. He served as academic dean of Pacific Union College before assuming the presidency of that school. Later he became president of Emmanuel Missionary and Walla Walla colleges. He continued teaching in retirement and served with his second wife, Ellen Gibson, in Taiwan.

CHRISTIAN RECORD. *See* Christian Record Services.

CHRISTIAN RECORD BENEVOLENT ASSOCIATION. *See* Christian Record Services.

CHRISTIAN RECORD SERVICES, INC. (CRS). A multinational, nonprofit corporation that develops, produces, and distributes free publications and services that help meet the educational, recreational, social, and motivational needs of the sight- and hearing-impaired and of those with other physical disabilities. It has its headquarters at 4444 South 52nd Street, Lincoln, Nebraska 68516.

History. *Beginnings of the Work for the Visually Impaired.* As early as 1897 the General Conference, in its awakening awareness of a duty to give the message of the Bible to all the world, gave consideration to reaching the visually impaired. In an effort to fulfill this recognized duty, the International Tract Society, with headquarters in Battle Creek, Michigan, purchased a stereotype machine for making plates for raised point print and issued a number of tracts. In 1899 a new era opened. A 27-year-old young man from Nebraska named Austin O. Wilson, sightless since the age of 9, and a former student of the Nebraska School for the Blind, enrolled at Battle Creek College and began to urge the church leaders to do more for the visually impaired. As a result, the General Conference Committee decided to publish a journal for the visually impaired, the *Christian Record,* a 10-page monthly that would present choice reading matter and Seventh-day Adventist doctrines to sightless readers. The first editors of the paper were L. A. Hoopes, secretary of the General Conference, and L. T. Nicola, of the International Tract Society. As far as possible, sightless persons were to be used to do the mechanical work necessary to print the magazine. Wilson was employed to put out the first number. The facilities were crude. After the embossing plates were made with the old stereotype machine, he and his wife (also sightless) used a common clothes wringer to print the sheets that made up the first issue of 75 copies printed in January 1900. The stated aim of the *Christian Record* was "to educate, and to suggest lines of work that would supply many blind people with an independent livelihood." The cover of the magazine carried ink-print advertisements of articles that would be good items for sightless salespersons.

Also called to service in the new venture in 1900 were two Nebraska friends of Wilson, L. N. Muck and his wife. They were graduates of the Nebraska School for the Blind, and she was a teacher in that institution. Together with the Wilsons, they worked on the production of the magazine the first few years. When Wilson spoke at the General Conference of 1901 in behalf of sending the new magazine to all schools and libraries for the visually impaired, the delegates showed keen interest in the new undertaking by the questions they asked. His recorded answers inform us that at that time an issue had 20 to 24 pages, each containing about half as much as the ordinary typewritten page, and that they were sending out about 200 copies a month. L. A. Hoopes, the editor, stated that already some converts had been won as a result of reading these publications for the visually impaired. The *Christian Record* was no more than well begun when the Review and Herald publishing plant burned in December 1902, destroying all the equipment, including the special facilities of the *Christian Record.* The work for the visually impaired was moved to College View, Nebraska, in May 1904. By 1905 the circulation had increased to between 600 and 700.

Means of Financial Support. When the paper was begun, church members were urged to make offerings for the support of the new missionary project. They also were urged to visit the visually impaired in their neighborhood and solicit their subscriptions to the *Record.* If the sightless person was too poor to subscribe, the solicitor was urged to give him or her the money ($1.50 at first) to pay for a subscription. At the General Conference session of 1909 it was recommended that the union and local conferences endeavor to place the *Christian Record* in the hands of every sightless person in their territories who could read it. Several unions appropriated $300, and each local conference was urged to raise 10 cents a member annually for the work. Accordingly, Muck visited camp meetings, promoting the work for the visually impaired and urging the conferences to raise their goals. At the Autumn Council of 1911 it was voted to support the *Christian Record* on the same basis as other mission work, by yearly appropriation. In 1912 the periodicals of the publishing house were accorded free mailing privileges in the United States; no subscription price was to be charged.

By 1915 a plan of public solicitation of funds from business firms and individuals for the support of the work had evolved. This in time became the permanent plan of support of the organization. Beginning in a small way with part-time solicitors or retired people, the solicitation program has grown as the increased services have demanded. It was enlarged during the administration of D. D. Rees, beginning in 1927. As a result, the finances of the institution have been placed upon a firm footing.

Beginning in 1960, Seventh-day Adventist churches in the North American Division give an offering every year to provide the denominational services; the public contributes the funds that provide the nonsectarian services.

Nature of Publications and Other Services. Very early the need of a circulating library was seen, especially as a means of making available the braille Bible, in 18 volumes, and other inspirational books. In 1909 C. N. Miller, a sightless editor, reported that such a library had been established. The library contains choice inspirational and religious volumes, circulated postage free, as is all matter for the visually impaired in the United States and Canada.

Mrs. C. W. Degering (1948-1958) and Mrs. C. G. Cross (1958-1974), both sighted librarians and skillful braillists, have been largely responsible for the rapid development of the institution's large lending library, which is considered to be not only the best but also the largest of its type.

By 1926 there were enough SDAs among the visually impaired to create a demand for braille Sabbath school lesson quarterlies. In response that year, the institution began publication of the Sabbath school lessons, including notes and helps (now called *The Student).*

In January 1937 a monthly magazine for the thousands of junior-age sightless children, called *The Children's Friend,* was begun. Under the leadership of C. W. Degering (1949-1958), an expanded program of publication was inaugurated. In 1951 the institution received permission to braille the magazine *Life and Health,* issued monthly.

Two evangelistic magazines—*The Bible Expositor* and later *These Times*—were published for some years, but these were dropped in the fifties in favor of Bible correspondence courses and doctrinal tracts. In 1954 a magazine for teenagers, *The Youth,* was begun.

In February 1955, in response to an obvious need, the *Christian Record Talking Magazine* was introduced. Issued quarterly on disks, this medium allows the visually impaired and others with physical disabilities to enjoy talking features: nature, adventure, and informative interviews relevant to current events. This method reaches those who cannot read braille.

During the fifties a number of inspirational books, such as *Thoughts From the Mount of Blessing, Steps to Christ,* and *The Desire of Ages,* by Ellen G. White, and *Alone With God,* by Matilda Andross, were recorded as talking books. These are distributed by the United States Library of Congress and its 50 regional libraries.

In January 1959 a magazine in large print was launched for those who, although legally sightless, are partly sighted and can read large print. Gauged for youth and young adults, it was called *Happiness.* In April 1961 the two magazines were combined under the name *Youth Happiness* and were brailled as well as published in large print. In January 1976 the magazine was renamed *Young and Alive.*

In 1959 a new experiment was made in the production of storybooks for sightless parents of sighted children. These books are trademarked FULL VISION books. The sightless parent reads the brailled story on the left-hand page while the child's attention is held by the picture on the right-hand page. The series of storybooks includes Bible stories, stories about nature, science, and patriotism, and poems for small children.

Projects include the printing of more material in large or sight-saving type for partially sighted readers. *Steps to Christ,* the first of these books, was completed in May 1965. Since 1962 considerably more talking books have been produced, including the Conflict of the Ages Series and many other books. In February 1961 the taped edition of *The Student* was started. It contained senior-division lessons, mission stories, and 30 minutes of articles from the church paper. Since 1972 *The Student* has been produced in braille and on flexible disc. It contains only the adult Sabbath school lesson quarterly information. In 1962 the tape-lending library was begun. Volunteers from many parts of the U.S.A. read assigned books onto tapes for the organization. These are duplicated and put into circulation in the tape-lending library.

Christian Record employs many area representatives in the United States. The representatives assist thousands of people each year who are sightless or have other physical disabilities. The representatives introduce people to the free services of CRS and assist them in making adjustments to a different way of life, both physically and spiritually.

Beginning in January 1965, a quarterly braille edition of the *Review and Herald* (now the *Adventist Review*) was issued for SDA braille-reading adults, to enable them to keep up with the progress of SDA activities in all parts of the world.

The institution makes no charge for any subscription, book, or other benefit. Students who have visual, hearing, or other physical disabilities, have the opportunity to receive scholarship money from CRS.

Having outgrown its plant, the institution

erected a larger plant with ample provision for expansion and occupied it the summer of 1963.

CRS helps SDA conferences overseas by sending publications and Bible courses. Most of the services are sent directly to English-speaking people in 70 countries.

Contracted Services. The original motive of the sightless people who encouraged establishing the *Christian Record* was to bring SDA teachings to the visually impaired. As time went on, it was decided to make the magazine nonsectarian, since many copies went to schools for the visually impaired and to others who were zealous members of other churches. The new policy was to use the *Christian Record* as a benevolent nonsectarian enterprise, and announce in its pages any tracts and other publications of a sectarian nature, which those interested could receive free upon request. Such sectarian work conducted by the Seventh-day Adventist Church, and paid for by the church at actual cost, is carried on the organization's books as "contracted services."

Longtime Workers. Among the sightless workers who have given long and faithful service to Christian Record are Mrs. Armenta Zadina (50 years), Albert Macy (35 years), Mrs. N. L. Muck (more than 25 years), N. L. Muck (more than 20 years), Lyle Harris (more than 20 years), and Mrs. A. O. Wilson (nearly 20 years).

Longtime sighted workers include Mrs. A. S. Bringle (more than 50 years) and Dean Duffield (40 years). D. D. Rees was editor and manager for the longest period—22 years. Among others who worked more than 30 years are E. R. Corder, F. G. Corder, Mrs. Ora F. Lightcap, Mrs. D. F. Bush, Mrs. J. L. Derby, and H. F. Drake.

Recent Developments. After the appointment on Mar. 1, 1958, of C. G. Cross as manager and editor, surveys were conducted dealing with the facts on, and trends among, sightless people and organizations serving the visually impaired. The information from these surveys and the work of the institution were studied by a committee appointed by the General Conference. The Christian Record Board voted favorably on the recommendations of this committee, and made them the framework for subsequent progress.

As a result, emphasis has been focused on reorganizing and developing the field work; dropping and combining certain magazines, and initiating new periodicals to meet specific needs; meeting the demands of the state and local permit-issuing organizations in order to qualify for the thousands of solicitation permits that are needed annually (the public is asked to pay for the nonsectarian services only; the Seventh-day Adventist Church pays for the sectarian services it promotes); launching publications in large print for people of dimming sight or with partial vision; greatly increasing the capacity of the free lending library of braille, recorded, and large-print books; encouraging closer cooperation with ministers in following up Bible interests; producing a new type of book for sightless parents who rear their young sighted children; developing more services specifically for visually impaired SDAs participating more actively in professional meetings within the industry; maintaining a constant public relations program both within the church and among the public; launching a new department of magazines, books, music, and special programs on magnetic tapes; inaugurating a system of volunteer workers in the plant and in the field; and producing more books on long-playing records, and cassettes.

An addition to services is CRS's National Camps for Blind Children. Since its beginning in 1967, more than 34,000 sightless campers have attended camps throughout the United States and Canada. Activities enhance self-confidence, boost morale, and offer hope. Since 1980 a winter camp at Winter Park, Colorado, has been offered. Approximately 45 campers participate in downhill skiing, snowmobiling, cross-country skiing, and many other winter sports.

The deaf services department serves more than 4,000 individuals, and programs are added each year to help those who are hearing-impaired. A videotape-lending library, youth camps, workshops, easy English publications with simple sentences for adults, coloring books for children, and Bible lessons are offered those with hearing impairments.

In 1963 the organization changed its name from Christian Record Benevolent Association, Incorporated, to Christian Record Braille Foundation, Inc., so as better to identify the organization.

In 1989 the organization changed its name from Christian Record Braille Foundation, Inc. to Christian Record Services, Inc. Because CRS offers services for deaf and others with physical disabilities, the name needed to encompass more than braille work.

As of June 1993 circulation of the publications of Christian Record were: *Christian*

Record, braille, 6,500; *Christian Record Talking Magazine*, flexible disk, 13,300; *Children's Friend*, braille, 3,400; *Deaf Light*, easy English, 3,800; *Encounter*, recorded, 6,300; *Lifeglow*, large print, 29,000; *New Dawn*, easy English, 700; *Review*, braille, 800; *The Student*, braille, 2,900; *The Student*, cassette, 150; *The Student*, recorded, 2,700; *Viva Radiante*, Spanish, large print, 1,000; *Young and Alive*, braille, 7,000; and *Young and Alive*, large print, 26,000.

Editors and Managers: L. A. Hoopes and L. T. Nicola, 1900-1902; L. N. Muck, 1902-1904; L. N. Muck, E. T. Russell, A. W. George, J. S. Hart, 1905-1907; B. E. Huffman, E. T. Russell, C. N. Roberts, J. S. Hart, 1908-1909; C. N. Miller, 1909-1911; L. N. Muck, Mrs. L. N. Muck, Mrs. A. O. Wilson, 1912-1913; Mrs. A. O. Wilson, 1914-1916; H. C. Lacey, Mrs. A. O. Wilson, 1917; H. C. Lacey, M. E. Willis, 1918; J. N. Anderson, M. E. Ellis, 1919-1920; J. N. Anderson, J. H. Jeys, 1921-1923; Roger Altman, 1924-1927; D. D. Rees, 1928-1949; C. W. Degering, 1949-1958; C. G. Cross, 1958-1973. Hereafter the managers did not serve as editors.

General Manager: A. W. Kaytor, 1973-1974.

Presidents: F. G. Thomas, 1974-1978; Eugene Stiles, 1978-1980; B. E. Jacobs, 1980-1982; Howard H. Voss, 1983-1985; Vernon L. Bretsch, 1985-1991; Clarence E. Hodges, 1991- .

CHRISTIAN RECORD TALKING MAGAZINE. *See* Christian Record Services, Inc.

CHRISTIANIA HEALTH HOME. *See* Kurbadet.

CHRISTIANIA PUBLISHING HOUSE. *See* Norwegian Publishing House.

CHRISTIANSEN, JAKOB (1848-1934). Missionary sailor. He was born in Norway and spent his youth on the seas as a sailor and as a teacher of navigation. He later emigrated to the United States, where he became a Seventh-day Adventist in 1866, and entered the colporter work. After attending a training school in Oregon in the school year 1887-1888 he became an evangelist. In 1890 he went out on the first cruise of the mission ship *Pitcairn* as a mate. After the death of Captain Marsh, he brought the ship back and then commanded it on its second cruise. In 1893 he came to New York and there served as ship missionary from the *Sentinel*, a mission boat in the New York Harbor. In 1896 he returned to Norway, where he worked as a colporter for two years, after which he was invited to take charge of the ship mission at Hamburg. Six years later, he went to Stettin (now Szczecin) and established a ship mission there. From 1906 to 1913 he worked in the Netherlands. During the winter months he repaired camp meeting and preaching tents at Friedensau. In 1914 he went to Friedensau to stay, and retired at the old people's home there in 1916. Unable to settle down, he went out to preach and organized congregations at Prenzlau and Ferdinandsdorf in Germany. In 1925 he returned to Norway and engaged in evangelism for the next four years. He finally gave in to age and retired in 1929, past the age of 80.

CHRISTMAN, HARRY KRUM (1892-1982). Publishing director, circulation manager. Born in Pennsylvania, the second of six children, he was educated at Mount Vernon College in Ohio. After graduating in 1914, he dedicated himself to the colporter ministry and accepted his first denominational position as publishing director for the West Pennsylvania Conference. He had planned to follow his father into the practice of medicine, but God had other plans. In 1915 he married Ruth Robbins, a musician. Continuing his ministerial career, he was asked in 1919 to join C. V. Leach in the Home Missionary Department of the General Conference. During the time that they worked together, the book *Christian Service* was compiled from the writings of Ellen White.

In succeeding years he labored in various conferences—Michigan, Pennsylvania, Ohio—and the Columbia Union before moving to Nashville to begin 26 memorable years as circulation manager for Seventh-day Adventist journals, seven years at Southern Publishing Association promoting *Watchman* magazine (later *These Times*), and 19 years at Pacific Press promoting *Signs of the Times*, where he worked closely with editor Arthur Maxwell. He retired in 1962 after 48 years of service for the church he loved.

CHRISTMAS. The Seventh-day Adventist Church does not follow the Christian, or church, year of festivals and fasts, and hence does not celebrate Christmas as an ecclesiastical festival. However, it is customary in some SDA congregations to have a special program or special music with a Nativity theme on the

Sabbath that falls on or near December 25.

SDAs have ignored Christmas as a church festival because of the absence of any divine command to observe the day. Furthermore, Christ's birth date is unknown, and December 25 was chosen by the Roman churches late in the fourth century, to coincide with the "birthday of the sun," the pagan solstice festival. On the other hand, SDAs have utilized the spirit of the Christmas season to direct people to the biblical teachings concerning Christ's birth and have encouraged the giving of liberal offerings to missionary purposes.

In SDA publications apparently the first mention of Christmas in connection with the story of Christ's birth is a poem by Jane Gay entitled "A Christmas Lyric," which appears in the *Review and Herald* (15:30, Dec. 15, 1859). A few years later, in the same periodical, the following advertisement by J. M. Aldrich, secretary of the SDA Publishing Association, appeared: "CHRISTMAS AND NEW YEARS COMING!—The little folks of course must be remembered on these occasions. This is right. I would suggest, however, that, instead of filling the children's stockings with candy, sugar-birds, and rubber-dogs, and telling them that that mythical creature—*old Santa Claus*—came down the chimney or through the keyhole, and paid such respect to their suspended hosiery, you had far better send to this office and procure for them one or more of the following named, really beautiful, interesting and valuable little books: viz: *Bethlehem and Her Children; Morning Star; Sweet Story of Old; Promised One; Joseph and His Brethren; History of Paul; Sketches From Jericho*" *(ibid.* 27:8, Dec. 5, 1865).

In the 1870s it appears that it became customary in some SDA churches to have a Christmas tree in church, on which offerings were placed.

In 1879 there was considerable discussion in the *Review and Herald* with regard to the use of these Christmas trees for raising money for church projects. The following question, answered apparently by James White, sparked the dialogue: "Is it right to have Christmas trees and festivals? Is there any authority in the Bible for so doing?

"Ans. We do not see any necessary connection between Christmas trees and festivals. . . . We can have Christmas trees without . . . [a festival]. Such trees as were provided in Battle Creek and Oakland, and we trust in many other of our churches, last Christmas, to bear our gifts to some important enterprises in the Lord's cause, we believe are all right. Is there anything in the Bible against so doing?" *(ibid.* 53:24, Jan. 16, 1879).

In the discussion that followed, Uriah Smith wrote that he thought that it was all right to celebrate the *occasion* of Christ's birth on December 25 without any particular regard for the day *(ibid.* 53:28, Jan. 23, 1879). E. Lanphear, apparently a layman, remarked: "It is a question whether Christ is honored by the practice of celebrating the day as people generally are accustomed to celebrate it" *(ibid.* 53:43, Feb. 6, 1879). S. N. Haskell took the position that it is all right to celebrate the event of Christ's birth with a Christmas tree and a religious service *(ibid.* 53:64, Feb. 20, 1879). J. P. Logan, apparently a layperson, suggested that it might be better not to have Christmas trees at all, "especially as its disuse would injure no one, while its use does hurt the weak" *(ibid.* 53:163, May 22, 1879).

The next December Ellen White recommended various books as Christmas gifts to children in place of "candies and useless toys." She also pointed out that while many people spend the Christmas season "in frivolity and extravagance, gluttony and display . . . it is our privilege to depart from the customs and practices of this degenerate age" *(ibid.* 54:189, Dec. 11, 1879). In regard to the Christmas tree, she made no specific comment on its use in the home, but stated that "there is no particular sin in selecting a fragrant evergreen, and placing it in our churches" *(ibid.).* Gifts for the church were to be placed upon its branches.

In 1888 in an announcement of the Week of Prayer, the suggestion was made that on the Sabbath preceding Christmas a meeting should be conducted to lay plans for the Week of Prayer and also for the "Christmas meeting." "Daily readings" for the Week of Prayer and "Christmas programs" had been sent out to the churches.

In 1890 the Week of Prayer was announced as coming during the Christmas season from December 20 to 27, and the General Conference president reminded SDAs that "it will be a time when the world around us is indulging in much feasting and folly. . . . Let us deny ourselves . . . and bring large contributions to the foreign missions" *(ibid.* 67:745, 746, Nov. 26, 1890).

On the matter of gifts, Ellen White said: "It is pleasant to receive a gift, however small, from those we love. It is an assurance that we are not forgotten, and it seems to bind us to them a little closer.

"Brethren and sisters, while you are devising gifts for one another I would remind you of our heavenly Friend, lest you should be unmindful of His claims. . . .

"While urging upon all the duty of first bringing their offerings to God, I would not wholly condemn the practice of making Christmas and New Year's gifts to our friends. It is right to bestow upon one another tokens of love and remembrance if we do not in this forget God, our best friend. We should make our gifts such as will prove a real benefit to the receiver" *(ibid.* 59:788, 789, Dec. 26, 1882).

CHRISTOFFERS, SIEGFRIED (1912-1959). Editor and publishing house administrator. He was born in a Seventh-day Adventist minister's home in Hungary and received his education at Neandertal Missionary Seminary. After leaving school, he served as colporteur and preacher in Germany until 1937, when he joined the Hamburg Publishing House as archivist. In 1939 he studied at the SDA Theological Seminary in Washington, D.C. During World War II he attempted to return home via the Far East, but was stranded in Japan for about five years. After returning to Germany, he was appointed in 1947 as head of the Editorial Department of the Advent-Verlag (Hamburg). It fell to him to restore SDA writing and editing in Germany and after 1950 to rebuild and develop the publishing plant of which he had become manager. His motto in this work was taken from Hosea 10:12: "Break up your fallow ground: for it is time to seek the Lord, till he come and rain righteousness upon you." He was killed in an automobile accident in 1959.

CHRISTOLOGY. That branch of theological study that deals with the person, attributes, and mission of Jesus Christ. The Greek word *Christos,* "Christ," was originally a title, equivalent to the Hebrew *Mashîach,* "Messiah," but came to be used as a name, or surname, of Jesus. Hence, while Christology might be expected to deal more specifically with Jesus' Messiahship, in actual use it includes every phase of His person and work. Seventh-day Adventists hold that "forever truly God, [Jesus] became also truly man. . . . He was conceived of the Holy Spirit and born of the virgin Mary. He lived and experienced temptation as a human being, but perfectly exemplified the righteousness and love of God" *(Church Manual* [1990], p. 24).

The role of Jesus Christ is suggested by the title "Lord," which is frequently applied to Him. NT scholars commonly recognize that the simple declaration "Jesus is Lord" was the earliest confession of Christian faith (Acts 2:36; Rom. 10:9, 10; 1 Cor. 12:3; Phil. 2:11), made, perhaps, by every convert at baptism. But this simple declaration by no means implies a simple Christology. The Greek-speaking Jews referred to God as *Kurios,* "Lord." In the Septuagint, *Kurios* is not only a translation of the Hebrew word *'Adonai*, "Lord," but also of God's covenant name Yahweh, or "Jehovah." Therefore to any reader of the Septuagint, *Kurios,* "Lord," was a common title for the God of the OT, denoting His power over the world and humans as Creator, Ruler, and Giver of life. By designating Jesus as "Lord," Christians attributed deity to Him, and ascribed to Him supreme authority and power.

It is evident in the NT that Jesus was regarded as both God and human being. But no attempt was made to interrelate these two phases of His nature. The NT stresses Jesus' mission and work, and attempts no explanation of the mystery of His nature. But the historical Christ is set forth as at once fully God and fully human.

By the second century, however, the church felt compelled by one-sided distortions to work out the philosophical implications of the Incarnation. The heretical Ebionites, for example, conceived of Christ as a merely human Messiah and denied His divine nature. The Docetists and Gnostics, on the other hand, denied the reality of His humanity, for they believed that matter is evil. The church had to meet these heresies.

The Christological controversies of the fourth and fifth centuries centered on two main problems: the relation of the nature of Christ to that of God, and the relation between the divine and the human nature in the person of Christ. Arius (250-336) denied the eternity and absolute deity of Christ, and made Him the first and highest of created beings. The Council of Nicea (325) adopted a creed asserting that Jesus is of one substance (*homoousios*) with the Father. Apollinaris the Younger (d. c. 390), on the other hand, being especially concerned to maintain the deity of Christ, denied the integrity of His human nature. He taught that in the Incarnation the divine Logos was united with the purely animal elements present in human nature, without the mind or soul. Theodore of Mopsuestia (d. 428) and his pupil Nestorius (d. after 451) separated the divinity and humanity in Christ almost to the point of making Him into two persons, a view that was condemned by the Council of Ephesus in 431. Eutyches (d. after 454) held that although before the Incarnation there were two natures in Christ, at the Incarnation they were coalesced into one. The Council of Chalcedon in 451 formally defined the church's position, that in the person of Christ there was an abiding union of Godhood and humanity without the integrity of either being impaired: "one . . . Christ . . . in two natures, inconfusedly, unchangeably, indivisibly, inseparably."

Some of the earliest Seventh-day Adventists—for example, James White and Joseph Bates—had formerly been members of the "Christian Connection" (later part of the Congregational Christian Church, now merged into the United Church of Christ), a church that at that time held to a form of the Arian belief concerning Christ's nature. These people did not deny that Christ was divine, the Creator of heaven and earth, Son of God, Lord, and Saviour; they mostly argued that the terms "Son" and "Father" indicated that the Son had a beginning, even though in the inconceivably remote past. Upon becoming SDAs they retained this belief, which found expression in their writings. But not all Seventh-day Adventists held this view, and it was not an essential part of the SDA doctrine. For nearly a half century, difference of opinion on this point persisted, but open controversy was avoided and the anti-Trinitarian view died a natural death. The two leading anti-Trinitarians, James White and Uriah Smith, changed their opinions considerably. James White, for instance, had at first rejected the "old trinitarian" idea "that Jesus Christ is the very and Eternal God" *(Review and Herald* 3:52, Aug. 5, 1852), although he believed in Christ's divinity *(ibid.* 4:66, Sept. 8, 1853); he later wrote that SDAs "hold the divinity of Christ so nearly with the trinitarian" position that very little real difference existed (*ibid.* 48:116, Oct. 12, 1876), and that the Son "was equal with the Father in creation, in the institution of law, and in the government of created intelligences" *(ibid.* 56:56, July 15, 1880). Uriah Smith, in the first edition of his *Thoughts on Revelation* (1867, p. 59), called the preexistent Christ "the first created being." But he soon came more nearly into harmony with his brethren by modifying this statement by the time the first combined edition of *Daniel and the Revelation* came out (1882), in which he explained (p. 488) that the Only-begotten of God could hardly be "any being created in the ordinary sense of that term." He later spoke against degrading Christ to a created being *(Looking Unto Jesus,* [1898], p. 12). Other early Adventist leaders who showed Arian tendencies were J. H. Waggoner, his son, E. J. Waggoner, and W. W. Prescott, who, as late as 1896 *(Review and Herald* 73:232, Apr. 14, 1896), spoke of Christ as having had two births—one in eternity, and one in the flesh.

Early SDA anti-Trinitarians opposed the Trinitarian concept on the basis that such a belief was contrary to common sense and to NT statements indicating Christ's subordination to the Father, that it was of pagan origin, and that it depreciated the personality of Christ and the importance of His vicarious death. It was largely through the writings of Ellen White that the Trinitarian view finally prevailed. Although never trained in the intricacies of theology, she carefully avoided, through the years, the pitfalls of the Christological controversies of past generations.

She apparently did not find it necessary to take issue with her close associates on Christology, but she repeatedly asserted Christ's equality with God, as early as 1869, and increasingly in the 1870s and 1880s (1869: 2T 200; 1875: 3T 566; 1880: 4T 458; and many other statements). She described Christ as "the Majesty of heaven, . . . equal with God" (1883: 1SM 69); "Sovereign of heaven, one in power and authority with the Father" (1888: GC 459); "of one substance, possessing the same attributes" with the Father *(Signs of the Times* 20:54, Nov. 27, 1893); "the only-begotten Son of God, who was with the Father from eternal ages" (1895: FE 382); "The Lord God . . . clothed with the habiliments of humanity" (1895: FE 379); "Infinite and omnipotent"; "the eternal, self-existent Son" (Ev 615). In her masterpiece *The Desire of Ages* (1898) she wrote: "In Christ is life, original, unborrowed, underived" (DA 530; also in an article of the year before, *Signs of the Times* 23:214, Apr. 8, 1897). Later, she said: "He did not cease to be God when He became man. . . . The Godhead was still His own" (1903: Ellen G. White, in SDACom 5:1129). In 1906 she wrote: "Christ was God essentially, and in the highest sense. He was with God from all eternity," "a distinct person, yet one with the Father" *(Review and Herald* 83:8, Apr. 5, 1906).

With reference to the relationship between the two natures, she declared that Christ "did not cease to be God when He became a man.

The human did not take the place of the divine, nor the divine of the human. . . . The two expressions . . . were, in Christ, closely and inseparably one, and yet they had a distinct individuality" *(Signs of the Times* 25:2, May 10, 1899).

Overemphasis on the deity of Christ is sometimes pressed to the point that it obscures His real and true humanity, with the result that He ceases to be an example of how we in our humanity can, through Him, overcome as He overcame.

"It would have been an almost infinite humiliation for the Son of God to take man's nature, even when Adam stood in his innocence in Eden. But Jesus accepted humanity when the race had been weakened by four thousand years of sin. Like every child of Adam He accepted the results of the working of the great law of heredity" (DA 49).

"Our Saviour took humanity, with all its liabilities. He took the nature of man, with the possibility of yielding to temptation. We have nothing to bear which He has not endured" *(ibid.* 117).

Christ was tempted by Satan as we are tempted, but "on not one occasion was there a response to his manifold temptations" (Ellen G. White, in SDACom 5:1129).

"He took upon Himself human nature, and was tempted in all points as human nature is tempted. He could have sinned; He could have fallen, but not for one moment was there in Him an evil propensity" *(ibid.* 5:1128).

He was tempted "like as we are, yet without sin" (Heb. 4:15).

CHRONOLOGY. Seventh-day Adventists always have been interested in biblical chronology, both historical and prophetic. The founders had participated in the Millerite movement, and had belonged to the segment that after 1844 still held that the 2300 prophetic days of Dan. 8:14 were fulfilled on Oct. 22, 1844, although they abandoned the Second Advent as the expected event for that day. Seventh-day Adventists believe that no time prophecies extend beyond the 2300 days; they thus set no dates for the Second Advent.

In historical biblical chronology, SDA scholars generally hold that the time statements in the Bible are valid but not necessarily all-inclusive; that exact B.C. dates cannot be assigned, for example, to the Creation or to any biblical events before the time of the later Hebrew kings (see SDACom 1:196). Formerly, SDA publications, like others, cited Ussher's seventeenth-century chronology (as printed in Bible margins since 1701); this scheme was once useful, as an approximation for the later periods of biblical history, but is now superseded by better attested dates in historical chronology as established by archaeology, and in some cases fixed by astronomy. Newer denominational textbooks employ these more exact findings. Seventh-day Adventists do not, however, accept the vast periods of the prehistoric time scale based on the evolutionary theory *(see* Evolution).

SDA scholars have made contributions to knowledge in the field of biblical and historical chronology—for example, Edwin R. Thiele, *The Mysterious Numbers of the Hebrew Kings* (Chicago: University of Chicago Press, 1951), a Judah-Israel chronology; and Siegfried H. Horn and Lynn H. Wood, *The Chronology of Ezra 7* (Washington, D.C.: Review and Herald, 1953). There are several summaries and discussions of biblical and historical chronology in this Reference Series (see SDACom 1:174-196; 2:36, 77, 124-164; 3:45, 85-110, 326-327; 4:17-24; 5:227-266; 6:97-107; also SDADic, "Chronology"). For SDA interpretations of certain chronological prophecies, *see* Twenty-three Hundred Days; Year-Day Principle.

CHRZESCIJANSKI INSTYTUT WYDAWNICZY ZNAKI CZASU. *See* Polish Publishing House.

CHUHARKANA HOSPITAL DISPENSARY. A medical institution operated variously as a clinic, a dispensary, and a hospital, at Chuharkana Mandi, about 30 miles (50 kilometers) west of Lahore in Pakistan, by the Pakistan Union.

Seventh-day Adventist medical work in the area began in 1914, when F. H. Loasby and V. L. Mann, a physician, toured the villages surrounding Lahore Punjab by oxcart, preaching and treating the sick. When it was decided to establish a medical center to which the sick could be brought and where workers could be trained to operate village dispensaries, land was purchased in 1916 at Chuharkana. During the next two years bungalows, a hospital, and a dispensary building were erected. Dr. Olive Smith and her husband were called to assist and later to succeed Dr. Mann, who returned to the United States in 1919. Dr. Smith became ill and left in 1920, and with no other doctor available, E. R. Reynolds, a young licentiate with some medical training, took charge of the dispensary until Ilma Dowling, an Australian nurse, arrived. In 1923 the hospital building was converted into a school, and only the dispensary work was continued. However, from 1930 to 1936, SDA medical services were available to the residents of the area at Chichoki Mallian, 15 miles (25 kilometers) from Chuharkana, where Dr. R. C. Lindholm was operating a hospital.

In 1946 Dr. Carrie J. A. Robbins, and her husband, C. W. Robbins, arrived in Chuharkana and opened a hospital there. In 1949 C. W. Robbins died, and a short time later Dr. Robbins returned to the United States. Robert Shrewsbury, M.D., succeeded her and developed the hospital into a 20-bed unit. After he left in 1955, the medical work again was limited to a dispensary, with K. E. Deweltz and his wife in charge.

In 1968 the Deweltz family departed, and since that time the institution has been limited to a school clinic staffed by a faculty nurse. *See also* Pakistan Adventist Seminary.

CHUHARKANA MANDI ELEMENTARY SCHOOL. *See* Pakistan Adventist Seminary.

CHULUMANI HOSPITAL. *See* La Paz Adventist Clinic.

CHUNG HUA SAN YÜ YEN CHIU SHE. *See* China Training Institute.

CHURCH (local organization). The basic organizational unit of the church at large, a group of baptized believers united by their common faith (*see* Church, Nature of), and also by an organization based on the New Testament pattern of church government. The local Seventh-day Adventist church acts either through its elders, deacons, and other officers constituting the church board, or by vote of the whole congregation, in matters of local administration, the admission and dropping of members, the operation of a church school, and the election of its officers. It works in cooperation with its pastor, who guides the church activities, and it belongs to a group of churches organized into a conference, under relations defined in the constitution and bylaws of the conference (or mission, or some other such unit). The handbook for the guidance of the local church is the *Church Manual*.

I. Church Membership. 1. *Admission.* There are three prerequisites for admission to membership in the Seventh-day Adventist Church: (1) conversion, (2) acceptance of the principles and doctrines of the SDA Church, (3) baptism by immersion. Those complying with these prerequisites are granted membership by vote of the members. For those requesting admission by baptism, the vote may be taken prior to baptism (that is "subject to baptism") or after baptism. Those requesting membership who have previously been baptized by immersion may be received on their profession of faith. In this category come those who have been members of other denominations that practice baptism by immersion, and who wish to be received on their former baptism. SDAs whose membership records are unavailable may also be received on profession of faith. In their case, a careful study is made of the circumstances, usually in consultation with the conference president. If it is found that the person applying for membership on profession of faith is still a member of another church in the denomination, he or she cannot be received unless granted a letter from the church to which he or she belongs (see "Transfer of Membership" below). If the church refuses such a letter and the member regards the refusal as unfair, he or she may appeal to the conference committee. Rebaptism is required of those who have been disfellowshipped and wish to regain their membership.

Because church membership involves a spiritual relationship to God and to humanity, only those who have experienced regeneration should seek entrance into the church. The minister is urged to give due emphasis to this requirement.

Candidates for baptism are fully instructed in the church's doctrinal beliefs and the principles of conduct, which are summarized in the *Church Manual* (1990 ed., pp. 179-182). Preceding baptism, the candidates, in the presence of the church, or, if that is not practicable, before the church board, take the baptismal vow as given in the *Church Manual* (1990 ed., pp. 44, 45).

2. *Transfer of Membership.* Church members moving to a new locality where they expect to stay longer than six months are expected to transfer membership to the church near their new location or, if there is no church nearby, to the conference church. They make request for transfer to the clerk of the church they desire to join; the clerk then notifies the clerk of the church where membership is held, who transmits the notification, through the minister or church elder, to the church board. If the board deems these members to be in good and regular standing, the request for transfer is

presented to the church the first time in what is called a first reading, that is, the first presenting of the members' names in a duly called meeting of the church (usually the Sabbath service). Upon a second reading, usually a week later, a vote on whether to grant a letter of transfer is taken. The interval allows opportunity for any objection, which is usually made privately to the pastor or elder.

The letter, if granted, is sent to the clerk of the church the member proposes to join. There the member's request is submitted through the pastor or elder to the church board, and finally to the church, which votes on the request after a second reading, as in the case of the church granting the letter. If the vote is affirmative, the member is enrolled as a member and a notification is returned to the clerk of the church from which the member has been transferred. Until the clerk receives this notification of acceptance the member retains his or her former membership. If because of disrupted communications it is impossible to receive a letter from the member's previous church, the local church may accept the member by vote without a letter after taking counsel with the local conference or mission.

If a church declines to receive a member seeking admission by letter, the clerk returns the letter to the church that issued it, with a full explanation for the refusal of membership.

Letters are not granted to members who are under church discipline (qualifying statements being out of order). Under no circumstances may a letter be granted or accepted by a church without the request of the member involved. Members can never be added or removed (except in case of death) without a vote of the church. On the dismissal of members, *see* Church Discipline.

II. Church Administration. Every church member has a voice in electing the local church officers, who, with the pastor, lead in the administration of church affairs.

1. *Pastor.* The pastor is primarily the spiritual leader of the church, but is also the leader and adviser of the officers, ranking above the local elder, and is usually the chair of the church board. But the pastor is not an elected officer of the church; all pastors and assistant pastors are appointed by the executive committee of the conference (or mission) to which the church belongs. The minister is responsible for the church services and for the planning of all church activities, with the assistance of the elders. If the pastor is a licensed minister *(see* Licentiate) rather than an ordained minister, the local elder presides at the Lord's Supper and at business meetings, but an ordained minister presides at all meetings unless that individual appoints the elder to do so on occasion. The pastor leads and instructs the officers and the membership in evangelistic activities.

2. *Church Officers.* The church elder(s) and the deacon(s) are the leaders in the spiritual and practical functions, respectively. Other general officers are deaconess(es), church clerk, and church treasurer. Under some circumstances a very small or incompletely organized church may have a church leader instead of an elder. The Sabbath school and other auxiliary organizations and departments of the church have their own officers, but all are elected annually by vote of the church.

In the broadest sense the term *church officers* includes all persons chosen in the annual church election. Following is a typical list:

Elder or elders
Deacon or deacons
Deaconess or deaconesses
Clerk
Treasurer
Assistant treasurer or treasurers
Church chorister, or song leader
Church organist or pianist
Church education secretary
Family life director
Personal ministries leader
Personal ministries secretary
Interest coordinator
Community Services director
Sabbath school superintendent
Assistant Sabbath school superintendent
Sabbath school secretary
Assistant Sabbath school secretary
Sabbath school extension division secretary
Sabbath school division leaders
Sabbath school Investment secretary
Sabbath school chorister, or song leader
Sabbath school organist or pianist
Sabbath school Vacation Bible School director
Leader of Home and School Fellowship
Assistant leader of Home and School Fellowship
Secretary of Home and School Fellowship
Leader of Dorcas Society
Dorcas Society secretary-treasurer
Adventist Youth Society leader
Associate Adventist Youth leader
AYS sponsor
Adventist Junior Youth Society superintendent

Assistant AJY superintendent(s)
AYS secretary-treasurer
Assistant AYS secretary-treasurer
AYS music director
AYS pianist or organist
Pathfinder Club director
Pathfinder Club deputy director
Religious liberty secretary
Health and temperance secretary
Communication secretary
Stewardship secretary
Church board
Church school board
Such other officers as the church may deem advisable

Officers are elected annually Nominations are made by a nominating committee that is chosen by a special committee elected by vote of the church. This special committee may be chosen in one of two ways: By nominations from the floor or by voting to authorize the church board, together with five to seven persons nominated from the floor, to recommend the personnel of the nominating committee. The nominating committee prepares a list of names to submit to the church for officers and assistants. Any member of the church may appear before the committee during its sessions to make suggestions or objections. When the nominating committee is ready to render its report, the report of this committee may be presented at the Sabbath service or at a specially called meeting of the church.

It is the right of any member to raise an objection to the nominating committee's report. He may move that the whole report be referred back to the committee for further consideration. If the motion carries, the member making the objection, or any other member who desires to do so, may appear before the committee to make objections to any name. When the committee makes its final report to the church, the church proceeds to vote. The election is by the majority vote of those present and voting.

If an office of the church becomes vacant during the year, the church board nominates a successor to fill the vacancy and submits the nomination to the church for election.

For the beginnings of local church officers in the Seventh-day Adventist Church, *see* Church Elder; Deacon; Organization.

3. *Church Board.* The representative administrative body of the local church is the church board, elected annually. It customarily includes the elder or elders, the head deacon, the head deaconess, the treasurer, the clerk, the personal ministries leader, the personal ministries secretary, the Sabbath school superintendent, the Community Services leader, the AYS leader, and such other members as may be deemed advisable. The pastor serves as chair, but may arrange for the elder to preside at the board meeting. The number that will constitute a quorum should be determined at a church business meeting. It is recommended that church board meetings be held at least once a month.

The church board, as the governing body of the church, considers details of the church business, is concerned with anything that pertains to the spiritual life of the members, and is responsible for coordinating the various activities of the church. It may delegate authority to persons or committees. It receives requests for letters of transfer and makes recommendations to the church concerning the names, but it cannot disfellowship members, grant letters of transfer, or receive or dismiss members; that must be done by vote of the church.

4. *Church Business Meetings.* Church business meetings are held annually, or may be called more often as the need may arise. They are customarily announced in advance at a regular Sabbath morning service. Any matters pertaining to the business or other affairs of the church are taken up, and, in addition, in the annual meeting, reports may be received from the church clerk, reporting on membership and perhaps certain board actions; the personal ministries secretary, on the missionary activities of the church; the treasurer, on funds received and disbursed for the church; the deacons on visitation and any other matters that come under their care; the Adventist Youth Society secretary, on the activities of the society; the Sabbath school secretary on membership and other Sabbath school items; the principal or teachers on any developments in the church school; and the Home and School Fellowship leader on the activities and needs of that organization.

The pastor usually presides at church business meetings, although an elder may do so. The routine operations of the church are directed by the church board, but major items are taken to the church business meetings, usually after study by the board.

III. Organizing or Disbanding a Church. 1. *Procedure of Organizing.* The formation of a new church is presided over by an ordained minister—either the president of the conference or mission or a minister designated by him. If among the group desiring to form a church there are members of the conference church or of other SDA churches, these should bring with them to the meeting of organization letters of transfer from their churches. Such persons form the nucleus of the new church, and vote on the names of persons joining the Seventh-day Adventist Church for the first time. If there are none with previous church membership, then, under the direction of the presiding minister, three newly baptized believers of good reputation are selected by the officiating minister to form the nucleus, and they proceed to vote on the names of the other candidates for membership. Each of these, upon being voted in, may vote on accepting the remaining candidates.

When all have been received into membership, a nominating committee is chosen, with the officiating minister as chair, to bring in names for the various offices to be filled. After election of the officers and the ordination of the elder and deacon (if not already ordained), an action may then be taken requesting the conference (or its equivalent unit) to receive the new church into the family of churches at its next session. For the organization of a company as a preliminary step toward organizing a church, *see* Company.

As early as 1883, it was recognized *(Review and Herald* 60:393, June 19, 1883) that, in order to safeguard the unity of the church, a local church body should be organized only in consultation with the state conference committee. Before any conference organizations existed, only an ordained minister was considered competent to perform the work of organization. For some years a key step in the procedure of church organization was the signing of a church covenant by the charter members. A typical early procedure is that outlined in the 1861 "Address" submitted to the newly organized Michigan Conference (see *Review and Herald* 18:156, Oct. 15, 1861).

2. *A Union of Two Churches.* Sometimes a new church is formed by the union of two existing congregations. For such a step, approval of the conference committee is first obtained, and then a meeting of each church is called, the conference president or the pastor presiding, that each church may vote on the proposed union. After an affirmative vote by both churches, they hold a joint meeting under the leadership of the conference president or someone appointed by the conference. A written agreement is drawn up, stating the conditions of union (such as disposal of property, financial obligations, the name of the new church, etc.) and providing for release from office of all the officers of both churches. After this, a nominating committee brings in names for officers of the united church, and a copy of the agreement is filed with the local conference.

No member of either church may be dropped at the time of the uniting. The new church is then received into the conference at its next session.

3. *Disbanding a Church.* Churches may be disbanded because of loss of members, for disciplinary reasons, or for apostasy. When loss of members threatens the existence of the church, the conference committee customarily takes action recommending its disbanding. Before such a step is taken, the remaining members are given opportunity to transfer their membership to other churches, either by letters voted by the church, if enough members remain, or upon recommendation of the conference committee.

Rarely is a church disbanded for disciplinary reasons. The conference studies the proposal to disband and presents the case to the union committee; then the matter is referred to the church in question. Action to disband should be by a majority vote of the members.

In a case of apostasy of a majority of the members of a church, or their refusal to submit to order and discipline, the conference committee customarily presents a statement of the case to a conference session, which, by majority vote, may expel the offending church from the sisterhood of churches. If there are remaining loyal members, they may establish a new church or be recommended for membership in other churches by vote of the conference committee.

IV. Denomination-wide Relationships. The local church aids the pastor in evangelism, and under the pastor's leadership and under the counsel of departmental leaders from the conference and higher organizations it carries on lay evangelism and other local activities; and it is the local church that receives the new recruits into a fellowship of worship and work that embraces older members, new members, and prospective members. But the local church is an integral part of a worldwide organization.

A group of local churches forms a conference (or mission, or section, or otherwise named unit); and a group of these units forms a union conference. The unions, grouped under divisions, form the General Conference organization.

The church, being a constituent unit of a conference, participates in conducting the conference affairs by sending its delegates to the biennial sessions to help elect the conference officers and other members of the conference executive committee and to transact business. In this standing conference committee is vested the delegated authority of all the constituent churches.

The local churches send their tithes and offerings, except those funds given for local expenses, to the conference (or mission, or other such unit), and the conference provides the pastors and evangelists. The conference holds title to all local church properties, and the conference and higher units of organization may contribute to building funds and to the operation of the church school.

The conference president is the chief elder, or overseer, of all the churches, and each of them has access to the president's counsel and to the counsel of the departmental secretaries of the conference. Local church schools are under the guidance of a conference educational superintendent. Union and General conference leaders and departmental staffs furnish counsel and promote projects for the work of the local church. Thus the local unit bears responsibilities toward, and receives aid from, the entire church body.

CHURCH (territorial organization). In some parts of the world, a term used in phrases such as the Bulgarian church, Spanish church, or the Seventh-day Adventist Church in Canada, designating the units of SDA organization in those respective areas. More commonly such organizational units are designated as conference, mission, section, or field.

CHURCH ADMINISTRATION. *See* Church (local organization); Organization.

CHURCH AND STATE. The Seventh-day Adventist denomination from its very beginning has been a staunch advocate of church-state separation, especially in the United States, where there is clear constitutional provision for such separation, holding that the distinction between church and state is drawn in the New Testament: "Render therefore unto Caesar the things which are Caesar's; and unto God the things that are God's" (Matt. 22:21). On the one hand, civil government is ordained of God (Rom. 13:1-4); therefore, whether the civil authority is wielded by a Christian, a Jew, a Muslim, or a pagan, it finds its source in God; all citizens are under the protection of, and are subject to, the civil power. Civil government's legitimate concern relates to temporal affairs; the Bible says that in this sphere it is ordained by God. On the other hand, the church was given spiritual authority, and Christ was careful to emphasize that the authority of the church was distinct from temporal power (Matt. 18:17, 18; John 18:36). Only those citizens who have professed allegiance to Christ can be counted as subjects of the spiritual kingdom of Christ. The church concerns itself, as a matter of priority, with the soul and conscience of the individual.

History reveals that frequently the state has used the church to gain its ends and that conversely, in other instances, the church has dominated the state. In either case persecution has resulted. Therefore, Seventh-day Adventists believe that the distinctly different purposes of Caesar's kingdom and of Christ's kingdom are best achieved when neither is subservient to the other and neither encroaches in the area that belongs to the other.

The 1948 Autumn Council of the General Conference Committee issued the following statements regarding church and state relationships: "We believe in civil government as divinely ordained to protect men in the enjoyment of their natural rights, and to rule in civil things, and that in this realm it is entitled to the respectful and willing obedience of all.

"We believe that all legislation which unites church and state is subversive of human rights, potentially persecuting in character, and opposed to the best interests of the church and of the state: and therefore, that it is not within the province of human government to enact such legislation.

"We believe it to be our duty to use every lawful and honorable means to prevent the enactment of legislation which tends to unite church and state, and to oppose every movement toward such union, that all may enjoy the inestimable blessings of religious liberty . . ." (*Actions of the Autumn Council of the General Conference Committee* [1948], p. 13).

The committee passed the following resolutions: "*Relation of Church and State.* WHEREAS, 'The union of the church with the state, be the degree never so slight, while it may appear to bring the world nearer to the church, does in reality but bring the church nearer to the world' (GC 297), and,

"WHEREAS, The state should never invade the distinctive realm of the church to affect in any way the complete freedom of conscience, or the right to profess, practice, and promulgate religious beliefs; and the church should never invade the distinctive realm of the state,

"*We recommend,* 1. That we, the representatives of the Seventh-day Adventist Church in biennial Autumn Council assembled, reaffirm our full belief in the historic doctrine of the separation of church and state, and our resolute purpose as a church to maintain that doctrine unimpaired in our relations with all earthly governments, remembering always that the trend toward union may be gradual and subtle.

"*Loyalty to Government:* WHEREAS, Governments have been set up among men, under God, to regulate human relationships (Rom. 13:1-3; 1 Peter 2:13-17); and,

"WHEREAS, Civil government includes the exercise of the police powers inherent in sovereignty, to prevent whatever may jeopardize the health, morals, safety and general welfare of society;

"*We recommend,* That we reaffirm our loyalty to civil government, pledging our sincere obedience to its laws, and praying for the peace of the country and for all those in authority. That we reaffirm, however, at the same time, our inalienable right to worship God according to the dictates of our own conscience and to promulgate our religious beliefs among all men (Acts 5:29; Mark 16:15)" *(ibid.,* pp. 14, 15).

For other Seventh-day Adventist statements on the subject of church and state, *see* Religious Liberty.

Church-State Separation in the United States. The Constitution of the United States erected safeguards to ensure the separation of church and state—a policy rare among eighteenth-century governments—and this separation has promoted prosperity and harmony for both the churches and the civil government in the United States.

Separation of church and state is most often tested where money is involved. Complete separation of church and state means that state money, which is tax money, is intended for the support of legal and recognized activities that belong to the state. It means that church money, the tithes and offerings of believers, is intended for the support of the religious activities of the church.

Church Schools and the State. Perhaps the greatest area of concern in church-state relations in the United States is in education. As the number of students has multiplied, and as the cost of education has increased, church-affiliated institutions have found it increasingly difficult to support their schools. When government funds became available, the temptation was great for the church to accept them.

The argument against the use of government funds for a church-controlled school is twofold:

1. These government funds, received through the taxing power of the state, would be used to teach religious doctrines in which many of the taxpayers do not believe.

2. Control usually follows subsidy. If the church school accepted state money, it would sooner or later have to accept an unwarranted degree of government control.

When a religious organization tries to dip into the public treasury to support its church school system (teach its distinctive beliefs), it invites the state to trespass in an area that belongs to God and not to Caesar. Parents who refuse the education public schools offer their children and patronize a religious school, in the United States at least, should assume the responsibility of financing that religious-oriented education.

Therefore, to protect religious freedom the Seventh-day Adventist Church opposes the use of government funds to teach religion. The official action of the General Conference regarding state aid to SDA schools reads: "WHEREAS, The Seventh-day Adventist Church in the United States is in full accord with the principles of the separation of church and state as set forth in the federal Constitution, and has through the years supported this principle;

"*We recommend,* That in the United States the denominational policy for our schools of all grades shall be to refrain from accepting gifts of money, land, buildings, or equipment from government; or grants from public tax money for the salaries of teachers; or the maintenance, operation, or support of the services that the schools supply.

"This shall not be construed to prejudice the acceptance of the regular functions of the Public Health Department, such as public health nurses' services, vaccinations, inoculations, or tuberculosis surveys; nor shall it forbid the acquisition, for a consideration, of war surplus" *(ibid.* [1949], p. 26).

Medical Institutions. The same principles apply to the church's medical institutions. In the official action referring to the medical work a careful distinction is made between capital development and operating expenses.

The policy reads: "WHEREAS, Our medical institutions are an integral part of our denominational program;

"*We recommend,* 1. That in the United States our medical institutions refrain from accepting any government aid for operating or maintaining these institutions.

"2. That inasmuch as our medical institutions render a recognized service to the medical needs of the communities in which they are located, government grants for capital development may be accepted. However, it shall be understood that a grant shall be received only after careful study by the operating board, and approval by the union and General Conference committees" *(ibid.,* pp. 26, 27).

A Complex Situation. Relations between church and state in recent years have been distinguished by an ever-increasing complexity of new problems for which no precedent exists. Frequently it is difficult to discover the line between involvement and separation, for instance, in the proposals of government loans at low interest to parochial schools, tax exemption for tuition payments to church schools, the donation of government equipment to church-affiliated college laboratories, government subsidies for teaching certain subjects in private colleges, and other plans, such as tuition vouchers paid from tax funds to be used by parents or students at the schools of their choice.

Areas in which church-state problems may be encountered include public aid to sectarian schools; religious exercises in public schools; shared time or released time for religious instruction; censorship; chaplaincies; divorce; birth control; Sunday laws; ambassador to and from the Holy See; tax exemption for church properties; government aid to church and clergy; immigration quotas and naturalization requirements; military service; state aid to church-affiliated charity and welfare organizations; adoption regulations; and nondiscrimination in church employment.

In many countries of the world additional difficulties between church and state are: Saturday attendance at state schools, compulsory religious services in the armed forces, restrictions on the holding of religious services, evangelistic work, sale of religious literature, baptism of converts, operation of religious institutions, visits by church leaders living in other countries, and publishing of religious literature.

Principles and Application. SDAs support the principle of church-state separation even though in the application of the principle in the complex issues and conditions of many lands they allow differences in practice. Where church-state separation does not exist or where, as in some countries, the governments to a large extent depend on Christian mission institutions to render public services in educational or medical areas, subsidies are accepted. It is recognized, however, that the acceptance of aid involves the risk of encountering government control or of a setback through the sudden loss of the financial aid. In some countries, governments have given land and property for institutions, or have aided in the operation of schools, hospitals, or clinics where such facilities would otherwise be lacking, or where the medical help or welfare work was greatly needed for the benefit of the local people.

Regarding the application of the principle of church-state separation in other countries the General Conference Executive Committee in the Autumn Council of 1948 recommended: "That we reaffirm our belief that this fundamental principle of the separation of church and state should be worldwide in application; recognizing, however, that the applying of certain details of the principle may be different in different parts of the world, due to varied forms of government.

"That in view of these considerations, it must, therefore, be left to the discretion of Division Committees to determine just how this principle shall be applied in their respective fields; but maintaining that in any overlapping of activities, the state should not enter the spiritual realm of the church nor the church the civil rights of the state" *(Action of the Autumn Council of the General Conference Committee* [1948], p. 14).

Thus, although there may be differences in application, the basic Seventh-day Adventist doctrine is the same around the globe: The church member is a loyal citizen, rendering to his or her government "the things that are Caesar's," and he or she is equally a loyal follower of Christ, rendering to his or her Maker "the things that are God's." The church asks religious liberty for its members and for all others. It regards its function as that of calling people to their duty toward God and fellow humans and to their privileges as children of God—not as that of gaining preferred position or material advantage from the state. *See also* Religious Liberty; Sunday Laws.

CHURCH BOARD. *See* Church (local organization).

CHURCH BUILDINGS. Throughout their history Seventh-day Adventists have erected various types of church buildings. The first church in which a group of Adventists became Sabbathkeepers in 1844 was one erected in 1842 or 1843 by the Christian Brethren of Washington, New Hampshire. (A group of 15 organized the SDA church there in 1862, but it was many years before Seventh-day Adventists had full ownership of the building.)

This church is a simple rectangular frame building 30' x 40' (9 m. x 12 m.), with clapboard exterior and a plain gable roof. There are two separate entrance doors at the front, leading into a small vestibule, from which two more doors open into the church auditorium, and a narrow stairway leads up to a small balcony. The interior walls are plastered, and there is a series of plain glass windows on two sides, one of which overlooks the church cemetery about 75 feet (25 meters) away. The church seats about 120.

This simple style of architecture is typical of many early SDA church buildings. Even in Battle Creek, Michigan, where SDAs had the largest numbers, the first three church buildings, erected 1855, 1857, and 1866, and the first Review and Herald building were constructed in the same simple architectural style as the Washington, New Hampshire, church.

The large central church in Battle Creek, called the Dime Tabernacle, built 1878-1879, was finished outside with a brick veneer over frame construction. There was a tall spire, or belfry, a balcony, and a basement. Movable partitions in the main auditorium permitted the closing off of certain sections for committee rooms when the building was used for General Conference sessions. There were four entrances, one at each corner. The building, 130' x 105' (40 m. x 32 m.) and seating 3,200 people, burned in 1922, and has been replaced by a substantial light-brick, square-looking building of modest but dignified design.

Seventh-day Adventists never developed a distinctive style of architecture. In fact, variety in style and design is the vogue in churches, educational buildings, sanitariums, publishing houses, and conference buildings. However, the newer buildings are much more functional than their earlier prototypes. The larger churches are designed to care not only for the spiritual but also for the social and educational needs of its members. Such buildings are equipped with modern conveniences such as baptistries, with heated water; air-conditioning; acoustical systems so all can hear the speaker; glassed-in noise-proof rooms in which mothers with small children may see and hear the services; separate rooms for Sabbath school classes; offices for the pastor and treasurer; perhaps libraries and auxiliary rooms with kitchens for cooking classes or social occasions; and in some cases rooms for elementary schools and Community Services rooms for the missionary activities of the church.

The building may be of stone, of a simplified Neo-Gothic design, with open vaulted ceiling, buttresses, and colored rose window. The Alexandria, Virginia, church is an example of brick Colonial, while the church in Grasonville, Maryland, is of ultramodern design, with a tall, pointed roof descending almost to the ground on the sides. Brick and cement block, built around a steel frame, are commonly used in the newer buildings. The Covina, California, church, a modern structure, is built with its church school and other accommodations around an open court.

In various countries institutional architecture is determined largely by the means available, the climate, and the building-construction methods of each country, ranging from the simplest forms of thatch and bamboo, through sunbaked brick, frame construction, and stucco; and in Europe brick or stone from traditional to very modern pattern, the cross forming a part of the design. The beliefs of the church are reflected in certain features of its buildings, such as the absence of altars and the presence of baptistries for immersion.

CHURCH CALENDAR. Special days designated annually by the General Conference to be observed by the churches for the study or promotion of the work of the various departments of the church, and for the receiving of offerings for specified purposes. (Seventh-day Adventists do not follow the church year, or Christian year, used by the liturgical churches and increasingly by other denominations.)

In the preparation of the calendar, ordinarily the General Conference departments make their recommendations to the Annual Council, and if there are any special problems involved, a committee of the General Conference studies the recommendations before they are presented to the council. After being passed by the council, the list is published from time to time in the various church papers and annually in the *Yearbook.*

The plan goes back at least to Nov. 14, 1918, when the General Conference Committee, on the recommendation of the treasurer and the departmental secretaries of the General Conference, voted 11 special offerings to be received in the ensuing year, for Intensive Training, European Relief, Rural Schools, Religious Liberty, Colored Work, Midsummer and Annual Offerings (for missions), and four Thirteenth Sabbath Offerings. Five special days were set apart for the Missionary Volunteer Department, Medical Department, Sabbath School Rally, and the Education Department (two). Much earlier than that the fourth (now the first) Sabbath of each month was designated for the promotion of local missionary work, and the second Sabbath for the promotion of worldwide missions.

By 1923 there were 23 special days, weeks, and offerings designated in the calendar, and on Apr. 25, 1935, it was noted by the General Conference that the calendar was becoming overcrowded, and the plan was restudied. However, the calendar for 1965 listed 39 special days, weeks, and offerings, in addition to the four Thirteenth Sabbath Offerings taken in the Sabbath school.

By 1994 this had increased considerably. Following is the church calendar published for 1994:

Jan. 1	Outreach/Church Budget
Jan 8*	Inner City/World Budget
Jan. 8-15*	Religious Liberty Week
Jan. 15*	Religious Liberty
Jan. 22	Local Conference Advance
Jan. 29	Church Budget
Feb. 5	Outreach/Church Budget
Feb. 12*	Adventist TV Ministries/ World Budget
Feb. 19	Church Budget
Feb. 19-26*	Christian Home and Marriage Week
Feb. 26*	Local Conference Advance
Feb. 26*	Temperance Sabbath (*Listen*, *Winner*)
Mar. 5	Outreach/Church Budget
Mar. 12*	Adventist World Radio/ World Budget
Mar. 12-19*	Adventist Youth/Week of Prayer
Mar. 19	Church Budget
Mar. 26	Local Conference Advance
Mar. 26	Health Ministries Sabbath
Apr. 2	Outreach/Church Budget
Apr. 2*	Missionary Magazines (*Signs*, *Message*, *El Centinela*, *La Sentinelle*)
Apr. 9*	Andrews University/World Budget
Apr. 9	Stewardship Sabbath
Apr. 16	Church Budget
Apr. 16*	Literature Evangelism Sabbath
Apr. 23	Local Conference Advance
Apr. 23*	Education Sabbath
Apr. 30	Church Budget
May 7	Outreach/Church Budget
May 7	Community Services Sabbath
May 14*	Disaster and Famine Relief/ World Budget
May 14	Community Relations Sabbath
May 21	Church Budget
May 28	Local Conference Advance
May 28	Youth Sabbath
June 4	Outreach/Church Budget
June 11*	Adventist Service Members Support/World Budget
June 18	Church Budget
June 25	Local Conference Advance
July 2	Outreach/Church Budget
July 9*	Christian Record Services/ World Budget
July 16	Church Budget
July 23	Local Conference Advance
July 30	Education Sabbath
Aug. 6	Outreach/Church Budget
Aug. 13*	Oakwood College/World Budget
Aug. 20	Church Budget
Aug. 27	Local Conference Advance
Sept. 3	Outreach/Church Budget
Sept. 10*	Missions Extensions/ World Budget
Sept. 10-17	Nurture Periodicals (*Adventist Review*, *Insight*, *Guide*, *Primary Treasure*, *Little Friend*)
Sept. 17	Church Budget
Sept. 17-24*	Family Togetherness Week
Sept. 24	Local Conference Advance
Oct. 1	Outreach/Church Budget
Oct. 1-8*	Health Education Week (*Vibrant Life*)
Oct. 8*	Voice of Prophecy/World Budget
Oct. 15	Church Budget

Oct. 15*	Spirit of Prophecy Sabbath
Oct. 22	Local Conference Advance
Oct. 29	Church Budget
Oct. 29*	Pathfinder Sabbath
Nov. 5	Outreach/Church Budget
Nov. 5*	Ingathering Campaign Begins
Nov. 5-12*	Week of Prayer
Nov. 12*	Annual Sacrifice/World Budget
Nov. 19	World Budget
Nov. 19	Stewardship Sabbath
Nov. 19	SDA Human Relations Sabbath
Nov. 26	Local Conference Advance
Nov. 26*	Bible Sabbath
Dec. 3	Outreach/Church Budget
Dec. 3*	Ingathering Sabbath
Dec. 10*	Health and Temperance Sabbath/World Budget
Dec. 17	Church Budget
Dec. 24	Local Conference Advance
Dec. 31	Church Budget
Dec. 31	Ingathering Campaign ends

THIRTEENTH SABBATH OFFERINGS—1994

Mar. 26	South American Division
June 25	Eastern Africa Division
Sept. 24	Trans-European Division
Dec. 17	Euro-Africa Division

* Special materials provided

CHURCH CLERK. A local church officer who is the secretary of all the business meetings of the church, including its board meetings, and keeps up to date the church record book containing a record of these meetings and the membership list. The clerk adds or drops names from the membership list, but only by vote of the church (except when a member dies, then the clerk records the date of death without church action). The clerk also carries on the correspondence in connection with transfer of members to or from other churches.

In addition, the clerk keeps a record of special services, fills out the credentials for delegates to the conference session, and furnishes certain reports requested by the conference, among these, reports of membership from the clerk's records.

CHURCH COMMUNICATION SECRETARY. A local church's representative in its relations with the public through the use of the press and other news-distributing agencies.

If several churches in a city arrange for a central publicity committee, each communication secretary may be a member, and works in harmony with any general plan that will best facilitate the handling of news for the several churches.

CHURCH COMPASS *(Kyohoi Chinam)* (1916- ; monthly; published by Korean Publishing House in Seoul, Korea). The official organ of the Korean Seventh-day Adventist Church. This 44-page Korean language magazine contains Korean Seventh-day Adventist Church religious news and inspiration, "Week of Prayer" readings for church members, and promotional material for all departments of the organization.

The *Church Compass* was launched on Jan. 20, 1916. In December 1941, during the period of Japanese occupation, its name was changed to *Church Guide.* In August of 1941 the publication was discontinued. In December 1945, soon after Japanese occupation ceased, publication began again.

The present format was adopted in July 1969. It originally contained the general articles and the Morning Watch devotional articles. It was later separated into general articles from the Morning Watch devotional book according to the needs of the Korean church. The *Church Compass* consecutive numbers are No. 1 through No. 834 through December 1993.

Editors: Mimi Scharffenberg, 1916-1918; E. J. Urgchart, 1918-1922; Theodora Wangerin, 1923-1925; E. J. Urgchart, 1926-1930; Theodora Wangeren, 1931-1939; Kim Chang Jip, 1940; Yoo Yung Soon, 1941; Koh Hee Kyung, 1942-1944; Chung Tong Shim, 1945-1946; Theodora Wangerin, 1947-1951; S. Y. Oh, 1958-1965; Kim Tong Ki, 1966-1967; Lee Yung Hee, 1968-1971; Kim Tong Ki, 1971-1980; Chun Se Won, 1980- .

CHURCH DEVELOPMENT SERVICE. A service developed to provide fund-raising counseling and direction to local Seventh-day Adventist churches throughout North America. The first such service was established in 1957 by the Southwestern Union Conference. William J. Hubert, with background experience in professional fund-raising, served as the director. The success of this program in aiding church and school construction led the General Conference Committee to establish such a service for the churches throughout the North American Division.

Hubert was called to the General Conference to direct the training of personnel in the various local and union conferences for the establishment of this plan.

During the 1959 spring meeting the General Conference Committee adopted the title "Seventh-day Adventist Church Development Service" for this fund-raising service. An intensive training program was begun, and by the 1962 General Conference session 21 Church Development Service directors in union and local conferences of the North American Division had conducted every-member canvasses that raised more than $15 million for local conference and academy building projects.

In such a "directed" canvass the local church was provided with a director from the union or local conference office for a period of two to five weeks, depending on the size of the church. He was a denominational worker trained in counseling churches in approved methods to raise funds for capital improvement. The director, who was responsible for the supervision and management of the canvass, trained the lay leaders and the pastor in spiritual methods of fund-raising through the preparation, organization, education, and solicitation phases of an every-member-canvass program. To assure the successful collection of pledged funds, the director also maintained a close contact with the church through a follow-up service.

The Church Development Service not only helped the churches raise funds for building projects but also, through emphasis on education in stewardship, promoted increased interest in the general church program. Surveys revealed that such increased giving most often brought an increase in other offerings of the church.

The Church Development Service no longer exists, but the work is carried on by stewardship directors.

CHURCH DIRECTORIES. *See* Directories.

CHURCH DISCIPLINE. The action of the church in dealing with erring members. After every effort to reclaim an erring member has failed, and discipline becomes necessary to preserve the reputation of the church, two procedures are open: a vote of censure or a vote to disfellowship (to drop from membership). A vote of censure is taken when the offense is considered serious enough to warrant the disapproval of the church but not grievous enough to warrant loss of membership. It is intended to impress the member with the need of amending his or her life and to grant a period of time to do so. This action may be taken at any duly called meeting of the church, and the offending member may be present. A member is placed under censure for a stated period of time, during which he or she cannot hold any church office, vote on church affairs, or have public part in any of the exercises of the church, such as teaching a Sabbath school class. He or she may not transfer membership to another church while under censure. If at the end of the period of censure the member gives evidence of satisfactory conduct, he or she will be considered in good standing; if not, his or her case must be reconsidered.

Among the causes for disfellowshipping are denial of faith in the fundamentals of the gospel and in the cardinal doctrines of the church; fraud or willful misrepresentation in business; disorderly conduct that brings reproach on the church; persistent refusal to recognize properly constituted church authority; the use, manufacture, or sale of alcoholic beverages; the use of tobacco or addiction to narcotic drugs; open violation of the law of God, such as worship of idols, murder, adultery, fornication, stealing, profanity, Sabbathbreaking, willful falsehood, and remarriage of divorced persons except the innocent party in a divorce for adultery.

No minister, church, or conference has the right to set up tests of fellowship other than those agreed upon by the entire church. Action to disfellowship may be taken only at a duly called meeting of the church and by majority vote. The church board cannot disfellowship, and the member has the right to be heard in his or her own defense. Members cannot be dropped for nonattendance at church services nor for failure to render financial support to the church.

The members are urged to manifest friendship and love toward a disfellowshipped member and endeavor to win that individual back. He or she may be reinstated upon confession, evidence of repentance and amendment of life, and after rebaptism.

The one who has been disfellowshipped has a right of appeal to the committee of the conference in which the church is located. If the conference feels that injustice has been done, it may recommend reinstatement. If the church declines to receive him or her, the conference may then recommend him or her to membership in some other church.

The disfellowshipping of members seems

to have been practiced from the time churches were organized. In the *Review and Herald* of Nov. 25, 1851, James White reported that the brethren in Washington, New Hampshire, had withdrawn fellowship from one in doctrinal error (2:52). J. H. Waggoner in 1853 made an official statement in the *Review and Herald* concerning an action taken by the church at Alden, Illinois, withdrawing fellowship from a certain W. A. Raymond for an unchristian course taken, and for accusing the church of injustice. This was written in semilegal terms, and was ordered by, and in behalf of, the Alden church (4:184, Dec. 13, 1853).

Later W. H. Littlejohn stated that there is no such thing as "dropping names" in the Seventh-day Adventist Church. There are three methods only by which a name is removed from the church list: by death, by letter of transfer, or by "withdrawing the hand of fellowship" *(ibid.* 62:427, July 7, 1885).

CHURCH ELDER. The highest officer in the local church, outranked only by the minister. He or she is elected by the church for a term of one year, and may be reelected for additional terms. After the initial election, the elder must be ordained to the office by an ordained minister *(see* Ordination), but does not have to be reordained when accepting the same office in another church. The elder also may act as a deacon without ordination to that office.

In the absence of the pastor, the elder is responsible for the church services, either conducting them or arranging for them. The elder also may conduct the Communion service. While the pastor usually is chair of the church board, the local elder may act in that capacity if it seems advisable (see *Church Manual* [1990], pp. 57-61, 88).

The work of a local elder is confined to the church electing him or her, although the elder may serve more than one church if other churches elect him or her. By special arrangement with the president of the conference or mission the elder may conduct a baptismal service when an ordained minister is not available. The elder is not authorized to conduct the marriage ceremony.

It is the church elder's duty to foster all the activities of the church, to cooperate with the conference, to see that the various officers carry out their responsibilities, and that delegates to conference sessions are elected. The elder is not a delegate ex officio to such sessions.

The earliest Seventh-day Adventist churches did not elect elders; the deacon appears to have been the only church officer. But as early as 1854 Joseph Bates in an article "Church Order" spoke of two kinds of elders in the New Testament church: those who rule and those who preach the Word *(Review and Herald* 6:22, 23, Aug. 29, 1854). The next year J. B. Frisbie, a pioneer minister in Michigan, wrote, in a two-part article under the same title, of (1) the elders who had the spiritual oversight of all the churches—the "traveling elders"—and (2) the "local elders" who had the pastoral care of one church. These he distinguished from the deacons, who were to look after the temporal affairs of the church *(ibid.* 6:155, Jan. 9, 1855). In the January 23 issue (p. 164), in answer to a question by John Byington as to whether elders and deacons were to be appointed in every church, James White urged that the New Testament church order be adopted and that in "every church where the numbers, and talents, and graces of individuals are sufficient," the officers of the church should be appointed. Further articles on "Church Order" by Frisbie appeared in June and July 1856. In the Oct. 15, 1861, issue of the *Review and Herald,* an address on church organization by J. N. Loughborough, Moses Hull, and M. E. Cornell appears. They state in the introduction (28:156): "The subject of organization having been referred to us by the late general conference, with the request that we hold a Bible class thereon, and address you through the *Review,* we have accordingly had the subject under investigation, and submit the following thoughts for your consideration.

"In the address the election and ordination of elders as well as deacons in the churches are clearly prescribed" *(ibid.,* pp. 156, 157).

A series of articles in 1874 by G. I. Butler, entitled "Thoughts on Church Government," further defined the office and work of church elders. While the office of elder was recognized as the principal one in the church, his powers were regarded as merely advisory, since the body of the church was the deciding authority *(ibid.* 44:69, Aug. 18, 1874). However, "the work of correcting, admonishing, and overseeing in the church" belonged to the elder far more than to anyone else *(ibid.* 44:92, Sept. 8, 1874), and the minister and the members were to support the elder against gossip and against idle complaints *(ibid.* 44:101, Sept. 15, 1874).

In a later article by H. A. St. John, the chief duties of church elders were again delineated (*ibid.* 46:165, Nov. 25, 1875). They should visit the members and seek the wandering, baptize, and conduct the ordinances in the absence of the evangelist, and call business meetings before the conference session, at the close of the year, and at other times when necessary. If the church had no deacon, the elder was to act in his place, look after the Sabbath school, and attend all meetings if possible. Elders should keep records of their work and the meetings.

By 1885 the work of the church elder was defined very much as it is at the present time. For example, in the report of the General Conference proceedings, beginning Nov. 18, 1885, at Battle Creek (*SDA Yearbook*, 1886, p. 47), the rule was laid down that a local elder if reelected, or if properly elected as elder of another church, need not be reordained. Apparently this rule was not immediately followed universally, because as late as 1896 the following question and answer appeared in the *Review and Herald:* "If a local elder moves to another church and is there chosen elder, does he need to be reordained?" "Yes; we think he should be ordained again, because his ordinations are local" (*Review and Herald* 73:121, Feb. 25, 1896).

CHURCH GOVERNMENT (or church polity). A system for directing the affairs of the church in an orderly manner. Only a primitive organization existed in the early Christian church, for the obvious reason that organization came only when the growth of the church demanded it. In the New Testament church the bond of union was the common faith of the believers and the personal guidance of apostles themselves. The Jews, who accepted Christ at first, worshiped at the Temple (Acts 2:46; 3:1) and separated from the body of Judaism only when forced to. But it was not long before an elementary church government was established.

The setting apart of Matthias to take the place of Judas might be considered the first organized act of the Christian church body (Acts 1:23-26). Another major act was the appointment of seven deacons for the ministry of tables as distinct from the ministry of the Word (Acts 6:1-8). The council at Jerusalem (Acts 15:6-29), sometimes referred to as the first General Conference, represented a significant concerted effort by the church.

Paul's instruction with regard to the office of elders (1 Tim. 3:1-7) and to that of deacons (vs. 8-13) revealed a developing organization. Two Greek words described the leaders selected to supervise the New Testament churches: *presbuteros,* "elder," referring to a position of dignity, and *episkopos,* "overseer," referring to the responsibility to superintend.

As the church expanded rapidly in the postapostolic period, and as churches united in given areas, the "overseers," or bishops, assumed wider powers, and in time archbishops appeared, exercising still wider authority. The papal system of church government was the outcome. The bishop of Rome held that his peculiar authority rested on divine origin and sanction. This system has also been called *monarchical* or *hierarchical.* In it the supreme power is vested in the pope, who is the head of the various orders of priesthood.

Other systems of church government that developed were:

1. The congregational system, sometimes called "independent." It has the highest powers residing in the local congregation. No other authority can legislate for it or direct its life.

2. The presbyterian system. This provides for government by elected representatives, by teaching elders (ministers), and by ruling elders (laymen), functioning in such representative bodies as presbyteries, synods, and a general assembly as the supreme governing body.

3. The episcopal system. This centers in the bishops, who are successors of the apostles and have governing power in the church.

The polity of the Seventh-day Adventist Church contains both presbyterian and congregational elements. Its authority springs from the members, whose representatives govern through a five-stage organization—local church, conference, union, division, and General Conference. Beyond the local church level there is limited lay representation in the governing bodies, but the local church, in which every member has a vote, has distinct prerogatives of its own. The polity may be described as a *representative system. See* Organization.

CHURCH LEADER. A term used to describe a person elected in a new or small church in which no one possesses the experience or qualifications is necessary for an elder, or no one with such experience or qualifications is willing to assume the position of elder. The leader is to be "responsible for the services of the church, including the business meetings. The leader must either conduct these or arrange for someone else to do so. A church leader may not preside at any of the church ordinances, administer baptism, conduct the

Lord's Supper, perform the marriage ceremony, or preside at business meetings when members are disciplined. A request should be made to the conference president for an ordained minister to preside at such meetings" *(Church Manual* [1990], p. 61).

CHURCH LETTER. *See* Church (local organization).

CHURCH MANUAL. An official handbook, issued by the General Conference, dealing with matters of local church organization, services, and operation, church officers, church membership, standards of conduct, and relationships of the church to conference officers, and workers. The *Church Manual* is to be distinguished from the *Manual for Ministers.*

The first serious attempt at a church manual was made in 1882, when a committee consisting of W. H. Littlejohn, J. O. Corliss, and H. A. St. John was appointed by the General Conference to prepare a church manual, to be printed first serially for discussion and criticism (13 articles came out in the *Review and Herald* from June 5 to Aug. 28, 1883). It covered such matters as the organizing of churches; the duties of church officers; the admission, transferring, and dropping of members; church trials; and the conducting of quarterly business meetings and the ordinances. However, the next General Conference, in November 1883, decided against publishing a church manual because it was deemed to be undesirable to take any step that could be construed as leading to a creed or discipline other than the Bible, or toward formalism. G. I. Butler, president of the General Conference, explained the action taken, in an article in the *Review and Herald* (60:745, Nov. 27, 1883).

In subsequent years a number of books or pamphlets were published by different writers on the work of the church and the duties of church officers, the most important being J. N. Loughborough's *The Church, Its Organization, Order and Discipline* (1907), a personal undertaking, but long considered the standard manual on church order. It was not until 1932 that an official Seventh-day Adventist *Church Manual* appeared, issued by the General Conference.

Revisions in the *Manual* were made in 1934 and 1940 to keep the contents in step with the developments of the world work. An extensive revision was made in 1951. Concerning this, the preface to the 1951 edition states: "There are two reasons why a new revision of the manual is now being issued. One is that actions taken in the General Conference sessions of 1946 and of 1950 have made necessary some very significant changes in what was contained in previous editions of the manual. Another reason is that our work has grown so remarkably in various parts of the world, and is meeting problems peculiar to certain areas, that it was felt necessary to have a general church manual setting forth basic matters of denominational policy and practice, with certain details of local application left to the division committees to decide and to present to their workers in written form. The General Conference Committee, therefore, in its Autumn Council held at Denver, Colorado, October 18-27, 1948, authorized a complete revision of the *Church Manual,* and in doing so provided that each division of the General Conference might publish a supplement to it. The action was as follows:

" 'That this new *Church Manual* be the manual for the world field, and that the divisions take in hand the matter of making it available in the languages of their respective language areas.

" 'That each division, including the North American Division[,] of the world field prepare a "Supplement" to the new *Church Manual,* not in any way modifying it, but containing such additional matter as is applicable to the conditions and circumstances prevailing in the division; the manuscripts of these "Supplements" to be submitted to the General Conference Committee for endorsement before being printed *(Autumn Council Actions* [1948], p. 1187).'

"This revision has been prepared by a body of men appointed by the General Conference Committee. The members of this special committee have had access to correspondence from the field and also to the latest developments in our denominational policies. These materials, together with what has been previously published, have been classified, and appear in the present volume. The contents of this manual deal with general matters of policy pertaining to church government. Details of application, as they might vary in the different divisions of our work, have been left to the handling of the division committees through supplements in accordance with the General Conference action cited" (pp. 19, 20).

The 1946 General Conference session took action that all changes and revisions of the *Church Manual* must be authorized by the General Conference in session. The 1963 edition incorporated all revisions and additions through the 1962 General Conference session. The revisions voted by the 1970 General Conference session were incorporated in the 1972 edition of the *Church Manual.* At the 1975 General Conference session in Vienna, Austria, further and numerous revisions covering the entire *Church Manual* were approved. Many of these were purely verbal changes made in the interests of style and lucidity. Others, though important in clarifying and enlarging certain areas, cannot be said to have constituted a basic revision of the *Manual.* They are incorporated in the 1976 edition of the *Church Manual.*

The 1980 General Conference session took action to make an in-depth editorial revision of the 27 fundamental beliefs of the Seventh-day Adventist Church. Prior to the action at the session there was a wide participation and input from the *Church Manual* Committee, the Administrative Committee of the General Conference, an ad hoc committee, all the divisions of the world, the Annual Council of the General Conference, and an editing committee appointed by the session to make recommendations for the final decision of the GC session. Changes were mostly in the way the beliefs were expressed, not in their content.

Probably the most important action regarding the *Church Manual* at the 1985 General Conference session was related to the organization of the church. This defined four constituent levels in the organization of the Seventh-day Adventist Church—local church, local conference or local field/mission, union conference or union field/mission, and the General Conference. Divisions are not constituent levels, but are sections of the General Conference with administrative responsibility assigned for a particular geographical area of the world. Other small revisions or amendments affected funds of the local church and conference/missions, Sabbath schools, Home and School Association, Health and Temperance Department, and administration of the local church. On this last item, conference officers were given the right to attend business meetings of local churches, and conference presidents to attend local church board meetings.

The 1990 General Conference session incorporated a new section establishing the proper procedure to make amendments or revisions in the *Church Manual.* Suggested revisions should be submitted to the General Conference *Church Manual* Committee through constituent levels of the church. The level on which the amendment originates will give study and consideration to it and, if approved, will send it to the next constituent level for wider study and counsel. If the amendment is approved, the suggested revisions are submitted to the next level for further evaluation. The *Church Manual* Committee will consider all recommended amendments or revisions and, if approved, will prepare them for presentation to the Annual Council and to the General Conference in session, which is the only body with authority to make any changes in the *Church Manual.* Other amendments include a rewriting of the baptismal vow to update the language, a definition that local elders can be ordained only by an ordained minister with credentials "from the local conference," an exception allowing licensed or commissioned ministers ordained as local elders to perform marriage ceremonies in divisions in which their administrative committees have approved it, and a rewriting of the section on the Communion service to make its content more easily understood, in a more comprehensive way.

CHURCH MEMBERSHIP. *See* Church (local organization).

CHURCH MEMBERSHIP, NECESSITY OF. *See* Church, Nature of.

CHURCH MINISTRIES DEPARTMENT. Department created at the 1985 General Conference session in New Orleans, formed from a merger of four former departments and a service of the General Conference (namely, Lay Activities, Sabbath School, Stewardship and Development, Youth, and the Home and Family Service).

As explained at the 1985 General Conference session, the action to bring these former entities together into one department would apply "only to the General Conference and its divisions." Later it could "be implemented at the union and then the local conference levels." It was not intended to change the organization of departments at the local church level. (See *Adventist Review* 162:29, July 2, 1985, pp. 10, 11.)

Philosophy. The Department of Church Ministries shares the responsibility for developing a global evangelistic strategy in consultation and harmony with administration and other departments of the church. It challenges the world church with objectives, goals, and plans to take the gospel to all the world. All of its activities are intended to be coordinated into a master strategy for soul winning and for nurturing the church membership.

The philosophy undergirding the department includes the following elements: (1) it is a support ministry to the church; (2) its support is developed through modeling spiritual leadership and training, producing resource materials, and providing consultant services; (3) its assignment is to integrate and coordinate the necessary groupings of specialty functions comprehended within the department: children's ministries, family ministries, lay activities/personal ministries, stewardship and development ministries, Sabbath school ministries, and youth ministries; (4) its responsibility is to foster a wholistic ministry that involves worship, fellowship, nurture, stewardship, and outreach in order to provide a coordinated emphasis for the church.

The church ministries staff incorporates qualified personnel selected on the basis of their knowledge, skills, and abilities to care for the specialized functions, activities, and responsibilities encompassed by the work of the Department of Church Ministries. Their coordinated teamwork increases the potential for the best possible analysis, planning, material development, and implementation of plans to meet the needs of the target audience.

Early History: 1985-1990. Delmer Holbrook served as director from the inception of the department in 1985 until his retirement in June 1988. His expertise in the fields of management, leadership, and education equipped him with the skills necessary to work for unity of purpose and to provide a climate conducive to good interpersonal relationships. GC vice president Kenneth Mittleider served as the department's liaison with administration.

Early issues included the development of the departmental philosophy and working policies. Considerable debate surrounded the extent to which the new department was an integration of the former entities, a coordination of their functions, or some combination of the two. Were the departmental associates to be generalists in church ministries or specialists in the work of the former departments and service? Would there be a universal model for presenting the various functions of the department? If so, what would such a model look like?

Delmer Holbrook conducted leadership seminars in the various divisions for the new CM staffs. A world advisory held at the General Conference headquarters in January 1987 brought division church ministries directors together for team-building and consultation on the issues facing the new department. Considerable freedom was given to the world divisions to develop approaches suitable for their particular needs.

"Ministries" became the standard term to describe the functions of the former departments and service. In addition to family ministries, lay activities/personal ministries, Sabbath school ministries, stewardship ministries, and youth ministries, two new ministries emerged. Children's ministries received its impetus from the vision and prompting of Helen Craig, former Sabbath school associate director for children's Sabbath school, Vacation Bible School, and child evangelism. The emergence of music ministries was stimulated by the enormous talent and enthusiasm of singing evangelist and Sabbath school specialist Charles L. Brooks. Under his leadership the *Seventh-day Adventist Hymnal* was produced in 1985, and the songbook for primaries, *Sing for Joy*, was published in 1989. His untimely death in that same year brought a great loss to the department, including the fledgling music ministry.

Representatives from each of the former departments and service comprised focus groups, which were established for each of the ministries. These focus groups enabled an integrative working relationship and the development of a sense of unity among personnel of the various ministries.

AMiCUS, a joint venture of Church Ministries, Education, and Adventist Chaplaincy Ministries, was formed in 1987 as a worldwide outreach and support ministry for college and university students in non-Seventh-day Adventist institutions.

Delmer Holbrook, longtime educator in the church, elevated the religious education aspects of the department. Curriculum specialist Charles Betz and his wife, Harriet, served as consultants during 1987 to help the department develop curriculum frameworks for each of the ministries. Stopping short of an integrated curriculum for the department, this effort acknowledged that the General Conference model would have a strong educational base and would be a coordination of functions of the former departments and service.

Alternative approaches took shape in some of the world divisions. For example, the North American Division configured church ministries along an age-level, developmental model featuring adult ministries, youth ministries, and children's ministries, while the South Pacific Division offered an integrated thematic perspective with a four-part focus: worship, fellowship, nurture, and mission.

When Delmer Holbrook retired in 1988, George Knowles became the department director, serving until his retirement at the 1990 General Conference session. Knowles continued the building process, working through a number of committees to address the various structural aspects of the new department, encouraging the continuing development of a coordinated model and preparing for *Church Manual* changes to reflect the work of church ministries.

Serving the Church Ministries Department during the 1985-1990 quinquennium were the following: Malcolm Allen, youth; Maurice Bascom, personal ministries/general church ministries; Charles L. Brooks, Sabbath school/music (deceased 1989); Helen Craig, children's ministries (retired 1989); Gilbert Bertochini, Sabbath school; Don Crane, stewardship; Karen Flowers, family ministries; Ronald Flowers, family ministries; Erwin Gane, editor, *Adult Sabbath School Lessons* (appointed in 1986); Robert Grady, Sabbath school; Betty Holbrook, family ministries (retired in 1988); Delmer W. Holbrook, director (retired in 1988); George Knowles, lay activities/personal ministries (elected director in 1988); Israel Leito, youth (elected in 1986); Samuel Monnier, lay activities/personal ministries; Leo Van Dolson, department editorial director and editor, *Adult Sabbath School Lessons* (retired in 1987); Paul Smith, stewardship; Virginia Smith, children's ministries (elected in 1989); Michael Stevenson, youth (deceased 1993). James Joiner and Laurell Peterson were assistant directors.

After 1990. Israel Leito, formerly associate for senior youth, was elected director at the Indianapolis General Conference session of 1990 and served until Dec. 31, 1993, when he became president of the Inter-American Division. In addition to continuing in his responsibility as codirector of family ministries, Ronald Flowers was elected to serve as department director from Jan. 1, 1994, until the end of the quinquennium. Vice presidential adviser Matthew Bediako emphasized a close working relationship with General Conference administration.

With the provisional status of the Church Ministries Department lifted at the 1990 General Conference session, efforts were undertaken in earnest to prepare *Church Manual* documents and working policies for official action at the next General Conference session. In the face of a decrease in the number of specialists in the various aspects of church ministries throughout the world field and a downsizing of the General Conference Church Ministries Department itself, a higher profile was given to the six ministries dealing with children, youth, family, lay activities/personal ministries, Sabbath school, and stewardship. Smaller ministry committees replaced the larger focus groups, and associates in the department were given the title of director or in some cases codirector of their ministries. A world advisory held in February 1991 brought together division directors and associates with the headquarters team. The world staff shaped the agendas for their ministries for the quinquennium.

Closer ties and interfacing with other departments were also fostered. In cooperation with the Ministerial Association, a manual for local church elders was developed, and in 1993 the Year of the Pastor was promoted.

Major activities undertaken by the department included the Year of Youth Evangelism (1993), launched with the International Congress on Youth Evangelism, held in Prague, Czechoslovakia, in August 1992, which led to some 400,000 baptisms through youth efforts in 1993. The year 1994, named the Year of the Family, following the United Nations designation, led to a number of initiatives by family ministries. Research designed to provide demographic data as well as specifics about the functioning of SDA families was initiated in the world divisions. Regional consultations, such as the Pan-African Consultation on the Family in Kenya in 1992, in which 21 countries were represented, encouraged a proactive approach by the church in assisting families. The work of stewardship and development received new impetus at the Annual Council of 1993 with the mandate to establish stewardship commissions at the various organizational levels of the church.

Publications. A new publication, the *Church Ministries Worker,* was begun in 1985 under the acting editorship of Leo Van Dolson. Graham Bingham became editor in 1986, and the publication was discontinued in 1990. By 1994 in addition to a wide variety of training and resource manuals, regular publications by the various ministries included the Sabbath school/personal ministries quarterly *Action*, the family ministries annual *Planbook*, stewardship's monthly *Resource*, youth ministries quarterly publications *Accent* and *Journal of*

Adventist Youth Ministry, and AMiCUS's quarterly publication *Dialogue*. Sabbath school teacher and student editions of quarterlies and publications produced in cooperation with the Review and Herald and Pacific Press publishing associations included the *Adult Sabbath School Lessons* (standard, large print, and easy English editions), *Collegiate Quarterly*, *Cornerstone Connections*, *Junior Sabbath School Lessons*, *Earliteen Sabbath School Lessons*, *Primary Sabbath School Lessons*, *Kindergarten Sabbath School Lessons*, and *Mission* (adult, teen, and children's editions). The department also produced program helps for cradle roll, primary, and junior/earliteen Sabbath school leaders.

The General Conference Church Ministries Department staff during 1990-1995 included Malcolm Allen, youth; Lyndelle Chiomenti, editor, *Adult Easy English Sabbath School Lessons*, and associate editor, standard *Adult Sabbath School Lessons*; Don Crane, stewardship; Karen Flowers, family; Ronald Flowers, family (elected director in 1994); Erwin Gane, editor, *Adult Sabbath School Lessons*; Charlotte Ishkanian, editor, *Mission* (appointed in 1993); Murray Joiner, personal ministries (resigned in 1993); Janet Kangas, editor, *Mission* (resigned in 1993); Andrea Kristensen, editor, *Junior* and *Earliteen Sabbath School Lessons*; Israel Leito, director, 1990-1993; Calvin Smith, Sabbath school/personal ministries; Virginia Smith, children's ministries; Michael Stevenson, youth/music (deceased 1993); Gary Swanson, editor, *Collegiate Quarterly*, *Cornerstone Connections*; David Wong, youth (elected in 1993); James Zachrison, personal ministries/ Sabbath school (elected in 1994). Patricia Habada, curriculum specialist, and Laurell Peterson, Sabbath school production manager, were assistant directors.

CHURCH MINISTRIES WORKER (formerly *Sabbath School Worker;* 1885-1990; monthly; R&H). A journal designed for Sabbath school teachers and officers. It contained lesson helps for the teachers of the seven divisions, also articles on teaching methods, and on special topics such as Rally Day, Visitors' Day, branch Sabbath schools, Vacation Bible Schools, Sabbath school Investment, and child evangelism. From 1985 it contained material for all church ministries officers. It was replaced by *Action* in 1990.

In 1885 the *Sabbath School Worker* began as a 16-page quarterly printed in Battle Creek, Michigan (at 25 cents a year), providing no lesson helps, only articles on organization and teaching methods. In 1887 and 1888 in the interests of economy these articles were put into the *Youth's Instructor* as a supplement, but thereafter the *Worker* appeared again, printed this time in Oakland, California, by the Pacific Press. In 1890 it was made a 24-page monthly, including lesson helps and missions stories (the latter transferred in 1912 to a separate *Missions Quarterly*).

In 1901, when the International Sabbath School Association was reorganized as the Sabbath School Department of the General Conference, the *Worker* articles were combined with the *Advocate of Christian Education;* then from 1904 the *Sabbath School Worker* was resumed and published continuously by the Review and Herald.

At first brief lesson helps were given on only two levels; gradually they were expanded and subdivided. By 1923 lesson helps appeared for senior and youth divisions, and one section for the children's divisions in three subsections for junior and primary, kindergarten, and cradle roll. Later the helps for all these divisions were separated, and one added for earliteens.

The period from 1961 to 1970 was a time of great increase in size of the *Worker*. In 1961 a *Worker* of 56 pages was published; in 1964, 64 pages; and in 1970, 112 pages every month. About 80 of these pages were lesson helps. The year of the big change was 1971. The lesson helps had expanded to a point where they were too bulky and could serve better as separate loose-leaf entities for each division. During 1971 the journal reverted to material of a more general nature and the name was changed to *Worker, Journal of Sabbath School Action.*

After 1971 the *Worker* was a 16-page monthly and contained only promotional, inspirational, statistical, and instructional material. *The Program Helps* and *Teaching Aids* had become separate publications.

In 1985, when the Sabbath School Department became part of the new Church Ministries Department, the name was changed to *Church Ministries Worker* and it became a 32-page magazine. In 1990 it became *Action*.

Editors: Publishing committee, first named was W. C. White, 1885-1887; publishing committee, first named, C. H. Jones, 1889-1890; Mrs. C. H. Jones, 1890-1891; F. M. Wilcox, 1891-1893; M. H. Brown, 1893-1900; L. Flora Plummer, January-October 1904; G. B. Thompson, November 1904-August 1905;

L. Flora Plummer, August 1905-1935; J. A. Stevens, 1936-1950; L. L. Moffitt, 1950-1958; G. R. Nash, 1958-1970; Fernon Retzer, 1970-1975; H. F. Rampton, 1975-1985; Leo Van Dolson (acting), 1985-1986; Graham Bingham, 1986-1990.

CHURCH MINISTRY, INSTITUTE OF. *See* Institute of Church Ministry.

CHURCH, NATURE OF. "Church" is a translation of the Greek *ekklēsia,* literally, "a calling out." This was a common Greek word for any called or summoned assembly, and reflects the fact that people were called to public meetings by heralds. The Septuagint uses *ekklēsia* to translate the Hebrew *qahal,* which in the OT designates Hebrew assemblies or all Israel, as a community. In the NT *ekklēsia is* used to designate (a) Christians gathered for worship (1 Cor. 11:18; 14:3, 28); (b) local congregations consisting of all Christians living in one place (Matt. 18:17; Acts 5:11; 8:3; etc.); (c) the entire body of Christians, the church universal to which believers in all places belong (Matt. 16:18; 1 Cor. 10:32; 12:28; Heb. 12:23; etc.). The nature of the church is clarified by the words used in the NT to describe it. Among these are body, temple, household, family, assembly, and by extension, fellowship.

Jesus Christ is the head of the church; the church is His body (Eph. 1:22, 23; 5:23). Thus Christ is Lord of the church and preeminent over it (Col. 1:18). If the church is fully subject to its divine Head, He can sanctify and cleanse it so that it will be holy and without blemish (Eph. 5:23-27). As head of the church, the seat or source of direction and intelligence, Christ will guide it in all its plans and activities, coordinating all parts and supplying wisdom and vital force to every member of the body so that all can work together effectually (Eph. 4:15, 16; Col. 2:19).

Jesus Christ "builds" His church (Matt. 16:18) into a holy temple "fitly framed," exceedingly beautiful and symmetrical, with Christ Himself as the chief cornerstone and the apostles and prophets as the foundation (Eph. 2:21; cf. 1 Peter 2:6-8). The Christian church was founded when Jesus called the apostles. It grew as the Holy Spirit, through the apostles' preaching and the witness of members, carved out other living stones (1 Cor. 3:16, 17; 1 Peter 2:5), which were to become the "habitation of God through the Spirit" (Eph. 2:22), a "spiritual house" in which men and women who have accepted Jesus as their Lord and Saviour offer "spiritual sacrifices acceptable to God" (1 Peter 2:5).

Converted men and women—living stones—become members of the "household of God" (Eph. 2:19), and are no longer strangers or foreigners in a revolted world, but a part of the "whole family in heaven and earth" (Eph. 3:15). "Believers on the earth and the beings in heaven who have never fallen constitute one church" (6T 366). Others in this household include the angels, the Holy Spirit, Jesus, the Father, and, doubtless, unfallen beings from other worlds (Heb. 12:22-24).

All the members of Christ's church on earth constitute "the general assembly and church of the firstborn, which are written in heaven" (verse 23). Twice-born, faithful members of every local church are a part of this great universal church, "all that in every place call upon the name of Jesus Christ" (1 Cor. 1:2). They enjoy communion and fellowship with others who accept Christ as the head of the church (1 John 1:3).

Jesus Christ is founder of the church universal, in the inclusive sense of the whole family of God from Adam to the end of the world, and in the particular sense of the Christian church established during His incarnation. In rejecting Christ, literal Israelites, collectively as a nation, were cut off like dead branches from the true stock of Abraham. True Israel was then the faithful remnant that accepted the Messiah, and to this original stock Gentile Christians were grafted (Rom. 11:5, 17, 24, 26; cf. 9:6). Thus the tree now includes the spiritual, as well as literal, children of Abraham who believe in Jesus Christ (Gal. 3:16, 26-29).

Christ provided divine guidance for His church in the form of an inspired record of His own life and of His will as revealed through prophets and apostles (John 16:13; Heb. 1:1, 2; 1 John 1:1-3). He sent the Holy Spirit as His representative and as a helper for the church; He provides the church with a teaching ministry and other necessary spiritual gifts, manifested through various members of the church (Eph. 4:8-16; 1 Cor. 12:4-12, 28; Rom. 12:5-8); and He gave the church a commission to go into all the world proclaiming Christ, teaching all men to observe all that He commanded, making disciples and then baptizing into Christian fellowship those who would accept Him and obey His Word (Matt. 28:18-20). To the church He gave authority to ordain teachers (Acts 13:1-3), to admit members into the church, and to expel from it those who apostatized (John 20:22, 23; Matt. 16:19; 18:15-18).

It is apparent, therefore, that the church is a brotherhood of believers, a spiritual communion, a loving fellowship of those who accept Christ as Lord, who take up His cross and obey His Word, and who are thus accepted by God as His sons and daughters. God's universal church is more than an association or organization of people; it is a community of believers consisting of His elect of every land and age who have been united to Him by faith, forgiven by grace, and ennobled by the indwelling Spirit. This union with Christ's body is signified by baptism and is expressed visibly by participation in His ordinances, by meeting together for worship, and by service for His cause. Finite men and women cannot determine who is or is not numbered as part of the church universal, for the essence of the church is Jesus Christ existing in the minds, or hearts, of those who have accepted Him as their Saviour, who love Him and one another, and who obey His Word as they understand it. The essence of the church is a life union between Christ and His people, created by the mysterious working of the Holy Spirit.

From time to time, in order to convey to all people a particular message of warning or instruction, or to lead them to a more complete understanding of His will, God has raised up special movements. God's Spirit has manifested Himself through human instrumentalities, leading them to associate together to advance His purpose for humanity. Seventh-day Adventists believe that God raised up the Advent movement in the last days, immediately prior to the second coming of Christ, to this end. They believe their movement to be a fulfillment of prophecy (Rev. 14:6-12; 12:17). They also hold the basic evangelical truths, in common with conservative Christians generally, but believe that their special function in God's purpose is to draw the attention of the world to the imminent second coming of Christ and to God's holy law, both of which sublime truths are largely ignored by the world. Neglect of God's law has also obscured the seventh-day Sabbath of the fourth command of the Decalogue, the memorial of the creation of the world and of personal salvation through Christ. The accomplishment of this task demanded more than the devotion of a host of Christians scattered among many denominations. It called for a united, organized body dedicated to the common task and working together in unison to achieve the goal described in the prophecy. That prophecy specified how the people fulfilling it could be recognized, and what their task would be (Rev. 12:17; 14:6-12).

Seventh-day Adventists believe that the church is both visible and invisible—visible in a body of people God calls out and commissions to accomplish His purpose at a given period of history, and invisible in the multitude of sincere and devoted men and women of all churches, or no church, who worship Him in spirit and in truth to the extent of their knowledge of truth.

While they believe that the prophecies of Rev. 14:6-12 and 12:17 point specifically to their history and work, Seventh-day Adventists do not believe that they alone constitute the true children of God today. While they hold that the SDA movement is the visible organization through which God is proclaiming the last special message for the world at this time, they also heartily accept the words of Jesus, "Other sheep I have, which are not of this fold" (John 10:16).

They believe that God works in and through all organizations whose leaders are willing to accept divine guidance in their decisions, and to the extent that they do so. They believe, also, that the message they as SDAs are bearing to the world—and which, indeed, gave rise to the Seventh-day Adventist Church—was divinely ordained for this time, and that this sublime commission constitutes the Seventh-day Adventist Church, in a unique way, God's visible church on earth today. They believe that while the leaders and ministers of the church, like other dedicated Christians, are subject to human limitations and that they may at times err in judgment, God nevertheless guides in the decisions they make, and overrules when an error in judgment or action would be fraught with grave consequences for the church. Furthermore, they believe that the General Conference in session, with representatives of the church from around the world present, constitutes the agency through which God guides and directs His cause on earth today.

Finally, they believe it to be God's purpose to recover the remnant of His people, the multitude of earnest sincere believers in every church who are living up to all the light they have. All these are potential members of that final "remnant" described in Rev. 12:17. In the spirit of Christian humility SDAs consider it their solemn task and privilege to complete the work begun at the time of the Protestant

Reformation in the sixteenth century by calling attention to certain great truths of Scripture that Christendom as a whole has lost sight of, and, by giving to the world God's last great message recorded in Rev. 14:6-12, to reach all open-minded men and women with the announcement of Christ's soon coming to earth in power and glory, and to help them prepare to meet Him in peace.

CHURCH OF GOD (ADVENTIST). *See* Adventist Bodies; Marion Party.

CHURCH OF GOD (SEVENTH DAY). *See* Marion Party.

CHURCH OFFICERS. *See* Church Elder; Church (local organization); Deacon; Organization.

CHURCH OFFICERS' GAZETTE (1914-1951; monthly; R&H, 1914-1918, and SPA, 1948-1951; files, AU, AUC, LLU, UC, CoUC, R&H). A magazine not intended for general circulation, but subscribed to by local churches to "furnish a medium for communicating the plans, policies, and instruction of the North American Division Committee to the church officers" to help them in building up their work.

It included programs for MV Society meetings, sermon and program material for the monthly and weekly church missionary services, special material for MV Week in the spring of each year (beginning 1922), poetry, discussions regarding the MV Reading Courses, and information to help plan the services and activities of the local church and to promote missions offerings; also, beginning September 1942, a section containing material for the Home and School Association. It was superseded by three new specialized periodicals—*GO; MV Program Kit;* and *Adventist Home and School.*

Editors: Edith M. Graham and Matilda Erickson, 1914, 1916; C. L. Benson and Edith Graham, 1915; edited by the Home Missionary Department and the Missionary Volunteer Department, 1916-1919; T. E. Bowen, 1919-1942; Roger Altman, 1942-1945; J. I. Robison, 1945-June 1951.

CHURCH ORDINANCES. *See* Baptism; Foot Washing; Lord's Supper.

CHURCH RADIO (AND TV) SECRETARY. In North America the local church officer whose duty it is to lead the members in distributing announcements of Seventh-day Adventist radio and television programs and in securing enrollments to the Bible correspondence schools; to promote the annual radio and television offerings; and to work with the church communication secretary in arranging with local stations for radio or television programs.

CHURCH SCHOOL. In Seventh-day Adventist education, a day school conducted by a local church or by a group of churches (occasionally by a denominational institution) providing Christian training and general elementary education. The term *church school* is generally used synonymously with the term *elementary school,* although some churches conduct a nine- or 10-grade school, which is officially called an intermediate school, but in common usage a junior academy. *See* Schools, SDA.

CHURCH SCHOOL BOARD. The administrative body of an elementary or intermediate school operated by a church or group of churches. This body may be the church board or a separate school board elected by the church or a school committee of the church board appointed by the church board. Where two or more churches unite to operate a school, there is a union school board. *See* Schools, SDA.

CHURCH SCHOOLS—STATE AND FEDERAL AID. *See* Church and State.

CHURCH SERVICES. *See* Services, Church.

CHURCH TREASURER. The custodian of all church funds. These include the tithe; funds designated for local, institutional, mission, or conference purposes, all collections and offerings from the Sabbath school, the Adventist Youth Society, Community Services center, and other departments of the church. He or she issues receipts for all monies received in church envelopes; he or she remits to the conference each month the tithe and various offerings given for missions or general work, but holds in a bank account in the name of the church all funds contributed to the local church or to its departments and societies, and any income from rentals or other sources. Funds that he or she may be holding for the church school or for the Adventist Youth Society, the Community Services center, and other church organizations are disbursed by him or her on the order of the school board or of the executive committee of the group concerned. Expenditures for local missionary work may be authorized by the Personal Ministries Council, if there is one. Otherwise, funds are disbursed by order of the church board in a regular meeting.

The church treasurer's books are audited annually by the conference treasurer or by someone appointed by the conference committee. The books and records of the church treasurer may be inspected only by the conference auditor, the pastor, the church elder, or one authorized to do so by the church board.

CIENCIA DE LOS ORIGENES. *See* Geoscience Research Institute.

CIMINDI ACADEMY (Sekolah Lanjutan Advent). A day high school operated by the West Java Mission and Cimindi church. The school has been functioning since July 1983, having begun as a primary school and junior high. All class activities are conducted within the premises of the Indonesia Publishing House. Because of limited classroom space, classes are operated in the afternoon. There are 14 teachers in this school and two nonteaching staff members. Two of the teachers are not Seventh-day Adventists.

Principals: B. Bangun, 1983-1985, K. A. Siregar, 1986-1994; D. H. Siregar, 1994- .

CIREBON ACADEMY. An educational institution located in Cirebon, one of the major cities in western Java. The school is operated by the local church under the auspices of the West Java Mission. It has been in continuous operation since it first began operating as an elementary school in 1968. The junior high grades were added in 1970 and the senior high grades in 1973.

Principals: R. K. Siahaan, Efron Batubara, Y. U. Silalahi, Plagius Dompas.

CITIZENS, SEVENTH-DAY ADVENTISTS AS. *See* Church and State; Noncombatancy; Religious Liberty.

CITY MISSIONS. A term applied in Seventh-day Adventist history to establishments of two different types.

a. Centers for evangelism and distribution of publications.

b. Welfare missions of one kind or another, ministering to the underprivileged.

Evangelistic Type. Beginning about 1883, Seventh-day Adventists established a number of so-called city missions for the purpose of promoting evangelism in the large cities. These were, as J. H. Waggoner said, quite in contrast with what were (and are) generally known as city missions, of the welfare type; rather they were prototypes, in a sense, of the modern evangelistic centers. S. N. Haskell, who promoted these evangelistic missions, described their function as a center for pastoral work, the distribution of publications, the giving of Bible readings, and also the maintaining of good relations with the press (*Review and Herald* 61:278, Apr. 29, 1884; cf. 61:410, June 24, 1884, and 61:807, 808, Dec. 23, 1884).

Pioneer city missions were opened in New York, Chicago, and San Francisco. The Chicago mission was sponsored by the International Tract and Missionary Society for a year (1884) on an experimental basis and financed by the Michigan and Wisconsin conferences, then it was turned over to the Illinois Conference. Missions of this kind came to be established also in key cities in other conferences. Generally located in a residential area, such a mission provided a reading room or small lecture room, also living quarters for the staff, who distributed tracts, took subscriptions for periodicals, sold books, and thus found interested persons to whom they gave Bible studies in the homes or at the mission, and whom they invited to public meetings in the mission. Converts were organized into Sabbath schools to form the nuclei of future churches. (This was the method of beginning SDA work in Washington, D.C., for example. *See* Potomac Conference.)

Almost from the beginning, these missions gave in-service training in city evangelism to workers, especially to those who gave Bible readings, and who soon came to be known as Bible workers—later called Bible instructors.

These missions were intended to be supported by the colporteur work of the staff and by donations of food supplies or money from church members elsewhere. However, they proved to be such a heavy financial burden to the conferences that few lasted past the 1880s. In Chicago, the training function was carried on in the Central Bible School.

Welfare Type. After the evangelistic-type of city missions was discontinued the term was used in the next decade for establishments to serve the needy. Beginning in 1893, an extensive slum mission work was conducted in Chicago under the sponsorship of the SDA (later, International) Medical Missionary and Benevolent Association, led by Dr. Kellogg of the Battle Creek Sanitarium, for which workers were trained in several medical missionary training schools operated by the Battle Creek Sanitarium *(see Yearbook of the International Medical Missionary and Benevolent Association,* 1896, pp. 116-133; General Conference *Bulletin,* 1901, p. 175). The Chicago medical missionary institutions included a workingmen's home, where a penny-a-meal cafeteria, inexpensive overnight lodging, and supplies of clothing were provided for poor and homeless men; a rest home for unwed and destitute mothers; an evangelistic mission among the poor; several dispensaries; a community health and recreation center for mothers and children in the stockyards district of the city; an employment agency for released prisoners; and a mail-order catalog store, the profits of which helped to cover the expenses of the charitable work and at the same time provide goods at lower prices to customers in isolated communities. The mission published a monthly promotion magazine, the *Life Boat.* Missions of a similar type were established by SDAs in many other places.

The General Conference *Bulletin* of the fourth quarter 1900 reports city missions in 24 cities in 17 states and three countries outside the United States (Australia, New Zealand, and Sweden). Emphasis came to be placed on well-organized public evangelism, which resulted in the formation of many city churches. However, so great was the investment of money and effort in these missions that Ellen White warned against overinvesting in such work at the expense of the main emphasis of the church on the proclamation of the SDA message. By 1903, when the Battle Creek medical organization began to drift from denominational control, interest in slum missions had waned.

Welfare work was continued by the Dorcas Welfare Societies, and in recent years has been sponsored by the Department of Church Ministries in Community Services centers conducted by local churches.

CIVIL DEFENSE. *See* Community Services.

CIVIL WAR, SEVENTH-DAY ADVENTISTS IN. *See* Noncombatancy.

CLAREMONT SANITARIUM. A 51-room medical institution operated from 1897 to 1905 near Claremont, a suburb of Cape Town, South Africa, under the direction of the International Medical Missionary and Benevolent Association of Battle Creek Michigan (the organization headed by J. H. Kellogg). No expense was spared to make it the best-equipped medical institution south of the equator, the total cost amounting to £50,000, of which the Wessels family contributed £30,000. The first medical director was R. S. Anthony, M.D. (a former pioneer colporteur), who was later assisted by Kate Lindsay, M.D., who came from Battle Creek Sanitarium. Within a week of opening every bed was filled and it became necessary to rent adjacent buildings.

Early in 1900, while the Anglo-Boer War was raging, the British imperial government requisitioned half of the sanitarium building for the use of army officers sent south from the battlefields to convalesce. As a result the standards of the institution were rapidly broken down, particularly after the army set up a bar in its section of the building.

The war having brought heavy financial losses, members of the Wessels family who had invested heavily in the sanitarium requested and obtained permission to operate the institution and retain the profit. However, with the postwar depression, patronage dropped. For a time the institution was operated as a hotel, but ultimately it went into bankruptcy. In 1905 the four-story building burned to the ground.

CLAREMONT UNION COLLEGE. *See* Helderberg College.

CLARK, GRACE AGNES (1898-1955). Missionary. She was born in Gloucester, England. In 1921 she was a member of a large party of missionaries who sailed from the British Isles for East Africa to reestablish Seventh-day Adventist mission stations disrupted during World War I. Among the first places she was assigned was Kamagambo Mission, in Kenya, where she was active in establishing and developing a strong girls' school, of which she was headmistress for 12 years. Then she moved 14 miles (22 kilometers) north to Nyanchwa Mission, where, for four years, she pioneered girls' work. In 1937 she was appointed secretary-treasurer of the Kenya Union Mission, and held this position until Uganda, Tanganyika, and Kenya were merged into a new union in 1942.

During her years of service at Kamagambo

and Nyanchwa, Miss Clark had become thoroughly familiar with the vernacular languages, particularly the Luo. In 1943, when the Advent Press at Gendia was expanding its facilities at a time when there was an ever-increasing demand for vernacular literature, she joined the staff as official translator, and held that position to the time of her death. Because she had become recognized throughout Kenya as an outstanding authority on the Luo language, she was invited by the British and Foreign Bible Society to participate in the work of translating the Bible into that tongue. For her contribution she was made a life member of that society.

CLAUSEN, NIELS (1851-1925). Minister, editor. Born in Denmark, he emigrated to the United States at the age of 19. He attended Battle Creek College (1874-1877), preached in Wisconsin, Iowa, and Nebraska, and was ordained in 1879. From 1883 to 1886 he edited a Seventh-day Adventist Danish-Norwegian paper in Battle Creek, and then went to Norway to edit its Norwegian paper and to assist in evangelistic work. He returned to the U.S. in 1906, engaged in self-supporting work for two years, and then preached in Oklahoma for the next 10 years. He retired in 1917.

CLEMENT, LORA E. (1890-1958). Editor. After graduating from Union College in 1908, she became secretary to M. E. Kern in Washington (1908-1911). She then joined the *Youth's Instructor* staff under Fannie Dickerson Chase, and became associate editor in 1918. She became editor in 1923 and held that position until 1952. Her Let's Talk It Over column was a notable feature of the paper for many years. From 1952 to 1958 she was librarian of the Review and Herald Publishing Association. Her death occurred as the result of a traffic accident.

CLERK. *See* Church Clerk.

CLIFFORD, FRANCIS GEORGE (1899-1972). Administrator in Trans-Africa and Australia. Francis Clifford was born in Bath, England, and was baptized in 1913. Educated at Stanborough Park College and later Spion Kop College in South Africa, he completed the ministerial course in 1922. Commencing his service as an evangelist, he continued in the work until 1933, when he was called to departmental leadership. He served efficiently in this area at both union and division levels. In 1941 he was called to administrative responsibility as president of the South African Union Conference. In 1946 he became secretary of the South African Division, which position he held until his appointment to the presidency of the Australasian Division in 1954. In 1962 he retired from his responsibilities and returned to South Africa.

CLÍNICA ADVENTISTA ANA STAHL. *See* Ana Stahl Adventist Clinic.

CLÍNICA ADVENTISTA DE BARQUISIMETO. *See* Barquisimeto Adventist Clinic.

CLÍNICA ADVENTISTA DE JULIACA. *See* Juliaca Adventist Clinic.

CLÍNICA ADVENTISTA DE LA PAZ. *See* La Paz Adventist Clinic.

CLÍNICA ADVENTISTA DE LOS ANGELES. *See* Los Angeles Adventist Clinic.

CLÍNICA ADVENTISTA DE MIRAFLORES. *See* Miraflores Adventist Clinic.

CLÍNICA ADVENTISTA DE MONTERREY. *See* Mexico.

CLÍNICA ADVENTISTA DE QUITO. *See* Quito Adventist Clinic.

CLÍNICA ADVENTISTA DE SÃO ROQUE. *See* São Roque Adventist Clinic.

CLÍNICA AMERICANA (Juliaca). *See* Juliaca Adventist Clinic.

CLÍNICA AMERICANA (Quito). *See* Quito Adventist Clinic.

CLÍNICA MÉDICA ADVENTISTA BELGRANO. *See* Belgrano Adventist Medical Clinic.

CLINICS AND DISPENSARIES. In general, medical facilities offering treatment or medicines to outpatients but not bed or house care. There is not always a clear line of distinction between the Seventh-day Adventist clinic and the dispensary; there is of necessity some overlapping. In general, it can be said that a clinic is a medical facility operated by an established hospital; it may be in close proximity to the hospital or remote from it. The work done at the clinic may or may not be charitable in nature; however, the word ordinarily connotes a reduction in the charges made. In contrast, dispensaries are operated in more remote areas, and the service, generally speaking, is either free or at a reduced rate. Either of these facilities may have physicians and nurses in attendance or they may be operated only by nurses and local helpers (called dressers in some areas).

First North American Clinic or Dispensary. The first attempt by SDAs to set up an institution for free medical service was made in Chicago in 1893 by J. H. Kellogg, M.D., noted as the director of the Battle Creek Sanitarium, Battle Creek, Michigan. He was assisted in this venture by Drs. W. B. Holden and David and Mary Paulson and opened the Chicago Medical Mission on Custom House Place. (Later the Paulsons moved to Hinsdale, Illinois, a suburb of Chicago, and eventually developed what is now the Hinsdale Sanitarium and Hospital.) From this beginning other dispensaries were developed in the Chicago area, which were known by such names as Life Boat Mission, the Maternity Free Dispensary, and Life Boat Rescue Service.

First Overseas or Foreign Clinic or Dispensary. What is said to have been the first clinic established outside the United States was opened in Guadalajara, Mexico, in 1894 by Dr. Lillis Wood and a nurse, Ida Crawford. The site for it had been selected in 1893 by D. T. Jones, representing the SDA Foreign Mission Board. The clinic prospered, and eventually a 50-bed sanitarium was established.

From these humble beginnings SDA clinics and dispensaries have spread until they belt the globe. At the close of 1993, statistics showed nearly 300 separate clinics and dispensaries, including some mobile clinics, plus medical launches and airplanes These facilities, which treat more than 1 million patients annually, are found in Africa, the Far East, Europe, North America, South America, Mexico, India, Myanmar, Pakistan, and the South Pacific Islands. The mode of transportation ranges from the airplane to the oxcart; the accommodations range from the most up-to-date buildings and equipment to the rude shelters of bush clinics on the plateaus of the Andes or of Africa, where in some cases the only protection from the sun is the shade of a spreading tree. With modest facilities, each of these clinics or dispensaries treats daily up to 100 or more patients suffering with a wide variety of diseases such as leprosy, sleeping sickness, malaria, and many others.

Medical Launch. A specialized type of traveling medical facility is used in areas devoid of roads but having navigable waterways. In such areas, where live people who desperately need medical help, floating dispensaries bring help to remote villages and isolated families (*see* Missionary Vessels).

List. Following is the list of clinics, dispensaries, health centers, and aid posts as listed in the 1994 *Yearbook.*

Africa-Indian Ocean Division:

Adventist Health Services-Nigeria, Nigeria
- Aiyetoro Ekiti Dispensary, Nigeria
- Arum Tumara Dispensary, Nigeria
- Igbobini Clinic, Nigeria
- Ilishan Remo (ASWA) Health Centre, Nigeria
- Maigamo Dispensary, Nigeria
- Ramin Kura Health Centre, Nigeria
- Ugbo Clinic, Nigeria

Antananarivo Adventist Dental Clinic, Madagascar
Asamang Adventist Health Centre, Ghana
ASSABU (Association des Services de Sante Adventistes au Burundi), Burundi
- Buganda Clinic, Burundi
- Ndora Clinic, Burundi
- Nyanza-lac Health Center, Burundi
- Nyarunasi Health Center, Burundi
- Rutsindu Health Center, Burundi

ASSAR (Association des Services de Sante Adventistes au Rwanda), Rwanda
- Gitwe Dispensary, Rwanda
- Karora Dispensary, Rwanda
- Kaslala/Lubero Health Center, Zaïre
- Kigali Dental Clinic (Cabinet Dentaire Adventista de Kigali), Rwanda
- Kinunu Dispensary, Rwanda
- Mudende Health Centre, Rwanda
- Nyarwungo Dispensary, Rwanda
- Rwankeri Health Centre, Rwanda

Bakwa-Tombe Dispensary, Zaïre
Bandalungwa Dispensary, Zaïre
Bazega Dispensary (Dispensaire de Bazega), Burkina Faso
Beni Dispensary, Zaïre
Bere Health Centre, Chad
Bigobo Dispensary, Zaïre
Buea Dispensary, Cameroon
Buramba Dispensary, Zaïre
Bushonga Dispensary, Zaïre
Dibuko Dispensary, Zaïre

Divuma Dispensary, Zaïre
Dogba Dispensary, Cameroon
Glei Adventist Clinic, Togo
Kabinda Dispensary, Zaïre
Kamina Dispensary, Zaïre
Kanyabayongo Dispensary, Zaïre
Kanyatsi Dispensary, Zaïre
Kasolo Dispensary, Zaïre
Katalaya Dispensary, Zaïre
Kayna Dispensary, Zaïre
Kikamba Dispensary, Zaïre
Kinshasa Dental Clinic, Zaïre
Kirundu Dispensary, Zaïre
Lubilu Dispensary, Zaïre
Lubumbashi Adventist Dental Clinic (Clinique Dentaire Adventiste), Zaïre
Lukanga Dispensary, Zaïre
Lulengele Dispensary, Zaïre
Manjakaray Dispensary, Madagascar
Mokambo Dispensary, Zaïre
Nanga-Eboko Dispensary, Cameroon
Ndjokopunda Dispensary, Zaïre
Nebasa Dispensary, Zaïre
Niaguis Dispensary (Dispensaire de Niaguis), Senegal
Nkwanza Dispensary, Zaïre
Rwese Dispensary, Zaïre
Sangmelima Dispensary, Cameroon
Seventh-day Adventist Clinic, Ghana
Shanje Dispensary, Zaïre
Yaoundé Dental Clinic, Cameroon

Eastern Africa Division:
Abonza Clinic, Ethiopia
Adventist Dental Practice, Zimbabwe
Arusha Adventist Seminary and College Dispensary, Tanzania
Arusha Medical and Dental Clinic, Tanzania
Better Living Centre, Zimbabwe
Borabu Dispensary, Kenya
Botswana Adventist Medical Services, Botswana
Bugema Dispensary, Uganda
Busegwe SDA Dispensary, Tanzania
Bussi SDA Dispensary, Uganda
Bwasi Dispensary, Tanzania
Chambo Dispensary, Malawi
Chebwai Dispensary, Kenya
Chepareria SDA Health Centre, Kenya
Chikwariro Clinic, Zimbabwe
Chileka Dispensary, Malawi
Chipembe SDA Rural Health Centre, Zambia
Dar es Salaam Magomeni SDA Dispensary, Tanzania
Dar es Salaam Temeke SDA Dispensary, Tanzania
Dodoma SDA Dispensary, Tanzania
Endindeni Dispensary, Malawi
Eronge Dispensary, Kenya
Ethiopian Adventist College Clinic, Ethiopia
Gatumbi SDA Dispensary, Kenya
Gesusu Dispensary, Kenya
Green Lake Mission Clinic, Ethiopia
Guliso Clinic, c/o Gimbie Hospital, Ethiopia
Habiya SDA Dispensary, Tanzania
Hanke Clinic, Zimbabwe
Heru Juu Dispensary, Tanzania
Iganga Dispensary, Uganda
Ikizu Dispensary, Tanzania
Itibo Dispensary, Kenya
Kabokyek SDA Dispensary, Kenya
Kagana SDA Dispensary, Tanzania
Kagorogoro Dispensary, Uganda
Kagwa SDA Dispensary, Kenya
Kagwathi SDA Dispensary, Kenya
Kaigat Dispensary, Kenya
Kakoro SDA Dispensary, Uganda
Kamagambo Dispensary, Kenya
Kamageta SDA Dispensary, Tanzania
Kameya Dispensary, Tanzania
Karura SDA Dispensary, Kenya
Kasamwa Dispensary, Tanzania
Kasulu SDA Dispensary, Tanzania
Katikamu Dispensary, Uganda
Kebeneti Dispensary, Kenya
Kemera SDA Dispensary, Kenya
Kenya SDA Rural Health Services, Kenya
Kenyenya Dispensary, Kenya
Kigalama Dispensary, Uganda
Kireka Dispensary, Uganda
Kisongo SDA Dispensary, Tanzania
Kitundu SDA Dispensary, Kenya
Lake View Dispensary, Malawi
Likoni Road SDA Clinic, Kenya
Liumba Hill Dispensary, Zambia
Lobatsi Town Clinic, Botswana
Lower Gweru Clinic, Zimbabwe
Lunjika Dispensary, Malawi
Luwazi Dispensary, Malawi
Luzira Dispensary, Uganda
Makale Clinic, Ethiopia
Makanya Dispensary, Tanzania
Malabvi Dispensary, Malawi
Manyatta SDA Dispensary, Kenya
Matandani Dispensary, Malawi
Matare SDA Dispensary, Kenya
Mbeya SDA Dispensary, Tanzania
Mitandi Dispensary, Uganda
Mkundi SDA Dispensary, Tanzania
Morogoro Dispensary, Tanzania
Moshi SDA Dispensary, Tanzania

Moshupa Dispensary, Botswana
Mpanda SDA Dispensary, Tanzania
Mtwara SDA Dispensary, Tanzania
Mulodza Dispensary, Malawi
Musoma Dispensary, Tanzania
Mwagala SDA Dispensary, Tanzania
Mwakaleli SDA Dispensary, Tanzania
Mwanza SDA Dispensary, Tanzania
Mwerahari SDA Clinic, Zimbabwe
Nabingola SDA Dispensary, Uganda
Najjanankumbi Dispensary, Uganda
Namasalima Dispensary, Malawi
Nkhorongo Dispensary, Malawi
Nsambe Dispensary, Malawi
Nthenje Dispensary, Malawi
Ntusu SDA Dispensary, Tanzania
Nyabihore SDA Dispensary, Tanzania
Nyabikaye SDA Dispensary, Kenya
Nyabola SDA Dispensary, Kenya
Nyagesenda SDA Dispensary, Kenya
Nyanchwa SDA Dispensary, Kenya
Nyasore SDA Dispensary, Kenya
Nyazura Clinic, Zimbabwe
Oyani SDA Dispensary, Kenya
Parane Dispensary, Tanzania
Pemba SDA Health Service, Tanzania
Ranen SDA Dispensary, Kenya
Rangwe SDA Dispensary, Kenya
Riakworo SDA Dispensary, Kenya
Riokindo SDA Dispensary, Kenya
Rusaba SDA Dispensary, Tanzania
Sangilo Dispensary, Malawi
Segero Dispensary, Kenya
Senzani Dispensary, Malawi
Seventh-day Adventist Health Services, Kenya
Seventh-day Adventist Health Services, Tanzania
Seventh-day Adventist Orthodontic Services, Zimbabwe
Sironoi SDA Dispensary, Kenya
Sitoti Dispensary, Zambia
Soche Dispensary, Malawi
Solusi Clinic, Zimbabwe
Suji SDA Dispensary, Tanzania
Sumbawanga Dispensary, Tanzania
Tabora SDA Dispensary, Tanzania
Tarime SDA Dispensary, Tanzania
Tutuo SDA Dispensary, Tanzania
Twing Memorial Dispensary, Tanzania
Urambo SDA Dispensary, Tanzania
Utimbaru Dispensary, Tanzania
Watamu SDA Dispensary, Kenya
Wire Dispensary, Kenya
Wollega Adventist Academy Clinic, Ethiopia
Zanzibar SDA Health Services, Tanzania

Euro-Africa Division:
Cuale Dispensary, Angola
Italian Health Center, Italy
Lwena-Moxico Dispensary, Angola
Portuguese Health Center, Portugal
Quicuco Dispensary, Angola

Euro-Asian Division:
Adventist Health Center, Russia

Far Eastern Division:
Adventist Dental Clinic, Bangladesh
Balai Kesejahteraan Ibu Anak, Indonesia
Balai Pengobatan Advent (Bandar Lampung), Indonesia
Balai Pengobatan Advent (Sulawesi Utara), Indonesia
Balai Pengobatan Advent Ambon, Indonesia
Balai Pengobatan Advent Banjarmasin, Indonesia
Balai Pengobatan Advent Curup, Indonesia
Balai Pengobatan Advent Kasih, Indonesia
Balai Pengobatan Advent Kiaracondong, Indonesia
Balai Pengobatan Advent Kupang, Indonesia
Balai Pengobatan Advent, Loa Janan, Indonesia
Balai Pengobatan Advent Lubuk Linggau, Indonesia
Balai Pengobatan Advent Pangkal Pinang, Indonesia
Balai Pengobatan Advent Ponain, Indonesia
Balai Pengobatan Advent Pontianak, Indonesia
Balai Pengobatan Advent Samarinda, Indonesia
Balai Pengobatan Advent Samosir, Indonesia
Balai Pengobatan Advent UNAI, Indonesia
Bangkok Adventist Hospital Midwifery Clinic, Thailand
Chiangmai Dental Clinic, Thailand
Chiengkhong Clinic, Thailand
Guam SDA Clinic, Guam
Kaohsiung Adventist Clinic, Taiwan
Klinik Gigi Advent (Dental Clinic) (Bandar Lampung), Indonesia
Klinik Gigi Advent (Dental Clinic) (North Sumatra), Indonesia
Kwangju Clinic, Korea
Maetang Adventist Clinic, Thailand
Medan Adventist Hospital Clinic, Indonesia
Mountain View College Medical Clinic, Philippines
Padang Sidempuan Adventist Clinic, Indonesia
Palau SDA Clinic, Western Caroline Islands

Philippine Union College Health Service, Manila
Pokfulam Medical Clinic, Hong Kong
Saipan Adventist Clinic, Saipan
Taejeon Clinic, Korea

Inter-American Division:
Andrews Memorial Hospital Dental Clinic, Jamaica
Barquisimeto Clinic, Venezuela
Bella Vista Polyclinic, Puerto Rico
Caracas Adventist Dispensary, Venezuela
Catherine Hall SDA Health Clinic, Jamaica
Cave Memorial Clinic and Nursing Home, Barbados
Clinica del Noroeste, Mexico
Clinica Higuera de los Vega, Mexico
Dispensario Adventista de Barquisimeto, Venezuela
Dispensario Medico Adventista, Mexico
Family Therapy Clinic, Puerto Rico
Medica y Dental Escandon, Mexico
St. Kitts Dental Clinic, West Indies
St. Vincent Primary Health Care and Dental Unit, West Indies
St. Vincent SDA Dental Clinic, West Indies
Trench Town SDA Clinic, Jamaica
Walters, H. S., Health Clinic, Jamaica

North American Division:
Monument Valley Dental Clinic, Utah, U.S.
West Shores Medical Clinic, Arkansas, U.S.

South American Division:
ADRA-Ecuador Dispensary, Ecuador
Adventist Center for Assistance Development (Rio de Janeiro), Brazil
Adventist Center for Assistance Development (Campinas), Brazil
Adventist Community Development Center, East Region, Brazil
Adventist Community Development Center (Brooklin Paulista, São Paulo), Brazil
Adventist Community Development Center (Jardim Arpoador, São Paulo), Brazil
Adventist Community Development Center (Liberdade, São Paulo), Brazil
Adventist Medical Clinic, Brazil
Adventist Medical Dispensary, Ecuador
Adventist Welfare Center (Goiania), Brazil
Adventist Welfare Center (São Paulo), Brazil
Adventist Welfare Center, Olimpia, Brazil
Adventist Welfare Center, South Region, Brazil
Campinas Adventist Clinic, Brazil
Campinas Adventist Community Development Center, Brazil
Ellery Adventist Vocational Center, Brazil
Good Samaritan Clinic, Brazil
Healthy Living Adventist Center, Uruguay
Iguape Adventist Welfare Center, Brazil
Iguape Medical Base, Brazil
Indaial Medical Base, Brazil
La Paz Adventist Clinic, Bolivia
Pan de Azucar Dispensary, Uruguay
Quixada Adventist Medical-Dental Clinic, Brazil
Santa Catarina Conference Medical Base, Brazil
São Carlos Adventist Welfare Center, Brazil
Sobral Adventist Clinic, Brazil
Vida Integral Adventist Medical Center, Chile
West São Paulo Medical Clinic, Brazil

South Pacific Division:
Ambunti Clinic, Papua New Guinea
Aore Clinic, Vanuatu
Balalava Clinic, Solomon Islands
Batuna Clinic, Solomon Islands
Bereme Clinic, Papua New Guinea
Bisidia Aid Post, Papua New Guinea
Borokuni Clinic, Solomon Islands
Brisbane Adventist Medical Centre, Australia
Dalikona Clinic, Solomon Islands
Dovelle Clinic, Solomon Islands
Fundue Clinic, East Vanuatu
Hoiya Clinic, Papua New Guinea
Honoa Clinic, Solomon Islands
Kasterita Clinic, Papua New Guinea
Kauma Clinic, Kiribati
Kukudu Clinic, Solomon Islands
Kwailabesi Clinic, Solomon Islands
Madakacho Clinic, Solomon Islands
Middlebush Clinic, Vanuatu
Moruma Clinic, Papua New Guinea
Mount Diamond Clinic, Papua New Guinea
Ngarigohu Clinic, Solomon Islands
Nighilani Clinic, Papua New Guinea
Nodana Clinic, Solomon Islands
Nuatabu Clinic, Solomon Islands
Ota Clinic, Solomon Islands
Pacific Adventist College Clinic, Papua New Guinea
Paglum Clinic, Papua New Guinea
Port Quimie Clinic, Vanuatu
Port Resolution Clinic, Vanuatu
Redcliff Clinic, Vanuatu
Sango Clinic, Solomon Islands
Sonoma Adventist College Clinic, Papua

New Guinea
Uhu Clinic, Solomon Islands

Southern Asia Division:
Seventh-day Adventist Clinic, Nepal
Seventh-day Adventist Clinic, India
Spicer Memorial College Dispensary, India

Trans-European Division:
Adventpura Health Center, Pakistan
Helsinki Hydrotherapy Institute, Finland
Rural Health Education Center, Pakistan
Seventh-day Adventist Dental Services, Pakistan

Attached Fields—Southern Africa Union Conference:
Bridge Clinic, Lesotho
Emmanuel Clinic, Lesotho
Maluti Health Centre, Lesotho
Mapheleng Health Centre, Lesotho
Swazi Eye Services, Swaziland

CLINIQUE LA LIGNIÈRE. *See* Lake Geneva Sanitarium.

CLINTON THEOLOGICAL SEMINARY. An educational institution that operated at Clinton, Missouri, from 1910 to 1925 for a German-speaking constituency. Among the thousands of Germans who migrated to the United States during the nineteenth century and settled in the Midwest, many became Seventh-day Adventists and conducted worship in their native tongue. In order to educate German-speaking ministers, Union College (established in 1891) operated a German Training Department. Then, in 1910, a separate institution was established for this purpose at Clinton, Missouri, known as Clinton German Seminary, a junior college, with affiliated grade school and academy. It occupied the buildings of old Baird College. An emphasis was placed on the German language, and public meetings were held in German. From the first, interest on the part of the German-American youth was less than enthusiastic. They desired to become Americans and learn to use the English language without a handicap. The first year, 105 students were enrolled in the college and 17 in the junior department. From 1915 the *Statistical Report* listed the school as a senior college. The enrollment slowly climbed until in its peak year (1917) there were 210 students in grades 9 and above, but only 30 of these were in the important seminary years beyond the secondary level, where they would be trained especially for the German work. College enrollment reached an all-time high of 43 in 1922.

The anti-German feeling built up during World War I (reflected in the change of the name of the school to Clinton Theological Seminary in 1917), militated against teaching in German and further prejudiced the young people against segregation in a German school. After the war the shift of sentiment toward educating the young people in English, together with financial losses owing to small enrollment, caused the school to cease operation in 1925, at which time it united with Broadview College and Theological Seminary *(see* Broadview Academy).

CLIPPERTON ISLAND. *See* French Polynesia.

CLOSE OF PROBATION. *See* Probation.

COBBAN, FRANKE FLOWERS (1886-1974). Nurse and administrator. A native of South Dakota, she entered denominational work in 1904 at Battle Creek Sanitarium. In succeeding years, she served at Washington Sanitarium and Hospital, the Harding Rural Rest Home in Ohio, and the General Conference Medical Department. She became instructor of nurses at the White Memorial Hospital and Glendale Sanitarium and Hospital in California. She also worked as director of nurses at the St. Helena Sanitarium in California. In 1971 she was chosen for the Hall of Fame in the Northern California Chapter of ASDAN (Association of SDA Nurses).

COBBAN, HAROLD HENRY (1882-1962). Assistant treasurer, missionary. He graduated from Mount Vernon Academy (1904), and was married to Grace Thornton (1905). For the next two years he worked in the treasurer's office of the General Conference, and then spent a term of service in Jamaica, Panama, and Trinidad. He again took up his work in the General Conference treasurer's office and remained there until his retirement in 1951. He helped establish treasury offices in South America and the Far East.

COGGESHALL, RICHARD H. (1845-1930). Publishing house worker. Shortly after his baptism in 1867 he joined the staff of the Review and Herald publishing house as a compositor. In 1885 he was sent to Basel,

Switzerland, to assist in the establishment of a publishing house there. Two years later he was sent to Oslo, Norway, on a similar mission. On returning to the United States, he continued with the Review and Herald until 1902.

COLCORD, GEORGE W. (1843-1902). Educator, administrator. He was the founder of Milton Academy (1887) in Oregon, a forerunner of Walla Walla College (1892), and also of Graysville Academy (1892), which developed into the Southern Training School, Southern Missionary College, and now Southern College of Seventh-day Adventists. He was twice president of the Illinois Conference, and for the last several years of his life taught church school in Colorado.

COLCORD, WILLARD ALLAN (1860-1935). Minister, editor. Educated at Battle Creek College, he preached in Iowa (1886-1888) and engaged in editorial work for the General Conference (1888-1893). For two years during this period he served as secretary of the General Conference. He then went to Australia for editorial and administrative work (1893-1902). On returning to the United States, he taught for two years at Union College (1902-1904), then became a secretary (under the chair) of the Religious Liberty Department (1904-1910) and was also on the book committee of the Review and Herald publishing house (1907-1914). At this time he lost faith in the doctrines and leadership of the Seventh-day Adventist Church and disassociated himself from the church. About 20 years later, in 1934, he published a retraction of his position in the *Review and Herald* and was received back into church fellowship.

COLE, JOHN MARTIN (1862-1937). Missionary, administrator. He was born in Ireland, but grew up in Nebraska, U.S.A. He entered the ministry in 1884, preaching in the North Pacific Conference (Oregon and Washington), was ordained in 1890, and in 1893 went on the second cruise of the *Pitcairn* for mission service in Fiji and Norfolk islands. On returning to the United States, he again preached in Oregon (1897-1909), and then served as president of the South Australian Conference (1909-1911). After terms as president of the New Zealand Conference (1911-1915), of the North New Zealand Conference (1915-1916), and of the New South Wales Conference (1916-1926), he returned to the United States and preached in Illinois and western Washington (1926-1928). His last appointment was to the Leeward Islands Conference, where he served as president (1928-1930).

COLEGIO ADVENTISTA ANTILLIANO. *See* Cuba Adventist Seminary.

COLÉGIO ADVENTISTA BRAZILEIRO. *See* Brazil College.

COLEGIO ADVENTISTA CHILENO. *See* Chile Adventist Education Center.

COLEGIO ADVENTISTA DE ANTOFAGASTA. *See* Antofagasta Adventist Academy.

COLEGIO ADVENTISTA DE ASUNCIÓN. *See* Asunción Adventist Academy.

COLEGIO ADVENTISTA DE BOLIVIA. *See* Bolivia Adventist Educational Complex.

COLÉGIO ADVENTISTA DE BUTIÁ. *See* Paraná Adventist Academy.

COLEGIO ADVENTISTA DE CHILE. *See* Chile Adventist Educational Center.

COLEGIO ADVENTISTA DE CONCEPCION. *See* Concepcion Adventist Academy (Chile).

COLEGIO ADVENTISTA DE CUBA. *See* Cuba Adventist Seminary.

COLEGIO ADVENTISTA DE LAS ANTILLAS. *See* Antillian Adventist University.

COLEGIO ADVENTISTA DE LAS CONDES. *See* Las Condes Adventist Academy.

COLEGIO ADVENTISTA DE MIRAFLORES. *See* Miraflores Adventist Academy.

COLEGIO ADVENTISTA DE MUNGULUNI. *See* Mozambique Adventist Seminary.

COLEGIO ADVENTISTA DE PUERTO RICO. *See* Metropolitan Adventist Academy (Puerto Rico).

COLEGIO ADVENTISTA DE QUITO. *See* Quito Adventist Academy.

COLEGIO ADVENTISTA DE RESISTENCIA. *See* Resistencia Adventist Academy.

COLEGIO ADVENTISTA DE SAGUNTO. *See* Sagunto Adventist College.

COLEGIO ADVENTISTA DE SALVADOR. *See* Salvador Adventist Academy.

COLEGIO ADVENTISTA DE SAN CRISTÓBAL. *See* San Cristóbal Adventist Secondary School.

COLEGIO ADVENTISTA DE TITICACA. *See* Titicaca Adventist Academy.

COLEGIO ADVENTISTA DE UCAYALI. *See* Ucayali Adventist Academy.

COLEGIO ADVENTISTA DEL ECUADOR. *See* Ecuador Adventist Academy.

COLEGIO ADVENTISTA DEL PACÍFICO. *See* Pacific Adventist Academy.

COLEGIO ADVENTISTA DEL PLATA. *See* River Plate Adventist University.

COLEGIO ADVENTISTA DO HUAMBO. *See* Angola Academy.

COLEGIO ADVENTISTA DOMINICANO. *See* Dominican Adventist Academy.

COLEGIO ADVENTISTA EMMANUEL. *See* Emmanuel Adventist Secondary School.

COLEGIO ADVENTISTA ENRIQUILLO. *See* Enriquillo Adventist Secondary School.

COLEGIO ADVENTISTA JUAN PABLO DUARTE. *See* Juan Pablo Duarte School (Barahona); Juan Pablo Duarte School (San Juan de la Maguana); Juan Pablo Duarte Secondary School (San Pedro de Macorís).

COLEGIO ADVENTISTA LA PAZ. *See* La Paz Adventist Academy.

COLEGIO ADVENTISTA MARANATHA. *See* Maranatha Adventist Secondary School.

COLEGIO ADVENTISTA MARIA TRINIDAD SANCHEZ. *See* Maria Trinidad Sanchez Secondary School.

COLEGIO ADVENTISTA OZAMA. *See* Ozama Adventist Secondary School.

COLEGIO ADVENTISTA SANTIAGO SUR. *See* South Santiago Adventist Academy.

COLEGIO CAMERERO. *See* River Plate Adventist University.

COLÉGIO CRUZEIRO DO SUL. *See* Cruzeiro do Sul Adventist Academy.

COLEGIO DEL PACÍFICO. *See* Pacific Academy.

COLEGIO INDUSTRIAL COLOMBO-VENEZOLANO. *See* Colombia Adventist University.

COLÉGIO INTERNACIONAL DE CURITYBA. *See* Brazil.

COLEGIO LIBERTAD. *See* Liberty Secondary School.

COLEGIO LINDA VISTA. *See* Linda Vista Academy.

COLEGIO MAX TRUMMER. *See* Adventist Atlantic Secondary School.

COLEGIO MIXTO ADVENTISTA EL PROGRESO. *See* Progresso Adventist Coeducational School.

COLEGIO MODELO ADVENTISTA. *See* Colombian Islands Mission Secondary School.

COLEGIO MODELO CENTRAL. *See* Model Central Secondary School.

COLEGIO NICANOR GONZALEZ MENDOZA. *See* Nicanor Gonzalez Mendoza Secondary School.

COLEGIO PORTEÑO ADVENTISTA. *See* Adventist Port Academy.

COLEGIO RICARDO GREENIDGE.

See Richard Greenidge Academy.

COLEGIO SALUD Y SABER. *See* Health and Knowledge Secondary School.

COLEGIO UNION. *See* Union Adventist Educational Complex.

COLEGIO VOCACIONAL ADVENTISTA DE NICARAGUA. *See* Adventist Vocational School of Nicaragua.

COLEGIO VOCACIONAL DE AMERICA CENTRAL. *See* Central American Adventist University.

COLEGIO VOCACIONAL Y PROFESIONAL MONTEMORELOS. *See* Montemorelos University.

COLLÈGE ADVENTISTE ANTILLES-GUYANE. *See* Antilles Guyane Adventist Secondary School.

COLLÈGE ADVENTISTE D'ANTARANDOLO. *See* Antarandolo Adventist School.

COLLÈGE ADVENTISTE DE BOUAKÉ (Ivory Coast). *See* Bouaké Adventist Secondary School.

COLLÈGE ADVENTISTE DE DOGBA. *See* Dogba Secondary School.

COLLÈGE ADVENTISTE DE GITWE. *See* Gitwe Adventist Secondary School.

COLLÈGE ADVENTISTE DE KIVOGA. *See* Kivoga Secondary School.

COLLÈGE ADVENTISTE DE RWANKERI. *See* Rwankeri Adventist Secondary School.

COLLÈGE ADVENTISTE DE SANGMELIMA. *See* Sangmelima Adventist Secondary School.

COLLÈGE ADVENTISTE DE SOAMANANDRARINY. *See* Soamanandrariny Adventist Secondary School.

COLLÈGE ADVENTISTE DE SONGA. *See* Songa Institute.

COLLÈGE ADVENTISTE D'IVOAMBA. *See* Antarandolo Adventist School.

COLLÈGE ADVENTISTE DU CAP-HAITIEN. *See* Cap-Haitien Adventist Academy.

COLLEGE FOOD. A food factory that operates in cooperation with denominational educational institutions in Korea. Soonan Euimyung School has operated a farm and produced various agricultural products from its early days.

In 1914 the Soonan Euimyung School purchased farmland with the assistance of the denomination and established an industrial department. Through this industrial program the school has offered its students an opportunity to earn their school expenses and be self-supporting.

In May 1927 a food factory was built, and the work of production and sales of health foods commenced in earnest. The foods produced at the Euimyung School food factory quickly gained public acceptance in Korea and won second place in the countrywide bazaar conference for Korean products, which opened in Seoul in April 1928. This happened even though the Euimyung School products exhibit was closed on Sabbath.

At that time there were 50 outlets in Seoul, one in Japan, and one in China. The school was subsequently taken over by the Japanese government, and because of religious persecution and the dissolution of the church, production halted.

Once Korea was liberated from Japan, the church reorganized and our college reopened. Because of our concept of education, the college planned a farm and a ranch, and purchased six milk cows in 1948. Milk customers at that time were missionary families, government dignitaries, and foreign embassy personnel. The milk output in 1955 was 5,500-6,600 pounds (2,500-3,000 kilograms) a day, and the milk was delivered by carriage.

In May 1959 George S. Haley was appointed as College Industrial Department head. He erected a milk plant. In 1972 College Food developed and produced different flavors of ice cream (chocolate, vanilla, and strawberry) and processed various vegemeat products, as well as soy milk and peanut butter.

After Korean Sahmyook Food was established by the church in 1978, the college food company stopped producing foods and devoted itself to milk production. In 1984 a new milk plant of 16,000 square feet (1,487 square meters) was built. Daily output of milk was 88,000 pounds (40,000 kilograms) in 1987, with 60 outlets.

In 1988 the name was changed to College Food and its operation separated from the college. In December of the same year College Food purchased 7.9 million square feet (736,201 square meters) of forestland near Hongchun, Kangwon-do for a new pasture site. After that, College Food began marketing developed chocolate milk, light milk, and yogurt and put them on the market.

Milk production at the plant is now 110,000-132,000 pounds (50,000-60,000 kilograms) a day, and the number of outlets is 90, with 98 employees involved in the production of chocolate milk, skim milk, light milk, yogurt drink, and ice cream. College Food has contributed greatly to the development of Korean Sahmyook University.

COLLEGE HEALTH FOODS. *See* Inter-American Health Food Company, Trinidad.

COLLEGE OF ARTS AND SCIENCES. *See* Andrews University; La Sierra University.

COLLEGE OF MEDICAL EVANGELISTS. *See* Loma Linda University.

COLLEGE OF TECHNOLOGY. *See* Andrews University.

COLLEGE PRESS. *See* University Printers.

COLLÈGE VERTIÈRES. *See* Haitian Adventist College.

COLLEGE VIEW ACADEMY. A day school on the secondary level located in Lincoln, Nebraska, and closely associated with Union College. The faculty and staff numbered 13 in 1993. When Union College was founded in 1891, of the several hundred students enrolled, nearly all were taking work comparable to secondary or elementary grades. The courses were "English Preparatory Course," comparable to the junior high school course of today (grades 7, 8, 9); the "Preparatory Course" of three years, comparable to the senior high school course today (grades 10, 11, and 12); and the regular college courses. Students were allowed to range over the offerings, taking classes on different levels. In 1907 for the first time an academy curriculum of four years was offered. However, the administration was the same for college and academy, and the college teachers taught academy classes. In 1915, for the first time college students outnumbered academy students in some departments, and graduating classes were separated. In 1924 the academy was organized as a separate department, and in 1932 a separate principal was named for Union College Academy.

On July 1, 1962, the Helen Hyatt Elementary School and the academy began operating as the Seventh-day Adventist Schools of Lincoln under the joint management of the College View church and Union College. At that time the name was changed to College View Academy.

Ground was broken for a $285,000 academy building Sept. 3, 1961, and the building was occupied Feb. 17, 1963. In 1964 the Seventh-day Adventist churches in Lincoln united as constituents of the K-12 system, combining under the name of "The SDA Schools of Lincoln," with the College View Academy the cap sheaf of the system.

Principals: C. L. Newkirk, 1963-1964; G. E. Thompson, 1964-1970; Henry Wooten, 1970-1971; D. A. Potter, 1971-1973; Oren W. Hewitt, 1973-1975; G. G. Davenport, 1975-1977; Dean Holmes, 1977-1979; Gary Bollinger, 1979-1983; Kenneth Utt, 1983-1985; Gary Bollinger, 1985-1989; Michael Schwartz, 1989- .

COLLEGEDALE ACADEMY. A coeducational day and boarding school on the senior high school level, affiliated with Southern Missionary College, at Collegedale, near Chattanooga, Tennessee. It is owned and operated by the Georgia-Cumberland Conference. The parent institution, founded in 1893 as the Graysville Academy (later Southern Training School) at Graysville, Tennessee, was moved to Collegedale, Tennessee, and reopened in 1916 as Southern Junior College, which became a senior college in the spring of 1944 *(see* Southern College of Seventh-day Adventists).

Until 1936 grades 9 through 12 were organized as an integral part of the junior college program, but in that year the secondary school was given a separate status and renamed Collegedale Academy. In 1968 the Greater Collegedale School System was organized with its own board of trustees (made up of personnel from the Georgia-Cumberland Conference of Seventh-day Adventists, the Collegedale and Ooltewah Seventh-day Adventist churches), and since that time has carried the entire responsibility for the financial support and management of Collegedale Academy.

Collegedale Academy has been accredited since 1938 by the Tennessee State Department of Education, the Southern Association of Colleges and Secondary Schools, and the SDA Board of Regents. At the beginning of the 1992-1993 school year, the academy had an enrollment of 229 and a staff of 18 full-time teachers, 13 of whom hold master's degrees.

Principals: D. C. Ludington, 1944-1947; J. C. Gaitens, 1947-1949; M. J. Sorenson, 1949-1951; W. B. Higgins, 1951-1957; P. J. Hoar, 1957-1959; J. R. Siebenlist, 1959-1961; Kenneth Stewart, 1961-1964; F. H. Hewitt, 1964-1968; R. M. Barrow, 1968-1980; Dean E. Maddock, 1980-1987; Hamlet Canosa, 1987-1991; Kermise Rowe, 1991- . Before 1944 the academy was under the direction of the president of Southern Missionary College.

COLLEGES AND UNIVERSITIES. *See* Schools, Seventh-day Adventist; also names of specific institutions.

COLLEGIATE ADVENTISTS FOR BETTER LIVING (CABL). An organization formed in 1972 to stimulate campus interest in a temperate and well-balanced lifestyle. The organizational process took place at Southwestern Adventist College in Keene, Texas. Its objective is to serve as a collegiate version of the American Health and Temperance Society and to provide a forum for students to demonstrate positive convictions while building camaraderie and support for a healthful lifestyle. Overseen by the Health and Temperance Department of the North American Division, CABL sponsors rallies, oratorical competitions, and a wide variety of other programs and activities in the interest of drug prevention and positive living.

COLLONGES-SOUS-SALÈVE ADVENTIST INSTITUTE. *See* Salève Adventist Institute.

COLOMBIA. A republic in the northwestern part of South America. Included in its territory are the islands of San Andrés, Providencia, and Santa Catalina, in the Caribbean Sea about 130 miles (210 kilometers) from the coast of Nicaragua, and the islands of Malpelo and Gorgona in the Pacific Ocean. The mainland is bounded on the north by the Caribbean Sea, on the east by Venezuela and Brazil, on the west by the Pacific Ocean and Panama, and on the south by Ecuador and Peru. Colombia, with an area of 439,735 square miles (1.1 million kilometers), is the fourth-largest country in South America.

Although Colombia is situated in the tropics, its climate varies with altitude from hot near the sea level to temperate in the highlands and cold in the Andes, whose peaks are covered with perpetual snow. The population of the country (1994) is 35.6 million.

Colombia was inhabited largely by the Chibcha Indians before the arrival of Europeans. In 1499 Alonso de Ojeda, a Spanish explorer, discovered what is now Colombia, and Spanish domination was established in 1538 by Jiménez de Quesada. In 1564 Colombia became a part of the presidency of New Granada under the viceroyalty of Peru.

The wars of independence are usually dated from 1781, when new taxation laws caused an Indian uprising. The rebellion was crushed, but the spirit of revolt persisted. Independence was gained in 1819, and on Dec. 17, 1819, Simón Bolívar united Venezuela and New Granada under the name of Republic of Colombia. Soon afterward this union, which in time included Ecuador also, became known as Gran Colombia and lasted until 1830. Since independence there have been repeated changes of government.

The language of Colombia is considered by some to be the purest Spanish in Latin America. Freedom of worship is guaranteed by the constitution, but Roman Catholicism was restored to the position of the state religion in 1957, some 20 years after its disestablishment in 1936. Protestantism is well represented among the different classes of society.

Seventh-day Adventist Statistics. The territory of Colombia is a part of the Colombia Union Conference, which in turn is part of the Inter-American Division. Statistics (1993) for *Colombia:* churches, 448; members, 116,758; church or elementary schools, 71; ordained ministers, 113; licensed ministers, 73; teachers, 244. Headquarters address: Carrera 84, No. 33B-69, Medellín.

Statistics (1993) for the missions and conferences—*Atlantic Colombia Mission:* churches, 98; members, 26,261; church schools, 13; ordained ministers, 17; licensed ministers, 15; teachers, 13. Headquarters: Barranquilla. *Colombian Islands Mission:* churches, 7; members, 629; church schools, 2; ordained ministers, 3; teachers, 19. Headquarters: San Andrés Island. *East*

Colombia Conference: churches, 111; members, 32,108; ordained ministers, 21; credentialed missionaries, 18. Headquarters: Bucaramanga. *Pacific Colombia Conference:* churches, 91; members, 27,762; church schools, 12; ordained ministers, 24; teachers, 23. Headquarters: Cali. *Upper Magdalena Conference:* churches, 130; members, 34,831; church schools, 17; ordained ministers, 31; licensed ministers, 16; teachers, 13. Headquarters: Bogotá.

For territories of the conferences and missions, *see* Inter-American Division.

Institutions. Adventist Atlantic Secondary School; Colombia Adventist University; Colombian Islands Mission Secondary School; El Llano Adventist Vocational Institute; Emmanuel Adventist School; Liberty Secondary School; Pacific Adventist Secondary School.

Development of Seventh-day Adventist Work. *Beginnings.* The beginning of the work in mainland Colombia is usually dated about 1916 or 1917, although the area continued to be listed in the Adventist mission records as "unentered" until 1921. In 1894 Frank C. Kelley went from the United States to Bogotá as a self-supporting missionary, paying his expenses by teaching English and selling photographic goods. He returned to his homeland, married, and went again to Colombia, but his wife's health required their return to the homeland in 1899, before any fruitage of their work was evident. The Kelleys returned again to Colombia in December 1920, when they worked for two and a half years before taking permanent return in 1923. About the turn of the century SDAs entered the islands of San Andrés and Providencia, which belong to Colombia but are situated some 200 miles (320 kilometers) north of Colón, Panama, and are inhabited mostly by non-Catholic English-speaking people. In 1901 S. Parker Smith (son of Uriah Smith) and his wife opened a school on San Andrés. In 1908 Smith wrote in the *Review and Herald* that there was a church of 19 members on the first island and a larger one on the other, and that SDA work was carried largely through the school on the islands. These islands were assigned to the West Caribbean Conference at that time.

A report in the *Review and Herald* late in 1915 states concerning mainland Colombia that "self-supporting workers have been in this field; but until a few weeks ago no regular conference work had ever been opened there." Later reports show that B. E. Connerly, a minister of the West Caribbean Conference, had entered Colombia and had begun to prepare the field with health books for the eventual opening of a mission. He worked mainly in Barranquilla and Medellín. During 1916 and 1917, several colporteurs went into Colombia, among them Gilbert Schwerin, Harold C. Brown, and George A. Kneeland. They sold *Guía Práctica de la Salud* ("Practical Guide to Health"), *Heraldos del Provenir* ("Heralds of the Future"), and *El Rey que Viene* ("The Coming King").

When Schwerin was in Bogotá, he sold a book to a shoe store owner by the name of Salvador Plata, who later became interested in SDA teachings. In 1921 another colporteur, L. V. Cleaves, went to Bogotá and also made contact with Salvador Plata, who introduced him to his brothers, Eugenio and Carlos. Cleaves studied the Bible with them, and when others joined the group (among them Francisco and Manuel Hernandez, Joaquin Rincón, and the Lemoine family), a Sabbath school was formed. Late in 1921 E. Max Trummer, then president of the West Caribbean Conference, of which Colombia formed a part, visited Bogotá and held the first SDA public meetings in the country. Two years later, in 1923, Francisco Hernandez and Eugenio and Carlos Plata were baptized in Bogotá. Trummer organized a church there in 1923.

In 1921 a box of SDA books was sent to the seaport of Cartagena. When no one claimed it, the books were finally distributed among the members of the local Presbyterian congregation, whose pastor, Antonio Redondo, became interested in SDA doctrines through reading them.

In 1922 Trummer conducted the first baptism in Colombia, at which time Antonio Redondo and his wife and daughter were baptized in the Sinú River near a small town called Cereté. Thereafter, Redondo became a Bible instructor and went to Barranquilla, where he gathered Moisés Valdés, Manuel Martínez, Modesto Mayorga, Sebastián Meléndez, and Gonzalo Luna Escandón into the first group to be baptized there. They formed the nucleus of a church that was organized in Barranquilla in 1924, the second in the Colombian Mission.

Organization and Growth. In 1922 Colombia was organized as a mission in the Central American Mission (the next year in the Caribbean Union Mission), with Trummer as its first superintendent, and headquarters at Bogotá. In 1925 the territory of Colombia was divided into four local missions: the Atlantic

Colombia, with offices at Barranquilla; the Antioquian, with offices at Medellín; the Central Colombia, with offices at Bogotá; and the Pacific Colombia, with offices at Cali. However, it took several years to staff all these missions. Not until 1927 did George C. Nickle and his wife go to Cali to organize the work in that city.

In 1927 the Colombia Venezuela Union, composed of Colombia, Venezuela, and the island of Curaçao, was organized at a meeting held at the Inter-American Division office in Balboa, Canal Zone, Panama. The first union committee meeting in Colombia was held Aug. 15, 1929. The union headquarters were first established in Cali, Colombia. At that time H. E. Baasch was union president; J. B. Ross, secretary-treasurer; Fred Steeves, publishing secretary; and Carlos Plata, press secretary. On Feb. 23, 1930, the union offices were moved to Medellín, where they have remained. In 1932 the first church property in Bogotá was bought.

With minor variations, the territorial division of Colombia was maintained until on Jan. 17, 1941, the work on the mainland of Colombia was reorganized into three missions: the Upper Magdalena Mission, the Atlantic Colombia Mission, and the Pacific Colombia Mission, with headquarters in Bogotá, Barranquilla, and Cali, respectively.

In 1951 the Colombian Islands were transferred from the Central American Union to the Colombia-Venezuela Union and the Atlantic Colombia Mission. In 1955 they became a separate mission.

The Colombian Union Conference was reorganized in 1989 and in 1993, with five missions or conferences: the Atlantic Colombia Mission, the Colombian Islands Mission, the East Colombia Conference, the Pacific Colombia Conference, and the Upper Magdalena Conference.

Health, Education, and Welfare Work. In 1936 a union training school near the city of Medellín was established, later known as the Instituto Colombo-Venezolano, and now as Colombia Adventist University.

The *Voice of Prophecy* radio program is broadcast over several national radio stations and is favorably received by the public. Welfare activities fostered by the SDA Church are liberally supported by numerous merchants.

Seventh-day Adventists are well known in even the most isolated sections of the country for their health principles, clean living, and strict honesty. Except in the case of ecclesiastical opposition, which at times has developed into persecution during periods of political instability, government authorities generally grant liberty to SDAs to promote various activities.

COLOMBIA ADVENTIST UNIVERSITY (Corporacion Universitaria Adventista; formerly Colombia-Venezuela Union College). A coeducational boarding school on the junior college level situated in Santa Teresita, a suburb of Medellín, Colombia, on a 60-acre (25-hectare) farm known as El Noral. Operated by the Colombian Union Conference through a school board, the college serves a union constituency of more than 115,000 members.

The school year runs from February to October. Instruction is in Spanish. After operating on a yearly renewal of registration the school was granted an operating permit by the Colombian Ministry of Education on Dec. 19, 1958. Although the school was founded especially for the benefit of Seventh-day Adventist young people from Colombia and Venezuela, it receives a limited number of students of other faiths.

Established in 1936, the school opened on Feb. 15, 1937, with 12 students under the direction of G. W. Chapman, with Mrs. Chapman, R. D. Buckner, and Mercedes Castro on the faculty. Known as the Colegio Industrial Colombo-Venezolano (Colombia-Venezuela Industrial College), it occupied for one year a two-story house in a section of Medellín known as Aranjuez. Then for four years the school operated on a small rented farm known as La Mariela, five miles (eight kilometers) from Medellín, and the name was changed to Academia Colombo-Venezolano (Colombia-Venezuela Academy). The first class graduated in 1940.

In July 1941 the school was moved to El Noral (purchased for 21,000 pesos). Two concrete dormitories were built at the foot of a hill. During the first years the second floors served as dormitory rooms for students, and the ground floors were used as teachers' quarters, kitchen, dining room, chapel, and classrooms. Two teachers' cottages were also built, and farm buildings were remodeled to serve as a bakery, a carpenter and print shop, and a cottage for the caretaker.

In 1945 a reinforced concrete administration building was erected, the second floor housing an ample kitchen and a large dining room, and the first floor the administrative offices, classrooms, the laundry, and a small store. In 1948 the school adopted the name Instituto Colombo-Venezolano (also known as Colombia-Venezuela Union College and before 1948 as Colombia-Venezuela Union Training School).

In 1952 a large court for games and sports was built by student labor. The printshop and an elementary school were constructed in 1954. A new entrance to the school was opened in 1957, and was later paved. An auditorium was built in 1961 and furnished in 1962 with new benches and an electric organ. The organ was assembled on the campus and its cabinet built in the carpenter shop. Additional teachers' homes brought the total residences to 10.

The small-scale industries include a print shop, bakery, carpentry shop, book bindery, and farm.

The program followed for several years included five years of primary instruction, six years of secondary, plus one year of specialized training. In 1960 the addition of another year of specialized instruction gave the school junior college rating. During 1963 the school board standardized the graduation requirements of the ministerial, normal, secretarial, commercial, and music courses. Ninety percent of the SDA workers in the Colombia Union have graduated from this school.

The music building of the college was inaugurated Dec. 4, 1973. The facility provides four teaching studios, 10 practice rooms, a large hall for ensemble rehearsals and recital functions of the department, a group piano studio, a department office, and a broadcast/recording suite.

The school publishes a prospectus combined with the annual, called the *Omega*.

Presidents: G. W. Chapman, 1937-1940; R. O. Garner, 1941 (acting); G. W. Chapman, 1942; W. H. Wineland, 1943-1945; C. L. Powers, 1946-1948; Clyde Bushnell, 1949; W. E. Aeschlimann, 1949-1951; D. H. Baasch, 1952; F. H. McNeil, 1953; A. R. Monteith, 1954-1956; Gilberto Bustamante, 1957-1964; Guillermo Krieghoff, 1965-1970; Luis A. Flórez, 1971-1975; Donaldo J. Thomann, 1975-1976; Esteban Beleno, 1976-1979; Miguel Angel Lopez, 1979-1982; Edmundo Alva, 1982-1985; Esteban Baleno (acting), 1985-1986; Edgar Escobar, 1986-1990; Leonardo Suescun, 1990-1993; Edgardo Munoz, 1993-1994; Gamaliel Florez, 1994- .

COLOMBIAN ISLANDS MISSION. *See* Colombia; Inter-American Division.

COLOMBIAN ISLANDS MISSION SECONDARY SCHOOL (Colegio Modelo Adventista; formerly San Andrés Secondary School). A coeducational secondary school offering a complete national secondary program, situated on the island of San Andrés and serving the three small Colombian islands of San Andrés, Providencia, and Santa Catalina. The secondary students attending from Providencia board with families in San Andrés. Until 1973 the secondary school used part of the facilities of the primary school, but in 1974 two classrooms were added to help accommodate the secondary students. The school was established in 1964 under the direction of Jaime Perry, and is recognized by the SDA Board of Regents and the Colombian government. In 1993 the school functioned in a new installation in Bahia del Cove. In 1993 the school had a faculty and staff of 14.

Principals: Jaime Perry, 1964-1965; Prudence Ashley Grayman, 1965-1966; Jorge Newball, 1966-1967; Pablo Amaya, 1967-1968; Jorge Newball, 1968-1970; Félix Hurtado, 1970-1971; Lina Acosta, 1971-1972; Félix Hurtado, 1972-1973; Alonso Flórez, 1973-1974; Dorance Gordon, 1974-1975; Juan Alberto Díaz, 1976-1978; José E. García, 1979; Raúl Parra, 1980-1981; Esteban Beleño, 1982-1983; Lixberth Ruiz, 1984-1987; Wilson Rojas, 1988-1992; John Newlove, 1993-1994; Alejandro Veloza, 1994- .

COLOMBIAN UNION CONFERENCE. *See* Colombia; Inter-American Division.

COLORADO. *See* Central States Conference; Colorado Conference; Rocky Mountain Conference.

COLORADO CONFERENCE. A unit of church organization that included the state of Colorado and also San Juan County in New Mexico. (*See also* Central States Conference.) On Feb. 8, 1981, the Colorado Conference was merged with the Wyoming Conference to form the Rocky Mountain Conference. The Colorado Conference was part of the Central Union Conference.

History. 1. *Beginnings of the Work in Colorado.* Shortly after the gold rush to Colorado in the early 1860s a young Seventh-day Adventist girl came across the plains of Kansas and Colorado in a covered wagon and found work in the home of a miner in Denver. She later married a miner named Shaw and they made their home in Golden. Their son, J. L. Shaw, was for years the treasurer of the General Conference. The second SDA in Colorado was Mrs. Amy Dart, who settled in Boulder in 1872 and began to circulate SDA publications. That same year James and Ellen White spent some time in Colorado recuperating their health. They bought a 40-acre (15-hectare) tract in the mountains back of Boulder and made contact with the two lone SDAs in the state. D. M. Canright, who came to see the Whites in their retreat, visited the Shaws at Golden, and in August and September 1873 held meetings—the first Seventh-day Adventist evangelistic meetings in Colorado. Because of the resulting interests, the General Conference named Colorado a mission. In 1878 an experienced evangelist, M. E. Cornell, went to open work there. He held meetings at Boulder and Georgetown.

Because of the cold nights at that elevation, the meetings were closed Sept. 22, but as a result of the campaign two ministers accepted the SDA faith. Later that fall Cornell held meetings at Sunshine and won at least 15 converts. The next summer J. O. Corliss and A. O. Burrill joined him. They held meetings in Longmont, Boulder, Denver, St. Vrain, and Fort Collins. At Boulder on Aug. 2, 1879, a church of 26 was organized—the first in Colorado—and a Sabbath school of 40. At St. Vrain a church of 13 was formed in October. At Denver the membership increased from 3 to 30. James and Ellen White came and spoke at Boulder and Denver. At Denver Ellen White spoke at a temperance rally attended by more than 600. In 1881 the first Seventh-day Adventist church building in Colorado was completed at Boulder.

In the spring of 1880 A. J. Stover visited a group of adherents that had spontaneously arisen at Texas Creek as a result of reading the *Signs of the Times* and other SDA publications. Only one of the group had ever seen an SDA preacher. One had been a Methodist preacher in Missouri but was expelled for keeping the Sabbath. Nine "signed the covenant," and about eight expressed a desire for baptism.

After another series of meetings in Denver, begun on Aug. 18, 1880, a church of 21 members was organized. It met in a canvas tabernacle that accommodated the 60 persons who attended Sabbath school.

2. *Colorado Conference Organized.* The first Colorado camp meeting was held Sept. 26-Oct. 2, 1883, in the outskirts of Denver, with nine delegates representing four churches and "two classes," and with an attendance of from 100 to 150. At this meeting the Colorado Conference was organized, with E. R. Jones president, J. W. Horner secretary, and H. H. Pierce treasurer. The Colorado Conference territory consisted of Colorado, New Mexico, and Wyoming.

3. *Beginnings on the Western Slope.* The Rocky Mountains, running from north to south, divide Colorado into two dissimilar geographical sections, almost like two different states, with travel difficult between them. In the autumn of 1885 George O. States with his family settled on Surface Creek and preached the first SDA sermon on the Western Slope at Eckert, in the home of the first member in the conference living west of the mountains, a man named Castle.

The next spring States canvassed in Delta County, selling Uriah Smith's *Marvel of Nations* and Ellen G. White's *Great Controversy.* In the summer of 1886 States and George Cram held the first tent meetings on the Western Slope, at Montrose. Because of disturbances caused by a lynching mob attacking the neighboring jail, the meetings were disrupted, but evangelism in the area went forward through personal work.

A series of meetings at Crawford in 1887 won five; by 1888 the persevering States had increased the number to 21 and organized them into the first church on the Western Slope. Churches were organized at Aspen in 1895 and at Glenwood Springs in 1899. Other western Colorado churches organized in the 1890s were Uncompahgre, Pitkin, Fruita, Telluride, Durango, Paonia, Grand Junction, and Eckert. At Farmington, in San Juan County, New Mexico, a church had been organized by 1899, and the first SDA church building in New Mexico had been dedicated.

4. *Subsequent History.* In the meantime new churches east of the mountains had been admitted to the conference in the 1880s and 1890s: Silver Cliff, 1888; Pueblo, 1889; Colorado Springs, 1890; North Willow, Lyons, and Alamosa, 1894; Monte Vista, Idaho Springs, and Alma, 1895; La Veta, Bellevue, and Timpas Valley, 1896; Salida, Wentz, Hygiene, Fort Morgan, Cripple Creek, Florence, and Howard, 1897; Niwot, 1899; Canon City was also organized in the 1890s.

By 1902, when Colorado became part of the new Central Union Conference, the Colorado Conference, embracing Colorado and New Mexico, had 42 churches and nine companies, with a membership of about 2,000.

5. *Schools.* The Delta church operated a school in 1897-1898, which possibly was the first one in Colorado. In 1898 Boulder, Denver, and Longmont operated church schools.

Several churches west of the mountains, under the leadership of H.M.J. Richards, opened the Palisade school in the fall of 1904, out of which grew the Western Slope Industrial School. This was later called Colorado Western Slope Academy, which by 1907 was a 12-grade school with an enrollment of 85. In the meantime, on the Eastern Slope the Eastern Colorado Academy opened in 1907 at Campion *(see* Campion Academy). By 1913 the western school disappeared from the records.

6. *Inter-Mountain Conference, a Temporary Organization.* After a time the members on the Western Slope asked to organize their own conference. Their request was not immediately granted, but a vice president, resident on the Western Slope, was elected in 1903, and special camp meetings were held from time to time on the Western Slope. In 1908 the conference was split along the continental divide to make the new Western Colorado Conference, with headquarters at Grand Junction. The rest of the conference was renamed Eastern Colorado Conference, but in 1909 it took back the original name, Colorado Conference. (New Mexico, with the exception of San Juan County, had already been turned over to the Southwestern Union in 1907.) The Western Colorado Conference was enlarged in 1916 to take in Utah, renamed Inter-Mountain Conference, and joined to the Pacific Union Conference. In 1918 this new conference founded a new Western Slope Academy at Rulison, known as Inter-Mountain Academy. In 1920 the Inter-Mountain Conference was reorganized to include only the eastern part of Utah, western Colorado, and San Juan County, New Mexico, and was returned to the Central Union Conference. On Aug. 1, 1932, the Inter-Mountain Conference was dissolved, eastern Utah going back to the Pacific Union, and western Colorado and San Juan County, New Mexico, reuniting with eastern Colorado to re-form the Colorado Conference. The Western Slope membership had grown from 300 at the division, in 1908, to 697 in 1932 at the reunion. With the dissolving of the conference, Inter-Mountain Academy ceased to operate.

7. *Medical Institutions.* In 1893 John Fulton visited Boulder for his health, and soon afterward persuaded J. H. Kellogg, head of SDA medical work, to establish a sanitarium there. This later became the Boulder Memorial Hospital, under the control of the Central Union Conference. The Porter Memorial Hospital, although never owned by the Colorado Conference, was opened in Denver, a private gift to the Central Union Conference, in 1930.

8. *Evangelistic Projects and Methods.* By 1906 the Colorado Conference was supporting 12 missionaries in other countries; in 1908 the conference began sending one third of its tithe quarterly to the General Conference. Colporteur work began early in Colorado. In 1886 canvassing companies were organized, which worked together for moral support as they traveled from place to place, covering section after section. One feature in the later 1890s was a "colporteur wagon." The canvasser took his family in the wagon, and making a temporary headquarters, canvassed the area round about and then moved on to another base.

When in the 1880s the General Conference encouraged the establishment of urban centers for in-service training in evangelism, known as city missions, such an institution was opened in Denver in 1886 and operated for several years. In 1897 an 85-room building was rented and operated for several years as a "city medical mission and workingmen's home." The Bethel Mission, another center operated under the same management, was a rescue home for women. Another mission of the same type was opened in Boulder in 1893. Vegetarian cafés in Denver and Colorado Springs were prospering in 1902. Another training program for workers was the three-month Bible School. The one for 1894 taught various advanced grade and high school subjects and emphasized Bible, English, history, and canvassing.

9. *Growth in the Denver Area.* The membership in the city of Denver grew slowly from 21 members in one church in the fall of 1880 to 3,766 members in nine churches by 1974, as lay evangelism and branch Sabbath schools resulted in several churches around the periphery, and public evangelistic campaigns resulted in others. A Black church that belongs to the Central States Conference unites with the other local churches in support of the consolidated school. The first church school in Denver, a one-teacher school, opened in 1898-1899. In 1928 there were 10 grades, and by 1963 a full-fledged academy *(see* Mile High Academy).

Colorado was among the first conferences to have a young people's department. As early as 1894, the "Young People's Missionary Band of Denver" petitioned the conference for aid in extending young people's work through the conference. In time the Sabbath school department was given the responsibility of doing something for the young people. In 1904 the Central Union held a young people's convention at Union College. In 1905 before the General Conference Missionary Volunteer Department was founded, Meade MacGuire became the first field secretary of the young people's department for Colorado.

10. *Workers From the East.* Like other Western states, Colorado profited by numbers of SDA settlers coming from farther east. These did missionary work among their neighbors and aroused an interest that led to the establishing of several new churches.

Among the workers who came to Colorado for health and remained to work was G. W. Anglebarger, a minister of the Ohio Conference. Told that he could not live a year if he remained in a severe climate, he arrived at Denver in the late 1880s to take charge of the city mission, and remained to work, principally in Denver, for the next 40 years. F. M. Wilcox came with his wife to Boulder Sanitarium seeking to improve his health in 1895 and stayed as an employee of that institution 14 years. C. C. Holbrook, an unusual and influential man, not a conference worker, was judge of the twelfth judicial district of Colorado. Because his court did not convene on the Sabbath, he cleared a crowded docket by holding court in the evening. He held a ministerial license, was a member of the conference committee, and often preached.

11. *Recent Developments.* In 1950 the conference purchased Glacier View campsite, which now has 530 acres (215 hectares), a beautiful mountain lake, and 39 permanent structures. Construction of a new 660-seat chapel and a 52-room lodge housing 200 people was begun in the spring of 1974. The name was changed to Glacier View Ranch on Nov. 20, 1972.

A new conference office building near the Porter Memorial Hospital in Denver was occupied Jan. 1, 1958. A new wing was opened Sept. 1, 1971, to house the Adventist Book Center. On Apr. 1, 1963, the conference joined others in the support of the La Vida Mission for the Navajo Indians, 53 miles (85 kilometers) from Farmington, New Mexico.

By 1974 all non-English-speaking churches and companies had disbanded or joined English-speaking churches except for one Navajo and two Spanish churches.

The Rocky Mountain Conference, merging the Colorado and Wyoming conferences, was organized in 1981. See that listing for additional history and information.

12. *Presidents—Colorado Conference:* E. R. Jones, 1883-1885; W. Ostrander, 1885-1886; C. P. Haskell, 1886; E. H. Gates, 1886-1890; J. R. Palmer, 1890-1894; N. W. Kauble, 1894-1896; J. M. Rees, 1896-1900; G. F. Watson, 1900-1908; J. W. Lair, 1908-1909; C. R. Kite, 1909-1913; A. T. Robinson, 1913-1917; W. A. Gosmer, 1917-1922; M. B. Van Kirk, 1922-1923; M. L. Rice, 1923-1931; J. F. Piper, 1931-1933; J. J. Nethery, 1933-1937; V. G. Anderson, 1937-1939; G. F. Eichman, 1939-1945; N. C. Peterson, 1945-1955; R. S. Joyce, 1955-1963; H. V. Reed, 1963-1973; W. C. Hatch, 1973-1981.

Western Colorado Conference: W. F. Kenneth, 1908-1911; E. A. Curtis, 1911-1916.

Inter-Mountain Conference: E. A. Curtis, 1916-1917; H. E. Lysinger, 1917-1920; N. T. Sutton, 1920-1922; B. H. Shaw, 1922-1924; J. W. Turner, 1924-1930; B. M. Grandy, 1930-1932.

COLORADO SANITARIUM. *See* Boulder Memorial Hospital.

COLPORTEUR. *See* Literature Evangelist.

COLPORTEUR SCHOLARSHIPS. *See* Scholarships, Literature Evangelist.

COLTHEART, JOHN FREDERICK (1924-1974). Evangelist. A native of Tasmania, he was baptized into the church at 14 years of age. After graduation from Avondale College he received a call to labor in New Zealand. He left for that field immediately, saving money by sleeping on deck. In 1948 he married Raye Williams, and four years later he was ordained to the gospel ministry. He conducted large evangelistic campaigns in 10 countries, speaking to audiences as large as 10,000.

In 1967 he became evangelist for the Northern European Division. Later he served as secretary of the Ministerial Association. During this time he held successful campaigns in cities such as London, Bristol, Edinburgh, Rotterdam, Helsinki, and Oslo.

COLUMBIA ADVENTIST ACADEMY. A coeducational secondary school operated by a local constituency of 11 churches. It is situated on a 250-acre (100-hectare) tract in Meadow Glade, approximately 12 miles (20 kilometers) northeast of Vancouver, Washington, and 2.5

miles (four kilometers) southwest of Battle Ground, Washington. It is accredited by the state of Washington, the Seventh-day Adventist Board of Regents, and the Northwest Association of Secondary and Higher Schools.

The physical plant consists of an administration building, containing classrooms, science laboratories, library, registration and business offices; a classroom annex; a music conservatory-gymnasium; home economics building; shop; cafeteria; seven faculty cottages; two barns; loafing shed for cattle; machine shed; and industrial building.

The forerunner of the present academy was a church school established in 1899 in Vancouver, Washington, by John R. Clark and his wife, who had come from England. Myrtle Clark Atkins was the first teacher, and among other early teachers were John J. Clark and Nellie Clark. With the addition of a few boarding students in the fourth year, the Clarks moved to a large tract of land about 12 miles (20 kilometers) northeast of Vancouver. Of this tract they donated 20 acres (eight hectares) to the conference, in a wooded area, on which in 1903 the Meadow Glade school was begun in a building of rough boards. In 1906 the first permanent building was erected and the school was expanded to 10 grades, and about 1911 to 12 grades. Land north of the school was cleared in 1912-1913 by the schoolboys and the local church members.

Some of the early supporters of the school were L. D. House, a church elder; J. R. Clark and his son, John; L. F. Burdoin, board member and for 18 years business manager; H. W. Lashier; Joe Emmerson, Sr.; A. Elmer Fleck; John F. Gildersleeve; and G. E. Johnson, three times principal, whose leadership did much to mold the school.

In 1915 the Western Washington Conference placed the school under local church management. In 1922 the school was renamed Columbia Academy. Beginning in 1928, the principal's salary was paid by the Western Oregon Conference, to whose territory several southwest counties in the state of Washington had been transferred.

After years of hardship, including a fire in 1936 that destroyed the library, some of the boys' apartments, and the business office, the school came under the control of the newly formed Oregon Conference in 1939.

An extensive building program followed, including a girls' dormitory (1946, enlarged 1964), a church, a home-economics building, a laundry, a boys' dormitory, a combined music conservatory and gymnasium, service and industrial buildings, a masonry-and-steel barn housing an enlarged dairy herd and providing modern facilities for the dairy (operated from 1927 to 1986), a cafeteria and a classroom annex. Farmland and a new well and water tower were also added.

The school was renamed Columbia Adventist Academy in 1974. After three years of negotiations, planning, and preparation a Harris Pine Mills installation began production in 1975 and operated successfully until 1989.

Because of the cost of operating three boarding schools in the Oregon Conference and the decline in senior academy students, the Oregon constituency voted to make CAA a day academy beginning in the 1977-1978 school year. In the 1990s there was a school enrollment of 150 students.

Principals: G. E. Johnson, 1906-1908; L. G. Paap, 1908-1909; S. C. Hansen, 1909-1910; J. B. Clymer, 1910-1912; G. E. Johnson, 1912-1913; C. G. Clymer, 1913-1914; F. W. Fields, 1915-1916; C. G. Clymer, 1916-1917; George Bugbee, 1917-1919; G. E. Johnson, 1920-1924; D. E. Venden, 1924-1926; H. M. Lodge, 1927-1929; Frank Wallace, 1929-1930; W. R. Emmerson, 1930-1933; C. L. Witzel, 1933-1936; Arthur R. Tucker, 1936-1938; G. L. Beane, 1938-1944; B. M. Kurtz, 1944-1951; C. E. Davis, 1951-1955; G. Glenn Davenport, 1955-1959; W. L. Schoepflin, 1959-1960; H. T. Ochs, 1960-1966; L. B. Griffin, 1966-1970; Glen W. Davis, 1970-1975; V. Kaiser, 1975-1980; Ed Boyatt, 1980-1982; Floyd White, 1982-1985; Richard Serns, 1985-1988; Wayne Culmore, 1988-1991; Kelly Bock, 1991- .

COLUMBIA UNION COLLEGE. A coeducational four-year liberal arts college in Takoma Park, Maryland. Established as Washington Training College in 1904, it was renamed Washington Foreign Mission Seminary the same year. In 1913 its name was changed to Washington Missionary College, and to Columbia Union College in 1961. It is accredited by the Middle States Association of Colleges and Schools and by the SDA Board of Regents, and is a member of the American Association of Colleges. It is recognized by the State Board of Education of the state of Maryland for the preparation of elementary and secondary school teachers, by the National League for Nursing for its program in nursing, including public health nursing, and by the Committee on Allied Health Education and Accreditation of the American Medical Association for its medical laboratory technician and medical technology programs.

The campus comprises 20 acres (eight hectares) of land in the north-central area of the city of Takoma Park, on Carroll and Flower avenues. The 14 buildings include an administration building, residence halls, laboratories, library, and gymnasium. The total evaluation stands at more than $9 million.

The governing board is composed of not more than 38 members, including the president, executive secretary, treasurer, and director of education of the Columbia Union Conference; the presidents of the eight constituent conferences; the president of the college; the president of Washington Adventist Hospital; the pastor of the Sligo Seventh-day Adventist Church; and one trustee elected from among the principals of the senior academies of the Columbia Union Conference. Enrollment in 1993 was 1,159, and the staff numbered 125 (six administrators, 23 associate and assistant administrators, 47 instructors, four supervisory and 45 auxiliary personnel).

Washington Training College. The institution was founded when the denominational headquarters were moved to the Washington, D.C., area after two disastrous fires had destroyed the two largest institutions (Battle Creek Sanitarium, Feb. 18, 1902, and the Review and Herald publishing house, Dec. 30, 1902). Counseled by Ellen White not to rebuild in Battle Creek, but to find a favorable place in the Eastern states, the locating committee, composed of A. G. Daniells, W. W. Prescott, I. H. Evans, S. N. Haskell, H. W. Cottrell, S. N. Curtiss, J. E. Jayne, W. A. Spicer, C. D. Rhodes, and D. W. Reavis, investigated many properties from the Hudson River to the Potomac River. After weeks of searching and comparing, the committee selected and authorized the purchase, for $6,000, of the 50-acre (20-hectare) tract in Takoma Park on which Columbia Union College and the Washington Adventist Hospital now stand. The land was approved by Ellen White as the place for a college.

Their report was presented to a council convening in Washington, D.C., Oct. 7, 1903. The council recommended that a campaign be launched to raise $100,000 for the General Conference building, a school, and a sanitarium, and to pay for the land, moving, and equipment. By June 15, 1905, $103,054.20 had been received.

Thus, under the direct management of the General Conference, the construction of Washington Training College began June 1, 1904. Corporation papers were signed July 27, 1904, and the first college term began on Nov. 30, 1904, with 50 students and the following administration: James W. Lawhead, president; Benjamin G. Wilkinson, Bible and history; Mrs. B. G. Wilkinson, English; Mrs. M. H. Tuxford, matron and home economics; W. A. Colcord, English; J.A.L. Derby, science; Walton John, music; H. E. Rogers, business and shorthand.

During the first three years of the college's history, its spirit of sacrifice and devotion to missions manifested itself in the loyalty and unity of its faculty and students in a new venture in education. Three buildings, North Hall, Central Hall, and South Hall, now stood on the main campus. About a half mile (0.8 kilometers) away was a large dwelling house, the temporary residence of Ellen White, which served also in part as the women's residence hall. As more than an interested observer of a new educational institution, Mrs. White not only took an interest in the management, the faculty, and all the students of the college but she made it her personal duty to encourage the workmen who were constructing the walls and shaping the campus. She invited them to worship in the morning.

Washington Foreign Mission Seminary. At the biennial General Conference council of May 10, 1907, at Gland, Switzerland, the vexing problem confronting the delegates was the dearth of competent missionary personnel. To avoid sending out ineffectively prepared or unsuited missionary appointees to a foreign land, it was necessary to furnish preliminary training. The finger of circumstance pointed to Washington Training College as the most favorably situated for, and as most easily adaptable to, this special purpose. Thus in 1907 the Washington Foreign Mission Seminary was established, under the presidency of Homer R. Salisbury, who earlier had left the United States to be principal of Duncombe Hall Training College, London (*see* Newbold College), and from there had been assigned to the Levant Union Mission. The former principal of the denomination's school at Cape Town, South Africa, C. H. Hayton, was business manager. The members of the faculty were men with a variety of experiences and backgrounds, such as Arthur G. Daniells,

William A. Spicer, George A. Irwin, Eugene W. Farnsworth, and Frederick E. Griggs; and Drs. Harry W. Miller and Daniel H. Kress.

The enrollment for the year 1907-1908 was 77. That was a year of new ventures and many firsts for the college. The first missionary faculty member left the college to go as a missionary to China, taking with him three new missionary recruits. The first full-time faculty member sailed for mission duty in South America. The first on-campus ordination service was held. The first electrically driven printing press was installed. The first administration building, College Hall, later known as Science Hall, was completed.

The mission training program was intensive and covered such backgrounds as the geography, history, and culture of the various countries. Both John L. Shaw, returning from mission service in India, and Milton E. Kern headed the seminary for brief terms. By the close of 1913 there had gone from its halls 90 trainees to preach and teach in 27 countries of the earth.

A Liberal Arts College. In the autumn of 1914 the seminary resumed the status of a liberal arts college, for which it already had a charter, and took the name Washington Missionary College. A program was begun for defining academic departments. Because of the need for a distinct line of demarcation between college preparatory and college work, certain college prerequisites were set up. A summer school was put into operation for the first time. At the first commencement exercises, held May 22, 1915, five received the Bachelor of Arts degree.

In 1915-1916 the college, whose plant had been built for 150 students, reached an enrollment of 270, and the dormitory overflow had to be housed in tents. A fund-raising campaign for more college buildings was begun in which, on Jan. 20, 1916, faculty and students banded themselves into an organization known as the Students' Association and raised $7,500. In April 1916 the first issue of the *Sligonian,* a monthly college paper (called the *Columbia Journal* since 1981), appeared with two main interests—more students and more money for the building campaign. Despite the material shortages created by World War I, an administration building, named Columbia Hall, was erected, and dedicated free of debt on Feb. 20, 1919. By the end of the second decade, in the fall of 1924, the institution looked proudly at its increased enrollment, now 400, its enlarged dormitories, an addition to the dining room, new laboratory equipment, new industrial shops, a better home-economics department, and more books for the library; also at the faculty's scholarship level and its unified effort in fulfilling the religious and scholastic purposes for which the college was founded.

In establishing a separate junior college under the name of Columbia Junior College in June 1933, the board of trustees separated the lower freshman and sophomore classes from the senior college and assigned them to certain faculty members who, as the faculty of Columbia Junior College, taught junior-level terminal courses. An entirely new organization was set up, a separate bulletin was prepared, and separate scholarship requirements were enforced. The new junior college was accredited in due time by the Middle States Association. This accreditation, needed for premedical and teacher training courses, in no way jeopardized the possibilities for future senior college accreditation. The program, originated and advocated by John P. Neff, secretary of education for the Columbia Union Conference, went into effect in August 1933. Dr. Benjamin G. Wilkinson, dean of theology of the senior college (and one of the few faculty members with a Ph.D. degree), was elected dean of the junior college. The junior college operated until 1944.

In 1936 a revitalized college building program began, including a building (now H.M.S. Richards Hall, housing the department of religion) to house the elementary school and the teacher training program (1939), a central heating plant (1940), a new library building (1942), named the Theofield G. Weis Memorial Library in 1970 to honor his many years of service, and an addition to Science Hall (formerly College Hall). The institution received senior college accreditation with the Middle States Association in 1942.

The growth of the college continued with ever-increasing momentum during the next two decades. The institution passed successfully through rigid accreditation inspections and internal difficulties. Young and highly trained teachers were brought to the campus. An almost defunct alumni association was revitalized. Halcyon Hall, women's residence, was completed in 1947 (enlarged 1963). A gymnasium was erected in 1950 and a swimming pool was added to the same building in 1955.

The early 1960s saw several additions to the campus. In 1962 Morrison Hall, a new men's residence, was occupied. It was named in honor of the former president, Harvey A. Morrison, and its chapel was named in honor of G. Eric Jones (dean of men, 1927-1936). In the same year the interior of Columbia Hall was completely altered, except for the chapel, to accommodate the administrative offices and a modern self-service bookstore.

In 1963 a new wing was added to Halcyon Hall, housing an additional 110 women. Long-range plans were laid for new buildings to be added.

The college operates a department of behavioral science offering a degree in psychology, the first of its kind in the denomination. The campus radio station, WGTS-FM, with a power of 29,500 watts, covers the metropolitan area and reaches out as far as New Jersey, Pennsylvania, West Virginia, and central Virginia.

In 1950 the Washington Sanitarium and Hospital School of Nursing was reorganized and made a part of the college baccalaureate program in the Department of Nursing, but the sanitarium did not relinquish entire control of the nursing school until 1956. In 1961 full accreditation by the National League for Nursing, including public health nursing, was obtained, this in addition to the academic accreditation from the Middle States Association previously received.

In 1966 the Museum of Biblical Antiquities was dedicated in the H.M.S. Richards Hall of Religion. Also the John M. Keller Memorial Library was dedicated by the biology department.

Following the devastating fire that destroyed Columbia Hall on Feb. 19, 1970, the Campus Center was speedily completed and occupied. This new complex with 100,000 square feet (9,300 square meters) cost $3.1 million and houses the administrative offices, dining room, and some classrooms. It was renamed Wilkinson Hall in 1982 in honor of the first Bible/history teacher, B. G. Wilkinson.

Because of the tremendous need to provide for the burgeoning Medical Technology Department, the former press building has been renovated at a cost of $175,000. This new Health Sciences Building opened in November 1974, and was enlarged and renovated in 1983.

In 1984 the college began the adult evening program to meet the needs of adults in the community who are working full-time but wish to complete a baccalaureate degree.

In attempting to meet the needs of youth today who desire shorter college courses, eight two-year Associate of Arts degree programs are being offered. CUC is committed to providing the finest in Christian education in training its youth in the sciences, the arts, and the humanities. But its highest goal is to inspire them in spiritual commitment to Jesus Christ.

Presidents: James W. Lawhead, 1904-1907; Homer R. Salisbury, 1907-1910; John L. Shaw, 1910; Milton E. Kern, 1910-1914; John L. Shaw, 1914-1916; Benjamin F. Machlan, 1916-1921; Marion E. Cady, 1921-1922; Harvey A. Morrison, 1922-1927; Harry H. Hamilton, 1927-1935; Harvey A. Morrison, 1935-1936; Benjamin G. Wilkinson, 1936-1946; William H. Shephard, 1946-1959; Charles B. Hirsch, 1959-1965; Winton H. Beaven, 1965-1970; George H. Akers, 1970-1974; Colin Standish, 1974-1978; William Loveless, 1978-1990; N. Clifford Sorensen, 1990-1992; Charles Scriven, 1992- .

COLUMBIA UNION CONFERENCE. The North American administrative unit comprising the following local conferences: Allegheny East, Allegheny West, Chesapeake, Mountain View, New Jersey, Ohio, Pennsylvania, and Potomac. Headquarters: 5427 Twin Knolls Road, Columbia, Maryland. Official organ: *Columbia Union Visitor.* Statistics (1993): churches, 576; members, 92,622; church-related elementary schools, 122; ordained ministers, 386; licensed ministers, 58; Bible instructors, 17; teachers, 575.

Institutions. Blue Mountain Academy; Columbia Union College; Garden State Academy; General Conference of Seventh-day Adventists; Hackettstown Community Hospital; Highland View Academy; Home Study International/Griggs University; Kettering College of Medical Arts; Kettering Medical Center; Mount Vernon Academy; Pine Forge Academy; Reading Rehabilitation Hospital; Review and Herald Publishing Association; Shady Grove Adventist Hospital; Shenandoah Valley Academy; Spring Valley Academy; Takoma Academy; Washington Adventist Hospital.

The Columbia Union Conference was formed in 1907 by combining the former southern area of the Atlantic Union Conference with the Ohio Conference (formerly in the Lake Union Conference). At that time it had a total of 187 churches and 5,320 members.

Presidents: W. J. Fitzgerald, 1908; G. B. Thompson, 1909; B. G. Wilkinson, 1909-1918; F. H. Robbins, 1918-1932; H. J.

Detwiler, 1932-1941; F. H. Robbins, 1941-1946; D. A. Ochs, 1946-1957; V. G. Anderson, 1957-1958; L. E. Lenheim, 1958-1962; Neal C. Wilson, 1962-1966; Cree Sandefur, 1966-1973; W. B. Quigley, 1973-1978; Wallace O. Coe, 1978-1985; Ron M. Wisbey, 1985-1994; Ralph Martin, 1994- .

COLUMBIA UNION VISITOR (1896 until Mar. 18, 1906, as *Welcome Visitor;* semimonthly until Oct. 10, 1901; then weekly, published by the Ohio Conference; after Jan. 1, 1908, published by the newly organized Columbia Union Conference; name changed to *Columbia Union Visitor* beginning with Mar. 18, 1908, issue; weekly until Mar. 24, 1966, then every two weeks; since Aug. 3, 1972, issued as a supplement inserted in alternate issues of the *Review and Herald,* both magazines mailed to the membership of the Columbia Union; beginning Aug. 13, 1982, published semimonthly and mailed directly to Columbia Union members as a separate magazine; on Dec. 1, 1989, began including the *Adventist Review* in alternate issues, both magazines mailed to the membership in the Columbia Union; starting with the Feb. 1, 1991, issue, began inserting monthly newsletters from the eight conferences in its territory and *A Healing Ministry*, monthly newsletter prepared by the Adventist health-care institutions in the Columbia Union, alternating issues with the *Adventist Review;* files in GC). Official organ of the Columbia Union Conference in the North American Division. Prepared by the Columbia Union Communication Department; printed by the Review and Herald Publishing Association, Hagerstown, Maryland.

COMMANDMENTS, TEN. *See* Law; Law and Grace.

COMMISSION ON RURAL LIVING. *See* Adventist-Laymen's Services and Industries.

COMMISSIONS ON GRADUATE EDUCATION. *See* Education, Graduate, Commission on.

COMMITTEE ON BIBLICAL STUDY AND RESEARCH. *See* Biblical Research Institute.

COMMUNICATION, DEPARTMENT OF. A General Conference department formed by the merger of the Bureau of Public Relations and the Radio-Television Department in January 1973. The merger was suggested by the advisory committees of the two departments and approved at the 1972 Annual Council. At the 1990 General Conference session, the department's function was refocused to address primarily the press and media relations from the General Conference.

The Communication Department's concerns include the development and maintenance of a true image of the church, a clear understanding of the church's principles by the public, and the effective use of broadcast and audiovisual techniques and media in communicating the gospel to the world. To achieve this, the department utilizes every appropriate medium of public information and community relations.

The department offers services to its two primary publics, that of the church itself and of the church's various publics. Representing the entire church to the public media and the community at large, the department offers a variety of communication services—including media relations and broadcast and video productions—to other departments and entities. In this sense, it functions at headquarters much like an institutional public relations office. At the same time it maintains a departmental program throughout the world church along the same lines as other church departments, counseling and aiding the various church organizations and institutions on the corporate and local level in their communications and media programs.

Interests of the department are served by communication directors at division, union, local conference, and church levels.

The 1990 refocusing of the Communication Department established its primary function as that of the Office of News and Information. In 1994 the department included four units: (1) the Office of News and Information, with its Adventist News Network (ANN) serving the official press agency of the Seventh-day Adventist Church; (2) Media Services, a production center for video and information service broadcast programming; (3) SDAs On-line Forum on CompuServe; and (4) Public Relations and General Conference tours.

The General Conference Spring Meeting of 1993 established the Communication Strategy Commission to address the communication ministry of the Seventh-day Adventist Church. The commission had a fourfold purpose: (1) to establish an overall communication strategy/structure for the church to govern its broadcast media, public relations, and other communication activities both within the church and for the world at large; (2) to design this strategy for use at all levels and by all entities of the church; (3) to develop the strategy/structure in such a way that it will provide direction for all broadcast media, public relations, and communication activities; (4) to provide a basis in the strategy for all supporting ministries involved in communication activities to contribute to the overall communication strategy of the church.

See also Seventh-day Adventist Media Center.

Directors of the Bureau of Public Relations: W. L. Burgan, 1912-1940; C. B. Haynes, 1940-1942; J. R. Ferren, 1942-1954; D. H. Thomas, 1954-1956; H. B. Weeks, 1956-1962; E. W. Tarr, 1962-1973.

Secretaries of the Radio and Radio-Television Department: Paul Wickman, 1948-1953; E. R. Walde, 1953-1964; J. O. Iversen (acting), 1964-1966; J. J. Aitken, 1966-1971; W.R.L. Scragg, 1971-1973.

Directors of the Department of Communication: W.R.L. Scragg, 1973-1975; M. Carol Hetzel, 1975-1978; James E. Chase, 1979-1984; Robert W. Nixon, 1984-1988; Shirley A. Burton, 1988-1994; Ray Dabrowski, 1994- .

COMMUNICATION SECRETARY. *See* Church Communication Secretary.

COMMUNION. *See* Lord's Supper.

COMMUNITY HOSPITAL OF SEVENTH-DAY ADVENTISTS. A general acute hospital with a capacity of 61 beds and 10 bassinets, owned and operated by the Caribbean Union in Port-of-Spain, Trinidad, West Indies. The property consists of a modern, two-story, reinforced concrete structure situated on a leased five-acre (two-hectare) tract of land. The hospital, administered by a hospital administrator and a chief of staff, maintains medical, surgical, dental, and obstetrical departments.

The Community Hospital of Seventh-day Adventists developed out of an outpatient clinic opened by R. F. Dunlop in rented quarters at the corner of Charlotte and New streets, Port-of-Spain, Trinidad, on May 1, 1948, under the name of Port-of-Spain Seventh-day Adventist Clinic. Later in 1948 a building was purchased at 2A Mucurapo Road, and was used as a charity clinic. After a year the clinic was wholly self-supporting. After the need for inpatient facilities became apparent, a building was made available by the South Caribbean Conference in a desirable location at 7 Queen's Park West, and in these quarters a 16-bed nursing home, called the Seventh-day Adventist Medical Unit, was established on Apr. 19, 1953.

In 1955 R. F. Dunlop, medical secretary of the Caribbean Union, suggested a site at Cocorite, Western Main Road, controlled by the government of Trinidad, on which to construct a hospital plant. The site was leased, and construction began Feb. 1, 1960. The project was completed and patients were transferred from the nursing home on Sept. 17, 1962. At that time the institution was named Port-of-Spain Community Hospital. The first chairman of the board of directors was C. J. Ritchie.

On Sept. 3, 1970, the administrative structure of Port-of-Spain Adventist Hospital was changed from that of medical director-business manager to that of administrator and chief of staff. Mrs. Betty Robertson, M.A., who was director of nursing services, was appointed the first administrator of the hospital and Dr. W. H. Shea was appointed chief of staff. L. K. Hadley was appointed assistant administrator in charge of business.

On Nov. 30, 1973, the hospital board voted to change the official name of the hospital from Port-of-Spain Community Hospital of Seventh-day Adventists to Port-of-Spain Adventist Hospital. In 1994 the hospital's name was changed once again, to Community Hospital of Seventh-day Adventists.

In 1994 a staff of 23, including six physicians and dentists, served the hospital.

Medical Directors: R. F. Dunlop, 1962; V. J. Soloniuk, 1963-1964; W. H. Shea, 1964-1965; James Miyashiro, 1966-1967; Richard Larsen, 1968-1969; Daniel Patchin, 1969-1970.

Administrators: Betty Robertson, 1970-1974; Lloyd Gittens, 1974-1984; Lawrence Duncan, 1984-1991; Eric Murray, 1991- .

COMMUNITY SERVICES (formerly known as Health and Welfare Services). The generic name used to designate social and emergency services given by the church to individuals, families, and larger groups in the community. These services encompass giving material aid in such forms as clothing, bedding, furniture, and household furnishings. They sometimes take the form of small cash grants in emergency situations. Included also are adult-education classes in such areas as healthful cooking, home management and budgeting, dressmaking, child care, home nursing, first aid, and medical self-help. Other free services frequently offered are relief ministry to disaster victims, mobile health screening, and summer camping for inner-city children.

Community Services programs are promoted and directed by the Department of Personal Ministries, in cooperation with church administrative officers and other church departments. Program planning and decision-making are done through committees on local church, local conference, union conference, division, and General Conference levels.

On the General Conference level the board of the Adventist Development and Relief Agency (ADRA) deals with disaster relief assistance as well as international relief. On division, union conference, and local conference levels, Community Services planning and funding is the responsibility of a committee that serves as a subcommittee of the conference executive committee.

On the local church level the total Community Services program is under the direction of the church evangelism council. This council coordinates the outreach programs of all departments. It also is the planning committee for personal ministries, and it therefore makes all major decisions affecting church Community Services programs.

The particular subsidiary organizations within the Department of Church Ministries that are responsible for Community Services include: the Dorcas Society, an organization of church women, Adventist Men, and the Community Services center.

The Dorcas Society specializes in giving material aid to families and in supplying clothing and bedding for international disaster relief. Adventist Men, in addition to conducting lay preachers' evangelistic meetings, specialize in work for prisoners and their families and in disaster relief. The Community Services center not only serves as a vehicle for Dorcas Society distribution of life necessities, but is also the base for adult education.

Visiting in Community Services. Visiting homes in Community Services gives the program a community outreach. Three types of visits are made: the initial visit, intended to acquaint the family with Community Services plans and to find needy persons or those willing to donate materials; the pick-up call, to gather supplies to be distributed to the needy or to supply relief to the unfortunate; and the follow-up visit to homes, to give further aid and spiritual encouragement.

Every Member in Community Services. All members of the Seventh-day Adventist Church are encouraged to take part in Christian benevolence and welfare service. They are taught the biblical basis for their service in the example and the commission of Jesus (Matt. 4:23; 10:8; Luke 10:37) and the prophetic message of Isa. 58. Even before the organization of the General Conference in 1863 provision was made at Battle Creek, Michigan, for a fund to aid the poor *(Review and Herald* 16:192, Oct. 30, 1860). The early welfare ministry was carried out primarily by the deacons and deaconesses of the church.

After 1874 the organization of Dorcas Societies spread among the churches, beginning in North America. The activities of these women's societies were not confined to meeting the needs of church members, but reached out into the community. In her public messages and writings, Ellen White pointed out that "God calls upon every man to take up his neglected work," that is, the work of showing "mercy to the destitute, the suffering, the wounded, those who are ready to die" (WM 49).

Assignment of responsibility for this work to the Home Missionary Department in 1913, development of a Disaster and Famine Relief Service following World War II *(see* ADRA), and establishment of Health and Welfare centers beginning in the 1950s were all major factors in the growing support of Community Services by the whole church membership.

Ellen White wrote in 1913: "There is a wide field for service for women as well as for men. . . . The help of all is needed. . . . Even the children should be taught to do some little errand of love and mercy for those less fortunate than themselves" *(ibid.* 75).

The church's *Manual for Health and Welfare Services* outlines activities for all church members. Through such activities, young people are taught the spirit of sharing; the intuitive sympathies of the women are directed in caring for the sick, ministering to the poor, and comforting the sorrowing; and the talents of the men are challenged to equip centers to serve in disaster relief, and to teach skills in first aid.

Although the North American Division pioneered the SDA Community Services, other world division fields were quick to follow. The earliest welfare organization on record outside of America was an association founded in 1897 in Hamburg, Germany. Since 1928 the welfare agency of the church in Germany has been registered with and recognized by the Fifth Union and the German Liga, the organization of voluntary and public welfare agencies of Germany.

City Missions and Welfare Centers. Near the turn of the century Dr. J. H. Kellogg and others in the Battle Creek Sanitarium became interested in beginning welfare work in large cities. In 1893, with the assistance of a gift of $40,000 from John Wessels of South Africa, he opened in Chicago, Illinois, the Chicago Medical Mission. Connected with it in the city were about a dozen branch and associate institutions. From this beginning, for about a decade the work spread to many of the large cities of the United States. These centers were of various kinds, including not only the traditional city missions, places where persons received "soup, soap, and salvation," but also homes for orphans or delinquents and welfare centers of a more general type. In 1900 the denominational directory listed them in 24 cities in 17 states and three countries overseas. By 1904 there were few left outside the institutions in Chicago, which were backed by the Battle Creek medical group. In 1898 Dr. J. H. Kellogg began publishing a welfare magazine, *The Life Boat,* of which Dr. David Paulson, who later took charge of the Chicago mission, was editor for many years. It reached a circulation of 150,000 and was discontinued in 1932.

World Wars and Natural Disasters. The Dorcas Society remained as the principal SDA welfare agency. After World War II, which left millions homeless and destitute, appeals directed to the churches and Dorcas Societies for material aid met a substantial response in the form of food, clothing, and other supplies. Natural disasters demonstrated the need of preparation for Christian disaster relief service. In 1950 all churches were asked to stockpile food and clothing for emergency purposes. Most of the conferences in North America own mobile units for use in transporting and distributing clothing, bedding, and food.

The church has given help in many major disasters in the United States and in other countries. The international relief organization of the church, established in 1956, is now the Adventist Development and Relief Agency (ADRA). It is an internationally recognized, nongovernmental organization with offices throughout the world.

Community Services Centers. As the welfare work expanded, smaller churches were encouraged to secure a room in the church building or in a home in which clothing could be stored. The larger churches were encouraged to operate Community Services centers—usually separate buildings—where not only food, clothing, bedding, and first-aid supplies are stored, but where classes in first aid, home nursing, and mass feeding are taught. Community Services centers are under the charge of a director who is a member of the local Church Evangelism Council. Identifying pins, arm bands, and uniforms were adopted, and the name "Community Services Sponsored by Seventh-day Adventists" has come to be the official designation of the welfare services of the church.

Centers are open to the public on specified days and hours. Food, clothing, and bedding, and sometimes furniture and appliances are given to individuals and families on the sole basis of need. Medical and hospital equipment is lent without charge. Close cooperation is maintained with other agencies, public and voluntary, in order to avoid duplication, to help make possible more effective services, and to refer persons with special needs to the best sources of help that are available.

Civil Defense Training and Service. SDAs feel a special obligation to serve their country in noncombatant capacities such as Civil Defense. Since medical and welfare services are the special areas of Civil Defense in which the church is most deeply involved, training in rescue, first aid, home nursing, medical self-help, mass feeding, shelter management, and related activities have received special emphasis. These provide opportunity for all church members to serve the community and nation, to help preserve life and relieve human suffering.

On Apr. 6, 1942, the General Conference Committee voted to ask the Home Missionary Department to serve as the channel for promoting and exchanging information regarding Civil Defense by and in the churches. Later the same year, these activities were transferred to the Commission on National Service, but were returned in 1958 to what is now known as the Church Ministries Department.

At the Autumn Council of 1961 the General Conference Committee recommended that, in existing denominationally owned structures in North America, shelter areas be provided and stocked with the minimum water, food, and other necessities as recommended by Civil Defense authorities; that institutional personnel be organized and trained to provide protection in time of disaster and lay plans for disaster training; that members be encouraged to undertake similar protective measures for their families in their homes, and to enroll in first aid and similar training classes. The altruistic motive was thus stated: "That as the end of all things rapidly approaches we ourselves seek by the grace of God to be individually prepared and to do our utmost to help our fellowmen to prepare for the solemn events ahead" (Autumn Council, 1961).

COMOROS. A federal Islamic republic that became independent in 1978, Comoros lies between the northern tip of Madagascar and the African mainland. The area of the islands is 838 square miles (2,170 square kilometers). The population (1994) is 530,000, made up of Africans, Arabs, and Indians. The religion is Muslim, the languages are Arab, French, and Comoran, akin to Swahili. Agriculture is the chief occupation, with vanilla, cacao, and oils for the world perfume makers (ylang-ylang, citronella, jasmine) as the principal products.

The islands form part of the territory assigned to the Indian Ocean Union Mission, which is part of the Africa-Indian Ocean Division. In 1955 Sulleman Ali Pax from M'sapere, island of Mayotte, visited Diégo-Suaraez, Madagascar, and became acquainted with our message through Elie Fayard After many years of study and meditation he was baptized in Antananarivo, Madagascar, on June 9, 1965. Since 1967 and for a long time he has been the only Seventh-day Adventist on the island of Mayotte. Abner Ranaivoson, a former Islamic imam born in Comoros, converted to Seventh-day Adventism in Madagascar and went to Mayotte in 1986. He has helped many young Muslims in Mayotte through Bible correspondence courses. Fear has hindered decision-making. The first baptismal ceremony on the island took place in November 1992. In Comoros, SDA members immigrating from Madagascar have witnessed cautiously. The first baptism there was held in February 1991.

COMPANY. A group of believers in an area organized for fellowship and worship, but not on the level of organization of a church. It may be organized by a district pastor or by a minister appointed by the conference or mission. In consultation with the members, he or she appoints a leader and a treasurer. Other officers, such as for the Sabbath school, are elected by vote of those who have been baptized. All who have been baptized are members of the conference church.

Companies are formed when a group of believers in an area wishes to organize, but its number is too small to warrant a church organization, or when believers do not wish to take upon themselves the responsibilities of a fully self-administered church organization.

The leader is not ordained to his office and does not have the authority vested in an elder of a church. The treasurer keeps a record of the funds of the company, and sends all money, except that given for local purposes, to the conference or mission treasurer. The company cannot administer church discipline. Such matters must be referred to the conference committee and to the president, who is the elder of the conference church.

It is always hoped that the company will develop into a church; therefore its leadership has the duty of promoting the activities that are usually associated with regular churches.

COMPLEJO EDUCATIVO ADVENTISTA DE BOLIVIA. *See* Bolivia Adventist Education Center.

COMPLEJO EDUCATIVO ADVENTISTA UNION. *See* Union Adventist Educational Complex.

COMSTOCK, BELLE JESSIE (WOOD) (1880-1961). Physician, author. After teaching in public schools for seven years, she went to Battle Creek, Michigan, to study medicine. She married Dr. D. D. Comstock in 1907 and graduated in medicine at the University of Southern California in 1909. The Doctors Comstock spent seven years with the Glendale Sanitarium, where they initiated the visiting nurse organization and conducted health institutes. They were closely associated with the clinic of the medical school (now part of Loma Linda University). For more than 20 years Dr. Belle Comstock was in charge of the clinic in nutrition and endocrinology at the White Memorial Hospital.

She contributed many articles to health magazines, especially *Life and Health,* and wrote a number of books, including *All About the Baby, The Home Dietitian,* and *Physiology: The Human Body and How to Keep It in Health.* In collaboration with A. W. Spalding she wrote *The Days of Youth, Growing Boys and Girls,* and *Through Early Childhood.*

CONCEPCION ADVENTIST ACADEMY (Chile) (Colegio Adventista de Concepcion). A secondary educational institution located in Concepcion, Chile. Founded in 1942 as a primary school it was later expanded to include kindergarten. In 1982 all secondary grades were added. Secondary licensing was obtained in 1983.

Concepcion Adventist Academy operates in two areas of the city: the primary grades are taught at a location at Angol; secondary grades are taught at a location at Freire.

In 1992 the fiftieth anniversary of the school was celebrated. A total of 1,423 students in 1993 were distributed as follows: kindergarten, 56; elementary, 703; secondary, 664. There are 44 faculty members and 19 on the administrative staff.

Principals: Andrea de López, 1965-1966; Ruth Correa de Pozo, 1967-1973; George Araya Bishop, 1982-1987; Rolando Montoya Sierra, 1988- .

CONCEPCION ADVENTIST ACADEMY (Philippines). An educational institution begun in 1973 at Concepcion, Ilocos Sur, Philippines. It offers a complete national secondary program that admits graduates to institutions of higher learning. In 1993 the school had a staff and faculty of six.

Principals: Liwliwa L. Alawas, 1985-1986; Bernardo Castillo, 1986-1987; Imelda Estrada, 1987-1989; Mrs. Tomas Estrada, 1989-1992; Tomas Estrada, 1992- .

CONDITIONAL IMMORTALITY. *See* Death; Eternal Life; Immortality; Resurrection.

CONDITIONAL PROPHECY. *See* Israel, Prophecies Concerning; Bible, Interpretation of.

CONFERENCE. A term used variously in the Seventh-day Adventist Church. Most often the word, when used alone, refers to the unit of church administration called a *local conference,* in which a number of local churches are associated for administrative purposes *(see* Conference, [local]); it is also used for the area in which this organization operates. The term *conference* is used similarly of the *union conference* (or union), comprising several local conferences; also of the *General Conference,* comprising all the union organizations, and of its quinquennial session.

Among early SDAs the word was used loosely to describe "general meetings" (most often over a weekend) of local groups of churches or of individual members, led by one or more of the leading ministers for the purposes of strengthening the churches, reaching converts, or studying any problem of common interest (as, for example, the "Sabbath conferences" beginning in 1848). They even used the term *general conference* for sessions of that nature before there was any denominational organization; for example, those held in the 1850s at Battle Creek, Michigan, to which a general invitation was issued and to which a few came from outside the state.

CONFERENCE (local). A unit of Seventh-day Adventist Church organization composed of the local churches within a given area, such as a state. With other local conferences such a unit is a constituent member of a union conference. The conference officers are the president and the secretary-treasurer. The officers, together with the conference executive committee, form the administrative body.

Administration. The conference president is an ordained minister of experience and reputation, and is the ranking officer in the conference and in any of the churches within the conference at which the individual may be present. The president is at the head of the ministers in the conference and counsels in all their activities. A president has access to all the churches, their services and business meetings, and may preside over any of the meetings of the churches when it is deemed necessary. Although the president cannot set aside any of the duly elected officers of a church, they are bound to recognize this individual as the superior officer in the conference. The president is chair of the conference executive committee and of various other committees and boards, including boards of all conference institutions. The president is also a member of the union conference executive committee and the boards of union-operated institutions.

The conference secretary-treasurer is responsible for keeping the business records of the conference and for receiving and disbursing conference funds in harmony with conference policy or committee action. This individual also audits the books of the church treasurers within the conference, unless a regular auditor is appointed to that work.

Each conference has a legal association or corporation to carry on the financial transactions of the conference and to hold title to property. Church buildings and schools are held in the name of this legal association rather than in the name of the local church.

The executive committee (commonly referred to as the conference committee) is composed of from five to nine members and is elected at each regular session of the conference. The president is a member of the committee and is its chair. The ministry and the laity of the conference are also usually represented on the committee.

The conference issues credentials, licenses, and certificates to the various types of conference employees. *(See* Credentials, Licenses, Certificates.) It also directs the activities of the several departments. Its officers are also the officers of the conference church. It operates conference institutions, such as secondary schools, sanitariums, and hospitals, and subsidizes schools and church building projects. It pays the salaries of evangelists, local pastors (appointed to their churches by the conference committee), and Bible instructors *(see* Financial Policies). In cooperation with the local church school boards, it assigns elementary school teachers to these schools. (Most conferences receive the tuition collected by the churches and pay the church school teachers.)

Departments. The conference fosters various lines of denominational work among the churches through departments, at the head of which are directors or vice presidents, elected to their office at the biennial session of the conference and working under the direction of the conference committee. These directors do not have administrative authority; their relation to the field is advisory on matters that affect their own departments, unless otherwise requested by the conference president. While departmental directors are under the direction of the president and the executive committee, they also cooperate with the union departments, which in turn sustain a similar relation to the division or General Conference departments. *See* names of specific departments.

Sessions. A conference meets in session every two years, with delegates from the various churches represented. Such a session elects officers and the conference executive committee; receives new churches; hears reports on the work in the conference during the term then closing from the president, secretary-treasurer, and heads of conference departments; appoints the standing committees for the session; and acts on the recommendations of these committees.

The committee on nominations, with the union conference president (or one who has been designated by that individual) as chair and a General Conference representative meeting with it, recommends names for the officers, the departmental director, the executive committee, and institutional boards for the next biennial term. The committee on credentials and licenses makes recommendations on the renewing or issuing of credentials and licenses to conference workers. The committee on constitution and bylaws suggests changes in the constitution and bylaws. The plans committee studies and presents plans and policies for the promotion of the work of the conference during the ensuing term.

In addition, reports are presented to the delegates from the officers and departmental secretaries on the work in their charge.

Delegates to the conference session are elected by the churches on the basis of one delegate for each church and an additional delegate for a specified number of church members, as provided for by the constitution. There are no appointed or ex officio delegates.

Delegates are chosen to represent not only their church but the entire conference; hence it is not permissible for delegates to attempt to organize voting in blocs.

Under the present system a new conference is organized by the union conference, with the sanction of the division. For a history of the development of the local conference in the SDA denomination, *see* Organization. For other units of organization also composed of local churches, *see* District, Field, Mission, Section, Station.

CONFERENCE CHURCH. A church organization composed of scattered baptized members in a conference who do not live near enough to a local church to belong to it. The officers of this church are the officers of the conference. However, these conference officers have their membership in the church of the locality where they reside. The conference committee functions as the board of the conference church and the president as the church elder. It is not intended that aged or infirm or other persons who live near a local church but who are unable to attend its service should join the conference church, since it is considered the privilege of the local church to minister to them.

CONFERENCE COMMITTEE. *See* Conference (local).

CONFÉRENCE DES ÉGLISES ADVENTISTAS DU SEPTIÈME JOUR DU

QUEBEC. *See* Quebec Seventh-day Adventist Church Conference.

CONFERENCE DIRECTORIES. *See* Directories.

CONGO. An independent African state (capital, Brazzaville), which received its independence on Aug. 15, 1960. Congo is not to be confused with Zaïre, formerly also named Congo (capital, Kinshasa), which adjoins it on the south and east. Elsewhere it is bounded on the south also by Angola, on the north by Cameroon and the Central African Republic, and on the west by Gabon. It has an area of 132,046 square miles (342,000 square kilometers) and a population (1994) of 2.4 million, mainly Kongo. About 47 percent of the people are animists, and another 47 percent are Christians. The majority are engaged in agriculture, although important industries are developing. French is the official language.

The territory of Congo comprises the Republic of Congo Mission Station, a part of the Central African Union Mission, which in turn is a part of the Africa-Indian Ocean Division. In July 1972 Jean Kempf and his family were sent to Brazzaville to open the work in this country. Before this a young Congolese worker had begun to work in Brazzaville and had raised up a group of interested people. In 1978 the work in Congo was closed. Then in 1991 the church was reorganized by Gary Wagner. In 1993, in spite of many difficulties, there were 32 members.

CONGREGATION. Literally, a gathering; in common Protestant usage (a) a group of people gathered for worship and religious instruction, the group of people who habitually so gather; (b) in some countries the organized local unit of any denomination other than the state church or churches.

In sense (a) a *congregation* is thought of in contrast with a secular *audience:* a minister addresses the congregation in a service in the church, but speaks to an audience in a public lecture on religious liberty, or possibly to an audience of miscellaneous listeners in an evangelistic tabernacle. In sense (b) *congregation* is an organization of the "sect" type, in contrast with a "church"; for example, in Germany or Scandinavia one attends or joins a Catholic or a Lutheran church, but a Baptist, Methodist, or Seventh-day Adventist congregation.

CONLEY, ANNIE CHARLOTTE (1891-1990). Nurse, midwife. She was born in New South Wales, Australia, into the family of John and Charlotte Pocock. Her parents accepted the Seventh-day Adventist message under the ministry of Robert Hare and David Steed in Parramatta during 1892. In hard times Ellen White helped the Pocock family, and while Avondale College was being built, John stayed for some months in the White home. As a child Annie sometimes accompanied Mrs. White on visits in her horse-drawn vehicle, and she used to gather maidenhair fern for Mrs. White's table.

In 1911 Annie began the nursing course at Sydney Sanitarium and Hospital (now Sydney Adventist Hospital). After graduation she gained experience in Warburton, Victoria, and then established the Pine Hill Private Hospital near Avondale College. More than 1,000 children were born in her hospital or in their homes with the help of Annie's midwifery skills. Annie married Robert Conley on Oct. 12, 1926. Four children were born to this union.

CONNECTICUT. *See* Northeastern Conference; Southern New England Conference.

CONNERLY, BRENTON ERNEST (1869-1937). Pioneer worker in the Inter-American Division. As a young man he went to Colorado in search of fortune in the gold mines. While there he met a Seventh-day Adventist minister, accepted the SDA faith, joined the church by baptism, and entered the colporteur work. In 1900 he married Lillian Snyder, of the Chicago city mission. After his ordination several years later he worked first in Puerto Rico and then in Panama. He was the first SDA minister to work in Colombia. In 1919 he returned to the United States after 17 years of service in Latin America. For the next 18 years he pastored churches and preached in the Potomac Conference.

CONRADI, LOUIS RICHARD (1856-1939). Evangelist and administrator; in his last years a Seventh Day Baptist minister. Born in Karlsruhe, Germany, he began studies leading to the Roman Catholic priesthood, but migrated to America at the age of 17. After working at various jobs, he found employment clearing land on the farm of a Methodist merchant in Iowa. He was converted in 1878 to the Seventh-day Adventist faith in the home of James Burton, a farmer, where he boarded.

Applying himself diligently to his studies, he completed the four-year course at Battle Creek College in one third the usual time, at the same time working as a typesetter. He worked with energy for the German-speaking people of the Middle West and in 1882 was ordained.

In 1886 the General Conference sent him to work in Europe, with his headquarters in Switzerland. From there he traveled extensively in Russia and Germany. On an evangelistic journey to the Crimea the same year, he was accused of teaching Jewish heresy and was imprisoned for 40 days. After the General Conference session of 1888, he went in 1889 with a group of associates to work in Hamburg, Germany, where he made his home for the rest of his life. In 1891 Germany and Russia were separated from the Central European Conference and placed under the direction of Conradi. He became the first chairman of the General European Conference in 1901, and also vice president of the General Conference in 1903; he remained head of the work in Europe (later as president of the European Division) until 1922.

He traveled widely over Europe and visited Russia several times. He was often pursued by the police, but was never again arrested, although he was expelled from Romania, Turkey, and Hungary. He made repeated visits to Africa and the Middle East.

In 1909 and 1914 he traveled extensively in South America, where new conferences were being organized, and in 1926 he was invited to tour the Far East, where he fell seriously ill, but recovered.

His written works include a revision and enlargement of J. N. Andrews' *History of the Sabbath* and his own expositions (in German) of the books of Daniel and the Revelation, which were translated into several languages, also *The Impelling Force of Prophetic Truth,* and numerous pamphlets and articles including, through the years, many graphic reports of his missionary journeys published in the *Review and Herald.*

In 1932, at the age of 76, he separated from the Seventh-day Adventist Church and became a minister for the Seventh Day Baptists.

CONSCIENCE ET LIBERTÉ ("Conscience and Liberty," 1971-   ; twice yearly). A French magazine published by Vie et Santé, Dammarie-les-Lys, France. Three numbers were published in 1948 and 1949, edited by Dr. Jean Nussbaum. The magazine contains 128 pages and has a circulation of 8,500. It contains studies, documents, précis, and information concerning religious liberty around the world, and is the organ of the International Association for the Defense of Religious Liberty.

Editors: Pierre Lanarès, 1971-1982; Gianfranco Rossi, 1984- .

CONSCIENTIOUS OBJECTOR. *See* Noncombatancy.

CONSTITUTION. *See* General Conference Constitution and Bylaws.

CONVERSION. A supernatural transformation of the mind, affections, and life that restores the freedom, self-control, and spiritual union with God that were lost as a result of sin.

Conversion involves contrition and confession, that is, a recognition and acknowledgment of oneself as a sinner in need of forgiveness. It also involves an unconditional decision to reorient one's will, aims, and life to conform with the will of God, a corresponding effort to that end, and a willing dependence upon God for the necessities of life and eventually for the complete restoration of all that was lost as a result of sin.

A personal experience of conversion is essential to salvation. The Bible describes this experience by a variety of figurative expressions that call attention to various aspects of what is, in fact, a complex subjective (internal) experience accompanied by important objective (external) effects. It is described, on the one hand, as something a person does: a *turning* from one mode of life to another (Matt. 18:3; Acts 3:19; 11:21; 14:15; 26:18), a *repentance,* or change of mind (Acts 2:38; 3:19; 2 Cor. 7:9, 10). But it is also described as something done to or for a person: a *rebirth* (John 1:12, 13; 3:3-7; 1 Peter 1:3, 23; 2:2; 1 John 5:18), a *creation* (Gal. 6:15; Eph. 2:10; 4:24), a *resurrection* from spiritual death (Eph. 2:1, 5, 6; cf. Col. 2:12, 13), a *washing,* or *cleansing,* from sin (Titus 3:5; 2 Peter 1:9), and an *implanting* of a new system of values (Eze. 36:26; Jer. 31:33; Heb. 8:10). It is an experience of the mind, or "heart": a *coming to know* God or religious truth (John 8:32; 17:3; Col. 3:10), a *renewal* of the mind (Eph. 4:23; cf. Rom. 12:2). It produces a *new nature* (Eph. 4:24; Col. 3:10), and marks the beginning of a new life *in Christ* (2 Cor. 5:17).

The precise form conversion may take varies from one individual to another, as determined by such factors as one's temperament, psychological maturity, intellectual capacity, external circumstances, degree of behavioral change required, and cultural background. Accordingly, no particular pattern of experience may be considered normative, either as to duration or depth of emotional involvement.

Conversion presupposes, as a minimum, awareness of (1) God's existence and His involvement in human affairs, (2) the distinction between moral right and wrong, and (3) the need for external help. There can be no self-surrender where there is no sense of need and dependence. Early religious training and direct contact with the revealed Word and with human witnesses are not necessarily essential to conversion, for it has occurred when none of these was present; so long as the mind is free to exercise genuine volition, environmental factors cannot prevent conversion. The function of these external factors is to encourage the human response to the call of God's Spirit. The mission of the church is to increase the number, frequency, and intensity of these contributing factors.

Conversion marks the beginning of a continuing operation of the Holy Spirit in a process of spiritual growth. This growth consists of an improved understanding of God's will and the gradual elimination of residual tendencies to sin.

Evidence of genuine conversion is both subjective and objective. The subjective evidence that conversion has occurred includes consciousness of love for, and trust in, God, awareness of the supreme importance of religious and spiritual values, and enjoyment of Bible reading, prayer, and worship. Absence of the objective evidence—continuing growth toward perfection in Jesus Christ—is conclusive proof that genuine conversion has not occurred.

Conversion consists essentially in a transformation of the mind, of a man's attitude, and through the mind, of the entire life.

"The leaven of truth works secretly, silently, steadily, to transform the soul. The natural inclinations are softened and subdued. New thoughts, new feelings, new motives, are implanted. A new standard of character is set up—the life of Christ. The mind is changed; the faculties are roused to action in new lines. Man is not endowed with new faculties, but the faculties he has are sanctified. The conscience is awakened. We are endowed with traits of character that enable us to do service for God" (COL 98, 99).

Conversion begins with a reorientation of the mind to the will of Christ, and starts a person on the pathway that leads to a complete restoration, through the grace of Christ, of the divine character, which was lost when Adam sinned.

See also Justification; New Birth; Sin.

COOK ISLANDS. An archipelago lying in the south, central part of the Pacific Ocean, 1,800 miles (2,900 kilometers) northeast of New Zealand. It covers only 93 square miles (241 square kilometers), even though the islands are scattered over more than 620 miles (1,000 kilometers) from north to south. The northern group are coral atolls and include Manihiki, Nassau, Penrhyn, Pukapuka, and Rakahanga, while the southern islands are volcanic hills and include Aitutaki, Atiu, Mangaia, Mauke, Mitiaro, and Rarotonga, on which is located the capital of Avarua. The fertile soil of these southern islands produces an abundance of vegetables and tropical fruits that are at times exported by air to New Zealand. The climate is mild, and the islands and atolls support 18,552 people (1991), most of whom are brown-skinned Polynesians. Half this number live on the main island of Rarotonga. The southern islands are a popular tourist destination, and the people are known for their friendliness and hospitality.

In 1773 Capt. James Cook reached the southern islands, and in 1888 Britain took control until 1901, when administrative control passed to New Zealand. A new constitution gave the islanders authority over their internal affairs in 1965, with New Zealand retaining responsibility for defense and foreign affairs. Sir Albert Henry became the first prime minister in 1965, followed by Sir Thomas Davis in 1976. The prime minister in 1993 was Sir Geoffrey Henry. The country retains a queen's representative, Apinera Short (1993).

Christianity first came to the island of Aitutaki through two Raiatean teachers, Papeiha and Vahapata, who had been stationed there by John Williams in 1821. In 1823 two teachers from Tahaa were settled on the islands of Mitiaro and Mauke, and Papeiha introduced Christianity on Rarotonga. To assist these London Missionary Society national missionaries, Charles Pitman came from England in 1827. Henry Royal served on Aitutaki from 1839 to 1876. Pitman, Aaron Buzacott (1828), and Ta'unga contributed to the translation of the Bible into the Rarotongan language.

Seventh-day Adventist Statistics. The islands of the Cook group comprise the Cook Islands Mission, a section of the Central Pacific Union Mission, which in turn is a part of the South Pacific Division. Statistics (1992) for *Cook Islands:* churches, 15; members, 850; church schools, 3; ordained ministers, 6; licensed ministers, 4; teachers, 10. Headquarters of Cook Islands Mission: Titikaveka, Rarotonga, Cook Islands.

Institutions. Papaaroa College.

Seventh-day Adventist Work. On its first voyage the *Pitcairn* visited the islands of Mangaia, Rarotonga, and Aitutaki in April 1891. On Rarotonga books were sold by the Reads and the McCoys, with Francis Nicholas (Waugh), secretary to the islands' administrator making a purchase that eventually led to her acceptance of the SDA message. On the *Pitcairn's* third voyage, Dr. James Caldwell, Maude Young from Pitcairn Island, Dudley Owen, Mr. Wellman, and Lillian White were left on Rarotonga in June 1894. These self-supporting missionaries engaged in medical and educational (government) activities. J. D. Rice arrived on the *Pitcairn* in mid-1895, and taught in government schools. The first two Maori converts were baptized in April 1898.

Two Christmas days were observed in 1899 by order of the government, to enable the Cook Islands to correctly observe Western Hemisphere day sequence, as early missionaries hadn't made any day change on crossing the 180° meridian on their voyages eastward from Europe. Many Cook Islanders were reluctant to accept the change from Saturday to Sunday for their day of worship, and it took the threat of loss of land tenure to persuade them to keep the new day. For 75 years they had worshiped on the seventh-day Sabbath. Before the end of 1900 Edward Gates baptized 18 people at Titikaveka on Rarotonga, as some had still refused to keep the new day and had asked SDA missionaries to teach them Bible truth on the Sabbath. Some suffered for their stand, being fined and made to work on the roads. A. H. Piper, the first Avondale-trained missionary to enter service in the Pacific islands, arrived on Rarotonga on Oct. 31, 1900.

More Australian missionaries were added to teach school at Arorangi and Titikaveka: Evelyn Gooding, 1902-1905, and Mark Carey, 1906-1907. The first church building, erected by Piper and his supporters in Titikaveka, was dedicated by newly arrived missionary Griffiths Jones on May 23, 1904. George Sterling commenced work on Aitutaki island in 1912, and conducted the first baptism there in 1913. The first converts in the northern islands were made on Pukapuka in 1919.

In 1916 the Cook Islands became a section of the newly established Eastern Polynesian Mission, and remained in this organization until 1923, when they became a separate mission. In 1948 the mission became a part of the Central Pacific Union Mission.

COOK ISLANDS MISSION. *See* Cook Islands; South Pacific Division.

COOK ISLANDS MISSIONARY SCHOOL. *See* Papaaroa College.

COOK, J. B. (1804-1874). Baptist minister, Millerite preacher, and editor. After the disappointment in 1844 he joined J. D. Pickands in publishing a small sheet, the *Voice of the Fourth Angel,* at Cleveland, Ohio. For a time he held a "shut door" view. In 1846, in his paper the *Advent Testimony,* and in O.R.L. Crosier's *Day-Dawn,* he advocated the seventh-day Sabbath. However, by 1849 he was teaching that the Sabbath was not for Christians, but was a type of the millennial sabbath. He wrote extensively against the Sabbatarians in Joseph Marsh's *Advent Harbinger.* Some of his earlier writings were reprinted by Seventh-day Adventists, for example, in the second issue of the *Advent Review* 1:7-16, August 1850; and in the *Review and Herald* 2:4, Aug. 5, 1851; 2:97, Mar. 2, 1852.

COOKERY. *See* Diet; Health Evangelism.

COOPER, ALFRED (1867-1945). One of the pioneer Seventh-day Adventist workers in Mexico. He was born in England but later lived in the United States. After working as a colporteur for a while, he studied at Battle Creek College. In 1893 he married Lillian Froom, who had been a Bible instructor in the Illinois Conference. The two completed a nursing course at Battle Creek, then joined the first group of SDA workers in Mexico and helped to open a mission at Guadalajara; he, by assisting in the medical work, and his wife, by teaching the mission school. In 1898 they went to Mexico City, where they taught nursing at a government hospital for a while. In 1904 Lillian Cooper died. Later Cooper engaged in self-supporting work in Mexico, and operated a cannery at Mexico City. He died in California in his seventy-ninth year.

COOPER MEMORIAL HOSPITAL. *See* Seventh-day Adventist Cooper Memorial Hospital.

COPENHAGEN BIBLE SCHOOL. *See* Danish Junior College.

COPENHAGEN FOOD COMPANY. *See* Nutana.

COPENHAGEN PUBLISHING HOUSE. *See* Danish Publishing House.

COPPERBELT ZAMBIA FIELD. *See* Eastern Africa Division; Zambia.

COPTIC ADVENTIST DENOMINATION IN EGYPT. *See* Egypt, Arab Republic of.

COPTIC ADVENTIST THEOLOGICAL SEMINARY. *See* Nile Union Academy.

CORAL SEA UNION MISSION BIBLE WORKERS' TRAINING SCHOOL. *See* Papua New Guinea Union Mission Bible Workers' Training School.

CORAL SEA UNION MISSION COLLEGE (New Britain). *See* Kambubu Adventist High School.

CORAL SEA UNION MISSION COLLEGE (Papua New Guinea). *See* Kabiufa Adventist High School.

CORLISS, JOHN ORR (1845-1923). Evangelist, missionary. Left fatherless at 5, young Corliss developed an independent mind that later helped him in his pioneering work. At 16 he became a sailor and saw service in the Civil War. In 1866 he became a Freewill Baptist and in 1868 a Seventh-day Adventist, having lived with the James Whites for some time, and having been tutored in SDA beliefs by Joseph Bates.

In 1868 he became superintendent and chaplain of the Western Health Reform Institute at Battle Creek, Michigan. He engaged in public evangelism in Michigan (1871-1875, 1881-1883) and in Maine (1875). He pioneered SDA work in Virginia (1876 and 1877), in Colorado (1879), and in California (1884).

With S. N. Haskell and others he pioneered SDA work in Australia (1885-1887). Against considerable opposition, his evangelistic campaigns in Melbourne, Adelaide, and other cities won many converts, chiefly from the professional and business classes, including an unusually large number of entire families. In 1886 he became one of the managing editors of the *Bible Echo,* supporting the journal largely from his private means. Because of poor health he returned to California, where he engaged in editorial and religious liberty work (1887-1893); then he went again to Australia for another term of service (1893-1896).

Corliss and A. T. Jones were the first SDAs to appear before legislatures to plead the cause of separation of church and state. In 1889, as a member of a General Conference press committee, Corliss appeared before a Senate Committee on Education and Labor that was considering Sunday rest legislation. When he came before a committee of the Arkansas legislature, he was credited with bringing about the defeat of a bill to repeal a clause exempting Sabbathkeepers.

He served for a period as Bible teacher for the Battle Creek Sanitarium nurses' and medical classes (1897-1898), and in ministerial work in Canada (1898-1899). Then he worked in California until near the time of his death, with the exception of a term spent in England in school and evangelistic work (1902-1904). Having inherited some private means, he used it largely in paying tuition for young students attending SDA schools and in supporting other church enterprises.

CORNELL, MERRITT E. (1827-1893). Pioneer evangelist on the Pacific Coast. A former Millerite, and then a member of the *Advent Harbinger* group who taught the "age to come" doctrine *(see Messenger* Party), he was won to the Sabbatarian Adventists by Joseph Bates in 1852, and immediately set out with great energy to proclaim his new faith. At Battle Creek, Michigan, in 1854 he and Loughborough conducted the first Adventist meetings held in a tent.

His wife, Angeline, worked with him, sometimes remaining to instruct further those who had become interested in the meetings, while her husband went on to the next place. In a sense she was the forerunner of today's Bible instructors.

In 1871 Cornell worked with Loughborough in the first Seventh-day Adventist tent meetings in San Francisco, California, and in 1874 with Canright in Oakland. In 1875 he gave a series of lectures in Dallas, Texas.

Shortly after this, in 1876, he was disconnected from the organized work of the church, although he did some freelance preaching for several years. Then after some years of isolation he returned to Michigan from Maryland in 1889. A reconciliation was effected, and he again served in the ministry from 1890 until his death.

CORONELLA RETIREMENT VILLAGE/NURSING HOMES. Centers for the aged, owned and operated by the Victoria Conference of Seventh-day Adventists. In 1952 homes for the aged in the Victorian Conference had been established at Croydon and were known as Coronella Homes for the Aged, "Coronella" being the name of the guest house purchased to form the nucleus of the venture. On Jan. 19, 1958, the first units were opened at Nunawading, Victoria, Australia, adjoining the Victorian Conference campground. Additional units have been added as finances, including government subsidy, permitted. In 1993 each institution was operating in its own right, with a separate board of management. However, they operate under a single constitution and are answerable to the Victorian Conference. Some details of each of these retirement villages follow.

Alawara Retirement Village, Bendigo. Began with 20 units in 1976. In 1993 there were 20 single bedroom units, a 35-bed hostel, and an activity center. It had 56 residents.

Coronella Retirement Village, Nunawading. In 1993 Nunawading cared for 27 residents in a nursing home, 64 in a hostel, and 45 in 32 units (16 double and 16 single). Ladies' auxiliaries provide valuable aid.

Fernleigh Retirement Village, Ballarat. The homes in Ballarat began to be occupied as they were completed early in 1968. In 1993 there were 10 units with 10 residents.

Mountain View Retirement Village. The village, situated just below the Warburton Hospital, in 1993 had 10 one-bedroom self-care units with 13 residents and a 50-bed hostel.

These institutions are largely self-supporting.

CORPORACION UNIVERSITARIA ADVENTISTA. *See* Colombia Adventist University.

CORPORATIONS. Legally incorporated entities formed for the transaction of such legal and fiscal matters of the denomination as require corporate agents under the various laws of the places where the church might have its material interests. For example, corporations have been formed to hold real estate and other church assets, and to operate medical, educational, manufacturing, charitable, custodial, and evangelistic enterprises. In some countries incorporation of church bodies is a prerequisite to conducting any public activity.

In the United States and in many other places, the church itself is not an incorporated body, and neither are its ecclesiastical administrative organs (such as conferences, unions, and other such subdivisions). Instead, parallel to the ecclesiastical organization are legal corporations on the conference, union, and General Conference levels that transact the necessary legal business on behalf of the respective denominational units. The membership (constituency) of the corporation usually is the executive committee on the corresponding denominational unit or the delegates to the sessions of that unit. The officers of both entities are often the same persons.

In the Seventh-day Adventist Church the church edifices and real estate are not held in the name of individual congregations, and the holding of properties by trustees is discountenanced. Instead, local church properties are held by the conference corporations.

Most of the institutional activities of the church are conducted by separate, local corporations, and the board chair of each institution is usually the president of the respective church organizational unit. In ordinary usage an institution is referred to as being owned by a certain conference or union conference, but the actual ownership is vested in the corporation that is controlled by or affiliated with that conference or union conference.

On the General Conference level the 1993 *Yearbook* listed the following corporations or associations: Adventist Development and Relief Agency International (ADRA); Adventist Health System/Loma Linda, Inc.; Adventist Historic Properties, Inc.; Chan Shun International Foundation; Christian Record Services, Inc.; Ellen G. White Estate, Inc.; General Conference Corporation of Seventh-day Adventists; Gencon Insurance Service, Inc.; Gencon Insurance Company of Vermont; Gencon Financial Services, Inc.; Harris Foundation; Seventh-day Adventist Radio, Television, and Film Center (Adventist Media Center).

CORRESPONDENCE SCHOOLS. *See*

Bible Correspondence Schools; Home Study International.

CORSICA. *See* Euro-Africa Division; France.

COSMETICS. *See* Dress.

COSSENTINE, ERWIN EARL (1896-1984). Pioneer educator. Born in Minnesota, he helped to establish Eastern New York Academy (now Union Springs Academy). He also served as educational and MV secretary of the Carolina and Georgia conferences. He was called to serve overseas as principal of New Zealand Missionary College and president of Avondale, La Sierra, and Union colleges. For 20 years he was secretary of the General Conference Education Department.

COSTA RICA. A Central American republic, bounded on the north by Nicaragua, on the northeast by the Caribbean Sea, on the southeast by Panama, and on the southwest and west by the Pacific Ocean. It has an area of 19,575 square miles (50,699 square kilometers) and a population (1994) of 3.3 million. The inhabitants of Costa Rica are predominantly of Spanish ancestry, with a minority of Blacks and a few small, dwindling Indian tribes. The principal exports include coffee, bananas, and ornamental plants. The state religion is Roman Catholicism, but there are (1993) some 1 million Protestants of different denominations.

Seventh-day Adventist Statistics. The territory of Costa Rica constitutes the Costa Rica Mission, which is a part of the Central American Union Mission, which in turn is a part of the Inter-American Division. Statistics (1993) for *Costa Rica:* churches, 63; members, 17,333; church or elementary schools, 7; ordained ministers, 14; licensed ministers, 9; teachers, 36. Costa Rica Mission headquarters are at San José. The Seventh-day Adventist Church is the largest non-Catholic church group in Costa Rica.

Institutions. Central American Adventist University; Costa Rica Secondary School (Limón); Costa Rica Secondary School (San José).

Development of Seventh-day Adventist Work. For several years about the turn of the century, F. J. Hutchins, pioneer SDA missionary in Central America, made frequent visits to Costa Rica in the missionary schooner the *Herald,* and began work in Limón. About 1902 H. Louie Mignott, C. N. Moulton, and two other colporteurs named Horton and Brooks worked there. In 1903 I. G. Knight, who succeeded Hutchins, reported in the *Review and Herald* (80:15, Dec. 3, 1903) 10 baptisms and the organization of a church of 26, presumably at Pacuarito, some distance from Limón. The reports in the *Review and Herald* indicated that by 1906 there were several churches in the country and that a worker, T. M. Brown, was doing evangelistic work in San José, the capital city.

The first primary school was established at Limón in 1921, with D. P. Abbott as teacher. A secondary school, which later developed into Univeridad Adventista de Centro America (Central American University), was opened in October 1927, with G. S. Ray as the first principal. Also in 1927 SDA work in the republics of Costa Rica and Nicaragua, until then included in the West Caribbean Conference, was organized as the Costa Rica-Nicaragua Mission, a part of the Central American Union, with the officers of the union serving as administrators. There were eight churches and 216 members in the mission by the end of that year. In 1928 the work in Costa Rica became a separate mission with four churches and 148 members.

In 1973 a seven-acre (three-hectare) tract was obtained in Hatillo, a suburb of the capital, and construction began on an elementary school/evangelistic center complex. The following year the first buildings were started for a youth camp located on a 45-acre (18-hectare) site near Orotina.

COSTA RICA MISSION. *See* Costa Rica; Inter-American Division.

COSTA RICA SECONDARY SCHOOL (Limón) (Centro Educativo Adventista de Limón). An educational institution operated by the Costa Rica Mission in Limón, Costa Rica. It was established in 1984.

Principals: Verna Clark, 1988-1989; Carolin Dodd, 1989-1990; Faye Patterson, 1990- .

COSTA RICA SECONDARY SCHOOL (San José) (Centro Educativo Adventista de Costa Rica). A K-12 institution operated by the Costa Rica Mission in the heart of the capital city of San José.

In November 1974 the first classroom building with three rooms was inaugurated by R. H. Pierson, then president of the General Conference. In 1975 classes started at the elementary level with a total of 13 students and three teachers. The institution began under the name of Escuela Adventista de Hatillo.

Later junior high was added, and the enrollment increased to 339 students and seven teachers. In March 1984 grades 10 and 11 were added. The first graduation was held in that year, with a class of 12. Also, in 1984 the school was approved by the Ministry of Public Education to operate as a government-recognized institution under the name of Centro Educativo Adventista de Costa Rica.

In 1993, 472 students were enrolled on all levels. The staff includes 25 instructors, a chaplain, an adviser, a secretary, and an accountant-cashier.

Besides the academic program approved by the government, Costa Rica Secondary School offers English, Bible, and computer classes, the latter begun in 1993 in both the elementary and high school programs. The classrooms are distributed in four buildings covering a total area of more than 107,600 square feet (10,000 square meters).

Principals: Floribeth Moreira, 1975; Luisa Carr, 1976; Rodrigo Burgos, 1977-1981; Marjorie Carmona, 1982-1983; Verna Clark, 1984; Ivanhoe Sanchez, 1985; Eduardo Barr, 1986- .

CÔTE D'IVOIRE. A West African republic, which received independence on Aug. 7, 1960, but retained close ties with France. It has an area of 124,503 square miles (322,463 square kilometers), and a population (1994) of 14.3 million. The country (formerly known as the Ivory Coast) is bounded on the west by Liberia and Guinea, on the south by the Gulf of Guinea, on the north by Mali and Burkina Faso, and on the east by Ghana Agriculture is the chief occupation of the people, with yams, manioc, bananas, maize, rice, and millet the principal crops. The chief exports are coffee, cocoa, bananas, pineapple, and timber. The country has long been famous for its gracefully carved figurines made from elephant tusks, which gave this area its name. The majority of the people are animists.

Seventh-day Adventist Statistics. The territory of Côte d'Ivoire comprises the Côte D'Ivoire Mission, which is part of the Sahel Union Mission, which in turn is part of the Africa-Indian Ocean Division. Statistics (1992) for *Côte d'Ivoire:* churches, 31; members, 3,096; church or elementary schools, 5; secondary schools, 1; ordained ministers, 8; licensed ministers, 7; primary school teachers, 25; secondary school teachers, 41. Headquarters for the mission are at Abidjan.

Institutions. Bouake Adventist Secondary School.

Development of Seventh-day Adventist Work. The first SDAs to enter the Ivory Coast were two traders named Bley and Essien, who came from Ghana. Sometime after 1920, these two men settled at Tiemelekro and established a company of adherents. About the same time, Joseph Kouamé Djouman and Pierre Kouamé Adingrah, who were members of the Dida tribe of the southern part of the Ivory Coast, and who went to Ghana to learn to grow cocoa, met some Adventists there, accepted their doctrines, and returned to their home village preaching their newly discovered faith.

When the officers of the Ghana Mission heard about the interested companies in the Ivory Coast, they sent a national worker, J. K. Garbrah, to visit them. As a result of this visit, six persons later were baptized at Agbahou.

From 1937 until World War II, except for a visit made by Jesse Clifford, the president of the Ghana Mission, SDAs in the Ivory Coast had contact with the denomination only through the paper *Les Signes des Temps,* published in France.

The first national workers in the Ivory Coast were two young men, Felix Donkor and John Zakka, who were sent to Ghana to study. The work was organized in 1946 when the first foreign missionaries, G. M. Ellstrom and J. L. Jespersen came from the United States. When they arrived with their families, they were housed for several years in army surplus beach huts until they were given permission to purchase land and construct permanent houses. In 1953 the first national colporteur, Jacob Gbessin, started work. In the same year J. R. Buzenet, from France, and a converted Senegalese Muslim, Bah Amadou, opened a primary school in Bouake. A secondary school soon followed.

CÔTE D'IVOIRE MISSION. *See* Africa-Indian Ocean Division; Côte d'Ivoire.

COTTRELL, HAMPTON WATSON (1852-1940). Evangelist, administrator. After attending Battle Creek College, he engaged in business (1877-1885), and then opened a city mission in Cleveland, Ohio. Then for three years he was superintendent of the Maritime Mission (Canada), for two years, an evangelist in New England, and for five years, president of the

Atlantic Union Conference. During that period, he also represented the General Conference at numerous meetings in Europe, and assisted in the removal of the denominational headquarters to Washington, D.C. Following this, he was president of the Pacific Union (1905-1910), the Western Oregon Conference (1912-1922), and the North Pacific Union (1922-1923). Because of serious illness, he was forced in 1925 to take up less active work.

COTTRELL, ROSWELL F. (1814-1892). One of the early Adventists; writer, poet, minister. He descended from the Huguenots and was born in a Seventh Day Baptist family in the state of New York. Through reading the *Review and Herald* some time about 1851 and comparing its message with the Scriptures, he was led to join the developing group of Seventh-day Adventists and immediately began to contribute his talents as a writer and poet to the propagation of the faith that he had espoused. He wrote one of the earlier (1854) series of Bible lessons for the young people that was published in the *Youth's Instructor*. In 1855 these lessons were bound together into a book that served as a guide to biblical study among the churches for several years afterward. After the publication office of the *Review and Herald* was moved to Battle Creek in 1855, he served as a member of the editorial committee. As a minister he worked with J. N. Loughborough and W. S. Ingraham in New York and Pennsylvania. At the time of the organization of the denomination, he was among those opposed to a formal structure, and expressed his views through several mildly worded communications published in the *Review and Herald* that provoked heated rejoinders from James White. In the end he accepted the organization and continued through the years, almost to his death, actively working for the church. A number of his poems have been set to music, and three of them appeared in the *Church Hymnal*.

COTTRELL, ROY F. (1878-1970). Missionary, author, pastor. He was born in New York state into a family of Adventist pioneers. In 1902 he married Myrtie Ball, and six years later they sailed for China, where he served until 1920. During those years he wrote 10 books that were published in the Mandarin language. After returning to the United States, he continued to write, authoring 15 books and booklets, eight series of Sabbath school lessons, and hundreds of articles that appeared in church journals. During his later years he served as a pastor in the Southern California Conference. He gave 60 years of devoted service to the church.

COURVILLE, CYRIL BRIAN (1900-1968). Neuropathologist, teacher, author, founder of medical institutions. He was a native of Michigan and received his early education at Cedar Lake Academy and Emmanuel Missionary College. After completing his medical training at the College of Medical Evangelists, he took a three-year course in neuropathology, neurology, and neurosurgery, and returned to teach at his alma mater. He wrote nearly a score of books, one of which is the standard textbook on neuropathology. In 1934 he founded the Cajal Laboratory of Neuropathology and later helped with the organization of the Medical Cadet Corps. With fellow faculty members, he founded the forty-seventh General Hospital Unit, which served in New Guinea and the Philippines during World War II.

A physician at Johns Hopkins University referred to Dr. Courville as "the world's greatest neuropathologist." At the time of his death he was still serving on the faculty of Loma Linda University.

COVENANT. In Scripture, a term usually referring to the various agreements into which God has, from time to time, entered with individuals—Noah, Abraham, and Israel, for example. Jeremiah and the writer of Hebrews also speak of a "new covenant" God promised to make with His people (Jer. 31:31-33; Heb. 8:8-13).

A human covenant may be either a mutual agreement between equals who share in formulating its terms or one imposed by a superior upon an inferior. The parties to a divine-human covenant are not equals. The purpose and conditions of such a covenant are determined by God and voluntarily accepted by human beings. All covenants between God and humanity are based on the principle that obedience to the will of God means life; disobedience brings death. This was true before sin entered; it is true now. Because of the fallen nature inherited from Adam, men and women cannot render perfect obedience to the will of God by their own power. The covenants made with humanity since the Fall are designed to meet men and women in their fallen condition so as to enable them to achieve the obedience required of them through faith in Christ. The purpose and terms are basically the same in each divine-human covenant, but the form of statement and the mode of operation may vary according to the historical circumstances. From God's point of view there has ever been only one such agreement—the "everlasting covenant." But from humanity's point of view there seem to have been a number of covenants. This is because of the dissimilarity of the outward forms.

God's covenant with Abraham at the time of his migration to Palestine included the promise that his posterity would become a great nation, and appointed the patriarch an ally of Heaven in the task of bringing a knowledge of salvation to all men (Gen. 12:1-3). This covenant was formalized a few years later, as recorded in Gen. 15. At Mount Sinai Abraham's descendants voluntarily accepted God as their ruler, and their role as the chosen people (Ex. 19:5-8; 24:5-8; PP 370-373). The immediate objective of the covenant at Sinai was the establishment of the Hebrew nation in Palestine, and the ultimate objective, the evangelization of the world (Deut. 7:7-14; Isa. 49:3, 6, 8). Under the covenant, Israel became God's chosen people and He became their acknowledged ruler. The covenant was the basis of all His dealings with them. Their form of government under the covenant relationship was a theocracy. Their place of worship was the tent of the covenant. Their Sacred Scriptures were the book of the covenant.

The everlasting covenant between Christ and the Father for the salvation of humanity was formulated in eternity past (Eph. 1:4; Heb. 6:18). It became operative the moment sin entered, and was formally ratified by Christ's death on the cross. Even as Moses mediated the old covenant, Christ became the mediator of the new covenant (Heb. 9:15-17). It is a "better covenant" in that it is established on Christ's own eternal promise to die for sinners, instead of on the people's fickle promises, as with the old covenant (Heb. 8:6). Whereas under the covenant mediated at Sinai God's law was written upon tables of stone, the covenant mediated at Calvary is to be written in living letters on the heart, or mind, of all who accept the salvation afforded by the blood of the "everlasting covenant" (Heb. 13:20).

Early Seventh-day Adventist comment on the covenants arose out of the relationship of the Ten Commandments—and thus of the seventh-day Sabbath—to the old covenant. As early as 1857, Roswell F. Cottrell, formerly a Seventh Day Baptist minister, pointed out that far from abolishing God's law, the new covenant called for it to be inscribed in men's and women's hearts (Heb. 8:10, 11; *Review and Herald* 9:124, Feb. 19, 1857). D. M. Canright answered the contention of critics that the old covenant was a covenant of works and the new covenant one of faith thus: "We think that the connection between faith and works has ever been the same under both covenants. Faith in Christ was as necessary to salvation in the days of Noah, or Adam, as it is today" *(Review and Herald* 27:161, Apr. 24, 1866).

The fact that Abraham was justified by faith did not release him from obeying God's commands.

The first major exposition of the two covenants was a series of articles by J. O. Corliss in the *Review and Herald* between March and May 1883. He explained that the old covenant was an *agreement* made *with respect to* the Ten Commandments but that the two are separate and distinct (Deut. 10:2; cf. 31:26). In contrast, the Decalogue was a covenant *commanded* (Deut. 4:13; *ibid.* 60:196, Mar. 27, 1883). The old covenant was ratified by the shedding of blood *before* the Ten Commandments were engraved on the tables of stone. The new covenant, like the old, was made *with Israel* (Heb. 8:10; *ibid.* 60:213, Apr. 3, 1883).

N. J. Bowers listed 12 biblical reasons against the argument identifying the Ten Commandments with the old covenant, which was done away at the cross. The Decalogue was in existence long before the old covenant became effective at Mount Sinai. The covenant was made *with respect to* the Decalogue, not identical with it. The old covenant was made *with* the people, whereas they were *commanded* to keep the Ten Commandments. The old covenant consisted of divine and human promises, not commands (Ex. 24:7; cf. Heb. 8:6). The human promises were faulty, whereas the Ten Commandments were perfect (Heb. 8:7; cf. Rom. 7:12, 14). Under the new covenant the law is written on the believer's mind (Heb. 8:10). The old covenant ended at the cross, but the Ten Commandments did not (Matt. 5:17-20). He also called attention to the fact that Paul refers to the covenant and the law as distinct entities (Rom. 9:4; *ibid.* 62:579, 580, Sept. 15, 1885).

Uriah Smith discussed the old and the new covenants at considerable length in a series of eight editorials from September to November

1887. He referred to them as two editions of God's everlasting covenant with human beings *(ibid.* 64:584, Sept. 13, 1887). There is nothing in the nature of mutual agreement in the Ten Commandments; they were *commanded (ibid.* 64:600, Sept. 20, 1887). According to Deut. 5:3, "The Lord made not this [the old] covenant with our fathers, but with us, even us, who are all of us here alive this day." If Moses here refers to the Decalogue, its principles were not binding on men and women before Sinai; they were free to violate its precepts at will—an impossible situation *(ibid.* 64:617, Oct. 4, 1887). The new covenant, like the old, was made with Israel (God's people), not Gentiles, but the latter might be included in it by becoming spiritual children of Abraham (Gal. 3:29; *ibid.* 64:632, Oct. 11, 1887). On their part the Jews must believe in Christ in order to enjoy its blessings (Rom. 2:28, 29; Gal. 3:29; *ibid.* 64:648, Oct. 18, 1887). God's law is the basis of both covenants *(ibid.* 64:680, Nov. 1, 1887).

See also Sabbath.

COVENANT, CHURCH. A written pledge, at one time used to enroll members uniting to organize a local church; also a pledge signed by an individual convert upon taking his or her stand. In 1861, at the formation of the first Seventh-day Adventist conference organization, in Michigan, it was voted to recommend that churches in organizing use a covenant, a practice apparently common in other denominations at that time, and already followed by SDAs in some places. The form adopted was as follows:

"We, the undersigned, hereby associate ourselves together, as a church, taking the name, Seventh-day Adventists, covenanting to keep the commandments of God, and the faith of Jesus Christ" *(Review and Herald* 18:148, Oct. 8, 1861).

The essence of the covenant, as it concerned the individual, was the pledge "to keep the commandments of God, and the faith of Jesus Christ." There is also mention of a covenant to keep the Sabbath, which may have been identical, signed by converts before taking the step of becoming church members (see, for example, *Review and Herald* 60:694, Nov. 6, 1883).

CRAGER, CUNO PARKER (1886-1945). Mission administrator, educator. A graduate of South Lancaster Academy (1907), he was preceptor of Mount Vernon Academy (1907-1908); principal of Claremont Union College, Capetown (1909-1915); educational, Missionary Volunteer, and Sabbath school secretary of the Austral Union in Argentina (1916-1920). Ordained to the ministry in 1920, he was president of the Chile Conference (1920-1923); educational, Missionary Volunteer, and Sabbath school secretary of the South American Division (1923-1929); educational secretary of the Central Union (1929); associate educational secretary in the General Conference (1930-1935); superintendent of the Central American Union Mission (1935-1941); superintendent of the Central Colombia Mission (1941). He supervised erection of buildings for Colegio Vocacional y Profesional in Montemorelos, Mexico (1942); taught Bible in the Colegio Adventista de las Antillas (1943); and in 1945 became superintendent of the Puerto Rico Mission, but held this office for only four and a half weeks, when he became ill and died a month later.

CRAVEN, JOSEPH HARRISON (1906-1964). Treasurer and publishing house manager. He began denominational work in 1923 on the staff of the British Publishing House, where he served for 12 years. After this, he was treasurer of the Stanborough Hydro for 10 years, until his appointment in 1946 as secretary-treasurer to British Advent Missions, Ltd. In 1949 he became manager of the Stanborough Press, where he served until his death. Under his leadership the press acquired new departments that lifted it to much higher levels of technical skill and productivity.

CRAWFORD ADVENTIST ACADEMY (formerly Toronto Junior Academy). A K-12 educational institution located in Toronto, Canada. It was established in 1953 through the efforts of Dr. Erwin Crawford. Enrolled for the 1993-1994 school year were 227 elementary school students and 166 secondary school students. There were 34 teachers and staff.

Principals: Eugene W. Rau, 1980-1987; Vernon Langdon, 1987- .

CREATION. Seventh-day Adventists believe that the entire universe came into being through divine creative acts (Isa. 40:26; Ps. 19:1; 33:6), but that the narrative of Gen. 1 and 2 focuses primarily on this earth and life upon it. They consider the Creation to have been a direct, supernatural event by divine fiat in which both the Father and the Son participated, with the Son as the active agent (Gen. 1:26; Col. 1:16, 17). The Holy Spirit is also mentioned in connection with the Creation account (Gen. 1:2).

Since their beginning SDAs have held the doctrine of a literal creation in one week of time and have used the belief to support the doctrine of the Sabbath *(Review and Herald* 1:1, November 1850). They have considered the Sabbath as an institution inseparable from the Creation, "a safeguard against atheism and idolatry," "a weekly memorial of the living God," who created all things in six days of time *(ibid.* 5:101, Apr. 18, 1854).

SDAs have always affirmed belief in creation *ex nihilo*—that God was not indebted to previously existing matter when He brought the earth into existence. They have generally taken it for granted that it was on the first day of Creation week that He brought into existence the matter that composed the earth and that He proceeded immediately with the work of the six days. However, almost from the first, some SDAs have allowed that the Genesis account can be understood to mean that God spoke into existence the substance of the earth sometime prior to the events of the six literal days of creation. For example, as early as 1860 the *Review and Herald* reprinted a selection from *The Bible True,* in which appeared the statement that there is not "anything in revelation which forbids us to believe that the substance of the earth was formed long before it received its present organization" *(Review and Herald* 16:49, July 3, 1860).

On the other hand, J. N. Andrews declared in 1861: "On the first day of the week God created the heavens and the earth. The earth thus called into existence was without form and void" *(ibid.* 19:1, Dec. 3, 1861).

A few years later D. T. Bourdeau wrote: "The Bible says that God made heaven and earth as well as all that in them is, in six days. It is in the beginning of the first day, therefore, that God created the heaven and the earth, as spoken of in Gen. 1:1" *(ibid.* 29:98, Feb. 5, 1867).

Representing the other school of thought, J. P. Henderson wrote in 1887: "The creation of the material substance of the heaven and the earth may have been ages prior to the six days' work in which it was prepared for the abode of man, and yet do no violence to a single statement in the Bible" *(ibid.* 64:418, July 5, 1887).

Seven years later J. G. Matteson, leader of SDA work in Scandinavia, made the following observation: "In six days God created heaven and earth and all that in them is. Ex. 20:11. He created the heaven and the earth in the beginning. John 1:1. The solar system to which we belong, and the orb on which we live were consequently made on the first day of the week. Before that time there was nothing in this part of God's great universe. But the Lord spake, and it was done; He commanded and it stood fast. Ps. 33:9" *(ibid.* 71:722, Nov, 20, 1894).

While not denying observed facts, Seventh-day Adventists have rejected arguments from geology used to support the theory that the days of Creation week were actually long geologic periods *(see* Science and Religion). They point out that the integrity of the Creation week was attested when the law was given at Sinai (Ex. 20:8-11), and that there is no other satisfactory explanation for the origin of the weekly cycle. Since it is absurd to suppose that matter and energy can arise spontaneously out of nothing, the only reasonable solution is to postulate a Creator. SDAs have taken apparent purpose, intricate design, and order in nature as evidences of a Creator of infinite wisdom and limitless power.

SDAs consider the doctrine of a divine creation as the indispensable foundation for Christian and biblical theology. This fact is emphatically attested from Genesis to Revelation. God's position as Creator is often pointed to as distinguishing Him from all false gods (1 Chron. 16:24-27; Ps. 96:5, 6). The God of creation is the God of the moral law, in the heart of which the Sabbath is given as a sign, symbol, and memorial of His creative power (Ex. 20:8-11; 31:13-17; Eze. 20:20).

The God of creation is also the God of salvation and judgment (Ps. 89:11-15; 146:6-10; Rev. 14:7). He who has power to create has power to redeem, to restore, to create anew the heavens and the earth, to create within man a clean heart (Isa. 44:21-28; 65:17-25; Ps. 51:10). The Christ of creation is before all, He upholds all things by the word of His power, and by Him all things consist (Col. 1:16, 17; Heb. 1:1-3). He was in the beginning with God; He became flesh and dwelt among us with power to save (John 1:1-14). The great fact of Creation is thus essential to the fundamental facts of the Christian faith.

See also Evolution; Science and Religion.

CREDENTIALS, LICENSES, CERTIFICATES. Certificates issued to persons in various categories of denominational employment by a mission, a conference, a union, or the General Conference or its divisions. The most frequently issued certificates are: (1) ministerial credentials for ordained ministers; (2) ministerial licenses for unordained ministers; (3) commissioned minister credentials to employees with not less than five years' experience (divisions are free to bestow such a credential if they choose) for associates in pastoral care, Bible workers, treasurers, uncredentialed departmental directors, institutional chaplains, presidents or vice presidents of major institutions, auditors, and field directors of Christian Record Services (employees with less than five years' experience in these categories are issued commissioned minister licenses); (4) missionary credentials for unordained experienced employees, including elementary or secondary teachers; (5) missionary licenses for field medical, educational, and office workers, which may also be granted to miscellaneous office, institutional, and industrial workers who have been in denominational employ more than five years, who do not qualify for missionary credentials; (6) literature evangelist credentials for permanent colporteurs; and (7) literature evangelist licenses for beginning colporteurs with three months' experience. Some divisions also offer (8) teaching-ministry credentials for teachers having more than five years' experience (teaching-ministry licenses for those with less than five years); (9) ministerial internship certificates to college ministerial graduates during their ministerial internship years. All credentials and licenses are granted for a specified period and may be withdrawn in harmony with the constitutional provisions of the issuing organization.

Before the development of formal organization in the Seventh-day Adventist Church, cards signed by "the leading brethren" were issued to the church's ministers. When the first conference (Michigan) was organized, in 1861, it voted to issue its ministers certificates of ordination and annual "credentials to be signed by the chairman and clerk of the conference" *(Review and Herald* 18:148, Oct. 8, 1861). An individual desiring to preach was, after thorough examination, granted a license to preach, and after a year or more of acceptable ministry, was ordained. A clear distinction was made in the *Church Manual* articles of 1883 *(Review and Herald* 60:586, Sept. 11, 1883) between ministerial credentials and licenses, the former being for ordained persons only.

CREED. A formal, official statement of doctrinal beliefs, as for instance the Apostles' Creed or the Westminster Confession. Seventh-day Adventists have no formal creed, although a statement of beliefs may be found in the denominational *Yearbook* and *Church Manual* *(see* Doctrinal Statements). Seventh-day Adventists consider the entire Bible to be their creed: "The Holy Scriptures, Old and New Testaments are the written Word of God, given by divine inspiration through holy men of God who spoke and wrote as they were moved by the Holy Spirit. In this Word, God has committed to man the knowledge necessary for salvation. The Holy Scriptures are the infallible revelation of His will. They are the standard of character, the test of experience, and the authoritative revealer of doctrines, and the trustworthy record of God's acts in history" *(Church Manual,* p. 23).

This is in harmony with what James White declared as early as 1847: "The Bible is a perfect, and complete revelation. It is our only rule of faith and practice" *(A Word to the Little Flock,* p. 13). The earliest SDA periodical, *Present Truth,* made a similar declaration: "The Bible is our chart—our guide. It is our only rule of faith and practice, to which we would closely adhere" *(Present Truth* 1:46, December 1849).

The covenant signed by those organizing themselves into a church contained the simple declaration: "taking the name, Seventh-day Adventists, covenanting to keep the commandments of God, and the faith of Jesus Christ" *(Review and Herald* 18:148, Oct. 8, 1861).

CREWS, JOSEPH ARCHIE (1924-1994). Pastor, teacher, radio and television speaker. A son of the South, Crews was graduated in 1946 as president of the first class to graduate with a four-year bachelor's degree from Southern Missionary College. In 1947 he earned an M.A. in systematic theology from the SDA Theological Seminary. That year he also married Lu Ann Tunison and began a five-year ministry in Florida.

From 1952 to 1957 the Crewses did evangelistic work in India. Upon their return they pastored in Texas and Kentucky. In 1965 the Chesapeake Conference called Crews to develop a radio program that would generate interests for the conference's evangelistic outreach. The broadcast was named *Amazing Facts,* and it first aired during the spring of 1966 on WBMD, Baltimore, Maryland. Currently Amazing Facts airs radio and television programs on 120 stations around the world.

Crews was known for his inspiring, straightforward conservative preaching. He authored 58 books and many magazine articles, and he recorded 553 radio and television sermons. In July 1990 he received the American Broadcaster's Award for 25 years of gospel broadcasting. On Oct. 10, 1994, he succumbed to a cerebral hemorrhage.

CRIEFF NURSING HOME AND HEALTH INSTITUTE, LTD. *See* Roundelwood.

CRISLER, CLARENCE CREAGER (1877-1936). Secretary, mission administrator. He was born in Brooklyn, Iowa, and was reared in a Seventh-day Adventist home, his parents having accepted the SDA faith when he was 5 years old. He graduated from the Orlando, Florida, high school in 1892 and later taught in the Seventh-day Adventist academy in Graysville, Tennessee. He was baptized in 1893. For two years (1895-1897) he attended Battle Creek College. The next three or four years he worked in the General Conference office in Battle Creek as private secretary for such leaders as O. A. Olsen, G. A. Irwin, and A. G. Daniells.

In July 1901 he began working for Ellen White in her Elmshaven office in California and continued there until one year after her death in 1915. In 1916, while accompanying A. G. Daniells, the president of the General Conference, on a trip to the Orient, he was made general secretary of the Far Eastern Division. There I. H. Evans ordained him in 1922.

In 1930, when the China Division was organized, he became its secretary. He was editor of the Far Eastern Division *Outlook* and later of the *China Division Reporter* and was associate editor of the Chinese church paper. He contributed much to the development of books and pamphlets in the Chinese language. He also served as a member of the managing boards for the Chinese publishing house, the college, and the sanitarium.

In 1936 he was asked to go with G. J. Appel and other missionaries on a trip to Tibet. He seemed apprehensive of the long and hazardous journey, but willingly accepted his assignment. On Mar. 3, 1936, the group set out for but never reached Tibet. At Titao, Kansu, a little village six miles (10 kilometers) south of Lanchow, China. Crisler died of pneumonia and was buried in Lanchow.

He wrote two books published posthumously: one describing the work in the remote regions of China, entitled *China's Borderlands and Beyond;* another, on church administration: *Organization; Its Character, Purpose, Place, and Development in the Seventh-day Adventist Church.*

CRISTOBAL, JUAN D. (1909-1962). Church leader in the Philippines. He was born in the Philippines and joined the Seventh-day Adventist Church in 1927, after attending evangelistic tent meetings and about 1933 entered denominational service as a teacher in the East Visayan Mission. Later he was secretary of the Religious Liberty Department and of the Home Commission of the Mindanao Mission, the first there to hold this office. He was later secretary of the Education and Young People's departments of Southern Luzon Mission (1946-1949), president of the Southern Luzon Mission (1949-1953), and secretary of the Religious Liberty and Temperance departments of the North Philippine Union Mission (1953-1962). In 1962 he was killed in an automobile accident.

CROATIA. A republic in southeastern Europe bordered by Slovenia, Bosnia and Herzegovina, Yugoslavia, Hungary, and the Adriatic Sea. It has an area of 21,829 square miles (56,537 square kilometers), and a population (1994) of 4.7 million. The principal language is Serbo-Croatian; the main religion is Roman Catholicism.

For more than 800 years Croatia was politically aligned with Hungary. It was also under Turkish, French, and Austrian influence. In 1918 Croatia became part of the Kingdom of the Serbs, Croats, and Slovenes, which became Yugoslavia in 1929. Croatia declared independence from Yugoslavia in 1991, precipitating fighting between the Croats and the Yugoslavian army units and their Serbian supporters.

Seventh-day Adventist Statistics. Croatia is part of the Croatian-Slovenian Conference, an attached field of the Trans-European Division. In 1993 the *Croatian-Slovenian Conference* had 92 churches and a membership of 3,364. Headquarters are at Zagreb, Croatia.

Institutions. Adventist Seminary; Croatian-Slovenian Publishing House.

CROATIAN ADVENTIST SEMINARY. *See* Adventist Seminary (Croatia).

CROATIAN-SLOVENIAN CONFERENCE. *See* Croatia; Slovenia; Trans-European Division.

CROATIAN-SLOVENIAN PUBLISHING HOUSE. (Znaci Vremena) (Signs of the Times). A publishing organization operated since the early 1990s by the Croatian-Slovenian Conference at Zogreb, Croatia. Branch houses include Izdvastvo Adventistickug teoloskog fakulteta Marusevec (Adventist College of Theology Publishing), in Marusevec, Croatia; Zivot i Zdrarlje (Life and Health), in Zogreb; and Znamenja Casa (Signs of the Times), in Ljubljana, Slovenia. Languages in which publications are issued include Albanian, Croatian, Czech, and Slovenian. Prior to the 1990s the Croatian-Slovenian Publishing House was a branch of the Yugoslavian Publishing House. For the history of the Croatian-Slovenian Publishing House, *see* Yugoslavian Publishing House.

CROSIER (CROZIER), OWEN RUSSELL LOOMIS (1820-1913). Millerite preacher and editor, of Canandaigua, New York, first writer on what was to become the Seventh-day Adventist sanctuary doctrine. He was baptized in autumn 1843 by E. R. Pinney. As a young itinerant preacher he was associated with Hiram Edson and F. B. Hahn, and in March 1845 collaborated with Hahn in publishing, at Canandaigua, the *Day-Dawn,* a small Millerite paper. According to J. N. Loughborough, he was with Edson in the cornfield at Port Gibson on the morning after the sad vigil of Oct. 22, 1844. In any case, he accepted Edson's explanation of the Millerite disappointment, joined with Edson and Hahn in intensive Bible study in the winter of 1844-1845, and wrote out their joint findings on the subject of the sanctuary and its cleansing. As the concept of the sanctuary ministry of Jesus developed, a progression of increasingly clear articles came from the pen of Crosier during 1845 and 1846. The first was in the *Day-Dawn,* first published in March 1845 (it appears as a part of a Canandaigua newspaper, *Ontario Messenger,* Mar. 26, 1845). Articles on the sanctuary types by Crosier appeared in the *Day-Star* during the latter part of 1845; these culminated with a lengthy essay in the Feb. 7, 1846, *Day-Star Extra,* published in Cincinnati, Ohio. Crosier's exposition was endorsed by Edson and Hahn, who also provided funding for the special issue. Crosier's presentation convinced Joseph Bates, James White, and other New England Adventists. Bates, in turn, presented the Sabbath doctrine to the Port Gibson group in a conference at Edson's home. Crosier kept the Sabbath for a time and advocated it in the *Day-Dawn* in December 1846 (see *Review and Herald* 3:8, May 6, 1852), but soon repudiated it and his early sanctuary view. In 1847 he anticipated the "new view" of the daily. Crozier (as he spelled it after about 1850) served on the staff of Joseph Marsh's *Advent Harbinger,* 1847-1853. He placed the three angels' messages (and the Sabbath) after the Advent. In 1850 he, Marsh, and others taught a doctrine of the millennium ("the age to come") opposed by Adventists in general, a view foreshadowed only partly in one section of his sanctuary article of 1846. In 1858 he was an evangelist for the Michigan Conference of the Advent Christian Church.

CROSS, CHESTER G. (1913-1981). Administrator. A native of Des Moines, Iowa, he served the church for 45 years, mostly in the publishing work in the Northern and Central unions. He also served as publishing director of the Southern European Division. From 1958 to 1974 he was manager of Christian Record Braille Foundation. After that time he worked in the Trust Services Department of the Southern Union.

CRUZEIRO DO SUL ADVENTIST ACADEMY (Instituto Adventista Cruzeiro do Sul). A coeducational boarding and day school on the senior high school level, owned by the Rio Grande do Sul Conference and operated by a board representing that conference. It is situated on a 180-acre (75-hectare) tract of rich pasture land two miles (three kilometers) from the town of Taquara, state of Rio Grande do Sul, Brazil.

The plant consists of 22 buildings, including a large church auditorium, a school edifice, two dormitories, homes for teachers, a carpenter shop, a store, and a dairy.

The property originally belonged to Ernesto Bergold, who maintained a small clinic there, offering simple, natural treatments. In 1928 A. C. Harder obtained this property for the purpose of opening a school to be named Colegio Cruzeiro do Sul. Harder, investing his own money as well as his wife's inheritance, and receiving no salary, acted as principal and teacher and was aided in his efforts by Jose Mendes, another self-sacrificing teacher. By 1932 the school had two buildings, and in 1935 it became the property of the Rio Grande do Sul Conference. In 1937 the conference invited Dr. Otávio Espírito Santo, an engineer with considerable teaching experience, to administer the institution. Under his leadership the school was approved by the government in 1939 on the junior high school level and took the name Ginásio Adventista de Taquara. A commercial course was added in 1957 that conformed to the government standards, and as a result, the name of the school was changed in 1961 to Instituto Cruzeiro do Sul, with its present academic status.

Directors: Otávio Espírito Santo, 1937-1941; João Linhares, 1942; Dario Garcia, 1943-1946; José Alvaranga, 1947-1948; Renato Emir Oberg, 1948; Jacob Germano Streithorst, 1949-1950; Siegfried Hoffmann, 1951; Mario Roque, 1952-1954; João Rodriques dos Passos, 1955; Sesóstris César Souza, 1956; João Rodriques dos Passos, 1957-1959; Jacob Germano Streithorst, 1960; João Bork, 1960-1962; Henrique Marquart, 1963-1965; Leonid Bogdanow, 1965-1966; Darci M. Borba, 1967-1968; Carlos M. Borba, 1969-1970; Isaac P. Guimarães, 1971; Corino Pires da Silva, 1972-1974; Earle P. Linhares, 1975-1982; Moises Sanches, 1983-1984; Argemiro Fontoura, 1985; José O. de Oliveira Paula, 1986-1988; Lourival B. Preuss, 1988-1990; Milton Souza, 1990- .

CUBA. A republic occupying a large island and several small islands situated in the northern part of the Caribbean Sea, having an area of 44,218 square miles (114,524 square kilometers) and a population (1994) of 11 million. Spanish is the national language, with English widely used as a second language. Church and state are separate, though the population is predominantly Roman Catholic. In 1962 there were about 265,000 Protestants in Cuba. About half the island consists of flat or rolling terrain; the remainder is hilly or mountainous. The climate, except in the mountains, is semitropical, the temperature never varying more than about 10 degrees from an average of 77° F (25° C). Cuban economy is based largely on the exportation of sugar and tobacco, and until the present government (1994) assumed power in 1959, the island was generally recognized as being the world's largest producer of sugar.

Historical Background. Originally inhabited by Arawak Indians, Cuba was discovered by Columbus, Oct. 28, 1492. It was used by the Spaniards as a base, first for further exploration and later for the fleets of treasure ships returning to Spain. The island developed an agricultural economy, but relative prosperity came only after the Treaty of Ryswick (1697) ended the raids of the British, French, and Dutch buccaneers, which had seriously disrupted the economy. Even then Spain's policy of economic exploitation and monopolistic control, together with discrimination against the Creoles (Cubans of Spanish descent), fostered discontent, which erupted in several open revolts by the tobacco growers.

Cuba was held by the British from 1762 to 1763. During the American Revolution the island served as a base of operations for the French and Spanish allies against Great Britain.

The early nineteenth-century spirit of independence engendered in Spanish America by Napoleon's occupation of Spain was ruthlessly suppressed in Cuba, although not eradicated, by the Spanish forces on the island. The most notable unsuccessful revolt was the Ten Years' War (1868-1878).

Another revolution, in 1895, led by José Julián Marti, ended in American intervention and the Spanish-American War (1898). The United States occupied the islands until 1902, at which time the Republic of Cuba was formed, with the United States reserving the right to intervene to preserve Cuba's independence and stability. Under this provision, when in 1906 a revolution broke out, United States forces occupied the island until 1909. The provision was revoked in 1934.

For the most part, until 1952 the presidents and congress were elected. Since that time the government has been a dictatorship.

Seventh-day Adventist Statistics. Until 1967 the territory of Cuba consisted of the East Cuba and West Cuba conferences, part of the Antillian Union Mission, which in turn was a part of the Inter-American Division. Since 1967 the church has been reorganized in order to fulfill the requirements of the new system of government. For many years the church operated as the National Association of the Seventh-day Adventist Church in Cuba with three province offices, called delegations, to run the church's affairs in the provinces. From Apr. 21-24, 1989, the tenth National Association Congress of the Seventh-day Adventist Church in Cuba was held. It established the Cuban Union Conference with three delegations: Central, East, and West. Statistics (1992) for *Cuba:* churches, 112; members, 11,235; ordained ministers, 48; licensed ministers, 35. Cuban Union Conference Headquarters are in Havana.

Statistics (1992) for the delegations—*Central Delegation:* churches, 29; members, 2,739. Headquarters: Camaguey. *East Delegation:* churches, 47; members, 4,884. Headquarters: Holguin. *West Delegation:* churches,

38; members, 4,598. Headquarters: Habana.

Institutions. Cuba Adventist Seminary.

Seventh-day Adventist Work. *Beginnings.* In the winter of 1902-1903, W. A. Spicer spent a few days in Cuba. Returning, he urged Seventh-day Adventists to begin missionary work there *(Review and Herald* 80:15, Aug. 11, 1903). A few months later the first missionaries arrived and began self-supporting colporteur and medical work. Reporting in the *Review and Herald* (82:12, Mar. 9, 1905) on the work in this early period, Isaiah E. Moore, a self-supporting nurse, who with his wife arrived in Havana in May 1904, said: "Brother and Sister Hall and Brother and Sister Sterquel came to Cuba about two years ago [i.e. 1903] and settled at La Gloria. . . . Brother and Sister [Joseph] Clark [who also came in 1903] are holding up the banner at Ceballos, and have been distributing literature. . . . Brother Stytch, who has doubtless been on the island longer than any other Seventh-day Adventist, is now at Bahia Honda. . . .

"Brother and Sister O[tis] L. Dart, of Graysville, Tenn., arrived in Havana the last of November [1904]. They are all self-supporting workers."

The Cuban Mission was established in 1904 and organized in 1905, with E. W. Snyder as director. The first church was organized in 1905, in La Lisa, a suburb of Marianao, near Havana. This church became known as the Havana Adventist Church.

The first Cuban converts were Pedro Cruz and Manuel Avila. Cruz was the first to become interested in SDA teachings and invited his friend Avila to attend meetings that were being held in La Lisa. Together they studied the SDA doctrines with the missionaries, and were baptized May 18, 1907. Later the same year eight more became members by baptism (Oct. 26).

About that time a church was organized in eastern Cuba and another at Omaja, an American colony, 100 miles (160 kilometers) from Santiago. The Havana church was registered under the name Iglesia Adventista del Septimo Dia de Cuba (Seventh-day Adventist Church of Cuba). The next year this name became official.

In 1905 there were only six SDA members in Cuba, but by 1908 this number had grown to 53. From 1911 to 1914, work was developed among the Americans and English living in Cuba, and many joined the church. In 1911 H. A. Birbeck-Robinson came from Mexico to give strong leadership to the publishing work.

In 1917 there were 47 added by baptism, raising the total membership to 173. For the next 15 years there was a steady increase of members, so that at the end of 1932 there were 1,001 members reported. Churches were organized at Guanabacoa, El Cerro in Havana, Santiago, and other cities of the island.

The Cuban Mission was reorganized as the Cuban Conference, which, during its first session held in Havana from Jan. 31 to Feb. 9, 1935, elected as its president E. J. Lorntz, who had been president of the Cuban Mission since 1933.

From 1,001 at the end of 1932, membership rose to 2,108 by the end of 1937. Membership continued to rise, though a little more slowly, during the next three years. In a special conference session December 1940 to January 1941, the Cuban Conference was divided into the East Cuba Conference (provinces of Camagüey and Oriente) and the West Cuba Conference (provinces of Las Villas, Matanzas, Habana, and Pinar del Río).

Education. SDA educational work had its origin in a school on the San Claudio farm near the town of Cabañas, in Pinar del Río. The school's first principal was Mrs. S. H. Carnahan. This school was the forerunner of the Colegio de las Antillas, which was later transferred to Puerto Rico (1962), and of the Seminario Adventista de Cuba (now Cuba Adventist Seminary). Cuba had 40 elementary church schools before all private schools were prohibited by law in 1961.

Radio Work. Radio work in Cuba began in 1935 over a station in Havana. The program called *La Voz del Atalaya* ("The Voice of the Watchman") was broadcast Sundays (9:00 a.m.), with Miguel Vasquez as speaker. In 1942, when the General Conference Radio Department appointed Braulio Pérez to prepare and record Spanish radio programs to be transmitted to Spanish-speaking countries overseas, CMQ, the most important radio station in Cuba at that time, accepted the program to be broadcast on Sundays. Later, a radio Bible school was begun, which still functions, although the radiobroadcasts have been discontinued because of government restrictions that have been imposed.

CUBA ADVENTIST SEMINARY (Seminario Adventista de Cuba). A coeducational boarding school on the junior college level, situated on a 331-acre (134-hectare) site five miles (eight kilometers) from Santa Clara, approximately in the center of the island of Cuba. It is operated by the Cuban Union

Conference and serves the constituency of the church in Cuba. Until recently the elementary and secondary curriculum had state recognition. At present (1993) only the equivalent of grades 10 through 14 is permitted and mainly seminary courses are offered. Whereas the 1962 school enrollment was 313, it is now about 24. The total school staff numbers five.

The physical plant includes two dormitories, 14 classrooms, a library, a chapel, administrative offices, six industrial buildings, 14 homes for teachers and other employees, and 29 student apartments.

From the beginning of Seventh-day Adventist work in Cuba until 1922, several elementary schools were established in different parts of the island, but these were short-lived. In the summer of 1922 the first secondary school with boarding facilities and industries was established on a small farm in Oriente province, near the town of Bartle. Charles J. Foster was its founder and constructed the first buildings. The school grew slowly and eventually served the Spanish-speaking fields of the Antillian Union, becoming known as the Colegio Adventista (Antillano). However, its site on the extreme end of the island, the poor land, and the scarcity of water hindered normal development. When J. S. Marshall became principal of the school, he made plans for moving the institution to a more appropriate location.

In February 1940 the Antillian Union committee purchased the present site, and in May 1940 the school began to function in temporary quarters on the Santa Clara campus as the Colegio Adventista de las Antillas.

In 1945 the school was authorized to offer two years of advanced training in theology and elementary education, raising the school to junior college status. Two years later the first students graduated from these courses.

Under the administration of F. G. Drachenberg, who became principal in 1947, a canning industry was established, which was a principal source of student employment.

In 1949 commercial and secretarial courses were added to the curriculum to meet the need for workers in these areas in the Antillian Union. The following year the college, having fulfilled the requirements, became affiliated with the Department of Education of Union College, Lincoln, Nebraska. At the same time a junior college course for Bible instructors was established, and in 1952 a course in agriculture was added. At first only the elementary school was recognized by the Cuban government, but in 1952 the school received state recognition of its secondary classes.

In the summer of 1955 plans were completed for establishing a four-year college program to serve the needs of the Spanish-speaking constituency in the Inter-American Division. The senior college ministerial course was approved by the General Conference Department of Education and the Inter-American Division in May 1958. That year plans were also laid for offering a degree in elementary or secondary education, and these were first made available in the 1958-1959 school year.

One hundred additional acres (40 hectares) of land bordering the school property were purchased in 1959. This new addition expanded the work possibilities for students.

After the 1960-1961 school year senior college classes were not offered because of the difficulty of retaining trained professors in Cuba and of bringing in students from the other Spanish-speaking countries in the Inter-American Division. The senior college courses were subsequently offered at the Puerto Rico school, thus effecting a move of Antillian College to that country, leaving the Cuban school operating on the junior college level.

In February 1967 government representatives took possession of the institution's buildings, industries, land, cattle, and equipment, excepting the library books and the academic records. This action terminated 27 years of efforts and progress in what was up to that time the main educational institution of the Antillian Union.

After three years of negotiation with officials of Cuba's Ministry of Education, authorization was given for the opening of a very small institution strictly for seminary purposes, with a maximum enrollment of 20 men. School opened again in March 1970, downstairs in the former Antillian Union office building in Rancho Boyeros near the city of Havana.

In this new phase, the Cuban Adventist Seminary continues to operate at the 14-grade level.

Principals/Presidents: Charles J. Foster, 1922-1924; G. T. Vore, 1925; C. L. Pohle, 1926-1928; J. D. Livingston, 1928-1931; David E. Lust, 1931-1937; J. S. Marshall, 1937-1947; F. G. Drachenberg, 1947-1954; R. L. Jacobs, 1954-1955; Walton J. Brown, 1955-1960; Alfredo Aeschlimann, 1960-1961; Manuel Carballal, 1961-1962; Vicente Rodríguez, 1962-1967; Isaias de la Torre,

1970-1972; Pedro de Armas, 1973-1978; Alejandro Delgado, 1978-1984; Virgilio Zaldivar, 1984-1991. Recent *Yearbooks* list the position of principal as vacant.

CUBAN UNION CONFERENCE. *See* Cuba; Inter-American Division.

CULT. A system of religious belief and worship, especially one peculiar to a particular national or ethnic group. In this sense the religion of ancient Israel with its feasts and sacrifices has been referred to as a cult. Other ancient civilizations such as those of Phoenicia and Egypt had their cult worship. When applied to contemporary groups, the term is usually used in a derogatory sense and implies that the groups thus described deviate from what is considered to be the accepted norm of belief and practice.

Occasionally some ultraconservative writers classify Seventh-day Adventists as a cult, usually because of a misunderstanding of SDA teachings or a deliberate intent to misrepresent these teachings. SDAs do not consider that the term "cult" is accurately used of them, in view of the fact that they accept without reservation the historic tenets of the Christian faith, such as the inspiration of the Bible, the Bible as the Christian's sole rule of faith and practice, the Trinity, the deity and preexistence of Christ, His vicarious death, salvation by faith in Christ alone, and the second coming of Christ in power and glory to annihilate evil and to establish His eternal kingdom.

CUMBERLAND CONFERENCE. *See* Georgia-Cumberland Conference; Kentucky-Tennessee Conference.

CUMMINGS, JONATHAN (fl. c. 1852). A Millerite Adventist who began to preach in 1852 that the second coming of Christ was to take place in the autumn of 1853 or in the spring of 1854. After the passing of the set time, his followers, whose belief in the doctrine of conditional immortality separated them from the main body of Millerite Adventists, organized themselves into an Adventist body that since 1861 has borne the name Advent Christian Church, and which now is the largest of the Adventist bodies that do not observe the seventh-day Sabbath.

CURAÇAO. *See* Inter-American Division; Netherlands Antilles.

CURDY, JOSEPH (1862-1947). Swiss evangelist, editor, translator, teacher, and administrator. Born in a Catholic home, he became a Seventh-day Adventist in 1884 and the next year entered denominational work. It appears that he worked in the Waldensian valleys of northern Italy in the 1890s. In 1888 he married Amélie Jaquet. In 1896 he was ordained to the ministry. In the early years of the twentieth century he preached in Belgium. About the same time he was one of the editors of *Les Signes des Temps* and *Le Messager de la Prophétie.* In 1907 he became president of the French-Swiss Conference, an office he held until 1910. Afterward, he worked in France and Switzerland, and in 1920 went to Canada and took charge of the French Department of Oshawa Missionary College (now Kingsway College). Also in 1920 he married Emma Clerc, his first wife having died. While in Canada, he edited *Les Signes des Temps* (Canadian). He returned to Switzerland in 1926 and engaged in pastoral work there.

CURITIBA SCHOOL. *See* Brazil.

CURROW, MAY LACEY WHITE (1873-1969). Pioneer. She was born at Cuttack, near Calcutta, India. She attended school in England and traveled with her family to Tasmania at the age of 9.

Her family was converted to the Seventh-day Adventist Church in the late 1880s. Desiring to be a Bible worker, May attended the Seventh-day Adventist school at Melbourne. There she met W. C. White, a widower and son and helpmeet of Ellen White. At the time of their marriage May was 21 and Willie was 40. The marriage proved highly successful, with May becoming a real mother to Willie's two daughters, Ella, 13, and Mabel, 8. May herself became the mother of five children, including twin boys. She passed to her rest at Eden Valley, Colorado, just one day short of her ninety-sixth birthday.

CURTIS, ELI (fl. 1845-1851). A Millerite of New York City who wrote articles in the *Day-Dawn* (Canandaigua, New York) and the *Day-Star* (Cincinnati, Ohio), and published at least two ephemeral sheets of his own in New York (extant examples: the *Girdle of Truth Extra,* 1848, and the *Sharp Sword With Two Edges,* 1851). In 1845 he wrote letters to the *Day-Star,* indistinguishable from those of the Millerites advocating the "shut door," but by

1851 he was a full-fledged spiritist, reprinting alleged spirit messages intended to prepare the world for the Second Advent. Ellen White, who had seen some of his articles written before he was a spiritist, wrote to him in 1847 agreeing with him on some points (for example, the millennium beginning and ending with the two literal resurrections and followed by the new heavens and new earth), but disagreeing on other points (in James White's *A Word to the "Little Flock,"* pp. 11, 12). By 1848 he was reprinting some of her writings without her consent. His misuse of them in garbled form called forth her protest against his "inconsistent course for some time past" and "his [unfavorable] influence on the cause of truth" *(Present Truth* 1:80, May 1850).

CURTIS, JESSIE WEISS (1881-1972). Well-known minister in the Pennsylvania Conference. She received her education at Battle Creek, Michigan, and was the youngest student in her class. She began her work as a Bible worker in New Jersey, Washington, D.C., and Pennsylvania. During her early ministry she worked with H.M.J. Richards, father of H.M.S. Richards, of the Voice of Prophecy. Mrs. Curtis also worked with Ned Ashton, a former pastor of Sligo church in Takoma Park, Maryland, N. R. Dower of the General Conference, and F. H. Robbins, former president of the Columbia Union Conference. She conducted her own tent meetings throughout northeastern Pennsylvania, and as a result organized many new churches in the conference. The last three churches that she pastored were Beaumont, Tunkhannock, and Montrose, all three of which were built under her supervision. During her ministry she conducted an abundance of Bible studies, and as a result hundreds have become Seventh-day Adventists. Many young interns worked under her instruction. In 1932 she married John Curtis, a prominent businessperson who was generous to the denomination. He preceded his wife in death. Mrs. Curtis was still witnessing until shortly before her death.

CURTIS, WILL D. (1851-1907). Pioneer Seventh-day Adventist missionary in Australia. He accepted SDA beliefs when about 30 years old. Joining the church, he entered the ministry and in 1887 went to Australia. On the way there, he assisted with the establishment of SDA work in Hawaii, and visited in New Zealand. He returned to the United States in 1892 on the *Pitcairn.* He then served as superintendent of education for the Illinois and Indiana conferences and the Lake Union Conference.

CURTISS, SPENCER NELSON (1862-1925). Publishing house manager. He began serving an apprenticeship with the Review and Herald Publishing Association in 1881, graduated from Battle Creek College in 1882, joined the Pacific Press in 1887 as manager of the Book Department, and later became superintendent of the factory. In 1893 he established and managed the first Pacific Press branch at Kansas City, and later was transferred to the New York branch. From 1903 to 1912 he was manager of the Review and Herald Publishing Association. After again serving as manager of the Kansas City branch, he served as manager of the new international branch at Brookfield, Illinois (1916-1922).

CYPRUS. An island republic situated in the eastern end of the Mediterranean Sea, with a land area of 3,572 square miles (9,251 square kilometers) and a population (1994) of 730,000. Four fifths of the inhabitants are Greek Christians and most of the rest are Turkish Muslims. English, Greek, and Turkish are spoken on the island. In its history Cyprus passed through the hands of many empires. From 1878 until it achieved independence in 1960, Great Britain administered Cyprus. In 1964 and again in 1974 civil strife on the island interfered with Seventh-day Adventist missionary activities.

Seventh-day Adventist Statistics. Cyprus constitutes a section in the Middle East Union Mission, which is an attached union under the General Conference. Statistics (1993): churches, 1; members, 38. The headquarters are in Nicosia, Cyprus.

Development of Seventh-day Adventist Work. The first Seventh-day Adventist to go to Cyprus was Moses Boursalian, an Armenian who fled there with his family from Antioch, Turkey, about 1912. For years he quietly plied combs made by his family from village to village on donkey back and talked of his beliefs to his neighbors. Later his son John became the first SDA colporteur on the island. In 1930 there was a company of about 10 adherents in Nicosia.

Except for visits by SDA ministers to baptize new converts and hold Communion services, there was no official SDA work for many years. Finally in 1932 R. S. Greaves and his wife, former missionaries to Turkey and

Greece, made Cyprus their home and became pioneer workers on the island, having emigrated from Canada.

At the close of World War II A. N. Barlas and Aram Ashad and his wife arrived to establish the work on a more permanent basis. The small group of SDAs worshiped in their homes. In 1953 Fred Veltman, an American missionary, became president of the newly organized Cyprus Mission. The welfare work carried on by the SDAs included the rebuilding in Paphos of a home destroyed by an earthquake. In the mid-1950s a correspondence school was opened in Nicosia, and the first Seventh-day Adventist church building on the island was erected at Nicosia in 1956, and the church took part in the Cyprus International Fair.

The work on the island was directed from Beirut between 1956 and 1959. The first large-scale evangelistic meetings were held by Robert L. Mole in 1959, with simultaneous translations into Greek and Armenian. J. Sherwood Jones was appointed president in 1964, but did not move there until June 1965, because of political disturbances. Soon after, Moses Elmadjian, a Cypriot and the grandson of the first SDA in Cyprus, was appointed mission secretary-treasurer.

During the disturbances the church and offices were looted and damaged, and the workers were obliged to move to new quarters in Nicosia. Temperance work served as the main approach to the public, and in 1967 the first Five-Day Plan to Stop Smoking conducted in the Greek language was held in the capital, sponsored by the mayor of Nicosia. That same year the church was able to gain official recognition by the government. A new center was purchased and occupied in a residential area in Nicosia, which in 1993 was still serving as church headquarters. Attempts were made in 1970 to establish a dental clinic on the island, but these attempts were unsuccessful. Early in 1972 Manouk Benzatian pioneered work in the Turkish section of Cyprus by holding the first Five-Day Plan in that language on the island.

Dean McDaniel was the director of the work in Cyprus at the time of the 1974 civil strife. Unable to continue work, he was obliged to return to the United States.

Evangelist Dinos Mastromihalis came to Cyprus from Australia in 1992 to hold the first Greek evangelistic campaign in Nicosia. Approximately 250 people attended, some of whom are attending church services regularly.

Efforts have been very successful in the area of literature evangelism, stop-smoking plans, health and stress seminars, and Revelation seminars.

CYPRUS SECTION. *See* Cyprus; Middle East Union Mission.

CZECH REPUBLIC. A country in central Europe bounded on the north by Poland, on the east by Slovakia, on the south by Austria, and on the west by Germany. It has a territory of 30,344 square miles (78,591 square kilometers) and a population (1994) of 10.4 million.

The country of Czechoslovakia was formed after World War I out of the ancient Czech principalities of Bohemia, Moravia, and a part of Silesia, together with Slovakia, all of which were contained in the former Austro-Hungarian empire. The present Czech Republic was constituted in 1993. Ethnically the people are about 95 percent Czechs and 5 percent Slovaks, Germans, and Poles. Forty percent of the people belong to the Roman Catholic Church; 20 percent are Protestant, independent Catholic, Orthodox, or Jewish; and 40 percent are unchurched.

The present Czech Republic is one of the most advanced countries in Europe culturally and industrially, Prague (its capital) being the site of one of the oldest European universities. The Slavs in the territory of the present Czech Republic had established a great empire by the ninth century. About that time Christianity was introduced there by the Greek missionaries Cyril and Methodius, who not only preached but also gave the Slavs their written alphabet, the Cyrillic. Later the Roman Catholic Church caused the adoption of the Latin script in Czechoslovakia, but the Cyrillic was retained as the script of the countries of Russia, Bulgaria, and Serbia.

From the tenth century, the combined pressure of Magyars and Germans gradually eroded the Slavic state, although until the wars of the Reformation, which began in Bohemia, the Czechs maintained a considerable degree of local political and cultural independence. Near the beginning of the fifteenth century, the Reformation movement sprang up in Bohemia, where John Huss preached in the national language. He was burned as a heretic at Constance. In the Roman Catholic Counter Reformation that followed the Reformation, Protestantism was seriously weakened in Czechoslovakia.

Seventh-day Adventist Statistics. The territory of the Czech Republic constitutes the

Bohemian and Moravia-Silesian conferences, which are a part of the Czecho-Slovakian Union Conference, which in turn is a part of the Euro-Africa Division. Statistics (1992) for the *Czech Republic:* churches, 131; members, 7,223; ordained ministers, 49; licensed ministers, 7; Bible instructors, 18.

Statistics for the conferences—*Bohemian Conference:* churches, 57; members, 2,725; ordained ministers, 20; Bible instructors, 9. Headquarters: Praha. *Moravia-Silesian Conference:* churches, 74; members, 4,498; ordained ministers, 29; licensed ministers, 7; Bible instructors, 9. Headquarters: Ostrava.

Institutions. Adventist Bible Seminary; Czecho-Slovakian Publishing House.

Seventh-day Adventist Work. *Beginnings.* Seventh-day Adventist tracts in the Czech language were prepared as early as 1890 by the Hamburg Publishing House. A Czech Baptist in Hamburg by the name of Antonin Simon read these tracts, accepted the SDA doctrines the same year, and at once translated some other tracts. After returning to Bohemia, he settled in Roudnice and later in Malesice, near Prague. The members of the Simon family were active missionaries and soon made converts of many of their associates and neighbors. The son, Joseph Simon, entered the work in 1918 and later was principal of a school in Lodenice. In 1894 L. R. Conradi, of Germany, made arrangements for a Protestant publisher at Pardubice, Bohemia, to print a Czech-language edition of Ellen White's *Steps to Christ.* The next year Conradi reported visiting a group of adherents near Prague and celebrating the Lord's Supper with them, the first such celebration by SDAs in Bohemia.

The first Seventh-day Adventist minister to conduct systematic evangelistic work in Prague was J. P. Lorenz, who arrived there in 1901 and found a group of Sabbathkeepers. He organized a church that by 1902 had 20 members. The early converts developed into strong church workers; one of them, a man by the name of Skakal, living at Nymburk, became the first editor of the Czech paper *Hlasatel Pravdy* ("Herald of Truth"), when it was launched by the Hamburg Publishing House in 1906.

In 1907 and 1908 general meetings of SDAs in the old Austro-Hungarian empire were held in Prague. By 1911 the work in Bohemia and Moravia had become so well established that the territory was divided into the Bohemian Mission field, with 114 members, and the Moravian-Silesian Mission, with 135 members.

The government of the old Austro-Hungarian monarchy strongly opposed efforts to teach Protestant doctrines, especially through the circulation of publications. Early SDA colporteurs (among them, Josef Doubravsky, J. Popelka, and K. Polednik) were arrested several times while doing colporteur work in 1912. However, obstacles did not prevent the printing of books and papers. The Hamburg Publishing House continued the monthly paper *Hlasatel Pravdy* until World War I. In 1913 the same house printed a new Czech edition of *Steps to Christ,* and in 1915 Ellen G. White's *Thoughts From the Mount of Blessing,* as well as certain books by L. R. Conradi.

In 1919 the Czechoslovakian Union Conference, composed of the North Bohemian, the West Silesian-Moravian, and the Polish-Silesian conferences, and the Central Bohemian and the Slovakian missions, was organized, with E. E. Frauchiger, from Switzerland, as the first president. Its headquarters were established in Opava, Silesia. At the end of 1920, the union had 55 churches, with 1,691 members. In 1920, when the eastern part of Silesia was ceded to Poland, the consequent transfer of 535 members to the Polish Union reduced Czechoslovakia's membership.

A publishing house (listed in the *Yearbook* as the Czechoslovakian Publishing House) was established soon after the war, with F. Ludwig in charge. It issued publications in Bohemian, Slovakian, Polish, Slovenian, German, and Hungarian.

In 1921 the first training course was offered in Czechoslovakia. A permanent training school (listed in the *Yearbook* as Czechoslovakian Mission School) was opened in 1925 at Lodenice. Many evangelists trained in this school determined to continue the Reformation begun by John Huss and John Amos Komensky (Comenius), and to turn the people of Czechoslovakia to God.

During the years between the two world wars encouraging progress was made. At the outbreak of World War II in 1939 there were 97 churches, with 3,157 members, in Czechoslovakia. When Germany occupied Czechoslovakia, the activities of the Seventh-day Adventist Church were greatly hindered. The publishing house and the training school were closed. However, during the years between 1939 and 1945, baptisms took place, and despite adversity, the membership increased, although the majority of the German-speaking Seventh-day Adventists had to return to

Germany after the war.

After the war the publishing house flourished again, and plans were laid for its enlargement and the reestablishment of the training school. A property was bought in a suburb of Prague for this purpose, and building operations were proceeding well. In 1951 the local conference organizations were dissolved by the government. From 1952 to 1956 the public activities of our denomination were stopped, and the churches were closed. Nevertheless, the work continued, and in spite of many hardships new converts were baptized and the holy ordinances celebrated. In 1956 all Seventh-day Adventist churches were reopened. In 1968 the local conferences—Bohemian, Moravia-Silesian, and Slovakian—were reorganized, and the Czechoslovakian Bible Seminary and the Czechoslovakian Publishing House were reestablished in Prague.

In 1993, after the split of former Czechoslovakia into two independent states—the Czech Republic and Slovakia—the union was renamed the Czecho-Slovakian Union Conference and was granted complete freedom of operation.

Until 1938 Czechoslovakia was a part of the Central European Division, then of the Central European Division Section II. In 1946 it was made a part of the Southern European Division, now the Euro-Africa Division.

CZECHOSLOVAKIAN BIBLE SEMINARY. *See* Adventist Bible Seminary.

CZECHO-SLOVAKIAN PUBLISHING HOUSE (Advent-Orion Publishing House) (Vydavatelstvi a Nakladatelstvi Advent-Orion). A publishing house operated by the Czecho-Slovakian Union Conference in Prague. In the early years Seventh-day Adventist publications were imported from Hamburg, Germany, and the United States. After World War I the Czecho-Slovakian Publishing House was established, but before World War II the church was forced to close it, and only a few church publications were printed by a private company. In 1968 the publishing house was reestablished with its own printing and bindery facilities. The printing of the *Signs of the Times* and the Sabbath school quarterly was done by the government press, and other publications in the denominational facility. In addition to booklets, tracts, and periodicals *(Signs of the Times* and *Our Little Light* for children), many books have been printed, including *Patriarchs and Prophets, Prophets and Kings, The Desire of Ages, The Acts of the Apostles, The Great Controversy, Christian Service*, and two large hymnals (one with music and one without). Most publications are in the Czech language, but some are printed in the Slovakian and Hungarian. In 1990, after the fall of Communism in Czechoslovakia, the publishing house was reorganized and renamed. Following the split of the Czech and Slovak republics, the Slovakian branch was established in 1993.

Managers: F. Ludwig, 1920-1939; J. Cepl, 1940-1952; Jiri Drejnar, 1968-1980; K. Nowak, 1980-1989; M. Hlouch, 1990; J. Brodsky, 1991; P. Fürst, 1992- .

CZECHO-SLOVAKIAN UNION CONFERENCE. *See* Czech Republic; Euro-Africa Division; Slovakia.

CZECHOWSKI, MICHAEL BELINA (1818-1876). Converted Catholic priest who first carried the Seventh-day Adventist message to Europe. A Pole by birth, he was educated for the priesthood in Cracow, but was forced to flee his native land in the wake of revolutionary activities in that area. After considerable wandering throughout Europe, he became disillusioned with the Catholic Church, married, and came to America. For a while he attended Grand Ligne Mission, a French Baptist school, near Montreal, Canada, and then was sent as an evangelist to work among the French-speaking people across the border in the United States. Faced with reverses, he left the field and went west. He came upon an Adventist tent meeting at Findlay, Ohio, and there joined the Adventist Church in 1857. (His name then appeared in the *Review and Herald* as M. Belina Czechowski.) Thereafter, he worked in association with D. T. Bordeau in Canada, northern New York, and Vermont.

Czechowski had a great desire to go to Italy as a missionary for the denomination, but the leaders felt that the young Seventh-day Adventist organization was not yet ready for such an enterprise. Disappointed, but determined to carry out his plans, he sought assistance from another Adventist denomination. This enabled him to go to Europe in 1864, 10 years before the church sent J. N. Andrews as an official missionary to Europe. He came to Torre Pellice in a Waldensian valley in Piedmont, northern Italy, where he formed a company of believers whom he taught the SDA doctrines, even though he himself was no longer associated with the SDA Church. Encountering much opposition in Italy, he left the country after 14 months and went to Switzerland, where he worked for four years with great energy and perseverance, establishing a periodical entitled *L'Evangile Eternel* ("The Everlasting Gospel"), which was published for about two years.

Through his teaching and prolific writing, he proclaimed the Sabbath and the second coming of Christ, and as a result of his efforts several companies of believers were established in Switzerland, the largest being in Tramelan. The group in Tramelan has been later regarded as the first SDA church to be established in Europe. Czechowski's efforts formed a foundation on which to establish a European mission under Andrews' leadership.

From Switzerland he went to Romania, where he again preached Adventism and laid the foundation for future growth. He died in Vienna in 1876. Several libraries in the United States hold many original documents and Czechowski's correspondence with SDA leaders, including Ellen White, and political luminaries of the day.

Until 1975 it was not known where he was buried, but minutes before the adjournment of the 1975 General Conference session in Vienna, official word was received that the grave had been located in the Central Friedhof Cemetery in that city where he had been laid 99 years before.

In 1976 an international historical symposium held in Warsaw, Poland, studied Czechowski's life and work as an SDA "trailblazer" in Europe and published its conclusions.

D

DAHOMEY. *See* Benin.

DAIL, GUY (1871-1934). Minister, division secretary. He was converted in 1881 and baptized by M. Enoch the same year. From 1886 to 1891 he attended Battle Creek College, where, according to his own words, he was reconverted and rebaptized. Next he enrolled in Union College and in 1895 became its first graduate from the classical course with a B.A. degree.

From 1895 to 1901 he worked for the Seventh-day Adventist Foreign Mission Board in Battle Creek, Philadelphia, and New York. In 1901 he was called to Europe, where he served until 1904 as the recording and corresponding secretary of the German Union. Then from 1904 to 1920 he was secretary of the European Division, with headquarters in Hamburg. During a part of this time (1917-1920) he also was president of the German-Swiss Conference and had his residence in Bern. He was ordained in 1911.

In 1920 he returned to America and taught Bible at Pacific Union College until 1924, when he was urgently invited to return to Europe to head the Bible Department in the Baltic Union Training School. In 1928, when the old European Division was divided, he was elected secretary of the Central European Division, with headquarters in Berlin. He held this position until 1932, when he was appointed director of the Bulgarian Mission. He remained with the mission until 1934, when he returned to the Central European Division headquarters to serve as departmental secretary.

DAILY, THE. As used in the prophecy of Daniel, a cryptic term for what was taken away by a power described as "a little horn, which waxed exceeding great" in the vision of Dan. 8 and as the "king of the north" in Dan. 11. In each instance an apostate form of worship variously designated "the transgression of desolation" (Dan. 8:13) or "the abomination that maketh desolate" (Dan. 11:31; 12:11) is set up in its place. The Hebrew word translated "daily" is *tamîd.* Aside from its five occurrences in Daniel, it occurs nearly 100 times elsewhere in the OT, usually as an adverb but frequently as an adjective, and meaning "continual(ly)," "perpetual(ly)," "regular(ly)." In Daniel *tamîd* is an adjective used substantively; that is, no noun is supplied. Readers are left uncertain as to the noun that should be supplied to complete the sense. But *tamîd* is a key word in the visions of Dan. 8 and 11-12, and a correct understanding of it is relevant to the interpretation of these prophetic passages. The KJV translators supplied the English word "sacrifice": for example, "the daily *sacrifice* was taken away" (Dan. 8:11). The RSV renders the corresponding clause: "The continual *burnt offering* was taken away." The KJV and RSV renderings are identical in meaning, the translators holding that in Daniel *tamîd* referred to the "daily" or "continual" sacrifice offered in the Jewish temple every morning and every evening.

History of Interpretation. 1. *Literal and Symbolic Interpretations.* Through the centuries, long before the Advent movement *(see* Millerite Movement) of the 1840s, there had been two classes of interpretations of "daily," or "continual." The *literal* view saw the "daily" as meaning the Jewish sacrifices in the Temple, and the taking away of the "daily" as their interruption by Antiochus (2nd century B.C.), or by the Romans (A.D. 70), or by a last-day antichrist. In this view, the "two thousand three hundred evenings and mornings" (Dan. 8:14, margin) are 2,300 (or 1,150) literal days, and the 1290 days (Dan. 12:11) similarly literal days. The symbolic view, also widely held, saw the periods as symbolic days, that is, as literal years, extending into the Christian Era; and the "daily" as a symbol of true worship or sound doctrine in the church, taken away by either the Papacy or the Muslim conquest (or, from the Catholic side, as the sacrifice of the Mass abolished by Protestants, or by a future antichrist).

2. *Two Interpretations Among Seventh-day Adventists.* Adventist writers have given two symbolic interpretations of the "daily": (1) the so-called old view, inherited from the Millerite movement, namely, that the "daily" means ancient Roman paganism; and (2) the so-called new view, also advocated by at least one unnamed Millerite writer but not adopted by the others, that the "daily" represents Christ's priestly mediation in the heavenly sanctuary. Both of these views agree that the desolating little horn described as taking away the "daily" and treading down the sanctuary and the people of God represents the Papacy. According to the first view the "daily" that was taken away is the *first phase* of the Roman horn's oppressive power (paganism, replaced by the papal phase in the role of treading down God's sanctuary and people); but according to the second view the "daily" is the *object,* rather than the agent, of the little horn's attacks (the true mediation of Christ, our high priest, replaced by the false mediation of a human priesthood).

3. *Origin of the "Old" View.* The identification of the "daily" as paganism originated with William Miller. Seeking the meaning of the term as he found it in Daniel, he searched, with the aid of a concordance, in the King James Version of the Bible for other occurrences of the English word "daily." He described his search thus: "I read on and could find no other case in which it was found, but in Daniel. I then took those words which stood in connection with it, *'take away.'* He shall *take away* the daily, 'from the time the daily shall be *taken away,'* &c. I read on, and thought I should find no light on the text; finally I came to 2 Thess. ii. 7, 8. 'For the mystery of iniquity doth already work, only he who now letteth, will let, until he be *taken out of the way,* and then shall that wicked be revealed,' &c. And when I had come to that text, O how clear and glorious the truth appeared. There it is! that is 'the daily!' Well, now, what does Paul mean by 'he who now letteth,' or hindereth? By 'the man of sin,' and 'the wicked,' Popery is meant. Well, what is it which hinders Popery from being revealed? Why, it is Paganism: well, then, 'the daily' must mean Paganism" (William Miller, quoted in Apollos Hale, *Second Advent Manual,* p. 66).

Protestants before Miller had applied this text in Thessalonians to the replacing of Roman paganism by apostate Christianity; he now applied it thus: The "daily" (Roman paganism) was taken away and the place of its (pagan) sanctuary (Rome) was cast down, or polluted; and in its place the abomination (the papal system) was set up in the church. Then God's sanctuary, which was trodden down first by paganism and then by the Papacy, was to be cleansed. He at first identified this as "the temple at Jerusalem and the worshipers therein"; later as "the Earth and the Church." (See his *Evidence . . . on the Second Coming* ["Miller's Lectures"] [1838 ed.], pp. 36-38; *Letter . . . on the Cleansing of the Sanctuary* [1842], p. 8.)

Miller gave the date A.D. 508 as the time

when the "daily" would be taken away (explained as the triumph of the Roman church over Roman paganism) and the 1290 days (Dan. 12:11), counted as years, would begin. According to his reckoning, the date A.D. 508 also marked the end of a period of 666 years (arrived at by his application of the number 666 mentioned in Rev. 13:18), during which Roman paganism would dominate the people of God, first the Jews and later the Christians *(Evidence,* p. 81).

4. *Opposition to Miller's Interpretation.* Miller's explanation of the "daily" soon drew fire from his opponents on two scores: (1) his chronology and (2) his identification. His chronology was objected to on historical grounds and his identification of the "daily" on exegetical grounds—the latter especially from those who held the literal view that the "daily" and the time periods (1290 and 2300 days) meant literal sacrifices and literal days.

5. *Shift in Millerite Position.* Miller's colleagues generally accepted his identification of the "daily" but disagreed with his application of the number 666. The most widely used Millerite prophetic chart (designed by Fitch, 1842) omitted any explanation of 666 or any identification of the "daily." In 1843 a view at variance with Miller's appeared in the *Midnight Cry* (5:52, 53, Oct. 4, 1843). This view, which was disclaimed in an editor's note, identified the "daily" as the "continual mediation of Jesus Christ" taken away by the papal little horn, which "cast down the place of his gospel sanctuary" when it "cast down the sacraments and gospel truth" and "the true doctrine of the cross of Christ."

Yet in spite of differences of opinion on Miller's detailed interpretation, the Millerites stood united against the opponents who contended for the literal rather than the symbolic interpretation. Time and again Millerite writers insisted that the word "sacrifice" was not in the original Hebrew but was supplied by the translators, that therefore the "daily" did not mean the literal Jewish sacrifices taken away by Antiochus, and that the 2300 days were not literal days but years, to be dated from 457 B.C. Not until the period of confusion and division following the 1844 disappointment did a group arise (the "Age to Come" party) supporting the old literalist view, looking to literal sacrifices in the future at Jerusalem; and this view was repudiated by the majority of those who remained with Miller and Himes, and also by the small group that became the Seventh-day Adventists.

6. *Forerunner of Seventh-day Adventist Views.* When the Sabbatarian Adventists moved on, after 1844, to develop their new doctrine of the heavenly sanctuary, they left behind William Miller's identification of the sanctuary of Dan. 8:14, of the two beasts of Rev. 13, and of the number 666 as pertaining to the "daily," but they retained Miller's idea that the "daily" and the "transgression of desolation" were two successive phases of the Roman power, pagan and papal.

However, in the very beginning a suggestion was made in a new direction, when O.R.L. Crosier, after joint study with Hiram Edson and F. B. Hahn, wrote out the first exposition of the sanctuary doctrine. The first article appeared in the *Day-Dawn* in 1845. His article in the *Day-Star Extra,* Feb. 7, 1846, expressly stated that Daniel's various references to the sanctuary as being cast down (Dan. 8:11), polluted (Dan. 11:31), trodden underfoot (Dan. 8:13), and cleansed (v. 14) applied to the *heavenly* sanctuary of the new covenant. This, he said, can be trodden underfoot figuratively in the same way as the Son of God has been.

"This 'politico-religious' beast polluted the Sanctuary (Rev. 13:6) and cast it down from its place in heaven (Ps. 102:19; Jer. 17:12; Heb. 8:1, 2) when they called Rome the holy city (Rev. 21:2) and installed the Pope there with the titles 'Lord God the Pope,' 'Holy Father,' 'Head of the Church,' &c., and there, in the counterfeit 'temple of God' he professes to do what Jesus actually does in his Sanctuary; 2 Thess. 2:1-8. The Sanctuary has been trodden underfoot (Dan. 8:13), the same as the Son of God has; Heb. 10:29" *(Day-Star Extra,* Feb. 7, 1846, p. 38).

This was a definite step away from Miller's *two* sanctuaries, that of Dan. 11:31 as a pagan sanctuary belonging to the daily, and that of Dan. 8:13, 14 as the temple of God. He does not define Daniel's "daily." He does *(ibid.,* p. 39, col. 3) say, "The daily service described was a sort of continual intercession," but the context of this statement shows that he is clearly speaking of the Levitical sacrifices performed daily throughout the year in contrast with the special *yearly* service of the Day of Atonement. Crosier describes these services as a type of the heavenly priesthood of Christ, lasting from His ascension to the end of the 2300 years; not as Daniel's "daily," taken away when the Papacy was set up.

But by 1847 Crosier had clearly rejected Miller's "daily equals paganism" equation for a new definition. He read in Dan. 8:11 (taking the margin): *"from* him [Christ] the daily" was taken away. He defined the "daily" as the doctrine "that *Christ* 'WAS CRUCIFIED FOR US' " (cf. "true doctrine of the cross" in col. 1, sec. 5), replaced by the Papacy, "with its human merit, intercessions and institutions in place of Christ's" *(Day-Dawn* 2:2, Mar. 19, 1847). This was almost the later SDA "new view."

7. *Development of Seventh-day Adventist "Old" View.* Crosier had identified the sanctuary in Dan. 8:11, 13, 14 and 11:31 as the heavenly sanctuary. Adventist writers thereafter agreed that the sanctuary described in Dan. 8:14, the one to be cleansed after 2300 days, meant the heavenly sanctuary. In the other three passages, Adventist writers in general followed Crosier also (perhaps with the single exception of David Arnold) in applying the sanctuary described in Dan. 8:13, the one that was trodden underfoot, to the heavenly sanctuary, even though they continued to hold, with Miller, that the "daily" was paganism and that the sanctuary referred to in Dan. 8:11 and 11:31 (cast down, and polluted) belonged to the "daily," and represented a pagan sanctuary. Joseph Bates identified the "daily" as paganism in 1846 (*The Opening Heavens,* p. 31), so did J. N. Andrews in 1853 *(Review and Herald* 3:145, Feb. 3, 1853; cf. p. 129, Jan. 6, 1853), and later Uriah Smith *(ibid.* 24:180, Nov. 1, 1864) and James White ("The Time," in his *Sermons on the Coming and Kingdom of . . . Christ* [1870 ed.], pp. 116, 117; cf. pp. 108, 118, 122-125). In an early article *(Review and Herald* 1:28, 29, January 1851) White had followed Crosier in arguing at length that the sanctuary trodden down was the one in heaven, but he did not define the "daily" in this article. When he later did define it, he emphatically described "the daily, and the transgression of desolation" as "two desolating powers; the first paganism, then, Papacy" *(Sermons,* p. 116).

Other Adventist writers subsequently followed this interpretation, and Smith gave a more detailed exposition in *Thoughts on Daniel and the Revelation.*

8. *A Variant View and Its Results.* Oddly enough, however, an isolated and atypical interpretation had appeared in March 1850, in the earliest article on Dan. 8 in any Adventist periodical—an article by David Arnold *(Present Truth* 1:60). It was significant in relation to one of several attempts among the larger group of non-Sabbatarian Adventists—those who had abandoned the 1844 date—to find a new and later time reckoning for the 2300 years. A few of them, expecting the end of the period in 1850, were advocating that believers go to Jerusalem (among those who went was Mrs. Clorinda S. Minor).

Arnold opposed the 1850 expectation but appeared to echo some of the current Holy Land enthusiasm. Explaining the "daily" as meaning the literal Jewish sacrifices at Jerusalem that were taken away in A.D. 70, he equated the treading down of the host with the oppression of the Jews through the centuries, and saw the cleansing of the sanctuary as involving their deliverance.

It was the 1850 expectation, and its effect on a few Sabbatarian Adventists, that occasioned a statement by Ellen White in that year mentioning the "daily." She said that the word "sacrifice" is not in the original text and that the Millerites had held "the correct view" of it. (The Millerites, as already noted, had repeatedly emphasized this view of the word "sacrifice," namely, that the word had been added; they had insisted that the "daily," or continual, did not mean any actual Jewish sacrifices.) Mrs. White also warned against the setting of any new dates after 1844 and against looking for a gathering of the saints to old Jerusalem before the Second Advent *(Present Truth* 1:87, November 1850, reprinted in EW 74, 75).

9. *Ellen G. White on the "Daily."* Many years later Mrs. White's 1850 statement—after its setting, and the specific errors at which it was aimed, were forgotten—was cited (from EW 74, 75) in controversy as an endorsement of the prevalent Millerite *identification* of the "daily," namely, as paganism. When questioned, however, on the meaning of the "daily," Mrs. White "usually said that she has no clear light on the subject, and that our brethren would have to study the matter for themselves" (W. C. White letter to J. E. White, June 1, 1910, in White Archives, Ellen G. White Estate, Inc.). According to A. G. Daniells' report of an interview with her concerning the "daily," she made it clear that her 1850 statement was not intended to settle the identity of the "daily," which she did not profess to know, but to state that the Millerites had the right view of the "daily" as to that period of time (the 2300 days); that she had written with reference to the errors current at that time, especially the attempts to revise the dating of the 2300 days (statement of A. G. Daniells, Sept. 25, 1931, in White Archives). Time was the point at issue—as it had been between the

Millerites and their opposers who made the "daily" the literal Jewish sacrifices—not the identity of the "daily."

In 1910 Mrs. White rebuked those who differed over "the true meaning of 'the daily,'" saying that it was "a subject of minor importance," and that she "had no instruction on the point under discussion." Her advice was: "While the present condition of difference of opinion regarding this subject exists let it not be made prominent" (1SM 164-168).

10. *The "New" View.* Feeling the need of a more accurate linguistic and historical basis for interpreting the "daily," a growing number of SDA leaders set forth what came to be called—somewhat inaccurately—the "new view." Two flaws in the argument for paganism as "the daily" were pointed out (see for example, W. W. Prescott, "The Daily," pp. 9-11): first that the historical events cited for the taking away of the "daily"—the victory of Clovis, Catholic king of the Franks, over the Arian Visigoths—actually constituted a victory over Arianism, not paganism; and second, that Clovis' success did not occur in 508.

About 1900 L. R. Conradi, who soon thereafter became head of SDA work in Europe, wrote to Mrs. White in Australia, asking her to give him any light she might have on the subject, and if not he would proceed to publish what he and his associates had arrived at. Since she had none, he issued his work on the book of Daniel in German (see W. C. White letter to J. E. White, June 1, 1910, in White Archives). Conradi's work, the first SDA book to offer a substitute for the "daily = paganism" interpretation, was *Die Weissagung Daniels,* which was later translated into several European languages and was recommended in 1905 for circulation in America among foreign-speaking readers.

In a letter to Mrs. White, Apr. 17, 1906 (in White Archives), Conradi recalled how he came to his conclusions that: (1) the word "sanctuary" meant "the sanctuary of God as it was in type on earth and as it is in antitype now in heaven"; (2) the "daily," or continual, was the true sanctuary service; (3) the taking away of the "daily" was the papal church's displacement of "the true sanctuary service by its own human service," the Mass, setting "aside the true High Priest by placing the pope in His stead"; (4) the prophecy of the cleansing of the sanctuary assured Daniel, at a time when the Jerusalem Temple lay in ruins, "that not only would the typical service in the earthly sanctuary be restored, but that there would be a true service in heaven which should be carried on unto the end." He stated further that he was surprised to find that some of the Reformation writers thought "the idolatrous mass" "to be the abomination predicted in Daniel 8"; and thus he linked his "new" view with an interpretation much older than Miller's "old" view.

Conradi discussed his interpretation with A. G. Daniells (who in 1900 was passing through Europe en route to the 1901 General Conference session), H. P. Holser, W. W. Prescott, and W. A. Spicer. Daniells later reported hearing of it then from Conradi and further from Prescott. In America thereafter Prescott, and Daniells especially, and others advocated this interpretation.

Although for a time there was considerable controversy in ministerial circles, Mrs. White's counsel—to avoid divisive argument on a minor point—eventually prevailed. Debate on the subject has long since ceased.

DAKAR MISSION SCHOOL. *See* Senegal.

DAKOTA ADVENTIST ACADEMY (DAA). A coeducational boarding school on the senior high school level situated northwest of Bismarck, North Dakota, overlooking the Missouri River. The school is owned and operated by the Dakota Conference, under the jurisdiction of the Mid-America Union.

Jeannette Johnson received an academy scholarship for coming up with the name for the new academy—Dakota Adventist Academy. Dakota Adventist Academy opened its doors for the first school year September 1977 with a very incomplete building. The academy building houses classrooms, dorm rooms, chapels, gymnasium, and cafeteria all under one roof. The boys' and girls' dorms consist of three wings each on alternate sides of the building, with a total of 96 student rooms plus guest rooms. Each two-room unit is connected by an adjoining bathroom. Only two of the nine classrooms were finished, forcing teachers to meet with their classes in partially finished dormitory chapels, recreation rooms, and the dining room. Completion of the building went forward at an irregular pace until 1993, when it was mostly finished. During the summer of 1992, volunteers donated time and money to finish the library area in the basement of the atrium.

The school board and staff of the school made a concerted effort to meet the needs of both the college-bound and the non-college-bound students, but even with 180 students the first year, it was apparent that high school-age students were not often ready to make the choice of which track to emphasize. The four industries that were meant to provide work-study programs for the students all failed and left the decreasing enrollment with standard shop classes including some emphasis on auto mechanics and auto body.

One week before school was to start in 1987, the constituency voted to close the school until the accumulated bills and building costs could be paid. The students were encouraged to attend schools in surrounding states. The church members throughout the Dakota Conference and friends from all over the world helped raise the money to pay bills to the vendors and the nearly $1 million that was still owed on construction costs. The $100,000-plus that was owed to vendors was paid by January of 1988, and in April the constituents voted to reopen for the next school year if the $300,000 subsidy, needed to operate in the black, could be raised before June 30. With the help of the alumni associations of Sheyenne River Academy and Plainview Academy, the money was raised and school reopened in August of 1988.

The school continues to operate a strong academic program, and its graduates find they can compete on an equal basis with other students in the advanced schools of their choice. Starting in 1992-1993, the students were able to work as literature evangelists for their work-study program. Also, during that year students entered the Vocational Industrial Clubs of America Skills Olympics for the first time. Out of approximately 1,000 students from schools all over North Dakota that competed in auto body skills events, DAA students took second, third, and fourth place. A leadership skills contest also showed that DAA has quality education and students. DAA students received first place in the auto body written test and second place in extemporaneous speaking. The academy development program continues with the goal of raising approximately $300,000 in advance of each fiscal year. In 1993, 83 students registered at DAA, including three students from Japan, two from Australia, and other students from states as distant as Alaska and Oregon. From 1978 through 1993, 321 students received diplomas from Dakota Adventist Academy. Camp meeting is held annually at the academy along with other conference meetings, alumni gatherings, and training programs. The conference Adventist Book Center is a part of the main academy building. *See* Sheyenne River Academy for earlier information, as DAA replaced the school at Sheyenne River Academy.

Principals: J. Ray Bailey, 1977-1978; David Cochenour, 1979; Clayton Heinrich, 1979-1980; L. E. McClain, 1980-1984; Robert LeBard, 1984-1987; school closed 1987-1988; Larry Unterseher, 1988-1991; Steve Watson, 1991- .

DAKOTA CONFERENCE. The unit of church organization comprising the territory of the states of North Dakota and South Dakota. Statistics (June 1993): churches, 65; membership, 4,402; church or elementary schools, 12; ordained ministers, 19; licensed ministers, 8; elementary teachers, 15; secondary teachers, 8. Headquarters: 217 North Grand, P.O. Box 520, Pierre, SD 57501-0520; phone (605) 224-8868, fax (605) 224-7886. The conference forms a part of the Mid-America Union Conference.

Institutions: Dakota Adventist Academy, Pine Ridge Mission.

Local churches—*North Dakota:* Beach, Beulah, Bismarck, Bottineau, Bowdon, Bowman, Butte, Carrington, Cleveland, Dakota Adventist Academy, Dakota Conference Church, Devils Lake, Dickinson, Edgeley, Ellendale, Fargo, Gackle, Goodrich, Grand Forks, Grassy Butte, Harvey, Hebron, Hurdsfield, Jamestown, Kulm, Lehr, Linton, Lisbon, Mandan, Manfred, McClusky, Minot, New Home, New Leipzig, Ray, Stanley, Streeter, Turtle Lake, Valley City, Wahpeton, Watford City, Williston; *South Dakota:* Aberdeen, Bison, Bowdle, Custer, Hot Springs, Hurley, Huron, Interlakes (at Madison), Lemmon, Martin, Mitchell, Mobridge, Ortley, Pierre, Pine Ridge, Platte, Rapid City, Redfield, Sioux Falls, Spearfish, Watertown, Yankton.

History. *Beginnings of the Work in the Area.* On Oct. 12, 1980, the North Dakota Conference voted to merge with either or all of Minnesota, South Dakota, and/or Wyoming conferences. The South Dakota Conference voted on Apr. 26, 1981, to merge with the North Dakota Conference. A special merger committee consisting of the executive committees from both the North Dakota and the South Dakota conferences met and voted on May 6, 1981, that the merger of the two conferences would take effect on July 1, 1981. It was voted that the Adventist Book Center remain in North Dakota and the conference office would stay in South Dakota. On July 1, 1981, the North Dakota Conference had 45 churches and a membership of 3,316. The South Dakota Conference had 25 churches and a membership of 1,932. The two conferences had already been working together in support of secondary education in the building and funding of Dakota Adventist Academy near Bismarck, North Dakota. Dakota Adventist Academy was opened for the 1976-1977 school term.

The Dakota Conference has two youth campsites. Flag Mountain, near Hill City, South Dakota, and Northern Lights near Bottineau, North Dakota. Camps were operated at both camps during the summer months until 1991, when it was decided to rotate where camp was held each summer. Currently camp is held in South Dakota on odd-numbered years and in North Dakota on even years.

Pine Ridge Mission (South Dakota) has been in operation since 1969 in order to reach out to Native Americans. Up until 1988 the mission supported an elementary school. At that time a study was taken to see how many people who had gone through the school had actually joined or were involved in the Seventh-day Adventist Church. Also, a study was done to determine the best way to reach the Indian people. It was decided to try a pilot program with new methods of outreach. The school was closed at the end of the 1988 school year, and instead emphasis was placed on alcohol support groups, felt needs seminars, Bible studies, self-help classes, worship services, and home visitation. In 1993 the mission was staffed by five individuals, only one of which receives a full salary. Two people are full-time volunteers. The mission has been successful in reaching souls with this new emphasis of outreach. Several improvements to the mission occurred in the past few years, including a new bus barn. In 1993 an additional staff house was built. Each year groups from various academies and colleges bring groups of students to help paint and repair the mission as well as to provide Vacation Bible Schools and other special meetings for the Native Americans. Periodically Native American evangelists are also brought in to hold evangelistic meetings.

The Dakota Conference members have always been strong supporters of Christian education. This became apparent in the late 1980s. In 1987 the conference administrators felt a need to share with the constituents of the conference how deep in debt the conference was, primarily because of expenses incurred for Dakota Adventist Academy. The original cost estimates of DAA were $2.5 to $3 million. The General Conference and Mid-America Union put in $7.5 million toward the academy debt and left the rest to the conference to cover. Adding to the DAA debts was the fact that the conference had experienced a $130,000 loss in tithe for 1986. The conference no longer had the reserves to increase subsidies to the academy and was getting deeper in debt because of the interest. At the 1987 constituency meeting $90,671 was needed to pay off the industrial arts building, the farm owed $200,000 to denominational organizations, $925,000 was owed to the General Conference of Seventh-day Adventists, and bills to Bismarck vendors were also outstanding. The North American Division offered to match $200,000 if the conference could come up with the same amount by the end of 1987. The North American Division also agreed to pay the interest owed, which amounted to between $80,000 to $85,000, and promised to match funds for the next two years to help liquidate debts. Other conferences in the Mid-America Union had already been paying one half of 1 percent of tithe to apply to the debt. It was voted to raise the $200,000 by selling the Jamestown office, three empty parsonages, and Northern Lights Camp. (Enough money was raised without selling the camp. It was later voted to take Northern Lights off the market.) The industrial arts building debt was paid off with the sale of farm equipment and the cattle. After many meetings and much emotion, it was voted to close Dakota Adventist Academy for the 1987-1988 school year. The vote was 189 to 173. By Aug. 16, 1987, $354,439.82 had been raised for debt reduction and $72,228 had been raised for DAA operating, but $92,000 in accounts payable was still owed from the previous school year. At the close of 1987, debt reduction amounted to $706,259. The remaining DAA debt stood at $1,334,314. The Mid-America Union wrote off $105,000 owed them by the Dakota Conference in 1987. On Feb. 28, 1988, the constituency voted to reopen DAA in the fall of 1988 after being closed for one year. A development committee was formed, and $300,000 was raised before the school year began in order to cover the 1988-1989 operating expenses. By March of 1990, $2,828,000 had been paid in interest as well as money for operating expenses because of the strong support of the Dakota people. Each subsequent year through 1991-1992, the academy ended the fiscal year operating in the black.

Two new churches were built by Maranatha Flights International between 1983 and 1986. These churches were in Harvey, North Dakota, and McClusky, North Dakota. In 1986 the Devils Lake church was sold and the church from Langdon, North Dakota, was moved to Devils Lake to replace the previous church. The Ortley, South Dakota, church was organized in 1985. Because of district realignments, several parsonages were bought and sold between 1985 and 1993. Parsonages sold include the ones in Gackle, Beach, Turtle Lake, Beulah, Williston, and Pierre. New parsonages were bought in Wahpeton and Minot and two parsonages were built in Pierre to house conference workers. In 1993 the declining Gackle membership decided to sell their church and rent it instead. A new church was built in Aberdeen with the help of Maranatha in the fall of 1993.

Membership in the Dakotas has been declining since 1985, when the membership total was at 5,323, until in 1993 the membership stood at 4,402. Because younger members were leaving home in search of employment, smaller churches had to close their doors—including Killdeer, North Dakota, in 1986, Belle Fourche, South Dakota, in 1989, Max, North Dakota, in 1991, and Kenmare, North Dakota, in 1993. White River, South Dakota, was disbanded in 1990, although it had not been active for several years. Hoping to turn this trend around, several new outreach ministries were implemented in the nineties. The conference subsidized the Ken Cox videos to any members in the conference who were willing to use them. Several people have been won because of these videos. A Family Life Department and a Women's Ministries Department were formed to strengthen the homes of members and their friends. Special retreats for women have been held each fall since 1989. During the 1992-1993 school year student literature evangelists started canvassing near Bismarck, North Dakota, and toured several towns during the summer. The group had exceptional book sales and left a free *Desire of Ages* or *Great Controversy* in every home that bought any book. Also in 1993 student youth worked in the Pierre area doing community service projects. After several years of only part-time staffing in the trust department, a full-time trust director was hired for the conference in 1990. Since that time the Trust Department has been updating all of the conference trusts.

Besides reaching out to the Dakota people, constituents felt a burden to help when doors opened to receive the gospel in the Ukraine. During the summer of 1992, an evangelistic team went to the Ukraine totally supported by gifts from Dakota members. In 1993 another group went to the Ukraine to train sister churches how to conduct Sabbath school classes. *See also* North Dakota Conference and South Dakota Conference for historical information.

Presidents: Ben J. Liebelt, 1981-1986; John W. Thurber, 1986-1987; Don T. Shelton, 1987-1993; Robert G. Peck, 1993- .

DANCING. *See* Recreation and Amusements.

DANIEL, INTERPRETATION OF. The various interpreters of the prophecies of Daniel may be divided into three basic schools, according to their views of the events referred to in the book.

1. *Events in Ancient History.* Expositors of one school assign Daniel's depiction of great tribulation and deliverance mostly to an episode of Jewish history 2,000 years or more ago, under Antiochus Epiphanes, a tyrant who sought to abolish the Jewish religion in 168 B.C. Those who hold this view see Antiochus as the "little horn" of Dan. 7 and 8, and interpret the four kingdoms of Dan. 2 and 7 as culminating with the Greco-Macedonian Empire, which is considered to be the fourth.

Many of this group of expositors reject the validity of the predictive element in prophetic literature, and attribute the book of Daniel to an unknown writer who is supposed to have lived about 165 B.C., and who presumably employed the device of representing himself as Daniel, the prophet, to spur his fellow Jews in their revolt against Antiochus Epiphanes. They consider Daniel's predictions to be *vaticinum post eventum,* "predictions" actually made after the events "foretold" took place. The noteworthy resemblance between certain details of Daniel's prophecy and incidents during this critical episode in Jewish history, or later during the wars with Rome, gives this interpretation an appearance of plausibility. Some who accept the book of Daniel as authentic predictive prophecy likewise assign its climax to the time of Antiochus or to the Roman Empire of the first century of the Christian Era.

As for the Antiochus theory, despite certain similarities between some of the aspects of

Daniel's predictions and the events connected with the Antiochus Epiphanes episode, Seventh-day Adventists find compelling reasons for rejecting this interpretation. For one thing, Antiochus reigned about midpoint of the Hellenistic kingdoms that followed Alexander the Great, not "at the latter end of their rule," as Daniel specifies (Dan. 8:23, RSV). His oppression of the Jews was a temporary affair, and by no stretch of the imagination can it be said that he "prevailed over them, until the Ancient of Days came, and judgment was given for the saints of the Most High, and the time came when the saints received the kingdom," as Daniel explicitly declared the future tyrant would do (Dan. 7:21, 22, RSV). It is a simple historical fact that God did not establish His eternal, righteous reign on earth in the long ago when the Jews were still His chosen people. Antiochus did not prove to be the imposing personage required by the prophecies of Daniel, nor was his reign in any sense a prelude to the Messianic Age. Furthermore, the resurrection of Dan. 12:2, which was to take place immediately upon the downfall of the tyrant king, did not follow Antiochus' expulsion from Judea. No events connected with his oppression of the Jews correspond to the time periods of Daniel. In fact, the attempt to identify Antiochus Epiphanes as the tyrant prince of Daniel breaks down at every major point. As if to clinch the matter, two centuries *after* Antiochus, Christ categorically declared that the tyrant prince and the great tribulation of Daniel's prophecies were *still* in the future (Matt. 24:15-20). Thus, to apply Daniel's prophecy to Antiochus is to reject Christ's own interpretation.

2. *Gap Theory (Events in Ancient Times and at the End).* Another school of expositors splits the book of Daniel between ancient history and the future, finding Antiochus in the little horn of Dan. 8 but applying the little horn of Dan. 7 to a last-day antichrist (connected somehow with a Roman fourth kingdom). Most of these expositors are premillennialists of the variety known as dispensationalists *(see* Premillennialism), who hold that prophecy "is concerned only with history as it affects Israel and the Holy Land" *(Scofield Reference Bible,* note on Dan. 11:35), past and future. Holding that God's rejection of the Jewish nation at the cross was only temporary, they believe that Daniel's predictions were fulfilled in order up to the time of Christ, at the end of the sixty-ninth "week" of Dan. 9:27, at which time, according to their understanding, the clock of prophecy stopped, to resume only at or immediately preceding Christ's return. According to this theory, "the entire church age" intervenes "between the sixty-ninth week, after which Messiah was cut off, and the seventieth week, within which the 'little horn' of Dan. 7, will run his awful course," and in the midst of that future "seventieth week" the Jews, restored as a nation to their role as a chosen people, will undergo a three-and-one-half-year tribulation, during which their renewed Temple sacrifices will be taken away *(ibid.,* note on Dan. 9:24). Advocates of this theory point to the new state of Israel and to the return of some 2 million Jews to Palestine as the first steps toward the fulfillment of these prophecies and toward the bestowal of world dominion on the Jews in a 1,000-year Messianic world rule.

As for the gap theory, Seventh-day Adventists consider that only by removing the OT kingdom promises completely from their literary, historical, and covenant context can they be made to apply to literal Israel in the present or future. Taken at face value, the statements of the inspired writers themselves clearly preclude such an application. (See SDACom 4:25-38.) Adventists see the OT promises of restoration to covenant status, and of universal dominion, as strictly conditional (see Jer. 18:6-10). When the Jews rejected their Messiah, our Lord specifically rejected them as the chosen people (see Matt. 21:43; 23:38), but as individuals the Jews continued to be recipients of grace and could be saved by accepting Christ. Furthermore, the Scriptures nowhere support or provide for a gap of some 2,000 years postulated by this theory, between the sixty-ninth and seventieth "weeks" of Dan. 9:27.

3. *A Third View—Continuous Fulfillment.* A third school of expositors is that represented by the early church interpreters and those of the Protestant Reformation. They saw prophecy as fulfilling continuously in history. They identified the four empires of Dan. 2 and 7 as Babylon, Persia, Greece, and Rome; the 10 horns of Dan. 7 as the tenfold partition of the Roman Empire followed by antichrist. The early Christians expected the antichrist in the future. They did not believe in a "gap" that makes prophecy skip over the period of the church, but in continuous fulfillment, operating even in their day.

Jerome (c. A.D. 400), whose interpretation of Daniel was accepted as standard during the Middle Ages, believed the partitioning of the Roman Empire, then in progress, to be the fulfillment of the tenfold division of the fourth empire of prophecy. He listed several of the divisions by name. He expected the imminent overthrow of Rome to make way for the little horn, the antichrist who would reign in the church, oppressing the saints for three and one-half literal years, after which would come the judgment and the Second Advent. Augustine, however, a few years later, interpreted the stone kingdom—the kingdom of God—as the church in the present age.

The late Middle Ages saw a revival of interest in the historical fulfillment of the prophecies, with the addition of two new features—identification of the little horn of Dan. 7 with the Papacy (apparently introduced by Archbishop Eberhard II of Salzburg, Austria, in 1240), and the application of the year-day principle to the prophetic time periods.

Thus developed the idea of the little horn—identified with the NT antichrist and the "man of sin" connected with a great apostasy—as a religiopolitical power, successor to the Roman Empire, enforcing its authority on the people of God and continuing down to the last days. The three and one-half times of this horn were computed as 1260 years *(see* Year-Day Principle). There were various datings assigned to this period, but the capture and banishment of Pope Pius VI by the French in 1798 and his death without an immediate successor led a number of expositors to mark this as the ending of the 1260 year-days.

4. *The 2300 Days and the 70 Weeks.* During the decades following 1798, there was an increased interest in ascertaining the time when the 2300-day period of Dan. 8:14, counted as years, would end, and in discovering the relation of the 70 weeks of Dan. 9 to the 2300 days *(see* Twenty-three Hundred Days).

There had long been universal acceptance of the 70 weeks as "weeks of years," with Christ's death generally placed in the seventieth week. A large number of expositors who took part in the Old World Advent Awakening of the early decades of the nineteenth century followed Johann P. Petri (d. 1792) in using the 70 weeks of Dan. 9 as the key with which to unlock the 2300 "days" of Dan. 8:14, by beginning both synchronously. Many of them fixed upon 457 B.C. or thereabouts as the beginning, and A.D. 33 to 34 as the end of the 70 weeks with the cross either in the midst or at the end of the seventieth week. These looked for the end of the 2300 years in 1843, 1844, or 1847. Identifying the little horn of Dan. 8 as the Papacy or as Islam, they differed on the nature of the events to mark the close of the 2300 years, interpreting the cleansing of the sanctuary of Dan. 8:14 variously as the rescue of Palestine from the Muslims, the fall of the Papacy, the purification of the church, the restoration of the Jews, the beginning of a millennial kingdom, or the Second Advent.

The distinctive features of William Miller's message were his identification of this event as the cleansing of the earth by fire at the second coming of Christ, which he anticipated "about the year 1843"; and his rejection of the two popular interpretations of the kingdom of God on earth—(1) as a golden age preceding Christ's coming, and (2) as a kingdom set up after the Second Advent, with the restored Jews in a position of leadership. Instead, he saw the Second Advent as ending human probation and introducing the eternal kingdom of the glorified saints on a re-created earth. For the Millerite views *see* Millerite Movement.

The link between the Millerite and the Seventh-day Adventist interpretation of the cleansing of the sanctuary was furnished by Hiram Edson's explanation, following the 1844 Millerite disappointment (written out by O.R.L. Crosier after joint study with Hiram Edson and Dr. F. B. Hahn), that the heavenly sanctuary of the book of Hebrews is the one referred to in Dan. 8:14 *(Day-Star Extra,* Feb. 7, 1846).

5. *Daniel 11.* By the time of William Miller, expositors were largely agreed on the application of the earlier part of Dan. 11 to Ptolemies and Seleucids, but they differed on where to introduce Rome. Miller explained the willful king of Dan. 11:36 as the Papacy, but took the king of the north in v. 40 to represent England, and in vs. 40-45, Napoleon. There was division of opinion between recognizing the Papacy or the Turk in the interpretation of the latter part of Dan. 11 among SDAs for nearly a century. Some, such as James White, found the Papacy represented, while Uriah Smith identified Turkey as the power. His classic exposition, *Thoughts on Daniel,* which was printed in the *Review and Herald* from January 1869 to July 1871, perpetuated his view for three quarters of a century. Many SDAs today follow the position taken by White.

6. *Seventh-day Adventist Interpretation.* SDAs follow a continuous historical interpretation. (For the classical exposition of Daniel, see Uriah Smith, *Thoughts on Daniel and the Revelation;* for a contemporary exposition, see *SDA Bible Commentary* on Daniel.) SDAs

identify the nations of the metallic image of Dan. 2 as the Babylonian, Medo-Persian, Greco-Macedonian, and Roman empires, and the 10 toes as the barbaric kingdoms that succeeded Rome and grew into the nations of modern Europe. The "stone" that demolishes the image is Christ's eternal kingdom, the "great mountain" that fills the earth. This same succession of political powers is represented by the four beasts of Dan. 7, with the 10 horns as the kingdoms in the area of the old Roman Empire and the little horn of Dan. 7 as the Papacy. SDAs understand the great horn of the Grecian goat in Dan. 8 to represent Alexander the Great (the book itself explains the symbolic ram and he-goat of Dan. 8 as the Persian and Grecian kingdoms); and the four horns the Hellenistic kingdoms into which his empire was divided, with the little horn of Dan. 8, which grows exceeding great, as representing Rome in both imperial and papal phases, with emphasis on the latter. The cleansing of the sanctuary in v. 14 is understood to refer to the blotting out of confessed and forgiven sins from the books of record in the heavenly sanctuary, beginning at the close of the 2300 "evening and mornings" in A.D. 1844 (figured on the day-for-a-year principle of prophecy from 457 B.C.). *See* Investigative Judgment.

Seventh-day Adventists understand the angel's explanation of Dan. 9:24-27 to be the second installment of the explanation of the vision begun in Dan. 8, with emphasis on the "70 weeks," or 490 years, that were to be "cut off" as the first portion of the 2300 years of Dan. 8:14 and assigned to the Jewish nation. They consider that the carrying out, in 457 B.C., of Artaxerxes' decree authorizing the complete restoration of the Jewish law and administration in Jerusalem marks the beginning of the "70 weeks," or 490 years, and that this prophetic period terminated in A.D. 34, with Christ's crucifixion in A.D. 31 in the midst of the seventieth week of the prophecy (v. 27).

SDAs understand Dan. 11 to be a continuous delineation of history beginning with Daniel's time, with the kings of the "north" and "south" as the Seleucid and Ptolemaic dynasties of Syria and Egypt. Rome is usually understood to come into the picture from v. 14 onward, and vs. 36-39 are applied by some to the Papacy and to its persecution of God's people, by others to France during the Revolution. The closing verses are applied by some to the Papacy and to its persecution of God's people, by others to France during the Revolution. The closing verses are applied by many to the Papacy during the "time of the end," beginning in 1798, at the close of the three and one-half "times," or 1260 days, or years, of Daniel's prophecy, although others hold the view that these verses are still unfulfilled prophecy. Christ's standing up in Dan. 12:1 is understood to mark the termination of His ministry in the heavenly sanctuary at the close of probationary time. Christ's deliverance of His people foretold in Dan. 12:1 is correlated with the prophecies of Revelation.

Daniel was instructed to "shut up the words, and seal the book, until the time of the end" (Dan. 12:4), implying that it could not be understood until that time, but would be then, in terms of its actual fulfillment in history. Evidently not all was sealed, for the angel's explanation applied certain symbols to specific nations and persons (Dan. 8:20-22; 11:2). SDAs believe that the things revealed to Daniel were afterward complemented in the revelation made to John and recorded in the book of Revelation.

DANIELLS, ARTHUR GROSVENOR (1858-1935). Minister and administrator. He was born in Iowa, the son of a Union Army physician and surgeon, who died in the Civil War. At the age of 10 he was converted to the Seventh-day Adventist faith, and in 1875 entered Battle Creek College, remaining only one year because of ill health. After he and his wife taught in public schools for one year, he received a call to the ministry. Feeling timid and unprepared, he hesitated, but after praying earnestly, he came under conviction. He began his ministry in 1878 with Robert M. Kilgore in Texas. He was then secretary to James and Ellen White for one year, and later an evangelist in Iowa.

In 1886 he was called as pioneer SDA missionary to New Zealand, and remained in the antipodes for 14 years. From 1889 to 1891 he was president of the New Zealand Conference and from 1892 to 1895 of the Australian Conference. When Ellen White went to Australia in 1891, he became closely associated with her. On the formation of the Central Australian Conference in 1895, he became its first president. Later he was president of the Australasian Union Conference.

He assumed the presidency of the General Conference in 1901 at a difficult period in the history of the church, but he met with ability financial and organizational problems and the task of moving the headquarters of the denomination to Washington, D.C. He traveled extensively on all continents, convinced of the necessity of getting his information firsthand. The reforms and reorganization that took place during his period of office led to great expansion of the church throughout the world. In 1922 he relinquished the presidency of the General Conference and held the post of secretary for four years. During that time he visited Australia and New Zealand, lands to which he was warmly attached, and made the last of his many journeys to South America.

Daniells was concerned with the development of a spiritual ministry, and led in the formation of the Ministerial Association and *Ministry* magazine. He was one of the denomination's most dynamic leaders. He authored *The World War, A World in Perplexity, Christ Our Righteousness,* and *The Abiding Gift of Prophecy.*

DANISH FOOD FACTORY. *See* Nutana.

DANISH JUNIOR COLLEGE (Vejlefjordskolen). A coeducational boarding school on the junior college level, operated by the Danish Union of Churches located about six miles (10 kilometers) from Vejle, a town on the Danish mainland overlooking Vejle Fjord. Campus and orchard make up a 100-acre (40-hectare) estate. Besides the main building, which accommodates an assembly hall, dining room, kitchen, administrative offices, theological library, and student housing, there are dormitories for men and women, and a school building with offices, ordinary classrooms, facilities for the teaching of sciences, music, and modern languages, general library, and a swimming pool. In addition to these, there are buildings for faculty housing and the elementary school.

Enrollment in 1993 numbered approximately 300, including the 105 pupils of the elementary school. The faculty numbered 27 teachers including 10 part-time instructors.

After a seven-year elementary school course, there is a three-year course in secondary work *(realskole),* at the end of which students sit for government examinations. In 1972 another three-year course (*gymnasium*) was added, this leading up to university entrance requirements (*studentereksamen*). The language of instruction is Danish.

A mission and colporteur school was established by M. M. Olsen in Copenhagen in 1890. The student body consisted of 12 young men and women from Norway and Denmark and 10 Scandinavians from the United States. After four years 16 students had finished the twelfth grade and three took their student examination from the University of Copenhagen.

On Aug. 31, 1894, Olsen moved the school to a newly erected building in Frederikshavn, where it opened with an enrollment of 36. This school is listed in the *General Conference Bulletin* as Frederikshavn High School, but there have been references to it under the name of Frydenstrands School. In 1898 the school was discontinued. L. H. Christian and L. Muderspach reopened it in 1903 in Copenhagen, with 24 students, but later moved it to a large manor house, Hogholt, in north Jutland. After one year it was brought back to its previous site in Frederikshavn. On Sept. 13, 1908, Erik Arnesen opened the school in a large villa in Skodsborg, 10 miles (16 kilometers) north of Copenhagen. The following year it was moved into new quarters on the sanitarium grounds, where it remained for nine years. Then it was moved to Naerum, a site two miles (three kilometers) from the coast, where it made steady growth for 12 years. Until 1921 Denmark's schools served the Norwegian constituency also.

In October 1930 the school was transferred to its present site near Vejle Fjord. H. M. Johnson, who had come from La Sierra College in California, served as principal for eight years, building up the school and developing farm and garden work and a state-recognized scholastic program. In 1957 the school became a junior college. From 1952 to 1958, while there was no denominational school in Norway, the Vejlefjord School served as training school for Norwegian young people as well.

Principals: M. M. Olsen, 1890-1896; C. C. Hansen, 1896-1898; (no school, 1898-1903); L. Muderspach, 1903-1908; E. Arnesen, 1908-1917; L. Muderspach, 1917-1920; E. Arnesen, 1920-1925; P. A. Christiansen, 1925-1930; H. M. Johnson, 1930-1938; P. A. Christiansen, 1938-1947; K. A. Frederiksen, 1947-1948; C. A. Larsen, 1948-1952; A. Varmer, 1952-1957; H. Muderspach, 1957-1963; B. Olsen, 1963-1966; H. J. Schantz, 1966-1971; A. Wagenblast, 1972- .

DANISH-NORWEGIAN SEMINARY. *See* Hutchinson Theological Seminary.

DANISH PUBLISHING HOUSE (Dansk Bogforlag). A denominationally owned and operated publishing house, situated in Naerum,

Denmark. It has five employees in editorial-production and distribution.

In the early years Seventh-day Adventist publications in Denmark were imported, first from the United States, later from Norway. When *Tidernes Tegn* ("Signs of the Times") began to be printed in Kristiania (Oslo), Norway, in 1879 a number of copies went to Denmark, and in July 1881 *Sundhedsbladet* (health journal) was issued also for both countries.

In harmony with a vote taken at the second annual meeting of the Danish Conference (at Hellum, 1882), a depot for publications was opened at C. C. Hansen's home in Asaa, and in May 1886 a depot was opened in Copenhagen. In 1889 Denmark had four colporteurs, who met with strong opposition. A colporteur institute was held in 1892 under the leadership of H. L. Henriksen, and the work began to develop.

In 1893 C. C. Hansen and H. L. Henriksen organized a private firm, registered under the name C. C. Hansen and Company, which made a contract with the Norwegian Publishing House, Kristiania, to distribute its literature in Denmark. This firm, operated in Copenhagen, in the Ebenezer church building, continued until 1905, when the Danish Conference voted to establish a publishing house in Copenhagen, which they registered in the chamber of commerce under the name Dansk Bogforlag, København (Copenhagen Publishing House, also listed in the *Yearbook* as Denmark Publishing House). The first publishing committee was composed of the following: P. A. Hansen, chair; J. C. Raft; Jens Olsen, manager; L. Muderspach; H. L. Henriksen; N. P. Nelson; and P. Hansen, publishing secretary. In 1906 arrangements were made with the firm of C. C. Hansen and Company to transfer all assets to the Copenhagen Publishing House. In 1966 the publishing house was moved to Odense, where it is located in a new building. In 1993 it moved to Naerum, where accommodations already existed.

Periodicals: The house publishes *Tidernes Tegn* ("Signs of the Times"), *Sundhedsbladet* (health journal), *Adventnyt* (a church paper), Sabbath school lesson quarterlies for adults and children, missions quarterly, and an annual Ingathering paper.

Managers: J. G. Matteson, 1877-1881; C. C. Hansen, 1881-1893; C. C. Hansen and H. L. Henriksen, 1893-1905; Jens Olsen, 1905-1910; Chr. Hedebaek, 1910-1927; Johan Nielsen, 1927-1935; R. F. Jensen, 1935-1948; Viggo Thomsen, 1948-1958; W. S. Jensen, 1958-1966; Borge Olsen, 1966-1970; Aage Andersen, 1970-1971; W. S. Jensen, 1971-1977; Kaj Pedersen, 1977-1984; Erling Berg, 1984-1985; J. Madsen, 1985-1992; W. S. Jensen, 1992-1993; Tue Westing, 1993- .

DANISH UNION OF CHURCHES. *See* Denmark; Faroe Islands; Greenland; Trans-European Division.

DANSK BOGFORLAG. *See* Danish Publishing House.

DANUBE CONFERENCE. *See* Austria.

DAR ES SALAAM HOSPITAL ("The House of Peace" Hospital). A general hospital formerly owned and operated by the Middle East Division of the General Conference (from 1946 to 1959) at Baghdad, Iraq.

Seventh-day Adventist medical work began in Baghdad in the early 1930s when Marie Huehner, of Germany, opened a maternity home. Dr. E. G. Essery and Stanley Johnson began remodeling the premises of what had been one of Baghdad's busiest hotels into a temporary 25-bed hospital. Called to other work, these two were succeeded by Drs. Joseph Saaty and S. D. Karmy. Joined by two nurses, Joyce and Lucille Henderson, and Melville Seitz, they opened Dar es Salaam (also transliterated Dar El Salaam) Hospital and received the first patients in November 1946. A School of Nursing was founded in October 1948, with the first students coming from various countries in the Middle East. That same year the hospital registered 7,685 patient visits and admitted 347 persons.

In June 1951 the General Conference signed a 90-year lease with the Iraq government on 5.7 acres (23,000 square meters) of land in an exclusive section of Baghdad for the purpose of erecting a modern hospital building. On June 8, 1952, the minister of health of Iraq laid the cornerstone. The new Dar es-Salaam Hospital was dedicated Nov. 27, 1954.

Financial support for the hospital stemmed mainly from the church organization and its members, notably the brothers Bashir and Nasif Hasso, members of the Baghdad church.

Dar es Salaam Hospital was reputed to be the finest medical facility in Iraq. Village clinics conducted by the staff extended the services of the hospital. More than 1,000 patients were hospitalized in 1955, the first full year of operation in the new 46-bed unit. The total was 1,269 in 1956, 1,589 in 1957, and 1,761 in 1958. From the School of Nursing, recognized by the Iraq Ministry of Health in 1958, the total number of graduates reached 24. By the end of that year the hospital staff included 90 national employees and 12 foreign workers.

The revolution in Iraq, beginning July 14, 1958, brought a trend toward nationalization of medical services, which became readily apparent by early 1959. In May the Iraq government announced its intention to nationalize the Dar es-Salaam Hospital. It was closed in early June; late the following month, it was reopened as a government-managed hospital staffed by medical personnel from Eastern Europe. Several members of the former staff were transferred to the Benghazi Hospital in Libya.

Negotiations with the revolutionary government concluded with an agreement that provided for the recovery of a sizable percentage of the church's net capital investment.

Medical Directors: ———, 1946-1949; Clarence H. Schilt, 1949-1952; K. H. Pihl, 1952-1955; William Wagner, 1955-1959.

Administrators: M. V. Jacobson, 1949-1956; Richard G. Ubbink, 1956-1959.

Directors of the School of Nursing: Mrs. Joseph Saaty, 1948-1949; Evelyn Welch, 1949-1951; Evangeline Voth, 1951-1958; Gladys Hurd, 1958-1959.

DAR ES SALAAM SCHOOL. An educational institution on the secondary level that was located at Karadet Mariam, Baghdad, Iraq. The school was established in 1947. This school was nationalized, along with all other private schools in Iraq, in 1974.

DARK AGES. A standard historical term used by historians to mean the period of intellectual and cultural stagnation and decline in Europe lasting from the overthrow of the Roman Empire by the barbarians to the revival of learning (the Renaissance). Although some make the term equivalent to the Middle Ages as a whole (the thousand years from 500 to 1500 at the latest), most historians equate it with the *early* Middle Ages (roughly from the sixth to the eleventh centuries). The "darkness" began to be dispelled first in the Renaissance, and further in the Reformation and the age of exploration. With the sixteenth century we reach the beginnings of modern history. The phrase is sometimes misused in expositions of the historical fulfillment of the time prophecies.

DARK DAY. As defined in Merriam-Webster *Third International Dictionary* (1950 and earlier editions): "Any day characterized by great darkness, whether due to cloudiness, smoke, volcanic ashes, or the like; esp., May 19, 1780, when an unexplained darkness extended over all New England (possibly due to forest fires)." Because of its preeminence as the most outstanding occurrence of this sort, unequaled in intensity, extent, and duration—as dark as at "candle-lighting" for some hours in a large area of New England, and also because of its timing, the Dark Day of May 19, 1780, was cited by Millerites and by later Adventists as a fulfillment of certain prophecies (Matt. 24:29; Rev. 6:12). For eyewitness accounts describing the meteorological phenomena and the effect of this notable obscuration, see SB 562ff.

DARLING RANGE SCHOOL. *See* Carmel Adventist College.

DAUGHERTY, FRANK J. (1902-1984). Missionary, educator. He and his wife, Ila, served in Alaska at Shungnak from 1929 to 1934. It was considered one of the most isolated and run-down villages in the Arctic. Frank went as a community worker, but found himself wearing many hats.

From 1934 to 1937 he taught more than 100 children at Point Barrow while working for the United Press. During this period he organized the rescue party searching for Will Rogers and Wiley Post.

He next labored at Gambell, St. Lawrence Island, during the period of 1937-1944. He was both principal and teacher there, and organized the first group of Sabbathkeepers in the Arctic. There is now an organized church in this place.

In 1949 he was asked to reopen the Navajo Mission School at Holbrook, Arizona, where he served as principal, business manager, construction superintendent, teacher, and pastor. After 17 years of this his health began to fail, but he continued to do voluntary work at the mission until he passed away. He gave out more than 3,000 copies of *Steps to Christ* at tourist centers.

Daugherty was the key person in obtaining both Thunderbird Adventist Academy and Monterey Bay Academy properties from the government for $1 each.

DAVAO MISSION. *See* Far Eastern Division; Philippines.

DAVID, DEACON (1895-1954). Minister, pioneer worker in the Delta area of Burma (Myanmar). He was a son of David Hpo Hla (the first ordained Burmese SDA minister) and began work in the church in 1919 as a teacher at the Meiktila School. Later he was sent to a Seventh-day Adventist theological training school at Lucknow, India, and upon return was sent to open Adventist work in Bumah Chaung in the Delta area of Burma, where he spent many years as pastor-evangelist. A number of his converts there later became evangelists. In 1926 he married Daw Mya May. In 1931 he was ordained to the ministry. In 1941 he was elected as a delegate to the General Conference session, the first Burmese to attend the general council of the church. He spent the war years in Rangoon and afterward served as pastor of the Rangoon church and Bible teacher of Myaungmya Middle School. He retired because of poor health a few years before his death.

DAVIDIAN SEVENTH-DAY ADVENTISTS—SHEPHERD'S ROD. An offshoot launched by Victor T. Houteff, a member of a Seventh-day Adventist church in Los Angeles, California, in 1929, popularly called the "Shepherd's Rod," after the title of his first publication. His organization took the name of "Davidian Seventh-day Adventists" in 1942. Houteff, who regarded himself as a divinely inspired messenger of God, set forth succinctly the primary subject of his teaching in his first publication as follows: "This publication contains only one main subject with a double lesson; namely, the 144,000 [of Rev. 7:4-9; 14:1] and a call for reformation" (*The Shepherd's Rod,* first ed. [1930], vol. 1, p. 11).

In May 1935 Houteff and 11 followers (including children) migrated from California to Waco, Texas, and established a colony on a nearby farm, which they referred to thereafter as Mount Carmel Center. This center was intended to be the temporary headquarters for the assembling of the 144,000 sealed ones, preparatory to their transfer to Palestine as the re-established kingdom of David under a theocratic regime, there to direct the closing work of the gospel on earth prior to the second advent of Christ.

Prior to his death on Feb. 5, 1955, Houteff had appointed his wife to lead his flock until the Lord should choose another prophet to take charge of it. The Waco *Tribune-Herald* of Feb. 27, 1955, reported shortly after Houteff's death that at one time there had been as many as 125 persons living at the Mount Carmel Center, including children and some invalids in the rest home.

Immediately after Houteff's death the Shepherd's Rod party began to break up into splinter groups. The main body, under Mrs. Houteff's leadership, announced in print to the public that the prophetic period of 1260 days foretold in Rev. 11 would end on Apr. 22, 1959, and that on that date God would intervene in a remarkable manner in Palestine to clear out both the Jews and the Arabs for the establishment of the Davidic kingdom in that country. Responding to an official call to assemble at their Waco headquarters during Apr. 16-22, 1959, in readiness to move to Palestine as soon as Providence should indicate, several hundred persons gathered at the Mount Carmel Center to await the fulfillment of the prediction. When the date passed uneventfully, most of the people—disappointed, confused, and embarrassed—scattered slowly from Waco to begin life anew elsewhere as best they could. Some returned to the SDA Church, some lost all faith in the Bible and strayed off into the world, and some joined splinter groups, such as "the Branch" (which actually sent a few colonizers to Israel in a mission that has ended in failure). Some stayed with the Waco leaders to face the future.

Mrs. Houteff and her associate leaders frankly and publicly acknowledged in print on Dec. 12, 1961, and Jan. 16, 1962, that the Shepherd's Rod party and its peculiar teachings were not sound. Finally, on Mar. 11, 1962, they resigned, declared the Davidian Association dissolved, closed their Mount Carmel Center, and put the property up for sale. Having done this, they scattered.

Subsequent to Mrs. Houteff's disbanding of the organization, several groups persisted, each claiming to be the authentic successor to the Shepherd's Rod party. One of these groups, calling themselves Branch Davidian Seventh-day Adventists, established a center, again near Waco, which in 1984 came under the control of Vernon Howell, who in 1981 had been disfellowshipped from the Tyler, Texas, Seventh-day Adventist Church. Later Howell changed his name to David Koresh, a name adopted from the Semitic form of the name of Cyrus, the Persian ruler of the sixth century B.C. In addition to pressing his claim to the prophetic gift, he presented himself as a latter-day fulfillment of the roles of David and Cyrus as deliverers of God's people.

Howell (Koresh) traveled widely, recruiting members for his community, especially in Australia and Great Britain. His special teachings, based on an interpretation of Ezekiel 9 and the seven seals of Revelation, led to a heightened sense of impending attack, for which in preparation a large quantity of firearms was stockpiled in the Davidian headquarters.

On Feb. 28, 1993, the Davidian community was surrounded by law-enforcement authorities, leading to extensive gunfire and the death of several persons, both within the building and of officers outside. A tense state of siege continued, until on Apr. 19, 1993, during an attack by officers, fire broke out in the building, destroying the wooden structure and killing approximately 90 persons inside.

Since destruction of the Branch Davidian community, several other splinter groups remain as remnants of the Shepherd's Rod movement.

"DAVIS" INDIANS. *See* Davis, Ovid Elbert; Guyana.

DAVIS, MARIAN (1847-1904). Secretary to Ellen White. Prior to 1879, when she entered the employ of Ellen White as a literary assistant, she taught a country school for a short time, and worked as a proofreader in the Review and Herald printing office for several years. She accompanied Mrs. White in her travels in America, to Europe in 1885, and to Australia in 1891. She returned with Mrs. White to California in 1900.

DAVIS MEMORIAL HOSPITAL. A 54-bed general acute hospital situated in Georgetown, the capital and chief city of Guyana. It is owned and operated by the Caribbean Union Conference. It was named in memory of O. E. Davis, a pioneer Seventh-day Adventist missionary to the aboriginal Indian people of British Guiana (now Guyana), who died among them in 1911.

The present staff consists of one local and two overseas physicians, one local dental surgeon, two local dentists, 13 graduate national nurses, 18 practical nurses, three nurses' aides, one pharmacist, two X-ray technicians, and four laboratory technicians.

SDA medical work in Guyana dates from 1952, when the mission committee, with R. E. Delafield as chair, took action to build a clinic on the mission's Queenstown property in eastern Georgetown. Materials were secured from the United States air base nearby, and the construction was under the direction of F. Todd, a contractor. The cornerstone was laid on Nov. 9, 1952, by the mayor of Georgetown, R. B. Gajraj.

A physician, E. C. Duerksen, called to head the clinic, arrived on Feb. 24, 1954, and by the end of the year had treated a total of 5,295 persons, about half of them charity patients. At that time the staff totaled nine workers. An open house was held on Oct. 28, 1954, which was attended by the governor and a number of local dignitaries.

When the clinic proved inadequate for the needs of the area, early in 1955 a large house was rented, and on July 21, 1955, after another physician, O. J. Pogue, had joined the staff, a hospital was opened. The first surgery performed at the hospital was a hernia repair on a church member by the name of DeJonge, for which, in the absence of a surgery light, L. A. Kraner, mission president at the time, provided illumination by holding a gooseneck desk lamp. Until an autoclave was installed in 1956, sterilization of supplies was done at a government hospital. When the water supply improved in 1957, it was no longer necessary to pump water by hand. A part of a Thirteenth Sabbath Offering overflow in 1960, together with donations solicited locally and hospital earnings, provided a fund to finance the construction of a 40-bed hospital, which was opened in December 1965. It was not until Apr. 16, 1967, that the hospital was officially opened by the lord mayor, Mrs. Dorothy Bailey, in the presence of a capacity crowd, including the governor-general.

The present building houses a laundry, patient rooms, kitchen, surgery, labor and delivery rooms, laboratory, X-ray, Outpatient Department, and other essential units. It has two private rooms, three semiprivate rooms, four private wards, and four clinic wards.

This building, with ground floor and one story, was a dream of Dr. Oliver J. Pogue, who was instrumental in transforming the dream of a modern Davis Memorial Hospital into a reality.

In 1971 Shirley Field-Ridley, minister of health, opened the dental clinic. The audience included several officials of government and a good cross section of the community.

The institution was operated under a medical director/business manager form of administration until 1966.

Medical Directors/Administrators: E. C. Duerksen, 1954-1957; O. J. Pogue, 1957-1966; H. N. Gates, 1966-1971; R. D. Neufeld, 1971-1976; R. P. Woodruff (acting), 1976-1977;

Jess C. Holm, 1977-1978; Reynaldo L. Descalso, 1978-1980; Maxwell Blakeney, 1980-1983; Bertram Todd, 1983-1985; Erling Berg, 1985-1986; Ernest A. Burgess, 1986-1989; Mrs. Leila P. Julien, 1989-1992; Esther Premdas-Quashie, 1992- .

DAVIS, OVID ELBERT (1869-1911). Missionary to Guiana. A ministerial graduate from Emmanuel Missionary College, he began his service as a self-supporting missionary in Canada and Alaska. He pioneered the work among the Indians at Port Simpson, British Columbia, near the southern end of the Alaska panhandle, and on Dec. 11, 1903, established there the first Indian church in the province, and possibly in the Pacific Northwest. After working there for three or four years, and for a brief period in Washington and Michigan, he took charge of the Guiana Mission in 1906. He had established three stations among the Indians of the interior when he died of blackwater fever on a missionary trip to Mount Roraima. Because of his work among the Arecuna and Akawaio tribes, these Indians have been called "Davis" Indians by Seventh-day Adventists. One of their chiefs reported that he had had a vision telling him of the second coming of Christ, and promising him that a man with a "black book" would be sent to his tribe to teach them more about God and the seventh-day Sabbath.

DAVIS, THOMAS H. (d. 1911). One of the pioneer Seventh-day Adventist colporteurs who brought SDA publications to Chile and Ecuador. He and F. W. Bishop were sent to Chile in 1894. Ten years later, in 1904, he entered Ecuador and served as field secretary and colporteur until 1909. He died at the River Plate Sanitarium in Argentina.

DAVIS, WILLIAM C. (1760-1831). A Presbyterian minister, founder of an Independent Presbyterian Church (which had about a dozen congregations) in South Carolina, and apparently the first in America to explain (in his 1811 pamphlet *The Millennium*) the 70 weeks and the 2300 days as beginning together, the latter ending with 1847. This ending point, however, he allowed as possibly four years earlier, since, as he remarked, the Christian Era was generally thought to be four years too late. Thus he implied 1843, William Miller's date for the end of the 2300 years. Said Miller: "One or two in every quarter of the globe have proclaimed the news, and agree in the time," and mentioned Davis and several others who dated the end of the 2300 years in 1843 or 1847. But what Davis looked for was not the Second Advent but "the downfall of popery, and the dawn of the church's glory," that is, the millennium, which, like many other postmillennialists of his day, he explained (in his 1827 book *A Treatise on the Millennium)* as 360,000 years, to be followed by the Second Advent.

DAVY, WILLIAM LUDLOW (1886-1957). Missionary in Nyasaland (Malawi). He was born in Plymouth, England, where he received his grammar school education. During his boyhood years he was deeply impressed by reading the life and missionary experiences of David Livingstone. He also attended a lecture by John G. Paton, the famous missionary to the South Seas. These two things strongly influenced him to give himself to mission service some years later. At the age of 21 he emigrated to Canada, where he studied for three years at Battleford Academy. Shortly after this he married Elsie Annie Little.

In 1920 Davy and his wife traveled to Africa and spent the first four months at Solusi Mission. From there they went to Nyasaland, where Davy was appointed director of the Matandani Mission, a station some 70 miles (112 kilometers) west of the city of Blantyre. At this station they worked together for four years.

In 1924 Mrs. Davy became ill with blackwater fever. Because the exceptionally heavy rainy season that year had washed away the bridge over the Shire River, no medical help could reach her, and she died. Alone, Davy conducted his wife's funeral and the same year, with his three children, returned to the United States.

In 1926 he married Lydia Stickle, and together they went to Africa. After nine months in Bechuanaland, he returned to Nyasaland. For the next five years he was again stationed at Matandani, and afterward he was called to assist at the Malamulo Mission Training School. The first year there he taught in the school, and in 1935 acted as director of the mission. It was at Malamulo that he was ordained to the ministry by H. M. Sparrow.

After his return from furlough in 1936, Davy and his wife were sent to Luwazi, the northernmost SDA mission in Nyasaland, situated some 24 miles (38 kilometers) from Lake Nyasa, where they worked together for almost 20 years. Davy walked for hundreds of miles through the hills, established dozens of outschools, and watched churches grow. When failing health at length forced him to leave Africa, he retired in Modesto, California.

DAWN. *See* Deaf Persons, Work for.

DAY OF ATONEMENT. *See* Investigative Judgment; Sanctuary; Scapegoat.

DAY-DAWN (1845-1847). An Adventist (not Seventh-day Adventist) paper published, apparently irregularly, at Canandaigua, New York, by F. B. Hahn, and edited by O.R.L. Crosier. Its first issue appeared on Mar. 26, 1845, in the *Ontario Messenger.* The *Day-Dawn* was also published as a separate paper for distribution among Adventists. Only the *Ontario Messenger* article is known to be extant. The *Day-Dawn* was reported in the *Day-Star* 5:36, Apr. 15, 1845. The *Day-Dawn* carried the first sanctuary article that was closely connected with the "Bridegroom" concept as advocated by Joseph Turner and Apollos Hale in the January 1845 *Advent Mirror.* O.R.L. Crosier wrote his more definitive article on the sanctuary in the Feb. 7, 1846, *Day-Star Extra.* Later issues of the *Day-Dawn* carried Crosier's 1846 advocacy of the Sabbath (extract, *Review and Herald* 3:8, May 6, 1852); also more on the sanctuary (reprint: *ibid.* 1:78-80, May 5, 1851) and notes on his "new view" of the daily, both in March 1847.

DAYS OF FASTING AND PRAYER. *See* Fasting.

DAYS, SPECIAL. *See* Church Calendar.

DAY-STAR (1843-1847?). A Millerite periodical founded in Cincinnati as *The Western Midnight Cry,* with J. V. Himes as publisher; first edited by George Storrs, who was succeeded in December 1843 by Enoch Jacobs. After the disappointment of 1844 Jacobs took over publication of the paper and renamed it the *Day-Star,* beginning Feb. 18, 1845. Because the *Day-Star* dissented from Himes's *Advent Herald* in holding that the 1844 movement was valid and that the 2300 days had ended in October 1844, many of those who shared the *Day-Star* view, including James White and others who became the pioneers of the Seventh-day Adventist movement, read the *Day-Star* and wrote letters to its editor. In its columns appeared the first published communications from Ellen Harmon (White) and an extended exposition of the doctrine of the sanctuary written by O.R.L. Crosier (based on joint study with Hiram Edson and F. B. Hahn). Crosier had first written of the importance of the sanctuary in the March 1845 *Day-Dawn.* He began a more complete presentation of the types in the *Day-Star,* beginning on Sept. 26, 1845. This culminated in the publication of the *Day-Star Extra.*

SDA pioneers found themselves parting company with the *Day-Star* after Jacobs in 1846 went over to the "Spiritualizers," whose doctrine he had formerly denounced *(see* Spiritualism [1]). Soon afterward he joined the Shakers; the paper was moved to a Shaker settlement, Union Village, near Lebanon, Ohio, and in May 1847 became a Shaker publication.

DEACON. The local church officer next in rank to an elder. Deacons have care of the church's temporal business, are responsible for the care of the church property (all bills for upkeep are referred to the treasurer), assist the elders in the celebration of the Lord's Supper by receiving the bread and wine from the pastor or elder and serving the members, help in making the physical arrangement for the Communion service and the baptismal service, and have a particular charge of relieving the poor, the unfortunate, and the needy sick.

The deacon is elected to office by the church for a term of one year, and must be reelected if he is to continue in office. He must be ordained to his office *(see* Ordination) by an ordained minister holding credentials from the conference. A deacon once ordained need not be reordained upon reelection, provided he has maintained his church membership. If one who has been ordained as an elder is elected as deacon, he need not be ordained as a deacon, for his ordination in the one office qualifies him to function in the other as well. In a large church a board of deacons is organized, which is presided over by a head deacon.

The first reference to deacons in the Seventh-day Adventist Church is probably the mention of a committee of seven chosen at Washington, New Hampshire, in 1851 "to attend to the wants of the poor" *(Review and Herald* 2:52, Nov. 25, 1851). In 1853 the *Review and Herald* mentions two men, one in Fairhaven, Massachusetts, and the other in Dartmouth, Massachusetts, who were named deacons to administer the ordinances during the absence of a minister. These were approved by a full assembly of the churches and set apart by Frederick Wheeler by prayer and the laying on of hands (*ibid* 4:199, Dec. 27, 1853). Similarly the next year Charles Glover was chosen and set apart as a deacon at Sylvan, Michigan, and Cyrenius Smith at Jackson, Michigan. Apparently each church had only one officer, a deacon.

At first the office of deacon in the SDA Church seems to have combined the functions of deacon and elder. It was some time later that elders were appointed to carry the responsibilities outlined in Scripture, and deacons were assigned specifically to the temporal affairs of the churches.

It is generally thought that the incident mentioned in Acts 6:1-6 is a record of the origin of the office of a deacon in the Christian church. However, the seven men set apart are not called deacons; nevertheless their duties and responsibilities corresponded closely to those of the deacons whose qualifications Paul enumerated in 1 Tim. 3:8-13. The New Testament shows that the office of a deacon implied more than caring for the material needs of the church. *See* Church (local); Deaconess.

DEACONESS. A woman elected in a local church to perform functions analogous to those of a deacon. The term *deaconess* (Greek *diakonos*, which can refer to either males or females) occurs in Rom. 16:1, RSV, in a context (compare v. 2) that suggests that the office of deaconess may have been established by the time the Epistle to the Romans was written, toward the close of the sixth decade of the Christian Era. Deaconesses cooperate with the deacons in caring for the sick, poor, and unfortunate. They prepare the bread for the Lord's Supper and arrange the Communion table. They also take care of the towels and basins used in the ordinance of foot washing. They assist the women candidates in the baptismal service and take care of the baptismal robes. In larger churches, a board of deaconesses is formed, with a chairman and sometimes a secretary. In many churches deaconesses help at the regular Sabbath service by welcoming people to church, especially visitors.

DEAD, STATE OF THE. *See* Death.

DEADLY WOUND. *See* Revelation, Interpretation of.

DEAF LIGHT. *See* Christian Record Services, Inc.

DEAF PERSONS, WORK FOR. Seventh-day Adventist work for deaf persons is mentioned as early as 1879. At that time Ellen White wrote, "We were interested in Brother Kimbal, who is a mute and has been a missionary among the mutes" (4T 300).

Although for many years Seventh-day Adventists had no organized work for deaf individuals, there were persons who devoted their time to giving the SDA message to them. As early as 1914 Agatha Kroeker, of Lincoln, Nebraska, instructed a young deaf woman in the SDA message in exchange for instruction in the use of sign language. Miss Kroeker then proceeded to carry on active evangelistic work for deaf persons, and even published a small missionary paper, *The Best Friend of the Deaf.* In one year she had collected more than 4,000 names of deaf persons in the United States.

In 1949 E. H. Adams, an SDA minister, and his wife became burdened for deaf people, and began work among them in the Oakland, California, area.

At the General Conference session in 1950 a committee, consisting of A. V. Olsen, A. L. Ham, and E. D. Dick, was commissioned to make recommendations concerning a proposal presented by a young man, John Issler, that a mission for deaf persons be organized. In a letter to the General Conference two years earlier, he had stated that he had a burden to work for deaf people in the North American Division. He had been told that his burden was appreciated, but that at that time there were no plans to open a special department among deaf persons.

In 1953 the following recommendation was adopted by the General Conference as presented from the union conference presidents: "*We recommend,* That a survey be made in each local conference to secure names and addresses of deaf people, and that plans be laid in the conference to send them literature of the message" (North American Division Committee on Administration, *Minutes,* Apr. 13, 1953, pp. 53, 54).

In the meantime, from 1951 to 1953, Issler had canvassed in the Los Angeles, California, area and had collected 7,000 names of deaf persons.

The next year responsibility for directing work for deaf persons was assigned to the Home Foreign Committee. The General Conference recommended "that efforts be made to develop workers to preach the present truth in the sign language to the deaf-mutes, and that in North America the Home Foreign Committee be encouraged to study this problem with interested union conferences" *(General Conference Reports,* vol. 131, No. 29, p. 224).

At the 1958 General Conference session, held in Cleveland, Ohio, the following recommendations were made to enlarge the work for deaf persons:

"1. That the General Conference Committee study ways and means to strengthen the work on behalf of persons thus afflicted and to encourage the training of workers in the use of the sign language.

"2. That the responsibility of fostering our work among the deaf-mutes be assigned to one of the departments of the General Conference as may be determined by the General Conference Committee."

The same year (1958) Arthur W. Griffith, a lay worker for deaf persons, joined Issler in the development of a monthly newsletter for SDA deaf persons called *Dawn*, standing for Deaf Adventist Witness News. It is now called *New Dawn* and is published bimonthly by Christian Record Services.

About this time (1958) C. N. Kohler, an SDA minister, was called to work for deaf persons in the Central and Northern California conferences, especially in the Bay Area. He served in this phase of the work until 1960, when he returned to ministry for those with no loss of hearing.

In 1960 the North American Missions Committee was given the responsibility of the work for deaf persons. The same year (1960) Neil Davidson and his wife were invited by the Southern California Conference to fill the vacancy left by Issler, who resigned because of ill health. Arthur Griffith was called by the Oregon Conference committee to work for deaf persons part-time on salary. In July 1961 he was taken on as a full-time licensed minister to deaf individuals. In the same year Rex Rolls, a colporteur from Nevada, was invited by the Central and Northern California conferences to take up the work laid down by Kohler.

In 1968 Alfred Griffith, son of Arthur Griffith, graduated from Walla Walla College and was called to the Potomac Conference to work for deaf students in the Washington, D.C., area. He conducted a six-week evangelistic effort for deaf persons at Gallaudet College. By 1971, 20 students in that area had joined his group.

In 1970 Arthur Griffith was the first deaf person to be ordained to the gospel ministry, and, in addition to his work in Oregon, began spasmodic work for scattered deaf persons in Vancouver, British Columbia. In 1975 he was called to the Potomac Conference and continued the ministry at Gallaudet College. Rex Rolls then accepted a call to succeed Griffith in working for deaf persons in the Oregon Conference.

In 1979 the Northern California Conference called Alfred Griffith to work for deaf persons in the Bay Area. Alfred expanded his work to most parts of northern California. In 1993 Alfred was still working in northern California.

In 1980 the General Conference called Thompson Kay, who had taught at the Ohio State School for the Deaf and was then teaching at Alcy Junior Academy in Memphis, Tennessee, to start a deaf ministry. Kay became director of Deaf Services at what is now Christian Record Services. He worked with the *Adult Sabbath School Lesson* editors to produce an *Easy English Adult Lesson Quarterly* designed for those who had a limited vocabulary as a result of their hearing problem. Kay also was responsible for the production of such Easy English materials as *The Story of Redemption*, Amazing Facts, and sign language coloring books. He conducted numerous deaf awareness programs for SDA churches throughout the world field.

In 1987 a deaf layperson, Max Gallimore, was called to work for Deaf Services as editor. He edited *Deaf-Light*, an inspirational outreach magazine, and *New Dawn*, a newsletter for deaf persons.

In 1993 four deaf persons were working for the SDA Church: George Belser in the Oregon Conference, Raj Witteborg in the Potomac Conference, Paul Kelly in the New York Conference, and David M. Trexler as editor in the Deaf Services at Christian Record Services.

Church Membership and Population. The exact total of deaf members among the SDA churches in North America is not fully known, but CRS serves approximately 600 SDA deaf persons in North America. According to the 1990 census, there are 23 million deaf and hearing-impaired persons in the United States alone.

DEATH. The cessation of life and the state that follows. The Scriptures speak of: (1) the first death, the common lot of all humans as the natural result of Adam's sin (Rom. 5:12; 1 Cor. 15:22; Heb. 9:27); (2) "the second death," the "wages," or penalty of sin, at the end of the millennium (Rom. 6:23; Rev. 2:11; 20:14; 21:8); (3) spiritual death "in trespasses and sins," the condition of those who have never accepted

Christ, or who, having accepted Him, fall away (Rom. 8:6; Eph. 2:1, 5, 6; Col. 2:13; 1 Tim. 5:6); and (4) death to sin, which accompanies the new birth (Rom. 6:2-11; Gal. 2:20; Col. 2:13; 1 Peter 2:24; 1 John 3:14). This article is concerned with the first and second deaths.

Seventh-day Adventists conceive of humanity as an integral unity in which the component parts are interdependent. Upon the disintegration of this unity at the "first" death, conscious existence is no longer possible—the condition of humanity in death is "one of unconsciousness" *(Church Manual* [1990], p. 181). The second death is the consuming of the wicked *(ibid.,* p. 180). Seventh-day Adventists believe that men and women are by nature mortal beings, that immortality is conditional on accepting Christ, and that it will be bestowed simultaneously on all the saved of all ages, at the second coming of Christ (1 Cor. 15:22, 23, 51-54).

Origin and Development of the Seventh-day Adventist View. The majority of adherents to the Millerite movement believed that human beings are conscious in death, and that the wicked will suffer eternal punishment. However, through the influence principally of George Storrs, a Methodist minister, a number espoused the doctrine of unconsciousness in death. Storrs got his doctrine from Henry Grew, a devout and critical student of the Bible, who in 1835 published a tract titled *The Intermediate State.* This tract set forth the concept that all of humanity is subject "to the dominion of death, and that hope of all future existence must be founded on the glorious doctrine of the resurrection from the grave" (Henry Grew, *The Intermediate State* [1844], preface, p. 2).

Two years later (1837) Storrs read Grew's pamphlet, but was at first skeptical of its teachings. However, being a sincere and diligent Bible student, Storrs searched the Scriptures on this point and, after three years, finally espoused Grew's view. Soon after accepting this new teaching, he withdrew from the Methodist communion. He wrote three letters to an intimate friend, a prominent minister in the Methodist Church, in which he set forth his new convictions. A few months later Storrs had an interview with this minister, who advised him to publish the views expressed in the three letters. Taking his friend's advice, Storrs issued *An Enquiry; Are the Souls of the Wicked Immortal? In Three Letters* (1841). After further intensive investigation of the subject, he expanded this work, which appeared in 1842 as a book titled *An Enquiry; Are the Souls of the Wicked Immortal? In Six Sermons.* This work, popularly known as Storrs' *Six Sermons,* received wide circulation throughout the United States and exerted a profound influence on William Miller's followers.

Through the influence of Charles Fitch, a prominent Millerite leader, Storrs accepted, in mid-1842, the Millerite teaching concerning the imminence of the Second Advent. Later Storrs himself became prominent in the movement and led many of the Millerites to accept his views concerning humanity's unconscious condition in death and the ultimate extermination of the impenitent.

At first Storrs did not introduce his "peculiar" views directly into his public preaching, apparently so as not to distract attention from the more important message of the Lord's imminent return.

But as it was known that he held these views he was constantly met with inquirers, both ministers and private Christians, to whom he frankly stated his belief that "all the wicked will God destroy" *(Six Sermons on the Inquiry: Is There Immortality in Sin and Suffering?* [1855], p. 13).

When, on several occasions in the fall of 1842, the Millerite periodical *The Signs of the Times* censured a minister who felt it his duty to preach not only the coming of the Lord but also what the end of the wicked would be, Storrs felt that he should keep silent no longer, and so he published 5,000 copies of a revised edition of his *Six Sermons* and scattered them over the United States. The following year (1843) he started the *Bible Examiner,* a periodical issued occasionally, whose object was expressed by its motto, "No Immortality, or Endless Life Except Through Jesus Christ Alone" *(ibid.,* p. 17). In this journal he answered his critics and propagated his views.

On Jan. 25, 1844, Charles Fitch, who had convinced Storrs of the imminence of the Second Advent, took his stand for the doctrines of unconsciousness in death and the destruction of the wicked. Concerning this he wrote, as quoted by Storrs in the later edition of his *Six Sermons:* "As you have long been fighting the Lord's battles alone on the subject of the state of the dead and of the final doom of the wicked, I write this to say that I am at last, after much thought and prayer, and a full conviction of duty to God, prepared to take my stand by your side" *(ibid.,* p. 15).

Storrs' writings convinced many Millerites that his positions were correct. Many other ministers in various other parts of the country also came to the same view. With few exceptions, however, the leaders of the Millerite movement were strongly opposed to Storrs' teachings. This is clearly indicated in a letter by I. E. Jones, a Millerite preacher of Boston, to William Miller, dated Apr. 6, 1844: "I had the pleasure of seeing Brother Litch and Brother Whiting last week, and the last, and again this week, and they think as do our Boston brethren, Himes, Bliss and Hale, that something ought to be done to separate our influence from Brother Storrs' views of the end of the wicked; for, as it now is, he virtually wields from our silence, the whole, or almost the whole, advent influence" (quoted in F. D. Nichol, *The Midnight Cry,* p. 192).

It seems apparent that Storrs had a substantial following among the rank and file of the Millerites. But since the leaders as a whole were opposed to his views, opposition manifested itself. William Miller, among others, took Storrs to task for his views, and in a letter disclaimed "any connection, fellowship, or sympathy with Br. Storrs' views of the intermediate state, and the end of the wicked" *(Midnight Cry* 6:355, May 23, 1844).

Another opponent, Josiah Litch, editor, organizer, and preacher in the Millerite movement, became so agitated that he published a paper against Storrs' views, called the *Anti-Annihilationist.*

But in spite of opposition from various sources, Storrs' views took root. Among those who accepted them was Ellen G. Harmon (later Ellen G. White), who subsequently became a prominent leader and writer in the Seventh-day Adventist Church. In the book *Life Sketches . . . Experience and Extensive Labors of Elder James White and His Wife, Mrs. Ellen G. White* (1880) Mrs. White relates how she came to adopt the conditionalist view concerning death and the annihilation of the wicked. She says: "One day I listened to a conversation between my mother and a sister, in reference to a discourse which they had recently heard, to the effect that the soul had not natural immortality. Some of the minister's proof texts were repeated. . . .

"I listened to these new ideas with an intense and painful interest. When alone with my mother, I inquired if she really believed that the soul was not immortal. Her reply was that she feared we had been in error on that subject, as well as upon some others.

"'But, mother,' said I, 'do you really believe that the soul sleeps in the grave until the resurrection? Do you think that the Christian, when he dies, does not go immediately to heaven, nor the sinner to hell?'

"She answered: 'The Bible gives us no proof that there is an eternally burning hell. . . .'

"It was some months after this conversation before I heard anything further concerning this doctrine; but during this time my mind had been much exercised upon the subject. When I heard it preached, I believed it to be the truth" (pp. 170, 171).

The impact of Storrs' views on the Millerites may be judged by the fact that one of the 10 fundamental principles adopted at the conference held in Albany, New York, on Apr. 29, 1845, stated that the inheritance of the departed saints is not received at death but at the Second Advent. Also indicative of the influence of Storrs' views on the Millerites is the fact that in 1961 at least four of the five surviving religious bodies whose origins may be traced to the Millerite movement still held that man is unconscious in death, and at least three of the five held that the wicked will be destroyed in the second death. The exception is the Life and Advent Union, which holds that those who are not saved "will remain in their graves forever" (Frank S. Mead, *Handbook of Denominations in the United States* [1961], p. 23).

About the time that Ellen Harmon accepted the views of humanity's unconsciousness in death and of the destruction of the wicked, James White and Joseph Bates, Millerite preachers who later became prominent Seventh-day Adventist leaders, accepted them also. In *A Word to the Little Flock* (1847, pp. 3, 8, 10), one of the first publications of the group that later developed into the Seventh-day Adventist Church, White repeatedly speaks of the saints as being in their mortal state prior to the Second Advent, and Bates in his book *Second Advent Waymarks and High Heaps* (1847, p. 49) speaks of events that will come "after immortality" *(see* Immortality).

The first clear statement by a Seventh-day Adventist leader concerning humanity's unconscious condition in death appears to have been made by Roswell F. Cottrell, an early SDA leader, in the *Review and Herald* (4:157, Nov. 22, 1853), in which he declares: "'The dead know not anything,' and never will till they are raised from the dead, and that will not take place till Christ is seen in the clouds of heaven with power and great glory."

The first extended exposition of the SDA view on the end of the wicked appears to have been written by James White in a series of articles entitled "Destruction of the Wicked," beginning with the *Review and Herald* (6:82, 83) issue of Oct. 24, 1854, in which he proposed to "describe the different kinds of hell believed in by men," to "show the nature of the hell of the Bible," and to "prove from the Bible what will be the final destiny of the wicked." A year and a half later, he wrote in the *Review and Herald* (7:164, Feb. 21, 1856) that by the term *annihilation* he meant "destruction as conscious beings." In 1874 an article entitled "A Declaration of the Fundamental Principles of Seventh-day Adventists" declared that "the wicked" become "as though they had not been" *(Signs of the Times* 1:3, June 4, 1874).

The first SDA book dealing with the question of the first and second deaths was written by D. P. Hall, an SDA minister who later apostatized, and was titled *Man Not Immortal: The Only Shield Against the Seductions of Modern Spiritualism* (1854). This appeared first as a series of articles in the *Review and Herald* beginning in the Aug. 29, 1854, issue (6:17). These articles were followed a few months later by another series of articles by J. N. Loughborough, a pioneer leader, entitled "Is the Soul Immortal? An Examination of the Scripture Testimony Concerning Man's Present Condition and His Future Reward or Punishment," which first appeared in the Sept. 4, 1855, issue of the same periodical (7:33). These articles were published in book form in 1856 under the same title as the articles. By the mid-1850s SDA teachings concerning unconsciousness in death had become a settled doctrine.

Among early SDA books on this subject were: *Which? Mortal or Immortal? or An Inquiry Into the Present Constitution and Future Condition of Man,* by Uriah Smith (1860); *The Transgressor's Fate, or A Short Argument on the First and Second Deaths,* by Moses Hull (1861); *History of the Doctrine of the Immortality of the Soul,* by D. M. Canright (1871); and *Man's Nature and Destiny, or The State of the Dead, the Reward of the Righteous, and the End of the Wicked,* by Uriah Smith (1884).

Basis of the Seventh-day Adventist View. The Scriptures consistently teach that all created things subsist by the power of God (Acts 17:25, 28; Col. 1:16, 17). They continue to exist by virtue of the fact that God wills them to exist. God created human beings with a free will capable of choosing to disobey; thus they would reap the consequence—death (Gen. 2:16, 17). Continued existence was made contingent upon continuing obedience.

When Adam and Eve chose disobedience they would have been annihilated had not the Son of God in mercy offered to provide a vicarious atonement (Gal. 1:4; Titus 2:14; cf. Gen. 3:15; John 3:16). But the life that Adam and Eve—and their posterity—now had was a temporal, probationary life. It was henceforth "appointed unto men once to die" (Heb. 9:27; cf. Rom. 5:12).

However, this death, which is the common lot of all humanity, is not annihilation but a temporary unconscious state, until the resurrection. The Scriptures repeatedly and explicitly declare this intermediate state to be a period of unconsciousness. The following are some of the Bible passages that Seventh-day Adventists have used to support this view.

"In death there is no remembrance of thee: in the grave who shall give thee thanks?" (Ps. 6:5).

"The grave cannot praise thee, death cannot celebrate thee: they that go down into the pit cannot hope for thy truth" (Isa. 38:18; cf. Ps. 88:10-12).

"Put not your trust in princes, nor in the son of man, in whom there is no help. His breath goeth forth, he returneth to his earth; in that very day his thoughts perish" (Ps. 146:2-4).

"The dead praise not the Lord, neither any that go down into silence" (Ps. 115:17).

"[When a man dies] his sons come to honour and he knoweth it not; and they are brought low, but he perceiveth it not of them" (Job 14:21).

"The living know that they shall die; but the dead know not any thing" (Eccl. 9:5).

"There is no work, nor device, nor knowledge, nor wisdom, in the grave, whither thou goest" (v. 10).

SDAs also have used texts that refer to death as a "sleep," a figure, they believe, that implies unconsciousness:

"Now shall I sleep in the dust; and thou shall seek me in the morning but I shall not be" (Job 7:21).

"Man dieth, . . . and where is he? As the waters fail from the sea, and the flood decayeth and drieth up: so man lieth down, and riseth not: till the heavens be no more, they shall not awake, nor be raised out of their sleep" (Job 14:10-12).

"Lazarus sleepeth. . . . Lazarus is dead" (John 11:11, 13).

"They stoned Stephen. . . . And . . . he fell

asleep" (Acts 7:59, 60).

"They . . . which are fallen asleep in Christ" (1 Cor. 15:18).

For the second death, which represents complete cessation of being, *see* Hell. *See also* Immortality; Resurrection.

DEATH, SECOND. *See* Hell.

DE BEER, JOHANNES NICHOLAS (1881-1967). Colporteur, pioneer, missionary, administrator. Johannes was the grandson of the owner of the farm on which the Kimberley diamond mine was discovered. He was born in the Boshoff district of the Orange Free State and accepted the truth while very young. When he was 19 he went to Claremont Sanitarium, where he trained as a nurse and headed the Swedish Massage Department. After the old sanitarium closed he served the church as a colporteur for a time.

In 1910 Pastor and Mrs. De Beer went to Rhodesia, where for 12 years they served on various stations, pioneering the work in several areas. In 1922 he was called to the presidency of the Free State Conference.

In 1927 De Beer moved to Transkei and established the Cancele mission station. His work was always characterized by answered prayer and miracles of grace. Later he served as president of the Cape Field and the South Bantu Mission, where he labored until 1951.

He retired after more than 40 years of service to the church. During his retirement he ministered to a number of Cape churches.

DEBRE TABOR ADVENTIST CHURCH SCHOOL. A coeducational boarding school operated by the Northwest Ethiopia Field near Debre Tabor, 50 miles (80 kilometers) east of Lake Tana in northern Ethiopia. Known formerly as Begemder Mission School, it was the first school in Begemder province. This area is a Coptic Christian area, although there are some of other faiths.

The school was established in 1932 with about 20 students. Sheik Zekarias (or Zacharias), a Muslim, claiming a revelation from God, had predicted that people would come from abroad and teach the gospel more clearly and openly *(see* Ethiopia). This school was considered a fulfillment of his prediction.

Interrupted by the Italian war against Ethiopia, the school was reestablished, after five years, by G. Gudmundsen. Although originally a day school, it was soon made a boarding school, with about 20 boarding students. It grew gradually, until in 1973 there were 24 boarding and 197 day students. Debre Tabor Adventist School was nationalized in 1976.

Principals: E. E. Saarinen, 1957-1961; Rudolf Andersen, 1961-1964; Agedew Bezuneh, 1964-1966; Sherard Wilson, 1966-1970; C. Vander Mei, 1970-1973; Gebregziabier Guddaye, 1973-1976.

DEBRE TABOR HOSPITAL. *See* Haile Selassie I Hospital.

DECKER, HENRY W. (1837-1926). Administrator. Son of a pioneer Baptist minister in Wisconsin, he accepted the Seventh-day Adventist faith about 1859. In 1863 he was one of a committee of three in the Wisconsin Conference that appealed to the governor of the state on behalf of SDA service personnel in the Civil War. After his ordination in 1875, he was president of the Wisconsin Conference for a total of some 10 years, and for a short time headed the North Texas Conference. He preached in Illinois and then for many years preached and directed conferences in the Pacific Northwest. He was the chief promoter in the building of Walla Walla College and of the Portland Sanitarium.

DECREES, DIVINE. The doctrine that all events in the natural and spiritual realms were sovereignly determined by God from all eternity. According to Reformed theologians, the divine decrees are, in fact, part of one plan that embraces all human acts whether good or evil. In regard to evil, God's agency is said to be permissive.

On this subject the Seventh-day Adventist position approximates that of Arminian theology *(see* Arminianism), in contradistinction to the Calvinist. SDAs believe that God decreed a holy, happy life for all His creatures, and that sin was never part of God's sovereignly determined, eternal plan. The Reformed position, as John Wesley pointed out, brands God as responsible for the existence of sin, and produces antinomianism. "The doctrine of the divine decrees," wrote Ellen G. White, "unalterably fixing the character of men, had led many to a virtual rejection of the law of God" (GC 261).

God foresaw that some of the holy beings He planned to create would exercise their free wills, with which He endowed them, to sin. "From the beginning, God and Christ knew of the apostasy of Satan, and of the fall of man through the deceptive power of the apostate. God did not ordain that sin should exist, but He foresaw its existence and made provision to meet the terrible emergency" (DA 22).

In the eternal ages prior to Creation, on the basis of God's foreknowledge, it was decreed that Christ should pay the penalty for human transgression. Accordingly, God eternally decreed the availability of saving grace to all who should accept the proffered sacrifice, and that those who rejected it should eventually be annihilated, along with sin itself. Infinite wisdom devised a plan by which the universe would become forever secure; all who should choose to cooperate with the divine purpose should live forever, while those who refused to do so should cease to exist. But God endowed created beings with the power to choose, individually, the group with which they would be associated. Those who chose to be associated with the group predestined to annihilation would die an eternal death, while all who chose to be associated with the group predestined to life eternal would live forever.

DEDICATION, CHILD. *See* Child Dedication.

DEFENSE LITERATURE COMMITTEE. A committee instituted in 1943 by the General Conference Committee to study and answer publications against the church. At the request of the General Conference officers, this committee issued replies to attacks on the denomination and to teachings of offshoot groups. The name Defense Literature Committee was not adopted until some time after its founding. In 1969 this committee was merged with the Committee on Biblical Study and Research under the title Biblical Research Committee.

Chairs: L. H. Christian, 1943-1946; M. E. Kern, 1946-1952; W. E. Read, 1952-1958; H. W. Lowe, 1959-1969.

DE FLUITER, HENRY (1872-1970). Musician and pastor. A native of Holland, De Fluiter came to the United States in 1881. The following year he attended a meeting held by Dwight Moody and Ira Sankey and resolved to make the music field his lifework.

In 1902 he wrote his first hymn, "Matthew 24." Fifty-eight years later he wrote his last, "The Day Must Be Near." In the intervening years he wrote and published more than 200 hymns.

He associated with H.M.S. Richards in 1926, directing large choirs in crusades across the nation.

During his ministry he pastored numerous churches in southern California. Considered to be the Seventh-day Adventist Church's best-known hymn writer, his influence will continue through songs such as "Homesick for Heaven," "Longing," "Over Yonder," "Lord, Keep Us Faithful," and "Ride On, King Jesus."

DE FOREST, PERRY ALFRED (1867-1947). Leader of Seventh-day Adventist medical work in Switzerland. He was born in Canada. Losing his mother at the age of 4, he was placed in a foster home, where he remained until at the age of 18 he was converted and joined the Salvation Army. At the age of 20 he became an SDA, perhaps through the influence of his uncle, George King, a prominent colporteur. About the same time (1888), he married Amy H. Gee. He then went to Battle Creek Sanitarium, where he obtained a nursing diploma and soon thereafter enrolled in the medical school of the University of Cincinnati. With no material support but his hard work and strong will, he graduated in 1894 with a medical degree. He also obtained postgraduate diplomas in the areas of eye, ear, nose, throat, and dentistry. His aim was to become a mission doctor, but when it was decided to open health work in Switzerland, the General Conference in 1895 sent him there as medical superintendent. He opened Institut Sanitaire (Health Institute) at Basel in 1896 and started a school of nursing and a health food factory. Later, he assisted in the establishment of the Lake Geneva Sanitarium (La Lignière) and served first as its director and then as house doctor until his retirement in 1935.

In his first year in Switzerland, he edited a health journal, *Le Vulgarisateur* ("The Popularizer"), and later was the first editor of the German magazine *Gute Gesundheit* ("Good Health"), begun in 1897. He also authored a number of popular health and hygiene books in the French language.

DELAWARE. *See* Allegheny East Conference; Chesapeake Conference.

DELHOVE, DAVID E. (1882-1949). Belgian missionary to Africa. He was born into a Protestant family in Belgium. When he was 17 he accepted the Sabbath from a tract sent by an uncle in America. At 24 he was baptized. In 1909, wishing to go to Africa as a missionary, he went to England to study English. He attended Stanborough College and supported his family by working as a nurse's aide in the sanitarium.

In 1913 he was sent by the British Union to Kenya, East Africa. He left his family in Belgium, intending to return for them in two years. However, the following year war cut off all communication with Belgium. Delhove was quickly drafted into the Belgian Army, and served for four years as a reconnaissance officer. Traveling during this time across Ruanda-Urundi several times, he felt that it would make a fruitful mission field.

After a separation of more than five years, he was reunited with his family, and, while in Belgium, he persuaded Henry Monnier to go with him to Africa. Entering the former German territory of Ruanda-Urundi (now Rwanda and Burundi), which had been assigned to Belgium as a mandate in 1919, they were permitted to occupy three mission stations previously operated by a German Protestant society.

In 1921 Delhove founded the Gitwe Mission on a site where no Africans would live because it had been cursed by a previous chief. From Gitwe he pushed out in all directions, and encouraged the founding of the Rwankeri (1922) and Buganda (1925, later moved to Ndora) missions. The following year, Delhove was ordained.

He pioneered the work on several stations. In 1929 the Ruanda-Urundi field was taken over by the African Division and eventually joined to the Congo Union. After 10 years as mission director on Songa and Kirundu, Delhove was asked to pioneer the opening up of the Rwese Mission.

Although retired in 1944, he continued to live and work in the Congo until his death. Appreciated for his wide knowledge of local problems, he served as a member of the council of the governor-general of the Belgian Congo. Several children of the Delhove family, born in Ruanda-Urundi, later became second-generation missionaries in the Congo.

Delhove died of a heart attack at Rutshuru on Mar. 12, 1949. The doctor who was with him stated that only 10 minutes before taking his last breath Pastor Delhove was seeking to convert the native orderly attending him.

DELL RESIDENTIAL CARE HOME, THE. A home for aged Seventh-day Adventists, operated by the British Union Conference and situated near Lowestoft, Suffolk, England. The building and grounds, formerly a private home, were donated by a church member. The building was opened on July 3, 1953, with room for 15 residents, but later it was enlarged to accommodate 27. A matron and her husband are resident at the home and are responsible for 24 staff members, including care assistants, domestic, kitchen, and maintenance workers. Ten apartments for retired church members were built on the grounds in 1974.

DENMARK. A 1,000-year-old kingdom of 16,000 square miles (41,000 square kilometers) in Northern Europe with a population (1994) of a little more than 5 million. The Faroe Islands (population 47,500) and Greenland (population 57,000) belong to Denmark. Manufacturing and farming are the principal occupations. The teachings of Luther were introduced into Denmark during the early part of the sixteenth century. In 1536, after a series of civil struggles, Lutheranism became the state religion. More than 95 percent of the people are members of that church.

Seventh-day Adventist Statistics. The territory of Denmark constitutes the Danish Union of Churches, including the Faroe Islands, with Greenland as a separate mission, both within the Trans-European Division. It is divided into two local conferences. Statistics (1993) for the *Danish Union of Churches:* churches, 54; members, 3,072; church or elementary schools, 7; ordained ministers, 28; honorary ministers, 12; credentialed commissioned ministers, 10; credentialed missionaries, 11; literature evangelists, 2. Headquarters: Concordiavej 16 C.I., 2850 Naerum, Denmark. *Greenland Mission:* churches, 1; members, 13.

Institutions. Danish Junior College; Danish Publishing House; Old People's Home (Solbakken Plejehjem); Old People's Home (Sondervang Plejehjem); Skodsborg Physiotherapy School.

Development of Seventh-day Adventist Work. *Beginnings.* The SDA message reached Denmark from the United States in 1872 by means of the Danish monthly *Advent Tidende,* which John G. Matteson, a native son of Denmark, had started primarily for the Scandinavian people in America. During May of the same year, Matteson received a letter from a man who had already begun to keep the Sabbath and who was distributing the papers among his neighbors in order to win others. In June Matteson sent 20 taler ($11) to another man in Denmark and asked him to have a tract on the Sabbath printed and distributed. Later Matteson received word that 1,000 copies had been printed and given out, and also received many encouraging letters from readers of the *Advent Tidende* in Denmark, stating that they had begun to follow the teachings of the Bible as they had found them taught in the papers.

In 1875 M. A. Sommer wrote from Denmark that he had been reading the *Advent Tidende* for two years. As the printer of a monthly paper with a circulation of 4,000, he asked for and received permission of the officers in Battle Creek to incorporate articles from the *Advent Tidende* into his paper. But when he boldly attacked the ministers of the state church he was arrested and imprisoned for two months in 1876.

In March 1877 one of the interested readers wrote of some of his attempts to win others. "I hope that the Lord in His mercy will allow His workers to visit Denmark, so that souls also here may be won for the Lord." After receiving several such letters from different parts of Denmark, Matteson wrote to James White, the president of the General Conference, asking for permission to leave his work in the U.S. and take up missionary work in Denmark. His request was granted, and he was promised the prayers and financial support of American SDAs. Thus, 22 years after leaving his homeland, Matteson arrived in Denmark on June 6, 1877, as the pioneer SDA worker to all the Scandinavian countries. J. N. Andrews at that time had been in Switzerland for three years.

Soon after arriving, Matteson printed a hymnbook containing 70 psalms. He organized Sabbath schools wherever he found a few interested persons, and began the first temperance society in Denmark. After a few months, in spite of great opposition and even threats on his life, he baptized nine converts. In May 1878 he organized the first Seventh-day Adventist church in Denmark, the Alstrup church in Vendsyssel, with 27 members. This was the first SDA church in Northern Europe.

In September 1878 Knud Brorson arrived from America, having been sent by the General Conference to assist Matteson and thus release him to make frequent trips to Norway and Sweden, where he was fostering a growing work. To aid him further, Matteson selected qualified laymen whom he trained; others he taught how to sell books and papers. On July 1, 1881, Matteson sent out the first issue of *Sundhedsbladet,* an eight-page monthly health magazine, still being published. By this time Matteson had written 30 different pamphlets and tracts, which were being distributed all over Scandinavia.

At the time of the Denmark Conference session held in June 1906, there were in Denmark 18 churches with 746 church members. Although the membership and resources in Denmark were small, they joined other Scandinavian countries in opening mission work in Ethiopia. Seven years later Denmark sent two licensed ministers to the Faroe Islands as colporteur evangelists. In recent years work was opened in Greenland.

The first church school in Denmark was opened in Dronninglund in 1883. Seven years later another school was started at Hellum, which functioned for many years under the name of Jerslev Friskole, then in 1964 combined with another school to form the Jerslev-Ostervraa church school. By 1898 there were six church schools in Denmark, one in Copenhagen, and the others in Jutland.

In 1887 M. M. Olsen came from America and in 1890 started a mission school that became the Vejlefjord Højer Skole (Danish Junior College).

In September 1897 a small sanitarium was opened in Frederikshavn in north Jutland. Later the institution was sold to a private church member, who for years continued the medical work that the denomination had begun.

A second medical institution opened in 1898 at Skodsborg, 10 miles (16 kilometers) north of Copenhagen, in two small buildings that had once belonged to the royal family. Through the years this sanitarium grew to be one of the largest operated by SDAs anywhere in the world *(see* Skodsborg Sanitarium). There are also more than 60 private clinics scattered throughout Denmark. Shortly after the sanitarium was founded, a food factory was established in Copenhagen, which was operated at Bjaeverskov, near Ringsted *(see* Nutana). Both the sanitarium and food factory are still operating, but no longer belong to the church.

A publishing house was organized in 1905 to distribute literature printed in Norway, a function which had been handled by a private firm since 1893 *(see* Danish Publishing House).

Organization. Less than three years after his arrival in Denmark, on May 30, 1880, Matteson organized the first conference outside of North America—the Denmark Conference, with seven churches and 120 adherents, of whom 91 were baptized members.

From 1902 to 1931 the Denmark Conference was part of the Scandinavian Union Conference, which was made up of Sweden, Norway, Denmark, Finland, Iceland, and Greenland. At a session held Mar. 18-22, 1931, the Scandinavian Union was divided to form the East Nordic and the West Nordic Union conferences. The latter included the countries of Denmark and Norway. In the same year, Denmark was divided to form the East Denmark and the West Denmark conferences. In 1992 the West Nordic Union Conference was dissolved, and the Danish Union of Churches was formed.

DENMARK PUBLISHING HOUSE. *See* Danish Publishing House.

DENTAL EDUCATION. Interest in dentistry as part of a well-rounded program of professional training in the field of medicine and health education within the denomination was reflected in the charter of the College of Medical Evangelists (now Loma Linda University), which proposed the degree of Doctor of Dental Surgery. However, nothing was done about it. In the 1932 spring meeting of the General Conference Executive Committee it was voted to "explore the feasibility of establishing a school of dentistry in connection with the school of medicine of the College of Medical Evangelists, or of making a group arrangement with some standard dental college where our young people can have the safeguards of Christian home life."

To explore the possibilities, a committee of five was appointed, one of whom was Dr. J. Russell Mitchell, a practicing dentist on the faculty of the Atlanta (Georgia) Southern Dental College. On the recommendation of this committee to the Autumn Council in 1933, the General Conference Department of Education made arrangements with the Atlanta Southern Dental College to accept Seventh-day Adventist students and to grant them Sabbath privileges. The first group of SDA students was admitted in the fall of 1934.

In a 1938 meeting of the College of Medical Evangelists constituency, the feasibility of establishing a dental school was discussed, and later studies were made. Dr. Herbert G. Childs, chair of the Department of Stomatology of the medical school, in 1939 presented a report on the advisability of establishing an SDA dental school, using the existing facilities of the medical school, offering the first two years of basic sciences in Loma Linda and the two years of clinical training in Los Angeles. On seeing a brochure describing this plan, Dr. M. Webster Prince, an SDA layperson who was a practicing dentist in Detroit and a member of the Council on Dental Education (the accrediting agency for all dental schools within the United States), pointed out that the proposed plan was not in keeping with the council's policies on four major points: Dental education should be a university discipline, taught entirely on one campus, by a highly selective faculty, with preference given to well-qualified full-time teachers, and operated on an eleemosynary basis, with autonomy and adequate financial support. This evaluation resulted in discarding the then-existing plans.

When Atlanta Southern Dental College found it necessary to affiliate with Emory University, the effect was to rule out the SDA arrangement with the school. Serious study was undertaken again in 1944 for the establishment of an SDA dental school. In 1947 the General Conference Committee terminated the agreement with the Atlanta Southern Dental College and authorized the sale of the denominationally owned student home.

Four years later the General Conference Executive Committee launched new plans that resulted eventually in the establishment of an SDA School of Dentistry. The first class graduated in 1957. Presently, the total student body consists of 80 students enrolled in each year of the dental curriculum, 40 students each year in the dental hygiene curriculum, and 60 graduate dentists are enrolled in nine postdoctoral programs of dental specialty education.

The original physical plant (Prince Hall) was enlarged and remodeled in 1976, approximately doubling the size of the original structure.

The School of Dentistry offers more than 135 continuing education courses each year to practicing dentists. More than 6,000 enrollees each year include dentists from 15 or more countries outside the United States. *See* Loma Linda University.

DE NUNEZ, BERTHA LEON (1933-1984). Bible worker, nurse. She completed a two-year theology degree in 1953, and worked as Bible instructor in evangelistic campaigns. Wishing to serve people, she took nursing in 1955, and also used her talents in music to organize groups among the students. After finishing her nursing in 1958, she continued graduate studies at the San Marcos Major

University, where she also worked as supervisor. In 1960 she married Elias De Nunez and worked by his side in his ministry.

DENVER SOUTH CHURCH SCHOOL. *See* Mile High Adventist Academy.

DEPARTMENT OF EDUCATION. *See* Education, Department of.

DEPARTMENT OF HEALTH. *See* Health and Temperance Department.

DEPARTMENT OF PUBLIC AFFAIRS AND RELIGIOUS LIBERTY. *See* Public Affairs and Religious Liberty, Department of.

DEPARTMENT OF PURCHASE AND SUPPLY. *See* Institutional Services/ESDA.

DEPARTMENTS. Functional subdivisions of the denominational work on various administrative levels. In the General Conference there were, in 1994, seven departments and 31 services, corporations, and other organizations. In their respective territories, each division, union, conference, and mission also has departments in the same or similar categories, working under their respective executive committees but with the aid and guidance of the General Conference departments.

For the departments and their various spheres of service, *see* General Conference Departments; also names of specific departments.

DETACHED ORGANIZATION (conference, mission field, etc.). A unit of church organization not forming a part of the next higher unit. An example would be a detached mission that is not a part of any union mission but is operated directly by the division.

DETAMORE, FORDYCE W. (1908-1980). Educator, missionary, evangelist. Born in Minnesota, he attended Emmanuel Missionary College, and after graduating, he and his wife, Aletha, entered denominational work as teachers. Later they served in ministerial work in the Indiana and Michigan conferences, then accepted a call to the Far Eastern Division, where he served as educational superintendent in two unions.

In 1942 H.M.S. Richards, Sr., asked him to help out with the *Voice of Prophecy* as the broadcast went coast to coast. Detamore was responsible for originating many features at the Voice, such as the slogan "Forward in Faith," the *Voice of Prophecy News,* and the Book-of-the-Month Club. He also wrote the first lessons for the Bible school, including the junior course.

He was responsible for setting up telephone evangelism and assisted in the organization of the Voice of Prophecy evangelism association.

Later he worked as an evangelist in China and throughout the Far East and in the Texas and Florida conferences.

After retirement he volunteered his services for the Voice of Prophecy and worked full-time, including one campaign a year overseas in Manila, Hong Kong, Singapore, Indonesia, and Australia.

He passed to his rest in Orlando, Florida.

DETAMORE, FRANCIS ARTHUR (1872-1938). Missionary administrator in Malaya, minister, and teacher. He spent his early days on a farm in Minnesota and began his education in the public schools there. After being baptized into the Seventh-day Adventist Church at the age of 13, he attended a conference school in Minneapolis, Minnesota. Afterward he returned to his home community and taught in a public school, but became so impressed that SDA children should have the benefits of denominational education that in 1898 he taught the first Adventist church school in Minnesota without pay. He was principal of the Minnesota Industrial School (1899-1901), teaching in the winter, studying in the summer at Battle Creek College, and assisting in evangelistic meetings whenever possible. From 1898 to 1908 he served as educational secretary, field secretary, and pastor in the Minnesota Conference. Later he transferred to the Oregon Conference, where he served as educational secretary and also as principal of Laurelwood Academy (1909); and later (1910-1912) he worked in the Upper Columbia Conference. In 1912 he went to Southern Asia to superintend the Malay missions. There under his leadership, the Malaysian publishing house (now Southeast Asia Publishing House) was built, and the Singapore Training School (now Southeast Asia Union College) was established. After 10 years the condition of health in his family made a return to the homeland necessary. After his return, he worked in departmental offices in the Indiana (1923-1929), Upper Columbia (1929-1936), and Oregon (1936-1938) conferences.

DETWILER, HOWARD JOHNSON (1889-1951). Administrator. After graduating from Mount Vernon College, he worked as an evangelist in the East Pennsylvania Conference until 1920. Then he became Bible teacher at, and shortly afterward principal of, Mount Vernon Academy. He was president of the West Virginia Conference (1924-1928), the New Jersey Conference (1928-1932), the Columbia Union Conference (1932-1942), and the Potomac Conference (1942-1951).

DE-VAU-GE GESUNDKOSTWERK GmbH. *See* German Health Food Factory.

DE VINNEY, FREDERICK HENRY (1862-1943). Minister, missionary. Baptized in 1896, he engaged in colporteur work, then preached in New York State and New England (1898-1905). From 1906 to 1910 he was president of the Eastern New York Conference. Appointed superintendent of the Japan Mission in 1910, he later became vice president of the Asiatic Division (1917), and then president of the Southern China Union Mission (1918). On returning to the U.S. in 1926, he was elected president of the Louisiana-Mississippi Conference, an office he held until 1932. He was next appointed pastor of the Jackson, Mississippi, church, whose congregation he served until his retirement in 1938.

DEVOTIONAL CALENDARS. *See* Morning Watch.

M. C. DHAMANWALA ENGLISH HIGH SCHOOL OF SEVENTH-DAY ADVENTISTS. An institution that began as a church school in 1945, using a room at the Women's Wadia College just opposite the mission hospital campus in Surat, Gujarat, India. It was reorganized by Shalini Shinde in 1958. After relocation to the church vestry in 1966, where classes were held for 10 years, a temporary shed was erected to accommodate the expanding student body. Then in response to a challenge by the Central India Union committee, G. Jacob, the region director, and the principal, Pramod Gaikwad, set about raising funds that were to be matched by the union. The school building was completed in 1978 and named after the principal donor. During the next two years the staff quarters and another floor were added and the school was upgraded to ICSE level.

This institution, which started with less than 15 students in 1945, now serves not only the Seventh-day Adventist children in Surat, but also more than 3,500 students, both Christian and non-Christian. It is providing an education along the lines of Seventh-day Adventist principles.

Administrators: P. R. Macwan, 1945-1958; Shalini Shinde, 1958-1966; H. Jump, 1966-1970; Pramod Gaikwad, 1970-1978; B. Victor Sam, 1978-1983; George Luke, 1983; R. G. Waidande, 1984-1988; C. H. Prakash, 1988-1992; M. S. Jeremiah, 1992- .

DIAMANTE ACADEMY. *See* River Plate Adventist University.

DICK, EVERETT N. (1898-1989). Educator, developer. Born in Kansas, he is best known for establishing the Seventh-day Adventist Medical Cadet Corps as an alternative to bearing arms in the armed forces. The organization became worldwide after Dick took three globe-circling trips to establish it in other countries.

He joined the staff of Union College in 1930 and never officially retired.

DICKERSON, FANNIE M. *See* Chase, Fannie M.

DICKSON, LOUIS KLAER (1890-1963). Minister, conference administrator. Educated at Healdsburg College (1907-1908) and Lodi Normal Institute (1909-1910), he was baptized in 1908 and ordained in 1916. He was an evangelist in the California Conference (1910-1915), and continued in pastoral evangelism in the Western Oregon Conference (1915-1921), in the Southern California Conference (1921-1922), and in the Greater New York Conference (1922-1927). He served as president of the Greater New York Conference (1927-1933), then of the Florida Conference (1933-1936), the Northern California Conference (1936-1940), the Southeastern California Conference (1940-1941), and the Pacific Union Conference (1941-1945). In 1945 he was elected vice president of the General Conference for North America, and served as a general vice president of the General Conference from 1947 until his retirement in 1958.

DIET. The subject of diet has received strong emphasis among Seventh-day Adventists. This is because of the bearing of nutrition on the individual's mental, social, and spiritual welfare as well as the physical welfare, and consequently on the person's ability to serve God and humanity and to comprehend spiritual things. SDAs find both a scientific and a biblical basis for this emphasis: (1) the teaching of science that what we eat and drink affects not only our bodies but also our brains, and (2) biblical admonitions to the Christian to "glorify God in your body, and in your spirit, which are God's" (1 Cor. 6:20), and "whether therefore ye eat, or drink, or whatsoever ye do, do all to the glory of God" (1 Cor. 10:31).

Since SDAs, as creationists, accept the Genesis record as literal history, they believe that the diet there described was the original diet that God provided, and is therefore the best possible diet. This diet consisted entirely of the products of plants—grains, fruits, nuts, and vegetables (Gen. 1:29, 30; 3:18). A modification of this diet, permitting the use of flesh as food, occurred after all plant life had been destroyed by the Flood (Gen. 9:1-4). Further specific instruction was given to Moses regarding the unclean meats that were to be excluded from the diet (Lev. 11; Deut. 14:3-20). Because the original diet did not include the flesh of animals, the Seventh-day Adventist Church recommends a lacto-ovovegetarian diet, a diet consisting essentially of plant foods supplemented by a moderate use of milk and eggs—natural foods of animal origin. The recommendation of this type of diet is only a part of the comprehensive health program of the church. *See* Health Principles.

SDAs regard proper diet and a care for health as the Christian's duty. They advocate abstinence from harmful foods and drinks not on the basis of religious taboo, but on the basis of the law of cause and effect. They believe that the prohibition to the Hebrews of the flesh of certain animals, such as hogs, for food was based on the unfitness of the flesh of these animals for humanity's diet, and was not a mere ceremonial restriction. Abstinence from tobacco and alcohol and the abuse of drugs is required of SDAs, because these are poisons. On the other hand, vegetarianism, for example, is advocated as a way of health but has not been made a requirement of church membership. The SDA doctrine is that attention to diet is a Christian duty because of its effect on health.

Development of Seventh-day Adventist Position on Diet. In the middle of the nineteenth century, when the SDA Church was formed, the average American diet was a monotonous one of meats, fats, starches, and sweets, with fresh fruits and vegetables often limited to summer months. Impaired health and sickness because of poor dietary practice were prevalent. At a time when there was a marked dearth of the concept of healthful diet in the scientific world, the basic principles of healthful dietary were urged upon the church through the pen of Ellen White, beginning in 1863.

In more recent times basic principles advocated by Mrs. White have been fully substantiated and repeatedly emphasized by the scientific researches of such people as Henry C. Sherman, Elmer V. McCollum, Clive McCay, Frederick J. Stare, and many others whose outstanding studies have proved that the liberal use of whole-grain cereals, vegetables, fruits, and nuts is the proper means of enhancing and improving the dietary.

Counsels to the church from Mrs. White presented first the injurious effects of alcohol, tobacco, tea, and coffee, and then the undesirability of flesh foods, the free use of sugar, refined flour, "grease" (especially animal fats), rich foods, spices and condiments, overeating, irregularity in eating, and improper food combinations.

Those counsels recommended a diet without flesh foods, consisting of a liberal variety of fruits, whole grains, legumes, nuts, and vegetables prepared in a simple, appetizing manner, with some dairy products and eggs, when proper precautions were taken in regard to the latter two to lessen the risk of disease. Possible necessity of the eventual replacement of dairy products and eggs because of the increase of disease among animals was foreseen. The need for skill and intelligence to make the diet palatable and nutritious was recognized, and homemakers were encouraged to study and put into practice the principles of healthful cookery, based on the best scientific data currently available.

From the large body of instruction from Mrs. White on foods and dietetic practices for the church, a 477-page volume has been compiled, *Counsels on Diet and Foods.* The author (p. 198) set down broad principles regarding diet: "Those who understand the laws of health, and who are governed by principle, will shun the extremes, both of indulgence and of restrictions. Their diet is chosen, not for the mere gratification of appetite, but for the upbuilding of the body. They seek to preserve every power in the best condition for the highest service to God and man. The appetite is under the control of reason and conscience, and they are rewarded with health of body and mind. While they do not urge their views offensively upon others, their example is a testimony in favor of right principles."

Nutritional Adequacy of the Vegetarian Diet. During a period of many years, scientific studies have been made of meatless dietaries. Wherever well-controlled studies have been made not hampered by inability to obtain a full variety of food or by social customs that restrict proper choice, the results have shown the adequacy of a diet without flesh foods.

A lacto-ovovegetarian diet does not differ markedly from the average Western diet. The principal difference is that it replaces flesh foods with a greater variety of cereals, legumes, and nuts, supplemented by a moderate intake of milk and eggs.

The effects of such a diet have been tested by various methods, including studies of endurance, metabolic rate, blood constituents, growth and development of the young, adequacy for pregnancy, and maintenance of adults. One of the most thorough and comprehensive investigations yet reported was done by Mervyn G. Hardinge and Frederick J. Stare (1954), who made a comparative study of three types of dietaries—the lacto-ovovegetarian, pure vegetarian (no animal products), and nonvegetarian (meat diet). These scientists studied representative groups of adults, adolescents, and pregnant women. Although the average food intake varied widely among individuals, the average intake of the three groups approximated or exceeded the recommendations of the National Research Council of the National Academy of Sciences. Their findings indicated that a lacto-ovovegetarian diet is adequate as a lifetime program under normal as well as stress conditions. (See "Nutritional Studies of Vegetarians," *The American Journal of Clinical Nutrition* 2:73-88, March-April 1954.) Hardinge and Hulda Crooks prepared an extensive review of the subject of vegetarianism ("Non-Flesh Dietaries," *Journal of the American Dietetic Association* 43:545-558, December 1963; 45:537-542, December 1964).

Disease in Relation to Diet. In addition to nutritional diseases that stem from a lack of various food constituents, a number of illnesses are related in part to overnutrition and an imbalance of nutrients. The possible relationship between dietaries high in total calories, total fats, saturated fats, and cholesterol, and the frequency of diseases of the heart and blood vessels and cancer has been the subject of large-scale investigations.

Selection of Food. Nutritional research and human experience have shown that there is no indispensable food and that a good diet can be compounded in many ways. Moderation in calories in order to maintain the ideal body weight and the selection of a variety of wholesome unrefined foods without undue emphasis on, or extreme restriction of, any one nutrient, remain desirable nutritional goals in the light of instruction given to the church and of current scientific literature.

DIME TABERNACLE. A former large Seventh-day Adventist church, the fourth to be built in the city of Battle Creek, Michigan. Stonelaying for the foundation began on Aug. 19, 1878, and by the following February the name Dime Tabernacle had been acquired (denominational members had been invited to donate dimes for the project). The erection of the tabernacle was considered a fitting climax to the career of James White, who that year (1879) accepted for the last time the presidency of the General Conference.

Seating about 4,000, the tabernacle was considered the logical meeting place for the 1901 General Conference session, where worldwide expansion and organization plans were laid. The tabernacle continued to be a meeting place for large gatherings of SDAs until it was destroyed by fire in 1922.

DINBANDHU ADVENTIST HOSPITAL. The Dinbandhu Charitable Hospital Trust of Kholwad (12 miles [20 kilometers] north of Surat City, India) and the Surat Hospital Trust Association of Seventh-day Adventists combined to operate a hospital in Kholwad village. The Dinbandhu Charitable Hospital Trust constructed, furnished, and partially equipped a 50-bed hospital that it turned over to the Surat Hospital Trust Association to operate. However, because of a severe shortage of personnel and funds, the Surat Hospital Trust Association had to withdraw from this contract and turn back the running of the hospital and its programs to the Dinbandhu Charitable Hospital Trust in 1991. Thus the word "Adventist" was dropped from the title, and SDAs no longer had any responsibility in operating this hospital.

Medical Directors: A. T. Jonahs, 1988-1991; Mathew K. Philip, 1991.

DIRECTOR, DEPARTMENTAL. Formerly departmental secretary. A person in charge of one or more departments in a conference, union, or other unit of church organization. In some cases the term *secretary* is used. *See* Departments.

DIRECTORIES. The official directory of the denomination is the *Seventh-day Adventist Yearbook,* published by the General Conference. It covers the geographical and administrative subdivisions, from the General Conference organization and its departments, commissions, and services, down to local administrative offices; the various denominational institutions—educational, medical, publishing, and others; and a list of workers. In it also appear the General Conference constitution and bylaws, the Statement of Fundamental Beliefs, a list of countries with their organizational locations, and statistical summaries.

There are also church directories, listing the addresses of local churches, published by some world divisions.

The local conferences in North America have unpublished directories, which they circulate among those who have need for statistics and information on specific local conferences.

There are other directories, not of the church but of Seventh-day Adventist groups, such as the yearly directories of SDA physicians and dentists in the *Alumni Journal* of the Loma Linda University School of Medicine and the *Journal of the National Association of Seventh-day Adventist Dentists,* and the *Adventist Services and Industries Laymen's Directory.*

DIRKSEN, HENRY J. (1859-1929). Minister; one of the pioneer Seventh-day Adventist workers on the Canadian prairies. He was born in Europe, somewhere near the Black Sea, and at the age of 23 came to America with his parents, settling in South Dakota, where he married Mary Derkson in 1887. His name appears in the *Yearbook* in the list of workers first in 1893, as a licentiate in the Minnesota Conference (there spelled Duerkson), and the next year his address is given in North Dakota (still under the Minnesota Conference listing). He afterward worked in Wisconsin, Manitoba, Saskatchewan, and Washington. About 1905 he moved to Portland, Oregon, and with the exception of some time between 1912 and 1915, which he spent in Manitoba again, he lived in Portland the rest of his life. His son, Henry Dirksen, was one of the first SDA workers in Iran.

DISAPPOINTMENT, 1844. *See* Millerite Movement.

DISASTER RELIEF. *See* Adventist Development and Relief Agency International.

DISBANDING CHURCHES. *See* Church (local organization), III, 3.

DISCIPLINE. *See* Church Discipline.

DISFELLOWSHIPPING. *See* Church Discipline.

DISPENSARIES. *See* Clinics and Dispensaries.

DISPENSARIO MEDICO ADVENTISTA. *See* Quito Adventist Clinic.

DISPENSATION. A biblical term used by Christians in general, of the old and new dispensations, corresponding to the Old and New Testaments, or to the Jewish and the Christian systems, which are different, yet form part of one plan of salvation.

But the original two biblical dispensations were later expanded by some theologians. For example, there was some subdividing or adding of dispensations by ecclesiastical writers such as Tertullian and Origen, by Joachim in the Middle Ages, and by Cocceius in more modern times, yet nothing as far-reaching as the system of dispensations described in the present "dispensationalist" system of interpretation. Modern dispensationalism is the product of the elaborations of John N. Darby (founder of the Plymouth Brethren), and appears in its most popular form in the notes of C. I. Scofield in the *Scofield Bible.* This system partitions world history into seven ages, or "dispensations"—time periods—in each of which God is supposed to deal differently with humanity. In this scheme the "church age" (the Christian Era) is regarded as a "parenthesis," or gap, in prophecy; as an age of pure grace between a past Jewish dispensation of law and a future one in which the Jews will be again the people of God and will rule the nations under a restoration of the Mosaic code. This system of seven dispensations is claimed by its adherents as basic to or synonymous with premillennialism, so that in the public mind it is likely to be attributed mistakenly to several classes of premillennialists who do not hold it. It is in complete contrast to the Seventh-day Adventist type of premillennialism.

DISTRICT. A term used in Seventh-day Adventist Church organization in several senses:

1. Formerly (1889-1901), one of the six (later eight) areas called General Conference Districts, each comprising several conferences and/or missions, which were under the leadership of a superintendent. These districts, designated generally by number, though sometimes by name (such as No. 1, Atlantic; No. 2, Southern; etc.), were replaced by union conferences. *See* Organization, III, 2; IV, 2.

2. A group of neighboring churches served by one minister but not otherwise considered a unit.

3. An administrative unit smaller than or subordinate to a mission, a field, or a union, under a director, with whom may be associated a group of other ministers and/or missionaries. Such a district may comprise the area of an entire country, one or more subdivisions of a country, or a smaller unit.

DISTRICT OF COLUMBIA. *See* Allegheny East Conference; Potomac Conference.

DISTRICT OF COLUMBIA CONFERENCE. A former unit of church organization, existing from 1909 to 1924, embracing the District of Columbia and neighboring areas in Maryland and Virginia. In 1903 the District of Columbia and Takoma Park, Maryland, which had formerly belonged to the Chesapeake Conference, had been set up as a detached district, composed of three churches, and 300 members, administered directly by the General Conference. This was done soon after the General Conference moved its headquarters and the Review and Herald to Washington, D.C., and procured land in suburban Takoma Park, Maryland, for the erection of the Washington Sanitarium and Hospital and the school that is now Columbia Union College. Later this district was expanded to take in the Washington metropolitan area, including two adjacent counties in Maryland and six in Virginia, and was made a conference in 1909 under the Columbia Union Conference. In 1924, when it was last listed in the *Yearbook*, it included the District of Columbia, the Maryland counties of Montgomery, Prince Georges, Charles, and St. Marys, and the Virginia counties of Alexandria, Fairfax, Loudoun, Prince William, Fauquier, Stafford, Northumberland, King George, Westmoreland, Richmond, and Lancaster. In 1924 it was organized, with the rest of Virginia, as the Potomac Conference, with the headquarters remaining in Takoma Park.

DIVINE DECREES. *See* Decrees, Divine.

DIVISION. The largest geographical and administrational unit next to the General Conference, embracing a number of unions, missions. conferences, sections, etc. Theoretically, each division administration is the section of the General Conference that operates in that area; it is therefore called in the constitution a division section, although in customary use, the term *division* alone is sufficient. The president of the division is a vice president of the General Conference. For the development of the divisional administration, *see* Organization, V. For specific divisions and their constituent parts, *see* Africa-Indian Ocean Division; Eastern Africa Division; Euro-Africa Division; Euro-Asia Division; Far Eastern Division; Inter-American Division; North American Division; South American Division; South Pacific Division; Southern Asia Division; Trans-European Division.

DIVISION HEALTH FOOD COMPANY. *See* South American Division Health Food Company.

DIVORCE. The legal dissolution of marriage, which has for the Christian believer not only a social and a psychological impact but also a religious one. The following 11 points state as clearly as possible the position of the Seventh-day Adventist Church on the subject of divorce and remarriage:

"1. 'In the sermon on the mount Jesus declared plainly that there could be no dissolution of the marriage tie, except for unfaithfulness to the marriage vow.'—*Thoughts From the Mount of Blessing,* p. 63. (Matt. 5:32; see also Matt. 19:9.)

"When Jesus said, 'Let not man put asunder,' He established a rule of conduct for the church under the dispensation of grace which must transcend forever all civil enactments which would go beyond His interpretation of the divine law governing the marriage relation. He here gives a rule to His followers, who must adhere to it whether or not the state or prevailing custom allows larger liberty.

"2. Even though the Scriptures allow divorce for 'unfaithfulness to the marriage vow,' earnest endeavors should be made by those concerned to effect a reconciliation urging the innocent spouse to forgive the guilty one and the latter to amend his or her conduct, so that the marriage union may be maintained.

"3. In the event that reconciliation is not effected, the innocent spouse has the biblical right to secure a divorce, and also to remarry.

"4. A spouse found guilty of adultery by the church shall be subject to church discipline. Even though the transgressor may be genuinely repentant, he or she shall be placed under censure for a stated period of time, in order to express the church's abhorrence of such evil. The transgressor who gives no evidence of full and sincere repentance shall be disfellowshipped. In case the violation has been so flagrant as to bring public reproach on the cause of God, the church, in order to maintain its high standards and good name, shall disfellowship the individual even though there is evidence of repentance.

"5. A guilty spouse, who is divorced, has not the moral right to marry another while the innocent spouse still lives and remains unmarried and chaste. Should he or she do so, he or she, if a member, shall be disfellowshipped. The person whom he or she marries, if a member, shall also be disfellowshipped.

"6. When a divorce is secured by either spouse, or when both mutually secure a divorce on any grounds other than that of 'unfaithfulness to the marriage vow,' the party or parties securing the divorce shall come under the censure of the church except as provided later in this paragraph. In the event that either spouse who is a church member remarries—unless in the meantime the other party has remarried, committed adultery or fornication, or died—the one remarrying shall be disfellowshipped from the church. The person whom he or she married shall also be disfellowshipped. It is recognized, however, that sometimes there may be conditions that make it unsafe or impossible for husband and wife to continue to live together. In many such cases the custody of the children, the adjustment of property rights, or even personal protection may make necessary a change in marriage status. In such cases it may be permissible to secure what is known in some countries as a legal separation. However, in some civil jurisdictions such a separation can be secured only by divorce, which under these circumstances would not be condemned. But such a separation or divorce, in which 'unfaithfulness to the marriage vow' is not involved, does not give either one the scriptural right to remarry, unless in the meantime the other party has remarried, committed adultery or fornication, or been removed by death. Should a member who has been thus divorced remarry, he or she, if a member, shall be disfellowshipped; and the one whom he or she marries shall also be disfellowshipped from the church.

"7. A guilty spouse who has violated his or her marriage vow and has been divorced and disfellowshipped and who has remarried, or a person who has been divorced on other than the grounds set forth in section 1 and has remarried, and who has been disfellowshipped from the church, shall be considered as standing under the disapproval of the church and thus ineligible for membership except as hereinafter provided.

"8. The marriage contract is not only more sacred but also infinitely more complex than ordinary contracts in its possible involvements; for example, in the factor of the children who may be born. Hence, in a case where any endeavor by a genuinely repentant offender to bring his marital status into line with the divine ideal presents apparently insuperable problems, his or her plea for readmittance shall, before final action is taken, be brought by the church through the pastor or district leader to the conference committee for counsel and recommendation as to any possible steps that the repentant one, or ones, may take to secure such readmittance.

"9. Readmittance to membership of those who have been disfellowshipped for reasons given in the foregoing sections shall be on the basis of rebaptism.

"10. When a person who has been involved in divorce proceedings is finally readmitted to church membership, as provided in section 8, every care should be exercised to safeguard the unity and harmony of the church by not giving such a person responsibility as a leader; especially in an office which requires the rite of ordination, unless by very careful counsel.

"11. No Seventh-day Adventist minister has the right to officiate at the remarriage of any person who, under the stipulation of the preceding paragraphs, has no scriptural right to remarry" *(Church Manual* [1990], pp. 172-174).

In 1976 the General Conference established a set of guidelines and procedures to assist pastors and church administrators in the implementation of the instructions quoted above (cf. *Review and Herald* 154:7, Feb. 17, 1977).

DJIBOUTI. A country located on the east coast of Africa. It is about the size of New

Hampshire, with an area of 8,950 square miles (23,200 square kilometers) and a population (1994) of 413,000. Its neighbors are Ethiopia on the north and west and Somalia on the south. Djibouti gained independence from France on June 27, 1977. The country was formerly known as French Somaliland and the French Territory of the Afars and Issas. The great majority of the inhabitants are Muslim.

Seventh-day Adventist Statistics. In 1992 an agreement was signed between the republic of Djibouti and the Eastern Africa Division of Seventh-day Adventists to build a dental clinic in the city of Djibouti with a high priority of preventive care and appropriate health education for the general public.

Construction of the clinic was completed early in September 1992 on land given by the government. This medical ministry may well serve as a stepping-stone in spiritual ministry to the needs of the people.

The country of Djibouti is part of the Ethiopian Union Mission in the Eastern Africa Division.

DOCTRINAL STATEMENTS, SEVENTH-DAY ADVENTIST. Throughout their history Seventh-day Adventists have affirmed that "the Bible and the Bible only" should be the Christian's creed and that they have no creed but the Bible. However, over the years they have issued various statements of belief gradually moving toward the 27 fundamental beliefs published in the denominational *Yearbook* since 1981 and in the *Church Manual* (1990).

1. *James White's Informal Statement.* In August 1853 James White, as editor of the *Review and Herald,* replied to an inquiry from a Seventh Day Baptist in what was perhaps the first SDA statement of faith—merely the all-inclusive scriptural phrase "the commandments of God, and the faith of Jesus" (Rev. 14:12).

"As a people we are brought together from divisions of the Advent body [the Millerites], and from the various denominations, holding different views on some subjects; yet, thank Heaven, the Sabbath is a mighty platform on which we can all stand united. And while standing here, with the aid of no other creed than the Word of God, and bound together by the bonds of love—love for the truth, love for each other, and love for a perishing world—'which is stronger than death,' all party feelings are lost. We are united in these great subjects: Christ's immediate, personal second Advent, and the observance of all of the commandments of God, and the faith of his Son Jesus Christ, as necessary to a readiness for his Advent" (James White, in *Review and Herald* 4:52, Aug. 11, 1853).

In December of the same year, White proposed a "Charter" for gospel order in a series of four articles. The second article, on doctrine, explains the relationship of gospel order (church organization) to unity of belief. This was evidently a delicate subject, as numerous reproofs for "creed-making" were published in the *Review and Herald.* Carefully the editor suggested a basis for "doctrinal purity" as essential to order in the church: "Is the church of Christ," he asked, "to be left without a rule of faith? We answer, that she is provided with a creed that is sufficient. 'All scripture is given by inspiration of God'" *(ibid.* 4:180, Dec. 13, 1853).

2. Review and Herald *Masthead Statement.* A list of five "leading doctrines taught by the *Review*" was published in the masthead of the *Review and Herald* from Aug. 15 to Dec. 19, 1854. The author is not identified, and no reason was given for its omission in future issues. The doctrines read as follows:

"The Bible and the Bible alone, the rule of faith and duty.

"The Law of God, as taught in the Old and New Testaments, unchangeable.

"The Personal Advent of Christ and the Resurrection of the Just, before the Millennium.

"The Earth restored to its Eden perfection and glory, the final inheritance of the Saints.

"Immortality alone through Christ, to be given to the Saints at the resurrection."

3. *"Fundamental Principles."* In 1872 the press at Battle Creek issued a pamphlet containing 25 propositions, unsigned. The introductory statement reads in part: "In presenting to the public this synopsis of our faith, we wish to have it distinctly understood that we have no articles of faith, creed, or discipline, aside from the Bible. We do not put forth this as having any authority with our people, nor is it designed to secure uniformity among them, as a system of faith, but is a brief statement of what is, and has been, with great unanimity, held by them" ("A Declaration of the Fundamental Principles Taught and Practiced by the Seventh-day Adventists," p. 3).

These were reprinted in *Signs of the Times* (1:3, June 4, 1874); then in the last of four installments of Uriah Smith's "The Seventh-day Adventists . . ." in the *Review and Herald* (44:171, Nov. 24, 1874); again in *Signs of the Times* (1:108, Jan. 28, 1875); it appeared as a pamphlet, both as "Fundamental Principles" and as part of the reprint of all four articles in 1875 and later, for example, in 1877-1878, 1884, and 1888, under the same or slightly varied titles, and with identical or similar introductions, declaring that Seventh-day Adventists "have no creed but the Bible; but they hold to certain well defined points of faith, for which they feel prepared to give a reason" (1875 *Signs* reprint, and 1877-1878 complete pamphlet).

In the 1889 *Yearbook* of the denomination, which was a larger volume than usual, containing general information about the church and its activities, these "Fundamental Principles" were included in a slightly revised and expanded form in 28 sections (pp. 147-151). This was not continued in subsequent issues, but it was inserted again in the *Yearbook* in 1905 and continued to appear through 1914.

Twenty-eight "Fundamental Principles," "by the late Uriah Smith," were reprinted in the *Review and Herald* (89:4, Aug. 22, 1912). They also appeared in pamphlet form as No. 5 of the Words of Truth Series, with 29 sections, the additional one being No. 14, on religious liberty.

4. *Fundamental Beliefs—1931.* On Dec. 29, 1930, the General Conference Committee voted that a statement of beliefs be prepared by a committee of four, including the General Conference president and the editor of the *Review and Herald.* This was printed first in the 1931 *Yearbook* and the next year in the *Church Manual.* At the 1946 General Conference session it was voted that it, as well as any other portion of the *Church Manual,* should be revised only at a General Conference session. This statement, entitled "Fundamental Beliefs of Seventh-day Adventists," containing 22 sections, was still published with minor revisions in those two books until 1980. It was considered to be a summary of the principal features of Adventist beliefs.

5. *Fundamental Beliefs—1980.* During the General Conference session in 1980, in Dallas, Texas, the delegates from the world church approved a revised edition of the Statement of Fundamental Beliefs. The process of revision was initiated by the President's Executive Advisory and went to the *Church Manual* Committee. The chair of the committee and the president of the General Conference, Robert H. Pierson, following a recommendation from PRADCO, appointed an ad hoc committee, chaired by W. Duncan Eva, to work on the revision of the document. The first revised draft of the statement was circulated among a group of theologians for their input. This document was taken to the Annual Council in 1979 and voted in principle to recommend it to the General Conference session for final approval. The Annual Council also recommended that the statement "receive wide exposure to the world field" and that written suggestion should be welcome. Consequently, the document was sent to members of the division committees, to all the unions in North America, and to all the union colleges of the church. In addition, the statement was published in the *Adventist Review* (157:8, Feb. 21, 1980), inviting church members "to consider it carefully and to send comments or suggestions" to the committee. For the first time in the history of the church, the world church was actually involved in the revision of the Statement of Fundamental Beliefs.

Copies of the statement, incorporating the suggestions received from the world fields, were sent to the delegates to the GC session six weeks before the session convened in the summer of 1980. The statement was extensively discussed during the session and finally approved by the delegates. This statement is published in the *Church Manual* and the *Yearbook.* In its introduction it is stated that the fundamental beliefs "constitute the church's understanding and expression of the teaching of Scripture." It is also affirmed that the church has no creed except the Bible. Following is the statement as it appears in the 1994 *Yearbook* (pp. 5-8):

"Seventh-day Adventists accept the Bible as their only creed and hold certain fundamental beliefs to be the teaching of the Holy Scriptures. These beliefs, as set forth here, constitute the church's understanding and expression of the teaching of Scripture. Revision of these statements may be expected at a General Conference session when the church is led by the Holy Spirit to a fuller understanding of Bible truth or finds better language in which to express the teachings of God's Holy Word.

"1. The Holy Scriptures

"The Holy Scriptures, Old and New Testaments, are the written Word of God, given by divine inspiration through holy men of God who spoke and wrote as they were moved by the Holy Spirit. In this Word, God has committed to man the knowledge necessary for salvation. The Holy Scriptures are the infallible revelation of His will. They are the standard of character, the test of experience, the authoritative revealer of doctrines, and the trustworthy record of God's acts in history.

(2 Peter 1:20, 21; 2 Tim. 3:16, 17; Ps. 119:105; Prov. 30:5, 6; Isa. 8:20; John 17:17; 1 Thess. 2:13; Heb. 4:12.)

"2. The Trinity

"There is one God: Father, Son, and Holy Spirit, a unity of three co-eternal Persons. God is immortal, all-powerful, all-knowing, above all, and ever present. He is infinite and beyond human comprehension, yet known through His self-revelation. He is forever worthy of worship, adoration, and service by the whole creation. (Deut. 6:4; Matt. 28:19; 2 Cor. 13:14; Eph. 4:4-6; 1 Peter 1:2; 1 Tim. 1:17; Rev. 14:7.)

"3. The Father

"God the Eternal Father is the Creator, Source, Sustainer, and Sovereign of all creation. He is just and holy, merciful and gracious, slow to anger, and abounding in steadfast love and faithfulness. The qualities and powers exhibited in the Son and the Holy Spirit are also revelations of the Father. (Gen. 1:1; Rev. 4:11; 1 Cor. 15:28; John 3:16; 1 John 4:8; 1 Tim. 1:17; Ex. 34:6, 7; John 14:9.)

"4. The Son

"God the eternal Son became incarnate in Jesus Christ. Through Him all things were created, the character of God is revealed, the salvation of humanity is accomplished, and the world is judged. Forever truly God, He became also truly man, Jesus the Christ. He was conceived of the Holy Spirit and born of the virgin Mary. He lived and experienced temptation as a human being, but perfectly exemplified the righteousness and love of God. By His miracles He manifested God's power and was attested as God's promised Messiah. He suffered and died voluntarily on the cross for our sins and in our place, was raised from the dead, and ascended to minister in the heavenly sanctuary in our behalf. He will come again in glory for the final deliverance of His people and the restoration of all things. (John 1:1-3, 14; Col. 1:15-19; John 10:30; 14:9; Rom. 6:23; 2 Cor. 5:17-19; John 5:22; Luke 1:35; Phil. 2:5-11; Heb. 2:9-18; 1 Cor. 15:3, 4; Heb. 8:1, 2; John 14:1-3.)

"5. The Holy Spirit

"God the eternal Spirit was active with the Father and the Son in Creation, incarnation, and redemption. He inspired the writers of Scripture. He filled Christ's life with power. He draws and convicts human beings; and those who respond He renews and transforms into the image of God. Sent by the Father and the Son to be always with His children, He extends spiritual gifts to the church, empowers it to bear witness to Christ, and in harmony with the Scriptures leads it into all truth. (Gen. 1:1, 2; Luke 1:35; 4:18; Acts 10:38; 2 Peter 1:21; 2 Cor. 3:18; Eph. 4:11, 12; Acts 1:8; John 14:16-18, 26; 15:26, 27; 16:7-13.)

"6. Creation

"God is Creator of all things, and has revealed in Scripture the authentic account of His creative activity. In six days the Lord made 'the heaven and the earth' and all living things upon the earth, and rested on the seventh day of that first week. Thus He established the Sabbath as a perpetual memorial of His completed creative work. The first man and woman were made in the image of God as the crowning work of Creation, given dominion over the world, and charged with responsibility to care for it. When the world was finished it was 'very good,' declaring the glory of God. (Gen. 1:2; Ex. 20:8-11; Ps.19:1-6; 33:6, 9; 104; Heb. 11:3.)

"7. The Nature of Man

"Man and woman were made in the image of God with individuality, the power and freedom to think and to do. Though created free beings, each is an indivisible unity of body, mind, and spirit, dependent upon God for life and breath and all else. When our first parents disobeyed God, they denied their dependence upon Him and fell from their high position under God. The image of God in them was marred and they became subject to death. Their descendants share this fallen nature and its consequences. They are born with weaknesses and tendencies to evil. But God in Christ reconciled the world to Himself and by His Spirit restores in penitent mortals the image of their Maker. Created for the glory of God, they are called to love Him and one another, and to care for their environment. (Gen. 1:26-28; 2:7; Ps. 8:4-8; Acts 17:24-28; Gen. 3; Ps. 51:5; Rom. 5:12-17; 2 Cor. 5:19, 20; Ps. 51:10; 1 John 4:7, 8, 11, 20; Gen. 2:15.)

"8. The Great Controversy

"All humanity is now involved in a great controversy between Christ and Satan regarding the character of God, His law, and His sovereignty over the universe. This conflict originated in heaven when a created being, endowed with freedom of choice, in self-exaltation became Satan, God's adversary, and led into rebellion a portion of the angels. He introduced the spirit of rebellion into this world when he led Adam and Eve into sin. This human sin resulted in the distortion of the image of God in humanity, the disordering of the created world, and its eventual devastation at the time of the worldwide flood. Observed by the whole creation, this world became the arena of the universal conflict, out of which the God of love will ultimately be vindicated. To assist His people in this controversy, Christ sends the Holy Spirit and the loyal angels to guide, protect, and sustain them in the way of salvation. (Rev. 12:4-9; Isa. 14:12-14; Eze. 28:12-18; Gen. 3; Rom. 1:19-32; 5:12-21; 8:19-22; Gen. 6-8; 2 Peter 3:6; 1 Cor. 4:9; Heb. 1:14.)

"9. The Life, Death, and Resurrection of Christ

"In Christ's life of perfect obedience to God's will, His suffering, death, and resurrection, God provided the only means of atonement for human sin, so that those who by faith accept this atonement may have eternal life, and the whole creation may better understand the infinite and holy love of the Creator. This perfect atonement vindicates the righteousness of God's law and the graciousness of His character; for it both condemns our sin and provides for our forgiveness. The death of Christ is substitutionary and expiatory, reconciling and transforming. The resurrection of Christ proclaims God's triumph over the forces of evil, and for those who accept the atonement assures their final victory over sin and death. It declares the Lordship of Jesus Christ, before whom every knee in heaven and on earth will bow. (John 3:16; Isa. 53; 1 Peter 2:21, 22; 1 Cor. 15:3, 4, 20-22; 2 Cor. 5:14, 15, 19-21; Rom. 1:4; 3:25; 4:25; 8:3, 4; 1 John 2:2; 4:10; Col. 2:15; Phil. 2:6-11.)

"10. The Experience of Salvation

"In infinite love and mercy God made Christ, who knew no sin, to be sin for us, so that in Him we might be made the righteousness of God. Led by the Holy Spirit we sense our need, acknowledge our sinfulness, repent of our transgressions, and exercise faith in Jesus as Lord and Christ, as Substitute and Example. This faith which receives salvation comes through the divine power of the Word and is the gift of God's grace. Through Christ we are justified, adopted as God's sons and daughters, and delivered from the lordship of sin. Through the Spirit we are born again and sanctified; the Spirit renews our minds, writes God's law of love in our hearts, and we are given the power to live a holy life. Abiding in Him we become partakers of the divine nature and have the assurance of salvation now and in the judgment. (2 Cor. 5:17-21; John 3:16; Gal. 1:4; 4:4-7; Titus 3:3-7; John 16:8; Gal. 3:13, 14; 1 Peter 2:21, 22; Rom. 10:17; Luke 17:5; Mark 9:23, 24; Eph. 2:5-10; Rom. 3:21-26; Col. 1:13, 14; Rom. 8:14-17; Gal. 3:26; John 3:3-8; 1 Peter 1:23; Rom. 12:2; Heb. 8:7-12; Eze. 36:25-27; 2 Peter 1:3, 4; Rom. 8:1-4; 5:6-10.)

"11. The Church

"The church is the community of believers who confess Jesus Christ as Lord and Saviour. In continuity with the people of God in Old Testament times, we are called out from the world; and we join together for worship, for fellowship, for instruction in the Word, for the celebration of the Lord's Supper, for service to all mankind, and for the worldwide proclamation of the gospel. The church derives its authority from Christ, who is the incarnate Word, and from the Scriptures, which are the written Word. The church is God's family; adopted by Him as children, its members live on the basis of the new covenant. The church is the body of Christ, a community of faith of which Christ Himself is the Head. The church is the bride for whom Christ died that He might sanctify and cleanse her. At His return in triumph, He will present her to Himself a glorious church, the faithful of all the ages, the purchase of His blood, not having spot or wrinkle, but holy and without blemish. (Gen. 12:3; Acts 7:38; Eph. 4:11-15; 3:8-11; Matt. 28:19, 20; 16:13-20; 18:18; Eph. 2:19-22; 1:22, 23; 5:23-27; Col. 1:17, 18.)

"12. The Remnant and Its Mission

"The universal church is composed of all who truly believe in Christ, but in the last days, a time of widespread apostasy, a remnant has been called out to keep the commandments of God and the faith of Jesus. This remnant announces the arrival of the judgment hour, proclaims salvation through Christ, and heralds the approach of His second advent. This proclamation is symbolized by the three angels of Revelation 14; it coincides with the work of judgment in heaven and results in a work of repentance and reform on earth. Every believer is called to have a personal part in this worldwide witness. (Rev. 12:17; 14:6-12; 18:1-4; 2 Cor. 5:10; Jude 3, 14; 1 Peter 1:16-19; 2 Peter 3:10-14; Rev. 21:1-14.)

"13. Unity in the Body of Christ

"The church is one body with many members, called from every nation, kindred, tongue, and people. In Christ we are a new creation; distinctions of race, culture, learning, and nationality, and differences between high and low, rich and poor, male and female, must not be divisive among us. We are all equal in Christ, who by one Spirit has bonded us into one fellowship with Him and with one another; we are to serve and be served without partiality or reservation. Through the revelation of Jesus Christ in the Scriptures we share the same faith and hope, and reach out in one witness to all. This unity has its source in the oneness of the triune God, who has adopted us as His children. (Rom. 12:4, 5; 1 Cor. 12:12-14; Matt. 28:19, 20; Ps. 133:1; 2 Cor. 5:16, 17; Acts 17:26, 27; Gal. 3:27, 29; Col. 3:10-15; Eph. 4:14-16; 4:1-6; John 17:20-23.)

"14. Baptism

"By baptism we confess our faith in the death and resurrection of Jesus Christ, and testify of our death to sin and of our purpose to walk in newness of life. Thus we acknowledge Christ as Lord and Saviour, become His people, and are received as members by His church. Baptism is a symbol of our union with Christ, the forgiveness of our sins, and our reception of the Holy Spirit. It is by immersion in water and is contingent on an affirmation of faith in Jesus and evidence of repentance of sin. It follows instruction in the Holy Scriptures and acceptance of their teachings. (Rom. 6:1-6; Col. 2:12, 13; Acts 16:30-33; 22:16; 2:38; Matt. 28:19, 20.)

"15. The Lord's Supper

"The Lord's Supper is a participation in the emblems of the body and blood of Jesus as an expression of faith in Him, our Lord and Saviour. In this experience of communion Christ is present to meet and strengthen His people. As we partake, we joyfully proclaim the Lord's death until He comes again. Preparation for the Supper includes self-examination, repentance, and confession. The Master ordained the service of foot washing to signify renewed cleansing, to express a willingness to serve one another in Christlike humility, and to unite our hearts in love. The Communion service is open to all believing Christians. (1 Cor. 10:16, 17; 11:23-30; Matt. 26:17-30; Rev. 3:20; John 6:48-63; 13:1-17.)

"16. Spiritual Gifts and Ministries

"God bestows upon all members of His church in every age spiritual gifts which each member is to employ in loving ministry for the common good of the church and of humanity. Given by the agency of the Holy Spirit, who apportions to each member as He wills, the gifts provide all abilities and ministries needed by the church to fulfill its divinely ordained functions. According to the Scriptures, these gifts include such ministries as faith, healing, prophecy, proclamation, teaching, administration, reconciliation, compassion, and self-sacrificing service and charity for the help and encouragement of people. Some members are called of God and endowed by the Spirit for functions recognized by the church in pastoral, evangelistic, apostolic, and teaching ministries particularly needed to equip the members for service, to build up the church to spiritual maturity, and to foster unity of the faith and knowledge of God. When members employ these spiritual gifts as faithful stewards of God's varied grace, the church is protected from the destructive influence of false doctrine, grows with a growth that is from God, and is built up in faith and love. (Rom. 12:4-8; 1 Cor. 12:9-11, 27, 28; Eph. 4:8, 11-16; Acts 6:1-7; 1 Tim. 3:1-13; 1 Peter 4:10, 11.)

"17. The Gift of Prophecy

"One of the gifts of the Holy Spirit is prophecy. This gift is an identifying mark of the remnant church and was manifested in the ministry of Ellen G. White. As the Lord's messenger, her writings are a continuing and authoritative source of truth which provide for the church comfort, guidance, instruction, and correction. They also make clear that the Bible is the standard by which all teaching and experience must be tested. (Joel 2:28, 29; Acts 2:14-21; Heb. 1:1-3; Rev. 12:17; 19:10.)

"18. The Law of God

"The great principles of God's law are embodied in the Ten Commandments and exemplified in the life of Christ. They express God's love, will, and purposes concerning human conduct and relationships and are binding upon all people in every age. These precepts are the basis of God's covenant with His people and the standard in God's judgment. Through the agency of the Holy Spirit they point out sin and awaken a sense of need for a Saviour. Salvation is all of grace and not of works, but its fruitage is obedience to the Commandments. This obedience develops Christian character and results in a sense of well-being. It is an evidence of our love for the Lord and our concern for our fellowmen. The obedience of faith demonstrates the power of Christ to transform lives, and therefore strengthens Christian witness. (Ex. 20:1-17; Ps. 40:7, 8; Matt. 22:36-40; Deut. 28:1-14; Matt. 5:17-20; Heb. 8:8-10; John 15:7-10; Eph. 2:8-10; 1 John 5:3; Rom. 8:3, 4; Ps. 19:7-14.)

"19. The Sabbath

"The beneficent Creator, after the six days of Creation, rested on the seventh day and instituted the Sabbath for all people as a memorial of Creation. The fourth commandment of God's unchangeable law requires the observance of this seventh-day Sabbath as the day of rest, worship, and ministry in harmony with the teaching and practice of Jesus, the Lord of the Sabbath. The Sabbath is a day of delightful communion with God and one another. It is a symbol of our redemption in Christ, a sign of our sanctification, a token of our allegiance, and a foretaste of our eternal future in God's kingdom. The Sabbath is God's perpetual sign of His eternal covenant between Him and His people. Joyful observance of this holy time from evening to evening, sunset to sunset, is a celebration of God's creative and redemptive acts. (Gen. 2:1-3; Ex. 20:8-11; Luke 4:16; Isa. 56:5, 6; 58:13, 14; Matt. 12:1-12; Ex. 31:13-17; Eze. 20:12, 20; Deut. 5:12-15; Heb. 4:1-11; Lev. 23:32; Mark 1:32.)

"20. Stewardship

"We are God's stewards, entrusted by Him with time and opportunities, abilities and possessions, and the blessings of the earth and its resources. We are responsible to Him for their proper use. We acknowledge God's ownership by faithful service to Him and our fellowmen, and by returning tithes and giving offerings for the proclamation of His gospel and the support and growth of His church. Stewardship is a privilege given to us by God for nurture in love and the victory over selfishness and covetousness. The steward rejoices in the blessings that come to others as a result of his faithfulness. (Gen. 1:26-28; 2:15; 1 Chron. 29:14; Hag. 1:3-11; Mal. 3:8-12; 1 Cor. 9:9-14; Matt 23:23; 2 Cor. 8:1-15; Rom. 15:26, 27.)

"21. Christian Behavior

"We are called to be a godly people who think, feel, and act in harmony with the principles of heaven. For the Spirit to re-create in us the character of our Lord we involve ourselves only in those things which will produce Christlike purity, health, and joy in our lives. This means that our amusement and entertainment should meet the highest standards of Christian taste and beauty. While recognizing cultural differences, our dress is to be simple, modest, and neat, befitting those whose true beauty does not consist of outward adornment but in the imperishable ornament of a gentle and quiet spirit. It also means that because our bodies are the temples of the Holy Spirit, we are to care for them intelligently. Along with adequate exercise and rest, we are to adopt the most healthful diet possible and abstain from the unclean foods identified in the Scriptures. Since alcoholic beverages, tobacco, and the irresponsible use of drugs and narcotics are harmful to our bodies, we are to abstain from them as well. Instead, we are to engage in whatever brings our thoughts and bodies into the discipline of Christ, who desires our wholesomeness, joy, and goodness. (Rom. 12:1, 2; 1 John 2:6; Eph. 5:1-21; Phil. 4:8; 2 Cor. 10:5; 6:14-7:1; 1 Peter 3:1-4; 1 Cor. 6:19, 20; 10:31; Lev. 11:1-47; 3 John 2.)

"22. Marriage and the Family

"Marriage was divinely established in Eden and affirmed by Jesus to be a lifelong union between a man and a woman in loving companionship. For the Christian a marriage commitment is to God as well as to the spouse, and should be entered into only between partners who share a common faith. Mutual love, honor, respect, and responsibility are the fabric of this relationship, which is to reflect the love, sanctity, closeness, and permanence of the relationship between Christ and His church. Regarding divorce, Jesus taught that the person who divorces a spouse, except for fornication, and marries another, commits adultery. Although some family relationships may fall short of the ideal, marriage partners who fully commit themselves to each other in Christ may achieve loving unity through the guidance of the Spirit and the nurture of the church. God blesses the family and intends that its members shall assist each other toward complete maturity. Parents are to bring up their children to love and obey the Lord. By their example and their words they are to teach them that Christ is a loving disciplinarian, ever tender and caring, who wants them to become members of His body, the family of God. Increasing family closeness is one of the earmarks of the final gospel message. (Gen. 2:18-25; Matt. 19:3-9; John 2:1-11; 2 Cor. 6:14; Eph. 5:21-33; Matt. 5:31, 32; Mark 10:11, 12; Luke 16:18; 1 Cor. 7:10, 11; Ex. 20:12; Eph. 6:1-4; Deut. 6:5-9; Prov. 22:6; Mal. 4:5, 6.)

"23. Christ's Ministry in the Heavenly Sanctuary

"There is a sanctuary in heaven, the true tabernacle which the Lord set up and not man. In it Christ ministers on our behalf, making available to believers the benefits of His atoning sacrifice offered once for all on the cross. He was inaugurated as our great High Priest and began His intercessory ministry at the time of His ascension. In 1844, at the end of the prophetic period of 2300 days, He entered the second and last phase of His atoning ministry.

It is a work of investigative judgment which is part of the ultimate disposition of all sin, typified by the cleansing of the ancient Hebrew sanctuary on the Day of Atonement. In that typical service the sanctuary was cleansed with the blood of animal sacrifices, but the heavenly things are purified with the perfect sacrifice of the blood of Jesus. The investigative judgment reveals to heavenly intelligences who among the dead are asleep in Christ and therefore, in Him, are deemed worthy to have part in the first resurrection. It also makes manifest who among the living are abiding in Christ, keeping the commandments of God and the faith of Jesus, and in Him, therefore, are ready for translation into His everlasting kingdom. This judgment vindicates the justice of God in saving those who believe in Jesus. It declares that those who have remained loyal to God shall receive the kingdom. The completion of this ministry of Christ will mark the close of human probation before the Second Advent. (Heb. 8:1-5; 4:14-16; 9:11-28; 10:19-22; 1:3; 2:16, 17; Dan. 7:9-27; 8:13, 14; 9:24-27; Num. 14:34; Eze. 4:6; Lev. 16; Rev. 14:6, 7; 20:12; 14:12; 22:12.)

"24. The Second Coming of Christ

"The second coming of Christ is the blessed hope of the church, the grand climax of the gospel. The Saviour's coming will be literal, personal, visible, and worldwide. When He returns, the righteous dead will be resurrected, and together with the righteous living will be glorified and taken to heaven, but the unrighteous will die. The almost complete fulfillment of most lines of prophecy, together with the present condition of the world, indicates that Christ's coming is imminent. The time of that event has not been revealed, and we are therefore exhorted to be ready at all times. (Titus 2:13; Heb. 9:28; John 14:1-3; Acts 1:9-11; Matt. 24:14; Rev. 1:7; Matt. 24:43, 44; 1 Thess. 4:13-18; 1 Cor. 15:51-54; 2 Thess. 1:7-10; 2:8; Rev. 14:14-20; 19:11-21; Matt. 24; Mark 13; Luke 21; 2 Tim. 3:1-5; 1 Thess. 5:1-6.)

"25. Death and Resurrection

"The wages of sin is death. But God, who alone is immortal, will grant eternal life to His redeemed. Until that day death is an unconscious state for all people. When Christ, who is our life, appears, the resurrected righteous and the living righteous will be glorified and caught up to meet their Lord. The second resurrection, the resurrection of the unrighteous, will take place a thousand years later. (Rom. 6:23; 1 Tim. 6:15, 16; Eccl. 9:5, 6; Ps. 146:3, 4; John 11:11-14; Col. 3:4; 1 Cor. 15:51-54; 1 Thess. 4:13-17; John 5:28, 29; Rev. 20:1-10.)

"26. The Millennium and the End of Sin

"The millennium is the thousand-year reign of Christ with His saints in heaven between the first and second resurrections. During this time the wicked dead will be judged; the earth will be utterly desolate, without living human inhabitants, but occupied by Satan and his angels. At its close Christ with His saints and the Holy City will descend from heaven to earth. The unrighteous dead will then be resurrected, and with Satan and his angels will surround the city; but fire from God will consume them and cleanse the earth. The universe will thus be freed of sin and sinners forever. (Rev. 20; 1 Cor. 6:2, 3; Jer. 4:23-26; Rev. 21:1-5; Mal. 4:1; Eze. 28:18, 19.)

"27. The New Earth

"On the new earth, in which righteousness dwells, God will provide an eternal home for the redeemed and a perfect environment for everlasting life, love, joy, and learning in His presence. For here God Himself will dwell with His people, and suffering and death will have passed away. The great controversy will be ended, and sin will be no more. All things, animate and inanimate, will declare that God is love; and He shall reign forever. Amen. (2 Peter 3:13; Isa. 35; 65:17-25; Matt. 5:5; Rev. 21:1-7; 22:1-5; 11:15.)"

DOCTRINES, SEVENTH-DAY ADVENTIST. *See* Doctrinal Statements, Seventh-day Adventist; also names of specific doctrines.

DOGBA SECONDARY SCHOOL (Collège Adventiste de Dogba). A secondary institution established in 1972 at Maroua, Cameroon. It offers an incomplete secondary program.

DOMINASE ADVENTIST HOSPITAL. A 40-bed medical institution established in 1990 at Kumasi, Ghana, in West Africa. In 1994 Frank Abebrese was the staff physician.

DOMINICA. *See* Inter-American Division; Leeward and Windward Islands.

DOMINICA SEVENTH-DAY ADVENTIST SECONDARY SCHOOL. A coeducational nonresident high school operated by the East Caribbean Conference of Seventh-day Adventists. It is situated at Roseau, Dominica.

The school opened in September 1980 with

an enrollment of about 75 students. By 1988 the school's enrollment had grown to 179, and a five-year secondary education was offered to prepare students for the job market. In 1993 there were 13 staff members and a student enrollment of 220.

Principals: Hubert Taylor, 1980; Andrew Farrel, 1981; Anthony Ollivieirre, 1982; Elroy O'garro, 1983; Jeanette McDowell, 1983-1988; Donovan Rene, 1988- .

DOMINICAN ADVENTIST ACADEMY (Colegio Adventista Dominicana). A primary through college-level school founded in 1947 in the capital of the republic and later moved to Herrera, 12 miles (19 kilometers) from Santo Domingo. Its limited facilities served as classrooms, offices, and dormitories. By 1962 a total of 207 students were in attendance and in 1975 the school was moved to Bonao, where it still operates. Under the leadership of Jose Hernández the school was expanded to offer college-level courses. Until recently the college-level director served also as the principal for both primary and high school levels. In 1992 the academy level had a faculty of 10 and 116 high school students.

Principals: Donovan Olson, 1946-1947; Robert Maxson, 1947-1949; Charles Pierce, 1949-1950; L. A. Wheeler, 1950-1956; D. J. Thomann, 1956-1958; L. F. Moore, 1958-1963; Tulio Haylock, 1963-1966; Valentín Acosta, 1966-1967; J. W. Taylor, 1967-1968; César Puesán, 1968-1969; Luis F. Lescay, 1969-1971; Samuel E. Cole, 1971-1975; Jose Hernández, 1975-1978; Antonio Ceballos, 1978; Cami B. Cruz, 1978-1985; Ramón Araújo, 1985-1987; Wilson Roberts, 1987-1989; Luis Sánchez, 1989-1990; Letty D'Oleo, 1990; Amiris Gomez, 1991-1992; Letty D'Oleo, 1993- .

DOMINICAN ADVENTIST UNIVERSITY (Universidad Adventista Dominicana). An educational institution offering four years of postsecondary studies. The Dominican Adventist University had its beginnings in 1947 in Santo Domingo. Later it was moved to Herrera, some 12 miles (19 kilometers) from the center of the capital, where it functioned as a boarding academy. Its facilities provide classrooms, offices, and dormitories.

By 1962 the school had 207 students, and in 1975 it was moved to Bonao, some 44 miles (74 kilometers) from the capital, where it still operates. That same year the school began offering college-level courses in theology, education, and commerce, and a secretarial course.

In 1976 the college received accreditation from the Inter-American Evaluating Commission for the courses previously mentioned, and in 1978 the first official graduation of 20 students from the four courses offered at the time was celebrated.

In 1979 steps were taken to offer the full four-year college courses, and the Higher Education Commission of the General Conference gave a provisional authorization, adding secondary education to the list of courses previously offered.

In 1981 the Granix Industry was founded, providing an important source of work for students.

In 1982 the school adopted its official name. Through the years other courses have been added, such as psychology, computer sciences, secondary education, and others. The university is a member of the Council of Higher Education of the Dominican Republic. It has an affiliated campus functioning in the metropolitan area of the capital, Santo Domingo.

Presidents: Cami Cruz, 1978-1985; Ramón Araújo, 1985-1987; Wilson Roberts, 1987-1989; Luis Sánchez, 1989-1992; Oreste Natera, 1992- .

DOMINICAN CONFERENCE. *See* Dominican Republic.

DOMINICAN MISSION. *See* Dominican Republic.

DOMINICAN REPUBLIC. A Latin American country occupying the eastern two thirds of the tropical island of Hispaniola in the Caribbean Sea. It has an area of 18,704 square miles (48,500 square kilometers) and a population (1994) of 7.8 million. Its capital is Santo Domingo, the oldest city in the Americas, which for three centuries was the seat of Spanish power in the New World. The official language is Spanish and the established religion is Roman Catholic, but other forms of religion are permitted.

Seventh-day Adventist Statistics. The territory of the Dominican Republic constitutes the Dominican Union Mission, part of the Inter-American Division. Statistics (1992) for the *Dominican Republic:* churches, 295; members, 80,870; church or elementary schools, 41; ordained ministers, 43; licensed ministers, 99; teachers, 412. Dominican Union

Mission headquarters are at Respaldo Fantino Falco 1-A, Ensanche Plantini, Santo Domingo, Dominican Republic.

Statistics (1992) for the conferences and missions—*Central Dominican Conference*: churches, 119; members, 32,515; church or elementary schools, 13; ordained ministers, 16; licensed ministers, 20; teachers, 145. Conference headquarters are at Calle Juan Sánchez Ramírez 40, Santo Domingo, República Dominicana. *East Dominican Mission*: churches, 56; members, 16,231; church or elementary schools, 7; ordained ministers, 8; licensed ministers, 55; teachers, 62. Mission headquarters are at Avenida Circunvalación, Edificio Yagré, Apartamento 2A, IK, San Pedro de Macorís, República Dominicana. *North Dominican Conference*: churches, 85; members, 22,585; church or elementary schools, 18; ordained ministers, 12; licensed ministers, 17; teachers, 169. Conference headquarters are at Avenue Juan Pablo Duarte, Corner Avenue México, Santiago, República Dominicana. *South Dominican Mission*: churches, 35; members, 9,539; church or elementary schools, 3; ordained ministers, 7; licensed ministers, 7; teachers, 36. Mission headquarters are at Azua, República Dominicana.

Institutions. CEA Adventist Secondary School; Dominican Adventist University; Enriquillo Adventist Secondary School; Juan Pablo Duarte School (Barahona); Juan Pablo Duarte School (San Juan de la Maguana); Juan Pablo Duarte Secondary School; Las Palmos Children's Home; Maranatha Adventist Secondary School; Maria Trinidad Sanchez Secondary School; Metropolitan Adventist Academy (Santo Domingo); Ozama Adventist Secondary School; San Cristóbal Adventist Secondary School.

Development of Seventh-day Adventist Work. *Beginnings.* When Charles Moulton, a Jamaican, came to the Dominican Republic from Puerto Rico in 1907 as a colporteur, he found seven Sabbathkeepers already there. In 1908 a Sabbath school was organized at Central Consuelo, and the first Dominican converts, María Williams, her six sons, and a daughter, were baptized. The two older children, James and John, later became workers for the church. James became a colporteur and later a minister, and was the first to carry the SDA teachings to the south of the country. The second Sabbath school was organized about 1909 at a place called Cruz de Mendoza in the capital city of Santo Domingo, where Charles Moulton had worked as a colporteur and self-supporting minister. His first convert in that city was Casiano Carrión.

The first Seventh-day Adventist church was organized in the city of Santo Domingo in 1917, when H. D. Casebeer arrived to take charge of the work. Two years later the first church-owned building in Santo Domingo was erected at 89 Avenida Mella. On that same site a new church with seating capacity for 500 was built in 1962.

In 1918 Moulton went to the region of Cibao and began preaching in Santiago de los Caballeros. He later took up residence in Moca. His work there resulted in the organization of the second SDA church in the Dominican Republic, at Jábaba, in 1921. Its charter members included Luis Gómez and his family.

In 1922 James Phipps and his wife, national converts, went to Barahona to establish a primary school. With their help in April 1924, 16 persons were baptized and a church was organized. Among the converts were Andrea de González and her two daughters, Leonela and Caridad, who years before had bought SDA publications from James Williams. Another of the members baptized into the new group was Adolfo Moretta, who became a worker for the church.

Probably the first SDAs in San Juan de la Maguana were the Milanés family. Later a layperson, George Ogando, was sent there to preach, and in 1942 the San Juan church was organized.

Organization and Growth. The early SDA work in the Dominican Republic was administered from Puerto Rico. In 1924 the Dominican Mission (Santo Domingo Mission) was organized, with William Steele as its first superintendent. At that time there were 147 members in two organized churches. During Steele's administration O. A. Jones and his wife divided the city of Santo Domingo into several zones and founded numerous branch Sabbath schools, as a means of evangelism. In 1929 Peter Nygaard became the mission president. By 1936 the church membership reached 743 in 10 organized churches. In 1943 there were 21 organized churches, with 1,559 members. In 1950 there were 23 church groups and 2,000 members; in 1961 there were 40 organized churches and 3,998 members. Then came sudden growth. The year 1962 saw a remarkable advance of the SDA Church in the Dominican Republic, when by the end of that year the membership of the mission reached 5,248.

In 1964, 32 of the 40 churches met in their own church buildings. The *Voice of Prophecy* radio program was transmitted weekly over three stations, and there were several thousand active members enrolled in the radio Bible correspondence school.

On Aug. 1, 1963, the Dominican Mission achieved conference status and became the Dominican Conference, with Gabriel Castro as the first president. On Jan. 1, 1964 Eligio González became president.

At a special biennial session held on Jan. 1, 1972, the Dominican Conference was reorganized as the Central Dominican Conference and the North Dominican Mission. The Central Dominican Conference was established with 47 churches and 9,297 members. Its first president was E. Galvá. The North Dominican Mission was established with 30 churches and 4,242 members. Its first president was J. Espinosa. At the end of 1973 there were 52 churches, with 11,566 members, who contributed a total of $272,461.93 in tithe in the Central Dominican Conference; and 36 churches, with 6,749 members, who contributed a total of $100,813.34 in the North Dominican Mission.

In July of 1990 the North Dominican Mission was reorganized as the North Dominican Conference with 73 churches, and 21,614 members, with Oreste Natera as the first president.

On July 7, 1986, the South Dominican Mission, with 23 churches and 5,432 members, was organized. Diógenes Suero was the first president.

At a special session held in July 1990 the Central Dominican Conference was reorganized as the Central Dominican Conference and the East Dominican Mission. The East Dominican Mission was established in July 1990 with 45 churches and 12,918 members. Its first president was Feliberto Martínez.

At the end of 1992 there were 119 churches, with 32,515 members, who contributed a total of $1,431,876.06 in tithe in the Central Dominican Conference, and 56 churches, with 16,231 members, who contributed a total of $474,920.29 tithe in the East Dominican Mission.

In January 1994 the Antillian Union was reorganized into two unions: the Puerto Rico Union Conference and the Dominican Union Mission.

DOMINICAN UNION MISSION. *See* Dominican Republic; Inter-American Division.

DONGHAE ACADEMY (Donghae Sahmyook Joongkodeung Hakkyo). A secondary school offering a three-year course, operated in Donghae by the East Central Korean Conference. In 1952 the first class of the middle school was opened. Lee Yong Jin was appointed as the first principal. In 1981 the first class of the high school was opened upon the completion of a new building equipped with modern educational facilities.

In 1993 the thirty-ninth graduation ceremony of the middle school and the ninth graduation ceremony of the high school took place. The middle school consists of three classes and the high school six classes. There are 84 students in middle school and 203 students in high school, with 25 teachers.

Principals: Lee Yong Jin, 1952-1956; Lim Kyung Bum, 1956-1958; Yeon Kwan Heum, 1958-1959; Chung Han Yung, 1959-1962; Kim Jae Shin, 1962-1963; Chung Han Yung, 1963-1965; Cha Bae Hyun, 1965; Kim Ki Hyuk, 1965-1966; Moon Young Sik, 1966-1968; Min Byung Ho, 1968-1973; Kim Pyung Kook, 1973-1975; Lim Choon Taik, 1975-1984; Shin Seung Uk, 1984-1987; Cha Bae Hyun, 1987-1990; Kim Dae Sung, 1990-1992; Lee Jong Jik, 1992- .

DORCAS SOCIETIES. An organization of Seventh-day Adventist women established to minister to those in sickness and want. Its work and name were inspired by the life of Tabitha, or Dorcas (Acts 9:36). The first society (called "Dorcas and Benevolent Association") was formed in October 1874 and developed from a prayer band meeting in the home of Mrs. Henry Gardner in Battle Creek, Michigan. Eight women became charter members, and Mrs. George Amadon (daughter of the first General Conference president, John Byington) was the first president. When the Dime Tabernacle was dedicated (1878), society meetings were held in the northwest belfry. Activities included making garments and supplying food for needy families, caring for the fatherless and widows, and ministering to the sick. This pattern was followed by other churches in America and across the seas. With the organization of the Home Missionary Department in 1913, Dorcas Society work came under that department's direction.

Every church is encouraged to organize a Dorcas Society. By 1973 there were 10,425 societies in operation. Although the downplaying of reporting in recent years makes it impossible to give current statistics, the number continues to grow. Local officers include a leader, who is a member of the church board and of the Church Evangelism Council, and a secretary-treasurer. Membership is open to all ages and is not confined to church members.

Objectives and Services. The objective of the Dorcas Society is to help people physically and spiritually, in the name and spirit of Jesus. Its concern is for every case of need, irrespective of creed, class, nationality, or ethnic origin. The society attempts to meet emergency needs not provided by other agencies. The repair and distribution of good clothing is a specialty; surplus supplies are shipped abroad through ADRA. In addition to continuing services, it carries on occasional projects, such as supplying shoes for needy children and sending disadvantaged children to summer camps.

Each society is encouraged to secure at least one room for use as a welfare unit. It should provide work space and a place for storage of emergency supplies, including a reserve of clothing, blankets, food, etc., for use in disaster-relief service. Materials and funds are donated, and service is voluntary. Where the local church operates a Community Services center the society supplies a major part of the working force.

Federations. In 1934 the first Dorcas Welfare Federation was formed by the churches of the Chicago, Illinois, area. Such federations, composed of the individual Dorcas Societies and Community Services center personnel of a given area within the conference, offer opportunity for exchanging ideas, sharing experiences, combining forces in common projects, and unifying Community Services activities. Although such federations originated locally and are formed by local societies in counsel with pastors and conference lay activities secretaries, the General Conference Lay Activities Department has offered guidance and encouragement. Mrs. Grace D. Mace, who served the department for 28 years, first as office secretary and later as assistant secretary, played a major part in guiding the development of the Dorcas Welfare Societies and their organization into federations.

The federation exercises no authority over its constituent Dorcas Societies and centers, which work under the direction of their individual church officers. Federation officers are elected biennially.

Many conferences also appoint a conference federation president, who assists the conference lay activities secretary in directing Community Services activities for the entire conference.

The 1964 Fall Council recommended that a substantial portion of the church welfare fund be made available by the church board to the Dorcas Welfare Society for exclusive use in health and welfare projects benefiting non-SDA indigent families and disaster victims in the community.

The 1978 Annual Council recommended that a minimum of 30 percent of all solicited Ingathering Reversion funds returned to conferences be assigned to conference- or church-sponsored Community Services projects, including building or renting Community Services centers and the expense of operating these centers.

DOREMUS UNION SCHOOL. *See* Portland Adventist Academy.

DORLAND, OSCAR MILTON (1892-1964). Evangelist, pastor, administrator. He was born in the United States and went to England in 1911 to complete his ministerial training at the missionary college. He entered the ministry in 1914 and a year later became pastor of the Chiswick church. He served in South England until 1924, when he was asked to serve as president of the Welsh Mission. Following this, he served in the same capacity in the South and North England conferences. During World War II he engaged in pastoral work in the large Bristol district and became a well-known representative for Seventh-day Adventists of military age at the tribunals for conscientious objectors. After the war he once again served as president of the North England Conference until 1951. Thereafter, until his official retirement in 1958, he served as president of the Irish Mission. He and his wife retired near Reading, where he pastored the church and also taught in the Theology Department of Newbold College.

DÖRNER, FRIEDRICH AUGUST (1877-1961). Minister and conference administrator in Germany and Southeastern Europe. He was born in Germany and joined the Seventh-day Adventist Church in 1901. Shortly after his baptism he became a bookkeeper in one of the denominational offices. In 1908 he entered evangelistic work. The *Yearbook* listed him from 1909 first as secretary of the West German Conference and corresponding secretary of the German Union Conference, then as missionary licentiate in the Hungarian Conference, and the next year as licentiate. In 1911 he married Emilie Meitert, and was ordained. From 1913 until World War I he was listed as secretary and Sabbath school secretary of the Danube Union Conference, concurrently serving as secretary-treasurer of tract societies in the Mid-Hungarian and Transylvanian conferences, and in the Adriatic and Romanian missions and Sabbath school secretary of the Bulgarian, North Hungarian, Theiss-Save, and West Hungarian missions. From 1917 to 1919 he was listed as director of the West Hungarian Mission. In 1921 he was listed as secretary-treasurer and Sabbath school secretary of the East German Union. Between 1923 and 1946 he was listed as a minister in the Berlin Conference. He retired at the end of 1945.

DOUBRAVSKY, JOSEF (1890-1958). Minister and church administrator in Czechoslovakia. Converted from Catholicism in his youth, he was baptized in 1908. He attended a Seventh-day Adventist seminary for three semesters, and about 1912 sold Bibles and SDA periodicals in Czechoslovakia, for which he was imprisoned. In 1919 he began pastoral service in the church. In 1923 he became president of the Central Bohemian Conference; in 1926, of the Moravian-Silesian Conference; and from 1935 until his retirement in 1952, he was president of the Czechoslovakian Union Conference.

DRAGON OF REVELATION 12. *See* Revelation, Interpretation of.

DRAMA. *See* Recreation and Amusements.

DRANGMEISTER, HEINRICH (c. 1875-1939). Minister in Germany and missionary to German East Africa. He joined the Seventh-day Adventist Church in 1905 and afterward studied at the Friedensau Missionary Seminary in preparation for the ministry. In 1908 he was sent as a missionary to German East Africa, where in 1912 he was ordained at Friedenstal. Upon his return to Germany in 1919, he worked in several areas, and in 1928 settled in Hamburg, where he preached and served as transportation agent for the Central European Division.

DRESS. Seventh-day Adventists advocate neatness and simplicity in dress in harmony with good taste, and the avoidance of fashions that are detrimental to health. These principles have been summarized by Ellen White as follows: "I beg of our people to walk carefully and circumspectly before God. Follow the customs in dress so far as they conform to health principles. Let our sisters dress plainly, as many do, having the dress of good, durable material, appropriate for this age, and let not the dress question fill the mind. Our sisters should dress with simplicity. They should clothe themselves in modest apparel, with shamefacedness and sobriety. Give to the world a living illustration of the inward adorning of the grace of God" (CG 414).

Since early in their history Seventh-day Adventists have spoken out against improper dress. The editor of the *Review and Herald* inserted in the July 10, 1855, issue John Wesley's pronouncement on the evils of improper dress. At a conference held at Battle Creek, Michigan, May 27, 1856, Mrs. White delivered a message deploring the "conformity of some professed Sabbathkeepers to the world." These, she said, "have a disposition to dress and act as much like the world as possible, and yet go to heaven" (1T 131).

In 1858 John Byington, later elected first president of the General Conference, wrote: "Are sleeves which are largest at the *little* end, and round tires like the moon, (or hoops,) [Isa. iii, 18] articles of dress that are modest apparel? 1 Tim. ii, 9. If so, let them be recommended to the church generally."

These positions were taken at a time when the styles of women's dresses were unhealthful and extravagant. It was the day of the hoop skirt, trailing skirts, bustles, and whalebone corsets. Many besides SDAs were protesting against the fashions of the day. For example, M. Angeline Merritt, writing in 1852, declared in *Dress Reform Practically and Physiologically Considered:* "Every lady who has any experience in domestic life must understand the abundant inconvenience attendant upon a style of dress, the dimensions of whose *superfluities* may be adduced in yards and pounds. The utility of skirts for sweeping floors and sidewalks, and for mopping stairways and passages, has become a proverb" (p. 79).

In 1862 Ellen Beard Harman, another dress reformer, wrote in *Dress Reform: Its Physiology and Moral Bearings:* "Viewed in *any* aspect, the common style of dress for women is one of the *greatest barbarisms* ever known, especially considering the age in which we live. Only think of the women of the *nineteenth century* wearing apparel incompatible with the laws of their being—with health, comfort, and convenience, protection and neatness, disproportioned to the body, awkward and burdensome!" (p. 26).

In an endeavor to correct these evils, some reformers went to extremes in the invention of dress styles so radically different as to be offensive to good taste. One of the more popular such fashions became known as the "American costume," invented by a Ms. Austin, which has been described as being composed of mannish trousers covering the legs with a dress coming to the knees, and in some cases coming to midway between the hips and the knees. It was against both the extravagances of the prevailing dress styles and the fanatical extremes of some of the dress reformers that Ellen G. White wrote: "No occasion should be given to unbelievers to reproach our faith. We are considered odd and singular, and should not take a course to lead unbelievers to think us more so than our faith requires us to be.

"Some who believe the truth may think that it would be more healthful for the sisters to adopt the American costume, yet if that mode of dress would cripple our influence among unbelievers so that we could not so readily gain access to them, we should by no means adopt it, though we suffered much in consequence. But some are deceived in thinking there is so much benefit to be received from this costume. While it may prove a benefit to some, it is an injury to others.

"I saw that God's order has been reversed, and His special directions disregarded, by those who adopt the American costume. I was referred to Deuteronomy 22:5: 'The woman shall not wear that which pertaineth unto a man, neither shall a man put on a woman's garment: for all that do so are abomination unto the Lord thy God.'

"God would not have His people adopt the so-called reform dress. It is immodest apparel, wholly unfitted for the modest, humble followers of Christ" (1T 420, 421).

Seventh-day Adventists have considered proper Christian dress and ornamentation so important that a statement to that effect was included in the fundamental beliefs published in 1889: "XV. That the Scriptures insist upon plainness and modesty of attire as a prominent mark of discipleship in those who profess to be the followers of Him who was 'meek and lowly in heart,' that the wearing of gold, pearls, and costly array, or anything designed merely to adorn the person and foster the pride of the natural heart, is to be discarded, according to such scriptures as 1 Tim. 2:9, 10; 1 Peter 3:3, 4" *(SDA Yearbook* [1889], p. 150).

In the Statement of Fundamental Beliefs prepared by the Battle Creek church in 1894 the same ideas were expressed in a slightly modified form: "That the Scriptures insist upon plain and modest attire as a mark of discipleship in those who profess to be followers of Christ, and therefore that the wearing of gold, pearls, and costly array, merely for adornment, is contrary to Scriptures, and should not be indulged in by Christians."

The Statement of Fundamental Beliefs of 1931, although using a more general language, still expressed clearly the church's positions on this subject: "17. That the followers of Christ should be a godly people, not adopting the unholy maxims nor conforming to the unrighteous ways of the world, not loving its sinful pleasures nor countenancing its follies. That the believer should recognize his body as the temple of the Holy Spirit, and that therefore he should clothe that body in neat, modest, dignified apparel" *(SDA Yearbook* [1931], p. 379).

A year later the *Church Manual* (1932) dealt with the subject in a more explicit way. Among a list of principles of Seventh-day Adventism to be accepted by candidates for baptism the individual was to be asked: "17. In matters of dress will you follow the Bible rule of plainness and simplicity, abstaining from the wearing of gold as ornaments and costly array, observing the principles of modesty and Christian dignity?" (p. 78).

The revised Statement of Fundamental Beliefs approved during the 1980 General Conference session in Dallas, Texas, include, under the section entitled Christian Behaviour, this sentence: "While recognizing cultural differences, our dress is to be simple, modest, and neat, befitting those whose true beauty does not consist of outward adornment but in the imperishable ornament of a gentle and quiet spirit" *(SDA Yearbook* [1981], p. 7).

The statement was interested, like the previous one, in general principles. The more specific details were published in the *Church Manual* (1990). Relative to dress, it states: "Christians should avoid gaudy display and 'profuse ornamentation.' Clothing should be, when possible, 'of good quality, of becoming colors, and suited for service. It should be chosen for durability rather than display.' Our attire should be characterized by 'beauty,' 'modest grace,' and 'appropriateness of natural simplicity' *(Messages to Young People*, pp. 351, 352). That it may not be conspicuous, it should follow the conservative and most sensible styles of the time.

"The adoption of fads and extreme fashions in men's or women's dress indicates a lack of attention to serious matters. Regardless of how sensibly people generally may dress, there are always extremes in style that transgress the laws of modesty, and thus have a direct bearing on the prevalence of immoral conditions. Many who blindly follow the styles are at least partly unconscious of these effects, but the results are no less disastrous. The people of God should always be found among the conservatives in dress, and will not let 'the dress question fill the mind' *(Evangelism*, p. 273). They will not be the first to adopt the new styles of dress or the last to lay the old aside" (p. 143).

On the matter of adornment, referring to jewelry and ornaments, the *Church Manual* continues with this summary: "'To dress plainly, abstaining from display of jewelry and ornaments of every kind, is in keeping with our faith' *(Testimonies*, vol. 3, p. 366). It is clearly taught in the Scriptures that the wearing of jewelry is contrary to the will of God. 'Not with broided hair, or gold, or pearls, or costly array' is the admonition of the apostle Paul (1 Tim. 2:9). The wearing of ornaments of jewelry is a bid for attention which is not in keeping with Christian self-forgetfulness. . . .

"Let us remember that it is not the 'outward adorning' which expresses true Christian character, but 'the hidden man of the heart . . . a meek and quiet spirit, which is in the sight of God of great price' (1 Peter 3:3, 4). The use of cosmetics not in keeping with good taste and the principles of Christian modesty should be avoided. Cleanliness and Christlike deportment should be observed in the care and grooming of the individual who is seeking at all times to please and rightly represent Christ our Lord" (pp. 143, 144).

The wedding ring has never been condemned by the church in countries in which the ring was considered to be a criterion of virtue, a symbol of a commitment and not an ornament *(ibid.*, pp. 143, 144). In these countries it is considered imperative for married persons to wear a wedding band. Until recently, this was not regarded to be the case in the North American Division. However, changes in the understanding of the function of the wedding ring among church members in this division led the leaders to vote, in 1986, "to recognize that, in harmony with the position stated in the *Church Manual* (pp. 145, 146 [1986]), some church members in the North American Division as in other parts of the world feel that wearing a simple marriage band is a symbol of faithfulness to the marriage vow and to declare that such persons should be fully accepted in the fellowship and service of the church" *(Adventist Review* 165:31, Aug. 4, 1988).

In recent times many simpler and more healthful dress styles have been promoted, and the question of dress has become less of an issue among Seventh-day Adventists, but SDAs still are encouraged to dress in a manner that befits Christians, particularly Christians who are aware that they are living in the time of the final day of atonement (Ex. 33:5, 6; Lev. 16:29, 30).

DREW, GEORGE R. (1835-1905). Pioneer colporteur and ship missionary in England. He was an Englishman, who, after 15 years as sailor and ship captain, heard the Seventh-day Adventist message and accepted it while in San Francisco Harbor. For seven years he stayed in California studying the Bible and spreading his new faith. In 1882 he returned to England with John Loughborough and a group of SDA workers and engaged in the sale of publications and in ship missionary work at Liverpool. One of his first contacts was with a Finnish sea captain, A. F. Lundqvist, who is credited with introducing SDA work into Finland.

DRINHAUS, PAUL (1886-1930). Evangelist and administrator in Germany. He was born of Seventh-day Adventist parentage and educated at Friedensau Missionary Seminary. Upon graduation, he preached throughout Germany. He became president of the Saxon Conference in 1913, president of the West German Union in 1918, home missionary secretary of the European Division in 1926, and president of the East German Union in 1927. On a trip in West Africa, during which he investigated the opportunities of opening new work in Liberia, he died of malaria.

DRINHAUS, PETER (1889-1950). Pastor, missionary. Born in Germany, he was trained at Friedensau Missionary Seminary, did pastoral work in Germany for several years, then went in 1914 as a missionary to German East Africa, where he was interned during World War I. He returned to Germany, and in 1921 went to the Netherlands East Indies Union Mission, of which he later became president. In 1940 he was again interned, spending time in Java, Sumatra, and India, and upon his release in 1946 went to the United States. For a short time (1947-1948) he was pastor of the Brooklyn, New York, German church, then retired because of ill health.

DRUILLARD, ALMA (d. 1903). Early colporteur, missionary in South Africa. A businessman from the midwestern United States, he joined the Seventh-day Adventist Church about 1879, and entered colporteur work. In 1889 he and his wife, Nellie H., went to South Africa, where he worked for nearly six years, and where he is reported to have been a "favorite missionary" of Cecil Rhodes and Dr. L. Jameson. After his return to the United States in 1896, he served as treasurer of Boulder Sanitarium for several years. About 1901 he was on the staff of Emmanuel Missionary College.

DRUILLARD, NELLIE HELEN (RANKIN) (1844-1937). Founder of Riverside Sanitarium, cofounder of Madison College, financier. She was a member of the Rankin family that furnished a number of women church workers. A graduate of Wisconsin State Normal College, she superintended Boulder, Colorado, and Furnas County, Nebraska, public schools. Later she worked at Battle Creek Sanitarium. She was married to Alma Druillard, a businessman of means. In 1886 she served as Tract Society secretary in the Nebraska Conference, and in 1888 as treasurer of the Nebraska Conference. In 1889 she and her husband went to South Africa. While there she was treasurer and auditor of the conference and secretary of the Tract Society. She spent her spare time as a nurse in a small sanitarium opened by the Wessels family. She was also secretary of the South African Woman's Christian Temperance Union. Upon return to the United States in 1896, she served as matron and accountant for the Boulder Sanitarium, where her husband was treasurer. Later she served as treasurer of Emmanuel Missionary College until 1903.

In 1904, at the age of 60, she became one of the founders of a school. When her nephew, E. A. Sutherland, and Percy T. Magan, a young man to whose education she had contributed financially, left their positions at Emmanuel Missionary College to go South, she joined them in establishing a school at Madison, Tennessee (*see* Madison Institutions). She lent the money for the purchase of the land, and for 20 years afterward was the institution's treasurer and fiscal adviser. She was the organizer of the Madison Sanitarium and its School of Practical Nursing, in which she was the first instructor. At the age of 78 she was injured in an automobile accident in California, and while recuperating, she determined to do something specific for the Blacks in the southern United States. Returning to Tennessee, she established Riverside Sanitarium and School of Nursing and devoted more than 10 years of her life to its development before transferring it to General Conference management. Two years before her death she retired to the campus of Madison College and there, to the last days of her life, attended board meetings and counseled self-supporting institutions that grew around Madison.

DUFFIE, MALCOLM BRADLEY (1844-1919). Member of the "press committee" organized in 1888 to devise and carry out plans for the dissemination of information on civil and religious liberty, the first committee of this kind to be organized by Seventh-day Adventists. He was a veteran of the Civil War and for some years was employed in the editorial office of the Review and Herald. From 1891 to 1893 he was one of the editorial contributors to the *Youth's Instructor*.

DUNA CONFERENCE. *See* Hungary; Trans-European Division.

DUNBAR, ELDINE W. (1900-1989). Youth leader. He served as a denominational employee for nearly 44 years, including his last position as an associate secretary of the General Conference.

He is best known, however, for his work with youth for 39 years, becoming a youth leader in the General Conference in 1944. He led out in organizing the Pathfinder Club and was instrumental in setting standards for the youth organization's Master Guide level.

DUNCOMBE HALL MISSIONARY COLLEGE. *See* Newbold College.

DUNN, BRIAN MANSFIELD (1940-1965). Missionary nurse, the first expatriate Seventh-day Adventist to die violently in the South Pacific. Brian and Valmae Dunn, Sydney Sanitarium graduates, left Sydney on

Nov. 23, 1965, to begin work at the Malaita Hospital (now Atoifi Adventist Hospital). The fatal spear thrust was aimed out of the dark on the night of Dec. 16 when Brian was about to reenter his home after having attended to an urgent request for medicine for a patient he had been treating. He died a few days later, Dec. 19, after a difficult journey by native canoe, mission boat over rough seas, dinghy, airplane, and finally ambulance over rough roads, to the Honiara Hospital.

DUPUY, DANIEL HAMMERLY (1907-1972). Author, pastor-evangelist, educator. He was born in Gland, Switzerland, but moved to Uruguay at an early age. He was educated at River Plate College in Argentina, and later took advanced work in the United States. In 1970 Andrews University conferred on him the honorary title of Doctor of Divinity.

He served in many capacities during his 44 years of service to the church. He was the author of more than 60 books and pamphlets and hundreds of articles appearing in both denominational and nondenominational publications.

DUTCH GUIANA. *See* Suriname.

DYKES, EVA B. (1893-1986). Educator, author. Born in Washington, D.C., she received her Ph.D. from Radcliffe in 1921, specializing in English, Latin, German, and Greek language studies. She was the first Black woman to receive a doctorate in the United States. After teaching at Walden and Howard universities, she joined Oakwood College in 1944 as chair of the English and Humanities departments. She was the author of several magazine articles and books, including *The Negro in English Romantic Thought*. She was active in the movement leading to the formation of regional conferences. In 1973 she received the Certificate of Merit from the General Conference Department of Education. In 1975 she was granted the citation of excellence for her contribution to Seventh-day Adventist education. She served as a notable educator for more than 50 years.

E

E. D. THOMAS MEMORIAL HIGHER SECONDARY SCHOOL. *See* under Thomas.

EARLY RAIN. *See* Latter Rain.

EARTH, NEW. *See* Home of the Redeemed.

EAST ADVENTIST ACADEMY (Academia Regional Adventista del Este). A coeducational nonresident secondary school located in Rio Grande, Puerto Rico, operated by the East Puerto Rico Conference. It was opened in 1964 as the Rio Grande School. Jenny Perez, the wife of the local pastor, directed the two-room 30-student school.

By 1966, 60 students were enrolled, and Dora Gomez served as principal. In 1970 a new school was built on a large piece of land purchased by funds contributed by an anonymous donor. The two-story building housed 10 grades and 200 students. In 1979 eleventh and twelfth grades were added. In 1993 the school had 14 teachers and 317 students in grades K-12.

Principals: Hermino Garcia, Eli Toro, Jose Leer, Neftali Garcia, Otoniel Cabrera, Edith Perez, Eleuterio Ortega, Carlos Molina, Luis Gomez, Carlos Capote.

EAST AFRICAN PUBLISHING HOUSE. *See* Africa Herald Publishing House.

EAST AFRICAN UNION MISSION. *See* Eastern Africa Division; Kenya; Somalia.

EAST AFRICAN UNION TRAINING SCHOOL. *See* Bugema College.

EAST ASSOCIATION MISSION. *See* Angola; Euro-Africa Division.

EAST BANGLADESH REGION. *See* Bangladesh; Far Eastern Division.

EAST BOLIVIA CONFERENCE. *See* Bolivia; South American Division.

EAST BRAZIL ACADEMY. *See* Petropolis Adventist Academy.

EAST BRAZIL UNION CONFERENCE. *See* Brazil; South American Division.

EAST CAMEROON MISSION. *See* Africa-Indian Ocean Division; Cameroon.

EAST CARIBBEAN CONFERENCE. *See* Barbados; Inter-American Division; Leeward and Windward Islands.

EAST CARIBBEAN TRAINING SCHOOL. *See* Caribbean Union College.

EAST CENTRAL KOREAN CONFERENCE. *See* Far Eastern Division; Korea.

EAST CENTRAL MISSION. *See* Africa-Indian Ocean Division; Nigeria.

EAST COLOMBIA CONFERENCE. *See* Colombia; Inter-American Division.

EAST CONFERENCE. *See* Brazil.

EAST CUBA CONFERENCE. *See* Cuba.

EAST DELEGATION. *See* Cuba; Inter-American Division.

EAST DENMARK CONFERENCE. *See* Denmark.

EAST DOMINICAN MISSION. *See* Dominican Republic; Inter-American Division.

EAST INDIA SCHOOL. *See* Seventh-day Adventist High School (Khunti).

EAST INDIA SECTION. *See* India; Southern Asia Division.

EAST INDONESIA UNION MISSION. *See* Far Eastern Division; Indonesia.

EAST JAMAICA CONFERENCE. *See* Inter-American Division; Jamaica.

EAST JAPAN CONFERENCE. *See* Far Eastern Division; Japan.

EAST JAVA ACADEMY (Sekolah Lanjutan Advent). A boarding school on the senior high school level operated by the East Java Mission near Sukorejo, about 30 miles (50 kilometers) south of Surabaya, Java, Indonesia. Opened on Feb. 1, 1967, the school operates in rented buildings owned by one of the church members. The enrollment was 24 students. The East Java Mission had purchased a piece of land of 25 acres (10 hectares) located about 10 miles (15 kilometers) from Sukorejo. It was the plan to build permanent structures on the newly purchased property, but the government refused to give permission to build because the people living in the area were afraid that their children would be converted to Christianity. In 1972 the government gave permission for the school to be built on the property, and in September of the same year the academy moved to its present location.

It is at an elevation of 1,300 feet (400 meters), which gives it a cooler climate and a gentle breeze, making it more pleasant for the students to study and live there. The school has been able to add buildings and facilities and the campus has been landscaped and taken care of by the faculty and students. Presently it has a beautiful campus that well represents Seventh-day Adventist educational institutions.

In 1992, under the direction of Dr. S. Tabuchi, Far Eastern Division director of education, the Japan and Korean Teachers Association donated equipment for a water system that supplies the needs of students and teachers. The 1993 enrollment of junior and high school is 232 students. There are 121 boys and 111 girls; of these, 178 live in the dormitories on campus. Eighty-five percent of the students are Seventh-day Adventist. The staff comprises 14 full-time faculty, including administration and three part-time teachers.

Principals: C. Kainde, 1967-1968; C. E. Dompas, 1968-1974; Agus Ricky, 1975 (one semester); M. Pardosi, 1975-1978; Sukamto, 1978-1979; C. E. Dompas, 1979-1985; R. B. Matahari, 1986-1987; E. T. Panjaitan, 1988- .

EAST JAVA MISSION. *See* Far Eastern Division; Indonesia.

EAST KANSAS CONFERENCE. *See* Kansas Conference.

EAST KASAI FIELD. *See* Africa-Indian Ocean Division; Zaïre.

EAST MEDITERRANEAN FIELD. *See* Jordan; Lebanon; Middle East Union Mission; Syria.

EAST MICHIGAN CONFERENCE. *See* Michigan Conference.

EAST NIGERIA CONFERENCE. *See* Africa-Indian Ocean Division; Nigeria.

EAST NORWAY CONFERENCE. *See* Norway; Trans-European Division.

EAST PANAMA CONFERENCE. *See* Inter-American Division; Panama.

EAST PASCO MEDICAL CENTER. An 85-bed community hospital in Zephyrhills, Florida, owned and operated by Adventist Health System/Sunbelt Health Care Corporation with headquarters in Orlando.

Adventist Health System/Sunbelt acquired the former Jackson Memorial Hospital, a 53-bed doctor-owned facility in Dade City, Florida, in 1981. Shortly after this acquisition, ground was broken for an 85-bed hospital in nearby Zephyrhills. Within two weeks of opening on Jan. 23, 1985, the 85,000-square-foot (7,900-square-meter) hospital was full. Since then East Pasco Medical Center has had eight expansion programs. In addition to acute-care beds, it also has an 11-bed skilled nursing unit and a 10-bed observation unit where patients can stay for up to 23 hours.

In 1993 more than 30,000 square feet (2,800 square meters) were added to the hospital at a cost of approximately $14 million. The new area includes a state-of-the-art outpatient surgical center, an expanded wellness center, a Cardiopulmonary Department, a support services area, and physical, speech, and occupational therapy areas.

East Pasco Medical Center hosts a number of activities and programs to help members of its community learn to stay well and to acquaint them with the mission of Seventh-day Adventist health care.

Presidents: Robert A. Wade, 1981-1985; Roy Orr, 1985-1986; Bob A. Dodd, 1986- .

EAST PENNSYLVANIA CONFERENCE. *See* Pennsylvania Conference.

EAST PERU MISSION. *See* Peru; South American Division.

EAST POLISH CONFERENCE. *See* Poland; Trans-European Division.

EAST PUERTO RICO CONFERENCE. *See* Inter-American Division; Puerto Rico.

EAST RUSSIAN UNION MISSION. *See* Euro-Asia Division; Russia.

EAST RWANDA FIELD. *See* Africa-Indian Ocean Division; Rwanda.

EAST SÃO PAULO CONFERENCE. *See* Brazil; South American Division.

EAST SIBERIAN MISSION. *See* Euro-Asia Division; Russia.

EAST TANZANIA FIELD. *See* Eastern Africa Division; Tanzania.

EAST VENEZUELA MISSION. *See* Inter-American Division; Venezuela.

EAST VISAYAN ACADEMY (Bulacao). A coeducational boarding school on the senior high school level, operated by the Central Visayan Mission at Bulacao, Talisay, Cebu, Philippines. In 1974 the secondary enrollment was 245 and the staff numbered 11. The students are mostly Seventh-day Adventists.

The school opened June 23, 1931, on F. Ramos Street, Cebu City, with Mrs. W. Riffel and Silvestre Ygay as teachers, and with six students enrolled in the first year of high school. Classwork was not recognized by the government. The next year (1932-1933) the school operated in the Cebu City SDA chapel, with 47 pupils in the elementary grades and seven in the first and second years of high school. However, for the next three years it was only an elementary school.

In 1936 the Philippine Union Mission authorized operation as a government-accredited first year of high school. For the school year 1938-1939, the school was moved to the present site on approximately 20 acres (eight hectares) of land along the highway a few miles (several kilometers) south of the city of Cebu. About 30 students enrolled in the first three years of the high school course. An administration building, two dormitories, a dining hall, and teachers' cottages were constructed. During the 1939-1940 school year the institution became a four-year academy, serving the then East Visayan Mission and, until the Mindanao Mission Academy was established in 1947, also the Mindanao Mission.

During World War II the school was closed, but in 1946 the buildings were rebuilt and school was reopened, with U. M. Oliva as principal. Two years later the academy was granted full recognition by the Department of Education of the republic of the Philippines; it also became a member of the Far Eastern Association of SDA Colleges and Secondary Schools. The school has a small farm and a garden.

In 1978 the union and the mission decided to build a new two-story building to house the administrative offices, the library, the teachers' rooms, and the chapel. Upon completion of the building, enrollment in the elementary and secondary levels increased tremendously. The new edifice cost the organization a huge sum of money.

In 1990 the province of Cebu was struck by a super typhoon that brought immense destruction upon people and property. Even the seemingly strong edifices on the campus were not spared. The boys' and girls' dormitories, the cafeteria, the administration building, a number of teachers' cottages, and the elementary school building were badly hit. It took the school administration several months to rehabilitate the campus.

A year after the calamity, the mission and the school officials came up with a proposed rebuilding project that was presented during the constituency meeting of the mission in the summer of 1991. Construction of a large multipurpose auditorium soon began.

By the end of 1992 the new gymnasium was completed. This new structure has a seating capacity of 7,000 and cost the organization more than 4 million pesos. As a result, East Visayan Academy has become the center of huge gatherings, religious or secular in nature.

Principals: Mrs. W. B. Riffel, 1930-1931 (acting), 1931-1932; Luis Elumir, 1932-1936; Pedro Gatchalian, 1936-1937; P. C. Cabansag, 1937-1938; U. M. Oliva, 1938-1942; war years, 1942-1946; U. M. Oliva, 1946-1948; L. L. Quirante, 1948-1950; D. M. Hechanova, Jr., 1950-1953; A. A. Poblete, 1953-1956; B. G. Mary, 1956-1959; A. C. Segovia, 1959-1960; J. A. Ladion, 1960-1963; J. M. Atil, 1963-1968; Mrs. F. P. Penola, 1968-1972; S. M. Rasa, Sr., 1972-1974; Mrs. F. P. Penola, 1974-1976; D. A. Noval, 1976-1983; C. R. Colo, 1983-1985; I. T. Balacy (acting), 1985-1986; D. A. Noval, 1986-1987; I. T. Balacy, 1987-1990; D. S. Albite, 1990-1991; L. J. de los Santos, 1991-1993; J. T. Requillo, 1993- .

EAST VISAYAN ADVENTIST ACADEMY (Leyte). A coeducational boarding high school established in 1992 at Leyte, Philippines.

The members of the East Visayan Mission had long wanted a secondary school in their field. In the late 1980s they were able to purchase a 35-acre (14-hectare) plot of land for 200,000 pesos. Construction of the first building began in 1990, and the school was officially opened June 15, 1992. The beginning enrollment was 167, with six teachers.

Industries include farming and hollow brick making. The school owns a tractor, a turtle-type power tiller, a rice thresher, a rice mill, a truck, and welding equipment. Recently the academy was presented with a 20-passenger jeepney, the gift of Pastor and Mrs. S. Suzuki, visitors from Japan.

Principal: Elias M. Jucaban, 1992- .

EAST VISAYAN MISSION. *See* Far Eastern Division; Philippines.

EAST ZAÏRE FIELD. *See* Africa-Indian Ocean Division; Zaïre.

EAST ZAMBIA FIELD. *See* Eastern Africa Division; Zambia.

EAST ZIMBABWE CONFERENCE. *See* Eastern Africa Division; Zimbabwe.

EASTER. The annual festival celebrating the resurrection of Christ, which now falls on the first Sunday after the first full moon on or after the spring equinox (Mar. 21). The word "Easter" is from *Ēastre,* Anglo-Saxon name for the goddess of spring during whose month (April) the old Teutonic spring festival was observed. With the coming of Christianity the name was transferred to the Christian Passover, which fell at the same season.

The NT gives no clear evidence of a commemorative celebration of the Resurrection (in Acts 12:4, KJV, "Easter" is a mistranslation for

"Passover"). However, early Christians seem to have continued the observance of Passover (Acts 20:6) and may have thought of it as a memorial of the Passion (cf. 1 Cor. 5:7, 8). The apostles John and Philip are reported to have kept Passover in this way, and such a celebration seems definitely to have been an established practice from the time of Bishop Xystus I (c. A.D. 116-c. 125) of Rome.

About A.D. 150 the Quartodeciman ("fourteenth") controversy arose as to whether Easter should commemorate the Passion and fall always on the *fourteenth* day of Nisan, the Passover (as was the practice in Asia), or whether it should celebrate the Resurrection and come on a set annual Sunday, regardless of date, according to another tradition that by then had become general practice. These two points of view may reflect differences between the Pharisaic and the Qumran calendars. The controversy was finally resolved at the Council of Nicaea (A.D. 325) in favor of the latter view.

Regarding baptism as the biblical commemoration of the Resurrection (see Rom. 6:3-5), and mindful of the pagan origin of the day, early Seventh-day Adventists did not celebrate Easter. In 1887 Uriah Smith wrote that Easter "savors of the customs of the Protestant Church not wholly weaned from Mother Rome" *(Review and Herald* 64:179, Mar. 22, 1887). The next year *(ibid.* 65:217, Apr. 3, 1888) L. A. Smith gave as the reason for SDA nonobservance of the day the fact that "we find there [in the Bible] no mention of Easter, or of Lent, or of Good Friday, or of any of the numerous other feast and fast days which the Church of Rome has always made, and which Protestant churches are fast coming to make, so prominent."

EASTER ISLAND. *See* Chile.

EASTERN AFRICA DIVISION. A large unit of church organization to which is allotted the following territory: Botswana, Djibouti, Eritica, Ethiopia, Kenya, Malawi, Somalia, Tanzania, Uganda, Zambia, Zimbabwe. Statistics (1992): churches, 4,872; members, 1,106,988; church or elementary schools, 299; ordained ministers, 639; licensed ministers, 512; teachers, 424. Headquarters: Harare, Zimbabwe. Official organ: *Eastern Africa Division Outlook.*

The division was organized in 1970 as the Afro-Mideast Division and reorganized as the Eastern Africa Division in 1981 and 1983, with 240,311 members in 1,249 churches. *See* Afro-Mideast Division.

Constituent organizations. The Eastern Africa Division is comprised of seven union missions and three fields:

1. *East African Union Mission* (organized 1921; reorganized 1960, 1987). Territory: Kenya and Somalia. Statistics (1992): churches, 1,344; members, 314,739; church or elementary schools, 10; ordained ministers, 161; licensed ministers, 183; teachers, 49. Headquarters: Nairobi, Kenya.

Constituent organizations and their territories—*Central Kenya Conference* (organized 1906; reorganized 1953, 1981, 1986, 1989): Central, Eastern, and Nairobi provinces, and Kajiado, Laikipia, Nakuru (except Olenguruone division), and Samburu districts; *Kenya Coast Field* (organized 1986): Coast and North Eastern provinces; *Kenya Lake Field* (organized 1906; reorganized 1953, 1961, 1990): Kendu Bay and Oyugis divisions, parts of Mbita and Rangwe divisions, and Homa Bay district; *North Nyanza Field* (organized 1990): Kisumu and Siaya districts; *Ranen Field* (organized 1918; reorganized 1961): Central, Kehancha, Migori, and Western divisions of South Nyanza district; *South Kenya Conference* (organized 1906; reorganized 1953, 1981): Kisii, Narok, and Nyamira districts; *Western Kenya Field* (organized 1981): part of Rift Valley province, Western province, and Turkana district.

2. *Ethiopian Union Mission* (organized 1923; reorganized 1945). Territory: Djibouti and Ethiopia. Statistics (1992): churches, 337; members, 79,602; church or elementary schools, 17; ordained ministers, 48; licensed ministers, 19; teachers, 58. Headquarters: Addis Ababa, Ethiopia.

Constituent organizations and their territories—*Central Ethiopia Field* (established 1932): Hararge and Kaffa regions, the Shoa region north of Awash River, and part of Wollo region; *Northwest Ethiopia Field* (established 1929): Gojjam and Gonder regions, and part of Wollo region; *South Ethiopia Field* (established 1947): Arussi, Bale, Gemu-Goffa, and Sidamo regions, and the Shoa region south of Awash River; *West Ethiopia Field* (established 1925): Illubabor and Wollega regions, Gambela, and Asosa.

3. *Malawi Union Mission* (organized 1925). Territory: Malawi. Statistics (1992): churches, 732; members, 134,131; church or elementary schools, 11; ordained ministers, 74;

licensed ministers, 43; teachers, 100. Headquarters: Blantyre, Malawi.

Constituent organizations and their territories—*Central Lake Field* (organized 1964): central Malawi; *North Lake Field* (organized 1958; reorganized 1964): northern Malawi; *South Lake Field* (established 1958; reorganized 1964): southern Malawi.

4. *Tanzania Union Mission* (organized 1903; reorganized 1960). Territory: Tanzania. Statistics (1992): churches, 626; members, 124,270; ordained ministers, 102; licensed ministers, 63. Headquarters: Arusha, Tanzania.

Constituent organizations and their territories—*East Tanzania Field* (organized 1960; reorganized 1982, 1990): Dodoma, Lindi, Morogoro, Mtwara, Pwani, and Ruvuma regions, and the islands of Pemba and Zanzibar; *Mara Conference* (organized 1909; reorganized 1912, 1960, 1977, 1982, 1987, 1990): Mara region and Ukerewe Island; *North-East Tanzania Conference* (organized 1903; reorganized 1960, 1990): Arusha, Kilimanjaro, and Tanga regions; *South Nyanza Conference* (organized 1912; reorganized 1960, 1990): Mwanza and Shinyanga regions; *South-West Tanzania Field* (organized 1960; reorganized 1982, 1990): Iringa, Mbeya, and Rukwa regions; *West Tanzania Field* (organized 1990): Kagera, Kigoma, Singida, and Tabora regions.

5. *Uganda Union Mission* (organized 1987; reorganized 1989). Territory: Uganda. Statistics (1992): churches, 401; members, 75,725; church or elementary schools, 185; ordained ministers, 84; licensed ministers, 61; teachers, 217. Headquarters: Kampala, Uganda.

Constituent organizations and their territories—*Central Uganda Field* (organized 1927; reorganized 1982, 1989): political districts of Kalangala, Kampala, Kiboga, Luwero, Masaka, Mpigi, Mubende, Mukono, and Rakai; *Eastern Uganda Field* (organized 1989): political districts of Bukedi, Iganga, Jinja, Kamuli, Kapchorwa, Karamoja, Kotido, Kumi, Mbale, Moroto, Pallisa, Sebei, Soroti, and Tororo; *Northern Uganda Mission* (organized 1992): political districts of Apach, Arua, Gulu, Kitgum, Lira, and Nebbi; *Southwestern Uganda Field* (organized 1927; reorganized 1982, 1989): political districts of Bundibugyo, Bushenvi, Kabale, Kasese, Mbarara, Ntungamo, and Rukungiri, and parts of Kabarole district; *Western Uganda Field* (organized 1989): political districts of Hoima, Kabarole, Kibale, and Masindi.

6. *Zambesi Union Mission* (organized 1919). Territory: Zimbabwe. Statistics (1992): churches, 413; members, 180,553; church or elementary schools, 66; ordained ministers, 81; licensed ministers, 38. Headquarters: Bulawayo, Zimbabwe.

Constituent organizations and their territories—*Central Zimbabwe Conference* (established 1921; organized 1981): central Zimbabwe; *East Zimbabwe Conference* (organized 1964): eastern and northern Zimbabwe; *West Zimbabwe Conference* (organized 1981): western Zimbabwe.

7. *Zambia Union Mission* (organized 1972). Territory: Zambia. Statistics (1992): churches, 990; members, 185,120; church or elementary schools, 10; ordained ministers, 77; licensed ministers, 93. Headquarters: Lusaka, Zambia.

Constituent organizations and their territories—*Central Zambia Field* (organized 1988): Lusaka and Central provinces; *Copperbelt Zambia Field* (organized 1988): Copperbelt province; *East Zambia Field* (organized 1988): Eastern province; *North Zambia Field* (organized 1972): Luapula and Northern provinces; *South Zambia Field* (organized 1972): Southern province; *West Zambia Field* (established 1972; organized 1988): North Western and Western provinces.

8. *Attached fields—Eritrea Mission Field* (established 1907): Eritrea.

North Botswana Field (established 1921, organized 1951; reorganized 1984): Central, Chobe, Ngamiland, and North-East districts.

South Botswana Field (established 1984): Ghanzi, Kgalagadi, Kgatleng, Kweneng, Southern, and South-East districts.

Institutions. The following institutions are located in the Eastern Africa Division:

Educational Institutions: Akaki Seventh-day Adventist School (Ethiopia); Anderson School (Zimbabwe); Bugema Adventist College (Uganda); Bugema Adventist Secondary School (Uganda); Bulawayo Adventist Secondary School (Zimbabwe); Ethiopian Adventist College (Ethiopia); Hanke Adventist Secondary School (Zimbabwe); Ikizu Secondary School (Tanzania); Kamagambo High School and Teachers' College (Kenya); Kuyera Adventist Academy (Ethiopia); Lake View Seminary and Training Centre (Malawi); Lower Gweru Adventist Secondary School (Zimbabwe); Lunjika Secondary School (Malawi); Malamulo Secondary School (Malawi); Matandani Training School (Malawi); Maxwell Adventist Academy (Kenya); Nyazura Adventist

Secondary School (Zimbabwe); Parane Secondary School (Tanzania); Rusangu Secondary School (Zambia); Solusi Adventist Secondary School (Zimbabwe); Solusi University (Zimbabwe); Tanzania Adventist Seminary and College (Tanzania); University of Eastern Africa Baraton (Kenya); Wollega Adventist Academy (Ethiopia).

Hospitals and Sanitariums: Adventist Health Centre Lilongwe (Malawi); Blantyre Adventist Hospital (Malawi); Gimbie Hospital (Ethiopia); Heri Adventist Hospital (Tanzania); Ishaka Adventist Hospital (Uganda); Kanye Hospital (Botswana); Kendu Adventist Hospital (Kenya); Lusaka Adventist Clinic (Zambia); Malamulo Hospital (Malawi); Mwami Adventist Hospital (Zambia); Seventh-day Adventist Health Services (Kenya); Yuka Adventist Hospital (Zambia).

Publishing Houses: Africa Herald Publishing House (Kenya); Ethiopian Advent Press (Ethiopia); Malamulo Publishing House (Malawi); Tanzania Adventist Press (Tanzania); Upper Nile Press (Uganda); Zambia Adventist Press (Zambia).

For the history of the Seventh-day Adventist work in the Eastern Africa Division, see the specific names of the countries in the area.

Division Presidents: Bekele Heye, 1981-1991; L. D. Raelly, 1992- .

EASTERN ASIA DIVISION. *See* Asiatic Division; Far Eastern Division.

EASTERN CANADIAN MISSIONARY SEMINARY. *See* Kingsway College.

EASTERN CANADIAN UNION CONFERENCE. *See* Seventh-day Adventist Church in Canada.

EASTERN CAROLINE ISLANDS. *See* Guam and the U.S. Trust Territory of the Pacific Islands.

EASTERN COLORADO ACADEMY. *See* Campion Academy.

EASTERN COLORADO CONFERENCE. *See* Colorado Conference.

EASTERN HIGHLANDS SIMBU MISSION. *See* Papua New Guinea; South Pacific Division.

EASTERN HIGHLANDS TRAINING SCHOOL. *See* Kabiufa Adventist High School.

EASTERN NEW YORK ACADEMY. *See* Union Springs Academy.

EASTERN NEW YORK CONFERENCE. *See* New York Conference.

EASTERN OREGON MISSION. A unit of church organization existing from 1910 to 1911 embracing the counties of Morrow, Gilliam, Sherman, Wasco, Crook, Wheeler, Grant, Harney, and Lake in Oregon. It was set off in 1910 from the Upper Columbia Conference as a mission by the North Pacific Union Conference. In September 1911 it was decided to distribute this territory among the Western Oregon, Upper Columbia, and Southern Oregon conferences.

EASTERN PUBLISHING ASSOCIATION. *See* Middle East Press.

EASTERN SOLOMON ISLANDS MISSION. *See* Solomon Islands; South Pacific Division.

EASTERN TRAINING SCHOOL. *See* Seventh-day Adventist School (Singapore); Southeast Asia Union College/Southeast Asia Adventist Seminary.

EASTERN UGANDA FIELD. *See* Eastern Africa Division; Uganda.

EASTERN UKRAINIAN CONFERENCE. *See* Euro-Asia Division; Ukraine.

EASTERN UNION CONFERENCE. A North American administrative unit that existed for less than a year. In the organization of union conferences voted by the General Conference session of 1901, the territory of the old General Conference District No. 1 (12 conferences and missions: Maine, Vermont, New England, New York, Pennsylvania, Atlantic, Chesapeake, West Virginia, Virginia, Quebec, Maritime Provinces, and Newfoundland) became the Eastern Union Conference. In its first session, November-December 1901, its Canadian territory was separated to form, with Ontario, the Canadian Union Conference, and the rest was renamed the Atlantic Union Conference.

EASTERN ZIMBABWE FIELD. *See* Zimbabwe.

EASTMAN, WILLIAM WALTER (1867-1957). Publishing secretary. Ordained in 1897, he served in the publishing work in Nashville, Tennessee, and for some years as publishing secretary in the Texas Conference. From 1914 to 1930 he was associate publishing secretary of the General Conference. He later served as pastor of several churches in the Washington, D.C., area.

EBEYE SEVENTH-DAY ADVENTIST HIGH SCHOOL. A coeducational day school on the senior high school level operated by the Guam-Micronesia Mission of Seventh-day Adventists. It is located in the Kwajalein atoll, part of the republic of the Marshall Islands.

Educational work began on Ebeye in 1981 when a K-6 school was operated. The following year this was expanded into a K-9 school, and each successive year another grade was added, until in 1985 it became a full 12-grade high school, the first high school on this atoll. The spring of 1986 marked the first high school graduation experienced on Ebeye.

The institution serves as a true mission school, serving a community of about 12,000, where SDA students comprise only about 2 percent of the student body. Instruction is in English, the students' second language, and the teaching staff consists of SDA volunteers. The present enrollment (1993) is 230. Each year some students are baptized as a result of the ministry of this mission school, and these comprise about one third of the church membership.

The high school began under the direction of Jack Penner, who served as the first principal in 1982, the year the high school was started with grade 9.

Principals: Jack Penner, 1982; Steven Krunich, 1983; David Reynolds, 1984-1985; Verlin Leer, 1986-1987; William Fralick, 1988- .

ECCLES, JOHN (1850-1902). Pioneer Seventh-day Adventist medical missionary in Central America. He was born at Madras, India, of Irish parentage. When he was about 13 years of age his parents moved to Canada. From there he went to Michigan several years later. Entering Battle Creek Sanitarium as a patient in 1877, he became acquainted with the SDA message and was baptized. Shortly after that he married Martha Crane, of Sheboygan, Michigan. After working eight years at Battle Creek Sanitarium and several years elsewhere as a nurse, he entered the medical school of the University of Pennsylvania and graduated as a physician three years later, in 1896. In March 1900 he and his wife went to the Central American Mission Field as self-supporting Adventist medical missionaries and settled on the island of San Andrés, Colombia. From there he visited settlements along the coasts of Panama and Costa Rica. In September 1901 he fell ill of septicemia and died in January 1902 at the United Fruit Company's hospital at Bocas del Toro, Panama.

ECHO PUBLISHING COMPANY. *See* Signs Publishing Company.

ECKENROTH, MELVIN K. (1914-1975). Educator, evangelist, departmental chair, pastor, administrator. A native of Pennsylvania, he was orphaned at an early age and left in the care of his maternal grandmother. By the age of 13 he was preaching in local churches and meeting houses. After graduating from Shenandoah Valley Academy, where he early showed leadership ability, he enrolled at Washington Missionary College (now Columbia Union College). He arrived with 38 cents in his pocket, ready to commit his life to Christian endeavor. As a college senior he transferred to Emmanuel Missionary College (now Andrews University), from which he graduated in 1937. Subsequently he received his master's and Bachelor of Divinity degrees from the SDA Theological Seminary and his doctoral degree from Howard University.

In 1938 Eckenroth married Margaret Hope Lawry and that same year began his ministry as pastor of a 13-church district in Indiana. This was followed by pastorates in Florida and Michigan.

He later served as an evangelist in Minnesota, and in 1947 joined the General Conference Ministerial Association as an associate secretary, to that time the youngest person ever called to the General Conference. From 1951 to 1958 he was chair of the Department of Field Ministries at the Adventist Theological Seminary and also the teacher of Graduate Overseas Extension Schools for the church. During this time he became known as "Mr. Evangelism" around the world.

In 1959 he was called to be president of the New Jersey Conference, and four years later joined the faculty of Columbia Union College as chair of the Department of Religion and Philosophy, a position he held until his death.

During his years of service he wrote widely for church publications. He is listed in *Who's*

Who in American Education, Directory of American Scholars, Distinguished American Educators, Distinguished Americans of the South, and *Who's Who in Maryland.*

ÉCOLE ADVENTISTE. *See* Senegal.

ÉCOLE ADVENTISTE D'ANKAZAMBO. *See* Ankazambo Adventist School.

ÉCOLE DE SONGA. *See* Songa Institute.

ÉCOLE DES SCIENCES INFIRMIERES DE MUGONERO. *See* Mugonero School of Nursing Science.

ÉCOLE LA PERSEVERANCE DE BOISSARD. *See* Perseverance Boissard School.

ÉCOLE TOUSSAINT LOUVERTURE. *See* Cap-Haitien Adventist Academy.

ECUADOR. A republic situated on the northwest coast of South America, bounded on the south and east by Peru, on the north by Colombia, and on the west by the Pacific Ocean, with an area of about 105,000 square miles (270,670 square kilometers), according to the United Nations Statistical Office, though Ecuador claims an additional 112,000 square miles (290,000 square kilometers) held by Peru. Ecuador's population (1994) is 10.7 million. Since the Spanish conquest the Ecuadorians have been predominantly Roman Catholic, and the country traditionally has been one of the strongholds of Catholicism in Latin America. Though church and state are separate, the state still retains strong ties with the Vatican It was estimated (1991) that there are approximately 54,000 Protestants in the country. The official language is Spanish, which is spoken by 93 percent of the people, the remaining 7 percent speaking Quechua and other Indian languages. Some of the Indian tribes, such as the Jivaros and Aucas, live in primitive conditions.

Topographically Ecuador is divided into three distinct regions: (1) the *Costa,* a low, rolling coastal plain between the Pacific Ocean and the Andes; (2) the *Sierra,* formed by two parallel ranges of the Andes running north and south the length of the country, with a valley 70 to 180 miles (110 to 290 kilometers) wide between, where the bulk of the people live; and (3) the *Oriente,* which consists of humid jungles in the upper Amazon basin. The climate varies with the region; the eastern lowlands are hot and rainy, the highlands are temperate the year around, and the coastal plain is hot and humid from January to May and cool and dry throughout the rest of the year. The economy of the country is basically agricultural and pastoral. About 25 percent of the working population are employed in handicrafts and manufacturing.

Historical Background. The territory that is now Ecuador was inhabited originally by Indian tribes that came down from Central America. During the first half of the fifteenth century these tribes formed the kingdom of Quito, which after a bitter struggle was incorporated into the Inca Empire in 1493. Francisco Pizarro, the Spanish conqueror, began his conquest of the Inca Empire by landing with his forces at the Bay of San Mateo in Ecuador in 1531. In 1534 Sebastian de Belalcázar (Benalcázar), one of Pizarro's lieutenants, completed the conquest of the part of the Inca Empire that is now Ecuador and incorporated it into the viceroyalty of Peru. But being situated between this viceroyalty and that of New Granada, the territory was transferred from one to the other several times during the colonial period.

For many years the spirit of revolt, engendered by centuries of Spanish oppression, gave rise to a series of unsuccessful rebellions. The turning point in the struggle for independence was reached when the patriots gained control of Guayaquil in 1820, but it was not until the victory of Pichincha (May 24, 1822) that José de Sucre, at the head of the Ecuadorian army, with the assistance of troops from the neighboring countries, was able to throw off the Spanish yoke. It then joined Bolívar's short-lived republic of Greater Colombia (Gran Colombia), which embraced the territory of the former viceroyalty of New Granada and Peru. This republic lasted less than a decade, and on May 13, 1830, Ecuador declared its independence.

The next 30 years of Ecuadorian history were turbulent politically, reaching a climax between 1845 and 1860, when five different presidents succeeded one another in office and the constitution was changed several times. Finally a strong leader, Gabriel Garcia Moreno, emerged, who served as president for two periods (1861-1865 and 1869-1875). An austere Roman Catholic, he sought peace and consolidation for his country by strict religious discipline. The Roman Catholic Church was invested with complete control of education, and a concordat with the Vatican (1863) guaranteed to the church a large measure of control in civil affairs.

However, in spite of his assumed dictatorial powers, Moreno was unable to suppress the growing spirit of liberalism, which continued to develop after his second administration, and reached a climax in the revolution led by General Eloy Alfaro (1895), a liberal. This political turnover split the country into two main camps, which have persisted since, with the liberals dominating the coastal plain and the Catholic conservatives dominating the highlands. The result has been a succession of weak liberal administrations, which have not been able to enforce the religious freedom guaranteed in the constitution. However, recent Ecuadorian history has shown slow but steady progress toward democratic ideals and toward greater stability in government.

Seventh-day Adventist Statistics. Until 1985 Ecuador was part of the Ecuador Mission, a part of the Inca Union Mission. After that up until Jan. 6, 1993, the Ecuador Mission was a detached mission in the South American Division. On Jan. 7, 1993, Ecuador was divided into two missions. Statistics (1992) for *Ecuador:* churches, 41; members, 18,800; elementary schools, 11; ordained ministers, 20; licensed ministers, 13; credentialed missionaries, 17; teachers, 67. North Ecuador Mission headquarters are at Quito and South Ecuador Mission headquarters are at Guayaquil.

Institutions. Ecuador Adventist Academy; Pacific Adventist Academy; Quito Adventist Academy; Quito Adventist Clinic.

Seventh-day Adventist Work. *Beginnings.* The first SDA to come to Ecuador was Thomas H. Davis, a colporteur, who arrived in Guayaquil with his family about Aug. 30, 1904, and went to work selling SDA publications. On Nov. 7, 1905, George W. Casebeer, a minister, arrived with his wife to take charge of the interest aroused by Davis's work. A few months after Casebeer's arrival the South American Union Mission recommended that Ecuador be separated from the West Coast Mission (Chile, Bolivia, Peru, and Ecuador) and be made a separate mission, with Casebeer as its superintendent. The prospects for SDA work looked bright as in various places doors opened. Many seemed interested and several were keeping the Sabbath. The first convert to be baptized was C. E. Yepez, whom J. W. Westphal baptized at Ambato about the middle of 1907 (*Review and Herald* 84:18, Sept. 26; 84:14, Dec. 12, 1907). In a short time an English language school was opened.

The first blow to this encouraging prospect was the death of Mrs. Davis at Ambato on July 16, 1907. Soon afterward unrelenting persecution broke out. Added to these perplexing circumstances were the political instability of the country and the unhealthful climatic conditions along the coast. Before the end of 1908 both the Casebeer and the Davis families left the country and accepted calls to work in Chile. Their places were taken by Octavio Navarrete, a colporteur, and William Steele, who was appointed mission director. A short time later William W. Wheeler, a minister and practical nurse, arrived with his wife, but in a few months Mrs. Steele's illness forced the family to leave the country. They were replaced by John Osborne and his family, who arrived in Ecuador shortly before October 1910.

Early in 1911 Wheeler baptized what appears to be the second Ecuadorian convert, a "Brother Espinoza, of Machala" (*Revista Adventista* 11:10, April 1911). Slowly the work seemed to be gaining a foothold so that by the middle of the year a mission church of some seven or eight members, composed of the Sabbathkeepers in all of Ecuador, was organized (*ibid.* 11:10, July 1911). But again there were reverses. Before the end of 1911 both Osborne and Wheeler were taken ill with tropical diseases, and although Osborne recovered sufficiently to stay on for a time, Wheeler was compelled to leave Ecuador.

The Osbornes were joined by César Lopéz of Peru and Santiago Mangold of Argentina early in 1912, and on June 15 of that year what appears to be the first local Seventh-day Adventist church in Ecuador was organized in Quito with eight members (*ibid.* 2:8, October 1912). Again hopes revived that SDA work would prosper in Ecuador, but they were soon dashed when Mrs. Mangold became ill and died, and before the end of 1913 her husband and little daughter had to return to Argentina. For a time the Osbornes were the only foreign workers in Ecuador.

In the summer of 1914 two more missionary families arrived—C. E. Knight, originally from the United States, and Enrique Mangold of Argentina. Knight took over the superintendency of the mission from Osborne, who had been weakened by disease, and Mangold led in the canvassing work. However, their work was seriously hampered by a revolution that lasted for more than two years and by illness caused by unhealthful climatic conditions (*ibid.* 16:18, March-April 1916). SDA work in Ecuador came to a virtual standstill for the next several years. In 1916 there were 23 SDAs in the country; by 1921 this number had decreased to 20.

Later Developments. In 1921 Orley Ford, who had been working among the Indians of Peru for several years, was sent to Ecuador, where he began work among the Indians of Lake Colta, near the city of Riobamba, early in 1922. The work was popular with the Indians and with the government, but no converts were made, so that by 1924 SDA membership in Ecuador had dwindled to 17, and the foreign workers had decreased to two. Writing in the *Revista Adventista* of Nov. 12, 1928, Ford said: "For many years the work in Ecuador has progressed under serious difficulties and seeming failure, and the workers, on encountering the wall of opposition that rose up before them, have become discouraged" (p. 10). But a break came when in 1927 G. A. Schwerin arrived with his family to do evangelistic work. As a result of his work the membership, which stood at only 31 in 1927, more than doubled to 65 in 1928.

On Jan. 10, 1929, the Ford and Schwerin families, who were vacationing together at Colta Lake Mission Station, narrowly escaped death in an Indian uprising against Whites. Later that same year the Ford family came close to death at the hands of a fanatical mob in the town of San Miguel, Bolívar province.

By 1931 membership in Ecuador climbed to 108, and although for the next 10 years the figure remained around 120, there was never any doubt that SDA work in Ecuador had come to stay. In 1941 the foundations of the first SDA church building in Ecuador were laid in Quito.

Beginning with 1943, membership in Ecuador began to climb steadily. From 143 in that year the number increased to 262 in 1949. But the most significant rise in membership came after a series of evangelistic meetings held by Walter Schubert in the city of Guayaquil in 1950. At the end of that year membership stood at 395. By 1957 there were 1,035 members; in 1963, 1,639; in 1973, 4,236; and in 1992, 18,800.

Educational Institutions. In 1991 SDAs had three secondary schools in Ecuador. Ecuador Mission Academy, established at Guayaquil in 1961, is now a boarding academy known as Colegio Adventista del Ecuador (Ecuador Adventist Academy). There also are two day academies, one in Quito and the other in Guayaquil.

Medical Work. The Clínica Adventista de Quito (Quito Adventist Clinic), inaugurated in February 1961, is the only SDA medical institution in Ecuador. In 1990 property was purchased 37 miles (60 kilometers) from Quito on which a Better Living center was built in 1993.

ECUADOR ADVENTIST ACADEMY (Colegio Adventista del Ecuador). A boarding academy on the senior high school level, owned and operated by the Ecuador Mission. It is located on a 407-acre (165-hectare) property, 90 miles (145 kilometers) west of the capital city of Quito, about 160 miles (260 kilometers) north of Guayaquil and about nine miles (14 kilometers) from Santo Domingo de los Colorados. It is in a forest area, at an altitude of between 2,000 and 2,500 feet (610 and 760 meters) above sea level. Its climate is quite tropical and humid.

The school was first opened in Guayaquil as a day academy in 1961, and was moved to its present location in 1968. Since that time an attractive little campus has been developed, including an expanding boys' dormitory, a girls' dormitory, a multipurpose kitchen and dining room, an administration building, and two classroom buildings.

A yucca starch industry operated for a while, but had to be closed. There is a carpentry and a repair shop.

Principals: Nathan Merkel, 1968-1971; Grover Rose, 1971-1973; Bert Elkins, 1974; Augusto Rivas, 1975-1977; Hector Palacios, 1978-1979; Augusto Rivas, 1980-1983; Jaime Penna, 1984-1987; Augusto Rivas, 1987-1989; Hector Palacios, 1990- .

ECUMENISM. From the Greek *oikoumenē*, "the inhabited world," "the whole world," and thus "universal." Generally "ecumenism" is associated with the movement to bring the Christian churches together in united action and belief, and eventually in some form of organic union. However, as the end of the second millennium approached, the goal of most "ecumenists" was no longer organic unity, but "visible unity." *Oikoumenē* occurs 15 times in the NT, as, for example, in Luke 2:1 of the extent of the Roman registration mentioned and in Matt. 24:14 of the extent of the preaching of the gospel. During the nineteenth and early twentieth centuries Protestant ecumenical efforts began to focus on social service and foreign missions, through such organizations as the YMCA (founded in London in 1844), the Evangelical Alliance (formed in

London in 1846), the Federal Council of Churches (in America, 1900), and Christian World Communions, such as the Lutheran World Federation, World Methodist Council, Baptist World Alliance, and what is called the World Alliance of Reformed Churches. The world Missionary Conference at Edinburgh, Scotland, in 1910 is often referred to as the first important step in the ecumenical movement. Two Seventh-day Adventist delegates participated, including W. A. Spicer, secretary of the General Conference. Significant also was the International Missionary Council that met at Jerusalem in 1928, and at Madras in 1938. Since that time, ecumenism has focused on the home front. The organized ecumenical movement developed in three major streams: International Missionary Council, Faith and Order, and Life and Work. The Faith and Order Movement met at Lausanne, Switzerland, in 1927 and at Edinburgh in 1937. The other movement, known as Life and Work, had been sponsored since 1920 by Nathan Söderblom, the Lutheran archbishop of Uppsala, Sweden. Life and Work conferences were held at Stockholm, Sweden, in 1925 and at Oxford, England, in 1937. Ecumenical cooperation for Christian youth was considered at Oslo in 1947, and this was followed by a series of World Christian Youth conferences and the World Council for Christian Education.

The capstone of ecumenical effort came with the creation of the World Council of Churches (WCC) at Amsterdam in 1948 when the Faith and Order and Life and Work movements merged. The World Council met again at Evanston, Illinois, in 1954. The only requirement for membership in the World Council in those early years was acceptance of "our Lord Jesus Christ as God and Saviour."

At the New Delhi Assembly of the WCC in 1961, there were delegates from 197 member churches representing 300 million Christians in 90 countries. The Greek Orthodox Church already was a member of the council, and the Russian Orthodox Church, with 50 million members, was accepted for membership together with some other Orthodox churches. The International Missionary Council merged with the WCC at that time. The original simple prerequisite for membership was enlarged to read: "The World Council of Churches is a fellowship of churches which confess the Lord Jesus Christ as God and Saviour according to Holy Scripture and therefore seek to fulfill together their common calling to the glory of one God, the Father, Son and Holy Spirit."

This change was necessary in order to incorporate the Orthodox churches. Many Protestants doubt that organic unity is possible without theological unity, and fear that the attempt to present a united message to the world under such circumstances is contrary to the Protestant concept of the individual interpretation of Scripture. Ecumenism does not have the undivided support of the laity. However, the ecumenical movement has been gradually bringing some churches together in formal union ("union churches"), as well as in less formal but united action through such organizations as the National Council and the World Council of Churches. There are more than 100 national councils of churches, most of them associated with the WCC. The Roman Catholic Church is a member of more than one-third of these councils.

Several major Protestant denominations are not members of the World Council, including the Southern Baptist Convention, the Seventh-day Adventist Church, the Lutheran Church-Missouri Synod, and the great majority of Pentecostal churches. The Catholic Church appointed observers to attend the New Delhi meeting, this being the first official ecumenical gesture of the kind on the part of the Vatican, although unofficial Roman Catholic observers have attended most of the major ecumenical gatherings since the Edinburgh meeting in 1937.

Formerly aloof from matters of ecumenical concern, or even quite openly hostile (several warnings were issued by the Vatican), the Roman Catholic Church began to take an active interest in the ecumenical movement in connection with Vatican Council II, under Pope John XXIII, who appointed a Secretariat for the promotion of Christian Unity to promote closer relations with the non-Catholic churches. Through this Secretariat, which now has been upgraded to the level of a Council, arrangements were made for Protestant observers to attend the council and for them to express their opinion on matters before the council. A decree promulgated by Session III of the council, entitled "On Christian Unity," outlined the Catholic approach to the problem. Early in 1965 the World Council of Churches appointed a working group to enter into formal dialogue on matters of mutual interest and concern, with a similar group to be appointed by the Secretariat for the Promotion of Christian Unity.

However, high-ranking Catholic spokespersons have made it clear that Catholic concessions to facilitate unity cannot alter either the magisterium (the teaching authority of the church) or the papacy (its governing authority). Therefore, structural rapprochement between Protestantism and Catholicism will involve Protestantism's ultimate acceptance of the doctrine and authority of the Roman Catholic Church, including the primacy of the pope. The many and far-reaching concessions the Catholic Church is able and willing to make in order to bring about the reunion of Christendom will not affect the essential substantive factors that constitute *the* Catholic Church.

The General Conference Committee has never voted an official statement regarding the Seventh-day Adventist relationship to the ecumenical movement as such. A book has been written dealing at length with the subject (B. B. Beach, *Ecumenism—Boon or Bane?* [Review and Herald, 1974]), and a number of articles have appeared over the years in SDA publications, including the *Adventist Review*. Thus, while there is not exactly an official position, there are clear indications regarding the Seventh-day Adventist viewpoint.

Generally it can be said that, while the Seventh-day Adventist Church does not completely condemn the ecumenical movement and its main organizational manifestation, the World Council of Churches, it has been critical of various aspects and activities. Few would wish to deny that ecumenism has had laudable aims and some positive influences. Its goal is visible Christian unity. No SDA can be opposed to the unity Christ Himself prayed for. The ecumenical movement has promoted kinder interchurch relations with more dialogue and less diatribe and helped remove unfounded prejudices.

Through its various organizations and activities, the ecumenical movement has provided more accurate and updated information on churches, spoken for religious liberty and human rights, combatted against the evils of racism, and drawn attention to socioeconomic implications of the gospel. In all this the intentions have been good and some of the fruit palatable. However, in the total picture the banes tend to outweigh the boons.

On the basis of Bible prophecy and the writings of Ellen G. White, SDAs anticipate the eventual success in some form or another of the ecumenical movement, both in eliminating the divisions of Protestantism and in reuniting Christendom by bridging the gulf that separates non-Catholic communions from Rome. The ecumenical movement will then become a concerted effort to unite not only Christians but also the entire world and to secure universal peace and security by enlisting the power of civil government in a universal religiopolitical crusade to eliminate all dissent. Seventh-day Adventists envision this crusade as the great apostasy to which John the revelator refers as "Babylon the great." They understand also that God's last message of mercy to the world prior to the return of Christ in power and glory will consist of a warning against this great apostate movement, and a call to all who choose to remain loyal to Him to leave the churches connected with it. (See Rev. 13:15-17; 14:6-11; 16:12-14; 17:1-6; 18:1-4; GC 444, 445, 573, 588, 589, 615.)

F. D. Nichol, editor of the *Review and Herald,* has summarized the SDA attitude toward the ecumenical movement thus: "We can heartily agree with World Council leaders that the endless divisions in Christendom are a tragedy. Accordingly, we must agree that it is laudable to seek to remove these divisions and thus produce unity. That far we can go with them in their reasoning.

"We doubt the wisdom of the method they are employing to secure unity. And we take issue with the evident assumption that underlies their thinking; namely, that if the various religious bodies will adjust their government and doctrines here and there, they can be fitted together harmoniously. We believe that true unity is possible only in terms of Bible truth, and that any unity short of that is a deception. . . . God's true church in the world must be distinguished first and above all else by its devotion to the revealed will of God as found in the Holy Scriptures" *(Review and Herald* 131:14, Sept. 23, 1954).

In an editorial entitled "Why We Cannot Join" *(ibid.* 142:15, Mar. 18, 1965), Nichol explained why Seventh-day Adventists decline to participate in such organizations as the National Council of Churches: "At the heart of the ecumenical movement is the policy to soft-pedal what its communicants cannot agree on. How else could such a movement gain cohesion or make progress at all? At the very heart of the Advent movement is the conviction that we should emphasize our distinctive doctrines. . . . True, we hold certain prime Christian doctrines in common with all other Christian people, but let us never forget that it is not our theological points of agreement but our points of difference that justify our existence as a separate people. And it is only as we keep those points of difference clear that we protect against blurring out the edges of Adventism in a disordered world."

A person's attitude toward ecumenism will be determined by the individual's concept of the nature of the church. Seventh-day Adventists believe that all sincere Christians, of whatever communion, constitute the people of God. But they believe also that the SDA Church has been given a special message for the world in this generation—the message of Christ's imminent, personal, visible return to earth in power and glory to establish His universal, righteous, eternal reign, and of preparation for that event—and that eventually, sincere Christians everywhere will recognize the validity of this message and of the Seventh-day Adventist Church as God's remnant church. SDAs welcome Christian fellowship with other denominations but believe that the message with which they have been entrusted is for the entire world, and that the proclamation of this message is not compatible with membership in the World Council of Churches. Furthermore, in view of their conviction that the message they have to give must go to all the world, they could not accept the assignment of a limited area for missionary work. They regret that their sense of world mission makes membership in the National Council and the World Council impracticable. However, SDAs seek to work in fellowship with other Christians in every way that does not involve a compromise of what they understand to be their mission as a people.

SDAs are concerned regarding not only the ecumenical understanding of unity, but the approach of many ecumenists, especially in the setting of the World Council of Churches, to belief, understanding of Scripture and mission, sociopolitical responsibility, and eschatology.

Should SDAs cooperate ecumenically? SDAs should cooperate insofar as the authentic gospel is proclaimed and crying human needs are being met. The Seventh-day Adventist Church wants no entangling memberships and refuses any compromising relationships that might tend to water down its distinct witness. However, SDAs wish to be "conscientious cooperators." The ecumenical movement as an agency of cooperation has acceptable aspects; as an agency for organic unity of churches, it is much more suspect.

Back in 1926, long before ecumenism was in vogue, the General Conference Executive Committee adopted an important statement that is now a part of the General Conference *Working Policy* (075). This declaration has significant ecumenical implications. The concern of the statement was for the mission field and relationships with other "missionary societies." However, the statement has now been broadened to deal with "religious organizations" in general. It affirms that Seventh-day Adventists "recognize those agencies that lift up Christ before men as a part of the divine plan for evangelization of the world, and . . . hold in high esteem Christian men and women in other communions who are engaged in winning souls to Christ." In the church's dealings with other churches, "Christian courtesy, frankness, and fairness" are to prevail. Some practical suggestions are made in order to avoid misunderstandings and occasion for friction. The statement makes it very clear, however, that the "Seventh-day Adventist people" have received the special "burden" to emphasize the Second Coming as an event "even at the door," preparing "the way of the Lord as revealed in Holy Scripture." This divine "commission" makes it, therefore, impossible for SDAs to restrict their witness "to any limited area" and impels them to call the gospel "to the attention of all peoples everywhere."

Experience has taught that generally the best relationship to the various councils of churches (national, regional, world) is that of observer-consultant status. This helps the church to keep informed and to understand trends and developments. It helps to know Christian thinkers and leaders. SDAs are provided the opportunity to exert a presence and make the church's viewpoint known. Membership is not advisable. Those ecumenical organizations are usually not "neutral." They often have quite specific goals and policies, and play sociopolitical advocacy roles.

Today the World Council of Churches has as its goal not so much organizational union as "mutual recognition." What this means is that the different churches and denominations are to recognize each other's baptism, Communion service (Eucharist), and ordained ministry. During the last decade of the twentieth century a key ecumenical term is *koinonia*, that is, communion, fellowship, cooperation, and caring partnership.

It would appear that the organized ecumenical movement reached a pinnacle of enthusiasm and influence in the late sixties, in the immediate aftermath of Vatican II. Since then the WCC has gone into a period of ecumenical doldrums and even decline. Much ecumenical activity now takes place outside of the WCC on the local level in the form of unstructured interdenominational youth and lay Bible study and prayer groups, fellowships, and community service endeavors.

EDITORIAL SAFELIZ. *See* Safeliz Publishing House.

EDITURA CURIERUL ADVENTIST. *See* Romanian Adventist Publishing House.

EDIZIONI A.D.V. L'ARALDO DELLA VERITÀ. *See* Italian Publishing House.

EDMED, HERBERT JOHN (1864-1934). Evangelist, administrator, and missionary. He was born in Surrey, England, and while in his teens went to South Africa in an effort to build up his health. He became interested in Seventh-day Adventist teachings through reading a copy of *Daniel and the Revelation* sold to him by one of the pioneer colporteurs. Shortly after reading the book he attended a series of meetings by I. J. Hankins, and was baptized. He was married in 1890, and shortly after that opened a hardware store.

While visiting South Africa a few years later, S. N. Haskell was deeply impressed by Edmed's capabilities and persuaded him to enter the ministry. In spite of a depression, Edmed was able to sell his business profitably within three weeks. His first duties were pastoral and evangelistic. He held meetings in many of the principal cities and towns of South Africa, establishing groups of converts, which later became strong churches. Edmed was president of two conferences—the Natal Transvaal Conference and the Cape Conference.

He was ordained by W. W. Prescott in 1912. Except for several years in England as Bible teacher at Stanborough (now Newbold) College, he spent the rest of his working years in the West Indies. For a few years he served as an executive, and after that as pastor of various churches.

EDMER SCHOOL. A coeducational mission day school operated at Georgetown, Grand Cayman, Cayman Islands, West Indies, by a local school board. The 1993 enrollment was 67, with a teaching staff of five.

The school was named in memory of Mrs. Clara Edmer and George Merren, two early Seventh-day Adventist believers in the Cayman Islands who made substantial contributions to the support of Christian education.

Edmer School was founded in September 1968 as a junior high school, with permission to add forms until senior high school status was achieved. Edmer gained high school status, but discontinued operating as a high school in 1986, when the government of the Cayman Islands opened a middle school, attracting a number of students who had been attending the Edmer High School.

Principals: Mrs. J. Peace (acting), 1968-1969; Carl Henry, 1969-1970; Mrs. J. Peace, 1970-1971; R. Rose, 1971-1972; H. Shand, 1972-1973; L. V. McMillan, 1973-1974; V. Cato, 1974-1977; D. Tatum, 1978-1982; R. Rose, 1982-1983; Mrs. L. Smith, 1983-1986; K. Adderley, 1986-1987; G. Coke, 1987-1988; C. McLaughlin, 1988- .

EDO-DELTA MISSION. *See* Africa-Indian Ocean Division; Nigeria.

EDSON, HIRAM (1806-1882). A layman (later ordained) of Port Gibson, New York, the pioneer responsible for introducing, among those who became Seventh-day Adventists, the fuller understanding of the sanctuary and its cleansing. Edson was a respected Methodist steward in 1843 (or possibly 1844), when he accepted the message of the imminent Second Advent. As the Millerites' day of expectation approached, he held evening cottage meetings in his home. On Oct. 22 he invited the people to come to the last meeting, and bade goodbye to those who declined, never expecting to meet them again. Concerning this meeting he said, "We looked for our coming Lord until the clock tolled twelve at midnight. The day had then passed, and our disappointment became a certainty. Our fondest hopes and expectations were blasted" (Hiram Edson, fragment of a manuscript on his "Life and Experience," fol. 8v).

But Edson kept musing in his heart: "My advent experience has been the richest and brightest of all my Christian experience. . . . Has the Bible proved a failure? Is there no God, no heaven, no golden city, no Paradise?" *(ibid.,* fols. 8v, 9r).

After waiting and weeping until dawn, many of the Advent believers slipped away to their desolate homes. To some of those who remained Edson said, "Let us go to the barn" *(ibid.,* fol. 9r). They went into the almost-empty granary and prayed until the conviction came that their prayers had been heard and accepted, and that light would be given and their disappointment explained.

Later Edson said to one of his companions, "Let us go and see, and encourage some of our brethren" *(ibid.,* fol. 9v; according to Loughborough this second man was O.R.L. Crosier). They shunned the road, perhaps to avoid scoffers, and crossed Edson's field, where the corn was still in the shock and the pumpkins were on the vines. Suddenly Edson stopped. As he stood there an overwhelming conviction came over him "that instead of our High Priest *coming out* of the Most Holy of the heavenly sanctuary to come to this earth on the tenth day of the seventh month, at the end of the 2300 days, he for the first time *entered* on that day the second apartment of that sanctuary and that he had a work to perform in the Most Holy before coming to this earth. That he came to the marriage at that time [an allusion to the parable of the bridegroom in Matt. 25; *see* "Midnight Cry"]; in other words, to the Ancient of Days, to receive a kingdom, dominion, and glory; and we must wait for his return *from the wedding" (ibid.,* fol. 9v).

Edson's mind was also directed to Rev. 10, a chapter presenting the symbol of the sweet, then bitter, book. The Adventists' experience had indeed been as honey in their mouths. Now in the aftermath it had suddenly become as bitter as gall (Rev. 10:9, 10). The prophecy also indicated that they must testify again, and furthermore that when the seventh angel began to sound, the ark of his testament was seen in the temple of heaven (Rev. 11:19). These were the principal thoughts that coursed through Edson's mind as he stood there in rapt meditation. Meantime his companion—evidently Crosier—who had been accompanying him, likewise deep in study, suddenly noticed that Edson had stopped. He called back, asking why he had paused. And Edson responded, "The Lord was answering our morning prayer, giving light with regard to our disappointment" *(ibid.,* fol. 10r).

That concept threw a floodlight upon their disappointment. Christ had indeed fulfilled what the type had actually called for. It would be a while before He would complete this cleansing of the sanctuary, and not until then would He come forth as king.

Edson, Crosier, and their mutual friend Dr. Franklin B. Hahn agreed to meet as a study group to search the Bible intensively along these lines. Their study continued for some months. Their joint conclusions were published in articles by Crosier in the *Day-Dawn* of March 1845 (which appears as part of the Mar. 26, 1945, *Ontario Messenger),* a number of issues of the *Day-Star* in late 1845, and the *Day-Star Extra* of Feb. 7, 1846, published in Cincinnati, Ohio.

Crosier's presentation came into the hands of Joseph Bates, James White, and various other Eastern Adventists, and many readily accepted the position set forth. Thus was opened up correspondence between the New York trio and this New England group. Later a conference was appointed for Edson's place to which these Eastern brethren were invited. White was unable to be present, but Bates attended, and converted Edson (and Hahn) to the seventh-day Sabbath. Edson had already caught certain glimpses of the Sabbath through his study of the sanctuary, the ark, and the Ten Commandments and through reading certain lines from T. M. Preble, but he had not yet seen its importance. This was the first public instance of joining in united relationship the sanctuary and Sabbath positions, two distinctive tenets of faith characterizing the slowly forming body of Seventh-day Adventists. A little later, in 1848, one of a series of important conferences was held in Edson's barn.

Edson was not only a thoughtful Bible student and an earnest evangelistic helper but also a self-sacrificing contributor, putting his possessions into the upbuilding of the growing cause that he loved. He sold his farm in 1850 to help defray evangelistic expenses of the infant Sabbatarian movement. His next farm, in Port Byron, he likewise sold, two years later, and from the proceeds lent James White the money to purchase his printing press at Rochester.

Edson was ordained in 1855. Whether this ordination was understood at the time to be to a local or general ministry is not clear. He was awarded credentials in 1870. It was he who introduced young J. N. Loughborough to the Adventist ministry and traveled with him around the circuit of churches early in Loughborough's ministry.

EDUCANDÁRIO ESPÍRITO SANTENSE ADVENTISTA. *See* Espírito Santo Academy.

EDUCANDÁRIO NORDESTINO ADVENTISTA. *See* Northeast Brazil Academy.

EDUCATION, DEPARTMENT OF. In the General Conference, the branch that, with its director, associate directors, and staff, fosters and directs the worldwide Seventh-day Adventist educational system. The department counsels with the officers of the General Conference relative to educational matters and leads in formulating the major educational policies of the denomination; assists the General Conference Appointees Committee in selecting educational workers for overseas duty; makes recommendations to the General Conference Executive Committee relative to requests made by schools to offer programs on the tertiary level; issues promotional posters and leaflets; prepares annual analytical reports of the educational systems of SDA schools in various countries (known as the *World Report)* and assists school officials in evaluating the credits presented by foreign students through a publication known as *World Patterns of Seventh-day Adventist Education*; encourages teachers in maintaining high standards of instruction; develops standards for teacher education and issues; influences through its Board of Regents the standards and trends in secondary schools and tertiary schools, and accredits those that meet acceptable standards; conducts educational councils and workshops; maintains liaison with various governmental agencies that may affect the operation of SDA schools; publishes *The Journal of Adventist Education,* a professional periodical devoted to the interpretation of Christian education for the SDA teacher and school administrator; assists the schools and teachers in creating a strong spiritual atmosphere on the campuses of SDA schools in which children and youth may be nurtured in Christian growth; visits and inspects schools; assists in educational planning; and helps with educational meetings and councils in the various places around the world.

The director of the department is the chair of the Board of Regents.

Organizational units such as divisions, unions, and conferences each have an educational director.

History. The Department of Education goes back to 1887. Article II, section 1, of the constitution of that time states "the officers of this [General] Conference shall be a President, a Recording Secretary, a Corresponding Secretary, a Home Missionary Secretary, a Foreign Missionary Secretary, and an Educational Secretary, a Treasurer, and an Executive Committee of seven, of whom the President shall be one" (*Yearbook* [1888], p. 91).

Among the list of officers of the General Conference elected in November 1887 was "W. W. Prescott, Educational Secretary."

In the revised constitution adopted in 1889, the Bylaws, Article I, section 4, defined the work of the educational secretary as follows: "The Educational Secretary shall have the general supervision of the educational work of the denomination. It shall be his duty to visit the different educational institutions; and he may, with the concurrence of the Executive Committee, call teachers' institutes, when the circumstances seem to demand. It shall be his duty to suggest plans and devise means for the development of the educational work of the denomination. He shall also make a report to the General Conference at its sessions, of the progress of the work, and of the general standing of the educational institutions" *(ibid.* [1890], p. 116).

As the first educational secretary of the General Conference (1887-1897), W. W. Prescott, a graduate of Dartmouth College, gave vigorous leadership to the denomination's growing educational system, traveling back and forth across the continent promoting the cause of Christian education and counseling the boards and faculties of new schools. During part of his term as educational secretary he was also president of Battle Creek College (1885-1894) and the first president of two new colleges, Union College (1891-1893) and Walla Walla College (1892-1894). A principal in each of these three colleges cared for the daily administration of the school. He organized the first North American-wide teachers' institute for SDA educators, which met for six weeks in 1891 at Harbor Springs, Michigan, with more than 100 in attendance. Thirty had attended the first SDA teachers' institute held at Battle Creek, Michigan, June 21-26, 1888.

In 1897 the office of educational secretary was abolished by a change in the constitution, and the work of supervising the church's schools was assigned to the corresponding secretary of the General Conference. In the reorganization of 1901, by means of General Conference departments, a system was developed whereby the president of the General Conference and major officers could be assisted by full-time specialists in promoting and guiding various aspects of the church's life and activity.

Against this background the Department of Education was organized. The General Conference elected an educational committee of seven members who appointed their own chair and secretary. In the early years it was the secretary who reported to the General Conference session on the work of the department; the chair did not devote full time to the department, and sometimes did not even reside at the denomination's headquarters. However, when Frederick Griggs became chair (1904), that post became the major position, and he himself reported to the General Conference sessions. The provision for both a chair and secretary of the department continued until 1909, when Frederick Griggs, who had been chair since 1904, was appointed secretary of the department, and the position of chair was abolished. The new plan then adopted, under which the president of the General Conference is the head of all departments, has continued to the present. By 1914 an assistant secretary was added, and in following years associate and assistant secretaries were chosen to help carry the growing work of the department. The term *director* was substituted for *secretary* in 1974.

With minor variations resulting from financial problems or the capabilities and interests of the staff, since 1931 the organization of the department has been essentially as follows: the director of the department, who has general oversight of all departmental activities; and associate directors having specified responsibilities.

Under the reorganization of 1901 the duties of the Department of Education were outlined as follows:

"1. To act as a committee of reference in relation to all educational matters.

"2. To assist in an advisory way in supplying properly qualified teachers for the different schools.

"3. To suggest plans for promoting and properly representing the educational work at the camp meetings and other large gatherings.

"4. To act as a Book Committee in relation to the different educational books, providing for the securing and writing of books by suitable authors, and planning for the introduction of suitable books into our schools.

"5. To promote the development of church and conference schools in all fields" (tenth meeting of General Conference Committee, Battle Creek, Michigan, Apr. 25, 1901).

In 1903 the Department of Education called a nationwide conference of SDA educators at Union College, Lincoln, Nebraska, "to study all the phases of schoolwork which are general in character, and to devise and inaugurate plans that will be of universal application" (*General Conference Bulletin* [1903], p. 224). At that meeting "a general scheme for the organization of the school interests of our denomination was planned and adopted"; the Department of Education was asked to "advise and assist in the conduct of schools and to foster educational interests throughout the world" (*ibid.* [1909], p. 77). Plans were laid whereby each union and state conference would establish a department of education patterned after that of the General Conference. Each union conference was to establish a college or training school, and the local conferences were to assume responsibility for primary and intermediate schools.

The basic pattern then adopted for promoting and directing the SDA parochial (church school) system remains to the present. Within a few years after 1903, union and state conferences in North America set up departments of education, and a decade or two later, overseas Seventh-day Adventist conferences and missions had done likewise.

At various times since that first nationwide conference of SDA educators, the Department of Education of the General Conference has organized other conventions (some of them worldwide and some as joint councils with the Missionary Volunteer Department), which set the tone and direction of Christian education in the SDA denomination. The major conventions were held at Lincoln, Nebraska, 1903, 1904, and 1906; Berrien Springs, Michigan, 1910; St. Helena, California, 1915; Lincoln, Nebraska, 1917; Colorado Springs, Colorado, 1923; and Blue Ridge, North Carolina, 1937. The rapid increase in the number of schools and teachers has made it inadvisable to hold large conventions of that type in recent years.

The department assists the division departments of education in holding conventions and workshops in addition to holding at least one annual Institute for Christian Teaching in various world educational centers.

In 1993 the department functioned under the structure of a director, three associate directors, the editor of the *Journal of Adventist Education*, and three secretaries. The purposes and duties of the department are defined in the General Conference *Working Policy* and implemented through the following functioning committees and boards: General Conference SDA International Board of Education, Committee on Seventh-day Adventist Theological Education, and the Board of Regents.

Educational Secretaries of the General

Conference: W. W. Prescott, 1887-1897; L. A. Hoopes, 1897-1901.

Departmental Secretaries (called chairmen until 1909 and directors since 1974): J. H. Kellogg, 1901-1902; W. W. Prescott, 1902-1903; L. A. Hoopes, 1903-1904; Frederick Griggs, 1904-1910; H. R. Salisbury, 1910-1913; J. L. Shaw, 1913-1915; Frederick Griggs, 1915-1918; W. E. Howell, 1918-1930; C. W. Irwin, 1930-1933; W. E. Nelson, 1933-1936; H. A. Morrison, 1936-1946; E. E. Cossentine, 1946-1966; Charles B. Hirsch, 1966-1974; Walton J. Brown, 1974-1980; Charles R. Taylor, 1981-1985; George H. Akers, 1985-1990; Humberto M. Rasi, 1990- .

EDUCATION, GRADUATE, COMMISSION ON. Two commissions set up in 1961: the Commission on Graduate Education in the North American Division; the Commission on Graduate Education in Overseas Divisions. Primary functions of these two commissions were to guide and coordinate the graduate program in the denomination's higher schools, to pass upon requests for curriculum expansion, and to make recommendations to the General Conference Committee pertaining to graduate work. The North American section was merged into the North American Division Commission on Higher Education in 1967.

The Commission on Graduate Education in Overseas Divisions became what is known as the International Board of Education.

EDUCATION, SEVENTH-DAY ADVENTIST PHILOSOPHY OF. All philosophies of education tend ultimately to rest on the concept of the nature of human beings that is held by the founders of that particular educational system. It has been truly said that until what people are born *as* and what they are born *for* is known, a system of education that will meet people's needs and help them achieve the purpose for which they are destined, or of which they are capable, cannot be planned. Many education philosophies are based on the assumption that human beings are born good, and that the purpose of education is to develop the good latent in children. This premise naturally leads to a child-centered or subject-centered philosophy of education. Certain other educational systems are built on the premise that children are born to serve the state, and that therefore the educational program is designed to shape the product entirely for the ends of the government.

Seventh-day Adventists base their philosophy of education on the belief that the ultimate purpose of human beings is to love and serve God and others, and that all instruction and learning must be directed toward helping them achieve that end.

The Bible clearly teaches that since the Fall all people are born with a tendency toward evil; this tendency has strengthened with the passing centuries. Because SDAs hold this religious concept, they have no faith in the perfectibility of humanity through natural means of instruction. Fallen humans cannot achieve the purpose for which they were created without a God-centered education that teaches them to open their minds to the unseen but all-powerful Spirit of God, the only agency that can bring a rebirth of the original nature and an enduring reformation of life habits and mental outlook. Ellen G. White, who was the denomination's first and major writer on educational theory, states this viewpoint: "To bring man back into harmony with God, so to elevate and ennoble his moral nature that he may again reflect the image of the Creator, is the great purpose of all the education and discipline of life" (CT 49).

The same writer has set forth the basic educational philosophy of Seventh-day Adventists thus: "True education means more than the pursual of a certain course of study. It means more than a preparation for the life that now is. It has to do with the whole being, and with the whole period of existence possible to man. It is the harmonious development of the physical, the mental, and the spiritual powers. It prepares the student for the joy of service in this world and for the higher joy of wider service in the world to come" (Ed 13).

Accordingly, one of the major objectives of the SDA school system is to bring about the salvation of young people through acceptance of and faith in Jesus Christ as their personal Saviour, and following that, to help them achieve growth in character so that they will become God-fearing, honest, stable, and productive members of society. The curricula in SDA schools are designed to instruct the students in a biblical view of the origin of life, of humanity's duty, and of humanity's destiny; and to safeguard them from errors arising from humanistic and materialistic worldviews.

In order that young people may attend school in an atmosphere conducive to spiritual development, contemplation, and study undisturbed by the distractions of cities, efforts have been made to locate SDA schools, and particularly the boarding schools, in rural areas in which the students may have numerous opportunities for the study of nature. It is hoped that they will recognize early that the physical world, with its orderly laws and processes, is the handiwork of the divine Creator and Sustainer of all life. Wherever possible, agricultural enterprises are carried on in connection with SDA schools, and students are encouraged to work in these. The philosophy behind this is the value in learning the secrets of growing things, and becoming aware of the fact that the earth is the source from which comes all food as well as the storehouse of all raw materials from which people fashion their implements and machines, build their homes and factories, and obtain sources of power.

In order to allow adequate physical development before children undertake the duties of the schoolroom, which tax the eyes and the emotions, the church urges parents to provide a good home environment for growing children and not to send them to school until they reach a minimum age of 7 years.

Seventh-day Adventists hold that it is a right of all children of SDA parents to receive a Christian education, and that although a major share of the responsibility for providing it rests upon the parents, the local church too bears a responsibility to see that all children of the church are provided as much education in SDA schools as a young person desires or as can benefit him or her.

Generally speaking, SDA elementary schools *(see* Church School) are operated by the local churches in cooperation with the local conferences, the secondary schools by the local (state) conferences, the colleges by the union conferences, and graduate schools by the General Conference. *See* Schools, Seventh-day Adventist.

SDAs recognize the right of the government to require that children be educated to an extent that will enable them to fulfill their duties as citizens. However, since God has given children to parents, and not to the state, the parents have the right to determine where and how their children are to be educated. SDAs appreciate and financially support the public schools of the countries in which they reside. They believe these schools are doing an excellent work, but hold that religious instruction should not be a part of the public school curriculum *(see* Church and State). Hence, even though the worldwide system of SDA schools is costly, SDAs finance it gladly, believing that the results justify whatever the cost may be. SDA parents are urged to send their children to denominational schools wherever they can be operated, but no religious sanctions are used to force them to do so.

In order to implement this overall philosophy, SDAs endeavor to operate their schools in such a way that the curriculum, the extracurricular activities, and every school experience contribute to reaching the following objectives:

1. To maintain in each school a spiritual atmosphere in which prayer, worship, and doing the will of God will be, in the eyes of the majority of the students, the ideal and accepted pattern of living.

2. To make the Bible and the biblical worldview the center of all study and teaching.

3. To enable all students to achieve a Christian philosophy of life and to have opportunities to acquire the attitudes, knowledge, and skills necessary to express their philosophy in Christian character.

4. To promote a high level of scholarship, with emphasis on independent thinking and the highest achievement possible for each individual, and with reference to its practical application to the needs of the world.

5. To give students the opportunity to learn habits of healthful living, so that their physical development may be enhanced not so much by a program of games and competitive sports as by employment in school-related industries or agricultural enterprises in which they may learn a useful trade or skill, gain a sense of achievement, find in physical activity release from the tensions resulting from a heavy study program, learn a respect for the dignity and worth of physical labor, obtain a balanced view that will prevent the development of intellectual snobbery, and, at the same time, continue the educational process by developing habits of industry, promptness, reliability, accuracy, thoroughness, and self-reliance.

6. To promote social, cultural, and emotional growth, resulting in stable, balanced citizens who are a credit to their community, who are fitted to bear life's responsibilities, and who have developed insights and outlooks that make life worth living.

7. To give instruction in homemaking and in skills necessary to make and maintain happy marriages.

8. To encourage the students to make a personal commitment of their capacities and strength to the service of God, humanity, and their church, choosing professions that enable

them to serve others and to participate in the promulgation of the Christian faith.

EDUCATIONAL INSTITUTIONS. *See* Schools, SDA.

EDWARDS, EVA ELIZABETH (1884-1981). Musician, educator, dean. She was born in Auckland, New Zealand, of Seventh-day Adventist parents won to the faith by A. G. Daniells. Her father died when Eva was a girl, and her mother then moved to Avondale, Australia. Eva, as a teenager, worked in the home of Pastor J. E. Fulton, pioneer missionary to Fiji. In the Fulton home she caught a vision for mission service and went with them when they returned to serve in Fiji. A keen musician, Eva translated many hymns into Fijian. She was one of the first teachers at Buresala Training College (later Fulton College) in Fiji. She also taught at the Avondale church school and was secretary to the Tongan Mission. For many years she served in the Sabbath school departments of conferences in both Australia and New Zealand, finally becoming Sabbath school secretary (director) for the Australasian Division. Eva also served as dean of women at Western Australia Missionary College and Longburn Adventist College, New Zealand.

EDWARDS, JOSEPHINE CUNNINGTON (1904-1993). Author, educator, missionary, storyteller. Born in Muncie, Indiana, she received her B.A. degree from Andrews University, her M.A. from Vanderbilt University, and her Doctor of Humane Letters from Andrews. She married Lowell A. Edwards in 1923, and they served as missionaries to Africa, the source of many of her stories. Besides her two sons, she adopted three African children, including Alice Princess Siwundhla, for whom Josephine arranged a surprise appearance on the *This Is Your Life* nationwide television program. She was the author of more than 30 books and was known and loved internationally for her storytelling. A scholarship fund in journalism, education, and communication was established in her memory.

EDWARDS, OTIS BERNARD (1901-1971). Educator. A native of Florida, he accepted the Seventh-day Adventist doctrine at an early age and enrolled in Oakwood College to better prepare himself for the Lord's service.

His teaching career began in Montgomery, Alabama, in 1924, and two years later he was called to Oakwood, where he served in various positions, including director of music, dean of men, professor of history, dean of the college, and chair of the Department of Social Sciences.

In 1926 he married Roberta Adele Clairborne. He is the composer of the Oakwood College song, "To Thee, Our Dear Oakwood."

At the time of his retirement in 1968 he had served Oakwood College for 42 years. His death, on Oct. 23, was the result of a car accident.

EDWARDS, WILLIAM HERBERT (1854-1938). Secretary, treasurer. After his baptism in 1877 he joined the staff of the Review and Herald Publishing Association and served first as manager of the Book Department (1878-1888), and then as secretary and treasurer (1888-1891). Between 1891 and 1901 he served variously as treasurer of the General Conference, secretary and treasurer of the General Conference Association, and treasurer of the Foreign Mission Board. He was also for a time treasurer of the Michigan Conference. From 1901 to 1912 he was secretary-treasurer of the Lake Union, and then served as secretary-treasurer and auditor of the Northern Union (1912-1918). After 1918 he was in charge of the printshop at the General Conference.

EFFORT. In Seventh-day Adventist evangelistic usage, a word that crept into use as a technical term for a public evangelistic campaign. This sense may have been derived from, or at least developed out of, the frequent appearance of the word in Ellen White's urgent appeals, beginning in the 1880s, to evangelize the cities. Following are examples: "In efforts made in large cities one half of the effort is lost because they close up the work too soon" (Ev 328). "How much better if some of the same speakers who arouse the interest of the people during the largest attendance at the meeting would remain to follow up the work begun, by a thoroughly organized protracted effort" *(ibid.* 83). In her usage "making public effort" *(ibid.* 445; cf. 429) was equivalent to "holding public meetings." It was perhaps from this equivalence that the expression "hold efforts," arose among ministers and laity. However, in her terminology an effort was made, put forth, entered upon, or engaged in *(ibid.* 42, 325, 399, 457), not held. Today the rather incomprehensible phrase has generally been replaced; "campaign" or "program" supplants "effort" as a term for a series of meetings.

EGYPT ACADEMY. *See* Nile Union Academy.

EGYPT, ARAB REPUBLIC OF. A republic situated in Africa including the eastern Sahara, the Nile Valley, the isthmus of Suez, and the Sinai Peninsula. It has an area of 386,650 square miles (1 million square kilometers). Of the country's 59.3 million people (1994), most live in the Nile Valley.

The racial groups that through many centuries entered Egypt have been assimilated to produce an Arabic-speaking indigenous Egyptian race, basically Mediterranean-type, with Arab and Negroid elements. Many Armenian and Greek colonies are found in the cities and large towns. More than 90 percent of Egyptians are Muslims. The largest religious minority is the 8 million-strong Monophysite Christian community known as the Coptic Orthodox Church, dating from before the Muslim period. The Roman Catholic Church began missionary work in Egypt around the turn of the thirteenth century. It was not until the nineteenth century that Protestants took an active interest in Egypt. In 1993 there were about 750,000 Protestants in Egypt in no less than 17 denominations. The oldest university in the world is in Egypt, the Al-Azhar in Cairo.

Ancient Egypt, whose pyramids were already old in the days of Abraham, Joseph, and Moses, saw the last of its pharaohs in the closing period of the Old Testament, yet it still exists as a nation, outliving all the empires that successively ruled it—Persian, Macedonian, Roman, Byzantine, Arab, and Turkish.

In Alexandria, as a center of Hellenistic culture, were blended Greek and Eastern thought. There Jewish scholars produced the Septuagint—the Greek translation of the Old Testament that was used by the apostles. Alexandrian astronomers gave to Rome—and thence to us—the ancient Egyptian 365-day year; the early Alexandrian Church Fathers blended Greek philosophy with Christianity and developed their own brand of theology; and Egypt gave monasticism to the church.

In the seventh century the Egyptian Christians, oppressed by the Byzantines as heretics, welcomed the invading Arabs as liberators. Egypt accepted Islam and the Arabic language and became a stronghold of Muslim orthodoxy. However, a Christian minority held out; their present descendants in the Coptic Orthodox Church still use in their liturgy the old Coptic dialects, derived from the ancient Egyptian language. (The terms *Copt* and *Coptic,* now ordinarily applied specifically to indigenous Egyptian Christians, originally meant merely "Egyptian.")

Early in the nineteenth century the country began to move toward modernization. In 1882, after a massacre of foreigners in Alexandria, Britain stepped in, though Egypt remained a part of the Turkish Empire. World War I made Egypt a British protectorate; in 1922 it became a kingdom, under Fuad I; in 1953, a republic.

Seventh-day Adventist Statistics. The territory of the Arab Republic of Egypt constitutes the Egypt Field, part of the Middle East Union. Statistics (1993): churches and companies, 17; members, 1,300; ordained ministers, 4; licensed ministers, 6; teachers, 65. Egypt Field headquarters are in Heliopolis, Cairo, Egypt.

Institutions. Adventist Health Education Foundation (Egypt Food Factory); Nile Union Academy.

Development of Seventh-day Adventist Work. Egypt was the first of the Middle Eastern countries to be entered by the SDAs. Beginning sometime in 1877, the Italian SDAs in Naples sent the French paper *Signes des Temps* to their acquaintances among the Italians in Alexandria and corresponded with them about the SDA doctrines. In the spring of 1878 Romualdo Bartola, an Italian commercial traveler and self-supporting missionary, visited Alexandria on business and formed a group there, baptizing seven persons. In 1879 Dr. Herbert Panmure Ribton, a graduate of Dublin University, who was one of the first to be baptized in Italy and who pioneered the work in southern Italy, moved to Alexandria, then the largest commercial port on the Mediterranean, and began missionary work. He opened a school and had some tracts translated into Arabic. However, two years later, on June 11, 1882, he and two Italian converts, Giuseppe Rupp and one Aligretti, were killed in Alexandria during a riot against foreigners there. As a result, the group of members was scattered.

About 15 years afterward several Armenian SDA families from Turkey settled in Cairo and Alexandria and spread the SDA doctrines there. About the same time, J. Leuzinger, from Italy, went to Port Said to do ship missionary work. In 1899 Louis F. Passebois, and his wife and Ida Schlegel, trained nurses, were sent from Europe. They opened a health home and restaurant in Cairo. Their work resulted in several converts, and in 1901 L. R. Conradi of the European Division organized the first

Seventh-day Adventist church in Egypt

In 1902 the Oriental Union Mission, with headquarters in Cairo, was formed and placed under the direction of W. H. Wakeham, a Canadian-born missionary from the United States. Sometime before 1906 the publishing work was begun with the printing of a small book in Arabic on the prophecies of Daniel.

Between 1906 and 1908 the first national SDA minister in Egypt, Awaida Abd es-Shahid, was ordained. But apostasy among the Armenian members developed about that time and depleted the membership so that it was necessary to build up the work again. The work in Egypt was put under the Egyptian-Syrian Mission of the newly formed Levant Union Mission. George Keough, of Ireland, came in 1908 to take charge of the work, and set out to master the Arabic language.

Progress was slow. In 1912 there were only 18 members, with two ordained ministers, one Bible instructor, four colporteurs (at Cairo), and two nurses. But in the same year a group of upper Egyptian Christians, led by former Presbyterian Yacoub Beshai Yacoub, from the village of Beni Adi, near Assiut, learned about Keough, a White man who kept the Sabbath. They had been keeping the seventh-day Sabbath for about six years. When they invited him to visit, Keough found a ready-made community of Sabbath observers. He soon baptized 24 people, of whom 17 were men, and, in 1913, organized them into the first indigenous Seventh-day Adventist church in the country.

Shortly before World War I the country was divided into two missions: Lower Egypt, with headquarters in Cairo, led by W. K. Ising; and Upper Egypt, with headquarters in Beni Adi, with George Keough in charge. There were about 40 SDAs in Egypt, coming from the Greek, Armenian, and Coptic communities. During the war Ising, a German national, was interned, but Keough continued the work organizing churches in Tataliah and Deirut. When the Levant Union was dissolved in 1923, and the Egypto-Syrian Mission of the European Division was organized, with Keough in charge, there were 70 members in Egypt.

In 1923 plans were laid for the development of work among the Arabs and for opening a publishing work at Matariah, near Cairo. C. H. Rieckman was called to head the bookwork. An edition of 7,500 copies of *The Sure Word of Prophecy* was printed in Arabic, as well as smaller books. Five colporteurs worked in the field. The main SDA work was carried on at that time in Cairo, Beni Adi, Tataliah, and Deirut. There were members also in Masra, Sohag, and Luxor.

In 1927 the Arabic Union Training School was opened in Matariah, with V. E. Toppenberg as director and Ibrahim Khalil as a teacher, but continued only a few years. *(See* Nile Union Academy.)

Egypt was included in the territory of the Arabic Union Mission, which was organized in November 1927 as part of the European Division (from 1928, of the Central European Division). In the 1930s work was resumed in Alexandria by M. C. Grin. Twelve persons were baptized.

When the events leading up to World War II separated the work in Egypt from the Central European Division headquarters, American missionaries were sent in by the General Conference, and E. L. Branson became director of the Egyptian Mission. The northern Sudan was included in the Egyptian Mission, an arrangement that continued until 1950.

At the time of the organization of the Middle East Division in 1950, the Egypt Mission became part of the Nile Union Mission (to which was assigned the territory of Egypt, Libya, northern Sudan, that part of Arabia bordering on the Red Sea, and Aden). In 1955 the Egypt Mission was divided: the Lower (Northern) Egypt Mission came under the direction of Hilal Dose and the Upper Egypt Mission was directed by C. V. Brauer. The area was further divided in January 1957, when Hilal Dose was placed in charge of the Central Egypt Section, Hilmy Berbawy as president of the Upper Egypt Section, and W. R. Lesher in charge of the Delta Section. These divisions proved unwieldy, and by December 1958 the work was reunited in one Egypt Section. This was administered by the officers of the Nile Union. At the Nile Union biennial council of 1960 it was decided to Egyptianize the church organization. A new constitution was adopted that provided for a national church, called the Coptic Adventist Denomination in Egypt. Hilal Dose became the first national president.

In 1962 the Nile Union was discontinued, leaving the Middle East Division to deal directly with the Egyptian church.

In the reorganization of 1970 the administration of Egypt was placed under the Egypt Field, a part of the Middle East Union, which was, in turn, part of the Afro-Mideast Division.

In 1941 there were two schools, one at

Beni Adi and another at Tataliah. In a decade and a half the educational work grew to 12 schools. In 1946 the Egypt Training School (later the Nile Union Academy, now called in English the Adventist Theological Institute of Egypt and the Nile Union Academy, and in Arabic a name translated literally the "Coptic Adventist Theological Seminary") was established at Fayoum (Seila) and in 1954 moved to Gabal el-Asfar. When in the mid-1950s government curriculum requirements caused the church to close most of its schools, this school, along with the Heliopolis Adventist School, remained open. The Heliopolis elementary school was moved to property at nearby Zeitoun. In 1993 only the Nile Union Academy was still in operation.

Welfare work of various types has been developed in recent years. In 1947 an orphanage, named the Matariah Mercy Home, was established in Matariah, with Erna Kruger as matron. During 1963 the orphanage was rebuilt and its capacity doubled. Welfare centers have been established by the major churches. Special government awards were given in 1963 to the Seventh-day Adventist Welfare Societies in Fayoum and Assiut for outstanding service.

A limited medical work has been done in recent years. During the 1940s Erna Kruger did some medical missionary work in Cairo; Dr. Maher Bishai operated a small clinic in Heliopolis in 1953; and a small clinic was operated at Maghagha for a few months in 1956 by Dr. Youssiff Bishai.

About the end of 1959 an evangelistic center was opened in Cairo.

Beginning in 1971 steps were taken to establish a health food factory in Cairo. Land was purchased and construction began in 1974. The Adventist Health Education Foundation (Egypt Food Factory) was operating in 1993.

Work in Egypt has been carried on through the conducting of junior camps, Vacation Bible Schools, evangelistic meetings, and temperance programs.

EGYPT FIELD. *See* Middle East Union Mission; Egypt, Arab Republic of.

EGYPT FOOD FACTORY. *See* Adventist Health Education Foundation.

EGYPT TRAINING SCHOOL. *See* Egypt, Arab Republic of.

EGYPTO-SYRIAN MISSION. *See* Egypt, Arab Republic of.

EHLERS, WALDEMAR (1879-1929). One of the pioneer Seventh-day Adventist workers in Brazil. Born and educated in Germany, he began his service in the office of the Hamburg Publishing House in 1896, then in 1898 went to Brazil as a teacher, and in 1901 entered evangelistic work. He was the first president of the Santa Catarina and Paraná Conference (1906-1909) and later was president of the Rio Grande do Sul Conference (1909-1914). Failing health forced his return to Germany, where he taught at Friedensau for two years, then preached and was president of three different conferences until 1923, when he could no longer continue in active service and retired to Brazil.

1844 MOVEMENT. *See* Millerite Movement.

EIRE. *See* Ireland.

EKAMAI ADVENTIST SCHOOL. *See* Adventist Ekamai School.

EKDOTIKOS OIKOS PHAROS TIS ELLADOS. *See* Light House Publishing Company.

EKEBYHOLMSSKOLAN. *See* Swedish Junior College and Seminary.

ELDER (lay). *See* Church Elder.

ELDER (ordained minister). A title used by Seventh-day Adventists to designate an ordained minister, although "pastor" is more often used. However, "pastor" is also applied to licensed ministers. Believing that "reverend" belongs properly only to God (Ps. 111:9), SDAs do not address their ministers by this title. "Elder" as used in the Bible did not necessarily mean an old person, but one who has attained maturity and experience. In the OT the title was used for those of certain official rank and position, such as heads of families, households, or tribes (Gen. 50:7; Ex. 3:16; 2 Sam. 5:3). The NT applies *presbuteros* ("elder") also to church leaders *(see* Church Elder).

SDAs of the late 1840s and early 1850s did not use "elder" in referring to their own ordained ministers, preferring to call them "brother." They did, however, refer to non-SDA ministers by "elder." With the rise of church organization and the need for a fully qualified ministry, "elder," referring to an ordained minister, came into general use among Seventh-day Adventists in North America. In recent years "elder" has declined in popularity somewhat, but continues as an alternative for "pastor."

ELDRIDGE, CLEMENT (fl. 1885-1895). Publishing and religious liberty leader. His name first appears in the denominational *Yearbook* in 1887, when he was auditor at the Central Publishing Association (Review and Herald) in Battle Creek. In December 1888 he became a member of the first press committee appointed to bring the issue of religious liberty before the public. In 1889 he apparently was chair of the second committee that prepared the way for the founding of the National Religious Liberty Association, of which he became the first president. In that same year he was a member of the building committee for the schooner *Pitcairn*. In 1889 his name appeared also as the general manager of the Central Publishing Association, a position he held until 1892 or 1893, when he joined a private publishing firm in Chicago. In 1890 his name appeared as the first general canvassing agent for the International Tract and Missionary Society, thus making him a forerunner of the General Conference Publishing Department directors.

ELDRIDGE, RETHA HAZEL (1910-1990). Teacher, writer, missionary, linguist. After growing up in New York City, she graduated from Atlantic Union College in 1934. She and her minister husband, Paul H. Eldridge, accepted a call in 1937 to teach in Japan. Surviving World War II included internment in a Japanese prison camp and a dramatic rescue by American paratroops which provided material for her first book, *Bombs and Blessings*, published in 1946. Back in Japan again after the war, she began serving as director of the Voice of Prophecy Bible Correspondence School, and became the only Seventh-day Adventist woman to develop proficiency in reading Japanese. The publishing house asked her to make prepublishing comparison of translated materials to verify accuracy and ensure preservation of nuance. She read the entire handwritten Japanese manuscript for *The Desire of Ages*, a massive undertaking.

Her second book, *From the Rising of the Sun*, telling the story of the Voice of Prophecy in Japan, was published in 1964. Retiring in 1975 after serving 38 years in the Far Eastern Division, she produced her final literary work at the request of Home Study International—a course of study in prophetic guidance, published about 1978. Having completed a lifetime of service that included homemaking, teaching, accounting, writing, management roles, and loyal support of her husband, she died in 1990, shortly after her eightieth birthday.

ELECTION (of church officers). *See* Church (local organization), II, 2.

ELECTION (theological). *See* Arminianism; Foreknowledge; Free Will; Predestination.

ELK POINT ACADEMY. *See* Plainview Academy.

EL LLANO ADVENTIST VOCATIONAL INSTITUTE (Instituto Vocacional Adventista del Llano). A coeducational boarding institute located in the department of Meta, Colombia. It was established in 1976. In 1993 there was an enrollment of 140 and a faculty of 14.

Principals: Luis Cordenas, 1992; Heraldo Cordenas, 1993- .

ELLEN G. WHITE ESTATE, INCORPORATED. An organization created by the last will and testament of Ellen G. White to act as her agent in the custody of her writings, handling her properties, "conducting the business thereof," "securing the printing of new translations," and the "printing of compilations from my manuscripts." Her will, dated Feb. 9, 1912 (printed in its entirety as Appendix Q in F. D. Nichol's *Ellen G. White and Her Critics),* named five church leaders to serve as a board of trustees: Arthur G. Daniells, president of the General Conference; William C. White, her son; Clarence C. Crisler, a secretary; Charles H. Jones, manager of the Pacific Press; and Francis M. Wilcox, editor of the *Review and Herald.* Four of the five were members of the Executive Committee of the General Conference.

Appointment of the trustees was for life, Ellen White providing that "if a vacancy shall occur for any reason among said trustees, or their successors, a majority of the surviving or remaining trustees are hereby empowered and directed to fill such vacancy by the appointment of some other fit person"; or if this provision were to fail, the General Conference Executive Committee should appoint someone to fill such a vacancy. The will dedicated the major portion of the existing and potential royalty incomes from her books to the work of the trustees. (For additional information, see Appendix B, "The Settlement of Ellen G. White's Estate," in volume 6 of A. L. White's biography of Ellen White, *Ellen G. White: The Later Elmshaven Years.)*

At the death of Ellen White, July 16, 1915, this self-perpetuating board began to function. It soon sold Ellen White's real estate, consisting mainly of Elmshaven, her home property near St. Helena, California, then began the continued care of her literary properties. Under the terms of the will, such responsibilities fell into three areas: (1) possession of the copyrights to her writings and the care and promotion of her books in the English language; (2) preparation of manuscripts for, and the promotion of the translation and publication of her writings in other languages; and (3) custody of the files of manuscripts and other files, and the selection of matter from the E. G. White manuscript files for publication. The board now carries a fourth responsibility, which has developed naturally through the years—acquainting Seventh-day Adventists and others with Mrs. White and her work.

Organization. *The Original Board.* When the board was organized in 1915, A. G. Daniells served as president. The secretaryship, after being held for a short time by C. C. Crisler, passed to W. C. White, the only member of the board devoting full time to the work of the trustees. He filled this office until his death in 1937. From 1915 to 1937 the work was carried on at Elmshaven in a rented office building with a vault that was used to house the E. G. White materials.

During the 19 years they worked together, the original members, in addition to routine tasks, (1) published 10 posthumous compilations (for an annotated bibliography of the E. G. White books, *see* White, Ellen G., Writings of, and Appendix D in the *Comprehensive Index to the Writings of Ellen G. White);* (2) produced an 865-page *Comprehensive Index to the Writings of Ellen G. White,* published in 1926; (3) carried forward the thorough indexing of the Ellen G. White manuscript files; and (4) in counsel with the leading officers of the General Conference in 1933 and 1934, laid the foundation for continuing the trusteeship in perpetuity. The steps taken to ensure the perpetuation of the trusteeship were: *(a)* in 1933 the trustees, as the constituency, formed a corporation under the laws of the state of California "to carry out and perform the provisions of the charitable trust created by the last will and testament of Ellen G. White deceased"; *(b)* the General Conference agreed to provide adequate financial support for the work of the trustees in the form of an annual budget; the trustees, in turn, assigned to the General Conference all royalty incomes produced by the Ellen G. White books; *(c)* it was agreed to move the property and work of the trustees at some appropriate future time to Washington, D.C., thus placing it close to the world headquarters of the church.

Period of Transition. When three of the original trustees died—one in 1935 and two in 1936—the vacancies were filled in harmony with the provisions of the will and the bylaws of the 1933 corporation. The full-time secretary, W. C. White, died on Sept. 1, 1937. He was replaced by his son, Arthur L. White, who for nine years had served as his secretary and for four years as assistant secretary of the White Estate. The work of the White Estate was moved to the General Conference, Washington, D.C., in January 1938.

Present Organization. With the demands upon them increasing steadily with the growth of the church and numerous constituencies to be represented, in 1950 the trustees increased the board's membership from five to seven, and in 1958 amended the bylaws of the corporation to provide for a constituency and board of nine, seven to be life members and two to be elected for a term corresponding to that of General Conference elected personnel (originally four years, but now five). In 1970 the board was increased to 11; in 1980, to 13; and, in 1985, to 15. The number of life members has remained at seven. At quinquennial meetings the board also elects the secretary and associate secretaries, as well as officers of the corporation, as provided for in the bylaws.

Relationship to General Conference. Through the years a close working relationship has been obtained between the White trustees and the General Conference. Most of the trustees are members of the General Conference Executive Committee. Various matters, such as promoting the overseas publication of the Ellen G. White material, appropriation of funds to assist in the foreign language publication of Ellen G. White books, and overall planning of Spirit of Prophecy promotion, including preparation of materials for the annual Spirit of Prophecy Sabbath, although intimately related to the work of the White trustees, are beyond the sphere of their direct responsibility. These are handled by the General Conference Committee through a subcommittee known as the Spirit of Prophecy Committee. This committee includes several of the White trustees. The duties of this subcommittee and the working relationship between the General Conference Committee and the White Estate are currently set forth in a joint agreement adopted by the General Conference Committee and the White Estate trustees on Oct. 10, 1957. There is an interlocking and at times overlapping of responsibilities; nevertheless, a smooth and efficient working relationship between the two organizations is maintained.

The Work of the White Estate. *Routine Work.* The paid staff members (1) safeguard and maintain the records in the custody of the trustees, and the indexes thereto, in such a manner as to serve the church; (2) handle the copyrights to the Ellen G. White works; (3) conduct such research in these works and the related historical materials as may be called for; (4) respond to questions that may be directed to the White Estate in personal interviews and in a worldwide correspondence; (5) assemble, when authorized by the trustees, materials for compilations from Ellen G. White's writings; (6) foster, in conjunction with the Spirit of Prophecy Committee, the ever-widening publication of these writings in various languages and at times make selections or abridgments as called for and authorized; (7) fill assignments in church, institutional, and field visitation as the needs and best interests of the advancing work of the church require; (8) conduct tours of historical sites of denominational interest, especially in the New England states; and (9) prepare articles, correspondence lessons, and text materials.

Productions of special value to the church include the four-volume *Comprehensive Index to the Writings of Ellen G. White* (1962 1992); the six-volume facsimile reprints of the Ellen G. White *Present Truth* and *Review and Herald* articles; the four-volume Ellen G. White *Signs of the Times* articles; the Ellen G. White *Youth's Instructor* articles; the Periodical Resource Collection volumes; the six-volume biography of Ellen G. White, by A. L. White; and *The Published Writings of Ellen G. White on Compact Disc* (CD-ROM), a tool of inestimable value to users of computers.

Branch Offices and Research Centers. The White Estate maintains two branch office research centers—one at Andrews University, Berrien Springs, Michigan, and the other at Loma Linda University, Loma Linda, California. These offices contain duplicates of the Ellen White documents and other historical materials housed in the main office at General Conference headquarters. Beginning in 1974, the White Estate also has set up Ellen G. White-SDA Research Centers on the campuses of 11 Seventh-day Adventist colleges and universities outside North America, in the countries of Argentina, Australia, Brazil, England, India, Korea, Mexico, Nigeria, Philippines, Russia, and South Africa.

Use of E. G. White Manuscript Materials. During the later years of her life, Ellen White often drew upon her unique 50,000-page manuscript file in the preparation of published works. The White trustees have continued to draw upon this for the compilations made since her death. These manuscripts constitute an invaluable basic file of historical records and of counsel to the church. The copyright of these manuscripts resides solely with the White trustees.

While all of Ellen White's writings are available for research, the unpublished letters, manuscripts, and other materials in the Ellen G. White files do not constitute a public archive. The sacred nature of the files generally and the confidential nature of many of the communications in the files require that they be cared for and used responsibly. Even manuscripts whose primary value is historical in nature must not be used in a solely secular manner. "Spiritual things are spiritually discerned" *(The Desire of Ages*, p. 55; see also 1 Cor. 2:14). Because of this, during the first few decades following Ellen White's death, careful policies governing the use and release of unpublished materials were set up, ultimately resulting in the publication of 21 volumes known as *Manuscript Releases*. In recent years the earlier restrictive policies have been adapted to accommodate the needs of increased research.

Officers of the Board. The two chief officers of the board are the chair and the secretary. The chair is also president of the corporation. The secretary serves not only as secretary of the board but as executive secretary of the organization, being responsible for the day-to-day operations of the office and staff. Beginning in 1915, when the terms of Ellen White's will went into effect, the White Estate has had 10 chairs and four secretaries.

Chairs: A. G. Daniells, 1915-1935; J. E. Fulton, 1935-1936; J. L. Shaw, 1936-1937; F. M. Wilcox, 1938-1944; M. E. Kern, 1944-1951; D. E. Rebok, 1952; A. V. Olson, 1952-1963; F. D. Nichol, 1963-1966; W. P. Bradley, 1966-1980; Kenneth H. Wood, 1980- .

Secretaries: William C. White, 1915-1937; Arthur L. White, 1937-1978; Robert W. Olson, 1978-1990; Paul A. Gordon, 1990- .

ELLEN G. WHITE PUBLICATIONS. An unofficial title of the Ellen G. White Estate, Incorporated.

ELLINGWORTH, GEORGE ALBERT (1881-1942). English missionary to Africa. Born in Bedfordshire, England, he went to South Africa in 1902. After becoming a Seventh-day Adventist in 1904, he canvassed for a few months, then entered Claremont Union (now Helderberg) College. When an urgent need arose at Solusi Mission, he answered the call, returning to the college nine months later. About 1908 he accepted his first regular appointment, going to the Maranatha Mission in the Kaffirland field.

Called in 1909 to Nyasaland (Malawi), he worked there for 18 years, for many years as a teacher at Malamulo, at first with Joel C. Rogers, then from 1912 to 1920 with Christopher Robinson. While in Nyasaland he was joined by Mary Long, who became his wife. Many teachers trained in Ellingworth's classes went out to build up mission schools established throughout southern Nyasaland.

During World War I Ellingworth served for two years in the Medical Department of the British Army in Nyasaland. It was a time of real hardship for the Ellingworth family. A little daughter, Jessie, died of malaria. In 1920 Ellingworth succeeded Christopher Robinson in charge of the Nyasaland field, which in 1925 was separated from the Zambesi Union and organized as the Southeast African Union Mission, with headquarters at Malamulo, with Ellingworth as the first president.

In 1928 Ellingworth accepted a call to head the Tanganyika Field (Tanzania) and in 1937 became president of the Congo Union, with headquarters at Gitwe. In 1939, when failing health made it necessary for him to move to a lower elevation, he took charge of the South Congo Field, and in 1941 he moved to Songa Mission. The following year, while on a tour of the schools around Elisabethville, he died suddenly in April from a heart attack. He was buried in the Protestant cemetery of that city, the service being conducted by Bishop John M. Springer, of the Methodist Episcopal Church, according to the outline of the burial service as found in the SDA *Manual for Ministers,* which the bishop found in Ellingworth's briefcase.

ELLIOTT, HENRY THOMAS (1888-1967). Educator, departmental and General Conference secretary. Elliott was born in Wisconsin and received his education at Emmanuel Missionary College, graduating in 1912. He served as preceptor and teacher at Bethel Academy for a time and was principal of the school from 1914 to 1920. He was ordained to the ministry in 1920 and, after two years as MV secretary of the Lake Union, he became an associate secretary of the General Conference MV Department. In 1930 he was elected general secretary of the department, and three years later he became associate secretary of the General Conference, a position he held for 25 years.

ELLIOTT, WALTER PAUL (1892-1967). Administrator, departmental secretary, board chair. He was born in Illinois and received his education at Bethel Academy and Emmanuel Missionary College. He was married in 1911 to Alice Garton, and six years later began denominational service in Michigan. Beginning in 1922, he was in charge of the Haitian Mission for five years. Following this he served as assistant to the president of the Potomac Conference, and from 1929 to 1933 was president of that conference. From 1933 to 1946 he was connected with the Review and Herald Publishing Association, serving as general manager of that institution for 10 years. He then became publishing secretary of the General Conference. In 1950 he was elected chair of the board of trustees of the College of Medical Evangelists, where he served for nine years.

During this time the university established the School of Dentistry and Graduate School, and constructed the present White Memorial Medical Center in Los Angeles. During this period he also served as chair of the board of the Pacific Press Publishing Association. He retired in 1959.

ELMSHAVEN. *See* White, Ellen G.

ELMSHAVEN HOMES FOR THE AGED. *See* Seventh-day Adventist Retirement Village.

EL SALVADOR. The smallest but most densely populated of the Central American republics, bounded on the northeast and east by Honduras, on the east by the Gulf of Fonseca and Nicaragua, on the south by the Pacific Ocean, and on the northwest by Guatemala. It is about 160 miles (260 kilometers) long and 60 miles (100 kilometers) wide and covers 8,236 square miles (21,300 square kilometers). It is a land of lakes and volcanoes, of mountain ranges and fertile valleys. Its climate is tropical but not unbearably hot. It has been an independent republic since 1839.

The population of El Salvador (1994) is 5.7 million. The language is Spanish and the dominant religion is Roman Catholic, though the constitution provides religious liberty for all.

Seventh-day Adventist Statistics. The territory of El Salvador constitutes the El Salvador Conference, part of the Central American Union Mission, which in turn is part of the Inter-American Division. Statistics (1992) for *El Salvador:* churches, 194; members, 54,666; church or elementary schools, 11; ordained ministers, 16. The El Salvador Conference headquarters are strategically located in the heart of a new center of government buildings, corner of 19 Calle Poniente and 3rd Avenida Norte, Urbanización Guadalupe, San Salvador, El Salvador.

Institutions. Adventist Training School of El Salvador; Model Central Secondary School.

Development of Seventh-day Adventist Work. *Beginnings.* The first SDA missionaries in El Salvador were John L. Brown and his wife, who arrived there in the fall of 1915. Through the sale of publications, they introduced SDA teachings to the people, so that by the end of the year there were several Sabbathkeepers and many friends. Early in 1916 public meetings were held and 14 persons were baptized. The first church was organized at San Salvador, the capital, on Oct. 2[illegible], 1916, with a membership of 19, and soon afterward a church school was opened. Next Brown went to Santa Ana, the second-largest city, and held another series of evangelistic meetings. Soon a church was organized there also and a small church school opened. About this time U. M. Cooke went to El Salvador to begin the colporteur work, and several new converts were recruited. J. A. Bodle and his wife, who colporteured there, contributed much to the success of SDA work in Santa Ana.

C. F. Staben, who became director of the El Salvador Mission in 1918, reported a membership of 50 in that year. Thereafter, despite many political upheavals, SDA work grew steadily in El Salvador. All principal towns and many smaller towns and villages have well-organized SDA churches. Church schools were opened soon after the work was organized in San Salvador and continued with increasing success. In 1992 there were 70 teachers and 124 students. In 1944 the Voice of Prophecy broadcasts began, and the radio correspondence school was opened a few months later. The Dorcas Society has played an important part in the mission work in El Salvador. Youth camps and Voice of Youth broadcasts also helped the growth of the Seventh-day Adventist Church. In 1992 there were 337 Youth Societies and 40 Dorcas Societies in the country.

EL SALVADOR CONFERENCE. *See* El Salvador; Inter-American Division.

EMMANUEL ADVENTIST SECONDARY SCHOOL (Colegio Adventista Emmanuel). A coeducational day school offering six years of secondary school required by the Colombian system of education. The school is situated in a southern suburb of the city of Bogotá called Luna Park. In 1993, 1,193 students were in attendance. The school is owned and operated by the Upper Magdalena Conference and serves several churches of the city of Bogotá. The course of studies is approved by the Colombian government. The secondary school was established in 1954 under the leadership of Zita Robinson.

Principals: Zita Robinson, 1954-1955; Esther Vivanco, 1956; Carolina Cordero, 1957; Esteban Beleño, 1958-1960; David González, 1961; Joel Manosalva, 1962-1963; María I. de Vargas, 1964-1966; Héctor Larrota, 1967-1968; Benjamín Suescún, 1969; José Leal, 1970; Augustín Urrutia, 1971-1972; Beatríz de Krumbein, 1973-1974; Magda de Cárdenas, 1975-1976; Orlando Hurtado, 1977; Luis Pacheco, 1978-1982; Félix Hurtado, 1982; Orlando Hurtado, 1983-1986; Manuel Rojas, 1986-1988; Gladys Rojas, 1989; Magda de Cárdenas, 1990-1992; Gustavo Zapata, 1992- .

EMMANUEL MISSION SCHOOL. A boarding primary and secondary educational institution located in Lesotho in the Southern Africa Union Conference. Established in 1969, the school offers a complete secondary program leading to qualifications for admittance to institutions of higher learning. There were a faculty and staff of 18 in 1993.

Principals: M. E. Seteka, 1970; P. Kote, 1971; B. B. Mafuya, 1972-1973; M. E. Seteka, 1974-1977; E. P. Komota, 1978-1980; A. Mhaka, 1980-1981; J. M. Nkhethoa, 1981-1982; P. Moyo, 1982-1988; J. M. Nkhethoa, 1988-1989; J. L. Mafisa, 1989-1994; T. Pulumo, 1994- .

EMMANUEL MISSIONARY COLLEGE. *See* Andrews University.

EMPRESS ZAUDITU MEMORIAL ADVENTIST HOSPITAL. A 110-bed hospital operated for 44 years by the Ethiopian Union Mission in Addis Ababa, Ethiopia. The hospital was established in 1932 by Emperor Haile Selassie I. On the occasion of his being crowned (Nov. 2, 1930), the Scandinavian Union Conference of Seventh-day Adventists had sent him congratulations, and he had expressed a desire to present a gift to the SDA mission. Realizing the needs of his people, and being well acquainted with SDA medical work, he asked the church to operate the new hospital. Dr. George Bergman was appointed the first medical director.

The Italians took over the hospital about the beginning of 1939. In the last year of its operation during the Italian administration, the hospital was listed in the *Yearbook* as the Adventist Sanitarium and Hospital.

When the emperor returned in May 1941, Mrs. Della Hanson, wife of the mission superintendent, approached him regarding the restoration of the hospital. He turned it over to the mission at once. Nurses Lisa Johansen (Johannesson) and Rasmine Hofstad moved in, and beginning in 1942, they operated it with the help of a local eye specialist. Merlin G. Anderson, M.D., came in 1945 and served eight years as medical director.

On Jan. 26, 1971, the new Empress Zauditu Memorial Adventist Hospital was officially opened by Emperor Haile Selassie I. In addition to facilities offered by the old hospital, the new hospital had a sauna bath, hydrotherapy, inhalation therapy, Bacteriology Department, improved X-ray department, dental clinic, and a dresser school. A new nursing school complex, built with Norwegian aid in 1971, provided housing for 40 student nurses, and had a library, chapel, four classrooms, two offices, a lounge, and three apartments.

During the first six months of 1971, 20,750 new patients were seen in the outpatient clinic (return visits not included) and 7,823 patient visits were made in the appointment clinic.

Empress Zauditu Hospital was nationalized in 1976.

Medical Directors: George C. Bergman, 1932-1938; M. G. Anderson, 1945-1953; F. L. Artress, 1953-1954; C. E. Steen, Jr., 1954-1959; C. J. Houmann, 1959-1962; G. R. Rigsby, 1962-1969; A. P. Bokovoy, 1969-1974; J. C. Holm, 1974-1976.

EN MARCHA (Spanish). Organ of the Colombia-Venezuela Union Mission.

ENCOUNTER. An eight-page bimonthly published by the Stanborough Press, Ltd., Alma Park, Grantham, Lincolnshire, England.

ENCOUNTER SERIES (formerly Character Classics). A four-year plan of daily devotional reading and study from the Bible, correlated with the five volumes of the Conflict of the Ages Series, by Ellen G. White: *Patriarchs and Prophets, Prophets and Kings, The Desire of Ages, The Acts of the Apostles*, and *The Great Controversy*. It was prepared to add interest to the reading of the Bible and also to enable young people to gain a better understanding of Bible history, biography, doctrines, and prophetic fulfillments.

ENGLAND. *See* Great Britain and Northern Ireland; Trans-European Division.

ENGLISH LANGUAGE SCHOOLS (Far East). A name applied to church-sponsored community schools designed to assist indigenous people to learn the English language, and at the same time to teach them the message of the Seventh-day Adventist Church. Small schools of this kind have been operating on and off in most countries of the Far East ever since overseas missionaries first arrived.

The organized language school idea did not materialize until the colleges of North America started a student missionary program.

History. The organized English language school idea started in the fall of 1966 at the Osaka Center in Japan, when a young American evangelist, M. T. Bascom, discovered soon after he arrived in that city that one of the most effective evangelistic programs in the Osaka Center had been the English language classes started by Bobbie Jane Van Dolson when the center was opened and that most Japanese young people wanted to learn

English. Bascom and his wife started a school with an enrollment of 16. This grew very rapidly until it was necessary for him to call on students from the United States to assist with the program. The school continued to expand until, in early 1975, there were eight schools in Japan alone. Bascom returned to the United States to work on his doctorate, and a former student missionary, Bruce Bauer, took over as director of the language schools. He remained in that position until 1983, when Roy Castlebuono took over. In 1991 the language schools were reorganized and were directed from the English Language School Department at the Japan Union Conference. In 1993 Mark Duarte was serving as director.

In September 1969 Dean Hubbard, then finishing his Korean language study, started a similar school in Seoul, Korea, and it was an immediate success. A second school started shortly thereafter in Pusan, Korea. In 1973 the former city hall in Kwangju, Korea, was purchased by the Seoul school and thus a third school started in Korea. *See* Seventh-day Adventist Language Institutes, Korea.

The idea spread, and soon there were schools in Djakarta and Bandung, Java, Indonesia; Phnom Penh, Cambodia; Haad Yai, Thailand; and Menado, Celebes, Indonesia. In early 1975 there were 16 English language schools operating in the territory of the Far Eastern Division.

In the fall of 1974 the Far Eastern Division committee appointed a full-time English language school director for the division. The first director was Dr. M. T. Bascom.

ENOCH, GEORGE FRANCIS (1876-1944). Evangelist, missionary for 36 years. He was educated at Battle Creek College, Walla Walla College, and Pacific Union College. In 1898 he married Bertha Graham. In that same year he was appointed to the West Indies, where he worked for three years each in Jamaica, Trinidad, and Barbados. In 1907 he went to India, where he carried on aggressive evangelism in many centers, including Lucknow and Bombay, and for several years edited the *Oriental Watchman*.

ENRIQUILLO ADVENTIST SECONDARY SCHOOL. A 12-grade educational institution that is accredited by the Inter-American Division and the Department of Education of the Dominican Republic. It is situated in Jábaba, a small town some 2.5 miles (four kilometers) from Moca, the nearest city.

The school began in 1925 when Luis Gómez donated the land on which the school was constructed. The first teacher was Adolfo Miranda. It originally was named Academia Arturo Roth and functioned as a primary school until 1979, when the secondary school courses were started. It is interesting to note that this campus has one of the best vegetable gardens functioning in the entire North Dominican Conference. In 1993 a total of 230 students were in attendance and the school had seven teachers. Primary school principals have included Adolfo Miranda, Nena Cabrera, Ana Cabral, Salvador Alvarez, and Germania Gómez (28 years).

Principals: Ramon Alberto, 1980-1982; Gladys de Lora, 1982-1984; Moises Lora, 1984-1985; Daniel Fana, 1985-1990; Librael Gómez, 1990- .

ENTERPRISE ACADEMY. A coeducational boarding school on the senior high school level, situated on the south edge of the small town of Enterprise, Kansas, and overlooking the Smoky Hill River valley. Owned and operated by the Kansas-Nebraska Conference, it is one of three academies serving this conference of 10,964 members. During the school year of 1993-1994 there were 21 full- and part-time staff members, including the Industrial Department heads.

Immediate forerunners of Enterprise Academy were schools at Downs and Oswego, Kansas.

With the financial aid of local businesspersons, the conference expanded an existing two-teacher school in Oswego, an intermediate school operated since 1901, and opened the Strode Industrial Academy on Sept. 16, 1908. In addition to the regular academy subjects, the academy offered courses in practical training in agriculture and taught certain trades. N. W. Kauble, a former president of Union College and of Emmanuel Missionary College, was the first principal. In 1917 the name of the school was changed to Oswego Academy. After the East Kansas Conference and the West Kansas Conference, in existence since 1910, combined in 1914 to form the Kansas Conference, the leaders of the united conference considered it desirable to have one strong school in a central location. Accordingly, in 1919 a Methodist school property at Enterprise, Kansas, was purchased. At that time the property consisted of 23 acres (nine hectares), with four buildings.

An additional 47 acres (19 hectares) were purchased. All the original buildings have since been replaced. Enterprise Academy opened on Sept. 17, 1919.

Years of drought, causing many Seventh-day Adventists to move to other states that were not affected by the adverse weather conditions, brought losses in enrollment. With the establishment of an academy in Missouri in 1946, students from that state no longer attended Enterprise Academy. This brought a further decrease in enrollment.

Of the present buildings, the gymnasium was built in 1943, the cafeteria-chapel in 1946-1947, and the campus store in 1951. At a constituency meeting called in May 1959 to consider the future of the academy, it was voted overwhelmingly to rebuild the plant and continue to operate Enterprise Academy as the school for the Kansas Conference. Since that time, new buildings added were the girls' dormitory (completed in 1960), the administration building (completed in 1962), and the boys' dormitory (completed in 1963). A 12-room addition was added to the girls' dormitory in 1965, and in 1974 a new dean's quarters, worship room, and recreation room were added to the boys' dormitory, plus additional dormitory rooms.

A larger gymnasium was built in 1966, allowing the first gymnasium to house school industries until 1972, when a large industrial building was built to house them. The first gymnasium and an adjacent building are now a functional industrial education complex, which house classes in auto mechanics, welding, woodworking, and photography, as well as housing the Grounds/Maintenance Department.

Industries at Enterprise Academy include Midco Plastics and the academy farm. The 1,200-acre (500-hectare) farm grows feed grain, forage, hay, and wheat, plus maintaining a herd of 55 range cows plus calves.

Enterprise Academy is accredited by the SDA Board of Regents. The academy publishes the yearbook *Our Yesterdays* and the school paper *Our Todays.*

Principals: E. E. Pringle, 1919-1921; H. F. Saxton, 1921-1923; Lester O. Knowlton, 1923-1925; Vernon P. Lovell, 1925-1933; Everett D. Kirk, 1933-1935; R. R. Newman, 1935-1945; Ellis R. Maas, 1945-1947; O. L. Heinrich, 1947-1951; L. G. Barker, 1951-1955; Ben Trout, 1955-1957; E. C. Wines, 1957-1964; Don L. Weatherall, 1964-1969; Keith Wiseman, 1969-1971; W. F. Wright, 1971-1973; D. L. Carr, 1973-1979; Howard Barron, 1979-1983; Jack Francisco, 1983-1986; Miriam Kittrell, 1986-1989; Arnold Schnell, 1989-1991; Keith Hallam, 1991- .

EQUATORIAL AFRICAN PUBLISHING HOUSE. *See* Central African Publishing House.

EQUATORIAL GUINEA. The former Spanish Guinea, consisting of Río Muni, on the west coast of Africa (with several adjacent islands), and the islands of Bioko (formerly Fernando Póo; Macías Nguema) and Annobón. The total area is 10,831 square miles (28,000 square kilometers) in size and it has a population (1994) of 400,000. Agriculture is the chief occupation, with cocoa, coffee, wood, fruits, and vegetables the chief exports. Río Muni lies just north of the equator, bounded on the north by Cameroon, on the east and south by Gabon, and on the west by the Gulf of Guinea.

Equatorial Guinea comprises the Equatorial Guinea Mission, which is part of the Central African Union Mission, which in turn is part of the Africa-Indian Ocean Division. Statistics (1993) for *Equatorial Guinea:* churches, 6; members, 259; ordained ministers, 3; licensed ministers, 2.

Seventh-day Adventist Work. On Bioko there were 14 Seventh-day Adventist members and one ordained minister in 1963. The first missionary was sent in 1960, although two African SDA families from São Tomé had lived on this island for some time. José Lopez, minister and nurse, with his wife, also a nurse, arrived from Spain on Sept. 9 of that year and opened a dispensary and held meetings with the resident members. On May 19, 1962, the first two people were baptized, and in 1963 four more—two from São Tomé, one from Nigeria, and the fourth, a member of the indigenous Bubi tribe.

Because of the political situation, there were no foreign missionaries in Equatorial Guinea for some time after 1972. Four Equatorial Guineans carried on the work. In June 1974 a young graduate from the Bible course at the Séminaire Adventiste (Cameroon Training School) was sent to Bata, the capital of Río Muni. This was the first time that the SDA message entered the part of Equatorial Guinea on the African continent. Within a few months 25 were meeting regularly every Sabbath. By 1993 the membership was more than 250.

EQUATORIAL GUINEA MISSION. *See* Africa-Indian Ocean Division; Equatorial Guinea.

ERHOLUNGSHEIM FRIEDENSAU. *See* Friedensau Retreat.

ERHOLUNGSHEIM WALDPARK. *See* Waldpark Hohenfichte Retreat.

ERICKSON, J. M. (1854-1931). Minister, teacher. He was born in Dalsland, Sweden, and confirmed in the Swedish state church (Lutheran). While in the military school in Stockholm, he was converted and sought immediate release from the military, which was finally obtained with great difficulty. In the autumn of 1879 he sailed for America, and in Minneapolis became an active member of the Baptist Church. Convinced that God was calling him to the ministry, he spent three years in the Baptist Theological Seminary in Morgan Park, Chicago, Illinois. On completion of his studies, he accepted the pastorate of the Worcester, Massachusetts, Baptist Church. Feeling the need of more training, he returned to Sweden and enrolled as a student in Bethel Seminary in Stockholm. After finishing his studies, he returned to the United States and became pastor of the Baptist church in Campello, Massachusetts.

In 1886, through the work of D. M. Canright, Erickson accepted the Seventh-day Adventist faith and began to sell SDA books. In the fall of 1887 he entered South Lancaster Academy to become better acquainted with SDA doctrines. He was ordained in 1888 and began his preaching for the church in Boston and Providence. Before the end of the year he was invited by the General Conference to work in Sweden. Two years later he was called back to head the Swedish Department at Union College, where he remained six years (1890-1896). After this he worked as an evangelist in Connecticut, Michigan, and Massachusetts. Then in 1901 he was called back to Sweden again, where he preached for 10 years. In 1911 he returned to America and for 10 years headed the Bible Department in the Broadview Swedish Seminary at La Grange, Illinois. Then until 1928 he engaged in pastoral work in the cities of Chicago, Minneapolis, and Providence.

ERICKSON, MATILDA. *See* Andross, Anna Matilda (Erickson).

ERICKSON, MELVIN EDDY (1918-1976). Educator, administrator. He was born in Saskatchewan, Canada, and received a Bachelor of Theology degree from Canadian Union College in 1947. Erickson served as principal of Okanagan Academy in British Columbia and as a pastor in the same province. He married Lorna Joy Stickle and, following his ordination to the ministry in 1952, became youth director and superintendent of education for the Alberta Conference, later moving to New York in the same capacity. After receiving an administration degree from Syracuse University, he became superintendent of education of the Georgia-Cumberland Conference, a position he held until 1966, when he became secretary-treasurer of the Ontario-Quebec Conference. He later served as associate director of education for the Southern Union and earned his Ph.D degree from Georgia State University. Dr. Erickson was the author of an educational game, two books, and numerous articles. At the time of his death he was editor of a journal entitled *Focus on Education.*

ERITREA. An independent nation in eastern Africa whose neighbors include Ethiopia on the south, Djibouti on the east, the Sudan on the west, and the Red Sea on the north. Eritrea covers an area of 45,300 square miles (117,000 square kilometers) and has a population (1994) of 3.2 million. Eritrea declared its independence from Ethiopia in 1993.

Seventh-day Adventist Statistics. The territory of Eritrea constitutes the Eritrea Mission Field, an attached field of the Eastern Africa Division. Statistics (1994) for *Eritrea:* churches, 3; members, 450; ordained ministers, 2. Headquarters are at Asmera.

For development of Seventh-day Adventist work in Eritrea, *see* Ethiopia.

ERITREA MISSION FIELD. *See* Eastern Africa Division; Eritrea.

ERNST, LUIS (1874-1952). Pastor and administrator. He was born in Uruguay of Swiss descent and was the first student of River Plate College.

In 1898 Ernst sold his land and cattle, transferred the cheese factory he owned to his brother, and one Monday afternoon, probably Sept. 26, with a Bible in one hand and his suitcase in the other, presented himself before the leaders of the Seventh-day Adventist work gathered in Crespo, Entre Ríos, Argentina. His purpose was to attend the SDA school in Entre

Ríos, which did not yet exist. The mission committee decided to establish the school immediately, and Luis Ernst stayed in Entre Ríos.

He finished digging the first well for the school, and helped to build the first edifice. He later accompanied F. H. Westphal during his pastoral visits. Westphal used the time to teach him in return for Spanish lessons from the young man, who served as his translator.

He entered evangelistic work in 1903, and in 1905 was ordained to the ministry. He was the first president of the Alto Paraná Mission from 1906 to 1909. In 1907 he, with Ignacio Kalbermatter, raised a church with 12 members in Asunción, Paraguay. Later he worked in Bahía Blanca, Rosario, and other cities in the Argentine Conference, and from 1921 to 1935 he worked in Uruguay. He served as a worker until 1938, at which time he retired.

ERZBERGER, HEINRICH (1884-1953). Administrator, missionary. He was born in Basel, Switzerland, and was baptized in his boyhood. After he attended Friedensau Missionary Seminary for one year (1904-1905), he joined the staff of the East German Conference as Bible instructor, and for eight years served as an evangelist in eastern and western Germany. In 1913 he went to the Middle East as superintendent of the Syrian Mission. In 1917 he succeeded Emil E. Frauchiger as the head of the Levant Union Mission. Six years later, in 1923, he went to preach in Alsace, France, and in Italy. In 1926 he began a term of Bible teaching at Seminar Marienhöhe, near Darmstadt, Germany. From there he went in 1928 to Neandertal Missionary Seminary to serve as its president, then returned to head the Darmstadt school in 1935. From 1939 to 1947 he served as a minister in Germany, and was listed in the *Yearbook* in the South Bavarian Conference. In 1947 he returned to his native Switzerland, and after four years in the ministry there, he retired in 1951 after 46 years of service to the church. He married Louise Zange in 1912.

ERZBERGER, JAMES H. (1843-1920). First Seventh-day Adventist minister in Europe. His name is sometimes spelled Erzenberger or Ertzberger. He was born at Eltisberg, near Basel, Switzerland. In 1864 he entered a Protestant training school to prepare for ministerial work, and later worked for a short time as chaplain and evangelist. Before long he met a small group of Sabbathkeepers in Tramelan, Switzerland, who had been instructed by M. B. Czechowski, a converted Polish priest who had brought the SDA message from the United States to Switzerland. Erzberger joyfully accepted the SDA faith, and was baptized by Albert Vuilleumier late in 1868, six years before J. N. Andrews, the first SDA foreign missionary, arrived in Switzerland.

In 1869 the Swiss SDAs established by Czechowski sent Erzberger to the General Conference session, which convened in Battle Creek in May of that year, to plead for a minister. Unfortunately, he arrived too late for the session, but he remained 15 months in the United States, living most of the time in the home of James and Ellen White, who took a special interest in him. Early and late he worked to perfect his knowledge of the English language and to become acquainted with all phases of SDA work.

In September 1870 he returned to Switzerland, having first been ordained. Soon after J. N. Andrews arrived in Switzerland in 1874, Erzberger accompanied him on a visit to a group of Sabbathkeepers in Elberfeld, Rhenish-Prussia, who had accepted the Sabbath truth through the study of their Bibles. Andrews did most of the preaching while Erzberger, who was proficient in German, French, and English, did the translating.

Erzberger remained in Germany more than three years, and while there conducted the first baptism and organized the first church (1876) in Germany.

Thereafter, with the exception of the years 1905-1912, when he and his family lived in Hamburg, Germany, Erzberger made his home in Switzerland to the time of his death in 1920. His work carried him to France, Belgium, and other countries.

ESCOLA AGRÍCOLA ADVENTISTA DO AMAZONAS. *See* Agro-Industrial Adventist Trans-Amazon Academy.

ESCONDIDO ADVENTIST ACADEMY. A coeducational day school located in northern San Diego County. The school was established in 1985. In 1993 approximately 250 students were enrolled in grades K-12.

The school's history began nearly 100 years ago when the Seventh-day Adventist community started a neighborhood school in 1903. By 1963 the school had some 100 students in grades 1-10. In 1984 EAA was fully accredited as an academy, providing quality Christian education to students from 14 constituent churches. Its stated mission is to provide a Christ-centered environment in which together students, parents, and teachers can experience the presence of God, and to offer a progressive curriculum that equips students to serve and to work as moral, thinking, responsible citizens for their local and global community while preparing for Christ's return. In 1993 EAA had 35 faculty and staff members.

Principals: Kenneth Dunn, 1985-1987; Benn Nicola, 1987-1992; Martha Havens, 1992- .

ESCUELA ADVENTISTA DE HATILLO. *See* Costa Rica Secondary School.

ESCUELA AGRÍCOLA E INDUSTRIAL DEL PACÍFICO. *See* Pacific Academy.

ESCUELA AGRÍCOLA E INDUSTRIAL DEL SURESTE. *See* Linda Vista Academy.

ESCUELA AGRÍCOLA INDUSTRIAL MEXICANA. *See* Montemorelos University.

ESCUELA DE CAPACITACION ADVENTISTA SALVADORENA. *See* Adventist Training School of El Salvador.

ESCUELA INDUSTRIAL Y DE SALUD. *See* Mexico, IV, 2.

ESDA. *See* Institutional Services/ESDA.

ESDA HOME FOR THE INFIRM AGED. An old-age home situated between Brakpan and Springs, at Windhoek, South Africa. The institution was taken over by the Transvaal Conference on Nov. 1, 1973. During the following year extensive renovations were made on one section. In September of 1974 the 36 resident patients were transferred to the completed unit. In 1975 the institution had facilities for 67 patients. In 1993 the facilities were upgraded and extended to accommodate 77 residents in 30 rooms.

ESDAKOST FOOD COMPANY (AB Esdakost). A distributing company for import, sales, and distribution of health foods and related products produced by foreign Seventh-day Adventist factories and other non-SDA manufacturers, established in 1969 at Rimbo, Sweden.

General Manager: Lars Sandberg, 1969-1978; Bertil Utterback, 1978-1984; Carsten Warn, 1984-1986; Ulf Gustavsson, 1986-1990; Ilkka Kuivisto, 1990-1993; Bertil Utterback, 1993- .

ESPÍRITO SANTO ACADEMY (Educandário Espírito Santenes Adventista). A secondary-level boarding school established in 1963 at Colatina, Espírito Santo, Brazil, and owned by the Espírito Santo Conference. Pioneering the establishment of this school were Ernesto Roth and Edward Kanna. The campus is on the top of a beautiful hill on the banks of the Río Doce (Sweet River). In 1975 a three-year curriculum began to be offered on the secondary level.

Principals: Edward Kanna, 1963; Herbert Kurt Weber, 1964-1968; Rolf Belz, 1969; Azel R. Wegele, 1970-1971; Aluizio Gabriel, 1972-1973; Zizion Fonseca, 1974-1991; Josias Candido Lacerda, 1992- .

ESPÍRITO SANTO CONFERENCE. *See* Brazil; South American Division.

ÉTABLISSEMENT MEDICO-SOCIAL LE FLON. An old people's home operated by the French Swiss Conference at Oron-la-Ville, Switzerland. Through various gifts and an appropriation from the conference, a small property was purchased in 1961 located in the village of Oron-la-Ville, 12 miles (20 kilometers) from Lausanne. A building and a small garden were already on the property, making it possible to accept 15 residents immediately. In 1968 a modern addition increased the capacity to 24 beds and provided a comfortable chapel for church activities, as well as an attractive children's Sabbath School Department.

Directors: Elder and Mrs. Charles Monnier, 1962-1975; Adolf Kinder, 1975-1980; Sylvain Meyer, 1981-1987; Felix Berger, 1987-1990; Rene Augsburger, 1990- .

ESTONIA. A republic bounded by the Baltic Sea, Russia, and Latvia. Estonia occupies an area of 17,413 square miles (45,100 square kilometers), and has a population (1994) of 1.6 million. The official language is Russian. Evangelical Lutheranism is the most common religious affiliation.

Estonia was a Russian province before World War I, but was independent between the two great wars. It was conquered by the USSR in 1940, and declared itself "occupied territory."

Estonia declared full independence on Aug. 20, 1991.

Seventh-day Adventist Statistics. Estonia comprises the Estonian Conference, which is part of the Baltic Union Conference in the Trans-European Division. Statistics (1992) for *Estonia:* churches, 16; members, 1,663; ordained ministers, 12; Bible instructors, 3.

Seventh-day Adventist Work. *Beginnings.* SDA work gained a foothold in Estonia when two ministers, H. J. Loebsack and Gerhard Perk, visited Reval (now Tallinn) in the summer of 1897. They had been invited there by a woman living in St. Petersburg, then the capital of Russia, who requested them to visit her Baptist parents in Reval. The group of interested people gathered secretly in the home and later in an old barn in a backyard, where Perk preached in German with someone translating into Estonian. There were three converts, all women who in due course were baptized. On Sept. 5, 1897, Perk organized the first SDA church in Estonia, at Tallinn. Gradually new members were added.

In 1898 in Helsingfors (now Helsinki), Finland, the first SDA publication in the Estonian language was printed. It was a tract entitled *Taanieli Raamatu Seletus* ("Explanations of the Book of Daniel"). The first printing of SDA tracts within the confines of the Russian Empire proper (Finland was autonomous) was done in Riga, Latvia, in 1899. The languages were Latvian and Estonian, not Russian. This work was later suppressed by the government, and afterward all printing for Estonia was done in Germany at the Hamburg Publishing House. In 1905 came *Tee Kristuse Juurde* ("Steps to Christ"); in 1908, *Kristlik Kasinus* ("Christian Temperance"); in 1914, *Mõtted Õndsakskiitmise Mält* ("Thoughts From the Mount of Blessing")—all three by Ellen G. White. The magazine *Siioni Vahimees* ("Zion's Watchman") and the church paper *Siioni Tööline* ("Zion's Worker"), as well as Sabbath school quarterlies and other church papers, were also published there.

As the work spread throughout the country, churches were organized in several cities. In 1901, when the work in Russia was divided according to ethnic lines, Estonia, along with Latvia, Lithuania, and Poland, was included in the North Russian Mission, under D. P. Gaede. During the time Gaede worked in Tallinn about 1902, a number of talented young men joined the church, three of whom eventually trained at Friedensau Missionary Seminary and became the first national ministers.

Estonia Between the Wars. After the Russian revolution, Estonia acquired independence, and with it religious freedom. By that time the church numbered about 1,000 adherents, organized into the Estonian Conference. In 1917 the Estonian Publishing Department was organized, and from then until Estonia lost independence in 1940, SDA publications were printed within the country. Martin Bärengrub was in charge of the work. He with L. Hallang, Eduard Ney, Eduard Magi, and Harald Pild, served as editors of various magazines published during that time: *Tõe Sõnumud* ("Messages of Truth"), *Noorte Sõber* ("Friend of Youth"), *Meie Aeg* ("Our Time"), *Missioni Teated* ("Mission Records"), and *Noorte Juhised* ("Youth Instruction"). Thousands of tracts and books were also printed during this period. The books and periodicals produced by the publishing house found a ready market in the general public. Nevertheless, the work did not continue without difficulties. When outside pressures were removed, internal difficulties sprang up and led to a division within the church, caused by differences among the leaders. But at the first conference session held after the war, in 1920—attended by L. H. Christian and Aarne Rintala—the church was largely reunited. The work continued to grow rapidly. Public meetings were held in large cities, and for a number of years the church conducted a series of radiobroadcasts from Tartu by Eduard Magi. The membership grew to about 2,200, and the church acquired six church buildings, including two at Tallinn.

In 1923 the Estonian Conference was united with Latvia and Lithuania in the Baltic Union Conference. In that same year the Baltic Union School (Suschenhof) to train workers was opened at Riga, Latvia. From 1935 a small school was operated in the city of Tallinn, with about 60 to 80 students and six to eight teachers. In 1932 and again in 1935 Estonian young people participated in the Baltic Union youth congresses. Later, after the Baltic Union Mission School was closed by the Latvian government, the Estonian Conference opened its own theological school at Tallinn from 1937 to 1940. The school, headed by R. W. Vinglas, taught all subjects required by the state plus denominational theological subjects.

At the time when Estonia was incorporated into the Soviet Union in 1940, the church's institutions were closed, and its stock of literature was confiscated. However, the publications were found during the time of German occupation and bought back by the church as scrap paper. Needless to say, they were quickly distributed. For a time the churches were permitted the use, at a high rent, of their buildings, which had been nationalized. Then, after a time, the various churches were obliged to share buildings with other denominations, especially after some were bombed during the war. However, worship services were permitted. During the war SDAs were active in welfare work.

Later on, when small congregations were merged and the minimum size of a congregation was set at 50 members, this reduced the number of Seventh-day Adventist congregations to 13, in the charge of 13 ministers. Special permission was required for ministers to visit outside of their own churches. Because Sabbath school supplies were no longer available, the churches arranged for a Bible reading hour before the preaching service.

In 1944 the territory of Estonia became part of the Federation of Seventh-day Adventists in the Union of Soviet Socialist Republics. All denominational organizations except for local churches were dissolved in the 1960s. Although the Estonian Conference ceased to exist in the legal sense, it continued in a de facto sense. The Estonian Conference and the Baltic Union Conference were restored in 1989.

ESTONIAN CONFERENCE. *See* Estonia; Trans-European Division.

ESTONIAN MISSION SCHOOL (Adventusuühingute Usuteaduse Kool). A former training school with an elementary school department established in 1935 and operated by the Estonian Conference at Tallinn, Estonia. The *Yearbook* lists it from 1936 to 1946 and names R. Vinglas as its principal.

ETERNAL LIFE. The life without end promised those who believe in Jesus Christ and receive His saving grace (John 3:15, 16; Titus 1:2; 1 John 5:11). The Hebrew word *'ôlam,* commonly translated "eternal," or "everlasting," means, basically, "something hidden," and thus designates a long time whose limits are unknown, or "hidden." The duration of *'ôlam is* always relative to, and determined by, that to which it is applied. Thus *'ôlam* may refer to a lifetime (Ex. 21:6), or a period the beginning of which is lost in antiquity (Gen. 6:4; Joshua 24:2; Prov. 22:28). When used with the figure of sleep it means death (Jer. 51:39); when applied to God (Ps. 90:2; Isa. 40:28) its designation is limitless. The expression "everlasting life" *(chayyê 'ôlam)* occurs in the OT only in Dan. 12:2. Compare v. 7, where God is characterized as *chê ha-'ôlam,* "he who lives eternally." The contextual implication is thus that eternal life is a sharing in the life of God. The Hebrew mind conceived of God as living in limitless time, and not abstractly in the sense of being beyond time. The same mind also conceived of those whom God resurrects as living this way.

The Greek term corresponding to *'ôlam* is *aiōn,* also designating a long but relative extent of time, and thus an adequate translation of *'ôlam* in the LXX. However, with Plato *aiōn* came also to stand for the abstract, qualitative concept of "eternity" in contradistinction to time—a timeless situation to which the limitations of time do not apply. It has been suggested that the NT gives to *aiōn* both quantitative and qualitative dimensions, and that particularly in the Johannine writings, where the expression "eternal life" recurs frequently (John 3:16; 5:24; 17:2; 1 John 1:2; etc.), is this qualitative aspect salient.

Often eternal life is referred to simply as "life" *(zōē),* or "the life" (Gr. *hē zōē*). Eternal life is granted to those who "believe," that is, to those who have faith (John 3:16; 11:25, 26); to make it available to humanity is the particular object for which Christ came (John 6:51, 57, 58; 14:6, 19); to know God and His Son, Jesus Christ, is eternal life (John 17:3).

In John two dimensions of eternal life are especially intertwined: eternal life as a gift, in principle, when a person believes in Christ (John 5:24, that individual has eternal life), and as a literal possession to be bestowed in actuality at the Parousia (John 5:28, 29). Commenting on these two dimensions, Ellen White said: "'This is the record, that God hath given unto us eternal life, and this life is in His Son. He that hath the Son hath life.' And Jesus said, 'I will raise him up at the last day.' Christ became one flesh with us, in order that we might become one spirit with Him. It is by virtue of this union that we are to come forth from the grave—not merely as a manifestation of the power of Christ, but because, through faith, His life has become ours. Those who see Christ in His true character, and receive Him into the heart, have everlasting life. It is through the Spirit that Christ dwells in us; and the Spirit of

God, received into the heart by faith, is the beginning of the life eternal" (DA 388).

The Seventh-day Adventist point of view considers eternal life as "exclusively the property of God" (Ellen G. White, in SDACom 5:1130). It was given to Adam conditionally and mediated to him by the tree of life (Gen. 2:9; 3:22; PP 60). He forfeited eternal life by his sin, but it is restored by Christ on condition of "perfect righteousness, harmony with God, perfect conformity to the principles of His law" (MB 76). It is ours now if we are *in Christ* (1 John 5:11, 12). We possess it now on condition of maintaining our relationship to Christ.

In a sense, eternal life is a reward to the obedient, but it is not earned, for it is a "free gift" to those who believe in Christ as their personal Saviour (1SM 297). SDAs emphasize the literalness of the eternal life bestowed in the resurrection. Eternity is conceived of as endless time in which the saved will have ample opportunity to learn ever more concerning God's infinite purpose for them, to enjoy and study the wonders of the universe, and to realize their highest ambitions. *See* Immortality.

ETHIOPIA. An ancient independent empire, formerly governed by a constitutional monarchy and now governed by a transitional government, in northeast Africa, bounded on the east by Djibouti and Somalia, on the north by Eritrea, on the south by Kenya, and on the west by Sudan. It has an estimated area of 437,800 square miles (1,134,000 square kilometers) and a population (1994) of 58.7 million. Agriculture is the principal occupation of the people, the chief exports being coffee, pulses, oilseeds, hides, goatskins, and sheepskins.

Much of eastern Ethiopia is low, hot, and dry, with some territory below sea level. The western and northern areas are high, with 8,000-foot (2,400-meter) plateaus and mountain peaks as high as 15,000 feet (4,600 meters). There are many hot springs, craters from extinct volcanoes, and large areas of volcanic rock and soil. Addis Ababa, the capital, is in central Ethiopia at an elevation of about 8,000 feet (2,450 meters). The Blue Nile rises in north central Ethiopia. Amharic is the official language, but many other languages and dialects are spoken. The peoples of Ethiopia include the Amhara, the Tigrean, the Oromo, the Somali, the Falasha or Ethiopian Jew, and the Gurage. Southern areas are mostly Muslim; central and northern areas are Christian (constituting the majority). Emperor Haile Selassie I became regent in 1916 and was crowned emperor in 1930. In 1974 he was deposed, and a Provisional Military Administrative Council was established to govern the land.

Historical Background. Ethiopia has had a knowledge of God from ancient times. The former constitution of Ethiopia declared that the line of Haile Selassie I descended without interruption from the dynasty of Menelik, the son of the queen of Sheba and King Solomon of Jerusalem. Jewish priests, Levites, and workers are said to have been brought to Ethiopia at that time to assist in establishing the new religion and government. Jewish religious influence in Ethiopia in NT times is evident from the narrative of the Ethiopian courtier who was baptized by Philip (Acts 8:26-39). About A.D. 330 Frumentius and Aedesius, two young Christians who were shipwrecked on the Red Sea coast and brought to the king of Aksum, won him to Christianity. Frumentius, who brought this news to Alexandria, was proclaimed the first bishop of Ethiopia. Through the centuries until 1950, when an Ethiopian was consecrated archbishop, the Ethiopian Church was headed by Egyptians.

During the sixteenth century, under invasion by Muslim neighbors, Ethiopia invoked Portugal's assistance. Portuguese intervention repulsed Muslim attempts to subdue the highlands of Ethiopia, but the Catholic priests, builders, and artisans who came in with the Portuguese Army greatly influenced the religion of the country. In 1622 King Socinios accepted Catholicism. His decree prohibited the observance of Saturday, which the people had observed along with Sunday (see SB, Nos. 1462-1465), and a revolt resulted. In 1633 the Jesuits were expelled from Ethiopia, and the country closed its doors to foreign influences until the twentieth century.

Seventh-day Adventist Statistics. The territory of Ethiopia and Djbouti constitute the Ethiopian Union Mission, which is a part of the Eastern Africa Division. Statistics (1992) for *Ethiopia*: churches, 337; members, 79,602. Union headquarters are at Addis Ababa, Ethiopia. For the territories of the missions, *see* Eastern Africa Division.

Statistics (1992) for the missions—*Central Ethiopia Field:* churches, 23; members, 7,155; church or elementary schools, 7; ordained ministers, 7; licensed ministers, 10; teachers, 30. Headquarters are at Addis Ababa, Ethiopia. *Northwest Ethiopia Field:* churches, 8; members, 2,666; church or elementary schools, 2; ordained ministers, 2; teachers, 7. Headquarters are at Debre Tabor, Ethiopia. *South Ethiopia Field:* churches, 174; members, 31,913; church or elementary schools, 4; ordained ministers, 21; teachers, 23. Headquarters are at Awassa, Ethiopia. *West Ethiopia Field:* churches, 129; members, 37,182; church or elementary schools, 4; ordained ministers, 16; licensed ministers, 9; teachers, 21. Headquarters are at Gimbie, Ethiopia.

Institutions. Akaki SDA School; Ethiopian Advent Press; Ethiopian Adventist College; Gimbie Hospital; Kuyera Adventist Academy; Wollega Adventist Academy.

Development of Seventh-day Adventist Work. *Beginnings.* L. R. Conradi, General Conference vice president for Europe, is credited with first proposing SDA mission work in Ethiopia. In 1906 he reported visiting the Ethiopian church in Jerusalem, where services were held on Friday night, Sabbath, and Sunday.

What was called the Abyssinian Mission began in 1907 as a project of the Scandinavian Union Conference under the direction of the General Conference Committee in Europe. The first two missionaries sent out, P. N. Lindegren and J. Persson of Sweden, opened a mission station in Eritrea, then an Italian colony, since Ethiopia proper was not open to missionaries. In 1909 they were joined by Anol Grundset, V. E. Toppenberg, and Dr. F. W. Vasenius, and later Hans Steiner and E. J. Lorntz. The work was disrupted by World War I. The first three national converts were baptized in Eritrea in March 1914. Toppenberg was the first to enter Ethiopia proper in 1921, moving his family to Addis Ababa. There he purchased property for mission headquarters and a girls' school. In 1922 three Scandinavian missionaries came to Asmara, Eritrea, and established a dispensary and a school.

The first SDA doctor to work in Ethiopia was Dr. G. C. Bergman, who arrived in 1927 and opened the Taffari Makonnen Hospital in Dessie the following year. In 1933 he opened the Empress Zauditu Memorial Hospital in Addis Ababa, where Dr. T. C. Nicola joined him in 1934.

In the Debre Tabor district SDA missionaries made many converts from among the followers of one Sheikh Zacharias (or Zekarias), a Muslim trader who had been converted to Christianity of a sort after having had visions and dreams about the Sabbath (though he himself never became an observer of the Sabbath), the return of Jesus, and the coming of White missionaries with the Bible truth.

In 1923 the Ethiopian Union was organized, with V. E. Toppenberg as first president. It included the Eritrean, Central Abyssinian, and Gallaland missions. For a period after the conquest of Ethiopia by Italy in 1936, these areas became part of the Italian Union Mission. After the liberation the Ethiopian Union Mission was reorganized, but it was administered for several years from North America by the General Conference. In 1949 the mission was made a part of the Northern European Division, and in 1970 a part of the newly organized Afro-Mideast Division. It became part of the Ethiopian Union Mission in the newly formed Eastern Africa Division in 1983.

The Italian forces, who set up their administration in Addis Ababa in 1936, had as their objective the elimination of Protestant missions and the control of Catholic missions by Italians. By early 1939 all SDA institutions had been expropriated. Other Protestant missions were similarly treated. Moving into huts on the outskirts of the city, the SDA missionaries who remained, N. B. Nielsen, Rasmine Hofstad, and Lisa Johansen, attempted to carry on their work, and in 1940 the Hansons and Mae Mathews returned from furlough.

When Ethiopia was liberated in 1941, the union headquarters and school began to function again, and a few months later the Zauditu Memorial Hospital was reopened by two nurses. In 1943 H. M. Hanson opened a boys' school (moved from Addis Ababa) in Akaki, Ato Gobazei opened a school in Dessie, and G. Gudmundsen began the work in Debre Tabor *(see* Debre Tabor Adventist Church School; Haile Selassie I Hospital), where he was joined the next year by Nurse Shake' Nalkranian. M. J. Sorensen returned in 1945 and reopened the mission work in Ghimbi *(see* Gimbie Adventist Hospital; Wollega Adventist Academy). In 1947 V. E. Toppenberg, pioneering again in southern Ethiopia, established the Ethiopian Adventist Training School (now Ethiopian Adventist College) at Kuyera. Two visitors to the school in Kuyera, who were much impressed by the teachings of the blind pastor, Tekle-Haimanot, were from a group of Protestant converts who had carried on the work of their foreign missionaries expelled during the war and who had won thousands of converts. Soon a petition with many signatures and thumbprints arrived from a place in Wollaita called Sakie, asking for an evangelist. One of the students was sent down to Sakie during the summer vacation, and in 1955 evangelistic work was begun there by a pastor, Negarie Mulatta. In 1957 a church was organized with 293 members; and by 1959 there was a church building, a school, and a clinic. As work developed in the Wollaita and Cambatta districts, government permission was obtained in 1961 for the erection of a mission station in the latter, at Abonza, as a central station. Establishment of a number of churches, clinics, and schools throughout southern Ethiopia followed.

In Addis Ababa a modern church building was dedicated in February 1961, with Emperor Haile Selassie I and other members of the imperial family in attendance. In 1968 a boarding school, Wollega Adventist Academy, opened in Wollega province, and in 1970 the new Empress Zauditu Memorial Adventist Hospital was officially opened. It was nationalized in 1976.

By 1993 many of the six-grade schools had been taken over by the military regime, but 10 still were being operated, along with 10 eight-grade schools, three boarding academies, and one junior college. Eleven clinics were in operation. A small printing establishment was serving the field.

In 1993 Eritrea declared itself independent from Ethiopia, and the North Ethiopia Field became the Eritrea Field. *See* Eritrea.

ETHIOPIAN ADVENT PRESS. A publishing firm with printing facilities operated by the Ethiopian Union Mission in Addis Ababa, Ethiopia. The first Seventh-day Adventist book published in Amharic, the official language of Ethiopia, was Ellen G. White's *Steps to Christ,* which was sold by colporteurs from about 1930 until the Italian occupation in 1936. The book *The Bible Speaks* (in two volumes) was published in the 1940s. As a result of reading this book, entire companies of adherents have sprung up.

The Ethiopian Advent Press was built in 1955 largely through the interest and effort of W. S. Jensen from Denmark, secretary-treasurer of the Ethiopian Union Mission. In 1963 the firm had three small presses and a bindery, and employed eight people. Recently a new Minabinda was purchased, and a used Heidelberg offset press installed. These, together with three presses, a typesetter, folder, guillotine, stapler, and stitching machine, provide employment for 12 people. Since the Amharic language has more than 250 letters in its alphabet, typesetting and printing are extremely complicated.

In 1993 the Ethiopian Advent Press was publishing primary, youth, and adult Sabbath school lesson quarterlies; Ellen G. White's *Counsels for the Church, Steps to Christ,* and *The Story of Jesus,* as well as *Bible Truth, The Bible Made Plain, The Bible Speaks, Life at Its Best, Ways to Health and Happiness*, and a book on stewardship; also tracts and Voice of Prophecy correspondence lessons and union mission printing. A two-story addition to the front of the plant was constructed in 1974, and more recently a warehouse was completed.

In the earlier years this publishing house was listed in the *Yearbook* under the names of Ethiopian Press and Ethiopian Union Mission Publishing House.

Managers: W. S. Jensen, 1955-1958; H. Palm, 1959-1970; R. Burgess, 1971-1973; G. Bruce Vogt, 1974-1978; Damie Djeffar, 1979-1985; Moise Mariam, 1985-1988; Damie Djeffar, 1988- .

ETHIOPIAN ADVENTIST COLLEGE (formerly Ethiopian Adventist Training School). A coeducational day and boarding school on the senior high and junior college levels, situated at Kuyera, 150 miles (240 kilometers) south of Addis Ababa, at an elevation of 6,500 feet (2,000 meters). It holds 650 acres (260 hectares) of land under leases from the Ethiopian government and has a teaching staff (1993) of 27. The 10-acre (four-hectare) campus is dotted with more than 50 structures of wood and stone. Upon completion of the secondary school, the students sit for the Ethiopian School Leaving Certificate Examination (college entrance). The school now offers training on the college level (two years after grade 12) to prepare students for business, theology, education, and agriculture.

The school is supported by a denominational subsidy, fees, and industries. Work is provided for students in the usual school departments, a 500-acre (200-hectare) grain farm, a flour mill with a capacity of 1,000 pounds (450 kilograms) per hour, a garden, an orchard, a store, a furniture (wood and metal) factory, and a metal trailer factory. Water supply for irrigation comes from a river that flows through the property. In 1962 a well 385 feet (120 meters) deep was drilled, which supplies all of the domestic needs.

The school was established in 1947 by V. E. Toppenberg. It occupied old and temporary buildings until 1952, when the lease for the land was obtained. Immediately an extensive building program was begun, and more than 30,000 square feet (2,800 square meters) of educational, service, and industrial buildings, and dwellings were erected. Also in 1952, 12 students completed the first teacher-evangelist training class. The scholastic standard was raised for the two succeeding classes; in 1958 the first twelfth-grade class was graduated, and in 1966 the first college class graduated.

There have been continued improvements with the passing years—an *injera* (staple food) kitchen, boys' dormitory, a new science building, auto technology center, and improved farm. In 1970 the elementary section was moved across the road into an eight-room complex built with Swedish aid, providing further space for housing and classrooms on the main campus. Teacher training and junior college (two years of college) began in 1972, and in 1973 a course in mechanized farming was offered.

The college program was suspended in 1977 for political reasons, but reactivated in 1990. In 1993, 103 students were enrolled in the junior college program.

Principals: V. E. Toppenberg, 1947-1953; A. H. Hanson with L. Rasmussen (acting), 1953-1955; L. Rasmussen, 1955-1959; S. Berkeley, 1959-1962; Irene Eide (acting), 1962-1963; O. C. Bjerkan, 1963-1968. E. W. Marter (acting), 1968-1970; Dr. O. C. Bjerkan, 1970-1971; Dr. W. F. Riley (acting) 1971-1972; Per Naesheim (acting), 1972-1974; D. K. Griffith, 1974-1976; M. A. Morford, 1976-1978; I. K. Dulan, 1979-1982; Neal Scott (acting), 1982-1983; David Patterson 1983-1985; M. T. Graham, 1985-1987; Fanta Chelabo, 1987-1988; J. Fink, 1988- .

ETHIOPIAN MISSION TRAINING SCHOOL FOR BOYS. *See* Akaki Seventh-day Adventist School.

ETHIOPIAN UNION MISSION. *See* Djibouti; Eastern Africa Division; Ethiopia.

ETHIOPIAN UNION MISSION PUBLISHING HOUSE. *See* Ethiopian Advent Press.

EURO-AFRICA DIVISION. A large unit of church organization to which is allotted the following territory: Algeria, Andorra, Angola, Austria, Azores Islands, Belgium, Bulgaria, Canary Islands, Czech Republic, France, Germany, Gibraltar, Holy See, Italy, Liechtenstein, Luxembourg, Madeira Islands, Malta, Monaco, Morocco, Mozambique, Portugal, Romania, San Marino, São Tomé and Principe, Slovakia, Spain, Switzerland, Tunisia, and Western Sahara. Statistics (1992): churches, 3,289; members, 375,044; church or elementary schools, 17; secondary schools and colleges, 21; ordained ministers, 830; credentialed commissioned ministers, 35; licensed ministers, 531; credentialed missionaries, 240; licensed missionaries, 243; credentialed commissioned ministers of teaching, 4; elementary teachers, 78; secondary and college teachers, 315; medical institutions, 3; publishing houses, 12; dispensaries, 5; nursing and retirement homes, 13. Headquarters: Schosshaldenstrasse 17, 3006 Berne, Switzerland.

The organization of the Euro-Africa Division was approved by the 1971 Annual Council of the General Conference and began to function officially on Jan. 1, 1972. It was formed from the countries and geographical divisions formerly administered by the Central European and the Trans-Mediterranean (Southern European) divisions.

For the history of Seventh-day Adventist work in the Euro-Africa Division, see specific names of countries and island fields in the area.

Constituent Organizations. The Euro-Africa Division is comprised of six union conferences, two union missions, five unions of churches, and MISSERM.

1. *Angola Union Mission* (organized 1925; reorganized 1957). Territory: Angola and São Tomé and Principe. Statistics (1992): churches, 552; members, 140,130; ordained ministers, 82; licensed ministers, 167; credentialed missionaries, 13; licensed missionaries, 2; schoolteachers, 20; secondary schools, 1. Headquarters: Rua Teixeira da Silva, Huambo, Angola.

Constituent organizations and their territories—*Central Association Mission* (organized 1983): Benguela, Bie, Huambo, and Kwanza Sul; *East Association Mission* (organized 1985): Lunda Norte, Lunda Sul, and Moxico; *North Association Mission* (organized 1982; reorganized 1985): Bengo, K. Norte, Kabinda, Luanda, Malanje, Uige, and Zaïre; *São Tomé and Principe Mission* (established 1938; organized 1947; reorganized 1976, 1983): São Tomé and Principe; *South Association Mission* (organized 1984): Huila, K. Kubango, Kunene, and Namibe.

2. *Austrian Union of Churches* (organized 1947; reorganized 1967). Territory: Austria. Statistics (1992): churches, 44; members, 3,267; ordained ministers, 26; credentialed

commissioned ministers, 1; credentialed missionaries, 6; licensed missionaries, 25; teachers, 16; secondary schools, 1. Headquarters: Nussdorferstrasse 5, Vienna, Austria. Official organ: *Adventecho.*

3. *Bulgarian Union of Churches* (organized 1920). Territory: Bulgaria. Statistics (1992): churches, 70; members, 5,058; ordained ministers, 22; licensed ministers, 26. Headquarters: Solunska 10, Sofia, Bulgaria.

4. *Czecho-Slovakian Union Conference* (organized 1919; reorganized 1968). Territory: Czech Republic and Slovakia. Statistics (1992): churches, 169; members, 9,090; ordained ministers, 71; licensed ministers, 35. Headquarters: Zalesi 50, 14 200 Praha 4-Lhotka, Czech Republic.

Constituent organizations and their territories—*Bohemian Conference* (organized 1919; reorganized 1968): Bohemia; *Moravia-Silesian Conference* (organized 1913; reorganized 1968): Moravia and Silesia; *Slovakian Conference* (organized 1919; reorganized 1968): Slovakia.

5. *Franco-Belgian Union Conference* (organized 1928; reorganized 1955). Territory: Belgium, Corsica, France, Luxembourg, and Monaco. Statistics (1992): churches, 140; members, 10,758; ordained ministers, 74; credentialed commissioned ministers, 6; licensed commissioned ministers, 4; credentialed missionaries, 14; teachers, 29; elementary schools, 2; secondary schools, 1. Headquarters: 680-684 Avenue de la Liberation, Le Mee sur Seine, France. Official organ: *Revue Adventiste.*

Constituent organizations and their territories—*Belgian-Luxembourg Conference* (organized 1920): Belgium and Luxembourg; *North France Conference* (organized 1955; reorganized 1970): north France; *South France Conference* (organized 1955; reorganized 1970): south France, Corsica, and Monaco.

6. *Italian Union of Churches* (organized 1928; reorganized 1972, 1982). Territory: Holy See, Italy, Malta, and San Marino. Statistics (1992): churches, 88; members, 5,210; ordained ministers, 37; credentialed commissioned ministers, 10; credentialed missionaries, 32; licensed ministers, 10; licensed commissioned ministers, 2; licensed missionaries, 37; teachers, 29; elementary schools, 3; secondary schools, 3. Headquarters: Lungotevere Michelangelo 7, Rome, Italy. Official organ: *Messaggero Avventista.*

7. *Mozambique Union Mission* (organized 1933; reorganized 1972). Territory: Mozambique. Statistics (1992): churches, 478; members, 150,000; ordained ministers, 35; licensed ministers, 40; teachers, 9; seminary, 1. Headquarters: Avenida Maguiguana No. 300, Maputo, Mozambique.

Constituent organizations and their territories—*Central Mission* (organized 1972): Manica, Sofala, and Tete provinces; *North Mission* (organized 1935; reorganized 1957): Cabo Delgado, Nampula, Niassa, and Zambezia provinces; *South Mission* (organized 1972): Gaza, Inhambane, and Maputo provinces.

8. *North German Union Conference* (organized 1909; reorganized 1992). Territory: Berlin-Brandenburg, and the states of Bremen, Hamburg, Mecklenburg-Vorpommern, Niedersachsen, Nordrhein-Westfalen, Saxonia, Saxony-Anhalt/Thueringia, and Schleswig-Holstein. Statistics (1992): churches, 400; members, 20,404; ordained ministers, 176; credentialed missionaries, 25; licensed ministers, 42; licensed missionaries, 36. Headquarters: Fischerstrasse 19, Hannover, Federal Republic of Germany.

Constituent organizations and their territories—*Berlin-Brandenburg Conference* (organized 1909; reorganized 1954, 1992): Berlin and the state of Brandenburg; *Hansa Conference* (organized 1900; reorganized 1992): the states of Hamburg, Mecklenburg-Vorpommern, and Schleswig-Holstein; *Lower Saxonian Conference North* (organized 1902): the state of Bremen and the northern part of the state of Niedersachsen; *Lower Saxonian Conference South* (organized 1934): southern part of the state of Niedersachsen; *Northern Rhenish-Westfalian Conference* (organized 1989): the state of Nordrhein-Westfalen; *Saxonian Conference* (organized 1919; reorganized 1971, 1990): the state of Sachsen; *Saxony-Anhalt/Thueringia Conference* (organized 1948; reorganized 1971, 1990): the states of Sachsen-Anhalt and Theuringen.

9. *Portuguese Union of Churches* (organized 1904; reorganized 1972, 1982). Territory: Azores Islands, Madeira Islands, and Portugal. Statistics (1992): churches, 77; members, 7,451; ordained ministers, 33; credentialed missionaries, 61; licensed ministers, 16; licensed missionaries, 9; teachers, 49; elementary schools, 6; secondary schools, 2. Headquarters: Rua Joaquim Bonifacio 17, Lisboa Codex, Portugal.

10. *Romanian Union Conference* (organized 1919). Territory: Romania. Statistics (1992): churches, 897; members, 66,203; or-

dained ministers, 108; licensed ministers, 114; licensed missionaries, 16. Headquarters: Strada Plantelor 12, Bucharest, Romania.

Constituent organizations and their territories—*Banat Conference* (organized 1961; reorganized 1992): Arad, Bihor, Caras-Severin, Hunedoara, and Timis; *Moldavia Conference* (organized 1928; reorganized 1961): Bacau, Botosani, Galati, Iasi, Neamt, Suceava, Vaslui, and Vrancea; *Muntenia Conference* (organized 1928; reorganized 1961, 1992): Braila, Bucuresti, Buzau, Calarasi, Constanta, Dimbovita, Giurgiu, Ialomita, Ilfov, Prahova, and Tulcea; *North Transylvania Conference* (organized 1911; reorganized 1961, 1992): Alba, Bistrita Nasaud, Cluj, Maramures, Salaj, and Satu-Mare; *Oltenia Conference* (organized 1992): Arges, Dolj, Gorj, Mehedinti, Olt, Teleorman, and Vilcea; *South Transylvania Conference* (organized 1989; reorganized 1992): Brasov, Covasna, Harghita, Mures, and Sibiu.

11. *South German Union Conference* (organized 1912; reorganized 1970). Territory: the states of Baden-Wuerttemberg, Bavaria, Hessen, Rhineland-Palatinate, and Saarland. Statistics (1992): churches, 205; members, 13,957; ordained ministers, 90; credentialed missionaries, 29; licensed ministers, 17. Headquarters: Senefelderstrasse 15, Ostfildern-Ruit, Federal Republic of Germany. Official organ: *Adventecho.*

Constituent organizations and their territories—*Baden-Wuerttemberg Conference* (organized 1912; reorganized 1970): the state Baden-Wuerttemberg; *Central Rhenish Conference* (organized 1920; reorganized 1970): the states of Hessen, Rhineland-Palatinate, and Saarland; *North Bavarian Conference* (organized 1934): upper, central, and lower Franconia, and upper Palatinate; *South Bavarian Conference* (organized 1902; reorganized 1919): lower and upper Bavaria, and Swabia (including Regensburg).

12. *Spanish Union of Churches* (organized 1903; reorganized 1958, 1972, 1982). Territory: Andorra, Canary Islands, Gibraltar, and Spain. Statistics (1992): churches, 55; members, 5,964; ordained ministers, 34; credentialed commissioned ministers, 2; credentialed missionaries, 57; licensed ministers, 16; licensed missionaries, 58; teachers, 73; elementary schools, 4; secondary schools, 1. Headquarters: Calle Cuevas 23, Madrid, Spain.

13. *Swiss Union Conference* (organized 1928). Territory: Liechtenstein and Switzerland. Statistics (1992): churches, 57; members, 4,176; ordained ministers, 40; credentialed commissioned ministers, 15; credentialed missionaries, 3; licensed ministers, 6; licensed commissioned ministers, 1; licensed missionaries, 13; teachers, 8; elementary schools, 1; secondary schools, 1. Headquarters: Gubelstrasse 23, Zurich, Switzerland. Official organ: *Adventecho.*

Constituent organizations and their territories—*French Swiss Conference* (organized 1884): French- and Italian-speaking Switzerland; *German Swiss Conference* (organized 1901): Liechtenstein and German- and Romansh-speaking Switzerland.

14. *MISSERM* (under the direct supervision of the division) (organized 1928; reorganized 1966, 1993) (formerly North African Mission). Territory: Algeria, Morocco, and Tunisia. Headquarters: 63, Rue du Faubourg Poissonnière, Paris, France.

Institutions. Institutions in the Euro-Africa Division include the following:

Educational Institutions. Adventist Bible Seminary (Czech Republic); Adventist Private School (Switzerland); Bogenhofen Seminary (Austria); Friedensau Theological Graduate School (Germany); Italian Junior College (Italy); Lisbon Secondary School (Portugal); Marienhöhe Seminary (Germany); Mozambique Adventist Seminary (Mozambique); Oliveira do Douro Secondary School (Portugal); Romanian Adventist Theological Institute (Romania); Sagunto Adventist College (Spain); Saleve Adventist Institute (France).

Food Companies. German Health Food Factory (Germany); PHAG Food Factory (Switzerland); Spanish Food Factory (Spain).

Hospitals and Sanitariums. Berlin Hospital (Germany); Bongo Mission Hospital (Angola); Lake Geneva Sanitarium (Switzerland).

Retirement Homes and Orphanages. Basle Old People's Home (Switzerland); Berlin-Steglitz Old People's Home (Germany); Casa de Pensii si ajutoare a Bisericii Crestine Adventiste de Ziua a Saptea din Romania (Romania); Etablissement Medico-Social Le Flon (Switzerland); Forli Old People's Home (Italy); Friedensau Old People's Home (Germany); Haus Stefanie (Austria); Haus Wittelsbach Old People's Home (Germany); Lapi (Portugal); Maison de Retraite (France); Neandertal Old People's Home (Germany); Old People's Home (Switzerland); Spanish Old People's Home (Spain); Uelzen Old People's Home (Germany).

Media Centers. Adventist Foundation for

the Blind (Switzerland); Studio Media Production (France); Voice of Hope (Germany).

Publishing Houses. Advent Publishers (Switzerland); Angola Publishing House (Angola); Austrian Publishing House (Austria); Bulgarian Adventist Publishing House (Bulgaria); Czecho-Slovakian Publishing House (Czech Republic); Hamburg Publishing House (Germany); Italian Publishing House (Italy); Life and Health Publishing House (France); Mozambique Publishing House (Mozambique); Portuguese Publishing House (Portugal); Romanian Adventist Publishing House (Romania); Safeliz Publishing House (Spain).

Retreat Centers. Adventhaus Freudenstadt (Germany); Bergheim Muehlenrahmede (Germany); Friedensau Retreat (Germany); Waldpark Hohenfichte Retreat (Germany).

Global Mission. During the first three years of the 1990-1995 quinquennium the Euro-Africa Division baptized 82,931 souls (75 percent of their goal of 110,000) and established 733 new congregations.

Finance. The division leads the world field in the Annual Week of Sacrifice offering. Led by the German-speaking conferences, it provided more than US$1.3 million in 1992 to the world mission program.

Presidents: C. L. Powers, 1972-1975; Edwin Ludescher, 1975- .

EURO-ASIA DIVISION. A large unit of church organization comprised of the following territories: Armenia, Azerbaijan, Belarus, Georgia, Kazakhstan, Kyrgyzstan, Moldova, Russia, Tajikistan, Turkmenistan, Ukraine, and Uzbekistan.

Statistics (1994): churches, 803; members, 93,740; ordained ministers, 300; credentialed missionaries, 147. Headquarters: ul. Isakovskogo, No. 4 Korpus 1, Moscow, Russia.

The division was organized in 1990 with a membership of 34,338 members in 530 churches, being formed by 15 republics of the former USSR.

Constituent Organizations. The Euro-Asia Division is comprised of five union conferences and two attached fields.

1. *East Russian Union Mission* (organized 1994). Territory: Russia east of the Ural Mountains. Statistics (1994): churches, 73; members, 7,784; ordained ministers, 21. Headquarters: ul. Novo-Yamskaya 53, Irkutsk, Russia.

Constituent organizations and their territories—*East Siberian Mission* (organized 1993): Krasnoyarski Krai (including Evenkia, Khakassia, and Taimyr), Yakutia-Sakha republic, and the regions of Buryatia, Chita (including Achinski-Buryatski district), Irkutsk (including Ust'-Ordynski Buryatski district) and Tuva; *Far Eastern Mission* (organized 1992): Khabarovski Krai (including Jewish district) and Primorski Krai, and the regions of Amur, Kamchytka (including Koryaki), Magadan (including Tchukotka), and Sakhalin; *West Siberian Conference* (organized 1993): Altiiski Krai (including Gomo-Altaiiski district) and the regions of Kemerovo, Novosibirisk, Omsk, Tomsk, and Tyumen (including Khanty-Mansiisk and Yamalo-Nenetski districts).

2. *Moldova Union Conference* (organized 1989). Territory: Moldova. Statistics (1994): churches, 84; members, 7,417; ordained ministers, 29; credentialed missionaries, 36. Headquarters: ul. Bernardatsi 22, Kishinev, Moldova.

Constituent organizations and their territories—*Northern Moldova Conference* (organized 1989): northern part of Moldova; *Southern Moldova Conference* (organized 1989): southern part of Moldova.

3. *Southern Union Conference* (organized 1990; reorganized 1994). Territory: Kazakhstan, Kyrgyzstan, Tajikistan, Turkmenistan, and Uzbekistan. Statistics (1994): churches, 54; members, 4,417; ordained ministers, 31; credentialed missionaries, 15. Headquarters: ul. Tatarskaya 33, Almaty, Kazakhstan.

Constituent organizations and their territories—*Central Asia Conference* (organized 1978; reorganized 1994): Tajikistan, Turkmenistan, and Uzbekistan; *Kazakhstan Conference* (organized 1979; reorganized 1994): Kazakhstan regions of Akmola, Aktyubinsk, Almaty, Dzherhazgan, East Kazakhsky, Gyriev (Atyran), Karaganda, Kokchetav, Kustanai, North Kazakhsky, Pavlodar, Semipalatinsk, Taldy-Kurgan, and Uralsk; *Southern Conference* (organized 1978; reorganized 1994): southern regions of Kazakhstan (Chimkent, Dzhambul, and Kzyl Orda) and Kyrgyzstan.

4. *Ukrainian Union Conference* (organized 1977; reorganized 1988). Territory: Ukraine. Statistics (1994): churches, 378; members, 40,140; ordained ministers, 109; credentialed missionaries, 70. Headquarters: ul. Lukyanovskaya 9-B, Kiev, Ukraine.

Constituent organizations and their territories—*Bukovinskaya Conference* (Chernovtsy) (organized 1978): Chernovtsy region; *Central*

Ukrainian Conference (organized 1978; reorganized 1987): Cherkassy, Chernigov, Kiev, Poltava, and Sumy regions; *Eastern Ukrainian Conference* (organized 1981; reorganized 1987): Dnepropetrovsk, Donetsk, Kharkov, Lugansk, and Zaporozhye regions; *Podolsk Conference* (organized 1981): Khmelnitsky, Vinnitsa, and Zhitomir regions; *Southern Ukrainian Conference* (organized 1967; reorganized 1987): Crimea, Kherson, Kirovograd, Nikolayev, and Odessa regions; *Western Ukrainian Conference* (organized 1978; reorganized 1991): Ivano-Frankovsk, L'vov, Rovno, Ternopol, Volynsky, and Zakarpatsy regions.

5. *West Russian Union Conference* (organized 1994). Territory: Russia west of the Ural Mountains. Statistics (1994): churches, 185; members, 29,903; ordained ministers, 72. Headquarters: P.O. Box 51, Klimovsk, Moscow region, Russia.

Constituent organizations and their territories—*Central Conference* (organized 1994): Komi ASSR and the regions of Ivanovo, Kaliningrad, Kostroma, Moscow, Smolensk, Vladimir, and Yaraslavl; *North Caucasus Conference* (organized 1994): Krasnadarski Krai (including Adygeya) and Stavropolski (including Krarachyaero-Tcherkessia), the republics of Chechenо-Ingushetia, Dagestan, Kabardino-Balkaria, Kalmykia, and North Osetiya, and the Rostov region; *Northwestern Conference* (organized 1994): Karelija republic and the regions of Arhangelsk (including Nenetski district), Murmansk, Novgorod, Pskov, St. Petersburg, Tver, and Vologda; *Southern Conference* (organized 1994): the regions of Belgorod, Bryansk, Kaluga, Kursk, Lipetsk, Orlov, Riazan, Tambov, Tula, and Voronezh; *Ural Conference* (organized 1994): the republics of Bashkortostan and Udmurita and the regions of Chelyabinsk, Ekaterinburg, Kurgan, Orenburg, and Perm (including the Komi-Permyatski district); *Volga Conference* (organized 1994): the regions of Astrakhan, Penza, Samara, Saratov, Ul'yanovsk, and Volgograd; *Volgo-Vyatskaya Conference* (organized 1994): the republics of Chuvashia, Mari-El, Mordovia, and Tataria, and the regions of Kirov and Nijegorodskaya.

6. *Attached fields—Belarus Conference* (organized 1978): Belarus. Headquarters: 1 Tyrazhny per. 3, Minsk, Belarus.

Trans-Caucasus Field (organized 1994): Armenia, Azerbaijan, and Georgia.

Institutions. Source of Life Publishing House (Russia); Voice of Hope (Russia); Zaokski Theological Seminary (Russia).

History. For the history of the work in the Euro-Asia Division, see specific names of countries in the area of the division.

Presidents: M. P. Kulakov, 1990-1992; Ted N. C. Wilson, 1992- .

EUROPEAN DIVISION. A unit of church organization that functioned from 1913 to 1928.

Beginning in 1901, the European unions and their mission territories were treated as a unit, called the European General Conference (1901 to 1903), later in the *Yearbook,* the General European Conference (1904-1907). Since 1903 the General Conference had had a vice president for Europe. By 1909 this territory was referred to as the European Division, but the lack of definition led to the European request in 1912 for constitutional provision for a full-fledged organization of the European and other divisions. Consequently, at the 1913 General Conference session, action was taken to set up a pattern under which divisions were to operate as integral units of the General Conference organization, with full staffs and with presidents who were also vice presidents of the General Conference *(see* Organization). The European Division territory was defined as "Europe; the Russian and the Turkish possessions in Asia; Persia, Arabia, and Afghanistan; and that part of Africa not included in Rhodesia, British Central Africa, and the Union of South Africa." After the disruption of World War I the division was reorganized (1920). In 1928 it operated the Arabic, East African, Ethiopian, and West African Union missions, and other missions in Persia, Turkey, Madagascar, Mauritius, Faroe Islands, and Iceland. In 1928 it was divided into four divisions—the Northern European Division, Central European Division, Southern European Division, and what was known as the Federation of Seventh-day Adventists in the USSR. (Part of the Central European Division's mission territory became, many years later, in 1951, the Middle East Division.)

The president of the European Division until 1922 was L. R. Conradi. L. H. Christian was president from 1922 to 1928.

For Seventh-day Adventist history and institutions in these territories, see the successor divisions and their respective countries.

EUROPEAN INSTITUTE OF WORLD MISSION (EIWM). An institution founded in

1982 with the following objectives:

1. To review and reaffirm the mission of the church and to define the role of the interdivision worker in the fulfillment of that mission.

2. To acquaint newly appointed interdivision workers with the conditions and problems they will meet in their respective fields of service and prepare them to relate to these conditions and problems in a tactful and Christian manner.

3. To study current issues in world mission and how interdivision workers can relate to them successfully.

4. To inform interdivision workers of the general policies and procedures that will directly affect their term of overseas service. The EIWM serves and is governed by the two European-based divisions, namely, the Euro-Africa Division and the Trans-European Division, by operating annually four-week training courses for missionaries, called from Europe to serve in other parts of the Seventh-day Adventist world field, and also to acquaint personnel called from other divisions to work in Europe with the new cross-cultural situation in which they will find themselves. The four-week mission institute program covers such areas as mission theology, mission anthropology, area studies, church growth, mission structure and practice, the missionary family, missionary relationships, tropical health and hygiene, SDA Church policies and finances, ADRA, AWR, and other specialist subjects important for the missionary.

The European Institute of World Mission is accredited with Andrews University (through Newbold College) and grants both undergraduate and postgraduate credit to participants. The institutes are conducted alternately in the Euro-Africa Division and Trans-European Division territories on the campuses of Saleve Adventist Institute, Collonges, France, and Newbold College, England.

The EIWM is administered by a board consisting of the officers of the two European-based divisions, the principals of the host colleges, and the mission institute director, Borge Schantz. The European Institute of World Mission has produced two major readers for SDA evangelistic outreach programs, namely, "Adventist Missions Facing the 21st Century" (1990) and "Cast the Net on the Right Side" (1993), on crucial issues for witnessing to Western people.

EUROPEAN MISSION. *See* Angola.

EVANGELISM, PUBLIC. Seventh-day Adventists believe that evangelism—the proclamation of the gospel—is the very heart of Christianity. From the early days of the Seventh-day Adventist Church, public evangelism has played a major role in the growth and development of the denomination. It began with a handful of devoted preachers holding meetings among little groups of those who had taken part in the Millerite movement. As concepts widened, it was not long until the church realized its mission to carry the three angels' messages (Rev. 14:6-12) to "every nation, and kindred, and tongue, and people" (v. 6).

There were at first no settled pastors of churches. Congregations led by lay elders were expected to carry on lay evangelism with the occasional aid of the ministers. Today local pastors are still expected to hold evangelistic meetings from time to time.

Among the first generation of SDA evangelists may be listed Joseph Bates, James White, George W. Holt, and Samuel W. Rhodes.

As the membership of the church grew, public evangelism continued to be an important part of the soul-winning program of the church. Ellen White encouraged these efforts by her periodical articles, special testimonies, personal counsels, and addresses over the years, many of which have been collected and published as a book entitled *Evangelism.*

At the present time public evangelism is conducted by full-time itinerant evangelists, who move from place to place within a conference or union; by district pastors, who hold meetings within their districts; and by lay evangelists.

As times changed, methods also changed, and evangelism has come to include radio and television programs, correspondence lessons, and other methods, such as health evangelism programs, Revelation and Prophecy seminars, and Sequence Evangelism seminars.

International programs such as those produced by the Voice of Prophecy, Faith for Today, Breath of Life, and It Is Written are a focal point for evangelism. The Adventist Media Center sponsors the Adventist Evangelistic Association, directed by C. Lloyd Wyman, which coordinates the public evangelism emphasis of the various media programs, with evangelists conducting meetings throughout North America. It Is Written builds its program around the purchase of time on television stations, with local follow-up through personal visiting and public meetings.

Since 1972 a yearly coordinated evangelistic thrust has been adopted in many of the world divisions. These have been designated as MISSION '72, '73, '74, '75, Thousand Days of Reaping, Harvest 90, and Global Mission. MISSION '75 inaugurated an integrated health evangelism approach known as the Century 21 Better Living Institute. Later another health evangelism program known as Your Health and Your Future was developed by *Life and Health* magazine and the General Conference Ministerial Association. Every-member involvement in evangelism especially characterizes these approaches.

See also Evangelistic Centers; Lay Evangelism; Minister: Communication, Department of; Remnant Church.

EVANGELISTIC CENTERS. Institutions designed for big-city evangelism through multiple methods. The program of a center includes youth meetings, welfare activities, cooking schools, and other health education programs, regular weekly public evangelistic services, Bible classes, and usually a reading room. Often a church organization is connected with an evangelistic center, and regular Sabbath services are conducted. The supreme object of evangelistic centers is soul winning. Goodwill and pleasing public relations are maintained while every possible method and program in approaching the minds of men with the gospel of Jesus Christ are being employed.

Limited availability and high rentals of halls in large metropolitan areas, as well as the need for multiphase programs reaching mind, body, and spirit, led to the evangelistic center concept. After visiting such an evangelistic center developed by another denomination—the People's Church, in Toronto, Canada—H.M.S. Richards, of the *Voice of Prophecy* broadcast, suggested the incorporation of this idea in the Seventh-day Adventist program.

In 1952 the General Conference Spring Meeting allocated accumulated funds of the China Division for 1952, 1953, and 1954, which could no longer be used in China, for the establishment of evangelistic centers in London, New York, and Chicago. Centers also were established in other cities, such as Cairo, Egypt; Beirut, Lebanon; Osaka, Japan; Manila and Cebu, Philippines; and Djakarta, Indonesia. Most of the major centers had been sold by 1994, but a few continue to operate.

EVANS, ADELAIDE BEE (COOPER) (1870-1958). Editor of the *Youth's Instructor* from 1899 to 1904. She was born in the state of New York, and at the age of 13 began working at the Review and Herald publishing house at Battle Creek, Michigan, serving as proofreader and copy editor under Uriah Smith, G. G. Tenny, and A. T. Jones. In 1899 she became editor of the *Youth's Instructor.* Five years later she resigned to marry Irwin H. Evans, at that time manager of the Review and Herald Publishing Association. Later she shared in his missionary service in eastern Asia. She wrote several books for children and youth, among them *The Bible Year, Easy Steps in the Bible Story, The Children's Friend, Men of Might, Really Trulies, Stories of the Kings From David to Christ, Story of Esther,* and *Strange People and Customs.*

EVANS, IRWIN HENRY (1862-1945). Administrator, General Conference vice president, author. A second-generation Seventh-day Adventist, he was educated at Battle Creek College. He was licensed as a minister in Michigan in 1882, transferred to Kentucky in 1885, and was ordained in 1886. Returning to Michigan, he served as conference president from 1891 until he became president of the General Conference Association in 1897. His next assignment was president of the Mission Board (1899).

In 1900 Evans was sent to Europe to settle the business problems of the Christiania Publishing House, which was facing bankruptcy. The following year he began a four-year term as president and manager of the Review and Herald. He was treasurer of the General Conference (1903-1909), president of the Asiatic Division (1909-1913), North American Division (1913-1918), and Far Eastern Division (1919-1930). Then he served as a general vice president of the General Conference until 1936, and a field secretary from 1936 until his retirement in 1941. From 1931 to 1941 he was also head of the Ministerial Association.

Known as a forceful preacher and writer, he was the author of several books, *The Preacher and His Preaching, Ministry of Angels, The Way of Divine Love,* and *This Is the Way.*

He took a keen interest in the development of the SDA Theological Seminary, and on several occasions taught homiletics there. He was to a considerable extent responsible for the development of the *Church Hymnal,* and wrote the hymn "Welcome, Day of Sweet Repose."

EVANS, L. C. (1901-1983). Pastor, evangelist, administrator. He was born in Ohio and in 1920 married Lela Goldsmith. Shortly after their marriage they became Seventh-day Adventists, and in 1926 entered the literature ministry in Zanesville, Ohio. Soon the conference gave him three churches to pastor while continuing his canvassing. Later he served in full-time pastoral work in the Ohio Conference.

The Florida Conference called him to pastoral and evangelistic work in 1936. In the 1940s he was president of the Florida Conference. Later he served in this capacity in the Greater New York and Southern New England conferences. In 1952 he was invited to be president of the Southwestern Union Conference, where he served until his retirement in 1966. During his administration he launched and directed a strong development program for Southwestern Junior College, looking toward its becoming a senior college.

EVERSON, CHARLES THEODORE (1874-1956). Evangelist, missionary. During the early part of his ministry he served as chaplain in Chicago and San Francisco missions. From 1902 to 1909 he conducted evangelistic meetings in Italy and helped to organize the work in that country. Returning to the United States, he held evangelistic meetings in Chicago, New York, and other principal cities. He published a collection of his lectures, entitled *The Last Warning Message,* and several pamphlets.

EVIL, ORIGIN OF. Seventh-day Adventists believe that moral evil originated in heaven prior to the creation of our world, when Lucifer, most exalted of the angels, became jealous of the Son of God and rebelled against divine authority; that evil is thus defiance of God and a revolt against His righteous authority and goodness. They hold that although the Bible makes no propositional, definitive statement concerning the origin of evil, two OT passages allude to the event in highly figurative language. Under the figure of the king of Tyre, Eze. 28:12-19 portrays Lucifer, as Satan is known prior to his rebellion, as a covering cherub who, though "full of wisdom, and perfect in beauty," became "corrupted" and was cast "out of the mountain of God." Isa. 14:12-14 describes Lucifer under the figure of the king of Babylon. He was determined to establish his throne "above the stars of God," but has instead "fallen from heaven." Ultimately he is to "be brought down to hell, to the sides of the pit" (v. 15), or, in the words of Ezekiel, to be reduced to "ashes upon the earth."

The NT makes occasional reference to Satan as being the originator of evil (see John 8:44; 1 John 3:8). It suggests also that in his rebellion against God, Satan won the sympathy of a large number of the angels who shared his fate in being cast out of heaven, and who will be destroyed with him at the day of judgment (2 Peter 2:4; Jude 6). In a passage usually considered as describing the original conflict in heaven as well as a secondary clash at the time of Christ's crucifixion, John the revelator says that "there was war in heaven," in which "Michael and his angels" were victorious. Satan "was cast out into the earth, and his angels were cast out with him."

The writings of Ellen White provide additional details on the origin of evil that are in accord with the brief statements of Scripture. For instance, she declares that God was in no way responsible for evil, but that "sin began with Satan" *(Review and Herald* 63:145, Mar. 9, 1886). She enumerates three main causes of Lucifer's rebellion: (1) pride in his own glory, (2) jealousy of Christ's position and authority, and (3) resentment toward God's authority. In her various works she traces the origin of evil thus: "Little by little, Lucifer came to indulge a desire for self-exaltation. . . . Instead of seeking to make God supreme in the affections and allegiance of His creatures, it was Lucifer's endeavor to win their service and homage to himself. And coveting the honor which the infinite Father had bestowed upon His Son, this prince of angels aspired to power which it was the prerogative of Christ alone to wield. . . . Pride in his own glory nourished the desire for supremacy. . . . He gloried in his brightness and exaltation, and aspired to be equal with God" (GC 494, 495).

"When God said to His Son, 'Let us make man in our image,' Satan was jealous of Jesus. He wished to be consulted concerning the formation of man, and because he was not, he was filled with envy, jealousy, and hatred" (EW 145).

"Satan grew bold in his rebellion, and expressed his contempt of the Creator's law. . . . He claimed that angels needed no law but should be left free to follow their own will, which would ever guide them right; that law was a restriction of their liberty; and that to abolish law was one great object of his standing as he did" (SR 18, 19).

"God, in His great mercy, bore long with Lucifer. He was not immediately degraded from his exalted station when he first indulged the spirit of discontent, nor even when he began to present his false claims before the loyal angels. Long was he retained in heaven" (GC 495, 496).

"The heavenly councils pleaded with Lucifer. The Son of God presented before him the greatness, the goodness, and the justice of the Creator, and the sacred, unchanging nature of His law" *(ibid.* 494).

"Again and again he [Lucifer] was offered pardon, on condition of repentance and submission. . . . But pride forbade him to submit. He persistently defended his own course, maintained that he had no need of repentance, and fully committed himself, in the great controversy, against his Maker" *(ibid.* 496).

When the spirit of discontent and disaffection had ripened into open revolt, "all the heavenly host were summoned to appear before the Father" (SR 18).

"Satan unblushingly made known his dissatisfaction that Christ should be preferred before him. He stood up proudly and urged that he should be equal with God and should be taken into conference with the Father and understand His purposes. God informed Satan that to His Son alone He would reveal His secret purposes, and He required all the family in heaven, even Satan, to yield Him implicit, unquestioned obedience; but that he (Satan) had proved himself unworthy of a place in heaven. Then Satan exultingly pointed to his sympathizers, comprising nearly one half of all the angels, and exclaimed, 'These are with me! Will you expel these also, and make such a void in heaven?' He then declared that he was prepared to resist the authority of Christ and to defend his place in heaven by force of might, strength against strength. . . . Then there was war in heaven. The Son of God, the Prince of heaven, and His loyal angels engaged in conflict with the archrebel and those who united with him. The Son of God and true, loyal angels prevailed; and Satan and his sympathizers were expelled from heaven. All the heavenly host acknowledged and adored the God of justice. Not a taint of rebellion was left in heaven. All was again peaceful and harmonious as before" *(ibid.* 18, 19).

SDA belief concerning the origin of evil is essentially the same as that traditionally held by most other Christian churches. *See* Fall, The; Satan and His Angels.

EVOLUTION. *Mechanistic Evolution.* The theory of organic evolution holds that all living forms in the world, plant and animal, including humanity, are descendants of one or of a few simple organisms, which in turn arose by chance from nonliving matter. It is held that the present level of development has been accomplished by the cumulative effect of small changes from generation to generation over a vast period of time, possibly 4 billion years or more. Simple, primitive, archaic forms are supposed to have given rise to a variety of types, which by continued divergence would produce a branching treelike mosaic of life. The majority of present-day biologists hold that this process of descent with modification, whereby new species and basic types are supposed to have arisen, has occurred by a strictly random or chance process, with natural selection eliminating the less fit. This concept is called *mechanistic evolution,* or *materialism.*

Theistic Evolution. Because of the overwhelming complexity of even the simplest forms of life and the improbability of life arising spontaneously from inorganic matter, some allow that the original simple forms may have been specially created. Others hold that the entire evolutionary process has been under the guidance of a Supreme Being of infinite wisdom—that God has "created" all things by this method. A common view among both Catholic and Protestant scientists and theologians, including some evangelicals, is that when humanity had reached a certain evolutionary level—a few thousand years ago at the "creation week"—the Creator endowed humans with those characteristics by which they became moral beings capable of recognizing the difference between right and wrong, capable of sinning, and with the capacity for appreciation of esthetic, ethical, and spiritual values. These concepts are all forms of *theistic evolution.*

Seventh-day Adventist Position. SDA theologians and scientists reject both mechanistic and theistic evolution, on both scriptural and scientific grounds. In 1864 Ellen G. White pointed out that "when men leave the word of God in regard to the history of creation, and seek to account for God's creative works upon natural principles, they are upon a boundless ocean of uncertainty. . . . His creative works are just as incomprehensible as His existence" (3SG 93).

"The genealogy of our race, as given by inspiration, traces back its origin, not to a line of developing germs, mollusks, and quadrupeds, but to the great Creator" (PP 45).

Some years later L. A. Smith pointed out that any attempt to explain Creation by evolution is beset with "insurmountable difficulties" *(Review and Herald* 81:4, Sept. 15, 1904).

Advocates of the theory of evolution generally assume that the Bible precludes the possibility of any change of species, and that evidences of such change therefore disprove the Bible and confirm evolution. The typical attitude is reflected in a sentence from a letter written by Darwin in 1844 to a close friend and eminent botanist Joseph Hooker: "I am almost convinced (quite contrary to the opinion I started with) that species are not (it is like confessing a murder) immutable" (E. Nordenskiold, *The History of Biology,* pp. 463, 464). But while the Scriptures mention a great variety of different, complex animals and plants as being present at the end of Creation week, it does not indicate that changes would not take place, especially after sin entered the world. In fact, the curse of Gen. 3:17, 18 implies that unfavorable changes would occur. From the first, SDA writers have recognized change of species (G. W. Amadon, in *Review and Herald* 16:122, Sept. 4, 1860). But this, of course, is very different from the sort of change required for the origin of new higher categories—the orders, classes, and phyla of animals and plants.

Ellen White's reference in 1864 to the almost "endless variety of species of animals" indicates that new species have been formed (3SG 75). In 1902 G. M. Price noted that the real point of difference between the Genesis record and the Darwinian philosophy is not whether sufficient variation has occurred to "produce practically new and distinct species. The fossils show us that species have varied sufficiently to produce very distinct morphological and structural difference. . . . But the real question is whether the general run of these changes have not all been in the direction of degeneration" *(Outlines of Modern Science and Modern Christianity*, p. 199).

It might be noted that many of the most evident changes in nature—such as parasites with rudimentary digestive systems, flightless birds, and beetles with fused wing covers—represent reductions or loss of structures, or specializations.

Fundamental arguments against evolution used in recent years by SDA writers include: (1) the improbability of spontaneous generation of life from nonliving material, inasmuch as scientists still do not know what life is; (2) the inadequacy of known mechanisms of change to bridge the gulf between widely different structural and physiological characteristics by which the major groups of organisms differ from one another; (3) the unfitness for survival of hypothetical intermediates, incipient stages between many delicately balanced organ systems; (4) the tremendous preponderance of harmful or lethal effects in hereditary changes such as mutations and chromosomal aberrations; (5) the total absence of transitional series of forms connecting different major types in the fossil record of past life—higher categories such as classes, orders, and nearly all families as well (if the various phyla and orders arose by evolution, at least a few of the transitional sequences, or missing links, should have been preserved, but such series are not known to exist); (6) the presence in the lowest sedimentary rock layers in which an appreciable number of fossils occur in any abundance—the Cambrian—of a wide variety of highly complex animal forms wholly modern in structural detail; and (7) the existence of an evident design and purpose in nature, of features that exhibit a degree of complexity far beyond our ability to comprehend. Divine creation seems to be the only reasonable solution.

Analysis makes it abundantly clear that nearly all the valid scientific evidence for evolution is, in fact, evidence of change of the type that SDA creationists accept as having certainly occurred since the Creation as they conceive of its having occurred. Support for the more fundamental changes required by the theory of evolution is tenuous, uncertain, and completely inconclusive. No scientific discovery has yet given an informed creationist reason to doubt the Bible record of a fiat creation. It is the theories, not the observed facts, of the natural world that are in conflict with the Scripture record.

See Creation; Science and Religion.

EXCELSIOR ACADEMY. *See* Spain.

EXECUTIVE COMMITTEE. *See* General Conference Executive Committee.

F

FABRICA DE PRODUCTOS FRUITIGRAN. *See* South American Division Health Food Company.

FABRICA DE PRODUCTOS SUPERBOM. *See* South American Division Health Food Company.

FABRIQUE DE PRODUITS DIETETIQUES. *See* PHAG Food Factory.

FACULTY OF RELIGION. *See* Loma Linda University.

FAEROE ISLANDS. *See* Faroe Islands.

FAGAL, WILLIAM A. (1919-1989). Television pioneer. Born in Albany, New York, to a young couple who were already immersed in lay work in the Seventh-day Adventist Church, William, along with his brother, Harold, were early dedicated to the gospel ministry. Harold claims that as a child he was "baptized" countless times by his older brother.

With his goal of presenting to the world the news of a soon-coming Saviour, William was a "young man in a hurry." He rushed through public high school in three years and at 16 enrolled at Atlantic Union College, where he enthusiastically embraced his theology studies. He graduated in 1939 as president of his class and was hired by the New York Conference; he was then given full charge of six churches along a 150-mile (240-kilometer) stretch of the southern counties of that state. He was 20 years old.

In 1940 Fagal chose the little Corning church for his first effort, and within a year the membership had tripled to 90. In that same year he married his college sweetheart, Virginia Rittenhouse. She would later assist him on the nation's television screens as cohost of *Faith for Today*.

In the summer of 1941 Fagal was privileged to study evangelism under J. L. Shuler. In 1942 the 23-year-old pastor was ordained to the gospel ministry, and three days later he was asked to conduct a full-scale evangelistic campaign in the 3,000-seat Kleinhans Music Hall in Buffalo, New York. Despite his limited experience, and with only two months to prepare, Fagal accepted the challenge. Within 18 months 150 converts were baptized. He was then called to the Washington Avenue church in downtown Brooklyn, where he arrived on his twenty-fifth birthday.

During the next six years Fagal baptized between 50 and 100 per year. He also broadcast "live" each Sunday morning over station WHN.

In April 1950 a committee from the General Conference called on Fagal to produce a weekly television program. He had only six weeks to prepare the first *Faith for Today* telecast. Fagal's burden was for the unchurched, "to show them what God is really like." The result was true-to-life dramatized stories—modern parables that followed the example of Jesus, who "without a parable spake . . . not unto them" (Matt. 13:34).

By December of that first year the program's outreach had grown to an 11-station "live" network extending as far west as Nebraska and Texas, with Los Angeles and San Francisco being served by kinescope. By 1956 the filmed program was on scores of stations, and by 1967, 320 stations throughout the world were airing it, a large proportion of them free as a public service.

Fagal became a much-loved preacher to audiences throughout the country. He excelled in biographical preaching, bringing life to many Bible characters.

He wrote 21 books, and for a number of years wrote a weekly column for *Signs of the Times*. His full-message book *By Faith I Live* was designated the denomination's Book of the Year for 1966, selling more than 300,000 copies in the first six months. His book *Three Hours to Live* (also printed under the title *By God's Grace, Sam*) has circulated even more widely and has been translated into several languages.

In recognition of Fagal's service to the Seventh-day Adventist Church, Andrews University awarded him the Doctor of Divinity degree in 1967, and in 1980 he was the recipient of the Charles Weniger Award for Excellence. He preached to uncounted millions in his lifetime, but if asked how he wished to be addressed—whether as elder, doctor, or pastor—he would say pastor, for to him that simple term described how he felt about his mission in caring for the worldwide "flock" God had given him.

FAITH AND WORKS. In the NT the believer's confidence in and acceptance of what Christ has done to make reconciliation with God possible is called faith. Conversely, what someone may attempt to do, through compliance with ritual requirements or by charitable deeds, to earn merit with God as a means of salvation is called works. In this sense, faith and works are seen as mutually exclusive, as are light and darkness. Paul's Epistle to the Galatians is the apostle's classic reply to the theory that Christians, who presumably have found salvation by faith in Christ, can better their standing with God and become more eligible for His grace by efforts of their own—specifically, by complying with the ritual requirements of the Jewish religious system. Paul's categorical censure of the Galatians' attempt to find salvation by adding the works of the Jewish ritual law to faith in Christ is applicable to all in every age who suppose that they can earn merit toward salvation by compliance with any legal requirements, even those of the moral law.

In later centuries, however, the idea that ritual performance, penance, and charitable deeds sufficed to expiate a person's sins, and entitled that individual to salvation, eclipsed the NT concept of righteousness by faith alone. This great truth—that men and women are wholly dependent upon faith in Christ and His righteousness—was restored by the Reformation of the sixteenth century, and constitutes the very essence of Seventh-day Adventist belief and practice today.

Walking on earth as a man, Jesus exemplified perfect righteousness. Dying on the cross, He satisfied the law's demand, so that through faith repentant sinners may come into a right relationship to Christ. Outside of Christ, trusting in their own works, they would be confronted with the full demand of the law as the standard by which character is to be judged, and would be wholly unable to satisfy its claims upon them. Even perfect compliance with God's moral requirements subsequent to conversion, if such were possible, would not atone for a past life of sin; hence the sinner's need of faith in and utter dependence upon the vicarious death of Christ and His enabling power to live in harmony with the will of God. Christ's saving righteousness is complete and sufficient; humans can add nothing to it.

If the Galatians would abandon the works-righteousness prescribed by the ritual law and find salvation by faith in Christ, says Paul, the good works of the Holy Spirit would be manifest in their lives (Gal. 5:22, 23; 6:2), not as a means to salvation but as the result of it. And, as James explains, faith unaccompanied by this kind of works is dead (James 2:20; 3:13). Such "good works" are the inevitable product of genuine salvation by faith (Eph. 2:10; Heb. 8:10). They are the works of faith, not of the law. Without them a person's faith is utterly vain. Faith works by love to produce a life of obedience and fruits unto holiness. Faith results not only in a right relationship to God but also in a cooperation with Him that makes possible a likeness to Christ in both spirit and conduct. Where living faith exists there will always be corresponding works. Good works of faith manifest in the life of the believer prepare him or her to enjoy the fellowship of heavenly beings. They demonstrate that he or she chooses to walk in loving obedience to God here and so can be trusted in a perfect world *(Review and Herald* 92:10, Sept. 23, 1915). Such a life proves that the believer's profession of faith in Christ is not in vain. The absence of good works in a professing Christian's life is evidence that he or she is still under the dominion of sin, despite profession of faith in Christ. The loving and obedient response of good works reveals a sincere and complete surrender to God and to His will *(ibid.* 67:612, Oct. 7, 1890). The Holy Spirit is said to write God's moral law upon the heart (Heb. 8:10).

The gospel saves from sin and unto righteousness. Those who would dwell with God and the angels will not love darkness, nor will they indulge in works that are evil. The good works of faith are an expression of loving gratitude to God (John 14:15, 23). No one can give evidence of a living faith if there is an absence of good works, of victory over sin (Matt. 7:16-20). A professed Christian destitute of good works gives no evidence of having been saved by Christ, or of union with Christ.

In no small measure the debate about the relationship between faith and works is a matter of semantics—of differing definitions read into the words "works" and "law," of neglect to ascertain from the context of passages of

Scripture cited the sense in which the terms are used, and of failure on the part of those in dialogue to recognize these differences. Often, for instance, there is failure to recognize that by "law" the Bible writers usually mean the revelation of God's will as recorded in Scripture, particularly the Pentateuch (Ps. 119; Luke 24:44), but also at times (as in Gal. 3:2, 4) the Jewish religious system of rites and ceremonies (which is an integral part of "the law" in the former sense). Similarly "works" and "works of law," when used in the context of the Jewish religious system, always refer to the ritual requirements of this "law" (e.g., Gal. 2:16; 3:2). Often those on one side or the other of the law-grace, faith-works dialogue restrict the word "law" to the Decalogue. This is the sense in which SDAs usually speak of the "law." A discussion involving the terms "faith," "works," and "law" should begin with a clear definition of these words and a recognition of the sense in which the various Bible writers use them. In each use of one of these words, those in dialogue should make clear the sense intended.

Finding many passages of Scripture in which "the law" is spoken of in a favorable sense as "holy," "just," "good," and "perfect," and as enduring forever (for example, Ps. 34:7; Matt. 5:17, 18; Rom. 7:12, 14), Seventh-day Adventists usually think of "works" as voluntary obedience to the moral law, or Decalogue, on the part of one who has *already* found salvation by faith in Christ. Sometimes the antinomian in dialogue also uses the word "law" in the sense of "Decalogue." But reading the depreciative declarations of Paul in Galatians about "the law" (the apostle's term for the Jewish religious system), the antinomian mistakenly concludes that obedience to the commands of the Decalogue must be the "works of the law" against which Paul inveighs so vehemently (Gal. 2:16, 21; 5:1-4). At other times the antinomian in dialogue understands "law" in the same sense in which Paul uses it, but leaps to the erroneous conclusion that because the moral principles enunciated in the Decalogue were incorporated into the old covenant ritual system at Mount Sinai, the Decalogue itself must have lapsed with that system at the cross. This person forgets that these principles were also to be incorporated into the new covenant (Heb. 8:10, 11). Antinomians seem to be blind to the fact that the moral principles set forth in the Decalogue have always had an independent existence apart from the Jewish religious system, and were never dependent upon it nor subordinate to it. This independent existence, apart from the Jewish or any other religious system, is based on the fact that the commands of the Decalogue express God's infinite, righteous character and will in terms adapted to humanity's understanding in its fallen condition. These principles are not relative to anything else, but absolute in the same sense that God Himself is absolute. *See* Law.

In Galatians the idea of "law" as the Jewish religious system merges imperceptibly into that of law in an abstract sense to mean *any* law, and "works of law" to mean legalism as a way of salvation. When "law" is used to mean the Jewish religious system with its rites and ceremonies, which became obsolete at the cross, and "works" to mean compliance with these ritual requirements, SDAs agree that faith and works (in this sense, as Paul uses the words in Galatians) are mutually exclusive. The same would be true if the principle set forth in the Epistle to the Galatians is applied to the Ten Commandments, and "works of law" is construed to mean a legalistic compliance with the moral principles of the Decalogue as a means to salvation. But when, as Seventh-day Adventists usually use the words, "law" is a synonym for the Decalogue and "works" is understood to mean compliance with its moral precepts—not as a means of salvation but as willing obedience rendered by a grateful son to the expressed will of a beneficent Father—then the two words are complementary, not contradictory. This agrees with Paul's teaching in Gal. 5:22, 23; 6:2. It was in this sense that C. M. Snow wrote: "Thus we see that there is no conflict between the law and the gospel [faith]. The one reveals sin, the other reveals the remedy. The one reveals the character of God, the other reveals the only arrangement whereby we can have bestowed upon us a likeness of that character. The one reveals heaven's rule of government, the other reveals the only arrangement God has made to counteract the effect of Satan's rebellion against that government. Thus do the two work together and thus will they continue to work together until sin and all the results of sin have been eradicated from the universe. Then will the gospel cease, for salvation will have been completed; but the law will never cease" *(Review and Herald* 83:6, Oct. 18, 1906).

See also Justification; Law; Law and Grace; Legalism; Righteousness by Faith; Sanctification.

FAITH FOR TODAY. A religious television ministry sponsored by the Seventh-day Adventist Church. As television rapidly developed, Seventh-day Adventist leaders began to see in this means of mass communication a powerful medium for reaching people's hearts and minds with the gospel. In the spring of 1950, at the urgent request of the Atlantic Union, a committee was appointed by the General Conference to investigate the possibility of telecasting on one of the New York City television stations. With the signing of a 13-week contract with WJZ-TV for release of an SDA telecast at 9:30 each Sunday evening, William A. Fagal, a pastor in New York City, who had conducted a successful six-year program of radio and public evangelism in the area, pioneered this project.

After wide counsel both within and without the denomination, the "parable approach" program format was adopted, which allowed for a wide latitude in subject matter to be presented in story form: the portrayal of everyday problems of life, followed by the Bible's solution; then a five-minute sermonet by the pastor to solidify the discussion in the story. Several gospel songs were included, the program ending with an invitation by Mrs. Fagal, along with her husband, to enroll in the Bible correspondence course. The new program, named *Faith for Today,* was launched on May 21, 1950, and it enjoys the distinction of being the longest-running nonnews program currently being aired on television. Only *Meet the Press* has had a longer run.

Sixty-six letters came in as the result of that first telecast, all of them requesting the Bible course and other material offered on the program, and the mail response continued to grow.

Upon action by the General Conference Committee in Autumn Council, Faith for Today expanded to network status in December 1950, reaching New York, Washington, D.C., Detroit, Chicago, Philadelphia, Birmingham, Minneapolis, Omaha, and Fort Worth. After the Voice of Prophecy radio group had presented a similar TV program beamed to Los Angeles and San Francisco for several months, these two stations were also added to the Faith for Today network.

In June of 1951 the first full-time Faith for Today quartet was formed, with Harold Lickey, first tenor; Walter Isensee, second tenor; Herbert Hohensee, baritone; and Lyle Jewel, bass.

At first local conference Bible schools cared for the Bible School enrollees, but Faith for Today began to operate its own Bible correspondence school in January 1952. That spring when funds for the expansion of the program seemed to be nonexistent, a providential opening occurred. The television station in Utica, New York, requested the privilege of showing Faith for Today kinescopes without cost, as a public service. Other stations rapidly followed, and the United States armed services asked for kinescopes to show in far-flung Army and Air Force bases throughout the world. Eventually more than 300 stations were showing Faith for Today each week, a large proportion as a public service.

It was not long before denominational leaders in other countries began forward strides in television planning. In January 1955 DZAQ-TV in Manila, the Philippines, began to use Faith for Today kinescopes, with a local address inserted. In the fall of 1956 in the very first week that television came to Australia, Faith for Today was televised in Sydney and three weeks later in Melbourne, thus becoming the first religious program to be seen in Australia. It was the same on Guam, where Faith for Today began to be aired during the first week of television operations.

During the fall of 1960 denominational leaders in Nigeria took advantage of a providential opening to have Faith for Today released regularly from Ibadan. Thus it was the first religious program to be shown on what was then Africa's first and only TV station. Another "first" occurred in November 1962, when the South American Division began its own version of Faith for Today in Portuguese in São Paulo, Brazil—the first non-government-sponsored religious telecast to be seen in all South America. Bermuda, Puerto Rico, and Korea were also showing the programs.

Until January 1956 all telecasting had been done "live." Changing to film made it possible to provide stations with better picture quality than the kinescopes afforded. To the parable approach were added interviews with missionaries and other Christians with meaningful stories to tell. By 1963 Faith for Today went to color, making the program more desirable in the big city areas.

The mail response grew from the original 66 letters to a high of 10,000 in a single week. In the first decade of the Bible school the lessons were requested by more than 1 million. To the Faith for Today Bible Course were soon added courses based on *The Great Controversy* and *The Desire of Ages.* Other courses followed—Daniel and Revelation, health and nutrition, and lessons for juniors and youth. In 1974 a new Daniel and Revelation course called "Today's Life" was released, and also a new full-message course under the title "Living Faith."

By the time Faith for Today celebrated its twenty-fifth anniversary, the Bible school had graduated more than 183,000 students, resulting in more than 24,000 known baptisms.

In 1972, after being based in New York City for 22 years, the telecast moved its headquarters to Thousand Oaks, California. Quality control was greatly enhanced in the new location with the development of a dedicated staff of SDA technicians, working hand in hand with the technical/professional assistance readily available in Hollywood. At the close of 1974 Faith for Today joined other denominational media components in the new Seventh-day Adventist radio, television, and film center complex in Thousand Oaks.

Soon after the move to California, the Faith for Today staff saw the potential for reaching secular viewers through a hospital-based drama program. The *Westbrook Hospital* series proved highly successful. In 1975 Faith for Today produced its first hour-long film—on the life and martyrdom of Reformer John Huss. Later several prime-time specials reached thousands of homes, and a thriving Christian film rental market resulted.

The year 1980 marked a major transition for the program. Pastor Fagal continued to be active, but turned the leadership of the organization over to Daniel G. Matthews. Pastor Matthews had broad experience as a pastor, public relations director, and conference administrator. He hosted an entirely new format in 1985 entitled *Christian Lifestyle Magazine,* featuring interviews and mini-documentaries of people who put their faith into action to make a difference for good in a needy world.

Out of *Christian Lifestyle Magazine, Lifestyle Magazine* was born in 1991. Using this approach, Faith for Today reaches a North American television audience of up to 1 million people each week. The program is also shown over the United States Armed Forces Television Network in 56 countries and over regular television outlets in Greece. In addition, the program's audio version airs on the 13 stations of the Adventist Radio Network and over Adventist World Radio-Europe.

To follow up, Faith for Today has established the Lifestyle Learning Center, offering material dealing with basic themes of the Bible: keys to wellness, nutrition, marriage, relationships, and parenting. Faith for Today likes to think of the program as the health voice of the Seventh-day Adventist Church. Through these means Faith for Today utilizes "the right arm of the message," continuing to guide the seeker to a deeper appreciation of and commitment to spiritual values.

See Lifestyle Magazine.

FAITH HEALING. *See* Healing, Faith.

FALKLAND ISLANDS (Islas Malvinas). A British crown colony (claimed by Argentina), formed by two large and more than 200 small islands situated in the southwest Atlantic, near the Strait of Magellan, about 300 miles (500 kilometers) east from the coast of Patagonia. The archipelago has an area of 4,618 square miles (11,960 square kilometers) and a population (1991) of approximately 2,100, mostly of British descent. The two main islands, whose coasts are deeply indented by numerous bays, are separated by Falkland Sound. The terrain varies from rugged to undulating. The climate is moist and the vegetation luxuriant. Exports consist mainly of wool, leather, fur, and whale oil.

Historical Background. Some claim that the archipelago was discovered in 1520 by Estevão Gomes, a deserter from Magellan's expedition; others, that it was discovered in 1594 by the British navigator John Davys. The first recorded settlement of the islands was made by the French in 1764. French mariners of Saint-Malo gave the islands the name of Malouines, which name was adopted by the Spaniards, who referred to them as the Maluinas, or Malvinas. They were under the control of the Spanish from 1775 until the independence of the countries that had formed the Viceroyalty of Rio de la Plata. Argentine sovereignty over the archipelago, through governors subject to Buenos Aires, ended in 1833, when the British occupied the islands by force. After the expulsion of the Argentineans, the use of Spanish was abandoned, and English became the language of the islands.

Development of Seventh-day Adventist Work. The first Seventh-day Adventist to work in these islands was the colporteur C. A. Nowlen, in 1893. He reported "excellent success" in selling SDA books there, including Ellen White's *Great Controversy.* Apparently no other SDAs visited these islands until 1933-1934, when Roy Chamberlayne, an English SDA colporteur, worked there. He sold big and small books, and was informed in April 1934 from Port Stanley that an old widow had started to keep the Sabbath. The Austral Union had voted to send a missionary colporteur to the islands as soon as possible, and authorized W. F. Miller, president of the Magellan Mission, to visit the Falklands in 1930 and 1936, but there is no record that either of these visits was made.

In November 1974 Benoní Cayrús, director of the Public Relations and Stewardship departments in the Austral Union, became the first SDA pastor to visit the Falkland Islands. He stayed nine days, and on Sabbath, November 16, conducted the first baptism for Christopher R. Spall, the son of an SDA missionary nurse in Africa. With the merger of the Patagonia Mission and the Buenos Aires Conference in 1972, the Falkland Islands became part of what was then the South Argentine Conference, with headquarters in the city of Buenos Aires. At this time they again belong to the South Argentine Mission, part of the Austral Union of the South American Division.

FALL COUNCIL. *See* Annual Council.

FALL, THE. The event by which human beings, created in the image of God and ordained to reflect His sinless character, forfeited the state of innocence, incurred the penalty of death, and introduced into the world the disorders resulting from sin. By partaking of the forbidden fruit in the Garden of Eden, Adam and Eve, progenitors of the human race, rebelled against divine authority and fell into a state of spiritual depravity from which they were unable to extricate themselves.

The Biblical Account. According to Gen. 2 and 3, God "planted a garden eastward in Eden; and there he put the man whom he had formed." Except for "the tree of knowledge of good and evil," all the resources of this garden were for the use and enjoyment of Adam and Eve. Concerning this tree God said, "Thou shalt not eat of it: for in the day that thou eatest thereof thou shalt surely die." The tree was reserved by God as a test of humanity's loyalty and obedience.

But one day as Eve was alone in the vicinity of the tree she heard a serpent say, "Yea, hath God said, Ye shall not eat of every tree of the garden?" Attracted by the phenomenon of a serpent speaking, she engaged in conversation with the creature. At last, persuaded by the argument that she would attain to a higher state of knowledge and experience by partaking of the fruit, she yielded to temptation and ate. Next she offered the fruit to Adam, and he too ate.

As the immediate result of their disobedience Adam and Eve were afraid, and hid themselves from the presence of God. When God called them to account for their conduct, Adam confessed his guilt but blamed Eve for tempting him, and Eve in turn blamed the serpent. God placed a curse upon the serpent for its part in the temptation, then said: "I will put enmity between thee and the woman, and between thy seed and her seed; it shall bruise thy head, and thou shalt bruise his heel." This statement has usually been understood as a message of hope to the disobedient pair, a promise that sin would eventually be destroyed by divine intervention. God told Adam and Eve that their lot in life would now be difficult, and that eventually they would die. He then sent the sinful pair out of Eden, lest they continue to eat of the tree of life, and sin be immortalized. Entrance to the garden was barred by angels with flaming swords.

By disobeying God, human beings suffered a moral fall, with consequent disorder and degeneration, not only to themselves and their posterity, but to the plant and animal kingdoms as well. See Rom. 5:12; 8:22.

Seventh-day Adventist View. SDAs understand the Bible story of the Fall to be a literal historical account. This view was held widely by the Christians who joined the Millerite movement in the mid-1800s and who later united to form the Seventh-day Adventist Church, and it has been held by the denomination since. Ellen White has expanded the account of the Fall given in broad outline in the Bible. She explains that Adam and Eve were told of Lucifer's rebellion in heaven, and of his determination to lead them to follow him in transgression.

"If separated from each other they would be in greater danger than if both were together. . . . God would not permit Satan to follow the holy pair with continual temptations. He could have access to them only at the tree of knowledge of good and evil" (SR 31).

"In order to accomplish his work unperceived, Satan chose to employ as his medium the serpent—a disguise well adapted for his purpose of deception.

"Eve had wandered near the forbidden tree, and her curiosity was aroused to know how death could be concealed in the fruit of this fair tree. She was surprised to hear her queries taken up and repeated by a strange voice. 'Yea, hath God said, Ye shall not eat of every tree of the garden.' Eve was not aware that she had revealed her thoughts by conversing to herself aloud; therefore, she was greatly astonished to hear her queries repeated by a serpent" (*Review and Herald* 43:82, Feb. 24, 1874).

He told Eve that by eating the fruit they would become "as gods." The act of eating of the forbidden fruit involved more than disobedience—it revealed "distrust of God's goodness, disbelief of His word, and rejection of His authority" (Ed 25). Its effects are seen in nature as well as in man: "All nature is confused; for God forbade the earth to carry out the purpose He had originally designed for it. . . . The curse of God is upon all creation. Every year it makes itself more decidedly felt" (Ellen G. White, in SDACom 1:1085).

As to the consequences of Adam's transgression on him and on his posterity, Ellen White wrote: "They [Adam and Eve] were told that their nature had become depraved by sin; they had lessened their strength to resist evil, and had opened the way for Satan to gain more ready access to them" (PP 61).

"Man had become so degraded by sin that it was impossible for him, in himself, to come into harmony with Him whose nature is purity and goodness" (*ibid.* 64).

Regarding the consequences of parental wrongdoing upon children, Ellen White declared: "It is inevitable that children should suffer from the consequences of parental wrongdoing, but they are not punished for the parents' guilt, except as they participate in their sins. It is usually the case, however, that children walk in the steps of their parents. By inheritance and example the sons become partakers of the father's sin. Wrong tendencies, perverted appetites, and debased morals, as well as physical disease and degeneracy, are transmitted as a legacy from father to son, to the third and fourth generation" (PP 306).

See Evil, Origin of; Satan and His Angels.

FALLING OF THE STARS. A phrase used of "falling stars," or meteor showers, especially of the great shower of Leonid meteors seen in America Nov. 12-13, 1833, the most spectacular star shower on record. (The Leonids were visible in the Eastern Hemisphere in major showers of lesser magnitude in 1866 and again in the Western in 1867.) These meteors, because of their preeminence and their timing, were taken by many Millerites and by Seventh-day Adventists as fulfilling certain Bible prophecies of signs in the natural world heralding the last days (Matt. 24:29; Rev. 6:13). For eyewitness descriptions and astronomical explanations of the Leonids see SB, Nos. 730-746.

FALSE PROPHET, THE. *See* Revelation, Interpretation of.

FAMINE RELIEF. *See* Adventist Development and Relief Agency International.

FAR EASTERN ACADEMY. A coeducational boarding school on the senior high school level, operated by the Far Eastern Division at Singapore. The 1974 secondary enrollment was 93, and faculty numbered 13.

The school was established in 1926 in temporary quarters in Shanghai, China, to provide a central, fully accredited secondary school for the children of missionaries throughout the Far East. In 1927 the school was moved to a campus provided for it on Ningkuo Road. To existing buildings were later added a chapel-industrial building and a boys' dormitory. Charles Larsen served as first principal.

Because of political unrest in 1937-1938, classes were carried on at Castle Peak, New Territories, Hong Kong. In 1939 the faculty and student body returned to Shanghai. In 1940 the school opened in September, only to close in November when the political situation made it advisable for most of the missionaries to return to their homeland.

As missionaries returned to China after World War II, the school again opened in Shanghai in the fall of 1946. However, in 1948, with the general evacuation of missionaries from China, Far Eastern Academy moved back to Hong Kong and finished the school year.

In 1949 the academy reopened its doors, this time at Singapore in the Far Eastern Division office, with R. A. Figuhr as teacher. Opening enrollment was only three pupils. A part of the school library and some of the equipment was shipped to Singapore from Hong Kong. The academy ceased operation for two years for lack of enough students to fill it. Though the attendance has never been large, the school has remained open from 1952 to the present.

In 1958 the school was moved to a three-story administration building, which provided offices, classrooms, laboratory, and library on the main floor, and on the lower level a kitchen and dining room. Classrooms were on the second floor. Two duplex buildings provided housing for four faculty families and guest rooms.

A former overseas home on the campus was turned into a classroom building to house the typing, biology, home economics, and industrial arts classrooms.

In 1970 the Southern Asia Division closed Vincent Hill School in India. Thus a larger number of secondary overseas students matriculated at the academy in Singapore. A new four-story dormitory building that also provided apartments for deans, an assembly hall, and additional classrooms was completed.

In 1992 the boarding portion of the Far Eastern Academy was closed, and Far Eastern Elementary School joined Far Eastern Academy to become a grades 1-10 day school. Beginning with the school year 1993-1994, the school accepted students in grades 1-8 only.

Principals: Charles Larsen, 1926-1929; Harry H. Morse, 1929-1932; Charles Larsen, 1932-1936; Harry H. Morse, 1936-1937; W. E. Anderson, 1937-1941; Wilton H. Wood, 1946-1949; John F. Bohner, Jr., 1952-1953; Leeta Hemme, 1953-1954; James M. Davis, 1954-1957; L. A. Benzinger, 1957-1958; Floyd G. Wood, 1958-1963; D. F. Aldridge, 1963-1966; G. O. Thompson, 1966-1970; G. H. Fisher, 1970-1974; D. R. Halenz (acting), 1974-1975; Dean Maddox, 1975-1979; Ron Anderson, 1979-1981; Arthur W. Robinson, 1981-1987; Gary L. Affolter, 1988-1992; John Zollbrecht, 1992-1993; Carol Ryan, 1993- .

FAR EASTERN DIVISION. A large unit of church organization to which is allotted the territory of Bangladesh, Brunei, Cambodia, Democratic People's Republic of Korea, Hong Kong, Indonesia, Japan, Laos, Macao, Malaysia (including Sabah and Sarawak), Myanmar, Philippines, Republic of Korea, Singapore, Sri Lanka, Taiwan, Thailand, Vietnam, and islands of the Pacific north of the equator, west of the international date line, and south of 50° north latitude (including Wake Island but excluding Kiribati north of the equator). In 1985 Bangladesh, Myanmar, and Sri Lanka, formerly with the Southern Asia Division, were added to the Far Eastern Division. The division is divided into the Japan and Korean union conferences, the Bangladesh, Central Philippine, East Indonesia, Myanmar, North Philippine, South China Island, South Philippine, and West Indonesia union missions, the Sri Lanka Union of Churches, and the Guam-Micronesia Mission of Seventh-day Adventists. Statistics (1992): churches, 4,949; members, 917,089; church or elementary schools, 632; ordained ministers, 1,467; licensed ministers, 801; Bible instructors, 49; teachers in primary schools, 1,405; teachers in universities, colleges, and secondary schools, 2,028. Headquarters are at 800 Thomson Road, Singapore 1129, Republic of Singapore. Official organ: *Far Eastern Division Outlook.*

Constituent Organizations. The Far Eastern Division comprises nine union missions, two union conferences, one union of churches, and one attached mission.

1. *Bangladesh Union Mission* (organized 1919; reorganized 1938, 1979). Territory: Bangladesh. Statistics (1993): churches, 67; membership, 8,560; ordained ministers, 23. Headquarters: Adventpur, 149, Mirpur Road No. 1, Shah Ali Bagh, Mirpur, Dhaka 1216, Bangladesh.

Constituent organizations and their territories—*East Bangladesh Region* (organized 1984; reorganized 1988): Banbarban, Brahmanbaria, Chandpur, Chittagong, Comilla, Cox's Bazar, Dhaka, Feni, Gazipur, Khagrachari, Lakshmipur, Manikganj, Munshiganj, Narayanganj, Narshingdi, Noakhali, and Rangamati; *North Bangladesh Mission* (organized 1988): Hobiganj, Jamalpur, Kishorgang, Maulavi Bazar, Mymensingh, Netrokona, Sherpur, Sunamganj, Sylhet, and Tangail; *South Bangladesh Mission* (organized 1988): Bagerhat, Barguna, Barisal, Chuadanga, Faridpur, Gopalgonj, Jessore, Jhalokathi, Jheraidah, Khulna, Kushtia, Madharipur, Magura, Meherpur, Narail, Patuakhali, Pirojpur, Rajbari, Sariatpur, Satkhira, and Vola; *West Bangladesh Mission* (organized 1984; reorganized 1988, 1994): Bogra, Chapinawabgonj, Dinajpur, Gaibanda, Joypurhat, Kurigram, Lalmonirhat, Nator, Nilphamari, Noagaon, Pabna, Panchagarh, Rajshahi, Rangpur, Sirajgonj, and Thakurgaon.

2. *Central Philippine Union Mission* (organized 1951; reorganized 1964). Territory: Visayan Islands. Statistics (1993): churches, 609; members, 130,165; ordained ministers, 44. Headquarters: 112 Gorordo Avenue, Cebu City, Philippines. Official organ: *Gaceta sa Iglesya* ("Church Gazette"), in Cebuan.

Constituent organizations and their territories—*Central Visayan Mission* (organized 1914; reorganized 1965): provinces of Bohol, Cebu, Masbate, and Ticao Islands; *East*

Visayan Mission (organized 1914; reorganized 1965): provinces of Eastern Samar, Leyte del Norte, Leyte del Sur, Northern Samar, and Western Samar; *Negros Conference* (organized 1962; reorganized 1994): provinces of Negros Occidental and Negros Oriental, and the island of Siquijor; *West Visayan Mission* (organized 1914; reorganized 1962): provinces of Aklan, Antique, Capiz, Guima-ras, Iloilo, and Romblon.

3. *East Indonesia Union Mission* (organized 1964; formerly part of the Indonesia Union Mission). Territory: Irian Jaya, Maluku Sangihe, Talaud, and Sulawesi. Statistics (1993): churches, 467; members, 56,548; church or elementary schools, 68; ordained ministers, 152; licensed ministers, 59; Bible instructors, 3; teachers, 218. Headquarters: Jalan B. W. Lapian 38, Manado, Sulawesi Utara, Indonesia. For official organ *see* West Indonesia Union Mission.

Constituent organizations and their territories—*Central Sulawesi Mission* (organized 1965): Buol Toli-toli, Donggala, Luwuk-Banggai, and Posso; *Irian Jaya Mission* (organized 1950; reorganized 1955): Irian Jaya; *Maluku* (Ambon) *Mission* (organized 1929): Maluku; *North Minahasa Mission* (organized 1923; reorganized 1971): north Maluku and north Minahasa; *Sangihe and Talaud Island Mission* (organized 1964): Sangihe and Talaud; *South Minahasa Mission* (organized 1923; reorganized 1971): Bolaang Mongondow, Gorontalo, and South Minahasa; *South Sulawesi Mission* (organized 1939): Buton, Muna, south Sulwesi, and southeast Sulawesi.

4. *Japan Union Conference* (organized 1917; reorganized 1919; consolidated 1975; reorganized 1984). Territory: Japan. Statistics (1993): churches, 108; members, 13,557; ordained ministers, 88. Headquarters: 846 Kamikawai-cho, Asahi-ku, Yokohama 241, Japan. Official organ: *Adobenchisto Raifu* ("Adventist Life").

Constituent organizations and their territories—*East Japan Conference* (organized 1984): Hokkaido, main island north of Shizuoka and Nagano and Niigata prefectures; *Okinawa Mission* (organized 1984): Okinawa Islands, Naze City, and Oshimagun of Kagoshima prefecture; *West Japan Conference* (organized 1984): main island west of Aichi, Gifu and Toyama prefectures, and Kyushu and Shikoku islands.

5. *Korean Union Conference* (organized 1919; reorganized 1984). Territory: Democratic People's Republic of Korea and the Republic of Korea. Statistics (1993): churches, 527; members, 108,700; ordained ministers, 85. Headquarters: 66 Hoegi-dong, Dongdaemun-ku, Seoul, Korea. Official organ: *Church Compass.*

Constituent organizations and their territories—*East Central Korean Conference* (organized 1908; reorganized 1919, 1978, 1983): eastern part of Seoul, Kang Won (except the county of Chul Won), the counties of Ka Pyung, Ku Ri, Kwang Joo, Mi Keum, Nam Yang Ju, Sung Nam Si, and Yang Pyung in Kyung Ki, and the counties of Chei Chun and Tan Yang in North Choong Chung; *Middlewest Korean Conference* (organized 1963; reorganized 1971, 1983): North Choong Chung (except the counties of Chei Chun and Tan Yang), South Choong Chung, and Taejeon City; *North Korean Mission* (organized 1934): that portion of Korea lying north of the armistice line; *Southeast Korean Conference* (organized 1919; reorganized 1967, 1983): the cities of Pusan and Taegu, and North Kyung Sang and South Kyung Sang provinces; *Southwest Korean Conference* (organized 1952; reorganized 1971, 1983): Chejudo, North Chunla, South Chunla, and Kwangju-city; *West Central Korean Conference* (organized 1908; reorganized 1919, 1978, 1983): western part of Seoul, Kyung Ki (except the counties of Ka Pyung, Kwang Joo, and Yang Pyung), and the counties of Chul Won and Kang Won.

6. *Myanmar Union Mission* (organized 1919; reorganized 1938). Territory: Myanmar. Statistics (1993): churches, 147; members, 14,867; ordained ministers, 42. Headquarters: 68 U Wisara Road, Yangon 11191, Myanmar.

Constituent organizations and their territories—*Ayeyarwady Mission* (organized 1919; reorganized 1938): Ayeyarwady division; *Central Myanmar Mission* (organized 1967): Kayah, Rakhine, and Southern Shan states, the upper part of Kayin state, the lower part of Magway and Mandalay divisions, and the upper part of Bago division; *South East Mission* (organized 1919; reorganized 1938): Mon state, part of Southeast Bago division, part of Southern Kayin state, and Taninthayi division; *Upper Myanmar Mission* (established 1919): Chin Hills, Naga Hills, Kachin and Northern Shan states, the upper part of Magway and Mandalay divisions, and Sagaing division; *Yangon Attached District* (established 1977): parts of Southwest Bago and Yangon divisions.

7. *North Philippine Union Mission* (orga-

nized 1917; reorganized 1951). Territory: Abra, Albay, Aurora, Bataan, Batanes, Batangas, Benguet, Bulacan, Burias, Cagayan, Camarines Norte, Camarines Sur, Catanduanes, Cavite, Ifugao, Ilocos Norte, Ilocos Sur, Isabela, Kalinga-Apayao, La Union, Laguna, Marinduque, Mindoro, Mountain province, Nueva Ecija, Nueva Vizcaya, Palawan, Pampanga, Pangasinan, Quezon, Rizal, Sorsogon, Tarlac, Zambales, and the city of Manila. Statistics (1993): churches, 1,076; members, 165,538; ordained ministers, 196. Headquarters: 2059 Donada Street, Pasay City, Philippines. Official organ: *Mizpa.*

Constituent organizations and their territories—*Central Luzon Conference* (organized 1906; reorganized 1931): provinces of Aurora, Bataan, Bulacan, Cavite, Nueva Ecija, Palawan, Pampanga, Rizal, Tarlac, and Zambales, and the cities of Caloocan, Manila, Pasay, and Quezon; *Mountain Provinces Mission* (established 1939; organized 1956): Benguet, the eastern part of Ilocos Sur and Abra provinces, Ifugao, Kalinga-Apayao, and Mountain province; *Northern Luzon Mission* (organized 1919): Abra, Batanes, Cagayan, Ilocos Norte, Ilocos Sur, Isabela, La Union, part of Nueva Ecija, Nueva Vizcaya, Pangasinan, and part of Tarlac; *South-Central Luzon Mission* (organized 1931): provinces of Batangas, Laguna, Marinduque, Occidental Mindoro, Oriental Mindoro, and Quezon; *Southern Luzon Mission* (organized 1926): provinces of Albay, Burias, Camarines Norte, Camarines Sur, Catanduanes, and Sorsogon.

8. *South China Island Union Mission* (organized 1949). Territory: Hong Kong, Macao, Matsu, Pescadores, Quemoy, and Taiwan. Statistics (1993): churches, 60; members, 10,183; ordained ministers, 28. Headquarters: 40 Stubbs Road, second floor, Hong Kong. Official organ: *Last Day Shepherd's Call.*

Constituent organizations and their territories—*Hong Kong-Macao Conference* (organized 1949): Hong Kong and Macao; *Taiwan Mission* (organized 1950, reorganized 1976): Matsu, Pescadores, Quemoy, and Taiwan in the republic of China.

9. *South Philippine Union Mission* (organized 1951; reorganized 1964). Territory: island of Mindanao and Sulu archipelago. Statistics (1993): churches, 1,037; members, 256,739; ordained ministers, 144. Headquarters: Carmen Hills, Crossing Alta Tierra, 9000 Casgayan de Oro City, Philippines.

Constituent organizations and their territories—*Davao Mission* (organized 1965): provinces of Davao del Norte, Davao del Sur, and Davao Oriental, and Davao City; *Northeastern Mindanao Mission* (organized 1966): provinces of Agusan del Norte, Agusan del Sur, Surigao del Norte, and Surigao del Sur; *Northern Mindanao Conference* (organized 1937; reorganized 1966, 1988): provinces of Bukidnon, Camiguin, Cotabato, parts of Lanao del Norte, Lanao del Sur, and Misamis Oriental; *Southern Mindanao Mission* (organized 1950; reorganized 1965): provinces of Cotabato, Maguindanao, Sarangani, South Cotabato, and Sultan Kudarat; *Western Mindanao Mission* (organized 1958): Lanao del Sur, Misamis Occidental, Zamboanga del Norte, Zamboanga del Sur provinces, part of Lanao del Norte province, and the Sulu archipelago.

10. *Southeast Asia Union Mission* (organized 1917; reorganized 1929). Territory: Brunei, Cambodia, Laos, Malaysia, Singapore, Thailand, and Vietnam. Statistics (1993): churches, 262; members, 52,013; ordained ministers, 26. Headquarters: 251 Upper Serangoon Road, Singapore 1334, Republic of Singapore. Official organ: *The Messenger.*

Constituent organizations and their territories—*Peninsular Malaysia Mission* (organized 1914; reorganized 1988): Peninsular Malaysia; *Sabah Mission* (Masehi Advent Hari Ketujoa Sabah; reorganized 1961): Malaysian state of Sabah; *Sarawak Mission* (SDA Mission of Sarawak; reorganized 1961): Brunei and the Malaysian state of Sarawak; *Singapore Mission* (organized 1988): Singapore; *Thailand Mission* (organized 1919): Laos and Thailand; *Vietnam Mission* (organized 1937): Vietnam.

11. *Sri Lanka Union of Churches* (organized 1950): Sri Lanka. Statistics (1993): churches, 28; membership, 2,347; ordained ministers, 11. Headquarters: 7 Alfred House Gardens, Colombo 3, Sri Lanka.

12. *West Indonesia Union Mission* (organized 1964, formerly part of the Indonesia Union Mission). Territory: Java, Kalimantan (Indonesian Borneo), Lesser Sunda islands, Madura, Sumatra, and Timor. Statistics (1992): churches, 471; members, 69,099; schools, 76; ordained ministers, 183; licensed ministers, 99; Bible instructors, 9; teachers, 300. Headquarters are at Jalan M. T. Haryono Blok A, Kav 4 and 5, Jakarta 12810, Java, Indonesia. Official organ (for both Indonesia unions): *Warta Advent.*

Constituent organizations and their territories—*Central Sumatra Mission* (organized

1972): Riau province, West Sumatra province, and Tapanuli from Sipintupintu to the south; *East Java Conference* (organized 1913): Bali, central Java east of 110.0° east longitude, east Java (including SuraKarta), Lombok, and Madura; *Jakarta Conference* (organized 1913; reorganized 1973): West Java from 105.5° to 107.5° east longitude, including Jakarta; *Kalimantan Mission* (organized 1953): Kalimantan (Indonesian Borneo); *North Sumatra Mission* (organized 1917; reorganized 1937): Aceh, Sumatra East Coast, and North Tapanuli up to Sipintupintu; *Nusa Tenggara Mission* (organized 1956): Adonara, Alor, Flores, Kisar, Rote, Sabu, Solor, Sumba, Sumbawa, Timor, Timor Timur, and other smaller islands in the Lesser Sunda Islands; *South Sumatra Mission* (organized 1929): Bangka, Bengkulu, Jambi, Lampung, and Palembang; *West Java Mission* (organized 1913; reorganized 1973): west Java from 107.5° to central Java 110.5° east longitude, including Jokjakarta and excluding Surakarta.

13. *Attached Field—Guam-Micronesia Mission of Seventh-day Adventists* (organized 1948): islands of the Pacific north of the equator, west of the international date line, and south of 50° north latitude (including Wake Island but excluding Kiribati north of the equator).

Institutions. The following institutions operate in the Far Eastern Division:

Educational Institutions. Adventist Ekamai School and Ekamai International School (Thailand); Adventist International Institute of Advanced Studies (Philippines); Ayer Manis School (Sarawak, East Malaysia). Baesa Adventist Academy (Philippines); Bandung Academy (Indonesia); Bangladesh Adventist Seminary and College; Central Luzon Adventist Academy (Philippines); Central Philippine Adventist College; Chiang Mai Adventist Educational Center (Thailand); Cimindi Academy (Indonesia); Concepcion Adventist Academy (Philippines); Donghae Academy (Korea); East Java Academy (Indonesia); East Visayan Academy (Philippines); East Visayan Adventist Academy (Philippines); Ebeye Seventh-day Adventist High School (Marshall Islands); Far Eastern Academy (Singapore); Goshen Adventist Secondary School (Malaysia); Forest Hills Academy (Philippines); Guam Adventist Academy; Hahnkook Academy (Korea); Hiroshima Saniku Gakuin (Japan); Home Study School (Far East) (Singapore); Honam Academy (Korea); Hong Kong Adventist College; Hong Kong Sam Yuk Secondary School; Indonesia Union College; Irian Jaya Academy (Indonesia); Japan Missionary College; Kellogg-Mookerjee Memorial Seminary (Bangladesh); Klabat Academy (Indonesia); Korean Sahmyook University; Kowloon Sam Yuk Middle School (Hong Kong); Kwangchun Academy (Korea); Lake View Academy (Philippines); Lakpahana Adventist College and Seminary (Sri Lanka); Lipa Adventist Academy (Philippines); Maluku Academy (Indonesia); Marshall Islands Mission Academy; Matutum View Academy (Philippines); Medan Academy (Indonesia); Mindanao Mission Academy (Philippines); Mission College (Thailand); Mount Klabat College (Indonesia); Mountain View College (Philippines); Mountain View College Academy (Philippines); Myanmar Union Adventist Seminary; Naga View Academy (Philippines); Negros Mission Academy (Philippines); North Sulawesi Academy (Indonesia); North Sumatra Academy (Indonesia); Northeast Luzon Academy (Philippines); Northeastern Mindanao Academy (Philippines); Northern Luzon Adventist College (Philippines); Northern Luzon Adventist College Academy (Philippines); Nusa Tenggara Academy (Indonesia); Palau Mission Academy (Micronesia); Palawan Adventist Academy (Philippines); Pasay City Adventist Academy (Philippines); Pematang Siantar Academy (Indonesia); Philippine Union College; Philippine Union College Academy; Pohnpei Adventist High School (Micronesia); Sabah Adventist Secondary School (Malaysia); Sam Yuk Middle School (Hong Kong); Seoul Academy (Korea); Seventh-day Adventist School (Singapore); Singapore San Yu High School; South Sumatra Academy (Indonesia); Southeast Asia Union College (Singapore); Southern Mindanao Academy (Philippines); Sunny Hill College (Malaysia); Taejeon Middle School (Korea); Tai Po Sam Yuk Secondary School (Hong Kong); Taiwan Adventist Academy; Taiwan Adventist College; Tirad View Academy (Philippines); Toraja View Academy (Indonesia); West Visayan Academy (Philippines); Western Mindanao Academy (Philippines); Wonju Academy (Korea); Yungnam Academy (Korea).

Hospitals and Sanitariums. Adventist Medical Center (Okinawa); Bacolod Sanitarium and Hospital (Philippines); Bandung Adventist Hospital (Indonesia); Bangkok Adventist Hospital (Thailand); Cagayan Valley Sanitarium and Hospital (Philippines); Calbayog Sanitarium and Hospital (Philippines); Gingoog Sanitarium and Hospital (Philippines); Hongkong Adventist Hospital; Kobe Adventist Hospital (Japan); Lakeside Adventist Hospital (Sri Lanka); Manila Sanitarium and Hospital (Philippines); Medan Adventist Hospital (Indonesia); H. W. Miller Memorial Sanitarium and Hospital (Philippines); Mindanao Sanitarium and Hospital (Philippines); Palawan Adventist Hospital (Philippines); Penang Adventist Hospital (Malaysia); Phuket Adventist Hospital (Thailand); Pusan Adventist Hospital (Korea); Seoul Adventist Hospital (Korea); Taiwan Adventist Hospital; Tokyo Adventist Hospital (Japan); Tsuen Wan Adventist Hospital (Hong Kong); Youngberg Adventist Hospital (Singapore).

Food Companies. Japan Food Factory; Korean Sahmyook Food; Mission Health Food Co. (Thailand).

Publishing Houses. Bangladesh Adventist Publishing House; Indonesia Publishing House; Japan Publishing House; Kinsaung Publishing House (Myanmar); Korean Publishing House; Lakpahana Press of Seventh-day Adventists (Sri Lanka); Philippine Publishing House; Signs of the Times Publishing Association (Taiwan); Southeast Asia Publishing House (Singapore); Thailand Publishing House.

Retirement Homes and Orphanages. Shalom Nursing Home (Higashikurume); Shalom Nursing Home (Yokosuka).

History. The division was organized in 1919, after the old Asiatic Division was split into the Far Eastern (at first called the Eastern Asia) Division and two separate unions—the India Union Mission and the Australasian Union Conference. It was reorganized in 1931 when China became a separate division, and on Jan. 1, 1938, it took over the Far Eastern territory of the Central European Division, the Netherlands East Indies *(see* Indonesia).

For the history of the Seventh-day Adventist work in the Far Eastern Division, see specific names of the countries and islands in the area.

Division Presidents: I. H. Evans, 1919-1930; Frederick Griggs, 1931-1936; V. T. Armstrong, 1937-1941; W. P. Bradley (acting), 1942-1943; none, 1943-1945; V. T. Armstrong, 1945-1954; F. A Mote, 1954-1958; C. P. Sorensen, 1958-1966; P. H. Eldridge, 1966-1975; W. T. Clark, 1975-1985; Ottis C. Edwards, 1985-1992; Pyung Duk Chun, 1992- .

FAR EASTERN DIVISION OUTLOOK (1912-   ; 1912-1914 as *Newsletter for the Asiatic Division,* mimeographed; 1914-1917 as *Asiatic Division Mission News;* 1917-1924 as *Asiatic Division Outlook*; monthly; file in GC). Official organ of the Far Eastern Division, published at division headquarters, Singapore.

The paper continued to carry the name *Asiatic Division Outlook* until 1924 even though the name of the division was changed in 1919 to Far Eastern Division.

Because of the many languages spoken in the division, the *Outlook* has never served as a church paper. Circulation, beginning with 200 copies, has increased steadily through the years. It is sent out each month as a medium of communication among the mission fields to English-reading workers in the division, current and former missionaries, friends and relatives of the current workers, and to the various organizations in the world field for mission promotion.

FAR EASTERN ISLAND MISSION ACADEMY. *See* Guam Adventist Academy.

FAR EASTERN MISSION. *See* Euro-Asia Division; Russia.

FARGO, SALAM (1895-1974). Home missionary. During the two world wars, Salam supported the needy and fatherless on her own meager income. Married to a non-Seventh-day Adventist, she brought up her eight children to love the Lord, and all were baptized. In support of the work in Iraq, Salam distributed thousands of tracts and never missed an opportunity to share Jesus with others.

FARNSWORTH, CYRUS K. (c. 1822-1899). Younger brother of William Farnsworth; member and, it appears, a lay leader of the first group of Sabbathkeeping Adventists in Washington, New Hampshire *(see* Washington, New Hampshire, church), in whose home many of the early Adventist meetings took place. He married Delight Oakes, whose mother, Mrs. Rachel Oakes (later Preston), was instrumental in bringing the knowledge of the seventh-day Sabbath to Adventist believers of Washington.

FARNSWORTH, EUGENE WILLIAM (1847-1935). Evangelist, administrator. His father, William, was one of the first Sabbathkeeping Adventists, and Eugene was among the first born into a Sabbathkeeping Adventist family. At 19 he came under the spiritual influence of J. N. Andrews, and a short time later, when James and Ellen G.

White and J. N. Andrews conducted meetings in Washington, New Hampshire, Eugene Farnsworth was baptized in an opening cut through two feet of ice. Later, after moving to Iowa, he responded to the urging of G. I. Butler and others to enter the gospel ministry.

Licensed in 1874, he preached eloquently and vigorously to the settlers in the Midwest. In 1883 he was appointed president of the Iowa-Nebraska Conference, but continued in evangelistic work. Later he superintended the district comprising Nebraska, Iowa, Wisconsin, Minnesota, and South Dakota.

He was in demand as a speaker at camp meetings and general gatherings in most parts of the United States. Shortly after the establishment of Union College he became instructor in Bible, and during his first year baptized 100 of the 600 students. In 1896 he began eight years of pioneer evangelism in Australia and New Zealand, then went to London, England. Returning to the United States, he was for four years president of the Atlantic Union Conference, and then head of the Bible Department of what is now Columbia Union College for one year (1910). In 1911 he assumed the presidency of the California Conference, and several years later retired at Angwin, California. However, he was again brought into service, and spent several years visiting churches, schools, and camp meetings in the United States and Canada.

Following an illness and healing, he became active in responding to hundreds of requests to pray for the sick, and prepared a booklet entitled *Divine Healing*.

FARNSWORTH, VESTA JANE (CADY) (1855-1932). Teacher, Sabbath school administrator, editor. Between 1890, the year her first husband, A. D. Olsen, died, and 1893 she was corresponding secretary of the International Sabbath School Association. In 1893 she married E. W. Farnsworth, and a few years later they went to Australia, where they worked for nearly eight years. During part of that time she edited the *Bible Echo*. Upon returning to the United States, they worked in the Atlantic Union Conference and were associated with what is now Columbia Union College until 1911, when Farnsworth was called to the presidency of the California Conference. For a time Mrs. Farnsworth led in the Sabbath school work. She was the author of four books for children: *Friends and Foes in Field and Forest; Stories Mother Told; The Real Home; The House We Live In.*

FARNSWORTH, WILLIAM (1807-1888). Reputed to be "the first Seventh-day Adventist," that is, the first of the Adventists who kept the seventh-day Sabbath. He accepted the Adventist (Millerite) doctrine about 1840 and in 1844 declared himself a Sabbathkeeper, among the first of a small group from among the members of the Washington, New Hampshire, Christian Church who became the first Adventists to observe the seventh day as the Sabbath *(see* Washington, New Hampshire, church).

FAROE ISLANDS. A group of 18 islands situated in the Atlantic Ocean north of Scotland, lying approximately midway between Norway and Iceland. The combined area of the islands is 540 square miles (1,400 square kilometers), and the population (1994) is 47,500.

In the seventh century Celtic priests from Ireland discovered 18 lonely windswept islands in the North Atlantic Ocean between Iceland and Norway. These clerics stayed only for a short while. However, they left behind sheep that were able to find sustenance on the grass-covered rocks. Later, Vikings from Norway on their way to Iceland settled and named the newfound country Faroe Islands, meaning sheep islands.

The Faroe Islands were politically dependent upon Norway until 1380, when they became connected with Denmark. They have been self-governing in most matters since 1948, and have their own language and flag. Tórshavn is the capital.

Some scholars claim that the first settlers in the seventh century, the Celtic monks, were Sabbathkeepers. The national archives reveal that in the seventeenth century individual Lutherans were concerned with the Sabbath-Sunday issue.

Seventh-day Adventist Work. Except for some SDA publications sent to the Faroes, the SDA message did not reach these isolated islands until 1913, when two licensed ministers were sent to the islands from Denmark to sell SDA books and papers. At the Scandinavian Union Conference session that year the president had said: "We must not forget the Faroe Islands." Two years later Emanuel Christiansen (Westman), one of the two ministers, held a series of evangelistic meetings and won five converts. On Jan. 1, 1919, he reported 13 new members. The second canvasser, Valdemar Jacobsen, took charge of the work in 1920 and remained for six years. For a number of years, the islands were a part of the territory of the Iceland Conference, but in 1946 they were united with the East Denmark Conference.

Seventh-day Adventist fishermen from the Faroes first brought Advent literature to Greenland before this island was opened to the proclamation of the Advent message.

In 1959 a clinic for physiotherapeutical treatment (Skodsborgbadet) was opened in Tórshavn. In 1966 an SDA elementary school was opened. There are now 82 pupils, with five full-time and two part-time teachers. The school is a great asset in breaking down prejudice. It has a waiting list until the year 2000. The school is a feeder into Danish Junior College. Colporteur work has proved successful on the Faroes, and SDA literature is to be found in most homes. The Seventh-day Adventist Church is regularly on Faroese television, with divine services and evening worships.

Administratively, the Faroese Church is connected to the Danish Union of Churches.

FASNACHT, OSCAR (1888-1960). Business administrator in Switzerland. His education prepared him for a business career. He was employed in the civil service when in 1911 he joined the SDA Church. In 1912 he became manager of the Basel health food store and in 1917 assumed leadership also of the tract society in Basel. In the same year he married Ruth Guenin. From 1920 until 1932 he served as treasurer of the Romanian Union Conference; from 1932 to 1935 he was cashier of the Southern European Division. In 1935 he took charge of the Phag health food factory at Gland, Switzerland. His last position before retirement was that of treasurer of the German-Swiss Conference. He took an interest in the various affairs of the church and usually served as an elder of local congregations.

FASSETT, O. R. (fl. 1843-1880). A physician of Lockport, New York, who became a Millerite in 1843 and then a preacher, and later a minister of the group that became the Advent Christian Church. He was quoted in some of the early Seventh-day Adventist papers, for example, in the *Advent Review* 1 (No. 2): 2-4, August 1850.

FASTING. Voluntary abstinence, whether total or partial, from food for religious purposes. The principle behind fasting is that, when conducted judiciously, it contributes to good health and can increase spiritual sensitivity. In addition, it is an act of worship, a special outward and wholistic expression of the person's dependence on God's grace, power, and presence when confronting real or potential challenges and/or problems.

While there seems to be no divine command to fast (see SDADic 344, 345), the Bible gives many examples of individuals and groups who fasted for various reasons: Moses (Ex. 34:28), David (2 Sam. 12:21-23), Elijah (1 Kings 19:8), Daniel (Dan. 9:3), Nehemiah (Neh. 1:4), Esther (Esther 4:16), God's people (Esther 4:3, 16), Jesus (Matt. 4:2), Peter (Acts 10:30), the leaders at Antioch (Acts 13:2), and Paul and Barnabas (Acts 14:23).

Fasting has been practiced in a limited way by Seventh-day Adventists. Special days of fasting and prayer have been observed in the SDA Church since early in its history. Following are examples of announcements of days of fasting in the church paper:

A general call for such a day was signed by James White and M. E. Cornell: "We have consulted with brethren with whom we have recently associated, in regard to a day of fasting and prayer, in view of the want of faithful laborers in the wide harvest field; and also the feeble state of health of several who are now engaged in the work; and the suggestion meets the approbation of all. . . . By advice of brethren we appoint the first Sabbath in June as a day of fasting and prayer. . . . We recommend that all the churches be united in fasting and prayer on the day named, for the above object" *(Review and Herald* 6:228, May 15, 1855).

A fast day was recommended by the Battle Creek, Michigan, church: "We have submitted the subject of a day of fasting, humiliation, self-examination, confession and prayer to the Battle Creek church, who are unanimous in recommending Sabbath, August 3, 1861. . . .

"The Bible, especially the New Testament, is not very definite on the subject of fasting, whether we should entirely abstain from food, and how long. Feeble persons are generally very dependent on the small quantity of plain food which they take. These may have no duty in point of abstinence. We would recommend to all to abstain from their noon meal if consistent, and let the other two meals, if eaten, be plain" *(ibid.* 18:60, July 23, 1861).

In 1877 a fast day was appointed by the New York and Pennsylvania Conference and another in the same year by the Vermont Conference *(ibid.* 49:101, Mar. 29, 1877; 50:67, Aug. 23, 1877), but in general such a day is set by the General Conference. In 1866 the General Conference announced a four-day fast, and in 1882 a three-day one. (For descriptions of these as observed in local churches, see *Review and Herald* 28:5, June 5, 1866; 59:784, Dec. 12, 1882). However, fasts of such duration were unusual.

A modern example of collective fasting is the day of fasting appointed for the delegates of the General Conference session in 1954 *(ibid.* 131:16, May 25, 1954) and in 1958 (GCC [1958], p. 1137). The General Conference has occasionally invited the world church to fast and pray for specific purposes, e.g., for the work in China *(ibid.* [1959], pp. 229, 234), and for world peace *(ibid.* [1991], p. 8).

FATTEBERT, ULYSSES CHARLES (1871-1947). Physician, missionary. He was educated in Healdsburg and Battle Creek colleges, and the University of St. Louis (M.D., 1905). He married Ellen I. Burrill in 1906. After mission service in Mexico (1906-1913), he pioneered medical missionary work on Cebu and Mindanao in the Philippines (1913-1921). Later he engaged in private practice in Phoenix, Arizona.

FAYARD, MARCELO I. (1894-1966). Colporteur, editor, author. A native of France, he was educated in Switzerland and entered colporteur work in Spain in 1912. In 1914 he transferred to the Argentine Publishing House, where he became an editor. His last post of duty was at the Pacific Press Publishing Association in California. He was the author of 17 books and translated 13 Ellen White books into the Spanish language.

FAYOUM TRAINING SCHOOL. *See* Nile Union Academy.

FEATHER RIVER HOSPITAL. A medical institution in Paradise, California, originally founded by a group of dedicated physicians and businesspersons as the Feather River Sanitarium and Hospital. It opened Dec. 3, 1950, with a total of 15 patient beds. By 1959 it had expanded to 38 beds, and surgical services had been added.

Since December 1960 the hospital has been owned and operated by the Seventh-day Adventist Church. A new physicians' office building was completed in 1964 adjacent to the hospital, providing six office suites.

With the rapid growth of the community, it soon became apparent that a larger facility was needed. Plans were laid, and in 1968 a new complex, consisting of 51 acute beds (including eight maternity) and 97 convalescent beds, was completed and occupied.

With continued growth of the area, more acute beds were needed, and in a short time the convalescent care facility was converted to an acute medical unit and a 12-bed coronary-care unit. Other services now offered include respiratory therapy, rehabilitation, speech therapy, diagnostic laboratory and X-ray services, many sophisticated surgical procedures usually available only in larger centers, nuclear medicine, pharmacy, and emergency services.

Additional services available include same-day surgeries, a cardiac catheterization lab, and cardiac rehabilitation. The Feather River Home Health Agency provides in-home support services to numerous local residents. The Center for Women's Health, opened in September 1990, offers a wide variety of services, including diagnostic mammography, psychological counseling, nutritional counseling, perinatal services and childbirth education, a GYN nurse practitioner, and a wellness counselor.

In September 1992 the hospital opened the Paradise Pediatric Center, guaranteeing the availability of quality pediatric care to all local children.

The hospital cooperates with the California State University at Chico, Butte College, and Yuba College in providing clinical experience for students in nursing, inhalation therapy, and radiology. In addition, a very active in-service program for hospital personnel is carried on continually. A well-planned patient health education program is in operation.

Community service programs include various diabetes education programs offered at the Center for Women's Health; community updates offered by local physicians; and an annual health fair that provides various health screenings and tests to hundreds of local residents. Vegetarian cooking classes help local people to adopt a healthy lifestyle.

Administrators: M. D. Elkins, 1960-1964; A. G. Streifling (acting), 1964; C. H. Snyder, 1964-1966; H. A. Rudisaile, 1967-1970; E. D. Case, 1970-1973; L. R. Langworthy (acting), 1973-1974; L. E. Coy, 1974-1987; G. E. Pifer, 1987- .

FÉDÉRATION DES ÉGLISES ADVENTISTES DU SEPTIÈME JOUR DU

QUÉBEC. *See* Quebec Seventh-day Adventist Church Conference.

FEET WASHING. Erroneous term. *See* Foot Washing.

FEHR, JOHANN (1884-1959). Minister and conference administrator in Switzerland and France. He was the ninth child of a blacksmith in Guxhagen, Germany. As a youth in his native village he learned cabinetmaking, and while working at his trade at Kassel, Hesse, he began to study Seventh-day Adventist teachings and joined the church in 1902, at 17 years of age. He had determined, even before he was baptized, that he would become a minister, a goal that he later achieved.

He was called first to southern Germany in 1906, and in 1908 to Switzerland to work among the German-speaking people. In 1911 he married Clara Koch in Zurich, and in 1912 he was ordained to the ministry. From Switzerland he went to France, where he was president of the Alsace-Lorraine Conference from 1920 to 1922. Returning to Switzerland, he was president of the German-Swiss Conference from 1937 to 1947. He retired in 1952, but continued his ministry as he was able until his death in Zurich in 1959.

FELLOWSHIP, TESTS OF. *See* Church (local organization), I.

FENNER, HANS (1872-1948). Minister and church leader in Germany. He was baptized into the Seventh-day Adventist Church in January 1900, shortly after entering the colporteur work. In 1901 he began to preach, and in January 1906 he was ordained to the ministry. In the spring of the same year he married Maria Janert. According to the *Yearbook* he worked in the East German Conference (1903), Prussian Conference (1904-1906), East German Conference (1906), and West German Conference (1907-1909). From 1909 to 1912 he was president of the West German Conference. Afterward he was president of the South German Conference (1912- ? ; between 1917 and 1921 the *Yearbook* did not list changes in Central Europe), the Westphalian Conference (? - 1921), the Hessian-Westphalian Conference (1921-1927), Thuringian Conference (1927-1930), and finally the West German Union (1930-1940). After 10 years as president of the union, he retired from active service.

FENNER, HARRY E. (c. 1862-1940). One of the founders of Seventh-day Adventist Young People's societies. He was a youth of about 17 when in 1879 Luther Warren came to work on the Fenners' farm, and together they organized the young people of the Hazelton township church, Michigan, for missionary work. Until he died at the age of 78, Fenner remained an active lay member of the church.

FERGUSON, JACKSON (1832-1900). Lay preacher, farmer, miner, real-estate broker, postmaster, state assemblyman. He was born in Ohio, and at the age of 6 moved with his family to Indiana and then to Iowa, where he grew up and married Elizabeth Peugh. They eventually settled in California, and Ferguson was a well-established farmer near Santa Rosa when J. N. Loughborough arrived in San Francisco in 1868. Opposition to Loughborough and his message from other churches only increased Ferguson's interest.

After his baptism he lost no time in sharing the message, and soon received a license to preach. He traveled in the state somewhat until Ellen White told him that his missionary work should be done at home so as to help his wife train their children. The family moved about California, then to Saint Clair, Nevada, where meetings were held, resulting in baptisms. By 1878 a church of 29 members was established in Saint Clair. Next Ferguson and a trained evangelist held meetings in Reno, and a church was organized there. During this time Ferguson was elected to the state assembly, where he was respected for his firm belief in the Bible. Influenced, perhaps, by his zeal, the SDAs in the area became known as persistent missionaries. Later a company was formed in the Nevada town of Wadsworth, where Ferguson lived during his last years.

FERNSTRÖM, KARL ANTON (1852-1944). Minister in Sweden. Converted in a strong religious revival in his village about 1870, he joined the Swedish Missionary Society. In 1882 he moved to Stockholm, where he was influenced by public meetings conducted by J. G. Matteson and O. Jonsson. He and his wife were baptized on Feb. 22, 1885, and joined the Seventh-day Adventist Church. He became a colporteur, attended Matteson's Bible school in Stockholm, and later was elected elder of the Stockholm church. In 1890 he settled in Grythyttehed and the next year was ordained to the ministry at the annual meeting held there. For 50 years he was pastor of the Seventh-day Adventist congregation that met in a church building erected on his property. He traveled the country from north to south and walked through many villages, towns, and cities of Sweden preaching the gospel.

FERNWOOD ACADEMY. *See* Union Springs Academy.

FIELD, FRANK WILLIAM (1863-1944). An early church leader in Japan. He became a Seventh-day Adventist at the age of 19. During the 1890s he taught at Mount Vernon Academy. In 1901 he was ordained to the ministry and went to direct SDA work in Japan, where, under his leadership, a publishing house and a training school were established. In 1910 he returned to the United States and afterward taught at Pacific Union College, Meadow Glade Academy, and Southern Junior College.

FIELD (unit of church organization). The name used in some parts of the world for the unit of church organization corresponding to a local conference, a mission, or a section, or a national church; that is, a unit comprising local churches, stations, or districts, and itself forming, normally, a part of a union (the exception being a "detached" field not part of any union but operated directly under the division). "Mission field" has been used at times to designate a territory assigned to or worked by a conference or some other unit, but not yet organized as a mission. *See* Organization, Development of, in Seventh-day Adventist Church.

FIELD GLEANINGS FROM THE CARIBBEAN UNION. *See Caribbean Union Gleanings.*

FIELD MISSIONARY SECRETARY. *See* Publishing Department Director.

FIELD SECRETARY. General field secretaries of the General Conference are workers elected, in addition to the officers, to serve in carrying the field responsibilities of the General Conference, under the direction of the General Conference Executive Committee. They are assigned either to field service or to special projects and responsibilities as determined by the committee. Division field secretaries function similarly under the respective division committees.

Field responsibilities may include (1) promoting the general worldwide objectives of the church, (2) promoting specific lines of endeavor, (3) attending and giving assistance in general, union, or local gatherings of workers or church members, and (4) building the spiritual interests of the church.

FIELD TIDINGS. *See Southern Tidings.*

FIGUHR, R. R. (1896-1983). Missionary, administrator, fifteenth president of the General Conference. Born in Superior, Wisconsin, he attended Laurelwood Academy in Oregon, Pacific Union College, and Walla Walla College. He entered denominational work in 1915, serving in the Western Oregon Conference as a literature evangelist, teacher, evangelist, and pastor. He was ordained to the gospel ministry in 1918. Two weeks later he married May Belle Holt and entered the Army.

Beginning in 1923 he served in various capacities in the Philippines. In 1941 he was called to be president of the South American Division, a position he held until 1950, when he was called to the General Conference as a vice president. He was elected president of the General Conference in 1954 and served in that capacity until his retirement in 1966.

Figuhr's administrative skills were augmented by his linguistic ability, for he was fluent in German, Spanish, and Tagalog. He was noted as having a good balance between consecration and administration.

FIJI. A fully independent nation consisting of an archipelago situated in the South Pacific, between latitude 15° and 22° and astride the 180th meridian, having a combined area of about 7,055 square miles (18,270 square kilometers), and a population (1994) of 764,000. The population is made up largely of Fijians and Indians, with minorities of Europeans and Chinese and other Pacific Islanders. The majority of Fijians are either Methodists or Roman Catholics. The Indians are mainly Hindus, Muslims, and Sikhs.

The islands, mainly of volcanic origin, are mountainous. They are well watered and surrounded by coral reefs with openings into good harbors. Principal exports are sugar, copra, gold, and fruit. The capital, Suva, is on the south coast of Viti Levu, the largest island. Fiji, formerly a member of the British Commonwealth, is now an independent republic. The prime minister is head of the executive branch and presides over a cabinet of ministers. Fiji has a bicameral parliament with a house of representatives consisting of 70 members and a senate of 34 members. The islands were sighted by Abel Tasman, a Dutch navigator, in 1643. Capt. James Cook visited the Fiji group in 1774. Capt. William Bligh, of the *Bounty*, sighted most of the islands when he went through the archipelago after the famous mutiny. In 1874 King Cocobau ceded the islands to Great Britain. Fiji was brought under Christian influence between the years 1830 and 1850.

Seventh-day Adventist Statistics. The territory of Fiji was divided into the East and West Fiji missions until 1965, when they were combined to become the Fiji Mission, which is part of the Central Pacific Union Mission, which in turn is a part of the South Pacific Division. Statistics (1993) for *Fiji:* churches, 118; members, 15,908; church or elementary schools, 11; ordained ministers, 29; licensed ministers, 37; teachers, 48.

Institutions. Fulton College; Vatuvonu Vocational Training Centre.

Development of Seventh-day Adventist Work. The first SDA missionary to arrive in Fiji was John I. Tay in 1891 on the mission vessel *Pitcairn.* After a few months he became ill and died. In 1895 J. M. Cole from the United States began work in Levuka, then the capital of the islands. The same year, the islands were organized as a mission. In 1896 J. E. Fulton arrived in Suva and opened SDA work first at Tamavua, near the previous Central Pacific Union Mission headquarters. He later transferred to Suva Vou (new Suva) when Ratu Ambrose Roko Tui Suva, king of Suva, accepted the Sabbath. In 1900 Fulton began a small paper, the *Rarama* ("Light"). He also translated Ellen White's *The Great Controversy* (abridged) and a book of Bible readings. About the turn of the century the Australasian Union Conference accepted the responsibility of the South Pacific island field from the General Conference.

Under Fulton's ministry, two prominent Fijian nationals became SDAs. One of them was Ratu Meli, a high chief; the other Pauliasi Bunoa, who was ordained an SDA minister in October 1906.

In 1908 Peni (or Beni) Tavodi, the first Fijian foreign missionary, was sent to New Guinea. Through the years at least a dozen other Fijian families have gone as missionaries to other places in the South Pacific.

In 1912 Mrs. E. Meyers arrived in Fiji and began work among the many North and South Indians who had been brought from India to work on the sugar plantations. For several years this work for the North and South Indians was carried on as a separate mission, but later it was combined under one administration. There was a school for Indians at Samabula, near Suva.

In 1916 the Central Polynesian Conference was organized, with headquarters in Fiji. The territory included Fiji, Samoa, Tonga, and Niue. This form of organization was found impracticable and was shortly abandoned.

Because of large accessions in membership in inland Viti Levu in 1918 and 1919, educational facilities were increased—Navuso Central School was opened on the Wainibuka River in 1921 and the Vatuvonu Central School at Buca Bay, Vanua Levu, in 1932. In 1940 the Buresala Training School was transferred to the mainland of Viti Levu and later became Fulton Missionary College. School buildings at Samabula, Navuso, and Buresala were dismantled and used at Fulton.

When the Australasian Division was reorganized in 1949, Suva, the capital of the Fiji Islands, became the headquarters of the Central Pacific Union Mission, with the Fiji archipelago as one of the local missions of that union. At the same time, Fulton Missionary College became the central training institution for the union mission. At the union session in 1951 the Fiji Mission was divided into the East and West Fiji missions.

As the years passed and the number of children at educational level grew, it became apparent that the Fiji Mission needed another school. Because of this need the Navesau School, in the Wainibuka district, was established in 1964 to cater to pupils in the primary level.

As in other developing countries, the standard of education in Fiji has gradually risen in the past few years. Both Vatuvonu, in Buca Bay, and Navesau became junior secondary schools. Vatuvonu is currently a vocational training school. This has enabled both schools to cope with the standard of education and also to have a higher enrollment.

FIJI MISSION. *See* Fiji; South Pacific Division.

FINANCIAL POLICIES. The General Conference Executive Committee has from its beginning formulated financial policies to guide it and its subsidiary organizations in the conduct of their activities. Policies and methods are outlined in the *General Conference Working Policy.*

With regard to care and responsibility in financial operations, the *General Conference Working Policy* (1992-1993 ed., p. 439) states:

"*Cash Basis*—All activities of a recurring nature for which denominational financial support is involved shall be conducted on a cash basis. All funds necessary for such operations shall be in hand or provision shall be made before commencement of activities.

"*Financial Responsibility*—Neither the General Conference nor any of the individual divisions composing it shall be held financially responsible for any obligations it has not assumed by its own action. This is also the general policy of the union and local conferences/missions and other organizations and institutions of the denomination.

"*Budget Plan*—All denominational organizations shall follow the budget plan of financial operating. The annual operating budget shall be approved by the controlling committee. It shall be the responsibility of the officers of each level of organization to require subsidiary organizations in their territory to follow the budget plan.

"*Monthly Financial Reports*—Monthly financial reports showing the actual operating expenses and budgetary provision to date shall be prepared and studied by the organization's administrative officers. Treasurers shall keep controlling boards and committees informed by providing monthly financial statements except in the case of relatively inactive organizations in which case statements may be submitted quarterly. Boards and committees should compare these statements with the budget adopted at the beginning of the year and be prepared to act with the officers in increasing income and/or decreasing expenditures as may be necessary.

"*Authorization for Appropriations*—In the use of General Conference, division, union, and local conference/mission funds, appropriations to subsidiary organizations shall be made only by specific action of the controlling committees."

FINLAND. A republic in northern Europe with a total area of 130,120 square miles (337,000 square kilometers). Twelve percent of this area is occupied by lakes, for Finland is "the land of tens of thousands of lakes." Finland has a population (1994) of 5 million, of whom 296,000 are of Swedish extraction. Consequently, both Finnish and Swedish are the official languages of the country.

Finland is bounded on the east by Russia, on the north by Norway, and on the west by Sweden. Finland was under the suzerainty of Sweden from the time the Christian faith was brought to the country in the twelfth century until the year 1809. Then it passed under the control of Russia and so remained until it gained its independence in 1917. The principal occupations are farming, forestry, and industry.

In Finland 92 percent of the people are Lutherans, but there is also another state church, the Greek Orthodox Church, with about 56,000 members. There is full religious liberty.

Seventh-day Adventist Statistics. In Finland there are two conferences and one mission: the Finland Finnish Conference, the Finland Swedish Conference, and the Lapland Mission, comprising the Finnish Union Conference, which is a part of the Trans-European Division. Statistics (1992) for *Finland:* churches, 67; members, 6,126; church or elementary schools, 5; ordained ministers, 20; licensed ministers, 10; Bible instructors, 21; teachers, 26. Union headquarters: Uudenmaantie 50, 20720 Turku, Finland. Statistics for the conferences and the mission—*Finland Finnish Conference*: churches, 51; members, 5,684; church or elementary schools, 4; ordained ministers, 14; licensed ministers, 8; Bible instructors, 16; teachers, 12. Headquarters: Annankatu 7, 00120 Helsinki 12, Finland. *Finland Swedish Conference:* churches, 12; members, 276; ordained ministers, 1; licensed ministers, 2; Bible instructors, 2; teachers, 3. Headquarters: Annegatan 7 C 19, 00120 Helsingfors, Finland. *Lapland Mission*: churches, 4; members, 166; ordained ministers, l; Bible instructors, 3. Headquarters: Uudenmaantie 50, 20720 Turku, Finland.

Institutions. Adventtikirkon Vanhainkoti; Finland Junior College; Finland SDA Publishing House; Hopeaniemi Sanitarium.

Development of SDA Work. *Beginnings.* The first Seventh-day Adventist in Finland was a sea captain, A. F. Lundqvist. While at sea, he had been converted by the Plymouth Brethren and while in Liverpool in 1885 had purchased from an SDA colporteur, George Drew, Uriah Smith's book *Daniel and the Revelation.* He also bought Ellen G. White's book *The Great Controversy.* As a result of reading these books he immediately began to keep the Sabbath and became a Seventh-day Adventist, remaining faithful until his death in 1955, at the age of 97. After returning to his native country, he wrote on Nov. 10, 1885, to the Swedish magazine *Sanningens Harold* to call the attention of the Swedish SDAs to Finland. In 1891 the Swedish canvassing leader, Emil Lind, was sent to Finland to explore the possibilities of selling books there. He met many difficulties, and was even threatened with exile to Siberia, but he continued his work for a while. When in 1892 the General Conference promised financial help for the work in Finland, the Swedish Conference sent its president, Olof Johnson, and two Bible instructors, Augusta Larsson and Matilda Lindgren, to Finland. They went to Helsinki on July 21, 1892, where Johnson rented a suitable apartment. Because foreigners were not allowed to hold open public meetings, he began to hold worships in his own home, to which the people were invited. They also visited homes and distributed literature. More and more interested people came, and 30 children attended their Sunday school. The first convert was M. Lindqvist, a carpenter, who came to "convert" Olof Johnson, "the Jewish slave of the law," but returned home convinced, saying, "From now on I shall not work on Saturdays." His wife and his aged mother joined him in his newly found faith, and he became a canvasser. This beginning of SDA work in Finland was in the Swedish language.

Seventh-day Adventists began public preaching in Helsinki on Jan. 15, 1893, in the Temperance Hall. Six men and six women were baptized and celebrated the Communion service on May 27, 1893. The first Seventh-day Adventist church was organized in Helsinki on the Sabbath, Apr. 21, 1894, with 24 charter members. At that time there were about 50 to 60 adherents in Finland. Among the Finnish-speaking people the work began with the distribution of SDA publications.

The workers from Sweden discovered that no book could be brought into Finland and sold. However, since there was no law against giving publications away, the group distributed them by the hundreds. At the same time a number of pamphlets were translated into Finnish and printed by local publishers. By 1894, 14 colporteurs were selling them in many parts of Finland. In 1893 E. J. Waggoner's book *Christ and His Righteousness* was published as the first SDA book in Finnish.

Preaching in Finnish began in Turku in the autumn of 1894, when Olof Johnson used K. L. Östring as his interpreter.

At the annual meeting of SDAs in Finland in 1897, it was decided to found a publishing house and to print the magazine *Aikain Vartija* ("Watchman of the Times").

Early Organization and Growth. At the annual meeting in Helsinki, Oct. 5-10, 1909, it was voted to organize the Finland Conference as part of the Scandinavian Union. Fred Anderson, a Swedish American, was elected as the first president. When Anderson transferred to Sweden he was succeeded by Louis Muderspach from Denmark, who held large evangelistic campaigns in Helsinki and Tampere. As young Finnish-speaking workers such as Aarne Rintala, Vaino Kohtanen, and Kaarlo Soisalo entered the work, it made rapid progress, and new churches were organized all over the country. In 1917 the three-year "Missionary School" was founded in Hämeenlinna. In 1921 the conference headquarters were built in Helsinki and the "Hydro-Electric Institute" (physical therapy treatment rooms) was opened in the same building in 1926. In 1918 the Finnish Junior College was opened in Hämeenlinna, where it continued until 1929, when it ceased to operate for two years. In 1931 it reopened in Helsinki, where it continued for only one year before being transferred to its present site in Piikkio.

In 1943 the SDA denomination received official recognition, taking for its name Suomen Adventtikirkko ("Finnish Adventist Church").

Developments Toward the Finland Union. In 1929 the Finland Conference was divided into the Finnish and Swedish conferences. The Finnish Conference contained 1,127 members and the Swedish 314. Then in 1946 the Finnish Conference was divided into the East and West Finland conferences. Helsinki remained the headquarters of the East Finland Conference, which had 16 churches and 1,439 members. Tampere became the headquarters of the West Finland Conference, with 13 churches and 1,491 members.

At the quadrennial meeting in Stockholm of the East Nordic Union (to which Finland and Sweden had belonged since 1931) on June 14-19, 1955, it was voted to divide the union into the Swedish Union and the Finland Union. The Swedish Conference in Finland was joined to the Swedish Union, leaving the Finland Union with a membership of 4,568.

The SDA message has been preached in all the towns, in hundreds of villages, and in nearly all the centers of population in Finland. The

Bible correspondence school has operated with success, and the welfare and temperance work has attracted much attention. A beautiful campsite in central Finland is the summer center of the work for young people and church members.

In 1983 the Lapland Mission, formerly the northern part of the West Finland Conference, was established. The mission had 163 members in three churches. In the same year, the Finland Swedish Conference was incorporated into the Finland Union from the Swedish Union. It increased the union membership with 318 members and 12 churches. In 1991 the East Finland Conference and the West Finland Conference united to become one conference, the Finland Finnish Conference.

Special Phases and Features in the Work. Finland has passed through several difficult periods since the SDA message was first preached in the country. The first was the civil war, which brought independence in 1917. Then in 1939 Finland fought with Russia, and after a short time of peace fought again from 1941 to 1944. These wars, misfortunes, and distresses caused many to turn to God, thus presenting opportunities for evangelism. Meetings were held in spite of the air attacks. When the bombardment was over, the people would climb out of the cellars to continue the meeting.

One of the unique features characteristic of the work in Finland has been the prominent part played by women evangelists. Their service began when many ministers were called to serve their country. Among them was Elsa Luukkanen, who gathered large audiences. Hundreds of converts were baptized. Even though, since the war, the ministers have returned to their fields, several women evangelists are continuing their work with good success.

SDA temperance has risen to a recognized position in the country. The anti-smoking campaign has been well received. Smoking Sam has been demonstrated to approximately 750,000 schoolchildren throughout the country.

Community service work has been extended to the underprivileged areas of the country, and a systematic mass distribution of clothes and other needed materials has been organized. These activities, in cooperation with the local social officers, have been a means of bringing help to about 30,000 people annually.

The Bible correspondence school has since 1948 been an integral part of the SDA evangelistic work in Finland, and has had about 3,000 students every year, with approximately 45 baptisms annually. Because the radio and TV work is based under national control the church cannot combine the BCS work with broadcasting. The BCS is connected with the Church Ministries Department.

In central Finland, situated in the community of Laukaa, there is a permanent campsite, Kallioniemi, with permanent accommodations for 200. Since 1953 this camp has developed into an evangelistic center during the summer months. Camps for children and youth, adults, mothers, and workers are held, with attendances of about 2,000 annually.

FINLAND FINNISH CONFERENCE. *See* Finland; Trans-European Divison.

FINLAND JUNIOR COLLEGE (Toivonlinnan Yhteiskoulu). A coeducational boarding school operated by the Finland Union Conference, including comprehensive school on the junior and senior levels (forms 1-6 and 7-9) and three years of high school level. At intervals of years a seminary is also operated on campus. The constituency supporting the institution numbers about 6,000. Toivonlinna ("fortress of hope") is situated on the southwestern coast 14 miles (22 kilometers) from Turku, the oldest city in Finland, on the side of a hill overlooking a fjord connecting with the Gulf of Bothnia. The campus is part of a 120-acre (50-hectare) estate, of which 100 acres (40 hectares) are forest land. In 1993 there were 103 comprehensive school pupils and 85 upper secondary students, making a total enrollment of 187 instructed by 17 teachers.

History: The school has occupied three different sites. From 1918 to 1929 it was situated in Hämeenlinna, in the interior. In 1931, after a break of two years, it was located in Helsinki, the capital of Finland. After a year it was moved to its present campus in Piikkiö, where it was operated under the name of Toivonlinnan Lähertysopisto until the autumn of 1941, when the name was changed to Toivonlinnan Kristillinen Opisto. In 1963 the present name was introduced, and since 1960, a three-year gymnasium leading to the university was added to the program. Toivonlinna Seminary continued as a separate department on campus. Since 1960 Toivonlinna has issued state-accepted certificates. In 1958 the school began to get subsidies from the Finnish government, and since 1988 the law also obliges the municipalities the students come from to take part in operating costs.

Principals: W. Sucksdorff, 1918-1919;

V. Kohtanen, 1919-1920; A. Y. Rintala, 1920-1921; E. Hamara, 1921-1925; O. Angervo, 1925-1929; K. Soisalo, 1931-1932; A. Y. Rintala, 1932-1946; H. Karström, 1946-1961; V. Jaakkola, 1961-1971; M. J. Lahti, 1971-1978; S. Anttila, 1978- .

FINLAND OLD PEOPLE'S HOME. *See* Adventtikirkon Vanhainkoti.

FINLAND SDA PUBLISHING HOUSE (Kirjatoimi). A publishing firm with printing plant operated by the Finland Union Conference and situated on the outskirts of Tampere, Finland. Seventh-day Adventist publishing work in Finland began when in 1893 E. J. Waggoner's book *Christ and His Righteousness* was published and printed in Helsinki as the first SDA book in Finnish. A branch office, headed by Knut Sandberg from Stockholm, Sweden, was established in Helsinki in 1894. The first periodical published in Finland was the Swedish *Tidens Tecken* ("Signs of the Times") in 1896, and the following year the Finnish *Aikain Vartija* ("Watchman of the Times"), now entitled *Nykyaika* ("Our Times"), was begun. The publishing house was formally organized in Helsinki in 1897.

In 1961 the firm was moved from Helsinki to the present 50-acre (80-hectare) property, where buildings were erected for a complete publishing house with printing facilities. Essential machinery was donated by the Publishing Expansion Committee of the General Conference.

Publications are issued in Finnish and Swedish. Books, including several by Ellen White, have been widely sold by literature evangelists in Finland. *The Bible Story,* by Arthur S. Maxwell, 10 volumes in full color, is among the significant subscription books printed by the offset presses of the Finland Publishing House. In 1993 the following journals were published: *Nuori Usko* (a monthly youth paper), *Nykyaika* (a weekly missionary and general church paper; also a quarterly Braille edition), *Terveys* (a monthly health journal), and the Sabbath school lesson quarterlies for senior, junior, and primary ages.

Over recent years there has been a vigorous growth in production and distribution of literature. The Finland Publishing House has for several years had the second-highest sales among the denominational publishing houses in Europe.

Managers: Knut Sandberg, of Sweden, 1894-1901; Adolf Böttcher, of Germany, 1901-1906; Nils Hammar, of Sweden, 1906-1922; Yrjö Miettinen, 1922-1959; Aarne Unhola, 1959-1968; Joel Niininen, 1969-1986; Anna-Liisa Halonen, 1986-1989; Heimo H. Lempinen, 1989- .

FINLAND SWEDISH CONFERENCE. *See* Finland; Trans-European Division.

FINLAND UNION CONFERENCE. *See* Finland; Trans-European Division.

FIRE, ETERNAL. *See* Hell.

FIRESIDE CORRESPONDENCE SCHOOL. *See* Home Study International.

FIRST ANGEL'S MESSAGE. *See* Three Angels' Messages.

"FIRST-DAY ADVENTIST." A phrase used loosely by early Seventh-day Adventists to designate any non-Sabbatarian Adventists, that is, any of the other denominations originating from the Millerite movement. It is not the name of any denomination. *See* Adventist Bodies.

FIRST-DAY OFFERING. A freewill offering (now discontinued) for "foreign mission work" "laid aside [on Sunday] each week at home," and turned in quarterly through the tract society *(Review and Herald* 64:776, Dec. 13, 1887). The plan, inaugurated in 1887, continued for some years. For later methods of raising money for worldwide missions *see* Sabbath School Offerings; Second Sabbath.

FISHER, GEORGE SEPTIMUS (1872-1947). Manager of denominational health food manufacture in Australia. He was born in England and received his early schooling there. In 1893 he attended a Seventh-day Adventist camp meeting near Melbourne, Australia, where he heard Ellen White outline the future development of SDA institutions in that country. Three years later, in 1896, he joined the Seventh-day Adventist Church and became associated with the Echo Publishing Company as clerk. In 1904 he was transferred to the health food factory in Sydney and led out in its development and general management until 1933. He was then appointed manager of the Sydney Sanitarium and served there until his retirement in 1942. He was a founding member of the Australasian Conference Association, Limited, and until his death served on the committee of the Australasian Union Conference.

FITCH, CHARLES (1805-1844). Congregational minister, later Presbyterian minister, Millerite leader, the designer of the "1843 chart." Early in 1838 Fitch accepted Miller's views, producing a sensation with his sermons. But his ministerial associates treated the new doctrine with such searing ridicule and contempt that for a time he lost confidence in it, and lapsed into his former views of the world's conversion.

It was Josiah Litch, who had known of Fitch's experience, who brought him again to the definite acceptance of the Adventist faith. From then on he was one of the most fearless, aggressive, and successful Millerite leaders. Fitch, assisted by Apollos Hale, designed the widely used "1843" prophetic chart, painted on cloth, which he presented to the Boston General Conference of May 1842.

In the latter part of 1842 Fitch was asked to go to Cleveland, Ohio, and vicinity. Despite opposition, a definite interest in the Advent message developed at Oberlin College, where Fitch was given opportunity to deliver a series of lectures on the Second Advent in September 1843.

By 1843 Fitch was one of the most prominent of the Millerite leaders. In January of that year he began to edit a weekly journal called the *Second Advent of Christ.* In this he printed (July 26, 1843) his sermon (from Rev. 14 and 18) on the mighty angel who cried, "Babylon the great is fallen," and who was followed by the warning voice, "Come out of her, my people, that ye be not partakers of her sins, and that ye receive not of her plagues." In this Fitch contended that the term *Babylon* was no longer limited to the Roman Catholic Church, but now included also the great body of Protestant Christendom. He maintained that both branches of Christendom had, by their rejection of the light on the Advent, fallen from the high estate of pure Christianity. He contended that Protestantism was either cold to the doctrine of the Second Advent or had spiritualized it away. This address was put into pamphlet form and later reprinted in various Millerite papers.

Early in October 1844 Fitch accepted the "seventh month" concept, and looked to Oct. 22 as the time for the coming of Christ. He was ill in Buffalo at the time, and died on Oct. 14, shortly before the day of expectation, from pneumonia contracted after prolonged exposure while baptizing outdoors in cold weather.

FIVE-DAY PLAN TO STOP SMOKING. The original Seventh-day Adventist stop-smoking plan, originated by J. Wayne McFarland, M.D., and Elman J. Folkenberg. It was formally introduced to the church at the 1962 General Conference session in San Francisco. It has more recently been revised and updated by the General Conference Health and Temperance Department. *See* Breathe Free: The Plan to Stop Smoking.

FLAIZ MEMORIAL HIGHER SECONDARY SCHOOL OF SEVENTH-DAY ADVENTISTS (formerly Narsapur High School). A coeducational English language boarding school on the senior high school level, operated by the Central India Union section of the Southern Asia Division at the town of Narsapur (Narasapur) in the delta of the Godavari River, in northeast Andhra Pradesh state. The school is affiliated with the ICSE Council recognized by the Indian government. The enrollment in 1992 was 560 students, with a faculty of 57.

The school was opened in 1921 as the Telugu Intermediate School (later listed as Telugu Secondary School in 1928, and Telugu Mission High School, 1929-1930), in temporary thatch-roofed huts by T. R. Flaiz, then superintendent of the Telugu Mission. The early students themselves helped make and burn brick for the first permanent buildings. In 1925, when the enrollment reached 45, the school received its first full-time principal, C. A. Schutt. In succeeding years the plant was enlarged and modernized several times. Electricity was installed in the late 1950s.

A new boys' dormitory, built to accommodate 300 students, was formally opened in 1973. The money for this building, and for a new administration block, was received from a 1968 Thirteenth Sabbath Offering overflow. The administration building has 11 large classrooms, a library, science laboratory, and office rooms.

The school owns 44 acres (18 hectares) of land, half of which are arable, producing 70 percent of the rice eaten by the students.

In the 1930s the school was listed in the *Yearbook* as the Narsapur High School, but in 1947 the high school classes were discontinued and the students sent to the Lowry Memorial Higher Secondary School, which served the whole union. In the late 1940s and early 1950s the school was listed as the Narsapur Secondary Boarding School. In the early 1950s the school again offered full high school work and its students were prepared for the Andhra Pradesh State matriculation examination. From 1956 to 1978 it was again known as the Narsapur High School. In 1978 the present name was adopted.

Principals: T. R. Flaiz, 1921-1925; C. A. Schutt, 1925-1932; J. A. Nelson, 1932-1933; C. A. Randolph, 1933-1937; H. A. Hansen, 1937-1942; C. B. Williams, 1942-1948; G. A. Anandam, 1948-1951; E. N. Simon, 1951-1953; W. F. Zill, 1953-1956; R. E. Stahlnicker, 1956-1958; W. F. Zill, 1959-1962; R. H. Jones, 1962-1965; H. D. Erickson, 1965-1966; P. L. Parker, 1967-1968; I. Subhushanam, 1968-1969; M. D. Moses, 1969-1970; K. B. Rao, 1970-1979; D. Sukumaran, 1979-1981; P. Steven Kelly, 1981-1982; M. George Luke, 1982-1983; J. V. Prasada Rao, 1983-1985; I. D. Devadas, 1985-1988; M. George Luke, 1988- .

FLEMING, LORENZO D. (1808-1867). Minister, reformer, editor, and Millerite leader. Before accepting Millerism he was an active supporter of educational, temperance, and antislavery efforts, and for a time was acting editor of the *Emancipator.* As a Millerite he became editor of *Glad Tidings,* Rochester, New York (which later became the *Voice of Truth*), then assistant editor of the *Midnight Cry.* He wrote *New Testament Companion* (1839), *The Midnight Cry: A Synopsis of Evidences of the Second Coming* (1842), and *First Principles of the Second Advent Faith* (1844). His Casco Street Christian church in Portland, Maine, to which in 1840 he invited William Miller, was the church in which the family of Ellen Harmon accepted Miller's teachings.

FLETCHER ACADEMY AND HOSPITAL. *See* Madison Institutions.

FLETCHER, WILLIAM WARDE (1879-1947). Former evangelist and administrator in Australia and Southern Asia, born in Tasmania. He joined the Seventh-day Adventist Church in 1900, and the next year began to work as a colporteur. From 1902 to 1904 he was in charge of the Book Department of the Echo Publishing Company. In 1905 he began evangelistic work, and in 1906 went to Singapore. Leaving there, he later engaged in city mission work in Adelaide, South Australia, and in 1912 was ordained to the ministry. He was president of the South Australian Conference from 1912 to 1914; young people's, home missionary, and educational secretary of the Australasian Union Conference (1914); and vice president of the union in 1915. From there he went to India, where he served as president of the India Union Mission (1916-1919). Later he served as field secretary and then chair of the Southern Asia Division (1920-1922). Upon returning to Australia, he conducted evangelism, served as an administrative officer of the Australasian Union, and for a time taught Bible at Australasian Missionary College. About 1930, for doctrinal reasons, he severed his connection with the church and later was associated with the Sydney Bible Training Institute and the Free Evangelical Fellowship.

FLOOD. The universal deluge described in Gen. 6 to 9, in which, except for the occupants of the ark, all air-breathing animals of the "dry land" are said to have been destroyed. According to the biblical account, "the waters prevailed so mightily upon the earth that all the high mountains under the whole heaven were covered; the waters prevailed above the mountains, covering them fifteen cubits deep" (Gen. 7:19, 20, RSV). Seventh-day Adventists view the Bible account of the Flood literally (G. W. Amadon, in *Review and Herald* 16:122, Sept. 4, 1860; J. N. Andrews, in *Review and Herald* 60:472, July 24, 1883; G. M. Price, *The New Geology* [1923]; H. W. Clark, *The New Diluvialism* [1946]; etc.). The Scriptures declare that the purpose of the Flood was to destroy obdurate sinners and to permit a new beginning from the faithful remnant that survived. Bible writers confirm the record of Genesis (Isa. 54:9; 2 Peter 2:5; 3:6; Heb. 11:7), as does our Lord (Matt. 24:37; Luke 17:26).

From medieval times those who accept the Genesis account literally have commonly attributed fossils—the traces or remnants of animals and plants preserved in the rocks—to the Noachian deluge. At times a misguided faith led to hasty and premature conclusions by some not qualified to judge the nature of the fossil remains. For instance, notable theologians and preachers, such as Augustine and Cotton Mather, mistakenly identified teeth from fossil mammoths as those of a giant antediluvian race of human beings.

Of the many features from the fossil record that have been taken as suggestive of a flood that destroyed the earth, the following are typical: abundant fossil remains of marine animals in the rocks of many mountain chains and all continents have been taken as evidence for the widespread extent of the Flood; evidences in many instances of rapid, and at times catastrophic, circumstances of burial of plant and animal remains are taken as suggestive of flood burial; existence of tropical and warm temperate forms in rocks of high latitudes is felt by many to suggest a major climatic change in postdiluvian times.

The mute testimony of the rocks is often obscure and open to various views, and, as would be expected, there has not always been unanimity as to the interpretation of certain geologic features that may be related to the Flood. The degree to which a definite order or sequence exists in the fossil-bearing strata, the question whether certain topographic features are a result of the Flood or of other geologic events such as volcanism or glaciation, and the extent of pre- and post-Flood geologic activity are a few of the debated questions. (See A. T. Jones, *Review and Herald* 60:513, 514, Aug. 14, 1883; G. M. Price, *The New Geology* [1923]; H. W. Clark, *The New Diluvialism* [1946]; F. L. Marsh, *Studies in Creationism* [1950].)

From 1860 onward, articles defending the Genesis account of the Flood appeared in the *Review and Herald* at rather frequent intervals. A dozen or more times over the next 30 years the Babylonian cuneiform account of the Flood, then recently discovered, and the universal tradition of a great deluge were mentioned as confirming the Bible record of that event (18:173, Oct. 29, 1861; 18:180, Nov. 5, 1861; 41:61, Feb. 4, 1873; 44:139, Oct. 27, 1874; 68:602, Sept. 29, 1891; etc.). Other articles point to fossils, especially marine fossils high in the mountains, as evidence of a flood of great depth and extent *(ibid.* 16:122, Sept. 4, 1860; 18:173, Oct. 29, 1861; etc.). Foremost among SDA geologists in the twentieth century was George McCready Price, from whose pen came no less than 16 books on various aspects of creationism, evolution, and the Flood. (See especially *Common Sense Geology* and *The New Geology.)* From the biological viewpoint, biologists Harold W. Clark and Frank L. Marsh have considered fossil remains in relation to the Flood. The SDA-sponsored Geoscience Research Institute, in association with Andrews University in Berrien Springs, Michigan, is evidence of major denominational interest and effort in this area. This institute is devoted to a scientific study of the various branches of paleontology and to the correlation of scientific studies with the Bible. A recent readily available source for the SDA point of view with respect to the Flood from the viewpoint of geology is the article "Evidences of a Worldwide Flood," in volume 1 of *The SDA Bible Commentary* (pp. 64-97). *See* Evolution; Science and Religion.

FLORIDA. *See* Gulf States Conference; Florida Conference; South Atlantic Conference; South Central Conference.

FLORIDA CONFERENCE. A unit of church organization comprising the territory of the state of Florida except the counties of Bay, Calhoun, Escambia, Gulf, Holmes, Jackson, Okaloosa, Santa Rosa, Walton, and Washington, which belong to the Gulf States Conference. Statistics (1993): churches, 152; companies, 15; members, 34,499; church schools, 43; ordained ministers, 159; licensed ministers, 23; church school teachers, 155; credentialed missionaries, 47; licensed missionaries, 13; credentialed and licensed literature evangelists, 17. Headquarters: 655 Wymore Road, Winter Park, Florida. The conference forms part of the Southern Union Conference. *(See also* South Atlantic Conference.)

Institutions. East Pasco Medical Center; Florida Hospital; Florida Hospital College of Health Sciences; Florida Hospital/Waterman; Forest Lake Academy; Greater Miami Academy; Medical Center Hospital; Walker Memorial Hospital.

Local churches: All Nations, Altamone Springs, Apopka (Highland, Spanish), Arcadia, Avon Park (Spanish), Belleview, Bethel (French), Bonita Springs, Boynton-Delray, Bradenton, Bradmore (Spanish), Brandon (Brandon, Spanish), Brooksville, Bushnell, Carol City (Spanish), Carrollwood, Casselberry (Spanish), Clearwater, Clermont, Cocoa, Crawfordville, Cross City, Dade City, Daytona Beach, Deland, Deltona (First, Spanish), Ebenezer (Spanish), Eden, Filipino-American, Florida Hospital, Florida Living, Forest City (Spanish), Forest Lake, Fort Lauderdale (Fort Lauderdale, Spanish), Fort Meade, Fort Myers (Fort Myers, Spanish), Fort Myers Shores, Fort Pierce, Gainesville, Groveland Academy, Hernando, Hialeah (Spanish), High Springs, Hollywood (Spanish), Homestead (Homestead, Spanish), Homosassa, Inverness, Islamorada, Jacksonville (First, Mandarin, Orange Cove, Southpoint, Spanish), Jennings Lake, Jensen

Beach, Jupiter-Tequesta, Kendall, Key Largo, Key West, Kissimmee (Kissimmee, Spanish), Kress Memorial, Lady Lake, Lake City, Lake Placid, Lake View, Lake Wales, Lake Worth, Lakeland, Lauderhill, Leesburg, Madison, Maranatha, Marathon, Markham Woods, Melbourne (Melbourne, Spanish), Miami Beach (First Spanish), Miami (Central Spanish), Miami Springs, Miami Temple, Miramar, Mount Carmel, Mount Dora, Naples, New Port Richey, New Smyrna Beach, North Miami, North Miami Beach, North Port, Northwest Dade, Northwest Miami (Spanish), Ocala, Okeechobee, Opalocka (Spanish), Orlando (Central, Central Korean, Spanish, Vietnamese), Palatka, Palm Coast, Palmetto, Palm Springs (Spanish), Pem-Mar, Perry, Pine Hills, Pinellas (Spanish), Plantation, Plant City, Pompano Beach, Port Charlotte, Punta Gorda, Riverview, Royal Palm, St. Augustine, St. Petersburg, Sanford Meadows, Sarasota, Sebring, Shuler Memorial, Silver Springs Shores, South Brevard, South Broward, South Orlando, Spring Hill, Starke, Sunshine State, Tallahassee, Tampa (First, Korean, Spanish), Titusville, University, Venice-Nokomis, Vero Beach, Walker Memorial, Wauchula (Wauchula, Spanish), West Palm Beach (First, Spanish), Westchester (Spanish), Winter Garden, Winter Haven, Winter Springs, Zephyrhills.

Companies: Boca Raton, Canaan, Englewood, Fort Lauderdale (Portuguese), Gainesville (Spanish), Indiantown (Spanish), Interlachen, Jacksonville (Korean), Morija (French), Normandy (Spanish), Salem (French), Sebring (Spanish), Spring Hill (Spanish), Venice (Yugoslavian), Wimauma (Spanish).

History. *Beginnings of the Work in the Area.* S. N. Haskell reported an 1873 convert (place unmentioned), a Black man "who . . . then went to his people in Florida," where he found many of them eager for his books and tracts and some willing to adopt the Sabbath *(True Missionary* 1:56, July 1874). It is not known whether he won any permanent converts.

Beginning as early as 1876, news items from Florida appear in the *Review and Herald.* In that year a letter from Jacksonville refers to "a little company here, who have accepted the seventh day." The next year there is mention of six Seventh-day Adventists in St. Augustine and about the same number in Jacksonville. About the beginning of 1883 J. O. Corliss visited the few families of adherents scattered throughout the state, but the only evangelism reported was conducted by laypersons. One of these was Charles P. Whitford, from Vermont, who lived in Moultrie, a new settlement south of St. Augustine. In 1883 and 1884 he wrote of a few SDA families there and of new converts in that county (St. Johns).

The first SDA series of meetings in Florida, held early in 1885, was reported by G. G. Rupert, a minister sent by the General Conference. Preaching near Terra Ceia Bay, on the Gulf coast 40 miles (65 kilometers) south of Tampa, where about 20 SDAs from Michigan had settled, he added 10 converts and organized a church of 22 members. This oldest Seventh-day Adventist church in the state—and still the largest as late as 1895—was the forerunner of the present Palmetto church. Soon after leaving the Terra Ceia church, Rupert baptized six and organized a church at Sorrento, in central Florida. Here lived L. H. Crisler, who had heard SDA preaching in Iowa but had not accepted the faith until moving to Florida, and who was to be, a few years later, the first Florida Conference president. Two churches organized by Rupert in 1886—at Orlando and Jacksonville—were later disbanded because of their members moving away, but were reorganized in 1890 and 1898, respectively.

These two disbanded churches exemplify one of several difficulties met in the early work in Florida—a fluctuating population. Evangelists preaching to winter residents might find their best hearers leaving for their northern homes in the spring. Or small new churches could melt away almost overnight if their members were among that class of settlers who had arrived in Florida with much enthusiasm but little adaptability to the new climate or the unfamiliar requirements of soil and season, and who soon moved away to seek a better location or other employment. Because of the instability of the population in those early days, S. H. Lane, who was sent to Georgia and Florida in 1888, recommended to the General Conference a delay in the intended organization of a conference in Florida.

Yet the migratory habits of the population had one advantage, as Samuel Fulton had reported to the General Conference session of 1887 on his return from Florida. Most of the people in the cities and towns, having come recently from elsewhere and having broken their ties with the past to some degree, were more ready to take up new ideas. He reported a liberal spirit, a lack of prejudice. Others after him found this true, though in the more conservative localities active opposition could develop. It was in a backwoods post office that evangelist L. H. Crisler encountered an irate citizen who assaulted him viciously until restrained by bystanders.

Other hindrances to progress were the periodic yellow fever scares, which inhibited public meetings, and a freeze that brought economic disaster. For example, the threat of yellow fever epidemics prevented tent meetings scheduled in 1887 for Tampa, where there were nine members; kept people away from the 1888 meetings in Lake City; and canceled a camp meeting in the 1890s, although the epidemic did not actually enter peninsular Florida. The 1895 camp meeting was eliminated because of the economic depression consequent upon what was still remembered for more than a half century as "the big freeze," which not only wiped out the 1894-1895 citrus crop but killed many groves outright. For several years church budgets and colporteur sales suffered from the effects.

Organization in the Nineties. Despite setbacks, the 1890s were a decade of organization and progress. By 1890 organized or unorganized groups of adherents were reported at or near Apopka, Earlton, Fernandina, Gainesville, Jacksonville, Lake City, Moultrie, Orange Heights, Orlando, Palmetto, Pine Hill, St. Andrews Bay, St. Augustine, Sorrento, Tampa, and Waldo. Not all of these were permanent.

There were six churches represented in the meeting at Barberville in September 1893 that organized the Florida Conference and at the same time a tract society and a Sabbath school association. The new conference began life with three ordained ministers, two licentiates, and 139 members, with a territory comprising all of Florida. (There were two territorial changes later: in 1908 seven northwestern counties were given to the Alabama Conference, and two others in 1922; a tenth was transferred in 1932 to the new Alabama-Mississippi Conference.)

During the nineties several other firsts are reported: in 1892 the first "company of canvassers," supervised by canvassing agent S. T. Page, and the first SDA church building, erected by the members of Barberville (organized in February) and De Leon Springs; and in November 1894 the first camp meeting and regular session of the new conference, held at Tampa—said to be the first camp meeting of any denomination in that area. The campers, including 100 who came up the bay in two schooners from Terra Ceia and elsewhere in Manatee County, were housed in 50 tents and apartments. A. T. Jones spoke twice daily, and other speakers were G. I. Butler, former General Conference president, who had retired to Florida in 1888, and R. M. Kilgore, superintendent of the Southern District, who stayed over after the end of the meeting to organize the Tampa church.

During that decade efforts were made to evangelize several ethnic groups. House-to-house work for Blacks as well as Whites was reported at Lawtey (1891) and at Milton (1897). In 1897 reference is made to M. T. Ivory, a Black licentiate (later ordained), working since April in Orlando. In September 1899 Ivory reports preaching to White people for three weeks in Punta Gorda and working among the Blacks in various places all during the year, with the result that a church was organized in Orlando. (For Black Seventh-day Adventists in Florida and neighboring states, *see* South Atlantic Conference.)

There were hopes of beginning mission work among the Seminole Indians in south Florida through contacts made at Chokoloskee, when in 1896 W. L. Bird visited the little SDA group there on the southern Gulf coast at Ten Thousand Islands. In 1897 the conference president felt that the way seemed to be opening, yet nothing permanent appears to have come of it. Fifty years later there were reports of one SDA half-Seminole trying to reach these Indians—a woman whose tribal membership gave her access to them.

Likewise little was realized from hopes for a Tampa-based Cuban mission work. Immediately preceding the Spanish-American War in 1898, relief contributions were solicited for the Cuban refugees in Tampa, and plans were made to distribute Spanish publications to the "readers" in the local cigar factories (functionaries who were hired to read to the employees as they rolled cigars). Many years later some evangelistic work was carried on for the Spanish-speaking people in Tampa, but the few converts were absorbed into the English-speaking church. Only in recent years was a Spanish church organized in Miami.

Development in the Twentieth Century. On May 1, 1901, when the former General Conference District No. 2 (the Southern District) became the Southern Union Conference, the Florida Conference became one of its component conferences. In November 1901 the Florida Conference elected as president G. I. Butler, who had twice been

General Conference president. Because of his health he had retired to Bowling Green, Florida, in 1888, and then had remained long after his recovery to care for his invalid wife, who died just preceding this conference session. The following January, at the first session of the new Southern Union Conference, this former General Conference president was elected the union president, in addition to his Florida work. Thus until 1904 the Florida Conference had a president who lived in Nashville, Tennessee.

During the first 10-year period, the Florida Conference doubled its membership, growing to 12 churches and 286 members by 1903, and in the second decade, to 27 churches and 744 members in 1913. Among the churches organized by that time were those at St. Petersburg (1905), Daytona (1909), and Miami (1910). Meanwhile, the Florida Sanitarium had been opened in Orlando in 1908, and the conference headquarters moved there in 1910.

In a state with a steadily developing population, church membership continued to grow despite economic setbacks because of the collapse of the Florida "boom" and the great depression of the 1930s. Forest Lake Academy, near Orlando, was established in 1926, and its campus provided a permanent camp meeting site. In the forties and fifties several sanitariums and hospitals were opened (see list near the beginning of this article), also a youth campsite was acquired at High Springs (Camp Kulaqua), and a new conference headquarters building (opened January 1960) was erected.

Membership figures show one drop, which, however, was not an actual decrease. In 1945 the transfer of the Black membership to the newly organized South Atlantic Conference reduced the Florida Conference totals from 68 to 47 churches, and from 6,038 to 4,579 members. By the end of 1950 there were 51 churches, with 5,558 members, and at the end of 1974 the membership reached 16,154 with 89 churches. By the end of 1992 membership totaled 34,197 with 149 churches and 17 companies.

Presidents: L. H. Crisler, 1893-1901; George I. Butler, 1901-1904; C. B. Stephenson, 1904-1906; L. H. Crisler, 1906-1907; R. W. Parmele, 1907-1912; W. H. Heckman, 1913-1917; A. R. Sandborn, 1917-1919; C. B. Stephenson, 1919-1921; J. L. Shuler, 1921-1926; A. S. Booth, 1926-1933; L. K. Dickson, 1933-1936; L. E. Lenheim, 1936-1941; L. C. Evans, 1941-1947; R. H. Nightingale, 1947-1954; Don R. Rees, 1954-1957; H. H. Schmidt, 1957-1965; W. O. Coe, 1965-1973; H. J. Carubba, 1973-1984; Malcolm D. Gordon, 1985-1990; O. O. Graham, 1990- .

FLORIDA CONFERENCE ACADEMY. *See* Forest Lake Academy.

FLORIDA HOSPITAL. A 1,462-bed acute-care medical center with five campuses—Florida Hospital Orlando, Florida Hospital Altamonte, Florida Hospital Apopka, Florida Hospital East Orlando, and Florida Hospital Kissimmee. Florida Hospital serves Greater Orlando as a community hospital and is also a major tertiary referral hospital for central Florida and much of the Southeast, the Caribbean, and South America.

Florida Hospital opened in 1908, accommodating scarcely 20 patients. L. N. Sickler, M.D., served as medical director; Lydia E. Parmele, M.D., wife of the conference president, was house physician; and H. A. Shreve was the first business manager.

After three years of operation and gratifying growth under the shareholders' plan, the institution was placed under full conference control. A new hospital building was erected of concrete veneer, increasing the capacity to 60 beds. In 1913 the Nursing School graduated a class of five.

In 1940 a new building was erected, adding 18 hospital rooms, two operating rooms, a delivery room, and other facilities. By 1946 a court of patients' cottages was completed. In 1949 a north wing, a four-story concrete structure, was completed, doubing the capacity of the entire hospital. A nurses' training center built in the 1950s included a three-story education building with dormitory for 100 students, assembly hall, library, laboratories, classroom, administrative offices, and recreation rooms.

The hospital School of Nursing graduated a total of 480 from 1913 to 1958. In the mid-fifties Southern Missionary College, in Tennessee, began to offer a program in nursing leading to the B.S. degree, using this hospital for clinical practice. The first students graduated under this arrangement in 1960. A school of practical nursing, founded 1962, graduated its first 10 students in 1963.

A modern psychiatric wing was completed in 1958 to accommodate 31 patients. The Morgan Memorial Rehabilitation Center, a four-story concrete building housing 60 beds for pediatrics and a complete Physical Medicine and Rehabilitation Department, was constructed in 1962. Also during 1962 the original sanitarium and hospital buildings built between 1913 and 1918 were demolished to make way for a new 80,000-square-foot (7,500-square-meter) hospital building to house most of the ancillary departments and to add 100 beds. This building was completed in 1964.

In 1967 a new South wing was opened providing administrative offices as well as 132 additional beds. In 1970 a new West wing, adding 48 beds, was opened. During 1973 a 103-bed satellite hospital, eight miles (13 kilometers) north of the main plant, was completed.

Beginning early in 1974 an $11 million expansion added 168 beds to the main hospital as well as a new Trauma and Emergency Center, laboratory, Radiology Department, Engineering Service, and Food Service.

In the 1970s Florida Hospital and its medical staff led the effort to develop subspecialty services in Florida. During the decade the hospital saw the start of the region's first joint replacement surgery program and the beginning of the kidney transplant program. Florida Hospital continued to expand in the seventies with new programs, new equipment, and two new satellite hospitals in Altamonte and Apopka.

The 1980s brought more expansion to Florida Hospital. Florida Hospital Orlando gained 134 new patient beds, new office facilities and patient-care floors, as well as a helipad for emergency transports with the addition of an 11-story, 220,000-square-foot (20,500-square-meter) patient tower in 1985. In 1990 Florida Hospital added 197 new patient beds by bringing on another satellite—Florida Hospital East Orlando—and in 1993, 120 more patient beds were added with the acquisition of Florida Hospital Kissimmee. In 1992 Florida Hospital received national recognition for its commitment to quality health care.

Today unique specialty services in cardiology, orthopedics, rehabilitation, obstetrics, women's medicine, and microsurgery, as well as many special care nursing units, serve patients of all ages and all levels of care. With 43,000 inpatients, 130,000 outpatients, and 116,000 emergency cases each year, Florida Hospital treats more patients than any other hospital in central Florida—in fact, it has the second-highest volume in the state.

Business Managers/Administrators: H. A. Shreve, 1908-1911; Leroy T. Crisler, 1911-1919; W. J. Ewing, 1919-1922; E. L. Place, 1922-1926; O. A. Hudson, 1926-1929; C. A. Rottmiller, 1929-1933; W. E. Abernathy, 1933-1937; R. G. Bowen, 1937-1944; A. C. Larson, 1944-1950; L. T. Hall, 1950-1959; C. B. Hardin, 1959-1961; D. W. Welch, 1961-1973; Bob Scott, 1973-1979; Mardian J. Blair, 1979-1984; Thomas L. Werner, 1984- .

FLORIDA HOSPITAL COLLEGE OF HEALTH SCIENCES. A coeducational undergraduate institution located on the Florida Hospital Medical Center (FHMC) campus in Orlando, Florida. The college is accredited by the Seventh-day Adventist Board of Regents, is fully licensed by the Florida State Board of Independent Colleges and Universities, and has been awarded candidacy status by the Southern Association of Colleges and Schools. Hospitals used by the college for clinical experiences are accredited by the Joint Commission of Accreditation of Healthcare Organizations.

While the college itself is a new institution, some of its programs have been in place for a number of years. The Registered Nursing program was established in 1913 by what is now Florida Hospital Medical Center and was operated for 70 years as a three-year hospital-based nursing training program. In 1983 a two-year associate degree program was begun at FHMC under the sponsorship of Southern College of Seventh-day Adventists. In 1992 that program was transferred to Florida Hospital College of Health Sciences. At the same time, the college brought together three other educational programs (radiography, diagnostic medical sonography, and radiation therapy), two of which had been in existence at FHMC for some time.

The college offers two-year Associate of Science degrees in nursing, diagnostic medical sonography, radiation therapy, and radiography. Certificate programs are also available for practical nursing, radiation therapy, and diagnostic medical sonography.

Presidents: David E. Greenlaw, 1992- .

FLORIDA HOSPITAL/WATERMAN. A 182-bed acute-care hospital in Eustis, Florida, operated by Adventist Health System/Sunbelt Health Care Corporation.

In 1926, 10 doctors opened a small hospital in a wing of the Rowe Hotel in Umatilla, Florida. By 1933 it had become an 18-bed not-for-profit facility called Lake County Medical Center. The doctors moved the hospital into the Fountain Inn in nearby Eustis in 1938. The inn, built by Frank Waterman, president of the Waterman Fountain Pen Company, had suffered financial problems and was closed in

1936. Waterman turned over his famous resort to the doctors, and over the next 25 years the medical facility expanded. The name was changed to Waterman Memorial Hospital in memory of its benefactor.

In 1960 the Waterman Memorial Hospital Association was formed. This group of concerned citizens provided guidance and raised funds for hospital renovations. With aggressive planning, the hospital was soon expanded to include the following: additional patient rooms, new lobby, administrative offices, support services suites, a chapel, new laboratory, obstetrical unit, and business offices. Recent additions include a physical therapy rehabilitation center, outpatient services center, and expanded emergency room.

In 1992 the hospital became part of Adventist Health System/Sunbelt Health Care Corporation, and its name was changed to Florida Hospital/Waterman.

Presidents: Royce Thompson, 1992- .

FLORIDA LIVING NURSING CENTER. A 120-bed skilled nursing facility in Apopka, Florida, owned by the Florida Conference of Seventh-day Adventists and leased by Sunbelt Health Care Centers, a division of Adventist Health System/Sunbelt Health Care Corporation. The facility was officially opened July 15, 1970, with 15 patients. The facility grew over the years, with its most recent expansion added in 1989. The nursing center is conveniently located adjacent to the 90-unit Florida Living Retirement Center, also owned by the Florida Conference.

FLORIDA LIVING RETIREMENT COMMUNITY. A residential community operated by the Florida Conference primarily for Seventh-day Adventist members on a 20-acre (eight-hectare) property made available by K. A. Wright, a retired educator. The site is a spacious countryside setting adjacent to Forest Lake Academy and is within one mile (1.6 kilometers) of a small shopping area and post office. This facility was originally planned to provide for approximately 225 residents to be constructed in stages according to need and availability of funds. The first units were opened on Sept. 12, 1965. There are presently 10 apartment buildings with six to eight units in each, 34 single-room units, and an administrative building.

FLOWERS, A. E. (1853-1894). Pioneer Seventh-day Adventist worker in Trinidad, West Indies. He was converted in his youth, and in 1873 joined the Seventh-day Adventist Church. During the autumn of 1891 he and his wife engaged in evangelism in St. Louis, Missouri. In 1894 he was sent to Trinidad, but after working only a few months there he died of yellow fever.

FOLLETT, ORNO (1882-1960). Missionary to the American Indians for 40 years. He studied nursing at the St. Helena Sanitarium. In 1909 he married Agnes Wammack, and for several years engaged in evangelistic work in Kansas.

Having had two bouts with tuberculosis, he took a five-month trip in a covered wagon to look for a location for an Indian mission, and in 1916 established a mission among the Navajos at Thoreau, New Mexico. A mission home, school, and dispensary were built, and later, a small hospital. He spent 15 years working among this tribe, and aided in translation of parts of the Bible into Navajo. He also established several missions among the Indians of Arizona.

FOOD COMPANIES. Church-owned companies manufacturing health foods of various kinds, especially vegetarian protein foods and whole-grain cereal products. Seventh-day Adventist food manufacture began as a department of the Battle Creek Sanitarium, which produced granola and other cereals and wafers for the patients. Sales were a by-product of diet therapy, as patients ordered foods for their own use after leaving the institution. Thus originated the Battle Creek Sanitarium Health Food Company. The Kellogg brothers, John Harvey and W. K., set up a private business also, that later became famous for its products, but this was not church owned. As the system of Seventh-day Adventist sanitariums spread elsewhere, so did the health foods. Various plants were set up in connection with these medical institutions, and others separately. Following is a list of the companies now operating under church institutional management:

Adventist Health Education Foundation (Egypt Food Factory) (Cairo, Egypt)

Division Health Food Company (Brasilia, Brazil): Buenos Aires Health Food Company (Buenos Aires, Argentina); Brazil Food Factory (São Paulo, Brazil); Uruguay Factory (Productos Frutigran) (Canelones, Uruguay)

Esdakost Food Company (Rimbo, Sweden)

German Health Food Factory (Lueneberg, Germany)

Healthy Kitchen Food Company (Rimbo, Sweden)

Inter-American Health Food Company (Coral Gables, Florida, U.S.A.): Colombia Branch (Medellin, Colombia); Costa Rica Branch (Alajuela, Costa Rica); Haiti Branch (Port-au-Prince, Haiti); Jamaica Branch (Westico Foods) (Mandeville, Jamaica); Mexico-Montemorelos Branch (Montemorelos, Mexico); Mexico-Navojoa Branch (Navojoa, Mexico); Mexico Sales Branch (Montemorelas, Mexico); Puerto Rico Branch (Rio Piedras, Puerto Rico); Trinidad Branch (College Health Foods) (Port-of-Spain, Trinidad)

Japan Food Factory (Chiba-Kan, Japan)

Korean Sahmyook Food (Choongchung-nam-do, Korea)

Mission Health Food Company (Bangkok, Thailand)

PHAG Food Factory (Gland, Switzerland)

Sanitarium Health Food Company (Wahroonga, Australia): Adelaide Branch (Adelaide, Australia); Auckland Factory (Auckland, New Zealand); Brisbane Branch (Moorooka, Australia); Carmel Factory (Carmel, Australia); Christchurch Factory (Christchurch, New Zealand); Cooranbong Factory (Cooranbong, Australia); Melbourne Branch (Kilsyth, Australia); New Zealand Branch (Auckland, New Zealand); Palmerston North Factory (Longburn, New Zealand); Perth Branch (Victoria Park, Australia); Sydney Branch (Castle Hill, Australia); Warburton Factory (Warburton, Australia)

Philippine Union College Health Foods (Silang, Cavite, Philippines)

Spanish Food Factory (Sagunto, Spain)

Swedish Nutana Food Company (Rimbo, Sweden).

FOODS. *See* Diet; Health Principles.

FOOT WASHING. By washing the disciples' feet when He instituted the ordinance of the Lord's Supper, Jesus made use of a common practice of the day and gave it spiritual significance (John 13:1-17). By this act of humility He subdued the spirit of pride and the desire for supremacy that pervaded the disciples' hearts.

The ritual of foot washing was generally observed in the early church (cf. 1 Tim. 5:10). Later foot washing was sometimes practiced in connection with the love feast, or agape, in the apostolic church. Inasmuch as the agape provided an opportunity for feeding the poor, it also became an occasion for washing their feet. Later on, as a result of excesses, various church councils forbade the celebration of the agape, and this may provide a clue to the disappearance of foot washing as a general practice. The Council of Toledo (A.D. 694) recommended foot washing on Maundy Thursday (the Thursday preceding Easter). Foot washing was later used, in some instances, in connection with baptism or as a substitute for it, and sometimes even at marriages.

The earliest extant nonbiblical reference to foot washing is in Canon 48 of the Council of Elvira (A.D. 306), which forbids priests and clerics to wash the feet of newly baptized persons when they leave the baptismal font, a practice that was followed in Ireland, northern Italy, certain parts of Spain, and Gaul, but, according to the testimony of Ambrose, not at Rome. This rule was later incorporated into canonical law. See SB 763-767.

Commenting on John 13:1-17, early Church Fathers, such as Origen, usually considered the practice of foot washing a spiritual experience and a symbol of humility. But there were other opinions. Ambrose, bishop of Milan, explained that newly baptized persons were anointed on the head and their feet were washed, so that, as in the case of Peter, "hereditary sins might be done away with, for our sins are remitted by baptism" *(On the Mysteries,* NPNF, 2nd series, vol. 10, p. 321). In Ambrose' opinion, foot washing was also "a help towards humility." It also has a spiritual experience: "Wash the steps of my mind that I may not sin again. Wash the heel of my soul, . . . that I feel not the serpent's bite on the foot of my soul" *(Of the Holy Spirit,* NPNF, p. 95). For Augustine of Hippo, foot washing not only indicated humility among brethren but was to be practiced for mutual forgiveness. Especially on the occasion of foot washing, he said, "We know that of this also we were admonished . . . that we should confess our faults one to another, and pray for one another" *(On the Gospel of John,* NPNF, 1st series, vol. 7, p. 306). One reason that foot washing was not literally and mutually practiced was that many interpreted Christ's injunction spiritually; that is, they held that Jesus' example was to be considered merely a pattern of what the Christian should do and was not necessarily to be a mechanical, physical repetition of the washing of feet.

Early Adventists debated among themselves the question of foot washing. In 1845 advocates referred to this as "an example for *showing* our love to the brethren, by an act of humility on the part of the superior" *(Day-Star* 8:11, Oct. 25, 1845), and held that it was important to observe "*all* the commands of Jesus, even to washing one another's feet" *(ibid.* 8:1, Oct. 18, 1845). The practice was sometimes referred to as our Lord's "least commandment" *(ibid.* 7:8, Aug. 18, 1845). Opposers of the practices of foot washing and the "holy kiss" (Rom. 16:16, etc.) linked these rites with fanaticism, doubtless because they were practiced by some of the fanatics in New England who demonstrated their humility by bizarre methods.

In 1854 Ellen White warned that members had "not always moved as judiciously as they should," and spoke of avoiding the appearance of evil *(Supplement to the Christian Experience and Views of Ellen G. White* [1854], pp. 37, 38).

Seventh-day Adventists observe the ceremony immediately preceding the Lord's Supper, and therefore it is sometimes called the preparatory service. It is also called the ordinance of humility. It is suggested that participants correct misunderstandings and confess their faults one to another at this service. Men and women take part in the service separately. The exchange of a kiss by the two serving each other is often included, especially among the older members, but it is not considered necessary.

As to the significance of the service, the following is quoted from *The Desire of Ages* (p. 650) in the *Church Manual* (p. 82): "This ordinance is Christ's appointed preparation for the sacramental service. While pride, variance, and strife for supremacy are cherished, the heart cannot enter into fellowship with Christ. We are not prepared to receive the communion of His body and His blood. Therefore it was that Jesus appointed the memorial of His humiliation to be first observed."

Commenting further on the significance of the service in the context of the institution of the ordinance by Jesus, Ellen G. White says: "The service which Peter refused was the type of a higher cleansing. Christ had come to wash the heart from the stain of sin. In refusing to allow Christ to wash his feet, Peter was refusing the higher cleansing included in the lower. . . . These words ["He that is washed needeth not save to wash his feet, but is clean every whit"] mean more than bodily cleanliness. Christ is still speaking of the higher cleansing as illustrated by the lower. He who came from the bath was clean, but the sandaled feet soon became dusty, and again needed to be washed. So Peter and his brethren had been washed in the great fountain opened for sin and uncleanness. Christ acknowledged them as His. But temptation had led them into evil, and they still needed His cleansing grace. When Jesus girded Himself with a towel to wash the dust from their feet, He desired by that very act to wash the alienation, jealousy, and pride from their hearts. This was of far more consequence than the washing of their dusty feet. With the spirit they then had, not one of them was prepared for communion with Christ. Until brought into a state of humility and love, they were not prepared to partake of the paschal supper, or to share in the memorial service which Christ was about to institute. Their hearts must be cleansed. Pride and self-seeking create dissension and hatred, but all this Jesus washed away in washing their feet. A change of feeling was brought about" (DA 646).

FORD, HARRY EUGENE (1889-1938). Administrator. He was born in Indiana and attended Beechwood Academy, studied nursing at the Wabash Valley Sanitarium, and graduated with a B.S. degree from Purdue University (1913). Afterward he worked as laboratory technician at Lafayette, Indiana. After service in the Medical Corps of the Army during World War I, in 1919 he installed and afterward operated X-ray equipment at Hinsdale Sanitarium. After 17 years there, during which for a time he acted as secretary of the board of management, he became business manager of Riverside Sanitarium and Hospital (1936), an all-Black-staffed medical institution.

FORD, ORLEY (1893-1972). Missionary to South and Central America. After his graduation from Walla Walla College in 1917, Orley and his bride, the former Lillian Shafer, sailed for Peru, where they served for four years. Soon after their arrival an Indian came to the mission and said that his son had a "sore foot." Orley was horrified to see that gangrene had already set in and progressed to the young man's knee. Amputation was the only solution, and the young missionary, who had completed a four-month course in medical techniques, performed the surgery with the only instruments available—a butcher knife and an ordinary saw. Later he successfully performed two additional surgeries and also made the man a satisfactory wooden leg.

The Fords moved next to Ecuador, where they dedicated nine years of their lives to the people of that country. Beginning in 1930, they served in several Central American countries, where Ford carried the responsibility as president in three different missions for 27 years. The Fords retired in 1961, but elected to stay in El Salvador, where he remained active until his death. At the time of his passing he had set a record in Seventh-day Adventist mission history, having devoted 55 years to mission service. At his request he was buried in El Salvador, among the people he loved.

FOREIGN MISSION BOARD. *See* Mission Board.

FOREIGN MISSIONARY SEMINARY. *See* Columbia Union College.

FOREIGN MISSIONS. *See* Missions.

FOREKNOWLEDGE. The doctrine that God, possessing perfect knowledge, foresees all future events. The Scriptures offer abundant testimony of God's ability to predict the future, and offer this ability as an evidence of His claim to deity (Isa. 41:4, 22, 23; 42:9; 46:9, 10; Dan. 2:28; Acts 3:18). No other so-called god can do so.

Seventh-day Adventists recognize three broad categories of predictive prophecy as attesting God's foreknowledge. First are predictions of divine purpose independent of humanity's will. For instance, God predicted the atonement of Christ and the final triumph of righteousness (Gen. 3:15; Dan. 2:44; Rev. 11:15; 20:12-15; 11:27). The second class consists of predictions of humanity's actions, as, for example, the many OT prophecies of the behavior of the Jewish people toward Christ (Isa. 53). The Scripture reports a great many such prophecies of contingent events (1 Sam. 23:10-13; 1 Kings 13:20-26; 2 Kings 13:19). The third class consists of predictions of divine reward or punishment. Some of these are pronouncements of inevitable retribution for sins committed; others are of a conditional nature, in which the fulfillment will be reward in case of obedience or destruction in case of rebellion. Had Israel continued in obedience, the threats of retribution would never have been fulfilled (see Deut. 4:27, 40; 6:3, 18, 19; 28:58-68; Lev. 26:27-33).

In Reformed theology, which follows Calvin's lead, the divine decrees precede God's foreknowledge.

God has decreed all things and has decreed them with their causes and conditions in the exact order in which they come to pass; and His foreknowledge of future things (and also of contingent events) rests on His decree (L. Berkhof, *Systematic Theology,* pp. 67, 68). Seventh-day Adventists, distinguishing between foreknowledge and predetermination, deny categorically that the evil deeds of men were fixed by divine decree. God foresees and foretells, but "the prophecies do not shape the characters of the men who fulfill them" (Ellen G. White, in *Review and Herald* 77:721, Nov. 13, 1900). God "did not work to bring about a certain condition of things, but He knew that such a condition would exist" (Ellen G. White, in SDACom 6:1082). The SDA view of divine foreknowledge approximates the Arminian position.

FOREST HILLS ACADEMY. A coeducational boarding senior high school formerly operated on a 365-acre (150-hectare) tract of land in Magkiangkang, Bayugan, Agusan del Sur, about 30 miles (50 kilometers) from Butuan City, the timber city of Mindanao Island, South Philippines.

The school was a successor to the former Butuan City Mission Academy, established in 1969, which was situated in the heart of Butuan City. Its buildings were mainly of secondhand materials, splitboards, and round timbers purchased cheaply.

Work on the establishment of Forest Hills Academy began in 1972. Under the direction of T. C. Cabaluna, R. L. Cabaluna, and a group of laypersons, buildings of temporary materials were erected.

Forest Hills Academy served as a training school for the entire Northeastern Mindanao Mission field.

The school was closed in the mid-1970s.

Principals—Butuan City Mission Academy: P. Niere, 1969-1970; J. V. Emverda, 1970-1972; *Forest Hills Academy:* J. V. Emverda, 1972-1973; R. L. Cabaluna, 1973-1975; N. N. Macarine, 1975-1976.

FOREST LAKE ACADEMY. A coeducational day and boarding school on the senior high school level, situated 11 miles (18 kilometers) northwest of Orlando, Florida, and four miles (6.5 kilometers) east of Apopka (post office, Maitland, Florida). On the 385-acre (155-hectare) campus overlooking Mirror Lake are the boys' and girls' dormitories, administration building, gymnasium-auditorium, bindery-press, cafeteria, maintenance building, laundry, and faculty homes. Approximately 80 acres (30 hectares) are planted in citrus trees. The academy is fully accredited by the Southern Association of Colleges and Schools, the state of Florida, and the SDA Board of Regents.

Forest Lake Academy had two forerunners. The first Seventh-day Adventist secondary school in Florida was at Fort Ogden (1909-1912), called the Fort Ogden School, then the South Florida Intermediate School. In 1918, on the campus of the Florida Sanitarium and Hospital in Orlando, a new intermediate school called Winyah Lake School (later Academy) was established, and began its first year with an enrollment of about 50. This was a 10-grade school, which later became Forest Lake Academy.

In August 1925 a 160-acre (65-hectare) tract was purchased for $16,000 from the heirs of J. W. Emerson, and in 1925-1926 F. H. Parrish and his wife and 12 young people moved to the new property. The nine-room farmhouse was used as the girls' dormitory, dining room, kitchen, and administration building. The boys camped in the barn. This school was known at first as the Florida Conference Academy, or simply Florida Academy. In 1926 it became known as Forest Lake Academy. One dormitory was built in 1926-1927, and the second the following year. A part of the administration building was erected in 1936-1937; the rest of the structure was added during J. M. Howell's administration. A camp meeting tabernacle was built about 1930, later enlarged, and finally used for youth sessions. A gymnasium-auditorium was built in 1954.

In 1932-1933 Forest Lake Academy's first twelfth-grade class, 13 in number, was graduated. *The Reflector,* the school paper, was first published in 1929-1930, and the first yearbook, the *Mirror,* in 1945.

Under K. A. Wright's administration the original acreage was more than doubled by the purchase of additional land. A part of this land, planted in grapefruit trees, is still a source of income.

Because of the age of most of the buildings, the Florida Conference voted in 1962 to raise a million-dollar rebuilding fund over a five-year period. Under this program, which was under the direction of H. H. Schmidt, conference president, and William Fuchs, principal, a boys' dormitory, a maintenance building, a cafeteria, and a bindery-press were constructed, and a new girls' dormitory and a new administration building were scheduled and soon completed.

Principals: F. H. Parrish, 1925-1927; D. C. Ludington, 1927-1929; W. E. McClure, 1929-1932; C. A. Schutt, 1932-1933; W. E. McClure, 1933-1937; K. A. Wright, 1937-1938; J. E. Whelpley, 1938; K. A. Wright, 1939-1942; J. M. Howell, 1942-1948; H. M. Lodge, 1948-1950; J. M. Ackerman, 1950-1953; R. L. Osmunson, 1953-1955; W. E. McClure, 1955-1958; L. C. Strickland, 1958-1960; William Fuchs, 1960-1965; L. C. Stannard, 1965-1968; Stephen Yost, 1968-1971; R. H. Fox, 1971-1974; E. F. Armour, 1974; John Wagner, 1974-1976; H. D. Kinsey, 1976-1983; Robert Caskey, 1983- .

FORMOSA. *See* China, Republic of.

FORSYTH MEMORIAL SANITARIUM AND HOSPITAL. A 33-bed general hospital, owned and operated by the Florida Conference from 1947 to 1964. It was situated in the state capital, Tallahassee. The institution had facilities for medical, surgical, and obstetrical cases, also a diagnostic laboratory and X-ray facilities, and a Dietary Department to provide regular and special diets as ordered by the physicians. The hospital was licensed by the Florida State Board of Health as a general hospital and was a member of the American Hospital Association, the Florida Hospital Association, and the Northwest Florida Hospital Council.

Officers—Medical Directors: J. P. Chapin, 1947-1948; William E. Westcott, 1949-1962. *Business Managers:* G. C. Williamson, 1947-1948; F. G. Winters, 1949-1961; J. F. Medanich, 1961-1962. *Administrator:* J. F. Medanich, 1962-1964.

FORT OGDEN SCHOOL. *See* Forest Lake Academy.

FORTY-TWO MONTHS. *See* Revelation, Interpretation of.

FOSS, HAZEN (fl. 1844; d. 1893). A young man who experienced visions in the autumn of 1844. He is described as a man of fine appearance, pleasing address, and education. He lived at Poland, Maine, about 30 miles (50 kilometers) north of Portland.

Of the Millerite persuasion, Foss firmly believed that the second advent of Christ would take place on Oct. 22, 1844. In September or early October of that year he had a vision in which he saw the travels of the Adventists to the City of God and was instructed to deliver to them certain messages of warning. He also saw the trials and persecution that would come to him as the result of his faithfulness in telling what he had seen. Subsequently, he declined to relate the vision.

The disappointment of Oct. 22 left Foss with the feeling that he had been deceived. In a second vision he was warned that if he refused to relate it to others the burden would be taken from him and placed on one of the weakest of the Lord's children. As he contemplated his responsibility he dreaded the reaction should he declare that he had experienced visions, for the Millerite leaders had taken a stand against such manifestations. At one time a group assembled to hear him tell of what he had been shown, but he refused to relate it. Then one day very strange feelings came to him, and he heard a voice saying, "You have grieved away the Spirit of the Lord."

According to Ellen White's account (letter 37, 1890), when he heard the voice he was horrified at his stubbornness and rebellion and told the Lord he would relate the vision. Calling a meeting, he attempted to communicate it, but his mind could not recall the vision. After several attempts he cried out in despair, "It is gone from me; I can say nothing, the Spirit of the Lord has left me." The meeting was described by those who were present as "the most terrible meeting they were ever in."

In December 1844, after this experience, Ellen G. Harmon (later White) had her first vision. At the time Ellen Harmon knew nothing of the experience of Hazen Foss, but while visiting in Poland, Maine, in February 1845 she related at Maguire's Hill the first vision she had seen. Foss was invited to the meeting but would not come in. From outside the closed door he heard her account. The next day he called on her at her sister's home in Poland, and recounted his experience. As she reported it, he declared, "Ellen, . . . the Lord gave me a message to bear to His people. And I refused after being told the consequences, I was proud; I was unreconciled to the disappointment. I murmured against God and wished myself dead. Then I felt a strange feeling come over me. I shall be henceforth as one dead to spiritual things. I heard you talk last night. I believe the visions are taken from me, and given to you. Do not refuse to obey God, for it will be at the peril of your soul. I am a lost man. You are chosen of God; be faithful in doing your work, and the crown I might have had, you will receive" (Ellen G. White letter 37, 1890).

Foss lived until 1893, but from the time he refused to relate his visions he had no interest in religious matters.

FOUNTAIN HEAD ACADEMY. *See* Highland Academy.

FOUNTAIN HEAD SANITARIUM. *See* Highland Hospital.

FOUR BEASTS. *See* Daniel, Interpretation of, 6.

FOUR DK PLAN (usually written 4 DK Plan). Abbreviation for the Four Dimensional Key to the Cause of Alcoholism, a Temperance Department program developed in 1969 by Ernest H. J. Steed, General Conference temperance director, in cooperation with Dr. L. A. Senseman, of Glendale Adventist Medical Center.

This plan consisted of both educational preventive aspects and rehabilitative measures to meet the problem of alcoholism.

The 4 DK Plan was discontinued in 1980 when the GC Health and Temperance departments were joined.

FOUR EMPIRES OF DANIEL. *See* Daniel, Interpretation of, 6.

FOX RIVER ACADEMY. *See* Illinois Conference.

FOY, WILLIAM ELLIS (fl. 1840s). A Millerite preacher, of interest to Seventh-day Adventists because his name is occasionally mentioned as one who in 1842 and 1844 had visions relating to the Adventist (Millerite) movement. He was described as a tall, light-skinned Black man, an eloquent speaker. He lived in New England and as a young man in 1835 gave his heart to Christ. Sometime thereafter he became a member of the Freewill Baptist Church. However, in 1842 he was preparing to take holy orders as an Episcopal minister. It was at this time that he had two visions relating to the near advent of Christ and to last-day events. Prior to this, while deeply religious, he had been, by his own testimony, "opposed to the doctrine of Jesus' near approach," but after the visions he joined the Millerites in heralding the message of the expectation of Christ's coming.

The account of two initial visions of William Foy, together with a brief sketch of his Christian experience, was published in 1845 in pamphlet form in Portland, Maine. The first occurred Jan. 18, 1842, while he was attending a prayer service in Boston on Southark Street. According to eyewitnesses he was in vision two and a half hours. The pamphlet includes the statement of a physician who examined him during a vision and testified that he could find no appearance of life "except around the heart." As Foy declared: "My breath left me."

In the first vision, Foy saw the reward of the faithful and the punishment of sinners. Although he felt it his duty to tell what he had seen, he made the excuse that he had not been instructed to relate it. Finding no peace of mind, he had a description of the vision printed, but it was a "very imperfect sketch." In a second vision, on Feb. 4, 1842, in which he saw multitudes of those who had not died and those who had been raised from the dead being assembled to receive their reward, he heard the instruction that he was to reveal what he had seen and to warn his fellow creatures to flee from the wrath to come.

Foy's unwillingness to relate to others what he had seen stemmed not only from the prejudice of the Millerites against any who claimed to have divine revelations but also, he said, from "the prejudice among the people against those of my color." He questioned in his mind, "Why should these things be given to me, to bear to the world?"

On Feb. 6, 1842, the pastor of the Bloomfield Street church in Boston called upon Foy to relate the visions in his house of worship. He consented reluctantly, and the next afternoon he faced a large congregation. As he began to speak, his fear left him, and he related with great freedom the things he had seen.

After this he traveled for three months delivering his messages to crowded houses of many denominations. When speaking, he wore the robes of the Episcopal clergy. As he graphically described the heavenly world, the New Jerusalem, and the compassionate love of Christ, and exhorted the unconverted to seek God, many responded to his entreaties. However, because his family needed support, Foy, after three months, retired from public work to labor with his hands. Three months later, feeling impelled to deliver his message, he again took up his public ministry, expecting soon to see his Saviour.

Ellen Harmon heard Foy speak in Beethoven Hall in her home city, Portland, Maine, when she was but a girl. According to J. N. Loughborough, Foy had a third vision near the time of the expectation in 1844 in which he saw three platforms, which he could not understand in the light of his belief in the imminent coming of Christ. In perplexity he ceased public work.

Some have questioned the genuineness of William Foy's experience, but others have felt that the "visions bore clear evidence of being the genuine manifestations of the Spirit of God" (Loughborough, *The Great Second Advent Movement,* p. 146). Ellen White in a 1912 interview (EGW Document File 231) reported that she had talked with him once when he was present in a meeting in which she was relating her own early visions, and that he had said that her account was just what he had seen. She apparently regarded his experience as genuine.

FRÄKORNID-BÓKAFORLAG ADVENTISTA. *See* Iceland Publishing House.

FRANCE. A republic in Western Europe, with a land area of 220,668 square miles (571,500 square kilometers) (including the island of Corsica) and a population (1994) of 57.8 million. The majority of the people are of French nationality, but there are large groups of Italians, Spaniards, Poles, Portuguese, and North Africans. French is spoken universally, but the people also speak Breton in Brittany; a German dialect in Alsace and Lorraine; Spanish, Catalan, and Basque on the Spanish border; Flemish along the Belgian frontier in the northeast; and Italian in Corsica and in the southeast. The religion of the people is mainly Roman Catholic, but there are about 800,000 Protestants, chiefly Calvinist and Lutheran, about 700,000 Jews, and about 3 million Muslims from North Africa.

The peoples of what is now France (Romanized Gaul) had contacts with Christianity by the second century A.D. In the fifth century, after the Germanic invasions, the church served as the bond for the fusion of many tribes into the Frankish state, marking the beginning of many centuries during which the church played a powerful part in French society. The crowning of Charlemagne, the Frankish king, as the "Roman Emperor" by the pope in the year 800 symbolized this peculiar relation. But through the centuries there was opposition to the power of Rome, and southern

France was the home of reform movements, such as those of the Albigenses and the Waldenses, protesting against the practices of the Roman Church. The extermination of the Albigenses was the object of one of the crusades (1208-1213).

When the Reformation came to France it gained adherents among the simple and the noble people alike, but the church used the power of the state to suppress the Protestants. Later this alliance of the reactionary church with the absolutist state led to the union of their opponents, the liberal political groups and the anticlerical and antireligious movements. Toleration was granted the Protestants by the Edict of Nantes in 1598, but as the power of the state grew, the edict was revoked in 1685, and from then until the French Revolution only the Roman Catholic religion was allowed to exist in France. The revocation of the edict resulted in severe persecution and caused the mass flight of Protestant Huguenots from France, leaving entire localities desolate. The emigration deeply hurt the economy, because the country lost a high percentage of its artisan and commercial classes. The action of the church in this period led to the absolute rejection of the Christian religion by the leaders of France in the course of the French Revolution (1789). But the complete eradication of religion was not accepted by the masses, nor were various substitutes, such as theism, theophilanthropism, and the worship of reason. Under Napoleon the church was again called to support the state, and an understanding with Rome made the clergy the servants of the state. The Restoration retained this arrangement and it was continued until 1905, when finally the church was separated from the state. Still, numerous laws imposing control on the exercise of religion were retained, and the complete freedom of religion did not come until later in the century. The effect of the centuries-long struggle between the church and the state and between the forces of reaction and liberalism thoroughly secularized the French people.

Overseas Departments and Territories. A number of the overseas departments and territories of France are described in separate articles. *See* Comoro Islands; French Guiana; French Polynesia; Guadeloupe and dependencies; Martinique; New Caledonia and Loyalty Islands; Réunion; and Wallis Archipelago.

Seventh-day Adventist Statistics. The territory of France is part of the Franco-Belgian Union Conference, which in turn is part of the Euro-Africa Division. Statistics (1992) for *France:* churches, 114; members, 10,758; ordained ministers, 74; licensed ministers, 23. Headquarters for the Franco-Belgian Union: 680-684 Avenue de La Liberation, 77350 Le Mee sur Seine, France.

Statistics for the conferences—*North France Conference:* churches, 60; members, 5,286; ordained ministers, 26; licensed ministers, 2; teachers, 2; elementary schools, 1. Headquarters: 130 Boulevard de l'Hôpital, 75013 Paris, France. *South France Conference:* churches, 54; members, 3,925; ordained ministers, 23; licensed ministers, 3. Headquarters: Rue du Romarin, 34830 Clapiers, France.

Institutions. Life and Health Publishing House, Maison de Retraite (Le Foyer du Romarin), Salève Adventist Institute.

Seventh-day Adventist Work. *Beginnings in Southern France.* The work J. N. Andrews carried on among the French-speaking people in Switzerland after his arrival from the United States in October 1874 was a prelude to Seventh-day Adventist work in France. D. T. Bourdeau, also from the United States, joined Andrews in Switzerland in January 1876. His first work in what is now France began in what until after World War I was German territory. In the spring of 1876, even before he and Andrews launched the monthly *Les Signes des Temps* in Switzerland, copies of which were sent into France, he spent three weeks in what was then Alsace, Germany. He reported in the *Review and Herald* (47:181, June 8, 1876) that "while Brn. Andrews and Aufranc were making preparations for the work in Bâle [Basel] I came to Le Ban de la Roche, Alsace, a distance of seventy-five miles, to spend a few weeks aiding Bro. Scheppler, who had come here from Illinois on a visit, and to follow up the work of French tracts sent from America."

When he left, six had decided to keep the Sabbath. He merely visited interested families on this trip, but on his return for 10 days or more in August, he preached and baptized a few converts.

In October of the same year he settled with his family in southern France. There he preached in different places but especially in Valence, where 17 people were baptized. Because of many restrictions from the ecclesiastical authorities, Bourdeau and Andrews went to Paris in March 1877 to ask the government for permission to work with more liberty. Bourdeau left France in September 1877 and went to work in the country of Switzerland.

In 1878 Bourdeau reported in the *Review and Herald* that political changes made it easier to preach and distribute tracts than formerly. A lay evangelist of Valence, named Gabert, circulated publications, took subscriptions for *Les Signes,* and preached in three departments, at Crest, Beaufort, Ouste, Lyon, Villefort, and other places. D. T. Bourdeau joined him at St. Didier when strong opposition arose. Public evangelism was hindered by the French law that required such meetings to be held in a church building.

In 1884 D. T. Bourdeau held a series of meetings in Branges, a small village, baptized a number of people, and organized a church of 17 members. Later he went to Bastia, on the island of Corsica, where *Les Signes des Temps* had created an interest, and, after only about a month's work, established a church of 11 members. In the mid-1880s Jean-Pierre Badaut, a recent convert, sold SDA publications in France.

About 1890 an interest was awakened in several other towns and villages in the south of France, particularly Nîmes, in towns in the Department of Gard, and in Lacaze, Tarn. In 1893 a Sabbath school was established in Pierre-Ségade, near Lacaze. In 1894 work was begun in Besançon and in Lyon. In 1897 there were four workers in France.

About 1888 Emery P. Auger, a colporteur from the United States, had attempted to sell SDA publications, but it was not until 1897, when two colporteurs were active in the region of Montbéliard and in Saône-et-Loire, that any success in this undertaking was reported.

At the end of the century there were three more ministers in France: J. Curdy, T. Nussbaum, and D. Lecoultre, all from Switzerland. In 1900 L. P. Tièche was placed at the head of the work in southern France.

Northern France Entered. The capital of France was not forgotten. The financial report of the Central European Conference, September 1899, mentions a fund for establishing a mission in Paris. At a meeting of the conference that same year a pledge was made to establish a mission in Paris.

In April 1900 Paul Roth and his wife went to Paris, hoping to establish themselves in giving treatments in private homes. Two colporteurs were also sent to sell *Les Signes des Temps* and the health journal *Le Vulgarisateur,* but because entrance to homes for the work they were doing was forbidden, they had little success. A. L. Meyrat and Arnold Roth, from Switzerland, opened a health food enterprise at Clichy known as Pur-Aliment. Jean Vuilleumier, pastor and editor of periodicals, took an active part in these beginnings. On Apr. 6, 1901, at the end of the first SDA Communion service held in Paris, a church was organized.

In 1902 when the French-Latin Union Mission was organized, with B. G. Wilkinson as president, J. Curdy was made president of the French Mission. In the fall of 1902 Wilkinson settled in Paris and conducted a Bible course in 1902-1903, to train French evangelists. These students devoted part of their time to canvassing and personal evangelism.

By Sept. 10, 1902, there were about 10 churches and 130 members in France (which at that time did not include Alsace-Lorraine), and by Dec. 31, 1907, according to the *Statistical Report,* there were 16 churches and companies and 227 members.

The French Conference. In 1907 the French Mission was made a conference, with H. H. Dexter, of the United States, as president. But aside from the capital, the north of France had not been touched as yet. After the Latin Union session, held in Vergèze, Department of Gard, in 1909, an evangelist was sent to Rouen, and another to Lille. Paris had a separate organization as the Paris District. At the beginning of 1914, preceding World War I, there were 346 church members in France.

At a session in Nîmes in August 1918, the conference was reorganized, with Alfred Vaucher as president, and a few months later, at the end of the war, there were 439 members. Some 200 were added when Alsace-Lorraine was receded to France in 1919. The first church there had been organized in Mulhouse in 1901. Others were organized in Strassburg (1902), Metz (1907), Merlebach (1909), and Colmar (1910). The churches of this territory, formerly in the South German Conference, were organized in 1919 as the Alsace and Lorraine Conference and attached to the Latin Union Conference.

In 1923 the French Conference was divided into two, the North France and South France conferences, the dividing line being approximately the Loire River. Alsace-Lorraine was called the East France Conference.

Franco-Belgian Union. In 1928 the Latin Union Conference was dissolved and the Franco-Belgian Union Conference was formed, composed of the three French conferences and the Belgian Conference. Oscar Meyer was elected president, and headquarters were established in Paris. In 1949 a fourth conference, that of Southwest France, was organized with 200 members, with headquarters in Bordeaux. Altogether in France there were at that time 57 churches, with 2,500 members. In 1968 it was decided to combine the three French conferences into two: the North France Conference, under the direction of André Matton, with headquarters in Paris; and the South France Conference, under the direction of Elie Davy, with headquarters in Montpellier. In the same year, Luxembourg was attached to the Belgian Conference. The growth in membership proved the reorganization to have been a wise decision.

Churches and Institutions in the Paris Area. When the Franco-Belgian Union was organized in 1928, Paris had a church of about 120 members. Some 30 years were required to reach this number. In 1931 the church occupied new quarters on the Boulevard de l'Hôpital, in the union conference headquarters building. After World War II, when these quarters became too small for the members, a former Anglican church building was purchased in Neuilly, a residential suburb of Paris, and some of the members established a new congregation. Churches were also organized at Versailles and at the publishing house that operated since 1922 at Dammarie-les-Lys *(see* Life and Health Publishing House [France]). Since 1965 six more churches have been organized in the Paris area, four of them in their own buildings. The Paris area had about 1,500 members in 1974.

When Algeria became independent in 1962, many French SDAs returned to France, most of them settling in the southern part of the country.

Before World War II, most of the French SDA churches met in rented quarters, which were often inadequate for the work of the church. In 1960 extensive plans were laid for church construction, and by December 1969 nine new chapels had been built.

For years it had been felt that the SDA message should be proclaimed over the radio in the French language. Finally Charles Gerber began weekly broadcasts in May 1947 over Radio Luxembourg; in April 1948 talks were also introduced on Radio Monte Carlo. A radio recording studio was set up in Paris in the headquarters building in 1949. Maurice Tièche began educational talks over the French National network in 1950. In the studio in Paris, broadcasts in French and other languages were produced, transmitted mainly over Radio Luxembourg and Radio Monte Carlo until 1968, and in the 1970s, shortwave over Trans World Radio from Lisbon. In 1993 six radio stations in France were broadcasting the SDA message.

Bible correspondence courses in France began in 1948; several series are being offered at the present time by the Franco-Belgian Union. They are advertised over the radio and by leaflets distributed by the church members.

The circulation of publications is strongly promoted in France, as is also the work of the different departments in an atmosphere of religious liberty.

FRANCO-BELGIAN UNION CONFERENCE. *See* Belgium; Euro-Africa Division; France; Luxembourg; Monaco.

FRANCO-HAITIAN ADVENTIST SEMINARY. *See* Haitian Adventist College.

FRANKLIN, ERNEST EDWARD (1890-1956). Canadian-born leader in publishing work. He entered service as a student colporteur in 1908. After graduation from Emmanuel Missionary College in 1913 he became field missionary leader successively in the Indiana, Wisconsin, Atlantic Union, and Lake Union conferences. From 1930 to his retirement in 1954 he was associate secretary of the General Conference Publishing Department.

FRASER VALLEY ADVENTIST ACADEMY. A senior academy owned and operated by the British Columbia Conference and situated at 26026 48th Avenue, Aldergrove, British Columbia.

Fraser Valley Adventist Academy, located in British Columbia's rural Lower Fraser Valley region near metropolitan Vancouver, began operating as a consolidated school in 1972. At that time several churches in the valley united their small one- and two-room schools into a four-room four-teacher academy with an enrollment of 79 students. Within three years the school grew to a full senior secondary school with more than 150 students and nine teachers.

A volunteer work project, organized to expand facilities in 1974, led to the constituency's ability to build a $150,000 classroom complex for less than $100,000. By 1993 the constituency had grown to include seven churches, 200 students, and six bus routes, serving church youth living over an area of 600 square miles (1,550 square kilometers).

The school is denominationally accredited and is approved by the government of British Columbia. An enriched curriculum prepares students for university entrance anywhere.

Principal: D. Vanderwerff, 1972-1977; W. Matheson, 1977-1978; A. J. Sands, 1978-1982; I. Cheeseman, 1982-1987; E. Rau, 1988- .

FRAUCHIGER, EMIL E. (1865-1947). Minister and administrator in Europe and Turkey. Born in Lausanne, Switzerland, he was in the group of 22 who in 1886 accepted the Seventh-day Adventist faith in Lausanne as the result of the preaching of J. Erzberger and L. R. Conradi. He immediately entered the colporteur work, serving first in his homeland and two years later in Rhenish Prussia, where a group had begun to keep the Sabbath as a result of reading the Bible.

Proving himself to be successful in winning souls, he was called into evangelistic work in Germany. In 1907 he was elected president of the Rhenish-Prussian Conference. In 1909 he went to Constantinople as superintendent of the Turkish Mission. The following year he was appointed superintendent of the Levant Union Mission, with headquarters in Constantinople, where he remained through the dangers and horrors of World War I. From 1919 to 1923 he served as president of the Czechoslovakian Union Conference. From 1924 until his death he lived and worked, as his strength permitted, in Switzerland.

FREDERIKSHAVN HIGH SCHOOL. *See* Danish Junior College.

FREE WILL. The capacity with which the Creator endowed human beings that enables them to make choices as to whether to obey or to disobey God, to be subject to moral law or not to be subject to it. This endowment precludes the use of force on God's part to effect a change in human beings. God seeks to draw people to Him, but leaves each person free to decide for himself or herself whether or not to respond. If people choose to ally themselves with God, His will becomes omnipotent in their lives and nothing can keep them from following God's plan.

Calvinism and Arminianism propose two greatly differing views regarding free will. These views reach far back into church history. Augustine spoke of what he called God's irresistible grace and absolute foreordination, which would preclude a truly free will. Pelagius, a British monk living in Rome, rejected Augustinianism, declaring that people could rise up and determine to work out their own salvation in fear and trembling. Thus began the unending controversy over divine grace and human free will.

Calvin asserted that God, by an irrevocable decree, had destined certain persons to salvation and others to reprobation, irrespective of their personal choice or attitude. Those thus appointed to salvation would inevitably be saved, and all others as certainly damned. According to Calvin, Jesus Christ did not die for all, but only for those who had thus been elected by God to salvation. Those destined to salvation would be unable to resist the Spirit of God working in their hearts, whereas no desire or effort on the part of those predestined to eternal damnation could possibly avert that fate. To the strict Calvinist, election rests solely on the sovereign good pleasure of God, not on faith or works.

Arminianism, on the other hand, defines predestination as an everlasting decree, in Christ, to make everlasting life available to all sinners who, by His power and grace, accept Jesus Christ and persevere in the good fight of faith (Eph. 1:3-8). God will reject only those who voluntarily refuse the offer of divine grace. According to Arminius, Jesus died for all, and by virtue of His death all are eligible to accept pardon from sin, to find acceptance with God, to remain steadfast to the end, and to enter God's eternal kingdom. Sin deprived humanity of the capacity to exercise free will; by His death on the cross Christ restored that capacity. Apart from God's grace human beings are helpless. All good works are a result of this grace, which, though absolutely necessary, is not irresistible. Through this divine grace men and women can be victorious over sin, the world, and the devil.

Numerous modifications of the theories of Calvin and Arminius have come in since their day. Seventh-day Adventists find elements of biblical truth in both Calvinism and Arminianism. Both the OT and the NT stress the freedom of the human will (Deut. 28:1, 2, 13-15; Joshua 24:14-25; Isa. 1:19, 20; Jer. 18:7-10; 29:13, 14; Matt. 7:24-27; 23:37; Rom. 6:12, 13; 14:10-12; 2 Cor. 5:10; Rev. 22:17).

God, in grace and mercy, desires that all shall be saved through faith in Jesus Christ, but He leaves with humanity the choice of accepting or rejecting His gracious gift. Everyone is therefore responsible for his or her own destiny. The person who chooses to place his or her free will on the side of God's will, and who wills to keep it there, is invincible "in Jesus Christ." However, by voluntarily surrendering his or her will to the will of God, a person does not thereby lose the freedom of his or her will. The individual can still choose to break the union with Christ, though no force, temptation, coercion, or deception is able to wrest salvation from the one who chooses to serve the Master by a definite, continual committal and action of the will.

FREEMAN, MARGHERITA MARY (1884-1976). Physician. Born in Perth, Western Australia, she graduated from medicine at Sydney University and received further training at Rotunda Hospital, Belfast, Ireland. She served as a physician at the Avondale Adventist Health Retreat until 1912, when she married Dr. T. A. Sherwin and moved to Wahroonga, Sydney, where she and her husband served at the Sydney Adventist Hospital. She died at the Freeman Nursing Home in Perth, an institution named in honor of her lifetime of service to the church in Australia.

FREEMAN NURSING HOME. *See* Seventh-day Adventist Retirement Village.

FRENCH ADVENTIST SEMINARY. *See* Salève Adventist Institute.

FRENCH ANTILLES-GUIANA UNION MISSION. *See* French Guiana; Guadeloupe and Dependencies; Inter-American Division.

FRENCH CAMEROON TRAINING SCHOOL. *See* Nanga-Eboko Adventist Secondary School.

FRENCH CONFERENCE. *See* France.

FRENCH GUIANA. An overseas department of France with an area of 43,740 square miles (112,600 square kilometers), situated on the northeast coast of South America, bounded on the west by Suriname and on the south and east by Brazil. Between the ocean and the mountain ranges there is a coastal strip 10 to 30 miles (16 to 50 kilometers) wide. In 1946 French Guiana, which had until that time been a colony of France, terminated the penal settlement there and was reorganized as an overseas department. The majority of the 101,000 inhabitants (1991 estimate) are of African-American or mixed blood. In the interior there are several tribal groups of Indians. There are also several hundred freed convicts and political deportees from France.

Seventh-day Adventist Statistics. The territory of French Guiana constitutes the French Guiana Mission in the French Antilles-Guiana Union Mission, which in turn is part of the Inter-American Division. Statistics (1993) for *French Guiana:* churches, 4; companies, 8; members, 1,169; elementary schools, 2; ordained ministers, 4; teachers, 11. Headquarters: 39 Rue Schoelcher, Cayenne, French Guiana.

Seventh-day Adventist Work. The first Seventh-day Adventist worker in French Guiana was R. T. Colthurst, who after serving in Algeria and on the island of Mauritius for two terms conceived the idea of going into hitherto-unentered Guiana. Having received permission in 1938 from the Inter-American Division to go to the colony, he paid his own passage from his native Britain to the capital city of Cayenne, but because of the war in Europe he was refused entrance into French Guiana. He waited and worked for about two years in Suriname until the necessary permission was obtained.

Because it was impossible to find a place to carry on public evangelism in French Guiana, Colthurst went from door to door, visiting many of Cayenne's 14,000 inhabitants. He could not sell books, but he made friends. As a result, by the time he was called to British Guiana he had baptized one person and had interested a number of others.

In 1946 the Caribbean Union sent a licensed minister, A. H. Linzau, to continue the personal work begun by Colthurst. After two years in the area he won a group of converts that became the nucleus of the first SDA church. Eager to have their own church building, the members gathered large stones to build one. The president of the Caribbean Union, Robert Pierson, sold French Guiana stamp collections in the United States to raise cash. In 1964 that congregation had the only Protestant church building in Cayenne.

In 1952 Marcel Perau and Paul Joseph, who was a colporteur, opened work in St. Laurent du Maroni, the second-largest city of French Guiana. They also took the SDA message to the Carib Indian tribes that live in the area. The first SDA baptism among these Indians occurred in 1958, when S. B. Jean-Elie baptized nine candidates. The chief of one of the tribes that occupy the reservation of Paddock, to the north of St. Laurent, became a convert. In the late 1950s Jean-Elie gained the favor of the authorities and the people of Cayenne with his welfare work, by providing warm meals to the poor and the former prisoners of the penal colony.

In 1959, shortly after the organization of the French-speaking areas of the Inter-American Division into the Franco-Haitian Union, French Guiana was organized as a mission, with Ernest Veuthey as president. Five months later he was succeeded by Marcel Perau. In December 1962 Eugene Berle succeeded Marcel Perau, who began the work with some other tribes such as the Samamaca, the Bony, and the Bosh. At the same time, the work entered a remote area called St. George near the Brazilian border. Etienne Plumain and Luc Chandeler, successively, became president of the mission. Thomas Labetant is the current president. A secondary school is operated by the mission with the recognition of the government. On Jan. 10, 1974, the second church building of French Guiana was dedicated. At present there are five church buildings, the last having been dedicated on Mar. 28, 1993.

FRENCH GUIANA MISSION. *See* French Guiana; Inter-American Division.

FRENCH-LATIN UNION MISSION. *See* France.

FRENCH POLYNESIA. An overseas territory of France comprising the Gambier, Marquesas, Society, and Tubuaï islands, the Tuamotu archipelago, and Clipperton Island, between about 132° and 157° west longitude and 7° and 28° south latitude, except Clipperton Island, which is situated at about 109° west longitude and 10° north latitude. The territory has a combined area of 1,575 square miles (4,100 square kilometers), with a population (1991) of 188,814. The Tuamotus and Clipperton are low coral atolls, the other groups are made up of high basaltic lavas, each surrounded by a fringe or barrier of coral reefs. The chief products are copra, mother-of-pearl shell, vanilla, and phosphate. The islands produce an abundance of tropical fruits.

The islands were discovered by Europeans in April 1769, when Capt. James Cook was sent by the Royal Society of London to observe a transit of Venus across the sun's disk and to pursue geographic researches. He anchored in Matavai Bay, east of Papeete, now the capital of the territory, where the scientists made their observations.

Early Christian Missions. On Mar. 5, 1797, the London Missionary Society's ship, *Duff,* landed at Tahiti four ordained ministers, a number of artisans, five women, and two children. At first they were favorably received, but tribal fighting endangered their lives. One was murdered; four were maltreated. Most of the missionaries escaped from the island on passing vessels and went to New South Wales. Later they returned, and after the reigning chief, King Pomare, was converted to Christianity in the second decade of the nineteenth century, the entire population was brought under Christian influence. By 1836 the Bible had been translated into Tahitian by Henry Nott, a missionary of the London Missionary Society.

Seventh-day Adventist Statistics. The territory of French Polynesia comprises the French Polynesia Mission, which is a part of the Central Pacific Union Mission, which in turn is a part of the South Pacific Division. Statistics (1993): churches, 26; members, 3,607; ordained ministers, 6. Headquarters are at Papeete, Tahiti.

Seventh-day Adventist Work. The first Seventh-day Adventist to visit Tahiti was John I. Tay, a layperson, who in 1886 spent a few weeks on the island on his way to Pitcairn Island. A. J. Read and his wife, arriving on Tahiti on the first voyage of the *Pitcairn* in 1891, opened SDA work. They returned to the United States in 1895.

Arriving on the second voyage of the *Pitcairn* in 1893, B. J. Cady and his wife settled on Raiatea, which lies about 120 miles (200 kilometers) northwest of Tahiti. E. C. Chapman and his wife, who were on the same boat, assisted by printing literature in the Tahitian language. Cady opened a school in his home and later purchased a property for a school to train national workers. This school was conducted partly on industrial lines. Management and staff included the following missionary families: Close, George Beckner, and H. L. Fowler; also Anna Nelson.

In 1906 the Eastern Polynesian Mission was formed, composed of French Polynesia, Cook Islands, Easter Island, and Pitcairn Island, with headquarters at Raiatea, and with B. J. Cady as superintendent.

In 1908 George L. Sterling and his wife

took charge of the school. In 1909 F. E. Lyndon became mission director. In 1914 the mission reported 43 converts, with four church buildings on the islands of Tahiti, Raiatea, Huahine, and Moorea.

In 1916 the South Pacific mission field was reorganized into three areas: the Central Polynesian Conference, with headquarters in Fiji and C. H. Parker in charge; the Melanesian Mission, with G. F. Jones as superintendent; and the Eastern Polynesian Mission, with headquarters in Tahiti and F. E. Lyndon as superintendent. Later this arrangement was discontinued, and the Cook and other islands became separate missions. Tahiti continued to be the headquarters of the French territory.

In 1948, at a special session of the Australasian Union Conference, French Polynesia became part of the Central Pacific Union Mission. From 1949 to 1965 a number of French nationals—F.J.H. MacDougall, M. P. Nouan, E. J. Landa, Ernest Veuthey, Marcel Bornert, S. P. Jerome, R. V. Esposito, and J. Surel—served consecutively in the field. In 1958 new headquarters were built. In 1960 a new Papeete church was erected, seating 500, and in 1962 a new school on the primary level was opened in the islands.

In 1972 a youth center was erected on the island of Moorea; in 1973 a new president's home was built and extensive additions were made to the mission headquarters office. Several new church edifices have been built in recent years, notably on Moorea and Bora Bora.

FRENCH POLYNESIA MISSION. *See* French Polynesia; South Pacific Division.

FRENCH PUBLISHING HOUSE. *See* Life and Health Publishing House (France).

FRENCH SOMALILAND. *See* Djibouti.

FRENCH SWISS CONFERENCE. *See* Euro-Africa Division; Switzerland.

FRENCH, THOMAS MARION (1883-1949). Educator, missionary, administrator. He was educated at Battle Creek College. Beginning in 1908 he served as missionary in Sierra Leone and in Gold Coast (now Ghana), where his first wife, Lucinda Katherine Peabody, died at Axim, Gold Coast, in 1911. He left Africa and afterward taught Bible at Stanborough Park Missionary College (1915-1916), later directed the Religious Liberty Department in the West Virginia Conference, and still later headed the School of Theology at Emmanuel Missionary College (1918-1922). Afterward he went to Africa, where he was field, young people's, educational, and Sabbath school secretary of the African Division (1922-1929). He was editor of the African *Signs of the Times* (1925-1927) and later president of the Natal-Transvaal Conference (1927-1929). Upon returning to the United States, he served in the following positions: head of the School of Theology at Atlantic Union College, an associate editor of the *Review and Herald* for about four years (1934-1938), chair of the Bible Department at Walla Walla College, president of the West Virginia Conference (1939-1942), and president of the East Pennsylvania Conference (1942-1943).

FRENCH, WILLIAM ROBERT (1881-1968). Minister, Bible teacher. He was born in Cedar Grove, Texas, and was a member of the first graduating class at Keene. In 1899 he began nurse's training, and five years later he began his work in the ministry in Keene. He was a minister and a Bible teacher in several of our colleges, and a number of churches were built under his direction. He and his family served in India for one term of mission service.

FRESNO ADVENTIST ACADEMY. A coeducational day school on the senior high school level, with an elementary school, serving the churches of the Fresno, California, area. It is owned by the Central California Conference and is administered by a joint board consisting of representatives from supporting churches and the conference. The staff consists of the principal, registrar, accountant, secondary teachers, 11 elementary teachers, and a custodian. Elementary and secondary schools are on the same property, at 5397 E. Olive Avenue in Fresno. The academy is accredited by the SDA Board of Regents, is approved by the University of California, and is a member of the Western Association of Secondary Schools and Colleges.

The school began as an elementary church school that opened in a single room in the autumn of 1897 in the Fresno English church at Mariposa and O streets in downtown Fresno. Several years later the school was moved to a one-room house on White Avenue, and in 1907 to a two-room school at North Fruit and Napa streets on the western edge of the city. Some 10 years later George Driver donated a five-acre (two-hectare) site. The original plant consisted of an elementary unit and a building housing the secondary school. To this were later added a shop and a music building. The 12-grade program began in the fall of 1921, with a graduating class (1922) of three.

In 1941 a small Quonset-type auditorium, formerly used for evangelistic purposes, was moved to the property and named Driver Hall. It served the recreational needs of the community and the school, and for a time, after an earthquake in 1952 forced abandonment of the original Mariposa and O streets church structure, the church needs of the Fresno English church. Later additions were administrative offices (1943), cafeteria and home arts building (1946), library and commercial room space (1947), two houses for teacher occupancy (1948), and a two-classroom unit for grades 7 and 8 (1949).

Construction on Parkside Auditorium was begun in 1953. This large building provided for the school and church recreational needs and was used as a meeting place for the Fresno English church until November 1960, when a new church building was erected. Driver Hall, no longer needed, was removed.

At the business meeting of Nov. 9, 1964, the Fresno Central church voted to purchase a 40-acre (16-hectare) site for relocating the school. At the time of the purchase the property was in the country. In 1974 property, which formerly was a farm, was incorporated into the city limits.

The elementary classrooms were completed on the new site on Olive Avenue, and classes began in 1967. The first two buildings of the academy section were completed in the spring of 1971, and the junior high grades moved to the new location. Grades 9-12 moved to the new campus in the fall of 1972. The library and home economics buildings were completed in 1973. Two barns on the Olive Avenue site have been remodeled—one to serve as an industrial arts building, the other to serve as a temporary assembly room. The beautiful mansion built at the turn of the century has been renovated and houses the Music and Art departments. Presently a $1 million campaign for the building of a new gymnasium to serve school and community needs is being launched.

Principals: J. W. Winn, 1921-1923; A. D. Fields, 1923-1925; Robert Kitto, 1925-1932; J. E. Young, 1932-1937; Cecil I. Chrisman, 1937-1942; John W. Rhodes, 1942-1943; Alban W. Millard, 1943-1945; Paul G. Wippermann, 1945-1948; Otto Hancock, 1948-1951; Walter T. Will, 1951-1957; E. Kenneth Smith, 1957-1965; G. D. Bras, 1965-1967; Paul Plummer, 1967-1969; Jerry Lewis, 1969-1971; Derrell K. Smith, 1971-1975; Joel Noble, 1975-1980; William Pearson, 1980-1984; Winston R. Dennis, 1984-1987; Steve McKeone, 1987- .

FREUDENSTADT ADVENTIST RETREAT. *See* Adventhaus Freudenstadt.

FRIDLIN, MARIUS (1903-1972). Missionary, division secretary, administrator. After accepting the Seventh-day Adventist message in his native country, Alsace, in 1928 and spending three years preparing for the gospel ministry at the French Adventist Seminary, Fridlin began his service as dean of men at his alma mater and then as a young minister at Metz, France. He was ordained in 1935 and then spent 11 years guiding the mission program in Cameroon. In 1946 he was called to serve as secretary of the Southern European Division, and in 1958 he accepted the presidency of that field, where he served for 12 years. Although retired, he was active in the work until his death.

FRIEDENSAU BIBELLEHRBRIEFE. *See* Germany.

FRIEDENSAU OLD PEOPLE'S HOME. An institution operated by the North German Union on the campus of the theological high school at Friedensau, Germany, not far from Magdeburg.

It was established in 1907 by what was then the German Union. The money was raised through donations and through the sale of the book *The Ministry of Healing,* on which the author, Ellen G. White, had released all profits. At the opening, 60 aged people found their home in this new institution.

In 1949 the western wing of the former Friedensau Sanitarium was given to the old people's home. Thus the home has accommodations for about 90 residents. The main building was completely rebuilt in 1973/1974.

At present (1993) the manager is Roland Rudolph and the head nurse is Ute Schosnig.

FRIEDENSAU RETREAT (Erholungsheim Friedensau). A 100-bed rest center (formerly a sanitarium) operated by North German Union Conference. It was established in connection with the founding of Friedensau Seminary on a tract of 97 acres (40 hectares) near Burg, not far from Magdeburg, purchased in September 1899 by the then German Conference. The sanitarium was opened in July 1901 with a capacity of 30 patients. The first medical director was Dr. A. J. Hoenes, from the United States. The treatments given, employing natural remedies—air, sun, water, massage—became so popular that the sanitarium was enlarged in 1903 by the acquisition of a villa west of the original building, and again in 1907 by the addition of a wing, thus allowing the number of beds to be doubled.

In 1922 the Friedensau Sanitarium was changed into a convalescent home in the charge of a head nurse. In March 1924 the house was placed at the disposal of the Friedensau Missionary Seminary as the women's dormitory, and from 1924 to 1943 it was also occupied by a school of domestic science.

In 1949 the institution was reopened as a retreat center. The western wing was given to the Old People's Home. In 1956-1957 another wing with 36 rooms was built, and in 1968 a third floor was added above the main building. Thus the capacity was increased to accommodate 120.

The Erholungsheim Friedensau is a retreat for spiritual uplift and physical relaxation used in two-week periods for Seventh-day Adventists and friends. It serves also for ministerial retreats, layperson's meetings, and various committee meetings.

Directors: A. J. Hoenes, M.D., 1901-1907; E. Meyer, M.D., 1907-1922; J. Esser, 1922-1924; Else Dronsek, 1949-1968; Christa Schade, 1968-1979; Heinz Janus, 1979-1992; Anita Kabus, 1993- .

FRIEDENSAU THEOLOGICAL GRADUATE SCHOOL (Theologische Hochschule Friedensau). An educational institution offering study programs in theology and social work. It is situated seven miles (12 kilometers) east of Burg, near Magdeburg, Germany. Its buildings stand in a forest on a tract of field, pasture, and woodland. The school is operated by the Euro-African Division. In 1992 there were 48 students with a faculty of 10 and administration of five.

Action to establish a missionary school for the training of ministers and missionaries was taken by the then German Conference in July 1899. In September an estate of 93 acres (38 hectares), with an old water mill and farm buildings, was obtained, and on Nov. 19, 1899, school opened with one teacher and seven students, being the first Seventh-day Adventist ministerial training institution in Europe. The number increased to 29 students by the end of the year. For the maintenance of the school, and to provide earnings for the students, a bakery and a food factory were established in 1899, and in 1900 a joiner's workshop, a smithy, and a locksmith's workshop. Three temporary dormitories for the constantly growing number of German and foreign students were constructed. In 1902 the first larger building was erected, with three floors and housing 50 students. In 1904 the chapel and the north wing were added, doubling the student capacity and adding four classrooms. The continued growth of the student body necessitated the erection of what became known as the new school, which was built in 1909 and 1911, and provided four more classrooms, an assembly room, and apartments for teachers and students. In 1912-1913 about 250 students from the middle, northern, eastern, and southern parts of Europe attended. From 1900 to 1914 annual camp meetings were held on the college campus, with about 3,000 visitors attending toward the end of that period. When World War I broke out, the enrollment decreased considerably, and in September 1917, the college had to be closed down completely. From 1915 to 1917 some of the building space was used as a hospital for wounded soldiers. After a summer session in 1919 the school reopened in October with 60 students, and in spite of economic difficulties the number attending reached 200 in the school years of 1921-1922 and 1924-1925.

In the meantime a number of colleges were founded in other countries, and the other German unions had established their own schools. Hence Friedensau became the mission school of the East German Union only. The student body continued to be small, even though a series of new courses in teaching, home economics, commerce, and a preparatory course for nursing was introduced. The enrollment from 1928 to 1934 dropped from 150 to 100; from 1934 to 1938 it stood between 50 and 70; and from 1938 to 1943 it again rose to 100. Between the two world wars only a few camp meetings were conducted at Friedensau, which were with one exception MV Bible schools. In 1939 Friedensau became once more the ministerial training school of all three German unions and functioned as such until August 1943, when it had to be closed down again because of World War II. The buildings were again used as a military hospital (August 1943 to March 1947).

In July 1947 the school was opened for the third time, with four teachers and 18 young men attending. During this first school year after World War II the number of students increased to 67, and in 1950 to 100. Between 1956 and 1989 it has ranged from 60 to 90. The faculty has increased correspondingly.

In 1957 and in 1972 camp meetings were held at Friedensau for the youth, with more than 800 attending. The seventy-fifth anniversary was celebrated on July 6, 1974, when a new organ and the reconstructed chapel were dedicated.

With the drastic changes in Europe in 1989 and the eventual reunification of Germany, Friedensau obtained again its former historic position. In the 1980s foreign students came from various Socialist countries, and after the reunification Friedensau regained its greater international responsibilities. A new dining hall (Mensa) was completed in March 1992; the first renovated dormitory (Villa) was dedicated in November of that year.

The Division of Theology holds the Old and New Testament, Church History, Systematic and Pastoral Theology departments. In 1992 the Department of Church Development was added. The Division of Social Work is divided into five departments: Theology/Ethics, History/Political Sciences, Education/Behavioral Sciences, Administration/Law, and Social Work. Emphasis is given to social work in the developing countries.

Presidents: O. Lüpke, 1899-1914; E. Meyer, 1914-1917; J. Esser, 1917; W. Müller, 1919-1920; E. Meyer, 1920-1921; W. Müller, 1921-1925; B. Ohme, 1925-1928; W. Michael, 1928-1933; R. Dangschat, 1933-1934; W. Eberhardt, 1934-1939; W. Michael, 1939-1943; W. Eberhardt, 1947-1954; S. Lüpke, 1954-1968; F. Schönfeld, 1968-1982; M. Böttcher, 1982-1990; Bernhard Oestreich, 1990-1991; B. Pfeiffer, 1991- .

FRISBIE, JOSEPH BIRCHARD (1816-1882). Minister. He was licensed to preach for the Methodists in 1843 and was ordained in 1846. For years he was a bitter opponent of Adventist teachings, but in 1853, after he had been assigned by his bishop to debate the Sabbath question with Joseph Bates, he reversed his position and began to observe the Sabbath and to preach Adventist doctrines.

He built the first Seventh-day Adventist church in Battle Creek on his property, located at the corner of Cass and Van Buren streets, and served as pastor of that church during its early years.

Although for a period he became discouraged and left the ministry, he later returned to the work. He stopped preaching some time before his death because of ill health. He was a deep Bible student with an independent turn of mind. In several early articles he contributed to the development of the Seventh-day Adventist philosophy of church organization, systematic benevolence, and to the doctrine of the millennium.

FROOM, LE ROY EDWIN (1890-1974). Author, editor, teacher, departmental secretary. Froom was born in Illinois and received his training at Washington Training Center (now Columbia Union College), Pacific Union College, and Walla Walla College. He began his ministry in Cambridge, Maryland, in 1913. In 1915 he joined the Pacific Press Publishing Association as a trainee editor, and three years later went to China as editor of the Chinese *Signs of the Times.* When he returned to the United States he became editor of *Watchman* magazine. He was called to the General Conference headquarters, where he was first associate secretary and then secretary of the Ministerial Association from 1926 to 1950. During this time he founded *The Ministry* magazine and was its editor for 22 years. A specialist in historical research, Froom served also as professor of historical theology at Andrews University Seminary, where he taught during the summer quarter.

He was one of the most distinguished writers that the denomination has produced. Among the many books he left as a legacy to the church are the four-volume *The Prophetic Faith of Our Fathers,* the two-volume *The Conditionalist Faith of Our Fathers, Movement of Destiny, The Coming of the Comforter,* and *The Holy Spirit—Executive of the Godhead,* a manuscript nearly complete at the time of his death. He also contributed to various encyclopedias.

FRUITIGRAN PRODUCTS. *See* South American Division Health Food Factory.

FUKUINSHA. *See* Japan Publishing House.

FUKUZAWA, AIKO (1880-1979). Sabbath school director, teacher. Born in Kobe, Japan, she was adopted into the Fukuzawa family because of her mother's death. She mastered English and French at the prestigious Tsuda College in Tokyo. She came to know Seventh-day Adventists when she became ill and was treated at Kobe Sanitarium and Hospital.

She was baptized in 1906 and began teaching English. Several months later she met Magoji Suzuki, a minister. They were married in 1907. She set as her principle this statement: "I was privileged to be reared in a good environment. I have money that I can decide how to use. I always pray to God to show me the best way to use it." She generously helped many young believers and donated funds to Japan Missionary College.

After moving to Chiba she taught English at the college for a while, then became Sabbath school director. She translated English lessons into Japanese. Being fluent in English, she was able to explain the principles of Ellen White's writings to others in her country.

Her daughter Masu never attended state schools. Under her tutelage Masu became an accomplished musician and a highly educated worker in the church.

FULLER MEMORIAL HOSPITAL. A 82-bed psychiatric/substance abuse hospital located in South Attleboro, Massachusetts, eight miles (13 kilometers) north of Providence, Rhode Island. The institution is on a beautifully landscaped estate on U.S. 1 with easy access to Interstate 95 and other highways.

In the mid-1930s Alice Fuller Davenport, sole heir of Charles H. and Nellie A. Fuller, made available the 60-acre (25-hectare) Fuller estate for use as a hospital or sanitarium. Under the leadership of Julian C. Gant, M.D., from Boston, the Seventh-day Adventist Layman's Benevolent Association of New England, Inc., was formed and incorporated in 1937 to operate such an institution. The estate, with its mansion and several other buildings, was bequeathed to the association the same year and was named Fuller Memorial Sanitarium, a memorial to Charles and Nellie Fuller.

The early days of the sanitarium saw a real struggle to maintain its operation. The names of E. Opdyke, Margaret Spaulding, and Walter Spady are prominent in the early development of the institution. In 1938 Laurence A. Senseman, M.D., joined the staff of the fledgling hospital and became its leading spirit through the years.

From the care of a few patients, each in a spacious room of the mansion, the operation at Fuller grew until the larger rooms had to be converted into semiprivate rooms and wards. Another building to the rear of the mansion was remodeled to furnish living quarters for some of the staff, and then later converted into a Geriatric Department.

Because of an increasing number of patients and World War II draining off the available supply of nurses, an attendant nurse's course was started in 1940. This course, with affiliation in surgery and pediatrics at a nearby hospital, trained a number of practical nurses for sanitarium service. The course was discontinued after the close of the war relieved the nurse shortage.

In 1945 the basement of the main building was remodeled and the kitchen, staff cafeteria, and treatment rooms were moved to the new quarters, thus releasing more rooms upstairs for patient accommodations. Further expansion of the building supplied space for administrative offices and additional patient rooms. A modern kitchen was soon added to supply facilities for the serving of healthful and often specialized diets for the patients. The 1950s saw construction of the much-needed recreation hall with funds raised by the sanitarium personnel.

In 1956 a fund-raising drive was begun to raise the monies needed to construct a sizable addition to the main building. In 1957 Mrs. Davenport died, and the trustees of the estate, having noted the successful operation of the sanitarium, made a gift of a substantial endowment to the institution and also a sizable donation to the building fund, making possible immediate construction of the new west wing. Dedication of the addition took place in 1959. This expansion increased patient capacity to 55 beds and provided space for doctors' offices, a medical library and staff room, medical records office, administrative offices, laboratory, X-ray room, treatment rooms, and a new occupational therapy section.

Operation of the sanitarium was turned over to the Atlantic Union Conference of Seventh-day Adventists in 1964, and the board of directors was enlarged to include several of the administrators of the Atlantic Union and Southern New England conferences, with the Atlantic Union president as board chair. Shortly thereafter, in 1965, Harold Knox was named administrator. The following year Gerald E. Shampo was called to be administrator, and Dr. Senseman was named medical director. Recruitment of specialty staff and the expansion of the program and the physical plant to include new therapeutic techniques was the priority concern. Most important was the goal of further developing a program consistent with the needs of the surrounding communities.

In late 1970 a new wing was opened, increasing patient capacity to 75 and furnishing new and improved quarters for patient services including medical and patient libraries, an auditorium seating 100, and much-needed office space. A further needed expansion was initiated in 1972, and the child psychiatry unit was opened in 1975 in the greatly enlarged Fuller Lodge, which formerly housed the Geriatric Department. The new facility furnishes psychiatric services for children age 10 through 18.

The hospital also conducts a strong outpatient service and has a good working relationship with community mental health and medical facilities. A strong in-service training program is carried on at Fuller. Nursing students from other area hospital schools of nursing are sent to Fuller for their psychiatric nursing affiliation.

In 1973 the name was officially changed to Fuller Memorial Hospital. The hospital is fully licensed as a specialty hospital by Massachusetts, and in 1969 received full accreditation from the Joint Commission on Accreditation of Hospitals with special commendation for the quality of care provided. Subsequent renewals of accreditation included commendation for cleanliness and neatness. The hospital is a member of the Massachusetts Association for Private Psychiatric Hospitals, the American Hospital Association, the American Psychiatric Association, and the American Medical Association.

Medical Directors, Superintendents: Julian Gant, M.D., 1936-1938; L. A. Senseman, M.D., 1939-1969; David Johnson, M.D., 1969-1970; Arnold Nielsen, M.D., 1970-1981; Ronald Geraty, M.D., 1981-1987; M. Annette Hanson, M.D., 1987-1992; Robert G. M. Johnston, M.D., 1992- .

Business Managers, Administrators: E. Opdyke, 1937-1938; Mrs. Margaret Spaulding, 1938; L. A. Senseman, 1939-1964; Mrs. Strickler, 1940-1942; Walter Spady, 1942-1946; George Gohde, 1946-1965; Harold Knox, 1965-1966; Gerald E. Shampo, 1966-1980; Stephen O. Paden, 1980-1981; Ronald C. Brown, 1981-1990; Landon Kite, 1990- .

FULTON COLLEGE. A coeducational boarding school situated at Korovou, Tailevu, Fiji. The following training courses are offered: agricultural, commercial, primary and secondary teaching, social work, and ministerial.

The need for a training school in the Fiji Islands was recognized as early as the turn of the century by J. E. Fulton, a pioneer Seventh-day Adventist missionary. To meet this need he secured an estate of several hundred acres (80-120 hectares) known as Buresala, on the island of Ovalau in the central island group, and on it began a training school in 1904-1905. The school was under the directorship of S. W. Carr, a graduate of Avondale College. The first year a few married students and several young men attended the school. In 1909 there were 10 or 12 young women who enrolled also.

From this school soon came a small corps of national workers, several of whom were sent as pioneer missionaries to New Guinea to assist in opening SDA work in that field. In the early twenties the young women's section was transferred to Navuso, on Viti Levu Island, where a primary boarding school was established. This school, under European leadership, trained national women as teachers. About the same time, a boarding school was established at Samabula, near Suva, also under European leadership, to train Indians as teachers and workers. In 1932 Vatuvonu Central School for training Fijian teachers was established in East Fiji.

With rising standards of education in the years immediately prior to World War II, and government pressure for better qualified teachers, Seventh-day Adventists, after careful survey in 1939, decided to consolidate their educational work in the islands and bring all Seventh-day Adventist training schools in the Fiji group into one unit at a centrally situated campus. G. Branster, mission superintendent, with the mission committee, instructed a subcommittee consisting of A. E. Watts, Walter Ferris, and A. P. Dyason to search for a suitable site.

An estate of 400 acres (160 hectares) 30 miles (50 kilometers) from Suva, the capital of the islands, was secured, and early in 1940 building operations began on the new site under the supervision of A. P. Dyason. Teachers' dwellings and school buildings from Samabula, Wainibuka (Navuso), and Buresala were dismantled, transported to the new site, and reconstructed. A large dairy industry has been established at Fulton College in recent years. The profits from this industry are intended to improve and provide new buildings and plant for the college.

Early in 1941 Fulton College opened and began training men and women of all races. In succeeding years numbers of students from

Tonga, Samoa, and other fields who were eager to take advantage of the higher levels of Christian education have also attended.

When the Central Pacific Union Mission was established in 1949 with headquarters at Suva, Fulton College was made a union college to train workers for the entire Central Pacific Union Mission territory.

In 1959 a rebuilding program was begun with the erection of a dining hall, and in 1964 a new block consisting of a chapel, a library, 10 classrooms, and administrative offices was opened. A new primary school block was opened in 1971. Fulton College benefited from the third quarter Thirteenth Sabbath Offering overflow in 1973. The amount received was $229,000. With this money a new dormitory for young men was built and opened in 1975.

In 1990 Fulton upgraded its Ministerial Certificate to a three-year Diploma of Theology, and in 1991 the Certificate in Primary Teacher Education was also upgraded to a three-year diploma.

Principals: A. G. Stewart, 1941; A. P. Dyason, 1942-1949; L. S. Wood, 1949-1953; A. W. Martin, 1954-1958; A. P. Dyason, 1959-1964; John Cernik, 1965-1971; M. P. Cozens, 1972-1973; A. J. Sonter, 1974-1977; A. S. Currie, 1978-1979; J. L. Wilson, 1980-1983; J. Hammond, 1984-1985; A. G. Hedges, 1986-1989; J. Mea'ole, 1990-1991; N. W. Tausere, 1992- .

FULTON, JOHN EDWIN (1869-1945). Missionary, administrator. Born in Nova Scotia, he moved at the age of 6 to the United States. He attended Healdsburg College, and in 1891 married Susie Virginia Newlon. After serving as a minister in Oregon, Washington, and California, he engaged in evangelism in New Zealand for a year (1895-1896). With the exception of the year 1903, when he was Bible teacher at Australasian Missionary College, from 1896 to 1906 he served as an evangelist in Fiji. He was president of the New South Wales Conference (1906-1909), the Australasian Union Conference (1909-1916), the Asiatic Division, which at that time included China, Japan, India, and the East Indies (1917-1918), the Southern Asia Division (1918-1921), the Pacific Union Conference (1921-1922), the North American Division (1922), and the Australasian Division (1922-1926). Returning to the United States, he served as president of the Pacific Union Conference (1926-1932), and then for a short time was president of the Northern California Conference (December 1933-1936) and of the Southern California Conference (1936).

FUNDACION CETEBEDI. *See* Inter-American Health Food Company, Costa Rica Branch.

FUNDAMENTALISM. The ultraconservative wing of Protestantism, especially as represented by denominations that rejected, or rose in opposition to, the movement known as Modernism. The name is derived from a series of books entitled *The Fundamentals,* which were published in the United States, beginning in 1909, with the aid of two wealthy laymen by the Testimony Publishing Company, and reprinted in 1917 by the Bible Institute of Los Angeles. Fundamentalism itself, however, actually antedates this series of books. It is characterized by belief in the verbal inspiration of the Bible, miracles, a supernatural creation, the virgin birth, a substitutionary atonement, the bodily resurrection, and the literal second advent of Christ. To Fundamentalists, the Bible is literally true, and historically and theologically inerrant in its original autographs. Men and women are sinners who can be "saved" by a transforming new birth, after which they must live lives of sobriety and righteousness characterized by modest dress, wholesome entertainment, abstinence from alcoholic beverages and (often) tobacco, and by regular prayer, Bible study, and militant missionary work. Mass evangelism, radio preaching, and missions among non-Christian peoples are strongly emphasized by groups advocating this school of thought.

Fundamentalists founded numerous Bible institutes, some of which became Bible colleges and theological seminaries. A method of biblical interpretation known as dispensationalism *(see* Premillennialism) has had considerable popularity. The Holiness churches are all to be found here. The National Association of Evangelicals and the International Council of Christian Churches both include in their ranks Fundamentalist groups of different hues. Fundamentalists also have had considerable influence in British university circles.

Since about 1940 a group of Fundamentalist scholars has arisen calling for a more enlightened attitude toward modern culture, particularly in the areas of science and sound biblical scholarship. Those sympathetic to this trend called themselves Evangelicals. This group has produced significant biblical and theological works and well-respected scholars. The Evangelical Theological Society represents the views of these scholars. Their theology is accessible to a general religious audience through the journal *Christianity Today*, published in Washington, D.C., U.S.A.

The Fundamentalists have distinguished themselves from Evangelicals by being, according to them, more loyal to the biblical doctrines. Fundamentalism grew significantly in power and influence in America during the 1970s and most of the 1980s. Its adherents became activists against the social, moral, and economic evils of America and against secular humanism. Since then its influence has been felt even in political circles. Many religious programs by radio and television and multiple ministries came into existence transcending denominational barriers. During this period religious publishing houses operated by laypersons flourished. The general public could no longer perceive any significant difference between Fundamentalism and Evangelicalism. In fact, Evangelicalism became a very strong trans-denominational religious phenomenon.

By the end of the 1980s and the beginning of the 1990s, Evangelicalism continued to be quite influential. By then Evangelicals were quite concerned with the nature and authority of the Scriptures, and a strong debate was going on among themselves on these subjects. A group of them, called neo-Evangelicals, had accepted a limited definition of the doctrine of the inerrancy of the Bible. They considered the Scriptures to be inerrant and infallible on matters of faith and life but not on matters of science and history. This group rejected the historicity of the biblical Creation account (Gen. 1-3). Elements of the liberalism opposed by Fundamentalists after World War I seemed to have crept into some Evangelical circles.

Theologically, Seventh-day Adventists have a number of beliefs in common with Fundamentalists, but for various reasons have never been identified with the movement. More and more Evangelicals have come to recognize Seventh-day Adventists as orthodox, but the recognition is not universal. This is mainly because of the SDA teachings concerning the law and the Sabbath, the state of the dead and the fate of the wicked, the 2300 days of Dan. 8:14 and the investigative judgment, and the Spirit of Prophecy. On their part, Adventists reject as unbiblical a number of teachings held by many (though not all) Fundamentalists, such as antinomianism and dispensationalism, the natural immortality of the soul, the secret rapture, the restoration of the Jews as God's chosen people, and a temporal millennium on earth before the second coming of Christ. These theological differences have made cooperation between Seventh-day Adventists and Fundamentalists, in areas of mutual concern such as literal creation versus evolution, very difficult if not impossible.

FUTUNA ISLANDS. *See* South Pacific Division; Wallis Archipelago.

FUTURE LIFE. *See* Home of the Redeemed.

FUTURE PUNISHMENT. *See* Hell.

FUTURISM. *See* Historicism; Premillennialism; Prophetic Interpretation.

G

GABON. An independent republic situated on the Atlantic coast of central Africa, bounded on the north by Equatorial Guinea and Cameroon, on the east and south by the Congo, and on the west by the Atlantic Ocean. Gabon has an area of 103,346 square miles (268,000 square kilometers) and a population (1994) of 1.1 million, mainly Bantus. About 60 percent are Christian, the rest animists. Languages are French (official) and Bantu dialects.

Seventh-day Adventist Statistics. Gabon is one of the nine missions that make up the Central African Union, which in turn is part of the Africa-Indian Ocean Division. Statistics (1993) for *Gabon:* churches, 4; members, 906; ordained ministers, 1. The SDA Church was recognized officially by the government in 1981. Libreville and Port Gentil were entered that year under the direction of Daniel Cordas. The work developed slowly. In the 1990s the creative evangelism fostered by Max Pierre brought a sudden spurt in membership growth.

GABON MISSION. *See* Africa-Indian Ocean Division; Gabon.

GACETA (1961-   ; quarterly, in Cebuan). Organ of the Central and South Philippine Union missions, a 68-page church gazette issued in the vernacular language for Cebuan-speaking churches.

GAEDE, DAVID PETER (1867-1962). Minister, missionary. He was born to a Mennonite family in the Wohldemfürst (later Alexanderfeld) colony on the Kuban River in Caucasus, Russia. In 1879 he moved with his parents to Peabody, Kansas. At 15 he was baptized into the Mennonite Brethren Church, and in 1885, as the first of the large Gaede family, he joined the Seventh-day Adventist Church. He attended SDA schools in Lehigh and in Hillsboro, and there, on Apr. 14, 1889, he married Elizabeth Duerksen. When in 1890 Union College was established, he attended college in winter and canvassed in summer with religious books. Later three of his brothers joined him in college. After the second year, he and his brother Peter received permission to work in Kansas without salary to prove their calling as ministers. They worked on a farm to support themselves, and the following winter held meetings in Durham with good success. A year later they were regularly employed, with David working in Iowa and Peter in Kansas.

In 1898 D. P. Gaede was persuaded to accompany his parents, who had joined the SDA Church, to visit relatives and friends in Russia, the father paying his salary and expenses. They spent some time in the old colonies on the river Molotchnaya north of the Crimea and then went to the Caucasus. Everywhere Gaede found opportunities to hold meetings and to baptize new members.

After returning to Iowa, he offered to join the meager working force in the vast domain of the czars. Arriving in Russia with his family in the spring of 1900, he headed the North Russian Mission until 1907, then the West Russian Mission until 1909. Later he served as president of the South German Conference in the West German Union (1909-1911), and back in Russia as president of the Black Sea Mission until 1914, at the beginning of World War I, when he returned to the United States.

Upon his return Gaede served as a minister in South Dakota, in Nebraska, and in Wisconsin. His wife having died in 1918, he married in 1921 a widow, Bertha (Quade) Huecker, of Milwaukee, Wisconsin.

GALUSHA, ELON (1790-1856). Minister of the Lockport, New York, Baptist Church, who became a Millerite preacher. He was a son of the Vermont governor who had commissioned William Miller in the state militia during the War of 1812. He was known as a sound reasoner, an eloquent speaker, and a careful writer. In 1845 he presided at the Albany Conference, at which the main group of Millerites rallied to form a continuing Adventist body.

GAMBIA, THE. One of smaller independent nations on the African continent, surrounded by Senegal except for its Atlantic coast. The Gambia River separates the country into two sections. Its narrow strip of land is only 15 to 30 miles (25 to 50 kilometers) wide and stretches eastward from the Atlantic Ocean for 300 miles (475 kilometers). The Gambia was the oldest and most northerly of the former British West African dependencies, and the last crown colony and protectorate on the west coast to gain independence, on February 18, 1965.

Portuguese navigators first reached the Gambia River in 1456. For 200 years the Portuguese enjoyed a quiet monopoly of trade with the neighboring countries, but were challenged by other European powers in the seventeenth century. Portugal sold trading rights to the British in 1618. The British acquired the capital, Banjul (formerly Bathurst), in 1618, and administered both The Gambia and Sierra Leone from there until 1888, when they were separated.

The Gambia is widely recognized for its abundance of birds—some 500 species have been listed. Approximately 960,000 people (1994) live in The Gambia. Although the official language is English, all ethnic groups have their own language. The major religion is Islam (90 percent). Most of the rest are Christian. The people of Gambia may be divided into five ethnic groups: Mandinka, Wolof, Fula, Jola, and Serahuli. The climate is subtropical.

The Gambian economy is heavily dependent on peanuts and peanut by-products, which provide nearly 90 percent of export earnings. Trade consists mainly of export of manufactured goods and commodities (e.g., rice, sugar, textiles) to neighboring countries. In recent years the production of food crops such as millet, maize, cassava, and rice have steadily increased. Cotton is also a principle export product. Attempts are being made to diversify the agricultural base through promoting horticulture, livestock, and fisheries development. Tourism has become the fastest-growing sector of the Gambian economy.

Development of Seventh-day Adventist work. The Gambia constitutes the Gambia Mission Station. It was officially registered with the Gambian government in 1987. The Gambia Mission Station is part of the West African Union Mission which in turn is part of the Africa-Indian Ocean Division. Statistics (1992) for *The Gambia:* churches, 2; members, 248; elementary schools, 2.

Seventh-day Adventists entered Gambia officially in 1973 by sending Daniel Cudjoe from Ghana as a literature evangelist. Pastor Cartwright, an evangelist from the United States, despite much opposition, conducted an evangelistic campaign in Banjul in 1975. At the end of December 1979 there were 22 members.

In 1981 Louis C. Nielsen arrived as mission station director and was able to obtain a plot of land from the New Jeshwang/Ebou Town villages (1982) for the purpose of building a school in the urban area of Serekunda, thereby meeting an urgent need in the area of education.

In 1983 the Seventh-day Adventist Church opened the first SDA school in The Gambia, using temporary facilities in Kanifing. However, with development funds from Sweden, Canada, and the Netherlands, a complete new physical plant was built in New Jeshwang. One of the major achievements of this institution has been that prejudice has been broken down. As a result, the church has become widely recognized and respected for offering a quality education to more than 500 primary children. The Seventh-day Adventist Education Center is well-equipped and maintained, and has modern facilities. The Danish Children's Fund contributes significantly to the operation of the elementary school. In 1992 the Gambian government officially requested the church to consider the establishment of a middle and high school on the campus of the Seventh-day Adventist Education Center.

Through community-based development projects, ADRA has been able to penetrate the unentered regions.

GAMBIA MISSION STATION. *See* Africa-Indian Ocean Division; Gambia.

GAMBIER ISLANDS. *See* French Polynesia; South Pacific Division.

GAMBLING. *See* Recreation and Amusements.

GANDER, STANLEY HERBERT (1899-1969). Missionary to New Guinea. Born in Dorset, England, he migrated with his parents to Australia at the age of 13, and was baptized in 1916. He was a fitter and turner by trade, and also trained at the Sydney Sanitarium as a nurse. In 1922 he married Greta Tivey, and the next three years were spent as chef at the SDA Sanitarium Health Food cafés in Melbourne and Brisbane. This was followed by seven years in colporteur work. In 1932 he was called to mission service, first as principal of the Boliu School on Mussau, and then for two years at Kainantu in the Eastern Highlands of New Guinea. In 1936 he pioneered the work at Bena Bena, where he remained until the Japanese invasion in 1942. In that year he was ordained to the gospel ministry. He spent the war years back in Australia in the Lay Activities Department and then in evangelism in the North New South Wales Conference. On his return to New Guinea in 1947, he pioneered the work in the Western Islands, Madang, and the Sepik River area. In 1955 he became lay activities secretary for the Coral Sea Union Mission, with headquarters in Lae. His involvement in a plane crash in 1956 necessitated hospitalization for a year, after which he retired from active service.

GARCIA, DARIO (1912-1967). Teacher, educational administrator, departmental secretary. A native of Rio Grande do Sul, Brazil, he studied in state institutions in south Brazil. After accepting the Seventh-day Adventist message in 1933, he enrolled at Brazil College. While there he married Anna Ida Braun. From 1937 to 1941 he studied at Pacific Union

College in California, where he received his degree in elementary education.

Returning to Brazil, he taught for two years and was then called as principal of Taquara Academy, where he served until 1945. He returned to Brazil College as chair of the Educational Department and was later elected president of the institution.

At the General Conference session of 1950 he was elected educational and Missionary Volunteer secretary of the South American Division, and shortly thereafter was ordained as a minister of the church.

In 1955 he and his family returned to Brazil, where he served at Paraná Academy in Curitiba and again as president of Brazil College until 1961, when he began work on a graduate degree at Andrews University. In 1962 he received his master's degree and began work on a doctoral program.

At the time of his death he was under appointment as educational secretary of the South Brazil Union.

GARCIA, JERONIMO GRANERO (1903-1974). Evangelist, teacher, administrator, departmental secretary. He was born in Spain, and came to Brazil as a boy. He studied at Instituto Adventista de Ensino from 1920 to 1925, when he graduated. In 1926 he married Anna Klein de Araújo. From 1926 to 1936, he worked as a Bible worker, evangelist, and departmental secretary in São Paulo and Rio Grande do Sul. From 1936 to 1940 he was president and evangelist of the Northeast Brazil Mission. From 1940 to 1944 he served as a teacher and vice president in the Colégio Adventista (Brazil College).

He was the president of the Rio Grande do Sul Conference and evangelist in the São Paulo Conference from 1944 until 1949, when he returned to Brazil College as a teacher, and as president from 1951 to 1952. From 1954 to 1958 he was a departmental secretary in the South American Division and the South Brazil Union. In 1958 he returned to Brazil College as a teacher, where he served until the time of his retirement in 1966.

GARDEN STATE ACADEMY. A coeducational boarding school on the senior high school level, serving the New Jersey Conference, situated in rural Sussex County of northwest New Jersey near Tranquility, 60 miles (100 kilometers) north of Trenton. About one third of the 365-acre (150-hectare) property is forested hillside; the remainder is rolling farmland and open meadows with shade trees. There are also two lakes.

History. *Founding and Early Days.* The academy for New Jersey grew gradually from a church school into an academy. The school was first opened in the Babcock office building in Plainfield in the school year 1926-1927. The next year one ninth-grade pupil was enrolled. Each succeeding year another secondary grade was added, until in 1930-1931 the first class of seven seniors was graduated.

After several moves, the school settled down at 31 Rockview Avenue in North Plainfield. At first called the Plainfield Academy, it was renamed the North Plainfield Academy in 1934. Through all these years the school was sponsored by the Plainfield church.

Mrs. Mable Baker Dickson served as the first principal in 1927, when the first secondary grade was offered. In 1933 she resigned as principal but remained as teacher of English and language for 17 years. She and her husband were parents, teachers, and deans to the young people. Their home was opened as dormitory, gymnasium, and infirmary. Ruth Wilcox, the conference superintendent of education when the school began, is regarded as the founder; she spent many years with the school both during and after her term of superintendency.

The school was unique in its early days in that it was operated largely for the benefit of students who could not afford to go to a boarding academy. Students were placed in wealthy homes in Plainfield and were able to earn all expenses working in these homes and in nearby businesses. Beginning in 1933, Miss Wilcox spent her full time for many years placing students in homes and supervising them. Her constant recruitment helped build up enrollment. Benjamin Blinn, business manager from 1933 to 1936, is credited with putting the school, which had no money and owed many bills, on a paying basis. Aided by income from the placement students, the school was soon growing and healthy.

The Move to Eighth Street. On June 1, 1941, the academy moved to the former Nash home on 622 West Eighth Street, Plainfield, a 25-room brick building on a large corner lot in one of Plainfield's best residential sections. It became a conference school, and its name reverted to Plainfield Academy.

Reorganization and Relocation. For 22 years the new plant served well for classrooms, offices, chapel, dormitory, and teachers' housing, but by 1958 the school, crowded about by the city, needed to expand its facilities. The home-placement program, no longer satisfactory, was being abandoned in a gradual three-year changeover, with no new placement students being admitted. In the spring of 1958 Plainfield Academy was reorganized as a boarding school and was renamed Garden State Academy. All boarding students were gradually moved into new housing units. Plans were made to relocate in a rural area as soon as possible.

On May 5, 1963, a special constituency session voted to purchase the present property near Tranquility, and remodeling of the existing buildings began immediately. Garden State Academy opened its doors at the new rural site in September 1963. In that year there was a faculty of 12 and an enrollment of 82.

The girls' dormitory was added to the campus in 1968. It contains 48 double rooms, guest rooms, lounge, and a chapel with seating capacity for more than 200.

The all-purpose building, begun in the fall of 1972, was completed free of debt by the end of 1974. This building houses seven classrooms, a laboratory, the new library, the administration suite, shower and locker rooms, and an all-purpose room, which is used as the camp meeting auditorium. After a fire destroyed the cafeteria and the boys' dorm, two new structures were built to replace them in 1982. One wing of the cafeteria building serves as the Music Department. The 1992 enrollment was 86 students, with 15 on faculty and staff.

Principals: Mrs. Mable Baker Dickson, 1927-1933; I. U. Dodge, 1933-1934; A. N. Shafer, 1934-1936; Lloyd Klopfenstein, 1936-1939; J. R. Minesinger, 1939-1940; Mrs. C. C. Ellis, 1940-1943; H. J. Alcock, 1943-1945; W. G. McCready, 1945-1953; G. P. Katcher, 1953-1957; L. E. Poole, 1957-1962; G. H. Byers, 1962-1964; L. B. Kidder, 1964-1966; Merle Rouse, 1966-1968; C. G. Jackson, 1968-1973; James Clizbe, 1973-1979; J. D. Miller, 1979-1980; Alan Hurlbert, 1980-1984; Ivan Weiss, 1984-1988; David Mathi, 1988-1992; J. Tom Fogg, 1992- .

GARHWAL INDUSTRIAL SCHOOL. *See* India.

GARNER, OWEN T. (1901-1973). Administrator. A native of Illinois, he attended Emmanuel Missionary College and was ordained to the ministry in 1927. Many of his 43 years in the work were spent in administrative work. He served as president of the Kansas, Nebraska, New York, Montana, and South Dakota conferences.

GATES, EDWARD HARMON (1855-1940). Missionary, administrator. Having accepted the Seventh-day Adventist faith in 1874, he attended Battle Creek College and was ordained to the ministry in 1879. After engaging in evangelism and serving as president of the Colorado Conference (1888-1890), he went in October 1890 to the South Sea Islands on the mission ship *Pitcairn.* While the rest of the group went on to other islands, he and his wife remained on Pitcairn Island. Here he baptized 82 persons and organized a church, then spent 19 months visiting a number of South Sea islands, and on his return to Pitcairn established a school. At this time a typhus epidemic on the island caused great hardships and many deaths. He returned to the United States in 1894, but soon went to the East for 30 years of service. He opened work in Singapore, the East Indies, and the Philippines; was president of two conferences in Australia; and for a time was vice president of the Australasian Union Conference. He retired in California. He described his experiences in a book, *In Coral Isles* (1923).

GAUSSEN, LOUIS (1790-1863). Protestant minister and teacher of theology in Geneva; his full name was Francois Samuel Robert Louis Gaussen. He was one of the leaders of the evangelical movement in opposition to the prevalent rationalism of the day, and helped to form the Geneva Evangelical Society and its School of Theology. Gaussen became one of the leading representatives of conservative Protestantism on the Continent. He made a special study of prophecy, and in 1837 taught a course of lessons on Daniel to a group of children, which many adults attended. He held the standard Protestant historical view of prophecy as fulfilling through the ages, and expected the Second Advent soon, although he did not teach any date. His lessons, published as *Daniel le Prophéte* (1839), were translated into English and published by the Presbyterian Board of Publication in Philadelphia. Millerite writers cited Gaussen and reprinted one of his works. Seventh-day Adventists have considered him as one of the forerunners on the Continent in drawing attention to the Second Advent (see GC 364-366).

GEM STATE ADVENTIST ACADEMY. A coeducational boarding school on the senior high school level, 3.5 miles (six kilometers) south of Caldwell, Idaho, operated by the Idaho Conference. The school fulfilled the need for a boarding academy for the young people of the Idaho Conference after the Ames Academy, near Eagle, Idaho, was destroyed by fire. For a time the church at Caldwell tried to carry on a day school, known as Mountain View Academy, but at the Baker, Oregon, camp meeting, June 1918 a committee was chosen to select a site for a new school. After careful consideration, Caldwell, being geographically near the center of the conference territory, was chosen.

The school was situated on the corner of Indiana Avenue and Linden Street, a semirural section with an apple orchard nearby, approximately two miles (three kilometers) southeast of the Union Pacific depot. Construction was begun in the summer of 1918 under trying conditions caused by World War I.

At the laying of the cornerstone a Bible was cemented into the left pillar of the chapel steps. Work on the building, under the supervision of H. A. Green, was sufficiently completed to begin school in January of 1919 with 30 students and with A. G. Meiklejohn as principal.

In the 1920s a large barn was built back of the academy to house a small dairy and a woodwork shop. Later the upper floor was converted into a gymnasium. In 1944, the dairy, which had greatly expanded, was moved to a recently purchased farm nearby, on Linden Street, east of the academy buildings. In 1933 a small cannery was begun in the basement of the church school. It too expanded and for about 12 years provided work for a number of students. A bakery began operations in a building erected in 1934-1935. This industry prospered also, and it was necessary to construct a new building. In 1944 the old building was remodeled and made into an annex to the girls' dormitory.

Extensive improvements were made during the years 1940-1943, when T. W. Walters was the administrator. New constructions at that time included a wing for the girls' dormitory, a boys' dormitory, and a large gymnasium. George S. Belleau, conference president, secured financial help from the neighboring conferences in the North Pacific Union.

On May 2, 1960, with realization that the original buildings were sorely in need of replacement, and that it would be desirable to have the school in more rural surroundings, it was voted at a special conference session to build a new school plant south of Caldwell, on an elevation overlooking Boise Valley, with the snowcapped Boise Mountains in the background. Work was begun on the buildings in the summer of 1960, with M. E. Smith as supervisor. The buildings were occupied in the 1962-1963 school year.

Plants for the Champion Bake-N-Serve Industries were constructed on the new campus in 1963 and 1965, an industrial arts building in 1967, 13 homes for staff members between 1963 and 1967, administration building expansion and Marcia Ann Meyers Memorial Chapel in 1973. In 1978 a new section was added to the gym, almost doubling its size. In 1982 the administration building auditorium was transformed into a church. Administration building expansion continued in 1989 with the construction of a Christian radio station and additional Music Department facilities.

Principals: John E. Weaver (chosen as first principal, but was unable to serve because of the war); A. J. Meiklejohn, 1918-1919; A. N. Attebury, 1919-1922; W. C. Baldwin, 1922-1923; W. A. Gosmer, 1923-1924; G. E. Johnson, 1924; H. E. Weaver, 1925; J. L. Christian, 1925-1927; R. L. Hubbs, 1927-1929; F. E. Stratton, 1929-1931; W. S. Boynton, 1931-1938; W. G. McCready, 1938-1940; T. W. Walters, 1940-1943; K. E. Groves, 1943-1946; H. D. Schwartz, 1946-1949; G. L. Beane, 1949-1953; B. M. Kurtz, 1953-1959; R. T. Carter, 1959-1964; J. V. Peters, 1964-1965; C. L. Perkins, 1965-1966; W. W. Meske, 1966-1969; Arthur Nelson, 1969-1974; Clayton B. Breakie, 1974-1979; Cyril G. Connelly, 1979-1982; Wayne R. Wentland, Jr., 1982-1985; W. W. Meske, 1985-1986; Kelly B. Bock, 1986-1991; John F. Gatchet, 1991- .

GENCON FINANCIAL SERVICES, INC. *See* Risk and Insurance Management.

GENCON SELF-INSURANCES SERVICES. *See* Risk and Insurance Management.

GENERAL CONFERENCE. The central governing organization of the Seventh-day Adventist Church, composed of such union conferences, union missions, and unions of churches (either in organized division sections or without divisional affiliation) as have been or shall be properly organized and accepted by vote of the General Conference in session; together with such local conferences and properly organized local missions as are not included in any division, union conference, or union mission, or such local organizations directly attached to divisions as have been or shall be properly organized and accepted by vote of the General Conference in session.

The General Conference was organized on May 21, 1863, in Battle Creek, Michigan, where the headquarters remained until 1903. The present headquarters address is 12501 Old Columbia Pike, Silver Spring, Maryland 20904-6600, U.S.A.; the telex number is 440186 SDAY UI or 440632 SDAY UI; the fax number is (301) 680-6090.

General Conference sessions normally are held every five years, but sessions may be postponed up to two years by action of the Executive Committee during unusual world conditions. The voters of the General Conference are delegates at large (all members of the General Conference Executive Committee and certain others chosen by the Executive Committee) and regular delegates (representatives of the union and local conferences and missions). *See* General Conference Session.

The General Conference conducts its worldwide work through sections called divisions, each operating within a specified territory assigned by General Conference action. The division sections are: the Africa-Indian Ocean, China, Eastern Africa, Euro-Africa, Euro-Asia, Far Eastern, Inter-American, North American, South American, South Pacific, Southern Asia, Trans-European, and Middle East Union and Southern Africa Union. The divisions being, in fact, sections, or divisions, of the General Conference, are operated under the provisions of the General Conference Constitution, Bylaws, and *Working Policy*. Thus the Seventh-day Adventist Church is organized, not as a series of separate national or regional churches but as one worldwide, unified, international church, using one *Church Manual* and operating by one general policy. This concept is carried out in general in providing leadership for each division, whose chief executive officer, the division president, is also a vice president of the General Conference. (In China, leadership is provided within the country.)

The officers of the General Conference are (in 1993): the president, six general vice presidents and one vice president from each division, the secretary, an undersecretary, five associate secretaries, the treasurer, an undertreasurer, and five associate treasurers. There are also four general field secretaries, an auditor, and seven associate auditors. The number of associates in the above lists is variable, according to conditions and needs. There are seven regularly organized departments, offices, and associations in the General Conference, which foster the various phases of the work of the church through the union and local conference departments. These are: Church Ministries, Communication, Education, Health and Temperance, Ministerial, Public Affairs and Religious Liberty, and Publishing. Each of these has a director with one or more associates, and some in addition have assistants *(see* separate articles on these). Recent additions to activities of the General Conference are Global Mission, Adventist World Radio, and the Biblical Research Institute.

A number of services are operated by the General Conference in behalf of the headquarters organization and of subsidiary organizations, including a transportation bureau, an insurance service for denominational institutions and interests, Risk Management Services, Adventist Chaplaincy Ministries, Adventist Development and Relief Agency (ADRA) (an agency operated by a board in Washington, D.C., that provides help for development and welfare service to points of special need arising from disaster or famine throughout the world), and Home Study International/Griggs University. Also in the General Conference headquarters are the office of the Ellen G. White Estate, Incorporated, and the office of the president of the Adventist-Laymen's Services and Industries (ASI).

The constitution authorizes the organization by the General Conference of such incorporations as the development of the work may require. Three such incorporations are in existence, though only one, the General Conference Corporation, organized in 1904, is active. The two inactive incorporations kept in existence for legal reasons are the North American Conference Corporation of SDAs and the General Conference Association of SDAs. The function of these bodies is to hold property and to attend to other fiscal responsibilities as may be required in conducting the work of the General Conference, since the General Conference itself is not a legally incorporated body.

In the Seventh-day Adventist Church, missionaries are selected, sent out, and supported by the General Conference itself, since the church has no separate mission board. A

Foreign Mission Board, later called Mission Board, was organized in 1889 and operated as a church agency until the General Conference session of 1903 voted that its function, "the supervision of the missionary operations of the denomination," be assumed by the General Conference Executive Committee (*General Conference Bulletin,* Apr. 14, 1903, p. 195), although it was continued for some time as a legal entity for business transactions. *See* Mission Board. Thus the church in its central organization, and not in an agency apart from its central life, accepts the responsibility and carries the concern of bearing its distinctive message to every nation and people of the world.

Important in the operation of the General Conference is the role of the Executive Committee, which is made up of a large proportion of ex-officio members, together with up to 40 elective members who are chosen at the General Conference sessions or by the Executive Committee between sessions. The committee's ex-officio members include all who are elected at the General Conference sessions, whether serving in the headquarters office or in the division offices; also the presidents of all union conferences and union missions throughout the world, ex-presidents of the General Conference holding credentials from that conference, and designated representatives of certain general institutions. The Executive Committee has full administrative power during the intervals between the sessions of the General Conference, with authority to grant credentials and licenses to its workers, to fill vacancies that may occur through death, resignation, or otherwise in its offices, boards, committees, and agencies; and also to withdraw credentials and licenses by a two-thirds vote of the members present at any regular meeting. Because the General Conference is one worldwide organization, the Executive Committee is international. It meets twice a year at Spring Meeting and at Annual Council and at any other time at the call of the chair. Everyday business is carried on by the GC Administrative Committee (ADCOM), which meets once a week. *See* General Conference Executive Committee.

The General Conference is accepted by the members and all subsidiary organizations as the highest authority in the church, this authority being at its fullest in the General Conference in session. "The General Conference is not something apart from the churches and conferences and union organizations, but is the sum of all these, the uniting of all the parts for unity and cooperation in doing the work which Christ instituted His church to accomplish" (General Conference *Working Policy* [1962], pp. 37, 38; see also *Church Manual,* ch. 4).

Presidents: John Byington, 1863-1865; James White, 1865-1867; J. N. Andrews, 1867-1869; James White, 1869-1871; G. I. Butler, 1871-1874; James White, 1874-1880; G. I. Butler, 1880-1888; O. A. Olsen, 1888-1897; G. A. Irwin, 1897-1901; A. G. Daniells, 1901-1922; W. A. Spicer, 1922-1930; C. H. Watson, 1930-1936; J. L. McElhany, 1936-1950; W. H. Branson, 1950-1954; R. R. Figuhr, 1954-1966; R. H. Pierson, 1966-1979; Neal C. Wilson, 1979-1990; Robert S. Folkenberg, 1990- .

Secretaries: Uriah Smith, 1863-1873; S. Brownsberger, 1873-1874; Uriah Smith, 1874-1876; C. W. Stone, 1876-1877; Uriah Smith, 1877-1881, A. B. Oyen, 1881-1883; Uriah Smith, 1883-1888; D. T. Jones, 1888-1891; W. A. Colcord, 1891-1893; L. T. Nicola, 1893-1897; L. A. Hoopes, 1897-1901; H. E. Osborne, 1901-1903; W. A. Spicer, 1903-1922; A. G. Daniells, 1922-1926; C. K. Meyers, 1926-1933; M. E. Kern, 1933-1936; E. D. Dick, 1936-1952; D. E. Rebok, 1952-1954; W. R. Beach, 1954-1970; C. O. Franz, 1970-1980; G. Ralph Thompson, 1980- .

Treasurers: E. S. Walker, 1863-1865; I. D. Van Horn, 1865-1868; J. N. Loughborough, 1868-1869; E. S. Walker, 1869-1870; G. H. Bell, 1870-1871; Mrs. A. P. Van Horn, 1871-1873; E. B. Gaskill, 1873-1874; Harmon Lindsay, 1874-1875; Fredricka House, 1875-1876; Uriah Smith, 1876-1877; Mrs. M. J. Chapman, 1877-1883; A. R. Henry, 1883-1888; Harmon Lindsay, 1888-1893; W. H. Edwards, 1893-1897; A. G. Adams, 1897-1900; H. M. Mitchell, 1900-1903; I. H. Evans, 1903-1909; W. T. Knox, 1909-1922; J. L. Shaw, 1922-1936; W. E. Nelson, 1936-1950; C. L. Torrey, 1950-1966; K. H. Emmerson, 1966-1980; L. L. Butler, 1980-1985; Donald F. Gilbert, 1985- .

GENERAL CONFERENCE ARCHIVES. *See* Archives.

GENERAL CONFERENCE ASSOCIATION. *See* Corporations.

GENERAL CONFERENCE BIBLE SCHOOLS. A series of training schools sponsored by the General Conference between 1889 and 1896, offering winter courses in Battle Creek, Michigan (later in other places), designed for "ministers, licentiates, Bible workers, and elderly persons," but open to "any laborer, in any department of the cause, and those who desire to become laborers, who cannot take a regular course of study in any of our educational institutions" (General Conference Bible School announcement for 1893-1894).

The first session (called the Bible School for Ministers), held for 20 weeks in Battle Creek in 1889-1890, was an outgrowth of a 10-week institute held at Battle Creek College the preceding year. The announcement, outlining a two-year course, lists W. W. Prescott as principal, and the following serving on the faculty: Uriah Smith, A. T. Jones, E. J. Waggoner, E. W. Farnsworth, W. H. McKee, and W. A. Colcord. In 1893-1894 a 24-week term was offered in Battle Creek.

The 1895-1896 announcement outlines a three-year course; in that year, two 20-week schools were held, one in Battle Creek, with J. H. Durland as principal, and the other at Union College, Nebraska, with L. A. Hoopes as principal. Similar courses were given at Walla Walla and Healdsburg colleges and South Lancaster Academy.

The General Conference then discontinued these Bible schools because arrangements had been made for the regular schools to provide such training. Battle Creek College, for example, began in 1895-1896 to offer a two-year Bible course.

For other types of Bible schools, *see* Bible Schools and Institutes; Workers' Institutes.

GENERAL CONFERENCE BULLETIN (1895-1922; vols. 1 to 4, 1895 to 1903, quarterly with extras during the General Conference sessions of 1895 and 1901; vols. 5 to 9, 1903, 1909, 1913, 1918, and 1922, daily during sessions; published by the General Conference of Seventh-day Adventists; file in RH). In its first period it was a medium of communication from the General Conference to the public and contained statistics, general information concerning the work of the church, reports of meetings, records of proceedings, Week of Prayer readings, and directories of workers, institutions, and organizations. From 1895 to 1903 the *Bulletin* filled the place of the *Yearbook.*

In the second period it contained only the published record of proceedings of the General Conference. The record of other sessions of the General Conference is contained in the *General Conference Daily Bulletin* and in the *Review and Herald.*

GENERAL CONFERENCE COMMITTEE. *See* General Conference Executive Committee.

GENERAL CONFERENCE CONSTITUTION AND BYLAWS. The basic documents of the organization called the General Conference of Seventh-day Adventists. The General Conference is an unincorporated body brought into existence to administer the general affairs of the church, and especially to pursue its evangelistic aim, "to teach all nations the everlasting gospel of our Lord and Saviour Jesus Christ and the commandments of God" (Constitution, Art. II).

The adoption of the first constitution in Battle Creek, Michigan, on May 21, 1863, climaxed a decade or more of lively discussion among the members regarding the advisability of church organization. Those who opposed organization, or "order," argued that it would trespass upon the believers' individual Christian liberty, and some even said that such a church organization would immediately become Babylon. Those who set forth the benefits of organization pointed out that it would prevent confusion, control fanaticism, and make provision for the accrediting of the ministry, the holding of property, and the support of the work. Ellen White as early as 1853 urged the establishing of the church upon "gospel order." The Michigan Conference, the first of the state conferences, was organized Oct. 6, 1861. The General Conference was organized by delegates from six state conferences—Michigan, Wisconsin, Iowa, Minnesota, New York, and Ohio—meeting at Battle Creek in 1863. The 1863 constitution contains the following preamble: "For the purpose of securing unity and efficiency in labor, and promoting the general interest of the cause of present truth, and of perfecting the organization of the Seventh-day Adventists, we, the delegates from the several state conferences, hereby proceed to organize a General Conference, and adopt the following constitution for the government thereof" *(Review and Herald* 21:204, 205, May 26, 1863).

The constitution, which follows the above preamble, contains nine articles (for this constitution in full, *see* Organization), outlining the organization and touching on the following subjects: Article I, name; II, officers; III, duties of president and secretary; IV, duties of treasurer; V, duties of the Executive Committee, which include supervision of the work, distribution of laborers, and calling for funds for missionary work; VI, quota of delegates from state conferences; VII, term of office of the officers (one year); VIII, meetings of the conference; IX, amendments to the constitution.

In assigning financial responsibilities to the Executive Committee, the constitution (Art. V, Sec. 2) has made provision that "means for missionary operations may be received by donation from state conferences, churches, or individuals; and the committee are authorized to call for means when needed." Thus the first constitution made provision for the essential elements in the infant church—a simple organization with officers, and the means of financing its operations.

The present constitution is not an amended form of the original one; it is a new constitution adopted in 1901 (*see* Organization).

The constitution may be amended at any session of the General Conference. Through the years it has undergone considerable change to fit the requirements of a developing work. The latest text appears in the current *Yearbook,* also in the biennial editions of the General Conference *Working Policy.* The constitution describes the object of and outlines the membership of the conference; lists the officers, their duties, manner of election, and term of office; makes provision for the election of the Executive Committee, for the holding of sessions, for the organization of incorporations and the employment of agents, for the adoption of bylaws, and for the amending of the constitution and bylaws.

In 1889 bylaws were added to the constitution to elaborate further the organization and operation of the conference. In the bylaws in their present form the operation of the conference in division sections is delineated; the election of the standing committees of the sessions is outlined; the listing of officers is extended and their duties developed in greater detail; powers, organization, and meetings of the Executive Committee are more fully defined; division committees are provided; financial operations, together with a listing of funds and appropriations, are set forth; also miscellaneous items are touched upon, such as corporation boards, departments, audits, wages, and expense.

More detailed regulations are incorporated from time to time into the *Working Policy* of the General Conference.

Following is the constitution of the General Conference of Seventh-day Adventists as revised at the fifty-fifth session held in Indianapolis, Indiana, July 5-14, 1990.

"Article I—Name

"This organization shall be known as the General Conference of Seventh-day Adventists.

"Article II—Purpose

"The purpose of this General Conference is to teach all nations the everlasting gospel of our Lord and Saviour Jesus Christ and the commandments of God.

"Article III—Membership

"Sec. 1. The membership of the General Conference shall consist of:

"a. All union conferences and union missions that have been or shall be properly organized and accepted by vote of the General Conference in session.

"b. All conferences and missions and unions of churches directly attached to the General Conference, and all conferences and missions and unions of churches directly attached to a division that have been or shall be properly organized.

"Article IV—General Conference Sessions

"Sec. 1. The General Conference shall hold quinquennial sessions at such time and place as the Executive Committee shall designate and announce by a notice published in the *Adventist Review* in three consecutive issues at least four months before the date for the opening of the session. In case special world conditions make it imperative to postpone the calling of the session, the Executive Committee, in regular or special council, shall have authority to make such postponement, not to exceed two years, giving notice to all constituent organizations.

"Sec. 2. The Executive Committee may call special sessions of the General Conference at such time and place as it considers proper, by means of a notice as provided for in Sec. 1, and the transactions of such special sessions shall have the same force as those of the regular sessions.

"Sec. 3. The election of officers and the voting on all matters of business shall be by viva-voce vote, or as designated by the chairman, unless otherwise requested by a majority of the delegates present.

"Sec. 4. The delegates to a General Conference session shall be designated as follows:

"a. Regular delegates.

"b. Delegates at large.

"Sec. 5. Regular delegates shall represent the General Conference's member union conferences, union missions, member conferences, missions, and unions of churches as defined in Article III, Sec. 1, and shall be appointed with the objective that at least 25 percent be lay delegates as follows:

"a. Delegates representing union conferences shall be appointed by the respective unions.

"b. Delegates representing union missions and unions of churches having division affiliation shall be appointed by the respective division executive committees in consultation with the organizations concerned.

"c. Delegates representing conferences and missions attached to a division but not to any union conference or mission shall be appointed by the respective division executive committee in consultation with the organizations concerned.

"d. Delegates representing union conferences and union missions, (conferences and missions) and unions of churches attached to the General Conference but not to any division shall be appointed by the Executive Committee in consultation with the organizations concerned.

"Sec. 6. Regular delegates shall be allotted on the following basis:

"a. Each union conference and union mission shall be entitled to one delegate other than its president (who is a delegate at large), without regard to membership; and an additional delegate for each conference and mission in its territory without regard to membership.

"b. Each union of churches shall be entitled to one delegate, without regard to membership.

"c. Each conference and mission directly attached to a division or to the General Conference shall be entitled to one delegate, without regard to membership.

"d. Each union conference, union mission, union of churches, and attached conference and mission described in Sections 6-a, 6-b, and 6-c shall be entitled to additional delegates based upon its proportion of the world church membership. The total delegates under this provision shall not exceed 1,200.

"Sec. 7. Delegates at large shall represent the General Conference, its divisions, and its organizations, and shall be appointed on the following basis:

"a. All members of the Executive Committee.

"b. Four delegates from each division, without regard to membership, and one additional delegate for each 100,000, or major fraction thereof, of the division membership, such delegates to be appointed by the division executive committee and their credentials to be ratified by the General Conference in session. At least 50 percent of these delegates shall be laypersons, pastors, teachers, and nonadministrative employees.

"c. Those representatives of the church's general and division institutions and other entities, and those general workers, field secretaries, laypersons, and pastors who are selected by the Executive Committee of the General Conference and its divisions, the credentials for whom are to be ratified by the General Conference in session. The number of these delegates shall not exceed 20 percent of the total number of both regular delegates and other delegates at large herein provided for.

"Sec. 8. Credentials to sessions shall be issued by the General Conference to those appointed as provided for in harmony with the provisions of this article.

"Sec. 9. Calculations for all delegate allotments as provided for in this article shall be based upon the membership as of Dec. 31 of the second year preceding the General Conference session.

"Article V—Election

"Sec. 1. The following shall be elected at each regular session of the General Conference:

"a. A president, vice presidents, a secretary, an undersecretary, associate secretaries, division secretaries, a treasurer, an undertreasurer, associate treasurers, division treasurers, general field secretaries, division field secretaries, a director and associate directors of the General Conference Auditing Service, directors of division auditing services, a secretary and associate secretaries of the Ministerial Association, a director and associate directors of each duly organized General Conference department, namely, Church Ministries, Communication, Education, Health and Temperance, Public Affairs and Religious Liberty, Publishing, a director of Archives and Statistics, a director of Adventist Chaplaincy Ministries, a director and associate directors of Trust Services; division Ministerial Association secretaries, division departmental directors, division directors of Trust Services, and, for divisions in which special circumstances require it, any other departmental or service directors, upon the request of the division executive committee, and the approval of the General Conference Executive Committee.

"b. Other persons, not to exceed 80 in number, to serve as members of the Executive Committee, at least 30 of whom shall be laypersons from all the divisions.

"Article VI—Executive Committee

"Sec. 1. The Executive Committee of the General Conference shall consist of:

"a. Those elected as provided by Article V except the director and associate directors of the General Conference Auditing Service and directors of division auditing services.

"b. Presidents of union conferences, presidents of union missions, past presidents of the General Conference holding credentials from the General Conference, the manager of Adventist World Radio-Asia, the president of Andrews University, the director and associate directors of Biblical Research Institute, the president of Christian Record Services, the executive director of General Conference Risk Management Services, the director of Geoscience Research Institute, the president of Home Study International, the president of Loma Linda University, the president of Oakwood College, the president of Pacific Press Publishing Association, the director of Philanthropic Service for Institutions, the president of Seventh-day Adventist Radio, Television, and Film Center, the president of Review and Herald Publishing Association, the president/executive director of Adventist Development and Relief Agency International, the executive secretary of Adventist-Laymen's Services and Industries, the director of General Conference Personnel Administration, the editor and associate editors of *Adventist Review*, the president, secretary, undersecretary, and associate secretaries of Ellen G. White Estate, the speaker of Ayer, Hoy, y Mañana, the speaker of Breath of Life, the speaker of Faith for Today, the speaker of It Is Written, the speaker of Voice of Prophecy, and the speaker of La Voz de la Esperanza.

"Article VII—Officers and Their Duties

"Sec. 1. The officers of the General Conference shall be a president, vice presidents, a secretary, an undersecretary, associate secretaries, a treasurer, an undertreasurer, and associate treasurers.

"Sec. 2. President: The president or his designee shall preside at the sessions of the General Conference, act as chairman of the Executive Committee, and serve in the general interests of the General Conference, as the Executive Committee may advise, and perform such other duties as usually pertain to such office.

"Sec. 3. Vice Presidents: Each vice president shall assist the president in the general administrative work of the General Conference or preside over a division territory.

"Sec. 4. Secretary, undersecretary, and associate secretaries: It shall be the duty of the secretary to keep the minutes of the proceedings of the General Conference sessions and meetings of the Executive Committee, to maintain correspondence with church organizations, and to perform such other duties as usually pertain to such office. The undersecretary and the associate secretaries shall assist the secretary in this work.

"Sec. 5. Treasurer, undertreasurer, and associate treasurers: It shall be the duty of the treasurer to receive all funds of the General Conference and disburse them in harmony with the actions of the Executive Committee, to render such financial statements at regular intervals as may be desired by the president or by the Executive Committee, and to perform such other duties as usually pertain to such office. The undertreasurer and associate treasurers shall assist the treasurer in this work.

"Article VIII—Term of Office

"Sec. 1. All officers of the General Conference and those members of the Executive Committee provided for by Article V, Sec. 1-a, shall hold office from the time of election until the next ensuing regular session, or until their successors are elected and appear to enter upon their duties.

"Sec. 2. Members of the Executive Committee provided for by Article V, Sec. 1-b, shall serve from the time of their election until the next ensuing regular session.

"Article IX—Corporations and Agents

"Sec. 1. Corporations may be authorized by the General Conference in session or by the Executive Committee.

"Sec. 2. The General Conference Corporation is a legal entity formed to hold title to General Conference assets, to serve the General Conference in carrying out its purposes, and to receive gifts and legacies for the General Conference unincorporated.

"Sec. 3. At each regular session of the General Conference, the delegates shall elect the trustees of corporate bodies connected with this organization that may be required by the statutory laws governing each corporate body.

"Sec. 4. The Executive Committee shall appoint or employ agents and other persons as necessary to execute its work effectively.

"Article X—Bylaws

"At any regular or special session of the General Conference the delegates may enact, amend, or repeal bylaws. Such actions may embrace any provision not inconsistent with the constitution.

"Article XI—Amendments

"This constitution or its bylaws may be amended by a two-thirds vote of the delegates present and voting at any session, provided that, if it is proposed to amend the constitution at a special session of the General Conference, notice of such purpose shall be given in the call for that special session."

GENERAL CONFERENCE DAILY BULLETIN (1887, 1888, 1889, 1891, 1893, 1897, 1899; 1889-1893 as *Review and Herald Extras;* daily except Saturday during session; published by the General Conference at place of session; file in RH). Published record of the proceedings of the General Conference in session. Proceedings of earlier and later sessions are reported in the *Review and Herald* and in the *General Conference Bulletin* for the years 1895, 1901, 1903, 1909, 1913, 1918, and 1922. The first five volumes are numbered consecutively 1 to 5; that of 1897 is numbered volume 1, and the last volume, for 1899, is numbered volume 8.

GENERAL CONFERENCE DEPARTMENTS. The name given to designate major areas of the church's outreach. They are arranged to promote and guide specific phases of denominational activity. The department does not administer directly, but through the departments recommendations are made to the General Conference Executive Committee. Each department has a director, and one or more associate directors, assistants, and office staff as may be considered advisable. The departments provide counsel, promotional material, and supplies to the field, working in cooperation with the division, union, and local administrators and their departmental directors.

Each General Conference department is guided by an advisory committee, which meets periodically to assess the program of its department and to provide orientation in its overall thrust. Membership on the General Conference advisories is by General Conference Executive Committee action. The departmental director serves as chair of the advisory committee. A similar organization is followed in each world division and on union conference levels.

For articles on the activities of departments, *see* Church Ministries Department; Communication Department; Education Department; Health and Temperance Department; Public Affairs and Religious Liberty Department; Publishing Department; Trust Services.

The Ministerial Association, although not organized as a department, serves the church on the General Conference level.

Beginnings of Departmental Concept of Organization. Before the turn of the century the work of the denomination had grown to the extent that the General Conference president and secretary were no longer able to encompass all the demands of the field for counsel and direction. There were in operation separate denomination-wide associations, such as the medical, temperance, Sabbath school, and tract and missionary societies, but these were not a part of the General Conference administration. To meet the demands, the General Conference in 1887 added to its officers an educational secretary and a home mission secretary to guide in the conducting of workers' institutes and city missions, and provided for an international publishing committee to promote the general interests of the publishing work.

Departments Organized. At the General Conference session of 1901 the departments were first organized, each with a chair (a member of the General Conference executive committee), a secretary, and an appropriate staff *(see* Organization). In 1909 the chairs became secretaries; the General Conference president was considered the chair. These departments were not administrative bodies, for they were not directly responsible for such institutions as schools, the publishing houses, or the medical institutions. Established as the medium of communication, they were to bring the needs of the field or of the institutions to the attention of the administration of the General Conference, and to represent the desires, the purposes, and the policies of the General Conference to the field and to the institution. They were intended also to bring the various fields or institutions into coordination one with the other in matters of operation, unifying as far as practical or desirable the operation of institutions.

At first these departments were lightly staffed, but the expansion of the work in the field and the growth in the number and size of the institutions, the increase in the complexity of the work itself, the demand for materials, supplies, literature, and the study of plans and techniques all required the addition of personnel and the formation of additional departments.

By action of the General Conference session of 1985, the departments of Lay

Activities, Sabbath School, Adventist Youth, Stewardship, and the Home and Family Service were merged into one coordinated department—the Church Ministries Department.

GENERAL CONFERENCE DISTRICT. *See* District.

GENERAL CONFERENCE EXECUTIVE COMMITTEE. The administrative body of the Seventh-day Adventist Church in the intervals between sessions of the General Conference. It consists of all who are elected at the General Conference sessions to serve in the General Conference organization and in the divisions; also the presidents of union conferences and union missions, the ex-presidents of the General Conference holding credentials from the General Conference, the presidents of the two SDA universities, the editor of the *Adventist Review,* the presidents of the publishing houses in the United States, the president of Home Study International/Griggs University, and the executive director of the General Conference Insurance Service; also up to 80 others, elected at the sessions or by the General Conference Executive Committee between sessions. There are (1993) about 370 members of the Executive Committee. The term of office of all except the ex-officio members is from one regular General Conference session to the next, usually five years.

In 1991 the Annual Council reduced the weekly scheduled Executive Committee meeting to four required annual meetings, one each quarter. It also authorized the establishment of an Administrative Committee (ADCOM) with limited authority to care for routine items generally associated with the General Conference headquarters. Should a need arise necessitating a meeting of the Executive Committee, the General Conference president or a General Conference officer may call a meeting of the Executive Committee at any time. The 1993 Annual Council further reduced the required frequency of meetings to semiannual meetings, one in the spring (Spring Meeting) and the other in the fall (Annual Council).

GENERAL CONFERENCE MISSIONS DIVISION. A provisional organization formed by the General Conference Committee on Dec. 16, 1943, to foster the work in the mission fields that, because of World War II, were detached from their division organizations. A provisional committee administered the work in these fields from headquarters at Washington, D.C. This division is listed in the *Statistical Report* through 1945.

GENERAL CONFERENCE RISK MANAGEMENT SERVICES. *See* Risk and Insurance Management.

GENERAL CONFERENCE SESSION. The meeting (held quinquennially) of delegates representing the worldwide Seventh-day Adventist Church.

The first session, at which the General Conference of Seventh-day Adventists was organized, was held in Battle Creek, Michigan, May 20-23, 1863. Twenty delegates were in attendance—four from the state of New York, two from Ohio, 10 from Michigan (eight ministers and two laypersons), one from Wisconsin, two from Iowa, and one from Minnesota. Of the conferences then in existence, only the Vermont Conference was not represented. Committees on constitution, credentials, and nominations were duly appointed, and the constitution of the General Conference was adopted. It consisted of nine articles setting forth the usual features of organization and provided for representation from the constituent conferences to the yearly sessions. The conference's officers (president, secretary, and treasurer) were elected for the ensuing term of one year. In 1889 the constitution was amended to convene sessions biennially. From 1905 to 1970 the constitution provided for regular quadrennial sessions. Since 1970 sessions have been held every five years.

The importance of the quinquennial session in Seventh-day Adventist Church government is evident. This is the time when the highest organization in the administration of a worldwide work convenes to express the collective thinking and planning of the church. The final authority of this body is accepted by all subordinate organizations and interests in the various sections of the world. In a word, the General Conference quinquennial session synthesizes and implements church organization on a world scale.

This form of church government recognizes that authority rests in the church membership, which delegates executive responsibility to representative bodies and officers for the governing of the church and the promotion of church interests. These basic principles of authority and representation characterize the four steps in SDA organization leading from the individual believer to the world church. Within the framework of local responsibility and organization, members meet personally or through personal representation to ensure a united body and a united action. On the conference or local field level, the united body of churches in a state, province, or local territory organizes and directs the work. Local fields affiliate within a larger territory to form unions. The union organization likewise prosecutes the work within its territory. Then, finally, these union groupings unite in the General Conference as a body embracing the church in all parts of the world.

The quinquennial session operates, as did the first session in Battle Creek, on the basis of duly accredited delegates. These delegates and voters are designated: (a) delegates at large; and (b) regular delegates.

The delegates at large include all members of the General Conference Executive Committee (commonly called the General Conference Committee) and such other delegates as are recommended by it for seating at the session to represent general institutions and church interests *(see* General Conference Constitution, Art. IV, Section 7); the number of these others is not to exceed 20 percent of the total number of delegates in attendance otherwise provided for.

The regular delegates are appointed as outlined in Article IV, Section 6, of the General Conference Constitution.

The General Conference Committee issues credentials to the delegates appointed as provided for in Article IV, Section 8. Calculations for the delegate allotments are based upon the membership as of Dec. 31 of the second year preceding the General Conference session.

The delegates to the quinquennial session are able to bring to the officers in charge whatever matter they feel is worthy of attention. The assembly sets up a number of standing committees (Constitution and Bylaws, Credentials and Licenses, Finance, Nominations, and Plans) to prepare the regular business of the session and to process items or suggestions that are to come before the assembly. Special groups can be appointed to deal with specific items. During the quinquennium, technical committees prepare materials on certain aspects of the General Conference operation. The work of these committees comes likewise to the session through regular channels. Specific provision is made in the bylaws (Art. II, Sec. 2) for the number and choice of members that constitute the nominating committee.

Sessions of the General Conference are held quinquennially at the time and place determined by the General Conference Executive Committee, although they can be postponed for as long as two years during unusual world conditions. This committee may call special sessions at such a time and place as it deems proper by a notice like that for regular sessions, and the transactions of such special sessions have the same force as those of the regular sessions. The election of officers and the voting on all matters of business that come before the session are by viva-voce vote or as designated by the chair, unless otherwise requested by a majority of the delegates present. Currently the number of delegates at large and regular delegates in attendance at a quinquennial session approximates 1,900.

The foregoing outlines the essential role of the General Conference sessions in SDA Church administration. This role is further enhanced by the fact that the General Conference session symbolizes in SDA ranks the importance of organization in God's work. The church believes that organization is of God and is based on divine principles. The General Conference organization and session are intended to exemplify these principles and the order that should prevail in God's church.

SESSIONS OF THE GENERAL CONFERENCE OF SEVENTH-DAY ADVENTISTS

Session	Delegates	Opening Date	Place
1	20	May 20, 1863	Battle Creek, Mich.
2	20	May 18, 1864	Battle Creek, Mich.
3	21	May 17, 1865	Battle Creek, Mich.
4	19	May 16, 1866	Battle Creek, Mich.
5	18	May 14, 1867	Battle Creek, Mich.
6	15	May 12, 1868	Battle Creek, Mich.
7	16	May 18, 1869	Battle Creek, Mich.
8	22	March 15, 1870	Battle Creek, Mich.
9	17	Feb. 7, 1871	Battle Creek, Mich.
10	14	Dec. 29, 1871	Battle Creek, Mich.
11	18	March 11, 1873	Battle Creek, Mich.
12	21	Nov. 14, 1873	Battle Creek, Mich.
13	19	Aug. 10, 1874	Battle Creek, Mich.
14	18	Aug. 15, 1875	Battle Creek, Mich.
*	15	Mar. 31, 1876	Battle Creek, Mich.
15	16	Sept. 19, 1876	Lansing, Mich.
*	16	Nov. 12, 1876	Battle Creek, Mich.
16	20	Sept. 20, 1877	Lansing, Mich.
*	22	Mar. 1, 1878	Battle Creek, Mich.
17	39	Oct. 4, 1878	Battle Creek, Mich.
*	29	Apr. 17, 1879	Battle Creek, Mich.
18	39	Nov. 7, 1879	Battle Creek, Mich.
*	28	Mar. 11, 1880	Battle Creek, Mich.
19	38	Oct. 6, 1880	Battle Creek, Mich.
20	41	Dec. 1, 1881	Battle Creek, Mich.
21	47	Dec. 7, 1882	Rome, N.Y.
22	65	Nov. 8, 1883	Battle Creek, Mich.
23	67	Oct. 30, 1884	Battle Creek, Mich.
24	70	Nov. 18, 1885	Battle Creek, Mich.
25	71	Nov. 18, 1886	Battle Creek, Mich,
26	70	Nov. 13, 1887	Oakland, Calif.
27	91	Oct. 17, 1888	Minneapolis, Minn.
28	109	Oct. 18, 1889	Battle Creek, Mich.
29	125	Mar. 5, 1891	Battle Creek, Mich.
30	130	Feb. 17, 1893	Battle Creek, Mich.
31	150	Feb. 15, 1895	Battle Creek, Mich.
32	140	Feb. 19, 1897	College View, Nebr.
33	149	Feb. 15, 1899	South Lancaster, Mass.
34	268	Apr. 2, 1901	Battle Creek, Mich.
35	139	Mar. 27, 1903	Oakland, Calif.
36	197	May 11, 1905	Washington, D.C.
37	328	May 13, 1909	Washington, D.C.
38	372	May 15, 1913	Washington, D.C.
39	443	Mar. 29, 1918	San Francisco, Calif.
40	581	May 11, 1922	San Francisco, Calif.
41	577	May 27, 1926	Milwaukee, Wis.
42	577	May 28, 1930	San Francisco, Calif.
43	671	May 26, 1936	San Francisco, Calif.
44	619	May 26, 1941	San Francisco, Calif.
45	828	June 5, 1946	Washington, D.C.
46	943	July 10, 1950	San Francisco, Calif.
47	1,109	May 24, 1954	San Francisco, Calif.
48	1,160	June 19, 1958	Cleveland, Ohio

Session	Delegates	Opening Date	Place
49	1,314	July 26, 1962	San Francisco, Calif.
50	1,495	June 16, 1966	Detroit, Mich.
51	1,782	June 11, 1970	Atlantic City, N.J.
52	1,756	July 10, 1975	Vienna, Austria
53	1,696	Apr. 17, 1980	Dallas, Tex.
54	1,853	June 27, 1985	New Orleans, La.
55	1,943	July 5, 1990	Indianapolis, Ind.
56	2,352	June 29, 1995	Utrecht, Netherlands

*Special sessions

GENERAL CONFERENCE SESSION OF 1888. *See* Righteousness by Faith.

GENERAL CONFERENCE SESSION OF 1901. *See* Organization, IV.

GENERAL CONFERENCE *WORKING POLICY.* *See Working Policy.*

GENERAL COUNSEL, OFFICE OF. *See* Office of General Counsel.

GENERAL EUROPEAN CONFERENCE. *See* European Division.

GENERAL MEETING. In early Seventh-day Adventist practice a weekend meeting held usually by a local church for the local and neighboring members (also commonly called a conference), most often lasting from Friday afternoon to Sunday, combining a revival meeting and a business meeting for planning evangelism. An example is one announced under the heading Conference: "Providence permitting there will be a general meeting of Sabbath-keepers in Monterey, Allegan Co., Mich., Commencing Friday, Nov. 14th at 1 o'clock, P.M., and to hold over Sabbath and First-day.

"The wants of the cause in Allegan Co. will be considered at this meeting. Bro. Joseph Bates is especially requested to attend.

"In behalf of the church. M. E. Cornell" *(Review and Herald* 9:8, Nov. 6, 1856).

In this case members from five other places joined with the believers at Monterey. The meetings included "fervent prayers, pointed exhortations and cheerful songs of the brethren and sisters" and "the presentation of the sure word of prophecy" of Christ's coming, which "aroused and quickened his dear children in the meeting." There was also a baptismal service. Bates reported the meetings *(ibid.* 9:40, Dec. 4, 1856).

GENERAL SABBATH SCHOOL ASSOCIATION. *See* Sabbath School Department.

GEOLOGY. *See* Flood; Science and Religion.

GEORGE, WILLIAM AARON (1866-1950). Physician, administrator. He attended Battle Creek College, graduating in 1891, and was graduated from the University of Michigan Medical School in 1894. He also taught at Battle Creek College in 1894. When the American Medical Missionary College was opened in 1895, he was appointed professor of chemistry. After that he served as medical superintendent of Nebraska Sanitarium (1901-1907) and of Nashville Sanitarium (1907-1911). In 1911 he was appointed head surgeon at Loma Linda Sanitarium. He also taught anatomy at the College of Medical Evangelists. He retired from active service in 1934. He was also an ordained minister, prominent in church activities.

GEORGETOWN ADVENTIST ACADEMY. A former coeducational nonresident high school situated at 53 Hadfield Street, Georgetown, Guyana. The school began in 1949 under the principalship of K.J.E. Dummett in quarters at the back of the Georgetown Seventh-day Adventist Church on Church and Oronoque streets, with 10 students enrolled. Operations were suspended in 1951 and resumed in 1959 with Lindrey Niles as principal. Operated by the Guyana Mission, the school had a highest-ever enrollment of 216 in 1971-1972. The school offered five years of secondary instruction in preparation for the General Certificate of Education ordinary level examinations and was approved by the Guyana government. Along with basic academic subjects, the students were taught cooking, typing, and agriculture as practical subjects. The school closed around 1980.

Principals: K.J.E. Dummett, 1949-1951; Lindrey Niles, 1959-1961; Roy McGarrell, 1961-1962; Lynette Hinds, 1962-1964; Samuel Beckles, 1964-1965; Lloyd Le Gendre (acting), 1965; Vernon Grosvenor (acting), 1965; Henry A. Lewis, 1965-1966; Mrs. K. Cooper (acting), 1966; Errol Thompson, 1966-1967; Steve Wilsey, 1967-1968; Kenneth Gittens, 1968-1970; Dolwin Anderson, 1970-1976; Clement Teixeria, 1976-1980.

GEORGIA. *See* Georgia-Cumberland Conference; South Atlantic Conference.

GEORGIA. A European country bordered by the Black Sea, Russia, Turkey, Armenia, and Azerbaijan. It occupies an area of 26,911 square miles (69,700 square kilometers) and has a population (1994) of 5.7 million. Georgia was annexed to Russia in 1801 and entered the former USSR in 1922, becoming a constituent republic in 1936.

In 1989 strong feelings of nationalism led the USSR to a campaign of repression. On Apr. 9, 1991, Georgia declared its independence and became an independent state when the Soviet Union disbanded on Dec. 25, 1991.

Seventh-day Adventist Statistics. Georgia is a part of the Trans-Caucasus Field, an attached field of the Euro-Asia Division. Statistics (1992) for *Georgia:* churches, 4; members, 209. In 1904 Dr. Vagan Pampanjan, an Armenian, started to work among Armenians in the city of Tiflis (now Tbilisi) and its suburbs in Georgia. In 1906, after graduating from the SDA school in Friedensau, Albert Ozel, a physician, began to work among the Germans and the Letts. Soon he was able to organize a small church. After eight years the Czarist government exiled him to the Narinsky in Tomsk province, where he died from typhus two years later at 38 years of age.

In 1925 the first official meetings of the Transcaucasian Seventh-day Adventist churches took place in the city of Tiflis. Because of the bad condition of the roads and lack of funds, only 20 delegates were able to attend; they included Georgians, Armenians, Russians, and Germans. The meeting adopted the constitution of the Transcaucasian field with a membership of 233. Elder Galodzhajev was elected field chair; Elder Klimenko, secretary, and Brethren Istjagin, Volov, and Bogdasarjants were members of the field committee.

I. M. Droiling and P. I. Lagutov were working in Georgia in 1993. The international conflicts and enmity between various groups and political parties are hampering the spread of the gospel in the area.

The law concerning freedom of conscience was not in effect in the country in 1993. The patriarch of the Georgian Orthodox Church, Ilja II, personally handles the religious problems in the state.

GEORGIA CONFERENCE. *See* Georgia-Cumberland Conference.

GEORGIA-CUMBERLAND ACADEMY. A coeducational boarding school on the senior high school level, opened in 1965 and operated by the Georgia-Cumberland Conference near Calhoun, Georgia. Seven main buildings were erected on a 600-acre (250-hectare) tract known as the Hurlbutt Farms, formerly occupied by the Scott Sanitarium (a private enterprise).

Industries operating on campus in 1994 included Calhoun Greenhouses, Grafe Stained Glass, GCA Packaging, and Sample Barn (manufacture of carpet sample booklets/displays for the carpet industry).

Principals: Edward Reifsnyder, 1965-1968; W. A. Sowers, 1968-1970; James Clizbe, 1970-1973; L. C. Anderson, 1973-1977; R. M. Barrow, 1977-1978; Wayne McNutt, 1978-1982; Cyril Connelly, 1982-1988; Vic Kostenko, 1988-1989; John Thomas, 1989- .

GEORGIA-CUMBERLAND CONFERENCE. The unit of church organization comprising the territory of Georgia, Cherokee County in North Carolina, and eastern Tennessee to the eastern boundaries of the counties of Cannon, Clay, Coffee, Dekalb, Franklin, Jackson, and Smith. *(See also* South Atlantic Conference; South Central Conference.) Statistics (1992): churches, 123; members, 21,286; church schools, 63; ordained ministers, 98; licensed ministers, 11; Bible instructors, 1; teachers, 169. Headquarters: 255 Georgia Cumberland Conference Road NE, Calhoun, Georgia. The conference forms part of the Southern Union Conference.

Institutions. Atlanta Adventist Academy; Collegedale Academy; Georgia-Cumberland Academy; Southern College. Also located within the conference territory are Gordon Hospital; Jellico Community Hospital; Smyrna Hospital; and Takoma Hospital, all of which belong to the Adventist Health System/Sunbelt.

Local churches—*Georgia:* Albany,

Americus, Athens, Atlanta (Belvedere, First Hispanic, First Romanian, Georgia Central Korean, Korean, Metropolitan, North, North Hispanic, Southside), Augusta, Austell, Baxley, Boston, Brunswick, Calhoun, Carrolton, Cartersville, Cedartown, Cleveland, Cohutta, Columbus, Conyers, Dalton (Dalton, Hispanic), Douglasville, Dublin, Duluth, Ellijay, Fayetteville, Gainesville, Georgia-Cumberland Academy, Griffin, Hiram, Kingsland, LaGrange, Lakeland, Leesburg, Macon, Madison, Marietta (Marietta, Korean), Morganton, Moultrie, Oglethorpe, Peachtree City, Pine Mountain Valley, Ringgold, Rising Fawn, Rock Spring, Rome, Rossville, Savannah, Smyrna, Statesboro, Stone Mountain, Summerville, Thomaston, Thomasville, Tifton, Valdosta, Warner Robins, Waycross, Wildwood (New England, Wildwood Chapel), Woodstock.

North Carolina: Andrews, Murphy.

Tennessee: Apison, Athens, Beersheba Springs, Birchwood, Bristol, Chattanooga (First, Hamilton Community, St. Elmo, Standifer Gap), Cleveland (Bowman Hills, Ladd Springs), Coalfield, Coalmont, Collegedale (Collegedale, Korean, Spanish-American), Cookeville, Crossville, Dayton, Decatur, Deer Lodge, Dunlap, Graysville (Brayton, Graysville), Greeneville (Greeneville, South Green), Harriman, Hixson, Jasper, Jelico, Johnson City, Kingsport, Knoxville (First, Grace, Halls Crossroads), Laurelbrook, Lenoir City, Little Creek, Maryville, McDonald (McDonald Road, Village Chapel), McMinnville, Monteagle, Morristown, Mountain City, Newport, Oak Ridge, Ooltewah, Pikeville, Roan Mountain, Rogersville, Sevierville, Soddy-Daisy, Spencer, Spring City.

Companies—*Georgia:* Auburn, Douglas, Jasper, Milledgeville. *Tennessee:* Chattanooga (Tiftonia Spanish-American).

History. *Beginnings of the Work in the Area.* Seventh-day Adventist publications penetrated the territory of the present Georgia-Cumberland Conference in 1872, four years before the first SDA workers arrived, resulting in the conversion of J. A. Killingworth and his family, of Griffin, Georgia. Rufus Eugene Seagraves learned about the SDA health principles from a Dr. Irwin in 1875 and was baptized three years later by C. O. Taylor, the first denominational worker in Georgia. Taylor came to the south Georgia town of Quitman in the autumn of 1876. Knowing of no other SDAs in the state, he engaged in personal evangelism. The next spring he learned of the Killingworths through the *Review and Herald.* On his way north to visit them in 1877, he passed through Houston County, where he won J. S. Killen, a planter and lawyer, along with some of his friends and some employees who formerly had been his slaves *(see* South Atlantic Conference). (Later four of Killen's sons and three daughters entered the colporteur work, one of them receiving local ministerial credentials in the 1880s.)

In 1876, the same year that Taylor arrived in Georgia, a church was organized in the present Georgia-Cumberland Conference territory in Tennessee as a result of the work of Orlando Soule, who came to visit an SDA friend named Wetherby, who had moved from Michigan to Sparta, Tennessee, on the edge of the Cumberland Plateau. Asked to lecture there, Soule remained to preach in several places, was ordained by D. M. Canright in May, and built up the first church in the conference area, the Mount Gilead church, not many miles from Sparta. He organized the church in the autumn, with Patrick D. Moyers, his first convert, as elder. Moyers, one of the earliest Southern-born SDA preachers, was a strong pillar at Mount Gilead and later at Graysville, Tennessee.

Early in the history of the Quitman, Georgia, group of converts, one of the members, Samuel Mitchell, was arrested in July 1878 for plowing in his field on Sunday. In poor health, he could not endure the damp cell, and became ill after serving 15 days of his 30-day sentence. Refusing on the one hand to take money that a member of Congress offered for his release, and on the other to promise that he would not work on Sunday if he were released, he died a martyr to Sunday law enforcement on Feb. 4, 1879.

Two colporteurs, George A. King and Charles F. Curtis, came to Georgia in 1885 to sell the books *Daniel and the Revelation,* by Uriah Smith, and *Sunshine at Home,* and returned North with enthusiastic reports of future prospects for the South. At the 1886 General Conference session Curtis, a student at Battle Creek College, and his betrothed, whom he married shortly thereafter, were asked to work in Atlanta with George W. Anglebarger, who was to head a city mission. Curtis was to look after the canvassing work, Mrs. Anglebarger was to be the "mission mother," and Mrs. Curtis the Bible instructor. The two couples reached Atlanta Mar. 3, 1887, a few months after the arrival of Charles Bliss, the minister in charge of the Georgia mission field, who had already won one convert in meetings conducted at Jonesboro.

After five weeks of a damp spring in Atlanta, Anglebarger, whose health had failed, moved with his wife to Colorado. A few days later they were replaced by three Michigan Bible instructors, Clara Conklin, Anna Thomas, and Mrs. Charles Swartout, and Charles Swartout, a colporteur. Curtis took charge of the city mission.

The group conducted meetings in Atlanta and Fort Valley. On the advice of S. H. Lane, who replaced Bliss in Georgia and Florida in 1887, the Atlanta mission was closed because of a depression, and the workers moved to a less expensive home and in it conducted Sabbath and weeknight meetings. Later the headquarters were moved to the southeast section of the city, where a church was organized in the fall of 1888. Curtis, then Georgia Tract Society director, was also assigned Florida and South Carolina.

A Review and Herald office was established in Atlanta in 1889 and remained active until the Southern Publishing Association in Tennessee was formed in 1901.

Lane and his half brother, Dr. O. C. Godsmark, held a tent series in Athens, Georgia, in 1889. That same year Georgia's first SDA camp meeting, with about 60 in attendance, was held at Reynolds, where a few people were already observing the Sabbath. Also in that year, two ministers, M. G. Huffman, of Indiana, and L. T. Crisler, of Florida, conducted tent meetings at Alpharetta, Georgia, and organized a company, which later became a church.

With the help of P. D. Moyers and J. W. Scoles, E. R. Gillett built a church in Graysville, Tennessee, a small town 30 miles (50 kilometers) north of Chattanooga, to which he had moved in 1885. J. M. Rees organized a group of 10 members there on Sept. 8, 1888. The following year the General Conference Committee appointed R. M. Kilgore president of District No. 2 (Southern District), and in 1890 he came to the South with his secretary, Arthur W. Spalding, and made Graysville his headquarters. The town remained headquarters for the Southern District for the next 12 years.

Eastern Kentucky and eastern Tennessee were organized in 1889 as the Cumberland Mission. Georgia was part of the Southern Mission. G. T. Wilson, conducting tent meetings, was responsible for establishing a church in 1890 at Barwick, Georgia, not far from Quitman. The 1892 General Conference session authorized A. P. Heacock to conduct tent meetings in the Cumberland Mission and Wilson in Georgia.

The Southern Training School, founded at Graysville, Tennessee, in 1892 and later moved to Collegedale, Tennessee, was the parent of the present Southern College.

In 1893 churches were organized by J. W. Scoles at Webster, Roane County, Tennessee, by W. A. McCutchen at Gainesville, Georgia, and by Grant Adkins in Knoxville, Tennessee. Also at Knoxville, following quiet house-to-house Bible studies, a company of Black converts was organized. On Nov. 19 W. A. McCutchen and E. C. Keck, who had recently arrived from Battle Creek, were arrested for building benches for a new church school in Gainesville, Georgia, on Sunday. The case was tried twice and finally dismissed on the grounds that the labor performed by the men was not of their ordinary calling. The school was opened in 1893 and accepted children in elementary (and, for a time, in secondary) grades. By June 30, tithe for the previous 12 months in the Cumberland Mission had risen to $844 and in Georgia to $898.

Late in 1894, 20 Graysville and Dayton, Tennessee, members were jailed for Sunday labor and sentenced to the chain gang. The controversy temporarily closed the Graysville school.

Cumberland Conference and Georgia Conference Organized. At a camp meeting in Harriman, Tennessee, Sept. 14, 1900, the Cumberland Mission was organized into the Cumberland Conference, with Smith Sharp as president. There were 450 members, one ordained minister, and two licensed ministers. Tithe amounted to about $3,800 that year. Between Aug. 9 and 19, 1901, at a camp meeting at Austell, Georgia, the Georgia Conference, embracing the state of Georgia, was organized, with C. A. Hall as president.

A church was organized at Macon, Georgia, in 1898. Later, churches were organized in Tennessee at Brayton (1901), Cleveland (1903), Daylight (1904), and Chattanooga (1907). The Southern Sanitarium at Graysville was completed in 1904. Another denominational sanitarium was established in Atlanta in 1903 near the conference headquarters. During the next 10 years privately operated treatment rooms and sanitariums were opened in Knoxville, in Chattanooga, and at

East Lake in Atlanta, the last named operated by Dr. C. F. Curtis. The Cumberland Industrial School was established by Clifford G. Howell at McMinnville, Tennessee, in 1902, and in 1907 it had an enrollment of 23. In 1905 another intermediate school was developed from a church school at Alpharetta, Georgia, which in 1915 reverted to the local church.

When the Southeastern Union Conference was organized, Jan. 12, 1908, the Cumberland Conference was reduced to include only eastern Tennessee (with the western boundary on the west side of the counties of Clay, Jackson, Putnam, White, Warren, Grundy, and Marion), and was left with a membership of 530, with 12 churches and five elementary schools. By 1909 Dade, Walker, Catoosa, Whitfield, Murray, Fannin, and Gilmer counties, in northwest Georgia, and Dekalb, Smith, and Macon counties, in Tennessee, were also listed as belonging to the Cumberland Conference.

Churches were organized at Athens, Tennessee (1910), Savannah, Georgia (1911), Lenoir City, Tennessee (1912), Greeneville, Tennessee (1913), and Stonewall, Georgia (1914). Also in 1914 a self-supporting school was established at Reeves, Georgia, near Calhoun, with a church of 31 members, most of whom had moved there from California. In 1915 churches were organized at Fitzgerald, Georgia, and Johnson City and Bristol, Tennessee. Work in Johnson City dates back to the work of J. M. Rees in 1887.

As a result of large-scale evangelism in Atlanta by C. B. Haynes in 1912, 1914, 1917, and 1918, more than 150 were baptized and a new church was built. In 1915 there were 491 members in 15 Georgia Conference churches, and 604 members in 15 Cumberland Conference churches.

Territorial Changes. In 1918 the counties of Echols, Clinch, Charlton, Ware, Pierce, Wayne, Camden, Glynn, and McIntosh, in the southeast corner of Georgia, were transferred to the Florida Conference, and the northwest Georgia counties of Whitfield, Murray, Finnin, and Gilmer were returned from the Cumberland Conference. A year later 18 western counties of North Carolina were added to the Cumberland Conference (none of which were retained after 1932 except Cherokee). In 1922 the conference headquarters was established adjacent to the Atlanta First church on Cherokee Avenue. Then in 1924 seven more northwest Georgia counties went back to the Cumberland Conference.

Self-supporting medical institutions were prominent in several localities: a sanitarium at Reeves, Georgia, from 1915 to 1920, reorganized later as the Scott Sanitarium; the East Lake Rest Home, operated by Dr. C. F. Curtis, taken over by Dr. J. F. Schneider from 1923 to 1927, replaced by the Georgia Sanitarium, on the west side of Atlanta, until 1958; a sanitarium at Douglasville, Georgia, opened in 1918 by Charles Jones and his wife in connection with the Flat Rock School (1916-1923; from 1920 to 1923 a conference-owned school).

The General Conference, through Dr. J. R. Mitchell, arranged for SDA students to attend the Atlanta Southern Dental School in 1934 and operated a student home until 1948. Additional self-supporting hospitals, now active, include, in Tennessee, Little Creek Sanitarium, Hospital, and School (organized in 1940), at Concord; Laurelbrook Hospital and School, Dayton. Takoma Hospital at Greeneville, Tennessee, built by Dr. L. E. Coolidge in 1927, was given to the Southern Union in 1954. Wildwood Sanitarium was organized in 1942 at Wildwood, Georgia. In 1958 the conference assumed the operation of two county hospitals in Georgia—Watkins Memorial Hospital at Ellijay and Louis Smith Memorial Hospital at Lakeland. In 1993 most of the hospitals were part of the Adventist Health System/Sunbelt (*see* list above).

Georgia-Cumberland Conference Organized. The Cumberland Conference was combined with the Georgia Conference in March 1932, forming the Georgia-Cumberland Conference, with H. E. Lysinger as president, and with headquarters at 547 Cherokee Ave., SE., Atlanta, Georgia. The 24 churches in the Cumberland Conference and the 23 in Georgia made 47 churches, with a total membership of 2,490. In 1938 there were 49 White churches with 2,781 members and nine Black churches with 772 members. When on Jan. 1, 1946, the Black churches of Tennessee were taken into the South Central Conference, and the Black churches of Georgia and the Carolinas and all of Florida, except that portion lying west of the Apalachicola River, were taken into the South Atlantic Conference, there were 61 churches left to the Georgia-Cumberland Conference, with 3,000 members and 18 ordained ministers.

Conference properties acquired in the 1950s included a youth camp in the Blue Ridge Mountains of north Georgia (Atoka Springs Camp, 1955) and the Hurlbutt Farms (1959), with nearly 600 acres (250 hectares), where the

Scott Sanitarium had been situated. These were near Calhoun, Georgia, and were purchased for a site for the Georgia-Cumberland Academy, which was opened in 1965. In 1994 Cohutta Springs Center was dedicated debt-free.

Presidents—Georgia Conference: C. A. Hall, 1901-1903; R. M. Kilgore, 1903-1906; George W. Wells, 1906-1910; C. B. Stephenson, 1910-1912; L. T. Crisler, 1912-1913; N. V. Willess, 1913-1916; W. H. Branson (acting), 1916; B. J. White, 1916-1917; B. W. Brown, 1917-1918; W. F. McMahen, 1918-1919; B. W. Spire, 1919-1922; A. S. Booth, 1922-1926; B. F. Kneeland, 1926-1932; *Cumberland Conference:* Smith Sharp, 1900-1903; O. C. Godsmark 1903-1905; W. W. Williams, 1905-1907; J. F. Pogue, 1907-1910; P. G. Stanley, 1910-1913; W. H. Branson, 1913-1915; R. W. Parmele, 1916-1917; J. L. Shuler, 1917-1919; A. W. Coon, 1919-1921; B. F. Kneeland, 1921-1926; R. I. Keate, 1926-1932; *Georgia-Cumberland Conference:* H. E. Lysinger, 1932-1937; R. I. Keate, 1937-1943; I. M. Evans, 1943-1949; G. R. Nash, 1949-1956; A. C. Fearing, 1956-1958; N. C. Wilson, 1958-1960. A. C. McKee, 1960-1963; LeRoy J. Leiske, 1963-1964; Desmond Cummings, 1964-1980; Gary B. Patterson, 1980-1986; William A. Geary, 1986-1994; Gordon Bietz, 1994- .

GEOSCIENCE RESEARCH INSTITUTE. A research institute established in 1957 by action of the Annual Council for the purpose of making available to the Seventh-day Adventist Church competent advice concerning the relation of scientific evidence to inspired testimony. The institute focuses mainly on the biological, geological, and paleontological questions regarding the origin of life and the past history of our planet in the context of the Creation account given in the book of Genesis.

The institute conducts its work through laboratory, field, and literature investigation. It also devotes significant effort in communicating with the church and other entities through teaching, lecturing, geological field conferences, videos, and periodical publications. In 1974 the institute began publishing *Origins*, a semiannual technical publication. *Geoscience Reports*, which is designed for elementary and secondary educational levels, began publication in 1981. The Spanish periodical *Ciencia de los Origenes* has been in production since 1982.

The institute was first located on the campus of Andrews University. In 1980 it was moved to Loma Linda University in order to take advantage of the close proximity of significant geological features as well as the scientific environment of that institution. At Loma Linda the institute has laboratories and a 20,000-volume library. In 1991 the institute established two branch offices: one in Europe at the Saleve Adventist Institute in France, and one in South America at the River Plate Adventist University in Argentina.

Directors: Frank L. Marsh, 1957-1964; Richard M. Ritland, 1964-1971; Ariel A. Roth, 1971-1973; Robert H. Brown, 1973-1980; Ariel A. Roth, 1980-1994; L. James Gibson, 1994- .

GERBER, ROBERT (1893-1971). Administrator, treasurer, departmental secretary. He was born in Lajoux, Switzerland, and began denominational service in 1915 as a Bible worker. The following year he served at the publishing house in Gland, and for the next four years he was accountant at the Spanish Publishing House.

From 1920 to 1928 he was treasurer of the then Latin Union, and for the following six years served as president of the Iberian Union. After a term as hospital administrator at Gland, he served as president of the Swiss Union for eight years, followed by a two-year term as Sabbath school and MV secretary of the Southern European Division. He was then appointed treasurer of that division, which office he held until 1958. From that time until his retirement in 1962, he served as a division departmental secretary.

GERMAN HEALTH FOOD FACTORY (De-Vau-Ge Gesundkostwerk GmbH). A firm in Lüneburg, Germany, owned by the Euro-Africa Division, which makes a wide variety of products ranging from bread and cereal flakes to nut creams, vegetable spreads, meat analogs from soybeans, and diabetic food. The products are distributed through several channels, but mainly through health food stores. The factory was founded in 1899 at Friedensau, near Magdeburg, and began operation in an old mill under the management of Augusto Pages. But since the factory was too small and too far from markets and sources of imported raw materials, such as fruits and nuts, to operate economically, a new plant was built at Hamburg shortly before World War I.

In 1940 the political conditions in Germany forced the denomination to transfer the factory to four Seventh-day Adventist trustees—Willy Lühr, the former manager, A. Vollmer, O. Schildhauer, and H. Niemann—who continued to operate it as a private company until the building was almost completely destroyed in an air raid on July 28, 1943. Some 12 months later the factory resumed production, but on a diminished scale.

After World War II, in 1947, a new organization, formed by the former Central European Division, took over operation of the food factory from the remaining trustees. In 1966 a new building was constructed in north Hamburg, at Brödermannsweg 17. New soy products were developed, and a new sales force was organized. The rapid growth of sales, both in and outside Germany, made it necessary to lay plans for more space and greatly expanded facilities. Early in 1974 a new property was purchased in Lüneburg, an attractive industrial area of Germany. Shortly afterward the company moved to that location.

By 1993 the company employed more than 400 people and had a yearly turnover of $75 million. For decades, health food shops have been the main market. The German Health Food Factory holds about 8 percent of the market and is considered the most important health food producer in Germany, also supplying the health food market in many other European countries.

Besides the health food shop business, the company produces breakfast cereals, nut-nougat cream, dried fruit and nuts, and baby food under private label.

Managers: August Pages, 1899-1903; Wilhelm Krumm, 1903-1920; Hermann Hoth, 1920-1935; Willy Lühr, 1935-1947; Henry Niemann, 1947-1964; Erich Amelung, 1964-1970; Michael Makowski, 1970- .

GERMAN SWISS CONFERENCE. *See* Euro-Africa Division; Switzerland.

GERMANY. A republic with an area of 137,838 square miles (357,000 square kilometers) and a population (1994) of 81 million. It is bordered by Denmark on the north; the Netherlands, Belgium, Luxembourg, and France on the west; Switzerland and Austria on the south; and the Czech Republic and Poland on the east. Approximately 45 percent of the population is Protestant and 37 percent is Catholic.

Historical Background. Germans are successors of the ancient Teutonic tribes that inhabited Northern Europe at the time Caesar marched north of the Alps in the middle of the first century B.C. As early as the first century A.D. the Roman historian Tacitus wrote a book entitled *Germania,* in which he described the territory north of the Alps.

The origin of Germany can be traced to Charlemagne, who united much of Western and Central Europe under his rule and whom the pope crowned king of the Holy Roman Empire in A.D. 800. His successors divided the territory into several parts. The part that later became Germany and Austria retained the title of the Holy Roman Empire until the Napoleonic Wars. Until the beginning of the nineteenth century Germany consisted of a large number of small kingdoms, principalities, and free cities loosely associated within the Holy Roman Empire and governed by an elective emperor. After the beginning of the nineteenth century they were united in a German federation. The disunity of Germany for such a long period can be attributed in part to the outcome of the Thirty Years War, which assigned religious authority to the ruler of each domain, thus splitting the nation and preventing joint political development of areas representing differing religions. In the late 1800s Prussia assumed the leading role in the formation of a united Germany.

Following World War I, a republic replaced the empire. After World War II the Federal Republic of Germany was established in the west and the German Democratic Republic in the east.

Forerunners. Interest in the Second Advent was evident in Germany in the early nineteenth century. Scattered Sabbathkeepers and small groups of people who anticipated Christ's soon return appeared as early as 1844. There were Christians in the Tauber area of Bavaria who accepted the biblical Sabbath, inspired by the writings of Tennhardt, an eighteenth-century Nürnberg Bible student. In 1902 two Württemberg men who had been keeping the seventh-day Sabbath for more than 50 years were baptized into the Seventh-day Adventist Church.

In the second half of the nineteenth century a Baptist by the name of Stangnowsky in East Prussia led a group of people to keep the seventh-day Sabbath after he had become convinced that Sunday was introduced by the post-apostolic church. Most of this group later joined the SDA Church.

More direct predecessors of SDAs in Germany were groups formed by J. H. Lindermann, a weaver by trade, in Elberfeld, in the vicinity of Wuppertal in North-Rhineland,

Westphalia. In the midnineteenth century he concluded from his study of the Bible that Christ was coming soon. He preached the news to his neighbors, and soon a group joined him. In 1867 he also discovered through Bible study that the seventh day is the true Sabbath. He printed tracts on the Sabbath, the millennium (which he expected the saints to spend on the earth), and adult baptism, as well as a hymnbook reflecting the Advent hope and the Sabbath truth. He raised up groups in Vohwinkel, Solingen, Gladbach, and Rheydt.

Seventh-day Adventist Work. Word of these groups was brought to SDAs in Switzerland in the early 1870s by a wandering beggar. He gave the Swiss members the address of German Sabbathkeepers in the Rhineland who held similar beliefs. James Erzberger, the first ordained SDA minister in Europe, wrote to Lindermann and received an invitation to come and preach to the believers there. In 1875, the year after he arrived in Switzerland, J. N. Andrews went with Erzberger to visit the German Sabbathkeeping Adventists in their homes near Elberfeld. They found a company of about 50 believers. Lindermann, who could not accept the SDA interpretation of the millennium, did not join the SDA Church, but several of his followers at Vohwinkel formed the nucleus of one of the first SDA churches in Germany. Later some members of the Lindermann family became SDAs.

After spending five weeks visiting scattered companies and preaching in public and in private, Andrews returned to Switzerland, leaving Erzberger in Germany to carry on public evangelism. Soon Erzberger met Christians from East Prussia who held views similar to those of SDAs on baptism, the Second Advent, the seventh-day Sabbath, and temperance.

The first SDA baptism in Germany took place on Jan. 8, 1876, when Erzberger baptized eight persons at Solingen. There he soon organized the first SDA church in Germany, with 25 members. The church at Vohwinkel was organized at about the same time. Erzberger left in the late 1870s. In 1884 the churches at Solingen and Vohwinkel joined the newly organized Swiss Conference.

In 1886 the General Conference sent L. R. Conradi to Europe to carry on work among the Germans. When Ellen White came to Europe the following year, she visited the Vohwinkel and Gladbach churches in the Rhineland. Conradi prepared tracts, and in 1888 organized colporteur work in Germany. That same year Gerhard Perk, one of the first SDA converts in Russia who had to leave because of persecution, and Emil Frauchiger, a Swiss convert, came to Germany to sell *Das Leben Jesu,* a book by Ellen White on the life of Christ.

In 1889 Hamburg was chosen as the headquarters for SDA work in Germany. The first training institute to prepare workers for Germany was held there that summer. As a result of the work of the early colporteurs in Hamburg, 12 persons were baptized in 1889, the first SDA baptism in that city, followed by the organization of a church of 25 members. A branch of the Imprimerie Polyglotte (Switzerland) was opened in Hamburg under the name of International Tract Society, which issued publications not only in German but also in several of the languages of Eastern Europe. These publications were used to begin missionary work on ships in the Hamburg harbor.

With a total membership of about 100, the German church held its first general meeting in a suburb of Hamburg in 1891. At this time Germany and Russia were organized as one mission, with Conradi as president and Boettcher as secretary-treasurer. That same year G. Perk and Elise Plass (later Mrs. H. F. Schuberth) were sent to Berlin to do Bible and colporteur work. Soon converts were won for Christ.

In 1894, at a general meeting held in a tent behind the recently acquired headquarters property, it was decided to erect a building on the property to serve as chapel, school, and printing plant. In 1894 H. F. Schuberth arrived from the United States to take charge of the instruction of the 15 students in the newly organized school. This school trained ministers for Russia as well as Germany.

Expansion of the Work in Germany and Overseas. In 1894 the 11 members in Berlin were organized into a church. The International Tract Society in Hamburg took over the German work of the publishing house in Basel. Soon it was issuing four periodicals and printing literature in 14 languages. Churches were organized in eastern Germany, Magdeburg, and Königsberg in 1895. That same year evangelistic work was started among the Polish people, and the first German missionaries, H. Graf and B. Hedrich, were sent to Brazil.

In 1896 Emil Frauchiger conducted evangelistic meetings in Stuttgart, winning a number of converts. Others were won in Lüdenscheid by E. Enseleit. That year J. N. Loughborough, representing the American mission board, met with 200 members for Sabbath services at the seventh general meeting, held in Hamburg. Records show that by 1897, the German field had more than 1,000 members.

The mission was organized as a conference in 1898 with territory including Austria, Hungary, the Netherlands, Romania, Bulgaria, and Serbia. Conradi was elected president; H. F. Schuberth, secretary; and Bertha Severin, treasurer.

Captain Christiansen, formerly skipper of the *Pitcairn,* and Klaus von Fintel, a helmsman with long experience in the Hamburg harbor, used a motorboat to conduct missionary work for sailors. F. Stuhlmann, his wife, and a colporteur were the next ones sent as missionaries to Brazil in 1898.

During the autumn of 1899 a small estate was secured near the city of Magdeburg, where a training school named Friedensau (peaceful meadow) was opened. A sanitarium and a small health food factory were added.

Organization of the German Union Conference. By 1901 the SDA work in this field had grown to the place that it was organized into a union comprised of 149 churches and 3,843 members. In addition to Germany, the territory included Austria, Hungary, German Switzerland, Russia, the Balkan States, and the Netherlands.

To finance additional buildings at Friedensau, laypersons sold Ellen White's book *Christ's Object Lessons.* In 1902 G. W. Schubert conducted evangelistic work in Cologne, and soon a church was organized, which five years later had its own church building. By the end of 1905 this new union reported a membership of about 5,000. The publishing house in Hamburg reported sales of 50 million pages of tracts and books and more than 2.5 million copies of magazines in 12 different languages. The order for a half million copies of a single special edition of *Herold der Wahrheit,* the missionary periodical, was an encouraging indication of growth.

Educational Work. Until 1900 the educational work was concentrated at the Friedensau seminary and nursing school. Student nurses came from all the countries of the newly formed union, including Russia, until World War I.

Medical Work. The first SDA medical institution in Germany was opened in Friedensau in 1901. Three years later a nurses' home was opened in Berlin for missionary nurses doing private duty in Greater Berlin. Several years later, a similar home was opened in Breslau, in eastern Germany. Finally there were 18 such medical units scattered throughout Germany, employing 52 nurses—both men and women. Berlin and Friedensau in the east, and Wiesbaden, a prominent health resort in western Germany, were important SDA medical centers.

Foreign Missions. SDA missionaries went from Germany to South America in the 1890s, and later Germany became a home base for extensive mission work in Africa. To assist in spreading the gospel, some German missionaries reduced local native African languages to writing.

Post-World War I Reorganization. Departmental secretaries were chosen to promote the various departments of the church. In 1920 six mission fields were assigned to Germany, and missionaries were again sent to the Netherlands East Indies and Ethiopia. In Berlin, where there were nearly 2,000 SDAs, Waldfriede Sanitarium and Hospital was acquired in 1920, and a School of Nursing was added in 1922 (*see* Berlin Hospital). The first issue of *Jugendleitstern,* the youth magazine, appeared in 1920. A year later two training schools were opened in western Germany: the Central European Missionary Seminary at Kirchheim/Teck, in Württemberg, and the Neandertal Missionary Seminary near Düsseldorf, Rhineland (*see* Marienhöhe Seminary). A sanitarium was established at Bad Aibling, in upper Bavaria, which has since been converted into an old people's home (*see* Haus Wittelsbach Old People's Home).

In the autumn of 1925 the first SDA medical mission was opened in Russia, staffed by Kurt Klepzig, a German physician.

During the 1920s the church membership grew rapidly. Between 1920 and 1925, 9,645 new members were added. By 1927 the total membership numbered 36,000.

The first Seventh-day Adventist youth congress was held in 1928 in Chemnitz in Saxony, with an attendance of more than 3,000 delegates from the European Division. The congress idea, which has become a highlight of AY work, is one of the significant contributions made by the German field to the worldwide AY work.

Central European Division Formed. Berlin was chosen as headquarters of the newly formed Central European Division in 1928, one of the four divisions formed from the European Division. This new division included Germany, Austria, Czechoslovakia, Hungary, Greece, Albania, Bulgaria, Turkey,

Palestine, Syria, Iran, Iraq, Egypt, Liberia, Sudan, Arabia, Cyprus, Transjordan, the Spanish and Portuguese colonies in West Africa, and the Netherlands East Indies. Missionaries were sent out from Germany to many of these countries.

By 1929 Germany had eight nurses' homes with 70 missionary nurses serving the public. A welfare center in Berlin, called "Friedensheim," offered refuge to 100 people in need of food and lodging. An organization called "Hilfswerk Mutter und Kind" cared for young mothers and children. SDAs became known for their cooperation with national and other organizations in the care of the needy.

In spite of the economic and political problems of the 1930s, which led to the prohibition of canvassing work, 2,000 converts joined the church.

Because of currency regulations in 1935, the Central European Division was divided into two sections: the first comprised the three German unions, and the second made up the rest of the division territory. The headquarters of the second section was moved first to Basel, Switzerland, then to Washington, D.C., U.S.A., in 1937 and placed under General Conference administration in 1938. Because of government restrictions, the church paper, *Der Adventbote,* was stopped in 1941, and publication was not resumed until 1949.

Reorganization and Development After 1945. After World War II it was necessary to reorganize the Central European Division. Some of the territory previously administered from Germany was assigned to the Southern European Division and some to Northern Europe. The Central European Division then consisted of the South German Union, the West German Union, and the East German Union (from 1967 to 1971 the Union of Seventh-day Adventists in the German Democratic Republic). Berlin was divided into two conferences: Berlin East Conference and Berlin West.

Three thousand members were added to the church in 1946, largely as the result of lay evangelism. The statistical report for that year lists Germany with 707 churches and only 27 church buildings, 31,000 members, and 224 ministers. By 1974 more than 250 new churches had been built. A Bible correspondence school was begun by Max Busch in 1946.

The radiobroadcast called *Die Stimme der Hoffnung* ("Voice of Hope") was broadcast in German over Radio Luxembourg. Between 1947 and 1949 the three seminaries were reopened and the church paper resumed publication. A. Wicklein led 200 colporteurs to sell periodicals. SDA welfare groups were very active, helping more than 100,000 people annually.

Growing prosperity and an increasing tendency to formalism in the state church have made it more difficult to gain decisions involving changes in the pattern of life, but the church members have been active in distributing tracts and lending books, thus helping the ministers to find interested people. The Central European Division continued to function until Jan. 1, 1972, when it joined with the Trans-Mediterranean Division in forming the Euro-Africa Division.

Federal Republic of Germany After 1949. The Federal Republic of Germany was organized into the West German Union and the South German Union conferences. These unions formed a part of the Central European Division until January 1972, when the Trans-Mediterranean Division and the Central European Division merged, forming the Euro-Africa Division.

In 1949 the former East German Union was reorganized into the Union of Seventh-day Adventists in the German Democratic Republic, and comprised the area of this newly founded socialist state. Seven local conferences belonged to this union. The political situation made it necessary in 1954 to divide the former Berlin Conference (organized in 1909) into the West Berlin Conference and the East Berlin Conference, and in 1964 the West Berlin Conference was separated from the administration of the Union of Seventh-day Adventists in the German Democratic Republic. In July 1971 the seven conferences were reorganized into six local fields, following the state district areas, and the same union was changed to the German Democratic Republic Union Conference.

The denomination was a recognized religious body in the German Democratic Republic. The seminary property, four retreat centers, an old people's home, and the church properties were owned and administered by a legal association.

The publishing work, established in 1962, in cooperation with a state printing plant, developed from year to year. In addition to the Sabbath school quarterlies and other periodicals, three or four books and four to six tracts were printed annually. The union operated a Bible correspondence school called "Friedensau

Bibellehrbriefe," begun in 1965, the first in a socialist state.

Audiovisual institutes were conducted to provide material for evangelistic work and lay activities. The facilities of the Friedensau campus were used for youth camps, with more than 800 in attendance.

The reunited Germany after 1990. On Oct. 3, 1990, East and West Germany united to form the new Federal Republic of Germany. This led the Seventh-day Adventist Church in Germany to reorganize. While the South German Union remained unchanged, the East German Union (new name since October 1990) and the West German Union have joined the North German Union, with headquarters in Hannover. The theological education at Marienhöhe Seminary ceased in 1994, leaving the Friedensau Theological Graduate School (Theologische Hochschule Friedensau) the sole institution for theological training in Germany. The reunion of Germany has demanded financial sacrifices. In 1992, apart from the extension of the Friedensau Theological Graduate School, the Adventist Church in Germany donated DM 3.1 million for modernizing churches in the former East Germany.

The official church paper of the North German Union Conference is *Adventecho*, a 32-page monthly periodical published in Hamburg.

Seventh-day Adventist Statistics. Both German unions form a part of the Euro-Africa Division. Statistics (1993) for the *Federal Republic of Germany:* churches, 606; members, 34,280; ordained ministers, 312; licensed ministers, 81; Bible instructors, 3.

Statistics for the *North German Union Conference*: churches, 400; members, 20,330; ordained ministers, 212; licensed ministers, 49; Bible instructors, 1. Headquarters: Fischerstrasse 19, 30167 Hannover. Statistics for the conferences—*Berlin-Brandenburg Conference:* churches, 50; members, 2,656; ordained ministers, 35; licensed ministers, 8. Headquarters: Berlin. *Hansa Conference:* churches, 50; members, 2,747; ordained ministers, 25; licensed ministers, 7. Headquarters: Hamburg. *Lower Saxonian Conference North:* churches, 25; members, 1,842; ordained ministers, 12; licensed ministers, 4; Bible instructors, 1. Headquarters: Bremen. *Lower Saxonian Conference South:* churches, 28; members, 1,893; ordained ministers, 13; licensed ministers, 5. Headquarters: Hannover. *Northern Rhenish-Westfalian Conference:* churches, 77; members, 5,240; ordained ministers, 37; licensed ministers, 8. Headquarters: Mettmann. *Saxonian Conference:* churches, 99; members, 3,848; ordained ministers, 45; licensed ministers, 10. Headquarters: Dresden. *Saxony-Anhalt/Thueringia Conference:* churches, 71; members, 2,104; ordained ministers, 38; licensed ministers, 7. Headquarters: Erfurt.

South German Union Conference: churches, 206; members, 13,950; ordained ministers, 100; licensed ministers, 32; Bible instructors, 2. Headquarters: Senefelderstrasse 15, 73760 Ostfildern-Ruit. Statistics for the conferences—*Baden-Wuerttemberg Conference:* churches, 75; members, 5,358; ordained ministers, 34; licensed ministers, 15; Bible instructors, 2. Headquarters: Stuttgart. *Central Rhenish Conference:* churches, 62; members, 4,120; ordained ministers, 28; licensed ministers, 7. Headquarters: Frankfurt/Main. *North Bavarian Conference:* churches, 32; members, 1,821; ordained ministers, 12; licensed ministers, 3. Headquarters: Nürnberg. *South Bavarian Conference:* churches, 37; members, 2,651; ordained ministers, 19; licensed ministers, 7. Headquarters: München.

Since the end of World War II, 163 churches have been built or reconstructed in Germany, mostly by volunteers among the church membership. In 1987 the Adventist Development and Relief Agency (ADRA/Germany) was established in Darmstadt (now in Weiterstadt, near Darmstadt). In 1991 ADRA/Germany spent DM 7.8 million for humanitarian relief in 19 countries of the world. More than 2,000 tons (1,800 metric tons) of food, medicine, and essential hospital supplies were brought to the former Soviet Union.

Institutions. Adventhaus Freudenstadt; Bergheim Mühlenrahmede; Berlin Hospital; Berlin-Steglitz Old People's Home; Friedensau Old People's Home; Friedensau Retreat; Friedensau Theological Graduate School; German Health Food Factory; Hamburg Publishing House; Haus Wittelsbach Old People's Home; Neandertal Old People's Home; Uelzen Old People's Home; Voice of Hope; Waldpark Hohenfichte Retreat.

GEWISSEN UND FREIHEIT ("Conscience and Liberty"). A German magazine published twice yearly by the Hamburg Publishing House. Begun in the spring of 1973, the magazine contains 96 pages and has a circulation of 8,000. It contains studies, documents, précis, and information concerning religious liberty around the world, and is the organ of the International Association for the Defense of Religious Liberty.

Coeditors: Pierre Lanarès, Oswald Bremer, 1973-1983; Gianfranco Rossi, Baldur Pfeiffer, Oswald Bremer, 1984-1991; Gianfranco Rossi, Baldur Pfeiffer, 1992- .

GEYMET, JEAN DAVID (1842-1923). Colporteur, one of the earliest Seventh-day Adventist converts in Europe. He was working in a silk mill at Torre Pellice, the Waldensian stronghold in the Piedmont region of northern Italy, when M. B. Czechowski brought the SDA teachings to Italy in 1864. Geymet readily accepted the new teaching, was baptized, and accompanied Czechowski to Switzerland, doing some preaching and helping him establish churches, which later became the first Seventh-day Adventist churches in Europe. Toward the end of the decade Geymet, while working as a baker, in his spare hours translated Uriah Smith's books *Thoughts on Daniel* and *Thoughts on the Revelation* into French. In 1870 he married Theresa Trombotto and lived in Piedmont until 1886, in which year he reentered church work as a colporteur and continued for many years in this service. Of his colporteur experience he wrote: "Twice I went over the Piedmont valleys, and there is no settlement where I did not leave some books or publications." When he was 80 he wrote to the *Revue Adventiste:* "I still can make 20 kilometers [13 miles] on foot selling books. . . . I cannot conceive of how a true Adventist can remain inactive and silent about the second coming of Jesus Christ, and not impart this happy hope to the hearts of his fellow men by work and the printed page" (28:12, Feb. 1, 1924).

GHANA. A West African republic composed of the former British colony of the Gold Coast and the British trusteeship territory of Togoland. It gained independence on Mar. 6, 1957 (the first of the African nations south of the Sahara to attain independence after World War II), and adopted a republican constitution on July 1, 1960. It is bounded on the south by the Gulf of Guinea, on the east by Togo, on the west by the Côte d'Ivoire, on the north by Burkina Faso, and has an area of about 92,100 square miles (240,000 square kilometers) and a population (1994) of 17.2 million. Most of the people are supported by agriculture. Ghana used to be the world's largest producer of cacao, which is its most valuable export, followed by timber and gold. The country also contains valuable deposits of bauxite, diamonds, and manganese. The name was derived from that of a West African empire that flourished more than 1,000 years ago. A large portion of the African diaspora in the Americas traces its origins or ancestry to Ghana.

Seventh-day Adventist Statistics. The territory of Ghana constitutes the Central Ghana Conference, Mid-West Ghana Mission, North Ghana Mission, and South Ghana Conference which are part of the West African Union, which in turn forms part of the Africa-Indian Ocean Division. Statistics (1992) for *Ghana:* churches, 413; members, 153,389; ordained ministers, 96; licensed ministers, 94.

Statistics (1992) for the conferences and missions—*Central Ghana Conference:* churches, 225; members, 85,820; ordained ministers, 46; licensed ministers, 35. Headquarters: Kumasi. *Mid-West Ghana Mission:* churches, 71; members, 26,360; ordained ministers, 13; licensed ministers, 10. Headquarters: Sunyani. *North Ghana Mission:* churches, 4; members, 3,321; ordained ministers, 7; licensed ministers, 5. Headquarters: Tamale. *South Ghana Conference*: churches, 113; members, 37,888; ordained ministers, 30; licensed ministers, 44. Headquarters: Accra.

Institutions. Advent Press; Adventist Vocational Institute; Agona Seventh-day Adventist Secondary School; Asamang Seventh-day Adventist Hospital; Asokore Seventh-day Adventist Teacher Training College; Bekwai Seventh-day Adventist Secondary School; Dominase Adventist Hospital; Valley View College.

Development of Seventh-day Adventist Work. *Beginnings.* SDA work in West Africa began in 1888 when Francis I. U. Dolphijn, an African, began to keep the Sabbath after reading literature sent by the International Tract Society, which had been supplied to him by the captain of a ship anchored in Apam, in what is now Ghana. Raising up a group of believers, he continued to write to the General Conference requesting that missionaries be sent. In 1892 Lawrence C. Chadwick, president of the International Tract Society, spent several months with the group at Apam, and at the January 1893 General Conference session made an earnest plea for missionaries to be sent to West Africa.

The first SDA missionaries, Edward L. Sanford and Karl G. Rudolph, arrived at Apam on Feb. 22, 1894. Within five months frequent attacks of malaria forced Sanford's departure, but Rudolph continued another 18 months. On Oct. 3, 1895, Dudley U. Hale (the new mission superintendent), George and Eva Kerr (both nurses), and G. P. Riggs (a colporteur) arrived at Cape Coast, where they met Rudolph, who had previously moved there from Apam. During the following year a successful medical missionary program was conducted in Cape Coast. In August 1896 the Kerrs moved to the new mission site near Esiam, 23 miles (37 kilometers) inland from Salt Pond, where a building program that was planned to include the mission headquarters, a school and hospital, was started.

Unfortunately, their work was cut short by sickness. The two Kerr children died in 1896. After canvassing for eight months, illness forced Riggs's departure for Liverpool, where he died Jan. 8, 1897. Because of failing health, the Kerrs left for Cape Town, South Africa, on Apr. 16, 1897, and Hale departed on June 3. On Mar. 27, 1897, in the first Seventh-day Adventist baptism in West Africa, Hale baptized Francis I. U. Dolphijn, Fred and Isaac Dolphijn, and G. P. Grant.

In March 1903 Hale returned to Ghana with his family and Mr. and Mrs. J. M. Hyatt. The Hyatts worked in Cape Coast, while the Hales moved to a new mission site near Manso, on the railroad line between Sekondi and Tarkwa. About six months later Hale and his family had to leave a second time to save his life. The Hyatts continued in Cape Coast until they moved to Freetown, Sierra Leone, in 1905. In July 1905 David C. Babcock, with his family, was sent to take charge of the work in West Africa, which he supervised from Sierra Leone.

During the following years Babcock and C.E.F. Thompson, a Jamaican who joined the SDA Church in Sierra Leone, with the cooperation of C. A. Ackah, J. A. Bonney, D. N. Daharty, J. K. Garbrah, and J. A. Sackey, developed SDA work among the Nzima people of the Axim area. In 1910 Babcock baptized about 50 believers, organizing churches at Axim and Kikam. Early in January 1911 Prof. and Mrs. Thomas M. French went to the Gold Coast. In Axim, on Jan. 18, two weeks after their arrival, Mrs. French died of blackwater fever, and French, suffering from repeated attacks of malaria, returned to the United States. Thereafter, Thompson took charge of the Gold Coast work until he, broken in health, died on Mar. 25, 1912.

Early Organization and Growth. At a general meeting in Sierra Leone in 1913, W. H. Lewis was appointed to the Gold Coast. He and his family were ordered to go first to the Canary Island health base to get rid of fever. He came to the Gold Coast alone in September 1914, landing in Sekondi, while his family remained in the Canaries. With J.A.B. Davies, of Sierra Leone, he visited SDAs in Axim and Kikam. Davies was placed in charge while Lewis pushed on to Kumasi in Ashanti in search of a site for permanent headquarters. On Nov. 6, 1914, he reported that he had found favorable sites for two mission stations. In Agona, capital of a chiefdom 22 miles (35 kilometers) northeast of Kumasi, Lewis found an old European resthouse, which the chief offered until a headquarters station could be erected. The paramount chief of Agona, Nana Kwame Boakye, gave a larger plot of land, where Lewis erected a house and a school building with the assistance of the chief and his people. In the school there, which became the center of a group of schools, J. K. Garbrah, H. E. Boyce, J. J. Hyde, H. K. Munson, F. L. Stokes, and F. Edwards taught at various times. In 1914 Lewis listed 45 adherents who had been won in Agona, Assamang, and Ntonso. Shortly after this he was forced to return home because of serious injuries received in a motorcycle accident. Later T. Baker, L. F. Langford, and J. Clifford came to the Gold Coast, and with three African workers, J. K. Garbrah, J.A.B. Davies, and J. A. Bonney, spread the work to Kofiase, Bipoa, and other nearby towns. After World War I Langford was appointed general superintendent for the West African Combined Mission (organized 1918), which included Sierra Leone, Liberia, and the Gold Coast, with headquarters first at Waterloo, Sierra Leone, then at Agona, in the Gold Coast.

In January 1924 H. K. Munson joined the mission personnel. At the suggestion of the chief commissioner of Ashanti, the headquarters were moved from Agona into Kumasi. In 1927 they were returned to Agona. In 1930 the *Yearbook* lists the Agona Training School, with H. K. Munson as the first principal.

In 1931 J. Clifford, who had gone from the Gold Coast to Nigeria, returned to Agona to lead the Gold Coast Mission. In 1933 the field was reorganized into the Gold Coast Union Mission, with the Gold Coast, the Ivory Coast, Dahomey, Togoland, and Upper Volta as its territory. New headquarters were opened at Bekwai, South Ashanti, with its good rail, road, and postal communications. Under the leadership of F. L. Stokes, a center was opened in new territory at Koforidua, and a church established in the capital city, Accra, the center of the Ga-speaking people. Under T. Fielding and others the work at Agona stretched north to Kwame Danso, and a church and a school were established in Kumasi, the capital of Ashanti. J. B. Tekyi opened the work in the Tekyiman area and C. B. Mensah in the Mampong district. Members from the Gold Coast developed interests in the Ivory Coast in three different centers, and these were visited by J. K. Garbrah, S. B. Essien, and J. Clifford, conducting baptisms and organizing the work. In 1943 the Gold Coast Mission became part of the African West Coast (now West African) Union Mission.

Educational Work. New education laws made it necessary either to train teachers or to close the mission's schools. In 1939 C. A. Bartlett began training teachers to pass their External Teacher's Certificate. In 1945 permission was granted by the Education Department to open a recognized two-year teacher training college at Bekwai, with C. A. Bartlett as principal, which later became a four-year training college. Thus was realized the goal of training SDA young people to develop into missionary teachers and open church schools. From the beginning the students were trained in soul winning, often rising at 4:00 a.m. to conduct evangelistic campaigns in nearby villages. Bekwai Training College was phased out in July 1974 by order of the government.

In 1953 the Bekwai Secondary School was opened, with N. C. Maberly as headmaster. The school, under the leadership of C. Y. Kyereme as headmaster, has expanded and is now offering preuniversity courses in arts and sciences at the sixth-form (junior college) level.

The Asokore-Koforidua Teacher Training College was opened in 1962, with C. Y. Kyereme as the principal. Asokore is now the only SDA teacher training college in Ghana. Another teacher training college was opened in 1963 at Agona, Ashanti, the place where the work in central Ghana began, with L. H. Berlin as principal. In accordance with government policy the school completely converted into the SDA Secondary School, Agona, in September 1974 with I. K. Ansong as headmaster.

The Adventist Girls' Vocational Institute was opened in Techiman, Brong Ahafo region, as a day school by action of the Ghana Conference and the West African Union on Oct. 8, 1974, with Mrs. Emelia Kusi as headmistress. She was followed by Agnes Osei and Victoria Daaku. In the mid-1980s the school's name was changed to Adventist Vocational Institute; directors have included Nabi Donkor, A. P. Mensah, and C. A. Mensah. In October what is now Valley View College opened in Accra with Walton Whaley as principal.

Literature Ministry. After G. P. Riggs had spent a short time selling books in 1895, little was done in colporteur evangelism until A. Cook canvassed in 1933. He conducted a field school in salesexpertise for local recruits with whom he worked most of the large towns. Again there was little activity until 1949, when two Jamaicans, L. Davidson and E. L. Brown, were recruited to revive and reestablish the work.

Medical Work. To meet the medical needs of the people, the Kwahu Hospital was established in 1955 by Dr. J. A. Hyde and officially opened on July 28, 1957; later a School of Nursing was begun and a midwifery course was offered. This was nationalized by the government in 1973. During the 1980s and 1990s the Central Ghana Conference established new hospitals and clinics.

Recent History. In 1957 the Gold Coast Mission became the Ghana Mission, and in February 1959 C. B. Mensah (the first national Ghanaian worker to serve thus) was appointed president of the Ghana Mission.

On Dec. 25, 1970, the first Black conference in all Africa was organized at the eleventh constituency meeting, held at Asokore, Koforidua, with J. K. Amoah elected as president. Since that time it has financed its own operations, and its national workers are carrying forward an aggressive program of evangelism.

In 1985 Jacob J. Nortey of Ghana became the president of the Africa-Indian Ocean Division. At the 1990 General Conference session Matthew Bediako, a Ghanaian, became the first full-blooded African to serve the General Conference. He later became a General Conference vice president.

As a result of the Global Mission strategy adopted by the world church in 1990, baptized membership in Ghana in mid-1993 was 155,465.

GHANA CONFERENCE. *See* Ghana.

GIBRALTAR. A British colony 2.3 square miles (six square kilometers) in area on a peninsula on the southwest coast of Spain at the western entrance to the Mediterranean. The population (1992) of 29,650 is mainly of Italian origin. The majority are Roman Catholics. The languages are English and Spanish.

No regular Seventh-day Adventist work was carried on in Gibraltar until very recently. In 1934 G. F. Jones and his wife, pioneer missionaries in the South Pacific, lived there for a while. In 1993 some organized work had been started and there were seven church members living in that area. Gibraltar is assigned to the Spanish Union of Churches in the Euro-Africa Division.

GIDDINGS, HOMER ELI (1859-1939). Educator. A graduate of Battle Creek College in 1889, he entered educational work in Texas and participated in the development of Oak Hill church school, the nucleus for what later became Southwestern Union College. From 1892 to 1897 he was active in educational and evangelistic work in Missouri, and from 1897 to 1902 headed the Bible Department of Keene Academy. He then served as president of Fernando College, California (1902-1905), and as principal of Gravel Ford Academy, Oregon (1905-1906). He conducted evangelistic and religious liberty work in the Southwestern Union (1906-1908), preached in New Mexico (1908-1909), taught at Amarillo Academy (1909-1911) and at Hamby Academy (1911-1913), served as head of Manson Academy, British Columbia (1913-1915), took a rest for the next two years, and then came back into educational work, teaching in elementary schools in central California (1917-1920). Next he went to Hawaii, where he was principal of the Hawaiian Mission Academy from 1920 to 1924, after which he directed evangelistic work. He retired in 1927.

GIDDINGS, PHILIP (1865-1946). One of the early Seventh-day Adventists in the Caribbean, evangelist, pastor, and missionary. He was a native of British Guiana, and a teacher for many years. He learned about SDAs in 1885 through certain SDA publications that passed through the office of which he was the postal service manager. Having borrowed and studied them, he became convinced of their truthfulness and resigned his position in order to keep the seventh-day Sabbath. In 1891 he went to Battle Creek, where he studied nursing and Bible, graduating from the college in 1895. After that he returned to the Caribbean and served as evangelist and pastor in British Guiana, Dominica, and the French-speaking islands of Martinique, Guadeloupe, and Haiti, where he was associated with the SDA training college. In 1902 he married Louisa Peters, a graduate nurse from the Battle Creek Sanitarium and sister of George Peters, who later became secretary of the General Conference Negro Department.

GIEBEL, OTTO (1886-1936). Evangelist, pastor, and conference leader in Germany. He joined the Seventh-day Adventist Church at the age of 23, attended the Friedensau Missionary Seminary (1910-1911), and in 1911 began preaching in Berlin. After ordination he worked in the Hesse-Westphalian Conference and in 1923 was elected president of the Hansa Conference. In 1927-1928 he devoted a year to SDA work in Holland. From 1928 to 1934 he was president of the Hanover Conference, after which he assumed the presidency of the South Bavarian Conference, where an automobile accident ended his life and service early in 1936.

GIFFARD MEMORIAL HOSPITAL. A 110-bed general hospital at Nuzvid, Andhra Pradesh, India, about 32 miles (50 kilometers) northeast of Vijayavada with specialized eye and dental services. It is operated by the Central India Union of the Southern Asia Division. The hospital operates a government-accredited School of Nursing and offers a course in medical laboratory technology. It is administered by staff physicians and a medical director. It is situated on 23 acres (nine hectares) of land and has 17 hospital buildings and 35 staff residencies. In 1992 there were 2,000 inpatients and 40,000 outpatients. During that year there were 350 major surgeries, 750 minor surgeries, 400 deliveries, and 1,400 eye surgeries.

The hospital was established in 1925 by a trust agreement concluded between Sree Rajah Sobhanadri Apparao, zamindar of Telaprole, and the India Financial Association of Seventh-day Adventists. Under the terms of the agreement, largely negotiated by T. R. Flaiz, the zamindar turned over to the association control of approximately five acres (two hectares) of land, three uncompleted hospital buildings, and Rs.10,000 in cash. It was the wish of the donor that the hospital be named after his friend Giffard, an officer of the British India Army.

The hospital was opened on Sept. 15, 1925. A. E. Coyne, M.D., was superintendent; a staff of 12 included a midwife, a compounder (a medical assistant with some training in pharmacy), two dressers, three attendants, two gardeners, a caretaker, a laundryman, and a sweeper. The bed capacity was 21. In 1929 the number of beds was increased by 12, and by 1942 the hospital had 45 beds.

From May 1942 to August 1944 the hospital was inactive because of the evacuation of its overseas personnel, but a dispensary was successfully operated by B. S. Solomon, Y. Daniel, S. Joseph, and A. Grace. The hospital was reopened in August 1944 by Dr. Elizabeth J. Hiscox, and in 1945 a program was launched that resulted in the acquisition of more land, the expansion of the bed capacity to 108, and the establishment of a government-recognized nurse's training school. In 1955 a 20-bed maternity ward, financed largely by a gift from the zamindar of Elamarru, was opened.

From the beginning of the hospital's operation, informal nurse's training had been given, at first by Mrs. Coyne and later by Dr. Emma Hughes. In 1928 the managing committee authorized the setting up of a three-year nurse's training program and a two-year compounding training course, each with prerequisite of eighth-standard education (about second year of high school). Training was begun the next year and continued until 1942. After the reopening of the hospital in 1945, the first recognized higher-grade certificate course in nursing began in 1946. Government recognition by the Madras Nurses and Midwives Council was granted in 1947, but was made retroactive to 1946.

The one-year matriculate-level course in laboratory technology and a midwifery course for nurses was begun in 1952. The laboratory school was upgraded in 1974 and became a two-year course in 1990. The Nursing Council of India integrated the separate six-month midwifery course into a three-year A-grade nursing course in 1988.

The hospital's Community Health Department was started in 1956. Supported by government and voluntary health organizations, it provides five programs to selected villages: home deliveries, nutrition supplementary feeding program, immunization, health education, and family welfare. The Dental Department was added to the hospital in 1974.

In 1980, in partnership with Christffel-Blenden Mission of Germany, the hospital opened an Eye Department, which includes, besides eye treatments and cataract surgeries, comprehensive eye care for target villages and school children.

The hospital has a strong chaplain's program and has worked closely with the Global Mission program that has established more than 40 churches in the Nuzvid area.

Medical Directors (as indicated by the *Yearbook*): A. E. Coyne, 1924-1930; A. E. Clark, 1930-1932; D. W. Semmens, 1932-1937; H. G. Hebard, 1937-1938; D. W. Semmens, 1938-1942; temporarily suspended, 1942-1944; E. J. Hiscox, 1944-1945; T. R. Flaiz, 1945-1947; J. B. Oliver, 1947-1952; D. W. Smith, 1952-1953; J. B. Oliver, 1953-1958; P. S. Nelson, 1958-1962; J. B. Oliver, 1962-1967; C. A. Ninan, 1967-1972; N. S. Fernando, 1972; E. J. Hiscox, 1972-1974; K. P. George, 1974-1975; M. Jagannadha Rao, 1975-1976; E. J. Hiscox, 1976-1977; Philip Viruthan, 1978-1982; G. E. McWilliams, 1982-1984; Ronnie Gyi, 1984-1985; P. Mohan Chandrasekhar, 1986-1989; Narendra Rao, 1990; Pramod Hansdak, 1991; Ronnie Gyi, 1991- .

GIFTS OF THE SPIRIT. *See* Spiritual Gifts.

GILBERT AND ELLICE ISLANDS. *See* Kiribati; Tuvalu.

GILBERT AND ELLICE ISLANDS MISSION. *See* Kiribati; Tuvalu; South Pacific Division.

GILBERT AND ELLICE SDA MISSIONARY SCHOOL. *See* Kauma Adventist High School.

GILBERT, ANDREW C. (1880-1967). Administrator and educational pioneer. He was born in Minnesota and attended Battle Creek College. Baptized at 19, he began denominational work as a colporteur in Illinois and then taught church school in Minnesota. He entered the ministry in 1902 and was ordained five years later. Shortly after his marriage to Blanche Shaw he began his 17 years of service in Canada, where he served as president of the Saskatchewan and British Columbia conferences and the West Canadian Union. He was instrumental in establishing the first academy in Saskatchewan and Rest Haven Sanitarium in British Columbia.

Because of a visual problem he transferred to west Michigan, where it was hoped he could bear a lighter load of responsibility. But his eyesight continued to fail, causing him to give up denominational work.

GILBERT, FREDERICK CARNES (1867-1946). Evangelist to the Jews. Born in London, England, of Jewish parentage, he accepted the Seventh-day Adventist faith in Boston, Massachusetts, in 1889 and attended South Lancaster Academy (1890-1894). In 1896 he married Ella M. Graham. Ordained in 1898, he served in the ministry in the Atlantic Union Conference until 1911, when he joined the North American Division staff. He worked unceasingly for the conversion of Jews. In 1918 he became secretary of the Jewish Department of the General Conference, and in 1922 a field secretary. His worldwide evangelistic work took him to various places in Europe, Asia, and Central and South America.

His published works include *Messiah in His Sanctuary, Judaism and Christianity, Divine Predictions of Mrs. Ellen G. White Fulfilled,* and the autobiographical works *From Judaism to Christianity* and *Gospel Work Among the Hebrews.*

GILLIS, WALTER EMSLIE (1874-1954). Missionary, treasurer. He was born in Canada and educated at Walla Walla College. After a short period in the ministry in British Columbia, he worked at the Pacific Press (1901-1908), for a short period at the Mexican publishing house, and briefly as educational secretary of the West Washington Conference. In 1910 he went to China, where he served as manager of the Signs of the Times Publishing House and was secretary of the China Union Mission, secretary-treasurer of the East China Mission, and treasurer of the North China Union for brief periods. In 1918 he moved to Singapore to help to establish the Malaysian Signs Press there. Upon returning to China, he was superintendent of the mission work in Shensi, and then home missionary secretary of the East China Union. From 1930 until his retirement in 1940 he was manager of the publishing house in Seoul, Korea.

GIMBIE HOSPITAL. A 70-bed hospital operated by the Ethiopian Union Mission and situated on the headquarters compound of the West Ethiopia Field in Gimbie, Wollega province, about 300 miles (500 kilometers) west of Addis Ababa, capital of Ethiopia. The hospital usually is staffed by two overseas physicians and four nurses. There are 98 national employees, some of whom are trained as nurses and health assistants.

Although Gimbie is only about 8 degrees north of the equator, its 6,000-foot (1,850-meter) elevation gives it a favorable climate. The town is the largest in that region, and is in the heart of the coffee-growing area of Ethiopia. Although the people are poor, they have a cash income for a few months each year. Most of the peoples of Ethiopia are of Semitic origin; however, there are a few Black tribes in the lower areas near Gimbie. The predominant religions in the country are Islam and Ethiopian Orthodox.

Before the Italian occupation Seventh-day Adventists operated a small clinic in Gimbie under the direction of an Ethiopian national, but the Italians took over the property, and while controlling it built several new buildings on it. After the war the Ethiopian government returned the property, which now had the additional buildings, to the mission. A hospital was opened by Dr. Claude Steen, Jr., in 1947. Shortly thereafter a new clinic was built to meet the increasing need.

The hospital staff supervises several clinics operated by nurses and health assistants. Many of these workers are active in evangelistic work.

Medical Directors: Claude Steen, Jr., 1947-1952; Roland K. Nielsen, 1952-1955; H. F. Sturges, 1955-1958; M. G. Anderson, 1960-1961; K. W. Saunders, 1961-1966; L. R. Zachary, 1967-1969; J. H. Friend, 1970-1972; L. N. Wright, 1972-1973; W. C. Richli, 1974-1978; Kr. Hogganvik, 1978-1981; J. Roca, 1981-1982; Silas Gomes, 1982-1984; E. Block, 1984-1985; M. Gebru, 1985-1988; A. F. Lasta, 1988-1989; H. Giebel, 1989- .

GIMBIE MISSION SCHOOL. *See* Wollega Adventist Academy.

GINGOOG SANITARIUM AND HOSPITAL (formerly Gingoog Community Hospital). A 30-bed secondary general hospital operated by South Philippine Union Mission in the city of Gingoog in northern Mindanao Island, Philippines. A member of Adventist Health Services-Asia (AHSA), it has a workforce of two staff physicians, three visiting physicians, five nurses, and 15 other regular workers.

On June 7, 1962, the Mindanao Sanitarium and Hospital contracted to take over the operation of the 12-bed medical clinic of Dr. Paterno Primero for seven years. In May 1969 the South Philippine Union Mission committee took an action making it a separate entity from the Mindanao Sanitarium and Hospital. It continued to operate in rented quarters until the end of

May 1970, when it transferred to a 12-bed hospital unit on a lot purchased for about $9,600. On Dec. 11, 1972, it moved to its present site.

The hospital changed its name from Gingoog Community Hospital to Gingoog Sanitarium and Hospital on Nov. 5, 1992.

Presidents: A. P. Roda, 1962-1967; W. M. Torres, 1968; G. D. Poblador, 1969-1985; J. J. Postrero, 1985- .

GINTER (HINTER), JOHANN F. (d. 1919). Minister, administrator. He was born to a German Protestant family in southern Russia at Velikoknyasheskoye, east of the Don River and north of the Caucasus. After becoming a Seventh-day Adventist, he worked as a colporteur, selling publications imported from Switzerland and America in the German colonies in Russia. At the German Union session at Friedensau, in July 1904, he was asked to transfer to the Balkan States. At Bucharest, Romania, he found a group of 16 members. He also worked in Rustchuk, Romania.

In 1907 his wife, who had been baptized in Russia 15 years earlier, died (age 34). Early in 1909, when he was compelled by the authorities to leave the country because the growth of the church was considered a threat to the prosperity of the Greek Orthodox Church, he settled in Bulgaria near the Romanian border.

In the same year, he was sent back to Russia to head the East Russian Mission. In 1910 he headed the Volga Mission. Between 1911 and 1916 he was part-time director of the Ural and Volga missions. At the end of World War I he went to southern Russia as president of the East Russian Union Conference. On Feb. 25, 1919, in Rostov-on-Don, he died of typhus in the postwar famine and epidemic.

GITWE ADVENTIST SECONDARY SCHOOL (Collège Adventiste de Gitwe). A coeducational boarding school in Rwanda, offering six years of secondary training. The school is situated about 10 miles (16 kilometers) north of the town of Nyanza in the central part of Rwanda. The school is operated by a board of managers chosen from the Rwanda Union. The school is situated on a 125-acre (50-hectare) tract of land. Student enrollment has greatly increased over the years, especially from 1991. In 1993 there were approximately 650 students and 26 teachers.

The plant consists of an administration block with five offices and seven classrooms completed in 1971, a unit of nine other classrooms built in 1973, two dormitories accommodating 450 students, a dining hall seating 500, a church with a seating capacity of 800, and several homes for the administrative personnel and teachers.

The school offers scientific training, a teacher-training course, and general high school subjects that are taught according to the curriculum outlined by the Government Education Department, except for Bible. Most of the students are Rwandan, but there are also a number from neighboring Burundi. The language of instruction is French.

The present school was originally formed by the merging of two earlier schools. The Gitwe mission station was established with a primary school in 1921 by D. E. Delhove, formerly a worker in Kenya. In 1931 the school began to train teachers for the Ruanda-Urundi field, with F. M. Robinson as the first principal, who was followed by A. Matter.

Meanwhile, in 1923, in the Katanga province of the Belgian Congo, the Katanga Mission had been established near Elisabethville by A. C. LeButt, with African helpers sent from Nyasaland and Northern Rhodesia (James Malinki and Jonah Kapalasha), who already had begun to erect temporary buildings. In August 1923 W. H. Branson reported a number of African converts of some education in Elisabethville who were waiting to enter a training school at Katanga (*African Division Outlook* 21, Aug. 15, 1923, p. 1). By Dec. 28, 1924, when B. E. Schaffner arrived to take charge of the school, there were 40 students in school preparing to go out as teachers and evangelists. W. R. Vail was in charge of this school from 1931 to 1935. Beginning in 1931, it appeared in the *Statistical Report* as the Séminaire Adventiste du Congo.

Realizing that there were more students in Rwanda than in Zaire, the leaders transferred the seminary from Katanga to Gitwe in 1934. The school, however, served the three countries under Belgian colonial rule under the name Adventist Seminary of the Belgian Congo and Ruanda-Urundi. An American missionary named R. L. Jones acted as director of both the school and the mission field from 1934 until 1940. During this time two years of teacher training were established. The first graduation was held in 1936.

From this time on, those who finished their schooling were used in the countries bordering Rwanda as teacher-evangelists. The missionary work was greatly extended throughout Rwanda under the direction of Jones. During the 1940s many students were able to finish the three years of post-primary teacher training. To achieve this goal, the school had to function in the summer.

Much of the time principals of the college served also as directors of the Gitwe Mission, which had a large district and many schools to administer. As a result the actual operation of the training school fell to a large extent upon the headmasters, among whom were W. R. Vail, P. Howe, and E. L. Tarr.

The separation of the school and the mission took place in 1947. This action permitted principals to devote themselves solely to school affairs.

In 1963 A. L. Hands initiated a two-year vernacular ministerial course that A. M. Long took over in 1968, teaching in French. This was discontinued in 1981.

In 1966, under the leadership of M. Graham, a full secondary level consisting of a three-year general course and a scientific section was initiated and completed by the first graduates in 1972. During this six-year period the seminary status was changed into that of an academy, the program outlined by the government was followed, and most of the above-mentioned facilities were finished. However, the diplomas offered to Gitwe graduates were not officially recognized. State recognition occurred in 1976, with retroactive effect from the year before.

In 1981, with the implementation of government education reform, the scientific section and the teacher training course were extended to six years.

Principals: R. L. Jones, 1935-1940; K. F. Ambs, 1941-1942; A. Matter, 1942-1943; K. F. Ambs, 1943-1946; P. S. Marsa, 1946-1948; E. I. Edstrom, 1948-1955; L. C. Robinson, 1955-1957; B. P. Wendell, 1957-1959; M. J. Church, 1959-1962; A. G. Roth, 1963-1965; A. L. Hands (acting), 1965; M. Graham, 1965-1972; R. Davidian, 1972-1973; A. Raitt, 1973-1974; R. D. Jordan, 1974-1978; C. Rochat, 1978-1979; P. Ramseier, 1980-1981; D. Vanderwerff, 1981-1984; S. Niyibizi, 1984-1985; A. Nzahumunyurwa, 1985-1989; S. Maniraguha, 1989-1990; M. Mugemana, 1990-1991; M. Pollin, 1991- .

GJORDING, JOHN GODFRED (1890-1954). Missionary to China, minister, and administrator. He was born in a family of Danish Mormons who soon after his birth migrated to Utah in the United States, where they all joined the Seventh-day Adventist Church. After training at Union College and at Hutchinson Theological Seminary, he went to China in 1915. There he helped to organize SDA work in Manchuria, serving as home missionary secretary, field missionary secretary, and secretary-treasurer (1915-1918). Later he was in charge of the financial and then of the overall management of the Signs of the Times Publishing House in Shanghai (1918-1921). Still later he was director of the East China Union Mission (1922-1928). From China he went to superintend the Malayan Union Mission (1929-1937), and concluded his service by pastoring churches in the Northern California, Florida, Tennessee, Washington, and Oregon conferences.

GLEANER. *See Atlantic Union Gleaner;* North Pacific Union *Gleaner.*

GLENDALE ADVENTIST ACADEMY. A coeducational day school on the senior high school level (with associated K-9 school) at 700 Kimlin Drive, Glendale, California, serving a constituency of 18 churches under the direction of the Southern California Conference and the Pacific Union Conference. It is accredited by the SDA Board of Regents (1936), the University of California (1947), and the Western Association of Schools and Colleges (1992). During 1992-1993 the enrollment in grades 9-12 was 282.

The forerunner of Glendale Adventist Academy was the one-room Glendale church school with 15 pupils, opened in 1907 in the basement of the gymnasium of the old Glendale Sanitarium on Isabel Street, Glendale. Mrs. B. B. Davis was its first teacher.

In 1908-1909 a one-room building was erected across the street at a cost of $500, and painted green. The next year the green building was moved across the street onto the sanitarium grounds, and enlarged to two rooms. In 1911-1912 grade 9 was added.

In 1916 a new three-room building was erected one block north on the east side of Isabel Street at 234 North Isabel Street, and grade 10 was added; then in 1920 grade 11.

In 1921-1922 the school became a regular 12-grade school, and was named Glendale Academy. Max Hill was its first principal. In that year the school published its first school bulletin, entitled *Glendale Annual Announcement,* and the first annual, *The Stepping Stone;*

it also graduated its first class, of five members. By 1922-1923 it became urgent to find a new site for the Glendale Academy, with ample room for growth. Yet the church had no funds, and the conference was trying to solve the problem of replacing San Fernando Academy.

When about 40 acres (15 hectares) of land in Sycamore Canyon became available for $37,000, with a required down payment of $10,000, 10 lay members who were interested in the future of the academy, and were willing to take a risk, negotiated a loan by each signing a personal note for $1,000 and thus made the down payment. Then they had the property surveyed for subdividing. The sale of part of the property paid for the development and left 18 acres (seven hectares) higher up, which provided a school site free of debt, although no profit was made on the venture. W. Byron Dart and his workers erected the present building.

In the fall of 1923 Glendale Academy opened on the new site, with Dan Ochs serving as principal. The old green building was moved to the new campus, to serve as the woodwork shop (until 1941), and the grade school building from Isabel Street served as the grade school (until 1945). In 1924 the name was changed to the Glendale Union Academy. In that year the printshop was built, and in 1928-1929 a new two-room building for the seventh and eighth grades. A building to provide the gymnasium, the vocational arts rooms, and the band room was erected in 1941, and a new 10-room grade school in 1945. Then the building that had housed the seventh and eighth grades was moved and enlarged to provide a cafeteria for all grades. The library building, which serves also as the study hall, was built in 1955. During the summer of 1962 a four-classroom building was added to the elementary section.

The year 1967 saw the completion of a shower and locker room facility to meet the needs of grades 7-12. In 1962 the academy began the development of a new campus master plan, which called for the replacement of the original academy building built in 1922. Two new secondary buildings completed in 1971 provide classroom facilities for most of the academic content areas. The remodeling of the library facility into a media center was completed in 1974. In addition, the academy owns seven faculty and staff cottages acquired from 1950 to 1988.

In the period from 1907 to 1992, the one-teacher church school with 15 pupils grew to an enrollment of 489 in grades K-8, and 282 in grades 9-12; and from one teacher to a teaching staff of 21 in grades K-8, and 20 in grades 9-12.

In 1965 "Union" was dropped from the school name.

Academy Principals: Max Hill, 1921-1922; Dan Ochs, 1922-1927; W. L. Avery, 1927-1928; Lee R. Marsh, 1928-1936; John Young, 1936-1938; C. D. Striplin, 1938-1942; J. Alfred Simonsen, 1942-1947; N. L. Parker, 1947-1957; Charles E. Watkins, 1957-1977; Edward Boyatt, 1977-1980; Kenneth Phillips, 1980-1982; Kenneth von Hof, 1982-1984; Frank Skoretz, 1984-1986; Michael Conner, 1986-1988; Douglas Ammon, 1988-1991; Harold Hampton, 1991- .

GLENDALE ADVENTIST MEDICAL CENTER. A 464-bed general hospital and medical center with a medical staff of 500 physicians and more than 2,000 employees, situated on a 32-acre (13-hectare) tract in Glendale, California. It is the largest hospital in Adventist Health System/West. The medical center provides care for 15,000 admissions, 27,000 emergency room visits, and 30,000 home health visits each year. The medical center provides medical education through residency programs in family practice and obstetrics/gynecology and through clinical facilities for several college and university schools of nursing. It is accredited by the Joint Commission for the Accreditation of Health Care Organizations and the Commission on the Accreditation of Rehabilitation Facilities, and is a member of the Hospital Council of Southern California and the California Association of Hospitals and Health Systems.

Specialized centers of excellence include Behavioral Medicine, Cancer Services, Cardiac Services, Outpatient Services, Rehabilitative Medicine, and Women's Services. Through an affiliation with Loma Linda University Medical Center, Glendale Adventist's Center for Cancer Services provides patients access to the area's most powerful linear accelerator, the world's first proton beam accelerator, and other advanced technologies.

Glendale Adventist provides ongoing community outreach programs, including the Health Match physician referral and health education phone line; PhoneFriend, which provides support for latchkey children; ASSIST, which provides transportation, meal and grocery delivery, and other support services on a short-term urgent basis; the GAMC Thrift Shop; Top Dog, a pet therapy program for patients; KidPrint, which provides fingerprint and photo identification for children; and many free and low-cost community education classes.

Glendale Adventist Medical Center was established in August 1905 as Glendale Sanitarium. Early in 1904, under the direction of Ellen White, John Burden and a group of Adventist leaders began to search for a suitable location for a medical institution in southern California. One of two properties under consideration was the Glendale Hotel. This building of 75 rooms, situated eight miles (13 kilometers) north of Los Angeles in the country settlement of Glendale (population 500), had been built for about $60,000 during the California boom of 1880, but had been closed by the subsequent depression before hotel operation was begun. For a time the building was used by an Episcopal girls' school, and later by the Glendale High School. When the Seventh-day Adventist group explained to the owner, L. C. Brand, the purpose of their proposed institution, he reduced the price from $20,000 to $12,500. Accepting this as a sign of divine direction, they made the purchase.

Under the direction of the sanitarium's first medical superintendent, Dr. Abbie Winegar Simpson; the head nurse, Lenora Lacey; and the business manager, J. A. Burden, the hotel was converted into a health center. The sanitarium facilities were meager and equipment and methods primitive, but patients came from far and near. Following treatment, many patients who planned to settle in the area stayed on, making the sanitarium their temporary abode as they looked for a home. Civic organizations convened for meetings and banquets in the sanitarium's dining room, making it a hub of early community life.

A School of Nursing was established in 1905 under the direction of Lenora Lacey. It graduated two students in 1906 and five in 1907. Instrumental in the accreditation of the school in 1911 was the business manager, Harmon W. Lindsay.

Bed capacity was increased to 100 in 1917, and in 1920 a new one-story hospital on an adjacent piece of land provided facilities for medical, maternity, and surgical patients. By 1922, having become more than a treatment center, the institution was named the Glendale Sanitarium and Hospital. In order to serve more patients and to accommodate more complex functions, additional personnel, facilities, and equipment were required, and it became apparent to the conference committee that new quarters would be essential for expansion in a community already grown to 30,000.

Under the direction of Dr. H. G. Westphal, medical superintendent, and C. E. Kimlin, business manager, the second major step was taken in the development of this institution. The downtown sanitarium was sold, and a 30-acre (12-hectare) hill was purchased far out of town, situated between the San Rafael foothills and the Sierra Madres, and surrounded by unimproved land and apricot groves. On the crest a modern five-story building of fireproof construction was erected.

Advertised as offering the famous "Battle Creek treatment," the sanitarium was filled to capacity with advance reservations. Emphasis was placed upon the use of physical therapy, proper diet, and a balance of rest and exercise to restore the body to normal functioning. Available also were modern clinical and metabolic laboratories, operating rooms, X-ray, dental, and eye, ear, nose, and throat facilities, and two large hydrotherapy departments.

The third phase in the development of this institution into a major medical center came in 1955, on the fiftieth anniversary of its founding. An adjoining five-story 125-bed addition was completed. This provided 10 operating room suites, plus maternity, pediatric, and emergency facilities.

In 1961 the hospital entered its fourth phase of development—the construction of a 60-bed mental health center at the east end of the main hospital (opened in July 1963) and a physical medicine and rehabilitation center, with accommodations for 24 bed patients, on the north side. Funds were provided by the community and the institution.

Jan. 1, 1966, Glendale Sanitarium and Hospital officially became Glendale Adventist Hospital. It was the first Seventh-day Adventist institution to use the name "Adventist" in the title to indicate religious affiliation. "Sanitarium" was dropped because the hospital no longer had sanitarium-type beds.

The last nursing class graduated in 1967, and the hospital became the extended campus of Pacific Union College School of Nursing. The Glendale school graduated a total of 1,282 nurses.

The fifth phase of development began with the opening of the diagnostic and treatment center in December 1969. The $3.5 million center housed the clinic, radiology, pathology, pharmacy, and other treatment services. In January 1972 a new critical care center accepted its first patients. Located atop a multilevel parking structure, this addition brought the bed capacity to 452. The next development was a surgery expansion unit, with intensive care and data processing center, opening in October 1972.

The name was changed for the fourth time to Glendale Adventist Medical Center in May 1974. Civic advisory board chair Walter Stolrow explained the change. "The addition of services and educational programs has turned the former 'sanitarium' into a comprehensive medical center."

Construction began in November 1974 on the $24 million replacement for the 52-year-old main building housing 163 medical beds, dietary services, library, administration offices, and other departments. In 1993 the hospital opened the newly constructed Physician's Medical Terrace, a 70,000-square-foot (6,500-square-meter) medical office building, and a 400-space parking garage that provides medical offices with a direct link to the hospital.

Administrators: J. A. Burden, 1905-1907; J. J. Wessels, 1907-1909; W. Ray Simpson, 1909-1910; Harmon W. Lindsay, 1910-1914; V. H. Lucas, 1914-1924; J. A. Burden, 1924; E. G. Fulton, 1924-1932; C. E. Kimlin, 1932-1934; M. C. Lysinger, 1934; J. Howarth, 1934-1936; L. V. Clark, 1936-1940; E. G. Fulton, 1940; H. B. Thomas, 1940-1947; G. B. Nelson, 1947-1959; E. J. Rembolt, 1960-1973; L. W. Roth, 1973-1984; Bob Scott, 1984-1987; M. H. Jackson, 1987-1992; R. G. Carmen, 1992- .

GLENN, WILLIAM NEWTON (1837-1906). Publishing administrator and editor. He was born and educated in Pennsylvania, but while quite young went to the frontier territories of Kansas and Nebraska, where he kept a general store and learned the printing trade. During the Civil War he joined the Union Army and was stationed in California. After his release he joined the Baptist Church and went into newspaper work in Stockton, working on the *Independent* and the *Herald.* Poor health required a period of rest, during which he learned about Seventh-day Adventist beliefs, and he and his wife became members of the church in 1875. In 1876 he joined the staff of the Pacific Press at Oakland, California, and remained there for 30 years until his death, acting successively as proofreader, head of the typeroom, manager, and editor. His name was listed among those on the first editorial committee of *Our Little Friend* from 1890 to 1893 and as its editor from 1893 to 1901. For some years he was assistant editor of the *Signs of the Times* (1900-1906). He was chair of the editorial committees of the Apples of Gold Library and the Bible Students' Library (two series of pocket-sized monthly leaflets on gospel themes) and the Sentinel Library (a series of pamphlets on religious liberty issues). His articles on religious liberty appeared also in nondenominational magazines. He authored several tracts and a book, *Things Foretold.*

GLOBAL MISSION. An initiative to place, before the year 2000, a Seventh-day Adventist presence in every one of 5,234 population segments of 1 million constituting the world's population at the time of the General Conference session in 1990; also to foster growth in areas with established work, reaching unentered municipalities and ethnic and language groups. The idea was launched by N. C. Wilson at the Annual Council held in 1986 at Rio de Janeiro, Brazil, and developed by a committee with world representation for adoption at the 1989 Annual Council and the 1990 session. R. J. Kloosterhuis and C. R. Taylor assisted in the planning stages. M. L. Ryan was called to lead in the implementation, and H. L. Butler to assist in the development of funds through donations.

Because the major challenges lie in the Islamic, Hindu, and Buddhist populations of Asia and North Africa, study is needed to define approach and content, to unlock doors long closed to the gospel. For this purpose B. Schantz, J. Skariah, and C. Maberly were asked to direct study institutes to develop and test strategies for these three main bodies of religiously inclined people. The Center for International Relations was set up to facilitate placement of SDA lay professional people in government or business positions in countries in which the traditional type of missionary cannot obtain entry. The Global Mission Data Book, with input from all levels of organization, provided the point of departure, identifying location and numbers of Seventh-day Adventists in the world, and the 2,300 population segments of 1 million with no SDA members. More than 500 of these segments were involved in some kind of Global Mission activity by mid-1993.

As a secondary objective, the growth of the church in the four divisions with no unentered segments of 1 million is exemplified in the South American Division's targeting the

4,176 unentered municipalities in its territory. Unentered ethnolinguistic and socioeconomic "people groups" are also vivid examples of outreach encompassed under the name of Global Mission. More than 12,000 such targets had been selected and more than 4,000 of them had been entered as part of the program by mid-1993.

GNUTZMANN, LUCINDA HERMANN (1900-1988). Educator, missionary. Born in Rio Grande do Sul, Brazil, she was baptized in 1922 and attended Brazil College. In 1926 she married Joao Gnutzmann, and two years later they were called to work in Africa, the first Brazilian missionaries on that continent. Lucinda later pioneered a school at her birthplace.

GO: THE JOURNAL FOR ADVENTIST LAYMEN (July 1951-1971; monthly; RH since 1954; August 1965, circulation 14,511; files in AU, AUC, CoUC, LLU, LSC, UC). Formerly the official organ of the General Conference Home Missionary Department (published by Southern Publishing Association to March 1954), promoting its activities and containing articles and illustrations on successful lay soul-winning methods and other features of Christian service. This journal was authorized by the 1950 Autumn Council to replace the eight pages in *Church Officers' Gazette* formerly used by the Home Missionary Department for the weekly and monthly home missionary programs, the general department promotion, and the material formerly published in the *Lay Preacher* and the *Dorcas Letter.*

Editors: Adlai Albert Esteb, 1951-1970; L. A. Shipowick, 1970-1971.

See Adventist Layman.

GOA. *See* India.

GOD. The statement concerning the Deity in the Seventh-day Adventist summary of fundamental beliefs *(see* Doctrinal Statements, SDA) reads as follows: "There is one God: Father, Son, and Holy Spirit, a unity of three co-eternal Persons. God is immortal, all-powerful, all-knowing, above all, and ever present. He is infinite and beyond human comprehension, yet known through His self-revelation. He is forever worthy of worship, adoration, and service by the whole creation. (Deut. 6:4; Matt. 28:19; 2 Cor. 13:14; Eph. 4:4-6; 1 Peter 1:2; 1 Tim. 1:17; Rev. 14:7.)"

"God is a spirit; yet He is a personal being, for man was made in His image. As a personal being, God has revealed Himself in His Son" (Ed 132). He is not an abstract idea or ideal that has existence only in the human mind. He is the reality to whom the idea and the ideal point.

Long ago the question was asked of Job, "Canst thou by searching find out God? canst thou find out the Almighty unto perfection?" (Job 11:7). Finite wisdom and ingenuity are inadequate to comprehend an infinite God. Only to the extent that He reveals and self-authenticates Himself can we know Him. But we can properly say that we "know" Him in the incarnate Christ, for "God was in Christ" (2 Cor. 5:19), the Eternal Word made flesh.

One of the basic character traits of God is love, in the ultimate NT sense of the Greek word *agapē,* or infinite care and concern for the happiness and well-being of created beings. The supreme demonstration of this love is seen in the mission of God the Son to this world (John 3:16). God's love is not static, nor is it in any way influenced adversely by the reaction of created beings to it. When God loves He is being Himself, for "God is love" (1 John 4:8).

God is self-existent. All other life is from Him, as a gift. No creature has life apart from Him. It is in Him that "we live, and move, and have our being" (Acts 17:28). He gives all, and can receive nothing that He has not first given.

God is immutable. He never changes, or differs from Himself. He is perfect. He is not subject to changing moods or attitudes. His affection is constant, His love is sure. He is not coaxed into action. "I am the Lord, I change not" (Mal. 3:6).

God is omniscient. His knowledge is complete and perfect. It is impossible for Him to add to His knowledge, inasmuch as all knowledge originated with Him. He knows what was, what is, and what will be.

God is omnipresent. "The eyes of the Lord are in every place, beholding the evil and the good" (Prov. 15:3). There is no place to which a person can flee to escape from God's presence. God is ever near. See Ps. 139.

God is omnipotent. "Power belongeth unto God" (Ps. 62:11). He is sovereign ruler over all. His power is absolute and infinite. Nevertheless, God has bestowed upon created beings the power of choice with respect to their own destiny. God's infinite power, ever controlled by His infinite love and wisdom, is never used for selfish ends. His power is fully revealed in the change that takes place in the hearts and lives of individuals, transforming them from sinners into saints.

God is faithful. God cannot be unfaithful, because He is immutable. "Know therefore that the Lord thy God, he is God, the faithful God, which keepeth covenant and mercy with them that love him" (Deut. 7:9). He cannot cease to be what He is, and He is always consistent with Himself. Human beings become unfaithful as a result of selfish desire, fear, weakness, or loss of concern. But these traits are alien to the divine character.

God is holy. In being holy, God does not conform to a standard, for He is that standard. "Be ye holy; for I am holy" (1 Peter 1:16). The holiness that God demands of created beings is not the absolute holiness of Deity, which God Himself alone possesses. It is a relative holiness that He waits to impart to His creatures in their preparation for heaven. God alone can be absolutely holy, for He alone has an infinite comprehension of absolute perfection of character. "I am God, and not man; the Holy One" (Hosea 11:9).

The holiness that God expects of created beings is commensurate with what He has revealed to them and with their capacity to comprehend what has been revealed. Furthermore, divine grace provides that in Christ the sincere, repentant sinner may have access to the perfect holiness of Christ and to divine power that will enable him or her to overcome imperfections of character.

See Christology; Holy Spirit.

GODHEAD. *See* God.

GOG AND MAGOG. *See* Revelation, Interpretation of.

GOLD COAST. *See* Ghana.

GOLDEN GATE ACADEMY. A coeducational day school instructing in grades 1-12 and serving the eastern Bay Area, operated by the Northern California Conference on a wooded 15-acre (six-hectare) site in the East Oakland hills (3800 Mountain Boulevard, Oakland, California). The school is accredited by the SDA Board of Regents, the University of California, and the Western Association of Schools.

The school opened in 1923 under the direction of A. C. Nelson and a staff of nine teachers, in a former public school unit in Berkeley, purchased by the Northern California Conference. The main building contained classrooms, offices, a cafeteria, and a library. In addition, there was a chapel and a two-story industrial building. Principal Nelson's administration (1923-1929) saw the growth of graduating classes from six to 16, the establishment of a printing press, and the adoption of girls' uniforms of blue skirts and white middy blouses with blue collars (the girls' uniform was abolished in 1944).

By 1929 all debts were paid, and despite increased financial problems during the Depression, by 1932 Golden Gate Academy had been accredited by the University of California. By 1937 the library contained 5,000 volumes, an increase of 2,000 since 1929. The year 1938 set a new record, with 23 students in the graduating class. During the next few years students led in campaigns for a new gymnasium, the paving of the schoolyard, and the addition of a new stove to the cafeteria (which, in 1940, advertised a "very simple yet nourishing meal for 11 cents"). In 1941 the yearbook, *Anchor*, was launched. The present *Golden Cable* was begun in 1948, after several short-lived school newspapers. Because of the exigencies brought on by World War II, beginning in 1942 every student was expected to take medical cadet training. The 1946 *Anchor* listed 87 former students who had served in the armed forces, including three who had given their lives.

To meet the needs of the growing school, the present site in Oakland was purchased in 1946. The new academy buildings were under construction in the fall of 1948 and opened in 1949. Students showed their enthusiasm by fund-raising activities. The academy section consisted of six classrooms (enlarged to eight in the 1950s), library, and administrative offices; a separate elementary section contained six classrooms (enlarged to eight in the 1950s). Another two-story building provided a gymnasium, cafeteria, shop, and temporary chapel for both academy and elementary use.

From 1950 to 1952 finishing work was continued on several buildings. Landscaping was undertaken, and a home was built for the principal. In 1963 two additional faculty homes were purchased and moved onto the campus, and the printshop was expanded. In 1965 a new chapel was completed. The Goldenaires, a choral group, and the present academy band were organized in 1954. Plans to improve the plant began in 1973, with each constituent church and the Northern California Conference joining their resources to repave the parking lot, reroof the gymnasium, replace gutters and downspouts, plan and install effective drainage, replace ceilings in 16 classrooms and the library, and make general improvements. The 1992-1993 enrollment was 34 in the academy and 130 in the elementary school. The faculty numbered seven for the academy and six for the elementary school; the staff numbered four.

Principals: A. C. Nelson, 1923-1929; Gerald E. Miles, 1929-1932; K. R. Rasmussen, 1932-1937; R. B. Prout, 1937-1938; W. O. Baldwin, 1938-1942; E. J. Henning, 1942-1943; W. B. Amundsen, 1943-1948; P. G. Wipperman, 1948-1949; P. G. Wipperman and J. D. Hardt, 1949-1950; S. W. Johnson, 1950-1952; F. D. Fisher, 1952-1956; D. M. Warren, 1956-1960; Walter Comm, 1960-1962; W. P. Thurber, 1962-1964; Paul Plummer, 1964-1967; James Costa, 1967-1970; Darryl Comstock, 1970-1972; C. C. Blackburn, 1972-1976; William Wright, Jr., 1976-1979; C. C. Blackburn, 1979-1980; Pennie Lister, 1980-1984; Ronald Williams, 1984-1987; Birdie Williams, 1987-1992; Joyce Lee, 1992- .

GONTAR, A. E. (c. 1857-1933). One of the early Russian Seventh-day Adventists and a pioneer of the Advent message among his people, first as a colporteur, later as a minister. Beginning in 1893 he served as church elder in various churches in the Ukraine. In 1907 he worked in Kiev, the capital of the Ukraine. On a number of occasions he was arrested for his activities and sentenced to prison. From 1907 to 1911 he worked in the East Russian Mission and afterward, until World War I, in the Little Russian Mission. He spent the war years in exile in Siberia, as did a number of other SDA preachers. After the revolution he worked in the East Ukrainian Conference. About 1924 he retired and settled in the city of Melitopol in southern Russia, where he served the local church. On May 13, 1933, four days before his death, he preached his last sermon to the church. Returning home on May 17, he called the brethren and his family to his bedside and admonished them to remain true to the Bible truth and to continue to show sinners the way to Christ.

GONZALEZ, GONZALO (1909-1957). Blind minister in Costa Rica; one of the first Costa Ricans ordained to the Seventh-day Adventist ministry. He was a carpenter before he lost his sight in an accident. While in deep discouragement over his affliction, even to the point of attempting suicide, he was invited by an SDA friend to attend meetings at the friend's church, which he joined in 1933. In order to support his family he began to sell *El Centinela* (an evangelistic journal in Spanish). Later, moved by a zeal to spread SDA teachings, he worked as a Bible instructor, memorizing the texts of his studies. In 1952 he was ordained, and until his death he pastored churches in Costa Rica.

GOOD HEALTH (1866-1953; 1866-1878, as *Health Reformer;* 1912-1914, as *Good Health Magazine;* monthly; Good Health Publishing Co., Battle Creek, Michigan). The first Seventh-day Adventist-sponsored popular journal devoted to health education. It was lost to the denomination with the separation of Dr. J. H. Kellogg from the church. It was last listed in the *Yearbook* in 1906.

Editors: H. S. Lay, 1866-1868; editorial committee, 1868-1871; James White, 1871-1874; J. H. Kellogg, 1874-1906.

GOOD HEALTH ASSOCIATION (SCOTLAND) LIMITED. *See* Roundelwood.

GOOD HOPE CLINIC. *See* Miraflores Adventist Clinic.

GOOD HOPE CONFERENCE. *See* South Africa, Republic of.

GOOD HOPE HIGH SCHOOL. A coeducational day and boarding school on the high school level, operated by the Good Hope Conference to meet the educational needs of the Good Hope Conference constituency. It is situated on a 139-acre (55-hectare) tract of land at Kuils River, about 15 miles (25 kilometers) from Cape Town. In 1974, when it was a junior college, there was an enrollment of 192 in the primary school, 235 in the high school, and 20 in the college, with a teaching staff of 25.

Good Hope College developed from a church school opened in 1929 at the Salt River church, with Adeline V. Sutherland as principal. The school was moved in 1930 to a newly purchased six-acre (2.5-hectare) farm at Athlone, Cape, and became a training school. During the following 30 years it developed into a full high school, which also offered theological and normal training. By 1932 secondary work was being offered, and college work in 1956. During the years the school has provided many workers for the Good Hope Conference. When the campus lost its rural character, a new tract of 169 acres (70 hectares) was bought at Kuils River. In 1963 the high school and college departments moved to the new site, leaving on the campus a seven-grade elementary school. In that year there was an enrollment of 86 in the high school and two in the college, with a teaching staff of 11.

In 1963 the physical plant consisted of a two-story dormitory for 40 students, a dining room and kitchen unit, a small laundry, and the first section of the administration building. Students worked at raising vegetables, flowers, fruit, and chickens, and cared for a herd of Jersey cows. In 1965 the second section of the administration building was completed, providing accommodation for the high school teaching program, and in 1969 the Cyril Bender Hall was opened to provide a library and classrooms for the college teaching. Other developments have included the erection of a school hall seating 1,800 in 1970, a science block in 1972, and a men's industrial unit in 1974. In 1969 the young women transferred from the old dormitory, in which both sexes had been accommodated, to a new two-story building of their own, thus increasing the overall dormitory accommodation by a further 40 students.

Most students commute by train or bus from all parts of the Cape Peninsula. High school students sit for public examinations on completing grade 12. In 1992 a new swimming pool was opened. In 1993 the enrollment was 197 in the high school, with 67 living in the dormitory. There were 16 teachers, four administrative assistants, and six on the support staff.

Principals: Adeline V. Sutherland, 1930-1932; R. A. Buckley, 1933-1934; P. H. Mantell, 1935-1940; W. H. Hayter, 1941-1943; G. S. Glass, 1944-1947; O. B. Hanson, 1948-1952; D. M. Swaine, 1953; C. C. Marais, 1954-1960; G.J.E. Coetzee, 1961-1964; A. J. Raitt, 1965-1972; W. A. Hurlow, 1973-1976; B. H. Parkerson, 1976-1977; Mrs. L. R. Peterson, 1978-1982; B. H. Parkerson, 1983-1989; P. P. Plaatjes, 1990- .

GOOD SAMARITAN. *See* Systematic Benevolence.

GOOD SAMARITAN CLINIC. *See* Brazil.

GOODRICH, HIRAM CARLETON (1849-1933). Missionary to Central America. He was the son of a Baptist minister, and was instructed in Seventh-day Adventist beliefs in the home of his future wife. He was baptized in 1870. He attended Battle Creek College in 1873, married Anna Elizabeth Hafer in 1874, and in 1887 began his service for the church as tract and missionary director in Michigan. In 1892 he was licensed to preach, and in 1894 was ordained to the ministry. In 1900 he went to Central America as superintendent of the Central American Mission, with headquarters in the Bay Islands. From 1902 to 1907 he was in charge of work in Spanish and British Honduras, and from 1907 until 1914 he was president of West Caribbean Conference. When he became too old to carry the responsibilities of executive work, he settled on the Isle of Pines and carried on missionary work until 1929, when he retired to Nashville, Tennessee.

GOPALGANJ BOYS' SCHOOL. *See* Kellogg-Mookerjee Memorial Seminary.

GOPALGANJ HOSPITAL. A former medical institution of the Bangladesh Union Section at Gopalganj, in the Delta of the Ganges River. Dispensary work operated by evangelists and national nurses began in 1905 or 1906 and continued to 1929 when a physician, C. F. Schilling, took charge of the work. Two years later he moved the medical work to Jalirpar, 19 miles (30 kilometers) away. He was succeeded by H. G. Hebard, followed by J. Johannes, who moved the work back to Gopalganj in 1939 and built a 20-bed hospital there. Because of the war, in 1942 the hospital was closed and the dispensary was cared for by a national staff (among them S. N. Arinda, C. R. Bol, and A. C. Bol).

A woman physician, M. R. Young, repaired and reequipped the hospital during 1961 and 1962. The dispensary work was continued into 1963 by Harold Googe. Then L. N. Powrie continued until the arrival of another woman physician, F. P. Noecker, in December 1967. This period saw improvements in buildings and equipment and a limited medical launch work started with the 39-foot (12-meter) M.L. *Adventist,* which was ready for service in 1965. After 10 months Noecker's work was cut short by illness. Powrie continued the dispensary with the assistance of a national staff until another physician, J. Van Blaricum, arrived in 1970. He served one year, improving the hospital facility and rebuilding its reputation. Because of unsettled conditions during the independence movement of 1971, the hospital was again closed, but the dispensary was continued by Powrie and then maintained by the national staff until the arrival of a Filipino physician, F. D. Solivio, who revitalized the hospital early in 1973. He was soon joined by another physician, A. Osario. The nursing staff was augmented by Bengali nurses from Karachi early in 1974.

Because of rapid development, it was decided to expand the facility to 50 beds. As a first stage in this plan a 30-bed wing was completed in 1974. Because the medical launch work could not be maintained, the M.L. *Adventist* was sold in 1973, and in its place three village dispensaries were in operation.

The hospital averaged an almost 100 percent bed occupancy. Up to 150 patients were seen in the outpatient clinic daily. The hospital provided the best medical and surgical facilities for more than 3 million people living within a 50-mile (80-kilometer) radius. It was closed in the mid-1980s.

GORDON HOSPITAL. A 65-bed health-care facility in Calhoun, Georgia, operated by Adventist Health System/Sunbelt Health Care Corporation, Orlando, Florida.

After World War I, Gordon County had one physician, Zebulon V. Johnston. Wilbur D. Hall joined him in 1935, and within months they opened a small hospital, which they shared with a drugstore and the Atlanta Gas Company. Patients were transported by a hand-operated elevator between the operating room on the second floor and patient rooms on the third floor. Office visits were $1, home visits $3, a bed in the ward—including everything from meals to medicines—was $3, and a private room $5.

A new county hospital was built in 1953. It was replaced in 1979 by the present 65-bed facility on Red Bud Road. In 1981 Adventist Health System/Sunbelt Health Care Corporation entered into a lease/purchase contract with Gordon County to operate the hospital. It exercised its purchase option in 1993.

The medical staff of 45 represents a wide range of specialties. The hospital provides such sophisticated services as computerized tomography (CT) scanning, lithotripsy, cardiac catheterization, and magnetic resonance imaging (MRI).

The Gordon Hospital Foundation Board established a $125,000 scholarship fund in 1990 for students pursuing nursing and allied health careers. By 1993 it had awarded 17 scholarships.

Presidents: Lawrence Payne, 1981-1986; Robert Trimble, 1986-1989; Dennis Kiley, 1989- .

GORLE, RUTH THOMAS (1899-1971). Educator. Born in Rhodesia of pioneer stock, she learned the Ndebele language while young and became well acquainted with the customs of the local people. This was to stand her in good stead in later years.

In 1924 she was married to Robert Vaughan Gorle, and the young couple moved to Salisbury. Through the efforts of a student colporteur, Ernest Marter, and an evangelist, Arthur Ingle, Ruth and her husband accepted the Seventh-day Adventist truth and became charter members of the Salisbury church. Immediately they began to press for a church school, and for a while the Gorles paid the teacher's salary themselves.

Widowed in 1937, Ruth took her family of three young children to Helderberg College, where she worked her way through school and thus obtained the professional training needed to support the family. After receiving a master's degree she taught in the English Department of the college and served as librarian for eight years. In 1957 she accepted a call to Solusi College, where she was responsible for laying the foundation for the college program.

For more than 30 years Ruth was closely connected with the college training program in the Trans-Africa Division, and the majority of the national workers of the division passed either through her classroom or under her sphere of influence.

GOSHEN ADVENTIST SECONDARY SCHOOL (Sekolah Menengah Advent Goshen). A coeducation boarding school operated by the Sabah Mission. It is located about 100 miles (160 kilometers) north of Kota Kinabalu, the capital of Sabah, Malaysia. As a result of the pioneering work of J. T. Pohan and the northward "migration" of Adventists led by Salag Gaban from mid-Sabah to the Marudu Bay area, the number of church members mushroomed at the newly named village of Goshen (after the biblical Israelite province in Egypt) in the early 1950s. The need arose for the opening of the one-teacher Goshen Church School in 1952, with Mandatang Gaban as its first teacher.

In 1969 the name Goshen Adventist

Secondary School was adopted when it began offering lower secondary classes. It produced its first form 3 (Lower Certificate of Education) graduates in 1971. In 1980 it was upgraded to offer form 4 classes and by the following year produced its first form 5 graduates. In 1992 the school was upgraded again to offer form 6 classes, thus becoming a full-fledged high school, preparing matriculation students for university candidacy, while at the same time operating kindergarten and elementary sections under the same administration. The total enrollment in 1993 was 350.

Goshen started with the English medium of instruction but had to switch to the Bahasa Malaysia medium in 1976. It remains a church school today by virtue of the fact that its students are comprised predominantly of Seventh-day Adventist members and children of church members. About one fourth of the present workers and teachers of the Sabah Mission are graduates or former students of the school.

Principals: Mandatang Gaban, 1952-1955; Leopold Peter, 1956-1958; G. Y. Dizon, 1959-1965; Mary Mun, 1966-1967; Joseph Thia, 1969-1971; Miun Lundoh, 1972-1975; Nelton Bingku, 1976-1981; James Lai, 1982-1984; Nelton Bingku, 1985-1991; Daniel Bagah, 1992- .

GOSPEL HERALD [1] (1898-1903; monthly, at first irregular, afterward weekly; Gospel Herald Publishing Company, later SPA; absorbed by *These Times,* 1903; files in White Publications). At first the organ of the Southern Missionary Society, promoting and reporting missionary work among the Black people in the South. It began as a private project, edited and printed by J. E. White (the first nine issues on board his mission boat *Morning Star)* at Yazoo City, Mississippi, then at Battle Creek, Michigan. Beginning with the first number of volume 4, January 1901, the paper was issued in Nashville, Tennessee, where White had moved his Gospel Herald Publishing Company. Under a new policy it became an evangelistic journal for the Southern states, carrying general religious articles. The reports of the Black mission work were continued for a time in a separate supplement, optional to subscribers. In the spring of that year its publication was taken over by the Southern Publishing Association (SPA), newly formed in Nashville by the merger of J. E. White's Herald Publishing Company and the Atlanta branch of the Review and Herald Publishing Association. Then in 1903 the *Gospel Herald* was suspended after five numbers and absorbed by the SPA's *Southern Watchman* (later *These Times);* it should not be confused with a second journal called the *Gospel Herald (see Gospel Herald* [2]).

GOSPEL HERALD [2] (1904-1923; monthly; five preliminary undated issues in 1903, and volume 1, 1904, as *Southern Missionary;* published by Southern Missionary Society, later North American Negro Department; irregularities in numbering of volumes; files in White Publications).

The second organ of the Southern Missionary Society, launched in Nashville, Tennessee, by J. E. White for the purpose of reporting and promoting the Black mission work in the South—after the original *Gospel Herald (see Gospel Herald* [1]) had been changed to a church paper for the Southern Union Conference. This second journal, called the *Southern Missionary* in volume 1, resumed with volume 2 the old title left unused after the merger of the original *Gospel Herald* with the *Southern Watchman* (later *These Times*). In 1910 this second *Gospel Herald* became the organ of the newly formed Negro Department (later the North American Regional Department) of the General Conference, and the printing was taken over by the press of Oakwood College, Huntsville, Alabama. From then on it became primarily a news journal for the Black churches in North America—the function later performed by the *North American Informant.*

Editors: James E. White, 1904-1910; A. J. Haysmer, 1910-1913; T. A. Jeys, 1913-1917; W. L. Bird, 1917-1923; J. A. Tucker, 1923 (August-October).

GOSPEL OF HEALTH. *See Medical Missionary.*

GOSPEL SICKLE, THE (1886-1888; semimonthly; RH on behalf of the International Missionary Society; files in GC). A missionary paper "to be used in ship and city missions, in distributors, and wherever a small paper will best serve the wants of the cause" (minutes of the International Tract Society, Dec. 6, 1885). In its first issue, Feb. 1, 1886, the president of the General Conference, George I. Butler, wrote: "*The Gospel Sickle* is designed for sharp work. We intend it shall bristle all over with the pointed truths of the last message. . . . We want this journal to be *blazing hot* with truth."

The Gospel Sickle appeared in a setting of vigorous debate in the church over the interpretation of "law" in Galatians. On Feb. 18, 1887, Ellen White wrote [to A. T. Jones and E. J. Waggoner]: "A pain comes to my heart every time I see the *Sickle*. . . . If there is a difference upon any parts of the understanding of some particular passage of Scripture, then do not be with pen or voice making your differences apparent and making a breach when there is no need of this" (Letter 37, 1887; quoted in *Counsels to Writers and Editors,* pp. 78, 79).

The Sickle ceased publication with volume 3, no. 24, dated Dec. 15, 1888, because of a considerable decline in circulation.

Editorial Committee: Uriah Smith, George I. Butler, W. H. Littlejohn, D. M. Canright, R. F. Cottrell, 1886-1888.

GOSPEL'S WORD PUBLISHING HOUSE. *See* Romanian Publishing House.

GÖTTING, FRIEDRICH (1865-1956). Minister and conference administrator in Germany. Joining the Seventh-day Adventist Church in 1901, he worked as colporteur until 1905. In 1906 he entered evangelistic work and served first as a Bible instructor (listed in 1907 *Yearbook*) and later as a licensed minister (1909) in the North German Conference. He was ordained to the ministry in 1910. Between 1910 and 1928 he was president of the Silesian Conference, the Pomeranian Conference, and the Brandenburg Conference. From 1929 to 1932 he was a minister in the Pomeranian Conference. He was married to Johanna Huss.

GOVERNMENT, CHURCH. *See* Church Government.

GRACE. God's free favor exercised toward undeserving sinners. It is entirely spontaneous on His part and not conditioned on human merit (John 3:16; Eph. 1:3-11). It is an expression of the redeeming, loving attitude of God. In exercising grace, God gives before He requires. The exercise of saving grace results in forgiveness, pardon, justification, and sanctification. From a human point of view the most remarkable quality of God is His infinite patience and unchangeable love for sinners in spite of their unfaithfulness and rebellion (Eph. 2:8).

Human beings are saved wholly by grace, which comes to them as a free gift from God. Salvation is by grace alone, to the entire exclusion of human merit, power, or wisdom. *Grace* is largely a NT word. The OT has no precise equivalent for the NT word, yet everywhere the OT reflects the grace of God in His dealings with sinners. People in the OT times were saved by grace as surely as they were in NT times.

Redeeming grace is possible only in and through the work of Christ (Rom. 3:24; 5:20, 21). God could not forgive sinners apart from the saving work of Christ. The supreme expression of grace is what God did in and through Christ. Grace is unlimited; it embraces all humanity; it is for all persons (1 Tim. 2:4; Titus 2:11; 2 Peter 3:9). Nevertheless, people can resist God's grace as they do the influence of the Holy Spirit. To be saved by grace is to be saved wholly from within the heart of God.

"Grace is God's hand extended to miserable sinners. Faith is the sinner's hand stretched up to clasp the offered hand of God" (H. W. Lowe, in *Review and Herald* 130:6, Sept. 3, 1953).

"God's grace extends mercy to those who do not deserve mercy, and He adopts into His family those who do not belong there by natural birth" (W.G.C. Murdoch, in *Review and Herald* 137:7, Apr. 21, 1960).

GRADUATE SCHOOL. *See* Loma Linda University.

GRAF, HULDREICH F. (1855-1946). Evangelist, missionary. He was born in Germany and died in Brazil. In 1869 he came with his parents to the United States and settled on a farm near Good Thunder, Minnesota. There with other members of the family he became a member of the Seventh-day Adventist Church. In 1889 he entered the ministry in the Minnesota Conference, and in 1891 he was ordained. He taught Bible in the German language in Union College from 1893 to 1895.

In 1895 he was sent by the General Conference to Brazil, where he engaged in evangelistic work (1895-1903) and served as president of the Brazilian Mission (1902-1905). Upon the organization of the South American Union in 1906 he became president of the Rio Grande do Sul Conference. During his 12 years in Brazil he baptized more than 1,400 converts and organized more than a score of churches. With extremely limited means he started several schools that finally developed into the SDA college near São

Paulo. He was also instrumental in establishing the first SDA publishing house in Brazil.

In 1907 he returned to the United States and worked in Minnesota (1907-1908), Ohio, central California, and Wisconsin. He retired about 1915 and returned to Brazil to be near some of his children.

GRAF, JULIUS J. (1851-1927). Minister. He was born in Posen, Germany, and came to the United States at the age of 19 and settled in Good Thunder, Minnesota. He became a Seventh-day Adventist in 1884 as a result of the work of W. B. Hill. When a church was organized in Good Thunder, he was chosen to be its first elder. He spent most of his time working among the German-speaking people in the Northern and Central Union conferences and established a number of churches. He was the father of Otto J. Graf and Alma Graf, both of whom made significant contributions in SDA educational institutions.

GRAF, OTTO JULIUS (1879-1950). Educator. He received his B.A. from Union College and his M.A. from the University of Nebraska. He served for one year as educational secretary of the Northern Union Conference, and one year as history teacher at Union College. From 1908 to 1917 he was president of Emmanuel Missionary College and exerted upon the college a molding influence. Because of ill health he retired permanently in 1918.

GRAHAM, EDITH M. (d. 1918). Treasurer, administrator. She accepted the Seventh-day Adventist faith during a voyage from England to New Zealand. In 1895 she became treasurer of the Australian Conference and its tract society, later of the Australasian Union Conference. In 1913 she attended the General Conference in the United States and remained to take charge of the home missionary branch of the Publishing Department of the General Conference (later organized as the Home Missionary Department).

GRAHAM, SYLVESTER (1794-1851). Presbyterian minister, health reformer, and lecturer on temperance and dietetics who advocated vegetarian diet and introduced into general use graham bread, made of coarse wheat flour. He studied at Amherst College and was ordained to the ministry in the Presbyterian Church. Ellen White made references to his bread and whole-wheat flour in her works. *See* Health Principles.

GRAINGER, W. C. (1844-1899). First American Seventh-day Adventist missionary to Japan, minister, teacher, and college president. A convert of Abram La Rue in California in the 1870s, soon after conversion he conducted evangelistic meetings in that state. He later taught in, and was president of, Healdsburg College. In 1896 he was asked by the Foreign Mission Board to open SDA mission work in Japan. Accompanied by a former student of his of Japanese descent, T. H. Okohira, he went to Tokyo and began work among the young people, mainly university students, by giving them English lessons, using the Bible as a text. In 1899 he started the monthly *Owari no Fukuin* ("The Gospel for the Last Days"), the first SDA Japanese language periodical.

GRAND LEDGE ACADEMY. A coeducational day school that was located on the large Michigan Conference campground 10 miles (16 kilometers) west of Lansing near the intersection of State Highways 43 and 100.

The school opened in September 1958, with 88 students, to fill the need for a boarding academy for 10 counties in southwestern Michigan, which were being served by two day academies, Emmanuel Missionary College Academy and Battle Creek Academy. G. E. Hutches, then president of the Michigan Conference, led in its establishment. No new buildings were erected for the operation of the school, although camp meeting buildings were remodeled extensively to provide proper facilities. A craft shop was also opened to provide labor for the students. By 1973 it was producing nearly $1 million in sales yearly. On Sunday morning, Oct. 1, 1967, the wooden girls' dormitory was completely gutted by fire while the students were away on a weekend camping trip. At a full constituency meeting in Battle Creek, Feb. 25, 1968, it was voted to close the school as a conference-sponsored boarding academy. However, the 13 churches of the Lansing district accepted the responsibility to continue to operate it as a day school. In May 1970 a conference-built gymnasium-auditorium was completed to meet educational and camp meeting needs. It was the first new building constructed for the school.

A full program for grades 9-12 was offered from the opening of the school in September 1958. Course offerings were divided in 1963-1964 into two curricula: a college preparatory course and a general course, with separate diplomas.

It ceased operating as a boarding academy in the spring of 1968. The local churches ran it as a day academy until 1982. In 1982 it was consolidated with the Lansing school. The last secondary graduation was held in 1985, with two students graduating. From 1985 to 1989 it was operated as a 10-grade school. The buildings were sold along with the sale of the Grand Ledge campgrounds in 1989.

Principals: Ralph P. Bailey, 1958-1962; H. D. Lawson, 1962-1964; C. L. Newkirk, 1964-1968; D. A. Potter, 1968-1971; James Stephan, 1971-1974; Ray Brooks, 1974-1976; Harold Oetman, 1976-1981; Ronald Adams, 1981-1983; David E. Pearson, 1983-1984; Larry D. Blackmer, 1984-1986; James P. Larsen, 1986-1989.

GRANOSE FOODS LIMITED (British Health Food Factory). A health food factory situated in Stanborough Park, Watford, Hertfordshire, England, manufacturing several varieties of vegetarian protein foods and breakfast cereal biscuits, one of the latter being called Sunny Bisk. The Seventh-day Adventist health food work in Great Britain was begun by a group of laypersons who, under the name London Health Food Company, purchased health foods from Dr. J. H. Kellogg, of Battle Creek, Michigan, and distributed them to the public. After a few years SDA leaders in Great Britain sent J. Heide, a master baker, to Battle Creek to learn how to make the foods. In 1899 a manufacturing company was formed under the name International Health Association Limited; it was changed in 1926 to Granose Foods Limited. The company purchased a flour mill in Salford, near Redhill, Surrey, to serve as the factory. Disused plant equipment obtained from Battle Creek, together with machinery purchased in Great Britain, formed the nucleus from which the present business has grown. W. T. Bartlett was the first manager and secretary, and A. Rodd was the first factory superintendent.

Before electricity was available, candles were often used, a practice that led to a fire that burned the factory to the ground in 1900. Health foods were again temporarily imported from the United States, but gifts and loans from SDAs reestablished the company, in Birmingham.

In 1907 all Seventh-day Adventist institutions in England, including the food factory, were centralized at Stanborough Park, Watford. In July 1986 a decision was taken to erect a purpose-built factory at Newport Pagnell on a site some 30 miles (50 kilometers) north of Watford. Trading began from the new site in January 1989. The business was sold in January 1991.

Managers: S. S. Barnard, 1907-1908; W. C. Sisley, 1908-1913; W. R. White, 1913-1917; W. C. Sisley, 1917-1918; M. N. Campbell, 1918-1922; W. R. Raitt, 1922-1923; H. Osborne, 1923-1935; J. Rigby, 1935-1946; G. E. Adair, 1946-1951; G. E. Norris, 1951-1963; G. E. Norris and B. Goulstone, 1963-1964; B. Goulstone, 1964-1969; A. H. Evans, 1969-1976; R. Poulton, 1976-1979; I. H. Carter, 1979-1980; K. H. Adair, 1980-1983; Peter J. Archer, 1984-1991.

GRANOVITA. *See* Spanish Food Factory.

GRANT, MILES (1819-1911). An Advent Christian minister and evangelist, editor of the *World's Crisis,* 1856-1876. In 1871, when he was in California, Seventh-day Adventists helped to sponsor his meetings since he preached conditional immortality and views on the prophecies somewhat similar to theirs, but the cooperative venture proved unsuccessful. Later Grant became an active opponent of Seventh-day Adventists. Ellen White encountered his opposition when she was in the Waldensian country of northern Italy, about the end of 1885.

GRÃO PARÁ ADVENTIST ACADEMY (Instituto Grão Pará). A coeducational day school, which originally was conducted on the junior high school level except for the *curso comercial* ("commercial course"), which was on the senior high school level. It is situated in Marco, a suburb of Belém, capital of the state of Pará, Brazil. It is owned by the North Brazil Union Mission and operated by a board of 11 members, which includes representatives from each of the conferences and missions that comprise the union. The school year runs from February to December, with a month's vacation in July.

In 1954 H. E. Walker, educational secretary for the union, seeing the need for a secondary school in the Amazon region, with the support of W. J. Streithorst, union president, laid plans for a day school, which was to serve as a pilot project for a boarding academy to be built later. Construction began in 1960, and the inauguration ceremony was held Feb. 21,

1961, attended by government officials. The representative of the federal Ministry of Education, who was present, commended Pará Academy for being the first educational institution opened in Belém that conformed from its beginning to the government building code for such schools. The school facilities consist of eight large classrooms, a library, a science laboratory, an applied arts room, a teachers' room, and three administrative offices These are situated on a plot of land near the starting point of the Belém-Brasília Highway.

Classes began Feb. 23, 1961, with 411 enrolled in the academy. Two years later a gymnasium with a seating capacity of 3,000 was constructed. The school was upgraded to full secondary in 1974 and was served by a staff of 13. In 1993 there were 68 teachers serving 1,844 students.

Principals: Gerson Pires de Araujo 1961-1962; Claudomiro Fonseca, 1963-1965; Gerson Pires de Aroujo, 1965-1967; N. A. Reichembach, 1967-1968; Claudomiro Fonseco. 1968; W. P. Araujo, 1968-1974; C. L. Feitosa 1974-1977; Joao V. Kuntze, 1978-1980; Lilis T. Nunes, 1981-1983; Wilson Schenfeld, 1984-1985; Sonia A. Reis, 1986-1988; Nazaré de Fátima Mota, 1989-1991; Roberto W. A. Faustino, 1992; Kleber Abreu, 1993; Edir K. Wolff, 1993- .

GRAYSVILLE ACADEMY [1]. *See* Southern College of Seventh-day Adventists.

GRAYSVILLE ACADEMY [2]. A 10-grade boarding school operated from 1916 to 1930 at Graysville, Tennessee. It was established on the site of the former Southern Training School, after the training school was moved to Ooltewah, Tennessee. The academy was operated first by the local church and later by the Cumberland Conference.

GRAYSVILLE SANITARIUM. *See* Southern College of Seventh-day Adventists.

GREAT BRITAIN AND NORTHERN IRELAND. The United Kingdom, including England, Scotland, Wales, and Northern Ireland, also the Channel Islands and the Isle of Man, covering an area of about 94,000 square miles (243,500 square kilometers), with a population (1994) of 58 million.

Historical Background. Britain was invaded by Julius Caesar in 55 B.C In A.D. 43 it was made a Roman province under Claudius. Julius Agricola, the general who pushed the Roman frontier as far north as Scotland, erected a series of fortresses across the country from the Firth of Forth to the Firth of Clyde. The emperor Hadrian (A.D. 117-138) built a wall from the Tyne to the Solway Firth, much of which remains today. Constantine was saluted by his troops as emperor in York in A.D. 306. After the Roman occupation ended, a century later, the country was successively raided and peopled from the Continent by Angles, Jutes, Saxons, Danes, and Normans.

Christianity was well established in Britain by the middle of the fifth century, but almost disappeared with the arrival of the pagan peoples from the coast of Europe. Roman Catholic Christianity, brought by Augustine and other monks, became dominant in Britain in the seventh century. In the middle of the sixteenth century, England and Scotland rejected the authority of the pope, and thereafter became strongholds of Protestantism. However, Ireland remained solidly Catholic except for the northern counties, which became predominantly Protestant in population after the British government in the seventeenth century sent in large numbers of Scottish and English settlers.

The Established Church of England is Episcopal, that of Scotland, Presbyterian, but various other denominations flourish, independently of state support. The majority in Northern Ireland are Presbyterian and Anglican.

In two respects Seventh-day Adventists may find forerunners in earlier British religious movements. From the Seventh Day Baptists of England went emigrants to New England in the sixteenth century. It was a New England Seventh Day Baptist who in 1844 introduced the observance of the Sabbath to a group of Adventists who later became part of the nucleus of the developing Seventh-day Adventist Church. The other forerunners were expositors of prophecy who anticipated certain points of prophetic interpretation taught by Seventh-day Adventists, although they differed from the American SDAs and had no direct connection with them. These were early nineteenth-century premillennialists, among various denominations in various parts of the United Kingdom, who proclaimed the Second Advent as near. For example, writers in England, Scotland, and Ireland had set forth 1843 or 1844 as the end of the 2300 days (of Dan. 8:14) before William Miller published his views in 1836. They and the Millerites participated in a widespread international awakening of interest in the Second

Advent. *See* Premillennialism.

Seventh-day Adventist Statistics. The territory of Great Britain constitutes the major part of the British Union Conference (which includes Ireland), a part of the Trans-European Division. Statistics (1993) for *Great Britain:* churches, 242; members, 18,193; schools, 9; ordained ministers, 116; licensed ministers, 39; Bible workers, 12; teachers, 93. Headquarters for the British Union Conference: Stanborough Park, Watford, Hertfordshire, England. The official organ is the *British Advent Messenger.*

Statistics (1993) for the missions and conferences—*Irish Mission:* churches, 11; members, 323; ordained ministers, 4; licensed ministers, 2. Headquarters: 9 Newry Road, Banbridge, Down, Northern Ireland. *North England Conference:* churches, 84; members, 5,622; ordained ministers, 31; licensed ministers, 11; Bible workers, 4; teachers, 11. Headquarters: 22 Zulla Road, Mapperley Park, Nottingham, England. *Scottish Mission:* churches, 10; members, 278; ordained ministers, 2; licensed ministers, 3. Headquarters: 5 Ochilview Gardens, Crieff, Perthshire, Scotland. *South England Conference:* churches, 122; members, 11,487; schools, 5; ordained ministers, 59; licensed ministers, 22; Bible workers, 8; teachers, 51. Headquarters: 25 St. Johns Road, Watford, Hertsfordshire, England. *Welsh Mission:* churches, 15; members, 483; ordained ministers, 6; licensed ministers, 1. Headquarters: Glan Yr Afon, 10 Heol Y Wern, Caerphilly, Mid Glamorgan, Wales.

Institutions. The Dell Residential Care Home; John Loughborough School; Newbold College; Roundelwood; Stanborough Press Limited; Stanborough School.

Development of Seventh-day Adventist Work. *Beginnings in England.* The first SDA worker in England was William Ings, a native of Hampshire, who had lived in the United States and had worked for the Review and Herald. Returning to England by way of Basel, Switzerland, and arriving on May 23, 1878, at Southampton, he began distributing tracts from door to door and selling magazines. After a brief stay he went to Switzerland but returned a short time later and within four months reported 10 persons keeping the seventh-day Sabbath. In response to his appeal for help, J. N. Loughborough and his wife were sent from the United States in December 1878. Loughborough held meetings in Shirley Hall and later preached to groups of interested persons in a house called Ravenswood, which was procured to provide a meeting room and living quarters.

Seeing the importance of building a strong base in Britain, the General Conference made an appeal in the *Review and Herald* for $100,000, with which to support and advance the work in that and other British countries. In April 1879 Maud Sisley, who had been in Switzerland, came to assist Loughborough in his evangelistic work as Bible instructor and colporteur. By this time a Sabbath school of 17 members was organized in Southampton. That summer Loughborough preached in a tent that he had pitched on a convenient lot in the city. Impelled by curiosity, many came to listen, but were slow to accept the message preached by the American evangelist. Briefly that same summer J. N. Andrews assisted Loughborough. A national Tract and Missionary Society was organized on Feb. 5, 1880, and 1,000 copies of the *Signs of the Times* were distributed during the year. On Feb. 8, 1880, Loughborough baptized six converts in the first Seventh-day Adventist baptismal service in England.

In 1882 Adelbert A. John began to work in Great Grimsby, a seaport town in Lincolnshire. In 1884 a small printing plant was set up in this town, which became the headquarters in the north. In Ulceby (a country village about 10 miles [16 kilometers] northwest of Grimsby) and in Southampton church buildings were provided in 1888.

When Loughborough returned to England from the General Conference session of 1881, he was accompanied by a group of workers, including George R. Drew, who subsequently spent 22 years as a colporteur in England. Drew worked in Liverpool on the west coast in 1883, and one of his first converts was a ship's captain, A. F. Lundqvist, a Finn who introduced SDA teachings into Finland.

J. N. Loughborough reported in the *Review and Herald* (60:632, Oct. 9, 1883) that on Sept. 2 and 3, 1883, a church of about 20 members was organized in Southampton. This was apparently the first Seventh-day Adventist church in Great Britain. On Oct. 1, 1883, there were 100 SDAs in England. In 1884 George I. Butler, General Conference president, visited the country, and M. C. Wilcox arrived to edit the *Present Truth,* first published at Grimsby in May 1884. A thousand copies were distributed in the first year of publication. Also in 1884 a second church, one in Grimsby, was organized.

In May 1885 S. H. Lane and Robert F. Andrews joined the workers in England. In August of the same year Ellen White, on her way to Switzerland, spent two weeks in Britain visiting the churches in Grimsby, Ulceby, Riseley, and Southampton.

In the early summer of 1887 S. N. Haskell arrived to conduct evangelistic work. The Chaloners, a double-fronted house in northern London, was purchased to serve as general headquarters. Three Bible instructors assisted Haskell, and the first baptism in London took place on June 9, 1888. The small plant that had been printing *Present Truth* in Grimsby was transferred to London in 1887. It was here that W. A. Spicer served his apprenticeship as an editor, with E. J. Waggoner, before Spicer went to India in 1898 to edit the *Oriental Watchman.*

Beginnings in Northern Ireland. In 1885 a group of SDA colporteurs entered Ireland. In 1891 the first church was organized in Banbridge, Northern Ireland. Joseph Watson, the church clerk, thus reported: "A meeting of the Seventh-day Adventists of Ireland was called by Elder D. A. Robinson on Sunday, July 5, 1891. The meeting was held in Parkmount House, Banbridge, there being representatives from Banbridge, Tanderagee, Clones [in what is now Ireland, or Eire], Coleraine, and Belfast. Prayer was offered by Brother Hutchinson, which was followed by an address on organization from Elder Robinson."

Twenty-six names were appended to the church covenant. R. W. Whiteside and R. Mussoen, working in the north area, organized a company in Kilmoyle.

SDA progress has been slow in Ireland. In 1993 there were 11 churches in Ireland, with a membership of 323. These four churches in Northern Ireland and the one in Ireland form the Irish Mission (organized 1902; reorganized 1952), coordinating the two separate political entities. *(See* Ireland.)

Scotland. The first attempt to open SDA work in Scotland appears to have been made early in 1886 by S. H. Lane and R. F. Andrews. After visiting three places, they held meetings in a hall at Lochmaben, a town of 2,000 in southern Scotland. Although they advertised extensively and called on nearly every family, the attendance was low, varying from 15 to 70 *(Review and Herald* 63:252, Apr. 20, 1886).

In the summer of 1888 S. N. Haskell visited Scotland. From his report *(ibid.* 65:520, Aug. 14, 1888) it is evident that thousands of SDA publications had been sent to Scotland before his visit, as a result of which some "were on the point of keeping the Sabbath."

In 1891 N. Z. Town took a group of canvassers to Scotland to sell SDA publications *(ibid.* 68:374, June 16, 1891). The results of their work are not known.

Then in 1893 a member from Northern Ireland named Hollingsworth went with his daughter to Glasgow, Scotland, selling Ellen White's book *Patriarchs and Prophets.* A Bleasby family—the mother, two sons, and two daughters—accepted the SDA doctrines, and the first company of adherents in Scotland was formed. John McAvoy, continuing the work, won a family named Barr. In 1901 H. E. Armstrong baptized 20 converts and organized the first Seventh-day Adventist church in Scotland.

Scotland and all the adjacent islands make up the Scottish Mission, which was organized in 1902 and reorganized in 1928 and 1991. In 1993 there were churches in 10 Scottish towns and a membership of 278.

Wales. SDAs entered Wales in 1888, when A. A. John preached in a tent near Aberystwyth. In 1895 in the village of Troedrhwgwair, W. H. Meredith (who later became the first British president of the British Union) was won by the witness of a colporteur. He was baptized the next year in the city of Bath, in England. The Welsh Mission was organized in 1902, and with the other fields within the British Union was reorganized in 1928.

In 1896 J. S. Washburn baptized 47 converts after evangelistic meetings in Cardiff, but no church was organized at the time. In April 1903 in Pontypridd the first Welsh church was organized, composed of 20 converts won by W. H. Meredith. A few months later a church was organized in Cardiff. In 1993 there were 15 churches in the Welsh Mission and a membership of 483.

British Union Conference. In 1902 the British Union Conference was organized, with O. A. Olsen as the first president. It included the South England and North England conferences (both organized in that same year, with E. J. Waggoner and E. E. Andross, respectively, serving as the first presidents) and three missions—Ireland, Scotland, and Wales (with William Hutchinson, H. E. Armstrong, and A. F. Ballenger, respectively, as directors). Several territorial changes have been made since 1902. According to the present territorial alignment (1993), the South England Conference comprises all the counties south of the Wash and includes the Channel Islands, the Isles of Scilly, and the Isle of Wight. The North England Conference includes the Isle of Man and all the counties north of the Wash, east of Wales, but excluding the border counties of Hereford, Worcester, and Shropshire, which are included in the Welsh Mission.

In 1906 the British Union Conference purchased a 55-acre (25-hectare) estate at Watford known as Stanborough Park, some 17 miles (30 kilometers) from the center of London. On this estate, which included a manor house, institutions were erected that have served the British Union—the Stanborough Press, a factory for the manufacture of health foods (*see* Granose Foods), and the first headquarters building for the union conference (opened in 1923). The manor house was first used as a junior college, then was converted into a medical institution, which continued until its close in 1968 (*see* Stanboroughs Nursing and Maternity Home).

As the work expanded, the headquarters building proved too small. A new and spacious block of offices, erected in 1962 and extended in 1990, cares adequately for the officers of the union, the missions, and the Voice of Prophecy Bible School. The building occupied by the former union junior college (*see* Newbold College) housed the Stanborough School until its demolition in 1991, when a new building was erected (a six-classroom primary school was built on Stanborough Park, separate from the secondary school, during 1974).

The publishing house burned in 1964, and new quarters were built at Grantham, Lincolnshire, and opened in 1967.

Through the years many SDA evangelists have preached in Britain, some with marked success. After G. E. Vandeman's 1952 evangelistic campaign in London in the Coliseum and Stoll theaters, the General Conference provided funds that made possible the leasing in 1953 of the Crown property known as the New Gallery Cinema, on Regent Street, near Picadilly Circus. This was remodeled as an evangelistic center, with an auditorium seating about 1,400 and adjacent rooms for chapel, reading room, and offices (*see* Evangelistic Centers). In 1991 the Crown Commissioners bought back the lease, and a new center has been purchased near Marble Arch.

Among those who have gone from the British field to serve overseas are: G. F. Jones, George Keough, S. G. Maxwell, W. T. Bartlett, Dr. G.A.S. Madgwick, W. McClements, H. W. Lowe, W. G. Till, J. Clifford, F. G. Clifford, E. G. Essery, S. Bull, A. S. Maxwell, and many others. For the SDA educational program, the British Union has contributed such individuals as E. E. White (Euro-Africa Division), W.G.C. Murdoch (Andrews University), E. E. Heppenstall (Loma Linda University), S. Bull (La Sierra College), W. T. Hyde (Pacific Union College), and W.R.A. Madgwick (Atlantic Union College).

GREAT LAKES ADVENTIST ACADEMY. A coeducational boarding school on the senior high school level. On Nov. 2, 1986, a special constituency meeting of the Michigan Conference of Seventh-day Adventists voted to merge Adelphian Academy and Cedar Lake Academy. This vote set into motion the process that culminated in the establishment of Great Lakes Adventist Academy on the grounds of what was formerly Cedar Lake Academy. It officially started on Aug. 31, 1987.

This school is centrally located on M-46, three miles (five kilometers) east of the village of Edmore, 17 miles (27 kilometers) west of Alma. This rural setting encourages the development of an appreciation and love for nature. The spacious grounds and modern buildings provide the students with a comfortable atmosphere in which to live and learn.

When Great Lakes Adventist Academy opened its doors for the 1987-1988 school year, it did so with a commitment to continue the more than 170 combined years of service that characterized Adelphian and Cedar Lake.

Even though Great Lakes Adventist Academy is Michigan's newest boarding academy, in a very real sense it is also the oldest. The school is dedicated to the purpose of carrying on the traditions begun by Cedar Lake in 1898 and Adelphian in 1904. *See* Adelphian Academy; Cedar Lake Academy; Grand Ledge Academy.

Principals: Gregory Gerard, 1987-1989; Ray Davis, 1989- .

GREATER BOSTON ACADEMY. A coeducational day school on the senior high school level at 20 Woodland Road, Stoneham, Massachusetts. It is owned by the Southern New England Conference and is operated by a board with representation from six churches in the Greater Boston area with a constituency of about 1,000 members. There is an average student enrollment of 90. In 1958 Greater Boston Academy was accredited by the New England Association of Colleges and Secondary Schools. Its curriculum is essentially college preparatory, although courses in applied arts are also available. The chief school publication is the yearbook, *The Mayflower*.

Greater Boston Academy is an outgrowth of earlier beginnings on the elementary level. As early as 1916 a church school was conducted in Everett, Massachusetts, by Ruth Meleen, and for the next three years a small school was maintained in the Everett-Malden district. The fall of 1920 marked the beginning of the Boston Intermediate School, which employed three teachers. By 1924 classes were held in the newly acquired Boston Temple, at Warren Avenue and West Canton Street, Boston. In 1940 the school was transferred to a dwelling at 325 Harvard Street, Cambridge, Massachusetts, and renamed the Boston Temple Junior Academy. Robert W. Hall and his wife taught together from 1929 until Hall's death in 1942.

Under the pastoral leadership of Norval F. Pease, the twelfth grade was added in 1944, and the high school, now separate from the elementary grades, took the name of Greater Boston Academy. In 1946, with the purchase of school property from the Middlesex University, the academy was relocated at the Newbury Street address. In the spring of 1963 this building was sold; a new school plant was erected at the Woodland Road address in Stoneham, on the grounds of the New England Sanitarium and Hospital, and was first used in the autumn of 1965.

Principals: Richard J. Hammond, 1944-1948; Edwin C. Harkins, 1948-1952; Richard J. Hammond, 1952-1971; Alfred P. Aastrup, 1971-1976; Theodore Lunde, 1976-1978; Arnold Farenick, 1978-1980; Henri Marais, 1980-1985; Donald Watson, 1985-1986; Joelle Andre, 1986-1989; Pierre Ramseier, 1989-1992; Bill Arnold, 1992- .

GREATER MIAMI ACADEMY. A coeducational day school on the senior high school level, operated with its grade school on a five-acre (two-hectare) campus in Miami, Florida, and supported by several Miami churches. In 1962 the academy reported an enrollment (including the grade school) of 248 and a teaching staff of 20. The buildings provide 13 classrooms and an auditorium, and there are outdoor recreational and parking areas.

The year 1962 was the fiftieth anniversary of the founding of the parent church school. In 1912 Miami's Seventh-day Adventist congregation (formed in 1910) opened a school in a tent at the rear of the church building, which was then under construction. The first teacher, Miss Grady Lea (Mrs. David L. Wiltse), had between 20 and 25 pupils. Classes were later moved to the church building, which was sold in 1925.

The school was later operated as the Miami Junior Academy in church-owned property on NW. 30th Street and 3rd Avenue. From two classrooms, two teachers, and 86 pupils, the school grew to five classrooms and 115 pupils in 10 grades by 1950. A year later the school board, which represented the constituent churches, bought an undeveloped city block, and in 1952 Miami Junior Academy moved into two new buildings of three classrooms each at 18th Avenue.

In 1960, after the addition of six new classrooms, a music studio, and a large auditorium, the school became the 12-grade Greater Miami Academy. Plans for 1962-1965 included new elementary classrooms separated from the present buildings, also full teacher certification and academy accreditation. In 1970 a library and vocational building were added to the school plant.

In 1992 Greater Miami Academy celebrated its eightieth anniversary on its new 10-acre (four-hectare) campus, built in 1989. The 1992 enrollment was 437.

Principals: Lester Stannard, 1960-1962; James Shepard, 1962-1965; Howard Kennedy, 1965-1969; Eugene Armour, 1969-1971; James Shepard, 1971-1974; J. K. Herman, 1974-1981; Norman French, 1981; Royce Spalding, 1981-1983; Julio Tabuenca, 1983-1985; Steve Watson, 1985-1986; Jack Stiles, 1986-1989; Manuel R. Fuentes, 1989- .

GREATER NEW YORK ACADEMY. A coeducational day school on the senior high school level, operated by the Greater New York Conference, and situated in Woodside, Queens, New York. The school is accredited by the Seventh-day Adventist Board of Regents and by the University of the State of New York. In 1992 the enrollment was 190; the faculty numbered 14.

By 1920 an SDA grade school in the Bronx had grown to the point where the services of three teachers were required. In that year, because of overcrowded conditions, and because of the need for classes on the high school level, the former Temple Israel, at Lenox Avenue and 120th Street, New York City, was purchased. Besides serving as a school, this new property became the home of the uniting congregations of the New York First church and the Bronx company, which then assumed the name of City Temple church. The new school, called Temple Academy and offering grades 9 and 10, was opened with 36 enrolled, and with H. H. Morse as principal. The name was changed to Greater New York Academy in 1922. The first school paper, *The Student,* began in 1923.

After the City Temple was sold early in 1926, the academy was operated for two years in a rented church building at 122 West 76th Street, and later in the former Second Presbyterian Church on West 96th Street. In 1929 the Brooklyn SDA Church acquired new and commodious property at 484 Washington Avenue, Brooklyn, and this became the home of the academy.

In 1935 the school was able to meet the exacting requirements for a charter from the New York Board of Regents. In 1945 the academy moved into the former Labor Temple at 41-32 58th Street in Woodside, Queens, New York, which with a minimum of remodeling became an up-to-date home for the wandering school. In 1966 the General Conference Welfare Center located next door to the academy moved to new quarters. That building was purchased and remodeled into an academy gymnasium. A 4,300-square-foot (400-square-meter) new wing housing five additional classrooms was completed in August 1988.

Principals: H. H. Morse, 1920-1925; C. E. Owens, 1925-1926; Rowena E. Purdon, 1926-1928; Titus Kurtichanov, 1928-1929; S. W. Tymeson, 1929-1932; X. P. Walton, 1932-1936; C. E. Wittschiebe, 1936-1937; Duane Cowin, 1937-1940; H. J. Alcock, 1940-1943; L. E. Smart, 1943-1947; G. H. Gibson, 1947-1949; J. H. Nylander, 1949-1950; Lee Taylor, 1950-1955; William Fuchs, 1955-1960; LaRue L. Cook, 1960-1964; Ronald Goodall, 1964-1965; Rudolph Knauft, 1965-1967; Anthony DeFranco, 1967-1969; Clyde Newmyer, 1969-1975; David A. Cadavero, 1975-1985; John Hill, 1985-1986; David F. Santos, 1986-1991; Del Metellus, 1991- .

GREATER NEW YORK CONFERENCE. A unit of church organization comprising the territory of New York City and that portion of New York State consisting of the counties of Columbia, Dutchess, Greene, Nassau, Orange, Putnam, Rockland, Suffolk, Sullivan, Ulster, and Westchester. *(See also* Northeastern Conference.) Statistics (1992): churches, 89; members, 14,414; church or elementary schools, 12; ordained ministers, 76; licensed ministers, 2; Bible instructors, 11; teachers, 35. Headquarters: 7 Shelter Rock Road, Post Office Box 5029, Manhasset, New York 11030. The conference forms part of the Atlantic Union Conference.

Institutions. Greater New York Academy.

Local churches—*New York City,* borough of *Brooklyn:* Brooklyn, Dunamis, Ebenezer, French Bethesda, French Gethsemane, French Jerusalem, French Mahanaim, French Mount Sinai, French Peniel, Maranatha, New Haven, New Jerusalem, Spanish Bay Ridge, Spanish Central Brooklyn, Spanish East New York, Spanish South Brooklyn, Spanish Williamsburg; borough of *Bronx:* Co-op City, Emmanuel, First Ghana (African), Grand Concourse, Living Waters, Morris Park, North Bronx, Philadelphia, Spanish Fordham, Spanish Intervale, Spanish Mott Haven, Spanish Prospect, Spanish Soundview, Spanish University, Spanish Washington, Tabernacle of Joy, Victory; borough of *Manhattan:* Advent Hope, Crossroads, Hungarian, Manhattan, Portuguese, Spanish Broadway, Spanish Central Manhattan, Spanish Delancey, Spanish Dyckman, Spanish Fort Washington, Spanish Manhattan, Ukrainian, Washington Heights; borough of *Queens:* Alpha East Elmhurst, Astoria, Flushing, French Bethsaida, Jackson Heights, Korean New York, Korean Queens, Jackson Heights, New York Chinese, Ozone Park, Portuguese Queens, Ridgewood, Romanian, Spanish Astoria, Spanish Far Rockaway, Spanish Queens, Spanish Richmond Hill, Spanish Woodside; borough of *Staten Island:* Korean Staten Island, Manor Road, Spanish Staten Island; other counties: Antioch, Babylon, Five Towns, French Ephraim, French Sychar, Hartsdale, Hempstead, House of Prayer (Van Center), Huntington, Kingston, Korean Bronx, Korean Pearl River, Livingston, Macedonia, Mamaroneck, Middletown, Monticello, Newburgh, Old Westbury, Patchogue, Pearl River, Peekskill, Port Jervis, Poughkeepsie, Riverhead, Spanish Bay Shore, Spanish Glen Cove, Spanish Haverstraw, Spanish Hempstead, Spanish Huntington, Spanish New Rochelle, Spanish Patchgoue, Spanish Rockville Center, Spanish West Babylon, Spanish Yonkers, Yonkers, Youngsville.

History. *Forerunners.* The Adventist message came to the New York area when William Miller gave a course of lectures in New York City in the spring of 1840. On Oct. 25, 1841, the third general conference of the Millerites convened in Broadway Tabernacle. Intense interest led to the publication of the Adventist views through the *Midnight Cry,* which was printed in the city, first as a daily and then as a weekly, and was distributed across the country.

On Feb. 6, 1844, J. V. Himes, a Millerite leader, attended an Adventist conference held at Franklin Hall. This was followed by Miller's lectures at Broadway Chapel to an overflow audience described as "solemn and attentive."

Seventh-day Adventist Work. *Beginnings.* In 1848 James and Ellen White visited New York City and held meetings in a certain Brother Moody's house in Brooklyn. J. K. Bellows reported to James White in 1851 a group of converts numbering 13. Early evangelistic work was reported by M. B. Czechowski, a converted Catholic priest, who organized a church and who rented a chapel in Brooklyn in 1860. He held several services on Sabbath, and meetings in French, Polish, and English on Sunday. He also reported work among the Italians, Swedes, and Germans.

Because the New York City area is the main gateway to the nation, the early growth of Seventh-day Adventist churches there suffered from the constant outflow of the westward movement. Furthermore, the members were scattered and engulfed by a vast populace composed of many divergent nationalities. Reports of meetings held in New York City appeared only sporadically in the church journals from 1850 to 1880.

The year 1883 marked the beginning of the New York city mission, which employed a staff of two in 1885. The Brooklyn city mission was established in January 1886 under the direction of the General Conference.

H. E. Robinson reported tent meetings conducted in 1888 in the city of Newburg with the assistance of M. C. Wilcox. Also in that year the Pacific Press Publishing Association established its eastern plant in New York City. Here the religious liberty periodical *American Sentinel* was published from 1890 to April 1900, and from December 1901 to October 1903 (as the *Sentinel of Christian Liberty*). This publishing branch continued until 1903. Missionary work was also conducted by a harbor boat called the *Sentinel,* which plied among the incoming and outgoing ships *(see* Missionary Vessels).

Early Organization. Because SDAs in the New York City area felt more attached to the New England SDAs than to those belonging to the upstate New York churches, they and groups situated in Pleasantville and Williamsburg (Brooklyn) requested in August 1873 to unite with the New England Conference. A portion of the present conference area, New York City, Long Island, Staten Island (plus New Jersey), was organized into a tract society district of the New England Tract and Missionary Society, with W. J. Boynton as superintendent.

On Sept. 26, 1889, the areas of New York City, Long Island, Staten Island, and the counties of Westchester and Rockland, which formerly had been part of the New England Conference, were made part of the newly formed Atlantic Conference. When the Eastern Union Conference was formed early in 1901, the Atlantic Conference was included under its jurisdiction.

Churches. In 1894 H. G. Thurston reported that 14 were keeping the Sabbath in the upstate city of Middletown. In 1898 J. N. Loughborough reported that there was one English church in New York City, one English church and one Scandinavian church in Brooklyn, and two English churches in Jersey City, with a combined membership of nearly 500. The New York City church was situated on 125th Street and had been organized with 18 members by E. E. Franke. S. N. Haskell spent two years strengthening this church and working in the city area. Subsequently this church became known as the New York No. 1 church. Oldest of the midcity English churches, it became known in 1920 as the City Temple after absorbing the Bronx English congregation. After the absorption the new church had a membership of more than 500. In 1948 the church was relocated in lower Manhattan, and its name changed to Manhattan Seventh-day Adventist Church. The Jamaica church (Queens) was organized in December 1927.

When the Washington Avenue (Brooklyn) church was relocated in Jackson Heights (Queens), the Woodside (Queens) church was absorbed and the new group became known as the Jackson Heights church on June 30, 1959. A portion of the Washington Avenue membership also formed the New York Center church, organized Jan. 9, 1960. Another merger occurred in March 1964 when the Bay Ridge (Brooklyn) and the Italian American (Brooklyn) churches merged to form the Brooklyn church.

Foreign Language Work. The city area's vast and diversified foreign language population has posed many problems in communicating the SDA message. Work among the Scandinavians began in earnest when John F.

Hansen held meetings in 1887. As a result of his work among the Swedes a Swedish church was formed in Brooklyn in 1894. In 1898 Carl Swenson began work among the Swedes in the city, which resulted in the organization of a church of 22 in 1903. In 1911 two churches, one Danish-Norwegian and the other Swedish, were formed from the Brooklyn group.

What appears to have been the first SDA German church in the area was formed in 1899, with a membership of 16.

After conference organization SDA work among the foreign language populace increased sharply. Growth in membership among the German, Danish-Norwegian, and Swedish members was rapid. Shortly after 1900 Rosario Calderone, a converted priest, began house-to-house work among the Italians of the city. Under the sponsorship of the General Conference, L. Zecchetto also worked in the city. Extensive distribution of Czechoslovakian literature in 1906 led to the baptism of nine Czechoslovaks in June 1907, and to the formation of a church in that same year. Joseph Spicer worked among the Yugoslavians. A devout Catholic, he had picked up a wet copy of *The Watchman* along the railroad tracks near the waterfront, and the magazine ultimately led him to accept the SDA message and to enter its ministry. Hungarians in the city were first evangelized by John Sivak and others, and then organized into the first Hungarian SDA church in America in July 1910.

Further advances in the foreign language work began in 1920 when the Italian church was organized with a membership of 17. Significant progress among the Spanish-speaking people in New York City began with the efforts of Lewis Sebastian, a layperson from Puerto Rico. His work was largely among those who had left the SDA Church after their arrival in this city. In June 1929 these reclaimed members formed the nucleus of the first Spanish church in the city and the parent church for several other Spanish congregations. Since then the Spanish work has progressed to more than 5,000 in more than 30 churches. Russian-speaking persons were organized into a church in March 1930.

Greater New York Conference Organized. In a special session of the Atlantic Conference held in December 1901, Greater New York, Long Island, and the counties of Putnam, Rockland, and Westchester were formed into the Greater New York Conference, to become effective Jan. 1, 1902. The organization of the Greater New York area into a separate conference was endorsed by specific counsel from Ellen White. The new conference was made a part of the new Atlantic Union Conference. The headquarters of the new conference were situated at 400 West 57th Street in Manhattan. In the transition the members of the New York church accepted the responsibility for reestablishing a children's home that had formerly been situated in Paterson, New Jersey, and had been operated by the SDAs there.

The president of the newly created Greater New York Conference was H. W. Cottrell, who also served as president of the Atlantic Union Conference. At this time the Greater New York Conference area had a population of 4,515,810 in an area of 308 square miles (800 square kilometers). The conference had ten congregations (four in Brooklyn, four in New York City, and two in Jersey City), with a combined membership of 527. However, only one congregation owned a church building; seven of the congregations held their services in rented quarters. At the time another church, in the Bronx, was in process of organization. The conference employed five ordained ministers, two licensed ministers, three canvassers, and nine other workers. One church school with an enrollment of 20 was in operation.

By 1903 the conference had been enlarged to include the counties of Dutchess, Orange, and Ulster. In 1911 a certificate of incorporation was registered with the state. In 1912 Sullivan County (formerly part of New York Conference) became part of the Greater New York Conference. In 1922 Delaware County (also formerly part of the New York Conference) became part of the Greater New York Conference. In 1950 it was returned to the New York Conference. In 1922 the counties of Greene and Columbia were transferred from the New York Conference to the Greater New York Conference.

Later History. In 1911 the conference membership stood at 1,051. By 1920 this number had risen to 2,721, a gain of about 160 percent. By the end of 1928 there were 3,113 members in 26 churches under the leadership of 15 ordained ministers. At the time the Northeastern Conference organized in 1945, 1,817 of the total membership of 4,386 were transferred to the new conference. (For the development of Black churches, *see* Northeastern Conference.) By late 1964 the Greater New York Conference had more than regained this membership loss, reporting 4,654 members organized in 45 churches under 32 ordained ministers.

In January 1965 the conference headquarters were moved to North Hills, adjacent to the Long Island Expressway at New Hyde Park Road, North Hills, Manhasset, New York. The property included more than ten acres and a residence, which was converted into offices. A guest room and two apartments were included in the three-story structure.

Increasing commercialization and the risk of being taxed for the undeveloped land led the administration to look elsewhere for office property. An estate was purchased in Manhasset, New York, not far from the other office. A large addition, which included room for an Adventist Book Center and an attractive chapel in which workers' meetings could be held, was built. There is adequate office space for present and future needs. The move to this office was completed during 1975.

Evangelism. The great evangelistic challenge of the metropolitan area has been the continuing concern of church leadership on the General, union, and local conference levels. Ellen White gave frequent counsel regarding the direction of the work among the masses of the city. Early conference leaders, such as S. N. Haskell, H. W. Cottrell, and their successors, wrestled with problems unique to this large city. Frequent letters and visits by A. G. Daniells, General Conference president (1901-1922), characterized the continuing involvement on the part of the General Conference through counsel and specific aid in many forms.

Greater New York evangelists have used diversified methods and new techniques to reach the populace. The tent meeting was the popular summer rallying point in the early days. Later the city's many halls, auditoriums, and theaters, including Carnegie Hall were focal points for evangelism. Major evangelistic campaigns were held by Charles Everson (1914), Jesse C. Stevens (1917), C. B. Haynes (1919), and Louis K. Dickson (1922).

Powerful media of communication, first radio and then television, were used to broadcast the SDA message to the city. Through the years many SDA workers presented series of programs on radio. In May 1950 Faith for Today, directed by W. A. Fagal, then pastor of the Washington Avenue church, began on TV. The influence of this program spread rapidly and is now felt throughout North America and overseas.

After outgrowing several headquarters locations, the telecast moved to Carle Place, Long Island, in 1963. In the early seventies broadcasting and production studios began concentrating their activities in California more than in New York. In May 1972 Faith for Today moved its operation to the Seventh-day Adventist Radio, Television, and Film Center in Newbury Park, California. This gave much better access to the studios and production centers.

The ever-present need for an evangelistic center in the heart of New York City resulted in a grant in 1954 by the General Conference toward the establishment of a center at 227 West 46th Street, off Times Square. This all-purpose facility had auditoriums, chapels, offices, and accommodations for transient missionaries and other church-employed workers. The center was sold in 1979 and replaced by the Adventist Information Center at 12 West 40th Street, off Fifth Avenue. The new facility has an Adventist Book Center and two chapels that host the Ukrainian and Hungarian congregations, as well as an information center.

From 1933 to 1945 S. A. Kaplan pioneered the work among the Jewish people of the city. After a gap of about four years, during which he worked at the General Conference and was in charge of work for the Jews, he resumed his work in the New York City area, and in 1949 established the Bronx Community Chapel, replaced in 1958 by the Times Square Center at 410 West 45th Street, near Times Square, in a building purchased and renovated within a year. In 1948 J. N. Hoffman was appointed director of the Jewish work. In 1950 a Ukrainian church was established as a result of the work carried on by Miroslav Roshak.

Institutions. Secondary church school education was fostered in the city with the establishment in 1920 of Temple Academy, forerunner of Greater New York Academy. Harlem Academy was also begun in 1920 with eight (later 12) grades (now Northeastern Academy, serving the constituency of the Northeastern Conference).

In 1955 the Adventist Home for the aged was established in Livingston, New York. It was a member of the SDA Association of Self-Supporting Institutions. In 1966 the Greater New York Conference was asked to assume full operation of the institution. In 1973 the Adventist Nursing Home was constructed and occupied. It was a 120-bed nursing care facility on the same grounds with the Adventist Home. Although not fully owned by the church, it was managed and operated by the Greater New York Conference. By the mid-

1980s both the Adventist Home and the Adventist Nursing Home were no longer under the conference management.

Facilities. In 1962 the Eagle Lake campground near Sloatsburg, New York, was sold and the Berkshire Country Club at Wingdale was purchased. There are 282 acres (115 hectares) and full facilities for camp meetings and youth camping programs. The facilities are frequently used by the Atlantic Union and other groups outside Greater New York. A meeting hall seating 2,500 was completed in 1964, replacing the auditorium, which had been destroyed by fire. Since becoming conference property, additions to the operating facilities represent a total expenditure of more than $2 million.

In 1975 the conference committee voted to enlarge the medical missionary work being carried on by its health screening van by expanding to five vans.

The New York Korean church was established in Queens and a Romanian company was organized in 1977 in Ridgewood. A company of Chinese believers also was established that year. A Pakistani congregation, speaking Urdu, was established in Manhattan in 1979. The year 1981 marked the start of SDA work among Haitians and other French-speaking people in the Greater New York Conference.

In 1980 the conference was forced to repossess their former property in North Hills, Long Island. This additional space allowed for expansion of the community health services and van ministry.

During the 1990s a satellite dish was constructed in North Hills that makes it possible to cover all of North America and part of South America with television. On Nov. 1, 1992, the SDA Good News Television Network officially came on the air. Later the FCC gave permission to operate the channel 29 station in the Greater New York area.

Presidents: H. W. Cottrell, 1902-1903; C. H. Edwards, 1903-1908; M. L. Andreasen, 1908-1909; R. D. Quinn, 1909-1913; J. L. McElhany, 1913-1915; J. E. Jayne, 1915-1922; C. B. Haynes, 1922-1926; E. K. Slade (acting), 1926-1927; L. K. Dickson, 1927-1933; W. H. Heckman, 1933-1936; W. A. Nelson, 1936-1942; C. M. Bunker, 1942-1947; L. C. Evans, 1947-1950; E. L. Branson, 1950-1959; G. E. Jones, 1959-1965; L. L. Reile, 1965-1973; D. J. Sandstrom, 1973-1978; G. M. Kretschmar, 1978-1994; Charles Griffin, 1994- .

GREATER SYDNEY CONFERENCE. *See* Australia; South Pacific Division.

GREECE. A small republic situated on a peninsula jutting into the Mediterranean Sea, bounded on the north by Albania, Macedonia, and Bulgaria, on the extreme northeast by Turkey, on the east by the Aegean Sea, and on the west by the Ionian Sea. Its total area is 50,547 square miles (131,000 square kilometers), and its population (1994), 10.6 million. The country is mountainous. The main sources of employment are farming, shipping, trade, and industries. The official national religion is Greek Orthodox. Only a small percentage of the people are non-Orthodox (Catholics, Protestants, Jews, and a few Muslims in the northern provinces and islands).

Of the various states of Europe, Greece has the longest history and has been considered the cradle of European civilization. Its culture reached its highest point in the fifth century B.C., but it was in the fourth century B.C., under Alexander the Great, that Greek culture and political institutions influenced wide areas and became dominant in the eastern Mediterranean world, and subsequently infiltrated the Roman West. After a period of decline, it was revitalized when, in A.D. 330, the capital of the Roman Empire was transferred to Constantinople, the site of the ancient Greek colony of Byzantium, where the Greeks gradually gained control of the court and of the government so that the Byzantine Empire became essentially an empire of the Greeks. There ensued a cleavage between the forms of Christianity in the West and in the Greek East, which led to the schism in the church between Rome and Constantinople in 1054. When Constantinople fell to the Turks in 1453, Greece became a Turkish province and regained its independence only in the beginning of the nineteenth century. Since then its territory has expanded northward and also includes some islands in the Aegean Sea. These expansions have brought a varied non-Greek population into the state.

Seventh-day Adventist Statistics. The SDA Church in Greece constitutes the Greek Mission, which is attached to the Trans-European Division. Statistics (1993) for *Greece:* churches, 8; members, 250; ordained ministers, 4; licensed ministers, 2; credentialed missionaries, 7. Greek Mission headquarters: Keramikou 18, Athens, Greece.

Institutions. Light House Publishing Company.

Seventh-day Adventist Work. *Beginnings.* As early as 1878 there is reference in the *Review and Herald* to "fruit" from publications that had been sent to Greece. An Italian SDA, a commercial traveler named Bertola, went to Greece in 1879 and shared his faith as the opportunity was afforded him, but there is no record of any permanent results of his work. In 1899 the Mission Board sent over H. A. Henderson, a licensed minister, probably chosen because he had taught Greek (in South Lancaster Academy). He reported from Nauplia in the *Review and Herald* in 1899 and 1900 that he had made contacts and had found interests, but he made no reference to converts.

In 1907, after the General Conference biennial session at Gland, Switzerland, another professor of ancient Greek, W. E. Howell, was sent to Greece. He settled with his family in a suburb of Athens and began to study the modern language, but in 1909 he was recalled to America to resume educational work. While in Greece he had supervised the translation of some tracts into modern Greek.

The first known Seventh-day Adventist convert in Greece was George Brakas, of Vostina (a town then belonging to Albania), who had learned of the Sabbath and observed it several years before hearing in 1908 of a small Sabbathkeeping church in Constantinople. Every 15 days he sent a letter addressed to "the church which keeps the Sabbath." In 1909 he was visited by R. S. Greaves from the SDA Turkish Mission. Brakas, his wife, and his eldest daughter were baptized. In 1912 the remaining three members of his family were baptized.

On another trip to this area, early in 1910, Greaves stopped at Athens to baptize S. Fameliari, the first SDA in Athens, who had accepted the faith through reading publications sent to him from the United States.

Late in the same year, Greaves was sent to head the new Grecian Mission. He went first to Ioánnina, later to Patras and Thessaloníki. Times were hard because of tension between Greece and Turkey. When World War I began, the Greaves family left Greece. Remaining were F. Scior, a ministerial licentiate, and Alexandra Keanides, a Greek nurse from Turkey. The Greaves family returned to Thessaloníki from 1921 to 1926.

However, in 1921 events combined to strengthen the work. Because of political unrest, about 2 million Greeks fled from Turkey to Greece as refugees. Among these were 10 or 12 SDA families, some Greek, others Armenian. Some of these families settled in Thessaloníki, others in Piraeus and Athens. In 1923 a church was organized, and an orphanage for the refugee children was opened in Thessaloníki. Greaves was mission director, and A. H. Larson was in charge of the orphanage, which unfortunately had to be closed in 1926.

During 1923 a group was organized in Piraeus and met in the home of Mable Kalfa. The first missionary to do evangelistic work in the Athens area was M. C. Grin, who came from Switzerland and worked in Greece from 1925 to 1932. The first church in Athens was organized in 1927 with 15 members, most of whom belonged to the family of A. Christoforides. In 1926 E. Hennecke became director. He organized a church in Berea and remained in Greece until 1932, when he and M. C. Grin were compelled to leave the country, and A. N. Stabellos became acting president of the Greek Mission.

When C. A. Christoforides became the director of the mission (1939) the headquarters were moved from Thessaloníki to Athens. At the end of World War II a church and headquarters building was erected in Athens and dedicated in 1950. Three years later a church was built in Níkaia, a suburb of Piraeus. After a brief period of leadership by Nick Poulos, Nick Germanis became president of the Greek Mission in 1958.

From 1928 to 1938 the Greek Mission belonged to the Central European Division and from 1938 to 1940 to Section II of that division. From 1940 to 1945 it was part of the mission territory administered by the General Conference, and in 1946 it became a mission of the Southern European Division. In 1972 the Greek Mission was attached to the Southern European Union Mission, within the newly formed Euro-Africa Division.

In the fall of 1972 a secondary day school was begun in Athens, with Nick Germanis as principal. It was the first school SDAs organized in Greece, and it constituted a major step forward in the training of the youth for the service of God. The students lived in the Athens area. The school was closed in 1982.

During the month of October 1971, 15-minute radiobroadcasts were introduced six nights a week in the Greek language. These programs were transmitted from the Trans-Europe station in Lisbon, Portugal. The best reception of these broadcasts were in the large industrial centers of Europe, where hundreds of thousands of Greeks live and work. Three of these broadcasts were on religious topics, two were educational, and one presented health subjects. The production of shortwave broadcasts was halted in the 1980s because of lack of response. In 1993 a new production studio opened in order to produce local radio programs.

The Five-day Plan to Stop Smoking and other health seminars, initiated by Nick Germanis, became a significant outreach method in the Athens area. A Better Living center in Athens and *Lifestyle Magazine* TV programs in Attica, Corinth, Epirus, and Macedonia continue this form of outreach and present SDAs as a caring church.

GREEK MISSION. *See* Greece; Trans-European Division.

GREEK PUBLISHING HOUSE. *See* Light House Publishing Company.

GREEN, WILLIAM HAWKINS (1871-1928). Minister, department secretary. A graduate in law and theology from Shaw University, he practiced law in Charlotte and Elizabeth City, North Carolina, and in Washington, D.C. He became a Seventh-day Adventist in 1901. After further study he preached in Pittsburgh, Pennsylvania, from 1905 to 1909, and then for a few months in Atlanta, Georgia. After a period as pastor of the Ephesus church, Washington, D.C. (1909-1912), he built up the Hartford Avenue SDA Church in Detroit, Michigan (1912-1918). From 1918 to 1928 he was secretary of the North American Negro Department of the General Conference, the first Black to hold that office.

GREEN RIVER ORDINANCES. Local laws in a number of cities in the United States prohibiting all door-to-door solicitation without prior invitation of the occupant. They are named after Green River, Wyoming, where in 1931 one of the first such laws was enacted.

In *Martin v. Struthers,* 319 U.S. 141 (1943), the Supreme Court of the United States held that a municipality could not forbid the free distribution of brochures "advertising a religious meeting." In *Breard v. Alexandria,* 341 U.S. 622 (1951), the Court upheld a Green River ordinance in a case involving solicitors for subscriptions to secular magazines such as *Saturday Evening Post* and *Newsweek.* The Court said the ordinance was a valid exercise of the city's police power to regulate commerce.

Some commentators suggest the *Breard* case allows Green River ordinances to be used to bar the work of literature evangelists. But in Louisiana, where the *Breard* case arose, it had already been held that literature evangelists do not fall within the ordinance because they are neither "solicitors, peddlers, hawkers, itinerant merchants or transient vendors" (*Shreveport v. Teague,* 200 La. 679, 8 So.2d 640 [1941]). In *Green River v. Martin,* 61 Wyo. 81, 254 P.2d 198 (1953), the language of the ordinance was held to be directed only to commercial activities. In *City of Anchorage v. Berry,* 145 F.Supp. 868 (1956), the court pointed out that the *Breard* case involved a "transaction of a commercial nature" and that the literature evangelist makes door-to-door calls "for the primary purpose of preaching his religion in an attempt to proselyte followers for his religious beliefs and congregation; thus, the sale, if it can be considered such, was incidental to this method of preaching."

As the Supreme Court of Wyoming said in the *Martin* case: "There is an extraordinary diversity of opinion among the courts as to the validity" of Green River ordinances as applied to religious solicitors.

Green River ordinances have been used at times to try to prevent door-to-door selling of religious literature. But most city governments have recognized the right of the church to propagate the gospel by this method. The church is opposed to such ordinances when they are applied to the selling of religious literature, holding that it violates the First Amendment guarantee of the free exercise of religion, a part of which is the preaching of the gospel through means of selling the printed page.

The *Breard* case noted that First Amendment protection does not extend "to colporteurs offending . . . state trespass laws by distributing, after notice to desist, like publications to the tenants in a private apartment house."

GREENLAND. A large island lying mainly within the Arctic Circle; a Danish colony until 1953, but since then an integral part of Denmark. Since 1979 Greenland has been ruled by its own magistrate and has two representatives in the Danish Folketing. It has an area of about 840,000 square miles (2.2 million square kilometers), but only the coastline is inhabited. Its population (1994) is 57,000. Greenland's technically correct name is Kalaallit Nunaat; Nuuk is the capital. The principal sources of income are fish, seals, sheep, minerals, reindeer, and furs.

Greenland was sighted by Gunnbjørn Ulfssøn of Iceland in A.D. 975. European settlement began with Eric the Red, who was banished from Iceland about 982. His son Leif Ericsson introduced Christianity into Greenland from Norway in 1000. In 1410 all connections between Scandinavia and Greenland ceased, and the colonists disappeared. A new Danish-Norwegian settlement was made early in the eighteenth century, primarily through the initiative of the Lutheran priest Hans Egede, who, from 1721 to 1736, was known as the apostle to Greenland. A majority of the inhabitants profess Lutheranism, although the Moravians, who had a mission on the island as early as 1733, are also represented there.

Development of Seventh-day Adventist Work. The first SDA contacts were made through publications brought by fishermen from the Faeroe Islands. In 1953 Andreas Nielsen of Denmark was appointed to begin evangelism in Greenland, and went there the following year. Later that year he baptized Amon Berthelsen, the first SDA convert in Greenland. Nielsen was joined in 1957 by a nurse, Ella Praestiin. In 1959 Anna Hogganvik, a physiotherapist, opened the Skodsborg Clinic in Godthaab. It was operated by the mission until 1992, when a new health system in Greenland forced the clinic to close.

The Greenland Mission is part of the Danish Union of Churches, which is a part of the Trans-European Division. In 1992 there were 13 members and one church building in Godthaab. In recent years the field has been served by self-supporting missionaries.

GREENLAND MISSION. *See* Greenland; Trans-European Division.

GREER, GEORGE W. (1895-1967). Musician and teacher. Born in California, he was reared in a Christian home and educated at Pacific Union College. In 1917 he was married to Hazel McElhany, and after further education was called to teach music at Lodi Academy. In 1926 the family returned to Pacific Union College, where Greer formed and toured with the first a cappella choir to be organized in any Seventh-day Adventist college. During his career he served at Washington Missionary College, Atlantic Union College, Avondale College, and the SDA Theological Seminary. In 1943 he took a three-year leave from teaching to work with the Voice of Prophecy radiobroadcast. In 1956 he returned to Pacific Union College, where he taught voice and conducted the choirs until his retirement in 1960, at which time the college board of trustees conferred on him the rank of professor emeritus of music.

GREGG, LIZZIE M. (1875-1957). Departmental secretary and administrator. Born in England, she served as tract society secretary in several conferences in the Australasian Union, as Missionary Volunteer and Sabbath school secretary of the New Zealand Conference, and as assistant in the Home Missionary Department of the General Conference. She later was assistant to the manager of the Periodical Department of the Review and Herald (1915), assistant periodical secretary of the Canadian Watchman Press (1920), and registrar of the Home Study Institute (1926-1941).

GREGORY, ABEL LANDERS (1867-1950). Pioneer Seventh-day Adventist self-supporting missionary physician to Latin America. He joined the SDA Church at the age of 21, and some time later, began the study of medicine at Hahnemann Hospital and College in California. Two years after completing the course, he and his wife, Lulu, daughter of J. O. Corliss, volunteered to go to Brazil as self-supporting medical missionaries. He worked there for seven years (1902-1909), then at the River Plate Sanitarium in Argentina for a brief period (1909-1910). Returning to the United States, he took charge of the Graysville Sanitarium (1910-1911), but soon went to Mexico and was in charge of treatment rooms at Guadalajara Sanitarium (1912-1914). In 1914 he went to Florida and superintended the Orlando Sanitarium for a year, then worked with an evangelistic group in Florida (1917-1919). After working briefly in Cuba (1919) and in California (1919-1921), he left for his last post of missionary service, in Honduras, where he spent more than a quarter century as a self-supporting medical evangelist. Besides practicing medicine, he helped found the Honduras Industrial Academy.

GRENADA (pronounced Gren-ay-dah). A former British Associated State with limited self-government that became fully independent Feb. 7, 1974. It is the smallest independent nation in the Western Hemisphere and lies southernmost in the long arc of the Windward

Islands in the southeast Caribbean, 90 miles (145 kilometers) north of the Venezuelan coast.

The area comprises 133 square miles (345 square kilometers) and has a population (1994) of 94,000, more than 50 percent of which are of African descent. More than half the people are Roman Catholic. The economy is agricultural, mainly nutmegs, bananas, cocoa, sugar, and rum.

Seventh-day Adventist Statistics. Grenada is a mission that is a part of the Caribbean Union Conference, which is in turn a part of the Inter-American Division. *See also* Leeward and Windward Islands. Statistics (1993) for the *Grenada Mission:* churches, 28; members, 6,577; elementary schools, 2; ordained ministers, 9; licensed ministers, 3; teachers, 24. Headquarters: Advent Avenue, Grand Bras, St. Andrew's, Grenada.

Institutions. Grenada Seventh-day Adventist Comprehensive Secondary School.

GRENADA MISSION. *See* Grenada; Inter-American Division.

GRENADA SEVENTH-DAY ADVENTIST COMPREHENSIVE SECONDARY SCHOOL (Mount Rose Secondary School). A coeducational nonresident high school situated at Mount Rose, Grenada, West Indies. The school was begun in September 1958, with an enrollment of 19. Henry Bourgeois was principal. Operated at first by the Mount Rose Seventh-day Adventist Church, it became conference-operated and state-aided in 1973. It offers secondary level courses in the humanities, physical sciences, domestic science, woodwork, and secretarial sciences, and prepares students to write the Caribbean Examination Council examination at ordinary level.

Principals: Henry Bourgeois, 1958-1960; Eglon Wilson, 1960-1961; Willie Joseph, 1961-1967; Lincoln Bernard, 1967-1972; Alvin Ham-Ying (acting), 1972-1973; James Bourgeois, 1973; Alvin Ham-Ying, 1973-1974; Lee Buddy, 1974-1976; Phillip Finlay, 1976-1980; Thompson Fleary, 1980-1982; Bacter Fanwar, 1982-1983; Jaswant Kapur (acting), 1983; Carol Odle, 1984; Martha Jeffrey, 1985- .

GRENADINES. *See* Inter-American Division; Leeward and Windward Islands.

GRIFFITH, DORLIN KNOWLES (1921-1990). Pastor, educator, administrator. Born in Oklahoma, he married Consuelo Hernandez when he was 20 and soon after began a tour of service in the medical corps of the United States Army.

In 1953 he received a B.A. degree from Pacific Union College and in 1961 earned an M.A. from Andrews University. He began his denominational service as a pastor/teacher in Oxnard, California. He also served as youth pastor and pastor in the Los Angeles area. After ordination in 1957, he taught school and became principal of San Fernando Valley Academy.

In 1966 he and his family moved to Atlanta, where he became superintendent of education for the Georgia-Cumberland Conference. In 1971 he served in the same capacity in the Florida Conference.

In 1974 the Griffiths moved to Africa, where D. K. was president of Ethiopian Adventist College. Upon their return to the United States he was called to be superintendent of education in the Gulf States Conference and later served in that office for the Southern Union Conference.

Following his semi-retirement in 1987, he served as interim superintendent of education for the Georgia-Cumberland Conference and continued for the remainder of his life as an associate superintendent.

GRIGGS, DONALD EZRA (1901-1967). Physician, missionary, teacher. He was born to Prof. and Mrs. Frederick Griggs in South Lancaster, Massachusetts. In 1922 he graduated from Emmanuel Missionary College and two years later received his M.D. degree from the College of Medical Evangelists. Following internship, he and his wife, the former Loice Adamson, went to China, where he served at Peking University and as superintendent of the Shanghai Sanitarium until 1931. After special training in London and Vienna, he returned to the United States, where he joined the faculty of Loma Linda University. He was honored there as Alumnus of the Year in 1958. At that institution he served in various capacities. At the time of his death he was clinical professor of medicine. During his active career he was awarded some of the highest honors and posts afforded in the medical field.

GRIGGS, FREDERICK (1867-1952). Educator and administrator. He was educated at Battle Creek College, the University of Buffalo, and Washington Missionary College. He married Blanche Eggleston in 1892. While principal of the preparatory school of Battle Creek College (1890-1899), he strongly advocated the establishing of a teacher-training school, and became the first head of such a school connected with Seventh-day Adventist colleges (1896).

He was principal of South Lancaster Academy (1899-1907), and at different times chair or secretary of the General Conference Department of Education (1903-1910 1915-1918). From 1910 to 1914 he was president of Union College, and later of Emmanuel Missionary College (1918-1925). He served overseas as field secretary (1925-1930) and then president (1931-1936) of the Far Eastern Division, and of the China Division (1936-1938).

After returning to the United States in 1938, Griggs held for 11 years the chair of the board of trustees of the College of Medical Evangelists and of the Pacific Press. In 1940 he married Mabel Shaffer Murrin.

GRIGGS UNIVERSITY. *See* Home Study International/Griggs University.

GROESCHEL, OTTO MAX (1896-1962). Manager of Book and Bible Houses in Brazil, secretary-treasurer. He was born in Germany and was trained in Brazil. From 1912 to 1920 he was an accountant at the Brazil Publishing House. Afterward, from about 1921 on, he served as secretary of the tract society in the Rio Grande do Sul Conference in Brazil. Later he was secretary-treasurer and manager of book depositories of the East Minas Mission (1924-1927), the Rio Espírito Santo Mission (1927-1934), the Northeast Mission (1934-1937), the Bahia Mission (1937-1950), and the Northeast Brazil Mission (1950-1957).

GRUNDSET, OLE J. (1886-1957). Minister, one of the pioneer workers in Manchuria, China. He received his education at Maplewood Academy, Hutchinson Theological Seminary, and Union College. After working as a colporteur in North Dakota, he entered ministerial training and later was engaged in evangelistic work in Minnesota, Wisconsin, and Iowa. In 1912 he attended Washington Foreign Mission Seminary, and in 1913, after marrying Anna Sorensen, went to China, where he and Bernhard Petersen opened an SDA mission in Manchuria in 1914. While in China, he was ordained to the ministry. About 1921 he returned to the United States and took the medical course and graduated in medicine at Loma Linda in 1927. When the condition of his wife's health prevented his returning to the mission fields, he entered private practice.

GUADALAJARA SANITARIUM. *See* Mexico.

GUADELOUPE AND DEPENDENCIES. An overseas department of France consisting of a number of islands in the Lesser Antilles archipelago in the Caribbean Sea: Guadeloupe, Marie-Galante, Les Saintes, and Désirade (all situated between Montserrat and Dominica); and St. Barthélemy and St.-Martin (French section), situated some 140 miles (225 kilometers) to the north.

Guadeloupe consists of two islands: Basse-Terre (otherwise known as Guadeloupe proper), a volcanic island whose highest elevation is 4,869 feet (1,500 meters), and low-lying Grande-Terre, separated from Basse-Terre by a narrow channel called Rivière Salée (Salt River). The total area of the two islands is 660 square miles (1,700 square kilometers), and the population (1994) is about 395,000. The town of Basse-Terre is the capital, but Pointe-à-Pitre, on Grande-Terre, is the principal port and commercial center. The population, composed of Blacks and the descendants of Norman and Breton settlers who came there in the seventeenth century, is largely Roman Catholic in religion. There are several Protestant bodies in the country, including Seventh-day Adventists, "La Mission Evangelique," Jehovah's Witnesses, Baptists, and Pentecostals.

Seventh-day Adventist Statistics. The territory of Guadeloupe and its close-lying dependencies was organized into the Guadeloupe Mission of Seventh-day Adventists in January 1966. In 1994 the Guadeloupe Conference was part of the French Antilles/Guiana Union Mission, which is part of the Inter-American Division. Statistics (1993) for *Guadeloupe and dependencies*: churches, 44; members, 8,753; secondary schools, 1; elementary schools, 4; ordained ministers, 14; credentialed missionaries, 28; licensed ministers, 6; licensed missionaries, 18; credentialed and licensed literature evangelists, 10. Headquarters: Morne Boissard, Pointe-à-Pitre, Guadeloupe.

Institutions. Persévérance Boissard School.

Seventh-day Adventist Work on Guadeloupe. The first SDA missionary to Guadeloupe was Philip Giddings, who visited the island in 1908, while he was working in the Leeward Islands Mission. In 1914 he went with his family to Pointe-à-Pitre and opened the first Protestant mission on the island. He held worship services at his house and organized a Sabbath school. Visiting villages and towns, and sleeping in the homes of the people who received him, he sold books, gave Bible studies, held cottage meetings, and distributed tracts. The first persons he baptized were four members of the Flipps family in Pointe-à-Pitre and four members of the James family of Capesterre. When he left Guadeloupe in 1924, there were about 12 baptized members (mostly of British descent), but almost all of them left the country after the hurricane of 1928. The first SDA church building was erected at Grippon in 1930 by Maxine Herisson, who sold her property to pay its cost. After Giddings left, no workers were stationed on the island until 1932, when two Martiniquan colporteurs, E. Berle and S. B. Jean-Elie, went to Guadeloupe. The first church was organized at Pointe-à-Pitre in 1935 with 25 members instructed by those colporteurs. In September 1938, when the first general meeting of the members was held, there were three churches and three companies. At that time Eugene Berle was ordained, and became the first SDA minister to be ordained in the French West Indies.

The first church school was opened at Pointe-à-Pitre in 1947, with Joseph Bigord as director. By 1993 it had become an important 12-grade primary and secondary school, called "La Perseverance," with an enrollment of more than 536 pupils (270 in the secondary grades) in a four-story building.

Dependencies. On Marie-Galante, 16 miles (25 kilometers) southeast of Guadeloupe (area, 58 square miles [150 square kilometers]; population [1993], 15,000), most of the people are Roman Catholic, but there are 170 SDA adherents.

On St.-Martin (French section), 142 miles (225 kilometers) northwest of Guadeloupe (area, 20 square miles [50 square kilometers]; population [1982], 8,000), the first SDAs were baptized in 1934. In 1993 there were 272 adherents on the island.

On Désirade, six miles (10 kilometers) southwest of Grande-Terre (area, 10 square miles [25 square kilometers]; population [1993], more than 1,600), the first SDAs were baptized in 1973. There were 19 adherents on the island. The other dependencies, predominantly Catholic in population, were still barely touched by SDA work in 1993. They are Les Saintes, a group of islands seven miles (11 kilometers) south of Basse-Terre, with 10 SDA adherents, and St. Barthélemy, 130 miles (200 kilometers) northwest of Guadeloupe.

GUADELOUPE CONFERENCE. *See* Guadeloupe; Inter-American Division.

GUAM AND MICRONESIA. Territory in the western Pacific covering 3 million square miles (7.8 million square kilometers) of water and land immediately north of the equator, extending 2,400 miles (3,850 kilometers) from east to west and 1,700 miles (2,700 kilometers) from north to south. In this vast area there are 2,141 islands with a total land area of only about 1,000 square miles (2,600 square kilometers) and a population of approximately 275,000. Micronesia means "tiny islands" and includes the Federated States of Micronesia (Yap, Chuuk, Pohnpei, and Kosrae), Guam (an unincorporated United States territory), the commonwealth of the Northern Mariana Islands (Saipan is the district center), republic of Palau (or Belau), and the emerging nation of the Marshall Islands.

The predominant religion in Guam and the Marianas is Roman Catholic; in the Eastern Carolines and Western Carolines (both part of Micronesia) and the Marshall Islands the Protestant denominations are prominent. English is the official language and is also the language used in all schools.

Seventh-day Adventist Statistics. The territory of Micronesia constitutes the Guam-Micronesia Mission, an attached field of the Far Eastern Division. Statistics (1992) for *Guam-Micronesia Mission:* churches, 17; members, 2,562; church schools, 15; ordained ministers, 20; licensed ministers, 9; teachers, 142. Headquarters: Agana Heights, Guam.

Institutions. Ebeye Seventh-day Adventist High School (Marshall Islands); Guam Adventist Academy (Guam); Marshall Islands Mission Academy (Marshall Islands); Palau Mission Academy (Western Caroline Islands). (There are also three clinics: Guam Seventh-day Adventist Clinic [Guam]; Palau Seventh-day Adventist Clinic [Western Caroline Islands]; Saipan Adventist Clinic [Northern Mariana Islands]. *See* Guam SDA Clinic.)

Development of Seventh-day Adventist Work. *Western Caroline Islands.* The first SDA in the area was James G. Gibbon, an English sailor who adopted Koror (Palau district), in the Western Carolines, as his home. He accepted SDA beliefs after reading tracts sent on a merchant vessel in the 1890s from Hong Kong by the pioneer self-supporting missionary Abram La Rue.

In the late 1920s, according to an account by V. T. Armstrong *(Review and Herald* 124:18, Dec. 18, 1947), William Gibbon, a son of James G. Gibbon, living on the island of Palau, sought to establish contact with SDAs and wrote a letter addressed to "Armstrong, Tokyo." In response to this appeal, SDA workers visited the island in 1930 and 1932—V. T. Armstrong, S. Ogura, and S. Miyake. William Gibbon was baptized, later 20 persons, after a series of evangelistic meetings, and at a later time seven more. On July 7, 1934, J. O. Bautista and his wife, sponsored by the Missionary Volunteer societies of the Philippine Islands, arrived on this island. In 1939 W. S. Ogura joined them for a month, and 10 more persons were baptized.

During World War II two SDA Japanese missionaries in the Western Carolines were interned by the Japanese administrators for refusal to bear arms, and one of these, Seiichi Yamamoto, succeeded in interesting Toribiong Uchel, one of his jailers, in SDA beliefs. After the war Toribiong Uchel was baptized and in 1956 became the first ordained Palauan Seventh-day Adventist minister; he met a tragic death by drowning in 1965 while on a mission trip among the islands.

In 1949 P. L. Williams, division treasurer, and Robert E. Dunton conducted baptisms on Koror and Babelthaup. In the autumn of 1949 J. L. Bowers and his wife came from the China Division to head the work on Koror.

Guam. The first known Sabbathkeeper on the island was Guillermo Flores, a Baptist minister on Guam, who had believed and kept the seventh-day Sabbath since 1926 without ever having seen any other Sabbathkeeper. He was later dismissed for his sabbatarian views. In 1948 he united with the Seventh-day Adventist Church and later entered its ministry. Seventh-day Adventist influence on Guam was strengthened on Sept. 9, 1944, when Henry Metzker, of Sutherlin, Oregon, a pharmacist's mate, first class, U.S.N.R., inquired at the home of Guam congressman Manuel Ulloa of Dededo as to where the Seventh-day Adventist church was situated. At that time there was no church on the island, but the Ulloa family became interested, and a year later, in the autumn of 1945, while A. N. Nelson and F. R. Millard, on their way to Japan as interpreters for a special mission, were delayed on Guam by typhoon weather ahead, the Ulloas with five of their children and a nephew were baptized. The Ulloa home became a place of worship every Sabbath. In the second baptism, on Dec. 25, 1947, six more were baptized.

In May 1948 the first SDA missionary to Guam, Robert E. Dunton, arrived. A church was organized May 30. A month later he learned that his permit to live on Guam was valid for 10 more days only, and that he would have to return to the United States unless the mission had property and a home for the missionary on the island. With the help of mission officials who visited Guam, he was able to arrange for the purchase of property and for the erection of a dwelling on it. The house was completed in time for his family to join him in September of the same year. Mrs. Dunton became the first SDA colporteur there.

As the work progressed, Ray Turner and C. G. Oliver joined the Guam staff. The first church building was erected in Dededo in 1949, and at the first mission session, held in Agana, Guam, in March 1950, the mission was formally organized, with R. E. Dunton as president and C. G. Oliver as secretary-treasurer.

Since August 1954 the Voice of Prophecy radio program has been on the air regularly. The weekly Faith for Today television program is also being sponsored.

Northern Mariana Islands. In 1950 interested people on Saipan sent a request to the mission for a teacher. Guillermo Flores worked with R. E. Dunton in early evangelism in the Marianas, becoming the first regular SDA worker on Saipan. Two Quonsets were purchased for the first meeting hall and workers' home. Flores lived on Saipan during 1950-1951 and 1955-1956. For the next 20 years pastors from Guam churches visited the members on Saipan periodically, but there was little progress until a layperson, Robert Larsen, arrived to work for the U. S. Trust Territory government. A company was formed and a regular Sabbath school conducted. In 1970 the Guam SDA Clinic leased land and made plans to open a dental-medical clinic. The first dentist to work in the Trust Territories, Dr. Steven Fisher, arrived in January 1973. The dental clinic was successful from the first week. Sabbath services were then moved to the clinic building. In August 1974 the second resident pastor, George Wright, a ministerial intern, began working on Saipan.

Eastern Caroline Islands. On the island of Pohnpei lived a doctor and dentist who accepted

SDA beliefs and were baptized while attending school in Fiji. Land large enough for a house and church was found on Pohnpei in 1966. A house was constructed by Frank Taitague, who was appointed district pastor for the Eastern Carolines. For a cement block church to be built, sand had to be obtained from the bottom of the lagoon, the workers diving, filling baskets with sand, and loading it into boats. A church building seating 200 was finished and dedicated Oct. 12, 1968.

GUAM ADVENTIST ACADEMY. A K-12 day school operated by the Guam Micronesia Mission of Seventh-day Adventists. The academy is located 12 miles (20 kilometers) south of the capital city of Agana. GAA has a school population (1993) of 245 students: 190 in the elementary and 55 in the secondary level. The student body is a homogeneous mix of peoples from the Pacific islands, the Philippines, and the United States. GAA basically follows the Pacific Union curriculum, and all instruction is in English.

The forerunner of Guam Adventist Academy, and the first SDA school on Guam, was founded in the village of Dededo in 1949 by Robert E. Dunton, first president of the mission, and Ray Turner, who gathered materials from an Army dump and erected a two-room Quonset hut. Mrs. Maria Ulloa and Mrs. Magdalena Flores taught the 26 students that year.

In 1951 a second school was opened in the southern village of Talofofo in a purchased Quonset hut. In August 1953 the Dededo school moved to Agana Heights near the present site of the mission headquarters. In 1957 the Talofofo school merged with the Agana Heights school, which by then had added grades 11 and 12 to its curriculum.

In 1964 the school transferred to its current location in beautiful Windward Hills and the school name was changed from Far Eastern Island Mission Academy to Guam Mission Academy. In 1972 a new gymnasium was built. A new two-story classroom and chapel building was added in 1974, tripling the classroom space of the academy. In 1987 the students moved into four new classrooms added to the east side of the main facility. In 1980 the school's name became Guam Adventist Academy.

Principals: C. G. Oliver, 1954-1955; V. G. Barlett, 1955-1957; F. A. Crofoot, 1957-1959; R. R. Greve, 1959-1962; J. F. Bohner (acting), 1962-1963; R. R. Greve, 1963-1965; L. G. Sibley, 1965-1967; L. C. Hagele, 1967-1969; Virgil Easterdy, 1969-1972; P. J. Easton, 1972-1976; Gerhard Koehn, 1976-1978; Arthur Robinson, 1978-1981; David Gouge, 1981-1983; James Nick, 1984-1985; David Gillham, 1985-1989; Clyde Henderson, 1989-1991; Jerry N. Kiser, 1991-1993; Robert Stahlnecker, 1993- .

GUAM-MICRONESIA MISSION OF SEVENTH-DAY ADVENTISTS. *See* Far Eastern Division; Guam and Micronesia.

GUAM SEVENTH-DAY ADVENTIST CLINIC. A modern medical-dental clinic located near the business and tourist center of Guam on a 10-acre (four-hectare) site. The clinic has 10 physicians, four dentists, and three optometrists on its staff. It offers a full range of services, including family practice, obstetrics, gynecology, pediatrics, internal medicine, ophthalmology, surgery, preventive medicine, lab, X-ray, pharmacy, dentistry, and optometry, and sees about 90,000 patients annually. The clinic is owned and operated by the Guam-Micronesia Mission of Seventh-day Adventists.

History. In 1953 Dr. R. H. Barker was called to open the Guam Clinic. Because facilities were difficult to obtain, Dr. Barker worked full-time for the government hospital while he supervised construction of the first clinic building and getting it furnished and supplied. In 1956 Dr. L. A. Smart arrived and opened the clinic, which met considerable religious opposition, but after a few months was successful. A Dental Department was added in 1966. Dr. W. N. Young was the first dentist. The clinic grew and expanded until it took over the mission office next door. When there was no possibility of further expansion in the Agana Heights area, the clinic purchased a 10-acre (four-hectare) piece of land in Tamuning for future building.

In 1962 Typhoon Karen, with winds of 220 mph (350 kph), devastated the island of Guam, destroying 90 percent of all buildings. During the typhoon Dr. Walter Thompson, a clinic doctor, rushed to Guam Memorial Hospital to help patients and was the only physician to stay with them for the duration of the storm, even though the hospital employed staff physicians. At the height of the storm Dr. Thompson delivered a baby and led 30 mothers with babies from the hospital's fourth floor, which was being destroyed by the typhoon, to safety on the first floor. As a result of his efforts, no lives were lost and no one was injured. On Jan. 25, 1963, Dr. Thompson received a citation from the Seventh Guam Legislature commending him for his "courage, calmness, and fortitude" during the typhoon. Included in the resolution was an expression of gratitude to the Guam SDA Clinic for "providing low cost medical assistance to all in the territory needing the same, without regard for race, color, or creed, all of which is in the highest traditions of the American Missionary Movement."

In 1969 Merritt Crawford was called to build a new clinic. The dental section was completed and opened in 1971, and the medical section was completed the next year. The clinic was built in such a way that a small hospital could be added. Seeking to expand its medical missionary work to other islands of Micronesia, the Guam clinic opened a branch dental clinic in Saipan in January 1973 with Steve Fisher, D.D.S., as the director. Dr. Fisher served more than 16 years at the Saipan clinic developing it into a highly successful, fully equipped, modern dental facility.

On Mar. 29, 1978, the Guam clinic opened a second branch clinic by transferring Dr. and Mrs. Robert Baker to Palau. Dr. Baker, an optometrist, oversaw the construction of the clinic, which was initially to provide eye services only. In 1990 the Palau clinic was moved to a larger building donated by Mr. Roman Tmetuchl, a prominent SDA Palauan businessperson. The expanded clinic offered medical, dental, and eye services. Dr David Allen, an internist, was called to oversee its construction and serve as its first director.

In 1991 and 1992 the Guam clinic received requests from the governor and legislators of Chuuk to start a branch medical clinic in Moen, the most populous island of Chuuk state. Plans were laid to start a branch clinic in Chuuk in 1994.

Medical Directors: R. H. Barker, 1953-1956; L. A. Smart, 1956-1959; R. Gloor, 1959-1962; W. C. Thompson, 1962-1964; T. E. Gibson, 1964-1970; C. A. Renschler, 1970-1972; A. W. Olson, 1972-1976; J. S. Shank, 1976-1978; Y. P. Aoyagi, 1978-1982; E. B. Holm, 1982-1987; L. K. Hanson, 1987-1988; C. J. Rick, 1988-1991; S. W. Hildebrand, 1991-1992; B. A. Geslani, 1992- .

GUATEMALA. The most westerly of the Central American republics, bounded on the west and north by Mexico and on the east by Belize, Honduras, and El Salvador. The country is mountainous, the interior being crossed by elevated mountain ranges, with many active and inactive volcanoes. It contains some of the most fertile soil in America, and is primarily an agricultural country, with coffee being the principal export. Guatemala, situated in the tropics, presents a great diversity of climate, with three well-marked climatic zones: cold, temperate, and hot. Its area is 42,042 square miles (110,000 square kilometers). The population (1994) of 10.7 million is composed mainly of mestizos and Indians. Most of the inhabitants live in the highland regions, with small concentrations in the coastal lowlands.

Spanish is the official language, but it is unknown to thousands who speak one or another of the various Indian dialects. Roman Catholicism is the predominant religion, but freedom of worship is accorded to all.

Seventh-day Adventist Statistics. The territory of Guatemala constitutes the Guatemala Mission in the Central American Union Mission, which forms a part of the Inter-American Division.

Statistics (1993) for *Guatemala:* churches, 202; members, 53,727; church or elementary schools, 13; ordained ministers, 30; licensed ministers, 14. Mission headquarters are at 1-a, Calle 18-24, Zona 15, Vista Hermosa 2, Guatemala, Guatemala.

Institutions. Progreso Adventist Coeducational School.

Development of Seventh-day Adventist Work. E. L. Cardey and C. A. Nowlen began work in the city of Guatemala in 1908. They acquired an English language school and converted it into a missionary enterprise under the name Guatemala English School. The school had seven teachers, with whom they organized the first Sabbath school.

In 1913 J. B. Stuyvesant and his family arrived in Guatemala to direct the English school, which was disconnected from the mission the following year. When the Guatemala Mission was organized in 1913, he became its first president, serving until 1917. Under his leadership the work was begun in several towns adjacent to the capital.

E. W. Thurber arrived in Guatemala in October 1917 and assumed the presidency of the mission in January 1918. Under his administration the property where the former Guatemala Mission offices and the main church in the city of Guatemala are situated was acquired. According to the mission records, some of the first church members were: Abrahan Espinosa, José Angel López, María Anita de López, X. Molina, Julio

Molina, and Adrian Alcantara.

Fred Owen established the work in the city of Quezaltenango with a major evangelistic campaign, which resulted in another Sabbath school. From 1925 to 1927 the El Salvador Mission and the Guatemala Mission were both administered by one president, with headquarters in Guatemala. These fields were both part of the Aztec Union until 1926, at which time the Central American Union was organized. Orley Ford (who became director in 1931) extended the work to other departments of the country.

Evangelism among the Maya Quiche Indians was begun under the leadership of Moisés Tahay. A school was organized in 1948, known as the Centro Cultural Indigenista ("Indian Cultural Center"). As a result there are several Indian workers, with 12 churches, 14 organized groups, and many branch Sabbath schools among this large section of the Indian population.

The Asociacion Cultural de Guatemala ("Cultural Association of Guatemala"), established in 1948, is a legal association authorized by the government to hold denominational properties. The Seventh-day Adventist Church was first registered in Guatemala as an organization in 1956.

Medical work was begun in 1962 at a rural clinic known as Vista Hermosa, near San Cristobal, Totonicapán, established by Drs. Antonio Solares and Felícito Fernando especially for the treatment of rural communities. Later another rural clinic opened in Santa Ana, Momostenango.

The first colporteurs came in 1911. The first church and MV Society were organized in 1913, and the first Dorcas Welfare Society in 1931. In 1965 there were five elementary schools. Other phases of the work include radiobroadcasting, AY camps, Pathfinder Clubs, and active temperance programs.

GUATEMALA MISSION. *See* Guatemala; Inter-American Division.

GUENIN, JULES CESAR (1883-1965). Evangelist, teacher, author, and administrator. He was born in Switzerland and was baptized into the Seventh-day Adventist Church in 1898. Four years later he began work as a colporteur and also attended a Bible School conducted in Geneva. From 1904 to 1905 he attended the Latin Union School at Gland. Later he served as evangelist in France, director of the North Africa Mission, Algeria (1914-1919), principal of the Latin Union School at Îmes, France (1919-1920), director of the Portuguese Mission (1924-1925), teacher at the Séminaire Adventiste du Salève (1928-1931), president of the South France Conference (1938-1945), president of the Franco-Belgian Union (1945-1950), and president of the French-Swiss Conference (1950-1953). After retirement he looked after the interests of the Bible correspondence school and also taught at Séminaire Adventiste. He was married to Marguerite Jauvert in 1907. Throughout his life he was a regular contributor to the French language denominational periodicals. He also wrote textbooks on the Bible for use in seminary classes.

GUGEL, EMIL (1879-1958). Pioneer minister and leader in Germany. He began his missionary career as a literature evangelist in 1904 in the Rhineland, then from 1905 to 1911 served as traveling preacher in western Germany. In 1911 he was ordained to the ministry and soon afterward was elected president of the Württemberg Conference. Subsequently he was president of the German-Swiss Conference (1919-1925), and from 1925 to 1934, successively, of the South Bavarian Conference, Central European Union, and South German Union. In 1934 he became president of the German Inter-Union Association and from 1937 until his retirement in 1948 served as field secretary and secretary of the ministerial association of the Central European Division (Section I).

GUIDE (1953-   ; Oct. 7, 1953-Dec. 25, 1963, as *Junior Guide;* weekly; RH; 1994 circulation, 34,000; file in RH; indexed in the SDA Periodical Index, 1971-   ). A paper for readers aged 10 through 14. The first official action that led to the publishing of *Guide* was probably a meeting of the officers of the General Conference during the Autumn Council in 1951, from which came a recommendation to "give study to the adjusting of the content of our existing children's and youth's papers so as to provide a journal especially adapted to the junior age group."

On Apr. 9, 1952, during the spring meeting of the General Conference Committee, it was voted "that a journal be provided for junior youth" from 10 years to 15. On Oct. 20 it was voted that the Review and Herald should be the publisher, and on Nov. 20 it was voted to call Lawrence Maxwell from the Northern

California Conference to be the editor.

Through a contest announced in the pages of the *Youth's Instructor,* the title *Junior Guide* (submitted by 225 out of 1,600 entries) was adopted.

The first issue, dated Oct. 7, 1953, contained 16 pages. There were three stories, an editorial, an article on the MV Honor in stars, instructions on making a crystal radio set and a tight-line telephone, news of Pathfinder activities, and the junior Sabbath school lesson.

Beginning with volume 2 in January 1954, the number of pages was increased to 24, and the size was reduced. Further reductions were made Jan. 4, 1967, and July 4, 1973. The printing was in one color until January 1967, when a second color was added to each issue.

Beginning with the first issue of 1964, the name was changed to *Guide* and the earliteen Sabbath school lessons were added. A switch to offset printing and an increase to 32 pages were accomplished with the Mar. 18 issue.

Each issue uses several communication methods and styles of writing. These include true stories, parables and allegories, Christian humor, and truth-conveying fiction. Along with life-changing stories, young readers enjoy special columns that provide honest answers to tough questions today's juniors are asking, encourage readers to react from a biblical perspective to current events, give problem-solving advice from Christian counselors, and help readers find their way through the Bible. The first issue of each month is specially crafted for sharing with a friend who may not know Jesus. Twice a year the entire issue is a cover-to-cover story that invites the reader to choose Jesus as Saviour and Friend.

Editors: Lawrence Maxwell, 1953-1970; Lowell Litten, 1970-1983; Penny Estes Wheeler, 1983-1986; Jeannette Johnson, 1986-1994; Carolyn Rathbun, 1995- .

GUILD, CECIL BENNETT (1908-1974). Missionary, treasurer, administrator. The son of a Seventh-day Adventist minister, he was born in Michigan and studied at Cedar Lake Academy and Emmanuel Missionary College. After graduating in 1931, he married Nora Dunn, and the following year they sailed for China. After three years of language study, Guild was appointed manager of the West China Training Institute. The following year he became director of the West Szechwan Mission. During this period of leadership, 1938, he was ordained to the ministry.

When China was invaded during World War II, Guild was director of the Honan Mission. The family evacuated to Chungking, where he carried on evangelistic work. Later he was made superintendent of West China Union Mission. In 1949, while he was serving the Voice of Prophecy work in China, the Communists encircled Shanghai. The Guilds then joined the Southern Asia Division, where he took up the presidency of the Western India Union until 1952, when he became president of the Burma Union. In 1962 he was appointed treasurer of the Southern Asia Division, and in 1966 he became secretary of the division.

GUIMARAES, RUTH OBERG (1912-1975). Educator. She attended Brazil College in São Paulo, Brazil, graduating in 1933 with a degree in teaching and in theology. In 1938 she married Jose Guimaraes, who also taught at the college. Mrs. Guimaraes taught at all levels at Brazil College in a variety of disciplines. She composed the college hymn and translated hymns for the school's Carlos Gomes choir.

GUINEA. A republic on the west coast of Africa, independent since 1958, bounded by Guinea-Bissau, Senegal, and Mali on the north, by Côte d'Ivoire on the east, and by Liberia and Sierra Leone on the south. The capital is Conakry. It has an area about 95,000 square miles (250,000 square kilometers), and a population (1994) of 6.4 million, mainly Blacks. Eighty-five percent are Muslims; 8 percent are Christians.

Seventh-day Adventist Statistics. The territory of Guinea constitutes the Guinea Mission Station, part of the Sahel Union Mission, which in turn is part of the Africa-Indian Ocean Division. Statistics (1992): churches, 1; companies, 8; members, 300; licensed ministers, 2. Headquarters are in Conakry.

Development of Seventh-day Adventist Work. In 1987 and 1988 a lay SDA couple from Europe quietly witnessed to their faith. In April 1992 the first war refugees from Liberia arrived in Guinea, including a number of Seventh-day Adventists and a licensed pastor, W. Oloysius. They soon began witnessing for their faith. ADRA/Guinea is the most important nongovernment organization in the country. The work is being strengthened further by workers from Adventist Frontier Missions, who are learning the Mandingo language.

GUINEA-BISSAU. A former Portuguese

colony that became independent in September 1974. Lying on the extreme west coast of Africa, it has an area of 13,948 square miles (36,300 square kilometers), with a population (1994) of 1.1 million. The capital is Bissau. The principal occupation of the people is agriculture, with rice, palm oil, peanuts, coconuts, and timber the chief exports.

Seventh-day Adventist Statistics. The territory of Guinea-Bissau constitutes the Guinea-Bissau Mission, part of the territory of the Sahel Union Mission, which is a part of the Africa-Indian Ocean Division. Statistics (1992): churches, 1; members, 145; ordained ministers, 1; licensed ministers, 2. Headquarters are in Bissau.

Development of Seventh-day Adventist Work. In 1963 there were only two adherents to the SDA faith in the country—a woman and her niece. Without knowing of the existence of the Seventh-day Adventist Church, the aunt had begun to keep the Sabbath in 1955, after reading a borrowed book, *A Nossa Epoca e o Destino do Mundo,* a translation of *Our Day in the Light of Prophecy,* by W. A. Spicer. Without doubt one of the colporteurs from Portugal, who have periodically worked in Guinea-Bissau, placed that book. Later the director of the Cape Verde Mission made plans to send a missionary. In November 1955 G. S. Rosa brought his family to Bissau, the capital, hoping to work as a traveling salesperson and to begin missionary work. His request for residence was refused on the grounds that there were not a sufficient number of adherents to his religion to warrant admission. In 1973 a missionary, Francisco Cordas, was sent from Portugal with his family. At the beginning of 1974 a church of 15 members was organized in Bissau. Guinea-Bissau was organized as a mission in 1985.

GUINEA-BISSAU MISSION. *See* Africa-Indian Ocean Division; Guinea-Bissau.

GUINEA MISSION STATION. *See* Africa-Indian Ocean Division; Guinea.

GUJARAT REGION. *See* India; Southern Asia Division.

GULF SECTION. *See* Bahrain; Kuwait; Middle East Union Mission; Oman; United Arab Emirates.

GULF STATES CONFERENCE. A unit of church organization comprising the territory of Alabama, Mississippi, and the following 10 counties of northwestern Florida, west of the Apalachicola River: Bay, Calhoun, Escambia, Gulf, Holmes, Jackson, Okaloosa, Santa Rosa, Walton, and Washington. *(See also* South Central Conference.) Statistics (1993): churches, 68; members, 7,040; church schools, 18; ordained ministers, 31; licensed ministers, 9; church school teachers, 32. Headquarters: 6450 Atlanta Highway, Montgomery, Alabama. The conference forms part of the Southern Union Conference.

Institutions. Bass Memorial Academy. (Oakwood Academy and Oakwood College, at Huntsville, Alabama, are listed under the South Central Conference.)

Local churches—*Alabama:* Andalusia, Anniston, Athens, Birmingham (First, Roebuck), Clanton, Decatur, Dothan, Eufaula, Fairhope, Floral Crest, Florence, Fort Payne, Gadsden, Gilbertown, Guntersville, Hanceville, Hueytown, Huntsville, Jackson, Mobile (Bearfork Road, First), Montgomery, Opelika-Auburn, Ownbey Chapel, Pell City, Phenix City, Phil Campbell, Selma, St. Elmo, Sylacauga, Troy, Tuscaloosa, Uchee Pines; *Florida:* Bonifay, Crestview, DeFuniak Springs, Fort Walton Beach, Marianna, Milton, Panama City, Pensacola; *Mississippi:* Bass Memorial, Brookhaven, Columbia, Columbus, Corinth, Florence, Greenville, Gulfport, Hattiesburg, Jackson, Laurel, McComb, Meridian, Natchez, Olive Branch, Pascagoula, Pine Forest, Quitman, Southaven, Tupelo, Vicksburg, Water Valley.

Companies—*Alabama:* Scottsboro, Valley; *Mississippi:* Greenwoods, Newton.

History. *Beginnings in Alabama.* Seventh-day Adventist evangelism in Alabama was begun by Jesse Morgan Elliott (sometimes spelled Ellett), a Southern Unionist who had fought in the Federal army and had been discharged when he lost his eyesight. Having embraced the SDA faith while in the North, and having returned to his home in Alabama after the war, he went about teaching his new beliefs. He awakened a great interest among the people and gathered groups of converts. A call for an SDA minister sent in May 1873 to E. B. Lane, an evangelist in Edgefield Junction, near Nashville, Tennessee, remained unanswered for several years for lack of someone to send. In 1876 D. M. Canright briefly visited Alabama. By 1878, when A. O. Burrill and his wife came to Bladon (Bladen) Springs, there were already 50 or 60 converts in the state of Alabama, nearly all the fruit of Elliott's work. Burrill organized a church at Bladon Springs and held evangelistic meetings. Then early in 1880 C. O. Taylor spent three weeks there. In December 1880, J. O. Corliss, who had been sent to visit the churches in the South, ordained J. M. Elliott to the ministry and licensed J. R. Waite to preach. Interest was further developed in this area through personal work, Bible studies, the colporteur work, and through copies of the *Review* sent from the North and West.

As early as 1885 Peter H. Clark established himself in the Gulf City Hotel in Mobile, Alabama, opened a reading room, and carried on personal evangelism through distributing publications. In 1894 the second SDA church in Alabama was organized in Montgomery. In Birmingham a mission established in February 1887 by S. S. Smith and C. W. Olds was succeeded by a church organized in 1898. Early evangelists used schools, halls, and private homes for meeting places. In 1896 a school was opened in Huntsville for Black young people; it later became Oakwood College.

Alabama Conference Organized. The Alabama Conference was organized in 1901, covering that state; by 1908 the territory included also seven counties in western Florida: Calhoun, Escambia, Holmes, Jackson, Santa Rosa, Walton, Washington; in the 1920s two more were added (Bay and Okaloosa). The first officers of the conference were: president, W. L. McNeely; secretary, A. C. Bird; treasurer, C. E. Giles; secretary of education, W. L. Bird; state (canvassing) agent, C. J. Dart. There were four ministers and two licentiates. The Alabama Conference continued until 1932, when the Alabama-Mississippi Conference was formed. Alabama headquarters were variously in Selma, Birmingham, Fort Payne, and Clanton.

Beginnings in Mississippi. SDAs were found in Mississippi as early as the beginning of 1880. One was Peter H. Clark, in Jackson County, who had heard the SDA message in Texas at least two years earlier and whom C. O. Taylor urged to preach. J. M. Elliott, of Alabama, preached at Otho, Jasper County, in 1880, where C. O. Taylor baptized seven in 1881. Taylor preached also at Ellisville, in Jones County. In 1885 R. B. Hewitt held a series of meetings at Beauregard, gathering a company of 15 believers, and organizing a Sabbath school. There was a church in Hatley in 1898, and groups of adherents met also at Amory, Tupelo, and Burnsville.

Around the turn of the century J. E. White and a group of workers, including W. O. Palmer and Fred Rogers, operated the river steamer *Morning Star* (built in 1894 by White in Allegan, Michigan) on the Mississippi from its base at Vicksburg, Mississippi, and later on the Cumberland, from its new base at Nashville, Tennessee, as a private mission enterprise and worked for the Black people. (For the beginnings of the Black work in Mississippi *see* South Central Conference; Southern Missionary Society.)

Work among the White people of Vicksburg was begun in November 1902 by F. R. Rogers, who had come to Mississippi to superintend the Black schools conducted by J. E. White's Southern Missionary Society. There was much prejudice, but Rogers and his wife showed themselves friendly to their White neighbors, especially to the children, and opened a small school. At first their son Chester was the only pupil, but interest increased and the school began to grow. A Sunday school was also begun, which drew 40 to 50 adults and children. In a short time Rogers had gained 11 adult converts, with five children. Later 10 miles (16 kilometers) in the country he held meetings under the trees and aroused much interest. To aid him in his evangelism he sold or gave away, besides books, many copies of *Signs of the Times, Our Little Friend, Life Boat,* and *Good Health.* His work resulted in the organization of several home Sabbath schools.

Mississippi Conference Organized. The Mississippi Conference was organized at the camp meeting held at Hatley, July 26 to Aug. 4, 1901, with R. M. Kilgore presiding. In that year there were three churches, five companies, and 182 members. A constitution was adopted, and Rodney S. Owen was elected conference president; W. J. Blake, secretary-treasurer; F. R. Rogers, Sabbath school secretary and superintendent of schools; and H. W. Pierce, state (canvassing) agent. Owen and Pierce were the only ordained ministers. An Ellisville-Laurel church was organized in 1904. A charter member reports that the Hattiesburg church stems from a company formed in 1905 with 21 members, which was organized as a church in 1914.

The first SDA church in Jackson, the state capital, was organized in 1912 with 13 charter members. More members were added the same year as the result of evangelistic meetings conducted in the conference office building by

C. S. Wiest, the incoming conference president. (Until 1917 the conference president served also as pastor of the Jackson church.) At the end of 1912 the Mississippi Conference had six churches and 159 members.

Louisiana-Mississippi Conference. From 1920 to 1932 the Mississippi and Louisiana conferences were united as the Louisiana-Mississippi Conference, with the headquarters for the new conference remaining at Jackson, Mississippi. The first president of this combined conference was William Randolph Elliott, son of Jesse M. Elliott, the pioneer evangelist of Alabama and Mississippi. (For Louisiana, *see* Arkansas-Louisiana Conference.)

Alabama-Mississippi Conference Organized. In 1932, when the Louisiana section was transferred to the Southwestern Union Conference, the states of Alabama and Mississippi were united into one conference, retaining the nine counties of northwest Florida, which had previously made up a part of the Alabama Conference, and adding Gulf County. R. I. Keate became the first president of the newly organized Alabama-Mississippi Conference. Shortly after the organization the headquarters were moved from Jackson to Meridian, Mississippi. In 1946 the Black constituency of Alabama-Mississippi Conference separated to become part of the South Central Conference.

Many of the churches organized in the Alabama-Mississippi Conference in recent years were the result of evangelistic campaigns conducted by district pastors. From 1955 through 1962 the conference membership increased about 40 percent; 21 new church organizations were added, and about as many new church buildings. During this same period a $2 million school, Bass Memorial Academy (opened in September 1961), was built in southern Mississippi as a result of a gift from I. H. Bass of Lumberton.

The years 1963 to 1975 were years of both consolidation and continued growth. During this period 22 congregations acquired new church plants. Eight new churches were organized. The million-dollar mark in tithe was first reached in 1972, and in 1973 total conference membership passed the 5,000 mark.

In 1968 the conference acquired a 60-acre (25-hectare) peninsula on Lake Martin, near Dadeville, Alabama, and proceeded to develop Camp Alamisco. Buildings constructed included: lodge with family rooms, dining hall, and chapel; five camper and staff cabins; a headquarters-gymnasium complex; and various storage buildings. There are housing accommodations for the camp ranger.

The conference headquarters was moved from Meridian, Mississippi, to Montgomery, Alabama, in 1973, after careful study indicated the entire territory could best be served from the new location. Building of a new office, prominently located on a suburban five-acre (two-hectare) lot seven miles (11 kilometers) east of downtown Montgomery, was begun in the fall of 1974. The $300,000 plant was completed in the spring of 1975.

Gulf States Conference. In 1984 the constituency voted to rename the conference in order that Florida constituents would also be included in the name.

Presidents—Alabama Conference: W. L. McNeely, 1901-1905; A. J. Haysmer, 1906-1909; J. R. Bagby, 1910; E. G. Hayes, 1911-1912; A. L. Miller, 1912-1918; J. F. Wright, 1918-1921; S. G. Haughey, 1921-1922; C. B. Stephenson, 1922-1927; A. B. Russell, 1927-1931; N. S. Ashton, 1931-1932. *Mississippi Conference:* Rodney S. Owen, 1901-1903; H. G. Thurston, 1904-1905; F. R. Shaeffer, 1906-1907; W. S. Lowry, 1909-1912; C. S. Wiest, 1912-1916; C. J. Buhalts, 1916-1919; W. R. Elliott, 1919-1920. *Louisiana-Mississippi Conference:* W. R. Elliott, 1920-1926; F. H. DeVinney, 1926-1932. *Alabama-Mississippi Conference:* R. I. Keate, 1932-1937; H. W. Walker, 1937-1941; H. J. Capman, 1941-1949; I. M. Evans, 1949-1954; L. J. Leiske, 1954-1962; Wallace O. Coe, 1962-1965; W. D. Wampler, 1965-1981; W. A. Geary, 1981-1984. *Gulf States Conference:* W. A. Geary, 1984-1985; R. R. Hallock, 1985-1992; J. O. Greek, 1992- .

GUTZEIT, ELZA (1900-1982). Educator, pioneer missionary. After graduating from Brazil College with a degree in education, she left with her husband for Barnunal Island, where they opened a mission compound for the Indians of the Carajá tribe. She also served as dean of women and the first teacher at Espírito Santo Academy.

In 1950, after her husband's death, she moved to the Trans-Amazon area, where she helped to establish the Agro-Industrial Adventist Trans-Amazon Academy. When nearly 80 years old, she continued to teach Bible and English. After her retirement in 1980, she led 23 neighbors to baptism during an evangelistic effort.

GUYANA. The only English-speaking co-operative republic in the world; formerly British Guiana. Having gained its independence from Great Britain on May 26, 1966, Guyana became a cooperative republic on Feb. 23, 1969. Guyana is situated on the northeast coast of South America on the Atlantic Ocean, between Suriname on the east, and Venezuela on the west. Brazil is on the south and west. It covers an area of 83,000 square miles (215,000 square kilometers), and has a population (1994) of 730,000, composed of Indians (of India heritage), Blacks, and those of mixed race. Most of the people live along the coast. The chief products of the country are sugar, rice, bauxite, timber, gold, and diamonds. The area was occupied by the Dutch in the seventeenth century, but in 1814 three colonies, Berbice, Essequibo, and Demerara, came under British administration. In 1831 they were joined into a single colony and called British Guiana, which is the only English-speaking country on the mainland of South America.

Christianity was brought to the country in the early days of settlement, but the slaves learned little of it until the eighteenth century, when Moravian missionaries became active in the area. During the nineteenth century thousands were brought from India to work on the sugar plantations, and thus Hinduism and Islam both have a large number of adherents.

Seventh-day Adventist Statistics. The territory of Guyana constitutes the Guyana Conference, part of the Caribbean Union Conference, which in turn is part of the Inter-American Division. Statistics (1992) for *Guyana:* churches, 105; companies, 30; members, 28,492; ordained ministers, 13; licensed ministers, 17. Headquarters: Georgetown, Guyana.

Institutions. Davis Memorial Clinic and Hospital.

Development of Seventh-day Adventist Work. *Beginnings.* Seventh-day Adventist teachings reached British Guiana in 1883, making it the first country on the continent of South America to receive the SDA message. According to early accounts, W. J. Boynton, a worker at the International Tract Society office in New York, in that year gave a bundle of SDA papers to the captain of a ship bound for Georgetown, requesting him to distribute them when he arrived there. On reaching the port, the captain scattered them on the wharf, saying, "I have fulfilled my promise." A man standing by gathered some of the papers, read them, and lent them to his neighbors. Soon there was a group keeping the seventh-day Sabbath.

The new converts corresponded with the International Tract Society and a colporteur was found who proceeded to British Guiana and distributed SDA publications sent to him. Presumably this colporteur was T. E. Amsterdam, a recent convert, who in 1886 reported having held Sabbath services and weekday public meetings for Bible study in several places, and having organized the South American Tract Society, with branches in several communities.

In 1887 the General Conference responded to requests from British Guiana by sending a minister, G. G. Rupert. During his stay of three or four months he baptized 30 persons and organized the first Seventh-day Adventist church and Sabbath school in Georgetown. George King, an early SDA colporteur, accompanied Rupert and sold about $800 worth of books. In 1891 another of the pioneer SDA colporteurs, William Arnold, canvassed the territory. In 1892 L. C. Chadwick visited the country for 22 days, during which he encouraged the members and baptized 24 persons. When he left, the members in British Guiana numbered 41. The first resident minister, W. G. Kneeland, arrived at Georgetown late in December 1893. Two years later, in 1895, he organized another church at Bootooba, situated about 90 miles (145 kilometers) from Georgetown.

In 1895 Philip Giddings, who had been among the first converts in British Guiana, returned from training at Battle Creek College and became the first national evangelist. At the same time, an attempt was made to open medical work, but it was unsuccessful because of the lack of a physician with British certification.

Responding to a plea for a missionary, O. E. Davis, superintendent of the mission, who had been in British Guiana since 1906, in 1910 pioneered the work among the Indians in the interior. In 1911 he reached Mount Roraima on the British Guiana-Venezuela-Brazil border and attempted to establish a mission there, but weakened by repeated attacks of malaria, he died after having made some converts. About 1925 C. B. Sutton and W. E. Baxter were sent to search out these Indians. They found them still singing "Jesus knows all about our struggles" and other hymns that Davis had taught them. In 1927 A. W. Cott established work there. Because of Davis's work among them, these Indians, belonging chiefly to the Akawaio (or Accawai) and Arecuna tribes, are known among SDAs as the "Davis" Indians. In 1929 or 1930 Joseph Gonsalves and A. W. Cott and his wife reported meeting with Indians in the same area who had known about the seventh-day Sabbath, clean foods, and temperate living as a result of a vision seen by their chief some years before Davis's trip. Many of the Mount Roraima Indians were baptized after 1930 and a mission school was later established in the area.

Educational Work. In 1907, the year following the organization of the British Guiana Conference, the *Statistical Report* listed two small schools. The next year it listed three. According to the account given by Wesley Amundsen in his book *The Advent Message in Inter-America,* about 1909 two schools were operated in the suburbs of Georgetown especially for the children of India heritage and a third, situated up the Essequibo River, was taught by Johannah H. Daw, later Mrs. E. E. Parchment. He related that there were no regular budgets for the educational work, and that it was supported by contributions from people concerned with Christian education. For example, for more than seven years the school on the Essequibo River was supported by an SDA layperson in North America. A school established at Bootooba on the Demerara River some years later was in 1963 the oldest continuously operating school in the mission. The government no longer allows private schools.

Medical Work. In 1908 R. N. Graves, a national of British Guiana, returned home with a British medical diploma and practiced for some time. After an interval the work was reestablished in 1952. E. C. Duerksen, a physician, arrived in 1954 to take charge of the medical work, and was joined in 1955 by Oliver J. Pogue, also a physician. In July 1955 the Davis Memorial Clinic and Hospital in Georgetown began taking in patients.

Development of Organization. The British Guiana Mission began in 1894 with the arrival of the resident minister. The first step in formal organization was taken late in 1897, when the mission work in the Caribbean area was coordinated as the West Indian Mission Field, with A. J. Haysmer as superintendent. In 1903 the East Caribbean Conference, including British Guiana, was organized. A further step was taken in 1906 when the West Indian Union Conference was formed and British Guiana became one of its five organized conferences. Sometime later the territory was linked with the South Caribbean Conference. In 1924 the three Guianas—British, Dutch, and French—became one mission, with D. C. Babcock as superintendent. They were organized into the Guiana Conference in 1926. In January 1945 the Guianas were divided into three separate fields, the territory of British Guiana becoming the British Guiana Mission, under the Caribbean Union Mission.

GUYANA CONFERENCE. *See* Guyana; Inter-American Division.

H

HAAD YAI MISSION HOSPITAL. A general hospital with a capacity of 30 beds and eight bassinets, formerly operated by the Southeast Asia Union at Haad Yai, a town on the Bangkok-Singapore railway line, about 20 miles (30 kilometers) southwest of Songkhla, in the southern part of Thailand, near the Malaysian border.

Seventh-day Adventist work in Haad Yai was begun by Ronald C. Gregory, M.D., who on Oct. 5, 1949, opened a medical clinic in a small rented hotel, where he and his family lived. Beginning as a branch of the Bangkok Sanitarium and Hospital, the clinic grew rapidly, and plans were soon drawn to build a hospital. In 1953 the foundation for a 20-bed brick hospital building was laid on a two-acre (.8-hectare) plot of land donated by Chee Kim Joong, and on July 1, 1954, Haad Yai Mission Hospital opened its doors.

In 1959 a wing was added to the building, making a 30-bed hospital, including outpatient facilities. In 1971 a clinic was opened in downtown Haad Yai, where all outpatients were treated.

In addition to the workers' living quarters built on the donated land, a modest chapel with a seating capacity of 100 was built in 1956. When the hospital was established, it was the only such institution in town. By the early 1980s it faced keen competition from seven other hospitals, including a large teaching facility in Haad Yai. As a result, it incurred heavy operating losses for several years.

In October 1985 it was decided that Haad Yai should operate as a satellite of Bangkok Adventist Hospital for a trial period of two years. In February 1986 the Bangkok facility took over control of the smaller hospital. A three-story building was purchased and renovated for use as a city clinic, which opened for business on Apr. 22, 1986. Because of a lack of administration staff and physicians, Bangkok Adventist Hospital turned the operation of Haad Yai back to the Southeast Asia Union Mission on Aug. 1, 1987. Because of a lack of funds and personnel, the hospital closed its doors on Feb. 15, 1988.

Medical Directors: R. C. Gregory, 1949-1954; Byron Eller, 1954-1955; R. C. Gregory, 1955-1964; Frank Crider, 1964-1967; James C. Jay, 1967-1968; R. C. Van Arsdell, 1968-1973; R. C. Gregory, 1973-1976; A. L. Elumir, 1976-1978; W. V. Donato, 1979-1982; R. E. Bartolome, 1982-1986; C. Kootanasan, 1986-1987; Henry Martono (acting), 1987-1988.

HABENICHT, HERALD AMBROSE (1906-1974). Teacher and administrator. A native of Argentina, he graduated from Emmanuel Missionary College and the University of Michigan. After serving on the faculties of Indiana and Shenandoah Valley academies, he became director of Montemorelos College in Mexico. Later he served in the same capacity at the Central American Vocational College in Costa Rica.

Returning to the United States, he joined the faculty of Adelphian Academy and later was called to a position on the La Sierra College faculty.

HABENICHT, ROBERT H. (1866-1925). Physician, missionary. Educated at Battle Creek College, he entered the ministry in Iowa in 1888. From 1893 to 1898 he spent the summers in ministerial work and the winters in taking the medical course at Iowa State University. After his graduation he was appointed director of the Iowa Sanitarium (1899). From 1901 to 1922 he engaged in ministerial and medical work in Argentina and founded the River Plate Sanitarium in 1908. After a period in the United States, although feeble in health, he later returned to Brazil with the hope of continuing his work, but died shortly after arriving in São Paulo.

HACKETT, WILLIS J. (1915-1993). Pastor, evangelist, missionary, administrator. Born in Mullen, Nebraska, he attended Union College, graduating in 1939 with a degree in theology. He met his wife Margaret at Boulder Sanitarium, and they were married in 1937. Two sons were born of this union. The first 19 years of his ministry were spent in pastoral, evangelistic, and departmental work in the United States. In 1952 he was called to the Far East, where he served in the division and as president of the North Philippine Union.

In 1958 the family returned to the United States, where Willis served as president of Atlantic and Pacific union conferences. He became a vice president of the General Conference in 1968, in which position he served until retirement in 1980. Part of his duties consisted of serving on and chairing many boards, including the Loma Linda University and Andrews University boards.

After his wife's death in 1987, he married Thelma Trude. They lived and served in the Northwest until Willis's sudden death in 1993.

HACKETTSTOWN COMMUNITY HOSPITAL. A fully accredited, 106-bed acute health-care facility set amid the rolling hills of northwestern New Jersey, about one hour west of New York City.

Hackettstown Community Hospital came about as the result of a dream that started in the 1940s. As the years passed, an entire community purposed to work together to make that dream a reality.

The going was not easy. Financial roadblocks seemed almost insurmountable following a long period of frustration during which changing hospital regulations caused plans to be drawn and redrawn, and costs to go higher and still higher. Providence intervened in 1967 during an Ingathering visit between two Seventh-day Adventist ministers and a Hackettstown banker. The discussion turned to the worldwide chain of SDA-operated hospitals. The arrival on the scene of one of the proposed hospital's board members prompted the banker to suggest that the SDA Church build a hospital in Hackettstown. Subsequent discussions and events led the hospital board, unable to see their way around funding difficulties, to invite the Columbia Union Conference to assume ownership, control, and management of the hospital-to-be.

The Seventh-day Adventists and the community then took on the task of financing and building the hospital together as a team—individuals, families, small businesses, large corporations, foundations, service clubs, and government and SDA Church representatives. Through pledges, grants, fund drives, the "Bucket Brigade," and other sources, amounts large and small poured in. Ultimately, thanks to God's providence and the vision and dedication of many people, the hospital opened its doors in February 1973.

Small yet innovative, Hackettstown Community Hospital offers services and technology available at much larger hospitals, while offering a dimension of caring and personal attention these might find difficult to offer.

The range of services includes traditional and laser surgery, 24-hour emergency care, approved cancer care, new operating/recovery area, new intensive care/coronary care and intermediate telemetry units, same-day surgery program, family-centered maternity care, laboratory/pathology area, Radiology Department featuring CT scanner, nuclear medicine and approved mammography program, physical therapy and other rehabilitative services, substance abuse services, sleep disorder program, pain management center, and more.

True to its SDA heritage, Hackettstown Community Hospital goes to great lengths to instill in people an attitude of illness prevention so they'll never have to come to the hospital to get well. This they accomplish through educational programs offered through the year to residents, local corporations, schools, and community groups. Strong efforts are also put forth through a variety of screenings to help identify health problems before they become life-threatening. While it is true that every department at Hackettstown Community Hospital has as its ultimate mission the salvation of patients, its Pastoral Care Department officially carries forward the spiritual component of the healing process. Among the ongoing activities and projects are an active literature distribution program, the ministry of a staff singing group that cheers patients daily, grief recovery programs, 24-hour SDA television programming, and daily staff worships.

Hackettstown Community Hospital is committed to joining other SDA health-care institutions in assisting Christ as He continues His ministry of healing sick bodies, minds, and souls.

Hackettstown Community Hospital is part of Adventist Healthcare Mid-Atlantic Corporation.

Administrators: Charley O. Eldridge, 1973-1975; Henry Scoggins, 1975-1985; Gene C. Milton, 1985- .

HACKMAN, EARL FREDRICK (1898-1951). Conference administrator, home missionary leader. Upon graduation from the Mount Vernon Academy in 1918, he entered home missionary work, first as an assistant secretary and later as secretary of the department in the Ohio Conference (1919-1920). Still later he served as home missionary secretary of the Southeastern Union (1920-1924) and as assistant and associate home missionary secretary of the General Conference (1924-1934). After that he served as president of the Southeastern California Conference (1934-1940), the Northern California Conference (1940-1943), the Southern Union (1943-1947), and the Inter-American Division (1947-1950).

HADLEY MEMORIAL HOSPITAL. A former nonprofit 80-bed general hospital incorporated, owned, and operated by the Columbia Union Conference of Seventh-day Adventists, situated on a hill overlooking the Potomac River at 4601 Martin Luther King, Jr., Avenue SW., Washington, D.C. It was accredited by the Joint Commission on Accreditation of Hospitals and was a member of the American Hospital Association. It received patients from far and near, regardless of race, creed, color, national origin, or sex, ranging from the diplomatic to the indigent.

The hospital grew out of the work of the Washington Sanitarium Mission Hospital (commonly called "the clinic"), which opened in 1914 under the direction of Dr. L. E. Elliott in the historic Thomas Law house at 1252 Sixth Street SW. The clinic was operated by the Washington Sanitarium (now Washington

Adventist Hospital), and in the beginning, also, the Foreign Missionary Seminary (now Columbia Union College). Its purpose was to minister to the indigent and to serve as a training center for postgraduate nurses and foreign mission appointees.

Dr. Henry G. Hadley and his wife were placed in charge of the work in 1919. In 1923 the Hadleys purchased the building, built up a self-supporting work, and in the spring of 1930, gave the property to the General Conference. Again from 1933 until it closed in 1961, Dr. Hadley carried on the clinic and in connection with it an active research program in the immunization field.

In 1945 Dr. Hadley purchased six acres (2.5 hectares) on Nichols Avenue SW. in the name of the General Conference. On it he erected Hadley Memorial Hospital, a three-story brick structure, completely air-conditioned, with all the modern facilities of a general hospital. It was opened on July 29, 1952, with the transfer of seven patients from the old clinic (which continued separately until 1961), and was dedicated free of debt in 1955. All the money needed for this new institution, except about 1 percent given by friends, was raised from the earnings of the Sixth Street clinic, which had a large paying clientele in addition to the indigent patients. In 1952 the ownership of the property was transferred to the Potomac Conference and in 1957 to the Columbia Union Conference.

In 1992 the hospital was sold to a nondenominational group.

Administrators: H. G. Hadley, 1952-1962; Harvey A. Rudisaile, 1962-1967; C. O. Eldridge, 1967-1969; James Suzuki, 1969-1985; Albert L. Dudley, 1986-1992.

HAFFNER, GOTTFRIED F. (1867-1920). Minister. He was born in Tscherbakowski, Russia, and at the age of 9 came with his parents to the United States and settled in Lehigh, Kansas, where he accepted the Seventh-day Adventist faith. After spending three years in Battle Creek College and one year in the Bible Institute in Milwaukee, Wisconsin, he began preaching in the Missouri Conference in 1889. Shortly thereafter he went to the Oregon Conference and worked among the German-speaking people. After about two years he was transferred to the Washington Conference, where he worked for eight years, establishing a number of German churches. About 1899 he was transferred to the Oklahoma Conference, where after one year in pastoral and evangelistic work he was elected president of the conference, which position he held from 1902 to 1905. Until 1917, when failing health led to his resignation, he was leader of the German work in North America.

HAHN, FRANKLIN B. (1809-1866). Physician of Canandaigua, New York, president of the village corporation, and secretary of the Ontario County Medical Society, and a Millerite. As a good Bible student he joined Crosier and Edson in intensive study of the sanctuary doctrine in the winter of 1844-1845. It was at his house that Crosier wrote out their joint findings on the subject.

Hahn published the *Day-Dawn* (which Crosier edited) in 1845, and in 1846, with Edson, financed the *Day-Star Extra* containing Crosier's article. He accepted the Sabbath with Edson, but by 1851 he had apparently reverted to the Sundaykeeping majority.

HAHNKOOK ACADEMY (Hahnkook Sahmyook Joongkodeung Hakkyo) (Korean College Academy). A coeducational boarding and day school on the junior and senior high school levels, located on the Korean Sahmyook University campus, Seoul, Korea. Owing to disruptions of World War II, the secondary school in Seoul, which had opened in 1938, was closed. It was reopened in the fall of 1947, with 113 students. In 1949 the school secured 210 acres (85 hectares) of land from the Yee Dynasty Estates and moved to its present location.

During the Korean War four students were killed and four others were captured by the North Koreans, and the school was transferred to Cheju Island. At the end of 1952 the school was reopened in Seoul.

The school received the title of "Outstanding Academy" from the provincial government for its ideal environment and high quality of education. In 1980 the main school building was constructed, an auditorium followed in 1986, a new school building in 1991, and a language lab in 1992. There are 60 faculty members and 1,350 students.

Principals: Lee Sung Euy, 1938-1941; Kwak Pyung Soo, 1941-1943; James M. Lee, 1947-1953; Chung Dong Shim, 1953-1954; D. S. Lee, 1954-1959; Kim Yung Do, 1959-1965; Lee Kyung Il, 1965-1970; Kwon Hyuk Chong, 1970-1972; Kim Yung Do, 1972-1975; Kim Joon Pal, 1975; Kim Jae Shin, 1975-1976; Kim Hong Ryang, 1976-1978; Lee Seong

Chin, 1978-1984; Lim Choon Taek, 1984-1990; Kim Hyo Seong, 1990- .

HAILE SELASSIE I HOSPITAL. A 46-bed hospital operated for 41 years by the Ethiopian Union Mission in Debre Tabor, Ethiopia. Debre Tabor is situated 9,000 feet (2,750 meters) above sea level in Begemder Province, about 50 miles (80 kilometers) east of Lake Tana, the source of the Blue Nile. Many of its 7,000 inhabitants are very poor.

The task of establishing a mission station and hospital at Debre Tabor was assigned to G. Gudmundsen, a veteran missionary from Norway. His assignment was difficult: the terrain was mountainous, and there were no roads. All iron sheets for the roof and some other materials had to be transported on mules from Addis Ababa, a six-week round trip. The hospital was finished in 1934. The main building was a stone structure having seven rooms on each side of a center corridor. Emperor Haile Selassie I gave the project his name and 30,000 silver dollars (about US$20,000).

Upon completion of the hospital building, Erik Palm, a pioneer Seventh-day Adventist missionary in Ethiopia, began clinic work, which was interrupted, however, by the Italian war. After the war much work had to be done to restore the building, such as installing new doors and windows. At the same time the floors were set with cement and tile.

Regular hospital work began in 1947, when Roland Nielsen, M.D., from Denmark, became the first physician to direct the institution. The local people showed increasing confidence in the hospital. In 1973 the number of outpatients treated was 4,664, of whom 1,036 were admitted to the hospital. Although the collection of fees was difficult and much charity work was done, the hospital was on its way to becoming self-supporting.

A new clinic building of stone was completed in 1964, providing three more rooms for inpatients in addition to facilities for the care of outpatients—a waiting room, a reception room with connection to an examining room, a treatment room, a laboratory, and a room for minor surgery.

Nurses included Shake Nalkranian, an Armenian; Margit Halvorsen, a Norwegian; Else Schantz Christensen, a Dane; Margot Sponghagen, a Swede; and Carolyn Stuyvesant, an American. In 1973 a clinic was established in Addis Ager, an SDA community located 22 miles (35 kilometers) from Debre Tabor.

Haile Selassie I Hospital was nationalized in 1975.

Medical Directors: Roland Nielsen, 1947-1949; Kristian Hogganvik, 1949-1970; F. J. Myers, 1971-1973; Kristian Hogganvik, 1974-1975.

HAITI. A Caribbean republic occupying the western third of the large island of Hispaniola, the rest of the island being the Dominican Republic. The island became a Spanish colony after it was discovered by Columbus in 1492, but late in the seventeenth century it was ceded to France and became her most prosperous possession, exporting considerable amounts of sugar and other tropical products. After the original Indian population had been decimated, the Spaniards and the French brought over large numbers of African slaves, whose descendants now populate the country. The French Revolution brought freedom to the slaves, and a later attempt to return them to slavery led to an armed resistance and the proclamation of independence in 1804. In 1820 the island became the world's first Black republic. Twenty-four years later, in 1844, the eastern part of the island declared its independence as the Dominican Republic, and since then Haiti has maintained its present boundaries.

The area of Haiti is 10,579 square miles (27,400 square kilometers), three fourths of which is mountainous. The population (1994) is 6.5 million. Haiti is the most densely populated country in Central America, with 600 persons per square mile (230 per square kilometer). Ninety-five percent of the people are Black. White residents, mostly foreigners, number about 2,000. The official languages of Haiti are French and Creole, a mixture of early French and African tongues with an addition of English, Spanish, and Indian words. The official religion is Roman Catholicism, but Haiti practices religious freedom, and there are several Protestant bodies in the country, including Baptists, Anglicans, Pentecostals, Seventh-day Adventists, and others. Voodoo, a mixture of ceremony and African superstition, is still practiced.

Seventh-day Adventist Statistics. The territory of Haiti comprises the Haitian Union Mission, which in turn is part of the territory of the Inter-American Division, and is divided into two missions—the North Haiti Mission and the South Haiti Mission. Statistics (1993) for *Haiti:* churches, 239; members, 164,053; elementary schools, 270; ordained ministers,

49; credentialed missionaries, 123; licensed missionaries, 58; teachers, 640; licensed ministers, 49. Headquarters: Ruelle Ganot 78, Port-au-Prince, Haiti.

Statistics (1993) for the missions—*North Haiti Mission:* churches, 122; members, 85,190; church and elementary schools, 127; ordained ministers, 14; licensed ministers, 21; credentialed missionaries, 30; licensed missionaries, 17; teachers, 275. Headquarters: Cap-Haitien. *South Haiti Mission:* churches, 117; members, 78,863; church or elementary schools, 143; ordained ministers, 26; licensed ministers, 26; credentialed missionaries, 30; licensed missionaries, 17; teachers, 275. Headquarters: Port-au-Prince.

Institutions. Adventist Hospital of Haiti; Haitian Adventist College; Inter-American Health Food Company, Haiti Branch.

Development of Seventh-day Adventist Work. *Beginnings.* SDA doctrines first penetrated Haiti in 1879. In that year John N. Loughborough, then living in Southampton, England, and William Ings sent a box of books and tracts to Cap Haitien. Since they did not address it to anyone specifically, the steamship company delivered the box to the Episcopal missionary stationed in the city, who in turn distributed its contents among other Protestant missions nearby. On the following Sunday the Baptist missionary gave these publications to his congregation. Two young Jamaicans, Henry Williams and his wife, studied the tracts and began to keep the Sabbath. They procured other reading material from the publishers and circulated it among neighbors. More than 10 years later—in 1892—they met an SDA for the first time, L. C. Chadwick, who visited Haiti and in course of time baptized them. For many years, until several others joined them at the turn of the century, they apparently were the only SDAs in Haiti.

About 1904 or 1905 Michel Nord Isaac, a Methodist preacher and teacher who was longing for more spiritual light, knelt one day in a corner of his office and asked the Lord to help him find the truth. While he was still in prayer, someone knocked on the door. It was one of his pupils, who said: "Teacher, I have found among my father's books at home one entitled *The History of the Sabbath.* Would you like to read it?" Isaac regarded this incident as a direct answer to prayer and was soon convinced that all he learned from the book was the truth.

Determined to live up to his knowledge, he began at once to preach his new beliefs, and published and circulated a tract in their defense. One of his friends helped him make contact with Henry Williams. Because of Isaac's work, when the first SDA evangelist, W. Jay Tanner, went to Haiti in the fall of 1905, he found several groups of Sabbathkeepers waiting for him, including an entire congregation from one of the Protestant churches.

In December 1905 Tanner held the first baptisms. By the end of the year, about 40 to 50 persons, most of them well-educated and influential, had joined the church. During 1906 some 30 persons were added to the church, and Isaac entered the new areas of Limbé and Port Margo, preaching and organizing companies of converts.

Early in 1907 E. Fawer, a French-speaking worker, arrived from Europe to aid in the work. In November the first Seventh-day Adventist church in Haiti was organized at Grande Rivière, with 25 members; by the end of the year its membership had increased to 40, while the total membership stood at more than 80.

After Tanner left the field in 1911, Isaac, who had become a fervent and zealous preacher, served as leader during that time. By the end of the year there were four churches and five companies, with a total membership of about 190. The first church school was reported in that year also. In 1912 Albert F. Prieger took charge of the mission. In 1914 he was joined by E. A. Curdy, a French-speaking evangelist from Europe, and the church extended to new areas, among them Port-au-Prince, Saint-Marc, Trou du Nord, Gonaïves, and Saint-Michel-de-l'Atalaye.

Organization and Growth. Until 1914 the Haitian Mission was under the direction of the West Indian Union Conference, but in that year the mission was placed under General Conference direction as part of the Northern Latin American Missions group. The statistical report for that year listed eight churches, 273 baptized members, one ordained minister, two licensed ministers, two licensed missionaries, four colporteurs, and 14 Sabbath schools. Two years later, in 1916, the Haitian Mission counted 11 churches, 322 members, with 98 persons baptized during that year. The number of workers had increased to 11. By 1920 there were three ordained ministers, four licensed ministers, and six licensed missionaries, and the membership had increased to 617 baptized members meeting in 15 organized churches and several companies.

With the opening of Séminaire Adventiste

d'Haiti (Haitian Seminary) with eight students and two teachers, under the leadership of Herminie Roth in 1921, the educational work on the secondary level began in Haiti. About that time the MV work also began, with the organization of a society of 28 members.

From 1918 to 1922 the work was headed by Pastor Andre G. Roth, who came from Switzerland. When he left, W. P. Elliott was appointed president and M. D. Howard, secretary-treasurer. In 1922 the Haitian Mission was assigned to the Inter-American Division. The work entered new areas, such as Jacmel and Plaisance, and the canvassing work grew under the direction of C. G. Parkins and D. Apollon. In 1924 the work was well spread across the land of Haiti, with churches or groups in Port-de-Paix, Gonaïves, Limonade, Jacmel, Ranquitte, Cerca-la-Source, Pignon, Bahon, Thomassique, and Cerca-Carvajal. From 1924 the Haitian Mission was under the direction of the Antillian Union Mission. By the end of that year the statistical report showed 23 churches, 750 baptized members, 16 workers, and 24 Sabbath schools, with a membership of 944.

In 1925 the Lay Activities Department was organized under the leadership of J. A. Decaenel. In the same year there were six church schools operating with nine teachers and an enrollment of 240. In this year the work entered Ouanaminthe. In 1928 Elliott was replaced by J. A. Decaenel. In 1930 the mission had 25 churches with a total membership of 1,561, and 45 Sabbath schools with 2,221 members. In 1932 the headquarters of the mission were transferred from Cap Haitien to Port-au-Prince. About that time two ministers, Dorce Dorsainvil and F. D. Apollon, entered the Cayes and held a series of meetings.

The statistical report of Dec. 31, 1947, listed 36 churches, 6,937 members, 126 Sabbath schools with 10,260 members, and 17 church schools. The welfare work was begun in 1947 under the direction of E. Veuthey, then president of the Haitian Mission. In April 1948 the first Voice of Hope Bible correspondence course was offered. As of Dec. 31, 1962, there were 7,846 students taking the three available courses offered in the French language.

In 1959 the Haitian field was divided into two missions: the North Haiti Mission, with headquarters at Cap Haitien, and the South Haiti Mission, with headquarters at Port-au-Prince.

As early as 1935 action was taken regarding the establishing of medical work in Haiti but the action became a reality only in April 1960, when the South Haiti Mission opened a small clinic near the Franco-Haitian Seminary. At present one polyclinic and one hospital, Adventist Hospital of Haiti, are being operated in Port-au-Prince and one health and welfare center in Cap-Haitien.

Franco-Haitian Union. In 1958 Haiti became part of the Franco-Haitian Union, formed of the French-speaking areas in the Caribbean: Haiti, which had been part of the Antillian Union, and French Guiana, Guadeloupe and dependencies, and Martinique, which had been part of the Caribbean Union. A. O. Dunn was chosen to be the first president of the Franco-Haitian Union, serving until July 1960.

In 1989 the Haitian Union Mission was formed, with Asser A. Jean-Pierre as its first president.

HAITI ADVENTIST HOSPITAL. *See* Adventist Hospital of Haiti.

HAITI FOOD FACTORY. *See* Inter-American Health Food Company, Haiti Branch.

HAITIAN ADVENTIST COLLEGE (Université Adventiste d'Haiti). A coeducational boarding school on the senior college level, situated about five miles (eight kilometers) from Port-au-Prince, Haiti, and operated by the Haitian Union to serve a constituency of 164,053 (June 1993). At that time the secondary enrollment was 936 and the university enrollment was 571. These were served by 30 faculty members. In 1959 the Haitian government authorized the school to offer classwork leading toward the baccalaureate (U.S. high school) level. In the same year the General Conference Department of Education authorized work on the junior college level. In 1992 the university received official recognition from the government.

Two of the main industries are a printshop and a technical service. In July 1993 the school offered a master's degree in religion as an extension program of Andrews University.

The school opened as the Séminaire Adventiste d'Haiti (Adventist Seminary of Haiti, also called Haitien Seminary) in October 1921, with Herminie L. Roth as directror. There were eight students and two teachers. The school plant consisted of four buildings on the Vaudreuil estate of 15 acres (six hectares), five miles (eight kilometers) southwest of Cap Haitien. Only grades 9 through 12 were offered at that time. In 1926 the addition of the elementary grades resulted in total student enrollment of 50. Because of financial reverses the enrollment dwindled to 28 in 1927, and to 22 in 1930. However, during these years several faculty homes and industrial buildings were constructed. After reorganization, the 1932 school year began with 13 faculty members and 110 students. Because of the Depression, the institution did not operate during 1933-1934.

In 1934 the school was moved to Port-au-Prince, a more central site, nearer to markets for school industries as well as to the mission headquarters. Consequently, for the next two years the school was operated as a day school in a rented house in the northeast section of Port-au-Prince. The school's printshop was installed in this building, and the woodwork shop in rented quarters on Rue du Centre. In 1935 the school was moved to a stone-and-wooden-frame building at the eastern end of the mission property on Avenue Joseph Nicolas and Magloire Ambroise. This structure housed the printshop and the woodwork shop. In the latter part of that year the Haitian government authorized the school to offer full secondary work, thus permitting students to sit for the official state examinations leading to the baccalaureate certificate. As a result of this recognition the enrollment in 1936 increased as follows: elementary, 103; secondary, 19; junior college, six. The name was changed from Séminaire Adventiste d'Haiti to Collège Vertières. The school remained on this site for 10 years, but during the latter part of this period the enrollment again declined and heavy indebtedness was incurred.

In 1945, under M. D. Howard as board chair, the college was transferred to a 78-acre (32-hectare) tract at Diquini, about four miles (six kilometers) southwest of Port-au-Prince. The funds were obtained by the sale of the Vaudreuil property. When the Franco-Haitian Union was organized in 1959, the school became the union college with the name of Franco-Haitian Seminary. In 1961 R. E. Perrin was called to be the president. Under his leadership the enrollment increased and has maintained a steady growth. In 1974, 500 students were distributed among the elementary, secondary, and college levels. To meet the need of the French fields, authorization was granted in June 1973 by the General Conference Education Department to the Franco-Haitian Seminary to offer 16 grades in theology. The staff has been greatly improved by sending the teachers to Andrews University and France to get further graduate-level training.

Principals: Herminie L. Roth, 1921-1923; W. P. Elliott, 1923-1924; Hermininie L. Roth, 1924-1925; H. H. Thompson, 1925-1926; A. O. Dunn, 1926-1928; H. G. Patchett, 1929-1930; H. L. Higgins, 1930-1934; A. G. Roth, 1934-1939; Mrs. A. G. Roth, 1939-1941; A. L. Christensen, 1941-1942; A. G. Roth, 1942-1943; R. H. Howlett, 1943-1945; Paul Evers (acting), 1945-1946; M. E. Moore, 1946-1947; Paul Evers (acting), 1947-1948; A. L. Christensen, 1948-1950; A. G. Roth, 1950-1952; A. L. Rochat, 1952-1959; R. J. Kloosterhuis, 1959-1960.

Presidents: R. E. Perrin, 1961-1968; T. E. Wade, 1969-1971; P. G. Miller, 1971-1976; Alberto Dos Santos, 1976-1982; Mario Collins, 1983-1984; Michel Lamartine Porcena, 1985-1986; Amos Bossous, 1986-1987; Serge Vernet, 1987-1991; Mike Lekic, 1991-1993; Ezechias Jean, 1993- .

HAITIAN UNION MISSION. *See* Haiti; Inter-American Division.

HALE, APOLLOS (fl. 1844). Methodist minister, Millerite preacher and writer, associate editor of *Signs of the Times* and its successor, the *Advent Herald.* A deep thinker and a careful and critical writer, he was noted for his clarity and logic. He assisted Fitch in preparing the "1843 chart" used by Millerite preachers and wrote articles, pamphlets, and a *Second Advent Manual.*

Along with others, Hale concluded that Miller's "Jewish year 1843" should end, not at the 1844 spring equinox, but at the new moon of April, according to the old Karaite Jewish calendar. He also concluded that the end of the 2300 years would fall within the following Jewish year and looked for their ending on the tenth day of the Jewish seventh month in the autumn.

For a time after the Oct. 22 disappointment he held to the validity of the "true midnight cry" and joined with Joseph Turner (coeditor of the *Hope of Israel* in Portland, Maine) in issuing the *Advent Mirror* (vol. 1, No. 1, January 1845), which presented their joint personal interpretation of the parable of the ten virgins, namely, that the coming of the bridegroom to the wedding did not, as they had thought, signify the coming of Christ as king, but rather His coming to the Ancient of Days to receive His kingdom before coming to the earth for His saints, and that this was what had taken place at the end of the 2300 days.

"The coming of the bridegroom would point out some change of work or office, on the part of our Lord, in the invisible world; and the [virgins'] going in with him a corresponding change on the part of his true people. With him it is within the veil—where he had gone to prepare a place for us, with them it is outside the veil, where they are to wait and keep themselves ready till they pass in to the marriage supper" (p. 3).

The Adventists, they explained, having gone forth to meet their Lord in 1843, slumbered as the Bridegroom delayed, and then trimmed their lamps in response to the "true midnight cry" of the "seventh month" message. Since Oct. 22 they had been waiting for the Bridegroom to return from the wedding or had gone to buy oil; the Bridegroom could be expected any moment.

Soon after, Hale wrote an article in the *Advent Herald* explaining this view and adding that the parable does not end with the events that are to take place at the actual coming of Christ, for when He appears it is to execute judgment. "It would seem to coincide much more naturally with the judiciary *trial* which precedes the execution (the judgment which begins at the house of God)" (reprinted in *Review and Herald* 2:25-27, Sept. 16, 1851).

After the spring of 1845 Hale was identified with the majority group of Adventists and apparently ceased to teach these distinctive views.

HALE, DUDLEY UPTON (1865-1949). One of the pioneer Seventh-day Adventist workers on the west coast of Africa and in British Guiana, South America. He became an SDA at the age of 23 and shortly afterward entered the ministry in Texas. He was ordained in 1895. On Oct. 4, 1895, he led a party of SDA missionaries ashore at Cape Coast Castle, Gold Coast (Cape Coast in what is now Ghana), and established the first Seventh-day Adventist mission in West Africa. In 1897 repeated attacks of malaria drove him out of the country, and after a brief stay in Texas he went to superintend the work in British Guiana (1897-1900). From 1900 to the end of 1902 he was an evangelist in Texas. In 1903 he returned to West Africa, but was again forced by malaria to leave almost immediately. Afterward he served as a minister and evangelist in the Texas Conference (1903-1907), and as president in the Missouri (1907-1908), Southern Missouri (1908-1911), Wyoming (1911-1914), Nebraska (1914-1916), and Northern New England (1920-1926) conferences.

HALL, D. P. *See Messenger* Party.

HALL, HARRY HARVEY (1871-1934). Publishing house administrator. After a term of service in the Kansas Conference and tract society, he went in 1894 to the Pacific Press publishing house and worked there for 26 years. He began in the Sales Department, later managed the Book Department, and for years was vice president of the association. Assigned to the development of branch houses, he was largely responsible for the establishing of a branch printing office in the Canal Zone, Panama.

In 1920 Hall was released temporarily to the General Conference to give special attention to the operation of publishing houses overseas and to methods of promoting the publishing work. This assignment took him to Europe, Asia, Africa, Australia, South America, and Central America. Appointed as secretary of the General Conference Publishing Department in 1930, he continued to promote all lines of the publishing work in various parts of the world field.

HALL, ORRIN A. (1878-1959). Missionary, educator. A graduate of Union College (1899), he taught a church school in Missouri, then engaged in ministerial work (1900-1904). From 1904 to 1907 he was principal of the Northwestern Training School, Manitoba, Canada, and from 1907 to 1909 MV secretary of the Nebraska Conference. He went to China in 1909 as mission director and principal of the training school in Honan province. After the removal of the school to Shanghai, he taught there for several years.

He was superintendent of the East China Union Mission for nine years, and then of the Central China Union Mission. Because of his wife's health, he returned to the United States, where he did pastoral work for five years in California. Returning again to the mission field, he served in the South China Union. After five years in Hong Kong he worked for the division's Ministerial Association and as an editor, then again became superintendent of the East China Union. He was one of the last Seventh-day Adventist missionaries to be evacuated from Shanghai. After returning to the United States, he engaged in pastoral work in the Northern California Conference for five years.

HALLANG, LUDVIG NIKKAR (1886-1965). Pastor, administrator, editor. Born in Tallinn, Estonia, Hallang became a Seventh-day Adventist in 1896. He attended the missionary seminary at Friedensau, Germany, for three years. In 1910, he became a pastor in Estonia and led out in the building of the first church in that country. Before his ordination in 1914 he had organized the first Seventh-day Adventist church on the island of Ösel. He was the first editor of the Estonian *Message of the Truth.* After serving as president of the Far-East Siberian Conference, he returned to Estonia, where he was assistant editor of *Our Times* and served as a pastor. From 1928 to 1930 he was president of the Estonian Conference. At the time of his death he had completed 62 years of service to the church.

HALLIWELL, LEO BLAIR (1891-1967). Medical missionary to Brazil. A native of Odessa, Nebraska, Halliwell accepted the truth under the efforts of O. O. Bernstein and became a Bible instructor in Iowa. During this time he organized a Sabbath school that developed into the Charles City church.

In 1921 he and his wife, the former Jessie Rowley, were called to serve in Brazil, the site of their labor for the next 38 years.

After seven years in the state of Bahia, the Halliwells were called to east Brazil and then to north Brazil, where there were only three other church members in the immense area around Belém. On a get-acquainted trip by riverboat and canoe up the Amazon, the young missionary was dismayed to discover the poverty, superstition, and disease of the people of his district.

Deeply impressed that a launch would be most effective in reaching the 2 million people living along the 40,000 miles (65,000 kilometers) of navigable rivers forming the Amazon River basin, Halliwell made appeals for such a launch, and the funds were donated by the MV Societies of North and South America.

After spending part of his furlough in 1930 taking a course in tropical diseases, Halliwell returned to Brazil. He sketched the design for a shallow draft 30-foot (nine-meter) boat with a 10-foot (three-meter) beam and hacked out the hull himself from Amazonian hardwoods. He also installed the engine and wiring and then began a 30-year stint of steering his aquatic clinic, the *Luzeiro,* up and down the 1,000-mile (1,600-kilometer) stretch of river between Belém and Manaus, covering some 12,000 miles (19,000 kilometers) a year. Together Leo and Jessie treated more than a quarter million Brazilians and Indians for a host of tropical and other diseases, as well as spreading the message among the grateful people.

At first the nationals living along the river were frightened by the huge "canoe," but the sound of phonograph music soon had them creeping from their hiding places in amazement. They were just as amazed at the effects of quinine on the malaria raging in their villages.

At first Halliwell bought medicine from slender mission resources. Later he was kept supplied by doctors and pharmaceutical houses in the United States and the public health departments of the states of Pará and Amazonas. One of his greatest services was the awakening of the Brazilian government to the fact that its people are the most important of its rich natural resources and the understanding that the state of health of these people could well decide the future prosperity of the country. In recognition of the Halliwells' service, the Brazilian government awarded them the distinguished National Order of the Southern Cross.

In 1942, with no funds available, Halliwell realized a dream of long standing when he opened a tiny clinic in Belém, staffed by a Brazilian doctor. In 15 years it was a fully equipped 40-bed hospital.

At age 65 Halliwell accepted a call to Rio de Janeiro, to supervise the well-developed work of the SDA medical launches in South America.

HAM, ALLEN L. (1889-1974). Missionary, vice president of the General Conference. In 1909 he completed a course in engineering at Walla Walla College and with his wife attended the Foreign Mission Seminary in Washington, D.C., as a mission appointee. In 1913 they began work in Hong Kong. A year later he became director of the Cantonese Mission, serving in that capacity for 20 years. He was ordained to the ministry in 1917. In 1935 he became superintendent of the South China Union Mission, serving until taken prisoner by the Imperial Japanese Army on Christmas Day 1941.

After repatriation in 1942 he became vice president of the General Conference for the Southern Asia Division until 1950. He then served as general field secretary for the General Conference for four years, after which he became a vice president until his retirement in 1958. During his various terms in the General Conference he served as chair of the boards of Madison College and Hospital, Oakwood College, Riverside Sanitarium, and Southern Publishing Association.

After retirement he served for a term on the board of Loma Linda University and was active in the Elmshaven church (Deer Park, California) as first elder and chair of the church school board.

HAMBURG PUBLISHING HOUSE (Saatkorn-Verlag GmbH). A publishing institution composed of five legal companies: Advent-Verlag GmbH, ES-TE-A, Saatkorn-Verlag GmbH, Grindeldruck GmbH, and Dr. med. Schneider GmbH. All are under one manager. The plant is situated in Hamburg, Germany.

The house publishes Seventh-day Adventist books and the following periodicals in German: *Adventecho* ("Advent Echo"; prior to 1973, *Der Adventbote* ["Advent Messenger"]; prior to 1920, Zions-Wächter ["Watchman of Zion"]); *Besser Leben* ("Better Living"); Sabbath school lesson quarterlies for children, juniors, and seniors; and *Zeichen der Zeit* ("Signs of the Times"; prior to 1973, *Ruf in die Zeit* ["Message for Our Time"]; prior to 1959, *Herold der Wahrheit* ["Messenger of Truth"]).

The publishing house at Hamburg grew out of a branch of the Imprimerie Polyglotte (established in Basel, Switzerland, by J. N. Andrews), which was opened in Hamburg in 1889 under the name Internationale Traktatgesellschaft ("International Tract Society") in two rented rooms at the SDA mission headquarters at 41 Sophienstrasse.

In 1893 the Hamburger Verein der STA (Hamburg SDA Association) was organized and acquired a building at Grindelberg 15a, where the publishing branch was moved, and where the SDA headquarters in Germany were established. Because of certain difficulties in supplying German publications from outside the country, the whole German Department of the Imprimerie Polyglotte was transferred to Hamburg on Aug. 27, 1895. From this date the Hamburg Publishing House began its independent existence, though at first it retained the name Internationale Traktatgesellschaft in Hamburg. From 1895 until it was made a separate company in 1900 it was legally and financially a part of the Hamburger Verein. The buildings and land of the publishing house are still owned by the Hamburger Verein, which erected a separate building to house the press in 1912.

Foreign Language Work. The Hamburg branch of the Imprimerie Polyglotte quickly became a center for the SDA publishing work in central and east European languages. By the time it acquired separate status in 1895, it was issuing publications in 14 languages, and some years later the number of languages used increased to 20: German, Dutch, Lithuanian, Latvian, Estonian, Russian, Polish, Wendish, Bohemian, Slovakian, Hungarian, Serbian, Croatian, Bulgarian, Romanian, Spanish, Portuguese, Yiddish, Swahili, and Chasu.

Beginning in 1903 the Hamburg Publishing House established several branches throughout central and eastern Europe: in Basel, Switzerland (1903); in Riga, Russia (Latvia, 1908); in Constantinople (Istanbul), Turkey (1909); at The Hague, Netherlands (1924); in Vienna, Austria (1924); in Budapest, Hungary; and in Bucharest, Romania. Most branches were only distributing agencies, but some also printed magazines, books, tracts, and other denominational publications. The Hamburg house provided the branches in Budapest, Bucharest, and Riga with printing equipment, technicians, and supplies. When because of World War I separate publishing houses were established in Yugoslavia, Romania, Czechoslovakia, Poland, Estonia, Latvia, Hungary, Bulgaria, and the Netherlands, the Hamburg house left the stock of publications on hand to them without charge.

In 1922 the publishing work was organized in Hamburg as Advent-Verlag E. V. ("Advent Publishing House Registered Association"). After the Nazi government made it impossible for the denomination to operate the press, the house was turned over to private hands. In 1938 the firm was renamed Advent-Verlag Vollmer and Bentlin KG ("Adventist Publishing House, Vollmer and Bentlin, Limited Partnership"), and in 1939 it was again renamed as Vollmer and Bentlin KG ("Vollmer and Bentlin, Limited Partnership"). A. Vollmer and W. Bentlin acted as trustees of the denomination and were personally responsible for the affairs of the publishing house for eight years. During part of this time, in consequence of Nazi laws and of war conditions, it was impossible to produce publications for the church; only job printing was permitted. In July 1943 all the buildings dating from the 1890s, which included the business and editorial offices, the archives of the European work of the SDA denomination, and the adjoining church building, were burned to the ground in an air raid.

In 1947 the publishing house was returned to the denomination, and in September of that year it received a license to print denominational publications. Since past experience had shown that it would be convenient to separate the management of the publishing house from that of the press, the printing plant became a separate legal entity, first bearing the name Vollmer and Bentlin GmbH ("Vollmer and Bentlin, Ltd."), and then, since 1954, Grindeldruck GmbH ("Grindel Printing Co., Ltd."); the Publishing Department was reorganized as the Advent-Verlag GmbH ("Adventist Publishing House, Ltd."). In 1948 this firm organized the production of publications for the general public into a new department under the name of Saatkorn-Verlag ("Saatkorn Publishing House"). The new department grew so fast that it could be organized as a separate firm in 1963.

The work was carried on in the remaining buildings until 1960, when a new wing with six floors was erected for the Press Department, and the building that it had occupied for 48 years (since 1912) was repaired and renovated.

In 1952 on the same grounds the foundation was laid for a church building and guest room accommodations for the publishing house. The basement of this building was completed to provide space for paper stock.

Progress of the Publishing House. Prior to 1895 there were two employees engaged in publishing work in Hamburg. When the German Department of the Imprimerie Polyglotte was transferred to Hamburg in 1895, the number of workers increased to 10, and the sales for that year amounted to 64,000 marks (about $16,000). In 1900 there were 22 workers and the sales were 160,000 marks. In 1910 there were 58 workers and the sales amounted to 480,000 marks. In 1928, the best year before World War II, the sales totaled more than 1 million marks. After World War II the employment rose to more than 150 in 1950, and in 1952 the volume of sales was greater than ever before, even though the population served by the house decreased considerably, being limited only to West Germany. In 1957 the volume of sales passed 2 million marks, and in 1962 it reached almost 4 million marks. In 1963 the house employed about 200 people. Since then more modern equipment has been installed to avoid the high labor costs.

Publishing House Equipment. Before 1900 only the composing was done at the publishing house; the printing was done elsewhere. In 1900 the first printing presses and a folding machine were installed, thus enabling the house to print and bind magazines, tracts, booklets, and brochures. The quality of the work of the publishing house earned a gold medal at the International Exhibition of the Printing and Publishing Trade and of the Graphic Arts in Leipzig in 1914. Since the 1920s the Hamburg house has been equipped to manufacture all its books and magazines.

In 1928 the publishing house was given honorable mention at the International Exhibition in Cologne because of its efficiency. In 1933 it acquired music type, which enabled it to manufacture hymnbooks. At that time the equipment in the printshop and book bindery was completely up-to-date, but during the next 25 years it was impossible to replace any machinery. Since World War II the obsolete equipment has been replaced. An innovation was the installation of offset equipment in 1962. As the result of a special process invented at the plant, the publishing house became known throughout Germany.

In 1963 several one- and two-color presses of different sizes enabled the plant to produce multi-color prints at a reasonable price. Modern linotypes and one monotype with keyboard and caster were used in the Composing Department. Following the trend of the time, two perforators and one pacesetter (Photon) for composing were installed in 1974. In addition, the press has two typing machines with RCO-types, which supply the manuscript for automatic reading machines.

In 1992, after the reunification of Germany, the Publishing Association of the German Democratic Republic was integrated into the Hamburg Publishing House.

Managers: H. Hartkop, 1900-1924; A. Vollmer, 1924-1938; A. Vollmer and W. Bentlin, 1938-1950; S. Christoffers and W. Bentlin, 1950-1959; H. E. Morenings, 1959-1975; R. Rupp, 1976-1990; E. Boettge, 1991- .

HAMMERLY DUPUY, DANIEL (1907-1972). Pastor, professor, author. He was native of Switzerland. His parents took him to Argentina in 1908, when they were called as nurses to River Plate Sanitarium and Hospital, and the following year to Uruguay. He went to primary and secondary schools in Uruguay and Argentina, received his theological training at River Plate College, and later studied at Potomac University, where he obtained his Master of Arts degree in 1955, and in 1956 his Bachelor of Divinity degree. In 1970 Andrews University conferred on him an honorary Doctor of Divinity degree.

In 1929 he married Angélica Peverini, and in 1937 was ordained to the ministry. During his 44 years of work in the Seventh-day Adventist Church, he served as publishing department director (1928-1929), local pastor and evangelist (1930-1943), Austral Union evangelist (1944-1948), public relations director (1950-1956), professor at River Plate College (1956-1957), writer of textbooks and evangelist (1958-1960), university students' counselor (1961-1962), and professor at Inca Union College, Peru (1963-1972).

He was an untiring reader in Spanish, French, and English, and a dedicated researcher during his trips throughout the Americas, Europe, Africa, and Asia. He wrote more than 60 books and smaller works, not counting his numerous articles for our magazines on anthropology, ethnology, archaeology, chronology, biology, paleontology, history, geography, religion, and ethics.

One could say that Dr. Hammerly passed away with his pen in hand. His posthumous work, *Guide to Study the Bible (Guía para estudiar la Biblia),* was published in 1973.

HANFORD COMMUNITY MEDICAL CENTER. A 54-bed general acute hospital located at 450 Greenfield Avenue, Hanford, California, with an active medical staff of 73 physicians and more than 500 full-time employees. The institution had an average daily occupancy of 46.9 patients in 1993.

Licensed by the state of California, it is a member of the California Association of Hospitals and Health Systems, Healthcare Reform, and Hospital Council of Northern and Central California, and is fully accredited by the Joint Commission on Accreditation of Hospitals.

The present facility was built in 1965 and opened as a denominational institution in the summer of that year. A full range of services is provided, including an intensive care unit, cardiac catheterization lab, outpatient services, 24-hour emergency services, and a maternity center.

The Kerr Outpatient Center was opened in June 1993. This is a freestanding outpatient center that houses lab, radiology, mammography, cardiopulmonary function lab, and the outpatient surgical services. It was named after Edwin E. Kerr, a member of the HCMC active medical staff, who has given many years of service to Kings County.

An ordained staff chaplain ministers to the needs of patients and employees alike, stressing the spiritual healing that is part of serving the whole person.

Administrators: Henry Bergh, 1965-1968; Henry Friesen, 1969-1972; Virgil P. Morris, 1972-1982; Fred Manchur, 1983-1987; Charles Ricks, Sr., 1987-1992; Stan Berry, 1992- .

HANKE ADVENTIST SECONDARY SCHOOL. A boarding school operated on the senior high level, located at Shurugwi, Zimbabwe, Africa.

In 1911 Chief Mudzengi, brother of retired worker Paul Pimbono, gave the Hanke property to the Seventh-day Adventist mission. The following year a church was constructed and a stone house, which is still in use. A small outdoor school was begun by Pastor Ngono. This has developed into the largest primary school in the Zambesi Union. The January 1993 enrollment was 283 secondary school students with 17 teachers, and 670 primary school pupils with 19 teachers.

The present primary school dates from 1941. In the 1950s the school was upgraded, and in 1969 the institution advanced to junior secondary level. In 1974 it was upgraded to full secondary status, with emphasis on industrial arts.

Water has been a problem and was first brought from the river about a half mile (.3 kilometers) away. A well was dug in 1925, but this and subsequent wells proved inadequate. Recently a new source has been discovered.

Principals: R. A. Burns, 1956-1957; W.C.H. Outwaite, 1957-1958; S. T. Palvie, 1959-1961; J. W. Christensen, 1962-1964; K. Farnsworth, 1965; C. T. Bannister, 1966; B. A. Roberts, 1967-1970; R. R. Adams, 1972-1976; J. Whitehurst, 1977; P. W. Chiduku, 1977-1978; Z. S. Serere, 1978-1979; P. W. Chiduku, 1981-1982; A. P. Sibanda, 1983-1994; A. J. Dhliwayo, 1994- .

HANKINS, IRA JOHN (1854-1937). Missionary. After attending Battle Creek College from 1876 to 1878, he entered the ministry in Iowa in 1879. In 1888 he became the third Seventh-day Adventist minister to enter South Africa, C. L. Boyd and D. A. Robinson having preceded him by a few months. After a brief period as president of the Indiana Conference (1901-1903), he returned to South Africa to take the presidency of the Cape Conference. His first wife, née Clara Tracy, having died, he was married in 1903 to Eva Perkins Miller, the widow of Eli B. Miller. In addition to his other duties, he was editor of the *Sentinel* (later the *Signs of the Times*), with his wife as assistant. He retired from active service in 1921, and in 1923 returned to the United States.

HANKINS, WINFERD CAMERON (1880-1968). Missionary, pastor, evangelist. He was born in Iowa and studied at Washington Missionary College prior to going to China in 1905. He and his family served as missionaries for 18 years and then returned to the United States, where he served as a pastor and evangelist in the Michigan Conference for 20 years. In 1945 he moved to the Arizona Conference and retired in 1961.

HANSA CONFERENCE. *See* Euro-Africa Division; Germany.

HANSEN, LOUIS A. (1872-1969). Pioneer medical missionary. He was a native of Denmark and moved to the United States at an early age. In 1889 he served as colporteur and licensed minister in the Indiana Conference. After completing the nurse's course at Battle Creek in 1896, he and his wife began treatment rooms in Nashville, Tennessee. Later he became one of the founders of the Florida Sanitarium and was manager of three sanitariums—Nashville, Tennessee; Graysville, Tennessee; and Washington, D.C. He is considered the first Seventh-day Adventist self-supporting medical missionary.

For 24 years, he served with *Life and Health* magazine as assistant, associate, and chief editor. He was also an associate secretary of the General Conference Medical Department for several years. While in this position, he developed a central purchasing bureau that later became ESDA. He retired in Florida in 1946.

HANSON, DELLA F. (1897-1981). Missionary. She and her husband, Herbert Hanson, served in Norway, then were invited to go to Ethiopia. Emperor Haile Selassie I, after five years of exile in Great Britain, was looking for a person to restore order in his palace, which the Italian invaders had used as their army headquarters. In his search he called on the Seventh-day Adventist mission. Della Hanson was selected for the job. Of the 40 years the Hansons spent in Ethiopia, Della spent 30 of them in service in the royal palace. This was the most unusual foreign mission service in the history of the Seventh-day Adventist Church. Because of this relationship, the emperor donated the land and much of the operating expense for the secondary school that was started and operated under the Hansons' supervision. Della stayed on in service to the emperor for eight years after her husband's death, leaving only when the government was overthrown.

HANSON, HERBERT MARTIN (1894-1966). Pioneer and missionary. He was born in Minnesota of parents who had recently emigrated from Norway. He attended Maplewood Academy and Hutchinson Theological Seminary, graduating in 1921. In June of that year he was married to Della Thompson, and the young couple sailed for Norway, where they helped to establish the first Seventh-day Adventist academy in that country.

Hanson served as principal of the school for 11 years and then answered a call to Ethiopia. The family first located in Addis Alem, where he took over the principalship of the mission school. Because of the Italian invasion the school soon closed, but was reopened several months later. Since he was not allowed to teach English, Hanson studied ahead of his pupils and taught Italian.

When Haile Selassie I returned to Ethiopia from exile, Hanson was urged to start a school in Addis Ababa, which he did. In 1943 the emperor gave a site for the Akaki school, where Hanson served periodically as principal, teacher, and builder.

Twice the Hansons left Ethiopia expecting never to return, but each time the longing for the people brought them back. After a period of ill health Herbert passed to his rest at the Empress Zauditu Memorial Hospital. The emperor provided the royal hearse for the service, which was attended by many members of the royal family and several ministers of state.

After Herbert's passing, Della Hanson remained at her post as housekeeper to His Imperial Majesty, Haile Selassie I, a position she held for 17 years.

HAPPINESS (Braille). *See* Christian Record Services, Inc.

HAPUR ELEMENTARY BOARDING SCHOOL. A coeducational English language elementary boarding school, operated near Hapur, Uttar Pradesh, about 35 miles (55 kilometers) east-northeast from Delhi, by the Northwestern Indian Union under the Southern Asia Division.

Forerunner of the school was the North India Girls' School, opened by M. M. Mattison on Jan. 12, 1919, with eight students. The next year the girls were moved to Lucknow and a boys' school was operated (listed in the *Yearbook* first in 1921 as the North India Boys' School established in 1917). The *Yearbook* lists it in 1922 as the Northwest Union Mission Training School, in 1923 as the North India Anglo-Vernacular Boys' Middle School, and between 1924 and 1929 as the United Provinces School for Boys. Urdu and Hindi were the languages of instruction. In December 1929 the Hapur school was amalgamated with the Northwest India Union Training School at Roorkee and the former North India Girls' School (then known as the United Provinces Girls' School) was brought back to Hapur. During the thirties the girls' school at Hapur was listed in the *Yearbook* as North Agra Mission Girls' School. The Hapur Elementary School first appeared in the *Yearbook* in 1939 in place of North Agra Mission School, and at the same time the name Roorkee High School appears for the Northwest India Union Training School.

In 1956 the Roorkee school and the Hapur school were put under one management. Later the school at Hapur became a coeducational institutional institution under the name Union Elementary School. The present school dates from 1961, when an English language boarding school was established.

In 1964 the boarding section of the school was joined with the school at Roorkee, and Hapur became an English Medium Day School. In 1974, the boarding section was reopened with assistance from the Christian Children Fund. The enrollment in 1974 was 460, including 130 boarders.

See Seventh-day Adventist High School (Roorkie).

Principals: M. M. Mattison, 1919-1920; F. W. Smith, 1920-1924; L. E. Allen, 1924-1929; Mrs. F. H. Loasby, 1929-1930; Mrs. R. L. Kimble, 1930-1932; Mrs. H. D. Strever, 1932-1933; Miss C. A. Craggs, 1933-1934; Mrs. O. O. Mattison, 1934-1936; Mrs. P. K. Simpson, 1936-1938; Mrs. R. P. Morris, 1938-1941; H. C. Alexander, 1941-1943; T. R. Torkelson, 1943-1948; Mrs. R. P. Morris, 1948-1949; R. F. Juriansz, 1949-1952; G. J. Christo, 1952-1954; D. H. Skau, 1954-1955; B. M. Shad, 1955-1960; P. E. Howard, 1960-1961; G. J. Christo, 1961-1962; M. C. Stanley, 1962-1963; C. A. Chacko, 1963-1964; Mrs. W. Storz, 1964-1966; S. J. Phasge, 1966-1972; S. Mishal, 1972-1973; N. Curtis, 1973-1974; O. V. Jonathan, 1974.

HARBERT HILLS ACADEMY AND SANITARIUM. *See* Madison Institutions.

HARDINGE, MOLLY ELLEN MIRIAM PETAVEL (1908-1993). Author, educator, missionary, musician. Born in Neuchâtel, Switzerland, even as a young girl she had questions about the seventh-day Sabbath. At 14 she wanted to be a nun, but her Swiss godmother became a Seventh-day Adventist and offered to pay for Molly's education at Stanborough College in England. Molly was baptized two years later. While at school she became a coworker with Arthur Maxwell at Stanborough Press and was "Auntie Miriam" to children reading *Present Truth.* She taught piano and speech at Stanborough College and married Leslie Hardinge in 1935. One daughter was born to them.

Moving to the United States in 1946, the Hardinges worked together at three American colleges as well as at Newbold College in England and at the SDA Theological Seminary in the Far East. She organized "Evangeline Clubs" to train ministers' wives for their future work. In 1948 Eric B. Hare invited Molly to prepare Sabbath school lessons for juniors around the world. In 22 years she wrote 88 quarterlies. Among the books that she wrote was *Begin Today With God*, the first Seventh-day Adventist devotional for juniors.

HARE, EDWARD (1847-1948). First colporteur leader in New Zealand. Probably the first to accept the Seventh-day Adventist faith in New Zealand, he was taught the SDA doctrines by S. N. Haskell, who stayed in his house while visiting Auckland in 1885. Soon after accepting the new faith, he began to distribute SDA publications in New Zealand, eventually organizing a number of colporteurs. He also invited S. N. Haskell to visit other members of his family and bring the SDA beliefs to them.

HARE, ERIC B. (1894-1982). Missionary, writer, administrator, storyteller. Born in Victoria, Australia, the second son of Pastor and Mrs. Robert Hare, he graduated from Australasian Missionary College in 1913 and took a two-year nurse's course at Sydney Sanitarium. He married Agnes Fulton, daughter of Pastor and Mrs. J. E. Fulton. He served as a missionary nurse in Burma from 1915 to 1917 and then directed the Tenasserim Mission of Burma until 1934. At that time he was called to become Sabbath school and youth director of the Northern California Conference. He also served in the Southern California Conference, in the Burma Union, the Southeastern California Conference, and the Pacific Union Conference. From 1946 until his retirement in 1962, he was an associate director in the Sabbath School Department of the General Conference.

A prolific writer of books, he is best known for the vivid way he told character-building stories to small children.

HARE, REUBEN ETHELBERT (1889-1976). Minister, missionary, administrator. Born in Gisborne, New Zealand, he was the son of pioneer New Zealand Adventist Robert Hare. Reuben Hare served in the Australasian (now South Pacific) Division and the Southern Asia Division. In recognition of his many years of volunteer service to the St. John's Ambulance Association, Hare was elected as a knight of the venerable Order of Saint John of Jerusalem, which order was bestowed on him by Queen Elizabeth II at Buckingham Palace.

HARE, ROBERT (1858-1953). Member of a pioneer Seventh-day Adventist family in New Zealand, veteran evangelist, poet, writer, and editor in Australia and New Zealand. He was born in Northern Ireland but when a child he emigrated to the antipodes. In 1885, when S. N. Haskell visited New Zealand, Hare was engaged in a boat-building business and also preached. Having accepted the seventh-day Sabbath, he gave up the business and traveled to America to attend Healdsburg College. In 1888 he graduated, was ordained, married, and returned to New Zealand to assist A. G. Daniells in tent evangelism. In 1890 Hare went to Australia, where he engaged largely in evangelism until his retirement in 1928. From 1899 to 1902 he edited the *Bible Echo,* and between about 1908 and 1911 and again between about 1914 and 1920 he taught Bible at Avondale College. He spent several months on Pitcairn Island.

Hare was a gifted poet and wrote more than 2,000 poems in his lifetime. Some of these were published by the Review and Herald in a little volume, *Along Life's Journey.* His articles appeared in SDA periodicals over a number of years. His sons, Reuben and Eric B., were active in SDA work in Australia and elsewhere.

HARE, ROBERT A. (1889-1965). School and hospital administrator, physician, editor. He was born in New Zealand, but moved to the United States as a youth. He received his B.A. degree from Union College in 1910 and became principal of Maplewood Academy. In 1918 he became head of the English Department at Pacific Union College and a year later went to Lodi Academy as principal. He received his master's degree from the University of California. For the next four years he attended the College of Medical Evangelists, graduating as president of the class of 1925. He practiced medicine for two years at the Hinsdale Sanitarium and Hospital. In 1938 he became medical director of the Washington Sanitarium and Hospital, a position he held until 1957. He was a consulting editor of *Life and Health* and served as medical secretary of the Columbia Union for eight years.

HARGREAVES, HENRY ELLISON (1898-1958). Physician; missionary to Iran. Born and educated in England, he went as a medical missionary to Iran in 1925. In 1930, while in England for further training in ophthalmology, he married Gwendolyn Constance Brown. She died in 1936, and he remarried in 1938. He supervised the Arak Mission Hospital (also called Sultanabad Hospital) 1931-1934 and c. 1945-1949. In 1937 he opened an eye clinic. Between 1939 and 1945 he was president of the Iran Mission. In 1950 he went to Australia as medical secretary of the Australasian Inter-Union Conference, where he served until 1953.

HARLAN, RUSSELL M. (1914-1972). Artist. He was a native of Takoma Park, Maryland, and lived there all his life. The great-grandson of J. N. Andrews (the first Seventh-day Adventist foreign missionary), he spent his entire adult life in the employ of the Review and Herald Publishing Association. He was the fourth generation of his family to serve in this organization. He became one of the denomination's top artists, and during his 38-year career did illustrations, many of which were in color, for scores of magazines and books, including *The Bible Story* and *Bedtime Stories.*

HARLEM ACADEMY. *See* Northeastern Academy.

HARMON, ELLEN. *See* White, Ellen G.

HARMON HIGH SCHOOL. A coeducational day school on the senior high school level, situated at Scarborough, Tobago, West

Indies, and operated by the South Caribbean Conference. It is under the direction of a general policymaking board of management, which meets once a year, and an executive board, which meets monthly. The school offers five years of secondary instruction in preparation for the Caribbean Examination Council (CXC) and is approved by the Trinidad and Tobago government. The school occupied a building on Bacolet Street connected with the Scarborough Seventh-day Adventist Church. The school first opened under local church control in January 1952. The 14 secondary students were taught by Merille McKenzie, with the assistance of Lloyd Gittens, an elementary teacher. At the end of four years the first five students who sat for the Cambridge School Certificate Examination were all successful. This success led to a growth in the enrollment. The Harmon School (called Scarborough Seventh-day Adventist High School until 1957) came under direct conference control in April 1960. In September 1969 the school was moved to new premises on six acres (2.5 hectares) of land at Rockly Vale, Scarborough, Tobago. During the 1992-1993 academic year the school had a staff of 22 and a total enrollment of 423. In 1992 it was accredited for three years by the Inter-American Division Commission on Accreditation and the General Conference Board of Regents.

Principals: Merrille McKenzie, 1952-1956; John Ambrose, 1956-1959; Merrille McKenzie, 1959-1961; Hollibert Phillips, 1961-1963; Nathaniel Moore (acting), 1963-1964; John Ambrose, 1964-1969; Ruthven Prime, 1968-1970; Nathaniel Moore, 1970-1971; Hollis James (acting), 1972-1973; Philbert Hislop (acting), 1973-1974; Rupert Ryan, 1974-1978; Peter Archer, 1978-1988; Philbert Hislop, 1988- .

HARPER, WALTER (1854-1937). Pioneer colporteur. He became a Seventh-day Adventist in 1879 and began selling SDA publications in 1881 in California. At that time he sold *Home Hand-Book of Domestic Hygiene and Rational Medicine,* by J. H. Kellogg, reportedly the first subscription book handled by SDA colporteurs. Later he handled *Thoughts on Daniel and the Revelation* and other large subscription books as they were prepared. Through the 1880s he worked on the Pacific Coast, delivering in his banner year 3,000 large books. Later he worked in all states west of the Mississippi River. It has been estimated that during the more than 50 years of his work as a colporteur he sold and delivered more than $100,000 worth of SDA books. Ellen White addressed personal communications to him encouraging him in his work.

HARRIS, CLYDE HEATH (1890-1968). Businessperson. He was born in Oregon and enjoyed a Christian home, although he did not join the church until 1914. In 1913 he opened a small box factory in Milton, Oregon. By 1916 he had added a sawmill and in 1924 branched out further. In the years of operation, only 1932 saw no profit for the Harris enterprises. The Harris furniture factory became one of the largest producers of unfinished furniture in the nation. In all his business dealings, Harris relied heavily upon the Lord and did his utmost to conduct his affairs in a manner pleasing to God.

After prayerful consideration, he and his wife, Mary, were convinced that they should donate their multimillion-dollar holdings to the church, which they did in 1951.

HARRIS PINE MILLS. A taxable wood products manufacturing corporation with its main offices and plant on a 70-acre (30-hectare) site at Pendleton, Oregon, and with branch plants throughout the United States. It was owned and operated by the General Conference for the benefit of Seventh-day Adventist work and was a gift from its original owners to the church.

The company operated four main divisions: lumber, furniture, cutstock, and redwood products. The furniture and redwood divisions had branch operations in 14 states other than the Oregon home base. The company was a fully integrated industry, handling all parts of the process from the growing of trees to the delivery of finished products to the customer. Besides its offices and plants, the corporation held a large quantity of timber and timberlands, and equipment for building and maintaining logging roads. A number of branches and subsidiaries were situated on or near SDA school campuses for the purpose of providing work for students.

The company originated in 1913 when Clyde Harris and his brother invested about $2,000 in the establishment of a box factory at Milton, Oregon, which they named the Milton Box Company. Soon afterward Clyde and his wife became SDAs. As business prospered, a sawmill was added in 1916.

In 1939 the company was moved to Pendleton, Oregon, and named the Harris Pine Mills. In 1942 Clyde Harris and his wife bought out the brother's interest and became sole owners. By 1951 the company was considered to be among the nation's largest producers of unfinished furniture. That year the Harrises decided to donate the business to the church. Harris related his decision in the *Review and Herald* (130:4, Jan. 8, 1953) in these words: "As I began to approach the age which many regard as the retirement age, I pondered as to what disposition I should make of my property. I thought of the wealthy men whom I had noticed when I was young. What had they accomplished? I bore in mind that all must soon pass. Why should I wait until I was old and no longer had the zest of life before I made my decision? My wife and I considered the matter seriously. We decided we wanted the Lord to have the business."

The company was turned over to the General Conference of Seventh-day Adventists in 1951 and continued to grow and prosper. In 1953 Harris Pine Mills was valued at $8.5 million; grossed $5.5 million; processed nearly 4 million board feet of lumber; employed 450 people, of whom 50 were students from Walla Walla College; and had two branch offices. Six years later (1959) Harris Pine Mills was valued at $10.5 million; grossed $8.6 million; processed nearly 51 million board feet of lumber; employed 648 people, of whom 205 were students; and had four branch offices. By the end of 1964 Harris Pine Mills was valued at $17.5 million; grossed $13.7 million; processed 90 million board feet of lumber; employed 1,202 people, of whom 575 were students; and had 12 branch plants. In 1973 there were 23 plants, with a gross volume of $40 million. Labor on a part-time basis was extended to 2,700 students.

The positive financial operations of Harris Pine Mills declined from 1980 until 1986. On Dec. 6 of that year the General Conference placed the company in bankruptcy to stop continued losses. There were sufficient assets to pay all creditors and retirement benefits, with the exception of a debt owed to the General Conference. Closure of Harris Pine Mills was a great loss to the church and its educational institutions, as it had provided considerable student labor and had been a blessing and benefit to many young people.

Prior to closing, the sales during the five-year period 1980-1985 were $321,442,985 and trending downward. Students earned approximately $50 million during the years of operation. Full-time employees also enjoyed the benefits of work provided by the mills. The company was completely liquidated and did not operate as a church entity after the closure on Dec. 6, 1986. Four and a half years after its closure by the church, in May 1991, the last owner sold all the assets and permanently closed the doors of this enterprise.

HARRISON, CHARLES (1888-1986). Physician, administrator. Born in Indiana, he studied medicine in the United States, London, and Edinburgh, gaining the M.R.C.S., L.R.C.P., and F.R.C.S. degrees. For more than 30 years he was medical director of the Sydney Sanitarium and Hospital (now Sydney Adventist Hospital). Not only was he a highly skilled surgeon and physician; he was also loved and respected by staff and patients. He was greatly appreciated as a teacher and lecturer.

When he returned to the United States, he became professor of anatomy at Loma Linda University. The Charles Harrison Memorial Home at Cooranbong, Australia, is a tribute to his contribution to Adventism in the South Pacific.

HARRISON, MARGARET (fl. 1890s). A Scotswoman living in Jamaica, she read literature distributed by James Palmer, a pioneer worker. She later opened her home to Palmer for Sabbath meetings. In 1893 Mrs. Harrison went to Battle Creek Sanitarium for treatments. While there, she attended the 1893 General Conference session and made an appeal for missionaries to Jamaica. Soon after, the first Jamaican believers were baptized and a church was organized. The second church was located in Mrs. Harrison's home.

HARRISON MEMORIAL HIGH SCHOOL. A coeducational day school on the senior high school level, operated at 3 Cottage Road, Montego Bay, Jamaica, West Indies, by a local school board. The 1992 secondary school enrollment was 261, with a teaching staff of 25. An eight-grade elementary school is conducted in connection with the high school.

The school was named in memory of Mrs. Margaret Harrison, one of the first Jamaican Seventh-day Adventists. In 1894 Mrs. Harrison paid her own way to attend the General Conference session at Battle Creek and pleaded that workers be sent to Jamaica. As a result, James Patterson, a colporteur, was sent, followed later by J. A. Haysmer.

Harrison Memorial High School was opened on Jan. 12, 1953, with 23 students in three grades and five teachers. The first principal was I. B. Benson, who served until September 1955. The first school board served under the chairmanship of H. S. Walters, then president of the West Jamaica Conference.

This school provides courses on the spiral system, preparing students for the General Certificate of Education examinations held by Cambridge University and the Caribbean Examination Council examination. Courses are adapted to the requirements of the denominational school system. The curriculum includes courses in Bible, social sciences, modern languages, literature, natural sciences, mathematics, health education, and applied arts.

Principals: I. B. Benson, 1953-1955; Joe Fletcher, 1955-1957; Mrs. E.C.H. Reid (acting), 1957-1959; A. L. Dwyer, 1959-1966; Mrs. E.C.H. Reid (acting), 1967-1968; J. Haakmat, 1968-1969; C. Perry (acting), 1969-1971; A. L. Dwyer, 1971-1974; C. Jones, 1974-1975; M. Chapman, 1975-1977; W. H. Gunter, 1977-1979; Mrs. Lunnette Wright, 1979-1984; Mrs. M. Reid, 1984- .

HART, JOSIAH SIDNEY (1843-1932). Pioneer traveling minister. He was a native of Vermont who came with his family to Nebraska, where he resided for 40 years. In 1872 he married Alice C. Perrigo. He attended Battle Creek College, where he prepared for the gospel ministry and was ordained later to that work. He devoted 30 years to ministerial work, traveling extensively in the area and raising up many churches by his faithful labor.

HARTKOP, JOHANN HEINRICH FREDERICH (1872-1925). Business administrator. He joined the Seventh-day Adventist Church in 1893 and served successively as a worker, bookkeeper, assistant manager, and manager (1900-1924) of the Hamburg Publishing House.

HARTMAN, GEORGE ERNEST (1879-1951). Missionary, administrator. He joined the Seventh-day Adventist Church with his parents when he was young. He studied at South Lancaster Academy and supplemented his education by correspondence courses. From 1897 to 1908 he worked successively as stenographer for the General Conference Publishing Association, as stenographer and bookkeeper in the offices of the Pennsylvania Conference, and as treasurer and manager of Pennsylvania Sanitarium. In 1909 he sailed for South America, where he served as secretary-treasurer of the South American Union (1909-1915), treasurer of the Austral Union (1915-1925), and manager of the Buenos Aires Publishing House (1909-1920). After his first furlough he moved to Brazil, where he was treasurer of the South Brazil Union (1926-1940) and treasurer of the Brazil Publishing House for a brief period. He retired in 1941 in the United States and died at Lincoln, Nebraska.

HARVEST INGATHERING. *See* Ingathering.

HARVEY, RUSSELL JACK, M.D. (1922-1972). Missionary physician. He was born in the Cape province of South Africa and spent his early years in Johannesburg, where he received his secondary education.

During World War II he served in the South African Air Force. Upon cessation of hostilities, he returned to his home city for medical training.

After his conversion to the Seventh-day Adventist faith, he was married to Maureen Kilroe Smith, and together they served effectively at the former Nokuphila Hospital in Johannesburg, Kendu Hospital in Kenya, Ishaka Hospital in Uganda, and Malamulo Hospital in Malawi. In this latter institution he instituted a flying-doctor service, which cared for various clinics and dispensaries across the country. His wife predeceased him in 1967. In 1971 he married Irene Ingheim, a missionary nurse. Because of his 16 years of service in Malawi, he was known to many as "Dr. Malamulo."

He was killed on Dec. 10, 1972, while attempting to land his light aircraft.

HARVEY INDUSTRIAL SCHOOL. *See* Sheyenne River Academy.

HASEL, GERHARD FRANZ (1935-1994). Educator, scholar, author, administrator. Born in Vienna, Austria, he was the third child in a devout Seventh-day Adventist family. His father, Franz Joseph, a colporteur and minister, was early drafted into the Wehrmacht and assigned to the Russian front, His mother, Helene, took a firm stand that none of her four children would attend school on Sabbath, no matter what the cost to herself.

After completing his secondary education, Gerhard entered trade school in Frankfurt and in 1953, at the age of 18, was declared the best engineering apprentice in the state and received a full college scholarship.

Feeling a direct call to work for the Lord, he relinquished the scholarship and enrolled at the Marienhöhe Seminary, where he completed the four-year licentiate program in 1958. During those summers, and during many that followed, he did colporteur work to meet expenses.

In 1958 he attended Atlantic Union College, and the following year found him at Andrews University, where he earned a master's degree in one year.

He married Hilde Schafer in 1961. Three children were born to them.

Gerhard completed his B.D. in 1962 and began a 27-year teaching career at Andrews University in 1967. He received his Ph.D. from Vanderbilt University, specializing in Old Testament.

In 1976 he became chair of the seminary's Old Testament Department and director of the Ph.D. and Th.D. programs. In 1981 he became dean of the seminary, a position he held for seven years.

He authored 14 books, four of which were reviewed 39 times in various scholarly journals, and wrote more than 300 articles, including one written by invitation for the *Anchor Bible Dictionary.*

At the time of his death, in an automobile accident while traveling to a camp meeting, he was working on two volumes, Amos and Hosea, for Eerdman's *New International Commentary on the Old Testament.* He was also serving as the first John Nevins Andrews professor of Old Testament and biblical theology at the seminary, and was an active member in seven learned societies.

HASKELL, HETTY (HURD) (1857-1919). Teacher of Bible instructors. She was converted at the age of 8, but five years later, when her father died, she lost interest in religious things. In 1884, while teaching a school at Lemoore, California, she reluctantly agreed to attend a Seventh-day Adventist camp meeting at Oakland. While there she was converted again and joined the church. The next year she attended one of the first SDA schools for Bible instructors, which was opened in San Francisco. Afterward she worked as Bible instructor and teacher of other instructors in California, England (1887-1892), South Africa (1892-1897), and Australia (1897-1899). While in Australia she married S. N. Haskell, and afterward helped him in his widespread evangelistic and Bible educational work.

HASKELL, STEPHEN NELSON (1833-1922). Evangelist, administrator. He began preaching for the non-Sabbatarian Adventists in New England in 1853, and later the same year began to observe the Sabbath. In 1850 he married Mary How, who in 1869 assisted in organizing the first Vigilant Missionary Society. After doing self-supporting work in New England, in 1870 he was ordained and became president of the New England Conference (1870-1876, 1877-1887). In 1870 he organized the first conference Tract and Missionary Society and subsequently organized similar societies in various parts of the eastern United States. He was president of the California Conference (1879-1887) and also of the Maine Conference (1884-1886) during that period, and part of that time was out of the country.

In 1885 he was in charge of a group that was sent to open denominational work in Australia. His preaching in New Zealand was climaxed by the forming of the first group of Seventh-day Adventists in that country. In 1887 with three Bible instructors he began SDA work in London, England, and organized a church there. He made a world tour on behalf of missionary work in 1889-1890, visiting western Europe, Southern Africa, India, China, Japan, and Australia. In 1918, some 28 years later, in a report to the General Conference, he related that on that world tour he baptized one individual in China and another in Japan, the first in these countries (see *Review and Herald* 99:17, Dec. 14, 1922). No other reports of these baptisms are extant, nor do later historians on SDA denominational history mention them. He was again president of the California Conference from 1891 to 1894. His first wife died in January of that year. Again in Australia (1896-1899), he engaged in evangelistic work and taught Bible at the Avondale school. While there he married Hetty Hurd in February 1897. Another of Haskell's "firsts" was the organization of the first African-American SDA church in New York City (1902). After this, he conducted a series of Bible training schools and evangelistic series in Tennessee and California, and once again served as president of the California Conference (1908-1911).

He led in temperance work in Maine (1911), began printing books for the blind (1912), and assisted in the development of the White Memorial Hospital (1916). Until near the time of his death he attended institutes and camp meetings, and promoted the general work of the denomination. His written works include *The Story of Daniel the Prophet, The Story of the Seer of Patmos,* and *The Cross and Its Shadow.*

HASTINGS INTERMEDIATE SCHOOL. *See* Platte Valley Academy.

HASTINGS, LEONARD W. (d. c. 1882). Prominent layperson of New Ipswich, New Hampshire. He and his wife, Elvira (1808-1850), were close friends of James and Ellen White. J. N. Loughborough *(Great Second Advent Movement,* pp. 166, 167) relates how Hastings' potatoes, left in the ground in October 1844 because he was expecting his Lord, escaped the rot that ruined the early-dug potatoes in that area. Ellen White tells of the healing of Mrs. Hastings and her infant by prayer (LS 122, 123). Hastings served on nominating and auditing committees at the organization of the New England Conference *(Review and Herald* 36:78, Aug. 23, 1870) and was vice president of the New England Tract and Missionary Society, New Ipswich, New Hampshire *(ibid.* 45:110, Apr. 1, 1875).

HATZFELDHAVEN RURAL HEALTH CENTRE. A former colony that accommodated 300 Hansenide (leprosy) patients (TB patients were also treated). It was situated 75 miles (120 kilometers) northwest of Madang on the coast of Papua New Guinea.

In 1949 negotiations were entered into with the government of Papua New Guinea to build a Hansenide colony to be staffed by mission personnel. An advance party, including the president of the Madang Mission, T. F. Judd, H. W. Nolan, medical secretary of the Coral Sea Union Mission, and A. S. Page-Dhu, superintendent elect, landed with equipment to lay out the site and begin building operations. K. C. Mitchell superintended the work.

In 1974 this institution became the Hatzfeldhaven Rural Health Centre, with Hansenide, tuberculosis, and general hospital patients. It was also responsible for general administration of a number of village aid posts and domiciliary treatment of both Hansenide and tuberculosis patients.

Hatzfeldhaven was nationalized by the government in 1980.

Officer in Charge: Peter Tutua, 1974-1979.

HAUGHEY, STEPHEN GERARD (1869-1958). Evangelist and conference administrator. After his education at Mount Vernon College and Battle Creek College he served as an evangelist in Ohio, Florida, and Tennessee, then went to Ireland (1899) and to Scotland for two years, then became president of the North England Conference. Returning to the United States in 1921, he served as president of the Alabama Conference (1921-1922) and the Nebraska Conference (1922-1932). After this he engaged in pastoral-evangelistic work in Nebraska, Minnesota, and Kentucky-Tennessee. From 1938 to his retirement in 1944, he assisted in the Editorial Department of the Southern Publishing Association.

HAUS STEFANIE (Stefanie Old People's Home). An old folks' home in Austria accommodating about 40 guests. It is able to accommodate 60 additional guests during church meetings, or holiday gatherings of church members. It is operated under church control and is located in Semmering, a famous health resort some 60 miles (100 kilometers) south of Vienna. This property, formerly the Spa Hotel Stefanie, was purchased in May 1970 by a legal society.

Managers: Josef Stöger, 1970-1973; Engelbert Hatzinger, 1973-1983; Karl Lana, 1983- .

HAUS WITTELSBACH OLD PEOPLE'S HOME. A home accommodating about 200 persons, operated by the South German Union at Bad Aibling (a town about 30 miles [50 kilometers] southeast of Munich), Upper Bavaria, Germany.

It was established in 1954 in the renovated 100-room former Wittelsbach Spa Hotel, which had been acquired for the Seventh-day Adventist Church in 1919 by the Deutscher Verein für Gesundheitspflege, Bad Aibling ("German Association for Health Services, Bad Aibling"). It operated in the summers between 1920 and 1943 as the Bad Aibling Sanitarium, offering a variety of water treatments, especially mud baths, under the direction of Rosa Staerr. The institution had 40 rooms for patients, with a total capacity of 60 beds. The profits of the sanitarium were distributed in free treatments to needy patients. Between 1922 and 1925 the sanitarium buildings were used during the winter months by the Aibling Seminary *(see* Marienhoehe Seminary). After World War II, until 1953, the property was used as a refugee camp. In 1954, after thorough renovation, the building was reopened as the Bad Aibling Sanitarium and Old People's Home.

The old people's home includes a nursing department with 64 beds, a department for physical therapy, and a doctor's office (internal medicine and natural remedies). Young people are being trained in several professions, including Bible and health instruction, bookkeeping, housing, nursing, and cooking.

Superintendents: K. Hasenknopf, 1953-1956; A. Sachsenmeyer, 1956-1963; H. Thieme, 1963-1973; Karl Fleck, 1974; Johannes Klingeberg, 1974-1984; Helmut Haubeil, 1984- .

HAWAII CONFERENCE. The unit of church organization comprising the territory of the state of Hawaii and the military installation of Johnston Island. The Hawaiian Islands were formerly designated the Sandwich Islands by Capt. James Cook, who named them after the earl of Sandwich.

The population of Hawaii (1993) is 1.2 million, of whom nearly 900,000 are living in Honolulu, the capital. The other populated islands are Hawaii, Kauai, Maui, Molokai, Lanai, and Niihau. Statistics (1994): churches, 23; companies, 2; members, 4,869; church or elementary schools, 9; ordained ministers, 28; licensed ministers, 2; teachers, 60. Headquarters: 2728 Pali Highway, Honolulu, Hawaii. The conference is part of the Pacific Union Conference.

The current governor (1994) of the state of Hawaii is John David Waihee III, a 1964 graduate of Hawaiian Mission Academy. After completing studies at Andrews University, he continued with studies at the University of Hawaii's School of Law. In the intervening years he was involved with the state constitutional convention, and prior to becoming governor was lieutenant governor of the state. Governor Waihee is now serving his second term.

Institutions. Castle Memorial Hospital; Hawaiian Mission Academy.

Local churches: Aiea, Hauula, Hilo, Honokaa, Honolulu (Central, Diamond Head, Japanese, Korean, Samoan-Tokelau), Kahului, Kailua, Kaneohe, Kapaa, Kohala, Kona, Lahaina, Lawai Valley, Molokai, Puna, Wahiawa, Waianae, Waimanalo, Waipahu.

Companies: Kihei, Lanai.

History. *Beginnings of the Work in Hawaii.* Seventh-day Adventist influence first reached the Hawaiian Islands in 1883 or 1884, when Abram La Rue and L. A. Scott went from California to sell SDA literature on Oahu. On Dec. 27, 1885, W. M. Healey, sent by the General Conference, arrived in Honolulu with his wife and 10-year-old daughter, having traveled steerage class for $25 each to conserve funds. The two colporteurs had stirred up considerable interest in the capital city by the time Healey began evangelistic meetings on Jan. 15, 1886, in a 50-foot (15-meter) tent pitched on the corner of Vineyard and Fort streets. When he left Honolulu four months later, there was a company of nine baptized believers. A. J. Cudney followed Healey to Oahu, and on July 22, 1888, he organized the nine charter members in Honolulu as the first SDA church in Hawaii. A few days later, on July 31, 1888, Cudney left Honolulu on a sailboat to go to Pitcairn Island, but his ship and all on board were lost at sea. Since his tragic death occurred before he had had opportunity to report the organization of the church, the church was not officially recognized by the General Conference until its reorganization in 1896.

On Nov. 19, 1891, while en route to Australia on the ship *Alameda,* Ellen White and a party of five stopped briefly in Honolulu. During the 19 hours the ship was in port Mrs. White spoke to a large audience in the YMCA chapel. The sizable attendance was largely the fruit of the efforts of G. B. Starr and his wife, who had arrived about six weeks earlier and had stirred up considerable interest there by holding meetings. The Starrs continued on with Mrs. White to Australia.

E. H. Gates arrived in 1895, and in February 1896 he reorganized the church in Honolulu. Mrs. Gates taught a small church school in their home. About this time Dr. Preston Kellogg (brother of W. K. Kellogg of cornflakes fame and of J. H. Kellogg of the Battle Creek Sanitarium) opened a sanitarium in downtown Honolulu, but it was short-lived.

Also in 1895 H. H. Brand and his wife opened a school for Chinese boys, and later (1897) a boarding school known as the Palama Chinese School, which later became the Anglo-Chinese Academy (discontinued 1903), a forerunner of the present Hawaiian Mission Academy. In June 1897 the Brands went to Hilo on the island of Hawaii, where they opened the Hilo Chinese Mission School (discontinued 1903).

During the administration of C.D.M. Williams (1905-1913), the first SDA church building in Honolulu was erected, a frame building constructed by the members at a cost of about $1,450, including the lot. On Sept. 26, 1908, Williams baptized the first two converts on the island of Hawaii at Hilo. In 1913 the first MV Society and Tract Society were organized in Honolulu.

In October 1915 L. T. Heaton and his family arrived in answer to a call in the *Review and Herald* for someone to go to the Hawaiian Islands to foster the colporteur work there. Heaton had been in charge of the colporteur work in Canada before going to Hawaii. After four years he returned to Canada for health reasons, but worked in the islands again from January 1930 until April 1946.

The first permanent elementary school in the islands, known as the Bethel Grammar School, was begun in 1914. With the addition of secondary grades, this school developed into the present Hawaiian Mission Academy, with a special English Department, which has continued through the years as a strong and important part of the educational work in Hawaii.

On Feb. 26, 1921, the Hilo church of 22 charter members was organized, with S. T. Hare as pastor. Hawaii thus became the second island to have an organized church. The island of Maui became the third island with an organized church, as a congregation of 15 members was organized on Mar. 16, 1929, by Robert McKeague, the son of one of the charter members of the first church to be organized in Hawaii.

In 1929 Hawaii became part of the Pacific Union Conference. Prior to that it had been a detached mission administered by the Foreign Mission Board of the General Conference.

Because its population comprises people of many races and different backgrounds, Hawaii has often been called "the melting pot of the Pacific." Several nationalities are represented in the membership of each of our churches. However, since most islanders speak English, this has become the principal language in the SDA churches in Hawaii.

The Hawaiian Conference carries on the work of the church in all five of the principal islands in the group.

The radio has been a factor of prime importance in evangelism. In 1931 C. R. Webster began the first radiobroadcast. The last 15 minutes of each broadcast was given to brief messages in either the Hawaiian language, by Robert McKeague, or the Japanese language, by Shohei Miyake. after he arrived from Japan in 1934. Broadcasts were expanded to include those of the Voice of Prophecy (first heard in Hawaii in 1942), the Voice of Hope (in the Ilocano language), and the Japanese Voice of Prophecy. Faith for Today also telecasts.

Land was purchased in 1966 for a youth camp to be located in the Waianae Valley. By 1974 seven cabins, restroom facilities, and a cafetorium had been erected and in use. The new mission office building was completed and occupied in early 1972.

Superintendents/Presidents: E. H. Gates, 1895-1897; H. H. Brand (acting), 1897-1898; B. L. Howe, 1898-1901; J. H. Behrens, 1901-1904; C.D.M. Williams, 1904-1913; F. H. Conway, 1913-1918; R. W. Smith (acting), 1918; L. L. Hutchinson, 1918-1926; C. L. Lingenfelter, 1926-1929; W. E. Atkins, 1929-1930; C. R. Webster, 1930-1936; C. S. Prout, 1936-1939; J. E. Fulton, 1939-1940; G. E. Taylor, 1940-1944; W. J. Harris, 1944-1949; C. E. Andross, 1949-1955; Cree Sandefur, 1955-1960; B. W. Mattison, 1960-1965; A. G. Streifling, 1965-1971; Lawrence Davidson, 1971-1978; Thomas Mostert, 1978-1979; Shigenobu Arakaki, 1979-1987; Charles Sandefur, 1987-1993; J. Lynn Martell, 1993- .

HAWAIIAN MISSION ACADEMY. A coeducational boarding school on the senior high school level in Honolulu, operated by the Hawaiian Conference of Seventh-day Adventists.

Several schools were operated in Hawaii before the founding of the Hawaiian Mission Academy. In 1895 H. H. Brand and his wife, sent by the General Conference, established a school in Honolulu for Chinese boys. After two years, at the request of leading Chinese residents, a boarding school was established to teach English, the higher studies, and "the Bible, just as it reads." It was housed in the former residence of a Hawaiian chief by the name of Nawahi. The property, being a part of the royal lands and unpurchasable, was leased to a Chinese, who subleased it to the school, which became known as the Palama Chinese School. In the spring of 1897 the W. E. Howells and Mrs. Sophia B. Kinner, of Healdsburg College in California, arrived to replace the Brands, who proceeded to the island of Hawaii, where they opened the Hilo Chinese Mission School.

In the fall of 1898 a public program performed in English by the students awakened such an interest that the resulting increase in applications necessitated larger school facilities. So enthusiastic were the Chinese patrons that in June 1899 a group of Chinese merchants agreed to purchase a lot (on North Kukui Street), erect the necessary buildings, and maintain the school so long as the church would supply an adequate teaching staff.

The building program was interrupted by an outbreak of bubonic plague in the Chinese section of Honolulu, and almost one school year was lost before the enlarged school, which became known as the Anglo-Chinese Academy, could occupy its new facilities. Then major differences among the sponsoring Chinese merchants brought on a crisis in the fall of 1903 that resulted in a mortgage foreclosure sale, thus ending the SDA mission operation of this school and dooming the Hilo Chinese Mission School as well. All the teachers returned to the mainland except the principal, I. C. Colcord, and his wife, who continued teaching the school under Chinese management until 1905.

In 1913, after a period without an SDA school in Hawaii, F. H. Conway, who was in charge of the church work in Hawaii, promoted plans for a church school in the basement of the mission home. As a result, Matilda Tampka launched the Bethel Grammar School in the fall of 1914 with more than 30 pupils. Much of the classroom furniture during the first year was composed of gasoline cases.

In September 1916 the Bethel Grammar School was operated in Kaimuki on the site of the present Aliiolani School. Two years later the arrival of a new teacher, Juliette Kaiuaola, who was part Hawaiian, held the school together, and in a second emergency, in 1919, other temporary teachers stepped into the breach. Despite interruptions, the Bethel Grammar School grew and attracted increasing interest among non-SDAs. New property was purchased in 1919 at 1426 Young Street and a ninth grade was added in 1920. Further growth made the Young Street quarters inadequate.

In the autumn of 1921 the school, then situated on the White property at 1417 Makiki Street, offered a full four-year high school course. Because it served all the islands, it was named the Hawaiian Mission Academy. Despite additional construction on the adjoining property at 1409 Makiki Street (both tracts totaling 46,152 square feet [4,300 square meters]), the school was hard pressed to house its student body, which had grown from 59 in 1921 to 153 in 1922. The extraordinary increase in the number of students of Japanese ancestry (from five to 95, of whom 69 were foreign-born) was attributed to the academy's strong English program.

Because of the large number of students deficient in English, a noncredit special language department for English drill was added in 1924. It operated continuously until 1943 and reappeared as the Special English Department in the fall of 1948. Between 40 and 80 students, mainly foreign-visa students coming from various parts of Asia and the islands of the Pacific, come yearly to learn to read, write, and speak English well enough to continue further studies in American high schools and colleges. The work of the Special English Department has created much local goodwill, especially in the business community, and it is recognized for its contribution by American consulates throughout the Orient.

The fortunes of Hawaiian Mission Academy were varied in the 1920s. The year 1923 saw an enlargement of faculty, an expansion of classroom space, and the peak enrollment (187) of the decade. Then the enrollment dwindled, until in 1928, after the mission board, for financial reasons, had reduced the academy to a 10-grade school, it reached a low of less than 120. However, the eleventh grade was resumed in 1929 and the twelfth in 1930.

From 1930 to 1939 the attendance grew from 131 to 280. There were also important changes in the physical plant, notably a new administration building, with an auditorium seating 250, fronting on Makiki Street. In 1937 advanced courses in teacher training and in ministerial and Bible instructor training were added, comparable with the first two college years as given at La Sierra and Pacific Union colleges. Because of an insufficient demand, the second year of the Advanced Training School was abandoned in 1941, and by 1952 all advanced training was discontinued.

Additional land on the corner of Keeaumoku and Matlock streets was purchased in 1941, giving room for the expanding elementary program, for World War II more than doubled the attendance. In 1946 the mission board purchased a royal estate, situated at 1438 Pensacola Street, from the heirs of Princess Kawananakoa. In December 1949 the administrative offices and the secondary and special English classes were transferred to the new property, making room for the entire elementary division at the Makiki site. The Keeaumoku-Matlock property, no longer needed, was disposed of.

A completely new plant of concrete and tile now stands on the old royal estate.

Two classroom units, comprising seven classrooms, teachers' offices, and complete laboratory facilities for chemistry, physics, and biology, were completed in 1949. The administration and library buildings were completed in 1953. A two-story home economics and classroom unit was occupied during the 1954 school year. The cafeteria, laundry, and bakery are housed in the George H. Miranda building, completed in 1957.

A second-story addition completed in 1966 added new classrooms, a language laboratory, teachers' conference room, and additional restroom facilities.

The completion of McKeague Hall in 1968 added gymnasium facilities for physical education, along with additional rooms to provide a place for music and industrial education.

The school cafeteria occupies the site of Princess Kawananakoa's home, which was long a landmark in Honolulu and the social center of many picturesque royal celebrations, where world diplomats and visiting royalty were entertained. Only the old garden, with tropical verdure in its natural state, is kept intact for student programs. As a memento of an international past, this garden is also a fitting symbol of Hawaiian Mission Academy's international student body, whose large non-SDA composition has been a fruitful field for evangelization through the years.

The doors of a new two-story dormitory complex were opened to welcome the residents for the school year 1986-1987. This facility provides a home away from home for students from the neighboring islands, mainland, and foreign countries.

Principals: W. E. Howell, 1898-1901; I. C. Colcord, 1901-1905; H. E. Giddings, 1920-1924; P. A. Webber, 1924-1925; S. C. Rockwell, 1925-1928; J. A. Simonson, 1928-1940; F. E. Rice, 1940-1945; D. J. Bieber, 1946-1949; A. W. Millard, 1950; A. R. Tucker, 1950-1951; J. F. Knipschild, 1952-1953; E. J. Digneo, 1953-1959; H. E. Voth, 1959-1965; G. L. Plubell, 1965-1968; C. O. Roy, 1968-1971; W. J. Bourbeau, 1971-1973; W. H. Claus, 1973-1975; R. A. Atkins, 1975-1979; R. L. Smith, 1979-1981; R. K. Among, 1981-1983; J. R. Ward, 1983-1987; H. P Winn, 1987-1989; D. E. Maddock, 1989-1991; W. R. Wentland, 1991- .

HAY, MARIAN MARGARET (1908-1983). Educator, editor. Born in New Zealand, she received her early education from the New Zealand Government Correspondence School. She studied at New Zealand Missionary College from 1924 to 1926 and at Avondale College from 1928 to 1931, graduating from the ministerial course. She entered denominational service in 1931 as a Bible instructor in the North New South Wales Conference and served as Sabbath school and youth director of that conference from 1933 to 1935, when she joined the Signs Publishing Company as editor of *Our Little Friend,* a position she held until her retirement in 1968.

HAY, ROY EDGAR (1887-1935). Minister, missionary. Educated at Union College, he went in 1913 to the Philippine Islands and did pioneer work among the Ilocano people. In 1917 he was placed in charge of the newly organized Northern Luzon Mission. Returning to the United States after eight years, he engaged in home missionary and Sabbath school work in the Nebraska Conference, and later worked in Colorado, Kansas, Oregon, and California.

HAYNES, CARLYLE BOYNTON (1882-1958). Evangelist, administrator, author. He was converted at the age of 18 and was ordained in 1908. In his Baltimore evangelism in 1911, he consistently made use of the public press, under the guidance of one of his converts, a newspaperman, Walter L. Burgan. One result of this was the setting up of the General Conference Press Bureau, with Burgan in charge. From 1912 to 1918 he was evangelist for the Southeastern Union, and from 1919 to 1923 for the Greater New York Conference. In his many years as an evangelist (from 1908 to 1923) he conducted vigorous campaigns in such cities as Atlantic City, Chattanooga, Wilmington, Baltimore, Washington, D.C., and New York. From 1918 to 1919 he was secretary of the War Service Commission. He was president of the Greater New York Conference (1922-1926), the South American Division (1926-1930), and the Michigan Conference (1934-1940). From 1940 until his retirement (1955), he was director of the SDA War Service Commission. He was one of the better-known Seventh-day Adventist writers on Bible doctrines for lay readers. He wrote 45 religious books, some of which have been translated into various languages. They include *The Other Side of Death, The Divine Art of Preaching, Living Evangelism, Our Times and Their Meaning, The Return of Jesus,* and *Christianity at the Crossroads.*

HAYS MEMORIAL HOSPITAL. *See* Central Texas Medical Center.

HAYS NURSING CENTER. A 120-bed nursing center situated in the beautiful hill country of south central Texas at 1900 Medical Parkway, San Marcos, Texas. Opened in October 1988, the facility is owned and operated by the Southwestern Union Conference of Seventh-day Adventists. Located near Central Texas Medical Center, HNC offers a full range of nursing services.

Revenues in 1992 totaled $2,141,000. The center employs 80 full- and part-time personnel.

Administrators: Daniel Swinyar, 1988-1990; Russell Weaver, 1990-1993; Raymond Alway, 1993- .

HAYSMER, ALBERT JAMES (1861-1950). Pioneer Seventh-day Adventist worker in the Caribbean. In 1878 he began to work at Battle Creek Sanitarium and there joined the School of Hygiene, the first class in medical training sponsored by the denomination. For the next nine years he worked as a nurse at the sanitarium. In 1883 he married Sadie Crandall, who died a few years later. In 1888 he married Mrs. Dora Wellman.

In the autumn of 1887 he entered the ministry in Michigan, and in 1893 went to Jamaica as the first SDA minister on the island. Later he served as superintendent of the West Indian Mission (1897-1905). After 12 years in the Caribbean he returned to the United States, where he served as president of the Alabama Conference until 1909 and as secretary of the North American Negro Department of the General Conference (1909-1913).

Later he was president of the West Indian Union Conference for five years (1913-1918). In 1918 he returned to North America and served as president of the Alberta Conference (1918-1920), and then worked in the Minnesota Conference as president (1920-1923), home missionary secretary (1926-1929), and pastor. He retired about 1937. For a time afterward he pastored the Stoneham church in Massachusetts.

HEALDSBURG COLLEGE. *See* Pacific Union College.

HEALEY, WILLIAM MAYHEW (1847-1932). Evangelist, administrator. In 1874 he began preaching in California and for many years was an able and successful evangelist. Sent in 1885 to Honolulu, he followed up the interest created by the literature distribution of his friend Abram La Rue, and baptized the first Adventist believers in the islands. From 1894 to 1897 he was president of the North Pacific Union Conference. The rest of his working life he preached in the Western states and for a number of years was religious liberty secretary of the Southern California Conference.

HEALING, FAITH. The cure of disease by supernatural means, through faith in divine power. The role of faith healing in the Christian church is based on numerous examples in the OT—Naaman and Hezekiah, for example (2 Kings 5:14; 20:5-7)—and in the NT, especially acts of healing performed by our Lord (Mark 1:30-34, 40-42; 2:1-12; etc.; John 9:1-7) and the apostles (Acts 3:1-11; 9:32-41; 14:8-10). The power to heal was one of the special gifts of the Spirit entrusted to the church (1 Cor. 12:28-30; cf. Mark 16:17, 18), and the sick were invited to ask for special prayer by the elders for healing (James 5:14, 15). It is evident, however, that God did not see fit in all instances to grant the request for healing, even when the petitioner was worthy and had, presumably, met all the conditions (2 Cor. 12:7-10).

From the first, Seventh-day Adventists have recognized faith healing as "a doctrine that the Lord taught" *(Review and Herald* 4:100, Oct. 4, 1853; cf. 74:10, Jan. 5, 1897), and occasionally specific instances of such healing have been reported in the *Review and Herald* (17:204, May 14, 1861; 26:166, Oct. 24, 1865; 27:198, May 22, 1866; etc.). From time to time there have been articles on the Bible principles of faith healing and warnings against counterfeits *(ibid.* 24:67, July 26, 1864; 62:331, May 26, 1885; 64:35, Jan. 18, 1887; 68:642, Oct. 20, 1891).

On the importance of discriminating between the true and the false, G. C. Tenney wrote in an editorial: "While we believe fully in the ability and willingness of God to hear the prayer of faith, and that He can and often does restore the sick in answer to prayer, still we are bound to say that we have no confidence that a very great deal that passes for faith healing is what it pretends to be" *(ibid.* 72:230, Apr. 9, 1895).

He cautions that Satan is able, under certain circumstances, to perform miracles of healing, and that in many cases of reputed faith healing the basic cause of the malady is a state of mind. It is "misleading," he said, to credit these "mind cures" to divine power. He warned against the danger that the sick may be led "to ignore rational measures for recovery" *(ibid.)*.

Various writers have discussed the principles on which faith healing can occur. In 1901, L. A. Smith stressed the importance of cooperating with the laws of health: when a sick person "is violating these laws, and from such violation suffers in health, he cannot reasonably expect the Lord to remove the consequences until he himself removes that which brought on the consequences." The man who "refuses to do what he can do for himself, and tries to have it performed by prayer" is expecting the impossible. "This is not faith. . . . God does for man what man cannot do for himself" *(ibid.* 78:474, 475, July 23, 1901).

Of the prerequisite experience of those who pray for the healing of others, E. Hilliard wrote: "*Divine* healing is not done through those who are living in open transgression of the moral law. Restoration to health, through the agency of those who knowingly disregard the requirements of heaven, is not from God" *(ibid.* 97:8, Aug. 5, 1920).

Other writers point out the importance of seeking competent medical counsel and help, and the fact that the answer to prayer for healing may come as a gradual process or by the application of principles of healthful living and the use of natural remedies, and often through the skill of competent doctors.

Probably the most extensive coverage of the subject was a series of five articles by Roy F. Cottrell in the *Review and Herald* from May 12 to June 9, 1949. This series discusses the example of Christ, human beings as the temple of the Holy Ghost, health principles and the dedication of one's physical faculties to God, the prayer of faith, conditions for answered prayer, faith versus presumption, the ministry of pain, and the marks of "Healing, Counterfeit and Genuine." Cottrell also dealt with the psychosomatic relationship between the physical and the spiritual.

Seventh-day Adventists believe that the invitation and promise of James 5:14, 15 are valid today, and that authentic instances of healing still take place. However, SDAs also believe in the principle known as "the economy of miracle"—that, at least under ordinary circumstances, God does not employ supernatural means to accomplish that which humans themselves may achieve by natural means at their command. These natural means include intelligent cooperation with the principles of healthful living and the use of natural remedies and medical knowledge now available. Therefore, special prayer should be accompanied by an intelligent use of the aforementioned means. This does not in any way demonstrate a lack of faith, and it may be that God ordains healing to take place as human effort cooperates with divine power. Furthermore, in general only those who purpose to order their lives in all respects in harmony with God's revealed will may expect God to hear their prayers.

The extensive medical and health work of SDAs around the world—sanitariums, hospitals, and clinics; schools of medicine, dentistry, nursing, and various fields of medical technology; health education and publications—testify to the church's belief in the importance of health as one aspect of the gospel message and of Christian living, and of their practical concern for health and healing.

Seventh-day Adventists believe that special prayer for healing should be accompanied by heart searching and renewed dedication of the life. There should be not only full and firm faith in God's willingness and power to heal but also complete resignation to God's will, and willingness to accept what His infinite goodness and wisdom shall deem to be best. The ultimate miracle—restoration of the sinner—ought always to be expected even when restoration of the body may not come to pass.

Seventh-day Adventists do not believe that the claims of the popular "faith healers" are valid, or that their methods are worthy of the name Christian or in harmony with the principles of faith healing set forth in Scripture. In view of the scriptural warning against false miracles, especially in the last days (2 Thess. 2:9, 10; Rev. 13:13, 14), it is always well to test presumed cases of healing closely by the principles concerning faith healing set forth in Scripture.

HEALTH. *See Vibrant Life.*

HEALTH AND KNOWLEDGE SECONDARY SCHOOL (Colegio Salud y Saber). An educational institution located in Tijuana, Mexico. It began operation in 1949, and by 1958 was offering both kindergarten and elementary classes.

During the 1970s the school operated at the preparatory level under the name Omega Preparatory School. In the early 1980s the school was known as Tijuana Secondary School; its present name was adopted in 1983.

In 1993 the school served 20 area churches.

Principals: Paula de Quijada, 1949-?; Tomas Ortega, 1958-1960; Apolonio Díaz, 1960-1966; Dina Barceló, 1966-1968; Rodolfo Bracamontes, 1968-1971; Ramón Aguilar, 1971-1975; Enoc Márquez, 1975; Isaías Medrano, 1976; Nohemí Soto, 1977-1978; Danie Suárez, 1978-1979; Atanasio Soto, 1980-1981; Abel Alvarez, 1981-1982; Hermelinda Quijada, 1983-1986; Adán Velázquez, 1988-1991; Daniel Cortés, 1991.

HEALTH AND TEMPERANCE. *See Vibrant Life.*

HEALTH AND TEMPERANCE ASSOCIATION. *See* American Health and Temperance Association; International Health and Temperance Association.

HEALTH AND TEMPERANCE DEPARTMENT. The department of the General Conference that, with its director, associate directors, and staff, fosters, counsels, evaluates, maintains close contact with, and aids Seventh-day Adventist medical work and institutions throughout the world, promoting temperance and health education in churches, schools, and to the public, and encouraging higher levels of health and well-being.

History of Health Department—*The Forerunner of the Department.* The earliest organization sponsored by Seventh-day Adventists for the overall guidance of the denomination's medical work was the Seventh-day Adventist Medical Missionary and Benevolent Association (later the International Medical Missionary and Benevolent Association). This organization was incorporated in 1893, with J. H. Kellogg, M.D., as president, A. J. Read as secretary, and H. J. Rand as treasurer. Unlike the present department, this association was both a property-holding organization and an administrative organization, intended originally for the control and oversight of all SDA medical institutions. Under the leadership of Kellogg, the Benevolent Association was active in the establishment of medical institutions in North America and, to a lesser extent, overseas.

Later an attempt of the General Conference to bring this more or less independent body into closer denominational control resulted in the withdrawal of the association from its denominational connection. Of the major medical institutions affected by this withdrawal, only the Battle Creek Sanitarium was permanently removed from denominational control.

Medical Department Organized. Profiting by its experience with the strong International Medical Missionary and Benevolent Association, the General Conference proceeded, in its 1905 session, to organize a medical department within the General Conference.

In the eighteenth meeting of the 1905 General Conference session, held May 22, W. A. George, M.D., was elected chair and J. E. Froom, M.D., secretary and executive officer, and the department was named the Medical Missionary Department (or Council) of the General Conference. The department name was later changed to the Medical Department of the General Conference, and in the late sixties the name was changed to Health Department. In 1980 it was voted to combine the departments of Health and Temperance.

Administrative Changes: Administrative function is shown by changes that occurred in the department through the years. In 1920 Franke Cobban was added to the staff for the direction of nursing education and service. In 1934 a secretary on medical placement was established and largely functioned at Loma Linda to more effectively encourage distribution of its graduates. In 1946 J. Wayne McFarland, M.D., was added as secretary of health and medical evangelism. Joyce Wilson (now Hopp) was added to the staff in 1956 to serve the department in the areas of health education and school health. To strengthen overseas recruitment and placement, E. E. Randolph was called as a new associate secretary in 1958. Also in 1958 Harley Rice was added to provide hospital administration expertise to the staff, and Eldon E. Carman, D.D.S., added dental expertise in 1971.

The 1950s and 1960s were years of major transition from closed-staff denominational sanitariums to open-staff community hospitals. By the mid-1970s the church in North America had formed five regional organizations to manage its health-care work. In 1982 a national organization, the Adventist Health Systems/U.S.A., was formed, separate from the Health Department, but in 1991 this was reversed, and the coordinating function for all health-care work was moved back to the Health and Temperance Department. In 1993 the church's health-care work in North America was operated by nine regional health-care corporations.

Other concurrent trends have also been seen in the health work of the church. The 1970s saw a much stronger emphasis placed on public health and health education/health evangelism. In the 1980s, however, a strong trend toward consolidation of departments and decreasing the size of the Health Department became evident. Since 1985 the total staff of Health and Temperance decreased from 37 to 10. Despite this downsizing, however, the department continues to serve an important function in such areas as AIDS awareness, drug treatment and prevention, and helping to develop for the church consensus papers on such ethical issues as abortion. The Christian View of Human Life Committee, chaired by the Health and Temperance Department director, has been particularly active and has published consensus statements in the *Adventist Review* and *Ministry* magazines.

Recognizing the importance of looking at alternatives to traditional medical care and the need to adapt to changing times, the department convened on June 19-23, 1993, in Silver Spring, Maryland, a major conference of representatives from around the world. Entitled Health 2000 and Beyond: A Study Conference on Adventist Theology, Philosophy, and Practice of Health and Healing, the proceedings have been published by the department, and recommendations for strengthening the impact on the SDA health program have been formulated.

Areas of Concern and Responsibility. The Department of Health and Temperance, at all levels of church organization, currently:

1. Serves as a resource for information and counsel on health and temperance affairs.
2. Advises the church and its departments and related agencies, in the development and administration of health- and/or temperance-related policies and programs.
3. Promotes a healthful lifestyle among church members through literature, programs, and Sabbath services.
4. Provides, through publications, services, and programs, an ongoing witness to the world concerning the detrimental physical, mental, and spiritual effects of tobacco, alcohol, and other harmful substances.
5. Sponsors and/or organizes societies to effectively involve church and nonchurch organizations in united endeavors to promote the nonuse of tobacco, alcohol, and other harmful substances.
6. Encourages involvement in the evangelistic thrust of the church by developing and using health and temperance programs and media that will gain the trust and confidence of people.
7. Provides support of Seventh-day Adventist health-care institutions, clinics, and health/temperance programs at each level of church organization. This is done through memberships on boards, inspections, assistance in recruiting personnel, cooperation with community programs, and support for spiritual ministries, including the work of chaplains.
8. Maintains liaison with Seventh-day Adventist health personnel-related organizations such as dentists, dietitians, nurses, optometrists, and physicians.
9. Promotes and/or sponsors health and temperance seminars and workshops.
10. Develops and/or catalogs resource material for health and temperance education and programs.

Secretaries/Directors: W. A. George, M.D. (chair), 1905-1909; W. A. Ruble, M.D. (secretary), 1909-1910; D. H. Kress, M.D., 1910-1911; George Thomason, M.D., 1912; W. A. Ruble, M.D. (secretary), 1913; L. A. Hansen (nurse, assistant secretary), 1913; W. A. Ruble, M.D. (secretary), 1919; L. A. Hansen (nurse, assistant secretary), 1919-1922; A. W. Truman, M.D., 1922-1926; L. A. Hansen, C. E. Rice (assistants), 1926-1928; A. W. Truman, M.D., 1928-1936; H. M. Walton, M.D., 1937-1946; T. R. Flaiz, M.D., 1946-1966; R. F. Waddell, M.D., 1966-1975; E. A. Crawford, M.D., 1975-1976; Samuel L. DeShay, M.D., 1976-1980; Mervyn G. Hardinge, M.D., 1980-1985; G. Gordon Hadley, M.D., 1985-1990; Albert S. Whiting, M.D., 1990- .

HEALTH AND TEMPERANCE MISSIONARY SCHOOL. A school formed by the Battle Creek Sanitarium in 1889 to prepare leaders and instructors in the health and temperance work of the church. It was a major part of the health education campaign that the sanitarium was created to carry on. Later its objectives were taken over by the American Medical Missionary College.

Background of the Educational Work of the Sanitarium. The work of educating the church membership and the public in the principles of health and hygiene stemmed from Ellen G. White's counsels in 1863 and 1865 *(see* Health Principles), on her insistence on the need for this work, and on her suggestion that an institution would become necessary to accomplish this task. In 1866 delegates to the General Conference pledged themselves to use their best influence to impress the importance of health principles upon others. In that year a journal for the promotion of health principles, *Health Reformer,* was begun.

Two years later, at the General Conference held in May 1868, the delegates noted that "the cause of health reform among our people demands that labor and attention which our preachers cannot bestow in connection with their other arduous labors" *(Review and Herald* 31:356, May 26, 1868). Consequently, a graduate physician, M. G. Kellogg, was appointed to present lectures on healthful living among the churches. However, after appointments at three churches where the lectures were highly appreciated, the doctor received no further invitations. A few months later he left for California.

During the next eight years the promotion of health education was carried with more or less success through the pages of the *Health Reformer,* lectures at the Health Reform Institute, and the efforts of ministers. The possibilities of a united educational campaign on the part of ministers and physicians was not well understood, and the matter was again brought to the attention of the leaders through the counsels of Ellen G. White in the latter part of 1876. Attention was called to the fact that Jesus combined the work of healing the sick with that of preaching the gospel. It was recognized that if His method was to be carried out in the Seventh-day Adventist Church, laypersons and ministers must have the opportunity of receiving a broader education in health principles. Attention was turned to the physicians at the sanitarium for leadership in such training.

The School of Hygiene. In 1877 a "School of Hygiene" was announced. S. N. Haskell wrote: "We speak in behalf of this hygienic school. We believe it is needed. There should be connected with every church individuals who understand what to do in the sickroom. They should know how to give packs, baths, etc." *(Review and Herald* 50:197, Dec. 20, 1877).

The school was intended to supply the need for lecturers in the field who would educate the people on the subject of health. The school was unique in America, if not in the world. Dr. Kellogg said about its objectives: "It is not intended in any sense to take the place of a regular medical course, but simply to give to individuals wishing to commence the study of medicine a basis for a broad, liberal, thorough, and practical medical education, and to supply to those desiring only a limited amount of medical knowledge an opportunity to become familiar with a large share of the practical knowledge in the hands of the profession divested of its technical dress, simplified, and put in shape to be readily utilized" *(Health Reformer* 12:380, 381, December 1877).

The school was opened Jan. 14, 1878, with an initial enrollment of 75 students, which soon grew to 150. The course continued for 20 weeks, with daily classes. Studies collateral to hygiene, such as anatomy, physiology, chemistry, physics, and mental philosophy (what today would be called psychology), were included in the course. The course of study given in the school of hygiene was accepted by medical colleges in the United States as a part of the regular medical course. The cost of tuition was $25. Room and meals were offered at the Sanitarium Students' Club for $1.60 a week, and some could earn their school expenses by working at the sanitarium.

Hundreds of students attended this course of health instruction during the several years that it was offered at the sanitarium. According to D. E. Robinson, many of these afterward gave substantial assistance to the organization and work of the health and temperance associations that were by this time flourishing all over the country, and a number of them devoted their lives to medical missionary work *(The Story of Our Health Message,* p. 244).

The First Seventh-day Adventist School of Nursing. In the spring of 1883 the sanitarium announced that it could give a three-month course of training to a few young women in "nursing, massage, the use of electricity, and other branches of the practical medical department," to be followed by a period of service at the sanitarium from two to five years. But apparently the opportunities of service in the nursing profession had not yet been appreciated by SDA young people, for only two applied for this course, the first attempt of the sanitarium to offer a course for the training of its own nurses.

In the autumn of that year another provision for a course to train nurses was made, and at that time applicants swamped the facilities. This time the course was to run for six months, giving the students knowledge in "all the branches of practical and theoretical study necessary to qualify competent persons to become first-class professional nurses." At the end of the first term the course was extended to two years, and that became the standard term of training at Battle Creek Sanitarium.

The Nurses Adopt a Missionary Objective. In 1888 a group of eight nurses dedicated their lives to missionary work. Their example influenced others of their class to combine the service of health with the promotion of religion. The idea of public health education as a part of the church's mission again came into prominence. Moreover, the network of medical institutions staffed by the graduates of the sanitarium grew and began to spread abroad.

The Health and Temperance Missionary School Established. By 1889 the need for efficient and consecrated workers in the various phases of the health and temperance program of the church outran the supply. Dr. Kellogg suggested that in addition to the need for competent medical personnel for service in medical institutions, there was a need for instruction in the principles of hygiene and healthful cooking at large camp meetings and other places where the people gathered.

To meet these needs, the sanitarium, with the approval of the General Conference Committee, opened in the autumn of 1889 the Health and Temperance Missionary School. It is indicative of the scope of the new school that at that time the committee recommended that the managers of schools, city missions, camp meetings, and other denominational institutions should select their matrons, cooks, and nurses from those who had received special training for the work at the sanitarium. At the same time it also recommended that the conferences should select suitable young men and women to take this special training.

Dan T. Jones, the secretary of the General Conference at that time, commented: "One reason why the health and temperance work has not been received more favorably by our people and others is because it is not understood, and its principles have been abused by those who have had the will to carry them out in their daily living, but have not been taught how to do so properly. If competent cooks could be selected in each conference, and educated, and then allowed to visit different churches and teach the sisters to prepare their food healthfully and in a palatable manner, it would do much toward advancing the interests of health reform" (quoted in Robinson, p. 247).

The new undertaking was highly successful. At the end of the four-month period of training it was reported that the average daily attendance was about 100 and that 20 were ready to enter the work immediately.

According to Robinson, among those enrolled in that first class were several persons who later became prominent in the denominational service: W. H. Wakeham, for many years secretary of the American Health and Temperance Association, A. A. John, J. B. Beckner, G. H. Baber, W. L. Bird, M. A. Altman, and Mrs. D. H. Kress *(ibid.).*

In succeeding years the school was known as the Health Missionary School and Medical Missionary School. The latter was operated in Chicago in conjunction with the American Medical Missionary College and apparently ceased to exist as a separate entity when its training program became a part of the curriculum of the college about 1901.

HEALTH AND WELFARE CENTERS. *See* Community Services.

HEALTH CONNECTION, THE. The official resource center for the General Conference and North American Division Health and Temperance departments; previously known as Narcotics Education, Inc. Materials produced by the Health and Temperance Department are distributed through the Health Connection via a direct-mail catalog and through Adventist Book Centers. Since 1990 the Health Connection has been operated by the Review and Herald Publishing Association in Hagerstown, Maryland.

The Health Connection has dual missions and markets. It is also commissioned to operate on a nondenominational basis for the purpose of placing in public school systems educational material on the subjects of alcohol, tobacco, and other drugs. This is accomplished by producing materials and by screening products available from other organizations ensuring that the best drug-prevention videos, software, displays, posters, pamphlets, puppet programs, and other educational material are offered through the Health Connection's catalog. *Winner* and *Listen* magazines, printed by the Review and Herald Publishing Association, are also marketed to public schools through the Health Connection. All materials offered promote a drug-free rather than a responsible-use message.

HEALTH EDUCATION. *See* Health Evangelism.

HEALTH EVANGELISM. The aspect of gospel work that presents basic health principles and offers practical instruction in health and sensible health habits as an avenue to a more abundant life and a sound Christian faith. Health evangelism may be defined as Christian health education. From the 1860s the Seventh-day Adventist Church has promoted health evangelism through its ministry, its medical institutions, and its professional personnel.

Concerning the evangelistic role of physicians, Ellen White wrote: "Let the medical workers present the important [SDA] truths . . . from the physician's viewpoint Physicians of consecration and talent can secure a hearing in large cities at times when other men would fail. As physicians unite with ministers in proclaiming the gospel in the great cities of the land, their combined labors will result in influencing many minds in favor of the truth for this time" (MM 248).

Many Seventh-day Adventist evangelists make health and nutrition a part of their public program. But beyond this, Ellen White was given the message that every minister should become involved in medical missionary work: Medical missionary work "is to be connected with the gospel ministry. It is the gospel in practice. . . . I wish to tell you that soon there will be no work done in ministerial lines but medical missionary work. The work of a minister is to minister. Our ministers are to work on the gospel plan of ministering. . . . You will never be ministers after the gospel order till you show a decided interest in medical missionary work, the gospel of healing and blessing and strengthening. . . . The Lord wants every one of His ministers to come into line. Take hold of the medical missionary work, and it will give you access to the people. Their hearts will be touched as you minister to their necessities" (CH 532, 533).

In 1868 Dr. M. G. Kellogg was sent to visit the churches to promote an interest in health, and in 1878 Dr. John Harvey Kellogg opened a school of hygiene for the training of health lecturers (see Health and Temperance Missionary School). Leaders of the denomination gave health lectures at sanitariums, and SDA medical institutions have carried on a continuous program of health education. Health courses are taught in SDA schools and colleges.

In 1866 the first Seventh-day Adventist health paper, the *Health Reformer* (later called *Good Health*), was published. The *Pacific Health Journal and Temperance Advocate*, published first in 1885, continued to 1904, when it became *Life and Health*, a monthly magazine. *Health*, begun in 1934, merged with *Life and Health* in 1948. *Life and Health* has since become *Vibrant Life*.

Nutrition Schools. Through all its medical institutions, the SDA Church has endeavored to offer a continuing education program in diet, cookery, and nutrition. To implement a specific program in union and local conferences, Dr. J. W. McFarland, of the Medical Department, in 1954 arranged for Dr. and Mrs. H. W. Vollmer to conduct nutrition and cooking schools in major institutions, with the objective of preparing competent instructors in conferences and local churches to teach the basic principles of good nutrition and to avoid the extremes of faddists. Since that time, other Health and Temperance Department associate directors have fostered this program. Currently many different forms of vegetarian cooking classes are being conducted for the public.

Other Programs. Other programs of health outreach that are evangelistic include home nursing classes, stressing simple home treatments, first-aid classes, weight control, physical fitness, dietary control of heart disease, stress management, and other classes and seminars designed to meet people's felt needs. Materials for use in such programs are available through the North American Distribution Center, the General Conference Health and Temperance Department, or the School of Public Health of Loma Linda University.

Health correspondence lessons and special health features are a part of the Voice of Prophecy, Faith for Today, and It Is Written radio and television programs.

Since early 1970 more and more SDA medical institutions have carried on strong health evangelistic programs, employing full-time graduates of the School of Health, Loma Linda University, as health educators to coordinate evangelistic programs with chaplains, doctors, and nurses both in North America and overseas.

Education Against Alcohol, Tobacco, and Narcotics. Since abstinence from the use of tobacco and alcohol, as well as narcotics, is a requirement for church membership among Seventh-day Adventists, there is a continuing program of education against their use. The General Conference Health and Temperance and Ministerial departments cooperate to help victims of the tobacco habit to stop smoking through the Breathe Free stop-smoking plan, conducted by minister-doctor teams.

HEALTH JOURNALS. In the year of the founding of the first Seventh-day Adventist health institution (which became Battle Creek Sanitarium), the first SDA health journal was launched. It was called the *Health Reformer*, later *Good Health;* however, it was lost to the denomination when Dr. J. H. Kellogg and the Battle Creek Sanitarium were separated from the church. It was last listed in the 1906 *Yearbook.* However, by that time there were seven other health journals. Three of these—*Life and Health,* Washington, D.C.; *Australasian Good Health,* Wahroonga, Australia; and *Good Health,* London—were in English; the following were in other languages: *Gute Gesundheit* ("Good Health"), Hamburg; *La Salud* ("Health"), Guadalajara, Mexico; *Sundhedsbladet* ("Health Journal"), Copenhagen; and *Le Vulgarisateur et Messager de l'Hygiene* ("The Popularizer and Messenger of Hygiene"), Geneva.

Through the years the doctrine of health has been an important part of the SDA message, and these publications serve to inculcate the principles of healthful living and wholesome diet and the basic methods of home care of the sick.

The current health journals, listed in the 1993 *Yearbook,* are as follows:

In English:

Good Health, Warburton, Australia.

Health and Home, Manila, Philippines.

Herald of Health, The, Pune, India.

Vibrant Life, North America.

In other languages:

Danish: *Sundhedsbladet* ("Health Journal"), Odense, Denmark.

French: *Vie et Santé* ("Life and Health"), Dammarie-les-Lys Cedex, France.

German: *Besser Leben* ("Better Living"), Hamburg, Germany.

Leben und Gesundheit ("Life and Health"), Hamburg, Germany.

Hindi: *Swasthya Aur Jeevan* ("Life and Health"), Pune, India.

Indonesian: *Rumah Tangga dan Kesehatan* ("Home and Health"), Bandung, Java, Indonesia.

Italian: *Vita e Salute* ("Life and Health"), Florence, Italy.

Kannada: *Arogyavani* ("Life and Health"), Pune, India.

Korean: *Home and Health,* Seoul, Korea.

Norwegian: *Sunnhetsbladet* ("Health Journal"), Oslo, Norway.

Portuguese: *Alcool, Fumo e Saude* ("Smoke Signals"), Tatui, Brazil.

Sande e Lar ("Health and Home"), Sacavem Codex, Portugal.

Vida e Saúde ("Life and Health"), Tatui, Brazil.

Serbian: *Zivot i Zdravlje* ("Life and Health"—Cyrillic alphabet), Belgrade, Yugoslavia.

Spanish: *Vida Feliz* ("Happy Life"), Buenos Aires, Argentina.

Swedish: *Liv i Nutid* ("Life Today"), Gavle, Sweden.

Tamil: *Nalwazhi* ("The Good Way"), Pune, India.

Telegu: *Margadarsi* ("Pathfinder"), Pune, India.

Urdu: *Sehat* ("Health"), Lahore, West Pakistan.

HEALTH PRINCIPLES. Seventh-day Adventists believe that Christians should have a concern for health, not because of any ceremonial or legalistic significance, but for the practical reason that only in a sound body can they render the most effective service to God and to others. The reason for emphasis on health principles is health. Health is related to religion in that it enables people to have a clear mind with which to understand the will of God and a strong body with which to do the will of God.

Seventh-day Adventists believe that at the Fall all three aspects of humanity's nature—the physical, the intellectual, and the spiritual—were affected; and that Jesus, who said He had come to restore that which was lost (Luke 19:10), seeks to save the whole person. In His ministry Christ touched these three aspects: He preached the gospel of the kingdom (spiritual), He healed those who were mentally deranged (intellectual), and He restored those afflicted with disease (physical).

Apart from this divine example of our Lord, SDAs find elsewhere in the New Testament a recognition of the importance of a healthy, sound body. For example, Paul declares: "I beseech you therefore, brethren, by the mercies of God, that ye present your bodies a living sacrifice, holy, acceptable unto God, which is your reasonable service" (Rom. 12:1). "What? know ye not that your body is the temple of the Holy Ghost which is in you, which ye have of God, and ye are not your own? For ye are bought with a price: therefore glorify God in your body, and in your spirit, which are God's" (1 Cor. 6:19, 20). He further taught that belief in the soon coming of Christ calls for a dedication of the complete man to God: "The very God of peace sanctify you wholly; and I pray God your whole spirit and soul and body be preserved blameless unto the coming of our Lord Jesus Christ" (1 Thess. 5:23).

Accountability for Health. On these biblical bases rests the belief that there is an accountability to God for the preservation of health, and that the person who knowingly violates simple health principles, thereby bringing on ill health, disease, or disability, is living in violation of the laws of God. The smoker who brings upon himself or herself cancer of the lungs; the drinker who develops cirrhosis of the liver; the irregular eater, or the overeater, or the one who indulges in excessive quantities of heavy or rich food and develops serious digestive disease; the corpulent, intense, nonexercising business or professional person who is overtaken with a heart attack—all these are in greater or less measure responsible for the ills they suffer and bear some guilt for neglect of the bodies entrusted to them. This fact makes our relationship to the entire question of health a highly practical one, not an emotional or a legalistic one. If, as SDAs believe, Christians have the same responsibility to preserve the health as they have to preserve their character, then promotion of a wider understanding of basic health principles assumes an important role in religion and theology.

It is in the light of these facts that SDAs concern themselves with the care of the sick, helping to bring relief to those who suffer. They further endeavor to promote through education desirable habits and practices of health whereby disease is lessened or prevented and the body preserved in health.

Health Reform and Seventh-day Adventist Leaders. The emphasis on healthful living and the sense of responsibility for the individual's body as a Christian duty arose in the SDA movement in the same year in which the General Conference was organized. It was natural that a people who endeavored to apply biblical precepts to their daily lives should consider seriously the physical aspect of life.

However, many years before, at least one of the pioneer leaders, Captain Joseph Bates, practiced what was known as health reform. Emphasizing health principles as part of his message, he preached abstinence from stimulants and narcotics, though he did not urge on others his dietary habits.

James and Ellen White brought the subject of healthful living as an issue before the Adventists. As early as 1848 Ellen G. White spoke of the harmful effects of tobacco, tea, and coffee. In 1853 and 1855 James White reprinted in the *Review and Herald,* of which he was editor, articles against tobacco (4:178, Dec. 13, 1853; 7:9, July 24, 1855). J. N. Andrews in 1856 wrote that the use of tobacco was "a sin against God." In 1854 Ellen White admonished SDAs to adopt a simple, wholesome diet without grease and rich foods. In January 1863, during a diphtheria epidemic, James and Ellen White applied successfully to their two sick children the home treatments recommended in a newspaper article by Dr. James C. Jackson, of Dansville, New York, who emphasized the importance of healthful diet, fresh air, and water treatments.

Health principles as part of the Seventh-day Adventist emphasis may be dated from June 1863, when Mrs. White set forth in greater detail the cultivation of health as a part of the Christian's duty: "It is not safe nor pleasing to God to violate the laws of health, and then ask Him to take care of our health, and keep us from disease, when we are living directly contrary to our prayers" (MS 1, 1863).

"I saw that it was a sacred duty to attend to our health, and arouse others to their duty. . . . We have a duty to speak, to come out against intemperance of every kind—intemperance in working, in eating, in drinking, in drugging, and then point them to God's great medicine, water, pure soft water, for diseases, for health, for cleanliness, for luxury. . . . We should not be silent upon the subject of health, but should wake up minds to the subject" *(ibid.).*

At the same time, she spoke against drugs and flesh meats, and urged the importance of pure air and a proper diet. She published these principles in the summer of 1864 in *Spiritual Gifts,* volume 4 (pp. 120-151), and prepared six articles entitled "Disease and Its Causes" that were to form parts of a tract series, *How to Live* (1865). It was not until she had sketched out these articles that she read some of the writings of J. C. Jackson, R. T. Trall, Sylvester Graham, and others who were protesting against the popular customs in diet and dress, and the prevalent medical practices that now seem rather barbarous. Some of these "health reformers" held a number of extreme views from which she strongly dissented, but she was surprised to find agreement on many points. Mrs. White incorporated extracts from some of these health reformers, along with her own articles, in the six tracts *How to Live,* selecting and rejecting on the basis of the principles she had set forth *(Review and Herald* 30:260, Oct. 8, 1867).

When her husband suffered a stroke in 1865, she placed him in Dr. Jackson's Dansville health institution, but took him away because she disapproved of some of the treatments prescribed for him.

Regarding the health principles outlined during this early period by Ellen White, which were far in advance of medical practices prevalent in that day, J. H. Waggoner wrote: "We do not profess to be pioneers in the general principles of the health reform. The facts on which this movement is based have been elaborated, in a great measure, by reformers, physicians, and writers on physiology and hygiene, and so may be found scattered through the land. But we do claim that by the method of God's choice it has been more clearly and powerfully unfolded, and is thereby producing an effect which we could not have looked for from any other means.

"As mere physiological and hygienic truths, they might be studied by some at their leisure, and by others laid aside as of little consequence; but . . . it comes to us as an essential part of *present truth,* to be received with the blessing of God, or rejected at our peril" *(ibid.* 28:77, Aug. 7, 1866).

Again in 1865 Ellen White stressed the essential nature of health principles and their relation to other truths of the Bible. She wrote: "We as a people must make an advance move in this great work. Ministers and people must act in concert. . . . There are but few as yet who are aroused sufficiently to understand how much their habits of diet have to do with their health, their characters, their usefulness in this world, and their eternal destiny. . . . Sabbathkeepers who are looking for the soon appearing of their Saviour should be the last to manifest a lack of interest in this great work of reform. Men and women must be instructed, and ministers and people should feel that the burden of the work rests upon them to agitate the subject" (1T 485-489).

Furthermore, she urged the 4,000 members of the SDA Church that the progress of health principles was not to depend wholly upon teaching the principles from the desk and by means of publications. The SDA church must establish an institution for the treatment of the sick on rational principles, and for teaching the patients how to preserve their health: "We should provide a home for the afflicted and those who wish to learn how to take care of their bodies that they may prevent sickness. We should not remain indifferent and compel those who are sick and desirous of living out the truth to go to popular water cure institutions for the recovery of health, where there is no sympathy for our faith" *(ibid.* 489).

The result was the founding of the forerunner of the Battle Creek Sanitarium. Ellen White pointed out that such an institution, if rightly conducted, would be a means of helping the patients spiritually as well as physically; that while their bodies were being treated their minds might be opened to spiritual truths and their lives brought into a closer relation with the will of the heavenly Father. In addition, she proposed a plan whereby such an institution might assist the poor: "Those to whom God has intrusted means should provide a fund to be used for the benefit of the worthy poor who are sick and not able to defray the expenses of receiving treatment at the institution" *(ibid.* 494, 495).

Thus the gospel of health became a part of the Seventh-day Adventist message, "just as closely connected with it as are the arm and hand with the human body" *(ibid.* 486).

HEALTH REFORM. *See* Diet; Health Evangelism; Health Principles; Health Work.

HEALTH REFORM INSTITUTE. *See* Battle Creek Sanitarium.

HEALTH SECRETARY. A physician, nurse, qualified layperson, or a church elder whose duty it is to promote the health program of the Seventh-day Adventist Church in his or her respective area, on either the conference or the local church level. The health secretary sponsors general health education classes, cooking and nutrition schools, home nursing classes, school health education, and temperance activities. In close cooperation with the lay activities leader, he or she participates in the operation of local Community Services centers.

HEALTH WORK. A phrase common in Seventh-day Adventist usage, meaning not only the profession of medicine, but other phases of the healing arts such as nursing, dentistry, dietetics, the various paramedical techniques, and health education. The following categories may be enumerated:

a. Education of health professions and allied health professionals.

b. Preventive medicine and health education, Better Living centers.

c. Clinical medicine and dentistry.

d. Health evangelism.

e. Health care institutions and other facilities.

For reasons Seventh-day Adventists pay

significant attention to questions of health, *see* Health Principles.

Seventh-day Adventists hold that it is in the very nature of Christian life and faith to exercise compassion toward those who need help, to aid both soul and body. This concept is tersely stated in the motto of the Loma Linda University School of Medicine: "To make man whole." It is this high motivation that leads Christian people to give emphasis to various forms of medical ministry.

The many kinds of SDA medical work as listed above are employed under varying circumstances to conform to the requirements of each country, as resources are available. In larger metropolitan centers of more advanced countries, modern, well equipped hospitals are developed in keeping with local standards and needs. Except where the larger facilities are developed to be used as teaching centers, small towns or rural areas of newly developed countries are well served by smaller hospitals or by well-equipped clinics or dispensaries. In certain areas, medical units in some instances take the form of medical launches *(see* Missionary Vessels).

In the non-Christian countries of the world, medical work of some form may be the only Christian activity permitted. Hospitals, clinics, maternity centers, well-baby clinics, or simple dispensaries are cordially accepted where the minister is not allowed to go.

Any ministry to the sick in the spirit of Christ is a communication understood by all. It is for this reason that in many instances medical ministry of some form is the medium of choice for entry into new or difficult lands. More and more, effort in health education and public health, which emphasizes healthful living, is receiving governmental favor where curative medicine alone may be regarded as competitive with local practitioners.

On the lay level, church members are encouraged to learn simple health principles and to engage in local health and welfare work.

Education for Medical Work. Professional education to train physicians nurses, dentists, dietitians, administrators, and many types of technical workers is needed to sustain the widespread medical work to which Seventh-day Adventists are committed.

Professional education in most of these categories is available in the universities of most countries. Graduates from these secular universities are now staffing most SDA medical institutions.

The SDA Church currently operates three universities that provide medical education. Loma Linda University in Loma Linda, California, is a General Conference health science university that operates Schools of Nursing, Medicine, Dentistry, Allied Health Professions, and Public Health, as well as a Faculty of Religion.

The Inter-American Division operates Montemorelos University in Montemorelos, Mexico, which provides training in the biomedical sciences in such areas as medicine, dental technology, nursing, and public health.

River Plate University in Argentina is currently opening the denomination's third medical school in addition to the Nursing School operating there.

In India there has been a special relationship for many years between the Seventh-day Adventist Church and the Christian Medical College at Vellore. In return for the provision by the church of faculty and financial assistance, the interdenominational medical college has accepted a quota of qualified SDA applicants to the College of Medicine. Also, in recent years the church has provided support through Loma Linda University to Kasturba Medical College in Manipal, where a quota of SDA medical, dental, and other health-related professional students are also accepted.

Nurse training is provided in many SDA colleges and hospitals. Midwifery training is offered in connection with several of the overseas nurse training programs. Especially well known is the program in Bangkok, Thailand, now being operated through the new Mission College. Different types of medical technology are offered at several Adventist colleges and universities. Physical therapy training is offered at Loma Linda, Kettering, and Andrews University, and until recently, at Skodsborg, near Copenhagen in Denmark.

HEALTHY KITCHEN FOOD COMPANY, THE (AB Halsans kok). A distributing company for import, sales, and distribution of frozen health food products manufactured by different factories. It was established in 1983 at Rimbo, Sweden.

Healthy Kitchen is a joint stock company. The Swedish Union Conference is the sole shareholder.

The company is located close to Swedish Junior College, near Rimbo.

General Managers: Bertil Utterback, 1983-1984; Carsten Warn, 1984-1986; Ulf

Gustavsson, 1986-1990; Ilkka Kuivisto, 1990-1993; Bertil Utterback, 1993- .

HEARERS' CLASS. A class of those contemplating joining the Seventh-day Adventist Church, which is conducted among primitive peoples in certain parts of Africa. Indoctrination continues for one year, after which the "hearers" join the baptismal class for an additional year of instruction before baptism is administered and church membership is granted. A similar system is employed in some other parts of the world: for example, in the Pacific islands, where a preparatory class precedes the baptismal class. In pidgin English it is sometimes called "class make-ready."

HEAVEN. *See* Home of the Redeemed.

HEAVENLY SANCTUARY. *See* Sanctuary; Twenty-three Hundred Days.

HEBREW SCRIPTURE ASSOCIATION. *See* Israelite Heritage Institute.

HELDERBERG COLLEGE. A senior college operated by the Southern Africa Union, an attached union of the General Conference, Helderberg College is situated three miles (five kilometers) from Somerset West and 30 miles (50 kilometers) from Cape Town in the Republic of South Africa. Located on the same campus but no longer under college administration are the Helderberg High School and Helderberg Primary School. The college has a staff of 52 full-time and part-time lecturers and administrative and auxiliary personnel with a wide background of training and education. The student body (1993 enrollment: 295) reflects the rich diversity of the Republic of South Africa and includes students from 25 other countries. The academic year runs from February to November. The college is situated on 370 acres (150 hectares) of land on the slopes of Helderberg Mountain.

Helderberg College is the successor of Claremont Union College and Spion Kop College.

History. *Claremont Union College.* The Claremont school, situated on a 23-acre (nine-hectare) farm at Claremont, eight miles (13 kilometers) from Cape Town, began its first school year in February 1893 as the first SDA college in Africa, as well as the first college operated by the Seventh-day Adventist denomination outside North America. With funds provided by the South African members, Pieter Wessels in particular, a very representative three-story building was erected, which provided the kind of accommodation required for a coeducational institution with an enrollment of 65. It had classroom space for about 120. Primary and secondary education, and later a one-year missionary course, were offered. The church decided to run a nonracial, nonsectarian school in an attempt to recognize liberty of conscience, and about half the students were non-SDAs.

The college provided training in practical skills and industries such as shoemaking and repairing, laundry work, carpentry, and gardening.

Financial problems plagued the school during the early years of the twentieth century. The deep depression that gripped South Africa after the close of the Boer War cut deeply into the enrollment. Although fees were set extremely low in order to attract students, the enrollment ran at half the capacity of the college; at one time there were only 30 boarding students in attendance.

Some of the problems that the college experienced arose from the need to harmonize the principles of education brought in from the United States with the practical necessity in South Africa of preparing students to meet public examination requirements. Many parents felt that they had to safeguard their children's future by having them meet the national academic standards, and therefore did not send them to the college, whose administrators were unable to solve the dilemma. Nevertheless, the 31 graduates of those years have served the church in many varied and responsible capacities.

Spion Kop College. Because the expansion of the suburbs of Cape Town brought the city atmosphere ever nearer the school, and because there was insufficient land to allow the raising of the necessary food for the school by the students, it was voted in 1916 to move the school to Spion Kop Mission Farm (on a former SDA Zulu mission) in Natal, where the influences of the city would be eliminated and there would be a better opportunity for the institution to become self-sufficient.

School was closed in 1918 while the necessary buildings were being erected at Spion Kop. Early in 1919 the new institution, first known as the South African Training School, later (1922, when a more advanced course of study was offered) Spion Kop College, opened with J. I. Robinson as principal. Industries consisted of the farm on which maize and beans were grown, a small dairy that supplied the school and its staff with milk, and a factory in which clothing was manufactured by student labor.

The medium of instruction was English; however, Dutch, superseded in 1924 by Afrikaans (modified Dutch), and Zulu (a main African language) were taught. Thirty-two graduates were sent out from Spion Kop College. The enrollment never exceeded 100.

If Claremont had been too near the city, Spion Kop was too isolated from its constituency. It was decided to move the school to a more favorable location. The buildings at Spion Kop were placed at the disposal of the South African Union, which transferred to this site the Bantu Normal School from Bethel and reopened it as the Spion Kop Training Institution for the training of African workers.

Helderberg College. In 1928 the college was moved to Somerset West, its present site. There followed immediate and steady enrollment growth, and the number of graduates rose to an average of about 20 a year.

When the college opened, the total plant consisted of two three-story student residences and two staff cottages erected the preceding year by O. R. Shreve. The women's residence, later given the name of Meade House, served also as kitchen, dining hall, and laundry. The men's residence, named Salisbury House, included at that time the administrative offices, classrooms, and assembly hall. The administration building, Branson Hall, was erected by the students during 1929, and other buildings were built by the same means from year to year as the enrollment grew. Anderson Hall, built in 1951, contained an auditorium, several classrooms and offices, and the library. Glanz Hall provides a dining room and kitchen on the ground floor and a gymnasium above.

The church, with seating capacity for 1,000, was completed in 1976. A new women's residence, Anne Visser House, was occupied in 1977 and has accommodation for 134 ladies, with 12 of the rooms currently in use as guest rooms. Meade House was remodeled in 1979 and now serves as the Pieter Wessels Library (1993 holdings: 53,000 volumes). It also houses the E. G. White Research Centre, opened in 1983, and the Heritage Room.

At present the Business and Secretarial departments use lecturing facilities in the administration building, which also provides classrooms for the high school until it is relocated to its own campus on the Helderberg property. The Arts and Education Department and the Theology Department use facilities in the College Block, which originally provided boarding facilities and classroom space for the primary school. Additional recreational facilities were added during the eighties: tennis courts, swimming pool funded through student initiative, and extended gymnasium facilities. The student center, completed in 1988, has two squash courts, and provides room for social activities, student representative council facilities, and a snack shop. An imposing new entrance arch was erected by the Alumni Association in 1993, the centenary year of the college.

Through affiliation with Andrews University, Helderberg College offers a Bachelor of Arts in theology for the training of ministers and a Bachelor of Arts with communication, English, history, psychology, and religion as possible majors. The Business Department offers a Bachelor of Business Administration degree with accounting and management as majors, and also a number of diploma courses in business studies and public relations. These diploma courses vary in length from one to four years and are accepted by a number of national bodies. The Secretarial Department offers choices of emphasis in its diploma courses as well. Computer science is taken in conjunction with the other programs. The prerequisite for degree programs is matriculation or its equivalent, which is the standard university entrance requirement.

Helderberg College also serves as an extension campus for Andrews University for the offering of the M.A. in religion, where students can complete the work in four years by taking one quarter at the end of each year. To date, 49 have graduated from this program.

The college industries consist of the farm, dairy, and a maintenance and motor body shop. Through the provision of work/study bursaries, the college makes available opportunities for 80 students to earn part of their fees and gain valuable experience in the various departments. The college makes available 20 housing units for married students, and half of the single students are in boarding.

The total number of graduates from Helderberg College over the past 100 years is 1,371.

Principals of Claremont Union College: E. B. Miller, 1893-1894; Mrs. A. Druillard, 1895; Miss E. Peck, 1896; J. L. Shaw, 1897-1900; W. A. Ruble, 1901-1902; C. H. Hayton, 1902-1907; W. S. Hyatt, 1907; J. F. Olmstead,

1908; C. P. Crager, 1909-1915; W. E. Straw, 1916-1917.

Principals of Spion Kop College: J. I. Robinson, 1919; U. Bender, 1920-1921; J. D. Stickle, 1922; E. D. Dick, 1923-1927.

Principals of Helderberg College: M. P. Robinson, 1928-1933; G. E. Shankel, 1934-1941; W. E. McClure, 1942-1946; M. P. Robinson, 1947-1948; W. E. McClure, 1949-1954; E. L. Tarr, 1955-1961; P. J. van Eck, 1961-1964; H. E. Marais, 1965-1972; A. O. Coetzee, 1973-1978; D. Birkenstock, 1979- .

HELDERBERG HIGH SCHOOL. A coeducational multiracial school operated by the Cape Conference of Seventh-day Adventists.

The school was established not merely to teach the sciences, but for the purpose of giving instruction in the great principles of God's Word and in the practical duties of everyday life. To this end, the opportunities are here given whereby students can be fitted for a useful life and at the same time receive the proper education of the mind and heart.

The high school was part of Claremont Union College, established in 1893, as well as Spion Kop College in Natal from 1919 to 1927.

In 1928 the college and the high school were moved to its present premises on the Helderberg College campus on the slopes of Helderberg Mountain, just outside Somerset West.

In 1935 a system was started whereby pupils were prepared for the government matriculation examinations. The years 1935-1939 saw great advancement and consolidation become possible because of strong and dedicated commitment to the work of Christian education.

As of 1953 all standard 10 pupils were entered for the Joint Matriculation Board or National Senior Certificate examinations.

In 1974 Helderberg High School administratively separated from the college with the appointment of J.J.W. Muller as principal. This gave the high school and the college separate identities, with their own staff and a minimum of shared facilities. The high school also changed over to writing the Cape Senior Certificate examination under the auspices of the Cape Education Department.

At present Helderberg High School has no facilities of its own, the facilities being occupied by the high school being rented from the college. A fund-raising project is presently under way for the construction of a new high school on the Helderberg campus.

Principals: J.J.W. Muller, 1975-1979; O. J. Campbell, 1980- .

HELL. The place and state of punishment and destruction, by eternal fire in the second death, of those who reject God and the offer of salvation in Jesus Christ. The Heb. *she'ôl* and the Gr. *hadēs,* both translated "hell," refer to the unseen world, or world of the dead. The Gr. *geenna* denotes the "hell" of fiery punishment. The Gr. verb *tartaroō,* "to cast [down] to hell," occurs but once (2 Peter 2:4). Inasmuch as in the Bible the English word "hell" is used to connote a place of punishment for the impenitent, as well as the realm of the dead (*geenna* as well as *she'ôl* and *hadēs*), confusion often results. Recognizing the difference in meaning, the RSV and other modern translations prefer to transliterate the Heb. *she'ôl* into English as Sheol and the Gr. *hadēs* as Hades. Of the 11 times *hadēs* occurs in the NT, in nine instances the RSV retains the Gr. transliteration. In one of the other instances (Matt. 16:18), the RSV translates the words of Christ rendered in the KJV as "the gates of hell," as "the powers of death," and in the other (1 Cor. 15:55) it renders *hadēs*, "death." In the four occurrences of *hadēs* in Revelation, the term is in each instance connected with the word for death in the twin expression "death and Hades" (RSV). The word *hadēs* appears on many ancient tombstones in Asia Minor with reference to the grave of the person there buried.

The Gr. term denoting a place of punishment, *geenna*, is used 12 times in the NT. It is derived from the Heb. *Gê Hinnom,* or "Valley of Hinnom," the deep valley immediately to the south of Jerusalem. From OT references (Joshua 15:8; 2 Kings 23:10; Jer. 7:31) and from the description of its position in 1 Enoch 26:1-5, it has been identified with the present *Wâdī er-Rabâbeh.* Jeremiah (2:23; 7:31, 32) indicates that the valley was the site where the barbaric heathen rite of burning children to Molech was conducted. Wicked King Ahaz seems to have instituted this devilish practice (2 Chron. 28:3; cf. PK 57). Manasseh, a grandson of Ahaz, restored this rite (2 Chron. 33:1, 6; cf. Jer. 32:35). Years later good King Josiah formally desecrated the high places in the Valley of Hinnom (2 Kings 23:10), thus bringing the practice to a halt. Jeremiah announced that because of this wicked practice the valley was to be called "valley of slaughter," because there the enemies of the Jews would kill the fleeing inhabitants of Jerusalem and leave their bodies unburied (Jer. 7:32; 19:6, 7).

In the postexilic period, with the development of a definite doctrine of eschatology, the idea of a fiery hell as the place of punishment for sinners became a part of popular Jewish belief. *Gê Hinnom* was regarded first as the entrance to hell, and then as a term for hell itself. See also 1 Enoch 67:6; 90:26; 98:3. The tradition that makes the Valley of Gehenna a place of burning rubbish, and thus a type of the fires of the last day, appears to have originated with Rabbi Kimchi, a Jewish scholar of the twelfth and thirteenth centuries. Ancient Jewish literature knows nothing of the idea. The earlier rabbis cite Isa. 31:9 for the concept of Gehenna's being a type of the fires of the last day.

Three times in the Sermon on the Mount, Jesus referred to *geenna* (Matt. 5:22, 29, 30). He also spoke of Him who is "able to destroy both soul and body in hell *[geenna]"* (Matt. 10:28), and warned the Pharisees of "the damnation of hell *[geenna]"* (Matt. 23:33). He said that it is better to be maimed and gain eternal life than to be cast whole into *geenna* (Mark 9:43, 45, 47). Luke 12:5 clearly indicates that the *geenna* experience lies beyond death.

As to the nature and effect of hellfire, Bible teaching is clear. In Matt. 3:12 sinners are compared to chaff that is burned with "unquenchable fire" (cf. Mark 9:43-48; Luke 3:9). In Matt. 25:41 the wicked are represented as being consigned to "everlasting *[aiōnios]* fire." And in Matt. 5:22 Jesus referred to the final judgment on the wicked as "hellfire." All three passages refer to the fires of the last day that will devour the wicked and all their works. This fire will purge the earth (2 Peter 3:10-12; Luke 3:17). It will be ignited after all the finally impenitent who come up in the second resurrection (Rev. 20:5) are marshaled under Satan around the New Jerusalem (v. 9). (In other words, it is not burning now.) The devil, his evil confederates, and all who have been deceived by them are cast into this lake of fire (vs. 10, 14, 15).

Seventh-day Adventists have generally avoided the use of the word "annihilation" because of the connotation some have given it, such as that the wicked forever cease to exist at the first death. The SDA view is that "the unrighteous dead will . . . be resurrected, and with Satan and his angels will . . . [be consumed by] fire from God" *(Church Manual* [1990], p. 31). This is the second death, from which there will be no resurrection. The word *aiōnios,* usually translated "everlasting" or "eternal," and once "forever," means literally, "lasting for an age," in the sense of being continuous and not subject to capricious change. The English words "everlasting" and "eternal," on the other hand, imply duration *unlimited.* The duration signified by *aiōnios* must be determined by the nature of the person or thing it describes. In the NT *aiōnios* is used to describe both the fate of the wicked and the reward of the righteous. Following the above principle, we find that the reward of the righteous is life to which there is no end, whereas the reward or judgment of the wicked is death to which there is no end (cf. Rom. 6:23). In John 3:16 "everlasting life" stands in contrast to "perish."

The word "unquenchable" may be similarly understood. Jeremiah predicted that God would kindle a fire in Jerusalem that would "not be quenched" (Jer. 17:27). This prediction was fulfilled when the city was destroyed by Nebuchadnezzar (2 Chron. 36:19-21). Obviously that fire is not burning today. It was unquenchable in the sense that the Jews were unable to *put* it out; it burned until it destroyed their city and *went* out.

This has been the Seventh-day Adventist position from the first. James White, one of the founders, wrote in 1850: "To those on his left hand the King will say, 'Depart from me, ye cursed, into everlasting fire prepared for the devil and his angels.' This 'everlasting fire' is that which 'comes down from God out of heaven,' and DEVOURS them. It will 'BURN THEM UP, saith the Lord of hosts, that it shall leave them neither root nor branch.' This everlasting fire, which will not be quenched until the whole host of Gog and Magog are devoured, which was prepared for the devil and his angels, will burn up, not only the 'root,' the devil, but the branch, or branches, his children, not a scrap left, thank heaven! Then God will have a clean universe and there will be no more tempting devil to annoy the saints, or holy beings of other worlds" *(Advent Review* 1:50, September 1850).

Uriah Smith, for many years editor of the official church organ, the *Review and Herald,* wrote a series of articles in 1859 under the title "Mortal or Immortal, Which?" He made a thorough investigation of texts bearing on the subject, and in his concluding article stated that the doctrine of eternal punishment in hell, unless proof is found in Scripture, should be rejected "as most dangerous and destructive error."

Seventh-day Adventists have also pointed to the inconsistency of the doctrine of eternal torment with the character of God as revealed in the Bible.

"How repugnant to every emotion of love and mercy, and even to our sense of justice, is the doctrine that the wicked dead are tormented with fire and brimstone in an eternally burning hell; that for the sins of a brief earthly life they are to suffer torture as long as God shall live. . . .

"Where, in the pages of God's Word, is such teaching to be found? Will the redeemed in heaven be lost to all emotions of pity and compassion, and even to feelings of common humanity? Are these to be exchanged for the indifference of the stoic, or the cruelty of the savage? . . .

"What would be gained to God should we admit that He delights in witnessing unceasing tortures; that He is regaled with the groans and shrieks and imprecations of the suffering creatures whom He holds in the flames of hell? Can these horrid sounds be music in the ear of infinite Love? . . .

"It is beyond the power of the human mind to estimate the evil which has been wrought by the heresy of eternal torment. The religion of the Bible, full of love and goodness, and abounding in compassion, is darkened by superstition and clothed with terror. When we consider in what false colors Satan has painted the character of God, can we wonder that our merciful Creator is feared, dreaded, and even hated? The appalling views of God which have spread over the world from the teachings of the pulpit have made thousands, yes, millions of skeptics and infidels" (GC 535, 536).

As to Jesus' story of the rich man and Lazarus, which is often presented as proof that the soul goes to its reward at death, SDAs believe that it was a parable and that Jesus was using an argument *ad hominem* based on the Pharisees' erroneous concept of the condition of men and women in death.

This concept is reflected in Josephus' discourse concerning Hades, in which he sets forth Hades as a place wherein the souls of all—both righteous and unrighteous—are confined until a proper season, which God has determined, when all will be resurrected from the dead. He pictures it as a subterranean region shrouded in darkness. In this region, he says, a place has been set apart as a lake of unquenchable fire, where the wicked will eventually be cast. At the gate of this region, presumably, stands an archangel, with a group of guards. Passing through the gate, the just are conducted to the right by their respective angels, to a place of light. Here in bliss and rejoicing, basking in the smiles of their forebears, they rest, awaiting the resurrection and eternal new life in heaven. This imaginary place is called "the bosom of Abraham."

Josephus goes on to explain that as the unjust reach the gate, the angels drag them to the left into the neighborhood of hell itself. There they hear the noise of hell and feel its hot vapor, while awaiting in fearful expectation the horrors of the lake of fire. They may also look in the opposite direction and see the righteous enjoying the bliss of Abraham's bosom. Between the two groups, however, there is a deep chasm which cannot be crossed by either the just or the unjust ("An Extract Out of Josephus's *Discourse to the Greeks Concerning Hades,*" in his *Works,* Whiston translation, Philadelphia [1853], pp. 524-526).

HEMINGFORD INTERMEDIATE SCHOOL. *See* Wyoming Conference.

HENRIKSEN, HANS LUDVIG (1896-1973). Treasurer and publishing house manager. A native of Denmark, he served the church for 45 years in his homeland, in Switzerland, France, and Madagascar. His work was primarily as a treasurer and a manager of publishing houses. He served on the conference, union, and division levels.

HENRY, ARCHIBALD R. (1839-1909). Treasurer of the General Conference (1883-1888) and a financial officer and adviser of many early Seventh-day Adventist institutions, such as the Central SDA Publishing Association, Health Reform Institute (later known as the Battle Creek Sanitarium), Battle Creek College, Colorado Sanitarium, Union College, Nebraska Sanitarium, International Medical Missionary and Benevolent Association, and American Medical Missionary College. Born in Iowa, son of a Methodist minister, he was educated at Simpson College at Indianola, Iowa, and became president of a bank at Indianola.

In 1882, shortly after he joined the SDA Church, he was called to assist in the financial management of the SDA Publishing Association at Battle Creek, Michigan. He held this position of treasurer continuously until 1897, except between 1885 and 1887, when he was vice president of the association. Between 1893 and 1895 he was both treasurer and manager of the institution.

In 1883 he was elected to serve also as a treasurer of the General Conference. In 1889 he was president of the General Conference Association of SDAs, in 1890-1891 its vice president, in 1892 its auditor, and in 1893 its treasurer. Simultaneously he was a member of governing boards of nearly all early SDA medical and educational institutions in the Western states.

HENRY, SAREPTA MYRENDA (IRISH) (1839-1900). Writer, temperance worker, one of the early leaders of the Woman's Christian Temperance Union, Seventh-day Adventist leader in women's work. She was born into the family of a Methodist minister who did much pioneering work in Illinois. Being too frail, in her father's opinion, to work at the household chores, Sarepta spent her childhood and youth accompanying him on his itineraries. In her youth she attended Rock River Seminary. In 1861 she married James W. Henry, a teacher, who died 10 years later, leaving her with three small children. She supported her family by teaching and by writing stories and poetry for publication.

Appalled one day in the spring of 1874 that her child had been enticed to enter a saloon, she set out to organize the Christian women of Rockford, Illinois, to active promotion of temperance. Gradually her sphere of action enlarged, and she became a national evangelist for the newly organized Woman's Christian Temperance Union. In the second half of the 1880s she became ill, and by 1895 sank into complete invalidism with a heart ailment. During the late summer of 1896, while a patient in the Battle Creek Sanitarium, she accepted the SDA teachings. Shortly afterward she was healed while in prayer, and resumed her WCTU work.

In 1898 she conceived a plan for what she called "woman ministry." Lecturing on the role of the mother in the moral education of society, she stressed this from coast to coast in the United States and Canada. She also presented her plan to SDA congregations. A. W. Spalding remarked later that in the work instituted in the Seventh-day Adventist Church by Mrs. Henry came "the first semblance of an organized effort to train parents and to give help in their problems" *(Origin and History of Seventh-day Adventists,* vol. 3, p. 200).

She wrote numerous articles for the *Review and Herald,* and among her published books and pamphlets are: *The Abiding Spirit; Good Form and Christian Etiquette; How the Sabbath Came to Me; The Marble Cross and Other Poems; The Spirit of Burning; Studies in Christian Principles; Studies in Home and Child Life; The Unanswered Prayer; The Way, the Truth, the Life;* and *What and How to Answer.* Her biography has been written by several authors, among them her daughter, Mary Rossiter, *My Mother's Life;* and her granddaughter, Margaret R. White, *Whirlwind of the Lord;* and by Ava Covington Wall, in *They Also Served.*

HEPPENSTALL, EDWARD (1901-1994). Pastor, author, teacher. Born in Great Britain, he served his church both in his homeland and in the United States. After attending college in Yorkshire, Heppenstall began his service for the denomination in 1928 as a teacher in the British Union.

In the thirties he transferred to Michigan, where he graduated from Emmanuel Missionary College in 1933. He then served as a teacher and MV secretary for the Michigan Conference. From 1941 to 1955 he was head of the Bible Department at La Sierra College.

He furthered his formal education by earning an M.A. in history from the University of Michigan and later a Ph.D. in theology and philosophy from the University of Southern California.

In 1955 he joined the faculty of the SDA Theological Seminary, where he taught and later chaired the Department of Theology and Christian Philosophy. From 1967 to 1970 he was on the instruction faculty of the Division of Religion at Loma Linda University,

Dr. Heppenstall was known for his warmhearted personality and vigorous teaching in which he frequently used the Socratic method. He encouraged careful thought, progressive attitudes, and loyalty to the church.

Heppenstall authored numerous articles and papers for the SDA Church, as well as the following books: *In Touch With God, Is Perfection Possible? The Man Who Is God, Our High Priest,* and *Salvation Unlimited.*

He was 93 years old at the time of his death, leaving behind his wife, Margit Strom Heppenstall, an author of note in the SDA Church.

HERALD OF TRUTH PUBLISHING HOUSE, THE. *See* Italian Publishing House.

HERALDO PUERTORRIQUENO (1932-

1940, 1942-1972; before 1945 as *El Heraldo Antillano;* 1945-1950 as *Heraldo Adventista,* monthly, in Spanish; 1972-1994 as *El Heraldo de las Antillas;* since 1994 as *Heraldo Puertorriqueno;* incomplete files in GC). The official organ of the Puerto Rican Union. When the Antillian Union headquarters was transferred from Cuba to Puerto Rico, the publication was moved to Puerto Rico. When the Antillian Union was split into the Dominican and Puerto Rican unions, the publication became part of the Puerto Rican Union.

HERI ADVENTIST HOSPITAL. A 70-bed general hospital, which also conducted some leper work until 1976. It is situated near Lake Tanganyika in western Tanzania, a few miles from the Burundi border and about 45 miles (70 kilometers) from Kigoma. It is operated by the Tanzania Union and serves the Ha tribe primarily, but draws patients from other tribes as well.

W. Sparrow began construction in 1947. Before the buildings were completed, a clinic was opened in June 1949, with Dr. W. H. Taylor, F.R.C.S., in charge and Alice Jensen as nurse. Petro Morwa was the first ministerial worker in the area. In the same year work was begun for 20 lepers, the government supplying the necessary drugs. The number of lepers later increased to 500, most of them outpatients.

The hospital opened officially in June 1953. The plant consists of an administration block, a men's ward, a women's ward, a surgical unit with X-ray equipment, an Outpatient Department, utility buildings, and staff housing.

The present nursing staff is made up of nationals. It consists of a nursing director, two registered male nurses, two registered nurse midwives, and one psychiatric nurse. The beds are usually filled, and the average daily outpatient load is 40. In addition to the work at the hospital, five outclinics are operated, at Heru Juu, Kasulu, Rusaha, Kagunga, and Mpanda.

The Division of Public Health and Tropical Medicine of Loma Linda University has graduated a number of African workers through the years. Evangelism has been fostered at Heri, and a church building was dedicated in 1961. In 1993 there were 10 organized churches, with 2,236 members. As a result, a field was organized to carry the work forward in the western zone of Tanzania.

Medical Directors: W. H. Taylor, 1949-1958; W. E. Birkenstock, 1959-1962; C. L. Wical (acting), 1962-1964; C. Blaine, 1964-1967; N. Ashton, 1967-1970; B. Nelson (acting), 1970-1971; J. A. Twing, 1971-1972; F. Mtango (acting), 1972-1973; R. G. Thomas, 1973-1976; P. L. Laguno, 1976-1977; Dan N. Holm, 1977-1980; Alvin Rocero, 1980-1984; Ferran Sabate, 1984-1986; Aguido Magdadaro, 1986-1988; E. Kraft, 1988-1989; N. Katondo, 1989- .

HERITAGE ACADEMY (formerly Little Creek Academy). *See* Madison Institutions.

HERITAGE GREEN SENIOR CENTRE. A senior retirement community comprised of a 110-apartment complex, a 20-bed retirement lodge, and an 87-bed nursing home. The complex is located in southern Ontario, Canada, in a quiet country setting in the city of Stoney Creek. It is designed and operated to help seniors live a more comfortable, fulfilling life in a Christian, homelike atmosphere. It is a nonprofit institution owned and operated by the Ontario Conference of the Seventh-day Adventist Church. An Adventist church is located on site to serve residents and the community.

HETZE, GOTTLIEB (1848-1927). A pioneer Seventh-day Adventist worker in Russia. He was born in the German settlement of Dreispitz, on the Volga River in Russia, and in 1883 emigrated to the United States, where he lived in Kansas and later in Oklahoma. After becoming an SDA he went to Russia in 1902 at his own expense and worked as a self-supporting evangelist. Later he was ordained to the ministry and served in the Volga River area, the Caucasus, the Urals, and the Crimea. For a time he carried departmental responsibilities in the conferences. In 1922 he returned to America. His death was brought about as a result of a fall that he sustained while helping to erect a church building at Okeene, Kansas (he had been a carpenter by trade).

HETZELL, MARGARET CAROL (1917-1978). Departmental director, writer. Born in New Jersey, she accepted the Seventh-day Adventist message as a teenager. She was encouraged by Pastor Horace Shaw to attend Washington Missionary College, where she worked her way through in the proofroom of the College Press.

Her first work with the church was in the proofroom at the Review and Herald Publishing Association. Her hobby of photography came to the attention of the General

Conference Bureau of Public Relations, predecessor of the Communication Department, and in 1951 she became a staff member of the bureau. In 1954 she became assistant director and in 1962 associate director. At the General Conference session in 1975 she assumed the responsibilities of director of the department.

Hetzell wrote scores of articles for SDA publications and non-SDA magazines. She produced workbooks in communication, and numerous film and program scripts and articles appearing in many countries. She was editor of *Tell* for more than 20 years. Her book, *The Undaunted*, published in 1967, told of the miraculous things that happened to people spreading the good news of the gospel.

She was listed in *Who's Who of American Women, Who's Who in Public Relations, Foremost Women in Communications*, and several other biographical publications.

HEWITT, DAVID (1805-1878). First Seventh-day Adventist convert in Battle Creek, Michigan. He is prominent in SDA history mainly because of the interesting story of his first meeting with SDAs. A traveling peddler by occupation and a Presbyterian by profession, he was pointed out to Joseph Bates in 1852 as the most honest man in the town of Battle Creek. He accepted the Seventh-day Adventist doctrines, being one of the earliest non-Millerites to join the movement. He was baptized in the same year together with J. P. Kellogg. He preached occasionally, it seems, although Bates called him one of the "professed public teachers" in Michigan. He wrote several letters to, and contributed short doctrinal articles for, the *Review and Herald*. At the time the denominational name was formally discussed, he was the first to move that "we take the name Seventh-day Adventists," though the motion was later withdrawn and rephrased.

HIDALGO VERACRUZ CONFERENCE. *See* Inter-American Division; Mexico.

HIGH SCHOOLS. *See* Schools, Seventh-day Adventist.

HIGHLAND ACADEMY. A coeducational boarding school on the senior high school level located in the north central part of the state of Tennessee. Situated 40 miles (65 kilometers) north of Nashville, on State Highway 109 between Gallatin and Portland, the school is owned and operated by the Kentucky-Tennessee Conference of Seventh-day Adventists. It received accreditation with the Seventh-day Adventist Board of Regents on July 1, 1949, and with the state of Tennessee on Aug. 11, 1961. The current curriculum is accredited and includes courses that offer the students a choice of general or college preparatory programs.

The school operates on a 387-acre (160-hectare) property on which can be found an administration-classroom building, two dormitories, a large gymnasium, a music-fine arts building, a lighted athletic field, and several faculty homes, all attractive and set in the midst of a tree-shaded campus. Highland Manor, a nursing home facility; Wilks Publications; and a newly established packing industry are also on campus, providing work opportunities for the students.

Highland Academy is the successor of the privately owned Fountain Head Rural School and Sanitarium. This school was established when Forrest F. West and his family, accompanied by his mother and his sisters, Edna and Bessie West, moved from Springfield, Missouri, in January 1907. They were joined by Braden Mulford, brother of Mrs. F. West, who had assisted in the founding of Madison College. The group felt strongly that a school should be established at Fountain Head, near Portland, and a hospital be built that would not only benefit the community but also provide employment for boys and girls to work their way through school.

Some of the first industries included a farm, dairy, orchard, woodworking shop, cannery, and also a sawmill, which furnished lumber for the first school building, which was erected in 1908.

B. N. Mulford headed the school from 1907 to 1942. It offered only grades 1-8 during the first five years, added two secondary years in 1912, and became a complete secondary school in 1940.

F. F. West was in charge of agriculture in the early years. The Mulfords, both registered nurses, were also instrumental in founding the first sanitarium, in 1907.

Transfer to Conference. In 1945 the academy and sanitarium, administered as one institution, were taken over by the Kentucky-Tennessee Conference and the Alabama-Mississippi Conference and operated jointly until 1948, when the institution became the property of the Kentucky-Tennessee Conference. In October 1945 the school's name was changed from Fountain Head Rural School to Highland Academy.

The Student Association sponsors the publication of the school newspaper, the *Highlander,* and the yearbook, the *Chimes,* both published since 1949.

Principals: M. E. Moore, 1945-1946; William Sandborn, 1946-1947; M. E. Moore, 1947-1948; W. F. Ray, 1949-1951; J. H. Bischoff, 1951-1952; L. C. Strickland, 1952-1956; H. D. Lawson, 1956-1962; C. U. Dunbebin, 1962-1966; J. T. Durichek, 1966-1969; D. Weatherall, 1969-1973; D. W. McNutt, 1973-1976; L. H. Opp, 1976-1977; Gerald Coy, 1977-1980; Eugene Brewer, 1980-1984; H. D. Lawson, 1984-1987; Richard Stevenson, 1987-1988; Melvin Eisele, 1988-1989; Jim Ingersoll, 1989- .

HIGHLAND HOSPITAL. *See* Tennessee Christian Medical Center—Portland.

HIGHLAND VIEW ACADEMY. A coeducational school on the senior high school level operated by the Chesapeake Conference. It is situated on the western slope of South Mountain, six miles (10 kilometers) east of Hagerstown, Maryland, on Mount Aetna Road.

Prior to 1947 the Seventh-day Adventist congregations in the area maintained independent church schools, but the need was felt for a strong consolidated school. In September of that year the Black Rock Junior Academy, offering the ninth and tenth grades, was begun in the Smithsburg church. The next year the eleventh grade was added. In 1948 a 292-acre (120-hectare) tract at South Mountain was purchased, half to be sold as homesites to help finance the new school building, and plans were drawn for a one-story, four-room school of modern design. The Chesapeake Conference purchased about 20 acres (eight hectares) for an MV summer camp. In the fall of 1949 Mount Aetna Academy was opened as a full 12-grade school.

In 1950 a gymnasium and two more classrooms were added. SDAs began to move in, forming a rural community adjacent to the school. In 1958 a new water system, from springs, was installed, supplying 37 homes, Mount Aetna Academy, and the campsite.

In 1965 the Chesapeake Conference committee voted to establish a conference boarding academy at Mount Aetna. The name Highland View Academy was announced in October 1965.

As of 1992 the academy has two dormitories, a large cafeteria, and an administration building with a new library. A new church has just been built on the campus. Two commercial bakeries, run by Hadley Farms and Davita Foods, provide work opportunities for the students. Enrollment is generally between 150 and 200 students.

Principals: Mrs. Lincoln Cox, 1949-1952; C. B. Mosher, 1952-1956; Carl Shafer, 1956-1958; James Davis, 1958-1959; William Joost, 1959-1960; Merle Rouse, 1960-1961; Wesley Moore, 1961-1964; John Wright, 1964-1965; E. W. Kier, 1965-1968; A. D. Holmes, 1968-1971; D. R. Keele, 1971-1974; J. R. Bailey, 1974-1976; Harvey Bristow, 1976-1979; Harvey Byram, 1979-1987; Harry Mayden, 1987-1992; Morgan Hellgren, 1992- .

HILLIARD, WILLIAM IRA (1888-1971). Missionary and treasurer. He was born in South Dakota and graduated as a nurse from the Glendale Sanitarium in California. In 1916 he married a classmate, Jessie Allen, and that summer they sailed for China, where he assisted in establishing our first medical institution in Shanghai. He spent a total of 46 years in overseas service to the church. This included various capacities of service, but was predominantly in the field of finance. Included also were three and a half years in Japanese concentration camps.

HILO CHINESE MISSION SCHOOL. *See* Hawaiian Conference; Hawaiian Mission Academy.

HIMALAYAN CHURCH. A former unorganized unit of church territory (most of it unentered) assigned to the Northeast Union, which is a part of the Southern Asia Division; it was listed in the *Yearbook* from 1956 through 1964. It comprised Bhutan, Nepal, Sikkim, Tibet, and an area in northeast India.

HIMALAYAN REGION. *See* Bhutan; Nepal; Southern Asia Division.

HIMES, JOSHUA VAUGHAN (1805-1895). The great publicist, promoter, and organizer of the Millerite movement, and in many ways its leading figure. He was born in Rhode Island and went to New Bedford, Massachusetts, to learn a trade. In 1825 he entered the ministry in the Massachusetts Christian Conference. He fought the liquor traffic energetically and was an assistant to William Lloyd

Garrison in a battle against slavery. His Chardon Street Chapel in Boston became the headquarters for all kinds of reform meetings.

In November 1839 Himes invited William Miller to hold a series of meetings in his church. Himes became convinced of the general points of Miller's teaching and felt a burden to get the new doctrine before the people. He asked Miller why he had not gone to the large cities. Miller responded that he went only where he was invited. Himes then told him to prepare for a great campaign—that the doors would be opened in every state in the Union east of the Mississippi.

Himes launched *The Signs of the Times* in 1840, without patrons or a single subscriber, and with only a dollar of capital. He brought out a second and a third edition of Miller's *Lectures,* and was thenceforth in charge of the publication and the distribution of Adventist literature. He published charts, pamphlets, books, tracts, songbooks, broadsides, and handbills.

In New York City Himes established a daily paper, the *Midnight Cry* (1842), in connection with a great evangelistic series. Ten thousand copies were printed daily for a number of weeks and hawked by newsboys. When the meetings closed, the paper continued publication as a weekly.

Himes was back of the call issued by an authorizing committee, headed by William Miller, for the first "General Conference on the Second Coming of Christ" (1840). He led in inaugurating the series of Millerite camp meetings, and he undertook the task of securing a giant tent, large enough to accommodate several thousand people, to be used in cities where no churches or halls were open for Millerite lectures.

He took no part in the "seventh-month" movement that looked to Oct. 22, 1844, as the date for the Advent, but like Miller, he acknowledged its validity shortly before that date.

After the October disappointment Himes held to the Advent hope, but repudiated the seventh-month movement, or "true Midnight Cry," which he had been slow to accept.

Himes played a leading part in the Albany Conference of 1845, in which the main body of Adventists attempted to form a permanent organization. For some years after Miller's death, he was the leader of the mainline group called the American Millennial Association (later known as the Evangelical Adventists, but now long defunct). In 1863, having embraced the doctrine of conditional immortality, he joined the other main group, the Advent Christian Church, and edited the paper later called the *Advent Christian Times.* However, in the 1870s he separated from that body and entered the Episcopal ministry, in which he remained until his death. In these later years he maintained generally friendly relations with the Seventh-day Adventists.

HINDSON, ANNA L. (INGELS) (1862-1933). Editor, conference secretary. In 1883, shortly after accepting the Seventh-day Adventist faith, she joined the Pacific Press staff, beginning a term of service for the church that continued uninterrupted for 50 years. For nine years she was secretary of the California Tract Society, and in 1893 was appointed to a similar position in Australia. Several years later she became secretary of the Australasian Union Conference and held that office until she married James Hindson in 1898. Together they then organized the tract society in western Australia. At the same time he began the health food work and she acted as secretary-treasurer of the West Australian Mission. For 34 years she was editor of the *Australasian Record,* and for 18 years she edited the *Missionary Leader.* She served for eight years as secretary of the union conference's Young People's Department. Her 30 years as secretary of the Australasian Union Sabbath School Department have been regarded as her outstanding contribution to the church.

HINSDALE HOSPITAL. A 459-bed general acute-care hospital located in the village of Hinsdale, some 17 miles (30 kilometers) west of Chicago's major business district. It is the largest and oldest hospital in DuPage County, Illinois, where it has served the community for 90 years.

The hospital offers a wide range of services. In addition to medical and surgical patient units, the hospital contains a mental health unit, a three-phase newborn nursery, intensive-care and coronary-care units, a children's unit, and units for orthopedic, maternity, and minimal-care patients.

Among facilities and services available at the hospital are a level II trauma center; a regional poison control center; the Opler Cancer Center for advanced and leading-edge treatment of cancer patients; the Rooney Heart Institute for coronary care; New Day Center, DuPage County's oldest chemical dependency program of its kind; and the Paulson Rehab Network, the largest physical rehabilitation network in the area. In addition, the hospital facilitates a medical residency program on campus.

Community outreach efforts each year draw more than 5,000 people from northern Illinois to such programs as screenings for diabetes, glaucoma, heart disease, and cancer; classes in weight control, nutrition, and stress management.

The medical staff of nearly 640 physicians represents all major specialties, with emphasis on primary care. Approximately 2,400 full- and part-time employees staff the hospital. A corps of more than 500 volunteers, which includes some 150 junior volunteers from the community, supplement the paid staff by providing patient-related services within the hospital.

The hospital also operates a School of Medical Technology, a School of Radiologic Technology, and a full family practice residency program, training medical professionals from local colleges and universities, and from around the world, in the latest medical techniques and knowledge, while giving them practical experience in a Seventh-day Adventist Christian hospital environment.

History. In 1899 Dr. David Paulson, a graduate of Bellevue Medical College, left the Battle Creek Sanitarium to pioneer the medical work among the indigent of Chicago. Later he began to consider the need for a sanitarium outside the city limits. C. B. Kimball, a prominent Chicago businessman and friend, made available an abandoned country estate in the village of Hinsdale at a low figure without interest and with long-term payments. Lacking in funds but not in faith, Dr. Paulson and his wife, Mary, also a physician, moved onto the property and began to gather a staff. In October of that year the Hinsdale Sanitarium and Benevolent Association was organized and a board of trustees named. On June 6, 1905, before the rooms were finished, the first patient, a young woman who had been an invalid for years, arrived. She went home cured and later became a physical culture teacher. Shortly after the dedication on Sept. 20, 1905, all rooms were filled.

The year 1907 brought hard times to the country, and much of the director's time was spent in the making and repaying of loans. When the board voted a salary of $75 a month for Dr. Mary Paulson, she refused to accept it, stating that her former salary of $65 a month was entirely adequate. Dr. David Paulson was receiving $40 a week, and nurses were paid 15 and 17 cents an hour.

In 1908 the first nursing class was graduated. In 1910 Dr. W. H. Wolfsen was employed as assistant to Dr. Paulson, bringing to four the medical staff, referred to as the "medical faculty" because they functioned as teachers as well as physicians.

By the close of the first decade (1914), the sanitarium conducted, in addition to the regular program, the School of Nursing, the Good Samaritan Inn for indigent patients, the rescue home for girls, the gospel program for prisoners, the health education work, medical evangelistic tours, and the continuing of the medical mission in Chicago. To encourage young people to work at the sanitarium without sacrificing their education, Hinsdale Academy was established in the area.

Subsequent History. By 1917 the institution was placed under the jurisdiction of the Lake Union Conference, but without financial control or obligation. A year later a deed of trust furnished funds for a large, three-story fire-resistant addition, completed in 1920.

During the great depression of the early 1930s, many businesses closed, but by reducing the working force, curtailing inventory supplies, and cutting wages, the sanitarium weathered the storm.

By 1945 it appeared desirable to replace the antiquated original buildings, and the constituency asked the Lake Union Conference to assume ownership and supervision, and to give financial assistance in the rebuilding program.

While plans for building were in the embryonic stage, a severe polio epidemic struck the area, with 53 active cases in the county. In the crisis, Eugene Kettering and his wife, local residents, helped provide the hospital with the latest equipment for combating the disease, and workers labored around the clock, until the emergency passed. This prompt and efficient response to a need heightened community interest in the hospital. A group of leading citizens met in the Kettering home to lay plans for organizing the community to help finance the new $3 million, 195-bed hospital building. On Sept. 27, 1953, 8-year-old "Chucky" Richards, one of the 1949 polio victims, cut a ribbon to open the new institution.

Community interest in the hospital continued to grow; a civic advisory board was formed in 1950 as a link between hospital and community leaders. As demands for hospital services increased, the hospital began experiencing crowded conditions. In 1960 a capital funds campaign was launched toward construction of a seven-level addition. The north wing was dedicated May 12, 1963, nearly doubling the size of the hospital and eventually bringing its capacity to 360 beds.

During the 1960s the hospital opened its first intensive-care unit, purchased a cobalt therapy unit with community gifts, acquired a computer, upgraded X-ray and laboratory instruments, and conducted its first Five-Day Plan to Stop Smoking.

As the suburbs near Hinsdale swelled in size, crowded conditions, especially in the ancillary departments, began to put pressure on the hospital to expand facilities once more.

In 1972 the brick veneer structure that had served as the main hospital building from 1920 until 1953 was demolished to make way for a new five-level south wing. Again the community responded, this time giving $1.5 million in cash and pledges.

In 1974 the hospital established the office of medical education to coordinate continuing education for staff physicians and to organize and direct a family practice residency.

In the 1980s the hospital continued to grow, eventually reaching its current 459-bed capacity. The hospital built upon its strong primary care base, adding advanced tertiary services. In addition, the hospital revamped its operating rooms, opening 10 new suites. The hospital began operating two magnetic resonance imaging machines, one in the hospital itself and one off-campus, aiding doctors in diagnosis and working with surgeons on advanced surgical techniques, such as stereotactic neurosurgery. The hospital also revamped its computer system with the addition of an HBO CareNet system that allows precise tracking of patient data and needs.

An open heart center was established, the Rooney Heart Institute. The institute has opened a cardiac surgical suite with advanced multimedia ability to help doctors review cases and teach procedures. The Rooney Heart Institute also became one of the first facilities in the area to perform the latest in balloon angioplasty procedures, the procedure that uses a cagelike device to help keep clogged arteries open.

A center for advanced cancer treatment and study, the Opler Cancer Center, was opened. This center is one of the few in the nation certified to use cutting-edge and experimental treatments for cancer. There are some 92 experimental treatment protocols in use at the hospital, and the hospital has recently opened a molecular pathology lab to help in the diagnosis and the treatment of its many patients.

The hospital's birth-care center is one of the busiest in the state, with some 3,000 babies born each year. The unit offers full neonatology and neonatal intensive-care services. For children, the pediatrics unit recently opened a Pediatric Special Care Unit designed to care for children in need of intensive hospital monitoring.

During the early 1990s the hospital implemented the Patient Centered Care (PCC) model of operations. In the PCC model, hospital services are brought to the patient rather than the patient to the services, as in traditional hospital models. All patient supplies and some diagnostic functions are performed without the patient leaving the room. In addition, caregivers are cross-trained in disciplines, allowing greater flexibility in giving care. Doctors and nurses will also have access to patient records and the hospital computer system from within a patient's room, allowing doctors and nurses to spend more time with the patient.

Administrators: David and Mary Paulson, cofounders; H. E. Hoyt; A. C. Gaylord; Julius Paulson; C. E. Rice; I. V. Roberson; Verah MacPherson; W. E. Abernathy; L. M. Bowen; G. C. Hoskins; B. C. Marshall, 1945-1948; R. H. Hervig (acting), 1948-1950; N. C. Taylor, 1950-1954; A. C. Larson, 1954-1963; M. J. Blair, 1963-1970; W. H. Wilson, 1970-1976; L. E. Laurence, 1976-1977; Irwin C. Hansen, 1977-1980; Donald L. Hanson, 1980-1986; Kenneth W. Bauer, 1986- .

HINTER, J. F. *See* Ginter, J. F.

HIROSHIMA SANIKU GAKUIN (Hiroshima Saniku Senior High School). A secondary school located in Hiroshima-ken, Daiwa-cho, Japan. It is nestled on a hillside of 84 acres (34 hectares) surrounded by evergreen hills, abundant in trees and seasonal flowers. It is ideal for study, self-reflection, and prayer. From Hiroshima city this ideal location is about a 45-mile (70-kilometer) drive along a scenic country road.

There are three separate programs carried out on the school campus, namely, the senior high school, junior high school, and elementary school. Each is headed by a principal under the directorship of the president, who coordinates the functions of these three independent schools. About 99 percent of the total academy, senior and junior enrollment, live in the dormitories. The school is far from the concentration of church members.

This institution maintains high standards and quality in comprehensive living, learning, and working programs. Especially strong are the traditions of Bible study and work education while maintaining a high quality of academic programs. As of 1993 there were 173 students in the junior high school, 304 students in the senior high school, and 73 teachers and staff members. The majority of the students are from Seventh-day Adventist homes. After transferring the school site to the present Hiroshima Saniku Gakuin campus, the number of graduates has grown to more than 1,500.

Religious activities consist of worship and other meetings on Sabbath, chapel hours and Weeks of Prayer in spring and fall, Bible study groups, musical services for surrounding churches, branch Sabbath schools, distribution of literature, and visitation.

To provide work education, the school has more than 27 areas, including agriculture, grounds work, woodwork, maintenance, ironwork, bakery, custodial, cafeteria, store, home economies, library, horticulture, office work, and dormitory work. Hiroshima Saniku Gakuin exists to provide a balanced education in harmony with the standards and ideals of the Seventh-day Adventist Church, the development of Christian character, and a Christian philosophy of life.

Presidents: Shigenobu Arakaki, 1977-1979; Kenji Soneda, 1980-1992; Tetsuya Yamamoto, 1992- .

HISTORICAL (HISTORICIST) VIEW OF PROPHECY. *See* Historicism.

HISTORICAL RESEARCH COMMITTEE. A committee authorized by the General Conference Committee in 1938 that functioned from time to time until 1953 investigating certain historical, archaeological, and chronological topics connected with the Seventh-day Adventist application of the 70 weeks and the 2300 days of Daniel 8 and 9. The group was generally called merely the Research Committee, but later, after the formation of the Committee on Biblical Study and Research, the older committee was given the adjective "Historical." It sponsored the publication of *The Chronology of Ezra 7,* by Siegfried H. Horn and Lynn H. Wood (1953).

HISTORICISM. This term is used to describe a school of prophetic interpretation that conceives the fulfillment of the prophecies of Daniel and Revelation as covering the historical period from the time of the prophet to the establishment of the kingdom of God on earth. These prophecies were given in visionary circles that recapitulate the content of the previous vision, adding new information or providing a slightly different perspective of the same historical period. Thus, for instance, Dan. 2, 7, 8-9, and 10-12 are parallel prophecies covering basically the same historical period. In Revelation the same type of recapitulation is employed in the interpretation of the messages to the seven churches, the seven seals, the seven trumpets, and Rev. 12-14.

The validity of historicism as a method for the interpretation of Daniel and Revelation is provided by the fact that the angel interpreter in Daniel used this method in explaining the meaning of the visions to the prophet. In a dream he is informed that the dream of the king in Dan. 2 represents four kingdoms that will arise in human history before the kingdom of God is established (verses 36-45). The four beasts of Dan. 7 represent those same kingdoms, after which God will give the kingdom to the saints (verses 18, 19). The first kingdom was identified as Babylon (verses 36-38). In Dan. 8 two animals are used as symbols to represent the Medo-Persian and Greek empires (verses 19-21). The fourth kingdom is not identified in Daniel, but Jesus takes it to be Rome (Matt. 24:15). According to Daniel, this kingdom was to be divided, and a little horn would exercise political and religious control over the people. In the time of the end the horn is to be destroyed and God's kingdom established forever.

Jesus used this method when He interpreted Dan. 9:26, 27 as referring to the future destruction of Jerusalem in A.D. 70 (Luke 21:20-22). Paul also speaks about a series of successive prophetic events to be fulfilled within history before the second coming of Christ (2 Thess. 2:1-12). Historicism as a method of interpretation is found in the Bible itself, and it provides the key for the interpretation of the apocalyptic books of Daniel and Revelation.

The historicist approach to prophetic interpretation was used by the early Church Fathers up to the fifth century A.D. LeRoy E. Froom has shown that a significant shift in prophetic interpretation occurred when Augustine defined the kingdom of God as the Christian church and spiritualized the millennium, making it a symbol of the Christian Era *(The Prophetic Faith of Our Fathers*, vol. 1, pp.

473-491). His views prevailed during the Middle Ages, until the period of the Protestant reform. The Reformers restored historicism as the method to be used in the interpretation of Daniel and Revelation, and identified the papacy as a manifestation of the antichrist predicted in those books.

The Counter-Reformation developed a new system of prophetic interpretation that came to be known as preterism. This method was developed by a Spanish Jesuit named Luis de Alcazar (d. 1613). According to him, the prophecies of Revelation were fulfilled during the first six centuries of the Christian Era. He identified Nero with the antichrist *(ibid.,* vol. 2, pp. 506-508). Preterism was later adopted by many Protestants and has become today the prevailing method of prophetic interpretation among religious scholars in general. According to them, Daniel deals with events that took place during the time of the Maccabbeans, and Revelation deals with the situation of the church during the time of John.

Among more conservative Protestants, historicism has been replaced by futurism. Futurism applies the prophecies of Revelation mainly to events that will take place within a seven-year period just before the second coming of Christ. This is the position taken by most dispensationalists.

Seventh-day Adventists believe that historicism is the right method of prophetic interpretation to be used in the interpretation of the books of Daniel and Revelation. The method is supported by the Scriptures itself and was in use during the early church period. Moreover, they feel that in using this method they are also preserving an important aspect of the Reformers' work of restoration.

HLIDARDALSSKOLI. *See* Iceland Secondary School.

HOBART ADVENTIST SCHOOL (formerly Moonah Seventh-day Adventist School). A coeducational day school on the primary and secondary level, situated on Cheviot Road, West Moonah, a suburb of Hobart, Tasmania, Australia. It is owned and operated by the Tasmanian Conference and is administered by a school board composed of members of supporting metropolitan churches and conference administration. In 1959 the state's Education Department granted the school full secondary registration for courses of study leading to the Tasmanian Certificate of Education in academic and practical subjects. The enrollment in 1993 was 115; there were six full-time teachers and two part-time instructors.

The school was relocated to its present site in 1983, replacing one that had operated on Fleet Street, Moonah, since 1933, and prior to that by the City Seventh-day Adventist Church on Warwick Street, Hobart. Twenty-four pupils were enrolled by the first teacher, P. N. Sheppard. Accommodation was gradually increased, until on Feb. 20, 1955, a new high school unit was dedicated. In February 1957 a third primary schoolroom was added to the original unit, and a science classroom/laboratory was built in 1971.

A completely new school, erected on the present site, was officially opened and dedicated on May 22, 1983. Two more classrooms and a canteen were added in 1993.

Principals: A. Westerman, 1934-1937; W. Whisker, 1938; G. Maywald, 1939-1940; E. A. Butler, 1941; D. Dyson, 1942-1946; Miss E. Stewart, 1947; Miss J. Davis, 1948-1949; I. Harvey, 1950; L. M. Davis, 1951-1954; W. G. Litster, 1955-1959; J. G. Litster, 1960-1962; M. P. Cozens, 1963-1964; B. Howell, 1965-1969; R. A. Spoor, 1970-1974; G. H. Blum, 1975-1976; A. Savage, 1977-1979; V. Hill, 1980-1981; G. H. Perry, 1982-1986; G. M. Coe, 1987- .

HOFFMAN, BENJAMIN PHILIP (1889-1967). Missionary, pastor, administrator, teacher. Hoffman studied at Pacific Union College, the University of Southern California, and the Foreign Mission Seminary in Washington, D.C. After his ordination in 1912, he and his wife sailed for Japan, where he served as pastor and district director in Kobe. In 1917 he became president of the Japan Conference and later served as president of the Japan Union Mission. A gifted scholar, Hoffman mastered the Japanese language to such a degree that the national people, when hearing him speak on the radio, presumed that they were listening to someone who had known Japanese from birth.

Upon his return to the United States in 1921, he served as secretary of miscellaneous languages in the Bureau of Home Missions of the General Conference and later as head of the Bible Department at Pacific Union College and as a professor in the Theological Seminary in Washington, D.C.

During 1951 and 1952 he did literary work for the Japan Publishing House and also served with the Central California Conference.

His final service to the church was as pastor to churches in the Central California Conference. Among these were the churches of the people so dear to his heart—the Japanese congregations in Mountain View and San Francisco.

HOHENAU ADVENTIST SANITARIUM (Sanatorio Adventista Hohenau). A medical institution situated in south Paraguay, near the border with Argentina, and 22 miles (35 kilometers) from Encarnación, the second-largest city in Paraguay. The work was started by Benoní Cayrús, when he was president of the Paraguay Mission, and Dr. Carlos Drachenberg.

In 1962 they obtained 7.5 acres (three hectares) of land from the Hohenau German Community, and with donations received from the residents were able to construct the first building, the foundation stone of which was laid in 1963.

Even though Dr. Carlos E. Drachenberg had been appointed as director of the sanitarium in 1963, medical work did not begin until 1965. In 1966 a committee was named to study plans for the sanitarium; the second stage of construction was begun, adding 30 beds and other facilities.

The inauguration of the new building and an airstrip took place in 1971, when an acute economical crisis affected the whole area and the sanitarium. Physicians from River Plate Sanitarium and Hospital, from Chaco Sanitarium and Hospital, and from Paraguay Adventist Sanitarium traveled to Hohenau, taking turns in attending the medical necessities of the institution. This situation ended in 1973.

In 1993 there were six doctors and 11 nurses. The 22 beds of the sanitarium render good service, and the present facilities will suffice to cope with the necessities of the area and the work in that place for the next decade.

Medical Directors: Carlos Drachenberg, 1965-1967; G. Wensell, 1968; Arnold Treiyer, 1969-1971; there was no medical director during 1971-1973; Rubén Rostán Rhiner, 1974-1978; Miguel Ibanez, 1979-1980; Eduardo Hellvig, 1980-1987; Enrique Stoletniy, 1987-1994; Omar Loose, 1995- .

HOLBROOK SEVENTH-DAY ADVENTIST INDIAN MISSION SCHOOL. A 12-grade coeducational boarding school for Native Americans situated 2.5 miles (four kilometers) southwest of Holbrook, Arizona. The school officially opened in September 1946 with an opening enrollment of 26. It was born of the vision of Marvin and Gwen Walter, who helped establish the school on 300 acres (120 hectares) just off the Navajo reservation.

Throughout the years many changes have taken place on the campus. In 1955 work was completed for a new girls' dormitory. The church was built in 1963, and in 1965 a new boys' dormitory was completed. A new cafeteria was built in 1972 by the building trades class from Pacific Union College. In 1973 Maranatha Flights International constructed the vocational trades building, housing facilities for a home economics lab, a computer lab, and classroom space for auto mechanics, welding, drafting, and electrical training. The gymnasium was built in 1984, and in 1985 Maranatha returned to build a new administration building.

In addition to changes in the physical plant, curriculum has changed as well. In the late 1950s several grades were added, first the ninth, the next year the tenth, and then the eleventh. In 1971 the twelfth grade was added.

Holbrook Seventh-day Adventist Indian Mission School is the only 12-grade SDA "mission" boarding school serving North American Native Americans, starting with first through third graders who reside in their own "little boys'" and "little girls'" dormitories. The school is accredited by the Board of Regents of the General Conference and offers a basic curriculum.

Marvin Walter was the first principal and Josephine Holmes the first teacher. Sponsored jointly by the Arizona Conference and the Pacific Union Conference, with the Arizona Conference supervising, this school is intended to train Native American students to bring the gospel to their own people.

Principals: Marvin Walter, 1946-1948; John Gilchrist, 1948-1949; Frank J. Daugherty, 1949-1966; King Hooper, 1966-1969; Earl Spaulding, 1969-1978; Carl Rose, 1978-1983; David James, 1983-1986; Douglas Hayes, 1986-1987; Eugene Schneider, 1987-1989; Duane Anderson, 1989-1992; Donald Wright, 1992- .

HOLDEN, WILLIAM BURROUGHS (1873-1955). Physician, administrator. Educated at Battle Creek College, the University of Michigan, and Rush Medical College, he received his M.D. degree in 1897. In 1903 he joined the medical staff at the Portland Sanitarium and Hospital, and was medical superintendent of that institution for the greater part of his 52 years' association with it.

HOLDEN, WILLIAM HENRY (1874-1968). Administrator. He was born in New York State and entered the colporteur work following his graduation from Potsdam State Normal College. He began ministerial work in Montana and served as principal of Bozeman Intermediate School for two years. Soon after his marriage to Sadie Marie Rittenhouse in 1906, he was called to be dean of men at Walla Walla College. In 1909 he was elected president of the Vermont Conference and in the succeeding years served as president of the following conferences: Eastern New York, Southern Illinois, Eastern and Western Michigan, Wisconsin, and Lake Union. He served the denomination actively for 45 years.

HOLINESS. *See* Sanctification.

HOLLEY, ROGER (1914-1985). Missionary, evangelist. Born in Michigan, he graduated from Washington Missionary College in 1939. He went immediately to the Far East, where he served briefly in Japan before the outbreak of World War II, then went on to the Netherlands East Indies (Indonesia). He escaped from there on the last ship out in 1941, narrowly missing being sunk by a German U-boat.

Returning to the United States, he served as pastor-evangelist in the Iowa and Carolina conferences from 1942 to 1954. He was married to Joan Bollman in 1944.

In 1954 he joined the Fordyce Detamore evangelistic team in the Texas Conference as campaign manager. In 1958 he entered full-time evangelism, serving in several conferences.

In 1974 he went to the Afro-Mideast Division as evangelist. One eight-week campaign in Kenya resulted in the baptism of 3,000 persons. Returning to the United States in 1977, Holley served as pastor of the Burleson, Texas, church until his retirement in 1979.

HOLSER, HENRY P. (1856-1901). One of the early church administrators in Europe. He was born in Michigan, and at the age of 18 joined the Seventh-day Adventist Church. In 1882 he entered evangelistic work, serving apprenticeship in Iowa under A. G. Daniells. After three years he was ordained to the ministry and the next year served as secretary-treasurer of the Minnesota Conference. In 1887 he went to Europe (Switzerland), where a year later he became president of the Central European Conference (1888-1899) and was head of the European Mission from 1895 to 1899. During the late 1890s he became ill and spent the winter of 1899 in Egypt, both to improve his health and to establish SDA work in that country. When his health failed to improve, he returned to the United States and died shortly after.

HOLT, GEORGE W. (1812-1877). A Millerite minister of Connecticut, then one of the first to embrace the new sanctuary and Sabbath positions. In 1850 he was associated with James White in publishing the *Advent Review* and traveled considerably in northeastern Canada, New York, and Ohio, and later in Michigan, Illinois, and Wisconsin.

HOLY FLESH HERESY. A teaching that arose in Indiana in 1900 involving the conference president and certain other workers, according to which Christ attained "holy flesh" in Gethsemane like that of Adam before the Fall; likewise, believers, when revived by the Holy Spirit, would never sin again and would never die. Their preaching was accompanied by shouting and falling prostrate (2SM 34). Ellen White spoke vigorously against this movement, which she said was similar to an early fanaticism in one segment of the Adventists at the end of 1844 *(ibid.* 31-35; *General Conference Bulletin* [1901], p. 421). The movement soon died down.

HOLY SEE. *See* Vatican City.

HOLY SPIRIT. Seventh-day Adventists believe that the Holy Spirit is a personal being, the third member of the Godhead, or Trinity ("Fundamental Beliefs of Seventh-day Adventists," *Church Manual* [1990], p. 179). The Holy Spirit was present to seal Christ's baptism (Matt. 3:16, 17). He is named with the Father and the Son in the Great Commission and baptismal formula (Matt. 28:19; cf. 2 Cor. 13:14), and likewise at Pentecost (Acts 2:33). The relationship between the three persons of the Godhead is clearest in the teachings of Christ (John 14:16, 26; 15:26; 16:13-15). Among the Holy Spirit's personal characteristics are knowledge (1 Cor. 2:11), will (1 Cor. 12:11), mind (Rom. 8:27), love (Rom. 15:30), communion (2 Cor. 13:14), grief (Eph. 4:30). He can be insulted (Heb. 10:29) and lied to (Acts 5:3, 4).

The Holy Spirit convicts hearts of the heinousness of sin, of the desirability of righteousness, and of the certainty of judgment (John 16:8-11). He convicts, woos, and wins people to Christ. His mission is to guide into all truth, for He is the "Spirit of truth" (John 16:13; 14:26). The Bible was written under His guidance and inspiration (2 Peter 1:20, 21). While on earth, Christ's personal presence was localized. But by virtue of His very nature, the Holy Spirit can be, and is, everywhere present. The Holy Spirit is Christ's true vicar, or representative, on earth. He applies to individuals the benefits of the atoning sacrifice of Calvary, making effectual in us that which Jesus did *for us.* He applies Christ's mediatorial work to responsive human hearts, regenerating, justifying, sanctifying, and communicating to us the very life of our risen Lord as we await Christ's second, personal return. He enables Christians to bear "the fruit of the Spirit" in their lives (Gal. 5:22, 23). He selects and fits individuals for service, and qualifies them with power for witnessing (Acts 1:8; 13:2-4; 15:28). He imparts to men and women the various spiritual gifts (1 Cor. 12:7-11).

The Apostles' and Nicene creeds make a simple affirmation of faith in the Holy Spirit as a member of the Trinity, the latter stating that He "proceedeth from the Father" (Henry Bettenson, *Documents of the Christian Church,* p. 37). The Arian heresy, on the other hand, denied deity to the Spirit. Athanasius and others affirmed belief that the Spirit was of the same substance as the Father and the Son (E. H. Klotsche, *The History of Christian Doctrine* [1945], p. 70). The mainstream of Christianity has always accepted the unqualified deity and personality of the Holy Spirit.

More than a century ago, during the formative period of Seventh-day Adventist doctrine, there were differences of opinion on the Holy Spirit and on certain other matters. The pioneer SDAs of those early years were dedicated Christians who had come from many different denominations, and some diversity of opinion was to be expected. It seems that many believed that the Holy Spirit was only a "power" or "influence" and not a person. J. H. Waggoner, for instance, refers to the Holy Spirit as "that awful and mysterious power which proceeds from the throne of the universe" *(The Spirit of God: Its Offices and Manifestations,* p. 9). Uriah Smith similarly spoke of the Spirit as "a mysterious influence emanating from the Father and the Son, their representative and the medium of their power" *(The Biblical Institute* [1878], p. 184). During these formative years, emphasis in preaching and in church publications was on the distinctive features of the Advent message, and there was some tendency to take the great fundamental tenets of Christianity for granted. Furthermore, there was no official creed, and on some matters difference of opinion persisted for a number of years. Unity of belief was eventually achieved, not by ecclesiastical fiat, but by cooperative study and the conviction of the Holy Spirit, with the confirmatory witness of the Spirit of Prophecy. By the end of the nineteenth century there was general unanimity of opinion in favor of the view that the Holy Spirit is a personal being, the third member of the Trinity. Ellen White repeatedly refers to the Holy Spirit as "the Third Person of the Godhead" (DA 671) and as "a divine person" (Ev 617).

SDAs believe that the Holy Spirit is a person as verily as the Father and Son are persons of the Godhead (L. E. Froom, *The Coming of the Comforter* [1928], pp. 41, 42). He is Christ's true successor on earth *(ibid.,* p. 25). He is "another Comforter" (that is, in addition to Christ; John 14:16, 26; 15:26; 16:7), whom Christ promised to send in His stead, and who came at Pentecost to make redemption through Christ personally efficacious to those who accepted the proffered salvation.

The Holy Spirit is the divine presence, the divine instructor, the divine convictor, the divine comforter, of Christians, individually and as a church, imparting the life of Christ and imbuing the receiver with Christ's attributes. The Holy Spirit influences; He is not a mere influence, power, or energy. He is not only comforter but also advocate, representative, intercessor, pleader, and consoler. He is not simply a mysterious "divine afflatus" (Uriah Smith, *Looking Unto Jesus,* p. 10) emanating from the Father, an invisible principle of life, but a divine person—the third person of the Godhead.

Furthermore, SDAs believe that the Holy Spirit is, next to Christ Himself, God's greatest gift to humanity. His coming as Christ's successor made provision for the believer's every need. He convicts, converts, guides, reproves, teaches, watches, witnesses, enables, comforts, helps, illuminates, transforms, sanctifies, intercedes, unifies, and strengthens. He implants grace and reveals and impresses truth. He imparts the very life of Christ and restores the image of God to the soul. He illuminates the mind, fosters spiritual growth, molds the character, energizes the life, activates the conscience, and impels to service.

Some classical Seventh-day Adventist works on the Holy Spirit are: L. E. Froom, *The Coming of the Comforter* (1928); W. H. Branson, *The Holy Spirit* (1933); G. B. Thompson, *The Ministry of the Spirit* (1914); Francis M. Wilcox, *The Early and the Latter Rain* (1938).

HOME AND FAMILY SERVICE. A family service organized in 1975 and functioning as a service organization of the world church, with headquarters in the General Conference. In 1985 its activities were merged with those of several other departments in the new Department of Church Ministries.

Home and Family Service came into existence as a direct result of the increasingly urgent need to build stronger, more stable Seventh-day Adventist homes. Although Seventh-day Adventists have always promoted strong marriages and successful Christian families, the influences of the rapidly deteriorating social conditions in the 1960s and 1970s caused increasing concern among SDAs. It became apparent that new tools, approaches, and methods were needed.

HFS traces its roots back to 1913. Ellen White convinced Arthur Spalding to commit his life to work for families. The Home Commission began its work in 1922 under Spalding's leadership. Books, courses, and study materials were developed, and by 1942 Spalding's efforts had successfully established recognition and acceptance of family life education within the church both in North America and overseas.

During the next three decades, marriage and family life programs were promoted through the Education Department by such leaders as Archa Dart and John Cannon.

In late 1974 a committee was set up under the leadership of W. Duncan Eva to study the current problems of the SDA home and to search for solutions and develop recommendations. Betty Holbrook, a member of the committee, designed a plan called Home and Family Service, which was accepted by the General Conference session in Vienna in 1975.

A few months later Delmer and Betty Holbrook were asked to organize and lead the new effort for SDA marriages and families. The original team of the Holbrooks and their administrative secretary, Wanda Tate, was joined in 1980 by Ronald and Karen Flowers. Delmer Holbrook served as HFS director from 1975 until 1982 and was succeeded by Betty Holbrook as director until 1985, when HFS was merged with Church Ministries.

During its 10-year existence before becoming a part of Church Ministries, HFS produced a variety of instructional manuals and materials that covered a broad spectrum of family life issues. Topics included parenting, marriage preparation, marriage enrichment, singleness, single-parent families, family finance, family worship, sexuality, self-worth, communication, conflict resolution, and temperaments.

A Bible and Spirit of Prophecy base for family life education was developed. Both an understanding of family needs and an awareness of the principles and methods of Adventist Family Life training were widely accepted throughout the world church. The development of several specialized approaches to marriage and family ministry were also fostered by HFS—including Marriage and Family Commitment, developed by John and Millie Youngberg; Seventh-day Adventist Marriage Encounter, founded by Albert and Betty Brendel; and Adventist Marriage Enrichment, established by Edward and Letah Banks.

The Holbrook and Flowers team organized and conducted training seminars for administrators, pastors, and laity in every world division.

Throughout its history the Home and Family Service cosponsored annual training seminars with Andrews University (Family Life Workshop began in 1975) and Loma Linda University (Family Life Workshop West began in 1978). An infrastructure of family life educators and conference, union, and division directors began to develop throughout the world field.

During the short period of 10 years Home and Family Service achieved a remarkable measure of success in reaching the varied cultures of earth with the SDA answers to the worldwide breakdown of family life. The goal of raising the consciousness of the church toward the needs of its families was achieved, and an ongoing program of SDA family life education was set in place.

HOME AND HEALTH *(Ka Jung Koa Kun Kang,* 1990-   ; published bimonthly by Korean Publishing House in Seoul, Korea). The health and culture magazine for believers and nonbelievers in Korea. This 40-page magazine deals with various topics such as eating habits, drugs, drinking, smoking, mental health, geriatric diseases, marriage, and education. It presents God's special messages about health, home life, and education, as given to us through Ellen White.

Eighteen thousand copies of *Home and Health* were published quarterly from January 1990, changing to bimonthly January 1992. The magazine is in color, and 50,000 copies were published beginning December 1993. The *Home and Health* consecutive numbers are No. 1 through No. 20 up to December 1993.

Editor: Chun Se Won, 1990- .

HOME AND SCHOOL (1909-1938; 1909-1915 as *Christian Education,* 1915-1922 as *Christian Educator;* earlier bimonthly, later monthly, during the school year; RH, for Department of Education complete files: AU, UC). A magazine for teachers and parents, used in connection with the Home and School Association. Its place was filled from 1942 to 1951 by a section in the *Church Officer's Gazette,* then from 1951 on by the *Adventist Home and School.* This journal, now discontinued, was superseded by the *Home and School Leader.*

Editors: Frederick Griggs, 1909; H. R. Salisbury, 1910-1913; J. L. Shaw, 1913-1914; W. E. Howell, 1914-1916; Frederick Griggs, 1916-1918; W. E. Howell, 1918-1930; Flora Williams, 1930-1938.

HOME AND SCHOOL FELLOWSHIP (formerly Home and School Association). A society formed in the local church and coordinated through the North American Division Department of Education, with the purpose of fostering good home and school relationships. It was first called the Parent-Teacher Association. In 1922 the work was divided: the section that gave special attention to parent education was called the Home Commission, and the section that fostered good home and school relationships was given the name Home and School Association.

The Home Commission was sponsored originally by the Education, Young People's Missionary Volunteer, Home Missionary, Sabbath School, and Medical departments. In 1941 the work of the Home Commission was integrated with the Department of Education, and the term Home and School Association was used for societies with schools and Christian Home Council for societies without schools. In 1956 the name Home and School was chosen to cover both types of organizations.

The society was concerned with the infant, the preschooler and schoolchild, the teenager, the young adult, and the husband and wife.

This association was charged with the promoting and fostering of home and parent education as a regular part of the work of the education departments at the General, union, and local conference levels.

The Home and School Association served elementary and intermediate church schools and day academies, and promoted the enrollment of every Seventh-day Adventist child in one of these schools. It was concerned with pupil motivation, teachers' welfare, parents' interests, financial aid, and with establishing good working relations between the home and the school, between the parent and the teacher.

The founder and mainspring of organized parent education among Seventh-day Adventists was A. W. Spalding, who served the General Conference as full-time secretary of the Home Commission for 19 years (1922-1941). Mrs. Florence Rebok served as Parent and Home Education secretary from 1941 to 1947 (during which time *The Adventist Home* and *Child Guidance* were compiled), and Mrs. Arabella Moore Williams from 1947 to 1954; Archa O. Dart served from 1954 to 1970, and W. J. Cannon from 1970 to 1975, when the work was taken over by Home and Family Service.

HOME COMMISSION. *See* Home and School Fellowship.

HOME EDUCATION. The need for sound Christian instruction for children and parents has been recognized by this movement since the early days of its history. To supply this need and to coordinate all the church's efforts in this regard, the General Conference requires its Department of Education to sponsor, foster, and encourage the interests of both home and school.

In 1919 (reorganized 1922) the Home Commission of the General Conference was born and continued as constituted until 1941. During this period it was cosponsored by most departments of the General Conference. In 1941 the responsibility fell to the Department of Education. For a time it was represented in the field by two organizations—the Home and School Association and the Christian Home Council. The journal *Adventist Home and School* was the official organ of communication and covered the needs of both of the aforementioned organizations.

As the needs developed, *Adventist Home*

and School became two journals: the *Adventist Home* magazine and the *Home and School Leader*. The former became a subscription magazine filling the needs of the general membership, and the *Home and School Leader* supplied materials for the monthly meetings of the Home and School Fellowship.

The Home and School Fellowship was originally called the Home and School Association. The Home and School Association was a society formed in the local church, and coordinated through the General Conference Department of Education, with the purpose of fostering good home and school relationships. It was first called the Parent-Teacher Association. In 1922 the work was divided: the section that gave special attention to parent education was called the Home Commission (which became part of the Department of Education in 1941), and the section that fostered good home and school relationships was given the name Home and School Association. In later years the name Home and School Association was changed by action of the Department of Education staff to Home and School Fellowship *(see* Home and School Fellowship).

At the 1975 General Conference session Home Education became a part of Home and Family Service, with D. W. Holbrook and his wife, Betty, sharing the responsibility.

Currently all available materials for Home Education or the Home and School Association are in the charge of the various divisions' education departments.

HOME HELP. A former church member temperance activity for the meeting of alcohol, tobacco, drug, and weight-control problems. Initiated and designed in 1971 by Ernest H. J. Steed, General Conference temperance director, the Home Help visitation plan consisted of using specially prepared films and literature and cassettes in personalized contact within the confines of the home.

Home Help visitors, in representing Seventh-day Adventists and providing a public service, were encouraged to go two by two then to continue until practical benefits were seen. If desired, a spiritual program could be further provided. Entitled Christ Speaks to Modern Man, it consisted of a Bible study plan, the showing of six films, and the loan of literature.

Home Help was requested via media announcements or from friends. Many made choices through this program to live rewarding lives without alcohol, tobacco, or drugs.

HOME MISSIONARY. *See Missionary Magazine.*

HOME MISSIONARY DEPARTMENT. *See* Church Ministries, Department of; Lay Activities, Department of.

HOME NUTRITION INSTRUCTOR'S PROGRAM. *See* Vegetarian Cuisine Instructor's Program.

HOME OF THE REDEEMED. Seventh-day Adventists believe that the redeemed will be transported to heaven—the "Father's house"—at the Second Advent (John 14:1-3; 1 Thess. 4:13-18; cf. Heb. 11:16), where they will live for a thousand years. At the close of the thousand years the redeemed will return to this earth, which will be renovated after the destruction of sin and sinners *(see* Hell; Millennium) and become the eternal abode of the redeemed.

SDAs believe that, in a large part, conditions in the new earth will be as they would have been on earth had sin never entered. They therefore look forward to living on this planet with resurrected glorified bodies resembling the ones that Adam and Eve possessed before they sinned, and to carrying on pursuits such as humanity would have engaged in had sin not entered. They apply to this future restoration the passage "And thou, O tower of the flock, the strong hold of the daughter of Zion, unto thee shall it come, even the first dominion" (Micah 4:8). They also apply literally the passage "Behold, I create new heavens and a new earth. . . . And they shall build houses, and inhabit them; and they shall plant vineyards, and eat the fruit of them" (Isa. 65:17-21). To them the future life is not some spirit existence in an ethereal heaven.

Furthermore, because SDAs do not believe in a conscious existence between death and the resurrection, they do not believe that the redeemed go to heaven at death. They maintain that the "spirit" that goes back to God at death (Eccl. 12:7) is not conscious, but represents the personal identity, which is preserved until the resurrection so that in the resurrection every individual will have his or her own character (see SDACom 5:1093). They believe also that resurrected bodies will bear resemblances to the former bodies, so that friend will recognize friend.

The capital of that new earth will be the New Jerusalem, which, after the millennium, descends from heaven and is established upon this earth (Rev. 21:1, 2, 10; Heb. 11:10, 14-16). This city is described in detail in Rev. 21 and 22. The presence of the city signifies the presence of God, for after John saw the Holy City descending he "heard a great voice out of heaven saying, Behold, the tabernacle of God is with men, and he will dwell with them, and they shall be his people, and God himself shall be with them, and be their God" (Rev. 21:3).

Among conditions that will not exist, John mentions the following: "There shall be no more death, neither sorrow, nor crying, neither shall there be any more pain: for the former things are passed away" (v. 4).

As a warning against spiritualizing the scriptural statements regarding the future life, Ellen G. White has remarked: "A fear of making the future inheritance seem too material has led many to spiritualize away the very truths which lead us to look upon it as our home" (GC 674, 675).

Far from being a state of idleness, the future life will be one of creative activity. "Every faculty will be developed, every capacity increased. The acquirement of knowledge will not weary the mind or exhaust the energies. There the grandest enterprises may be carried forward, the loftiest aspirations reached, the highest ambitions realized and still there will arise new heights to surmount, new wonders to admire, new truths to comprehend, fresh objects to call forth powers of mind and soul and body" *(ibid.* 677).

Despite what has been recorded in the Scriptures of the glories of that future abode, Seventh-day Adventists believe that not all has been revealed. "Eye hath not seen, nor ear heard, neither have entered into the heart of man, the things which God hath prepared for them that love him" (1 Cor. 2:9).

They anticipate that the glories of that world will far exceed their fondest expectations, and they find in a contemplation of future glories a strong motivation for Christian dedication.

HOME STUDY INTERNATIONAL/ GRIGGS UNIVERSITY. A correspondence school organized in 1909 that offers preschool, elementary, secondary, college, and adult education. Home Study International (HSI) has the following objectives: 1. Complete and improved elementary courses for the child who cannot study in a regular schoolroom situation. Preschool courses are guided by parents. 2. Constantly revised and updated secondary courses to aid the student who is temporarily out of school, needs extra credit, or for some other legitimate reason needs to study by correspondence; to aid the secondary school administration in resolving scheduling conflicts; to use in extension classes when no certified teacher is available; and to provide new courses, which some schools may be unable to provide because of lack of finances or instructors. 3. New courses as well as constantly revised college-level courses to aid the college student with scheduling or other difficulties; to provide acceptable credits for college students temporarily out of school; to aid adults and others who wish to work toward graduation but cannot do full-time resident study; to provide courses for the specialized needs of small groups of college students when classes do not fill or no qualified teacher is available. 4. A variety of professional educational courses for classroom teachers who need to meet certification requirements. 5. Correspondence courses for foreign mission appointees. 6. Adult education-type noncredit courses for the lay members of the church. These courses include classes in biblical studies and courses for general cultural improvement and recreational pursuits. 7. Extension classes to be conducted in the churches, supervised by pastors or qualified laity. 8. Specialized courses designed for in-service training or as self-improvement studies for all church employees. 9. Development of foreign branches of HSI to provide all the above services to the church overseas. 10. Through the Collegiate Division, Griggs University offers college degree programs in religion that provide training opportunities to church workers unable to attend a college campus. 11. Reliable, high-quality coursework for all educational levels. Courses are open to anyone who can reasonably profit from correspondence study, regardless of church affiliation or nationality.

In 1962 HSI became a member of the National University Continuing Education Association. Among the 193 members of this organization, HSI occupies a unique position. It is the only accredited correspondence school offering courses on the elementary level as well as secondary, college, and adult education.

The National Home Study Council, the only government-recognized organization for correspondence schools, accredited HSI on Dec. 1, 1967. HSI is also a member of the International University Consortium and the Association of College Registrars and Admissions Officers.

Organized in 1909, Home Study International was first known simply as the Correspondence School and was founded by Prof. Frederick Griggs, one of the early educational leaders of the Seventh-day Adventist Church. He attended a convention in Atlanta, Georgia, early in 1909, where he heard President Charles Van Hise, of the University of Wisconsin, describe the fast-developing correspondence school concept in that state. Launched on July 18, 1909, the school had as its first president W. E. Howell, who served in that capacity until C. C. Lewis succeeded him; the latter was principal for 10 years. During this time the name was changed to Fireside Correspondence School. In 1931 the school was incorporated by the District of Columbia under the name Home Study Institute. It became Home Study International in the mid-1980s.

In the early days of the school, the central office occupied one room in the General Conference building. In 1920 the office was transferred to Columbia Hall at Washington Missionary College (now Columbia Union College); it was later returned to the General Conference building and in 1942 given space in the Seventh-day Adventist Theological Seminary building. Three years later the school was assigned a two-story residence on Carroll Avenue, across the street from the Review and Herald Publishing Association. When this space proved inadequate, a new three-story air-conditioned building was erected on the same lot; an addition to this building, which doubled its work space, was completed in 1972. It now occupies space in the new General Conference headquarters.

By Oct. 4, 1909, 62 students had registered. Today Home Study International is teaching thousands of students worldwide.

In 1990 Home Study International expanded its contribution to the global mission of the Seventh-day Adventist Church by founding a new degree-granting division—Griggs University. Named in honor of Frederick Griggs, the university offers religion degree programs at both the Associate of Arts and Bachelor of Arts levels.

Until 1924, financial matters had been handled under the general control of the treasurer of the General Conference. Schoolwork was under the guidance of the Department of Education through a board appointed by the General Conference Committee. Beginning Jan. 1, 1924, this division of responsibility was discontinued, and a new board took control. The principal, now known as the president, was given full authority, both as literary head and business manager, with a separate bank account for the school.

As early as 1918 the principal reported students in nearly every state and province of the United States and Canada, besides a few students in India, China, Japan, Korea, Java, the Philippines, Fiji, Australia, Brazil, and Chile. In 1919 the General Conference Committee empowered the board of the Fireside Correspondence School to establish a branch upon request in any division or union conference outside North America.

There are presently five active branches, located in Africa, Australia, England, Singapore, and South Africa.

Confidence in the work and credits of the school have been strengthened by a resolute program of improving instruction and maintaining satisfactory relationships with Seventh-day Adventist resident schools and colleges. HSI does not attempt to compete, but only to act as the extension arm of these schools in the ways stated at the beginning of this article.

One of the most popular programs of the school is its kindergarten course, which is designed to be taught by mothers, with supervision from the resident teachers at HSI.

Home Study International is currently assisting Columbia Union College's external degree program by providing student services. The program allows persons who cannot become residents at a college to enroll for individually prepared curriculums leading to a bachelor's degree. No residence is required.

In its determination to offer the most effective instruction, Home Study International is constantly revising syllabuses and updating its textbooks.

Principals: W. E. Howell, 1911-1913; C. C. Lewis, 1913-1924.

Presidents: M. E. Olson, 1924-1946; W. H. Teasdale, 1946-1965; D. W. Holbrook, 1965-1985; Charlotte Conway, 1985-1986; George Babcock, 1986-1989; Joseph Gurubatham, 1989- .

HOMMEL, FRANK LEWIS (1875-1964). Founder of Seventh-day Adventist medical work in western Canada. He was born at Rochester, New York. In 1896, when about 21 years old, he became a Seventh-day Adventist. Afterward he attended South Lancaster Academy, studied nursing at Battle Creek Sanitarium (1898-1899), and engaged in medical missionary work in Chicago part of the time. In 1900 he was a member of a city mission in New York City, and from 1902 to 1903 was in charge of men's treatment rooms at Battle Creek Sanitarium. In 1903 a classmate invited him to visit Alberta. There he saw an opportunity for providing hydrotherapy treatments, and engaged in self-supporting medical missionary work for the next six years. While in Alberta he married Larena Belle Carpenter, the second church school teacher in the province. In 1909 the Alberta Conference made plans to establish a sanitarium at Lacombe. As secretary-treasurer of the conference, Hommel solicited funds with which to buy land and erect the building.

But difficulties developed, and the project at Lacombe was abandoned in favor of treatment rooms in Calgary. He then went to Calgary to open the establishment there (1911). From there he went to Washington, D.C., where he served as house manager at the Washington Sanitarium for about a year (1912-1913), then returned to Alberta as treasurer, teacher, and dean of boys at Alberta Industrial Academy and auditor of Western Canadian Union Conference. From 1918 to 1921 he was manager of the Alberta (later, Bethel) Sanitarium and in 1921 became the first manager of the Rest Haven Sanitarium in British Columbia. Ill health forced his retirement in November 1924.

HON, ERIC (1908-1980). Health educator. Of Australian-Chinese origin, he left his family business at 31 years of age to work for the Chinese community in Sydney. Thereafter, he began the first Community Services center, the first Seventh-day Adventist adoption agency, and the first cooking and nutrition schools and clinics attached to local churches. He ultimately became the first health director of the Trans-Tasman Union Conference, in 1963. In the late 1970s he led the Metro Ministry program in Greater New York. This was followed by several years of service at Weimar College, where he prepared students for medical missionary work.

HONAM ACADEMY (Honam Sahmyook Joongkodeung Hakkyo). A coeducational boarding school on the junior and senior high school levels, operated by the Southwest Korean Conference at a campus outside the city of Kwangju. In 1993 it had an enrollment of 464 and a teaching staff of 26. Five percent of the students are non-Seventh-day Adventists.

The academy takes its name from the Honam Mission, which was formed in 1952 when the territory of the former South Korean Mission was divided into the Southeast Korean and Southwest Korean missions (in Korea, the Yungnam and Honam missions). After the Korean War, a church in Kwangju was established and became the headquarters of the Honam Mission. The members of that area opened church schools and in 1952 requested an academy.

Plans for building the institutions of the Korean Union Mission after the Korean War included the addition of three new academies, one to be in Honam Mission territory. Classes began in 1953. A tract of about seven acres (three hectares) of land was acquired outside the city in 1955, United States Army tents were purchased, and the school was moved to the new site in Sansoo-dong. A variety of fruit trees were planted. Industrial training included fruit farming, gardening, poultry raising, and dairying. The high quality of work done has been recognized by the government educational department. In 1958 the school received senior high school accreditation from the government and the Far Eastern Division. In 1969 new land was purchased, and in 1970 the school was moved to Chuwoel-dong. A new school building was completed, and in 1988 a new dormitory building was erected on the campus as a memorial of the eightieth anniversary of the gospel proclamation in Korea.

Principals: Huh Man Sik, 1953-1954; Kim Ki Bang, 1954-1959; Kang Cain Ha, 1959-1962; Kim Tal Kon, 1962-1964; Choi Myung Hwan, 1964-1967; Lee Sung Jin, 1967-1969; Kim Seung, 1969-1973; Kim Joon Pal, 1973-1975; Kim Hyo Sung, 1975-1978; Kim Jae Shin, 1978-1984; Lee Sung Jin, 1984- .

HONDURAS. A Latin American republic situated in the heart of Central America, bounded on the west by Guatemala, El Salvador, and the Pacific Ocean, on the north by the Caribbean Sea, and on the east and the south by Nicaragua. It has an area of 43,277 square miles (112,000 square kilometers) and a population (1994) of 5.3 million. Honduras gained its independence from Spain in 1821 and from 1838 has maintained a republican form of government. Roman Catholicism is the predominant religion, but the constitution guarantees freedom of worship. The climate ranges from moderate in the highlands to wet tropical in the jungles in the lowlands. The official language is Spanish; however, there are a few tribes that speak their own dialects, and the people of the Bay Islands, ceded to Honduras by Great Britain in 1861, speak English.

Seventh-day Adventist Statistics. The territory of Honduras constitutes the Honduras Mission in the Central American Union Mission, which is a part of the Inter-American Division.

In July 1988 the Honduras Mission territory was divided in two, giving birth to the Bay Islands Mission. The mainland mission is now known as the Seventh-day Adventist Mission of Continental Honduras.

Statistics (1993) for *Honduras:* churches, 85; groups, 45; members, 41,781; church schools, 9; ordained ministers, 12; licensed ministers, 13; Bible instructors, 1. Headquarters are at Tegucigalpa, Honduras.

Institutions. Adventist Educational Center; Valley of the Angels Hospital.

Development of Seventh-day Adventist Work. *Beginnings.* Seventh-day Adventist teachings first penetrated Honduras when Mrs. E. Gauterau, who had joined the Seventh-day Adventist Church while in California, returned to her home in the Bay Islands of Honduras, bringing with her many SDA publications, which she shared with her neighbors. In 1887 T. H. Gibbs, a minister from New Orleans, made an exploratory visit to the Bay Islands and distributed more tracts and books. Some of the people who became interested carried on correspondence with the International Tract Society for a number of years. By the time L. C. Chadwick, president of the International Tract Society, visited Bay Islands in 1891, about 20 persons were ready for baptism.

In that same year the first resident minister, Frank J. Hutchins, arrived and established his headquarters on the island of Roatan. In 1892 baptisms were held and a Sabbath school was organized on the island of Bonacca (Guanaja). In that same year a baptism and a "general meeting" of all the believers was held on Roatan. In 1893 one of the first church buildings owned by SDAs in Central America was acquired on Guanaja through buying out the minority shareholders of what was first intended to be a union church. The membership of the church at that time was 25, and about 60 people attended the Sabbath school. The building still stands, and with the additions that the growth in membership has required, it is the largest Seventh-day Adventist church building in the Honduras Mission.

Toward the close of the same year, C. L. Emmerson joined Hutchins in the work on the islands. With the arrival of W. A. Miller a mission school was opened on July 4 on Bonacca. By the end of the year, there were three companies of SDAs in the Bay Islands, with total membership of more than 100. Plans were made to build a 50-foot (15-meter) mission schooner, and funds were contributed by the Sabbath schools for this purpose. In 1897 the boat was commissioned and named *Herald.* It was used for conducting missionary work not only in the Bay Islands but also in Nicaragua, Costa Rica, Panama, and even Colombia.

Organization and Growth. In the beginning of the mission work in this Caribbean area the republic of Honduras, with its Bay Islands, and British Honduras were considered a single mission field, which was referred to as the Central American Mission, and their statistics were reported together. In 1905 the combined membership, most of it in the Bay Islands, was 160, organized in five churches and five companies. In 1906 the field was included in the West Indian Union Conference. In 1908 its area was extended to include Guatemala and El Salvador, and the whole was organized as the Central American Conference, with a membership of 333. In 1913 the Central American Conference was reduced to the size of the original mission, and the next year it, along with some other areas in the Caribbean, was transferred to the General Conference as a detached mission, the whole group being named the Northern Spanish American Missions. In 1918 Honduras and British Honduras were organized as the Honduras Mission, with a membership of 267. In 1922 the Honduras Mission, with a membership of 300 in 13 churches, was included in the newly formed Inter-American Division as a part of the Central American Mission. Then in 1923 it was attached to the Aztec Union Mission, but in 1926 was joined with the Central American Union Mission. This structure of organization was maintained until January 1930, when the work on the mainland of Honduras was placed in a separate mission. In 1937 the mission assumed its present territorial boundaries. By the end of that year there were 15 churches, with 624 members.

Recent Developments. In recent years the church has undertaken religious radiobroadcasts and has established a Bible correspondence school. For the Cariban tribe, 50,000 of whom live along the seacoast, *Steps to Christ* has been translated.

Primary schools have been established in Santa Barbara, Choluteca, and on Roatan. The Santa Barbara school has been used as a means of evangelistic outreach. The modern, well-equipped school on Roatan was donated by Kern Hyde and his father, Captain Merl Hyde. These laypersons dedicated the profits from one of their fishing boats to the $17,000 project. A hospital was begun in Valley of the Angels, 17 miles (30 kilometers) from the capital city, during the administration of Robert Folkenberg.

In 1992 George Grieve, with his Yesterday, Today, and Tomorrow team, held a nationwide crusade in which 1,150 souls were baptized. The local workers continued their efforts after the team departed and launched other crusades, baptizing approximately 1,350 souls. Eight additional churches were organized in formerly unreached territories of mainland Honduras.

HONDURAS MISSION. *See* Honduras; Inter-American Division.

HONG KONG. A crown colony of the United Kingdom, situated on the southern coast of China, and consisting of the island of Hong Kong and the tip of the Kowloon Peninsula, which were ceded to the United Kingdom in 1841 and 1860, respectively, and the rest of the peninsula, leased from China in 1899. With the joint declaration between the Sino-British governments, the colony will be returned to China on July 1, 1997, but will be allowed to keep its capitalist system for another 50 years. The total area of the colony is 413 square miles (1,100 square kilometers), most of which is uninhabitable rock, but its population (1992) was estimated at 5.8 million people, overwhelmingly Chinese. Both the Chinese and English languages are used in the colony. Hong Kong is an important commercial and industrial center in the Far East. Many mission societies have churches, schools, and charitable organizations in Hong Kong.

Seventh-day Adventist Statistics. The territory of Hong Kong, along with Macao, forms the Hong Kong-Macao Conference in the South China Island Union Mission, which forms a part of the Far Eastern Division. Statistics (1992) for the *Hong Kong-Macao Conference* (including one church and one mission school in Macao): churches, 17; companies, 5; members, 3,724; church schools, 4; mission schools, 3; ordained ministers, 16; Bible instructors, 1; teachers, 67. Headquarters: 26-28 Hillwood Road, Kowloon, Hong Kong.

Institutions. Hong Kong Adventist College; Hong Kong Sam Yuk Secondary School; Hongkong Adventist Hospital; Kowloon Sam Yuk Secondary School; Sam Yuk Middle School; Tai Po Sam Yuk Secondary School; Tsuen Wan Adventist Hospital.

Development of Seventh-day Adventist Work. *Beginnings.* Seventh-day Adventist work in eastern Asia began at Hong Kong with the arrival in 1888 of Abram La Rue from the United States. He opened a mission for the sailors of the many ships that came to Hong Kong. His home also served as a distribution center for SDA publications in several languages. La Rue never learned the Chinese language, but he became acquainted with, and developed the friendship of, a Chinese translator at the colonial court, who translated for La Rue into Chinese a tract called *The Judgment* and the chapter from Ellen G. White's *Steps to Christ* entitled "The Sinner's Need of Christ"—the first Seventh-day Adventist publications in Chinese. La Rue worked alone until the arrival in Hong Kong in 1902 of the first SDA mission appointees to China, J. N. Anderson and his family and Ida Thompson. La Rue died in 1903, leaving most of his life savings to benefit the China Mission. The first baptism in Hong Kong occurred on Mar. 1, 1902, when Anderson baptized seven of La Rue's English converts.

In 1916 Hong Kong became the site for the Seventh-day Adventist headquarters in South China, but in 1920 there were in the colony, in addition to the three families of union mission workers (F. H. De Vinney, B. R. Owen, and R. M. Milne), only two members—a Chinese woman and a colporteur. In 1927 property was purchased on Stubbs Road, and a two-story headquarters building, consisting of four apartments, was erected and named La Rue Villa in honor of Abram La Rue, Hong Kong's first Seventh-day Adventist missionary.

Later Developments. In 1937 a church school was opened by the Mongkok church, and land was bought at Clearwater Bay on the mainland for the South China Training Institute, which at the time operated at Canton, China. The campus was ready in 1939, and in the same year the Pioneer Memorial church was built and became the headquarters church for work in the area. In connection with it a church school was opened, largely for the benefit of refugees. For several years World War II interrupted the development of the SDA work, but after the war it was resumed with new vigor. Evangelism spread throughout the territory, the Voice of Prophecy Bible Correspondence School was begun, and work was started at Yuen Long in 1948. In 1949 the China Division office and many of its staff were transferred to Hong Kong as well as the collegiate classes of the China Training Institute. By 1954 there were 10 churches in the Hong Kong-Macao area. By the end of 1958 there were about 1,600 members in Hong Kong. By September 1959 the combined enrollment of five schools reached 1,700 pupils. Fifteen years later, in 1974, the combined enrollment reached 2,900. By December of 1992 there were 3,724 members, and the combined enrollment of students was 3,126 from the college. In addition there were four secondary schools, four church schools, and two kindergartens. Most of the students come from non-SDA homes.

Funds were solicited to build a hospital at Tsuen Wan, and the building was opened May 22, 1964. Seven years later another hospital at Stubbs Road was opened. In 1992 there were 16 church buildings in Hong Kong.

HONG KONG ADVENTIST COLLEGE. A coeducational boarding school on the senior college level operated by the South China Island Union Mission on a 40-acre (16-hectare) site not far from Kowloon City, Hong Kong. In 1993 it had an enrollment of 197 (secondary and college students) and a staff of 40.

Hong Kong Adventist College developed from the first Seventh-day Adventist school taught in the Chinese language. In 1903, near the close of the Ching dynasty, Ida Thompson, one of the first SDA missionaries in China, opened in Canton what came to be known as the Bethel School for Girls, and a few months later E. H. Wilbur established a school for boys. Both were taught in Chinese on the elementary level, and both were situated immediately outside the South Gate of old Canton. The boys' school was closed for a time, but in 1915 A. L. Ham reopened it under the name of Sam Yuk School (Threefold Education School), with 12 students. By 1914 the Bethel Girls' School had been relocated in Tungshan, a suburb of Canton; in 1917 the boys' school also moved.

In 1920 Ida Thompson, who had been absent for a time, returned and resumed her position as principal of the Bethel School. By 1922, when coeducation had become accepted in China, the two schools merged as an intermediate school called the Sam Yuk Middle School (listed in *Yearbooks* as Cantonese Intermediate School; later as Canton Middle School). It served the Kwangtung, Hakka, and Kwangsi missions.

Instead of dividing the six-year secondary course into three years of junior and three of senior high school, the Sam Yuk Middle School divided the course into four years and two years, to give students who stopped at the junior high school level a more adequate education. The last two secondary grades offered training in various fields to meet the student's individual interest or talent as well as the denomination's need. Graduates were thus prepared for either higher education or employment. Later, farms, factories, and science laboratories were added, preparatory schools were established, and ministerial, business, and home economics courses were set up. In 1935 the institution, then called the Canton Training Institute, came under the direct supervision of the South China Union Mission, which aimed to raise the school to a higher educational level and enlarge its services.

When the Canton Sanitarium and Hospital was built on the school grounds, overcrowding resulted, and it was decided to find a more suitable place for the school that would allow for development. In 1937 about 40 acres (15 hectares) were purchased, and construction began on a completely new campus in the Clear Water Bay area, about seven miles (10 kilometers) from the central business districts of Hong Kong.

The new campus had not been completed when the Sino-Japanese War reached Canton, making an immediate move necessary. This move marked the beginning of a decade of uncertainty and constant moving. For two years the school occupied a large rented mansion in Sha Tin, Kowloon. Then in September 1939 the school, renamed the South China Training Institute, was able to operate at its new home at Clearwater Bay. But two years later, when war came to Hong Kong, the school was again moved, this time to a place called Lao Lung, in the interior of Kwangtung province. After World War II lack of transportation kept the school in the interior until the summer of 1946; then, because of the damage done to the campus at Clearwater Bay, the institution returned for a year to its former crowded site in Tungshan, in Canton. Finally, in 1947 the school returned to its home in Clearwater Bay, where it has since remained.

The school continued to grow, and a new curriculum was set up at the beginning of the 1958-1959 school year, the faculty was enlarged, and facilities added. In 1962, when a complete collegiate curriculum was introduced, the name of the school was changed to South China Union College.

In 1970 the constituents of South China Island Union Mission decided to combine South China Union College and Taiwan Missionary College in Taiwan to form one college under one administration, with the name South China Adventist College for both campuses. For legal and other reasons, even though these two campuses continued to be under one administration, in 1973 the name of the college was changed back to South China Union College for the Hong Kong campus, while the Taiwan campus was renamed Taiwan Adventist College.

In 1981 the constituency of the South China Island Union Mission separated the secondary and college sections and adopted the name of Hong Kong Adventist College. The college was subsequently registered and approved by the Education Department of Hong Kong as a postsecondary institution.

In 1982 the college established an affiliation with Loma Linda University, which enables students on the Hong Kong campus to receive B.A. degrees in religion or theology granted by Loma Linda University. In the same year, the college received full accreditation from the Board of Regents of the General Conference of Seventh-day Adventists.

In 1991 the affiliation agreement was transferred from Loma Linda University to La Sierra University.

During the 90 years of the school's existence thousands of young people have enrolled in its classes. Through the years students from this school have held key positions in denominational work.

Principals/Presidents: Ida Thompson, 1903-1922; E. H. Wilbur, 1905-1911; A. L. Ham, 1915-1917; H. B. Parkers, 1917-1922; A. L. Ham, 1922-1925; L. C. Wilcox, 1925-1928; A. L. Ham, 1929-1931; L. C. Wilcox, 1931-1934; M. Y. Sum, 1928-1929; H. S. Leung, 1934-1938; Paul Quimby, 1938-1939; C. A. Carter, 1939-1941; H. S. Leung, 1942-1949; T. S. Geraty, 1949-1950; H. S. Leung, 1950-1952; T. M. Lei, 1952-1953; D. W. Curry, 1953-1962; Samuel Young, 1962-1968; M. D. Lee, 1968-1970; D. K. Brown, 1970-1972; W. K. Nelson, 1972-1973; Samuel Young, 1973-1978; Charles H. Tidwell, Sr., 1978-1981; Wong Yew Chong, 1981-1983; Eugene Hsu, 1983-1986; Rudolf E. Klimes, 1986-1989; Handel Luke, 1989-1991; Roger P. W. Li, 1991- .

HONG KONG-MACAO CONFERENCE. *See* Far Eastern Division; Hong Kong.

HONG KONG SAM YUK SECONDARY SCHOOL. A coeducational day school in Hong Kong operated on the senior high school level in English (with an elementary school conducted in Chinese), under the direction of the Hong Kong-Macao Conference. The students, most of them Chinese, are 15 percent Seventh-day Adventist. The school is registered with the Education Department of Hong Kong, and its graduates, before leaving school, take the Certificate of Education Examination conducted by the local government.

The secondary school originated in 1948, three years after the close of World War II, when SDAs in Hong Kong were less numerous than now. It began as a church school conducted in the Chinese language, with only nine pupils, under the direction of Warren Hilliard and T. M. Chu, pastors of the Pioneer Memorial church. The school was first known as the Pioneer Memorial Church School, in memory of Abram La Rue, a self-supporting colporteur-Bible worker, who landed on the island of Hong Kong in 1888.

In September 1949, when the mission committee authorized the organization of a mission school, the name was changed to Sam Yuk Primary School. (In Chinese, *Sam Yuk* refers to the threefold education of head, heart, and hand.) Harry H. Morse, then union mission treasurer, was appointed supervisor and Alice Morse principal. In September 1950 Samuel Young was appointed head teacher. Before long the enrollment increased to 300, with a faculty of 11. In 1953 D. W. Curry was appointed supervisor.

In 1955, when a new classroom building was completed, classwork was extended to the ninth grade. The enrollment increased to 450. In 1957 the school system was changed to Anglo-Chinese. In 1960 a second classroom building, Morse Hall, was completed. The 1961 *Yearbook* lists it as the Sam Yuk Middle School, Happy Valley Branch.

In 1963 the name of the school was changed to Hong Kong Sam Yuk Secondary School. The school is tuition-supported.

Principals: Alice Morse, 1949-1953; D. W. Curry, 1953-1959; Mrs. R. M. Milne, 1959-1961; Handel Luke, 1961-1966; C. H. Tang, 1966-1980; Handel Luke, 1980-1989; Anna Lee, 1989-1992; Joseph Heun Bing Kuen, 1992- .

HONGKONG ADVENTIST HOSPITAL. A 150-bed hospital located on Stubbs Road in Hong Kong. In 1959 the Far Eastern Division asked Dr. Harry W. Miller to come to Hong Kong to establish medical work. Dr. Miller was accompanied by veteran China missionaries Ezra L. Longway and Robert M. Milne, who raised funds through public solicitation.

The health-care work in Hong Kong comprises two general hospitals located 14 miles apart, originally under one administration. The first hospital, now renamed Tsuen Wan Adventist Hospital, opened May 22, 1964, in Tsuen Wan, a satellite town in Kowloon, Hong Kong.

In 1970 fund-raising was begun to build a second hospital at 40 Stubbs Road in the mid-levels of Hong Kong island. The property was acquired in 1927 and was used first as church headquarters, then later as staff housing. Dr. Chan Shun, former chair and managing director of Crocodile Garments Limited, gave the first $1 million to the project. Many companies and individuals have contributed and are still contributing to the growth and development of the hospital.

On May 4, 1971, the Hongkong Adventist Hospital was declared open by Dr. Gerald Choa, director of health services, and Mrs. Chan Shun. In 1984 the two hospitals became separate organizations.

The Hongkong Adventist Hospital, referred to locally as "The Adventist," is a modern circular-shaped eight-story steel and concrete building with central air-conditioning. Its unique design helps provide quick and efficient service to all of its patients, and fits in with the hospital's standard of high quality health care.

In March of 1985 the Heart Center was opened, and the open-heart surgery and catheterization lab services began operation. In addition to a broad range of general services in the outpatient and specialty clinics, this 110-bed hospital also offers neurosurgery, a full rehab program (including sports medicine), as well as dental and dental laboratory facilities. The Diagnostic Imaging Department has been progressively upgraded to include CT scanning, nuclear medicine, and magnetic resonance imaging. The Heart Center and the health promotion/wellness programs are what the hospital is best known for in Hong Kong. There is also a clinic at the Baguio Villa Estates in Pokfulam, on the western side of the island.

A 12-story staff apartment building adjacent to the hospital also houses an eight-grade elementary school for children of the hospital staff, as well as the local offices of the South China Island Union Mission.

Administrators: R. W. Burchard, 1970-1979; D. L. Dunfield, 1979-1983; Mervyn Leicester, 1983-1984; James McAlvin, 1984-1985; Virgil P. Morris, 1985-1988; Henry P. Friesen, 1988- .

HONOLULU CHINESE DAY SCHOOL. *See* Hawaiian Mission Academy.

HONORS. *See* Pathfinder Honors.

HOOPES, L. A. (1859-1925). Educator, editor, missionary. He was educated at the University of Nebraska and taught there and at other schools for several years before accepting the Seventh-day Adventist faith in 1882. He began work for the church as an evangelist, was ordained in 1885, and was elected president of the Nebraska Conference in 1889. Shortly afterward he taught Bible at Union College, and later served as secretary of the General Conference for four years (1897-1901). He was president of Union College from 1901 to 1904, and for some time served as coeditor of the *Christian Record* (a braille magazine) before going to Australia, where he served in educational work for nearly nine years. Returning to the United States, he was Bible teacher at Graysville Academy and then principal of Oak Park Academy from 1916 to 1919. From 1920 until his death he was chaplain at the Hinsdale Sanitarium.

HOPE OF ISRAEL [1] (1844-1845[?]; weekly; Portland, Maine). An Adventist paper published by John Pearson, Jr., at first with Joseph Turner, later alone. It was not a Sabbatarian journal, but in it was published T. M. Preble's discussion of the Sabbath in February 1845 (later reprinted as a tract), the first printed advocacy of the seventh day among Adventists. It was this article that convinced Joseph Bates that he ought to observe the seventh day. In June 1845 Pearson, then the sole editor, announced that he could not bring it out weekly, but would issue it irregularly, whenever possible. At least one more number was issued two or three months later, printed this time at Boston, announcing Pearson's abandonment of the view that the parable of the Bridegroom had been fulfilled in the Millerite movement, and his return to the *Advent Herald* party, the majority group of Adventists.

HOPE OF ISRAEL [2] (1863-1865, 1866-19?). A paper first published in Michigan by a disaffected group of Seventh-day Adventists led by Samuel Davidson and Gilbert Cranmer (Enos Easton, editor). It was revived at Marion, Iowa, in 1866 by another dissident movement led by B. F. Snook and W. H. Brinkerhoff *(see* Marion Party) that was later organized as the Church of God (Adventist). After several changes of name the journal was still published in 1936 as the *Bible Advocate and Herald of the Coming Kingdom.*

***HOPE OF ISRAEL* PARTY** (1858). *See* Marion Party.

HOPE WITHIN THE VEIL (1845; weekly; Portland, Maine). An Adventist (not Sabbatarian) journal begun about June 1, 1845 (the second number was issued June 23), by C. H. Pearson (brother of John Pearson, Jr., editor of the *Hope of Israel)* and Emily C. Clemons. Late in August the first issue of the second volume was stopped in midprinting because the editor and publisher (and also the chief printer, W. H. Hyde) abandoned their belief that the parable of the Bridegroom had any application to the 1844 experience; they reverted to the majority view of the *Advent Herald* party. In that unfinished issue was O.R.L. Crosier's second article on the sanctuary doctrine *(Day-Star* 7:50, Oct. 11, 1845)—either the article that was printed in the *Day-Star* as an Extra in February 1846, or a shorter draft of this article preceding its final form.

HOPEANIEMI SANITARIUM. A 105-bed medical institution operated by the Finland Union Conference 30 miles (50 kilometers) from Helsinki, Finland.

The Hopeaniemi Sanitarium was opened for the first time in 1943 as the first year-round Seventh-day Adventist-owned sanitarium in Finland. The beautiful property was purchased by the Finland Swedish Conference, and work commenced with extremely limited resources under the direction of Dr. V. Sucksdorff, Jr. Through additions and rebuilding, the sanitarium capacity increased from 15 to 40 patients by 1957.

Facilities and property continued to expand. Innovative methods of treatment, particularly in the fields of hydrotherapy and dietetics, were presented. In 1973 plans were made for a grand-scale updating of the whole institution. In 1975 the Finland Union Conference purchased the sanitarium from the Finland Swedish Conference, and since that time it has been operated by the Finland Union Conference. After much effort and financial sacrifice on the part of church members, a new and modern complex began operation in 1979 under the management of Reijo Olin, business manager. It was called by the present name. The 105-bed capacity was achieved with the completion of a new wing extension in 1984.

This new institution now offers one of the most versatile hydrotherapy and rehabilitation programs in Finland. Apart from the fully equipped Physiotherapy Department, facilities include a swimming pool, exercise pool, gymnasium, training therapy center, hobbies and crafts room, cooking instruction kitchen, medical laboratory, and auditorium.

The natural forest setting on the edge of a lake creates an ideal relaxing environment with opportunities for a variety of outdoor activities, including hiking, swimming, rowing, tennis, and cross-country skiing in winter.

For a number of years Hopeaniemi has trained rehabilitation assistants in its independent government-approved school. Of the more than 455 graduates at Hopeaniemi, many have continued serving the institution, and some have opened private clinics in different parts of the country.

Medical Directors: V. Sucksdorff, Jr., M.D., 1943-1963; M. Miettinen, 1964-1971; P. O. Pylkkanen, M.D., 1972-.

HÔPITAL ADVENTISTE DE KOZA. *See* Koza Adventist Hospital.

HÔPITAL ADVENTISTE D'HAITI. *See* Adventist Hospital of Haiti.

HÔPITAL DE MUGONERO. *See* Mugonero Hospital.

HÔPITAL DE SONGA ET LEPROSERIE. *See* Songa Adventist Hospital.

HORN, SIEGFRIED H. (1908-1993). Archaeologist. A native of Germany, Horn received his college training in Germany, England (where he studied under Lynn H. Wood), and Walla Walla College. He then served as a minister in Holland (1930-1932), and as a missionary in Java and Sumatra (1932-1940). During World War II he was interned in Sumatra and India for six and a half years, during which he studied ancient languages, as well as biblical, historical, and archaeological subjects in which he was especially interested. After the war he took up graduate studies at the SDA Theological Seminary under Wood, and at Johns Hopkins University under W. F. Albright. Transferring to the University of Chicago, he was granted a Ph.D. degree in Egyptology in March 1951, with a dissertation entitled "Relations Between Egypt and Asia During the Egyptian Middle Kingdom." In that year he became chair of the Department of Archaeology and History of Antiquity in the SDA Theological Seminary, and continued to serve as professor of archaeology until retirement. Horn also taught courses in archaeology in seminary extension schools in Mexico, France, the Philippines, Germany, Japan, Australia, and Austria, repeatedly spending periods of study in the Near East; conducted three guided tours for ministers and Bible teachers through the Bible lands (1957, 1959, and 1966); and in 1960 became a staff member of the Drew-McCormick archaeological expedition, which, under the direction of G. Ernest Wright, of Harvard University, excavated biblical Shechem in Jordan. Horn served as a supervisor on the expedition during the three seasons (1960, 1962, 1964), and prepared some of the Shechem material for publication. One fruit of this work was the publication, in the *Journal of Near Eastern Studies,* January 1962, January 1966, and July 1973, of all scarabs found at the Shechem up to 1968.

After he became a teacher at the seminary, Horn wrote numerous articles on the popular level for various SDA periodicals, authored three books on the same level—*Light From the Dustheaps* (1955), which also appeared in German, Italian, and Korean translations; *The Spade Confirms the Book* (1957), which was also published in separate German editions in West and East Germany; and *Records of the Past Illuminate the Bible* (1963). He also wrote numerous archaeological and historical articles for *The SDA Bible Commentary,* and was the principal author (furnishing nearly three fourths of all articles) of the *SDA Bible Dictionary* (1960). With Wood he coauthored *The Chronology of Ezra 7,* and an article on the fifth century B.C. calendar of the Jews at Elephantine, which appeared in the *Journal of Near Eastern Studies* (January 1954). He also wrote papers for various other journals. From 1962 to 1974 he served as editor of the *Andrews University Seminary Studies,* the first volume of which appeared in 1963. Beginning with the summer of 1968, Andrews University has sponsored an archaeological expedition to biblical Heshbon in Jordan. The first three seasons of excavations (1968, 1971, 1973), which were supported also by the American Center for Oriental Research in Amman and by Calvin Theological Seminary in Grand Rapids, Michigan, were directed by Horn. These, along with a season in 1974, provided opportunities for practical training in field archaeology to Bible teachers, ministers, and ministerial students interested in biblical archaeology. He also made a tremendous contribution to a large number of students and colleagues at the SDA Theological Seminary and a number of extension schools, as well as at the archaeological digs. More than a few of these have been quite active in professional archaeology through their publications and fieldwork. In 1978 Andrews University's archaeological museum was renamed the Horn Archaeology Museum in his honor.

HORTON, SANFORD BYERLY (1858-1927). First president of the Louisiana Conference (1901-1908). He was a Louisiana lawyer whose political ambition brought him to Washington, D.C., where he joined the Seventh-day Adventist Church in 1890. In 1891 he entered its ministry, preaching throughout the Eastern states before becoming the first president of the Louisiana Conference in 1901. He was religious liberty secretary for the Southern Union (1908-1910), Atlantic Union (1911), Columbia Union (1914-1915), Lake Union (1920-1924), and West Michigan Conference (1913, 1916-1919). He closed his service in the ministry in the East Michigan Conference.

HOSPITAL ADVENTISTA DE BELÉM. *See* Belém Adventist Hospital.

HOSPITAL ADVENTISTA DE MANAUS. *See* Manaus Adventist Hospital.

HOSPITAL ADVENTISTA DE NICARAGUA. *See* Nicaragua Adventist Hospital.

HOSPITAL ADVENTISTA DE SÃO PAULO. *See* São Paulo Adventist Hospital.

HOSPITAL ADVENTISTA DE VALLE DE ANGELES. *See* Valley of the Angels Hospital.

HOSPITAL ADVENTISTA DE VITÓRIA. *See* Vitória Adventist Hospital.

HOSPITAL ADVENTISTA DO BONGO. *See* Bongo Mission Hospital.

HOSPITAL ADVENTISTA DO PÊNFIGO. *See* Pênfigo Adventist Hospital.

HOSPITAL ADVENTISTA SILVESTRE. *See* Silvestre Adventist Hospital.

HOSPITAL DEL SURESTE. *See* Southeast Hospital.

HOSPITAL UNIVERSITARIO DE MONTEMORELOS. *See* Montemorelos University Hospital.

HOSPITALS. *See* Sanitariums and Hospitals; names of specific institutions.

HOUR OF PROPHECY. An evangelistic agency affiliated with and owned by the Texas Conference Association of Seventh-day Adventists, with offices located on Highway 67, Keene, Texas. It was established in 1965 under the direction of Bob Thrower, at that time an evangelist of the Texas Conference, and under the supervision of Charles Dart, conference president. Thrower continues to be director of the Hour of Prophecy, public evangelist, radio speaker, and editor of the agency's *Hour of Prophecy News,* a monthly tabloid.

"HOUSE OF PEACE" HOSPITAL. *See* Dar es Salaam Hospital.

HOWELL, WARREN EUGENE (1869-1943). Educator, missionary. He was baptized in 1884 and received his B.A. from Battle Creek College in 1894 and an honorary M.A. from Emmanuel Missionary College in 1919. He was a student of history, Greek, and biblical interpretation, and author of *Gospel Key Words* and a *Grammar Manual.* He taught at Healdsburg College (1894-1897) and for four years was principal of Palama Chinese School in Honolulu. Then he taught at Emmanuel Missionary College until 1903, and one year at Healdsburg College, where he was president for two years.

He became the first president of the Loma Linda College of Evangelists, but after one year he was sent, in 1907, as a Seventh-day Adventist missionary to Greece. Returning in 1909, he served as principal of the Fireside Correspondence School (now Home Study International) for four years, then for four years was assistant secretary and then secretary for 12 years in the General Conference Department of Education, during which time he traveled widely in America and abroad. He was an associate editor (1909-1914) and editor (1914-1916 and 1918-1930) of *Christian Education,* whose name was changed to *Christian Educator* in 1915 and *Home and School* in 1922, in which he emphasized the SDA principles of education as advocated by Ellen White.

Howell was chair of the committee appointed to revise the book *Daniel and the Revelation,* and secretary of the Spirit of Missions Committee, which promoted and directed college and seminary mission language study. From 1930 until his death he was secretary to the president of the General Conference.

HOWLAND, STOCKBRIDGE (1801-1883). Pioneer Adventist layperson in Topsham, Maine, whose home, which was often referred to as "Fort Howland" or "Advent Fort," offered hospitality to many early Adventist workers. In his house James and Ellen White set up their first housekeeping in 1847. Later they left their infant son, Henry, with the Howlands for five years. Howland's daughter, Frances, healed in answer to a prayer of faith, was an early example of divine healing among Adventists.

Howland had been a deacon of the Congregational Church when he accepted Millerite views in 1841 and was actively engaged in the propagation of these views around Topsham. As a result, he was ridiculed by some of his associates, who, declaring him mentally incompetent, succeeded in gaining the appointment of a legal guardian over his affairs. Soon after, however, when the community needed a good bridge and could not find a better builder and designer than Howland, the guardianship was terminated. He spent the last 11 years of his life in Battle Creek, Michigan.

HPO HLA, DAVID (d. 1929). First ordained Burmese Seventh-day Adventist minister; also a teacher, translator, and editor. He was one of the first to accept Seventh-day Adventist teachings in Burma, where H. H. Votaw had gone in 1905. From then until his death he served as a preacher, language teacher at the Meiktila School for the missionaries, language instructor, and translator and editor of an SDA Burmese magazine.

HRESSINGARHEIMILI HLIDARDALSKOLA. *See* Iceland Summer Sanitarium.

HRISCANSKA ADVENTISTICKA CRKVA. *See* Macedonia; Macedonian Mission; Trans-European Division.

HUAMBO ADVENTIST SEMINARY. *See* Bongo Adventist Seminary.

HUENERGARDT, JOHN F. (1875-1955). Pioneer Seventh-day Adventist worker in Hungary, conference administrator, minister, teacher, and editor. Born in a German colony in Russia, he came to Kansas in childhood and graduated from the German Bible course at Union College in 1897. He entered church work as a licentiate at Hamburg, Germany, in 1898 and was sent to Hungary to begin the work there. In 1900 he was ordained at Friedensau, Germany, and became superintendent of the Hungarian and Balkan States Mission Field in 1902, and president of the Hungarian Conference in 1907 and of the Danube Union Conference in 1912. He came to New York in 1919 to work for the Hungarians there. In 1921 he joined the faculty of the Broadview College and Theological Seminary and began editorial work on German language papers. Between 1925 and 1929 he was associate secretary of the Bureau of Home Missions of the General Conference and then was president of the Yugoslavian Union Conference. He returned to the United States in 1935 and retired in 1936. After retirement he pastored German churches in Lodi and Los Angeles, California, until 1949 and was associate editor of an SDA German language paper until shortly before his death.

HUGHES, CASSIUS BOONE (1859-1921). Educator. He became a Seventh-day Adventist at the age of 16, was educated at Battle Creek College, and entered the ministry about 1885 in Kansas. When Walla Walla College was opened, he became its Bible teacher and dean of men. He was ordained in 1893 and in 1894 became the first principal of Keene Academy. About 1897 he went to Australia as the first principal of the Avondale School (now Avondale College) and remained there until about 1902, when he joined the staff of Oakwood Industrial School (now Oakwood College) at Huntsville, Alabama, but was soon recalled to Keene Academy. After three and a half years he went to Jamaica to establish a school there (West Indian Training School). Returning to the United States two or three years later, he served as principal of Keene Academy for another six years (1909-1915). He served as dean of men at Pacific Union College for a year and a half, then headed a new academy at Battleford, Saskatchewan, for nearly two years (1916-1918), after which he went to the West Indies for two years (1918-1920) to reestablish the school there. Ill health forced his return to the United States, where he was briefly associated with an intermediate school at Loma Linda, California.

HUGULEY MEMORIAL MEDICAL CENTER. A 213-bed hospital involving the total health concept, located in south Fort Worth, Texas. Owned by the Southwestern Union, the new institution, incorporated in August 1972, is part of Adventist Health System/Sunbelt. It was named after Herbert Taylor Huguley, a dentist and real estate investor of Dallas, Texas, who left his $6 million estate to the Seventh-day Adventist Church to build a hospital in honor of his parents.

In 1984 a 40,000-square-foot (3,720-square-meter) fitness center and education building was built on the campus, adjoining Huguley. More recently a two-year, $16 million expansion plan included the construction of a new cardiac catheterization laboratory, outpatient surgery center, physicians' office building and underground parking garage, renal dialysis clinic, lobby and patient registration area, along with the enlargement of the Radiology Department and remodeling of other service areas, including emergency.

Huguley Hospice Care was established in 1987. Along with Huguley Home Health Agency, it provides in-home care for terminally ill or homebound patients.

Future planned expansion includes a water fitness complex, a hospice house, and a new, relocated chapel offering greater capacity.

Huguley is accredited by the Joint Commission on Accreditation of Healthcare

Organizations.

Administrators: William Wiist, 1972-1978; John Koobs, 1978-1987; Desmond Cummings, Jr., 1987-1990; Donald W. Welch, 1990-1992; A. David Jimenez, 1992- .

HUGULEY NURSING CENTER. A 178-bed nursing center located on the Huguley Memorial Medical Center campus at 301 Huguley Blvd., Burleson, Texas. Opened in 1988, the facility was built by and is owned and operated by the Southwestern Union Conference of Seventh-day Adventists. The center accommodates residents with needs from custodial care to skilled nursing care and offers a full range of therapy programs. The center has 130 employees. Fiscal year 1992 revenues exceeded $4 million.

Administrators: Maxine Smith, 1988-1989; Leroy Leiske, 1989-1990; David Hannah, 1990- .

HUGULEY PLACE RETIREMENT CENTER. A 144-unit full-service retirement community owned by Huguley Memorial Medical Center and featuring a blend of independent living with security. The facility opened in July 1988. It is part of Huguley's total care campus concept, together with Huguley Nursing Center and Huguley Health Club. One-bedroom, two-bedroom, and studio apartments are available. Three meals a day are provided, and transportation is furnished. Planned activities, both cultural and spiritual, are emphasized. Huguley Place provides jobs for 35 employees. It is presently operating at capacity, with a three-month waiting list.

Administrators: Leroy Leiske, 1988; Steve Hayes, 1989; Jim Hamilton, 1990; Arnie Loven, 1991; Arthur Loignen, 1992- .

HULL, MOSES (1836-1907; fl. 1860). A onetime Seventh-day Adventist minister who defected. In the early 1850s he became a member first of the United Brethren Church and later of the first-day Adventists. There is some evidence that he accepted the Seventh-day Adventist faith in a series of tent meetings conducted in Greenvale, Illinois, in July 1857, although he may have been led to the truth by a layman, Solomon Myers. He preached his first sermon in connection with the Greenvale meetings. Shortly thereafter he preached in tents and halls in Iowa, and was ordained in August 1858.

Hull was an eloquent and convincing preacher who attracted multitudes to his meetings, and consequently was in great demand. He was an interesting writer as well. Among his tracts were: *Mark of the Beast, Infidelity and Spiritualism,* and *The Transgressor's Fate.* The latter was one of the earliest Seventh-day Adventist expositions of the unconscious state of the dead *(see* Death). He also produced a work of 182 pages entitled *The Bible From Heaven.* Preaching in many states from the Midwest to the Atlantic coast, he was often challenged to debates, which he usually won, even against spiritualists. With ever-increasing success he began to depend more and more on self and less and less on God. On Nov. 5, 1862, and again in June 1863, Ellen White wrote appeals to him to look away from self to the Lord. She also warned him against friendship with spiritualists, and added, "Never should one man be sent forth alone to combat with a spiritualist" (1T 428). Notwithstanding this warning, he accepted a challenge to another debate with some spiritualists. During the debates he became confused, made certain concessions, and lost the battle. It was reported that he said, "From now on I am a spiritualist." A few days afterward he made a confession to the church and was granted another chance, but on condition that he work with Loughborough. This he did for some months, but he was never the same. In September 1863 he preached his last SDA sermon, then joined the spiritualists and became a lecturer and writer for them.

HULTAFORS HEALTH CENTRE AND HOSPITAL (Hultafors Halsocenter). A 165-bed medical institution situated 33 miles (53 kilometers) east of Gothenburg, Sweden, operated by the Swedish Union Conference. There are two physicians and 98 other employees. The health center receives patient referrals from Boras city; the Greater Gothenburg Metropolitan Health Planning Commission; Forsakringskassan, the state-operated insurance system; and the Alvsborgs Provincial Council. Combined, the referrals account for approximately 70 percent of occupancy. The remaining 30 percent are self-paying private patients.

The 365-acre (150-hectare) sanitarium property is situated 800 feet (245 meters) above sea level on a wooded mountain ridge overlooking beautiful Lake Viared some 300 feet (90 meters) below. The institution serves as a rehabilitation center for patients with medical and psychiatric problems of many kinds. It has a well-functioning clinical laboratory, an occupational therapy facility, a gym and exercise center, and an eight-floor addition completed in 1972 that houses a modern Physical Therapy and Hydrotherapy Department. This building features a large indoor swimming pool on the top floor, which commands a breathtaking view of the lake and forests below.

The sanitarium property was acquired by the church in March 1926, mainly through the efforts of G. E. Nord, then president of the Scandinavian Union Conference, and C. V. Anderson, then president of the Swedish Conference. In the same year the Hultafors Seventh-day Adventist Church was established and a Sabbath school organized.

After extensive renovation of the existing buildings, the main one having been built in 1907, the sanitarium opened its doors in early June 1926. From the beginning the number of patients was so large that a 16-room annex was added in the spring of 1927, and a three-story building containing offices and some 20 rooms was added in 1932-1933. The church congregation, which previously had met in temporary quarters, in 1937 occupied a new church seating 250. Between 1936 and 1938 further large improvements were put into effect. The kitchen was modernized, the large dining room enlarged, and the lounge remodeled.

A step forward was taken in 1943 when a new wing containing 33 guest rooms and two large sun porches was added. A special section for 20 bed patients was provided (later enlarged to 40 beds). This expansion required enlarged facilities for the doctors and nurses, which were provided in 1951.

In 1962 another building was completed, containing facilities for physical exercise and rehabilitation, three offices, and four patient rooms. In addition, the sanitarium had over the years acquired six houses for the staff. Two large buildings containing 18 apartments have been constructed, the second in 1960. A new apartment building for single employees was constructed in 1974.

A totally new kitchen was added in 1986 together with a total renovation and expansion of the cafeteria. At the same time, a new reception area was added, giving visitors a much better first impression when they arrive at Hultafors.

In 1991 market pressures became so strong that Hultafors faced the risk of having to close. The biggest challenge facing Hultafors is how to best reflect Christ's concern for wellness in today's dynamic health-care market. Sweden represents one of the world's most completely socialized medical systems. What Hultafors provides is a complement to social medicine. Here the individual has the right to choose qualified rehabilitation with a distinctive Christian perspective.

Medical Directors: Isak Unhall, 1932-1964; N. Blomstedt, 1964-1984; Christer Joreteg, 1984-1988; Lenna Laitinen, 1989; Gunnar Roslin, 1989-1993; Hans Lofgren, 1993- .

HUMAN RELATIONS, OFFICE OF. The North American Office of Human Relations, with its director and its advisory committee, is concerned chiefly with the strengthening of the bonds of unity among the diverse people groups within the churches and institutions of the North American Division. It is a service that works with division and union administration in the work of reaching people within its assigned territory and helping to transform the diverse racial and ethnic people groups of the church in North America into a new people, a new community, and a new society based on love and peace.

The office sees four major objectives as essential to its work: (1) promoting fundamental belief 13 as the church's official statement of oneness and encouraging the membership to take aggressive steps to achieve unity; (2) promoting Policy C-50 as the church's official position on the harmonious blending of its diverse membership in the total life of the church, and affirming the seven principles of this policy as (a) those by which the North American Division will conduct the activities of the church, (b) those to which its employees will ascribe, and (c) those that the NAD will encourage among its membership; (3) developing a multicultural relationship model and working for its acceptance as a new paradigm for achieving oneness in the fellowship; and (4) promoting the Conciliation and Dispute Resolution Procedures model as a tool for settling differences that occur among the body.

Organizationally, the office works with the division and union leaders in the promotion of human relations goals, objectives, and activities, but its work is not limited to these areas. The office does share information and provide counsel and guidance to persons on the local level as well as in the churches when such is sought.

Statistics. The following statistics were compiled by the Office of Human Relations, Archives and Statistics, and other departments in the General Conference and North American Division in 1991. The membership statistics for multicultural groups and other data relative to administrative and support employees of the division are customarily compiled by the Office of Human Relations.

In 1991 the membership of the division was reported as 776,848, with statistics for the multicultural groups as follows: members of African descent, 223,599, or 28.78 percent; members of Asian descent, 19,898, or 2.56 percent; members of Caucasian descent, 462,552, or 59.54 percent; members of Hispanic descent, 66,418, or 8.54 percent; Native Americans, 1,757, or .22 percent; others, 2,635, or .34 percent.

In the North American Division area (total population about 285 million), the African-American population is more than 30 million. Churches and companies that are of African-American descent and located within the nine regional conferences of the NAD were 773. The membership for the regional conferences (along with the African-American work in the Pacific and North Pacific unions and Bermuda) in 1991 was 200,836. Other data include church schools, 177; ordained ministers, 435; licensed ministers, 85; Bible instructors, 40; teachers, 515.

Tithe income in 1991 was $75,777,066; world mission offerings, $2,270,209. Baptisms were 10,850 for that year.

Institutions. Northeastern Academy; Oakwood College; Pine Forge Academy. There are junior academies in the following cities: Birmingham, Huntsville, Mobile, Montgomery, Selma, Alabama; Little Rock, Pine Bluff, Arkansas; Hartford, Connecticut; Wilmington, Delaware; Fort Lauderdale, Hialeah, Jacksonville, Ocala, St. Petersburg, West Palm Beach, Florida; Albany, Atlanta, Augusta, Columbus, Lithonia, Macon, Savannah, Georgia; Chicago, Waukegan, Illinois; Gary, Indianapolis, Indiana; Kansas City, Kansas; Louisville, Kentucky; Alexandria, Baton Rouge, Hammond, Pineville, Shreveport, Louisiana; Baltimore, Hyattsville, Maryland; Cassopolis, Detroit, Flint, Inkster, Michigan; Jackson, Mississippi; Kansas City, St. Louis, Missouri; Omaha, Nebraska; Hillside, Trenton, New Jersey; Bronx, Brooklyn, Buffalo, Laurelton, New Rochelle, Newburgh, Rochester, New York; Charlotte, High Point, La Grange, Raleigh, Wilmington, Winston-Salem, North Carolina; Cleveland, Cincinnati, Ohio; Anderson, Florence, Greenville, Greenwood, Orangeburg, Sumter, South Carolina; Chattanooga, Memphis, Nashville, Tennessee; Dallas, Houston, Round Rock, Texarkana, Texas; Newport News, Richmond, Virginia; Milwaukee, Wisconsin.

Regional Conferences. There are nine North American regional conferences, most of them organized in 1945 or 1946, that have a leadership and constituency largely African-American. These are called regional because of their distinctive geographical arrangement. Each regional conference is organized with the existing administrative structure of a union conference, and covers not merely one portion of the union area, but all the African-American churches in the entire region of the union, except in the Southern and Columbia unions, which contain two regional conferences.

The nine regional conferences in North America are: the *Allegheny East Conference,* embracing the Black congregations in the territory of Delaware, the District of Columbia, and New Jersey, and eastern portions of Maryland, Pennsylvania, Virginia, and West Virginia (office: Pine Forge, Pennsylvania); the *Allegheny West Conference,* embracing the Black congregations in the territory of Ohio and western portions of Maryland, Pennsylvania, Virginia, and West Virginia (office: Columbus, Ohio); the *Central States Conference,* embracing the Black congregations in the territory of Colorado, Iowa, Kansas, Minnesota, Missouri, Nebraska, North Dakota, South Dakota, and western New Mexico (office: Kansas City, Kansas); the *Lake Region Conference,* embracing the Black congregations in the territory of Illinois, Indiana, Michigan, Minnesota, and Wisconsin (office: Chicago, Illinois); the *Northeastern Conference,* embracing the Black congregations in the territory of Connecticut, Maine, Massachusetts, New Hampshire, New York, Rhode Island, and Vermont (office: St. Albans, New York); the *South Atlantic Conference,* embracing the Black congregations in North Carolina and South Carolina and northern Georgia (office: Atlanta, Georgia); the *South Central Conference,* embracing the Black congregations in the territory of Alabama, Kentucky, Mississippi, Tennessee, and western Florida (office: Nashville, Tennessee); the *Southeastern Conference,* embracing the Black congregations in the territory of eastern Florida and northern Georgia (office: Altamonte Springs, Florida); the *Southwest Region Conference,* embracing the Black congregations in the territory of Arkansas, Louisiana, Oklahoma, Texas, and eastern New Mexico (office: Dallas, Texas).

The North Pacific and Pacific unions and the Seventh-day Adventist Church in Canada have no regional conferences, but the Pacific Union Conference has a Regional Affairs Department serving in an advisory capacity to all the conferences in which there is a considerable African-American membership, and the North Pacific Union Conference has a Health and Temperance and Regional Affairs Department, as well as Multi-cultural Ministries and Native Ministries Northwest departments, serving in a similar advisory capacity. In Canada there are separate Black congregations as well as churches with Black constituents in their memberships; in Bermuda most of the churches have a majority of Blacks. Missionaries called from responsibilities in the regional conferences have gone to India, South America, Africa, Asia, and the West Indies.

The regional conferences were formed in the hope that the new organizations might, with concentration on work within a specific ethnic group, achieve greater results in a shorter space of time than would be achieved under the previously existing organizations (in some cases under a departmental or mission arrangement). The plan has been responsible for an evangelistic penetration into the African-American community that had not been possible under the organizations that formerly administered the work among the nation's African-American membership. The regional conferences also have created more opportunities for leadership and participation by gifted and trained African-American young people of the church, whose selection in the same or similar capacities had not worked out in the years prior to the formation of the regional conferences. Another practical result has been that African-American members of the SDA Church have been more readily and more naturally represented in elected offices and on boards and committees outside the regional conferences than appears to have been true formerly.

History. *Origin of Work Among Black Americans.* Before SDAs existed as a group, there were African-American adherents of the Adventist (Millerite) movement.

Adventist leaders in the beginning were identified as antislavery in sentiment. Some of them had actively aided Blacks in their struggle against the severe system of slavery: both John P. Kellogg (father of Dr. John Harvey Kellogg) and John Byington, who was later the first president of the General Conference, had operated stations of the Underground Railroad on their farms in Michigan and New York, respectively, and thus aided fleeing slaves to reach freedom in Canada. Byington was well acquainted with Sojourner Truth.

The first Black Seventh-day Adventists were probably in the North, where the church originated, but they are not noted separately in the early accounts, since they would naturally be members of the same churches with the White people, according to the social pattern in that region. Not until SDAs began to move into the South did they encounter Blacks in any number and in a social pattern of segregation. In trying to fulfill the primary objective of the church—to preach the message "to every creature"—these newcomers made converts from both Whites and Blacks and carried on work in some places especially for the latter.

For the work for African-Americans in the South, begun in Tennessee as early as 1871, *see* South Central Conference; in Texas and Georgia as early as 1876, *see* Southwest Region Conference and South Atlantic Conference. In North Carolina the work was begun in 1877 by papers sent through the mail.

In the West, C. M. Kinney, reputed to be the first African-American ordained as an SDA minister, was won in 1878 by J. N. Loughborough in Nevada, and became a charter member of the Reno church. Later he preached in the South.

No Black Churches at First. In entering the South, the White evangelists encountered a social system based on the separation of the races, though at that early time (the 1870s) the separation was less complete than later. C. O. Taylor, the first SDA minister to go into Georgia, preached in a rural Baptist church in which he found Blacks attending along with the Whites, though seated separately *(Review and Herald* 49:8 [i.e., 7], Jan. 4, 1877). D. M. Canright, preaching in Kentucky, reported three Black Sabbathkeepers, "members of the church with the others" *(ibid.* 47:174, June 1, 1876).

James Edson White, apostle to the African-American communities along the lower Mississippi River, remarked that for Blacks to be members of White churches had been the custom in pre-Civil War days, when slave church members had belonged to their masters' congregations *(ibid.* 78:265, Apr. 23, 1901), and it was after the war that Blacks formed their own churches and employed their own ministers *(Gospel Herald,* February 1906, p. 6).

But by the time White reached the South, in the 1890s, he noted that a separation in terms of race was on the increase and that because of opposition—both by local Whites who opposed the education of Blacks, and by Blacks who did not trust Whites and feared exploitation—the work of the Southern Missionary Society became increasingly difficult *(ibid.)*. In one place in 1899 his work was practically closed, and the society had to staff its Mississippi schools with African-American teachers because of local opposition to Whites teaching Blacks *(ibid.,* October 1899, p. 87; July 1900, p. 63).

In Texas in 1876 D. M. Canright reported that there was no objection to his working for the African-American people so long as he worked among them only *(Review and Herald* 47:166, May 25, 1876). In 1887 J. M. Rees in Tennessee reported that there was no trouble regarding White and Black members in the SDA Church, but that if ministers tried to preach to both races in their meetings for the general public, they would have no White people to speak to *(General Conference Bulletin,* Nov. 14, 1887, p. 2). When O. C. Godsmark and his brother attempted to preach to both in Georgia, their evangelistic meetings were deserted by both White and Black listeners. On the other hand, even many years later, Black evangelists sometimes preached successfully to White and Black congregations. J. G. Thomas reported such meetings in Jackson, Mississippi; Gainesville, Florida; Chattanooga, Tennessee; and Columbus, Georgia, where 90 Blacks and 37 Whites were baptized from his meetings. F. S. Keitts, in Nashville; W. W. Fordham, in Jacksonville; and L. B. Baker, in El Paso, reported similar experiences.

Increasing Opposition in the Nineties. The early attempts at interracial churches in the South were abandoned in the face of opposition from outside. J. E. White, in explaining why the Southern Missionary Society conducted work for Whites and Blacks separately, declared that they had been forced by necessity to adopt that policy. "We preferred to live and work in such lines as we could than to force the issue and be cut off from the work" (*Gospel Herald,* January 1901, supplement, p. 4). He added that Seventh-day Adventists, who teach an unpopular doctrine, "cannot do work in many lines that would be tolerated in others," and remarked that racial feeling was deepening *(ibid.)*. It may be assumed that much of the problem encountered by White and others stemmed from the fact that they were Northerners coming South to work for Blacks, but it is also a matter of record in American history that in the 1890s, in a period of economic and political unrest, segregation increased sharply, and many legal restrictions date from that time.

Increased opposition to the work in the South was noted by Ellen White, who for many years had urged the evangelism and education of the African-American people. In 1891 she read a manuscript, "Our Duty to the Colored People" (released Mar. 20, 1891, and later printed as a pamphlet by J. E. White), to the General Conference Committee at Battle Creek. In this she said that Black members should be received into the White churches (p. 11). Speaking of the White members, she said that "if a Colored brother sits by their side they will not be offended or despise him," for they are journeying to the same heaven (p. 9). "If Jesus is abiding in our hearts we cannot despise the Colored man who has the same Saviour abiding in his heart" (p. 9).

But by 1895 she urged caution in the South, saying that in the future the missionary work among Black people "would have to be carried on along lines different from those followed in some sections of the country in former years" (9T 206).

The reason given repeatedly by Mrs. White for the change of method was the strengthening opposition *(ibid.* 205) from outside the church. She used phrases such as "danger of closing the door" to the work *(ibid.* 214); "we shall find our way blocked completely" *(ibid.)*; "Do nothing that will unnecessarily arouse opposition" *(ibid.* 208).

Separate Churches a Concession to Necessity. On the one hand, she laid down the principle of unity in Christ, who "laid the foundation for a religion by which Jew and Gentile, black and white, free and bond, are linked together in one common brotherhood, recognized as equal in the sight of God" (7T 225).

"The religion of the Bible recognizes no caste or color. It ignores rank, wealth, worldly honor. God estimates men as men with Him, character decides their worth. And we are to recognize the Spirit of Christ in whomsoever it is revealed. . . . He who is living in the atmosphere in which Christ lives will be taught of God and will learn to put His estimate on men" (9T 223).

She looked forward to a time "when the Holy Spirit is poured out," when "human hearts will love as Christ loved. And the color line will be regarded by many very differently from the way in which it is now regarded. To love as Christ loves lifts the mind into a pure, heavenly, unselfish atmosphere. He who is closely connected with Christ is lifted above the prejudice of color or caste" *(ibid.* 209).

On the other hand, in the face of an increasing racial feeling, she also warned that discretion is the better part of valor. She cautioned against contention or inviting opposition unnecessarily, for Adventist workers would have enough opposition from other sources *(ibid.* 211).

"The time has not come for us to work as if there were no prejudice. . . . If you see that by doing certain things which you have a perfect right to do, you hinder the advancement of God's work, refrain from doing these things" *(ibid.* 215).

She counseled that, on account of the changed situation, the Black believers should have their own houses of worship, "not to exclude them from worshiping with white people," but "that the progress of the truth may be advanced" *(ibid.* 206, 207). She advised providing separate churches as "the course of wisdom," "where demanded by custom or where greater efficiency is to be gained" *(ibid* 208), and "until the Lord shows us a better way" *(ibid.* 207).

A. W. Spalding reported that the method of dealing with the evangelism of African-Americans had been debated in General Conference sessions from time to time, "most speakers maintaining that as God is no respecter of persons, Christians should not allow social questions to affect their church polity" *(Origin and History of Seventh-day Adventists,* vol. 2, p. 188), although no action was taken. In fact, the 1877 session voted not to take action on the subject. Spalding records that when R. M. Kilgore (an Iowan who had preached some years in Texas) was made head of the SDA work in the South about 1890, "though brought up with the Northern conception of the problem," he "advocated the separation of white and colored churches. In the end this view prevailed" *(ibid.).*

Spalding wrote, around 1924 (in an unpublished manuscript, "Lights and Shades in the Black Belt," p. 142), that the church had taken the position that it should "recognize and conform to existing conditions which do not involve transgression of God's law." This attitude, he explained, though apparently "shaped by policy instead of principle," was "built upon the principle of policy" that the church in its social relations should defer to public opinion so "that the gospel may not be hindered."

The policy of separation, at first adopted for the sake of advancing the gospel, eventually came to be so taken for granted that probably a majority of SDA members in areas where segregation was the custom believed it to be a fundamental teaching of the church. The carrying out of this "principle of policy" over a period of years was not always understood by African-American members. As a consequence, some individuals and groups *(see* United Sabbath Day Adventists) became disaffiliated with the church, although many of those who went out returned to the original body.

Because, as Mrs. White pointed out, "in different places and under varying circumstances, the subject will need to be handled differently" (9T 213), the practice of separate African-American congregations has not been uniformly followed. In many parts of the country there are no separate churches, and even in areas in which the regional conferences operate, not all African-American members are in the regional churches. In some places the Black congregations were established by members who chose to withdraw from White congregations in order to have their own groups and work better for African-American evangelism; in other places, "where demanded by custom," the separation was the result of local necessity.

Development of Black Churches. The first African-American churches originated in the 1880s, and the next few in the 1890s, in the period of increased separation that resulted in the change of SDA method.

The first congregation of African-American Seventh-day Adventist believers was organized as a company in November 1883 and as a church in 1886 at Edgefield Junction, Tennessee. Its pastor was Harry Lowe, formerly a Baptist preacher. The second church of African-American believers, with 10 charter members, was established in Louisville, Kentucky, Feb. 16, 1890, where the work had been begun by A. Barry, who had accepted SDA teachings through reading the *Review and Herald.* The third was organized at Bowling Green, Kentucky, in June 1891. These first three, and also the fifth congregation, which was organized at Nashville, Tennessee, in September 1894, were in what is now the South Central Conference. The fourth, established by C. M. Kinney in New Orleans (organized June 1892), was the first in the present Southwest Region Conference.

Southern Missionary Society. The work of the Southern Missionary Society (incorporated in 1898) began in 1895 in Mississippi. It was founded by James Edson White, who went south in his Mississippi steamer *Morning Star* with a group of dedicated colporteurs, teachers, physicians, and Bible instructors from churches in the North, to bring the SDA message to African-American people along the Mississippi River. They were successful in establishing small churches and schools in Mississippi and other states. For the story, see *Gospel Herald; Morning Star;* Southern Missionary Society. White's printing firm was a forerunner of the Southern Publishing Association.

Other developments in the South included the establishing in 1895 of a school *(see* Oakwood College) and for a time (1906-1923) a sanitarium at Huntsville, Alabama, and two attempts at the establishment of a sanitarium in Nashville, Tennessee, between 1901 and 1909 *(see* Riverside Hospital).

Meantime work was beginning in earnest in cities of the East, beginning in New York City in 1902 *(see* Allegheny East Conference; Northeastern Conference).

Work in the West began in Los Angeles in 1906, when Jennie Ireland, a member of the White congregation in the city, began missionary work among the Black population and gave Bible studies to interested people, with the result that in 1908 the first Black church west of Ohio was formed *(see* Southern California Conference). Among those interested by Miss Ireland's work was the Temple family, whose daughter Ruth later attended medical school at Loma Linda and became noted as the original promoter of the idea of Health Week in the Los Angeles municipality's Health Department. Another was the Troy family, whose son Dr. Owen A. Troy became a pastor and evangelist in the West and Midwest, then associate secretary of the General Conference Sabbath School Department.

Departmental Organization. In 1894 there were about 50 Black SDAs in the United States. When the membership reached 900 in 1909, it was felt that to make a more noticeable impact on the growing African-American population some form of organization should be effected. Hence, at the General Conference held that year the North American Negro Department was organized. J. W. Christian, A. J. Haysmer, and C. B. Stephenson, in that order, were the first departmental secretaries. In 1918 the secretary reported that there were a total of 3,500 African-American members in the United States.

When the General Conference department was set up, union and local departments or missions were organized also. In the Southern Conference, the Southern Missionary Society formed the nucleus for the organization of a Southern Union Mission. The Southeastern Union set up a union Negro Mission Department, and for a time the Southwestern Union had a Southwestern Union Mission for Blacks. Most local conferences in these unions had a African-American department or a committee.

The first Black minister to head the General Conference department was W. H. Green, formerly a lawyer in the District of Columbia who had argued cases before the United States Supreme Court. He held the position from 1918 until his sudden death in October of 1928. To fill the vacancy, the Autumn Council of 1929 appointed George E. Peters as departmental secretary. After serving briefly, Peters went to New York City to stabilize the work there because of the grave situation after the United Sabbath Day Adventist crisis. Peters was succeeded by Frank L. Peterson, a pastor in Boston, Massachusetts. Peters was again elected to the position in 1941, and in 1951 was made a field secretary of the General Conference, the first Black to serve thus.

The name of the department was changed at the Autumn Council of 1942 from Negro Department to Colored Department, as the nation grew more concerned over integrating its African-American minority into the main current of American life. The term *Colored* somehow appeared less harsh, less divisive. To help with the medical needs of the various schools served by the department, Geneva Bryan, R.N., was made an assistant secretary of the department in 1942 and served until 1947.

Regional Conferences Organized. In 1944 the recommendation was made to organize full-fledged conferences of the African-American churches, a plan that had been requested some years earlier by Black leaders but had not then been considered feasible. The General Conference Committee in its Spring Meeting voted: "*We recommend,* 1. That in unions where the colored constituency is considered by the union conference committee to be sufficiently large, and where the financial income and territory warrant, colored conferences be organized.

"2. That these colored conferences be administered by colored officers and committees.

"3. That in the organization of these conferences the present conference boundaries within each union need not be recognized.

"4. That colored conferences sustain the same relation to their respective union conferences as do the white conferences" *(Actions of the Spring Meeting of the General Conference Committee,* Apr. 10-16, 1944, pp. 15, 16).

The first to act was the Lake Union Conference, which called a meeting of the African-American constituency in September to organize the Lake Region Conference (begun Jan. 1, 1945). Others followed, until in 1946 there were five such conferences. Two missions (Central States and Southwestern), which soon became conferences also, each with a full staff of officers and departmental secretaries, started in 1947.

In 1951 the North American Colored Department was enlarged by the addition of an associate secretary, Calvin E. Moseley, Jr., who succeeded G. E. Peters in 1953, both as secretary of the department and as a field secretary of the General Conference.

In 1954 Frank L. Peterson became secretary of the department and also associate secretary of the General Conference. Moseley was named associate secretary. The same year the name was changed from Colored Department to Regional Department as a further attempt to soften terms that seemed primarily to designate members on the basis of color.

In 1962 Frank L. Peterson was made a general vice president of the General Conference, and Harold D. Singleton, former president of the Northeastern Conference, became the Regional Department secretary, with Frank L. Bland, former president of the South Central Conference, as associate secretary.

In 1966, when Frank L. Bland succeeded the retiring Frank L. Peterson as vice president, Walter W. Fordham, president of the Central States Conference, was elected associate secretary of the Regional Department.

Recent Events. In many places in which the social pressures have lessened, previously all-White congregations have opened their membership in recent years. In the 1961 Autumn Council, the General Conference Committee voted a statement on human relations, quoting three of the extracts previously cited in this entry (7T 225; 9T 223, 209); and in the Spring Meeting of 1965 voted recommendations as follows: "*We recommend,* That the following principles and practices be adopted and carried out in our churches and institutions:

"1. Membership and office in all churches and on all levels must be available to anyone who qualifies, without regard to race.

"2. In our educational institutions there should be no racial bias in the employment of teachers or other personnel, nor in the admission of students.

"3. Hospitals and rest homes should make no racial distinction in admitting patients or in making their facilities available to physicians, interns, residents, nurses, and administrators who meet the professional standards of the institution.

"It is further recommended that these recommendations be given very serious consideration and that every effort be put forth to implement them as rapidly as is consistently possible" (Actions of the Spring Meeting of the General Conference Committee, Apr. 13, 14, 1965, in *Review and Herald* 142:8, Apr. 29, 1965).

In 1970 the General Conference Committee, at its spring session, in response to the desire among Black Seventh-day Adventists for a fuller involvement in leadership, passed what is generally referred to as the "16 points." Among these is an action stating:

"8. On the union conference level positive steps should be taken to open doors in the area of administrative and departmental leadership for those who have demonstrated their ability and qualifications to serve all segments of the church. In unions where there are Regional conferences or where there is an organized Regional department, the administrative officer level should include black leadership."

As a result, the seven unions with large Black memberships have elected officers and departmental secretaries from among their Black constituencies.

Another of the "16 points" provided for a Regional Presidents' Council, which meets twice a year under North American leadership and deals with problems distinctive to the regional work.

In 1975 the General Conference staff in Washington, D.C., included 17 persons elected to their positions from the Black constituency of North America, including two vice presidents and an associate secretary. There were also two persons in appointed positions.

Departmental Secretaries: J. W. Christian, 1909-1910; A. J. Haysmer, 1910-1914; C. B Stephenson, 1914-1918; W. H. Green, 1918-1928; G. E. Peters, 1929-1930; F. L. Peterson, 1930-1941; G. E. Peters, 1941-1953; C. E. Moseley, Jr., 1953-1954; F. L. Peterson, 1954-

1962; H. D. Singleton, 1962-1975.

Director of the Office of Regional Affairs: W. W. Fordham, 1975-1978.

Director of the Office of Ethnic Relations: W. S. Banfield, 1978-1979.

Director of the Office of Human Relations: W. S. Banfield, 1979-1989; Rosa T. Banks, 1989- .

HUMANITY, DOCTRINE OF. Humanity is the crowning work of Creation, made in God's image "both in outward resemblance and in character" (Gen. 1:26, 27; PP 45; GC 645). Believing in Creation, Seventh-day Adventists reject the theory that human beings evolved by slow degrees from the lower forms of life. They hold that the evolutionary philosophy "lowers the great work of the Creator" to the level of humanity's "narrow earthly conceptions" and that evolutionists degrade humans, and defraud them of the dignity of their origin (PP 45).

In their original state, man and woman possessed the possibility of unending life and continuous advancement. Their natural tendency was to live in harmony with the Creator's will and purpose for them. But human beings fell from their high estate and became mortal and sinful. Thenceforth, their natural tendency was contrary to God's will and purpose. Jesus Christ came to restore what had been lost as a result of sin (Luke 19:10). At His first advent Christ provided for the restoration of humanity's character; and at His second advent He will bestow upon those whose characters have been thus transformed the gift of immortality and the privilege of once more living in the divine presence.

George Storrs, a well-known Millerite preacher, advocated the doctrine of the mortality of humanity among his fellow Millerites, though it did not become a majority view among them until after 1844. Early in their history Seventh-day Adventists adopted the view that humans, when created, were given the opportunity of living forever, but that sin made them mortal (for the development of this view, *see* Death).

The Sept. 26, 1854, issue of the *Review and Herald* (7:53) printed a letter from John Byington of Buck's Bridge (near Potsdam), New York, who was later to become the first president of the General Conference. In it he described a conversation with a man concerning the question of spiritism, whether it was from the devil. This letter contains a fair summary of what was to become the Seventh-day Adventist view on humanity's nature and destiny: "God was infinitely holy and happy and it would be benevolent and good in Him to make a being capable of enjoying this blessedness. This goodness was manifest in creating [humanity] in His own image, capable of knowing and holding communion with . . . God." But, Byington maintained, since humans were "created, dependent" beings, they were therefore under their Maker's government; thus, God gave them His law, which "embraced all His will" concerning them. "Law given to a being possessing liberty and intelligence implies power to obey or disobey. To [humanity's] existence, therefore, is attached probation; and this implies a day of settling accounts, or a day of judgment."

Here Byington links the image of God with being "capable of knowing and holding communion with God," and affirms that humanity was endowed with free will "to obey or disobey." The letter closes with a typical description of the final, blessed state that human beings are to enjoy: "The devil and all his works [will] have an entire destruction. The curse is now removed from the earth, and God has a clean universe and a race of intelligent beings for ever to praise and glorify Him; which He would not have had, had He not have made [humans]" *(ibid.)*.

Seventh-day Adventists believe that humanity inherited a sinful nature with a propensity to sin, and their writings either reject or fail to stress the idea that human beings inherit the guilt of Adam's transgression.

SDAs point out that the concept that holds men and women to be a combination of mortal body and immortal soul arose from the speculations of pagan philosophers, and is contrary to the teachings of the Bible. A letter from R. F. Cottrell to the *Sabbath Recorder* (Seventh Day Baptist), quoted in the *Review and Herald* for Nov. 22, 1853, declares: "The Romans had the doctrines of purgatory and immortality of the soul before they ever heard of the Christian religion. Those who doubt this have only to consult Virgil and other ancient writers to be satisfied of it. . . . We know that heathen philosophers taught, very anciently, the immortality of the soul. I cannot say positively, but it was probably taught as long ago as the days of Solomon" (p. 157).

Seventh-day Adventists reject the view that men and women are merely or only or simply animals. This is shown by SDAs' vigorous opposition to Darwin's views on the descent of humanity, which, as stated earlier, degrades humans, who were made in the image of God. They do not believe that men and women differ from animals only in having more highly organized bodies. On the question whether human beings are material or spiritual, SDAs would say that, in ordinary language, they are both. Their intelligence and conscience are not usually understood as material functions, and the SDA Church has never taught that they should be so labeled. These functions are sometimes called "spiritual," and SDAs understand and accept this adjective in this sense. Seventh-day Adventists do not equate the biblical terms *soul* and *spirit* with the metaphysical concept of spirit, insisting that this technical term is foreign to both OT and NT and belongs in the realm of speculative philosophy rather than biblical theology.

The desire to impose the Aristotelian (matter-form) metaphysics on scriptural statements concerning humanity is not shared by SDAs. They prefer to retain biblical usage.

The terms *spirit* and *soul* are used in the Bible with different meanings and in many different scriptural contexts. In their use of the biblical terms, Seventh-day Adventists prefer to confine themselves to the meanings clearly intended in these passages, none of which ever speaks of "immortality" as being humanity's innate possession.

The mind-body or matter-spirit philosophical controversy, which teaches that body or matter is evil, and mind or spirit is good, is foreign to the thought world of the Bible. According to the Bible, God is the Creator of all things, and He called everything He made "good." These good things can all be used for evil purposes, however, because human beings, who were given dominion over creation, were also given the power of choice. Thus, because humans chose evil, both their material bodies and their spiritual intellects or consciences have come under the dominion of sin.

HUMILITY, ORDINANCE OF. *See* Foot Washing.

HUNDRED FORTY-FOUR THOUSAND. *See* One Hundred Forty-four Thousand.

HUNGARIAN OLD PEOPLE'S HOME. *See* Tass Old People's Home.

HUNGARIAN PUBLISHING HOUSE. *See* Adventist Publishing House; Hungary.

HUNGARIAN SEMINARY. A training school for ministers operated by the Hungarian Union Conference at Budapest, Hungary, since 1957. It is directed by the church president and has a staff of three teachers. The seminary offers a course by correspondence.

The need for the training of Hungarian Seventh-day Adventist ministers in Hungary was felt as early as 1903, but at that time it was not possible to establish a school in that country. Therefore, a number of young people were sent to the Friedensau Missionary Seminary in Germany (in 1910 seven Hungarian young people studied there), and after World War I some went to England. An action to establish a school in Hungary was taken at the conference session in September 1920, but it was not possible to execute it.

The Hungarian school project finally materialized in 1948 in a temporary program that lasted from Oct. 25, 1948, to Apr. 30, 1950. Twenty students attended the classes. After 1957, when the Seventh-day Adventist denomination was given official recognition, the training of ministers in Hungary finally became possible. Regular courses began in the autumn of 1957. In 1962 the school was replaced by a correspondence school.

In September 1967 systematic ministerial training came under the coordination of the Council of the Free Churches. A correspondence-type teaching program proceeded in six subjects: Old Testament, New Testament, systematic theology, practical theology, church history, and church and society. The special SDA subjects—dogmatics, church order, and interpretation of prophecy—were taught by the three participating SDA teachers. According to an agreement in 1972 concluded between the Council of the Free Churches, the Lutheran Theological Academy at Debrecen, and the Lutheran Theological Academy at Budapest, the seminary granted an academic degree to its students.

In 1989 the Hungarian Union withdrew from the Council of the Free Churches and reorganized the ministerial training. The Hungarian government recognized the seminary as a college in 1993. The Trans-European Division regards the seminary as a union college.

Principals: Jozsef Szakacs, 1971-1978; Jeno Szigeti, 1978-1984; Laszlo Hangyas, 1984-1989; Arpad Szollosi, 1989- .

HUNGARIAN UNION CONFERENCE. *See* Hungary; Trans-European Division.

HUNGARY. A people's republic in Central Europe, bounded by Slovakia and the Ukraine on the north, Romania on the east, Slovenia, Yugoslavia, and Croatia on the south, and Austria on the west. It has an area of 35,919 square miles (93,000 square kilometers), and its population (1994) is 10.3 million. About 90 percent of the people are of Hungarian origin. Two thirds of the people adhere to the Roman Catholic Church; other religious bodies include the Reformed Church, Lutheran, Orthodox, Unitarian, Baptist, Seventh-day Adventist, Methodist, and Jewish. All religious bodies have equal standing before the law.

The Hungarians are the descendants of the Ugro-Finnish people who migrated from Asia in the ninth century and established an independent kingdom by the year 1000. Soon thereafter they accepted Western Christianity, and for the next several centuries were in constant conflict with their neighbors and with the Turks, who finally occupied almost all of Hungary in the sixteenth century. The Reformation spread rapidly in Hungary, and soon its eastern and central part (Transylvania, now a part of Romania) became a bulwark of Protestantism in Eastern Europe. But the Counter-Reformation regained the lost position for the Catholic Church and nearly exterminated Protestantism in the western regions; only the Turkish occupation prevented its complete success. After the Turks were expelled near the end of the seventeenth century, Austria dominated Hungary; then in the 1800s the dual monarchy of Austria-Hungary was set up, and continued until the end of World War I, when Hungary became an independent state.

Seventh-day Adventist Statistics. The territory of Hungary constitutes the Hungarian Union Conference within the Trans-European Division. Statistics (1992) for *Hungary:* churches, 115; members, 4,462; ordained ministers, 23; licensed ministers, 25. Hungarian Union Conference headquarters: Szekely Bertalan u. 13, 1062 Budapest, Hungary.

Statistics (1992) for the two local conferences—*Duna Conference:* churches, 60; members, 2,284. Headquarters: Budapest. *Tisza Conference:* churches, 56; members, 2,156. Headquarters: Debrecen.

Institutions. Advent Publishing House; Hungarian Seminary; Tass Old People's Home.

Development of Seventh-day Adventist Work. *Beginnings.* M. B. Czechowski, a Polish ex-Catholic priest, became a Protestant in Switzerland and was baptized an SDA when he went to the United States in 1857. After raising up a Sabbathkeeping group in Tramelan, Switzerland, in 1867, he traveled through Europe, including Hungary, spreading the Sabbath truth. Seventh-day Adventists began their work in Hungary in Transylvania, a section later transferred to Romania. L. R. Conradi visited this area in 1890, and in a short time a woman convert went from there to the Hamburg Publishing House, where, according to contemporary accounts, she translated several Bible studies into Hungarian and took charge of their distribution by mail throughout Hungary (*Review and Herald* 69:773, Dec. 13, 1892). By 1893 there were 30 small tracts published in Hungarian.

In 1898 J. F. Huenergardt arrived from America to pioneer in Hungary and in the Danube basin. On his way to Klausenburg (now Cluj), in Transylvania, where he was to establish his headquarters, he visited in Budapest on Aug. 21, 1898, the first-known SDA in Hungary proper, a woman by the name of Anna Nagy, who had moved there from Transylvania. In the autumn of 1901 a recent convert of Huenergardt's, Michael B. Osz, went to Budapest and began to work there.

In March 1902 the first general meeting of Hungarian SDAs was held at Klausenburg, and at that time the foundations for the Seventh-day Adventist organization in Hungary were laid. The next year the first church in Hungary was organized in Békéscsaba. During the autumn of 1903 Huenergardt moved to Budapest, held meetings, and baptized several converts. In addition, interest in SDA beliefs spread through the work of colporteurs.

Reporting on a visit to Hungary in 1904, Jean Vuilleumier, of Switzerland, wrote: "During a recent trip to Hungary I met four or five of our workers in that country. In Budapest, the headquarters, meetings that started ten months ago have already resulted in about 15 baptisms, several candidates being Hungarian and others German. . . . There are companies of believers in several cities along the railway line crossing the country from North to South. . . . The work in Hungary began only six or seven years ago, and there are nearly 200 members" (*Le Messager* 8:88, November 1904).

Huenergardt trained workers and book evangelists, and began to issue some publications in the Hungarian language. In 1910 German ministers and evangelists came to his help; in 1911 a small Hungarian publishing house was established in Budapest as a branch of the Hamburg Publishing House. Later this house grew into an independent institution, with a printing plant under the management of Bela Gyarmati. It operated until the end of 1949, when it was nationalized by the government. In 1989 the Advent Publishing House was established in Budapest, and has continued in operation to the present.

Organization and Later Developments. In 1907 the work in Hungary was organized as the Hungarian Conference. In 1912 the Danube Union Conference, with headquarters in Budapest, was organized, with J. F. Huenergardt as president. It embraced Bulgaria, Hungary, Romania, and the area of the former Yugoslavia. The Hungarian Seventh-day Adventist Church at that time comprised the Middle Hungarian Conference, the North Hungarian Mission, and the West Hungarian Mission. After the territorial changes that followed World War I, the Hungarian Conference was reorganized within the European Division, with about 450 members and with Adolf Minck as president. By 1925 the membership had risen to about 1,000, and the church in Hungary was organized into a union conference with two local conferences. A building was constructed in Budapest with a chapel seating 500, offices for the union, and also living quarters. In 1928 Hungary was included in the Central European Division.

At that time ministerial students went for training to the Friedensau and Marienhöhe schools in Germany, and later to Watford, England. SDA papers published in Budapest were: *Az Arato* ("The Reaper"), *Az Idök Jelei* ("Signs of the Times"), and a health paper, *Boldog Elet* ("Happy Life"); of Ellen White's books, the Conflict of the Ages series and other writings were translated and printed. In 1936 the Hungarian Union Conference was reorganized with three local missions (referred to as conferences after World War II)

In 1938 the union acquired an old estate and a castle, transforming the property into a senior citizens' home for 80 to 100 people. Unfortunately, under government pressure, it had to be sold in 1941.

Through the years new headquarters were established successively in Miskolc, Szekesfehervar, and Szeged. Chapels were built or bought in Debrecen, Békéscsaba, Pécs, and other places.

In 1940 the Hungarian SDA churches were dissolved by order of the Ministry of War, and their activities prohibited, but in 1941 they were reopened by government permission under the name of Church of the Bible Followers. At about the same time the SDA work in Hungary came under the direction of the Southern European Division.

In 1940 parts of Transylvania, Slovakia, and Yugoslavia were again incorporated into Hungary and belonged to it until 1945. This change gave opportunities for building up the Hungarian-speaking churches in those areas. In 1958 the local conference organizations were disbanded and the union became a single organization.

In 1984 the Hungarian Union was reorganized with two conferences, and in that year Mark Finley conducted a public campaign that brought about a new beginning in the post-Communist life of Hungarian Seventh-day Adventists.

HUNT, WILLIAM (fl. c. 1880). A miner who, having heard J. N. Loughborough preach in California in the 1870s, carried Seventh-day Adventist literature with him to the diamond fields at Kimberley, South Africa, and thus introduced Seventh-day Adventist teachings into South Africa.

HUNTLEY, MARIA L. (1847-1890). Leader and instructor in lay missionary work. Born in a pioneer Seventh-day Adventist family at Washington, New Hampshire, she became secretary of the South Lancaster, Massachusetts, Vigilant Missionary Society. In 1874, when the General (later International) Tract and Missionary Society was first organized, she became its secretary and held that post through the rest of her life. She also taught at various times at South Lancaster Academy, Battle Creek College, and Healdsburg College, and at the time of her death was assistant principal and instructor in missionary correspondence at the Central Bible School for home and foreign missionaries at Chicago.

HUNTSVILLE TRAINING SCHOOL. *See* Oakwood College.

HURD, HETTY. *See* Haskell, Hetty (Hurd).

HURLOW, WILLIAM HENRY (1889-1972). Missionary nurse, singing evangelist, departmental secretary, administrator. He was born into a Seventh-day Adventist family in Wales and at an early age received a call to connect with the Cape Sanitorium in Plumstead, where he graduated from the nurses' course in 1914. He went immediately to the Malamulo Mission in Malawi to take charge of the school and dispensary there. Later he continued his mission service at Emmanuel Mission in Basutoland.

In 1919 he was called into European work, connecting with an evangelistic effort in Kimberley. While there he was married to Emma Irene Staples. Later he was called as a departmental secretary in the Cape Conference.

Working with the union evangelistic team, he served as singing evangelist in some of the major towns in South Africa.

In 1936 he was called to the presidency of the Cape Conference and four years later became secretary of the Missionary Volunteer, Home Missionary, and Medical departments of the South African Union. In 1950 he became president of the Rhodesia Conference, where he served for three years. At his retirement in 1962, he had given a total of 50 years of service to the cause in southern Africa.

HUTCHINS, ALFRED S. (fl. 1885). Pioneer minister and conference administrator. For some five years prior to joining the Adventists in 1852, he had been a Freewill Baptist minister. He was ordained together with J. N. Andrews in 1853 and was one of the leaders of Seventh-day Adventist work in Vermont throughout most of the rest of his life. Some have called him the "father of the Vermont Conference." For a time he was chaplain at Battle Creek Sanitarium. He also preached in Michigan, Illinois, Pennsylvania, Ohio, and throughout New England and eastern Canada. His name appears for the last time in the directory of 1894.

HUTCHINS, FRANK J. (1869-1902). Pioneer Seventh-day Adventist evangelistic and medical missionary in Central America. He was brought into the Seventh-day Adventist Church at an early age as the result of tent meetings in California and studied for the ministry at Healdsburg and Battle Creek colleges. Soon after graduation he was offered ministerial work in Oregon, but he chose to take a medical course at the University of Michigan instead. However, a few weeks after matriculation he accepted an appointment to the Bay Islands in Central America, where he and his wife pioneered SDA work in 1891. On his advice, the General Conference built a small schooner, the *Herald,* with which mission work could be carried on more expeditiously among the islands of that area, and this served as the mission home for several years. He soon found that there was a serious need for dentists in that area, and there being none, he secured books and some instruments, and after a while became a proficient dentist. Not only was his dental work helpful in reaching the people, but, along with the sale of publications, it contributed toward meeting the expenses of the mission. After 11 years of service, he died of a tropical disease at Bocas del Toro, Panama.

HUTCHINSON THEOLOGICAL SEMINARY. An educational institution that was operated (originally under the name Danish-Norwegian Seminary) at Hutchinson, Minnesota, from 1911 to 1928 for the education of church workers in the Danish and Norwegian languages. The original plan was to train workers in foreign languages at Union College, but by 1909 that institution had become so crowded that it was voted to establish separate schools. L. H. Christian found at Hutchinson the buildings of a defunct Danish Lutheran institution, which were owned by the city of Hutchinson. After arranging for the purchase for $11,000, he visited 11 Danish and Norwegian members, who each gave $1,000 for the new undertaking. M. L. Andreasen, the first president, chose a faculty and opened the school in 1910, with an enrollment of 93 academy and upper-grade school students the first year. Although intended to operate on the college level, it had no college students until 1914. The number of college students rose from four to a maximum of 68 in 1919, then declined to 25 the last year of operation. While this enrollment was insufficient for the operation of a college, the academy averaged 112 per year.

As a result of the antiforeign feeling during World War I, the name of the school was changed in 1919 to Hutchinson Theological Seminary. By that time immigration had almost stopped, Scandinavian-American young people wished to be educated in the English language, and the need for foreign language schools was decreasing. Then, too, the competition between foreign and English schools for students from the same territory was keen. When the school closed in May 1928, the Minnesota Conference took over the plant and moved Maplewood Academy to the site.

H. W. MILLER MEMORIAL SANITARIUM AND HOSPITAL. *See* Miller.

HYATT, WILLIAM S. (1857-1936). Administrator and missionary. He was born at Williamstown, New York, and attended Battle Creek College, where he met Sadie Armitage, whom he married in 1882. That same year he took up ministerial work in New York, and was ordained to the ministry in 1885.

For a number of years Hyatt worked in Wisconsin, then for 10 years he served as conference president: four years in Texas (1888-1892), four in Missouri (1892-1896), and two in Kansas (1896-1897). In 1898 Hyatt and his family went to South Africa, where he took over the presidency of the conference (raised to union status after 1901) from A. T. Robinson. During the years of economic depression following the Anglo-Boer War, his considerable financial ability was taxed to the utmost to maintain the large institutions that had been launched in more prosperous times.

In expanding the mission fields to the north, Hyatt traveled extensively by oxcart and donkey wagon. Frequently when a missionary family went on furlough, he, even though president of the South African Union, took over the station.

Hyatt served as president of the Natal-Transvaal Conference from 1913 to 1921. On their first and only furlough to the homeland (1924-1929), the Hyatts spent four years going from church to church telling the story of African missions.

Returning to South Africa where his children were living and working, Hyatt served as pastor at Pretoria. When failing health forced him to seek a lower elevation, he went to Durban for pastoral work and spent the remaining years of his life in missionary work, writing hundreds of letters, attending camp meetings, and conducting Weeks of Prayer in the schools.

HYDE, CONRAD THOMAS JAMES (1907-1965). Missionary, teacher, administrator, departmental secretary. He was born in London to a family that produced five ordained Seventh-day Adventist ministers. In 1927 he completed the nurses' course at Stanborough Park Sanitarium, then took a two-year ministerial course at Stanborough College.

He began his work for the church at Kendu Hospital in Africa in 1930. In 1932 the family moved to the Kamagambo Training School, where the boys' boarding school was started. In 1940 he moved to Kandoto Mission, where he served as mission director until 1943. In this year he was ordained. From 1943 to 1947 he served at Kisii Mission Station, and then was called to head the Theological Department at Bugema College and later served as principal of the school. In 1958 he became president of the Tanzania Union, and in 1963 the family moved to Salisbury, where he became a departmental secretary and later field secretary for the division.

He was the first Master Guide in East Africa and mastered the Luo and Swahili languages to the point that he was issued a diploma for proficiency in these vernaculars by London University.

HYDE, JOHN ASHFORD (1923-1969). Missionary, physician, administrator. John was born in Plymouth, England, and at 9 years of age went with his parents to north Nigeria. At 16 he matriculated and was accepted for medical training at University College Hospital. In 1946 he married Myrtle Richter and went to the same area that his parents had pioneered in his youth.

His early surgeries were performed on a scrubbed kitchen table, utilizing kettles as sterilizers. During his years as a medical missionary, he never neglected spiritual care for the souls of his patients, and in 1951 he was ordained to the gospel ministry. He then served as president of the North Nigeria Mission until called to the Gold Coast (now Ghana) to help organize and open Kwahu Hospital. Jengre Hospital also stands as a memorial to his labors.

After completing advanced studies, he was called as medical secretary of the Northern European Division.

On one of his trips he was stricken with a sudden illness and passed to his rest in Vienna, Austria.

HYDE, JOHN JACOB (1893-1968). Missionary to Africa. A native of England, he was the oldest of 13 children. At the age of 15 he began his service to the church at the International Tract Society, which later became the Stanborough Press. After attending college, he entered evangelism in the South England Conference. Soon after his ordination in 1924, he received a call to mission service in Sierra Leone, known in those days as the "White man's grave." After a period of service, he and his wife, the former Louise Ashford, were transferred to the Gold Coast (now Ghana), where John headed the work. Winning the confidence of the warlike Ashanti people, the Hydes healed the sick, taught the young, and acted as arbitrators in tribal conflicts. For this service he was recognized by an official letter of thanks from the chief commissioner of the Ashanti region of the Gold Coast.

In 1930 Hyde was called to pioneer new work in north Nigeria. During his years in Africa he served as president of the Sierra Leone, Ghana, north Nigeria, and west Nigeria fields.

At his retirement in 1957, he had actively served the church for 45 years. In retirement he continued to work as a pastor until 1966, then as a church elder and a counselor to all who sought his guidance.

HYDE, WILLIAM H. (fl. 1845). An Adventist in Maine. In the spring of 1845 he was healed by prayer and a short time later was present when Ellen Harmon had a vision of the new earth. After hearing her description he wrote the hymn "We Have Heard From the Bright, the Holy Land" (1T 67-71; cf. EW 17-20), which was soon published in several "Second Advent papers" and in Himes's songbook *Advent Harp* (1849 edition).

This vision of the new earth, at which Hyde was present, was not Ellen Harmon's first vision (at which only five women were present; see 2SG 30; 1T 58), but occurred in the spring of 1845 *(Present Truth* 1:88, November 1850), more than two weeks, according to her own account, after her return from three months of travel (2SG 52; cf. 38, 50-52; see also 1T 58-67). It was published in 1846, together with the first vision without separation, in a broadside, "To the Little Remnant"; it is still printed without separation in *Early Writings,* where it begins with the last paragraph on page 17 (see W. C. White, in *Review and Herald* 112:7, Mar. 7, 1935).

If this Hyde was the W. H. Hyde who was the "chief printer" of *Hope Within the Veil,* published by C. H. Pearson at Portland, he did not remain with the little group that was forming one of the nuclei of the future Seventh-day Adventist Church, but about the end of August 1845 reverted to the views of the majority group of Adventists, known as the *Advent Herald* party.

HYDROTHERAPY. *See* Physical Therapy.

HYMNODY. The early hymnody of Sabbathkeeping Adventists laid heavy stress on the distinctive doctrines of the church—the Sabbath and the Second Advent. Beginning in 1849 with *Hymns for God's Peculiar People That Keep the Commandments of God and the Faith of Jesus,* James White edited five hymnals and four supplements for his fellow believers prior to the organization of the church in 1863. In addition, his sister, Anna White, compiled *Hymns for Youth and Children* in 1854.

While these early hymnals drew heavily on existing Protestant worship music, Adventists themselves wrote about 5 percent of the hymns they published during this era. Annie R. Smith and Roswell F. Cottrell were the most prolific Adventist hymnwriters of the period.

The first Sabbathkeeping Adventist hymnal to contain music was *Hymns for Those Who Keep the Commandments of God and the Faith of Jesus* (1855). The music in the earliest hymnals was derived from three sources: psalm tunes, Lowell Mason and his school, and folk hymns or White spirituals. Closely akin to the latter category were popular tunes for which Adventists supplied religious words. Uriah Smith's "Land of Light," written to fit Stephen Foster's tune "Swanee River," appeared in an 1858 supplement.

The second generation of pioneers, notably J. Edson White and his cousin Frank Belden, added variety if not quality to Seventh-day Adventist hymnody. Edson White was the first SDA printer to learn to set the musical type for hymnals. He published a number of temperance and Sabbath school songbooks, sometimes collaborating with Belden. Both men were composers, and a number of Belden's hymns still survive in SDA hymnody.

Since 1886 three volumes have dominated SDA hymnody. The first was *Hymns and Tunes.* Officially titled *The Seventh-day Adventist Hymn and Tune Book for Use in Divine Worship,* the collection was compiled between 1884 and 1886 by a special committee of the General Conference.

At the turn of the century F. E. Belden published *Christ in Song.* This hymnal supplanted *Hymns and Tunes* and remained the most popular collection among SDAs until 1941, when the *Church Hymnal* was published.

In 1981 the General Conference set up a 19-member Church Hymnal Committee to compile a new hymnal. The committee was chaired by C. L. Brooks, an associate director of the Sabbath School Department of the General Conference and an accomplished soloist. Wayne Hooper, formerly with the King's Heralds Quartet and the Voice of Prophecy, served as executive secretary. The committee included music teachers, choir leaders, organists, composers, writers, editors, soloists, evangelists, pastors, and church administrators.

Issued in 1985, the new hymnal retained 300 of the 1941 hymnal's selections, but two thirds of them were pitched lower to make them easier for congregations to sing. About 160 "new" hymns were introduced, drawn from Protestant hymnody as well as from new compositions and other SDA hymnals. In the Composers and Arrangers index of the new hymnal, several members of the compiling committee were acknowledged for their contributions. Wayne Hooper provided six original hymn tunes and arranged 19 others, while Melvin West wrote three new tunes and arranged 31. Other members contributing tunes were Allen Foster, James Bingham, and John Read. A pair of Sabbath hymn texts were contributed by Gem Fitch and Ottilie Stafford.

A number of hymn texts were altered slightly to avoid obsolete language, make theological corrections, or eliminate gender-exclusive language. A much-improved section of Scripture readings and worship aids was provided by Merle Whitney and his associates on a worship aids committee.

HYPNOTISM. The practice of inducing a state of hypersuggestibility in which susceptible persons may be led to accept and act uncritically upon suggestions given by others who thus in a measure control them. A trance state is characteristic of some levels of hypnosis but may or may not be obvious. The kinds of procedures that are now generally classified under the name hypnotism were known in the nineteenth century by a number of nebulous terms such as mesmerism, Braidism, mind cure, and animal magnetism.

The leaders of the Seventh-day Adventist Church have from the first rejected the use of hypnotism, considering it unethical and vulnerable to influence by unseen sinister forces. Ellen White recognized hypnotism as a science that "may appear . . . very valuable," through which "temporary relief may be felt"; but she spoke of it as leaving the subject of hypnosis more or less permanently weakened (MM 112, 116), and she referred to it as "the science by which satanic agencies work." She also spoke out against the practice on the ethical grounds that "no individual should be permitted to take control of another person's mind" *(ibid.* 115). Hypnotism deprives the subject of the free use of the will and takes the individual from the world of reality into a realm of fantasy in which he or she may experience enhanced visual and auditory imagery, automatic writing, depersonalization, various types of disorientation, and acceleration or inhibition of physiological functions *(Encyclopaedia Britannica* [1971], vol. 11, p. 996). Satan teaches the science of taking captive the minds of others and thus deprives them of the privilege of choosing to accept Jesus Christ (MM 110).

The General Conference Committee, in the 1955 Autumn Council, while recognizing the indispensable place of psychosomatic medicine and the appropriate application of psychology and psychiatry, took action on hypnotism, recommending that "we as a denomination recognize hypnotism as a dangerous procedure, and warn Seventh-day Adventists against employing or seeking its use," and that "we take a decided stand against the teaching or practicing of hypnotism in the Seventh-day Adventist institution."

Seventh-day Adventists, by and large, have followed Mrs. White's counsel and the direction of the church in this regard, and have felt that some of the more recent pronouncements by ethically sensitive investigators as well as the caution advised by many psychiatrists have tended to confirm the wisdom of this position.

I

IBADAN TEACHER TRAINING SCHOOL. *See* Seventh-day Adventist Training College (Ihie).

ICELAND. A large island in the North Atlantic with an area of about 37,000 square miles (96,000 square kilometers) and a population (1994) of about 265,000. Fishing and farming are the main industries. The interior, which consists of mountains and high plateaus, is uninhabited. There are many volcanoes and hot springs, the latter being used for heating homes and greenhouses. Because of the influence of the Gulf Stream, the climate is oceanic, with cool summers and comparatively mild winters. Iceland was settled by Norwegian Vikings and by some Irish and Scottish people in the ninth and tenth centuries. In the thirteenth century Iceland came under Norwegian and later Danish rule. Early in the sixteenth century, when Denmark became Protestant, Lutheranism also spread to Iceland. The first complete Icelandic Bible translation was published in 1584. Iceland has been an independent republic since 1944. The Lutheran Church is the state church, but there is complete freedom of religion. The inhabitants are completely literate and enjoy a high standard of living.

Seventh-day Adventist Statistics. The territory of Iceland constitutes the Iceland Conference, an attached field within the Trans-European Division. In 1993 there were seven churches, a membership of 503, four ordained ministers, and seven teachers.

Institutions. Iceland Publishing House; Iceland Secondary School.

Development of Seventh-day Adventist Work. *Beginnings.* The first-known Seventh-day Adventist in Iceland was the Norwegian minister O. J. Röst. According to a report by J. C. Raft in the *Review and Herald* of Feb. 11, 1915, Röst went to Iceland in the summer of 1893. Arriving there, he sailed around the island, stopped at various ports, and at Eskifjördur convinced a Lutheran minister of the Sabbath. Although this minister never became a member of the SDA Church, he kept the Sabbath to the end of his days and in spite of opposition from his own church retained his ministerial position.

In November 1897 David Östlund of Sweden was sent by the Denmark Conference to be the first Seventh-day Adventist missionary to Iceland. On the ship taking him to his field, Östlund was surprised to meet a Sabbathkeeping Icelander who was returning from Denmark to his homeland. This Icelander had been led to keep the Sabbath by reading a copy of *The Great Controversy,* but he and his wife had not yet been baptized. Having read in the *Evangeliets Sendebud* that a missionary was being sent to begin SDA work in Iceland, he and his wife decided to return home, hoping to be of assistance to the new missionary when he began his work. Östlund regarded this meeting on the ship as a hopeful augury for a successful mission in Iceland. He began his work by publishing and circulating books, the first of which were *The Second Coming of Christ,* by James White, and *Steps to Christ,* by Ellen White, both printed in 1898. Östlund, who was a printer himself, established his own press and in the year 1900 began to publish a semimonthly magazine called *Fraekorn* ("The Seed"), which for a time had the widest circulation of any paper in the country.

In 1903 Nils Anderson, a colporteur from Sweden, was sent to Iceland, where he worked as a pioneer canvasser until 1916.

The first church was organized May 19, 1906, in Reykjavik. A church building erected in 1905 was destroyed by fire in 1910, but rebuilt and dedicated early in 1912.

In the summer of 1911 the Scandinavian Union sent to Iceland a new missionary family, O. J. Olsen and his wife.

Organization and Growth. The mission in Iceland was supported by the General Conference until 1901, when it came under the General European Conference, later called the European Division (*Review and Herald* 92:14, Feb. 11, 1915). Three years later it was placed under the Scandinavian Union Conference. From 1923 to 1928 it was again a detached mission of the European Division, then of the Northern European Division. In 1930 the work in Iceland and the Faroe Islands was united and formed into the Iceland Faroes Conference, becoming in 1931 a part of the West Nordic Union. O. J. Olsen served as the conference president from 1931 to 1947, except for three years (1933-1936), when he stayed in Norway, and O. Frenning served as a vice president of the field. During World War II Iceland had scarcely any connection with Scandinavia. After the war the Faroe Islands were assigned to the East Denmark Conference, and Iceland was again linked directly to the Northern European Division as the Iceland Conference. In 1947 O. J. Olsen was called to serve as a field secretary of the Northern European Division.

Educational Work. A church school was opened by D. Östlund in 1905 but was discontinued after only a few years of operation. Two church schools were opened in 1928, one in Reykjavik and the other in the Westman Islands. Because of volcanic eruption in the Westman Islands in 1972, the school was forced to close in the middle of the school year. It reopened in 1974. In 1967 the school in Reykjavik was closed because of lack of facilities. In 1976 it was reopened in temporary accommodations. In 1990 it moved to a fine new building that also serves as an evangelistic center for the Greater Reykjavik area. The building was erected partly from a share of the Thirteenth Sabbath Offering for the third quarter of 1989 and accommodates also the conference office and the Iceland Publishing House. Iceland Secondary School was opened in 1950.

Private treatment rooms were opened in Reykjavik in 1911 (operated for more than 30 years) and in the Westman Islands in 1923. Treatment rooms have been operated in other places for longer or shorter periods of time. At the academy a guest home, Hressingarheimili Hlidardalsskoli, accommodating 50 patients for two and a half months during the summer vacation, offered hydrotherapy and electrotherapy administered by a qualified physiotherapist. It was discontinued in 1964.

Welfare societies, started in 1923, operate in five churches. These welfare societies donate to the poor annually in cash and supplies close to $50,000.

Bible Correspondence School and Radio. The Bible correspondence school, which was begun in 1948, has reached thousands of people and has won several converts. The government exercised control over radio broadcasting on the island for many years. However, in 1963 the church was given written permission to broadcast nationally one service a year. In 1986 broadcasting was decontrolled.

The publishing work has been a prominent feature of Seventh-day Adventist work in Iceland. Of the 60 books that have been published, including seven by Ellen White, many deal directly with biblical doctrines, while others foster the Christian home and provide stories for children and young people.

ICELAND CONFERENCE. *See* Iceland; Trans-European Division.

ICELAND PUBLISHING HOUSE (Fräkornid—Bókaforlag Adventista). A publishing firm without printing plant operated at Reykjavik, Iceland, by the Iceland Conference. This institution was established in 1932, but even before that the sale of publications was a prominent feature of Seventh-day Adventist work in Iceland. In 1898, a year after the arrival of the first missionary (David Östlund, who had been a printer), two books had begun to be circulated—*The Second Coming of Christ,* by James White, and *Steps to Christ,* by Ellen White. From 1900 until he left the country in 1914, Östlund edited a semimonthly magazine called *Fraekorn* ("The Seed"), which achieved marked popularity and had for a time a wider circulation than any other magazine in the country. Setting up his own press, he printed, besides his paper, books and tracts. Two books were published at the beginning of the century: *The Prophecies of Our Lord* and *The Revelation,* both by J. G. Matteson. Nils Anderson, from Sweden, pioneer colporteur in Iceland, worked untiringly from 1903 to 1916, riding his pony to the remotest corners of the land. Through the years about 40 books have been circulated among Iceland's scattered population. Its people, proud of their old Icelandic literature, the Sagas, have always had a great interest in reading.

The present publishing house, established in 1932, operated a small printing press and a small offset press for many years until all printing at its own facility was discontinued and the presses sold in 1989. The presses of our publishing houses in the neighboring Scandinavian countries and the Stanborough Press in England have carried out much of the printing work, such as the four volumes of the *Footprints of Jesus* in Icelandic, as well as the 10 volumes of the *Bible Stories,* by Arthur S. Maxwell. Thousands of them have been sold in the country. *Counsels for the Church,* by Ellen

White, was published in 1974, along with a study guide. In that same year the missionary paper *Signs of the Times* (Takn timanna) was published for the first time. *The Great Controversy* was retranslated and published in 1976, *Counsels on Stewardship* in 1984, and two Morning Watch books by Ellen White: *My Life Today* in 1979 and *Maranatha, the Lord Is Coming* in 1984. Many other titles have been published through the years for the church and the general public. Presently plans are under way to publish a retranslation (the fourth) of *Steps to Christ* and to publish the Conflict of the Ages series in its entirety.

Managers: O. J. Olson, 1932-1933; M. Helgason, 1933-1949; J. Gudmundsson, 1949-1959; M. Helgason, 1959-1966; R. Burgess, 1966-1969; O. Kristinsson, 1969-1976; T. Sveinsson, 1977-1989; J. Johannsson, 1989-1991; E. V. Arason, 1991-1994; Elias Theodorsson, 1994- .

ICELAND SECONDARY SCHOOL (Hlidardalsskoli). A coeducational boarding school on the senior high school level, situated 30 miles (50 kilometers) east of Reykjavik, owned and operated by the Iceland Conference. The property, which covers an extensive area of mountain and lava fields, totals 30,000 acres (12,000 hectares), of which about 100 acres (40 hectares) are tillable land. Widespread sections are suitable as pasturage for sheep.

The work of constructing the school building began on June 8, 1949. In the autumn of 1950 the school opened with 19 students, one teacher, and the principal, who was also the conference president. The building was dedicated on Sept. 24, 1951, by A. F. Tarr, then president of the Northern European Division.

Since the enrollment soon exceeded 40, the number for which the building was planned, work was begun early in 1956 on a new dormitory, which was occupied by 40 boys in the fall of 1959. It was officially dedicated in 1960, on the tenth anniversary of the school's opening.

The school employs four teachers; the student capacity is 80.

The farm had about 20 head of cattle and about 350 sheep and 600 chickens, but in 1989 farming was discontinued and the farm rented out to a church member.

During the summer months, while school is in recess, the buildings at the school were used for a sanitarium until 1964. Since then they have been used for various summer activities for children. For four summers the buildings were rented to the city of Reykjavik as a camp for children with mental disabilities, and twice the church has conducted camps and Vacation Bible Schools during the recess.

In 1967 a share of the Thirteenth Sabbath Offering overflow made possible an experimental drilling for hot water, of which there is plenty in the vicinity. The drilling proved successful—a miracle, according to the geologists; an answer to prayer, according to the church. This underground thermal steam about 250° F (120° C) was harnessed, and since then it has provided all the heat necessary for heating and leaves much water and steam unused. Part of this surplus heat is used for an outdoor swimming pool and for a greenhouse.

Most of the students at the school do not come from Seventh-day Adventist homes. For several years applications to enter the school have exceeded the accommodations available, which resulted in many being turned away.

The school operated grades 8 to 10, which led the pupils to the Grunnskólapróf (General Certificate of Education), which gives right to college entrance.

Principals: Julius Gudmundsson, 1950-1951; O. J. Olsen, 1951-1952; Julius Gudmundsson, 1952-1954; Sigfus Hallgrimsson, 1954-1955; Julius Gudmundsson, 1955-1960; Sigurdur Bjarnason, 1960-1964; Jon H. Jonsson, 1964-1972; Julius Gudmundsson, 1972-1974; Björgvin Snorrason, 1974-1979; Gudmundur Ólafsson, 1979-1982; Árni Hólm, 1982-1984; Einar V. Arason, 1984-1985; Jon H. Jonsson, 1985-1988; Erling B. Snorrason, 1988-1993; Björgvin Snorrason, 1993-1994; Asta Gudjonsdottir, 1994- .

ICELAND SUMMER SANITARIUM (Hressingarheimili Hlidardalsskola). A medical institution operated at Ölfus, Iceland, in the Hlidardalsskoli (Iceland Mission School), during the summer vacation. It was operated from 1954 to 1964.

A physiotherapist gave massage, electric treatments, and Finnish and several other kinds of baths according to prescriptions from a physician in Reykjavik, who visited the patients regularly.

IDAHO. *See* Idaho Conference; Upper Columbia Conference.

IDAHO CONFERENCE. The unit of church organization comprising the portion of

Idaho lying south of latitude 45° (including Lemhi County), and the counties of Baker, Grant, Harney, Malheur, Union, and Wallowa in Oregon. Statistics (1993): churches, 39; members, 5,030; church schools, 14; ordained ministers, 17; licensed ministers, 2; church school teachers, 30. Headquarters 7777 Fairview Avenue, Boise, Idaho. The conference constitutes part of the North Pacific Union Conference.

Institutions. Gem State Adventist Academy.

Local Churches—*Idaho:* Boise, Buhl, Caldwell (English, Spanish), Cambridge, Eagle, Eden, Emmett, Fruitland (Spanish), Gem State Adventist Academy, Heyburn, Homedale, Idaho Falls, Kuna, McCall, Meridian, Mountain Home, Nampa, New Plymouth, Parma, Payette, Pocatello, Salmon, Twin Falls, Weiser (Maranatha, Spanish), Wood River Valley (in Hailey). *Oregon:* Baker City, Burns, Cove, Elgin, Enterprise, John Day, La Grande, Long Creek, Ontario, Richland, Vale.

History. *Beginnings of Work in the Area.* Seventh-day Adventist teachings were introduced into Idaho about 1884. J. G. Smith was assigned the unworked territory of southern Idaho. During the first year he raised up several small Sabbath schools: one in Boise; one in High Valley, 12 miles (20 kilometers) north of Boise; and one in Franklin, 20 miles (32 kilometers) south of Boise. In November of 1885 Smith died of peritonitis, at the age of 42. In 1885 the General Conference sent D. T. Fero to carry on the work in Idaho. He reported to the *Review and Herald* that on his arrival there in December he found two Sabbath schools and an inactive tract society, and that in 1886 he combined the Sabbath schools and organized a church. This was the first official Seventh-day Adventist church in Idaho. It had 13 charter members. Although they could not all drive the necessary distance to meet together every Sabbath, they felt the need of a common church home. A building at Seventh and Front streets was located and rented for Sabbath services. In 1891 the membership had grown to 32, and the need for a larger meeting place was apparent. A building at Thirteenth and State streets was purchased and remodeled into an attractive church home. A room in the building was converted into the first SDA church school in Idaho. In 1917 a beautiful building at Sixth and Main streets was purchased and remodeled. It provided space for a spacious church plus rooms for the rapidly growing school. The rooms facing Main Street were used by the Idaho Conference for its offices. In 1951 A. E. Hempel, pastor of the Boise church, took on the task of building a new church on the corner of Wilson and Irving streets.

Jan. 16, 1993, was the date of the grand opening of the new church building at 1115 N. Cloverdale Road, constructed under the leadership of Don Driver.

Other areas where the Seventh-day Adventist message was preached early include Franklin, Idaho, where in 1886 Fero reported organizing a church of 19, and Moscow, Idaho, where a church was organized in 1887. In 1890 O. A. Johnson held meetings in the Methodist church in Salmon, Idaho, which were followed 12 years later by a series of meetings held there by John and Will Holbrook. However, it was not until 1908 that a company with about 20 members was organized at Salmon. After S. H. Kime preached at Long Creek, Oregon, in 1895, a church of seven was organized the next year (moved in 1908 to Fox Valley, but in 1916 returned to the original site). Other churches were founded at Baker, Oregon (organized in 1897 with 13 charter members), where Enid Sparks, lifetime teacher and author of juvenile books, was a member; at La Grande, Oregon (1898, with 18 members); at Cambridge, Idaho (1902, with 10 members); and at Parma, Idaho (1905, with 19 members).

The work in Caldwell, Idaho (organized in 1905, with eight members), was begun by O. K. Butler. This congregation, first meeting in the home of A. C. Bird, erected its first church building in 1909; its third is a modern structure serving a congregation of more than 400 members.

Organization of Conference. At a session of the Upper Columbia Conference held at College Place, Washington, on June 6, 1907, resolution 11 was voted as follows: "Whereas, experience has taught that more thorough and effective work can be done in a conference whose territorial area is small, and that much time and expense can be saved thereby in travel; and whereas, the territory of the Upper Columbia Conference is so large that it is difficult to secure proper representation at the regular conference sessions by churches remote from the place of meeting; and whereas, southern Idaho and eastern Oregon form part of the territory of the Upper Columbia Conference with a constituency sufficiently large to maintain a conference; therefore we recommend: (1) that a new conference be organized within the present territorial limits of the Upper Columbia Conference; (2) that the territory of this new conference be composed of the state of Idaho south of the parallel of 45 north latitude, and the counties Wallowa, Union, Baker, and Malheur in eastern Oregon. Your committee appointed to agree upon boundary lines for the proposed division of the conference would respectfully report that we think best to divide the conference on the lines proposed in resolution 11."

This committee was also authorized to name the time and place of a camp meeting, where this organization was perfected.

At this camp meeting, held at Weiser, Idaho, July 11-21, 1907, and presided over by G. E. Langdon, the Southern Idaho Conference was organized, a constitution was adopted, and officers were elected: W. W. Steward, president; J. M. Willoughby, vice president; T. L. Copeland, secretary-treasurer and missionary secretary; A. C. Bird, educational superintendent; and A. D. Guthrie, field secretary. (Later, at the fifth annual session of the conference, an amendment to the constitution eliminated the office of vice president.) At a subsequent session of the North Pacific Union Conference the counties of Grant and Harney in Oregon were added to the territory of the new Southern Idaho Conference. The 15 churches voted into the new organization—eight of them in Oregon, and seven in Idaho—with their respective memberships were as follows—in *Oregon:* Baker (45), Cove (14), Elgin (8), Halfway (18), La Grande (26), Ontario (25), Union (55), Wallowa (14); in *Idaho:* Blackfoot (16), Boise (110), Caldwell (43), Cambridge (60), Meridian (13), Parma (23), Twin Falls (16). There were also eight companies with a combined membership of 68, making a total of 554 members at the time of conference organization.

A list of denominational workers who have been members of the Boise church includes Drs. W. F. and G. E. Norwood, both on the medical faculty of Loma Linda University; L. A. Reed, former editor of the *Signs of the Times;* L. E. Froom, editor, preacher, and writer; the Christian family, including Hervey, John, Rolland, and Marie; Homer and George Casebeer and families; T. Lloyd Copeland; and many others. The Caldwell church has also produced an impressive list of former and present workers, among whom are Lela Simpson Perkins (Japan); Marie Simpson McNiel (South and Central America); Zoral and Elga Coberly (China); Raleigh and Edna Garner (India); Oral Garner (South America); and more recently M. Wesley and Joan Shultz (Pakistan). A member of the Caldwell church until her death was Mrs. Frank Steunenberg, whose husband, the governor of Idaho, was murdered by Harry Orchard (who experienced a miracle of conversion, and whose subsequent influence, while he lived and after his death, led to the baptism of several other inmates of the state prison).

Among other churches that produced denominational workers are the following: Twin Falls, Idaho, missionaries Wilma Leazer (Indonesia) and Harold Drake (Africa); Union, Oregon (now disbanded), G. F. Wolfkill, later a college president; and John E. Weaver, well known in the field of education; Mountain Home, Idaho, W. R. Beach, who retired (1975) as General Conference vice president; Filer, Idaho (organized 1924, originally composed chiefly of persons of German extraction from North Dakota), two ministers and a teacher, from the Kurtz family; Aberdeen, Idaho, two ordained ministers and a teacher from the Cornforth family; Buhl, Idaho, an ordained minister and a sanitarium business manager from the Johnson family; Cove, Oregon, the Bell sisters, one a conference Sabbath school secretary and the other a church school teacher who once taught Reuben R. Figuhr, who later became General Conference president.

The work in the conference through the years has moved rather slowly, especially in the eastern section of Idaho, and the membership has fluctuated. The conference was reorganized in 1930 and is now known as the Idaho Conference.

Through the years there have been many expansions of the facilities of the conference. About 1951 the building housing the conference office, the Boise school, and the church was sold, and another building that was bought and remodeled now serves as the conference office. A new church was built in one area of the city and a new church school in another (since replaced by one containing four modern classrooms, a large gymnasium, a Pathfinder room, a kitchen, and a manual training room). In this same period, the conference has built seven new churches and seven new schools, and built or acquired five parsonages and three Dorcas Society centers. In 1964 the entire Gem State Adventist Academy was rebuilt on a new 300-acre (120-hectare) campus. The conference also owns a summer camp known as Idahaven, consisting of 11.3 acres (4.5 hectares), situated at Payette Lakes, McCall, Idaho.

In 1969 the conference headquarters and Adventist Book Center moved into a newly constructed office building in a prominent location on the western edge of Boise.

Presidents—Southern Idaho Conference: W. W. Steward, 1907-1909; J. M. Willoughby, 1909-1912; A. M. Dart, 1912-1914; J. J. Nethery, 1914-1916; T. G. Bunch, 1916-1917; J. W. Norwood, 1917-1923; H. G. Thurston, 1923-1925; W. A. Gosmer, 1925-1930. *Idaho Conference:* W. A. Gosmer, 1930-1931; L. E. Esteb, 1931-1932; J. W. Turner, 1932-1938; G. S. Belleau, 1938-1945; C. C. Kott, 1945-1951; A. J. Gordon, 1951-1963; George W. Liscombe, 1963-1970; F. W. Bieber, 1970-1979; Bruce Johnston, 1979-1985; Paul W. Nelson, 1985-1988; Stephen L. McPherson, 1988- .

IGNACIO MANUEL ALTAMIRANO EDUCATIONAL CENTER (Centro Educativo Ignacio Manuel Altamirano). A secondary educational institution located on 91 Prosperidad Street, Colonia Escandón, in the Delegación Miguel Hidalgo of Mexico City. It serves the Mexican Union, and received authorization to function as an elementary school in 1963. By 1980 secondary levels had been added. The school now operates on the junior college level also.

The center has 14 classrooms in a three-level building. It is equipped with a laboratory and library, administrative offices, and assembly hall that serves as a board room and music classroom.

In 1993 classes were offered at the preelementary and kindergarten levels. The school employs a staff of 25 teachers and two secretaries. The present enrollment is 458.

Principals: Neftali Rodriguez, 1980-1984; Jacob Tadeo, 1984-1985; Eliasib Sanchez, 1985-1988; Lorenzo Tello, 1988-1990; Celia Rosas, 1990-1993; Orley Sanchez, 1993-1994; Josefina Mora, 1994- .

IKIZU SECONDARY SCHOOL. A coeducational boarding school on the high school level, operated by the Tanzania Union among the Wa-Ikizu tribe, 40 miles (62 kilometers) east of Musoma, a port on Lake Victoria. For a number of years the school conducted a teacher training program, and more recently a two-year evangelists' course. However, with the phasing out of the teacher training course, and with the ministerial course being moved to the Tanzania Adventist Seminary and College in Arusha, Ikizu became a secondary school only. In 1993 the school had a staff of 16 national teachers and an enrollment of 492.

About 1912 a mission station and primary school were established among the Ikizu tribe. At the outbreak of World War I the station was left in the hands of national teachers. Later the houses were looted by roving bands of Africans. In 1922 the station and primary school were reopened by missionaries sent out by the British Union. In 1928 Millie Morgan, a trained teacher from England, who was on the staff from 1926 to 1934, opened a teacher training course. Thus the school became known as the Ikizu Training School. Through the years many faithful African teachers have worked at the school, such as S. Magembe, and Yolam Kamwendo, who came from Nyasaland; S. Dea and R. Megera. The school has made steady progress, with periodic additions to its physical plant. Carpentry and agriculture are taught to the boys and home economics to the girls in modestly equipped laboratories. By 1965 Ikizu was a full secondary school registered with the government as a center for Cambridge (and later National) certificate examinations.

The teacher training course supplied the Seventh-day Adventist primary schools in Tanzania with a steady stream of certificated teachers, many of whom have taken further ministerial courses and are now holding responsible positions in the union. Particular attention was given to Bible teaching and practical evangelism, and every qualifying teacher received at his or her graduation teacher-evangelist credentials. Because of the government's decision to nationalize all teacher training colleges, this course was closed at the end of 1967.

Principals: F. G. Reid, 1940-1942; D. K. Short, 1943-1945; F. E. Schlehuber, 1946-1952; J.G.E. Coetzee, 1953-1956; H.W.E. Beavon, 1957-1958; R. L. MacGhee, 1959-1961; J. T. Bradfield, 1962-1964; George Dunder, 1964-1969; T. R. Lisso, 1970; E. M. Luyeho, 1971-1972; E. Okeyo, 1972-1977; L. Kanda, 1977-1979; A. D. Otieno, 1980; Joel Oola, 1981-1984; Elton Lusingu, 1984-1992; George Mwasumbi, 1992-1994; George Kusekwa, 1994- .

ILAM LODGE. A home for the aged at Christchurch, New Zealand, owned and operated by the South New Zealand Conference. A two-story residence, purchased in 1958 and enlarged in 1962, that provides for a total of 26 aged persons, all housed on the ground floor in single rooms. Additional semiindependent accommodation for 12 people is situated adjacent to the lodge. Occupational therapy and the services of a trained nurse are available. The administrative staff consists of a manager (nonresident) and a resident matron, assistant matron, and house manager. The home is situated immediately adjoining the Ilam church.

ILE-IFE SEVENTH-DAY ADVENTIST HOSPITAL. *See* Seventh-day Adventist Hospital Ile-Ife.

ILLINOIS. *See* Illinois Conference; Lake Region Conference.

ILLINOIS CONFERENCE. A unit of church organization in the state of Illinois. *(See also* Lake Region Conference.) Statistics (1993): churches, 98; members, 11,705; church schools, 24; ordained ministers, 60; church school teachers, 68. Headquarters: 3721 Prairie Avenue, Brookfield, Illinois. The conference forms part of the Lake Union Conference.

Institutions. Broadview Academy; Chicago SDA Academy; Hinsdale Hospital.

Local churches: Aledo, Alton, Aurora (English, Hispanic), Berwyn (Czechoslavakian), Bloomington (All Nations), Bolingbrook, Bradley (New Jerusalem), Broadview, Broadview Academy, Brookfield, Burbank, Cairo, Canton, Carthage, Caseyville (Oakhill), Centralia, Champaign, Chicago (Beverly Hills, Central [Hispanic], Korean, Goshen, Humboldt Park [Hispanic], Hungarian, Lakeview [English, Hispanic], Little Village [Hispanic], North [Hispanic], North Shore, Pilsen [Hispanic], Polish, Romanian, South [Hispanic], Wicker Park [Hispanic], Yugoslavian), Cicero (Hispanic), Danville, Decatur (Sunnyside), DeKalb, Des Plaines (Northwest [Korean]), Donnellson, Downers Grove, Du Qyoin, Eldorado, Elgin, Elmhurst, Fox Valley (Hispanic), Freeport, Galesburg (Parkview), Glen Ellyn, Harvey (New Heights), Hinsdale (English, Burr Ridge, Filipino-American), Jacksonville, Joliet (Hispanic), La Grange, Lockport (Joliet), Lincoln, Marion, Mattoon, Metropolis, Moline, Mount Vernon, Noble, North Lake (West Suburban [Hispanic]), Northbrook, Oak Park (West Central), Ottawa, Palatine (Forest Glen), Paris, Peoria (Knoxville Avenue), Petersburg, Princeton, Quincy, Richton Park (South Suburban), Rock Falls, Rockford (English, Hispanic), Saint Elmo, Savanna, Schaumburg (Korean), Sheridan, Springfield First, Stewardson, Streator, Tinley Park (West Park), Waukegan, West Frankfort, West Frankfort (Herrin), Westmont (Korean).

Companies: Aurora (Randall West [Hispanic]), Chicago (Korean American), Pontiac (Fairbury [Hispanic]), Rockford (Beacon of Light), Round Lake, Thompsonville.

History. The Sabbath doctrine was first proclaimed inside Illinois' borders in 1850 by Samuel W. Rhodes, 32 years after Illinois was accepted into the Union as a state. The state's population had reached approximately 55,000 by that time. Two years later Joseph Bates preached in the northwestern corner of Illinois, near the town of Galena, an area formerly the home of the Sac and Fox Indians, now settled mostly by farmers. As Bates visited this area at various times between 1852 and 1854, he met with much opposition from the "age to come" and "no law" people of the area. Bates toured northern Illinois again from Jan. 17 to Mar. 29, 1854, preaching in schoolhouses and halls, distributing books, and acting as subscription agent for the *Review and Herald* and *Youth's Instructor.* The *Review* carried this note: "The interest of the last message of mercy is deepening and widening all around. Souls are embracing the Sabbath of the Lord our God, saying it is truth" (5:4, Feb. 14, 1854).

During this time Bates spent some time at Round Grove in Whiteside County, where the westward surge of the Advent movement began to focus in this northwest corner. It was fertile farmland, but also the "iron horse" (the Galena and Chicago Union Railroad) stopped there on its way to Morrison. Most of the well-known pioneers helped open the work here. Two lay farmers must be singled out, for they spent minimum time planting and maximum time sowing the seeds of truth. Elon Everts was from New Hampshire and came west to Round Grove in 1855 with his wife and daughter after witnessing the ordination of J. N. Andrews and others in his home in 1853. This family was the focus of several of Ellen White's visions while she was in Round Grove. He tried hard to pull free from worldly wealth and drew strength from his friend, Josiah Hart, who came from Northfield, Vermont, in the early spring of 1856. These two formed a tireless evangelistic duo.

Josiah Hart witnessed to Ivory Colcord, the teacher of the first school in the Genesee Grove area, in the home of William Wick. Ivory's son, G. W. Colcord, and his wife were baptized by James White there in 1858. G. W. Colcord became an educator, founding Milton Academy in Oregon, the forerunner of Walla Walla College, and later opened the first school in the south at Graysville, Tennessee, the parent of Southern College. In January of 1858 Hart held meetings in Freeport, convincing two German families of the Sabbath truth. These conversions laid the groundwork for John Matheson in 1871 to open the foreign work in Illinois and Wisconsin.

Both Hart and Everts worked themselves into early graves. Hart passed away Aug. 17, 1858. Joseph Bates conducted the funeral and wrote in the *Review,* "We have just returned from the silent grave, leaving him beside Brother Everts" (12:16, Sept. 2, 1858).

J. N. Loughborough first came to Illinois in June 1853 after getting on a steamer at Grand Haven, Michigan, thinking it was headed for Wisconsin. By 1856 he had dropped out of the work and moved to Waukon, Iowa, where he was later revived by James and Ellen White's trip from Round Grove in the snow and across the frozen Mississippi. The horses and sleigh were driven by Josiah Hart and Elon Everts. Loughborough returned with them and began a series of meetings the next night in the Hittleson schoolhouse three miles (five kilometers) north of Round Grove.

In March 1857 at a meeting in Round Grove it was voted to purchase a tent for evangelism. Hart and Everts were on the committee, and Loughborough was the first to preach in it. On Aug. 14 it was pitched in Lyndon for 30 lectures. Earlier in the year Loughborough began the first Sabbath school and Bible class for new believers in Round Grove. Other evangelists, such as Isaac Sanborn and W. S. Ingraham, braved opposition and persecution. Both later became president of the conference, then Illinois-Wisconsin Conference.

Between 1856 and 1861 Round Grove was often the home of the Whites, who made at least six trips there to foster the work. Their Western tour brought them to Round Grove on Nov. 21, 1856. James had just published his wife's testimony to the church, No. 5, "Testimony to the Laodicean Church." On the twenty-fourth he preached on the "Seven Churches." The cry was "Be zealous and repent." It was just the needed boost to revive the work in Illinois. Several weeks later, in the midst of snowstorms, a conference was held at the Hittleston School with the Whites leading out. It was attended by John Byington, a former Methodist minister from Buck's Bridge, New York. Later he became the first General Conference president. By 1862 the railroad had moved on, as did the pioneers. (Today there are but a few buildings and gently rolling farmland silently witnessing the history-making efforts of many people.) Late in September 1868 the second camp meeting ever held by Seventh-day Adventists was convened at Clyde, Illinois.

At the request of the General Conference, Daniel Thompson went to Chicago in February 1883 and began the work of distributing literature in the rapidly growing metropolis. In that same year, as recommended by the General Conference, a mission was opened on Madison Street. It provided food and shelter for the needy and served as a training school in city mission work for young people from the college in Battle Creek, Michigan, and for others who desired experience in this type of work. Ten years later the Life Boat Mission was launched.

In 1895 Dr. J. H. Kellogg established the American Medical Missionary College on South Wabash Avenue. Fifteen years later the college was merged with the University of Illinois, but while it was under SDA auspices, about 200 physicians received their medical training. This college was a forerunner of the College of Medical Evangelists *(see* Loma Linda University). In 1904 Drs. David and Mary Paulson organized the Hinsdale Sanitarium and Benevolent Association, and opened a sanitarium at Hinsdale, near Chicago, the next year. The Hinsdale church was accepted into the Northern Illinois Conference on Feb. 6, 1908.

Conference Organization. On Sept. 27, 1862, at a meeting held at Avon, Wisconsin, the Illinois and Wisconsin State Conference was formed. In a division of territory in 1870 the Illinois Conference was formed *(Review and Herald* 36:31, July 12, 1870), which became a part of the Lake Union Conference in 1901, when the union was organized. In 1902 the state was divided between the Northern Illinois Conference, with offices in Chicago, and the Southern Illinois Conference, with offices first in Stewardson and later in Springfield. Late in 1918 there was another reorganization, and the Illinois Conference was reestablished, including the whole state except the counties of Cook, DuPage, Will, Lake, McHenry, Kane, Kendall, Grundy, and Kankakee; these were assigned to a new Chicago Conference (which included also

Lake County, Indiana). However, in 1931 the entire state was reunited into one conference (in November, Lake County, Indiana, was returned to the Indiana Conference). Offices for the reorganized Illinois Conference were first on Wacker Drive in Chicago, then after May 1932 in a building in Brookfield owned by the Pacific Press, and since March 1954 in a new office building in Brookfield.

Expansion of the Work. One of the earliest Seventh-day Adventist churches in Illinois was at Aledo, in the western part of the state. Robert F. Andrews, at that time president of the Illinois Conference, held meetings there in the early part of 1871, and in the same year organized a church of 30 members. A church building was erected at a cost of $1,365 and was dedicated on Oct. 12, 1884. The first church school teacher, Elizabeth Longacre, had an enrollment of five pupils in 1896.

In the southern part of the state, in the summer of 1878, G. H. Colcord and C. H. Bliss held tent meetings in Du Quoin, and 20 persons began keeping the Sabbath. On June 14, 1879, the Du Quoin church was organized.

Several institutions operated in the area of the conference for a time. The Tri-City Sanitarium in Moline, which opened in March of 1902, won fame for pioneering the treatment of such illnesses as poliomyelitis and rheumatism. It served the area until about 1924, when it was felt that the health program could be carried on adequately at the Hinsdale Sanitarium. The Moline church was organized on Feb. 27, 1904.

In 1900 the Sheridan Industrial Academy, later known as the Fox River Academy, was established, and in 1926 the Chicago Conference Academy. For a time academies were also operated at Hinsdale and at Du Quoin. The Fox River and Chicago academies were closed in 1933 and consolidated with the school at Broadview, which at that time was an academy and junior college. In 1934 the Broadview school became an academy only, and has been the academy for Illinois since that time. The school was moved in 1958 to Lafox. Broadview College and Theological Seminary, originally the Broadview Swedish Seminary, was the forerunner of Broadview Academy. A branch of the Pacific Press Publishing Association operated at Brookfield for many years.

A work for foreign-speaking peoples in Chicago was begun early. Beginning in 1863, a young Danish Baptist preacher, John G. Matteson, who had accepted the SDA doctrines, spent some time in Illinois, preaching to Scandinavian Americans. In 1871 he organized a church among a group of Norwegian people, who built, on Erie Street, the first Seventh-day Adventist church building in Chicago. In 1890 J. M. Erickson, A. J. Stone, and Carl Norlin conducted meetings for Swedish-speaking people, and in 1892 a Swedish SDA church was organized. Work was also conducted among the Chinese. J. N. Loughborough reported at the Plano camp meeting on Aug. 23, 1894: "The Chinese work in Chicago, although conducted under difficulties, is not without interesting results. Though we are not able to point to souls who have fully identified themselves with the truth, yet there are scores who are interested in the study of the Bible and are being drawn toward the Lord and His people" *(Illinois Recorder,* Oct. 22, 1894).

A Chinese school was conducted each Sunday evening, with some 26 students who learned to read and write English; the more advanced studied the Bible. Having 17 teachers, the pupils received a high degree of individual attention. The German work was established in 1909 as a result of meetings held by Henry Schulz. Rosario Calderone opened the work among the Italians of Chicago in 1912. One of the first two converts was Anthony Catalano, who later became the pastor of the Italian church and worked with his people for 50 years. At present the Chicago area has numerous foreign-language churches.

In 1983 the Hinsdale Filipino-American church was formed, and their new sanctuary was dedicated in 1991. For the past 10 years the Hispanic work has grown to where the Hispanic population is now 17 percent of the total Illinois Conference membership.

The first Hungarian congregation in the Greater Chicago area was organized in the fall of 1918 to proclaim the everlasting gospel and the three angels' messages to the Hungarian population. The Korean church now includes six congregations. Work continues among the Polish people, and the Romanian church, as well, is growing significantly. The work among Yugoslavians has grown, and they dedicated their new facility in 1991.

The first Black SDA church in the Chicago area was opened in 1910 with the help of a special offering given by the churches of the Lake Union Conference. In 1944 the Black constituency of the Lake Union organized its own conference, the Lake Region Conference, which began to function Jan. 1, 1945.

Recent Developments. The Illinois

Conference has recently reported progress in several areas. Whereas in 1910 the largest total of Ingathering solicited by one person was $47, for years the Illinois Conference has averaged $25 or more per capita for the entire conference membership. This increase has been attributed in part to the extensive welfare program carried on by the conference.

The now worldwide group organizations of local Dorcas societies began in Illinois, with the Dorcas Federation idea being initiated and developed by Mrs. Herman Kleist, with the cooperation of E. R. Potter and C. S. Joyce, conference and union home missionary secretaries. The first Dorcas Federation was organized officially at a meeting in the Chicago South Side church, and the first regular meeting was held in April 1934 in the Hinsdale church. In June 1935 the federation was accepted as part of the conference program.

From 1958 to 1986 Little Grassy Lake Camp, in southern Illinois, near Carbondale, has provided a delightful and rugged atmosphere for junior camps, teenage camps, senior camps, and family camps. Prior to that, from 1931 junior camps were held at various rented areas, then at Camp Reynoldswood, at Dixon, for several years.

Presidents—Illinois and Wisconsin Conference: W. S. Ingraham, 1862-1863; Isaac Sanborn, 1863-1867; R. F. Andrews, 1867-1870.

Illinois Conference: R. F. Andrews, 1870-1875, 1879-1885; R. M. Kilgore, 1885-1891; J. N. Loughborough, 1891-1895; S. H. Lane, 1895-1899; N. W. Kauble, 1899-1901; Allen Moon, 1901-1902.

Northern Illinois Conference: Allen Moon, 1902-1904?; N. W. Kauble, 1904?-1905; L. H. Christian, 1905-1906; William Covert, 1906-1912; G. E. Langdon, 1912-1916; W. A. Westworth, 1916-1917; J. H. Schilling, 1917-1919.

Southern Illinois Conference: S. H. Lane, 1902-1903; J. M. Rees, 1903-1906; W. D. Parkhurst, 1906-1908; S. E. Wight, 1908-1910; E. A. Bristol, 1910-1914; A. J. Clark, 1914-1917; E. F. Petersen, 1917-1919.

Chicago Conference: A. J. Clark, 1919-1923; J. W. Christian, 1923-1930; R. E. Harter, 1930.

Illinois Conference: W. H. Holden, 1919-1923; W. A. Westworth, 1923-1927; S. N. Rittenhouse, 1927-1931.

Illinois Conference (reunited): R. E. Harter, 1931-1934; M. A. Hollister, 1934-1937; M. V. Campbell, 1937-1942; L. E. Lenheim, 1942-1947; Theodore Carcich, 1947-1951; J. L. McConaughey, 1951-1955; Wayne B. Hill, 1955-1960; W. A. Nelson, 1960-1971; John L. Hayward, 1971-1980; Everett Cumbo, 1980-1988; Bjarne Christensen, 1988-1993; James L. Brauer, 1993- .

ILLINOIS-WISCONSIN CONFERENCE. *See* Illinois Conference; Wisconsin Conference.

ILOCANO JUNIOR MIDDLE SCHOOL. *See* Northern Luzon Academy.

IMAGE OF DANIEL 2. *See* Daniel, Interpretation of.

IMAGE TO THE BEAST. *See* Revelation, Interpretation of.

IMMERSION. *See* Baptism.

IMMORTALITY. The state or quality of not being subject to death; from the Gr. *athanasia,* "deathlessness," and *aphtharsia,* "incorruptibility." Seventh-day Adventists believe that human beings are mortal, that is, that they are subject to death, and that death is a state of complete unconsciousness *(see* Death). "Immortality" occurs five times in the KJV and the RSV. "Immortal" (Gr. *aphthartos)* occurs once in the KJV and twice in the RSV. The Scriptures ascribe immortality to God alone (1 Tim. 6:16). He alone is declared to be immortal (Rom. 1:23, RSV; 1 Tim. 1:17). The Christian seeks immortality (Rom. 2:7), which Christ brought to light "through the gospel" (2 Tim. 1:10), and which the believer is to "put on" at the "last trump" (1 Cor. 15:52-54). The Scriptures nowhere describe immortality as a quality or state that a man or woman—or his or her "soul" or "spirit"—possesses inherently. The terms usually rendered "soul" and "spirit" (Heb. *nephesh* and *ruach;* Gr. *psuchē* and *pneuma*) in the Bible occur more than 1,600 times, but never in association with the words "immortal" or "immortality."

The doctrine that immortality is dependent upon acceptance of salvation by faith in Christ is called conditional immortality, and the belief in that doctrine is sometimes called "conditionalism." Many Christians throughout the centuries have held this view (see SB Nos. 850-856).

The idea that a person has an immortal soul, or spirit, was introduced into the

Christian church by pagan philosophy, especially Platonic philosophy. As Greek philosophy infiltrated the early church, belief in the immortality of the soul became the prevailing view in Christendom and continues to be the predominant view today.

The vast majority of the followers of William Miller held the common belief that man by nature has an immortal soul. However, through the influence of George Storrs, a prominent Millerite preacher, a significant minority accepted conditionalism along with the belief that a person is unconscious between death and the resurrection, and these beliefs became a prominent feature of the SDA bodies after 1844. Many of them reasoned that if human beings went to their reward at death, there would be no need for a second coming, a resurrection, or a final judgment.

See Death; Eternal Life.

IMPRIMERIE ADVENTISTE. *See* Adventist Printing House (Madagascar).

IMPRIMERIE ADVENTISTE "IMA." *See* Central African Publishing House.

IMPRIMERIE "LES SIGNES DES TEMPS." *See* Maison d'Edition Vie et Sante.

IMPRIMERIE POLYGLOTTE. *See* Maison d'Edition Vie et Sante.

INCA UNION ACADEMY. *See* Union Adventist Educational Complex.

INCA UNION MISSION. *See* Bolivia; Ecuador; Peru; South American Division.

INCA UNION TRAINING SCHOOL. *See* Inca Union University.

INCA UNION UNIVERSITY. *See* Union Adventist Educational Complex.

INCARNATION. *See* Christology.

INDIA. A federal republic in southeastern Asia situated on the Indian peninsula. It is bordered by Pakistan on the west, China, Nepal, and Bhutan on the north, and Myanmar on the east. Its eastern part surrounds Bangladesh on three sides. India is the world's second most populous country, with a population (1994) of about 920 million. In area, 1.2 million square miles (3.2 million square kilometers), it is the seventh-largest country in the world and is about one third of the area of the 50 states of the United States.

India is divided topographically into three regions. Along its northern border are the Himalayan Mountains, the highest in the world; immediately south of them lies the great plain formed by the valleys of the Indus, the Ganges, and the Brahmaputra rivers; and to the south of this plain lies the great Indian peninsula, a low plateau surrounded by coastal mountain ranges. The climate of India is characterized by extremes. For the greater part of India there are only three seasons: a cool winter, from October to February; an intensely hot season, from March to June; a rainy season, from June to September. There are also dry and wet parts of the country: while the arid desert of Rajasthan in the west may have only a trace of precipitation, totaling less than five inches (13 centimeters) in a year, at Cherrapunji, in Assam (the easternmost state), the average rainfall is more than 35 feet (11 meters) a year. The northern areas have frost in the winter, but the temperature there may reach 120° F (48° C) of heat in the summer, when high humidity is also prevalent throughout most of the country.

The ethnic composition of the people is extremely complex and is reflected in the many languages of the country. There are many national scripts in India, and some languages can be written in two or three different scripts. At the present time English is widely used for official and business purposes.

Historical Background. India, one of the world's oldest inhabited countries, had a well-advanced civilization at the time the better-known Sumerian and Egyptian societies flourished. It is uncertain who were the earliest inhabitants of India or whence they came. Dravidians occupied the peninsula of India before the earliest recorded invasions of the Aryan people.

It seems fairly certain that when the Indo-Aryans penetrated the valleys along the Indus and Ganges, the Deccan Plateau was not affected by their movements. The Dravidians there developed their distinct form of civilization.

The time of the Aryan invasion is not known but is thought to have been about the middle of the second millennium B.C. The first accurate historical date in the history of India is the invasion of Alexander the Great in 327-326 B.C. There followed other invasions by fair-skinned people. From the eighth century A.D. and continuing to the sixteenth century,

Muslims invaded the land. Afghans, Persians, Turks, and Mongols also penetrated into the plains of Hindustan. The Mongol invaders of the sixteenth century established a powerful Mogul empire under their ruler Akbar, a contemporary of Queen Elizabeth I. Akbar tried to create a united India, even attempting to unite the two great religions of Hinduism and Islam.

In 1498 Vasco de Gama, a Portuguese navigator, reached the southwestern coast of India. During the next 200 years all great European powers struggled for the trade of India, until in the mid-nineteenth century Britain had assumed control of most of the area. After World War II the independence movement reached its peak and the British withdrew in 1947, leaving behind them two new states: India (largely Hindu) and Pakistan (largely Muslim). In 1962 India incorporated Goa, Daman, and Diu, former Portuguese possessions on the western side of the Indian peninsula.

Religions of India. Religion has played an important role in the formation of Indian culture and today still controls every activity of the people. About 740 million of the population are Hindus. Hinduism, a religious philosophy resulting from the amalgamation of concepts held by the Indo-Aryan invaders and the Dravidians, dates from the sixth or seventh century B.C. The sacred books of the Hindus, the Vedas, were produced more than 1,000 years before Christ. The most prominent characteristics of this philosophy are (1) the doctrine of transmigration of souls, (2) division of people into castes (Brahmans—scholars and priests; Kshatriyas—warriors and rulers; Vaisyas—traders and artisans; and Sudras—farmers and laborers; and below these the outcastes, "the untouchables," who performed the most menial tasks), and (3) the obligation of all to do their duty in the state in which they were born. These doctrines account largely for the inherent religious conservatism in India and the reluctance to accept new teachings.

Other religious groups represented in India are Muslims, of whom there are about 100 million; Sikhs, a group holding a reformed Hinduistic philosophy, numbering about 20 million adherents; Jains, with about 3.5 million followers; Buddhists, whose religion began in India six centuries B.C., now numbering 5 million; Zoroastrians, about 120,000; and Christians, about 20 million adherents, three quarters of whom are Roman Catholic.

Early Christian Missions. There is a tradition that the apostle Thomas preached the gospel to the peoples of India and established the Nestorian Christian church in the south. There is historical evidence that national Christians existed in India since the fourth century. Upon the arrival of the Portuguese in the sixteenth century, the Roman Catholic missionaries began work in southern India. In the seventeenth century the Danes acquired Tranquebar as a trading post in southern India, and there the first Protestant missionaries went soon after. Some years later, in 1706, two missionaries from Germany, named Ziegenbalg and Plutschau, landed at Tranquebar, and having mastered the Tamil language in spite of many difficulties, they established schools and preached in the villages. Before Ziegenbalg died in 1719 he translated into Tamil the whole of the New Testament and the Old Testament up to the book of Ruth. It seems that this was the first translation of any Scriptures into an Indian language.

During the eighteenth century the great figure in missionary history of South India was Christian Frederick Schwartz. He lived among the people, going from village to village, preaching to all classes. He went to the Hindu temple cities of Trichinopoly, Madurai, and Tinnevelly with the gospel, and as a result of his work they became strongholds of Christianity.

William Carey, born in England in 1761, did for the north of India what Schwartz had done for the south in the cause of missionary endeavor.

In 1793 Carey and a physician named Thomas were appointed to India as missionaries of the "Baptist Society for Propagating the Gospel Among the Heathen." Since at that time the East India Company, which controlled India, did not favor missionary activities, Carey eventually settled in Serampore, a Danish possession, and began work.

During the next 34 years Carey and his colleagues translated or published the Scriptures in 40 languages and dialects. They also established a printing house so that the printed page could reach the many parts of India that were not accessible to direct missionary activity. After an 1833 act of Parliament opened all British India to missionaries of any nationality, the Protestant missionary endeavors in India began on a large scale. By 1900 there were at work in various parts of India 73 denominations or missionary societies, with a combined Protestant membership of nearly 1 million. In the twentieth century several Protestant denominations (Anglican, Methodist, Presbyterian,

Dutch Reformed, and Congregationalist) joined together to form the Church of South India.

Seventh-day Adventist Statistics. The territory of India, which constitutes the major part of the Southern Asia Division, is divided into four unions: the Central India Union Section, which is divided into three sections and three regions; the Northeast India Union Section, which is divided into one conference, two sections, and one region; the Northern India Union Section, which is divided into four sections; the South India Union, which is divided into five sections; and one attached field. Statistics (1992) for *India:* churches, 894; members, 184,397; ordained ministers, 430.

Statistics for the unions and missions—*Central India Union Section:* churches, 242; members, 69,234; ordained ministers, 48. Headquarters: Post Box 1413, Marketyard P.O., Pune. *Gujarat Region*: churches, 10; members, 1,237. Headquarters: Gujarat. *Maharashtra Section:* churches, 46; members, 9,411. Headquarters: Bombay. *North Andhra Section:* churches, 86; members, 25,601. Headquarters: Hyderabad. *Orissa Region:* churches, 11; members, 1,215. Headquarters: Orissa. *South Andhra Section*: churches, 78; members, 22,024. Headquarters: Vijayawada. *Zaheerabad Region:* churches, 11; members, 9,746. Headquarters: Zaheerabad.

Northeast India Union Section: churches, 108; members, 18,624. Headquarters: "Santana," Laitumkhrah, Shillong, Meghalaya. *Assam Region:* churches, 14; members, 2,379. Headquarters: Guwahati. *Manipur/Nagaland Section:* churches, 30; members, 5,006. Headquarters: Imphal. *Meghalaya Section:* churches, 25; members, 4,902. Headquarters: Shillong. *Mizo Conference:* churches, 39; members, 6,337. Headquarters: Aizawl.

Northern India Union Section: churches, 132; members, 21,060. Headquarters: 11 Hailey Road, New Delhi. *East India Section:* churches, 64; members, 8,668. Headquarters: Ranchi. *Madhya Bharat Section:* churches, 21; members, 1,848. Headquarters: Jaipur. *North India Section:* churches, 21; members, 7,558. Headquarters: Jalandhar. *Upper Ganges Section:* churches, 25; members, 2,880. Headquarters: Hapur.

South India Union Section: churches, 409; members, 75,352. Headquarters: 38/1 Coles Road, Fraser Town, Bangalore. *Karnataka Section:* churches, 66; members, 22,581. Headquarters: Bangalore. *North Kerala Section:* churches, 40; members, 7,237. Headquarters: Trichur. *North Tamil Section:* churches, 66; members, 13,849. Headquarters: Tiruchirapalli. *South Kerala Section:* churches, 145; members, 16,083. Headquarters: Trivandrum. *South Tamil Section:* churches, 92; members, 15,602. Headquarters: Madurai.

Attached fields—Andaman and Nicobar Island Region: churches, 1; members, 106. Headquarters: Post Box 638, Haddo, Port Blair, Andaman and Nicobar Islands.

Himalayan Region: churches, 3; members, 273. Headquarters: Kathmandu, Nepal.

Institutions. *Educational*—Adventist Training School; Bangalore Seventh-day Adventist Higher Secondary School; M. C. Dhamanwala English High School of Seventh-day Adventists; Flaiz Memorial Higher Secondary School of Seventh-day Adventists; James Memorial Higher Secondary School; Lowry Memorial Junior College; Manipur Boarding School; Raymond Memorial High School; Seventh-day Adventist High School (Khunti); Seventh-day Adventist High School (Khurda); Seventh-day Adventist High School (Madurai); Seventh-day Adventist High School (Roorkee); Seventh-day Adventist High School (Tiruchirapalli); Seventh-day Adventist Higher Secondary School (Kottarakara); Seventh-day Adventist Higher Secondary School (Madras); Seventh-day Adventist Higher Secondary School (Lasalgaon); Seventh-day Adventist Higher Secondary School (Thiruvella); Spicer Memorial College; Spicer Memorial College Higher Secondary School; E. D. Thomas Memorial Higher Secondary School.

Medical—Giffard Memorial Hospital; Milton Mattison Memorial Hospital; Ottapalam Seventh-day Adventist Hospital; Pune Adventist Hospital; Ranchi Hospital; Ruby Nelson Memorial Hospital; Seventh-day Adventist Hospital; Simla Sanitarium and Hospital; Surat Hospital.

Retirement Homes and Orphanages—Elim Adventist Home; Sunshine Children's Home.

Publishing—Oriental Watchman Publishing House.

Seventh-day Adventist Work. *First Contacts, 1890-1895.* It is not known precisely when SDA teachings were first introduced into India, or when evangelism began. It is known that in 1890 S. N. Haskell and P. T. Magan crossed India from Calcutta to Bombay on their mission survey journey around the world.

Traditionally the beginning of Seventh-day Adventist work in India has been dated from 1893, when William Lenker and A. T. Stroup (or Strop, as Lenker refers to him in his accounts), two colporteurs from America, landed in Madras and began canvassing for SDA subscription books among the English-speaking inhabitants of the major cities of India, traveling the length and breadth of the country in the course of two succeeding years. However, in his first report, written on his way to India, Lenker stated that "while in London, my heart was made to rejoice to learn that the truth has gone before to India, and that good work has begun with encouraging omens" (*Review and Herald* 70:686, Oct. 31, 1893). A year later he reported in the *Review and Herald* that "shortly before our arrival at Madras [November 1893], sister Anna P. Gordon, who had been in Bombay for nearly a year," died. He identified her in his communication as a "faithful worker" and a teacher of Seventh-day Adventist doctrines in India (72:5, Jan. 1, 1895).

If she was the "Miss G" to whom D. A. Robinson referred, writing from London (*ibid.* 70:5, Jan. 3, 1893), she had begun to observe the Sabbath in London in 1892 through contact with SDAs while she was en route from the United States to India to work in that country as a self-supporting missionary.

In the same report Lenker mentioned that in the autumn of 1894 there were five workers in India, presumably colporteurs (one each at Madras, Mysore, and Hyderabad, and two at Calcutta), three of whom came from Australia. In his *Origin and Progress of Seventh-day Adventists* (p. 517) M. E. Olsen mentions only two from Australia, a retired British India Army captain by the name of Masters, who returned with his wife to India after they had become SDAs. However, in her recollections, Georgia Burrus Burgess identified them as coming from New Zealand (*Eastern Tidings* 36:2, May 8, 1941).

The early colporteur work met with outstanding success, the people welcoming SDA publications and at times buying duplicate copies and also volunteering to sell to their friends. Lenker reported that his first year's sales amounted to $4,000, and that other colporteurs had met with similar success. Very early the people asked that the books be translated into the local languages, one man volunteering to translate them into Tamil (*Review and Herald* 71:84, Feb. 6, 1894). A pamphlet containing Bible readings on the life of Christ, prepared by S. N. Haskell, was translated and published by an independent Protestant mission at Poona in 1894 (*ibid.* 72:5, Jan. 1, 1895).

In an article entitled "A Comprehensive Survey of the Early Work [in India]," L. G. Mookerjee, writing in 1941, mentions another early development: "We are told that before any Seventh-day Adventist work was opened in India, Dr. J. H. Kellogg of Battle Creek, Michigan, U.S.A., was supporting a Bengali Christian, B. N. Mitter by name, who was connected with the American Baptist Mission. When D. A. Robinson came to India, arrangements were made, and the Seventh-day Adventist Mission took over B. N. Mitter and family in their work at the orphanage in Calcutta" (*Eastern Tidings* 36:7, May 8, 1941).

Opening the Mission. The first regular SDA worker to reach India under appointment by the Mission Board was Georgia Burrus (later Georgia Burgess), a young Bible instructor from California, who arrived in Calcutta on Jan. 23, 1895.

It had been planned that she would accompany D. A. Robinson, the leader of the projected mission to India, but when he was delayed in England, Georgia Burrus proceeded alone, aiming to work as a self-supporting worker until the regular mission could be established, the Mission Board paying only her fare. Captain Masters and his wife met her at the dock and helped her establish herself in a strange land.

Georgia Burrus found lodgings during her first year in Calcutta at the YWCA home, where her vegetarian diet called forth much favorable comment and brought her a reduction in the charge made for meals. Engrossed in the study of the Bengali language, she found little time to work for her support, and consequently was soon short of funds. On learning this, her teacher volunteered to continue instructing her without a fee, but at that time she received a letter from someone in Africa whom she did not even know, promising her financial support for one year.

On Nov. 8, 1895, Dores A. Robinson and another Bible instructor, Martha May Taylor, arrived in Calcutta, and opened a regular Seventh-day Adventist mission in a house on Bow Bazar Street, rented and prepared for them by Georgia Burrus.

In March 1896 a school for Hindu girls was opened on the first floor of the mission house under the supervision of Georgia Burrus and May Taylor, with a well-educated Bengali woman as a teacher. The schoolwork helped the young women to master the language and provided the opportunity to visit the homes of the students, where they could teach Christianity to the women secluded in the zenanas (women's quarters) of large families. It was while visiting the zenanas in the neighborhood of the school that Georgia Burrus met Nanibala Biswas, who later became the first Seventh-day Adventist convert from Hinduism and adopted Burrus as her last name, after the one who acquainted her with Christianity.

Then about the beginning of December 1896 Robinson began conducting regular Sunday night meetings in the mission hall on the topic "The Christianity of Jesus Christ: What It Is and What It Is Not," and held several temperance meetings as well. From the beginning the meetings were intended for the English-speaking Indians rather than for the Europeans, though both groups were present. As the meetings progressed the attendance increased. When the mission house was closed for repairs after an earthquake, a theater was secured, and from July through the next winter the meetings were held there, the audience contributing enough to cover the expenses.

Also in 1896 SDA publishing work began in India in Calcutta. In that year the International Tract Society, which gave its address as 154 Bow Bazar Street, issued the first brochure of the International Series, a four-page tract entitled "Can All Be Saved?" Later in that year, an article by Ellen White, "The Coming of Christ," was published as a tract in the Bengali language. The printing on these first publishing ventures was done by the commercial presses in Calcutta. The publishing work was aided by the local converts. One of them, A. C. Mookerjee, translated and printed SDA tracts into Bengali at his own expense.

In 1896 three nurses—Samantha Whiteis, Margaret Green, and G. P. Edwards—with Edwards' wife arrived. A month later O. G. Place, M.D., came and opened treatment rooms for the middle-class Hindus on the first floor of the mission house. Soon he also had a number of Indian young men and women in training as assistants and nurses. Meanwhile, as the schoolwork expanded, a second school was opened (Mar. 3) at the request of parents in the neighborhood, taught by Kheroda Bose, a young Christian widow recommended by Baptist missionaries. Shortly afterward she became the first Indian convert. In the spring the schools had about 70 students, but in the autumn, about 200 girl pupils, ranging in age from almost babyhood to about 10 years, the age when girls customarily left the school to be married.

In July of that year an orphanage called the Home for Destitute Indian Children was opened with about 30 youngsters, most of them boys, in a house adjoining the mission compound on Bow Bazar Street.

Soon several European and Indian families joined the Seventh-day Adventists, among them the Belchambers, the Meyers, and the Mookerjees, according to an account given by L. G. Mookerjee *(Eastern Tidings* 36:7, May 8, 1941). These various accessions occurred in 1896, although the first mention of these converts in the *Review and Herald* appeared only some two years later, in May 1898 (75:334, May 24, 1898), by which time Robinson could report four European families and four or five Bengali families among the new members.

In mid-March of 1898 William A. Spicer, who had been connected with the publishing work in England for a few years, arrived at Calcutta. Almost immediately he set out to establish and edit the *Oriental Watchman,* an evangelistic magazine of the Indian Mission. The first issue of 1,500 copies, published in May, was distributed free. Soon colporteurs from overseas arrived to sell it, notably Ellery Robinson from England *(Eastern Tidings* 36:4, May 8, 1941), who worked in Bengal and Bombay; R. W. Yeoman, who worked in southern India and on Ceylon; I. D. Richardson, who went into the northwest and into Kashmir; W. W. Quantock, who traveled through East Bengal and the Central Provinces; and Herbert B. Meyers, a recent convert, who took the magazine to Burma and the Malay States. Their work swelled its paid circulation to 4,000 copies monthly (at an annual subscription rate of Rs.1-8-0).

About the time that Spicer arrived (he recalled later), the mission published tracts in English, Bengali, and Hindi, which they distributed with the help of coolies who went to different sections of the town, leaving at every home the tracts in appropriate languages with a small handwritten note, "I think these will interest you." Among the large books sold by the colporteurs in the early days were *The Great Controversy, The Desire of Ages,* and *Patriarchs and Prophets,* by Ellen White; *Daniel and the Revelation,* by Uriah Smith; *From Eden to Eden,* by J. H. Waggoner; *Prophetic Lights,* by E. J. Waggoner; and *Home Handbook of Domestic Hygiene, Man the Masterpiece,* and *Ladies' Guide,* by Dr. J. H. Kellogg.

Entering New Areas. During late 1898 or early 1899 the first SDA mission station in the Indian countryside was opened at Karmatar, about 170 miles (270 kilometers) northwest of Calcutta. The work began as a medical dispensary, but in the winter of 1899-1900 the orphanage was moved to a farm at Karmatar and was renamed the Orphanage Industrial School. In charge of the school were D. A. Robinson and F. W. Brown, the latter a former missionary of another denomination, who arrived in 1899.

During the summer of 1899 Robinson held a series of evangelistic meetings in a town hall at Darjeeling, then the site of the government offices during summer months, situated in the foothills of the Himalayas north of Calcutta. In the autumn of that year reports came from northwest India that Sabbathkeepers had sprung up there as the result of the work of colporteurs.

When an epidemic of smallpox broke out among the children soon after the transfer of the orphanage, SDA work in India suffered its first casualties in the deaths of Robinson and Brown. Thereafter the medical work at Karmatar was discontinued, and instead the workers were concentrated at Calcutta, where a sanitarium was developing.

In 1899 the first church school for the English-speaking children was opened in the mission building at Calcutta under the supervision of May Taylor and Mrs. Brown; however, it appears that the school functioned only one year and then was discontinued for a while.

Expansion of the Work. Between 1900 and 1910 the Seventh-day Adventist work spread throughout India, developing in the east, reaching the west, becoming established in the south, and extending to the northwest, where the headquarters were established to bring them nearer to new fields. After the death of Robinson, the leadership of the work fell to Spicer, the only ordained Seventh-day Adventist minister in India. In 1901 Spicer was recalled to the General Conference and was succeeded by J. L. Shaw, former president of the Claremont Union College, in South Africa. Soon after his arrival he reported the organization of the first Seventh-day Adventist church in India, at Calcutta.

Throughout the decade the number of workers increased. New mission stations were opened, new medical enterprises were begun, the educational structure was strengthened, the foundations for many of the present institutions were laid, and the number of SDA publications was enlarged. In 1902 the workers in India, who had come from different backgrounds and had had little opportunity for association with one another since their arrival, gathered for their first training and refresher institute at Calcutta in order to exchange experiences and to strengthen the evangelistic work. The proportion of women medical and colporteur workers during that early decade in India was perhaps greater than that in any other Seventh-day Adventist mission field. The names of Georgia Burrus (later Mrs. Burgess), Anna Orr, Anna Knight (a Black American teacher, colporteur, and nurse), Thekla Black, Grace Kellogg, and some others recur again and again in the missionary accounts from India. Interest in the work in India was demonstrated also by the women of the Southwestern Union Conference in America, who endeavored to create a fund for the support of zenana workers.

In 1904 the first general meeting of workers in Southern Asia was held at Calcutta. At that time there were 130 SDAs in the area. At first the work was conducted in English and Bengali, but by 1907 the Hindi, Santali, Urdu, and Tamil languages had been added. In 1909 there were 230 SDAs in the territory of the Indian Mission (including Ceylon).

The young people's work also received attention, and in 1909 the MV Standard of Attainment course in Bible doctrines and denominational history was introduced to the Young People's Societies.

New Missions: East. In 1900 the second SDA station in India was opened at Simultala, some 30 or 40 miles (48 or 64 kilometers) west of Karmatar, where W. A. Barlow, a former missionary for another Protestant body who became an SDA in 1900, opened an industrial school for the Santali people. At first Barlow assumed financial responsibility for the work there, but in 1903 the station became a part of the regular mission program of the church. In 1904 the first three Santali converts were baptized. In 1905 Barlow sent one of his students to teach in a school at Babumohal, a village some distance away where Barlow built a chapel and a school building.

In 1902 an attempt was made to establish a station at Chandernagore, some 30 miles (50 kilometers) north of Calcutta. A clinic was opened; however, after a short time the supervising nurse was moved elsewhere. In 1909 the first meeting of the Bengali church members was held at Gopalganj, now in Bangladesh, which had been opened in 1906 by L. G. Mookerjee.

New Missions: West. According to L. G. Mookerjee *(Eastern Tidings* 36:8, Sept. 1, 1941), among the early resident SDA workers in western India were a physician, Lucinda Marsh, who practiced at Bombay in 1906 (the available records do not relate what was the result of her work), and C. A. Hansen, who began preaching in Bombay in 1905, but who was forced to leave India the next year because of ill health. About two years later, in 1908, George F. Enoch came to the area. Mookerjee related that after learning the Marathi language Enoch selected Panvel, near Kalyan, to the northeast of Bombay, as the site of his station. There in 1911 he operated a girls' school with 43 students, half of them from Jewish homes. At the same time he translated tracts into the local language, and in 1910 translated *Steps to Christ,* by Ellen White, into Marathi. In 1913 he published a "fairly large" book of Bible readings.

In 1911, when other workers joined Enoch in West India, a Sabbath school was conducted at Lonavla (Lonauli), some 35 miles (60 kilometers) northwest of Poona.

New Missions: South. Seventh-day Adventist work in the south of India began after certain Sabbathkeeping Tamil merchants, who had met an SDA evangelist in Colombo, Ceylon, in 1904, invited SDA ministers to visit them. In 1906 J. S. James was assigned to that field and in 1907 went to Bangalore to study the language. In December 1907 Shaw, Enoch, and James went to the Tinnevelly (Tirunelveli) district, near the southern tip of India, on their first visit to the Tamil Sabbathkeepers. While the missionaries were there, the leaders of this Sabbathkeeping community asked the church to open a school and a mission among them. James settled there in March 1908, living for a while in a schoolhouse in the middle of the village.

In order to help the many sick in that area James and his wife opened a dispensary on the veranda of their house. During their first year an epidemic of cholera broke out, and the missionaries spent most of their time working for the sick. In 1908 Belle Shryock, a nurse, joined the workers. On two acres (.8 hectare) of land outside the village, given by the people, a brick-and-mortar residence was erected in 1909, the first mission bungalow built in India with SDA mission funds.

From the beginning of the work in the south, a number of national young people were trained to help the missionaries in medical, educational, and evangelistic work. One of these, E. D. Thomas, a well-educated youth whose father was connected with the Church of England training school at the nearby village of Nazareth, became James's helper and interpreter. On Apr. 2, 1910, James baptized the first converts from this area, 14 men and 6 women, Thomas among them. From then on the work continued to grow rapidly.

New Missions: Northwest. In the second half of the first decade of the twentieth century, SDA work extended into the northwestern areas of the country. In 1906 L. J. Burgess and his wife (the former Georgia Burrus) pioneered evangelistic work in the Hindi language in Almora, a town northeast of Delhi, not far from the Nepal border, and near Naini Tal, the summer center of many Protestant missions, where evangelistic work in English had been conducted by Brown some years previously. There they translated Seventh-day Adventist tracts into Hindi and Urdu. The next year they moved to Dehra Dun, farther to the northwest, and three years later, in 1910, opened an industrial school for Garwahli youth in that vicinity. S. N. Haskell told the readers of the *Review and Herald* that the Burgesses chose to conduct their pioneering work without charge to the Indian mission budget, and financed their expenditures by the sale of subscriptions to the *Bible Training School* magazine while on furlough in America.

In 1907 a property was purchased in Mussoorie, in the foothills of the Himalayas above Dehra Dun, about 120 miles (192 kilometers) north of Delhi, for a school *(see* Vincent Hill School), a sanitarium, and a place where the workers could go for a rest from the hot and humid climate of coastal cities and the torrid heat of the interior. Late in 1907 the work of the Calcutta Sanitarium was transferred there.

In 1909 Lucknow became the site of the printing house and of the mission headquarters, and early in 1909 the first organized Hindustani SDA church in the mission was established there.

Medical Work, 1900-1910. Medical work continued to develop throughout the decade. In 1900 the treatment rooms in Calcutta, operated for some time on Wellesley Street by Drs. R. S. and Olive Ingersoll, were moved to a larger place at 51 Park Street, and there came to be called the Medical and Surgical Sanitarium. In the next year the institution was moved to still larger quarters at 50 Park Street, and there became known as the Calcutta Sanitarium. The vacated quarters were occupied by the newly established Sanitarium Health Food Company, which continued the preparation of health foods begun in a small way by D. A. Robinson early in the history of the medical work in India. In 1901 the Karmatar dispensary, which had suspended operations after Brown's death, was reopened with May Quantock (the former May Taylor) in charge. She was succeeded by Thekla Black. Dr. R. S. Ingersoll came twice a month to take care of the more complicated cases. In 1902 a medical station was opened at Chandernagore, some 30 miles (50 kilometers) north of Calcutta, where Samantha Whiteis and Grace Kellogg, a newly arrived worker, administered simple treatments.

In January 1903 the Calcutta Sanitarium became self-supporting. At that time it was reported that a nursing class was being taught. In 1907 the Calcutta Sanitarium was reduced to treatment rooms, and the main medical work in India shifted to the more healthful climate of Mussoorie, where Dr. H. C. Menkel opened the Mussoorie Sanitarium in 1908 and operated it until 1910. In 1906 Dr. Lucinda Marsh conducted medical work in the city of Bombay, but she became ill after a few months and left the area. In 1908 treatment rooms were opened in Lucknow.

As a rule medical work was conducted at all Seventh-day Adventist missions and even where the missionaries were not medically trained. The demand for medical assistance was so great that simple treatments were given everywhere.

Educational Work, 1900-1910. Seventh-day Adventist education in India during the first decade of the twentieth century expanded from one school at Karmatar, the Orphanage Industrial School, to at least five in various areas of the country. In 1900 Barlow opened a school at Simultala, where about a score of Santali young men were trained in various trades and in better methods of farming as well as in evangelistic and teaching methods. In 1902 a boarding school was opened for the English-speaking students at Karmatar, under the supervision of Thekla Black. Anna Orr was the teacher of the first group of 12 students. It appears from the records that it was an elementary school and that after two or three years it was moved to Calcutta, where it met for a time in the home of one of the workers. There does not seem to be any mention of this school between 1905 and 1910. The 1905 *Statistical Report* lists one elementary and one intermediate school in the India Mission, with a total enrollment of 25. In 1904 one of the first Santali converts, a young man trained in Barlow's school, went to teach at the newly established Babumohal mission school some distance from the Simultala mission.

The beginning of schoolwork in southern India dates from 1909, when according to the *Outline of Mission Fields* (page 119), a school, staffed at first with non-Adventist teachers, was opened under the supervision of James at Nazareth near the community of Sabbath-keeping Tamil Christians.

In 1910 an industrial school was opened by L. J. Burgess and his wife in the vicinity of Dehra Dun, in northern India. This was listed in the *Yearbook* until 1926, first under the name of Garhwal Industrial School, and later as "Open View" Mission School.

Publishing Work, 1900-1910. SDAs began their publishing work almost as soon as the mission was established. For a number of years they conducted it under the name International Tract Society. The first printing press owned by the church in India was set up in 1903, when the Watchman Press was established at 38 Free School Street in Calcutta. Its largest project was to print the *Oriental Watchman,* the circulation of which reached 5,000 copies a month in 1902. At the first general meeting of workers held at Calcutta in December 1904 it was decided to move the printshop to Karmatar, where it remained until 1909, when it was moved to Lucknow in northern India.

After the press was established, the quantity of literature available for the Indian readers steadily increased. In 1901 the Mission Board reported nine tracts available in the national languages of India. Many of these were translated by the converts and printed at their own expense. In 1903 Barlow reported that the new mission press had printed 2,000 copies each of the three tracts that he had translated into Santali, and that three more were ready for the press. Sometime in 1904 an Indian in the southern part of the country translated SDA tracts and articles from the *Oriental Watchman* into Kanarese and had them printed at his own expense, without having met an SDA. In 1902 the English language health magazine printed in England (whether there was a special Indian edition is not quite certain) was introduced and its circulation grew rapidly among the vegetarian Hindus, who welcomed it and were intrigued by the health principles that it advocated. In 1904 the *Review and Herald* reported that *Steps to Christ,* by Ellen White, was available in Bengali. In 1910 Dr. Menkel founded the *Herald of Health.*

The church organ *Eastern Tidings* (now *Southern Asia Tidings)* was founded in 1902. At first it was mimeographed, but after 1903 it was printed. In 1909 the first SDA evangelistic magazine in an Indian language, *Yuga Lakshan,* in Bengali, was founded at Calcutta, with L. G. Mookerjee as editor.

Organization of the India Union Mission and Subsequent Growth. Until 1909 the work in India, Pakistan, Burma, and Ceylon was administered directly as a detached mission by the General Conference. Then for a brief period, it was administered by the Asiatic Division, but by 1910, when the work had spread throughout these countries, it was thought best to decentralize the administration. In a reorganization the Indian work was divided into four missions: the Bengali Mission, comprising the Bengali, Oriya, Santali, and Assamese language areas; the North India Mission, comprising the Hindi (Hindustani, Bihari, Rajasthani, Punjabi, and Sindhi) language areas; the South India Mission, comprising the Tamil, Telegu, Kanarese, Malayalam, and Singhalese language areas; and the Western India Mission, comprising the Marathi and Gujarati language areas. These, together with the Burma Mission and Ceylon (then a part of the South India Mission), were formed into the India Union Mission. J. L. Shaw, superintendent of the work in India since 1901, became the first union superintendent.

After the reorganization the work advanced in ever-increasing tempo. In 1914 the total number of SDAs in the India Union Mission was about 450. Five years later, in 1919, when the India Union Mission (which between 1915 and 1918 had been a part of the Asiatic Division) was reorganized into the Southern Asia Division, there were 978 members.

Progress in South India. Progress was especially rapid in the south, where Christianity had made its greatest impact, and where consequently, the people were better prepared to accept the SDA doctrine. A number of strong national workers developed there. For example, after a Tamil language magazine, whose title is translated "Present Truth," began publication in 1912, a group of nine Tamil colporteurs was trained and sent out to present SDA publications to their fellow citizens. One of them, Suvisasha Muthu, pioneered in what is now the state of Kerala. An entire village where he had worked was later converted and a church was established there; thereupon the village changed its name to Adventpuram, "the place of Adventists," and later became the center for the work in that area. In the spring of 1917 the first national Seventh-day Adventist minister in India, E. D. Thomas, who had worked with James and Lowry from the beginning in southern India, was ordained.

To help train men several schools were established in the course of years. In 1915 Gentry G. Lowry established a high school at Coimbatore for the Tamil young people, which, after several changes in location, developed into Spicer Memorial College and Lowry Memorial High School. A school at Narsapur, on the east coast of southern India on the Godavari River delta, was opened in 1921 by T. R. Flaiz. Five or six years later H. G. Woodward (a former worker for another denomination who had joined the SDAs in India) opened the Malayalam mission in southwestern India. A school was opened at Kottarakara in 1925. In the same year the Tamil school at Prakasapuram offered high school courses for the first time. Besides, there were many village elementary schools staffed by national teachers.

Also in 1925 two hospitals were established in South India: one at Nuzvid, Andhra Pradesh, near Vijayawada, in the delta of the Krishna River *(see* Giffard Memorial Hospital), and another at Narsapur. In the early 1930s a third hospital was opened at Bobbili, southwestern Orissa, about 60 miles (96 kilometers) north of Vishakhapatnam in Andhra Pradesh, near the eastern coast. After World War II only the Giffard Memorial Hospital was still in operation, but later, about 1950, a clinic was conducted for several years at the city of Tiruchirappalli (Trichinopoli) on the Coleroon River (called Nalwazhi Clinic).

In 1940 the church members in southern India received their own church organ, the *Southern India Observer.* In 1948 *Marga Darsi* ("Pathfinder"), a health journal in the Telegu language, was founded, and in 1950 another health journal, *Kerala Deepam* ("Light of Kerala"), was begun in the Malayalam language.

In 1941 the predecessor of the Bangalore Seventh-day Adventist High School was founded, and in 1953 the E. D. Thomas Memorial High School was formed out of the high school division of the James Boarding School and established on its own campus at Kudikadu, near Thanjavur. The growth of the educational work was shown in the enrollment figures of the schools appearing in the *Statistical Report.* The 1925 *Report* listed a total of 30 schools in the South India Union

Mission, with an enrollment of 819. Five years later, in 1930, there were 25 schools, with 1,033 students. Ten years later, in 1935, there were 24 schools, with 900 students. In 1940 there were 24 schools, with 1,063 students; in 1950 there were 29 elementary schools, with an enrollment of 1,111, and four secondary schools, with a total of 370 students; in 1963 there were 33 elementary schools, with 998 pupils, and seven secondary schools, with 1,199 students. In 1970 there were 22 elementary schools, with 4,331 students, and five secondary schools, with 729 students; in 1981 there were 88 elementary schools, with 30,318 students, and five secondary schools, with 1,367 students; and in 1992 there were 129 elementary schools, with 59,158 students, and six secondary schools, with 3,474 students.

Church membership in South India also grew. In 1911 the total for the South India Union was 124. At the end of 1931 the membership was 1,408. Another 20 years later it was 5,207; in 1974 it was 31,578; and in 1992 it was 80,484.

Progress in Western India. After the organization of the India Union more workers arrived to develop the work in western India. Among them were M. D. Wood, a former missionary for another denomination, who opened a school at Kalyan, near Bombay, while his wife, a medical missionary, operated a dispensary there, beginning about 1912. She also taught nursing at the Marathi Training School for Nurses (which was established about 1915 at Kalyan but apparently closed shortly afterward). In the same year G. W. Pettit came to conduct evangelism among the English-speaking people in Bombay, assisted the next year by F. H. Loasby. In 1914 a church was organized in Bombay. In 1915 Roland E. Loasby began village evangelism in the vicinity of Lasalgaon, a town 150 miles (240 kilometers) northeast of Bombay. In 1921 the Kalyan school, relocated at Lasalgaon, became a training institution for the Western India Union.

Also in 1921 the headquarters of the Southern Asia Division were moved to the Salisbury Park compound (named in memory of H. R. Salisbury, second superintendent of the India Union, who lost his life while returning to India during World War I) in Poona, Maharashtra, a city in the hills about 75 miles (120 kilometers) southeast of Bombay. Three years later, in 1924, the Oriental Watchman Publishing House was moved there also.

In 1936 medical work was begun in Surat, a city near the western coast, 160 miles (260 kilometers) north of Bombay, by George A. Nelson. He opened a small clinic which later, in 1942, by popular request and with financial assistance from local sources, became the Surat Hospital.

In the course of World War II the college section of the Spicer Junior College was moved from Bangalore to its present campus at Kirkee, near Poona *(see* Spicer Memorial College). The progress of educational work in western India is shown by the figures that appeared in the *Statistical Report.* In 1911, a year after the organization of the India Union, western India had two church schools with 68 pupils; by 1936 there were seven church schools, with an enrollment of 134; in 1963 there were 16 elementary schools, with 486 students, two secondary schools, with 177 students, and one senior college, with 291 students; and in 1970 there were 13 elementary schools, with 1,095 students, one secondary school, with 300 students, and one senior college, with 769 students.

Church membership in the area, which in 1911 was 20, was 517 in 1936, 1,843 in 1963, and 3,074 in 1970. In 1955 the union paper, *Gateway Messenger,* the organ of the Western India Union, was begun. This union is distinctive in that it was the first in India to elect a national as its president (M. D. Moses, 1962).

Progress in Northern India. Evangelistic work in northern India began in the upper valley of the Ganges about the time the India Union headquarters were transferred to Lucknow in north-central India in 1909. After 1910 S. A. Wellman, M. M. Mattison, I. F. Blue, and others promoted the development of Seventh-day Adventist work. About 1911 Vera Chilton began work among the Hindu women at Lucknow, and soon thereafter a residence for Christian women was constructed so that those who were driven out by their relatives for accepting Christianity could have a place to live. About the same time an Urdu language school was conducted at Dehra Dun by Alice O'Connor, a resident of India, a convert who had an excellent knowledge of Urdu. Later she joined with two nurses, Misses Kurtz and Shryock, in the operation of a school and dispensary at Najibabad, near Dehra Dun. In 1914 treatment rooms were opened at Simla, a summer resort in the foothills of the Himalayas, by H. C. Menkel, a physician, who operated treatment rooms at Simla, in the mountains, during the summers and at Delhi, on the plains, during the winters.

In 1915 one of the earliest training schools for Indian workers was established at Lucknow under the name of Indian Christian Training School *(see* Seventh-day Adventist High School [Roorkee] for its successors). In 1919 M. M. Mattison opened a girls' school at Lucknow *(see* Hapur Elementary School). At first the work centered on the headquarters at Lucknow, but later a secondary center developed at Hapur, about 30 miles (48 kilometers) east of Delhi, where a North India Boys' School was established in 1917, which later became a training school for the Northwest India Union *(see* Seventh-day Adventist High School [Roorkee]). In 1911 an English language school was opened at Mussoorie; many of the children of the overseas workers in Southern Asia received their secondary education and for a time some college education there. *See* Vincent Hill School.

The work was not carried on without opposition or persecution. In 1911 a national, John Last, an earnest evangelist, was beaten to death by a mob in a city of Patiala in Punjab.

Progress in Northeast. The work in the province of Bihar was begun with the orphanage at Karmatar in 1899 and was later carried to Ranchi, where the North East India Union Training School was situated from about 1920 until the 1930s. In 1917 the first Bengali worker, L. G. Mookerjee, was ordained to the ministry. The work continued to develop in the 1920s when R. J. Borrowdale and W. B. Votaw conducted village evangelism throughout the area. About 1930 a hospital was opened at the Karmatar station under the supervision of H. G. Hebard, which, however, was soon closed. An elementary school opened in 1936 at Khunti, about 20 miles (32 kilometers) south of Ranchi, had initial difficulties, but became a strong factor in the work in the northeastern part of India. After medical work in the area had been carried on largely in several dispensaries, R. V. Shearer in 1949 opened a small hospital at Ranchi, which since then has grown to 85-bed capacity.

In 1927 E. R. Osmunson went to Cuttack, in the delta of the Mahanadi River, and began the study of the Oryia language preparatory to opening a mission station at Khurda. Because of primitive conditions, the missionaries lived in a tent for almost a year before their home was ready.

The work east of the Brahmaputra River was pioneered by Burgess and his wife. Planning to retire in India, they settled near Shillong, in Assam (now in Meghalaya), and there aroused an interest. Later, in 1941, a training school was established in that part of India. In 1949 W. G. Lowry, a second-generation worker in India, entered the area of the Lushai Hills in Assam, on the southeastern border with Burma, and in 1950 established an industrial boarding school at Aijal.

The official organ of the church in northeast India was the *Northeast Broadcast.* In 1951 the name was changed to *Northeast Union Visitor.*

Publishing Work. As noted earlier, the publishing work in India began soon after a mission was established there, with tracts and a monthly magazine in English, the *Oriental Watchman.* Later were issued a number of tracts on religious themes, developed gradually after the formation of the India Union Mission, by which time there was also a monthly health journal, *Herald of Health,* and a Bengali evangelistic quarterly *Juga Lakshan* ("Signs of the Times"). In 1912 an evangelistic quarterly magazine called the *Present Truth* was begun for the Tamil readers. The 1915 *Yearbook* listed also Hindi and Urdu *Signs of the Times.* During World War I the publication of English-language magazines was suspended. By 1920 there were eight periodicals in the national languages of India issued by the SDA publishing house at Lucknow: *Juga Lakshan,* a Bengali bimonthly; *Pralai Kalana Chinho,* a Gujerati quarterly; *Kalyug ke Chinha,* a Hindi bimonthly; *Pralai Kalachi Chinha,* a Marathi quarterly; *Nikalkala Sattium,* a Tamil quarterly; *Nishinati-i-Quiyamat,* an Urdu bimonthly; and quarterly issues of *Present Truth* in Malayalam, Telegu, and Kanarese (the latter not listed as published by the house).

The largest SDA book in the national languages at that time was *Bible Readings.* In the early 1920s, experienced colporteurs were brought from overseas to sell large English-language subscription books, such as *The Great Controversy,* by Ellen White, *Daniel and the Revelation,* by Uriah Smith, and *Heralds of the Morning,* by Asa O. Tait, and in 1924 the first subscription book designed for sale by Indian colporteurs, *Health and Longevity,* by Dr. A. C. Selmon. Colporteurs soon thereafter were selling health books in all the principal dialects, but the sales of religious books were small. *Our Day in the Light of Prophecy,* by W. A. Spicer, was among the first religious books published (the late 1920s or in the early 1930s). Before 1945 one Hindi and four English printings of a book by R. B.

Thurber, *Toward a Better Day*, were sold, and also two printings of an abridgment of *The Ministry of Healing,* by Ellen White, which was published under the title *Health and Healing.* Since then sales of religious publications have been increasing, as colporteurs have gained experience. In 1962 *Counsels for the Church* (an abridgment of *Testimonies for the Church,* by Ellen White) was published in Hindi. According to a report in the *Review and Herald* (142:14, Oct. 21, 1965), in 1964 SDAs were printing in 24 of the languages of India, Pakistan, Ceylon, and Burma.

Later Progress. In 1950 the church began to use another avenue of communication—radio evangelism, which was begun with several weekly broadcasts over Radio Ceylon. Even though at the beginning the Bible correspondence school could not be announced, the public was made aware of it through the newspapers. Within a decade and a half the Voice of Prophecy School enrolled 2.4 million who were studying their lessons in 15 languages. Although Radio Ceylon later was closed to purely religious broadcasts, *The Radio Doctor,* a program of health evangelism, was continued.

After Goa was incorporated into India in 1962, N. G. Mookerjee began work there by giving Bible studies.

In 1964 India's Spicer Memorial College was the site of a division-wide youth congress. Almost 1,000 delegates were in attendance. Later in the year India's first course in the Five-Day Plan to Stop Smoking was conducted at Bangalore.

In the Voice of Prophecy work India has benefited from the fact that in 1971 broadcasts over Radio Sri Lanka again began after a silence of 10 years. As a result seven language broadcasts plus an English broadcast reach out to a potential audience of more than 1 billion people.

In 1974 Sikkim, on India's northern border, was entered and a small medical clinic set up.

In 1989 the Southern Asia division headquarters was moved to Tamil Nadu.

INDIA UNION MISSION. *See* Southern Asia Division.

INDIAN CHRISTIAN TRAINING SCHOOL. *See* Spicer Memorial College.

INDIAN OCEAN PUBLISHING HOUSE. *See* Adventist Printing House (Madagascar).

INDIAN OCEAN UNION MISSION. *See* Africa-Indian Ocean Division; Comoros; Madagascar; Mauritius; Réunion; Seychelles.

INDIAN OCEAN UNION TRAINING SCHOOL. *See* Soamanandrariny Adventist Secondary School.

INDIAN PUBLISHING HOUSE. *See* Oriental Watchman Publishing House.

INDIANA. *See* Indiana Conference; Lake Region Conference.

INDIANA ACADEMY. A coeducational boarding school on the senior high school level, operated at Cicero, Indiana, by the Indiana Conference. The academy is fully accredited by the Seventh-day Adventist Board of Regents, its most current certification having been issued in 1990. It was also granted "Continuous Commission" accreditation by the Department of Public Instruction of the state of Indiana in April of 1989.

Indiana Academy originated in 1902 as Boggstown Manual Training Academy (changed to Beechwood Manual Training Academy in 1905), at Boggstown, Indiana, on four acres (1.6 hectares) of land donated by William Applegate. Its first class graduated in 1908, with 11 members.

Eventually it was felt that a more centrally located site with adequate room for expansion and with better communication facilities should be found. After extended investigation the present property, a farm of 95 acres (40 hectares) near Cicero, was selected. In later years, the following properties were purchased: the Johnson farm, the Barnhiser farm, the Bowser farm, the Crumm farm, and the Miller farm. Additional property was purchased in 1974 and in the 1980s, making a present total of approximately 420 acres (170 hectares).

On Aug. 17, 1919, ground was broken for the girls' dormitory, and during that school year the academy was moved and was renamed Indiana Academy. The class of 1923 was the first class to have spent all four years at Indiana Academy. Roscoe Moore, later president of the New York Conference, was president of the class; Lowell Edwards, vice president; Thelma Chew, valedictorian; and Josephine Cunnington, class poet. The first annual, *The Ciceronian,* was published that year, with Josephine Cunnington as editor in chief.

After some difficult years serious consideration was given to closing the school in 1934, but it survived and resumed a natural order of progress.

The academy has been blessed with many opportunities for the students to earn tuition dollars while they learn academically. It has been served by such companies as Harris Pine Mills (1960), Hoosier Plastics and Packaging (1969), American Color (1980), American Leisure—Little Lakes (1983), and currently has Zee Medical on the campus.

The most current construction includes two mini-dorms built in 1974. These small dorms have 30 students each and help to lend a more homestyle atmosphere to the boarding school campus. A new girls' dorm was built in 1981. It houses approximately 48-50 girls comfortably. In 1985-1986 the Indiana Conference undertook the renovation of the gymnasium, which is utilized by the school for physical education, gymnastics, and recreation. It is also used by the conference for a camp meeting site. Approximately $450,000 was spent in the upgrading to provide a beautiful and comfortable facility. At present a new music/chapel complex is nearing completion.

Principals: B. F. Machlan, 1902-1907; C. L. Stone, 1907-1908; C. L. Taylor, 1908-1911; W. L. Avery, 1911-1913; E. A. von Pohle, 1913-1916; J. G. Lamson, 1916-1919; Charles W. Marsh, 1919-1925; Louis P. Thorpe, 1925-1930; J. W. Craig, 1930-1933; V. P. Lovell, 1933-1937; W. A. Nelson, 1937-1941; E. E. Bietz, 1941-1945; V. C. Hoffman, 1945-1948; C. M. Willison, 1948-1955; Dyre Dyresen, 1955-1959; V. L. Bartlett, 1959-1968; C. L. Newkirk, 1968-1970; James R. Nash, 1970-1977; Alan Bohman, 1977-1982; W. G. Nelson, 1983-1985; Harold Grosboll, 1985-1992; Nick E. Minder, 1992-1994; Steven Aust, 1994- .

INDIANA CONFERENCE. A unit of church organization comprising the state of Indiana. *(See also* Lake Region Conference.) Statistics (1993): churches, 71; members, 5,600; church schools, 15; ordained ministers, 38; licensed ministers, 9; church school teachers, 27. Headquarters: Meridian Street, Carmel, Indiana. The conference forms part of the Lake Union Conference.

Institutions. Indiana Academy.

Local churches: Alexandria, Anderson, Angola, Bedford, Bloomfield, Bloomington, Brownsburg, Chapel Hills, Cicero, Columbus, Connersville, Crown Point (Northwest), East Chicago (Spanish), Elkhart, Evansville, Fort Wayne, Frankfort, Greencastle, Greenfield, Greenwood Fellowship, Hammond, Hartford City, Huntingburg, Indianapolis (Chapel West, Glendale, Hispanic, Irvington, Northwest, South Side), Jeffersonville, Knox, Kokomo, Lafayette, La Porte, Lewis, Logansport, Madison, Marion, Markle (Chapel Hill), Martinsville, Michigan City, Monticello, Muncie, New Albany, New Castle, New Harmony, Noblesville, North Vernon, Paoli, Plymouth, Richmond, Rochester, Scottsburg, Seymour, Shelbyville, South Bend, Spencer, Tell City, Terre Haute, Valparaiso, Vincennes, Wabash, Warsaw, Washington, Wolf Lake.

History. *Beginning of the Work in the Area.* Joseph Bates, from Fairhaven, Massachusetts, was undoubtedly the first Seventh-day Adventist scout and missionary to enter Indiana on behalf of the Adventist faith, in July 1849. However, the earliest evangelistic teams heralding the Adventist message to former Millerites, and eventually to the populace at large, came the next year, 1850. Bates, with Abraham A. Dodge, of Battle Creek, Michigan, visited and preached in July; and Samuel W. Rhodes, from Oswego, New York, with John C. Bowles, of Jackson, Michigan, came in September and stopped long enough at Kingsbury, near La Porte, to convince Joseph and Jemima Catlin.

There is some evidence that in the autumn of 1851 John N. Andrews, of Poland, Maine, may have visited the state. During 1853 the far-ranging Bates came as far south as Lawrenceburg and Sullivan to confirm William Gould and Richard Moran in the faith, and John N. Loughborough, of Rochester, New York, and Merritt E. Cornell, of Michigan, won adherents—prominently, Joel and Lydia Locke—with meetings at Salem Center and Kingsbury.

An early group emerged around the Daniel Carpenter family at North Liberty from 1855 to 1858, when George Smith of Ohio, an artisan, came to work and witness near La Porte. Two of his converts—Peter Palmbad, from Sweden, and a man named Swartz, from Wittenberg, Germany—had been Adventists of a sort about 1844. These three teamed with Loughborough and won James and Addie Harvey, a man named Rupert, and others at North Liberty.

During the Civil War, when progress was slow, the converts pleaded with denominational leaders at Battle Creek for "preaching brethren." Accordingly, well-recognized ministers of the period (Joseph Bates, Moses Hull, J. H. Waggoner, J. N. Loughborough, John Byington, W. S. Ingraham, D. M. Canright, R. J. Lawrence) appeared on tours almost yearly to preach and stabilize, principally in the northern counties.

In October 1861 Salem Center organized the first church. Near South Bend in August 1864 the first series of tent meetings, by Waggoner and Ingraham, was conducted. The North Liberty congregation in 1868 erected the first meetinghouse. For the time being these churches were accepted into the Michigan Conference. By 1870 "bands" had coalesced also at Sullivan, Russiaville, Cicero, Tipton, Spencer, Patricksburg, Fairfield, Erwin, Lancaster, Bowling Green, and Sulphur Springs.

A new, better-planned era opened when two brothers, Elbert B. and Sands H. Lane, from near Battle Creek, came to conduct "lectures" as fledgling ministers in 1869. The first state camp meetings, held near Tipton and Fairfield in 1870 and 1871, strengthened the idea of organizing a conference.

Organization. Final impetus for organization developed when a windstorm in June 1872 ruined the (Michigan) tent and cut short an evangelistic series by Waggoner and E. B. Lane, at Gosport. In order to have a tent of their own for camp meeting, stalwarts in the churches (W. R. Carpenter, J. Harvey, Jacob Styles, D. F. Randolph, Charles Seaward, W. Covert, Isaac Zirkle, Noah Carahoof, Anson Worster) gathered money, bought a new tent, set up camp meeting west of Kokomo, and there on Sept. 20 convened a business meeting.

With General Conference president G. I. Butler in the chair, Harvey successfully moved to form the Indiana Conference. To keep the Lanes preaching, however, the organizers chose only local men as officers: president, William Covert; secretary, James Harvey; treasurer, Isaac Zirkle. Constituent churches were Alto, Erwin, North Liberty, Patricksburg, and Salem Center.

Progress to 1900. For the remainder of the century the dominant purpose of organized Adventism in Indiana was statewide evangelism, and preaching was carried on in more than 300 recorded places. To captain this vast undertaking, reliance was put chiefly upon three able presidents—Covert, S. H. Lane, and Starr—and upon dedicated evangelistic workers, such as Arthur W. Bartlett, William and John Covert, J. P. Henderson, William Hill, N. W. Kauble, David H. Oberholtzer, Joseph M. Rees, F. M. Roberts, J. S. Shrock, Victor and Luzerne Thompson, and W. A. Young. These men worked long in building young churches in their state.

Many of these early churches do not now exist, because of mergers, deaths, removals, and lukewarmness, yet a surprising number do (some disbanded and later reestablished). They are listed here in order of initial dates: Marion, 1876; Lafayette, 1877; Alexandria, Noblesville, Bloomington (as Smithville to 1871, then as Unionville to 1916), and Wolf Lake, 1878; Hartford City, Kokomo, and Northfield, 1883; Middletown, 1884; Plymouth, 1885; Sullivan (as Dugger to 1892, then as Salem to 1937), 1886; Boggstown, Rockford (as Barber's Mill to 1932), Rochester, and Wabash, 1887; Indianapolis, 1888; Angola, 1889; Terre Haute, 1892; Knox, 1893; Elnora, 1895; Monon (as Honey Creek to 1929), 1896; Fort Wayne, Tell City (as Mount Zion to 1917), 1897; Anderson, 1898; Connersville, Muncie, and South Bend, 1900.

It was arduous work to establish scores of churches with few workers and a scanty budget. Thus J. M. Rees, in bringing out a church in Terre Haute, borrowed $600 and reported, "I am almost broken down under it [the weight of the work]." E. E. Marvin, N. W. Kauble, and "Willie" Gray were stoned three times while holding meetings at Kempton, and also P. G. Stanley, S. S. Davis, and R. H. Sparks were threatened at Connersville. Nevertheless, these men established churches. Sands Lane was well along in a series at Wolf Lake when someone broke into the church and stole his charts from the wall in order to show that the law had been abolished. When his audience learned of the loss they raised money to buy new ones. A church emerged there.

In 1877 Bartlett's crowded meetings at Deedsville had to be moved from a church to a school, then to a barn, which became so packed that he had to enter through a window. A congregation was organized there. When Lane and Bartlett were holding meetings at Thorntown a windstorm ripped and flattened their tent, but community friends showered them with money to repair and reraise it. A church resulted there.

When Lane and W. W. Sharpe entered Sevastopol in 1879 to gather a church, they attracted so many from that farming hamlet to Sabbath services that "it made quite a change in the village—a merchant left his store, the shoemaker, harness maker, and the undertaker closed shop. Men came from the country with work, but were told they could not get it done till the next day" *(Review and Herald* 54:102, Sept. 18, 1879). A church resulted there.

Resourceful evangelists utilized their special skills. As early as 1888 John Covert conducted afternoon children's meetings at Rigdon, which attracted overflow audiences of adults to the evening services. In 1893 and 1894 at Priam and Farmersburg, Stanley prefaced his meetings with cooking demonstrations that brought out the curious to view this masculine and educational oddity. Converts were won in these places.

Often a series of meetings was conducted in a church of another denomination; this frequently resulted in opposition and eventually in locked buildings. Thereupon the SDA minister usually turned to house-to-house visiting.

On many occasions opposers demanded debates. Bartlett had five of these encounters at Wabash. Probably the most spectacular was the one that lasted four days between Lane and a Disciples' pastor at Farmersburg in the midsummer of 1883. This brought out 1,000 town and countryside listeners. Churches were begun in this vicinity.

Work in Indianapolis was started when Bartlett, as yet a teacher, formed a small Sabbath school in the spring of 1876. Finally in 1883 the conference, awaking to the strategic position of the city, authorized further endeavors. Various members, ministers, Bible instructors, colporteurs, and artisans played parts in this campaign, led by Bartlett and William Covert. At the outset, a "city mission" and lecture room were opened at 32 Cherry Street (1885); later a church was erected on Central Avenue (1887) and a church body was organized (1888). Early the next year Ellen White and A. T. Jones came and, with spiritual sermons, sparked the drive for converts. In 1888, 1892, 1893, and 1894 camp meetings were held on the north side of the city. By 1901 the membership approached 200.

The denomination thrived comparatively well in Indiana during the first half century of its history. By the end of the 1870s membership had increased from 150 to 522 and churches from 5 to 24. In 1890 there were 1,179 members in 50 churches; and by 1900 there were 2,226 in 69 churches. In sum, this forthright, earnest, horse-and-buggy generation of SDAs doubled its numbers every 10 years—a rate of growth not matched until the 1930s.

Since 1900. Indiana's membership from 1900 to 1930 remained close to 2,000. These decades were difficult ones for the conference. At the outset the "holy flesh" doctrine of 1900-1901 caused a stir that resulted in the resignation of the entire Indiana Conference committee, and consequent unrest that was calmed only by the ministrations of Ellen White, A. G. Daniells, O. S. Hadley, A. W. Bartlett, and a later conference president, W. J. Stone (1903-1909).

When the Lake Union Conference was organized in 1901, Indiana became a constituent member. A large percentage of the membership in the state is concentrated north of the Shelbyville moraine.

During the early period the conference consistently put a great deal into nurturing its own young people. As early as 1892 the youth of the Indianapolis church organized a "young people's society," and other churches followed the precedent. In 1897 two churches began church schools—Farmersburg (with Maude Atherton as teacher) and Salem (with Mattie Pease). By 1930 about 20 of these schools existed. The conference operated a secondary school near Boggstown known as Beechwood Academy (1903-1919), which was continued near Cicero as Indiana Academy of Seventh-day Adventists. Grants were made to Emmanuel Missionary College, which was the Lake Union college at Berrien Springs, Michigan. Moreover, the Wabash Valley Sanitarium at Lafayette (established 1906) also helped train young people.

In 1917 the northern tier of seven counties was transferred to the West Michigan Conference. At the end of 1918 the westernmost part of the Lake County was given to the newly formed Chicago Conference and in 1931 became briefly a part of the reunited Illinois Conference. When at the end of 1931 it and the other northern counties came "home" again, they contained sizable churches not there before—that is, Hammond, Michigan City, and Gary.

Through the years as some old churches disbanded, new ones were established, some of which endure to the present—two prior to 1910, Elkhart and Logansport; three in the next decade, Cicero, Indianapolis South Side, and Vincennes; eight during the twenties, Bedford, Evansville, Frankfort, New Albany, New Castle, New Harmony, North Vernon, and Shelbyville.

The years of the Depression and of World War II and its aftermath were soul-searching ones for Seventh-day Adventists in Indiana. Between 1930 and 1950 churches increased from 47 to 68 (though six Black churches were transferred in 1945 to the newly formed Lake Region Conference), and membership doubled to more than 4,000. This advance was planned by conference administrators and spearheaded by evangelists, but the ranks were well bolstered with active laymen. The operational base was broadened by the addition of more churches: Bloomfield, Columbus, Converse, Elizabeth, Glezen, Huntington, Jeffersonville, Livonia, Martinsville, Rensselaer, Seymour, Valparaiso, and Versailles.

An example of the strategic methods is furnished by Indianapolis. At the depth of the Depression, in 1932, the members rallied to operate a penny-a-dish cafeteria for humanity's sake (611 were served on Thanksgiving), then girded themselves to help their ministers win converts. In doing this they expanded the membership in their churches to one seventh of the conference total, and set a pattern of progress. Many-faceted evangelism included preaching crusades, radio programs, Bible study classes, and Vacation Bible Schools. (The older use of camp meetings for evangelistic purposes in unworked areas had ended around 1920, and in 1949 a permanent camp meeting site and facilities were established on the Indiana Academy premises.) Thus through a period of hard times and war conditions, the two, then the four, metropolitan churches climbed in membership from 350 to 735.

The decade of the 1950s was one of only moderate gains. Membership in the 72 churches advanced to 5,000. This increase was obtained by adhering to the "Indianapolis pattern" in the larger cities, especially the holding of vigorous evangelistic series. Youthful churches of this decade were Brownsburg, East Chicago (Spanish), Indianapolis, Irvington, Monticello, Portland, Scottsburg, Warsaw, and Washington.

By 1960, therefore, in the 26 large-city churches were concentrated half of the SDAs in the state. South Bend was the largest, with nearly 400 members. In earlier years this congregation had included personnel of the Review and Herald branch office and warehouse (1908-1937) and of the Lake Union Conference office (1903-1915). After 1945 and repeated evangelistic campaigns, it rapidly expanded to first place.

However, since 1885, because of its central location, Indianapolis has usually been the headquarters of the conference. (Before this, conference officers conducted business from their own home, as some did even afterward.) Some 10 changes were made (it was at Cicero from 1923 to 1930), but in October 1955 it was moved from near the center of Indianapolis to 1405 Broad Ripple Avenue, near the suburbs, where it occupied a contemporary-style office building. In 1975 it was moved to 15250 North Meridian Street, Carmel.

Indiana's latest undertaking was the purchase (1961), development, and operation of Timber Ridge Camp on 207 acres (84 hectares) of woodland and lake near Spencer. Youth camps, which do much to stabilize young people in the faith, had been conducted since 1931 on rented properties.

More and more the old landmarks, such as churches of wood, are being replaced with brick or Indiana-limestone edifices; more adequate budgets are possible (the conference debt, unpaid since 1900, was liquidated in 1942).

Presidents: William Covert, 1872-1874; James Harvey, 1874-1877; Sands H. Lane, 1877-1884; William Covert, 1884-1888; F. D. Starr, 1888-1894; J. W. Watt, 1894-1897; W. B. White, 1897-1898; R. S. Donnell, 1898-1901; I. J. Hankins, 1901-1903; W. J. Stone, 1903-1909; Morris Lukens, 1909-1911; O. Montgomery, 1911-1913; E. A. Bristol, 1913-1916; W. A. Westworth, 1916-1918; C. S. Wiest, 1919-1926; F. A. Wright, 1926-1931; M. A. Hollister, 1931-1934; S. E. Wight, 1934-1940; F. O. Sanders, 1940-1943; S. E. Wight, 1943-1947; C. M. Bunker, 1947-1954; Arthur Kiesz, 1954-1960; T. E. Unruh, 1960-1963; R. S. Joyce, 1963-1969; R. L. Dale, 1969-1975; G. W. Morgan, 1975-1981; Robert Thompson, 1981-1985; John Loor, 1985-1992; David Wolkwitz, 1992- .

INDIANS, AMERICAN. *See* Native Americans.

INDONESIA. A republic in Southeast Asia occupying most of the islands between the mainland of Asia and Australia, including Sumatra, Java, Sulawesi (Celebes), the southern part of Borneo, called Kalimantan, the western half of New Guinea, called Irian Jaya (incorporated in 1963), and East Timor, a former Portuguese colony that was integrated into Indonesia on July 17, 1979. Indonesia has some 17,000 islands, of which 6,000 are named and 1,000 are permanently settled. It stretches from 95° to 135° east longitude, a distance of about 3,125 miles (5,000 kilometers) from east to west, and from about 6° north of the equator to about 11° south of the equator, a distance of about 1,250 miles (2,000 kilometers). The republic has a total area of 735,268 square miles (1.9 million square kilometers) and is inhabited (1994) by 200 million people. Two thirds of them live on Java; thus this island is one of the most densely populated areas in the world. Ethnically, Indonesians belong to the Malay race and are related to the indigenous peoples of the neighboring areas of Asia and Polynesia; there are also significant groups of Chinese and other continental Asians.

The great majority of the people of Indonesia are Muslims, but there are Hindus, Christians, and pagans, and among the Chinese, Buddhists and Confucianists. The constitution of the country guarantees religious freedom to all. The official language of Indonesia is Bahasa Indonesia, developed quite recently from the Malay and local dialects, with words from Dutch, English, Arabic, and Sanskrit. English, which has become the second language of the republic, is taught in all high schools. For more than three and a half centuries the Dutch controlled the territory of Indonesia, first through the medium of the United East Indies Company and later directly through government administration. However, after World War II nationalists gained control of the country and proclaimed independence in 1945. In 1949 Indonesian independence was formally recognized by the Netherlands. In 1976 the eastern part of Timor was integrated to the territory of Indonesia.

Seventh-day Adventist Statistics. The territory of Indonesia forms the East and West Indonesia union missions in the Far Eastern Division. For the respective territories of the unions and the missions, *see* Far Eastern Division.

Statistics (1992) for *Indonesia:* churches, 945; members, 135,647; ordained ministers, 335; licensed ministers, 158; Bible instructors, 12; church or elementary schools, 235; teachers, 1,300.

Statistics (1992) for the unions and missions:

1. *East Indonesia Union Mission:* churches, 474; members, 66,548; ordained ministers, 152; licensed ministers, 59; Bible instructors, 3; church or elementary schools, 103; teachers, 628. Headquarters: Jalan B. W. Lapian 38, Manado, Sulawesi Utara. *Central Sulawesi Mission:* churches, 36; members, 3,853; ordained ministers, 10; licensed ministers, 4; church or elementary schools, 12; teachers, 30. Headquarters: Palu. *Irian Jaya Mission:* churches, 40; members, 8,281; ordained ministers, 21; licensed ministers, 21; church or elementary schools, 12; teachers, 36. Headquarters: Jayapura. *Maluku Mission:* churches, 28; members, 3,075; ordained ministers, 10; licensed ministers, 6; church or elementary schools, 2; teachers, 17. Headquarters: Ambon. *North Minahasa Mission:* churches, 113; members, 18,191; ordained ministers, 37; licensed ministers, 14; church or elementary schools, 34; teachers, 321. Headquarters: Manado. *Sangihe and Talaud Island Mission:* churches, 44; members, 3,190; ordained ministers, 6; licensed ministers, 3; church schools, 2; teachers, 12. Headquarters: Tahuna. *South Minahasa Mission:* churches, 179; members, 27,290; ordained ministers, 28; licensed ministers, 6; church or elementary schools, 37; teachers, 184. Headquarters: Tomohon. *South Sulawesi Mission:* churches, 34; members, 2,668; ordained ministers, 20; licensed ministers, 3; church or elementary schools, 4; teachers, 28. Headquarters: Ujung Pandang.

2. *West Indonesia Union Mission:* churches, 471; members, 69,099; church or elementary schools, 132; ordained ministers, 183; licensed ministers, 99; teachers, 672. Headquarters: Jalan M. T. Haryono Blok A, Kav. 4, 5, Jakarta, Java. *Central Sumatra Mission:* churches, 50; members, 4,773; church or elementary schools, 5; ordained ministers, 10; licensed ministers, 10; teachers, 44. Headquarters: Sibolga. *East Java Conference:* churches, 60; members, 10,605; church or elementary schools, 13; ordained ministers, 29; licensed ministers, 5; teachers, 69. Headquarters: Surabaya. *Jakarta Conference:* churches, 62; members, 11,620; church or elementary schools, 22; ordained ministers, 44; licensed ministers, 16; teachers, 75. Headquarters: Jakarta. *Kalimantan Mission:* churches, 30; members, 4,521; church or elementary schools, 6; ordained ministers, 13; licensed ministers, 19; teachers, 30. Headquarters: Balikpapan. *North Sumatra Mission:* churches, 147; members, 18,140; church or elementary schools, 56; ordained ministers, 21; licensed ministers, 11; teachers, 271. Headquarters: Pematang Siantar. *Nusa Tenggara Mission:* churches, 48; members, 6,565; church or elementary schools, 5; ordained ministers, 9; licensed ministers, 6; teachers, 43. Headquarters: Kupang. *South Sumatra Mission:* churches, 41; members, 4,796; church or elementary schools, 5; ordained ministers, 9; licensed ministers, 6; teachers, 43. Headquarters: Palembang. *West Java Mission:* churches, 33; members, 4,733; church or elementary schools, 19; ordained ministers, 22;

licensed ministers, 2; teachers, 92. Headquarters: Bandung.

The official organ of the East and West Indonesian union missions is *Warta Advent.*

Institutions. Bandung Academy; Bandung Adventist Hospital; Cimindi Academy; East Java Academy; Indonesia Publishing House; Indonesia Union College; Irian Jaya Academy; Klabat Academy; Maluku Academy; Medan Academy; Medan Adventist Hospital; Mount Klabat College; North Sulawesi Academy; North Sumatra Academy and Indonesia Union College Extension; Nusa Tenggara Academy; Pematang Siantar Academy; South Sumatra Academy; Toraja View Academy.

Development of Seventh-day Adventist Work. *Beginnings.* The first Seventh-day Adventist to visit Indonesia may possibly have been Abram La Rue, who is reported to have been in Java sometime between 1888 and 1903. SDA work in Indonesia began in 1900, when R. W. Munson, formerly a missionary for another denomination at Singapore, and well acquainted with the language of the people, opened a mission at Padang, on the west coast of Sumatra. One of his first converts was Tay Hong Siang, a Christian preacher, a Chinese who as an orphan had been in Munson's orphanage in Singapore a number of years previously.

Three years later, in 1903, the East Indian archipelago was made a mission field of the Australasian Union Conference. In 1905 Immanuel Siregar, a Christian from Batakland, accepted the SDA faith after Bible studies with R. W. Munson. He then returned to the uplands of North Sumatra, land of the cannibal Bataks, taking the doctrine to his own people.

Other early missionaries were G. A. Wantzlick and his family in Sumatra; G. A. Teasdale and his family, Petra Tunheim, and Anna Nordstrom in Surabaja, East Java. Sim Gee Nio, who came from Singapore, proved a great help as a translator.

A workers' council for Java was held on Oct. 22, 1908, with J. E. Fulton, from Singapore, presiding. Publishing work was begun in Sukabumi, West Java, with printing equipment that had been brought over from Singapore in February 1910, and the publication of a quarterly periodical, *Utusan Kebenaran Melayu* ("Malay Messenger of Truth"), was begun. In 1911 the press was moved to Jakarta. This led to developing a church in that city. This church, organized in 1912 by G. F. Jones, the intrepid ship captain-missionary of the Pacific islands, was the first SDA church to be established on Java. Five souls were baptized in the first baptism in Java, which took place Mar. 29, 1911, at Sukabumi. One of the first to be baptized by R. W. Munson was Samuel Rantung, who pioneered the work in North Celebes.

Malaysian Union Mission. At a workers' meeting about the beginning of 1913, held at Sumber Wekas, a small hill station about 40 miles (65 kilometers) south of Surabaja, the missions in the East Indies field were organized as a union mission field, with F. A. Detamore as superintendent of the field. Three of the local missions included in it were the Sumatra, East Java, and West Java missions.

At a meeting of the Malaysian Mission workers at Sumber Wekas, Feb. 15-20, 1917, it was reported that there were two missions in Sumatra and two in Java—the East and the West. There were small companies in Kediri, Jogjakarta, and Semarang. In that year the Malaysian Union Conference was organized, including these missions in Indonesia. Melvin Munson, son of R. W. Munson, arrived in Java to be editor of the press. Instead of the former quarterly, the monthly *Pertandaan Zaman* ("Signs of the Times") was published. Literature was printed in Siamese, Batak, Nias, and Arabic Malay.

Workers from Europe began arriving in Indonesia during 1921. In that year A. H. Zimmerman and his wife came from Europe in September, and Peter Drinhaus and Friedrich Dittmar and their families in October. P. J. Raubenheimer and his wife came from South Africa.

Samuel Rantung, a Jakarta convert who had gone to Singapore to attend the training school and who later served as a teacher in that school, returned to his home in Ratahan, Menado, North Celebes, on a leave of absence in October 1920. His parents and relatives accepted his faith, and 22 people were baptized on Dec. 30, 1921, by F. A. Detamore. The next day the first church on the Celebes was organized with 25 members. Samuel Rantung and M. E. Diredja remained in the Celebes to foster the new interests.

In his report to the General Conference session in 1922, F. A. Detamore gave the following statistics for the Malaysian Union Mission: From a membership of 337 in 1917, four years later the number had almost doubled, increasing to 660.

In 1924, after a three-month series of evangelistic meetings in the city of Medan, northern Sumatra, by I. C. Schmidt, 32 baptized members were reported. These were chiefly from the Ambonese, Bataks, and Chinese. Colporteur work was the only means of evangelism outside the city of Medan. A Sabbath school was organized in Kutaradja, Atjeh, and another on the island of Sabang, off the northern tip of Sumatra. The latter had 35 members of whom 12 had been baptized.

Public evangelistic meetings in Java, held by J. S. Yates in a tent in Jakarta late in 1923 in 3 languages—Malay, Dutch, and Chinese—resulted in 20 baptisms.

The West Java Mission held its first mission session in Jakarta in December 1923. Delegates were present from five churches, representing a combined membership of more than 250. The church building there had been erected from funds collected locally. A mission school was in operation with two teachers and 60 students. At a mission session six years later, reports showed a membership of 530, and seven schools, all self-supporting, with 626 students enrolled. The mission operated 18 outstations.

East Java held a mission session in January 1929 and reported a membership of 385 in six churches and companies. At that time a Dutch-Chinese school with 170 students enrolled at Surabaja, and a Javanese school with 62 students was reported. In Samarang a Dutch-Chinese school with 200 students was directed by I. C. Schmidt.

At the end of 1924 Albert Munson (brother of Melvin) reported more than 500 believers in the Celebes, of whom 188 had been baptized. Early in 1925 P. Pietersz and a colporteur, J. Liklikwatil, went to Ambon. They met bitter opposition, but on Oct. 3 Albert Munson came from Menado and baptized 22 persons, the first SDA baptism in Ambon. In 1926 Samuel Rantung found 53 converts on the island of Saparua. During 1927 more than 100 persons had been baptized in Ambon, and the island of Banda was entered. Early in 1926 permission was given to SDAs to work in North Celebes.

Netherlands East Indies Union Mission Organized. In 1929 the territory of Indonesia was organized as the Netherlands East Indies Union Mission (since 1947 the Indonesia Union Mission), and transferred from the Far Eastern to the Central European Division. It was first reported as divided into six missions (Batakland Mission, North Sumatra Mission, South Sumatra Mission, West Java Mission, East Java Mission, and North Celebes Mission) and the Ambon and Padang districts (all eight listed as missions by the end of the year). There were then 48 churches and companies in Indonesia, with 1,736 members, and 13 schools, with 1,309 students. The officers of this new union mission were B. Ohme, superintendent, and H.E.R. Schell, secretary-treasurer.

Batakland Mission. Having been appointed to take charge of the Batakland field at the annual meeting in Singapore, Mar. 2-12, 1920, and being unable to conduct evangelistic work, D. S. Kime opened an English school at Sipogu. This school became an entering wedge into Batakland. Its students, who had come from all parts of the country, took the SDA message back to their own people. Eight were baptized in the first public baptism in Batakland, conducted by G. B. Youngberg on Mar. 23, 1929.

In January 1930 Kime called Karel Tambunan from Medan to work for 800 emigrant families from northern Batakland who had settled at Sajur Matinggi, in the Angkola and Sipirok district. In April 1931 S. Ritonga was sent there to open a mission school. G. A. Wood succeeded Kime as director, and on July 2, 1931, dedicated a church and school building. At that time there were 35 baptized members there.

In November 1932 permission was given to SDAs to work in all of Batakland. Immediately public evangelism was launched in different places. In spite of opposition 50 persons joined the church at Balige and 17 at Porsea.

At the 1936 session of the Batakland Mission, 13 churches were reported and 10 new churches were received into church fellowship at the session. The membership had grown to 443 by the end of 1935, and more than 1,000 persons were attending Sabbath schools.

In 1937 this mission was merged with the North Sumatra Mission.

South Sumatra Mission. A small company had been organized at Palembang when F. Dittmar went there early in 1929. Medical missionary work was begun by Maria Muster, a midwife from Germany. In December 1933 there were six national evangelists and four colporteurs in the field. By the end of 1940 the membership had reached 336.

West Java Mission. At the annual meeting in 1932 the West Java churches sent 54 delegates; at that time the Chinese church in Jakarta was accepted into fellowship. The mission then had a membership of 489. By 1935 there were 702 members. The West Java Training School gave diplomas to its first three graduates in

1936 (*see* Indonesia Union College).

East Java Mission. At the end of 1930 the East Java Mission had 12 churches and companies, 14 Sabbath schools, and three mission schools, with 585 students. In 1934 two more churches were accepted into fellowship.

Sangihe and Talaud Island Mission. Alex Lengkoan was born to Lutheran parents in Kakas, Tondano, July 4, 1900. Graduating from the nursing school, he worked as a nurse in Manado from 1922-1926. In Manado he met another nurse, Marie Lumabaeng. They studied SDA doctrines and were baptized and got married in 1926. Alex left nursing to become a colporteur. In 1928 a group of believers were worshiping in the village of Salurang, which was Marie's hometown. This became the first SDA church in the Sangihe and Talaud Island Mission. Alex later became a Bible teacher and then an ordained minister. From Salurang the work expanded to Tamako, Minanga, Tagulandang, and throughout the mission.

North Celebes Mission. When Ambon and South Celebes were made a separate district under the supervision of the union mission in 1929, this left the North Celebes Mission with a membership of only 477. However, by the end of 1930 its membership had increased to 600 in 13 churches, eight new churches having been accepted into the mission in 1930. Two of their most successful colporteurs were sent to New Guinea to work among "the Papuans and other inhabitants" of the island.

By July 1934 there were 42 churches, and the membership had grown to 1,155. The church at Menado was dedicated at the annual meeting of the North Celebes Mission in 1935, and 18 persons were baptized. A colporteur, J. Moroisa, pioneered the work on Morotai. A Missionary Volunteer convention, held at Langowan, Menado, on June 6, 1937, was attended by more than 1,100 young people from the North Celebes. At the end of that year there were 54 churches in that mission.

Ambon Mission. Three colporteurs entered Ambon in 1922, and scattered many books and periodicals throughout the islands. Permission to do missionary work was finally granted in December 1928, and soon a church in Ambon was organized. The next March 41 were baptized there, among them four from Banda and nine from Saparua. The church at Ambon dedicated its newly erected church building on Nov. 6, 1935.

By the end of 1937 permission had not as yet been received to do missionary work on the Tanimbar Islands, although SDAs had visited these islands.

South Celebes. In February 1929 South Celebes was made a separate district under the direct supervision of the union mission at Bandung. Samuel Rantung was sent to Ujung Pandang, and on Apr. 4, 1930, the first baptism was held and a church was organized.

From Torajaland, about 180 miles (290 kilometers) north of Makassar (now Ujung Pandang), four persons came to Makassar on Mar. 29, 1935, in order to receive baptism.

From 1937 Through World War II. At the close of 1937 the following statistics were given for the union: membership, 4,554 (an increase of 2,818 in nine years); churches and companies, 130; Sabbath schools, 134; membership, 5,497. MV Societies, 60; membership, 1,496; a training school with 15 students; other schools, 18 with 1,166 students; colporteurs, 62. There was no work as yet in the Lesser Sunda Islands, Borneo, and West New Guinea (now Irian Jaya).

Because conditions with the approach of World War II made it difficult for the Central European Division to administer the work in Indonesia, the Netherlands East Indies Union Mission was transferred back to the Far Eastern Division on Jan. 1, 1938. However, the general form of the union mission organization was maintained. The work continued to grow. By the second quarter of 1939 the North Celebes Mission had 1,926 members and Ambon had 267, and converts were found on many of the neighboring islands. The number of ordained ministers in the union had grown to eight, and national leaders were gradually assuming leadership of the work.

South Celebes was organized into a local mission during the session held at Bandung in 1939. In the Celebes, A. Londa baptized five candidates at Gorontalo in August of that year.

When the Nazis invaded the Netherlands during World War II, the Dutch interned all the German missionaries in Indonesia. In 1941 K. Tilstra was appointed union mission superintendent, but at the time of the occupation by the Japanese he was interned. In spite of the war the work of God went forward.

Postwar Developments. *Reorganization, 1947.* At the first union mission session after the war, held in Jakarta from Mar. 22 to 26, 1947, union mission appointments were made as follows: K. Tilstra, president (D. S. Kime acting as president while Tilstra was on furlough to the United States); secretary, Leo

Hogendorp; acting treasurer, W. U. Hutapea. Changes were also made in the administration of local missions. Administrators were appointed as follows: D. S. Kime, West Java; M. Kauntul, East Java; A. Londa, North Celebes; A. Pasuhuk, South Celebes; R. O. Walean, Ambon; and S. H. Pandjaitan, Central Java, being stationed at Samarang.

At this first postwar union mission session, six nationals were ordained; thus the total number of national ordained ministers was increased to 20.

Irian Jaya (West New Guinea). In 1928 Albert Munson and V. L. Beecham made a short visit to the northwest coastal area of New Guinea. In 1941 two Indonesian colporteurs, A. Kadir and I. Tuamulia, were sent in; they reported one convert, a Chinese. After the interruption of World War II, D. A. Dompas was sent to Sorong in 1948, and later D. van Waardenburg went to Manokwari. In 1951 the Indonesia Union Mission sent E. H. Vijsma to organize the West New Guinea Mission. After independence for Indonesia came, many SDA members from Indonesia, mainly Dutch citizens, moved to New Guinea, and churches were organized in Sorong, Manokwari, and Hollandia (later renamed Kotabaru, still later Sukarnapura, and now Jayapura), where the first SDA church was built in 1954.

In 1953 the West New Guinea Mission was placed under the direct supervision of the Far Eastern Division, with Klaas Tilstra as president. In March 1955 the mission had 96 members.

In 1957 the first church composed entirely of indigenous members was organized in the coastal village of Mambui. In the same year SDA medical work was begun by Mrs. K. Tilstra, a registered nurse, and a training school was opened at Dojo Baru on Dec. 2, 1957, with L. E. Keizer in charge. Early in 1961 Dr. N. Twijnstra opened a dental clinic, which because of political conditions was closed in 1963. In 1963 the first Irian minister, J. Bindosano, was ordained.

Work among the primitive tribes of the Tor River area, near Sarmi, was begun in 1958, after a visit there by Dr. G. Oosterwal, an SDA missionary-anthropologist. Village schools were opened, and in 1962 the first convert from these primitive tribes was baptized.

Publishing Work. The first SDA missionary to Indonesia, R. W. Munson, was also the first to translate SDA publications into the Malay language. He translated a series of small tracts and a collection of hymns. A 30-page booklet, *Second Advent of Christ,* was published, and parts of Ellen White's *Great Controversy* were translated and prepared for printing in Arabic characters.

With the establishment of the Indonesia Publishing House (1949), production of much-needed publications was increased, opening the way for a large group of colporteurs to spread the SDA message in printed form rapidly throughout the many islands.

Among the Spirit of Prophecy books that have been printed are *Counsels to the Church* (four volumes), *Steps to Christ, The Desire of Ages, The Great Controversy,* and *Messages to Young People.*

Radio and Television. The Voice of Prophecy correspondence courses were introduced by Mrs. H.E.R. Schell in Cimindi in 1948. In 1950 the headquarters were moved to Bandung. In 1954 Bible correspondence courses were available for Voice of Prophecy students in Indonesian, Chinese, Dutch, and English. During the first nine years of operation 214,358 applicants requested lessons and 10,152 completed the courses. Baptisms reported as a result of these studies totaled 3,260.

A monthly TV program on a Dakarta station was introduced on Jan. 24, 1963, produced by J. T. Manullang, radio-TV secretary of the Indonesia Union Mission. It was the first live regularly scheduled SDA television broadcast in the Far Eastern Division.

Muslim Evangelism. At the 1926 General Conference session it was reported that 100 converts with a Muslim background had been won in Indonesia. For the nine-year period 1954-1962, the number of baptisms from among Muslims totaled 844. These baptisms were the result of Voice of Prophecy lessons, personal evangelism, and public evangelistic meetings.

Recent Growth. The Indonesia Union Mission passed the 10,000 membership mark during the year 1952. Although it took a half century to gain the first 10,000 converts, the second 10,000 required less than a decade.

As the Lord's work grew in the 1960s in Indonesia, it became necessary to reorganize the union. By the end of 1972, 15 local missions spread along the equator for more than 3,000 miles (5,000 kilometers). Thus it was that in January of 1964 the Indonesia Union Mission was divided into two unions. The East Indonesia Union Mission included Maluku, Sangihe, Talaud, and Sulawesi; and the West Indonesia Union Mission included Sumatra; South Borneo (now Kalimantan); Java;

Madura; Bali, Lombok, and the Nusa Tenggara group (now Lesser Sunda Islands); Timor; and West Irian (West New Guinea). In 1972 West New Guinea, now known as Irian Jaya, became a part of the East Indonesia Union Mission.

Shortly after this reorganization a number of new missions were organized. In the East Indonesia Union the Sangihe-Talaud Mission was organized in 1964, and the Central Sulawesi Mission in 1965. The former included the Sangihe and Talaud islands, and the latter Buol Toli-Toli, Donggala, Luwuk-Banggai, and Posso. As the work grew in the North Celebes (or Sulawesi) Mission it became necessary to reorganize the mission. Thus, in 1971 two missions were formed from the former North Celebes Mission and became the North and South Minahasa missions. The North Minahasa Mission included Ternate, Morotai, and North Minahasa, while the South Minahasa Mission was comprised of Bolaang Mongondow, Gorontalo, and South Minahasa.

Later the West Indonesia Union Mission reorganized several missions within its territory. In December 1971 the West Kalimantan (Borneo) Mission became a district of the West Java Mission. In 1972 the island of Kalimantan (Borneo) was reorganized and became one mission, the Kalimantan Mission, its territory being the Indonesia section of the island of Borneo, with mission headquarters in Balikpapan.

In 1971 the North Sumatra Mission was also divided into two missions. Early in 1972 the Central Sumatra Mission was organized with the following territory: part of North Sumatra province from Sipintu-pintu to the south, West Sumatra province, and Riau province. The North Sumatra Mission then had part of the North Sumatra province from Sipintu-pintu to the north and Aceh province. In 1973 the two missions in Java were reorganized to form three missions, East Java, Central Java, and West Java. The West Java Mission was also to include Purwakarta Bogor, Cianjur, and Sukabumi. In the early 1980s the West Java Mission took over the territory of the Central Java Mission, and the Jakarta Mission was formed from the territory that had previously been the West Java Mission. In 1994 the East Java and Jakarta missions became conferences.

In 1992 total membership for the West Indonesia Union Mission was 69,099, with 66,548 in the East Indonesia Union Mission; or a total of 135,647 members and 157,733 Sabbath school members. Headquarters for the union were moved to a new strategic location in 1991.

The educational work has advanced rapidly, with two colleges and 13 senior academies in Indonesia. Of the latter, seven are boarding academies. The church school program has also been doing well.

With the arrival of two mission planes in Indonesia, based in Irian Jaya (western New Guinea), the prospects in this area are bright for rapid growth.

The Health Department of the East Indonesia Union Mission began a rural health program in 1988. Dr. Kathleen Kuntaraf, FED health director, conducted a training program for rural health student missionaries (RHSM) for the union. Since that time 14 RHSMs have been sent to various missions in the union territory. The effort was blessed with 57 baptisms, including the establishment of a company in the Maluku Mission.

INDONESIA PUBLISHING HOUSE (Percetakan Advent Indonesia). A publishing house with printing plant operated at Bandung, Java, Indonesia, by the West and East Indonesia union missions as an interunion institution, through a board of directors representing both unions. No commercial printing is accepted. Publications are issued in the Indonesian language.

As early as February 1910 the Australasian Union Conference had established a small printing plant at Sukabumi, Java, called the Java Mission Press. It was under the supervision of R. W. Munson, who had served in Sumatra earlier and had also been employed at the Avondale Press, Australia, for some time. He was assisted at the Java Mission Press by E. K. Hungerford and a man from Singapore named Lee; later by Immanuel Siregar, who had been his first Indonesian convert while working in Sumatra, and Samuel Rantung, one of the first converts to the Seventh-day Adventist Church in Jakarta, Java.

The Java Mission Press issued a quarterly Malay periodical called *Utusan Kebenaran Melayu* ("Messenger of Truth"); several Malay tracts ("Daniel 7," "About Opium Smoking," "Cigarettes," "The Lord's Sabbath," "The End of the World"); two Sundanese tracts ("The Love of God"—the first chapter of *Steps to Christ,* by Ellen White—and "Creation," by J. E. Fulton); and *Christ Our Saviour,* by Ellen White, all of which had been translated by R. W. Munson and formerly printed at the

Avondale Press in Australia. Another book was also prepared by R. W. Munson containing a series of Bible studies, and it was called *Pelajaran Kitab Alkudus,* later *Saksi Kebenaran.* It was a translation of a book on doctrines by G. B. Starr.

After the Dutch government refused to grant permission for Seventh-day Adventists to do missionary work in Sukabumi, the press was moved to Jakarta in April 1911. It was later sold and a larger printing plant erected in Singapore, which was dedicated on Mar. 10, 1920.

Because it was less expensive and more convenient to print in Indonesia, the editorial staff was transferred to Bandung, Java, in March 1929 and located at Naripan 72; there was a publishing house board, a manager, and a book depot that distributed the publications through the Adventist Book Centers, but the printing was done by commercial firms.

After years of operation in this manner, a new building for offices and factory was constructed in Cimindi, a western suburb of Bandung, in 1954. The publishing house staff moved in during January 1955, and the plant was dedicated Feb. 18. The building was substantially enlarged in 1967, and again in 1974. An auditorium was added in 1978.

The one-story brick-and-concrete building faces the main east-west highway through Bandung. The various departments function in separate rooms; an assembly hall seats more than 100; a small English-Indonesian library is available; and a conference room was recently developed. One truck is used for delivery and pickup.

The pressroom operates one Heidelberg SORD, and two Heidelberg KORDs; and one Heidelberg cylinder press—all one color. New equipment has also been purchased for use in the composition room, offset section, and the bindery. These include a Roland Patva 2C (one color) in 1976; a Hamada (one color) in 1990; a Mueller (two colors), eight computers, a camera, and gang stitching machine in 1991.

The house served approximately 1,000 literature evangelists in 1992 and more than 120,000 church members. Subscription literature includes a monthly health journal, *Rumah Tangga dan Kesehatan,* and a list of 72 titles including *Kebahagiaan Sejati* ("Steps to Christ"); *Kerinduan Segala Zaman* ("Desire of Ages"); *Narkotik; Menu Sehat* ("Vegetarian Cookbook"); *Penjaga Kesehatan* (medical book); *Sahabat Anakanak* ("My Bible Friends"). Also included are stop-smoking, AIDS, and family planning materials; *The Great Controversy; Bible Readings;* and *Maranatha.*

The house attempts to meet the needs of the constituency of both Indonesian unions by providing Sabbath school lesson quarterlies, mission quarterlies, visual aids, church songbooks, and departmental supplies as well as the monthly church paper.

Managers: W. Köster, 1929-1937; H.E.R. Schell, 1938; A. I. Krautschick, 1939; I. E. Gillis, 1940-1941; H.E.R. Schell, 1942, 1945-1946; E. van Alphen, 1947-1948; H.E.R. Schell, 1949-1952; E. A. Pender, 1953-1958; L. E. Barber, 1959-1965; J. H. Lesiasel, 1965-1973; B. T. Styadi, 1973-1978; Nootje Sasela, 1979; Kaleb Onsoe, 1980-1984; Lambok Silitonga, 1985-1988; Djinan Sinaga, 1989- .

INDONESIA UNION COLLEGE (Universitas Advent Indonesia). A coeducational boarding school on the senior college level, operated by the West Indonesia Union Mission on an estate of about 52 acres (20 hectares), 12 miles (20 kilometers) north of Bandung, Java. In 1993 the school had an enrollment of 910 and a staff of 90 (50 of them teachers). The students are mostly Indonesians, with some students from Malaysia. More than 80 percent are from Seventh-day Adventist homes; the rest are non-Christians or from other Christian groups.

History. *Training School.* The first SDA school for the training of workers in Indonesia was opened in 1929 at Tjimindi, near Bandung, Java. It was named the Opleidingsschool der Advent-Zending (listed in the *Yearbook* as Tjimindi Training School; after 1939, as Netherlands East Indies Training School). Earlier, when the Netherlands East Indies (now Indonesia) was a part of the Malayan Union Mission, with headquarters in Singapore, all Indonesian workers were trained in Singapore.

When the school opened (under the direction of H. Eelsing, with L.M.D. Wortman and K. Mandias as teachers), only a two-year ministerial training course was offered. At the first graduation, held in the fall of 1931, seven of the original 16 students received diplomas.

From 1929 to 1942 the school had an average enrollment of fewer than 30 students. When in 1936 an orphanage, which had been opened in Bandung the preceding year, was moved to Tjimindi and operated in connection with the school, it became evident that the Tjimindi property was not large enough for future development. Consequently a larger tract of land was purchased at Gadobangkong, a village a short distance west of Bandung. Buildings were erected, and the school was moved to the new campus in 1938. The orphanage remained at Tjimindi and was later closed. The new facilities enabled the school to accept more students. World War II forced it to close in 1942. Several of the teachers were placed in concentration camps, where two of them, L.M.D. Wortman and M. van Emmerick, subsequently died.

When peace returned, the buildings were quickly rehabilitated. In 1948 the school reopened under a new name, Indonesia Union Seminary. Under the instruction of Isaac C. Schmidt, a two-year ministerial course was again offered. The student body numbered 45, of whom four were young women.

Junior College. Up until this time the main aim of the school had been to train ministerial workers. In 1949 the entire educational system was revised in order to provide an education for all SDA young people. To accomplish this, a four-year secondary school was opened, which later expanded to a six-year program in harmony with the Indonesian government's educational system. Also in 1949 the ministerial training program was incorporated into a regular junior college curriculum. The college department also offered a normal course under the leadership of Lloyd W. Mauldin.

With the enlarged curriculum, the annual enrollment increased rapidly. Two factors contributed to this: a growing appreciation for Christian education and a steadily increasing church membership. However, the five-acre (two-hectare) tract of land at Cadobangkong was not large enough to provide for the needed expansion, so in 1953 the present school site of 57 acres (22.7 hectares) of fertile soil was purchased, about 12 miles (20 kilometers) north of Bandung near the village of Cisarua. Some abandoned dairy barns near the site were rented for use as temporary dormitories, classrooms, and teachers' homes, and in January 1954 the school opened. As the students watched the new buildings being erected across the valley from their barn homes, they called the new site the Promised Land, and longed for their "exodus from Egypt." By the spring of 1957 the last of the students had moved out of the cow barns.

Senior College. After that there was growth both in physical plant and in enrollment. A fourth year in the ministerial course was authorized, and in 1964 the school was recognized by the General Conference as a four-year senior college, with majors in theology, education, and accounting, and minors in the same subjects, and also a two-year curriculum in secretarial science, elementary education, and home economics. The Indonesian government approved the status of the college and the university in 1982.

Most of the younger denominational workers and leaders in Indonesia are graduates of this college. Graduates are serving overseas also.

Principals/Presidents: H. Eelsing, 1929-1931; L.M.D. Wortman, 1931-1943; I. C. Schmidt, 1948-1949; A. M. Bartlett, 1949-1953; B. A. Aaen, 1953-1955; L. A. Benzinger, 1955-1957; B. A. Aaen, 1957-1962; Percy Paul, 1962-1963; Bryce Newell, 1963-1965; G. H. Fisher, 1965-1970; A. Simorangkir, 1970-1974; R. H. Tauran (acting), 1974; D. R. Halenz, 1975; R. A. Nainggolan, 1976-1978; U. Aritonang, 1979-1980; R. A. Hutagaol, 1981-1990; T. L. Tobing, 1990-1992; R. A. Hutagaol, 1992- .

INDUSTRIAL INSTITUTE. *See* Union Adventist Educational Complex.

INDUSTRIAS COVAC SA. *See* Inter-American Health Food Company, Costa Rica Branch.

INFANT DEDICATION. *See* Child Dedication.

INFORMANT. *See North American Regional Voice.*

INGATHERING (known formerly as Harvest Ingathering; also called in various parts of the world by other names). An annual worldwide denominational appeal to, and gathering in of funds from, the general public. The campaign serves a double purpose: (1) it provides funds to aid a world program that includes medical, educational, welfare, and evangelistic projects, which bring relief and uplift to humanity and a living Christ to the world, and (2) it is a means of making contacts in millions of homes, whose occupants are presented with a special issue of a magazine that describes the worldwide work of Seventh-day Adventists and that offers the opportunity of enrolling in a Bible correspondence course. This solicitation has been conducted every year since 1903 and has been extended to all countries where there is SDA work, where permitted by the government. Solicitors are unpaid volunteers from among the church members in all walks of life.

The Seventh-day Adventist humanitarian program of welfare, medical, educational, and evangelistic projects is the church's attempt to follow the example of Jesus Christ, who went about doing good, healing the sick, teaching the people, and preaching the gospel. In North America increasingly larger amounts of the Ingathering funds are being used each year for Community Services that extend emergency relief irrespective of race, creed, or color.

Funds sent to overseas countries provide for many projects, such as clinics, dispensaries, leper colonies, mission schools—often the only facilities available to large populations. At the same time, about one third of the total funds collected in the Ingathering campaigns is contributed by donors in overseas countries. In many of these countries, significant projects have been carried out with such funds. For example, in China several hospitals were established with funds raised locally.

The funds gathered in this campaign comprise only about 10 percent of the total annual budget of the General Conference, the major source of funding being the tithes and offerings of SDA members.

Origin. The idea of giving away magazines and asking, in return, for contributions for the mission program originated with Jasper Wayne, a traveling salesperson of nursery stock, who lived in Sac City, Iowa. As he related the experience in 1903, he ordered 50 copies of a special issue of the *Signs of the Times.*

Receiving them at the post office, he unwrapped them and began to hand them out to people standing in the lobby, saying that any money received would go to the cause of foreign missions. To his surprise he disposed of them immediately and received more than $4 for missions.

About 10 days later another package of 50 papers arrived, sent by mistake. He took these papers with him in his buggy to use as occasion offered. The first man he approached gave 15 cents and the next 18 cents, and then a woman gave 25 cents. This gave him courage to suggest 25 cents thereafter; some gave larger sums. Receiving about $26 by distributing these 50 papers and realizing the possibilities in this plan of securing money for missions, he at once ordered 400 copies more to carry with him. In about a year he had raised about $100 with them and had greatly enjoyed explaining the work of the church.

In 1904, at a camp meeting held at Omaha, Nebraska, he interested the president of the Nebraska Conference in his plan. Though reluctant to speak before a large audience, he mustered his courage and explained his method at one of the meetings. Also, he had a talk with Ellen White, who was present at the camp meeting. She manifested a deep interest and gave the plan her endorsement *(Christian Service,* pp. 167-177).

In 1908 the General Conference recommended the Ingathering plan to all churches, approving the use of a special Thanksgiving number of the *Review and Herald* for informing the public of SDA work, and in gathering Thanksgiving gifts for missions.

Objectives and Goals. The Ingathering program, promoted by the GC Church Ministries Department, with financial aspects managed by the GC Treasury Department. The program has five objectives: (1) 100 percent membership participation, (2) total coverage of territory, (3) searching for persons interested in the gospel, (4) increased offerings, and (5) a thorough follow-up of interests.

During the early years of Ingathering no specific financial objectives were set. In 1915 members were encouraged to set for themselves voluntary individual goals as to the total amount raised. The principle of an individual goal was recommended to all divisions of the world field, and in 1934 it was recommended that conferences assign Ingathering goals for each church. In 1935 the Autumn Council recommended the Minute Man goal, representing appropriations from North America to maintain the work overseas for one minute. Beginning in 1948, the Bible correspondence school advertisement and coupon became a regular feature in the Ingathering magazines. In 1959 the Minute Man goal was replaced by the individual Silver Vanguard objective of $25.

Methods. The campaign, officially limited to a maximum of six weeks, is conducted by various methods—street solicitation, visits to places of business and to homes, singing bands, Christmas caroling, and correspondence.

Results. Through 1992, $509,380,626 had been gathered in the countries of the world. The sum of $67,247,599 was raised in the five-year period 1988-1992.

INGERSOLL, OLIVE GRACE (PERRY) (1873-1955). Medical missionary to India; wife of Dr. Robert S. Ingersoll. At the age of 10 she was baptized by the Free Will

Baptists, but her parents shortly afterward accepted the Seventh-day Adventist faith, and she was rebaptized in 1886. In 1892 she began work as corresponding secretary of the Michigan Tract Society, and in 1893 worked at the Battle Creek Sanitarium. The next year she enrolled in the medical course at the University of Michigan, from which she graduated in 1898. That same year she married Robert S. Ingersoll, a fellow graduate, went with him to India, and there shared his work. Upon their return to the United States she joined the staff of the Washington Sanitarium, then helped her husband operate a private sanitarium and later practiced privately with him and their son.

INGERSOLL, ROBERT STEPHENSON (1874-1955). Medical missionary to India. His parents became Seventh-day Adventists shortly after his birth, and he joined the church at the age of 14. In 1898 he graduated from the medical course at the University of Michigan, married a fellow graduate, Olive Perry, and sailed to India, where the two doctors joined the pioneer SDA medical missionary O. G. Place in Calcutta. After Place returned to the United States, the Ingersolls carried on the work of the Calcutta Sanitarium and helped to expand SDA medical work in India. Returning about 1909, Dr. Robert Ingersoll became superintendent of the Washington Sanitarium. Later, after briefly operating a private sanitarium, he headed the Florida Sanitarium at Orlando. From 1918 to 1930 he was superintendent of the Madison, Wisconsin, Sanitarium, after which he practiced privately in Wisconsin.

INGS, WILLIAM (d. 1897). Publishing house worker, minister. He was born in Hampshire County, England, but grew up in the United States. As a young man he entered the employ of the Review and Herald publishing house in Battle Creek. In 1877 he was sent to Switzerland to assist J. N. Andrews in equipping and organizing the new publishing house in Basel. On May 23, 1878, he went to England, the land of his birth, for a short vacation in Southampton. Before returning to Basel two weeks later he had won two converts to the Seventh-day Adventist faith. When Andrews heard the result of this brief visit, he arranged for Ings to return to England to establish the work there in that country.

Back in Southampton, Ings began distributing SDA publications and holding meetings. After 16 weeks he reported 10 people keeping the Sabbath. In answer to his earnest appeals for an experienced man to help him the General Conference sent J. N. Loughborough in December 1878 to take charge of the work in the British Isles. After this Ings left most of the preaching to Loughborough while he devoted most of his time to the circulation of SDA publications. The first baptism took place on Feb. 8, 1880.

In 1882 Ings returned to the United States and entered the work in the California Conference, where he was ordained in 1884. In 1886 he was called back to England to help establish a publishing house in London. In 1889 he returned to his post in California and remained there until his death in 1897.

INISHA COMMUNITY MEDICAL CENTRE. A 46-bed medical institution that has grown out of the missionary activities of Ile-Ife Hospital *(see* Seventh-day Adventist Hospital Ile-Ife) in Nigeria. It is owned by the Inisha community, but the church operates the institution.

The clinic became a hospital in the early seventies when Dr. Gulleng was the medical director. The facilities (January 1993) include two wards, an Outpatient Department, one X-ray building, a medical laboratory, stores, kitchens, and two resident houses for medical doctors. In 1993 Inisha had 30,000 patients, 200 prenatal visits, and 300 deliveries.

Medical Directors: J. Sodeko, 1985-1991; J. O. Dare, 1992-1994; E. O. Aremu, 1994- .

INSIDE REPORT, THE (1983-). An illustrated two-color monthly magazine. Its circulation is 35,000, and it is free upon request. *The Inside Report* is sent automatically to anyone who donates $5 or more to Amazing Facts. The magazine contains articles of inspiration, poems, evangelism and radio/TV schedules, and news about Amazing Facts. It is published by Amazing Facts, P.O. Box 680, Frederick, Maryland. Managing editor, Debra J. Hicks.

INSIGHT (1970- ; weekly [except June-August 1974, 1975]; RH, 1994 circulation, 20,000; file in RH). A 16-page paper for readers ages 14 through 19.

Publication of *The Youth's Instructor* ceased in April 1970 under Editor Walter T. Crandall. A new youth magazine, *Insight,* began publication in May 1970. *Insight* developed from a special committee set up by the General Conference when it became apparent that the church needed to update its senior youth magazine.

The emphasis of *Insight* is the mission of Jesus Christ and its implications for young Christians. It offers practical ways of understanding Scripture and living the Christlike life. Helping young people live successfully through the trials and confusion of the last days is a prime objective.

Insight encourages reader involvement and builds Christian commitment and a sense of community for Seventh-day Adventist teens through a blend of feature articles, short stories, poetry, question-and-answer columns, youth testimonials, Bible explanation, youth service reports, and how-to articles. Articles are approximately 50 percent assigned and 50 percent freelance.

Editors: Donald Yost, 1970-1971; Roland Hegstad (acting), 1971-1972; Michael Jones, 1972-1975; Donald John, 1975-1981; Dan Fahrbach, 1982-1985; Christopher Blake, 1986-1993; Lori Tripp Peckham, 1993- .

INSIGHT/OUT (1988- ; monthly; RH; file in RH). A 16-page outreach paper for readers ages 14 through 19.

Insight/Out is a monthly edition of the weekly *Insight* subscription. It focuses on Christian life-changing themes while avoiding SDA jargon. *Insight* subscribers are encouraged to share this edition with non-SDA relatives, neighbors, classmates, workmates, and acquaintances and to order subscriptions for outreach to nonbelieving teens.

INSPIRATION OF SCRIPTURE. In their statement of fundamental beliefs Seventh-day Adventists set forth their position on the inspiration of Scripture as follows: "The Holy Scriptures, Old and New Testaments, are the written Word of God, given by divine inspiration through holy men of God who spoke and wrote as they were moved by the Holy Spirit. In this Word, God has committed to man the knowledge necessary for salvation. The Holy Scriptures are the infallible revelation of His will. They are the standard of character, the test of experience, the authoritative revealer of doctrines, and the trustworthy record of God's acts in history (2 Peter 1:20, 21; 2 Tim. 3:16, 17; Ps. 119:105; Prov. 30:5, 6; Isa. 8:20; John 17:17; 1 Thess. 2:13; Heb. 4:12)" *(Church Manual* [1990], p. 23).

SDAs do not believe in verbal inspiration, according to the usual meaning of the term, but in what may properly be called thought inspiration. The SDA point of view on this matter has best been set forth by Ellen White: "The Bible is written by inspired men, but it is not God's mode of thought and expression. It is that of humanity. God, as a writer, is not represented. Men will often say such an expression is not like God. But God has not put Himself in words, in logic, in rhetoric, on trial in the Bible. The writers of the Bible were God's penmen, not His pen. Look at the different writers.

"It is not the words of the Bible that are inspired, but the men that were inspired. Inspiration acts not on the man's words or his expressions but on the man himself, who, under the influence of the Holy Ghost, is imbued with thoughts. But the words receive the impress of the individual mind. The divine mind is diffused. The divine mind and will is combined with the human mind and will; thus the utterances of the man are the word of God" (1SM 21).

"The Bible, with its God-given truths expressed in the language of men, presents a union of the divine and the human. Such a union existed in the nature of Christ, who was the Son of God and the Son of man. Thus it is true of the Bible, as it was of Christ, that 'the Word was made flesh, and dwelt among us' (John 1:14).

"Written in different ages, by men who differed widely in rank and occupation, and in mental and spiritual endowments, the books of the Bible present a wide contrast in style, as well as a diversity in the nature of the subjects unfolded. Different forms of expression are employed by different writers; often the same truth is more strikingly presented by one than by another. And as several writers present a subject under varied aspects and relations, there may appear, to the superficial, careless, or prejudiced reader, to be discrepancy or contradiction, where the thoughtful, reverent student, with clearer insight, discerns the underlying harmony.

"As presented through different individuals, the truth is brought out in its varied aspects. One writer is more strongly impressed with one phase of the subject; he grasps those points that harmonize with his experience or with his power of perception and appreciation; another seizes upon a different phase; and each, under the guidance of the Holy Spirit, presents what is most forcibly impressed upon his own mind—a different aspect of the truth in each, but a perfect harmony through all. And the truths thus revealed unite to form a perfect whole, adapted to meet the wants of men in all the circumstances and experiences of life" (GC vi).

The original autographs of Scripture have, of course, long since been lost, and the sacred documents have passed through the hands of countless copyists, redactors, and translators. Naturally, there have been certain modifications but, almost without exception, these have been of relatively minor importance. The Bible has been transmitted to us with vastly greater accuracy and reliability than any other similar ancient document. Of textual changes such as these, Ellen White wrote: "I saw that God had especially guarded the Bible; yet when copies of it were few, learned men had in some instances changed the words, thinking that they were making it more plain, when in reality they were mystifying that which was plain, by causing it to lean to their established views, which were governed by tradition. But I saw that the Word of God, as a whole, is a perfect chain, one portion linking into and explaining another. True seekers for truth need not err" (EW 220, 221).

"Some look to us gravely and say, 'Don't you think there might have been some mistake in the copyist or in the translators?' This is all probable, and the mind that is so narrow that it will hesitate and stumble over this possibility or probability would be just as ready to stumble over the mysteries of the Inspired Word, because their feeble minds cannot see through the purposes of God. . . . All the mistakes will not cause trouble to one soul, or cause any feet to stumble, that would not manufacture difficulties from the plainest revealed truth" (MS 16, 1888; *The Testimony of Jesus*, pp. 12 13).

We should not "lament that these difficulties exist, but accept them as permitted by the wisdom of God." The Bible "is plain on every point essential to the salvation of the soul" (5T 706).

Despite the finite limitations of human language, and of the human writers, and of those through whose hands the sacred documents have since passed, the Scriptures as we have them today are sufficient to convey a knowledge of God's infinite purpose for humanity and to lead all to salvation in Jesus Christ. Essential truth, perhaps obscure in one passage, shines forth with clear luster elsewhere. In their present state, and taken as a whole, the Scriptures are altogether adequate, for all practical purposes, to fulfill the purpose for which they were intended by their divine Author.

INSTITUT ADVENTISTE DE LUKANGA. *See* Lukanga Adventist Institute.

INSTITUT ADVENTISTE DU SALÈVE. *See* Salève Adventist Institute.

INSTITUT DE RWAMIKO. *See* Rwamiko Institute.

INSTITUT DE SONGA. *See* Songa Institute.

INSTITUT SANITAIRE. *See* Lake Geneva Sanitarium.

INSTITUT TECHNIQUE DE LUKANGA. *See* Lukanga Adventist Institute.

INSTITUTE OF ART AND GRAPHIC PRINTING. *See* Romania.

INSTITUTE OF CHURCH MINISTRY. An official department of the Seventh-day Adventist Theological Seminary at Andrews University, founded in 1979 as the Institute of Church Ministry by Desmond Cummings, Jr. The purpose of this new institute was to share the expertise and resources of Andrews University with the SDA Church in North America, thus aiding denominational decision-makers and facilitating the larger church in the accomplishment of its goals. As such, ICM serves as the North American Division strategic resource center, with a sustaining grant from the division. In 1993 ICM became the home of the Center for Latino Research on Religion and Society, also sponsored by the North American Division. In addition to its ongoing relationship with NAD, ICM provides services on a fee basis for other denominational entities. It lists the General Conference, local conferences and churches, and SDA journals among its clients.

The work of ICM is based on the belief that the tools of social science can join with biblical and theological insights in advancing the objectives of the church. Its mission is conducted through field-based research, preparing marketing reports based on census data, publications, preparation of various materials, information processing, and consultation. Some of the areas in which ICM has been active are a 10-year longitudinal study of the retention of youth in the SDA Church, lay member involvement in local congregations, the most effective training for pastoral ministry, SDA Church growth factors, SDA ministerial morale, human relations, youth drug usage, church giving patterns, preferences of readers of the *Adventist Review,* SDA women in leadership, SDA Hispanics, and attitudes of SDA members in a variety of areas. The information gained has been shared with the church through published books, manuals, pamphlets, journal articles, and research reports. Some findings have been shared with the wider world through publications in scholarly journals. Institute personnel also make presentations at church conventions, ministers' meetings, teachers' meetings, camp meetings, and in local congregations.

In addition to full-time staff, ICM employs students to assist in the various tasks. These include seminary students in training for ministry, who gain valuable practical experience relevant to their future vocation. ICM also consults with other Andrews University faculty members in departments such as marketing, communications, and behavioral science when their expertise can prove beneficial in meeting a challenge. Desmond Cummings, Jr., served as director of the institute from 1979 to 1984. Roger L. Dudley has served as director from 1984.

INSTITUTE OF WORLD MISSION. An entity of the Seventh-day Adventist Church that came into existence by Annual Council action in 1956. Because the missionary situation was radically changing at the time, it was felt that missionaries needed better training to cope with the new and ever-changing challenges of cross-cultural missions. It was voted that all newly appointed missionaries, missionaries on furlough, and national workers returning to their home fields would receive an intensive missionary training of six weeks' duration in such areas as missionary anthropology, the Adventist message in a changing world, health and hygiene, principles of Adventist mission work, and specific area studies.

The Annual Council action of 1956 was first implemented in the summer of 1966, when Myrl O. Manley and Gottfried Oosterwal led out in a four-week intensive training institute. It was conducted on the campus of Andrews University and attended by 21 newly appointed and furloughing missionaries.

From that year on, intensive training sessions on Adventist world mission have been conducted every summer. They became known as the Summer Institute of World Mission. At first they were of four weeks' duration. In 1971 an extra week was added, and the next year the Annual Council action of 1956 was fully implemented when another week was added to the program. In that same year the name Summer Institute of World Mission was dropped and the name Institute of World Mission adopted. Soon after the first training began, mission administrators in the field saw the great difference this new missionary training made in the life and work of the missionaries. They insisted that all missionaries should attend these institutes before departing for their fields of labor. In 1972 another institute was added, conducted in the winter. As the number of missionaries grew in this heyday of Adventist overseas missions, a third was added in 1975. From that year until the present three intensive missionary training programs have been conducted every year in North America: one in the summer, one in the fall, and one in the spring.

The effectiveness of such missionary training showed itself in many different ways: a sharp decline in the number of missionaries returning prematurely, an increase in the number of those who stayed longer than one term of service, less suffering from culture shock, and greater effectiveness in missionaries' work, including language learning.

As North America was not the only home base of missionaries at the time, areas such as Europe and Australia also showed an interest in offering better training for their missionaries. First in 1972, then in 1975, and again in 1978, Gottfried Oosterwal, who in 1969 had been appointed the director of the Institute of World Mission, led out in missionary training institutes in Europe. The first two were held on the campus of Newbold College, England, and the last one at the seminary at Collonges, France. Three years later these institutes led to the establishment of the European Institute of World Mission under the direction of Borge Schantz. In the same way, the Institute of World Mission spawned the Australian Institute of World Mission. Dr. Oosterwal first led out in a special missionary training program at Avondale College in 1981, and then every year from 1983 on. In 1993 the Australian Institute of World Mission was established with its own director, John Gate, and its own board.

At first the Institute of World Mission was organizationally linked to the newly established Department of World Mission at the SDA Theological Seminary, of which Gottfried Oosterwal was the founder and first chair (1969). As the institutes continued to grow in size and in number, and as new functions were added to their operation, a separate organization was needed for a more efficient operation. This happened in 1981 when what is now known as the Seventh-day Adventist Institute of World Mission was established, with its own board (chaired by the secretary of the General Conference), its own budgets, its own staff, and its own building. Dr. Oosterwal was called to lead out in this new and expanded venture of the institute. Besides the training of missionaries around the world, other functions given to the Institute of World Mission included research and publications on missions, missionary consultations in the field, and the promotion of missions in the SDA Church, worldwide.

As the institute grew in size, tasks, and functions, more staff were added. In 1971 Russell Staples joined Gottfried Oosterwal as a staff member of the Institute and the Department of World Mission. Four years later Werner Vyhmeister was called to join the staff, and in 1980 Nancy Vyhmeister was invited to join. After the separation of the Institute of World Mission from the Department of World Mission at the SDA Theological Seminary, Gottfried Oosterwal and Werner Vyhmeister stayed with the institute, while Russell Staples and Nancy Vyhmeister remained with the department.

In 1987 the institute ventured out into a new endeavor: the training of nonchurch workers for their assignment in cultures other than their own. This included business leaders, health personnel, educators, and people in technical aid and development. To accomplish this new venture, a separate organization was called into existence: the Center for Intercultural Relations. Structurally, this center is part of Andrews University. Gottfried Oosterwal is its director.

As of January 1993 the staff of the institute consisted of Gottfried Oosterwal, director; Jon Dybdahl, associate director; Reinder Bruinsma, staff member; and Mrs. Pam Swanson, administrative assistant. The institute is located in the Sutherland House on the campus of Andrews University, Berrien Springs, Michigan.

INSTITUTES OF SCIENTIFIC STUDIES FOR THE PREVENTION OF ALCOHOLISM. Organizations set up in various parts of the world to carry on research work and provide training in all phases of the alcohol problem. Sponsored by the National Committees for the Prevention of Alcoholism in the respective countries, these institutes carry on educational programs for the prevention of alcoholism through publications, films, forums, and radio and television programs.

Educationally, the institute conducts sessions at which instruction is given on the graduate level. The institute course of study is not designed primarily for the layman, though many civic-minded laymen attend the courses; it is intended for people on the professional level, such as teachers, educators, law-enforcement officials, public and mental health leaders, physicians, editors, social and welfare workers, and religious leaders.

Each session consists of lectures, discussion periods, seminars, forums, workshops, and field trips. Nationally and internationally known authorities lecture in their special fields. The scientific facts and basic information gained qualify the graduates of the sessions to work more effectively toward the prevention of alcoholism. In some of the sessions the students receive graduate university credit for their study. Selected lectures are transcribed and made available for permanent reference, and basic materials are published in reprint form for professional use.

The first Institute of Scientific Studies was established in 1950 at Loma Linda, California, at the Loma Linda University medical school. Since that time more than 1,000 students have pursued the annual course of study offered by that institute. In 1961 this institute began to offer a unique annual service to professional groups, the first Medical Seminar on Alcoholism being conducted that year in Los Angeles and in the same year the first in-service training workshop for public school teachers.

The second institute, established at American University in Washington, D.C., in 1956, became known as the Washington Institute of Scientific Studies.

The All-European Institute, sponsored by the European Bloc of the International Commission in cooperation with the International Bureau Against Alcoholism, was launched in 1955. Its first four sessions were held in Geneva, with subsequent sessions being held in various cities, including Vienna, Paris, Lausanne, Warsaw, London, Amsterdam, and Oslo. This organization is now called the International Council on Alcohol and Alcohol Addicts. The ICPA, apart from this cooperation, conducts seminars in the European area.

The All-Asian Institute, sponsored by the

Southern Asia Bloc of the International Commission, was launched in 1956, and was conducted on the Wilson College campus in Bombay, India. Many prominent Indian leaders serve on the institute committee and take part in seminars.

The Australian Institute, plans for the launching of which were laid at the organizational meeting of the Australian National Committee on Oct. 13, 1958, conducted its first session on the medical college campus of the University of Sydney, Jan. 18-29, 1960.

The South African National Committee was organized on Sept. 14, 1959. Its first session was conducted on the campus of the Witwatersrand University, Jan. 2-13, 1961.

The first session of the Philippine Institute, conducted under the auspices of the Philippine National Committee, was conducted on the campus of the University of the Philippines, Apr. 10-21, 1961. This committee has continued to hold annual institutes and seminars throughout the Philippines with great success.

Other national institutes and seminars as a part of the ICPA program have been held in Mauritius, Cameroon, Kenya, Tanzania, Malagasy, Turkey, Korea, Japan, Sri Lanka, Israel, Iran, Zambia, Central African Republic, Togo, Brazil, and Yugoslavia. The First World Congress of the ICPA was held in Afghanistan in 1972.

INSTITUTION MEDICALE "VIE ET SANTE." *See* Life and Health Medical Institution.

INSTITUTIONAL CONSULTING SERVICE. *See* Philanthropic Service for Institutions.

INSTITUTIONAL RESEARCH. An activity that collects and analyzes data to provide information for administrative decision-making. Currently serving the Board of Higher Education, this service was begun in 1972 with the formation of the Board of Higher Education and since 1988 has been directed by Dallas Kindopp.

INSTITUTIONAL SERVICES/ESDA. The former purchasing agency of the General Conference designed to serve the denomination's institutions and its workers in the United States and overseas. It was administered by a general manager, assistant managers (East and West Coasts, U.S.A.), and treasurers, and had ordering, sales, automobile, export, and shipping departments. The sales department also distributed supplies, books, and syllabuses sponsored by the Educational, Health, Ministerial, Publishing, and Youth departments of the General Conference.

ESDA History. ESDA was a trade name, the significance of which is no longer known, but is believed to be the acronym for Seventh-day Adventist prefixed with an E, either for euphony or standing for "East," since there was an East Coast as well as a West Coast branch of the organization. The agency originated in 1920 as the Purchasing Bureau composed of H. H. Cobban, J. J. Ireland, L. A. Hansen, C. W. Irwin, H. H. Hall, and a member each from the Review and Herald, Pacific Press, and Southern Publishing associations.

Previous to this a small store had been operated for a time in the basement of the General Conference office primarily for the handling of packaged foodstuffs for the office workers. L. A. Hansen, of the General Conference Medical Department, sensing that the overseas institutions, particularly sanitariums, needed help with their purchases, had made contact with various firms for discount purchasing. Later, schools and conference offices and institutions in foreign countries also were invited to channel their purchasing through the bureau, thus enabling all to receive lower prices.

In 1946 the name of Bureau was changed to Department of Purchase & Supply. In February 1947 the department was moved from two rooms in the basement of the General Conference building to what was then called the Northwestern Building (later renamed ESDA Building, at 107 Carroll Street, Takoma Park, Maryland).

During the early postwar years, when many articles were scarce, an unusually large amount of purchasing was carried on by ESDA for both overseas and North American organizations. As materials and products became more plentiful after the war years, the sales reached a level of approximately $2 million per year.

In 1950 the trade name of ESDA Sales & Service was adopted. Operation continued in the Northwestern Building until March of 1969 when the building was torn down to make way for the new General Conference office building, called the North Building. The administrative offices were moved to what had formerly been Dr. Queen's house at 7112 Willow Avenue. The rooms were remodeled and offices set up for the manager, export, and treasury sections. The store section was moved to the end of the warehouse building so as to continue to serve the local area on a limited basis. In June 1972, after the completion of the North Building, the administrative offices were moved to its fifth floor, with N. W. Litchfield, manager.

Institutional Services History. In 1956 John Knipschild, then superintendent of schools for the Southern California Conference, approached his conference president, R. R. Bietz, about experimenting in a new way of purchasing so as to save SDA schools and other SDA institutions purchasing funds by pooling the buying strength. Upon approval in the summer of 1956, bids were placed with leading manufacturers and distributors to supply for the school year 1956-1957, sanitary supplies, classroom paper supplies, sporting and playground equipment. As a result of the initial bid, more than $8,000 was saved over the preceding average five years of yearly purchasing. This was the beginning of developing a concept of buying to save metropolitan, urban and rural, large and small SDA institutions in their purchasing needs of all types of hardware and software supplies. This procedure was expanded and refined during the years that John Knipschild was superintendent of schools in the Southern California and Northern California conferences.

In 1968 the Pacific Union Conference invited Knipschild to join the Pacific Union as a full-time coordinating purchaser for the schools, churches, hospitals, rest homes, camps, and administrative office in its territory. At the same time, the North Pacific and Southwest unions requested to be a part of these pioneering services. The North Pacific employed James Costa to promote and clear orders for its union to Institutional Services/SDA—its first official name.

IS/ESDA History. During the summer of 1973 John Knipschild was invited by the General Conference to take over the management of ESDA and reorganize the denominational purchasing procedures so as to incorporate buying and distribution procedures for the whole world field. In August 1973 the ESDA nomenclature was expanded to its current official title of Institutional Services/ESDA (abbreviated IS/ESDA), which merged the two organizations into one facility to provide expanded services to the world field through its headquarters office located in the General Conference North Building. IS/ESDA eventually became Adventist World Purchasing Service, which continued purchasing for the world field for a number of years. AWPS was closed in 1992 after the General Conference determined that each division and institution could handle its own purchasing.

Purchasing Agents and Managers of ESDA: F. B. Knight, 1945-1950; J. McCartney, 1950-1956; O. A. Blake, 1956-1970; N. W. Litchfield, 1970-1973.

Purchasing Agents and Managers of IS/ESDA: J. F. Knipschild, 1973-1977; Erwin H. Mack, 1977-1982; John M. Stephenson, 1982-1992.

INSTITUTO ADVENTISTA AGRO-INDUSTRIAL. *See* Adventist Agricultural-Industrial Academy.

INSTITUTO ADVENTISTA BRASIL CENTRAL. *See* Central Brazil Academy.

INSTITUTO ADVENTISTA CRUZEIRO DO SUL. *See* Cruzeiro Do Sul Adventist Academy.

INSTITUTO ADVENTISTA DE BALCARCE. *See* Balcarce Adventist Academy.

INSTITUTO ADVENTISTA DE ENSINO. *See* Brazil College.

INSTITUTO ADVENTISTA DE ENSINO DE MINAS GERAIS. *See* Minas Gerais Adventist Academy.

INSTITUTO ADVENTISTA DE ENSINO DO NORDESTE. *See* Northeast Brazil College.

INSTITUTO ADVENTISTA DE LOS ANDES. *See* Andes Adventist Academy.

INSTITUTO ADVENTISTA DE MANAUS. *See* Manaus Adventist Academy.

INSTITUTO ADVENTISTA DE MORÓN. *See* Morón Adventist Academy.

INSTITUTO ADVENTISTA DE RESISTENCIA. *See* Resistencia Adventist Academy.

INSTITUTO ADVENTISTA DE SANTA FE. *See* Santa Fe Adventist Academy.

INSTITUTO ADVENTISTA DEL URUGUAY. *See* Uruguay Adventist Academy.

INSTITUTO ADVENTISTA FLORIDA. *See* Buenos Aires Adventist Academy.

INSTITUTO ADVENTISTA GRÃO PARÁ. *See* Grão Pará Adventist Academy.

INSTITUTO ADVENTISTA JUAN BAUTISTA ALBERDI. *See* Northeast Argentine Academy.

INSTITUTO ADVENTISTA LOS POLVORINES. *See* Los Polvorines Adventist Academy.

INSTITUTO ADVENTISTA PANAMEÑO. *See* Panama Adventist Institute.

INSTITUTO ADVENTISTA PARANÁENSE. *See* Paraná Adventist Academy.

INSTITUTO ADVENTISTA SÃO PAULO. *See* São Paulo Adventist Academy.

INSTITUTO ADVENTISTA TRANSAMAZONICO AGRO-INDUSTRIAL. *See* Agro-Industrial Adventist Trans-Amazon Academy.

INSTITUTO ADVENTISTA VELEZ SARSFIELD. *See* Velez Sarsfield Adventist Academy.

INSTITUTO ADVENTISTA VICTOR AMPUERO MATTA. *See* Victor Ampuero Matta Adventist Academy.

INSTITUTO BIBLICO. *See* Mexico; Universidad de Montemorelos.

INSTITUTO COLOMBO-VENEZOLANO. *See* Colombia Adventist University.

INSTITUTO COMERCIAL PROSPERIDAD. *See* Mexico.

INSTITUTO CRUZEIRO DO SUL. *See* Rio Grande Do Sul Academy.

INSTITUTO DE ESTUDIOS POR CORRESPONDENCIA. *See* River Plate Adventist University.

INSTITUTO EDUCACIONAL E AGRÍCOLA PETRÓPOLIS. *See* Petrópolis Adventist Academy.

INSTITUTO INDUSTRIAL (Peru). *See* Union Adventist Educational Complex.

INSTITUTO INDUSTRIAL BOLIVIANO ADVENTISTA. *See* Bolivia Adventist Educational Complex.

INSTITUTO JUAN BAUTISTA ALBERDI. *See* Northeast Argentina Academy.

INSTITUTO MÉDICO ADVENTISTA. *See* Chile.

INSTITUTO PETRÓPOLITANO ADVENTISTA DE ENSINO. *See* Petrópolis Adventist Academy.

INSTITUTO RURAL ADVENTISTA DO NORDESTE. *See* Northeast Brazil Academy.

INSTITUTO TEOLÓGICO ADVENTISTA. *See* Petrópolis Adventist Academy.

INSTITUTO UNIVERSITARIO ECLESIÁSTICO ADVENTISTA. *See* Venezuelan Adventist Ecclesiastical University.

INSTITUTO VICENTE SUAREZ. *See* Vicente Suarez Institute.

INSTITUTO VOCACIONAL ADVENTISTA DEL LLANO. *See* El Llano Adventist Vocational Institute.

INSTITUTO VOCACIONAL DE VENEZUELA. *See* Venezuela; Venezuelan Adventist Ecclesiastical University.

INSTITUTUL THEOLOGIC ADVENTIST. *See* Romanian Adventist Theological Institute.

INSURANCE, PROPERTY. *See* Risk and Insurance Management.

INSURANCE SERVICE OF THE GENERAL CONFERENCE. *See* Risk and Insurance Management.

INTER-AMERICAN DIVISION. A large unit of church organization to which is allotted the following territory: Anguilla, Antigua and Barbuda, Aruba, Bahamas, Barbados, Belize, British Virgin Islands, Cayman Islands, Colombia, Costa Rica, Cuba,

Dominica, Dominican Republic, El Salvador, French Guiana, Grenada, Guadeloupe, Guatemala, Guyana, Haiti, Honduras, Jamaica, Martinique, Mexico, Montserrat, Netherlands Antilles, Nicaragua, Panama, Puerto Rico, St. Kitts and Nevis, St. Lucia, St. Vincent and the Grenadines, Suriname, Trinidad and Tobago, Turks and Caicos Islands, United States Virgin Islands, and Venezuela.

Statistics (1992): churches, 4,617; members, 1,385,517; primary schools, 688; ordained ministers, 1,133; licensed ministers, 830; teachers, 3,274. Headquarters: 760 Ponce de Leon Boulevard, Coral Gables, Florida. Official organ: *Inter-American News Flashes* (in three languages).

In the territory that now comprises the Inter-American Division, various groups of church organizations have existed—such as the West Indian Union Conference, the Northern Spanish American Missions, the Northern Latin American Missions (unorganized), and the North Latin-American Group—with various changes in names and territories. The Inter-American Division was formed in 1922 by combining the former North Latin-American Group, the Mexican and Central American missions, and certain unattached conferences, among them the Jamaica, South Caribbean, and West Caribbean conferences. At the time of formation the new division embraced the Caribbean Union Mission and the Central American Mission.

The division was organized in 1922 with 221 churches and 8,146 members.

Constituent Organizations. The Inter-American Division comprises 12 union missions and conferences.

1. *Caribbean Union Conference* (organized 1926; reorganized 1945, 1966, 1975, 1983, 1986). Territory: Anguilla, Antigua and Barbuda, Barbados, British Virgin Islands, Dominica, Grenada, Guyana, Montserrat, St. Kitts and Nevis, St. Lucia, St. Vincent and the Grenadines, Suriname, Trinidad and Tobago, United States Virgin Islands, Saba, St. Eustatius, and St. Maarten (Dutch section) in the Netherlands Antilles. Statistics (1992): churches, 415; members, 127,036; primary schools, 38; ordained ministers, 128; licensed ministers, 91; teachers, 316. Headquarters: 7 Rookery Nook, Maraval, Trinidad, West Indies. Official organ: *Caribbean Union Gleanings.*

Constituent organizations and their territories—*East Caribbean Conference* (organized 1926; reorganized 1945, 1960, 1975): Barbados, Dominica, St. Lucia, and St. Vincent and the Grenadines; *Grenada Mission* (organized 1983): Carriacou, Grenada, and Petit Martinique; *Guyana Conference* (organized 1926; reorganized 1945): Guyana; *North Caribbean Conference* (organized 1975): Anguilla, Antigua and Barbuda, British Virgin Islands, Montserrat, St. Kitts and Nevis, United States Virgin Islands, and the islands of Saba, St. Eustatius, and St. Maarten (Dutch Section) in the Netherlands Antilles; *South Caribbean Conference* (organized 1903; reorganized 1945, 1950, 1975): Trinidad and Tobago; *Suriname Mission* (organized 1945): Suriname.

2. *Central American Union Mission* (organized 1926). Territory: Belize, Costa Rica, El Salvador, Guatemala, Honduras, Nicaragua, and Panama. Statistics (1992): churches, 775; members, 237,089; primary schools, 77; ordained ministers, 139; licensed ministers, 85; teachers, 425. Headquarters: Costado Norte del Estadio de Alajuela, Urbanización Montenegro, Etapa No. 3, Alajuela, Costa Rica.

Constituent organizations and their territories—*Bay Islands Mission* (organized 1988): Honduras Bay Islands and the department of Gracias a Dios on the mainland; *Belize Mission* (organized 1929; reorganized 1937): Belize; *Costa Rica Mission* (organized 1927): Costa Rica; *East Panama Conference* (organized 1906; reorganized 1990): Cocle, Colón, Comarca de San Blas, Darien, Herrera, Los Santos, and Panama provinces of Panama; *El Salvador Conference* (organized 1915; reorganized 1927): El Salvador; *Guatemala Mission* (organized 1913; reorganized 1927): Guatemala; *Honduras Mission* (organized 1918; reorganized 1937): Honduras, except for the department of Gracias a Dios and the Bay Islands; *Nicaragua Mission* (organized 1928): Nicaragua; *West Panama Mission* (organized 1990): Bocas del Toro, Chiriqui, and Veraguas provinces of Panama.

3. *Colombian Union Conference* (organized 1927; reorganized 1989). Territory: Colombia. Statistics (1992): churches, 455; members, 116,758; primary schools, 74; ordained ministers, 113; licensed ministers, 73; teachers, 361. Headquarters: Carrera 84, No. 33B-69, Medellín, Colombia.

Constituent organizations and their territories—*Atlantic Colombia Mission* (organized 1925): the Colombian provinces of Atlántico, Antioquía (north of latitude 7°), Bolívar, Cesar, Choco (north of latitude 7°), Córdoba, La Goajira, Magdalene, and Sucre; *Colombian*

Islands Mission (organized 1955): Colombian islands of Providencia, San Andrés, and Santa Catalina; *East Colombia Conference* (organized 1985: the Colombian provinces of Arauca, Boyaca (northeast section), Casanare (east section), Norte de Santander, Santander, and Vichada; *Pacific Colombia Conference* (organized 1941; reorganized 1978): the Colombian provinces of Antioquia (south of latitude 7°), Caldas, Cauca, Choco (south of latitude 7°), Narino, Putumayo, Quindio, Risaralda, and Valle; *Upper Magdalena Conference* (organized 1926; reorganized 1930): the Colombian provinces of Amazonas, Boyaca (except northeast section), Caqueta, Casanare (except east section), Cundinamarca, Guaviare, Huila, Meta, Putumayo, Tolima and Vaupes.

4. *Cuban Union Conference* (established 1905; reorganized 1941, 1968, 1979, 1989). Territory: Cuba. Statistics (1992): churches, 112; members, 11,235; ordained ministers, 48; licensed ministers, 35. Headquarters: Calle 168, No. 31504, Reparto Lutgardita, Rancho Boyeros, Santiago de las Vegas, Havana, Cuba.

Constituent organizations and their territories—*Central Delegation* (organized 1989): Camaguey, Ciego de Avila, Cienfuegos, Sancti Spiritus, and Villa Clara; *East Delegation* (organized 1989): Granma, Guantanamo, Holguin, Las Tunas, and Santiago de Cuba; *West Delegation* (organized 1989): Condad Habana, La Habana, Mantanzas, Pinar del Rio, and Municipio Especial Isla de la Juventud.

5. *Dominican Union Mission* (organized 1994). Territory: Dominican Republic. Statistics (1992): churches, 295; members, 80,870; primary schools, 41; ordained ministers, 43; licensed ministers, 99; teachers, 412. Headquarters: Respaldo Fantino Falco 1-A, Ensanche Plantini, Santo Domingo, Dominican Republic.

Constituent organizations and their territories—*Central Dominican Conference* (organized 1924; reorganized 1963, 1972): National District and Peravia province, east to the Nizao River, of the Dominican Republic; *East Dominican Mission* (organized 1990): east region of the Dominican Republic; *North Dominican Conference* (organized 1972): north and northeast regions of the Dominican Republic; *South Dominican Mission* (organized 1986): southwest region of the Dominican Republic.

6. *French Antilles-Guiana Union Mission* (organized 1989). Territory: French Guiana, Guadeloupe and dependencies (including St. Barthélemy and St.-Martin [French Section]), and Martinique. Statistics (1992): churches, 102; members, 22,124; primary schools, 10; ordained ministers, 33; licensed ministers, 23; teachers, 58. Headquarters: 46 Rue Emile Zola, Terres Sainville, Fort-de-France, Martinique, French West Indies.

Constituent organizations and their territories—*French Guiana Mission* (organized 1945; reorganized 1959): French Guiana; *Guadeloupe Conference* (organized 1965; reorganized 1977): Guadeloupe and dependencies (including Desirade, Les Saintes, Marie-Galante, St. Barthélemy, and St.-Martin [French Section]); *Martinique Conference* (organized 1974): Martinique.

7. *Haitian Union Mission* (organized 1989). Territory: Haiti. Statistics (1992): churches, 239; members, 158,726; ordained ministers, 49; licensed ministers, 49; teachers, 640; primary schools, 162. Headquarters: Ruelle Ganot 78, Port-au-Prince, Haiti.

Constituent organizations and their territories—*North Haiti Mission* (organized 1905; reorganized 1959): departments of North, Northeast, and Northwest; *South Haiti Mission* (organized 1905; reorganized 1959): departments of Artibonite, Centre, Gran d'Anse, South, South East, and West.

8. *North Mexican Union Conference* (organized 1923; reorganized 1977, 1985). Territory: the states of Aguascalientes, Baja California Norte, Baja California Sur, Chihuahua, Coahuila, Colima, Durango, Guanajuato Jalisco, México, Michoacán, Nayarit, Nuevo León, Queretaro, San Luis Potosí, Sinaloa, Sonora, Tamaulipas, and Zacatecas, and the Federal District. Statistics (1992): churches, 336; members, 83,016; primary schools, 67; ordained ministers, 99; licensed ministers, 85; teachers, 271. Headquarters: Aparto 280, Montemorelos, Nuevo Leon, Mexico.

Constituent organizations and their territories—*Baja California Conference* (organized 1988): the states of Baja California Norte and Baja California Sur, and the northern section of Sonora; *Central Mexican Conference* (organized 1924; reorganized 1975): Federal District and the state of Mexico; *North Mexican Mission* (organized 1988): the states of Chihuahua and Durango, and the Lake region; *Northeast Mexican Conference* (organized 1924; reorganized 1977, 1988): the states of Coahuila, Nuevo Leon, San Luis Potosí, and Tamaulipas; *Northwest Mexican Conference* (organized 1924; reorganized 1977): the states of Sinaloa and Sonora; *West Mexican Mission* (organized 1975): the states of Aguascalientes, Colima, Guanajuato, Jalisco, Michoacán, Nayarit, Queretaro, and Zacatecas.

9. *Puerto Rican Union Conference* (organized 1994). Territory: Puerto Rico. Statistics (1992): churches, 252; members, 28,747; primary schools, 17; ordained ministers, 80; licensed ministers, 42; teachers, 194. Headquarters: 1188 Verona Street, Villa Capri, Rio Piedras, Puerto Rico.

Constituent organizations and their territories—*East Puerto Rico Conference* (organized 1909; reorganized 1948, 1969): Puerto Rico (east of Highway No. 149) and the islands of Culebra and Vieques; *West Puerto Rico Conference* (organized 1909; reorganized 1948, 1969): Puerto Rico (west of Highway No. 149).

10. *South Mexican Union Conference* (organized 1985). Territory: the states of Campeche, Chiapas, Guerrero, Hidalgo, Morelos, Oaxaca, Puebla, Quintana Roo, Tabasco, Tlaxcala, Veracruz, and Yucatán. Statistics (1992): churches, 844; members, 294,331; primary schools, 110; ordained ministers, 118; licensed ministers, 176; teachers, 333. Headquarters: Uxmal 431, Colonia Narvarte, México.

Constituent organizations and their territories—*Central Chiapas Conference* (organized 1989): central part of the state of Chiapas; *Hidalgo Veracruz Conference* (organized 1989): the states of Hidalgo and Veracruz (except the south); *Mayab Mission* (organized 1948; reorganized 1985): the states of Campeche, Quintana Roo, and Yucatán; *North Chiapas Conference* (organized 1989): northern part of the state of Chiapas; *Oaxaca Mission* (organized 1988): the state of Oaxaca; *Soconusco Mission* (organized 1983): southern part of the state of Chiapas; *South Pacific Conference* (organized 1989): the states of Guerrero, Morelos, Puebla, and Tlaxcala; *South Veracruz Conference* (organized 1988): southern part of the state of Veracruz; *Tabasco Conference* (organized 1948; reorganized 1975, 1981, 1985): the state of Tabasco.

11. *Venezuela-Antilles Union Mission* (organized 1927; reorganized 1989). Territory: Aruba, Venezuela, and the islands of Bonaire and Curaçao in the Netherlands Antilles. Statistics (1992): churches, 241; members, 58,653; primary schools, 31; ordained ministers, 85; licensed ministers, 48; teachers, 248. Headquarters: Calle Casiquiare, Qta. U.V.A., El Marques, Distrito Sucre, Estado Miranda, Venezuela.

Constituent organizations and their territories—*Central Venezuela Conference* (organized 1989): the states of Aragua, Guarico, and Miranda, San Fernando in the state of Apure, Federal District, and the federal territory of Amazonas; *East Venezuela Mission* (organized 1989): the states of Anzoategui, Bolivar, Delta Amacuro, Monangas, Nueva Esparta, and Sucre; *Netherlands Antilles Conference* (organized 1934): Aruba and the islands of Bonaire and Curacao in the Netherlands Antilles; *West Central Venezuela Conference* (organized 1992): the states of Barinas, Carabobo, Cojedes, Lara, Portuguesa, Yaracuy, and the central part of the state of Apure, after the dividing line bordering the towns of El Samon de Apure, Yaguai, Medano Alto, Santa Rosa, and Puerto Paez and the border towns of Palmarito, La Trinidad, and Elurza, and up to the south of the stream of the Arauca River; *West Venezuela Mission* (organized 1992): the states of Falcón, Mérida, Tachira, Trujillo, and Zulia, the western part of the state of Apure, and the federal dependencies.

12. *West Indies Union Conference* (organized 1944). Territory: Bahamas, Cayman Islands, Jamaica, and Turks and Caicos Islands. Statistics (1992): churches, 550; members, 166,836; primary schools, 67; ordained ministers, 121; licensed ministers, 62; teachers, 119. Headquarters: Mandeville, Jamaica, West Indies.

Constituent organizations and their territories—*Bahamas Conference* (organized 1909): Bahamas; *Cayman Islands Mission* (organized 1944; reorganized 1954): the islands of Cayman Brac, Grand Cayman, and Little Cayman; *Central Jamaica Conference* (organized 1962): Clarendon, Manchester, St. Ann, St. Catherine, and St. Mary; *East Jamaica Conference* (organized 1903; reorganized 1944, 1962): East St. Mary, Kingston, Portland, St. Andrew, and St. Thomas; *Turks and Caicos Islands Mission* (organized 1965; reorganized 1988): Turks and Caicos Islands; *West Jamaica Conference* (organized 1903; reorganized 1944, 1962): Hanover, St. Elizabeth, St. James, Trelawny, and Westmoreland.

Institutions. The following institutions operate in the Inter-American Division:

Educational Institutions: Adventist Atlantic Secondary School (Colombia); Adventist Educational Center (Honduras);

Adventist Training School of El Salvador (El Salvador); Adventist Vocational School of Nicaragua (Nicaragua); Andrews High School (Trinidad); Antigua Seventh-day Adventist School (Antigua); Antilles Guyane Adventist Secondary School (Martinique); Antillian Adventist University (Puerto Rico); Bahamas Academy (Bahamas); Barbados Seventh-day Adventist Secondary School (Barbados); Bates Memorial High School (Trinidad); Belize Adventist College (Belize); Bequia Seventh-day Adventist Secondary School (Bequia); Cap-Haitien Adventist Academy (Haiti); Caribbean Union College (Trinidad); CEA Adventist Secondary School (Dominican Republic); Central Adventist Academy (Puerto Rico); Central American Adventist University (Costa Rica); Colombia Adventist University (Colombia); Colombian Islands Mission Secondary School (Colombia); Costa Rica Secondary School (Limón) (Costa Rica); Costa Rica Secondary School (San José) (Costa Rica); Cuba Adventist Seminary (Cuba); Dominica Seventh-day Adventist Secondary School (Dominica); Dominican Adventist University (Dominican Republic); East Adventist Academy (Puerto Rico); Edmer School (Grand Cayman); El Llano Adventist Vocational Institute (Colombia); Emmanuel Adventist Secondary School (Colombia); Enriquillo Adventist Secondary School (Dominican Republic); Grenada Seventh-day Adventist Comprehensive Secondary School (Grenada); Haitian Adventist College (Haiti); Harmon High School (Tobago); Harrison Memorial High School (Jamaica); Health and Knowledge Secondary School (Mexico); Ignacio Manuel Altamirano Educational Center (Mexico); Juan Pablo Duarte School (Barahona) (Dominican Republic); Juan Pablo Duarte School (San Juan de la Maguana) (Dominican Republic); Juan Pablo Duarte Secondary School (San Pedro de Macoris) (Dominican Republic); Kingsway High School (Jamaica); Liberty Secondary School (Colombia); Linda Vista Academy (Mexico); Maranatha Adventist Secondary School (Dominican Republic); María Trinidad Sánchez Secondary School (Dominican Republic); Metropolitan Adventist Academy (Dominican Republic); Metropolitan Adventist Academy (Puerto Rico); Model Central Secondary School (El Salvador); Montemorelos University (Mexico); Mountain View Adventist Academy (St. Vincent); Nicanor González Mendoza Secondary School (Mexico); North Adventist Academy (Puerto Rico); Northwestern Adventist Academy (Puerto Rico); Ozama Adventist Secondary School (Dominican Republic); Pacific Academy (Mexico); Pacific Adventist Secondary School (Colombia); Panama Adventist Institute (Panama); Perseverance Boissard School (Guadeloupe); Port Maria High School (Jamaica); Portland High School (Jamaica); Progreso Adventist Coeducational School (Guatemala); Richard Greenidge Academy (Venezuela); St. Ann's Bay High School (Jamaica); St. Croix Seventh-day Adventist Secondary School (St. Croix); St. Lucia Seventh-day Adventist Academy (St. Lucia); St. Thomas-St. John Seventh-day Adventist Secondary School (St. Thomas); San Cristóbal Adventist Secondary School (Dominican Republic); Savanna-La-Mar High School (Jamaica); Southern Academy (Trinidad); Venezuela Vocational Institute (Venezuela); Vincente Súarez Institute (Mexico); West Adventist Academy (Puerto Rico); West Indies College (Jamaica); Willowdene High School (Jamaica).

Food Companies: Inter-American Health Food Company.

Hospitals and Sanitariums: Adventist Hospital of Haiti (Haiti); Andrews Memorial Hospital (Jamaica); Antillean Adventist Hospital (Netherlands Antilles); Barquisimeto Adventist Clinic (Venezuela); Bella Vista Hospital (Puerto Rico); Buena Vista Clinic (Mexico); Cave Memorial Clinic and Nursing Home (Barbados); Davis Memorial Clinic and Hospital (Guyana); Montemorelos University Hospital (Mexico); Port-of-Spain Adventist Hospital (Trinidad); Southeast Hospital (Mexico); Valley of the Angels Hospital (Honduras).

Retirement Homes and Orphanages: Las Palmas Children's Home (Dominican Republic); Linda Vista Retirement Home (Puerto Rico); Los Pinos Children's Home (Guatemala).

Publishing Houses: Inter-American Publishing Association.

History. For the history of the work in the Inter-American Division, see specific names of countries and islands in the area of the division.

Presidents: E. E. Andross, 1922-1936; G. A. Roberts, 1936-1941; Glenn Calkins, 1941-1947; E. F. Hackman, 1947-1950; Glenn Calkins, 1951-1954; A. H. Roth, 1954-1962; C. L. Powers, 1962-1970; B. L. Archbold, 1970-1980; G. W. Brown, 1980-1994; Israel Leito, 1994- .

INTER-AMERICAN HEALTH FOOD COMPANY. The management company for the church health food industries in the Inter-American Division. Owned and operated by the Inter-American Division, its purpose is to promote the manufacture and sale of health foods in the division territory, to provide employment and training for students in the colleges and schools of the division, to support the Seventh-day Adventist health message, and to emphasize and support educational and benevolent institutions of the church. The companies associated with the Inter-American Health Food Company produce bread and bread products, breakfast cereals, protein foods, textured soy proteins, soy milk, and assorted spreads. The company also operates one restaurant and three printing presses, and manages farms in Mexico, Jamaica, and Colombia.

In 1992 there were 14 branches of the company operating in seven countries, with group turnover in excess of US$9 million. More than 400 students were employed division-wide, along with 290 full-time employees. There are five branches operating in Mexico, four in Colombia, and one each in Costa Rica, Trinidad and Tobago, Puerto Rico, Haiti, and Jamaica. More than 340 products are manufactured in the associated factories.

History. The Inter-American Health Food Company was established in 1977 in order to become the coordinating and management organization for the newly emerging food factories that were then beginning to be established as separate institutions on the campuses of the Adventist senior colleges and universities in the Inter-American Division. The company headquarters were located at the division office in Miami, Florida.

Factories located in Navojoa, Mexico (Alimentos Colpac), Costa Rica (Fundacion CETEBEDI) and Jamaica (Westico Foods) were the first to join the Inter-American Health Food Company, presenting their first balance sheets in 1977. The Medellin Branch in Colombia joined in 1978. Montemorelos (Panificadora la Carlota) was established in 1980, and the Monterrey Restaurant opened its doors in 1985. The year 1987 saw the opening of the Trinidad Branch and the incorporation of the old Pacific Press printing plant into the operations of the company. The Mexico Sales Branch was organized in 1989. The Puerto Rico Branch was also established in 1989. The food work in Colombia expanded with the opening of the Cali (Viva Mejor) Branch in 1989, the starting up of the Bucaramanga (Viva Mejor) Branch in 1991, and the establishment of a farm and rice processing factory in Los Llanos in 1993.

Managing Directors: Alejo Pizarro, 1977-1984; Emilio Wandersleben, 1984-1985; Sidney Cole, 1985- .

INTER-AMERICAN HEALTH FOOD COMPANY, ALINSA (Mexico Sales Branch). A distributor of health foods that has operated in the Mexican territory since 1986. Alinsa stands for Alimentos Integronaturales ("wholesome natural foods"). It was created by the Inter-American Division for the purpose of distributing health foods to Mexico and improving service to clients of the Navojoa, Sonora, and Montemorelos, Nuevo León, factories. At first its territories were divided into the western zone, with headquarters situated in Guadalajara; and the central zone, with headquarters in Mexico City. In 1989 the company extended its activity to cover the rest of the country of Mexico, and set up five more distribution centers in the cities of Tijuana, Chihuahua, Pichucalco, Monterrey, and Torreon. As a result of this expansion, Alinsa is able to serve more than 500 health stores as well as many of the supermarket chains spread throughout Mexico. Annual sales are approximately US$1.8 million.

Managers: Cesar Campos, 1986-1988; Juan Martin Meza, 1989- .

INTER-AMERICAN HEALTH FOOD COMPANY, COLOMBIA BRANCH (Productos Icolpan). A bakery started in Colombia in 1978 that was incorporated into the Inter-American Division Health Food Company in 1979. *See* Inter-American Division Health Food Company.

INTER-AMERICAN HEALTH FOOD COMPANY, COSTA RICA BRANCH (Fundacion CETEBEDI). The Costa Rica food factory of the Inter-American Health Food Company and the philanthropic foundation (Fundacion CETEBEDI) that owns and operates it.

In 1954, under the leadership of Manuel Carvajal and the manager, Francisco Arroyo, the Vocational College of Central America, located in La Ceiba, City of Alajuela, Costa Rica, began a bakery with the purpose of creating a source of assistance for students with low incomes. The first bakery was so small that only one person was needed to distribute the bread on a bicycle with baskets attached to it, front and back.

In 1960 Israel González was inspired by Miguel Drachenberg, who on his arrival began to promote the production of protein products. Drachenberg had established similar factories in Jamaica and Mexico.

Between 1974 and 1975 Kenneth Fleck brought about a more industrious and competitive tone to the operation of the bakery. Equipment was purchased in the United States, and managers were contracted to train the personnel working in the factory.

In 1980 the factory began to produce soy milk and other products based on soybeans, with the assistance of machinery that was imported from Mexico. These products were well accepted by the people in Costa Rica. Even high-ranking government officials became interested in how the soybean could be turned into milk and other useful healthy products.

In July 1980 a new building was constructed for the bakery and for the manufacture of soy proteins under the industry name Industrias COVAC SA. In October 1987 the name was changed to Fundacion CETEBEDI, which implies objectives of education and the use of resources in the training of students. The new name better fitted the purpose for which the industry was started. Fundacion CETEBEDI also operates a printing press that serves the Central American Union as well as the needs of Costa Rica. Many of the workers in the Central American Union have been able to complete their studies because of the benefits provided by the bakery and the press.

INTER-AMERICAN HEALTH FOOD COMPANY, HAITI BRANCH. A food company located on the grounds of the Haitian Adventist College campus in Carrefour, Port-au-Prince, Haiti.

Planning for its installation commenced early in the 1980s. In 1986 commercial baking equipment was donated by ADRA/Holland through VIWOS. Political unrest caused a long delay, but after a break of several years, construction of the factory building commenced in 1991. ADRA/Canada provided substantial assistance toward the cost of this construction. The first manager, Lawrence Fowler, came from Australia in 1991 and completed the building equipment and installation.

Production commenced in July 1993. Initial products included a range of breads plus bottled potable water.

Boulangerie Adventiste is operated by the Inter-American Division and the Haitian Union for the benefit of the youth studying at Haiti Adventist College.

Manager: Lawrence W Fowler, 1991- .

INTER-AMERICAN HEALTH FOOD COMPANY, MEXICO-MONTEMORELOS BRANCH (Panificadora la Carlota). A health food industry that is an active member of the Inter-American Health Food Company, with headquarters in Miami, Florida. It is situated in the heart of the citrus zone of Mexico, Montemorelos, in the state of Nuevo León, about 45 minutes from the northern city of Monterrey, on the campus of the Montemorelos University.

The factory area is approximately 15,000 square feet (1,400 square meters) including warehouses, work area, workshop, and offices. There are five principal lines of products: breakfast cereal products, cookies and bread, canned products, packaged products, and texturized products.

The history of Panificadora la Carlota is divided into two major stages—the period before it became a member of the Inter-American Division Health Food Company, and the time since it joined the Inter-American Division Health Food Company in 1979.

Before 1979 the bakery was a local industry serving only the community of Montemorelos and the students of the then Vocational and Professional College of Montemorelos, which later became Montemorelos University. Despite its local nature, the industry was always noted for its good bread.

When the Inter-American Health Food Company took over the management of the industry, it became an industry of influence both in the local and regional areas, and during the period 1979-1985 supplied a large portion of the bread for Montemorelos and Monterrey.

In 1985 Panificadora la Carlota began to diversify its production and became an industry selling its products throughout the country of Mexico. Breakfast cereals and whole-grain cookies and crackers were developed. Health food products were packaged and canned meat substitutes were made, and finally, with the gift of an extruder from the food company in Australia, the factory began to attend to the growing need for texturized soy protein in Mexico.

Panificadora la Carlota has specialized in employing students. Yearly it employs an average of 60 students studying at the University of Montemorelos, fulfilling the SDA ideal of combining study and work programs.

Managers: Meliquiades Sosa, 1979-1982; Emilo Wandersleben, 1982-1986; Cesar Campos, 1986-1987; Raul Pairo, 1987-1988; Juan Martin Mendoza, 1988-1990; Adolfo Ruiz, 1990- .

INTER-AMERICAN HEALTH FOOD COMPANY, MEXICO-NAVOJOA BRANCH (Alimentos Colpac). A health food factory working principally with health foods based on soybeans. It is located at Pacific Academy (Colegio del Pacifico), in Navojoa, Sonora, in northwest Mexico. Alimentos Colpac operates on an irrigated farm of 700 acres (285 hectares) Forty acres (15 hectares) are set aside for citrus crops and another plot for vegetables. There is also a manufacturing plant.

Alimentos Colpac originated in 1968 when Paul Allred commenced work with foods based on gluten and texturized soy protein. At its beginning the factory was administered by Pacific Academy, but for financial reasons the Colpac became part of the Inter-American Division Food Company on July 2, 1975.

This date marked the beginning of the second stage of development of Alimentos Colpac, during which its installations and equipment have been greatly improved. Its products are based on texturized soy protein, with variations in flavors, shapes, and sizes. Colpac also manufactures soy milk, breakfast cereals, and a wide variety of cookies, crackers, and whole-wheat products.

The production capacity of the factory can yield seven tons (6.5 metric tons) of texturized soy protein per day and up to 30,000 whole-grain cookies. Annual sales are in excess of $1 million.

The founder of the factory was Paul Allred; Pedro Midguet Sanchez helped in the area of production.

Managers: Jesus E. Ferreyra, 1975-1978; Filiberto Verduzco, 1979-1984; Juan M. Meza, 1984-1987; Adaias Rivas, 1988-1989; Manuel Rubio, 1990- .

INTER-AMERICAN HEALTH FOOD COMPANY, TRINIDAD BRANCH (College Health Foods). A food factory on the campus of Caribbean Union College. Nestled in a beautiful valley, at just about the middle of the northern range, it was set up because exchange control restrictions made it difficult to import vegetarian foods.

This industry began operations in August 1987. It is owned by the Inter-American Division and the Caribbean Union Conference. The college is a recipient of the profits and benefits from industrial rents and student labor.

The products, which are well accepted by the islands of the Caribbean and the home base, consist of bakery items, granola, oats, bran, wheat germ, peanut butter, fruit mixes, nut mixes, dried soy products, frozen soy products, and nut meat.

A large portion (65-70 percent) of the workforce comes from student labor. The full-time staff range between 22 and 25 persons through the year.

The industry's first manager, Isaac Mohamed, is still at the helm, providing the leadership that gives stability, and is responsible for the steady growth rate of this potential giant.

INTER-AMERICAN MESSENGER *(Mensajero Interamericano).* (1927-1973; monthly, then quarterly; Spanish). Organ of the Inter-American Division for its Spanish-speaking members until 1974, when it was replaced by the Spanish edition of the world *Review and Herald, La Revista Adventista,* in a special monthly edition for the Inter-American Division. The Spanish-speaking members of the division also receive the monthly, four-page *Chispazos de Interamerica.*

The *Mensajero Interamericano* was nearly a duplicate of the English *Inter-American Messenger,* as seemed advisable. Beginning with the February 1937 issue, the *Mensajero* adopted the same volume and number as that of the *Messenger.*

The translating and printing of the *Mensajero* were done at the Pacific Press Branch in the Canal Zone until 1948, when the printing was given to the press at Antillian Junior College. The *Mensajero* was then edited and translated in the Inter-American Division office in Miami, Florida, and printed at the Montemorelos Vocational and Professional College in Montemorelos, Mexico, until it ceased to be published at the close of 1973. It had a circulation of 21,000 and was sent free to Spanish-speaking members.

INTER-AMERICAN NEWS FLASHES (1924- ; 1927-1962 as *Inter-American Division Messenger;* monthly until 1970; quarterly since then, supplemented by the fortnightly, two-page *Inter-American Messenger Flashes;* file in GC). Official organ of the

Inter-American Division. The first issue, a 12-page magazine bearing the date April 1924, was published to be a "channel of inspiration and blessing to the workers" of the newly organized Inter-American Division.

The *Inter-American Messenger* reported the activities, growth, and plans for future development of the work of the Seventh-day Adventist Church in the territory of the Inter-American Division and carried articles of an inspirational and instructional nature. The magazine was sent to church members in the English-speaking areas of the division and to a few readers in other divisions who have ties with Inter-America.

The *Messenger* was printed first at the Pacific Press Branch in the Canal Zone, from 1948 to 1953, at the Antillian Junior College in Cuba, then at the Caribbean Union College in Port of Spain, Trinidad. The periodical is edited at the Inter-American Division headquarters, which are situated in Miami, Florida.

A Spanish edition, *Mensajero Inter-Americano,* was issued monthly, and then quarterly, for Spanish-speaking members until replaced by the Spanish edition of the world *Review and Herald,* and a French edition, *Messager de la Division Inter-Americaine,* at the same frequency for French-speaking members. *The Inter-American News Flashes* appears in Spanish (*Chispazos de Interamerica*) and French (*Eclair D'Inter-Amerique*).

INTER-AMERICAN PUBLISHING ASSOCIATION (Asocíacion Publicadora Interamericana). A publishing association with editorial and administration staff that coordinates the publishing of books and periodicals in the Inter-American Division. It has no printing facilities. A warehouse stores books printed by other denominational publishers or contracted printing companies.

The publishing house was established in January 1983, when Pacific Press Publishing Association, because of monetary restrictions among the countries of the Inter-American Division, passed on this responsibility to the IAD administration. This publishing association serves the three main languages of the IAD: Spanish, English, and French. The headquarters are located in Miami, Florida, and the editorial staff is located in Mexico. The printing work is done in Mexico, Colombia, Argentina, Spain, the United States, and the United Kingdom.

The publishing association markets on a worldwide basis. Finished goods are purchased from other publishers, or the plant negotiates the publishing rights of other books and magazines to be printed locally whenever the quality and the printing costs suit the needs.

In the beginning the administrative offices were located in one of the offices of the IAD headquarters in Miami, Florida. Later they were moved to a rented premises, and since 1991 the plant has had its own building at 1890 NW. 95th Avenue, Miami, Florida. It contains 19,000 square feet (1,770 square meters), of which 3,000 square feet (280 square meters) are dedicated to office space and 16,000 square feet (1,500 square meters) are for warehouse purposes.

The Inter-American Publishing Association serves its 950,000 Spanish-speaking members with trade books, missionary magazines, and subscription books for 4,000 regular and student colporteurs. It also provides subscription books for 550 French-speaking and 576 English-speaking regular and student colporteurs. Ninety percent of the English trade books are channeled by the publishing association from books printed by Pacific Press, Review and Herald, and other denominational publishers. The French constituency of the IAD is supplied for the most part with trade books printed at the Life and Health Publishing House in France. The entire division's sales operations for 1992 exceeded $6 million.

Because this is a division organization, the IAD president is the president of the board. The members are the division administrators, all the union presidents, and two division departmental directors. Day-to-day operations are overseen by a general manager and three associates.

Manager: Juan C. de Armas, 1983- .

INTERMEDIATE STATE. *See* Death.

INTER-MOUNTAIN CONFERENCE. A former unit of church organization existing from 1916 to 1932. It comprised the former territory of the Utah and Western Colorado conferences (the state of Utah, Colorado west of the Continental Divide, and San Juan County, New Mexico). It was a part of the Pacific Union Conference through 1919, when it was transferred to the Central Union Conference, its Utah territory reduced to the counties of Daggett, Uinta, Duchesne, Carbon, Emery, Grand, and San Juan. In 1932 it was dissolved, its Utah counties were transferred to the Nevada-Utah Conference, in the Pacific

Union Conference; and western Colorado and San Juan County, New Mexico, were made part of the Colorado Conference, under the Central Union Conference.

Presidents: E. A. Curtis, 1916; H. E. Lysinger, 1917-1920; N. T. Sutton, 1920-1922; B. H. Shaw, 1922-1924; J. W. Turner, 1924-1930; B. M. Grandy, 1930-1932.

INTERN, MINISTERIAL. *See* Minister.

INTERNATIONAAL ADVENT ZENDINGSGENOOTSCHAP. *See* Boekenhuis "Veritas."

INTERNATIONAL ASSOCIATION OF ADVENTIST EDITORS. *See* Adventist Editors International.

INTERNATIONAL AUDIO-VISUAL SERVICE (AVS). A service developed in 1972 by the General Conference of Seventh-day Adventists as one of the four components in what was then the Adventist Radio, Television, and Film Center. *See* Adventist Media Center.

INTERNATIONAL BOARD OF EDUCATION. *See* Education, Department of.

INTERNATIONAL COMMISSION FOR THE PREVENTION OF ALCOHOLISM. An organization established in 1950 to help unite the efforts of leading citizens of various nations interested in solving the problems arising from beverage alcohol. In harmony with the trend of modern medicine, the emphasis of the commission is toward prevention rather than cure. Though the organization, whose program is exclusively of an educational nature, is recognized as nonsectarian and nonpolitical, Seventh-day Adventists took a leading part in launching the organization.

The commission consists of approximately 250 members chosen from every country on the basis of its respective population. Thomas R. Neslund now serves as ICPA executive director; Lincoln Steed is associate director.

The immediate objective of the commission is the setting up of affiliated National Committees in all major countries. W. A. Scharffenberg, instigator of the ICPA, along with Dr. Andrew C. Ivy and Dr. Haven Emerson, established the first National Committee in the United States in 1952. The major objective of each National Committee is to set up an Institute of Scientific Studies in strategic areas that will provide scientific training and conduct research work in all phases of the alcohol problem. Many such institutes have been established.

The commission also prepares and publishes authoritative materials for teachers and professional temperance workers, and for use in general educational work, and fosters a worldwide program for the prevention of alcoholism through films, forums, and radio and television programs. A book, *Toward Prevention,* has been published, featuring the best lectures during a 10-year period, and a series of basic scientific articles has been prepared in brochure form for distribution among professional groups. The organization sponsors a newsletter known as the *ICPA Reporter,* designed to keep members of the commission informed on the latest methods being used to check the rise and spread of alcoholism.

The commission endeavors to put the spotlight of science on alcohol in order to show alcohol's effects on the individual and the nation, and to encourage and publicize the educational, legislative, and social measures that have been effectively used against alcohol in various parts of the world.

INTERNATIONAL EDUCATIONAL RECORDING ORGANIZATION. *See* Campbell, Alexander John.

INTERNATIONAL HEALTH AND TEMPERANCE ASSOCIATION. The organization set up by the General Conference to launch, foster, and coordinate the church's temperance program conducted throughout the world, both within the church and outside the church. Its constitution was adopted by General Conference action at the Autumn Council of 1947, at which time representatives from the world divisions were present.

The principal objectives of the International Health and Temperance Association are to enlighten the peoples of the various countries of the world concerning the effects of the use of alcoholic beverages, tobacco, and narcotics, to enlist the active participation of all church members and other interested persons in temperance endeavor, and to encourage the habits of better living.

The Executive Committee of the General Conference, and the presidents and executive secretaries of the various division and national societies affiliated with the International

Health and Temperance Association, comprise the board of governors, which meets annually in connection with the Annual Council and quinquennially at the time of the General Conference session.

Membership in the International Health and Temperance Association consists of such division or national societies as may be sponsored by Seventh-day Adventist conference organizations throughout the world. Each division is encouraged to organize a society within its area, which in turn organizes and fosters a national society in each country in the division territory.

Members of the division committee and the presidents and executive secretaries of all the national societies affiliated with the division society serve as the board of governors for the division society.

Financial support for the International Health and Temperance Association comes from offerings and special contributions; 10 percent of the funds received through the annual Health and Temperance Offering is remitted to the association international headquarters for support of the worldwide work.

The International Health and Temperance Association uses its resources in educational and promotional programs of the world church, including Global Mission projects, Adventist Youth to Youth programs, and various training seminars.

Annually, the International Health and Temperance Association promotes the World Health and Temperance Day, at which time the basic health and temperance beliefs of the church are emphasized for church members, and the challenge of the church's temperance program for the church and the public is presented.

Presidents: J. L. McElhany, 1948-1950; W. H. Branson, 1950-1954; A. V. Olson, 1954-1958; H. L. Rudy, 1958-1960; M. V. Campbell, 1960-1962; R. S. Watts, 1962-1970; M. S. Nigri, 1970-1975; F. W. Wernick, 1975-1980; M. G. Hardinge, 1980-1983; F. W. Wernick, 1983-1985; W. O. Coe, 1985-1989; R. J. Kloosterhuis, 1989-1990; L. S. Ranzolin, 1990- .

Executive Directors: W. A. Scharffenberg, 1948-1964; E. J. Folkenberg, 1964-1968; E.H.J. Steed, 1968-1982; Albert S. Whiting, 1983-1985; DeWitt S. Williams, 1985-1987; Thomas R. Neslund, 1987- .

INTERNATIONAL HEALTH ASSOCIATION LIMITED. *See* Granose Foods Limited.

INTERNATIONAL HEALTH FOOD ASSOCIATION. A General Conference service organization made up of Seventh-day Adventist Church-owned food companies from around the world. The director coordinates the various phases of denominational food production and marketing activities throughout the world field. (For a brief history of Seventh-day Adventist food manufacture, *see* Food Companies.) The association received its current name in 1987 when the food companies, meeting in Brazil, recommended the adoption of a name that better described the aims and objectives of the church's food companies, which up to that time had been coordinated in their activities by the General Conference World Foods Service, which was established in 1968 by vote of the General Conference Autumn Council.

The association is a service of the General Conference for church-owned food companies that have separate institutional status. The officers of the association are appointed by the General Conference. The purpose of the association is to coordinate manufacturing and sales activities, to promote interchange of ideas and information among members, and to help establish standards for the types of foods produced and the manner in which food company business is run.

The association promotes the manufacture and distribution of health foods and supports SDA health principles as a way to better health. It also encourages the extension of church-operated food companies to new areas by encouraging members to contribute annually to a development fund, which is used to assist in the establishment of new industries. The association also provides technical assistance to church-owned industries that do not yet qualify for separate institutional status.

In 1992 there were 49 food factories affiliated with the International Health Food Association. These factories operated in 25 countries and had a combined annual turnover in excess of $285 million. They employed a total of 708 students and had 3,800 full-time employees.

For a list of the companies now operating under church institutional management, *see* Food Companies.

Secretaries: E. W. Howse, 1969-1974.

Directors: E. W. Howse, 1969-1980; Lance Butler, 1980-1983; Eric Fehlberg, 1983-1992; Sidney Cole, 1992-1994; Eugene Grosser, 1994- .

INTERNATIONAL MEDICAL MISSIONARY AND BENEVOLENT ASSOCIATION. A legal corporation founded in 1893 under the name Seventh-day Adventist Medical Missionary and Benevolent Association (renamed International Medical Missionary and Benevolent Association in 1896). It was dissolved in 1904. The association aimed to promote the medical activities of the denomination and to hold the properties of the church's medical and charitable enterprises. The objectives of the association, specifically, were "to erect and manage homes for orphan children and for friendless aged persons, also hospitals and sanitariums for the treatment of the sick poor and others, the same to be either self-supporting or supported in whole or in part by funds secured for the purpose; to establish dispensaries in cities, medical missions at home and abroad, visiting nurses' work, Christian Help work; to educate missionary physicians and nurses; to provide for the needy poor; to promulgate the principles of health and temperance and to do good in a variety of ways" *(Yearbook of the International Medical Missionary and Benevolent Association,* 1896, pp. 58, 59).

Although the association was intended to be a holding corporation for the several Seventh-day Adventist sanitariums and other enterprises, in practice it became a consultative body with a constituency composed of the General Conference Committee, presidents of local conferences, several men appointed for two-year terms by the General Conference in session, all donors of $1,000 or more to its treasury, and delegates from the various sanitariums and subsidiary organizations. On the administrative side, it became the employing agency for the Seventh-day Adventist medical missionaries. Dr. J. H. Kellogg was its prime mover and president. The activities of the association were taken over largely by the Medical Department (now Health and Temperance Department) of the General Conference that was created in 1905.

INTERNATIONAL PUBLISHING ASSOCIATION. *See* Pacific Press.

INTERNATIONAL RELIGIOUS LIBERTY ASSOCIATION. An organization founded to disseminate the principles of religious liberty throughout the world, and to defend the right of all men to worship (or not to worship) as their consciences shall dictate; and incorporated to hold title to property or to receive bequests to be used to achieve the objectives of this corporation.

The association was formally incorporated Aug. 16, 1946, in the District of Columbia by S. A. Wellman, E. W. Dunbar, and H. H. Votaw.

The IRLA board of trustees is elected at biennial sessions. Provision is made in the bylaws for an unlimited number of members, including Seventh-day Adventists and others interested in the aims of the organization. The board elects a president, vice presidents, a secretary-general, associate secretaries, and a treasurer. This association developed out of an earlier International Religious Liberty Association, organized in 1893, which in turn was a development of the National Religious Liberty Association organized in 1889. The offices were in New York City until, in March 1898, the office was moved to Chicago, Illinois, where it remained until the transfer of denominational headquarters to Washington, D.C., in 1904.

Affiliated religious liberty associations have also been organized in a number of countries, most recently in India, Romania, Russia, Poland, Hungary, and Croatia.

The International Association for the Defense of Religious Liberty, located in Bern, Switzerland, is a sister organization with which the IRLA closely cooperates. The latter is in consultative status with the United Nations Economic and Social Council.

The most visible activity of the IRLA has been the organization of world congresses in Amsterdam (1977), Rome (1984), and London (1989); and regional congresses in New Delhi (1986), Nairobi (1991), and Suva, Fiji (1993). It has also cosponsored religious liberty conferences in Parma (1988), Budapest (1992), and Moscow (1993). The first international conference regarding human rights to be held in Albania after atheistic rule was cosponsored by the IRLA and the University of Tirane in 1992.

Presidents: L. K. Dickson, 1952-1958; H. L. Rudy, 1958-1959; M. V. Campbell, 1960-1969; W. J. Hackett, 1969-1970; N. C. Wilson, 1971-1976; W. J. Hackett, 1976-1980; N. C. Wilson, 1980-1985; W. O. Coe, 1985-1988; C. Mau, 1988-1990; D. Lotz, 1990-1992; L. S. Ranzolin, 1992- .

INTERNATIONAL SABBATH SCHOOL ASSOCIATION. *See* Sabbath School Department.

INTERNATIONAL SERVICE COMMISSION. *See* National Service Organization.

INTERNATIONAL TEACHER SERVICE (ITS). A special department of the General Conference whose function is to recruit and train people to teach English abroad, and to establish English language schools in countries where it is feasible to do so.

It was established in November 1990 under the direction of M. T. Bascom and Treva Burgess. Mrs. Burgess and her husband, Robert, were the first individuals officially invited by the Chinese government to direct ADRA projects and teach in a government university.

Since its inception, ITS has placed teachers in China, the Commonwealth of Independent States, Turkey, and Poland. The objectives of ITS are to share the gospel as Jesus did by contacting people, making friends with them, gaining their confidence, and then sharing with them the good news.

INTERNATIONAL TRACT AND MISSIONARY SOCIETY. *See* Tract and Missionary Societies.

INTERNSHIP, MINISTERIAL. *See* Minister.

INVESTIGATIVE JUDGMENT. A Seventh-day Adventist term for the preliminary phase of the great final judgment by which God intervenes in human affairs to bring the reign of sin to a close and to inaugurate Christ's eternal reign of righteousness (see Dan. 7:9, 10, 13, 14). This opening phase is called an investigative judgment because it consists of an examination of the life records of all who have ever professed to accept salvation in Christ and whose names are therefore inscribed in "the Lamb's book of life." Its purpose is to verify their eligibility for citizenship in God's eternal kingdom. At the close of the investigative judgment the sins of those who have endured to the end are "blotted out" from the books of record and the names of all others are stricken from the book of life (Ex. 32:32, 33; Rev. 3:5; 20:12, 15; 22:19). Seventh-day Adventists teach that in view of the fact that at His second coming Christ rewards "every man according as his work shall be" (Rev. 22:12; cf. Rom. 2:5-11), it is evident that this investigation of the life record takes place *before* He returns to earth to gather the elect. The divine proclamation "Fear God, and give glory to him; for the hour of his judgment is come," is specifically presented as *preceding* the Advent (Rev. 14:7; cf. v. 14).

To be sure, God does not need to investigate the records in order to learn or to determine who is eligible to be saved. It is for the benefit of all created beings that the facts with respect to each person's fate should be known, as an assurance to all that justice has been done and as a guarantee of the eternal stability of the divine government. The Bible writers speak of "books" in which God keeps a record of character—of good and evil deeds as measured by a person's knowledge of, and voluntary relationship to, divine grace and God's revealed will (Ex. 32:32; Mark 16:16; Phil. 4:3; James 4:17; Rev. 20:12, 13; 22:11, 12).

The doctrine of the investigative judgment is an integral part of the sanctuary doctrine, and relates especially to the fulfillment in antitype of the ancient Day of Atonement service. In brief, the Day of Atonement consisted, in figure, of a review of the individual records of God's people—of their personal relationship to God through the sanctuary ministration. At the close of the special service of the day a final disposal of all sins that had been confessed, forgiven, and transferred in figure to the sanctuary during the preceding year was made; the sanctuary was "cleansed" of the record of these sins removed (see Lev. 16).

Persons whose sins were included in this work of cleansing were released from further responsibility for their past record of sin, and their status under the covenant relationship was revalidated. Those no longer eligible to continue in the covenant relationship were to be "cut off" from Israel. The ancient Day of Atonement was thus a day on which the eligibility of each individual Israelite to continue under the covenant relationship was reviewed, and it was therefore a day of judgment (see SB, Nos. 111-118; SDADic, "Atonement, Day of").

Development of Seventh-day Adventist View. William Miller based his 1843/1844 message chiefly on the text (Dan. 8:14) "Unto two thousand and three hundred days; then shall the sanctuary be cleansed," holding that the period of time here specified terminated in that year (*see* Sanctuary; Twenty-three Hundred Days). He understood this cleansing of the sanctuary to involve a work of judgment and to consist in the purification of this earth by the fires of the last day, at the second coming of Christ in power and glory. When, after the disappointment of 1844, those who later became Seventh-day Adventists reviewed Miller's interpretation of Dan. 8:14, they became convinced of the validity of Miller's exposition of the time period, but concluded that the sanctuary here referred to is the sanctuary in heaven, mentioned in the book of Hebrews, where Christ now ministers as our great high priest. Inasmuch as the earthly sanctuary and its services were types of the heavenly sanctuary (Heb. 8:2, 5; 9:6-9, 23; cf. Ex. 25:8, 9), as the earthly sanctuary was cleansed on the ancient Day of Atonement (Lev. 16), and as the earthly sanctuary ceased to exist in A.D. 70, early SDAs concluded that the cleansing of the sanctuary foretold in Dan. 8:14 must refer to a counterpart of the ancient Day of Atonement to be conducted in the heavenly sanctuary. The SDA understanding of a cleansing of the heavenly sanctuary, of a great antitypical day of atonement, and of an investigative judgment is based on this analogy drawn in the book of Hebrews between the earthly and heavenly sanctuaries.

The view that the sanctuary to be cleansed in 1844 is the one in heaven was first written out by Owen R. L. Crosier, in the *Day-Dawn* in 1845 and in the *Day-Star Extra* of Feb. 7, 1846. Crosier emphasized two aspects of the antitypical cleansing—the blotting out of sins and the disposal of sins by placing them, in figure, on the head of the scapegoat. This he based on Acts 3:19: "Repent ye therefore, and be converted, that your sins may be blotted out, when the times of refreshing shall come from the presence of the Lord."

Crosier connected this blotting out of sins with the cleansing of the sanctuary from the sins of the people on the ancient Day of Atonement. "A little attention to the law will show that the sins were borne from the people by the priest, and from the priest by the goat. 1st, They are imparted to the victim. 2nd. The priest bore them in its blood to the Sanctuary. 3rd, After cleansing them from it on the 10th day of the seventh month, he bore them to the scape-goat. And 4th, The goat finally bore them away beyond the camp of Israel to the wilderness. This was the legal process, and when fulfilled the author of sins will have received them back again, (but the ungodly will bear their own sins,) and his head will have been bruised by the seed of the woman" *(ibid.* 43).

About the time Crosier was first writing his view concerning the heavenly sanctuary William Miller wrote a letter (Mar. 20, 1845) in which he applied the judgment-hour message to the closing ministry of Christ in the heavenly sanctuary: "That the prophetic numbers did close in 1844, I can have but little doubt. What then was there worthy of note that could be said to answer to the ending of the periods under these numbers so emphatically describing the end? I answer. The first thing I will notice is, 'The hour of his Judgment is come.' I ask, is there any thing in the scriptures to show that the hour has not come, or in our present position to show, that God is not now in his last Judicial character deciding the cases of all the righteous, so that Christ (speaking after the manner of men) will know whom to collect at his coming or the angels may know whom to gather when they are sent to gather together the elect, whom God has in this hour of his Judgment justified? Rom. 8:33. . . . It also seems by John's description of this event, Rev. 19:1, 2, 11, that the scene of the Judgment begins in heaven, and the first thing mortals on earth will see will be the messenger of God, Rev. 20:1, who is Jesus Christ, descending from God, to execute the Judgment written in heaven, and fulfill the decrees and promises made in heaven by him who sitteth on the great white throne. . . . If this is true, who can say God is not already justifying his Sanctuary, and will yet justify us in preaching the time?" *(Day-Star* 5:31, Apr. 8, 1845).

Judging by their writings, Adventists who later formed the Seventh-day Adventist Church did not notice William Miller's suggestion relating the judgment of Rev. 14:6, 7 to the cleansing of the sanctuary mentioned in Dan. 8:14.

In his initial explanation of the October 1844 disappointment, Hiram Edson had spoken of Christ's having "a work to perform" in the heavenly sanctuary after the end of the 2300 days and before His return, but he gave no further explanation. Crosier's expanded discussion of the sanctuary in his 1846 article did not connect the cleansing of the sanctuary with the judgment. The nearest approach to the idea was an allusion to "the breast-plate of judgment" worn over the heart of the high priest when he went into the Holy of Holies on the Day of Atonement, "that he may bear their judgment" *(Day-Star* 9:40, *Extra,* Feb. 7, 1846).

He may or may not have derived this from Enoch Jacobs, who in November 1844 spoke of the names of the children of Israel on the "breast-plate of judgment" as typifying the people whose sins are put away before Christ personally returns, and suggested the possibility that on the antitypical Day of Atonement, the tenth day of the seventh month, Jesus had begun to sit in judgment and was on His way to execute the judgment in person *(Western*

Midnight Cry 4:19, Nov. 29, 1844).

Neither is it clear whether Jacobs derived this idea of the final putting away of sins from a letter he had received from William Miller (dated Nov. 22) in which Miller, replying to an inquiry, wrote that Christ would come as judge, to bear our sins away; "that our sins cannot be blotted out until Christ comes to judge His people is evident from . . . Rom. 14:10; 2 Cor. 5:10; Rom. 2:6" *(ibid.* 4:26, Dec. 21, 1844).

Nor is it possible to find a connection between the SDA view and the earlier reference by Josiah Litch *(Prophetic Expositions* [1842], vol. 1, pp. 49-54) to a preliminary phase of the judgment—the examination, or trial, of every person preceding the resurrection, and the execution of the judgment at the Second Advent. The various elements—the blotting out of sins, the putting away of sins, the examination of the books, the cleansing of the sanctuary from the sins—were all present in Millerite thinking, but the synthesis cannot be traced exactly.

By 1849, when the early Seventh-day Adventist group had well established its identity, Ellen White wrote: "I saw that Jesus would not leave the Most Holy Place until every case was decided either for salvation or destruction" *(Present Truth* 1:22, August 1849; reprinted in EW 36), yet she did not call it the judgment.

In the same year David Arnold *(Present Truth* 1:43-45, December 1849) and the next year Joseph Bates *(Review and Herald* 1:22, December 1850) echoed the phrase "breastplate of judgment," and carried the idea further, to equate the coming of the Bridegroom to the wedding with the entrance of the high priest into the Holy of Holies on the Day of Atonement, blotting out the sins of those whose names are on the breastplate (in the antitype, the Israel of God), but neither mentions the judgment. James White did not mention the breastplate of judgment in his article in *Present Truth* 1:75-79, May 1850; and in another discussion of the sanctuary doctrine *(Review and Herald* 1:29, January 1851), he mentioned only the removal of sins by placing them on the head of the scapegoat. In 1853 J. N. Andrews wrote a series of articles on the sanctuary. When he came to the cleansing on the Day of Atonement, he mentioned only the blotting out of sins and the transfer of sins to the scapegoat *(Review and Herald* 3:147, 148, Feb. 3, 1853).

However, in 1854 J. N. Loughborough, like William Miller in 1845, connected the cleansing of the sanctuary as a work of judgment with the message of the first angel of Rev. 14: "The hour of his judgment is come." He asked: "What was that work of cleansing? Is the work of cleansing the Sanctuary fitly heralded by the first angel's message? in other words, Is it a work of judgment? For light on this subject, we shall be obliged to go to the type. Let us look at the type. See the high priest preparing himself to cleanse the Sanctuary; almost the first thing he did was to gird upon him the breastplate of judgment. For what does he put that on? It certainly looks as though he was going to do a judgment work. . . .

"Now read 1 Pet. iv. Verse 5 declares that Christ is ready to judge the quick and the dead. Verse 7. 'But the end of all things is at hand.' Verse 11. 'If any man speak let him speak as the oracles of God.' (Oraclesten commandments. See Acts vii, 38.) Why speak as the oracles of God? Because the oracles are the duty brought out by the third angel's message. Verse 17. 'The time is come that judgment must begin at the house of God: and if it first begin at us, what shall the end be of them that obey not the gospel of God.' Verse 19. Commit the keeping of your souls to God. 1 Tim. v, 24. 'Some men's sins are open before-hand going before to judgment.' We see by this what the judgment is that the first angel of Rev. xiv refers to" *(ibid.* 4:30, Feb. 14, 1854).

The next year Uriah Smith formally developed the idea of judgment, building also on the connection between the cleansing of the sanctuary and the judgment-hour message: "The work of cleansing the earthly sanctuary was a work of judgment. The high priest went into the most holy place, bearing the breast-plate of judgment, and on that breast-plate the names of the twelve children of Israel, to make an atonement for the holy sanctuary, and for all the people of the congregation. Lev. xvi, 33. This prefigured a solemn fact; namely, that in the great plan of salvation, a time of decision was coming for the human race; a work of atonement, which being accomplished, God's people, the true Israel, should stand acquitted, and cleansed from all sin. . . . We read in Dan. vii, 10, that the *judgment* was set, and the *books* were opened. Again in Rev. xx, 12, the books were opened, and the dead were judged out of those things written in the books, *according to their works.* From this we learn that a record is kept of the acts of all men; and from that record, their reward is given them according to their deserts. There is no judgment in this sense of the term, independent of these books of record; but we read [1 Pet. iv, 17] that there is a time when judgment must begin at the house of God; when some men's sins are open beforehand, going before to judgment; [1 Tim. v, 24;] and if, says Peter, it first begin at us what shall the end be of them that obey not the gospel of God. This must be a judgment of the same nature and can refer to no other work than the closing up of the ministration of the heavenly Sanctuary, hence that work must embrace the examination of individual character; and we conclude that the lives of the children of God, not only those who are living, but all who have ever lived, whose names are written in the Lamb's book of life, will during this time pass in final review before that great tribunal. We see, therefore, how in this respect, the work of the type is infinitely surpassed by that of the antitype. . . .

"The first angel proclaimed, Fear God and give glory to him; for the hour of his Judgment is come. At the end of the 2300 days, when that message closed, had that time come? If the judgment scene which takes place in the second apartment of the Sanctuary, to which this proclamation doubtless refers, did not then commence, it had not come; and the first angel with his message, was too fast. But we believe that work did there commence; that there was the time when judgment began at the house of God, and the time came when Daniel, and all the righteous in the person of their Advocate should stand in their lot" (*ibid.* 7:52-54, Oct. 2, 1855).

Finally, in 1857, James White rounded out the doctrine, using "investigative judgment": "The time is come that judgment must begin at the house of God, and if it first begin at us, what shall the end be of them that obey not the gospel of God? And if the righteous scarcely be saved, where shall the ungodly and the sinner appear? 1 Pet. iv, 17, 18.

"This text we must regard as prophetic. That it applies to the last period of the church of Christ seems evident from verses 5-7, 12, 13. In the judgment of the race of man, but two great classes are recognized—the righteous and the sinner, or ungodly. Each class has its time of judgment; and, according to the text, the judgment of the house, or church, of God comes first in order.

"Both classes will be judged before they are raised from the dead. The investigative judgment of the house, or church, of God will take place before the first resurrection; so will the judgment of the wicked take place during the 1000 years of Rev. xx, and they will be raised at the close of that period.

"It is said of all the just, 'Blessed and holy is he that hath part in the first resurrection,' therefore all their cases are decided before Jesus comes to raise them from the dead. The judgment of the righteous is while Jesus offers his blood for the blotting out of sins. Immortal saints will reign with Christ 1000 years in the judgment of the wicked. Rev. xx, 4; 1 Cor. vi, 2, 3. The saints will not only participate in the judgment of the world, but in judging fallen angels. See Jude 6.

"'Some men's sins [the righteous] are open before hand, going before to judgment, and some men [the wicked] they follow after.' 1 Tim. v, 24. That is, some men lay open, or confess their sins, and they go to judgment while Jesus' blood can blot them out, and the sins be remembered no more; while sins unconfessed, and unrepented of, will follow, and will stand against the sinner in that great day of judgment of 1000 years.

"That the investigative judgment of the saints, dead and living, takes place prior to the second coming of Christ seems evident from the testimony of Peter. 'Who shall give account to him that is ready to judge the quick [living] and the dead.' . . . 1 Pet. iv, 5-7.

"It appears that the saints are judged while some are living and others are dead. To place the investigative judgment of the saints after the resurrection of the just, supposes the possibility of a mistake in the resurrection, hence the necessity of an investigation to see if all who were raised were really worthy of the first resurrection. But the fact that *all* who have part in that resurrection are 'blessed and holy,' shows that decision is passed on all the saints before the second coming of Christ. . . .

"When will the cases of the living saints pass in review in the investigative judgment of the house of God? This is a question worthy the candid and most solemn consideration of all who have a case pending in the court of heaven, and hope to overcome. In the order of heaven, we must look for their judgment to follow that of the dead, and to occur near the close of their probation" ("The Judgment," *ibid.* 9:100, Jan. 29, 1857).

Summary of Seventh-day Adventist View. The best presentation of the investigative judgment in current SDA literature is the chapter entitled "The Investigative Judgment," in *The Great Controversy,* by Ellen White, from which the following summarizing sentences are taken:

"The work of the investigative judgment and the blotting out of sins is to be accomplished before the second advent of the Lord" (p. 485).

"He comes to the Ancient of days in heaven . . . at the termination of the 2300 days in 1844. . . . Our great High Priest enters the Holy of Holies, and there appears in the presence of God, to engage in the last acts of His ministration in behalf of man—to perform the work of investigative judgment" (p. 480).

"Jesus will appear as their [His people's] advocate, to plead in their behalf before God" (p. 482).

"The intercession of Christ in man's behalf in the sanctuary above is as essential to the plan of salvation as was His death upon the cross" (p. 489).

"In the great day of final atonement and investigative judgment, the only cases considered are those of the professed people of God" (p. 480).

"Beginning with those who first lived upon the earth, our Advocate presents the cases of each successive generation, and closes with the living" (p. 483).

"Every man's work passes in review before God, and is registered for faithfulness or unfaithfulness" (p. 482).

"The books of record in heaven, in which the names and the deeds of men are registered, are to determine the decisions of the judgment" (p. 480).

"The law of God is the standard by which the characters and the lives of men will be tested in the judgment" (p. 482).

"All who have truly repented of sin, and by faith claimed the blood of Christ as their atoning sacrifice, have had pardon entered against their names in the books of heaven; as they have become partakers of the righteousness of Christ, and their characters are found to be in harmony with the law of God, their sins will be blotted out, and they themselves will be accounted worthy of eternal life" (p. 483).

"When any have sins remaining upon the books of record, unrepented of and unforgiven, their names will be blotted out of the book of life, and the record of their good deeds will be erased from the book of God's remembrance" (p. 483).

"When the work of the investigative judgment closes, the destiny of all will have been decided for life or death" (p. 490).

"When the investigative judgment closes, Christ will come, and His reward will be with Him to give to every man as his work shall be" (p. 485).

INVESTMENT FUND. *See* Sabbath School Offerings.

INYAZURA MISSION SCHOOL. *See* Nyazura Adventist Secondary School.

IOWA. *See* Central States Conference; Iowa Conference; Iowa-Missouri Conference.

IOWA CONFERENCE. A unit of church organization that existed from 1863 to 1980. The Iowa Conference was a part of the Northern Union Conference in 1980. In that year the Iowa Conference merged with the Missouri Conference. These are the statistics reported in early 1980: churches, 60; members, 4,473; church schools, 18; church school teachers, 31; ordained ministers, 16; licensed ministers, 9.

Local churches at the time of the merger in 1980 were Albia, Ames, Atlantic, Audubon, Bedford, Bloomfield, Boone, Burlington, Cedar Rapids, Centerville, Charles City, Cherokee, Clinton, Council Bluffs, Creston, Davenport, Delphos, Des Moines, Dubuque, Estherville, Exira, Fairfield, Forest City, Fort Madison, Glenwood, Greenfield, Grinnell, Guthrie Center, Hampton, Harlan, Hawarden, Hawkeye, Humboldt, Indianola, Iowa City, Keokuk, Knoxville, Lake City, Marshalltown, Mason City, Missouri Valley, Muscatine, Nevada, Newton, Onawa, Osceola, Oskaloosa, Ottumwa, Ruthven, Sioux City, Spencer, Spirit Lake, Toledo, Ute, Village Creek, Washington, Waterloo, Waukon, and Winterset.

Early History. Early contact with Iowa is indicated in a letter to the *Review and Herald* (editorial office dated Feb. 17, 1856), in which Alvarez Pierce of Hardin County, Iowa, stated that although he was isolated, he was a faithful member and appreciated receiving the *Review*. Probably the first evangelistic sermons in Iowa were delivered by Joseph Bates in response to an invitation from W. and H. Bates, who had recently moved to Iowa from Illinois. Beginning Apr. 24, 1856, he gave a course of lectures at a schoolhouse in Pony Hollow, Clayton County, and also preached at a number of other places.

On May 1 Bates went to Waukon, in Allamakee County, and was welcomed by a group of about 30 Seventh-day Adventists who had moved there recently from New England

and New York, including the families of Andrews, Butler, Stevens, and Loughborough. Some of these families had felt hurt over the removal of the place of publication of the *Review and Herald* from the East to Battle Creek, and J. N. Andrews and J. N. Loughborough, ministers among the group, were discouraged.

In December 1856 James and Ellen White drove through snow and ice across the Mississippi River to Waukon to encourage Andrews and Loughborough to enter the field again. This resulted in a revival at Waukon and the return of the two ministers to the work.

The preceding summer Jesse Dorcas had made a lecture tour through the southern part of the state. In the latter part of 1857 Moses Hull conducted the first sustained evangelistic campaign in Iowa. The members at Decatur City were so well pleased with his services that they rented a home for him and presented him with a horse and buggy.

E. B. Saunders, in April 1858, eager to spread the Word of God in Iowa, appealed to the leading brethren of the denomination to send an evangelistic tent, guaranteeing transportation expenses and offering to spend at least half of his time working as a tent hand. In response to this appeal Vermont sent its tent (there were only three in the denomination at this time), and thus the Adventist believers held their first Iowa tent meetings in Lisbon that summer. J. H. Waggoner, who led in these meetings, reported that preachers were busy circulating falsehoods against Adventists and stirring up bitter prejudice, but that the people were listening gladly. The tent was moved to Iowa City later that summer, where James White came and preached.

On Feb. 15, 1859, Hiram Westover of Afton, Iowa, sent an appeal for a minister and wrote that W. H. Brinkerhoff, a lawyer by training, was preaching. He told of hard times and of his gratitude for the *Review* even though he was unable to pay for it. Westover, who owned two farms, was willing to sell one in order to secure the services of Moses Hull, but he could not find a buyer, nor could he find any money to borrow. Under the leadership of Jesse Dorcas, representatives of several companies organized the southern Iowa tent committee and made pledges for the purchase of a tent for Iowa.

With this tent, in the summer of 1859 M. E. Cornell and Moses Hull held a series of meetings at Knoxville. Widespread rumors that the ministers were Mormon polygamists only served to arouse an interest; attendance averaged 600 to 800. A church of 50 was organized, which by April of the next year reported a membership of about 100. When James and Ellen White visited there in March 1860, opponents accused them of being Mormons and threatened to tar and feather them. After a few meetings, however, the ill feelings melted and the crowds grew to such a size that it was necessary to take the windows out of the courthouse, where the meetings were held, in order for those outside to hear. It was here, at a time when the Sabbath school idea was new among Adventists, that the first Sabbath school in Iowa was organized with 70 members. Knoxville thus became the stronghold of Adventism in Iowa.

A hindrance to growth was found in the difficulty of separating the orthodox from the extremist, since no organization had been provided for by the leaders at Battle Creek—not even a name. The church at Fairfield, Iowa, organized with 48 members in June 1860, called themselves "The Church of the Living God"; and the Marion brethren, numbering 50, organized in July as the "Church of Jesus Christ." The first company to organize with the name Seventh-day Adventists was the one at Richmond with 31 members.

Organization of the Iowa Conference. When Brinkerhoff, now a minister, proposed organizing two conferences in Iowa, James White endorsed the idea, and Brinkerhoff called the meeting to organize the Southern Iowa Conference at Knoxville, on Mar. 16, 1862. Thirteen delegates, representing seven churches, chose H. C. Whitney president and R. S. Patterson secretary. A line from Council Bluffs to Des Moines and thence to the Mississippi River was the territorial boundary for the Northern and Southern Iowa conferences. The Northern Iowa Conference was organized at Marion on May 10, 1862, with nine delegates from six churches. They elected J. T. Mitchell president and M. B. Smith secretary.

Before a year had rolled around, however, the two-conference setup was dissolved, and at a meeting at Fairview on Jan. 25, 1863, delegates from nine churches (Waterloo, West Union, Waukon, Marion, Lisbon, Millersburg, Knoxville, Dayton, and Fairview) organized themselves into the Iowa State Conference of Seventh-day Adventists, with J. T. Mitchell as chair and M. B. Smith as secretary. Another meeting was called for autumn. In May the General Conference was organized, and on

September 20, when the Iowa delegates met again at Pilot Grove, they adopted the constitution recommended by the General Conference and elected B. F. Snook as the first conference president and W. H. Brinkerhoff as secretary-treasurer.

Subsequent History. The year 1865 saw a division in Iowa. Snook and Brinkerhoff returned from the General Conference session in the spring of that year with a critical attitude toward James and Ellen White and other leaders, and began to spread their disaffection among the churches. At the Iowa Conference session later in the year efforts of the Whites to conciliate them seemed to succeed, yet shortly afterward the old objections loomed large once more. One of their criticisms was that the counsels of Mrs. White during the Civil War had not given them the help needed in a time of crisis but dealt with less important matters. Their real objections seem to have been their loss of confidence in the leaders and an unwillingness to support the Whites. A change of leadership in Iowa was needed and the Iowa Conference elected as president George I. Butler, then still a layman, elder of the Waukon church. An open revolt resulted, with about half the Marion church following the dissidents into a new movement with headquarters at Marion. H. E. Carver, elected conference secretary, soon joined the Marion Party. Finally the Marion group was disfellowshipped in 1866. After this severe blow to the youthful conference, the General Conference sent seasoned workers, A. C. and D. T. Bourdeau and W. S. Ingraham, who brought prosperity out of chaos in Iowa.

In 1868, only a few weeks after the first Seventh-day Adventist camp meeting at Wright, Michigan, the first Iowa camp meeting was held at Pilot Grove in Washington County. On the last day of the meeting J. N. Andrews baptized 32.

Congregations increased rapidly in the seventies. Osceola, Ruthven, Cherokee, Union, Davis City, Fremont, Bentonsport, and Buffalo Grove joined the sisterhood of churches. Of the 13 companies of Scandinavians scattered in various parts of Iowa, 12 organized their own churches.

The group of adherents at Nevada, which was destined to play a prominent part in Iowa Conference history, was gathered again at this time. (Some Adventists who had looked for the Lord in 1844 and had welcomed Moses Hull when he held tent meetings there in 1858, had formed a company of Seventh-day Adventists then.) On Oct. 15, 1876, R. M. Kilgore organized the present church, with a charter membership of 15.

During the eighties churches were established in numerous places, including Forest City, Webster City, Algona, Fontanelle, Grinnell, Castana, Montezuma, Boonesborough, Council Bluffs, Exira, Alexander, Walnut City, Delphos, Atalissa, Milton Junction, Logan, Harlan, and Audubon. A church was founded in Des Moines in 1885. In the fall of that year A. G. Daniells and a group of young workers started a city mission in that city for the purpose of using it as a training facility. The next year the Iowa Conference purchased a building in Des Moines that served as the mission home, the conference headquarters, and the church. In 1899 a home for unwed mothers was established, and in the same year, the Iowa Sanitarium (later moved to the town of Nevada) and a health food factory. The year 1928 saw a noteworthy advance in Des Moines. As a result of a campaign by F. W. Johnson and his Bible instructor 126 persons were baptized. In the same year a new church school, called the Norman Wiles School, after the South Seas missionary, was dedicated.

The 1890s saw churches established at Cedar Rapids, Urbana, Milford, Sheldon, Muscatine, Davenport, and Dubuque.

In 1902 Iowa became a member of the newly formed Central Union Conference. However, in 1907 it was transferred to the Northern Union.

The worldwide Ingathering program originated from the 1903 project of Jasper Wayne, a nurseryman of Sac City, who traveled about the county selling nursery stock and who conceived the idea of giving away papers and asking for mission offerings.

In 1903 Iowa Industrial Academy, later called Stuart Academy, was established in Stuart. It was moved in 1911 to Nevada, Iowa, and renamed Oak Park Academy.

In the early part of the twentieth century, the Iowa Conference, at the suggestion of the General Conference, shared some of her experienced workers with weaker conferences and overseas areas, continuing to pay their salary for some years.

Later Developments. In the 1940s churches in the following places were organized: Newton, Washington, Ames, Spencer, Greenfield, Estherville, and Toledo. During the same decade two evangelistic campaigns in

Des Moines resulted in the adding of 301 new members. In 1948 the Black church of Des Moines was transferred to the Central States Mission (now the Central States Conference) when that mission was expanded to include the territory of Iowa. During the later 1960s and early 1970s the church of Delphos was reestablished and organized again, which had started back in the 1880s, and a church was established in Bedford.

The Iowa Conference office was first located in Des Moines. However, from 1909 to 1940 it was in Nevada. In 1944 it was moved back to Des Moines and located at 504 42nd Street until 1969. At that time the clubhouse for the Des Moines Golf and Country Club became available, and a generous donation made it possible to purchase it in 1970. This provided adequate facilities for a new office.

On July 20, 1980, the Iowa constituency voted to merge with the Missouri Conference.

Presidents—Southern Iowa Conference: H. C. Whitney (chair), 1862.

Northern Iowa Conference: J. T. Mitchell (acting), 1862.

Iowa Conference: J. T. Mitchell, 1863; B. F. Snook, 1863-1865; G. I. Butler, 1865-1871.

Iowa and Nebraska Conference: G. I. Butler, 1871-1872; H. Nicola, 1872-1876; G. I. Butler, 1876-1877; E. W. Farnsworth, 1877-1878.

Iowa Conference: L. McCoy, 1878-1879; E. W. Farnsworth (acting), 1879; G. I. Butler, 1879-1882; H. Nicola, 1882-1883; E. W. Farnsworth, 1883-1884; O. A. Olsen, 1884-1885; G. I. Butler, 1885-1886; J. H. Morrison, 1886-1892; C. A. Washburn, 1892-1893; E. G. Olsen, 1893-1896; Clarence Santee, 1896-1900; E. E. Gardner (vice president), 1900-1901; L. F. Starr, 1901-1907; M. N. Campbell, 1907-1912; A. R. Ogden, 1912-1920; W. H. Clark, 1920-1923; H. H. Hicks, 1923-1928; C. F. McVagh, 1928-1932; R. S. Fries, 1932-1935; D. S. Osgood, 1935-1941; D. N. Wall, 1941-1942; J. D. Smith, 1942-1946; W. A. Dessain, 1946-1951; D. C. Butherus, 1951-1959; M. D. Howard, 1959-1963; Kimber Johnson, 1963-1969; E. L. Marley, 1969-1976; Don Holland, 1976-1980.

IOWA INDUSTRIAL ACADEMY. *See* Oak Park Academy.

IOWA-MISSOURI CONFERENCE. A unit of church organization comprising the states of Iowa and Missouri. Statistics (1993): churches, 114; members, 10,040; church schools, 27; pastoral staff, 50; Bible instructors, 1; church school teachers, 39. Headquarters: 1005 Grand Avenue, West Des Moines, Iowa. The conference is part of the Mid-America Union.

Institutions. Sunnydale Academy.

The states of Iowa and Missouri each had its own conference until the summer of 1980 when the two conferences merged. The Missouri Conference office in Kansas City closed when this merger occurred, and the office in Des Moines now serves as headquarters for the new two-state conference. Information on the history and development of both the Iowa and the Missouri conferences is presented in separate articles under each name.

Both states had their own academies until the spring of 1980 when circumstances made it necessary to close the Iowa school, Oak Park Academy. Later that summer when the Iowa and Missouri conferences merged, Missouri's Sunnydale Academy in Centralia, Missouri, began to provide high school education for the church members in both states. Information on both of these schools is provided in separate articles under Oak Park Academy and Sunnydale Academy.

Through the decade of the 1970s both the Iowa and the Missouri conferences had their share of financial difficulties. Early in 1980 both conferences reviewed these needs at various conference meetings. A committee was set up to study which locations would be best for administrative offices, the academies, and the youth camp. The leaders from both conferences discussed their options and felt it would be a benefit to the Lord's work to merge the two conferences.

On June 1 the Missouri Conference voted that they were favorable to a merger with Iowa. On June 29 the Iowa Conference voted that they also were favorable. On July 20 at a special joint session, delegates from the Iowa and the Missouri conferences met in Des Moines to finalize a merger. The officers chosen to lead the new two-state conference were Ralph Watts, Jr., president; Robert Peck, secretary; and John Amick, treasurer. Watts and Amick served for only one year. Don Gilbert became treasurer in August 1981, and W. D. Wampler became president in November 1981.

Not long after the merger the leadership discovered they had some tremendous financial challenges. The faithful constituency of both Iowa and Missouri arose to the need, and after a decade this indebtedness has been paid off. During this same time significant improvements costing more than $1 million have been made to Sunnydale Academy and Camp Heritage without incurring additional indebtedness. At the same time a strong evangelism program has been carried out, funded by a strong conference budget program as well as a newly instituted annual evangelism offering.

Ten churches were added since the merger in 1980: Bolivar, Chillicothe, Kansas City Southland, Kansas City Central (Spanish), Marshall, Richville, St. Louis Northwest, St. Louis West County, and Troy, Missouri, and Fort Dodge, Iowa.

Presidents: R. S. Watts, Jr., 1980-1981; William D. Wampler, 1981- .

IOWA SANITARIUM. A medical institution formerly operated by the Iowa Conference, established first at 603 East 12th Street, Des Moines, in 1899. In connection with it, a health food plant was opened the first year, and shortly thereafter a nurse's training program was set up. By 1905 the institution was in difficulty, apparently because of a lack of outstanding medical leadership, a decline in patronage, and the difficulty of collecting accounts. Although the patient capacity was 50, by 1908 patronage had declined to 304 for the year.

The "sanitarium plan" at that time called for the patient to stay at the institution for some time, relax, take walks amid nature, and learn new health habits. Since the city location, amid sundry noises, was not ideal, a tract of land a mile (1.6 kilometers) south of Nevada, Iowa, was purchased, and $47,118 pledged by the members toward an anticipated cost of $60,000. In August 1909 the building was dedicated. The nurse's training program was moved with the sanitarium, and the program was operated until 1929 with from 20 to 30 student nurses each year. Once again the institution began to run behind financially. It has been suggested that failure to change from sanitarium to hospital method, and failure to change to an open staff of local doctors, spelled its downfall. When on Jan. 30, 1943, the institution burned to the ground, with the loss of one life, no attempt was made to rebuild the sanitarium.

IRAN. An Islamic republic in the Middle East, bounded by Turkey and Iraq on the west, the republics of Armenia, Azerbaijan, and Turkmenistan on the north, Afghanistan and Pakistan on the east, and the Persian Gulf on the south. It comprises 636,293 square miles (1.6 million square kilometers), and has an estimated population (1994) of 66 million.

Most of the population is of Aryan descent, speaking the Farsi language; about one fifth is of Turkish origin. There are also groups of Arabs, Armenians, and Assyrians. Almost 99 percent of the people adhere to Shiism. Zoroastrian, Jewish, and Christian minorities are also found in Iran.

Iran, known formerly as Persia, has had a long history. The empire of the Medes and Persians, founded in the sixth century B.C. by Cyrus the Great, extended at its height from the river Indus to the Aegean Sea. Persia appears in biblical history as the land of Cyrus, Darius, and Artaxerxes, who helped the Jews reestablish themselves after the Babylonian exile, and as the land of Esther and Ahasuerus. It was also the cradle of Zoroastrianism and its derivative Mithraism—the sun worship that competed with early Christianity in the Roman Empire. Despite numerous invasions by foreign armies throughout its history, Persia always maintained its identity.

During the period of Arab conquest Persia accepted Islam, but retained its own language. In modern Persia reaction to British and Russian influence resulted in nationalism and a constitutional government, which began a program of modernization. The country is still mainly agricultural, but has rich oil deposits. Since 1935 it has been known as Iran, its ancient Iranian name.

Seventh-day Adventist Statistics. The territory of Iran constitutes the Iran Field, part of the Middle East Union, which is an attached field under the General Conference. Statistics (1992) for *Iran:* churches, 3; members, 52. The Iran Field headquarters are in Tehran, Iran.

Development of Seventh-day Adventist Work. Iran was entered by the SDAs in 1911, when F. F. Oster and Henry Dirksen (both Americans) went there from Germany and settled at Reẕā'iyeh (Urmia) in northwestern Iran near the Turkish border and worked among the many Christians (Armenians and Nestorian Assyrians) living in the area. In 1913 Dirksen left. In the same year Oster married, and with his wife moved to Marāgheh, where there were no other Protestant missionaries. Sometime about 1914 the first converts, a Russian musician and his wife, were baptized. Shortly after World War I broke out, Oster made a preaching tour of the region.

During the war, when all Christians in the area had to flee from the marauding Kurdish tribesmen, the Osters retired to Tabriz. By the time they left on furlough in 1919, there were two Sabbathkeeping families in Iran. Three years later, when the Osters returned to Tabriz, their teachings attracted much attention and led to the first baptism of nationals in Iran, on May 26, 1923. On the same date the first Seventh-day Adventist church in Iran was organized with 22 charter members. The Sabbath school, organized earlier in the year, had an average attendance of 130, and a Young People's Missionary Volunteer Society had about 70 members. The next winter two church schools were opened, one for the Assyrian and one for the Armenian children. Early in 1926 Oster reported that the enrollment in the school at Tabriz was about 120, and that there were six other schools in the country (*Review and Herald* 103:24, Apr. 22, 1926). At the time there were about 150 members in the northwestern part of Iran. In 1925 Dr. H. E. Hargreaves arrived from England to begin medical missionary work. During 1926 Dr. Arsen Arzoo, a Loma Linda graduate, began medical work at Julfa and later in Isfahan, in central Iran, and O. Olson came and took charge of the educational work that was growing rapidly, the enrollment having increased to about 500 students, mostly orphans and children of the refugees. At present the denomination operates no educational institutions in Iran, as both the academy and elementary schools were appropriated by the government.

There was a great need for Seventh-day Adventist publications in the national languages of the people. In Armenian there were only a few tracts, a collection of the Bible readings, and Ellen White's *Steps to Christ;* in Assyrian there were a few tracts, but reports mention no publications in Farsi, the language of the majority. In 1928 Dr. Arzoo moved to Sultanabad (now Arāk), a predominantly Farsi-speaking community, and opened a dispensary (later supervised by Dr. Hargreaves, it appears). The coming of SDAs was welcomed there, and at the request of the leaders of the Muslim community a school was opened in December 1929 with 35 students. By the close of the school year there were 50, and in 1931 there were 126, coming mostly from the Muslim families. In the 1930s, when the educational laws of the country were changed, the mission schools closed. The schools in Iran had served the double role of educating the young people and of creating a reservoir of teachers who could be called upon as national evangelists, of whom there were six in 1928.

As time went on, the work in Iran was carried on in many languages among its many national groups (for example, a station at Resht, opened in 1932, required someone familiar with Syriac, Farsi, Turkish, and Russian); yet, it was for many years largely limited to minority groups, such as Armenians, Russians, and Assyrians. But with the introduction of the Voice of Prophecy Bible Correspondence School in 1948, all the people of Iran came for the first time within the scope of SDA work.

In 1946 the Iran Training School, later called the Iran Adventist Academy, was opened. In 1963 it offered a full high school curriculum authorized by the Ministry of Education. On Mar. 4, 1962, the SDA physical therapy clinic (Tehran Physiotherapy Clinic) was officially opened in Tehran.

A new elementary school was built and dedicated in 1969, and under the principalship of Anoosh Keshishzadeh, grew to a full eight-grade school, with plans to expand to intermediate grades before it was nationalized by the government. Work was begun in Shiraz in 1965 and continued for about five years.

In 1967 the organization in Iran began to change its approach to meet the needs of the non-Christian peoples there. Temperance work was used successfully in the conducting of Five-Day Plans, film projections in schools, and television appearances. In 1971 the provinces of southern Iran were declared unentered territory and set aside for experimental evangelism for Muslims.

Organization. Seventh-day Adventist work in Iran was first organized as a mission of the European Division. For a time after World War I it was part of the Levant Union and then was returned to the European Division. In 1928 it was assigned to the Central European Division, and was later a part of its Section II. In 1932 it was divided into the East and West Persian missions, then in 1935 reunited to form the Iran Mission with headquarters at Tehran. Later the Iran Mission became a part of the Middle East Union, and, still later, of the Middle East Division upon its organization in 1951. In the reorganization of 1970 it became the Iran Field, again under the Middle East Union, and part of the Afro-Mideast Division.

At present the Middle East Union operates as an attached field to the General Conference.

IRAN ADVENTIST ACADEMY. A boarding school for boys on the secondary level, formerly operated by the Iran Mission on a seven-acre (three-hectare) piece of choice property about eight miles (13 kilometers) north of Tehran, Iran, in the foothills of the Alborz Mountains. The curriculum was that prescribed by the Iran Ministry of Education, with the exception of religion.

The school was founded by Paul C. Boynton in Darband in 1946 under the name of Iran Training School, as a coeducational high school, unlicensed by the government. After two years of operation at Darband, high rental costs, among other factors, forced the school to move to the mission building in Tehran. During the furlough of P. C. Boynton, the Iran Mission officers took over responsibilities of running the school until the arrival of C. L. Gemmell, who carried on under extremely adverse political conditions until the school was forced to close down. Thereupon the principal and a few students as well as the budget were transferred to Middle East College in Beirut, Lebanon.

The Iran school was revived under the principalship of M. E. Adams in October 1955 as a vocational junior high school with government recognition.

The Thirteenth Sabbath Offering overflow for the first quarters of 1955 and 1957 provided sufficient funds for the purchase of property and the construction of two buildings for a permanent home. During the first three years the school acquired a boys' dormitory, a teacher's cottage, a 230-foot (70-meter) well, and an elevated water-storage tank. On Nov. 27, 1958, R. R. Figuhr, president of the General Conference, preached at the dedication of the new administration building. In 1959 M. H. Morovati was elected as the first national principal of the school. Thereafter several additions were made to the physical plant, among them a chapel and a teachers' duplex. A notable milestone was passed when on Apr. 14, 1962, the minister of education signed the official permit to operate the school as a full-scale high school under its new name, Iran Adventist Academy. The first twelfth-grade class graduated in 1965. The academy was later appropriated by the government.

Principals: P. C. Boynton, 1946-1950; C. L. Gemmell, 1951-1952; M. E. Adams, 1955-1958; Kenneth Oster, 1958-1959; M. H. Morovati, 1959-1965; Vigain Marcarian, 1965-1966; M. H. Morovati, 1966-1970; Johnny Manassian, 1970-1977; Daniel Manassian, 1977-1990.

IRAN FIELD. *See* Iran; Middle East Union Mission.

IRAN LITERATURE SOCIETY. *See* Middle East Press.

IRAQ. A republic in the Middle East, centering in the Tigris and Euphrates River valleys (Mesopotamia), and bounded by Iran on the east, the Persian Gulf and Kuwait on the south, Saudi Arabia on the southwest, Jordan on the west, Syria on the northwest, and Turkey on the north. It has a territory of 173,259 square miles (448,740 square kilometers) and a population (1994) of 20 million.

The Arabs predominate in the population, but there is a significant minority of Kurds in the north. There are also groups of Turkomans, Assyrians (Nestorian Christians), and Armenians; the Jews, who before the founding of modern Israel numbered about 100,000, have almost all left the country. More than 90 percent of the people are Muslims, belonging either to the Sunni or the Shia sect. The latter has its international headquarters in Iraq. There are about 300,000 Christians and about 40,000 Yezidis (those of a sect worshiping an angel believed to have been formerly the author of evil). Christians are found in all of the main towns, but are concentrated chiefly in the Mosul district. There are the ancient Nestorian, Gregorian, Armenian Orthodox, and Jacobite churches, as well as some Eastern rite groups in union with the Roman Catholic Church, and a few Protestants.

The official language of Iraq is Arabic, but the minority groups have their own languages, and English is widely used for business purposes. The territory of Iraq has been called the cradle of civilization, for it was the land of Sumer, Babylon, and Assyria. It was the home of Abraham, the land of the exile of Israel and Judah, the scene of the long career of Daniel under the kings of Babylon and under Cyrus after the Persian conquest of Babylonia. During the Hellenistic period, in the priestly schools of Mesopotamia, Babylonian and Greek learning fused to produce scientific astronomy—and also astrology, with its planetary week and day of the sun. In the seventh century A.D. the land was conquered by the Arabs, who developed centers of learning and culture in the city of Baghdad before they were overrun by the Mongols in the thirteenth century.

From the sixteenth century until the end of World War I the area was a part of the Ottoman Empire; then after a brief period of British administration it became an independent kingdom in 1932. In 1958 it became a republic.

Seventh-day Adventist Statistics. The Iraq Field is under the Middle East Union, which is in turn an attached union under the General Conference. Statistics (1993) for *Iraq:* churches, 4; members, 152; ordained ministers, 1; licensed ministers, 2. The Iraq Field headquarters are at Baghdad.

Development of Seventh-day Adventist Work. SDA beliefs were introduced into Iraq by a native of Mosul, Bashir Hasso, who was baptized in 1911 in Beirut, having read Uriah Smith's *Daniel and the Revelation* while he was a student at the American University there, and having been instructed further by W. K. Ising, the SDA missionary in Beirut. Although isolated from contact with the church during World War I, he had seven persons ready for baptism when Ising visited Iraq (then called Mesopotamia) in 1923.

During Ising's visit, the Mosul church was organized (Mar. 17, 1923). In 1924 James McGeachy went to Mosul, and three years later reported 19 church members. A. L. Barr came to Mosul in 1927. By 1931 a church school had been opened. Secondary school classes were added in 1945, so that by 1958 the enrollment reached 125. Early in 1955 a Mosul church and school building containing eight classrooms and an auditorium seating 250 was dedicated. Mosul was the first church in Iraq to have its own building, but during the political instability of the early 1960s in northern Iraq most of the church members left and the school (Iraq Training School) was closed. A small company was revived there by Fuad Ashkar in 1957.

The commercial contacts of the first Iraqi Seventh-day Adventists in Baghdad led to the development of a group of SDAs there by 1929. In 1946 the Dar es-Salaam Hospital was opened at Baghdad, and soon it earned a reputation as providing the best medical service in the country. (In June 1959 the hospital was nationalized, and was reopened in July as a government-managed hospital.) In 1947 a school was opened in Baghdad, which with the later addition of secondary school classes became one of the major SDA schools in the Middle East. The school was nationalized in 1974, but SDA teachers staff it and have Sabbath privileges. In the late fifties two churches were established in Baghdad. A major portion of the cost of their construction was raised locally.

Seventh-day Adventist groups were established also at Basra and Kirkuk. In 1936 Sabel Baghdassarian began a Sabbath school at Basra, and in 1948 Rose Haddad opened an elementary school there, which was closed a few years later when no suitable building was available. In 1959 land was purchased and plans were made for the erection of a church (completed 1965) and school building there. At Kirkuk a school was opened in temporary quarters in 1954. Later the school building was purchased and remodeled, providing a chapel seating 80 persons. That same year the Kirkuk school had an enrollment of 230.

Ingathering campaigns have been held since 1952, with Iraq leading the Middle East Division for several years in the amount of funds raised. The first camp meeting in Iraq was held in the summer of 1954 at Behbad. In 1955 the Dar es-Salaam Association, a welfare society, was organized and officially recognized. The same year the first summer camps for juniors were conducted. A Book and Periodical House was established in 1956. Between 1951 and 1960 membership grew from 127 to 163.

Organization. SDA work in Iraq was organized in 1923 as the Mesopotamian Mission of the European Division. In 1928 the mission became part of the Central European Division. Later it was a part of the Arabic Union, then of the Middle East Union of the General Conference Missions Division, and was placed in the Middle East Division in 1951. In 1970 it became the Iraq Field under the Middle East Union. It is the only self-supporting field in the Middle East.

The first Iraqi to direct the church, Behnam Arshat, elected president in 1957, administered the work during the 1958 national revolution, and in 1959 was able to secure official recognition of the church as a national religious organization, the Seventh-day Adventist Church of Iraq.

The work was directed for many years by Ghanem Fargo, a lay businessman in the Baghdad church. In 1992 Basim Aziz was elected president although he is residing in Amman, Jordan.

IRAQ FIELD. *See* Middle East Union; Iraq.

IRAQ TRAINING SCHOOL. *See* Iraq.

IRELAND. A republic comprising the southern portion of the island called Ireland, situated in the northern Atlantic Ocean and separated from England by the Irish Sea. It has an area of 26,600 square miles (68,900 square kilometers), and a population (1994) of 3.5 million, of whom more than 90 percent are

Roman Catholic. Agriculture is the main industry of the republic.

Until some time after the English Reformation, the religion of Ireland was Roman Catholic. During the seventeenth century, as a result of the British sending in settlers, the counties of Northern Ireland became predominantly Protestant. The southern counties, which remained Roman Catholic, became increasingly dissatisfied with British rule, and Irish patriots made many efforts to break the alien yoke. However, all attempts to gain political independence failed until the twentieth century. In 1922 the 26 southern counties were constituted as the Irish Free State with dominion status. In 1937, under a new constitution, this territory became known as Ireland (Eire in the Irish language), and in 1948 it proclaimed itself a republic and withdrew from the Commonwealth. It was accepted into the United Nations, and in 1973 into membership in the European Economic Community. The capital city is Dublin, with a population of more than 500,000; Cork, the next city in size, has a population of 136,000, and only three other cities have a population of more than 20,000.

Seventh-day Adventist Statistics. The territory of Ireland is part of the Irish Mission (which also includes the six counties of Northern Ireland), which is part of the British Union Conference, which in turn is part of the Trans-European Division. Statistics (1993) for *Ireland:* churches, 2; companies, 2; members, 77; ordained ministers, 1. Irish Mission headquarters are at 9 Newry Road, Banbridge, Co. Down, Northern Ireland.

Development of Seventh-day Adventist Work. *Beginnings.* In 1861 the *Review and Herald* published letters from Ireland reporting that five persons had begun keeping the seventh-day Sabbath as a result of receiving books and papers from relatives in the United States. Late in 1885 R. F. Andrews, a native-born Irishman who had gone to the United States and returned on a visit to relatives and friends, preached in Clones and other places, winning one convert. The following year he and S. H. Lane spent four weeks in Ireland preaching in various places including Clones. In 1888 S. N. Haskell, on a visit to that country, reported finding interested persons in Dublin. That same year J. H. Durland came to Ireland, where he spent a month. With Andrews he went to Clones for five days, and baptized a husband and wife.

In 1898 M. A. Altman began work in Dublin, where seven were baptized and organized into a company. During 1902 and 1903 William Hutchinson entered Limerick and Cork. One person accepted the SDA message in Limerick, and remained faithful.

In 1902 the Irish Mission was formed under the presidency of Hutchinson. By 1908 there were 21 members in southern Ireland, 20 of whom were in Dublin. In 1913, the Dublin church, with an organized membership of 15, was received into the fellowship of the Irish churches in Ulster.

Although the civil war of 1916 to 1922 restricted evangelistic activity, growth was steady. In 1928, when the membership stood at 33, the first church building was purchased.

IRIAN JAYA. *See* Indonesia.

IRIAN JAYA ACADEMY (formerly West New Guinea Mission Training School). A coeducational senior boarding academy offering six years of high school (grades 7-12), operated by the Irian Jaya Mission and situated at Doyo Baru, 28 miles (45 kilometers) inland from Jayapura (formerly Hollandia). The school had a 1993 enrollment of 245 students. In addition to the accredited curriculum, the academy has 100 acres (40 hectares) of vegetables, coconuts, and cash crops; offers vocational training in mechanics, carpentry, and farming; is headquarters for training lay evangelists to primitive areas; and operates a two-teacher church school (grades 1-6) of 40 students.

Land for a training school was purchased in January 1954, and in March six young men from the Waropen coast enrolled, although there were neither buildings nor faculty. However, the mission personnel, K. Tilstra, E. H. Vijsma, and their wives, held classes in the back of the unfinished church building in Hollandia. Later two more enrolled. When the school year closed, six received certificates, and several of them entered denominational employment in 1956. One, Jacobus Bindosan, was sent to his own village to do evangelistic work. Others were sent out later to open schools in the interior among the primitive people.

When a flood damaged the original land, a new property, in a large grove, was purchased in February 1956. There were still no regular teachers. In November 1957 Leslie E. Keizer arrived with his family from Indonesia and opened the school six days later with eight students. Soon 60 were enrolled (in grades 4-6). In 1959 a church school was added for grades 1-3, taught by Gloria E. Keizer. In 1963 the European staff was replaced by Indonesians and Filipinos, with D. Kawai becoming the first Irian teacher. A 1965 Thirteenth Sabbath Offering overflow made possible the construction of the first permanent building, a boys' dormitory. From 1967 to 1969 two cement-block staff houses and a cafeteria were added. The school was granted full senior academy status in 1971. An overseas pilot's home, hangar, and airstrip were developed in 1972, making the academy base for the mission's aviation program. The S. Amprimo family returned to Australia in 1973 with the longest record of service to the school (12 years). In the late 1970s a permanent 10-classroom and administration building was constructed.

In 1993 the academy had an enrollment of 89 and a faculty and staff of 10.

Principals: K. Tilstra, 1956-1962; G. Oosterwal, 1962-1963; Chris Dompas, 1963-1967; Chris Mangowal, 1967-1969; Y. S. Maramis, 1969-1970; H. Pasuhuk, 1970-1972; A. Wahongan, 1973-1977; F. Kairupan, 1977-1978; J. Jakob, 1979-1981; J. S. Dimara, 1982-1986; Max Mantiri, 1987; C. Yoafifi, 1988-1989; H. Karubaba, 1990- .

IRIAN JAYA MISSION. *See* Far Eastern Division; Indonesia.

IRISH MISSION. *See* Great Britain and Northern Ireland; Ireland; Trans-European Division.

IRVING, EDWARD (1792-1834). Scottish minister in London, a popular and eloquent preacher on the prophecies. A Presbyterian, he was expelled from his pulpit in 1832 for his unorthodox teachings and founded the "Holy Catholic Apostolic Church." However, this church soon went to extremes that brought him discredit, though he was always respected personally as a devout Christian. He participated in the interdenominational Albury Conferences (1826-1830) and Powerscourt Conferences (1830 and later), for the study of prophecy, out of which grew the modern futurist type of premillennialism. Between 1826 and 1832 he preached in both England and Scotland, and drew large crowds to hear his sermons on the Second Advent. Although his views on the events connected with the Second Advent were vastly different from those of the Seventh-day Adventists, he is regarded as one of those who in the first half of the nineteenth century proclaimed the nearness of the Second Advent.

IRWIN, CHARLES WALTER (1868-1934). Educator; son of George A. Irwin. He received his A.B. from Battle Creek College (1891), his M.A. from the University of Nebraska (1927). After teaching Greek and Latin at Union College (1891-1898), he became principal of the Southern Industrial School in Graysville, Tennessee (1898-1900). From 1903 to 1908 he served in Australia as principal of the school that became Avondale College. This was the pioneer Seventh-day Adventist school in the Southern Hemisphere, and Irwin contributed much to its development.

Returning to the United States, he served as the first president of Pacific Union College (1909-1921), then as associate secretary, and later head (1930-1933) of the Education Department of the General Conference.

IRWIN, GEORGE A. (1844-1913). Administrator. While imprisoned in Andersonville during the Civil War, he read Baxter's *Saint's Everlasting Rest,* which led to his conversion. He later joined the Congregational and then the Methodist Church. In the winter of 1884-1885 he accepted the Seventh-day Adventist faith. Shortly thereafter he entered denominational employment and served successively as district director, treasurer of the Ohio Conference, and president of the Ohio Conference (1889-1895). In 1895 he was appointed president of District No. 2 and in 1897 he was elected president of the General Conference. In 1901 he was chair at the opening of the General Conference when far-reaching changes were made in the organization of the church. After serving as president of the Australasian Union Conference (1901-1905), he served as vice president for North America (1909-1911) and head of the North American Foreign Department. He was president of the Pacific Union Conference (1910-1912), and then served as president of the board of directors of the College of Medical Evangelists (now Loma Linda University's School of Medicine) and as vice president of the Pacific Union Conference.

ISAAC, DANIEL (1871-1956). Minister, administrator. He was educated at Union College, and began preaching in July 1897, in the South Dakota Conference. The following summer he and his wife went to Battle Creek, where they spent two years taking a nurse's course. In

January 1901 he resumed his work in the South Dakota Conference and remained there four years, during which time he was ordained.

In the autumn of 1904 Isaac was called to Europe, where for one year he engaged in evangelistic work in Germany. Then he was sent to Russia, where he served as a conference president from October 1905 until June 1921. After a year of furlough to recuperate his health he entered the employ of the Wisconsin Conference and remained until September 1927, when he transferred to the Oklahoma Conference. Because of sickness he was forced to retire in 1929.

ISAAC, FRANK R. (1880-1962). Minister, administrator. He was born at Parker, South Dakota, and received his B.A. degree from Union College in 1915. Later he did postgraduate work in the Colorado University.

From 1904 to 1912 he worked in the South Dakota Conference, first as a teacher, then as conference treasurer, and later as principal of Elk Point Academy (later Plainview Academy). From 1912 to 1914 he was dean of men at Union College. One year, 1915-1916, he was president of Southwestern Junior College, at Keene, Texas. From there he was called to the presidency of Clinton Theological Seminary at Clinton, Missouri, where he remained until 1923. He was educational and Missionary Volunteer secretary of the Southeastern Union Conference (1923-1930), and of the Lake Union Conference (1930-1937). The next two years he served as president of Oshawa Missionary College at Oshawa, Ontario, Canada. From 1939 to 1950 he was chaplain, pastor, and teacher at the Boulder Sanitarium in Boulder, Colorado. At the age of 70 he retired to California.

ISAAC, JOHN (1873-1956). Minister, administrator, teacher. He attended Union College in Nebraska, where he was converted to the Seventh-day Adventist faith. He immediately prepared for the ministry and began preaching in South Dakota in June 1897, and remained there until 1901 when he was called to Wisconsin. From May 1902 to August 1905 he worked in the Ontario Conference in Canada. From August 1905 to April 1906 he worked in Germany. The next seven years he taught German at Walla Walla College. From July 1913 to September 1918 he served as president of the Oklahoma Conference, after which he spent two years teaching in the Clinton Theological Seminary in Missouri. From June 1920 to August 1922 he worked in the West Oregon Conference. In 1922 he was called to Europe, where he served as president of the Polish Union Conference until April 1931. Returning to the homeland after nine years of taxing labor, he soon found it necessary to retire from active service.

ISHAKA ADVENTIST HOSPITAL. An 85-bed general hospital situated about 40 miles (65 kilometers) from Mbarara on the Fort Portal road in western Uganda. It is owned and operated by the East African Union. The present plant consists of two general wards, a simple maternity ward, two simple private wards, a semiprivate ward plus outpatient and operating blocks, and suitable housing for the staff. There is also a beautiful church building on the hospital grounds.

The current work of the hospital consists of general medical, surgical, pediatrics, obstetrics, and gynecology. Ishaka Adventist Hospital is the emergency and referral medical center of the Bushenyi district. Its community work consists of primary health care, including immunization, family planning services, and counseling, as well as antenatal and other maternal and child health services. AIDS care and counseling are available.

A deliberate spiritual outreach ministry is undertaken in conjunction with the local Adventist church. A primary school and a secondary school are located on the hospital campus. A nurse training program, which was initiated in 1976 but halted in 1977 because of oppressive political conditions, was vigorously revived in 1987, and government accreditation is now being sought for it.

Ishaka Adventist Hospital was located in western Uganda because of the medical needs of the then Ankole district. The omugabe (king) of Ankole made a grant of land for this purpose to the Uganda Field in the late 1940s.

Construction was begun in 1948 by S. Musa, a Kikuyu Seventh-day Adventist, assisted by another African, D. Senyonga, who, being a mechanic, was able to give valuable help, especially in transporting materials. R. J. Wieland, president of the Uganda Field, gave general supervision until 1949, when Dr. D. L. Stilson, under appointment for Ankole, made frequent journeys from Kampala to oversee the construction. A ministerial worker already on the scene began evangelistic work in a temporary chapel.

Medical work was opened in 1950 with

only half of the plant complete. However, within a year the second half was opened and occupied. Else Brandt, of Denmark, served as matron. Dr. D. L. Stilson was assisted by his wife, Dr. Mildred Stilson, and during the years he served as medical director the hospital attained a high reputation throughout Uganda. Constant improvement of the physical plant was made as funds became available.

Medical Directors: D. L. Stilson 1950-1961; W. H. Taylor, 1961-1964; R. M. Buckley, 1964-1967; A. S. Whiting, 1967-1968; E. C. Kraft, 1969-1971; E. J. Shidler, 1971-1972; S. I. Biraro, 1972-1977; hospital under oppressive regime of Idi Amin from September 1977 until April 1979; Sam I. Biraro, 1979-1980; R. Guerrero (hospital administrator), 1980-1982; E. K. Mpora, 1982-1985; A. Rocero, 1986-1987; Sam I. Biraro, 1987-1991; T. Fesaha, 1991-1992; J. M. Omwega, 1993- .

ISING, WALTER KONRAD WILHELM (1881-1950). Missionary to the Middle East, administrator. He was born in Danzig, Germany, accepted the Seventh-day Adventist faith in tent meetings held in Friedensau, Germany, in 1903, and was baptized by E. Frauchiger in Berlin the next year. In 1904 he was drafted into military service, court-martialed and imprisoned for refusing to serve on the Sabbath. In January 1905, after being discharged from the army, he became secretary of the German Union Conference and editor of the *Zions Wächter*. From 1909 to 1920 he was leader of the Syrian-Egyptian Mission, with headquarters in Beirut, Lebanon, although during World War I he was interned on the Isle of Malta for 61 months, during which his health suffered.

From July 1920 to December 1928 Ising was secretary of the old European Division, and from then until 1936 he was superintendent of the Arabic Union Mission. He opened SDA work in Iraq. In 1937 he became secretary of the General Conference branch office in Basel. The next year he was associate secretary of the General Conference Sabbath School Department in Washington. From 1946 until his retirement in 1950 he was a general field secretary. He spent much time and effort finding homes and occupations for European refugees displaced by World War II, and visiting German-speaking members in the United States and Canada. He translated George McCready Price's book *Q. E. D.* and wrote *Among the Arabs in Bible Lands.*

ISLAMIC STUDIES. *See* Seventh-day Adventist Global Centre for Islamic Studies.

ISLE OF MAN. *See* Great Britain and Northern Ireland.

ISLE OF WIGHT. *See* Great Britain and Northern Ireland.

ISOLATED MEMBERS. *See* Conference Church.

ISRAEL. A republic in the Middle East bounded on the north by Lebanon, on the east by Syria and Jordan, on the south by the Gulf of Aqaba, on the southwest by the Arab Republic, and on the west by the Mediterranean Sea. The country is 265 miles (425 kilometers) long, 70 miles (110 kilometers) wide at its widest point, and 12 miles (20 kilometers) at its narrowest point. Its population (1994) is about 5 million. In 1993 there were approximately 120,000 Christians and 36,000 Druzes. These minorities are largely of Arabic origin. Most Christians are Greek Orthodox or Catholic. Since 1948 between 3 and 4 million Jews have immigrated to Israel.

In addition to the areas known as Galilee, the Valley of Jezreel, the coastal plains of Sharon and Philistia, Judea, and the Negev, at the time of the Israeli-Arab war of June 1967, Israel occupied the Syrian Heights of Golan, Samaria (also known as the West Bank), the Gaza Strip, and the Desert of Sinai.

On Mar. 26, 1979, a peace treaty between Israel and Egypt was signed, and on Sept. 13, 1993, Israel and the Palestine Liberation Army agreed on recognition of each nation, bringing autonomy for the Gaza Strip and Jericho.

The territory was the home of the Hebrews from the period of the gradual conquest of the land following the exodus from Egypt in mid-second millennium B.C.; and after the brief united kingdom under David and Solomon (about 1000 B.C.) was divided into the kingdoms of Israel in the north and Judah in the south. It was lost to Assyria and Babylon (eighth to sixth centuries B.C.) then reoccupied under the overlordship of the Persians, the Ptolemies, and the Seleucids. In the second century B.C. it was the seat of an independent Jewish state ruled by the Hasmonaean priest-kings; then it came under the power of Rome shortly before New Testament times.

Palestine remained the homeland of the Jews until the final dispersion under the Roman emperors of the first and second centuries. The area was taken over by the Arabs in the seventh century, and Jerusalem became one of the centers of Islam. Groups of Jews remained in the country through the centuries under Muslim rule (on the same basis as the Christian minorities), but there was no large-scale immigration of Jews until modern times. In the Middle Ages, for several centuries, the Crusaders struggled for control over the country, but eventually the land came under the rule of the Turks. The Turkish Empire held it until World War I, after which Palestine was made a mandate of Great Britain. In the course of that war the British government issued the Balfour declaration recommending "the establishment in Palestine of a national home for the Jewish people." This declaration encouraged the Zionist dream of an independent Jewish state in Palestine, and spurred large-scale immigration of Jewish settlers into the area. When the British mandate lapsed, and the United Nations voted for the partition of Palestine, the ensuing Jewish-Arab war resulted in the present boundary, drawn as an armistice line, between Israel and Jordan. Thus the history of the present-day state of Israel dates from 1948 when Great Britain surrendered its mandate over Palestine and an independent Israeli state was proclaimed.

The official languages of Israel are Hebrew (developed from biblical Hebrew and enriched by a modern technical and cultural vocabulary borrowed partly from Western European sources) and Arabic. Most of the people, speaking the various languages of the countries from which they came, had to learn Hebrew almost as a foreign tongue. Although Israel is a Jewish state, religious freedom is accorded by law. Many Christian monks and pilgrims throng the monasteries established to preserve various traditional sites of the Holy Land.

Seventh-day Adventist Statistics. The territory of Israel constitutes the Israel Mission, which is an attached field of the Trans-European Division. Statistics (1993) for *Israel:* churches, 5; members, 128; ordained ministers, 1; licensed ministers, 2. Headquarters: Advent House, 4 Rehov Abraham Lincoln, Jerusalem, Israel.

Seventh-day Adventist Work. *Beginnings.* The first Seventh-day Adventist to come to Israel (which was then Palestine) was Clorinda S. Minor, who came from the United States in 1849. She lived with some other SDAs working at rehabilitating the land, planting groves, and helping people, especially Jews, who were among the first returning to the land of their forefathers. She firmly believed that this was part of God's plan in the return of Jesus in glory.

According to extant records, another of the first SDAs to visit Palestine was G. C. Tenney, in 1892 *(Review and Herald* 70:106, Feb. 14, 1893). However, no work was begun at that time. Abram La Rue, the pioneer SDA lay missionary in the Far East, visited Jerusalem sometime between 1890 and 1897, but there is no record of any missionary work conducted there by him. SDA work in Palestine, in the area of Israel, began with the visit of Henry P. Holser, the superintendent of the European Mission, to Haifa, Jaffa, Sarona (near Jaffa), and Jerusalem early in 1898. He made the acquaintance of some of the German colonists settled near these cities, distributed literature among them, and took subscriptions to an SDA health journal. On his return to Europe he made an appeal at a general meeting held in Hamburg for volunteers to work in Palestine. J. H. Krum, a German SDA from the United States, responded, and with his wife went to Jaffa (biblical Joppa) in the same year and conducted colporteur work among the German colonists. Toward the end of 1899 F. Hörner, a male nursing graduate of the Basel Sanitarium, went to Jaffa and opened treatment rooms there. A few months afterward Miss Hausmann, a nurse, who later married Hörner, joined him in the medical work. According to a report that appeared in the *Review and Herald* of Nov. 26, 1901 (78:771), in the preceding 12 months these nurses had given 1,260 treatments. By 1901 Krum had moved to Jerusalem and had begun medical work there in the old city, joined by S. Jespersson and his wife, from Basel.

While on a visit to Palestine in 1904 L. R. Conradi, then director of the European work of the church, baptized three converts in Jaffa about the end of February and organized the Jaffa-Jerusalem church *(Review and Herald* 81:12, July 21, 1904), composed largely of workers' families and German converts. Four years later the total membership was about 20.

In 1908 the medical institution in Jerusalem reported that Europeans, Arabs, and Jews were seeking remedial treatments there.

In 1911 a tent meeting was held in a German colony that had established itself on Mount Carmel.

Interruption by World War I. In 1914, at the outbreak of World War I, several German missionaries (among them W. K. Ising) in Syria and Palestine were either interned, or forced to leave the field. Henry Erzberger, superintendent of the Syrian Mission from 1913 to 1917, who was a Swiss citizen, continued to live for a time in Jerusalem.

Reestablishment of the Work. Little is known about the development of the work from 1918 until 1929, when Ising returned to Beirut (in Lebanon) and took charge of the work in Palestine. In 1929 the medical institution in Jerusalem, confiscated by the Turks in the course of World War I, was reestablished by Bror Färnström and his wife, both physical therapists trained in the Skodsborg Sanitarium in Denmark. They found, left over from the pre-1914 institution, a sign "Wasserbehandlungen" (water treatments), a small faradic apparatus, and a book of statistics. They opened in rented quarters in a house outside the Damascus Gate, in what is now Israel. They remodeled the interior of the house to fit it for use, but the facilities were meager. The housing and facilities were not so good as before, but the situation improved considerably when in 1934 the treatment rooms were moved into a building erected by the mission on a site acquired in 1930 near the YMCA building, west of the walled city, and hence also in what is now Israel. The building, containing apartments, a meeting hall, and a basement for treatment rooms, was officially dedicated on Apr. 19, 1935. A workers' meeting was held on that occasion, attended by 35 missionaries and other workers from the Middle East countries.

About 1934 the headquarters of the Arabic Union Mission, which had been in Beirut, Lebanon, were transferred to Haifa. At Haifa another institute for massage, hydrotherapy, and electric treatments was established, and operated by two nurses, Alfred Piorr and his wife. Along with the medical work, Erich Schubert conducted evangelistic campaigns.

In 1935 the first thorough house-to-house canvassing with SDA books was conducted by a colporteur named Hamed Abeid, a national of the country who had accepted the SDA faith while in Cuba and had returned to Palestine. In the course of the 10 weeks that it took him to cover Jerusalem he sold 700 books in different languages, one third of them religious. He sold many copies of the book *Health and Longevity,* by Dr. A. C. Selmon.

In 1936 an interesting reference to Seventh-day Adventists in Jerusalem was made in a meeting of a standing committee of the British House of Commons. In the official report of the proceedings of Mar. 24, 1936, it is stated that "in Jerusalem they are well established and well known for their works of charity, and are held in deservedly high repute."

World War II and After. When World War II broke out the situation in the Middle East became most difficult for the SDA Church. Afterward, when the British mandate lapsed and Israel became an independent state in 1948, the church lost all its Arab members, who found refuge in the Arab countries. A few of Jewish origin remained. For the next several years the number of SDAs in Israel increased gradually, mostly through the immigration of SDA refugees of Jewish origin from Bulgaria and some from Shanghai. All through this period the Färnströms remained in charge, and when they left in 1952 for the SDA hospital in Karachi, Pakistan, there were about 12 members in Israel.

In 1950, on the occasion of a visit by an SDA minister of Jewish origin from Europe, a general meeting of all members was convened in Jerusalem for the purpose of reorganizing the church and celebrating the Lord's Supper. Many of the members could not understand each other, having come from various countries, so that it was necessary to use interpreters during services. On the occasion of a visit by E. E. Roenfelt in 1951, the translations were made into the Russian, Bulgarian, German, and Hebrew languages.

This territory was a part of the Central European Division until its subdivision into Sections I and II in 1935, when it was assigned to Section II, with headquarters in Basel, Switzerland. In 1937 the headquarters were moved to Washington, D.C. In 1938 the mission was placed directly under the administration of the General Conference, where it remained until the organization of the Middle East Division in 1951.

Because of restrictions on travel to and from the Arab countries, a change became necessary, and in 1955 the Israel Field became a part of the Euro-Africa Division. Since the Israeli-Arab War (1967), the Arab East Center in Jerusalem has been attached to the field. As a result of further realignment of territories at the time of the 1985 General Conference session, the Israel Field became part of the territory of the Trans-European Division, in 1986. At this time the Arab East Center in Jerusalem was remodeled and is now the much-appreciated Jerusalem Study Center, operated by Andrews University.

ISRAEL, MENDEL CROCKER (1834-1921). Evangelist, missionary. Born in Nova

Scotia, he moved in his early 20s to New England, and in 1858 to Oregon. In 1874, while in Massachusetts doing carpentry work with his brother, John, an ardent Seventh-day Adventist, he accepted the SDA faith. The next year he attended a biblical institute in San Francisco conducted by James White, Uriah Smith, and J. H. Waggoner, and was encouraged to enter evangelistic work. He was ordained in 1878 and spent many years in evangelism in the California Conference.

In 1885, 10 years after Ellen White had urged the establishing of a mission in Australia, Israel went with the first group of SDA workers and conducted vigorous evangelistic campaigns in Melbourne, Adelaide, and other cities. After a conference was established in 1888, he did pioneering work in Tasmania, went to New Zealand in 1889, and later was president of the conference for several years. In 1896 he returned to evangelistic work in California and retired in 1905.

ISRAEL FIELD. *See* Israel; Trans-European Division.

ISRAEL, PROPHECIES CONCERNING. OT predictions concerning the role of ancient Israel under the covenant relationship, here considered especially with respect to Israel's witness to the true God, to the coming of Messiah, and to the establishment of the Messianic kingdom. Seventh-day Adventists regard these predictions as a declaration of the divine purpose with respect to Israel as the covenant people and as conditional upon their cooperation with God's purpose for them as a nation.

Origin of the Seventh-day Adventist View. *Millerite Interpretation.* William Miller and his associates firmly rejected the then popular millennarian belief (of Literalist premillennialism) that the prophecies of the Bible predicted the last-day "return of the Jews, as such, either before, at, or after the Advent of Christ, to Palestine, to possess that land a thousand years" (Josiah Litch, in *Advent Shield* 1:47, 48, May 1844). All of them shared the conviction that Christ's return to this earth was imminent and that His coming would end human probation and that He would purify the earth by fire and set up His eternal kingdom.

J. V. Himes is quoted as saying in 1850 that the Millerites had always battled against the prevailing "Judaizing notions" in regard to the age to come, because "Judaism and Adventism are two different things" (Isaac C. Wellcome, *History of the Second Advent Message,* p. 592). By "Judaism" and "Judaizing notions" he was referring to the belief that the coming age would see the Jews restored not only to Palestine but also as God's chosen nation, ruling over mortal nations in a millennial kingdom on earth, in which sin and death would continue. That opposition to this was a distinctive point of Adventist doctrine from the first is seen from the recommendation of the twelfth Millerite Second Advent Conference (in 1842) that "all persons who reject the doctrines of temporal millennium and the restoration of the Jews to Palestine, either before or after the Second Advent, and who believe the Second Advent of Christ and the *first* resurrection to be the next great events of prophetic history, be invited to enroll their names as member[s] of this conference" *(The Signs of the Times* 3:69, June 1, 1842; see SB No. 1083).

It is also affirmed: "No portion of the New Testament scriptures [gives] the most indirect intimation of the literal restoration of the Jews to old Jerusalem; we believe that the arguments drawn from the Old Testament prophecies are based on a mistaken view of those prophecies" *(ibid.).*

Branding the millennarian view a "vain supposition," William Miller declared: "There is not a text, promise or prophecy, written or given of God" to support the application of OT prophecies concerning a future restoration of the Jews *(Views of . . . William Miller,* ed. 1842 by J. V. Himes [Second Advent Library, No. 1], p. 233).

Early Seventh-day Adventist writers differed from the Millerites in expecting the renewal of the earth, not at the Second Advent, but at the end of the millennium, but with them held that the Second Advent and the first resurrection will end human probation and usher in the reign of the glorified saints—all the redeemed, both Jew and Gentile—and that this allows no place for a post-Advent kingdom of restored Jews in the mortal state. Not much appears in SDA publications on the subject until the "Age to Come" disaffection of the early 1850s brought the topic into discussion. Probably the first major treatment of the subject was part of a series of articles by J. H. Waggoner in early 1856 (see *Review and Herald* 7:177, Mar. 6; 7:185, Mar. 13; etc.).

Reasons Given in SDA Writings. Reasons given by Miller and early SDA writers for rejecting the millennarian view as unscriptural may be summarized as follows:

1. The OT prophecies were a declaration of

God's *purpose* for literal Israel, and their fulfillment to literal Israel was strictly *conditional* upon Israel's cooperation with the divine purpose.

"All of God's purposes of grace to man are conditional, [and] as the blessings set before them [the Jews] were conditional, they could *claim* them only on the fulfillment of the conditions. . . . We consider that this was a conditional prophecy, the promises of which have been forfeited" (J. H. Waggoner, *The Kingdom of God* [1859], pp. 87-109).

"This [the old] covenant was made at Horeb, and was conditional, as recorded in Ex. xix. The Lord said to them, '*If* ye will obey my voice indeed, and keep my covenant, *then* ye shall be a peculiar treasure unto me above all people' " (J. H. Waggoner, in *Review and Herald* 9:77, Jan. 8, 1857).

"The promise to Abraham and to his seed of the possession of the literal land of Canaan was conditional [Deut. 4:1, 2; 5:32, 33; 6:1-3; 8:1 cited in proof]" (A. S. Hutchins, in *Review and Herald* 9:197, Apr. 23, 1857).

On this point of conditionality, Ellen White comments: "Through the Jewish nation it was God's purpose to impart rich blessings to all peoples" (COL 286).

"[But] the glorious possibilities set before Israel could be realized only through obedience to God's commandments" (*ibid.* 305 cf. PP 118, 368, 369).

"These promises were conditional on obedience" (PK 704).

"As they would obey the divine laws, they would receive the divine blessing" (in SDACom 2:998).

"The promises and the threatenings of God are alike conditional" (Ev 695).

2. The promises to literal Israel were based on the old covenant relationship, and because of the nation's failure to comply with the conditions God attached to the promises, the Jewish people forfeited their right to those promises.

"Do the Scriptures teach that the natural descendants of Jacob are entitled to any special privileges or blessings under the new covenant [either now or in the future]? We affirm that they do not, and appeal to the testimony of God's word" (J. H. Waggoner, *The Kingdom of God* [1859], p. 88). "The promises of the kingdom . . . were forfeited under the old covenant" (*ibid.*, p. 101).

"They could *claim* them only on the fulfillment of the conditions. . . . Therefore it must be admitted that they can receive nothing in the future for any consideration in the past" (*ibid.*, p. 87).

At Sinai, Israel "entered into a solemn covenant with God, pledging themselves to accept Him as their ruler, by which they became, in a special sense, the subjects of His authority" (PP 303).

"God had separated them from the world, that He might commit to them a sacred trust. He had made them the depositaries of His law, and He purposed, through them, to preserve among men the knowledge of Himself. Thus the light of heaven was to shine out to a world enshrouded in darkness, and a voice was to be heard appealing to all peoples to turn from their idolatry to serve the living God" (*ibid.* 314).

They were thus to "stand forth under His wise and holy rule as an example of the superiority of His worship over every form of idolatry" (*ibid.*).

"All who . . . turned from idolatry to the worship of the true God were to unite themselves with His chosen people. As the numbers of Israel increased they were to enlarge their borders, until their kingdom should embrace the world" (COL 290).

"If Jerusalem . . . had heeded the light which Heaven had sent her, she might have stood forth in the pride of prosperity, the queen of kingdoms. . . . She might through Him have been . . . the mighty metropolis of the earth" (DA 577).

"Had Israel as a nation preserved her allegiance to Heaven, Jerusalem would have stood forever, the elect of God" (GC 19).

"Had Israel remained true to God, this glorious building [the Temple] would have stood forever, a perpetual sign of God's especial favor to His chosen people" (PK 46).

"Christ would have averted the doom of the Jewish nation if the people had received Him. . . . [But] they rejected the Light of the world, and henceforth their lives were surrounded with darkness as the darkness of midnight. The doom foretold came upon the Jewish nation" (*ibid.*, p. 712).

"A nation's sin and a nation's ruin were due to the religious leaders" (DA 738).

"When Christ should hang upon the cross . . . , Israel's day as a nation favored and blessed of God would be ended" (GC 21).

3. The restoration promises were made prior to, or in connection with, the return from Babylonian captivity, and applied to the restoration period.

"There is not a text, promise or prophecy written or given of God, which was not given before their return from Babylon, and I believe was then literally fulfilled" (William Miller, *Views,* p. 233).

"Had Israel been true to God, He could have accomplished His purpose through their honor and exaltation" (DA 28).

"The captivity would not have been necessary" (PK 564).

The covenant promises might "have met fulfillment in large measure during the centuries following the return of the Israelites from the lands of their captivity" *(ibid.* 703, 704).

4. The Jews are now entitled to salvation on the same basis as the people of every other nation, and OT promises not already fulfilled to them belong now in principle to the church, the spiritual seed of Abraham from all nations, in so far as they are applicable to the new historical situation. The Boston Second Advent Conference went on record to the effect that "the Old Testament prophecies . . . have been fulfilled in what the gospel has already done, or remain to be fulfilled in the gathering of all the spiritual seed of Abraham into the New Jerusalem" *(The Signs of the Times* 3:69, June 1, 1842; see SB, No. 1083).

"There are other [OT] prophecies that cannot apply in the first dispensation, but to a state more glorious than the present, where death and mortality cannot enter" (F. M. Bragg, in *Review and Herald* 9:11, Nov. 13, 1856).

The Israelite people "forfeited their blessings as His chosen people." Nevertheless "the glorious purposes which He had undertaken to accomplish through Israel were to be fulfilled. All who through Christ should become the children of faith were to be counted as Abraham's seed; they were inheritors of the covenant promises" (PP 476).

"That which God purposed to do for the world through Israel, the chosen nation, He will finally accomplish through His church on earth today" (PK 713, 714).

The prophecies of the OT concerning Israel's Messianic role "are today meeting fulfillment in the advancing lines of mission stations that are reaching out into the benighted regions of earth" *(ibid.* 375).

5. For a valid application of OT prophecies in the new NT historical situation to the Christian church, we must look to the inspired writers of the NT for guidance. The Boston Second Advent Conference of 1842, as has been noted, based its rejection of a literal application of the OT prophecies to a future kingdom of the Jews in Palestine for a thousand years on the fact "that no portion of the New Testament scriptures" contains even an "indirect intimation of the literal restoration of the Jews to old Jerusalem."

The same point is made in an early SDA book: "All of *our views* of the Old Testament promises and prophecies must bow to the expositions in the New Testament" (Waggoner, *The Kingdom of God* [1859], p. 97).

Biblical Basis of Seventh-day Adventist View. *Promises to Israel Based on the Covenant.* All of God's dealings with the Israelites in OT times were based on the covenant that had originally been ratified between God and Abraham (Gen. 12:1-3; 15:18; 17:2-7). At Mount Sinai, more than four centuries later, Israel took an oath of allegiance to God, accepting Him as their sovereign and becoming in a special sense subjects of His authority (Ex. 19:5-8; 24:3-8; Deut. 7:6-14). This covenant continued in force until the leaders of the nation formally rejected Jesus as the Messiah and declared before Pilate their allegiance to "no king but Caesar" (Matt. 21:43-45; 23:36-38).

Under the covenant relationship the people of Israel pledged themselves to obey God (Ex. 19:1-8; 24:3-8), and He, on His part, promised to give them the land of Palestine as their inheritance (Gen. 15:18; Deut. 1:7, 8) and to endow them with unique physical, intellectual, and material blessings designed to render them the greatest nation upon the face of the earth. Among these covenant blessings were health, vigor, and immunity to sickness and disease (Ex. 15:26; Deut. 7:12-15); superior mental acuity and sound judgment (Deut. 4:6); skill in the cultivation of the soil that would gradually restore their land to the fertility and beauty of Eden, and bring prosperity to their flocks and herds (Deut. 7:13; 28:3-5, 8, 12; Isa. 51:3; Mal. 3:10, 11). As a result of obedience Israel would enjoy unparalleled prosperity and reach the highest standard of living of any nation (Deut. 8:18; 28:11-13), and become the greatest nation on the face of the earth (Deut. 4:6-8; 7:14; 28:1, 2, 10, 13; Jer. 33:9; Mal. 3:12). All of these blessings were predicated on Israel's wholehearted cooperation with the revealed will of God, and to their best effort He would add Heaven's rich blessing (Deut. 4:9; 28:1, 13, 14; 30:9, 10). Israel was thus to be a living example and a witness to the world of the infinite superiority of the worship and service of the true God (Deut. 4:6-9; 7:12-15; 28:1-13; Isa. 49:3, 6; 61:9; 62:1, 2), and one by one the nations would unite with Israel in serving Him (Isa. 2:2, 3; 11:10; 14:1; 19:18-22; 45:14; 55:5; 56:6, 7; 60:1-12; Jer. 3:17; 16:19; 33:9; Zech. 2:11; 8:20-23).

But as a result of apostasy, Israel forfeited possession of the land of Canaan, which was theirs only by virtue of the covenant relationship, and spent 70 years as captives in Babylon (2 Chron. 36:14-17; Isa. 5:1-7; Jer. 25:5-7; 29:18, 19; 32:21-23; Eze. 7:2-9; 12:3-28; 20:28, 35-38; 21:25-32; 36:18-23; Micah 2:10; cf. Hosea 9:3, 15), where they were to learn in adversity the lessons they had failed to learn during times of prosperity (Jer. 25:5-7; 46:28; Eze. 20:35-38).

Restoration After the Exile. After the Captivity, God renewed His covenant with Israel, restored them to their own land, and promised that all the covenant promises might yet come to pass if they would be loyal to Him (Jer. 31:3-38; 33:3-26; Eze. 36:8-11, 21-38; 43:10, 11; Micah 4:8-12; Zech. 1:17; 2:12; 6:15; 10:6). It is significant that all OT promises looking forward to a time of restoration for the Jews as the covenant people *anticipated their return from Babylonian captivity* (Isa. 14:1-7; 27:12, 13; Jer. 16:14-16; 23:3-8; 25:11; 29:10-14; 30:3-12; 32:37-44; Eze. 34:11-16; 37; Amos 9; Micah 2:12, 13). A probationary period of 490 years was allotted to Israel in which to measure up to God's purpose for them as a nation (Dan. 9:24-27; cf. Jer. 12:14-17). This period of time was to culminate with the coming of Messiah and the establishment of His kingdom.

The Kingdom Forfeited in the Rejection of the Messiah. At the time appointed Messiah came, but His own people "received him not" (John 1:11). Three days prior to the crucifixion Christ pronounced Heaven's verdict upon the Jewish nation: "The kingdom of God shall be taken from you, and given to a nation bringing forth the fruits thereof"; "your house is left unto you desolate" (Matt. 21:43; 23:38).

The Babylonian captivity did not mark "a full end" of Israel's role as the covenant people (Jer. 4:27; 5:18; 46:28), but when the Jews rejected their Messiah there was no assurance of reinstatement; this rejection was permanent and irrevocable (cf. Jer. 12:14-17).

The Kingdom Transferred. With the irrevocable rejection of Israel as the covenant people at the cross, the rights, privileges, promises, and blessings of the covenant relationship passed to the Christian church as God's chosen representative on earth (Matt. 28:19, 20; 2 Cor. 5:18-20; Acts 10:34, 35; Gal. 3:9, 27-29; 1 Peter 2:9, 10; Rom. 9:24-26, 30, 31; 10:12, 13). Like everyone else, individual Jews could still find salvation, but they must do so as believers in Christ and not as descendants of Abraham (Rom. 9:6; 11:1, 2, 11, 15, 22-26). NT writers often reinterpret OT prophecies originally addressed to literal Israel, in terms of the new historical situation, applying them to the church (Acts 2:17-21; 15:15-17; Rom. 9:25-29; 1 Cor. 9:9, 10; Gal. 3:11, 16; 4:22-31; Heb. 4:1-10; 8:8-12; 1 Peter 2:9, 10. Many OT prophecies—such as those affirming Israel's worldwide mission and the ingathering of the Gentiles, and those pointing forward to the eternal rest in Canaan—never were, and now never can be, fulfilled to Israel as a nation.

The concept that the covenant promises must be fulfilled to literal Israel is based on a misconception of the conditional nature of prophecy. Since the Jews forfeited their special status as the covenant people, there is no valid scriptural basis for relating the present-day return of the Jews to Palestine, and the modern state of Israel, to the OT covenant promises.

Fulfillment Under the New Testament. After the transfer of the covenant relationship to the church, many OT promises not already fulfilled to literal Israel would never be fulfilled because they were strictly conditional upon Israel's retaining its status as the covenant people. Others would be fulfilled to the Christian church, as spiritual Israel, *in principle*—but not necessarily in detail, because of the fact that many details of the prophecies were made with respect to Israel as a literal nation situated in the land of Palestine, whereas the Christian church is a spiritual "nation" scattered all over the world. Obviously, such details cannot apply to the church, at least in a literal sense.

Inasmuch as all the OT promises originally applied to literal Israel, it is only when a later inspired writer applies them to the new historical situation, in which the church is God's chosen instrument, that we can be positive of the validity of this application. Details that depended upon the Jews continuing as God's chosen people in the land of Palestine have lapsed by default. To lift selected passages out of their literary and historical context in the OT and to apply them arbitrarily to our day is not valid exegesis.

In summary, the OT prophecies concerning Israel constitute a declaration of God's *purpose* with respect to the Jews as the covenant people; these prophecies were strictly *conditional* upon their cooperation; by rejecting Jesus as the

Messiah the Jewish nation withdrew from the covenant relationship and forfeited its special relationship to God under the covenant; the covenant promises and privileges were permanently transferred to the Christian church as the new covenant people, to be fulfilled to the extent that they are applicable under the new historical situation; details dependent on literal Israel retaining its status as the covenant people, resident in Palestine, have lapsed by default; we are dependent upon later inspired writers for a valid application of these OT predictions to the church.

ISRAEL, RESTORATION OF. *See* Israel, Prophecies Concerning.

ISRAEL, "SPIRITUAL." *See* Israel, Prophecies Concerning.

ISRAELITE. *See Shabbat Shalom.*

ISRAELITE HERITAGE INSTITUTE. An organization to which was assigned, by action of the General Conference Committee, the work of fostering Seventh-day Adventist work among the Jewish people through Bible correspondence lessons, radio programs, a quarterly periodical, and also evangelistic work—either by public meetings, where advisable, and/or personal activities, such as house-to-house visitation.

Hebrew Scripture Association. The forerunner of the Israelite Heritage Institute, the Hebrew Scripture Association, was formed in 1955 with W. E. Read as its president. The work of the association was, in the main, initiatory and advisory, for its activities were carried on largely through the regular channels of the union and local conferences. The association was composed of 19 members, but its routine work was cared for by an executive committee of seven, operating from the denominational headquarters on budgets voted by the annual Autumn Council of the General Conference.

Earlier efforts to win Jewish converts had been included in the program of the Bureau of Home Missions (organized in 1905 as a department of the General Conference to promote gospel work among the foreign language population of the United States and Canada), because large numbers of the Jews in these countries at that time spoke Yiddish. About 1911 F. C. Gilbert, an English-born Jew converted to Christianity in America, who had become an SDA minister, was appointed to supervise the Jewish work. Gilbert for some time had been an editor of evangelistic publications for Jews, and under his supervision the development of SDA publications and fieldwork on behalf of the Jews had been begun.

Later S. Kaplan, his successor, also a convert from Judaism, became concerned about the need for literature for the Jewish people and initiated a quarterly journal named *The Sabbath Exponent* (now *Shabbat Shalom).* Other Jewish workers helped in caring for the work in different parts of the field.

The approach to Jewish people has been varied according to circumstances, and practically all who have been won have come in through personal ministry. There has never been any mass evangelism of the Jews. In recent years reports have come from all parts of the world regarding Jews accepting Jesus as the Messiah.

The Times Square Center, 410 W. 45th Street, New York City, was opened as an evangelistic center for Jewish work in 1959. Lectures on healthful living given by Jay Hoffman, an SDA minister of Jewish ancestry, attracted as many as 400 Jewish persons at one time.

The Spirit of Prophecy states that many Jews will be converted in the last days.

ISTITUTO AVVENTISTA VILLA AURORA SCUOLA MEDIA E LICEO SCIENTIFICO SEMINARIO DI TEOLOGIA. *See* Italian Junior College.

IT IS WRITTEN. A plan of global evangelism that centers on 30-minute videotapes (films until 1969) produced in color for television release. It combines mass communication with public evangelism and personal contacts made by laypeople.

The plan was developed in 1955 when George Vandeman, an associate secretary of the Ministerial Association (later a general field secretary of the General Conference), was asked to explore the possibilities of a new approach to city evangelism.

With an initial appropriation from the 1955 Autumn Council, the first films were made in California. Production moved to the East Coast in the fall of 1956. Two laymen, Dr. J. W. Field and Don Loveridge, contributed heavily to the new project. The General Conference was headquarters for production until the end of 1971 when It Is Written moved to Thousand Oaks, California, where the Seventh-day Adventist Media Center is now located.

During the early years It Is Written (IIW) operated with an extremely small staff.

Marjorie Lewis Lloyd assisted with both scripts and production through 1971. At that time David L. Jones assumed production responsibilities. In 1993 the staff included 15 persons serving in production, field services, public relations, and prayer ministries.

Until 1992 the telecast featured George Vandeman as speaker, with a unique semidocumentary format. The series was supplemented by a blend of doctrinal, health, and felt-needs telecast messages designed to appeal to a broad secular audience. With an inventory of more than 550 Scripture-based programs, It Is Written produces each year approximately 36 additional telecasts to assure that material remains as up-to-date as possible.

Viewers are invited to telephone or write for free books or other materials. Interested individuals are guided through a Bible course by local conference laypeople or pastors. With careful follow-up, the program is a continuing source of baptisms.

Mark Finley became the speaker/director of IIW in September 1992. Ministerial secretary for the Trans-European Division from 1985-1990, Finley founded the North American Division Evangelism Institute in 1979. Vandeman continued with the ministry as speaker emeritus and consultant.

It Is Written has the distinction of producing the first religious telecast regularly broadcast in color. It has been aired at various times throughout Australia and Europe. A French It Is Written telecast, with George Hermans as speaker, covered eastern Canada from 1974-1990. In 1992 the It Is Written Foundation in Canada merged with the Destiny telecast and began producing programs for Canada exclusively, using Mark Finley as speaker and Henry Feyerabend as associate speaker.

After the collapse of Communism in the former Soviet Union, IIW blanketed the Commonwealth of Independent States with programs dubbed into Russian. During that same time a group of laypersons in Brazil funded the production of the Vandeman programs dubbed into Portuguese and using Brazilian musicians taped on the IIW set. In 1992, IIW was rated as the top religious program in Brazil. Nielsen ratings in the United States reflect favorable response to the programs throughout the country. The programs have garnered 17 Angel awards from Excellence in Media since 1978.

ITALIAN JUNIOR COLLEGE (Istituto Avventista Villa Aurora Scuola Media e Liceo Scientifico Seminario di Teologia). A coeducational boarding school on the junior college level operated by the Italian Union of Churches, serving a constituency numbering 5,236 (1993). The school is situated on a 50-acre (20-hectare) estate on the outskirts of Florence.

The school was opened in 1940 when World War II prevented the Italian students from attending the French seminary at Collonges. It was then housed in the building occupied by the Italian Union Mission and Publishing House in Florence. In the summer of 1947 the school was transferred to newly acquired property at Via del Pergolino 12. Alongside the central building, which is a large villa dating from the sixteenth century, a new dormitory for boys has been erected.

Courses offered are middle school, three years, recognized by the Italian educational authorities; secondary school, five years, officially recognized; the fifth year, introduced in 1975-1976; theology, three years, the remaining portion being completed at the French Adventist seminary at Collonges-sous-Salève. Bible subjects are also taken by resident students who are at the same time enrolled in the University of Florence.

Principals: G. Cupertino, 1940-1952; B. B. Beach, 1952-1958; S. Agnello, 1958-1963; Franco Santini, 1963-1964; Henri Long, 1964-1968; Michele Buonfiglio, 1968-1970; Alfredo Romano, 1970-1972; Francesco Santini, 1972-1980; Pierre Winandy, 1980-1985; Raul Posse, 1985-1990; Vittorio Fantoni, 1990- .

ITALIAN MISSION. *See* Italy; Malta; San Marino.

ITALIAN PUBLISHING HOUSE (Edizioni A.D.V. L'Araldo della Verità). A publishing house operated at Florence, Italy. Although the Seventh-day Adventist message first came to Italy in 1864, many years elapsed before a solid work could be established. Impressed that publications in Italy would help to stabilize the work, J. N. Andrews and other pioneer workers in Europe took a keen interest in the preparation of literature in Italian. As early as 1884 a 16-page Italian quarterly, *L'Ultimo Messaggio* ("The Last Message"), appeared in Basel, Switzerland, the center at that time. Later the paper was printed in Genoa, Italy, and from 1909 to 1914 in Florence.

In 1921 a book depository was opened in Florence at the Italian Mission headquarters. A new monthly paper appeared entitled *L'Araldo della Verità* ("The Herald of Truth").

With the help of funds from Big Week, a building lot was bought in 1925 in Florence, and in 1926 a building was erected, which housed the Italian Publishing House (without printing plant) and the Italian Mission, with three second-floor apartments. At that time there were four employees: the manager (who was also the secretary-treasurer of the mission), the editor, one assistant, and the man in charge of the stockroom. Besides *L'Araldo della Verità* (which was published regularly until 1943, when it was discontinued because of World War II restrictions), a church paper, *Messaggero Avventista* ("Adventist Messenger"), was published.

In 1949, when conditions had improved, the offices of the Italian Union Mission were transferred to Rome, thus giving the publishing house full use of the building in Florence. In 1951 a bindery was set up, and in 1952 the Publishing Rehabilitation Fund of the General Conference equipped the press. Gradually new modern machines have been added, including, in 1956, an Intertype C-4 typesetting machine.

Expansion of the plant became necessary in 1966, but because of legal limitations only an underground and ground floor could be built for paper storage and bindery. In 1970 the first offset press was introduced, and in 1972, a second one. During 1974 an automatic assembler and a three-knife trimming stitcher were purchased for periodicals and tracts.

The Italian Publishing House produces various books and tracts, and three monthly papers: *Messaggero Avventista* ("Adventist Messenger") for the church; *Segni dei Tempi* ("Signs of the Times") since 1946—in place of *L'Araldo della Verità;* and *Vita e Salute* ("Life and Health").

At the present time (1993), the Italian Publishing House has 15 employees. The sales in 1993 amounted to L921,038,211.

Managers: L. Mair, 1926-1928; Giovanni Fenz, 1929-1954; Giuseppe Ferraro, 1954-1958; Silvano Cortesi, 1958-1962; Silo Agnello, 1962-1964; Ismaele Rimoldi, 1964-1982; Giuseppe De Meo, 1982-1986; Gaetano Pispisa, 1985-1990; Franco Evangelisti, 1990- .

ITALIAN UNION OF CHURCHES. *See* Euro-Africa Division; Italy; Malta; San Marino.

ITALY. A republic in Southern Europe occupying principally the boot-shaped peninsula extending southeastward into the Mediterranean Sea, and bounded on land by France, Switzerland, Austria, and Slovenia. It includes the islands of Sicily to the south and Sardinia to the west, and other small islands. Within Italy, but independent of it, are the sovereign states of San Marino and Vatican City. The total area is 116,303 square miles (301,225 square kilometers); the population (1994) is 5.8 million.

The terrain and climate of Italy are diversified, varying from the frigid heights of the Alps in the northwest to the semitropical southern tip. The peninsula has the typical Mediterranean climate of rainy winters and dry summers. Ninety percent of the area is farmland or forest. Principal agricultural products are cereals, garden produce, wines, and olives. In industry, textiles are the most important. Industrial requirements for fuel and minerals cannot be met without imports, but hydroelectric power is plentiful and well developed.

The Italian people are a blend of the ancient Umbrians, Ligurians, Latins, Etruscans, Greeks, Spaniards, and others from Roman times, and the later Goths, Lombards, and even Saracens, with a German-speaking minority group in the Tyrol region. The vast majority speak Italian. They are 99 percent Catholic; the largest Protestant groups being the Waldensians, the Pentecostals, and the Baptists.

Once the proud homeland of the Roman Empire that ruled the Mediterranean world, Italy was overrun by successive barbarian invaders and remained dismembered through the Middle Ages, ruled in various areas by foreign kings, emperors, popes, and powerful nobles, later by princes of modern European states—Spain, Austria, France—and by princes of Italian principalities. Finally in the mid-nineteenth century arose a nationalist movement for liberation and unification that resulted in 1870 in the creation of modern Italy as a constitutional monarchy under the House of Savoy.

The incorporation of the Papal States and the city of Rome into the new nation left the pope without territory and at odds with the Italian government until the reconciliation of 1929. The Lateran treaty of 1929 made the pope a ruler again over Vatican City.

In World War I Italy sided with the Allies, and in World War II, under the rule of Mussolini, with Germany. In 1946, after the Italian people voted against the monarchy, Italy became a republic. In the constitution of 1948 all religions were declared equal, and freedom of worship was guaranteed.

Seventh-day Adventist Statistics. The territory of Italy, plus the two enclaves (unentered) of San Marino and Vatican City, and the island of Malta, constitutes the Italian Union of Churches, which is part of the Euro-Africa Division. Statistics (1993) for *Italy:* churches, 89; members, 5,236; ordained ministers, 41; credentialed commissioned ministers, 3; credentialed missionaries, 25. Headquarters for the Italian Union are at Lungotevere Michelangelo 7, Rome. The national territory is divided into four fields: North Field, Central Field, South Field, and Sicilian Field.

Institutions. Forli Old People's Home; Italian Junior College; Italian Publishing House.

Development of Seventh-day Adventist Work. *Beginnings.* Italy occupies a unique place in denominational history in that it was the first country in Europe in which SDA doctrines were preached. The herald was M. B. Czechowski, a Polish ex-Catholic priest who had been baptized in Findlay, Ohio, by M. E. Cornell in the summer of 1857, and had later worked with D. T. Bourdeau among French-speaking people in America, but had failed to persuade the Seventh-day Adventists to send him to Europe. Going under the sponsorship of another Adventist denomination, but not regarded by them as one of their regular missionaries, he arrived in Torre Pellice, in the Waldensian valleys of Piedmont, northern Italy, in 1864. He rented a hall, preached, and carried on religious discussions on the Bible. He also extended his activities to Turin, Milan, Bergamo, Venice, and Brescia. In some of these cities he may have won some converts. He taught the Sabbath, and his first converts in Torre Pellice and in Switzerland later became connected with the SDA Church. Catherine Revel and J. D. Geymet were the first to accept the Sabbath. Geymet became the first SDA colporteur in Europe, and worked in Italy, Switzerland, and France from 1864 to 1921. The Torre Pellice church provided a number of SDA workers, such as Alfred Vaucher (grandson of Catherine Revel), who for many years was the Bible teacher in the French college at Collonges-sous-Salève; Elie Bertalot, minister in Italy from 1910 to 1945; and Albert Long, missionary in Madagascar from 1928 to 1948.

In 1877 J. N. Andrews, the first missionary sent by Seventh-day Adventists to Europe, came from Switzerland to Naples and baptized H. P. Ribton, M.D., and his wife and daughter in the Bay of Naples near Pozzuoli (biblical Puteoli). Dr. Ribton held meetings in Naples and soon reported five converts; by 1878 there were 22 converts there. Ribton translated several tracts into Italian. Dr. Ribton came in contact with Ercole Volpi, a former minister of the Italian Free Church, who had become a pastor of the Baptist Church in Bari. This minister accepted the Sabbath truth and baptized a number of people into the SDA message. Volpi had lengthy correspondence with J. N. Andrews in Basel.

Beginning sometime in 1877, the Italian SDAs in Naples sent the French paper *Signes des Temps* to their acquaintances among the Italians in Alexandria, Egypt, and corresponded with them about SDA doctrines. In the spring of 1878 Romualdo Bertola, an Italian commercial traveler and self-supporting missionary, visited Alexandria on business and formed a group there, baptizing seven persons. He also visited other Mediterranean countries, including Turkey, Greece, and Malta, where he found others interested in the message. Italy was then the center of an extensive missionary movement in the Mediterranean area. A tract, *Il Giorno del Signore* ("The Day of the Lord"), was published in Naples in 1884 as a reply to the tract *Il Sabato Cristiano* ("The Christian Sabbath"), written by Daniel Wilson against the Sabbath.

In 1884 D. T. Bourdeau visited Italy and organized a church in Naples (10 members). He secured the help of A. Biglia and held meetings in Barletta and Bari. In 1885 A. C. Bourdeau settled in Torre Pellice, where there were a few adherents. Ellen White visited Torre Pellice in 1885. *L'Ultimo Messaggio* ("The Last Message") was the first SDA Italian periodical. It was printed in Basel, Switzerland, about 1884 and was circulated by A. Biglia. In 1895 H. P. Holser visited Naples, Turin, Torre Pellice, and Genoa and mentions that a Swiss SDA, J. Leuzinger, was doing missionary work in Genoa and on the ships.

As early as 1900 there were a "few Sabbathkeepers" in Rome, but no SDA worker had been sent there. In 1902 C. T. Everson and his wife and Mrs. J. R. Schell were sent from California to take up work in Italy, and settled in Rome. The first convert, named Lattoni, held meetings in Italian in 1904 in Rome, the first public SDA evangelism in the "Eternal City." A. Fant and D. Gaeta, baptized by C. T. Everson during his stay in Rome, assisted in the propagation of the faith in Italy before 1910. Another convert in Rome, Miss L. Chiellini, a member of the Waldensian aristocracy, later assisted in the translation of SDA publications into Italian, especially being involved with the translation of Ellen White's book *Steps to Christ.*

In 1909 Everson was replaced as director of the Italian Mission Field by L. Zecchetto from America. Settling in Genoa, Zecchetto arranged for the periodical *L'Ultimo Messaggio* to be printed in Florence. Maria Cambiaso, a lay member found in Genoa by D. Gaeta while canvassing and baptized in 1910, was instrumental in winning converts in Genoa, Montaldo Bormida, and elsewhere. At the time of the 1909 General Conference session, there were 52 members in Italy.

Work in Florence was begun in 1910 and in Pisa in 1912 by G. L. Lippolis. At this time two members of the Gravina church, where P. Creanza had come in 1908, entered the work—G. Sabatino in Florence and N. Cupertino in Naples.

By December 1918 there were seven churches and 110 members in Italy. In 1920 members are mentioned in Torre Pellice, Bolzano, Montaldo Bormida, Genoa, Pisa, Bari, Gravina, and Firmo. Since Italy was a mission of the European Division, workers were sent from Austria, Germany, and Switzerland.

In 1922 the first general meeting and first colporteur institute were held. In 1923 V. Speranza came from the United States as publishing secretary. The publishing house "L'Araldo della Verità" was established in Florence in 1926 *(see* Italian Publishing House).

In 1928 the Italian Union Mission was established, with headquarters at Florence. It comprised the North, Central, and South Italian missions, with 19 churches and 410 members. G. L. Lippolis was elected president and served until 1934.

The Italian armed forces, who were in control in Addis Ababa in 1936, had as their objective the elimination of Protestant missions and the control of Catholic missions by Italians. In 1938 Giuseppe Cupertino took charge of the Ethiopian Mission, which was then part of the Italian Union Mission.

During World War II, Italy was separated from the division office in Berne. Quite a few of the Italian workers were on their own because war had interrupted communications within the country. Luigi Beer, president of the Italian Union Mission from 1934 to 1959, tried to keep in touch with the workers. In the Piedmont area, Riccardo Bongini prepared and mimeographed his own Sabbath school quarterlies. In the north some ministers had to be paid directly by the local church treasurers. In spite of difficulties, the publishing work steadily increased. The membership grew from 845 members in 1939 to 1,213 in December 1945. No other church in Italy grew so rapidly during the war years.

In 1959 Giuseppe Cavalcante became president of the Italian Union Mission, followed in 1964 by Silo Agnello. He held this position until 1971 when the Italian Union Mission was incorporated as a mission in the Southern European Union Mission.

Sicily. Sicily was entered in 1916 with the return of sisters M. and D. Infranco from the United States. In September 1920 R. Calderone came and baptized six people. In May 1921 the first church in Sicily was organized at Montevago. In September 1921 G. L. Lippolis had two discussions with G. Raimondo, professor of sacred eloquence in the Seminary of Palermo. As a result of these discussions Catholics published a tract entitled "Brevi risposte agli Avventisti del Settimo Giorno" ("A Brief Answer to the Seventh-day Adventists"), by G. Amodeo, to which G. L. Lippolis replied with the tract "La luce dirada le tenebre" ("The Light Dispels the Darkness"). R. Valerio, converted in the United States, became an evangelist and established a church in Palermo in 1928, and companies in Catania, Piazza Armerina, and San Michele di Ganzaria.

By 1940 it became necessary to have an Italian training school to accommodate the young people who had been attending the Séminaire Adventiste in Collonges, France, since 1925. Thus a training school was established, first housed in the union and publishing headquarters in Via Trieste, Florence, but later transferred to Villa Aurora *(see* Italian Junior College). A recently purchased Methodist chapel became the temporary headquarters of the union. Later, property was purchased in Rome for the offices of the Italian Union, where they were transferred in 1949.

The Bible correspondence course, organized in 1947, had by 1973 served a total of 119,304 registered students, of whom 7,634 had finished the course and 995 had been baptized. Radio programs were broadcast in Italian over the local radio Bologna for nearly three years, from 1947 to 1950, and over radio Montecarlo from 1950 to 1957; also over radio Cagliari (Sardinia) from 1947 to 1952. It has not been possible to broadcast over the national network.

Religious Freedom. There is more freedom today than in the past, when religious authorities seriously opposed the work. The Italian government has recognized SDA ministers and, by decree, has granted them permission to celebrate marriages as state functionaries. It gives Sabbath free to those in military service, and to pupils in public schools and also releases them from attendance at Catholic religion classes. However, because of the difficulty of finding work with the Sabbath free, many people are hindered from accepting the SDA message.

The work is carried on by meetings in regular places of worship and by Bible studies in the homes of interested people. Colporteur work, the entering wedge in the early days, is still highly effective.

From April 27 to May 1, 1989, a national congress took place at Rimini celebrating 60 years of the Italian Union. Starting in 1990 the Seventh-day Adventist Church is included on 30 million income tax returns as part of the 8 percent campaign. In cooperation with ADRA International, the Adventist Church has carried out four promotional campaigns, with ads on radio, television, and in magazines, that have exposed the church to 55 million Italian citizens. The Public Affairs and Religious Liberty Department had the responsibility for this activity.

IVORY COAST. *See* Côte d'Ivoire.

IVORY COAST SECONDARY SCHOOL. *See* Bouaké Adventist Secondary School.

IZDAVASTVO ADVENTISTICKOG TEOLOSKOG FAKULTETA MARUSEVEC (Adventist College of Theology Publishing). *See* Croatian-Slovenian Publishing House; Yugoslavian Publishing House.

J

JACKSON, SAMUEL ELLIS (1873-1930). Missionary in the Philippines, conference administrator and teacher. Orphaned before the age of 7, he went to live with a Seventh-day Adventist family and soon accepted their beliefs. He attended Battle Creek College, canvassed, and taught school before he entered evangelistic work in the Minnesota Conference in 1902. Five years later, in 1907, he was ordained to the gospel ministry and soon after was elected president of the Minnesota Conference. In 1906 and again in 1912 he taught Bible at Maplewood Academy. He was president of the North Dakota Conference (1913-1918) and after that went to the Philippine Islands to be superintendent of the Philippine Union Mission. In 1929 his health failing, he returned to the United States and retired.

JACOBS, ENOCH (fl. 1845). A non-Sabbatarian Adventist, a one-time Methodist Protestant minister, editor of the *Day-Star* at Cincinnati. After the passing of Oct. 22, 1844, when the major Millerite papers, such as the *Advent Herald,* abandoned that date as marking the end of the 2300 days of Dan. 8:14, Jacobs held that the prophetic period had indeed ended at that time (perhaps with Christ sitting in judgment before His return), although he opposed the contention of the "spiritualizers" that the Second Advent had taken place and that it was not personal but spiritual, and invisible except to the eye of faith *(see* Spiritualism [1]).

Because Jacobs' paper supported the validity of the 1844 movement, a number of the Adventists who later formed the nucleus of the Seventh-day Adventist Church wrote in its columns in 1845 and early 1846 *(see Day-Star).*

However, in 1846 Jacobs adopted the "spiritualist" view that he had formerly opposed. This view was rejected emphatically by Ellen Harmon (see EW 77) and James White and their group. Before long Jacobs moved his family to a Shaker village, and he and his wife joined the Shakers. The *Day-Star* became a Shaker journal in 1847.

JACOB'S TROUBLE, TIME OF. In Seventh-day Adventist terminology a brief period of extreme tribulation through which the church is to pass immediately prior to the Second Advent. The expression is based on Jacob's experience at the brook Jabbok upon his return to Palestine after 20 years of exile in Haran, as recorded in Gen. 32:22-30, and on Jeremiah's application of the term to ancient Israel's experience in Babylonian captivity prior to their liberation and restoration to their own land (Jer. 30:3, 7-9, 11).

When Jacob was returning with his wives, children, flocks, and herds, he learned that his brother Esau was coming to meet him with 400 armed men, evidently bent on murder. Greatly alarmed, Jacob spent the night in prayer at the Jabbok, wrestling with an unknown assailant whom at first he probably thought to be one of Esau's retainers but who proved to be a celestial being (Gen. 32:6-30). Jacob emerged from this crisis with a new name—Israel, meaning "God contends"—and with divine assurance of protection. The meeting with Esau proved to be a cordial reunion (Gen. 33:1-4).

Jeremiah's use of the expression "the time of Jacob's trouble" occurs in Gen. 30:7, following his prediction that the Captivity was to continue for 70 years (Gen. 29:10), and that at its close the people would be restored to their homeland (Gen. 30:1-3). However, in the land of their captivity Israel's prospect of restoration would appear hopeless (vs. 5-7)—as a similar restoration had to Jacob at the Jabbok. It is in this setting that Jeremiah declares: "Alas! for that day is great, so that none is like it: it is even the time of Jacob's trouble; but he shall be saved out of it" (Gen. 30:7).

With these OT experiences in mind, Seventh-day Adventists have applied the expression "the time of Jacob's trouble" to the future experience of the church during the eschatological "time of trouble" referred to in Dan. 12:1—after the close of human probation, while the seven last plagues are falling (LS 117)—immediately preceding the deliverance of the saints at Christ's second coming. In SDA eschatological thinking the setting of this experience is described as follows: "As Satan influenced Esau to march against Jacob, so he will stir up the wicked to destroy God's people in the time of trouble. And as he accused Jacob, he will urge his accusations against the people of God. He numbers the world as his subjects; but the little company who keep the commandments of God are resisting his supremacy. If he could blot them from the earth, his triumph would be complete. . . . They afflict their souls before God, pointing to their past repentance of their many sins. . . . Their faith does not fail because their prayers are not immediately answered. Though suffering the keenest anxiety, terror, and distress, they do not cease their intercessions. They lay hold of the strength of God as Jacob laid hold of the Angel; and the language of their souls is, 'I will not let thee go, except thou bless me.'

"Had not Jacob previously repented of his sin in obtaining the birthright by fraud, God would not have heard his prayer and mercifully preserved his life. So, in the time of trouble, if the people of God had unconfessed sins to appear before them while tortured with fear and anguish, they would be overwhelmed; despair would cut off their faith, and they could not have confidence to plead with God for deliverance. But while they have a deep sense of their unworthiness, they have no concealed wrongs to reveal. Their sins have gone beforehand to judgment, and have been blotted out; and they cannot bring them to remembrance" (GC 618-620).

Deliverance follows the scenes of affliction and distress: "At that time thy people shall be delivered, every one that shall be found written in the book" (Dan. 12:1).

JAKARTA CONFERENCE. *See* Far Eastern Division; Indonesia.

JALIRPAR SECONDARY BOARDING SCHOOL. *See* Kellogg-Mookerjee High School.

JAMAICA. An English-speaking island nation in the Caribbean. It is 90 miles (145 kilometers) south of Cuba and has an area of 4,411 square miles (11,400 square kilometers) and a population (1994) of 2.6 million. The island was discovered by Columbus in 1494 and remained in the possession of the Spaniards until it was taken in 1655 by the English, who controlled it until 1962.

The population, according to the latest statistics, is 76 percent pure African (Blacks were first imported into Jamaica in 1517, and until slavery was finally abolished in 1838 the island was one of the greatest slave markets in the world), 15 percent Afro-European, and the remaining 9 percent numerous racial mixtures, hence the motto on the coat of arms: "Out of many one people."

Agriculture is the basic industry. Nearly

every tropical product can be grown there, though the chief economic crops are sugar, bananas, citrus, cocoa, coconuts, ginger, tubers and pimento (allspice). Cattle raising is extensive. The country is rich in minerals, and is among the world's largest exporter of bauxite. Gypsum and marble, and deposits of copper, zinc, lead, and manganese are found in fairly large quantities. The discovery of bauxite and the swift growth of the tourist industry have greatly strengthened the economy of the island.

Jamaica has a high standard of education. The University of the West Indies, founded in 1946, is situated on Jamaica, and medicine, the arts, education, and the natural and social sciences are taught. There are several private and government-subsidized colleges and high schools providing education to the level of the General Certificate of Education and Caribbean Examination Council Examinations. These schools are open to all.

Religion. There is no established church on the island, although the Seventh-day Adventist Church constitutes the largest single denomination. The Roman Catholic Church came with the Spaniards. Protestant denominations include the Church of England, introduced in 1662; the Moravians, whose missionaries arrived in 1754 and became the first to teach Christianity to the slaves; the Baptists, who founded their mission in 1782; the Methodists, who came in 1789; the Presbyterians, organized in 1819; the Congregationalists, formed in 1876; the Seventh-day Adventists, who began work about 1890; and many other less numerous Protestant bodies.

Seventh-day Adventist Statistics. The territory of Jamaica constitutes a large part of the West Indies Union Conference, which is in the Inter-American Division. Statistics (1992) for *Jamaica:* churches, 503; members, 153,341; church or elementary schools, 19; ordained ministers, 100; licensed ministers, 58; Bible instructors, 19; teachers, 284. Headquarters for the West Indies Union Conference are in Mandeville, Jamaica. Official organ for this union: *West Indies Union Visitor.*

Statistics (1992) for the conferences—*Central Jamaica Conference:* churches, 206; members, 57,680; church or elementary schools, 6; ordained ministers, 29; licensed ministers, 23; Bible instructors, 8; teachers, 45. Headquarters: 58 Brunswick Avenue, Spanish Town, Jamaica. *East Jamaica Conference*: churches, 116; members, 53,941; church or elementary schools, 5; ordained ministers, 29; licensed ministers, 16; Bible instructors, 5; teachers, 38. Headquarters: 74 Constant Spring Road, Kingston 10, Jamaica. *West Jamaica Conference*: churches, 181; members, 41,683; church or elementary schools, 8; ordained ministers, 26; licensed ministers, 17; Bible instructors, 11; teachers, 43. Headquarters: Catherine Hall, Montego Bay, Jamaica.

Institutions. Andrews Memorial Hospital; Harrison Memorial High School; Kingsway High School; Port Maria High School; Portland High School; St. Ann's Bay High School; Savanna-La-mar High School; West Indies College; Willowdene High School.

Development of Seventh-day Adventist Work. *Beginnings.* Interest was aroused by the introduction of SDA publications. About 1889 or 1890 William Arnold, a colporteur, went to the West Indies, and on the Island of Antigua sold a book to a man who sent it to his son, James Palmer, in Kingston, Jamaica. James Palmer wrote to the International Tract Society for more publications, which, when they arrived, he distributed in the city. Some of the tracts he had received he gave to a doctor at a public hospital, who, not being interested, gave them (including the tract *Elihu on the Sabbath)* to Mrs. Margaret Harrison, an Englishwoman who devoted much of her time to visiting the sick and helping the unfortunate. Although she became convinced through her reading that the seventh day was the Sabbath, she decided to put away the thought of keeping it. However, while attending church one Sunday, at which the Ten Commandments were being read, the fourth commandment arrested her attention. Impressed by the plain teaching of the divine command, she decided that she would keep God's holy day. She also began correspondence with the International Tract Society. Meanwhile the Palmers had interested four or five other families in Seventh-day Adventist teachings. When Mrs. Harrison learned of these people, she opened her home for their meetings. This group constituted the first company of Sabbathkeepers on Jamaica.

In 1892 L. C. Chadwick from the International Tract Society visited the group, and James Patterson and B. B. Newman began work as colporteurs in Jamaica, and eventually placed hundreds of books and magazines in the homes of the people. In 1893 Mrs. Harrison went to Battle Creek for treatment. While there she attended the General Conference session and appealed for a missionary for Jamaica. In response to her plea, A. J. Haysmer and his family were sent to establish a mission from funds raised through the Sabbath school offering, which in 1892 had been allocated to the West Indies. Landing in Kingston in May 1893, they found six adherents waiting to welcome them. Haysmer conducted public evangelistic meetings, and in March 1894 organized the first Seventh-day Adventist church on the island, with 37 members. Several months later a church building was acquired in Blue Mountain Valley.

In March 1895 another minister, F. I. Richardson, joined Haysmer on Jamaica. In midyear the *Review and Herald* reported a membership on the island of 102. Several factors contributed to rapid growth in membership. The church members, active in circulating SDA publications throughout the island, lent or gave away large numbers of *Signs of the Times*, tracts, and pamphlets. Many of the young men and women who joined the church trained as colporteurs and sold Seventh-day Adventist books in every parish. As a result of this aggressive promotion of the SDA teaching the membership increased to 300 in 1896. Among the converts were ministers of other denominations who in many instances led some of their congregations with them. These ministers in turn helped to spread Seventh-day Adventist beliefs, and attracted persons who later became prominent workers in the church.

Organization and Growth. In November 1897 the first general meeting of workers for the West Indies was held in Kingston, and the West Indian Mission was organized with its headquarters in Jamaica. In 1903, during the visit of W. A. Spicer, then secretary of the Foreign Mission Board, the 1,200 Jamaican adherents were organized into the Jamaica Conference under J. B. Beckner, the first conference in the West Indies to be organized. The next year Jamaican churches sent out their first missionary, a young man, Nathan Moulton, directing him to go to Puerto Rico. Later others were sent out, opening the work in the Turks and Caicos Islands, and the Cayman Islands.

In 1906 the West Indian Union Conference was organized, with headquarters at Kingston, Jamaica. In 1907 the first union conference meeting was held at Kingston with more than 400 delegates from the Caribbean field. This meeting was in session when an earthquake destroyed the city, but no one in the building was injured. The next year the union headquarters were moved to Colón, Canal Zone, but they were returned to Jamaica in 1911. In 1908 the first national Seventh-day Adventist ministers, A. N. Durrfant, Hubert Fletcher, M. Jones, W. H. Randle, and Linton Rashford, were ordained.

In 1919 there were 2,200 members in 50 churches in Jamaica. In 1923, the year in which the Jamaica Conference (including the Cayman Islands) became a part of the newly organized Antillian Union Mission, its membership was 2,216 in 56 churches. By the end of 1943 the membership had grown to 9,255 in 150 churches. With this increase in membership, the Jamaica Conference was divided into two missions, which in 1944 were organized into conferences. At the same time a new union was organized, the British West Indies Union Mission, comprising Jamaica, the Bahama Islands, the Cayman Islands, Turks and Caicos Islands, and British Honduras, with headquarters in Jamaica. In 1952 Allan C. Stockhausen, a Jamaican, was the first national to become president of this union. The union's name was changed in 1959. In January 1962 the two Jamaican conferences were reorganized into the present three conferences: the Central, East, and West Jamaica conferences. At the time the total membership was 31,309.

The membership at the end of 1992 was 153,314 in 503 churches. If a cross were laid down the full length of the island, with the crossbeam at the widest part and the churches were strung out on these two lines, these churches would be less than a half mile (.8 kilometer) apart. The North Street church in Kingston is one of the largest SDA congregations in the world. Each Sabbath day in 1992 more than 190,000 persons met in the island's Sabbath schools, which meant that there was one Sabbathkeeper for every 15 persons in Jamaica.

Institutions and Departmental Activities. Seventh-day Adventist medical work in Jamaica began in 1913, when D. E. Wellman opened treatment rooms in Kingston with four nurses (one man and three women). For lack of funds, this work was discontinued in 1918. After that, classes in home nursing were conducted from time to time at the West Indies College. In 1944 property was purchased in an attractive suburb of Kingston, and the next year medical work was reestablished when Andrews Memorial Hospital opened it doors. West Indies College, in conjunction with Andrews Memorial Hospital, operates a nursing program offering the bachelor's degree.

The West Indian Training School, offering

courses on the secondary level for the whole Caribbean area, was opened at Riversdale, Jamaica, in 1907 with C. B. Hughes in charge. To help finance the institution, the General Conference Committee donated 3,000 copies of Ellen White's book *Christ's Object Lessons*, which were to be sold and the proceeds given to the school. In 1913 the school was closed. In 1919 a new school, also named West Indies Training School, was opened at Mandeville. This later became a junior and still later a senior college.

In 1947 the Voice of Prophecy programs were put on the air and a Bible correspondence school was opened, marking the beginning of radio work on the island. In the first 15 years of the correspondence school's operation, 144,000 persons enrolled for study and 3,000 had joined the SDA Church through baptism. The program still continues to play an important role in the union evangelism program. Over the past 10 years some 40,000 persons enrolled and 1,654 joined the church through baptism.

Literature evangelism, as the bedrock on which the work started in this union, continues to grow and expand. Between 1960 and 1990 more than 1,000 souls have been baptized as a direct result of the work of colporteurs. During this period approximately US$20 million worth of books have been sold by colporteurs and the Adventist Book Centers.

Lay evangelism has held an important place in SDA work in Jamaica. Having been encouraged to share their faith with their neighbors, the church members have brought into being most of the churches on the island. The ministers each usually hold two to three evangelistic campaigns a year, and in 1992 there were 29 ministers, each of whom baptized 100 or more; one baptized more than 300, and four more than 200.

The combined church ministries activities for 1992 were as follows: Bible studies, 40,712; units of Seventh-day Adventist publications distributed, 43,273; value of articles given away, $1,483,728.96.

JAMAICA FOOD FACTORY. *See* Inter-American Health Food Company.

JAMES, GEORGE (c. 1860-1894). First Seventh-day Adventist missionary to the indigenous people of Africa. As a young violinist in London, playing for concerts and in places of amusement but not satisfied with his future prospects, James decided to emigrate to the United States in the 1880s. Not long after his arrival he attended a series of evangelistic meetings and was baptized into the Seventh-day Adventist Church. In order to gain a more thorough knowledge of the Bible that he might share his faith more effectively, he attended Battle Creek College.

While at the college James became interested in foreign missions. Only a few years before, the first group of SDA workers had gone to Australia and the islands of the Pacific. James decided that he too wanted to work among people not reached by the gospel, and that he would follow in the footsteps of Judson, Moffat, and Livingstone. When a foreign mission band was formed at the college, he joined, and in time became its leader. In 1890 he asked the Foreign Mission Board to send him to Africa. The board replied that funds were limited, and they did not feel that the time had come to open up work among the pagans in Africa. Determined to follow his convictions, James sold all he had except his violin to pay his own way to Africa.

Arriving at Cape Town by January 1893, he set out for Nyasaland (now Malawi). He went by steamer to Durban and Chinde, at a mouth of the Zambezi River; by whaleboat, with a crew of 10 Africans, up the Zambezi and Shire rivers for 18 days; then by hammock 28 miles (45 kilometers) to Blantyre. Near there, at the nonsectarian mission of a Mr. Booth (apparently Joseph Booth, later at Malamulo), James introduced Sabbathkeeping and spent some time teaching the Seventh-day Adventist message.

Little is known of the activities of the young missionary during the next two years. He passed from village to village, mingling freely with the African people, preaching the gospel and treating the sick. Once he went to the assistance of a tribe in danger of being enslaved. Wherever he went, he carried with him the "box that could sing," as the Africans called his violin. He loved the people, and they loved him. Many years later W. H. Anderson met some Nyasaland Africans who described the very features of George James. They told about his violin, and about his keeping "the right day" as his day of rest.

In 1894 James was thrilled to hear of the mission station being opened for the indigenous people in Matabeleland, near Bulawayo. Feeling that he could accomplish more by linking up with other workers, he bade farewell to his weeping converts, promising to return soon with other missionaries, and took a river steamer bound for the coast. On the way he was stricken with malaria and died. The steamer stopped briefly for a hasty burial in a lonely unmarked spot.

JAMES, JUDSON S. (1879-1965). Pioneer missionary, departmental secretary, publishing house manager, editor. He was born in Iowa and entered denominational work as a colporteur. He became field secretary, serving in Illinois, West Virginia, and the Northern Union. In 1906 he and his family went to India, where they opened up the work among the Tamil Sabbathkeepers. In 1917 and 1918 he was vice president of the China Division and after this served as home missionary secretary for the Central Union and associate Sabbath school secretary of the General Conference. In 1926 he became manager of the publishing house at Poona, India, and editor of the *Oriental Watchman.* He served as president of the West India Union in 1930. The James Memorial High School in Prakasapuram, South India, is named in his honor.

He returned to the United States in 1936 and for five years edited the *Southern Tidings.*

JAMES MEMORIAL HIGHER SECONDARY SCHOOL. A coeducational boarding school operated at Prakasapuram, Tamil Nadu, India, by the South Tamil Section of the South India Union in the Southern Asia Division. It is named for J. S. James, who with his wife pioneered in the area among a group of Tamil Sabbathkeepers in 1908. A small day school was opened in 1909, in the charge of a Mrs. Joseph. In 1912 the school, then called Tamil Day and Boarding School, and taught by E. D. Thomas, had 92 students, including 12 boarders. It served as a middle school for several terms, being known in 1921 as the Tamil Mission School and later as the Tamil Intermediate School. Beginning in 1925, high school work was offered for about 18 years, under several names: first, Tamil High School, the Prakasapuram High School, later Prakasapuram Secondary Boarding School, and still later James Secondary Boarding School. In 1953 overcrowding of the campus caused the transfer of the high school grades to Kudikadu, where E. D. Thomas Memorial High School was established.

It continued as an elementary school for several years, and now it has become James Memorial Higher Secondary School, with an enrollment of 342 students and 21 staff members. Plans have been laid for several new classrooms, a dining hall, and an adequate kitchen.

Principals: Monickam Dhason, 1957-1958; D. P. Thomas, 1958-1959; Y. G. Thomas, 1959-1962; D. P. Thomas, 1962-1964; V. Joseph, 1964-1965; J. Monickam, 1965-1966; V. Joseph, 1966-1968; C. P. Jonahs, 1968-1970; H. Theodore (acting), 1970-1971; Y. R. Samraj, 1971-1973; K. I. Varghese, 1973-1976; M. E. Joseph, 1976-1977; T. J. Lazarus, 1977-1985; Ebenezer Samuel, 1985; K. Arthur Immanuel, 1985-1987; S. Sundaram, 1987-1990; V. K. Baby, 1990-1993; R. John, 1993- .

JAMES WHITE MEMORIAL HOMES. *See* Retirement Homes and Orphanages.

JAPAN. A nation with a democratic form of government that occupies a chain of islands lying off the eastern edge of the continent of Asia and consists of four main islands, Hokkaido, Honshu, Kyushu, Shikoku, plus the Ryukyu islands. On its total land area of 143,574 square miles (371,857 square kilometers) (slightly smaller than the state of California) live 125.1 million people (1994). The nation was formerly a kingdom with an emperor, but at the close of World War II the emperor became a symbol or figurehead, and his position results from the agreement of the people who hold the sovereign power. The population is largely homogenous, of a decidedly Mongoloid type, though there are indigenous Ainu peoples living on the island of Hokkaido who have some Caucasian features, which distinguish them from the Japanese, and there are also significant immigrant communities of Koreans and Chinese.

The authentic history of Japan dates from the fourth century A.D., when the Japanese came under the influence of the Chinese civilization and religion. The culture of Japan has been characterized through the centuries by its capacity to assimilate foreign influences. The Chinese provided a foundation for its development, supplying Japan with the literary language, and with Buddhism and Confucianism, but the Japanese built upon these contributions their own literary and religious systems; for example, by the end of the sixteenth century there was in Japan a specific brand of Buddhism. During the period when the national state was formed, religion was subordinated to the needs of the state and gradually developed into

Shintoism, which became the state religion in the latter part of the nineteenth century. After World War II the support of religion by the state was discontinued. Buddhism and Shintoism are still predominant, and the ethics of Confucianism still permeate the social structure, but an interest in Christianity has developed.

The first Christian missionary to enter Japan was the Jesuit Francis Xavier, who arrived in 1549. His work and that of his successors met with remarkable success. It is estimated that at the end of 30 years there were 150,000 converts in 200 churches. However, political unrest and a growing mistrust of the real objectives of the missionaries led to the loss of official favor, to opposition, and to persecution, and thousands suffered martyrdom. Finally, all priests were expelled, the Christian faith was banned, and in 1624 Japan virtually closed its doors to the outside world. Jesuit records intimate that before the opposition was aroused there were a half million converts.

The isolation lasted for 230 years. The end of the period was marked by the arrival in the Bay of Yedo on July 8, 1853, of four American ships of war under the command of Commodore Matthew Calbraith Perry. Perry presented a letter from the president of the United States, and on a second visit a treaty was signed at Yokohama on Mar. 31, 1854, opening two ports to American ships. This opened the way for relations with other nations. Before long the island kingdom was reopened both to foreign trade and to missionary activity.

Government edicts against Christianity were removed from public bulletin boards in 1873, though laws restricting Christianity were not immediately repealed. In 1889 the emperor Meiji granted his people a constitution containing a religious liberty clause. That clause soon became a dead letter, because the militarists took control of the government and persecution of the Christians returned.

The new postwar constitution enacted in 1947 guarantees religious freedom for all and stipulates that the state "is to refrain from religious education or any other religious activity." Japan now enjoys as much religious liberty as almost any other country, and Christianity has taken its place as one of Japan's religions, with about 1 million members, 56 percent of them Protestants (1992).

Seventh-day Adventist Statistics. The territory of Japan constitutes the Japan Union Conference, part of the Far Eastern Division. Statistics (1993) for *Japan:* churches, 108; members, 13,557; ordained ministers, 88; licensed ministers, 29; Bible instructors, 9; teachers of high school and college, 67. Headquarters for the Japan Union Conference: 846 Kamikawai-cho, Asahi-ku Yokohama 241, Japan. Official organ of the union: *Adobenchisto Raifu* ("Adventist Life").

At the twenty-eighth session of the Japan Union Mission, held in December 1974, the union was reorganized into sections with administrative supervision and management at the union level rather than in local missions. The sections were as follows: Hokkaido, Tohuku, Kanto, Chubu-Kansai, Nishi Nippon, and Okinawa.

At the thirtieth session of the union mission in 1983, an action was voted to organize into two conferences and one mission. In the next year, at the extraordinary session of the Japan Union Mission, it was voted to organize a union conference, the second in the Far Eastern Division. From then on, the Japan Union Conference has had as its substructure the East Japan Conference, West Japan Conference, and the Okinawa Mission.

Statistics (1993) for the conferences and mission—*East Japan Conference:* churches, 55; members, 7,087; ordained ministers, 33; licensed ministers, 12. Headquarters are at Tokyo. *Okinawa Mission:* churches, 16; members, 1,840; ordained ministers, 9; licensed ministers, 4. Headquarters are at Okinawa. *West Japan Conference:* churches, 37; members, 4,630; ordained ministers, 24; licensed ministers, 8. Headquarters are at Osaka.

Institutions. Adventist Medical Center; Hiroshima Saniku Gakuin; Japan Food Factory; Japan Missionary College; Japan Publishing House; Kobe Adventist Hospital; Shalom Nursing Home (Higashekurme); Shalom Nursing Home (Yokosuka); Tokyo Adventist Hospital.

Seventh-day Adventist Work. *Beginnings.* As early as the spring of 1889, not long after reaching Hong Kong, Abram La Rue, the pioneer self-supporting missionary to the China coast, made a number of trips to Japan and distributed SDA publications in Yokohama and Kobe. S. N. Haskell visited Japan in 1890. Writing from Hong Kong July 16, he reported, "We baptized one man in Japan. There are others there who are interested; and we learned that the Sabbath question has been discussed among the Japanese, and that there are some of them keeping the Sabbath" *(Review and Herald* 67:518, Aug. 26, 1890).

The first Seventh-day Adventist missionaries sent to Japan were W. C. Grainger, of California, former president of Healdsburg College, and T. H. Okohira, a native of Japan, a former Healdsburg student. They reached Tokyo on Nov. 19, 1896, and began work by conducting the Shiba Bible School, which soon had an attendance of 60 young men. One of these young men was Hide Kuniya, who was in the first group of four Japanese to be baptized in Japan, and who later became one of the first two Japanese ordained SDA ministers, the other being Okohira. Until his death in 1962, this veteran worker was instrumental in bringing large numbers of converts into the church. He had been brought to the Bible school by a friend, a fellow soldier—an army doctor, M. Kawasaki, who entered practice in Tokyo and helped Kuniya take his training for the ministry. Dr. Kawasaki set out to learn SDA methods of treatment in order to become a medical missionary.

In November 1897 Grainger's wife and younger daughter joined him. Other workers soon followed—B. O. Wade and his wife, W. D. Burden and his wife (a daughter of the Graingers), and S. Hasekawa, a Japanese who had attended Healdsburg College. In January 1899 a second Bible school was opened in Tokyo.

The first SDA church was organized in Tokyo, June 4, 1899, with a membership of 13. In July a monthly church paper, *Owari no Fukuin* ("The Gospel for the Last Days"), was launched and paid for by profits from the sale of health foods to foreigners. It was renamed *Toki no Shirushi* ("Signs of the Times") in June 1917.

Grainger died Oct. 31, 1899. Late in 1901 F. W. Field, of Mount Vernon, Ohio, was sent with his family to be superintendent of the mission. At that time the Tokyo church had about 25 members, and there were several awaiting baptism at Wakamatsu and Nagasaki. One book had been printed in Japanese and two had been translated and were awaiting publication.

A sanitarium was opened in Kobe on June 1, 1903, with Dr. S. A. Lockwood in charge, assisted by Dr. Kumashiro (later Mrs. Noma) and later by Dr. Kawasaki, both Japanese physicians. Kobe Sanitarium operated until the end of February 1909. In 1908 other Japanese doctors under the leadership of Dr. Kiku Noma opened a privately owned sanitarium that carried on SDA medical work in Kobe for many years.

The first SDA tent meeting in Japan was held in Tokyo in 1905. That same year two churches were organized, one in Tokyo and the other in Kobe. In 1906 there were 126 adherents in Japan. The first general meeting for workers was held in January 1907, in the Kobe church, and was presided over by W. W. Prescott of the General Conference. In 1908 Hakodate, the chief city on the northern island of Hokkaido, was entered, and by the end of 1909 there were five churches and about 168 members. In 1911 the first evangelistic campaign on the island of Shikoku was undertaken.

A training school was opened in Tokyo in 1908, headed by Harry F. Benson, who had arrived in Japan in 1906. In 1913 J. N. Herboltzheimer and his wife, both nurses, who had worked with the Japanese doctors at their sanitarium in Kobe for a time, opened treatment rooms in Yokohama.

With the arrival of more missionaries in 1912 (B. P. Hoffman, A. N. Anderson, and P. A. Webber, and their wives) the emphasis was placed upon the necessity of acquiring a good knowledge of the Japanese language. In 1914 a publishing house was established and the first mission headquarters building was erected in the western part of Tokyo. Members then numbered 243.

In 1915 Japan reported work in three new places and a new church organized at Nagoya. The first church school, under tentative permission, was opened at the mission headquarters early in September 1915. It was later closed by the authorities, and there were no church schools in Japan until April 1949, when one was opened at Ogikubo in Tokyo.

Organization. In 1917 the work in Japan was organized into the Japan Conference, with B. P. Hoffman, who had superintended the work, as president.

The spring council of the Asiatic Division Committee held in Shanghai in 1919 recommended further reorganization of the Japan field. Accordingly, at a conference session held the next August at Gotemba, near the foot of Mount Fuji, the Japan Union Mission was formed, comprising six local missions: Hokkaido, Tohoku, Kanto, Kansai, Chugoku, and Kyushu. B. P. Hoffman became the first union mission president. At that time there were 14 churches and 305 members.

Beginning in 1923 the following large denominational books were published in Japanese—Ellen White's *Patriarchs and Prophets, The Great Controversy,* and *Christ's Object Lessons,* and Uriah Smith's *Thoughts on Daniel* and *Thoughts on the Revelation.*

Under the leadership of E. J. Kraft, union mission publishing secretary, the colporteur work in Japan grew rapidly.

In 1926 the training school was moved from the congested Tokyo compound to 35 rural acres (14 hectares) at Naraha in the province of Chiba and was reorganized. Students and teachers did all the work of building, farming, and running the school plant. The program of mental, physical, and spiritual education, alternating earnest study with practical work, attracted the favorable attention of the public and the national and provincial leaders.

With the arrival of Dr. E. E. Getzlaff and his wife in Japan on Dec. 1, 1927, a 20-bed hospital was built on the union mission compound in Tokyo, and was opened on May 1, 1929.

Seventh-day Adventists in Wartime Japan. After the "Shanghai incident" of July 1937, which was a harbinger of war, the government control over the lives of the people tightened. Detectives continually visited Christian churches in Japan, keeping watch over the movements of ministers and laity alike. It was not long until foreign missionaries were unwanted in the country, and by 1941 the General Conference had withdrawn all overseas SDA workers.

Because of their earlier close contacts with the West, the national workers and believers came to feel more and more the suspicion thrown on Christians by the officials and people. In 1943 the Seventh-day Adventist Church was dissolved because of its emphasis on the doctrine of the second coming of Christ, which clashed with the current national policy of extending the reign of the imperial house throughout the world.

On Sept. 20, 1943, the Japanese government in one day imprisoned 36 leaders and six laypersons. Church buildings, the publishing house, the school, and the hospital were ordered to be sold. It seemed that a deathblow had been dealt SDA work in Japan.

Seventh-day Adventists in Postwar Japan. With the surrender of the Japanese forces and the occupation of Japan by the Allied Powers in the fall of 1945, old restrictions were removed and new liberties given, which meant the beginning of a new era for SDAs. One of the first actions of Gen. Douglas MacArthur as supreme commander of the Allied Powers was the release of political prisoners, which included SDA workers. Subsequently he issued a directive that properties wrongfully transferred be returned, under which three former missionaries, who returned to Japan immediately after the surrender, were able to get SDA properties returned. E. J. Kraft arrived in September 1945, and F. R. Millard and A. N. Nelson came in October. Millard was appointed first postwar president of the Japan Union Mission on Nov. 18, 1945.

With a new constitution, after the war Japan became a democratic nation. Church members reunited and missionary activities began. The General Conference allocated rehabilitation funds for Japan and sent over many workers. Churches were rebuilt, the college was reopened, and the work began to prosper more than before.

At the fifteenth session of the Japan Union Mission held in May 1948 the union mission, which since the war had operated as a single mission, was divided into the North and South Japan missions. President and secretary-treasurer of the North Japan Mission were P. H. Eldridge and Tsuruji Hasegawa, respectively. For the South Japan Mission the leading officers were V. E. Kelstrom and Kensaku Yasui. Three years later, in 1951, Okinawa was organized as a regular mission in the Japan Union Mission, with E. E. Jensen as president. In December 1965 the Hokkaido Mission was organized with five churches under the leadership of W. I. Hilliard, president. In December 1966 the Japan Union Mission office building was moved from Tokyo to Yokohama.

The Japanese Voice of Prophecy Bible Correspondence School, set up in Tokyo late in 1947, operated for some years before the first radio program was put on the air (on Aug. 2, 1952). In 1963 Japanese broadcasts were put on the air not only in Japan but also in Okinawa, Hawaii, the United States, and South America. During the 46 years of operation, the Voice of Prophecy Bible correspondence school recorded a total of 809,413 applications, 224,682 enrollments, and 93,812 graduates, which resulted in 8,751 baptisms.

Whereas cottage meetings were all that could be attempted before 1941, the postwar interest in Christianity brought people flocking to evangelistic meetings. In a 20-night series of meetings held in Tokyo during 1947 the average attendance was more than 600, even though the meeting hall was on the sixth floor of an unheated building that had no elevator and the time was the dead of winter.

Toward the end of 1950 the Japan Publishing House was moved to a new location on the outskirts of Yokohama. Sixteen books by Ellen White, newly translated into the

Japanese language, have been published since the war. The work of literature evangelism has prospered. Every summer more than 100 students from the college are out selling publications to earn part- or full-time scholarships. As of 1992 there were 27 full-time literature evangelists and 272 working part-time.

In 1952 an evangelistic center was opened in Tokyo, comprising the Tokyo Central church, North Japan Mission office, Voice of Prophecy offices, and a clinic operated by the Tokyo Adventist Hospital. When the Japan Union Mission moved to its present location, the Voice of Prophecy also relocated on the union compound. The clinic was relocated on the compound of the Tokyo Adventist Hospital in 1973.

In 1959 an evangelistic center was dedicated in Osaka, with Leo Van Dolson serving as its first director. The main-floor auditorium had a seating capacity of 250 and was well furnished with musical and visual-aid equipment. On the second floor, space was provided for a clinic and a dental office. On the third floor were classrooms. There was a round-the-calendar program of evangelism. In this center an English language school program was started, taught by a group of student missionaries and AVSC volunteers. (The center was relocated to another site in Osaka in 1990.) As of 1992 English language schools were operated in Osaka, Kobe, Himeji, Hiroshima, Kagoshima, Tokyo, and Chiba, with a total enrollment of almost 1,000 students for the year.

As for educational institutions, Japan Union Conference has five kindergartens, 10 elementary church schools, three junior high schools, one senior high school, and one college (1992). Japan Missionary College (Saniku Gakuin College) offers five courses—theology, Christian studies, education, English, and nursing education. The college choir is well known for its beautiful performance of sacred music, and the Choral Arts Society made a concert tour of the United States in 1966. There are three medical institutions, with a total of 326 beds—Tokyo Adventist Hospital, Kobe Adventist Hospital, and Adventist Medical Center in Okinawa—operated by the Japan Union Conference. These institutions offer such community services as stop-smoking plans and welfare services that are much appreciated by the community.

Health food production is one of the unique activities in Japan. Saniku Foods for a long time was a part of the Work Education Department of Japan Missionary College, but in 1970 the management was transferred from the college to the Japan Union Mission, and Saniku Foods became a union institution. Sales in 1992 amounted to approximately $1 million. Soy milk, vegetable protein, whole-wheat bread, and cookies are the main products, many of which are exported to other countries.

Two nursing homes for the aged were established, one in 1984 and the other in 1992. The first, Shalom Nursing Home (Yokosuka), was established with 50 beds for the aged with disabilities and 50 beds for the aged with dementia. It is also used as a day-care center for those who are living in the nearby districts and have needs to be cared for. The second, Shalom Nursing Home (Higashikurume), is located in Tokyo. It has 50 beds for those with disabilities and 30 beds for those with dementia. It is also used as a day-care center. These nursing homes are managed in a Christian manner and are appreciated by those in need of their services.

JAPAN FOOD FACTORY (San-iku Foods). Food industry of the Japan Union Conference. An institution begun as the Health Food Department of Japan Missionary College. After several years of expanding production, it was set up as a separate institution of the Japan Union Conference and given the present name. In 1993 it was situated in Sodegaura City. The factory has five departments. In 1992 there were 76 employees. Factory equipment was valued at US$5.2 million, and total assets listed as US$10.4 million. Control of this institution is vested in a board of directors that is elected by the Japan Union Conference committee. The board of management, consisting of the conference officers, plus several key members of San-iku Foods, handles the regular activities of the food program.

The Sanitarium Health Food Company in Australia has contributed greatly to the expansion of the health food program in Japan. Besides financial loans, L. A. Piper was sent from Australia to put the program on a commercial basis. Dr. H. W. Miller also contributed to the production of Soyalac, which is an important product of San-iku Foods.

Managers: M. Yoshimura, 1949-1959; H. Imura, 1959-1962; N. Nemoto, 1962-1969; A. Cree, 1969-1972; M. Uruma, 1973-1992; S. Kudo, 1992- .

JAPAN MISSIONARY COLLEGE (Saniku Gakuin College). A coeducational boarding school on a senior college level, operated by the Japan Union Conference, near Naraha, 50 miles (80 kilometers) from Tokyo, across the bay from Yokohama.

Seventh-day Adventist educational work in Japan began on Jan. 1, 1898, with the opening in Tokyo of a Japanese-English Bible school, with some 80 students, by William C. Grainger, a former president of Healdsburg College, California. His interpreter was Teruhiko H. Okohira, a Japanese-born convert who had been a Healdsburg student. The two had arrived in Japan more than a year earlier. Okohira later became one of the first Seventh-day Adventist ordained Japanese ministers. Grainger's enthusiasm for the Bible made such an indelible impression on his Tokyo students that only a few months later, on Apr. 30, 1898, a baptism was conducted in the Meguro River, the first SDA baptismal service in Japan. Among those baptized was a young man, Hide Kuniya, who later became the first Seventh-day Adventist convert in Japan to be ordained to the ministry.

The work of the school progressed steadily, but on Oct. 31, 1899, after having been in Japan only two years and eleven months, Grainger died. His work was continued by William D. Burden, and two years later by Frank W. Field, director of the Japan Mission, who also fostered the work of training young people for service. In 1910 he was succeeded by F. H. DeVinney.

From 1908 to 1913 Harry F. Benson directed a training course for workers, including Bible, history, biology, English, and other subjects. During these years the school was operated at the mission headquarters in the Sendagaya district of Tokyo. In 1914, when the headquarters of the Japan Mission were moved from Sendagaya to Amanuma, on the outskirts of Tokyo, the school was moved to the same site and was called the Nihon Dendo Gakko (Japan School of Evangelism). It was primarily a workers' training institute, offering courses in Bible, history, language, and music.

The school operated until the spring of 1917. On Oct. 1, 1919, it was reorganized as Amanuma Gakuin, with an initial student body of 32, under the direction of Perry A. Webber as president and Andrew N. Nelson as manager. Within a short time the institution included an elementary school of six years, a secondary school of five years, and a junior college of three years.

There came a growing conviction that, in harmony with the SDA philosophy of education, the school should be situated away from the city in a place where students could engage in agriculture, building, and other practical arts. After careful search, 35 acres (14 hectares) (later increased to 44 acres [18 hectares]) of woodland and farmland were secured at Naraha, in Chiba Prefecture, on the eastern side of Tokyo Bay, some 50 miles (80 kilometers) from Tokyo. On May 2, 1926, the first group of teachers and students (boys only) arrived at the school site and began erecting buildings and cultivating the fields. The students and teachers were responsible for most of the work done in building the school.

On Oct. 14, 1926, opening ceremonies were held, with Frederick Griggs from the Far Eastern Division as speaker. The school, for boys only, was called in Japanese, Nihon San-iku Gakuin ("Japan Threefold Educational School," with reference to the mental, physical, and spiritual aspects of true education). At the same time a similar school for girls was started in Tokyo.

The school at Naraha offered a six-year secondary course and a two-year junior college course. The president of the new school, Andrew N. Nelson, organized several strong work departments—carpentry, health food manufacture, commercial art, house painting, and agriculture. All teachers and students engaged in this work program, which also included landscaping the grounds and running the various service industries. During the difficult prewar years, while Francis R. Millard was in charge, the school successfully withstood government demands that conflicted with SDA principles.

During World War II, Christianity was restricted and the Seventh-day Adventist Church suppressed. The school was closed by a Chiba Prefectural order in December 1943. When the war ended, plans to reopen the school were made, and on Jan. 23, 1947, students were again admitted. To begin with, a sequence of subjects in training for evangelism on the high school level was offered. The girls' school at Tokyo was moved to Naraha and merged with the boys' school in one of Japan's early successful coeducational experiments. As life returned to normal in Japan, the school resumed its prewar curriculum, then expanded both program and facilities. On July 1, 1953, the college was recognized by the General Conference as a full senior college. Since that time, course work leading to the Bachelor of Arts degree has been offered.

As requirements of accreditation in Japan are difficult to meet, there was a feeling of real accomplishment when the college received government recognition for both the junior and senior high school on Aug. 31, 1948; for the primary school on June 14, 1950; for the school of theology on Dec. 22, 1950; and more recently for the junior college department of English on Jan. 27, 1971.

Relocation of the college sector took place in August 1978. It was moved south of the old campus to Otaki-machi in Chiba Prefecture, about 80 miles (130 hectares) southeast of Tokyo. In 1987, when the Nursing Department received government accreditation as a junior college with a three-year program, the college was reorganized as a junior college with two departments (English and nursing), and a senior college with two departments (theology and education). Since 1988 the Theology Department has offered a five-year B.Th. degree program. During the 1992 school year the enrollment reached an all-time high of 350.

Principals/Presidents: A. N. Nelson, 1926-1935; F. R. Millard, 1936-1937; P. A. Webber, 1937-1939; F. R. Millard, 1939-1940; H. Yamamoto, 1940-1942; K. Otsuki, 1942-1943; closed, 1943-1947; W. W. Konzack, 1947-1950; F. R. Millard, 1950-1951; R. S. Moore, 1951-1956; T. Yamagata, 1956-1969; R. E. Klimes, 1969-1973; G. Hirokawa, 1973-1974; S. Arakaki, 1974-1976; S. Nagakubo, 1976-1994; S. Tabuchi, 1994- .

JAPAN PUBLISHING HOUSE (Fukuinsha). A publishing organization with its own printing plant operated by the Japan Union Conference at Yokohama. It issues books and the following periodicals: *Sainzu obu za Taimuzu* ("Signs of the Times"), *Ansokunichi Gakko Shotoka Kyoka* ("Primary Sabbath School Lesson Quarterly"), *Ansokunichi Gakko Chuto Kyoka* ("Junior Sabbath School Lesson Quarterly"), *Ansokunichi Gakko Kyoka* ("Sabbath School Lesson Quarterly").

In 1899, when the first church was organized in Japan, a publishing house, called Owari no Fukuinsha (literally, "Gospel for the Last Days Publishing House"), was established, though it did not have its own presses. Teruhiko Okohira and two of the first four men baptized, Mokutaro Kawasaki and Hide Kuniya, did the editorial work on the first paper published, *Owari no Fukuin* ("Gospel for the Last Days"), which later became *Jicho (Sainzu obu za Taimuzu),* the Japanese *Signs. Steps to Christ,* by Ellen White, was the first denominational book published in Japan (1901 or 1902).

In 1907 or 1908 W. D. Burden placed a hand press in the basement of his residence and began to print magazines and tracts. In 1914 a publishing house was built near the mission headquarters in the western part of Tokyo. To existing equipment were added in 1916 a new press, oil engine, and paper cutter. In 1922 the brick building was remodeled, a second story added, and a heating plant installed, making it, according to H. H. Hall, "the best plant we have in the Orient." Subsequently a number of books were published, including abridged editions of Ellen White's *Gospel Workers* (1920) and *Patriarchs and Prophets* (1922). A book on the Sabbath was published in 1923.

In the great earthquake of Sept. 21, 1923, the two-story publishing house was partially destroyed. The presses continued to operate in the old building until a new plant was ready early in 1924. The typecases were put into the Amanuma church building, and typesetting was carried on there for a few months.

When the Seventh-day Adventist work was suppressed in 1943, the publishing house was taken over by a secular publisher.

In 1946 the Fukuinsha (Gospel Press), as the publishing house has since been known, came back into denominational operation, but difficulties were experienced in securing adequate supplies of paper, ink, and other materials. Furthermore, the printing equipment was in very poor condition, and in 1947 there was only one worker with previous experience. In view of the situation, the three publishing houses in North America and the General Conference Publishing Rehabilitation Committee made appropriations for equipment over a period of years totaling $56,500, and the Far Eastern Division provided $25,000 for a new factory building. In later years appropriations were made through the budget committee, so that by the end of 1953 this committee had voted a total of $61,000 for building and operating funds. The new plant was built at Asahi-ku, near Yokohama, to which the publishing work was moved in 1948. To increase production, a large offset press and platemaking equipment were purchased in 1955.

After the war it was necessary to retranslate and reprint all denominational books in order to meet government requirements for simplifying written Japanese, but despite this delay the work has gone forward. At the first postwar union mission colporteur institute the colporteurs had only one small book, *So Little Time,* and the journal *Signs of the Times* for single sales.

By 1974 the house had published 16 of Ellen White's books in Japanese: *Education,* in 1953; *The Story of Redemption,* in 1955; *Counsels on Sabbath School Work*, in 1956; *The Ministry of Healing, Messages to Young People,* and *Your Home and Health,* in 1957; *The Impending Conflict,* in 1961; *Steps to Christ,* in 1962; *The Desire of Ages* and *Thoughts From the Mount of Blessing,* in 1963; *The Adventist Home* and *Colporteur Ministry,* in 1965; *Christ's Object Lessons,* in 1967; *Christian Service,* in 1970; *Patriarchs and Prophets,* in 1971; and *The Great Controversy,* in 1974.

It has also published 84 other books by various authors, ranging from children's books to introductory books to Christianity which are designed to acquaint the non-Christian Japanese readers with the basics of Christianity.

The funds that came from the sale of a portion of the press property to the Highway Authority in 1972 and 1973 helped the house to upgrade with a new two-color offset press, a small offset press, a perfect binder, a camera set, a cutter, and other items.

Heads of the Editorial Department since World War II: T. Yamagata, 1946-1948; Y. Seino, 1948-1950; K. Kuniya, 1950-1958; T. Saito, 1958-1968; Minoru Inada, 1968-1974; Minoru Hirota, 1975-1984; Yonezo Okafuji, 1985-1991; Kenji Soneda, 1992- .

Managers (approximate dates for early years): W. D. Burden, 1908-1911; C. N. Lake, 1911-1912; W. D. Burden, 1913; Clarence C. Hall, 1914-1915; Albert B. Cole, 1916-1931; a committee of V. T. Armstrong, H. J. Perkins, and Shokei Miyake, 1931-1933; Harvin P. Evens, 1933-1940; W. E. Guthrie, 1940-1941; Vinston E. Adams, 1947-1950; Kenneth W. Tilghman, 1950-1956; Martin C. Bird, 1956-1964; Robert Pohle, 1965-1972; H. F. Meyer, 1972-1974; H. Yasukochi, 1974-1988; Yonezo Okafuji, 1989-1992; Kenji Soneda, 1993- .

JAPAN SANITARIUM. *See* Kobe Adventist Hospital.

JAPAN SCHOOL OF EVANGELISM. *See* Japan Missionary College.

JAPAN UNION CONFERENCE. *See* Far Eastern Division; Japan.

JAPAS, SALIM (1921-1992). Evangelist, educator, author. Born in Argentina, he accepted Christ at age 16 and was baptized into the Seventh-day Adventist Church. He was the only Adventist in his family, but this only fixed in him a strong faith and love for the truth. After graduating from River Plate College, he entered denominational service in the South American Division in 1946, where he served as pastor, departmental director, and evangelist until 1966. After a brief tenure in the North American Division, he went to the Middle East Division as an evangelist, serving from 1967 to 1970.

Japas arrived in the Inter-American Division in 1970 and served as professor and head of the Theology Department at Antillian College in Puerto Rico until 1985, when he became ministerial secretary and evangelist for the division. He retired in 1990 after 44 years of service to the church.

Japas authored six books and many magazine articles, all of which spoke of hope, trust, and security.

JARO MIDDLE SCHOOL. *See* West Visayan Academy.

JAVA. *See* Indonesia.

JAVA MISSION PRESS. *See* Indonesia Publishing House.

JAY MEMORIAL ADVENTIST HOSPITAL. A former 30-bed hospital situated in Jay, Oklahoma, operated under lease by the Oklahoma Conference.

The Jay community erected the building and in addition raised more than $20,000 to launch the hospital. On June 20, 1965, the hospital, fully equipped, was opened to the public. L.E.C. Joers, M.D., was the medical director and surgeon. On Aug. 11, 1965, Ethel M. Walker-Heras, M.D., joined the staff as a second physician, with offices in the hospital.

In 1970 an addition known as the East Wing was made to the hospital at a cost of approximately $84,000. This section housed the doctors' offices and clinic. From 1980 to 1985 Jay Memorial Adventist Hospital was operated by the Adventist Health System/Sunbelt.

Administrators/Presidents: L.E.C. Joers, 1965-1973; W. C. McConnell, 1973-1977; Billie Beesley, 1977-1980; Douglas Langley, 1980-1984; Robert E. Trimble, 1984-1985.

JEFFERSON ADVENTIST ACADEMY. A coeducational boarding school on the senior high school level, situated on 18 acres (seven hectares) of land in the "Pines" of eastern Texas, a short distance off Highway 49, five miles (eight kilometers) northwest of Jefferson, Texas, in Marion County. It is operated by the Jefferson Seventh-day Adventist Church. Students come from other parts of Texas and the states of Arkansas and Louisiana, and some from a much greater distance.

Jefferson Academy grew out of the Jefferson Intermediate School established in 1914, with James H. Ball as the first principal. The first annual calendar, announcing 10 grades, tells of the origin of the school thus: In 1913 the Progressive Club of Jefferson approached the Southwestern Union and North Texas conferences, seeking the establishment of a Seventh-day Adventist colony and school in that section. W. A. McCutchen, president of the North Texas Conference, made arrangements for the purchase of an 1,800-acre (750-hectare) plantation to provide land for the school and land for subdivision into tracts of 10 to 100 acres (four to 40 hectares) for SDA families. The original school building was paid for by a gift of $2,000 from the citizens of Jefferson. The school appears as Berea Intermediate Academy in the 1919 *Statistical Report* and as Berea Intermediate School in the *Yearbook* from 1920 to 1928. It underwent varied experiences of growth over a period of years, operated under various names (Berea Junior Academy, Jefferson Junior Academy, Jefferson Rural Academy), and offered at different times 10 grades, 11 grades, and 12 grades, then in the 1950s returned to 10 grades.

In 1960 the school was reactivated as a 12-grade boarding academy. The original school building was enlarged to provide office space for the administrative functions of the school. A house, which was moved to vacate space for a new church building, was converted into a girls' dormitory, and barracks from an army installation were converted into a boys' dormitory. A new industrial arts building was completed in 1961, a food services building was put into service in 1962, and a new elementary school was completed in 1963. New dormitories and a gymnasium were erected in 1965. With these increased facilities, the enrollment was expected to increase to 100 boarding students plus another 25 to 40 day students.

In 1972 the local community church members reassumed the operation of Jefferson Academy.

Jefferson Academy offers courses in both college preparatory and vocational fields. Instruction is given in Bible, English, mathematics, science, home arts, commercial subjects, and other one-year courses.

Publications of the school are the *Whispering Pines* (eight issues per year) and the school annual, the *Pine Cone*.

Principals: J. W. Hiser, 1960-1962; M. W. Perkins, 1962-1963; Earl Adams, 1963-1966; Floyd Eccles, 1966-1968; Stuart Crook, 1968-1970; Leroy Steck, 1970-1972; Richard Claridad, 1972-1973; Kenneth Jameson, 1973-1974; Duane Lemon, 1974-1975; Harvey Byram, 1975-1976; Paul Tooley, 1976-1977; Robert Warren, 1977-1979; John Baker, 1979-1980; Vernon Kaiser, 1980-1981; George Smith, 1981-1984; George Parry, 1984-1985; G. Charles Dart, Jr., 1985-1988; Ron Adams, 1988-1991; Michael Furr, 1991-1992; Gaston Wallace, 1993-1994; Jerry Austin, 1994- .

JEFFES, NORMAN FISHER (1896-1963). Businessperson, school board member, and chair. A native of Australia, he accepted the Seventh-day Adventist message at the age of 11 and later attended Australian Missionary College. He was known for his industry in developing plants for the manufacture of Weetbix breakfast cereal. After developing three such plants in Australia and New Zealand, which were sold to the Sanitarium Health Food Company, he went to South Africa and established a similar industry.

He served as a church elder in both Australia and South Africa for more than 40 years and was a member of the Helderberg College board and the Cape Conference executive committee for 25 years. He played a leading role in developing Hillcrest Secondary School in Mowbray, Cape, South Africa, and also led out in the erection of the Plumstead church.

JELLICO COMMUNITY HOSPITAL. A 54-bed acute-care hospital located in Jellico, Tennessee, operated by Adventist Health System/Sunbelt Health Care Corporation since 1974. A medical staff of three in 1974 grew to 15 by 1993. The hospital employs about 250 persons. It serves 20,000 patient visits per year, of which 18,000 are outpatient visits. Approximately 300 babies are born at Jellico Community Hospital every year.

The hospital expanded services in 1983 to include an intensive care unit. In 1984 the hospital was accredited by the Joint Commission on Accreditation of Health Care Organizations. A home health care agency was established in 1985.

Ground was broken in 1993 for a $3.8 million expansion project to include a new emergency center, expanded surgery suites and recovery room, expanded laboratory and diagnostic imaging facilities, gift shop, modern obstetrics unit, chapel, and new waiting rooms and lobby.

Administrators/Presidents: H. D. Sanderford, 1974-1978; P. B. Mitchell, 1979; James Thompson, 1979-1981; Keith Hausman, 1982-1991; Kenneth Mattison, 1991- .

JELØY BAD OG DIETTKURSTED (Jeløy Clinic). A former institution opened in 1938 by Skodsborg graduate physiotherapists Einar and Ellen Fahlberg, who operated it until the Seventh-day Adventist Church took over on Jan. 1, 1971. The bed capacity was then 34. This was increased to 68.

The institution accepted patients who were in need of hydrotherapy and physiotherapy. Even though most of the clients were not Seventh-day Adventists, the institution, with its vegetarian food, was a popular place for rehabilitation. Two physicians, one with a specialty in rheumatology, were connected with the various departments.

Jeløy is an island in the Oslo Fjord, and it is part of the town of Moss, located about 40 miles (65 kilometers) south of Oslo. The institution was located in a park of approximately two acres (one hectare). A nature park with forest and seashore borders the property.

An extension of the institution in several stages was completed. This included treatment rooms, patient rooms, and administrative offices.

The Norwegian Union sold Jeløy in 1994 because of the considerable financial commitment it took to maintain the hospital's first-class accreditation.

Administrators: Frithjof Asheim, 1971-1991; Erling G. Olsen, 1991-1994.

JENGRE SEVENTH-DAY ADVENTIST HOSPITAL. A 103-bed general acute hospital situated at Jengre, a village north of Jos, northern Nigeria, owned and operated initially by the North Nigerian Mission but transferred to the West African Union Mission in 1959. In 1973 the hospital was staffed by one doctor, two midwives, one nurse, and one technician, all from overseas; three national midwives, five national nurses, and two laboratory technicians. Twenty-nine thousand patients attended the clinics, and 405 surgeries were done, mostly hernia and hydrocele. Formerly the hospital specialized in leprosy treatment.

J. J. Hyde and his wife began work in northern Nigeria in 1931. At the time there was an epidemic of jiggers (chiggers) in the country, and Mrs. Hyde, a nurse trained at The Stanboroughs, in England, opened a dispensary. In 1947 their son, Dr. J. Ashford Hyde, who had been with them as a boy in northern Nigeria, was appointed to enlarge the medical work and to establish a hospital. Capital investment in 1947 was $300. In 1948 a ward was established with a grant of $2,500 by the West African Union Mission, and the next year the hospital was completed with funds from a Thirteenth Sabbath Offering overflow. In 1971 a new ward with theater and maternity unit was in use.

The hospital was taken over by the Plateau state government in 1976; but it was handed back to the church with full compensation in 1980.

Medical Directors: J. Ashford Hyde, 1947-1955; H. Lamp, 1955-1957; R. E. Davenport, 1957-1958; D. I. Peterson, 1959-1960; A. M. Owens, 1960-1961; P. Genstler, 1961-1963; A. M. Owens, 1963-1967; K. L. Kellin, 1967-1971; F. R. Bland, 1971-1972; D. E. Courser, 1972-1974; G. Wedon, 1974-1976; under government control, 1976-1980; E. Olewe, 1980-1983; H. Oladini, 1983-1984; A. Obisanya, 1984-1985; A. Saguan, 1986-1987; M. A. Jibrin, 1987-1989; A. Obisanya, 1989-1991; E. O. Eke, 1991-1994; A. Obisanya, 1994- .

JESPERSSON, SVEN (1864-1927). Medical missionary in Palestine and Algeria. As a young man he went to Germany from his native Sweden and there in 1891 became a Seventh-day Adventist. He immediately began ship missionary work in Hamburg harbor and about a year later was sent by the mission to Battle Creek Sanitarium to take the nursing course. From there he went to Switzerland to help establish the Institut Sanitaire, later returned to Sweden, where he was associated with the training school, and then returned to Switzerland. After marrying Lydia Roumajon in 1901, he and his wife went to Jerusalem to serve as medical missionaries in the treatment rooms established by J. H. Krum. Because of a serious attack of malaria he returned to Switzerland four years later. There he taught at the newly opened Latin Union school at Gland for a year and then went to Algeria to begin

Seventh-day Adventist medical missionary work there. Plagued by persistent malarial attacks, he gave up his mission work in 1909 and went to the United States, where he studied medicine. Upon completing his course, he was associated with Battle Creek Sanitarium for about 10 years, after which he practiced in the city of Battle Creek, Michigan.

JESUS CHRIST. *See* Atonement; Christology; Sanctuary; Virgin Birth.

JEWELL, FREDERICK BURTON (1875-1967). Nurse and missionary. A native of Ithaca, New York, he was converted to the Seventh-day Adventist faith at 21 years of age and trained as a nurse at the old Battle Creek Sanitarium. In 1902 he told his wife, the former Elnora Van Horn, that he was offering his services to Africa. So began 43 years of service to the people of that continent. The Jewells settled first at Inyazura, then spent a short time in Zambia, but Solusi was to be their home. Here Jewell was in charge of the clinic, which soon drew patients from long distances. His particular interest was the maternity ward, and he studied constantly to improve his knowledge of safe methods of delivery. He set himself a goal of being able to cope with any complication so as to save the lives of the mothers and babies who were so precious to him. He delivered more than 1,350 babies and cycled thousands of miles through the veld to visit patients in their homes.

The Jewells returned to the United States only once during their 43 years of service in Africa. He passed to his rest at Bulawayo, Rhodesia, on May 16 and was buried at Solusi Mission.

JEWELRY. *See* Dress.

JEWS, EVANGELISM OF. *See* Israelite Heritage Institute; North American Division Multilingual Ministries.

JEWS, RESTORATION OF. *See* Israel, Prophecies Concerning.

JOHANSON, J. M. (1860-1928). Danish-born conference administrator, publishing house manager, colporteur leader, and college president. He was living in Tasmania when he began reading Seventh-day Adventist publications, as a result of which he began observing the Sabbath in 1891. Soon thereafter he met SDAs for the first time, left his cabinetmaking business, and together with his wife began canvassing. Eventually he became the canvassing leader of the Australasian Union Conference. After several years in this post he became associated with the Echo (later Signs) Publishing Company as sales manager, director, and later, general manager. In 1913 he was ordained and in 1915 was called to the presidency of the Australasian Missionary College. He left after two years to take charge of Seventh-day Adventist missions in Japan, Korea, and Manchuria. In 1919 he returned to the Signs Publishing Company in Australia and while managing it helped to establish a branch of the Sanitarium Health Food Company at Warburton. In 1926 he was elected general manager of the Australasian Conference Association.

JOHN, ADELBERT ALLEN (1856-1921). One of the pioneer Seventh-day Adventist workers in England, medical missionary to Mexico. Converted at the age of 17, he entered SDA ministerial work about 1877 in his native Illinois and in 1882 was sent by the Mission Board to England four years after the Loughboroughs first went to that country. He worked in England and Wales for about eight years, and was elected secretary of the first "European Council." Upon his return to the United States he worked in Iowa for a time, but having become interested in medical missionary work, he enrolled in 1894 in the medical course at the University of Michigan and graduated from Northwestern University in 1898. While at Chicago he was active in the work of the city mission there. After graduation and postgraduate work, he was sent to Mexico as medical superintendent of Guadalajara Sanitarium. After a year he took up private practice in Mexico. In 1912 he returned to Illinois and established a private sanitarium.

JOHN G. MATTESON INSTITUTE OF EVANGELISM (Mattesonskolen). Established September 1986 at the Norwegian Publishing House, Oslo, on the initiative of Gunnar A. Gustavsen and Willy Hugstmyr, publishing directors in the West Nordic Union. The institute is situated in Mysen, about 50 miles (80 kilometers) southeast of Oslo.

The institute is not a school, but rather an activity or a training program that is run by the Church Ministries Department in the union. It has an advisory committee that helps plan the activities and recommends the operating budget. The program has only one salaried employee, the director of the program. The Matteson Institute owns no property or facilities, and its operation is financially based on regular and special appropriations made by the union and the local conferences. It is also supported by "Granheim-stiftelsen," an independent, nonprofit corporation.

The program of the Matteson Institute of Evangelism is designed to train young volunteer workers so that they may be of help to the local pastors in their evangelistic outreach programs in the different local conferences in the union.

The training program includes field experience in the literature ministry for four or six weeks in the summer. The regular training program begins at the end of August with a five-week seminar, with special emphasis on the prophecies in Daniel and the Revelation. The fieldwork experience, which lasts from October through May, is interrupted by four 10-day seminars on topics related to personal evangelism. One of the highlights of the program is the New Year rally, which lasts for six days. As many as 150 young people have been assembled at these gatherings where the Advent message and its implications for "present time" have been studied. Such gatherings are planned and conducted by the young people connected with the program.

Director: Gunnar A. Gustavsen.

JOHN LOUGHBOROUGH SCHOOL. A secondary institution established in 1980 on Holcombe Road in London. In 1993 there were 169 students and a staff of 27.

Principals: Orville Woolford, 1984-1985; Keith Davidson, 1985-1993; Clinton A. Valley, 1994- .

JOHNS, ALGER FRANCIS (1918-1972). Teacher and author. A native of Missouri, he took his secondary education at Maplewood Academy in Minnesota. He received his Bachelor of Arts degree from Pacific Union College and his master's degree from the Seventh-day Adventist Theological Seminary. In 1959 he earned his Ph.D. degree from Johns Hopkins University. He taught in three denominational colleges and served on the staff of the SDA Theological Seminary from 1955 to the time of his death.

His published writings include contributions to *The SDA Bible Commentary* and the *SDA Bible Dictionary* and *A Short Grammar of Biblical Aramaic.*

JOHNSON, LEWIS (1851-1940). Minister, administrator. He was born at Nyborre, on the island of Moen, Denmark, and came to the United States in 1869, settling in Boone County, Iowa. As a young man he was converted and joined the Methodist Church. Soon thereafter he was granted a license and sent out to preach. In 1875 he attended several lectures by the Seventh-day Adventist evangelist J. F. Hanson. As a result, he accepted the SDA faith, was baptized, and became the elder of a newly organized church.

At a camp meeting held in Marshalltown, Iowa, in June 1876, he was granted a ministerial license and began to preach. The rest of that year and the next he worked in Iowa and in the Dakotas, and in 1878 and 1879 in Illinois, mostly in Chicago. During a camp meeting held in Bloomington, Illinois, in August 1878, he was ordained by George I. Butler.

At the invitation of the General Conference, Johnson left the United States Jan. 1, 1889, for Christiania (Oslo), Norway, to replace O. A. Olsen, who had been elected president of the General Conference. For 10 years he remained in Scandinavia, serving as president of three conferences, most of the time simultaneously (10 years of Norway, seven years of Sweden, and nine years of Denmark). During this period the membership more than doubled, increasing from 900 to 2,100.

When Johnson returned to the United States in September 1899, he was given charge of the Danish-Norwegian work in North America, with his home and office in College View, Nebraska. In 1912 he was elected president of the Washington Conference, a post he held for four years. Finishing his term as president, he continued working in this conference until the time of his retirement in 1927 at the age of 76.

JOHNSON, O. A. (1851-1923). Educator, administrator. Born in Ottawa, Illinois. In 1854 his family moved to Jefferson County, Wisconsin, where they joined several other Norwegian families, including that of O. A. Olsen, in the observance of the Sabbath. In the spring of 1860 this company was organized into a church, the first Norwegian church in the denomination. Johnson was baptized at the age of 13, and when 19 attended the Seventh Day Baptist College at Milton, Wisconsin, for one year. Then for four years he attended Battle Creek College. He established his first church in 1874 and was ordained in 1876.

Johnson preached in Wisconsin till 1882, when he was transferred to Nebraska to work among the Scandinavians. In 1888 he was transferred to Montana to open the work in that state, and in a short time organized a church in Livingston. Later that year he joined J. G. Matteson in conducting a training school in Chicago. In the fall of 1891 he went to Union College to take charge of the newly opened Scandinavian Department.

In 1894 Johnson was elected president of the Wisconsin Conference and served two years. He was then invited by the General Conference to attend camp meetings and other important gatherings in the Northern and the Central Union conferences. In the autumn of 1897 he was called again to head the Scandinavian Department of Union College. After three years in this post he was called to Europe to serve as president of the Norway Conference. During the school year of 1904-1905 he conducted a training school for workers in Christiania.

In 1908 Johnson accepted a call to head the Bible Department at Walla Walla College, where he remained until 1922. Because of failing health he resigned, but continued to attend camp meetings and to perform other duties as his strength permitted.

JOHNSON, OLAF (1843-1919). Evangelist, administrator. He was born in Vittensten, Vermland, Sweden. At the age of 33 he was baptized and joined the Baptist Church. About two years later he heard of, and accepted, the Seventh-day Adventist faith in Oslo, Norway, as a result of the work of J. G. Matteson, who had been sent to Europe in June 1877 to open the work in the Scandinavian countries. Shortly after becoming a Seventh-day Adventist, Johnson returned to Sweden to share his newfound faith with the people of his homeland. In the early years of his ministry the pioneer workers shared in common. He received no salary, and had to depend on the sale of books and papers and the meager earnings of his wife for the support of himself and family. He was ordained at the conference session in June 1883, and was soon regarded as the leading preacher in Sweden.

From 1889 to 1893 Johnson served as president of the Swedish Conference. In July 1892 he accepted the invitation to pioneer the work in Finland. During the years he spent there he laid a solid foundation for SDA work in that country. On his return to Sweden in 1901, he was again elected president of the Swedish Conference. In 1907 he undertook to pioneer the work in northern Sweden.

JONES, ALONZO T. (1850-1923). Minister, editor, author. He was born in Ohio. At the age of 20 he enlisted in the Army and for three years served his country. While most of his comrades spent their free time finding various pleasures he was in the barracks poring over his books—large historical works, Seventh-day Adventist publications that had fallen into his hands, and the Bible. Thus he was laying a strong foundation of knowledge for his later work as a preacher and a writer. After his discharge in 1873, he was baptized and began preaching on the West Coast for the SDAs. In May 1885 he became assistant editor of the *Signs of the Times,* and a few months later he and E. J. Waggoner became editors. This position he held until 1889.

These two men in 1888 stirred the General Conference session in Minneapolis with their preaching on righteousness by faith, and for several years afterward were sent by the General Conference Committee to preach on that subject from coast to coast at camp meetings and other large gatherings, in workers' meetings, in ministerial institutes, and in SDA institutions. Ellen White accompanied them to many of these places until she left for Australia in December 1891. Also for a number of years the two were principal speakers at the biennial sessions of the General Conference.

In 1897 Jones became a member of the General Conference Committee. From 1897 to 1901 he was editor in chief of the *Review and Herald,* with Uriah Smith as associate editor.

In 1889 Jones, with J. O. Corliss, spoke before a committee in Washington to oppose the Breckinridge Bill, intended to compel Sunday observance in the District of Columbia. The bill was defeated, and Jones soon became recognized as the denomination's most prominent speaker for religious freedom. At the time he was serving as editor of the *American Sentinel (see Sentinel of Christian Liberty),* the forerunner of *Liberty.* He also wrote voluminously for other Seventh-day Adventist papers and authored a number of books.

Feeling out of harmony with certain administrative policies, he resigned late in 1899 as a member of the General Conference Committee, but at the 1901 session he accepted membership again. While president of the California Conference (1901-1903), he accepted an invitation from Dr. J. H. Kellogg, who was then actively seeking to separate the Battle Creek Sanitarium from denominational control, to join his staff. Against the counsel of Ellen White he accepted the invitation.

Shortly after the removal of the General Conference headquarters from Battle Creek to Washington, D.C., in August 1903, Jones was invited to join the General Conference staff to work in the area of religious liberty and in other areas for which he was fitted. He accepted, but soon returned to Battle Creek, apparently for the purpose of helping Dr. Kellogg see the error of his way. However, he became sympathetic with the doctor in his warfare against the General Conference. This resulted in separation from denominational employment and, finally, in loss of church membership.

At the 1909 General Conference session, a supreme effort was made to bring him back. Three afternoons in succession he met with a large committee of leaders. At the last of the meetings, after an extended appeal for reconciliation, A. G. Daniells, the president of the General Conference, reaching his hand across the table, pleaded with Jones, saying, "Come, Brother Jones, come." Evidently moved, Jones arose, slowly extended his hand toward the outstretched one, then suddenly pulled it back and declared, "No, never," as he sat down.

Jones remained a Sabbath observer and was loyal to most of the other fundamental doctrines of the church. He died without a following.

JONES, CHARLES HARRIMAN (1850-1936). Publishing house manager. Previous to joining the Review and Herald at Battle Creek, Michigan, in 1871 and running the first power press operated by the Seventh-day Adventist denomination, he had worked as state printer in Manchester, New Hampshire. In 1879 he became an assistant in the Pacific Publishing plant in Oakland, California, and later, manager, and held that position except for a brief period of retirement until 1923. He directed the removal of the press to Mountain View, California, in 1904, retired briefly from the institution, but when the building burned to the ground in 1906 he returned as manager at the urgent request of Ellen White and the press leaders. In addition to his administrative work, he led in establishing publishing work in England and Canada.

Jones also took a leading part in the development of Sabbath school work and, with the exception of a few months, was president of the International Sabbath School Association from 1887 to 1898. He was also prominent in building the ship *Pitcairn*.

JONES, DAN T. (1855-1901). Minister, conference administrator, and leader of the first group of Seventh-day Adventist missionaries to Mexico. He joined the SDA Church in 1876. In 1881 he received a license to preach and was elected secretary of the Missouri Conference, and in 1882 became its president. In 1888 he left Missouri to become secretary of the General Conference and early the next year served on the committee that prepared the constitution of the National Religious Liberty Association. But the climate of Battle Creek and the heavy responsibilities were too burdensome for his health. In 1891 he went West to take charge of the Pacific Coast District (Number 6). In 1893, advised to seek a more southerly climate, he led the first group of Seventh-day Adventist teachers and medical missionaries into Mexico, where he established a mission school and the medical work that became Guadalajara Sanitarium.

JONES, GRIFFITHS FRANCIS (1864-1940). Master mariner, missionary. Born at Hamefyl, Wales, early in life he took to seafaring, and subsequently qualified as a Master of the Mercantile Marine. Shortly after he accepted the Seventh-day Adventist faith, in 1893, he was associated with the Doctors Kress in medical missionary work in England. In 1900 he went to the United States and entered Keene Academy, where he graduated from the Bible Instructors' course. Then he went to the Society Islands, and began a period of devoted mission service in the Far East and throughout the South Pacific.

In 1904 he pioneered the work in Singapore, and subsequently in Java, Sumatra, Borneo, and the Malay states. He entered the Western Solomon Islands in 1914 and won many of the heathen inhabitants. He worked on many islands, such as New Caledonia, New Guinea, and Lord Howe Island. Because of a remarkable facility with foreign languages he was able to work in many different lands. Later in life he engaged for a time in city mission work in London, then went abroad again and worked in Algiers, Spain, Gibraltar, and South Africa.

In all, he and his wife worked in 38 different countries and islands, representing some 34 languages.

JONES MISSIONARY COLLEGE. *See* Kambubu Adventist High School.

JONES, ROBERT LLEWELLYN (1903-1940). Missionary in Cameroon and the Congo. He was educated at Pacific Union College, Walla Walla College, and Washington Missionary College (B.A., 1927), and while a student he worked as an X-ray technician at the Walla Walla Hospital and the Washington Sanitarium. In 1925 he married Charlotte Boyd Jewell. In January 1927 he and his wife sailed for missionary service in Equatorial Africa, stopping en route for a year in Europe to learn the French language. In 1928 he opened Seventh-day Adventist work in Cameroon, settling at the Nanga-Eboco station, selected previously by the pioneer missionary W. H. Anderson.

In 1929, when the work in Cameroon was transferred from the African Division to the Southern European Division, Jones went to the Congo, where he took charge of the Songa, Kirundu, and Gitwe missions, and directed the Gitwe Training School. He was ordained in 1934. While on furlough he received an M.A. degree from the University of Southern California in 1935. Late in 1940 he went to the Bikobo Hill Mission and while there was attacked and mauled by a wild buffalo and died from the complications that set in.

JONES, WILLIAM MEAD (1818-1895). Prominent Seventh Day Baptist minister and scholar; editor of the *Sabbath Memorial* (London, England). He was the pastor of the historic Mill Yard church in London at the time Seventh-day Adventists began their work in Europe. J. N. Andrews and other early missionaries in Europe maintained cordial relationships with him.

JORDAN. A constitutional monarchy in the Middle East, officially called the Hashemite Kingdom of Jordan (before 1947, the Emirate of Transjordan), situated in the northwestern part of the Arabian Peninsula east of the Jordan River. Until the six-day Arab-Israeli war in June 1967, it also included Jerusalem and the West Bank of Palestine. The area is 37,500 square miles (97,100 square kilometers). The population is mostly Arab. Most of the citizens are Sunni Muslims.

The present country of Jordan includes various regions described in the Bible—lands traversed by Abraham in his wanderings, inhabited at the time of the Exodus by the Ammonites, Moabites, Edomites, Canaanites, and Amorites, and occupied in large part by the Israelites at the height of their power. Jordan's capital, Amman, is the site of ancient Rabbath-Ammon, taken by David about 1000 B.C.

The land was overrun by the Assyrians and the Babylonians in the eighth and sixth centuries B.C., and the Hebrews taken into exile. The western part was resettled by the Samaritans, and after the Babylonian captivity by the returning Jews. Thereafter the land was ruled successively by the Persian, Macedonian, and Roman empires, and the south and east were part of a flourishing Semitic Nabataean kingdom.

Jordan embraces parts of what in New Testament times was called Perea and Decapolis.

The area of what is now Jordan and the West Bank became largely Christianized in the early centuries. After the Muslim Arabs defeated the Byzantine emperor Heraclius at the Yarmuk River in the seventh century, the country became overwhelmingly Muslim. The Crusader kingdom that occupied a large part of the country in the twelfth century did not change the basic Arab and Muslim character of the country. Later came centuries of Turkish overlordship, until 1917. After World War I the area came under British control, the western portion a part of the mandate of Palestine and Transjordan as a constitutional state (an emirate) under British tutelage. After World War II the latter became an independent monarchy and Emir Abdullah its king. In the partition of Palestine in 1948, Transjordan took over the Arab remainder of Palestine and the country was renamed Jordan.

Seventh-day Adventist Statistics. Jordan is part of the territory of the East Mediterranean Field, which is a part of the Middle East Union, an attached field reporting directly to the General Conference. Statistics (1992) for *Jordan:* churches, 5; members, 150; church or elementary schools, 2; ordained ministers, 2; licensed ministers, 2; teachers, 7. East Mediterranean Field headquarters are in Jdeidet El Matn, Lebanon.

Institutions. Amman Adventist Secondary School; Amman Care Home.

Development of Seventh-day Adventist Work. *Beginnings, in Palestine.* Until the partition of Palestine in 1948, the work of Seventh-day Adventists on both sides of the Jordan River was directed from Jerusalem, headquarters of the Palestine-Transjordan Mission. However, the armistice line divided the city, and the mission headquarters with its book depot and hydrotherapy and electrotherapy clinic were included in the Zionist-occupied sector. Afterward new headquarters were established at Amman. The same missionaries worked in various places in what are now Jordan, Israel, Lebanon, and Syria; and sometimes the records are difficult to separate geographically.

Seventh-day Adventist work in Jerusalem dates from the beginning of the century when J. H. Krum, originally from America, who had come from Germany to Jaffa in 1898, moved to Jerusalem and opened treatment rooms about the beginning of 1901. He was joined in November 1901 by S. Jespersson and his wife, from Basel, Switzerland. Apparently this establishment was inside the walled city. In 1904 a Jerusalem-Jaffa church was organized, composed largely of workers' families and German converts. Jespersson had many opportunities to talk on medical and hygienic subjects to the foreign settlers at Jerusalem, and also to preach to small groups. But the work was not without sacrifice. In 1904 Krum left because of ill health, and that summer J. G. Teschner, a nurse from Germany, died of fever only a few months after his arrival at Jerusalem to replace the Jesperssons, who had to leave because of fever.

By 1908 the health institution, patronized by people of many nationalities, was almost self-supporting, and in 1910 it was moved to a better location, where it was carried on until 1916, when it was closed by the Turkish government.

In 1910 Marie Meyer, a German colonist, was baptized by W. K. Ising in a stream traditionally identified with the Brook Cherith, where Elijah was fed while hiding from Ahab. Frederich Gregorius worked among the villages north of Jerusalem. The town fathers of one of these, Et-Taiyibeh (possibly to be identified with ancient Ophrah), presented in 1911 a petition for a school, but for many years his request could not be granted because no workers were available. However, from Et-Taiyibeh came the first Arab convert in Palestine, a woman teacher, baptized in 1930. In 1931 G. W. Schubert baptized three Arabs in the Jordan, in the same general area where John the Baptist administered the rite. Two of these were young people from Et-Taiyibeh and the third a woman, the first convert from Bethlehem. Other Arab converts were won at Ram Allah, 10 miles (16 kilometers) north of Jerusalem, and at Beit Jala, near Bethlehem, where evangelism and branch Sabbath school work were reported by 1946.

East of the Jordan. In 1912 Tigran Zacharian (Brother Zachary), an Armenian colporteur who was working around Jerusalem, made a trip beyond the Jordan, and among other places left publications at Es-Salt. The next year Ibrahim el-Khalil (who later married Marie Meyer) held evangelistic meetings there but had to leave because of the war. However, as a result of his work Michael Hilal el-Haddad began to keep the Sabbath and pay tithe. Contact was reestablished in 1922. On Apr. 2, 1926, George Keough baptized 12 persons in the nearby river Jabbok and organized a church. A church building was erected later, but it was sold in 1954 after the members had moved to Amman.

Schools. By 1931 a school was operating in El-Husn, and from 1932 to 1939 Ibrahim el-Khalil pioneered the work. The school was closed in 1948 for lack of a worker but was reopened by Najeeb Azar in 1951. A school building and church auditorium was constructed in 1956, but it closed in 1963. Another school was operated at Es-Salt from 1934 till 1938. In 1942 a girls' school was opened at Amman by Ruby Williams and Farid Srour. Hana Jubran was named principal of this school in 1948, and classes were gradually added until in 1959 the first class of girls finished the secondary school (twelfth grade).

Additional classrooms were built in 1958, and a large auditorium was added in 1964. Mousa Azar attempted to operate a boys' school at Amman in 1948 and Ibrahim Ayoub in 1952, but these were not long continued. Later land was purchased and a school for boys again planned. Najeeb Azar opened a school in El-Karak in 1955 after the baptism there of Isbir Midinatt, a man who had observed the Sabbath since 1927, but who until 1954 had been unknown to Seventh-day Adventists. This school closed in 1962. Today the Amman Adventist Secondary School is in full operation.

Sabbath Schools and Evangelism. In the 1950s active Sabbath schools were established not only in the churches and schools at Amman, El-Husn, and El-Karak, but also in the homes of members at Amman Station and Ram Allah, and in small chapels, used also for evangelistic meetings, rented at Zerqa, Irbid, Sareeh, Khanzira, Beit Jala, Bethlehem, Jerusalem, Abboud, and Et-Taiyibeh. By 1955 Sabbath school membership was reported at 500, four times the church membership. Church membership also climbed steeply from 50 in 1950 to 164 in 1957.

In recent times literature evangelism has been carried on by the students working in the summer. There has been no medical work in the country since the operation of a massage clinic in the city of Amman for a few months in 1939.

At present a Bible correspondence school is being operated in Amman.

Notable Events. Noteworthy in the development of the work in Jordan were the printing of Sabbath school lesson quarterlies at Jerusalem in 1925 and 1926, the first printed in Arabic; the establishment of the Seventh-day Adventist Church as a legal association in Trans-jordan in 1936 with its own religious court (this was reaffirmed in 1961 when the church was recognized as a national denomination); the first MV junior camps in the Middle East Division, directed by Anees Haddad (1954); the ordination of the first Jordanian minister, Moussa Azar (1954); the first Arab president of the Jordan church, Chafic Srour (1957); the purchase of land in Jerusalem for the erection of a church auditorium (1960); the first decoration of the Christmas tree at Manger Square in Bethlehem (1960); the establishment of a Bible correspondence school in Amman (1963); the Jordan Welfare Society organized (1964); the first stop-smoking plans in the Middle East conducted by A. A. Haddad and H. C. Lamp (1965). The headquarters of the Jordan Section were moved to Jerusalem in 1966, but were moved back to Amman after the war in 1967.

A new orphanage was built and opened in Amman in 1969; but before it could begin operation, legal problems forced its closing. Efforts to reopen it were successful in 1974, and Kameel Haddad was appointed as the director.

JOST, HULDA (1887-1938). Welfare worker and leader in Germany. From her childhood she was interested in helping the unfortunate. At the age of 16 she entered a School of Nursing and later worked in the medical service of the German Navy at Wilhelmshaven. After World War I she was a social worker in the Ruhr area. In 1926 she joined the Seventh-day Adventist Church and, beginning in 1926, led in the welfare work, first in the West German Union, and from 1929 in the Central European Division.

JOURNAL OF ADVENTIST EDUCATION, THE (February 1939- ; bimonthly, October through June; GC Department of Education, printed by Southwestern Color Graphics; 1993 basic circulation, 7,400; file in the department library). A professional educational journal published primarily for teachers and other educational personnel in the Seventh-day Adventist school system worldwide. It contains general articles on educational philosophy and practice, and specialized articles written specifically for teachers of all levels. It is a member of the Educational Press Association of America.

Editors: W. Homer Teesdale, 1939-1946; Keld J. Reynolds, 1947-1955; Richard Hammill, 1955-1963; T. S. Geraty, 1963-1970; Garland J. Millet, 1970-1978; Victor S. Griffiths, 1978-1990; Beverly J. Rumble, 1991- .

JOURNAL OF THE ADVENTIST THEOLOGICAL SOCIETY (1990- ; published twice yearly by the Adventist Theological Society). A journal that serves as a vehicle for publishing the papers presented at the meetings of the Adventist Theological Society. In 1994 the circulation was 10,000.

Editors: Leo Van Dolson, 1990-1992; Frank Holbrook, 1993- .

JOWAI SECONDARY BOARDING SCHOOL. *See* Adventist Training School.

"JOY OF SERENITY AND SALVATION, THE." *See* Celebrations of Recovery.

JUAN PABLO DURARTE SCHOOL (Barahona). A 12-grade educational institution located in Barahona in the southern region of the Dominican Republic.

The school was founded in the year 1922 by James Phipps. Even though its beginnings were rather slow because the school was located in an area of poor economic resources, it has been greatly blessed.

The secondary level (grades 9-12) is accredited by the Education Commission of the Inter-American Division. It has 200 students on the secondary level, with nine teachers.

Some of the school directors have been Norma Familia, Magdalena Lizardo, Migdalia Lizardo, Maritza Manzanillo, Rosario Poueriet, Andrés Molina, Juan Reynaldo Rodríguez, and Elisa Mejía. The present director is Ariel de la Cruz.

JUAN PABLO DUARTE SCHOOL (San Juan de la Maguana). A secondary school belonging to the South Dominican Mission. It is accredited by the country's Education Department. In 1993 it had 127 students and a faculty of seven.

The school had its beginnings in the year 1957 and is still at its original location on General Cabral Street The first facility was a small room owned by the local Seventh-day Adventist church. The one teacher Elida Amparo, had 50 students in first and second grades. By 1967 there were eight grades and 250 students.

In 1981 the school began offering secondary school grade 9. Grade 10 was offered in 1982, and 11 and 12 were offered by 1984.

The school building has eight classrooms on the first floor and two on the second. The church, situated across from the school building, is used for general meetings.

Principals of the school have included German Lorenzo, María Celeste Reyes, Estherdreda Arrindell, Rafael Solís, Guillermo Rosario, and Juan Acevedo.

JUAN PABLO DUARTE SECONDARY SCHOOL. A 12-grade educational institution located in San Pedro de Macorís, Dominican Republic. The school had its beginnings in the year 1923 and obtained government recognition in 1925. Its first teacher was Juan Rivera.

The school is community-oriented, conducting patriotic and antidrug marches, conferences, concerts, and other activities.

In 1966, under the leadership of Arístides González, the school's first building was constructed. In 1993 the school had 830 students in both the primary and secondary levels, and 20 teachers along with seven nonteaching staff.

Recent Principals: Aurora Mateo de Rosario, 1966; Dorothy Young, 1967-1972; Rocío Frías, 1973-1984; Antonia Alcántara, 1985-1987; Carmen Baptista 1988-1990; Salvador Oviedo, 1991- .

JUDGMENT. The eschatological process by which God intervenes in human history to reward "every man according as his work shall be," to eradicate sin and its results from the universe, and to establish the righteous, universal, eternal reign of Christ. Seventh-day Adventists understand that the great final judgment involves three steps: (1) an investigative judgment, by which those eligible to eternal life are separated from those who are not eligible in a pre-Advent investigation; (2) an examination of the individual cases of the wicked by the righteous, during the millennium, to assure the latter that justice is being done in each case and to determine the sentence to be meted out in each case; and (3) the executive judgment, which takes place at the close of the millennium, when sentence is executed in the fires of hell.

In Millerite preaching, emphasis was placed on Christ's coming to execute judgment upon sin and sinners, at His appearing. A strong emphasis in the 1844 message was the pronouncement that "the hour of his judgment is come" (Rev. 14:7). But as early as 1841 the idea of a two-phase judgment began to be taught. Josiah Litch in that year published an *Address to . . . the Clergy,* in which he spoke of "the judicial scene of judgment" preceding the resurrection (p. 39) and of the execution of the judgment following it (p. 38). The next year he explained at length the distinction between the two: "1. It [the verb *judge]* is used in the Bible in the sense of a trial according to law and evidence; the idea being drawn from a civil or criminal court. The term is used in this sense in Luke xix. 22. . . .

"2. It signifies a penal judgment; or the execution of judgment; and is so used, Acts vii. 7. . . . The terms are both used in reference to the judgment of the human race. 1. All men will be brought to trial, or into judgment, and all their deeds and their moral characters will be examined and their everlasting states will be determined by the evidence produced from God's books, including the book of life. . . . No human tribunal would think of executing judgment on a prisoner until after his trial; much less will God. He will bring every work into judgment, with every secret thing, whether it be good or evil.

"But the resurrection is the *retribution* or *execution of judgment,* for 'they that have done good shall come forth to the resurrection of life'" (Josiah Litch, *Prophetic Expositions,* vol. 1, pp. 49, 50).

"God, 'The Ancient of Days,' Will Preside in the Trial.

"1. Daniel vii. 9, 10, presents the Ancient of days coming on his throne of fiery flame; the judgment is set and the books opened. He is distinct from the Son of man, spoken of in the 13th verse, when he comes to the Ancient of days.

"The Son of Man Will Execute the Judgment.

"Thus the Saviour declares, John v. 27: 'And hath given him authority to *execute judgment* also, because he is the Son of man'" *(ibid.,* p. 52).

Of the phase of the judgment that takes place during the millennium Ellen White wrote that Christ and the saints "judge the wicked, comparing their acts with the statute-book, the Bible, and deciding every case according to the deeds done in the body. Then the portion which the wicked must suffer is meted out, according to their works; and it is recorded against their names in the book of death" (GC 661; see 1 Cor. 6:2, 3).

Concerning the executive phase of the judgment the Scriptures declare, "Fire came down from God out of heaven, and devoured them" (Rev. 20:9). Commenting on the effects of this fire, Ellen White declares: "Some are destroyed as in a moment, while others suffer many days. All are punished 'according to their deeds.' . . . His [Satan's] punishment is to be far greater than that of those whom he has deceived. After all have perished who fell by his deceptions, he is still to live and suffer on. In the cleansing flames the wicked are at last destroyed, root and branch" (GC 673).

"This was the *execution of the judgment*" (E. G. White, in *Present Truth* 1:86, November 1850).

An early Bible description of the great final judgment is that of Joel 3. Here, God delivers His people and sits in judgment on the nations that have oppressed them, and annihilates them (Joel 3:1, 2, 11-17, 19-21). Daniel develops the idea further in his description of "the Ancient of days" sitting in judgment upon the little horn. "The judgment was set, and the books were opened." As a result, the "fourth beast, dreadful and terrible," was "slain, . . . destroyed, and given to the burning flame." The Ancient of days then awards the dominion of this earth to the "Son of man," that "all people, nations, and languages, should serve him; his dominion is an everlasting dominion," and "to the people of the saints of the most High, whose kingdom is an everlasting kingdom, and all dominions shall serve and obey him" (Dan. 7:9-14, 26, 27). John describes a similar scene at the close of the millennium, with the wicked dead of all ages raised to life and arraigned before the bar of divine justice to receive sentence and to be "cast into the lake of fire" (Rev. 20:7-15).

The apostle Paul declares that God has appointed a day in which He will judge the world, and that all human beings, living and dead, must appear before the judgment seat of Christ, to be rewarded for what they have done in the flesh (Acts 17:30, 31; Rom. 14:10; 2 Cor. 5:10; 2 Tim. 4:1; cf. 1 Peter 4:6). The judgment is closely associated, in point of time, with Christ's second appearing and the establishment of His kingdom (2 Tim. 4:1; cf. Dan. 7:9, 10, 13, 14; Jude 14). In the judgment every deed will be considered (Eccl. 12:13, 14; Rev. 20:12). God's moral law is the standard of judgment (James 2:10-12). The books of record in heaven include the book of life and the records of individual lives (Dan. 7:10; 12:1; Mal. 3:16; Rev. 20:12). God the Father and Christ the Son participate in the work of judgment (John 5:26, 27; Rom. 2:16; 2 Tim. 4:8; Jude 14, 15). The premillennial phase of the judgment of the wicked is described in Rev. 14:14-20 and 19:11-21. Prior to the executive judgment, at the close of the millennium, the unjust of all ages will be raised to life to hear sentence pronounced (Rev. 20:12-15). The earth is then purified of sin and sinners and created anew to be the eternal abode of the righteous (2 Peter 3:7-12; Rev. 20:14, 15; 21:1-5; 22:5).

Christ represented the judgment in the parables of the dragnet (separation of the righteous from the wicked), Matt. 13:47-50; of the talents (rewards), Matt. 25:14-30; and of the sheep and the goats (separation), Matt. 25:31-46; and of the man without a wedding garment (investigation of the guests, separation of the just and the unjust, and execution of the sentence), Matt. 22:2-14.

JULIACA ADVENTIST CLINIC (Clínica Adventista de Juliaca). A 21-bed general hospital owned and operated by the Inca Union Mission in Juliaca, department of Puno, in southeastern Peru. This was the first medical institution operated by Seventh-day Adventists in the Inca Union.

Seventh-day Adventist medical work in the highlands of Peru and Bolivia was started by F. H. Stahl, a missionary nurse, who went to this region in 1911 and worked there for many years. In 1922 Dr. S. Theron Johnston made his headquarters at the Platería Mission, and was the first SDA physician to enter the Lake Titicaca area. On Mar. 21, 1923, he rented a house in Juliaca, a more accessible center than the mission, and opened a small hospital. At that time the Southern Railway, one of Peru's two principal railway systems, made a contract with him to be its company doctor. Later the Social Security Service took over professional attention for all the workers' organizations in the area, including the railways, and amplified their contract with the hospital, signifying a considerable increase in the clinic's work. Fifty percent of operations performed are for patients affiliated with this state organization.

In 1927 the Inca Union Mission purchased, with money from the Missions Extension Fund, property on Loreto Street in Juliaca, one block from the central square; and under the direction of Dr. M. Bernard Graybill, a Loma Linda graduate, a one-story 20-bed hospital was constructed of adobe bricks. However, despite repeated attempts, Dr. Graybill was unsuccessful in obtaining a license from the government to practice medicine in Peru, and in 1928 the clinic was closed to White Peruvian clientele, with the exception of railroad and mine employees, with whom it had contracts, and cases specifically referred to it by recognized Peruvian physicians. However, within two weeks the local authorities requested that the clinic be reopened to the general public, and Dr. Graybill was guaranteed the necessary authorization to carry on his work. The original hospital building was modified and enlarged through the years and in 1961 was replaced by the present structure.

The clinic's area of influence extends not only to the approximately 100,000 inhabitants living in the surrounding area. In 1974 it became the center of the Juliaca Medical Association. At the initiative of Dr. Hugo Velarde, a specialized library, which renders invaluable service to all medical workers of that area, was founded. The clinic has established a nurse's aide program in connection with the Lake Titicaca Training School.

Medical Directors: S. Theron Johnston, 1923-1925; M. Bernard Graybill, 1925-1930; R. R. Reed, 1930-1935; R. O. Ingham, 1936; H. L. Dixon, 1937; Clayton R. Potts, 1939-1944; Elmer E. Bottsford, 1944-1948; David P. Duffie, 1948-1953; Howard C. Smith, 1953-1957; Erwin O. Beskow, 1957-1961; Eleodoro Alayza, 1961-1963; Rodolfo Alfaro, 1964; Gunnar Wensell, 1964-1966; Carlos Balarezo, 1967-1969; Werner Leibold, 1970-1972; Felix Galdos, 1973; Percy Cuba, 1974-1975; Juan Barrientos, 1975-1977; Victor Ramos, 1978-1982; Walter Campuzano, 1982-1983; Daniel Ludi, 1983-1984; Donavon Schwisow, 1984-1986; Daniel Ludi, 1986-1987; Francisco Condori, 1987-1989; Jose Medina, 1989-1990; Humberto Perales, 1990-1992; Francisco Condori, 1992- .

JUNIOR CAMP. *See* Camping.

JUNIOR GUIDE. *See Guide.*

JUNIOR MISSIONARY VOLUNTEERS. *See* Adventist Youth Societies; MV Societies.

JUSTIFICATION. Justification is the divine act of acquittal, of declaring a repentant sinner released from the guilt of sin and restored to divine favor. In the NT the term occurs only in Rom. 4:25 and 5:16, 18, where justification is said to have been made possible by Christ's vicarious death on the cross and His resurrection. It is the atonement that makes justification possible. Justification involves grace on the part of God and faith on the part of humanity. The verb *dikaiō,* "to justify," "to acquit," "to reckon," occurs some 40 times in the NT, the majority of these being in the Epistles of Paul. This fact implies that the doctrine of justification is basically a Pauline theme. It is the foundation upon which depend our relationship to God in this life and our hope for eternal life.

In the NT "to justify" means to pronounce or to declare a person to be right, or just, as, for example, in Luke 7:29, the publicans "justified God"; and in Rom. 3:4, where Paul says, "That thou mightest be justified in thy sayings." The term also means "to acquit" those of charges brought against them, as, for example, in Acts 13:39, "justified from all things, from which ye could not be justified by the law of Moses." In the case of God justifying sinners, He does so by virtue of His favorable disposition toward them and His gracious purpose with respect to them.

Justification does not impart to the recipients, in their own right, the moral quality of being right, nor does it vest them with that quality. It simply vindicates them of the claims of the moral law against them because of their unlawful acts. It grants them the legal status of being considered as if they had never committed unlawful acts. Their new status is one they enjoy only by virtue of their new relationship to Jesus Christ, and can retain only by maintaining that relationship. But justification comprehends more than pardon alone. It not only declares a sinner righteous, but entitles him or her to all the rewards and benefits that properly belong to the righteous.

The Jew of Paul's day commonly thought of righteousness objectively, as a legalistic and meticulous observance of the requirements of the law of Moses. The apostle presents the matter subjectively, as an inward disposition of heart and mind that leads to right action in harmony with "the law" as magnified by Jesus Christ and exemplified by His life on earth. When a person accepts Jesus Christ as his or her Saviour, he or she stands accepted before God, and enters into a new status, that of righteousness. But to begin with, this righteousness is more *ideal* than it is *actual*. It does not, as yet, consist of perfect fulfillment of the divine will, but primarily the individual has been accorded the right to an acceptable standing before God.

From first to last, this right status depends upon faith, not simply an intellectual faith (which even devils have; James 2:19), nor even merely trust (which is so often a mere passive dependence upon a superior power), but an ardent, vitalizing grasp of an intimate, personal relation to a personal Saviour. Often the apostle designates the relationship with God through Christ of one who has been justified by the expression "in Christ," meaning a personal relationship with Christ (Rom. 8:1; etc.). Thus, believers are sons of God by virtue of their faith (Gal. 3:26). They live, metaphorically, within Christ, and literally within the orbit of His will. Justification is never attained by presumed works of merit, whether those prescribed by the law of Moses or by ecclesiastical legislation or by personal choice. "A man is not justified by the works of the law, but by the faith of Jesus Christ" (Gal. 2:16; cf. Gal. 3:11). Justification is not an objective relation to a legal system of ethics, with the expectation of thereby meriting and obtaining divine approval and award (see Rom. 4:6-8; 5:17-19). The one who stands justified shall be eternally saved from wrath at Christ's second coming (Rom. 5:9, 10). God credits us with the life of perfect obedience our Lord lived on earth.

Justification carries with it the gift of peace with God (Rom. 5:1); it prepares the way for sanctification and glorification. Justification is ever a means to an end, not an end in itself. Paul sometimes uses the word "reconciled" to signify an experience similar to that of being "justified" (Rom. 5:10, 11). Unless God did something to change our status, He would be obliged to treat us as enemies.

The Seventh-day Adventist view of justification was set forth by James White in a *Review and Herald* editorial in 1869, in which he wrote: "How shall man be just with God? Or to speak still more definitely, how shall a sinner become just in God's sight? There is but one answer that can be returned to this. His is clearly the case of that class who are justified by faith without works. But how shall the man who is thus justified maintain his justification before God? By faith which produces good works. His justification is therefore, maintained as James insists, by faith and works" (34:16, July 6, 1869).

To one who misunderstood the Seventh-day Adventist position Uriah Smith replied: "Who claims that we are to be justified by the deeds of the law? We certainly do not. Justification by faith is our sole dependence, and ever has been. . . . Do you believe you have liberty now to commit any of the sins forbidden by the ten commandments? You do not; neither do we. Do you expect to be justified by faith while living in the commission of those sins? You would not. Neither do we. This is the real question in this matter; and in this we are agreed" (*ibid.* 37:140, Apr. 18, 1871).

Of the relationship between justification and obedience D. M. Canright wrote: "The Gospel is not given to succeed the law, but to save men from their sins, the violations of the law. Hence faith in Christ and obedience to the commandments of God should always go together. . . . Be it understood, then, that we are not seeking to be justified by the law, but by faith, as was Abraham, Rom. 4:1-4; and yet we keep God's law as did Abraham the father of the faithful" (*ibid.* 43:106, Mar. 17, 1874).

Ellen White has described justification in these words: "If you give yourself to Him [Christ], and accept Him as your Saviour, then, sinful as your life may have been, for His sake you are accounted righteous, Christ's character stands in place of your character, and you are accepted before God just as if you had not sinned" (SC 62).

"The righteousness by which we are justified is imputed; the righteousness by which we are sanctified is imparted. The first is our title to heaven, the second is our fitness for heaven" (MYP 35).

"When the sinner believes that Christ is his personal Saviour, then, according to His unfailing promises, God pardons his sin, and justifies him freely. The repentant soul realizes that his justification comes because Christ, as his substitute and surety, has died for him, is his atonement and righteousness" (1SM 367).

Seventh-day Adventists believe in justification by faith alone, but also that those who have been justified by faith will aspire to make the perfection of Christ as reflected in the moral law their own pattern of life and conduct—not as a means to justification but as a result of it, out of dedicated appreciation for His infinite gift of love (John 15:10).

See also Faith and Works; Law; Law and Grace; New Birth; Righteousness by Faith; Sanctification.

K

KABIUFA ADVENTIST HIGH SCHOOL (Papua New Guinea). A coeducational boarding secondary school situated on 250 acres (100 hectares) of fertile soil at Kabiufa, about seven miles (12 kilometers) from the town of Goroka on the Highlands Highway, at an elevation of 5,480 feet (1,670 meters). The students come mostly from mainland New Guinea.

Land for the mission station at Kabiufa was purchased by L. I. Howell and H. W. Nolan in 1947. This was the first attempt by Seventh-day Adventists to open up mission work in the area, and it became the site for the Eastern Highlands Training School. After union mission boundary adjustments it became, in 1953, the Coral Sea Union Mission College. The Coral Sea Union College was first established at Kambubu on the island of New Britain in 1950. In 1953 that became the location for the college (subsequently renamed Jones Missionary College) for the newly formed Bismarck Solomons Union Mission, and Kabiufa became the location of the college for the Coral Sea Union Mission.

Early in the history of Kabiufa, a sawmill had been established, and this became a valuable asset to the new college. A joinery industry and maintenance department gave practical instruction to many of the senior students. Courses offered included ministerial training, teacher training, and building construction. In 1968 the training courses were discontinued at Kabiufa and combined with those at Kambubu. Kabiufa then became, and still is, Kabiufa Adventist High School.

Through the years Kabiufa has established a reputation for the production of vegetables in the school gardens. A significant contribution to better production methods was made by J. K. Mittleider in the mid-1960s. This work was carried on by A. L. Voigt. The gardens provide excellent food for the school, for local demands, and for distribution within Papua New Guinea.

Principals: L. R. Thrift, 1949-1952; K. J. Gray, 1953-1955; A. G. Chapman, 1956-1957; J. R. Lee, 1958-1964; M. P. Cozens, 1965-1969; I. B. Rankin, 1970-1972; J. L. Wilson, 1973-1976; A. Steel, 1977-1981; G. Webster, 1982; L. Meintjes, 1983-1984; W.D.T. Potter, 1985-1986; R. M. Ferguson, 1987-1989; S. Kuku, 1990-1993; J. Barrons, 1993-1994; S. A. Barons, 1994- .

KAINE, JAMES (1933-1989). Preacher, administrator. Born in Costa Rica, he became a Seventh-day Adventist in 1942. He was married to Olga Palmer.

In 1958 he began working as a minister in Siquirres, Costa Rica, and was ordained in 1961. In 1965 he became treasurer of the British Honduras Mission (now Belize Mission), of which he later became president. He was transferred to Honduras and later returned to Costa Rica to further his education. He was then called to labor as a pastor in the Bay Islands of Honduras and later went to Honduras as manager of the Valley of the Angels Hospital.

He served the church for more than 30 years.

KA JUNG KOA KUN KANG. *See Home and Health.*

KALAKA, DAVID (c. 1844-1904). Pioneer preacher, colporteur, translator, the first African Seventh-day Adventist in Basutoland, South Africa. Educated in a French Evangelical mission school, he worked for 15 years in a printing plant and assisted in translating the Bible into the Sesuto language.

In 1895, while serving as guide and interpreter for S. N. Haskell, who spent several weeks visiting Basutoland, Kalaka became interested in the seventh-day Sabbath, and after many discussions he decided to keep it. After the trip was over, Haskell arranged for Kalaka to translate Ellen White's book *Steps to Christ* into the Sesuto language (this was one of the earliest translations of this book into a pagan tongue) and to attend a general SDA meeting in Kimberley. There Kalaka was baptized. He then returned to his own country to tell others of his newly found faith.

When J. M. Freeman entered Basutoland in 1899 as the first appointed Seventh-day Adventist missionary, Kalaka became his assistant and worked under him for five years. In 1902 Kalaka took a supply of *Steps to Christ* in Sesuto and traveled far back into the mountains, where in three weeks he visited 20 villages and sold many copies of the book. He later went on similar trips to various places. When he died at about the age of 60, he left a son who was teaching in a mission school and who became an SDA minister.

KALIMANTAN ACADEMY (Perguruan Advent Kalimantan). A day school operated by the Seventh-day Adventist Church under the control of Kalimantan Mission. The school, which is located in east Kalimantan, Indonesia, was started in 1964 with elementary and junior high classes. The senior high school was added in 1982. The government's accreditation granted in 1985 for junior and senior high school was recognized as the registered status.

Kalimantan Academy particularly serves three churches in the Balikpapan district; however, some of the students come from Manado, Ujungpandang, and several other cities within the Kalimantan Mission territory.

Principals: Hany Sualang, 1989- .

KALIMANTAN MISSION. *See* Far Eastern Division; Indonesia.

KAMAGAMBO HIGH SCHOOL AND TEACHERS' COLLEGE. A coeducational boarding school on the senior high school level, operated by the East African Union, 14 miles (22 kilometers) south of the town of Kisii, the administrative headquarters of the South Nyanza district in Kenya, East Africa. It is situated on 60 acres (25 hectares) of land lying one-half mile (.8 kilometer) from the main road to Tanzania, and has an elevation of 5,000 feet (1,525 meters) and an annual rainfall of about 60 inches (150 centimeters). Swahili, the lingua franca of East Africa, is used with English in the classrooms. The school serves a constituency of 314,739 church members in Kenya, and the majority of the students are adherents of the Seventh-day Adventist Church. In 1993 the teaching staff was all African with an enrollment of 548 teachers-in-training, 38 ministerial students, and 134 in the secondary school.

History. The predecessor of the training school was a mission school opened on a site given by the chief and his elders in 1913 to A. A. Carscallen and Petro Oyier, an African mission worker. This tract, covered with bush and trees, was a kind of buffer zone between two tribes and had been used by them as a battleground. The government hoped that by getting this particular piece of land for the missionaries peace might be preserved between the two tribes. D. E. Delhove spent a few months in 1913 helping Carscallen get the school started. Evangelistic work conducted in connection with the school resulted in the baptism of six persons in 1918. Illiterate adult converts were taught to read and write.

In 1921 E. R. Warland began teaching additional subjects, and in 1922 Grace Clarke began a boarding school for girls. The first girls were so timid that they had to be induced to attend by promises of clothing. In 1928 a teacher training course was begun, which the government agreed to recognize. In 1933 a boarding school was opened for boys. In 1965 the elementary classes of the boys' school were moved to another site in order to make room for the addition of the first two years of high school work. In 1962 the eleventh year of work was added, and in 1963 the twelfth year. At present the school offers full secondary education for both boys and girls. A two-year primary teacher training course is offered after the twelfth year of schooling. A two-year ministerial course is also offered.

The buildings are permanent brick and stone structures, and there is a good water supply, which is piped into all the houses. Lights are supplied by a generating plant. There is a church, for the use of the school only, which seats 1,000 people. A modern cafeteria, elementary school block, and office quarters add to the efficiency of the school plant.

Principals: E. R. Warland, 1928-1936;

S. W. Beardsell, 1936-1947; V. E. Robinson, 1948-1953; R. G. Pearson, 1954-1955; F. E. Schlehuber, 1957-1958; W. W. Oakes, 1959-1960; R. A. Marx, 1961-1965; Timothy Gorle, 1965-1967; F. N. Chase, 1967-1973; J. N. Kyale, 1973-1982; G. Y. Mgeni, 1982-1986; L. M. Dull, 1986-1987; G. O. Angíenda, 1987-1991; E. E. Njagi, 1991- .

KAMBUBU ADVENTIST HIGH SCHOOL (Papua New Guinea). A coeducational boarding secondary school situated on nearly 5,000 acres (2,000 hectares) of land on the south coast of the island of New Britain approximately 35 miles (55 kilometers) southeast of Rabaul. In 1993 a faculty and staff of 22 served the students.

The students come from the islands of the Bismarck Archipelago and Bougainville. The school caters for the first four years of secondary education, and a number of young men are trained in building construction. Food for the students is grown on the school property, the gardens being cared for by the students during the afternoon work period. The staple crops are *kau kau* (sweet potato), manioc, and a variety of taro.

The school operates a joinery shop where some of the students learn skills in handling tools and making furniture for sale in Rabaul. Transportation between the school and Rabaul is by the school launch, M.V. *Kambubu.* There is access by road, but an unbridged river, which is crossed by canoe, is a handicap.

Land for the school was purchased in 1936, £4,000 being provided by the Sanitarium Health Food Company. A school known as the Put Put Training School was begun, and A. R. Hiscox was the headmaster. Others who helped in developmental work were G. Peacock, H. R. Steed, A. J. Campbell, L. M. Maxwell, H. White, A. Gallagher, R.R.D. Marks, A. Harrison (builder), and E. Cherry (sawmiller).

When Japan entered World War II and penetrated southward. Hiscox was evacuated to Australia and the school was discontinued. The school site was occupied by the Japanese during the war, and all the buildings were destroyed.

The work of rebuilding began in 1946 and in 1947 the school was reopened as the Kambubu Training School, the name derived from a small river flowing through the property. In 1950 it was decided that the Kambubu Training School should become the college for the Coral Sea Union Mission. In 1953, when the Coral Sea Union was divided into two unions, it became the college for the Bismarck-Solomons Union Mission and was renamed the Adventist Union College. When this name proved generally unacceptable, it became in 1954 the Jones Missionary College, named after G. F. Jones, a pioneer SDA missionary to the South Pacific Islands. Training courses for ministers and teachers continued until 1968 when Sonoma Adventist College was established. Jones Missionary College then became Kambubu Adventist High School, the name it now bears.

Principals: E. Tonkin, 1946-1949; J. K. Aitken, 1950; L. N. Lock, 1951-1957; I. R. Harvey, 1958-1960; R. W. Richter, 1961; D. C. Sutcliffe, 1962-1965; K. J. Bullock, 1966-1969; K. E. Satchell, 1970-1972; D. A. Caldwell, 1973-1978; R. Wilkinson, 1979-1981; G. Dawkins, 1982; A. Hay, 1983; B. Bidmead, 1984-1986; D. Edgeworth, 1987; S. Kuku, 1988-1989; S. Panda, 1990-1992; J. Ponduk, 1993-1994; Noah Pune, 1994- .

KANDANA SEVENTH-DAY ADVENTIST HIGH SCHOOL. A coeducational day school on the elementary and secondary level, operated by the Sri Lanka Union of Churches of the Far Eastern Division. It is located in Kandana, Gampaha district, about nine miles (15 kilometers) north of Colombo beside Airport Road. It offers classes from preschool to grade 10 in the Sinhala language. English is taught as a second language. At the elementary level Tamil is also taught. When students complete grade 4 level, they sit for the government scholarship selection examination. Many pass the examination and are selected for prestigious schools in Colombo. At the end of grade 10, students sit for the GCE (O/L) examination, which is conducted by the Department of Examinations, Sri Lanka. Apart from the regular curriculum, special English classes are conducted in the afternoon for students who are interested in learning more English.

The main school campus is located on a one-acre (.5-hectare) site. Presently there is one two-story building with 11 classrooms, a library, and office space. A three-story building is in progress for another 11 classrooms and a science laboratory. In addition to this, there are classroom facilities at the premises of Kandana and Ja-Ela Seventh-day Adventist churches. In January 1993 the total enrollment was a little more than 1,000 students.

In 1961 Mrs. D. M. Fernando started a preschool, with an enrollment of six children, in the Voice of Hope Auditorium at 52, Negombo Road, Kandana. It was under the direction of D. M. Fernando, who was the pastor of the Enderamulla church and in charge of the work in Kandana. In 1963 Mrs. J. D. Peter was the teacher. The school has continued to grow, and many improvements have been added. Mr. H.G.M. Fernando was elected principal in 1987. Since then there have been more improvements, including the completion of the second floor with six classrooms, the library, and a staff room. Additional land was purchased and other physical improvements were made, including a miniscience lab. In 1988 the school received approval to present examinations conducted by the Department of Examinations, Sri Lanka.

Principals: Donald M. Fernando, 1961-1962; J. D. Peter, 1963; Marcia Abeywardana, 1964-1965; Irene Kulasekera, 1966-1968; Tudor Perera, 1969-1970; Mary Perera, 1971-1973; Luxmi Dissanayake, 1974-1979; Peter Munasinghe, 1980-1983; Gration Perera, 1983-1984; Sepalika de Silva, 1984-1987; H.G.M. Fernando, 1987- .

KANSAS. *See* Central States Conference; Kansas Conference; Kansas-Nebraska Conference.

KANSAS CONFERENCE. A former unit of church organization that included the state of Kansas. *(See also* Central States Conference.) Statistics in 1980 at the time of the merger with the Nebraska Conference: churches, 57; members, 4,697; church schools, 11; ordained ministers, 23; licensed ministers, 5; church school teachers, 22.

The conference formed part of the Central Union Conference.

Institutions that operated in the Kansas Conference included Enterprise Academy and Shawnee Mission Medical Center, located in Shawnee Mission, Kansas.

History. *Beginnings of the Work in the Area.* As early as the 1860s there were scattered groups of Seventh-day Adventists, immigrants from Eastern states, in Kansas. In 1866 several of these isolated pioneers, who often numbered no more than two or three in one place, wrote to the Review and Herald expressing their desire for other Seventh-day Adventists to join them and for ministerial help. In answer to these requests, other conferences sent workers to hold meetings, stimulate interest, and organize churches. These hardy preachers, holding meetings in tents or schoolhouses, worked under difficulties and often against opposition and prejudice.

The first tent meetings in Kansas appear to have been held by John Matteson during the fall of 1869. In October he preached in the area south of Mound City in Linn County, where there were already four members. Three were baptized, among the first in the state.

The following spring and summer found Matteson again in Linn County, holding meetings in Mapleton, Centerville, and Farlinville. In July 1870 he reported J. H. Cook's ordination as an elder of the Mound City church, and a three-day grove meeting at Farlinville.

Other outstanding early leaders in Kansas were D. J. Rousseau, Joseph Lamont, George Kennedy, J. N. Ayers (first Kansas Conference president), L. D. Santee, N. W. Vincent, D. T. Bourdeau, Smith Sharp, John Gibbs, R. G. Ranton, George W. Page, R. J. Lawrence, and George I. Butler.

Missouri-Kansas Conference. At the first camp meeting held in Kansas, at Pleasanton, in October 1870 (at which James and Ellen White were present), the Missouri-Kansas Conference was organized, with R. J. Lawrence as president. Two Kansas churches were taken into the new conference—Mound City and Centerville. Only a few of the widely separated members attended this camp meeting, but of those who did, some came amazing distances, leaving their sod houses and making the journey in covered wagons. One Kansan drove his team 270 miles (430 kilometers), and a wagonload of Missourians traveled six days. From a small beginning in 1870, including only five fully organized churches in both states, the membership increased to 22 churches by 1874.

The Kansas Conference Organized. At the Missouri-Kansas camp meeting held at Mound City, Kansas, in September 1875 the conference was divided into the Missouri Conference and the Kansas Conference, each having more than a dozen churches and about 300 members. The Kansas camp meeting held at Melvern in 1876 was described by James White as almost a miracle, considering the youth of the conference in the new state and the poverty of the people as a result of the drought and the grasshopper scourge. That year there were 235 members. By 1888, after active evangelism and the influx of many Adventists from the older Western states—Wisconsin, Illinois, and especially Iowa—the Kansas Conference was the second largest in the denomination, with a membership of 2,000. Although there was an exodus of settlers to Oklahoma and other states during the early nineties, by 1896 there were 85 churches and 3,000 members. During 1893 alone 148 were baptized at the four Kansas camp meetings.

Progress was not constant, however. Although the churches grew rapidly, there was occasional apostasy. George I. Butler in 1873 expressed concern for the spiritual condition of the cause in Kansas, fearing that some of the brethren were becoming too much involved in land speculation and profit. Then drought, distance, and discouragement plagued the pioneers. The dry weather of the late eighties and early nineties compelled many of the settlers to mortgage their farms, and many returned to the East. Whole sections of western Kansas were depopulated.

In general, the work in the early period was confined to small towns and rural schoolhouses, but prior to 1900 three now prominent city churches were founded: Topeka (12 members, 1882), Wichita (20 members, 1887), and Kansas City (1890).

The German language work had a most phenomenal growth in western Kansas. In Rush County, where there was a large settlement of German people of various faiths, the work of L. R. Conradi and S. S. Shrock resulted in the Otis church (organized about 1883). From this German church families moved west and formed other churches at Shaffer and Nekoma in Rush County, and Bazine in Ness County, also at Garden City and Great Bend. In the winter of 1884, Conradi and Shrock established a church at Hillsboro, which by May of 1885 had 123 members.

About this time work began among the Black population (*see* Central States Conference).

During the late eighties the need for a denominational school was expressed. A preparatory school was opened at Ottawa late in 1888. Courses included "the common branches," bookkeeping, and Bible, and students paid $2 a week for board and room with SDA families. L. J. Rousseau and his wife were the first teachers in this conference-operated school. A German school had operated at Lehigh and had closed by 1889, and one was opened at Otis in 1894.

To fill the needs of this frontier territory during the middle and late nineties, short-term workers' institutes trained colporteurs and others desiring to engage immediately in some branch of evangelistic work. One such session held in 1894 at Ottawa, in the eastern part of the state, had about 60 in attendance. In 1896 a five-week school was held at El Dorado, offering three general lines of study besides preaching services each night for the benefit of the general public. No tuition was charged. To those already in the work, and those who planned to enter the work for at least six months, room, heating stove, and fuel were free, while meals were given at cost. Those who could not attend were urged to send a young man or woman; such were boarded for $6 for the five weeks. During the session an urgent appeal was made for donations or for the loan of horses and rigs for use by the young women canvassers.

Kansas became one of the leaders in the canvassing work. Shortly after the introduction of subscription-book sales, Kansas colporteurs were organized in each county into a band of five or six members, including a leader to encourage them, order their books, assist them in deliveries, and meet with them each Sabbath and Sunday. The June 1887 report states that about 100 working canvassers in the state had sold 7,000 books in two or three months.

During the severe drought of 1888, when the farmers had little money, canvassers suffered severely. Hardships notwithstanding, some 60,000 families were visited during that year.

Subsequent History. Statistics in 1902 showed 2,559 members, 100 churches, and 11 schools, with a total enrollment of 242. By the end of 1909 Kansas had 87 churches. Tithes in 1909 amounted to nearly $40,000, with offerings of about $18,000. Book sales during 1908 totaled $12,304.27.

In 1902 treatment rooms were opened at Wichita, which later became known as the Kansas Sanitarium. The sanitarium prospered for a time but by 1928 had accumulated a debt of more than $100,000 and was closed that year. In 1907 and 1908 Kansas had 20 church schools, but had no provision for education beyond the eighth grade. Because graduates could not all be accommodated at Union College, it seemed imperative to open a conference school. In 1908 an intermediate school at Oswego was made an academy (later, 1919, moved and renamed Enterprise Academy).

Another intermediate school opened between Downs and Portis in western Kansas on Nov. 15, 1910. It was named Hill Agricultural Academy. Z. M. Hill and his wife donated the

40-acre (15-hectare) site.

East and West Kansas Conferences. In 1910 Kansas was divided into two conferences, with L. W. Terry as president of the East Kansas Conference and N. T. Sutton as president of the West Kansas Conference. The two were reunited in 1914 as the Kansas Conference, and headquarters were established at Wichita.

Later Developments. The conference membership decreased from 2,863 in 1902 to 2,205 members 20 years later, with 67 churches, nine ordained ministers, and 18 church schools. After a fluctuating upward trend during the twenties and early thirties, the membership by 1935 had reached 3,012 (64 churches, 10 ordained ministers, and 12 church schools). For 15 years the figures remained almost constant. The 1951 statistical report showed 3,507 members (with 62 churches, 18 ordained ministers, and 10 church schools) and a peak of 3,720 in 1955 (with 15 ordained ministers and 11 elementary schools, though fewer churches).

Disaster struck twice during the fifties. In 1951 five churches were damaged by high water, and in 1956 (and again in 1961) the boys' dormitory at Enterprise Academy was extensively damaged by fire. By the early sixties the school had a new plant.

On Jan. 1, 1981, the Kansas Conference merged with the Nebraska Conference to become the Kansas-Nebraska Conference.

Conference Presidents—Missouri-Kansas Conference: R. J. Lawrence, 1870-1873; J. H. Rogers, 1873-1875; *Kansas Conference:* J. N. Ayers, 1875-1879; Smith Sharp, 1879-1882; J. H. Cook, 1882-1887; A. G. Miller, 1887-1888; C. Hall, 1888-1893; C. McReynolds, 1893-1896; W. S. Hyatt, 1896-1897; J. W. Westphal, 1897-1901; E. T. Russell, 1901-1902; C. McReynolds, 1902-1905; I. Crane, 1906; R. C. Porter, 1906-1907; Charles Thompson, 1907-1909; W. Thurston, 1909-1910; *East Kansas:* L. W. Terry, 1910-1911; W. F. Kennedy, 1911-1913; W. H. Clark, 1913-1914; *West Kansas:* N. T. Sutton, 1910-1914; *Kansas:* W. D. MacLay, 1914-1917; W. H. Clark (acting), 1917; Morris Lukens, 1917-1918; F. W. Stray, 1918-1920; B. G. Wilkinson, 1920-1922; C. G. Bellah, 1922-1924; M. A. Hollister, 1924-1926; C. S. Wiest, 1926-1933; A. H. Rulkoetter, 1933-1935; O. T. Garner, 1935-1937; T. B. Westbrook, 1937-1938; J. H. Roth, 1938-1948; D. R. Rees, 1948-1954; F. O. Sanders, 1954-1962; H. C. Klement, 1962-1966; S. S. Will, 1966-1977; A. C. McClure, 1977-1978; J. O. Tompkins, 1978-1980.

KANSAS SANITARIUM. A former medical institution opened at Wichita, Kansas, in 1902, when the Nebraska Sanitarium, at Lincoln, sent two nurses, L. C. Christofferson and his wife, to open treatment rooms in Wichita. The Kansas Conference adopted the project, and in 1903 Dr. G. A. Droll joined the undertaking. A nurse's training class was opened in 1905. Later a 20-acre (eight-hectare) plot two miles (three kilometers) west of the heart of the city was purchased, and a four-story brick-veneer structure with a capacity of 30 patients was constructed. Toward this the citizens of Wichita raised $10,000 to match a similar amount from the conference, and on June 14, 1905, the new institution was opened. A 1909 report states that the patronage was good, that the financial condition of the institution was in good order, and that 22 nurses were in training. In 1911 as many as 50 patients were crowded into the institution. In 1923 the name was changed to Kansas Sanitarium and Hospital, and four years later, in 1927, to Wichita Sanitarium.

After the peak year, 1917, when 1,000 patients were treated, the average ran about 700 a year, until in the middle twenties patronage began to decline. This was attributed to a constant changing of medical superintendents, together with the failure to change to modern hospital organization with an open staff. To save the institution when a debt of more than $100,000 had accumulated, the Central Union Conference took over in 1927; but it was too late. On Oct. 16, 1928, it was voted to close the institution. The plant was later sold to the county for $60,000.

KANSAS-NEBRASKA CONFERENCE. A unit of church organization comprising the states of Kansas and Nebraska. *(See also* Central States Conference.) Statistics (1992): churches, 104; members, 10,945; church schools, 18; ordained ministers, 53; licensed ministers, 6; teachers, 46. Youth Camps: Broken Arrow Ranch, Olsburg, Kansas; and Camp Arrowhead, Lexington, Nebraska. The conference forms a part of the Mid-America Union Conference.

Institutions. College View Academy, Enterprise Academy, Platte Valley Academy, Shawnee Mission Medical Center, Union College.

Local churches—*Kansas:* Abilene, Arkansas City, Atchison, Bazine, Belleville, Chanute, Coffeyville, Dodge City, Downs, El Dorado, Emporia, Enterprise, Eureka, Fort Scott, Fredonia, Galena, Garden City, Goodland, Great Bend, Harper, Hepler, Hutchinson, Independence (Independence, South 18th), Iola, Junction City, Kansas City (Chapel Oaks, Maranatha), Kingman, LaCrosse, Larned, Lawrence, Leavenworth (Shiloh, Zion), Liberal, McPherson, Manhattan, Marysville, Newton, Norton, Oberlin, Olathe, Oswego, Otis, Ottawa, Overland Park, Paola, Parsons, Pittsburg, Pleasanton, Pratt, Salina, Sedan, Shawnee Mission, Thayer, Topeka, Troy, Wellington, Wichita (South, Spanish, Three Angels). *Nebraska:* Albion, Alliance, Aurora, Beatrice, Beaver City, Benkelman, Bridgeport, Broken Bow, Chadron, Columbus, Crawford, Curtis, Elm Creek, Fairbury, Falls City, Fremont, Gordon, Gothenburg, Grand Island, Hastings, Hay Springs, Heartwell, Hemingford, Holdrege, Holland, Hyannis, Kearney, Lexington, Lincoln (Capital View, College View, Northside, Piedmont Park, Spanish), Lynch, McCook, Nebraska City, Neligh, Nelson, Norfork, North Platte, Ogallala, Omaha (Bethesda, Golden Hills, Omaha Memorial, Sharon), Oshkosh, Scottsbluff (English, Spanish), Seward, Shelton, Sidney, Springview, Tekamah, Valentine, York.

History. *See* Kansas Conference; also Nebraska Conference. In the fall of 1980 the Kansas Conference and the Nebraska Conference merged to become the Kansas-Nebraska Conference, effective Jan. 1, 1981. The combined membership was 10,736 with 113 churches. There were 47 ordained ministers, 17 licensed ministers, and 51 teachers.

Presidents: J. O. Tompkins, 1981-1983; L. S. Gifford, 1983-1986; Gordon Retzer, 1986-1989; Jim Hoehn, 1989- .

KANYE HOSPITAL. A 167-bed medical institution situated in Kanye, Botswana. It is operated by the Zambesi Union, with financial aid from the Botswana government.

Kanye was the first Seventh-day Adventist hospital started for Africans and the first mission hospital to be established in Botswana. It is one of the oldest Seventh-day Adventist institutions in this part of Africa. It was opened in 1921 by Dr. A. H. Kretchmar, who received permission to do medical work at Kanye on condition that no preaching be done. Through the popularity, tact, and influence of Dr. Kretchmar, permission was obtained to hold religious meetings, which opened the way for evangelistic work among the Botswanas, near the area where Livingstone started his first mission station, Kolobeng (about 25 miles [40 kilometers] from Kanye). W. H. Anderson was the first missionary-evangelist to be stationed at Kanye, and he helped to establish the mission program.

In 1947 a nurses' training school was opened. Throughout the years more than several hundred nurses have completed their training. These trainees are serving at Kanye Hospital and at other institutions in Botswana. Two courses of training—a two-year enrolled nurses' course, and a four-year state registered nurses' course—are offered, both recognized by the Botswana government and the Nursing Council of Botswana, Lesotho, and Swaziland.

The hospital is responsible for the greater part of the health-care delivery in the southern district of Botswana, and a large portion of the Kalahari district. Monthly air trips, lasting three to five days, are undertaken in the mission plane, the *Quiet Hour.* When airfields (mainly dry salt lakes) are waterlogged, trips at six-week intervals are undertaken by truck. These trips last six to eight days and 500 to 1,100 patients are seen in the desert. Roads are primitive, often consisting of only two deep ruts in the desert sand.

In 1963 a new two-story 100-bed wing was completed. The daily census, including newborns, ran just under 150 for the first eight months of 1974, compared with 15 in 1950 and about 100 in 1961.

During 1974 a new dispensary with 10 maternity beds was erected at Moshupa, a village 16 miles (25 kilometers) from Kanye. This facility was staffed by five national workers. Another dispensary at Tshane in the Kalahari Desert was staffed by two national workers.

Two permanent church buildings have been built and companies organized in the Kalahari Desert, at Lehututu and Hukuntsi, as a result of the medical work in this area.

Medical Directors: Arthur Kretchmar, 1921-1925; H. A. Erickson, 1928; A. Huse, 1930-1932; Archie Tonge, 1933; J. Janzen, 1934-1935; D. H. Abbott, 1936-1937; E. G. Marcus, 1938-1941; C. P. Bringle, 1943-1947; R. W. Royer, 1948-1949; J. A. Hay, 1950-1960; C. J. Birkenstock, 1961-1965; K. Seligmann, 1966-1968; F. J. Innocencio, 1969-1970; C. L. Wical, 1971-1973; K. Seligmann, 1973-1979; M. Westermeyer, 1979-1980; R. F. Snide, 1980-1982; Russell H. Hanson, 1982-1983; Anthony

A. Rockwell, 1984-1986; Francis D. Solivio, 1986-1988; Antonio do Couto, 1988-1989; D. A. Brueske, 1989-1992; A. Lasta, 1992- .

KARACHI ADVENTIST HOSPITAL. A modern general hospital in Karachi, Pakistan, with a capacity of 158 beds controlled and operated by the Pakistan Union as part of the Trans-European Division. The hospital operates a dental clinic, a School of Nursing, a School of Midwifery, as needed a School of Medical Technology, a School of Physiotherapy, and a School of X-ray Technology. It has a Community Outreach Department affiliated with ADRA, currently running an ADRA-Rural Health and Education project and a portable water project.

Forerunner of the hospital was a clinic opened in 1949 by Dr. Genevieve Joy Ubbink and her husband, Richard Ubbink, who later served as the business manager of the hospital.

The clinic had two doctors' offices, a laboratory, a pharmacy, a surgery unit, and a small maternity ward. R. H. Dunn, M.D., took charge of the clinic in October 1950. Later, Beverly Bunnell came as the nursing superintendent. Other members of the early staff were G. Branganza and Miss Maher, nurses; Lal Baz, pharmacist; and Cecil Stout, laboratory technologist.

The great need for medical service in Pakistan influenced the mission to establish a fully equipped hospital. The main building was erected in 1951, and the hospital, with an 80-bed capacity, was officially opened in October of that year (four years after construction had begun), with George A. Nelson as the first medical director. A new wing added in 1961 increased the hospital capacity to 120 beds. Partial remodeling in 1989 increased the bed capacity to 138.

The hospital in 1993, 42 years after its establishment, had 30 private/semiprivate rooms, 14 general wards, three labor rooms, an ICU, major and minor operating rooms, a delivery room, and support services, including laboratory, X-ray, physiotherapy, and respiratory therapy.

In 1992 an average of 173 outpatients visited the hospital, and there were 102 inpatients. Overseas staff included one medical doctor, one dentist, and eight support staff. National workers included 40 full- and part-time physicians, 68 staff nurses, midwives, and 286 support staff. Approximately 23 percent of outpatients and 35 percent of admissions were given charity.

Karachi Seventh-day Adventist Hospital had the distinction in 1963 of having the first heart surgeries performed when a team from Loma Linda, having been invited by the government of Pakistan and supported by USAID, spent five weeks doing 41 heart surgeries.

The School of Nursing opened in 1956 and held its first graduation in 1961. Since its inception 555 students have been enrolled. A School of Midwifery was established in 1962 with a total of 195 students to date having been enrolled. Giebal Hall, a four-story Nursing School and dormitory for 90 residents, was completed in 1977. A modern dental clinic staffed by the expatriate dentist is part of the hospital complex.

The overall plan calls for replacing the existing 42-year-old structure in four phases with a new modern facility as funds are available.

Medical Directors: Robert H. Dunn, 1950-1951; G. A. Nelson, 1951-1955; J. C. Johannes, 1955-1956; S. L. Wilkinson, 1956-1959; K. W. Saunders, 1959-1960; R. I. McFadden, 1960-1966; Heath Rowsell, 1966-1967; W. R. Chapman, 1967-1970; Harald G. Giebel, 1970-1980; Peter Tung, 1980-1988; Robert H. Dunn, 1989-1990; Walter Ordelheide, 1991-1992; Edgar Archbold, 1993- .

Administrators: Clarence H. Hamel (associate), 1977-1980; Eric J. Johanson, 1980-1983; Les K. Bone, 1983-1986; Allen Fowler, 1986-1990; Helge A. Andvik, 1990-1994; Edgar Archbold, 1994- .

KAREN SCHOOL. *See* Myanmar.

KARLMAN, ALF MARCUS (1903-1965). Treasurer of various fields. He was a native of Sweden and accepted the Seventh-day Adventist message when he was 21. He immediately enrolled in the Nyhytten School, which in those days was the training center for Swedish workers. Upon completion of his course in 1927 he entered the organized work as treasurer of the publishing house in Stockholm. He remained there until 1937, when he was appointed treasurer of what was then the East Nordic Union Conference, where he served until 1947. At this time he was appointed treasurer of the provisionally reorganized Northern European Division, with headquarters in Stockholm, Sweden. In a further reorganization in 1951 he became assistant treasurer of the division, which position he held until 1958, when he became treasurer. He was ordained in late 1963 and the following year requested release from his work because of failing health.

KARMATAR MIDDLE ENGLISH SCHOOL. *See* Raymond Memorial High School.

KARMATAR MISSION PRESS. *See* Oriental Watchman Publishing House.

KARNATAKA SECTION. *See* India; Southern Asia Division.

KASAI TRAINING SCHOOL. *See* Institute Adventiste de Songa.

KASTIORITA HOSPITAL. A 12-bed medical institution operated at Inus, Bougainville, Papua New Guinea. It was established in 1966. In the early 1970s the director was R. D. Donaldson; later A. R. Craig became director, with one nurse, Pepi Jonah, assisting. At this time it operated only as a small clinic and was subsequently funded by the government, thereby ceasing operations as an institution of the church in 1978.

KATA RANGOSO. *See* Rangoso, Kata.

KATANGA TRAINING SCHOOL. *See* Gitwe Adventist Secondary School.

KAUBLE, NELSON WALKER (1857-1927). Educator, editor, administrator. He began to teach school at the age of 19, and while teaching studied to prepare himself for ministry in the United Brethren Church. His studies led him to the conviction that the seventh day of the week was the true Sabbath. Joining the Seventh-day Adventist Church, he began preaching in Indiana in 1885. About 1890 he went to South Dakota in ministerial and religious liberty work. Afterward he was president of the Colorado Conference (1894-1896), of Union College (1897-1898), and of the Illinois Conference (1899-1901); helped to found Fox River Academy and for a while served as principal of it (1901-1904); was president of Emmanuel Missionary College (1904-1908); edited the *Advocate of Christian Education* (1904-1905); and was principal of Strode Industrial Academy (1908-1911). In 1912 he became head of the Bible Department at Lodi Academy. Later he served the Northern California Conference as a minister and as religious liberty secretary until his death.

KAUMA ADVENTIST HIGH SCHOOL. A 7- to 11-grade coeducational boarding and day school, situated on the Kauma estate, a tract of some 35 acres (14 hectares) on the northern strip of Abemama Island in the island nation of Kiribati. This school has a staff of 13 teachers and an enrollment of 207 students. Although difficult to operate because of the problem of growing food and the lack of opportunity for earning income, the school has nevertheless been worthwhile as an evangelizing agency.

The school, consisting originally of primer classes, was established in 1949 on the site of the original mission headquarters. It was opened by Mrs. J. T. Howse and her daughter, Joan, assisted by Samuel, a native of the Ellice group, who had been educated in the training school in Samoa. It grew steadily, with the addition of further classes, until in 1952 the school was relocated on its present site, on which buildings of native materials were erected. During 1953 and 1954 Forms I and II were added and a boarding department was operated.

Form III was added to the secondary section in 1970. This allowed for further preparation before the students attend Fulton College.

W. M. Dawson, who became principal in 1955, was successful in having the school registered with the government. In 1957 the boarding department was enlarged; in 1959 a concrete and brick classroom and office block was erected, and a permanent boys' dormitory in 1960. The development of the estate was continued by further planting of coconuts and such other food crops as can survive in the poor atoll soil and the droughts, which are frequent.

Valuable service has been rendered to the school by national headmasters from various Pacific territories, namely Tavita Niu from Samoa, Henry Moala from Tonga, and Marika Tuivawa from Fiji, as well as by a number of local assistant teachers.

From the school, numbers have gone on for further training to Fulton College in Fiji, while others have been baptized as a result of their school experience.

More permanent buildings were begun in 1974 with the construction of two new classrooms, a store, and a new home for the principal.

More recently new dormitories, a chapel, and a dining hall, all in concrete block, have been added, as well as permanent staff homes.

Principals: Mrs. J. T. Howse, 1949-1952; F. W. Gifford, 1953-1954; W. M. Dawson, 1955-1956; A. J. Sonter, 1957-1961; R. N. Sutcliffe, 1962-1968; A. W. Clover, 1969-1971;

R. L. Cole, 1972-1974; W. Lawson, 1975-1980; D. Potter, 1981-1983; T. Ribabaiti, 1984-1985; C. Viva, 1986-1988; T. Ribabaiti, 1989- .

KAZAKHSTAN. An Asian country bordered by Russia, China, Uzbekistan, Kyrgyzstan, Turkmenistan, and the Caspian Sea. It occupies an area of 1,049,200 square miles (2,700,000 square kilometers) and has a population (1994) of 17.3 million.

The region came under the Mongols in the thirteenth century and gradually came under Russian rule during the years 1730-1853. It was admitted to the USSR as a constituent republic in 1936. Kazakhstan declared independence on Dec. 16, 1991, and became an independent state when the Soviet Union dissolved on Dec. 26, 1991.

Seventh-day Adventist Statistics. The territory of Kazakhstan comprises the Kazakhstan Conference and part of the Southern Conference, which are part of the Southern Union conference of the Euro-Asia Division. In 1992 there were 36 local churches and 142 companies in *Kazakhstan,* where the membership is 2,096. Many church buildings were constructed during the 1980s, but many members migrated to Germany, which hampered the progress of the work.

Seventh-day Adventist Work. Andrei Lubchenko, a participant in World War I, was the first to spread the Seventh-day Adventist message in northern Kazakhstan after his return from the war. Soon his fellow villager, N. I. Krikun, from the village of Chernigovka (Kustanai region), accepted the message. After the revolution some Kustanai ministers visited them and conducted several home church services. These visits resulted in the conversion of the Bedenko, Velgosha, and two Pavelko families. A Bible worker, Fjodor Cherkassky, was appointed minister of the local church. This church took as their example the first apostolic church and united into one agricultural cooperation, but because of crop failure in 1921 it was disbanded.

In 1922 Adolf Rebein moved to Kustanai but was murdered the same year while visiting the remote villages. I. I. Stieben and A. Paal worked in this field after him. In 1924 at the Seventh-day Adventist Congress in the village of Annovka, Elders Kurilko and A. D. Kalashnikow were elected ministers.

Samson Ratnikov worked as a pastor in Kustanai in 1928. Under his leadership, the local church grew and a choir was organized. But a lot of people left the place when the repression started. Ratnikov moved to Altai, where he was repressed in 1937-1939 and died in prison, as did many other brethren. Many widows and children were left. Holding worship services was prohibited, and if two families gathered together they were severely punished.

Some revival of the preaching activity started in the 1950s. The first was in the Kushmurun station under the leadership of I. I. Koner, who was later ordained.

Michael Kulakov, at the age of 26 years, was discharged from prison and exiled to Kazakhstan. He gave great support to the restoration and development of the SDA message in the country. After Stalin's death he was freed from exile, and in 1955 he moved to Alma-Ata. He managed to reorganize the church there in a very short time. Kulakov gathered together the members of the formerly repressed and separated SDA families (Pronevich, Chizhov, Pavelko, Frolov, Lebsok, Rybalko, Butenko, etc.) and some Povolzhsky (down the Volga River) Germans and others who had accepted Jesus Christ. Kulakov worked under the leadership of an experienced minister, Kzimir A. Korolenko, who was responsible for the work in Central Asia and Kazakhstan.

At the time of Khrushchev's repressions local churches were dispersed, so the members met in small groups. Korolenko was arrested and taken to prison. Kulakov moved to Uzbekistan and lived in the city of Kokand, where there were no SDAs.

During the mid-1960s the repression was stopped, and Seventh-day Adventist missionary work was immediately activated. People started to build and purchase church buildings, new congregations were established, and different contacts were developed. At the end of 1968 Alf Lohne, from the General Conference, visited this region. Later on, Kulakov had an invitation from his relatives to visit the United States, and while on this visit he established friendships with Robert Pierson and Alf Lohne. These men received an invitation to visit the USSR. Lohne visited Alma-Ata several times the same year.

The state has adopted the law of religious liberty by which any denomination has equal rights and the citizens may choose any religion or none at all.

KAZAKHSTAN CONFERENCE. *See* Euro-Asia Division; Kazakhstan.

KEEM LAW. *See* Law Keem.

KEENE INDUSTRIAL ACADEMY. *See* Southwestern Adventist College.

KEENE SANITARIUM. A small medical institution formerly operated by the Texas Conference at Keene, Texas, a Seventh-day Adventist community built around Keene Academy (now Southwestern Adventist College). The sanitarium began in 1901 under the supervision of D. Edson Garvin, M.D., but apparently was not fully operative until late in 1902, when Dr. Pliny F. Haskell and his wife took charge.

Other physicians connected with the institution in later years were D. C. Ross and Thomas J. Leach. The sanitarium ceased operations sometime in 1907 and its building was taken over by the school. For several years the sanitarium was known as the Lone Star Sanitarium.

KEH NGA PIT (fl. 1904-1928). First ordained Chinese Seventh-day Adventist minister. Member of a Chinese Christian family living in the vicinity of Amoy, Fukien, southern China, he was educated (reportedly on a collegiate level) in the English Presbyterian schools in that city and became principal of the Presbyterian Theological Seminary there. In 1904 he met Timothy Tay, a young Seventh-day Adventist worker, who had gone to Amoy to perfect his knowledge of the local dialect. Seeking to correct Tay, he studied the Bible with him and as a result became an SDA. In the spring of 1906 he was ordained to the ministry by J. N. Anderson *(Review and Herald* 83:16, Aug. 23, 1906). He wrote several pamphlets and expositions of prophecies in Chinese and devoted much of his time to propagating the gospel among his own people and among the different ethnic groups in the Fukien province. In the *SDA Yearbook* his name appears for the last time in 1928.

KELLER, FLORENCE ARMSTRONG (1875-1974). Physician and missionary. Keller was born in Missouri and as a young child lived with her family in Arkansas. When Keller was 10 the family moved by covered wagon to the state of Washington, where she grew up among the Indian children.

Later they moved to Walla Walla, where Keller was a member of the first class to matriculate there at the new college. From Walla Walla she went to Battle Creek to study nursing. She worked for Dr. J. H. Kellogg, who encouraged her to study medicine.

Keller graduated from the American Medical Missionary College, precursor of the College of Medical Evangelists. She had the distinction of being the first woman physician to be sent overseas by the church. In Australia she was married to her college sweetheart, Dr. Peter Martin Keller. Shortly after marriage they went to New Zealand, where they served for 19 years. During this time Dr. Keller was physician to the Maori royal family and became the first woman and first physician to be elected to the board of management of all hospitals in Auckland, although she was not a citizen of the country.

Upon returning to her homeland, Dr. Keller joined the faculty of the new College of Medical Evangelists. She spearheaded a campaign to raise funds to build the White Memorial Medical Center, which was officially opened in 1918. Many honors came to her during her 67 years as a physician and surgeon. At the age of 92, she was still doing surgery and seeing patients six days a week. She retired from active practice in 1967.

KELLOGG, JOHN HARVEY (1852-1943). Surgeon, inventor of surgical instruments, pioneer in physiotherapy and nutrition. He was born on a farm in Tyrone township in Livingston County, Michigan, one of 16 children. When he was young the family moved to Jackson, Michigan, and two years later to Battle Creek, Michigan, where the father established a broom factory. At 10 John worked in the broom factory, and at 12 he learned the printing business; at 14 he was proofreader, and at 16 a public school teacher. When he was 17 he attended high school one year and graduated. Early in life he exhibited boundless energy for work and for obtaining knowledge. From his boyhood he burned midnight oil. In 1873, encouraged by James and Ellen White to take a medical course, he enrolled as a student in Bellevue Hospital Medical College in New York. In his determination to acquire all the knowledge possible, he arranged with leading professors to give him private lessons in subjects not covered in the regular courses. It is said he spent more money for tutors than for tuition. In addition to his overcharged study program, he served as editor of the *Health Reformer* (later *Good Health),* a position he held throughout his life.

In 1876, shortly after having finished his

two-year medical course, he was appointed superintendent of the Western Health Reform Institute in Battle Creek. This institution had been opened 10 years before in answer to a call from Ellen White that Seventh-day Adventists should provide "a home for the sick, where they could be treated for their diseases, and also learn how to take care of themselves so as to prevent sickness."

The institution, although small at first, had already attracted considerable attention. Under the skillful management and the abounding enthusiasm of a young doctor it entered upon a new era of prosperity and expansion. In order to accommodate the rapidly growing list of patients, it soon became necessary to erect a large, modern well-equipped sanitarium and hospital building that sprouted wings and additional buildings as needed. When the institution burned to the ground in 1902, Kellogg immediately set about to erect a larger, more modern, and better-equipped sanitarium building. A School of Nursing was established and a large staff of qualified doctors was built up. Later he had a leading part in organizing the American Medical Missionary College, which began to function in 1895 and in which many SDA young people received their medical training. He himself made several trips to Europe to study surgery under the world's most famous surgeons in London, Paris, Berlin, and Vienna. It was not long before he became known in the United States and across the seas as one of the ablest surgeons of his time. Rich and poor, high and low, including royalty, came from far and near to be treated by him. However, it was not surgery alone that gave the Battle Creek Sanitarium its universal favorable reputation; it was also adherence to principles set forth by Ellen White for its operation—proper diet, natural remedies, and simple treatments, with faithful, loving care. Dr. Kellogg did much in the development of therapeutic principles and methods.

Dr. Kellogg was a confirmed vegetarian and an enthusiastic advocate of the principles of health and temperance. It was he who invented the cornflakes and other dry cereal breakfast foods now available the world over. He also invented Protose and other meat substitutes. Furthermore, he was the inventor of the electric cabinet, numerous other electric appliances, and machines for the treatment of various ailments. Many of these instruments are now in use in hospitals around the world. He was fully as interested in preventive medicine as in the healing art. In teaching healthful living, he freely paid tribute to the principles set forth in the writings of Ellen White, principles that were being confirmed by the findings of scientific research.

In addition to being an able physician and a famous surgeon, he was also a great writer. He wrote more than 50 books, most of them large scientific works, and numerous articles for medical journals, besides serving as editor of *Good Health*. He was also an interesting and instructive lecturer on health and temperance and a good preacher. He was always in demand at camp meetings and other large gatherings.

Shortly after the turn of the century Dr. Kellogg came into conflict with the leaders of the General Conference over his attempt to get control of all SDA medical institutions with which he had been associated. He finally did succeed in getting control of the Battle Creek Sanitarium, the Battle Creek Food Company, and the health institution in Mexico. He also began teaching strange doctrines. His book *The Living Temple* was permeated with the principles of pantheism.

Everything was done to help him see his error. Ellen White worked with him personally and sent him many messages, but in vain. In 1907 he lost his membership in the church. Only a few intimate friends followed him.

In 1927, some years after the break and against the instruction he had received, he and his associates built a mammoth addition to the Battle Creek Sanitarium and in so doing involved the institution in an indebtedness running into millions of dollars.

The depression that broke upon the United States in 1929 threw the institution into great financial perplexity, resulting ultimately in bankruptcy. When the United States became involved in World War II, an opportunity came in 1942 to the receivers to sell the institution to the government for an amount sufficient to meet all obligations and leave to the sanitarium corporation a surplus of funds.

The sanitarium business was moved across the street into smaller buildings that the corporation held. Conflicts soon arose over the true ownership of the surplus funds received from the sale of the large building. The conflict climaxed in a lawsuit, instigated by the doctor against the Seventh-day Adventist Church and its leaders, which was ultimately settled by a division of certain assets between the sanitarium corporation and the General Conference corporation. This resulted in about $650,000 being reverted to the church.

Dr. Kellogg took a great interest in the welfare of children and young people. He and his wife had no children of their own, but they provided the funds for the education of many young people, virtually rearing 40 boys and girls, and adopting many of them.

From his earliest connection with the organized work of the church, Dr. Kellogg manifested a deep interest in starting and developing new health institutions and treatment rooms in different parts of America and across the seas. On at least two occasions he was sent to Europe to help the leaders there establish medical institutions in their fields.

During his connection with the church Dr. Kellogg doubtless did as much as any man in the denomination, if not more, to bring the name and work of Seventh-day Adventists favorably before the world. Had he remained loyal, he could have continued as a mighty tower of strength. Many hoped and prayed that he would return. At times he seemed friendly. At his invitation the General Conference Executive Committee held its Autumn Councils in the Battle Creek Sanitarium in the years 1926, 1932, 1933, 1934, 1937, and 1941. He passed away in his Battle Creek home, Dec. 14, 1943, without having returned to the church.

KELLOGG, JOHN PRESTON (1807-1881). Cofounder of institutions. The father of Dr. Merritt Kellogg; Dr. John Harvey Kellogg; Will K. Kellogg, the cornflake king; and 13 other children. At the age of 29 he settled on a farm in a pioneer settlement in Tyrone township, Livingston County, Michigan. Being religiously inclined, he took the lead in arranging with his neighbors for calling a minister and establishing a place of meeting.

In 1852, while Kellogg was raking hay, a neighbor, M. E. Cornell, a young Adventist minister, who had just learned about the seventh-day Sabbath from Joseph Bates, leaped over the fence, and poured out the joyful news to him. Going to hear Bates, Kellogg became fully convinced and gladly accepted the Adventist message. From that moment he always manifested a deep interest in the progress of the Adventist movement. He became a strong pillar in the young movement and a liberal contributor to its many growing needs.

In 1855 Kellogg together with Henry Lyon, Dan Palmer, and Cyrenius Smith provided a fund of $1,200 for the purchase of ground and the erection of a building to house the Review and Herald publishing work, which they proposed should be moved from its rented quarters in Rochester, New York, to Battle Creek, Michigan. This proposal was gladly accepted by James White and his associates. It was the first step toward anchoring the headquarters of the denomination in the city of Battle Creek.

At a conference held in Battle Creek May 20, 1856, Kellogg was appointed a member of a committee of five, of which he was made treasurer, to manage the tent operations in the state of Michigan. At the same gathering he was made a member of a committee of three to manage the affairs of the newly established publishing house. In this capacity he served until May 1861, when he became one of the incorporators of the Seventh-day Adventist Publishing Association and served on the board of trustees till 1863.

In 1867 Kellogg joined nine others in signing articles of incorporation for the Health Reform Institute (later known as the Battle Creek Sanitarium), which had been opened in September 1866. He headed the list with the largest subscription—$500—to its capital stock. He was elected a member of the board of directors and served in that capacity until 1869.

Because of increasing infirmity, the later years of Kellogg's life were spent in comparative retirement. To the end, which came May 10, 1881, he maintained a sustaining trust in God and an abiding confidence in the faith he had espoused nearly 30 years before.

KELLOGG, MERRITT GARDNER (1832-1922). Physician, missionary. He was the oldest son of John P. Kellogg. Accepting the Adventist faith at the age of 20, he became active in the organization of the Battle Creek Sabbath school and was elected its first superintendent. In 1859 he moved to California, being probably the first Seventh-day Adventist in the state. In 1861 he gave a course of lectures in San Francisco and baptized 14 converts. In 1867 he returned to the East and took a short medical course at Troll's Hygieo-Therapeutic College in New Jersey. At the General Conference session in May 1868 he made a stirring appeal for workers to be sent to California. In response, J. N. Loughborough and D. T. Bourdeau were sent. The doctor joined these two men in their evangelistic campaigns, speaking especially on health subjects. It was with considerable satisfaction that he was able to report to the General Conference that the work in California was self-supporting.

In 1870, when he and Loughborough were conducting evangelistic meetings in Bloomfield, California, an epidemic of smallpox broke out. They immediately closed their meetings and went to work caring for the sick, using water treatments and diet. Kellogg lost only one patient, an infant, out of 11 cases, while another doctor using drugs lost four out of five. This experience gave the doctor and his drugless treatments a high standing in California. His work for the next six years was largely evangelistic. In 1877 and 1878 he helped to establish the Rural Health Retreat, later St. Helena Sanitarium, near St. Helena, California. As soon as doctors with more advanced training were available he withdrew in their favor.

In 1893 the General Conference sent Kellogg out to the South Sea Islands as a medical missionary. He sailed on the mission ship *Pitcairn* on her second trip and worked on several of the islands in the Tonga group. Later he was in Australia, where he designed and superintended the building of the Sydney Sanitarium.

Returning to America from Australia in 1903, he made his home in Healdsburg, California, and resided there the rest of his days. Because of failing sight and hearing, most of the last 19 years of his life were spent in retirement.

KELLOGG, WILL KEITH (1860-1951). Cornflakes manufacturer. He was born in Battle Creek, Michigan, the seventh son of John P. Kellogg, and brother of Drs. M. G. and J. H. Kellogg. From his boyhood he worked in his father's broom factory, and at 14 was traveling salesperson for the company. At 19 he was asked by James White to go to Texas to manage a broom factory that White and George King had set up in Dallas.

In 1879 Kellogg returned to Battle Creek. In 1880 he finished a business course in Kalamazoo, Michigan, married, and entered the employ of the Battle Creek Sanitarium, of which his brother, Dr. J. H. Kellogg, was the medical superintendent. For the next 25 years Will was connected with this institution, filling various positions from janitor to business manager. This was the time during which the doctor invented and developed numerous health foods, including cornflakes. The original idea came from the doctor, but it fell to the lot of Will Kellogg to carry on the research and the experiments required to perfect a food that would be palatable and wholesome. The production of these foods was carried on as a department of the sanitarium, and was primarily for the patients, with no thought of developing it into a commercial enterprise. But as former patients sent in orders for the health foods, the business grew to such proportions that the erection of a factory became a necessity. When the sanitarium board refused to launch out in the heavy expense involved, Dr. J. H. Kellogg decided to go into business for himself and established the Sanitas Food Company. The sanitarium continued to handle the old line of foods and retained the profits from them, while the doctor received the profits accruing from his new venture.

To the many duties already carried by Will Kellogg was now added the work of business manager of the Sanitas Food Company. In lieu of salary, he was granted 25 percent of the profits from the new enterprise. In 1899, when the Sanitas Food Company was incorporated, Will was given a written contract confirming the arrangement.

However, the two brothers began to differ radically regarding the operation of the food business. There were frequent serious misunderstandings, until at the age of 46 Will Kellogg decided to part company with his older brother. He bought from him the patent right to manufacture and sell cornflakes, and on Feb. 19, 1906, the Battle Creek Toasted Corn Flake Company was incorporated. Funds being scarce, the new enterprise started operation in a "shanty" on Bartlett Street. But with hard work, wise management, and liberal advertising the business grew rapidly into a large, prosperous affair. With two expanding businesses operating virtually side by side, the two brothers soon found themselves in conflict with each other. Each instituted court proceedings against the other. Legal battles dragged on for years, and the courts finally decided in favor of Will. On the proposal of John, Will agreed to waive all claims for damages, whereas the doctor paid all the legal expenses for both sides, which amounted to $225,000.

Under the driving energy and the wise management of Will Kellogg, his cornflake business grew to fabulous proportions. In addition to the enormous plant in Battle Creek and three other factories in the United States, the company established plants in Canada, Australia, England, South Africa, and Mexico, with branches in other lands. Will Kellogg became a multimillionaire.

Instead of leaving all his wealth to his

heirs, Will Kellogg in 1930 set up a foundation, the main purpose of which was "the promotion of the health, education, and welfare of mankind, but principally of children and youth." Commenting on this humanitarian act, *Time* magazine in its issue of Dec. 8, 1930, said: "Will Keith Kellogg . . . again belied the general impression that he is a dour moneymaker. He created the W K. Kellogg Foundation, gave it $1,000,000 for immediate use and promised for it a total of $50,000,000 if and when needed." In 1956 it was reported that this foundation had assisted more than 1,500 projects on three continents with a total expenditure of nearly $50 million. The annual grants at that time approximated $4 million.

In his youth Will Kellogg had become a member of the Seventh-day Adventist church in Battle Creek, but soon after his marriage he discontinued church attendance. When he finally was dropped from the membership list, he said the church could hardly do otherwise, seeing that he had not attended services in his own or any other church for 27 years. Although he did not frequent the church, he remained loyal to its principles of health and temperance. Although the food company, of which he was the principal stockholder, operated on the Sabbath, he claimed he personally kept the Sabbath. In his home the household servants were urged to have all preparations made before the setting of the sun Friday evening. He believed in God and had no sympathy with the atheists and pantheists of his time.

In his declining years, especially after he lost his sight in 1941, he spent much time on his expansive estate near Pomona, California, but the last few months of his long life were spent in his beloved hometown, Battle Creek, where his ashes were buried in Oak Hill Cemetery.

KELLOGG-MOOKERJEE MEMORIAL SEMINARY. A coeducational boarding school on the junior high school level, at Jalirpar, a village on the Lower Ganges in Bangladesh, operated by the South Bangladesh Mission. The school is situated on a 22.5-acre (nine-hectare) tract, much of which is used for agricultural purposes.

The school is named in honor of Grace Kellogg Mookerjee, an early American teacher at the school, and her husband, L G. Mookerjee, the pioneer worker in Bengal. The present enrollment of the Kellogg-Mookerjee Memorial Seminary is 475. The faculty consists of 22 members.

This school is a successor to the Gopalganj Boys' School opened in 1920 at Gopalganj, the first Seventh-day Adventist mission in Bangladesh, in a town situated on the Madhumati River in Faridpur District, East Bengal (Bangladesh), by Mookerjee, the superintendent of the field. In 1929 Dr. C. F. Schilling, who came to Gopalganj to open medical work, took charge of the school. Soon thereafter, when a Bengali girls' school was transferred from Hooghly, near Calcutta, to Gopalganj, the school became coeducational.

In 1931 the school was made a full high school under the direction of LeRoy Hunter. H. H. Mattison came in 1938, and the next year the school was transferred from Gopalganj to Jalirpar, 18 miles (30 kilometers) away on the Madaripur-Madhumati Canal, exchanging places with a hospital that had been established there in 1931 *(see* Gopalganj Hospital). The vacated Jalirpar Hospital building provided school and dormitory accommodation. On its new campus it was known first as Jalirpar Secondary Boarding School; then, since 1946, as the Kellogg-Mookerjee Memorial Seminary.

A building program begun in 1957 provided a boys' dormitory, a girls' dormitory, a chapel, kitchen, press building, industrial building, and four duplex homes for teachers. All the buildings are of brick construction.

In recent years capital developments have taken place. A new chapel building has been built, a three-story boys' dormitory was constructed, and a two-story orphanage center was built. It is presently accommodating 118 orphans.

A bakery has also been added along with a storage building and staff quarters. In addition, two shallow pumps were installed for school drinking water and for irrigation.

Principals: L. G. Mookerjee, 1920-1923; Mrs. L. G. Mookerjee, 1923-1926; C. A. Larsen, 1926-1927; Mrs. A. G. Youngberg, 1927-1928; Mrs. C. F. Schilling, 1929-1930; Mrs. L. G. Mookerjee, 1930-1931; LeRoy Hunter, 1931-1937; H. H. Mattison, 1937-1940; LeRoy Hunter, 1940-1942; P. C. Gayen, 1942-1944; S. K. Haldar, 1944-1945; P. C. Gayen, 1945-1947; N. G. Mookerjee, 1947-1948; R. N. Dass, 1948-1950; P. K. Gayen, 1950-1951; S. K. Haldar, 1951; P. C. Gayen, 1952; I. R. Thomas, 1953-1955; B. J. Jacques, 1955-1959; M. W. Shultz, 1959-1963; N. K. Baroi (acting), 1963; K. S. Brown, 1964; P. Durichek, 1965-1968; N. C. Dewri, 1969-1972; S. K. Bairagee, 1973-1974; Sukrit K.

Dass, 1975-1980; Byron B. Bol, 1981-1987; Swapon Halder, 1988-1992; Simson Biswas, 1993- .

KELOWNA INTERMEDIATE SCHOOL. *See* Okanagan Academy.

KENDU ADVENTIST HOSPITAL. A 164-bed general hospital situated three miles (five kilometers) from Kendu Bay on Lake Victoria, in Kenya. Owned and operated by the East African Union, it ministers to the medical needs of the Luo and Kisii peoples, who live principally in the thickly populated South Nyanza district of Kenya.

In 1974 the staff consisted of three doctors and five to seven European nurses, besides the following Africans: eight medical assistants, one laboratory technician, four midwives, one accountant, and one African business manager. Medical, surgical, and obstetrical services are provided, with X-ray, laboratory, and some physiotherapy facilities.

In 1993 the staff consisted of four doctors, 50 enrolled nurses, eight registered nurses, 23 medical assistants, two laboratory assistants, two technicians, two technician assistants, two accountants, one X-ray technician, and two physiotherapists.

The hospital provides general medical, surgical, pediatric, and obstetrical services. Outreach programs include maternal child care and immunization, family planning, and AIDS prevention education. Evangelistic activities are carried on through the chaplain's office.

In 1948 a medical assistants' course was started. This course has been changed to a nursing course. From 1984 the school has been training enrolled community nurses recognized by the Kenya's Nurses and Midwives Council. The present enrollment is about 16 students a year. In addition, the hospital has entered into affiliation with the University of Eastern Africa Baraton to provide a clinical facility for the B.S.N. of the University. It is hoped that this association will be expanded and upgraded.

Kendu Adventist Hospital School of Nursing graduates serve in many parts of the country and even in other countries of East and Central Africa. The hospital in the past has operated several dispensaries, but these are now managed under Seventh-day Adventist Rural Health Services.

Kendu Hospital was planned when G.A.S. Madgwick, of England, arrived at Gendia Station to pioneer the medical work in 1921. Pending the erection of suitable buildings at Gendia, he went to Kanyadoto Station for two years. By the time Dr. Madgwick returned from furlough in 1925, the builder, F. Solway, had made good progress and the hospital opened shortly as the Kenya Hospital. (The name was changed a few years later to Kendu Hospital.) The first nurses, Karen Nielsen and Carentze Olsen, both from Skodsborg Sanitarium in Denmark, arrived in December 1925. Both gave more than 25 years of service to Kendu Hospital and other medical centers in East Africa.

The most common medical problems at Kendu Hospital are malaria, bilharzia, gastroenteritis, and other parasitic infestations, as well as malnutrition. Tuberculosis, tetanus, and meningitis are still common, and measles is endemic. Because the old superstitions and African medicines have lost much of their grip on the people, modern medical care is generally accepted and appreciated. A small leprosarium was operated for a number of years but was closed for lack of space.

Most of the time there has been one doctor, but since 1966 there have been generally at least two doctors, and at times three, on the staff. With the arrival of a doctor couple in 1971, it has been possible to have three full-time doctors serving the hospital. Much credit must be given to the Africans who have served at the Kendu Hospital. An ordained African chaplain provides for the spiritual needs of the patients.

Kendu Adventist Hospital has added to its compound a hospital airstrip, a 30-bed maternity ward, female and private wards, administrative offices, a new laboratory, and a large warehouse or store for medicines and supplies. The old maternity ward was renovated into a new school and library. Many patients are served through the outpatient clinic, which operates every day except Sabbath. Prenatal, well-baby, and family planning clinics are held every week.

Medical Directors: G.A.S. Madgwick, 1925-1940; L. Ermshar, 1941-1942; L. P. Foster, 1943-1944; D. H. Abbott, 1944-1951; B. E. Ammundsen, 1950-1953; M. W. Fowler, 1953-1954; B. E. Ammundsen, 1954-1956; S. A. Kotz, 1956-1960; W. W. Oliphant, 1961-1962; E. A. Calkins, 1962-1963; A. W. Perepelitza, 1963-1966; K. H. Sturdevant, 1966-1969; R. M. Buckley, 1969-1970; D. W. Harrison (acting), 1970-1971; E. C. Kraft, 1971-1979; P. Llaguno, 1979-1980; A. Osorio, 1981-1983; E. C. Kraft, 1984-1986; A. Rocero, 1986-1989; E. C. Kraft, 1989-1990; E. Odira, 1990- .

KENNEBEC MANOR. A 70-bed nursing home operated in Canada by the Maritime Conference. The institution opened in May 1980. Ben Hort was the administrator in 1994.

KENTUCKY. *See* Kentucky-Tennessee Conference; South Central Conference.

KENTUCKY CONFERENCE. *See* Kentucky-Tennessee Conference.

KENTUCKY-TENNESSEE CONFERENCE. A unit of church organization comprising the state of Kentucky and approximately the western half of Tennessee, to the eastern boundaries of the counties of Cannon, Clay, Coffee, De Kalb, Franklin, Jackson, and Smith. (For the Black churches, *see* South Central Conference.) Statistics (1992): churches, 79; members, 10,681; church schools, 23; ordained ministers, 40; licensed ministers, 7; church school teachers, 53. Headquarters: 850 Conference Drive, Goodlettsville, Tennessee. The conference forms part of the Southern Union Conference.

Institutions. Highland Academy; Madison Academy; Memorial Hospital; Tennessee Christian Medical Center—Nashville (formerly Madison Hospital); Tennessee Christian Medical Center—Portland (formerly Highland Hospital).

Local churches—*Kentucky:* Ashland, Beaverdam (Ohio County), Belcher, Bowling Green, Bowling Green (Sand Hill), Columbia, Covington, Cynthiana, Drakesboro (Powderly), Elizabethtown, Franklin, Glasgow, Gratz, Harlan, Henderson, Hopkinsville, Jamestown, Kings Mountain (Grove), Lawrenceburg (Frankfort/Lawrenceburg), Leitchfield, Lexington, London, Louisville (First, South), Madisonville, Manchester, Mayfield, Middleton (St. Matthews), Morehead, Murray, Owensboro, Paducah, Pewee Valley, Prestonsburg, Richmond, Stearns, West Somerset (Somerset), Williamsburg, Winchester; *Tennessee:* Adamsville (Overbrook), Ashland City, Cedar Grove (Leach), Centerville, Clarksville, Columbia, Columbia (Covington), Cross Plains, Dechard, Dickson, Dyersburg, Franklin (Kingfield), Gallatin, Hendersonville, Jackson, Lawrenceburg, Lobelville, Madison (Boulevard, Campus), Memphis (First, Raleigh), Murfreesboro, Nashville (Bordeaux, First, Korean), Obion (Lane), Paris, Parsons, Portland (Portland, Highland), Pulaski, Ridgetop, Savannah, Smithville, Somerville, South Fulton, Tullahoma, White House, Woodbury.

Companies—*Kentucky:* Burkesville, Campton (Breathitt), Louisville (Korean), Middleboro, Shelbyville; *Tennessee:* Cave Springs, Chestnut Hill, Hohenwald, Madison (Spanish), Waynesboro.

History. *Beginnings of the Work in the Area.* Apparently the first Seventh-day Adventist minister to preach in what is now the Southern Union Conference was Elbert B. Lane, who was sent in March 1871 to Edgefield Junction, Tennessee, a few miles north of Nashville, to visit and baptize a small group of converts won through reading SDA publications. His reports in the *Review and Herald* (May 2, 1871, and later) tell how he held public meetings in the railroad station, the White listeners occupying one room and the Black another; as the crowd grew they used the freight room and the platform.

Before leaving the state in May, Lane had baptized five and had others interested. By autumn a letter from R. K. McCune describes the group as consisting of four White families and one Black preacher (a Baptist, convinced by reading after Lane's departure). Two years later Lane returned for a short time, baptized seven, and organized a church of 13 in May 1873. (It was at Edgefield Junction in the 1880s that the first Black Seventh-day Adventist church was organized. *See* South Central Conference.)

The earliest recorded evangelistic meetings in Kentucky began also in 1871, with the visit of Squier Osborn, who later became the first president of the Kentucky and Tennessee Conference. Osborn, a native Kentuckian living in Iowa, and not yet ordained, held meetings in his home county of Greenup, at Springville, Kentucky, across the river from Portsmouth, Ohio. About the beginning of 1872 he was joined for a month by J. Hare (both were commissioned by the Iowa Conference). Osborn left 11 converts by April 1. (The Springville, Kentucky, church was organized in 1874.) D. T. Bourdeau, sent by the General Conference at the same time, visited Hardin County, Kentucky, south of Louisville, where contacts had been made by J. B. Brown of California. Bourdeau's frequent reports from Nolin and Locust Grove tell of his 65 lectures in three places, from January through May 1872; of his visits in the homes; of his debate with an opposing preacher; and of the little Sabbath school begun at Locust Grove. A year later

Osborn held meetings at Locust Grove, baptized seven, and organized the first Seventh-day Adventist church in Kentucky (1873).

Kentucky and Tennessee Conference (1876-1879). The first conference organization, set up in 1876 with S. Osborn as president, was the Kentucky and Tennessee Conference, which lasted only three years.

Kentucky Conference and *Tennessee Conference* (1879-1889). The two-state combination was divided in 1879 into two conferences, with Osborn as president in Kentucky and G. K. Owen in Tennessee. However, Owen moved to Michigan soon after. Until his successor, Samuel Fulton, came in 1882, Osborn visited the Tennessee Conference occasionally and acted as president pro tem.

On one of these Tennessee trips, in 1881, Osborn reports visiting the Cross Plains, Edgefield Junction, Ridge, and Springville churches. This Springville, Tennessee, church, which had been organized as a result of Owen's evangelistic meetings in 1878 (and which was later moved to nearby Mount Vista, then to Parvo, and in 1935 to Paris), was soon to receive widespread attention in the press. Beginning in 1885, an intermittent series of prosecutions of SDAs, under the state Sunday law, during the eighties and nineties involved nearly every man in the Springville church. A number of these men were convicted and sentenced to fines or imprisonment, and in some instances to road labor on the chain gang. Several of these Springville cases, and notably that of R. M. King in another county, resulted in winning public sympathy for the accused. The obvious prejudice of the complainants, the character of the defendants, and the reputation of several of the attorneys who defended them combined to draw nationwide attention to the principles of religious liberty and church-state separation. From this Springville-Paris church came three foreign missionaries.

In 1882 Kentucky had two ordained ministers, two licensed ministers, and five churches, with 84 members; Tennessee had one ordained minister, three licensed ministers, and five churches, with 54 members.

In those days an evangelist sometimes faced not only legal but physical opposition. For example, when S. Fulton, president of the Tennessee Conference, held meetings in 1883 in the Leach community, a rural area 25 miles (40 kilometers) east of Jackson, Tennessee, opposers burned down his tent and threatened him with bodily harm. Undaunted, he continued preaching in the open air. Friends came with a volunteer guard of 12 armed men, gave offerings for a new tent, and built a log church. Two months later he held the Tennessee camp meeting there in the new tent, and organized a church. From this organization came one of the early conference presidents, W. R. Burrow.

In 1887 churches were organized in Bowling Green, Kentucky, and in Lane, Tennessee, where a church school was opened in 1891.

Tennessee River Conference and *Cumberland (Mission* and*) Conference* (1889-1908). The Tennessee River Conference, organized in 1889 with E. E. Marvin as its first president, included, roughly, the western half of both Kentucky and Tennessee. The eastern half of both states became the Cumberland Mission, administered by the Southern District of the General Conference. In 1891 the Tennessee River Conference had two ministers, seven scattered churches, and 172 members, while the Cumberland Mission had two ordained ministers, one licentiate, and two churches, with 37 members. In 1900 this mission became the Cumberland Conference, and in 1901 these two conferences became members of the new Southern Union Conference. In 1900 the Tennessee River Conference reported two ordained and four licensed ministers, 13 churches, and 400 members, while the Cumberland Conference reported a similar staff, with six churches and 400 members. The boundary between them was the western line of the Kentucky counties of Bullitt, Nelson, LaRue, Green, Metcalfe, and Monroe, and the Tennessee counties of Clay, Jackson, Putnam, White, Warren, Grundy, and Marion.

The Tennessee River Conference organized churches during this period at Trezevant (1889), Memphis (1895), Nashville (1895), Madison (1906), and Jackson (1906) in Tennessee, and at Sand Hill in Kentucky (1897). Between 1897 and 1908 churches were reported as being organized in Lexington (1901 or after), Louisville (1905); the Grove church was organized (1907), seven miles (11 kilometers) from Kings Mountain, Kentucky, in the Cumberland Conference.

Nashville, Tennessee, where there were Seventh-day Adventists as early as 1881, was destined to become an institutional center. About the turn of the century J. E. White made it the headquarters for his river steamer *Morning Star* and his Southern Missionary Society, through which he conducted work among Blacks, also for his Gospel Herald Publishing Company, which was soon to become part of the nucleus of the Southern Publishing Association. Near Nashville, under Ellen White's personal direction, E. A. Sutherland and P. T. Magan in 1906 founded the educational and medical institutions that became Madison Sanitarium and Madison College. Near Nashville also later was founded the Riverside Sanitarium and Hospital, an all-Black hospital.

Kentucky Conference and *Tennessee River Conference* (1908-1932). In 1908 another change in conferences took place. To form the Kentucky Conference, western Kentucky (except eight counties in the southwest) was taken from the Tennessee River Conference, and eastern Kentucky from the Cumberland Conference. (Then the Cumberland Conference, reduced to east Tennessee alone, became part of the Southeastern Union Conference, which was separated from the Southern Union from that year until 1932; *see* Georgia-Cumberland Conference.)

The Tennessee River Conference was left with 15 churches and 408 members. The new Kentucky Conference, organized in February 1908, with A. O. Burrill as president, had 14 churches and 263 members, with the conference office in Louisville. One small change came in 1909 when three Tennessee counties (De Kalb, Smith, and Macon) were transferred to the Cumberland Conference, thus leaving the eastern boundary of the Tennessee River Conference at the eastern line of Sumner, Trousdale, Wilson, Cannon, Coffee, and Franklin counties. Another change, in 1922, added six Kentucky counties (Trigg, Christian, Todd, Logan, Simpson, and Allen) to the Tennessee River Conference.

Churches organized in the Kentucky Conference during this period (1908-1932) included those of Sewellton (1915), which became in 1962 the Jamestown church; Belcher (1919); Covington (1919); Hill Top (about 1912), later disbanded and organized as the Stearns church (1922); Pewee Valley (1925), meeting in the Pewee Valley Sanitarium; and Ashland (1925). Churches organized in this period by the Tennessee River Conference included, in Kentucky: Paducah (1915); in Tennessee: Fountain Head (1907, now Highland, in connection with what are now Highland Hospital and Highland Academy); Lawrenceburg (1912); Bordeaux (1919); Murfreesboro (1923); and Dyersburg (1929).

Kentucky-Tennessee Conference. In 1932—the year in which the Southeastern and Southern Union conferences were reunited—the Kentucky Conference and the Tennessee River Conference were combined to form the Kentucky-Tennessee Conference, with headquarters at Nashville and C. L. Butterfield as the first president. This conference, including all of Kentucky and the western portion of Tennessee, began with 2,562 members, 43 churches, 10 ordained ministers, and four licensed ministers. In 10 years, by 1942, the membership grew to 4,326 (a yearly average increase of 168), with 54 churches (five composed of Black members, totaling 645) and 18 ordained ministers (four of whom served the Black Department). The tithe for 1932 was $41,262; the yearly tithe doubled in five years, and by 1943 was $196,064.

The conference lost about 600 members in 1946 in connection with the formation, in most of the union conferences of North America, of self-administered conferences composed of the Black congregations. The five Black churches in the Kentucky-Tennessee Conference joined the new South Central Conference, one of two such "regional" conferences covering the territory of the Southern Union.

This left the Kentucky-Tennessee Conference with 46 churches, 3,808 members, and 18 ordained ministers at the close of 1946. Ten years later it had 71 churches, 34 ordained ministers, 15 licensed ministers, 46 church school teachers, 21 colporteurs, and a membership of 5,338. The tithe for 1956 was $547,470. The year 1962 closed with these statistics: tithe, $738,851; 77 churches; 6,333 members; 32 ordained ministers; seven licensed ministers; 38 teachers; and 16 full-time colporteurs. At the end of 1992 these statistics were reported: tithe, $6,867,484.93; 79 churches; 10,681 members; 40 ordained ministers; seven licensed ministers; 53 teachers; and 10 full-time literature evangelists.

Later Developments. In 1945 the conference office in Nashville was moved from the corner of 24th Avenue, North, and Seifried Street to 3208 West End Avenue, and in 1959 to three and a half miles north of Madison, Tennessee.

Also in 1959 the conference bought 34.5 acres (14 hectares) for a youth camp on Center Hill Lake, about six miles (10 kilometers) northwest of Smithville, Tennessee, in De Kalb County (which, with several other border counties, was transferred to the Kentucky-Tennessee Conference territory; *see* beginning paragraph of this article for the boundaries). Four permanent camp buildings were finished by 1963. During the following 10 years 24 permanent buildings were added, which include a chapel, gymnasium, and a home for the camp ranger.

In 1967 the Adventist Book Center erected a new building on the campus near Madison Academy and Madison Hospital.

In 1979 the conference office moved from Gallatin Road in Madison to its present location in Goodlettsville, Tennessee. Twenty-nine new church buildings have been built since 1974, and the youth camp has been provided with a home for the camp director, with guest rooms on the lower level, a cafeteria with additional guest rooms, laundry, and staff lounge, and a swimming pool.

The Adventist Book Center moved its location next door to the conference office.

Presidents—Kentucky and Tennessee Conference: S. Osborn, 1876-1879; *Kentucky Conference:* S. Osborn, 1879-1884; G. G. Rupert, 1884-1886; J. H. Cook, 1886-1888; *Tennessee Conference:* G. K. Owen, 1879-1881; S. Fulton, 1882-1886; J. M. Rees, 1886-1888; William Covert, 1888-1889; *Tennessee River Conference:* E. E. Marvin, 1889-1890; C. L. Boyd, 1891-1896; F. D. Starr, 1896-1898; C. P. Bollman, 1898-1899; W. J. Stone, 1899-1903; N. W. Allee, 1903-1906; W. R. Burrow, 1906-1911; C. P. Bollman, 1911-1912; E. L. Maxwell, 1912-1913; J. W. Norwood, 1913-1914; W. R. Elliott, 1914-1919; I. M. Martin, 1919-1920; M. A. Hollister, 1920-1925; H. E. Lysinger, 1925-1932; *Cumberland Conference:* Smith Sharp, 1900-1903; O. C. Godsmark, 1903-1905; W. W. Williams, 1905-1907; J. F. Pogue, 1907-1908 *(see* Georgia-Cumberland Conference); *Kentucky Conference:* A. O. Burrill, 1908-1911; B. W. Brown, 1911-1916; R. I. Keate, 1916-1921; C. W. Curtis, 1921-1926; F. G. Ashbaugh, 1926-1930; J. A. Leland, 1930-1932; *Kentucky-Tennessee Conference:* C. L. Butterfield, 1932-1934; V. G. Anderson, 1934-1937; C. V. Anderson, 1937-1943; T. L. Oswald, 1943-1946; W. E. Strickland, 1946-1954; R. H. Pierson, 1954-1956; E. L. Marley, 1956-1969; K. D. Johnson, 1969-1977; E. S. Reile, 1978; A. C. McClure, 1978-1980; C. R. Farwell, 1980-1984; C. L. Shankel, 1985-1992; R. R. Hallock, 1992- .

KENYA. An East African republic, formerly a British protectorate and colony but independent since December 1963. The country is bounded on the north by Ethiopia and Sudan, on the east by Somalia and the Indian Ocean, on the south by Tanzania, and on the west by Uganda. The equator crosses it, yet the 17,000-foot (5,180-meter) Mount Kenya, lying a few miles south of the equator, is covered with perpetual ice and snow. It has an area of 224,960 square miles (582,650 square kilometers), and a population (1994) of 28.2 million, the majority of whom are Christians.

Agriculture is the principal occupation of Kenya's people, the principal domestic crops being maize and beans. Large quantities of tea, coffee, sisal, pyrethrum, and cashew nuts are exported annually.

Seventh-day Adventist Statistics. The territory of Kenya constitutes part of the East African Union, which in turn forms a part of the territory of the Eastern Africa Division. Statistics (1993) for *Kenya:* churches, 1,344; members, 314,739; ordained ministers, 161; licensed ministers, 183; teachers, 49. Headquarters: Milimani Road, Nairobi, Kenya, East Africa. For the territories of the unions and fields, *see* Eastern Africa Division.

Statistics (1992) for the fields—*Central Kenya Conference:* churches, 203; members, 27,308. Headquarters: Nairobi. *Kenya Coast Field:* churches, 42; members, 4,117. Headquarters: Mombasa. *Kenya Lake Field:* churches, 215; members, 60,201. Headquarters: Kendu Bay. *North Nyanza Field:* churches, 86; members, 17,588. Headquarters: Kisumu. *Ranen Field:* churches, 223; members, 61,210. Headquarters: Ranen. *South Kenya Conference:* churches, 384; members, 106,791. Headquarters: Kisii. *Western Kenya Field:* churches, 173; members, 29,005. Headquarters: Eldoret.

Institutions. Africa Herald Publishing House; Kamagambo High School and Teachers' College; Kendu Adventist Hospital; Maxwell Adventist Academy; Seventh-day Adventist Health Services; University of Eastern Africa Baraton.

Development of Seventh-day Adventist Work. The first Seventh-day Adventist missionary to Kenya was Canadian-born A. A. Carscallen, who arrived from Britain in 1906. With the assistance of E. C. Enns, a German missionary from Pare in Tanzania, he chose as the site for the first mission station a five-acre (two-hectare) plot at Gendia Hill, about two miles (three kilometers) inland from Kendu Bay of Lake Victoria. This site was among the Luo people in what is now South Nyanza.

Working with Carscallen was Peter

Nyambo, a Seventh-day Adventist worker originally from Malawi who had come with him from England. Within 14 months Carscallen reported that he had erected the basic mission buildings and had learned the Luo language, which had never before been reduced to writing. Later, he made a Luo translation of the Gospel of Matthew, which was accepted for publication in 1913 by the British and Foreign Bible Society of London.

In 1907 Carscallen was joined by J. D. Baker and his wife, who in 1909 opened a new station about 15 miles (25 kilometers) from Gendia. On May 21, 1911, the first 10 Luo believers were baptized. In 1912 four new stations were opened. At Nyanchwa Mission I. R. Evanson began work among the Kisii people. Records indicate that the work was difficult and no real impact had been made by the time World War I closed the station. After the war L.E.A. Lane, assisted by a Luo worker, Yakobo Olwa, reopened the station and built a school. Not until 1922 were the first two Kisii baptized. Later, the work in Kisii expanded rapidly. Paulo Nyamweya, one of the early converts, became the first African worker in Kenya to become a mission station director.

The Karungu Mission Station was opened by E. B. Phillips of England at a former government administrative post on Lake Victoria. Because the climate of the region was unhealthful and the population was decreasing, the station was soon closed, the buildings dismantled, and the materials used to build the Kanyadoto Mission, from which the work in the Karungu area was then cared for.

Work began at Kanyadoto in 1912 when a layman, J. H. Sparks, camped and preached under a large fig tree until land could be secured and temporary buildings erected. Mariko Otieno, a Luo worker, assisted in the early years at Kanyadoto, and in 1914 A. A. Matter and his wife, and Swiss workers, came to take charge. A. Watson opened work on the island of Rusinga in Lake Victoria. In 1913 Carscallen moved some 40 miles (65 kilometers) inland, southeast of Gendia, and opened the Kamagambo Station and was assisted for a short time by D. E. Delhove.

When the Germans invaded South Nyanza during World War I, the missionaries were evacuated to a camp near the Kaimosi Station of the Society of Friends, not far from Kisumu. None of the missionaries except Matter and Carscallen got back to their stations before 1916. When they did, they found the stations had been thoroughly looted and the buildings badly damaged. The large house at Gendia had caught fire while occupied by the military. The missionaries, many with furloughs long overdue, set about the uphill task of rebuilding and of recovering their scattered flocks.

Chaotic conditions following the end of the war prevented sending out replacements before 1920. In that year a large group of fresh recruits were sent from Britain to relieve the tired veterans. There were 10 in the first group, led by W. T. Bartlett. Of them Bartlett and W. H. Matthews stayed at Gendia, which served as headquarters; E. A. Beavon went to Nyanchwa Mission; W. W. Armstrong to Kanyadoto; S. G. Maxwell to Kamagambo; and T. G. Belton to Wire Hill Station. All were faced with an urgent rebuilding program. Before leaving Kenya, Carscallen handed over to Bartlett detailed maps showing the location of the various missions in Kenya and Western Tanzania.

Another group of new missionaries arrived in 1921, among them Dr. G.A.S. Madgwick, who in 1925 opened the Kendu Hospital about two miles (three kilometers) from Gendia Mission. E. R. Warland went first to Kanyadoto, later to Kamagambo. Also in this second group were Mrs. Bartlett and her daughter, Margery, who taught at Gendia, and Grace Clarke, who went first to Wire Hill, then to Kamagambo to build a girls' school. Miss Clarke developed a proficiency in Luo and Swahili that enabled her later to make a valuable contribution as a translator.

Prior to 1930 little had been done outside an area around Lake Victoria, but in 1933 the Karura Station was opened near Nairobi, with W. W. Armstrong as the first director. This became a base for work among the two principal tribes of Central Kenya, the Kikuyu and the Kamba. In 1934 W.C.S. Raitt, sent to begin work on the coast of Kenya, opened the Changamwe Station, near Mombasa, close to the main Mombasa-Nairobi road two and a half miles (four kilometers) from the center of the city. Work in this predominantly Muslim area developed slowly, as it did among the Kikuyu and Kamba peoples, but a number of churches and companies were established.

During 1930 to 1935 a number of new workers went to Kenya, among them C.T.J. Hyde, who worked first at Kendu Hospital, later at the Kamagambo school; and Jean Schuil, who gave nearly 20 years to the work of training teachers at Kamagambo.

Education. From the first, Seventh-day

Adventist missionaries in Kenya, as elsewhere in Southern Africa, sought to build a strong school system, believing that literacy was necessary to develop strong church members and trained workers to care for them. The central stations developed schools offering up to five or six years' education, which were fed by numerous two- or three-grade "bush" schools. During the late 1920s Kamagambo Training School (now Kamagambo High School and Teachers' College) was made the teacher training center for SDA work in Kenya. This training program received government recognition, its graduates sitting for government examinations before being sent out as teacher-evangelists. Schools for girls were established at Kamagambo, Nyanchwa, and Karura.

Hundreds of teachers went out to establish village schools, most of which clustered around the principal missions, which were concentrated in South Nyanza, bordering the lake. The typical schoolhouse was the place of worship on the Sabbath day for the village church, and the teacher of the school usually served as the leader of the company.

In 1947 the European constituency in East Africa, whose children were attending public schools, requested a church school to be established in Nairobi. The school (since 1962 called the Maxwell Preparatory School) was opened in 1949 with a hostel for boarders. Currently it is divided into Maxwell Adventist Preparatory School (elementary) and Maxwell Adventist Academy.

Problem of Government Aid. Government grants-in-aid were offered to managers of these SDA schools in the district of South Nyanza. These funds came from the annual tax levied on every male, for the government operated no schools, finding it more economical to make cash gifts to the missions that provided education for the indigenous inhabitants. This was a common practice of the British in various parts of the empire.

The grants-in-aid were of two kinds: (1) capital, available to directors of the larger missions for providing buildings and other educational facilities; and (2) recurring, made on behalf of all certificated teachers working in mission schools in Kenya, European and African alike.

The system eventually created problems. As the government wage scale rose rapidly, particularly after World War II, it became difficult to explain why a young man just out of school should receive considerably more than the mission could pay an experienced pastor. Probably more serious was the result that many of the teachers, in view of the source of their salaries, came to regard themselves as government rather than mission employees.

The pros and cons of accepting government aid were debated in Kenya church committees for more than two decades. The problem was also considered by the Southern African Division committee, which finally decided that no SDA organization should accept further government financial assistance for educational purposes after 1956 (this did not exclude grants made for medical work).

The results were far-reaching. SDA missions in Kenya entered upon an extremely difficult time. The East African Union did not have funds to operate the schools that had been receiving the grant. Many of them were either turned over to other mission societies or operated as independent African schools, the teachers continuing to receive salaries from the local government. Some of the teachers remained faithful to the church; others did not.

More recently the church members in the South Nyanza, Kisii, Migori, and Nyamira districts (which comprises a majority of the Kenya Seventh-day Adventist constituency) advocated a return to the practice of receiving government grants for educational work. After careful consultation with higher authorities, the union voted its approval as from 1962. This, however, did not apply to schools on central Kenya mission stations.

Organization and Growth. Originally the mission stations in Kenya, in what was then British East Africa, were under the sponsorship of the British Union Conference. From 1909 to 1912 the *Yearbook* lists the British East African Mission as "under the direction of the General Conference Committee in Europe," from 1912 to 1918 as part of the European Division, from 1918 to 1923 as part of the British Union.

In 1921 Kenya became part of the East African Combined Mission, with headquarters at Gendia Mission Station, Kenya. In 1924 Kenya is listed in the East African Union Mission, which after the formation of the Northern European Division in 1928 became a part of that. In the 1934 *Yearbook* four Kenya missions are listed; in 1938 there were five missions composing the Kenya Union Mission, with S. G. Maxwell as president; thereafter headquarters were in Nairobi.

Since World War II made it difficult for the

Northern European Division to administer the East Africa missions, these were transferred in 1941 to the Southern African Division. In 1943 a new East African Union emerged, which included Kenya, with H. M. Sparrow as president. Headquarters were in Kisumu, a town central to SDA work in Kenya, then from 1950 in Nairobi.

With the continued growth of membership it was decided in 1953 to set up once more field organizations within Kenya much as it had been when Kenya was a union. These were South Kenya (Kisii, Masai), Kenya Lake (Luo), and Central Kenya (areas outside of Nyanza province); in 1961 another field was formed known as the Ranen Field, also in Luo, Kuria, and Abasuba country.

Today African workers are carrying most of the work and also holding executive positions. In November 1972 D. K. Bazarra was appointed the first national president of the East African Union. Now all of the Kenya fields are administered by African presidents.

In 1981 the Western Kenya Field was organized, serving the Luhyas and Kalenjins of the Western Province of Kenya. In 1981 the South Kenya Field was organized into the South Kenya Conference. In 1986 the Kenya Coast Field was organized to serve the tribes of the Coast and North Eastern provinces. In 1989 the Central Kenya Field was organized into Central Kenya Conference. In 1990 the North Nyanza Field was organized to serve the Luo people.

KENYA COAST FIELD. *See* Eastern Africa Division; Kenya.

KENYA HOSPITAL. *See* Kendu Adventist Hospital.

KENYA LAKE FIELD. *See* Eastern Africa Division; Kenya.

KENYA TRAINING SCHOOL. *See* Kamagambo High School and Teachers' College.

KEOUGH, G. ARTHUR (1909-1989). Educator, administrator, missionary. Born in Cairo, Egypt, he served the church for 57 years on four continents. He founded Middle East College and later served as its president. He was the author of four books, several adult Sabbath school lesson quarterlies, and numerous articles.

In 1981 he was awarded the Citation of Excellence from the General Conference, one of the highest honors given to any Seventh-day Adventist educator. In his last position he served in the Religion Department of Columbia Union College. Upon retirement, he was named professor emeritus.

KEOUGH, GEORGE D. (1882-1971). Missionary and educator. A native of Crieff, Scotland, he entered the ministry in South England in 1905. Three years later he answered a call to mission service in Egypt. He mastered the Arabic language, and for the next 21 years he worked for the Muslims. In 1929 the Keoughs returned to England, where he taught Bible at Newbold College until 1937, when he was sent again to work another five years among the Arabic-speaking people.

When plans were laid for the preparation of missionaries for Islam, he was called to the Theological Seminary in Washington, where he taught Arabic and Bible from 1942 to 1946. At this time he returned once more to the Middle East to care for the newly established Voice of Prophecy organization in Beirut, Lebanon. Retiring in 1955, he returned to Britain and again taught at Newbold, continuing until 1965.

KERLYS. *See* Martinique.

KERN, MILTON EARL (1875-1961). Educator and youth leader. He was educated at Union College, Lincoln, Nebraska, and in 1900 married Florence Pierce.

For four years, from 1900 to 1904, Kern was head of the Bible and history departments at Union College, and because of his promotion of student missionary activities he was appointed secretary of the young people's department of the Central Union Conference in 1904, the first young people's secretary in the denomination. He had previously organized a "Young People's Society of Christian Service" in response to appeals from Ellen White to provide missionary opportunities for the youth of the church (1893).

At a General Conference Council held in Switzerland in 1907, when the Young People's Department of the General Conference was set up, Kern became the first chair, with Matilda Erickson as secretary. Later in the year at Mount Vernon, Ohio, the new organization was named the Young People's Missionary Volunteer Department, and Kern became its first secretary.

From 1910 to 1914 Kern was also president of the Foreign Mission Seminary (now Columbia Union College) at Washington. During the 1920s he spent most of his time overseas building the Missionary Volunteer Societies. In 1922, when the Home Commission was established by the General Conference Kern became chair. He was elected associate secretary (1930), then secretary (1933), of the General Conference.

In 1933 he entered another phase of his lifework when he was made dean of the Advanced Bible School. When in 1936 this school became the Seventh-day Adventist Theological Seminary (later a part of Andrews University), he became its first president. In 1943 he became field secretary of the General Conference and president of the board of trustees of the Ellen White Publications. He retired in 1950, remembered as the pioneer head of the youth movement in the Seventh-day Adventist Church.

KETRING, HERMAN FEASTER (1873-1913). Pioneer missionary on the west coast of South America. His parents became Seventh-day Adventists when he was a boy, and he was baptized at the age of 14. At the age of 18 he began canvassing in Arkansas and Kansas. Later, he studied for the ministry, first at Union College (1892-1894), and then at the General Conference Bible School (1894-1895). Between 1894 and 1901 he worked as an evangelist in Kansas and Wyoming. He was ordained in 1899 by G. A. Irwin. In 1901 he volunteered for service in South America and was sent to Chile. While there, he edited *Señales de los Tiempos* and for a time was superintendent of the West Coast Mission. Returning to the United States in 1905, he preached in Kansas, then became president of the Central New England Conference (1906-1909). Shortly after this he contracted tuberculosis, from which he never recovered. About 1910 he went to Denver, Colorado, and for a time was pastor of a church. Later he sought to recover his health in California.

KETTERING COLLEGE OF MEDICAL ARTS. *See* Kettering Medical Center.

KETTERING MEDICAL CENTER. A complex of service, education, and research institutions including Charles F. Kettering Memorial Hospital, Sycamore Hospital, Kettering College of Medical Arts, and Sycamore Glen Retirement Community. The medical center is an integral part of the health-care mission of the Seventh-day Adventist Church and is dedicated in perpetuity to serving the Greater Dayton, Ohio, community. There are 673 patient beds in total—482 at the Charles F. Kettering Memorial Hospital and 191 at Sycamore Hospital. Seven hundred and twenty-five college students, 79 medical residents, and a staff of research scientists complement the 3,700 employees that make up KMC on the campuses situated in Kettering and Miamisburg, south of Dayton, Ohio.

Its beginning dates back to 1958, when Eugene W. Kettering and his wife, Virginia, announced plans for building a 100-bed hospital on the family estate as a memorial to Eugene's father, Charles F. Kettering, renowned inventor, scientist, and humanitarian. The Ketterings agreed to underwrite 100 additional beds if the community would provide funds for a matching number. In a short time a team of interested community leaders raised approximately $2 million. With the matching Kettering funds, the capacity was thus tripled.

Impressed by previous contacts with the Hinsdale Sanitarium and Hospital, the Ketterings selected the Seventh-day Adventist Church to build and operate the new hospital. The Columbia Union on Nov. 13, 1959, took action establishing the charter and organization of the new hospital, and appointed George B. Nelson as executive officer. On Dec. 21, 1959, a nonprofit corporation was formed, and the church agreed to provide funds for construction of a School of Nursing and for initial operating costs.

Construction began after a groundbreaking ceremony on July 7, 1961. In December 1963 the family of O. Lee Harrison, longtime personal friend and professional associate of Charles F. Kettering, presented a gift of $800,000 to the hospital. This was immediately supplemented by another $1 million from the Ketterings for the purpose of adding a fifth floor. This floor, containing 100 beds for medical-surgical patients, was completed in 1965, bringing the hospital's bed capacity to more than 400. Medical, surgical, and pediatric services began on Mar. 3, 1964, and the Obstetrical Department was opened early in 1965. A broad complement of ancillary services, including a large Rehabilitative Medicine Department, is provided for both inpatients and outpatients. In 1993 there were 3,761 employees and a medical staff of 767 and 650 volunteers. The hospital and college represent a total investment of $30 million.

College Established. The educational programs of the medical center were developed between 1964 and 1967 under the direction of George Nelson, Anna May Vaughan, and Dr. William C. Sandborn.

Late in 1965 the board approved the funds and plans for the correlation of all the educational activities of the hospital into the academic structure of an associate degree college with special emphasis on health careers. In 1966 it was officially named Kettering College of Medical Arts. It enrolled its first students in 1967 in five allied health curriculums: nursing, radiology, respiratory therapy, environmental management, and medical record technology. In 1993 the college offered associate degrees in nursing, biomedical electronics technology, physician assistant, audiological sciences and imaging, general diagnostic radiologic technology, diagnostic special procedures technology, medical sonography-abdominal/obstetrics gynecologic, cardiovascular-nuclear medicine technology, respiratory care, preprofessional, and general education. Four additional curriculums were added in succeeding years: clinical dietetic technology, biomedical equipment technology, medical office assisting, and physician's assisting.

Campus Church. In December 1963, as the staff of the hospital was being assembled, a church was organized with 141 charter members. It first met in the hospital auditorium but soon moved to the gymnasium. In 1971 the congregation moved into a new church building constructed on land donated by Mr. and Mrs. Kettering. The congregation has grown to 1,010 members as of 1993. The growth of the churches in Dayton has been significant since the establishment of the medical center, growing to 16.5 percent of the conference membership.

Governance. As an Ohio nonprofit corporation and an integral part of the health-care mission of the Seventh-day Adventist Church, Kettering Medical Center is dedicated to serving the Greater Dayton, Ohio, community.

Governance of the institution is directly effected through the board of trustees, which is composed of 18 individuals, six ex officio representing union, conference and medical center administration, six community trustees who are members of the Seventh-day Adventist Church, and six community trustees who are not members of the church.

Presidents of the Medical Center: George B. Nelson, 1959-1968; Marlowe H. Schaffner, 1968-1979; Robert L. Willett, 1979-1994; Frank J. Perez, 1994- .

KETTLE FALLS ACADEMY. *See* Upper Columbia Conference.

KHALIL, IBRAHIM (c. 1870-1946). One of the first national Seventh-day Adventists in Lebanon; evangelist and minister. He was a Kurd from north Syria brought up as a Muslim, but came into contact with Christianity and accepted it. Fearing for his life, he changed his name to Ibrahim el-Khalil (or al Khalil) and fled to a village in the mountains of Lebanon. There W. K. Ising found him and studied the Bible with him. As a result Khalil became an Adventist in 1911. Afterward he preached in Egypt (he is listed first in the 1912 *Yearbook),* Lebanon, and Jordan (both Palestine and Transjordan), pioneering Adventist work in some places. He was ordained to the ministry about 1935. In 1924 he married Marie Meyer, one of the earliest SDA members in Palestine. He taught Arabic in the school that later became the present secondary school in Egypt. He retired about 1940 and was last listed in the 1946 *Yearbook.*

KHMER REPUBLIC. *See* Cambodia.

KHUNTI ADVENTIST HIGH SCHOOL. *See* Seventh-day Adventist High School (Khunti).

KHURDA ADVENTIST HIGH SCHOOL. *See* Seventh-day Adventist High School (Khurda).

KIDDER, FLORENCE M. (1885-1967). Educator. A native of Canada, she lost her mother at an early age and grew up in a foster family in Massachusetts. She graduated from South Lancaster Academy in 1903, and from that time on taught elementary school for 65 consecutive years. During this time she took her bachelor's degree from Emmanuel Missionary College. Her last post of service was the school at Pittsfield, Massachusetts. She passed away in her sleep on Dec. 21, just after closing school for the Christmas vacation.

KIEN KHUONG MATERNITY HOME. A medical institution operated from 1940 to 1961, part of the time by the Vietnam Mission. It was situated for about a year in Phnom Penh,

French Indochina (now the capital of Cambodia), thereafter for 20 years in Cholon, a suburb of Saigon, Vietnam. It was opened in Phnom Penh under the direction of Mrs. Robert Bentz and Mrs. Chen Keng Huy, with 20 beds and 15 workers, including three midwives and three students. It carried its name over the entrance in four languages—French, Cambodian, Vietnamese, and Chinese.

The maternity clinic averaged 100 deliveries a month until war broke out in Southeast Asia and the Bentzes were forced to leave Phnom Penh for Saigon. In the fall of 1941 the clinic was reestablished in Cholon, Vietnam. During the war years when all outside income was cut off, the operating gains of the maternity clinic provided subsidies for the continued operation of the mission.

After Mrs. Bentz returned to France following World War II, Mrs. Chen carried on with the help of local midwives until 1955, when Wong Mo Sun was called from Hong Kong. She stayed until 1959. Because of decreasing patronage and the danger of incurring heavy indebtedness, the maternity home was sold in September 1961.

KILGORE, ROBERT MEAD (1839-1912). Evangelist, administrator. Returning home from an army captaincy in 1865, he found his parents observing the seventh-day Sabbath, and soon joined them. Three years later he joined the evangelistic team of G. I. Butler and M. E. Cornell as tentmaster. Shortly afterward James White ordained him.

After working in the Eastern states for a time, he was sent by the General Conference in 1877 to Texas. A year or two later A. G. Daniells worked with him as his tentmaster. Within two years 200 persons had been won, and in 1878 Kilgore became the first president of the Texas Conference.

He was at different times president of the Illinois Conference, superintendent of General Conference District No. 2 and District No. 5; for one year he was president of the Southern Union Conference, and for four years its vice president. While holding these offices, he continued to engage actively in evangelism.

KILGORE, ROCHELLE PHILMON (1887-1993). Educator. Born on a cotton plantation in Georgia, she began teaching at age 17 for $15 a week. She graduated from Graysville Academy (forerunner of Southern College) in 1904 and received her master's degree from the University of Georgia in 1924. In 1929 she married Charles Kilgore and moved to South Lancaster, Massachusetts, where she worked on her doctorate at Boston University. In 1936 she was hired as a "temporary" teacher by Atlantic Union College, where she stayed for 25 years. She was known as a mentor of students, and more than 90 made their temporary homes with her. During World War II she was deeply committed to helping Seventh-day Adventist servicemembers, and corresponded with hundreds of them, encouraging them to finish college. She attended 25 consecutive retreats for servicemembers at Berchtesgaden, Germany. Retiring in 1960, she continued to teach part-time and was active in alumni affairs. She retired from alumni work just prior to her one hundredth birthday. Atlantic Union College bestowed upon her its first honorary doctorate in 1977. Dr. Kilgore devoted 75 years to SDA education, 50 of which were at Atlantic Union College.

KING, GEORGE ALBERT (1847-1906). Pioneer canvasser who developed the idea of subscription sale of Seventh-day Adventist books. A native of Canada, he came to the United States as a young man in search of fortune. Having accepted SDA beliefs, he desired to preach, but was discouraged by James White, who did not regard him a promising candidate. Eventually a Seventh-day Adventist layperson, "Uncle Richard" Godsmark, advised him to try selling SDA tracts and magazines. This he did with much success in both the United States and Canada. In 1878 and 1879 he was selling books and subscriptions to *Good Health* and *Signs of the Times* in Ontario (*Review and Herald* 53:54, Feb. 13, 1879). According to the recollection of C. F. Wilcox, another pioneer colporteur, King and he sold J. H. Kellogg's *Home Hand-Book of Domestic Hygiene and Rational Medicine,* a substantial book of more than 1,600 pages, in 1880, and thus gained experience in selling large books to the public.

At the 1881 General Conference session King urged those assembled to carry out the counsel given by Ellen White in 1879 that Seventh-day Adventist books should be sold widely among the public, and forcefully argued that two small books written by Uriah Smith, *Thoughts on Daniel* and *Thoughts on the Revelation,* could be published together in an attractive form for sale by canvassers to the public. As a result of his appeal, these were reprinted together, with new illustrations, by the Review and Herald early in 1882. D. W. Reavis relates that by way of demonstration King sold him the first copy of this edition of *Thoughts on the Book of Daniel and the Revelation* the very morning it was off the press Apr. 3, 1882. The book had good sale and was followed by other subscription books.

There is some uncertainty among SDA historians about the dating of this edition. M. E. Olsen *(Origin and Progress of Seventh-day Adventists,* p. 427) and Spalding *(Captains of the Host,* p. 416) give the date of the General Conference session as 1880, while J. N. Loughborough (in the *Rise and Progress of Seventh-day Adventists,* pp. 330, 331, and in a letter to W. W. Eastman in the *Review and Herald* 97:8, July 15, 1920), Matilda E. Andross *(Story of the Advent Message,* p. 124), and King's obituary *(Review and Herald* 83:19, Dec. 6, 1906) place this event at the 1881 session. The 1881 date appears more likely because there was a General Conference resolution on canvassing in that session, Dec. 12, 1881. Therefore this special subscription edition does not seem to be the first time that *Thoughts on Daniel* and *Thoughts on the Revelation* were offered to the public in a single binding, for at King's request, trial copies of the combined books had been made before the end of 1881 by putting together into one binding the already printed sheets of the two separately paged books plus a newly printed index. (See *Review and Herald* 96:332, Mar. 13, 1919; cf. *Review and Herald* 59:32, Jan. 10, 1882; General Conference proceedings, Dec. 12, 1881, in *Review and Herald* 59:10, Jan. 3, 1882, col. 2.)

In 1887 King visited British Guiana in South America, where there was no permanent SDA work at that time, and sold about $900 worth of books. After that he canvassed in the city of New York for about 19 years until his death in 1906. Throughout his life he was an enthusiastic recruiter and instructor of other canvassers.

KING, GEORGE DONALD (1903-1966). Evangelist, departmental secretary, administrator. A native of England, King graduated from Stanborough Missionary College in 1923 and became publishing department secretary of the North England Conference. In 1924 he and his wife went to West Africa for two years, followed by six years of evangelism in Scotland and North England. He was asked to serve as president of the Welsh Mission in 1932, and in 1936 he became publishing department secretary of the British Union. In the years that followed he served in administrative and secretarial capacities in the South England Conference, British Union Conference, and Northern European Division. In 1962 he suffered a stroke that left him unable to serve the church longer in an active way. In spite of this, he maintained a lively interest in the work of the denomination.

KING, R. M. (1856-1891). Tennessee farmer whose prosecution for plowing his field on Sunday attracted wide attention. He accepted the Seventh-day Adventist faith in 1884, one of the first in his community. In 1889 he was charged with violating Sunday laws, convicted, and imprisoned. His case was appealed to the Tennessee Supreme Court and to the United States district court. It was hoped to make his a test case in the United States Supreme Court on the constitutional principle relating to the establishment of religion by law, but his untimely death ended the proceedings.

KINGDOM OF GOD. In the Bible this phrase refers primarily to the kingly rule or sovereignty of God, which according to the NT, He exercises through Jesus Christ. The dominant theme in the teachings of Jesus as set forth in the Synoptic Gospels—His early preaching (Matt. 4:17; Luke 4:43), in the Sermon on the Mount (Matt. 5-7), in the early parables (Matt. 13), and at the Last Supper (Luke 22:29, 30)—is the kingdom of God.

The actual phrase does not occur in the OT, though "kingdom" in relation to God is found referring almost always to His authority or kingly rule (Ps. 22:28; 45:6; 103:19; 145:11, 13; Dan. 4:34; 6:26; etc.). In the Gospels, "kingdom of God" is used 15 times in Mark, 33 times in Luke, two times in John, and five times in Matthew. The phrase "kingdom of heaven" occurs 29 times in Matthew and once in some of the manuscripts of John 3:5. The two phrases are used synonymously. Matthew reflects the Jewish practice of substituting a reverent periphrasis, "heaven," for the sacred name, to avoid using the latter unnecessarily. The two phrases are used interchangeably in Matt. 19:23, 24. "Kingdom of God" is found seven times in Acts, nine times in Paul's writings, and once in the book of Revelation. In addition, such equivalent expressions as "thy kingdom," "his kingdom," "the kingdom," "my Father's kingdom," and "the kingdom of their Father" occur in the Synoptics. The kingdom of God is also the kingdom of Christ (Matt. 13:41; 16:28; Luke 22:30; John 18:36; Col. 1:13; 2 Peter 1:11; Rev. 11:15; 12:10).

The basic meaning of the Hebrew and Greek words for kingdom *(malkûth* and *basileia)* is kingly authority or sovereignty rather than the realm, or sphere, in which this authority operates. This primary meaning is reflected, for example, in Jesus' parable of the nobleman who went into a far country to receive a kingdom; that is, to receive regal power and authority (Luke 19:11, 12). The kingdom of God, then, is God's kingship, His sovereignty, His rule, His authority. When one seeks the kingdom (Matt. 6:33), or receives the kingdom (Mark 10:15), that kingdom has reference to God's sovereign rule over his or her life. God's kingdom is to be found where He is recognized as king.

There is a sense, of course, in which God is always and everywhere king (Ps. 47:2; 103:19; 145:13; Dan. 4:25). But His reign has not yet become a reality in history. Our world is in revolt against God, and Satan has usurped the rulership. However, God has not relinquished His sovereignty.

Jesus Christ entered earthly history to restore God's rulership on this earth (Dan. 2:44; 7:14; 1 Cor. 15:24, 25). This new manifestation of power and sovereignty is now the kingdom of God. God has taken the initiative in defeating Satan and in restoring mankind to willing subjection to His authority. Jesus came to our world as the head of this great kingdom, which is freeing men and women from bondage to Satan and making them citizens of a heavenly commonwealth (Phil. 3:20, 21).

This kingdom has two phases—"the kingdom of grace" and "the kingdom of glory." Although these terms are not used in the Bible, the Scriptures do speak of "the throne of grace" (Heb. 4:16) and "the throne of glory" (Matt. 25:31, 32), and thrones represent kingdoms. The throne of grace implies the existence of a kingdom of grace, and the throne of glory represents the future kingdom of glory.

The kingdom of grace, the soteriological phase, was present in the days of Jesus (Mark 1:15; Luke 16:16; 17:20, 21; Matt. 21:31; Col. 1:13f), and was manifested in Him as the Messiah. Individuals can enter this realm of grace here and now by acknowledging Him as ruler of their lives. This is the great spiritual kingdom of God's grace and righteousness. The controlling principles in this kingdom are not power and force, but justice, mercy, and love. Jesus' healings were part of the work of bringing this kingdom to humanity (Luke 11:20). Christ fully established this phase of the kingdom by His death. Where Satan had set his throne, Christ raised up His cross. Individuals enter the kingdom of divine grace by repenting, believing, and accepting the new birth (Matt. 18:3; John 3:5), and by submitting voluntarily to Christ's rule. This kingdom is established "by the implanting of Christ's nature in humanity through the work of the Holy Spirit" (DA 509). The ethical principles for citizens of the kingdom are set forth in the Sermon on the Mount. They are to make the kingdom supreme in their affections and devotions (Matt. 6:33).

But the kingdom is also future and eschatological. God's will and reign will never be perfectly realized in this age. They will not be fully realized until our Lord steps again into human history, asserts His universal rule, and puts an end to rebellion (Matt. 13:41-43). "When the Son of man comes in his glory, and all the angels with him, then he will sit on his glorious throne" (Matt. 25:31, RSV). As there are two advents of Christ, so there are two manifestations of His kingdom. It was for this second phase of the kingdom that Jesus taught the disciples to pray (Matt. 6:10). This kingdom is to be set up at the Second Advent and the resurrection of the just. Since this is a glorious, incorruptible, and everlasting kingdom, humans in their present state cannot enter it. "Flesh and blood cannot inherit the kingdom of God; neither doth corruption" (1 Cor. 15:50). Hence the nature of the living and of those who are resurrected is changed from corruptibility and mortality to incorruptibility and immortality. To those who experience this change the King of glory will say: "Come, ye blessed of my Father, inherit the kingdom prepared for you from the foundation of the world" (Matt. 25:34).

KINGDOM PROPHECIES. *See* Israel, Prophecies Concerning.

KINGSWAY COLLEGE (formerly Oshawa Missionary College). A coeducational boarding high school, operated by the Seventh-day Adventist Church in Canada on a tract of land at Oshawa, Ontario, 30 miles (50 kilometers) east of Toronto.

The high school is accredited by the Department of Education of the province of Ontario and by the Seventh-day Adventist

Board of Regents (1992). The 1992-1993 enrollment was 217; the faculty numbered 19, and the total staff, 40.

The school was originally (1903) called Lornedale Academy, later Buena Vista Academy, Eastern Canadian Missionary Seminary, Oshawa Missionary College, and Kingsway College. Motivation for the establishment of the school was the fact that many of the Canadian SDA young people who were attending Battle Creek College, in Michigan, were not returning to Canada. (Until 1899, when the SDA churches of the province of Ontario were organized as the Ontario Conference, the area had been a mission field of the Michigan Conference.) The school was established on a 50-acre (20-hectare) farm at Lorne Park, about 15 miles (25 kilometers) from Toronto, with Eugene Leland and his wife as the first teachers. For the first few years the school was operated like a large family enterprise, with the farm as the only industry, producing chiefly fruit and offering seasonal employment. The buildings consisted of a large stone house, a smaller house, and a large barn. In 1906 an addition to the old farmhouse provided a chapel, offices, and additional student rooms. The academy prospered as equipment was donated piece by piece. Appeals for cash and needed articles brought ready response. Those who had time but not money to give took their families to Lornedale and donated labor in the construction of the 1906 annex. The rooms were furnished at $25 each through individual pledges. The school had no electricity, no steam heat, no plumbing. The water supply was a local well.

In 1906 there were approximately 25 students, most of them from Ontario. Grades 1-11 were offered by 1908, and grade 12 was added in 1910. School expenses amounted to only $2.50 per week, and each student was required to work at least one hour a day. Under a scholarship plan a student could pay for a year's schooling by selling $150 worth of Ellen White's *Christ's Object Lessons.*

Early teachers included Walter Hancock, Mabel Patterson, Blanche Walker, and L. A. Jacobs. Although the school was called an industrial school, the influence of the classical schools of the day was strong. Hira T. Curtis, who came from Keene, Texas, as principal in 1908, taught Latin, German, mathematics, and history. M. E. Kern's *New Testament History* was used, as well as G. H. Bell's English texts.

Because the work provided by the fruit farm was seasonal, the Lornedale property was sold and the school was moved in the summer of 1912 to its present location at Oshawa, on a farm of 128 acres (50 hectares). The total acreage became 240 (100 hectares), when C. D. Terwillegar, the first SDA in Oshawa, offered his property to the school. The school was appropriately named Buena Vista Academy for its beautiful view of the surrounding countryside and Lake Ontario.

The first new structure was a small building, which for two years housed the classrooms, the printing press, and the business office. Later the school laundry and bakery operated in this building. The original farm building housed some of the students. Other students temporarily lived in tents.

A new multipurpose building was completed in 1914, toward the cost of which $4,000 was contributed at the 1912 Ontario camp meeting. This building was large and housed the assembly hall, classrooms, the business office, and living quarters for the staff and students.

Upon the advice of the General Conference, the school was turned over in May 1914 to the Eastern Canadian Union Conference. The following year Buena Vista Academy was chosen as the training center for French-speaking workers in North America, and the French Department of South Lancaster Academy was moved to Oshawa.

Herminie L. Roth had charge of this French Department for the first two years. She was followed by Jean Vuilleumier until 1920, when Joseph Curdy, of France, came to head the department. Subjects taught in French were grammar, rhetoric, literature, Old and New Testament history, Bible doctrines, and general history. Later E. A. Curdy joined the staff (see *Review and Herald* 97:30, Nov. 25, 1920). During this time Sabbath services were conducted in French for the French-speaking students. However, a steadily declining attendance of French-speaking students during the depression of the 1930s brought an end to the plan.

To identify the school with its purpose of training denominational workers, the name Buena Vista Academy was changed to Eastern Canadian Missionary Seminary in 1916. In 1919 an administration building was erected, providing space for carpentry rooms, offices, classrooms, a chapel, and piano rooms. During the 1920s the school, incorporated under the name of Oshawa Missionary College (1920), strengthened its academic program. Courses were offered in Bible, history, languages, sciences, commerce, music, and teacher training on the junior college level. Vocational training included, at different times, agriculture, carpentry, domestic science, hydrotherapy, nursing, and sewing.

The early years of the college followed the typical SDA pattern of industry combined with education. The woodwork industry, established in September 1921, has been, and is, the backbone of the industrial program.

After a lull in expansion caused by the economic problems of the early 1930s and by the Second World War, a college auditorium was built in 1949, which served as a church for the college and the community until 1960, when the new $350,000 College Park church, seating 1,200, was built.

In 1958 the college entered a new phase of expansion. The women's dormitory and the administration building were completely remodeled. The secretarial department was improved by the addition of new equipment and new classrooms. Additional music facilities were provided in a new building and the Home Economics Department expanded its quarters and equipment.

In 1958 the enrollment reached 200. In 1960 the first year of a three-year nursing course was offered, in affiliation with the newly established North York Branson Hospital in Toronto. The first class of nurses was graduated in 1963. Greater opportunities for student employment were provided by the completion of a 40,000-square-foot (3,750-square-meter) college woodwork factory. In 1965 a 14-room science and classroom building was completed.

In 1973 a new women's dormitory complex was built, including a cafeteria and dining room, and a student chapel with a seating capacity of 350. The former elementary school building was remodeled in 1974 to provide a Family Studies Department and a fine arts ceramics workshop. An industrial education building, also housing plant services, was added in 1980.

A new administration building was completed in 1988, and in 1989 the A. E. King Memorial Physical Fitness Complex was opened. This facility includes a large gymnasium, kitchen, seminar room, shower and change areas, weight room, squash and racquet ball courts, and serves both the school and the local community.

The school name was changed once again in 1966 to Kingsway College to reflect the total academic program offered by the institution. In the late 1970s the college section of the school was transferred to Canadian Union College in Alberta, the nursing program was phased out because of changing government regulations, and Ontario grade 13 was added to the academic program. In 1989 the Ontario Department of Education replaced grade 13 with courses designated as Ontario Academic Credits. Kingsway College graduates currently receive the Ontario Secondary School Diploma.

Throughout its history the school has served the constituency of eastern Canada, although, especially since the late 1950s, it has drawn its students from all of Canada and many parts of the world. Its alumni have given outstanding service to the church and community in many lands.

Presidents: Eugene Leland, 1903-1906; W. E. Hancock, 1906-1907; Eugene Leland, 1907-1908; H. T. Curtis, 1908-1910; W. J. Blake, 1910-1914; T. D. Rowe, 1914-1916; F. A. Spangler, 1916-1917; A. J. Olson, 1917-1921; K. L. Gant, 1921-1925; L. N. Holm, 1925-1930; C. W. Degering, 1930-1937; F. R. Isaac, 1937-1939; C. W. Shankel, 1939-1947; C. H. Casey, 1947-1948; Todd Murdoch, 1948; C. L. Smith, 1949-1950; W. A. Sowers, 1950-1958; P. W. Manuel, 1958-1968; Percy Paul, 1968-1971; W. F. Easterbrook, 1971-1975; A. N. White, 1976-1977; Malcolm Graham, 1977; Leroy Kuhn, 1978-1983; Ralph Janes, 1983- .

KINGSWAY HIGH SCHOOL. A coeducational day school on the senior high school level, operated by the East Jamaica Conference at 10-12 Osbourne Road, Kingston 10, Jamaica, West Indies. It was established in 1943 under the direction of W. F. Atkin, then president of the Jamaica Conference. The first principal was Vernon E. Berry, who was on loan from the Antillian Union, where he served as educational secretary. The school has an enrollment of 540 and a teaching staff of 23. The course of instruction is approved by the Jamaican government.

The school was known as New Hope College until 1946, when its present name was adopted. Construction of a new school building was begun in 1954 and completed in 1957. The need for more classroom space led to the acquisition of neighboring property in 1961. In 1974 a new building to accommodate 250 pupils was completed for the preparatory department of the school. In 1989 a new wing housing the kindergarten and grade 6 classrooms was constructed and a plan was drawn for the construction of an upper floor, which was completed in 1991, consisting of a science laboratory, a staff room, and two extra classrooms.

Graduates from this school are now working in the three conferences in which Jamaica is divided.

Principals: V. E. Berry, 1943; E. E. Parchment, 1943; Stanley Bull, 1944-1946; J. I. Crawford, 1946-1948; W. A. Holgate 1948-1951; V. H. Percy, 1951-1956; O. S. Rugless, 1956-1957; H. A. Mills, 1957-1958; V. H. Percy, 1958-1970; S. G. Campbell, 1970-1972; E. C. Pryce, 1972-1974; Mrs. A. White (acting), 1974-1976; H. Maynard-Reid, 1976-1977; L. Roo McKenzie, 1977-1979; D. A. Bignall (acting), 1979-1980; F. M. Davis, 1980-1983; E. H. Thomas (acting), 1983-1984 Mrs. L. Wright, 1984-1989; Ms. V. Ferguson, 1989- .

KINGSWAY PUBLISHING ASSOCIATION. *See* Pacific Publishing Association.

KINNEY (KINNY), CHARLES M. (1855-1951). Evangelist. As a youth he worked his way to Reno, Nevada. While there he attended evangelistic services conducted by J. N. Loughborough, accepted the Seventh-day Adventist faith, and became the first Black member of the Reno, Nevada, church. After two years' attendance at Healdsburg College (1883-1885) he entered the colporteur work in Kansas. He was assigned by the General Conference in 1889 to work in Louisville, Kentucky, and was ordained the same year, being apparently the first Black SDA to be ordained. His wife's invalidism eventually made it impossible for him to carry on full ministerial work. He retired in 1911. It was his privilege to see the Black membership of the Seventh-day Adventist Church in North America swell to 26,500.

KINSAUNG PUBLISHING HOUSE. A publishing house, with printing plant, operated by the Burma (now Myanmar) Union in Dagon until 1969 and then moved to Kanbe, about four miles (six kilometers) away from the mission headquarters.

After World War II the Kinsaung Publishing House was established. A substantial two-story brick building was erected at 72 U Wisara Road, Dagon, and printing work began May 28, 1950. With help from the Review and Herald Publishing Association and from the General Conference Publishing Rehabilitation Fund the plant acquired a Babcock No. 5 cylinder press, a smaller cylinder speed press, two Chandler and Price presses, a folder, a cutter, and suitable type and equipment.

The first manager was J. O. Wilson, who had been closely connected with the prewar publishing work. Later, supervisors trained at the Oriental Watchman Publishing House in Poona began carrying this responsibility. U Saw U, a member of Bamar's earliest Seventh-day Adventist family, led out during both prewar and postwar periods in editing and translating. From 10 to 13 workers are employed. Publications are issued in Bamar, Chin, English, Pwo Kayin, and Sgaw Kayin.

Managers: J. O. Wilson, 1950-1953; Pein Gyi, 1953-1957; C. B. Guild, 1957-1962; W. L. Murrill, 1962-1965; Doe Doe Shin, 1965-1980; BaKhin, 1981-1983; Kyaw Balay, 1984; Kyaw Sein Pe, 1985-1989; Cyrus Brown, 1990- .

KIRGHIZIA. *See* Kyrgyzstan.

KIRIBATI. An island country in the Micronesian Island group that encompasses 266 square miles (690 square kilometers), slightly smaller than New York City. The population (1994) is nearly 80,000. The citizens speak Gilbertese and English, which is the official language. Kiribati's nearest neighbors are Nauru, Tuvalu, and Tokelau. The economy is based on the exportation of copra and phosphates.

Christianity first came to this area around 1840, and at the present time the population is almost equally divided between Roman Catholics and Protestants.

Seventh-day Adventist Statistics. Kiribati, along with Nauru, comprises the Kiribati Mission, which is a part of the Western Pacific Union Mission, which is in turn a part of the South Pacific Division. Statistics (1993) for the *Kiribati Mission:* churches, 6; members, 1,116. Headquarters: Bairiki, Tarawa, Kiribati.

Institutions. Kauma Adventist High School.

Seventh-day Adventist Work. Seventh-day Adventist work in the Gilbert and Ellice Islands, of which Kiribati was a part, began in 1947. On May 31 of that year John T. Howse, an SDA pastor from Fiji, arrived at Funafuti in the Ellice Islands on the mission ship M.V. *Fetu Ao* ("Morning Star" in Samoan). He was met by Tavita Niu, a Samoan, who had arrived a few months earlier to begin work in the Ellice group. Persecution later made it necessary for Tavita to transfer to Abemama in the Gilberts, where he joined the staff of the Gilbert and Ellice Islands Missionary School.

After some time on the Ellice Islands, Howse proceeded to the Gilberts and secured a lease on Abemama, where he settled with his family, Oct. 6, 1947.

The first Sabbath school was organized on July 10, 1948, with a membership of 26. The first baptism was conducted at Abemama on Jan. 29, 1949, when five people were accepted into the mission church. SDA work spread from island to island, and qualified converts were placed in charge of the work.

The work of translating began soon after the missionaries arrived, the first project being the translation of the Voice of Prophecy Bible correspondence lessons.

In later years teachers from Fiji staffed church schools on the Gilbert Islands, while ministers from Samoa have been the district directors on the Ellice Islands.

KIRIBATI MISSION. *See* Kiribati; South Pacific Division.

KIRJATOIMI. *See* Finland Publishing House.

KIRUNDU STATION. *See* Zaïre.

KIVOGA SECONDARY SCHOOL (Lycée Maranatha de Kivoga). A coeducational boarding institution established in 1964 with 36 students and three teachers. Situated about 10 miles (16 kilometers) from Bujumbura, the capital of the republic of Burundi, on 126 acres (50 hectares) of freehold property. In September 1993 the school began offering high school level courses. There is also a primary school. Enrollment (1993): 321 primary, 618 secondary. Staff: 32 secondary and 12 primary. For 12 years the school was taken over by the government, but was given back in 1992.

Principal: U. Habingabwa, 1992- .

KIVU ADVENTIST COLLEGE. *See* Lukanga Adventist Institute.

KLABAT ACADEMY (SMA Advent Klabat). A senior academy located in Manado, Indonesia, to accommodate graduates from four Seventh-day Adventist junior academies in this city. It began operation in 1981. There were 110 students enrolled in two courses: social studies and sciences, in five classes taught by four full-time teachers and three part-time instructors. The school operated in the afternoon and made use of the renovated Tikala's Elementary and Junior Academy School building.

In 1982 a new temporary school building was built at Pall II (next to the mission office), and the school was operated in the morning. Later, in 1986, the school moved to Tikala Baru (the present site) in a permanent building. At present there are 160 students enrolled in three courses: social studies, science, and mathematics, in seven classes taught by nine full-time teachers.

Principals: F. Kairupan, 1981-1986; J. A. Raranta, 1986-1989; H. G. Neman, 1989- .

KLEIN, JACOB (fl. 1890). Pioneer Seventh-day Adventist minister in Russia. Few details of his life have been preserved. It is known that he was born in a German settlement on the Volga River in eastern Russia and that he emigrated to the United States, where he became a Seventh-day Adventist. He is listed in the 1888 *Yearbook* as a missionary worker in Nebraska. In 1889 he went to Hamburg, Germany (reportedly from Kansas, where lived many of the earliest German-American converts to Seventh-day Adventist beliefs), together with J. T. Boettcher and L. R. Conradi. There, after a short training at the newly established missionary school, he was ordained to the ministry and proceeded to his native area on the Volga River.

There he began missionary work, apparently not only among the German settlers but also among their Russian neighbors, for he was promptly arrested on the accusation of proselyting the members of the state church. After a detention of several weeks he was confined to the settlements and their immediate vicinity. During two years of his enforced stay in the area he established a group of strong adherents to the SDA faith. Later he served congregations, baptized new members, and organized churches in the Caucasus region, along the river Don, in the Crimea, and in the Mennonite colonies on the north shore of the Black Sea. In 1893 he attended a general meeting of the workers in Hamburg in company with H. J. Loebsack, who was probably one of his converts from the Volga, and who later led the SDA work in Russia for many years.

In 1895 Klein and his wife visited their aged parents in Kansas, but returned to Russia the same year. After his return he was listed in

1898 as president of the Sabbath School Association for the Russian field. Thereafter his name disappeared from the *Yearbook.*

KLEUSER, LOUISE CAROLINE (1890-1976). A native of Germany, she came with her parents to the United States at the age of 9. Ten years later she united with the Seventh-day Adventist Church. Her work for the church includes service as a Bible instructor, pastor of several churches, departmental secretary, teacher, writer, second lieutenant in the SDA Medical Cadet Corps (she was the first woman to complete this training course), and finally, associate secretary of the General Conference Ministerial Association, a post she held for 16 years, until her retirement in 1958.

She was the author of *The Bible Instructor,* a book used in teaching the art of personal soul winning.

KLINGBEIL, REINHOLD GUSTAV (1868-1928). Evangelist, pastor, and administrator. Brought as a child from his native Germany to the United States, he accepted Seventh-day Adventist beliefs at an early age and attended Union College. In 1893 he was sent by the General Conference to Europe, where he worked as an evangelist, first in Germany, then about 1893 in the Netherlands.

Klingbeil was ordained in Hamburg in 1896. In the course of the next 30 years he helped to establish the Seventh-day Adventist Church organization in the Netherlands and among the Flemish people of Belgium, serving as an evangelist, conference president, and for a time editor of the Dutch-language paper *Zions-Wachter.* During World War I he remained with his family in Brussels, where one of his daughters fell victim to wartime privations. Upon his return to the United States in 1926 he held the pastorate of a church in Michigan until his death.

KNEELAND, WARREN GEORGE (1867-1943). Missionary to Central America. Born into a pioneer Seventh-day Adventist family in Michigan, he attended Battle Creek College and was given a license to preach in 1890. In 1892 he married Mary E. Benton. The next year he was ordained to the ministry and went to British Guiana to organize SDA work there. Three years later an illness in the family forced their return to the United States, where he worked two or three years in the Dakota Conference. In 1901 he went to Trinidad as superintendent of the field and pioneered the work in Tobago and Grenada. From 1907 to 1909 he was president of the Jamaica Conference. Returning to the United States, he preached in Michigan, West Virginia, and New Jersey. In 1914 he was called to the presidency of the West Caribbean Conference, and during his term of service there he led in the pioneering of Seventh-day Adventist work in Colombia. Another illness sent him home, where he assumed the pastorate of churches in the Lake Union Conference. In 1921 he went to Bahama Islands, where he stayed three years. Back in the homeland, he pastored churches in Florida, Tennessee, and Georgia until his retirement in 1941.

KNIGHT, ANNA (1874-1972). Educator, missionary nurse, Bible and departmental worker, author. As a child in Mississippi, Anna found educational opportunities for a Black child to be almost nonexistent. On Sundays she would play with some White neighbor children, and by listening to them read and spell she soon learned the basic skills. Having no paper or pencil, she practiced her writing by scratching the earth with a stick. By the time she was in her teens she had completed the common branches taught in the country schools of the time, though she had never been inside a schoolhouse.

After writing to a New England newspaper requesting that reading materials be sent to her, she received the *Signs of the Times* from a reader of that paper and was converted to the Seventh-day Adventist faith. Through the help of a conference worker in Tennessee, Anna was able to attend Mount Vernon Academy in 1894. In 1898 she graduated from Battle Creek College as a missionary nurse and returned to her home state to operate a self-supporting school in Jasper County for Black children.

In 1901 she was appointed a missionary to India, where she served six years. In 1909 she was called by the Southeastern Union to work in Atlanta. Her duties included nursing, teaching, and Bible work. When the Southeastern Conference and Southern Conference merged she served in the Educational Department until regional conferences were formed, at which time she retired.

She was the author of *Mississippi Girl,* the story of her life. At 98 years of age she was serving as president of the National Colored Teachers' Association. A few months before her death she was awarded the Medallion of

Merit Award for extraordinary meritorious service to Seventh-day Adventist education.

KNOWLTON SANITARIUM. A medical institution formerly operated at Knowlton, Quebec, some 75 miles (120 kilometers) east of Montreal, with a capacity of 20 patients. It was operated by the Quebec Conference between 1903 and 1908. Connected with it was the first Seventh-day Adventist nursing school in Canada, which graduated its first class of six students in 1905. Dr. W. H. White served as its first superintendent, from 1903 to 1906; then it was directed by a non-SDA physician, R. M. McDonald, and was eventually closed because there was no physician available who could qualify for provincial certification.

KNOX, WALTER TINGLEY (1858-1931). Administrator, General Conference treasurer. He was born in Pittsburgh, Pennsylvania. At the age of 21 he was converted and joined the Methodist Church. He became a Seventh-day Adventist in 1889 in California and almost immediately entered denominational employment. As early as 1894 he is listed as an ordained minister. From 1897 to 1900 he was president of the California Conference. At the 1901 General Conference session he was elected president of the newly organized Pacific Union Conference when it comprised all California, Nevada, Utah, Alaska, the Hawaiian Islands, and Mexico, which position he held until 1904. In 1905 and 1906 he served as president again of the California Conference (called the California-Nevada Conference in the 1905 and 1906 *Yearbooks).*

Being a keen businessperson and an able administrator, in 1909 Knox was elected to serve as treasurer of the General Conference. In this position there fell to him the responsibility of working out the details of a financial program that would provide a steady flow of means into the mission treasury for the support of a rapidly expanding work.

In 1922 his request for release from his position to undertake less strenuous work was granted. He returned to his home in Mountain View, California, and for a number of years served as chair of the board of the College of Medical Evangelists. He also was a member of the board of the Pacific Press Publishing Association.

KOBE ADVENTIST HOSPITAL (Kobe Adobenchisuto Byoin). A 116-bed medical institution situated on a four-acre (1.6-hectare) plot of land in the northern suburbs of Kobe, a thriving port city of central Japan.

Medical work began in Kobe in 1903 when a small sanitarium was operated there for six years. Shortly before World War II, a small Seventh-day Adventist hospital opened for a brief period. These modest beginnings were the forerunners of a clinic begun by E. H. Krick, M.D., in downtown Kobe in 1967 as a branch of the Tokyo Sanitarium and Hospital. This clinic has now become the Kobe Adventist Hospital and has been transferred to a more ideal location. Dedicated on Oct. 30, 1973, the hospital has made continuous growth.

In 1988 the first major building plan was completed, bringing the number of patient beds to 116. Doctors' offices, laboratory facilities, a physical therapy unit, and a patients' business office were also added.

In 1992 a second major renovation and expansion provided more space for diagnostic radiology, dietary service, and administrative offices, as well as space for the hospice service, which began on June 1, 1992.

Another unique program is a health promotion center building that provides space for various programs that promote the Seventh-day Adventist lifestyle. The building was completed in 1983, and accreditation was given as a health center from the Labor Department on Apr. 1, 1992.

Medical Directors: C. D. Johnson, 1973-1974; J. Henmi, 1974- .

KOELLING, WILHELM JOHN (1888-1963). Missionary in East Africa and in Indonesia. He was born and brought up in Hamburg, Germany, baptized in 1903 or 1904, and studied at Friedensau Missionary Seminary (1904-1907). In 1907 he worked as Bible instructor at Cassel (in the West German Union Conference) and in 1908 went to German East Africa (now Tanzania) as a missionary. He returned in 1914 and worked as a minister in Germany until 1920, when he went as a missionary to Ethiopia. In 1929 he was assigned to the Netherlands East Indies (now Indonesia), where he was in charge successively of several missions. During World War II he was interned in Sumatra and in India and afterward retired in the United States.

KOFORIDUA DAY-TEACHER TRAINING COLLEGE. *See* Ghana; Asokore Seventh-day Adventist Teacher Training College.

KOILPILLAI, V. D. (1899-1957). Teacher, evangelist, and administrator. He was born into a family that belonged to a community of Sabbathkeeping Hindu Christians in the Tinnevelly district in southern India. His father was one of the prominent leaders of the group. When in 1907 these Sabbathkeepers heard of Seventh-day Adventist missionaries in India, they invited them to visit and to work among them. Since the Hindu Christian church did not offer schooling in the English language, Koilpillai's father arranged private tuition for a group of children in the community, but when the accommodations became too small, the SDA Mission took charge of the school and moved it to a larger building. Koilpillai attended this school, then the first SDA boarding school in India, and after that the South India Training School, from which he graduated in 1917. In that year he entered denominational work as a teacher in the Prakasapuram school and from then on occupied several important positions, such as headmaster, circle leader, principal of Prakasapuram school; president of the Tamil and Malayalam fields; union Sabbath school and home missionary secretary; and South India Union field secretary. He died while in an evangelistic campaign in Tanjore.

KONIGMACHER, SAMUEL M. (1877-1952). He was born at Ephrata, Pennsylvania, of Seventh Day Baptist parents who, while Samuel was a child, joined the Seventh-day Adventist Church. After two years at South Lancaster Academy he went to Battle Creek, where he took the nurse's course. Returning to Massachusetts, he worked as a nurse at the New England Sanitarium. Here he met and married Ruth Mason, who was likewise a nurse. Together they went to Battle Creek Sanitarium, then on to St. Helena Sanitarium, where they worked until called to Africa in 1907.

Konigmacher's first field was Nyasaland (now Malawi), where for a time he worked in the Malamulo Mission. Then he and his wife were sent to pioneer the work at Matandani Mission up in the Neno Hills, some 70 miles (110 kilometers) west of Blantyre. Here they worked for about five years. During that time they lost two infant sons, James and Martin, both stricken by malaria.

From Nyasaland the Konigmachers were called to Northern Rhodesia (now Zambia), and this remained their field of labor for 25 years. After a year at Rusangu during the absence on furlough of W. H. Anderson (c. 1917), they pioneered the work at Musofu Mission, near the Congo border. Here they buried their third son. During this period Konigmacher was ordained to the ministry (c. 1921).

Early in the 1920s the Konigmachers were asked to pioneer yet a third station far up the Zambezi River in Barotseland, Zambia. To reach this mission they proceeded up the river for two weeks by riverboat. For the next 18 years Barotseland was their home. At times, particularly when the river was in flood, they found it extremely difficult to secure essential supplies. The sandy nature of the country made it necessary to walk nearly everywhere. A number of outschools were established and a firm foundation was laid for the strong work that is now conducted in Barotseland.

Failing health compelled the Konigmachers to return to America, but their one living son, Arthur, remained in Africa. Accustomed to the warmth of Africa, Konigmacher sought a mild climate, and this he found in the Hawaiian Islands, where he died.

KONOLA ACADEMY. A coeducational boarding school on the senior high school level, formerly operated at Konola, 14 miles (22 kilometers) from Kakata, Liberia. The 75-acre (30-hectare) site, granted by the government, is in the heart of the rubber-growing area of Liberia and on the main road leading into the interior. It was one of four schools above the primary level operated by the Liberia Mission. The student body included Muslims, Catholics, and members of several Protestant churches, besides Seventh-day Adventists.

Konola Academy offered (on the American pattern) a four-year college preparatory course requiring 24 units to graduate. By special arrangement students who were unable to complete the basic academic subjects could take a course in trades-apprenticeship worked out on an individual basis. This gave young Africans an opportunity to learn a trade in the atmosphere of a Christian institution. Most of the school land was under cultivation, producing rice, vegetables, citrus fruits, bananas, and oil palms.

Established in 1937 by German missionaries as a primary training school for mission workers, Konola grew into an accredited high school recognized by the denomination and the Liberian government. The first classes were held in a mud building that served as school, dormitory, dining room, and church. At first only boys were accepted. In 1948 the first cement-block structure was erected, which provided classrooms, dormitory, and dining room. In 1951 girls were admitted for the first time, and a new dormitory was erected for boys.

In 1954 a new classroom block was completed, and in 1955 a new boys' dormitory constructed, giving room for the girls in the building vacated by the boys. Boarding was introduced in 1962.

A poultry farm and livestock were added to the farm in 1964. In 1965 an electric pump and water tower were installed and a woodwork shop was built.

In 1971 the building of a new cafeteria was begun, under Principal Fred Webb. It was used for the first time in March 1974, after extensive equipment was secured through K. Lethbridge.

A permanent and impressive church was built mainly under the initiative of J. King. It was dedicated in 1974.

Through a Swedish relief organization, funds were made available for the building of a primary school on the campus in 1974 under the supervision of S. Larsson. Also in 1974 a new staff house was added to the school. The same year 1,500 books were donated to the library, negotiated for by Miss E. Eckerman.

The academic program in Konola was greatly strengthened since 1972 through student missionaries and Volunteer Service Corps workers. The Konola Academy Choir gained national recognition for its excellent performances in 1973-1974 under the leadership of Roseclaire Musson.

In 1974 Principal T. Jarry opened a rice farm for Konola Academy near the Kavalla River. A rice milling machine was installed through D. Harrison. It served both school and public, thus providing a source of income to the institution.

For years the school taught grades 1-8, but in the 1949 *Statistical Report* Konola Mission School is listed among the training schools, with nine grades; in 1951 with 10 grades. Konola Academy as a full senior academy had its first high school graduation in 1958. The first senior class to register for the national examination was that of 1961.

The following buildings were constructed after the year 1961: four new additional staff houses for overseas and African workers, including a clinic, were completed in the early 1980s under the initiative of Principal B. A. Roberts, and a modern library was erected by Principal R. D. Gibbon. The library was dedicated in January 1990.

Because of civil unrest, the school is not able to function at the present time.

Principals: K. Noltze, 1937-1941; T. N. Ketola, 1941-1942; I. W. Harding, 1942-1946; P. E. Giddings, 1946-1954; T. W. Cantrell, 1955-1958; J. D. Johnson, 1958-1962; L. C. Nielsen, 1962-1965; L. H. Berlin, 1965-1967; Fred L. Webb, 1968-1971; T. Kudar Jarry, 1972-1975; B. A. Roberts, 1976-1979; M. I. Harding, 1980-1981; Carl Jonsson, 1982-1983; R. D. Gibbon, 1984-1988; Francis Chase, 1989-1990.

KONSTRUKCJA. *See* Poland.

KOREA. A peninsula of the Asian continent, lying between the Yellow Sea and the Sea of Japan, that is divided into two political entities, the Democratic People's Republic of Korea (North Korea) and the Republic of Korea (South Korea). Numerous small adjacent islands are part of these countries. Korea's continental boundaries, which run along the Yalu and Tumen rivers, separate it from China to the northwest and Russia to the northeast. It has an area of 85,286 square miles (220,900 square kilometers), and a population of about 66 million. The people are of the Mongolian race. The Korean language belongs to the Ural-Altaic group and is similar to Japanese in its grammar, but has a distinct vocabulary. It uses a phonetic alphabet consisting of 10 vowels and 14 consonants, but employs along with its alphabet Chinese ideographs. Their religions are animism, Buddhism, Confucianism, Christianity, and Chondokyo (a mixture of the other four).

The economy of South Korea is essentially agricultural, but since 1963 the country has made tremendous industrial growth. Modern highways, industrial complexes, and modern buildings have been constructed. The standard of living has been raised considerably.

Historical Background. *National Development.* The recorded history of Korea (Chosen) dates from the first century B.C., when its people were organized into three kingdoms. The Mongols invaded the country in A.D. 1231, but withdrew a century and a third later. In the mid-seventeenth century the Chinese placed Korea into a tributary relation, but Korea did not really lose its independence until it was annexed by Japan in 1910.

During most of its history Korea was under the Chinese cultural influence and could boast of a high state of learning. Some 50 years before the invention of printing in Europe, the Koreans used movable type to print Chinese characters, and by the middle of the fifteenth century an indigenous phonetic alphabet was developed. Their contacts with the West began in the middle of the seventeenth century, but they resisted all approaches of foreigners until Japan began foreign diplomatic relations in 1876.

The United States was the first Western nation to conclude a treaty with Korea (1882). In the early years of the present century, Japan acquired control of the country, and between 1910 and 1945 Korea was a part of the Japanese Empire. During this period Japanese was the official language, and the use of Korean was discouraged. The annexation had some beneficial results in the expansion of the educational system and in the industrialization of the country.

After World War II Korea was divided along the 38th parallel into two zones of occupation, the United States occupying the south and the USSR the north. The southern and northern parts have since developed their own governments, which are mutually hostile. The Korean War, fought between 1950 and 1953, devastated the country, but failed to reunite the northern and southern parts of Korea.

Entrance of Christianity. Christian books circulated in Korea in the seventeenth century. In the eighteenth century, Korean ambassadors and merchants came in direct contact with Christianity (Catholic) in Beijing, China. Thereafter tracts on the Catholic religion were circulated and the doctrine spread rapidly. However, the social leaders resented Christianity, and in 1789 an edict of suppression was promulgated, which was enforced for three years. Thousands of Christians were tortured and killed, but the faith was not destroyed. The last great persecution came as late as 1866.

In 1832 Dr. K.F.A. Gutzlaff, a Protestant translator of the Bible into several Asian languages, visited Korean schools while serving as a surgeon and an interpreter on an English trading vessel, and distributed Chinese Bibles. In 1866 Robert J. Thomas, representing the American Bible Society in China, arrived on the American schooner *General Sherman* and tossed portions of the Chinese Scriptures and some tracts to the Koreans on the bank of the river below Pyungyang. Infuriated, the people attacked the ship, killing the crew, Thomas among them. But the Bibles he had thrown ashore were taken and read, and thus the knowledge of the gospel came to many in that area. When Korea opened her doors to the West by making treaties with the United States in 1882 and with Britain and Germany in 1883, embassies were opened in Seoul. Dr. H. N. Allen, a Presbyterian minister in China, who came in 1884 as a doctor for the embassies and for the royal court, became the first resident missionary in Korea.

In 1885 H. G. Underwood, a Presbyterian, and H. G. Appenzeller, a Methodist, from America, arrived in Korea, the first of a large number of Protestant missionaries who since that time have rendered service there. The New Testament in the Korean language had preceded them. In 1863 John Ross, a Scottish Presbyterian missionary in Mukden, Manchuria, China, had become so interested in the Korean people that he learned the Korean language, and he made the first translation of the New Testament into the Korean script. In 1882, 3,000 copies of the Gospel of Luke and 3,000 of the Gospel of John were published in Mukden; Yun Soh Sang, the first Korean Bible colporteur, brought some of these to Korea. Later 5,000 copies of the New Testament were distributed. As a result of this work, when Protestant missionaries came to northern Korea they found whole communities professing Christianity, even though they had never met a Protestant missionary.

Seventh-day Adventist Statistics. The territory of Korea constitutes the Korean Union Conference, which constitutes a part of the territory of the Far Eastern Division and is divided into five conferences and one mission. Statistics (1992) for *Korea:* churches, 537; members, 111,673; church or elementary schools, 10; ordained ministers, 304; credentialed missionaries, 153; licensed ministers, 231; teachers, 412. Headquarters for the Korean Union Conference: 66 Hoegi-dong Dongdaemun-ku, Seoul, Korea. For the territories of the missions, *see* Far Eastern Division.

Statistics (1992) for the conferences—*East Central Korean Conference:* churches, 115; members, 38,268; church or elementary schools, 4; ordained ministers, 70; licensed ministers, 54; teachers, 158. Headquarters: 232-1 Chungryang-ri-Tongdaimoon-ku, Seoul, Korea. *Middlewest Korean Conference:* churches, 106; members, 13,169; church or elementary schools, 2; ordained ministers, 42; licensed ministers, 29; teachers, 55. Headquarters: 47-8 Mok Dong, Jung-ku, Taljeon, Korea. *Southeast Korean Conference:* churches, 101; members, 15,524; church or elementary schools, 2; ordained ministers, 39; licensed ministers, 28; teachers, 35. Headquarters: 59-2 Dae Myung-dong, Nam-ku, Taegu, Korea. *Southwest Korean Conference:* churches, 69; members, 11,476; church or elementary schools, 1; ordained ministers, 29; licensed ministers, 21; teachers, 27. Headquarters: 317-38 Juwol-dong, Seo-ku, Kwangju, Korea. *West Central Korean Conference:* churches, 120; members, 32,370; church or elementary schools, 1; ordained ministers, 62; licensed ministers, 71; teachers, 55. Headquarters: 74-2 Gyunji-dong, Jongro-gu, Seoul, Korea.

Estimated figures for the *North Korean Mission:* churches, 26; members, 866.

Institutions. Donghae Academy; Hahnkook Academy; Honam Academy; Korean Publishing House; Korean Sahmyook Food; Korean Sahmyook University; Korean vocational Training Institute; Kwangchun Academy; Pusan Adventist Hospital; Seoul Academy; Seoul Adventist Hospital; Taejeon Middle School; Wonju Academy; Yungnam Academy.

Development of Seventh-day Adventist Work. *Beginnings.* The Seventh-day Adventist message was introduced into Korea shortly after the turn of the century. At this time many Koreans were emigrating to Siberia, Manchuria, Hawaii, and Mexico. One day in May 1904 a Korean, waiting for his ship to Hawaii, was walking along a street in Kobe, Japan. He was attracted by a signboard that read in Chinese characters (Korean, Japanese, and Chinese use common ideographs), "The Seventh-day Sabbath Jesus Second Coming Church."

Being a Protestant, he became interested in this new church. He met Hide Kuniya, the evangelist, and a conversation began by means of writing the Bible texts in Chinese characters. Thus they studied the Seventh-day Adventist message. The next day the Korean brought a fellow Korean to study these new doctrines. These two men soon became convinced that the SDA teachings were biblical, and the evening before the first Korean, Lee Eung Hyun, was to leave for Hawaii, the two men requested baptism. It was past midnight when the two Korean converts, escorted by a group of Japanese believers, went up to the pool below Nunobiki Falls, were baptized, and became the first Seventh-day Adventists from among the Korean people.

Lee Eung Hyun left for Hawaii, but the second man, Son Heung Cho, returned to Korea. On shipboard he met Im Ki Pan, a Korean returning from Hawaii, and imparted to him the knowledge he had gained from Hide Kuniya. Im Ki Pan accepted these truths and proposed to give them to his people. Son Heung Cho went down to Pusan, and there he began to spread the new message. Soon about 35 persons were keeping the Sabbath. Meanwhile, Im Ki Pan continued up the west coast of Korea to the port of Chinnampo, where he created a great interest among the Christian Koreans. An urgent plea, signed by 36 persons, was sent to Hide Kuniya asking him to come over to teach them the Bible more fully.

In answer to this call, Hide Kuniya arrived in Korea on Aug. 10, 1904. He soon called for F. W. Field, of Japan, to help him organize churches. They visited many interested people, baptized 71 persons, and organized four churches, at Sondol, Kangdemuro, Yongdong, and Pamegi. They discovered in all some 140 Sabbathkeepers. Four charter members at Sondol—Kim Kyu Hyuk, Kim Ye Choon, Lee Keun Ok, and Kim Suk Yung—later developed into strong church workers. In September 1904 the work in Korea was put in the charge of Im Ki Pan.

Early Mission Work. To fill the need for a resident missionary who could speak Korean, W. R. Smith from the United States arrived late in 1905, and spent that winter in Seoul studying the Korean language. In the spring of 1906 he moved to Chinnampo to be near the Seventh-day Adventist churches. In the summer he moved to Sunan, where a new group of 22 baptized church members lived.

In January 1907 Mimi Scharffenberg, another SDA missionary from the United States, arrived in Sunan. During that summer a schoolhouse was built, and in the fall Smith and Mimi Scharffenberg opened a church school for boys and also began a workers' training course in which eight men and five women enrolled. Responding to calls for a doctor and other workers, Dr. Riley Russell and his wife, C. L. Butterfield and his family, and Helen May Scott, a qualified teacher, arrived in Sunan in 1908. Dr. Russell set up his clinic in one section of the schoolhouse. Later he also took charge of the boys' school.

In the fall of 1908 I. H. Evans, of the General Conference, and F. W. Field, of Japan, visited Korea. At a council held at that time the Korean Mission was organized, with Butterfield as superintendent and Smith as secretary-treasurer. A committee was appointed to find a site for the mission headquarters, a publishing house, and a sanitarium. There were then five churches with 105 baptized members in Korea.

At first, SDA publications in Korean were printed in Japan. In 1909 an old proof press was set up in the schoolhouse in Sunan, and in that year 18,000 tracts and also some of G. H. Bell's Bible lessons and Sabbath school lessons were printed. During the summer the first colporteur went out to sell these publications to a much interested public. Also in 1909 a girls' school was opened at Chinnampo under the supervision of Mimi Scharffenberg.

In September of 1909 Butterfield and Mimi Scharffenberg moved to Seoul, where for a time the work was carried on in rented quarters outside West Gate. Several Korean workers were also moved to Seoul to assist in the publishing and evangelistic work. A Sabbath school was organized in Seoul in 1909, and later, in January 1911, a church with 31 members.

R. C. Wangerin and his wife (sister of Mimi Scharffenberg) came to Korea in October 1909, and H. A. Oberg and his wife arrived a month later. Oberg served as secretary-treasurer and publishing secretary. Howard M. Lee and his wife (sister of May Scott) arrived in Sunan, Apr. 5, 1910, to take charge of the educational work.

In August 1910 I. H. Evans, president of the Asiatic Division of the General Conference, and F. W. Field, of Japan, met with the missionaries and Korean workers for study and counsel. The group laid plans to print a missionary paper at once, of which Mimi Scharffenberg was to be editor. Also at this meeting Dr. Riley Russell was ordained, and two Koreans, Lee Keun Ok and Kim Sung Won, were added to the mission committee.

The name chosen for the monthly magazine was *Gospel for the Last Days*. When government authorities objected to this name (Korea having been annexed to Japan in August 1910), the title *Three Angels' Message* was chosen. In January 1911 all missionaries, workers, and students joined in a sales campaign that extended from Busan to Wiju and sold more than 36,000 copies. In addition, 30,000 pages of leaflets were given away. In January 1917 the name of the magazine was changed to *Shi Jo* ("Signs of the Times").

In 1911 an acre (.4 hectare) of land was purchased at Kyung San, a county seat some 10 miles (16 kilometers) south of Taegu, on which a 28-foot-square (six-meter-square) tent was pitched. Wangerin and his family lived in one part of the tent while the other half was used for evangelistic meetings conducted by Butterfield, Wangerin, and Kim Kyu Hyuk. The next May a church of 30 members was organized there. During the summer of 1911 a camp meeting was held in Chinnampo.

After much searching in the environs of Seoul, a suitable place to locate the mission headquarters was found three miles (five kilometers) outside the East Gate. At this place three mission homes, a church, the publishing house, and mission offices were erected in the summer of 1912. While the buildings were under construction, the families connected with the mission work lived there in tents. On the first Sabbath in February 1913 the mission compound was dedicated. Present was H. R. Salisbury, representing the General Conference. During the summer of 1913 new school buildings and a dispensary were erected in Sunan.

In 1915 A. G. Daniells, president of the General Conference, attended the general meeting of the mission held at Sunan, at which two Korean workers, Lee Keun Ok and Chung Mun Kuk, were ordained to the ministry. This greatly encouraged the Korean members. That same year Oberg and Wangerin were ordained at the Asiatic Division meeting in Shanghai, China.

Organization of the Conference. At the 1917 meeting of the mission, at which A. G. Daniells was present, the Chosen Conference was organized, with C. L. Butterfield as president and B. R. Owen as secretary-treasurer. Another Korean worker, Kim Kyu Hyuk, was ordained at the time of this meeting.

After Wangerin died in 1917, his wife became the secretary of the Sabbath School and Missionary Volunteer departments, and later she served as editor of the *Signs of the Times* for nearly 20 years, also of the church paper *Kyo Hoi Chi Nam.*

In 1919 the Chosen Conference became a union mission with three local units: West Chosen Conference, Central Chosen Mission, and South Chosen Mission.

A food factory was opened at the school at Sunan in 1927, with L. I. Bowers in charge. A small clinic was opened in Seoul in 1931 and plans were laid to establish a hospital there. The present Seoul Sanitarium opened its doors early in 1936 *(Review and Herald* 113:21, Sept. 24, 1936), under the direction of Dr. G. H. Rue, who came to Korea in 1929, and gave almost continuous medical missionary service at that institution until his return to the United States in 1967.

World War II. As World War II approached the Far East, the United States government advised all American missionaries to leave Korea. In response, the missionaries left in the spring of 1941, but not before organizing the Korean workers to carry on the work. In February 1943 the leaders of the church, Choi Tai Hyun (or Chae Tae Hyun), Oh Yung Sup, Kim Sang Chil, Lee Sung Eui, Pak Chang Uk, and Kim Nae Chun were arrested by the Japanese police and held in prison until the end of the year. Choi Tai Hyun died as a result of torture inflicted in prison. Two of the others, Kim Nae Chun and Lee Sung Eui, were released from prison but, their health broken, they died soon after. Lee Myung Choon died also. In all, some 40 Seventh-day Adventists were imprisoned for their faith.

Because of suppression and persecution many of the workers and members fled to the mountains. There Kim Myung Kil shepherded many of these refugees and baptized 153. Cho Kyung Chul was another stalwart shepherd. One group went into the mountain ranges of central Korea, maintaining themselves by cutting wood and selling charcoal. The Bible and the books of Ellen White that had been translated into Korean were of great comfort to them at that time.

At the close of the war, Aug. 15, 1945, the members came out of their hiding places. In October 1945 Seventh-day Adventists from all parts of Korea gathered in Seoul for a 10-day general meeting. Here they shared the joy of reunion and expressed gratitude for God's protection. They also elected temporary officers for the union mission: Im Sung Won, president; Oh Syuk Yung, secretary-treasurer; Lee Ryu Sik, departmental secretary. Afterward they set out to recover the mission properties.

The first postwar missionaries, Ralph S. Watts, who returned as president of the union mission, and his wife, came in January 1947; in April Dr. G. H. Rue, James M. Lee, and Leland Mitchell were permitted to return to aid in the restoration of the medical and educational work.

In June 1947 the South Korean and the Central Korean missions were organized and staffed with Korean workers. Im Sung Won had already been appointed director of the North Korean Mission (north of the 38th parallel) in the spring of 1946.

In 1947 Mrs. Theodora Wangerin returned to resume the editorial work; Irene Robson arrived to be the director of nurses in the Seoul Sanitarium; R. C. Mills to be secretary-treasurer of the union mission; later Dr. R. W. Pearson came to work at the Seoul Sanitarium and Hospital.

Korean War. The work was developing rapidly when on June 25, 1950, the North Koreans invaded South Korea, and the missionaries were evacuated to Japan. During the war the Christians suffered greatly. Although less than 50 Seventh-day Adventists lost their lives, many others lost all their possessions, and many churches were destroyed.

Many members who had lived in North Korea came south during the winter of 1950, thus adding to the church membership in South Korea.

Meanwhile, the missionaries who had been evacuated to Japan began active evangelism in Osaka, where there was a large Korean population, with James M. Lee and George Munson conducting evangelistic campaigns. These resulted in many baptisms, and a church building was erected in Osaka for the Korean converts. The first baptism among these Koreans took place in Kobe at the foot of Nunobiki Falls, where the first two Korean converts had been baptized in 1904.

At the Far Eastern Division Council held in February 1951, Pak Chang Uk was appointed secretary-treasurer of the union mission. In the fall of that year Clinton W. Lee returned to Korea as president of the union mission and led in the restoration of the work that had been severely disrupted by war.

Postwar Growth. In 1951 a period of rapid growth in membership began in Korea. Although there were few overseas missionaries, at times only three, and there were neither offices nor secretarial staff, the average membership gains for those years was almost 25 percent a year. With more baptisms each year and thousands of new converts joining the Sabbath schools, C. H. Davis, who in 1958 came to Korea as president of the union mission, and the Korean leaders found it impossible to provide the funds needed to build churches to house the growing congregations. Many groups met in private homes, makeshift shelters, army tents, on the open hillsides, and under trees. Humble halls were built for worship in some farming areas where the people pooled their meager resources. Congregations more than doubled in a few months. Consecrated laymen left the larger cities to carry the message to unentered areas, pagan islands, and mountain villages. Colporteurs carrying publications into every office, factory, and home surpassed previous sales records year after year.

Thousands of young men and women spent their summer and winter vacations holding evangelistic meetings and conducting Vacation Bible Schools. Ten young overseas missionaries with their families joined the Korean workers and laypersons in the effort to print more books and magazines, organize more schools, guide more young people into mission service, enlarge the medical program, broadcast more radio programs, and reach out into new fields of evangelism.

In commemoration of the seventieth anniversary of the Korean Union Mission the Korean Publishing House (Shi Jo Sa) in 1974 printed 42,000 copies of *The Great Controversy* in a one-volume paperback edition. There were approximately 100 literature evangelists selling Spirit of Prophecy books, the *Signs of the Times,* and a Korean vegetarian cookbook.

When the Voice of Prophecy Bible correspondence school started in 1948, one series of Bible lessons was offered. In 1974 five different courses were available, including a braille Bible course. Approximately 500 enrolled in the different sets of lessons each month. Since 1948, 103,488 have graduated and 11,422 have been baptized. In 1957 radiobroadcasts were begun once a week. By 1974 the Voice of Prophecy was broadcasting over 22 stations each week.

The first Koreans to serve in other fields were two nurses, Oh Hei Cha and Cho Chung Cha, who were sent to Benghazi, Libya, in 1968. In December 1968 a Korean pastor, Shin Byung Hoon, was sent to São Paulo, Brazil, to serve the São Paulo Korean Seventh-day Adventist Church. Up to March 1993 another nurse and 23 more pastors were sent overseas to serve in foreign countries. In 1982 Kim Tong Choon was elected as the secretary of the Far Eastern Division. In 1992 Chun Pyung Duk was elected as president of the division. As many as 14 Korean pastors are serving in such countries as Germany, Paraguay, Russia, Saipan, Kazakhstan, Argentina, Philippines, Singapore, Japan, and China.

Active lay workers in the Central Korean Mission and the Southwest Korean Mission have formed layperson's associations for the purpose of raising money to help lay workers become established as self-supporting lay pastors in various areas where no regular worker is located. Approximately 1 million won (US$2,500) was contributed for this each year by these groups.

English language school evangelism opened in Korea in the fall of 1969. Dean Hubbard, then ministerial secretary, led out in the opening of this new school, patterned after the one in Osaka, Japan, which was reinstituted in 1966 by M. T. Bascom.

A section of a new building near the union mission headquarters in Seoul was leased and a laboratory constructed along with a number of classrooms. This school became the largest English school in the Far Eastern Division, with nearly 1,400 students enrolled. Teachers for this school were student missionaries from colleges in North America.

By 1992 a total of 15 institutes were opened in the major cities of Korea, making a total enrollment in 1992 of 64,388 students, taught by a staff of 113 volunteers. Language institutes have proved to be a great evangelistic outreach. Not only are English, Japanese, and Russian classes offered, but also Bible classes. Continuous evangelistic meetings harvest the interests created by the work of the volunteers.

In March 1978 the Central Korean Mission was divided into two missions—East Central Korean Mission and West Central Korean Mission. This accelerated the church growth. As a result, all of the five South Korean missions became conferences in 1983.

The English language schools have proved to be a great evangelistic outreach. Not only are English classes offered but also Bible classes. Continuous evangelistic meetings in the language-school chapels harvest the interests created by the work of the student missionaries.

KOREAN COLLEGE ACADEMY. *See* Hahnkook Academy.

KOREAN INDUSTRIAL SCHOOL. *See* Korean Sahmyook University.

KOREAN PUBLISHING HOUSE (Sijosa) (Signs of the Times Publishing House; in 1965 it was renamed Korean Publishing House). A publishing organization with its own printing facilities, operated by the Korean Union Mission at Seoul, Korea. It issues Seventh-day Adventist books and the following periodicals: *Shi Jo* ("Signs of the Times"); *Kyo Hoi Chi Nam* ("Church Compass"); *Home and Health;* senior, earliteen, and primary Sabbath school lesson quarterlies; and *Sabbath School Helper.*

The publishing house was established in the spring of 1909, when a printshop was set up in one of the rooms of the three-room schoolhouse in Soonan. Its printing equipment included a George Washington handpress and a small font of type, a gift from the Japan Mission. The first publications produced there were the Sabbath school lesson quarterly and 18,000 copies of three tracts that had been translated into Korean. They were followed by G. H. Bell's *Bible Lessons,* Nos. 1 and 2 (1,000 copies of each), "Helps to Bible Study," and other Sabbath school materials. Mimi Scharffenberg was the first editor.

In the summer of 1909 the publishing house and the mission office were moved to Seoul, the capital of Korea. For a time the work was conducted there in rented quarters outside the West Gate.

Late in 1912 a permanent location for SDA institutions was found at Hoi Ki Dong, near the East Gate of Seoul. There the buildings were erected, and in January 1913 the first printing was done in the new plant. On Jan. 24, 1930, that building was burned to the ground.

A new building 63' x 81' (19 m. x 25 m.) was erected. It was occupied in April 1931 and is still in use. In this building there are six offices, two storage rooms, vault, bindery room, and the factory in which are four presses, a typecaster, and other small equipment. On Sept. 11, 1963, a new German Heidelberg giant automatic cylinder press was dedicated.

A new two-story addition to the main building was occupied in May 1966, housing offices, library, chapel, and an enlarged printing plant. New German Original Heidelberg automatic one-color offset presses were added in 1965 and 1969. In 1974 a Japanese Sha-Ken photocomposing press was installed.

The printing done is a combination of Korean script and Chinese characters. Printing is also done in English.

Quite early in the publishing work it was decided to print an eight-page monthly missionary journal. This later became known as the *Shi Jo* ("Signs of the Times"). The church paper, the *Church Compass*, was begun about 1916. More than 22 of Ellen White's books have been translated, as well as evangelistic books, church hymnals, and the *Church Manual.* In 1994 the Korean Publishing House also was printing *Home and Health* magazine, the Sabbath school lesson quarterlies, and the *Sabbath School Helper*.

In 1973 the Korean Publishing House received a certificate from the Ministry of Culture and Information of Korea in honor of *Shi Jo*, the *Signs of the Times,* the oldest continuously published magazine in Korea, in both the religious and secular field. In 1974 the Korean Publishing House published more than 40,000 copies of *The Great Controversy* in a special paperback edition.

Managers: C. L. Butterfield, 1909-1910; Kim Seung Won, 1910-1912; Frank Mills, 1912-1914; Brownie R. Owen, 1915-1917; L. I. Bowers, 1917-1923; Earl L. Woods, 1923-1927; W. E. Gillis, 1927-1928; H. A. Anderson, 1928-1929; Pak Chang Uk, 1929-1930; W. E. Gillis, 1930-1940; James M. Lee, 1940; Pak Chang Uk, 1940-1941; Kim Chang Chip, 1941-1943; dissolution; G. W. Munson, 1947-1950; Donald S. Lee, 1950; Korean War; C. A. Williams, 1952-1954; V. E. Adams, 1954-1958; Chung Tae Hyuk (acting), 1958-1959; R. L. Sheldon, 1959-1966; H. R. Kehney, 1966-1970; C. C. Lee, 1970-1971; P. W. Im (acting), 1972-1973; Han Ki Cho, 1973-1978; Chung Pyung Duk, 1978-1982; Lee Bo Duk, 1982-1992; Kim Tong Choon, 1992- .

KOREAN SAHMYOOK FOOD. A health food factory located at Panjeong-ri, Jiksan-myun, Chunan-gun, Choongchungnam-do, 50 miles (80 kilometers) from Seoul, Korea. It is operated by the administrative board of the Korean Union Conference, under the supervision of the Far Eastern Division.

Sahmyook Food Company was established in 1978, when it began producing gluten foods developed by a team at Sahmyook University Industry. This food company, as a profitable company of the legal association of Sahmyook Hakwon, has as its purpose giving financial support to the education work and providing employment for Seventh-day Adventist youth.

In 1985 other products such as soy milk, Soyalac, and Soycool were added to the industry. In late October 1992 research was completed for the Sahmyook Melon Juice that is prepared with melon juice and soy milk. In 1985 the factory developed a soy milk drink with the help of Japan Food Factory and started to sell it in the market. This made the factory grow fast, and allowed them to extend their factory building and install many different types of modern machines. The following comparative figures indicate the factory's rapid expansion between 1981 and 1993: the number of employees increased from seven to 192, and buildings from one small structure to several, including a machine shop, a boiler house, and storage rooms. In 1992 the factory produced more than 26.8 million tons (24.3 million metric tons) of soy milk, and the total sales stood at US$21.8 million. One half of all profit was used to support the Korean Union Conference.

A second factory has been added and is located in the Southwest Korean Conference. This factory will produce mainly a health ion drink. A third factory located in the Southeast Korean Conference will produce a type of instant noodles (*ramyun*) and breakfast cereals.

The union executive committee appointed Lee Bo Duk as the first manager. He devoted himself to buying land for the food factory building site in 1978. Yoon Choong Yuh, a full-time business administration director of the Korean Sahmyook University, was appointed general manager in 1981. Mr. Yoon erected a factory building and installed the various machines needed, and started to provide and sell gluten foods such as vegeburger and vegemeat. On Mar. 19, 1990, Mr. Yoon received an award from the South Korean prime minister for supporting enterprise.

General Managers: Lee Bo Duk, 1978-1981; Yoon Chung Yuk, 1981- .

KOREAN SAHMYOOK UNIVERSITY (Sahmyook Taehakkyo). A coeducational boarding institution featuring college and graduate levels, operated by the Korean Union Conference, and situated on a 200-acre (80-hectare) site on the northeastern boundary of Seoul. In 1993 university enrollment was approximately 2,700, with a full-time faculty of more than 80. More than 400 elementary and 1,300 secondary pupils attend school on the same campus.

Early History. In September 1917 a two-year ministerial course for older students was introduced to provide qualified workers for the newly established Chosen Conference. Classes in theology were taught by C. L. Butterfield, conference president, at the Chosen Industrial School in Soonan—immediately north of P'yŏngyang in North Korea—which in 1911 replaced a boys' and a girls' school established in 1907 and 1909, respectively.

After the formation of the Chosen Union Mission in 1919, with headquarters in Seoul, the Chosen Industrial School became the Chosen Union Training School. During several years in the next decade, some course work was offered beyond the twelfth-grade level, but in general the school operated on the secondary level. In the fall of 1928 Clinton W. Lee joined the faculty and developed a curriculum.

In the spring of 1931 the ministerial school was separated from the Chosen Union Training School (which appears in the *Statistical Reports* through 1936; then is replaced by the Soonan Academy in 1937, 1938), and was moved to the union mission headquarters in Seoul. Because of financial problems, however, it did not operate from the summer of 1932 until May 1937. During this interim the students and some of the workers studied correspondence courses conducted by Clinton W. Lee. The reopened school was called the Chosen Union Workers' Training Institute. The faculty was increased, and Clinton W. Lee served as principal.

When World War II forced the overseas personnel to leave Korea in 1941, the work at the training institute was carried on for a year by Principal Lee Sung Eui and other nationals. However, under pressure from the Japanese police, it closed in May 1942. Up to this point, the school had produced more than 100 graduates, many of whom became pillars of the work in Korea.

Post-World War II Period. The school, listed in the *Yearbook* as Korean Union Seminary, reopened in September 1947, with 42 students. Ralph S. Watts, Sr., was principal and Lee Ryu Sik dean. Teachers included James M. Lee, Pak Chang Uk, Leland Mitchell and his wife, Betty (née Rue).

In November 1949 the school was moved from the city to its present site, about 12 miles (20 kilometers) from downtown Seoul. When the Korean War broke out in 1950, students were scattered and many of the buildings under construction were damaged or destroyed. In November 1951 the school, called Korean Union Training School, opened with about 40 students. Because of the damage to the buildings, some classes were conducted in the open air. Students bathed and washed their clothes in a creek that flowed through the school property. Secondary work, which had been offered by the Seoul Junior Training Institute—a secondary school established in the late 1930s—was now combined with seminary work on one campus.

Post-Korean War Period. In 1954 the school received a government permit to operate a college. During the ensuing years there was peaceful growth, and college industries prospered. Leading educators in Korea looked to the Adventist educational system as a pattern.

In February 1961 the Korean Ministry of

Education gave Korean Union College a permit to operate as a four-year theological college and to grant degrees at the bachelor's level. In 1962 the government approved the addition of an industrial junior college, specializing in agriculture for young men and home economics for young women. In 1964 the General Conference Educational Department recognized the school as a four-year senior college.

In 1966 *theological* was dropped from the Korean name of the college, and it began operation as a liberal arts school, with home economics and agriculture departments added to the curriculum. Also in 1966 the junior college was closed, and from 1968 an English major was offered. In 1973 a two-year industrial school on the junior college level was begun with George Haley as principal. Courses in dairy science and food and nutrition were offered. In that same year the government granted permission for the college to begin a four-year baccalaureate nursing course, which was implemented in 1974.

In 1975 the higher educational institutions in the Korean Union Mission were united under an integrated board of management, administration, and faculty, and began to operate as a university under one school system. The Graduate School was established in 1981.

Korean Sahmyook University in 1993. The university offers an Associate of Arts degree in dairy science, food technology, office automation, early childhood education, applied music, auto maintenance, and tourism English language interpretation. The senior college offers baccalaureate degrees in theology, English language and literature, business administration, music education, nutrition, chemistry, biology, horticulture, dairy farming resources, nursing, pharmacy, and rehabilitation therapy.

The Graduate School features the master's program in theology, religious education, pharmacy, and chemistry, and a doctorate (Ph.D.) in theology. The Theological Seminary, which started in 1990, offers an M.A. in theology for ministers. The School of Lifelong Learning—offering adult and continuing education courses—is a recent addition to the university curricula. The E. G. White-SDA Research Center and Northern Missionary College, and the extension school on the Sakhalin Island (Russia) are also newly inaugurated features of the university.

The college foods industry, begun in 1955 under the direction of Lee Mitchell, for many years supplied dairy products and garden produce to the Eighth U.S. Army and the Seoul foreign community. Dairy products are delivered daily to 90 distribution points throughout the Seoul area. In addition to the university's off-campus dairy farms and rice properties, vineyards, orchards, and garden areas are features of the main campus.

Principals and Presidents: Howard M. Lee, 1917-1920; J. E. Riffel, 1920-1924; Howard M. Lee, 1924-1937; Lee Kyung Il, 1937-1938; Clinton W. Lee, 1938-1940; Lee Sung Eui, 1940-1941; Chai Tai Hyun, 1941-1942; R. S. Watts, 1947-1949; James M. Lee, 1949-1953; Chung Tong Shim, 1953-1954; Donald S. Lee, 1954-1960; Tate V. Zytkoskee, 1960-1965; Rudy Klimes, 1965-1969; Kim Chong Wha, 1969-1973; Song Kwon, 1973-1974; Lee Key Ton, 1975-1976; Kim Chong Wha, 1977-1990; Kim Hong Ryang, 1990- .

KOREAN UNION COLLEGE. *See* Korean Sahmyook University.

KOREAN UNION CONFERENCE. *See* Far Eastern Division; Korea.

KOREAN UNION WORKERS' TRAINING INSTITUTE. *See* Korean Sahmyook University.

KOREAN VOCATIONAL TRAINING INSTITUTE (Sahmyook Gisul Hak-won). A coeducational boarding institution on the senior high school level, operated by the Korean Union Conference at Seoul, Korea. The institute was founded in July 1970 at Yungnam Academy at Kyongsan near Taegu, a provincial capital between Seoul and Pusan, Korea.

In 1968 the vocational training center opened in Yungnam Academy to the many students who had not gone on to college. As the program was successful, it was opened to the students of all the seven academies in Korea and had a new start as a vocational training institute under the direction of the Korean Union Conference. The Korean Vocational Training Institute was founded in 1979 with the help of $10,000, the overflow offering of one of the Thirteenth Sabbath offerings in 1979. In 1984 the institute was moved from Kyongsan to Seoul.

Korean Vocational Training Institute welcomes all junior high school graduates. Normal graduation requires three years' attendance. A work program enables students to provide for their tuition and living expenses. The curriculum offers mechanical engineering, electronical engineering, construction and computer programming. Students receive a national technician's license, approved by the government, and a certificate of credit that is comparable to that of a senior high school diploma.

Directors: Yoon Ok Jin, 1970-1973; Jo Sung Ki, 1974- .

KOSENA (GOSHEN) COLLEGE. *See* Samoa Adventist College.

KOSOVO. *See* Yugoslavia.

KOTTARAKARA SEVENTH-DAY ADVENTIST HIGH SCHOOL. *See* Seventh-day Adventist Higher Secondary School (Kottarakara).

KOTTAWA HIGH SCHOOL. *See* Lakpahana Adventist College and Seminary.

KOTZ, SIEGFRIED ARTHUR (1915-1967). Physician, medical administrator, and secretary. He was born in Africa of missionary parents and his childhood years were spent there and in Switzerland and Germany. When he was 10 the family moved to the United States, where the influence of denominational schools led him to Loma Linda University, from which he graduated as an M.D. in 1940. He was in general practice in Maryland for several years and served on the staff of the Washington Sanitarium and Hospital. Then he and his wife, the former Ethel Carr, and their children left for Africa, where he served at the Malamulo Hospital and Leprosarium at Malawi and then at Kendu Hospital at Kendu Bay, Kenya. During this time he was ordained to the ministry. In 1961 the family returned to the United States, where he earned a master's degree in public health from Yale University. In 1963 he was called as medical secretary for the Australasian Division.

KOWLOON SAM YUK SECONDARY SCHOOL. A coeducational day school on the senior high school level, situated in Kowloon, on the mainland across the strait from the island of Hong Kong, and operated by the Hong Kong-Macao Conference.

Kowloon Sam Yuk Secondary School began as a kindergarten and primary school in 1937 when many refugees, including numerous Seventh-day Adventists, poured into Hong Kong at the outbreak of the Sino-Japanese War. To meet the need for educating the children, a church school, sponsored by the local Mongkok church, was opened on the second floor of a rented house at 13 Fa Yuen Street, Kowloon. S. S. Ha, the first teacher, taught primary 1 to 4. By the time of the Japanese invasion of Hong Kong, December 1941, which resulted in the closing of the school, instruction had expanded to primary 6. K. C. Lo was the teacher at that time.

When a new chapel was built at 52 Boundary Street, Kowloon, in 1950 to replace the former building at Tung Choi Street, plans were laid by W. P. Chung, the pastor, and his members to restore the school. As a result of liberal contributions for furniture and equipment, school opened Feb. 12, 1951, with 76 pupils and five teachers in three classrooms. The next year enrollment grew to 182, and each succeeding year saw an increase in the number of students.

With more room in a five-story building, completed in 1956 with funds received mainly from Ingathering solicitation, the school was upgraded to the junior middleschool level (seventh grade) and the enrollment rose to 542.

In 1961, by permission of the Far Eastern Division, the school was upgraded to senior middle level (tenth grade).

In 1967, to meet the need for education in English by the community, the school began to operate an Anglo-Chinese section, using English as the teaching medium. Students may choose to study in either of these two sections.

In 1978 the Hong Kong government introduced the nine-year compulsory education program, which made it necessary to buy places in local private schools. Sam Yuk participated in the program. The project to develop the north wing of the school building for the primary church school was launched. In 1983 Sam Yuk became a "Caput" school, which enabled school facilities and staff salaries to be upgraded.

A new building was completed in 1988. In 1989 the school was officially named Kowloon Sam Yuk Secondary School. Further improvements have been made. For more efficient administration the Chinese secondary section ended in September 1991. The summer of 1992 saw the opening of form 6 (twelfth grade) and in 1993 form 7 opened to prepare students for tertiary education.

In 1993 there were 191 students enrolled. A total of 20 classes were looked after by a 39-member teaching staff, 19 of whom are Seventh-day Adventists. The school always has been and remains a strong evangelizing agency for winning souls. More than 688 students have been baptized.

Principals: Lo Hing So, 1960-1981; Tang Chung Huen, 1981-1987; Liang Wai Hong, 1987-1989; Mrs. Doris Foo, 1989- .

KOZA ADVENTIST HOSPITAL (Hôpital Adventiste de Koza). A 140-bed general hospital owned and operated by the Central African Union Mission at Koza, Cameroon, near the northern tip of the republic. Nestled in the mountains, it is 680 miles (1,100 kilometers) by air from the Guinea Gulf coast, and 160 miles (260 kilometers) south of Lake Chad, in the most densely populated area.

Seventh-day Adventist mission work at Koza was begun in 1949 by R. Bergstrom, from Sweden. A Thirteenth Sabbath Offering overflow in 1950 helped to provide funds for a hospital, although construction was delayed several years. Dr. F. W. Brennwald and his wife, who arrived in August 1953, conducted their medical work under the trees for some months, and then continued it in a temporary dispensary. In the summer of 1955 they had an eight-room dispensary with operating room, obstetrical unit, and pharmacy. A. Bodenmann, a Swiss missionary-builder, did most of the permanent construction. Dr. A. R. Bergman and his wife worked on the staff from December 1955 to 1961. Nurses were drawn from France, Switzerland, Germany, and Austria. Besides the doctor there are usually two European nurses.

In 1974 a new maternity ward with 12 beds and a surgical unit was inaugurated. These very modern additions are contributing to more efficient medical care. Thanks to this institution, the work of evangelism in northern Cameroon is progressing in spite of the strong Muslim influence.

Medical Directors: F. W. Brennwald, 1955-1964; W. E. Westcott, 1965-1968; Marc Kanor, 1968-1970; A. E. Boyce, 1970-1971; Ewald Axt, 1971-1974; Kohlia Stéveny, 1972-1981; Alain Tieche, 1981-1983; Eric Davy, 1986-1987; Paul Gheorghe, 1987-1991; Sergio Maldonado, 1991-1992; Meguille Daniel, 1992-1993; Sergio Maldonado, 1993- .

KRANKENHAUS WALDFRIEDE. *See* Berlin Hospital.

KRANZ, ALFRED F. JOHN (1900-1993). Born in South Australia, he studied at Adelaide University, Avondale College, and the Seventh-day Adventist Theological Seminary, where he earned his master's in theology in 1948.

He taught at the Adelaide Adventist School in 1921 and spent the following year in evangelism. He returned to teaching for two years in the North New Zealand Conference, and then served as preceptor and Bible teacher in New Zealand Mission College from 1923 to 1929. He was called to Avondale College as Bible teacher from 1930-1939 and then became principal of Western Australian Missionary College for six years. After his retirement in 1965 he continued to serve at that school for a number of years in a voluntary capacity.

KRESS, DANIEL HARTMAN (1862-1956) and **LAURETTA (EBY)** (1863-1955). Physicians. Kress was born in Ontario, Canada, and Lauretta in Michigan. They married in 1884, took their medical training together in the University of Michigan, and graduated in 1894. They had three children and adopted and educated 11 others. Before becoming a Seventh-day Adventist (1887), Daniel Kress had been a Baptist minister in Michigan.

After a period of service at the Battle Creek Sanitarium, the Kresses went to England in 1898 to establish Seventh-day Adventist medical work there. The first year they gave lectures, began health schools, and started a magazine called *Life and Health,* which was published for nearly a year. Appointed to Australia in 1900, they laid the foundation for a strong medical work there. After working in New Zealand for a time, they returned to Australia, and in 1907 to America. Daniel Kress became the first medical superintendent of the newly established Washington Sanitarium and Hospital; his wife was staff physician.

Daniel Kress specialized in health education and internal medicine, and from the time of his conversion was an ardent crusader against tobacco. In 1947 the Kress Memorial Foundation was set up in Washington, D.C., to promote research in narcotics.

In 1939 the Kresses intended to retire, but were called into service for a time as staff physicians at the Florida Sanitarium and Hospital. They wrote an autobiography entitled *Under the Guiding Hand* (1941).

KRESSVILLE HOMES FOR THE AGED. *See* Adventist Retirement Village, Inc.

KRIEGHOFF, CARLOS ENRIQUE (1870-1969). Pioneer worker in South America. Krieghoff was born in Switzerland and at the age of 15 emigrated to Chile with his family. After reading the book *Daniel and the Revelation,* he accepted the Seventh-day Adventist faith and was baptized in 1897. In 1902 he and his wife gave 45 acres (18 hectares) of land for the building of a school in Pua, Chile. The school began operation in 1906, and by the next year a building was erected with a capacity of 100 students. Krieghoff was the carpenter-builder, and also the first president of this training school, which eventually became Chile College.

In 1908 he was called as secretary-treasurer of the Chile Conference. After his ordination in 1912, he again served as president of the school in Pua until 1916 when he was assigned the work of secretary-treasurer for the newly formed Argentine Conference. Following this he was appointed superintendent of the Uruguay Mission and in later years he was secretary-treasurer of the Central Argentine Conference. In 1937 he retired in Argentina, in the city of Rosario, where he served as elder of the Central church for 12 years.

KRUM, JOHN HARRY (1866-1949). Minister, pioneer Seventh-day Adventist missionary to Palestine. He was born at Reamstown, Lancaster County, Pennsylvania. He joined the Seventh-day Adventist Church in 1890, and through his efforts a sister and her husband became SDAs. The following year he became a colporteur. During 1892-1893 he attended Union College, Lincoln, Nebraska. In December 1893 he was sent to Germany, where, following one year's training at Hamburg, he conducted evangelistic meetings in Berlin and other cities. One of his converts, Leontine Hulda Michaeli, became his bride in 1897.

In 1898 he was asked to pioneer the work of Seventh-day Adventists in Palestine, as the first European SDA worker sent to the Holy Land. At first he sold publications to settlers in German colonies at Jaffa and other cities. Later, employing the medical knowledge acquired from a two-year course at Baltimore Medical College, Baltimore, Maryland, five years of experience as a pharmacist, and a special course in hydrotherapy and electrical treatments taken at the Basel Sanitarium, Switzerland, he opened medical missions in Jaffa and Jerusalem, the mission in the latter city continuing for 14 years. He worked in both Palestine and Syria (the Lebanon area).

He endeavored to carry the SDA message also to the Armenians, Greeks, and Turks of Asia Minor, where he traveled extensively, working where the apostle Paul had labored, and experiencing similar dangers and narrow escapes. Despite persecution and prejudice, he won a number of converts before his health forced him to return to America in June 1904.

Subsequently he worked as a pastor in many states, among them Pennsylvania, Oklahoma, Texas, Arkansas, Tennessee, Ohio, and Florida, where he spent the last 25 years of his long term of denominational service.

KRUMM, WILHELM (c. 1861-1932). Business leader. In 1894 his wife joined the Seventh-day Adventist Church, and a few years afterward he followed her. In 1901 he gave up a profitable business to manage the business of the Friedensau institutions *(see* Friedensau Theological Graduate School). He stayed there until the school was closed at the onset of World War I in 1914. He then assumed leadership of the SDA Hamburg food factory, Nährmittelfabrik des Deutschen Vereins für Gesundheitspflege *(see* German Health Food Factory). In 1920 he returned to Friedensau and managed the affairs of one or another of its institutions until a stroke incapacitated him in 1929. He also managed an old people's home, and served as elder of the local congregation and as a member of conference and union committees.

KUCERA, LOUIS FRANK (1877-1959). The first Seventh-day Adventist Czechoslovakian colporteur in the United States through whose efforts the work among the Czechs and Slovaks of North America began. He was born in Czechoslovakia. About 1906, when in the New York area, he was given a German pamphlet entitled "Which Day and Why?" As a result of reading it he began to keep the seventh-day Sabbath. Later, he had three SDA tracts translated and printed for distribution among the Czech- and Slovak-speaking people. From 1909 to 1913 he looked after a Czechoslovak church in the New York area, then worked as a colporteur for two years and later took charge of a Czechoslovak church in Chicago. In 1919 he joined the international branch of the Pacific Press Publishing Association at Brookfield, Illinois, as a linotype operator for the Slavic languages, and continued with this work until he retired in 1948.

KUHN, MAY GILMAN COLE (1882-1964). Poet, missionary, teacher. A native of Massachusetts, she graduated from South Lancaster Academy in 1903 and became principal of a nine-grade school in Brooklyn, which later developed into an academy. She later received her B.A. degree from Washington Missionary College and her M.A. from the University of Southern California. She taught at Washington Missionary College, Union College, Emmanuel Missionary College, La Sierra College, Shanghai Missionary College, and the Home Study Institute. In 1909 she became educational secretary for the Atlantic Union Conference and then taught for a time in the Bermuda Islands. After returning to the United States, she studied nursing. In 1911 she married Pastor Otto B. Kuhn, and in 1916 they went to China, where they served until 1937. After returning home, she taught for a time at Loma Linda Academy. She was the author of several books, a number of articles, and many poems.

KUNIYA, HIDE (1872-1962). Pioneer Japanese Seventh-day Adventist minister, first Japanese to be baptized in Japan. During the Sino-Japanese War he was with the paymaster corps of the Japanese Army in China and there met Christians. Upon his return to Japan he met Japanese Christians, and one of them invited him to read tracts published by the first Seventh-day Adventist missionaries in that country. Later he met these missionaries, attended their Bible school in Tokyo, and joined the SDA Church in 1899. Soon thereafter, he took up the colporteur work and began to preach. In 1904 he was instrumental in introducing the Seventh-day Adventist work into Korea. In 1907 he was ordained. For 61 years he served the church as colporteur, pastor, editor, or mission director. After his retirement he was largely responsible for establishing two churches in Tokyo.

KUNZ, AUGUST (d. 1906). Teacher and editor. He was born in Germany and came to America about 1867. His name appears in the bulletin of Battle Creek College in 1879, and so far as is known he taught Hebrew and New Testament Greek until 1881. In this capacity, he taught Uriah Smith, C. C. Lewis, and L. R. Conradi. Later he taught German and Greek language and literature. He taught at Battle Creek until 1887 or 1888, and apparently at the same time carried on German language missionary correspondence for the General Conference, because Gerhard Perk, one of the earliest Seventh-day Adventists in Russia, reported in 1909 that he had correspondence with Kunz in 1882 and that it was Kunz who sent out German publications from the United States. His name first appeared in the *Yearbook* (listed as a licentiate) in 1883.

Late in 1887 or early in 1888 he went to Europe (the fifth European Council held in June 1888 passed a resolution that Kunz continue in the German work in Europe). Later, notations in the *Yearbooks* indicate that besides serving as a secretary of the German Department of the Central European Conference he was engaged in editorial work. He translated into German several books, such as Ellen White's *Great Controversy* and *Steps to Christ,* and Uriah Smith's *Daniel and the Revelation.* In 1892 and 1893 he is listed as a teacher at Battle Creek College. From 1892 to 1894 he was one of the editors at the Central Seventh-day Adventist Publishing Association (Review and Herald) at Battle Creek.

About 1895 he joined the faculty of Keene Academy and taught there for about seven years. From 1904 to 1906 he taught at Union College, laying down his work only in the last stages of cardiac illness.

KURBADET (Oslo Health Home). A 25-bed clinic and hospital formerly operated in Oslo, Norway, by the West Nordic Union. The institution conducted a department for outpatients and employed one medical doctor who was a specialist in rheumatism, 10 physiotherapists, and 28 other workers. During 1974 Kurbadet's vegetarian restaurant was enlarged, and it served more than 200 meals a day.

Seventh-day Adventist health work in Oslo began July 4, 1898, when a clinic was opened by two graduates of Battle Creek Sanitarium, Alma Andersen and her sister, Emma Fleischer. They were followed in 1900 by O.J.O. Røst, who was trained at St. Helena Sanitarium, California, and later by managers C. M. Scott, Chr. Tobiassen, Bjarne Røst, Ola Stavdahl, and Arne Dyresen. (For a number of years the institution was listed in the *Yearbook* as Christiania Health Home.)

Kurbadet ceased operation in 1992.

KUWAIT. A small Arab state located on the northwest coast of the Persian Gulf between Iraq and Saudi Arabia, with an area of about 6,200 square miles (16,100 square kilometers) and a population (1994) of 1.8 million.

Its people are Arabs, but Indians and non-Kuwaiti Arabs are employed in large numbers. The oil fields employ several thousand Europeans and Americans. The official religion is Islam, with about three fourths of the population being Sunni and the rest Shia.

In 1963 there were two Sabbath schools in Kuwait, one at Kuwait, the capital, and another at Ahmadi. A church meeting hall was rented in 1964 and work there officially opened. The first baptism in Kuwait was conducted early in 1965 at a cove near Fahahil. Three were baptized.

The work in Kuwait has been carried on principally through student literature evangelism in the selling of health books, Ingathering solicitation, and temperance work in the showing of films and conducting of stop-smoking plans. Kuwait's church was organized in 1979. In 1983 the church was attached to the Middle East Union. In 1985 Kuwait was added to the East Mediterranean Field. By 1988 the membership was 188. Most of the constituency are Indians and Filipinos, with some Middle Easterners.

In the middle of 1988 the Gulf Section was organized, and Kuwait became a part of it.

KUYERA ADVENTIST ACADEMY. A coeducational boarding school located in Kuyera, Ethiopia. It was established in 1950 and reestablished in 1992. In 1994 there was a faculty and staff of 25.

Presidents: Jerrell Fink, 1992- .

KWAHU HOSPITAL. A general acute hospital of 140-bed capacity, operated by the West African Union Mission until it was nationalized by the government of Ghana on Sept. 16, 1974. It was situated near Mpraeso, Ghana, and was built with funds donated by the Ghana government, whose officials felt at that time that the Seventh-day Adventists could run a hospital efficiently and could give the nurses a moral as well as a medical training. The hospital, which was of pavilion-type construction, had separate units for male and female patients, a pediatrics ward, and a 50-bed obstetrical wing with 38 bassinets. It had facilities for medical and surgical cases, an X-ray Department, and a Department of Physiotherapy, and operated a School of Nursing and a School of Midwifery. The total capital investment in the institution was approximately $1 million. It served a population of about 50,000.

The hospital was opened in 1955, and Dr. J. Ashford Hyde, who was transferred from the Jengre Hospital, Nigeria, became its first medical director. L. Acton-Hubbard, also from Jengre, was director of nursing services, and Amy Horder was director of the School of Nursing. In 1961 the first business manager, B. J. Powell, came from England.

The School of Nursing, which operated from the founding of the hospital, was accredited by the Nursing Council of Ghana from its inception. The School of Midwifery was accredited by the Midwives' Council of Ghana in 1962.

Medical Directors: J. Ashford Hyde, 1955-1963; John Lennox, 1963-1970; R. E. Krum, 1970-1971; C.L.O. Allen (acting), 1971-1972; R. W. Royer, 1972-1973; S. A. Nagel, Jr., 1973-1974.

KWANGCHUN ACADEMY (Kwangchun Sahmyook Joongkodeung Hakkyo). A coeducational boarding school on the secondary level operated by the Middlewest Korean Conference at Kwangchun, Korea.

The school was established in 1954 as a junior academy. In 1964 it became a senior academy. Buildings include an administration building, auditorium, dining hall, two dormitories, and seven faculty homes.

Principals: Son Jae Rin, 1954-1955; Kim Hyung Rak, 1955-1956; Im Kyung Bum, 1956-1959; Hong Hyun So, 1959-1961; Kim Pyung Kook, 1961-1967; Choi Myung Hwan, 1967; Kim Seung Oh, 1967-1968; Kim Yung Do, 1968-1972; Lee Sung Jin, 1972-1978; Shin Seung Uk, 1978-1984; Kim Byeong Kuk, 1984-1987; Kim Hyo Sung, 1987-1989; Lim Chun Taiki, 1989- .

KYOHOI CHINAM. *See Church Compass.*

KYRGYZSTAN. A republic that occupies a land area of 76,642 square miles (198,500 square kilometers). Its neighbors include China, Uzbekistan, Tajikistan, and Kazakhstan. The population (1994) is 4.7 million.

The region was inhabited around the thirteenth century by the Kirghiz. It was annexed to Russia in 1864. After 1917 it was nominally an autonomous area that was reorganized in 1926 and made a constituent republic of the USSR in 1936. Kyrgyzstan declared independence on Aug. 31, 1991. It became an independent state when the Soviet Union disbanded on Dec. 25, 1991.

Kyrgyzstan comprises a part of the Southern Union Conference, in the Euro-Asia Division.

In 1993 there were 10 Seventh-day Adventist churches in Kyrgyzstan, with a membership of 667.

L

LABRADOR. *See* Seventh-day Adventist Church in Newfoundland and Labrador.

LACEY, HERBERT CAMDEN (1871-1950). Educator. Born in England, he moved with his family to India, and when 11, to Tasmania, where his family accepted the Seventh-day Adventist faith in 1887.

Coming to the United States, he graduated from Healdsburg College in 1892, then finished the classical course at Battle Creek College. After marrying Lillian Yarnell in 1895, he joined the first faculty of what is now Avondale College, where he taught Bible and Greek, and engaged in summer evangelism.

Returning to Healdsburg College, he taught Bible and ancient languages (1902-1904); then he became head of the Bible and Greek departments (1904-1913), and also president (1907-1913), of Stanborough Park Missionary College, which was to become Newbold College, England.

He taught Bible and biblical languages at Union College (1913-1918) and at what is now Columbia Union College (1918-1920), and then spent 15 months assisting in holding conventions in the Far East. Later he was pastor of churches in New York City and in southern California. For a time he was also professor of biblical exegesis at what is now Loma Linda University.

LACUNZA, MANUEL DE (1731-1801). A Jesuit of Chile and Italy, writer on the prophecies. Born in Santiago, he was admitted to probation in the Jesuit Order in his youth, became celebrated locally as a preacher, and took his vows in 1766. But in 1767 he was expelled from Chile, with all other Jesuits, when the order was suppressed in the Spanish dominions. Going first to Cádiz, Spain, and then settling at Imola, near Bologna, in central Italy, he began to study the Church Fathers and then the biblical prophecies, reading all the commentaries he could find. In 1779 he devoted himself solely to the study of the Scriptures.

The fruit of 20 years' study was his *La Venida del Mesías en Gloria y Magestad* ("The Coming of the Messiah in Glory and Majesty"), written in Spanish about 1791 under the pen name of Juan Josafa Ben-Ezra, supposedly a Christian Hebrew. The book emphasized the Second Advent at the beginning of the millennium.

There were no printed editions of his treatise before his death, but it soon became popular in manuscript form and was circulated in Spain and all the way "from Havana to Cape Horn."

The book was first printed in 1810 or 1811 near Cádiz, the printing being done secretly. It was subsequently printed in Spain in 1812, in London in 1816 (at the expense of General Belgrano, of Argentina), in Mexico in 1821-1822, in Paris in 1825, and again in London in 1826. Prominent Catholic writers either attacked or defended the work. In 1824 it was placed on the Index of Prohibited Books because Lacunza had exalted Scriptures above tradition, had taught that the antichrist was not an individual, had not acceptably venerated Catholic exposition, and had invited criticism by writing in the vernacular. In 1827 Edward Irving issued a two-volume English translation in London, as a result of which the book became well known in Britain.

Lacunza helped to turn the attention of many to the second advent of Christ. In this sense, he was regarded as a forerunner of William Miller. However, his interpretations of prophecies differed from Miller's on many points, and his futurism influenced the trend of British premillennialism into modern futurist dispensationalism.

LAKE GENEVA SANITARIUM (Clinique La Lignière). A 98-bed medical, dietetic, and physiotherapeutic institution held by the Société Philanthropique de "La Lignière," Inc., Gland, Vaud, Switzerland, and operated by the Euro-Africa Division. There are four full-time physicians employed by the institution, including the medical director. The total number of employees is about 84. The yearly gross income is in the neighborhood of $6.5 million.

The institution was established in Basel in 1895 in the building vacated when the printing plant was closed because of the enforcement of Sunday laws, and was called the Institut Sanitaire (also listed as Basel Sanitarium). P. A. De Forest, M.D., a Canadian who had studied at Battle Creek, arrived with his wife and two little daughters in August 1895, and opened the institution at the beginning of 1896. Operating with the sanitarium was a school of nursing, training both men and women.

In 1904 a property of 90 acres (35 hectares) was purchased on the shores of Lake Geneva in La Lignière, Gland, Vaud, halfway between Lausanne and Geneva. Some of the buildings on the property were quickly adapted to meet immediate needs, and it was possible to move the medical institution and the school of nursing from Basel to Gland in June 1905. Dr. De Forest continued in charge, but since he was a foreigner without a Swiss diploma, a Swiss physician was legally responsible. The institution in Gland took the name Sanatorium du Léman (Lake Geneva Sanitarium). A large addition was erected in 1911 for treatment rooms. During World War I an operating room was added under the supervision of Dr. L. E. Conradi. There have been other expansions through the years. The equipment has been constantly improved in keeping with modern requirements. There is no longer a surgical section or nursing school.

A new wing was opened in 1955 and another in 1968. Reconstruction of the original building and the main entrance was completed in 1972. In 1962 a new chapel was dedicated. The nurses' home was completed two years later. During the years apartment houses have been constructed to house staff members. In 1978 the first cardiovascular rehabilitation center of French-speaking Switzerland was established. In the 1980s the building was substantially renovated.

Adjacent to the sanitarium, a horticultural unit and a farm provide flowers, vegetables, and fruit for the well-being of the patients.

Business Managers: Henri Révilly, 1895-1906; Charles Reihlen, 1906-1908; Jules Robert, 1908-1926; Vital Monnier, 1926-1935; Robert Gerber, 1935-1939; Dr. H. Müller, 1939-1949; Charles Wehrli, 1949-1955; A. G. Roth, 1955-1962; Sylvain Meyer, 1962-1974; Paul Traphagen, 1975-1980; Adolf Kinder, 1981-1989; Dr. Eric Davy, 1989- .

Medical Directors: P. A. De Forest, 1895-1924; Hermann Müller, 1924-1964; F. W. Brennwald, 1964-1973; C. P. Jaggi, 1974-1986; Marie-Therese David, 1986- .

LAKE GROVE MISSION SCHOOL. *See* Native Americans.

LAKE PLACID MEDICAL CENTER. *See* Walker Memorial Medical Center.

LAKE REGION CONFERENCE. A unit of church organization comprising the territory of Indiana, Illinois, Michigan, Minnesota, and Wisconsin, composed largely of the Black and Hispanic congregations of this area. Statistics (1993): churches, 83; members, 21,397; church schools, 8; ordained ministers, 43; licensed ministers, 8; Bible instructors, 4; teachers, 47. Headquarters: 8517 South State Street, Chicago, Illinois 60619. The conference forms part of the Lake Union Conference.

Institutions. Chicago Seventh-day Adventist Academy (formerly Shiloh Academy), Peterson-Warren Academy (formerly F. L. Peterson School).

Local churches—*Illinois:* Champaign (Park Avenue), Chicago (African, Altgeld Gardens, Beacon of Joy, Bethlehem French, Hyde Park, Independence Boulevard, Logan Square, Morgan Park, New Life, Roscoe Village Spanish, Shiloh, Sion French, South Shore Spanish, Spanish Northwest, Straford Memorial), Chicago Heights (Emmanuel), Danville (Gethsemane), Decatur (Lebanon), Downers Grove (All Nations Fellowship), East St. Louis (New Jerusalem), Evanston (First, Nouvelle Jerusalem), Harrisburg (Emmanuel), Maywood (Maywood Community), Hopkins Park (Ephesus), Peoria (Mt. Sinai), Robbins, Springfield (SDA Bible Chapel), Waukegan (Shalem, Waukegan Spanish); *Indiana:* East Chicago (Bethel), Elkhart (Bethany Chapel), Evansville (Metropolitan), Fort Wayne (Body of Christ), Gary (Brunswick Heights, Mizpah), Indianapolis (Capitol City, Eastside, Haughville, Korean), Jeffersonville (Harrison Avenue), Marion (Ephesus), Michigan City (Voice of Hope), Muncie (Philadelphia), Newbergh, South Bend (Berean, Iglesia Hispana Adventista), Terre Haute (Mount of Olives); *Michigan:* Battle Creek (Berean), Belleville (Belleville Heights), Benton Harbor (Highland Avenue), Berrien Springs (All Nations), Cassopolis (Calvin Center), Detroit (Burns, City Temple, Conant Gardens, Detroit Center, Maranatha), Dowagiac (Faith), Ecorse, Flint (Fairhaven), Grand Rapids (Bethel), Idlewild, Ikster (Sharon), Jackson (Summit), Kalamazoo (Trinity Temple), Lansing (Bethel), Maybee (London), Mt. Clemens

(Cornelius), Muskegon Heights (Wood Street), Niles (Philadelphia), Pontiac (Southside), Saginaw (Ephesus), Southfield, Ypsilanti; *Minnesota:* Minneapolis (Glendale), St. Paul (Sharon); *Wisconsin:* Milwaukee (Sharon, Milwaukee Spanish).

History. *Beginnings of the Work Among Blacks in the Area.* At the time of the Civil War most Seventh-day Adventists lived in the North and for the most part were strongly against slavery. In SDA evangelism Black converts were brought into the churches with the Whites, and separate congregations were not at first formed. In churches where the Black membership was relatively small there was no inclination to form separate congregations, but Black churches were organized in some of the large cities.

In Chicago in 1905 a group of Blacks, members of the Southside church, organized a neighborhood church, with J. R. Buster, a literature evangelist, as W. D. Forde, who was made pastor in February 1910, recalls finding the group meeting in a rented store building on State Street, near Root Street. Later the congregation, which continued to grow, purchased a building on Dearborn Street, then in 1918 moved to larger quarters on Prairie Avenue. During these years several successful tent meetings were conducted. When a new church was built in 1925 on the site of G. E. Peters' evangelistic meetings, the congregation took the name Shiloh Seventh-day Adventist Church. With a membership nearing 500, the church was the largest in the Chicago Conference. M. G. Nunez, Herbert D. Greene, O. A. Troy, Harry E. Ford, T. H. Allison, Samuel Meyers, and H. W. Kibble are some of the workers who contributed to the work in the Chicago area. The 1993 membership was 3,036. Fifteen Chicago area churches began at Shiloh.

In Detroit, Michigan, the work began with J. W. Owens, who in July 1910 systematically distributed tracts and small books, hoping to find openings for Bible studies. By Dec. 31, 1910, he had organized a group of 17. The work later developed under the leadership of such men as W. H. Green (later secretary of the North American Negro Department of the General Conference), T. B. Buckner, under whose leadership the Hartford Avenue church was constructed, U. S. Willis, J. H. Laurence, and L. H. Bland. The Hartford Avenue church became mother to at least seven churches in the Detroit area.

In Indianapolis, Indiana, in 1907, L. W. Browne held tent meetings and won about 15 converts. One of his assistants was William A. Green, who had been a worker on the *Morning Star,* J. E. White's Mississippi riverboat, which had been used in the missionary venture that developed extensive Black work in the South. The Indianapolis church purchased its first building in 1911, but in 1938 erected a new brick building on Capitol Avenue (the church is presently located on East Forty-ninth Street). E. L. Campbell, Sydney Scott, W. D. Forde, E. A. Jarreau, and J. H. Laurence were among those who built up the cause in the Indianapolis area. By 1915 a church had been established also in Springfield, Illinois.

The various congregations that had been established opened church schools. From these large centers the work extended into the smaller cities. Membership increased as Southern SDAs joined in the great wave of Black migration from the Southern states to the Northern industrial centers during and after World War I. By the end of 1944 membership among Blacks in the Lake Union Conference area had grown to about 2,500.

Lake Region Conference Organized. The General Conference in its Spring Meeting, Apr. 10, 1944, recommended: "That in unions where the Colored constituency is considered by the union conference committee to be sufficiently large, and where the financial income and territory warrant, Colored conferences be organized."

The Lake Union Conference executive committee adopted the recommendation of the General Conference on July 17. Then a special meeting of the African-American constituents of the Lake Union Conference was called for Sept. 26, 1944. In this meeting, held at the Shiloh church in Chicago, the Lake Region Conference was formed. It was so named because this one conference encompassed the whole region of the Lake Union Conference. J. G. Dasent was elected president; F. N. Crowe, secretary-treasurer; Virgil Gibbons, publishing secretary; W. J. Kisack, MV and educational secretary; L. B. Baker, Book and Bible House manager; J. E. Johnson, Sabbath school and home missionary secretary. The Lake Region Conference began to function as such Jan. 1, 1945.

Soon after organization, the new conference purchased a tract of 120 acres (50 hectares) in Cass County, Michigan, for camp meeting purposes. The property has been constantly improved, until at the present time the total value of buildings and land is in excess of $2 million.

Since its founding, the Lake Region Conference has continued to grow. By 1993 the conference membership increased from about 2,500 at its inception to 20,905. In 1960 a new conference office building was constructed, replacing the old building that had served since its organization. This structure is valued at $105,000.

Presidents: J. G. Dasent, 1945-1949; T. M. Fountain, 1949-1951; H. W. Kibble, 1951-1961; C. E. Bradford, 1961-1970; J. R. Wagner, 1970-1977; C. D. Joseph, 1977-1987; L. R. Palmer, 1987-1990; R. C. Brown, Sr., 1990-1994; Norman K. Miles, 1994- .

LAKE TITICACA MISSION. *See* Peru; South American Division.

LAKE TITICACA TRAINING SCHOOL. *See* Titicaca Adventist Academy.

LAKE UNION CONFERENCE. The unit of church administration in North America comprising the following local conferences: Illinois, Indiana, Lake Region, Michigan, and Wisconsin, with headquarters at 8903 U.S. 31, Berrien Springs, Michigan. Official organ: *Lake Union Herald.* Statistics (1992): churches, 473; members, 66,497; ordained ministers, 253; licensed ministers, 37; Bible instructors, 5; teachers, 412 (K-12).

Institutions. Andrews University; Battle Creek Academy; Broadview Academy; Chicago SDA Academy; Great Lakes Adventist Academy; Indiana Academy; Peterson-Warren Academy; Wisconsin Academy. Organizations in the Hinsdale Health System are: Adventist Health Resources, Inc.; Chippewa Valley Hospital and Oakview Care Center; GlenOaks Medical Center; Health Care at Home Management Corporation; Health Ventures, Inc.; Hinsdale Hospital.

When the Lake Union Conference was formed in 1901, the territory was made up of the East Michigan, Indiana, Northern Illinois, North Michigan, Ohio, Southern Illinois, West Michigan, and Wisconsin conferences, and the Superior Mission. The Ohio Conference was transferred to the Columbia Union Conference in 1907.

Presidents: A. G. Daniells, 1901-1904; Allen Moon, 1904-1914; L. H. Christian, 1914-1918; William Guthrie, 1918-1928; W. H. Holden, 1928-1937; J. J. Nethery, 1937-1946; L. E. Lenheim, 1946-1951; M. L. Rice, 1951-1957; Jere D. Smith, 1957-1968; F. W. Wernick, 1968-1975; L. L. Bock, 1975-1980; Robert H. Carter, 1980-1994; Don C. Schneider, 1994- .

LAKE UNION HERALD (1908- ; monthly; files in GC). Official organ of the Lake Union Conference. It is circulated to the church members in the territory of the Lake Union Conference from funds members contribute to the church.

LAKE VIEW ACADEMY. A senior high school operated by the Northern Mindanao Conference of the Seventh-day Adventist Church at Don Carlos, Bukidnon, Philippines. It was established in 1967 at a site in the center of the town. In 1989 the school was transferred to its new campus overlooking Lake Pinamaloy. A denominationally accredited academy, it is working toward government accreditation.

Principals: Serafin Fadri, 1967-1969; R. L. Cabaluna, 1969-1970; R. E. Guanzoa, 1970-1971; A. G. Tiangha, 1971-1978; G. B. Mendoza, 1978-1982; Charles Aguilar, 1982-1988; Eliezer Saberola, 1988-1991; Moises Rafanan, 1991-1992; I. F. Faigmani, 1992- .

LAKE VIEW SEMINARY AND TRAINING CENTRE. A ministerial training school operated by the Malawi Union and located near Mlangeni in central Malawi, halfway between the two principal cities of Blantyre and Lilongwe. Lake View Seminary opened in 1980 under the leadership of H. H. Mattison, veteran missionary to India and Africa, with W. L. Masoka and G. R. Doss as instructors. Initially accepting students with junior secondary qualifications, Lake View now requires full secondary completion. The ministerial course takes two years and covers the ministry-related classes included in a college program. Lake View has a faculty of two regular workers and one volunteer.

Principals: H. H. Mattison, 1980-1981; B. L. Wright, 1981-1986; B. D. Wheeler, 1986-1987; G. R. Doss, 1987- .

LAKESIDE ADVENTIST HOSPITAL (formerly Lakeside Medical Centre). A 40-bed medical institution located at Kandy, Sri Lanka. Land was purchased in 1963 opposite the world-famous tooth temple of the Buddha. The hospital actually began as an outdoor clinic in 1964 under the direction of Dr. and Mrs. Noel Fernando. A Thirteenth Sabbath Offering overflow assisted in erecting a new building. In

1993 the hospital offered in-patient and out-patient departments, laboratory, X-ray, surgery, physiotherapy, pharmacy, and free health-education facilities. The present staff is approximately 80 percent Seventh-day Adventist.

Medical Directors/Presidents: Drs. Merle and Betty Fernando, 1967-1985; Henry Wiebe, 1985-1986; Mrs. Shivanthy Kamble, 1986-1987; Mrs. M. Aballada Guerreros, 1987-1988; Rodrigo R. Caagbay, 1988-1989; Percy Dias, 1989- .

LAKESIDE CLINIC. *See* Mindanao Sanitarium and Hospital.

LAKPAHANA ADVENTIST COLLEGE AND SEMINARY (Light of Sri Lanka Training Institute). A coeducational boarding school on the elementary, secondary, and junior college levels, operated by the Sri Lanka Union of the Southern Asia Division at Mailapitiya, Kandy district, Sri Lanka (near the center of the island, about 85 miles [135 kilometers] from Colombo). The school's name means "Light of Sri Lanka." It offers preschool through the General Certificate of Education examinations conducted by the Education Department of the Sri Lanka government. The school owns 168 acres (68 hectares) of land. Buildings constructed with the help of the Thirteenth Sabbath Offering overflow of June 1955 include an administration building housing offices, classrooms, library, science block, and chapel; men's dormitory; women's dormitory; 18 staff residences; and various industrial buildings providing facilities for approximately 220 students.

One hundred twenty acres (50 hectares) planted to coconut provide opportunity for student labor. Additional work opportunities are provided in the poultry, carpentry, and dairy industries.

The institute had its beginning in a mission school, which was opened in Moratuwa, near Colombo, in 1923, with an enrollment of 18. After opposition from the government and from the Buddhists of the neighborhood, the school was transferred to Kottawa, Pannipitiya, 12 miles (20 kilometers) from Colombo, and under the management of Miss Goonetilleke, was operated there as a boarding school, named Sinhalese Primary School, or Ceylon Mission School. In 1926 the school was transferred to a seven-acre (2.8-hectare) coconut estate. This school in 1950 became the Ceylon Union High School, which was moved in 1952 to Mailpitiya, its present site, and was renamed the Lakpahana Training Institute. Later it was renamed Lakpahana Adventist College and Seminary.

Principals: A. F. Jessen, 1928-1942; P.A.T.C. Tobo, 1942-1944; E. L. Juriansz, 1944-1957; A. W. Robinson, 1957-1964; F. E. Schlehuber, 1965-1968; T. B. Sadler, 1968-1976; R. E. Stahlnecker, 1977-1980; C. E. Ondrizek, 1981-1983; F. C. Oshiro, 1984-1986; R. G. Burton, 1987; U. D. Aloysius, 1988; D. S. Gibbs, 1988-1990; Peter Munasinghe, 1990- .

LAKPAHANA PUBLISHING HOUSE OF SEVENTH-DAY ADVENTISTS. A publishing plant with printing facilities that began as a student industry at Lakpahana High School and Seminary in 1966. In 1970 it was moved to rented quarters near Colombo, Sri Lanka, and enlarged with the aid of press rehabilitation funds. In 1974 a building was constructed and additional equipment added. In recent years it has been modernized with both offset and letterhead printing facilities. Recently a Macintosh desktop publishing capability was added.

Managers: Rex Rabot, 1974-1977; Norman Jansz, 1977-1985; A. O. Peries, 1985-1988; A.B.J. de Pinto, 1988-1989; P. P. Ambikapalau, 1989-1992; R.E.A. Emerson, 1992- .

LALE, DONALD (1931-1981). Educator, missionary, martyr. Reared on the Isle of Wight, he joined the Royal Air Force and was stationed on Mauritius, where a French family studied the Bible with him. He was baptized after returning to England and attended Newbold College. Later he took further training at Stoke Rochford College. With his wife, Ann, also a teacher, who had been born and reared a Seventh-day Adventist and had graduated as a Bible instructor from Newbold College, he answered a call to Rhodesia (now Zimbabwe), where they taught at Lower Gwelo College for two years. During the years of war for independence, they moved to Anderson School for three years.

In 1980, with Zimbabwe newly independent, the Lales moved to Inyazura Secondary School to teach Bible and English. There Don and Ann were cruelly murdered by terrorists less than two months after their arrival, leaving their two sons orphaned.

LA LIGNIÈRE. *See* Lake Geneva Sanitarium.

LA LOMA FOODS. *See* Loma Linda Foods/La Loma Foods.

LA MARNIÈRE. *See* Maison de Retraite (La Marnière).

LAMB SHELTERS. Inexpensive Sabbath school rooms constructed for the use of children. They are used extensively in the Far Eastern Division.

The first lamb shelter was dedicated on Mar. 4, 1967, at the Togop church in Sabah, Borneo. The idea originated with Mrs. Paulene Barnett, who in 1967 was serving as Sabbath school secretary of the Southeast Asia Union Mission. At a presidents' annual committee meeting in Singapore, George Munson, president of the Borneo Mission, was given $100 for the building of the first lamb shelter. Church buildings consisting of one room in some missions of the Far Eastern Division were for adults only. Mrs. Barnett insisted that the "lambs must be fed too!"

As a direct result of the fourth quarter's Thirteenth Sabbath Offering in 1971, 161 lamb shelters were built. Forty-nine more were provided by a subsidy by the Far Eastern Division, and 92 others were built as a result of special donations received from the United States. This made a total of 302 in 1974, but many more have been built of which we have no accurate records.

All labor in building the lamb shelters is the responsibility of the members. Subsidies are granted by the mission. Each shelter is a simple building 12' x 18' (4 m. x 5 m.). Minimum standards for construction are: cement floor, zinc or aluminum roof, wood siding, door that can be locked, wire mesh screening over window areas, benches, exterior painting and creosoting of all wood framing, adequate storage for supplies. Double lamb shelters should be divided by a permanent partition and contain a minimum size for either side of 200 square feet (20 square meters).

Lamb shelters, started in the Far Eastern Division, have become popular in many other areas of the world field.

LAMSON, MARY ELIZABETH (1875-1969). Educator. She was born in Michigan and received her early education in local schools. In 1895 she began teaching, a career that was to span 40 years.

In 1898 the first summer school for the training of teachers for Seventh-day Adventist schools was started. Mary borrowed the $5 entrance fee from her brother and enrolled. That fall she lived in the home of Dr. J. H. Kellogg and taught six of his adopted children, all ninth graders.

She served for two years as preceptress of Battle Creek College. She enjoyed the work, but when the college moved to Berrien Springs she remained in Battle Creek, where she taught church school for five years.

In 1918 she was invited by newly elected president Frederick Griggs to serve as preceptress of Emmanuel Missionary College and held this position until her retirement in 1935. During this time she took graduate studies and received her B.A. degree in 1928. Lamson Hall, residence for young women at Andrews University, is named in her honor.

LAMSON, PHOEBE (fl. 1860s). Physician. Born in New York, she was an alumnus of the Dansville, New York, Health Reform and Hydrotherapy Center. She was one of the first physicians at the Western Health Reform Institute at Battle Creek, and knew personally John Harvey Kellogg and James and Ellen White. It was noted that she gave herself unreservedly to the care and nurture of her patients.

LANCASTER JUNIOR COLLEGE. *See* Atlantic Union College.

LANDMARKS. An expression taken apparently from Prov. 22:28 ("Remove not the ancient landmark, which thy fathers have set" (cf. Prov. 23:10; see also Deut. 19:14) and used by Seventh-day Adventists to describe the doctrines that have made them a distinct religious group. These doctrines are commonly understood to be those relating to the sanctuary, the three angels' messages of Rev. 14, the Second Advent, the millennium, death, the seventh-day Sabbath, and the Spirit of Prophecy. Among other terms used with a meaning similar to landmarks are: "waymarks," "special points," "pillars of our faith," "the foundations," "pegs," and "pins." In SDA thinking, the landmarks are doctrines of such vital importance that they cannot be altered without changing the nature of the SDA Church.

Among the early Sabbathkeeping Adventists the term *landmarks* was used with reference to the ending of the 2300 days of Dan. 8:14. It was later that the expression came to denote other doctrines that have made SDAs a distinct religious group.

The earliest appearance of the term *landmarks* in an SDA publication was James White's use of it in connection with the 1844 ending of the 2300 days of Dan. 8:14 *(A Word to the "Little Flock"* [1847], p. 5).

Another of the early occurrences of the expression in Seventh-day Adventist writings is a letter by Ellen White (in *The Present Truth* 1:64, March 1850) in which those who abandoned Miller's chronology of the 2300 days and set a new date for the end of the period are said to "have removed the landmarks."

In a statement about a year later, those who were setting new times for the ending of the 2300 days were again warned that they were removing the landmarks. "Do not think us harsh and unchristian when we, honestly and in love, tell you that this work of removing the 'landmarks,' and following on from one point of time to another to find the end of the 2300 days, like a man following his shadow, dishonors the Advent cause, destroys true faith, offends God, and if persisted in, will lead to certain ruin" (James White, in *Review and Herald* 1:52, March 1851).

An article entitled "Removing the Landmarks" appeared in the *Review and Herald* of June 9, 1853, written by E. R. Seaman, of Rochester, New York, deploring the fact that some who had acted a conspicuous part in giving the judgment-hour message had ranked themselves "among the number who were still removing the landmarks," because they persisted in fixing new dates "for the termination of the days." As SDA doctrines developed, the term came to include other distinctive Adventist teachings. In retrospect in 1889 on the ancient landmarks Ellen White wrote: "The passing of the time in 1844 was a period of great events, opening to our astonished eyes the cleansing of the sanctuary transpiring in heaven, and having decided relation to God's people upon the earth, [also] the first and second angels' messages and the third, unfurling the banner on which was inscribed, 'The commandments of God and the faith of Jesus.' One of the landmarks under this message was the temple of God, seen by His truth-loving people in heaven, and the ark containing the law of God. The light of the Sabbath of the fourth commandment flashed its strong rays in the pathway of the transgressors of God's law. The nonimmortality of the wicked is an old landmark. I can call to mind nothing more that can come under the head of the old landmarks" *(Counsels to Writers and Editors,* pp. 30, 31).

On several occasions Ellen White warned concerning attempts to remove the landmarks of the Seventh-day Adventist faith. "After the truth has been proclaimed as a witness to all nations, every conceivable power of evil will be set in operation, and minds will be confused by many voices crying, 'Lo, here is Christ, Lo, he is there. This is the truth, I have the message from God, he has sent me with great light.' Then there will be a removing of the landmarks, and an attempt to tear down the pillars of our faith" *(Review and Herald* 69:769, Dec. 13, 1892).

"Spurious scientific theories [pantheism] are coming in as a thief in the night, stealing away the landmarks and undermining the pillars of our faith. . . . The most specious temptations of the enemy are coming in on the highest, most elevating plane. These spiritualize the doctrines of present truth until there is no distinction between the substance and the shadow" *(General Conference Bulletin,* Apr. 6, 1903, p. 87).

LANE, ELBERT B. (1840-1881). Evangelist. Selling his farm, he began to preach in Michigan in 1868. In 1869 he and his brother, S. H. Lane, engaged in evangelism in Indiana, which was then a mission, but which he left a conference. In 1871 he spent some time in Tennessee near Nashville, being the first Seventh-day Adventist minister to enter the South. The church he established at Edgefield Junction was the first Seventh-day Adventist church in the South. During his illness, his wife, Ellen, took his place in the pulpit and in visiting, and from then on preached independently with marked success.

In 1872 he returned to evangelism in Michigan, and two years later entered the Seventh Day Baptist college in Milton, Wisconsin, to further his knowledge of Hebrew and Greek. He then worked in Ohio and New England, and in 1876 he and J. O. Corliss began work in Virginia, where there were no SDAs at that time. Two years later he was recalled to Michigan for evangelistic and pastoral work, and remained there until his death.

LANE, ELLEN S. (1800s). Health and temperance worker, preacher. Married to Elbert B. Lane, a minister, Ellen was able to preach in his place during his illness. She was the first Seventh-day Adventist woman to receive a ministerial license. This was issued to her by the Michigan Conference. The Lanes worked together in Pennsylvania and in the Shenandoah Valley of Virgina, where they lectured around the New Market area and helped develop the New Market church. Ellen spoke mostly on health and temperance subjects and worked from house to house, holding prayer meetings in the homes. Her license was renewed in 1878. She continued working with her husband until his death in 1881, then labored alone until 1889.

LANE, SANDS HARVEY (1844-1906). Evangelist. He was employed as a youth in the printshop of the Review and Herald, but in 1869 joined his brother, E. B. Lane, in evangelistic work in Indiana. Some years later (1877) he became president of the Indiana Conference. Called to England in 1885 he engaged in evangelistic work in England and for a time in Ireland. He was president of the New York (1889-1895, 1903-1906), Illinois (1895-1899), and Southern Illinois conferences (1902-1903). He was president of the board of the Seventh-day Adventist Publishing Association (1899-1900), and also of the board of trustees of the General Conference Association (1901-1903).

LANTERN. *See South African Union Lantern.*

LAODICEA. *See* Revelation, Interpretation of.

LAOS. A small People's Democratic Republic bordered by Thailand, China, Myanmar, Vietnam, and Cambodia, with a population (1994) of 4.7 million and an area of 91,428 square miles (236,800 square kilometers). Buddhism is the state religion and is practiced by the lowland Lao; the inland tribal people are animists. Christian missions are working in a number of areas.

The territory of Laos is a part of the Thailand Mission in the Southeast Asia Union of the Far Eastern Division. The first Seventh-day Adventist mission station was opened in 1957 by Richard C. Hall and his family at Nam Tha, the center of one of the northwestern provinces. A short time later Nai Mun Lansri and Abel Pangan and his wife joined them, and by 1961 a church with 44 members, mostly from the Maeo tribe, had been organized.

Because of war, all mission personnel were evacuated from Laos early in 1962. Shortly after their departure military forces overran Nam Tha, and the mission buildings were destroyed.

A Filipino missionary was called to reopen the work in 1967. A. G. Biton and his family arrived in the field in 1968. By 1974 two churches were organized—one at Nam Yawn, with 73 members, and the other at Vientiane, with 14 members. In 1975, because of Communist advances in Southeast Asia, all SDA contact with Laos was cut off until Laos opened her border with Thailand in 1984. At that time Rungsit Saejang was able to enter the country and survey the situation. He found two churches still active: the Laos church in the capital city of Vietianne and a Hmong church at Nam Yawn.

Because the Laotian government would not allow a Thai pastor to work there, it was not until 1991 that Pastor Houmphanh, a former refugee repatriated from France, was assigned to oversee the work. In 1993 there were 120 church members and Sabbath school attendees in Laos.

LA PAZ ADVENTIST ACADEMY. A K-12 coeducational institution located in Villa Juana, Santo Domingo, Dominican Republic, and operated under the auspices of the Central Dominican Conference.

The La Paz Adventist Academy was founded Jan. 7, 1960. Its founders were Wilson Roberts and Cami Cruz and two teachers, Sira Bastardo and Ginovio Eustaquio.

By 1963 the school had 200 students in grades 1 to 8 with Ginovio Eustaquio as its principal. In 1993 the school had 304 students and nine teachers. It has had 14 principals. In 1993 Petronila Santana was principal.

LA PAZ ADVENTIST CLINIC (Clínica Adventista de La Paz). A service begun in 1980 in a building near the headquarters of the West Bolivia Mission offices. It began as a pharmacy and served the area where the Chulumani Hospital had operated before closing in 1970. The mission had maintained the Adventist Ambulant Clinic in answer to the needs of the community.

The La Paz Adventist Clinic was officially opened on Nov. 19, 1989. The effect has been the relief of pain and illness for many people as well as a promotion of the gospel message.

Administrators: Guido Ayala, 1989-1990; Armando Rios, 1991-1993; Roberto Catacora, 1993- .

Medical Directors: A. Carpintero, 1989-1992; J. Flores, 1993- .

LA PERSÉVÉRANCE DE BOISSARD SCHOOL. *See* Persévérance Boissard School.

LAPLAND MISSION. *See* Finland; Trans-European Division.

LA REVISTA ADVENTISTA. *See Revista Adventista.*

LA RUE, ABRAM (1822-1903). Pioneer self-supporting lay missionary in eastern Asia. Born in New Jersey, he spent his early manhood in California and Idaho, where he amassed and lost a considerable fortune in gold mining. He spent some time in the Hawaiian Islands, returned to California, and there, while working as a sheepherder, he accepted the Seventh-day Adventist faith. Immediately the new convert requested a mission appointment to China. The General Conference declined because of his advanced age and advised that he go to one of the Pacific islands. After spending a term in Healdsburg College, he worked his way to Honolulu, arriving in 1883 or 1884 with another colporteur, and sold books in the city and on the ships in port, with the result that W. M. Healey was sent in 1885 to establish Adventist work in the islands.

In 1888 La Rue went to Hong Kong. He set up a seamen's mission and for 14 years did colporteur work, mainly on the ships in Hong Kong harbor, but during that time he also made trips to Shanghai, Japan, Borneo, Java, Ceylon, Sarawak, Singapore, and once even to Palestine and Lebanon, selling books and distributing tracts wherever his ship stopped.

Although he worked in Hong Kong chiefly for Europeans, he did circulate two tracts in Chinese, translated for him by a Chinese friend, a colonial court translator. In 1902 J. N. Anderson arrived in Hong Kong and baptized seven of La Rue's converts, including six British Navy seamen.

Until the time of his death in Hong Kong, La Rue was a man of tireless energy, with a rare gift in meeting people and conveying his own religious convictions.

LASALGAON HIGH SCHOOL. *See* Seventh-day Adventist Higher Secondary School (Lasalgaon).

LAS CONDES ADVENTIST ACADEMY (Colegio Adventista de Las Condes). A coeducational institution offering the two last years of primary school and the complete secondary course. It belongs to the Central Chile Conference and is situated in Santiago, the capital city of the country. The staff is composed of three administrative workers and 17 teachers. The 1993 school year ended with 143 students in the high school section and 180 in the primary section.

In 1962, before the existence of the Chile Union, a request was submitted to the South American Division via the Austral Union to organize a day academy for the first three years of secondary classes. In 1963 the school began to function, and in 1968 authorization was requested to add the second cycle of secondary-level courses, which began in 1969.

In 1971 land was purchased in Las Condes municipal district, with an area of 81,420 square feet (7,567 square meters) providing 14,000 square feet (1,300 square meters) of construction suitable for the academy. Two years later two additional classrooms with a total area of 1,500 square feet (140 square meters) were built. In 1993 the library contained about 2,000 books.

Principals: Sergio Olivares, 1963-1964; Oscar Yáñez, 1965-1968; Graciela Carvajal, 1969-1970; Francisco Aguilera, 1971-1972; Marcelo Carvajal, 1973-1975; Abner Soto, 1976-1979; Edgard Araya, 1980-1982; Graciela Carvajal, 1983; Marcelo Carvajal, 1984-1987; Aurelio Vega, 1988; Abner Soto, 1989-1991; Luis Contreras, 1992- .

LA SIERRA ADVENTIST ACADEMY. A coeducational day school on the senior high school level at Riverside, California. Along with an elementary school under the administration of a principal, it is operated by a board representing 15 constituent churches, La Sierra University, and the Southeastern California Conference. Both academy and elementary teachers are considered members of the college staff by virtue of their responsibility in the Department of Education as supervising instructors. The early history and circumstances of its establishment are covered in detail under La Sierra University.

La Sierra Academy was originally founded in 1922 at the site of the present college campus; in 1925 it was renamed La Sierra Academy and Normal School; in 1927 it became Southern California Junior College, and in 1939 La Sierra College. During these years of rapid growth, the grades of the secondary level were referred to as La Sierra Academy, but under the varied titles of the parent institution.

In 1940 the secondary grades, under the title of La Sierra College Preparatory School, were provided with separate classrooms in the basement floor of Hole Memorial Auditorium, and the lower chapel in the same building was used for assembly. So far as possible, the secondary students were housed apart from the college students, and the preparatory school staff had no control over the government of the dormitories.

The need for separate academy facilities was recognized by Elmer Digneo, on the academy staff since 1940 and principal from 1947 to 1953. During the administration of G. T. Anderson, the college board purchased nine and a half acres (four hectares) next to the La Sierra College demonstration (elementary) school and the Loma Linda Food Company for the erection of new and separate facilities for the elementary and secondary grades. A single administrator, as principal and manager, was to coordinate the teacher education program with the college Department of Education and to provide for the community needs of the constituent churches, and also to handle the funds. The academy moved to the new location during Christmas vacation of the school year of 1954-1955.

In 1958-1962 a long-range development plan was made and implemented so that the elementary and secondary schools are contained entirely on the new premises. The La Sierra church sponsored a development program amounting to about $100,000, providing a well and an irrigation-sprinkler system, a woodshop and equipment, slab and surfaced courts with fully equipped shower and locker facilities. A gymnasium-cafeteria building was completed in 1967, and a vocational building was erected in 1968. That same year a science building and an administration building were completed.

The La Sierra College Demonstration School and the La Sierra College Preparatory School combined in 1962 to become the La Sierra Academy and Elementary School. In 1987 "Adventist" was added to the school's name. More than 3,700 students have graduated from the twelfth grade at La Sierra Adventist Academy during the 71 years of its existence.

Principals: La Sierra Academy: James I. Robison, 1922-1925. *La Sierra Academy and Normal School:* Louis C. Palmer, 1925-1927. *Southern California Junior College:* Willis W. Ruble, 1927-1928; H. Martin Johnson, 1929-1930; Erwin E. Cossentine, 1930-1939. *La Sierra College Preparatory School:* N. L. Parker, 1940-1947; Elmer J. Digneo, 1947-1953; Max M. Williams, 1953-1956; Floyd Wood, 1956-1958; W. G. Nelson, 1958-1962. *La Sierra Academy:* W. G. Nelson, 1962-1963; Reuben L. Hilde, 1963-1970; Andrew Peters, 1969-1976; Grant Macaulay, 1976-1984; Wendel Tucker, 1984-1987. *La Sierra Adventist Academy:* Wendell Tucker, 1987-1989; Lyle Botimer, 1989-1991; Bud Moon, 1991- .

LA SIERRA COLLEGE. *See* La Sierra University; Loma Linda University.

LA SIERRA UNIVERSITY. A coeducational institution of higher learning located in Riverside, California. In 1993 approximately 1,800 students were enrolled in the university's various on- and off-campus programs; these students were served by some 250 faculty and staff. The center of the university is the College of Arts and Sciences, which offers undergraduate and graduate instruction in 17 fields. It also comprises Schools of Business and Management, Education, and Religion, each of which offers undergraduate and graduate degrees, along with a Center for Lifelong Learning, designed to meet the higher educational needs of adults.

According to the university's mission statement, its Seventh-day Adventist heritage and commitment provide "a perspective for its educational programs and projects, a motivation for its intellectual vitality and rigor, a framework for its moral values and lifestyle, and a basis for its social consciousness and public service." The integration of religious belief with academic study is fostered by the requirement that a student in almost any degree program complete a course focusing on the relationship between religion and the issues confronted in connection with the field of study. The central function of Christian faith in the life of the campus is evinced by its weekly chapel services; on-campus, student-led religious programs; and ongoing community-involvement efforts. An annual Community Service Day has drawn positive media comment since its inception in 1989, and the university is involved in a number of other projects, including: prison ministries, Adopt a Grandparent, housing repair and painting for the needy elderly and disabled, counseling services for local juvenile offenders, outreach to Mexico, and various other programs for children and churches. The Resurrection Pageant, a dramatic indoor/outdoor portrayal of the Passion of Christ, draws more than 5,000 people to the campus each year.

The Seventh-day Adventist Church's first student missionary was sent abroad from La Sierra for a full-year term in 1964. This was the beginning of a continuing program of volunteer service that soon expanded to involve numerous students in yearlong mission stints around the globe. A major form of student mission service has traditionally been teaching in mission-operated English-language schools. Since 1990 La Sierra students have also assisted with overseas service projects under the auspices of the Adventist Development and Relief Agency in such locations as Kenya, Tanzania, and Nicaragua. As of mid-1993, 261 La Sierra students had served traditional student mission assignments, and an additional 56 had worked as ADRA volunteers.

Various campus resources add to the quality of the university's educational programs and enhance its ability to contribute to the life of the church and the local community. The Brandstater Gallery regularly features work by significant contemporary artists and provides a genteel setting for university cultural programs. The World Museum of Natural History features, among other things, one of the world's largest and finest collections of mineral spheres as well as notable taxidermy displays of crocodilians, turtles, tortoises, lizards, snakes, and Southeast Asian birds (the work of world-class taxidermist and La Sierra alumnus E. A. "Billy" Hankins III). The John Hancock Center for Youth Ministry supports the Seventh-day Adventist Church's local and global efforts to meet the spiritual needs of its young people. And the Fernando and Ana Stahl Center offers opportunity for the university community to promote the cause of world service in a variety of ways.

The university library's holdings include some 175,000 books, 35,000 bound journal volumes representing more than 1,500 currently received journal titles, and extensive microfilm and microfiche collections. The Heritage Room provides members of the university community and others with access to invaluable information about SDA history; a particular strength of the Heritage Room collection is its array of materials related to the origin and development of SDA education. The William M. Landeen Collection on the history of Christianity contains items significant for the study of the Protestant Reformation.

Among the university's publications are *Adventist Heritage*, a journal of Seventh-day Adventist history *La Sierra Today*, a magazine for alumni and friends; *Musings*, a literary and cultural journal; and various specialized newsletters. By 1993 the University Press had issued 13 volumes—among them the principal report on the Valuegenesis study, designed to aid the church in eliciting and retaining the commitment of young people to Adventism and its values. (V. Bailey Gillespie, La Sierra professor of theology and Christian personality, served as a principal Valuegenesis investigator.)

Campus diversity is a longstanding element of the university's heritage. At the beginning of the 1990s, undergraduate students represented 34 states and 75 different countries. In 1992-1993 African-Americans and other Blacks made up 7.6 percent of the on-campus student body; Native Americans and Alaska Natives, 0.4 percent; Caucasians, 40.5 percent; Hispanics, 15 percent; persons from the Indian subcontinent, 2.8 percent; persons from the Middle East, 2 percent; and East Asians and Pacific Islanders, 31 percent. This diverse student body is served by faculty and staff members from numerous ethnic and cultural backgrounds.

University faculty contribute to progress in their disciplines and enrich their teaching by engaging in research and other professional development activities. The number of professional presentations and publications has increased strikingly in recent years, as has university funding of research grants; in 1989-1990 university faculty members made some 140 presentations related to their areas of study. Recently published books by LSU faculty have focused on such diverse areas as the relationship between faith and reason and the development of Central American railways.

History. 1. *La Sierra Academy.* When the Southeastern California Conference was formed (1915), it had no academy. The Southern California Conference had, since 1902, operated San Fernando Academy, at San Fernando (as Fernando College, 1901-1907; Fernando Academy, 1907-1914). By 1920 it had outgrown its antiquated buildings, which had been purchased from a Methodist school of theology. In view of this, the presidents of the Southern and Southeastern California conferences, W. M. Adams and J. J. Nethery, began looking for a suitable site for a new academy to serve both conferences. After the failure of joint efforts to find a site at reasonable cost, the Southeastern California Conference purchased in 1922, at the cost of $112,500, 330 acres (135 hectares) of land from the Hole estate near Riverside.

Meanwhile, in May 1922 this conference had organized the new school, named La Sierra Academy, with J. I. Robison as principal and R. F. Emerson as general manager. On July 1, 1922, Robison announced the opening on Oct. 3 of a full-fledged 12-grade school. He later described the situation: "We did not have a building. We did not have a book in our library, nor a test tube for the laboratory. We did not have a desk or a chair. We did not even have a faculty. . . . But we did have faith. . . . And so with faith and courage and loyal cooperation and united effort we stepped forward, facing every difficulty, confident that the Lord was leading, and that we would open school on October 3, as we had advertised."

By Oct. 3, 1922, the boys' dormitory, including classrooms on the first floor, was ready. The girls' dormitory was only half plastered, and with the stairs not in, the girls had to climb ladders to get to their unfinished rooms. The building was completed before the end of the school year. Oil and wood stoves were used for heating, and oil lamps or candles for lighting. School opened with 84 students.

Plans were made immediately for two-year commercial and teacher-training curriculums beyond the academy level. In 1923, with the closing of San Fernando Academy, students from the Southern California Conference were encouraged to attend La Sierra Academy. The administration building was finished during the second year of the school's existence. That year La Sierra Academy had 204 students, with 31 graduates.

From 1925 the academy was operated jointly by the Southern and Southeastern California conferences. Enrollment growth was slow because five nonboarding academies were developing in the two conferences.

The problem of adequate water for the institution was solved in the fall of 1925, when W. J. Hole, former owner of the property, gave the school one of his wells in the valley and $5,000 with which to construct a pipeline to the institution. He later contributed two additional wells. *(See also* La Sierra Academy.)

2. *Southern California Junior College.* In 1927 La Sierra Academy became Southern California Junior College, whose first president and general manager was W. W. Ruble. To provide for the needs of the enlarged institution, major additions were made in office space, laboratory equipment, heating facilities, and the library, and an elementary school was built on the north side of the campus. During the next three years other facilities and the industrial program of the college were improved.

A critical period came when, because of the economic depression and the founding of new academies in the area, the academy enrollment decreased from 250 in 1928 to 95 in 1935. At the same time the junior college enrollment grew but slowly. Yet the improvement of the scholastic program and the physical plant continued in spite of the 1930s depression. The weekly newspaper, *The College Criterion,* was published for the first time in 1929. Also, during this time an efficient program of student recruitment was organized. In 1930 a "college day" program, the first in any SDA college, was held, in which academy seniors from the two conferences visited the campus. The associated student organization was established in the winter of 1931-1932. A new science hall was constructed in 1932, the addition of which led the Northwest Association of Colleges and Secondary Schools to accredit the junior college on May 1, 1933. A swimming pool, a camp meeting auditorium, and Hole Memorial Auditorium were constructed between 1935 and 1937.

3. *La Sierra College.* La Sierra College was accredited as a three-year college in 1939 by the Northwest Association of Colleges and Secondary Schools. This three-year accreditation granted by the association was unique and was designed to strengthen the premedical curriculum. In 1939 and 1940 a new men's dormitory and a new women's dormitory were constructed on the campus; a cafeteria building was completed in 1941. The increase in enrollment to 480 by 1940 made necessary the rapid expansion of the physical plant and the staff. In that same year the preparatory school was separated from the college.

With the coming of World War II and the resultant freezing of educational programs in Seventh-day Adventist colleges, the advance of La Sierra College to full college status was delayed. The war brought other critical problems. A personal appeal by the college president prevented a camp directly in front of the campus. The Navy manifested interest in taking over the school, but fortunately did not. In 1944 the General Conference authorized La Sierra College to offer four years of work, and in 1945 the college conferred its first degrees. One year later, in 1946, the institution was accredited as a four-year college by the

Northwest Association of Secondary and Higher Schools.

The postwar period was marked by rapid advancement. The college enrollment grew steadily after 1942, and in a boom period it reached 919 during the winter term of 1947-1948. New buildings erected in this period were the library-administration building (1946), the college church (1947), an industrial arts building, and a science building.

The 1950s saw continued growth of the physical plant, the increase of enrollment, and the continued strengthening of the college staff. In 1953 the college was accredited by the Western College Association. In order to protect the water supply of the college, 86 acres (35 hectares) of land to the south of the campus were acquired in 1954. By 1962 there were added a modern physical education facility, which included shower rooms, swimming pool, and tennis courts; a modern dairy; and poultry buildings.

By 1974 further major construction on the La Sierra campus included, besides additions to existing buildings, a high-rise men's residence hall housing 284 students, classroom-office buildings to house the departments of consumer-related sciences and agriculture, a gymnasium-auditorium (known as the Alumni Pavilion), and a library designed to accommodate 235,750 volumes and 550 patrons plus facilities for audiovisual services and a curriculum laboratory.

After World War II, the college saw a marked increase in cultural diversity among its students. Professors such as Edward Heppenstall encouraged creative reflection on the SDA heritage. And the growing appreciation for the serious thinking fostered at La Sierra was matched by the recognition that the college was establishing a unique link with the nearby College of Medical Evangelists (CME). SDA students began to look to La Sierra to provide them with the skills and contacts needed to make them successful applicants for admission to the church's health-science school. (The 1966 Danforth Foundation study, "Church-sponsored Higher Education in America," noted that a higher percentage of La Sierra graduates had received M.D. degrees in the years 1950-1959 than those of any other church-related institution of higher learning in the United States.) Academic programs flourished; by 1965 La Sierra College had a graduate division, and the faculty were cultivating an institutional vision that promoted postbaccalaureate studies in more than a half dozen fields.

La Sierra College's relationship with Loma Linda University, as CME was renamed in 1961, came under close scrutiny as church leaders considered options for converting Loma Linda University from a health sciences institution to a comprehensive university. Rejecting plans to create a competitive liberal arts college in Loma Linda, LLU's leaders pressed for a merger with La Sierra College, which occurred in 1967 when La Sierra became LLU's Riverside campus. Productive scholarly interchange and creative synergy resulted from the merger. However, after a 1986 meeting of the university constituency, at which concerns regarding university organization and operations surfaced, church and university administrators began to explore the possibility of consolidating all university programs in Loma Linda. But the cost of relocation together with on-campus and community support for retention of La Sierra in its current location led the trustees to abandon plans for consolidation.

Following further discussions of LLU's structure, the trustees voted to recommend a complete organizational separation between the La Sierra and Loma Linda campuses (officially effected at a meeting of the LLU constituency on Aug. 25, 1990). Fritz Guy, a 1952 graduate of La Sierra College and a former dean of the College of Arts and Sciences, was provisionally named to head the institution, identified temporarily as Loma Linda University, Riverside.

Broad-based alumni and community support led the trustees of the new university to adopt the name La Sierra University for the fledgling institution on Mar. 7, 1991. Their resolution noted that by opting to include the word "university" in La Sierra's name, they had "taken a policy position affecting, at the least, resources and governance." With this commitment clear, and with a new administration in place, La Sierra University began the task of charting a course toward the future.

Under its new name, La Sierra continued its progressive commitment to teaching, scholarship, and service and began to reestablish an independent identity. Especially important in this process was Global Village '92, a yearlong series of programs, organized in conjunction with ADRA International, that accented global service and responsibility and garnered significant attention from national and international news media.

Educational sociologist Garland Dulan,

formerly of Oakwood College, assumed the newly created position of provost in 1992. Fritz Guy decided to return to the classroom at the conclusion of the 1992-1993 academic year. To succeed him the trustees named Lawrence T. Geraty, an internationally noted archaeologist who was serving at the time as president of Atlantic Union College.

In 1993 anticipated projects included a proposed science center, a major library addition, and expansion of the University Commons. The university's current property holdings included 520 acres (210 hectares) of land, of which approximately 300 were available for potential development. University policy dictates that proceeds from the development of land assets be invested to preserve the principle in perpetuity and that only a portion of the income be used to fund university operations and capital improvements. Thus, the proceeds from the development of any land will become an endowment that will provide a permanent source of income for the university.

Current Academic Programs. *College of Arts and Sciences.* The purpose of the College of Arts and Sciences is to provide an environment for learning and personal growth that challenges and enables students to develop their intellects and their intellectual skills, to examine their values, and to mature in character and in Christian commitment. The college offers coursework in the traditional liberal arts and sciences (the humanities and fine arts, the natural sciences and mathematics, and the social and behavioral sciences) as well as in various areas of applied study (physical education, office management, and social work).

In 1993-1994, 17 departments of instruction offered 15 Bachelor of Arts degrees, 17 Bachelor of Science degrees, a Bachelor of Music degree, a Bachelor of Social Work degree, a Bachelor of Fine Arts degree, six Associate in Arts degrees, and two Associate in Science degrees. Graduate study—leading in some cases to the master's degree—is possible in art, chemistry, English, history, modern languages, music, office management, health and physical education, and psychology. The college offers course work leading to admission to professional curricula and programs at various levels; and it cooperates with the School of Education in offering graduate programs in teaching.

School of Religion. The Department of Religion at La Sierra College was consistently an active contributor to the life of the campus. It became part of Loma Linda University's Division of Religion when La Sierra and LLU merged in 1967. Twenty years later, in 1987, the division became the School of Religion, the name change serving to highlight the diversity of the school's academic roles and the importance of religious instruction within the university. Loma Linda University's La Sierra-based religion programs and faculty became the La Sierra University School of Religion when La Sierra became an independent university in 1990; La Sierra's School of Religion also assumed responsibility for all graduate programs in religion offered by Loma Linda University at the time of La Sierra's separation from Loma Linda.

The School of Religion provides general religious studies for all students in every school of the university. It prepares undergraduate majors for the ministry and for graduate and professional study. It offers graduate education for teachers and other Christian workers. And it supports the university, the church, its institutions, and the discipline of religious studies with research and publication and various programs of interest to the church and the community.

The school offers B.A. degrees in ministerial studies (with emphases in pastoral ministry, bilingual ministry, and educational ministry) and religion, and M.A. degrees in systematic theology, Christian ethics, church history, mission studies, church and ministry, and biblical studies. It also offers continuing education classes in various parts of the Pacific Union.

School of Education. In 1968 La Sierra's Department of Education became Loma Linda University's School of Education, which was retained as part of La Sierra University when the university came into being in 1990. The school seeks to enable students to gain the knowledge, skills, and attitudes required for success in their chosen areas of study in education; to help educators build sound philosophies of education in theological, historical, and sociological contexts; and to promote useful educational research.

Curricula are offered leading to B.A., M.A., Ed.S., and Ed.D. degrees in such areas as elementary and secondary teaching, educational administration and leadership, educational psychology and counseling, and educational foundations. Programs offered at the baccalaureate and postbaccalaureate levels qualify students for teaching credentials issued by the General Conference Department of Education and the California Commission for

Teacher Preparation and Licensing.

School of Business and Management. The Business Department of the College of Arts and Sciences became the School of Business and Management in 1986. The school's purpose is to provide students with the variety of skills necessary to success in the business environment. The school offers baccalaureate degrees with majors in business and management, accounting, management, management information systems, and marketing; and the M.B.A. in accounting, financial management, health administration, human resources and industrial relations, and marketing.

Center for Lifelong Learning. The Center for Lifelong Learning serves the educational needs of adult students 25 years of age and older. It coordinates programs leading to undergraduate degrees, with flexible requirements combining general education and career-related courses. Students at the center may receive credit not only for traditional academic achievement but also for prior experiential learning.

The center offers the Associate in Arts degree in human services; the Bachelor of Arts degree in liberal arts and business administration; the Bachelor of Science in health science; and the Bachelor of Social Work.

The university is accredited by the Western Association of Schools and Colleges and the North American Division Commission on Accreditation of the Board of Regents of the General Conference of Seventh-day Adventists. The School of Education's teacher-training curriculum is accredited by the California State Commission on Teacher Credentialing, and the School of Religion is working to secure accreditation by the Association of Theological Schools for the School of Religion. The university is a member of the American Council on Education, the Association of American Colleges, and the Association of Independent California Colleges and Universities. The program in social work is fully accredited by the Council on Social Work Education.

Principals and Presidents of La Sierra University (and its predecessors): La Sierra Academy: James I. Robison, 1922-1925. *La Sierra Academy and Normal School:* Louis C. Palmer, 1925-1927. *Southern California Junior College:* Willis W. Ruble, 1927-1928; H. Martin Johnson, 1929-1930; Erwin E. Cossentine, 1930-1939. *La Sierra College:* Erwin E. Cossentine, 1939-1942; Lowell E. Rasmussen, 1942-1946; Godfrey T. Anderson, 1946-1954; Norval F. Pease, 1954-1960; William M. Landeen, 1960-1962; Fabian A. Meier, 1962-1963; William M. Landeen, 1964-1965; David J. Bieber, 1965-1967. *Loma Linda University:* David J. Bieber, 1967-1974; V. Norskov Olsen, 1974-1984; Norman J. Woods, 1984-1990. *La Sierra University:* Fritz Guy, 1990-1993; Lawrence T. Geraty, 1993- .

LAST DAY SHEPHERD'S CALL, THE *(Mo Shih Mu Sheng)* (1921-   , with interruptions; monthly). Church paper and official organ of the South China Island Union Mission, first published for the China Division by the Signs of the Times Publishing House in Shanghai, China, in 1921. When the Pacific war broke out in 1941, the paper was discontinued for about one year. After that it was divided into two separate papers, one printed in Shanghai, China, and the other in Chungking, Szechuan, China. In 1946, when the China Division was reorganized, the two papers were again merged and published in Shanghai. After two years the political disturbances in China increased, and, as a result, the paper was discontinued.

In July 1954 the Signs of the Times Publishing Association of the South China Island Union Mission *(see* Signs of the Times Publishing Association [Taiwan]) began printing *The Last Day Shepherd's Call* at the Taiwan Missionary College Press, Taipei, Taiwan, until the publishing work moved to rented quarters adjacent to South China Island Union Mission office. At present the magazine is supplied to Chinese Seventh-day Adventists throughout the world.

LATIN-AMERICAN ADVENTIST THEOLOGICAL SEMINARY (Seminario Adventista Latinoamericano de Teologia). An institution of higher learning established in 1979 in São Paulo, Brazil, in conjunction with colleges and universities in Brazil, Chile, Peru, and Argentina.

The school offers limited graduate work in its own name. It offers bachelor's and master's degrees in religion and theology and has a Bible instructor course.

Presidents: Mario Veloso, 1982-1986; Enrique Becerra, 1986-1991; Wilson H. Endruveit, 1991- .

LATIN UNION CONFERENCE. A unit of church organization in Europe formed in 1902. It is listed in the *Yearbook* from 1904 to 1907 as the Latin Union Mission, then to 1928 as Latin Union Conference. The following countries were included in the union, at least during part of its existence: Algeria, Belgium, France, Italy, Morocco, Portugal, Spain, and Switzerland. The union formed the core of the Southern European Division, organized in 1928.

LATIN UNION PUBLISHING HOUSE. *See* Life and Health Publishing House.

LATIN UNION SCHOOL. *See* Salève Adventist Institute.

LATTER RAIN. Literally the spring rains at the close of the wet season in Palestine that matured winter grain for the harvest (Deut. 11:14), in contrast with the "early," or "former," rain the preceding autumn (Joel 2:23; Jer. 5:24; James 5:7) that germinated the seed and gave the crop a start before the onset of winter; theologically, in a metaphorical sense, the outpouring of the divine Spirit upon God's people to prepare them for the figurative harvest of the world at the end of time (cf. Hosea 6:3).

With respect to the gospel commission that Christ entrusted to His church on earth (Matt. 28:19, 20; Acts 1:8), Seventh-day Adventists refer to the experience at Pentecost as the "early," or "former," rain, and to the divine favor that will accompany the efforts put forth by consecrated believers under the guidance of the Holy Spirit at the end of time as the "latter rain"—in other words, to the seedtime and harvest of the gospel: "The outpouring of the Spirit in the days of the apostles was the beginning of the early, or former, rain. . . . But near the close of earth's harvest, a special bestowal of spiritual grace is promised to prepare the church for the coming of the Son of man" (AA 54, 55).

"The outpouring of the Holy Spirit on the day of Pentecost was the former rain, but the latter rain will be more abundant" (COL 121).

Ellen White describes the relationship between the two as thus: "As the 'former rain' was given, in the outpouring of the Holy Spirit at the opening of the gospel, to cause the upspringing of the precious seed, so the 'latter rain' will be given at its close, for the ripening of the harvest. . . . The great work of the gospel is not to close with less manifestation of the power of God than marked its opening. The prophecies which were fulfilled in the outpouring of the former rain at the opening of the gospel are again to be fulfilled at its close. Here are 'the times of refreshing' to which the apostle Peter looked forward when he said [Acts 3:19, 20 quoted]" (GC 611, 612).

The early rain is also applied to a preparatory personal experience prerequisite to receiving the latter rain. As a result of the early rain experience of the individual, the heart is "emptied of every defilement, and cleansed for the indwelling of the Spirit" (TM 507). The latter rain, in turn, qualifies the church for bearing witness in the "loud cry" and to stand firm during the last great time of trouble: "The ripening of the grain [as a result of the latter rain] represents the completion of the work of God's grace in the soul. By the power of the Holy Spirit the moral image of God is to be perfected in the character. We are to be wholly transformed into the likeness of Christ. The latter rain, ripening earth's harvest, represents the spiritual grace that prepares the church for the coming of the Son of man. But unless the former rain has fallen there will be no life, the green blade will not spring up. Unless the early showers have done their work, the latter rain can bring no seed to perfection" (*ibid.* 506).

The latter rain "revives and strengthens" God's people "to pass through the time of trouble" and fits them for translation (1T 353; 2SG 226).

"The latter rain is coming—the refreshing from the presence of the Lord. Those will receive it, in the church already gathered by the third angel's message [*see* Three Angels' Messages], who are prepared for it; and honest ones without will, under its influence, soon be gathered in" (Roswell F. Cottrell, in *Review and Herald* 31:280, Apr. 14, 1868).

LATVIA. A republic on the Baltic Sea whose neighbors include Estonia and Lithuania, Belarus, and Russia. It has an area of 24,900 square miles (64,491 square kilometers) and a population (1994) of 2.7 million. More than half the people are Latvians, who belong to the Baltic branch of Indo-European peoples; of the remainder, Russians, whose proportion has increased in the past 20 years, constitute the largest group. The area shows a strong imprint of German colonization, the land having been controlled by the Teutonic Knights for several centuries. About half the population is Lutheran; there is also a strong representation of Roman Catholics. Before World War II there were many Jews.

Seventh-day Adventist Statistics. Until the separation of Latvia from the Soviet Union, the territory was a part of the West Russian Union. Afterward the Latvian Conference was organized, and in 1923 the Baltic Union Conference was formed. After the absorption of Latvia by the Soviet Union, the work there became a part of the Federation of Seventh-day Adventists in the Union of Soviet Socialist Republics. Latvia now is in the Latvian Conference, a part of the Baltic Union, which is a constituent of the Trans-European Division. Statistics (1993) for *Latvia:* churches, 35; members, 2,808.

Seventh-day Adventist Work. *Beginnings.* The work in Latvia began in the middle 1890s when several colporteurs and Gerhard Perk worked in the Baltic cities. In 1895 Perk went to Riga, the capital of Latvia, to begin evangelistic work. On May 14, 1896, L. R. Conradi organized a church of 12 members in that city. When the Russian Union was organized in 1907, its headquarters were established in Riga, where the largest group of Adventists in the area were congregated. Over the years Seventh-day Adventists found Latvia a most fruitful evangelistic territory. Consistently the largest Baltic membership was found there.

Evangelism in Latvia. Little is known about evangelistic work in Latvia for a period after Perk left the country in the last years of the nineteenth century. In 1908, when the Russian Union and the Baltic Conference were organized, the Baltic Conference, which also included Estonia and St. Petersburg and Pskov and their environs, had 383 members in three churches.

In 1898 the first local colporteurs, J. Schneider and H. Meyer, began to work there. In the 1900s H. J. Lebsuc began working in Riga.

The church in Liepaja was founded in 1905 (the building was built in 1912). In 1908 churches were begun in Jelgava and Ventspils. In 1909 a worker went to the city of Libau (now Liepaja), where he found 15 members. Within three years their number had increased to 93 and they were building a chapel of their own. In the same three years a group of 100 members was gathered in Mitau (Jelgava), and the Riga group doubled its membership from 150 to 300.

This growth occurred under stringent governmental regulations that allowed no meetings for the public—only the regular church services were permitted. Despite the adverse conditions, in 1910 there were 445 baptisms in the Baltic Conference outside the area of Riga, many of them in Latvia.

After Latvia became an independent republic and complete religious freedom prevailed, the church work prospered. In 1924, although Latgale, the eastern province, inhabited mostly by Catholic and Greek Orthodox farmers, was not yet entered, there were in Latvia 34 churches and 1,800 members using Latvian, German, or Russian in their services. In 1927, in the city of Riga alone, there were 800 members in five churches—Latvian, German, and Russian. The chapel completed in Riga in 1928 had two auditoriums, one seating more than 600, and another seating 250.

Evangelism took different forms. In 1927 the Baltic Union School conducted a Vacation Bible School for the children of patrons of the summer resort. The next year a Russian evangelist came to work specifically among the many Russians in the Baltic states.

Membership continued to increase, until by 1931 Riga had more than 1,000 members. In 1932 there were seven churches in that city. In 1934 the membership of the Latvian conferences reached 2,113 (its territory had been divided into two conferences some time previously). A new chapel and a conference office were built in the city of Jelgava, for which the woodwork was made by the students of the Baltic Union School.

The rapid growth of the church in Latvia resulted from active lay participation in evangelism. One church elder in a community where there was no regular minister won a total of 37 converts. These lay evangelists, including many young people, were trained with the help of two manuals published at about that time, entitled *How Shall I Give Bible Studies?* and *Gospel Sales Manual.*

But by 1935 conditions had changed: all public lectures were required to be registered beforehand and the material was to be censored. Nevertheless, church membership continued to grow.

In 1937 there were 3,199 members in 60 churches, served by 15 ministers. Then in 1940 the area was incorporated into the Soviet Union.

Publishing Work in Latvia. The circulation of publications played a prominent role in the growth of the church. In Latvia the first SDA publications to be printed in Russia were produced in 1899 when a number of Latvian and Estonian tracts were published in Riga. Books published included *Christian Temperance* (1898), *Christ and His Righteousness* (1899), *Steps to Christ* (1905), and many others. After several years the publishing enterprise of the church was suppressed, but the tracts continued to be issued by private firms organized by evangelists in their own names. About the end of the first decade of this century, there are references in church papers to the publishing house in Riga. Actually the full development of publishing work was achieved only after the country became independent of the police control and religious totalitarianism of czarist Russia. In 1910 there were only 14 regular colporteurs in Latvia, and no work could be organized because of the restrictions. Then in 1922 a publishing house was established, and the sales began to grow. In 1924 there were 40 colporteurs in the field, and their number was limited only by the small size of the country. Among the 1.5 million people of Latvia at that time, colporteurs placed some 30,000 copies of Ellen White's *Great Controversy*, or about one copy for every 50 people.

Work for the Youth. Much of the success of the SDA message in Latvia is credited to the role that youth evangelism played in the history of the church. Although Latvia did not operate church schools, it did provide a high school for the training of evangelistic workers. This school, called the Baltic Union School, was opened in 1923 with 34 or 35 students on an estate called Suschenhof on a lake near Riga. Because most of the students were poor and the members were not wealthy enough to support the school, it was forced to operate on an almost self-supporting basis.

There were several industries—such as a dairy, a poultry farm, a soap factory, a woodworking shop, and several other enterprises—where students learned a trade and were able to earn their educational expenses. In 1927 the first graduates came out of the school; most of them were absorbed into the evangelistic force. Even during the most difficult years of the 1930s depression, the conference employed the school's graduates for evangelistic work The school also operated a summer resort in order to use its facilities during the summer. The clientele, mostly Jewish, was highly pleased with the service.

By 1930 the first two missionaries had gone from the Baltic Conference to Africa. In 1932 the first youth congress in the union was held on the grounds of the Baltic Union School. Some 500 young people attended the four-day session and covered their travel expenses by giving a choral and instrumental public concert in the city.

In 1934 the first SDA youth paper in Latvia was published by the young people themselves, without cost to the church. It was a 24-page monthly called *Jaunatnes Vadonis* ("Youth Leader"). One evangelist organized special youth Bible classes, a choral society, and an orchestra, in which membership was conditioned on high standards of behavior. After four years of careful training, the young people were ready for participation in a countrywide evangelistic campaign. They toured the land, providing music for evangelistic services and at the same time giving public concerts that provided more than enough funds for the expenses of the trip. In 1935 another unionwide youth congress was held in Riga.

Other Activities. During the great financial depression in the thirties, the Seventh-day Adventist Church organized welfare services, providing, among other things, meals for the unemployed and a day nursery and a summer camp for the underprivileged children of Riga.

Workers. Among the prominent leaders in Latvia were Janis Sprogis, Jacob Schneider, Janis Birzinsh, Karlis Sutta, Aleksandrs Eglitis, Arturs Jurkevics, Janis Oltinsh, Ernests Klotinsh, Arvids Cholders, and many others.

The Period After World War II. The last legal Seventh-day Adventist Church congress was held in Riga in May 1944, and E. Klotinsh was elected as a leader. Later when Latvia was absorbed by the Soviet Union, no church congresses were allowed. The Union Council, which was elected in 1944, continued its work until 1949. Then began a period of repression and arrests of the leaders of the church by the government.

The Seventh-day Adventist Russian church appointed A. Cholders supervisor of the work in 1950. As a member of the Union Seventh-day Adventist Church in the USSR he was authorized to lead the work in Latvia. His assistants were J. Oltinsh and E. Pavasars.

In 1960 the Russian Seventh-day Adventist Church Center was abolished by the state powers together with its accredited post in Latvia. All further work was to be carried out only in accordance with the Religion Department Council in Latvia. The council appointed J. Oltinsh to this work in 1964. He was also elected as a local council leader in the 1970s and completed his work in 1986, when official permission to organize a Seventh-day Adventist Latvian church congress was received after a 45-year break, and Valdis Zilgalvis was elected as conference president. When the Baltic Union was formed in 1989, V. Zilgalvis was elected as president of the union and Victor Geide was elected as president of the Latvian Conference. The next Seventh-day Adventist Latvian church congress was held in 1992, and V. Geide was reelected to the post of conference president.

Church membership in Latvia dropped from 2,058 in 1965 to 1,665 in 1988. Because of freedom to evangelize again, two large evangelistic campaigns were conducted by Jack Colon in 1991 and by Kenneth Mittleider in 1992.

LATVIAN CONFERENCE. *See* Trans-European Division; Latvia.

LATVIAN CONFERENCE SCHOOL (Adventes Misijas Seminars). A former training school operated by the Latvian Conference in Riga, Latvia, listed in the *Yearbook* from 1938 to 1946. It succeeded the Baltic Union School, also operated in Riga, after the Estonian Conference established its own school in 1935. World War II necessitated its closure.

LAUBHAN, CONRAD (1838-1923). The earliest Seventh-day Adventist worker in Russia. He was born in a settlement of German colonists at Tscherbakovka, on the Volga River, in Russia. In 1861 he married Katherine Sophia Meier, and in 1878 they emigrated to America, settling in Kansas, where, responding to the preaching of L. R. Conradi, they joined the Seventh-day Adventist Church. Soon afterward he became an evangelist and was listed in the 1886 *Yearbook* as a licentiate with an address at Lehigh, Kansas. In May 1886 he went to Russia and began preaching among the German colonies along the Volga River. He was ordained to the ministry in July 1887 at Basel, Switzerland. Later he worked in the Caucasus, the Don region, the Crimea, and in other areas of southern Russia. For 12 years he preached under most trying circumstances. Proselyting among the Orthodox Russians was regarded as a crime, and the other Protestants were ever ready to turn him over to the authorities. His health finally failed, and he returned to the United States, where he lived first in Oklahoma and later at College View, Nebraska.

LAUNCHES, MEDICAL AND MISSIONARY. *See* Missionary Vessels.

LAURELBROOK SCHOOL AND SANITARIUM. *See* Madison Institutions.

LAURELWOOD ADVENTIST ACADEMY. A former coeducational boarding senior high school, situated at the western foot of the Chehalem Hills, 4 miles (seven kilometers) southeast of Gaston, 25 miles (40 kilometers) southwest of Portland, Oregon, owned and operated by the Oregon Conference until 1986.

The school was located on 483 acres (200 hectares) under cultivation. There were 17 major buildings, including a 15,000-square-foot (1,400-square-meter) gymnasium and an outdoor athletic field. There was an instructional emphasis on agriculture.

History. In 1904 the board of the Western Oregon Conference voted to establish a secondary school for students in the 16 church schools then operating. The original 58 acres (25 hectares) were purchased Aug. 5, 1904, and construction was begun immediately. The entire neighborhood turned out to help in the work of tree clearing and erecting the first one-story building, used for a music studio, grammar school, and laundry. The second building, a two-story frame structure, later became the administration building.

At the camp meeting in 1905 money was raised for the girls' dormitory, a three-story building, with the kitchen and dining room on the lower floor. A barn was added the same summer, and a dairy begun, which supplied grade A milk for the school and for Portland Sanitarium. The water system was installed the next year, but a boys' dormitory was not built until 1921.

The school began as an intermediate school, teaching the first nine grades; the first tenth grader was graduated in 1906. At the conference session of 1909, the school, which now taught grades 7-12, was named Laurelwood Academy, after the community that residents had named Laurelwood because of the abundance of laurel in the vicinity.

In 1918 Laurelwood Academy became Laurelwood Junior College. A Normal Department was added, industries were established, and vocational training, including typing, was emphasized. Campus improvements, such as paving and electric lights, were effected. The junior college section was discontinued in 1925, since it was felt there were not enough students to supply both Laurelwood and Walla Walla College.

Extensive reconstruction plans began in 1942. Because no construction permits could be secured during the war, funds were temporarily invested in Series G war bonds. Less than a month after the war ended in 1945, construction began on an administration building and a new dormitory to accommodate 150 girls.

The school was renamed Laurelwood Adventist Academy at the time of the triennial constituency meeting held April 28, 1974. Increasing operating costs and decreasing enrollment led to the school being closed in 1985.

Principals: R. W. Airey, 1904-1909; R. W. Detamore, 1909; J. L. Kay, 1910-1921; F. S. Bunch, 1921-1925; H. E. Westermeyer, 1925-1931; F. J. Wallace, 1931-1934; H. R Miller, 1934-1938; G. H. Simpson, 1938-1942; C. D. Striplin, 1942-1943; T. W. Walters, 1943-1949; P. E. Limerick, 1949-1954; E. L. Gammon, 1954-1958; V. H. Fullerton, 1958-1965; A. T. Wiegardt, 1965-1969; W. W. Meske, 1969-1973; D. H. Lee, 1973-1976; Charles Hanson, 1976-1983; Hal Hampton, 1983-1985.

LAVANCHY, FRANCIS (1899-1973). Evangelist, departmental secretary, administrator. He began evangelistic work in Le Havre, France, and later became a departmental secretary in France. He served as president of three European conferences: Belgian, Swiss-French, and Franco-Belgian Union, holding the latter position for 16 years.

LA VOZ DE LA ESPERANZA ("Voice of Hope"; Spanish Voice of Prophecy). A syndicated weekly Spanish broadcast with a Bible correspondence school, video production, and music and daily radio programs, all under the same name. The weekly program can be heard in most of the Spanish-speaking countries over more than 400 radio stations, including Adventist World Radio-Latin America. Its main offices are in Thousand Oaks, California, with 32 branch locations in Spanish-speaking countries. Even though it is sponsored by the General Conference as one of the components of the Adventist Media Center, its financial support comes primarily from direct contributions.

The weekly broadcast began in 1942 as a subsidiary of the Voice of Prophecy, with speaker Braulio Perez Marcio, a Spanish evangelist and writer who throughout three decades of broadcasting became one of the most outstanding, trusted, and loved preachers for both Seventh-day Adventist and non-Seventh-day Adventist listening audiences.

First to air the weekly broadcasts were the former KOWL in Santa Monica, California, and CMQ in Havana, Cuba. Beginning in 1943, the program could be heard across Latin America, primarily over the former Pan American Broadcasting Company. A former vice president of Peru called it "the father of Spanish Christian radio programs."

Since 1971 Dr. Milton Peverini has led La Voz (first as associate speaker and later as director-speaker) into becoming a corporation independent of the Voice of Prophecy. He also has led in the producing of many new programs, videos, and books, and in assisting with evangelistic campaigns in North, Central, and South America.

The La Voz Correspondence School, through its full spectrum of courses on doctrines, family, health, and youth counseling, has graduated more than 1 million students. Since 1953 thousands of church members serving as *carteros misioneros* ("missionary mail carriers") have been key participants, using these courses for promoting both the radio program and the gospel.

LAW. Seventh-day Adventists have always distinguished the moral law, or Ten Commandments, from the ceremonial law, or the ritual requirements of the Jewish religious system. The moral law is a transcript in human language of the character and will of God, and of the principles by which His creatures are to live. Because the moral law comes from God and expresses His character, and because God's character is changeless, the principles this law sets forth are likewise eternal.

Both the OT and the NT sum up the 10 precepts of the moral law, though often worded in the form of two great commandments—love to God (the first four), and love to our fellowman (the last six; Deut. 6:5; Lev. 19:18; Matt. 22:34-40). In the Sermon on the Mount, Christ explained some of the principles of the moral law and made a practical explanation of them to life situations. Originally God implanted these principles in the very fiber and being of Adam and Eve, together with a natural inclination to live in harmony with them. The Creator also endowed humanity with the faculty of free choice; people might choose to acknowledge the lordship of the Creator by voluntary obedience, or they might choose to disobey. Obedience would guarantee eternal life; disobedience would incur condemnation and death. Humanity would find true liberty through obedience motivated by love. The moral law has never been against humanity; it is our guarantee of freedom in Christ.

The moral law requires righteousness and condemns unrighteousness. By His perfect life as a man, Christ met all the requirements of the law and demonstrated that it is just and good. By His vicarious death on the cross He satisfied the righteous demands of the law upon transgressors. By His grace He exchanges His own perfect righteousness for humankind's unrighteousness, and enables people to overcome every sinful tendency and to grow up, point by point, into the fullness of Christ's perfect character. All of this is accomplished by faith, apart from works of law.

In the heart of the repentant, forgiven sinner, transformed by divine grace, there will be a sincere desire, motivated by love, to live in harmony with all the divine requirements—not in order to be saved by any supposed works of merit on his or her part, but because he or she has already found salvation by faith in the infinite grace of Christ. "Do we then make void the law through faith? God forbid: yea, we establish the law" (Rom. 3:31). Forgiveness for past transgressions of the divine law does not carry with it a plenary indulgence to keep on transgressing that law. "God forbid. How shall we, that are dead to sin, live any longer therein?" (Rom. 6:2).

The principles set forth in the moral law are eternal. As we have seen, the Creator implanted these principles in the hearts of our first parents when He created them. At Mount Sinai He set forth these principles in the form of 10 explicit commands, in language suitable to the condition of humanity, fallen in sin. These commands He uttered with His own voice and inscribed with His own finger upon two tables of stone.

Subsequently He revealed to Moses the ceremonial code, whose types and symbols were designed to point forward to Christ and to help humanity understand and lay firm hold on redemption through the infinite sacrifice of Christ. Its rites and sacrifices could neither actually take away sin nor set the conscience free, but they could lead to faith in the coming Redeemer, in whom they all met fulfillment and reality. Without faith in that one great Sacrifice, divinely provided and promised, they were meaningless (Heb. 9:8-15).

The moral law is spiritual and can be kept only by those whose hearts have been renewed by the Spirit of God. Never in any age has its Author sought from humanity a mere outward response to the letter of the law. The moral law exercises its authority upon the inner person. It reveals sin as a conscious violation of the known will of God, thereby compelling sinners to acknowledge themselves as such, and thus to prepare to seek for, and receive, the mercy of God in Christ. It forbids not only outward acts of transgression, but every thought and motive that would lead to such acts. It requires submission of heart as well as life to God, and in so doing exposes sin at its source and in all its forms, and points the sinner to Christ for forgiveness. All attempts to earn righteousness by adhering scrupulously to legal requirements, even those of the moral law, are futile.

Christ's life and His teachings were altogether in harmony with the moral law. He vindicated this law, established it, confirmed it, and honored it by perfect obedience to its requirements. Those who choose to follow Christ will seek to become like Him. God's moral law will be written on their hearts and minds. All who have been truly converted and saved by grace will find their supreme joy in loving submission to the divine authority of the moral law, for in acknowledging that authority they acknowledge the authority of its Author, Jesus Christ.

The proper function of the moral law is to make a clear-cut distinction between right and wrong, to make known to humanity the standard of conduct of which God approves, to condemn all conduct that falls short of that standard, to convict those guilty of such conduct, and to convince sinners of their need for salvation by faith in the grace of Christ. But the moral law cannot justify sinners who violate it, nor can it provide either the desire or the ability to live in harmony with its precepts, nor does observance of it ingratiate a person with God. These are improper uses of the moral law and constitute what is known as legalism, which is the belief and attempt to find salvation and acceptance with God by one's own effort to keep the law, in contradistinction to salvation by grace alone. SDAs insist that there can be no salvation by works of law (*see* Legalism).

The gospel brings a change, but that change is not in the moral law. It is the transformation of believers by virtue of their new relationship to Christ. The gospel releases believers from the penalty of the law, but not from their obligation to live in harmony with its precepts.

In general, Protestants have affirmed belief in the binding force of the moral law, or Ten Commandments (see SB, Nos. 970-986), a position SDAs recognize as being in harmony with the teachings of Scripture. But when

SDAs insisted that the fourth commandment requires observance of the seventh day of the week as the Sabbath as a logically inevitable corollary, they encountered the vigorous assaults of certain groups who insisted that such Pauline passages as Col. 2:14-17 indicate the abolition of all OT law in the Christian Era, including the moral law. SDAs, in turn, called attention to the sharp distinction between the moral and the ceremonial law, as to character, function, and binding force in the Christian Era. For instance, in a book entitled *The Law of God* (1854) J. H. Waggoner called attention to the following: "Under the Jewish dispensation were incorporated two kinds of laws. One was founded on obligations growing out of the nature of men, and their relations to God and one another, obligations binding before they were written, and which will continue to be binding upon all who shall know them to the end of time. Such are the laws which were written by the finger of God on the tables of stone, and are called *moral laws.*

"The other kind, called *ceremonial laws,* related to various outward observances which were not obligatory till they were commanded, and then were binding only on the Jews till the death of Christ" (pp. 120, 121).

Elsewhere he says of these two laws: "By comparison, we find that two different laws are spoken of in the New Testament: one which is not made void through faith in Christ, which he came not to destroy; and another which he blotted out, and nailed to his cross" (*ibid.*, p. 73; cites Matt. 5:17, 18 and Col. 2:14-16 to illustrate this distinction).

Concerning these two laws, J. N. Andrews wrote: "The law within the ark was that which demanded atonement; the ceremonial law which ordained the Levitical priesthood and the sacrifices for sin was that which taught men how the atonement could be made" (*The Two Laws,* p. 28).

"Surely these two codes should not be confounded. The one was magnified, made honorable, established, and is holy, just, spiritual, good, royal; the other was carnal, shadowy, burdensome; and was abolished, broken down, taken out of the way, nailed to the cross, changed, and disannulled on account of the weakness and unprofitableness thereof. Those who rightly divide the Word of truth will never confound these essentially different codes, nor will they apply to God's royal law the language employed respecting the handwriting of ordinances" (*ibid.*, pp. 31, 32).

See also Faith and Works; Law and Grace; Legalism; Justification; Righteousness by Faith; Sanctification.

For a discussion of the Hebrew and Greek terms translated "law" (*tôrah* and *nomos*) see SDADic 641, 642.

LAW AND GRACE. Grace is divine favor extended to those who stand guilty and condemned to die before divine law. The necessity for divine grace arises from the sinner's inability to satisfy the demands of the law, except by his or her own death. Were it possible to change or abolish the divine law, there would be no need for grace. The sinner cannot bridge the gulf that his or her transgression of the law has made; the sinner cannot restore himself or herself to favor with God.

Law and grace are not contrary to each other. They are not mutually exclusive. Grace offers salvation from the penalty of the law, through the righteousness of Christ. It preserves both the honor and the majesty of the divine law and government, while giving life to those who have violated the law and rebelled against the government of heaven. Grace is not emancipation from the law, but it is emancipation from sin and from the penalty of the law. Grace provides salvation not by canceling the requirements of the law, but by cooperating with the law. The law condemns the transgressor; grace meets the penalty and sets the sinner free. Grace honors the law by presenting the perfect obedience of Christ in place of the sinner's disobedience. Grace does not lessen the authority of the law, but recognizes and maintains its authority by satisfying its claims. Grace forgives, but it leads those who have been forgiven to serve God in newness of life, according to His righteous will. Grace delivers the sinner from the condemnation of the law in order that he or she may obey and honor the law by a new and holy life. The Christian is to "grow" within the sphere of God's grace.

Of the relationship between law and grace as determining a person's preparation for eternal life, M. B. Smith wrote: "In this life we are justified freely by His grace. . . . But in the judgment grace is not the rule by which men are justified, but they will then be judged 'according to their works, whether they be good or bad' " (*Review and Herald* 20:15, June 10, 1862).

To some who misunderstood the Seventh-day Adventist concept of law and grace, James White replied: "Those who represent Sabbathkeepers as going away from Jesus, the only source of justification, and rejecting His atoning blood, and seeking justification by the law, do it either ignorantly or wickedly. . . . One may observe the letter of all ten of them [the Ten Commandments] and, if he is not justified by faith in Jesus Christ, never have right to the tree of life. The gospel arrangement is plain. God's law convicts of sin, and shows the sinner exposed to the wrath of God, and leads him to Christ, where justification for past offenses can be found alone through faith in His blood. The law of God has no power to pardon past offenses, its attribute being justice, therefore the convicted transgressor must flee to Jesus" *(ibid.* 3:24, June 10, 1852).

While believing that the born-again Christian will obey all of God's requirements, motivated by love, SDAs have always repudiated the idea that their obedience is a means to salvation, and clearly affirm that this is by grace alone: "Let it be distinctly understood that there is no salvation in the law. There is no redeeming quality in law. Redemption is through the blood of Christ" *(Signs of the Times* 3:378, Dec. 20, 1877).

"You may observe all these precepts, to the best of your ability, conscientiously; but if you look no further than the law for salvation, you can never be saved. The hope of eternal salvation hangs upon Christ" *(ibid.* 379).

See also Faith and Works; Justification; Law; Legalism; Sanctification.

LAW KEEM (1867-1919). Pioneer medical missionary in China. He was born in Kwangtung, China, and in 1882 went to the United States to obtain an education. While there he accepted Seventh-day Adventist beliefs and subsequently attended Healdsburg College and California Medical College (1896-1900). For several years Law Keem operated a private sanitarium in California. In 1904 he married Edith Miller, a graduate nurse, and in 1905 they became the fifth family to be sent by the mission board to China. There he promoted SDA work by opening chapels and dispensaries in several places in the southern and southwestern provinces. He died at his station at Nanning, Kwangsi province.

LAWHEAD (LOUGHHEAD), JAMES WHITE (1860-1937). Educator and administrator. Educated at Battle Creek College, he was teaching at his alma mater when he was chosen in 1891 to be the resident principal of the newly established Union College, whose president, W. W. Prescott, was simultaneously in charge of Battle Creek College and Union College. Lawhead served as its president from 1893 to 1896. Later he was principal of Mount Vernon Academy (1896-1904) and in 1904 became president of the newly founded Washington Training College, Takoma Park, Maryland (now Columbia Union College). Failing health led to his resignation and retirement in 1907.

LAY ACTIVITIES DEPARTMENT (formerly Home Missionary Department, now part of Church Ministries Department). The department of the General Conference that, with its secretary, associate secretaries, and staff, fostered the activities of laity in any line of local missionary service anywhere in the world. By "missionary" service is meant personal or public evangelism or Community Services (formerly Health and Welfare Service). There were corresponding departments in the divisions, unions, and conferences. *See* Church Ministries Department; Personal Ministries.

LAY EVANGELISM. The lay member's sharing of his or her faith with others, singly or in groups, by public speaking or private witness, by word or deed; especially the presentation and communication of the good news about Jesus Christ to others by way of opening to them the Word of God. The Seventh-day Adventist Church, recognizing that much of the growth of the church has been the result of lay evangelism, promotes lay evangelism by various methods, chiefly through the General Conference Church Ministries Department.

Personal Evangelism. Every committed SDA is expected to be a personal evangelist. Opportunities for missionary endeavor begin among friends, relatives, neighbors, and contacts in the workplace and include such ministry as personal house-to-house visitation, comforting the sick and mourners, helping the poor and afflicted, speaking peace to the disconsolate, and also giving Bible studies in the homes. SDAs are taught that it is the church's responsibility to carry the Word of God to every person's door. SDAs are offered training courses in the local church and shown that there are many opportunities for personal evangelism—in the home, in hotels and rooming houses, within prison walls, at the bedside of the sick, in parks, on ships, in public conveyances, in public places, in business offices, and at social gatherings.

A variety of well-tested audiovisual aids and materials are available for use by laypersons. Bible studies and evangelistic series have been prepared on filmstrips, cassette tapes, and videotapes. Several Bible courses are available. There are Picture Rolls, pictorial aids, and Bible-marking plans available. Laypersons also accept the call to lay preaching as a challenge.

In the fastest-growing divisions most of the outreach is done by laypersons trained, organized, and encouraged by pastors. Several divisions have strong programs for developing lay evangelists.

In 1979 Samuel Monnier introduced an eight-day Lay Evangelists' Training Seminar. These seminars have become annual events in many fields around the world. Training is provided in every area of lay evangelism, including on-the-job training in house-to-house visitation.

Another program, called Lay Bible Ministers, follows a curriculum that is taught on three or four weekends each year. Both programs provide the opportunity of returning for additional training after field experience.

Coordinated Evangelism. In recent years there has been a reemphasis on "coordinated evangelism"—the united efforts of laypersons and ministers conducted through the cooperation of the departments of the conference and the local church, and of the laity and pastor, in the common objective of winning souls to Christ.

A number of unions in North America and several world divisions have outlined a coordinated evangelism program and prepared booklets presenting steps to be taken by the departments, churches, and members.

Lay Training. From early times the denomination has offered training in evangelism, open to laypersons as well as workers, in the form of Bible schools and institutes.

The first division-wide lay congress was held in Grand Ledge, Michigan, Aug. 29 to Sept. 2, 1951, with delegates representing the churches in the North American Division. Training and demonstration workshops in the methods of soul winning and the first commissioning of the "120" were the highlights of this meeting. In the united lay advance that followed this congress there was a simultaneous launching of 4,237 lay evangelistic meetings on Sunday, Nov. 11, 1951.

Lay congresses overseas followed in 1953 and onward, some of the largest being held in eastern Asia in 1956 and in New Zealand and Australia in 1959. Other lay congresses offered also a decision and problem clinic and classes in the following: audiovisual aids, contemporary groups, leadership, lay preaching, and branch Sabbath schools. Beginning in 1979 in four different parts of the division, Inter-America has had large Festivals of the Laity once a quinquennium. Many lay evangelists attending consistently lead more than 100 a year to baptism. Lay congresses have trained thousands of laypersons in effective evangelistic methods, have given impetus to missionary activity, and have increased soul-winning results.

Some significant Annual Council recommendations and events influencing lay evangelism in the latter part of the twentieth century include:

1975—Publication of *Witnessing for Christ* as a joint project of the Ministerial Association and the following GC departments: Lay Activities, Sabbath School, Temperance, and Youth.

1976—The "Evangelism and Finishing the Work" document, and the recommendation "challenging every family to accept a territorial assignment."

1980—The Prayer Offensive, encouraging each church family/member to pray daily for their neighborhood and a specific unentered territory.

1982—The recommendation to appeal to members to dedicate two or more hours a week to working for others.

1986—The challenge to develop a global strategy to fulfill our global mission.

1987—Sabbath School Action Units. From the early days of the SDA movement inspired counsel emphasized the potential of the Sabbath school, with its small groups, as an effective soul-winning instrument. This has been dramatically demonstrated in some world divisions. Since 1987 Calvin Smith, of the Church Ministries Department, developed and systematized a plan that worked in North America and then spread worldwide. In each small class there is a care coordinator and a discussion group leader who share the hour of class time.

1994—The *Adult Sabbath School Lesson Quarterly* featured lessons on personal evangelism.

LAY, HORATIO S. (1828-1900). Pioneer Seventh-day Adventist physician and editor of the *Health Reformer*. He was born in the state of New York and reared in Pennsylvania, where he was apprenticed to a physician for the study of medicine. Having graduated from

Western Reserve College at Cleveland and from Detroit Medical College, he began his practice at Allegan, Michigan. In 1852 he married Julia M. Barber, and about four years later joined the Seventh-day Adventist Church through the influence of M. E. Cornell. In the early 1860s he took his wife, who had become ill, to a "water-cure" institution operated by Dr. J. C. Jackson at Dansville, New York, and apparently at the same time joined its staff and acquired practical experience in what was termed "rational medicine." Some three years later he returned to his practice, but was called in 1866 to head the newly established SDA health institution, the Western Health Reform Institute—later named Battle Creek Sanitarium—and to edit the first SDA health journal, the *Health Reformer.* He remained at the head of the institute for about four years. After that he practiced at Allegan and Petoskey, Michigan, until 1884, when he entered the ministry in the Michigan Conference. In the early 1890s he contracted tuberculosis, which resulted in his death at the age of 71.

LAYMAN FOUNDATION. *See* Madison Institutions.

LEACH, CLARENCE VICTOR (1889-1965). Pastor, departmental secretary, administrator. He was converted under the preaching of W. C. Moffett. For many years he gave faithful service to the church in the following capacities: pastor and publishing secretary of the West Virginia and Columbia Union conferences, home missionary secretary of the General Conference, and president of the West Virginia, East Pennsylvania, Ohio, Chesapeake, and Minnesota conferences.

LEBANON. A republic in the Middle East situated on the eastern shore of the Mediterranean Sea and bounded by Syria on the north and east and by Israel on the south. Its area is 4,015 square miles (10,400 square kilometers); its population, representing nearly every nationality of the Middle East, has been estimated (1994) at 3.6 million. Seventy percent of the people of Lebanon are Muslims; the other 30 percent are Christians. Arabic is the official language, but the minorities use their own languages—French is the second language of many Christians, and English is rapidly gaining ground throughout the country.

Trade provides two thirds of the national income. Half the workers are employed in agriculture, the chief crops being apples, citrus fruits, olives, tobacco, grapes, vegetables, and cereals. Manufacturing is also rapidly developing.

There is a correspondence between modern Lebanon and ancient Phoenicia. The Phoenicians were Canaanites who were pushed northward by the Hebrew conquest of Palestine. They in turn influenced the Hebrews; for example, Hiram of Tyre furnished cedars from the Lebanon mountains and craftsmen to build Solomon's Temple at Jerusalem; Jezebel, the queen of Israel who promoted Baal worship in Israel, was a Phoenician princess; and her daughter Athaliah, queen of Judah, promoted Baal worship in Judah.

Seafaring Phoenicians, traders and colonizers in distant lands, carried the alphabet to Greece and spread Eastern culture to Europe. The Phoenician city-states were, like Israel, tributary to Egypt, Assyria, Babylon, and Persia, successively, and later formed a part of the Seleucid Empire and the Roman province of Syria. Early Christianized, Lebanon provided a mountain stronghold for Maronite Christians seeking refuge from Byzantine orthodoxy and Muslim rule. Here through the centuries several kinds of Christians and Muslims, in nearly equal numbers, have preserved an equilibrium. After many centuries of Turkish rule, Lebanon became in 1921 a mandated territory under French administration, at first as part of Syria, later as a separate area. It became an independent republic in 1941.

Seventh-day Adventist Statistics. Lebanon is part of the East Mediterranean Field, part of the Middle East Union, an attached field of the General Conference. Statistics (1993) for the *East Mediterranean Field:* churches, 8; members, 1,371; ordained ministers, 2; credentialed missionaries, 26. Headquarters: Sabtieh, Jdeidet El Matn, Lebanon.

Institutions. Armenian Adventist School; Boushrieh Adventist Secondary School; Middle East College; Middle East Press; Mouseitbeh Adventist Secondary School.

Development of Seventh-day Adventist Work. *Beginnings.* Before any organized work was begun in Lebanon, Seventh-day Adventists had visited there. In 1897 H. P. Holser, of the Central European Conference, reported that Abram La Rue, pioneer missionary to the China coast, had spent a short time in Beirut and had left some publications there. In 1898 Holser visited there with a view to making plans for publishing in Arabic. About 1902 a

Syrian who had lived in the United States visited his parents in Lebanon, bringing a copy of *Bible Readings,* and convinced the Presbyterian pastor in his town of the claims of the seventh-day Sabbath. The pastor, Elias Zarub, not knowing that there were SDAs in the Middle East, went to the United States and spent six months in Berrien Springs, Michigan, then in 1903 returned to Beirut as an SDA worker. With J. H. Krum, head of the mission that included Syria (with Lebanon) and Palestine, he went among his friends and won converts. However, Zarub seems to have joined another religious group in 1908

Sabbathkeepers were reported in Beirut as early as 1904. Near the end of 1905 W. H. Wakeham, superintendent of the Egyptian Mission, visited the area and baptized Anistas Khouri, a woman who had begun to keep the Sabbath five years before, while on a visit in New York, and who was teaching a private school at Schwaifat, near Beirut; he also baptized a former Catholic priest in the village of Magdouche, near Sidon. At that time there were several adherents in Malaka, near Beirut, and Deir Mimas, near Mount Hermon, and in Beirut a German masseur named Haussman and his wife, who was a nurse from the Basel Sanitarium, were engaged in private health work. Haussman was a convert of the Krums in Jaffa. In 1908 W. K. Ising arrived from Germany, and in 1909 he became head of the Syrian-Egyptian Mission, which was then organized, with headquarters in Beirut. There were possibly seven or eight members in the city at that time. Early in 1910 a canvasser, T. Zachary, was working in Beirut, an Armenian who had come from Persia to Cairo and had there become an SDA in 1909.

Ising rented a house near what is now the American University of Beirut and gathered a group of young men, some of whom were students, for Bible lessons in his home. In 1911 he baptized five persons, including Ibrahim el-Khalil, an ex-Muslim, who later became a minister in Palestine and elsewhere; Shukri Nowfel, later the first Arab-speaking national to be ordained in the Arabic Union Mission; and Bashir Hasso, pioneer layman in Iraq.

In 1912 Ising reported some keeping the Sabbath in three places in Lebanon, one a Protestant Bible woman, who joined the church the next year. He also reported two canvassers at work. In 1913, while Ising was away in Mesopotamia for nine months, Zachary and Khalil worked in Lebanon.

Henry Erzberger, who came to Beirut from Switzerland about this time, remained throughout the period of the war, during which time the members held their Sabbath services at Bhamdoun, in the mountains and at the Erzberger home in Ras Beirut. In 1915 the Beirut church had 10 members. The 1917 *Yearbook* lists Erzberger for Jerusalem and does not name a worker for Beirut. No mission director was listed for the Syrian Mission until 1923, when Nils Zerne, from Berne, was named. The original membership seems to have dwindled or scattered.

Later Developments. In 1923, 10 SDA Armenian refugees from Turkey formed the beginning of the Beirut Armenian church, and Erzberger baptized Armenian converts.

The first elementary school was opened in Beirut in 1929, with Hana Jubran Nasr as headmistress. In 1953 it offered some secondary schoolwork and then was renamed the Beirut Junior Academy. Later it became a 12-grade secondary school and was again renamed Museitbeh Adventist Secondary School.

In the autumn of 1939 a training school for national workers, which later became Middle East College, was opened in Beirut.

In 1939 Neshan Hovhannessian founded a school for the Armenian Adventist children in Khalil Badawy, Beirut. This grew into a mission school, with facilities connected to the Bourj-Hammoud church, which was completed in 1965.

Sabbath school lessons in Arabic were printed in Beirut in 1928, but it was not until 1947 that the Middle East Press was established to issue SDA publications in the area. The first colporteur in the country, Zachary, who worked in Beirut about 1910, was joined later by Michael Ghafaryo. They sold SDA publications in most of the major mountain villages, especially in the popular resort towns frequented by visitors from all parts of the Middle East. Colporteurs continued to sell SDA publications in these towns, making Lebanon an important center for distribution to the other countries in the area.

By 1938 Armenian and Arabic congregations in Beirut had places of worship, but it was not long before these were overcrowded. On July 30, 1955, a new church for the Armenian believers, constructed on property adjoining the school, was dedicated. A new Arabic church was built at Museitbeh in 1959, the building including office space for the headquarters of the Lebanon Section. Hostile political conditions in the neighborhood of the Armenian church threatened the lives of worshipers and forced them to move to the other side of the Beirut River. A new church auditorium was completed in Bourj Hammoud in 1965, the largest Seventh-day Adventist church building in the Middle East.

Work was begun in southern Lebanon, at Aramoun, by a lay member, Nabeeha Nowfel Khoury. In the mid-1940s an elementary school was established there. For a time there was a worker at Marj'youn.

In 1948 W. E. Olson opened work in the el-Koura district of northern Lebanon. A school was begun that autumn at Shekka, with about 60 students, but it was shortlived. But in 1955 a church seating 125 persons was dedicated at Bishmezzine. The next year a school was opened there.

An Arabic branch Sabbath school, conducted by Edith Davis and students from Middle East College in the neighborhood of the college, grew until a small evangelistic center was opened there in 1954. When members of the branch Sabbath school were denied education privileges because of their interest in the Sabbath, it was decided to conduct an elementary school for them near Middle East College. School opened Oct. 12, 1956, as a laboratory for teacher-training students, under the auspices of the Education Department of Middle East College. It was upgraded to a high school affiliated with the college, and in 1969 was separated from the college and moved to its present location in Boushrieh.

By 1957 the branch Sabbath school had, through the efforts of Miss Davis and the college ministerial students, become a regular Sabbath school, and church services were held. In 1960 these meetings were conducted in the college chapel after the English services, and in 1965 they moved to the men's dormitory worship room, with Samir Shahine as the first pastor. Later the group moved to the Boushrieh district, and in 1970 the Boushrieh Seventh-day Adventist Church was dedicated.

An evangelistic center in Beirut was completed in 1959. It provided space for the Voice of Prophecy Bible Correspondence School, a physical therapy clinic, a large auditorium, and rooms for cooking and Bible classes. The clinic was opened in the autumn of 1960, with Leif Jensen in charge, but it closed when he left in 1968. Harry E. Robinson presented there the first series of public meetings in Arabic by an SDA missionary from the United States. A church was organized at the center on Oct. 7, 1961.

The Voice of Prophecy Bible Correspondence School was opened at Beirut in 1948. Seven years later a recording studio for preparing broadcasts was constructed on the campus of Middle East College. From 1956 to 1959, Dr. Clifford Anderson's health lectures translated into Arabic were broadcast regularly by the Lebanese national radio. The first Vacation Bible Schools in Lebanon were conducted at four places during the summer of 1957. During the summer of 1953 an MV leaders' training camp was conducted, and since then summer camps for juniors have operated annually. The first senior camp was organized in 1959. In 1963 the Lebanon Section became the first mission in the Middle East to purchase an MV campsite—mountain property forested with cedars in northern Lebanon. Government regulations, which required military training in the schools, led to the formation of Medical Cadet Corps camps in the summers of 1956 and 1957, and for a few years civil defense classes were taught throughout the school year.

Organization. During the formative period of SDA work in the Middle East, a single organization guided the work in the area, including Lebanon, Palestine, Iraq, Jordan, and Egypt, and was first known as the Syrian-Egyptian Mission, then as the Syro-Arabic Field, and later as the Egypto-Syrian Mission. After that the work in Lebanon was directed by the Syrian Mission, with headquarters in Beirut. In 1948 this was renamed the Lebanon-Syria Mission, and by 1958 was called the Lebanon-Syria Section. In 1959 this was divided into the Lebanon Section and the Syria Section. In 1970 it was reorganized as part of the East Mediterranean Field under the Middle East Union.

In 1967 the emphasis in missions began to be placed on the outreach of the church to non-Christians, and a program was inaugurated at the Beirut Adventist Center by Harley Bresee. Work was also pioneered in the mountain village of Bikfaiya by Jerald Whitehouse in 1970. In the northern Lebanon city of Tripoli an experimental evangelistic program was conducted among the non-Christians of the city by the Middle East Union TEAM.

Work in Lebanon is carried on principally by regular church evangelism programs, summer youth camps, temperance programs, and the mission schools. With the increasing shift to health evangelism approaches, an Adventist Health Education Foundation was formed to serve this need in 1974.

Having survived the 16-year-long civil war in Lebanon (1975-1991), the Seventh-day Adventist Church continues to carry on its multifaceted program in this challenging area.

LECOULTRE, DAVID (1863-1951). Pioneer evangelist in Switzerland, France, and Belgium. As a young child of 5, he lost his father, a Swiss contractor. Later his stepfather, who had become interested in Seventh-day Adventist doctrines through the preaching of James Erzberger in Orbe, Switzerland, introduced him to Seventh-day Adventism. He was baptized at the age of 15. In 1889 he married Adele Hirschy. Although he had had training in public school, he enrolled in 1893, when he was 30 years old, in one of the earliest training schools conducted by Seventh-day Adventists outside North America, which operated at Peseux, Switzerland, and there spent two years. Receiving a license as a minister, he worked as a colporteur and conducted public evangelism. He was the first SDA evangelist to preach in Paris, arriving there in 1900 during the time of the World's Exposition. Though he was never ordained, he helped to found several churches in Switzerland, among them those at Moudon, Payerne, Chateau-d'Oex, and Fleurier.

LEDGEVIEW MEMORIAL HOME. A 79-bed nursing home formerly operated at West Paris, Maine, by the Northern New England Conference. It was the wish of Mr. and Mrs. Adelbert Bowen to have a well-equipped, up-to-date nursing home in the West Paris area. In 1967 a group of Seventh-day Adventist laypersons formed a nonprofit corporation, received a $5,000 bank loan, and purchased a five-acre (two-hectare) tract of land. Contributions were given from the surrounding communities, and excavation began in 1969. In 1970 the project was given to the Northern New England Conference and, through the special efforts of Erland Thurlow and other workers, the nursing home opened on Sept. 13, 1971. The home was opened with a licensed capacity of 74 beds. Remodeling was done in 1973, allowing for the addition of five more beds. In 1974 a farm, which borders the nursing home property, was purchased. In 1988 the Northern New England Conference sold the nursing home to Mr. and Mrs. Lawrence A. Wilday.

LEE, FREDERICK (1888-1988). Missionary, administrator, editor. Born in Michigan, he and his wife Minnie served as missionaries to China for nearly 30 years, where he was director of various missions, superintendent of the North China and Central Union missions, and Ministerial Association director for the China Division. He edited the Chinese *Signs of the Times* and was later associate editor of the *Review and Herald* for 19 years. After the death of his wife, he married Emma Iversen Paul. His son Milton followed in his footsteps as a long-term missionary to China.

LEE KEUN OK (also transliterated Ne Kun Ok, Lee Keun Uk, and either K. U. or K. O. Lee, 1881-1932). Korean minister and administrator; one of the earliest Seventh-day Adventists in Korea; one of the first two ordained Korean Seventh-day Adventist ministers. He was baptized by Hide Kuniya in 1906 and attended the SDA school at Sunan, where he later taught from 1908 to 1910. In 1910 he began evangelistic work; in 1915 he was ordained to the ministry; in 1925 he became president of the West Chosen Conference, and about 1930 he was appointed director of the Central Chosen Mission, from which office he retired, because of failing health, shortly before his death.

LEE, LEONARD CROSWELL (1900-1974). Minister, author, radio speaker. A native of North Dakota, he graduated from Emmanuel Missionary College in 1927. That year he married Audra Reichenbach, who served with him in Michigan, Iowa, Louisiana, Ohio, West Virginia, and New York.

During his ministry he authored seven books, one of which was published in eight languages. He also wrote hundreds of articles appearing in church publications. He conducted a weekly radio program at Des Moines, Iowa, and served as the Faith for Today Bible School director for five years before his retirement.

LEEWARD AND WINDWARD ISLANDS. A group of islands in the West Indies. The Leeward Islands group includes Anguilla, Antigua and Barbuda, the British Virgin Islands, Guadeloupe and dependencies (including Désirode, Les Saintes, Marie-Galante, St. Barthélemy, and St.-Martin [French Section]), Montserrat, St. Christopher (St. Kitts) and Nevis, and Saba, St. Eustatius, and St. Maarten (Dutch Section) in the Netherlands Antilles. The Windward Islands include Dominica, Grenada, St. Lucia, and St. Vincent and the Grenadines. The total area of the islands, which are scattered along a 450-mile-long (720-kilometer-long) northwest-southwest curve between the Atlantic Ocean and the Caribbean Sea, is about 3,000 square miles (8,000 square kilometers), and the total population is about 2 million. The official language is English, but in the southern islands French is spoken. Sugar cane is the principal economic resource of the area.

Seventh-day Adventist Statistics. The territory of the Leeward Islands group is included in the North Caribbean Conference, part of the Caribbean Union Conference, and the Guadeloupe Conference, part of the French Antilles-Guiana Union Mission, all of which are part of the Inter-American Division. Statistics (1992) for the *North Caribbean Conference:* churches, 59; members, 16,685; elementary schools, 6; ordained ministers, 26; credentialed missionaries, 29; licensed ministers, 15; licensed missionaries, 36. Headquarters: Christiansted, St. Croix. Statistics (1993) for the *Guadeloupe Conference:* churches, 44; members, 8,753; secondary schools, 1; elementary schools, 4; ordained ministers, 14; credentialed missionaries, 28; licensed ministers, 6; licensed missionaries, 18; credentialed and licensed literature evangelists, 10. Headquarters: Morne Boissard, Point-à-Pitre, Guadeloupe.

The territory of the Windward Islands group is included in the East Caribbean Conference and the Grenada Mission, which are part of the Caribbean Union Conference, which in turn are part of the Inter-American Division. Statistics (1992) for the *East Caribbean Conference:* churches, 114; members, 32,902; elementary schools, 11; ordained ministers, 29; credentialed missionaries, 84; licensed ministers, 16; licensed missionaries, 66. Headquarters: St. Michael, Barbados. Statistics (1993) for the *Grenada Mission:* churches, 28; members, 6,577; elementary schools, 2; ordained ministers, 9; licensed ministers, 3; teachers, 24. Headquarters: St. Andrew's, Grenada.

The percentage of SDAs on a number of the Leeward and Windward islands is quite high.

Institutions. Antigua Seventh-day Adventist School (Antigua and Barbuda); Bequia Seventh-day Adventist Secondary School (St. Vincent and the Grenadines); Dominica Seventh-day Adventist Secondary School (Dominica); Grenada Seventh-day Adventist Comprehensive Secondary School (Grenada); Mountain View Adventist Academy (St. Vincent and the Grenadines); Saint Lucia Seventh-day Adventist Academy (St. Lucia).

SDA Work. SDA work on these islands began in the 1880s. In 1888 a Mrs. A. Roskruge from the island of Antigua became an SDA, while on a visit to England. Returning the next year to her home, she interested some of her friends and neighbors in her new beliefs and with them formed a Sabbath school. About that time William Arnold, a colporteur, made a trip through the islands of the Caribbean selling SDA books. He reported selling as many as 30 books in one day and 300 in one month. From 1890 to 1892 D. A. Ball, an ordained minister, preached on the islands from St. Thomas in the north to Grenada in the south and organized a company on the island of Antigua in 1890. In 1896 two colporteurs, T. Critchlow and J. Lewis, went to Monserrat, and two others from Barbados, W. F. Cozier and R. N. Batson, went to Antigua. In 1895 E. Van Duesen, who was stationed on Barbados, preached on the neighboring islands and began work on St. Vincent.

In 1897 the work on the islands was organized into the West Indian Mission, with A. J. Haysmer as superintendent, and a year later A. Palmquist and his wife were assigned to the Lesser Antilles Islands. In 1899 J. A. Morrow began work on the island of St. Kitts. Palmquist moved northward, and in 1900 entered the Virgin Islands with SDA books, and the next year Haysmer went there.

The number of workers in the area increased rapidly after the turn of the century. In 1901 D. E. Wellman went to Antigua, S. A. Wellman was assigned to the Lesser Antilles in general, and L. E. Wellman began work on Tortola in the British Virgin Islands. In 1904 W. G. Kneeland pioneered on Grenada, and in the same year the pioneer Inter-American worker P. Giddings, from British Guiana, opened SDA work in the island of Dominica. With the work by that time having become almost self-sustaining, in 1903 the Lesser Antilles islands were organized into the East Caribbean Conference. By 1907, when the first meeting of the West Indian Union Conference was held at Kingston, Jamaica, the work had been well established on Antigua, Dominica, St. Lucia, St. Vincent, Grenada, Tortola, St. Kitts, and Nevis.

In 1910 the mission operated a motor launch in the Virgin Islands and the surrounding area, then superintended by H.C.J. Walleker. In 1911 A. N. Durrant preached in tents on the Grenadines. This is the first time this area is mentioned in the reports, which also note that on Grenada one third of the members were Indians.

In the 1920s I. G. Knight established his headquarters on the islands of St. Kitts. There is also a report that much of the work on the islands was done by lay members, especially on the predominantly Catholic island of St. Lucia.

In the early 1930s there were four ministers in the Leeward Islands, 1,427 members, 25 organized churches, 30 Sabbath schools, and 23 young people's societies. Work on the island of Anguilla is first mentioned in 1933, when C. G. Van Putten preached there. By 1937 two companies were ready to be organized into churches. In 1934 there were six churches on Antigua, two churches on Nevis, and several elsewhere on the islands. The colporteur work continued to play an important role in the advancement of the SDA work throughout the area.

Work was started in the British Virgin Island of Virgin Gorda by L. D. Brathwaite, and in 1972 I. I. Berkel began work in Saba. The first welfare center was opened in 1973 on the island of Antigua in the capital of St. John's. In Antigua there is one SDA to every 25 of population.

In 1973 St.-Martin (French Section) and St. Barthélemy were turned over to the Guadeloupe Mission (now Guadeloupe Conference) of the Franco-Haitian Union Mission (now French Antillies-Guiana Union Mission).

The Leeward Islands have been part of the North Caribbean and Guadeloupe conferences, and the Windward Islands part of the East Caribbean Conference, since the mid-1970s. In 1983 Grenada left the East Caribbean Conference and became part of the Grenada Mission.

LE FLON OLD PEOPLE'S HOME. *See* Établissement Medico-Social Le Flon.

LEGAL ASSOCIATIONS. *See* Corporations.

LEGAL SERVICE (GENERAL CONFERENCE). *See* Office of General Counsel (General Conference).

LEGALISM. The view that salvation can be achieved or merited through compliance with a legal code. NT writers, particularly Paul, staunchly oppose such a view. Especially in his Epistles to the Romans and to the Galatians, Paul seeks to prove that no one can be justified in the sight of God by the works of the law. He sees legalism as the great shortcoming of Judaism, as he knew it in his time.

"Israel who pursued the righteousness which is based on law did not succeed in fulfilling that law. Why? Because they did not pursue it through faith, but as if it were based on works" (Rom. 9:31, 32, RSV).

To Paul, legalism was impossible as a means to salvation.

In contrast with faith, which requires a positive relationship toward God, legalism represents a negative attitude. It is at this point, ultimately, that the question of whether a person is a legalist or not must be settled. Theologically a person may hold that righteousness is by faith, but if his or her way of life and attitude toward God are basically structured in terms of a mere checklist code of do's and don'ts, he or she is still a legalist—"the letter killeth, but the spirit giveth life." Christian freedom does not mean that the Christian no longer observes God's requirements; it means that he or she does so through faith, in thankfulness for the salvation God has given. Having received salvation, the Christian obeys as an act of love and thanksgiving, out of a desire to comply with God's will. This view rules out any possible basic approach to religion in terms of a legal code.

See Faith and Works; Justification; Law; Law and Grace; Righteousness by Faith; Salvation; Sanctification.

LELAND, JAMES ARTHUR (1871-1951). Missionary, administrator. Trained at Battle Creek College, he entered evangelism in Colorado in 1893, married Hattie Emma Green (1869-1950) in 1894, and was ordained several years later. In 1898 in Argentina, he and N. Z. Town established the first Seventh-day Adventist school in Argentina (now River Plate Adventist University). He served briefly in Uruguay, then in Mexico as an evangelist and as a dentist at the Guadalajara Sanitarium (1901-1904). He worked especially among Spanish-speaking people in Albuquerque, New Mexico, and in Colorado (to about 1909) and Texas (1909-1917) among both English and Spanish congregations. Between 1913 and 1922 he was president successively of the South Texas, Virginia, and East Pennsylvania conferences, and later (1928-1932) of the Chesapeake and Kentucky conferences. During another mission term he was superintendent of the Aztec (1923) and Antillian

(1923-1927) unions. Later he pastored churches in Florida. His wife served as Bible instructor in Colorado; teacher in New Mexico, Texas, and Washington, D.C.; and Sabbath school and MV secretary in the Chesapeake and Kentucky-Tennessee conferences and in the Mexican and Antillian unions.

LE MÊME, ROSINA (ROSE, ROSA) (c. 1880-1919). First Seventh-day Adventist on the island of Mauritius. From her childhood she was deeply interested in spiritual things and in works of mercy. About the time she was 26 or 27, she decided that since she could not find satisfaction for her heart's longing on the island, she would go to Europe. This she did in 1910. After traveling in England and France, she went to Lausanne, Switzerland, where someone left at her door an announcement of a series of evangelistic meetings conducted by SDAs. She attended, and soon was baptized by H. H. Dexter, then superintendent of the French-Swiss Conference. In 1912 she returned to Mauritius, where she shared her new faith with her sisters. Despite much opposition from other relatives and former friends, she traveled throughout the island to tell of the soon coming of Christ. Soon she wrote to Europe that there were 24 persons studying the Bible with her. In response to her appeals for a minister, Paul Badaut went to the island in 1914, baptized those who had accepted the SDA faith, and established an SDA church there. She and her sister used part of the funds from their inheritance to build a chapel for the congregation. She devoted the rest of her life to spreading the Bible message among the people of the island.

The story of her life was related in the *Youth's Instructor* of Apr. 22, 1958.

LE MESSAGER DE LA DIVISION INTER-AMERICAINE. *See Messager de la Division Inter-Americaine, Le.*

LENKER, WILLIAM (1864-1945). Colporteur. When 20 years of age and attending Battle Creek College, he was invited by Uriah Smith to devote his life to the colporteur work. Subsequently he worked in England, Burma, China, and Japan, and started the colporteur work in India.

LEPRA. *See* Malawi.

LESOTHO (formerly Basutoland). Previously a British protectorate from 1868-1966, when it became an independent country completely surrounded by the republic of South Africa, bounded by the Orange Free State on the west and north, by Natal on the north and east, and by the Cape Province on the south. It has an area of 11,716 square miles (30,344 square kilometers). In 1994 the population was 1.9 million, almost all Sotho. The country is extremely mountainous (elevation 5,000 to 11,000 feet [1,500 to 3,300 meters]). Agriculture is the principal occupation. The exports are wool, mohair, beans, and peas. Labor forms an important export from Lesotho, 90,000 leaving each year to work in the republic of South Africa, chiefly in the mines. About 80 percent are Christian, 75 percent of these being Roman Catholic. Sesotho is the principal language, but both English and Sesotho are official. King Letsie III has since 1990 been the head of the Lesotho nation, which is governed by parliament, through a prime minister.

Seventh-day Adventist Statistics. The territory of Lesotho constitutes the Lesotho Field, which falls under the jurisdiction of the Southern Africa Union, an attached field of the General Conference. Statistics (1993) for *Lesotho:* churches, 20; members, 2,580; ordained ministers, 6; church schools, 6; high schools, 1; secondary schools, 1; teachers, 31. Headquarters: Maseru.

Institutions: Emmanuel Mission School; Maluti Adventist Hospital.

Development of Seventh-day Adventist Work. Seventh-day Adventist work in Lesotho began in the year 1896 when a Mosotho, David Kalaka, on a visit to Kimberley, became the first Mosotho SDA convert. He learned SDA teachings while serving as a guide for S. N. Haskell on a trip to Basotoland. In 1899 J. M. Freeman, in company with David Kalaka, established the first Seventh-day Adventist Basotoland mission at Kolo. This site was personally allocated to them by Lerothli, the paramount chief of Basotoland. The second mission, Emmanuel Station, was established in 1910 by H. C. Olmstead and has continued ever since.

LESOTHO FIELD. *See* Lesotho; Southern Africa Union.

LEVANT UNION MISSION. A unit of church organization in the eastern Mediterranean area listed in the *Yearbook* from 1907 to 1923 as attached to the European Division. The following countries were at some time part of the mission: Arabia, Bulgaria, Egypt, Ethiopia, Greece, Iran, Iraq, Israel, Jordan, Lebanon, Sudan, Syria, and Turkey. Before 1907 the unit had been the Oriental Union Mission. Much of its territory is now included in the Middle East Division.

LEWIS, CHARLES CLARKE (1857-1924). Educator. He was born at Lisbon, New York. At the age of 8 he moved with his parents to a farm at Buck's Bridge, New York. He began to teach at the age of 16. In 1877 he became a Seventh-day Adventist and the same year entered Battle Creek College, from which he was graduated in 1882. During his last year in college, he taught several classes and served as secretary to Uriah Smith, the editor of the *Review and Herald.* After graduation he spent the summer canvassing and assisting two evangelists with tent meetings. Then he taught public school for one year. From 1883 to 1887, he taught in Battle Creek College, after which he was called to head the Minneapolis Conference School.

In 1890-1891 he studied at Yale University. On leaving Yale, he was invited to teach in Union College, where he remained until 1896, after which he was made principal of Keene Academy at Keene, Texas. In 1892 while serving in Union College, he was ordained. After several years at Keene, he was elected president of Walla Walla College, where he served until 1904, when he accepted the presidency of Union College, which position he occupied until 1910. During the next three years he was professor of education and philosophy at Pacific Union College. From there he was called to fill the same position in Washington Missionary College and at the same time to head the Fireside Correspondence School This work he carried till the time of his death.

LEWIS, ELIZABETH ANN WILEY (1857-1915). Educator, Sabbath school worker, editor, writer. Born in Toronto, Canada, of Scottish-Irish parents, she attended Battle Creek College. She married Charles C. Lewis, a graduate of the college, and they both taught at Sumner, Michigan. Later they returned to Battle Creek, where he taught and she was part-time preceptor. She developed the first kindergarten Sabbath school class at the Battle Creek Tabernacle and introduced the idea wherever she went.

They taught in Minneapolis and then moved on to Union College, where she started a monthly paper, *Early Education.* Later they both worked at the Keene Academy in Keene, Texas, then while he served as president of Walla Walla College, she helped establish the elementary school. Back at Union College, she again complemented her president-husband by serving as dean of women and teacher. Later they spent three years in St. Helena, California. In 1912 the General Conference asked her to edit the Home Education Department's publication *Christian Education*, the forerunner of *Journal of True Education.*

LIBERIA. A West African republic with an area of 38,250 square miles (99,000 square kilometers) and a population (1994) of 3 million. The country is bounded on the south and west by the Atlantic Ocean, on the north by Sierre Leone and Guinea, and on the east by Côte d'Ivoire. Agriculture is the principal occupation of the people, with rubber, iron, cacao, and coffee the principal exports.

Liberia has a low coastline stretching 350 miles (550 kilometers) along the Atlantic Ocean and a hinterland extending into the interior for some 200 miles (300 kilometers). The climate is hot and humid. English is the official language, but approximately 28 different dialects are spoken. Since 1847 Liberia has been an independent Black republic.

In the early nineteenth century, when the pangs of conscience began to trouble the minds of Europeans and Americans and forceful appeals were made for the abolition of slavery, the American Colonization Society decided that the Liberian coast would make a suitable home for repatriated Blacks. Since that time hundreds of freed slaves and their descendants migrated there so that by 1925 there were about 25,000 American Liberians in the country.

Seventh-day Adventist Statistics. The territory of Liberia constitutes the Liberia Mission in the West African Union Mission, which forms a part of the Africa-Indian Ocean Division. Statistics (1993) for *Liberia:* churches, 34; membership, 11,492; ordained ministers, 5; credentialed missionaries, 5. Headquarters: P.O. Box 52, 1000 Monrovia.

Institutions. Seventh-day Adventist Cooper Memorial Hospital.

Development of Seventh-day Adventist Work. *Beginnings.* The *GC Daily Bulletin* of Oct. 24, 1889, contains a reference to "Bro. Gaston from Liberia, who recently embraced the truth, and has gone back to his country to sow the seeds of precious truth among his kindred." Later reports reveal that he was of the

Washington, D.C., church. In reporting his 1892 visit to West Africa at the January 1893 General Conference session, Lawrence C. Chadwick appealed that a missionary be sent to open a mission "at or near the home of Brother Gaston" *(GC Daily Bulletin* 5:2, Jan. 29, 1893). However, Liberia was to wait another 33 years for its first Seventh-day Adventist missionaries.

In 1926 the European Division sent R. Helbig and E. Flammer from Germany to Liberia, where, with L. F. Langford, of England (who had worked in the Gold Coast), they found a suitable site for the first SDA mission inland in Grand Bassa County, at Seahn. The next year Helbig and Flammer, making final arrangements for the piece of land, secured from the government a grant of 100 acres (40 hectares) of land for 99 years, on which were built the first school, church, and dispensary. Early in 1927 K. Noltze arrived from Germany to assist in the work in Liberia and remained there for 15 years.

On Apr. 30, 1930, the first four SDA converts were baptized at Seahn. Among them was Willie Helbig, who later became the first Liberian ordained minister. Later D. K. Reider arrived to join the missionary families. Noltze and Reider were sent to Liiwa, in the Gbarnga district, to begin another mission station.

In 1935 K. Noltze established the Konola Mission, where in 1937 he opened a boarding school for boys, which later became an accredited boarding academy for both boys and girls *(see* Konola Academy). N. S. During, an African pastor from Sierra Leone, was sent to Liberia in 1937 for schoolwork at Konola, and stayed there until 1939.

In 1936 T. N. Ketola, from Finland, arrived at the Konola Station and was moved to Liiwa Station in the following year. In 1941, after Noltze returned to Germany, Ketola moved back to Konola. In 1942 he bought property for new mission headquarters at Monrovia, the capital city of Liberia, and began the work there. He prepared buildings and made contacts with leaders and with the people before going to the United States in 1943. At that time the church membership in the entire country was 303.

In the meantime, in 1933, I. W. Harding, an African, had been sent as a missionary from neighboring Sierra Leone to Lower Buchanan in Liberia. When during World War II the overseas missionaries had to leave Liberia, Harding became, in 1942, the first African president of the Liberia Mission, a post he held until 1945. Under his leadership the work was expanded into Lower Buchanan and Monrovia, the capital city. By 1940 there were three mission stations and a baptized membership of 137 in the Liberia Mission.

Late in 1945 three Black American families appointed by the General Conference arrived in Liberia. G. N. Banks became president and secretary-treasurer of the mission; P. E. Giddings, the principal of the Konola School; and C. D. Henri, evangelist and leader in the Bassa district. Since 1945 Black missionaries from the United States have held the leadership of the field.

The temperance work progressed in Liberia, with successful use of stop-smoking plans and radio and television programs.

On Dec. 24, 1989, civil unrest developed, and since then more than half the population have become refugees. Many church members and pastors have been scattered to remote areas of Liberia and to neighboring countries. During this period 11 new churches have been raised up in Liberia and in neighboring countries.

LIBERIA MISSION. *See* Africa-Indian Ocean Division; Liberia.

LIBERTY (1906-   ; bimonthly; 1994 circulation, 190,614; files in R&H). A magazine of religious freedom; a publication of the North American Division, sponsored by the Public Affairs and Religious Liberty Department of the General Conference. It is successor to *Sentinel of Christian Liberty* (originally the *American Sentinel),* founded and first published in January 1886 as a monthly by the Pacific Press, at that time in Oakland, California.

At first a 32-page quarterly, *Liberty* became a bimonthly with the January 1959 issue. *Liberty* was launched in 1906, two years after its predecessor, *Sentinel of Christian Liberty*, had ceased publication. It was published for the Religious Liberty Bureau of the General Conference "as a medium for disseminating the principles of Christian Liberty." Its first issue carried the subtitle "A magazine of religious freedom, devoted to the American idea of religious liberty exemplified in the complete separation of church and state." The current issues carry a "Declaration of Principles of the Religious Liberty Association of America," which "was organized in 1889 by the General Conference of Seventh-day Adventists. Dedicated to the preservation of religious freedom, the association advocates no political or economic theories."

Editors: L. A. Smith, 1906-1909; C. M. Snow, 1909-1912; W. W. Prescott, 1912-1913; C. S. Longacre, 1913-1942; H. H. Votaw, 1942-1954; F. H. Yost, 1955-1958; J. A. Buckwalter, 1959; R. R. Hegstad, 1959-1993; Clifford R. Goldstein, 1993- .

LIBERTY SECONDARY SCHOOL (Colegio Libertad). A coeducational secondary school located at Bucaramanga, Colombia. It was established in 1940 and became a 12-grade secondary school in the early 1980s. In 1992 there was a total enrollment of 627 and a faculty and staff of 28.

Directors: Manuel Ignacio Mejia, 1980-1981; Cecilia Reyes, 1981-1982; Nahun Rojas, 1982-1983; Eliseo Bustamante, 1983-1984; Juan Alberto Diaz, 1984-1990; Salvador Poveder, 1990-1991; Manuel Sierra, 1991-1993; Wilson Rojas, 1993- .

LIBRAIRIE-IMPRIMERIE ADVENTISTE. *See* Adventist Publishing House (Madagascar).

LIBRAIRIE (IMPRIMERIE) POLYGLOTTE. *See* Life and Health Publishing House.

LIBRARY PROGRAM. A plan launched in 1939 to acquaint the reading public with Adventists and their message by supplying to public, seminary, college, university, and Bible institute libraries a selected group of denominational books that set forth the fundamental tenets held by Seventh-day Adventists.

Thousands of copies have been distributed through this plan. For public libraries the cost is shared equally by the local conference and church or churches. For university and seminary libraries the cost is shared equally by the General Conference, union conference, local conference, and publishing house concerned. Introduced in North America, it is now being fostered in other divisions.

LIBYA. An Arab republic on the north coast of Africa. It borders on Egypt and Sudan to the east, on Chad and Niger to the south, and on Algeria and Tunisia on the west. Its area is 679,359 square miles (1,750,000 square kilometers) and its population (1994) of 5 million consists primarily of Arab-Berbers. Arabic is the language of the country.

Orthodox Islam is the state religion, and though freedom of conscience has been provided by law, the making of converts is proscribed. In Greek and Roman times Libya was a thriving agricultural land, but by the twentieth century it had become a desert and a part of the Turkish Empire. In 1911 Italy occupied the country. In 1951, in accordance with a United Nations resolution, Libya became independent. In 1969 it became a republic.

Seventh-day Adventist Work. After the territory of Libya was assigned to the newly formed Southern European Division in 1928, colporteurs selling Italian publications visited Benghazi and Tripoli. When the Middle East Division was organized in 1951, Libya was assigned to the Nile Union of that division. The territory is now assigned to the Middle East Union.

After an exploratory visit early in 1952, Seventh-day Adventist representatives in 1953 were granted a permit to open medical work—the first time a Protestant organization was allowed to work in Libya—although all evangelistic activity or proselyting was proscribed. Subsequently Dr. Roy S. Cornell, from the United States, opened a hospital on May 21, 1956, at Benghazi.

From the hospital, welfare work was promoted through the distribution of food and clothing, especially during 1957, and through providing free medicines and clinical treatment. Also, temperance lectures and films were presented throughout the country during December 1957 and January 1958.

The medical work grew until in 1968 a new 65-bed hospital, financed principally by the oil companies in Libya, was opened, with D. Clifford Ludington as the medical director. In November 1969 the hospital was nationalized by the Revolutionary Command Council of Muammar el-Qaddafi.

On Aug. 13, 1960, a church was organized at Benghazi, consisting of 17 members from the hospital staff.

A first in the work in Libya was a Vacation Bible School conducted in 1964. Another first was the junior camp held in 1969. After the nationalization of the hospital, all workers left Libya and the work closed except for the occasional visits of literature evangelists. Only a few SDAs live in Libya, all non-Libyans from North Africa and Asia. Little contact has been made since the 1970s. There is no knowledge that SDAs are meeting as groups.

LICENTIATE (licensed minister). One

who has been granted a ministerial license by the conference. He or she is authorized to preach, assist in a spiritual way in any church activities, and lead in missionary work, and especially to engage in evangelism.

He or she may be elected as a local elder of a particular church and ordained as such, provided special arrangements have been made with the conference. In such a case he or she is vested with the authority of a local elder, but no more. This ordination as local elder qualifies him or her to serve only in such churches as have elected him or her as their local elder, and then only on the advice of the conference committee or president.

Conference committees do not have the right to authorize a licensed preacher to go from church to church baptizing or performing other church rites pertaining to the functions of an ordained minister. A conference committee action cannot be substituted for church election or ministerial ordination. *See also* Minister.

LICEO ADVENTISTA DE SANTIAGO. *See* Las Condes Adventist Academy.

LICEO ADVENTISTA DE TEMUCO. *See* Temuco Adventist Academy.

LICKEY, ARTHUR EDWIN (1895-1974). Educator, pastor, author. He was a native of Missouri and took his secondary education at Keene Industrial Academy in Texas. In his early ministry he labored in evangelistic and educational work in south Texas and New Mexico. Later he served as MV secretary for the Southern California Conference. He also worked in Colorado, Washington, and Oregon. He later served in a pastoral capacity in a number of large cities. He is the author of the Twentieth Century Bible Lessons and the book *God Speaks to Modern Man.*

LIECHTENSTEIN. A small independent principality (area, 62 square miles [160 square kilometers]); population (1994), 30,000. It is situated between Switzerland and Austria, united with Switzerland by monetary and customs union. The language is German and the religion about 85 percent Roman Catholic, 10 percent Protestant, 5 percent others.

The territory of Liechtenstein is assigned to the German Swiss Conference, part of the Swiss Union Conference, which in turn is part of the Euro-Africa Division.

Seventh-day Adventists have never had a church in Liechtenstein. Church members have lived there from time to time, but have moved away. In 1993 eight members lived there. Those living there generally attend church services in the nearby village of Buchs, Switzerland. The towns of Liechtenstein are visited annually for the Ingathering campaign, and by literature evangelists from time to time.

Since 1985 special evangelistic activities and efforts have been conducted. In 1993 regular home Bible studies were being conducted, with about 20 participants and interested friends.

LIFE AND HEALTH. *See Vibrant Life.*

LIFE AND HEALTH MEDICAL INSTITUTION (Institution Medicale "Vie et Sante"). A former 37-bed institution, situated in South France at Labastide-Villefranche, near the thermal springs of Salies-de-Béarn, at the foot of the Pyrénées. Before World War II an effort was made to reestablish the medical work in the Franco-Belgian Union Conference. In 1967 and again in 1969 the delegates to the Franco-Belgian Union Conference sessions voted that study should be given to the opening of a sanitarium. In March 1970 a commission appointed by the union committee began its task by going to the Spirit of Prophecy for guidance in establishing a medical work. The Lord led step-by-step.

The union chose a beautiful property of about 57 acres (23 hectares) with an old mansion and a lake. After it was voted by the union committee to make the purchase of this property on Sept. 27, 1971, church members donated the necessary funds (approximately $70,000). A young couple, Gérard and Colette Chartres (he, a civil engineer, and she, a medical doctor) were placed in charge of the new institution. Under their direction the existing building was remodeled.

In May 1971 the institution opened with 32 beds. From the start there was not enough room for those who wished to come. In July 1971 three rooms were added, providing an additional five beds. Plans were made to build a 35-bed addition, but the institution closed in 1976.

LIFE AND HEALTH PUBLISHING HOUSE (France) (Maison D'Edition Vie et Santé). A publishing firm at Dammarie-les-Lys, France, operated under the supervision of the Euro-Africa Division. There are 54 regular employees and one apprentice. Besides books, pamphlets, and tracts, the plant regularly prints three important periodicals: one for evangelism, *Signes des Temps* ("Signs of the Times"); a health paper, *Vie et Santé* ("Life and Health"); a church paper, *La Revue Adventiste* ("The Advent Review"); and also Sabbath school quarterlies.

Beginnings of publications in the French language can be traced to Switzerland. A French paper, *L'Evangile Eternel* ("The Everlasting Gospel"), was published monthly (with a few exceptions) from June 1866 to December 1868, together with various tracts, by M. B. Czechowski, who was the first to preach Seventh-day Adventist doctrines in Europe, even though sent there by another denomination.

When J. N. Andrews, the first Seventh-day Adventist representative, arrived in Switzerland in 1874, he immediately produced French tracts and laid plans for a periodical. With the assistance of D. T. Bourdeau he launched *Les Signes des Temps* ("The Signs of the Times") in July 1876 in Basel. It was published monthly, at first with eight pages, 12" x 16" (30 cm. x 41 cm.), changed in June 1880 to 16 pages, 8" x 13" (20 cm. x 33 cm.). This monthly periodical is still being published.

The publishing house began to operate in 1885 on Weiherweg Street, Basel, in a building erected mainly as a printing plant. For 10 years it produced many books and tracts in French and German as well as other languages, working under the name of Librairie (Imprimerie) Polyglotte ("Polyglot Bookstore"), listed in the *Yearbook* as Basel Publishing House. In addition to *Les Signes,* in 1890 a monthly health paper, *Le Vulgarisateur* ("The Popularizer"), was introduced, which became *Vie et Santé* in 1923.

When the plant had to be closed because of Sunday laws in 1895, the building was occupied by a medical institution. But the publishing office continued in Basel until 1903, though all the printing had to be done by other firms. When the printing plant was closed, the publishing house assumed the name of Société Internationale de Traités (International Tract Society), listed in the *Yearbook* as Latin Union Publishing House, and its future publications were limited to the French language. It was transferred to Geneva in 1903, and a branch office was opened in Paris, functioning there until 1905. In 1910 the publishing house was moved to Gland (Vaud), Switzerland, and a printing plant added in 1914 under the direction of L. E. Borle (manager 1910-1915). For many years the publishing house had been under the direction of Jules Robert, and he was again in charge from 1915 to 1922.

When at the close of World War I it was felt that the French language publishing house should be in France, the publishing house and printing plant were transferred from Gland in 1922 to a property acquired in the town of Dammarie-les-Lys (Seine-et-Marne), near the city of Melun and some 30 miles (50 kilometers) southeast of Paris. It then took the name of Maison d'Edition Les Signes des Temps. It is now called Maison d'Edition Vie et Sante.

Equipment: To meet increasing demands from the field, the equipment was updated from time to time, and new facilities were added, such as an electric generating plant. In 1924 additions were built on the factory and the administrative offices, and further additions were made to the printing plant in 1935 and 1954. Besides the administrative and editorial staffs (four editors, one layout artist and designer), the publishing house includes a printing plant. The photocomposition section is equipped with a monophoto with a clavier, a photo laboratory, and a mounting room. The books are no longer printed and bound in the publishing house, but the pressroom still contains an offset press for small work.

Circulation: After reduced activity during World War II, the French Publishing House revived with the reorganization of the colporteur work in France. In addition to the magazines referred to above, it publishes church and trade books, with special promotion for sets of books, *The Practical Guide to Life* (seven volumes on health and family living) and *The Spiritual Guides to Life* (the Bible and the five-volume Conflict of the Ages Series). French Publishing House publications are sold in all the French-speaking countries of the world.

Managers: G. A. Huse, 1922-1923; L. E. Borle, 1923-1925; H. L. Henriksen, 1926-1933; Ernest Meyer, 1933-1940; Georges Haberey, 1940-1948; Robert Erdmann, 1948-1952; Maxime Duplouy, 1952-1954; Elisée Bénézech, 1954-1968; Eugène Vervoort, 1968-1970; André Garsin, 1970-1980; Jean Scippa, 1980-1985; Alain Menis, 1985-1993; Aldo Monet, 1993- .

LIFE BOAT. *See* City Missions.

LIFE BOAT MISSION. *See* City Missions.

LIFE IN CHRIST. *See* Eternal Life; Immortality.

LIFEGLOW. *See* Christian Record Services, Inc.

LIFESTYLE MAGAZINE. A magazine-format program launched in 1985 by Faith for Today. First known as *Christian Lifestyle Magazine,* it featured interviews and stories of people who are making a difference by doing. The name was changed to *Lifestyle Magazine* in 1991. Topics range from such issues as AIDS, incest, and domestic violence to nutrition and drug addiction and therapy. It also focuses on relationships—in marriage, parenting, and with God.

Dan Matthews, as host and executive producer of *Lifestyle Magazine,* serves as moderator between on-camera guests, the 200-plus studio audience, and the thousands in the weekly listening audience. Drs. Rebekah Cheng and Edwin Nebblett help make up the regular team of medical professionals, and Dr. John McDougall often fields questions about nutrition.

Lifestyle Magazine has received many media honors and reaches a potential audience of 40 million homes each week. During the February 1992 Nielsen ratings, the program tied for first place in the devotional category for numbers of households per broadcast station. In June 1993 the Nielsen ratings ranked the program number one in its time slot in metropolitan New York City—the largest market in the world. Since November 1992, 13 new radio stations have been added to the list of television stations carrying the program when an audio version was offered to the Adventist Radio Network stations. In addition to being carried over the Armed Forces Television Network, *Lifestyle Magazine* was being broadcast twice each week over Adventist World Radio-Europe in 1994 and is telecast by a station in Athens that also serves the areas of Corinth and Thessalonica.

LIGHT (1951-1994; monthly; file in GC). Organ of the Northern Europe-West Africa, Northern European, and Trans-European divisions; superseded the *Advent Survey,* 1929-1941, the publication of which closed because of war conditions. From 1951 to 1970 and from 1980 to 1985 it was called *Northern Light.*

LIGHT HOUSE PUBLISHING COMPANY (Ekdotikos Oikos Pharos tis Ellados). A publishing enterprise, without a printing plant, conducted by the Greek Mission at Athens, Greece. The need for Seventh-day Adventist publications in the Greek language to help in evangelism was sensed by E. Hennecke, who was mission director from 1926 to 1932. Since it was difficult at that time to have SDA literature printed in Greece, he imported from America a number of books printed in Greek, whose English titles are: *The Bible Made Plain, Steps to Christ, Words of Comfort, His Second Coming,* and *Fighting Illness.* About the same time *World Empire* and *Pictures From Life* were printed in Greece. Young people from the SDA orphanage, formerly operated (1923-1926) at Thessaloníki, were the first colporteurs to circulate these publications in various parts of Greece.

The publishing house was formally established in 1930. N. S. Pappastamoulis, a Greek who had come from North America, supervised this department of the work for many years, during which time many books were sold.

After World War II new books were produced in Greece, mostly Greek translations of English books such as *The Ministry of Healing, Steps to Christ, His Cross and Mine, We and Our Children, God Speaks to Modern Man,* and a variety of tracts.

The publishing work was reorganized under the direction of Nick Tallios, who in 1961 took charge both of the publishing house and the colporteur work.

In the years that followed as many as 35 colporteurs worked for the Book and Bible House. When Nick Tallios left, Nick Germanis became manager. Later Eleftherios Dialektakis took over with Nick Giantzaklides as leader of the colporteur work.

Although new books were published, *The Desire of Ages,* and later *Christ's Object Lessons,* the publishing work came to a virtual standstill. In 1992 Christoforos Christoforides' book *The Revelation* was published, and efforts are being made to reopen the publishing work with a bookshop in Athens.

A LIGHT IN THE WAY PRODUCTIONS (Producciones "Una Luz en el Camino"). A communication center organized Apr. 19, 1972, and situated at Echeverría 1452, Florida, Buenos Aires, Argentina. The name of the institution corresponds to the radio and TV program *Una Luz en el Camino* ("A Light in the Way"), which is broadcast throughout the three countries of the Austral Union Conference (Argentina, Paraguay, and Uruguay). The radio version is a five-minute program created in 1964 and transmitted daily, free of charge, by 140 radio stations (in 1993), mostly in Argentina, but also in Paraguay and Uruguay, and in the territory of the Inca Union. The TV version begun in 1970 is 10 minutes in length, and is broadcast weekly by some 650 TV channels free of charge.

The center also produces religious music, records, and cassettes. The Bible correspondence school has thousands of active students, from this program and *The Voice of Hope.*

Facilities and Equipment. The two-story building has a film and recording studio, and technical control; also a reception area, storage, and several offices. Some equipment is rented according to need, and part is owned by the institution, such as recording machines, tape duplicators, control console, monitors, and scenography.

Evangelization. The institution offers its support and collaboration in all forms of evangelism, including "Una Luz en el Camino" publications, a set of books published by the Buenos Aires Publishing House.

Director. Since its beginning, Enrique Chaij has been director of the program and of the institution.

LIGHT OF SRI LANKA TRAINING INSTITUTE. *See* Lakpahana Adventist Seminary and College.

LILONGWE HEALTH CENTRE. *See* Seventh-day Adventist Health Centre (Lilongwe).

LILYDALE ADVENTIST ACADEMY. A coeducational boarding school on the secondary level, situated near Lilydale, at Mooroolbark, Victoria, Australia, about 30 miles (50 kilometers) from Melbourne, the capital of Victoria, and a similar distance from the Seventh-day Adventist community at Warburton. It offers courses preparatory to entry to Avondale College or any Australian university.

The estate on which the school stands comprises 40 acres (16 hectares) of good farming land and is beautifully situated on the hills overlooking the Shire of Lilydale and a portion of the Yarra Valley. In recent years an ornamental tree industry has enhanced the estate, providing income to the academy. The school opened February 1964, and among the initial 100 enrolled were representatives from all the eastern states of Australia and from Papua New Guinea. Enrollment in 1992 was 339.

The main buildings are the administrative block, dormitories, science laboratories, manual arts building, dining room, kitchen, and staff homes. A sports center was opened in 1993. The administrative section includes nine classrooms, a music studio, a library, and the office of administration.

During the first two years all students follow the same general course, and after that, certain core subjects designed to aid the development of a balanced personality are required of all. Other subjects are added according to the special abilities and objectives of the individual student.

Principals: W. J. Gilson, 1964-1965; A. C. Reye, 1966-1971; M. B. Durrant, 1972-1974; R. A. Spoor, 1975-1979; L. Bartlett, 1980-1985; R. A. Reid, 1986-1989; A. S. French, 1990- .

LIMA CLINIC. *See* Miraflores Adventist Clinic.

LIMA DAY ACADEMY. *See* Miraflores Adventist Academy.

LIMA TRAINING SCHOOL. *See* Union Adventist Educational Complex.

LINDA VISTA ACADEMY (Colegio Linda Vista). A coeducational boarding school situated on a 1,200-acre (500-hectare) ranch property in Pueblo Nuevo, Solistahuacan, Chiapas, Mexico. It is owned and operated by the Asociación Civil Filantrópica y Educativa de Mexico (the Civil Association of Seventh-day Adventists in Mexico). The school is accredited by the state of Chiapas and from its beginning has had the support of the local educational authorities. Classwork is offered from the primary through the equivalent of the twelfth grade. Beginning with the 1972-1973 school year, the school has offered the first year in the theological program as an affiliate of Montemorelos University. All instruction is in the Spanish language.

The school site consists of pine and oak woodland interspersed with meadows and a few small areas suitable for cultivation. A number of springs provide water, and the annual rainfall is about 70 inches (180 centimeters). The climate is cool, with little seasonal change in temperature.

Linda Vista Academy was established in September 1957 as a training school to serve the growing constituency in southern Mexico. It is considered the successor of a primary boarding school (the Escuela Agrícola e Industrial del Sureste) in Teapa, Tabasco, which had served the constituency of the Southeast Mexican Mission since 1948.

When construction on the new school

began, part of the staff and a small group of older students were invited to help in constructing the plant. Horace Kelley was called to serve as principal and to direct the building program. The school plant was built largely with materials produced on the property and with student labor under the direction of the teachers. Using the existing buildings, which consisted of a large stone house without windows and an adobe chapel, plus tents, the school opened in June 1958 with 60 students. Classes were held six days a week.

The first class graduated from the three-year secondary course in 1960, and a year later the first group of four completed the Bible instructor's training course. These four, in addition to those who later finished the Bible instructor's training course, became denominational workers in the Mexican Union. A large portion of the workers of the Mexican Union are graduates of Linda Vista or have studied there for several years.

Principals: H. K. Lucas, 1957-1960; D. S. Vargas, 1960-1961; H. K. Lukas, 1961-1963; D. S. Vargas, 1964; J. A. Fuentes, 1964-1968; D. S. Vargas, 1968-1970; Eloy Wade, 1971-1973; Edmundo Alva, 1973-1976; Felipe Presenda, 1976-1977; Filiberto Perez, 1977-1978; Ismael Castillo, 1978-1985; Gener Aviles, 1985-1990; Ezequiel Reyes, 1990- .

LINDSAY, HARMON (1835-1919). Financial administrator. He was treasurer of the General Conference from 1874 to 1875 and from 1888 to 1893, and participated in the establishment and development of Battle Creek College and Oakwood College. He also served as treasurer of several other church institutions, among them the Central SDA Publishing Association (now Review and Herald Publishing Association) in the 1890s. Later in his life he left the Seventh-day Adventist Church and joined the Christian Scientists.

LINDSAY, KATHERINE (1842-1923). Physician, founder of the first Seventh-day Adventist nurse's training school. After receiving some training in nursing and attending college for six years, she entered, in 1870, the University of Michigan Medical College. In 1875 she was graduated at the head of her class, with the first group of women to receive the college's degree. In early life she had been deeply influenced by reading the story of Florence Nightingale and by watching the development of nurse's training in England.

Joining the staff of the Battle Creek Sanitarium, "Dr. Kate" vigorously set about establishing there the first SDA school of nursing. Through the introduction of thorough classwork, she became known as a foremost teacher of student nurses.

In 1895 she went to South Africa. She worked in Claremont Sanitarium at Cape Town, became a leading consultant, and traveled under most difficult conditions to mission stations in the interior. En route to the United States, she traveled extensively in Europe, and in 1900 began 20 years as an active member of the medical staff and faculty of the Colorado Sanitarium in Boulder, devoting special interest to the Nursing School. She retained her unusual mental vigor until the time of her death.

LINDSEY, SARAH A. HALLOCK (late 1800s). Preacher. She was converted to Seventh-day Adventism in 1860 and married John Lindsey, a lay preacher. Their joint ministry held the Pennsylvania and New York churches together during a difficult time of apostasy and lack of good leadership. In 1872, along with her husband, Lindsey was licensed to preach, hold evangelistic meetings, and lead out in church business and committee sessions.

LINE ISLANDS. A Pacific island group running south-southeast from the Hawaiian Islands to the northern part of the French Polynesian group. The islands that comprise this group are Kingman (U.S.), Palmyra (U.S.), and Jarvis (U.S.), as well as Washington, Fanning, Christmas, Malden, Starbuck, Caroline, Vostok, and Flint, which are part of Kiribati. They have a total area of 255 square miles (660 square kilometers), and the population on the following islands (1994) is Washington, 936; Fanning, 1,309; Christmas, 2,537; and Kanton, 45, for a total population of 4,827, the rest being uninhabited.

They all were uninhabited for many years, until immediately prior to World War II, when most of them were garrisoned by United States forces. Today Christmas Island is run as a copra plantation by the Kiribati government, and is under special study as a development area for deep-sea sport fishing. Flint and Caroline islands are leased to a Tahitian merchant. Malden, Starbuck, and Vostock do not support even trees.

The group, including Christmas Island, is assigned to the Kiribati Mission in the Western Pacific Union Mission, which forms part of the

South Pacific Division. A Seventh-day Adventist minister serves the 98 members on Christmas Island. *See also* Kiribati.

LIPA ADVENTIST ACADEMY. A boarding academy operated at Bugtong, Lipa City, Philippines, by the South-Central Luzon Mission of the North Philippine Union. In 1975 Lipa Adventist Academy opened with 98 students. The school was previously known as South-Central Luzon Academy, which began in 1969.

From 1975 to 1992, 3,984 students attended the four high school levels, and 832 seniors have graduated from the school.

Principals: J. B. Villagomez, 1969-1970; Wilfredo Loriezo, 1970-1971; A. A. Arit, 1971-1973; W. T. Martinez, 1973-1975; R. A. Budayao, 1975-1976; F. E. Yulip, 1976-1977; W. T. Martinez, 1977-1979; A. M. Salazar, 1979-1980; R. G. Evangelista, 1980-1981; A. G. Labro, 1981-1984; N. G. Castillo, 1984-1986; F. E. Yulip, 1986-1988; B. A Bico, 1988-1991; N. S. Basit, 1991-1992; N D. de Chavez, 1992-1994; S. T. Molina, 1994- .

LIPKE, JOHN (1875-1943). Pioneer missionary in Brazil; teacher, administrator, and physician, who helped to establish Adventist publishing, educational, and medical work there. He was born in Berlin, Germany, and was named Johannes Rudolf Berthold Lipke. After studying for the ministry, he canvassed for three or four years. About 1896 he went to the United States and studied at Battle Creek Sanitarium. In 1897 he went to Brazil as a missionary teacher and taught in various centers. Recognizing the need for publications produced locally, from about 1902 to 1905 he promoted and edited a German-language magazine, naming it *Der Missionarbeiter*. In 1904 he made a trip to the United States urging the establishment of an Adventist press in Portuguese-speaking Brazil. Gifts gathered on this trip helped to establish the Brazil Publishing House. From 1905 to 1907 he taught and preached. In 1907 he was ordained and the next year took charge of the Rio Grande Mission. Three years later, in 1910, he became superintendent of the East Brazil Mission, and the same year edited a short-lived youth magazine, *Der Jugendfreund*. Beginning in 1913 or 1914, he superintended the São Paulo Mission, and while carrying this post developed and directed the Adventist Seminary at São Paulo. In 1918 he became superintendent of the North Brazil Union Mission. In 1920 he went to the United States and took the medical course at the College of Medical Evangelists. After graduation in 1925, he returned to Brazil and practiced medicine in Rio de Janeiro for 10 years, until an illness forced his retirement. He died at São Paulo.

LISTEN (subtitled "A Journal of Better Living") (1948- ; monthly; R&H; 1994 circulation c. 40,000; file in editorial office). A temperance journal published by the Review and Herald Publishing Association, Hagerstown, Maryland. It is the largest of all temperance publications, both in size and in circulation, and is now widely quoted, not only in the United States but in some 50 other countries of the world.

Originally a quarterly (through 1957), *Listen* continued as a bimonthly through 1965, changing to a monthly with the January 1966 issue.

Listen was inaugurated (1) to help launch and foster a worldwide educational program in behalf of total abstinence; (2) to publicize facts and data from current scientific and medical research on the effects of the use of alcoholic beverages and other narcotics on the physical, mental, and moral powers of the individual, and on the social, economic, political, and religious life of the nation; (3) to counter misleading and fallacious propaganda for alcoholic beverages in the press, on the billboards, and over radio and television, by the publication of facts proved by laboratory experiments and authentic surveys and studies; (4) to cooperate with other organizations and movements working for the elimination of intemperance from personal, family, and national life; (5) to encourage alcohol education in the schools and to advocate all other reasonable means of saving young people from the danger of alcohol and other narcotics, and to influence them toward sane, wholesome, and temperate living; (6) to offer aid and inspiration to those suffering from alcoholism or who are tempted to drink, pointing them to the true Source of help in divine power; (7) to aid in the dissemination of basic health principles, since true temperance is intimately connected with the development of a "sound mind in a sound body," thus to promote good mental health habits, a well-rounded personality, and emotional stability, along with methods of strengthening self-control, overcoming wrong habits, and developing a positive, healthy approach to life.

Editorial material in *Listen* focuses primarily on positive alternatives to an intemperate way of life, especially for young readers of high school age.

Color cover designs for *Listen* feature prominent personalities in various walks of life who have strong convictions about temperance. Among those featured have been cabinet members, governors, members of Congress, business and professional leaders, outstanding youth personalities, and well-known leaders in the world of sports and entertainment.

Listen is youth-slanted and circulated chiefly in high schools and among youth organizations. It is used by Community Crusades Against Drugs in a national program of introducing temperance materials into public school systems. It is unique in its field in being officially approved for use in the public school curriculum by about three fourths of the states through their commissioners of education. A teaching guide for classroom use is provided with each issue.

Listen magazine is the youth drug education publication of the International Commission for the Prevention of Alcoholism and Drug Dependency (ICPA), a nongovernmental organization of both the United Nations and the World Health Organization. Through the ICPA *Listen* articles and information are circulated throughout the world.

Listen produced and sponsored the film *I Took the High Road,* a story of contemporary youth who found the solution to their drug problems in a spiritual conversion and belief in the second coming of Christ.

Another extension of *Listen's* services was added in 1972 in the form of the *Listen* Fingertip Data Service. This consists of approximately 80 reference cards a month containing carefully selected facts on alcohol, tobacco, and drugs. These are available on a regular subscription basis.

A series of books containing reprint materials from *Listen* forms *Listen's* Better Living Library. Among them are *Invasion Upstairs* (alcohol); *If You Smoke, What Have You?* (tobacco); and *To Go to Pot, or Not?* (marijuana). These books are intended primarily for reference purposes, have wide circulation in school libraries, and are used extensively for classroom study. Frequently reprints of *Listen* articles are used in local option elections and for general circulation.

Listen has been awarded the National Safety Council's Public Interest Award for exceptional service to safety.

Editors: J. A. Buckwalter, 1948-1953; Francis A. Soper, 1953-1984; Gary B. Swanson, 1984-1990; Lincoln E. Steed, 1990- .

LITCH, JOSIAH (1809-1886). Methodist minister, the first well-known minister in New England to take his stand with William Miller, later a physician. He had a vigorous mind, a bent for investigation, and the courage to advocate what he believed to be truth. In the early days of slavery and temperance agitation, he was constantly in the forefront. He was a power in the pulpit and equally forceful with his pen, both as an editor (associate on *The Signs of the Times*) and as an author on prophecy.

Having accepted Miller's views in 1838, he wrote a 48-page synopsis of them entitled *Midnight Cry or; A Review of Mr. Miller's Lectures.* In the same year he wrote a 200-page book, *The Probability of the Second Coming of Christ About A.D. 1843.* In 1841 his Methodist Conference investigated his views, decided that he held nothing contrary to Methodism—though he went in some points beyond it—and permitted him to retire from the itinerant ministry. This allowed him to devote his time to the dissemination of the Second Advent doctrine.

Soon, however, Litch became a full-time traveling "general agent" of the Millerite Committee of Publication. He also became one of the editors of *The Signs of the Times* and of another Millerite paper in Philadelphia, the *Trumpet of Alarm.* He traveled extensively and preached on the prophecies with great effect. His prediction in 1838, based on prophetic interpretation, of a loss of Turkish power in August 1840 aroused widespread interest and spurred the study of prophecy. His *Address to . . . the Clergy* moved many ministers to examine the Adventist doctrine candidly, persuading not a few of them.

Litch was a pioneer in several points of prophetic interpretation that later were adopted by Seventh-day Adventists: that there was to be a "judicial scene of judgment" *(Address to . . . the Clergy* [1841], pp. 38, 39; cf. *Prophetic Expositions* [1842], vol. 1, pp. 49-54) preceding the resurrection, and separate from the execution of judgment *(see* Investigative Judgment); that the seven plagues were still future (*Prophetic Expositions,* vol. 1, p. 175). His expositions of the historical fulfillment of prophecy had considerable influence on Uriah Smith's interpretations.

Although Litch had earlier thought that "the door of mercy" would close some time preceding the Second Advent, he refused after the disappointment of 1844 to believe that any door was shut *(see* Open and Shut Door), and in consequence he abandoned the belief that the 2300 days ended in 1844. For a time he remained with that branch of the Adventists who did not accept the doctrine of conditional immortality, but in later years he left all connection with any Adventists. Wellcome says that Litch became a futurist, expecting nearly all the prophecies of Revelation after the fifth chapter to be fulfilled in the future, immediately preceding the Second Advent (Isaac C. Wellcome, *History of the Second Advent Message* [1874], p. 678 note).

LITERATURE. *See* Periodicals; Publishing Work.

LITERATURE EVANGELIST (colporteur). A Seventh-day Adventist who regularly sells denominational books and magazines from house to house to the public. He or she is considered a gospel worker whose efforts are coordinated with those of the other evangelistic workers of the church. The work is a sacred one and partakes of that of a minister, a teacher, and a salesperson. Going directly into the homes of all classes of people, literature evangelists (LEs) tell their customers of the way of salvation and pray with them, hoping that God will impress them as the books they leave in the homes are read and studied. Many are thus led into fuller understanding, spiritual conviction, and then into church fellowship through the influence of the press. Thousands of people who become interested in the SDA teachings first, in this way, enroll in Bible correspondence schools or attend evangelistic meetings and become members of the Seventh-day Adventist Church.

Literature evangelists receive a commission on their sales and also certain financial benefits if they meet stipulated requirements set forth in denominational policies.

History of the Work of the Literature Evangelist. Probably the first book evangelists worked in Europe during the 1860s. These men, Jean David Geymet, Sigismond Hanhardt, James Erzberger, and Michael B. Czechowski, although not under the sponsorship of the General Conference in Battle Creek, nevertheless proclaimed the Advent message, including the seventh-day Sabbath. Their ministry covered portions of Italy, Switzerland, and France.

In 1879 Ellen White began urging the two publishing houses, the Review and Herald and the Pacific Press publishing associations, to sell doctrinal books to the public through house-to-house canvassers. In 1880 Dr. J. H. Kellogg wrote a large book on health, *Home Handbook* (1,600 pages), which he sold by this method in advance of publication. One of the men who sold this book was a Canadian, George A. King, who had already canvassed several years, selling tracts, small books, and subscriptions to periodicals such as *Good Health.* King's success with Kellogg's subscription book may have been what fired him with the desire for a large volume setting forth SDA beliefs, published in an attractive subscription edition for the general public.

King once had a desire to become a preacher. James White, who was skeptical of King's abilities, requested Richard Godsmark to take King out to the Godsmark farm near Battle Creek, Michigan, and let him practice preaching, and then report on him. As the story is told, King would often be heard in his room praying early in the morning. At other times he would place his charts in the living room and preach to empty seats. One day after a Sabbath school conducted in the Godsmark home, he preached his trial sermon and made a miserable failure. Godsmark informed him that he would never make a minister, but encouraged him to try selling SDA publications to the people in their homes, and offered to supply him with some tracts and pamphlets. King went out with these and sold them, thus proving that he could sell SDA publications. This incident must have occurred some time before 1878, because in 1878 King had been canvassing for periodical subscriptions and for books in Ontario *(Review and Herald* 53:54, Feb. 13; 53:78, Aug. 28, 1879, etc.).

In 1881 he came to Battle Creek again, this time not asking to preach, but asking to put into systematic operation Mrs. White's plan of evangelistic bookselling. Having found that he could sell Uriah Smith's two small books on Daniel and the Revelation, he urged the Review and Herald to print the two books as one in a subscription edition in a larger size. The publishing house finally agreed to print 5,000 copies of the combined book, *Thoughts on Daniel and the Revelation,* in improved format, if King would assume responsibility for 1,000 copies. First, they made up sample copies by binding together already existing sections of the two books. After King and others sold these successfully, the two books were reprinted together with continuous paging in a larger size, and with illustrations. On Apr. 3, 1882, King sold the first copy of this new *Daniel and the Revelation* to D. W. Reavis for $2.50.

The story of the beginning of the work of the Seventh-day Adventist Church in many parts of the world is the story of literature evangelists preparing the way for the preacher.

In all the South American countries except Peru, the SDA work began either through SDA publications being sent into the countries or through the work of LEs. The first SDA LE or colporteur on South American soil was George King, who in 1887 canvassed for several months in British Guiana and sold 400 books.

In 1891 the General Conference sent three colporteurs, Elwin W. Snyder, C. A. Nowlen, and A. B. Stauffer, to open up the work in South America. Their original plan was to begin work in Montevideo, Uruguay, but after a "thorough looking over" they decided to go to Buenos Aires, Argentina *(Home Missionary* 4:46, February 1892). Stauffer went to the northern part of Argentina and worked among the Germans, and his two companions began their work in Buenos Aires. After four months, they had sold about 200 books and made a number of converts, among them Lionel Brooking, an immigrant from England. In July 1892 Brooking sold books in the Gran Chaco of Paraguay *(General Conference Bulletin,* Mar. 4, 1895, pp. 461, 462). At that time it was extremely difficult to sell books there. Early in 1893 Stauffer and Snyder returned to Uruguay to sell SDA publications. Stauffer sold *The Great Controversy* and other books and gave Bible studies to several families in the German-Swiss colonies, while Snyder worked in Montevideo. In 1896 F. H. Westphal baptized 18 converts and organized the first SDA church in Uruguay *(Review and Herald* 74:89, Feb. 9; 74:507, Aug. 10, 1897).

The first SDA to enter Ecuador was the literature evangelist Thomas Davis, who with F. W. Bishop had previously (1894) helped C. A. Nowlen initiate the work in Chile. In spite of many difficulties, great opposition, and the death of his wife, Davis canvassed for four years (1904-1908), working among the towns and villages along the railway that runs from Guayaquil to Iquitos. One year after his arrival, in 1905, the first Seventh-day Adventist preacher arrived in Ecuador.

R. A. Caldwell pioneered the book work in the Philippines, as well as in Malaysia and China. He remained in the Philippines for several years, being joined by other colporteurs, first of whom was Floyd Ashbaugh.

The Chinese province of Shaanxi was entered in 1915. This province, in the interior bordering the Yellow River, is the oldest site of Chinese civilization and culture, and here, at Sianfu, was the first capital of China. A colporteur found there a town called Gospel Village, which had been built 30 years before by a company of Christians emigrating from Shantung. Here his literature was gladly received, and the SDA faith made steady progress.

At the beginning of the SDA work in Australia and New Zealand, the leader of forces was S. N. Haskell, a strong promoter of literature distribution. In his company was William Arnold, one of the earliest and most successful SDA colporteurs, who, in the face of initial difficulties, led in putting this work on a paying basis there.

The Publishing Department of the General Conference, organized in 1902, laid plans to build publishing houses in strategic areas over the world, so as to serve the different language areas; secure proper publishing leadership; and recruit literature evangelists. Today more than 23,000 literature evangelists go from door to door selling the products of 59 publishing houses. Their retail sales annually in the world field exceed $100 million.

But the work of the literature evangelist is evangelistic. For example, these men and women annually distribute millions of pieces of free literature and pray in nearly 1 million homes. Baptisms each quinquennium as a result of contacts by literature evangelists total approximately 150,000.

Training of Literature Evangelists. Throughout the history of the Seventh-day Adventist Church the training of literature evangelists has received much attention, and many SDA educational institutions, especially outside North America, trace their beginnings to training schools for colporteurs and Bible instructors.

The current program for training literature evangelists in North America includes a short indoctrination session usually held at one of the publishing houses. Through lectures, training filmstrips, and the reading of training materials, the candidate is introduced to the elements of book production, the purposes and methods of SDA book distribution, and the principles of effective salesmanship of health and religious literature. This is usually followed by a period of individual on-the-job training by the conference publishing department secretary or one of his assistants. In many countries outside North America, literature ministry seminaries conduct three- to five-week training courses for literature evangelists, creating more professional workers.

The literature evangelist in the field is kept in touch with the developments in his line of work through periodical bulletins issued by local and union conference publishing departments and the quarterly, *Literature Evangelist,* issued by the Publishing Department of the General Conference. The LE also attends three or four district LE sales meetings a year and an annual LE institute, where additional training is given.

An increasingly important role in the training of literature evangelists is being played by the LE clubs on the campuses of SDA colleges and academies. Special student LE training classes are planned by conference publishing leaders before the students go out for their vacation-time work. Some of these students later become full-time literature evangelists or leaders in the publishing work.

LITHUANIA. A Baltic republic whose neighbors include Latvia, Poland, and the Russian Federation. Lithuania formally declared itself independent from the USSR on Mar. 11, 1990. It has a land area of 25,170 square miles (65,190 square kilometers), and a population (1994) of 3.8 million. The people are akin to the Latvians, and the great majority of them are ardent Roman Catholics. Their language, which retains traces of Sanskrit, is among the most ancient in Europe.

Lithuania was an important kingdom in Eastern Europe in the early Middle Ages, then for many centuries was joined to Poland, and together with Poland was divided between the Russian and the German empires, Germany holding the area of Klaipeda (Memel) to the end of World War I.

Seventh-day Adventist Statistics. Lithuania forms the Lithuanian Field, which is part of the Baltic Union of the Trans-European Division. In 1994 there were 539 members in eight churches.

Seventh-day Adventist Work. SDA work within the present boundaries of Lithuania began in the city of Memel and its environs some time before World War I, while the country was a part of Prussia. Churches developed at Memel, Heydekrug, Didshen, Pogegen, and Wilkishken. In addition, there were probably a few SDAs in other areas of Lithuania as well.

After Lithuania became independent in 1919, W. Strohl, a young German-speaking native of Jelgava, Latvia, who had become an SDA in St. Petersburg, Russia, was invited by a small group of recent SDA converts at Zagare, on the Latvian border, to preach in Lithuania. Arriving there, he reported that these were the only Seventh-day Adventists in the country outside of a group in Memel. Strohl earned his living by teaching English and bookkeeping for four and a half days a week. The other two and a half days he devoted to evangelistic work. Since he could not speak Lithuanian, his sermons and Bible studies were translated from Russian by one of the local church members.

Some time after the war several SDAs native to the area returned home after their wartime absence and, together with the group already in Zagare, formed the first Seventh-day Adventist church in Lithuania outside Memel.

In 1920 the work in Lithuania was attached to the East German Union and placed under the direction of E. Enseleit. In 1921 the first general meeting of Seventh-day Adventists took place at Memel. Two years later Strohl, returning from ministerial training at the Friedensau Missionary Seminary, began work in Siauliai, the second-largest city of the country. In two years a church of 17 members was organized there. In 1923 Lithuania became a mission field in the Baltic Union Conference. About 1924 SDAs entered Kaunas, the capital, and about two years later a church was organized there. By that time Strohl had mastered enough of the language to preach in Lithuanian. By mid-1924 there were 130 members in the mission.

In 1925 a book depository was established in Lithuania under the name of Lietuvas Knygas Leidings "Uola," under the direction of Enseleit. A periodical titled *Krisciones Namu Prietelis* ("Christian Friend of the Home") was published, which was replaced from 1930 until World War II by *Dabarties Klausimai* ("Problems of the Present Day"), under the editorship of M. Gnedinas, W. Strohl, V. Kavaliauskas, and K. Stradauskas.

A measure of religious freedom prevailed in Lithuania between the two world wars. In 1927 the 160-member church received recognition as a religious society and acquired corporate rights. Many of the SDA publications, including the monthly paper, Sabbath school quarterlies, the Ingathering pamphlet *Piuties Padeka,* and the Week of Prayer readings were printed in a government-operated printing establishment. In 1929 a hymnbook, *Kankliu*

Aidai, containing some 160 hymns was issued.

Among the books printed over the years were the following: *Kekias i Kristu* ("Steps to Christ"), by Ellen White; *Pasaulio krizio isvakarense* ("On the Eve of the World's Crisis"), by C. B. Haynes; *Busimasis Pasaulio karas* ("The Coming World War"), by J. Birsin; *Kuomet ayeis geresni laikai* ("When to Expect Better Times"), also by J. Birsin; and *Kova pries Dieva* ("The Struggle Against God"), by C. L. Taylor. About 10 colporteurs were engaged in the distribution of SDA publications throughout the country.

A number of national workers were trained at the Friedensau Missionary Seminary in Germany or in the Suschenhof school of the Baltic Union. When the foreign workers were forced to leave in the course of World War II, the work was left in the charge of two national ministers, who, it appears, could function only as elders of local churches.

Persecution following World War II caused many members of German and Latvian origin to leave Lithuania. That left only a few members of Lithuanian origin and two pastors—A. Virbitskas in Shaulyai and E. Kantauchunas in Kaunus. Most of those baptized during that period were in the 45-to-80-age bracket. In 1981 D. Ojalis took the post held until then by A. Virbitskas, and new people began to join the church.

After N. Link replaced E. Kantauchunas, who died in 1988, he worked with D. Ojalis in evangelistic campaigns in Panevejis, Shaulyai, and Ionava. Don Barnt and Ben Owing from the United States held evangelistic meetings the same year in Vilnius, organizing a church of 172 members there.

Since 1990 church literature and periodicals have been translated and published, and some of the young workers have been sent for training to the Zaokski Theological Seminary in Russia.

LITHUANIAN FIELD. *See* Lithuania; Trans-European Division.

LITTLE CREEK ACADEMY. *See* Madison Institutions.

LITTLE HORN. *See* Daniel, Interpretation of.

LITTLE ROCK SANITARIUM. *See* Arkansas-Louisiana Conference.

LITTLE TIME OF TROUBLE. A relatively brief time of adversity and persecution immediately prior to the close of human probation. The phrase "little time of trouble" is based on an explanatory statement in the 1854 supplement to Ellen White's first book, *A Sketch of the Christian Experience and Views of Ellen White,* first published in 1851. She had written: "At the commencement of the time of trouble, we were filled with the Holy Ghost as we went forth and proclaimed the Sabbath more fully" (p. 17). Incorrectly identifying this "time of trouble" with that mentioned in connection with the standing up of Michael in Dan. 12:1 (taken to be Christ's standing up at the close of probation), some pointed out the futility of going forth to proclaim the Sabbath at all after probation had closed.

In the supplement Ellen White explained that "the time of trouble" to which she referred would be immediately prior to the close of probation. She wrote: "'The commencement of that time of trouble,' here mentioned, does not refer to the time when the plagues shall begin to be poured out, but to a short period just before they are poured out, while Christ is still in the sanctuary" (EW 85).

This "short period," accordingly, came to be known as "the little time of trouble," in contrast with the "great time of trouble" spoken of by Daniel. Mrs. White wrote further: "At that time, while the work of salvation is closing . . . the nations will be . . . held in check. . . . The 'latter rain' . . . will come, to give power to the loud voice of the third angel, and prepare the saints to stand in the period when the seven last plagues shall be poured out" *(ibid.).*

For those who remain loyal to the expressed purposes of Heaven, the little time of trouble will thus be a time of intensive evangelistic endeavor.

See also Latter Rain; Loud Cry; Probation; Three Angels' Messages; Time of Trouble.

LITTLEJOHN, WOLCOTT HACKLEY (1834-1916). Minister, author. He was educated at Kalamazoo College and the University of Michigan, but left the latter in his sophomore year because of an infection in the eyes, which left him totally blind 15 years later. He became a Seventh-day Adventist in 1866, later entered the ministry, and was appointed pastor of Battle Creek Seventh-day Adventist Church in 1883. Shortly afterward he served as president of Battle Creek College (1883-1885). From that time on he devoted himself chiefly to writing on biblical subjects. Numerous articles for denominational papers, tracts, and pamphlets came from his pen. He was on the committee that prepared the articles (1882) that were the forerunner of a church manual. He was the author of *The Coming Conflict, Rome in Prophecy,* and other works. In the discussions on righteousness by faith conducted near the turn of the century, he staunchly defended the position of Uriah Smith, as opposed to that taken by E. J. Waggoner and A. T. Jones.

LITTLETON HOSPITAL. A general, acute, 105-bed hospital operated at Littleton, Colorado, by the Mid-America Union Conference. It is accredited by the Joint Commission on Accreditation of Healthcare Organizations and has an open staff of 310 active physicians and 486 employees. The hospital features such services as obstetrics and gynecology, pediatrics, medical/surgical, radiology, cardiopulmonary, rehabilitation, and 24-hour emergency care. All of its rooms are private, billed at semiprivate rates. Its Family Life Center offers a wide variety of classes and programs, and the hospital serves the community with ASK-A-NURSE, a 24-hour free health information and physician referral service. The hospital is a member of Rocky Mountain Adventist Healthcare.

History. Littleton Hospital was established in 1989 by Porter Memorial Hospital to meet the needs of the rapidly growing southern corridor of metropolitan Denver. It opened an 85-bed facility on Apr. 9, 1989. In November 1990 the vacant sixth story of this facility was finished, allowing for 26 additional patient rooms, and in January 1992 the birthing center was expanded to 40 beds. The emergency center was expanded in 1991, adding five additional procedure rooms.

President: Richard Hale, 1989- .

LIVINGSTON, JOHN DOUGLAS (1894-1967). Missionary, administrator, and teacher. He was born in Kansas and educated at San Fernando Academy and Pacific Union College in California. In 1915 he began more than 40 years of dedicated service to the church by teaching church school in Oakland and Mountain View. After his marriage in 1918 to Mabel Swanson, the young couple left for Cuba, where Livingston served as evangelist and mission superintendent for five years. Back in his homeland he taught at La Sierra and Phoenix academies, and then returned to Cuba as director of the Antillian school for several years. Later he was called to River Plate College in Argentina, where he headed the Theology Department from 1931 to 1948. In 1949 he received his M.A. degree at the SDA Theological Seminary and his B.D. degree from the same institution in 1950. From 1949 until his retirement he taught Bible and biblical languages at Columbia Union College and also served on the staff of what was then the Home Study Institute. After retiring he continued to teach Bible doctrines in Spanish for Home Study Institute until the day of his death.

LIVRARIA DA IGREJA ADVENTISTA DO SETIMO DIA DE MOCAMBIQUE. *See* Mozambique Publishing House.

LLOYD, ERNEST (1880-1985). Editor. Born in Canada, he attended school at Battle Creek College and the New England Sanitarium. After serving in various publishing positions and teaching posts, he joined Pacific Press in 1917. He became editor of *Our Little Friend* in 1924, a position he held until 1949.

LLOYD, MARJORIE LEWIS (1911-1985). Author, composer. She was born in Nebraska; her education was cut short by illness after only six weeks at Walla Walla College, but she worked with Seventh-day Adventist broadcasting from its inception in 1956 until shortly before her death. For almost 29 years she assisted in the preparation of scripts and books for the *It Is Written* television ministry.

Two of her major projects written for television audiences were the book *The Cry of a Lonely Planet* and *The Truth for the End-Time* Bible study series. Her personal testimony is contained in the book *If I Had a Bigger Drum.*

She was also a prolific writer of poems and songs; her grave marker bears the title of her best-known gospel song, "Jesus, Take My Hand."

LOASBY, ROLAND E. (1890-1974). Missionary, evangelist, educator. A native of England, he emigrated to the United States at 18 years of age and was a member of the 1915 graduating class of Washington Missionary College in Maryland. From 1910 to 1912 he served as a missionary in Bermuda. After his marriage in 1913 to Bernice Manuel, they went to India, where they spent 23 years in evangelistic and educational work. In 1938 he became chair of the New Testament Department of the Seventh-day Adventist Theological Seminary, a post he held for 22 years. From 1960 to 1969 he engaged in part-time teaching.

LODI ACADEMY. A coeducational day school operated by the Northern California Conference on a 38-acre (15-hectare) tract just inside the southeast corner of the city limits of Lodi, California. Students come from the two churches in Lodi, the Galt church, and three churches in Stockton. In 1992-1993 there were 19 staff members, and the enrollment in grades 9 to 12 was 136.

The school is listed by the University of California as an approved college preparatory secondary school, and it is accredited by the Seventh-day Adventist Board of Regents and the Western Association of Schools and Colleges (WASC).

Lodi Academy was established in 1908 by a stock corporation. The members of the first corporate board were Elton D. Sharpe, president; W. A. Williams, secretary; C. P. Moon, business manager; Sylvia Sharpe; and Lula Moon. The project was financed by the sale of stock to the amount of some $8,000, by $7,500 in donations, by heavy bank and individual loans, and by $8,500 worth of land contributed by the Lodi Chamber of Commerce.

Originally called Western Normal Institute, the school was established to specialize in teacher education, for neither Healdsburg College nor San Fernando Academy was meeting the demand for teachers. Since Healdsburg College closed in the spring of 1908, and Pacific Union College did not open until the fall of 1909, Western Normal Institute offered some advanced college courses. Charles E. Nixon, B.A. in 1909, was apparently the only person who received a degree from Lodi. The following in teacher education was offered over the years: 1908-1910, four-year college normal course; 1910-1911, subjects in grades 11 and 12; 1911-1914, two-year teachers' course beyond the academy; 1914-1915, only the second year of the teachers' course (graduating the class that had already begun); 1916-1924, one teachers' subject in grade 11 and one in grade 12; 1924-1932, two-year teachers' course beyond the academy; 1932 to the present, no teachers' training.

The name of the institution changed as follows: 1908-1910, Western Normal Institute; 1910-1911, Lodi Normal Academy; 1911-1914, Lodi Normal Institute; 1914-1925, Lodi Academy; 1925-1932, Lodi Academy and Normal; 1932-1967, Lodi Academy; 1967-1968, Lodi Union Academy; since 1968, Lodi Academy.

The institution was controlled by the Northern California Conference from 1911 until June 1914, then came under the control of the Pacific Union Conference until 1918; from 1919 to 1929 it was under the Northern California Conference and the Central California Conference, and since 1949 under the Northern California Conference.

In 1967 and 1968 the dormitories were closed, the original buildings demolished, and a new plant built to serve day students only. The new construction consists of five units, four being of modular design, housing classrooms, library, and administrative offices; and a chapel with seating for 400, with an adjacent music department.

Other buildings are a gymnasium/auditorium seating 4,000, a warehouse, an industrial arts building, and eight homes for staff, three of which are duplexes.

The two publications are the *Gateway,* a monthly newspaper published during the school year since May 1928, and the school annual, the *Lodian Light,* published since 1950.

Principals: E. D. Sharpe, 1908-1910; I. C. Colcord, 1910-1913; J.A.L. Derby, 1913-1914; J. H. Paap, 1914-1919; R. A. Hare, 1919-1920; D. D. Lake, 1920-1922; E. E. Farnsworth, 1922-1924; C. E. Kellogg, 1924-1926; V. V. Wolfkill, 1926-1927; D. A. Ochs, 1927-1931; H. E. Westermeyer, 1931-1937; L. R. Rasmussen, 1937-1941; E. F. Heim, 1941-1949; H. D. Schwartz, 1949-1950; L. M. Stump, 1950-1953; L. W. Roth, 1953-1956; W. T. Will, 1956-1961; V. H. Koenig, 1961-1965; H. E. Voth, 1965-1970; L. P. Weischadle, 1970-1972; G. E. Rhoads, 1972-1986; Elwood Ross, 1986-1988; Stanley Baldwin, 1988-1994; Samir Berbawy, 1994- .

LOEBSACK, HEINRICH J. (d. 1938). Evangelist and administrator; the first Seventh-day Adventist to be ordained as a minister in Russia (in 1894). He was born in a German colony on the Volga. He became an SDA as a young man and soon after, early in 1890, went to Hamburg, Germany, where he attended an SDA mission school for six months. On his return to Russia in August 1890 he worked as a colporteur in the German Volga colonies.

In 1895 on his way to a workers' meeting in Switzerland, Loebsack held meetings in the Crimea, then in Volhynia (near Romania), and found hundreds of interested people. After working for about six months in Germany, he visited Riga, Latvia, where work had been begun some months earlier; he baptized several people there and also in Poland. In 1897, while in the Volga colonies, he received calls from various Mennonite settlements on the border of Siberia.

By World War I Loebsack had worked in the Caucasus, Crimea, Volhynia, Poland, and the Ukraine, and had been president of the Southern Russian Conference. During the war he was president of the Little Russian Conference, which included Kiev, Poltava, and Chernigov provinces, and Poland. When O. E. Reinke died in 1921, Loebsack succeeded him as president of the Russian Union. In the early 1920s Loebsack led in reorganizing the conferences and missions. He became the first president of the All Russia Federation of Seventh-day Adventists.

When the Soviet government changed its policy on religious freedom in 1929, communications between conferences, workers, and churches were disrupted. The conference offices were closed, and many ministers and lay members in all parts of Russia were arrested, imprisoned, and exiled. By 1934 Loebsack was left alone in Moscow, because all his coworkers had been exiled. Upon applying to the government for permission to get help, he was asked to submit names with biographies. Thus permission was granted to call G. Grigoriev from Novosibirsk in Siberia. Soon after Grigoriev's arrival, Loebsack was arrested and sentenced to three years of isolated imprisonment in the city of Yaroslav, northeast of Moscow. Afterward his term was extended indefinitely. He died in prison in 1938. His wife died in 1961 in Alma Ata, Kazakhstan. His eldest daughter, Amalie Galladshev, died in exile.

He was editor of *Adventbote* ("Advent Messenger"), published in Moscow 1925 to c. 1929, and *Golos Istiny* ("Voice of Truth"), both monthly papers. He wrote a history of the early SDA work in Russia, but the unpublished manuscript, sent to the Hamburg Publishing House, was destroyed in the bombings of World War II.

LOHNE, ALF (1915-1993). Administrator, writer. Born in Kristiansand, Norway, he studied at Onsrud Missionary College in Norway, Newbold College in England, and the Seventh-day Adventist Theological Seminary in Washington, D.C. While a student he spent summers canvassing. In 1935 he began his denominational service as a Bible worker and literature evangelist in the East Norway Conference, and then served that conference and the North Norway Conference as evangelist.

After further studies at Newbold College, he married Agnes Plata Torkelsen in 1940. In his capacity as a departmental secretary in the West Nordic Union and later in the Northern European office, he made an outstanding contribution to the church in that part of the world, particularly in the field of communications.

In 1951 he was called to serve as president of the East Norway Conference, where he had begun in the work. He held this position until 1967, when he was first secretary and then president of the Northern Europe-West Africa Division. At the General Conference session in 1975, he was elected a general vice president of the General Conference. His main responsibility was to coordinate the work of the church in the Soviet Union and other Eastern European countries. With the help of other administrators he accomplished the delicate task of bringing about a reconciliation among differing factions of the church in the Soviet Union at a time when religious worship was restricted. During those years a strong foundation was laid that bore much fruit after restrictions were removed.

A prolific and gifted writer, his articles in denominational periodicals always attracted many readers and kept local church members in touch with the progress of the message around the world, particularly in the Soviet Union. He authored several books, the most popular of which was *Tomorrow Begins Today*, which went through a number of editions and was translated into several languages. His last book, *Adventists in Russia*, has also been widely read. It gives insights into the beginnings of Seventh-day Adventist work in that important area of the world, as well as intriguing stories of his visits there.

LOMA LINDA ACADEMY. A coeducational K-12 day school comprised of three divisions: the elementary school, the junior high school, and the senior high school. The academy is operated by 11 constituent churches, which have a combined membership of 12,914. The 19 buildings are situated on a 28.5-acre (11.5-hectare) campus at 10656 Anderson Street, Loma Linda, California, approximately one quarter mile north of Loma Linda University.

The academy is accredited by the Seventh-day Adventist Board of Regents, and in 1962 the high school became a charter member of the Western Association of Schools and Colleges. It is on the list of approved schools of the University of California.

The total 1992-1993 enrollment was 1,511. There were 531 enrolled in grades 9-12, 208 in grades 7 and 8, and 772 in grades K-6; 55 of the staff of 116 served the elementary school, 11 served the junior high level, and 32 were members of the secondary staff. The remaining 18 comprise the K-12 support staff.

The school is descended from the original Loma Linda church school, opened in 1906 in a tent pitched on the side of the sanitarium hill. Among the six original students were F. D. Nichol, former editor of the *Review and Herald,* and his two sisters. The following year, with 12 students, the school met in the building later known as Alumni Hall, and the next year, with 46 students, it occupied a new school building at the foot of the hill on Mound Street, northeast of the sanitarium. During the principalship of James I. Robison (1910-1913), later a missionary in Africa and an associate secretary of the General Conference, the school moved to a new building situated north of the present site, across San Timoteo Creek, and became a 10-grade school.

The list of board members in those early days included the names of J. A. Burden, W. A. George, G. M. Price, and Clarence Santee.

The school year of 1920-1921, under the principalship of Elson H. Emmerson, was the first year in which 12 grades were offered by Loma Linda Academy. A class of six graduated in the spring of 1921. However, in 1922 the academy was reduced to 10 grades, and the students for the eleventh and twelfth grades commuted to the new La Sierra Academy. The school again became a 12-grade academy in the fall of 1930, at the beginning of the principalship of W. C. Flaiz.

The first building on the present site was an elementary school unit built in 1931. The next year, 1932, the old school buildings were moved and reassembled on the present academy site, and the dedication of the new plant took place at the beginning of the 1932 school year.

The high school library and chapel, built in 1946, were saved when the rest of the administration building burned in March of 1946. The structure was rebuilt in time for the opening of school that fall. Flaiz Hall, the science-mathematics building, was completed in 1965.

In February of 1969 a flood caused extensive damage to the campus of the academy. In May of 1969 the Loma Linda Academy constituency voted, in view of projected enrollment growth and the severe flood damage done to the property, to initiate a comprehensive building program consisting of four phases: (1) gymnasium-classroom complex; (2) industrial education and academy classroom and administration complex; (3) elementary classroom complex; (4) preschool facilities. The first phase was completed in the spring of 1971, the second in 1974. In 1988 a new elementary school plant was completed south of the original campus. The new plant includes classrooms, offices, auditorium, gymnasium, food service facility, and specialty use rooms.

The high school student association publishes a paper, *The Mirror,* and a yearbook, *The Lomasphere*. The junior high school publishes a yearbook, *Reflections*, and the elementary school publishes a yearbook, *Footprints*.

Principals: E. H. Emmerson, 1920-1922; Mrs. O. J. Graf, 1922-1926 (10-grade school); W. F. Hardt, 1926-1930 (10-grade school); W. C. Flaiz, 1930-1935; A. C. Madsen, 1935-1940; J. A. Simonson, 1940-1942; H. H. Morse, 1942-1944; P. E. Limerick, 1944-1949; P. G. Baden, 1949-1959; E. J. Digneo, 1959-1967; H. L. Jensen, 1967-1968; A. H. Johns, 1968-1970; G. E. Thompson, 1970-1977; K. R. Lorenz, 1977-1982; J. G. Kerbs, 1982-1988; G. E. Rhoads, 1988- .

LOMA LINDA ADVENTIST SANITARIUM (Chaco Sanitarium and Hospital; Sanatorio Adventista Loma Linda). A medical institution situated 1.2 miles (two kilometers) from the city of Presidencia Roque Sáenz Peña (60,000 inhabitants), province of Chaco, Argentina.

In 1964 Mrs. Esther Leiva, who had been an inpatient at the River Plate Sanitarium and Hospital and was much impressed by the Christian assistance given by its personnel, desired that a similar sanitarium be founded in her city. She began to work among the inhabitants of Presidencia Roque Sáenz Peña, and captured the interest of Dr. Juan Carlos Moroni, who had been her doctor at River Plate Sanitarium, and of Dr. Arturo Weiss. They presented the idea to the leaders of the work.

In 1966 Drs. Weiss and Moroni were sent to establish a clinic in the city prior to the initiation of the sanitarium. A medical director and an administrator for the clinic and future sanitarium were appointed. The following year plans were laid for the building to be constructed in three stages. The third stage was begun in 1973.

By 1993 the sanitarium was serving a large area in north Argentina. There were 43 beds, 7 full-time doctors, and 15 nurses.

Medical Directors: Arturo J. Weiss, 1966-1980; Enrique Manrique, 1980-1981; Juan Carlos Moroni, 1981-1984; Rene A. Leichner, 1984-1991; Harold Cecotto, 1991- .

LOMA LINDA COLLEGE OF EVANGELISTS. *See* Loma Linda University.

LOMA LINDA FOODS/LA LOMA FOODS. A nonprofit corporation manufacturing and distributing health foods in the United States and Canada. It was owned and operated by the General Conference of Seventh-day Adventists for the purposes of (a) furthering by all proper means a better knowledge of the laws of healthful living, (b) manufacturing and selling healthful foods and related products, and (c) encouraging and supporting benevolent, educational, and religious enterprises of the Seventh-day Adventist Church. The main office, factory, and headquarters were at 11503 Pierce Street, Riverside, California; the second factory (featuring the production of soy milk in liquid and powdered form) was on Wooster Road, Mount Vernon, Ohio. Products included vegetarian protein foods (canned and frozen), soy milk, cereal coffee, gravy mixes, and canned soybeans.

History. Forerunner of Loma Linda Foods was the Loma Linda Sanitarium bakery, which began operation in 1905. It was called the Sanitarium Food Company, and its plant was situated on Anderson Street in Loma Linda. At first it manufactured a variety of breads and wafers, but it soon added other health food items. On Feb. 6, 1933, the name "Loma Linda Food Company" was adopted, and on July 1, 1935, the first articles of incorporation were filed for a perpetual, nonprofit organization with a 12-member board of directors elected every two years by a General Conference-selected constituency, the Pacific Union Conference, each local conference in the Pacific Union Conference, and the board of Loma Linda University. On Nov. 14, 1937, groundbreaking ceremonies for a factory building were held on a nine-acre site donated by the Southern California Junior College (now La Sierra College) at Arlington (Riverside). The new factory began operations on July 16, 1938, the main product being Ruskets, a flaked whole-wheat biscuit cereal, but later more than 30 other products were added, the main emphasis being upon the development and perfection of high-protein foods of vegetable origin. The company also distributed related food items processed and packaged by others under the Loma Linda Foods label.

On Jan. 1, 1951, Loma Linda Foods took over the business of the International Nutrition Laboratories, Inc., Mount Vernon, Ohio, purchased from Harry Willis Miller, M.D. Charles Percy Miles was named manager. The Canadian Division of Loma Linda Foods was established at Oshawa, Ontario, in 1962 on a site donated by Oshawa Missionary College (now Kingsway College). Frank L. Wessely was appointed its manager. It was closed in 1965. In 1951 the original corporation was liquidated and the ownership of the business was transferred to the Pacific Union Association. It was presented to the General Conference as a gift from the Pacific Union Conference on June 30, 1970. The affairs of the General Conference Corporation doing business as Loma Linda Foods was directed by a general board of management consisting of 25 members elected by the General Conference Executive Committee. The composition of the general board includes General Conference, union and local conferences, as well as Loma Linda Foods and church laity personnel.

Loma Linda Foods began with limited capital, and as the company grew, much of the earnings were invested in necessary buildings and machinery. Considerable sums were devoted to market development, to nutritional and product research, and to public nutrition education programs. Loma Linda Foods also afforded financial support to the Seventh-day Adventist Dietetic Association and provided fellowships to selected postgraduates of the School of Dietetics of Loma Linda University. By Jan. 1, 1965, it had also contributed to the denominational mission program more than $300,000 through the Loma Linda Foods label-saving plan for Sabbath school Investment.

In 1989 Loma Linda Foods sold its name and infant formula business to another company and renamed the remaining organization La Loma Foods. In 1990 La Loma was sold to Worthington Foods, an organization owned mainly by Seventh-day Adventist laypersons.

General Managers: G. T. Chapman, 1938-1962; C. P. Miles, 1963-1973; M. E. Dake,

1973-1976; L. Delmer Wood, 1976-1980; F.V.L. Bateman, 1980-1984; Eric Fehlberg, 1984-1986; Alejo Pizarro, 1986-1990.

LOMA LINDA SANITARIUM. *See* Loma Linda University.

LOMA LINDA SCHOOL OF NURSING. *See* Loma Linda University.

LOMA LINDA UNIVERSITY. A Seventh-day Adventist coeducational health sciences institution in inland southern California, 60 miles (100 kilometers) east of Los Angeles (in the San Bernardino, Redlands, area).

I. General Features. Professional curriculums are offered by the Schools of Allied Health Professions, Dentistry, Medicine, Nursing, and Public Health. Graduate programs are offered through the Graduate School.

There are 870 full-time faculty. Part-time and voluntary teachers, especially clinicians in the professional curriculums, bring the total to more than 1,900. Approximately 90 nations and virtually all of the states of the Union are represented in the annual enrollment of more than 3,000 students. Health science curriculums are offered for the Associate in Science (A.S.), Associate in Arts (A.A.), Bachelor of Science (B.S.), undergraduate and graduate certificates, Master of Science in Public Health (M.S.P.H.), Master of Health Administration (M.H.A.), Master of Public Health (M.P.H.), Master of Social Work (M.S.W.), Master of Physical Therapy (M.P.T.), Master of Science (M.S.), Master of Arts (M.A.), Doctor of Physical Therapy (DPT), Doctor of Public Health (Dr.P.H.), Doctor of Dental Surgery (D.D.S.), Doctor of Medicine (M.D.), and Doctor of Philosophy (Ph.D.) degrees.

The university was founded as the Loma Linda College of Evangelists in 1905 and chartered as the College of Medical Evangelists in the state of California in 1909. It was accredited by the Northwest Association of Secondary and Higher Schools in 1937, a relationship that was voluntarily surrendered in favor of the Western Association of Schools and Colleges in 1960 (prior to January 1962, Western College Association). The institution became Loma Linda University on July 1, 1961.

The professional schools and curriculums are approved by their own national accrediting organizations.

The Del E. Webb Memorial Library is the main library for the institution. The building was completed in 1981. Attached to it is the Vernier Radcliffe Wing, which houses the Heritage Room and the stacks. Also a part of the library building is the Randall Visitors' Center. This houses an amphitheater and the Jorgensen Learning Center, as well as the Robert M. Ricketts collection.

As of 1994 the holdings of the library included more than 375,000 books, bound periodicals, and audiovisual materials, and 2,500 current subscriptions. Special collections of Seventh-day Adventist and health sciences materials enrich the holdings and include the Clark, Lebowitz, Peterson, and Remondino collections. This is augmented with the Ellen White Estate Branch Office. The library is a depository for books published by the Pacific Press Publishing Association and the Review and Herald Publishing Association. Administratively separate departmental libraries exist on campus.

Several cooperative arrangements with other libraries give students and faculty access to their collections. These include the five largest libraries as well as most of the other academic libraries in the area. The library also participates in the Pacific Southwest region of the National Network of Libraries of Medicine, serving as one of the resource libraries.

Besides the traditional library services, the library faculty participate in course-integrated bibliographic instruction and work with the various schools to assure that the library is filling their information needs. The library has joined with the Medical Library and Information Center (MLIC) of the Loma Linda University Medical Center to move toward a local implementation of the Integrated Academic Information Management System concept, endorsed by the National Library of Medicine.

The publications of the university include the bulletins of the schools of the university; student handbooks and directories; *Scope* and the *Today* (successors to *The Medical Evangelists,* 1908-1962, and the *University Observer*, 1962-1988), as interpretative media for students, parents, alumni, faculty, and institutional family; a student newspaper; and the alumni publications of the schools of the university. *(Medical Arts and Sciences,* a quarterly scientific journal reflecting research and clinical investigation at the university, was published from 1947 to 1974.)

The Drayson Center is a 100,000-square-foot (9,300-square-meter) state-of-the-art fitness/wellness facility. It serves as the focal point for out-of-class campus life at Loma Linda. Students, faculty, at staff at Loma Linda and employees at Loma Linda University Medical Center may participate in the multi-faceted programs involving the wholistic concept of social, intellectual, physical, emotional, and spiritual wellness that supports Loma Linda's motto, "To make man whole."

The closing of the Norton Air Force Base (in San Bernardino, three miles [five kilometers] from the Loma Linda campus) in the early 1990s turned into a great opportunity for Loma Linda. After negotiations the clinic located on the base was donated to Loma Linda, along with a lot of clinic equipment. The Social Action Community Health System (SACHS) is centered in the 42,300 square feet (4,000 square meters) of clinic space. All of the Loma Linda health professional schools are intrinsically involved in providing interdisciplinary, comprehensive primary care for the uninsured in communities surrounding Loma Linda. SACHS also has several satellite clinics in neighboring communities. The roots of SACHS are found deep in the missionary outreach activities of Loma Linda University, Loma Linda University Medical Center, the University church, and the Southeastern California Conference.

1. *University Administration and Control.* Loma Linda University is a nonprofit corporation organized and existing under the laws of the state of California. The president of Loma Linda University is the president of the corporation. The Foundation, a division of the corporation, manages investment properties and securities, annuities, trust agreements, and life-income contracts.

Total land, buildings, and equipment are valued at more than $51 million. The Loma Linda campus consists of 142 acres (60 hectares). Adjacent reserve land totals 220 acres (90 hectares); other properties owned by the university in the community amount to 47 acres (20 hectares). Employees total approximately 1,300.

The institution is supported by the General Conference and, in addition, receives other financial support. Six of the 23 members of the board of trustees are elected from among the General Conference administrative staff. Also serving as members of the board are the president of the North American Division and up to four presidents of union conferences in the North American Division. Other trustees include alumni and laypersons.

The university, consisting of six schools and the faculty of religion, is administered by the president of the university, who represents the entire institution on the board of trustees and is responsible for all operations. There are five vice presidents in specific areas of operation: academic and research affairs, financial affairs, advancement, public affairs, and medical affairs. In addition to the school deans, there is a dean of student affairs, two special assistants to the president of the university in the area of diversity and international affairs. The medical center, although a separate corporation, is used in the educational function of the university.

2. *Consolidation of the School of Medicine.* A most significant event in the development, location, and expansion of the university involved the consolidation of the School of Medicine and the paramedical programs. From its inception as a medical school, the first two years of the medical curriculum were offered at Loma Linda. Because of the paucity of clinical material and the lack of proper clinical facilities at Loma Linda, the third and fourth years were taught at Los Angeles, at what is now the White Memorial Medical Center and with the excellent affiliation at the Los Angeles County General Hospital. Clinical teaching and medical research were carried on at these locations until the middle 1960s.

In time and after prolonged urging by the accrediting groups concerned, the School of Medicine was consolidated on a single campus at Loma Linda. The construction of a new 500-bed medical center, including a research wing, made this consolidation possible. This new facility was opened in July 1967. In addition, affiliations with other medical institutions in the vicinity of Loma Linda have been utilized.

3. *Relationship of La Sierra University With Loma Linda University.* When the Loma Linda trustees voted to unite the four years of medicine on the Loma Linda campus, the need was felt to undergird the professional studies on that campus with expanded offerings in the liberal arts. Various ways of implementing this action were given consideration. The eventual decision of the trustees was to merge La Sierra College, located 20 miles (30 kilometers) away, with Loma Linda University, which arrangement became effective July 1, 1967. The La Sierra College campus assumed the name Riverside Campus of Loma Linda University. In 1990 the Loma Linda University Board of Trustees voted to separate the two campuses as

independent corporations. This was done in order to allow each campus to more clearly focus on its distinctive mission. The Riverside campus is now known as La Sierra University. *(See* La Sierra University.)

4. *Humanitarian Outreach.* Loma Linda University is and always has been a part of the Seventh-day Adventist global mission. This is why the university was founded, and this is why it exists. If each Loma Linda University presence was represented by a dot, there would be 70 such dots on a world map emphasizing the global outreach of the university. Some of these dots represent university-wide projects, and others the program of a single school of the university, or even one individual. During the decade from 1984 to 1993 there was a significant and progressive increase in international activities at Loma Linda University. This encompassed all of the schools of the University in both faculty and student groups. To complement the activities within the schools there is also a steady stream of international visiting professors averaging 150 in number every year. All of this is in harmony with the global mission thrust that is the foundation of Loma Linda University. Only some of the varied activities of the university will be mentioned.

For many years the medical students and dental students have had opportunity to go on mission electives. This program continues to flourish, and through the years these students have gone to mission stations in almost 50 different countries as part of their professional education. Another active student group is Students for International Mission Service (SIMS). The SIMS groups go outside the United States to all parts of the world, and from 1985 through 1994, 2,247 students participated in different teams. These trips take place during vacation periods and are made up of multidisciplinary teams, with faculty supervision providing medical, dental, allied health, and public health assistance.

Since early in the 1980s Loma Linda University has had an agreement with Kasturba Medical College and the other schools of that university located in Manipal, India. This agreement has provided a way for Seventh-day Adventist students in India to receive their medical education there. Loma Linda University reciprocates with faculty exchange programs from all the different schools of the university. This program has been quite successful, and each year five Seventh-day Adventist Indian students graduate from medicine and/or dentistry, ready to serve local health needs. A similar program is in place at Obafemi Awolowo University in Ile Ife, Nigeria.

Another university-wide project is the Overseas Heart Surgery Team, which has functioned since 1963. From 1963 through 1992 the team has made 23 trips to 12 countries. Through the years thousands of patients have had lifesaving surgery and hundreds of local medical personnel have been trained. In many cases the ideal goal has been achieved, and the local country has been able to continue the same type of work after the team has left. In some countries self-sufficiency in cardiac surgery required a continuing program that was started with health-care personnel being rotated from Loma Linda University. From 1963 through 1992, 837 individuals were sent from Loma Linda University to carry out these services in the various countries.

The School of Medicine, using the experience obtained from the demonstration of the heart team, has encouraged the various departments to develop their individual overseas projects. Scores of such independent teaching missions have been sent to many countries, with results that are mutually beneficial. Ophthalmology, plastic and reconstructive surgery, and urology are just a few such participants. In each of the schools of the university there is an extensive faculty and medical exchange with countries throughout the world.

The School of Allied Health Professions has been active in assisting in curriculum development and faculty preparation in many countries, including India, China, Puerto Rico, and Jamaica. The Department of Cardiopulmonary Sciences has organized the School of Respiratory Therapy in Riyadh, Saudi Arabia. This is a unique situation, with Loma Linda University granting a degree in respiratory therapy to Saudi Arabian students who have been taught the same material that they would have received in Loma Linda. The first graduating class finished in 1990, and the program continues to flourish.

The School of Public Health provides extended programs that have now functioned well in more than 10 countries. This is a mechanism whereby the local people can obtain a public health degree from Loma Linda University by attending intensive summer sessions over a four-year period. This enables Loma Linda to extend its borders geographically and to be of greater assistance to other countries. The School of Public Health at

Loma Linda has just been designated as a collaborating center by the World Health Organization (WHO). This honor carries with it the opportunity to serve as an overseas consultant under the auspices of WHO.

The School of Dentistry has a strong continuing education program that is active both domestically and overseas. They have conducted courses in more than 20 countries and continue to expand their offerings. There is also an active faculty and medical exchange throughout the school with other dental schools in many countries. The most innovative program in the dental school, as regards the global mission, has been the international dentist program. This is designed to allow qualified dentists educated in other countries to earn an American Doctor of Dental Surgery degree. This program has been in place for the past several years, and more than 100 students have come from 30-plus countries. This program helps to develop strong ties with the countries of origin of these students.

As Loma Linda University is now a health sciences university, it has become more of a focal point for visitors from other nations. This gives an opportunity for the Loma Linda faculty to share not only their scientific expertise but their desire to use global outreach as a vehicle for "making man whole."

II. Historical Backgrounds: Loma Linda and Los Angeles. 1. *Forerunners and Beginnings.* The nucleus on which the university was formed in 1961 was the College of Medical Evangelists. This was the second Seventh-day Adventist medical college, but there was no organizational or legal connection between it and its predecessor, the American Medical Missionary College (1895-1910). The latter was connected with the Battle Creek Sanitarium, and both went out from denominational control about 1907. Even before that time Loma Linda was chosen as one of several sites for medical institutions in southern California. In 1900, soon after her return from Australia, Ellen White made her home at St. Helena, California, where a sanitarium had been established in 1878, and began to urge that medical institutions be established in southern California. She enlisted the assistance of a minister, John A. Burden, who in 1904 began to canvass the region for suitable sanitarium locations.

When Burden surveyed the coastal plains and valleys of southern California, he found for sale many tourist hotels and health resort buildings, which stood as mute evidence of the real-estate boom and subsequent debacle of the 1880s. Two of these were purchased privately on the advice of Mrs. White, and in time they came to be denominationally operated as the Paradise Valley Sanitarium at National City and the Glendale Sanitarium at Glendale, a suburb of Los Angeles.

Another of these was the Victorian-styled Loma Linda resort hotel, constructed in 1887-1888 as part of the Mound City development, which collapsed with the end of the great boom. It was bought in 1900 by the Loma Linda Association, a group of Los Angeles businessmen and physicians, the latter hoping to establish a health resort. The association remodeled and richly furnished the hotel, adding five patient cottages and a recreation hall, and landscaping the hill, raising the total investment above $150,000. This venture also failed, and by 1904 the luxury hotel stood almost empty. So matters stood early in 1905 when Ellen White, charmed by the beauty of the San Bernardino Valley and impressed by its possibilities as a location for a country sanitarium, instructed John A. Burden to look for a site. Burden found Loma Linda (Spanish for "Hill Beautiful"), including the hotel, the ancillary buildings, and 76 acres (30 hectares) of land, for sale for $110,000.

The owners of Loma Linda, desperate to sell and hoping to sell to someone who could be expected to succeed where they had failed in creating a health resort, lowered the price to $40,000, which Mrs. White instructed Burden to accept. The option was signed on May 26, 1905, with a down payment of $1,000, and two months later, on July 26, the indenture was signed, in which the Loma Linda Association, the party of the first part, sold and conveyed to John A. Burden, the party of the second part, the property known as Loma Linda, including all lands, buildings, furnishings, equipment, wells, insurance policies; 20 shares of capital stock in the Big Bear Water and Pipe Company, and 15 shares of capital stock in the Bryn Mawr Water Company—without which valley land would have been almost worthless in those days. Money came from unexpected sources, and by Apr. 15, 1906, the entire purchase price (discounted to $38,900) had been paid, and a dedication service was held on the sanitarium grounds. On June 20, 1905, the Southern California Conference of Seventh-day Adventists had agreed to accept the property as a denominational institution, which became a fact when the corporation was formed. In the beginning John Burden was the chairman of the board, president of the corporation, manager, and chaplain of the sanitarium.

2. *The First Schools at Loma Linda.* During the summer and fall preceding the opening of the sanitarium, young people began to arrive in anticipation of taking the nursing course at Loma Linda, for in those days it was taken for granted that an SDA sanitarium should have its own school of nursing. In November, with the arrival of Julia A. White, M.D., recruited by Mrs. White to be the sanitarium's obstetrician and head of the training program for nurses, it was announced that instruction in nursing would begin early in January of 1906. Actually, informal instruction had probably begun with the arrival of the students.

A council representing the Pacific Union Conference and the Southern California Conference in April 1906 gave substance to the educational program. Warren E. Howell was elected "president of the faculty" and instructed to gather a faculty and construct nursing, general collegiate, and evangelistic-medical curriculums. The school was named the Loma Linda College of Evangelists. Howell and his staff put together a prospectus for the college, then Howell departed for a mission appointment in Greece in the spring of 1907, and George Knapp Abbott, M.D., became head of the school in his place.

The curriculum in nursing was constructed along conventional Adventist lines for the first two years of the course, after which the students were eligible to take the first year of the evangelistic-medical course. Nine years of school were required for admission to the course in nursing. There were seven in the first class, all transfer students, which made possible their graduation on July 10, 1907.

Putting together a curriculum in medicine was a more difficult matter for the administration, which was plagued with uncertainties as to philosophy, and therefore content, in addition to uncertainties about the relationship between them and the sanitarium. On Dec. 9, 1909, under a new name, the College of Medical Evangelists received from the state of California a charter authorizing the granting of academic and professional degrees.

In 1910 the College of Medical Evangelists took definite shape in a series of decision-making conferences. In January the Pacific Union Conference in biennial session at Mountain View, California, heard an appeal from Loma Linda leaders for broader support and for assistance with planning for medical education. A committee appointed at this session secured from Ellen White a statement, dated Jan. 27, 1910, calling for quality medical education. In response, the conference recommended that CME offer a full medical course, that the controlling board be enlarged to include representation from the General Conference and the union conferences in North America, and that the financial support be equally broad. In April the Spring Council of the General Conference voted to approve the Pacific Union Conference recommendation and suggested three General Conference members for the CME board, including President A. G. Daniells.

Finally, a representative council met at Loma Linda, May 6-10, 1910, to give substance to the developing concept of CME. As a final result, the college and the sanitarium became one corporation. A board of 10 members was selected, including the president of the General Conference and the presidents of the Pacific Union Conference and the Southern California Conference. An appropriate financial base was approved, and operating funds for the next school year were voted. CME had become a General Conference institution. Formal instruction in medicine began over the year-end of 1909-1910, and the first class of six members was graduated on June 11, 1914.

The future of the College of Medical Evangelists appeared to hang in the balance when the Autumn Council met in Loma Linda in 1915. The denomination did not adequately understand the nature and objectives of the educational program. War clouds were gathering and institutional costs were rising, and despite the heroic efforts of the administration the American Medical Association had given the medical curriculum the poorest of all possible ratings. However, the College of Medical Evangelists had a new leader, a medical scientist and educator of distinction and experience, Newton G. Evans, M.D. Under his leadership, and with the loyal support of Arthur G. Daniells, president of the General Conference, I. H. Evans, and others, the council declared the denomination in favor of the expansion of the Loma Linda programs, including a fully accredited medical school.

Plans had to be laid for clinical practice on a wider scale than Loma Linda provided. As early as the fall of 1913, some months before the graduation of the first class in medicine, a clinic had been opened in Los Angeles, and the way was clear for limited student instruction at the Los Angeles County General Hospital. In 1915 Percy T. Magan, M.D., an experienced educator and administrator, was added to President Evans' staff as dean of the Los Angeles Division. Shortly thereafter land was purchased in Boyle Heights for the cottage-type original White Memorial Hospital, where upperclassmen in medicine received their clinical training under denominational auspices.

Changes in the constitution and bylaws, organizational structure, and administrative staff, as well as growth and progress in physical facilities, educational conception, and spiritual perception, have characterized the passing decades since the college in 1915 became more certain of its future course. From a very small institution with overlapping curriculums and uncertain objectives, it came to be, under the General Conference aegis, the denomination's largest and most complex institution. It became Loma Linda University in 1961.

3. *Loma Linda University Medical Center.* On Oct. 1, 1905, a few persons began to prepare Loma Linda Sanitarium for the admission of patients. Various dates have been given for the opening. On Oct. 9 Burden notified Mrs. White that "Loma Linda is now open to receive patients. Doctor Abbott is with us, and a number of other workers." Although the official patient register lists the first admission as on Oct. 12, Burden, the first manager, officially fixed Nov. 1 as the date of opening and issued his financial statements accordingly. There were as many as 55 patients at one time during the first winter season.

Because of the need for practical instruction in the care of surgical and critically ill patients, authorization was given in 1910 to raise $25,000 for the construction of a small hospital on the campus site, west of "the hill." This was occupied in 1913, but by 1915 it was apparent that the patronage was not sufficient to satisfy educational needs.

The transfer of Loma Linda Sanitarium assets to the College of Medical Evangelists on June 15, 1910, made Loma Linda Sanitarium legally an integral part of the college. However, the sanitarium, because of its independent origin and the recognized necessity of establishing a teaching hospital in Los Angeles, came to be less intimately related to undergraduate medical education, though it continued as the primary training facility for the School of Nursing. Its steady growth reflected a well-earned reputation as a popular community hospital in the San Bernardino Valley and a health center in the Pacific Southwest.

In May 1923 the trustees adopted a plan for a new building to be constructed on top of the hill. Construction on a one-story hospital facility was near completion in January 1924, but for lack of funds it was not furnished and occupied until the following August. A plan to add a second floor to the new hospital unit and to remove the two top floors of the sanitarium was abandoned in favor of constructing a new three-story sanitarium building adjacent to the hospital unit. Construction began in April 1928. Although the finished building cost only $2.52 a square foot, the money was hard to secure. Completion and occupancy came in March 1929, and the official opening on April 7. The upper floors of the old building were removed, and the modified structure was demoted to an annex status.

Full patronage soon created a demand for additional beds. Funds earned by the institution were sufficiently augmented to finance a half-million-dollar hospital unit, which was added to the east end of the new sanitarium building. The 1924 unit was converted into additional bed space and doctors' offices. Except for laboratory and radiology additions to the main structure, there were no major additions to the sanitarium and hospital until it was completely renovated in 1968 for classrooms, laboratories, and offices for the Schools of Health and Allied Health Professions.

In late 1962 the university trustees voted to consolidate on one campus at Loma Linda, including the programs that had previously been conducted partially in Los Angeles. To accommodate the heavier programs in professional curricula that the consolidated arrangement would require at Loma Linda, they launched plans to erect a new, larger hospital-medical center complex there.

Actual construction of the nine-story structure, with two levels underground, was begun soon after formal groundbreaking ceremonies on June 6, 1964. In July 1967 it was completed and occupied.

In the early 1980s Loma Linda University Medical Center became the only state-designated, level 1, regional trauma center for Inyo, Mono, Riverside, and San Bernardino counties, an area covering approximately one fourth of California.

Loma Linda University Medical Center is staffed by 4,500 employees and provides services for more than 23,000 inpatients annually.

Outpatient visits total more than 500,000 each year. In 1993 the medical center was licensed for more than 700 beds. Its community hospital (with 120 beds) and its Behavioral Medicine Center (an 89-bed psychiatric hospital) take the total to more than 900 beds.

Up to 35 percent of the medical center's patients are served in eight intensive-care units: surgical/trauma, neurosurgical, cardiothoracic surgery, pediatric cardiothoracic surgery, coronary, medical, neonatal, and pediatrics. It is one of the busiest university medical centers in the western United States. The medical center is licensed for 72 neonatal intensive-care beds for premature or sick babies, one of the largest facilities of its kind in the world. Half of the neonatal intensive-care unit's patients are transferred to Loma Linda from outlying community hospitals, and half of those transferred arrive by helicopter. An average of four helicopters a day fly into one of LLUMC's two heliports.

Loma Linda University Medical Center is best known around the world for its pioneering infant heart-transplant program, under the direction of Leonard L. Bailey, M.D., chair of the Department of Surgery. On Nov. 20, 1985, Baby Moses (Eddie Anguiano), at 4 days of age, became the youngest person in the world to undergo heart transplantation. To date, 150 babies under 6 months of age have received new hearts at LLUMC, with an overall success rate of approximately 80 percent. The tiny hearts weigh about one ounce. The youngest heart-transplant patient was baby Paul Holc, a Canadian, transplanted on Oct. 16, 1987, when he was just 3 hours old. He became the youngest person ever to receive an organ transplant of any kind.

The world's first hospital-based Proton Treatment Center was opened at LLUMC in October 1990, under the direction of James M. Slater, M.D., chair of the Department of Radiation Medicine. Patients at the Proton Treatment Center are now receiving a form of radiation therapy capable of irradiating cancerous tumors more precisely than conventional radiation, with far less of the debilitating side effects associated with conventional radiation.

LLUMC's proton accelerator, built by the U.S. Department of Energy's Fermi National Accelerator Laboratory, is the world's smallest synchrotron. The accelerator, producing up to 250 million electron volts of energy, and its proton guidance system, standing three stories tall, weigh 400 tons (360 metric tons).

"Loma Linda has taken a very courageous step by being the first medical institution in the world to bring the practical medical treatment to what has been, up until now, highly scientific research," says United States Congressman Jerry Lewis of California. "It is characteristic of Loma Linda University Medical Center to be in the forefront of this type of medical research and to have the vision to provide this sophisticated technology to cancer patients. The pioneering work is critical to our efforts to effectively treat and cure cancer. I believe this state-of-the-art facility at Loma Linda will be a model for the world medical community to emulate in future years."

The opening of the Loma Linda University Children's Hospital in 1993 is a response to the expanding need for specialized neonatal and pediatric care in the fastest-growing region in North America. With 275 beds, it is one of the largest children's hospitals in the United States.

Hanging on the east wall of the main lobby is Sallman's famous painting, *Head of Christ.* From the inspiration of the Great Physician, the institution chose as its motto, "To Make Man Whole," to emphasize a Christian philosophy that the human body is the temple of God (1 Cor. 6:19, 20).

Loma Linda University Medical Center. Medical Directors/Administrators: J. A. Burden, 1905-1910; T. J. Evans, M.D., 1910-1917; A. W. Truman, 1917-1918; H. W. Vollman, M.D., 1918-1923; A. N. Donaldson, M.D., 1923-1928; Daniel Burgeson, M.D., 1928-1929; M. S. King (acting), 1929-1930; H. M. Walton, M.D., 1930-1937; A. D. Butterfield, M.D., 1937-1949; H. M. Walton, M.D., 1949-1951; J. M. Nies, 1951-1953; C. A. Miller, 1953-1967; C. Victor Way, 1967-1974; H. H. Hill, 1974-1977; John D. Ruffcorn, 1977-1987; David B. Hinshaw, Sr., 1987-1994; J. David Moorhead, 1994- .

III. School of Nursing. Informal instruction in nursing for a group of transfer students who had been accepted in the fall of 1905 was the first educational activity in Loma Linda. The School of Nursing was officially opened in January of 1906 by Julia A. White, M.D., the first superintendent of nurses. The first graduate nurse to serve as superintendent of nurses was Mrs. Emma Martha Pallant Semmens (1913-1914), who had entered the nurse's training course at the Battle Creek Sanitarium in 1887 under the direction of Kate Lindsay, M.D.

After the opening of the White Memorial Hospital in Los Angeles in 1918, its facilities were used by student nurses from the training school at Loma Linda until mid-1966. From 1923 to 1948, two separate hospital schools of nursing were in operation—one at the Loma Linda Sanitarium and the other at the White Memorial Hospital. Both schools were under the same director from 1923 to 1926. One year of college prenursing curriculum was required for admission by both schools after 1932.

In 1948 the trustees authorized the organization of a single collegiate School of Nursing to use facilities at both campuses, to be administered by a dean, and to offer a curriculum leading to the Bachelor of Science degree, based upon one year of prescribed college courses before admission. The first class under this program graduated in June 1952. The class of 1959 was the first to receive public health nurse certification. Advanced instruction for the Master of Science degree was first offered in 1954 *(see* under VIII).

When the Associate of Science program was transferred from the College of Arts and Sciences on the La Sierra campus, the affiliation with the White Memorial Hospital was resumed for a short period from 1970-1975. Two specialty programs that could be started during the senior year of the baccalaureate program were begun in 1971: the pediatric nurse associate and the nurse midwifery programs. The pediatric nurse associate program was moved into the graduate program in 1978 and the curriculum revised as a postbaccalaureate program to prepare pediatric nurse practitioners. An adult nurse practitioner program was added at that time. The midwifery program was phased out in 1975. The pediatric and adult nurse practitioner programs were closed to new admissions in 1982.

In 1986 the School of Nursing reaffirmed its primary goal of preparing professional nurses at the baccalaureate level. The Associate of Science program was made an option that could be completed by the end of the junior year, at which time the student would also be ready for the state licensing examination, NCLEX-RN. Since 1990 the graduate program has offered clinical nurse specialist/practitioner programs in neonatal and pediatric critical care.

School of Nursing total number of graduates (through 1994): 5,417.

Loma Linda Sanitarium School of Nursing. Superintendents and Directors: Julia A. White, 1906-1913; Emma M. Semmens, 1913-1914; Julia A. White, 1915; Daisy L. Harding, 1915-1916; Irene V. Frisbie, 1916; Elizabeth Chapman, 1916-1920; Nora Whitney, 1921; Elizabeth Chapman, 1922-1923; Winifred F. Lindsay, 1923-1926; Elva L. Wallack, 1926-1927; Elsie B. King, 1927; Daisy E. Walton, 1928-1934; Ethel J. Walder, 1934 -1944 (dean, 1936-1939); Catherine N. Graf, 1944-1949.

White Memorial Hospital School of Nursing. Superintendents and Directors: Winifred F. Lindsay, 1923-1926; Martha E. Borg, 1926-1942; Ellen Vogel (acting director), 1942-1943; Mary C. Monteith, 1943-1947; Maxine Atteberry, 1947-1949.

Deans (since 1949): Kathryn J. Nelson, 1949-1956; Maxine Atteberry, 1956-1969; Marilyn J. Christian Smith, 1969-1981; Helen Emori King, 1981- .

IV. School of Medicine. 1. *Charter, 1909.* The School of Medicine may be said to date from Dec. 9, 1909, the date of the corporate act authorizing the College of Medical Evangelists to give academic and professional degrees. Ten students had begun the medical curriculum shortly before, not knowing precisely whether the college had a legitimate lease on life. By the time school opened on Sept. 29, 1910, a five-year curriculum had been developed, consisting of 6,109 clock hours of "didactic, laboratory, and clinical" subjects, and 1,037 hours in "biblical subjects." Students of the previous year were given credit for the work they had finished. Among these 10 were the six students who received the first Doctor of Medicine degrees in June 1914.

Students entering in 1909 were required to have only a high school diploma. But in 1910 a baccalaureate degree or, in lieu of it, a high school diploma plus a collegiate transcript certifying a limited number of required preprofessional subjects was required. An applicant also was eligible scholastically if he or she presented a certificate from the California State Board of Medical Examiners indicating that on examination the candidate had demonstrated a satisfactory knowledge of specific premedical subjects. The annual tuition was $100; a matriculation fee of $5 was paid on entering the first year only. Board and room were available at $3 a week.

2. *Early Clinical Instruction.* The original faculty roster listed 14 basic science teachers, with George K. Abbott, M.D., as dean. One of the 14, Alfred Q. Shryock, continued on the faculty until his death in 1950. Edward H. Risley joined the faculty in 1911 and continued until his death in 1943.

Facing the necessity of providing a clinical faculty in 1912, the school began recruitment immediately. Without the dedicated, continuing support of a nucleus of SDA physicians and a relatively larger number of other physicians who were leaders in their respective specialties, many of whom served the school from its beginning in Los Angeles until their retirement or death, the institution could not have attained its stability and growth. Numbered among this group of clinicians were George Thomason, Clinton A. Burrows, Wilburn H. Smith, Daniel D. Comstock, R. Manning Clarke, and August H. Larson.

Affiliation with the Los Angeles County General Hospital, with increasing use of its teaching facilities, began in 1913. By 1914 the officers of the college were keenly aware that the institution must have control of more clinical facilities than the Loma Linda Sanitarium could offer, if the medical school was to have more than a class "C" rating. This need led to the establishment of the White Memorial Hospital and Clinic in Los Angeles as a home for the clinical division, used by those in the third and fourth years of the curriculum.

3. *White Memorial Hospital and Clinic.* In October 1913 a one-room store building at 941 East First Street in Los Angeles was rented and readied for the conducting of a clinic. Dr. August H. Larson was the first full-time director of this First Street clinic.

The 1915 Autumn Council, meeting at Loma Linda, authorized the constituency to raise $61,000 to build and equip a teaching hospital. In 1916 half a city block was purchased in the 300 block on the east side of North Boyle Avenue in Los Angeles. In order that the entire block might be available when needed for the hospital, the remaining half of the block was purchased with private funds and later transferred to institutional ownership when the college was financially able to make the purchase. In 1917 the First Street clinic was housed in quarters on the newly acquired site and was known for some years as the Boyle Avenue Dispensary.

On Jan. 7, 1918, White Memorial Hospital received its first patient. The official dedication of the completed hospital was held on the afternoon of Apr. 21, 1918. The plant was enlarged in 1937 with the completion of a five-story, steel-and-concrete, fire- and earthquake-proof building, increasing the bed capacity to approximately 200. A seven-story wing incorporating surgeries, central services, and approximately 200 beds was completed in 1955 and dedicated on March 14. The demolition of certain old structures that housed patients left a total capacity of 256 patient beds and 40 bassinets.

The White Memorial Clinic served for many years as the largest private part-pay and charity clinic in the Los Angeles metropolitan area. It was a valuable facility for the education of nurses, technologists, therapists, medical students, interns, and resident physicians that was fully used until the phasing out of university teaching in Los Angeles began in 1964.

The White Memorial Hospital and Clinic continued under the ownership and control of the university until Jan. 1, 1964, at which time it became the property of the Southern California Conference and was renamed the White Memorial Medical Center. At the present time the university uses the White Memorial facilities, but the relationship is that of an affiliation. (*See also* White Memorial Medical Center.)

4. *The Climb to "A" Rating.* The first inspection of the medical school by a representative of the Council on Medical Education of the American Medical Association resulted in a "C" classification in February 1915. President Evans' forthright report to the Autumn Council in 1915 on the institution's deficiencies in medical education stimulated the decision to give earnest support to upgrading the college. The rise to a "B" rating was stimulated by sheer necessity in 1917, when the school was faced with the loss of all its male students to the draft. Selective service regulations permitted medical students in only class A and class B schools to continue their studies.

The coveted "A" rating was received on Nov. 14, 1922, and retained until the Council on Medical Education and Hospitals in 1929 began classifying all medical schools as *approved* or *unapproved.* The School of Medicine has continued on the list of approved medical schools without interruption.

5. *Innovative Programs.* A 12-month internship as prerequisite to obtaining the M.D. degree became a requirement for the class that entered in 1922.

An experimental program in medical education, known as the cooperative plan, was inaugurated in 1924. According to this program, students in the first two years were divided into two equal groups and spent alternate months in employment in some occupation related directly or indirectly to medicine. It was believed that the plan had educational virtue as well as economic value for the student. On recommendation of the Council of Medical Education and Hospitals of the American Medical Association and the Association of American Medical Colleges in 1935, the cooperative plan was eliminated and a conventional curriculum schedule was established.

When the United States entered World War II, all medical schools went on an accelerated program, making it possible to graduate four classes in three years. As a protection against interruption of medical training by the draft, most of the students enlisted in the Army or Navy and were assigned to respective medical military units that were established on the campus. It is significant that the contractual agreements with the military organizations took cognizance of SDA beliefs and practices. Even before the war, the School of Medicine had become the official sponsor of the 47th General Hospital of the United States Army Medical Reserves, which it staffed in large part from the faculties in medicine and nursing. Called to active duty in 1942, the unit served in New Guinea and the Philippines until the close of the war.

6. *Consolidation on One Campus.* Beginning as early as 1935, the difficulties associated with a divided campus became increasingly apparent and were repeatedly noted with emphasis by visiting committees representing the Council on Medical Education and Hospitals of the American Medical Association and the Association of American Medical Colleges. Between 1952 and 1963, the pros and cons of consolidation, and of consolidation on this campus or that campus, were thoroughly considered. The recommendation of the trustees and the decision of the church was to locate the School of Medicine in Loma Linda.

Because of its vital interest in the work of the White Memorial Hospital as an accessory of the church in the Los Angeles area, the Southern California Conference assumed ownership and control of the hospital on Jan. 1, 1964. The transfer of ownership included provision for the continuing for a time of several university schools in Los Angeles and for an educational affiliation between the university and the hospital for as long as this should be mutually beneficial.

In order to provide adequate clinical facilities for the School of Medicine students at Loma Linda, construction of the University Medical Center at Loma Linda commenced in 1964 and the initial phase of 320 beds was completed in 1967. Additional beds were opened over the next few years, bringing the total to 546 by the mid-1970s. In subsequent years additional wings were added, including the Schumann Pavilion, which houses the International Heart Institute and the medical center library for use by students and faculty. The Behavioral Medicine Center opened in nearby Redlands in 1990, providing an excellent facility for rotations in psychiatry. In 1990 the Proton Treatment Center opened, providing the opportunity for medical students to experience the application of this revolutionary technology to the therapy of cancer. Instruction in pediatrics is greatly enhanced by the Children's Hospital, which was completed in 1993. New facilities for cancer research and for a major conference center were begun in the mid-1990s. The School of Medicine's administrative offices will also be housed in this new building.

7. *Curriculum.* The curriculum in medicine consists of four academic years. Instruction is on the quarter system. The first six quarters are oriented to the sciences basic to the practice of medicine, including recent advances in such areas as cell and molecular biology and immunology. This portion of the curriculum is currently increasing emphasis on new methodologies for instruction, such as problem-based learning in small groups and computer-based graphics and databases. The remaining two academic years are made up of clinically oriented core instruction and five months of clinical electives. Clinical instruction takes place in the University Medical Center, the Jerry L. Pettis Veterans Memorial Hospital, and many affiliated hospitals, including Riverside and San Bernardino County hospitals, the White Memorial Medical Center, and Glendale Adventist Hospital.

Personal and professional growth for the student in whole person care in medicine is the focus of all disciplines in the school and of faculty in both the School of Medicine and the Faculty of Religion. Courses and contents are offered to emphasize biblical, ethical, and relational aspects of the practice of medicine. The core for "whole person formation" consists of 12 quarter hours of religion and ethics, and is completed during the first two years of the curriculum; clinical application of these principles is modeled by faculty during the junior and senior years of the curriculum.

In addition to the professional curriculum for the M.D. degree, the school collaborates with the medical center in providing opportunities for residencies and fellowships in all major medical and surgical specialties. A conjoint M.D./Ph.D. program is also available through the medical scientist training program, offered in collaboration with the Graduate School graduate programs in the basic medical sciences.

School of Medicine total number of graduates (through 1994): 7,703.

Deans: George K. Abbott, 1910-1914; Alfred Q. Shryock, 1914-1915; Percy T. Magan (Los Angeles division), 1916-1928; Edward H. Risley (Loma Linda division), 1924-1935; Newton G. Evans (Los Angeles division), 1928-1931; Llewellyn C. Kellogg (Los Angeles division), 1931-1932; Arthur E. Coyne (Los Angeles division), 1932-1935; Walter E. Macpherson (Loma Linda division), 1935-1936; Walter E. Macpherson (Los Angeles division), 1936-1942; Edward H. Risley, 1935-1942; Newton G. Evans, 1943-1944; E. Harold Shryock (Loma Linda division), 1945-1951; William F. Norwood (Los Angeles division), 1945-1951; E. Harold Shryock, 1951-1954; Walter E. Macpherson, 1954-1962; David B. Hinshaw, 1962-1975; Harrison S. Evans, 1975-1977; G. Gordon Hadley, 1977-1986; B. Lyn Behrens, 1986-1991; A. Douglas Will, 1991-1994; Brian S. Bull, 1994- .

V. Faculty of Religion. Because religious instruction has occupied a central place in all curriculums, the faculty and the course offerings in religion have been correspondingly enlarged as the university has expanded. In 1953 the program in religion was organized as a major division of the university, and in 1967 when the schools on the La Sierra campus united with the university, the Division of Religion continued to offer religious instruction, and in 1987 became the School of Religion.

In the configuration of Loma Linda University as a health sciences university in 1990, the role of religion as integrative in each of the programs of the university is mandated and continuously affirmed by university administration and the Loma Linda University board of trustees.

To assist in this integration, the Faculty of Religion (formerly the School of Religion) was established in July 1990.

The Faculty of Religion is committed to following four tasks, as defined by the teachings and practice of the Seventh-day Adventist tradition and mission:

1. To focus Christian wholeness for faculty and students in their personal and professional lives and witness.

2. To provide a religion curriculum with the following emphases:

a. Foundational studies (biblical, theological, and historical).

b. Ethical studies (personal, professional, and social).

c. Relational studies (personal, professional, and missions).

3. To foster and support research in the foundational, ethical, and relational disciplines.

4. To serve the university, the church, and the larger world community by personal involvement in fostering deeper spirituality, theological integrity, and social justice.

Directors/Deans: A. L. Bietz, 1944-1961; A. Graham Maxwell, 1961-1976; Walter Specht, 1976-1978; Kenneth Vine, 1978-1989; Niels-Erik Andreasen, 1989-1990; Wilber Alexander, 1990-1993; Gerald Winslow, 1993- .

VI. School of Dentistry. The 1909 charter of the College of Medical Evangelists had listed the degree of Doctor of Dental Surgery among the professional and academic degrees authorized, although the first such degree was not given until 1957. Through the years, administrators of the College of Medical Evangelists, denominational leaders, and special committees had at different times considered the feasibility of establishing a dental school.

Meanwhile, through the efforts of J. Russell Mitchell, D.D.S., and Gerald Alexander Mitchell, D.D.S., members of the faculty of Atlanta Southern Dental College, an arrangement was made in 1934 for that institution to enroll and give Sabbath privileges to a limited number of SDA students. This arrangement was terminated in 1947 when the dental college was merged with Emory University. (For these preliminary years, *see* Dental Education.)

In 1941 J. Russell Mitchell and M. Webster Prince, D.D.S., a well-known Detroit dentist and SDA layperson who had served eight years as a member of the Council on Dental Education of the American Dental Association, were appointed to a General Conference committee to pursue the subject further. Two years later (1943) the National Association of Seventh-day Adventist Dentists (NASDAD) was organized to promote the founding of a dental school; it has since become a large professional society and continues to be a strong supporter of the School of Dentistry.

In April 1951 a new committee was appointed, with R. R. Figuhr as chair and

M. Webster Prince, J. Russell Mitchell, T. R. Flaiz, Walter E. Macpherson, W. P. Elliott, C. L. Torrey, Keld J. Reynolds, E. D. Dick, and W. H. Branson as members. This committee's report to the Autumn Council in Cleveland, Ohio, Oct. 21, 1951, was accepted, and the Autumn Council recommended that definite plans be laid for the launching of a Seventh-day Adventist School of Dentistry as an integral part of the College of Medical Evangelists. Prince was appointed to serve as dean.

The school accepted its first class in the fall of 1953 in temporary quarters in Loma Linda and moved in 1955 into its own new building, a structure with 48,500 square feet (4,500 square meters) of floor space. The building was expanded in 1976 to double the amount of floor space so that the current facility has approximately 100,000 square feet (9,300 square meters) of net useable space. Basic science courses are provided by faculty who are shared with the School of Medicine and other health science schools on the Loma Linda campus.

The School of Dentistry is accredited by the Commission on Dental Accreditation and is a member of the American Association of Dental Schools.

In 1959 the School of Dentistry established a dental hygiene curriculum leading to a Bachelor of Science degree. From 1968 through 1986 a dental assisting curriculum was offered, leading to an Associate in Science degree; this program was terminated for reasons of fiscal exigency. Advanced (postdoctoral) education programs are offered in dental anesthesiology, endodontics, oral implantology, oral surgery, orthodontics, pediatric dentistry, periodontics, and prosthodontics. These postdoctoral programs are conducted through the administrative aegis of the Graduate School, under the operational control of the School of Dentistry.

School of Dentistry total number of graduates (through 1994): 4,193.

Deans: M. Webster Prince, 1951-1960; Charles T. Smith, 1960-1971; Judson Klooster, 1971-1994; Charles Goodacre, 1994- .

VII. School of Allied Health Professions. The School of Allied Health Professions was established in 1966 (under the name School of Health-Related Professions, 1966-1971) to consolidate the administration of the following individual curriculums that the university had already begun earlier: medical technology, 1937; physical therapy, 1941; medical radiography, 1941; occupational therapy, 1951; health information administration (formerly medical record administration curriculum), 1963.

Curriculums added since the school was established are nuclear medicine technology, 1970; radiation therapy technology, 1970; cardiopulmonary sciences (formerly respiratory therapy), 1971; nutrition and dietetics, 1972; medical sonography, 1976; special imaging technology, 1976; cytotechnology, 1982; coding specialist, 1987; occupational therapy assistant, 1988; physical therapist assistant, 1989. The curriculum in speech-language pathology and audiology, initiated in 1965 under the auspices of the College of Arts and Sciences of La Sierra University (formerly Loma Linda University), was transferred to the School of Allied Health Professions in 1987.

The goals of the School of Allied Health Professions are as follows:

1. To provide opportunity, instruction, and guided experience by which the student may acquire the basic knowledge and attain the skills essential to the practice of a chosen profession.
2. To help the student accept responsibility for integrity, ethical relationships, and empathic attitudes that can contribute to the welfare and well-being of patients.
3. To help the student develop a background of information and attitudes conducive to interprofessional understanding and cooperation.
4. To encourage the student to cultivate habits of self-education that will foster lifelong growth.
5. To engender and nurture in the student the desire to serve mankind, and in particular to serve as needed in the medical centers sponsored by the Seventh-day Adventist Church both in this country and elsewhere.

Total number of graduates (through 1994): 6,650.

Deans: Ivor C. Woodward, 1966-1986; Joyce W. Hopp, 1986- .

VIII. Graduate School. Instruction in the various health sciences and professions progressively assumed the role of academic disciplines during the second quarter of the twentieth century. A natural result was a demand for graduate instruction in the areas basic to the maintenance of these professions, as well as in related areas capable of enriching the preparation of professional men and women.

The postdoctoral hospital internship in preparation for general practice was established at an early date in the hospitals of the university. Also, the professional schools offer from time to time postgraduate and refresher courses for specialists as well as for general practitioners. In addition, the School of Medicine, especially at the White Memorial Hospital prior to 1964, organized graduate residencies in the principal clinical fields meeting the requirements for certification by the respective American specialty boards.

In 1946, to meet the postwar educational needs of returning medical veterans, the institution organized a Graduate School of Medicine under the deanship of Harold M. Walton, M.D., which established a nine-month basic science course as a foundation for residencies in surgery, medicine, obstetrics and gynecology, and orthopedics. A student who completed such a course, with an approved thesis, qualified for the Master of Medical Science degree. When this program gradually gave way to residencies enriched by basic science and research, the Graduate School of Medicine and its courses were terminated.

In 1953 a conventional graduate program was inaugurated in the basic science departments of the School of Medicine. In 1954 graduate instruction was offered in the School of Nursing leading to the Master of Science degree, under the direction of R. Maureen Maxwell, Ed.D. At the same time a School of Graduate Studies was authorized; in 1961 it was officially designated as the Graduate School. The following year instruction leading to the Doctor of Philosophy degree was authorized in certain basic medical sciences. Graduate instruction in nutrition was first offered in 1956-1957, and in dentistry in 1960-1961.

The Graduate School has extended its offerings into the following liberal arts areas: anthropology; biology; communicative disorders; English; history; marriage, family, and child counseling; mathematical sciences; Middle Eastern studies; religion; and sociology. Programs also leading to a master's degree are offered in medical technology and psychiatry. The Doctor of Philosophy is given in anatomy, biochemistry, biology, mathematical sciences, microbiology, pharmacology, and physiology.

The nursing program now offers a graduate curriculum with a nursing administration major and various clinical nurse specialist/practitioner options. The dental graduate programs cover endodontics, oral implantology, oral and maxillofacial surgery, orthodontics, and periodontics.

The Graduate School has extended its offerings into the following areas: biology, marriage and family therapy/family life education, and speech-language pathology. Programs also leading to a master's degree are offered in biomedical and clinical ethics, clinical ministry, and social work. The Doctor of Philosophy is given in anatomy, biochemistry, biology, microbiology, pharmacology, and physiology.

Graduate School total number of graduates (through 1994): 2,630.

Deans: Keld J. Reynolds (acting), 1957-1961; Thomas A. Little, 1961-1964; J. Paul Stauffer, 1964-1975; Norman J. Woods (acting), 1975-1977; Victor Griffiths, 1977-1978; Maurice Hodgen, 1978-1987; William Allen (acting), 1987-1988; W. Baron Rippon, 1988- .

IX. School of Public Health. The School of Public Health had its beginning with the organization in 1948 of the School of Tropical and Preventive Medicine, the purpose of which was to provide a base for research and teaching. After its reorganization in 1961, the Division of Public Health and Tropical Medicine began to offer master's programs through the Graduate School. Harold N. Mozar, M.D., was the director from 1948 to 1964; Mervyn G. Hardinge, M.D., Ph.D., Dr.P.H., became the director of the Division of Public Health in 1964.

The establishment of a School of Public Health was authorized in 1964, and plans were made for faculty and facilities to meet the requirements of the Committee on Professional Education of the American Public Health Association. Dr. Hardinge became the dean in July 1967. In October 1970 the name of the school was changed to School of Health. Authorization was given to offer work leading to the degrees of Master of Public Health and Master of Science in Public Health.

In 1972 the school was authorized to offer the Doctor of Health Sciences degree. Subsequently the Doctor of Public Health degree was authorized, with the first Dr.P.H. in epidemiology being granted in 1980. Students were first admitted to the Dr.P.H. program in health education in 1981 and to the Dr.P.H. program in nutrition in 1987. The Doctor of Health Sciences degree program was restructured to a Dr.P.H. in preventive care in 1991.

In the fall of 1979 the school was approved to begin a preventive medicine residency. An M.P.H. degree in a selected area is an integral part of the residency program.

The original name, School of Public Health, was readopted in 1987. In 1991 the School was reorganized to include the Center for Health Promotion and the Preventive Medicine Faculty Practice. The school provides the services of the Department of Preventive Medicine for the School of Medicine.

The instructional, research, and service programs within the school are organized and administered by six academic departments and three centers. The academic departments are Environmental and Occupational Health, Epidemiology and Biostatistics, Health Administration, Health Promotion and Education, International Health, and Nutrition. The three centers are the Center for Health Promotion (CHP), the Center for Health Research (CHR), and the Center for Health and Development (CHD).

A large spectrum of programs are offered by CHP, including weight management, executive health, stress management, smoking cessation, nutrition, exercise, and alcohol and drug dependency. Group sessions, individual counseling, and health assessment are conducted in the community or in corporate settings. CHP serves more than 10,000 clients per year and is a major training center for students.

The Center for Health Research opened in 1990 and reflects the school's growing involvement in public health research. The school is active in research projects involving preventive medicine, epidemiology, health education, nutrition, and other aspects of public health. Most notably, it has directed the Adventist Health Study, internationally recognized as a pathbreaking project in health research. CHR administers a research endowment fund and provides technical support for faculty projects in the school. It provides consultation to researchers throughout the university and surrounding community.

The newest center in the school, CHD, coordinates and directs all of the service and community development programs in the school that have a cross-cultural emphasis. It has four components. It directs the university Students for International Missions Service (SIMS), providing short-term mission opportunities around the world as well as in local communities. It also directs the Social Action Corps (SAC), which operates medical and dental clinics in the surrounding area for persons who cannot afford adequate health care. This provides a valuable community service through which students gain experience and understanding. The center also assists faculty in arranging international consulting projects with a variety of organizations and works with World Health Organization and its primary health-care projects.

Majors are offered in the following areas: biostatistics, environmental health, epidemiology, health administration, health promotion and education, international health, occupational health, nutrition, and preventive care.

Through its off-campus program, the school was a pioneer in bringing graduate education in public health to health professionals who could not leave their place of employment for full-time education. Courses have been offered in Canada, the Far East, Inter-America, as well as several sites in the United States. The first off-campus class graduated in 1978, and 814 persons (through December 1992) have received their public health degrees through this program. Of these, 252 were in international settings.

School of Public Health number of graduates (through 1994): 3,416.

Directors/Deans: Harold N. Mozor, M.D., 1948-1964; Mervyn G. Hardinge, M.D., Ph.D., Dr.P.H., 1964-1976; James M. Crawford, D.D.S., M.P.H., 1977-1980; Andrew P. Haynal, M.D., M.P.H., 1980-1983; James M. Crawford, 1983-1986; Edwin H. Krick, M.D., M.P.H., 1986-1990; Richard H. Hart, M.D., Dr.P.H., 1990- .

X. University Administration. *Presidents of Loma Linda University* (and its predecessors): *Loma Linda College of Evangelists:* Warren E. Howell, 1906-1907; George K. Abbott, 1907-1909. *College of Medical Evangelists:* Wells A. Ruble, 1910-1914; Newton G. Evans, 1914-1927; Edward H. Risley, 1927-1928; Percy T. Magan, 1928-1942; Walter E. Macpherson, 1942-1948; George T. Harding III, 1948-1951; Walter E. Macpherson, 1951-1954; Godfrey T. Anderson, 1954-1961. *Loma Linda University:* Godfrey T. Anderson, 1961-1967; David J. Bieber, 1967-1974; V. Norskov Olsen, 1974-1984; Norman J. Woods, 1984-1990; B. Lyn Behrens, 1990- .

General Officers of the College of Medical Evangelists: Vice Presidents: Walter E. Macpherson, 1948-1952; William Frederick Norwood, 1952-1955. *Dean of the Faculties:* Keld J. Reynolds, 1955-1959. *Vice President for Academic Affairs:* Keld J. Reynolds, 1959-1962. *General Business Manager:* John C. Shull, 1955-1962.

Vice Presidents of Loma Linda University: Vice Presidents for Academic Affairs: Keld J. Reynolds, 1962-1964; Robert E. Cleveland, 1964-1973; Norman J. Woods, 1974-1984; Helen Ward Thompson, 1984-

1989; Ian M. Fraser, 1991- .

Vice Presidents for Student Affairs: William G. Nelson, 1968-1969; Tracy R. Teele, 1970-1983.

Vice Presidents for Medical Affairs: Walter E. Macpherson, 1962-1967; Harrison S. Evans, 1976-1979; Marlowe H. Schaffner, 1979-1982; Harrison S. Evans, 1982-1986; David B. Hinshaw, Sr., 1986- .

Vice Presidents for Financial Affairs: Robert L. Cone, 1962-1970; Robert J. Radcliffe, 1970-1974; George G. O'Brien, 1974-1979; W. J. Blacker, 1979-1984; James A. Greene, 1984-1989; Donald G. Pursley, 1990- .

Vice Presidents for Foundation Affairs: Robert J. Radcliffe, 1974-1979.

Vice Presidents for Public Relations and Development: Jerry L. Pettis, 1962-1964; Howard B. Weeks, 1964-1971.

Vice Presidents for Development: David J. Bieber, 1974-1976; Don G. Prior, 1976-1979; Edward C. Wines, 1979-1985; W. Augustus Cheatham, 1985-1987.

Vice President for Public Affairs: W. Augustus Cheatham, 1987- .

Vice Presidents for Advancement: Robert Leonard, 1987-1988; Don G. Prior, 1988- .

Vice President for Health Services: J. David Moorhead, 1994- .

Vice President for Clinical Faculty: Brian S. Bull, 1994- .

Total Graduates of Loma Linda University (from its inception through 1994): 30,009.

LOMA LINDA UNIVERSITY HOSPITAL. *See* Loma Linda University.

LOMA LINDA UNIVERSITY MEDICAL CENTER. *See* Loma Linda University.

LONDON HEALTH FOOD COMPANY. *See* Granose Foods, Limited.

LONDON PUBLISHING HOUSE. *See* Stanborough Press Limited.

LONG BEACH ACADEMY. *See* Los Angeles Adventist Academy (California).

LONGACRE, CHARLES SMULL (1871-1958). Minister, evangelist, school administrator, editor, author. He was born Dec. 1, 1871, at Valley Forge, Pennsylvania. His ancestors came from Zurich, Switzerland, and had been Mennonite preachers for six generations prior to his father's. After graduating from State Teachers College, Kutztown, Pennsylvania, he taught in the public schools.

Longacre first heard of Seventh-day Adventist doctrines through Oliver Thompson, a colporteur who in 1895 brought copies of *Signs of the Times* to the Longacre home. A short time later two SDA ministers, J. G. Matteson and Lee S. Wheeler, conducted Sunday night meetings east of Norristown, which Longacre's parents and sisters attended from the first. Longacre himself, who did not attend until some time later, heard R. A. Underwood, a guest minister, deliver two lectures on the prophecies of Daniel. He became so interested that he dropped the law course he was taking at night school, and two weeks later, when Matteson planned to close the evangelistic meetings, Longacre suggested that he be permitted to continue the meetings and teach the people what he had heard and read in SDA books. Matteson accepted this offer, and Longacre continued the meetings all winter. That spring he had eight converts ready for baptism. These eight, with Longacre and others, were baptized and became charter members of the Norristown, Pennsylvania, Seventh-day Adventist Church.

During the summer of 1896 Longacre sold religious books in and around Norristown, Valley Forge, and Phoenixville, to earn money to attend Battle Creek College, Battle Creek, Michigan. He enrolled that fall and completed the ministerial course in May 1898 (he was granted a Bachelor of Arts degree by Emmanuel Missionary College, Berrien Springs, Michigan, in 1914). In June of that year he was employed by the Pennsylvania Conference to assist Lee S. Wheeler in evangelistic work at Pittsburgh.

On June 7, 1899, at Battle Creek, Longacre and Florence Martha Hughes were married by Uriah Smith. Two children, Ethel Elizabeth and Clarence Hughes, were born, the latter dying in infancy. Longacre continued evangelistic work in Pennsylvania until Dec. 31, 1907, and established SDA churches in Pittsburgh, Greensburg, Uniontown, Connellsville, and Washington. For nine years he was also religious liberty secretary of the Pennsylvania Conference. His personal appearance at house and senate hearings helped to defeat Sunday law bills that came before the state legislature at Harrisburg.

On Jan. 1, 1908, Longacre moved to South Lancaster, Massachusetts, to teach Bible and history at South Lancaster Academy. The next year he became principal of the academy, a position he held until Jan. 1, 1913.

From South Lancaster, Longacre moved to Washington, D.C., where on Jan. 1, 1913, he became associate secretary of the Religious Liberty Association. Later in the year he became its secretary and held that position to 1936 (in the meantime the name of the association was changed to Religious Liberty Department). Afterward he again was an associate secretary of the department until 1950. He edited *Liberty,* the association's journal, from 1914 to 1942 and was on the editorial staff at the time of his death. From 1932 to 1941 he also was secretary of the American Temperance Society. From 1943 until his retirement on Dec. 31, 1950, he was associate secretary of the Religious Liberty Association.

In 1916 George Washington University in Washington, D.C., granted him a Master of Arts degree in philosophy, with a minor in international law. He completed a three-year law course by correspondence with the La Salle Extension University in Chicago.

In 1919 he served as secretary of the General Conference Home Missionary Department.

In 1931 he was sent to Geneva, Switzerland, by the International Religious Liberty Association to oppose the World Calendar, backed by George Eastman.

He wrote many articles for SDA and other periodicals. He was author of the following books: *Freedom: Civil and Religious, The Church in Politics, Religious Liberty and Civil Government, Roger Williams—His Life, Work, and Ideals.* He also edited *American State Papers,* a compilation of documents on the separation of church and state.

In 1955, 1956, and 1957 Longacre received medals from Freedoms Foundation, Valley Forge, Pennsylvania, "for outstanding achievement in bringing about a better understanding of the American Way of life." In 1956 he received a citation from Protestants and Other Americans United for Separation of Church and State "in appreciation of his decades of distinguished service on behalf of religious freedom."

For a biography of Longacre, see Nathaniel Krum's *Charles S. Longacre, Champion of Religious Liberty.*

LONGBURN ADVENTIST COLLEGE. A coeducational boarding school, years 6-12, situated at Walker's Road, Longburn, four miles (six kilometers) from Palmerston North, on the North Island of New Zealand. It is owned by the Trans-Tasman Union Conference and is operated by a board of management with representation from the two New Zealand local conferences and the union conference. The enrollment, averaging 140, includes students from New Zealand, Australia, the Pacific Islands, and some Asian countries. In 1993 the school had a staff of 19, including 13 teachers and administrators.

History. Advanced schoolwork in New Zealand began in February 1908 when the Pukekura Training School opened its doors in a beautiful rural setting of 170 acres (70 hectares), four miles (six kilometers) southwest of Cambridge, in the northern portion of the North Island. The first board of control, with S. M. Cobb, president of the New Zealand Conference, as chairman, was elected at the annual conference at Cambridge, Jan. 9-19, 1908. The first principal was F. L. Chaney.

As the spread of Seventh-day Adventist work to south New Zealand made a more central site for the school advisable, the school was moved in April 1913 to a 30-acre (12-hectare) site near Longburn, in a quiet rural district. For a time the institution was called the Oroua Missionary School, later New Zealand Missionary College. The school property, comprising some of the richest farming land in the Dominion, provides an opportunity for training in dairying, vegetable growing, orcharding, and poultry farming. Through the generosity of G. F. Wright, the owner of adjoining property and for many years a member of the board, the original acreage was increased to 60 (25 hectares) by 1933, and further purchases in 1952 and 1961 brought the total to 132 acres (55 hectares). In addition, the school owns a block of 144 acres (58 hectares) of grazing land at Oroua Downs, about 12 miles (20 kilometers) away. In 1952 the Sanitarium Health Food Company built a food factory close to the campus, providing employment for a number of students.

In 1974 the college buildings consisted of two separate residences for the young men and young women, a classroom and administration building with a well-equipped library and science laboratory, a spacious modern church with seating for 400, a woodwork and engineering shop, and a laundry. The kitchen, dining room, and chapel remain in the original building. Recreational facilities include a swimming pool; tennis, basketball, and volleyball courts; and a playing field. During 1974 an additional science laboratory was erected, and future plans provide for the erection of a larger social hall and indoor sports center. Thirteen residences are provided for faculty and staff families, and in 1974 a block of four apartments for single staff members was opened.

More recently the following additions have been constructed: gymnasium (1978), industrial arts complex (1978), second story added to main building used as classrooms, home economics lab, seminar rooms, and staff offices (1980), and cafeteria and lounge (1981).

Scholastic Standards. Longburn College is registered as a secondary school with the New Zealand Ministry of Education and completes the work of the secondary grades, preparing students for the New Zealand School Certificate and the university entrance examinations. Students are also prepared for the Form Six Certificate, University Bursary and Scholarship, and the Higher School Certificate. A one-year postsecondary course in English as a foreign language is provided for students from the Pacific Islands and Asia.

In 1970 a new course was established to train primary school teachers. The nontheological subjects are those prescribed by the New Zealand Education Department for the internal Trained Teachers' Certificate examination. This course was discontinued in 1992.

Principals: F. L. Chaney, 1908-1910; W. J. Smith, 1911; J. Mills, 1912-1919; E. Rosendahl, 1920-1921; H. Kirk, 1922-1923; E. E. Cossentine, 1924-1927; E. Rosendahl, 1928-1933; G. H. Greenaway, 1934-1938; C. S. Palmer, 1939-1944; L. V. Wilkinson, 1945-1950; E. G. McDowell, 1951-1954; A.F.J. Kranz, 1955-1964; R. C. Syme, 1965; Walter Scragg, 1965-1966; R. A. Vince, 1967-1968; E. G. Krause, 1969-1972; L. M. Davis, 1973-1979; D. J. Cooke, 1980-1985; J. G. Hammond, 1986-1989; P. N. Devine, 1990-1992; P. V. Hann, 1993- .

LOPEZ MIRANDA, RAFAEL (d. 1922). First Puerto Rican Adventist colporteur and missionary. He was running a laundry business at Santurce, Puerto Rico, when a colporteur sold him the book *The Coming King* in Spanish. Earlier he had read the Spanish paper *El Centinela.* He readily accepted the doctrines contained in these publications and soon entered the colporteur work himself, working not only in his homeland but in Santo Domingo (Dominican Republic) and in Venezuela. On one of his pioneering trips in Venezuela he was assassinated by unknown assailants.

LORD HOWE ISLAND. A dependency of New South Wales, Australia, situated 436 miles (700 kilometers) northeast of Sydney. The island has an area of five square miles (13 square kilometers) and a population of 260.

Seventh-day Adventist Work. There is one church on the island, with a membership of 22, belonging to the Greater Sydney Conference in Australia.

Seventh-day Adventists first visited the island in 1895-1896, when J. M. Cole stopped there on his way from Norfolk Island to Sydney on the schooner *Oscar Robinson.* Then "in 1912 the light from Norfolk kindled a spark at Lord Howe Island" (E. H. Gates, *In Coral Isles,* p. 167), and a church of nine charter members was organized on May 11, 1913. In April 1920 the first Seventh-day Adventist church building on the island, erected by A. H. Ferris, was dedicated. In 1959 a new home for the minister was erected, and in 1960 a new church building was completed.

LORD'S SUPPER. The symbolic meal Jesus instituted on the night of His betrayal to commemorate His death and to foreshadow His coming kingdom; from the Gr. *kuriakon deipnon* (1 Cor. 11:20).

Seventh-day Adventist Practice. The "Outline of Doctrinal Beliefs" appearing in the *Church Manual* [1990] states: "The ordinance of the Lord's Supper commemorates the Saviour's death; and participation by members of the body is essential to Christian growth and fellowship. It is to be preceded by the ordinance of foot washing as a preparation for this solemn service" (p. 182; *see* Foot Washing).

In general, Seventh-day Adventists observe the Lord's Supper once each quarter. A typical service would be as follows: A short sermon precedes the ordinance of foot washing, for which the men and women meet separately. The church then reassembles, and the minister and elder(s) officiate at the Communion table. The bread is uncovered, 1 Cor. 11:23, 24 is read, and the prayer of blessing offered; the bread is then broken by the elders and distributed to the congregation by deacons. A similar procedure is followed for the wine, after the reading of 1 Cor. 11:25, 26. In each instance the congregation waits until all have been served, and partakes of the emblem simultaneously. The service is completed by the singing of a hymn and prayer.

Only unleavened bread and unfermented wine are used, leaven being considered a symbol of sin (1 Cor. 5:7, 8), and fermented wine an unworthy representation of the blood of

Christ. Seventh-day Adventists practice open Communion: "Christ's example forbids exclusiveness at the Lord's Supper. It is true that open sin excludes the guilty. . . . But beyond this none are to pass judgment. God has not left it with men to say who shall present themselves on these occasions. . . . There may come into the company persons who are not in heart servants of truth and holiness, but who may wish to take part in the service. They should not be forbidden" (DA 656; cf. *Church Manual,* p. 81).

Communion services are conducted only by ordained ministers and ordained church elders who are elected to office by the church in which they serve *(ibid.,* p. 83). Pastors who are not ordained ministers do not conduct the Lord's Supper unless they have been elected and ordained as local elders by the congregation in which the service is being celebrated.

Historical Development in the Seventh-day Adventist Church. The Lord's Supper has been a part of SDA services of worship from the beginning. For example, it is recorded that those attending the early Sabbath conference held in Volney, New York, beginning Aug. 18, 1848, celebrated it (2SG 97f.). As organization developed, it became a regular part of what was termed the "quarterly meeting." With members often widely scattered, this meeting was a major institution in organized church life. According to recommendations, it was opened with the reading of the membership roll by the church clerk, each member giving testimony regarding his Christian experience as his name was called (a form of this practice is sometimes still followed in smaller congregations). Next the church record for the previous quarter was read and corrected. Then if an ordained minister or elder was present, the Lord's Supper was celebrated. After sunset, or the next day, a church business meeting was held. Absence from quarterly meeting without report for nine months was grounds for dismissal from the church. While other aspects of this meeting have largely disappeared, in many congregations the Lord's Supper is still commonly referred to as quarterly meeting.

Throughout SDA history there appears to have been little change in understanding of the meaning of the Lord's Supper. The bread and wine have been seen as symbols of the body and blood of Christ, as reminders of Christ's passion and death. The Lord's Supper is also a witness to the believer's acceptance of Christ as his Saviour and of his faith in the Second Advent (cf. 1 Cor. 11:26). In the Communion service Christ meets with His people and the Spirit is present to seal them as His (DA 149, 659).

The Lord's Supper in the NT. The institution of the Lord's Supper is recorded in Matt. 26:20-29, Mark 14:17-25, Luke 22:14-20, and 1 Cor. 11:23-25. In both the Gospels and Paul's Epistle the words of institution contain the same three themes—substitution, covenant, and eschatology. Each of these is found in the background of the NT: Jesus repeatedly compares His mission to the OT figure of the vicariously suffering Servant (cf. Isa. 53:12; Mark 14:24; Luke 22:37); the "blood of the covenant" and the "new covenant" are familiar OT themes (Ex. 24:8; cf. Mark 14:24; Jer. 31:31; cf. Luke 22:20; 1 Cor. 11:25), as is also that of the eschatological banquet (Isa. 25:6-8; cf. Rev. 19:9; 21:3, 4, 9-14).

This eschatological orientation of the Lord's Supper as an anticipation of the Messianic banquet in the coming kingdom of God finds a particularly relevant parallel in the communal meals at Qumrân (see especially IQSa II, 1ff.). After describing the entrance of the members of the community to their sacramental meal, "The Messianic Rule" states: "When the common table shall be set for eating and the new wine [poured] for drinking, let no man extend his hand over the first-fruits of bread and wine before the Priest; for [it is he] who shall bless the first-fruits of bread and wine, and shall be the first [to extend] his hand over the bread. Thereafter, the Messiah of Israel shall extend his hand over the bread, [and] all the Congregation of the Community [shall utter a] blessing, [each man in the order] of his dignity" (G. Vermès, *The Dead Sea Scrolls in English* [1962], p. 121).

This is reminiscent of Luke 22:21 ("The hand of him who betrays me is with me on the table" [RSV]), and the information is interesting from the Seventh-day Adventist viewpoint that the wine used at Qumrân was "new wine" (Heb. *tîrôsh).* The broader significance of this meal is especially important: as in the Lord's Supper, the Qumrân meal represents at once both the present community and the future banquet of the elect. Thus the eschatological aspect of the Lord's Supper seems to have had a clear background in contemporary Judaism (F. M. Cross, *The Ancient Library of Qumrân* [1958], p. 64). This does not mean that the rite was simply borrowed from Qumrân; rather, we see both in Qumrân and in the NT similar developments, in the late Jewish milieu, of basic OT themes.

LORENZ, JOHN P. (1872-1917). Pioneer Seventh-day Adventist worker in Austria and Czechoslovakia. He was born in Messer, a German settlement in Russia. At the age of 4 he was brought to the United States, where he grew up near Lehigh, Kansas, and later attended Union College. He entered colporteur and evangelistic service before he was 20 years old. About 1900 he went to central Europe, where he pioneered Seventh-day Adventist work in Czechoslovakia (1901) and in Austria (1902), being the first ordained minister there. After four years in Europe he returned to America and taught at Keene Academy for two years and for some time preached in Texas, Oklahoma, and Missouri. In 1911, having graduated from the St. Louis College of Physicians and Surgeons, he entered private practice in Oklahoma.

LORNEDALE ACADEMY. *See* Kingsway College.

LOS ANGELES ADVENTIST ACADEMY (California) (formerly Lynwood Adventist Academy and Los Angeles Union Elementary School). A coeducational day school on the senior high school level, formerly situated in Lynwood, California. It is owned by the Southern California Conference and is operated by a board with representation from the churches in the southern portion of Los Angeles County, which it serves.

Forerunners of Lynwood were Los Angeles Seventh-day Adventist Academy (founded 1923), at 3210 Post Street in Los Angeles; and Long Beach Academy (established 1925), at 1880 Dawson Avenue in Long Beach. The last chairs of the two boards were, respectively, C. E. Kellogg, M.D., and Scott Donaldson. In 1937 David Voth, president of the Southern California Conference; B. M. Emerson, conference treasurer; C. D. Striplin, principal of Los Angeles Academy; and W. S. Potts, principal of Long Beach Academy, actively promoted plans for the combined school. Construction began in November under leadership of F. W. Paap, building superintendent; C. J. Kjose, contractor; and Clinton Nourse, architect. The cafeteria and manual arts building, the administration building, and the large camp meeting pavilion and school gymnasium were completed before the school was opened on Sept. 6, 1938. Work soon began on Rupp Memorial Chapel—a gift from Mrs. Emma Rupp in memory of her late husband, John Rupp, a Los Angeles businessman—which provided, besides the school chapel, facilities for the Lynwood church and the Music Department. There followed an auto mechanics building (1939), physical education locker and shower rooms (1953 and 1954), and a two-classroom unit (1962). Buildings are of Spanish architecture, in cream-colored stucco with red roofs. Throughout the years the conference used these facilities, school buildings, and grounds for its annual camp meetings.

In June 1963 the Rupp Memorial Chapel was destroyed by fire of undetermined origin. The Lynwood Seventh-day Adventist Church and the academy shared the costs of rebuilding.

Earlier school papers, *The Breakers* (Long Beach) and *Los Angeles Academy Broadcaster,* were succeeded in December 1938 by the *Lynwood Log* (eight issues a year). The school annual, *The Shipmate,* was first published in 1948.

When the Lynnwood site was sold to the Lynnwood Unified School District through eminent domain, the academy was moved to the Los Angeles Union Elementary School location in 1993 and renamed Los Angeles Adventist Academy.

Principals: W. B. Dart, 1938-1957; N. L. Parker, 1957-1966; W. D. Minder, 1966-1969; Eldon E. Stratton, 1969-1974; Roland L. McKenzie, 1974-1978; Harold Rich, 1978-1980; Cecil Gemmell, 1980-1982; William R. Wright, 1982-1988; James P. Willis II, 1988-1993; Glen F. McKnight, 1993- .

LOS ANGELES ADVENTIST ACADEMY (Chile) (Centro Educacional Adventista de Los Angeles). A coeducational secondary school located in sector El Alamo, Camino Antuco, Los Angeles, Chile, and operated by the South Chile Conference. It began operating in 1978.

The following secondary-level programs were offered in 1993: scientific humanities—four courses per level; professional technician—seven courses, including computation, agricultural mechanics, and chemistry analysis.

That year the following number of students were enrolled: 116 in the humanities and 194 professional technicians, for a total of 310. There were 22 secondary teachers. The library has 3,302 volumes.

Principals: Augusto Wandersleben, 1978-1980; Edwin Araya, 1981; Juan Pérez, 1982-1984; Rolando Montoya, 1985-1987; Alex Ojeda, 1988-1991; Manuel Gutiérrez, 1992- .

LOS ANGELES ADVENTIST CLINIC (Clínica Adventista de Los Angeles). A 23-bed medical institution located in Los Angeles, Chile. In the early 1970s decisive plans took shape to initiate medical work in the southern part of Chile; thus in 1976 attention was given to the city of Los Angeles. In 1977 a preliminary construction plan was approved that would be carried out in Los Angeles itself; on Aug. 15, 1979, the first stage was inaugurated, with the name Los Angeles Adventist Sanitarium. The institution began its services and became a government authorized institution in 1981.

In 1976 the first donation of equipment was received from Germany. In 1979 X-ray equipment was acquired from the United States, and in 1980, 14 boxes with medical equipment was also received as a donation from the United States. X-ray services began in February 1980, and in March of the same year the clinical laboratory was started.

In 1993 the Los Angeles Adventist Clinic offered the following services: general medicine, internal medicine, general surgery, OB-GYN, pediatrics, ophthalmology, dermatology, ENT and digestive endoscopy exams, kinesiatrics, laboratory, dentistry, radiology, inpatient, surgeries, childbirth and hospitalization, nursing, outpatient procedures.

These activities were enhanced by chaplaincy ministry as well as guidance given by the administrators. Plans are to develop a healthful living center to demonstrate the advantages of the Adventist lifestyle to the community.

Directors: Sergio Maldonado, 1979-1989; José W. Rodriguez, 1989; Eugenio Garrido, 1989- .

Managers: Arturo Opazo, 1979-1988; Jorge Jiménez, 1988-1993; Rene Pérez, 1993- .

LOSEY, LEON BIRD (1887-1974). Educator and administrator. A native of North Dakota, he began denominational work in 1921 as a minister in the Upper Columbia Conference. He served as principal of Grainger Academy for three years, following which he became educational and MV secretary of the Upper Columbia Conference. He was principal of Auburn Academy in Washington for a two-year term. From 1930 to 1939 he served in the Southern Asia Division as a principal. Returning to the United States, he was dean of men at Walla Walla College for 12 years.

LOS POLVORINES ADVENTIST ACADEMY (Instituto Adventista Los Polvorines). An academy located in Los Polvorines, a city in Buenos Aires province, Argentina. It belongs to the Buenos Aires Conference.

It began as an elementary school in 1983, but later added a secondary school program. The three first years are unified; the fourth and fifth years are diversified, and offer a commercial course with a specialty in taxation. Thirty teachers were employed in 1993. The first graduation took place in 1987.

The campus is located on 32,300 square feet (3,000 square meters), and the buildings are located on 12,900 square feet (1,200 square meters). The library has 3,470 books. There is also a workshop with six tables and 36 chairs, and a brand-new lab.

Principals: Delia Schimpf Fonseca, 1983-1984; Gustavo Laco, 1985-1987; Victor Bruchon, 1988-1989; Donaldo Leichner, 1990- .

LOUD CRY. The proclamation of the message of Rev. 18:1-4, represented as proclaimed by an angel who came "down from heaven, having great power," and with whose glory "the earth was lightened." The phrase reflects the statement that this angel "cried mightily with a strong voice." The message proclaimed by the angel is God's final call to those of His people still in mystical Babylon to "come out of her" in order to avoid being "partakers of her sins, and . . . of her plagues." This message is evidently given prior to the close of probation, inasmuch as there is still an opportunity for people to find salvation by fleeing from Babylon. It is also Heaven's final appeal to humanity, the last such message recorded in Scripture, for it immediately precedes the fearful scenes of divine retribution that mark the transition from the kingdoms of this world to the kingdom of Jesus Christ.

Seventh-day Adventists understand that the angel of Rev. 18 unites his voice with that of the third angel of Rev. 14:9-11, in view of the fact that the message proclaimed by the latter, in its context, is also God's last message to man and immediately precedes the coming of Christ and the final judgments of God upon this earth. This angel also spoke "with a loud voice." Accordingly, Seventh-day Adventists sometimes blend the two into one message, to which they refer as "the loud cry of the third angel." The first angel of Rev. 14 announces the hour of divine judgment; the second angel, the spiritual fall of mystical Babylon. The third angel warns against Babylon's counterfeit gospel.

"The work of this angel comes in at the

right time to join in the last great work of the third angel's message as it swells to a loud cry" (EW 277).

"These announcements [Rev. 18:1-4], uniting with the third angel's message [Rev. 14:9-11], constitute the final warning to be given to the inhabitants of earth" (GC 604).

"It is a message from Heaven uttering a final warning against a corrupt and backslidden Christianity, and going forth with such power that the whole earth is lightened with its glory" (James White, in *Review and Herald* 55:40, Jan. 15, 1880). "The third message is to ripen the harvest of the earth" *(ibid.* 18:20, June 11, 1861).

As for the literal application of this symbolic prophecy, Uriah Smith wrote: "The angel is not a literal angel, and we are not to suppose that we are to hear a literal voice sounding through the land giving the warning of this proclamation. It is to be simply the truth making its way into all parts of the earth" *(ibid.* 51:36, Jan. 31, 1878).

Ellen White described this future development in more detail as follows: "Servants of God, with their faces lighted up and shining with holy consecration, will hasten from place to place to proclaim the message from heaven. By thousands of voices, all over the earth, the warning will be given. . . . Thus the inhabitants of earth will be brought to take their stand" (GC 612).

People everywhere will come out of the apostate churches that compose mystical Babylon and unite with God's remnant people (EW 33). All who "had not heard and rejected the three messages obeyed the call and left the fallen churches" *(ibid.* 278).

Of the crisis in which the loud cry culminates, Mrs. White wrote further: "Fearful is the issue to which the world is to be brought. The powers of earth, uniting to war against the commandments of God, will decree that all, 'both small and great, rich and poor, free and bond,' shall conform to the customs of the church by the observance of the false sabbath. All who refuse compliance will be visited with civil penalties, and it will finally be declared that they are deserving of death. On the other hand, the law of God enjoining the Creator's rest-day demands obedience, and threatens wrath against all who transgress its precepts. With the issue thus clearly brought before him, whoever shall trample upon God's law to obey a human enactment receives the mark of the beast; he accepts the sign of allegiance to the power which he chooses to obey instead of God" (GC 604).

Compare Rev. 13:13-17. "When this last loud blast of the gospel trumpet is given," wrote M. E. Cornell, "probation will end, and the eternal decree go forth [Rev. 22:11 cited]. The destiny of all will then be irrevocably fixed" *(Review and Herald* 6:72, Oct. 10, 1854). Probation closes, and the seven last plagues fall.

See also Latter Rain; Three Angels' Messages.

LOUGHBOROUGH, JOHN NORTON (1832-1924). Pioneer evangelist and administrator. He first heard the present truth preached by J. N. Andrews in September 1852 at Rochester, New York, and was immediately convinced of the seventh-day Sabbath. For three years prior to this he had preached, as a lay preacher, the doctrines of the first-day Adventists, but had become dissatisfied. He took a public position to keep the Sabbath in October of 1852 and immediately began to proclaim his new belief. He had preached and supported himself by working, but in December 1852 he devoted himself to full-time ministry. He was ordained in 1854, and for several years conducted evangelistic work in Pennsylvania, New York State, and the Middle West. He pioneered the selling of Adventist literature in quantity when in 1854 he began selling it at 35 cents a packet at one of his tent meetings in Michigan. After a brief period of discouragement in 1856 because of financial straits, he returned with great zeal to his work, although for some time he still labored under difficult circumstances.

As the result of a serious illness brought on by overwork (1865), he became deeply interested in health reform and wrote a book called *Hand Book of Health; or a Brief Treatise on Physiology and Hygiene* (1868).

In 1868 with D. T. Bourdeau, he pioneered Seventh-day Adventist work in California, and by 1871 had helped establish five churches in Sonoma County, one of them in Santa Rosa, where the first Seventh-day Adventist church building west of the Rockies was erected in 1869. He baptized the first three SDA members in Nevada in 1878.

The same year (1878) he was sent by the General Conference to open SDA work in England, although the field had been prepared previously by the work of William Ings, a colporteur. Loughborough's five years in England resulted in the baptism of 37 persons and the establishing of a church in Southampton.

After his return to America (1883), he traveled as a representative of the General Conference in the North Pacific region, visiting camp meetings and strengthening members who had become confused because of apostate movements.

He was president of the Michigan Conference (1865-1868), treasurer of the General Conference (1868-1869), and for six years (1890-1896) was superintendent of several General Conference districts. He was also first president of the California Conference (1873-1878; again, 1887-1890), and of the Nevada Association (1878), the Upper Columbia Conference (1884-1885), and the Illinois Conference (1891-1895).

In 1892 he published *The Rise and Progress of Seventh-day Adventists,* the first denominational history (revised in 1905 as *The Great Second Advent Movement*). He published a number of other books, among them *The Church, Its Organization, Order, and Discipline* (1907), which for many years served in place of the church manual, and wrote many articles for denominational papers and edited the *Pacific Health Journal* for a time.

Loughborough made a world tour in 1908, including Europe, Africa, Australia, and New Zealand in his itinerary, which closed his active service, with the exception of occasional preaching at camp meetings and attendance at General Conference sessions.

LOUGHHEAD, JAMES WHITE. *See* Lawhead, James White.

LOUISIANA. *See* Arkansas-Louisiana Conference; Southwestern Union Conference; Southwest Region Conference.

LOUISIANA CONFERENCE. *See* Arkansas-Louisiana Conference.

LOUISIANA-MISSISSIPPI CONFERENCE (1920-1932). *See* Arkansas-Louisiana Conference; Gulf States Conference.

LOVELESS, WILLIAM C. (1897-1974). Pastor, writer, dean, teacher. A native of Missouri, he was educated at Southwestern Union College. He taught at Oshawa Missionary College in Canada and Columbia Union College in Maryland. As director of youth activities he was a pioneer promoter of youth congresses and junior camps in a number of areas. He served as educational secretary in Colorado and promoted the development of Mile High Academy in that state.

LOWE, HARRY (d. 1908). Probably the first Black American Seventh-day Adventist minister. He was born a slave, but by the time E. B. Lane came to preach SDA doctrines in Tennessee in 1871 *(see* South Central Conference), he had become a Baptist minister. He accepted the SDA faith and began to work for Black converts in his section of the state. The Tennessee Conference granted him a ministerial license in 1881. In 1883 he became the leader of a Black Seventh-day Adventist company formed at Edgefield Junction, Tennessee, which was organized as a church in 1886, the first Black Seventh-day Adventist church. In 1884 and 1888 the *Yearbook* lists him as a licentiate, but in 1886 and 1889 as a regular minister, although there is no record of his ordination in the SDA Church.

LOWE, HARRY W. (1893-1990). Minister and administrator. Born in Southampton, England, on Aug. 14, 1893, Harry W. Lowe became a pastor in Great Britain and served as president of the conference in the British Isles until 1947, when he moved to the United States. He took up work with the General Conference as associate Sabbath school director. Later he became a general field secretary, which post he held until 1971, when he retired and moved to Napa Valley, California. He died on July 31, 1990, in Calistoga, California.

LOWER AMAZON MISSION. *See* Brazil; South American Division.

LOWER GWERU ADVENTIST SECONDARY SCHOOL (formerly Lower Gwelo College). A coeducational boarding school operated by the Zambesi Union. It is situated 22 miles (35 kilometers) from the town of Gweru, Zimbabwe. In 1993 it had an enrollment of 665 in the primary course, including a number of blind boys and girls; 594 in the secondary school; and 44 in the Teacher Training Department.

History. The forerunner of the college was an elementary school at Somabula Mission Station. The site for the mission was chosen by F. B. Armitage, who in 1901, with his family and a group of African teachers headed by Harry Sibagobe, left Solusi Mission to open up a new mission east of Bulawayo. Because the site was within the African reserve, the land had to be leased, and could not be bought. A school was opened in 1902, and in 1904 eight students were baptized. When the site proved unhealthful, the station was moved to its present location, on land granted by Chief Bunina, and renamed the Lower Gwelo Mission.

In 1952 the Teacher Training Department formerly conducted at Solusi was transferred to Lower Gweru Mission Training School. In 1955 when the Southern Rhodesia Field headquarters were moved to the town of Gweru (they had been intermittently at Lower Gweru from 1923 to the early thirties and then continuously until 1955), Lower Gweru became the center of the teacher-training work for the entire Zambesi Union, and a higher course of teacher training was added to the former lower course. In 1963 secondary education was added to the lower and higher primary work, which had existed from the early years of the station. The school then became known as the Lower Gwelo Training College until 1978 when the teacher training school was discontinued because of the war. A school for the blind was opened in 1967. After learning to read and type in Braille, the pupils are integrated into the normal classes in the primary school. They use specially prepared textbooks, and all assignments are typed in Braille. This is known as the open system.

In 1980 the school was renamed Lower Gweru Adventist Secondary School. In 1992 it became the first SDA school to be granted A-level status. The church had been expanded, and a large auditorium and dormitories have been added.

Principals: W. R. Quittmeyer, 1952; P. B. Fairchild, 1953; J. Korgan, 1953-1954; H. M. Coy, 1955-1957; S. W. Beardsell, 1957-1965; K. B. Cronje, 1966; S. W. Beardsell, 1967; R A. Burns, 1968-1973; M. A. Lawson, 1974-1977; S. P. Mathema, 1978-1982; J. Fink, 1983; R. E. Kacelenga, 1984-1985; G. B. Nyathi, 1986-1994; A. P. Sibanda, 1994- .

LOWER SAXONIAN CONFERENCE NORTH. *See* Euro-Africa Division; Germany.

LOWER SAXONIAN CONFERENCE SOUTH. *See* Euro-Africa Division; Germany.

LOWRY, GENTRY GEORGE (1884-1942). Missionary to India, teacher, preacher, author, and administrator. His father was one of the pioneer Seventh-day Adventist ministers in the southern United States. He received his ministerial training at Southern Training School at Graysville, Tennessee, from which he graduated in 1908. While in school he took an active part in the evangelistic work of the church by canvassing and serving as tentmaster for the Haskell-Butler meetings at Nashville, Tennessee, in 1906. In 1907 he received a license to preach, and after his graduation served as principal of the Pine Grove Industrial Academy for a year. At the Mississippi camp meeting of 1909 he was ordained, his father being among the officiating ministers. In the same year he married Bertha Burrow and went to southern India, where he worked as vernacular evangelist among the Tamil-speaking peoples until 1912. While on furlough in 1913 he served as Sabbath school and home missionary secretary of the North Carolina Conference. He returned to India in 1914 and soon after became principal of the South India Training School. Between 1917 and 1926 he superintended mission work in the south of India, and in 1919 led out in the reorganization of the field into the South India Union Mission. Between 1926 and 1934 he was superintendent of Northeast India Union, and from 1934 to 1936 he supervised the Northwest India Union Mission as well. In 1937 he served for a few months as principal of the Meiktila Industrial School in Burma, and then was elected to lead the South India Union Mission again. Early in 1941 he was elected acting president of the Southern Asia Division and later became its president. He died shortly after, however, of a stroke.

An accomplished linguist, he preached in several national languages and wrote numerous articles describing life and work in India as well as tracts on SDA beliefs. He organized the first Sabbath school in southern India and wrote the first Bible lessons used in SDA schools there. Among his larger works is *Korada, a Child Widow of India* (1931).

LOWRY MEMORIAL HIGH SCHOOL, JUNIOR COLLEGE, AND TEACHER TRAINING INSTITUTE. An English language coeducational boarding school operated by the South India Union of the Southern Asia Division at Bangalore, in southern India. The school property comprises 59 acres (25 hectares) of farmland and 32 buildings. The school farm produces grains, vegetables, coconuts, and bananas, and supplies the staff with milk from a dairy herd. To provide work opportunities for its students, the school operates the following services and industries: bakery, dairy, food preparation, farm, janitorial, metalcraft, press, security, store, and woodcraft.

Lowry Memorial Junior College curriculum consists of six major programs: preuniversity college, teacher's training college, high school, computer training, data processing center, and work education. These are recognized by the Department of Education of the Southern Asia Division of Seventh-day Adventists and the Department of Public Instruction and Department of Education of the government of Karnataka.

Lowry Memorial is committed to educational opportunities for young men and women and does not discriminate on the basis of caste, sex, state, or religion among those seeking admission.

History. The school began in 1915, when Elder G. G. Lowry established it in Coimbatore, Madras. In 1916 the name Higher Secondary School was changed to South India Training School. In 1917 the school was moved to rented quarters in Bangalore cantonment.

In 1931 another boarding school was started at Basavanagudi, Bangalore, for the purpose of training Kannada-speaking people. It was closed in 1932, and its student body was invited to become part of the training school at Krishnarajapuram. The South India Training School steadily grew to become Spicer Memorial College, situated in Poona.

In 1942 the campus was taken away by the government for military purposes. The school was relocated at Kollegal, where it remained until 1945, when the school had to change its location to Channapatna. In 1946 the school property was relinquished to the government again, and the school was moved for the last time to its present location. Following the addition of the high school section, the school was renamed Lowry Memorial High School in honor of the late G. G. Lowry, a noted educator and social worker of the Seventh-day Adventist Church in Southern Asia.

At present there are 177 teaching and nonteaching members on the staff, and an enrollment of 1,990.

Principals: R. H. Shephard (acting), 1946; W. F. Storz, 1946-1948; H. A. Walls, Jr., 1948-1950; R. S. Lowry, 1950-1951; O. A. Skau, 1951-1953; G. Gurubatham, 1953-1954; D. H. Skau, 1954-1956; A. F. Jensen, 1956-1961; R. H. Jones, 1961-1963; S. G. David, 1963-1964; Arno Kutzner, 1964-1967; J. M. Curnow, 1967-1969; W. F. Easterbrook, 1969-1971; S. G. David, 1971-1974; A. M. Job, 1974-1975; K. I. Varghese, 1975-1980; S. A. Kodan, 1980-1982; N. Y. Reddy (acting), 1982; D. Sukumaran, 1982-1983; Mrs. E. S. James, 1983-1984; K. I. Varghese, 1984-1986; N. Sharath Chandra, 1986-1989; T. J. Lazarus, 1989-1993; J. Robert Donald, 1993-1994; T. J. Lazarus, 1994- .

LOYALTY ISLANDS. *See* New Caledonia and Loyalty Islands.

LUDINGTON, DON C. (1888-1971). Educator and missionary. He was a native of Kentucky. In 1913, following graduation from Emmanuel Missionary College, he became principal of Battle Creek Academy. From 1914 to 1923 he served as director of a school in Meiktila, Burma. After returning to the homeland, he served as MV and educational secretary of the Florida Conference. He was a founder and principal of Forest Lake Academy in that state. He was invited to join the staff of Southern Missionary College in 1929 and served there until his retirement in 1954.

LUGENBEAL, EDWARD NEWTON (1906-1949). Missionary administrator. After graduation from Emmanuel Missionary College (1927) and evangelistic work and teaching in Indiana (1927-1929), he served as Bible teacher at Philippine Junior College (1929-1931), then as director of the Northern Luzon Mission (1931-1939) and of the East Visayan Mission (1939-1941).

In 1942 he served in South America for three years as president of the Austral Union Conference. After a year as superintendent of the Mexican Union Mission, he became superintendent of the Inca Union Mission (1947-1949). He met accidental death by drowning.

LUKANGA ADVENTIST INSTITUTE (Institut Adventiste de Lukanga). A coeducational institution (formerly Kivu Adventist College) operated by the Zaïre Union. In 1959 a property was purchased at Lukanga. In 1969 an extensive building program on this property resulted in an attractive campus that provides for secondary and higher education.

The school was officially recognized by the government in 1975, and the students were then allowed to write the government examination and receive diplomas in pedagogy. In the same year two theology courses were added with the help of Elton Wallace, who was then rector of the Adventist University of Central Africa.

A technical school was established in 1990 (Institut Technique de Lukanga). The schools operate independently of each other. There is also a primary school on the compound where students do their practice teaching. Total enrollment of the combined schools is 776.

Directors: H. M. Peak, 1965-1971; J. H. Wright, 1971-1972; A. dos Santos, 1972-1975; D. Walther, 1975-1977; R. Ross, 1977-1978; T. Korson, 1979-1981; R. Prouty, 1981-1983; D. Saguan, 1983-1985; R. Perrin, 1985-1986; J. Pondexter, 1986-1988; N. Ruhaya, 1992; S. Bisika, 1993-1994; B. M. Safari, 1994- .

LUKENS, MORRIS (1871-1933). Conference administrator. Shortly after accepting the Seventh-day Adventist faith in 1892, he was appointed field secretary of the Pennsylvania Conference. Ordained in 1898, he engaged in evangelism in Pennsylvania. He served as president of the Chesapeake Conference (1906-1908), as manager of the Book Department of the Review and Herald Publishing Association, and then for two years as president of the Indiana Conference (1909-1911). From 1911 to 1917 he served in Australia as conference president and as union conference vice president.

On returning to the United States, he became president of the Kansas Conference for one year, then president of the Southwestern Union Conference (1918-1923). Unable for health reasons to accept a call to the presidency of the Inter-American Division in 1922, he was appointed president of the North Pacific Union Conference in 1923. From 1932 to 1933 he was president of the Northern California Conference.

LULENGELE TRAINING SCHOOL. *See* Songa Institute.

LUNDQUIST, HARRY B. (1891-1973). Educator, missionary, and administrator. After graduation from Emmanuel Missionary College in 1917, he married Hazel May Murray and began denominational work as a tentmaster in Indiana. Later he served as camp pastor for Seventh-day Adventist soldiers. From 1918 to 1921 he was principal of the Lima Training School in Peru, and for the next 16 years he was educational and MV secretary of the Inca and Austral unions and carried other responsibilities in the South American Division. Beginning in 1937, he served for two years as president of the Inca Union. Later he was educational secretary of the Southern Union Conference and a teacher at Pacific Union and Southwestern Union colleges. He served for 11 years in the Inter-American Division as president of the Antillian Union and Bible teacher at Antillian College.

After his wife's death in 1961, he married Grace Evans Green. When he returned to the United States from Inter-America in 1966, he did part-time teaching at Southern Missionary College.

LUNJIKA SECONDARY SCHOOL. A coeducational boarding school offering the complete secondary course. It is situated on a 184-acre (75-hectare) tract below the Viphya Plateau. Owned and operated by the South-East Africa Union, it serves the constituency of Malawi. English is the medium of instruction.

In 1993 the primary school had 300 students enrolled and a staff of eight teachers. The secondary school had 288 students, nine teachers, and 11 on the nonteaching staff.

The school developed from a village school begun by a Malawian national, James Malinki, in 1932. In 1962 a junior secondary school was started, and in 1966 a two-year ministerial training school. The ministers are now trained at Lake View Seminary in central Malawi.

At first known as Mombera, it was renamed Lunjika Secondary School in 1976, after the majestic peak that towers over the mission campus. It became a senior secondary school in 1982.

Principals: James Malinki, 1931-1933; S. M. Mbawala, 1933-1947; A. K. Phillips, 1947-1949; G. A. Otter, 1949-1960; W. D. Pierce, 1961-1965; A. K. Phillips, 1965-1968; P. A. Parks, 1968-1969; B. L. Wright, 1969-1973; F. K. Nyasulu, 1973-1975; W. W. Khonje, 1975-1977; S. R. Mfune, 1977-1980; H. J. Tsoka, 1980-1984; G. S. Moyo, 1984-1986; R. E. Thombozi, 1986-1987; R. R. Mzumara, 1987-1994; M. A. Mugaba, 1994- .

LÜPKE, OTTO (1871-1914). Educator and minister in Germany. He met Adventists in the mid-1890s, and after joining the church, entered the colporteur work in western Germany. Later he was ordained to the ministry, and in 1899 helped to found and then took charge of Friedensau Missionary Seminary, continuing as its head until his death in 1914. According to the *Yearbook*, he also served for periods as a recording secretary of the West German Conference, as a minister in western Germany, and as young people's department secretary of the East German Union.

LUXEMBOURG. An independent grand duchy in Western Europe bounded by Belgium, France, and Germany, with an area of 998 square miles (2,600 square kilometers) and a population (1994) of 402,000, predominantly Roman Catholic. French is the official language, but German is also spoken, and the common speech is in Letzeburgesch, the original local dialect.

The territory of Luxembourg was assigned to the French Conference, but since 1968 it has been a part of the Belgian-Luxembourg Conference, part of the Franco-Belgian Union, which in turn is a part of the Euro-Africa Division.

From 1924 to 1931 Charles Kamm, a Seventh-day Adventist minister from Alsace, eastern France, was assigned to Luxembourg to work under the direction of the Belgian Conference. He baptized a small group in 1926 and more in 1927 and 1929, but the converts were never organized into a church. In 1928 at least two young women from Luxembourg attended the Seminaire Adventiste du Salève in Collonges, France.

In 1947 an active lay member living in France near the border attempted to hold some meetings in Luxembourg, but this was not permitted by the authorities. An SDA minister from the Saar held some lectures in the 1950s, but with small attendance and without visible results. Colporteur work is forbidden. Three families were won by a lay member from Germany and met each Sabbath in the home of R. Tanson, a civil engineer.

During the fall of 1968 a series of 13 religious programs was telecast over Radio-Luxembourg. In January 1969 a short public effort was held by Pierre Lanarès and Raymond Meyer, from France, in a public hall. In the spring of 1969, a hall was rented in a hotel, and ministers from Belgium conducted weekly Sabbath meetings to follow up the public effort. In 1971 Marc Cools, a young Belgian missionary who had returned from Cameroon to finish his studies, was sent to Luxembourg by the Belgian-Luxembourg Conference to organize a church with 13 members. He and his family stayed in Luxembourg for 10 years. In 1993 there were 55 members in Luxembourg. For many years Luxembourg's powerful, privately owned radio station has broadcast SDA programs in many languages.

LUZ MISSION. *See* Angola.

L'VOV, IVAN ALEXANDROVICH (d. 1957 or 1958). Minister, editor, and Seventh-day Adventist church leader in Russia. A native of the St. Petersburg area, he trained for the ministry at Friedensau Missionary Seminary and returned about 1909 as a missionary licentiate. In 1912 he was ordained to the ministry at Reval (Tallinn), and two years later founded and edited, with S. Efimov, the evangelistic magazine *Blagaya Ves't'*. Shortly before World War I he was transferred to Moscow. In the 1920s he was president of the Ukrainian Union and in 1925 established in Kiev a publishing house called Patmos, that issued evangelistic magazines and other SDA publications. In 1928, with H. J. Loebsack and J. J. Wilson, he attended the council of the European Division held at Marienhöhe, Germany, the first time that representatives of the Federation of Seventh-day Adventists in the USSR had met with other SDA leaders since the federation was formed. Because of his active role in the promotion of SDA teachings by word and pen, he was exiled to Kazakhstan. After five years he was released during the general amnesty in the middle 1950s. He returned to Moscow, where he died soon after.

LYCÉE MARANATHA DE KIVOGA. *See* Kivoga Secondary School.

LYNWOOD ADVENTIST ACADEMY. *See* Los Angeles Adventist Academy (California).

LYSINGER, HARRY E. (1884-1966). Departmental secretary and administrator. He began his denominational work in 1906 as a colporteur in Missouri, where he entered the ministry in 1907. He was asked to serve as publishing secretary in the Wyoming Conference in 1908, but returned to the ministry in the Missouri Conference in 1909, where he continued until 1912. For the next five years he labored in Nebraska and northern California, and from 1917 to 1920 he served as president of the Intermountain Conference. Following this, he was home missionary secretary of the Central Union Conference for four years. In 1925 he became president of the

Tennessee River Conference, which position he held until 1932, when he was called to the same position in the Georgia-Cumberland Conference. From 1937 to 1943 he was president of the Carolina Conference, from which position he retired because of ill health.